D0559298

A Dictionary of
Writers and their Works

A Dictionary of
Writers and their Works

Edited by
MICHAEL COX

OXFORD
UNIVERSITY PRESS

Great Clarendon Street, Oxford OX2 6DP

Oxford University Press is a department of the University of Oxford.
It furthers the University's objective of excellence in research, scholarship,
and education by publishing worldwide in

Oxford New York
Athens Auckland Bangkok Bogotá Buenos Aires Calcutta
Cape Town Chennai Dar es Salaam Delhi Florence Hong Kong Istanbul
Karachi Kuala Lumpur Madrid Melbourne Mexico City Mumbai
Nairobi Paris São Paulo Shanghai Singapore Taipei Tokyo Toronto Warsaw

with associated companies in Berlin Ibadan

Oxford is a registered trade mark of Oxford University Press
in the UK and in certain other countries

Published in the United States
by Oxford University Press Inc., New York

First published 2001

British Library Cataloguing in Publication Data
Data available

Library of Congress Cataloging in Publication Data
Data available

ISBN 0-19-866249-1

1 3 5 7 9 10 8 6 4 2

Typeset by RefineCatch Limited, Bungay, Suffolk
Printed in Great Britain by T.J. International,
Padstow, Cornwall

For Dizzy junior

Contents

Preface

'I've got a little list – I've got a little list'
W.S. Gilbert, *The Mikado* (1885)

This dictionary has been compiled with the simple purpose of providing an easy-to-use source of basic information on writers and their works—on *who* wrote *what*. When memory fails, it can often be frustratingly difficult to identify the name of an unremembered (or misremembered) author from a known title. At the same time, discursive works of reference do not always provide the kind of unadorned factual data that may often be needed by students, teachers, or other specialist readers—for instance, to confirm the order in which a writer's works were published. The aim of the present work, therefore, has been to provide an extensive aide-mémoire, enabling readers to match the title of a work to its author and also to review, at a glance, that author's principal works in a single list. Thus the dictionary's indexes will tell you that the author of *Chitty-Chitty-Bang-Bang* was Ian Fleming, creator of James Bond, and also that Trollope's last novel published in his lifetime was *Marion Fay*.

The main part of the dictionary is arranged in two linked sections. The first, ordered alphabetically by author, allows readers to see immediately what works an author is best known for and in what order they were published. It consists of a brief description of each writer followed by a **select** list of his/her works by date of publication (or date of first performance, if earlier, in the case of plays). Here everything becomes a hostage to opinion. My judgement of what should and should not be included has not been entirely subjective; it has been tested against what writers and works have merited inclusion in a number of standard reference sources and supplemented, in the case of contemporary writers, by such indicators as review coverage. On the other hand, it is in the end a personal—sometimes an instinctive—choice, and all I can do is hold my hands up at the outset and admit that there are omissions, both deliberate and unintentional. That cannot be helped in a work of this type and I must crave indulgence from eagle-eyed readers who discover that their favourite author, or favourite book, has not been listed. So much to select from. So little space.

For writers of indisputably major canonical status, such as Shakespeare, Dickens, or Kingsley Amis, the list of works provided may indeed be complete; and because of the relative difficulty of locating title information, it is also sometimes the case that a fairly full list of titles is given for writers of (arguably) lesser literary standing (e.g. Mary Elizabeth Braddon, author of *Lady Audley's Secret*). But it is important to emphasize that completeness in all cases has not been the objective. The aim rather has been to complement titles that have genuine cultural resonance and celebrity (*Little Women, A Man for All Seasons, The Prisoner of Zenda, Breakfast at Tiffany's, A Taste of Honey*) with many others that are broadly representative of a wide range of writers from all periods (Dr Dee's *Monas Hieroglyphica*, for example, or Tom Taylor's *Our American Cousin*). It has been a particular objective to include generous coverage of titles from authors on whom basic title information is difficult to find without recourse to specialist sources. Thus, for instance, the works of the late Victorian novelist 'John Ackworth' (Frederick R. Smith) are not usually to be found mentioned in general works of reference, but a selection is listed here on the grounds that some readers engaged in literary research or study may need to know, or be reminded, that Ackworth was the author of the once reasonably well known *Clogshop Chronicles*.

The second of the dictionary's two major indexes lists all the works included in Section 1 in a single alphabetical sequence. This is the section to use if readers wish to identify authors whose names they have forgotten from a known title. It can also be used quickly to find out or confirm publication dates. (Authors themselves may find this index useful for checking whether someone else has already made use of a title they are thinking of using.)

The dictionary contains information on well over 25,000 titles from nearly 3,000 authors. The generally accepted canon of English literature from the fifteenth century to the year 2000 (ignoring for present purposes the vexed question of whether a canon does or should exist) predominates. However, effort has been made to include substantial coverage of American writers, especially those who are well known to British readers, as well as more select coverage of Canadian, Australian, and Anglo-Indian authors and major European and classical figures. As far as European writers are concerned, the selection has been based on those authors with whom the generality of British readers might be expected to be familiar with by name and reputation and whose works are available in translation. Thus, Dumas but not Djian; Flaubert but not Fourré; Balzac but not Bloy; Goethe but not Adolf Glassbrenner; Cervantes but not Jerónimo de Cuéllar. The dictionary also includes a large number of titles from popular genres (crime fiction, supernatural fiction, science fiction, historical romance) as well as coverage of works for children. Finally, to supplement the two main indexes, a select list of literary characters provides information on fictional names that crossword solvers, quiz fanatics, and others may need to identify.

I would like to acknowledge the valuable help of Vicki Rodger and Ruth Langley at OUP. Ruth, in particular, provided sterling support during the latter stages of compilation. It hardly needs saying that any errors and omissions are mine alone.

MAC

January 2001

Abbreviations

ANTH	Anthology
CH	Works for Children
D	Drama
DIC	Dictionary
EDN	Edition
F	Fiction
MISC	Miscellaneous
MUS	Music
NF	Non-Fiction
PER	Periodical
SS	Short Stories
V	Verse/Poetry

attrib.	attributed to
biog.	biography
bk(s)	book(s)
c.	circa
ed.	edited (by)
edn.	edition
inc.	including
orig.	originally
perf.	performed
prtd	printed
pt.	part
pub.	published
repub.	republished
rev.	revised
ser.	series
tr.	translated (by)
trn	translation
vol./vols	volumes(s)

Author Index

A

ABERCROMBIE, Lascelles (1881–1938)
British poet, dramatist, and critic
Interludes and Poems (1908) V
Emblems of Love (1912) V
Thomas Hardy (1912) NF
Deborah (1913) D
Speculative Dialogues (1913) NF
The Epic (1914) NF
An Essay Towards a Theory of Art (1922) NF
Four Short Plays (1922) D
Phoenix (1923) D
Principles of English Prosody (1923) NF
The Theory of Poetry (1924) NF
The Idea of Great Poetry (1925) NF
Romanticism (1926) NF
Twelve Idylls, and Other Poems (1928) V
The Sale of St Thomas (1930) D
Poetry: Its Music and Meaning (1932) NF
Lyrics and Unfinished Poems (1940) V

ABISH, Walter (1931–)
American novelist
Duel Site (1970) V
Alphabetical Africa (1974) F
Minds Meet (1975) F SS
In the Future Perfect (1977) F SS
How German Is It? (1980) F
99: The New Meaning (1990) F
Eclipse Fever (1993) F

ABRAHAMS, Peter (1919–)
South African novelist
Song of the City (1943) F
Mine Boy (1946) F
Path of Thunder (1948) F
Wild Conquest (1951) F
A Wreath for Udomo (1956) F
A Night of Their Own (1965) F
This Island Now (1967) F
The View From Coyoba (1985) F

ABSE, Dannie [Daniel] (1923–)
British poet, novelist, and dramatist
After Every Green Thing (1949) V
Ash on a Young Man's Sleeve (1954) F
Fire in Heaven (1956) D
Tenants of the House (1957) V
Poems, Golders Green (1962) V
Three Questor Plays (1967) D
A Small Desperation (1968) V
O Jones, O Jones (1970) F
Funland, and Other Poems (1973) V
A Poet in the Family (1974) NF
Way Out in the Centre (1981) V
A Strong Dose of Myself (1983) NF
Ask the Bloody Horse (1986) V
White Coat, Purple Coat (1989) V
Remembrance of Crimes Past (1990) V
There Was a Young Man From Cardiff (1991) NF
On the Evening Road (1994) V
Arcadia, One Mile (1998) V

ACHEBE, Chinua (1930–)
Nigerian novelist
Things Fall Apart (1958) F
No Longer at Ease (1960) F
The Sacrificial Egg, and Other Stories (1962) F SS
Arrow of God (1964) F
A Man of the People (1966) F
Beware, Soul-Brother (1971) V
Girls at War, and Other Stories (1972) F SS
Morning Yet on Creation Day (1975) NF
Anthills of the Savannah (1987) F
Hopes and Impediments (1988) NF

ACKER, Kathy (1948–)
American novelist
The Childlike Life of the Black Tarantula (1975) F
The Adult Life of Toulouse Lautrec by Henri Toulouse Lautrec (1978) F
Kathy Goes to Haiti (1978) F
Great Expectations (1982) F
Blood and Guts in High School (1984) F
Hello, I'm Erica Long (1984) F
Algeria (1985) F
Don Quixote: Which Was a Dream (1986) F
Empire of the Senseless (1988) F
In Memoriam to Identity (1990) F
Portrait of an Eye: Three Novels (1992) F
Pussy, King of the Pirates (1996) F
Bodies of Work: Essays (1997) NF

ACKERLEY, J[oseph] R[andolph] (1896–1967)
British dramatist and author
The Prisoners of War (1925) D
Hindoo Holiday (1932) NF
My Dog Tulip (1956) NF
We Think the World of You (1960) F
My Father and Myself (1968) NF

ACKLAND, Rodney (1908–1991)
British dramatist
Dance With No Music (1930) D
Improper People (1930) D
Strange Orchestra (1932) D
Birthday (1934) D
After October (1936) D
The Dark River (1941) D
Before the Party (1949) D
A Dead Secret (1957) D

ACKROYD, Peter (1949–)
British novelist, biographer, and poet
London Lickpenny (1973) V
Notes for a New Culture (1976) NF
Country Life (1978) V
Dressing Up: Transvestism and Drag (1979) NF

Ezra Pound and His World (1980) NF
The Great Fire of London (1982) F
The Last Testament of Oscar Wilde (1983) F
T.S. Eliot (1984) NF
Hawksmoor (1985) F
Chatterton (1987) F
The Diversions of Purley, and Other Poems (1987) V
First Light (1989) F
Dickens (1990) NF
English Music (1992) NF
The House of Doctor Dee (1993) F
Dan Leno and the Limehouse Golem (1994) F
Blake (1995) NF
Milton in America (1996) F
The Life of Thomas More (1998) NF
The Plato Papers (1999) F
London: The Biography (2000) NF

'ACKWORTH, John' [Frederick R. Smith] (1845–1919?)
British novelist
Clogshop Chronicles (1896) F
Beckside Lights (1897) F SS
The Snowcroft Critics (1898) F SS
Doxie Dent (1899) F
The Mangle House (1902) F

ACORN, Milton (1923–)
Canadian poet
Jawbreakers (1963) V
I've Tasted My Blood (1969) V
I Shout Love, and On Shaving off His Beard (1971) V
More Poems for People (1972) V
The Island Means Minago (1975) V
Jackpine Sonnets (1977) V
Captain Neal MacDougal and the Naked Goddess (1982) V
Dig Up My Heart (1983) V

ACTON, Eliza (1799–1859)
British cookery writer
Modern Cookery, in All its Branches (1845) NF

ACTON, Sir Harold [Mario Mitchell] (1904–1994)
British writer and aesthete
Aquarium (1923) V
An Indian Ass (1925) V
Humdrum (1928) F
This Chaos (1930) V
The Last Medici (1932) NF
Peonies and Ponies (1941) F
Memoirs of an Aesthete (1948) NF
The Bourbons of Naples 1734–1825 (1956) NF
The Bourbons of Naples 1825–61 (1961) NF
More Memoirs of an Aesthete (1970) NF
Tit for Tat, and Other Tales (1972) F SS

ACTON, John Emerich Edward Dalberg, 1st Baron Acton (1834–1902)
British historian
The War of 1870 (1871) NF
Historical Essays and Studies (1907) NF
The History of Freedom, and Other Essays (1907) NF
Lectures on the French Revolution (1910) NF
A Lecture on the Study of History (1895) NF

ADAM, Paul [Auguste Marie] (1862–1920)
French novelist
Chair Molle ['Weak Flesh'] (1885) F
Robes rouges ['Red Dresses'] (1891) F
Le Vice filial ['Filial Vice'] (1891) F
Le Mystère des foules ['The Mystery of the Masses'] (1895) F
La Force du mal ['The Force of Evil'] (1896) F
La Force ['The Power'] (1899) F
L'Enfant d'Austerlitz ['The Child of Austerlitz'] (1902) F

ADAMS, Andy (1859–1935)
American novelist
The Log of a Cowboy (1903) F
The Outlet (1905) F
Cattle Brands (1906) F SS
Reed Anthony, Cowman (1907) F
Wells Brothers (1911) F
The Ranch on the Beaver (1927) F

ADAMS, Arthur Henry (1872–1936)
New Zealand novelist and poet
Tussock Land (1904) F
The New Chum, and Other Stories (1909) F SS
Galahad Jones (1910) F
My Friend, Remember (1914) V
The Australians (1920) F
A Man's Life (1929) F

ADAMS, Douglas [Noel] (1952–)
British novelist and scriptwriter
The Hitch-Hiker's Guide to the Galaxy (1979) F
The Restaurant at the End of the Universe (1980) F
Life, the Universe and Everything (1982) F
So Long, and Thanks for all the Fish (1984) F
Dirk Gently's Holistic Detective Agency (1987) F
The Long Dark Tea-Time of the Soul (1988) F

ADAMS, Francis [William Lauderdale] (1862–1893)
Australian-born novelist and poet
Leicester (1885) F
Songs of the Army of Night (1888) V
John Webb's End (1891) F
Australian Life (1892) F
The Melbournians (1892) F
A Child of the Age (1894) F

ADAMS, Hannah (1755–1831)
American author
A Summary History of New England (1799) NF
The Truth and Excellence of the Christian Religion Exhibited (1804) NF
The History of the Jews (1812) NF

ADAMS, Henry [Brooks] (1838–1918)
American historian and man of letters
Democracy (1880) F
Esther (1884) F

History of the United States (1889–1991) NF
Memoirs of Marau Taaroa, Last Queen of Tahiti (1893) NF
Mont-Saint-Michel and Chartres (1904) NF
The Education of Henry Adams (1907) NF

ADAMS, Richard [George] (1920–)
British novelist
Watership Down (1972) F
Shardik (1974) F
The Plague Dogs (1977) F
The Girl in a Swing (1980) F
The Iron Wolf, and Other Stories (1980) F SS
Maia (1984) F
Traveller (1988) F
The Day Gone By (1990) NF
The Outlandish Knight (1999) F

ADAMS, Sarah Fuller, *née* Flower (1805–1848)
British poet and hymn-writer
Vivia Perpetua (1841) V

ADAMSON, Robert [Henry] (1943–)
Australian poet
Canticles on the Skin (1970) V
The Rumour (1971) V
Swamp Riddles (1974) V
Theatre I–XIX (1976) V
Cross the Border (1977) V
Where I Come From (1979) V
The Law at Heart's Desire (1982) V
The Clean Dark (1989) V
Wards of the State (1992) V P

ADCOCK, A[rthur] St John (1864–1930)
British critic and novelist
An Unfinished Martyrdom, and Other Stories (1894) F SS
Beyond Atonement (1896) F
East End Idylls (1897) F
The Consecration of Hetty Fleet (1898) F
In the Image of God (1898) F
In the Wake of War (1900) F SS
Songs of the War (1900) V
The Luck of Private Foster (1900) F
Admissions and Asides About Life and Literature (1905) NF
Love in London (1906) F
Billicks (1909) F
A Man With a Past (1911) F
Seeing it Through (1915) F
Gods of Modern Grub Street (1923) NF
The Glory That Was Grub Street (1928) NF

ADCOCK, [Kareen] Fleur (1934–)
New Zealand-born poet
The Eye of the Hurricane (1964) V
Tigers (1967) V
High Tide in the Garden (1971) V
The Scenic Route (1974) V
Below Loughrigg (1979) V
The Inner Harbour (1979) V
Hotspur (1986) V
The Incident Book (1986) V
Meeting the Comet (1988) V
Time Zones (1991) V
Looking Back (1997) V
Poems 1960–2000 (2000) V

ADDISON, Joseph (1672–1719)
English poet, essayist, dramatist, and statesman
The Campaign (1705) V
Remarks on Several Parts of Italy (1705) NF
Rosamund (1707) D
Cato (1713) D
The Drummer; or, The Haunted House (1716) D
A Discourse on Antient and Modern Learning (1734) NF

ADE, George (1866–1944)
American humorist and dramatist
Fables in Slang (1899) F
Forty Modern Fables (1901) F
The Sultan of Sulu (1902) D MUS
People You Know (1903) F
The College Window (1904) D
Just Out of College (1905) D
Hand-Made Fables (1920) F

'Æ' see George William Russell

AESCHYLUS (525–456 BC)
Greek tragic poet
The Persians (472 BC) D
Seven Against Thebes (467 BC) D
The Suppliants (463 BC) D
Agamemnon; Choephori; Eumenidies [Oresteia trilogy] (458 BC) D
Prometheus Bound D

AGARD, John (1949–)
Guyanese poet and children's author
Shoot Me With Flowers (1973) V
Man to Pan (1982) V
Limbo Dancer in Dark Glasses (1983) V
Lovelines for a Goat-Born Lady (1990) V

AGATE, James Evershed (1877–1947)
British journalist, drama critic, and novelist
Responsibility (1919) F
Alarums and Excursions (1922) NF
At Half-past Eight (1923) NF
Blessed are the Rich (1924) F
Agate's Folly (1925) NF
The Common Touch (1926) NF
Gemel in London (1928) F
Ego (1935) NF
Kingdoms for Horses (1936) NF
Bad Manners (1938) NF
Noblesse Oblige (1944) NF
Around Cinemas (1946) NF
Thus to Revisit (1947) NF

AGEE, James (1909–1955)
American novelist, poet, and screenwriter
Permit Me Voyage (1934) V
Let Us Now Praise Famous Men [photographs by Walker Evans] (1941) NF

The Morning Watch (1951) F
A Death in the Family (1957) F

AGUILAR, Grace (1816–1847)
British novelist, poet, and Jewish historian
The Magic Wreath (1835) V
Records of Israel (1844) F
The Women of Israel; or, Characters and Sketches from the Holy Scripture (1845) NF
The Jewish Faith (1846) NF
Home Influence (1847) F
The Vale of Cedars; or, The Martyr (1850) F
Woman's Friendship (1850) F
A Mother's Recompense (1851) F
The Days of Bruce (1852) F
Home Scenes and Heart Studies (1853) F SS

AHLBERG, Alan (1938–)
British children's author
Burglar Bill (1977) F CH
Cops and Robbers (1978) F CH
Each Peach Pear Plum (1978) V CH
Mr Biff the Boxer (1980) F CH
The One True Santa (1985) F CH
The Jolly Postman (1986) F CH

AICKMAN, Robert [Fordyce] (1914–1981)
British supernatural fiction writer
Dark Entries (1964) F SS
Powers of Darkness (1966) F SS
Sub Rosa (1968) F SS
Cold Hand in Mine (1975) F SS
Tales of Love and Death (1977) F SS
Intrusions (1980) F SS

AÏDÉ, Charles Hamilton (1826–1906)
British novelist, poet, and musician
Eleanore, and Other Poems (1856) V
Rita (1856) F
Confidences (1859) F
Carr of Carrlyon (1862) F
Mr and Mrs Faulconbridge (1864) F
The Romance of the Scarlet Leaf, and Other Poems (1865) V
The Marstons (1868) F
Penruddock (1873) F
Poet and Peer (1880) F
Songs Without Music (1882) V
Introduced to Society (1884) F
Passages in the Life of a Lady in 1814–1815–1816 (1887) F
A Voyage of Discovery (1892) F
Elizabeth's Pretenders (1895) F
Jane Treachel (1899) F

AIDOO, Ama Ata (1942–)
Ghanaian dramatist, novelist, short-story writer, and poet
The Dilemma of a Ghost (1964) D
Anowa (1970) D
No Sweetness Here (1970) F SS
Our Sister Killjoy (1977) F
Someone Talking to Sometime (1985) V
The Eagle and the Chicken, and Other Stories (1986) F SS
Changes (1991) F

AIKEN, Conrad Potter (1889–1973)
American poet, short-story writer, and novelist
Earth Triumphant (1914) V
The Jig of Forslin: A Symphony (1916) V
Turns and Movies (1916) V
Nocturne of Remembered Spring (1917) V
The Charnel Rose; Senlin: A Biography; and Other Poems (1918) V
Scepticisms: Notes on Contemporary Poetry (1919) NF
The House of Dust: A Symphony (1920) V
Punch: The Immortal Liar (1921) V
Priapus and the Pool (1922) V
The Pilgrimage of Festus (1923) V
Bring! Bring! (1925) F SS
Blue Voyage (1927) F
Costumes by Eros (1928) F SS
John Deth (1930) V
The Coming Forth by Day of Osiris Jones (1931) V
Preludes for Memnon (1931) V
Great Circle (1933) F
Among the Lost People (1934) F SS
Landscape West of Eden (1934) V
King Coffin (1935) F
Time in the Rock (1936) V
A Heart for the Gods of Mexico (1939) F
And in the Human Heart (1940) V
Conversation; or, Pilgrims' Progress (1940) F
Brownstone Eclogues (1942) V
The Soldier (1944) V
The Kid (1947) V
Skylight One (1949) V
Ushant [reissued 1971] (1952) NF
A Letter From Li Po (1955) V
Sheepfold Hill (1958) V
The Morning Song of Lord Zero (1963) V

AIKEN, Joan Delano (1924–)
British children's author and novelist
All You've Ever Wanted, and Other Stories (1953) F CH
The Wolves of Willoughby Chase (1962) F CH
Black Hearts in Battersea (1964) F CH
Nightbirds in Nantucket (1966) F CH
Hate Begins at Home (1967) F
The Whispering Mountain (1968) F CH
A Small Pinch of Weather, and Other Stories (1969) F CH
The Cuckoo Tree (1971) F CH
Died on a Rainy Sunday (1972) F CH
A Harp of Fishbones, and Other Stories (1972) F CH
Midnight is a Place (1974) F CH
Castle Barebane (1976) F CH
The Faithless Lollybird, and Other Stories (1977) F CH
Go Saddle the Sea (1977) F CH
The Lightning Tree (1980) F
The Shadow Guests (1980) F CH
Bridle the Wind (1983) F CH

Mansfield Revisited (1984) F
Up the Chimney Down (1984) F CH
A Goose on Your Grave (1987) F CH
Blackground (1989) F
The Haunting of Lamb House (1991) F

AIKIN, Lucy (1781–1864)
British poet, biographer, and children's author
Epistles on Women (1810) V
Lorimer (1814) F
Memoirs of the Court of Queen Elizabeth (1818) NF
Memoirs of the Court of King James the First (1822) NF
Memoirs of the Court of King Charles the First (1833) NF

AINSWORTH, William Francis (1807–1896)
British geologist, traveller, and author
Travels in the Track of the Ten Thousand Greeks (1844) NF

AINSWORTH, William Harrison (1805–1882)
British novelist and editor
December Tales (1823) F SS
Sir John Chiverton (1826) F
Rookwood (1834) F
Crichton (1837) F
Jack Sheppard (1839) F
The Tower of London (1840) F
Guy Fawkes; or, The Gunpowder Treason (1841) F
Old Saint Paul's (1841) F
The Miser's Daughter (1842) F
Modern Chivalry; or, A New Orlando Furioso (1843) F
Windsor Castle (1843) F
Saint James's; or, The Court of Queen Anne (1844) F
James the Second; or, The Revolution of 1688 (1848) F
The Lancashire Witches (1849) F
Auriol (1850) F
The Flitch of Bacon; or, The Custom of Dunmow (1854) F
The Star-Chamber (1854) F
Ballads (1855) V
The Spendthrift (1857) F
The Life and Adventures of Mervyn Clitheroe (1858) F
The Combat of the Thirty (1859) F
Ovingdean Grange (1860) F
The Constable of the Tower (1861) F
The Lord Mayor of London; or, City Life in the Last Century (1862) F
Cardinal Pole; or, The Days of Philip and Mary (1863) F
John Law (1864) F
The Spanish Match; or, Charles Stuart at Madrid (1865) F
The Constable de Bourbon (1866) F
Old Court (1867) F
Myddleton Pomfret (1868) F
Hilary St Ives (1870) F
Talbot Harland (1870) F
The South-Sea Bubble (1871) F
Tower Hill (1871) F
Boscobel; or, The Royal Oak (1872) F
The Good Old Times (1873) F
Merry England; or, Nobles and Serfs (1874) F
The Goldsmith's Wife (1875) F
Preston Fight; or, The Insurrection of 1715 (1875) F
Chetwynd Calverley (1876) F
The Leaguer of Lathom (1876) F
The Fall of Somerset (1877) F
Beatrice Tyldesley (1878) F
Beau Nash; or, Bath in the Eighteenth Century (1879) F
Stanley Brereton (1881) F

AIRD, Thomas (1802–1876)
Scottish poet
Murtzoufle (1826) V
The Captive of Fez (1830) V
Orthuriel, and Other Poems (1840) V

AKENSIDE, Mark (1721–1770)
British poet and physician
A British Philippic (1738) V
An Epistle to Curio (1744) V
The Pleasures of Imagination (1744) V
Friendship and Love: A Dialogue (1745) V
Odes on Several Subjects (1745) V
An Ode to the Right Honourable the Earl of Huntingdon (1748) V
An Ode to the Country Gentlemen of England (1758) V
An Ode to the Late Thomas Edwards (1766) V

'AKHMATOVA, Anna' [Anna Andreevna Gorenko] (1889–1966)
Russian poet
Evening (1912) V
The Rosary (1914) V
The White Flock (1917) V
Ecstasy Collection (1918) V
Anno Domini MCMXXI (1921) V
Plantain (1921) V
From Six Books (1940) V
Poem Without a Hero (1960) V
Requiem (1964) V

AKINS, Zoë (1886–1958)
American dramatist and novelist
Déclassé (1919) D
Daddy's Gone A-Hunting (1921) D
The Varying Shore (1921) D
The Texas Nightingale [rev. 1923 as *Greatness*] (1922) D
The Greeks Had a Word For It (1929) D
The Old Maid (1935) D
O, Evening Star (1936) D
Forever Young (1941) F

AKSAKOV, Sergei Timofeyevich (1791–1859)
Russian novelist
The Blizzard (1834) F
A Family Chronicle (1846–1856) F
Childhood Years of Bagrova-grandchild (1858) F

'ALAIN-FOURNIER' [Henri-Alban Fournier] (1886–1914)
French novelist
Le Grand Meaulnes (1913) F

ALBEE, Edward [Franklin] (1928–)
American dramatist
The Zoo Story (1958) D
The Death of Bessie Smith (1959) D
The American Dream (1960) D
The Sandbox (1960) D
Who's Afraid of Virginia Woolf? (1962) D
Tiny Alice (1964) D
A Delicate Balance (1966) D
Box (1968) D
Quotations from Chairman Mao Tse-Tung (1968) D
All Over (1971) D
Seascape (1975) D
Counting the Ways (1976) D
Listening (1976) D
The Lady from Dubuque (1979) D
Finding the Sun (1982) D
The Man Who Had Three Arms (1982) D
Walking (1984) D
Three Tall Women (1992) D

ALCOTT, Louisa May (1832–1888)
American novelist and children's author
Hospital Sketches (1863) NF
Moods (1865) F
Little Women (1868) F CH
Good Wives (1869) F CH
An Old-Fashioned Girl (1870) F CH
Little Men (1871) F CH
Work (1873) F CH
Eight Cousins; or, The Aunt-Hill (1875) F CH
Rose in Bloom (1876) F CH
A Modern Mephistopheles (1877) F
Under the Lilacs (1878) F CH
Jack and Jill (1880) F CH
Spinning-Wheel Stories (1884) F CH
Jo's Boys, and How They Turned Out (1886) F CH

ALDINGTON, Richard [Edward Godfrey Aldington] (1892–1962)
British poet, critic, and novelist
Images 1910–15 (1915) V
Images of Desire (1919) V
Images of War (1919) V
Exile, and Other Poems (1923) V
A Fool i' the Forest (1925) V
French Studies and Reviews (1926) NF
Death of a Hero (1929) F
Roads to Glory (1930) F SS
The Colonel's Daughter (1931) F
Stepping Heavenward (1931) F
Soft Answers (1932) F SS
All Men Are Enemies (1933) F
The Eaten Heart, and Other Poems (1933) V
Women Must Work (1934) F
Life Quest (1935) V
The Crystal World (1937) V
Very Heaven (1937) F
Portrait of a Genius, But . . . (1950) NF
Lawrence of Arabia (1955) NF

ALDISS, Brian Wilson (1925–)
British novelist and short-story writer
The Brightfount Diaries (1955) F
Space, Time, and Nathaniel (1957) F SS
Non-Stop (1958) F
The Canopy of Time (1959) F SS
The Airs of Earth (1963) F SS
The Dark Light Years (1964) F
Earthworks (1965) F
The Saliva Tree, and Other Strange Growths (1966) F SS
An Age (1967) F
Report on Probability A (1968) F
Barefoot in the Head (1969) F
The Hand-Reared Boy (1970) F
The Moment of Eclipse (1971) F SS
A Soldier Erect (1971) F
Billion Year Spree (1973) NF
Frankenstein Unbound (1974) F SS
The Malacia Tapestry (1976) F
Enemies of the System (1978) F
A Rude Awakening (1978) F
Moreau's Other Island (1980) F
Helliconia Spring (1982) F
Helliconia Summer (1983) F
Helliconia Winter (1985) F
Ruins (1987) F
Forgotten Life (1988) F
Bury My Heart at W.H. Smith's (1990) NF
Dracula Unbound (1991) F
Remembrance Day (1993) F
The Detached Retina (1994) NF
Somewhere East of Life (1995) F
Forgotten Life (1998) F
Life in the West (1998) F
The Twinkling of an Eye: My Life as an Englishman (1998) NF

ALDRICH, Thomas Bailey (1836–1907)
American novelist, poet, and journalist
The Bells (1855) V
Pampinea (1861) V
The Story of a Bad Boy (1870) F
Marjorie Daw and Other People (1873) F SS
Cloth of Gold (1874) V
Prudence Palfry (1874) F
Flower and Thorn (1877) V
The Queen of Sheba (1877) F
The Stillwater Tragedy (1880) F
Friar Jerome's Beautiful Book (1881) V
From Ponkapog to Pesth (1883) NF
Mercedes, and Later Lyrics (1884) V
Wyndham Towers (1890) V
An Old Town by the Sea (1893) NF
Two Bites at a Cherry, with Other Tales (1894) F SS
Judith and Holofernes (1896) V
Ponkapog Papers (1903) NF

ALEXANDER, Mrs A[nnie] H[ector], *née* French (1825–1902)
British novelist
Kate Vernon (1854) F
Agnes Waring (1856) F
Look Before You Leap (1865) F
The Wooing O't (1873) F
Ralph Wilton's Weird (1875) F
Her Dearest Foe (1876) F
A Life Interest (1888) F
The Snare of the Fowler (1892) F
A Ward of Chancery (1894) F
Barbara, Lady's Maid and Peeress (1897) F
Brown, V.C. (1899) F
Through Fire to Fortune (1900) F
Kitty Costello (1904) F
The Crumpled Leaf (1911) F

ALEXANDER, Mrs C[ecil] F[rances] (1818–1895)
British poet and hymn-writer
The Baron's Little Daughter, and Other Tales (1848) F
Hymns for Little Children (1848) V
The Lord of the Forest and His Vassals (1848) V
Moral Songs (1849) V
Narrative Hymns for Village Schools (1853) V
Hymns Descriptive and Devotional for the Use of School (1858) V
The Legend of the Golden Prayers, and Other Poems (1859) V

ALEXANDER, Sir William, Earl of Stirling (1567?–1640)
Scottish poet
The Tragedy of Darius (1603) D
Aurora (1604) V
The Monarchick Tragedies (1604) D
A Paraenesis to the Prince (1604) V
An Elegy on the Death of Prince Henry (1612) V
Doomsday; or, The Great Day of the Lord's Judgement (1614) V
An Encouragement to Colonies (1624) NF
Recreations with the Muses (1637) V

ALEXANDER, William (1826–1894)
Scottish novelist
Johnny Gibb of Gushetneuk in the Parish of Pyketillim (1871) F

ALFIERI, Vittorio (1759–1803)
Italian poet and dramatist
Saul (1782) D
On Tyranny (1789) NF

ALGER, Horatio (1832–1899)
American novelist and children's author
Luck and Pluck (1867) F CH
Ragged Dick (1867) F CH
Tattered Tom (1871) F CH

ALGREN, Nelson (1909–1981)
American novelist
Somebody in Boots (1935) F
Never Come Morning (1942) F
The Neon Wilderness (1947) F SS
The Man With the Golden Arm (1949) F
A Walk on the Wild Side (1956) F
The Devil's Stocking (1983) F

ALISON, Archibald (1757–1839)
British clergyman and author
Essays on the Nature and Principles of Taste (1790) NF
Principles of the Criminal Law of Scotland (1832) NF

ALISON, Sir Archibald (1792–1867)
British historian
History of Europe During the French Revolution (1832–1842) NF
Practice of the Criminal Law in Scotland (1833) NF

ALLBEURY, Ted [Theodore Edward le Bouthillier] (1917–)
British spy novelist
A Choice of Enemies (1973) F
Snowball (1974) F
Palomino Blonde [US: *Omega Minus*] (1975) F
Moscow Quadrille (1976) F
The Man with the President's Mind (1977) F
The Alpha List (1979) F
The Other Side of Silence (1981) F
Shadow of Shadows (1982) F
The Judas Factor (1984) F
The Reckoning (1999) F

ALLEN, [Charles] Grant [Blairfindie] (1848–1899)
British novelist and short-story writer
Strange Stories (1884) F SS
For Mamie's Sake (1886) F
In All Shades (1886) F
The Beckoning Hand, and Other Stories (1887) F SS
The Devil's Die (1888) F
This Mortal Coil (1888) F
Dr Palliser's Patient (1889) F
The Tents of Shem (1889) F
Dumaresq's Daughter (1891) F
What's Bred in the Bone (1891) F
The Duchess of Powysland (1892) F
Blood Royal (1893) F
Ivan Greet's Masterpiece, and Other Stories (1893) F SS
The Scallywag (1893) F
An Army Doctor's Romance (1894) F
At Market Value (1894) F
The British Barbarians (1895) F
The Woman Who Did (1895) F
Moorland Idylls (1896) F
A Splendid Sin (1896) F
An African Millionaire (1897) F SS
The Type-Writer Girl (1897) F
The Incidental Bishop (1898) F
Linnet (1898) F
Miss Cayley's Adventures (1899) F
Twelve Tales (1899) F SS
Hilda Wade, Hospital Nurse (1900) F SS

Sir Theodore's Guest, and Other Stories (1902) F SS
Under Sealed Orders (1895) F

ALLEN, James Lane (1849–1925)
American novelist and short-story writer
Flute and Violin (1891) MISC
A Kentucky Cardinal (1894) F
Aftermath (1896) F
Summer in Arcady (1896) F
The Choir Invisible (1897) F
The Reign of Law (1900) F
The Mettle of the Pasture (1903) F
The Bride of the Mistletoe (1909) F
The Doctor's Christmas Eve (1910) F
The Sword of Youth (1915) F
The Kentucky Warbler (1918) F
The Alabaster Box (1923) F
The Landmark (1925) F SS

ALLEN, Paula Gunn (1939–)
American poet, novelist, and critic
The Blind Lion (1974) V
Coyote's Daylight Trip (1978) V
A Cannon Between My Knees (1981) V
Starchild (1981) V
Shadow Country (1982) V
The Woman Who Owned the Shadows (1983) F
Skins and Bones (1988) V
Grandmothers of the Light (1991) V

ALLEN, Walter Ernest (1911–1995)
British novelist and critic
Innocence is Drowned (1938) F
Blind Man's Ditch (1939) F
Living Space (1940) F
The Black Country (1946) F
Rogue Elephant (1946) F
Reading a Novel (1949) NF
Dead Man Over All [US: *The Square Peg*] (1950) F
The English Novel (1954) NF
The Novel Today (1955) NF
All in a Lifetime [US: *Threescore and Ten*] (1959) F
Tradition and Dream (1964) NF
As I Walked Down New Grub Street (1981) NF
The Short Story in English (1981) NF
Accosting Profiles (1989) F

ALLEN, [William] Hervey (1889–1949)
American novelist
Anthony Adverse (1933) F

ALLENDE, Isabel (1942–)
Chilean novelist
The House of the Spirits (1982) F
Of Love and Shadows (1984) F
Eva Luna (1987) F
The Infinite Plan (1993) F
Paula (1995) F
Aphrodite (1998) F
Enduring Spirit (1998) F
Daughter of Fortune (1999) F

ALLINGHAM, Margery [Louise] (1904–1966)
British crime writer
The Crime at Black Dudley [the first Albert Campion mystery] (1929) F
Look to the Lady [US: *The Gyrth Chalice Mystery*] (1931) F
Death of a Ghost (1934) F
Flowers for the Judge [US: *Legacy in Blood*] (1936) F
Dancers in Mourning [US: *Who Killed Chloe?*] (1937) F
The Fashion in Shrouds (1938) F
Traitor's Purse (1941) F
The Tiger in the Smoke (1952) F
The Beckoning Lady [US: *The Estate of the Beckoning Lady*] (1955) F

ALLINGHAM, William ['Giraldus', 'Patricius Walker'] (1824–1889)
British poet and anthologist
Day and Night Songs (1854) V
Peace and War (1854) V
The Music-Master (1855) V
Nightingale Valley [as 'Giraldus'] (1860) V
The Ballad Book (1864) V
Laurence Bloomfield in Ireland (1864) V
Fifty Modern Poems (1865) V
Rambles by Patricius Walker (1873) NF
Evil May-Day (1882) V
The Fairies (1883) V
Rhymes for Young Folk (1887) V
Flower Pieces, and Other Poems (1888) V
Life and Phantasy (1889) V

ALSOP, Mary O'Hara *see* MARY O'HARA

ALTHER, Lisa (1944–)
American novelist
Kinflicks (1976) F
Original Sins (1981) F
Other Women (1985) F
Bedrock (1990) F
Five Minutes in Heaven (1995) F

ALVAREZ, Alfred (1929–)
British critic, poet, and novelist
The End of It (1958) V
The Shaping Spirit (1958) NF
The New Poetry (1962) ANTH
The School of Donne (1962) NF
Beyond All This Fiddle (1968) NF
Apparition (1971) V
The Savage God (1971) NF
The Legacy (1972) V
Her (1974) F
Autumn to Autumn and Selected Poems 1953–1976 (1978) V
Hunt (1978) F
The Day of Atonement (1991) F

AMADI, Elechi (1934–)
Nigerian novelist and dramatist
The Concubine (1966) F
The Great Ponds (1969) F

The Slave (1978) F
Estrangement (1986) F

AMBLER, Eric (1909–1998)
British thriller writer
The Dark Frontier (1936) F
Uncommon Danger [US: *Background to Danger*] (1937) F
Cause for Alarm (1938) F
Epitaph for a Spy (1938) F
The Mask of Dimitrios [US: *A Coffin for Dimitrios*] (1939) F
Journey into Fear (1940) F
Judgement on Deltchev (1951) F
The Schirmer Inheritance (1953) F
The Night-Comers [US: *State of Siege*] (1956) F
Passage of Arms (1959) F
The Light of Day [US: *Topkapi*] (1962) F
A Kind of Anger (1964) F
Dirty Story (1967) F
The Intercom Conspiracy (1970) F
The Levanter (1972) F
Doctor Frigo (1974) F
Send No More Roses [US: *The Siege of Villa Lipp*] (1977) F
The Care of Time (1981) F

AMIS, [Sir] Kingsley William (1922–1995)
British novelist, poet, and short-story writer
Bright November (1947) V
Lucky Jim (1953) F
That Uncertain Feeling (1955) F
A Case of Samples (1956) V
I Like It Here (1958) F
Take a Girl Like You (1960) F
New Maps of Hell (1961) NF
The Evans Country (1962) V
One Fat Englishman (1963) F
The James Bond Dossier (1965) NF
The Anti-Death League (1966) F
A Look Round the Estate (1967) V
Colonel Sun (1968) F
I Want It Now (1968) F
The Green Man (1969) F
What Became of Jane Austen? and Other Questions (1970) NF
Girl, 20 (1971) F
The Riverside Villas Murder (1973) F
Ending Up (1974) F
The Alteration (1976) F
Jake's Thing (1978) F
The New Oxford Book of Light Verse (1978) ANTH
Russian Hide-and-Seek (1980) F
Stanley and the Women (1984) F
The Old Devils (1986) F
Difficulties With Girls (1988) F
The Folks That Live on the Hill (1990) F
Memoirs (1990) NF
The Russian Girl (1992) F
Mr Barrett's Secret, and Other Stories (1993) F SS
You Can't Do Both (1994) F
The Biographer's Moustache (1995) F

AMIS, Martin [Louis] (1949–)
British novelist
The Rachel Papers (1973) F
Dead Babies (1975) F
Success (1978) F
Other People (1981) F
Money (1984) F
The Moronic Inferno, and Other Visits to America (1986) NF
Einstein's Monsters (1987) F SS
London Fields (1989) F
Time's Arrow (1991) F
Visiting Mrs Nabokov and other Excursions (1993) NF
The Information (1995) F
Night Train (1997) F
Heavy Water, and Other Stories (1998) F SS
Experience [memoirs] (2000) NF

AMMONS, A[rchie] R[andolph] (1926–)
American poet
Ommateum with Doxology (1955) V
Expressions of Sea Level (1964) V
Corsons Inlet (1965) V
Northfield Poems (1965) V
Tapes for the Turn of the Year (1965) V
Uplands (1970) V
Briefings (1971) V
Sphere: The Form of a Motion (1974) V
Diversifications (1975) V
Highgate Road (1977) V
The Snow Poems (1977) V
A Coast of Trees (1981) V
Worldly Hopes (1982) V
Lake Effect Country (1983) V
Sumerian Vistas (1987) V
Garbage (1993) V

AMORY, Thomas (1691?–1788)
Irish novelist
Memoirs: Containing the Lives of Several Ladies of Great Britain (1755) F
The Life of John Buncle, Esq. (1756) F

ANAND, Mulk Raj (1905–)
Indian novelist, short-story writer, and critic
The Lost Child, and Other Stories (1934) F SS
Untouchable (1935) F
The Coolie (1936) F
Two Leaves and a Bud (1937) F
Lament on the Death of a Master of Arts (1939) F
The Village (1939) F
Across the Black Waters (1940) F
The Sword and the Sickle (1942) F
India Speaks (1943) D
The Barber's Trade Union, and Other Stories (1944) F SS
The Big Heart (1945) F
Reflections on the Golden Bed (1947) F SS
The Tractor and the Corn Goddess, and Other Stories (1947) F SS
Seven Summers (1951) F
Private Life of an Indian Prince (1953) F

The Power of Darkness, and Other Stories (1958) F SS
The Old Woman and the Cow [repub. as *Gauri*, 1960] (1960) F
The Road (1961) F
Death of a Hero (1963) F
Lajwanti, and Other Stories (1966) F SS
Morning Face (1968) F
Between Tears and Laughter (1973) F SS
Confession of a Lover (1976) F
Conversations in Bloomsbury (1981) NF
The Bubble (1984) F
Little Plays of Mahatma Gandhi (1990) D

ANDERSEN, Hans Christian (1805–1875)
Danish writer of fairy tales
The Improvasitore [Eng. trn, 1845] (1835) F
Tales Told for Children (1835) F SS

ANDERSON, Jessica (1925–)
Australian novelist
An Ordinary Lunacy (1963) F
The Last Man's Head (1970) F
The Commandmant (1975) F
Tirra Lirra by the River (1978) F
The Impersonators [US: *The Only Daughter*] (1980) F
Stories From the Warm Zone (1987) F SS
Taking Shelter (1989) F

ANDERSON, Maxwell (1888–1959)
American dramatist and journalist
White Desert (1923) D
What Price Glory? (1924) D
The Buccaneer (1925) D
First Flight (1925) D
You Who Have Dreams (1925) V
Saturday's Children (1927) D
Gods of the Lightning (1928) D
Elizabeth the Queen (1930) D
Night Over Taos (1932) D
Both Your Houses (1933) D
Mary of Scotland (1933) D
Valley Forge (1934) D
Winterset (1935) D
The Masque of Kings (1936) D
The Wingless Victory (1936) D
High Tor (1937) D
The Star Wagon (1937) D
Knickerbocker Holiday [music by Kurt Weill] (1938) D
Key Largo (1939) D
Journey to Jerusalem (1940) D
Candle in the Wind (1941) D
The Eve of St Mark (1942) D
Storm Operation (1944) D
Joan of Lorraine (1947) D
Anne of the Thousand Days (1948) D
Lost in the Stars (1948) D
Barefoot in Athens (1951) D
The Bad Seed (1955) D

ANDERSON, Robert W[oodruff] (1917–)
American dramatist and novelist
All Summer Long (1953) D
Tea and Sympathy (1953) D
Silent Night, Lonely Night (1959) D
The Days Between (1965) D
You Know I Can't Hear You When the Water's Running (1967) D
I Never Sang for My Father (1968) D
Solitaire/Double Solitaire (1971) D
After (1973) F
Getting Up and Going Home (1978) F
Free and Clear (1983) D

ANDERSON, Sherwood (1876–1941)
American novelist and short-story writer
Windy McPherson's Son (1916) F
Marching Men (1917) F
Mid-American Chants (1918) V
Winesburg, Ohio (1919) F SS
Poor White (1920) F
The Triumph of the Egg (1921) F SS
Horses and Men (1923) F SS
Many Marriages (1923) F
Dark Laughter (1925) F
Tar: A Midwest Childhood [fictionalized autobiography] (1926) F
Alice and the Lost Novel (1929) F SS
Hello Towns! (1929) NF
Nearer the Grass Roots (1929) NF
Perhaps Women (1931) NF
Beyond Desire (1932) F
Death in the Woods (1933) F SS
Kit Brandon (1936) F
Home Town (1940) NF

ANDREWES, Lancelot (1555–1626)
British prelate and scholar
The Wonderful Combat Between Christ and Satan (1592) NF
Scala Coeli (1611) NF
Institutiones Piae; or, Directions to Pray (1630) NF
A Pattern of Catechistical Doctrine (1630) NF
The Moral Law Expounded (1642) NF
The Private Devotions [*Preces Privatae*] (1647) NF

ANDREWS, Cicily Isabel *see* REBECCA WEST

ANDREWS, Virginia (1933–1986)
American novelist
Flowers in the Attic (1979) F
Petals on the Wind (1980) F
If There Be Thorns (1981) F

ANGELOU, Maya (1928–)
American autobiographer, poet, and dramatist
I Know Why the Caged Bird Sings (1970) NF
Just Give Me a Cool Drink of Water 'fore I Die (1971) V
Gather Together in My Name (1974) NF
Oh Pray My Wings Are Gonna Fit Me Well (1975) V
Singin' and Swingin' and Gettin' Merry Like Christmas (1976) NF

And Still I Rise (1978) V
The Heart of a Woman (1981) NF
Shaker, Why Don't You Sing? (1983) V
All God's Children Need Traveling Shoes (1986) NF
Now Sheba Sings the Song (1987) V
I Shall Not Be Moved (1990) V
On the Pulse of the Morning (1993) V
Wouldn't Take Nothing For My Journey Now (1993) NF

ANOUILH, Jean (1910–1987)
French dramatist
The Ermine [*L'Hermine*] (1932) D
Traveller Without Luggage [*Le Voyageur sans bagage*] (1937) D
The Restless Heart [*La Sauvage*] (1938) D
The Thieves' Carnival [*Le Bal des Voleurs*] (1938) D
Léocadia (1940) D
Antigone (1944) D
Medea [*Médée*] (1946) D
Roméo et Jeannette (1946) D
Ring Round the Moon [*L'invitation au chàteau*] (1947) D
Ardèle (1948) D
The Rehearsal [*La Répétition*] (1950) D
Colombe (1951) D
Waltz of the Toreadors [*La Valse des toréadors*] (1952) D
The Lark [*L'Alouette*] (1953) D
Ornifle (1955) D
Poor Bitos [*Pauvre Bitos*] (1956) D
Becket (1959) D
Dear Antoine [*Cher Antoine*] (1969) D
The Arrest [*L'Arrestation*] (1974) D

ANSTEY, Christopher (1724–1805)
British poet and satirist
The New Bath Guide (1766) V
Speculation; or, A Defence of Mankind (1780) V
Liberality; or, The Decay'd Macaroni (1788) D
The Farmer's Daughter (1795) V
The Monopolist; or, The Installation of Sir John Barleycorn, Knight (1795) V

'ANSTEY, F.' [Thomas Anstey Guthrie] (1856–1934)
British novelist and humorist
Vice Versa; or, A Lesson to Fathers (1882) F
The Black Poodle, and Other Tales (1884) F SS
The Giant's Robe (1884) F
The Tinted Venus (1885) F
A Fallen Idol (1886) F
The Pariah (1889) F
Voces Populi [1st ser.] (1890) F
Tourmalin's Time Cheques (1891) F
The Talking Horse, and Other Tales (1892) F SS
The Travelling Companions (1892) F
The Man From Blankley's, and Other Sketches (1893) F SS
Mr Punch's Pocket Ibsen (1893) MISC
Under the Rose (1894) F
Lyre and Lancet (1895) F
Baboo Jabberjee, B.A. (1897) F
Puppets at Large (1897) NF
Love Among the Lions (1898) F
Paleface and Redskin, and Other Stories for Boys and Girls (1898) F CH
The Brass Bottle (1900) F
A Bayard from Bengal (1902) F
Salted Almonds (1906) F
In Brief Authority (1915) F
A Long Retrospect (1936) NF

'ANTHONY, Evelyn' [Evelyn Bridget Patricia Ward-Thomas, *née* Stephens] (1928–)
British historical novelist
Imperial Highness (1953) F
Elizabeth (1960) F
Victoria (1960) F
Clandara (1963) F
Assassin (1970) F
The Tamarind Seed (1971) F
The Poellenberg Inheritance (1972) F
The Occupying Power (1973) F
The Grave of Truth (1979) F
No Enemy But Time (1987) F

ANTHONY, Michael (1932–)
Trinidadian novelist
The Games Were Coming (1963) F
The Year in San Fernando (1965) F
Green Days by the River (1967) F
Cricket in the Road, and Other Stories (1973) F SS
Streets of Conflict (1976) F
All That Glitters (1981) F

'APOLLINAIRE, Guillaume' [Wilhelm de Kostrowitsky] (1880–1918)
French poet and art critic
The Decaying Magician [*L'Enchanteur pourrissant*] (1909) V
Le Bestiaire ['The Bestiary'] (1911) V
Alcools (1913) V
Les Peintres cubistes ['The Cubist Painters'] (1913) NF
Calligrammes (1918) V
Les Mamelles de Tirésias ['The Breasts of Tiresias'] (1918) V D
L'Esprit nouveau et les poètes ['The New Spirit and the Poets'] (1946) NF

APPERLEY, Charles James [Nimrod] (1779–1843)
British sporting writer
Nimrod's Hunting Tours (1835) NF
Nimrod's Northern Tour (1838) NF
Hunting Reminiscences (1842) NF
The Life of a Sportsman (1842) NF

APULEIUS, Lucius (fl. *c.* AD 155)
Roman author
Metamorphoses [English trn as *The Golden Ass*] (1566) F

AQUINAS, St Thomas (*c.* 1225–1274)
Italian philosopher and theologian
Summa Contra Gentiles NF
Summa Theologica [written 1265-after 1271] NF

ARAGON, Louis (1897–1982)
French poet, novelist, essayist, and journalist
Feu de joie ['Bonfire'] (1921) F
Les Aventures de Télémaque (1922) F
Le Mouvement perpétuel ['Perpetual Motion'] (1926) V
Le Paysan de Paris ['The Peasant of Paris'] (1926) F
Traité du style ['Treatise on Style] (1928) NF
Le Crève-Coeur ['Heartbreak'] (1941) V
Cantique à Elsa ['Song to Elsa'] (1942) V
Les Yeux d'Elsa ['Elsa's Eyes'] (1942) V
Aurélien (1944) F
Elsa (1959) V
Blanche (1967) F

ARBUTHNOT, John (1667–1735)
British medical writer, essayist, dramatist, and miscellaneous writer
'The History of John Bull' [5 separate pamphlets] (1712) NF
The Memoirs of the Extraordinary Life, Works and Discoveries of Martinus Scriblerus (1741) NF

ARCHER, Jeffrey [Howard] (1940–)
British popular novelist
Not a Penny More, Not a Penny Less (1976) F
Shall We Tell the President? (1976) F
Kane and Abel (1979) F
First Among Equals (1984) F
Honour Among Thieves (1993) F
Twelve Red Herrings (1994) F SS
The Proprietors (1996) F
To Cut a Long Story Short (2000) F

ARCHER, William (1856–1924)
British dramatic critic and journalist
English Dramatists of Today (1882) NF
Henry Irving, Actor and Manager (1883) NF
About the Theatre (1886) NF
Masks or Faces? (1888) NF
The Theatrical 'World' (1895) NF
Play-Making (1912) NF
God and Mr Wells (1917) NF
The Green Goddess (1921) D
The Old Drama and the New (1923) NF

ARDEN, John (1930–)
British dramatist and novelist
The Waters of Babylon (1957) D
Serjeant Musgrave's Dance (1959) D
The Workhouse Donkey (1963) D
Armstrong's Last Goodnight (1964) D
Left-Handed Liberty (1965) D
The Hero Rises Up (1968) D
The Island of the Mighty (1972) D
The Non-Stop Connolly Show (1977) D
To Present the Pretence (1977) NF
Silence Among the Weapons (1982) F HF
Books of Bale (1988) F
Cogs Tyrannic (1991) F SS
Jack Juggler and the Emperor's Whore (1996) F SS

ARIOSTO, Ludovico (1474–1535)
Italian poet
The Pretenders [*I Suppositi*] (1509) D
Orlando Furioso (1516–32) V

ARISTOPHANES (*c.* 445–*c.* 385 BC)
Greek comic poet
The Archarnians (425 BC) D
The Knights (424 BC) D
The Clouds (423 BC) D
The Wasps (422 BC) D
Peace (421 BC) D
The Birds (414 BC) D
Lysistrata (411 BC) D
Thesmophoriazusae (411 BC) D
The Frogs (405 BC) D
Plutus (382 BC) D

ARISTOTLE (384–322 BC)
Greek philosopher
Organon [6 treatises] NF
Metaphysics NF
Nicomachean Ethics NF
Eudemian Ethics NF
Politics NF
Rhetoric NF
On the Heavens NF
Historia animalium NF
On the Soul NF

ARLEN, Michael [Dikran Kouyoumdjian] (1895–1956)
Anglo-Armenian novelist and short-story writer
The London Venture (1920) F
The Romantic Lady, and Other Stories (1921) F SS
These Charming People (1923) F SS
The Green Hat (1924) F
May Fair (1925) F SS
Men Dislike Women (1931) F
Hell! Said the Duchess (1934) F
The Crooked Coronet, and Other Misrepresentations of the Real Facts of Life (1937) F SS

ARMIN, Robert (1565?–1610)
English actor and dramatist
Fool upon Fool; or, Six Sorts of Sotts (1600) F
Quips upon Questions; or, A Clown's Conceit on Occasion Offered (1600) V
A Nest of Ninnies (1608) D
The History of the Two Maids of More-clack (1609) D
The Italian Taylor, and his Boy (1609) V

ARMITAGE, Simon (1963–)
British poet
Zoom! (1989) V
Kid (1992) V
Xanadu (1992) Poem film
Book of Matches (1993) V
The Dead Sea Poems (1995) V
CloudCuckooLand (1997) V
All Points North (1998) NF

Killing Time (1999) V
Short and Sweet (1999) V

ARMSTRONG, John (1709–1779)
British physician and poet
The Economy of Love (1736) V
The Art of Preserving Health (1744) V
Taste (1753) V
A Day (1761) V

ARMSTRONG, Terence Ian Fytton *see* JOHN GAWSWORTH

ARNOLD, Dr Thomas (1795–1842)
British schoolmaster, religious writer, and historian
Principles of Church Reform (1833) NF
History of Rome (1838–43) NF

ARNOLD, Sir Edwin (1832–1904)
British poet and translator
The Feast of Belshazzar (1852) V
Griselda: A Tragedy; and Other Poems (1856) V
The Wreck of the Northern Belle (1857) V
The Light of Asia; or, The Great Renunciation (1879) V
Pearls of the Faith; or, Islam's Rosary (1883) V
With Sa'di in the Garden; or, The Book of Love (1888) V
The Light of the World; or, The Great Consummation (1891) V
Potiphar's Wife, and Other Poems (1892) V
Adzuma; or, The Japanese Wife (1893) D
The Tenth Muse, and Other Poems (1895) V
The Voyage of Ithobal (1901) V

ARNOLD, Edwin Lester [Linden] (1857–1935)
British novelist
The Wonderful Adventures of Phra the Phonecian (1891) F
The Constable of St Nicholas (1894) F
The Story of Ulla, and Other Tales (1895) F SS
Lepidus the Centurion (1901) F
Lieut. Gulliver Jones, His Vacation (1905) F

ARNOLD, Matthew (1822–1888)
British poet and critic
Alaric at Rome (1840) V
Cromwell (1843) V
The Strayed Reveller, and Other Poems (1849) V
Empedocles on Etna, and Other Poems (1852) V
Poems: A New Edition (1853) V
Poems: Second Series (1855) V
Merope (1858) V
England and the Italian Question (1859) NF
On Translating Homer (1861) NF
On Translating Homer: Last Words (1862) NF
A French Eton; or, Middle Class Education and the State (1864) NF
Essays in Criticism [1st ser.] (1865) NF
New Poems (1867) V
On the Study of Celtic Literature (1867) NF
Schools and Universities on the Continent (1868) NF
Culture and Anarchy (1869) NF
St Paul and Protestantism (1870) NF
Friendship's Garland (1871) NF
Literature and Dogma (1873) NF
God and the Bible (1875) NF
Last Essays on Church and Religion (1877) NF
Mixed Essays (1879) NF
Irish Essays, and Others (1882) NF
Discourses in America (1885) NF
Essays in Criticism [2nd ser.] (1888) NF
Essays in Criticism: Third Series (1910) NF

ARNOLD, William Delafield (1828–1859)
Anglo-Indian official and novelist
Oakfield; or, Fellowship in the East [by 'Punjabee'] (1853) F

ARNOW, Harriette (1908–1986)
American novelist
The Mountain Path (1936) F
The Hunter's Horn (1949) F
The Dollmaker (1954) F

ARTAUD, Antonin (1896–1948)
French actor, director, and dramatic theorist
L'Ombilic des limbes [*The Umbilicus of Limbo*] (1925) V
The Theatre and its Double [*Le Thétre et son double*] (1938) NF

ASCHAM, Roger (1515–1568)
British author
Toxophilus (1545) NF
The Schoolmaster (1570) NF

ASH, John (1948–)
British poet
Casino (1978) V
The Bed, and Other Poems (1981) V
The Branching Stairs (1984) V
The Burnt Pages (1991) V

ASHBERY, John [Lawrence] (1927–)
American poet
Turandot (1953) V
Some Trees (1956) V
The Tennis Court Oath (1962) V
Rivers and Mountains (1966) V
Sunrise in Suburbia (1968) V
Fragment (1969) V
A Nest of Ninnies (1969) F
The Double Dream of Spring (1970) V
Self-Portrait in a Convex Mirror (1975) V
Houseboat Days (1977) V
As We Know (1979) V
Shadow Train (1981) V
A Wave (1984) V
April Galleons (1987) V
Flow Chart (1991) V
Hotel Lautréamont (1993) V
Girls on the Run (2000) V

ASHFORD, Daisy [Margaret Mary Julia, later Mrs James Devlin] (1881–1972)
British child author
The Young Visiters [*sic*] (1919) F

ASHLEY, Bernard (1935–)
British children's author
The Trouble with Donovan Croft (1974) F CH

Terry on the Fence (1975) F CH
All My Men (1977) F CH
A Kind of Wild Justice (1978) F CH
Dodgem (1981) F CH
Linda's Lie (1982) F CH
High Pavement Blues (1983) F CH
Janey (1985) F CH
Running Scared (1986) F CH

ASHMOLE, Elias (1617–1692)
English antiquary
Theatrum Chemicum Britannicum [in Latin] (1652) NF
The Way to Bliss (1658) NF
A Catalogue of the Peers of the Kingdome of England (1661) NF
The Institution, Laws and Ceremonies of the Most Noble Order of the Garter (1672) NF
Memoirs of the Life of Elias Ashmole (1717) NF
The Antiquities of Berkshire (1719) NF

ASHTON, Winifred *see* CLEMENCE DANE

ASHTON-WARNER, Sylvia (1908–1984)
New Zealand novelist
Spinster (1958) F
Incense to Idols (1960) F
Teacher (1963) F
Bell Call (1965) F
Greenstone (1966) F
Myself (1967) F

ASIMOV, Isaac (1920–1992)
Russian-born American science fiction author
I, Robot (1950) F SS
Pebble in the Sky (1950) F SS
Foundation (1951) F
The Currents of Space (1952) F
Foundation and Empire (1952) F
Second Foundation (1953) F
The Caves of Steel (1954) F
The End of Eternity (1955) F
The Naked Sun (1957) F
The Gods Themselves (1972) F
The Bicentential Man, and Other Stories (1976) F SS
Foundation's Edge (1982) F
Foundation and Earth (1986) F
Nemesis (1989) F

ASTLEY, Thea (1925–)
Australian novelist
Girl with a Monkey (1958) F
A Descant for Gossips (1960) F
The Well Dressed Explorer (1962) F
The Slow Natives (1965) F
A Boat Load of Home Folk (1968) F
The Acolyte (1972) F
A Kindness Cup (1974) F
Hunting the Wild Pineapple (1979) F SS
An Item From the Late News (1982) F
Beachmasters (1985) F
It's Raining in Mango (1988) F
Reaching Tin River (1990) F
Vanishing Points (1992) F

ATHERSTONE, Edwin (1788–1872)
British poet
The Last Days of Herculaneum (1821) V
A Midsummer Day's Dream (1824) V
The Fall of Nineveh (1828) V
The Sea-Kings in England (1830) F
Israel in Egypt (1861) V

ATHERTON, Gertrude [Franklin], *née* Horn (1857–1948)
American novelist
Before the Gringo Came (1894) F
The Californians [rev. 1935] (1898) F
The Conqueror (1902) F
The Splendid Idle Forties (1902) F
Rezánov (1906) F
Julia France and Her Times (1912) F
The Sisters-in-Law (1921) F
Black Oxen (1923) F

ATWOOD, Margaret [Eleanor] (1939–)
Canadian novelist, poet, short-story writer, and critic
The Circle Game (1966) V
The Animals in That Country (1968) V
The Edible Woman (1969) F
The Journals of Susanna Moodie (1970) V
Procedures for Underground (1970) V
Power Politics (1971) V
Surfacing (1972) F
Survival: A Thematic Guide to Canadian Literature (1972) NF
Lady Oracle (1976) F
Dancing Girls (1977) F SS
Two-Headed Poems (1978) V
Life Before Man (1979) F
Bodily Harm (1981) F
True Stories (1981) V
Bluebeard's Egg, and Other Stories (1983) F SS
Unearthing Suite (1983) F SS
Interlunar (1984) V
The Handmaid's Tale (1985) F
Cat's Eye (1988) F
The Robber Bride (1994) F
Good Bones (1994) F SS
Alias Grace (1996) F
The Blind Assassin (2000) F

AUBIN, Penelope (*c.* 1685–1731)
English novelist
The Life of Madam de Beaumont (1721) F
The Strange Adventures of the Count de Vinevil and his Family (1721) F
The Life and Amorous Adventures of Lucinda (1722) F
The Noble Slaves; or, The Lives and Adventures of Two Lords and Two Ladies (1722) F
The Life of Charlotta du Pont (1723) F
The Life and Adventures of the Lady Lucy (1726) F

The Life and Adventures of Young Count Albertus (1728) F

AUBREY, John (1626–1697)
English antiquary
Miscellanies (1696) NF
Lives of Eminent Men ['Brief Lives'] (1813) NF

AUCHINLOSS, Louis [Stanton] (1917–)
American novelist, short-story writer, and critic
The Indifferent Children (1947) F
The Injustice Collectors (1950) F SS
Sybil (1952) F
A Law for the Lion (1953) F
The Romantic Egoists (1954) F SS
The Great World and Timothy Colt (1956) F
Venus in Sparta (1958) F
Pursuit of the Prodigal (1959) F
The House of Five Talents (1960) F
Portrait in Brownstone (1962) F
The Rector of Justin (1964) F
The Embezzler (1966) F
A World of Profit (1968) F
A Writer's Capital (1974) F
The Dark Lady (1977) F
Watchfires (1982) F
The Book Class (1984) F
Honorable Man (1985) F
Diary of a Yuppie (1986) F
The Golden Calves (1987) F
Skinny Island (1987) F SS
The Lady of Situations (1990) F
Three Lives (1993) F SS

AUDEN, W[ystan] H[ugh] (1907–1973)
British poet, dramatist, and critic
The Orators (1932) V
The Dog Beneath the Skin; or, Where is Francis? (1935) D
The Ascent of F.6 [with Christopher Isherwood] (1936) D
Look, Stranger! (1936) V
Letters From Iceland (1937) NF
On the Frontier (1938) D
Another Time (1940) V
Some Poems (1940) V
New Year Letter [US: *The Double Man*] (1941) V
For the Time Being (1945) V
The Age of Anxiety (1948) V
The Enchafed Flood; or, The Romantic Iconography of the Sea (1951) NF
Nones (1952) V
Homage to Clio (1960) V
The Dyer's Hand, and Other Essays (1963) NF
About the House (1966) V
City Without Walls (1969) V
Secondary Worlds (1969) NF
Academic Graffiti (1971) V
Epistle to a Godson (1972) V
That You Fog: Last Poems (1974) V

AUEL, Jean M[arie], *née* Untinen (1936–)
American novelist
The Clan of the Cave Bear (1980) F
The Valley of Horses (1982) F
The Mammoth Hunters (1985) F
The Plains of Passage (1990) F

AUERBACH, Erich (1892–1957)
German philologist
Mimesis: The Representation of Reality in Western Literature (1953) NF

AUGUSTINE OF HIPPO, St (354–430)
Philosopher and theologian
Confessions (*c.* 400) NF
De Trinitate (400–416) NF
The City of God [*De Civitate Dei*] (413–426) NF

AUSTEN, Jane (1775–1817)
British novelist
Sense and Sensibility (1811) F
Pride and Prejudice (1813) F
Mansfield Park (1814) F
Emma (1815) F
Northanger Abbey; and Persuasion (1818) F
Lady Susan [in J.E. Austen-Leigh's *Memoir*; written 1793–4] (1871) F
The Watsons [in J.E. Austen-Leigh's *Memoir*; written *c.* 1804] (1871) F

AUSTER, Paul (1947–)
American novelist, poet, essayist, and screenwriter
Squeeze Play (1982) F
The Invention of Solitude (1982) NF
City of Glass (1985) F
Ghosts (1986) F
The Locked Room (1986) F
In the Country of Last Things (1987) F
Moon Palace (1989) F
The Music of Chance (1990) F
The Art of Hunger (1991) NF
Leviathan (1992) F
Mr Vertigo (1994) F
Timbuktu (2000) F

AUSTIN, Alfred (1835–1913)
British Poet Laureate and novelist
Five Years of It (1858) F
An Artist's Proof (1864) F
The Poetry of the Period (1870) NF
The Golden Age (1871) V
Interludes (1872) V
The Tower of Babel (1874) V D
The Human Tragedy (1876) V
Leszko the Bastard (1877) V
Savonarola (1881) D
Soliloquies in Song (1882) V
At the Gate of the Convent, and Other Poems (1885) V
Prince Lucifer (1887) V
Fortunatus the Pessimist (1892) D
The Garden That I Love (1894) NF
In Veronica's Garden (1895) NF
The Conversion of Winckelmann, and Other Poems (1897) V
Lamia's Winter-Quarters (1898) V
Songs of England (1898) V
Haunts of Ancient Peace (1902) F

Flodden Field (1903) D
Sacred and Profane Love, and Other Poems (1908) V

AUSTIN, J[ohn] L[angshaw] (1911–1960)
British philosopher
How to Do Things with Words (1962) NF
Sense and Sensibilia (1962) NF

AUSTIN, Mary (1868–1934)
American novelist and essayist
The Land of Little Rain (1903) NF
Isidro (1905) F
Santa Lucia (1908) F
A Woman of Genius (1912) F
The Ford (1917) F

AVERY, Gillian [Elise] (1926–)
British children's writer
The Warden's Niece (1957) F CH
Trespassers at Charlecote (1958) F CH
James Without Thomas (1959) F CH
The Elephant War (1960) F CH
To Tame a Sister (1961) F CH
The Greatest Gresham (1962) F CH
The Peacock House (1963) F CH
The Italian Spring (1964) F CH
Call of the Valley (1968) F CH
Ellen's Birthday (1971) F CH
A Likely Lad (1971) F CH
Ellen and the Queen (1972) F CH
The Lost Railway (1980) F
Onlookers (1983) F

AVISON, Margaret [Kirkland] (1918–)
Canadian poet
Winter Sun (1960) V
The Dumbfounding (1966) V
Sunblue (1978) V
No Time (1990) V

AWDRY, Revd W[ilbert] V[ere] (1911–1997)
British children's author
The Three Railway Engines (1945) F CH
Thomas, the Tank Engine (1946) F CH
James, the Red Engine (1948) F CH
Henry, the Green Engine (1951) F CH
Toby, the Tram Engine (1952) F CH
Gordon, the Big Engine (1953) F CH
Edward, the Blue Engine (1954) F CH
Percy, the Small Engine (1956) F CH
Oliver, the Western Engine (1969) F CH
Duke, the Lost Engine (1970) F CH

AYCKBOURN, Alan (1939–)
British dramatist and children's author
Relatively Speaking (1965) D
How the Other Half Loves (1969) D
Time and Time Again (1971) D
The Norman Conquests [*Table Manners*; *Living Together*; *Round and Round the Garden*] (1973) D
Sisterly Feelings, [and] *Taking Steps* (1979) D
Way Upstream (1982) D
A Chorus of Disapproval (1984) D
Woman in Mind (1985) D
A Small Family Business (1987) D
Man of the Moment (1988) D
The Revenger's Comedies (1989) D
Wildest Dreams (1991) D
Time of My Life (1992) D
Communicating Doors (1995) D
Things We Do for Love (1998) D

AYER, [Sir] Alfred Jules (1910–1989)
British philosopher
Language, Truth and Logic (1936) NF
The Foundations of Empirical Knowledge (1940) NF
The Problem of Knowledge (1956) NF
The Concept of the Person, and Other Essays (1963) NF
Metaphysics and Common Sense (1969) NF
The Central Questions of Philosophy (1973) NF

AYRES, Pam (1947–)
British poet and children's writer
Some of Me Poetry (1976) V
Some More of Me Poetry (1976) V
Thoughts of a Late-Night Knitter (1978) V
Bertha and the Racing Pigeon (1979) F CH
The Ballad of Bill Spinks' Bedstead (1981) V
The Crater (1992) F CH

AYRES, Ruby Mildred, later Pocock (1883–1955)
British novelist
Castles in Spain (1912) NF
Richard Chatterton, VC (1915) F
Paper Roses (1916) F
For Love (1918) F
The One Who Forgot (1919) F
The Woman Hater (1920) F
The Love of Robert Dennison (1921) F

AYTOUN, William Edmonstoune [Bon Gaultier] (1813–1865)
British poet, parodist, and novelist
Poland, Homer, and Other Poems (1832) V
The Book of Ballads (1845) V
Lays of the Scottish Cavaliers, and Other Poems (1849) V
Firmilian; or, The Student of Badajoz (1854) V
Bothwell (1856) V
The Ballads of Scotland (1858) V
Poems and Ballads of Goethe (1859) V
Norman Sinclair (1861) F

B

BABBIT, Irving (1865–1933)
American critic
Literature and the American College (1908) NF
The New Laokoon (1910) NF
Masters of Modern French Criticism (1912) NF
Rousseau and Romanticism (1919) NF
Democracy and Leadership (1924) NF
On Being Creative (1932) NF
The Spanish Character, and Other Essays (1932) NF

BACON, Francis, Baron Verulam, Viscount St Albans (1561–1626)
English statesman and philosopher
Essays (1597) NF
The Advancement of Learning, Divine and Human (1605) NF
Essays (1612) NF
The Wisdom of the Ancients (1619) NF
Novum Organum (1620) NF
The History of the Reign of King Henry the Seventh (1622) NF
Apophthegms New and Old (1625) NF
The Essays or Counsels, Civil and Moral (1625) NF
Sylva Sylvarum; or, A Natural History [inc. *The New Atlantis*; pub. sep. 1627] (1626) NF
The New Atlantis (1627) F
The Elements of the Common Laws of England (1630) NF
The History of Life and Death (1638) NF
The Confession of Faith (1641) NF
The Felicity of Queen Elizabeth and Her Times (1651) NF
The Natural and Experimental History of Winds (1653) NF

BAGE, Robert (1728–1801)
British novelist
Mount Henneth (1781) F
Barham Downs (1784) F
The Fair Syrian (1787) F
James Wallace (1788) F
Man as He Is (1792) F
Hermsprong; or, Man as He is Not (1796) F

BAGEHOT, Walter (1826–1877)
British economist, historian, and critic
Estimates of Some Englishmen and Scotchmen (1858) NF
Parliamentary Reform (1859) NF
The History of the Unreformed Parliament and its Lessons (1860) NF
Count Your Enemies and Economise Your Expenditure (1862) NF
The English Constitution (1867) NF
Physics and Politics; or, Thoughts on the Application of the Principles of 'Natural Selection' and 'Inheritance' to Political Society (1872) NF
Lombard Street (1873) NF
Literary Studies (1879) NF
Economic Studies (1880) NF
Biographical Studies (1881) NF

BAGLEY, Desmond (1923–1983)
British thriller writer
The Golden Keel (1963) F
Wyatt's Hurricane (1966) F
Landslide (1967) F
The Vivero Letter (1968) F
The Spoilers (1969) F
Running Blind (1970) F
The Freedom Trap (1971) F
The Tightrope Men (1973) F
The Snow Tiger (1975) F
The Enemy (1978) F
Flyaway (1979) F
Bahama Crisis (1980) F
Windfall (1982) F
A Diary Without Dates (1918) NF

BAGNOLD, Edith [Algerine] [Lady Jones] (1889–1981)
British dramatist, novelist, and poet
The Sailing Ships, and Other Poems (1918) V
The Happy Foreigner (1920) F
Serena Blandish; or, The Difficulty of Getting Married (1924) F
Alice and Thomas and Jane (1930) F
'National Velvet' (1935) F
The Squire (1938) F
The Loved and Envied (1951) F
The Chalk Garden (1956) D

BAIL, Murray (1941–)
Australian short-story writer and novelist
Contemporary Portraits, and Other Stories (1975) F SS
Homesickness (1980) F
Holden's Performance (1987) F
Longhand (1989) NF

BAILEY, H[enry] C[hristopher] (1878–1961)
British novelist
My Lady of Orange (1901) F
Karl of Erbach (1903) F
The Master of Gray (1903) F
Raoul, Gentleman of Fortune (1907) F
Springtime (1907) F
Colonel Stow (1908) F
The God of Clay (1908) F
Storm and Treasure (1910) F
The Lonely Queen (1911) F
The Suburban (1912) F
The Gentleman Adventurer (1914) F
The Highwayman (1915) F
Call Mr Fortune (1920) F SS
Mr Fortune's Practice (1923) F SS
Garstons (1930) F
Mr Fortune Objects (1935) F SS
The Great Game (1939) F
The Bishop's Crime (1940) F

BAILEY, Hilary (1936–)
British novelist, short-story writer, and critic
Polly Put the Kettle On (1975) F
All the Days of My Life (1984) F
As Time Goes By (1988) F
Connections (2000) F

BAILEY, Nathan or Nathaniel (d. *c.* 1742)
English dictionary compiler
An Universal Etymological Dictionary (1721) NF

BAILEY, Paul (1937–)
British novelist and critic
At the Jerusalem (1967) F
Trespasses (1970) F
A Distant Likeness (1973) F

Peter Smart's Confessions (1977) F
Old Soldiers (1980) F
An English Madam (1982) NF
Gabriel's Lament (1986) F
An Immaculate Mistake (1990) NF
Sugar Cane (1993) F
Kitty and Virgil (1998) F

BAILEY, Philip James (1816–1902)
British poet
Festus (1839) V
The Angel World, and Other Poems (1850) V
The Mystic, and Other Poems (1855) V
The Age (1858) V
Universal Hymn (1867) V

BAILLIE, Joanna (1762–1851)
British poet and dramatist
Plays on the Passions (1798, 1802, 1812) D
De Montfort (1807) D
The Family Legend (1810) D
Metrical Legends of Exalted Characters (1821) V
The Martyr (1826) D
The Bride (1828) D

BAIN, Alexander (1818–1903)
Scottish philosopher and founder-editor of *Mind*
The Senses and the Intellect (1855) NF
The Emotions and the Will (1859) NF
Mental and Moral Science (1868) NF
Mind and Body (1873) NF

BAINBRIDGE, Beryl [Margaret] (1934–)
British novelist
A Weekend with Claude (1967) F
Another Part of the Wood (1969) F
Harriet Said . . . (1972) F
The Dressmaker (1973) F
The Bottle Factory Outing (1974) F
Sweet William (1975) F
A Quiet Life (1976) F
Injury Time (1977) F
Young Adolf (1978) F
Winter Garden (1980) F
Watson's Apology (1984) F
Mum and Mr Armitage (1985) F SS
Filthy Lucre (1986) F
An Awfully Big Adventure (1989) F
The Birthday Boys (1991) F
Every Man for Himself (1996) F
Master Georgie (1998) F
According to Queenie (2000) F

BAKER, 'Augustine' [originally **David]** (1575–1641)
English mystic
Sancta Sophia; or, Directions for the Prayer of Contemplation (1657) NF

BAKER, Nicholson (1957–)
American novelist
The Mezzanine (1989) F
Room Temperature (1990) F
U and I (1991) NF
Vox (1992) F
The Fermata (1994) F
The Size of Thoughts (1996) NF

BAKER, Sir Samuel White (1821–1893)
British explorer and author
The Rifle and Hound in Ceylon (1854) NF
Eight Years' Wanderings in Ceylon (1855) NF
The Nile Tributaries of Abbyssinia, and the Sword Hunters of the Hamran Arabs (1867) NF
Cast Up by the Sea (1868) F
Ismailia (1874) NF

BALCHIN, Nigel [Marlin] (1908–1970)
British novelist
Lightbody on Liberty (1936) F
Darkness Falls From the Air (1942) F
The Small Back Room (1943) F
Mine Own Executioner (1945) F
Lord, I Was Afraid (1947) F
A Sort of Traitors (1949) F
In the Absence of Mrs Petersen (1966) F
Kings of Infinite Space (1967) F

BALDWIN, James (1924–1987)
African-American novelist and essayist
Go Tell It on the Mountain (1953) F
The Amen Corner (1955) D
Notes of a Native Son (1955) NF
Giovanni's Room (1956) F
Nobody Knows My Name (1961) NF
Another Country (1962) F
The Fire Next Time (1963) NF
Blues for Mister Charley (1964) D
Going to Meet the Man (1965) F SS
Tell Me How Long the Train's Been Gone (1968) F
No Name in the Street (1972) NF
One Day, When I Was Lost (1973) D
If Beale Street Could Talk (1974) F
The Devil Finds Work (1976) NF
Just Above My Head (1979) F
The Price of the Ticket (1986) NF

BALDWIN, Louisa [Mrs Alfred], *née* Macdonald (1845–1925)
British novelist and short-story writer
A Martyr to Mammon (1886) F
The Story of a Marriage (1889) F
Where Town and Country Meet (1891) F
Richard Dare (1894) F
The Shadow on the Blind, and Other Ghost Stories (1895) F SS

BALE, John (1495–1563)
Bishop of Ossory, dramatist, and polemicist
The Examination and Death of the Martyr Sir John Oldcastle (1544) NF
The Acts of English Votaries (1546) NF
God's Promises (1547) D
John the Baptist's Preaching (1547) D
The Temptation of Our Lord (1547) D
The Three Laws (1548) D
The Chief Promises of God unto Man (1577) D

BALESTIER, [Charles] Woolcott (1861–1891)
American author and publisher
A Fair Device (1886) F
Benefits Forgot (1892) F

BALFOUR, Arthur James, OM, 1st Earl of Balfour (1848–1930)
British statesman and philosopher
A Defence of Philosophic Doubt (1879) NF
The Religion of Humanity (1888) NF
The Foundations of Belief (1895) NF
Decadence (1908) NF
Questionings on Criticism and Beauty (1909) NF
Theism and Humanism (1915) NF
Theism and Thought (1915) NF
Essays Speculative and Political (1920) NF
Chapters of an Autobiography (1930) NF

BALFOUR, Clara Lucas, *née* Liddell (1808–1878)
British novelist and temperance activist
'Scrub'; or, The Workhouse Boy's First Start in Life (1860) F
The Victim; or, An Evening's Amusement at the 'Vulture Tavern' (1860) F
Drift (1861) F
Passages in the History of a Shilling (1862) F

BALL, John (1911–)
American novelist
In the Heat of the Night (1965) F

BALLANTINE, James (1808–1877)
Scottish novelist, poet, and artist
The Gaberlunzie's Wallet (1843) F
The Miller of Deanhaugh (1844) F
Lilias Lee, and Other Poems (1871) V

BALLANTYNE, R[obert] M[ichael] (1825–1894)
Scottish novelist
Hudson's Bay; or, Every-day Life in the Wilds of North America (1848) NF
Snowflakes and Sunbeams; or, The Young Fur Traders (1856) F
The Coral Island (1858) F
Martin Rattler; or, A Boy's Adventures in the Forests of Brazil (1858) F
Ungava (1858) F
The World of Ice; or, Adventures in the Polar Regions (1859) F
The Dog Crusoe (1861) F
The Golden Dream; or, Adventures in the Far West (1861) F
The Gorilla Hunters (1861) F
The Red Eric; or, The Whaler's Last Cruise (1861) F
The Wild Man of the West (1863) F
Gascoyne, the Sandal-Wood Trader (1864) F
The Lifeboat (1864) F
The Lighthouse (1865) F
Shifting Winds (1866) F
Deep Down (1867) F
Fighting the Flames (1867) F
Silver Lake; or, Lost in the Snow (1867) F
Erling the Bold (1869) F
The Floating Light of the Goodwin Sands (1870) F
The Iron Horse; or, Life on the Line (1871) F
The Norsemen in the West; or, America Before Columbus (1872) F
The Pioneers (1872) F
Black Ivory (1873) F
Life in the Red Brigade (1873) F
The Pirate City (1874) F
Rivers of Ice (1875) F
In the Track of the Troops (1876) F
The Settler and the Savage (1876) F
Under the Waves; or, Diving in Deep Waters (1876) F
Jarwin and Cuffy (1878) F
The Lonely Island; or, The Refuge of the Mutineers (1880) F
Philosopher Jack (1880) F
Post Haste (1880) F
The Red Man's Revenge (1880) F
The Giant of the North; or, Pokings Round the Pole (1882) F
The Battery and the Boiler; or, Adventures in the Laying of Submarine Electric Cables (1883) F
The Madman and the Pirate (1883) F
Dusty Diamonds Cut and Polished (1884) F
The Young Trawler (1884) F
The Island Queen; or, Dethroned by Fire and Water (1885) F
The Rover of the Andes (1885) F
Twice Bought (1885) F
The Prairie Chief (1886) F
Red Rooney; or, The Last of the Crew (1886) F
The Big Otter (1887) F
The Fugitives; or, The Tyrant Queen of Madagascar (1887) F
Blue Lights; or, Hot Work in the Soudan (1888) F
The Middy and the Moors (1888) F
Blown to Bits; or, The Lonely Man of Rakata (1889) F
The Crew of the Water Wagtail (1889) F
The Eagle Cliff (1889) F
Charlie to the Rescue (1890) F
The Buffalo Hunters (1891) F
The Coxswain's Bride; or, The Rising Tide (1891) F
The Hot Swamp (1892) F
Hunted and Harried (1892) F
Personal Reminiscences in Book-Making (1893) NF
The Walrus Hunters (1893) F
Reuben's Luck (1896) F

BALLARD, J[ames] G[raham] (1930–)
British novelist and short-story writer
The Drowned World (1963) F
The Four-Dimensional Nightmare (1963) F SS
The Terminal Beach (1964) F SS
The Drought (1965) F
The Crystal World (1966) F
The Disaster Area (1967) F SS
The Atrocity Exhibition (1970) F
Crash! (1973) F
Concrete Island (1974) F
High Rise (1975) F
Low-Flying Aircraft, and Other Stories (1976) F SS

The Unlimited Dream Company (1979) F
The Venus Hunters (1980) F SS
Hello America (1981) F
Myths of the Near Future (1982) F SS
Empire of the Sun (1984) F
The Day of Creation (1987) F
Running Wild (1988) F
War Fever (1990) F SS
The Kindness of Women (1991) F
Rushing to Paradise (1994) F
Cocaine Nights (1996) F
Super-Cannes (2000) F

BALZAC, Honoré de (1799–1850)
French novelist
The Chouans [*Les Chouans*] (1829) F
Gobseck (1830) F
Sarrasine (1830) F
Colonel Chabert [*Le Colonel Chabert*] (1832) F
The Priest of Tours [*Le Curé de Tours*] (1832) F
The Wild Ass's Skin [*La Peau de chagrin*] (1832) F
Eugénie Grandet (1833) F
Old Goriot [*Le Père Goriot*] (1835) F
César Birotteau (1837) F
Lost Illusions [*Illusions perdues*] (1837–43) F
Ursule Mirouët (1841) F
Sons of the Soil [*Les Paysans*] (1844) F
Cousin Bette [*La Cousine Bette*] (1846) F
Cousin Pons [*Le Cousin Pons*] (1846) F
History of the Thirteen [*Histoire des Treize*] (1883–85) F

BANGS, John Kendrick (1862–1922)
American humorist
Tiddledywink Tales (1891) F SS
The Idiot (1895) F SS
A Houseboat on the Styx (1896) F SS

BANIM, John (1798–1842)
Irish novelist
The Celt's Paradise (1821) V
Damon and Pythias (1821) D
Revelations of the Dead-Alive (1824) F
Tales, by the O'Hara Family [1st ser.] (1825) F
The Boyne Water (1826) F
Tales by the O'Hara Family [2nd ser.] (1826) F
The Anglo-Irish of the Nineteenth Century (1828) F
The Denounced; or, The Last Baron of Crana (1830) F
The Chaunt of the Cholera (1831) V
The Smuggler (1831) F
The Bit o' Writin', and Other Tales (1838) F SS

BANIM, Michael (1796–1874)
Irish novelist and short-story writer
The Croppy (1828) F
The Ghost-Hunter and His Family (1833) F
The Mayor of Windgap (1835) F
Father Connell (1842) F
The Town of the Cascades (1864) F

BANKS, Iain [Menzies] (1954–)
Scottish novelist and science fiction writer
The Wasp Factory (1984) F
Walking on Glass (1985) F
The Bridge (1986) F
Consider Phlebas (1987) F
The Player of Games (1988) F
The Crow Road (1992) F
A Song of Stone (1997) F
The Business (1999) F

BANKS, Isabella, *née* Varley [Mrs G[eorge] Linnaeus Banks] (1821–1897)
British novelist and poet
Daisies in the Grass (1865) V
God's Providence House (1865) F
Stung to the Quick (1867) F
The Manchester Man (1876) F
Glory (1877) F
Forbidden to Marry (1883) F
Bond Slaves (1893) F

BANKS, Lynne Reid (1929–)
British novelist, dramatist, and children's writer
The L-Shaped Room (1960) F
The Backward Shadow (1970) F
Two is Lonely (1974) F
The Indian in the Cupboard (1980) F CH
The Warning Bell (1984) F
The Broken Bridge (1994) F
Fair Exchange (1998) F

BANKS, Russell (1940–)
American novelist
Family Life (1974) F
Searching for Survivors (1975) F SS
Hamilton Stark (1978) F
The Book of Jamaica (1980) F
The Relation of My Imprisonment (1983) F
Continental Drift (1985) F
Success Stories (1986) F SS
Affliction (1989) F
The Sweet Hereafter (1991) F
Rule of the Bone (1995) F

BANNERMAN, Helen (1863–1946)
British children's writer
The Story of Little Black Sambo (1899) F CH
The Story of Little Black Mingo (1901) F CH
The Story of Little Black Quibba (1902) F CH
Little Degchie-Head (1903) F CH
Pat and the Spider (1904) F CH
The Story of Little Black Quasha (1908) F CH
The Story of Little Black Bobtail (1909) F CH

BANVILLE, John (1945–)
Irish novelist and short-story writer
Long Lankin (1970) F SS
Nightspawn (1971) F
Birchwood (1973) F
Doctor Copernicus (1976) F
Kepler (1981) F
The Newton Letter (1982) F
Mefisto (1986) F
The Book of Evidence (1989) F
Ghosts (1993) F
Athena (1995) F

The Untouchable (1997) F
Eclipse (2000) F

BARAKA, Imamu Amiri *see* LeRoi Jones

BARBAULD, Mrs Anna Laetitia, *née* Aikin (1743–1825)
British poet, editor, and anthologist
Sir Bertram (1773) F
Lessons for Children of Two to Three Years Old (1778) NF
Hymns in Prose for Children (1781) NF
Civic Sermons to the People (1792) NF
Evenings at Home; or, The Juvenile Budget Opened [with John Aikin] (1792) MISC
Sins of the Government, Sins of the Nation (1793) NF
The British Novelists (1810) F
The Female Speaker; or, Miscellaneous Pieces in Prose and Verse (1811) MISC
Eighteen Hundred and Eleven (1812) V
A Legacy for Young Ladies (1826) MISC

'BARBELLION, W[ilhelm] N[ero] P[ilate]' [Bruce Frederick Cumming] (1889–1919)
British diarist
The Journal of a Disappointed Man (1919) NF

BARBER, Margaret Fairless *see* Michael Fairless

BARBEY-d'AUREVILLY, Jules-Amédée (1808–1889)
French novelist, critic, and short-story writer
Le Chevalier des touches (1864) F
Les Diaboliques (1874) F
L'Ensorcelée (1854) F

BARBOUR, John (*c.* 1320–1395)
Scottish poet, churchman, and scholar
The Bruce (1571) V

BARBUSSE, Henri (1873–1935)
French novelist
Under Fire [*Le Feu*] (1916) F
Le Couteau entre les dents ['Knife Between the Teeth'] (1921) F
Le Judas de Jésus ['Jesus' Judas'] (1927) F

BARCLAY, Alexander (1475–1552)
English poet, scholar, and monk
The Castle of Labour [from Pierre Gringore] (1505) V
The Ship of Fools [from Sebastian Brant] (1509) V
Saint George [from Baptista Spagnuoli ('Mantuan')] (1515) V
Jugurthine War [from Sallust] (1520) NF
Codrus and Mynalcas (1521?) V
The Mirror of Good Manners [from Mancinus] (1523) V
Eclogues (1530?) V

BARCLAY, Florence [Louisa], *née* Charlesworth (1862–1921)
British novelist
Guy Mervyn (1891) F
Jane Annie; or, The Good Conduct Prize (1893) F
The Rosary (1909) F
The Mistress of Shenstone (1910) F
The Following of the Star (1911) F
The Upas Tree (1912) F
The Broken Halo (1913) F
My Heart's Right There (1914) F

BARCLAY, John (1582–1621)
English author
Icon Animorum [Latin; tr. into English 1631 as *The Mirror of Minds*] (1614) NF
Argenis [Latin; tr. into English 1625] (1621) F

BARCLAY, Robert (1648–1690)
English Quaker apologist
A Catechism and Confession of Faith (1673) NF
The Anarchy of the Ranters and Other Libertines (1676) NF
Quakerism Confirmed; or, A Vindication of the Doctrines and Principles of the Quakers (1676) NF
An Apology for the True Christian Divinity (1678) NF
Apology for the True Christian Divinity Vindicated (1679) NF
Truth Triumphant Through the Spiritual Warfare (1692) NF

BARDWELL, Leland (1928–)
Irish novelist and poet
The Mad Cyclist (1970) V
Girl on a Bicycle (1977) F
The Fly and the Bed Bug (1984) V
Different Kinds of Love (1987) F SS
There We Have Been (1989) F

BARFOOT, Joan (1946–)
Canadian novelist
Abra (1978) F
Dancing in the Dark (1982) F
Duet for Three (1985) F
Family News (1990) F

BARHAM, R[ichard] H[arris] (1788–1845)
British humorist and poet
Baldwin; or, A Miser's Heir (1820) F
The Ingoldsby Legends; or, Mirth and Marvels [1st ser.] (1840) MISC
Some Account of My Cousin Nicholas [by 'Thomas Ingoldsby'] (1841) F
The Ingoldsby Legends [2nd ser.] (1842) MISC
The Ingoldsby Legends [3rd ser.] (1847) MISC

BARING, Maurice (1874–1945)
British novelist, short-story writer, dramatist, and poet
Triolets (1893) V
The Black Prince, and Other Poems (1903) V
Orpheus in Mayfair, and Other Stories and Sketches (1909) F SS
Dead Letters (1910) F
The Glass Mender, and Other Stories (1910) F SS
Lost Diaries (1913) F
The Puppet Show of Memory (1922) NF
'C' (1924) F
Cat's Cradle (1925) F
Half a Minute's Silence, and Other Stories (1925) F SS
Daphne Adeane (1926) F

The Coat Without Seam (1929) F
Robert Peckham (1930) F
In My End is My Beginning (1931) F
The Lonely Lady of Dulwich (1934) F

BARING-GOULD, S[abine] (1834–1924)
British novelist and miscellaneous writer
The Path of the Just: Tales of Holy Men and Children (1857) F SS
Curious Myths of the Middle Ages (1866) NF
Through Flood and Flame (1868) F
In Exitu Israel (1870) F
The Vicar of Morwenstow (1876) NF
Mehalah (1880) F
John Herring (1883) F
Court Royal (1886) F
The Gaverocks (1887) F
Red Spider (1887) F
Eve (1888) F
Richard Cable the Lightshipman (1888) F
The Pennycomequicks (1889) F
Arminell (1890) F
The Book of Were Wolves (1890) NF
Grettir the Outlaw (1890) F
Jacquetta, and Other Stories (1890) F SS
Margery of Quether, and Other Stories (1891) F SS
Urith (1891) F
In the Roar of the Sea (1892) F
Cheap Jack Zita (1893) F
Mrs Curgenven of Curgenven (1893) F
Kitty Alone (1894) F
The Queen of Love (1894) F
Noémi (1895) F
The Broom-squire (1896) F
Dartmoor Idylls (1896) F
Bladys of the Stewponey (1897) F
Guavas the Tinner (1897) F
Perpetua (1897) F
Domitia (1898) F
The Crock of Gold (1899) F
Pabo the Priest (1899) F
Winefred (1900) F
The Frobishers (1901) F
Royal Georgie (1901) F
Miss Quillet (1902) F
Nebo the Nailer (1902) F
Chris of All-Sorts (1903) F
A Book of Ghosts (1904) F SS
In Dewisland (1904) F
Monsieur Pichelmère, and Other Stories (1905) F SS

BARKER, A[udrey] L[ilian] (1918–)
British novelist and short-story writer
Innocents (1947) F SS
Apology for a Hero (1950) F
Novelette, with Other Stories (1951) F SS
The Joy-Ride and After (1963) F SS
Lost Upon the Roundabouts (1964) F SS
A Case Examined (1965) F
John Brown's Body (1969) F
Femina Real (1971) F SS
A Source of Embarrassment (1974) F
A Heavy Feather (1978) F
Life Stories (1981) F SS
Relative Successes (1984) F
The Gooseboy (1987) F
The Woman Who Talked to Herself (1989) F
Any Excuse for a Party (1991) F
Element of Doubt (1992) F SS
The Haunt (1999) F

BARKER, Clive (1952–)
British horror fiction writer
Books of Blood [vols i-iii] (1984) F
Books of Blood [vols iv-vi] (1985) F
The Damnation Game (1985) F
Weaveworld (1987) F
Cabal (1988) F
The Hellbound Heart (1988) F
The Great and Secret Show (1989) F
Imajica (1991) F
The Thief of Always (1992) F CH
Sacrament (1996) F
Galilee (1998) F

BARKER, George [Granville] (1913–1991)
British poet and novelist
Alanna Autumnal (1933) F
Thirty Preliminary Poems (1933) V
Janus (1935) F SS
Calamiterror (1937) V
Elegy on Spain (1939) V
Lament and Triumph (1940) V
Eros in Dogma (1944) V
The Dead Seagull (1950) F
News of the World (1950) V
The True Confession of George Barker (1950) V
A Vision of Beasts and Gods (1954) V
The View From a Blind I (1962) V
Dreams of a Summer Night (1966) V
The Golden Chains (1968) V
Runes and Rhymes and Tunes and Chimes (1969) V
Poems of Places and People (1971) V
Anno Domino (1983) V

BARKER, Howard (1946–)
British dramatist
Cheek (1970) D
Faceache (1971) D
Stripwell, [and] *Claw* [pub. 1977] (1975) D
Fair Slaughter (1977) D
That Good Between Us (1977) D
The Hang of the Gaol (1978) D
The Love of a Good Man (1978) D
The Loud Boy's Life (1980) D
No End of Blame (1981) D
The Power of the Dog (1984) D
Scenes From an Execution (1984) D
Crimes in Hot Countries (1985) D
Women Beware Women (1986) D
The Possibilities (1987) D
The Last Supper (1988) D
Seven Lears (1990) D
Rome (1992) D

All He Fears (1993) D
Hated Nightfall; [and] *Wounds to the Face* (1994) D

BARKER, Pat (1943–)
British novelist
Union Street (1982) F
Blow Your House Down (1984) F
The Century's Daughter (1986) F
The Man Who Wasn't There (1989) F
Regeneration (1991) F
The Eye in the Door (1993) F
The Ghost Road (1995) F
Another World (1998) F
Border Crossing (2000) F

BARLEY, Nigel (1947–)
British writer on anthropology and travel
The Innocent Anthropologist (1983) NF

BARLOW, Jane (1857–1917)
Irish novelist, short-story writer, and poet
Bog-Land Studies (1892) V
Irish Idylls (1892) F
The End of Elfintown (1894) V
Kerrigan's Quality (1894) F
Maureen's Fairing, and Other Stories (1895) F SS
Mrs Martin's Company, and Other Stories (1895) F SS
Strangers at Lisconnel (1895) F
A Creel of Irish Stories (1897) F
From the Land of the Shamrock (1901) F
Ghost-Bereft, with Other Stories and Studies in Verse (1901) V
By Beach and Bog-Land (1905) F SS
Irish Neighbours (1907) F SS
Irish Ways (1909) F
Doings and Dealings (1913) F
In Mio's Country (1917) F

BARNARD, Lady Anne, *née* Lindsay (1750–1825)
British poet
The History of Old Robin Gray (1783) V
Journal of a Residence at the Cape of Good Hope (1840) NF

BARNES, Barnabe (1571–1609)
English poet and dramatist
Parthenophil and Parthenophe (1593) V
A Divine Century of Spiritual Sonnets (1595) V
The Devil's Charter (1607) D

BARNES, Djuna (1892–1982)
American novelist, dramatist, and poet
A Book (1923) MISC
Ryder (1928) F
A Night Among the Horses (1929) MISC
Nightwood (1936) F
The Book of Repulsive Women (1948) V
The Antiphon (1958) V D
Vagaries Malicieux (1975) F
Smoke, and Other Early Stories (1982) F SS

BARNES, Julian [Patrick] (1946–)
British novelist
Duffy [as 'Dan Kavanagh'] (1980) F
Metroland (1980) F
Fiddle City (1981) F
Before She Met Me (1982) F
Flaubert's Parrot (1984) F
Putting the Boot In (1985) F
Staring at the Sun (1986) F
Going to the Dogs [as 'Dan Kavanagh'] (1987) F
A History of the World in $10\frac{1}{2}$ Chapters (1989) F
Talking It Over (1991) F
The Porcupine (1992) F
Letters From London (1995) NF
Cross Channel (1996) F SS
England, England (1998) F
Love, Etc (2000) F

BARNES, Margaret Ayer (1886–1967)
American novelist and dramatist
Years of Grace (1930) F
Within This Present (1933) F
Edna, His Wife (1935) F
Wisdom's Gate (1938) F

BARNES, Peter (1931–)
British dramatist
The Ruling Class (1969) D
Leonardo's Last Supper; [and] *Noonday Demons* (1970) D

BARNES, William (1801–1866)
British poet
Poetical Pieces (1820) V
Orra (1822) V
Poems of Rural Life in the Dorset Dialect (1844) V
Poems, Partly of Rural Life (1846) V
Hwomely Rhymes (1859) V
The Song of Solomon in the Dorset Dialect (1859) V
Poems of Rural Life in Common English (1868) V

BARNETT, Correlli [Douglas] (1927–)
British historian
The Desert Generals (1960) NF
The Swordbearers (1963) NF
Britain and Her Army (1970) NF
The Collapse of British Power (1972) NF
The Great War (1979) NF
The Audit of War (1986) NF
Engage the Enemy More Closely (1991) NF
The Lost Victory (1995) NF

BARR, Amelia [Edith], *née* Huddleston (1831–1919)
British-born novelist
Jan Vedder's Wife (1885) F
Between Two Loves (1886) F
The Bow of Orange Ribbon (1886) F
A Daughter of Fife (1886) F
Remember the Alamo (1888) F
Love For an Hour is Love Forever (1892) F
Bernicia (1895) F
A Knight of the Nets (1896) F
The Maid of Maiden Lane (1900) F
The House on Cherry Street (1909) F

BARR, Robert (1850–1912)
British novelist and short-story writer
The Adventures of Sherlaw Kombs [as 'Luke Sharp'] (1892) F SS
In a Steamer Chair, and Other Shipboard Stories [as 'Luke Sharp'] (1892) F SS
From Whose Bourne (1893) F SS
The Face and the Mask (1894) F SS
In the Midst of Alarms (1894) F
The Mutable Many (1897) F
The Countess Tekla (1899) F
Jennie Baxter, Journalist (1899) F
The Victors (1902) F
Over the Border (1903) F
The Triumphs of Eugene Valmont (1906) F SS
Stranleigh's Millions (1909) F SS

BARRÈS, [Auguste] Maurice (1862–1923)
French novelist
Sous l'oeil des barbares (1888) F
Un Homme libre (1889) F
Le Jardin de Bérénice (1891) F
Les Déracinés (1897) F
L'Appel au soldat (1900) F
Leurs figures (1902) F
Au service de l'Allemagne (1905) F
Colette Baudoche (1909) F
La Colline inspirée (1913) F
Le Génie du Rhin (1921) F
Un Jardin sur l'Oronte (1922) F

BARRIE, [Sir] J[ames] M[atthew] OM (1860–1937)
British novelist and dramatist
Better Dead (1887) F
Auld Licht Idylls (1888) F
When a Man's Single (1888) F
A Window in Thrums (1889) F
My Lady Nicotine (1890) F
The Little Minister (1891) F
Richard Savage (1891) D
Scotland's Lament (1895) V
Margaret Ogilvy (1896) F
Sentimental Tommy (1896) F
Tommy and Grizel (1900) F
The Little White Bird (1902) F
Peter Pan in Kensington Gardens (1906) F
Walker London (1907) D
Peter and Wendy (1911) F
Quality Street (1913) D
The Admirable Crichton (1914) D
The Greenwood Hat (1937) F

BARSTOW, Stan[ley] (1928–)
British novelist, short-story writer, and dramatist
A Kind of Loving (1960) F
The Desperadoes, and Other Stories (1961) F SS
Ask Me Tomorrow (1962) F
Joby (1964) F
The Watchers on the Shore (1966) F
A Raging Calm (1968) F
The Human Element, and Other Stories (1969) F SS
A Season with Eros (1971) F SS
A Casual Acquaintance, and Other Stories (1976) F SS
The Right True End (1976) F
The Glad Eye, and Other Stories (1978) F SS
A Brother's Tale (1980) F
Just You Wait and See (1986) F
Give Us This Day (1989) F
Next of Kin (1991) F

BARTH, John [Simmons] (1930–)
American novelist and short-story writer
The Floating Opera (1956) F
The End of the Road (1958) F
The Sot-Weed Factor (1960) F
Giles Goat-Boy; or, The Revised New Syllabus (1966) F
Lost in the Funhouse (1968) F
Chimera (1972) F SS
Letters (1979) F
Sabbatical: A Romance (1982) F
The Friday Book (1984) NF
The Tidewater Tales (1987) F
The Last Voyage of Somebody the Sailor (1991) F

BARTHELME, Donald (1931–1989)
American short-story writer and novelist
Come Back, Dr Caligari (1964) F SS
Snow White (1967) F
Unspeakable Practices, Unnatural Acts (1968) F SS
City Life (1970) F SS
Sadness (1972) F SS
Guilty Pleasures (1974) F SS
The Dead Father (1975) F
Amateurs (1976) F SS
Great Days (1979) F SS
Sixty Stories (1981) F SS
Overnight to Many Distant Cities (1984) F SS
Paradise (1986) F
Forty Stories (1987) F SS
The King (1990) F

BARTON, Bernard (1784–1849)
British Quaker poet
Metrical Effusions; or, Verses on Various Occasions (1812) V
The Convict's Appeal (1818) V
A Day in Autumn (1820) V
Napoleon, and Other Poems (1822) V
Verses on the Death of Percy Bysshe Shelley (1822) V
Poetic Vigils (1824) V
Devotional Verses (1826) V
A Widow's Tale, and Other Poems (1827) V
A New Year's Eve, and Other Poems (1828) V
The Reliquary (1836) V
Household Verses (1845) V
Sea-Weeds (1846) V
Ichabod! (1848) V

BATES, Henry Walter (1825–1892)
British naturalist
The Naturalist on the Amazon (1863) NF

BATES, H[erbert] E[rnest] (1905–1974)
British novelist and short-story writer
The Two Sisters (1926) F
Day's End, and Other Stories (1928) F SS
Catherine Foster (1929) F
Seven Tales and Alexander (1929) F SS
Charlotte's Row (1931) F
The Black Boxer (1932) F SS
The Fallow Land (1932) F
The House with the Apricot, and Two Other Tales (1933) F SS
The Woman Who Had Imagination, and Other Stories (1934) F SS
Cut and Come Again (1935) F SS
The Poacher (1935) F
A House of Women (1936) F
Something Short and Sweet (1937) F SS
The Flying Goat (1939) F SS
My Uncle Silas (1939) F
The Beauty of the Dead, and Other Stories (1940) F SS
The Greatest People in the World, and Other Stories (1942) F SS
In the Heart of the Country (1942) NF
How Sleep the Brave, and Other Stories (1943) F SS
Fair Stood the Wind for France (1944) F
The Cruise of the Breadwinner (1946) F
The Purple Plain (1947) F
The Bride Comes to Evensford, and Other Tales (1949) F SS
The Jacaranda Tree (1949) F
Colonel Julian, and Other Stories (1951) F SS
Love for Lydia (1952) F
The Feast of July (1954) F HF
The Daffodil Sky (1955) F SS
The Sleepless Moon (1956) F
Death of a Huntsman (1957) F
Sugar for the Horse (1957) F SS
The Darling Buds of May (1958) F
A Breath of French Air (1959) F
The Watercress Girl, and Other Stories (1959) F SS
An Aspidistra in Babylon (1960) F
When the Green Woods Laugh (1960) F
Now Sleeps the Crimson Petal, and Other Stories (1961) F SS
A Crown of Wild Myrtle (1962) F
Oh! To Be in England (1963) F
The Fabulous Mrs V (1964) F SS
A Moment in Time (1964) F
The Wedding Party (1965) F SS
The Four Beauties (1968) F SS
The Vanished World (1969) NF
A Little of What You Fancy (1970) F
The Blossoming World (1971) NF
The Song of the Wren (1972) F SS
The World in Ripeness (1972) NF
The Yellow Meads of Asphodel (1976) F SS

BATESON, F[rederick] N[oel] W[ilse] (1901–1978)
British critic, editor, and agricultural correspondent
The Cambridge Bibliography of English Literature (1940) NF
English Poetry (1950) NF
Wordsworth (1954) NF
Essays in Critical Dissent (1972) NF

BAUDELAIRE, Charles [Pierre] (1821–1867)
French poet, art and literary critic, translator, and essayist
La Fanfarlo (1847) F
Les Fleurs du mal ['Flowers of Evil'; first book publication] (1857) V
Les Épaves (1866) V
L'Art romantique ['Romantic Art'] (1869) NF
Petits poèmes en prose ['Little Poems in Prose'] (1869) V

BAUM, L[yman] Frank (1856–1919)
American journalist, dramatist, and children's writer
Mother Goose in Prose (1897) F CH
The Wonderful Wizard of Oz (1900) F CH
Dot and Tot of Merryland (1901) F CH
The Marvellous Land of Oz (1904) F CH
Ozma of Oz (1907) F CH
Dorothy and the Wizard of Oz (1908) F CH
The Scarecrow of Oz (1915) F CH
The Lost Princess of Oz (1917) F CH

BAUM, Vicki [originally Hedvig] (1888–1960)
Austrian-born American novelist
Grand Hotel (1930) F
Falling Star (1934) F
Headless Angel (1948) F
The Mustard Seed (1953) F
Ballerina (1958) F

BAWDEN, Nina [Mary], *née* Mabey (1925–)
British adult and children's novelist
Who Calls the Tune (1953) F
The Odd Flamingo (1954) F
Change Here for Babylon (1955) F
The Solitary Child (1956) F
Devil by the Sea (1957) F
Just Like a Lady (1960) F
In Honour Bound (1961) F
Tortoise by Candlelight (1963) F
Under the Skin (1964) F
A Woman of My Age (1967) F
The Birds on the Trees (1970) F
Anna Apparent (1972) F
Carrie's War (1973) F CH
The Peppermint Pig (1975) F CH
Afternoon of a Good Woman (1976) F
Familiar Passions (1979) F
Walking Naked (1981) F
The Ice House (1983) F
Circles of Deceit (1987) F
Keeping Henry (1988) F CH
Family Money (1991) F

BAXTER, James K[eir] (1926–1972)
New Zealand poet, dramatist, and critic
Beyond the Palisade (1944) V
In Fires of No Return (1958) V
Howrah Bridge (1961) V
Pig Island Letters (1966) V
The Band Rotunda (1967) D
The Devil and Mr Mulcahy (1967) D
The Sore-Footed Man (1967) D
Jerusalem Sonnets (1970) V
The Temptations of Oedipus (1970) D
Autumn Testament (1972) V

BAXTER, Richard (1615–1691)
English divine and devotional author
The Saints' Everlasting Rest (1650) NF
Gildas Salvianu (1656) NF
The Crucifying of the World, by the Cross of Christ (1658) NF
A Holy Commonwealth; or, Political Aphorisms (1659) NF
The Life of Faith, as it is the Evidence of Things Unseen (1660) NF
Now or Never (1662) NF
The Divine Life, in Three Treatises (1664) NF
Catholick Theologie (1675) NF
A Breviate of the Life of Margaret Baxter (1681) NF
Reliquiae Baxterianae (1696) V
Erin, and Other Poems (1822) V
Perfection; or, The Lady of Munster (1836) D

BAYLY, [Nathaniel] Thomas Haynes (1797–1839)
British songwriter, novelist, and dramatist
Parliamentary Letters, and Other Poems (1818) V
Weeds of Witchery (1837) V
Human Toll (1902) F

BAYNTON, Barbara Jane, *née* Lawrence (1857–1929)
Australian novelist and short-story writer
Bush Studies (1902) F SS

BEACH, Edward (1918–)
American novelist
Run Silent, Run Deep (1955) F

BEAMAN, S[ydney] G[eorge] Hulme (1886–1932)
Children's writer and illustrator
Tales of Toytown (1928) F CH

BEARDSLEY, Aubrey [Vincent] (1872–1898)
British illustrator and author
Last Letters (1904) NF
Under the Hill, and Other Essays in Prose and Verse (1904) MISC
The Story of Venus and Tannhäuser (1907) NF

BEATTIE, James (1735–1803)
Scottish poet and philosophical writer
Original Poems and Translations (1760) V
The Judgment of Paris (1765) V
An Essay on the Nature and Immutability of Truth (1770) NF
The Minstrel; or, The Progress of Genius [bk i] (1771) V
The Minstrel; or, The Progress of Genius [bk ii] (1774) V
Dissertations Moral and Critical (1783) NF
Evidences of the Christian Religion (1786) NF
Elements of Moral Science (1790) NF

BEAUCHAMP, Kathleen Mansfield
see KATHERINE MANSFIELD

BEAUMARCHAIS, Pierre Augustin Caron de (1732–1799)
French dramatist
Eugénie (1767) D
The Two Friends [*Les Deux Amis*] (1770) D
The Barber of Seville [*Le Barbier de Séville*] (1775) D
The Marriage of Figaro [*Le Mariage de Figaro*] (1784) D
Tavare (1787) O
The Guilty Mother [*L'Autre Tartufe; ou, la Mère coupable*] (1792) D

BEAUMONT, Francis (1585?–1616)
English poet and dramatist
Salamacis and Hermaphroditus (1602) V
The Woman Hater (1607) D
The Knight of the Burning Pestle (1613) D
Cupid's Revenge (1615) D
The Scornful Lady (1616) D
A King and No King (1619) D
The Maid's Tragedy (1619) D
Phylaster; or, Love Lies a Bleeding (1620) D
Wit Without Money (1639) D
The Wild-Goose Chase (1652) D
The Beggar's Bush (1661) D

BEAUMONT, Joseph (1616–1699)
English divine and poet
Psyche; or, Loves Mystery in XX Canto's (1648) V

BEAUVOIR, Simone de (1908–1986)
French novelist, philosopher, autobiographer, and feminist
She Came to Stay [*L'Invitée*] (1943) F
The Blood of Others [*Le Sang des autres*] (1945) F
All Men Are Mortal [*Tous les hommes sont mortels*] (1946) F
The Second Sex [*Le Deuxième Sexe*] (1949) NF
The Mandarins [*Les Mandarins*] (1954) F
The Long March [*La Longue Marche*] (1957) NF
Memoirs of a Dutiful Daughter [*Mémoires d'une jeune fille rangée*] (1958) NF
Force of Circumstance [*La Force des choses*] (1963) NF
Les Belles Images (1966) F
The Woman Destroyed [*La Femme rompue*] (1968) F SS
All Said and Done [*Tout compte fait*] (1972) NF

BEAVER, Bruce (1928–)
Australian poet and novelist
Under the Bridge (1961) V

Seawall and Shoreline (1964) V
The Hot Spring (1965) F
You Can't Come Back (1966) F
Open at Random (1967) V
Letters to Live Poets (1969) V
Lauds and Plaints: Poems, 1968–72 (1974) V
Odes and Days (1975) V
Death's Directives (1978) V
As It Was (1979) V
Charmed Lives (1988) V

BECKE, George Louis (1855–1913)
Australian-born novelist
By Reef and Palm (1894) F
A First Fleet Family (1896) F
His Native Wife (1896) F
The Mutineer (1898) F
Edward Barry, South Sea Pearler (1900) F
Helen Adair (1903) F
The Adventures of a Supercargo (1906) F
The Call of the South (1909) F

BECKETT, Gilbert Abbott à (1811–1856)
British humorist and dramatist
The Revolt of the Workhouse (1834) D
A Comic Blackstone (1846) F
A Comic History of England (1847) F
A Comic History of Rome (1852) F
The Modern Arabian Nights (1877) F

BECKETT, Samuel [Barclay] (1906–1989)
Irish dramatist, poet, and novelist
Whoroscope (1930) V
Proust (1931) NF
More Pricks Than Kicks (1934) F SS
Echo's Bones and Other Precipitates (1935) V
Murphy (1938) F
Watt (1953) F
Molloy [pub. in French 1951] (1955) F
Waiting for Godot [pub. in French 1952] (1955) D
Malone Dies [pub. in French 1951] (1956) F
All That Fall (1957) D
Endgame [pub. in French 1957] (1958) D
Krapp's Last Tape; Embers (1959) D
Happy Days (1961) D
How It Is (1964) F
Come and Go (1965) D
Imagine Dead Imagine (1965) F
Eh Joe, and Other Writings (1967) D
No's Knife (1967) F
Lessness [pub. in French 1969] (1971) F
The Lost Ones [pub. in French 1971] (1972) F
First Love [pub. in French 1970] (1973) F
Mercier and Camier [pub. in French 1970] (1974) F
For To End Yet Again, and Other Fizzles (1976) F
Four Novellas (1977) F
All Strange Away [limited edn 1976] (1979) F

BECKFORD, William (1760–1844)
British novelist and author
Dreams, Waking Thoughts and Incidents (1783) NF
Vathek [first pub. in French 1786] (1786) F
Modern Novel Writing, or, The Elegant Enthusiast (1796) F
Azemia (1797) F
The Story of Al Raoui (1799) F
Italy; with Sketches of Spain and Portugal (1834) NF
Recollections of an Excursion to the Monasteries of Alcobaça and Batalha (1835) NF

BEDDOES, Thomas Lovell (1803–1849)
British poet and dramatist
The Improvisatore, in Three Fyttes, with Other Poems (1821) V
The Bride's Tragedy (1822) V
Death's Jest-Book; or, The Fool's Tragedy (1850) V

BEDE, Cuthbert *see* EDWARD BRADLEY

BEDFORD, Sybille [Sybille von Schoenebeck] (1911–)
German-born British novelist and essayist
The Sudden View [reissued as *A Visit to Don Otavio*, 1960] (1953) NF
The Legacy (1956) F
A Favourite of the Gods (1963) F
A Compass Error (1968) F
Aldous Huxley (1973) NF
Jigsaw (1989) F
As It Was (1990) NF

BEER, Patricia (1924–1999)
British poet, dramatist, critic , and novelist
Loss of the Magyar, and Other Poems (1959) V
The Survivors (1963) V
Just Like the Resurrection (1967) V
The Estuary (1971) V
Spanish Balcony (1973) V
Reader, I Married Him (1974) NF
Driving West (1975) V
Moon's Ottery (1978) F
The Life of the Land (1983) V
Friend of Heraclitus (1993) V

BEERBOHM, [Sir Henry] Max[imilian] (1872–1956)
British essayist, caricaturist, and novelist
Caricatures of Twenty-Five Gentlemen (1896) NF
The Happy Hypocrite (1897) NF
More (1899) NF
The Poets' Corner (1904) NF
A Book of Caricatures (1907) NF
Yet Again (1909) NF
Zuleika Dobson (1911) F
A Christmas Garland (1912) NF
Fifty Caricatures (1913) NF
Seven Men (1919) F SS
And Even Now (1920) NF
Rossetti and his Circle (1922) NF
Things New and Old (1923) NF
Observations (1925) NF
Mainly On the Air (1946) NF

BEETON, Isabella Mary, *née* Mayson (1836–1865)
British journalist and domestic writer
The Book of Household Management (1861) NF

The Englishwoman's Cooking-Book (1862) NF
A Dictionary of Every-Day Cookery (1865) NF

BEHAN, Brendan [Francis] (1923–1964)
Irish dramatist
The Quare Fellow (1954) D
The Big House (1958) D
Borstal Boy (1958) NF
The Hostage (1958) D
Confessions of an Irish Rebel (1965) NF
The Scarperer (1966) F

BEHN, Aphra (1640?–1689)
English dramatist, poet, and novelist
The Forc'd Marriage; or, The Jealous Bridegroom (1670) D
The Amorous Prince; or, The Curious Husband (1671) D
The Dutch Lover (1673) D
Abdelazar; or, The Moor's Revenge (1676) D
The Town-Fop; or, Sir Timothy Tawdrey (1676) D
The Rover; or, The Banished Cavaliers (1677) D
Sir Patient Fancy (1678) D
The Feign'd Curtizans; or, A Night's Intrigue (1679) D
The Young King; or, The Mistake (1679) D
The False Count; or, A New Way to Play an Old Game (1681) D
The Round-Heads; or, The Good Old Cause (1681) D
The Second Part of the Rover (1681) D
The City-Heiress; or, Sir Timothy Treat-All (1682) D
Love-Letters Between a Noble-man and His Sister [pt. i] (1684) F
Love-Letters Between a Nobleman and His Sister [pt. ii] (1685) F
The Lucky Chance; or, An Alderman's Bargain (1686) D
The Amours of Philander and Sylvia [*Love-letters Between a Nobleman and his Sister* pt. iii] (1687) F
The Emperor of the Moon (1687) D
The Fair Jilt (1688) F
Oroonoko; or, The Royal Slave (1688) F
The History of the Nun; or, The Fair Vow-Breaker (1689) F
The Widdow Ranter; or, The History of Bacon in Virginia (1689) D

BEITH, John Hay *see* IAN HAY

BELASCO, David (1853–1931)
American dramatist, director, and theatre manager
Madame Butterfly (1900) D

BELL, Adrian [Hanbury] (1901–1980)
British novelist
Corduroy (1930) F
Silver Ley (1931) F
The Path by the Window (1952) F SS
My Own Master (1961) NF

BELL, [Arthur] Clive [Heward] (1881–1964)
British art critic
Art (1914) NF
Since Cézanne (1922) NF
Civilization (1928) NF
Proust (1928) NF
Old Friends (1956) NF

BELL, Gertrude [Margaret Lowthian] (1868–1926)
British traveller and author
The Desert and the Sown [US: *Syria: The Desert and the Sown*] (1907) NF
The Thousand and One Churches (1909) NF
Amurath to Amurath (1911) NF
The Palace and Mosque at Ukhaidir (1914) NF

BELL, Julian Heward (1908–1937)
British poet
Winter Movement, and Other Poems (1930) V
Work for the Winter, and Other Poems (1936) V

BELL, Lady Florence Isabel Eveleen [Mrs Hugh Bell], *née* Oliffe (1851–1930)
British novelist, dramatist, and author
The Story of Ursula (1895) F
Miss Tod and the Prophets (1898) F
The Arbiter (1901) F
The Dean of St Patrick's (1903) D
At the Works (1907) NF

BELLAMY, Edward (1850–1898)
American novelist
Six to One: A Nantucket Idyl (1878) F
Dr Heidenhoff's Process (1880) F
Miss Ludington's Sister (1884) F
Looking Backward: 2000–1887 (1888) F
The Blindman's World, and Other Stories (1898) F SS

BELLOC, [Joseph] Hilaire [Pierre René] (1870–1953)
British historian, poet, and critic
The Bad Child's Book of Beasts (1896) V CH
More Beasts—For Worse Children (1897) V CH
The Modern Traveller (1898) V
Danton (1899) NF
The Moral Alphabet (1899) V CH
Paris (1900) NF
Robespierre (1901) NF
The Path to Rome (1902) NF
Avril (1904) NF
Emmanuel Burden, Merchant (1904) F
The Old Road (1904) NF
Esto Perpetua (1906) NF
Hills and the Sea (1906) NF
Cautionary Tales for Children (1907) V CH
Mr Clutterbuck's Election (1908) F
On Nothing and Kindred Subjects (1908) NF
A Change in the Cabinet (1909) F
On Everything (1909) NF
The Pyrenees (1909) NF
On Anything (1910) NF
On Something (1910) NF
Pongo and the Bull (1910) F
First and Last (1911) NF
The French Revolution (1911) NF
The Girondin (1911) F
More Peers (1911) V

The Green Overcoat (1912) F
The Servile State (1912) NF
This and That and the Other (1912) NF
The Second Year of the War (1916) NF
The Free Press (1918) NF
Europe and the Faith (1920) NF
The Jews (1922) NF
The Contrast (1923) NF
The Cruise of the 'Nona' (1925) NF
Mr Petre (1925) F
A Companion to Mr Wells's Outline of History (1926) NF
Mr Belloc Still Objects to Mr Wells's Outline of History (1926) NF
Mrs Markham's New History of England (1926) NF
Short Talks with the Dead and Others (1926) NF
The Haunted House (1927) F
Oliver Cromwell (1927) NF
Belinda (1928) F
A Conversation with an Angel, and Other Essays (1928) NF
Survivals and New Arrivals (1929) NF
New Cautionary Tales (1930) V
A Conversation with a Cat and Others (1931) NF
Essays of a Catholic Layman in England (1931) NF
Ladies and Gentlemen (1932) V
Milton (1935) NF
The Crisis of Our Civilization (1937) NF
An Essay on the Nature of Contemporary England (1937) NF
On the Place of Chesterton in English Letters (1940) NF
The Silence of the Sea, and Other Essays (1940) NF

BELLOW, Saul (1915–)
American novelist
Dangling Man (1944) F
The Victim (1944) F
The Adventures of Augie March (1947) F
The Wrecker (1954) D
Seize the Day (1956) F
Henderson the Rain King (1959) F
Herzog (1964) F
Mr Sammler's Planet (1964) F
The Last Analysis (1965) D
Mosby's Memoirs, and Other Stories (1968) F SS
Humboldt's Gift (1975) F
To Jerusalem and Back (1976) NF
The Dean's December (1982) F
Him With His Foot in His Mouth, and Other Short Stories (1984) F SS
More Die of Heartbreak (1987) F
A Theft (1988) F
The Bellarosa Connection (1989) F
Something to Remember Me By (1993) F SS
It All Adds Up (1994) NF
Ravelstein (2000) F

BEMELMANS, Ludwig (1898–1962)
Austrian-born humorist, novelist, and children's writer
Madeline (1938) F CH

BENCHLEY, Peter Bradford (1940–)
American popular novelist
Jaws (1974) F
The Deep (1976) F
The Island (1979) F
The Girl of the Sea of Cortez (1982) F

BENCHLEY, Robert [Charles] (1889–1945)
American drama critic, humorist, and actor
Of All Things (1921) NF
Love Conquers All (1922) NF
Pluck and Luck (1925) NF
The Early Worm (1927) NF
20,000 Leagues Under the Sea; or, David Copperfield (1928) NF
The Treasurer's Report (1930) NF
From Bed to Worse (1934) NF
My Ten Years in a Quandary (1936) NF
After 1903—What? (1938) NF
Inside Benchley (1942) NF
Benchley Beside Himself (1943) NF

BENÉT, Stephen Vincent (1889–1943)
American poet, short-story writer, and novelist
The Beginning of Wisdom (1921) F
Young People's Pride (1922) F
The Ballad of William Sycamore (1923) V
Jean Huguenot (1923) F
King David (1923) V
Tiger Joy (1925) V
Spanish Bayonet (1926) F
John Brown's Body (1928) V
Thirteen O'Clock (1937) F SS
The Devil and Daniel Webster [libretto] (1939)
Tales Before Midnight (1939) F SS
Nightmare at Noon (1940) V
Western Star (1943) V
The Last Cycle (1946) F SS

BENÉT, William Rose (1886–1950)
American poet and critic
Merchants from Cathay (1913) V
The Falconer of God (1914) V
The Great White Wall (1916) V
The Burglar of the Zodiac (1918) V
Moons of Grandeur (1920) V
Man Possessed (1927) V
Rip Tide (1932) V
The Dust Which Is God (1941) V
Day of Deliverance (1944) V

BENLOWES, Edward (1602–1676)
English Royalist poet
Theophilia; or, Love's Sacrifice (1652) V

BENNETT, Alan (1934–)
British dramatist
Beyond the Fringe (1962) D
Forty Years On (1968) D
Getting On (1971) D
Habeas Corpus (1973) D
The Old Country (1977) D
Enjoy (1980) D

An Englishman Abroad (1982) D
A Private Function (1985) D
The Writer in Disguise (1985) D
The Insurance Man (1986) D
Prick Up Your Ears (1987) D
Single Spies (1988) D
The Lady in the Van (1990) NF
The Madness of George III (1992) D
Writing Home (1994) NF
Talking Heads (1998) D
Talking Heads 2 (1998) D

BENNETT, Enoch Arnold (1867–1931)
British novelist
Journalism for Women (1898) NF
A Man From the North (1898) F
Polite Farces for the Drawing-Room (1899) D
Fame and Fiction (1901) NF
Anna of the Five Towns (1902) F
The Grand Babylon Hotel (1902) F
The Gates of Wrath (1903) F
Leonora (1903) F
A Great Man (1904) F
Teresa of Watling Street (1904) F
The Loot of Cities (1905) F SS
Sacred and Profane Love (1905) F
Tales of the Five Towns (1905) F SS
Hugo (1906) F
The Sinews of War (1906) F
Whom God Hath Joined (1906) F
The City of Pleasure (1907) F
The Ghost (1907) F
The Grim Smile of the Five Towns (1907) F SS
Buried Alive (1908) F
How to Live on 24 Hours a Day (1908) NF
The Human Machine (1908) NF
The Old Wives' Tale (1908) F
The Statue (1908) F
Cupid and Commonsense (1909) D
The Glimpse (1909) F
Literary Taste (1909) NF
What the Public Wants (1909) D
Clayhanger (1910) F
Helen With the High Hand (1910) F
The Card (1911) F
Hilda Lessways (1911) F
The Matador of the Five Towns, and Other Stories (1912) F SS
Milestones (1912) D
Those United States (1912) NF
The Great Adventure (1913) D
The Regent (1913) F
The Author's Craft (1914) NF
The Price of Love (1914) F
Over There (1915) NF
The Lion's Share (1916) F
These Twain (1916) F
The Pretty Lady (1918) F
The Roll-Call (1918) F
The Title (1918) D
Sacred and Profane Love (1919) D
Things That Have Interested Me [1st ser.] (1921) NF
Lilian (1922) F
The Love Match (1922) D
Mr Prohack (1922) F
Riceyman Steps (1923) F
Elsie and the Child (1924) F SS
London Life (1924) D
The Clayhanger Family (1925) F
Lord Raingo (1926) F
Mr Prohack (1927) D
The Woman Who Stole Everything, and Other Stories (1927) F SS
Imperial Palace (1930) F
Journal, 1929 (1930) NF

BENSON, A[rthur] C[hristopher] (1862–1925)
British essayist, biographer, and short-story writer
Lord Vyet, and Other Poems (1895) V
Lyrics (1895) V
Life of Edward White Benson (1899) NF
The Professor, and Other Poems (1900) V
The Hill of Trouble, and Other Stories (1903) F
The House of Quiet (1904) F
The Isles of Sunset, and Other Stories (1904) F
Rossetti (1904) NF
Edward Fitzgerald (1905) NF
Peace, and Other Poems (1905) V
The Thread of Gold (1905) NF
The Upton Letters (1905) F
From a College Window (1906) NF
Walter Pater (1906) NF
The Altar Fire (1907) F
Beside Still Waters (1907) NF
The Letters of Queen Victoria (1907) NF
At Large (1908) NF
The Gate of Death (1909) F
The Silent Isle (1910) F
The Leaves of the Tree (1911) NF
Paul the Minstrel, and Other Stories (1911) F SS
Ruskin (1911) NF
The Child of the Dawn (1912) F
Thy Rod and Staff (1912) F
Along the Road (1913) NF
Joyous Gard (1913) NF
Watersprings (1913) F
The Orchard Pavilion (1914) F
Where No Fear Was (1914) F
Father Payne (1915) F
Hugh (1915) NF
The Trefoil (1923) NF
Memories and Friends (1924) NF
The House of Menerdue (1925) F
Basil Netherby (1926) F SS

BENSON, E[dward] F[rederic] (1867–1940)
British novelist, short-story writer, and biographer
Dodo (1893) F
Six Common Things (1893) F SS
The Rubicon (1894) F
The Judgement Books (1895) F
Limitations (1896) F
The Babe, B.A. (1897) F

The Money Market (1898) F
The Vintage (1898) F
The Capsina (1899) F
Mammon & Co (1899) F
The Princess Sophia (1900) F
The Luck of the Vails (1901) F
Scarlet and Hyssop (1902) F
An Act in a Backwater (1903) F
The Relentless City (1903) F
The Challoners (1904) F
The Image in the Sand (1905) F
The Angel of Pain (1906) F
Paul (1906) F
The Climber (1908) F
A Reaping (1909) F
Daisy's Aunt (1910) F
The Osbornes (1910) F
Account Rendered (1911) F
Juggernaut (1911) F
Mrs Ames (1912) F
The Room in the Tower, and Other Stories (1912) F SS
Thorley Weir (1913) F
The Weaker Vessel (1913) F
Dodo the Second (1914) F
David Blaize (1916) F
The Freaks of Mayfair (1916) F
Mike (1916) F
Mr Teddy (1917) F
David Blaize and the Blue Door (1918) F
Across the Stream (1919) F
The Countess of Lowndes Square (1920) F SS
Our Family Affairs (1920) NF
Queen Lucia (1920) F
Dodo Wonders (1921) F
Miss Mapp (1922) F
Peter (1922) F
Colin (1923) F
Visible and Invisible (1923) F SS
Alan (1924) F
David of King's (1924) F
Colin II (1925) F
Mother (1925) F
Rex (1925) F
Pharisees and Publicans (1926) F
Lucia in London (1927) F
Spook Stories (1928) F SS
The Male Impersonator (1929) F
Paying Guests (1929) F
As We Were (1930) NF
The Inheritor (1930) F
Mapp and Lucia (1931) F
As We Are (1932) F
Secret Lives (1932) F
Travail of Gold (1933) F
More Spook Stories (1934) F SS
Raven's Brood (1934) F
Lucia's Progress (1935) F
Final Edition (1940) NF

BENSON, R[obert] H[ugh] (1871–1914)
British novelist and priest
The King's Achievement (1905) F
The Queen's Tragedy (1906) F
The Sentimentalists (1906) F
The Conventionalists (1908) F
The Necromancers (1909) F
None Other Gods (1910) F
The Coward (1912) F
Loneliness (1915) F

BENSON, Stella (1892–1933)
British novelist and short-story writer
I Pose (1915) F
Twenty (1918) V
Living Alone (1919) F
The Poor Man (1922) F
Pipers and a Dancer (1924) F
The Little World (1925) F
Hope Against Hope, and Other Stories (1931) F SS
Tobit Transplanted [US: *The Far-Away Bride*] (1931) F
Christmas Formula, and Other Stories (1932) F SS

BENTHAM, Jeremy (1748–1832)
British writer on jurisprudence
A Fragment on Government (1776) NF
Defence of Usury (1787) NF
An Introduction to the Principles of Morals and Legislation (1789) NF
Panopticon; or, The Inspection-House (1791) NF
A Plea for the Constitution (1803) NF
Chrestomathia (1816) NF
Papers Upon Codification and Public Instruction (1817) NF
The Influence of Natural Religion upon the Temporal Happiness of Mankind (1822) NF
Book of Fallacies (1824) NF
The Rationale of Evidence (1827) NF
Official Aptitude Maximised—Expense Minimised (1831) NF
Deontology; or, Science of Morality (1834) NF

BENTLEY, E[dmund] C[lerihew] (1875–1956)
British inventor of the clerihew and detective novelist
Biography for Beginners (1905) V
Trent Intervenes (1913) F SS
Trent's Last Case [US: *The Woman in Black*] (1913) F
Those Days (1940) NF
Clerihews Complete (1951) V

BENTLEY, Phyllis [Eleanor] (1894–1977)
British novelist
Environment (1922) F
Cat-in-the-Manger (1923) F
Inheritance (1932) F
A Modern Tragedy (1934) F
The Whole of the Story (1935) F SS
Sleep in Peace (1938) F
Take Courage [US: *The Power and the Glory*] (1940) F
The Rise of Henry Morcar (1946) F
Life Story (1948) F
Quorum (1950) F
Noble in Reason (1955) F
Love and Money (1957) F SS

Crescendo (1958) F
A Man of his Time (1966) F

BENTLEY, Richard (1662–1742)
English classical scholar
A Confutation of Atheism from the Structure and Origin of Humane Bodies (1692) NF
A Confutation of Atheism from the Origin and Frame of the World (1692) NF
The Folly of Atheism (1692) NF
Matter and Motion Cannot Think (1692) NF
A Dissertation upon the Epistles of Phalaris (1697) NF
Remarks upon a Late Discourse of Free-thinking (1713) NF
A Sermon upon Popery (1715) NF

BERENSON, Bernard (1865–1959)
Lithuanian-born American art historian
The Venetian Painters (1894) NF
The Florentine Painters (1896) NF
The Central Italian Painters (1897) NF
The North Italian Painters (1907) NF
The Italian Painters of the Renaissance [prev. 4 titles collected] (1930) NF

BERESFORD, J[ohn] D[avys] (1873–1947)
British novelist and short-story writer
The Early History of Jacob Stahl (1911) F
The Hampdenshire Wonder [US: *The Wonder*] (1911) F
A Candidate for Truth (1912) F
Goslings (1913) F
The House in Demetrius Road (1914) F
The Invisible Event (1915) F
Nineteen Impressions (1918) F SS
The Impertubable Duchess, and Other Stories (1923) F SS
The Meeting Place, and Other Stories (1929) F SS
The Next Generation (1932) F
The Camberwell Miracle (1933) F
Blackthorn Winter, and Other Stories (1936) F SS

BERGER, John [Peter] (1926–)
British critic, novelist, and artist
A Painter of Our Time (1958) F
Permanent Red [US: *Towards Reality*] (1960) NF
The Foot of Clive (1962) F
Corker's Freedom (1964) F
The Moment of Cubism, and Other Essays (1969) NF
G (1972) F
Ways of Seeing (1972) NF
Pig Earth (1979) F
About Looking (1980) NF
Once in Europa (1987) F SS
Lilac and Flag (1990) F
To the Wedding (1995) F
King (1999) F

BERGER, Thomas [Louis] (1924–)
American novelist
Crazy in Berlin (1958) F
Reinhart in Love (1962) F
Little Big Man (1964) F
Killing Time (1967) F
Regiment of Women (1973) F
Sneaky People (1975) F
Who is Teddy Villanova? (1977) F
Arthur Rex (1978) F
Neighbors (1980) F
Reinhart's Women (1981) F
The Feud (1983) F
Nowhere (1985) F
Being Invisible (1987) F
The Houseguest (1988) F
Changing the Past (1990) F
Orrie's Story (1990) F
Meeting Evil (1992) F
Robert Crews (1994) F

BERGONZI, Bernard (1929–)
British literary critic, poet, and novelist
The Early H.G. Wells (1961) NF
Heroes' Twilight (1965) NF
T.S. Eliot (1972) NF
Reading the Thirties (1978) NF
The Romaine Persuasion (1981) F
The Myth of Modernism and Twentieth-Century Literature (1986) NF
Exploding English (1990) NF
Wartime and Aftermath (1993) NF

BERGSON, Henri (1859–1941)
French philosopher
Time and Free Will [*Essai sur les données immédiates de la conscience*] (1889) NF
Matter and Memory [*Matière et mémoire*] (1896) NF
Creative Evolution [*L'Évolution créatice*] (1907) NF

BERKELEY, Anthony *see* ANTHONY BERKELEY COX

BERKELEY, George (1685–1753)
British philosopher
An Essay Towards a New Theory of Vision (1709) NF
A Treatise Concerning the Principles of Human Knowledge (1710) NF
Passive Obedience (1712) NF
Three Dialogues Between Hylas and Philonous (1713) NF
An Essay Towards Preventing the Ruin of Great Britain (1721) NF
Alciphron; or, The Minute Philosopher, in Seven Dialogues (1732) NF
The Querist (1735) NF
Siris (1744) NF

BERKOFF, Steve[n] (1937–)
British actor and dramatist
East (1975) D
Decadence (1981) D
Sink the Belgrano! (1986) D

BERLIN, Sir Isaiah (1909–1997)
Latvian-born British philosopher and historian of ideas
Karl Marx (1939) NF
Historical Inevitability (1954) NF

Two Concepts of Liberty (1959) NF
Concepts and Categories (1978) NF
Russian Thinkers (1978) NF

BERRIDGE, Elizabeth (1921–)
British novelist and short-story writer
Upon Several Occasions (1953) F
Rose Under Glass (1961) F
Across the Common (1964) F
Sing Me Who You Are (1967) F
Family Matters (1980) F SS

BERRY, James (1924–)
Jamaican poet and novelist
Fractured Circles (1979) V
Lucy's Letters and Loving (1982) V
Chain of Days (1985) V
The Girls and Yunga Marshall (1987) F SS
Hot Earth, Cold Earth (1995) V
Playing a Dazzler (1996) V

BERRYMAN, John (1914–1972)
American poet
The Dispossessed (1948) V
Homage to Mistress Bradstreet (1956) V
His Thought Made Pockets and the Plane Buckt (1958) V
77 Dream Songs (1964) V
Berryman's Sonnets (1967) V
Short Poems (1967) V
His Toy, His Dream, His Rest (1968) V
The Dream Songs (1969) V
Love and Fame (1970) V
Delusions, etc. (1972) V
Recovery (1973) F
The Freedom of the Poet (1976) MISC
Henry's Fate (1977) V
We Dream of Honour (1988) NF

BESANT, Annie, *née* Wood (1847–1933)
British Theosophist and educationist
On the Deity of Jesus of Nazareth (1873) NF
On the Nature and Existence of God (1875) NF
The Gospel of Atheism (1877) NF
Reincarnation (1892) NF
An Autobiography (1893) NF
The Self and its Sheaths (1895) NF
The Ancient Wisdom (1897) NF
Esoteric Christianity (1901) NF
Theosophy and the New Psychology (1904) NF
Thought Power (1911) NF
Lectures on Political Science (1919) NF
Shall India Live or Die? (1925) NF

BESANT, Sir Walter (1836–1901)
British novelist
Studies in Early French Poetry (1868) NF
Ready-Money Mortiboy [with James Rice] (1872) F
My Little Girl [with James Rice] (1873) F
With Harp and Crown [with James Rice] (1875) F
The Case of Mr Lucraft, and Other Tales [with James Rice] (1876) F SS
The Golden Butterfly [with James Rice] (1876) F
This Son of Vulcan [with James Rice] (1876) F
Such a Good Man [with James Rice] (1877) F
By Celia's Arbour [with James Rice] (1878) F
The Monks of Thelema [with James Rice] (1878) F
Sweet Nelly, My Heart's Delight [with James Rice] (1879) F
'Twas in Trafalgar Bay, and Other Stories [with James Rice] (1879) F SS
The Seamy Side [with James Rice] (1880) F
The Chaplain of the Fleet [with James Rice] (1881) F
The Ten Years' Tenant, and Other Stories [with James Rice] (1881) F SS
All Sorts and Conditions of Men (1882) F
The Revolt of Man (1882) F
All in a Garden Fair (1883) F
The Captain's Room (1883) F SS
A Glorious Fortune (1883) F
The Art of Fiction (1884) NF
Dorothy Forster (1884) F
In Luck at Last (1884) F
Uncle Jack (1885) F
Children of Gibeon (1886) F
Katharine Regina (1887) F
The World Went Very Well Then (1887) F
Herr Paulus (1888) F
The Bell of St Paul's (1889) F
For Faith and Freedom (1889) F
To Call Her Mine (1889) F
Armorel of Lyonesse (1890) F
The Demoniac (1890) F
The Holy Rose (1890) F SS
St Katherine's by the Tower (1891) F
The Ivory Gate (1892) F
Verbena Camellia Stephanotis (1892) F
The Rebel Queen (1893) F
Beyond the Dreams of Avarice (1895) F
In Deacon's Orders (1895) F SS
The City of Refuge (1896) F
The Master Craftsman (1896) F
A Fountain Sealed (1897) F
The Changeling (1898) F
The Orange Girl (1899) F
The Alabaster Box (1900) F
The Fourth Generation (1900) F
The Lady of Lynn (1901) F
Autobiography (1902) NF
A Five Years' Tryst, and Other Stories (1902) F SS
No Other Way (1902) F
As We Are and As We May Be (1903) NF
Essays and Historiettes (1903) NF
London in the Nineteeth Century (1909) NF

BETHAM, Mary Matilda (1776–1852)
British poet and author
A Biographical Dictionary of the Celebrated Women of Every Age and Country (1804) NF
The Lay of Marie (1816) V
Vignettes: In Verse (1818) V

BETHAM-EDWARDS, Matilda [Barbara] (1836–1919)
British novelist, poet, and woman of letters
The White House by the Sea (1857) F

Now or Never (1859) F
Doctor Jacob (1864) F
Kitty (1869) F
Minna's Holiday; or, Country Cousins, and Other Stories (1876) F SS
Bridget (1877) F
Brother Gabriel (1878) F
Friends Over the Water (1879) F
Six Life Studies of Famous Women (1880) NF
Pearla (1883) F
Love and Mirage; or, Waiting on an Island, and Other Tales (1885) F SS
Next of Kin Wanted (1887) F
The Parting of the Ways (1888) F
For One and the World (1889) F
The Curb of Honour (1893) F
A Romance of Dijon (1894) F
The Dream-Charlotte (1896) F
The Lord of the Harvest (1899) F
A Suffolk Courtship (1900) F
Martha Rose, Teacher (1906) F
A Close Ring; or, Episodes in the Life of a French Family (1907) F
Hearts of Alsace (1916) F

BETJEMAN, Sir John (1906–1984)
British poet, writer on architecture, and broadcaster
Mount Zion; or, In Touch with the Infinite (1931) V
Ghastly Good Taste; or, A Depressing Story of the Rise and Fall of English Architecture (1933) NF
Continual Dew (1937) V
An Oxford University Chest (1938) NF
Old Lights for New Chancels (1940) V
New Bats in Old Belfries (1945) V
First and Last Loves (1952) NF
A Few Late Chrysanthemums (1954) V
Poems in the Porch (1954) V
Summoned by Bells (1960) V
High and Low (1966) V
A Nip in the Air (1974) V
Church Poems (1981) V

BEYLE, Henri Marie *see* STENDHAL

BHATTACHARYA, Bhabani (1906–1988)
Indian novelist
So Many Hungers (1947) F
Music for Mohini (1952) F
He Who Rides the Tiger (1954) F
A Goddess Named Gold (1960) F
Shadow From Ladakh (1967) F
Steel Hawk (1968) F SS
A Dream in Hawaii (1978) F

BICKERSTAFFE, Isaac (1733–1808?)
Irish dramatist
Love in a Village (1762) D
The Maid of the Mill (1765) D
The Padlock (1768) D

BIERCE, Ambrose [Gwinett] (1842–1914?)
American journalist, short-story writer, and poet
The Fiend's Delight (1873) MISC
Cobwebs From an Empty Skull (1874) MISC
Tales of Soldiers and Civilians [UK: *In the Midst of Life*] (1891) F SS
Black Beetles in Amber (1892) V
The Monk and the Hangman's Daughter (1892) F
Can Such Things Be? (1893) V SS
Shapes of Clay (1903) V
The Shadow on the Dial (1909) NF
The Devil's Dictionary [first pub.1906 as *The Cynic's Word Book*] (1911) NF

BILLINGTON, [Lady] Rachel [Mary], *née* Packenham (1942–)
British novelist
All Things Nice (1969) F
Lilacs Out of the Dead Land (1971) F
A Painted Devil (1975) F
A Woman's Age (1979) F
Theo and Matilda (1990) F
Bodily Harm (1992) F

BINCHY, Maeve (1940–)
Irish romantic novelist
Light a Penny Candle (1982) F
Firefly Summer (1987) F
Circle of Friends (1990) F
The Copper Beach (1990) F
The Glass Lake (1994) F
Tara Road (1998) F
Scarlet Feather (2000) F

BINYON, [Robert] Laurence (1869–1943)
British poet, dramatist, and art historian
Lyric Poems (1894) V
The Praise of Life (1896) V
Porphyrion, and Other Poems (1898) V
The Death of Adam, and Other Poems (1903) V
Attila (1907) V D
England, and Other Poems (1909) V
The Winnowing-Fan (1914) V
The Anvil, and Other Poems (1916) V
The New World (1918) V
Six Poems on Bruges (1919) V
The Secret (1920) V
Arthur (1923) V D
Boadicea (1927) V D
The Idols (1928) V
The North Star, and Other Poems (1941) V
The Burning of the Leaves, and Other Poems (1944) V

BIRD, Robert [Montgomery] (1806–1854)
American novelist and dramatist
The Gladiator (1831) D
Oralloossa, Son of the Incas (1832) D
The Broker of Bogotá (1834) D
Calavar; or, The Knight of the Conquest (1834) F
The Hawks of Hawk-Hollow (1835) F
The Infidel; or, The Fall of Mexico (1835) F
Sheppard Lee (1836) F
Nick of the Woods; or, The Jibbenainosay (1837) F
The Adventures of Robin Day (1839) F

BIRNEY, [Alfred] Earle (1904–1995)
Canadian poet and novelist
David, and Other Poems (1942) V
Now is Time (1945) V
Strait of Anian (1948) V
Turvey (1949) F
Trial of a City (1952) V D
Down the Long Table (1955) F
Ice Cod Bell and Stone (1962) V
November Walk Near False Creek Mouth (1964) V
Rag and Bone Shop (1971) V
Alphbeings and Other Seasyours (1976) V
Fall by Fury (1978) V

BIRRELL, Augustine (1850–1933)
British statesman and essayist
Obiter Dicta [1st ser.] (1884) NF
The Life of Charlotte Bronte (1887) NF
Obiter Dicta [2nd ser.] (1887) NF
Res Judicatae (1892) NF
In the Name of the Bodleian, and Other Essays (1905) NF
A Rogue's Memoirs (1912) NF
More Obiter Dicta (1924) NF
Et Cetera (1930) NF

BISHOP, Elizabeth (1911–1979)
American poet
North and South (1946) V
A Cold Spring (1955) V
Questions of Travel (1965) V
Geography III (1976) V

BLACK, William (1841–1898)
Scottish novelist
James Merle (1864) F
Love or Marriage? (1868) F
In Silk Attire (1869) F
Kilmeny (1870) F
A Daughter of Heth (1871) F
The Monarch of Mincing Lane (1871) F
Mr Pisistratus Brown, M.P. in the Highlands (1871) F
The Strange Adventures of a Phaeton (1872) F
The Maid of Killeena, and Other Stories (1874) F SS
A Princess of Thule (1874) F
Three Feathers (1875) F
Lady Silverdale's Sweetheart, and Other Stories (1876) F SS
Madcap Violet (1876) F
Green Pastures and Piccadilly (1877) F
Macleod of Dare (1878) F
Sunrise (1880) F
White Wings (1880) F
Shandon Bells (1883) F
Yolande (1883) F
Judith Shakespeare (1884) F
White Heather (1885) F
The Wise Women of Inverness, a Tale, and Other Miscellanies (1885) F SS
Sabina Zembra (1887) F
In Far Lochaber (1888) F
The Strange Adventures of a House-Boat (1888) F
The Penance of John Logan, and Two Other Tales (1889) F SS
The New Prince Fortunatus (1890) F
Donald Ross of Heimra (1891) F
Stand Fast, Craig-Royston! (1891) F
The Magic Ink and Other Tales (1892) F SS
Wolfenburg (1892) F
The Handsome Humes (1893) F
Highland Cousins (1894) F
Briseis (1896) F
Wild Eelin (1898) F

BLACKMORE, R[ichard] D[oddridge] (1825–1900)
British novelist and poet
Poems by Melanter (1853) V
Epullia, and Other Poems (1855) V
Clara Vaughan (1864) F
Cradock Nowell (1866) F
Lorna Doone (1869) F
The Maid of Sker (1872) F
Alice Lorraine (1875) F
Cripps the Carrier (1876) F
Erema; or, My Father's Sin (1877) F
Mary Anerley (1880) F
Christowell (1882) F
The Remarkable History of Sir Thomas Upmore, Bart., M.P. (1884) F
Springhaven (1887) F
Kit and Kitty (1889) F
Perlycross (1894) F
Fringilla (1895) V
Tales from the Telling House (1896) F SS
Dariel (1897) F

BLACKMORE, Sir Richard (1654–1729)
English physician and author
Prince Arthur (1695) V
King Arthur (1697) V
A Satyr Against Wit (1700) V
Eliza (1705) V
Advice to the Poets (1706) V
The Kit-Cats (1708) V
The Nature of Man (1711) V
Creation (1712) V
Redemption (1722) V
Alfred (1723) V
Natural Theology; or, Moral Duties Consider'd Apart from Positive (1728) NF

BLACKMUR, R[ichard] P[almer] (1904–1965)
American critic and poet
The Double Agent (1935) NF
From Jordan's Delight (1937) V
The Expense of Greatness (1940) NF
The Second World (1942) V
The Good European (1947) V
Language as Gesture (1951) NF
The Lion and the Honeycomb (1955) NF
Eleven Essays in the European Novel (1964) NF

BLACKSTONE, Sir William (1723–1780)
British jurist and author
The Pantheon (1747) V
An Analysis of the Laws of England (1756) NF
A Discourse on the Study of Law (1758) NF
Commentaries on the Laws of England (1765) NF

BLACKWOOD, Algernon [Henry] (1869–1951)
British supernatural fiction writer
The Empty House, and Other Ghost Stories (1906) F SS
The Listener, and Other Stories (1907) F SS
John Silence: Physician Extraordinary (1908) F SS
The Education of Uncle Paul (1909) F
Jimbo (1909) F
The Human Chord (1910) F
The Lost Valley, and Other Stories (1910) F SS
The Centaur (1911) F
Pan's Garden (1912) F SS
Incredible Adventures (1914) F SS
Day and Night Stories (1917) F SS
The Promise of Air (1918) F
Ancient Sorceries, and Other Tales (1927) F SS
Shocks (1935) F SS

BLAIR, Eric Arthur *see* George Orwell

BLAIR, Hugh (1718–1800)
Scottish scholar and critic
A Critical Dissertation on the Poems of Ossian, the Son of Fingal (1763) NF
Lectures on Rhetoric and Belles Lettres (1783) NF

BLAIR, Robert (1699–1746)
British poet
The Grave (1743) V

BLAISE, Clark (1940–)
Canadian novelist and short-story writer
A North American Education (1973) F SS
Tribal Justice (1974) F SS
Lunar Attractions (1979) F
Lusts (1983) F
Resident Alien (1986) MISC

BLAKE, Nicholas *see* C. Day Lewis

BLAKE, William (1757–1827)
British poet and artist
Poetical Sketches (1783) V
All Religions Are One [1788?] NF
There is No Natural Religion [1788?] NF
The Book of Thel (1789) V
Songs of Innocence (1789) V
The French Revolution (1791) V
America (1793) V
The Marriage of Heaven and Hell [1793?] V
Visions of the Daughters of Albion (1793) V
Europe (1794) V
The First Book of Urizen (1794) V
Songs of Innocence and of Experience, Shewing the Two Contrary States of the Human Soul (1794) V
The Book of Ahania (1795) V
The Book of Los (1795) V
The Song of Los (1795) V
Jerusalem (dated 1804) V
Milton (dated 1804) V

BLATTY, William Peter (1928–)
American novelist
The Exorcist (1971) F

BLEASDALE, Alan (1946–)
British dramatist and novelist
Scully (1975) F
Having a Ball (1981) D
The Boys from the Black Stuff (1985) D

BLESSINGTON, Marguerite, Countess of, *née* Power (1789–1849)
Novelist and editor
Journal of a Tour Through the Netherlands to Paris in 1821 (1822) NF
The Magic Lantern; or, Sketches and Scenes in the Metropolis (1822) NF
The Repealers (1833) F
Conversations of Lord Byron with the Countess of Blessington (1834) NF
The Two Friends (1835) F
The Confessions of an Elderly Gentleman (1836) F
The Victims of Society (1837) F
The Confessions of an Elderly Lady (1838) F
The Governess (1839) F
The Idler in Italy (1839) NF
The Belle of a Season (1840) V
The Idler in France (1841) NF
The Lottery of Life (1842) F
Meredith (1843) F
Strathern; or, Life at Home and Abroad (1845) F
The Memoirs of a Femme de Chambre (1846) F
Marmaduke Herbert; or, The Fatal Error (1847) F
Country Quarters (1850) F

BLIND, Mathilde (1841–1896)
British poet
The Prophecy of St Oran (1881) V
Tarantella (1885) F
The Ascent of Man (1889) V
Dramas in Miniature (1891) V
Songs and Sonnets (1893) V
Birds of Passage (1895) V

BLISH, James (1921–1975)
American science fiction writer and critic
Jack of Eagles (1952) F
Earthman, Come Home (1955) F
The Seedling Stars (1957) F SS
A Case of Conscience (1958) F
The Triumph of Time (1958) F
Doctor Mirabilis (1964) F
Cities in Flight (1970) F
The Day After Judgment (1970) F

BLIXEN, Karen Christentze *see* Isak Dinesen

BLOCH, Robert [Albert] (1917–)
American thriller and horror writer
The Scarf (1947) F

The Kidnapper (1954) F
Shooting Star (1958) F
Psycho (1959) F
Firebug (1961) F
Terror (1962) F
The Star Stalker (1968) F
American Gothic (1974) F
There is a Serpent in Eden (1979) F
Psycho II (1982) F
Night of the Ripper (1984) F
Unholy Trinity (1986) F

BLOK, Aleksandr Aleksandrovich (1880–1921)
Russian Symbolist poet, dramatist, and critic
The City (1904–8) V
The Night Violet (1906) V
The Puppet Show (1906) D
Faina (1906–8) V
The Snow Mask (1907) V
Native Land (1907–16) V
The Terrible World (1907–16) V
The Italian Verses (1909) V
Carmen (1914) V

BLOOM, Harold (1930–)
American literary critic
Shelley's Myth-Making (1959) NF
The Visionary Company (1962) NF
The Anxiety of Influence (1973) NF
The Flight to Lucifer (1979) F
Ruin the Sacred Truths (1989) NF
The Western Canon (1994) NF

BLOOMFIELD, Robert (1766–1823)
British regional poet
The Farmer's Boy (1800) V
Rural Tales, Ballads and Songs (1802) V
Good Tidings; or, News from the Farm (1804) V
Wild Flowers; or, Pastoral and Local Poetry (1806) V
Nature's Music (1808) V
The Banks of Wye (1811) V
May Day with the Muses (1822) V
Hazelwood Hall (1823) V

BLUME, Judy (1938–)
American novelist and children's writer
Are You There, God? It's Me, Margaret (1970) F CH
Then Again, Maybe I Won't (1971) F CH
It's Not the End of the World (1972) F CH
Tales of a Fourth Grade Nothing (1972) F CH
Deenie (1973) F CH
Blubber (1974) F CH
Forever (1975) F CH
Superfudge (1980) F CH

BLUNDEN, Edmund Charles (1896–1974)
British poet and critic
Pastorals (1916) V
The Waggoner, and Other Poems (1920) V
The Shepherd, and Other Poems of Peace and War (1922) V
Masks of Time (1925) V
English Poems (1926) V
Japanese Garland (1928) V
Retreat (1928) V
Undertones of War (1928) MISC
Nature in English Literature (1929) NF
Near and Far (1929) V
A Summer's Fancy (1930) V
Votive Tablets (1931) NF
The Face of England (1932) NF
Fall In, Ghosts (1932) NF
Halfway House (1932) V
Choice or Chance (1934) V
The Mind's Eye (1934) NF
An Elegy, and Other Poems (1937) V
Shells by a Stream (1944) V
Shelley (1946) NF
After the Bombing, and Other Short Poems (1949) V
Poems of Many Years (1957) V
A Hong Kong House (1962) V

BLUNT, Wilfrid Scawen (1840–1922)
British poet, traveller, and Arabist
Sonnets and Songs by Proteus (1875) V
Proteus and Amadeus (1878) V
The Love Sonnets of Proteus (1880) V
The Future of Islam (1882) NF
The Wind and the Whirlwind (1883) V
Ideas About India (1885) NF
A New Pilgrimage, and Other Poems (1889) V
Esther, Love Lyrics, and Natalia's Resurrection (1892) V
The Love Lyrics and Songs of Proteus (1892) V
Griselda (1893) V
Satan Absolved (1899) V

BLY, Robert [Elwood] (1926–)
American poet and critic
Silence in the Snowy Fields (1962) V
The Light Around the Body (1967) V
Water Under the Earth (1972) V
Old Man Rubbing His Eyes (1975) V
This Body is Made of Camphor and Gopherwood (1977) V
Counting Small Boned Bodies (1979) V
This Tree Will Be Here for a Thousand Years (1979) V
The Man in the Black Coat Turns (1981) V
At the Time of Peony Blossoming (1983) V
The Moon on a Fencepost (1988) V
Iron John (1990) NF

BLYTHE, Ronald [George] (1922–)
British novelist and author
Akenfield (1969) NF

BLYTON, Enid (1897–1968)
British children's writer
Twins at St Clares (1941) F CH
Five on Treasure Island (1942) F CH
The Magic Faraway Tree (1943) F CH
First Term at Malory Towers (1946) F CH
Little Noddy Goes to Toyland (1949) F CH
The Secret Seven (1949) F CH

BOCCACCIO, Giovanni (1313–1375)
Italian author and humanist
The Decameron (1349–1351) F

BODKIN, Maud [Amy] (1875–1967)
British literary critic
Archetypal Patterns in Poetry (1934) NF

BOLAND, Eavan [Aisling] (1944–)
Irish poet
New Territory (1967) V
Night Feed (1982) V
The War Horse (1975) V
In Her Own Image (1980) V
The Journey, and Other Poems (1986) V
Outside History (1990) V
In a Time of Violence (1994) V

'BOLDREWOOD, Rolf' [Thomas Alexander Browne] (1826–1915)
Australian novelist
Robbery Under Arms (1888) F
A Colonial Reformer (1890) F
The Miner's Right (1890) F
The Squatter's Dream (1890) F
A Sydney-Side Saxon (1891) F
Nevermore (1892) F
A Modern Buccaneer (1894) F
The Crooked Stick; or, Pollie's Probation (1895) F
The Sphinx of Eaglehawk (1895) F
The Sealskin Cloak (1896) F
My Run Home (1897) F
Plain Living (1898) F
A Romance of Canvas Town, and Other Stories (1898) F SS
Babes in the Bush (1900) F
In Bad Company, and Other Stories (1901) F SS
The Ghost Camp; or, The Avengers (1902) F
The Last Chance (1905) F

BÖLL, Heinrich (1917–1985)
German novelist and short-story writer
And Never Said a Word [Und sagte kein einziges Wort] (1953) F
Billiards at Half-Past Nine [Billard um halb zehn] (1959) F
Group Portrait with Lady [Gruppenbild mit Dame] (1971) F
The Lost Honour of Katherina Blum [Die verlorene Ehre der Katherina Blum] (1974) F
Flowering Cherry (1957) D

BOLT, Robert [Oxton] (1924–1995)
British dramatist and screenwriter
A Man for All Seasons (1960) D
The Tiger and the Horse (1960) D
Gentle Jack (1963) D
Doctor Zhivago [screenplay] (1966) D
Vivat! Vivat Regina! (1970) D
State of Revolution (1977) D

BOND, Michael (1926–)
British children's writer
A Bear Called Paddington (1958) F CH
Here Comes Thursday (1966) F CH
The Tales of Olga da Polga (1971) F CH

BOND, [Thomas] Edward (1934–)
British dramatist, poet, and translator
The Pope's Wedding (1962) D
Narrow Road to the Deep North (1968) D
Bingo (1973) D
The Sea (1973) D
The Bundle; or, New Narrow Road to the Deep North (1978) D
The Woman (1978) D
Derek (1982) D
The War Plays (1985) D
Jackets (1989) D
September 1989 (1989) D

'BON GAULTIER' *see* W.E. Aytoun

BOOTH, Martin (1944–)
British novelist, poet, and critic
Hiroshima Joe (1985) F
The Industry of Souls (1998) F

BOOTH, William (1829–1912)
Founder of the Salvation Army
In Darkest England, and the Way Out (1890) NF

BOOTHBY, Guy [Newell] (1867–1905)
Australian novelist and short-story writer
A Bid for Fortune; or, Dr Nikola's Vendetta (1895) F
A Lost Endeavour (1895) F
Doctor Nikola (1896) F
Doctor Nikola's Experiment (1899) F
A Sailor's Bride (1899) F
A Maker of Nations (1900) F
A Cabinet Secret (1901) F
'Farewell, Nikola' (1901) F
The Mystery of the Clasped Hands (1901) F
A Bride from the Sea (1904) F
In Spite of the Czar (1905) F
The Lady of the Island (1909) F

BORGES, Jorge Luis (1899–1986)
Argentinian short-story writer, poet, and essayist
Fervour of Buenos Aires [Fervor de Buenos Aires] (1923) V
Luna de enfrente (1925) V
A Universal History of Infamy [Historia universal de la infamia] (1935) F
El jardín de senderos que se bifurcan (1941) F SS
Artificios (1944) F SS
Fictions [Ficciónes] (1945) F SS
The Aleph, and Other Stories [El Aleph] (1949) F SS
Dreamtigers [El Hacedor] (1960) MISC
Dr Brodie's Report [El informe de Brodie] (1971) F SS
The Book of Sand [El libro de arena] (1975) F SS

BORROW, George [Henry] (1803–1881)
British author and translator
Romantic Ballads, Translated from the Danish (1826) V

The Talisman (1835) V
Targum; or, Metrical Translations from Thirty Languages and Dialects (1835) V
The Zincali; or, An Account of the Gypsies of Spain (1841) NF
The Bible in Spain (1843) NF
Lavengro (1851) F
The Romany Rye (1857) F
Wild Wales (1862) NF
Romano Lavo-Lil (1874) NF

BOSTON, Lucy [Maria] (1892–1990)
British children's writer
The Children of Green Knowe (1954) F CH
The Chimneys of Green Knowe (1958) F CH
The River at Green Knowe (1959) F CH
A Stranger at Green Knowe (1961) F CH
An Enemy at Green Knowe (1964) F CH
The Sea Egg (1967) F CH
Nothing of the Sort (1971) F CH
The Fossil Snake (1975) F CH
The Stones of Green Knowe (1976) F CH

BOSWELL, James (1740–1795)
Scottish biographer of Samuel Johnson and author
The Cub at Newmarket (1762) F
Dorando (1767) F
An Account of Corsica (1768) NF
The Journal of a Tour to the Hebrides with Samuel Johnson (1785) NF
The Life of Samuel Johnson (1791) NF

BOTTING, Eirene *see* ANTONIA WHITE

BOTTOME, Phyllis (1884–1963)
British novelist
The Master Hope (1904) F
Broken Music (1914) F
The Common Chord (1914) F
Strange Fruit (1928) F SS
Private Worlds (1934) F
The Mortal Storm (1937) F
London Pride (1941) F

BOTTOMLEY, Gordon (1874–1948)
British poet and dramatist
Poems at White-Nights (1899) V
The Gate of Smaragdus (1904) V
Chambers of Imagery [1st ser.] (1907) V
Gruach (1921) V D
Poems of Thirty Years (1925) V
Scenes and Plays (1929) V
Lyric Plays (1932) V D
Choric Plays and a Comedy (1939) V D
A Stage for Poetry (1948) NF

BOUCICAULT, Dion[ysius] [Lardner] (1820?–1890)
Irish-born dramatist
London Assurance (1841) D
The Old Guard (1843) D
Old Heads and Young Hearts (1849) D
The Queen of Spades (1851) D
The Corsican Brothers (1852) D
The Colleen Bawn, or, The Brides of Garryowen (1860) D
Arragh-na-Pogue; or, The Wicklow Wedding (1864) D

BOULLE, Pierre (1912–1994)
French novelist and short-story writer
The Bridge Over the River Kwai [*Le Pont sur la Rivière Kwai*] (1952) F
Planet of the Apes [*La Planete des Singes*] (1959) F

BOURGET, Paul (1852–1935)
French poet, essayist, and novelist
La Vie inquiète ['The Anxious Life'] (1875) V
Essais (1883) NF
L'Irréparable (1884) F
Nouveaux essais de psychologie contemporaine ['New Essays on Contemporary Psychology'] (1886) NF
André Cornélis (1887) F
Le Disciple (1889) F
Cosmopolis (1893) F
L'étape ['The Halting-Place'] (1902) F
Un Divorce (1904) F
L'émigré ['The Emigrant'] (1907) F

BOWEN, Elizabeth [Dorothea Cole] (1899–1973)
British novelist, essayist, and short-story writer
Encounters (1923) F SS
Ann Lee's, and Other Stories (1926) F SS
The Hotel (1927) F
Joining Charles, and Other Stories (1929) F SS
The Last September (1929) F
Friends and Relations (1931) F
To the North (1932) F
The Cat Jumps, and Other Stories (1934) F SS
The House in Paris (1935) F
The Death of the Heart (1938) F
Look at All Those Roses (1941) F SS
The Demon Lover, and Other Stories [US: *Ivy Gripped the Steps*] (1945) F SS
The Heat of the Day (1949) F
A World of Love (1955) F
The Little Girls (1964) F
A Day in the Dark, and Other Stories (1965) F SS
Eva Trout; or, Changing Scenes (1968) F

'BOWEN, Marjorie' [Gabrielle Margaret Vere Campbell, later **Long]** (1886–1952)
British novelist and short-story writer
The Viper of Milan (1906) F
The Sword Decides! (1908) F
Black Magic (1909) F
I Will Maintain (1910) F
Defender of the Faith (1911) F
God and the King (1911) F
The Rake's Progress (1912) F
The Governor of England (1913) F
A Knight of Spain (1913) F
Prince and Heretic (1914) F
The Carnival of Florence (1915) F
Dark Ann, and Other Stories (1927) F SS

The Last Bouquet (1932) F SS
The Bishop of Hell, and Other Stories (1949) F SS

BOWLES, Caroline Anne, later **Southey** (1786–1854)
British poet
Ellen Fitzarthur (1820) V
The Widow's Tale, and Other Poems (1822) V
Solitary Hours (1826) MISC
The Cat's Tail (1831) V
Tales of the Factories (1833) V

BOWLES, Jane (1917–1973)
American novelist, short-story writer, and dramatist
Two Serious Ladies (1943) F
The Summer House (1954) D
Plain Pleasures (1966) F SS

BOWLES, Paul (1910–)
American novelist, short-story writer, and poet
The Sheltering Sky (1949) F
A Little Stone (1950) F SS
Let It Come Down (1952) F
The Spider's House (1955) F
Their Heads Are Green and Their Hands Are Blue (1963) NF
A Life Full of Holes (1964) F
Up Above the World (1966) F
The Thicket of Spring (1972) V
Next to Nothing (1981) V
A Delicate Episode (1988) F SS
Unwelcome Words (1989) F SS

BOWLES, William Lisle (1762–1850)
British poet and antiquary
Fourteen Sonnets, Elegaic and Descriptive (1789) V
Hope (1796) V
St Michael's Mount (1798) V
Song of the Battle of the Nile (1799) V
The Sorrows of Switzerland (1801) V
The Picture (1803) V
The Spirit of Discovery; or, The Conquest of Ocean (1804) V
The Missionary (1813) V
The Grave of the Last Saxon; or, The Legend of the Curfew (1822) V
Ellen Gray; or, The Dead Maiden's Curse (1823) V
Days Departed; or, Banwell Hill (1828) V
St John in Patmos; or, The Last Apostle (1835) V

BOWRA, [Sir Cecil] Maurice (1898–1971)
British scholar and critic
The Oxford Book of Greek Verse in Translation (1938) ANTH
The Heritage of Symbolism (1943) NF
The Creative Experiment (1949) NF
The Romantic Imagination (1949) NF

BOYD, Martin (1893–1972)
Australian novelist
Love Gods (1925) F
Brangane: A Memoir (1926) F
The Montforts [as 'Martin Mills'] (1928) F
Dearest Idol [as 'Walter Beckett'] (1929) F
Scandal of Spring (1934) F
The Lemon Farm (1935) F
The Painted Princess (1936) F
The Picnic (1937) F
Night of the Party (1938) F
Nuns in Jeopardy (1940) F
Lucinda Brayford (1946) F
Such Pleasure (1949) F
The Cardboard Crown (1952) F
A Difficult Young Man (1955) F
Outbreak of Love (1957) F
When Blackbirds Sing (1962) F
The Tea-Time of Love (1969) F

BOYD, William [Andrew Murray] (1952–)
British novelist, short-story writer, and dramatist
A Good Man in Africa (1981) F
On the Yankee Station, and Other Stories (1981) F SS
An Ice-Cream War (1982) F
Stars and Bars (1984) F
The New Confessions (1987) F
Brazzaville Beach (1990) F
The Blue Afternoon (1993) F
The Destiny of Nathalie 'X', and Other Stories (1995) F SS
Armadillo (1998) F

BOYER, Abel (1667–1729)
English historian
The Royal Dictionary (1699) NF
Achilles; or, Iphigenia in Aulis (1700) D
The History of the Reign of Queen Anne (1703) NF

BOYLAN, Clare (1948–)
Irish novelist and short-story writer
Holy Pictures (1983) F
A Nail in the Head (1983) F SS
Last Resorts (1984) F
Black Baby (1988) F
Concerning Virgins (1990) F SS
Home Rule (1992) F
That Bad Woman (1995) F SS
Room For a Single Lady (1997) F
Another Family Christmas (1998) F
Beloved Stranger (1999) F

BOYLE, Kay (1903–1993)
American novelist, short-story writer, and poet
Wedding Day, and Other Stories (1930) F SS
Plagued by the Nightingale (1931) F
Year Before Last (1932) F
The First Lover, and Other Stories (1933) F SS
Gentleman, I Address You Privately (1933) F
My Next Bride (1934) F
Death of a Man (1936) F
The White Horses of Vienna (1936) F SS
A Glad Day (1938) V
Monday Night (1938) F
The Youngest Camel (1939) F
The Crazy Hunter (1940) F SS
Avalanche (1943) F
American Citizen (1944) V
A Frenchman Must Die (1946) F

His Human Majesty (1949) F
The Smoking Mountain (1951) F SS
Seagull on the Step (1955) F
Generation Without Farewell (1959) F
Nothing Ever Breaks Except the Heart (1966) F SS

BOYLE, Roger, Baron Broghill and 1st Earl of Orrery (1621–1679)
English statesman and author
Parthenissa (1651) F
The Martyrdom of Theodora, and of Didymus (1687) F
Guzman (1693) D
Herod the Great (1694) D
The Tragedy of King Saul (1703) D

BRACKENBURY, Alison (1953–)
British poet
Dreams of Power (1981) V
Breaking Ground (1984) V
Christmas Roses (1988) V

BRACKENRIDGE, Hugh Henry (1748–1816)
American novelist, dramatist, and poet
The Battle of Bunkers Hill (1776) D
The Death of General Montgomery (1777) D
Six Political Discourses (1778) NF
Modern Chivalry (1792–1815) F

BRADBROOK, Muriel [Clara] (1909–1993)
British literary scholar
The School of Night (1936) NF

BRADBURY, Malcolm [Stanley] (1932–2000)
British novelist and critic
Eating People is Wrong (1959) F
Stepping Westward (1965) F
What Is a Novel? (1969) NF
The Social Context of Modern English Literature (1971) NF
Possibilities (1973) NF
The History Man (1975) F
Who Do You Think You Are? (1976) F SS
The Modern American Novel (1983) NF
Rates of Exchange (1983) F
Cuts (1987) F
My Strange Search for Mensonge (1987) NF
No, Not Bloomsbury (1987) NF
The Modern World (1988) NF
Dr Criminale (1992) F
Dangerous Pilgrimages (1994) NF
Diderot at the Hermitage (2000) F

BRADBURY, Ray[mond] [Douglas] (1920–)
American novelist, short-story writer, dramatist, and poet
Dark Carnival (1947) F SS
The Martian Chronicles [UK: *The Silver Locusts*] (1950) F SS
The Illustrated Man (1951) F SS
Fahrenheit 451 (1953) F
The Golden Apples of the Sun (1953) F SS
October Country (1955) F SS
Dandelion Wine (1957) F
A Meditation for Melancholy [UK: *The Day it Rained Forever*] (1959) F SS
R is for Rocket, S is for Space (1962) F SS
Something Wicked This Way Comes (1962) F
The Machineries of Joy (1964) F SS
The Wonderful Ice Cream Suit (1965) D
Twice Twenty-Two (1966) F SS
Any Friend of Nicholas Nickleby's is a Friend of Mine (1968) F SS
The Halloween Tree (1968) D
I Sing the Body Electric (1969) F SS
When Elephants Last in the Doorway Bloomed (1973) V
Where Robot Men and Robot Women Run Round in Robot Towns (1977) V
Death is a Lonely Business (1985) F
The Toynbee Convector (1988) F SS
A Graveyard for Lunatics (1990) F
The Smile (1991) F SS
Green Shadow, White Whale (1992) F

BRADDON, Mary Elizabeth, later Maxwell (1835–1915)
British novelist, short-story writer, and editor
Three Times Dead; or, The Secret of the Heath (1854) F
Garibaldi, and Other Poems (1861) V
The Lady Lisle (1861) F
Lady Audley's Secret (1862) F
Ralph the Bailiff, and Other Tales (1862) F SS
Aurora Floyd (1863) F
The Captain of the Vulture (1863) F
Eleanor's Victory (1863) F
John Marchmont's Legacy (1863) F
The Doctor's Wife (1864) F
Henry Dunbar (1864) F
Only a Clod (1865) F
Sir Jasper's Tenant (1865) F
The Lady's Mile (1866) F
Birds of Prey (1867) F
Circe (1867) F
Rupert Godwin (1867) F
Charlotte's Inheritance (1868) F
Dead Sea Fruit (1868) F
Run to Earth (1868) F
Fenton's Quest (1871) F
The Lovels of Arden (1871) F
Robert Ainsleigh (1872) F
To the Bitter End (1872) F
Lucius Davoren; or, Publicans and Sinners (1873) F
Milly Darrell, and Other Tales (1873) F SS
Strangers and Pilgrims (1873) F
Lost for Love (1874) F
Taken at the Flood (1874) F
A Strange World (1875) F
Dead Men's Shoes (1876) F
Joshua Haggard's Daughter (1876) F
Weavers and Weft, and Other Tales (1877) F SS
An Open Verdict (1878) F
The Cloven Foot (1879) F

Vixen (1879) F
Just as I Am (1880) F
The Story of Barbara (1880) F
Asphodel (1881) F
Flower and Weed (1882) F
Mount Royal (1882) F
Flower and Weed, and Other Tales (1883) F SS
The Golden Calf (1883) F
Phantom Fortune (1883) F
Under the Red Flag (1883) F
Ishmael (1884) F
Wyllard's Weird (1885) F
Mohawks (1886) F
One Thing Needful (1886) F
Under the Red Flag, and Other Tales (1886) F SS
Like and Unlike (1887) F
The Fatal Three (1888) F
The Day Will Come (1889) F
One Life, One Love (1890) F
Gerard; or, The World, the Flesh, and the Devil (1891) F
The Venetians (1892) F
All Along the River (1893) F
The Christmas Hirelings (1894) F
Thou Art the Man (1894) F
Sons of Fire (1895) F
London Pride; or, When the World Was Younger (1896) F
Under Love's Rule (1897) F
In High Places (1898) F
Rough Justice (1898) F
His Darling Sin (1899) F
The Infidel (1900) F
The Conflict (1903) F
A Lost Eden (1904) F
The Rose of Life (1905) F
The White House (1906) F
Dead Love Has Chains (1907) F
Her Convict (1907) F
During Her Majesty's Pleasure (1908) F
Our Adversary (1909) F
Beyond These Voices (1910) F
The Green Curtain (1911) F
Miranda (1913) F
Mary (1916) F

BRADFORD, Barbara Taylor (1933–)
British popular novelist
A Woman of Substance (1980) F
Voice of the Heart (1983) F
Hold the Dream (1985) F
Act of Will (1986) F
To Be the Best (1988) F
Where You Belong (2000) F

BRADLEY, A[ndrew] C[ecil] (1851–1935)
British critic and scholar
Shakespearean Tragedy (1904) NF
Oxford Lectures on Poetry (1909) NF

BRADLEY, Edward ['Cuthbert Bede'] (1827–1889)
British humorist
The Adventures of Mr Verdant Green, an Oxford Freshman (1853) F
The Further Adventures of Mr Verdant Green, an Oxford Undergraduate (1853) F
Love's Provocations (1855) F
Tales of College Life (1856) F
Mr Verdant Green, Married and Done For (1857) F
Our New Rector; or, The Village of Norton (1861) F
A Tour in Tartan-Land (1863) F
The White Wife (1865) F SS
Mattins and Muttons; or, The Beauty of Brighton (1866) F
Little Mr Bouncer and His Friend, Verdant Green (1873) F
Figaro at Hastings, St Leonards (1877) F

BRADLEY, F[rancis] H[erbert], OM (1846–1924)
British philosopher
Ethical Studies (1876) NF
The Principles of Logic (1883) NF
Appearance and Reality (1893) NF
Essays on Truth and Reality (1914) NF

BRADLEY, Henry (1845–1923)
British philologist and lexicographer
The Making of English (1904) NF

BRADSTREET, Anne, *née* Dudley (1612–1672)
English colonial poet
The Tenth Muse Lately Sprung Up in America (1650) V

BRAGG, Melvyn (1939–)
British novelist and broadcaster
For Want of a Nail (1965) F
The Hired Man (1969) F
A Place in England (1970) F
The Nerve (1971) F
Kingdom Come (1980) F
Love and Glory (1983) F
The Maid of Buttermere (1987) F
A Time to Dance (1990) F
Crystal Rooms (1992) F
Credo (1996) F
The Soldier's Return (1999) F

BRAINE, John [Gerard] (1922–1986)
British novelist
Room at the Top (1957) F
Life at the Top (1962) F
The Jealous God (1964) F
The Crying Game (1968) F
Stay With Me Till Morning (1970) F
The Queen of a Distant Country (1972) F
The One and Last Love (1981) F
The Two of Us (1984) F
These Golden Days (1985) F

BRAITHWAITE, E[dward] R[icardo] (1912–)
Guyanese writer and diplomat
To Sir, With Love (1959) F

A Kind of Homecoming (1962) NF
Paid Servant (1962) F
Choice of Straws (1965) F
Reluctant Neighbours (1972) F
Honorary White (1975) NF

'BRAMAH, Ernest' [Ernest Bramah Smith] (1868–1942)
British detective story writer and poet
The Wallet of Kai Lung (1900) F SS
Max Carrados (1914) F SS
The Eyes of Max Carrados (1923) F SS
The Specimen Case (1924) F SS
Kail Lung Unrolls His Mat (1928) F SS
Kai Lung Beneath the Mulberry Tree (1940) F SS

BRATHWAITE, Edward [Kamau] (1930–)
Caribbean poet and historian
Rites of Passage (1967) V
Masks (1968) V
Islands (1969) V
The Arrivants: A New World Trilogy [cont. *Rites of Passage, Masks, Islands*] (1973) V
Days and Nights (1975) V
Other Exiles (1975) V
Black and Blues (1976) V
Mother Poem (1977) V
Sun Poem (1982) V
Third World Poems (1983) V
History of the Voice (1984) NF
X-Self (1987) V

BRAUTIGAN, Richard (1935–1984)
American novelist and poet
The Galilee Hitch-Hiker (1958) V
The Octopus Frontier (1960) V
A Condeferate General from Big Sur (1964) F
All Watched Over by Machines of Loving Grace (1967) V
Trout Fishing in America (1967) F
In Watermelon Sugar (1968) F
The Pill Versus the Springfield Mine Disaster (1968) V
Rommel Drives on Deep into Egypt (1970) V
The Abortion: An Historical Romance (1971) F
Revenge of the Lawn (1971) F
The Hawkins Monster: A Gothic Western (1974) F
Willard and his Bowling Trophies: A Perverse Mystery (1975) F
Loading Mercury with a Pitchfork (1976) V
Sombrero Fallout: A Japanese Novel (1976) F
Dreaming of Babylon: A Private Eye Novel (1977) F
June 30th, June 30th (1978) V
The Tokyo-Montana Express (1980) F
So the Wind Won't Blow It All Away (1992) F

BRAY, Anna Eliza, *née* Kempe, later **Stothard** (1790–1883)
British novelist
De Foix; or, Sketches of the Manners and Customs of the Fourteenth Century (1826) F
The Protestant (1828) F
The White Hoods (1828) F
Fitz of Fitz-Ford (1830) F
The Talba, or Moor of Portugal (1830) F
Warleigh; or, The Fatal Oak (1834) F
Trelawny of Trelawne; or, The Prophecy (1837) F
Trials of the Heart (1839) F
Henry de Pomeroy; or, The Eve of St John (1842) F
Courtenay of Walreddon (1844) F
The Father's Curse; and The Daughter's Sacrifice (1848) F
The Good St Louis and His Times (1870) F
Hartland Forest (1871) F
Roseteague; or, The Heir of Treville Crewse (1874) F

BRAY, Mrs Caroline [Cara], *née* Hennell (1814–1905)
British novelist
Richard Barton; or, The Wounded Bird (1873) F
Paul Bradley (1876) F
Branded; or, The Sins of the Fathers Shall Be Visited on the Children (1888) F

BRAZIL, Angela (1869–1947)
British writer of school stories for girls
A Terrible Tomboy (1904) F CH
The Fortunes of Philippa (1906) F JF
The Third Class at Miss Kaye's (1908) F JF
The Nicest Girl in the School (1909) F JF
Bosom Friends (1910) F JF
The School on the Loch (1946) F JF

BRECHT, Bertolt (1898–1956)
German dramatist and poet
Baal (1922) D
Drums in the Night [*Trommeln in der Nacht*] (1922) D
Man is Man [*Mann ist Mann*] (1927) D
The Threepenny Opera [*Die Dreigroschenoper*] (1928) D
St John of the Stockyards [*Die heilige Johanna der SchlachthÖfe*] (1929–30) D
The Life of Galileo [*Leben des Galilei*] (1937–9) D
The Good Woman of Setzuan [*Der Gute Mensch von Sezuan*] (1938–41) D
Mother Courage [*Mutter Courage*] (1941) D
The Resistible Rise of Arturo Uri [*Der aufhaltsame Aufstieg des Arturo Uri*] (1941) D
The Caucasian Chalk Circle [*Der kaukasische Kreidekreis*] (1948) D

'BRENT OF BIN BIN' *see* MILES FRANKLIN

BRENT-DYER, Elinor M. (1894–1969)
British writer of school stories
The School at the Chalet (1925) F CH

BRENTON, Howard (1942–)
British dramatist, poet, and novelist
Christie in Love, and Other Plays (1969) D
Hitler Dances (1972) D
Plays for Public Places (1972) D
Brassneck (1973) D
Weapons of Happiness (1976) D
Epsom Downs (1977) D
The Romans in Britain (1980) D
Blood Poetry (1985) D

Pravda (1985) D
Dead Head (1987) D
Diving for Pearls (1989) F
Iranian Nights (1989) D
Moscow Gold (1990) D
Berlin Bertie (1992) D
Hot Irons (1995) NF

BRETON, André (1896–1966)
French poet, essayist, and critic
Clair de terre (1923) V
Les Pas perdus (1924) NF
Nadja (1928) F
Le Surréalisme et la peinture (1928) NF
Le Revolver à cheveux blancs (1932) V
Les Vases communicants (1932) F
L'Air de l'eau (1934) V
Point du jour (1934) NF
La Clé des champs (1953) NF

BRETON, Nicholas (1545?–1626?)
English poet
A Small Handful of Fragrant Flowers (1575) V
The Pilgrimage to Paradise (1592) V
The Arbour of Amorous Devises (1597) V
The Passions of the Spirit (1599) V
Pasquil's Mad-cap (1600) V
Pasquil's Mistress; or, The Worthy and Unworthy Woman (1600) V
The Mother's Blessing (1602) V
The Passionate Shepherd; or, The Shepherd's Love (1604) V
The Soul's Immortal Crown (1605) V
Wit's Private Wealth (1607) NF

BREWER, E[benezer] Cobham (1810–1897)
British miscellaneous writer and dictionary compiler
A Dictionary of Phrase and Fable (1870) NF

BRIDGES, Robert [Seymour] (1844–1930)
British Poet Laureate, critic, and dramatist
Carmen Elegiacum (1876) V
The Growth of Love (1876) V
Prometheus the Firegiver (1883) V
Eros and Psyche (1885) V
Nero: Part 1 (1885) V D
The Feast of Bacchus (1889) V
Achilles in Scyros (1890) D
The Christian Captives (1890) D
Palicio (1890) D
The Return of Ulysses (1890) D
Eden (1891) V
The Humours of the Court: A Comedy, and Other Poems (1893) V
Milton's Prosody (1893) NF
Nero: Part 2 (1894) V D
Invocation to Music (1895) V
John Keats (1895) NF
Ode for the Bicentenary Commemoration of Henry Purcell (1896) V
A Song of Darkness and Light (1898) V
Now in Wintry Delights (1903) V
Peace Ode Written on the Conclusion of the Three Years' War (1903) V
Demeter (1905) V
The Chivalry of the Sea (1916) V
Ibant Obscuri (1916) V
The Necessity of Poetry (1918) NF
Britannia Victrix (1919) V
October, and Other Poems (1920) V
New Verse Written in 1921 (1925) V
The Testament of Beauty (1929) V

'BRIDIE, James' [Osborne Henry Mavor] (1888–1951)
Scottish dramatist
The Switchback; The Pardoner's Tale; The Sunlight Sonata (1930) D
The Anatomist, and Other Plays (1931) D
A Sleeping Clergyman (1933) D
Storm in a Teacup (1936) D
The King of Nowhere, and Other Plays (1938) D
Susannah and the Elders, and Other Plays (1940) D
Plays for Plain People (1944) D
Tedious and Brief (1944) NF
The British Drama (1945) NF
Daphne Laureola (1949) D
John Knox, and Other Plays (1949) D
The Baikie Charivari; or, The Seven Prophets (1952) D

BRIGGS, Asa, Lord Briggs (1921–)
British social historian
Victorian People (1954) NF
Victorian Cities (1963) NF
A Social History of England (1983) NF
Victorian Things (1988) NF

BRIGGS, Raymond [Redvers] (1934–)
British writer and illustrator of children's books
Jim and the Beanstalk (1970) F CH
Father Christmas (1973) F CH
Father Christmas Goes on Holiday (1975) F CH
Fungus the Bogeyman (1975) F CH
The Snowman (1979) F CH
When the Wind Blows (1982) F
The Tin Pot Foreign General and the Old Iron Woman (1984) F

BRIGHOUSE, Harold (1882–1958)
British dramatist
Lonesome-Like (1911) D
The Odd Man Out (1912) D
Hobson's Choice (1915) D
Sack (1916) D

BRILLAT-SAVARIN, Anthelme (1755–1826)
French jurist and magistrate
The Physiology of Taste [Physiologie du goût ou Méditations sur la gastronomie transcendente] (1825) NF

BRINK, André [Philippus] (1935–)
South African novelist
Looking on Darkness (1974) F
An Instant in the Wind (1976) F

Rumours of Rain (1978) F
A Dry White Season (1979) F
A Chain of Voices (1982) F
Mapmakers (1983) NF
The Wall of the Plague (1984) F
States of Emergency (1988) F
An Act of Terror (1991) F
On the Contrary (1993) F

BRITTAIN, Vera [Mary] (1893–1970)
British author, pacifist, and feminist
The Dark Tide (1923) F
Testament of Youth (1933) NF
Testament of Friendship (1940) NF
Seeds of Chaos (1944) NF
Testament of Experience (1957) NF

BROAD, C[harlie] D[unbar] (1887–1971)
British philosopher
Perception, Physics and Reality (1914) NF
Scientific Thought (1923) NF
The Mind and its Place in Nature (1925) NF
Religion, Philosophy and Psychical Research (1953) NF
Lectures on Psychical Research (1962) NF

BRODKEY, Harold [Roy] (1930–)
American short-story writer and novelist
First Love and Other Sorrows (1958) F SS
Women and Angels (1985) F SS
Stories in an Almost Classical Mode (1988) F SS
The Runaway Soul (1991) F

BRODSKY, Joseph [Alexandrovich] (1940–1996)
Russian-born poet
Elegy for John Donne, and Other Poems (1967) V
A Part of Speech (1980) V
Less Than One (1986) NF
To Urania (1988) V
Marbles (1989) D
Watermarks (1992) NF
So Forth (1995) V

BROME, Richard (1590?–1652?)
English dramatist
The Northern Lasse (1632) D
The Antipodes (1640) D
The Sparagus Garden (1640) D
A Jovial Crew; or, The Merry Beggars (1652) D
The Queen's Exchange (1657) D

BROMFIELD, Louis (1896–1956)
American novelist, short-story writer, and dramatist
The Green Bay Tree (1924) F
Possession (1925) F
Early Autumn (1926) F
A Good Woman (1927) F
The House of Women (1927) D
Awake and Rehearse (1929) F SS
The Farm (1933) F
The Rains Came (1937) F
It Takes All Kinds (1939) F SS
Night in Bombay (1940) F
Wild is the River (1941) F
Mrs Parkinson (1943) F
The World We Live In (1944) F SS
Pleasant Valley (1945) F

BRONTË, Anne (1820–1849)
British novelist and poet
Agnes Grey (1847) F
The Tenant of Wildfell Hall (1848) F

BRONTË, Charlotte, later **Nicholls** (1816–1855)
British novelist and poet
Jane Eyre (1847) F
Shirley (1849) F
Villette (1853) F
The Professor (1857) F

BRONTË, Charlotte (1816–1855)**, Emily** (1818–1848)**, and Anne** (1820–1849)
Poems by Currer, Ellis and Acton Bell (1846) V

BRONTË, Emily Jane ['Ellis Bell'] (1818–1848)
British novelist and poet
Wuthering Heights; and Agnes Grey [by 'Ellis and Acton Bell'] (1847) F

BROOKE, Charlotte (1740?–1793)
British translator and anthologist
Reliques of Irish Poetry (1789) V

BROOKE, E[mma] F[rances] [E. Fairfax Byrrne] (1859?–1926)
British novelist
A Fair Country Maid (1883) F
Entangled (1885) F
Heir Without a Heritage (1887) F
A Superfluous Woman (1894) F
Transition (1895) F
Life the Accuser (1896) F
The Confession of Stephen Whapshare (1898) F
The Engrafted Rose (1899) F
The Poet's Child (1903) F
The Twins of Skirlaugh Hall (1903) F
The Story of Hauksgarth Farm (1909) F

BROOKE, Frances (1724–1789)
British novelist
Letters from Juliet, Lady Catesby (1760) F
The History of Lady Julia Mandeville (1763) F
The History of Emily Montague (1769) F
The Excursion (1777) F
The Siege of Sinope (1781) D
Rosina (1783) D
Marian (1788) D

BROOKE, Henry (1703–1783)
English poet, novelist, and dramatist
Universal Beauty (1735) V
The Earl of Essex (1761) D
The Fool of Quality; or, The History of Henry Earl of Moreland (1765) F
Redemption (1772) V
Juliet Grenville; or, The History of the Human Heart (1774) F

BROOKE, [Bernard] Jocelyn (1908–1966)
British novelist
The Military Orchid (1948) F
The Scapegoat (1948) F
A Mine of Serpents (1949) F
The Goose Cathedral (1950) F
The Passing of a Hero (1953) F
Conventional Weapons (1961) F

BROOKE, Rupert Chawner (1887–1915)
British poet
1914 and Other Poems (1915) V
John Webster and the Elizabethan Drama (1916) NF
Letters From America (1916) NF
The Collected Poems of Rupert Brooke (1918) V

BROOKE, Stopford Augustus (1832–1916)
British essayist, critic, and biographer
Primer of English Literature (1876) NF
On Ten Plays of Shakespeare (1905) NF
Studies in Poetry (1907) NF
Ten More Plays of Shakespeare (1913) NF
Naturalism in English Poetry (1920) NF

BROOKE-ROSE, Christine (1926–)
British novelist, critic, and translator
The Languages of Love (1957) F
The Sycamore Tree (1958) F
The Dear Deceit (1960) F
The Middlemen (1961) F
Out (1964) F
Thru (1975) F
A Rhetoric of the Unreal (1981) NF
Amalgamemnon (1984) F
Xorandor (1986) F
Verbivore (1990) F
Textermination (1991) F
Remake (1996) F

BROOKNER, Anita (1928–)
British novelist and art historian
A Start in Life (1981) F
Providence (1982) F
Look at Me (1983) F
Hotel du Lac (1984) F
Family and Friends (1985) F
A Misalliance (1986) F
A Friend From England (1987) F
Latecomers (1988) F
Lewis Percy (1989) F
Brief Lives (1990) F
A Closed Eye (1991) F
Fraud (1992) F
A Family Romance (1993) F
A Private View (1994) F
Incidents in the Rue Laugier (1995) F
Altered States (1996) F
Soundings (1997) NF
Visitors (1997) F SS
Undue Influence (1999) F SS

BROOKS, Charles William Shirley (1816–1874)
British novelist, dramatist, and journalist
Timour the Tartar! or, The Iron Master of Samarkand-by-Oxus (1850) D
The Exposition (1851) D
Aspen Court (1855) F
The Gordian Knot (1859) F
The Silver Cord (1861) F
Sooner or Later (1868) F
The Naggletons (1875) F

BROOKS, Cleanth (1906–)
American literary critic
Modern Poetry and the Tradition (1939) NF
The Well-Wrought Urn (1947) NF

BROPHY, Brigid [Antonia Susan] (1929–)
British novelist, biographer, and critic
Hackenfeller's Ape (1953) F
The King of a Rainy Country (1956) F
Flesh (1962) F
The Finishing Touch (1963) F
The Snow Ball (1964) F
In Transit (1969) F
Palace Without Chairs (1978) F

BROSTER, D[orothy] K[athleen] (1878–1950)
British novelist and short-story writer
The Flight of the Heron (1925) F
The Gleam in the North (1927) F
The Dark Mile (1929) F
A Fire of Driftwood (1932) F SS
Couching at the Door (1942) F SS

BROUGHAM, Henry Peter, 1st Baron Brougham and Vaux (1778–1868)
British statesman and historian
An Inquiry into the Colonial Policy of the European Powers (1803) NF
A Letter to Sir Samuel Romilly . . . Upon the Abuse of Charities (1818) NF
Practical Observations Upon the Education of the People (1825) NF
Thoughts on Negro Slavery (1826) NF
Thoughts Upon the Aristocracy of England (1835) NF
'We Can't Afford It!' (1835) NF
Historical Sketches of Statesmen in the Time of George III [1st and 2nd ser.] (1839) NF
Historical Sketches of Statesmen in the Time of George III [3rd ser.] (1842) NF
Practical Philosophy (1842) NF
Albert Lunel; or, The Chateau of Languedoc (1844) F
The British Constitution (1844) NF
The Life and Times of Lord Brougham Written by Himself (1871) NF

BROUGHAM, John (1810–1880)
Irish-born American actor and dramatist
Metamora; or, The Last of the Pollywoags (1847) D
Temptation; or, The Irish Immigrant (1849) D
A Row at the Lyceum; or, Green Room Secrets (1851) D

Columbus (1857) D
The Mustard Ball; or, Love at the Academy (1858) D

BROUGHTON, Rhoda (1840–1920)
British novelist
Cometh Up as a Flower (1867) F
Not Wisely But Too Well (1867) F
Red as a Rose is She (1870) F
Good-bye, Sweetheart (1872) F
Nancy (1873) F
Tales for Christmas Eve (1873) F SS
Joan (1876) F
Second Thoughts (1880) F
Belinda (1883) F
Doctor Cupid (1886) F
Alas! (1890) F
Mrs Bligh (1892) F
A Beginner (1894) F
Scylla or Charybdis? (1895) F
Dear Faustina (1897) F
The Game and the Candle (1899) F
Foes in Law (1900) F
Lavinia (1902) F
A Waif's Progress (1905) F
Mamma (1908) F
The Devil and the Deep Sea (1910) F
Between Two Stools (1912) F
Concerning a Vow (1914) F
A Fool in Her Folly (1920) F

BROWN, Charles Brockden (1771–1810)
American novelist
Alcuin: A Dialogue (1798) NF
Wieland; or, The Transformation (1798) F
Arthur Mervyn (1799) F
Edgar Huntly (1799) F
Ormond (1799) F
Clara Howard (1801) F
Jane Talbot (1801) F

BROWN, Christy (1932–1981)
Irish novelist, autobiographer, and poet
My Left Foot (1954) NF
Down all the Days (1970) F
A Shadow on Summer (1974) F

BROWN, George Douglas ['George Douglas'], (1869–1902)
British novelist
The House With the Green Shutters [as 'George Douglas'] (1901) F

BROWN, George Mackay (1921–1996)
Scottish poet, novelist, and short-story writer
Loaves and Fishes (1959) V
The Year of the Whale (1965) V
A Calendar of Love, and Other Stories (1967) F SS
A Time to Keep, and Other Stories (1969) F SS
Fishermen with Ploughs (1971) V
Greenvoe (1972) F
Magnus (1973) F
Hawkfall, and Other Stories (1974) F SS
Letters from Hamnavoe (1975) NF
The Sun's Net (1976) F SS
Winterfold (1976) V
Under Brinkie's Brae (1979) NF
Voyages (1983) V
Christmas Poems (1984) V
Time in a Red Coast (1984) F SS
The Scottish Bestiary (1986) V
The Keepers of the House (1987) F SS
The Wreck of the Archangel (1989) V
The Sea King's Daughter (1991) F SS
Brodgar Poems (1992) V
The Lost Village (1992) V
Vinland (1992) F SS
Beside the Ocean of Time (1994) F
For the Islands I Sing (1997) NF
The Island of the Women, and Other Stories (1998) F SS

BROWN, Oliver Madox (1855–1874)
British novelist
Gabriel Denver (1873) F
The Dwale Bluth, Hebditch's Legacy, and Other Literary Remains (1876) F

BROWN, Rita Mae (1944–)
American novelist and poet
The Hand That Cradles the Rock (1971) V
The Rubyfruit Jungle (1973) F
Songs to a Handsome Woman (1973) V
In Her Day (1976) F
Plain Brown Rapper (1976) NF
Six of One (1978) F
Southern Discomfort (1982) F
Sudden Death (1983) F
High Hearts (1986) F
Bingo (1988) F

BROWN, William Hill (1765–1793)
American novelist
The Power of Sympathy (1789) F
Ira and Isabella; or, The Natural Children (1807) F

BROWNE, Charles Farrar *see* Artemus Ward

BROWNE, Frances (1816–1879)
British novelist, poet, and children's writer
Granny's Wonderful Chair, and Its Tales of Fairy Times (1857) F CH
Our Uncle the Traveller's Stories (1859) F SS
The Castleford Case (1862) F
The Hidden Sin (1866) F

BROWNE, Sir Thomas (1605–1682)
English physician and author
Religio Medici (1643) NF
Pseudodoxia Epidemica (1646) NF
Hydriotaphia: Urn-Burial (1658) NF
Certain Miscellany Tracts (1683) NF
Christian Morals (1716) NF

BROWNE, Thomas Alexander *see* Rolf Boldrewood

BROWNE, William, of Tavistock (1590?–1645?)
English poet
Britannia's Pastorals (1613) V
The Shepherd's Pipe (1614) V
Britannia's Pastorals: The Second Book (1616) V

BROWNING, Elizabeth Barrett (1806–1861)
British poet
The Battle of Marathon (1820) V
An Essay on Mind (1826) V
Prometheus Bound (1833) V
The Seraphim, and Other Poems (1838) V
Casa Guidi Windows (1851) V
Aurora Leigh (1857) V
Poems Before Congress (1860) V
The Greek Christian Poets and the English Poets (1862) NF
Last Poems (1862) V

BROWNING, Robert (1812–1889)
British poet
Pauline (1833) V
Paracelsus (1835) V
Strafford (1837) V
Sordello (1840) V
Bells and Pomegranates i: Pippa Passes (1841) V
Bells and Pomegranates ii: King Victor and King Charles (1842) V
Bells and Pomegranates iii: Dramatic Lyrics (1842) V
Bells and Pomegranates iv: The Return of the Druses (1843) V
Bells and Pomegranates v: A Blot on the 'Scutcheon (1843) V
Bells and Pomegranates vi: Colombe's Birthday (1844) V
Bells and Pomegranates vii: Dramatic Romances and Lyrics (1845) V
Bells and Pomegranates viii and Last: Luria; and A Soul's Tragedy (1846) V
Christmas-Eve and Easter-Day (1850) V
Cleon (1855) V
Men and Women (1855) V
The Statue and the Bust (1855) V
Dramatis Personae (1864) V
The Ring and the Book [vols. i, ii] (1868) V
The Ring and the Book [vols. iii, iv] (1869) V
Fifine at the Fair (1872) V
Red Cotton Night-Cap Country; or, Turf and Towers (1873) V
Pacchiarotta and How He Worked in Distemper, with Other Poems (1876) V
Dramatic Idyls [1st ser.] (1879) V
Dramatic Idyls [2nd ser.] (1880) V
Jocoseria (1883) V
Ferishtah's Fancies (1884) V
Asolando (1890) V
New Poems (1913) V

BROWNJOHN, Alan [Charles] (1931–)
British poet and novelist
Travellers Alone (1954) V
The Railings (1961) V
The Lions' Mouths (1967) V
Sandgrains on a Tray (1969) V
Transformation Scene (1971) V
Warrior's Career (1972) V
She Made of It (1974) V
Philip Larkin (1975) NF
A Song of Good Life (1975) V
A Night in the Gazebo (1980) V
The Old Flea-Pit (1987) V
The Observation Car (1990) V
The Way You Tell Them (1990) F
In the Cruel Arcade (1994) V
The Long Shadows (1997) F

BRUCE, James (1730–1794)
British explorer and author
Travels to Discover the Source of the Nile (1790) NF

BRUCE, Mary Grant (1878–1958)
Australian children's writer
A Little Bush Maid (1910) F CH
From Billabong to London (1915) F CH
Jim and Wally (1916) F CH
Captain Jim (1919) F CH
Billabong's Daughter (1924) F CH
Billabong Adventures (1927) F CH
Bill of Billabong (1931) F CH

BRUNHOFF, Jean de (1899–1937)
French children's writer
The Story of Babar (1931) F CH

BRUNTON, Mary, *née* Balfour (1778–1818)
British novelist
Self-Control (1811) F
Discipline (1814) F
Emmeline (1819) F

BRUTUS, Dennis (1924–)
South African poet and political activist
Sirens, Knuckles, Boots (1963) V
Letters to Martha (1968) V
China Poems (1970) V
Poems From Algiers (1970) V
A Simple Lust (1973) V
Strains (1975) V
Stubborn Hope (1978) V
Salutes and Censures (1984) V
Airs and Tributes (1989) V

BRYCE, James, Viscount Bryce of Dechmont (1838–1922)
British statesman, historian, and traveller
The Holy Roman Empire (1864) NF
Trans-Caucasia and Ararat (1877) NF
The American Commonwealth (1888) NF
Impressions of South Africa (1897) NF
Studies in History and Jurisprudence (1901) NF
Studies in Contemporary Biography (1903) NF
South America (1912) NF
The Ancient Roman Empire and the British Empire in India (1914) NF
Modern Democrats (1921) NF

BRYDGES, Sir Samuel Egerton (1762–1837)
British poet, novelist, and bibliographer
Sonnets and Other Poems (1785) V
Mary de Clifford (1792) F
Topographical Miscellanies (1792) NF
Arthur Fitz-Albini (1798) F
Le Forester (1802) F
Censura Literaria (1805) NF
The British Bibliographer (1810) NF
The Ruminator (1813) NF
Bertram (1816) V
The Hall of Hellingsley (1821) F
Letters on the Character and Poetical Genius of Lord Byron (1824) NF
Odo, Count of Lingen (1824) V
The Lake of Geneva (1832) V
The Autobiography, Times, Opinions and Contemporaries of Sir Egerton Brydges (1834) NF

BUCHAN, John, 1st Baron Tweedsmuir (1875–1940)
Scottish novelist, biographer, and statesman
Sir Quixote of the Moors (1895) F
Scholar Gypsies (1896) NF
John Burnet of Barns (1898) F
Grey Weather (1899) F SS
A Lost Lady of Old Years (1899) F
The Half-Hearted (1900) F
The Watcher by the Threshold, and Other Tales (1902) F SS
Some Eighteenth-Century Byways, and Other Essays (1908) NF
Prester John (1910) F
The Moon Endureth (1912) F SS
The Thirty-Nine Steps (1915) F
Greenmantle (1916) F
The Power-House (1916) F
Poems, Scots and English (1917) V
Mr Standfast (1918) F
The Path of the King (1921) F SS
Huntingtower (1922) F
Midwinter (1923) F SS
The Three Hostages (1924) F
John Macnab (1925) F
The Dancing Floor (1926) F
Homilies and Recreations (1926) NF
Witch Wood (1927) F
Montrose (1928) NF
The Runagates Club (1928) F SS
The Courts of the Morning (1929) F
Castle Gay (1930) F
The Blanket of the Dark (1931) F
The Gap in the Curtain (1932) F
Sir Walter Scott (1932) NF
A Prince of the Captivity (1933) F
The Free Fishers (1934) F
Oliver Cromwell (1934) NF
The House of the Four Winds (1935) F
The Island of Sheep (1936) F
Memory-Hold-the-Door (1940) NF
The Long Traverse (1941) F
Sick Heart River (1941) F

BUCHANAN, George (1506–1582)
Scottish historian, scholar, and poet
The Admonition (1571) NF
A Detection of the Doings of Mary Queen of Scots (1571) NF
Paraphrase on the First Twenty Psalms (1627) V

BUCHANAN, Robert Williams (1841–1901)
British poet, dramatist, novelist, and critic
Undertones (1863) V
Idyls and Legends of Inverburn (1865) F
London Poems (1866) V
North Coast, and Other Poems (1868) V
The Fleshly School of Poetry, and Other Phenomena of the Day (1872) NF
The Shadow of the Sword (1876) F
God and the Man (1881) F
Ballads of Life, Love and Humour (1882) V
The Martyrdom of Madeline (1882) F
Annan Water (1883) F
Foxglove Manor (1884) F
The New Abelard (1884) F
The Master of the Mine (1885) F
A Look Round Literature (1887) NF
The City of Dreams (1888) V
The Heir of Linne (1888) F
The Moment After (1890) F
Woman and the Man (1893) F
Rachel Dene (1894) F
Red and White Heather (1894) MISC
Effie Hetherington (1896) F
A Marriage by Capture (1896) F
Father Anthony (1898) F
The Rev Annabel Lee (1898) F
The New Rome (1899) V

BUCK, Pearl S[ydenstricker] (1892–1973)
American novelist
East Wind, West Wind (1930) F
The Good Earth (1931) F
Sons (1932) F
All Men Are Brothers (1933) F
The Mother (1934) F
A House Divided (1935) F
The Spirit and the Flesh (1936) F
This Proud Heart (1938) F
Dragon Seed (1941) F
Kinfolk (1949) F
Imperial Women (1956) F

BUCKERIDGE, Anthony (1912–)
British writer of school stories
Jennings Goes to School (1950) F CH
Jennings Follows a Clue (1951) F CH
Jennings' Little Hut (1951) F CH
Jennings and Darbishire (1952) F CH
Jennings' Diary (1953) F CH
According to Jennings (1954) F CH
Our Friend Jennings (1955) F CH
Thanks to Jennings (1957) F CH

BUCKLE, Henry Thomas (1821–1862)
British historian
History of Civilization in England (1857–1861) NF

BUCKLER, Ernest (1908–1984)
Canadian novelist
The Mountain and the Valley (1952) F
The Cruelest Month (1963) F
Ox Bells and Fireflies (1968) F
The Rebellion of Young David, and Other Stories (1975) F SS

BUCKLEY, Vincent (1925–1988)
Australian poet and critic
The World's Flesh (1954) V
Masters in Israel (1961) V
Arcady and Other Places (1966) V
Golden Builders (1976) V
Late-Winter Child (1979) V
The Pattern (1979) V
Cutting Green Hay (1983) NF

BUKOWSKI, [Henry] Charles (1920–1994)
American poet, novelist, and short-story writer
It Catches My Heart in Its Hands (1963) V
Crucifix in a Deathhand (1965) V
The Days Run Away Like Wild Horses Over the Hills (1969) V
Post Office (1971) F
Life and Death in the Charity Ward (1973) F SS
Notes of a Dirty Old Man (1973) NF
South of No North (1973) F SS
Burning in Water, Drowning in Flame (1974) V
Factotum (1975) F
Love is a Dog From Hell (1977) V
Women (1978) F
Dangling in the Tournefortia (1981) V
Ham on Rye (1982) F
War All the Time (1985) V
The Last Night of the Earth Poems (1992) V

BULLOCK, Alan [Louis Charles], Lord Bullock (1914–)
British historian
Hitler: A Study in Tyranny (1952) NF
Hitler and Stalin (1991) NF

BULLOCK, Shan F[adh] [orig. **John William]** (1865–1935)
Irish novelist
The Awkward Squads, and Other Stories (1893) F SS
By Thrasna River (1895) F
Ring o' Rushes (1897) F SS
The Barrys (1899) F
Irish Pastorals (1901) F
The Squireen (1903) F
The Red Leaguers (1904) F
Dan the Dollar (1907) F
Robert Thorne (1907) F
Thomas Andrews, Shipbuilder (1912) F
The Race of Castlebar (1913) F
Mors et Vita (1923) V
The Loughsiders (1924) F
After Sixty Years (1931) NF

BULWER-LYTTON, Edward George Earle Lytton, 1st Baron Lytton (1803–1873)
British novelist and dramatist
Ismael: An Oriental Tale, with Other Poems (1820) V
Delmour; or, A Tale of a Sylphid, and Other Poems (1823) V
Falkland (1827) F
O'Neill; or, The Rebel (1827) V
The Disowned (1828) F
Pelham; or, The Adventures of a Gentleman (1828) F
Devereux (1829) F
Paul Clifford (1830) F
The Siamese Twins (1831) V
Eugene Aram (1832) F
Asmodeus at Large (1833) F
England and the English (1833) NF
Godolphin (1833) F
The Last Days of Pompeii (1834) F
The Pilgrims of the Rhine (1834) F
Rienzi, the Last of the Tribunes (1835) F
The Duchess de la Valliere (1836) D
Ernest Maltravers (1837) F
Alice; or, The Mysteries (1838) F
Leila; or, The Siege of Granada [and] Calderon the Courtier (1838) F
The Lady of Lyons; or, Love and Pride (1839) D
Richelieu; or, The Conspiracy (1839) D
The Sea-Captain; or, The Birth-Right (1839) D
Money (1840) D
Night and Morning (1841) F
Eva: A True Story of Light and Darkness; The Ill-Omened Marriage, and Other Tales and Poems (1842) F
Zanoni (1842) F
The Last of the Barons (1843) F
The Poems and Ballads of Schiller (1844) V
Lucretia; or, The Children of Night (1846) F
The New Timon (1846) V
Harold, the Last of the Saxon Kings (1848) F
The Caxtons (1849) F
King Arthur (1849) V
The Disowned (1852) F
'My Novel'; or, Varieties in English Life (1853) F
The Haunted and the Haunters (1857) F
What Will He Do With It? (1859) F
A Strange Story (1862) F
Caxtoniana (1863) NF
The Boatman (1864) V
The Lost Tales of Miletus (1866) V
The Rightful Heir (1868) D
The Coming Race (1871) F
Kenelm Chillingly (1873) F
The Parisians (1873) F
Pausanias the Spartan: An Unfinished Historical Romance (1876) F

BULWER-LYTTON, Rosina [Doyle], *née* Wheeler, Lady Bulwer-Lytton (1802–1882)
Irish novelist
Cheveley; or, The Man of Honour (1839) F
The Budget of the Bubble Family (1840) F
The Prince-Duke and His Page (1841) F
Bianca Capello (1843) F
Memoirs of a Muscovite (1844) F
The Peer's Daughters (1849) F
Miriam Sedley; or, The Tares and the Wheat (1851) F
The School for Husbands; or, Moliere's Life and Times (1852) F
Very Successful! (1856) F
The World and His Wife; or, A Person of Consequence (1858) F
The Household Fairy (1870) F

BUNBURY, Selina (1802–1882)
Irish novelist
The Abbey of Innismoyle (1828) F
Tales of My Country (1833) F
Coombe Abbey (1844) F
The Star of the Coast; or, The Maid of Honour and Queen of England, Anne Boleyn (1844) F
Evelyn (1849) F
Our Own Story; or, The History of Magdalene and Basil St Pierre (1856) F
Sir Guy D'Esterre (1858) F
Florence Manvers (1865) F

BUNIN, Ivan Alexeievich (1870–1953)
Russian novelist and poet
The Village (1910) F
Sukhodol (1911) F
The Gentleman from San Francisco (1914) F
The Life of Arsenev (1927–9) F
Dark Avenues (1946) SS

BUNTING, Basil (1900–1985)
British poet
Redimiculum Matellarum (1930) V
Poems: 1950 (1950) V
Loquitur (1965) V
The Spoils (1965) V
Briggflatts (1966) V
First Book of Odes (1966) V

BUNYAN, John (1628–1688)
English religious writer
Some Gospel-Truths Opened According to the Scriptures (1656) NF
A Vindication of the Book Called Some Gospel-Truths Opened (1657) NF
A Few Sighs from Hell; or, The Groans of a Damned Soul (1658) NF
The Doctrine of the Law and Grace Unfolded (1659) NF
Christian Behaviour; or, The Fruits of True Christianity (1663) NF
The Holy City; or, The New Jerusalem (1665) NF
The Resurrection of the Dead, and Eternal Judgement; or, The Truth of the Resurrection of the Bodies (1665) NF
Grace Abounding to the Chief of Sinners (1666) NF
A Confession of My Faith, and a Reason of My Practice (1672) NF
A Defence of the Doctrine of Justification, by Faith in Jesus Christ (1672) NF
The Barren Fig-Tree; or, The Doom and Downfall of the Fruitless Professor (1673) NF
Differences in Judgment About Water-Baptism, No Bar to Communion (1673) NF
Instruction for the Ignorant (1675) NF
Light for Them That Sit in Darkness; or, A Discourse of Jesus Christ (1675) NF
The Strait Gate; or, Great Difficulty of Going to Heaven (1676) NF
Come & Welcome to Jesus Christ (1678) NF
The Pilgrim's Progress From This World, To That Which is To Come (1678) NF
A Treatise of the Fear of God (1679) NF
The Life and Death of Mr Badman (1680) NF
The Holy War, Made by Shaddai Upon Diabolus, for the Regaining of the Metropolis of the World (1682) NF
A Case of Conscience Resolved (1683) NF
The Pilgrim's Progress From This World to That Which is To Come: The Second Part (1684) NF
A Discourse Upon the Pharisee and the Publicane (1685) NF
Questions About the Nature and Perpetuity of the Seventh-Day-Sabbath (1685) NF
A Book for Boys and Girls (1686) NF
Good News for the Vilest of Men (1688) NF
Solomon's Temple Spiritualized; or, Gospel Light Fetched Out of the Temple at Jerusalem (1688) NF

'BURGESS, Anthony' [John Anthony Burgess Wilson] (1917–1993)
British novelist, critic, and translator
Time for a Tiger (1956) F
The Enemy in the Blanket (1958) F
Beds in the East (1959) F
The Doctor is Sick (1960) F
The Right to an Answer (1960) F
Devil of a State (1961) F
A Clockwork Orange (1962) F
The Wanting Seed (1962) F
Honey for the Bears (1963) F
Inside Mr Enderby (1963) F
The Novel Today (1963) NF
The Eve of St Venus (1964) F
Nothing Like the Sun (1964) F
Here Comes Everybody (1965) NF
A Vision of Battlements (1965) F
Tremor of Intent (1966) F
The Novel Now (1967) NF
Enderby Outside (1968) F
Urgent Copy (1968) NF
Shakespeare (1970) NF
MF (1971) F
Joysprick (1973) NF
The Clockwork Testament; or, Enderby's End (1974) F

Napoleon Symphony (1974) F
Beard's Roman Women (1976) F
Abba Abba (1977) F
1985 (1978) F
Earthly Powers (1980) F
The End of the World News (1982) F
Enderby's Dark Lady (1984) F
Ninety-Nine Novels (1984) NF
Homage to QWERTYUIOP (1985) NF
The Kingdom of the Wicked (1985) F
The Pianoplayers (1986) F
Little Wilson and Big God (1987) NF
Any Old Iron (1989) F
The Devil's Mode, and Other Stories (1989) F SS
You've Had Your Time (1990) NF
Mozart and the Wolf Gang (1991) F
A Mouthful of Air (1992) NF
A Dead Man in Deptford (1993) F

BURGOYNE, [General] John (1722–1792)
British soldier and dramatist
The Maid of the Oaks (1774) D
The Lord of the Manor (1780) D
The Heiress (1786) D
Richard Coeur de Lion (1786) D

BURKE, Edmund (1729–1797)
British statesman and philosopher
A Vindication of Natural Society (1756) NF
A Philosophical Enquiry into the Origin of Our Ideas of the Sublime and Beautiful (1757) NF
Observations on a Late State of the Nation (1769) NF
Thoughts on the Cause of the Present Discontents (1770) NF
Speech on American Taxation (1775) NF
Speech on Moving his Resolutions for Conciliation with the Colonies (1775) NF
Letter to John Farr and John Harris on the Affairs of America (1777) NF
Two Letters to Gentlemen in the City of Bristol (1778) NF
Reflections on the Revolution in France (1790) NF
An Appeal from the New to the Old Whigs (1791) NF
Two Letters on the Proposals for Peace with the Regicide Directory of France (1796) NF
Three Memorials on French Affairs (1797) NF
Two Letters on the Conduct of Our Domestic Parties (1797) NF

BURKE, John (1787–1848)
British genealogical and heraldic writer
Peerage and Baronetage (1826) NF

BURNAND, Sir Francis Cowley (1836–1917)
British dramatist, novelist, and editor of *Punch*
Happy Thoughts (1866) NF
Happy-Thought Hall (1872) F
The New History of Sandford and Merton (1872) F
Chikkin Hazard (1881) F
Gone Wrong (1881) F
The Real Adventures of Robinson Crusoe (1892) F

BURNET, Gilbert (1643–1715)
English prelate, historian, and polemicist
A Discourse on the Memory of Sir Robert Fletcher of Saltoun (1665) NF
The Mystery of Iniquity Unvailed (1672) NF
The History of the Reformation of the Church of England [vol. i; vol. ii, 1681; vol. iii, 1715] (1679) NF
Some Passages of the Life and Death of the Right Honourable John Earl of Rochester (1680) NF
The Life and Death of Sir Matthew Hale (1682) NF
A Collection of Several Tracts and Discourses (1685) NF
A Discourse of the Pastoral Care (1692) NF
Four Discourses (1694) NF
An Essay on the Memory of the Late Queen (1695) NF
Bishop Burnet's History of His Own Time [vol. i; vol. ii, 1734] (1724) NF

BURNETT, Frances [Eliza], *née* Hodgson (1849–1924)
British novelist and children's writer
That Lass o' Lowries (1877) F
'Haworth's' (1879) F
Louisiana (1880) F
A Fair Barbarian (1881) F
Through One Administration (1883) F
Little Lord Fauntleroy (1886) F CH
Sara Crewe; or, What Happened at Miss Minchin's (1888) F CH
The One I Knew the Best of All (1893) F
Two Little Pilgrims' Progress (1895) F CH
A Little Princess (1905) F CH
Racketty Packetty House (1907) F CH
The Secret Garden (1911) F CH

BURNETT, W[illiam] R[iley] (1899–1982)
American novelist
Little Caesar (1929) F
High Sierra (1940) F
Nobody Lives Forever (1943) F
Tomorrow's Another Day (1945) F
The Asphalt Jungle (1949) F
Mi Amigo (1959) F

BURNEY, Frances [or Fanny, later **D'Arblay]** (1752–1840)
British novelist and diarist
Evelina; or, The History of a Young Lady's Entrance into the World (1778) F
Cecilia; or, Memoirs of an Heiress (1782) F
Brief Reflections Relative to the Emigrant French Clergy (1793) NF
Camilla; or, A Picture of Youth (1796) F
The Wanderer; or, Female Difficulties (1814) F
Memoirs of Dr Burney (1832) NF

BURNINGHAM, John [Macintosh] (1926–)
British children's writer and illustrator
Borka: The Adventures of a Goose with No Feathers (1963) F CH
Mr Gumpy's Outing (1970) F CH
Mr Gumpy's Motor Car (1973) F CH

Avocado Baby (1982) F CH
Grandpa (1984) F CH

BURNS, John Horne (1916–1953)
American novelist
The Gallery (1947) F
Lucifer with a Book (1949) F
A Cry of Children (1952) F

BURNS, Robert (1759–1796)
Scottish poet
Poems Chiefly in the Scottish Dialect (1786) V

BURROUGHS, Edgar Rice (1875–1950)
American popular novelist
Tarzan of the Apes (1914) F
The Return of Tarzan (1915) F
A Princess of Mars (1917) F
The Son of Tarzan (1917) F
The Land That Time Forgot (1924) F
Tarzan, Lord of the Jungle (1928) F
Escape on Venus (1946) F

BURROUGHS, William S[eward] (1914–)
American novelist
Junkie (1953) F
Naked Lunch (1959) F
The Soft Machine (1961) F
The Ticket That Exploded (1962) F
Dead Fingers Talk (1963) F
Nova Express (1964) F
The Wild Boys (1971) F
Exterminator! (1973) F
Port of Saints (1973) F
The Last Words of Dutch Schultz (1975) F
The Third Mind (1978) F
Blade Runner: A Movie (1979)
Cities of the Red Night (1981) F
The Place of the Dead Roads (1984) F
Queer (1985) F
The Adding Machine (1986) NF
The Western Lands (1987) F

BURTON, Isabel, Lady Burton, *née* Arundell (1831–1896)
British traveller and author
The Inner Life of Syria, Palestine, and the Holy Land (1875) NF
Arabia, Egypt, India (1879) NF
The Life of Captain Sir Richard F. Burton (1893) NF
The Romance of Isabel, Lady Burton (1897) NF

BURTON, Sir Richard [Francis] (1821–1890)
British explorer and translator
Personal Narrative of a Pilgrimage to El-Medinah and Meccah (1855) NF
Book of the Sword (1884) NF
The Arabian Nights' Entertainments (1885) NF

BURTON, Robert (1577–1640)
English author
The Anatomy of Melancholy (1621) NF

BURY, Lady Charlotte [Susan Maria], *née* Campbell (1775–1861)
British diarist, novelist, and poet
Self-Indulgence (1812) F
Flirtation (1827) F
Journal of the Heart (1830) F
Diary Illustrative of the Times of George the Fourth (1838) NF
The History of a Flirt, Related by Herself (1840) F
The Manoeuvring Mother (1842) F
The Wilfulness of Woman (1844) F
The Lady of Fashion (1856) F

BUTLER, Joseph (1692–1752)
English theologian
Fifteen Sermons Preached at the Rolls Chapel (1726) NF
The Analogy of Religion, Natural and Revealed, to the Constitution and Course of Nature (1736) NF

BUTLER, Robert Olen (1945–)
American novelist
The Alleys of Eden (1981) F
A Good Scent From a Strange Mountain (1992) F SS
They Whisper (1994) F

BUTLER, Samuel (1612–1680)
English satirist
Hudibras: The First Part (1663) V
Hudibras: The Second Part (1664) V
Hudibras: The Third and Last Part (1678) V

BUTLER, Samuel (1835–1901)
British philosopher and novelist
The Evidence for the Resurrection of Jesus Christ (1865) NF
Erewhon; or, Over the Range (1872) F
The Fair Haven (1873) NF
Life and Habit (1878) NF
Evolution, Old and New (1879) NF
Unconscious Memory (1880) NF
Ex Voto (1888) NF
The Authoress of the Odyssey (1897) NF
The Iliad of Homer, Rendered into English Prose (1898)
Shakespeare's Sonnets Reconsidered (1899) EDN
The Odyssey, Rendered into English Prose (1900)
Erewhon Revisited Twenty Years Later (1901) F
The Way of All Flesh (1903) F
Essays on Life, Art and Science (1904) NF
God the Known and God the Unknown (1909) NF
Hesiod's Works and Days (1913) NF
The Humour of Homer, and Other Essays (1913) NF

BUTOR, Michel [Marie François] (1926–)
French novelist and critic
Passage de Milan (1954) F
Passing Time [*L'emploi du temps*] (1956) NF
Le Génie du lieu ['The Spirit of Place'] (1958–1988) NF
Degrees [*Degrés*] (1960) F
Mobile (1963) F
The Stuff of Dreams [*Matière de rêves*] (1975–85) NF

BYATT, A[ntonia] S[usan], *née* Drabble (1936–)
British novelist, short-story writer, and critic
Shadow of a Sun (1964) F
The Game (1967) F
The Virgin in the Garden (1978) F
Still Life (1985) F
Sugar, and Other Stories (1987) F SS
Possession (1990) F
Passions of the Mind (1991) NF
Angels and Insects (1992) F
The Matisse Stories (1993) F SS
The Djinn in the Nightingale's Eye (1994) F SS
Babel Tower (1996) F
Elementals (1998) F SS
The Biographer's Tale (2000) F

BYRD, William (1543–1623)
English composer
Psalms, Sonnets, & Songs of Sadness and Piety (1588) V MUS
Songs of Sundry Natures (1589) V MUS
Psalms, Songs, and Sonnets (1611) V MUS

BYRNE, John Keyes *see* HUGH LEONARD

BYROM, John (1692–1763)
English poet and stenographer
Enthusiasm (1751) V
The Universal English Short-hand (1767) NF
Seasonably Alarming and Humiliating Truths (1774) V

BYRON, George Gordon, Lord (1788–1824)
British poet
Fugitive Pieces (1806) V
Hours of Idleness (1807) V
Poems Original and Translated (1808) V
English Bards, and Scotch Reviewers (1809) V
Childe Harold's Pilgrimage (1812) V
The Curse of Minerva (1812) V
The Bride of Abydos (1813) V
The Giaour (1813) V
Waltz (1813) V
The Corsair (1814) V
Lara: A Tale (1814) V
Ode to Napoleon Buonaparte (1814) V
Hebrew Melodies (1815) V
Childe Harold's Pilgrimage: Canto the Third (1816) V
The Prisoner of Chillon, and Other Poems (1816) V
The Siege of Corinth; Parisina (1816) V
The Lament of Tasso (1817) V
Manfred (1817) V D
Beppo (1818) V
Childe Harold's Pilgrimage: Canto the Fourth (1818) V
Childe Harold's Pilgrimage (1819) V
Don Juan [cantos i–ii] (1819) V
Mazeppa (1819) V
Don Juan [cantos iii–v] (1821) V
Marino Faliero, Doge of Venice; The Prophecy of Dante (1821) V
Sardanapalus; The Two Foscari; Cain (1821) V D
The Vision of Judgment (1822) V
The Age of Bronze (1823) V
The Blues (1823) V
Don Juan [cantos vi-xiv] (1823) V
The Island; or, Christian and His Comrades (1823) V
Morgante Maggiore di Messer Luigi Pulci (1823) V
Werner (1823) V D
The Deformed Transformed (1824) V D
Don Juan [cantos xv–xvi] (1824) V
Hints From Horace (1831) V

BYRON, Robert (1905–1941)
British traveller, art critic, and historian
Europe in the Looking-Glass (1926) NF
The Station (1928) NF
The Byzantine Achievement (1929) NF
First Russia, Then Tibet (1933) NF
The Road to Oxiana (1937) NF

BYRRNE, E. Fairfax *see* E[MMA] F[RANCES] BROOKE

C

CABELL, James Branch (1879–1958)
American novelist, critic, and poet
The Eagle's Shadow (1904) F
The Line of Love (1905) F SS
Gallantry (1907) F SS
Chivalry (1909) F SS
The Cords of Vanity (1909) F
The Soul of Melicent [revised 1920 as *Domnei*] (1913) F
The Rivet in Grandfather's Neck (1915) F
The Certain Hour (1916) F SS
From the Hidden Way (1916) V
The Cream of the Jest (1917) F
Jurgen (1919) F
Figures of Earth (1921) F
The High Place (1923) F
Straws and Prayer-Books (1924) NF
The Music From Behind the Moon (1926) F SS
The Silver Stallion (1926) F
Something About Eve (1927) F
The White Robe (1928) F
Sonnets from Antan (1929) V
The Way of Ecben (1929) F
Smirt (1934) F
Smith (1935) F
Preface to the Past (1936) NF
Smire (1937) F
The King Was in his Counting House (1938) F
Hamlet Had an Uncle (1940) F
First Gentleman of America (1942) F

CABLE, George Washington (1844–1925)
American novelist and short-story writer
Old Creole Days (1879) F SS
The Grandissimes (1880) F
Madame Delphine (1881) F
Dr Sevier (1885) F
Bonaventure (1888) F
John March, Southerner (1894) F

Strong Hearts (1899) F SS
The Cavalier (1901) F
Bylow Hill (1902) F

CAFFYN, Kathleen Mannington *see* 'IOTA'

CAHAN, Abraham (1860–1951)
American novelist
Yekl: A Tale of the New York Ghetto (1896) F
The Imported Bridegroom, and Other Stories (1898) F SS
The Rise of David Livinsky (1917) F

CAIN, James M[allahan] (1892–1977)
American novelist
The Postman Always Rings Twice (1934) F
Double Indemnity (1936) F
Serenade (1937) F
Mildred Pierce (1941) F
Love's Lovely Counterfeit (1942) F
Past All Dishonor (1946) F
The Butterfly (1947) F
The Moth (1948) F
Galatea (1953) F
Mignon (1962) F
Rainbow's End (1975) F
The Institute (1976) F
The Baby in the Icebox (1981) SS

CAINE, [Sir Thomas Henry] Hall (1853–1931)
British novelist
The Shadow of a Crime (1885) F
The Deemster (1887) F
A Son of Hagar (1887) F
The Bondman (1890) F
The Scapegoat (1891) F
Capt'n Davy's Honeymoon; The Last Confession; The Blind Mother (1893) F SS
The Manxman (1894) F
The Christian (1897) F
The Eternal City (1901) F
The Prodigal Son (1904) F
The White Prophet (1909) F
The Prime Minister (1918) D
The Master of Man (1921) F
The Woman of Knockaloe (1923) F

CAIRD, Edward (1835–1908)
British philosopher
A Critical Account of the Philosophy of Kant (1877) NF
Hegel (1883) NF
The Social Philosophy and Religion of Comte (1885) NF
The Critical Philosophy of Immanuel Kant (1889) NF
Essays on Literature and Philosophy (1892) NF
The Evolution of Religion (1893) NF
The Evolution of Theology in the Greek Philosophers (1904) NF

CALDER-MARSHALL, Arthur (1908–1992)
British novelist, biographer, and editor
Two of a Kind (1933) F
The Scarlet Boy (1961) F

CALDERÓN DE LA BARCA, Pedro (1600–1681)
Spanish dramatist
Belshazzar's Feast [*La cena del rey Baltasar*] (1632) D
Life is a Dream [*La vida es sueño*] (1635) D
Physician to His Own Honour [*El médico de su honra*] (1635) D
Secret Vengeance for Secret Insult [*A secreto agravio secreta venganza*] (1636) D
The Wonder-Working Magician [*El mágico prodigioso*] (1637) D
The Great Theatre of the World [*El gran teatro del mundo*] (1645–50) D
The Mayor of Zalamea [*El Alcalde de Zalamea*] (*c.* 1643) D

CALDWELL, Erskine (1903–1987)
American novelist and short-story writer
American Earth (1931) F SS
Tobacco Road (1932) F
God's Little Acre (1933) F
We Are the Living (1933) F SS
Journeyman (1935) F
Kneel to the Rising Sun (1935) F SS
Southways (1938) F SS
Jackpot (1940) F SS
Trouble in July (1940) F
All Night Long (1942) F
Tragic Ground (1944) F
House in the Uplands (1946) F
The Sure Hand of God (1947) F
This Very Earth (1948) F
A Place Called Estherville (1949) F
Episode in Palmetto (1950) F
The Courting of Susie Brown (1952) F SS
A Lamp for Nightfall (1952) F
Love and Money (1954) F
Gretta (1955) F
Gulf Coast Stories (1956) F SS
Claudelle Inglish (1958) F
When You Think of Me (1959) F SS
Jenny by Nature (1961) F
Sometimes Island (1968) F
The Weather Shelter (1969) F
Annette (1973) F

CALLAGHAN, Morley [Edward] (1903–1990)
Canadian novelist and short-story writer
Strange Fugitive (1928) F
A Native Argosy (1929) F SS
It's Never Over (1930) F
No Man's Meat (1931) F
A Broken Journey (1932) F
Such is My Beloved (1934) F
They Shall Inherit the Earth (1935) F
Now That April's Here (1936) F SS
More Joy in Heaven (1937) F
The Loved and the Lost (1951) F
The Many Colored Coat (1960) F
A Passion in Rome (1961) F
A Fine and Private Place (1975) F
Close to the Sun Again (1977) F

A Time for Judas (1983) F
A Wild Old Man on the Road (1988) F

CALVERLEY, C[harles] S[tuart] formerly **Blayds** (1831–1884)
British poet and translator
Verses and Translations (1862) V
Translations into English and Latin (1866) V
Theocritus Translated into English Verse (1869) V
Fly Leaves (1872) V

CALVINO, Italo (1923–1985)
Italian novelist and short-story writer
The Path to the Nest of Spiders [*Il sentiero dei nidi di ragno*] (1947) F
The Cloven Viscount [*Il visconte dimezzato*] (1952) F
The Baron in the Trees [*Il Barone rampante*] (1957) F
Building Speculation [*La speculazione edilizia*] (1957) F
The Non-Existent Knight [*Il cavaliere inesistente*] (1959) F
Invisible Cities [*Le città invisibili*] (1972) F
Palomar (1983) F

CAMBRIDGE, Ada [Mrs George Frederick Cross], (1844–1926)
British novelist and poet
The Two Surplices (1865) F
My Guardian (1878) F
In Two Years' Time (1879) F
A Mere Chance (1882) F
A Marked Man (1890) F
The Three Miss Kings (1891) F
A Humble Enterprise (1896) F
At Midnight, and Other Stories (1897) F SS
Materfamilias (1898) F
Path and Goal (1900) F

CAMDEN, William (1551–1623)
English antiquary
[*Britannia*] [tr. Philemon Holland; first pub. in Latin 1586] (1610) NF

CAMERON, [John] Norman (1905–1953)
British poet and translator
The Winter House (1935) V
Forgive Me, Sire, and Other Poems (1950) V

CAMOËNS, Luis de (1524–1580)
Portuguese poet
The Lusiads [*Os Luciadas*] (1572) V

CAMPBELL, Alistair (1925–)
New Zealand poet and novelist
Mine Eyes Dazzle (1950) V
Sanctuary of Spirits (1963) V
Wild Honey (1964) V
Kapiti (1972) V
Dreams, Yellow Lions (1975) V
The Dark Lord of Savaika (1980) V
Soul Traps (1985) V
The Frigate Bird (1989) F

CAMPBELL, David (1915–1979)
Australian poet and short-story writer
Speak With the Sun (1949) V
The Miracle of Mullion Hill (1956) V
Evening under the Lamplight (1959) F SS
The Branch of Dodona, and Other Poems (1970) V
Starting from Central Station (1973) V
Devil's Rock, and Other Poems (1974) V
Deaths and Pretty Cousins (1975) V
Flame and Shadow (1976) F SS
Words with a Black Orpington (1978) V
The Man in the Honeysuckle (1979) V
The Wayzgoose (1928) V
Adamastor Poems (1930) V
The Georgiad (1931) V
Flowering Reeds (1933) V
Broken Record (1934) NF
Mithraic Emblems (1936) V
Flowering Rifle (1939) V
Light on a Dark Horse (1951) NF

CAMPBELL, Joseph (1879–1944)
Irish poet and man of letters
The Garden of Bees (1905) V
The Rushlight (1906) V
The Gilly of Christ (1907) V
The Mountainy Singer (1909) V
Earth of Cualann (1917) V

CAMPBELL, [Ignatius] Roy[ston] [Dunnachie] (1901–1957)
South African poet and translator
The Flaming Terrapin (1924) V

CAMPBELL, Thomas (1777–1844)
British poet, historian, and biographer
The Pleasures of Hope, with Other Poems (1799) V
Gertrude of Wyoming: A Pennsylvanian Tale, and Other Poems (1809) V
Theodric: A Domestic Tale, and Other Poems (1824) V
Poland (1831) V
Life of Mrs Siddons (1834) NF
Letters From the South (1837) NF
The Pilgrim of Glencoe, with Other Poems (1842) V

CAMPBELL, Wilfred (1858–1918)
Canadian poet, dramatist, journalist, and novelist
Snowflakes and Sunbeams (1888) V
Lake Lyrics, and Other Poems (1889) V
The Dread Voyage (1898) V
Beyond the Hills of Dream (1899) V
Ian of the Orcades; or, The Armourer of Girnigoe (1906) F
A Beautiful Rebel (1909) F
Sagas of Vaster Britain (1914) V

CAMPION, Thomas (1567–1619)
English poet and musician
Observations in the Art of English Poesy (1602) NF
The First Book of Airs (1613) V
Two Books of Airs (1613) V
The Third and Fourth Book of Airs (1617) V

CAMUS, Albert (1913–1960)
French novelist, dramatist, and essayist
Caligula (1938) D
The Myth of Sisyphus [*Le Mythe de Sisyphe*] (1942) NF
The Stranger [*L'Étranger*] (1942) F
Cross Purpose [*La Malentendu*] (1945) D
The Plague [*La Peste*] (1947) F
The Rebel [*L'Homme révolté*] (1951) NF
The Fall [*La Chute*] (1956) F
Exile and the Kingdom [*L'Exil et le royaume*] (1958) F SS

CANETTI, Elias (1905–1994)
Bulgarian-born dramatist, essayist, and novelist
Auto da Fé [*Die Blendung*] (1935) F
Crowds and Power [*Masse und Macht*] (1960) NF

CANNAN, Gilbert (1884–1955)
British novelist and playwright
Peter Homunculus (1909) F
Devious Ways (1910) F
Little Brother (1912) F
Four Plays (1913) D
Round the Corner (1913) F
Old Mole (1914) F
Mendel (1916) F
Three Pretty Men (1916) F
The Stucco House (1917) F
Time and Eternity (1919) F
Annette and Bennett (1922) F
Seven Plays (1923) D

CANTOR, Jay (1948–)
American novelist and essayist
The Space Between Literature and Politics (1981) NF
The Death of Che Guevara (1983) F
Krazy Kat (1987) F
Giving Birth to One's Own Mother (1991) NF

CANTWELL, Robert (1908–1978)
American novelist
Laugh and Lie Down (1931) F
The Land of Plenty (1934) F

CAPELL, Edward (1713–1781)
Shakespearian commentator
Prolusions; or, Select Pieces of Ancient Poetry (1760) ANTH
Mr William Shakespeare His Comedies, Histories and Tragedies (1767) EDN
Notes and Various Readings to Shakespeare (1779) NF

CAPES, Bernard Edward Joseph (1850?–1918)
British novelist and short-story writer
Adventures of the Comte de la Muette During the Reign of Terror (1898) F
At a Winter's Fire (1899) F SS
Our Lady of Darkness (1899) F
From Door to Door (1900) F
Joan Brotherhood (1900) F
The Extraordinary Confessions of Diana Please (1904) F
A Jay of Italy (1905) F
Loaves and Fishes (1906) F SS
The Great Skene Mystery (1907) F
The Green Parrot (1908) F
Gilead Balm, Knight Errant (1911) F
The House of Many Voices (1911) F
The Pot of Basil (1913) F
The Story of Fifine (1914) F
The Fabulists (1915) F
The Skeleton Key (1919) F

CAPOTE, Truman (1924–1984)
American novelist, non-fiction writer, and short-story writer
Other Voices, Other Rooms (1948) F
Tree of Night (1949) F SS
Local Color (1950) NF
The Grass Harp (1951) F
The Muses are Heard (1956) NF
Breakfast at Tiffany's (1958) F
A Christmas Memory (1966) F
In Cold Blood (1966) NF
The Thanksgiving Visitor (1969) F
The Dogs Bark (1973) NF
Then it All Came Down (1976) NF
Music for Chameleons (1980) MISC
One Christmas (1983) NF
Answered Prayers (1986) F

CAREW, Thomas (1595–1640)
English poet
Coelum Brittanicum (1634) D

CAREY, Henry (1687?–1743)
English poet, musician, and dramatist
The Contrivances; or, More Ways Than One (1715) D
Hanging and Marriage; or, The Dead-Man's Wedding (1722) D
Amelia (1732) D
Teraminta (1732) D
The Tragedy of Chrononhotonthologos (1734) D
The Honest Yorkshireman (1735) D
The Dragon of Wantley (1737) D
Nancy; or, The Parting Lovers (1739) D

CAREY, Peter (1943–)
Australian novelist and short-story writer
The Fat Man in History (1974) F SS
War Crimes (1979) F SS
Bliss (1981) F
Illywhacker (1985) F
Oscar and Lucinda (1988) F
The Tax Inspector (1991) F
The Unusual Life of Tristan Smith (1994) F
Jack Maggs (1997) F

CAREY, Rosa Nouchette (1840–1909)
British novelist
Nellie's Memories (1868) F
Wee Wifie (1869) F
Not Like Other Girls (1884) F
For Lilias (1885) F
Esther (1887) F
Only the Governess (1888) F
Merle's Crusade (1889) F

Other People's Lives (1897) F SS
Rue With a Difference (1900) F
Herb of Grace (1901) F
A Passage Perilous (1903) F
'No Friend Like a Sister' (1906) F

CARLE, Eric (1929–)
American children's author and illustrator
The Very Hungry Caterpillar (1969) F CH

CARLETON, William (1794–1869)
Irish novelist
Father Butler; [and] *The Lough Dearg Pilgrim* (1829) F
Traits and Stories of the Irish Peasantry [1st ser.] (1830) F
Traits and Stories of the Irish Peasantry [2nd ser.] (1833) F SS
Tales of Ireland (1834) F SS
Fardorougha the Miser; or, The Convicts of Lisnamona (1839) F
The Fawn of Spring-Vale; The Clarionet, and Other Tales (1841) F SS
Art Maguire; or, The Broken Pledge (1845) F
Denis O'Shaughnessy Going to Maynooth (1845) F
Parra Sashta; or, The History of Paddy Go-Easy and His Wife, Nancy (1845) F
Rody the Rover; or, The Ribbonman (1845) F
Valentine M'Clutchy, the Irish Agent; or, Chronicles of the Castle Cumber Property (1845) F
The Black Prophet (1847) F
The Emigrants of Ahadarra (1848) F
The Tithe-Proctor (1849) F
Red Hall; or, The Baronet's Daughter (1852) F
The Squanders of Castle Squander (1852) F
Willy Reilly and his Dear Coleen Brawn (1855) F
Alley Sheridan, and Other Stories (1858) F SS
The Evil Eye; or, The Black Spectre (1860) F
The Double Prophecy; or, Trials of the Heart (1862) F
Redmond Count O'Hanlon, the Irish Rapparee (1862) F
The Silver Acre, and Other Tales (1862) F SS

CARLYLE, Thomas (1795–1881)
Scottish critic, historian, and biographer
Wilhelm Meister's Apprenticeship [trn from Goethe] (1824) F
The Life of Friedrich Schiller (1825) NF
German Romance (1827) NF
The French Revolution (1837) NF
Sartor Resartus [privately printed 1834] (1838) P
Chartism (1839) NF
Critical and Miscellaneous Essays (1839) NF
On Heroes, Hero-Worship, and the Heroic in History (1841) NF
Past and Present (1843) NF
Oliver Cromwell's Letters and Speeches (1845) NF
Latter-Day Pamphlets (1850) NF
The Life of John Stirling (1851) NF
Samuel Johnson (1853) NF
Burns (1854) NF
History of Frederick II of Prussia, called Frederick the Great [vols. i–iv] (1858) NF
History of Frederick II of Prussia [vols. v–vi] (1865) NF
Shooting Niagara: and After? (1867) NF
The Early Kings of Norway (1875) NF
Characteristics (1877) NF
Goethe (1877) NF
Reminiscences (1881) NF

CARMAN, [William] Bliss (1861–1929)
Canadian-born poet
Songs from Vagabondia (1894) V
Ballads of Lost Haven (1895) V
By the Aurelian (1895) V
Behind the Arras (1895) V
Last Songs from Vagabondia (1895) V
Low Tide on Grand Pré (1895) V
More Songs from Vagabondia (1895) V

CARPENTER, Edward (1844–1929)
British poet, essayist, and social reformer
Narcissus, and Other Poems (1873) V
Moses (1875) V
Towards Democracy [pt. i] (1883) V
Modern Society (1885) NF
England's Ideal (1887) NF
Civilization: Its Cause and Cure, and Other Essays (1889) NF
From Adam's Peak to Elephanta (1892) NF
Homogenic Love and its Place in a Free Society (1894) NF
Marriage in a Free Society (1894) NF
Woman, and Her Place in a Free Society (1894) NF
Love's Coming-of-Age (1896) NF
Angels' Wings (1898) NF
Iolaus (1902) V
The Art of Creation (1904) NF
The Intermediate Sex (1908) NF
My Days and Dreams (1916) NF

CARR, E[dward] H[allett] (1892–1982)
British historian
Dostoevsky (1931) NF
Karl Marx (1934) NF
The Twenty Years' Crisis (1939) NF
Conditions of Peace (1942) NF
The Soviet Impact on the Western World (1946) NF
A History of Soviet Russia (1950–78) NF
The New Society (1951) NF
What is History? (1961) NF
From Napoleon to Stalin (1980) NF

CARR, J[ames Joseph] L[loyd] (1912–1994)
British novelist, children's writer, and publisher
A Day in Summer (1963) F
A Season in Sinji (1967) F
A Month in the Country (1980) F
The Battle of Pollocks Crossing (1985) F

CARR, John Dickson ['Carter Dickson'] (1906–1977)
American-born detective novelist
Hag's Nook (1933) F

The Plague Court Murders (1934) F
The Arabian Nights Murder (1936) F
The Judas Window [as 'Carter Dickson'; US: *The Crossbow Murder*] (1938) F
The Department of Queer Complaints [as 'Carter Dickson'] (1940) F SS
The Case of the Constant Suicides (1941) F
The Emperor's Snuffbox (1942) F

'CARROLL, Lewis' [Charles Lutwidge Dodgson] (1832–1898)
British children's writer and mathematician
Alice's Adventures in Wonderland (1865) F CH
Phantasmagoria, and Other Poems (1869) V CH
Through the Looking-Glass, and What Alice Found There (1872) F CH
The Hunting of the Snark (1876) V CH
Sylvie and Bruno (1889) F CH
Sylvie and Bruno Concluded (1893) F CH

CARROLL, Paul Vincent (1900–1968)
Irish dramatist
The Things That Are Caesar's (1932) D
Shadow and Substance (1937) D
The Devil Came From Dublin (1951) D

CARSON, Rachel (1907–1964)
American zoologist
Under the Sea Wind (1941) NF
The Sea Around Us (1951) NF
The Edge of the Sea (1955) NF
Silent Spring (1963) NF

CARTER, Angela [Olive], *née* Stalker (1940–1992)
British novelist, short-story writer, essayist, and translator
Shadow Dance [US: *Honeybuzzard*] (1966) F
The Magic Toyshop (1967) F
Several Perceptions (1968) F
Heroes and Villains (1969) F
Love (1971) F
The Infernal Desire Machines of Doctor Hoffman [US: *The War of Dreams*] (1972) F
Fireworks (1974) F SS
The Passion of New Eve (1977) F
The Bloody Chamber, and Other Stories (1979) F SS
The Sadeian Woman (1979) NF
Nothing Sacred (1982) NF
Nights at the Circus (1984) F
Black Venus [US: *Saints and Strangers*] (1985) F SS
Wise Children (1991) F
Expletives Deleted (1992) NF
American Ghosts and Old World Wonders (1993) F SS
Burning Your Boats (1995) F SS

CARTER, Elizabeth (1717–1806)
British poet, classical scholar, and translator
Examination of Mr Pope's Essay on Man [from J.P. Crousaz] (1739) NF
Sir Isaac Newton's Philosophy Explained for the Use of Ladies [from F. Algarotti] (1739) NF
Memoirs of the Life of Mrs Elizabeth Carter (1807) NF

CARVER, Raymond (1939–1988)
American short-story writer and poet
Will You Be Quiet, Please? (1976) F SS
Furious Seasons (1977) F SS
What We Talk About When We Talk About Love (1981) F SS
Cathedral (1984) F SS
Fires (1984) MISC
Where I'm Calling From (1988) F SS

CARY, [Arthur] Joyce [Lunel] (1888–1957)
British novelist
Aissa Saved (1932) F
An American Visitor (1933) F
The African Witch (1936) F
Castle Corner (1938) F
Mister Johnson (1939) F
Charley is My Darling (1940) F
Herself Surprised (1941) F
A House of Children (1941) F
To Be a Pilgrim (1942) F
The Horse's Mouth (1944) F
Marching Soldier (1945) V
The Moonlight (1946) F
A Fearful Joy (1949) F
Prisoner of Grace (1952) F
Except the Lord (1953) F
Not Honour More (1955) F
Spring Song, and Other Stories (1960) F SS

CARY, Elizabeth, Viscountess Falkland, *née* Tanfield (c. 1585–1639)
English dramatist and translator
The Tragedy of Mariam, the Fair Queen of Jewry (1613) D

CARY, Henry Francis (1772–1844)
British poet and translator
Sonnets and Odes (1788) V
Ode to General Kosciusko (1797) V
The Inferno of Dante (1805) V
The Vision; or, Hell, Purgatory and Paradise of Dante (1814) V
The Birds of Aristophanes (1824) V
Pindar in English Verse (1833) V

CARY, Patrick (1624–1656)
English poet
Trivial Poems, and Triolets (1771) V

CASTIGLIONE, Baldassare (1478–1529)
Italian humanist
The Courtier [*Il libro del cortegiano*] (1528) NF

CASTLE, Egerton Smith (1858–1920) and **Agnes, *née* Sweetman** (*c.* 1860–1922)
British popular novelists
The Bath Comedy (1900) F
The Incomparable Bellairs (1904) F
French Nan (1905) F
Diamond Cut Paste (1909) F

CATHER, Willa [Sibert] (1873–1947)
American novelist
April Twilights (1903) V
The Troll Garden (1905) F SS
Alexander's Bridge (1912) F
O Pioneers! (1913) F
The Song of the Lark (1915) F
My Antonia (1918) F
Youth and the Bright Medusa (1920) F SS
One of Ours (1922) F
A Lost Lady (1923) F
The Professor's House (1925) F
My Mortal Enemy (1926) F
Death Comes for the Archbishop (1927) F
Shadows on the Rock (1931) F
Obscure Destinies (1932) F SS
Lucy Gayheart (1935) F
Not Under Forty (1936) NF
Sapphira and the Slave Girl (1940) F

'CAUDWELL, Christopher' [Christopher St John Sprigg] (1907–1937)
British Marxist critic, aeronautical author, and writer of detective fiction
Fatality in Fleet Street [as Christopher St John Sprigg] (1933) F
Illusion and Reality (1937) NF
Studies in a Dying Culture (1938) NF
Further Studies in a Dying Culture (1949) NF

CAUSLEY, Charles [Stanley] (1917–)
British poet
Farewell, Aggie Weston (1951) V
Hands to Dance (1951) V
Survivor's Leave (1953) V
Union Street (1957) V
Johnny Alleluia (1961) V
Underneath the Water (1968) V
Figure of 8 (1969) V
Here We Go Round the Round House (1976) V
Secret Destinations (1984) V
Early in the Morning (1986) V
A Field of Vision (1988) V

CECIL, Lord [Edward Christian] David [Gascoyne] (1902–1986)
British biographer and critic
The Stricken Deer; or, The Life of Cowper (1929) NF
The Young Melbourne (1939) NF
Two Quiet Lives (1948) NF
Lord M.; or, The Later Life of Lord Melbourne (1954) NF

'CÉLINE, Louis-Ferdinand' [L.F. Destouches] (1894–1961)
French novelist
Journey to the End of Night [*Voyage au bout de la nuit*] (1932) F
The Church [*L'Église*] (1933) D
Death on the Instalment Plan [*Mort à crédit*] (1936) F
Guignol's Band I (1944) F
Castle to Castle [*D'un château l'autre*] (1957) F
North [*Nord*] (1960) F
Guignol's Band II (1964) F
Rigodon (1969) F

CENTLIVRE, Susanna, *née* Freeman [sometimes called **Susanna Carroll**] (1669?–1723)
English dramatist
The Perjur'd Husband; or, The Adventures of Venice (1700) D
The Stolen Heiress; or, The Salamanca Doctor Outplotted (1702) D
Love's Contrivance; or, Le Médecin malgré lui (1703) D
The Basset-Table (1705) D
The Gamester (1705) D
Love at a Venture (1706) D
The Platonick Lady (1706) D
The Busie Body (1709) D
The Perplex'd Lovers (1712) D
The Wonder! A Woman Keeps a Secret (1714) D
The Cruel Gift (1716) D
A Bold Stroke for a Wife (1718) D

CERVANTES SAAVEDRA, Miguel de (1547–1616)
Spanish novelist and dramatist
La Galatea (1585) F
Don Quixote [*El ingenioso hidalgo Don Quixote de la Mancha*] [pt. i] (1605) F
Exemplary Novels [*Novelas ejemplares*] (1613) F
Don Quixote [pt. ii] (1615) F
The Travels of Persiles and Sigismunda [*Los trabajos de Persiles y Sigismunda*] (1617) F

CHALKHILL, John (*c.* 1594–1642)
English poet
Thealma and Clearchus (1683) V

CHALLANS, Eileen Mary *see* MARY RENAULT

CHAMBERLAYNE, William (1619–1689)
English physician, poet, and dramatist
Love's Victory (1658) D
Pharonnida (1659) V

CHAMBERS, Sir E[dmund] K[erchever] (1866–1954)
British literary scholar
The Mediaeval Stage (1903) NF
The Elizabethan Stage (1923) NF
William Shakespeare: A Study of Facts and Problems (1930) NF

CHAMBERS, R[aymond] W[ilson] (1874–1942)
British philologist and literary historian
Widsith (1912) NF
Beowulf (1921) NF
Man's Unconquerable Mind (1939) NF

CHAMBERS, Robert (1802–1871)
Scottish historian, antiquary, and publisher
Vestiges of the Natural History of Creation (1844) NF
Explanations (1845) NF

CHAMIER, Captain [Frederick] (1796–1870)
British nautical novelist
The Life of a Sailor (1832) F
The Unfortunate Man (1835) F
Ben Brace (1836) F
The Arethusa (1837) F
Jack Adams, the Mutineer (1838) F
The Spitfire (1840) F
Tom Bowling (1841) F

CHANDLER, Raymond [Thornton] (1888–1959)
American writer of detective fiction
The Big Sleep (1939) F
Farewell, My Lovely (1940) F
The High Window (1942) F
The Lady in the Lake (1943) F
The Little Sister (1949) F
The Long Goodbye (1953) F
Playback (1958) F

CHANNING, William Ellery (1780–1842)
American Unitarian clergyman and poet
Poems (1843) V
The Woodman (1849) V
Near Home (1858) V
The Wanderer (1871) V
Eliot (1885) V
John Brown and the Heroes of Harper's Ferry (1886) V

CHAPMAN, George (1559?–1634)
English poet, dramatist, and translator
The Shadow of Night (1594) V
Ovid's Banquet of Sense (1595) V
Achilles' Shield (1598) V
The Blind Beggar of Alexandria (1598) D
Seven Books of the Iliad of Homer, Prince of Poets (1598) V
A Humorous Day's Mirth (1599) D
All Fools (1605) D
Eastward Hoe (1605) D
The Gentleman Usher (1606) D
Monsieur D'Olive (1606) D
Sir Giles Goosecap, Knight (1606) D
Bussy D'Ambois (1607) D
Homer, Prince of Poets (1609) V
The Iliad of Homer, Prince of Poets (1611) V
May Day (1611) D
Petrarch's Seven Penitential Psalms (1612) V
The Widdow's Tears (1612) D
The Revenge of Bussy D'Ambois (1613) D
Homer's Odyssey (1614) V
The Divine Poem of Musaeus (1616) V
The Whole Works of Homer; Prince of Poets (1616) V
The Georgics of Hesiod (1618) V
Batrachomyomachia; or, The Battle of Frogs and Mice [from Homer] (1624) V
Caesar and Pompey (1631) D

CHAPONE, Hester [Mrs John], *née* Mulso (1727–1801)
British author
Letters on the Improvement of the Mind (1773) NF
Miscellanies in Prose and Verse (1775) MISC

'CHARTERIS, Leslie' [Leslie Charles Bowyer Yin] (1907–1993)
British-born American thriller writer
Meet the Tiger [first of the many Simon Templar/ 'Saint' novels] (1928) F
Enter the Saint (1930) F

CHASE, Mary (1907–1981)
American dramatist
Harvey (1944) D

CHATEAUBRIAND, François-René, Vicomte de (1768–1848)
French author and novelist
Essay on Revolutions [*Essai sur les révolutions anciennes et modernes*] (1797) NF
Atala (1801) F
The Genius of Christianity [*Le Génie du christianisme*] (1802) F
René (1802) F
The Martyrs [*Les Martyrs ou le Triomphe de la religion chrétienne*] (1809) F
Travels in Greece, Palestine, Egypt and Barbary [*Itinéraire de Paris à Jerusalem*] (1811) NF
The Last of the Abencérages [*Les Aventures du dernier des Abencérages*] (1826) F
History of France [*Histoire de France*] (1831) NF
Memories From Beyond the Grave [*Mémoires d'outre-tombe*] (1849–50) NF

CHATTERTON, Thomas (1752–1770)
British poet
The Execution of Sir Charles Baldwin (1772) V
Poems, Supposed to Have Been Written at Bristol, by Thomas Rowley, and Others, in the Fifteenth Century (1777) V
Miscellanies in Prose and Verse [Supplement pub. 1784] (1778) MISC
The Revenge: A Burletta (1795) D

CHATWIN, Bruce [Charles] (1940–1989)
British novelist and travel writer
In Patagonia (1977) NF
The Viceroy of Ouidah (1980) F
On the Black Hill (1982) F
The Songlines (1987) F
Utz (1988) F
What Am I Doing Here? (1989) NF

CHAUCER, Geoffrey (1340?–1400)
English poet
The Canterbury Tales [pub. by Caxton] (1477) V
The Parliament of Fowls (1477?) V
Queen Anelida and False Arcite (1477?) V
The Consolation of Philosophy [from Boethius] (1478?) NF
The House of Fame (1483) V
Troilus and Criseyde (1483?) V

The Canterbury Tales [pub. by Pynson] (1526) V
The Workes of Geffray Chaucer [ed. William Thynne] (1532) V
The Workes of Geffrey Chaucer [ed. John Stow] (1561) V
The Workes of Our Antient and Lerned English Poet, Geffrey Chaucer [ed. Thomas Speght] (1598) V

CHEEVER, John (1912–1982)
American short-story writer and novelist
The Way Some People Live (1943) F SS
The Wapshot Chronicle (1957) F
The Housebreaker of Shady Hill (1958) F SS
Some People, Places and Things That Will Not Appear in My Next Novel (1961) F SS
The Brigadier and the Golf Widow (1964) F SS
The Wapshot Scandal (1964) F
Bullet Park (1969) F
The World of Apples (1973) F SS
Falconer (1977) F
The Stories of John Cheever (1978) F SS
Oh What a Paradise It Seems (1982) F

CHEKHOV, Anton [Pavlovich] (1860–1904)
Russian dramatist and short-story writer
Ivanov (1887) D
The Seagull (1895) D
Uncle Vanya (1900) D
Three Sisters (1901) D
The Cherry Orchard (1904) D

CHESNEY, General Sir George Tomkyns, KCB (1830–1895)
British novelist
The Battle of Dorking (1871) F
A True Reformer (1874) F
The Dilemma (1876) F
The Private Secretary (1881) F
The Lesters; or, A Capitalist's Labour (1893) F

CHESNUTT, Charles W[addell] (1858–1932)
African-American short-story writer and novelist
The Conjure Woman (1899) F SS
The Wife of His Youth (1899) F SS
The House Behind the Cedars (1900) F
The Marrow of Tradition (1901) F
The Colonel's Dream (1905) F

CHESTERTON, G[ilbert] K[eith] (1874–1936)
British essayist, novelist, poet, and critic
Greybeards at Play (1900) V
The Wild Knight, and Other Poems (1900) V
The Defendant (1901) NF
Twelve Types (1902) NF
The Napoleon of Notting Hill (1904) F
The Club of Queer Trades (1905) F SS
Heretics (1905) NF
Charles Dickens (1906) NF
All Things Considered (1908) NF
The Man Who Was Thursday (1908) F
Orthodoxy (1909) NF
Tremendous Trifles (1909) NF
Alarms and Discursions (1910) NF
The Ball and the Cross (1910) F
What's Wrong With the World (1910) NF
The Ballad of the White Horse (1911) V
The Innocence of Father Brown (1911) F SS
Manalive (1912) F
A Miscellany of Men (1912) NF
The Victorian Age in Literature (1913) NF
The Flying Inn (1914) F
The Wisdom of Father Brown (1914) F SS
The Crimes of England (1915) NF
The Superstition of Divorce (1920) NF
The Uses of Diversity (1920) NF
The Ballad of St Barbara, and Other Verses (1922) V
Eugenics, and Other Evils (1922) NF
The Man Who Knew Too Much, and Other Stories (1922) F SS
What I Saw in America (1922) NF
Fancies Versus Fads (1923) NF
The Everlasting Man (1925) NF
The Superstitions of the Sceptic (1925) NF
The Catholic Church and Conversion (1926) NF
The Incredulity of Father Brown (1926) F SS
The Outline of Sanity (1926) NF
Culture and the Coming Peril (1927) NF
The Judgement of Dr Johnson (1927) D
The Queen of Seven Swords (1927) V
The Return of Don Quixote (1927) F
The Secret of Father Brown (1927) F SS
Generally Speaking (1928) NF
The Poet and the Lunatics (1929) F SS
Come to Think of It (1930) NF
Four Faultless Felons (1930) F SS
All is Grist (1931) NF
Chaucer (1932) NF
All I Survey (1933) NF
St Thomas Aquinas (1933) NF
The Scandal of Father Brown (1935) F SS
The Well and the Shallows (1935) NF
As I Was Saying (1936) NF
Autobiography (1936) NF
The Paradoxes of Mr Pond (1937) F SS
The Coloured Lands (1938) MISC

CHETTLE, Henry (1560?–1607)
English dramatist
Kind Harts Dreame (1593) NF
Piers Plainnes Seaven Yeres Prentiship (1595) NF
England's Mourning Garment (1603) V
Patient Grissill (1603) D
The Tragedy of Hoffman; or, A Revenge for a Father (1631) D

CHILDERS, [Robert] Erskine (1870–1922)
British novelist and politician
The Riddle of the Sands (1903) F

CHILLINGWORTH, William (1602–1644)
English Theologian
The Religion of Protestants a Safe Way to Salvation (1637) NF

CHOLMONDELEY, Mary (1859–1925)
British novelist
The Danvers Jewels (1887) F

Sir Charles Danvers (1889) F
Diana Tempest (1893) F
A Devotee (1897) F
Red Pottage (1899) F
Moth and Rust (1902) F
Prisoners, Fast Bound in Misery and Iron (1906) F
Notwithstanding (1913) F
The Romance of His Life, and Other Romances (1921) F SS

CHOMSKY, Noam [Avram] (1928–)
American linguist
Syntactic Structures (1957) NF
Aspects of the Theory of Syntax (1965) NF

CHOPIN, Kate, *née* O'Flaherty (1851–1904)
American novelist and short-story writer
At Fault (1890) F
Bayou Folk (1894) F SS
A Night in Acadie (1897) F SS
The Awakening (1899) F

CHRISTIE, [Dame] Agatha [Mary Clarissa] *née* Miller (1890–1976)
British detective novelist and dramatist
The Mysterious Affair at Styles (1920) F
Murder on the Links (1923) F
Poirot Investigates (1924) F SS
The Murder of Roger Ackroyd (1926) F
The Mystery of the Blue Train (1928) F
The Seven Dials Mystery (1929) F
The Murder at the Vicarage (1930) F
The Thirteen Problems [US: *The Tuesday Club Murders*] (1932) F SS
The Hound of Death, and Other Stories (1933) F SS
Murder on the Orient Express [US: *Murder on the Calais Coach*] (1934) F
Parker Pyne Investigates [US: *Mr Parker Pyne, Detective*] (1934) F SS
Why Didn't They Ask Evans? [US: *The Boomerang Club*] (1934) F
The ABC Murders (1936) F
Murder in Mesopotamia (1936) F
Death on the Nile (1937) F
Appointment with Death (1938) F
Ten Little Niggers [US: *And Then There Was None*] (1939) F
One, Two, Buckle My Shoe [US: *The Patriotic Murders*] (1940) F
Evil Under the Sun (1941) F
The Body in the Library (1942) F
Five Little Pigs [US: *Murder in Retrospect*] (1942) F
Taken at the Flood [US: *There is a Tide*] (1948) F
A Murder is Announced (1950) F
They Do it With Mirrors [US: *Murder With Mirrors*] (1952) F
A Pocketful of Rye (1953) F
Hickory, Dickory, Dock [US: *Hickory, Dickory, Death*] (1955) F
The Mousetrap (1956) D
4.50 From Paddington (1957) F
The Mirror Crack'd From Side to Side [US: *The Mirror Crack'd*] (1962) F
The Clocks (1963) F
A Caribbean Mystery (1964) F
At Bertram's Hotel (1965) F
By the Pricking of My Thumbs (1968) F
Elephants Can Remember (1972) F
Sleeping Murder (1976) F

CHURCH, Richard Thomas (1893–1972)
British poet and novelist
The Flood of Life (1917) V
Hurricane, and Other Poems (1919) V
The Dream and Other Poems (1927) V
Oliver's Daughter (1930) F
News From the Mountain (1932) V
The Porch (1937) F
Twentieth Century Psalter (1943) V
Over the Bridge (1955) NF
The Dangerous Years (1956) F
The Golden Sovereign (1957) NF
The Inheritors (1957) V
The Voyage Home (1964) NF
The Burning Bush (1967) V

CHURCHILL, Caryl (1938–)
British dramatist
Owners (1972) D
Light Shining in Buckinghamshire (1976) D
Vinegar Tom (1976) D
Cloud Nine (1979) D
Top Girls (1982) D
Fen (1983) D
Softcops (1984) D
Serious Money (1987) D
Ice Cream (1989) D
Hot Fudge (1990) D
Mad Forest (1990) D
The Skriker (1994) D

CHURCHILL, Charles (1731–1764)
Clergyman and satirist
The Apology (1761) V
Night (1761) V
The Rosciad (1761) V
The Ghost [bks i–ii; bk iii, 1762; bk iv, 1763] (1762) V
The Author (1763) V
The Conference (1763) V
An Epistle to William Hogarth (1763) V
The Prophecy of Famine (1763) V
The Candidate (1764) V
The Duellist (1764) V
The Farewell (1764) V
Gotham [bk i; bks ii-iii, 1764] (1764) V
Independence (1764) V
The Times (1764) V

CHURCHILL, Winston (1871–1947)
American novelist
The Celebrity (1898) F

CHURCHILL, Sir Winston Leonard Spencer (1874–1965)
British statesman, historian, and novelist
The Story of the Malakand Field Force (1898) NF
London to Ladysmith via Pretoria (1900) NF
Savrola (1900) F
The World Crisis (1923) NF
My Early Life (1930) NF
Thoughts and Adventures (1932) NF
Marlborough (1933) NF
Great Contemporaries (1937) NF
Into Battle (1941) NF
The Unrelenting Struggle (1942) NF
The End of the Beginning (1943) NF
Onward to Victory (1944) NF
The Dawn of Liberation (1945) NF
Victory (1946) NF
The Second World War (1948) NF
A History of the English-Speaking Peoples (1956) NF

CHURCHYARD, Thomas (1520?–1604)
Poet and miscellaneous writer
A Myrrour for Man (1552) V
Churchyard's Round (1566) V
Churchyardes Farewell (1566) V
A Discourse of Rebellion (1570) V
A Scourge for Rebels (1584) NF
The Epitaph of Sir Phillip Sidney (1586) V
Churchyards Good Will (1604) V

CIBBER, Colley (1671–1757)
English Poet Laureate, actor, and dramatist
Love's Last Shift; or, The Fool in Fashion (1696) D
Womans Wit; or, The Lady in Fashion (1696) D
Xerxes (1699) D
Love Makes a Man; or, The Fop's Fortune (1700) D
She Wou'd and She Wou'd Not; or, The Kind Impostor (1702) D
The Careless Husband (1704) D
The Double Gallant; or, The Sick Lady's Cure (1707) D
Ximena; or, The Heroick Daughter (1712) D
Cinna's Conspiracy (1713) D
The Secret History of Arlus and Odolphus (1714) F
The Non-Juror (1717) D
The Refusal; or, The Ladies Philosophy (1721) D
Caesar in Aegypt (1725) D
The Provok'd Husband; or, A Journey to London (1728) D
Love in a Riddle (1729) D
An Apology for the Life of Mr Colley Cibber, Comedian (1740) NF

CLAMPITT, Amy (1920–)
American poet
The Kingfisher (1983) V
What the Light Was Like (1985) V
Archaic Figure (1987) V
Westward (1990) V
A Silence Opens (1994) V

CLANCY, Tom (1947–)
American thriller writer
The Hunt for Red October (1984) F
Red Storm Rising (1986) F
Patriot Games (1987) F
The Cardinal of the Kremlin (1988) F
Clear and Present Danger (1989) F
The Sum of All Fears (1991) F

CLARE, John (1793–1864)
British poet
Poems Descriptive of Rural Life and Scenery (1820) V
The Village Minstrel, and Other Poems (1821) V
The Shepherd's Calendar; with Village Stories and Other Poems (1827) V
The Rural Muse (1835) V

CLARK, Alfred Alexander Gordon *see* CYRIL HARE

CLARK, Kenneth Mackenzie, Baron Clark (1903–1983)
British art historian and critic
The Gothic Revival (1928) NF
Landscape into Art (1949) NF
The Nude (1956) NF
Civilisation (1969) NF

CLARKE, Arthur C[harles] (1917–)
British science fiction novelist and short-story writer
Childhood's End (1953) F SF
Earthlight (1955) F SF
The City and the Stars (1956) F SF
The Deep Range (1957) F SF
Tales of Ten Worlds (1962) F SS
2001: A Space Odyssey (1968) F SF
Of Time and Stars (1972) F SS
Rendezvous with Rama (1973) F SF
Imperial Earth (1975) F SF
The Fountains of Paradise (1979) F SF

CLARKE, Austin (1932–)
Barbadian-born Canadian novelist and short-story writer
Survivors of the Crossing (1964) F
Amongst Thistles and Thorns (1965) F SS
The Meeting Point (1967) F
Storm of Fortune (1971) F
When He Was Free and Young and He Used to Wear Silks (1971) F
The Bigger Light (1975) F
The Prime Minister (1977) F
Growing Up Stupid Under the Union (1980) NF
Colonial Innocency (1982) NF

CLARKE, Gillian (1937–)
British poet
The Sundial (1978) V
Letter From a Far Country (1982) V
Letting in the Rumour (1989) V
The King of Britain's Daughter (1993) V

CLARKE, Marcus Andrew Hislop (1846–1881)
British novelist
His Natural Life (1875) F

CLARKE, Mary Victoria Cowden, *née* Novello (1809–1898)
British novelist, short-story writer, and Shakespeare scholar
The Complete Concordance to Shakespeare (1845) NF
Kit Bam's Adventures; or, The Yarns of an Old Mariner (1849) F CH
The Girlhood of Shakespeare's Heroines (1850) F CH
The Iron Cousin; or, Mutual Influence (1854) F
The Shakespeare Key (1879) NF

CLARKSON, Thomas (1760–1846)
British anti-slavery campaigner
An Essay on the Slavery and Commerce of the Human Species (1786) NF
A Portraiture of Quakerism (1806) NF
The History of the Abolition of the African Slave-Trade (1808) NF

CLAVELL, James (1924–1994)
British novelist, film director, and producer
King Rat (1962) F
Tai Pan (1966) F
Shogun (1975) F
Noble House (1981) F

CLEARY, Jon [Stephen] (1917–)
Australian novelist
You Can't See Round Corners (1947) F
The Long Shadow (1949) F
Just Let Me Go [repub. 1990 as *You, the Jury*] (1950) F
The Sundowners (1952) F
The Climate of Courage [also titled *Naked in the Night*] (1954) F
Justin Bayard [also titled *Dust in the Sun*] (1955) F
The Green Helmet (1957) F
Back of Sunset (1959) F
North of Thursday (1960) F
The Country of Marriage (1962) F
A Flight of Chariots (1963) F
Forests of the Night (1963) F
The Fall of an Eagle (1964) F
The High Commissioner (1966) F
The Pulse of Danger (1966) F
The Long Pursuit (1967) F
Season of Doubt (1968) F
Remember Jack Hoxie (1969) F
Helga's Web (1970) F
Mask of the Andes [also titled *The Liberators*] (1971) F
Man's Estate [also titled *The Ninth Marquess*] (1972) F
Ransom (1973) F
Peter's Pence (1974) F
The Safe House (1975) F
A Sound of Lightning (1976) F
High Road to China (1977) F
Vortex (1977) F
The Beaufort Sisters (1979) F
A Very Private War (1980) F
The Faraway Drums (1981) F
The Golden Sabre (1981) F
Spearfield's Daughter (1982) F
The Phoenix Tree (1984) F
City of Fading Light (1985) F
Dragons at the Party (1987) F
Now and Then, Amen (1988) F
Babylon South (1989) F
Murder Song (1990) F
Pride's Harvest (1991) F
Dark Summer (1992) F
Bleak Spring (1993) F

CLELAND, John (1709–1789)
British novelist
Memoirs of a Woman of Pleasure (1749) F
Memoirs of a Coxcomb; or, The History of Sir William Delamere (1751) F
The Surprises of Love (1764) F

CLEMENS, Samuel Langhorne *see* MARK TWAIN

CLEMO, Jack [Reginald John] (1916–1994)
British poet and novelist
Wilding Craft (1948) F
Confession of a Rebel (1949) NF
The Clay Verge (1951) V
The Map of Clay (1961) V
Cactus on Carmel (1967) V
The Marriage of a Rebel (1980) NF
A Different Drummer (1986) V
The Shadowed Bed (1986) F
Approach to Murano (1992) V
The Cured Arno (1995) V

CLEVELAND, John (1613–1658)
English poet
The Character of a London Diurnall (1644) V
The Idol of the Clownes; or, Insurrection of Wat the Tyler (1654) V

CLIFFORD, [Sophia] Lucy, *née* Lane, Mrs W[illiam] K[ingdom] Clifford (1853–1929)
British novelist, short-story writer, and dramatist
Anyhow Stories (1882) F CH
Mrs Keith's Crime (1885) F
Love-Letters of a Worldly Woman (1891) F
A Wild Proxy (1893) F
The Modern Way (1906) F
Sir George's Objection (1910) F
The House in Marylebone (1917) F

CLIVE, Caroline [Mrs Archer-Clive], *née* Meysey-Wigley ['V'] (1801–1873)
British poet and novelist
IX Poems by 'V' (1840) V
The Queen's Ball (1847) V
The Valley of the Rea (1851) V
The Morlas (1853) V
Paul Ferroll (1855) F
Why Paul Ferroll Killed His Wife (1860) F
John Greswold (1864) F

CLOETE, Stuart (1897–1976)
South African novelist
Turning Wheels (1937) F
The Curve and the Tusk (1953) F
The Abductors (1970) F
A Victorian Son (1971) NF

CLOUGH, A[rthur] H[ugh] (1819–1861)
British poet
The Bothie of Toper-na-Fuosich (1848) V
Ambarvalia (1849) V
Amours de Voyage (1858) V
Letters and Remains (1865) MISC

COBB, Richard [Charles] (1917–1996)
British historian and author
A Second Identity (1969) NF
Reactions to the French Revolution (1972) NF
Death in Paris 1795–1801 (1978) NF
Promenades (1980) NF
Still Life (1983) NF
A Classical Education (1985) NF
People and Places (1985) NF

COBBE, Frances Power (1822–1904)
British writer on religion, philosophy, and women's rights
Darwinism in Morals and Other Essays (1872) NF
The Duties of Women (1881) NF
The Modern Rack (1889) NF
Life of Frances Power Cobbe (1894) NF

COBBETT, William (1763–1835)
British essayist, politician, and agriculturalist
Rural Rides in the Counties of Surrey, Kent, Sussex . . . (1830) NF

COCKTON, Henry (1807–1853)
British novelist
The Life and Adventures of Valentine Vox, the Ventriloquist (1840) F
George St George Julian, the Prince of Swindlers (1841) F
Sylvester Sound, the Somnambulist (1844) F

COCTEAU, Jean (1889–1963)
French poet, novelist, dramatist, film director, and critic
Aladdin's Lamp [*La Lampe d'Aladin*] (1909) V
Parade [ballet] (1917) D
The Eiffel Tower Wedding Party [*Les Mariés de la Tour Eiffel*] (1921) D
The Grand Escort [*Le Grand Écart*] (1923) F
Thomas the Imposter [*Thomas l'Imposteur*] (1923) F
Les Biches [music by Darius Milhaud and Francis Poulenc] (1924) D
Orpheus [*Orphée*] (1927) D
Les Enfants terribles (1929) F
The Infernal Machine [*La Machine infernale*] (1934) D
Beauty and the Beast [*La Belle et la bête*; film] (1945)
The Crucifixion [*La Crucifixion*] (1946) V
The Eagle Has Two Heads [*L'Aigle a deux têtes*] (1946) D
Phèdre [music by Georges Auric] (1950) D

COE, Jonathan (1961–)
British novelist
The Accidental Woman (1987) F
A Touch of Love (1989) F
The Dwarves of Death (1990) F
What a Carve Up! (1994) F
The House of Sleep (1997) F

COETZEE, J[ohn] M[ichael] (1940–)
South African novelist
Dusklands (1974) F
In the Heart of the Country (1977) F
Waiting for the Barbarians (1980) F
The Life and Times of Michael K (1983) F
Foe (1986) F
White Writing (1988) F
Age of Iron (1990) F
Doubling the Point (1992) F
The Master of St Petersburg (1994) F
Boyhood: Scenes from Provincial Life (1997) NF
Disgrace (1999) F
The Lives of Animals (1999) F

COHEN, Leonard (1934–)
Canadian poet, novelist, and songwriter
Let Us Compare Mythologies (1956) V
The Spice Box of Earth (1961) V
The Favourite Game (1963) F
Flowers for Hitler (1964) V
Beautiful Losers (1966) F
Parasites of Heaven (1966) V
The Energy of Slaves (1972) V
Death of a Lady's Man (1978) V

COHEN, Matt (1942–)
Canadian novelist and short-story writer
Korsoniloff (1969) F
Johnny Crackle Sings (1971) F
Columbus and the Fat Lady (1972) F SS
The Disinherited (1974) F
Wooden Hunters (1975) F
The Colours of War (1977) F
Night Flights (1978) F
The Sweet Second Summer of Kitty Malone (1979) F
Flowers of Darkness (1981) F

COLE, G[eorge] D[ouglas] H[oward] (1889–1959)
British Fabian economist and novelist
The World of Labour (1913) NF
Self-Government in Industry (1917) NF
Chaos and Order in Industry (1920) NF
Social Theory (1920) NF
A Short History of the British Working Class Movement 1789–1925 (1925) NF
Politics and Literature (1929) NF
What Marx Really Meant (1934) NF
The Common People 1746–1938 (1938) NF
A History of Socialist Thought (1953) NF

COLEGATE, Isabel (1931–)
British novelist
The Blackmailer (1958) F
A Man of Power (1960) F
The Great Occasion (1962) F

Statues in a Garden (1964) F
Orlando King (1968) F
Orlando at the Brazen Threshold (1971) F
Agatha (1973) F
The Shooting Party (1981) F
Deceits of Time (1988) F
The Summer of the Royal Visit (1991) F
Winter Journey (1995) F

COLERIDGE, Christabel Rose (1843–1921)
British novelist
Lady Betty (1870) F
Hanbury Mills (1872) F
An English Squire (1881) F
Jack o'Lanthorn (1889) F
Amethyst (1891) F
A Bag of Farthings (1893) F
Waynflete (1893) F
The Daughters Who Have Not Revolted (1894) NF

COLERIDGE, Mary Elizabeth ['Anodos'] (1861–1907)
British poet and novelist
The Seven Sleepers of Ephesus (1893) F
Fancy's Following (1896) V
Fancy's Guerdon (1897) V
The King With Two Faces (1897) F HF
The Fiery Dawn (1901) F HF
The Lady on the Drawing-room Floor (1906) F

COLERIDGE, S[amuel] T[aylor] (1772–1834)
British poet and critic
The Fall of Robespierre (1794) D
Conciones ad Populum; or, Addresses to the People (1795) NF
Ode on the Departing Year (1796) V
Poems on Various Subjects (1796) V
The Watchman (1796) NF
Fears in Solitude [Inc. 'France, an Ode', and 'Frost at Midnight'] (1798) V
'The Rime of the Ancient Mariner' [in Wordsworth and Coleridge, *Lyrical Ballads*] (1798)
The Death of Wallenstein (1800) D
The Piccolomini; or, The First Part of Wallenstein (1800) D
The Friend (1809) NF
Omniana; or, Horae Otiosiores (1809) MISC
Remorse (1813) D
Christabel; Kubla Khan: A Vision; The Pains of Sleep (1816) V
The Statesman's Manual; or, The Bible the Best Guide to Political Skill and Foresight (1816) NF
Biographia Literaria; or, Biographical Sketches of my Literary Life and Opinions (1817) NF
Sybilline Leaves (1817) V
Aids to Reflection (1825) NF
The Devil's Walk (1830) V
On the Constitution of the Church and State (1830) NF
Table Talk (1835) NF

COLERIDGE, Sara (1802–1852)
British poet and fantasy writer
Phantasmion (1837) F

COLETTE, Sidonie-Gabrielle (1873–1954)
French novelist
Claudine at School [*Claudine à l'école*] (1900) F
Claudine in Paris [*Claudine à Paris*] (1901) F
Claudine Married [*Claudine en ménage*] (1902) F
Claudine and Annie [*Claudine s'en va*] (1903) F
Minne (1904) F
Retreat From Love [*La Retraite sentimentale*] (1907) F
The Gentle Libertine [*L'Ingénue libertine*] (1909) F
The Vagabond [*La Vagabonde*] (1910) F
Chéri (1920) F
The Last of Chéri [*La Fin de Chéri*] (1926) F
Sido (1929) NF
The Cat [*La Chatte*] (1933) F
Duo (1934) F
Julie de Carneilhan (1941) F
From My Window [*De ma fenêtre*] (1942) NF
Gigi (1944) F

COLLIER, Jeremy (1650–1726)
English Nonjuror and historian
A Short View of the Immorality, and Profaneness of the English Stage (1698) NF
A Defence of the Short View of the Profaneness and Immorality of the English Stage (1699) NF
A Second Defence of the Short View of the Profaneness and Immorality of the English Stage (1700) NF
An Ecclesiastical History of Great Britain [vol. i; vol. ii, 1714] (1708) NF
A Farther Vindication of the Short View of the Profaneness and Immorality of the English Stage (1708) NF

COLLIER, John [Henry Noyes] (1901–1980)
British short-story writer and novelist
His Monkey Wife; or, Married to a Chimp (1930) F
Presenting Moonshine (1941) F SS
Fancies and Goodnights (1951) F SS
Pictures in the Fire (1958) F SS
Of Demons and Darkness (1965) F SS

COLLINGWOOD, R[obin] G[eorge] (1889–1943)
British philosopher and historian
Religion and Philosophy (1916) NF
Speculum Mentis; or, The Map of Knowledge (1924) NF
An Essay on Philosophical Method (1933) NF
The Principles of Art (1938) NF
An Essay on Metaphysics (1940) NF
The Idea of History (1946) NF

COLLINS, Anthony (1676–1729)
English Deist
A Discourse of Free-thinking (1713) NF
Philosophical Enquiry Concerning Human Liberty (1715) NF
A Discourse of the Grounds and Reasons of the Christian Religion (1724) NF

COLLINS, Charles Allston (1828–1873)
British novelist
A New Sentimental Journey (1859) F

The Bar Sinister (1864) F
Strathcairn (1864) F
At the Bar (1866) F

COLLINS, Edward James Mortimer (1827–1876)
British poet and novelist
Who Is the Heir? (1865) F
Sweet Anne Page (1868) F
The Ivory Gate (1869) F
The Vivian Romance (1870) F
Two Plunges for a Pearl (1872) F
Squire Silchester's Whim (1873) F
Sweet and Twenty (1875) F
A Fight With Fortune (1876) F

COLLINS, Jackie (1939–)
British popular novelist
The World is Full of Married Men (1968) F
The Bitch (1979) F
Hollywood Wives (1983) F

COLLINS, John Churton (1848–1908)
British essayist, biographer, and critic
The Study of English Literature (1891) NF
Essays and Studies (1895) NF
Ephemera Critica; or, Plain Truths About Current Literature (1901) NF
Studies in Shakespeare (1904) NF
Studies in Poetry and Criticism (1905) NF

COLLINS, William Wilkie (1824–1889)
British novelist and short-story writer
Memoirs of the Life of William Collins (1848) NF
Antonina; or, The Fall of Rome (1850) F
Rambles Beyond Railways; or, Notes in Cornwall Taken A-Foot (1851) NF
Basil (1852) F
Mr Wray's Cash Box; or, The Mask and the Mystery (1852) F
Hide and Seek (1854) F
After Dark (1856) F SS
The Dead Secret (1857) F
The Queen of Hearts (1859) F SS
The Woman in White (1860) F
No Name (1862) F
Armadale (1866) F
The Moonstone (1868) F
Man and Wife (1870) F
Poor Miss Finch (1872) F
Miss or Mrs? and Other Stories in Outline (1873) F SS
The New Magdalen (1873) F
The Frozen Deep, and Other Stories (1874) F SS
The Law and the Lady (1875) F
The Two Destinies (1876) F
The Haunted Hotel [with 'My Lady's Money'] (1878) F
The Fallen Leaves—First Series (1879) F
A Rogue's Life, From His Birth to His Marriage (1879) F
Jezebel's Daughter (1880) F
The Black Robe (1881) F
Heart and Science (1883) F
'I Say No'; or, The Love Letter Answered (1884) F
The Evil Genius (1886) F
The Guilty River (1886) F
Little Novels (1887) F SS
The Legacy of Cain (1888) F
Blind Love (1890) F

'COLLODI, Carlo' [Carlo Lorenzini] (1826–1890)
Italian children's author
Pinocchio (1883) F CH

COLMAN, George, the Elder (1732–1794)
British dramatist
Polly Honeycombe (1760) D
The Jealous Wife (1761) D
The Deuce is in Him (1763) D
The Clandestine Marriage (1766) D
The English Merchant (1767) D
Man and Wife; or The Shakespeare Jubilee (1769) D
The Man of Business (1774) D

COLMAN, George, the Younger (1762–1836)
British dramatist
Ways and Means; or, A Trip to Dover (1788) D
The Iron Chest (1796) D
The Heir at Law (1797) D
John Bull; or, The Englishman's Fireside (1803) D

COLUM, Padraic (1881–1972)
Irish dramatist and poet
The Land (1905) D
The Fiddler's House (1907) D
Wild Earth (1907) V
Thomas Muskerry (1910) D
The King of Ireland's Son (1916) F CH
Flower Pieces (1938) V
Irish Elegies (1961) V

COLVIN, Sir Sidney (1845–1927)
British critic and biographer
Landor (1881) NF
Keats [*English Men of Letters* series] (1887) NF
John Keats (1917) NF
Memories and Notes of Persons and Places, 1852–1912 (1921) NF

COMBE, William (1742–1823)
British poet
The Diaboliad (1777) V
The World As It Goes (1779) V
The Devil Upon Two Sticks in England (1790) F
The Tour of Dr Syntax in Search of the Picturesque (1812) V
The Second Tour of Doctor Syntax, in Search of Consolation (1820) V
The Third Tour of Doctor Syntax, in Search of a Wife (1821) V
The History of Johnny Quae Genus, the Little Foundling of the Late Doctor Syntax (1822) V

COMFORT, Alex[ander] (1920–2000)
British biologist, poet, and novelist
The Song of Lazarus (1945) V
The Signal to Engage (1946) V

Barbarism and Sexual Freedom (1948) NF
Sexual Behaviour in Society [rev. 1963 as *Sex in Society*] (1950) NF
Haste to the Wedding (1962) V
The Joy of Sex (1972) NF
All But a Rib (1973) V
More Joy of Sex (1973) NF

COMPTON-BURNETT, [Dame] I[vy] (1884–1969)
British novelist
Dolores (1911) F
Pastors and Masters (1925) F
Brothers and Sisters (1929) F
Men and Wives (1931) F
More Women Than Men (1933) F
A House and its Head (1935) F
Daughters and Sons (1937) F
A Family and a Fortune (1939) F
Parents and Children (1941) F
Elders and Betters (1944) F
Manservant and Maidservant (1947) F
Two Worlds and Their Ways (1949) F
Darkness and Day (1951) F
The Present and the Past (1953) F
Mother and Son (1955) F
A Father and His Fate (1957) F
A Heritage and its History (1959) F
The Mighty and Their Fall (1961) F
A God and His Gifts (1963) F
The Last and the First (1971) F

COMTE, Auguste (1798–1857)
French philosopher
Cours de philosophie positive (1830–42) NF

CONDON, Richard (1915–1991)
American thriller writer
The Oldest Confession (1958) F
The Manchurian Candidate (1959) F
Some Angry Angel (1960) F
A Talent for Loving (1961) F
An Infinity of Mirrors (1964) F
Prizzi's Honor (1982) F
Prizzi's Family (1986) F

CONGREVE, William (1670–1729)
British dramatist and poet
Incognita; or, Love and Duty Reconcil'd (1692) F
The Double-Dealer (1693) D
The Old Bachelor (1693) D
Love for Love (1695) D
The Mourning Muse of Alexas (1695) V
The Mourning Bride (1697) D
Amendments of Mr Collier's False and Imperfect Citations, (1698) NF
The Birth of the Muse (1698) V
The Way of the World (1700) D

CONNELL, Evan S[helby], Jr (1924–)
American novelist, short-story writer, and poet
The Anatomy Lesson (1957) F SS
Mrs Bridge (1959) F
The Patriot (1960) F
Notes From a Bottle Found on the Beach at Carmel (1963) V
At the Crossroads (1965) F SS
The Diary of a Rapist (1966) F
Mr Bridge (1969) F
Points for a Compass Rose (1973) V
The Connoisseur (1974) F
Double Honeymoon (1976) F
A Long Desire (1979) NF
St Augustine's Pigeon (1980) F SS
The White Lantern (1980) NF
Son of the Morning Star (1984) NF
The Alchymist's Journal (1991) F

CONNOLLY, Cyril Vernon (1903–1974)
British essayist, editor, and critic
The Rock Pool (1936) F
Enemies of Promise (1938) NF
The Unquiet Grave (1944) NF
The Condemned Playground (1945) NF
Ideas and Places (1953) NF
Previous Convictions (1963) NF

CONQUEST, [George] Robert [Acworth] (1917–)
British poet and historian
A World of Difference (1955) F
Between Mars and Venus (1962) V
The Great Terror (1968) NF
Arias From a Love Opera, and Other Poems (1969) V
The Harvest of Sorrow (1986) NF
Reflections on a Ravaged Century (1999) NF

CONRAD, Joseph [Józef Teodor Konrad Nałęcz Korzeniowski] (1857–1924)
Polish-born novelist and short-story writer
Almayer's Folly (1895) F
An Outcast of the Islands (1896) F
The Nigger of the 'Narcissus' (1898) F
Tales of Unrest (1898) F SS
Lord Jim (1900) F
The Inheritors (1901) F
Youth (1902) F SS
'The Heart of Darkness' [in *Youth*] (1902) D
Romance (1903) F
Typhoon, and Other Stories (1903) F SS
Nostromo (1904) F
The Mirror of the Sea (1906) NF
The Secret Agent (1907) F
A Set of Six (1908) F SS
Under Western Eyes (1911) F
'Twixt Land and Sea (1912) F SS
Chance (1913) F
Victory (1915) F
Within the Tides (1915) F SS
The Shadow-Line (1917) F
The Arrow of Gold (1919) F
The Rescue (1920) F
Notes on Life and Letters (1921) NF
The Rover (1923) F
The Nature of a Crime (1924) F
Suspense (1925) F
Tales of Hearsay (1925) F

CONROY, Jack [John Wesley] (1899–1980)
American novelist and editor
The Disinherited (1933) F
A World to Win (1935) F

CONSTANT, Benjamin [Henri-Benjamin Constant de Rebecque] (1767–1830)
French novelist and autobiographer
Adolphe (1816) F
My Life [*Ma Vie (Le Cahier rouge)*] (1907) NF
Cécile (1951) F

CONSTANTINE, David [John] (1944–)
British poet, novelist, and translator
A Brightness to Cast Shadows (1980) V
Watching For Dolphins (1983) V
Mappa Mundi (1984) V
Davies (1985) F
Madder (1987) V
Back at the Spike (1994) F

COOK, Eliza (1818–1889)
British poet and journalist
Lays of a Wild Harp (1835) V
Melaia, and Other Poems (1840) V
New Echoes, and Other Poems (1864) V
Diamond Dust (1865) V

COOKE, John [Esten] (1830–1886)
American novelist
Leather Stocking and Silk (1854) F
The Virginia Comedians (1854) F
Henry St John, Gentleman (1859) F
Surry of Eagle's Nest (1866) F
Fairfax (1868) F
Hilt to Hilt (1869) F
Mohun (1869) F
The Heir of Gaymount (1870) F
Hammer and Rapier (1871) F
Her Majesty the Queen (1873) F
Canolles (1877) F
Fanchette (1883) F
My Lady Pokahontas (1885) F

COOKSON, Catherine [Ann], *née* McMullen (1906–1998)
British popular historical novelist
Kate Hannigan (1950) F
The Fifteen Streets (1952) F
Colour Blind (1953) F
A Grand Man (1954) F
Maggie Rowan (1954) F
The Lord and Mary Ann (1956) F
Rooney (1957) F
The Menagerie (1958) F
Fanny McBride (1959) F
Slinky Jane (1959) F
Love and Mary Ann (1961) F
Life and Mary Ann (1962) F
Hannah Massey (1964) F
Marriage and Mary Ann (1964) F
Mary Ann's Angels (1965) F
Katie Mulholland (1967) F
Mary Ann and Bill (1967) F
The Round Tower (1968) F
Feathers in the Fire (1971) F
Pure as the Lily (1972) F
The Mallen Girl (1973) F
The Mallen Streak (1973) F
The Mallen Litter (1974) F
The Gambling Man (1975) F
The Tide of Life (1976) F
The Cinder Path (1978) F
The Man Who Cried (1979) F
Tilly Trotter (1980) F
Tilly Trotter Wed (1981) F
Tilly Trotter Widowed (1982) F
The Black Velvet Gown (1984) F
Goodbye Hamilton (1984) F
A Dinner of Herbs (1985) F
Bill Bailey (1986) F
The Moth (1986) F
Bill Bailey's Lot (1987) F
The Parson's Daughter (1987) F
Bill Bailey's Daughter (1988) F
The Upstart (1996) F
The Thursday Friend (1999) F

'COOLIDGE, Susan' [Sarah Chauncy Woolsey] (1845–1905)
American children's writer
What Katy Did (1872) F CH
What Katy Did at School (1873) F CH
Eyebright (1879) F CH
A Jersey Lily (1880) F CH
What Katy Did Next (1886) F CH
Clover (1888) F CH
In the High Valley (1890) F CH

COOPER, James Fenimore (1789–1851)
American novelist
Precaution (1820) F
The Spy (1821) F
The Pilot (1823) F
The Pioneers (1823) F
Lionel Lincoln (1825) F
The Last of the Mohicans (1826) F
The Prairie (1827) F
The Red Rover (1827) F
The Wept of Wish-ton-Wish (1829) F
The Water Witch (1830) F
The Bravo (1831) F
The Heidenmauer (1832) F
The Headsman (1833) F
Home as Found (1838) F
Homeward Bound (1838) F
The Pathfinder (1840) F
The Deerslayer (1841) F
Ned Myers (1843) F
Afloat and Ashore (1844) F
Miles Wallingford (1844) F
The Chain Bearers (1845) F
Satanstoe (1845) F
The Redskins (1846) F

The Crater (1848) F
Jack Tier (1848) F
The Oak Openings (1848) F
The Sea Lions (1848) F
The Ways of the Hour (1850) F

COOPER, Jilly, *née* Sallitt (1937–)
British popular novelist
Emily (1975) F
Bella (1976) F
Harriet (1977) F
Octavia (1977) F
Imogen (1978) F
Prudence (1978) F
Lisa & Co (1981) F
Riders (1985) F
Rivals (1988) F
Polo (1991) F
Appassionata (1996) F
Score! (1999) F

COOPER, Lettice [Ulpha] (1897–1994)
British novelist
The Lighted Room (1925) F
We Have Come to a Country (1935) F
The New House (1936) F
National Provincial (1938) F
Black Bethlehem (1947) F
Fenny (1953) F
Three Lives (1957) F
Late in the Afternoon (1971) F
Unusual Behaviour (1986) F

COOPER, Thomas ['The Chartist', 'Adam Hornbrook'] (1805–1892)
British poet and novelist
The Purgatory of Suicides (1845) V
Wise Saws and Modern Instances (1845) F SS
Captain Cobler; or, The Lincolnshire Rebellion (1850) F
Alderman Ralph; or, The History of the Borough and Corporation of Willowacre [as 'Adam Hornbrook'] (1853) F
The Family Feud [as 'Adam Hornbrook'] (1855) F

'COOPER, William' [Harry Sumerfield Hoff] (1910–)
British novelist
Scenes From Provincial Life (1950) F
The Ever-Interesting Topic (1953) F
Disquiet and Peace (1956) F
Young People (1958) F
Scenes From Married Life (1961) F
Memoirs of a New Man (1966) F
Love on the Coast (1973) F
Scenes From Metropolitan Life (1982) F
Scenes From Later Life (1983) F
Immortality at Any Price (1991) F
Scenes From Death and Life (2000) F

COOVER, Robert [Lowell] (1932–)
American novelist and dramatist
The Origin of the Brunists (1965) F
The Universal Baseball Association, Inc., J. Henry Waugh, Prop. (1968) F
Pricksongs and Descants (1969) F SS
A Theological Position (1972) D
The Water Pourer (1972) D
The Public Burning (1977) F
A Political Fable (1980) F
Spanking the Maid (1982) F
Gerald's Party (1986) F
Whatever Happened to Gloomy Guts of the Chicago Bears? (1987) F

COPE, Wendy (1945–)
British poet
Across the City (1980) V
Making Cocoa for Kingsley Amis (1986) V
Does She Like Word-Games? (1988) V
Men and Their Boring Arguments (1988) V
Serious Concerns (1992) V

COPPARD, A[lfred] E[dgar] (1878–1957)
British short-story writer and poet
Adam and Eve and Pinch Me (1921) F SS
Clorinda Walks in Heaven (1922) F SS
Hips and Haws (1922) V
The Black Dog, and Other Stories (1923) F SS
Fishmonger's Fiddle (1925) F SS
The Field of Mustard (1926) F SS
Pelagea, and Other Poems (1926) V
Silver Circus (1928) F SS
Nixey's Harlequin (1931) F SS
Crotty Shinkwin (1932) F SS
Dunky Fitlow (1933) F SS
Cherry Ripe (1935) V
Polly Oliver (1935) F SS
Tapster's Tapestry (1938) F SS
Ugly Anna, and Other Tales (1944) F SS
Fearful Pleasures (1946) F SS
Lucy in Her Pink Jacket (1954) F SS

CORBETT, Jim [James Edward] (1875–1955)
British author and conservationist
The Man-Eaters of Kumaon (1946) NF

CORELLI, Marie [Isabella Mary], *née* Mills, later **Mackay** (1855–1924)
British novelist
A Romance of Two Worlds (1886) F
Vendetta!; or, The Story of One Forgotten (1886) F
Thelma (1887) F
Ardath (1889) F
Wormwood (1890) F
The Silver Domino; or, Side-Whispers, Social and Literary (1892) NF
The Soul of Lilith (1892) F
Barabbas (1893) F
The Sorrows of Satan; or, The Strange Experience of One Geoffrey Tempest, Millionaire (1895) F
Cameos (1896) F SS
The Mighty Atom (1896) F
The Murder of Delicia (1896) F
Jane (1897) F
Ziska (1897) F

Boy (1900) F
The Master-Christian (1900) F
'Temporal Power' (1902) F
God's Good Man (1904) F
The Treasure of Heaven (1906) F
Holy Orders (1908) F
The Life Everlasting (1911) F
Innocent (1914) F
The Young Diana (1918) F
The Love of Long Ago (1920) F
The Secret Power (1921) F
Love—and the Philosopher (1923) F
Open Confession (1925) NF

CORKERY, Daniel (1878–1964)
Irish critic, dramatist, novelist, and short-story writer
A Munster Twilight (1916) F SS
The Threshold of Quiet (1917) F
The Hounds of Banba (1920) F SS
The Labour Leader (1920) D
The Yellow Bittern, and Other Plays (1920) D
The Hidden Ireland (1925) NF
The Stormy Hills (1929) F SS
Earth Out of Earth (1939) F SS

CORMIER, Robert (1925–)
American children's writer
The Chocolate War (1974) F CH
I Am the Cheese (1977) F CH
After the First Death (1979) F CH
The Bumblebee Flies Anyway (1985) F CH

CORNEILLE, Pierre (1606–1684)
French dramatist
Mélite (1629?) D
Clitandre (1632?) D
Médée (1634/5) D
The Theatrical Illusion [L'Illusion Comique] (1636) D
Le Cid (1637) D
Cinna (1640) D
Horace (1640) D
Polyeucte (1641?) D
The Death of Pompey [La Mort de Pompée] (1643) D
The Liar [Le Menteur] (1643) D
Théodore (1645) D
Héraclius (1646) D
Andromède (1650) D
Nicomède (1651) D
Oedipus [Oedipe] (1659) D
Sophonisbe (1663) D
Othon (1664) D

'CORNWALL, Barry' [Bryan Waller Procter] (1787–1874)
British poet
Dramatic Scenes, and Other Poems (1819) V
Marcian Colonna (1820) V D
A Sicilian Story, and Other Poems (1820) V
Mirandola (1821) V D
The Flood of Thessaly, the Girl of Provence, and Other Poems (1823) V
English Songs (1832) V

CORNWELL, Bernard (1944–)
British popular historical novelist
Sharpe's Eagle (1981) F
Sharpe's Trafalgar (2000) F
Harlequin (2000) F

CORNWELL, David John Moore *see* JOHN LE CARRÉ

CORNWELL, Patricia (1956–)
American crime writer
Postmortem (1990) F
Body of Evidence (1991) F
All That Remains (1992) F
Cruel and Unusual (1993) F
The Body Farm (1994) F
From Potter's Field (1995) F
Cause of Death (1996) F
Hornet's Nest (1997) F
Unnatural Exposure (1997) F
Black Notice (1999) F
Southern Cross (1999) F

CORVO, Baron *see* FREDERICK WILLIAM ROLFE

CORY, William [Johnson] (1823–1892)
British poet, classicist, and schoolmaster
Ionica (1858) V
Ionica II (1877) V

CORYATE, Thomas (1577?–1617)
English traveller and author
Coryats Crudities (1611) NF
Coryats Crambe; or, His Colwort Twise Sodden (1611) NF

COTTON, Charles (1630–1687)
English poet, translator, and miscellaneous author
A Panegyrick to the King's Most Excellent Majesty (1660) V
Scarronides; or, Virgile Travestie (1664) V
The Compleat Gamester; or, Instructions How to Play at Billiards, Trucks, Bowls, and Chess (1674) NF
Burlesque upon Burlesque; or, The Scoffer Scoft (1675) V
The Planters Manual (1675) NF
The Wonders of the Peake (1681) V

COVENTRY, Francis (1725–1754)
British satirical novelist
The History of Pompey the Little; or, The Adventures of a Lap-dog (1751) F

COWARD, [Sir] Noel [Pierce] (1899–1973)
British dramatist and songwriter
Fallen Angels (1925) D
Hay Fever (1925) D
The Vortex (1924) D
Bitter Sweet (1929) D
Private Lives (1930) D
Cavalcade (1931) D
Design for Living (1933) D
Present Indicative (1937) NF
To Step Aside (1939) F SS
Blithe Spirit (1941) D

Present Laughter (1942) D
This Happy Breed (1942) D
'Peace in Our Time' (1947) D
Relative Values (1951) D
Quadrille (1952) D
Future Indefinite (1954) NF
South Sea Bubble (1956) D
Pomp and Circumstance (1960) F
Waiting in the Wings (1960) D
Pretty Polly Barlow, and Other Stories (1964) F SS
Bon Voyage, and Other Stories (1967) F SS

COWLEY, Abraham (1618–1667)
English poet
Poetical Blossomes (1633) V
Loves Riddle (1638) D
The Mistresse; or, Severall Copies of Love-Verses (1647) V
The Guardian (1650) D
Cutter of Coleman-Street (1663) D

COWLEY, Hannah (1743–1809)
British dramatist and poet
The Runaway (1776) D
Albina, Countess Raimond (1779) D
Who's the Dupe? (1779) D
The Belle's Stratagem (1780) D
The Maid of Aragon (1780) V
Which is the Man? (1782) D
A Bold Stroke for a Husband (1783) D
More Ways Than One (1783) D
A School for Greybeards; or, The Mourning Bride (1786) D
The Scottish Village; or, Pitcairn Green (1786) V
The Fate of Sparta; or, The Rival Kings (1788) D
The Town Before You (1794) D
The Siege of Acre (1801) V

COWPER, William (1731–1800)
British poet
Olney Hymns (1779) V
Anti-Thelyphthora (1781) V
The Diverting History of John Gilpin (1782) V
The Task (1785) V
The Iliad and the Odyssey, Translated into Blank Verse (1791) V
Latin and Italian Poems of Milton Translated into English Verse (1808) V

COX, Anthony Berkeley ['Anthony Berkeley', 'Francis Iles'] (1893–1971)
British crime writer
The Layton Court Mystery (1925) F
The Wychford Poisoning Case [as 'Anthony Berkeley'] (1926) F
The Silk Stocking Murders [as 'Anthony Berkeley'] (1928) F
The Poisoned Chocolates Case [as 'Anthony Berkeley'] (1929) F
The Second Shot [as 'Anthony Berkeley'] (1930) F
Malice Aforethought [as 'Francis Iles'] (1931) F
Before the Fact [as 'Francis Iles'] (1932) F
As For the Woman [as 'Francis Iles'] (1939) F

COX, William Trevor *see* WILLIAM TREVOR

COZZENS, James Gould (1903–1978)
American novelist
Confusion (1924) F
Michael Scarlett (1925) F
Cock Pit (1928) F
The Son of Perdition (1929) F
S.S. Perdition (1931) F
The Last Adam [UK: *A Cure of Flesh*] (1933) F
Castaway (1934) F
Men and Brethren (1936) F
Ask Me Tomorrow (1940) F
The Just and the Unjust (1942) F
Guard of Honor (1948) F
By Love Possessed (1957) F
Children and Others (1964) F SS
Morning, Noon and Night (1968) F

CRABBE, George (1754–1832)
British poet
Inebriety (1775) V
The Candidate (1780) V
The Library (1781) V
The Village (1783) V
The News-Paper (1785) V
The Borough (1810) V
Tales (1812) V
Tales of the Hall (1819) V

CRACE, Jim [James] (1946–)
British novelist, short-story writer, and dramatist
Continent (1986) F
The Gift of Stones (1988) F
Arcadia (1992) F
Signals of Distress (1994) F
Quarantine (1997) F
Being Dead (1999) F

CRACKANTHORPE, Hubert Montague, born **Cookson** (1870–1896)
British short-story writer
Wreckage (1893) F SS
Sentimental Studies, (1895) F SS
Vignettes (1896) F SS
Last Studies (1897) F SS

CRAIK, Dinah Maria, *née* Mulock (1826–1887)
British novelist and essayist
The Ogilvies (1849) F
Olive (1850) F
Alice Learmont (1852) F
Bread Upon the Waters (1852) F
The Head of the Family (1852) F
Agatha's Husband (1853) F
Avillion, and Other Tales (1853) F SS
John Halifax, Gentleman (1856) F
Nothing New (1857) F SS
A Woman's Thoughts About Women (1858) NF
A Life for a Life (1859) F
The Fairy Book (1863) F CH
Mistress and Maid (1863) F
Christian's Mistake (1865) F

A Noble Life (1866) F
Two Marriages (1867) F
The Woman's Kingdom (1869) F
A Brave Lady (1870) F
The Unkind Word, and Other Stories (1870) F SS
Hannah (1872) F
Miss Tommy (1884) F
King Arthur (1886) F

CRANE, [Harold] Hart (1899–1932)
American poet
White Buildings (1926) V
The Bridge (1930) V
Collected Poems (1933) V

CRANE, Stephen (1871–1900)
American novelist, short-story writer, and poet
Maggie: A Girl of the Streets (1893) F
The Black Riders (1895) V
The Red Badge of Courage (1895) F
George's Mother (1896) F
The Little Regiment [UK: *Pictures of War*] (1896) F SS
The Third Violet (1897) F
The Open Boat (1898) F SS
Active Service (1899) F
The Monster (1899) F SS
War is Kind (1899) V
Whilomville Stories (1900) F SS
Wounds in the Rain (1900) MISC

CRASHAW, Richard (1612/13–1649)
English poet
Steps to the Temple (1646) V
Carmen Deo Nostro, Te Decet Hymnus (1652) V

CRAWFORD, Francis Marion (1854–1909)
American novelist and short-story writer
Mr Isaacs (1882) F
Dr Claudius (1883) F
A Roman Singer (1884) F
To Leeward (1884) F
Zoroaster (1885) F
Paul Patoff (1887) F
Saracinesca (1887) F
Greifenstein (1889) F
Sant' Ilario (1889) F
A Cigarette-Maker's Romance (1890) F
The Witch of Prague (1891) F
The Children of the King (1893) F
Don Orsino (1893) F
Pietro Ghisleri (1893) F
The Ralstons (1895) F
Taquisara (1896) F
Corleone (1897) F
Soprano (1905) F
The Prima Donna (1908) F
The White Sister (1909) F
Uncanny Tales (1911) F SS

CRAYON, Geoffrey *see* WASHINGTON IRVING

CREASY, Sir Edward Shepherd (1812–1878)
British historian
Fifteen Decisive Battles of the World, From Marathon to Waterloo (1851) NF
The Rise and Progress of the English Constitution (1853) NF

CRESSWELL, Helen (1934–)
British children's writer
Jumbo Spencer (1963) F CH
Jumbo Back to Nature (1965) F CH
Jumbo Afloat (1966) F CH
Where the Wind Blows (1966) F CH
The Piemakers (1967) F CH
Jumbo and the Big Dig (1968) F CH
The Signposters (1968) F CH
The Night-Watchmen (1969) F CH
The Outlanders (1970) F CH
The Beachcombers (1972) F CH
The Bongleweed (1973) F CH
Lizzie Dripping (1973) F CH
Lizzie Dripping Again (1974) F CH
Lizzie Dripping and the Little Angel (1974) F CH
Lizzie Dripping by the Sea (1974) F CH
The Winter of the Birds (1975) F CH
Ordinary Jack (1977) F CH
Absolute Zero (1978) F CH
Bagthorpes Unlimited (1978) F CH
Bagthorpes v. the World (1979) F CH
Dear Shrink (1982) F CH
The Secret World of Polly Flint (1982) F CH
Bagthorpes Abroad (1984) F CH
Bagthorpes Haunted (1985) F CH
Moondial (1987) F CH

CRICHTON, Michael (1942–)
American novelist
The Andromeda Strain (1969) F
The Terminal Man (1972) F
Congo (1980) F
Sphere (1987) F
Jurassic Park (1990) F
Disclosure (1994) F
The Lost World (1995) F
Timeline (1999) F

'CRISPIN, Edmund' [Robert Bruce Montgomery] (1921–1978)
British detective novelist
The Case of the Gilded Fly [US: *Obsequies at Oxford*] (1944) F
The Moving Toyshop (1946) F
Buried For Pleasure (1948) F
Love Lies Bleeding (1948) F
Frequent Hearses [US: *Double Death*] (1950) F
The Long Divorce [US: *A Noose for Her*] (1951) F

CRISTOFER, Michael (1945–)
American dramatist
The Shadow Box (1975) D

CROCKETT, Samuel Rutherford (1860–1914)
Scottish novelist
The Stickit Minister and Some Common Men (1893) F SS
The Lilac Sunbonnet (1894) F
Mad Sir Uchtred of the Hills (1894) F HF

The Play Actress (1894) F HF
The Raiders (1894) F
Bog-Myrtle and Peat (1895) F SS
The Men of the Moss-Hags (1895) F
Cleg Kelly, Arab of the City (1896) F
The Grey Man (1896) F
Lads' Love (1897) F HF
Lochinvar (1897) F
The Red Axe (1898) F
The Standard Bearer (1898) F
The Black Douglas (1899) F HF
Kit Kennedy (1899) F
Joan of the Sword Hand (1900) F
Little Anna Mark (1900) F HF
The Stickit Minister's Wooing, and Other Galloway Stories (1900) F
The Silver Skull (1901) F
The Dark o' the Moon (1902) F
The Loves of Miss Anne (1904) F
Red Cap Tales (1904) F HF
The White Plumes of Navarre (1906) F
Red Cap Adventures (1908) F HF
The Men of the Mountain (1909) F HF
The Moss Troopers (1912) F
A Tatter of Scarlet (1913) F
Silver Sand (1914) F

CROFTS, Freeman Wills (1879–1957)
British detective novelist
The Cask (1920) F
Inspector French's Greatest Case (1925) F
Sir John Magill's Last Journey (1930) F
Death on the Way [US: *Double Death*] (1932) F

CROKER, T[homas] Crofton (1798–1854)
British author and antiquary
Fairy Legends and Traditions of the South of Ireland [vol. i; inc. 4 stories by William Maginn] (1826) F SS
Fairy Legends and Traditions of the South of Ireland [vols. ii, iii] (1828) F SS
The Adventures of Barney Mahoney (1832) F

CROLY, [Revd] George (1780–1860)
British clergyman, poet, and novelist
The Angel of the World: An Arabian Tale; Sebastion: A Spanish Tale: With Other Poems (1820) V
Salathiel (1828) F
Marston; or, The Soldier and the Statesman (1846) F

'CROMPTON, Richmal' [Richmal Crompton Lamburn] (1890–1969)
British children's writer and novelist
Just—William (1922) F
More William (1922) F
William Again (1923) F
William the Fourth (1924) F
Still William (1925) F
William the Conqueror (1926) F
William in Trouble (1927) F
William the Outlaw (1927) F
William the Good (1928) F
William (1929) F
William the Pirate (1932) F
William the Rebel (1933) F
William the Gangster (1934) F
William the Detective (1935) F
Sweet William (1936) F
William the Dictator (1938) F
William and A.R.P. (1939) F
William and the Evacuees (1940) F
William Does His Bit (1941) F
William and the Tramp (1952) F
William and the Witch (1964) F
William and the Pop Singers (1965) F
William the Superman (1968) F
William the Lawless (1970) F

CRONIN, A[rchibald] J[oseph] (1896–1981)
Scottish novelist
Hatter's Castle (1931) F
The Stars Look Down (1935) F
The Citadel (1937) F
The Keys of the Kingdom (1942) F
Shannon's Way (1948) F
The Spanish Gardener (1950) F
Beyond This Place (1953) F
The Northern Light (1958) F
The Judas Tree (1961) F
A Song of Sixpence (1964) F
A Pocketful of Rye (1969) F

CROSSLEY-HOLLAND, Kevin [John William] (1941–)
British poet and translator
The Dream House (1976) V
Waterslain (1986) V
The Painting Room (1988) V

CROWE, Catherine Ann, *née* Stevens (1790–1876)
British novelist, essayist, and short-story writer
Adventures of Susan Hopley; or, Circumstantial Evidence (1841) F
Men and Women; or, Manorial Rights (1844) F
The Seeress of Prevorst [from J.A.C. Kerner] (1845) NF
The Story of Lilly Dawson (1847) F
The Night-Side of Nature; or, Ghosts and Ghost-Seers (1848) F
Light and Darkness; or, Mysteries of Life (1850) F SS
The Adventures of a Beauty (1852) F
Linny Lockwood (1854) F
Ghosts and Family Legends (1859) F SS
Spiritualism, and the Age We Live In (1859) NF

CROWLEY, 'Aleister' [Edward Alexander] (1875–1947)
British occultist
The Diary of a Drug Fiend (1932) F

CROWNE, John (d. 1703)
English dramatist
Juliana; or, The Princess of Poland (1671) D

The History of Charles the Eighth of France (1672) D
Calisto; or, The Chaste Nymph (1675) D
The Destruction of Jerusalem by Titus Vespasian (1677) D
The Ambitious Statesman; or, The Loyal Favourite (1679) D
Thyestes (1681) D
City Politiques (1683) D
Sir Courtly Nice; or, It Cannot Be (1685) D
Darius, King of Persia (1688) D
The English Frier; or, The Town Sparks (1690) D
The Married Beau; or, The Curious Impertinent (1694) D
Regulus (1694) D
Caligula (1698) D

CRUDEN, Alexander (1701–1770)
Scottish concordance compiler
A Complete Concordance to the Holy Scriptures of the Old and New Testament (1738) NF

CUDWORTH, Ralph (1617–1688)
English divine
A Discourse Concerning the True Notion of the Lords Supper (1642) NF
The Union of Christ and the Church, in a Shadow (1642) NF
The True Intellectual System of the Universe (1678) NF
A Treatise Concerning Eternal and Immutable Morality (1731) NF

CULPEPER, Nicholas (1616–1654)
English herbalist and astrologer
The English Physitian Enlarged (1653) NF

CUMBERLAND, Richard (1732–1811)
British dramatist, novelist, and poet
The Brothers (1769) D
The West Indian (1771) D
The Fashionable Lover (1772) D
The Choleric Man (1774) D
The Carmelite (1784) D
The Natural Son (1784) D
Arundel (1789) F
Calvary; or, The Death of Christ (1792) V
The Jew (1794) D
First Love (1795) D
Henry (1795) F
The Wheel of Fortune (1795) D
The Sailor's Daughter (1804) D
A Hint to Husbands (1806) D
John de Lancaster (1809) F
Retrospection (1811) V

CUMMINGS, E[dward] E[stlin] (1894–1962)
American poet
The Enormous Room (1922) F
Tulips and Chimneys (1923) V
& (1925) V
XLI Poems (1925) V
is 5 (1926) V
him (1927) D
ViVa (1931) V
Eimi (1933) NF
No Thanks (1935) V
Tom [satirical ballet] (1935) D
I/20 (1936) V
50 Poems (1940) V
Χαῖρε (1950) V
95 Poems (1958) V
73 Poems (1963) V

CUNNINGHAM, Allan (1784–1842)
Scottish poet, novelist, and man of letters
Songs, Chiefly in the Rural Language of Scotland (1813) V
Sir Marmaduke Maxwell: A Dramatic Poem (1822) V
Traditional Tales of the English and Scottish Peasantry (1822) F
The Songs of Scotland, Ancient and Modern (1825) V
Paul Jones (1826) F
Sir Michael Scott (1828) F
Lives of the Most Eminent British Painters, Sculptors and Architects (1829) NF
The Maid of Elvar (1833) V

CURNOW, Allen (1911–)
New Zealand poet, dramatist, critic, and editor
Not in Narrow Seas (1939) V
Island and Time (1941) V
At Dead Low Water (1949) V
Poems 1949–57 (1957) V
A Small Room with Large Windows (1962) V
An Incorrigible Music (1979) V
You Will Know When You Get There (1982) V
The Loop in Lone Kauri Road (1986) V
Continuum (1988) V

CURZON, Robert, Lord de la Zouche (1810–1873)
British travel writer
Visits to Monasteries in the Levant (1849) NF
Armenia (1854) NF

CUSSLER, Clive [Eric] (1931–)
American thriller writer
Raise the Titanic (1976) F

CYRANO DE BERGERAC, Savinien (1619–1655)
French dramatist and burlesque writer
La Mort d'Agrippine (1653) D
Le Pédant joué (1653) D
Histoire comique des états et empires de la Lune (1656) F
Histoire comique des états et empires du Soleil (1661) F

D

DABYDEEN, David (1956–)
Guyanese poet, novelist, and art historian
Slave Song (1984) V
Hogarth's Blacks (1985) NF
Coolie Odyssey (1988) V
The Intended (1990) F

Disappearance (1993) F
Turner: New and Selected Poems (1994) V

DACRE, Charlotte later **Byrne** (1782?–1841?)
British novelist and poet
The Confessions of the Nun of St Omer (1805) F
Hours of Solitude (1805) V
Zofloya; or, The Moor (1806) F
The Libertine (1807) F
The Passions (1811) F
George the Fourth (1822) V

DAHL, Roald (1916–1990)
British children's author and short-story writer
Over to You (1946) F SS
Sometime Never (1948) F
Someone Like You (1953) F SS
Kiss Kiss (1960) F SS
James and the Giant Peach (1961) F CH
Charlie and the Chocolate Factory (1964) F CH
Fantastic Mr Fox (1970) F CH
Switch Bitch (1974) F SS
My Uncle Oswald (1979) F
Tales of the Unexpected (1979) F SS
More Tales of the Unexpected (1980) F SS
George's Marvellous Medicine (1981) F CH
The BFG (1982) F CH
The Witches (1983) F CH
Matilda (1988) F CH

DAHLBERG, Edward (1900–1977)
American novelist and critic
Bottom Dogs (1929) F
From Flushing to Calvary (1932) F
Those Who Perish (1934) F
Do These Bones Live? (1941) NF
Flea of Sodom (1950) NF
The Sorrows of Priapus (1957) NF
Truth is More Sacred (1961) NF
Because I Was Flesh (1964) NF
Cipango's Hinder Door (1966) V
The Carnal Myth (1968) NF
The Olive of Minerva (1976) F

DAICHES, David (1912–)
Scottish scholar and author
A Critical History of English Literature (1960) NF

DALLAS, E[neas] S[weetland] (1828–1879)
British journalist and author
Poetics (1852) NF
The Gay Science (1866) NF

DALLAS, R[obert] C[harles] (1754–1824)
British miscellaneous writer
Miscellaneous Writings (1797) MISC
Percival; or, Nature Vindicated (1801) F
Aubrey (1804) F
The Morlands (1805) F SS
The Knights (1808) F SS
Recollections of the Life of Lord Byron (1814) NF
Ode to the Duke of Wellington, and Other Poems (1819) V
Sir Francis Darrell; or, The Vortex (1820) F
Adrastus; Amabel; and Other Poems (1823) V

DALRYMPLE, Sir David, Lord Hailes (1726–1792)
Scottish jurist and historian
Edom of Gordon: An Ancient Scottish Poem (1755) V
Ancient Scottish Poems Published from the MS of George Bannatyne (1770) V
Remarks on the History of Scotland (1773) NF
Annals of Scotland [vol. i; vol. ii, 1779] (1776) NF

DAMPIER, William (1652–1715)
English explorer, buccaneer, and author
A New Voyage Round the World (1697) NF
Voyages and Descriptions (1699) NF
A Voyage to New Holland, in the Year 1699 (1703) NF

DANA, Richard Henry, Jr (1815–1882)
American social reformer
Two Years Before the Mast (1840) NF
The Seaman's Friend [UK: *The Seaman's Manual*] (1841) NF
To Cuba and Back (1859) NF

'DANBY, Frank' [Julia Frankau, *née* Davis] (1864–1916)
British novelist and art historian
Dr Phillips (1887) F
A Babe in Bohemia (1889) F
Pigs in Clover (1902) F
The Sphinx's Lawyer (1906) F
A Coquette in Crape (1907) F
The Heart of a Child (1908) F
An Incompleat Etonian (1909) F
Let the Roof Fall In (1910) F
Joseph in Jeopardy (1912) F
Concert Pitch (1913) F
Full Swing (1914) F
Twilight (1916) F
Mothers and Children (1918) F

'DANE, Clemence' [Winifred Ashton] (1888–1965)
British novelist and dramatist
Regiment of Women (1917) F
Legend (1919) F
A Bill of Divorcement (1921) D
Granite (1926) D
The Babyons (1928) F
Broome Stages (1931) F
Wild Decembers (1932) D
Fate Cries Out (1935) F SS
The Moon is Feminine (1938) F
The Arrogant History of White Ben (1939) F

DANIEL, Samuel (1562–1619)
English poet and dramatist
The Worthy Tract of Paulus Jovius (1585) NF
Delia (1592) V
Delia and Rosamond Augmented (1594) V
The First Fowre Bookes of the Civile Warres Betweene the Two Houses of Lancaster and Yorke (1595) V
The Poeticall Essayes of Sam. Danyel (1599) V
The Works of Samuel Daniel Newly Augmented (1601) V

A Panegyrike Congratulatory [inc. 'A Defence of Rhyme'] (1603) V
Certaine Small Poems Lately Printed (1605) V
A Funerall Poeme uppon . . . the Late Noble Earle of Devonshyre (1606) V
The Queenes Arcadia (1606) V
Certaine Small Workes (1607) V
The Civile Wares Betweene the House of Lancaster and Yorke Corrected and Continued . . . (1609) V
Tethys Festival (1610) D
The First Part of the Historie of England (1612) NF
Hymens Triumph (1615) V
The Whole Workes of Samuel Daniel Esquire in Poetrie (1623) V

DANNAY, Frederic *see* ELLERY QUEEN

D'ANNUNZIO, Gabriele (1863–1938)
Italian novelist, dramatist, and poet
The Child of Pleasure [*Il piacere*] (1890) F
The Triumph of Death [*Trionfo della morte*] (1894) F
The Maidens of the Rocks [*Le Vergini delle rocce*] (1896) F
The Dead City [*La Città morta*] (1898) D
Gioconda [*La Gioconda*] (1899) D
The Flame of Life [*Il fuoco*] (1900) F
Francesca da Rimini (1901) D
The Daughter of Jorio [*La figlia di Jorio*] (1904) D
The Martyrdom of St Sebastian [*Le Martyre de Saint Sébastien*; music by Debussy] (1911) D
Parisina [music by Mascagni] (1913) D

DANTE ALIGHIERI (1265–1321)
Italian poet
Vita Nuova (1290–4) V P
Convivio [unfinished] (1304–8) NF
Divina Commedia (1307–21?) V P
De Monarchia (1309–12) NF

D'ARCY, Ella (1851–1937?)
British short-story writer and novelist
Monochromes (1895) F SS
The Bishop's Dilemma (1898) F
Modern Instances (1898) F SS

DARK, Eleanor (1901–1985)
Australian novelist
Slow Dawning (1932) F
Prelude to Christopher (1934) F
Return to Coolami (1936) F
Sun Across the Sky (1937) F
Waterway (1938) F
The Timeless Land (1941) F
The Little Company (1945) F
Storm of Time (1948) F
No Barrier (1953) F
Lantana Lane (1959) F

DARLEY, George (1795–1846)
British poet, mathematician, and author
The Errors of Ecstasie (1822) V
The Labours of Idleness; or, Seven Nights Entertainments [as 'Guy Penseval'] (1826) P
The New Sketch Book [as 'Geoffrey Crayon jun.'] (1829) NF
Thomas a Becket (1840) D
Ethelstan; or, The Battle of Brunanburgh (1841) D

DARWIN, Charles Robert (1809–1882)
British naturalist
The Zoology of the Voyage of HMS Beagle (1838–43) NF
Journal of Researches into the Geology and Natural History of the Various Countries Visited by HMS Beagle (1839) NF
The Structure and Distribution of Coral Reefs (1842) NF
Geological Observations on the Volcanic Islands, Visited During the Voyage of HMS Beagle (1844) NF
Geological Observations on South America (1846) NF
On the Origin of Species by Natural Selection (1859) NF
The Variation of Animals and Plants Under Domestication (1868) NF
The Descent of Man, and Selection in Relation to Sex (1871) NF
The Expression of the Emotions in Man and Animals (1872) NF

DARWIN, Erasmus (1731–1802)
British physician, poet, and author
The Loves of the Plants (1789) V
The Botanic Garden (1790) V
The Golden Age (1794) V
Zoonomia; or, The Laws of Organic Life (1794) NF
Phytologia; or, The Philosophy of Agriculture and Gardening (1800) NF
The Temple of Nature; or, The Origin of Society (1803) V

DARYUSH, Elizabeth, *née* Bridges (1887–1977)
British poet
Charitesse (1911) V
Verses (1916) V
Verses: Sixth Book (1938) V
Collected Poems (1976) V

DASENT, Sir George Webbe (1817–1896)
British diplomat, Norse scholar, and novelist
Popular Tales from the Norse (1859) F
The Story of Burnt Njal (1861) F
The Story of Gisli the Outlaw (1866) F
Annals of an Eventful Life (1870) F
The Vikings of the Baltic (1875) F

D'AUBIGNÉ, Théodore-Agrippa (1552–1630)
French Huguenot leader and author
Les Tragiques (1616) V
Universal History [*Histoire Universelle*] (1616–20) NF
The Adventures of Baron de Faeneste [*Adventures du baron de Faeneste*] (1617) F
Confession de Sancy (1660) F

DAUDET, Alphonse (1840–1897)
French novelist and poet
The Lovers [*Les Amoureuses*] (1858) V
Le petit chose (1868) F

Letters From My Mill [*Lettres de mon moulin*] (1869) F SS
Tartarin of Tarascon [*Tartarin de Tarascon*] (1872) F
Monday Stories [*Contes du lundi*] (1873) F SS
Fromont Junior and Risler Senior [*Fromont jeune et Risler aîné*] (1874) F
The Nabob [*Le Nabab*] (1877) F
Numa Roumestan (1881) F
The Evangelist [*L'Évangéliste*] (1883) F
Sappho (1884) F
Tartarin in the Alps [*Tartarin sur les Alpes*] (1885) F
The Defence of Tarascon [*La Défense de Tarascon*] (1886) F
Port Tarascon (1890) F

DAVENANT, [or **D'AVENANT], Sir William** (1606–1668)
English poet and dramatist
The Tragedy of Albovine, King of the Lombards (1629) D
The Cruel Brother (1630) D
The Just Italian (1630) D
The Temple of Love (1635) D
The Platonick Lovers (1636) D
The Triumphs of the Prince d'Amour (1636) D
The Witts (1636) D
Britannia Triumphans (1638) D
Madagascar; with Other Poems (1638) V
Salmacida Spolia (1639) D
The Unfortunate Lovers (1643) D
Love and Honour (1649) D
Gondibert (1651) V
The Siege of Rhodes (1656) D
The Cruelty of the Spaniards in Peru (1658) D
The History of Sr Francis Drake (1659) D
The Tempest; or, The Enchanted Island [from Shakespeare] (1667) D
The Rivals (1668) D
The Man's the Master (1669) D
Macbeth [from Shakespeare] (1674) D
The Seventh and Last Canto of the Third Book of Gondibert (1685) V

DAVID, Elizabeth, *née* Gwynne (1913–1992)
British food writer
A Book of Mediterranean Food (1950) NF
Italian Food (1954) NF
English Bread and Yeast Cooking (1977) NF
An Omelette and a Glass of Wine (1984) NF

DAVIDSON, John (1857–1909)
British poet, dramatist, and novelist
Perfervid (1890) F
In a Music-Hall, and Other Poems (1891) V
Fleet Street Eclogues [1st ser.] (1893) V
Ballads and Songs (1894) V
Baptist Lake (1894) F
Plays by John Davidson (1894) D
A Full and True Account of the Wonderful Mission of Earl Lavender (1895) F
Fleet Street Eclogues [2nd ser.] (1896) V
Miss Armstrong's and Other Circumstances (1896) F SS
New Ballads (1897) V
Godfrida (1898) D
The Last Ballad, and Other Poems (1899) V
Self's the Man (1901) D
The Testament of a Man Forbid (1901) V
The Testament of a Vivisector (1901) V
The Testament of an Empire-Builder (1902) V
The Testament of a Prime Minister (1904) V
The Theatrocrat (1905) D
God and Mammon (1907) V
The Testament of John Davidson (1908) V
Fleet Street, and Other Poems (1909) V

DAVIE, Donald [Alfred] (1922–1995)
British poet and critic
Purity of Diction in English Verse (1952) NF
Articulate Energy (1955) NF
Brides of Reason (1955) V
A Winter Talent, and Other Poems (1957) V
Events and Wisdoms (1964) V
Essex Poems (1969) V
The Shires (1974) V
In the Stopping Train, and Other Poems (1980) V
To Scorch or Freeze (1989) V
Under Briggflats (1989) NF
Collected Poems (1990) V

DAVIES, Idris (1905–1953)
Welsh poet
Gwalia Deserta (1938) V
The Angry Summer (1943) V
Tonypandy, and Other Poems (1945) V

DAVIES, John, of Hereford (1565–1618)
English poet
Mirum in Modum (1602) V
Microcosmos (1603) V
Wittes Pilgrimage (1605) V
Bien Venu (1606) V
Summa Totalis; or, All in All (1607) V
The Holy Roode; or, Christs Crosse (1609) V
Humours Heav'n on Earth (1609) V
The Scourge of Folly (1611) V
The Muses Sacrifice (1612) V
The Muses-Teares for the Losse of Henry, Prince of Wales (1613) V
Wits Bedlam (1617) V

DAVIES, Sir John (1569–1626)
English lawyer, poet, and historian
Orchestra; or, A Poeme of Dauncing (1596) V
Hymns of Astraea, in Acrosticke Verse (1599) V
Nosce Teipsum (1599) [also 1602, 1619] V
A Discoverie of the True Causes Why Ireland was Never Entirely Subdued (1612) NF

DAVIES, W[illiam] H[enry] (1871–1940)
British poet and autobiographer
The Autobiography of a Super-Tramp (1908) NF
Nature Poems and Others (1908) V
Beggars (1909) NF
Farewell to Poesy, and Other Pieces (1910) V
Songs of Joy and Others (1911) V

The True Traveller (1912) NF
The Bird of Paradise and Other Poems (1914) V
Child Lovers, and Other Poems (1916) V
Collected Poems [1st ser.] (1916) V
A Poet's Pilgrimage (1918) NF
The Song of Life and Other Poems (1920) V
The Hour of Magic and Other Poems (1922) V
Collected Poems [2nd ser.] (1923) V
A Poet's Alphabet (1925) V
A Poet's Calendar (1927) V
Collected Poems (1928) V
Ambition, and Other Poems (1929) V
The Loneliest Mountain, and Other Poems (1939) V

DAVIES, [William] Robertson (1913–1995)
Canadian novelist, dramatist, and critic
The Diary of Samuel Marchbanks (1947) NF
Fortune, My Foe (1949) D
The Table Talk of Samuel Marchbanks (1949) NF
At My Heart's Core (1950) D
Tempest Tost (1951) F
A Jig for the Gypsy (1954) D
Leaven of Malice (1954) F
A Mixture of Frailties (1958) F
A Voice From the Attic (1960) NF
Samuel Marchbanks' Almanac (1967) NF
Fifth Business (1970) F
Hunting Stuart [written 1955] (1972) D
The Manticore (1972) F
World of Wonders (1975) F
The Enthusiasms of Robertson Davies (1979) NF
The Rebel Angels (1981) F
The Well-Tempered Critic (1981) NF
High Spirits (1982) F SS
What's Bred in the Bone (1985) F
The Lyre of Orpheus (1988) F
Murther and Walking Spirits (1991) F
The Cunning Man (1995) F

DAVIN, Dan[iel Marcus] (1913–1990)
New Zealand-born novelist and short-story
Cliffs of Fall (1945) F
For the Rest of Our Lives (1947) F
The Gorse Blooms Pale (1947) F SS
Roads From Home (1949) F

DAVIOT, Gordon *see* JOSEPHINE TEY

DAVIS, Dick (1945–)
British poet and translator
In the Distance (1975) V
Seeing the World (1980) V
The Covenant (1984) V

DAVIS, H[arold] L[enoir] (1896–1960)
American novelist
Honey in the Horn (1935) F
Harp of a Thousand Strings (1947) F
Beulah Land (1949) F

DAVIS, Rebecca [Blane] Harding (1831–1910)
American novelist and short-story writer
Margaret Howth (1862) F
Waiting for the Verdict (1868) F
John Andross (1874) F
Silhouettes of American Life (1892) F SS

DAVIS, Richard Harding (1864–1916)
American journalist, novelist, short-story writer, and dramatist
Gallegher, and Other Stories (1891) F SS
Van Bibber and Others (1892) F SS
The West From a Car Window (1892) NF
The Exiles (1894) F SS
Our English Cousins (1894) NF
The Rulers of the Mediterranean (1894) NF
About Paris (1895) NF
Three Gringos in Venezuela and Central America (1896) NF
Cuba in War Time (1897) NF
Soldiers of Fortune (1897) F
The Cuban and the Porto Rican Campaigns (1898) NF
The King's Jackal (1898) F
A Year From a Reporter's Note-Book (1898) NF
The Lion and the Unicorn (1899) F SS
With Both Armies in South Africa (1900) NF
Captain Macklin (1902) F
Ranson's Folly (1902) F SS
The Bar Sinister (1903) F
The Dictator (1904) D
Miss Civilization (1906) D
The Scarlet Car (1907) F SS
Vera the Medium (1908) F
The White Mice (1909) F
Notes of a War Correspondent (1910) NF
With the Allies (1914) NF
With the French in France and Salonika (1916) NF

DAVYS, Mary (1674–1732)
English novelist, dramatist, and poet
The Amours of Alcippus and Leucippe (1704) F
The Fugitive (1705) F
The Northern Heiress; or, The Humors of York (1716) D
The Reform'd Coquet (1724) F
The Accomplish'd Rake; or, Modern Fine Gentleman (1727) F

DAY, John (*c.* 1574–*c.* 1640)
English dramatist
The Ile of Guls (1606) D
The Travailes of the Three English Brothers (1607) D
Humour Out of Breath (1608) D
Law-Trickes; or, Who Woul'd Have Thought It (1608) D
The Parliament of Bees (1641) D
The Blind-Beggar of Bednal-Green (1659) D

DAY, Thomas (1748–1789)
British poet, novelist, and author
The Dying Negro (1773) V
The Desolation of America (1777) V
Reflections upon the Present State of England (1782) NF
The History of Sandford and Merton (1783) F CH

DAY LEWIS, C. [Cecil Day-Lewis] ['Nicholas Blake'] (1904–1972)
British poet, critic, and writer of detective fiction
Beechen Vigil, and Other Poems (1925) V
Country Comets (1928) V
Transitional Poem (1929) V
From Feathers to Iron (1931) V
The Magnetic Mountain (1933) V
A Hope for Poetry (1934) NF
Collected Poems 1929–33 (1935) V
A Question of Proof (1935) F
Revolution in Writing (1935) NF
A Time to Dance and Other Poems (1935) V
The Friendly Tree (1936) F
Noah and the Waters (1936) V
Thou Shell of Death [US: *Shell of Death*] (1936) F
Starting Point (1937) F
The Beast Must Die (1938) F
Overtures to Death, and Other Poems (1938) V
The Georgics of Virgil (1940) V
Poems in Wartime (1940) V
Word Over All (1943) V
The Poetic Image (1947) NF
Collected Poems 1929–36 (1949) V
The Aeneid of Virgil (1952) V
An Italian Visit (1953) V
Collected Poems of C. Day Lewis (1954) V
Pegasus, and Other Poems (1957) V
The Buried Day (1960) NF
The Gate, and Other Poems (1962) V
The Eclogues of Virgil (1963) V
The Room, and Other Poems (1965) V
The Whispering Roots (1970) V

DE BERNIÈRES, Louis (1954–)
British novelist
The War of Don Emmanuel's Nether Parts (1990) F
Señor Vivo and the Coco Lord (1991) F
The Troublesome Offspring of Cardinal Guzman (1992) F
Captain Corelli's Mandolin (1994) F

DE BOSSIÈRE, Ralph [Anthony Charles] (1907–)
Trinidadian-born Australian novelist
Crown Jewel (1952) F
Rum and Coca Cola (1956) F
No Saddles for Kangaroos (1964) F
Alice-For-Short (1907) F
Somehow Good (1908) F
It Can Never Happen Again (1909) F
An Affair of Dishonour (1910) F
A Likely Story (1911) F
When Ghost Meets Ghost (1914) F

DEE, Dr John (1527–1608)
English mathematician, astrologer, and occultist
Monas Hieroglyphica (1564) NF

DEEPING, [George] Warwick (1877–1950)
British novelist
Uther & Igraine (1903) F
Love Among the Ruins (1904) F
The Seven Streams (1905) F
Mad Barbara (1908) F
The Return of the Petticoat (1909) F
The Lame Englishman (1910) F
Sincerity (1912) F
The House of Spies (1913) F
The White Gate (1913) F
The Pride of Eve (1914) F
Countess Glika, and Other Stories (1919) F SS
Three Rooms (1924) F
Sorrell and Son (1925) F
Old Pybus (1928) F
Roper's Row (1929) F
Old Wine and New (1932) F
Two Black Sheep (1933) F
The Man on the White Horse (1934) F
Two in a Train, and Other Stories (1935) F SS
The Woman at the Door (1937) F
The Malice of Men (1938) F
The Man Who Went Back (1940) F
Corn in Egypt (1941) F
The Dark House (1941) F
Slade (1943) F
Paradise Place (1949) F

DEFOE, Daniel (1660–1731)
English journalist, pamphleteer, poet, and novelist
An Essay Upon Projects (1697) NF
An Enquiry into the Occasional Conformity of Dissenters (1698) NF
The Poor Man's Plea (1698) NF
The Pacificator (1700) V
The True-Born Englishman (1701) V
The Mock-Mourners (1702) V
Reformation of Manners (1702) V
The Shortest Way with the Dissenters (1702) NF
The Spanish Descent (1702) V
A Hymn to the Pillory (1703) V
The Shortest Way to Peace and Union (1703) NF
The Dissenters Answer to the High-Church Challenge (1704) NF
An Essay on the Regulation of the Press (1704) NF
A Hymn to Victory (1704) V
More Short-Ways with the Dissenters (1704) NF
The Dyet of Poland (1705) V
Caledonia (1706) V
Jure Divino (1706) V
A True Relation of the Apparition of one Mrs Veal (1706) NF
The Vision (1706) V
The History of the Union of Great Britain (1709) NF
An Essay on the History of Parties, and Persecution in Britain (1711) NF
An Essay on the South-Sea Trade (1711) NF
And What if the Pretender Should Come? (1713) NF
A General History of Trade (1713) NF
The Family Instructor (1715) NF
The Life, Adventures and Pyracies of the Famous Captain Singleton (1720) F
Memoirs of a Cavalier (1720) F
Serious Reflections During the Life and Surprising Adventures of Robinson Crusoe (1720) F

The Fortunes and Misfortunes of the Famous Moll Flanders (1722) F
A Journal of the Plague Year (1722) F
Religious Courtship (1722) F
The History and Remarkable Life of Colonel Jacque [Colonel Jack] (1723) F
The Fortunate Mistress [i.e. *Roxana*] (1724) F
A New Voyage Round the World (1724) F
A Tour Thro' the Whole Island of Great Britain (1725) NF
An Essay Upon Literature (1726) NF
The Political History of the Devil (1726) NF
A System of Magick; or, A History of the Black Art (1726) NF
An Essay on the History and Reality of Apparitions (1727) NF
The Life and Strange Surprizing Adventures of Robinson Crusoe (1719) F
The Farther Adventures of Robinson Crusoe (1719) F

DE FOREST, John W. (1826–1906)
American novelist
Seacliff; or, The Mystery of the Westervelts (1859) F
Miss Ravenel's Conversion from Secession to Loyalty (1867) F
Overland (1871) F
Kate Beaumont (1872) F
The Wetherel Affair (1873) F
Honest John Vane (1875) F
Playing the Mischief (1875) F
Justine's Lovers (1878) F
Irene the Missionary (1879) F
The Bloody Chasm (1881) F
A Lover's Revolt (1898) F

DEHAN, Richard *see* CLO GRAVES

DEIGHTON, Len [Leonard Cyril] (1929–)
British thriller writer
The Ipcress File (1962) F
Horse Under Water (1963) F
Funeral in Berlin (1964) F
The Billion Dollar Brain (1966) F
An Expensive Place to Die (1967) F
Only When I Larf (1968) F
Yesterday's Spy (1975) F
Twinkle, Twinkle Little Spy [US: *Catch a Falling Spy*] (1976) F
SS-GB (1978) F
Berlin Game (1983) F
Mexico Set (1984) F
London Match (1985) F
Spy Hook (1988) F
Spy Line (1989) F
Spy Sinker (1990) F
Mamista (1991) F
Faith (1994) F
Hope (1995) F

DEKKER, Thomas (1572?–1632)
English dramatist and pamphleteer
The Pleasant Comedie of Old Fortunatus (1600) D
The Shoemakers Holiday; or, The Gentle Craft (1600) D
Satiro-Mastix; or, The Untrussing of the Humorous Poet (1602) D
The Wonderfull Yeare (1603) F
The Honest Whore (1604) D
The Meeting of Gallants at an Ordinarie; or, The Walkes in Powles (1604) NF
Newes from Graves-end: Sent to Nobody (1604) V
The Double PP: A Papist in Armes (1606) V
Newes from Hell (1606) NF
The Seven Deadly Sinnes of London (1606) NF
The Famous History of Sir Thomas Wyat (1607) D
Jests to Make You Merie (1607) F
A Knights Conjuring (1607) F
North-ward Hoe (1607) D
West-ward Hoe (1607) D
The Whore of Babylon (1607) D
The Belman of London (1608) NF
Lanthorne and Candle-light; or, The Bellmans Second Nights Walke (1608) NF
Foure Birds of Noahs Arke (1609) NF
The Guls Horne-book (1609) NF
The Ravevens [sic] *Almanacke* (1609) NF
Worke for Armourours; or, The Peace is Broken (1609) NF
If It Be Not Good, the Divel Is In It (1612) D
Troia-Nova Triumphans, London Triumphing (1612) D
A Strange Horse-race (1613) NF
The Artillery Garden (1616) V
Dekker his Dreame (1620) V
A Rod for Run-awayes (1625) NF
The Second Part of the Honest Whore (1630) D
Match Mee in London (1631) D
Penny-wise Pound-foolish (1631) NF
The Wonder of a Kingdome (1636) D

'DELAFIELD, E.M.' [Edmée Elizabeth Monica de la Pasture] (1890–1943)
British novelist, short-story writer, and dramatist
Zella Sees Herself (1917) F
The Pelicans (1918) F
The Heel of Achilles (1921) F
Mrs Harter (1924) F
The Way Things Are (1927) F
Women Are Like That (1929) F SS
Diary of a Provincial Lady (1930) F
Turn Back the Leaves (1930) F
Challenge to Clarissa (1931) F
The Provincial Lady Goes Further (1932) F
The Provincial Lady in America (1934) F
Love Has No Resurrection, and Other Stories (1939) F SS
The Provincial Lady in War-Time (1940) F
Late and Soon (1943) F

DE LA MARE, Walter John (1873–1956)
British poet and short-story writer
Songs of Childhood (1902) V
Henry Brocken (1904) F
The Return (1910) F

The Three Mulla-Mulgars (1910) F CH
A Child's Day (1912) V
The Listeners, and Other Poems (1912) V
Peacock Pie (1913) V
The Sunken Garden, and Other Poems (1917) V
Motley, and Other Poems (1918) V
Poems 1901 to 1918 (1920) V
Memoirs of a Midget (1921) F
The Veil, and Other Poems (1921) V
Down-Adown-Derry (1922) V
Come Hither (1923) ANTH
The Riddle, and Other Stories (1923) F SS
Ding Dong Bell (1924) F SS
Broomsticks, and Other Tales (1925) F CH
The Connoisseur, and Other Stories (1926) F SS
Stuff and Nonsense, and So On (1927) V
Told Again (1927) F SS
On the Edge (1930) F SS
The Fleeting, and Other Poems (1933) V
Poems 1919 to 1934 (1935) V
The Wind Blows Over (1936) F SS
Memory, and Other Poems (1938) V
Behold, This Dreamer! (1939) ANTH
Bells and Grass (1941) V CH
The Traveller [US: *The Burning-Glass*] (1946) V
Collected Stories for Children (1947) F CH
Inward Companion (1950) V
Winged Chariot (1951) V
O Lovely England, and Other Poems (1953) V
Private View (1953) NF
A Beginning, and Other Stories (1955) F SS
Complete Poems (1969) V

DELANEY, Shelagh (1939–)
British dramatist
A Taste of Honey (1958) D
The Lion in Love (1960) D

DELANY, Samuel R[ay] (1942–)
African-American science fiction writer
Babel-17 (1966) F
The Einstein Intersection (1967) F
Nova (1968) F
Driftglass (1971) F SS
Dhalgren (1975) F
The Jewel-Hinged Jaw (1977) NF
The American Shore (1978) NF
Distant Stars (1981) F SS
Starboard Wine (1984) NF
Stars in My Pocket Like Grains of Sand (1984) F
The Bridge of Lost Desire (1987) F

DE LA PASTURE, Edmée *see* E.M. Delafield

DE LA RAMÉE, Marie Louise *see* Ouida

DE LA ROCHE, Mazo (1879–1961)
Canadian novelist, children's writer, and dramatist
Explorers of the Dawn (1922) F SS
Possession (1923) F
Delight (1926) F
Jalna (1927) F
Whiteoaks of Jalna (1929) F
Finch's Fortune (1931) F
The Master of Jalna (1933) F
Young Renny (1935) F
Whiteoak Harvest (1936) F
Growth of a Man (1938) F
Whiteoak Heritage (1940) F
Wakefield's Course (1941) F
The Building of Jalna (1944) F
Return to Jalna (1946) F
Mary Wakefield (1949) F
Renny's Daughter (1951) F
Whiteoak Brothers (1953) F
Variable Winds at Jalna (1954) F
Centenary at Jalna (1958) F
Morning at Jalna (1960) F

DELILLO, Don (1936–)
American novelist
Americana (1971) F
End Zone (1972) F
Great Jones Street (1973) F
Ratner's Star (1976) F
Players (1977) F
Running Dog (1978) F
The Names (1982) F
White Noise (1985) F
Libra (1988) F
Mao II (1991) F
Underworld (1997) F

DE LISSER, H[erbert] G[eorge] (1878–1944)
Jamaican novelist
Jane's Career (1914) F
Susan Proudleigh (1915) F
Triumphant Squalitone (1917) F
Revenge (1919) F
The White Witch of Rosehall (1929) F
Psyche (1952) F
Morgan's Daughter (1953) F

DELL, Ethel Mary (1881–1939)
British popular novelist
The Way of an Eagle (1911) F
The Prey of the Dragon (1912) F
The Knave of Diamonds (1913) F
The Swindler, and Other Stories (1914) F SS
The Keeper of the Door (1915) F
The Hundredth Chance (1917) F
The Lamp in the Desert (1919) F
Rosa Mundi, and Other Stories (1921) F SS
The Black Knight (1926) F
By Request [US: *Peggy by Request*] (1927) F

DELL, Floyd (1887–1969)
American novelist
Moon-Calf (1920) F
The Briary-Bush (1921) F
Janet March (1923) F
Runaway (1925) F
An Old Man's Folly (1926) F
An Unmarried Father (1927) F

DELONEY, Thomas (1543?–1600)
English ballad-maker and pamphleteer
A Most Joyfull Songe (1586) V
The Queenes Visiting of the Campe at Tilsburie (1588) V
The Gentle Craft (1597) NF
The Pleasant Historie of Jack of Newberie (1597) F
Strange Histories, or Songs and Sonets (1602) V
Thomas of Reading; or, The Sixe Worthy Yeomen of the West (1612) F
The Pleasant History of John Winchcomb (1619) F
The Garland of Good Will (1628) V

DE MORGAN, William [Frend] (1839–1917)
British novelist and designer
Joseph Vance (1906) F
Alice-For-Short (1907) F
Somehow Good (1908) F
It Can Never Happen Again (1909) F
An Affair of Dishonour (1910) F
A Likely Story (1911) F
When Ghost Meets Ghost (1914) F

DENHAM, Sir John (1615–1669)
English poet
Coopers Hill [unauthorized] (1642) V
The Sophy (1642) D
The Anatomy of Play (1651) NF
Coopers Hill [first authorized edn] (1655) V
The Destruction of Troy [from Virgil] (1656) V
On Mr Abraham Cowley His Death, and Burial (1667) V
The Second Advice to the Painter (1667) V
Poems and Translations (1668) V
Version of the Psalms (1714) V

DENNIS, John (1657–1734)
English critic, poet, and dramatist
Poems in Burlesque (1692) V
The Impartial Critic (1693) NF
The Court of Death (1695) V
A Plot and No Plot (1697) D
The Usefulness of the Stage (1698) NF
Rinaldo and Armida (1699) D
Iphigenia (1700) D
The Advancement and Reformation of Modern Poetry (1701) NF
The Monument (1702) V
The Grounds of Criticism in Poetry (1704) NF
Liberty Asserted (1704) D
The Person of Quality's Answer to Mr Collier's Letter (1704) NF
Gibraltar; or, The Spanish Adventure (1705) D
The Battle of Ramillia; or, the Power of Union (1706) V
An Essay on the Operas After the Italian Manner (1706) NF
Appius and Virginia (1709) D
An Essay Upon Publick Spirit (1711) NF
Reflections Critical and Satyrical, Upon An Essay Upon Criticism (1711) NF
An Essay upon the Genius and Writings of Shakespear (1712) NF
Remarks upon Cato, a Tragedy (1713) NF
A True Character of Mr Pope, and his Writings (1716) NF
Remarks upon Mr Pope's Translation of Homer (1717) NF
The Invader of His Country; or, The Fatal Resentment (1720) D
A Defence of Sir Fopling Flutter (1722) NF
The Stage Defended (1726) NF
Remarks on Mr Pope's Rape of the Lock (1728) NF

DENNIS, Nigel [Forbes] (1912–1989)
British novelist, dramatist, and critic
Boys and Girls Come Out to Play (1949) F
Cards of Identity (1955) F
Two Plays and a Preface [*Cards of Identity*, and *The Making of Moo*] (1958) D
A House in Order (1966) F

DE QUINCEY, Thomas (1785–1859)
British essayist and prose writer
Klosterheim; or, The Masque (1832) D
Autobiographic Sketches [i] (1853) NF
Autobiographic Sketches [ii] (1854) NF
Miscellanies [i and ii] (1854) NF
Confessions of an English Opium Eater (1856) NF
Sketches, Critical and Biographic (1857) NF
Essays Sceptical and Anti-sceptical (1858) NF
Leaders in Literature (1858) NF
Studies in Secret Records, Personal and Historic (1858) NF
Classic Records Reviewed or Deciphered (1859) NF
Critical Suggestions on Style and Rhetoric (1859) NF
Speculations, Literary and Philosophic (1859) NF
Letters to a Young Man Whose Education Has Been Neglected (1860) NF

DESAI, Anita (1937–)
Indian novelist
Voices in the City (1965) F
Bye-Bye Blackbird (1971) F
Where Shall We Go This Summer? (1975) F
Fire on the Moutain (1977) F
Games at Twilight (1978) F SS
Clear Light of Day (1980) F
The Village by the Sea (1982) F
In Custody (1984) F
Baumgartner's Bombay (1988) F
Journey to Ithaca (1995) F
Fasting, Feasting (1999) F
Diamond Dust (2000) F

DESANI, G[ovindas] V[ishnoodas] (1909–)
Indian novelist
All About H. Hatterr (1948) F

DESTOUCHES, Louis-Ferdinand *see* LOUIS-FERDINAND CÉLINE

DE VERE, Aubrey Thomas (1814–1902)
Irish poet and man of letters
The Waldenses; or, The Fall of Rora (1842) V

The Search After Prosperine, and Other Poems (1843) V
English Misrule and Irish Deeds (1848) V
May Carols; or, Ancilla Domini (1857) V
The Sisters; Inisfail, and Other Poems (1861) V
Inisfail: A Lyrical Chronicle of Ireland (1863) V

DE VRIES, Peter (1910–1993)
American novelist and poet
But Who Wakes the Burglar? (1940) F
The Handsome Heart (1943) F
No, But I Saw the Movie (1952) F SS
Tunnel of Love (1954) F
Comfort Me with Apples (1956) F
The Mackerel Plaza (1958) F
The Tents of Wickedness (1959) F
Through the Fields of Clover (1961) F
The Blood of the Lamb (1962) F
Reuben, Reuben (1964) F
Let Me Count the Ways (1965) F
The Vale of Laughter (1967) F
The Cat's Pyjamas, and Witch's Milk (1968) F
Mrs Wallop (1970) F
Into Your Tent I'll Creep (1971) F
Without a Stitch in Time (1972) F SS
Forever Panting (1975) F
The Glory of the Humming-Bird (1975) F
I Hear America Swinging (1976) F
Madder Music (1977) F
Consenting Adults; or, The Duchess Will Be Furious (1980) F
Sauce for the Goose (1981) F
Slouching Towards Kalamazoo (1983) F
The Prick of Noon (1985) F
Peckham's Marbles (1986) F

DEXTER, Colin (1930–)
British crime writer
Last Bus to Woodstock (1975) F
Last Seen Wearing (1976) F
The Silent World of Nicholas Quinn (1977) F
Service of all the Dead (1979) F
The Dead of Jericho (1981) F
The Riddle of the Third Mile (1983) F
The Secret of Annexe 3 (1986) F
The Wench is Dead (1989) F
The Remorseful Day [last 'Inspector Morse' novel] (1999) F

DIAPER, William (1685–1717)
English poet
Dryaides; or, The Nymphs Prophecy (1712) V
Nereides; or, Sea-Eclogues (1712) V
An Imitation of the Seventeenth Epistle of the First Book of Horace (1714) V

DIBDIN, Charles (1745–1814)
British actor, dramatist, and songwriter
The Shepherd's Artifice (1765) D
The Deserter (1773) D
The Waterman; or, The First of August (1774) D
The Quaker (1777) D
Poor Vulcan (1778) D
Hannah Hewit; or, The Female Crusoe (1792) F
The Younger Brother (1793) F
A Complete History of the English Stage (1797–1800) NF
The Professional Life of Mr Dibdin . . . (1803) NF

DIBDIN, Michael (1947–)
British crime novelist
Ratking (1988) F
Dirty Tricks (1991) F
The Dying of the Light (1993) F
Blood Rain (1999) F

DIBDIN, Thomas Frognall (1776–1847)
British bibliographer and author
An Introduction to Rare and Valuable Editions of the Greek and Roman Classics (1802) NF
The Bibliomania, or Book Madness (1809) NF
The Bibliographical Decameron (1817) NF
A Bibliographical Tour in France and Germany (1821) NF
The Library Companion (1824) NF
Bibliophobia (1832) NF
Reminiscences of a Literary Life (1836) NF
A Bibliographical Tour in the Northern Counties of England and in Scotland (1838) NF
Cranmer (1839) F

DICK, Kay (1915–)
British novelist and editor
Young Man (1951) F
Sunday (1962) F
Ivy and Stevie (1971) NF
They (1977) F

DICK, Philip K[endred] (1928–1982)
American science fiction writer
The World Jones Made (1956) F
The Man in the High Castle (1962) F
Martian Time-Slip (1964) F
Now Wait for Last Year (1966) F
Do Androids Dream of Electric Sheep? (1969) F
Flow My Tears, the Policeman Said (1974) F
A Scanner Darkly (1977) F
The Divine Invasion (1981) F
Valis (1981) F

DICKENS, Charles [John Huffham] ['Boz'] (1812–1870)
British novelist, journalist, and editor
Sketches by 'Boz' [1st ser.] (1836) F
The Posthumous Papers of the Pickwick Club (1837) F
Sketches by 'Boz' [2nd ser.] (1837) F
Oliver Twist; or, The Parish Boy's Progress (1838) F
The Life and Adventures of Nicholas Nickleby (1839) F
Master Humphrey's Clock [vol. i] (1840) F
Barnaby Rudge (1841) F
Master Humphrey's Clock [vols. ii, iii] (1841) F
The Old Curiosity Shop (1841) F
American Notes for General Circulation (1842) NF
A Christmas Carol in Prose (1843) F
The Chimes (1844) F

The Life and Adventures of Martin Chuzzlewit (1844) F
The Cricket on the Hearth (1845) F
The Battle of Life (1846) F
Pictures from Italy (1846) F
Dombey and Son (1848) F
The Haunted Man and the Ghost's Bargain (1848) F
The Personal History of David Copperfield (1850) F
Bleak House (1853) F
A Child's History of England (1853) NF
Hard Times, For These Times (1854) F
Little Dorrit (1857) F
A Tale of Two Cities (1859) F
Great Expectations (1861) F
The Uncommercial Traveller (1861) P
Our Mutual Friend (1865) F
The Mystery of Edwin Drood [unfinished] (1870) F
The Mudfog Papers (1880) F

DICKENS, Monica [Enid] (1915–1992)
British novelist
One Pair of Hands (1939) NF
One Pair of Feet (1942) NF
The Fancy (1943) F
My Turn to Make the Tea (1951) NF
No More Meadows (1953) F
The Heart of London (1961) F
Kate and Emma (1964) F
One of the Family (1993) F

DICKEY, James [Lafayette] (1923–)
American poet, novelist, and non-fiction writer
Into the Stone, and Other Poems (1960) V
Drowning with Others (1962) V
Helmets (1964) V
The Suspect in Poetry (1964) NF
Buckdancer's Choice (1965) V
Babel to Byzantium (1968) NF
Deliverance (1970) F
The Eye-Beaters (1970) V
Self-interviews (1970) NF
The Strength of Fields (1970) V
Sorties (1971) NF
The Zodiac (1976) V
The Poet Turns on Himself (1982) NF
Puella (1982) V
Night Hurling (1983) NF
Bronwen, the Traw, and the Shape-Shifter (1986) V
Alnilam (1987) F
To the White Sea (1993) F

DICKINSON, Emily [Elizabeth] (1830–1886)
American poet
Poems by Emily Dickinson (1890) V
Poems: Second Series (1891) V
Poems: Third Series (1896) V
The Single Hound (1914) V
Unpublished Poems (1936) V

DICKINSON, Goldsworthy Lowes (1862–1932)
British philosophical writer
The Greek View of Life (1896) NF
A Modern Symposium (1905) NF
Justice and Liberty (1908) NF

DICKINSON, Patric [Thomas] (1914–1994)
British poet
The Seven Days of Jericho (1944) V
The Sailing Race, and Other Poems (1952) V
The Scale of Things (1955) V
The World I See (1960) V
This Cold Universe (1964) V
More Than Time (1970) V
A Wintering Tree (1973) V
The Bearing Breast (1976) V
Our Living John, and Other Poems (1979) V
Winter Hostages (1980) V
A Rift in Time (1982) V
To Go Hidden (1984) V

DICKINSON, Peter [Malcolm de Brissac] (1927–)
British novelist and children's writer
Skin Deep [US: *The Glass-Sided Ant's Nest*] (1968) F
The Weathermonger (1968) F CH
Heartsease (1969) F CH
The Devil's Children (1970) F CH
The Green Gene (1973) F
The Poison Oracle (1974) F
King and Joker (1976) F
Tulku (1979) F CH
The Last House Party (1982) F
Skeleton-in-Waiting (1989) F

DICKSON, Carter *see* JOHN DICKSON CARR

DIDEROT, Denis (1713–1784)
French philosopher and man of letters
Philosophical Thoughts [*Pensées philosophiques*] (1746) NF
The Indiscreet Toys [*Les Bijoux indiscrets*] (1748) F
Encyclopedia [*Encyclopédie, ou Dictionnaire Raisonné des Sciences, des Arts et des Métiers*] (1751) NF
Thoughts on the Interpretation of Nature [*Pensées sur l'interprétation de la nature*] (1753) NF
The Natural Son [*Le Fils naturel*] (1757) D
The Father of the Family [*Le Père de famille*] (1758) D
James the Fatalist [*Jacques le fataliste*] (1796) F
The Nun [*La Religieuse*] (1796) F
Rameau's Nephew [*Le Neveu de Rameau*] (1804) NF

DIDION, Joan (1934–)
American essayist and novelist
Run, River (1964) F
Slouching Towards Bethlehem (1968) NF
Play it as it Lays (1970) F
A Book of Common Prayer (1977) F
The White Album (1979) NF
Democracy (1984) F
Essays and Interviews (1984) NF
Miami (1987) NF
After Henry (1992) NF

DIGBY, Sir Kenelm (1603–1665)
English diplomat and author
Observations upon Religio Medici (1643) NF

DIGBY, Kenelm Henry (1796?–1880)
British miscellaneous writer
The Broad-Stone of Honour; or, The True Sense and Practice of Chivalry (1822) NF
A Discourse Concerning the Vegetation of Plants (1661) NF

DILKE, Sir Charles Wentworth, 2nd Baronet (1843–1911)
British politician and author
Greater Britain (1868) NF
Problems of Greater Britain (1890) NF

DILLON, Wentworth, 4th Earl of Roscommon (1633–1685)
English poet and translator
Horace's Art of Poetry (1680) V
An Essay on Translated Verse (1684) V
Poems (1717) V

'DINESEN, Isak' [Karen Christentze Blixen, *née* Dinesen] (1885–1962)
Danish-born novelist and short-story writer
Seven Gothic Tales (1934) F SS
Out of Africa (1937) F
Winter's Tales (1942) F SS
Last Tales (1957) F SS
Anecdotes of Destiny (1958) F SS
Shadows on the Grass (1960) F

DISCH, Thomas M[ichael] (1940–)
American science fiction writer
The Genocides (1965) F
Camp Concentration (1968) F
Under Compulsion (1968) F SS
334 (1972) F SS
Getting into Death (1973) F SS
On Wings of Song (1979) F
Fundamental Disch (1980) F SS
The Man Who Had No Idea (1982) F SS

DISKI, Jenny [born **Jenny Simmonds**] (1947–)
British novelist
Nothing Natural (1986) F
Rainforest (1987) F
Like Mother (1988) F
Then Again (1990) F
Happily Ever After (1991) F
Monkey's Uncle (1994) F
The Dream Mistress (1996) F
Skating to Antarctica (1997) NF
Don't (1998) NF

DISRAELI, Benjamin, 1st Earl of Beaconsfield (1804–1881)
British statesman and novelist
Vivian Grey [vols. i, ii] (1826) F
Vivian Grey [vols. iii, iv, v] (1827) F
The Voyage of Captain Popanilla (1828) F
The Young Duke (1831) F
Contarini Fleming (1832) F
The Wondrous Tale of Alroy; The Rise of Iskander (1833) F
Henrietta Temple (1836) F
Venetia; or, The Poet's Daughter (1837) F
The Tragedy of Count Alarcos (1839) F
Coningsby; or, The New Generation (1844) F
Sybil; or, The Two Nations (1845) F
Tancred; or, The New Crusade (1847) F
Lothair (1870) F
Endymion (1880) F

D'ISRAELI, Isaac (1766–1848)
British poet and miscellaneous writer
Curiosities of Literature [1st ser., vol. i] (1791) NF
Curiosities of Literature [1st ser., vol. ii] (1793) NF
An Essay on the Manners and Genius of the Literary Character (1795) NF
Miscellanies; or, Literary Recreations (1796) NF
Vaurien; or, Sketches of the Times (1797) F
Narrative Poems (1803) V
Flim-flams!; or, The Life and Errors of My Uncle, and the Amours of My Aunt! (1805) F
Despotism; or, The Fall of the Jesuits (1811) F
Calamities of Authors (1812) NF
Quarrels of Authors; or, Some Memoirs for Our Literary History (1814) NF
Curiosities of Literature [1st ser., vol. iii] (1817) NF
A Second Series of Curiosities of Literature (1823) NF
Amenities of Literature (1841) NF

DIXIE, Lady Florence [Caroline], *née* Douglas (1857–1905)
British traveller and novelist
Across Patagonia (1880) NF
Gloriana; or, The Revolution of 1900 (1890) F
Isola; or, The Disinherited (1902) V D

DIXON, Richard Watson (1833–1900)
British poet and ecclesiastical historian
Christ's Company, and Other Poems (1861) V
Historical Odes, and Other Poems (1864) V
Last Poems (1905) V

DOBELL, Sydney Thompson (1824–1874)
British poet and critic
The Roman [as 'Sydney Yendys'] (1850) V
Balder (1853) V
England in Time of War (1856) V

DOBSON, [Henry] Austin (1840–1921)
British poet and critic
Vignettes in Rhyme (1873) V
Proverbs in Porcelain (1877) V
At the Sign of the Lyre (1885) V
Poems on Several Occasions (1889) V
The Ballad of Beau Brocade, and Other Poems of the XVIIIth Century (1892) V
Eighteenth Century Vignettes [1st ser.] (1892) NF
Eighteenth Century Vignettes [2nd ser.] (1894) NF
The Story of Rosina, and Other Verses (1895) V
Eighteenth Century Vignettes [3rd ser.] (1896) NF
Old Kensington Palace and Other Papers (1910) NF
At Prior Park, and Other Papers (1912) NF
Eighteenth-Century Studies (1912) NF
Rosalba's Journal, and Other Papers (1915) NF

DOCTOROW, E[dgar] L[awrence] (1931–)
American novelist
Welcome to Hard Times [UK: *Bad Man From Bodie*] (1960) F
Big as Life (1966) F
The Book of Daniel (1971) F
Ragtime (1975) F
Loon Lake (1980) F
Lives of the Poet: Six Stories and a Novella (1984) F SS
World's Fair (1985) F
Billy Bathgate (1989) F

DODDRIDGE, Philip (1702–1751)
English Nonconformist divine, author, and hymn-writer
Free Thoughts on Reviving the Dissenting Interest (1730) NF
Sermons on the Religious Education of Children (1732) NF
Submission to Divine Providence in the Death of Children (1737) NF
Of the Evidences of Christianity (1743) NF
The Principles of the Christian Religion (1743) V
The Rise and Progress of Religion in the Soul (1745) NF

DODGSON, Charles Lutwidge *see* LEWIS CARROLL

DONLEAVY, J[ames] P[atrick] (1926–)
Irish novelist and dramatist
The Ginger Man (1955) F
A Singular Man (1963) F
Meet My Maker the Mad Molecule (1964) F SS
The Saddest Summer of Samuel S. (1966) F
The Beastly Beatitudes of Balthasar B. (1969) F
The Onion Eaters (1971) F
A Fairy Tale of New York (1973) F
The Destinies of Darcy Dancer, Gentleman (1977) F
Schultz (1979) F
Leila (1983) F
Are You Listening, Rabbi Löw (1987) F
That Darcy, That Dancer, That Gentleman (1990) F
Wrong Information is Being Given Out at Princeton (1998) F

DONNADIEU, Marguerite *see* MARGUERITE DURAS

DONNE, John (1572–1631)
English poet and prose writer
Pseudo-Martyr (1610) NF
An Anatomy of the World (1611) V
Ignatius his Conclave (1611) NF
The First Anniversarie: An Anatomie of the World. The Second Anniversarie: Of the Progres [sic] *of the Soule* (1612) V
Encaenia (1623) NF
Three Sermons Upon Speciall Occasions (1623) NF
Devotions Upon Emergent Occasions (1624) NF
The First Sermon Preached to King Charles: 3 April 1625 (1625) NF
Foure Sermons Upon Speciall Occasions (1625) NF
Five Sermons Upon Speciall Occasions (1626) NF
Deaths Duell (1632) NF
Juvenilia; or, Certaine Paradoxes, and Problemes (1633) NF
Poems, by J.D. (1633) V
Six Sermons Upon Severall Occasions (1634) NF
LXXX Sermons (1640) NF
Biathanatos (1644) NF
Fifty Sermons (1649) NF
Essayes in Divinity (1651) NF
Letters to Severall Persons of Honour (1651) NF
Paradoxes, Problemes, Essayes, Characters (1652) NF
XXVI Sermons (1660) NF

DOOLITTLE, Hilda (1886–1961)
American poet and novelist
Sea Garden (1916) V
Hymen (1921) V
Heliodora, and Other Poems (1924) V
Hippolytus Temporizes (1927) D
Hedylus (1928) F
The Hedgehog (1936) F
The Ion of Euripides (1937) D
The Walls Do Not Fall (1944) V
Tribute to Angels (1945) V
Flowering of the Rod (1946) V
By Avon River (1949) MISC
Tribute to Freud (1956) NF
End to Torment [biography of Ezra Pound] (1958) NF
Bid Me to Live (1960) F
Helen in Egypt (1961) MISC
Hermetic Definition (1972) NF
Hermione (1981) F

DORN, Ed[ward] (1929–1999)
American poet
The Newly Fallen (1961) V
From Gloucester Out (1964) V
Hands Up! (1964) V
Geography (1965) V
The Rite of Passage (1965) F
The North Atlantic Turbine (1967) V
Gunslinger (1968–72) V
Hello La Jolla (1978) V
Abhorrence (1990) V
By the Sound (1991) V

DOS PASSOS, John [Roderigo] (1896–1970)
American novelist
One Man's Initiation: 1917 (1920) F
Three Soldiers (1921) F
A Pushcart at the Kerb (1922) V
Rosinante to the Road Again (1922) NF
Streets of Night (1923) F
The Garbage Man (1925) D
Manhattan Transfer (1925) F
Orient Express (1927) NF
Airways, Inc. (1928) D
The 42nd Parallel (1930) F
1919 (1932) F
In All Countries (1934) NF
The Big Money (1936) F
Journeys Between Wars (1938) NF

Adventures of a Young Man (1939) F
The Ground We Stand On (1941) NF
Number One (1943) F
State of the Nation (1944) NF
Tour of Duty (1946) NF
The Grand Design (1949) F
The Prospect Before Us (1950) F
Chosen Country (1951) F
Most Likely to Succeed (1954) F
The Theme is Freedom (1956) NF
Men Who Made the Nation (1957) NF
The Great Days (1958) F
Prospects of a Golden Age (1959) NF
Midcentury (1961) F
Brazil on the Move (1963) NF
Mr Wilson's War (1963) NF
Occasions and Protests (1964) NF
The Best Times (1966) NF
The Fourteenth Chronicle (1973) NF

DOSTOEVSKY, Fyodor Mikhailovich (1821–1881)
Russian novelist and author
Notes from the House of the Dead (1860–1) NF
The Insulted and the Injured (1861) F
Winter Notes on Summer Impressions (1863) NF
Notes From Underground (1864) NF
Crime and Punishment (1866) F
The Idiot (1868) F
The Devils (1872) F
The Brothers Karamazov (1880) F

DOUGHTY, Charles Montagu (1843–1926)
British traveller, poet, and advocate of purified English
Travels in Arabia Deserta (1888) NF
The Dawn of Britain (1906) V
Adam Cast Forth (1908) V

DOUGLAS, Lord Alfred [Bruce] (1870–1945)
British poet and friend of Oscar Wilde
The City of the Soul (1899) V
The Placid Pug, and Other Rhymes (1906) V
Sonnets (1909) V
Oscar Wilde and Myself (1914) NF
The Autobiography of Douglas (1929) NF
Lyrics (1935) V

DOUGLAS, Gavin [or Gawin] (1474?–1522)
Scottish poet and bishop
The Palice of Honour (1535) V

DOUGLAS, George *see* GEORGE DOUGLAS BROWN

DOUGLAS, [George] Norman (1868–1952)
British travel writer and novelist
Siren Land (1911) NF
Fountains in the Sand (1912) NF
Old Calabria (1915) NF
South Wind (1917) F
They Went (1920) F
Summer Islands (1931) NF
Looking Back (1933) NF
Late Harvest (1946) NF

DOUGLAS, Keith [Castellain] (1920–1944)
British poet
Alamein to Zem Zem (1946) NF
Collected Poems (1951) V

DOUGLASS, Frederick (1817–1895)
African-American writer
Narrative of the Life of Frederick Douglass [rev. 1892] (1845) NF
My Bondage and My Freedom (1855) NF
Life and Times of Frederick Douglass (1881) NF

DOWDEN, Edward (1843–1913)
British critic and poet
Mr Tennyson and Mr Browning (1863) NF
Shakespeare (1875) NF
Poems (1876) V
A Shakespeare Primer (1877) NF
Studies in Literature 1789–1877 (1878) NF
Southey (1879) NF
The Life of Percy Bysshe Shelley (1886) NF
Transcripts and Studies (1888) NF
New Studies in Literature (1895) NF
Robert Browning (1904) NF

DOWLAND, John (1563–1626)
English lutenist and composer
The First Booke of Songes or Ayres of Fowre Partes (1597) V MUS
The Second Booke of Songs or Ayres (1600) V MUS
The Third and Last Booke of Songs or Aires (1603) V MUS
A Pilgrimes Solace (1612) V MUS

DOWSON, Ernest [Christopher] (1867–1900)
British poet and novelist
A Comedy of Masks (1893) F
Dilemmas (1895) F SS
Verses (1896) V
The Pierrot of the Minute (1897) V
Adrian Rome (1899) F
Decorations in Verse and Prose (1899) MISC

DOYLE, [Sir] Arthur Conan (1859–1930)
British novelist and short-story writer
The Mystery of Cloomber (1888) F
A Study in Scarlet (1888) F
Micah Clarke (1889) F
Mysteries and Adventures (1889) F SS
The Captain of the Polestar, and Other Tales (1890) F SS
The Firm of Girdlestone (1890) F
The Sign of Four (1890) F
The White Company (1891) F
The Adventures of Sherlock Holmes (1892) F SS
The Doings of Raffles Haw (1892) F
The Great Shadow (1892) F
The Memoirs of Sherlock Holmes (1893) F SS
The Refugees (1893) F
The Parasite (1894) F
Round the Red Lamp (1894) F SS
The Stark Munro Letters (1895) F
The Exploits of Brigadier Gerard (1896) F SS
Rodney Stone (1896) F

Uncle Bernac (1897) F
Songs of Action (1898) V
The Tragedy of the Korosko (1898) F
A Duet With an Occasional Chorus (1899) F
The Great Boer War (1900) NF
The Green Flag, and Other Stories of War and Sport (1900) F SS
The Hound of the Baskervilles (1902) F
The War in South Africa (1902) NF
Adventures of Gerard (1903) F SS
The Return of Sherlock Holmes (1905) F SS
Sir Nigel (1906) F
Through the Magic Door (1907) NF
Round the Fire Stories (1908) F SS
The Crime of the Congo (1909) NF
The Last Galley (1911) F SS
The Lost World (1912) F
The Poison Belt (1913) F
The German War (1914) NF
The Valley of Fear (1915) F
The British Campaign in France and Flanders [vol. i] (1916) NF
The British Campaign in France and Flanders [vol. ii] (1917) NF
His Last Bow (1917) F
The British Campaign in France and Flanders [vol. iii] (1918) NF
Danger! and Other Stories (1918) F SS
The New Revelation (1918) NF
The British Campaign in France and Flanders [vols. iv, v] (1919) NF
The Guards Came Through, and Other Poems (1919) V
The Vital Message (1919) NF
The British Campaign in France and Flanders [vol. vi] (1920) NF
The Wanderings of a Spiritualist (1921) NF
The Coming of the Fairies (1922) NF
The Poems of Arthur Conan Doyle (1922) V
Tales of Adventure and Medical Life (1922) F SS
Tales of Long Ago (1922) F SS
Tales of Pirates and Blue Water (1922) F SS
Tales of Terror and Mystery (1922) F SS
Tales of the Ring and Camp (1922) F SS
Tales of Twilight and the Unseen (1922) F SS
Our American Adventure (1923) NF
Memories and Adventures (1924) NF
Our Second American Adventure (1924) NF
The Land of Mist (1926) F
The Case-Book of Sherlock Holmes (1927) F SS
The Complete Sherlock Holmes Short Stories (1928) F SS
The Complete Sherlock Holmes Long Stories (1929) F SS
The Maracot Deep, and Other Stories (1929) F SS

DOYLE, Roddy (1958–)
Irish novelist and dramatist
The Commitments (1987) F
The Snapper (1990) F
The Van (1991) F
Paddy Clarke Ha Ha Ha (1993) F
The Woman Who Walked into Doors (1996) F
A Star Called Henry (1999) F

DRABBLE, Margaret (1939–)
British novelist and biographer
A Summer Bird-Cage (1963) F
The Garrick Year (1964) F
The Millstone (1965) F
Jerusalem the Golden (1967) F
The Waterfall (1969) F
The Needle's Eye (1972) F
The Realms of Gold (1975) F
The Ice Age (1977) F
A Writer's Britain (1979) NF
The Middle Ground (1980) F
The Oxford Companion to English Literature (1985) NF
The Radiant Way (1987) F
A Natural Curiosity (1989) F
The Gates of Ivory (1991) F
The Witch of Exmoor (1996) F

DRAYTON, Michael (1563–1631)
English poet
The Harmonie of the Church (1591) V
Idea (1593) V
Ideas Mirrour (1594) V
Matilda (1594) V
Endimion and Phoebe: Ideas Latmus (1595) V
Mortimeriados (1596) V
The Tragicall Legend of Robert Duke of Normandy (1596) V
Englands Heroicall Epistles (1597) V
The Barrons Wars in the Raigne of Edward the Second (1603) V
To the Majestie of King James (1603) V
Moyses in a Map of his Miracles (1604) V
The Owle (1604) V
A Paean Triumphall (1604) V
Poems (1605) V
Poemes Lyrick and Pastorall (1606) V
The Legend of Great Cromwel (1607) V
Poly-Olbion [pt. i] (1612) V
The Second Part, or a Continuance of Poly-Olbion (1622) V
The Battaile of Agincourt (1627) V
The Muses Elizium, Lately Discovered (1630) V

DREISER, Theodore [Herman Albert] (1871–1945)
American novelist and non-fiction writer
Sister Carrie (1900) F
Jennie Gerhardt (1911) F
A Traveler at Forty (1913) NF
The 'Genius' (1915) F
A Hoosier Holiday (1916) NF
Plays of the Natural and the Supernatural (1916) D
Free (1918) F SS
Twelve Men (1919) NF
Hey Rub-a-Dub-Dub (1920) NF
A Book About Myself (1922) NF
The Color of a Great City (1923) NF
An American Tragedy (1925) F
Moods, Cadenced and Declaimed (1926) V

Chains (1927) F SS
Dreiser Looks at Russia (1928) NF
A Gallery of Women (1929) F SS
My City (1929) NF
Dawn (1931) NF
Tragic America (1931) NF
America is Worth Saving (1941) NF
The Bulwark (1946) NF

DREWE, Robert [Duncan] (1943–)
Australian novelist, short-story writer, and journalist
The Savage Crows (1976) F
A Cry in the Jungle Bar (1979) F
The Bodysurfers (1983) F SS
Fortune (1986) F
The Bay of Contented Men (1989) F SS
Our Sunshine (1991) F

DRINKWATER, John (1882–1937)
British poet and dramatist
The Death of Leander, and Other Poems (1906) V
Cophetua (1911) D
Poems of Men and Hours (1911) V
Poems of Love and Earth (1912) V
Cromwell, and Other Poems (1913) V
Swords and Ploughshares (1915) V
Pawns: Three Poetic Plays [The Storm, The God of Quiet, A Night of the Trojan War] (1917) D
Prose Papers (1917) NF
Tides (1917) V
Abraham Lincoln (1918) D
Loyalties (1919) V
Mary Stuart (1921) D
Oliver Cromwell (1921) D
Seeds of Time (1921) V
Robert E. Lee (1923) D
From an Unknown Isle (1924) V
Bird in Hand (1927) D
Christmas Poems (1931) V
Inheritance (1931) NF
Discovery (1932) NF

DRUMMOND, William Henry (1854–1907)
Canadian poet
The Habitant (1897) V
Phil-o-Rum's Canoe, and Madeleine de Verchères (1898) V
Johnnie Courteau, and Other Poems (1901) V
The Voyageur, and Other Poems (1905) V
The Great Fight (1908) V

DRUMMOND, William, of Hawthornden (1585–1649)
English poet, dramatist, and critic
Mausoleum (1613) V
Teares on the Death of Meliades (1613) V
Poems by William Drummond of Hawthornden (1614) V
Forth Feasting (1617) V
A Midnights Trance (1619) NF
Flowres of Sion (1623) V
The History of Scotland (1655) NF

DRYDEN, John (1631–1700)
English poet, dramatist, and critic
Three Poems Upon the Death of Oliver Lord Protector of England, Scotland, and Ireland (1659) V
Astraea Redux (1660) V
The Wild Gallant (1663) D
The Rival Ladies (1664) D
The Indian Emperour; or, The Conquest of Mexico by the Spaniards (1665) D
Annus Mirabilis: The Year of Wonders, 1666 (1667) V
Secret-Love; or, The Maiden Queen (1667) D
Sir Martin Mar-all; or, The Feign'd Innocence (1667) D
An Evening's Love; or, The Mock-Astrologer (1668) D
Of Dramatick Poesie (1668) NF
Tyrannick Love; or, The Royal Martyr (1669) D
The Conquest of Granada by the Spaniards (1670) D
The Assignation; or, Love in a Nunnery (1672) D
Marriage-à-la-Mode (1672) D
Amboyna (1673) D
Aureng-Zebe (1675) D
All for Love; or, The World Well Lost (1677) D
The State of Innocence, and the Fall of Man (1677) D
The Kind Keeper; or, Mr Limberham (1678) D
Oedipus (1678) D
Troilus and Cressida; or, Truth Found Too Late (1679) D
Ovid's Epistles (1680) V
The Spanish Fryar; or, The Double Discovery (1680) D
Absalom and Achitophel [pt. i] (1681) V
The Duke of Guise (1682) D
Mac Flecknoe (1682) V
The Medall (1682) V
Religio Laici; or, A Laymans Faith (1682) V
The Second Part of Absalom and Achitophel [mostly by Nahum Tate (1652)] (1682) V
Miscellany Poems (1684) V
Albion and Albanius (1685) D
Sylvae; or, The Second Part of Poetical Miscellanies (1685) V
Threnodia Augustalis (1685) V
The Hind and the Panther (1687) V
A Song for St Cecilia's Day (1687) V
Britannia Rediviva (1688) V
Amphityron; or, The Two Socia's (1690) D
Don Sebastian, King of Portugal (1690) D
King Arthur; or, The British Worthy (1691) D
Cleomenes, the Spartan Heroe (1692) D
Eleonora (1692) V
Examen Poeticum: Being the Third Part of Miscellany Poems (1693) V
The Satires of Decimus Junius Juvenalis (1693) V
The Annual Miscellany for the Year 1694: Being the Fourth Part of Miscellany Poems (1694) V
Love Triumphant; or, Nature Will Prevail (1694) D
De Arte Graphica: The Art of Painting [from C.A. de Fresnoy] (1695) NF
An Ode on the Death of Mr Henry Purcell (1696) V
Alexander's Feast; or, The Power of Musique (1697) V
The Works of Virgil (1697) V
Fables Ancient and Modern (1700) V

DU BARTAS, Guillaume de Salluste (1544–1590)
French poet
Judith (1574) V
The Week [*La Semaine*] (1578) V

DU BELLAY, Joachim (1522–1560)
French poet
Defence of the French Language [*La Deffence et illustration de la langue françoyse*] (1549) NF
L'Olive (1549–50) V

DU BOIS, W[illiam] E[dward] B[urghardt] (c. 1868–1963)
African-American author
The Philadelphia Negro (1899) NF
The Souls of Black Folk (1903) MISC
John Brown (1909) NF
The Negro (1915) NF
Darkwater (1920) MISC
The Gift of Black Folk (1924) NF
The Dark Princess (1928) F
Black Reconstruction (1935) NF
Dusk of Dawn (1940) NF
Color and Democracy (1945) NF
The Ordeal of Mansart (1957) F
Mansart Builds a School (1959) F
Worlds of Color (1961) F

DUCK, Stephen (1705–1756)
English poet
Poems on Several Subjects (1730) V
Truth and Falsehood (1734) V
Poems on Several Occasions (1736) V
The Vision (1737) V
The Year of Wonders (1737) V
Every Man in his Own Way (1741) V
Caesar's Camp; or, St George's Hill (1755) V

DUFFY, Carol Ann (1955–)
British poet
Fleshweathercock (1973) V
Standing Female Nude (1985) V
Thrown Voices (1986) V
Selling Manhattan (1987) V
Mean Time (1993) V
The World's Wife (1999) V

DUFFY, Maureen [Patricia] (1933–)
British novelist, poet, and dramatist
That's How It Was (1962) F
The Single Eye (1964) F
The Paradox Players (1967) F
Lyrics for the Dog Hour (1968) V
Love Child (1971) F
The Venus Touch (1971) V
I Want To Go To Moscow (1973) F
Evesong (1975) V
Housepy (1978) F
Memorials of the Quick and the Dead (1979) V
Gor Saga (1981) F
Londoners (1983) F
Occam's Razor (1993) F
Restitution (1998) F

DUGDALE, Sir William (1605–1686)
English antiquary
The Antiquities of Warwickshire Illustrated (1656) NF
The History of St Paul's Cathedral (1658) NF
The History of Imbanking and Drayning of Divers Fenns and Marshes (1662) NF
The Baronage of England (1675) NF
A Short View of the Late Troubles in England (1681) NF

DUMAS, Alexandre ['père'] (1802–1870)
French dramatist, novelist, and travel writer
Henry III [*Henri III et sa cour*] (1829) D
Antony (1831) D
Richard Darlington (1831) D
Isabelle de Bavière (1836) F
Othon the Archer [*Othon l'archer*] (1840) F
The Château d'Harmenthal [*Le Château d'Harmenthal*] (1843) F
The Count of Monte Cristo [*Le Comte de Monte-Cristo*] (1844) F
The Three Musketeers [*Les Trois Mousquetaires*] (1844) F
Margaret de Navarre [*La Reine Margot*] (1845) F
Twenty Years After [*Vingt ans après*] (1845) F
The Bastard of Mauleon [*Le Bâtard de Mauléon*] (1846) F
Joseph Balsamo (1846–8) F
The Regent's Daughter [*La Fille du régent*] (1847) F
The Forty-Five Guardsman [*Les Quarante-cinq*] (1848) F
The Vicomte de Bragelonne [*The Vicomte de Bragelonne*] (1848–50) F
The Queen's Necklace [*Le Collier de la reine*] (1849) F
The Black Tulip [*La Tulipe noire*] (1850) F
The Mouth of Hell [*Le Trou de l'enfer*] (1850–1) F
The Woman with the Velvet Necklace [*La Femme au collier de velours*] (1851) F
Ange Pitou (1853) F
The Mohicans of Paris [*Les Mohicans de Paris*] (1854–7) F
The Polish Spy [*Les Blancs et les Bleus*] (1868) F

DUMAS, Alexandre ['fils'] (1824–1895)
French dramatist and novelist
The Lady with the Camelias [*La Dame aux camélias*] (1848) F
Le Demi-monde (1855) D
Le Fils naturel (1858) D
The Clemenceau Affair [*L'Affaire Clemenceau*] (1864) F
Les Idées de Madame Aubray (1867) D
La Femme de Claude (1873) D
Monsieur Alphonse (1873) D
Denise (1885) D

DU MAURIER, [Dame] Daphne (1907–1989)
British novelist and short-story writer
The Loving Spirit (1931) F
The Progress of Julius (1933) F
Jamaica Inn (1936) F
Rebecca (1938) F
Come Wind, Come Weather (1940) F SS

Frenchman's Creek (1941) F
Hungry Hill (1943) F
The King's General (1946) F
My Cousin Rachel (1951) F
The Apple Tree [US: *Kiss Me Again, Stranger*] (1952) F SS
Mary Anne (1954) F
The Scapegoat (1957) F
The Breaking Point [inc. 'The Birds'] (1959) F SS
The Infernal World of Branwell Brontë (1960) NF
The Glass-Blowers (1963) F
The Flight of the Falcon (1965) F
The House on the Strand (1969) F
Not After Midnight, and Other Stories [US: *Don't Look Now*] (1971) F SS
Rule Britannia (1972) F
Growing Pains [US: *Myself When Young*] (1977) NF
The Rendezvous, and Other Stories (1980) F SS
The Rebecca Notebook, and Other Memories (1981) MISC

DU MAURIER, George [Louis Palmella Busson] (1834–1896)
British artist and novelist
Peter Ibbetson (1892) F
Trilby (1894) F
The Martian (1897) F

DUNBAR, William (1460?–1513?)
Scottish poet
The Tua Mariit Wemen and the Wedo (1507?) V
The Flyting of Dunbar and Kennedy and Other Poems (1508) V
The Golden Targe (1508) V

DUNCAN, Robert [Edward] (1919–1988)
American poet
Heavenly City, Earthly City (1947) V
Medieval Scenes (1950) V
The Opening of the Field (1960) V
Roots and Branches (1964) V
The Years as Catches (1966) V
Fictive Certainties (1985) NF
A Paris Visit (1985) V
Ground Work II: In the Dark (1987) V

DUNMORE, Helen (1952–)
British poet and novelist
The Apple Fall (1983) V
The Raw Garden (1988) V
Recovering a Body (1994) V
A Spell of Winter (1995) F
Talking to the Dead (1996) F
Love of Fat Men (1997) F SS
Your Blue-Eyed Boy (1998) F
Ice Cream (2000) F SS

DUNN, Douglas [Eaglesham] (1942–)
Scottish poet, short-story writer, and editor
Terry Street (1969) V
The Happier Life (1972) V
Love or Nothing (1974) V
Barbarians (1979) V
St Kilda's Parliament (1981) V
Europa's Lover (1982) V
A Rumoured City (1982) ANTH
Elegies (1985) V
Secret Villages (1985) F SS
Northlight (1988) V
Dante's Drum-Kit (1993) V
Boyfriends and Girlfriends (1994) F SS
Dressed to Kill (1994) V

DUNN, Nell [Mary] (1936–)
British novelist and dramatist
Up the Junction (1963) F
Poor Cow (1967) F
The Incurable (1971) F
The Only Child (1978) F
Steaming (1981) D
My Silver Shoes (1996) F

DUNNE, J[ohn] W[illiam] (1875–1949)
British philosopher
An Experiment with Time (1927) NF
The Serial Universe (1934) NF
The New Immortality (1938) NF
Nothing Dies (1940) NF

DUNNE, Mary Chavelita *see* GEORGE EGERTON

DUNNETT, [Lady] Dorothy, *née* Halliday (1923–)
British historical novelist and painter
Game of Kings (1962) F
Queens' Play (1964) F
The Disorderly Knights (1966) F
Dolly and the Singing Bird [US: *The Photogenic Soprano*] (1968) F
Pawn in Frankincense (1969) F
Dolly and the Cookie Bird [US: *Murder in the Round*] (1970) F
Dolly and the Doctor Bird [US: *Match for a Murderer*] (1971) F
The Ringed Castle (1972) F
Dolly and the Starry Bird [US: *Murder in Focus*] (1973) F
Checkmate (1975) F
Niccolò Rising (1986) F
The Spring of the Ram (1987) F
Gemini (2000) F

DUNSANY, Lord [Edward John Moreton Drax Plunkett, 18th Baron Dunsany] (1878–1957)
Irish fantasy novelist, short-story writer, and dramatist
Time and the Gods (1906) F
The Sword of Welleran, and Other Stories (1908) F SS
A Dreamer's Tales (1910) F SS
The Book of Wonder (1912) F
Fifty-One Tales (1915) F SS
Tales of Wonder (1916) F SS
Plays of Gods and Men (1917) D
Tales of War (1918) F SS
Tales of Three Hemispheres (1920) F SS
If (1921) D
The King of Elfland's Daughter (1924) F
Jorkens Remembers Africa (1934) F SS

His Fellow Men (1952) F
Jorkens Borrows Another Whiskey (1954) F SS

DUPIN, Aurore *see* GEORGE SAND

'DURAS, Marguerite' [Marguerite Donnadieu] (1914–)
French novelist and dramatist
The Impudent Ones [*Les Impudents*] (1942) F
The Tranquil Life [*La Vie Tranquille*] (1944) F
La Douleur (1945) F SS
The Sea Wall [*Un barrage contre le Pacifique*] (1950) F
The Sailor from Gibraltar [*Le Marin de Gibraltar*] (1952) F
The Little Horses of Tarquinia [*Les Petits Chevaux de Tarquinia*] (1953) F
Moderato cantabile (1958) F
Hiroshima mon amour [screenplay] (1959) D
Les Viaducs de la Seine-et-Oise (1960) D
Le Ravissement de Lol V. Stein (1964) F
The Vice-Consul [*Le Vice-Consul*] (1966) F
The English Lover [*L'Amante anglaise*] (1967) F
Destroy, She Said [*Détruitre, dit-elle*; text and film] (1969) F
Love [*L'Amour*] (1971) F
Nathalie Granger [text and film] (1972) F
India Song [text and film] (1973) F
The Lover [*L'Amant*] (1984) F

D'URFEY, Thomas (1653–1723)
English poet and dramatist
The Fool Turn'd Critick (1676) D
Madame Fickle; or, The Witty False One (1676) D
The Siege of Memphis; or, The Ambitious Queen (1676) D
A Fond Husband; or, The Plotting Sisters (1677) D
Squire Oldsapp; or, The Night-Adventurers (1678) D
Trick for Trick; or, The Debauch'd Hypocrite (1678) D
The Virtuous Wife; or, Good Luck at Last (1679) D
The Progress of Honesty; or, A View of a Court and City (1681) V
Sir Barnaby Whigg; or, No Wit Like a Womans (1681) D
Butler's Ghost; or, Hudibras, the Fourth Part (1682) V
The Injured Princess; or, The Fatal Wager (1682) D
The Royalist (1682) D
A New Collection of Songs and Poems (1683) V
Choice New Songs (1684) V
The Malcontent: A Satyr (1684) V
A Common-wealth of Women (1685) D
The Banditti; or, A Ladies Distress (1686) D
A Fool's Preferment; or, The Three Dukes of Dunstable (1688) D
Collin's Walk Through London and Westminster (1690) V
New Poems (1690) V
Love For Money; or, The Boarding School (1691) D
The Marriage-Hater Match'd (1692) D
The Richmond Heiress; or, A Woman Once in the Right (1693) D
The Comical History of Don Quixote: Part 1 (1694) D
The Comical History of Don Quixote: Part the Second (1694) D
The Comical History of Don Quixote: The Third Part (1696) D
The Intrigues at Versailles; or, A Jilt in all Humours (1697) D
The Campaigners; or, The Pleasant Adventures at Brussels (1698) D
A Choice Collection of New Songs and Ballads (1699) V
Wonders in the Sun; or, The Kingdom of the Birds (1706) D
Stories, Moral and Comical (1707?) MISC

DURRELL, Gerald [Malcolm] (1925–1995)
British zoologist and author
My Family and Other Animals (1956) NF

DURRELL, Lawrence [George] (1912–1990)
British novelist, poet, and travel writer
Ten Poems (1932) V
Transition (1934) V
Pied Piper of Lovers (1935) F
The Black Book (1938) F
A Private Country (1943) V
Prospero's Cell (1945) NF
Cities, Plains and People (1946) V
Cefal (1947) F
On Seeming to Presume (1948) V
Reflections on a Marine Venus (1953) NF
The Tree of Idleness, and Other Poems (1955) V
Bitter Lemons (1957) NF
Esprit de Corps (1957) F SS
Justine (1957) F
Balthazar (1958) F
Mountolive (1958) F
Stiff Upper Lip (1958) F SS
Clea (1960) F
Collected Poems (1960) V
The Alexandrian Quartet [*Justine, Balthazar, Mountolive, Clea*] (1962) F
The Ikons, and Other Poems (1966) V
Sauve qui peut (1966) F SS
Tunc (1968) F
Nunquam (1970) F
The Red Limbo Lingo (1971) V
Vega and Other Poems (1973) V
Lifelines (1974) V
Monsieur; or, The Prince of Darkness (1974) F
Livia; or, Buried Alive (1978) F
Constance; or, Solitary Practices (1982) F
Sebastian; or, Ruling Passions (1983) F
Quinx; or, The Ripper's Tale (1985) F

DWIGHT, Timothy (1752–1817)
American poet
The Conquest of Canaan (1785) V
The Triumph of Infidelity (1788) V
Greenfield Hill (1794) V
The True Means of Establishing Public Happiness (1795) NF
The Nature, and Danger, of Infidel Philosophy (1798) NF
Travels in New England and New York (1821–2) NF

DWORKIN, Andrea (1946–)
American feminist author and novelist
Woman Hating (1974) NF
Our Blood (1976) NF
Pornography: Men Possessing Women (1981) NF
Ice and Fire (1986) F
Intercourse (1987) NF
Mercy (1990) F
Scapegoat (2000) NF

DYER, George (1755–1841)
British poet and author
Poems (1792) V
The Complaints of the Poor People of England (1793) V
The Poet's Fate (1797) V
Poems and Critical Essays (1802) MISC

DYER, John (1699–1757)
English poet
The Ruins of Rome (1740) V
The Fleece (1757) V

E

EAGLETON, Terry (1943–)
British literary critic
Exiles and Emigrés (1970) NF
The Rape of Clarissa (1982) NF
Literary Theory (1983) NF
The Ideology of the Aesthetic (1990) NF
Ideology: An Introduction (1991) NF
Heathcliff and the Great Hunger (1995) NF

EARLE, John (1601?–1665)
English bishop, character writer, and poet
Micro-cosmographie (1628) NF

EASTMAN, Charles [Alexander] (1858–1939)
Native American writer
An Indian Boyhood (1902) NF
Red Hunters and Animal People (1904) NF
Old Indian Days (1907) NF
Wigwam Evenings (1909) NF
The Soul of the Indian (1911) NF

EASTMAN, Max [Forrester] (1883–1969)
American social critic, essayist, and poet
Enjoyment of Poetry (1913) NF
Marx, Lenin, and the Science of Revolution (1926) NF
The Literary Mind (1931) NF
Artists in Uniform (1934) NF
Enjoyment of Laughter (1936) NF
Marxism: Is it Science? (1940) NF
Stalin's Russia (1940) NF
Poems of Five Decades (1954) V
Reflections on the Failure of Socialism (1955) NF
Great Companions (1959) NF
Love and Revolution (1965) NF

EBERHART, Richard [Ghormley] (1904–)
American poet and dramatist
A Bravery of Earth (1930) V
Reading the Spirit (1937) V
Song and Idea (1942) V
Burr Oaks (1947) V
Brotherhood of Man (1949) V
An Herb Basket (1950) V
Undercliff (1953) V
Great Praises (1957) V
The Quarry (1964) V
Thirty-One Sonnets (1967) V
Shifts of Being (1968) V
Fields of Grace (1972) V
Poems to Poets (1976) V
The Long Reach (1984) V
Maine Poems (1988) V
Florida Poems (1989) V

ECO, Umberto (1932–)
Italian novelist and critic
The Name of the Rose [*Il nome della rosa*] (1980) F
Foucault's Pendulum (1988) F
How to Travel with a Salmon, and Other Essays (1994) NF
The Island of the Day Before (1994) F

EDEL, [Joseph] Leon (1907–1997)
American biographer
James Joyce: The Last Journey (1947) NF
Henry James (1953–72) NF
Bloomsbury: A House of Lions (1979) NF
The Stuff of Sleep and Dreams (1982) NF
Writing Lives (1984) NF

EDEN, the Hon. Emily (1797–1869)
British novelist and traveller
The Semi-Detached House (1859) F
The Semi-Attached Couple (1860) F
Up the Country (1866) NF

EDEN, Richard (1521?–1576)
Translator
A Treatyse of the New India (1553) NF
The Decades of the New Worlde or West India (1555) NF
The Arte of Navigation (1561) NF

EDGAR, David (1948–)
British dramatist
Baby Love (1973) D
Dick Deterred (1974) D
The National Theatre (1975) D
Destiny (1976) D
Saigon Rose (1976) D
Our Own People (1977) D
The Jail Diary of Albee Sachs (1978) D
Mary Barnes (1978) D
Teendreams (1979) D
Nicholas Nickleby (1980) D
Maydays (1983) D
Entertaining Strangers (1986) D
Plays: One (1987) D
Heartlanders (1989) D
Plays: Two (1989) D
Shorts (1989) D

The Shape of the Table (1990) D
Plays: Three (1991) D
Pentecost (1995) D

EDGEWORTH, Maria (1767–1849)
British novelist and children's author
Letters for Literary Ladies (1795) NF
The Parent's Assistant; or, Stories for Children (1796) F CH
Castle Rackrent (1800) F
Belinda (1801) F
Early Lessons (1801) F CH
Moral Tales for Young People (1801) F CH
Popular Tales (1804) F
The Modern Griselda (1805) F
Leonora (1806) F
Tales of Fashionable Life [vols. i-iii] (1809) F SS
The Absentee (1812) F
Tales of Fashionable Life [vols. iv, v, vi] (1812) F SS
Continuation of Early Lessons (1814) F CH
Patronage (1814) F
Comic Dramas, in Three Acts (1817) D
Harrington; and Ormond (1817) F
Memoirs of Richard Lovell Edgeworth (1820) NF
Rosamond (1821) F CH
Frank (1822) F CH
Harry and Lucy Concluded (1825) F CH
Tales and Miscellaneous Pieces (1825) F
Little Plays for Children (1827) D CH
Garry Owen; or, The Snow-Woman; and Poor Bob, the Chimney-Sweeper (1832) F CH
Helen: A Tale (1834) F
Orlandino (1848) F CH

EDGEWORTH, Richard Lovell (1744–1817)
British author
Practical Education (1798) NF
A Rational Primer (1799) NF
Essays on Professional Education (1809) NF
Readings on Poetry (1810) NF

EDMOND, Lauris (1924–)
New Zealand poet
In the Middle Air (1975) V
The Pear Tree (1977) V
Wellington Letter (1980) V
Catching It (1983) V
High Country Weather (1984) F
Summer Near the Arctic Circle (1988) V

EDWARDS, Amelia Ann Blanford (1831–1892)
British novelist, short-story writer, and travel writer
Barbara's History (1864) F
Miss Carew (1865) F SS
Half a Million of Money (1866) F
Debenham's Vow (1870) F
In the Days of My Youth (1873) F
Untrodden Peaks and Unfrequented Valleys (1873) NF
A Thousand Miles Up the Nile (1877) NF
Lord Brackenbury (1880) F
Pharaohs, Fellahs, and Explorers (1891) NF

EDWARDS, Jonathan (1703–1758)
American Puritan and religious writer
God Glorified in the Work of Redemption (1731) NF
Divine and Supernatural Light (1734) NF
A Faithful Narrative of the Surprising Work of God (1737) NF
Charity and its Fruits (1738) NF
The Distinguished Marks of a Work of the Spirit of God (1741) NF
Sinners in the Hands of an Angry God (1741) NF
Some Thoughts Concerning the Present Revival of Religion in New England (1742) NF
Treatise Concerning Religious Affections (1746) NF
A Vindication of the Gospel Doctrine of Justifying Faith (1746) NF
An Humble Attempt to Promote Visible Union of God's People (1747) NF
An Humble Inquiry into the Rules of the Word of God (1749) NF
A Careful and Strict Enquiry into the Modern Prevailing Notions of Freedom and Will (1754) NF
The Great Christian Doctrine of Original Sin Defended (1758) NF

EDWARDS, Richard (1523?–1566)
English poet and dramatist
Damon and Pithias (1571) D
The Paradyse of Daynty Devises (1576) V

EGAN, Pierce, the elder (1772–1849)
British sporting journalist and author
The Mistress of Royalty; or, The Loves of Florizel and Perdita (1814) V
Boxiana; or, Sketches of Ancient and Modern Pugilism (1818) NF
Life in London (1821) F
Anecdotes of the Turf, the Chase, the Ring and the Stage (1827) NF
Finish to the Adventures of Tom, Jerry and Logic (1828) F

EGAN, Pierce, the younger (1814–1880)
British novelist and illustrator
Wat Tyler (1841) F
Paul Jones, the Pirate (1842) F
Fair Rosamond (1844) F
Eve; or, The Angel of Innocence (1867) F

'EGERTON, George' [Dunne, Mary Chavelita, later **Higginson, Clairmonte,** and **Bright]** (1859–1945)
British short-story writer, novelist, and dramatist
Keynotes (1893) F SS
Discords (1894) F SS
Symphonies (1897) F SS
Fantasies (1898) F SS
The Wheel of God (1898) F
Rosa Amorosa (1901) F
Flies in Amber (1905) F SS

EGERTON, Sarah, *née* Fyge, later **Field** (1670–1723)
English poet
The Female Advocate (1686) V
Poems on Several Occasions (1703) V

EGGLESTON, Edward (1837–1902)
American novelist
The Hoosier Schoolmaster (1871) F
The End of the World (1872) F
The Mystery of Metropolisville (1873) F
The Circuit Rider (1874) F
The Hoosier Schoolboy (1883) F
The Graysons (1888) F
The Faith Doctor (1891) F

EGGLESTON, George Cary (1839–1911)
American novelist and editor
A Man of Honour (1873) F
Juggernaut (1891) F
Dorothy South (1902) F
The Master of Warlock (1903) F
Evelyn Byrd (1904) F

'ELIOT, George' [Mary Ann, later **Marian, Evans]** (1819–1880)
British novelist
The Life of Jesus, Critically Examined by Dr David Friedrich Strauss (1846) NF
The Essence of Christianity [as Marian Evans] (1854) NF
Scenes of Clerical Life (1858) F
Adam Bede (1859) F
'The Lifted Veil' [in *Blackwood's Edinburgh Magazine*] (July 1859)
The Mill on the Floss (1860) F
Silas Marner, the Weaver of Waveloe (1861) F
Romola (1863) F
'Brother Jacob' [in the *Cornhill Magazine*] (June 1864)
Felix Holt, the Radical (1866) F
The Spanish Gypsy (1868) V
Agatha (1869) V
Brother and Sister [as Marian Lewes] (1869) V
Middlemarch (1871) F
The Legend of Jubal, and Other Poems (1874) V
Daniel Deronda (1876) F
Impresssions of Theophrastus Such (1879) F

ELIOT, T[homas] S[tearns] (1888–1965)
British poet, dramatist, and critic
Prufrock and Other Observations (1917) V
The Sacred Wood (1920) NF
The Waste Land (1923) V
Homage to John Dryden (1924) NF
Poems 1909–25 (1925) V
Journey of the Magi (1927) V
For Lancelot Andrewes (1928) NF
A Song for Simeon (1928) V
Animula (1929) V
Dante (1929) NF
Ash-Wednesday (1930) V
Marina (1930) V
Triumphal March (1931) V
Selected Essays 1917–1932 (1932) NF
Sweeney Agonistes (1932) V D
The Use of Poetry and the Use of Criticism (1933) NF
After Strange Gods (1934) NF
The Rock (1934) D
Murder in the Cathedral (1935) D
Collected Poems 1909–1935 (1936) V
Essays Ancient and Modern (1936) NF
The Family Reunion (1939) D
The Idea of a Christian Society (1939) NF
Old Possum's Book of Practical Cats (1939) V
East Coker (1940) V
The Waste Land, and Other Poems (1940) V
Burnt Norton (1941) V
The Dry Salvages (1941) V
Later Poems 1925–35 (1941) V
Little Gidding (1942) V
Four Quartets (1944) V
Notes Towards the Definition of Culture (1948) NF
The Cocktail Party (1949) D
The Three Voices of Poetry (1953) NF
The Confidential Clerk (1954) D
The Elder Statesman (1959) D
Collected Poems 1909–1962 (1963) V
To Criticize the Critic, and Other Writings (1965) NF
Inventions of the March Hare (1998) V

ELKIN, Stanley [Lawrence] (1930–)
American novelist and short-story writer
Boswell (1964) F
Criers and Kibitzers, Kibitzers and Criers (1966) SS
A Bad Man (1967) F
The Dick Gibson Show (1971) F
Searches and Seizures (1973) SS
The Franchiser (1976) F
The Living End (1979) F
George Mills (1982) F
Rabbi of Lud (1987) F
The MacGuffin (1991) F

ELLIOTT, Ebenezer (1781–1849)
British poet
The Soldier, and Other Poems (1810) V
Night (1818) V
Peter Faultless to His Brother Simon (1820) V
Love (1823) V
Scotch Nationality (1824) V
The Village Patriarch (1829) V
Corn Law Rhymes: The Ranter (1830) V
The Splendid Village: Corn Law Rhymes, and Other Poems (1833) V

ELLIOTT, Janice (1931–1995)
British novelist
Cave with Echoes (1962) F
Angels Falling (1969) F
A State of Peace (1971) F
Private Life (1972) F
Heaven on Earth (1975) F
Secret Places (1981) F
Dr Gruber's Daughter (1986) F
The Sadness of Witches (1987) F

Necessary Rites (1990) F
The Noise From the Zoo (1991) F SS

'ELLIS, Alice Thomas' [Anna Margaret Haycraft, *née* Lindholm] (1932–)
British novelist
The Sin Eater (1977) F
The Birds of the Air (1980) F
The 27th Kingdom (1982) F
The Other Side of the Fire (1983) F
The Clothes in the Wardrobe (1987) F
The Skeleton in the Cupboard (1988) F
The Fly in the Ointment (1989) F
The Inn at the Edge of the World (1990) F
A Welsh Childhood (1990) NF
Pillars of Gold (1992) F
The Evening of Adam (1994) F SS

ELLIS, Bret Easton (1964–)
American novelist
Less Than Zero (1985) F
Rules of Attraction (1987) F
American Psycho (1991) F
The Informers (1994) F SS

ELLIS, George (1753–1815)
British literary scholar and satirist
Poetical Tales by Sir Gregory Gander (1778) V
Specimens of the Early English Poets (1790) ANTH
Specimens of Early English Metrical Romances (1805) ANTH

ELLIS, Henry Havelock (1859–1939)
British psychologist and essayist
Man and Woman (1890) NF
The New Spirit (1890) NF
The Nationalization of Health (1892) NF
Sexual Inversion (1897) NF
Affirmations (1898) NF
The Evolution of Modesty (1899) NF
The Nineteenth Century (1900) NF
Studies in the Psychology of Sex (1905) NF
The Problems of Race Degeneration (1911) NF
The World of Dreams (1911) NF
The Task of Social Hygiene (1912) NF
Essays in Wartime (1916) NF
Little Essays of Love and Virtue (1922) NF
The Dance of Life (1923) NF
More Essays of Love and Virtue (1931) NF
The Revaluation of Obscenity (1931) NF
Psychology of Sex (1933) NF
My Confessional (1934) NF
My Life (1939) NF

ELLIS, Mrs William *see* SARAH ELLIS

ELLIS, Sarah, *née* Stickney [Mrs William Ellis] (1812–1872)
British novelist and didactic writer
Home; or, The Iron Rule (1836) F
The Women of England (1839) NF
The Daughters of England (1842) NF
The Englishwoman's Family Library (1843) NF
Pique (1850) F
Northern Roses (1868) F

ELLISON, Ralph [Waldo] (1914–1994)
African-American novelist, essayist, and short-story writer
Invisible Man (1952) F
Shadow and Act (1964) NF
Going to the Territory (1986) NF

ELLMANN, Richard (1918–1987)
American literary scholar and biographer
Yeats: The Man and the Mask [rev. 1979] (1948) NF
The Identity of Yeats (1951) NF
James Joyce (1959) NF
Oscar Wilde (1988) NF

ELLROY, James (1948–)
American crime writer
Blood on the Moon (1984) F
Because the Night (1985) F
Suicide Hill (1986) F
The Black Dahlia (1987) F
The Big Nowhere (1988) F
L.A. Confidential (1990) F
White Jazz (1993) F
American Tabloid (1995) F
My Dark Places (1996) F
Crime Wave (1999) F

ELLWOOD, Thomas (1639–1713)
English Quaker, poet, and friend of Milton
Davideis: The Life of King David of Israel (1712) V
The History of the Life of Thomas Ellwood (1714) NF

ELSTOB, Elizabeth (1683–1758)
English Anglo-Saxon scholar
The Rudiments of Grammar for the English-Saxon Tongue, First Given in English (1715) NF

ELTON, G[eofrey] R[udolph] (1921–1994)
British historian
The Tudor Revolution in Government (1953) NF
England Under the Tudors (1955) NF
Policy and Police (1972) NF
Reform and Reformation (1977) NF
Return to Essentials (1991) NF

ELTON, Oliver (1861–1945)
British literary scholar
A Survey of English Literature 1780–1830 (1912) NF
A Survey of English Literature 1830–80 (1920) NF

'ÉLUARD, Paul' [Eugène-Emile Grindel] (1895–1952)
French Surrealist poet
Capitale de la douleur (1926) V
Les Dessous d'une vie ou la pyramide humaine (1926) V
L'Amour, la poésie (1929) V
La Vie immédiate (1932) V
La Rose publique (1934) V

ELYOT, Sir Thomas (1490?–1546)
English diplomat and author
The Educacion or Bringinge up of Children [from Plutarch] (1530) NF

The Governor (1531) NF
Pasquil the Playne (1532) NF
The Doctrinall of Princis (1534) NF
The Castle of Health (1537) NF
The Dictionary of Syr Thomas Eliot (1538) NF
The Banquet of Sapience (1539) NF
The Defence of Good Women (1540) NF
The Image of Governance (1541) NF
A Preservative Agaynste Deth (1545) NF

EMECHETA, [Florence Onye] Buchi (1944–)
Nigerian novelist
In the Ditch (1972) F
Second-Class Citizen (1974) F
The Bride Price (1976) F
The Slave Girl (1977) F
The Joys of Motherhood (1979) F
Destination Biafra (1982) F
Double Yoke (1982) F
The Rape of Shavi (1983) F
Gwendolen (1989) F
Kehinde (1994) F

EMERSON, Ralph Waldo (1803–1882)
American philosopher, essayist, and poet
Nature (1836) NF
The American Scholar (1837) NF
Essays (1841) NF
Addresses and Lectures (1849) NF
Representative Men (1850) NF
English Traits (1856) NF
The Conduct of Life (1860) NF
May-Day, and Other Pieces (1867) V
Society and Solitude (1870) NF
Letters and Social Aims (1876) NF
Natural History of Intellect (1893) NF

EMPSON, Sir William (1906–1984)
British poet and critic
Seven Types of Ambiguity (1930) NF
Some Versions of Pastoral (1935) NF
The Gathering Storm (1940) V
The Structure of Complex Words (1951) NF
Milton's God (1961) NF

ENGEL, Marian, *née* Passmore (1933–1985)
Canadian novelist and short-story writer
No Clouds of Glory [reissued as *Sara Bastard's Notebook*, 1974] (1968) F
The Honeymoon Festival (1970) F
Monodromos [reissued as *One-Way Street*, 1975] (1973) F
Inside the Easter Egg (1975) F SS
Joanne (1975) F
Bear (1976) F
The Glassy Sea (1978) F
Lunatic Villas [UK: *The Year of the Child*] (1981) F
The Tatooed Woman (1985) SS

ENGELS, Friedrich (1820–1895)
German philosopher
The Condition of the Working Class in England [*Die Lage der arbeitenden Klassen in England*] (1845) NF

ENRIGHT, D[enis] J[oseph] (1920–)
British poet, novelist, critic, and editor
Season Ticket (1948) V
The Laughing Hyena, and Other Poems (1953) V
Academic Year (1955) F
Bread Rather Than Blossoms (1956) V
Some Men Are Brothers (1960) V
Addictions (1962) V
The Old Adam (1965) V
Unlawful Assembly (1968) V
Daughters of Earth (1972) V
The Terrible Shears (1973) V
Sad Ires (1975) V
Paradise Illustrated (1978) V
A Faust Book (1979) V
Instant Chronicles (1985) V
The Alluring Problem (1986) NF
Fields of Vision (1988) NF
The Way of the Cat (1992) V
Old Men and Comets (1993) V
Collected Poems: 1948–1998 (1998) V
Play Resumed (1999) V

ERASMUS, Desiderius (*c.* 1467–1536)
Dutch humanist
Adages [*Adagia*] (1500) NF
Enchiridion Militis Christiani (1503) NF
The Praise of Folly [*Encomium Moriae*] (1511) NF
Colloquia (1518) NF

ERDRICH, Louise (1954–)
American novelist and poet
Jacklight (1984) V
Love Medicine (1984) F
The Beet Queen (1986) F
Tracks (1988) F
The Crown of Columbus (1991) F
The Bingo Palace (1994) F

'ERRYM, Malcolm J.' [James Malcolm Rymer] (1804–1882?)
English writer of popular fiction
Ada the Betrayed; or, The Murder at the Old Smithy [sometimes attrib. to T.P. Prest] (1842) F
The Black Monk; or, The Secret of the Grey Turret [sometimes attrib. to T.P. Prest] (1844) F
Varney the Vampire; or, The Feast of Blood [sometimes attrib. to T.P. Prest] (1847) F

ERVINE, [John] St John [Greer] (1883–1971)
Irish dramatist, novelist, and drama critic
Mixed Marriage (1911) D
Jane Clegg (1914) D
Mrs Martin's Man (1914) F
John Ferguson (1915) D
The First Mrs Fraser (1929) D
Robert's Wife (1938) D

ETHEREGE, Sir George (1635–1691)
English dramatist
The Comical Revenge; or, Love in a Tub (1664) D
She Wou'd If She Cou'd (1668) D
The Man of Mode; or, Sir Fopling Flutter (1676) D

EURIPIDES (480–406 BC)
Greek tragic poet
Medea (431 BC) D
Andromache (*c.* 426 BC) D
The Supplicants (*c.* 422 BC) D
The Trojan Women (415 BC) D
Electra (*c.* 413 BC) D
Helen (*c.* 412 BC) D
The Phoenician Women (*c.* 410 BC) D
Orestes (408 BC) D

EUSDEN, Laurence (1688–1739)
English poet and Poet Laureate
A Letter to Mr Addison, on the King's Accession to the Throne (1714) V
A Poem on the Marriage of his Grace the Duke of Newcastle (1717) V
Three Poems (1722) V
The Origin of the Knights of the Bath (1725) V

EVANS, Sir Arthur [John] (1851–1941)
British archaeologist
The Palace of Minos at Knossos (1922–35) NF

EVANS, [David] Caradoc (1878–1945)
Welsh short-story writer and novelist
My People (1915) F SS
Capel Sion (1916) F SS
My Neighbours (1920) F SS
Nothing to Pay (1930) F
This Way to Heaven (1934) F
Pilgrims in a Foreign Land (1942) F SS
Mother's Marvel (1949) F

EVANS, Mary Ann *see* GEORGE ELIOT

EVELYN, John (1620–1706)
English diarist, author, and translator
Of Liberty and Servitude (1649) NF
The State of France (1652) NF
An Essay on the First Book of De Rerum Natura (1656) V
The French Gardiner (1658) NF
An Apologie for the Royal Party (1659) V
A Character of England (1659) NF
The Golden Book of St John Chrysostom (1659) NF
Fumifugium; or, The Inconvenience of the Aer (1661) NF
A Panegyric to Charles the Second (1661) V
Sculptura; or, The History, and Art of Chalcography and Engraving in Copper (1662) NF
Sylva; or, A Discourse of Forest-Trees, and the Propagation of Timber (1664) NF
An Idea of the Perfection of Painting (1668) NF
A Philosophical Discourse of Earth (1676) NF
The Compleat Gard'ner (1693) NF
Numismata (1697) NF
Memoirs of John Evelyn [first edn of Evelyn's diary, ed. W. Bray] (1818) NF

EWART, Gavin [Buchanan] (1916–)
British poet and editor
Poems and Songs (1939) V
Londoners (1964) V
Pleasures of the Flesh (1966) V
The Deceptive Grin of the Gravel Porters (1968) V
Alphabet Soup (1972) V
An Imaginary Love Affair (1974) V
No Fool Like an Old Fool (1976) V
All My Little Ones (1978) V
The Collected Ewart 1933–1980 (1980) V
More Little Ones (1982) V
Capital Letters (1983) V
The Ewart Quarto (1984) V
Festival Nights (1984) V
Late Pickings (1987) V
Penultimate Poems (1989) V
Collected Poems 1980–1991 (1991) V
Like It Or Not (1992) V

EWING, Mrs J[uliana] H[oratia], *née* Gatty (1841–1885)
British children's writer
Melchior's Dream, and Other Tales (1862) F CH
Mrs Overtheway's Remembrances (1869) F CH
The Brownies and Other Tales (1870) F CH
A Flat Iron for a Farthing (1872) F CH
Lob Lie-by-the-Fire (1874) F CH
Six to Sixteen (1875) F CH
Jan of the Windwill (1876) F CH
Old Fashioned Fairy Tales (1882) F CH
Jackanapes (1883) F CH
Daddy Darwin's Dovecote (1884) F CH
The Story of a Short Life (1885) F CH
Dandelion Clocks, and Other Tales (1887) F CH
Verses for Children (1888) V CH

EZEKIEL, Nissim (1924–)
Indian poet
A Time to Change (1951) V
Sixty Poems (1953) V
The Third (1958) V
The Unfinished Man (1960) V
The Exact Name (1965) V
Hymns in Darkness (1976) V
Latter-Day Psalms (1982) V

F

FABER, Frederick William (1814–1863)
British poet and hymn-writer
The Cherwell Water-Lily, and Other Poems (1840) V
The Styrian Lake, and Other Poems (1842) V
Sir Lancelot (1844) V
The Rosary, and Other Poems (1845) V
Hymns (1848) V

FABYAN, Robert (d. 1513)
English chronicler
The New Cronycles of Englande and of Fraunce (1516) NF

FAINLIGHT, Ruth (1931–)
American-born Anglo-Russian poet
A Forecast, a Fable (1958) V
Cages (1966) V

Eighteen Poems From 1966 (1967) V
To See the Matter Clearly, and Other Poems (1968) V
Another Full Moon (1976) V
The Region's Violence (1976) V
Sybils and Others (1980) V
Two Wind Poems (1980) V
Climates (1983) V
Fifteen to Infinity (1983) V
The Knot (1990) V

FAIRFAX, Edward (c. 1580–1635)
English poet and translator
Godfrey of Bulloigne; or, The Recoverie of Jerusalem [from Tasso's *Gerusalemme Liberata*, 1580–1] (1600) V

'FAIRLESS, Michael' [Margaret Fairless Barber] (1869–1901)
British novelist and non-fiction author
The Gathering of Brother Hilarius (1901) F
The Roadmender, and Other Papers (1902) NF

FAITHFULL, Emily (1836–1895)
British feminist, publisher, and novelist
Change Upon Change [US: *A Reed Shaken with the Wind*] (1868) F

'FALCONER, Lanoe' [Mary Elizabeth Morwenna Pauline Hawker] (1848–1908)
English novelist and short-story writer
Cecilia de Noel (1891) F
The Hotel d'Angleterre, and Other Stories (1891) F SS
Mademoiselle Ixe (1891) F
Shoulder to Shoulder (1891) F
The Wrong Prescription (1893) F

FALCONER, William (1732–1769)
British poet
The Shipwreck (1762) V
The Demagogue (1764) V

FALKNER, John Meade (1858–1932)
British antiquarian and novelist
The Lost Stradivarius (1895) F
Moonfleet (1898) F
The Nebuly Coat (1903) F

FALLON, Padraic (1906–1974)
Irish poet, dramatist, and short-story writer
Poems (1974) V
Poems and Versions (1983) V
Collected Poems (1990) V

FANSHAWE, Sir Richard (1608–1666)
English diplomat, translator, and poet
Il Pastor Fido, The Faithfull Shepherd [expanded 1648] (1647) V
Selected Parts of Horace, Prince of Lyricks (1652) V
Querer por sola querer: To love only for love sake (1654) V
The Lusiad; or, Portugals Historicall Poem (1655) V

FARJEON, Benjamin Leopold (1838–1903)
British novelist
Grif (1870) F
Blade o'Grass (1871) F
Joshua Marvel (1871) F
London's Heart (1873) F
The Duchess of Rosemary Lane (1876) F
The House of White Shadows (1884) F
Great Porter Square (1885) F
In a Silver Sea (1886) F
A Secret Inheritance (1887) F
The Tragedy of Featherstone (1887) F
Devlin the Barber (1888) F
Toilers of Babylon (1888) F
The Mystery of M. Felix (1890) F
Aaron the Jew (1894) F
Miriam Rozella (1898) F
The Mesmerists (1900) F

FARJEON, Eleanor (1881–1965)
British children's writer
Nursery Rhymes of London Town (1916) V CH
Martin Pippin in the Apple-Orchard (1921) F V CH
The Glass Slipper (1944) D CH
The Little Bookworm (1955) SS CH

FARMER, Beverley (1941–)
Australian novelist and short-story writer
Alone (1980) F
Milk (1983) F SS
Home Time (1985) F SS
A Body of Water: A Writer's Notebook (1990) NF SS
The Seal Woman (1992) F

FARNOL, John Jeffery (1878–1952)
British novelist
My Lady Caprice [US: *The Chronicles of the Imp*] (1907) F
The Broad Highway (1910) F
The Money Moon (1911) F
The Amateur Gentleman (1913) F
The Honourable Mr Tawnish (1913) F
Beltane the Smith (1915) F
Our Admirable Betty (1918) F
Black Bartlemy's Treasure (1920) F
The Quest of Youth (1927) F
Gyfford of Weare (1928) F
The Shadow, and Other Stories (1929) F SS
John o' the Green (1935) F
The Crooked Furrow (1937) F
The Happy Harvest (1939) F
The King Liveth (1943) F
My Lord of Wrybourne (1948) F
Waif of the River (1952) F

FARQUHAR, George (1678–1707)
English dramatist
Love and a Bottle (1698) D
The Adventures of Covent-Garden (1699) F
The Constant Couple; or, A Trip to the Jubilee (1699) D
Love and Business (1701) MISC
Sir Harry Wildair (1701) D
The Inconstant; or, The Way to Win Him (1702) D
The Twin-Rivals (1702) D
The Stage-Coach (1704) D

The Recruiting Officer (1706) D
The Beaux' Stratagem (1707) D
Barcellona (1710) V

FARRAR, [Dean] Frederic W[illiam] (1831–1903)
British schoolmaster and author
Eric; or, Little by Little (1858) F
Julian Home (1859) F
St Winifred's; or, The World of School (1862) F
The Three Homes [as 'F.T.L. Hope'] (1873) F
The Life of Christ (1874) NF
Darkness and Dawn; or, Scenes in the Days of Nero (1891) F HF
Gathering Clouds (1895) F HF

FARRELL, J[ames] G[ordon] (1935–1979)
Anglo-Irish novelist
A Man From Elsewhere (1963) F
The Lung (1965) F
A Girl in the Head (1967) F
Troubles (1970) F
The Siege of Krishnapur (1973) F
The Singapore Grip (1978) F
The Hill Station (1981) F

FARRELL, James T[homas] (1904–1979)
American novelist and short-story writer
Young Lonigan: A Boyhood in Chicago Streets (1932) F
Gas-House McGinty (1933) F
Calico Shoes (1934) F SS
The Young Manhood of Studs Lonigan (1934) F
Guillotine Party (1935) F SS
A World I Never Made (1936) F
Can All This Grandeur Perish? (1937) F SS
No Star is Lost (1938) F
Tommy Gallagher's Crusade (1939) F
Father and Son (1940) F
Ellen Rogers (1941) F
My Days of Anger (1943) F
To Whom It May Concern (1944) F SS
The League of Frightened Philistines (1945) NF
Bernard Clare (1946) F
Literature and Morality (1947) NF
The Road Between (1949) F
An American Dream Girl (1950) F SS
This Man and This Woman (1951) F
Yet Other Waters (1952) F
The Face of Time (1953) F
Reflections at Fifty (1954) NF
French Girls Are Vicious (1956) F SS
A Dangerous Woman (1957) F SS
Boarding House Blues (1961) F
Side Street (1961) F SS
The Silence of History (1963) F
What Time Collects (1964) F
Lonely for the Future (1966) F
New Year's Eve, 1929 (1967) F
When Time Was Born (1967) F
Childhood is Not Forever (1969) F
Invisible Swords (1971) F
A Brand New Life (1972) F
Judith (1974) F SS
The Dunne Family (1976) F
The Death of Nora Ryan (1978) F

FARRELL, M.J. *see* MOLLY KEANE

FAST, Howard M[elvin] (1914–)
American novelist
Two Valleys (1933) F
The Children (1937) F
Conceived in Liberty (1939) F
The Last Frontier (1941) F
The Unvanquished (1942) F
Citizen Tom Paine (1943) F
Freedom Road (1944) F
The American (1946) F
Clarkton (1947) F
My Glorious Brothers (1948) F
Spartacus (1952) F
Moses, Prince of Egypt (1958) F
The Winston Affair (1959) F
April Morning (1961) F
Power (1963) F
The Crossing (1971) F
The Hessian (1972) F

FAULKNER, William [Cuthbert] (1897–1962)
American novelist, short-story writer, and poet
The Marble Faun (1924) V
Soldiers' Pay (1926) F
Mosquitoes (1927) F
Sartoris (1929) F
The Sound and the Fury (1929) F
As I Lay Dying (1930) F
Idyll in the Desert (1931) F SS
Sanctuary (1931) F
These 13 (1931) F SS
Light in August (1932) F
Miss Zilphia Gant (1932) F SS
A Green Bough (1933) V
Dr Martino (1934) F SS
Pylon (1935) F
Absalom, Absalom! (1936) F
The Unvanquished (1938) F
The Wild Palms (1939) F
The Hamlet (1940) F
Go Down, Moses (1942) F SS
Intruder in the Dust (1948) F
Knight's Gambit (1949) F SS
Requiem for a Nun (1951) F D
A Fable (1954) F
Big Woods (1955) F SS
Faulkner at Nagano (1956) NF
The Town (1957) F
New Orleans Sketches (1958) F SS
Faulkner in the University (1959) NF
The Mansion (1960) F
The Reivers (1962) F
Faulkner at West Point (1964) NF

FAULKS, Sebastian (1953–)
British novelist
A Trick of the Light (1984) F

The Girl at the Lion d'Or (1989) F
A Fool's Alphabet (1992) F
Birdsong (1994) F
Charlotte Gray (1998) F

FEINSTEIN, Elaine (1930–)
English poet, novelist, dramatist, translator, and biographer
In a Green Eye (1966) V
The Circle (1970) F
The Magic Apple Tree (1971) V
At the Edge (1972) V
The Celebrants, and Other Poems (1973) V
The Glass Alembic [US: *The Crystal Garden*] (1973) F
Children of the Rose (1975) F
The Ecstasy of Dr Miriam Garner (1976) F
Some Unease and Angels (1977) V
The Feast of Euridice (1980) V
The Survivors (1982) F
The Border (1984) F
Badlands (1986) V
Mother's Girl (1988) F
All You Need (1989) F
City Music (1990) V
Loving Brecht (1992) F

FELL, Alison (1944–)
Scottish novelist and poet
Kisses for Mayakovsky (1984) V
The Bad Box (1987) F
Mer de glace (1991) F

FELLTHAM, Owen (1602?–1668)
English essayist and poet
Resolves (1623) NF

FÉNELON, François de Salignac de la Mothe (1651–1715)
French theologian and educator
The Education of Young Gentlewomen [*Traité de l'education des filles*] (1678) NF
The Maxims of the Saints Explained [*Explication des maximes des saints sur la vie intérieure*] (1697) F
The Adventures of Telemachus [*Les Aventures de Télémaque*] (1699) F
Fables and Dialogues of the Dead [*Dialogues des Morts anciens et modernes*] (1713) F
Twenty-Seven Tales and Fables, French and English (1729) F

FENN, George Manville (1831–1909)
British novelist
The Sapphire Cross (1871) F
A Little World (1877) F
Middy and Ensign; or, The Jungle Station (1883) F CH
Nat the Naturalist; or, A Boy's Adventures in the Eastern Seas (1883) F CH
The New Mistress (1883) F
Bunyip Land (1884) F CH
The Golden Magnet (1884) F CH
Menhardoc (1884) F CH
Brownsmith's Boy (1886) F CH
The Devon Boys (1886) F CH
The Master of the Ceremonies (1886) F
Yussuf the Guide; or, The Mountain Bandits (1886) F CH
Dick o' the Fens (1887) F CH
This Man's Wife (1887) F
The White Virgin (1894) F
Cormorant Crag (1895) F

FENTON, Sir Geoffrey (1539?–1608)
English translator and statesman
Golden Epistles (1575) NF

FENTON, James [Martin] (1949–)
British poet
Our Western Furniture (1968) V
Terminal Moraine (1972) V
A Vacant Possession (1978) V
Dead Soldiers (1981) V
A German Requiem (1981) V
Memory of War and Children in Exile (1983) V
Manila Envelope (1989) V
Out of Danger (1993) V
Certaine Tragicall Discourses (1567) F
A Discourse of the Civile Warres in Fraunce (1570) NF
Monophylo (1572) NF
The Historie of Guicciardin, Conteining the Warres of Italie (1579) NF

FERBER, Edna (1885–1968)
American novelist
Dawn O'Hara, the Girl Who Laughed (1911) F
So Big (1924) F
Showboat (1926) F
Cimarron (1930) F
Saratoga Trunk (1941) F
Giant (1952) F

FERGUSON, Adam (1723–1816)
Scottish philosopher and historian
The Morality of Stage-Plays Seriously Considered (1757) NF
An Essay on the History of Civil Society (1767) NF
Institutes of Moral Philosophy (1769) NF
The History of the Progress and Termination of the Roman Republic (1783) NF
Principles of Moral and Political Science (1792) NF

FERGUSON, Sir Samuel (1810–1886)
Irish poet and antiquary
Lays of the Western Gael (1864) V

FERGUSSON, Robert (1750–1774)
Scottish poet
Auld Reekie (1773) V
Poem to the Memory of John Cunningham (1773) V
Poems (1773) V
Poems on Various Subjects (1779) V

FERLINGHETTI, Lawrence (1920–)
American poet, editor, artist, and publisher
Pictures From the Gone World (1955) V
A Coney Island of the Mind (1958) V
Her (1960) F
Starting from San Francisco (1961) V

Unfair Arguments with Existence (1962) D
After the Cries of the Birds (1967) V
The Secret Meaning of Things (1969) V
Tyrannus Nix (1969) V
Open Eye, Open Heart (1973) V
Who Are We Now? (1976) V
Endless Life (1981) V
Love in the Days of Rage (1988) F

FERMOR, Patrick [Michael] Leigh (1915–)
British travel writer, novelist, and translator
The Traveller's Tree (1950) NF
The Violins of Saint-Jacques (1953) F
Mani (1958) NF
Roumeli (1966) NF
A Time of Gifts (1977) NF
Between the Woods and the Water (1985) NF

FERRAR, Nicholas (1592–1637)
English theologian and translator
The Hundred and Ten Considerations of Signior John Valdesso (1638) NF

FERRIER, Susan Edmonstone (1782–1854)
Scottish novelist
Marriage (1818) F
The Inheritance (1824) F
Destiny; or, The Chief's Daughter (1831) F

FEUCHTWANGER, Lion (1884–1958)
German Jewish novelist
The Ugly Duchess [Die hässliche Herzogin] (1923) F
Jud Süss (1925) F

FEUERBACH, Ludwig (1804–1872)
German philosopher and Bible critic
The Essence of Christianity [Das Wesen des Christentums] (1841) NF

FICHTE, Johann Gottlieb (1762–1814)
German philosopher
Doctrine of Knowledge [Wissenschaftslehre] (1794) NF
Speeches to the German Nation [Reden an die deutsche Nation] (1814) NF
A Little Book of Profitable Tales (1889) V

FIELD, Eugene (1850–1895)
American journalist, poet, and bibliophile
A Little Book of Western Verse (1889) V
With Trumpet and Drum (1892) V

FIELD, Nathan (1587–1633)
English actor and dramatist
A Woman is a Weather-cocke (1612) D
Amends for Ladies (1618) D

FIELD, Sarah *see* SARAH EGERTON

FIELDING, Henry (1707–1754)
British novelist, dramatist, and journalist
Love in Several Masques (1728) D
The Masquerade (1728) V
The Author's Farce; and The Pleasures of the Town (1730) D
Rape upon Rape; or, The Justice Caught in His Own Trap (1730) D
The Temple Beau (1730) D
Tom Thumb (1730) D
The Letter-Writers; or, A New Way to Keep a Wife at Home (1731) D
The Covent-Garden Tragedy (1732) D
The Lottery (1732) D
The Mock Doctor; or, The Dumb Lady Cur'd (1732) D
The Modern Husband (1732) D
The Old Debauchess (1732) D
The Miser (1733) D
Don Quixote in England (1734) D
The Intriguing Chambermaid (1734) D
An Old Man Taught Wisdom; or, The Virgin Unmask'd (1735) D
The Universal Gallant; or, The Different Husbands (1735) D
Pasquin, a Dramatick Satire on the Times (1736) D
The Historical Register for the Year 1736 (1737) D
The Champion; or, The British Mercury (1739) PER
An Apology for the Life of Mrs Shamela Andrews (1741) F
A Full Vindication of the Dutchess Dowager of Marlborough (1742) NF
The History of the Adventures of Joseph Andrews (1742) F
Miscellanies (1743) MISC
The Wedding-Day (1743) D
The True Patriot (1745) PER
The History of Tom Jones, a Foundling (1749) F
Amelia (1751) F
An Enquiry into the Causes of the Late Increase of Robbers (1751) NF
The Journal of a Voyage to Lisbon (1755) NF
The Life of Mr Jonathan Wild the Great (1759) F

FIELDING, Sarah (1710–1768)
British novelist
The Adventures of David Simple (1744) F
Familiar Letters Between the Principal Characters in David Simple (1747) F
The Governess; or, Little Female Academy (1749) F CH
Remarks on 'Clarissa' (1749) NF
The Adventures of David Simple: Volume the Last (1753) F
The Cry (1754) F
The History of the Countess of Dellwyn (1759) F
The History of Ophelia (1760) F

FIENNES, Celia (1662–1741)
English author
The Journeys of Celia Fiennes [definitive edn, ed. Christopher Morris] (1947) NF

FIERSTEIN, Harvey [Forbes] (1954–)
American playwright, actor, and producer
Torch Song Trilogy (1981) D
Safe Sex (1987) D
Spook House (1987) D

FIGES, Eva (1932–)
German-born British novelist, cultural critic, and dramatist
Equinox (1966) F

Winter Journey (1967) F
Konek Landing (1969) F
Patriarchal Attitudes (1970) NF
Days (1974) F
Nelly's Version (1977) F
Light (1981) F
Sex and Subterfuge (1982) NF
The Seven Ages (1986) F
Ghosts (1988) F
The Tree of Knowledge (1990) F
The Tenancy (1993) F
The Knot (1996) F

FILMER, Sir Robert (1588?–1653)
English political writer
The Anarchy of a Limited or Mixed Monarchy (1648) NF
The Necessity of the Absolute Power of Kings (1648) NF
Observations Concerning the Originall of Government, Upon Mr Hobs Leviathan (1652) NF
Observations Upon Aristotles Politiques Touching Forms of Government (1652) NF
An Advertisement to the Jury-Men of England Touching Witches (1653) NF
Patriarcha (1680) NF

FINCH, Anne, *née* Kingsmill, Countess of Winchilsea (1661–1720)
English poet
Miscellany Poems on Several Occasions (1713) V

FINDLATER, Jane (1866–1946)
Scottish novelist
The Green Graves of Balgowrie (1896) F

FINDLATER, Mary Williamina (1865–1963) and **Jane** (1866–1946)
Scottish novelists and short-story writers
Crossriggs (1908) F
Penny Monypenny (1911) F
Beneath the Visiting Moon (1923) F

FINDLEY, Timothy (1930–)
Canadian novelist
The Last of the Crazy People (1967) F
The Butterfly Plague (1969) F
Can You See Me Yet? (1976) D
The Wars (1977) F
Famous Last Words (1981) F

FINE, Anne (1947–)
British novelist
The Killjoy (1986) F
Alias Madame Doubtfire (1987) F CH
Goggle Eyes (1989) F
Taking the Devil's Advice (1990) F
Flower Babies (1993) F
Telling Liddy: A Sour Comedy (1998) F

FINLAY, Ian Hamilton (1925–)
Scottish poet, artist, and short-story writer
The Sea-Bed, and Other Stories (1958) F SS
The Dancers Inherit the Party (1960) V
Glasgow Beasts an' a Burd (1961) V
Butterflies (1973) V
A Mast of Hankies (1975) V
The Errata of Ovid (1983) V

FIRBANK, [Arthur Annesley] Ronald (1886–1926)
British novelist
Odette d'Antrevernes; and A Study in Temperament (1905) F SS
Vainglory (1915) F
Inclinations (1916) F
Caprice (1917) F
Valmouth (1919) F
The Princess Zoubaroff (1920) D
Sorrow in Sunlight [US: *Prancing Nigger*] (1925) F
Concerning the Eccentricities of Cardinal Pirelli (1926) F
The Artificial Princess (1934) F

FISH, Simon (d. 1531)
English theologian and pamphleteer
A Supplicacyon for the Beggers (1529) NF

FISHER, St John (1459?–1535)
English cardinal
The Fruitful Sayings of David (1508) NF
A Mourning Remembrance (1509) NF
The Sermon of John the Bysshop of Rochester (1521) NF
A Godlie Treatise Declaryng the Benefites of Prayer (1560) NF
A Spirituall Consolation (1578) NF

FISHER, Roy (1930–)
British poet
City (1961) V
The Ship's Orchestra (1966) V
The Cut Pages (1971) V
Bluebeard's Castle (1972) V
Scenes From the Alphabet (1978) V
The Thing About Joe Sullivan (1978) V
Poems 1955–1980 (1980) V
Consolidated Comedies (1981) V
Turning the Prism (1985) V
Top Down Bottom Up (1990) V
Birmingham River (1994) V

FITZGERALD, Edward (1809–1883)
British poet and translator
Euphranor (1851) V
Six Dramas of Calderón (1853) D
Salámán and Absál (1856) V
The Rubáiyát of Omar Khayyám (1859) V

FITZGERALD, F[rancis] Scott [Key] (1896–1940)
American novelist and short-story writer
Flappers and Philosophers (1920) F SS
This Side of Paradise (1920) F
The Beautiful and the Damned (1922) F
Tales of the Jazz Age (1922) F SS
The Vegetable; or, From President to Postman (1923) D
The Great Gatsby (1925) F
All the Sad Young Men (1926) F SS
Tender is the Night (1934) F
Taps at Reveille (1935) F SS

The Last Tycoon (1941) F
The Crack-Up (1945) NF
Afternoon of an Author (1958) NF
The Pat Hobby Stories (1962) F SS

FITZGERALD, Penelope [Mary] (1916–2000)
British novelist and biographer
The Golden Child (1977) F
The Bookshop (1978) F
Offshore (1979) F
Human Voices (1980) F
At Freddie's (1982) F
Innocence (1986) F
The Beginning of Spring (1988) F
The Gate of Angels (1990) F
The Blue Flower (1995) F
The Means of Escape (2000) F SS

FITZGERALD, R[obert] D[avid] (1902–1987)
Australian poet
The Greater Apollo (1927) V
To Meet the Sun (1929) V
Moonlight Acre (1938) V
Heemskerck Shoals (1949) V
Between Two Tides (1952) V
This Night's Orbit (1953) V
South-most Twelve (1962) V
Of Places and Poetry (1976) NF
Product (1977) V

FITZMAURICE, George (1878–1963)
Irish dramatist
The Country Dressmaker (1907) D
The Pie-Dish (1908) D
The Magic Glasses (1913) D
Five Plays (1914) D

FLANAGAN, Mary (1943–)
American novelist and short-story writer
Bad Girls (1984) F SS
Trust (1987) F
Rose Reason (1990) F
The Blue Woman (1994) F SS

FLANNERY, Peter (1951–)
British dramatist
Savage Amusement (1978) D
Our Friends in the North (1982) D
Singer (1989) D

FLAUBERT, Gustave (1821–1880)
French novelist
Mémoires d'un fou (1838) F
November [*Novembre*] (1842) F
Madame Bovary (1857) F
Sentimental Education [*L'Éducation sentimentale*] (1869) F
The Temptation of Saint Anthony [*La Tentation de saint Antoine*] (1874) V D SS
Three Tales [*Trois contes*] (1877) F SS
Bouvard et Pécuchet [unfinished] (1881) F

FLAVIN, Martin [Archer] (1883–1967)
American dramatist and novelist
Children of the Moon (1923) D
Broken Dishes (1929) D
The Criminal Code (1929) D
Mr Littlejohn (1940) F
Corporal Cat (1941) F
Journey in the Dark (1943) F
The Enchanted (1947) F
Cameron Hill (1957) F

FLECKER, James [born **Herman] Elroy** (1884–1915)
British poet and novelist
The Bridge of Fire (1907) V
The Last Generation (1908) F
Thirty-Six Poems (1910) V
The Golden Journey to Samarkand (1913) V
The King of Alsander (1914) F
The Old Ships (1915) V
Collected Prose (1920) NF
Hassan (1922) D

FLECKNOE, Richard (c. 1620–1678)
English poet and dramatist
Miscellania (1653) V
Love's Dominion (1654) D
The Diarium, or Journall (1656) V
A Relation of Ten Years Travells (1656) NF
Enigmaticall Characters (1658) NF
Heroick Portraits (1660) MISC
Erminia; or, The Fair and Vertuous Lady (1661) D
Love's Kingdom (1664) D
The Damoiselles à la Mode (1667) D
Sir William D'Avenant's Voyage to the Other World (1668) V
Epigrams (1669) V

FLEMING, Ian [Lancaster] (1908–1964)
British novelist and creator of James Bond
Casino Royale (1953) F
Live and Let Die (1954) F
Moonraker (1955) F
Diamonds Are Forever (1956) F
From Russia With Love (1957) F
Dr No (1958) F
Goldfinger (1959) F
For Your Eyes Only (1960) F
Thunderball (1961) F
The Spy Who Loved Me (1962) F
On Her Majesty's Secret Service (1963) F
Chitty-Chitty-Bang-Bang: The Magical Car (1964) F CH
You Only Live Twice (1964) F
The Man With the Golden Gun (1965) F

FLEMING, [Robert] Peter (1907–1971)
British traveller and author
Brazilian Adventure (1933) NF
One's Company (1934) NF
News From Tartary (1936) NF
The Flying Visit (1940) F
A Story to Tell, and Other Tales (1942) F SS
My Aunt's Rhinoceros, and Other Reflections (1956) NF
Invasion 1940 (1957) NF

FLETCHER, Giles, the Elder (1549?–1611)
English ambassador and poet
Of the Russe Common Wealth (1591) NF
Licia; or, Poemes of Love (1593) V

FLETCHER, Giles, the Younger (1588?–1623)
English poet
Christs Victorie, and Triumph in Heaven, and Earth, Over, and After Death (1610) V
The Reward of the Faithfull (1623) NF

FLETCHER, John (1579–1625)
English dramatist
The Faithfull Shepheardesse (1610) D
The Tragedy of Thierry King of France, and his Brother Theodoret (1621) D
The Elder Brother (1637) D
The Bloody Brother (1639) D
Monsieur Thomas (1639) D
The Night-Walker; or, The Little Theife (1640) D
Rule a Wife and Have a Wife (1640) D

FLETCHER, John Gould (1886–1950)
American poet
Irradiations: Sand and Spray (1915) V
Goblins and Pagodas (1916) V
Breakers and Granite (1921) V
Branches of Adam (1926) V
The Black Rock (1928) V
The Two Frontiers (1930) NF
The Epic of Arkansas (1936) V
Selected Poems (1938) V
South Star (1941) V
The Burning Mountain (1946) V

FLETCHER, Phineas (1582–1650)
English poet
Locustae (The Locusts, or Apollyonists) [Latin and Eng.] (1627) V
Britain's Ida (1628) V
Sicelides a Piscatory (1631) D
Joy in Tribulation; or, Consolations for Afflicted Spirits (1632) NF
The Way to Blessedness (1632) NF
The Purple Island; or, The Isle of Man (1633) V

FLINT, F[rank] S[tuart] (1885–1960)
British poet
In the Net of the Stars (1909) V
Cadences (1915) V
Otherworld (1920) V

FLORIO, John (1553–1625?)
English translator and lexicographer
Florio His Firste Fruites (1578) MISC
Florios Second Frutes . . . (1591) MISC
A Worlde of Wordes, or Most Copious, Dictionarie in Italian and English (1598) NF
The Essayes or Morall Politicke and Millitaire Discourses [Montaigne] (1603) NF

FO, Dario (1926–)
Italian dramatist
Accidental Death of an Anarchist (1970) D
Can't Pay? Won't Pay! (1970) D

FOGAZZARO, Antonio (1842–1911)
Italian novelist and essayist
The Little World of the Past [*Piccolo mondo antico*] (1895) F
The Saint [*Il santo*] (1905) F
Leila (1910) F

FOLLETT, Ken[neth Martin] (1949–)
British thriller writer
Eye of the Needle [US: *Storm Island*] (1978) F
The Key to Rebecca (1980) F

FONBLANQUE, Albany de (1793–1872)
English novelist
Bad Luck (1877) F

FONTANE, Theodor (1819–1898)
German novelist
Frau Jenny Treibel (1892) F
Effi Briest (1895) F

FONTENELLE, Bernard le Bovier (1657–1757)
French man of letters
New Dialogues of the Dead [*Nouveaux dialogue des morts*] (1683) F
Discourse on the Plurality of Worlds [*Entretiens sur la pluralité des mondes*] (1686) NF
The History of Oracles [*Histoire des oracles*] (1687) NF
On the Origin of Fables [*De l'origine des fables*] (1724) NF

FOOTE, Samuel (1720–1777)
British actor and dramatist
The Roman and English Comedy Consider'd and Compar'd (1747) NF
Taste (1752) D
The Englishman in Paris (1753) D
The Englishman Returned from Paris (1756) D
The Author (1757) D
The Minor (1760) D
The Lyar (1762) D
The Orators (1762) D
The Patron (1764) D
The Taylors (1767) D
The Devil upon Two Sticks (1768) D
The Lame Lover (1770) D
The Bankrupt (1773) D
A Trip to Calais (1778) D

FORD, Ford Madox [Ford Hermann Hueffer] (1873–1939)
British novelist and poet
The Shifting of the Fire (1892) F
The Queen Who Flew (1894) F CH
Poems for Pictures and for Notes of Music (1900) V
Rossetti (1902) NF
The Face of the Night (1904) V
The Benefactor (1905) F
The Soul of London (1905) NF
The Fifth Queen and How She Came to Court (1906) F
The Heart of the Country (1906) NF
An English Girl (1907) F
From Inland, and Other Poems (1907) V

The Pre-Raphaelite Brotherhood (1907) NF
Privy Seal (1907) F
The Fifth Queen Crowned (1908) F
Mr Apollo (1908) F
The 'Half Moon' (1909) F HF
A Call (1910) F
The Portrait (1910) F
Songs From London (1910) V
Ancient Lights and Certain New Reflections (1911) NF
The Critical Attitude (1911) NF
Ladies Whose Bright Eyes (1911) F
The Panel (1912) F
Mr Fleight (1913) F
The Young Lovell (1913) F
Collected Poems (1914) V
Henry James (1914) NF
The Good Soldier (1915) F
The Marsden Case (1923) F
Some Do Not (1924) F
No More Parades (1925) F
A Man Could Stand Up (1926) F
Last Post (1928) F

FORD, John (1586–1640?)
English dramatist and poet
Fames Memoriall (1606) V
A Line of Life (1620) NF
The Lovers Melancholy (1629) D
The Broken Heart (1633) D
Loves Sacrifice (1633) D
'Tis Pity She's a Whore (1633) D
The Chronicle Historie of Perkin Warbeck (1634) D
The Fancies, Chast and Noble (1638) D
The Ladies Triall (1639) D
The Queen; or, The Excellency of Her Sex (1653) D
The Sun's-Darling (1656) D

FORD, Richard (1796–1858)
British travel author
A Hand-Book for Travellers in Spain, and Readers at Home (1845) NF

FORD, Richard (1944–)
American novelist and short-story writer
A Piece of My Heart (1976) F
The Ultimate Good Luck (1981) F
The Sportswriter (1986) F
Rock Springs (1987) F SS
Wild Life (1990) F
Independence Day (1995) F

FORESTER, C[ecil] S[cott] (1899–1966)
British novelist and creator of Hornblower
Brown on Resolution [US: *Single-Handed*] (1929) F
The Gun (1933) F
The African Queen (1935) F
The General (1936) F
The Happy Return [US: *Beat to Quarters*. The first Hornblower novel] (1937) F
The Captain From Connecticut (1941) F
The Ship (1943) F
The Commodore [US: *Commodore Hornblower*] (1945) F
Hornblower and the Atropos (1953) F
The Good Shepherd (1955) F
Hornblower in the West Indies [US: *Admiral Hornblower in the West Indies*] (1958) F
Captain Hornblower, R.N. (1965) F

FORSTER, Edward Morgan (1879–1970)
British novelist, short-story writer, and critic
Where Angels Fear to Tread (1905) F
The Longest Journey (1907) F
A Room With a View (1908) F
Howards End (1910) F
The Celestial Omnibus, and Other Stories (1911) F SS
The Story of the Siren (1920) F
Pharos and Pharillon (1923) NF
A Passage to India (1924) F
Anonymity (1925) NF
Aspects of the Novel (1927) NF
The Eternal Moment, and Other Stories (1928) F SS
Goldsworthy Lowes Dickinson (1934) NF
Abinger Harvest (1936) NF
What I Believe (1939) NF
Billy Budd [music by Benjamin Britten] (1951) Opera
Two Cheers for Democracy (1951) NF
The Hill of Devi (1953) NF
Maurice (1971) F
The Life to Come, and Other Stories (1972) F SS
Arctic Summer, and Other Fiction (1980) F SS
The Prince's Tale, and Other Uncollected Writings (1998) NF

FORSTER, John (1812–1876)
British journalist and biographer
Life and Adventures of Oliver Goldsmith (1848) NF
Historical and Biographical Essays (1858) NF
Walter Savage Landor (1869) NF
The Life of Charles Dickens (1872) NF

FORSTER, Margaret (1938–)
British novelist and biographer
Dame's Delight (1964) F
Georgy Girl (1965) F
The Travels of Maudie Tipstaff (1967) F
The Park (1968) F
Miss Owen is at Home (1969) F
Mr Bone's Retreat (1971) F
The Seduction of Mrs Pendlebury (1974) F
William Makepeace Thackeray (1978) NF
Mother Can You Hear Me? (1979) F
Marital Rites (1981) F
Private Papers (1986) F
Have the Men Had Enough? (1989) F
Lady's Maid (1990) F
The Battle for Christabel (1991) F
Daphne du Maurier (1993) NF
Mother's Boys (1994) F
Hidden Lives (1995) NF
The Memory Box (1999) NF

FORSYTH, Frederick (1938–)
British thriller writer
The Day of the Jackal (1971) F

The Odessa File (1972) F
The Dogs of War (1974) F
The Fourth Protocol (1984) F
The Phantom of Manhattan (1999) F

FOSCOLO, Ugo (1778–1827)
Italian poet, novelist, dramatist, and poet
Last Letters of Jacopo Ortis [*Ultime lettere di Jacopo Ortis*] (1802) F
Of Sepulchres [*Dei Sepolcri*] (1807) V

FOSTER, David [Manning] (1944–)
Australian novelist
North South West [three novellas] (1973) F
The Pure Land (1974) F
The Fleeing Atalanta (1975) V
The Empathy Experiment (1977) F
Escape to Reality (1977) F SS
Moonlite (1981) F
Plumbum (1983) F
Dog Rock (1985) F
The Adventures of Christian Rosy Cross (1986) F
Testostero (1987) F
The Pale Blue Crochet Coathanger Cover (1988) F
Hitting the Wall [two novellas] (1989) F
Mates of Mars (1991) F

FOTHERGILL, Jessie (1851–1891)
British novelist
Healey (1875) F
The First Violin (1877) F
Probation (1879) F
The Wellfields (1880) F
Kith and Kin (1881) F
Made or Marred (1881) F
Peril (1884) F
From Moor Isles (1888) F

FOURNIER, Henri-Alban *see* ALAIN-FOURNIER

FOWLER, Hon. Ellen Thorneycroft, later **Felkin** (1860–1929)
British novelist and poet
Concerning Isabel Carnaby (1898) F
A Double Thread (1899) F
The Farringdons (1900) F
Sirius, and Other Stories (1901) F SS
Miss Fallowfield's Fortune (1908) F
Her Ladyship's Conscience (1913) F

FOWLER, H[enry] W[atson] (1858–1933) and **F[rancis] G[eorge]** (1870–1918)
British lexicographers and grammarians
The King's English (1906) NF
The Concise Oxford Dictionary of Current English (1911) NF
A Dictionary of Modern English Usage (1926) NF

FOWLES, John [Robert] (1926–)
British novelist and essayist
The Collector (1963) F
The Magus (1965) F
The French Lieutenant's Woman (1969) F
The Ebony Tower [novellas] (1974) F
Daniel Martin (1977) F
Mantissa (1982) F
A Maggot (1985) F

FOX, George, the elder (1624–1691)
English mystic, founder of the Society of Friends, and author
The Vialls of the Wrath of God (1654) NF
A Declaration Against all Popery (1655) NF
The Great Mystery of the Great Whore Unfolded (1659) NF
An Answer to the Arguments of the Jews (1661) NF
Some Principles of the Elect People of God (1661) NF
Three General Epistles (1664) NF
The Arraignment of Popery (1667) NF
Concerning Revelation, Prophecy, Measures and Rule (1676) NF
Concerning the Living God of Truth (1680) NF
A Journal (1694) NF

FOX, Paula (1923–)
American novelist and children's writer
How Many Miles to Babylon? (1967) F
The Slave Dancer (1973) F
The Lost Boy (1987) F

FOXE, John (1517–1587)
English martyrologist
Actes and Monuments of these Latter and Perillous Dayes [known as *The Book of Martyrs*] (1563) NF
A Sermon of Christ Crucified (1570) NF

FRAME, Janet [Paterson] (1924–)
New Zealand novelist, short-story writer, and poet
The Lagoon (1951) F SS
Owls Do Cry (1957) F
The Edge of the Alphabet (1962) F
Faces in the Water (1962) F
Scented Gardens for the Blind (1963) F
The Adaptable Man (1965) F
The Reservoir, and Other Stories (1966) F SS
A State of Siege (1966) F
The Pocket Mirror (1967) V
The Rainbirds (1968) F
Intensive Care (1970) F
Daughter Buffalo (1972) F
Living in the Maniototo (1979) F
To the Island (1982) NF
You Are Now Entering the Human Heart (1983) F SS
An Angel at My Table (1984) NF
The Envoy From Mirror City (1985) NF
The Carpathians (1988) F

FRAME, Ronald (1953–)
British novelist, short-story writer, and dramatist
Winter Journey (1984) F
Watching Mrs Gordon (1985) F SS
A Long Weekend with Marcel Proust (1986) F SS
Sandmouth People (1987) F
A Woman of Judah (1988) F SS
Penelope's Hat (1989) F
Bluette (1990) F
Underwood and After (1991) F

Walking With My Mistress in Deauville (1992) F
The Sun on the Wall [three novellas] (1994) F
The Lantern-Bearers (1999) F

'FRANCE, Anatole' [Jacques-Anatole-François Thibault] (1844–1922)
French novelist and man of letters
Golden Poems [*Poèmes dorés*] (1873) V
The Crime of Sylvester Bonnard [*Le Crime de Sylvestre Bonnard*] (1881) F
My Friend's Book [*Le Livre de mon ami*] (1885) F
The Literary Life [*La Vie littéraire*] (1888–92) NF
Balthasar (1889) F SS
Thaïs (1890) F
The Opinions of Jerome Coignard [*Les Opinions de Jérôme Coignard*] (1893) F
The Red Lily [*Le Lys rouge*] (1894) F
Pierre Nozière (1899) F
Monsieur Bergeret in Paris [*Monsieur Bergeret à Paris*] (1901) F
The Isle of Penguins [*L'Île des pingouins*] (1908) F
The Gods Are Thirsty [*Les Dieux ont soif*] (1912) F
The Angels' Revolt [*La Révolte des anges*] (1914) F

FRANCIS, Sir Philip *see* 'JUNIUS'

FRANCIS, Dick [Richard Stanley] (1920–)
British crime writer
Dead Cert (1962) F
Flying Finish (1966) F
Enquiry (1969) F
Rat Race (1970) F
High Stakes (1975) F
In the Frame (1976) F
Whip Hand (1979) F
Hot Money (1987) F
Longshot (1990) F
To the Hilt (1996) F
Field of 13 (1998) F

FRANK, Waldo [David] (1889–1967)
American novelist and critic
The Unwelcome Man (1917) F
Our America (1919) NF
The Dark Mother (1920) F
City Block (1922) F
Rahab (1922) F
Holiday (1923) F
Chalk Face (1924) F
Salvos (1924) NF
Virgin Spain (1926) NF
The Re-Discovery of America (1928) NF
America Hispaña (1931) NF
Dawn in Russia (1932) NF
The Death and Birth of David Markand (1934) F
In the American Jungle (1937) NF
The Bridegroom Cometh (1939) F
Chart for Rough Water (1940) NF
Summer Never Ends (1941) F
South American Journey (1943) NF
The Jew in Our Day (1944) NF
Island in the Atlantic (1946) F
The Invaders (1948) F
Birth of a World (1951) NF
Bridgehead (1957) NF
Cuba: Prophetic Island (1961) NF

FRANKAU, Gilbert (1884–1952)
British novelist
The Woman of the Horizon (1917) F
The Seeds of Enchantment (1921) F
Masterson (1926) F
Martin Make-Believe (1930) F

FRANKAU, Julia *see* FRANK DANBY

FRANKAU, Pamela (1908–1967)
British novelist and short-story writer
The Marriage of Harlequin (1927) F
The Black Minute, and Other Stories (1929) F SS
She and I (1930) F
Women Are So Serious, and Other Stories (1932) F SS
Tassle-Gentle (1934) F
Fifty-Five, and Other Stories (1936) F SS
The Devil We Know (1939) F
Shaken in the Wind (1948) F
The Willow Cabin (1949) F
A Wreath for the Enemy (1954) F
The Bridge (1957) F
Slaves of the Lamp (1965) F

FRANKLIN, Benjamin (1706–1790)
American politician and author
A Dissertation on Liberty and Necessity, Pleasure and Pain (1725) NF
Poor Richard's Almanack (1733–58) MISC
A Proposal for Promoting Useful Knowledge (1743) NF
Plain Truth; or, Serious Consideration on the Present State of the City of Philadelphia (1747) NF
Proposals Relating to the Education of Youth in Pensilvania (1749) NF
Experiments and Observations on Electricity (1751–4) NF
An Historical Review of the Constitution and Government of Pennsylvania (1759) NF
The Interest of Great Britain Considered with Regard to Her Colonies (1760) NF
Cool Thoughts on the Present Situation of Our Public Affairs (1764) NF

FRANKLIN, [Stella Maria Sarah] Miles ['Brent of Bin Bin'] (1879–1954)
Australian novelist
My Brilliant Career (1901) F
Some Everyday Folk and Dawn (1909) F
Up the Country [as 'Brent of Bin Bin'] (1928) F
Ten Creeks Run [as 'Brent of Bin Bin'] (1930) F
Back to Bool Bool [as 'Brent of Bin Bin'] (1931) F
Old Blastus of Bandicoot (1931) F
Bring the Monkey (1933) F
All That Swagger (1936) F
Pioneers on Parade (1939) F
My Career Goes Bung (1946) F
Prelude to Waking [as 'Brent of Bin Bin'] (1950) F

Cockatoos [as 'Brent of Bin Bin'] (1954) F
Gentlemen at Gyang Gyang [as 'Brent of Bin Bin'] (1956) F

FRASER, George MacDonald (1925–)
Scottish novelist
Flashman (1969) F
Flash for Freedom (1971) F
Flashman at the Charge (1973) F
The Pyrates (1983) F
Flashman and the Mountain of Light (1990) F
Flashman and the Tiger (1999) F

FRASER, G[eorge] S[utherland] (1915–1980)
Scottish poet and critic
The Fatal Landscape, and Other Poems (1941) V
Home Town Elegy (1944) V
The Traveller Has Regrets, and Other Poems (1948) V
Leaves Without a Tree (1953) V
The Modern Writer and His World (1953) NF
Vision and Rhetoric (1959) NF
Conditions (1969) V

FRASER, Lady Antonia, *née* Packenham (1932–)
British biographer and novelist
Mary Queen of Scots (1969) NF
Quiet as a Nun (1977) F

FRAUNCE, Abraham (1558?–1592/3)
English poet
The Arcadian Rhetorike (1588) NF
The Lawiers Logike (1588) NF
The Countesse of Pembrokes Emanuel (1591) V
The Countesse of Pembrokes Ivychurch (1591) V
The Third Part of the Countesse of Pembrokes Ivychurch: Entituled Amintas Dale (1592) MISC

FRAYN, Michael (1933–)
British novelist, dramatist, and journalist
The Day of the Dog (1962) NF
The Tin Men (1965) F
The Russian Interpreter (1966) F
Towards the End of the Morning (1967) F
A Very Private Life (1968) F
The Two of Us (1970) D
Sweet Dreams (1974) F
Alphabetical Order (1975) D
Clouds (1976) D
Donkeys' Years (1976) D
Make and Break (1980) D
Noises Off (1982) D
Benefactors (1984) D
The Trick of It (1989) F
Look Look (1990) D
Audience (1991) D
A Landing on the Sun (1991) F
Now You Know (1992) F
Here (1993) D
Copenhagen (1998) D
Headlong (1999) F

FRAZER, Sir J[ames] G[eorge] (1854–1941)
Scottish social anthropologist
The Golden Bough (1890) NF

FREDERIC, Harold (1856–1898)
American novelist and short-story writer
Seth's Brother's Wife (1887) F
In the Valley (1890) F
The Lawton Girl (1890) F
The Return of the O'Mahony (1892) F
The Copperhead (1893) F
Marsena, and Other Stories (1894) F SS
The Damnation of Theron Ware (1896) F
March Hares (1896) F SS
Gloria Mundi (1898) F SS
The Market Place (1899) F SS

FREELING, Nicholas (1927–)
British crime writer (creator of Van der Valk)
Love in Amsterdam [US: *Murder in Amsterdam*] (1962) F
Because of the Cats (1963) F
The King of the Rainy Country (1966) F
Tsing-Boum (1969) F
A Long Silence (1971) F
Dressing of Diamond (1974) F
The Widow (1979) F
Sand Castles (1989) F
You Who Know (1994) F
A Dwarf Kingdom (1996) F

FREEMAN, E[dward] A[ugustus] (1823–1892)
British historian
Principles of Church Restoration (1846) NF
A History of Architecture (1849) NF
The Preservation and Restoration of Ancient Monuments (1852) NF
The History and Conquests of the Saracens (1856) NF
History of Federal Government (1863) NF
The History of the Norman Conquest of England (1867) NF
Historical Essays [1st ser.] (1871) NF
The Growth of the English Constitution from the Earliest Times (1872) NF
Historical Essays: Second Series (1873) NF
Historical Essays: Third Series (1879) NF
The Historical Geography of Europe (1881) NF
The Reign of William Rufus and the Accession of Henry the First (1882) NF
The Methods of Historical Study (1886) NF
Historical Essays: Fourth Series (1892) NF

FREEMAN, Mary [Eleanor] Wilkins (1852–1930)
American short-story writer and novelist
A Humble Romance, and Other Stories (1887) F SS
A New England Nun (1891) F SS
Giles Corey, Yeoman (1893) D
Jane Field (1893) F
Pembroke (1894) F
Jerome, a Poor Man (1897) F
The Heart's Highway (1900) F
The Portion of Labor (1901) F
The Wind in the Rose-Bush (1903) F SS
Edgewater People (1918) F SS

FREEMAN, Richard Austin (1862–1943)
British detective novelist and short-story writer
The Adventures of Romney Pringle (1902) F SS
The Red Thumb Mark (1907) F CF
John Thorndyke's Cases [US: *Dr Thorndyke's Cases*] (1909) F SS
The Eye of Osiris [US: *The Vanishing Man*] (1911) F SS
The Singing Bone [US: *The Adventures of Dr Thorndyke*] (1912) F SS
Dr Thorndyke's Case-Book [US: *The Blue Scarab*] (1923) F SS
The Jacob Street Mystery [the last Dr Thorndyke novel] (1942) F SS

FRENCH, Marilyn (1929–)
American novelist and critic
The Women's Room (1977) F
The Bleeding Heart (1980) F
Beyond Power (1985) NF
Her Mother's Daughter (1987) F
Our Father (1994) F

FRENEAU, Philip [Morin] (1752–1832)
American poet
The American Village (1772) V
General Gage's Confession (1775) V
General Gage's Soliloquy (1775) V
The British Prison Ship (1781) V
Poems (1786) V
Poems Written Between the Years 1768 and 1794 (1795) V
Letters on Various Interesting and Important Subjects (1799) V

FRERE, John Hookham (1769–1846)
British translator and poet
Prospectus and Specimen of an Intended National Work by William and Robert Whistlecraft (1817) V

FRIEDMAN, Milton (1912–)
American economist
Essays in Positive Economics (1953) NF
Capitalism and Freedom (1962) NF
Dollars and Deficit (1968) NF

FRIEL, Brian [Bernard Patrick] (1929–)
Northern Irish dramatist and short-story writer
The Saucer of Larks (1962) F SS
Philadelphia, Here I Come! (1964) D
The Gold in the Sea (1966) F SS
The Loves of Cass McGuire (1966) D
Lovers (1967) D
Crystal and Fox (1968) D
The Gentle Island (1971) D
The Freedom of the City (1973) D
Volunteers (1975) D
Living Quarters (1977) D
Faith Healer (1979) D
Translations (1980) D
The Communication Cord (1982) D
The Diviner (1983) F SS
Making History (1988) D
Dancing at Lughnasa (1990) D
Molly Sweeney (1994) D

FROST, Robert [Lee] (1874–1963)
American poet
A Boy's Will (1913) V
North of Boston (1914) V
Mountain Interval (1916) V
New Hampshire (1923) V
West-Running Brook (1928) V
Collected Poems (1930) V
A Further Range (1936) V
A Witness Tree (1942) V
A Masque of Reason (1945) D
A Masque of Mercy (1947) D
Steeple Bush (1947) V
In the Clearing (1962) V

FROUDE, J[ames] A[nthony] (1818–1894)
British historian, biographer, and novelist
Shadows of the Clouds [as 'Zeta'] (1847) F SS
The Nemesis of Faith [as 'Zeta'] (1849) F
History of England from the Fall of Wolsey to the Death of Elizabeth (1856) NF
The English in Ireland in the Eighteenth Century (1872) NF
Thomas Carlyle (1882) NF
Memorials of Jane Welsh Carlyle (1883) NF
Thomas Carlyle: A History of his Life in London 1834–8 (1884) NF
Oceana; or, England and Her Colonies (1886) NF
The English in the West Indies; or, The Bow of Ulysses (1888) NF

FROUDE, R[ichard] H[urrell] (1803–1836)
British poet and Tractarian
Remains [pt. i and pt. ii] (1838) MISC

FRY, Christopher [Christopher Fry Harris] (1907–)
British dramatist and poet
The Boy With a Cart—Cuthman, Saint of Sussex (1937) D
The Firstborn (1946) D
A Phoenix Too Frequent (1946) D
The Lady's Not for Burning (1948) V D
Ring Round the Moon [from Anouilh, *L'invitation au chateau*] (1950) D
Venus Observed (1950) D
A Sleep of Prisoners (1951) D
The Dark is Light Enough (1954) D
The Lark [from Anouilh, *L'alouette*] (1955) D
Tiger at the Gates [from Giraudoux, *La guerre de Troie n'aura pas lieu*] (1955) D
Duel of Angels [from Giraudoux, *Pour Lucrece*] (1958) D
Curtmantle (1961) D
A Yard of Sun (1970) D
One Thing More (1986) D

FRY, Roger [Eliot] (1866–1934)
British art critic
Vision and Design (1920) NF

Transformations (1926) NF
Cézanne (1927) NF
Characteristics of French Art (1932) NF
Reflections on British Painting (1934) NF
Last Lectures (1939) NF

FRYE, [Herman] Northrop (1912–1991)
Canadian literary critic
Fearful Symmetry: A Study of William Blake (1947) NF
Anatomy of Criticism (1957) NF
The Well-Tempered Critic (1963) NF
The Bush Garden: Essays on the Canadian Imagination (1971) NF
The Great Code (1982) NF

FUENTES, Carlos (1928–)
Mexican novelist
The Masked Days [*Los dias enmascarados*] (1954) F SS
Where the Air is Clear (1958) F SS
Aura (1962) F
The Death of Artemio Cruz (1962) F SS
A Change of Skin [*Cambio de piel*] (1967) F
Terra nostra (1975) F
Distant Relations (1980) F
The Old Gringo (1985) F
Constancia, and Other Stories for Virgins (1989) F SS

FUGARD, Athol [Harold Lanigan] (1932–)
South African playwright
No-Good Friday (1958) D
Nongogo (1959) D
The Blood Knot (1960) D
Hello and Goodbye (1965) D
Boesman and Lena (1969) D
Sizwe Banzi is Dead (1972) D
Statements After an Arrest Under the Immorality Act (1972) D
Dimetos (1976) D
A Lesson from Aloes (1979) D
Tsotsi (1980) F
Master Harold and the Boys (1982) D
The Road to Mecca (1984) D
A Place with the Pigs (1987) D
My Children! My Africa! (1989) D
Playland (1992) D
Township Plays (1993) D

FULLER, Henry Blake (1857–1929)
American novelist and short-story writer
The Chevalier of Pensieri-Vani [as 'Stanton Page'] (1890) F
The Chatelaine of La Trinité (1892) F
The Cliff-Dwellers (1893) F
With the Procession (1895) F
The Last Refuge (1900) F
Under the Skylights (1901) F
Waldo Trench and Others (1908) F SS
On the Stairs (1918) F
Bertram Cope's Year (1919) F
Gardens of This World (1929) F
Not on the Screen (1930) F

FULLER, John [Leopold] (1937–)
British poet, novelist, dramatist, and children's writer
Fairground Music (1961) V
The Tree That Walked (1967) V
Epistles to Several Persons (1973) V
The Mountain in the Sea (1975) V
Lies and Secrets (1979) V
The January Divan (1980) V
Flying to Nowhere (1983) F
The Adventures of Speedfall (1985) F SS
The Grey Among the Green (1988) V
The Burning Boys (1989) F
Look Twice (1991) F
The Mechanical Body (1991) V

FULLER, Roy [Broadbent] (1912–1991)
British poet, novelist, children's writer, and editor
Poems (1939) V
Epitaphs and Occasions (1940) V
The Middle of a War (1942) V
A Lost Season (1944) V
Counterparts (1954) V
Fantasy and Fugue (1954) F
Image of a Society (1956) F
Brutus's Orchard (1957) V
The Father's Comedy (1961) F
Collected Poems 1936–1961 (1962) V
Buff (1965) V
New Poems (1968) V
Owls and Artificers (1971) NF
Tiny Tears (1973) V
From the Joke Shop (1975) V
An Ill-Governed Coast (1976) V
The Reign of Sparrows (1980) V
Souvenirs (1980) NF
Vamp Till Ready (1982) NF
As From the Thirties (1983) V
Home and Dry (1984) NF
Mianserin Sonnets (1984) V
New and Collected Poems 1934–1984 (1985) V
Subsequent to Summer (1985) V
Outside the Canon (1986) V
Available for Dreams (1989) V
Spanner and Pen (1991) NF
Last Poems (1993) V

FULLER, Thomas (1608–1661)
English antiquarian and divine
Davids Hainous Sinne (1631) V
The Historie of the Holy Warre (1639) NF
Joseph's Party-coloured Coat (1640) NF
The Holy State (1642) NF
A Sermon of Reformation (1643) NF
Truth Maintained (1643) NF
Good Thoughts in Bad Times (1645) NF
Andronicus; or, The Unfortunate Politician (1646) NF
Feare of Losing the Old Light (1646) NF
The Cause and Cure of a Wounded Conscience (1647) NF
Good Thoughts in Worse Times (1647) NF
The Just Mans Funeral (1649) NF

A Pisgah-Sight of Palestine and the Confines Thereof (1650) NF
Abel Redevivus; or, The Dead Yet Speaking (1651) NF
The Church-History of Britain (1655) NF
The Best Name on Earth (1657) NF
The Sovereigns Prerogative (1657) NF
The Appeal of Injured Innocence (1659) NF
Mixt Contemplations in Better Times (1660) NF
The History of the Worthies of England (1662) NF

FULLERTON, Lady Georgiana Charlotte, *née* Leveson-Gower (1812–1885)
British novelist and poet
Ellen Middleton (1844) F
Grantley Manor (1847) F
Lady-Bird (1852) F
Laurentia (1861) F HF
Rose Leblanc (1862) F
Too Strange Not To Be True (1864) F
Constance Sherwood (1865) F
A Stormy Life (1867) F
Mrs Gerald's Niece (1869) F
The Gold-Digger, and Other Verses (1872) V
Seven Stories (1873) F SS
A Will and a Way (1881) F

FURNIVALL, F[rederick] J[ames] (1825–1910)
British literary scholar
Le Morte Arthur (1864)
Bishop Percy's Folio Manuscript (1867) V
Ballads from Manuscripts (1868) V
The Works of William Shakespeare (1904) EDN
The Century Shakespeare (1908) EDN

FURPHY, Joseph (1843–1912)
Australian novelist
Such is Life (1903) F
The Buln-Buln and the Brolga (1944) F
Rigby's Romance (1946) F

G

GABORIAU, Émile (1832–1873)
French writer of detective fiction
L'Affaire Lerouge (1866) F
Le Crime d'Orcival (1867) F
Le Dossier 113 (1867) F
Les Esclaves de Paris (1869) F
Monsieur Lecoq (1869) F
La Corde au cou (1873) F

GADDA, Emilio Carlo (1893–1973)
Italian novelist
The Castle of Udine [*Il castello di Udine*] (1934) F
Adalgisa (1944) F
That Dreadful Mess on the Via Merulana [*Quer pasticciaccio brutto de via Merulana*] (1957) F
The Cognizance of Sorrow [*Cognizione del dolore*] (1963) F

GADDIS, William (1922–)
American novelist
The Recognitions (1955) F
JR (1976) F
Carpenter's Gothic (1985) F
A Frolic of His Own (1994) F

GAINES, Ernest J. (1933–)
African-American novelist and short-story writer
Catherine Carmier (1964) F
Of Love and Dust (1967) F
The Autobiography of Miss Jane Pitman (1971) F
In My Father's House (1978) F
A Gathering of Old Men (1983) F
A Lesson Before Dying (1993) F

GAITSKILL, Mary (1954–)
American novelist and short-story writer
Bad Behaviour (1988) F SS
Two Girls, Fat and Thin (1991) F

GALBRAITH, J[ohn] K[enneth] (1908–)
American economist
American Capitalism (1952) NF
The Affluent Society (1955) NF
The Great Crash (1961) NF
The New Industrial State (1967) NF
Economics and the Public Purpose (1973) NF
The Nature of Mass Poverty (1979) NF
The Anatomy of Power (1983) NF
The Culture of Contentment (1992) NF
A Journey Through Economic Time (1994) NF

GALE, Zona (1874–1938)
American novelist and short-story writer
Romance Island (1906) F
Birth (1918) F
Miss Lulu Bett (1920) F
The Secret Way (1921) V
Preface to a Life (1926) F
Yellow Gentians and Blue (1927) F SS
Portage, Wisconsin (1928) NF
Borgia (1929) F
Bridal Pond (1930) F SS
Papa La Fleur (1933) F

GALLANT, Mavis, *née* Young (1922–)
Canadian short-story writer and novelist
The Other Paris (1956) F SS
Green Water, Green Sky (1959) F
My Heart is Broken [UK: *An Unmarried Man's Summer*] (1964) F SS
A Fairly Good Time (1970) F
The End of the World, and Other Stories (1973) F SS
The Pegnitz Junction (1973) F SS
From the Fifteenth District (1979) F SS
Home Truths (1981) F SS

GALLICO, Paul [William] (1897–1976)
American novelist
The Snow Goose (1941) F
The Lonely (1947) F
Jennie (1950) F
The Small Miracle (1952) F

Ludmilla (1955) F
Flowers for Mrs Harris (1958) F
Too Many Ghosts (1961) F
Scruffy (1962) F
The Hand of Mary Constable (1964) F
The Poseidon Adventure (1969) F

GALSWORTHY, John (1867–1933)
British novelist, dramatist, and short-story writer
From the Four Winds [by 'John Sinjohn'] (1897) F SS
Jocelyn [by 'John Sinjohn'] (1898) F
Villa Rubein [by 'John Sinjohn'] (1900) F
A Man of Devon [by 'John Sinjohn'] (1901) F
The Island Pharisees (1904) F
The Man of Property (1906) F
The Country House (1907) F
A Commentary (1908) F
Fraternity (1909) F
Strife (1909) D
Justice (1910) D
A Motley (1910) F SS
The Patrician (1911) F
The Inn of Tranquillity (1912) NF
The Dark Flower (1913) F
The Fugitive (1913) D
The Mob (1914) D
The Freelands (1915) F
The Little Man, and Other Satires (1915) F SS
Five Tales (1918) F SS
The Burning Spear (1919) F
Awakening (1920) F
In Chancery (1920) F
The Skin Game (1920) D
Tatterdemalion (1920) F SS
To Let (1921) F
The Forsyte Saga (1922) F
Loyalties (1922) D
Windows (1922) D
The White Monkey (1924) F
Escape (1926) D
The Silver Spoon (1926) F
Swan Song (1928) F
Exiled (1929) D
Four Forsyte Stories (1929) F SS
A Modern Comedy (1929) F
On Forsyte Change (1930) F SS
Soames and the Flag (1930) F
Maid in Waiting (1931) F
Flowering Wilderness (1932) F
Over the River (1933) F
End of the Chapter (1935) F

GALT, John (1779–1839)
Scottish novelist, biographer, and poet
The Battle of Largs (1804) V
Voyages and Travels in the Years 1809, 1810 and 1811 (1812) NF
Letters from the Levant (1813) NF
The Majolo (1815) F
The Crusades (1816) V
The Earthquake (1820) F
Glenfell; or, Macdonalds and Campbells (1820) F
A Tour of Europe and Asia (1820) NF
Annals of the Parish; or, The Chronicle of Dalmailing (1821) F
The Ayrshire Legatees; or, The Pringle Family (1821) F
The Provost (1822) F
Sir Andrew Wylie of That Ilk (1822) F
The Steam-Boat (1822) F
The Entail; or, The Lairds of Grippy (1823) F
Ringan Gilhaize; or, The Covenanters (1823) F
The Spaewife (1823) F
The Bachelor's Wife (1824) F
Rothelan (1824) F
The Omen (1825) F
The Last of the Lairds; or, The Life and Opinions and Malachi Mailings (1826) F
Lawrie Todd; or, The Settlers in the Woods (1830) F
The Life of Lord Byron (1830) NF
Bogle Corbet; or The Emigrants (1831) F
The Member (1832) F
Stanley Buxton; or, The Schoolfellows (1832) F
Autobiography (1833) NF
Eben Erskine; or, The Traveller (1833) F
The Stolen Child (1833) F
Stories of the Study (1833) F SS

GARCÍA LORCA, Federico (1898–1936)
Spanish poet and dramatist
Book of Poems [*Libro de poemas*] (1921) V
Gypsy Ballads [*Romancero gitano*] (1928) V
Blood Wedding [*Bodas de sangre*] (1933) D
Lament for the Death of a Bullfighter, and Other Poems [*Llanto por la muerte de Ignacio Sánchez Mejías*] (1934) V
Yerma (1934) D
The House of Bernada Alba [*La casa de Bernada Alba*] (1935) D

GARCÍA MÁRQUEZ, Gabriel (1928–)
Colombian novelist
Leaf Storm, and Other Stories [*La hojarasca*] (1955) F SS
No One Writes to the Colonel [*El coronel no tiene quien le escriba*] (1961) F
In Evil Hour [*La mala hora*] (1966) F
One Hundred Years of Solitude [*Cien años de soledad*] (1967) F
The Autumn of the Patriarch [*El otoño del patriarca*] (1975) F
Chronicle of a Death Foretold [*Crónica de una muerte anunciada*] (1981) F
Love in the Time of Cholera [*El amor en los tiempos de coléra*] (1988) F
Strange Pilgrims [*Doce cuentos peregrinos*] (1992) F SS
Of Love and Other Demons (1995) F

GARDAM, Jane [Mary], *née* Pearson (1928–)
British novelist and short-story writer
A Few Fair Days (1971) F
The Summer After the Funeral (1973) F
Black Faces, White Faces (1975) F SS

The Sidmouth Letters (1975) F SS
God on the Rocks (1978) F
The Hollow Land (1981) F CH
The Pangs of Love, and Other Stories (1983) F SS
Crusoe's Daughter (1985) F
Showing the Flag (1989) F SS
The Queen of the Tambourine (1991) F
Trio (1993) F SS
Going into a Dark House, and Other Stories (1994) F SS
Faith Fox (1996) F
Missing the Midnight (1997) F

GARDINER, S[amuel] R[awson] (1829–1902)
British historian
History of England 1603–16 (1863) NF
Prince Charles and the Spanish Marriage 1617–23 (1869) NF
The Thirty Years' War (1874) NF
A History of England Under the Duke of Buckingham and Charles I 1624–8 (1875) NF
The Personal Government of Charles I (1877) NF
Introduction to the Study of English History (1881) NF
Outline of English History (1881) NF
The Fall of the Monarchy of Charles I 1637–49 (1882) NF
History of England from the Accession of James I to the Outbreak of the Civil War 1603–42 (1883) NF

GARDNER, Erle Stanley (1889–1970)
American crime writer and creator of Perry Mason
The Case of the Velvet Claws [first Perry Mason novel] (1933) F
The Case of the Sulky Girl (1933) F
The Case of the Curious Bride (1934) F
The Case of the Shoplifter's Shoe (1938) F
The Case of the Haunted Husband (1941) F
The Case of the Black-Eyed Blonde (1944) F
The Case of the Lonely Heiress (1948) F
The Case of the Grinning Gorilla (1952) F
The Case of the Careless Cupid (1968) F
The Case of the Postponed Murder [last Perry Mason novel] (1977) F

GARDNER, [Dame] Helen [Louise] (1908–1986)
British literary scholar, critic, and editor
The Divine Poems of John Donne (1972) EDN
The New Oxford Book of English Verse 1250–1950 (1972) ANTH

GARDNER, John [Champlin, Jr] (1933–1982)
American novelist, short-story writer, children's writer, and critic
The Forms of Fiction (1961) NF
The Resurrection (1966) F
The Wreckage of Agathon (1970) F
Grendel (1971) F
The Sunlight Dialogues (1972) F
Jason and Medeia (1973) F
Nickel Mountain (1973) F
The King's Indian (1974) F SS
Dragon, Dragon (1975) F CH
October Light (1976) F
On Moral Fiction (1978) NF
Freddy's Book (1980) F
The Art of Living (1981) F SS
Mickelsson's Ghosts (1982) F

GARDNER, John [Edmund] (1926–)
British thriller writer
The Liquidator (1964) F
The Werewolf Trace (1977) F
The Dancing Dodo (1978) F
Golgotha [US: *The Last Trump*] (1980) F
Licensed Renewed (1981) F
The Secret Generations (1985) F
The Secret Houses (1988) F
The Secret Families (1989) F

GARFIELD, Leon (1921–)
British children's writer
Jack Holborn (1964) F CH
Devil-in-the-Fog (1966) F CH
Smith (1967) F CH
Black Jack (1968) F CH
Mr Corbett's Ghost (1968) F CH
The Boy and the Monkey (1969) F CH
The Drummer Boy (1969) F CH
The God Beneath the Sea (1970) F CH
The Strange Affair of Adelaide Harris (1971) F CH
The Ghost Downstairs (1972) F CH
The Golden Shadow (1973) F CH
The Sound of Coaches (1974) F CH
The Prisoners of September (1975) F CH
The Pleasure Garden (1976) F CH
Garfield's Apprentices [series of 12 short novels] (1976–8) F CH
The Confidence Man (1978) F CH
Bostock and Harris (1979) F CH
John Diamond (1980) F CH

'GARIOCH, Robert' [Robert Garioch Sutherland] (1909–1981)
Scottish poet
17 Poems for 6d. in Gaelic, Lowland Scots and English (1940) V
Chuckles on a Cairn (1949) V
The Masque of Edinburgh (1954) V D
The Big Music, and Other Poems (1971) V
Doktor Faust in Rose Street (1973) V

GARLAND, [Hannibal] Hamlin (1860–1940)
American short-story writer and novelist
Main-Travelled Roads (1891) F SS
Jason Edwards: An Average Man (1892) F
A Little Norsk (1892) F
A Member of the Third House (1892) F
A Spoil of Office (1892) F
Prairie Folk (1893) F SS
Crumbling Idols (1894) NF
Rose of Dutcher's Coolly (1895) F
Wayside Courtships (1897) F SS
Boy Life on the Prairie (1899) F SS
The Captain of the Gray-Horse Troop (1902) F
Cavanagh, Forest Ranger (1910) F
Other Main-Travelled Roads (1910) F SS

A Son of the Middle Border (1917) NF
A Daughter of the Middle Border (1921) NF

GARNER, Alan (1934–)
British children's writer
The Weirdstone of Brisingamen (1960) F CH
The Moon of Gomrath (1963) F CH
Elidor (1965) F CH
The Owl Service (1967) F CH
Red Shift (1973) F CH
The Stone Book (1976) F CH

GARNER, Helen (1942–)
Australian novelist and short-story writer
Monkey Grip (1977) F
Honour and Other People's Children [two novellas] (1980) F
Postcards from Surfers (1985) F SS
The Children's Bach (1986) F
Cosmo Cosmolino (1992) F

GARNER, Hugh (1913–1979)
Canadian novelist
Storm Below (1949) F
Cabbagetown [complete text pub. 1968] (1950) F
The Silence on the Shore (1962) F
A Nice Place to Visit (1970) F
The Sin Sniper (1970) F
Death in Don Mills (1975) F
The Intruders (1976) F
Murder Has Your Number (1978) F

GARNETT, David (1892–1981)
British novelist and critic
Lady into Fox (1922) F
A Man in the Zoo (1924) F
The Sailor's Return (1925) F
The Old Dovecote, and Other Stories (1928) F SS
The Grasshoppers Come (1931) F
Beany-Eye (1935) F
The Golden Echo (1953) NF
Aspects of Love (1955) F
The Flowers of the Forest (1955) NF
A Shot in the Dark (1958) F
The Familiar Faces (1962) NF
Ulterior Motives (1966) F

GARNETT, Edward (1868–1936)
British critic, satirist, and playwright
The Breaking Point (1907) D

GARNETT, Eve (1900–1991)
British children's writer
The Family From One End Street (1937) F CH
Further Adventures of the Family From One End Street (1956) F CH
Holiday at Dew Drop Inn (1962) F CH

GARNETT, Richard (1835–1906)
British biographer, poet, and short-story writer
Relics of Shelley (1862) NF
Carlyle (1887) NF
The Twilight of the Gods, and Other Tales (1888) F SS
Iphigenia in Delphi (1890) V
History of Italian Literature (1897) NF
Essays of an Ex-librarian (1901) NF
William Shakespeare, Pedagogue and Poacher (1905) D

GARRICK, David (1717–1779)
British actor and dramatist
The Lying Valet (1741) D
An Essay on Acting (1744) NF
Miss in Her Teens; or, The Medley of Lovers (1747) D
Romeo and Juliet, by Shakespear (1750) D
Every Man in His Humour, by Ben Jonson (1752) D
The Fairies [from Shakespeare's *A Midsummer Night's Dream*] (1755) D
Catherine and Petruchio [from Shakespeare's *The Taming of the Shrew*] (1756) D
The Tempest [from Shakespeare] (1756) D
Lilliput (1757) D
Florizel and Perdita [from Shakespeare's *A Winter's Tale*] (1758) D
The Guardian (1759) D
High Life Below Stairs (1759) D
Cymbeline [from Shakespeare] (1762) D
The Country Girl [from Wycherley] (1766) D
Cymon (1767) D
The Irish Widow (1772) D
Bon Ton; or, High Life Above Stairs (1775) D

GARTH, Sir Samuel (1661–1719)
English physician and poet
The Dispensary (1699) V
A Compleat Key to the Dispensary (1714) NF
Claremont (1715) V

GASCOIGNE, George (1542?–1577)
English poet and miscellaneous author
A Hundreth Sundrie Flowres Bounde up in One Small Poesie (1573) V
The Glasse of Governement (1575) D
The Noble Arte of Venerie or Hunting [from J. de Fouilloux; formerly attrib. to George Turbeville] (1575) NF
The Posies of George Gascoigne Esquire (1575) V
A Delicate Diet, for Daintiemouthde Droonkardes (1576) NF
The Droome of Doomes Day (1576) NF
The Spoyle of Antwerpe (1576?) NF
The Steele Glas: A Satyre; Togither with The Complainte of Phylomene (1576) V

GASCOYNE, David [Emery] (1916–)
British poet, translator, and novelist
Roman Balcony, and Other Poems (1932) V
Opening Day (1933) F
A Short Survey of Surrealism (1935) NF
Man's Life is This Meat (1936) V
Hölderlin's Madness (1938) V
Poems 1937–1942 (1943) V
A Vagrant, and Other Poems (1950) V
Night Thoughts (1956) V
Paris Journal 1937–9 (1978) NF
Journal 1936–1937 (1980) NF

GASKELL, Elizabeth Cleghorn (1810–1865)
British novelist, short-story writer, and biographer
Mary Barton (1848) F
Libbie Marsh's Three Eras (1850) F
The Moorland Cottage (1850) F
Cranford (1853) F
Ruth (1853) F
Lizzie Leigh, and Other Tales (1854) F SS
North and South (1855) F
The Life of Charlotte Brontë (1857) NF
Round the Sofa (1859) F SS
Right at Last, and Other Tales (1860) F SS
Lois the Witch, and Other Tales (1861) F SS
A Dark Night's Work (1863) F SS
Sylvia's Lovers (1863) F
Cousin Phillis, and Other Tales (1865) F SS
The Grey Woman, and Other Tales (1865) F SS
Wives and Daughters (1866) F

GASS, William H[oward] (1924–)
American novelist, short-story writer, and critic
Omensetter's Luck (1966) F
In the Heart of the Heart of the Country (1968) F SS
Fiction and the Figures of Life (1970) NF
Willie Masters' Lonesome Wife (1970) F
On Being Blue (1976) NF
Habitations of the World (1985) NF

GATTY, Margaret, *née* Scott [Mrs Alfred Gatty] (1809–1873)
British children's writer, poet, and editor
The Fairy Godmothers, and Other Tales (1851) F CH
'Worlds Not Realized' (1856) F
The Poor Incumbent (1858) F
Aunt Judy's Tales (1859) F CH
The Human Face Divine, and Other Tales (1860) F CH
Parables from Nature (1861) F CH
Aunt Judy's Letters (1862) NF CH
Red Snow and Other Parables from Nature: Third Series (1862) F CH
Aunt Sally's Life (1865) F CH
Parables from Nature, Third and Fourth Series (1865) F CH
The Book of Sun-Dials (1872) NF CH
The Mother's Book of Poetry (1872) V CH

GATTY, Mrs Alfred *see* MARGARET GATTY

GAUTIER, Théophile (1811–1872)
French poet, novelist, and critic
Albertus (1832) V
Mademoiselle de Maupin (1835) F
La Comédie de la mort ['The Comedy of Death'] (1838) V
Une Larme du diable ['A Tear From the Devil'] (1839) F SS
Caprices et Zig-zags ['Whims and Zig-Zags'] (1845) NF
Wanderings in Spain [*Voyage en Espagne*] (1845) NF
Émaux et camées ['Enamels and Cameos'] (1852) V
La Peau de tigre ['The Tiger's Skin'] (1852) F
Le Capitaine Fracasse (1863) F
La Belle Jenny ['Beautiful Jenny'] (1865) F SS
A Winter in Russia [*Voyage en Russie*] (1866) NF
Histoire du romantisme ['History of Romanticism'] (1874) NF
Portraits et souvenirs littéraires ['Literary Portraits and Recollections'] (1875) NF

'GAWSWORTH, John' [Terence Ian Fytton Armstrong] (1912–1971)
British poet and editor
Poems 1930–32 (1933) V
The Mind of Man (1940) V

GAY, John (1685–1732)
English poet and dramatist
Wine (1708) V
The Present State of Wit (1711) NF
The Mohocks (1712) D
Rural Sports (1713) V
The Wife of Bath (1713) D
The Fan (1714) V
The Shepherd's Week (1714) V
The What D'Ye Call It (1715) D
Three Hours After Marriage (1717) D
Poems on Several Occasions (1720) V
The Captives (1724) D
Fables (1727) V
The Beggar's Opera (1728) D
Polly (1729) D
Acis and Galatea [music by Handel] (1732) D
Achilles (1733) D
Fables: Volume the Second (1738) D
The Distress'd Wife (1743) D
The Rehearsal at Goatham (1754) D

GEE, Maggie [Mary] (1948–)
British novelist and dramatist
Dying, in Other Words (1981) F
The Burning Book (1983) F
Light Years (1985) F
Grace (1988) F
Where Are the Snows? (1991) F
Lost Children (1994) F

GEE, Maurice (1931–)
New Zealand novelist, short-story writer, and children's author
The Big Season (1962) F
In My Father's Den (1972) F
Plumb (1978) F
Meg (1981) F
Sole Survivor (1983) F
Prowlers (1987) F
The Burning Boy (1990) F

GELBART, Larry (1923–)
American stage, radio, television, and film writer
A Funny Thing Happened on the Way to the Forum (1961) D

GELBER, Jack (1932–)
American dramatist
The Connection (1959) D
The Apple (1961) D
Square in the Eye (1966) D

The Cuban Thing (1969) D
Sleep (1972) D
Rehearsal (1976) D
Starters (1980) D

GELLHORN, Martha (1908–)
American war correspondent and novelist
The Trouble I've Seen (1936) F
Two by Two (1958) F SS
The Face of War (1959) NF
Pretty Tales for Tired People (1965) F SS
The Lowest Trees Have Tops (1969) F
Travels with Myself and Another (1979) NF
The Weather in Africa (1980) F

GENET, Jean (1910–1986)
French novelist and dramatist
Our Lady of the Flowers [*Notre-Dame-des-fleurs*] (1944) F
The Maids [*Les Bonnes*] (1946) D
Miracle of the Rose [*Miracle de la rose*] (1946) F
Chants Secrets ['Secret Songs'] (1947) V
Funeral Rites [*Pompes funèbres*] (1947) F
Querelle de Brest (1947) F
Thief's Journal [*Le Journal du voleur*] (1949) NF
The Blacks [*Les Nègres*] (1958) D
The Screens [*Les Paravents*] (1961) D

GEORGE, Henry (1839–1897)
American writer on political economy
Progress and Poverty (1879) NF
The Irish Land Question (1881) NF
Social Problems (1884) NF
Science of Political Economy (1897) NF

GERARD, John (1545–1612)
English herbalist
Herball or Generall Historie of Plantes (1597) NF

GERHARDIE [originally GERHARDI] William [Alexander] (1895–1977)
British novelist
Futility (1922) F
The Polyglots (1925) F
Pretty Creatures (1927) F SS
Jazz and Jasper (1928) F
Pending Heaven (1930) F
Memoirs of a Polyglot (1931) NF
Resurrection (1934) F
Of Mortal Love (1936) F
My Wife's the Least of It (1938) F

GIBBON, Edward (1737–1794)
British historian
Critical Observations on the Sixth Book of the Aeneid (1770) NF
The History of the Decline and Fall of the Roman Empire [vol. i] (1776) NF
A Vindication of Some Passages in the Fifteenth and Sixteenth Chapters of the History of the Decline and Fall of the Roman Empire (1779) NF
The History of the Decline and Fall of the Roman Empire [vols. ii, iii] (1781) NF
The History of the Decline and Fall of the Roman Empire [vols. iv, v, vi] (1788) NF
Miscellaneous Works (1796) NF

GIBBONS, Stella [Dorothea] (1902–1989)
British novelist, short-story writer, and poet
The Mountain Beast, and Other Poems (1930) V
Cold Comfort Farm (1932) F
Bassett (1934) F
Roaring Tower, and Other Short Stories (1937) F
The Lowland Venus, and Other Poems (1938) V
Christmas at Cold Comfort Farm, and Other Stories (1940) F SS
Ticky (1943) F
Westwood; or, The Gentle Powers [US: *The Gentle Powers*] (1946) F
Conference at Cold Comfort Farm (1949) F
The Swiss Summer (1951) F
Here Be Dragons (1956) F
The Charmers (1965) F
Starlight (1967) F
The Woods in Winter (1970) F

GIBRAN, Kahlil (1883–1931)
Lebanese-born American poet and spiritual writer
The Prophet (1923) NF

GIBSON, Wilfrid [Wilson] (1878–1962)
British poet
The Stonefolds (1907) V
Fires (1912) V
Borderlands (1914) V
Battle (1915) V
Friends (1916) V
Livelihood (1917) V
Krindlesdyke (1922) V D
The Golden Room, and Other Poems (1928) V
Hazard (1930) V

GIBSON, William [Ford] (1948–)
American science fiction writer
Neuromancer (1984) F
Burning Chrome (1986) F
Count Zero (1986) F
Mona Lisa Overdrive (1988) F
Virtual Light (1993) F

GIDE, André [Paul-Guillaume] (1869–1951)
French novelist, essayist, critic, and dramatist
Les Cahiers d'André Walter (1891) F
Saül (1896) D
The Immoralist [*L'Immoraliste*] (1902) F
Strait is the Gate [*La Porte étroite*] (1909) F
The Vatican Swindle [*Les Caves du Vatican*] (1914) F
Two Symphonies [*La Symphonie pastorale*] (1919) F
The Counterfeiters [*Les Faux-Monnayeurs*] (1926) F
Voyage au Congo (1927) NF
Retour du Tchad ['Return to Chad'] (1928) NF
L'École des femmes (1929) F
Oedipe (1930) D
Robert (1930) F
Retour d l'URSS ['Return to the USSR'] (1937) NF
Thésée (1946) F

GIESEL, Theodor *see* 'DR SEUSS'

GIFFORD, William (1756–1826)
British critic and satirist
The Baviad (1791) V
The Maeviad (1795) V
Epistle to Peter Pindar (1800) V
The Satires of Juvenal (1802) V
The Satires of Persius (1821) V
Autobiography (1827) V

GILBERT, Martin [John] (1936–)
British biographer and historian
The European Powers, 1900–1945 (1965) NF
Sir Winston Churchill (1966–88) NF
The Emergence of Jewish Statehood (1978) NF
The Holocaust (1986) NF
The First World War (1993) NF

GILBERT, Sir Humphrey (1539?–1583)
English navigator
A Discourse of a Discoverie for a New Passage to Cataia (1576) NF

GILBERT, William (1544–1603)
English physician and scientist
De Magnete [in Latin] (1600) NF

GILBERT, [Sir] W[illiam] S[chwenck] (1836–1911)
British dramatist, librettist, and lyricist
The 'Bab' Ballads (1869) V
More 'Bab' Ballads (1873) V
Trial by Jury [music by Sir Arthur Sullivan] (1875) D
HMS Pinafore; or, The Lass That Loved a Sailor [music by Sir Arthur Sullivan] (1878) D
The Pirates of Penzance; or, The Slave of Duty [music by Sir Arthur Sullivan] (1879) D
Patience; or, Bunthorne's Bride [music by Sir Arthur Sullivan] (1881) D
Princess Ida; or, Castle Adamant [music by Sir Arthur Sullivan] (1884) D
Iolanthe; or, The Peer and the Peri [music by Sir Arthur Sullivan] (1885) D
The Mikado; or, The Town of Titipu [music by Sir Arthur Sullivan] (1885) D
Ruddigore; or, The Witch's Curse [music by Sir Arthur Sullivan] (1887) D
The Gondoliers; or, The King of Barataria [music by Sir Arthur Sullivan] (1889) D
Songs of a Savoyard (1890) V

GILCHRIST, Alexander (1828–1861)
British biographer
Life of Blake (1863) NF

GILCHRIST, Ellen (1935–)
American short-story writer and novelist
In the Land of Dreamy Dreams (1981) F SS
The Annunciation (1983) F
Victory Over Japan (1984) F SS
Drunk with Love (1986) F SS
The Anna Papers (1989) F
Light Can Be Both Wave and Particle (1989) F SS
I Cannot Get You Close Enough [novellas] (1990) F

GILCHRIST, Robert Murray (1868–1917)
British journalist and regional novelist
A Peakland Faggot (1897) F SS
Willowbrake (1898) F
Nicholas and Mary (1899) F
The Courtesy Dame (1900) F
Natives of Milton (1902) F SS

GILDON, Charles (1665–1724)
English dramatist, critic, and poet
Miscellany Poems upon Several Occasions (1692) V
Chorus Poetarum; or, Poems on Several Occasions (1694) V
The Roman Brides Revenge (1697) D
Phaeton; or, The Fatal Divorce (1698) D
A Grammar of the English Tongue (1699) NF
The Lives and Characters of the English Dramatick Poets (1699) NF
Measure for Measure; or, Beauty the Best Advocate [from Shakespeare] (1699) D
Love's Victim; or, the Queen of Wales (1701) D
A New Miscellany of Original Poems, on Several Occasions (1701) V
A Comparison Between the Two Stages (1702) NF
Examen Miscellaneum, Consisting of Verse and Prose (1702) MISC
The Patriot; or, The Italian Conspiracy [from Nathaniel Lee's *Lucius Junius Brutus* (1681)] (1703) D
The Deist's Manual; or, A Rational Enquiry into the Christian Religion (1705) NF
Libertas Triumphans (1708) V
The New Metamorphosis [trn of *The Golden Ass* by Apuleius] (1708) NF
The Golden Spy; or, A Political Journal of the British Nights Entertainment (1709) NF
The Life of Mr Thomas Betterton (1710) NF
A New Rehearsal; or, Bays the Younger (1714) NF
Canon; or, The Vision (1717) V
The Complete Art of Poetry (1718) NF
Memoirs of the Life of William Wycherley (1718) NF
The Life and Strange Surprizing Adventures of Mr D[aniel] DeF[oe], of London, Hosier (1719) NF
All for the Better; or, The World Turn'd Upside Down (1720) V

GILFILLAN, George (1813–1878)
Scottish Dissenting minister, poet, and critic
A Gallery of Literary Portraits [2nd ser., 1850; 3rd ser., 1854] (1845) NF

GILLETTE, William [Hooker] (1855–1937)
American actor and dramatist
Esmerelda (1881) D
The Private Secretary (1881) D
Held by the Enemy (1886) D
Too Much Johnson (1894) D
Secret Service (1895) D

Sherlock Holmes [adaptation of Conan Doyle stories] (1899) D
Clarice (1905) D

GILLIATT, Penelope [Ann Douglass] (1932–1993)
British novelist, short-story writer, dramatist, and film critic
One by One (1965) F
A State of Change (1967) F
What's It Like Out? and Other Stories (1968) F SS
Nobody's Business (1972) F SS
Splendid Lives (1977) F SS
The Cutting Edge (1978) F SS
Mortal Matters (1983) F SS
They Sleep Without Dreaming (1985) F SS
A Woman of Singular Occupation (1988) F
Luigo (1990) F SS

GILMAN, Charlotte Perkins (1860–1935)
American feminist author and novelist
'The Yellow Wallpaper' [*New England Magazine*] (May 1892)
This Our World (1893) V
Women and Economics (1898) NF
Concerning Children (1900) NF
The Home (1904) NF
Man Made World (1911) NF
Moving the Mountain (1911) F
Herland (1915) F
With Her in Ourland (1916) F
His Religion and Hers (1923) NF
The Living of Charlotte Perkins Gilman (1935) NF

GILPIN, William (1724–1804)
British topographical author
Lectures on the Catechism of the Church of England (1779) NF
Observations on the River Wye, and Several Parts of South Wales, &c (1782) NF
Observations, Relative Chiefly to Picturesque Beauty . . . Particularly the Mountains, and Lakes of Cumberland, and Westmoreland (1786) NF
Observations, Relative Chiefly to Picturesque Beauty . . . Particularly the High-lands of Scotland (1789) NF
An Exposition of the New Testament (1790) NF
Remarks on Forest Scenery and Other Woodland Views (Relative Chiefly to Picturesque Beauty) (1791) NF
Three Essays on Picturesque Beauty (1792) NF
Picturesque Remarks on Western Parts of England and the Isle of Wight (1798) NF

GINSBERG, Allen (1926–)
American poet and non-fiction writer
Howl, and Other Poems (1956) V
Empty Mirror (1960) V
Reality Sandwiches (1963) V
The Yage Letters [correspondence with William S. Burroughs] (1963) NF
Ankor Wat (1968) V
Planet News (1968) V
Indian Journals (1970) NF
The Fall of America: Poems of These States (1973) V
The Gates of Wrath (1973) V
Iron Horse (1973) V
Allen Verbatim (1974) NF
The Vision of the Great Rememberer (1974) NF
First Blues (1975) V
Sad Dust Glories (1975) V
As Ever (1977) NF
Journals (1977) NF
Mind Breaths (1977) V
Composed on the Tongue (1980) NF
Straight Hearts's Delight (1980) NF
Plutonian Ode (1981) V
White Shroud (1986) V

GIRALDUS *see* William Allingham

GIRAUDOUX, Jean (1882–1944)
French diplomat, novelist, and dramatist
Provinciales (1909) F
Retour d'Alsace, août 1914 ['Return from Alsace in August 1914'] (1916) NF
Simon le pathétique (1918) F
Bella (1926) F
Siegfried (1928) D
Amphitryon 38 (1929) D
Judith (1931) D
Intermezzo (1933) D
La Guerre de Troie n'aura pas lieu [tr. 1955 by Christopher Fry as *Tiger at the Gate*] (1935) D
Électre (1937) D
Ondine (1939) D
Sodom et Gomorrhe (1943) D
The Madwoman of Chaillot [*La Folle de Chaillot*] (1945) D
Pour Lucrèce [tr. 1958 by Christopher Fry as *Duel of Angels*] (1953) D

GISSING, George [Robert] (1857–1903)
British novelist
Workers in the Dawn (1880) F
The Unclassed (1884) F
Demos (1886) F
Isabel Clarendon (1886) F
Thyrza (1887) F
A Life's Morning (1888) F
The Nether World (1889) F
The Emancipated (1890) F
New Grub Street (1891) F
Born in Exile (1892) F
Denzil Quarrier (1892) F
The Odd Women (1893) F
In the Year of the Jubilee (1894) F
Eve's Ransom (1895) F
The Paying Guest (1895) F
Sleeping Fires (1895) F
The Whirlpool (1897) F
Charles Dickens (1898) NF
Human Odds and Ends (1898) F SS
The Town Traveller (1898) F
The Crown of Life (1899) F
By the Ionian Sea (1901) NF
Our Friend the Charlatan (1901) F
The Private Papers of Henry Ryecroft (1903) F
Veranilda [incomplete] (1904) F

Will Warburton (1905) F
The House of Cobwebs, and Other Stories (1906) F SS

GITTINGS, Robert [William Victor] (1911–1992)
British poet and biographer
The Roman Road, and Other Poems (1932) V
John Keats (1968) NF
American Journey (1972) V
Young Thomas Hardy (1975) NF
The Nature of Biography (1978) NF
The Older Hardy (1979) NF
Claire Clairmont and the Shelleys (1992) NF

GLADSTONE, William Ewart (1809–1898)
British statesman and author
The State in its Relations with the Church (1838) NF
Studies on Homer and the Homeric Age (1858) NF
The Odes of Horace (1894) V

GLANVILL, Joseph (1636–1680)
English philosopher and theologian
The Vanity of Dogmatizing (1661) NF
Lux Orientalis; or, An Enquiry (1662) NF
Plus Ultra; or, The Progress and Advancement of Knowledge Since the Days of Aristotle (1668) NF
Logoi Threskia; or, A Seasonable Recommendation and Defence of Reason in the Affairs of Religion Against Infidelity (1670) NF
The Way of Happiness (1670) NF
Philosophia Pia; or, A Discourse of the Religious Temper of the Experimental Philosophy (1671) NF
An Earnest Invitation (1673) NF
Essays on Several Important Subjects (1676) NF
An Essay Concerning Preaching (1678) NF
A Seasonable Defence of Preaching, and the Plain Way of It (1678) NF
Saducismus Triumphatus; or, Full and Plain Evidence Witches and Apparitions (1681) NF

GLASGOW, Ellen [Anderson Gholson] (1874–1945)
American novelist
The Descendant (1897) F
The Voice of the People (1900) F
The Battle-Ground (1902) F
The Freeman, and Other Poems (1902) V
The Deliverance (1904) F
The Wheel of Life (1906) F
The Ancient Law (1908) F
The Romance of a Plain Man (1909) F
The Miller of Old Church (1911) F
In Virginia (1913) F
Life and Gabriella (1916) F
The Builders (1919) F
One Man in His Time (1922) F
The Shadowy Third (1923) F SS
Barren Ground (1925) F
The Romantic Comedians (1926) F
They Stooped to Folly (1929) F
The Sheltered Life (1932) F
In Vein of Iron (1935) F
In This Our Life (1941) F

GLENDINNING, Victoria (1937–)
British biographer and novelist
Vita (1983) NF
Rebecca West (1987) NF
The Grown Ups (1989) F
Anthony Trollope (1992) NF
Electricity (1995) F
Jonathan Swift (1998) NF

GLOVER, Denis (1912–1980)
New Zealand poet
Six Easy Ways of Dodging Debt Collectors (1936) V
Sings Harry (1951) V
Arawata Bill (1953) V
Since Then (1957) V

GLOVER, Richard (1712–1785)
British poet and dramatist
Leonidas (1737) V
London; or, The Progress of Commerce (1739) V
Boadicea (1753) D
Medea (1761) D
The Athenaid (1787) V

GLYN, Elinor, *née* Sutherland (1864–1943)
British novelist
The Visits of Elizabeth (1900) F
The Reflections of Ambrosine (1902) F
The Damsel and the Sage (1903) F
The Vicissitudes of Evangeline (1905) F
Beyond the Rocks (1906) F
Three Weeks (1907) F
Elizabeth Visits America (1909) F
His Hour (1910) F
Halcyone (1912) F
The Contrast, and Other Stories (1913) F SS
The Career of Katherine Bush (1917) F
Man and Maid—Renaissance (1922) F
Six Days (1924) F
It, and Other Stories (1927) F SS
Saint or Satyr? and Other Stories [US: *Such Men Are Dangerous*] (1933) F SS
Did She? (1934) F
Romantic Adventure (1936) NF
The Third Eye (1940) F

GODDEN, [Margaret] Rumer (1907–1998)
British novelist and children's writer
Black Narcissus (1939) F
Gypsy, Gypsy (1940) F
A Fugue in Time (1945) F
The River (1946) F
A Candle for St Jude (1948) F
A Breath of Air (1950) F
The Greengage Summer (1958) F
The Battle of the Villa Fiorita (1963) F
In This House of Brede (1969) F
The Peacock Spring (1975) F
Thursday's Children (1984) F
A Time to Dance, No Time to Weep (1987) NF
A House with Four Rooms (1989) NF
Coromandel Sea Change (1991) F

Pippa Passes (1994) F
Cromartie v the God Shiva (1997) F

GODWIN, William (1756–1836)
British philosopher and novelist
Damon and Delia (1784) F
Imogen (1784) F
Italian Letters; or, The History of the Count de St Julian (1784) F
An Enquiry Concerning the Principles of Political Justice (1793) NF
Things as They Are; or, The Adventures of Caleb Williams (1794) F
The Enquirer (1797) NF
St Leon (1799) F
Antonio (1800) D
Thoughts Occasioned by Dr Parr's Spital Sermon (1801) NF
Life of Geoffrey Chaucer, the Early English Poet (1803) NF
Fables Ancient and Modern (1805) NF CH
Fleetwood; or, The New Man of Feeling (1805) F
Faulkener (1807) D
Essay on Sepulchres (1809) NF
Letters of Verax to the Editors of the Morning Chronicle (1815) NF
Mandeville (1817) F
Letters of Advice to a Young American (1818) NF
Of Population (1820) NF
History of the Commonwealth of England (1824) NF
Cloudesley (1830) F
Thoughts on Man, his Nature, Productions and Discoveries (1831) NF
Deloraine (1833) F
Lives of the Necromancers (1834) NF

GOETHE, Johann Wolfgang von (1749–1832)
German poet, novelist, and dramatist
Götz of Berlichingen with the Iron Hand [*Götz von Berlichingen mit der eisernen Hand*] (1773) D
Clavigo (1774) D
The Sorrows of Young Werther [*Die Leiden des jungen Werther*] (1774) F
Iphigenia inTauris [*Iphigenie auf Tauris*] (1787) D
Egmont (1788) D
Torquato Tasso (1790) D
Reynard the Fox [*Reineke Fuchs*] (1794) V
Roman Elegies [*Römische Elegien*; in Schiller's *Die Horen*] (1795) V
Wilhelm Meister's Apprenticeship [*Wilhelm Meisters Lehrjahre*] (1795) F
Hermann und Dorothea (1797) V
The Natural Daughter [*Die natürliche Tochter*] (1803) D
Faust [pt. i; pt. ii pub. 1832] (1808) D
Elective Affinities [*Die Wahlverwandtschaften*] (1809) F
Poetry and Truth [*Dichtung und Wahreit*; autobiography] (1811–33) NF
Der west-östliche Divan ['East-West Divan'] (1819) V
Wilhelm Meister's Travels [*Wilhelm Meisters Wanderjahre*] (1821) F

GOFFE, Thomas (1591–1629)
English dramatist
The Raging Turke; or, Bajazet the Second (1631) D
The Couragious Turke; or, Amurath the First (1632) D
The Tragedy of Orestes (1633) D
The Careless Shepherdess (1656) D

GOGARTY, Oliver St John (1878–1957)
Irish poet and author
The Ship, and Other Poems (1918) V
An Offering of Swans (1923) V
Wild Apples (1928) V
As I Was Going Down Sackville Street (1937) NF
Others to Adorn (1938) V
Elbow Room (1939) V
Tumbling in the Hay (1939) F
Perennial (1946) V
It Isn't This Time of Year at All! (1954) NF

GOGOL, Nikolai Vasilevich (1809–1952)
Russian novelist and short-story writer
Evenings on a Farm Near Dikanka (1831–2) F SS
Arabesques (1835) F SS
Mirgorod (1835) F SS
Revizor (1836) D
Dead Souls (1842) F

GOLD, Herbert (1924–)
American novelist
Birth of a Hero (1951) F
The Prospect Before Us (1954) F
The Man Who Was Not With It (1956) F
The Optimist (1959) F
Love and Like (1960) F SS
Therefore Be Bold (1960) F
Salt (1963) F
Fathers (1967) F
The Great American Jackpot (1969) F
The Magic Will (1971) F SS
My Last Two Thousand Years (1972) NF
Swiftie the Magician (1974) F
Waiting for Cordelia (1977) F
He/She (1980) F
Family (1981) F
True Love (1982) F
Mister White Eyes (1984) F
Stories of Misbegotten Love (1985) F SS
Lovers and Cohorts (1986) F SS
Dreaming (1988) F
Travels in San Francisco (1990) F SS

'GOLD, Michael' [Irwin Granich] (1894–1967)
American journalist and novelist
120 Million (1929) F SS
Jews Without Money (1930) F
Change the World (1937) NF

GOLDING, Arthur (1536–1606)
English translator
The Abridgement of the Histories of Trogus Pompeius (1564) NF
Caesar: Gallic Wars (1565) NF

Metamorphosis [from Ovid; bks i–iv] (1565) V
Metamorphosis [from Ovid; bks i–xv] (1567) V
A Tragedie of Abrahams Sacrifice [from Theodore Beza] (1577) D
The Trewnesse of the Christian Religion [from Philippe de Mornay; trn begun by Sir Philip Sydney] (1587) NF

GOLDING, [Sir] William [Gerald] (1911–1993)
British novelist, dramatist, and poet
Lord of the Flies (1954) F
The Inheritors (1955) F
Pincher Martin [US: *The Two Deaths of Christopher Martin*] (1956) F
The Brass Butterfly (1958) D
Free Fall (1959) F
The Spire (1964) F
The Hot Gates, and Other Occasional Pieces (1965) NF
The Pyramid (1967) F
The Scorpion God (1971) F SS
Darkness Visible (1979) F
Rites of Passage (1980) F
A Moving Target (1982) NF
The Paper Men (1984) F
An Egyptian Journal (1985) NF
Close Quarters (1987) F
Fire Down Below (1989) F
The Double Tongue (1995) NF

GOLDSMITH, Oliver (1728–1774)
British poet, dramatist, novelist, and essayist
The Memoirs of a Protestant, Condemned to the Galleys of France, for his Religion [trn from Jean Marteilhe] (1758) NF
The Bee (1759) NF
The Critical Review; or, Annals of Literature (1759) NF
An Enquiry into the Present State of Polite Learning in Europe (1759) NF
The Citizen of the World; or, Letters From a Chinese Philosopher Residing in London to his Friends in the East (1760) F
The Life of Richard Nash, of Bath (1762) NF
An History of England (1764) NF
An History of the Lives and Deaths of the Most Eminent Martyrs (1764) NF
Essays (1765) NF
The Traveller; or, A Prospect of Society (1765) V
The Vicar of Wakefield (1766) F
Poems for Young Ladies (1767) V
The Good Natur'd Man (1768) D
The Present State of the British Empire (1768) NF
The Roman History (1769) NF
The Deserted Village (1770) V
Life of Henry St John, Lord Viscount Bolingbroke (1770) NF
The Life of Thomas Parnell (1770) NF
The History of England (1771) NF
Threnodia Augustalis (1772) V
She Stoops to Conquer; or, The Mistakes of a Night (1773) D
The Grecian History (1774) NF
An History of the Earth and Animated Nature (1774) NF
Retaliation (1774) V
The Haunch of Venison (1776) V
A Survey of Experimental Philosophy (1776) NF

GOMBRICH, [Sir] E[rnst] H[ans Josef] (1909–)
Austrian-born British art historian
The Story of Art (1950) NF

GONCHAROV, Ivan Aleksandrovich (1812–1891)
Russian novelist
An Ordinary Story (1847) F
Oblomov (1859) F
The Ravine (1869) F

GONCOURT, Edmond de (1822–1896)
French novelist
Elisa [*La File Élisa*] (1878) F
Chérie (1885) F

GONCOURT, Edmond de (1822–1896) and **Jules de** (1830–1870)
French novelists
En 18.. (1851) F
Les Hommes de lettres ['The Men of Letters'] (1860) F
Sister Philomène [*Soeur Philomène*] (1861) F
Germinie Lacerteux (1864) F
Renée Mauperin (1864) F
Manette Salomon (1867) F
Charles Demailly (1868) F
Madame Gervaisais (1869) F

GOOGE, Barnaby (1540–1594)
English poet
The Zodiac of Life [bks i-iii; from Palingenius] (1560) V
The Zodiac of Life [bks i–vi] (1561) V
Eglogs, Epytaphes, and Sonettes (1563) V
The Zodiac of Life [bks i–xii] (1565) V
The Ship of Safeguard (1569) V
The Popish Kingdome, or Reigne of Antichrist [from Thomas Kirchmeyer] (1570) V
Foure Bookes of Husbandry [from Conrad Heresbach] (1577) V

GORDIMER, Nadine (1923–)
South African novelist and short-story writer
Face to Face (1949) F SS
The Lying Days (1953) F
A World of Strangers (1958) F
Occasion for Loving (1963) F
The Late Bourgeois World (1966) F
A Guest of Honour (1970) F
The Conservationist (1974) F
Burger's Daughter (1979) F
July's People (1981) F
A Sport of Nature (1987) F

GORDON, Adam Lindsay (1833–1870)
Australian poet
The Feud (1864) V
Ashtaroth (1867) V

Sea Spray and Smoke Drift (1867) V
Bush Ballads and Galloping Rhymes (1870) V

GORDON, Caroline (1895–1981)
American novelist and short-story writer
Penhally (1931) F
Aleck Maury, Sportsman (1934) F
The Garden of Adonis (1937) F
None Shall Look Back (1937) F
Green Centuries (1941) F
The Women on the Porch (1944) F
The Forest of the South (1945) F SS
The Strange Children (1951) F
The Malefactors (1956) F
How to Read a Novel (1957) NF
Old Red (1963) F SS
The Glory of Hera (1972) F

GORE, Mrs C[atherine Grace] F[rances], *née* Moody (1799–1861)
British novelist and dramatist
Romances of Real Life (1829) F
Women As They Are; or, The Manners of the Day (1830) F
Mothers and Daughters (1831) F
Pin-Money (1831) F
The Opera (1832) F
The Hamiltons; or, The New Era (1834) F
Mrs Armytage; or, Female Domination (1836) F
Stokeshill Place; or, The Man of Business (1837) F
The Woman of the World (1838) F
The Cabinet Minister (1839) F
The Dowager; or, The New School for Scandal (1840) F
Preferment; or, My Uncle the Earl (1840) F
Cecil; or, The Adventures of a Coxcomb (1841) F
Cecil a Peer (1841) F
Greville; or, A Season in Paris (1841) F
The Ambassador's Wife (1842) F
The Man of Fortune, and Other Tales (1842) F SS
The Banker's Wife; or, Court and City (1843) F
The Birthright, and Other Tales (1844) F SS
The Débutante; or, The London Season (1846) F
Men of Capital (1846) F
Peers and Parvenus (1846) F
Sketches of English Character (1846) F
Temptation and Atonement, and Other Tales (1847) F SS
The Dean's Daughter; or, The Days We Live In (1853) F
Progress and Prejudice (1854) F
Mammon; or, The Hardships of an Heiress (1855) F
The Bride of Zante, and Other Tales (1861) F SS

GORENKO, Anna Andreevna *see* ANNA AKHMATOVA

GORGES, Sir Arthur (1577?–1625)
English poet and translator
Pharsalia [Lucan] (1614) V

GORKY, Maxim [Aleksei Maksimovich Peshkov] (1868–1936)
Russian novelist and dramatist
Makar Chudra (1892) F
Chelkash (1895) F
Foma Gordeyev (1899) F
Twenty-Six Men and a Girl (1899) F
The Lower Depths (1902) D
Philistines (1902) D
Konovalov (1903) F
The Mother (1907) F
Childhood (1913) F
Among People (1915) F
The Life of a Useless Man (1917) F
My Universities (1923) F
The Artamonov Business (1925) F
The Life of Klim Samgin (1925–36) F

GOSSE, Sir Edmund [William] (1849–1928)
British critic, biographer, and poet
New Poems (1879) V
Studies in the Literature of Northern Europe (1879) NF
Gray (1882) NF
Seventeenth-Century Studies (1883) NF
A History of Eighteenth-Century Literature 1660–1780 (1889) NF
The Life of Philip Henry Gosse (1890) NF
Gossip in a Library (1891) NF
The Secret of Narcisse (1892) F
In Russet and Silver (1894) V
The Jacobean Poets (1894) NF
Jeremy Taylor (1903) NF
Sir Thomas Browne (1905) NF
Father and Son (1907) NF
The Autumn Garden (1908) V
The Collected Poems of Edmund Gosse (1911) V
Portraits and Sketches (1912) NF
The Future of English Poetry (1913) NF
Inter Arma (1916) NF
Leaves and Fruit (1927) NF

GOSSE, Philip Henry (1810–1888)
British zoologist
Rambles on the Devonshire Coast (1853) NF
The Romance of Natural History (1860) NF
Playes Confuted in Five Actions (1582) NF

GOSSON, Stephen (1554–1624)
English pamphleteer
The Ephemerides of Phialo (1579) F
The Schoole of Abuse (1579) NF

GOUDGE, Elizabeth (1900–1984)
British novelist
Island Magic (1934) F
A City of Bells (1936) F
Towers in the Mist (1938) F
The Bird in the Tree (1940) F
Green Dolphin Country (1944) F
The Herb of Grace (1948) F
Gentian Hill (1949) F
The Heart of the Family (1953) F
The Child From the Sea (1970) F

GOULD, Nathaniel (1857–1919)
British sporting novelist
The Double Event (1891) F
The Dark Horse (1899) F
The Chance of a Lifetime (1907) F
A Fortune at Stake (1913) F

GOWER, John (c. 1330–1408)
English poet
Confessio Amantis (1390) V

GOWERS, Sir Ernest [Arthur] (1880–1966)
British civil servant and grammarian
Plain Words (1948) NF
ABC of Plain Words (1951) NF

GRAFTON, Sue (1940–)
American crime novelist
Keziah (1967) F
The Lolly Madonna War (1969) F
'A' is for Alibi (1982) F
'B' is for Burglar (1985) F
'C' is for Corpse (1986) F
'D' is for Deadbeat (1987) F
'E' is for Evidence (1988) F
'F' is for Fugitive (1989) F
'G' is for Gumshoe (1990) F
'J' is for Judgment (1993) F
'K' is for Killer (1994) F
'L' is for Lawless (1996) F
'M' is for Malice (1996) F
'N' is for Noose (1998) F
'O' is for Outlaw (1999) F

GRAHAM, Robert Bontine Cunninghame (1852–1936)
Scottish politician, traveller, and author
Mogreb-el-Acksa (1898) NF
The Ipané (1899) MISC
Thirteen Stories (1900) F SS
Success (1902) F SS
Progress, and Other Sketches (1905) F SS
Faith (1909) F SS
Hope (1910) F SS
Charity (1912) F SS
Scottish Stories (1914) F SS

GRAHAM, W[illiam] S[ydney] (1918–1986)
Scottish poet
Cage Without Grievance (1942) V
The Seven Journeys (1944) V
Second Poems (1945) V
The White Threshold (1949) V
The Nightfishing (1955) V
That Ye Inherit (1968) V
Malcolm Mooney's Land (1970) V
Implements in Their Places (1977) V
Collected Poems 1942–1977 (1979) V

GRAHAM, Winston [Mawdsley] (1910–)
British novelist and creator of the Poldark series
Ross Poldark (1945) F
Marnie (1961) F

GRAHAME, Kenneth (1859–1932)
British children's author and essayist
Pagan Papers (1893) MISC
The Golden Age (1895) F SS
Dream Days (1898) F SS
The Wind in the Willows (1908) F CH

GRAINGER, Francis Edward *see* HEADON HILL

GRAINGER, James (1721–1766)
Scottish physician and poet
Ode on Solitude (1755) V
The Sugar-Cane (1764) V

'GRAND, Sarah' [Frances Elizabeth Bellenden McFall] *née* Clarke (1854–1943)
British novelist
Ideala (1888) F
The Heavenly Twins (1893) F

GRANGE, John (*c.* 1577–1611)
English poet
The Golden Aphroditis (1577) MISC

GRANICH, Irwin *see* MICHAEL GOLD

GRANT, James (1822–1887)
British novelist
Sketches in London (1838) F
The Romance of War; or, The Highlanders in Spain (1846) F
Adventures of an Aide-de-Camp; or, A Campaign in Calabria (1848) F
The Scottish Cavalier (1850) F
Bothwell; or, The Days of Mary Queen of Scots (1851) F
Jane Seton; or, The King's Advocate (1853) F
Philip Rollo; or, The Scottish Musketeers (1854) F
Frank Hilton; or, The Queen's Own (1855) F
The Yellow Frigate; or, The Three Sisters (1855) F
Harry Ogilvie; or, The Black Dragoons (1856) F
The Phantom Regiment; or, Stories of 'Ours' (1856) F
The Constable of France, and Other Military Historiettes (1866) F SS
First Love and Last Love (1868) F
The Cameronians (1881) F
Derval Hampton (1881) F
Miss Cheyne of Essilmont (1883) F
Colville of the Guards (1885) F
Playing with Fire (1887) F
The Madras House (1910) D
Rococo; Vote by Ballot; Farewell to the Theatre (1917) D
The Exemplary Theatre (1922) NF
Prefaces to the Players' Shakespeare (1923) NF
The Secret Life (1923) D
Prefaces to Shakespeare (1927) NF
His Majesty (1928) D
On Dramatic Method (1931) NF

GRANVILLE-BARKER, Harley (1877–1946)
British critic and actor
The Marrying of Ann Leete (1902) D
The Voysey Inheritance (1905) D
Waste (1907) D

GRASS, Günter [Wilhelm] (1927–)
German novelist and socialist
The Tin Drum [*Die Blechtrommel*] (1959) F
Cat and Mouse [*Katz und Maus*] (1961) F
Dog Years [*Hundejahre*] (1963) F
Local Anaesthetic [*Örtlich betäubt*] (1969) F
From the Diary of a Snail (1972) F
The Flounder [*Der Butt*] (1977) F
The Meeting at Telgte [*Das Treffen in Telgte*] (1979) F
The Rats [*Die Ratten*] (1987) F
The Call of the Toad [*Die Unkenrufe*] (1992) F
Wide Field (1995) F

GRAU, Shirley Ann (1929–)
American novelist and short-story writer
The Black Prince (1955) F SS
The Hard Blue Sky (1958) F
The House on Coliseum Street (1961) F
The Keepers of the House (1964) F
The Condor Passes (1971) F
Evidence of Love (1974) F

GRAVES, A[lfred] P[ercival] (1846–1931)
Irish essayist, poet, editor, and songwriter
Songs of Old Ireland (1882) V
Songs of Erin (1892) V
Irish Literary and Musical Studies (1913) NF
A Celtic Psaltery (1917) V
Songs of the Gael (1925) V
To Return to All That (1930) NF

GRAVES, Clo[tilde Inez Mary] ['Richard Dehan'] (1863–1932)
British novelist, journalist, and dramatist
Dragon's Teeth (1891) F
Maids in a Market Garden (1894) F
The Dop Doctor [as 'Richard Dehan'] (1896) F
A Well-Meaning Woman (1896) F
A Mother of Three (1909) D
The Headquarter Recruit, and Other Stories [as 'Richard Dehan'] (1913) F SS
The Cost of Wings, and Other Stories [as 'Richard Dehan'] (1914) F SS
Earth to Earth [as 'Richard Dehan'] (1916) F
A Sailors' Home, and Other Stories [as 'Richard Dehan'] (1919) F SS

GRAVES, Richard (1715–1804)
British poet and novelist
The Love of Order (1773) V
The Spiritual Quixote (1773) F
The Progress of Gallantry (1774) V
Euphrosyne; or, Amusements on the Road of Life [vol. i] (1776) V
Columella; or, The Distressed Anchoret (1779) F
Eugenius; or, Anecdotes of the Golden Vale (1785) F
Lucubrations (1786) MISC
Plexippus; or, The Aspiring Plebeian (1790) F

GRAVES, Robert [von Ranke] (1895–1985)
British poet, novelist, critic, and translator
Over the Brazier (1916) V
Fairies and Fusiliers (1917) V
Country Sentiment (1920) V
The Pier-Glass (1921) V
Whipperginny (1923) V
The Meaning of Dreams (1924) NF
Mock Beggar Hall (1924) MISC
John Kemp's Wager (1925) V D
My Head! My Head! (1925) F
Poetic Unreason, and Other Studies (1925) NF
Welchman's Hose (1925) V
Another Future of Poetry (1926) NF
Lars Porsena; or, The Future of Swearing and Improper Language (1927) NF
Lawrence and the Arabs (1927) NF
Poems 1914–26 (1927) V
A Survey of Modernist Poetry (1927) NF
Mrs Fisher; or, The Future of Humour (1928) NF
Goodbye to All That (1929) NF
The Shout (1929) F
But It Still Goes On (1930) NF
Poems 1926–1930 (1931) V
Poems 1930–1933 (1933) V
The Real David Copperfield (1933) F
Claudius the God and his Wife Messalina (1934) F
I, Claudius (1934) F
Count Belisarius (1938) F
Sergeant Lamb of the Ninth [US: *Serjeant Lamb's America*] (1940) F
Proceed, Sergeant Lamb (1941) F
The Story of Marie Powell, Wife to Mr Milton [US: *Wife to Mr Milton*] (1943) F
The Golden Fleece [US: *Hercules, My Shipmate*] (1944) F
King Jesus (1946) F
Poems 1938–1945 (1946) V
The White Goddess (1948) NF
The Common Asphodel (1949) NF
Seven Days in New Crete (1949) F
Poems and Satires (1951) V
Poems 1953 (1953) V
The Greek Myths (1955) NF
Homer's Daughter (1955) F
The Penny Fiddle (1960) V CH
More Poems (1961) V
New Poems (1962) V
Oxford Addresses on Poetry (1962) NF
Ann at Highwood Hall (1964) V CH
Man Does, Woman Is (1964) V
Majorca Observed (1965) NF
Mammon and the Black Goddess (1965) NF
Poetic Craft and Principle (1967) NF
Poems 1965–1968 (1968) V
The Crane Bag and Other Disputed Subjects (1969) NF

GRAY, Alasdair [James] (1934–)
Scottish novelist, short-story writer, and dramatist
Lanark (1981) F
Unlikely Stories, Mostly (1983) F SS
1982, Janine (1984) F
The Fall of Kelvin Walker (1985) F
Lean Tales (1985) F SS

Old Negatives (1989) V
Something Leather (1990) F
Poor Things (1992) F
Ten Tales Tall and True (1993) F SS
A History Maker (1994) F
Mavis Belfrage (1996) F SS
The Book of Prefaces (2000) NF

GRAY, John [Henry] (1866–1934)
British poet
Silverpoints (1893) V

GRAY, Simon [James Holliday] (1936–)
British playwright and novelist
Colmain (1963) F
Wise Child (1967) D
Butley (1971) D
Otherwise Engaged, and Other Plays (1975) D
The Rear Column, and Other Plays (1978) D
Close of Play (1979) D
Quartermaine's Terms (1981) D
The Common Pursuit (1984) D
Melon (1987) D
Hidden Laughter (1990) D
Cell Mates (1995) D

GRAY, Stephen (1941–)
South African poet and novelist
It's About Time (1974) V
Local Colour (1975) F
Visible People (1977) F
Hottentot Venus (1979) V
Caltrop's Desire (1980) F
Love Poems, Hate Poems (1982) V
Time of Our Darkness (1988) F
Born of Man (1989) F
Apollo Café (1990) V
Season of Violence (1992) V

GRAY, Thomas (1716–1771)
British poet
Ode on a Distant Prospect of Eton College (1747) V
An Elegy Wrote in a Country Church Yard (1751) V
Designs by Mr R. Bentley, for Six Poems by Mr T. Gray [inc. 'Ode on the Death of a Favourite Cat', 'Ode on a Distant Prospect of Eton College'] (1753) V
Odes (1757) V
Poems (1768) V

GREELEY, Horace (1811–1872)
American journalist and author
Glances at Europe (1851) NF
The American Conflict (1864–6) NF
Recollections of a Busy Life (1868) NF

'GREEN, Henry' [Henry Vincent Yorke] (1905–1973)
British novelist
Blindness (1926) F
Living (1929) F
Party Going (1939) F
Pack My Bag (1940) NF
Caught (1943) F
Loving (1945) F
Back (1946) F
Concluding (1948) F
Nothing (1950) F
Doting (1952) F

GREEN, J[ohn] R[ichard] (1837–1883)
British historian
A Short History of the English People (1874) NF
The Making of England (1881) NF

GREEN, Matthew (1696–1737)
English poet and Quaker
The Grotto (1733) V
The Spleen (1737) V

GREEN, Paul [Eliot] (1894–1981)
American dramatist, short-story writer, and novelist
White Dresses (1923) D
The Lord's Will, and Other Carolina Plays (1925) D
Lonesome Road (1926) D
The Field God (1927) D
In Abraham's Bosom [first version pub. 1924] (1927) D
In the Valley (1928) D
Wide Fields (1928) F SS
Tread the Green Grass (1929) D
The House of Connelly (1931) D
Your Fiery Furnace (1932) D
Roll, Sweet Chariot (1934) D
This Body the Earth (1935) F
Hymn to the Rising Sun (1936) D
Johnny Johnson (1937) D
The Highland Call (1941) D
The Hawthorn Tree (1943) NF
Salvation on a String (1946) F SS
Drama and the Weather (1958) NF
Plough and Furrow (1963) NF
Home to My Valley (1969) F SS
Land of Nod (1976) F SS

GREEN, Thomas Hill (1836–1882)
British idealist philosopher
Prolegomena to Ethics (1883) NF

GREENAWAY, Kate [Catherine] (1846–1901)
English illustrator and writer of children's books
Under the Window (1879) V CH
The Birthday Book for Children [verses by Mrs Sales Barker] (1880) V CH
Mother Goose; or, The Old Nursery Rhymes (1881) V CH
Marigold Garden (1885) V CH

GREENE, [Henry] Graham (1904–1991)
British novelist and short-story writer
Babbling April (1925) V
The Man Within (1929) F
The Name of Action (1930) F
Rumour at Nightfall (1931) F
Stamboul Train (1932) F
It's a Battlefield (1934) F
The Basement Room, and Other Stories (1935) F SS
England Made Me (1935) F

A Gun for Sale (1936) F
Journey Without Maps (1936) NF
Brighton Rock (1938) F
The Confidential Agent (1939) F
The Lawless Road (1939) NF
The Power and the Glory (1940) F
The Ministry of Fear (1943) F
Nineteen Stories (1947) F SS
The Heart of the Matter (1948) F
The Third Man; The Fallen Idol (1950) F
The End of the Affair (1951) F
The Lost Childhood, and Other Essays (1951) NF
The Living Room (1953) D
Loser Takes All (1955) F
The Quiet American (1955) F
Our Man in Havana (1958) F
The Potting Shed (1958) D
The Complaisant Lover (1959) D
A Burnt-Out Case (1961) F
In Search of a Character (1961) NF
A Sense of Reality (1963) F SS
The Comedians (1966) F
May We Borrow Your Husband? and Other Comedies of the Sexual Life (1967) F SS
Travels With My Aunt (1969) F
A Sort of Life (1971) NF
The Pleasure Dome (1972) NF
The Honorary Consul (1973) F
The Human Factor (1978) F
Dr Fischer of Geneva; or, The Bomb Party (1980) F
Ways of Escape (1980) NF
J'accuse (1982) NF
Monsieur Quixote (1982) F
The Tenth Man (1985) F
The Captain and the Enemy (1988) F
The Last Word, and Other Stories (1990) F SS
Reflections 1923–1988 (1990) NF

GREENE, Robert (1558–1592)
English poet, dramatist, and pamphleteer
Mamillia (1583) NF
Arbasto (1584) F
Gwydonius: The Carde of Fancie (1584) F
Morando the Tritameron of Love (1584) F
The Myrrour of Modestie (1584) F
Planetomachia; or, The First Parte of the Generall Opposition of the Seven Planets (1585) F
Euphues his Censure to Philautus (1587) F
Penelopes Web (1587) F
Pandosto (1588) F
Perimedes the Blacke-Smith (1588) F
Ciceronis Amor: Tullies Love (1589) F
Menaphon (1589) F
The Spanish Masquerado (1589) F
Greenes Mourning Garment (1590) NF
Greenes Never Too Late; or, A Powder of Experience (1590) NF
Greenes Farewell to Folly (1591) NF
A Notable Discovery of Coosenage [running-title: *The Art of Cony-catching*] (1591) NF
The Second Part of Conny-Catching (1591) NF
The Blacke Bookes Messenger (1592) NF
Greenes Groats-worth of Witte (1592) NF
Philomela (1592) F
The Third and Last Part of Conny-Catching (1592) NF
The Honorable Historie of Frier Bacon, and Frier Bongay (1594) D
The Comicall Historie of Alphonsus, King of Aragon (1599) D
Greenes Orpharion (1599) F

GREENWOOD, Frederick (1830–1909)
British journalist, editor, and novelist
The Path of Roses (1859) F
Margaret Denzil's History (1864) F

GREENWOOD, Walter (1903–1974)
British novelist and dramatist
Love on the Dole (1933) F
His Worship the Mayor (1934) F
Standing Room Only (1936) F
The Cleft Stick (1937) F SS
So Brief the Spring (1952) F

GREER, Germaine (1939–)
Australian critic and author
The Female Eunuch (1970) NF
The Obstacle Race (1979) NF
The Revolting Garden [as 'Rose Blight'] (1979) NF
The Mad Woman's Underclothes (1986) NF
Daddy We Hardly Knew You (1989) NF
The Change (1991) NF
Slip-Shod Sybils (1995) NF

GREG, [Sir] W[alter] W[ilson] (1875–1959)
British scholar and bibliographer
A Bibliography of the English Printed Drama to the Restoration (1939) NF
The Editorial Problem in Shakespeare (1942) NF
The Shakespeare First Folio (1955) NF

GREGORY, Lady [Isabella Augusta] (1852–1932)
Irish dramatist and translator
Poets and Dreamers (1903) MISC
Seven Short Plays (1909) D
Irish Folk-History Plays (1912) D
New Comedies [*The Bogie Men; The Full Moon; Coats; Damer's Gold; McDonough's Wife*] (1913) D
Our Irish Theatre (1913) NF
Visions and Beliefs in the West of Ireland (1920) D
Three Wonder Plays [*The Dragon; Aristotle's Bellows; The Jester*] (1922) D
Three Last Plays [*Sancho's Master; Dave; The Would-Be Gentleman* (from Molière)] (1928) D

GREVE, Felix *see* FREDERICK PHILIP GROVE

GREVILLE, Fulke, first Lord Brooke (1554–1628)
English statesman and poet
The Tragedy of Mustapha (1609) D
Certaine Learned and Elegant Workes (1633) MISC
The Life of Sir Philip Sidney (1652) NF
Remains (1670) V

GREY, [Pearl] Zane (1872–1939)
American novelist
Riders of the Purple Sage (1912) F

GRIERSON, [Sir] H[erbert] J[ohn] C[lifford] (1866–1960)
British literary scholar and editor
The Poems of John Donne (1912) EDN
Metaphysical Lyrics and Poems of the Seventeenth Century (1921) EDN
Cross Currents in English Literature of the XVIIth century (1929) NF
The Oxford Book of Seventeenth-Century Verse (1934) ANTH

GRIEVE, Christopher Murray *see* HUGH MACDIARMID

GRIFFIN, Gerald (1803–1840)
Irish novelist, dramatist, and poet
The Collegians (1829) F
The Invasion (1832) F
Tales of My Neighbourhood (1835) F SS
Gisippus; or, The Forgotten Friend (1842) D
Talis Qualis; or, Tales of the Jury-room (1842) F SS

GRIFFITHS, Trevor (1935–)
British dramatist
Occupations; The Big House (1970) D
The Party (1973) D
Comedians (1975) D
All Good Men; and, Absolute Beginners (1977) D
Oi for England (1982) D
Real Dreams (1984) D
The Gulf Between Us (1992) D
Thatcher's Children (1993) D

GRIGSON, Geoffrey [Edward Harvey] (1905–1985)
British poet, critic, editor, and topographical author
New Verse (1939) ANTH
Under the Cliff, and Other Poems (1943) V
The Isles of Scilly, and Other Poems (1946) V
The Harp of Aeolus, and Other Essays on Art, Literature, and Nature (1947) NF
Samuel Palmer: The Visionary Years (1947) NF
Poetry of the Present (1949) ANTH
The Crest on the Silver (1950) NF
English Excursions (1960) NF
A Skull in Salop, and Other Poems (1967) V
Ingestion of Ice-Cream, and Other Poems (1969) V
Poems and Poets (1969) NF
Sad Grave of an Imperial Mongoose (1973) V
Angels and Circles, and Other Poems (1974) V
The Contrary View (1974) NF
The Fiesta, and Other Poems (1978) V
History of Him (1980) V
The Cornish Dancer, and Other Poems (1982) V
Montaigne's Tower, and Other Poems (1984) V

GRIMALD, Nicholas (1519?–1562)
English poet and translator
Three Books of Duties [Cicero] (1556) NF

GRIMM, Jacob Ludwig Carl (1785–1863) and **Wilhelm Carl** (1786–1859)
German philologists and folklorists
'Grimm's Fairy Tales' [*Kinder- und Hausmärchen*; first pub. in Eng. as *German Popular Stories*] (1812–14) F CH

GRINDEL, Eugène-Emile *see* PAUL ÉLUARD

GRISHAM, John (1955–)
American novelist
A Time to Kill (1989) F
The Firm (1991) F
The Pelican Brief (1992) F
The Client (1993) F
The Chamber (1994) F
The Rainmaker (1995) F
The Runaway Jury (1996) F
The Partner (1997) F
The Street Lawyer (1998) F
The Brethren (2000) F

GROSE, Francis (1731–1791)
British antiquary, lexicographer, and draughtsman
The Antiquities of England and Wales (1773–6) NF
A Classical Dictionary of the Vulgar Tongue (1785) NF
The Antiquities of Scotland [inc. Burns's 'Tam O'Shanter'] (1789–91) NF

GROSSMITH, George (1847–1912) and **Walter Weedon** (1854–1919)
British humorous novelists
The Diary of a Nobody (1892) F

GROTE, George (1794–1871)
British historian
Analysis of the Influence of Natural Religion on the Temporal Happiness of Mankind [as Philip Beauchamp] (1822) NF
A History of Greece (1845) NF
Plato and the Other Companions of Sokrates (1865) NF

GROVE, Frederick Philip [born **Felix Paul Greve]** (1879–1948)
Canadian novelist and essayist
Over Prairie Trails (1922) F
The Turn of the Year (1923) F
Settlers of the Marsh (1925) F
A Search for America (1927) F
Our Daily Bread (1928) F
The Yoke of Life (1930) F
Fruits of the Earth (1933) F
Two Generations (1939) F
The Master of the Mill (1944) F
In Search of Myself (1946) F
Consider Her Ways (1947) F

GROVE, Sir George (1820–1900)
British music scholar and editor
A Dictionary of Music and Musicians AD 1450–1880, by Eminent Writers (1879) NF

GUARINI, Giovanni Battista (1538–1612)
Italian poet and dramatist
Il pastor fido ['Fido the Shepherd'] (1589) D

GUEDALLA, Philip (1889–1944)
British historian and biographer
Supers and Supermen (1920) NF
The Second Empire (1922) NF
A Gallery (1924) NF
The Duke (1931) NF
Middle East 1940–2 (1944) NF

GUILPIN, Everard or Edward (fl.1598)
English poet
Skialetheia; or, A Shadow of Truth, in Certaine Epigrams or Satyres (1598) V
The Whipper of the Satyre his Pennance in a White Sheete (1601) V

GUNN, Jeannie, *née* Taylor [Mrs Aeneas Gunn] (1870–1961)
Australian novelist
The Little Black Princess (1905) F
We of the Never-Never (1908) F

GUNN, Mrs Aeneas *see* JEANNIE GUNN

GUNN, Neil M[iller] (1891–1973)
Scottish novelist
Morning Tide (1930) F
Sun Circle (1933) F
Butcher's Broom (1934) F
Highland River (1937) F
The Silver Darlings (1941) F

GUNN, Thom[son William] (1929–)
British poet and editor
Fighting Terms (1954) V
The Sense of Movement (1957) V
My Sad Captains, and Other Poems (1961) V
Touch (1967) V
Moly (1971) V
Jack Straw's Castle, and Other Poems (1976) V
Talbot Road (1981) V
The Occasions of Poetry (1982) NF
The Passages of Joy (1982) V
The Man With Night Sweats (1992) V
Old Stories (1992) V
Boss Cupid (2000) V

GUNNING, Elizabeth, later **Plunkett** (1769–1823)
British novelist
Lord Fitzhenry (1794) F
The Packet (1794) F
The Foresters (1796) F
The Orphans of Snowden (1797) F
The Gipsy Countess (1799) F

GUNNING, Susannah, *née* Minifie (1740–1800)
British novelist
The Histories of Lady Frances S— and Lady Caroline S— (1763) F
Family Pictures (1764) F
The Picture (1766) F
Barford Abbey (1768) F
The Hermit (1770) F
Anecdotes of the Delborough Family (1792) F
Virginius and Virginia (1792) V
Memoirs of Mary (1793) F
Delves (1796) F
Love at First Sight (1797) F
Fashionable Involvements (1800) F

GURNEY, Ivor [Bertie] (1890–1937)
British poet and composer
Severn and Somme (1917) V
War's Embers (1919) V

GUSTAFSON, Ralph (1909–)
Canadian poet
The Golden Chalice (1935) V
King Alfred (1937) V D
Epithalamium in Time of War (1941) V
Lyrics Unromantic (1942) V
Flight into Darkness (1944) V
Rivers Among Rocks (1960) V
Rocky Mountain Poems (1960) V
Sift in an Hourglass (1966) V
Ixion's Wheel (1969) V
The Brazen Tower (1974) F SS
Fire on Stone (1974) V
Corners in Glass (1977) V
Soviet Poems (1978) V
Sequences (1979) V
Landscape Without Rain (1980) V
The Vivid Air (1980) F SS
Conflicts of Spring (1981) V
Gradations of Grandeur (1982) V

GUTHRIE, A[lfred] B[ertram] (1901–1991)
American novelist
The Big Sky (1947) F
The Way West (1949) F
Shane (1951) F
These Thousand Hills (1956) F
Arfive (1971) F
Wild Pitch (1973) F

GUTHRIE, Thomas Anstey *see* F. ANSTEY

H

HABINGTON, William (1605–1654)
English poet and author
Castara (1634) V
The Historie of Edward the Fourth (1640) NF
The Queene of Arragon (1640) D
Observations upon Historie (1641) NF

HAGGARD, Sir Henry Rider (1856–1925)
British novelist
Cetawayo and His White Neighbours (1882) NF
Dawn (1884) F
King Solomon's Mines (1885) F
The Witch's Head (1885) F
Allan Quatermain (1887) F
Jess (1887) F

She (1887) F
Colonel Quaritch, V.C. (1888) F
Maiwa's Revenge; or, The War of the Little Hand (1888) F
Mr Meeson's Will (1888) F
Allan's Wife, and Other Tales (1889) F SS
Cleopatra (1889) F HF
Beatrice (1890) F
The World's Desire (1890) F
Eric Brighteyes (1891) F
Nada the Lily (1892) F
Montezuma's Daughter (1893) F
The People of the Mist (1894) F
Joan Haste (1895) F
Heart of the World (1896) F
Doctor Therne (1898) F
A Farmer's Year (1899) NF
The Last Boer War (1899) NF
Swallow (1899) F
Black Heart and White Heart, and Other Stories (1900) F SS
Lysbeth (1901) F
Pearl-Maiden (1903) F HF
The Brethren (1904) F
Stella Frefelius (1904) F
Ayesha (1905) F
Benita (1906) F
The Way of the Spirit (1906) F
Fair Margaret (1907) F
The Ghost Kings (1908) F
The Lady of Blossholme (1909) F
The Yellow God (1909) F
Morning Star (1910) F
Queen Sheba's Ring (1910) F
The Mahatma and the Hare (1911) F
Red Eve (1911) F
Marie (1912) F
Child of Storm (1913) F
The Wanderer's Necklace (1914) F
The Holy Flower (1915) F
The Ivory Child (1916) F
Finished (1917) F
Love Eternal (1918) F
Moon of Israel (1918) F HF
When the World Shook (1919) F
The Ancient Allan (1920) F
Smith and the Pharaohs, and Other Tales (1920) F SS
She and Allan (1921) F
The Virgin of the Sun (1922) F
Wisdom's Daughter (1923) F
Heu-Heu; or, The Monster (1924) F
Queen of the Dawn (1925) F
Allan and the Ice-Gods (1927) F

HAILEY, Arthur (1920–)
Anglo-Canadian thriller writer
The Final Diagnosis (1959) F
In High Places (1962) F
Hotel (1965) F
Airport (1968) F
Wheels (1971) F
The Moneychangers (1975) F
Overload (1979) F
Strong Medicine (1984) F
The Evening News (1990) F

HAKLUYT, Richard (1552?–1615)
English geographer
Divers Voyages Touching the Discoverie of America (1582) NF
The Principall Navigations, Voiages and Discoveries of the English Nation (1589) NF

HALDANE, J[ohn] B[urdon] S[anderson] (1892–1964)
British geneticist and author
Daedalus; or, Science and the Future (1924) NF
Possible Worlds, and Other Essays (1927) NF
The Inequality of Man, and Other Essays (1932) NF
Fact and Faith (1934) NF
Heredity and Politics (1938) NF
The Marxist Philosophy and the Sciences (1938) NF
New Paths in Genetics (1941) NF

HALE, Sarah [Josepha Buell] (1788–1879)
American humanitarian
Northwood: A Tale of New England (1827) F
Sketches of American Characters (1829) F SS
Poems For Our Children [inc. 'Mary Had a Little Lamb'] (1830) V

HALE, Sir Matthew (1609–1676)
English judge
Contemplations, Moral and Divine (1678) NF

HALES, John ['the ever-memorable**']** (1584–1656)
English author
Schisme and Schismaticks (1642) NF
Golden Remaines (1659) NF
Several Tracts by the Ever Memorable Mr Sir John Hales (1677) NF

HALEY, Alex [Palmer] (1921–1992)
African-American biographer and novelist
Roots (1977) F
A Different Kind of Christmas (1988) F

HALEY, Russell (1934–)
New Zealand short-story writer and novelist
The Sauna Bath Mysteries (1978) F SS
Real Illusions (1985) F SS
The Settlement (1986) F
Beside Myself (1990) F

HALIBURTON, T[homas] C[handler] (1796–1865)
Canadian satirist and humorist
A General Description of Nova Scotia (1823) NF
A Historical and Statistical Account of Nova Scotia (1829) NF
The Clockmaker; or, The Sayings and Doings of Samuel Slick, of Slickville [1st ser.; 2nd ser., 1838; 3rd ser., 1840] (1836) F SS
The Letterbag of the Great Western; or, Life in a Steamer (1840) F SS
The Attaché; or, Sam Slick in England [1st ser.; 2nd ser., 1844] (1843) F SS

The Old Judge; or, Life in a Colony (1849) F SS
Sam Slick's Wise Saws and Modern Instances (1853) F SS
Nature and Human Nature (1855) F SS

'HALL, Adam' [Elleston Trevor] (1920–)
English writer of spy fiction
The Berlin Memorandum [US: *The Quiller Memorandum*] (1965) F
The 9th Directive (1966) F
The Striker Portfolio (1969) F
The Warsaw Document (1970) F

HALL, Anna Maria, *née* Fielding [Mrs S[amuel] C[arter] Hall] (1800–1881)
Irish novelist and woman of letters
Sketches of Irish Character (1829) NF
The Buccaneer (1832) F
The Outlaw (1835) F
Tales of Women's Trials (1835) F
Uncle Horace (1837) F
Marian; or, A Young Maid's Fortunes (1840) F
The White Boy (1845) F
Stories of the Irish Peasantry (1850) F
A Woman's Story (1857) F
The Lucky Penny, and Other Tales (1858) F SS
Can Wrong Be Right? (1862) F
Nelly Nowlan, and Other Stories (1865) F SS
Alice Stanley, and Other Stories (1868) F SS

HALL, John, of Durham (1627–1656)
English poet, essayist, and pamphleteer
Horae Vacivae; or, Essays (1646) NF
Paradoxes (1650) NF

HALL, Joseph (1574–1656)
English prelate and author
Virgidemiarum, Sixe Bookes (1597) V
The Anathomie of Sinne (1603) NF
The Kings Prophecie; or, Weeping Joy (1603) V
Meditations and Vowes Divine and Morall (1605) NF
The Arte of Divine Meditation (1606) NF
Heaven Upon Earth; or, Of True Peace and Tranquillitie of Minde (1606) NF
Holy Observations (1607) NF V
Characters of Vertues and Vices (1608) NF
Epistles the First Volume [vol. ii, 1608] (1608) NF
Salomon's Divine Arts (1609) NF
Contemplations Upon the Principall Passages of the Holy Storie (1612) NF
Quo Vadis? (1617) NF
The Olde Religion (1628) NF
Occasionall Meditations (1630) NF
Christian Moderation (1640) NF
Episcopacie by Divine Right. Asserted (1640) NF
An Humble Remonstrance to the High Court of Parliament (1641) NF
A Short Answer to the Tedious Vindication of Smectymnuus (1641) NF
The Devout Soul (1644) NF
The Peace-Maker (1645) NF
The Remedy of Discontentment (1645) NF
The Balme of Gilead (1646) NF
Select Thoughts, One Century (1648) NF
Of Resolutions and Decisions of Divers Practicall Cases (1649) NF
Susurrium Cum Deo (1651) NF
The Great Mysterie of Godliness (1652) NF
Holy Raptures (1652) NF
The Invisible World (1659) NF

HALL, [Marguerite] Radclyffe (1880–1943)
British novelist and poet
'Twixt Earth and Stars (1906) V
A Sheaf of Verses (1908) V
Poems of the Past and Present (1910) V
Songs of Three Counties, and Other Poems (1913) V
The Forge (1924) F
The Unlit Lamp (1924) F
A Saturday Life (1925) F
Adam's Breed (1926) F
The Well of Loneliness (1928) F
The Sixth Beatitude (1936) F

HALL, Mrs S[amuel] C[arter] *see* ANNA MARIA HALL

HALL, Rodney (1935–)
British-born Australian poet, novelist, and editor
Penniless Till Doomsday (1962) V
Forty Beads on a Hangman's Rope (1963) V
Eyewitness (1967) V
The Autobiography of a Gordon (1968) V
The Law of Karma (1968) V
Heaven, in a Way (1970) V
Romulus and Remus (1970) V
The Ship on the Coin (1972) F
A Soapbox Omnibus (1973) V
A Place Among People (1975) F
Black Bagatelles (1978) V
The Most Beautiful World (1981) V
Just Relations (1982) F
Kisses of the Enemy (1987) F
Captivity Captive (1988) F
The Second Bridegroom (1991) F
The Grisly Wife (1993) F

HALL, Roger (1939–)
New Zealand dramatist
Glide Time (1976) D
Middle-Aged Spread (1977) D

HALLAM, Arthur Henry (1811–1833)
British poet and essayist
Remains in Verse and Prose (1834) MISC

HALLAM, Henry (1777–1859)
British historian
View of the State of Europe During the Middle Ages (1818) NF
The Constitutional History of England from the Accession of Henry VII to the Death of George II (1827) NF
Introduction to the Literature of Europe in the Fifteenth, Sixteenth, and Seventeenth Centuries (1837) NF

HALLECK, Fitz-Greene (1790–1867)
American poet
Fanny (1819) V
Alnwick Castle, with Other Poems (1827) V

HALLIWELL-PHILLIPPS [orig. **HALLIWELL**], **J[ames] O[rchard]** (1820–1889)
British literary scholar
Shakesperiana (1841) NF
The Nursery Rhymes of England (1842) NF
A Dictionary of Archaic and Provincial Words (1846) NF
The Life of William Shakespeare (1848) NF
A Dictionary of Old English Plays (1860) NF

HALPER, Albert (1904–1984)
American novelist
Union Square (1933) F
The Foundry (1934) F
On the Shore (1934) F SS
Sons of the Father (1940) F
Little People (1942) F SS
Only an Inch From Glory (1943) F
The Golden Watch (1953) F
Atlantic Avenue (1956) F
The Fourth Horseman of Miami Beach (1966) F

HAMBURGER, Michael [Peter Leopold] (1924–)
German-born British poet, translator, and critic
Later Hogarth (1945) V
The Dual Cactus (1957) V
Weather and Season (1963) V
In Flashlight (1965) V
The Truth of Poetry (1969) NF
Ownerless Earth (1973) V
Palinode (1977) V
Roots in the Air (1991) V

HAMILTON, Anthony (1646?–1720)
English soldier, poet, and author
Memoirs of the Life of the Count de Grammont (1714) NF

HAMILTON, Charles Harold St John *see* FRANK RICHARDS

HAMILTON, Cicely Mary (1872–1952)
British novelist, dramatist, and suffragist
Diana of Dobson's (1908) F
Marriage as a Trade (1909) NF
Just to Get Married (1911) F
A Matter of Money (1916) F
William, an Englishman (1919) F

HAMILTON, Donald (1916–)
American crime writer, creator of Matt Helm
Date with Darkness (1947) F
Murder Twice Told (1950) F
Night Walker (1954) F
Line of Fire (1955) F
Death of a Citizen (1960) F

HAMILTON, Elizabeth (1758–1816)
British novelist and writer on education
Translation of the Letters of a Hindoo Rajah (1796) F
Memoirs of Modern Philosophers (1800) F
Letters on the Elementary Principles of Education (1801) NF
Letters to the Daughter of a Nobleman (1806) NF
The Cottagers of Glenburnie (1808) F

HAMILTON, Jane (1957–)
American novelist
A Map of the World (1994) F
The Book of Ruth (1998) F
The Short Story of a Prince (1998) F
Disobedience (2000) F

HAMILTON, Mary Agnes (1884–1966)
British novelist
Less Than the Dust (1912) F
Dead Yesterdays (1916) F
Special Providence (1930) F
Life Sentence (1935) F

HAMILTON, Patrick [Anthony Walter] (1904–1962)
British novelist and dramatist
Craven House (1926) F
The Midnight Bell (1929) F
The Siege of Pleasure (1932) F
The Plains of Cement (1934) F
Impromptu in Moribundia (1939) F
Hangover Square; or, The Man With Two Minds (1941) F

HAMILTON, [Robert] Ian (1938–)
British poet, critic, biographer, and editor
Pretending Not to Sleep (1964) V
The Visit (1970) V
Anniversary and Vigil (1971) V
A Poetry Chronicle (1973) NF
Robert Lowell (1981) NF
In Search of J.D. Salinger (1988) NF
Fifty Poems (1990) V
Keepers of the Flame (1992) NF
The Oxford Companion to Twentieth-Century Poetry in English (1994) ANTH
Walking Possession (1994) NF

HAMILTON, Thomas (1789–1842)
Scottish novelist
Cyril Thornton (1827) F

HAMILTON, Virginia [Esther] (1936–)
American children's writer
Zeely (1967) F CH
The House of Dies Drear (1968) F CH
The Planet of Junior Brown (1971) F CH
M.C. Higgins the Great (1974) F CH
Arilla Sun Down (1976) F CH

HAMMETT, [Samuel] Dashiell (1894–1961)
American crime writer
The Dain Curse (1929) F
Red Harvest (1929) F
The Maltese Falcon (1930) F
The Glass Key (1931) F
The Thin Man (1932) F

HAMMICK, Georgina (1939–)
British short-story writer
People for Lunch (1987) F SS
Spoilt (1992) F SS
The Arizona Game (1996) F

HAMMON, Jupiter (1720–1800)
African-American poet
An Evening Thought (1760) V
An Address to the Negroes of the State of New York (1787) NF

HAMMOND, Henry (1605–1660)
English theologian
A Practicall Catechisme (1644) NF
Of the Reasonableness of the Christian Religion (1650) NF
A Paraphrase, and Annotations Upon all the Books of the New Testament (1653) NF

HAMMOND-INNES, Ralph *see* HAMMOND INNES

HAMPTON, Christopher [James] (1946–)
British dramatist
When Did You Last See My Mother? (1966) D
Total Eclipse (1968) D
The Philanthropist (1970) D
Savages (1973) D
Treats (1976) D
Tales From Hollywood (1983) D
White Chameleon (1991) D
Alice's Adventures Under Ground (1994) D

'HAMSUN, Knut' [Knut Pedersen] (1859–1952)
Norwegian novelist, poet, and dramatist
Hunger (1890) F
Mysteries (1892) F
Pan (1894) F
Victoria (1898) F
Growth of the Soil (1917) F

HANLEY, James (1901–1985)
Irish novelist, short-story writer, and dramatist
Drift (1930) F
Boy (1931) F
The Furys (1935) F
The Secret Journey (1936) F
Hollow Sea (1938) F
People Are Curious (1938) F SS
Our Time is Gone (1940) F
The Ocean (1941) F
No Directions (1943) F
Sailor's Song (1943) F
Crilley, and Other Stories (1945) F SS
Winter Song (1950) F
Levine (1956) F
An End and a Beginning (1958) F
A Woman in the Sky (1973) F
A Kingdom (1978) F

HANNAY, James (1827–1873)
Irish novelist
Biscuits and Grog (1848) F
King Dobbs (1849) F
Singleton Fontenoy, RN (1850) F
Eustace Conyers (1855) F
Studies on Thackeray (1869) NF

HANRAHAN, Barbara (1939–1991)
Australian novelist and artist
The Scent of Eucalyptus (1973) F
Sea Green (1974) F
The Albatross Muff (1977) F
Where the Queens All Strayed (1978) F
The Peach Groves (1979) F
The Frangipani Gardens (1980) F
Dove (1982) F
Kewpie Doll (1984) F
Annie Magdalene (1985) F
Dream People (1987) F SS
A Chelsea Girl (1988) F
Flawless Jade (1989) F
Good Night, Mr Moon (1992) F
Iris in Her Garden (1992) F SS

HANSBERRY, Lorraine (1930–1965)
American dramatist
A Raisin in the Sun (1959) D
The Sign in Sidney Brustein's Window (1964) D

HARDY, Thomas (1840–1928)
British novelist, poet, and short-story writer
Desperate Remedies (1871) F
Under the Greenwood Tree (1872) F
A Pair of Blue Eyes (1873) F
Far From the Madding Crowd (1874) F
The Hand of Ethelberta (1876) F
The Return of the Native (1878) F
The Trumpet-Major (1880) F
A Laodicean; or, The Castle of the De Stancys (1881) F
Two on a Tower (1882) F
The Mayor of Casterbridge (1886) F
The Woodlanders (1887) F
Wessex Tales (1888) F SS
A Group of Noble Dames (1891) F SS
Tess of the d'Urbervilles (1891) F
Life's Little Ironies (1894) F SS
Jude the Obscure (1896) F
The Well-Beloved (1897) F
Wessex Poems, and Other Verses (1898) V
Poems of the Past and the Present (1901) V
The Dynasts [pt. i] (1904) V
The Dynasts [pt. ii] (1906) V
The Dynasts [pt. iii] (1908) V
Time's Laughingstocks, and Other Verses (1909) V
A Changed Man, The Waiting Supper, and Other Tales (1913) F SS
Satires of Circumstance (1914) V
Moments of Vision and Miscellanous Verses (1917) V
Late Lyrics and Earlier, with Many Other Verses (1922) V
The Famous Tragedy of the Queen of Cornwall at Tintagel in Lyonesse (1923) D
Human Shows, Far Phantasies, Songs and Trifles (1925) V
Winter Words in Various Moods and Metres (1928) V

HARE, Augustus [John Cuthbert] (1834–1903)
British biographer and guidebook writer
Walks in Rome (1871) NF
Wanderings in Spain (1873) NF
Walks in London (1878) NF

'HARE, Cyril' [Alfred Alexander Gordon Clark] (1900–1958)
British judge and detective fiction writer
Tragedy at Law (1942) F
With a Bare Bodkin (1946) F
When the Wind Blows [US: *The Wind Blows Death*] (1949) F
That Yew Tree's Shade [US: *Death Walks the Woods*] (1954) F
He Should Have Died Hereafter [US: *Untimely Death*] (1958) F

HARE, David (1947–)
British dramatist
Slag (1970) D
The Great Exhibition (1972) D
Knuckle (1974) D
Fanshen (1975) D
Teeth 'n' Smiles (1975) D
Licking Hitler (1978) D
Plenty (1978) D
A Map of the World (1982) D
The Secret Rapture (1990) D
Murmuring Judges (1991) D
Racing Demon (1991) D
Absence of War (1993) D
Skylight (1995) D
Amy's View (1997) D
The Judas Kiss (1998) D

HARINGTON, Sir John (1560–1612)
English poet and translator
Orlando Furioso in English Heroical Verse [from Ariosto] (1591) V
The Englishmans Docter; or, The Schoole of Salerne [from Joannes de Mediolano] (1607) V
Epigrams Both Pleasant and Serious (1615) V

HARLAND, Henry ['Sidney Luska'] (1861–1905)
American novelist and short-story writer
As It Was Written [as 'Sydney Luska'] (1885) F
Mrs Peixada [as 'Sydney Luska'] (1886) F SS
The Yoke of the Thorah [as 'Sydney Luska'] (1887) F
My Uncle Florimond [as 'Sydney Luska'] (1888) F SS
Grandison Mather (1889) F
A Latin-Quarter Romance, and Other Stories [as 'Sydney Luska'] (1889) F SS
Two Women or One (1890) F
Mea Culpa (1891) F
Mademoiselle Miss, and Other Stories (1893) F SS
Grey Roses (1895) F SS
Comedies & Errors (1898) F SS
The Cardinal's Snuff-Box (1900) F
The Lady Paramount (1902) F
My Friend Prospero (1904) F

HARPER, Frances E[llen Watkins] (1825–1911)
African-American poet
Poems on Miscellaneous Subjects (1854) V
Iola Lerot; or, Shadows Uplifted (1892) F
The Martyr of Alabama (1894) V

HARPUR, Charles (1813–1868)
Australian poet
Thoughts: A Series of Sonnets (1845) V
The Bushrangers . . . and Other Poems (1853) D V
The Tower of the Dream (1865) V

HARRADEN, Beatrice (1864–1936)
British novelist and suffragette
Ships That Pass in the Night (1893) F
In Varying Moods (1894) F SS
Hilda Strafford; and The Remittance Man (1897) F
The Fowler (1899) F
Katharine Frensham (1903) F
The Scholar's Daughter (1906) F
Interplay (1908) F
Out of the Wreck I Rise (1912) F
The Guiding Thread (1916) F
Our Warrior Women (1916) NF
Where Your Treasure Is (1918) F
Rachel (1926) F

HARRINGTON or **[HARINGTON] James** (1611–1677)
English political theorist and author
The Common-wealth of Oceana (1656) NF
An Essay Upon Two of Virgil's Eclogues (1658) V
The Prerogative of Popular Government (1658) NF
Aphorisms Political (1659) NF
Virgil's Aeneis: The Third, Fourth, Fifth and Sixth Books (1659) V
Political Discourses (1660) NF

HARRIOT [HARIOT] Thomas (1560–1621)
English mathematician and astronomer
A Briefe and True Report of the New Found Land of Virginia (1588) NF

HARRIS, Christopher Fry *see* CHRISTOPHER FRY

HARRIS, 'Frank' [James Thomas Harris] (1856–1931)
British journalist, novelist, short-story writer, and biographer
Elder Conklin, and Other Stories (1894) F SS
Montes the Matador, and Other Stories (1900) F SS
The Bomb (1908) F
The Man Shakespeare and His Tragic Life Story (1909) NF
Unpath'd Waters (1913) F SS
Great Days (1914) F
The Yellow Ticket, and Other Stories (1914) F SS
Oscar Wilde (1918) NF
My Life and Loves (1922) NF
Undream'd of Shores (1924) F SS

HARRIS, George Washington (1814–1869)
American short-story writer
Sut Lovingwood (1867) F SS

HARRIS, James Thomas *see* FRANK HARRIS

HARRIS, Joel Chandler (1848–1908)
American short-story writer
Uncle Remus: His Songs and Sayings (1881) F CH
Nights with Uncle Remus (1883) F CH
Mingo and Other Sketches in Black and White (1884) F SS
Free Joe and Other Georgian Sketches (1887) F SS
Uncle Remus and his Friends (1892) F CH
Mr Rabbit at Home (1895) F CH
Sister Jane: Her Friends and Acquaintances (1896) F
Tales of the Home Folks in Peace and War (1898) F SS
Gabriel Tolliver (1902) F
The Making of a Statesman (1902) F SS
The Tar-Baby and Other Rhymes of Uncle Remus (1904) V CH
Uncle Remus and Br'er Rabbit (1906) F CH

HARRIS, John Wyndham *see* JOHN WYNDHAM

HARRIS, [Theodore] Wilson (1921–)
Guyanese novelist and poet
Fetish (1951) V
Eternity to Season (1954) V
Palace of the Peacock (1960) F
The Far Journey of Oudin (1961) F
The Whole Armour (1962) F
The Secret Ladder (1963) F
Heartland (1964) F
The Eye of the Scarecrow (1965) F
The Waiting Room (1967) F
Tumatumari (1968) F
Ascent to Omai (1970) F
Black Marsden (1972) F
Companions of the Day and Night (1975) F
The Tree of the Sun (1978) F
The Angel at the Gate (1982) F
Carnival (1985) F
The Infinite Rehearsal (1987) F
The Four Banks of the River of Space (1990) F

HARRIS, Thomas (1940–)
American novelist
Black Sunday (1975) F
Red Dragon (1981) F
The Silence of the Lambs (1988) F
Hannibal (1999) F

HARRISON, Frederic (1831–1923)
British lawyer, critic, and philosopher
Order and Progress (1875) NF
The Present and the Future (1880) NF
The Choice of Books, and Other Literary Pieces (1886) NF
The Meaning of History, and Other Historical Pieces (1894) NF
Studies in Early Victorian Literature (1895) NF
Tennyson, Ruskin, Mill and Other Literary Estimates (1899) NF
John Ruskin (1902) NF
The Creed of a Layman (1907) NF
The Philosophy of Common Sense (1907) NF
National and Social Problems (1908) NF
Autobiographic Memoirs (1911) NF
The Positive Evolution of Religion (1913) NF
The German Peril (1915) NF
Obiter Scripta (1918) NF
Novissima Verba (1920) NF
De Senectute (1923) NF

HARRISON, Jane [Ellen] (1850–1928)
British classical scholar
Prolegomena to the Study of Greek Religion (1903) NF
Themis (1912) NF

HARRISON, Jim (1937–)
American novelist and poet
Wolf (1971) F
A Good Day to Die (1973) F
Farmer (1976) F
Legends of the Fall (1978) F SS
Warlock (1981) F
Sundog (1985) F
Dalva (1989) F SS
The Woman Lit by Fireflies (1991) F SS

HARRISON, Mary St Leger *see* LUCAS MALET

HARRISON, Tony (1937–)
British poet, dramatist, and translator
Earthworks (1964) V
The Loiners (1970) V
From the School of Eloquence, and Other Poems (1978) V
Continuous (1981) V
A Kumquat for John Keats (1981) V
The Fire-Gap (1985) V
V (1985) V
Anno Forty-Two (1987) V
The Mother of the Muses (1989) V
Losing Touch (1990) V
A Cold Coming (1991) V
The Gaze of the Gorgon (1992) V
Black Daisies for the Bride (1993) V
The Shadow of Hiroshima (1995) V

HARROWER, Elizabeth (1928–)
Australian novelist
Down in the City (1957) F
The Long Prospect (1958) F
The Catherine Wheel (1960) F
The Watch Tower (1966) F

HART, Sir Basil [Henry] Liddell (1895–1970)
British military historian and strategist
The Remaking of Modern Armies (1927) NF
Reputations (1928) NF
The Decisive Wars of History (1929) NF
The Real War 1914–18 (1930) NF
The British Way in Warfare (1932) NF
The Ghost of Napoleon (1933) NF
'T.E. Lawrence', in Arabia and After (1934) NF
Through the Fog of War (1938) NF
The Defence of Britain (1939) NF
This Expanding War (1942) NF
The Revolution in Warfare (1946) NF

The Other Side of the Hill (1948) NF
The Rommel Papers (1953) NF
Deterrent or Defence (1960) NF
Memoirs (1965) NF
History of the Second World War (1970) NF

HARTE, [Francis] Bret[t] (1836–1902)
American short-story writer and poet
Condensed Novels and Other Papers (1867) F SS
The Lost Galleon (1867) V
The Luck of the Roaring Camp, and Other Sketches (1870) F SS
Mrs Skagg's Husbands (1873) F SS
Tales of the Argonauts (1875) F SS
Gabriel Conroy (1876) F
Two Men of Sandy Bar (1876) D
Ah Sin (1877) D
An Heiress of Red Dog, and Other Sketches (1878) F SS
Jeff Briggs's Love Story (1880) F
A Sappho of Green Springs, and Other Stories (1891) F SS
Colonel Starbottle's Client, and Some Other People (1892) F SS

HARTLEY, David (1705–1757)
English philosopher
Observations on Man, his Frame, his Duty, and his Expectations (1749) NF

HARTLEY, L[eslie] P[oles] (1895–1972)
British novelist and short-story writer
Night Fears, and Other Stories (1924) F SS
The Killing Bottle (1932) F SS
The Shrimp and the Anenome (1944) F
The Sixth Heaven (1946) F
Eustace and Hilda (1947) F
The Travelling Grave, and Other Stories (1948) F SS
The Boat (1949) F
My Fellow Devils (1951) F
The Go-Between (1953) F
A Perfect Woman (1955) F
The Hireling (1957) F
Two for the River, and Other Stories (1961) F SS
The Brickfield (1964) F
The Betrayal (1966) F
The Novelist's Responsibility (1967) NF
Poor Clare (1968) F
The Love Adept (1969) F
Mrs Carteret Receives, and Other Stories (1971) F SS
The Will and the Way (1973) F

HARVEY, Christopher (1597–1663)
English poet
The Synagogue; or, The Shadow of the Temple (1640) V

HARVEY, Gabriel (1550–1631)
English scholar and poet
Three Proper and Wittie, Familiar Letters (1580) NF
Three Letters, and Certaine Sonnets (1592) MISC
A New Letter of Notable Contents (1593) NF
Pierces Supererogation; or, A New Prayse of the Old Asse (1593) NF
The Hat on the Letter O, and Other Stories (1978) F SS

HASLUCK, Nicholas [Paul] (1942–)
Australian novelist, short-story writer, and poet
Quarantine (1978) F
The Blue Guitar (1980) F
The Hand That Feeds You (1982) F
The Bellarmine Jug (1984) F
Truant State (1987) F
The Country Without Music (1990) F

HASSALL, Christopher [Vernon] (1912–1963)
British poet, librettist, and biographer
Glamorous Nights [music by Ivor Novello] (1935) D MUS
Poems of Two Years (1935) V
Crisis (1939) V
S.O.S. . . . 'Ludlow' (1940) V
The Slow Night, and Other Poems (1949) V
The Player King (1952) D
The Red Leaf (1957) V
Edward Marsh (1959) V
Bell Harry, and Other Poems (1963) V
Rupert Brooke (1964) NF

HASTINGS, James (1862–1922)
British biblical scholar and editor
A Dictionary of the Bible (1898) NF

HAWES, Stephen (d. 1523?)
English poet
The Example of Virtue (1504?) V
The Convercyon of Swerers (1509) V
The Pastyme of Pleasure (1509) V
The Comforte of Lovers (1515) V

HAWKER, Mary Elizabeth *see* LANOE FALCONER

HAWKER, R[obert] S[tephen] (1803–1875)
British poet and antiquary
Ecclesia (1840) V
Reeds Shaken with the Wind (1843) V
The Quest of the Sangraal (1863) V
Cornish Ballads, and Other Poems (1869) V

HAWKES, Jacquetta, *née* Hopkins (1910–1996)
British archaeologist and novelist
A Land [plates by Henry Moore] (1951) NF
Man on Earth (1954) NF
King of the Two Lands (1966) F
The Dawn of the Gods (1968) NF
The First Great Civilizations (1973) NF

HAWKINS, Sir Anthony Hope *see* ANTHONY HOPE

HAWKINS [or HAWKYNS] Sir John (1532–1595)
English naval commander
A True Declaration of the Troublesome Voyadge of J. Haukins to the Parties of Guynea and the West Indies (1569) NF

HAWTHORNE, Julian (1846–1934)
American novelist
Bresant (1873) F

Garth (1877) F
Archibald Malmaison (1884) F
A Fool of Nature (1896) F

HAWTHORNE, Nathaniel (1804–1864)
American novelist and short-story writer
Fanshawe (1828) F
Twice-Told Tales [enlarged 1842] (1837) F SS
Grandfather's Chair (1841) F CH
Liberty Tree (1841) F CH
Mosses From an Old Manse (1846) F
The Scarlet Letter (1850) F
The House of the Seven Gables (1851) F
The Snow-Image, and Other Twice-Told Tales (1851) F SS
The Blithedale Romance (1852) F
A Wonder Book (1852) F CH
Tanglewood Tales (1853) F CH
The Marble Faun (1860) F
Our Old Home (1863) NF
Septimus Felton (1872) F
The Dolliver Romance (1876) F
The Ancestral Footstep (1883) F
Dr Grimshawe's Secret (1883) F

'HAY, Ian' [John Hay Beith] (1876–1952)
British novelist and dramatist
'Pip' (1907) F

HAY, John [Milton] (1838–1905)
American statesman, novelist, and poet
Castilian Days (1871) V
Pike County Ballads (1871) V
The Bread-Winners (1884) F
'The Right Stuff' (1908) F
A Man's Man (1909) F
A Safety Match (1911) F
A Knight on Wheels (1914) F
The First Hundred Thousand (1915) F

HAYCRAFT, Anna Margaret *see* ALICE THOMAS ELLIS

HAYDON, Benjamin Robert (1786–1846)
British painter and autobiographer
The Life of Haydon, From His Autobiography and Journals (1853) NF
Correspondence and Table-Talk (1876) NF

HAYLEY, William (1745–1820)
British poet and biographer
A Poetical Epistle to an Eminent Painter (1778) V
Epistle to Admirall Keppel (1779) V
An Essay on History in Three Epistles to Gibbon (1780) V
The Triumphs of Temper (1781) V
An Essay on Epic Poetry in Five Epistles to Mason (1782) V
A Philosophical, Historical and Moral Essay on Old Maids (1785) V
The Young Widow; or, A History of Cornelia Sedley (1789) F
The National Advocate (1795) V
The Life of Milton (1796) NF
An Essay on Sculpture (1800) V
The Life and Posthumous Writings of Cowper (1803) MISC
The Triumph of Music (1804) V
Ballads [prints designed and engraved by William Blake] (1805) V
Memoirs (1823) NF

HAYWARD, Sir John (1564?–1627)
English historian
The First Part of the Life and Raigne of King Henrie the IIII (1599) NF
The Sanctuarie of a Troubled Soule [pt. i] (1601) NF
The Lives of the III Normans, Kings of England (1613) NF
Davids Teares (1622) NF
The Life, and Raigne of King Edward the Sixt (1630) NF

HAYWOOD, Eliza (c. 1693–1756)
English novelist, dramatist, and journalist
Love in Excess (1719) F
Ten Letters From a Young Lady of Quality [from Edmé Bursault] (1720) F
The Fair Captive (1721) D
The British Recluse; or, The Secret History of Cleomira, Suppos'd Dead (1722) F
Idalia; or, The Unfortunate Princess (1723) F
Lasselia; or, The Self-abandon'd (1723) F
A Wife to be Lett (1723) D
La Belle Assemblé; or, The Adventures of Six Days [from Madeleine, Mme de Gomez] (1724) F
The Fatal Secret; or, Constancy in Distress (1724) F
The Masqueraders; or, Fatal Curiosity (1724) F
Poems on Several Occasions (1724) V
Bath-Intrigues (1725) F
Fantomina; or, Love in a Maze (1725) F
Memoirs of a Certain Island Adjacent to the Kingdom of Utopia (1725) F
The Mercenary Lover; or, The Unfortunate Heiress (1726) F
Cleomelia; or, The Generous Mistress (1727) F
The Perplex'd Dutchess; or, Treachery Rewarded (1727) F
Philidore and Placentia; or, L'amour trop delicat (1727) F
The Secret History of the Present Intrigues of the Court of Caramania (1727) F
The Agreeable Caledonian; or, Memoirs of Signiora di Morella, a Roman Lady [pt. i] (1728) F
Irish Artifice; or, The History of Clarina (1728) F
The Fair Hebrew (1729) F
Frederick, Duke of Brunswick-Lunenburgh (1729) D
The Opera of Operas; or, Tom Thumb the Great (1733) V
The Dramatic Historiographer (1735) NF
The Adventures of Eovaai, Princess of Ijaveo (1736) F
The Fortunate Foundlings (1744) F
Life's Progress Through the Passions; or, The Adventures of Natura (1748) F
The History of Miss Betty Thoughtless (1751) F
The History of Jenny and Jemmy Jessamy (1753) F

HAZLITT, William (1778–1830)
British critic and essayist
An Essay on the Principles of Human Action (1805) NF
Free Thoughts on Public Affairs; or, Advice to a Patriot (1806) NF
The Eloquence of the British Senate (1807) NF
A Reply to the Essay on Population (1807) NF
Characters of Shakespear's Plays (1817) NF
The Round Table [inc. 12 essays by Leigh Hunt] (1817) NF
Lectures on the English Poets (1818) NF
A View of the English Stage; or, A Series of Dramatic Criticisms (1818) NF
Lectures on the English Comic Writers (1819) NF
Political Essays, with Sketches of Public Characters (1819) NF
Lectures Chiefly on the Dramatic Literature of the Age of Elizabeth (1820) NF
Table-Talk; or, Original Essays [vol. i] (1821) NF
Table-Talk; or, Original Essays [vol. ii] (1822) NF
Characteristics (1823) NF
Liber Amoris; or, The New Pygmalion (1823) NF
Select British Poets (1824) NF
The Plain Speaker (1825) NF
The Spirit of the Age; or, Contemporary Portraits (1825) NF
Notes of a Journey Through France and Italy (1826) NF
The Life of Napoleon Buonaparte [vols. i, ii] (1828) NF
Conversations of James Northcote (1830) NF
The Life of Napoleon Buonaparte [vols. iii, iv] (1830) NF
Essays on the Principles of Human Action (1836) NF

HAZZARD, Shirley (1931–)
Australian novelist and short-story writer
Cliffs of Fall (1963) F SS
The Evening of the Holiday (1966) F
People in Glass Houses (1967) F
The Bay of Noon (1970) F
Defeat of an Ideal (1973) NF
The Transit of Venus (1980) F
Countenance of Truth (1990) NF

HEAD, Bessie (1937–1986)
South African novelist
When Rain Clouds Gather (1968) F
Maru (1971) F
A Question of Power (1974) F
A Bewitched Crossroad (1984) F

HEAD, Richard (1637?–1686?)
English fiction writer
The English Rogue (1665) F
The Floating Island; or, A New Discovery (1673) F
The Western Wonder; or, O Brazeel [reissued 1675 as *O-Brazile*] (1674) F
The Life and Death of Mother Shipton (1677) F

HEANEY, Seamus [Justin] (1939–)
Irish poet and critic
Eleven Poems (1965) V
Death of a Naturalist (1966) V
Door into the Dark (1969) V
Wintering Out (1972) V
North (1975) V
Field Work (1979) V
Preoccupations (1980) NF
The Rattle-Bag (1982) ANTH
Station Island (1984) V
Sweeney Astray (1984) V
The Haw Lantern (1987) V
The Government of the Tongue (1988) NF
The Redress of Poetry (1990) NF
The Tree Clock (1990) V
Sweeney's Flight (1992) V
The Spirit Level (1996) V
Opened Ground (1998) V
Beowulf (tr.) (1999) V

HEARN, [Patricio] Lafcadio [Tessima Carlos] (1850–1904)
Irish-Greek journalist, travel-writer, novelist, and writer on Japan
Gombo Zhêbes (1885) NF
Chita (1889) F

HEARNE, Thomas (1678–1735)
English antiquary
Reliquiae Bodleianae; or, Some Genuine Remains of Sir Thomas Bodley (1703) NF
The Itinerary of John Leland the Antiquary (1710) NF
A Collection of Curious Discourses (1720) NF
Robert of Gloucester's Chronicle (1724) NF

HEATH-STUBBS, John [Francis Alexander] (1918–)
British poet and critic
Wounded Thammuz (1942) V
Beauty and the Beast (1943) V
The Divided Ways (1946) V
The Darkling Plain (1950) NF
The Swarming of the Bees (1950) V
The Faber Book of Twentieth-Century Verse (1953) ANTH
A Charm Against the Toothache (1954) V
Helen in Egypt, and Other Plays (1958) D
The Triumph of the Muse, and Other Poems (1958) V
The Blue-Fly in His Head (1962) V
Satires and Epigrams (1968) V
Four Poems in Measure (1973) V
A Parliament of Birds (1975) V
The Watchman's Flute (1978) V
Birds Reconvened (1980) V
Buzz Buzz (1981) V
The Immolation of Aleph (1985) V
A Partridge in a Pear Tree (1988) V
The Game of Love and Death (1990) V

HEBER, Reginald (1783–1826)
British poet and hymn-writer
Europe (1809) V
Poems and Translations (1812) V

Hymns, Written and Adapted to the Weekly Church Service of the Year (1827) V
Narrative of a Journey Through India 1824–5 (1828) NF

HECHT, Ben (1894–1964)
American dramatist and novelist
The Master Poisoner (1918) D
Erik Dorn (1921) F
Fantazius Mallare (1922) F
Gargoyles (1922) F
1001 Afternoons in Chicago (1922) F
The Florentine Dagger (1923) F
Broken Necks (1924) F SS
Humpty Dumpty (1924) F
The Kingdom of Evil (1924) F
Tales of Chicago Streets (1924) F
Count Bruga (1926) F
The Front Page (1928) D
A Jew in Love (1930) F
The Champion From Far Away (1931) F SS
20th Century (1932) D
The Great Magoo (1933) D
To Quito and Back (1937) D
A Book of Miracles (1939) F SS
Ladies and Gentlemen (1939) D
1001 Afternoons in New York (1941) F
A Guide for the Bedevilled (1944) NF
A Child of the Century (1954) NF
The Sensualists (1959) F
Perfidy (1961) NF
Gaily, Gaily (1963) NF

HECTOR, Annie French *see* Mrs A.H. Alexander

HEINE, Heinrich (1797–1856)
German poet
Gedichte ['Poems'] (1821) V
Lyrisches Intermezzo ['Lyrical Intermezzo'] (1823) V
Pictures of Travel [*Reisebilder*; vols. i, ii] (1826–7) NF
Book of Songs [*Das Buch der Lieder*] (1827) V
Pictures of Travel [*Reisebilder*; vols. iii, iv] (1830–1) NF
French Affairs (1833) NF
The Romantic School [*Die romantische Schule*] (1836) NF
Germany: A Winter's Tale [*Deutschland: Ein Wintermärchen*] (1844) V
New Poems [*Neue Gedichte*] (1844) V
Atta Troll, and Other Poems [*Atta Troll: Ein Somernachtstraum*] (1847) V
Romancero [*Romanzero*] (1851) V

HEINLEIN, Robert A[nson] (1907–1988)
American science fiction writer
The Man Who Sold the Moon (1950) F
The Green Hills of Earth (1951) F
Revolt in 2100 (1953) F
Double Star (1956) F
Methuselah's Children (1958) F
Starship Troopers (1959) F
Strangers in a Strange Land (1961) F
Orphans of the Sky (1963) F
The Moon is a Harsh Mistress (1967) F
Time Enough for Love (1973) F
The Number of the Beast (1980) F
Friday (1982) F

HELLER, Joseph (1923–1999)
American novelist and dramatist
Catch-22 (1961) F
We Bombed in New Haven (1968) D
Clevinger's Trial (1974) D
Something Happened (1974) F
Good as Gold (1979) F
God Knows (1984) F
Picture This (1988) F
Closing Time (1994) F
Portrait of the Artist as an Old Man (2000) F

HELLMAN, Lillian [Florence] (1907–1984)
American dramatist
The Children's Hour (1934) D
Days to Come (1936) D
The Little Foxes (1939) D
Watch on the Rhine (1941) D
The Searching Wind (1944) D
Another Part of the Forest (1946) D
The Autumn Garden (1951) D
Toys in the Attic (1960) D
An Unfinished Woman (1969) NF
Pentimento (1973) NF
Scoundrel Time (1976) NF

HELPS, Sir Arthur (1813–1875)
British civil servant, novelist, and author
Realmah (1868) F
Casimir Maremma (1870) F

HELWIG, David (1938–)
Canadian poet, novelist, and short-story writer
Figures in a Landscape (1967) V
The Sign of the Gunman (1969) V
The Streets of Summer (1969) F SS
The Day Before Tomorrow (1971) F
The Best Name of Silence (1972) V
A Book About Billie (1972) F
Atlantic Crossing (1974) V
The Glass Knight (1976) F
A Book of the Hours (1979) V
Jennifer (1979) F
The King's Evil (1981) F
It Is Always Summer (1982) F
A Sound Like Laughter (1983) F

HEMANS, Felicia Dorothea, *née* Browne (1793–1835)
British poet
England and Spain; or, Valour and Patriotism (1808) V
The Domestic Affections, and Other Poems (1812) V
The Restoration of the Works of Art to Italy (1816) V
Modern Greece (1817) V
Translations from Camoens and Other Poets, with Original Poetry (1818) V
Tales and Historic Scenes (1819) V

Wallace's Invocation to Bruce (1819) V
The Sceptic (1820) V
Dartmoor (1821) V
Welsh Melodies (1822) V
The Siege of Valencia, with Other Poems (1823) V
The Vespers of Palermo (1823) V D
The Forest Sanctuary, and Other Poems (1825) V
Lays of Many Lands (1825) V
Records of Woman, with Other Poems (1828) V
Songs of the Affections, with Other Poems (1830) V
Hymns for Childhood (1834) V
National Lyrics and Songs for Music (1834) V
Scenes and Hymns of Life, with Other Religious Poems (1834) V

HEMINGWAY, Ernest [Miller] (1898–1961)
American novelist and short-story writer
Three Stories and Ten Poems (1923) F V SS
In Our Time (1925) F SS
The Sun Also Rises (1926) F
The Torrents of Spring (1926) F
Men Without Women (1927) F SS
A Farewell to Arms (1929) F
Death in the Afternoon (1932) NF
Winner Take Nothing (1933) F SS
Green Hills of Africa (1935) NF
To Have and Have Not (1937) F
The Fifth Column and the First Forty-Nine Stories (1938) D SS
For Whom the Bell Tolls (1940) F
Across the River and Into the Trees (1950) F
The Old Man and the Sea (1952) F
A Moveable Feast (1964) NF
Islands in the Stream (1970) F

HENDRY, J[ames] F[indlay] (1912–1986)
Scottish poet, editor, and novelist
The New Apocalypse (1939) ANTH
The White Horseman (1941) ANTH
The Bombed Happiness (1942) V
The Orchestral Mountain (1943) V
Crown and Sickle (1944) ANTH
Marimarusa (1978) V
A World Alien (1980) V

HENLEY, Beth (1952–)
American dramatist
Crimes of the Heart (1978) D

HENLEY, W[illiam] E[rnest] (1849–1903)
British poet, critic, and journalist
Admiral Guinea (1884) D
Beau Austin (1884) D
Macaire (1885) D
A Book of Verses (1888) V
Deacon Brodie; or, The Double Life (1888) D
Views and Reviews (1890) NF
The Song of the Sword, and Other Verses (1892) V
London Volunteers, and Other Verses (1893) V
Hawthorn and Lavender (1899) V
For England's Sake (1900) V
Views and Reviews (1902) NF
A Song of Speed (1903) V

HENRI, Adrian [Maurice] (1932–)
British poet, dramatist, novelist, painter, and children's writer
Tonight at Noon (1968) V
Autobiography (1971) V
One Year (1976) V
City Hedges (1977) V
From the Loveless Matel (1980) V
Penny Arcade (1983) V
Holiday Snaps (1985) V
Box, and Other Poems (1990) V
The Cerise Swimsuit (1992) V
Not Fade Away (1994) V

'HENRY, O.' [William Sydney Porter] (1862–1910)
American short-story writer
Cabbages and Kings (1904) F SS
The Four Million (1906) F SS
Heart of the West (1907) F SS
The Trimmed Lamp (1907) F SS
The Gentle Grafter (1908) F SS
The Voice of the City (1908) F SS
Options (1909) F SS
Roads of Destiny (1909) F SS
Strictly Business (1910) F SS
Whirligigs (1910) F SS
Sixes and Sevens (1911) F SS
Rolling Stones (1913) F SS
Waifs and Strays (1917) F SS
Postscripts (1923) F SS

HENRYSON, Robert (*c.* 1430–*c.* 1505)
Scottish poet
Orpheus and Eurydice (1508?) V
The Morall Faibillis of Esope in Scottis Meter (1570) V
The Testament of Cresseid (1593) V

HENTY, G[eorge] A[lfred] (1832–1902)
British boys' novelist
Out on the Pampas; or, The Young Settlers (1870) F CH
The Young Franc-Tireurs and Their Adventures in the Franco-Prussian War (1872) F CH
Facing Death (1883) F CH
Under Drake's Flag (1883) F CH
With Clive in India (1884) F CH
True to the Old Flag (1885) F CH
The Dragon and the Raven; or, The Days of King Alfred (1886) F CH
With Wolfe in Canada (1887) F CH
The Cat of Bubastis (1888) F CH
By Pike and Dyke (1890) F CH
By Right of Conquest; or, With Cortez in Mexico (1891) F CH
The Dash for Karthoum (1892) F CH
Held Fast for England (1892) F CH
Redskin and Cowboy (1892) F CH
Beric the Briton (1893) F CH
In Greek Waters (1893) F CH
On the Irrawaddy (1897) F CH
With Buller to Natal (1900) F CH

With Roberts to Pretoria (1901) F CH
With Kitchener in the Sudan (1903) F CH

HERAUD, John Abraham (1799–1887)
British poet and dramatist
Salvator, the Poor Man of Naples (1845) V D
Videna; or, The Mother's Tragedy (1853) V D
Uxmal; Macée de Léodepart (1877) V
Holy Deadlock (1934) F

HERBERT, Edward, 1st Baron Herbert of Cherbury (1583–1648)
English philosopher, historian, and poet
Occasional Verses (1665) V
The Life of Edward Lord Herbert of Cherbury, Written by Himself (1764) NF

HERBERT, Frank (1920–1986)
American science fiction writer
The Dragon in the Sea (1956) F

HERBERT, George (1593–1633)
English poet
The Temple (1633) V
Hygiasticon; or, The Right Course of Preserving Life and Health unto Extream Old Age (1634) NF
Outlandish Proverbs (1640) NF
Remains (1652) NF
A Priest to the Temple; or, The Country Parson his Character, and Rule of Holy Life [first pub. in *Remains*, 1652] (1671) NF

HERBERT, James (1943–)
British horror writer
The Rats (1974) F
The Fog (1975) F
The Survivor (1976) F
Fluke (1977) F
The Spear (1978) F
Lair (1979) F
The Dark (1980) F
The Jonah (1981) F
Domain (1984) F
Moon (1985) F
The Magic Cottage (1986) F
Haunted (1988) F
The Ghosts of Sleath (1994) F

HERBERT, [Sir] A[lan] P[atrick] (1890–1971)
British author and humorist
The Bomber Gipsy, and Other Poems (1918) V
The Secret Battle (1919) F
Plain Jane (1927) V
Misleading Cases in the Common Law (1929) F
The Water Gipsies (1930) F
A Book of Ballads (1931) V
Bring Back the Bells (1943) V
Light the Lights (1945) V
Independent Member (1950) NF

HERBERT, Frank [Alfred Francis] Xavier (1901–1984)
Australian novelist
Capricornia (1938) F
Seven Emus (1959) F
Soldiers' Women (1961) F
Disturbing Element (1963) NF
Larger Than Life (1963) F SS
Poor Fellow My Country (1975) F
Dune (1965) F
Dune Messiah (1969) F
Children of Dune (1976) F
God-Emperor of Dune (1980) F
Heretics of Dune (1982) F
Chapter House: Dune (1985) F

HERBST, Josephine [Frey] (1897–1969)
American novelist and journalist
Nothing is Sacred (1928) F
Money for Love (1929) F
Pity Is Not Enough (1933) F
The Executioner Waits (1934) F
Rope of Gold (1939) F
Satan's Sergeants (1941) F
Somewhere the Tempest Fell (1947) F

HERGESHEIMER, Joseph (1880–1954)
American novelist
The Lay Anthony (1914) F
Mountain Blood (1915) F
The Three Black Pennys (1917) F
Gold and Iron (1918) F
Java Head (1919) F
Linda Condon (1919) F
Cytherea (1922) F
Balisand (1924) F
Tampico (1926) F
Swords and Roses (1929) F
The Limestone Tree (1931) F
Tropical Winter (1933) F
The Foolscap Rose (1934) F

HERNE, James A. (1839–1901)
American dramatist and actor
Chums [retitled *Hearts of Oak*, 1880] (1879) D
Margaret Fleming (1890) D
Shore Acres (1892) D
The Reverend Griffith Davenport (1899) D
Sag Harbor (1899) D

HERRICK, Robert (1591–1674)
English poet
Hesperides; or, The Works both Humane and Divine of Robert Herrick Esq. (1648) V

HERRICK, Robert [Welch] (1868–1938)
American novelist
The Man Who Wins (1897) F SS
The Gospel of Freedom (1898) F
The Web of Life (1900) F
The Real World (1901) F
The Common Lot (1904) F
The Master of the Inn (1908) F
Together (1908) F
The Healer (1911) F
One Woman's Life (1913) F
Clark's Field (1914) F

The World Decision (1916) F
Homely Lilla (1923) F
Waste (1924) F
The End of Desire (1931) F
Sometime (1933) F

HERRIOT, James (1916–1995)
British veterinarian and novelist
All Creatures Great and Small (1972) F
It Should Happen to a Vet (1972) F
Let Sleeping Vets Lie (1973) F
All Things Bright and Beautiful (1974) F
Vets in Harness (1976) F
Vets Might Fly (1976) F
All Things Wise and Wonderful (1977) F
The Lord God Made Them All (1981) F
Every Living Thing (1992) F

HERSCHEL, Sir John [Frederick William] (1792–1871)
British astronomer
Outlines of Astronomy (1841) NF

HERSEY, John (1914–1993)
American journalist and novelist
A Bell for Adano (1944) F
Hiroshima (1946) NF
The Wall (1950) F
The Child Buyer (1960) F

HERVEY, James (1714–1758)
British devotional writer
Meditations Among the Tombs (1746) NF
Meditations and Contemplations (1748) NF
Theron and Aspasio (1755) NF

HERVEY, John, 2nd Baron Hervey of Ickworth (1696–1743)
British pamphleteer and memoir writer
Observations on the Writings of the Craftsman (1730) NF
An Epistle from a Nobleman to a Doctor of Divinity (1733) V
Memoirs of the Reign of George the Second (1848) NF

HESSE, Hermann (1877–1962)
German-Swiss novelist
Peter Camenzind (1904) F
Under the Wheel [*Unterm Rad*] (1906) F
Gertrud (1910) F
Rosshalde (1914) F
Knulp (1915) F
Demian (1919) F
Siddhartha (1922) F
Steppenwolf [*Die Steppenwolf*] (1927) F
Death and the Lover [*Narziss und Goldmund*] (1930) F
Magister Ludi [*Der Glasperlenspiel*] (1943) F

HEWETT, Dorothy [Coade] (1923–)
Australian poet, dramatist, and novelist
Bobbin Up (1959) F
What About the People (1961) V
This Old Man Comes Rolling Home (1966) D
Windmill Country (1968) V
Late Night Bulletin (1969) V
The Chapel Perilous (1971) D
Bons-Bons and Roses for Dolly (1972) D
Rapunzel in Suburbia (1975) V
The Tatty Hollow Story (1975) D
Greenhouse (1979) V
The Man From Mukinupin (1979) D
Journeys (1982) V
Alice in Wormland (1987) V
A Tremendous World in Her Head (1989) V
Wild Card (1990) NF
The Toucher (1993) F

HEWLETT, Maurice Henry (1861–1923)
British novelist and poet
A Masque of Dead Florentines (1895) V
The Forest Lovers (1898) F
Little Novels of Italy (1899) F SS
The Life and Death of Richard Yea-and-Nay (1900) F
The New Canterbury Tales (1901) F SS
The Queen's Quair; or, The Six Years' Tragedy (1904) F
Fond Adventures (1905) F SS
The Fool Errant (1905) F
The Stooping Lady (1907) F
Halfway House (1908) F
The Spanish Jade (1908) F
Open Country (1909) F
Rest Harrow (1910) F
Bendish (1913) F
The Song of the Plow (1916) V

HEYER, Georgette (1902–1974)
British historical and detective fiction novelist
The Black Moth (1921) F
Devil's Cub (1934) F
Death in the Stocks [US: *Merely Murder*] (1935) F
Regency Buck (1935) F
Behold, Here's Poison! (1936) F
They Found Him Dead (1937) F
A Blunt Instrument (1938) F
No Wind of Blame (1939) F
Envious Casca (1941) F
Faro's Daughter (1941) F
Duplicate Death (1951) F
Detection Unlimited (1953) F
Venetia (1958) F
Lady of Quality (1972) F

HEYLYN, Peter (1600–1662)
English ecclesiastical writer
Microcosmus: or, A Little Description of the Great World (1621) NF
The History of the Sabbath (1636) NF
Cosmographie (1652) NF
Ecclesia Vindicata (1657) NF
Ecclesia Restaurata; or, History of the Reformation (1661) NF
Cyprianus Anglicanus (1668) NF
Aerius Redivivus; or, The History of Presbyterianism (1670) NF

HEYWARD, [Edwin] DuBose (1885–1940)
American novelist, dramatist, and poet
Porgy (1925) F
Mamba's Daughters (1929) F
Jasbo Brown (1931) V
Peter Ashley (1932) F
Star Spangled Virgin (1939) F

HEYWOOD, Jasper (1535–1598)
English Jesuit, dramatist, poet, and translator
Troas [from Seneca] (1559) D
Thyestes [from Seneca] (1560) D
Hercules Furens [from Seneca] (1561) D
Johan Johan (1533) D

HEYWOOD, John (1497?–1580?)
English dramatist
The Pardoner and the Friar (1533) D
The Play of the Wether (1533) D
A Play of Love (1534) D
The Foure PP (1544?) D
Two Hundred Epigrammes (1555) V
The Spider and the Flie (1556) V

HEYWOOD, Thomas (1574?–1641)
English dramatist
King Edward the Fourth (1599) D
A Good Wife from a Bad (1602) D
If You Know Not Me, You Know No Bodie; or, The Troubles of Queene Elizabeth (1605) D
If You Know Not Me, You Know No Bodie [pt. ii] (1606) D
The Fayre Mayde of the Exchange (1607) D
A Woman Kilde with Kindnesse (1607) D
The Rape of Lucrece (1608) D
The Two Most Worthy and Notable Histories [from Sallust] (1608) NF
Troia Britanica; or, Great Britaines Troy (1609) V
The Golden Age; or, The Lives of Jupiter and Saturne (1611) D
An Apology for Actors (1612) NF
The Brazen Age (1613) D
The Silver Age (1613) D
The Foure Prentises of London (1615) D
Gynaikeion; or, Nine Bookes of Various History. Concerninge Women (1624) V
The Arte of Love [from Ovid] (1625) D
Englands Elizabeth Her Life and Trouble (1631) NF
The Fair Maid of the West; or, A Girle Worth Gold [2 pts.] (1631) D
The Iron Age [2 pts.] (1632) D
The English Traveller (1633) D
A Mayden-head Well Lost (1634) D
The Hierarchie of the Blessed Angells (1635) V
Philocothonista; or, The Drunkard (1635) V
A Challenge for Beautie (1636) D
Loves Maistresse; or, The Queens Masque (1636) D
The Royall King, and the Loyall Subject (1637) D
The Wise-Woman of Hogsdon (1638) D
The Life and Death of Queen Elizabeth (1639) V
The Life of Merlin (1641) NF
Fortune by Land and Sea (1655) D

HIBBERD, Jack (1940–)
Australian dramatist and novelist
White with Wire Wheels (1967) D
Dimboola (1969) D
A Stretch of the Imagination (1972) D

HIBBERT, Eleanor Alice *see* JEAN PLAIDY

HICHENS, Robert Smythe (1864–1950)
British novelist and short-story writer
The Green Carnation (1894) F
An Imaginative Man (1895) F
The Folly of Eustace, and Other Stories (1896) F SS
Flames (1897) F
The Londoners (1898) F
The Slave (1899) F
Tongues of Conscience (1900) F SS
The Garden of Allah (1904) F
The Call of the Blood (1906) F
A Spirit in Prison (1908) F
Bella Donna (1909) F
The Dweller on the Threshold (1911) F CF
The Paradine Case (1933) F CF

HIGGINS, George V[incent] (1939–)
American thriller writer
The Friends of Eddie Coyle (1972) F
The Digger's Game (1973) F
Cogan's Trade (1974) F
A City on a Hill (1975) F
The Judgment of Deke Hunter (1976) F
Dreamland (1977) F
A Year or So with Edgar (1979) F
Kennedy for the Defense (1980) F
The Rat on Fire (1981) F
The Patriot Game (1982) F
A Choice of Enemies (1984) F
Penance for Jerry Kennedy (1985) F
Imposters (1986) F
Outlaws (1987) F
Wonderful Years, Wonderful Years (1988) F
Trust (1989) F
Victories (1990) F

'HIGGINS, Jack' [Harry Patterson] (1929–)
British thriller writer
Toll for the Brave (1971) F
The Eagle Has Landed (1975) F
The Cretan Lover (1980) F
Solo (1980) F
Luciano's Luck (1981) F
Touch the Devil (1982) F
Exocet (1983) F
Night of the Fox (1986) F
A Season in Hell (1989) F
Day of Reckoning (2000) F

HIGHSMITH, Patricia (1921–1995)
American novelist and short-story writer
Strangers on a Train (1950) F
The Blunderer (1954) F
The Talented Mr Ripley (1955) F
Deep Water (1957) F

This Sweet Sickness (1960) F
Ripley Under Ground (1971) F
Ripley's Game (1974) F
Found in the Street (1986) F
Ripley Under Water (1991) F
Small g: A Summer Idyll (1995) F

HIJUELOS, Oscar (1951–)
American novelist
Our House in the Last World (1983) F
The Mambo Kings Play Songs of Love (1989) F
The Fourteen Sisters of Emilio Monez O'Brien (1993) F
Mr Ives' Christmas (1995) F

HILL, Aaron (1685–1750)
English poet and dramatist
Elfrid; or, The Fair Inconstant (1710) D
The Fatal Vision; or, The Fall of Siam (1716) D
The Creation (1720) V
Advice to the Poets (1731) V
Athelwold (1731) D
Alzira (1736) D
The Tragedy of Zara (1736) D
The Tears of the Muses (1737) V
The Fanciad (1743) V
Free Thoughts on Faith; or, The Religion of Reason (1746) V
Gideon; or, The Patriot (1749) V
Meropé (1749) D

HILL, Geoffrey (1932–)
British poet and critic
For the Unfallen (1959) V
King Log (1968) V
Mercian Hymns (1971) V
Somewhere is Such a Kingdom (1975) V
Tenebrae (1978) V
The Mystery of the Charity of Charles Péguy (1983) V
The Lords of Limit (1984) NF
The Enemy's Country (1991) NF
Canaan (1996) V

'HILL, Headon' [Francis Edward Grainger] (1857–1927)
British journalist and writer of popular fiction
Clues From a Detective's Camera (1893) F SS
Zambra the Detective (1894) F SS
The Spies on the Wight (1899) F

HILL, [John Edward] Christopher (1912–)
British historian
Puritanism and Revolution (1958) NF
The Intellectual Origins of the English Revolution (1965) NF
The World Turned Upside Down (1972) NF

HILL, Reginald (1936–)
British crime writer
A Clubbable Woman [first Dalziel and Pascoe novel] (1970) F
An Advancement of Learning (1971) F
Ruling Passion (1973) F
A Pinch of Snuff (1978) F
The Spy's Wife (1980) F
Deadheads (1984) F
Under World (1988) F
Arms and the Women (2000) F

HILL, Rowland (1744–1833)
British preacher and hymn-writer
Village Dialogues (1810) NF

HILL, Susan [Elizabeth] (1942–)
British novelist, short-story writer, dramatist, and children's writer
The Enclosure (1961) F
Do Me a Favour (1963) F
Gentleman and Ladies (1968) F
A Change for the Better (1969) F
I'm the King of the Castle (1970) F
The Albatross, and Other Stories (1971) F SS
Strange Meeting (1971) F
The Bird of Night (1972) F
A Bit of Singing and Dancing (1973) F SS
In the Springtime of the Year (1974) F
The Magic Apple Tree (1983) NF
The Woman in Black (1983) F
Through the Kitchen Window (1984) NF
Through the Garden Gate (1986) NF
Family (1989) NF
Air and Angels (1991) F
The Mist in the Mirror (1992) F
Mrs De Winter [sequel to Daphne du Maurier's *Rebecca* (1938)] (1993) F
The Service of Clouds (1998) F

HILLERMAN, Tony (1925–)
American crime writer
The Blessing Way (1970) F
Fly on the Wall (1971) F
Dance Hall of the Dead (1973) F
Skinwalkers (1986) F
Talking God (1989) F
Sacred Clowns (1993) F
First Eagle (1999) F

HILLYER, Robert [Silliman] (1895–1961)
American poet, novelist, and critic
Sonnets and Other Lyrics (1917) V
Alchemy (1920) V
The Five Books of Youth (1920) V
The Hills Give Promise (1923) V
The Halt in the Garden (1925) V
The Happy Episode (1927) V
The Seventh Hill (1928) V
The Gates of the Compass (1930) V
Riverhead (1932) F
In Time of Mistrust (1939) V
Pattern of a Day (1940) V
My Heart for Hostage (1942) F
Poems for Music (1947) V
The Death of Captain Nemo (1949) V
The Relic (1957) V

HILTON, James (1900–1954)
British novelist
Catherine Herself (1920) F

Storm Passage (1922) F
The Dawn of Reckoning (1925) F
The Silver Flame (1928) F
And Now Good-bye (1931) F
Lost Horizon (1933) F
Good-Bye Mr Chips (1934) F
To You, Mr Chips (1938) F SS
Random Harvest (1941) F
Time and Time Again (1953) F

HIMES, Chester [Bomar] (1909–1984)
African-American novelist
If He Hollers Let Him Go (1945) F
Lonely Crusade (1947) F
Cast the First Stone (1952) F
Third Generation (1954) F
The Primitive (1955) F
For Love of Imabelle [reissued as *A Rage in Harlem* (1965)] (1957) F
The Crazy Kill (1959) F
All Shot Up (1960) F

HINES, [Melvin] Barry (1939–)
British novelist
A Kestrel for a Knave [repub. 1974 as *Kes*; film 1974] (1968) F
The Gamekeeper (1975) F
Looks and Smiles (1981) F

HITLER, Adolf (1889–1945)
Austrian-born German dictator
Mein Kampf (1925) NF

HOADLY, Benjamin (1676–1761)
English prelate, Bishop successively of Bangor, Hereford, Salisbury, and Winchester
The Reasonableness of Conformity to the Church of England (1703) NF
The Happiness of the Present Establishment (1708) NF
The Nature of the Kingdom, or Church of Christ (1717) NF
The Common Rights of Subjects, Defended (1719) NF
A Plain Account of the Nature and End of the Sacrament of the Lord's-Supper (1735) NF
Sixteen Sermons (1754) NF
Twenty Sermons (1755) NF

HOADLY, Benjamin, 'the younger' (1706–1757)
British physician and dramatist
The Suspicious Husband (1747) D

HOBAN, Russell [Conwell] (1925–)
American novelist and children's writer
The Mouse and his Child (1967) F CH
The Lion of Boaz-Jachin and Jachin-Boaz (1973) F CH
Turtle Diary (1975) F
Riddley Walker (1980) F
Pilgermann (1983) F
Angelica's Grotto (1999) F

HOBBES, Thomas (1588–1679)
English philosopher
Eight Books of the Peloponnesian War [from Thucidides] (1629) NF
A Briefe of the Art of Rhetorique [from Aristotle] (1637) NF
De Corpore Politico; or, The Elements of Law, Moral and Politick (1650) NF
Humane Nature; or, The Fundamental Elements of Policie (1650) NF
Leviathan; or, The Matter, Forme, and Power of a Common-Wealth Ecclesiasticall and Civill (1651) NF
Philosophical Rudiments Concerning Government and Society (1651) NF
Of Libertie and Necessitie (1654) NF
The Questions Concerning Liberty, Necessity and Chance (1656) NF
Three Papers Against Dr Wallis (1671) NF
The Travels of Ulysses (1673) V
A Letter About Liberty and Necessity (1676) NF
Decameron Physiologicum; or, Ten Dialogues of Natural Philosophy . . . (1678) NF
Behemoth; or, An Epitome of the Civil Wars of England (1679) NF
An Historical Narration Concerning Heresie and the Punishment Thereof (1680) NF

HOBSBAUM, Philip [Dennis] (1932–)
British poet and critic
The Place's Fault, and Other Poems (1964) V
In Retreat, and Other Poems (1966) V
Coming Out Fighting (1969) V
Women and Animals (1972) V
Tradition and Experiment in English Poetry (1979) NF

HOBSBAWM, Eric [John Ernest] (1917–)
British historian
Primitive Rebels (1959) NF
The Age of Revolution: Europe 1789–1848 (1962) NF
Labouring Men (1964) NF
The Age of Capital, 1848–1875 (1975) NF
The Age of Empire, 1875–1914 (1987) NF

HOCKING, Joseph (1860–1937)
British clergyman and novelist
Jabez Easterbrook (1890) F
Ishmael Pengelly: An Outcast (1893) F
And Shall Trelawney Die? (1897) F
The Madness of David Baring (1900) F

HOCKING, Silas Kitto (1850–1935)
British novelist
Her Benny (1879) F
God's Outcast (1898) F
The Strange Adventures of Israel Pendry (1899) F

HODGE, Jane Aiken (1917–)
British historical novelist and biographer
Maulever Hall (1964) F
Here Comes a Candle (1967) F
Greek Wedding (1970) F
Savannah Purchase (1971) F
Polonaise (1987) F

HODGINS, Jack (1938–)
Canadian novelist and short-story writer
Spit Delaney's Island (1976) F SS
The Invention of the World (1977) F
The Resurrection of Joseph Bourne (1980) F
The Barclay Family Theatre (1981) F SS

HODGSON, William Hope (1877–1918)
British novelist and short-story writer
The Boats of the 'Glen Carrig' (1907) F
The House on the Borderland (1908) F
The Ghost Pirates (1909) F
The Night Land (1912) F
Carnacki the Ghost-Finder (1913) F SS
Men of Deep Waters (1914) F

HOFF, Harry Summerfield *see* WILLIAM COOPER

HOFFMAN, Charles Fenno (1806–1884)
American novelist, poet, and journalist
A Winter in the West (1835) NF
Greyslaer (1840) F
The Vigil of Faith (1842) V
The Echo (1844) V
Love's Calendar (1847) V

HOFFMANN, E[rnst] T[heodor] A[madeus] (1776–1822)
German Romantic author and music critic
Ritter Gluck (1809) F
Don Juan (1813) F
The Golden Pot [*Der goldene Topf*] (1814) F
Fantasies [*Fantasiestücke*] (1814–15) F SS
The Devil's Elixir [*Die Elixiere des Teufels*] (1815–16) F
Undine (1816) D
Night-Pieces [*Nachtstücke*] (1817) F SS
The Serapion Brothers [*Die Serapionsbrüder*] (1819–21) F
Opinions of the Tomcat Murr [*Lebensansichten des Katers Murr*] (1821–2) F

HOFFMANN, Heinrich (1809–1874)
German physician and children's author
Straw Peter [*Struwwelpeter*] (1847) F CH

HOFMANNSTHAL, Hugo von (1874–1929)
Austrian poet, dramatist, and essayist
Gestern ['Yesterday'] (1891) D
The Death of Titian [*Der Tod des Tizian*] (1892) D
Electra [*Elektra*] (1903) D
Oedipus and the Sphinx [*Oedipus und die Sphinx*] (1906) D
Der Rosenkavalier ['The Knight of the Rose'; music by Richard Strauss] (1911) D
Ariadne auf Naxos ['Ariadne on Naxos'; music by Richard Strauss] (1912) D
Everyman [*Jedermann*] (1912) D
Die Frau ohne Schatten ['The Woman Without a Shadow'; music by Richard Strauss] (1919) D
The Difficult Man [*Der Schwierige*] (1921) D
Das Salzburger grosse Welttheater ['The Salzburg Great Theatre of the World'] (1922) D
The Tower [*Der Turm*] (1925) D

HOGG, James (1770–1835)
Scottish poet and author
Scottish Pastorals, Poems, Songs, etc. (1801) V
The Mountain Bard (1807) V
The Queen's Wake (1813) V
The Hunting of Badlewe (1814) V
The Pilgrims of the Sun (1815) V
Madoc of the Moor (1816) V
The Brownie of Bodsbeck, and Other Tales (1818) F SS
Winter Evening Tales (1820) F SS
The Royal Jubilee (1822) V D
The Three Perils of Man; or, War, Women and Witchcraft (1822) F
The Three Perils of Woman; or, Love, Leasing and Jealousy (1823) F
The Private Memoirs and Confessions of a Justified Sinner, Written by Himself (1824) F
Queen Hynde (1825) V
The Shepherd's Calendar (1829) NF
The Domestic Manner and Private Life of Sir Walter Scott (1834) NF
Tales of the Wars of Montrose (1835) F SS

HOGGART, Richard (1918–)
British scholar and critic
The Uses of Literacy (1957) NF
A Local Habitation (1988) NF
A Sort of Clowning (1990) NF
An Imagined Life (1992) NF

HOLCROFT, Thomas (1745–1809)
British novelist, poet, and dramatist
Alwyn; or, The Gentleman Comedian (1780) F
Duplicity (1781) D
The Family Picture; or, Domestic Dialogues on Amiable and Interesting Subjects (1783) F
Tales of the Castle; or, Stories of Instruction and Delight (1785) F SS
Caroline of Lichtfield [from the French] (1786) F
Seduction (1787) D
Anna St Ives (1792) F
The Road to Ruin (1792) D
The Adventures of Hugh Trevor [vols. i–iii] (1794) F
The Adventures of Hugh Trevor [vols. iv–vi] (1797) F
A Tale of Mystery (1802) D
Memoirs of Bryan Perdue (1805) F
Memoirs of the Late Thomas Holcroft (1816) NF

HOLDEN, Molly [Winifred], *née* Gilbert (1927–1981)
British poet
To Make Me Grieve (1968) V
Air and Chill Earth (1971) V
The Country Over (1975) V

HÖLDERLIN, [Johann Christian] Friedrich (1770–1843)
German poet and novelist
Hyperion (1797–9) F

HOLINSHED, Raphael [or **Ralph**] (d. 1580?)
English chronicler
Chronicles of England, Scotlande, and Irelande (1577) NF

HOLLAND, Philemon (1552–1637)
English translator
The Romane Historie [from Livy] (1600) NF
Natural History [from Pliny] (1601) NF
The Philosophie, Commonlie Called, the Morals [Plutarch: *Moralia*] (1603) NF
The History of Twelve Caesars [from Suetonius] (1606) NF
The Roman Historie [from Ammianus Marcellinus] (1609) NF
The Institution and Life of Cyrus [Xenophon: *Cyropaedia*] (1632) NF

HOLLINGHURST, Alan (1954–)
British poet and novelist
Confidential Chats With Boys (1982) V
The Swimming-Pool Library (1988) F
The Folding Star (1994) F
The Spell (1998) F

HOLME, Constance (1881–1955)
British regional novelist
Crump Folk Going Home (1913) F
The Lonely Plough (1914) F
The Old Road From Spain (1916) F
Beautiful End (1918) F
The Splendid Fairing (1919) F
The Trumpet in the Dust (1921) F
The Things Which Belong (1925) F
The Wisdom of the Simple, and Other Stories (1937) F SS

HOLMES, Oliver Wendell (1809–1894)
American essayist, novelist, and poet
Songs in Many Keys (1826) V
The Autocrat of the Breakfast Table (1858) NF
The Professor at the Breakfast-Table (1860) NF
Elsie Venner (1861) F
Soundings From the Atlantic (1864) NF
The Guardian Angel (1867) F
The Poet at the Breakfast-Table (1872) NF
Songs of Many Seasons (1875) V
The Iron Gate (1880) V
Pages From an Old Volume of Life (1883) NF
A Mortal Antipathy (1885) F
Before the Curfew (1888) V
Over the Teacups (1891) NF

HOLMES, Richard (1945–)
British biographer
Shelley: The Pursuit (1974) NF

HOLROYD, Michael [de Courcy Fraser] (1935–)
British biographer and novelist
Lytton Strachey: The Unknown Years (1967) NF
Lytton Strachey: The Years of Achievement (1968) NF
Augustus John: The Years of Innocence (1974) NF
Augustus John: The Years of Experience (1975) NF
George Bernard Shaw: The Search for Love (1988) NF
George Bernard Shaw: The Pursuit of Power (1989) NF
George Bernard Shaw: The Lure of Fantasy (1991) NF
George Bernard Shaw: The Last Laugh (1992) NF
Lytton Strachey: The New Biography (1994) NF
Basil Street Blues: A Family Story (1999) NF

HOLTBY, Winifred (1898–1935)
British novelist, poet, and journalist
Anderby Wold (1923) F
The Crowded Street (1924) F
The Land of Green Ginger (1927) F
Poor Caroline (1931) F
Mandoa! Mandoa! (1933) F
Truth is Not Sober (1934) F SS
The Frozen Earth, and Other Poems (1935) V
South Riding (1936) F

HOME, Henry, Lord Kames (1696–1782)
Scottish judge and author
Essays Upon Several Subjects Concerning British Antiquities (1747) NF
Essays on the Principles of Morality and Natural Religion (1751) NF
Introduction to the Art of Thinking (1761) NF
Elements of Criticism (1762) NF
Sketches of the History of Man (1774) NF
Loose Hints Upon Education (1781) NF

HOME, John (1722–1808)
Scottish dramatist
Douglas (1757) D
Agis (1758) D
The Siege of Aquileia (1760) D
The Fatal Discovery (1769) D
Alonzo (1773) D
Alfred (1778) D

HOME, William Douglas (1912–1992)
British dramatist
The Chiltern Hundreds (1947) D
'Now Barabbas . . .' (1947) D
The Manor of Northstead (1954) D
The Reluctant Peer (1964) D
The Secretary Bird (1968) D
Lloyd George Knew My Father (1972) D
The Dame of Sark (1974) D
The Kingfisher (1977) D

HOMER, (8th century BC)
Supposed author of the *Illiad* and the *Odyssey*
The Iliad V
The Odyssey V

HOOD, Hugh (1928–)
Canadian novelist and short-story writer
Flying in a Red Kite (1962) F SS
White Figure, White Ground (1964) F
Around the Mountain (1967) F SS
The Camera Always Lies (1967) F
A Game of Touch (1970) F
The Fruit Man, the Meat Man, and the Manager (1971) F SS
You Can't Get There From Here (1972) F
The Swing in the Garden (1975) F
Dark Glasses (1976) F SS
A New Athens (1977) F
Reservoir Ravine (1979) F

None Genuine Without this Signature (1980) F SS
Black and White Keys (1982) F

HOOD, Thomas (1799–1845)
British poet
Whims and Oddities in Prose and Verse [1st ser.] (1826) MISC
National Tales (1827) V SS
The Plea of the Midsummer Fairies (1827) V
Whims and Oddities in Prose and Verse [2nd ser.] (1827) MISC
The Epping Hunt (1829) V
The Dream of Eugene Aram (1831) V
Tylney Hall (1834) F
'The Song of the Shirt' [pub. in *Punch*] (1843) V
Whimsicalities (1844) MISC

HOOK, Theodore Edward (1788–1841)
British novelist and wit
The Man of Sorrow [as 'Alfred Allendale'] (1808) F
Sayings and Doings [1st ser.] (1824) F
Maxwell (1830) F
Gilbert Gurney (1836) F
Jack Brag (1837) F
Gurney Married (1838) F
Births, Deaths and Marriages (1839) F
Precepts and Practice (1840) F
Peregrine Bunce; or, Settled at Last (1842) F

HOOKER, Richard (1554–1600)
English theologian
Of the Lawes of Ecclesiasticall Politie [fifth book pub. 1597] (1593) NF
A Learned Discourse of Justification (1612) NF
A Learned Sermon of the Nature of Pride (1612) NF
A Remedie Against Sorrow and Feare (1612) NF

HOOPER, J[ohnson] J[ones] (1815–1862)
American lawyer, journalist, and novelist
Some Adventures of Captain Simon Suggs, Late of the Tallapoosa Volunteers (1846) F

'HOPE, Anthony' [Sir Anthony Hope Hawkins] (1863–1933)
British novelist
A Man of Mark (1890) F
Father Stafford (1891) F
A Change of Air (1893) F
Half a Hero (1893) F
Sport Royal, and Other Stories (1893) F SS
The Dolly Dialogues (1894) F
The God in the Car (1894) F
The Indiscretion of the Duchess (1894) F
The Prisoner of Zenda (1894) F
The Chronicles of Count Antonio (1895) F
Comedies of Courtship (1896) F SS
The Heart of Princess Osra, and Other Stories (1896) F SS
Rupert of Hentzau (1898) F
Simon Dale (1898) F HF
Quisanté (1900) F
Tristram of Blent (1901) F
The Intrusions of Peggy (1902) F
Sophy of Kravonia (1906) F
Tales of Two People (1907) F
The Great Miss Driver (1908) F
A Young Man's Year (1915) F
Lucinda (1920) F

HOPE, Christopher (1944–)
South African-born novelist and poet
Cape Drives (1974) V
A Separate Development (1981) F
Kruger's Alp (1984) F
White Boy Running (1988) NF
Moscow, Moscow (1990) NF
Serenity House (1992) F

HOPKINS, Gerard Manley (1844–1889)
British Catholic priest and poet
Poems [ed. Robert Bridges] (1918) V
Poems: Second Edition, with Additional Poems [ed. Charles Williams] (1930) V

HOPLEY, George *see* CORNELL WOOLRICH

HORACE, [Quintius Horatius Flaccus] (65–8 BC)
Roman poet
Satires [bk i] (35 BC) V
Satires [bk ii] (30 BC) V
Epodes (30 BC) V
Odes [bks i-iii] (23 BC) V
Epistles [bk i] (20 BC) V
Epistles [bk ii] (14 BC?) V
Odes [bk iv] (14 BC?) V
Ars Poetica [*The Art of Poetry*] (8 BC?) P

HORGAN, Paul (1903–1995)
American novelist
The Fault of Angels (1933) F
No Quarter Given (1935) F
Far From Cibola (1938) F
Figures in a Landscape (1940) F SS
The Habit of Empire (1941) F
A Distant Trumpet (1960) F
Things As They Are (1965) F
The Peach Stone (1967) F SS
Everything to Live For (1968) F
Whitewater (1970) F
The Thin Mountain Air (1977) F
Mexico Bay (1982) F
Under the Sangre de Cristo (1985) F

HORNBY, Nick [Nicholas] (1957–)
British novelist
Fever Pitch (1992) F
High Fidelity (1995) F
About a Boy (1998) F
Speaking with the Angel (2000) F

HORNE, Richard Henry [or **Hengist]** (1803–1884)
British poet
The Spirit of Peers and People (1834) V
Cosmo de'Medici (1837) V
The Death of Marlowe (1837) D
Gregory VII (1840) V D
The History of Napoleon (1841) NF
Orion (1843) V

A New Spirit of the Age (1844) NF
Ballad Romances (1846) V
Memoirs of a London Doll, Written by Herself [as 'Mrs Fairstar'] (1846) F CH
Judas Iscariot (1848) V
The Dreamer and the Worker (1851) F
Prometheus the Fire-Bringer (1864) V D
Psyche Apocalypté (1876) V
Bible Tragedies (1881) V

HORNUNG, E[rnest] W[illiam] (1866–1921)
British novelist and short-story writer
A Bride from the Bush (1890) F
Tiny Luttrell (1893) F
The Boss of Taroomba (1894) F
The Unbidden Guest (1894) F
The Rogue's March (1896) F
My Lord Duke (1897) F
Young Blood (1898) F
The Amateur Cracksman (1899) F SS
Dead Men Tell No Tales (1899) F
Peccavi (1900) F
The Black Mask (1901) F
Raffles (1901) F SS
The Shadow of the Rope (1902) F
Stingaree (1905) F SS
A Thief in the Night (1905) F SS
Mr Justice Raffles (1909) F
Witching Hill (1913) F
Notes of a Camp-Follower on the Western Front (1919) NF

HOROVITZ, Frances [Margaret], *née* Hooker (1938–1983)
British poet
Water Over Stone (1980) V
Snow Light, Water Light (1983) V

HOROVITZ, Michael (1935–)
British poet, translator, and editor
High Notes From When I Was Rolling in Moss (1966) V
Bank Holiday (1967) V
Children of Albion (1969) ANTH
The Wolverhampton Wanderer (1971) V
Midsummer Morning Jog Log (1986) V

HOUGHTON, [William] Stanley (1881–1913)
British dramatist
The Younger Generation (1910) D
Hindle Wakes (1912) D

HOUSEHOLD, Geofrey [Edward West] (1900–1988)
British novelist and short-story writer
The Third Hour (1937) F
The Salvation of Pisco Gabar (1938) F SS
Rogue Male (1939) F
A Rough Shoot (1951) F
Watcher in the Shadows (1960) F
Dance of the Dwarfs (1968) F
Rogue Justice (1982) F

HOUSMAN, A[lfred] E[dward] (1859–1936)
British poet and classicist
A Shropshire Lad (1896) V
Last Poems (1922) V
The Name and Nature of Poetry (1933) NF
More Poems (1936) V

HOUSMAN, Laurence (1865–1959)
British poet, novelist, and dramatist
Green Arras (1895) V
Gods and Their Makers (1897) F
Spikenard (1898) V
Rue (1899) V
An Englishwoman's Love Letters (1900) F
John of Jingalo (1912) F
Angels and Ministers (1921) D
Little Plays of St Francis [2nd ser., 1931] (1922) D
Trimblerigg (1924) F
The Unexpected Years (1937) NF
Victoria Regina (1937) D
Palestine Plays (1942) D
Cynthia (1947) V
Strange Ends and Discoveries (1948) F SS

HOVEY, Richard (1864–1900)
American poet
Along the Trail (1898) V
The Holy Graal (1907) V

HOWARD, Bronson [Crocker] (1842–1908)
American dramatist
Saratoga (1870) D
Old Love Letters (1878) D
Baron Rudolph (1881) D
Mrs Winthrop (1882) D
One of Our Girls (1885) D
The Henrietta (1887) D
Shenandoah (1888) D
Aristocracy (1892) D

HOWARD, Edward (1793?–1841)
British nautical novelist
Rattlin the Reefer (1836) F
The Old Commodore (1837) F
Outward Bound; or, A Merchant's Adventures (1838) F
Jack Ashore (1840) F

HOWARD, Elizabeth Jane, *née* Liddon (1923–)
British novelist and short-story writer
The Beautiful Visit (1950) F
We Are For the Dark (1951) F SS
The Long View (1956) F
The Sea Change (1959) F
After Julius (1965) F
Something in Disguise (1969) F
Odd Girl Out (1972) F
Mr Wrong (1975) F SS
Getting It Right (1982) F
The Light Years (1990) F
Marking Time (1991) F
Confusion (1993) F

Casting Off (1995) F
Falling (1999) F

HOWARD, Robert E[rvin] (1906–1936)
American fantasy writer
Conan the Barbarian (1954) F

HOWARD, Sir Robert (1626–1698)
English dramatist, poet, and politician
Four New Plays [The Surprisal, The Committee, The Indian Queen, The Vestal Virgin] (1665) D
The Duell of the Staggs (1668) V
The Great Favourite; or, The Duke of Lerma (1668) D

HOWATCH, Susan [Ellizabeth], *née* Sturt (1940–)
British novelist
The Dark Shore (1965) F
Penmarric (1971) F
Glittering Images (1987) F
Glamorous Powers (1988) F
Ultimate Prizes (1989) F
Scandalous Risks (1990) F
Mystical Paths (1992) F
Absolute Truths (1994) F
A Question of Integrity (1994) F
The High Flyer (1999) F

HOWE, E[dgar] W[atson] (1853–1937)
American novelist and editor
The Story of a Country Town (1883) F
The Confession of John Whitlock (1891) F
Country Town Savings (1911) F

HOWE, Julia Ward (1819–1910)
American poet and lecturer on social reform
Passion Flowers (1854) V
'The Battle Hymn of the Republic' [in the *Atlantic Monthly*] (1862) V
Sex and Education (1874) NF

HOWELL, Thomas (fl.1568)
English poet
The Arbor of Amitie (1568) V

HOWELLS, William Dean (1837–1920)
American novelist, journalist, and critic
Venetian Life (1866) NF
Their Wedding Journey (1872) F
A Chance Acquaintance (1873) F
A Foregone Conclusion (1875) F
The Lady of the Aroostock (1879) F
The Undiscovered Country (1880) F
Dr Breen's Practice (1881) F
A Fearful Responsibility (1881) F
A Modern Instance (1882) F
A Woman's Reason (1883) F
The Rise of Silas Lapham (1885) F
Indian Summer (1886) F
The Minister's Charge (1887) F
April Hopes (1888) F
Annie Kilburn (1889) F
A Hazard of New Fortunes (1890) F
Criticism and Fiction (1891) NF
The Quality of Mercy (1892) F
An Imperative Duty (1893) F
My Year in a Log Cabin (1893) NF
The World of Chance (1893) F
A Traveler From Altruria (1894) F
Impressions and Experiences (1896) NF
The Landlord at Lion's Head (1897) F
An Open-Eyed Conspiracy (1897) F
Ragged Lady (1899) F
Their Silver Wedding Journey (1899) F
Literature and Life (1902) NF
The Son of Royal Langbrith (1904) F
Through the Eye of a Needle (1907) F
The Leatherwood God (1916) F

HOWITT, Mary, *née* Botham (1799–1888)
British author and translator
The Forest Minstrel, and Other Poems (1823) V
The Desolation of Eyam, and Other Poems (1827) V
The Book of the Seasons; or, The Calendar of Nature (1831) V
The Seven Temptations (1834) V
Sketches of Natural History (1834) V
Tales in Prose (1836) F CH
Wood Leighton; or, A Year in the Country (1836) F
Birds and Flowers and Other Country Things (1838) V
Hymns and Fire-side Verses (1839) V
The Neighbours [from Frederika Bremer] (1842) F
The Home; or, Family Cares and Family Joys [from Frederika Bremer] (1843) F
Wonderful Stories for Children [from Hans Christian Andersen] (1846) F CH
Ballads and Other Poems (1847) V
Brothers and Sisters [from Frederika Bremer] (1848) F
The Cost of Caergwyn (1864) F

HOYLE, Sir Fred[erick] (1915–)
British astronomer and science fiction author
A for Andromeda (1962) F

HOYT, Charles Hale (1860–1900)
American dramatist
A Bunch of Keys (1883) D
A Trip to Chinatown (1891) D

HUDSON, William Henry (1841–1922)
British novelist and nature writer
The Purple Land that England Lost (1885) F SS
A Crystal Age (1887) F
Fan [as 'Henry Harford'] (1892) F
The Naturalist in La Plata (1892) NF
Birds in a Village (1893) NF
Idle Days in Patagonia (1893) NF
Birds in London (1898) NF
Nature in Downland (1900) NF
El Ombú, and Other Tales (1902) F SS
Hampshire Days (1903) NF
Green Mansions (1904) F
Afoot in England (1909) NF
A Shepherd's Life (1910) NF
Far Away and Long Ago (1918) NF

HUEFFER, Ford Hermann *see* FORD MADOX FORD

HUGHES, Ted [Edward James] (1930–1998)
British poet, dramatist, editor, and translator
The Hawk in the Rain (1957) V
Lupercal (1960) V
Woodwo (1967) MISC
The Iron Man (1968) F CH
The Coming of the Kings, and Other Plays (1970) D
Crow (1970) V
Gaudete (1977) V
Cave Birds (1978) V
Moortown (1979) V
Remains of Elmet (1979) V
Under the North Star (1981) V
River (1983) V
Tales of the Early World (1988) V
Wolfwatching (1989) V
Rain-Charm for the Duchy (1992) V
Shakespeare and the Goddess of Complete Being (1992) NF
Winter Pollen (1994) NF
Tales from Ovid (1997) V
Birthday Letters (1998) V
Phedre (1998) V
Aeschylus: The Oresteia (1999) V
Alcestis [from Euripides] (1999) V

HUGHES, [James] Langston (1902–1967)
African-American novelist, short-story writer, dramatist, and poet
The Weary Blues (1926) V
Fine Clothes to the Jew (1927) V
Not Without Laughter (1930) F
Dear Lovely Death (1931) V
The Negro Mother (1931) V
The Dream Keeper (1932) V
Scottboro Limited (1932) V D
The Ways of White Folk (1934) F SS
Mulatto (1936) D
A New Song (1938) V
The Big Sea (1940) NF
Shakespeare in Harlem (1941) V
Fields of Wonder (1947) V
One-Way Ticket (1949) V
Simple Speaks His Mind (1950) F SS
Montage of a Dream Deferred (1951) V
Simple Takes a Wife (1953) F SS
I Wonder as I Wander (1956) NF
Simple Stakes a Claim (1957) F SS
Tambourines to Glory (1958) F
Ask Your Mama (1961) V
Something in Common (1963) F SS
Simple's Uncle Sam (1965) F SS

HUGHES, Richard [Arthur Warren] (1900–1976)
British novelist, dramatist, and poet
The Sisters' Tragedy, and Three Other Plays (1924) D
Confessio Juvenis (1925) V
A Moment of Time (1926) F SS
A High Wind in Jamaica [US: *The Innocent Voyage*] (1929) F
In Hazard (1938) F
The Fox in the Attic (1961) F
The Wooden Shepherdess (1973) F
Into the Lap of Atlas (1979) F SS

HUGHES, Thomas (1822–1896)
British novelist and biographer
Tom Brown's Schooldays (1857) F
The Scouring of the White Horse; or, The Long Vacation Ramble of a London Clerk (1859) F
Tom Brown at Oxford (1861) F
The Manliness of Christ (1879) NF

HUGO, Victor[-Marie] (1802–1885)
French poet, novelist, and dramatist
Odes (1822) V
Han of Iceland [*Han d'Islande*] (1823) F
The Slave King [*Bug-Jargal*] (1824) F
Odes et Ballades (1826) V
Cromwell (1827) D
Hernani (1830) D
Les Feuilles d'automne ['Autumn Leaves'] (1831) V
The Hunchback of Notre-Dame [*Notre Dame de Paris*] (1831) F
Marion Delorme (1831) D
Le Roi s'amuse [basis of Verdi's *Rigoletto*] (1832) D
Lucretia Borgia [*Lucrèce Borgia*] (1833) D
Marie Tudor (1834) D
Angelo (1835) D
Songs of Twilight [*Les Chants du crépuscle*] (1835) V
Les Voix intérieures ['Inner Voices'] (1837) V
Ruy Blas (1838) D
Les Rayons et les ombres ['Sunlight and Shadows'] (1840) V
Les Châtiments ['The Punishments'] (1853) V
Les Contemplations ['Contemplations'] (1856) V
La Légende des siècles ['Legend of the Centuries'] (1859) V
Les Misérables (1862) F
Toilers of the Sea [*Les Travailleurs de la mer*] (1866) F
L'Année terrible ['The Terrible Year'] (1872) V
Ninety-Three [*Quatre-vingt-treize*] (1873) F
Le Pape ['The Pope'] (1878) V
Les Quatre Vents de l'esprit ['The Four Winds of the Spirit'] (1881) V
Torquemada (1882) D

HULME, Keri (1947–)
New Zealand novelist, short-story writer, and poet
The Bone People (1984) F
Lost Possessions (1985) V
Te Kaihu: The Windeater (1986) F SS
Strands (1992) V

HULME, T[homas] E[rnest] (1883–1917)
British philosopher, poet, and aesthetician
An Introduction to Metaphysics [by Henri Bergson] (1913) NF
Speculations (1924) NF

HUME, David (1711–1776)
British philosopher and historian
A Treatise of Human Nature (1739) NF

Essays Moral and Political [vol. i] (1741) NF
Essays Moral and Political [vol. ii] (1742) NF
Philosophical Essays Concerning Human Understanding (1748) NF
Three Essays, Moral and Political (1748) NF
An Enquiry Concerning the Principles of Morals (1751) NF
Political Discourses (1752) NF
Essays and Treatises on Several Subjects (1753–6) NF
The History of Great Britain [vol. i] (1754) NF
Four Dissertations (1757) NF
The History of Great Britain [vol. ii] (1757) NF
The History of England, Under the House of Tudor (1759) NF
The History of England, from the Invasion of Julius Caesar to the Accession of Henry VII (1762) NF
The Life of David Hume (1777) NF

HUME, Fergus[on] [Wright] (1859–1932)
New Zealand writer of detective fiction
The Mystery of a Hansom Cab (1886) F
The Piccadilly Puzzle (1889) F
Monsieur Judas (1891) F
The Mystery of Landy Court (1894) F
The Dwarf's Chamber, and Other Stories (1896) F SS
Hagar of the Pawn-Shop (1898) F
The Silent House in Pimlico (1899) F
The Bishop's Secret (1900) F
The Lady from Nowhere (1900) F
A Traitor in London (1900) F
The Jade Eye (1903) F
Lady Jim of Curzon Street (1905) F
The Dancer in Red, and Other Stories (1906) F SS
The Mystery of a Motor Cab (1908) F

HUMPHREY, William (1924–)
American novelist and short-story writer
Home From the Hill (1958) F
The Ordways (1965) F
A Time and a Place (1968) F SS
Proud Flesh (1973) F
Hostages to Fortune (1984) F
No Resting Place (1989) F

HUNT, [Isobel] Violet (1866–1942)
British society hostess and author
The Maiden's Progress (1894) F
A Hard Woman (1895) F
The Way of Marriage (1896) F
Unkist, Unkind! (1897) F
The Human Interest (1899) F
Affairs of the Heart (1900) F SS
The Celebrity at Home (1904) F
The Workaday Woman (1906) F
White Rose of Withered Leaf (1908) F
The Wife of Altamont (1910) F
Tales of the Uneasy (1911) F SS
The Celebrity's Daughter (1913) F
Zeppelin Nights (1916) F

HUNT, [James Henry] Leigh (1784–1859)
British poet, essayist, and journalist
Critical Essays on the Performers of the London Theatres (1807) NF
An Attempt to Shew the Folly and Danger of Methodism (1809) NF
The Prince of Wales v The Examiner (1812) NF
The Feast of the Poets (1814) V
The Descent of Liberty (1815) V
The Story of Rimini (1816) V
Foliage; or, Poems Original and Translated (1818) V
Literary Pocket-Book (1818) MISC
Hero and Leander, and Bacchus and Ariadne (1819) V
Amyntas [from Tasso] (1820) V
The Months (1821) V
Ultra-Crepidarius (1823) V
Bacchus in Tuscany [from the Italian] (1825) V
Lord Byron and Some of His Contemporaries (1828) NF
Christianism; or, Belief and Unbelief Reconciled (1832) NF
Sir Ralph Esher; or, Adventures of a Gentleman of the Court of Charles II (1832) F
Captain Sword and Captain Pen (1835) V
A Legend of Florence (1840) D
The Seer; or, Common-Places Refreshed [pt. i; pt. ii, 1841] (1840) NF
The Palfrey (1842) V
Imagination and Fancy (1844) NF
Stories from the Italian Poets (1846) MISC
Wit and Humour (1846) NF
Men, Women, and Books (1847) NF
A Jar of Honey from Mount Hybla (1848) V
The Town (1848) NF
Readings for Railways (1849) MISC
Autobiography (1850) NF
Table Talk (1851) NF
The Old Court Suburb; or, Memorials of Kensington (1855) NF
Stories in Verse (1855) V
A Saunter Through the West End (1861) NF

HUNTER, Evan *see* Ed McBain

HURSTON, Zora Neale (1903–1960)
African-American novelist and folklorist
Jonah's Gourd Vine (1934) F
Their Eyes Were Watching God (1934) F
Seraph on the Suwanee (1948) F

HUTCHINSON, R[ay] C[oryton] (1907–1975)
British novelist
The Answering Glory (1932) F
The Unforgotten Prisoner (1933) F
Shining Scabbard (1936) F
Testament (1938) F
The Fire and the Wood (1940) F
The Stepmother (1955) F
A Child Possessed (1964) F
Johanna at Daybreak (1969) F

Origins of Cathleen (1971) F
Rising (1976) F

HUTTON, R[ichard] H[olt] (1826–1897)
British theologian, journalist, and critic
The Relative Value of Studies and Accomplishments in the Education of Women (1862) NF
Essays Theological and Literary (1871) NF
Criticisms on Contemporary Thought and Thinkers (1894) NF

HUXLEY, Aldous [Leonard] (1894–1963)
British novelist, short-story writer, poet, and essayist
The Burning Wheel (1916) V
The Defeat of Youth, and Other Poems (1918) V
Leda (1920) V
Limbo (1920) F SS
Crome Yellow (1921) F
Mortal Coils (1922) F SS
Antic Hay (1923) F
On the Margin (1923) NF
Little Mexican, and Other Stories (1924) V
Along the Road (1925) NF
Those Barren Leaves (1925) F
Jesting Pilate (1926) NF
Two or Three Graces, and Other Stories (1926) F SS
Proper Studies (1927) NF
Point Counter Point (1928) F
Arabia Infelix, and Other Poems (1929) V
Holy Face, and Other Essays (1929) NF
Brief Candles (1930) F SS
The Cicadas, and Other Poems (1931) V
Music at Night, and Other Essays (1931) NF
Brave New World (1932) F
Eyeless in Gaza (1936) F
The Olive Tree, and Other Essays (1936) NF
After Many a Summer [US: *After Many a Summer Dies the Swan*] (1939) F
The Art of Seeing (1943) NF
Time Must Have a Stop (1944) F
The Gioconda Smile (1948) D
Ape and Essence (1949) F
Themes and Variations (1950) NF
The Devils of Loudon (1952) F
The Doors of Perception (1954) NF
The Genius and the Goddess (1955) F
Adonis and the Alphabet, and Other Essays (1956) NF
Heaven and Hell (1956) NF
Brave New World Revisited (1958) NF
Island (1962) F

HUXLEY, Elspeth [Josceline] (1907–)
British detective novelist and autobiographer
Murder on Safari (1938) F
Death of an Aryan [US: *The African Poison Murders*] (1939) F
The Flame Trees of Thika (1959) NF

HUXLEY, [Sir] Julian [Sorell] (1887–1975)
British zoologist, philosopher, and public servant
Essays of a Biologist (1923) NF
Religion Without Revelation (1927) NF
What Dare I Think? (1931) NF
The Captive Shrew, and Other Poems of a Biologist (1932) V
If I Were a Dictator (1934) NF
We Europeans (1935) NF
The Uniqueness of Man (1941) NF
Evolution (1942) NF
On Living in a Revolution (1944) NF
Soviet Genetics and World Science (1949) NF
Evolution in Action (1953) NF
Essays of a Humanist (1964) NF
Memories [vol. i; vol. ii, 1973] (1970) NF

HUXLEY, Thomas Henry (1825–1895)
British scientist and author
On the Educational Value of the Natural History Sciences (1854) NF
On Races, Species and their Origin (1860) NF
Evidence as to Man's Place in Nature (1863) NF
David Hume (1878) NF
Science and Culture and Other Essays (1881) NF
Social Diseases and Worse Remedies (1891) NF
Evolution and Ethics (1893) NF

HUYSMANS, J[oris]-K[arl] (1848–1907)
French novelist
Les Soeurs Vatard ['The Vatard Sisters'] (1879) F
En ménage (1881) F
Against Nature [*Arebours*] (1884) F
En rade (1887) F
Là-bas (1891) F

HYDE, Douglas (1860–1949)
Irish poet, literary historian, and statesman
Beside the Fire: A Collection of Irish and Gaelic Folk Stories (1890) F SS
The Love Songs of a Connacht (1893) V
The Story of Early Gaelic Literature (1895) NF
A Literary History of Ireland (1899) NF
The Religious Songs of a Connacht (1906) V

'HYDE, Robin' [Iris Guiver Wilkinson] (1906–1939)
New Zealand novelist and poet
Passport to Hell (1936) F
Persephone in Winter (1937) V
Nor the Years Condemn (1938) F
Dragon Rampant (1939) NF
Houses by the Sea (1952) V

HYNE, C[harles] J[ohn] Cutcliffe (1865–1944)
British popular novelist and short-story writer
Four Red Nightcaps (1890) F
The Adventures of Captain Kettle (1898) F SS
The Further Adventures of Captain Kettle (1899) F SS
The Lost Continent (1900) F
The Derelict (1901) F
Empire of the World (1910) F

I

IBSEN, Henrik (1828–1906)
Norwegian dramatist
Brand (1865) D

Peer Gynt (1867) V D
A Doll's House (1879) D
Ghosts (1881) D
An Enemy of the People (1882) D
The Wild Duck (1884) D
Rosmersholm (1886) D
The Lady From the Sea (1888) D
Hedda Gabler (1890) D
The Master Builder (1892) D
Little Eyolf (1894) D
John Gabriel Borkman (1896) D
When We Dead Awaken (1899) D

ILES, Francis *see* ANTHONY BERKELEY COX

IMLAY, Gilbert (1754–1828)
American author and soldier
The Emigrants; or, The History of an Expatriated Family (1793) F
A Mogul Tale; or, The Descent of the Balloon (1784) D

INCHBALD, Elizabeth, *née* Simpson (1753–1821)
British novelist, dramatist, and actress
Appearance is Against Them (1785) D
Such Things Are (1787) D
A Simple Story (1791) F
Every One Has His Fault (1793) D
Nature and Art (1796) F
Wives as They Were and Maids as They Are (1797) D
Lovers' Vows (1798) D
The Wise Men of the East [from the German of Kotzebue] (1799) D
The British Theatre; or, A Collection of Plays, with Biographical and Critical Remarks (1808) D

INGE, William (1913–1973)
American dramatist and novelist
Farther Off From Heaven (1947) D
Come Back Little Sheba (1950) D
Picnic (1953) D
Bus Stop (1955) D
The Dark at the Top of the Stairs (1957) D
A Loss of Roses (1959) D
Natural Affection (1963) D
Where's Daddy? (1966) D
Good Luck, Miss Wyckoff (1970) F
My Son is a Splendid Driver (1971) F

INGE, W[illiam] R[alph] (1860–1954)
British theologian
Christian Mysticism (1899) NF
The Philosophy of Plotinus (1918) NF
Outspoken Essays [1st ser.] (1919) NF
Outspoken Essays [2nd ser.] (1922) NF
England (1926) NF
Lay Thoughts of a Dean (1926) NF
Christian Ethics and Modern Problems (1930) NF
God and the Astronomers (1933) NF
Modernism in Literature (1938) NF
Mysticism in Religion (1947) NF
The End of an Age (1948) NF

INGELOW, Jean (1820–1897)
British poet, novelist, short-story writer, and children's writer
A Rhyming Chronicle of Incidents and Feelings (1850) V
Allerton and Dreux; or, The War of Opinion (1851) F
Poems (1863) V
Studies for Stories (1864) F
Stories to be Told to a Child (1865) F CH
A Story of Doom, and Other Poems (1867) V
Mopsa the Fairy (1869) F CH
Off the Skelligs (1872) F
Fated to be Free (1875) F
Sarah de Berenger (1879) F
Don John (1881) F
Poems: Third Series (1885) V
John Jerome: His Thoughts and Ways (1886) F
Laura Richmond (1901) F CH

'INNES, Hammond' [Ralph Hammond-Innes] (1913–)
British thriller writer
Wreckers Must Breathe (1940) F
Attack Alarm (1941) F
Dead and Alive (1946) F
Killer Mine (1947) F
The White South (1949) F
The Angry Mountain (1950) F
Campbell's Kingdom (1952) F
The Strange Land (1954) F
The Mary Deare (1956) F
The Doomed Oasis (1960) F
Atlantic Fury (1962) F
The Strode Venturer (1965) F
The Conquistadors (1969) F
Levkas Man (1971) F
North Star (1974) F
Solomon's Seal (1980) F
Medusa (1988) F

INNES, Michael *see* J.I.M. STEWART

IONESCO, Eugène (1909–1994)
Romanian-born French dramatist
The Bald Soprano (1950) D
The Lesson (1951) D
The Chairs (1952) D
Victims of Duty (1953) D
Amédée (1954) D
The Killer (1958) D
Rhinoceros (1960) D
Hunger and Thirst (1964) D
Macbett (1972) D
Journey Among the Dead (1981) D

'IOTA' [Kathleen Mannington Caffyn] (1855?–1926)
Irish novelist and short-story writer
A Yellow Aster (1894) F
A Comedy in Spasms (1895) F
Poor Max (1898) F

Anne Mauleverer (1899) F
Dorinda and Her Daughter (1910) F
The Fire-Seekers (1911) F

IRELAND, David (1927–)
Australian novelist and dramatist
Image in the Clay (1964) D
The Chantic Bird (1968) F
The Unknown Industrial Prisoner (1971) F
The Flesheaters (1972) F
Burn [adaptation of *Image in the Clay* 1964] (1974) F
The Glass Canoe (1976) F
A Woman of the Future (1979) F
City of Women (1981) F
Archimedes and the Seagle (1984) F
Bloodfather (1987) F

IRELAND, [Samuel] William-Henry (1777–1835)
British Shakespeare forger, poet, and novelist
An Authentic Account of the Shakespear Manuscripts (1796) NF
The Abbess (1799) F
Vortigern, an Historical Tragedy [supposedly written by Shakespeare] (1799) D
Mutius Scaevola; or, The Roman Patriot (1801) D
The Angler (1804) V
The Confessions of William-Henry Ireland (1805) NF
Scribbleomania (1815) NF

IRISH, William *see* CORNELL WOOLRICH

IRVING, John [Winslow] (1942–)
American novelist
Setting Free the Bears (1969) F
The Water-Method Man (1972) F
The 158-Pound Marriage (1974) F
The World According to Garp (1978) F
The Hotel New Hampshire (1981) F
The Cider House Rules (1985) F
A Prayer for Owen Meaney (1989) F
Trying to Save Peggy Sneed (1993) F SS
A Son of the Circus (1994) F
A Widow for One Year (1998) F

IRVING, Washington ['Geoffrey Crayon'] (1783–1859)
American essayist and short-story writer
'The Letters of Jonathan Oldstyle, Gent.' [pub. in the *Morning Chronicle*] (1803) F
Salmagundi; or, The Whim-Whams and Opinions of Launcelot Langstaff, Esq., and Others (1807–8) F SS
A History of New York [by 'Diedrich Knickerbocker'] (1809) F
The Sketch Book [by 'Geoffrey Crayon'] (1819–20) MISC
Bracebridge Hall; or, The Humorists [by 'Geoffrey Crayon'] (1822) F SS
Tales of a Traveller (1824) F SS
History of the Life and Voyages of Christopher Columbus (1828) NF
A Chronicle of the Conquest of Granada (1829) F
The Alhambra (1832) MISC
The Crayon Miscellany (1835) MISC
Astoria (1836) F
The Adventures of Captain Bonneville, USA (1837) F
Oliver Goldsmith (1840) NF
Wolfert's Roost (1855) F SS
Life of Washington (1855–9) NF

IRWIN, Margaret [Emma Faith] (1889–1967)
British historical novelist and short-story writer
Still She Wished For Company (1924) F
Royal Flush (1932) F HF
Madame Fears the Dark (1935) F SS
Mrs Oliver Cromwell, and Other Stories (1940) F SS
Bloodstock, and Other Stories (1954) F SS

ISHERWOOD, Christopher [William Bradshaw] (1904–1986)
British novelist and dramatist
All the Conspirators (1928) F
The Memorial (1932) F
Mr Norris Changes Trains [US: *The Last of Mr Norris*] (1935) F
Sally Bowles (1937) F
Lions and Shadows (1938) NF
Goodbye to Berlin (1939) F SS
Journey to a War (1939) NF
Prater Violet (1945) F
The Berlin Stories (1946) F
The Condor and the Cows (1948) NF
The World in the Evening (1954) F
Down There on a Visit (1962) F
A Single Man (1964) F
Exhumations (1966) MISC
A Meeting by the River (1967) F
Christopher and His Kind 1929–39 (1977) NF

ISHIGURO, Kazuo (1954–)
Japanese-born novelist
A Pale View of Hills (1982) F
An Artist of the Floating World (1986) F
The Remains of the Day (1989) F
The Unconsoled (1995) F
When We Were Orphans (2000) F

J

JACKS, L[awrence] P[earsall] (1860–1955)
British Unitarian clergyman, philosopher, and theological writer
Mad Shepherds and Other Human Studies (1909) NF
The Alchemy of Thought (1910) NF
All Men Are Ghosts (1913) NF
From Authority to Freedom (1920) NF
Legends of Smokeover (1922) F
Responsibility and Culture (1925) NF
Heroes of Smokeover (1926) F
The Education of the Whole Man (1931) NF
The Last Legend of Smokeover (1939) F

JACKSON, Helen Hunt (1830–1885)
American poet, novelist, and children's writer
Ramona (1884) F

JACKSON, Holbrook (1874–1948)
British literary historian and critic
Bernard Shaw (1907) NF
Romance and Reality (1911) NF
The Eighteen Nineties (1913) NF
Dreamers of Dreams (1948) NF

JACKSON, Shirley [Hardie] (1919–1965)
American novelist and short-story writer
The Road Through the Wall (1948) F
The Lottery (1949) F SS
Hangsaman (1951) F
The Bird's Nest (1954) F
The Witchcraft of Salem Village (1956) F CH
The Sundial (1958) F
The Haunting of Hill House (1959) F
We Have Always Lived in the Castle (1962) F

JACOB, Naomi [Ellington] (1884–1964)
British novelist
Four Generations (1934) F
The Lenient God (1937) F
This Porcelain God (1939) F

JACOBS, W[illiam] W[ymark] (1863–1943)
British short-story writer, novelist, and dramatist
Many Cargoes (1896) F SS
The Skipper's Wooing, and The Brown Man's Servant (1897) F SS
Sea Urchins (1898) F SS
A Master of Craft (1900) F SS
Light Freights (1901) F SS
The Lady of the Barge, and Other Stories [contains 'The Monkey's Paw'] (1902) F SS
Dialstone Lane (1904) F
Captains All (1905) F SS
Short Cruises (1907) F SS
Salthaven (1908) F
Sailors' Knots (1909) F SS
Ship's Company (1911) F SS
Night Watches (1914) F SS
Sea Whispers (1926) F SS

JACOBSON, Dan (1929–)
South African novelist and short-story writer
The Trap (1955) F
A Dance in the Sun (1956) F
The Price of Diamonds (1957) F
Evidence of Love (1960) F
Beggar My Neighbour (1964) F SS
The Beginners (1966) F
The Rape of Tamar (1970) F
The Wonder-Worker (1973) F
The Confessions of Joseph Baisz (1977) F
Through the Wilderness (1977) F SS
Her Story (1987) F

JACOBSON, Howard [Eric] (1942–)
British novelist
Coming From Behind (1983) F
Peeping Tom (1984) F
Redback (1986) F
The Very Model of a Man (1992) F
No More Mister Nice Guy (1998) F
Getting Licked (1999) F
The Mighty Waltzer (1999) F

JAGO, Richard (1715–1781)
British poet
Edge-Hill; or, The Rural Prospect Delineated and Moralised (1767) V
Labor and Genius (1768) V
His Majesties Poeticall Exercises at Vacant Houres (1591) V
Daemonologie (1597) NF
The True Lawe of Free Monarchies (1598) NF
Basilikon Doron (1599) NF
A Counter-blaste to Tobacco (1604) NF

JAMES, Clive [Vivian Leopold] (1939–)
Australian author and broadcaster
Unreliable Memoirs (1980) NF
Falling Towards England (1985) NF
May Week Was in June (1990) NF

JAMES, C[yril] L[eonard] R[obert] (1901–1989)
Trinidadian essayist and journalist
Minty Alley (1936) F
Beyond a Boundary (1963) NF

JAMES, G[eorge] P[ayne] R[ainsford] (1799–1860)
British novelist
Richelieu (1829) F
Darnley; or, The Field of the Cloth of Gold (1830) F
De l'Orme (1830) F
Philip Augustus; or, The Brothers in Arms (1831) F
Henry Masterton; or, The Adventures of a Young Cavalier (1832) F
The String of Pearls (1832) F SS
Mary of Burgundy; or, The Revolt of Ghent (1833) F
The Life and Adventures of John Marston Hall (1834) F
The Gipsy (1835) F
One in a Thousand; or, The Days of Henri Quatre (1835) F
Attila (1837) F
The Robber (1838) F
The Gentleman of the Old School (1839) F
The Huguenot (1839) F
The Jacquerie; or, The Lady and the Page (1841) F
Eva St Clair, and Other Collected Tales (1843) F SS
The False Heir (1843) F
Agincourt (1844) F
Arabella Stuart (1844) F
The Smuggler (1845) F
The Castle of Ehrenstein (1847) F
The Woodman (1849) F
Henry Smeaton (1851) F
Agnes Sorel (1853) F
Ticonderoga; or, The Black Eagle (1854) F
Leonora d'Orco (1857) F

JAMES, Henry (1843–1916)
American novelist, short-story writer, and essayist
A Passionate Pilgrim, and Other Tales (1875) F SS
Transatlantic Sketches (1875) NF

Roderick Hudson (1876) F
The American (1877) F
Daisy Miller (1878) F
The Europeans (1878) F
French Poets and Novelists (1878) NF
Watch and Ward (1878) F
An International Episode (1879) F
The Madonna of the Future, and Other Tales (1879) F SS
Confidence (1880) F
The Portrait of a Lady (1881) F
Washington Square (1881) F
Portraits of Places (1883) NF
Tales of Three Cities (1884) F SS
The Author of Beltraffio (1885) F SS
Stories Revived (1885) F SS
The Bostonians (1886) F
The Princess Casamassima (1886) F
The Aspern Papers (1888) F SS
Partial Portraits (1888) NF
The Reverberator (1888) F
A London Life (1889) F SS
The Tragic Muse (1890) F
The Lesson of the Master (1892) F SS
Essays in London and Elsewhere (1893) NF
Picture and Text (1893) NF
The Private Life (1893) F SS
The Real Thing, and Other Tales (1893) F SS
Terminations (1895) F SS
Embarrassments (1896) F SS
The Other House (1896) F
The Spoils of Poynton (1897) F
What Maisie Knew (1897) F
In the Cage (1898) F
The Two Magics [inc.'The Turn of the Screw'] (1898) F SS
The Awkward Age (1899) F
The Soft Side (1900) F SS
The Sacred Fount (1901) F
The Wings of the Dove (1902) F
The Ambassadors (1903) F
The Better Sort (1903) F SS
William Wetmore Story and His Friends (1903) NF
The Golden Bowl (1904) F
English Hours (1905) NF
The American Scene (1907) NF
Views and Reviews (1908) NF
Italian Hours (1909) NF
The Finer Grain (1910) F SS
The Outcry (1911) F
A Small Boy and Others (1913) NF
Notes of a Son and Brother (1914) NF
Notes on Novelists (1914) NF
The Ivory Tower (1917) F
The Middle Years (1917) NF
The Sense of the Past (1917) F
Within the Rim, and Other Essays (1919) NF

JAMES, M[ontague] R[hodes] (1862–1936)
British scholar and ghost-story writer
Ghost Stories of an Antiquary (1904) F SS
More Ghost Stories of an Antiquary (1911) F SS
A Thin Ghost, and Others (1919) F SS
The Five Jars (1922) F CH
A Warning to the Curious, and Other Ghost Stories (1925) F SS
Eton and King's (1926) NF

JAMES, P[hyllis] D[orothy], *née* White, Baroness James of Holland Park (1920–)
British crime novelist
Cover Her Face (1962) F
A Mind to Murder (1963) F
Unnatural Causes (1967) F
Shroud for a Nightingale (1971) F
An Unsuitable Job For a Woman (1972) F
The Black Tower (1975) F
Death of an Expert Witness (1977) F
Innocent Blood (1980) F
The Skull Beneath the Skin (1982) F
A Taste for Death (1986) F
Devices and Desires (1989) F
Original Sin (1994) F
A Certain Justice (1997) F

JAMES, William (1842–1910)
American philosopher
The Principles of Psychology (1890) NF
The Varieties of Religious Experience (1902) NF
Pragmatism (1907) NF
The Meaning of Truth (1909) NF
A Pluralistic Universe (1909) NF

JAMES I [James VI of Scotland] (1566–1625)
English king
The Essayes of a Prentise, in the Divine Art of Poesie (1584) V
His Majesties Poeticall Exercises at Vacant Houres (1591) V
Daemonologie (1597) NF
The True Lawe of Free Monarchies (1598) NF
Basilikon Doren (1599) NF
A Counter-blaste to Tobacco (1604) NF

JAMESON, Anna Brownell, *née* Murphy (1794–1860)
Irish-born literary and art critic
Loves of the Poets (1829) NF
Memoirs of the Celebrated Female Sovereigns (1831) NF
Characteristics of Women, Moral , Poetical and Historical (1832) NF
Visits and Sketches at Home and Abroad (1834) NF
Winter Studies and Summer Rambles in Canada (1838) NF
Legends of the Saints (1848) NF
Legends of the Monastic Orders (1850) NF
Legends of the Madonna (1852) NF
Sisters of Charity (1855) NF
The Communion of Labour (1856) NF

JAMESON, [Margaret] Storm (1897–1986)
British novelist, poet, and critic
The Pot Boils (1919) F

Lady Susan and Life (1923) F
The Lovely Ship (1927) F
The Voyage Home (1930) F
A Richer Dust (1931) F
The Triumph of Time (1932) F
Company Parade (1934) F
Love in Winter (1935) F
None Turn Back (1936) F
The Novel in Contemporary Life (1938) NF
Cousin Honoré (1940) F
Cloudless May (1943) F
The Moment of Truth (1949) F
The Green Man (1952) F
A Cup of Tea for Mr Thorgill (1957) F
The Road From the Monument (1962) F
The Early Life of Stephen Hind (1966) F
The White Crow (1968) F
Journey From the North (1969) NF
There Will Be a Short Interval (1972) F

JANOWITZ, Tama (1957–)
American novelist
American Dad (1981) F
Slaves of New York (1986) F SS
A Cannibal in Manhattan (1987) F SS
The Male Cross-Dresser Support Group (1992) F SS

JARRELL, Randall (1914–1965)
American poet and critic
Blood for a Stranger (1942) V
Little Friend, Little Friend (1945) V
Losses (1948) V
The Seven-League Crutches (1951) V
Poetry and the Age (1953) NF
The Woman at the Washington Zoo (1960) V
A Sad Heart at the Supermarket (1962) NF
The Lost World (1965) V

JEFFERIES, [John] Richard (1848–1887)
British naturalist, journalist, and novelist
The Scarlet Shawl (1874) F
Restless Human Hearts (1875) F
The World's End (1877) F
The Gamekeeper at Home (1878) NF
The Amateur Poacher (1879) NF
Wild Life in a Southern County (1879) NF
Greene Ferne Farm (1880) F
Hodge and His Masters (1880) F
Wood Magic (1880) F
Bevis (1882) F
The Story of My Heart (1883) NF
The Dewy Morn (1884) F
The Life of the Fields (1884) NF
Red Deer (1884) NF
After London; or, Wild England (1885) F
The Open Air (1885) NF
Amaryllis at the Fair (1887) F
Field and Hedgerow (1889) NF

JEFFERS, [John] Robinson (1887–1962)
American poet
Flagons and Apples (1912) V
Californians (1916) V
Tamar, and Other Poems (1924) V
The Women at Point Sur (1927) V
Cawdor, and Other Poems (1928) V
Dear Judas, and Other Poems (1929) V
Descent to the Dead (1931) V
Thurso's Landing, and Other Poems (1932) V
Give Your Heart to the Hawks, and Other Poems (1933) V
Solstice, and Other Poems (1935) V
Such Counsels You Gave to Me, and Other Poems (1937) V
Be Angry at the Sun (1941) V
Hungerfield, and Other Poems (1945) V
The Double Axe (1948) V
The Beginning and the End (1963) V

JELLICOE, [Patricia] Anne (1927–)
British dramatist and director
The Sport of My Mad Mother (1956) D
The Knack (1961) D

JENKINS, Alan [Fitzgerald] (1955–)
British poet and editor
In the Hot-House (1988) V
Greenheart (1990) V
Harm (1994) V

JENKINS, [John] Robin (1912–)
Scottish novelist and short-story writer
The Cone-Gatherers (1955) F
Guests of War (1956) F
The Changeling (1958) F
Dust on the Paw (1961) F
A Toast to the Lord (1972) F
Fergus Lamont (1979) F
The Awakening of George Darroch (1985) F
Poverty Castle (1991) F

JENNINGS, Elizabeth [Joan Cecil] (1926–)
British poet
A Way of Looking (1955) V
A Sense of the World (1958) V
Song For a Birth or a Death, and Other Poems (1961) V
Recoveries (1964) V
The Mind Has Mountains (1966) V
Hurt (1970) V
Growing Points (1975) V
Consequently I Rejoice (1977) V
Moments of Grace (1979) V
A Dream of Spring (1980) V
Extending the Territory (1985) V
Times and Seasons (1992) V
Familiar Spirits (1994) V
In the Meantime (1997) V

JEPSON, Edgar [Alfred] (1863–1938)
British novelist
Sibyl Falcon (1895) F
The Keepers of the People (1898) F
The Dictator's Daughter (1902) F
The Admirable Tinker, Child of the World (1904) F

The Lady Noggs, Peeress (1906) F
Lady Noggs Intervenes (1908) F

JEROME, J[erome] K[lapka] (1859–1927)
British novelist, dramatist, and journalist
The Idle Thoughts of an Idle Fellow (1886) NF
Stage-Land (1889) NF
Three Men in a Boat (To Say Nothing of the Dog) (1889) F
Diary of a Pilgrimage (and Six Essays) (1891) NF
Told After Supper (1891) F SS
Novel Notes (1893) NF
John Ingerfield, and Other Stories (1894) F SS
Sketches in Lavender, Blue and Green (1897) F SS
The Second Thoughts of an Idle Fellow (1898) NF
Three Men on the Bummel (1900) F
The Observations of Henry (1901) F SS
Paul Kelver (1902) F
Tea-Table Talk (1903) NF
American Wives, and Others (1904) NF
Tommy and Co. (1904) F
Idle Ideas in 1905 (1905) NF
The Passing of the Third Floor Back, and Other Stories (1907) F SS
The Angel and the Author—and Others (1908) NF
They and I (1909) F
Malvina of Brittany (1916) F SS
All Roads Lead to Calvary (1919) F
Anthony John (1923) F
A Miscellany of Sense and Nonsense (1923) MISC
My Life and Times (1926) NF

JERROLD, Douglas [William] (1803–1857)
British dramatist, humorist, and journalist
Black-Eyed Susan; or, All in the Downs (1829) D
Sally in Our Alley (1830) D
The Rent Day (1832) D
Beau Nash, the King of Bath (1834) D
Men of Character (1838) NF
Cakes and Ale (1842) F SS
Punch's Letters to His Son (1843) F
The Story of a Feather (1844) F
Punch's Complete Letter-Writer (1845) NF
Time Works Wonders (1845) D
The Chronicles of Clovernook (1846) F
The Life and Adventures of Miss Robinson Crusoe (1846) F
Mrs Caudle's Curtain Lectures (1846) F
A Man Made of Money (1849) F
The History of St Giles and St James (1851) F

JESSE, F[ryniwyd] [Wynifried Margaret] Tennyson (1888–1958)
British novelist and dramatist
The Lacquer Lady (1929) F
A Pin to See the Peepshow (1934) F

JEWETT, Sarah Orne (1849–1909)
American novelist and short-story writer
Deephaven (1877) F SS
A Country Doctor (1884) F
A Marsh Island (1885) F
A White Heron (1886) F SS
The King of Folly Island (1888) F SS
A Native of Winby (1893) F SS
The Life of Nancy (1895) F SS
The Country of the Pointed Firs (1896) F SS
The Tory Lover (1901) F

JEWSBURY, Geraldine [Endsor] (1812–1880)
British novelist and woman of letters
Zoe (1845) F
The Half-Sisters (1848) F
Marian Withers (1851) F
The History of an Adopted Child (1852) F
Constance Herbert (1855) F
Angelo; or, The Pine Forest in the Alps (1856) F
The Sorrows of Gentility (1856) F
Right or Wrong (1859) F

JHABVALA, Ruth Prawer (1927–)
British novelist, screenwriter, and short-story writer
To Whom She Will (1955) F
The Nature of Passion (1956) F
Esmond in India (1958) F
The Householder (1960) F
A New Dominion (1972) F
Heat and Dust (1975) F
How I Became a Holy Mother, and Other Stories (1976) F SS
In Search of Love and Beauty (1983) F
Three Continents (1987) F
Poet and Dancer (1993) F
Shards of Memory (1995) F
East into Upper East (1998) F SS

JOAD, C[yril] E[dwin] M[itchinson] (1891–1953)
British philosopher
Essays in Common Sense Philosophy (1919) NF
Common-Sense Ethics (1921) NF
Introduction to Modern Philosophy (1924) NF
Thrasymachus; or, The Future of Morals (1925) NF
The Mind and its Workings (1927) NF
Guide to Modern Thought (1933) NF
Liberty To-day (1934) NF
The Dictator Resigns (1936) NF
Guide to Modern Wickedness (1939) NF
Journey Through the War Mind (1940) NF
A Critique of Logical Positivism (1950) NF
The Recovery of Belief (1952) NF

JOHNS, W[illiam] E[arle] (1893–1968)
British boys' novelist and creator of Biggles
The Camels Are Coming (1932) F CH
The Cruise of the Condor (1933) F CH
Biggles Flies Again (1934) F CH
Biggles of the Camel Squadron (1934) F CH
Biggles Flies East (1935) F CH
Biggles in Africa (1936) F CH
Biggles Flies West (1937) F CH
Biggles Flies South (1938) F CH
Biggles Flies North (1939) F CH
Biggles in the Baltic (1940) F CH
Biggles—Secret Agent (1940) F CH
Biggles Sees It Through (1941) F CH

Worrals of the WAAF (1941) F CH
Biggles in the Jungle (1942) F CH
Biggles in Borneo (1943) F CH
Biggles in the Orient (1945) F CH
Biggles Sees Too Much (1970) F CH

JOHNSON, B[ryan] S[tanley William] (1933–1973)
British novelist, dramatist, and poet
Travelling People (1963) F
Albert Angelo (1964) F
Trawl (1966) F
The Unfortunates (1969) F
House Mother Normal (1971) F
Christie Malry's Own Double Entry (1973) F

JOHNSON, Charles (1679–1748)
English dramatist
Love and Liberty (1709) D
The Force of Friendship (1710) D
The Successful Pyrate (1712) D
The Victim (1714) D
The Sultaness (1717) D
Love in a Forest (1723) D
The Tragedy of Medea (1730) D

JOHNSON, Edward (1599?–1672)
English-born historian of New England
The Wonder-Working Providence of Sion's Saviour in New-England (1654) NF

JOHNSON, [Emily] Pauline (1861–1913)
Canadian poet
The White Wampum (1895) V
Canadian Born (1903) V
Legends of Vancouver (1911) V
Flint and Feather (1912) V
The Moccasin Maker (1913) V
The Shagganappi (1913) V

JOHNSON, James Weldon (1871–1938)
African-American novelist, poet, civil rights leader, and educator
The Autobiography of an Ex-Colored Man (1912) F

JOHNSON, Linton Kwesi (1952–)
Jamaican-born poet
Voices of the Living and the Dead (1974) V
Dread Beat and Blood (1975) V
Inglan is a Bitch (1980) V
Tings and Times (1991) V

JOHNSON, Lionel [Pigot] (1867–1902)
British poet and critic
The Book of the Rhymers' Club (1892) V
Ireland, and Other Poems (1897) V
Poetry and Ireland (1908) NF
Post Liminium (1911) NF

JOHNSON, Pamela Hansford (1912–1981)
British novelist, dramatist, and critic
This Bed Thy Centre (1935) F
Blessed Above Women (1936) F
Girdle of Venus (1939) F
Too Dear For My Possessing (1940) F
The Trojan Brothers (1944) F
An Avenue of Stone (1947) F
A Summer to Decide (1948) F
Catherine Carter (1952) F
An Impossible Marriage (1954) F
The Unspeakable Skipton (1959) F
An Error of Judgement (1962) F
Night and Silence! Who is Here? (1963) F
Cork Street, Next to the Hatter's (1965) F
The Survival of the Fittest (1968) F
A Bonfire (1981) F

JOHNSON, Samuel (1709–1784)
British lexicographer, poet, novelist, and critic
London (1738) V
An Account of the Life of Mr Richard Savage (1744) NF
Miscellaneous Observations on the Tragedy of Macbeth (1745) NF
The Plan of a Dictionary of the English Language (1747) NF
Irene (1749) D
The Vanity of Human Wishes (1749) V
A Dictionary of the English Language (1755) NF
The Prince of Abissinia [Rasselas] (1759) F
The Plays of William Shakespeare (1765) EDN
The False Alarm (1770) NF
The Patriot (1774) NF
A Journey to the Western Islands of Scotland (1775) NF
The Works of Richard Savage (1775) EDN
Prefaces, Biographical and Critical, to the Works of the English Poets ['Lives of the Poets'] (1779) NF
Skyscrapers in the Mist (1946) NF
Journey Through Tomorrow (1947) NF

JOHNSTON, George [Henry] (1912–1970)
Australian novelist
Moon at Perigee [UK: *Monsoon*] (1948) F
The Cyprian Woman (1955) F
The Darkness Outside (1959) F
Closer to the Sun (1960) F
The Far Road (1962) F
My Brother Jack (1964) F
The Far Face of the Moon (1965) F
The Australians (1966) NF
Clean Straw for Nothing (1969) F
A Cartload of Clay (1971) F

JOHNSTON, Jennifer [Prudence] (1930–)
Irish novelist and dramatist
The Captain and the Kings (1972) F
The Gates (1973) F
How Many Miles to Babylon? (1974) F
Shadows on Our Skin (1977) F
The Old Jest (1979) F
Fool's Sanctuary (1987) F
The Invisible Worm (1991) F

JOHNSTON, [William] Denis (1901–1984)
Irish dramatist
The Moon in the Yellow River (1931) D
A Bride for the Unicorn (1933) D
The Golden Cuckoo (1939) D

JOHNSTONE, Charles (1719?–1800)
British novelist
Chrysal; or, The Adventures of a Guinea (1760) F
The Reverie; or, A Flight to the Paradise of Fools (1762) F
The History of Arsaces, Prince of Betlis (1774) F
The Pilgrim; or, A Picture of Life (1775) F
The History of John Juniper, Esq, alias Juniper Jack (1781) F
The Adventures of Anthony Varnish; or, A Peep at the Manners of Society (1786) F

JOLLEY, Elizabeth (1923–)
British-born Australian novelist and dramatist
Five Acre Virgin (1976) F SS
The Travelling Entertainer (1979) F SS
Palomino (1980) F
The Newspaper of Claremont Street (1981) F
Miss Peabody's Inheritance (1983) F
Mr Scobie's Riddle (1983) F
Woman in a Lampshade (1983) F SS
Milk and Honey (1984) F
Foxybaby (1985) F
The Well (1986) F
The Sugar Mother (1988) F
My Father's Moon (1989) F
Cabin Fever (1990) F
Central Mischief (1992) NF
The George's Wife (1993) F

JONES, Diana Wynne (1934–)
British children's writer
Wilkins' Tooth (1973) F CH
Dogsbody (1975) F CH
Eight Days of Luke (1975) F CH
Charmed Life (1977) F CH
The Magicians of Caprona (1980) F CH
Fire and Hemlock (1985) F CH

JONES, Ernest Charles (1819–1869)
British poet, novelist, and Chartist
The Student of Padua (1836) V MUS
De Brassier (1852) F
The Maid of Warsaw; or, The Tyrant Czar (1854) F
The Battle Day, and Other Poems (1855) V
Women's Wrongs (1855) F SS
The Revolt of Hindoostan; or, The New World (1857) V
Corayda: A Tale of Faith and Chivalry, and Other Poems (1860) V

JONES, Henry Arthur (1851–1929)
British dramatist
The Silver King (1882) D
Saints and Sinners (1884) D
Judah (1890) D
The Case of Rebellious Susan (1894) D
The Liars (1897) D
Mrs Dane's Defence (1900) D

JONES, James (1921–1977)
American novelist
From Here to Eternity (1951) F
Some Came Running (1957) F
The Pistol (1959) F
The Thin Red Line (1962) F
Go to the Widow-Maker (1967) F
The Ice-Cream Headache (1968) F SS
The Merry Month of May (1971) F
A Touch of Danger (1973) F
Whistle (1978) F

JONES, LeRoi [Imamu Amiri Baraka] (1934–)
American dramatist, poet, novelist, and essayist
A Good Girl is Hard to Find (1958) D
Cuba Libre (1961) NF
Dante (1961) D
Preface to a Twenty Volume Suicide Note (1961) V
Blues People (1963) NF
The Dead Lecturer (1964) V
Dutchman (1964) D
The System of Dante's Hell (1965) F
Home (1966) NF
Slave Ship (1967) D
Black Magic (1969) V
In Our Terribleness (1971) V
Raise Race Rays Raze (1971) NF
Spirit Reach (1972) NF
Reggae or Not! (1981) V
Daggers and Javelins (1984) NF

JONES, Madison [Percy Jr] (1925–)
American novelist
The Innocent (1957) F
Forest of the Night (1960) F
A Buried Land (1963) F
An Exile (1967) F
A Cry of Absence (1971) F
Passing Through Gehenna (1978) F
Season of the Strangler (1982) F SS

JONES, [Walter] David [Michael] (1895–1974)
British poet and graphic artist
In Parenthesis (1937) V
The Anathemata (1952) V
The Tribune's Visitation (1969) V
The Sleeping Lord, and Other Fragments (1974) V
The Kensington Mass, and Other Fragments (1975) V
The Dying Gaul, and Other Writings (1978) NF

JONG, Erica [Mann] (1942–)
American novelist and feminist
Fear of Flying (1974) F
How To Save Your Own Life (1977) F
Fanny (1980) F
Witches (1981) F
Parachutes and Kisses (1984) F
Serenissima (1987) F
Any Woman's Blues (1994) F
Fear of Fifty (1994) F

JONSON, Ben[jamin] (1572–1637)
English dramatist and poet
The Case is Altered (1598?) D
Every Man in His Humor (1598) D
Every Man Out of his Humor (1599) D

The Fountaine of Selfe-love; or, Cynthias Revells (1600) D
Poetaster; or, The Arraignment (1601) D
Sejanus his Fall (1603) D
Hymenaei; or, The Solemnities of Masque, and Barriers (1606) D
Volpone; or, the Foxe (1606) D
Epicoene; or, The Silent Woman (1609/10) D
The Alchemist (1610) D
Catiline his Conspiracy (1611) D
Love Restored (1612) D
Bartholomew Fayre [with *The Divell is an Asse* and *The Staple of Newes*; first pub. in Jonson's *Works* 1616] (1614) D
Christmas, his Masque (1616) D
The Golden Age Restor'd (1616) D
Mercurie Vindicated (1616) D
The Vision of Delight (1617) D
The Gypsies Metamorphos'd (1621) D
Newes from the New World Discover'd in the Moone (1621) D
The Fortunate Isles and their Union (1625) D
The New Inne; or, The Light Heart (1629) D
Execration Against Vulcan (1640) V

JORDAN, Neil (1950–)
Irish short-story writer, novelist, and film director
Night in Tunisia, and Other Stories (1976) F SS
The Past (1980) F
Sunrise with Sea Monster (1995) F

JOYCE, James [Augustine Aloysius] (1882–1941)
Irish novelist and poet
Chamber Music (1907) V
Dubliners (1914) F SS
Portrait of the Artist as a Young Man (1916) F
Exiles (1918) D
Ulysses [prtd in France] (1922) F
Pomes Penyeach (1927) V
Anna Livia Plurabelle (1928) F
Finnegans Wake (1939) F
Stephen Hero (1944) F
Ulysses [definitive text] (1986) F

'JUNIUS' [probably **Sir Philip Francis** (1740–1818)]
British politician and author
The Political Contest [pt. i, pt. ii] (1769) NF
*Two Letters from Junius to the D*** of G******* (1769) NF
Junius: Stat Nominis Umbra (1772) NF

K

KAFKA, Franz (1883–1924)
Austrian novelist
'The Metamorphosis' ['Die Verwandlung'] (1915) SS
The Trial [*Der Prozess*] (1925) F
The Castle [*Das Schloss*] (1926) F
America [*Amerika*] (1927) F

KÄSTNER, Erich (1899–1974)
German children's writer, novelist, and poet
Emil and the Detectives [*Emil und die Detektive*] (1928) F CH

KAVANAGH, Julia (1824–1877)
British novelist and essayist
Madeleine (1848) F
Nathalie (1850) F
Daisy Burns (1853) F
Rachel Gray (1856) F
Adele (1858) F
Seven Years, and Other Tales (1860) F SS
French Women of Letters (1862) NF
English Women of Letters (1863) NF
Sybil's Second Love (1867) F
Dora (1868) F
Silvia (1870) F

KAVANAGH, Patrick [Joseph] (1904–1967)
Irish poet and novelist
Ploughman and Other Poems (1936) V
The Green Fool (1938) NF
The Great Hunger (1942) V
A Soul For Sale (1947) V
Tarry Flynn (1948) F
Collected Pruse [*sic*] (1967) NF

KAVANAGH, P[atrick] J[oseph Gregory] (1931–)
British poet, novelist, and editor
One and One (1959) V
The Perfect Stranger (1966) NF
On the Way to the Depot (1967) V
A Song and Dance (1968) F
About Time (1970) V
A Happy Man (1972) F
Edward Thomas in Heaven (1974) V
Life Before Death (1979) V
Only By Mistake (1986) F
Presence (1987) V
An Enchantment (1991) V

KAYE, M[ary] M[argaret] (1908–)
British novelist
Shadow of the Moon (1957) F
The Far Pavilions (1978) F

KAYE-SMITH, Sheila (1887–1956)
British novelist
The Tramping Methodist (1908) F
Starbrace (1909) F
Willows Forge, and Other Poems (1914) V
Sussex Gorse (1916) F
Tamarisk Town (1919) F
Green Apple Harvest (1920) F
Joanna Godden (1921) F
The End of the House of Alard (1923) F
The Mirror of the Months (1925) F
Joanna Godden Married, and Other Stories (1926) F SS
Iron and Smoke (1928) F
Shepherds in Sackcloth (1930) F
Faithful Stranger, and Other Stories (1938) F SS

Kitchen Fugue (1945) F
Mrs Gailey (1951) F

KAZANTZAKIS, Nikos (1883–1957)
Greek novelist
Zorba the Greek (1946) F
The Last Temptation of Christ (1955) F

KEANE, Molly [Mary Nesta] ['M.J. Farrell'] (1905–1996)
Irish novelist and dramatist
Taking Chances [as 'M.J. Farrell'] (1929) F
Mad Puppetstown [as 'M.J. Farrell'] (1931) F
Devoted Ladies [as 'M.J. Farrell'] (1934) F
The Rising Tide [as 'M.J. Farrell'] (1937) F
Two Days in Aragon [as 'M.J. Farrell'] (1941) F
Good Behaviour (1981) F
Time After Time (1983) F
Loving and Giving (1988) F

KEARY, Annie (1825–1879)
British novelist and children's writer
The Heroes of Asgard (1857) F CH

KEATES, Jonathan (1946–)
British novelist, travel writer, and biographer
Allegro Postillions (1983) F SS
Handel: The Man and his Music (1985) NF
The Strangers' Gallery (1987) F
Italian Journeys (1991) NF
Stendhal (1994) NF
Venice (1994) NF
Purcell (1995) NF
Smile Please (2000) F

KEATING, H[enry] R[aymond] F[itzwalter] (1926–)
British crime writer
Zen There Was Murder (1960) F
A Rush on the Ultimate (1961) F
The Perfect Murder [the first 'Inspector Ghote' novel] (1964) F
Inspector Ghote's Good Crusade (1966) F
Murder Must Appetize (1975) NF
Inspector Ghote Draws a Line (1979) F
The Murder of the Maharajah (1980) F
Dead on Time (1988) F
The Iciest Sin (1990) F

KEATS, John (1795–1821)
British poet
Poems (1817) V
Endymion (1818) V
Lamia, Isabella, The Eve of St Agnes, and Other Poems (1820) V

KEBLE, John (1792–1866)
British clergyman and poet
The Christian Year (1827) V
National Apostasy in a Sermon (1833) NF
Primitive Tradition Recognized in Holy Scriptire (1836) NF
The Psalter or Psalms of David in English Verse (1839) V
Lyra Innocentium (1846) V
Sermons, Academical and Occasional (1847) NF
On Eucharistic Adoration (1857) NF
Sermons, Occasional and Parochial (1868) NF

KEILLOR, Garrison (1942–)
American short-story writer, novelist, and humorist
Happy to Be Here (1981) F SS
Lake Wobegon Days (1985) F SS
Leaving Home (1987) F SS
We Are Still Married (1989) F SS
Radio Romance (1991) F
The Book of Guys (1993) F

KELLY, George [Edward] (1887–1974)
American dramatist
The Torch-Bearers (1922) D
Craig's Wife (1925) D
Daisy Mayme (1926) D

KELLY, Hugh (1739–1777)
Irish dramatist and novelist
Memoirs of a Magdalen; or, The History of Louisa Mildmay (1767) F
False Delicacy (1768) D
A Word to the Wise (1770) D
Clementina (1771) D
The School for Wives (1773) D

KELMAN, James (1946–)
Scottish novelist and short-story writer
Not Not While the Giro (1983) F SS
The Busconductor Hines (1984) F
A Chancer (1985) F
Greyhound for Breakfast (1987) F SS
A Disaffection (1989) F
The Burn (1991) F SS
How Late it Was, How Late (1994) F

KEMBLE, Frances [Fanny] Anne, later **Butler** (1809–1893)
British actress, dramatist, and poet
Francis the First (1832) V D
Journal (1835) NF
Record of a Girlhood (1878) NF
Notes Upon Some of Shakespeare's Plays (1882) NF
Records of Later Life (1882) NF
Far Away and Long Ago (1889) F
Further Records (1890) NF

KEMP, William (fl.1600)
English comic actor and dancer
Kemps Nine Daies Wonder (1600) NF

KEN, Thomas (1637–1711)
English prelate and poet
A Manual of Prayers for the Use of Scholars of Winchester College (1674) NF
An Exposition on the Church-Catechism; or, The Practice of Divine Love (1685) NF

KENEALLY, Thomas [Michael] (1935–)
Australian novelist
The Place at Whitton (1964) F
The Fear (1965) F

Bring Larks and Heroes (1967) F
Three Cheers for the Paraclete (1968) F
The Survivor (1969) F
A Dutiful Daughter (1971) F
The Chant of Jimmie Blacksmith (1972) F
Blood Red, Sister Rose (1974) F
Gossip From the Forest (1975) F
Season in Purgatory (1976) F
A Victim of the Aurora (1977) F
Ned Kelly and the City of the Bees (1978) F CH
Confederates (1979) F
Passenger (1979) F
The Cut-Rate Kingdom (1980) F
Schindler's Ark (1982) F
A Family Madness (1985) F
The Playmaker (1987) F
Act of Grace [as 'William Coyle'] (1988) F
Towards Asmara (1988) F
Chief of Staff [as 'William Coyle'] (1991) F
Flying Hero Class (1991) F
The Place Where Souls Are Born (1992) NF
Woman of the Inner Sea (1992) F
Jacko (1993) F

KENNAWAY, James [Peeble Ewing] (1928–1968)
Scottish novelist and dramatist
Tunes of Glory (1956) F
Household Ghosts (1961) F
Some Gorgeous Accident (1967) F

KENNEDY, A[lison] L[ouise] (1965–)
Scottish novelist and short-story writer
Night Geometry and the Garscadden Trains (1990) F SS
Looking For the Possible Dance (1993) F
Now That You're Back (1994) F SS
So I Am Glad (1995) F
Original Bliss (1997) F
Everything You Need (1999) F

KENNEDY, John Pendleton (1795–1870)
American novelist and essayist
Swallow Barn [as 'Mark Littleton'] (1832) F SS
Horse-Shoe Robinson (1835) F
Rob of the Bowl (1838) F

KENNEDY, Margaret Moore (1896–1967)
British novelist
The Constant Nymph (1924) F
The Fool of the Family (1930) F
Troy Chimneys (1952) F

KENNEDY, William Joseph (1928–)
American novelist, short-story writer, journalist, and film critic
The Ink Truck (1969) F
Legs (1975) F
Billy Phelan's Greatest Game (1978) F
Ironweed (1983) F

KER, W[illiam] P[aton] (1855–1923)
Scottish literary scholar and critic
Epic and Romance (1897) NF

KERMODE, [Sir John] Frank (1919–)
British literary scholar and critic
The Romantic Image (1957) NF

KEROUAC, Jack (1922–1969)
American novelist
The Town and the City (1950) F
On the Road (1957) F
The Dharma Bums (1958) F
The Subterraneans (1958) F
Doctor Sax (1959) F
Maggie Cassidy (1959) F
Mexico City Blues (1959) V
Lonesome Traveler (1960) NF
Tristessa (1960) F
Big Sur (1962) F
Visions of Gerard (1963) F
Desolation Angels (1965) F
Vanity of Duluoz (1968) F
Pic (1971) F

KESEY, Ken (1935–)
American novelist
One Flew Over the Cuckoo's Nest (1962) F
Sometimes a Great Notion (1964) F

KESSON, Jessie (1916–1994)
Scottish novelist and dramatist
The White Bird Passes (1958) F
Glitter of Mica (1963) F
Another Time, Another Place (1983) F
Where the Apple Ripens (1985) F SS

KEY, Francis Scott (1779–1843)
American lawyer and poet
'The Star-Spangled Banner' [pub. in the *Baltimore Patriot*] (1814) V

KEYES, Frances Parkinson (1885–1970)
American novelist
The Old Gray Homestead (1919) F
Dinner at Antoine's (1948) F
I, the King (1966) F

KEYES, Sidney [Arthur Kilworth] (1922–1943)
British poet
The Iron Laurel (1942) V
The Cruel Solstice (1943) V

KEYNES, John Maynard, 1st Baron Keynes (1883–1946)
British economist
The Economic Consequences of the Peace (1919) NF
A Revision of the Treaty (1922) NF
A Tract on Monetary Reform (1923) NF
The Economic Consequences of Mr Churchill (1925) NF
A Treatise on Money (1930) NF
Essays in Persuasion (1931) NF
Essays in Biography (1933) NF
The General Theory of Employment, Interest and Money (1936) NF

KICKHAM, Charles [Joseph] (1828–1882)
Irish novelist
Sally Cavanagh; or, The Untenanted Graves (1869) F

KILLIGREW, Thomas (1612–1683)
English dramatist
The Prisoners, and Claracilla (1641) D
Comedies and Tragedies [inc. *The Parson's Wedding*] (1664) D

KILLIGREW, Sir William (1606–1695)
English dramatist and author
Pandora (1662) D
Three Playes [*Selindra*, *Pandora*, and *Ormasdes*] (1665) D
The Imperial Tragedy (1669) D
Mid-night Thoughts (1681) NF
Mid-night and Daily Thoughts (1694) MISC

KILROY, Thomas (1934–)
Irish novelist and dramatist
The Big Chapel (1971) F
Talbot's Box (1977) D
Double Cross (1986) D

KING, Francis [Henry] (1923–)
British novelist, short-story writer, dramatist, and editor
The Dividing Stream (1951) F
The Dark Glasses (1954) F
The Firewalkers [as 'Frank Cauldwell'] (1956) F
The Man on the Rock (1957) F
So Hurt and Humiliated, and Other Stories (1959) F SS
The Custom House (1961) F
The Japanese Umbrella, and Other Stories (1964) F SS
A Domestic Animal (1970) F
The Needle (1975) F
Hard Feelings, and Other Stories (1976) F SS
The Action (1978) F
Indirect Method, and Other Stories (1980) F SS
Act of Darkness (1982) F
Voices in an Empty Room (1984) F
The Woman Who Was God (1988) F
Visiting Cards (1990) F
The Ant Colony (1991) F
Yesterday Came Suddenly (1993) NF
The One and Only (1994) F
Dead Letters (1997) F

KING, Henry (1592–1669)
English prelate and poet
An Elegy Upon the Most Incomparable King Charles the I (1648) V
Poems, Elegies, Paradoxes, and Sonnets (1657) V

KING, Stephen [Edwin] (1947–)
American horror writer
Carrie (1973) F
Salem's Lot (1975) F
Night Shift (1976) F
The Shining (1976) F
The Stand (1978) F
The Dead Zone (1979) F
Firestarter (1980) F
Cujo (1981) F
Danse Macabre (1981) F
The Gunslinger (1982) F
Christine (1983) F
Skeleton Crew (1985) F
It (1986) F
Misery (1987) F
The Tommyknockers (1988) F
The Dark Half (1989) F
Four Past Midnight (1990) F
Needful Things (1991) F
Hearts in Atlantis (1999) F

KING, William (1663–1712)
English poet and miscellaneous writer
Dialogues of the Dead (1699) NF
The Furmetary (1699) V
The Transactioneer (1700) V

KINGLAKE, A[lexander] W[illiam] (1809–1891)
British historian and travel writer
Eothen; or, Traces of Travel Brought Home from the East (1844) NF
The Invasion of the Crimea [vols. i, ii] (1863) NF
The Invasion of the Crimea [vols. iii, iv] (1868) NF
The Invasion of the Crimea [vol. v] (1875) NF
The Invasion of the Crimea [vol. vi] (1880) NF
The Invasion of the Crimea [vols. vii, viii] (1887) NF

KINGSLEY, Charles (1819–1875)
British poet, novelist, and controversialist
The Saint's Tragedy; or, The True Story of Elizabeth of Hungary (1848) V D
Twenty-Five Village Sermons (1849) NF
Alton Locke, Tailor and Poet (1850) F
Yeast (1851) F
Phaeton; or, Loose Thoughts for Loose Thinkers (1852) NF
Sermons on National Subjects [1st ser.] (1852) NF
Who Are the Friends of Order? (1852) NF
Hypatia; or, New Foes with an Old Face (1853) F
Sermons on National Subjects: Second Series (1854) NF
Glaucus; or, The Wonders of the Shore (1855) NF
Sermons for the Times (1855) NF
Westward Ho!; or, The Voyages and Adventures of Sir Amyas Leigh (1855) F
The Heroes; or, Greek Fairy Tales for My Children (1856) F CH
Two Years Ago (1857) F
Andromeda, and Other Poems (1858) V
The Good News of God (1859) NF
Miscellanies (1859) NF
The Gospel of the Pentateuch (1863) NF
The Water-Babies (1863) F
'What, Then, Does Dr Newman Mean?' (1864) NF
Hereward the Wake (1866) F
The Water of Life, and Other Sermons (1867) NF
Discipline, and Other Sermons (1868) NF
Plays and Puritans, and Other Historical Essays (1873) NF

Prose Idylls, New and Old (1873) NF
Westminster Sermons (1874) NF

KINGSLEY, Henry (1830–1876)
British novelist and younger brother of Charles Kingsley
The Recollections of Geoffrey Hamlyn (1859) F
Ravenshoe (1862) F
Austin Elliot (1863) F
The Hillyars and the Burtons (1865) F
Leighton Court (1866) F
Silcote of Silcotes (1867) F
Mademoiselle Mathilde (1868) F
Stretton (1869) F
Hetty, and Other Stories (1871) F SS
Hornby Mills, and Other Stories (1872) F SS
Reginald Hetherege (1874) F
Number Seventeen (1875) F
The Grange Garden (1876) F

KINGSLEY, Mary (1862–1900)
British traveller and author
Travels in West Africa (1897)

'KINGSMILL, Hugh' [Hugh Kingsmill Lunn] (1889–1949)
British anthologist, biographer, novelist, critic, and parodist
A Will to Love (1919) F
Blondel (1927) F
Matthew Arnold (1928) NF
After Puritanism 1850–1900 (1929) NF
Samuel Johnson (1933) NF
The Sentimental Journey (1934) NF
The Fall (1940) F
The Progress of a Biographer (1949) NF

KINGSTON, W[illiam] H[enry] G[iles] (1814–1880)
British boys' novelist
The Prime Minister (1845) F
Peter the Whaler (1851) F CH
Salt Water (1857) F CH
The Cruise of the Frolic (1860) F CH
The Fire Ships (1861) F CH
Ben Burton (1871) F CH
The Three Midshipmen (1873) F CH
The Three Lieutenants (1874) F CH
The Three Admirals (1877) F CH
The Two Supercargoes (1877) F CH

KINSELLA, Thomas (1928–)
Irish poet, translator, and editor
The Starlit Eye (1952) V
Another September (1958) V
Downstream (1962) V
Wormwood (1966) V
Nightwalker, and Other Poems (1967) V
Butcher's Dozen (1972) V
Notes From the Land of the Dead (1972) V
The Good Fight (1973) V
Songs of the Psyche (1985) V
Out of Ireland (1987) V
Fifteen Poems From Centre City (1990) V
Madonna, and Other Poems (1991) V
From Centre City (1994) V

KIPLING, [Joseph] Rudyard (1865–1936)
British novelist, short-story writer, and poet
Departmental Ditties, and Other Verses (1886) V
In Black and White (1888) F SS
The Phantom 'Rickshaw, and Other Tales (1888) F SS
Plain Tales From the Hills (1888) F SS
Soldiers Three (1888) F SS
The Story of the Gadsbys (1888) F SS
Under the Deodars (1888) F SS
Wee Willie Winkie, and Other Child Stories (1888) F SS
Life's Handicap (1891) F SS
The Light That Failed (1891) F
Barrack-Room Ballads, and Other Verses (1892) V
Many Inventions (1893) F SS
The Jungle Book (1894) F CH
The Second Jungle Book (1895) F CH
The Seven Seas (1896) V
'Captains Courageous' (1897) F
The Day's Work (1898) F SS
From Sea to Sea, and Other Sketches (1899) NF
Stalky & Co. (1899) F
Kim (1901) F
Just So Stories for Little Children (1902) F CH
The Five Nations (1903) V
Traffics and Discoveries (1904) F SS
Puck of Pook's Hill (1906) F CH
Actions and Reactions (1909) F SS
Rewards and Fairies (1910) F CH
Songs From Books (1912) V
A Diversity of Creatures (1917) F SS
The Years Between (1919) V
Letters of Travel 1892–1913 (1920) NF
Debits and Credits (1926) F SS
Limits and Renewals (1932) F SS

KIRKUP, James [Falconer] (1923–)
British poet, dramatist, and travel writer
The Drowned Sailor, and Other Poems (1947) V
The Submerged Village, and Other Poems (1951) V
A Correct Compassion, and Other Poems (1952) V
The Descent into the Cave, and Other Poems (1957) V
The Only Child (1957) NF
The Prodigal Son (1957) V
The Love of Others (1962) F
These Horned Islands (1962) NF
Refusal to Conform (1963) V
Paper Windows (1968) V
A Bewick Bestiary (1971) V
The Body Servant (1971) V
Zen Garden (1973) V
Scenes From Sesshu (1978) V
Steps to the Temple (1979) V
No More Hiroshimas (1982) V
Shooting Stars (1992) V
Blue Bamboo (1994) V

KITCHIN, C[lifford] H[enry] B[enn] (1895–1967)
British novelist
Streamers Waving (1925) F
Mr Balcony (1927) F
Death of My Aunt (1929) F
The Auction Sale (1949) F
Jumping Joan (1954) F SS
The Book of Life (1960) F

KNIGHT, Ellis Cornelia (1758–1837)
British novelist and miscellaneous author
Dinarbas (1790) F
Marcus Flaminius; or, A View of the Military, Political and Social Life of the Romans (1792) F

KNIGHT, G[eorge Richard] Wilson (1897–1985)
British Shakespeare scholar and critic
The Wheel of Fire (1930) NF
The Imperial Theme (1931) NF
Principles of Shakespearian Production (1936) NF
The Burning Oracle (1939) NF
The Starlit Dome (1941) NF
The Crown of Life (1947) NF
Lord Byron: Christian Virtues (1952) NF
Laureate of Peace (1954) NF
The Mutual Flame (1955) NF

KNIGHTS, L[ionel] C[harles] (1906–)
British Shakespeare critic
How Many Children Had Lady Macbeth? (1933) NF
Drama and Society in the Age of Jonson (1937) NF
Explorations (1946) NF
Some Shakespearean Themes (1959) NF
An Approach to 'Hamlet' (1960) NF
Further Explorations (1965) NF

KNOLLES, Richard (1550?–1610)
English historian
The Generall Historie of the Turkes (1603) NF

KNOWLES, James Sheridan (1784–1862)
British dramatist, poet, and novelist
The Welch Harper (1796) V
Fugitive Pieces (1810) V
Brian Boroihme; or, The Maid of Erin (1812) D
Caius Gracchus (1815) D
Virginius; or, The Liberation of Rome (1820) D
William Tell (1825) D
The Hunchback (1832) D
The Wife (1833) D
The Love-Chase (1837) D
The Secretary (1843) D
George Lovell (1846) F
Fortescue (1847) F

KNOX, E[dmund George] V[alpy] (1881–1971)
British humorist
The Brazen Lyre (1911) V
A Little Loot (1920) MISC
'Parodies Regained' (1921) V
Fiction As She Is Wrote (1923) NF
These Liberties (1923) V P
Poems of Impudence (1926) V
Folly Calling (1932) V

KNOX, John (1505–1572)
Scottish reformer and historian
The First Blast of the Trumpet Against the Monstruous Regiment of Women (1558) NF
The History of the Reformation of Religion Within the Realm of Scotland (1587) NF

KNOX, [the Rt Revd Monsignor] Ronald [Arbuthnott] (1888–1957)
British Catholic priest and author
Naboth's Vineyard in Pawn (1913) NF
The Church in Bondage (1914) NF
Absolute and Abitofhel (1915) V
The Essentials of Spiritual Unity (1918) NF
A Spiritual Aeneid (1918) NF
Memories of the Future (1923) F
Aeneid Books VII to IX (1924) EDN
Sanctions (1924) F
The Viaduct Murder (1925) F
Other Eyes Than Ours (1926) F
The Three Taps (1927) F
The Footsteps at the Lock (1928) F
Caliban in Grub Street (1930) NF
Broadcast Minds (1932) NF
The Body in the Silo (1933) F
Still Dead (1934) F
Barchester Pilgrimage (1935) F
The Holy Bible [abridgement and rearrangement] (1936) BIB
Double Cross Purposes (1937) F
Let Dons Delight (1939) F
God and the Atom (1945) NF
The New Testament of Our Lord and Saviour Jesus Christ (1945) BIB
The Old Testament [tr. from the Latin Vulgate] (1949) BIB
The Trials of a Translator (1949) NF
Enthusiasm (1950) NF
The Holy Bible [trn from the Latin Vulgate] (1955) BIB
Autobiography of a Saint (1958) NF

KOCH, C[hristopher] J[ohn] (1932–)
Australian novelist
The Boys in the Island [rev. 1974] (1958) F
Across the Sea Wall [rev. 1982] (1965) F
The Year of Living Dangerously (1978) F
The Doubleman (1985) F
Crossing the Gap (1987) NF

KOCH, Kenneth [Jay] (1925–)
American poet and dramatist
Ko; or, A Season on Earth (1959) V
Thank You (1962) V
Bertha, and Other Plays (1966) D
The Pleasures of Peace (1969) V
A Change of Hearts (1973) D
The Art of Love (1975) V
The Duplications (1977) V

The Burning Mystery of Anna in 1951 (1979) V
On the Edge (1986) V

KOESTLER, Arthur (1905–1983)
Anglo-Hungarian novelist, essayist, and journalist
Darkness at Noon (1940) NF
Scum of the Earth (1941) NF
Arrival and Departure (1943) F
The Yogi and the Commissar, and Other Essays (1945) NF
Thieves in the Night (1946) F
The Age of Longing (1951) F
Arrow in the Blue (1952) NF
The Invisible Writing (1954) NF
The Trail of the Dinosaur, and Other Essays (1955) NF
The Sleepwalkers (1959) NF
The Lotus and the Robot (1960) NF
The Ghost in the Machine (1967) NF
The Call-Girls (1972) F
The Roots of Coincidence (1972) NF

KOONTZ, Dean (1945–)
American horror writer
The Crimson Witch (1971) F
Hanging On (1974) F
Prison of Ice (1976) F
Night Chills (1977) F
Whispers (1980) F
The Mask (1981) F
Phantoms (1983) F
Darkness Comes (1984) F
Strangers (1986) F
Twilight Eyes (1987) F
Watchers (1987) F
Lightning (1988) F
Midnight (1989) F
The Bad Place (1990) F
Hideaway (1992) F
Mr Murder (1993) F
Winter Moon (1993) F
Intensity (1995) F
Tick-Tock (1996) F

KOSINSKI, Jerzy (1933–1991)
Polish-born American novelist and essayist
The Painted Bird (1965) F

KOSTROWITSKY, Wilhelm de *see* GUILLAUME APOLLINAIRE

KOUYOUMDJIAN, Dikran *see* MICHAEL ARLEN

KRANTZ, Judith (1928–)
American popular novelist
Scruples (1968) F
Princess Daisy (1980) F
Mistral's Daughter (1982) F
I'll Take Manhattan (1986) F
Dazzled (1990) F

KUMIN, Maxine [Winokur] (1925–)
American poet, novelist, and short-story writer
Halfway (1961) V
The Privilege (1965) V
Through Dooms of Love (1965) F
The Passions of Uxport (1968) F
The Nightmare Factory (1970) V
The Abduction (1971) F
Up Country (1972) V
The Designated Heir (1974) F
House, Bridge, Fountain, Gate (1975) V
The Retrieval System (1978) V
To Make a Prairie (1979) NF
Our Ground Time Here Will Be Brief (1982) V
Why Can't We Live Together Like Civilized Human Beings? (1982) F SS
Closing the Ring (1984) V
The Long Approach (1985) V
In Deep Country (1987) NF
Nurture (1989) V
Looking for Luck (1993) V

KUNDERA, Milan (1929–)
Czech novelist
The Joke (1967) F
Life is Elsewhere (1973) F
The Farewell Party (1976) F
The Unbearable Lightness of Being (1984) F

KUNITZ, Stanley J[asspon] (1905–)
American poet
Intellectual Things (1930) V
Passport to the War (1940) V
The Testing-Tree (1971) V
The Wellfleet Whale (1983) V
Next-to-Last Things (1985) V NF

KUREISHI, Hanif (1954–)
British screenwriter and novelist
My Beautiful Launderette (1986) D
The Buddha of Suburbia (1990) F
The Black Album (1995) F
Intimacy (1998) F
Midnight All Day (1999) F

KYD, Thomas (1558–1594)
English dramatist
The Spanish Tragedie (1592) D
Cornelia [from Robert Garnier] (1594) D

KYNASTON, Sir Francis (1587–1642)
English poet
Leoline and Sydanis (1642) V

L

LABRUNIE, Gérard *see* GÉRARD DE NERVAL

LA FAYETTE, Marie-Madeleine Pioche de Lavergne, Comtesse de (1634–1693)
French novelist
The Princess of Montpensier [*La Princesse de Montpensier*] (1662) F
Zaïde (1670) F
The Princess of Cleves [*La Princesse de Cleves*] (1678) F

LA FONTAINE, Jean de (1621–1695)
French poet and fabulist
Fables [*Fables choisies, mises en vers*; vol. ii, 1679–94] (1668) V

LAING, R[onald] D[avid] (1927–1989)
Scottish psychiatrist and author
The Divided Self (1960) NF
The Self and Others (1961) NF
The Politics of Experience (1967) NF
Knots (1970) V

LAMB, Charles ['Elia'] (1775–1834)
British poet, dramatist, critic, and essayist
Blank Verse (1798) V
A Tale of Rosamund Gray and Old Blind Margaret (1798) F
John Woodvil (1802) D
Tales from Shakespear [14 pieces by Mary Lamb (1764)] (1807) F JF
Mrs Leicester's School; or, The History of Several Young Ladies (1808) F JF
Specimens of English Dramatic Poets (1808) V
Poetry for Children (1809) V
The First Book of Poetry (1810) V
Prince Dorus; or, Flattery Put Out of Countenance (1811) V
Mr H.; or, Beware a Bad Name (1813) D
Elia: Essays [1st ser.] (1823) NF
Elia: Essays [2nd ser.; unauthorized] (1828) NF
Album Verses, with a Few Others (1830) V
The Last Essays of Elia (1833) NF

LAMB, Lady Caroline (1785–1828)
British novelist and poet
Glenarvon (1816) F
Verses from Glenarvon (1819) V
Graham Hamilton (1822) F
Ada Reis (1823) F

LAMBURN, Richmal Crompton *see* RICHMAL CROMPTON

LAMMING, George [Eric] (1927–)
Barbadian novelist
In the Castle of My Skin (1953) F
The Emigrants (1954) F
The Pleasures of Exile (1960) NF
Season of Adventure (1960) F
Natives of My Person (1972) F

L'AMOUR [originally **LaMOORE] Louis** (1908–1988)
American popular novelist
Hopalong Cassidy and the Riders of High Rock [as'Tex Burns'] (1951) F
Hondo (1953) F

LAMPEDUSA, Giuseppi [Tomaso] (1896–1957)
Italian novelist
Pillar to Post (1938) NF
The Leopard [*Il Gattopardo*] (1958) F

LANCASTER, [Sir] Osbert (1908–1986)
British cartoonist and author
Homes, Sweet Homes (1939) NF
Classical Landscape with Figures (1947) NF
Drayneflete Revealed (1949) NF
Sailing to Byzantium (1969) NF

LANDON, Letitia Elizabeth ['L.E.L.'] (1802–1838)
British poet and novelist
The Fate of Adelaide, and Other Poems [as 'L.E.L.'] (1821) V
The Improvisatrice, and Other Poems [as 'L.E.L.'] (1824) V
The Troubador, Catalogue of Pictures, and Historical Sketches [as 'L.E.L.'] (1825) V
The Golden Violet, and Other Poems [as 'L.E.L.'] (1827) V
The Venetian Bracelet, and Other Poems [as 'L.E.L.'] (1828) V
Romance and Reality [as 'L.E.L.'] (1831) F
Francesca Carrara [as 'L.E.L.'] (1834) F
The Vow of the Peacock, and Other Poems [as 'L.E.L.'] (1835) V
Traits and Trials of Early Life [as 'L.E.L.'] (1836) F V
Ethel Churchill; or, The Two Brides [as 'L.E.L.'] (1837) F
Duty and Inclination (1838) F
Lady Anne Granard; or, Keeping Up Appearances (1847) F

LANDON, Perceval (1869–1927)
British barrister and journalist
Raw Edges [inc. the ghost story 'Thurnley Abbey'] (1908) F SS

LANDOR, Walter Savage (1775–1864)
British poet and essayist
Gebir (1798) V
Poems from the Arabic and Persian (1800) V
Poetry by the Author of Gebir (1802) V
Simonidia (1806) V
Count Julian (1812) V
Imaginary Conversations of Literary Men and Statesmen [vols. i, ii] (1824) F
Imaginary Conversations of Literary Men and Statesmen [vol. iii] (1828) F
Imaginary Conversations of Literary Men and Statesmen: Second Series [vols. iv, v] (1829) F
The Letters of a Conservative (1836) NF
Pericles and Aspasia (1836) V
The Pentameron and Pentalogia (1837) NF
Andrea of Hungary, and Giovanna of Naples (1839) D
Fra Rupert (1840) D
The Hellenics (1847) V
Imaginary Conversation of King Carlo-Alberto and the Duchess Belgioioso (1848) NF
The Italics (1848) V
Imaginary Conversations of Greeks and Romans (1853) F
The Last Fruit Off an Old Tree (1853) V NF
Antony and Octavius (1856) V
Dry Sticks, Fagoted (1858) V
Heroic Idyls (1863) V

LANG, Andrew (1844–1912)
Scottish poet, scholar, and folklorist
Ballads and Lyrics of Old France, with Other Poems (1872) V
The Odyssey of Homer, Done into English Prose (1879)
xxii Ballades in Blue China (1880) V
Helen of Troy (1882) V
Custom and Myth (1884) NF
The Princess Nobody (1884) F CH
Rhymes à la Mode (1885) V
Books and Bookmen (1886) NF
In the Wrong Paradise, and Other Stories (1886) F SS
Letters to Dead Authors (1886) NF
The Mark of Cain (1886) F
Aucassin and Nicolete (1887) V
Myth, Ritual and Religion (1887) NF
Grass of Parnassus (1888) V
The Blue Fairy Book (1889) ANTH
Prince Prigio (1889) F CH
Old Friends (1890) NF
The Red Fairy Book (1890) ANTH
The Green Fairy Book (1892) ANTH
Homer and the Epic (1893) NF
Prince Ricardo of Pantouflia (1893) F CH
Cock Lane and Common-Sense (1894) NF
The Yellow Fairy Book (1894) ANTH
My Own Fairy Book (1895) F CH
The Book of Dreams and Ghosts (1897) NF
The Life and Letters of J.G. Lockhart (1897) NF
Modern Mythology (1897) NF
Pickle the Spy; or, The Incognito of Prince Charles (1897) NF
The Pink Fairy Book (1897) ANTH
The Companions of Pickle (1898) NF
The Making of Religion (1898) NF
The Homeric Hymns (1899) MISC
Letters on Literature (1899) NF
The Grey Fairy Book (1900) ANTH
Parson Kelly (1900) F
Magic and Religion (1901) NF
The Mystery of Mary Stuart (1901) NF
The Violet Fairy Book (1901) ANTH
The Disentanglers (1902) V
The Brown Fairy Book (1904) ANTH
New Collected Rhymes (1905) V
The Puzzle of Dickens's Last Plot (1905) NF
Homer and His Age (1906) NF
The Orange Fairy Book (1906) ANTH
The Origins of Religion, and Other Essays (1908) NF
The Lilac Fairy Book (1910) ANTH
Shakespeare, Bacon and the Great Unknown (1912) NF

LANGBAINE, Gerard [the Younger] (1656–1692)
English dramatic critic and biographer
An Exact Catalogue of all the Comedies That Were Ever Printed or Published (1680) NF

LANGLAND, William (c. 1330–c. 1386)
English poet
The Vision of Pierce Plowman [*Piers Plowman*; first printing of the B-text] (1550) V

LARDNER, Ring[old] [Wilmer] (1885–1933)
American short-story writer
You Know Me, Al: A Busher's Letters (1914) F SS
Bib Ballads (1915) V
Gullible's Travels (1917) F SS
Treat 'Em Rough (1918) F
The Big Town (1921) F
How to Write Short Stories (1924) F SS
What of It? (1925) F SS
The Love Nest (1926) F SS
Round Up (1929) F SS
First and Last (1934) F SS

LARKIN, Philip [Arthur] (1922–1985)
British poet, novelist, and editor
The North Ship (1945) V
Jill (1946) F
A Girl in Winter (1947) F
The Less Deceived (1955) V
The Whitsun Weddings (1964) V
All What Jazz (1970) NF
The Oxford Book of Twentieth-Century Verse (1973) ANTH
High Windows (1974) V
Femmes Damnées (1978) V
Required Writing (1983) NF

LASKI, Harold [Joseph] (1893–1950)
British political scientist
A Grammar of Politics (1925) NF
Communism (1927) NF
The Dangers of Obedience, and Other Essays (1930) NF
Parliamentary Government in England (1938) NF
The Danger of Being a Gentleman, and Other Essays (1939) NF
Reflections on the Revolution of Our Time (1943) NF
Faith, Reason and Civilization (1944) NF
Reflections on the Constitution (1951) NF

LASKI, Marghanita (1915–1988)
British novelist and critic
Love on the Supertax (1944) F
Tory Heaven (1948) F
The Victorian Chaise-Longue (1953) F

LAUD, William, (1573–1645)
English prelate and Archbishop of Canterbury
A Relation of the Conference Betweene William Lawd . . . and Mr Fisher (1639) NF
Seven Sermons Preached upon Severall Occasions (1651) NF
A Summarie of Devotions (1667) NF
The History of the Troubles and Tryal of William Laud (1695) NF

LAURENCE, [Jean] Margaret, *née* Wemys (1926–1987)
Canadian novelist
This Side Jordan (1960) F
The Tomorrow-Tamer (1963) F SS
The Stone Angel (1964) F
A Jest of God [UK: *Now I Lay Me Down*] (1966) F

The Fire-Dwellers (1969) F
A Bird in the House (1970) F SS
The Diviners (1974) F SS
Heart of a Stranger (1976) NF

LAVER, James (1899–1975)
British poet, novelist, and art critic
His Last Sebastian, and Other Poems (1922) V
Portraits in Oil and Vinegar (1925) NF
English Costume of the Eighteenth Century (1931) NF
Nymph Errant (1932) F
Background for Venus (1934) F
The Laburnum Tree, and Other Stories (1935) F SS

LAVIN, Mary (1912–1996)
Irish short-story writer and novelist
Tales From Bective Bridge (1942) F SS
The Long Ago (1944) F SS
The Becker Wives (1946) F SS
Mary O'Grady (1950) F
The Greater Wave (1967) F SS
The Shrine, and Other Stories (1977) F SS
A Family Likeness (1985) F SS

LAW, William (1686–1761)
English theological and mystical writer
The Bishop of Bangor's Late Sermon Answer'd (1717) NF
The Absolute Unlawfulness of the Stage-Entertainment (1726) NF
A Practical Treatise upon Christian Perfection (1726) NF
A Serious Call to a Devout and Holy Life (1728) NF
The Case of Reason; or, Natural Religion, Fairly Stated (1731) NF
The Grounds and Reasons of Christian Regeneration (1739) NF
The Spirit of Prayer [pt. i; pt. ii 1750] (1749) NF
The Spirit of Love (1752) NF
The Way to Divine Knowledge (1752) NF
The Second Part of the Spirit of Love (1754) NF
Of Justification by Faith and Works (1760) NF

LAWLER, Ray[mond] [Evenor] (1921–)
Australian dramatist
Summer of the Seventeenth Doll (1955) D

LAWLESS, [Hon.] Emily (1845–1913)
Irish novelist and poet
A Chelsea Householder (1882) F
Hurrish (1886) F
Major Lawrence, F.L.S. (1887) F
Plain Frances Mowbray, and Other Tales (1889) F SS
With Essex in Ireland (1890) F
Grania (1892) F
Maelcho (1894) F HF
With the Wild Geese (1902) V
The Inalienable Heritage, and Other Poems (1914) V

LAWRENCE, D[avid] H[erbert] (1885–1930)
British novelist, poet, and short-story writer
The White Peacock (1911) F
The Trespasser (1912) F
Love Poems and Others (1913) V
Sons and Lovers (1913) F
The Prussian Officer, and Other Stories (1914) F SS
The Rainbow (1915) F
Amores (1916) V
Twilight in Italy (1916) NF
Look! We Have Come Through (1917) V
New Poems (1918) V
Bay (1919) V
The Lost Girl (1920) F
Tortoises (1921) V
Women in Love (1921) F
Aaron's Rod (1922) F
England, My England [UK: *1924*](1922) F SS
Birds, Beasts and Flowers (1923) V
Fantasia of the Unconscious (1923) NF
Kangaroo (1923) NF
The Ladybird; The Fox; The Captain's Doll (1923) F SS
Psychoanalysis and the Unconscious (1923) NF
Studies in Classic American Literature (1924) NF
St Mawr, Together with The Princess (1925) F
The Plumed Serpent (1926) F
Mornings in Mexico (1927) NF
Cavalleria Rusticana and Other Stories [from Giovanni Verga] (1928) F SS
Lady Chatterley's Lover [privately prtd in Florence] (1928) F
The Woman Who Rode Away, and Other Stories (1928) F SS
Pansies (1929) V
Pornography and Obscenity (1929) NF
A Propos of Lady Chatterley's Lover (1930) NF
Assorted Articles (1930) NF
Nettles (1930) V
The Virgin and the Gypsy (1930) F
The Man Who Died (1931) F
Etruscan Places (1932) NF
Lady Chatterley's Lover [1st expurgated English edn] (1932) F
The Lovely Lady (1932) F SS
Last Poems (1933) V
Phoenix [posthumous papers] (1936) NF
Lady Chatterley's Lover [1st unexpurgated English edn] (1960) F

LAWRENCE, G[eorge] A[lfred] (1827–1876)
British novelist
Guy Livingstone; or, Thorough (1857) F
Sword and Gown (1859) F
Barren Honour (1862) F
Border and Bastille (1863) NF
Maurice Dering; or, The Quadrilateral (1864) F
Sans Merci; or, Kestrels and Falcons (1866) F
Brakespeare; or, The Fortunes of a Free-Lance (1868) F
Breaking a Butterfly; or, Blanche Ellerslie's Ending (1869) F
Anteros (1873) F
Silverland (1873) F
Hagarene (1874) F

LAWRENCE, T[homas] E[dward] (1888–1935)
British soldier, Arabist, and author
Seven Pillars of Wisdom (1926) NF
Revolt in the Desert (1927) NF
Oriental Assembly (1939) NF

LEACOCK, Stephen (1869–1944)
Canadian humorist
Literary Lapses (1910) MISC
Nonsense Novels (1911) F
Sunshine Sketches of a Little Town (1912) F
Arcadian Adventures with the Idle Rich (1914) F
Further Foolishness (1916) MISC
Frenzied Fiction (1918) F
The Hohenzollerns in America (1919) MISC
Winsome Winnie, and Other Nonsense Novels (1920) F
My Discovery of England (1922) NF

LEAR, Edward (1812–1888)
British artist and nonsense poet
A Book of Nonsense (1846) V
Illustrated Excursions in Italy (1846) NF
Journals of a Landscape Painter in Albania, Illyria etc (1851) NF
Journals of a Landscape Painter in S. Calabria (1852) NF
A Book of Nonsense and More Nonsense (1862) V
Journal of a Landscape Painter in Corsica (1870) NF
Nonsense Songs, Stories, Botany and Alphabets (1871) V
More Nonsense, Pictures, Rhymes Botany (1872) V
Laughable Lyrics (1877) V

LEAVIS, F[rank] R[aymond] (1895–1978)
British literary critic, teacher, and educationist
New Bearings in English Poetry (1932) NF
For Continuity (1933) NF
Revaluation (1936) NF
The Great Tradition (1948) NF
The Common Pursuit (1952) NF
D.H. Lawrence, Novelist (1955) NF
Scrutiny: A Retrospect (1963) NF
Anna Karenina, and Other Essays (1967) NF
English Literature in Our Time and the University (1969) NF
Dickens the Novelist (1970) NF
Thought, Words and Creativity (1976) NF

'LE CARRÉ, John' [David John Moore Cornwell] (1931–)
British writer of spy fiction
Call for the Dead (1961) F
A Murder of Quality (1962) F
The Spy Who Came in From the Cold (1963) F
The Looking-Glass War (1965) F
A Small Town in Germany (1968) F
Tinker, Tailor, Soldier, Spy (1974) F
The Honourable Schoolboy (1977) F
Smiley's People (1980) F
The Little Drummer Girl (1983) F
A Perfect Spy (1986) F
The Russia House (1989) F
The Secret Pilgrim (1991) F
Our Game (1995) F
Single & Single (1999) F
The Constant Gardener (2000) F

LECKY, W[illiam] E[dward] H[artpole] (1838–1903)
British historian
The Religious Tendencies of the Age (1860) NF

LEE, [Nelle] Harper (1926–)
American novelist
To Kill a Mockingbird (1960) F

LEE, Harriet (1756–1851)
British novelist
The Errors of Innocence (1786) F
Canterbury Tales for the Year 1797 (1797) F SS
Clara Lennox; or, The Distressed Widow (1797) F

LEE, Laurie (1914–1997)
British poet and author
The Sun My Monument (1944) V
The Bloom of Candles (1947) V
The Voyage of Magellan (1948) V D
My Many-Coated Man (1955) V
A Rose for Winter (1955) NF
Cider With Rosie [US: *The Edge of Day*] (1959) NF
As I Walked Out One Midsummer Morning (1969) NF
I Can't Stay Long (1975) NF
A Moment of War (1991) NF

LEE, Manfred, B. *see* ELLERY QUEEN

LEE, Nathaniel (1649?–1692)
English dramatist
Nero, Emperour of Rome (1674) D
Sophonisba; or, Hannibal's Overthrow (1675) D
Gloriana; or, The Court of Augustus Caesar (1676) D
The Rival Queens; or, The Death of Alexander the Great (1677) D
Mithridates King of Pontus (1678) D
Caesar Borgia Son of Pope Alexander the Sixth (1679) D
Lucius Junius Brutus, Father of his Country (1680) D
Theodosius; or, The Force of Love (1680) D
The Princess of Cleve (1680/81) D
Constantine the Great (1683) D
The Massacre of Paris (1689) D
On the Death of Mrs Behn (1689) V

LEE, Sir Sidney (1859–1926)
British biographer and literary historian
A Life of William Shakespeare (1898) NF
Queen Victoria (1902) NF
Shakespeare and the Modern Stage, with Other Essays (1906) NF
The Place of English Literature in the Modern University (1913) NF
King Edward VII: A Biography [vol. i only] (1925) NF

LEE, Sophia (1750–1824)
British poet, novelist, and dramatist

The Recess; or, A Tale of Other Times [vol. i; vols. ii and iii, 1785] (1783) F
A Hermit's Tale (1787) V
Almeyda, Queen of Granada (1796) D
The Life of a Lover (1804) F

'LEE, Vernon' [Violet Paget] (1856–1935)
British critic, novelist, and short-story writer
Studies of the Eighteenth Century in Italy (1880) NF

LE FANU, Joseph Sheridan (1814–1873)
Irish novelist, and short-story writer
The Cock and Anchor (1845) F
The Fortunes of Colonel Torlogh O'Brien (1847) F
Ghost Stories and Tales of Mystery (1851) F SS
The House by the Churchyard (1863) F
Uncle Silas (1864) F
Wylder's Hand (1864) F
Guy Deverell (1865) F
All in the Dark (1866) F
The Tenants of Malory (1867) F
Haunted Lives (1868) F
A Lost Name (1868) F
The Wyvern Mystery (1869) F
Checkmate (1871) F
Chronicles of Golden Friars (1871) F SS
The Rose and the Key (1871) F
In a Glass Darkly (1872) F SS
Willing to Die (1873) F
The Purcell Papers (1880) F SS
The Watcher, and Other Weird Stories (1894) F SS
Madam Crowl's Ghost, and Other Tales of Mystery [ed. M.R. James] (1923) F SS

LE GALLIENNE, Richard (1866–1947)
British poet and essayist
My Lady's Sonnets (1887) V
Volumes in Folio (1889) V
English Poems (1892) V
The Religion of a Literary Man (1893) NF
Robert Louis Stevenson, and Other Poems (1895) V
The Quest of the Golden Girl (1896) F
Retrospective Reviews (1896) NF
Young Lives (1899) F
Sleeping Beauty, and Other Prose Fancies (1900) P
The Life Romantic (1901) NF
Little Dinners with the Sphinx, and Other Prose Fancies (1909) NF
New Poems (1910) V
The Lonely Dancer, and Other Poems (1914) V
The Silk-Hat Soldier, and Other Poems (1915) V
Vanishing Roads, and Other Essays (1915) NF
The Romantic Nineties (1926) NF

LÉGER, Marie René Saint-Léger *see* SAINT-JOHN PERSE

LE GUIN, Ursula K[roeber] (1929–)
American novelist, poet, and critic
A Wizard of Earthsea (1968) F CH
The Tombs of Atuan (1971) F CH
The Farthest Shore (1972) F CH
Wild Angels (1974) V
The Dispossessed (1975) F
Dramas Must Explain Themselves (1975) NF
The Wind's Twelve Quarters (1975) F SS
Orsinian Tales (1976) F SS
The Language of the Night (1978) NF
Tenth Millennium: The Beginning Place (1979) F
Interfaces (1980) F SS
Hard Words (1981) V
The Compass Rose (1982) F SS
Always Coming Home (1986) F
Tehanua (1990) F CH

LEHMANN, Rosamond [Nina] (1903–1990)
British novelist
Dusty Answer (1927) F
A Note in Music (1930) F
Invitation to the Waltz (1932) F
The Weather in the Streets (1936) F
The Ballad and the Source (1944) F
The Echoing Grove (1953) F
A Sea-Grape Tree (1970) F

LEHMANN, [Rudolph] John [Frederick] (1907–1987)
British poet and editor
A Garden Revisited, and Other Poems (1931) V
The Noise of History (1934) V
Evil Was Abroad (1938) F
The Sphere of Glass, and Other Poems (1944) V
The Age of the Dragon (1951) V
The Open Night (1952) NF
The Whispering Gallery (1955) NF
I Am My Brother (1960) NF
The Ample Proposition (1966) NF
A Nest of Tigers (1968) NF
In the Purely Pagan Sense (1976) F
Thrown to the Woolfs (1978) NF

LEIBER, Fritz [Reuter, Jr] (1910–1992)
American short-story writer and novelist
Conjure Wife (1953) F
The Wanderer (1964) F
A Spectre is Haunting Texas (1969) F
Our Lady of Darkness (1977) F
Ship of Shadows (1979) F SS

LEIGH, Mike (1943–)
British dramatist and film director
Nuts in May (1976) D
Abigail's Party (1979) D

LEITHAUSER, Brad (1953–)
American poet, novelist, and short-story writer
Hundreds of Fireflies (1982) V
Equal Distance (1985) F
The Cats of the Temple (1986) V
Hence (1989) F
The Mail From Anywhere (1990) V

'L.E.L', *see* LETITIA ELIZABETH LANDON

LELAND, John (1506?–1552)
English antiquary
The Laboryouse Journey and Serche of Johan Leylande for Englandes Antiquitees (1549) NF

LEMON, Mark (1809–1870)
British journalist, humorist, dramatist, and novelist
The Enchanted Doll (1849) F CH
Wait for the End (1863) F
Loved at Last (1864) F
Falkner Lyle; or, The Story of Two Wives (1866) F
Leyton Hall, and Other Tales (1867) F SS
Golden Fetters (1868) F

LENNOX, Charlotte, *née* Ramsay (1720–1804)
American-born English novelist, poet, and dramatist
The Life of Harriot Stuart, Written by Herself (1750) F
The Female Quixote; or, The Adventures of Arabella (1752) F
Henrietta (1758) F
Philander (1758) V D
Sophia (1762) F
The History of the Marquis of Lussa and Isabella (1764) F
The Sister (1769) D
Euphemia (1790) F

LEONARD, Elmore [John] (1925–)
American novelist and short-story writer
The Bounty Hunters (1953) F
Hombre (1961) F
Valdez is Coming (1969) F
Unknown Man No. 89 (1977) F
The Switch (1978) F
City Primeval (1980) F
Gold Coast (1980) F
Split Images (1982) F
La Brava (1983) F
Stick (1983) F
Glitz (1985) F
Bandits (1987) F
Touch (1987) F
Freaky Deaky (1988) F
Killshot (1989) F
Get Shorty (1990) F
Maximum Bob (1991) F
Riding the Rap (1995) F
Cuba Libre (1998) F
Be Cool (1999) F
The Tonto Woman, and Other Stories (1999) F SS

'LEONARD, Hugh' [John Keyes Byrne] (1926–)
Irish dramatist and author
Stephen D. [adapted from James Joyce] (1962) D
The Patrick Pearse Motel (1971) D
Da (1973) D
Summer (1974) D
Home Before Night (1979) NF
A Life (1979) D
Out After Dark (1989) NF
Parnell and the Englishwoman (1990) F

LEONARD, Lionel Frederick *see* FREDERICK LONSDALE

LE QUEUX, William [Tufnell] (1864–1927)
British popular novelist
Strange Tales of a Nihilist (1892) F
The Great War in England in 1897 (1894) F
The Eye of Istar (1897) F
England's Peril (1899) F
Secrets of Monte Carlo (1899) F
The Veiled Man (1899) F
Secrets of the Foreign Office (1903) F SS
The Man from Downing Street (1904) F
The Mask (1905) F
The Invasion of 1910 (1906) F
The Mysterious Mr Miller (1906) F
The Lady in the Car (1908) F
Spies of the Kaiser (1909) F
The Money-Spider (1911) F
Revelations of the Secret Service (1911) F
Beryl of the Biplane (1917) F

LERMONTOV, Mikhail [Yurevich] (1814–1841)
Russian novelist and poet
A Hero of Our Time (1840) F
Masquerade (1842) V D

LEROUX, Gaston (1868–1927)
French novelist
Le Mystère de la chambre jaune ['The Mystery of the Yellow Room'] (1907) F
The Phantom of the Opera [*Le Fantôme de l'Opéra*] (1911) F

LESAGE, Alain-René (1668–1747)
French novelist
Le Diable boiteux ['The Devil with a Limp'] (1707) F
Gil Blas (1715–35) F

LESSING, Doris [May], *née* Tayler (1919–)
British novelist, short-story writer, and dramatist
The Grass is Singing (1950) F
This Was the Old Chief's Country (1951) F SS
Martha Quest (1952) F
A Proper Marriage (1954) F
A Ripple From the Storm (1958) F
The Golden Notebook (1962) F
African Stories (1964) F SS
Landlocked (1965) F
Nine African Stories (1968) F SS
The Four-Gated City (1969) F
Briefing For a Descent into Hell (1971) F
The Story of a Non-Marrying Man [US: *The Temptation of Jack Orkney*] (1972) F SS
The Summer Before the Dark (1973) F
The Memoirs of a Survivor (1974) F
Re: Colonised Planet 5, Shikasta (1979) F
The Marriages Between Zones Three, Four and Five (1980) F
The Sirian Experiments (1981) F
The Making of the Representative for Planet 8 (1982) F
The Diary of a Good Neighbour [as 'Jane Somers'] (1983) F
Documents Relating to the Sentimental Agents in the Volyen Empire (1983) F
If the Old Could [as 'Jane Somers'] (1984) F
The Good Terrorist (1985) F
The Fifth Child (1988) F

London Observed (1990) F SS
Under My Skin (1994) NF
Love, Again (1996) F
Walking in the Shade (1997) NF
Mara and Dann: An Adventure (1999) F
Ben, in the World (2000) F

LE SUEUR, Meridel (1900–1996)
American feminist critic, novelist, and poet
The Girl (1939) F
Salute to Spring, and Other Stories (1940) F SS
North Star Country (1945) F SS
Conquistadors (1973) NF
The Mound Builders (1974) NF
Song for My Time (1977) NF

LEVER, Charles [James] (1806–1872)
Irish novelist
The Confessions of Harry Lorrequer (1839) F
Charles O'Malley, the Irish Dragoon (1841) F
Arthur O'Leary (1844) F
Tom Burke of 'Ours' (1844) F
Jack Hinton, the Guardsman (1845) F
The O'Donoghue (1845) F
St Patrick's Eve (1845) F
Tales of the Trains [as 'Tilbury Tramp'] (1845) F SS
The Knight of Gwynne (1847) F
Confessions of Con. Cregan, the Irish Gil Blas (1849) F
Roland Cashel (1850) F
The Dodd Family Abroad (1854) F
The Fortunes of Glencore (1857) F
Davenport Dunn; or, The Man of the Day (1859) F
Maurice Tiernay, The Soldier of Fortune (1861) F
One of Them (1861) F
Barrington (1863) F
A Day's Ride (1864) F
Luttrell of Arran (1865) F
Tony Butler (1865) F
Sir Brooke Fossbrooke (1866) F
The Bramleighs of Bishop's Folly (1868) F
Paul Gosslett's Confessions in Love, Law, and the Civil Service (1868) F
Lord Kilgobbin (1872) F

LEVERSON, Ada [Esther], *née* Beddington (1862–1933)
British novelist, short-story writer, and journalist
The Twelfth Hour (1907) F
Love's Shadow (1908) F
The Limit (1911) F
Tenterhooks (1912) F
Bird of Paradise (1914) F
Love at Second Sight (1916) F

LEVI, Peter [Chad Tigar] (1931–)
British poet and biographer
The Gravel Ponds (1960) V
Water, Rock and Sand (1962) V
Private Ground (1981) V
The Echoing Green (1983) V
Shadow and Bone (1989) V
The Rags of Time (1994) V
Reed Music (1998) V

LEVI, Primo (1919–1987)
Italian author
If This Is a Man [*Se questo è un uomo*] (1947) NF
If Not Now, When? [*Se non ora, quando?*] (1982) NF
The Periodic Table [*Il sistemo periodico*] (1984) NF

LEVIN, Ira (1929–)
American novelist and dramatist
A Kiss Before Dying (1953) F
Rosemary's Baby (1967) F
The Stepford Wives (1972) F
The Boys From Brazil (1976) F

LEVY, Amy (1861–1889)
British poet and novelist
Xantippe, and Other Verse (1881) V
A Minor Poet, and Other Poems (1884) V
Reuben Sachs (1888) F
The Romance of a Shop (1888) F
A London Plane-Tree, and Other Verse (1889) V
Miss Meredith (1889) F

LEWES, G[eorge] H[enry] (1817–1878)
British author, critic, and journalist
Ranthorpe (1847) F
Rose, Blanche, and Violet (1848) F
Comte's Philosophy of the Sciences (1853) NF
The Life and Works of Goethe (1855) NF
Aristotle (1864) NF
The Foundations of a Creed (1873) NF
Problems of Life and Mind (1873) NF
On Actors and the Art of Acting (1875) NF

LEWIS, Alun (1915–1944)
Welsh poet, novelist, and short-story writer
The Last Inspection (1942) F SS
Raiders' Dawn, and Other Poems (1942) V
Ha! Ha! Among the Trumpets (1945) V
In the Green Tree (1948) F SS

LEWIS, C[live] S[taples] (1898–1963)
British literary scholar, critic, and children's writer
The Pilgrim's Regress (1933) NF
The Allegory of Love (1936) NF
Out of the Silent Planet (1938) F
Rehabilitations, and Other Essays (1939) NF
The Problem of Pain (1940) NF
Broadcast Talks (1942) NF
A Preface to Paradise Lost (1942) NF
The Screwtape Letters (1942) NF
Christian Behaviour (1943) NF
Perelandra (1943) F
Beyond Personality (1944) NF
That Hideous Strength (1945) F
Miracles (1947) NF
Arthurian Torso (1948) V NF
Transposition and Other Addresses (1949) NF
The Lion, the Witch, and the Wardrobe (1950) F CH
Prince Caspian (1951) F CH
Mere Christianity (1952) NF
The Voyage of the Dawn Treader (1952) F CH
The Silver Chair (1953) F CH
English Literature in the Sixteenth Century (1954) NF

The Horse and His Boy (1954) F CH
The Magician's Nephew (1955) F CH
Surprised by Joy (1955)NF
The Last Battle (1956) F CH
Till We Have Faces (1956) NF
Reflections on the Psalms (1958) NF
The Four Loves (1960) NF
An Experiment in Criticism (1961) NF
A Grief Observed [as 'N.W. Clerk'] (1961) NF
The Discarded Image (1964) NF
Letters to Malcolm, Chiefly on Prayer (1964) NF
Screwtape Proposes a Toast, and Other Pieces (1965) NF
Christian Reflections (1967) NF

LEWIS, Janet (1899–1998)
American novelist and poet
The Invasion (1932) F
The Wife of Martin Guerre (1941) F
The Trial of Sören Qvist (1947) F
The Ghost of Monsieur Scarron (1956) F

LEWIS, M[atthew] G[regory] (1775–1818)
British novelist, poet, and dramatist
The Monk (1796) F
Village Virtues (1796) V
The Castle Spectre (1797) D
The Minister (1797) D
The East Indian (1799) D
The Love of Gain (1799) V
Rolla; or, The Peruvian Hero (1799) D
Tales of Terror (1799) F SS
Adelmorn the Outlaw (1801) D
Alfonso, King of Castile (1801) D
Tales of Wonder (1801) F SS
The Bravo of Venice (1805) F
Adelgitha; or, The Fruits of a Single Error (1806) D
Romantic Tales (1808) MISC

LEWIS, Norman (1918–)
British travel writer and novelist
Within the Labyrinth (1950) F
A Dragon Apparent (1951) NF
Golden Earth (1952) NF
A Single Pilgrim (1953) F
The Volcanoes Above Us (1957) F
A Small War Made to Order (1966) F
The Sicilian Specialist (1974) F
Cuban Passage (1982) F
Voices of the Old Sea (1984) NF
Jackdaw Cake (1985) NF
The Missionaries (1988) NF
An Empire in the East (1993) NF

LEWIS, [Percy] Wyndham (1882–1957)
British author and artist
Tarr (1918) F
The Art of Being Ruled (1926) NF
The Lion and the Fox (1927) NF
Time and Western Man (1927) NF
The Wild Body; A Soldier of Humour, and Other Stories (1927) F SS
The Childermass (1928) F
Paleface (1929) NF
The Apes of God (1930) F
Enemy of the Stars (1932) D
Filibusters in Barbary (1932) NF
Snooty Baronet (1932) F
Men Without Art (1934) NF
Left Wings Over Europe; or, How to Make a War About Nothing (1936) NF
Blasting and Bombarding (1937) NF
The Revenge for Love (1937) F
The Mysterious Mr Bull (1938) NF
The Hitler Cult, and How It Will All End (1939) NF
The Jews (1939) NF
The Vulgar Streak (1941) F
America and Cosmic Man (1948) NF
Rude Assignment (1950) NF
Rotting Hill (1951) F SS
The Writer and the Absolute (1952) NF
The Demon of Progress in the Arts (1954) NF
Self-Condemned (1954) F
Monstre Gai; Malign Fiesta (1955) F
The Red Priest (1956) F
The Roaring Queen (1973) F
Unlucky for Pringle (1973) F SS
Mrs Duke's Million (1977) F SS

LEWIS, [Harry] Sinclair (1885–1951)
American novelist
Our Mr Wrenn (1914) F
The Trail of the Hawk (1915) F
The Innocents (1917) F
The Job (1917) F
Main Street (1920) F
Babbitt (1922) F
Arrowsmith (1925) F
Elmer Gantry (1927) F
The Man Who Knew Coolidge (1928) F
Dodsworth (1929) F
Ann Vickers (1933) F
Work of Art (1934) F
It Can't Happen Here (1935) F
The Prodigal Parents (1938) F
Bethel Merriday (1940) F
Gideon Planish (1943) F
Cass Timberlane (1945) F
Kingsblood Royal (1947) F
The God Seeker (1949) F
World So Wide (1951) F

LIGHTFOOT, Joseph Barber (1828–1889)
British theologian and biblical scholar
Commentary on St Paul's Epistle to the Philippians (1868) NF
The Apostolic Fathers [pt. i, pt. ii, 1885] (1869) NF
Commentary on St Paul's Epistle to the Colossians (1875) NF
The Apostolic Age (1892) NF

LILLO, George (1693–1739)
English dramatist
Silvia; or, The Country Burial (1730) D

The London Merchant; or, The History of George Barnwell (1731) D
The Christian Hero (1735) D
Fatal Curiosity (1736) D
Marina (1738) D
Britannia and Batavia (1740) D
Elmerick; or, Justice Triumphant (1740) D

LILLY, William (1602–1681)
English astrologer
Merlinus Anglicus Junior: The English Merlin Revived (1644) NF
The Starry Messenger (1645) NF
Christian Astrology (1647) NF

LINDGREN, Astrid (1907–)
Swedish children's writer
Pippi Longstocking (1945) F CH
Bill Bergsen, Master Detective (1946) F CH

LINDSAY, David (1876–1945)
British-born Scottish novelist
A Voyage to Arcturus (1920) F

LINDSAY, Jack (1900–1990)
Australian poet, dramatist, novelist, and critic
Fauns and Ladies (1923) V
Life Rarely Tells (1958) NF
The Roaring Twenties (1960) NF
Fanfrolico and After (1962) NF
Decay and Renewal (1976) NF
The Blood Vote (1985) F

LINDSAY, Norman [Alfred William] (1879–1969)
Australian novelist, artist, and children's writer
A Curate in Bohemia (1913) F
The Magic Pudding (1918) F CH
Creative Effort (1920) NF
Hyperborea (1928) NF
Madam Life's Lovers (1929) NF
Redheap [US: *Every Mother's Son*] (1930) F
The Cautious Amorist (1932) F
Miracles by Arrangement [US: *Mr Gresham and Olympus*] (1932) F
Pan in the Parlour (1933) F
Saturdee (1933) F
Age of Consent (1938) F
The Cousin from Fiji (1945) F
Halfway to Anywhere (1947) F
Dust or Polish? (1950) F
The Scribblings of an Idle Mind (1966) NF
Rooms and Houses (1968) F

LINDSAY, [Nicholas] Vachel (1879–1931)
American poet
General William Booth Enters into Heaven, and Other Poems (1913) V
The Congo, and Other Poems (1914) V
The Chinese Nightingale, and Other Poems (1917) V
The Daniel Jazz (1920) V
The Golden Whales of California (1920) V
The Candle in the Cabin (1926) V
Johnny Appleseed (1928) V

LINGARD, John (1771–1851)
British historian
The Antiquities of the Anglo-Saxon Church (1806) NF
The History of England to the Accession of Henry VIII (1819) NF

LINKLATER, Eric [Robert Russell] (1899–1974)
Scottish novelist and short-story writer
White-Maa's Saga (1929) F
A Dragon Laughed, and Other Poems (1930) V
Juan in America (1931) F
The Men of Ness (1932) F
Magnus Merriman (1934) F
God Likes Them Plain (1935) F SS
Ripeness is All (1935) F
Juan in China (1937) F
Private Angelo (1946) F
Sealskin Trousers, and Other Stories (1947) F SS
Laxdale Hall (1951) F
The House of Gair (1953) F
A Year of Space (1953) NF
The Dark of Summer (1956) F
A Sociable Plover, and Other Stories and Conceits (1957) F SS
Roll of Honour (1961) F
A Man Over Forty (1963) F
A Terrible Freedom (1966) F

LINTON, Eliza Lynn, *née* Lynn (1822–1898)
British novelist and journalist
Azeth the Egyptian (1847) F
Amymone (1848) F
Realities (1851) F
Witch Stories (1861) F SS
Grasp Your Nettle (1865) F
Lizzie Lorton of Greyrigg (1866) F
Sowing the Wind (1867) F
The Girl of the Period (1868) NF
Ourselves (1870) NF
The True History of Joshua Davidson (1872) F
The Mad Willoughbys, and Other Tales (1875) F SS
Patricia Kemball (1875) F
The Atonement of Leam Dundas (1876) F
The World Well Lost (1877) F
Under Which Lord? (1879) F
The Rebel of the Family (1880) F
With a Silken Thread, and Other Stories (1880) F SS
'My Love!' (1881) F
The Girl of the Period, and Other Social Essays (1883) NF
Ione (1883) F
The Autobiography of Christopher Kirkland (1885) F
Stabbed in the Dark (1885) F
Paston Carew, Millionaire and Miser (1886) F
Through the Long Night (1888) F
The One Too Many (1894) F
In Haste and at Leisure (1895) F
Dulcie Everton (1896) F
'Twixt Cup and Lip (1896) F SS
My Literary Life (1899) NF
The Second Youth of Theodora Desanges (1900) F

LIPPARD, George (1822–1854)
American novelist
The Monks of Monk Hall (1844) F
Blanche of Brandywine (1846) F
New York: Its Upper Ten and Lower Million (1853) F

LIVELY, Adam (1961–)
British novelist
Blue (1988) F
The Burnt House (1989) F
The Snail (1991) F
I Sing the Body Electric (1993) F

LIVELY, Penelope [Margaret], *née* Greer (1933–)
British novelist, short-story writer, and children's writer
Astercote (1970) F CH
The Ghost of Thomas Kempe (1973) F CH
A Stitch in Time (1976) F CH
The Road to Lichfield (1977) F
Nothing Missing But the Samovar, and Other Stories (1978) F SS
Treasures of Time (1979) F
Judgement Day (1980) F
Next to Nature, Art (1982) F
Perfect Happiness (1983) F
According to Mark (1984) F
Corruption (1984) F SS
Pack of Cards (1986) F SS
Moon Tiger (1987) F
Passing On (1989) F
City of the Mind (1991) F
Cleopatra's Sister (1993) F
Oleander, Jacaranda (1994) NF
Heat Wave (1996) NF
Spiderweb (1998) F

LIVINGSTONE, David (1813–1873)
British missionary and explorer
Missionary Travels and Researches in South Africa (1857) NF

'LLEWELLYN, Richard' [Richard Daffyd Vivian Llewellyn Lloyd] (1907–1983)
Welsh novelist and dramatist
How Green Was My Valley (1939) F
None But the Lonely Heart (1943) F
A Few Flowers for Shiner (1950) F
Up, Into the Singing Mountain (1963) F
Down Where the Moon is Small (1966) F
Green, Green My Valley Now (1975) F

LLOYD, Richard Daffyfd Llewellyn *see* RICHARD LLEWELLYN

LOCHHEAD, Liz (1947–)
Scottish poet and dramatist
Memo for Spring (1972) V
Islands (1978) V
The Grimm Sisters (1981) V
Blood and Ice (1982) D
Dreaming Frankenstein and Collected Poems (1984) V
Silver Service (1985) D
True Confessions and New Clichés (1985) V
Mary Queen of Scots Got Her Head Chopped Off; (1987) D
Bagpipe Muzak (1991) V

LOCKE, John (1632–1704)
English philosopher
A Letter Concerning Toleration (1689) NF
An Essay Concerning Humane Understanding (1690) NF
A Second Letter Concerning Toleration (1690) NF
Two Treatises of Government (1690) NF
A Third Letter for Toleration (1692) NF
Some Thoughts Concerning Education (1693) NF
The Reasonableness of Christianity (1695) NF

LODGE, David [John] (1935–)
British novelist and critic
The Picturegoers (1960) F
Ginger, You're Barmy (1962) F
The British Museum is Falling Down (1965) F
The Language of Fiction (1966) NF
Out of the Shelter (1970) F
The Novelist at the Crossroads, and Other Essays on Fiction and Criticism (1971) NF
Twentieth-Century Literary Criticism (1972) NF
Changing Places (1975) NF
How Far Can You Go? [US: *Souls and Bodies*] (1980) F
Working with Structuralism (1981) NF
Small World (1984) F
Write On (1986) NF
Modern Criticism and Theory (1988) NF
Nice Work (1988) F
After Bakhtin (1990) NF
The Writing Game (1990) D
Paradise News (1991) F
Therapy (1995) F

LODGE, Thomas (1558–1625)
English poet, dramatist, pamphleteer, and fiction writer
An Alarum Against Usurers (1584) MISC
Scillaes Metamorphosis (1589) V
Rosalynde: Euphues Golden Legacie (1590) F
Robert Second Duke of Normandy, Surnamed Robin the Divell (1591) F
Euphues Shadow, the Battaile of the Sences (1592) F
The Life and Death of William Long Beard (1593) F
Phillis (1593) V
The Wounds of Civill War (1594) D
A Fig for Momus (1595) V
A Margarite of America (1596) F
A Treatise of the Plague [from F. Valleriole] (1603) NF

LOFTING, Hugh (1886–1947)
British children's writer
The Story of Dr Dolittle (1920) F CH
The Voyages of Dr Dolittle (1922) F CH
Dr Dolittle's Post Office (1923) F CH
Dr Dolittle's Circus (1924) F CH
Dr Dolittle's Zoo (1925) F CH
Dr Dolittle's Return (1933) F CH

LOFTS, Norah, *née* Robinson (1904–1983)
British popular historical novelist
I Met a Gypsy (1935) F SS
Here Was a Man (1936) F
The Town House (1959) F
The House at Old Vine (1961) F
The House at Sunset (1963) F

LOGUE, Christopher (1926–)
British poet and dramatist
Wand and Quadrant (1953) V
First Testament (1955) V
Devil, Maggot and Son (1956) V
Songs (1959) V
Logue's ABC (1966) V
Hermes Flew to Olympus (1968) V
New Numbers (1970) V
Urbanal (1975) V
War Music (1977) D
Red Bird (1979) V
Ode to the Dodo (1981) V
Kings (1990) D
The Husbands (1994) D
Prince Charming: A Memoir (1999) NF

'LONDON, Jack' [John Griffith Chaney] (1876–1916)
American novelist
The Son of the Wolf (1900) F SS
A Daughter of the Snows (1902) F
The Call of the Wild (1903) F
The People of the Abyss (1903) NF
The Sea-Wolf (1904) F
The Game (1905) F
War of the Classes (1905) NF
Before Adam (1906) F
White Fang (1906) F
Love of Life (1907) F SS
The Iron Heel (1908) F
Martin Eden (1909) F
Burning Daylight (1910) F
Lost Face (1910) F SS
South Sea Tales (1911) F SS
Smoke Bellew (1912) F
John Barleycorn (1913) F
The Valley of the Moon (1913) F
The Human Drift (1917) NF
Jerry of the Islands (1917) F
On the Makaloa Mat (1919) F SS

LONGFELLOW, Henry Wadsworth (1807–1882)
American poet
Outre-Mer: A Pilgrimage Beyond the Sea (1833–4) NF
Hyperion (1839) F
Voices of the Night (1839) V
Ballads and Other Poems (1841) V
Poems on Slavery (1842) V
The Spanish Student (1843) V D
The Belfry of Bruges, and Other Poems (1845) V D
Evangeline (1847) V
Kavanagh (1849) F
The Seaside and the Fireside (1849) V
The Golden Legend (1851) V
Hiawatha (1855) V
The Courtship of Miles Standish (1858) V
Tales of a Wayside Inn [1st ser.; 2nd ser., 1873; 3rd ser., 1874] (1863) V
Christus (1872) V
The Masque of Pandora (1875) V
Kéramos (1878) V
Ultima Thule (1880) V
In the Harbor (1882) V

LONGFORD, Elizabeth [Elizabeth Pakenham, Countess of Longford] (1906–)
British biographer
Victoria R.I. (1964) NF
Years of the Sword (1969) NF
Pillar of State (1972) NF

LONGLEY, Michael [George] (1939–)
Ulster poet
No Continuing City (1969) V
An Exploded View (1973) V
Man Lying on a Wall (1976) V
The Echo Gate (1979) V
Patchwork (1981) V
Gorse Fires (1991) V
Ghost Orchid (1995) V

'LONSDALE, Frederick' [Lionel Frederick Leonard] (1881–1954)
British dramatist
Aren't We All? (1923) D
On Approval (1926) D
Canaries Sometimes Sing (1929) D

LOOS, Anita (1893–1981)
American novelist and dramatist
Gentlemen Prefer Blondes (1925) F
But Gentlemen Marry Brunettes (1928) F
No Mother to Guide Her (1961) F

LORENZINI, Carlo *see* CARLO COLLODI

'LOTI, Pierre' [Julien Viaud] (1850–1923)
French novelist
Aziyadé (1879) F
Rarahu (1880) F
The Romance of a Spahi [*Le Roman d'un Spahi*] (1881) F
My Brother Yves [*Mon frère Yves*] (1883) F
An Iceland Fisherman [*Pêcheur d'Islande*] (1886) F
Madame Chrysanthème (1887) F
Matelot (1893) F
Ramuntcho (1897) F

LOVECRAFT, H[oward] P[hillips] (1890–1937)
American horror, fantasy, and science fiction writer
The Shadow Over Innsmouth (1936) F
The Outsider and Others (1939) F SS
Beyond the Wall of Sleep (1943) F
The Dunwich Horror and Others (1963) F SS
At the Mountain of Madness (1964) F
Dagon, and Other Macabre Tales (1965) F SS

LOVER, Samuel (1797–1868)
Irish novelist, songwriter, and portrait painter
Rory O'More (1837) F
Handy Andy (1842) F
L.S.D.; or, Treasure Trove (1844) F
Metrical Tales, and Other Poems (1860) V

LOWELL, Amy [Lawrence] (1874–1925)
American poet
A Dome of Many-Coloured Glass (1912) V
Sword Blades and Poppy Seed (1914) V
Men, Women, and Ghosts (1916) V
Tendencies in Modern American Poetry (1917) NF
Can Grande's Castle (1918) V
Pictures of the Floating World (1919) V
Legends (1921) V
A Critical Fable (1922) V
What's O'Clock? (1925) V
East Wind (1926) V
Ballads for Sale (1927) V

LOWELL, James Russell (1819–1891)
American poet, critic, and journalist
A Year's Life (1841) V
The Biglow Papers [1st ser.; 2nd ser., 1867] (1848) V
A Fable for Critics (1848) V
Poems: Second Series (1848) V
The Vision of Sir Launfal (1848) V
Fireside Travels (1864) NF
The Cathedral (1869) V
Among My Books [1st ser.; 2nd ser., 1876] (1870) NF
My Study Windows (1871) NF
On Democracy (1884) NF
Political Essays (1888) NF
Latest Literary Essays and Addresses (1891) NF

LOWELL, Robert [Traill Spence, Jr] (1917–1977)
American poet
Land of Unlikeness (1944) V
Lord Weary's Castle (1946) V
The Mills of the Kavanaughs (1951) V
Life Studies (1959) V P
Imitation (1961) V
For the Union Dead (1964) V
The Old Glory (1965) D
Near the Ocean (1967) V
Notebooks 1967–68 (1969) V
Dolphins (1973) V
For Lizzie and Harriet (1973) V
History (1973) V
Day by Day (1977) V

LOWES, John Livingstone (1867–1945)
American scholar and critic
Convention and Revolt in Poetry (1919) NF
The Road to Xanadu (1927) NF

LOWNDES, Marie [Adelaide Julie Elizabeth Renée] Belloc (1868–1947)
British novelist
The Heart of Penelope (1904) F
Barbara Rebell (1905) F
The Uttermost Farthing (1908) F
Studies in Wives (1909) F SS
Jane Oglander (1911) F
Mary Pechell (1912) F
The Lodger (1913) F
Studies in Love and Terror (1913) F SS
The End of Her Honeymoon (1914) F
Lilla (1916) F
The Red Cross Barge (1916) F
Love and Hatred (1917) F
The Lonely House (1920) F
Duchess Laura (1929) F

LOWRY, [Clarence] Malcolm [Boden] (1909–1957)
British novelist
Ultramarine (1933) F
Under the Volcano (1947) F
Hear Us, O Lord, From Heaven Thy Dwelling Place (1961) F SS
Dark As the Grave Wherein My Friend is Laid (1968) F
Lunar Caustic (1968) F

LUBBOCK, Percy (1879–1965)
British biographer and critic
The Craft of Fiction (1921) NF
Earlham (1922) NF
Roman Pictures (1923) F
Shades of Eton (1929) NF
Portrait of Edith Wharton (1947) NF

LUCAS, E[dward] V[errall] (1868–1938)
British essayist and topographical writer
The War of the Wenuses (1898) F
The Open Road (1899) ANTH
A Wanderer in Holland (1905) NF
Fireside and Sunshine (1906) NF
Listener's Lure (1906) F
A Wanderer in London (1906) NF
Character and Comedy (1907) NF
Over Bemerton's (1908) F
A Wanderer in Paris (1909) NF
Mr Ingleside (1910) F
Old Lamps for New (1911) NF
London Lavender (1912) F
A Wanderer in Florence (1912) NF
Loiterer's Harvest (1913) NF
Landmarks (1914) F
A Wanderer in Venice (1914) NF
Cloud and Silver (1916) NF
London Revisited (1916) NF
The Vermilion Box (1916) F
His Fatal Beauty; or, The Moore of Chealsea (1917) D
A Rover I Would Be (1928) NF
Traveller's Luck (1930) NF
Reading, Writing and Remembering (1932) NF

LUCAS, F[rank] L[aurence] (1894–1967)
British scholar, critic, poet, and novelist
Seneca and Elizabethan Tragedy (1922) NF
Authors Dead and Living (1926) NF

Eight Victorian Poets [enlarg. as *Ten Victorian Poets* 1940] (1930) NF
The Wild Tulip (1932) F
The Awakening of Balthazar (1935) V
The Decline and Fall of the Romantic Ideal (1936) NF
The Woman Clothed with the Sun, and Other Stories (1937) F SS
Doctor Dido (1938) F
Journal Under the Terror 1938 (1938) NF
Literature and Psychology (1951) NF
The Search for Good Sense (1958) NF
The Art of Living (1959) NF
The English Agent (1969) F

LUCIE-SMITH, [John] Edward [McKenzie] (1933–)
British poet, art historian, anthologist, translator, and novelist
A Tropical Childhood, and Other Poems (1961) V
Confessions and Histories (1964) V
Paul Claudel: Five Great Odes (1967) V
Towards Silence (1968) V
The Well-Wishers (1974) V

LUDLUM, Robert (1927–)
American thriller writer
The Scarlatti Inheritance (1971) F
The Osterman Weekend (1973) F
The Holcroft Covenant (1977) F
The Bourne Identity (1980) F
The Parsifal Mosaic (1982) F
The Bourne Supremacy (1986) F
The Icarus Agenda (1988) F
The Bourne Ultimatum (1990) F

LUNN, Hugh Kingsmill *see* HUGH KINGSMILL

LURIE, Alison (1926–)
American novelist, short-story writer, and critic
Love and Friendship (1962) F
The Nowhere City (1965) F
Imaginary Friends (1967) F
Real People (1969) F
The War Between the Tates (1974) F
Only Children (1979) F
The Language of Clothes (1981) NF
Foreign Affairs (1984) F
The Truth About Lorrin Jones (1988) F
Don't Tell the Grown-Ups (1990) NF
Women and Ghosts (1994) F SS
The Last Resort (1998) F

LUSKA, Sidney *see* HENRY HARLAND

LYALL, Gavin [Tudor] (1932–)
British thriller writer
The Most Dangerous Game (1963) F
Midnight Plus One (1965) F
Venus With Pistol (1969) F
Blame the Dead (1973) F
Judas Country (1975) F
The Secret Servant (1980) F
The Conduct of Major Maxim (1983) F
Honourable Intentions (1999) F

LYDGATE, John (1370?–1449)
English poet
Stans Puer ad Mensam (1476?) V
The Chorle and the Birde [written *c.* 1400] (1477?) V
The Horse the Ghoos & the Sheep [written post 1436] (1477?) V
The Temple of Glas [written *c.* 1403] (1477?) V
The Lyf of Our Lady (1484) V
The Fall of Princes [trn *c.* 1431–8 from Boccaccio] (1494) V
The Storye of Thebes [adapted *c.* 1421–2 from a French source] (1497?) V
The Assembly of the Gods [written post 1422] (1498) V
The Virtue of the Mass (1500?) V
The Complaint of the Black Knight (1508) V
Proverbs [written *c.* 1431–8] (1510?) V
The Governaunce of Kynges [trn *c.* 1370 from Aristotle; also known as *Secrets of the Old Philisoffres*] (1511) V
The Hystorye, Sege and Dystruccyon of Troye [paraphrased from Guido delle Colonne] (1513) V
The Testament of John Lydgate (1515?) V

LYLY, John (1554–1606)
English dramatist and author
Euphues (1578) NF
Euphues and his England (1580) NF
Alexander, Campaspe, and Diogenes (1584) D
Sapho and Phao (1584) D
Endimion, the Man in the Moone (1591) D
Gallathea (1592) D
Midas (1592) D
Mother Bombie (1594) D
The Woman in the Moone (1597) D
Loves Metamorphosis (1601) D

LYTTELTON, George, 1st Baron Lyttelton (1709–1773)
British statesman and poet
Blenheim (1728) V
An Epistle to Mr Pope (1730) V
The Progress of Love (1732) V
Advice to a Lady (1733) V
Letters from a Persian in England to his Friend at Isphahan (1735) F
Dialogues of the Dead (1760) V

LYTTON, Edward Robert Bulwer, 1st Earl of Lytton ['Owen Meredith'] (1831–1891)
British statesman and poet
Clytemnestra, The Earl's Return, The Artist, and Other Poems [as 'Owen Meredith'] (1855) V
The Wanderer [as 'Owen Meredith'] (1857) V
Lucile [as 'Owen Meredith'] (1860) V
The Ring of Amasis [as 'Owen Meredith'] (1863) V
Chronicles and Characters (1868) V
Orval; or, The Fool of Time (1869) V
Fables in Song (1874) V
Glenaveril; or, The Metamorphoses (1885) V

After Paradise; or, Legends of Exile (1887) V
King Poppy (1892) V
Ottilie (1883) F
Euphorion (1884) NF
Miss Brown (1884) F
A Phantom Lover (1886) F
Hauntings (1890) F SS
Vanitas (1892) F SS
Renaissance Fancies and Studies (1895) NF
Limbo, and Other Essays (1897) NF
Genius Loci (1899) NF
Hortus Vitae (1904) NF
Pope Jacynth, and Other Fantastic Tales (1904) F SS
The Enchanted Woods and Other Essays on the Genius of Places (1905) NF
The Spirit of Rome (1906) NF
Gospels of Anarchy, and Other Contemporary Studies (1908) NF
Laurus Nobilis (1909) NF
Vital Lies (1912) NF
The Tower of the Mirrors, and Other Essays on the Spirit of Places (1914) NF
Satan, the Waster (1920) F
For Maurice (1927) F SS

M

MABBE [or **MAB**] **James** (1572–1642?)
English translator
The Rogue; or, The Life of Guzman de Alfarache [from Matheo Alemán] (1622) F
The Spanish Bawd [from Fernando de Rojas] (1631) F
Exemplarie Novells (1640) F

Mac A'GHOBHAINN, Iain *see* IAIN CRICHTON SMITH

MACAULAY, [Dame Emilie] Rose (1881–1958)
British novelist, essayist, and travel writer
Abbots Verney (1906) F
The Secret River (1909) F
The Two Blind Countries (1914) V
Non-Combatants and Others (1916) F SS
Three Days (1919) V
Potterism (1920) F
Dangerous Ages (1921) F
A Casual Commentary (1925) NF
Crewe Train (1926) F
They Were Defeated (1932) F
Going Abroad (1934) F
They Went to Portugal (1946) NF
Fabled Shore (1949) NF
Pleasure of Ruins (1953) NF
The Towers of Trebizond (1956) F

MACAULAY, T[homas] B[abington], 1st Baron Macaulay (1800–1859)
British statesman, historian, essayist, and poet
Pompeii (1819) V
Evening (1821) V
Lays of Ancient Rome (1842) V
Critical and Historical Essays (1843) NF
The History of England from the Accession of James II [vols. i, ii] (1849) NF
Speeches Corrected by Himself (1854) NF
The History of England from the Accession of James II [vols. iii, iv] (1855) NF

'McBAIN, Ed' [Evan Hunter] (1926–)
American crime writer
The Blackboard Jungle [as Evan Hunter] (1954) F
Cop Hater (1956) F

MACBETH, George [Mann] (1932–1992)
British poet, novelist, and editor
The Broken Places (1963) V
A Doomsday Book (1965) V
The Night of Stones (1968) V
The Burning Cone (1970) V
The Orlando Poems (1971) V
Shrapnel (1973) V
Buying a Heart (1977) V
Poems of Love and Death (1980) V
The Cleaver Gardens (1986) V
The Anatomy of Divorce (1988) V
Trespassing (1991) V
The Patient (1992) V

MacCAIG, Norman [Alexander] (1910–1996)
Scottish poet
Far Cry (1943) V
The Inward Eye (1946) V
Riding Lights (1955) V
The Sinai Sort (1957) V
A Common Grace (1960) V
A Round of Applause (1962) V
Surroundings (1966) V
Rings on a Tree (1968) V
The World's Room (1974) V
Tree of Strings (1977) V
The Equal Skies (1980) V
Voice-Over (1988) V

MacCARTHY, [Sir Charles Otto] Desmond (1877–1952)
British journalist and dramatic critic
Remnants (1918) NF
Portraits (1931) NF
Criticism (1932) NF
Drama (1940) NF
Memories (1953) NF
Theatre (1954) NF

McCARTHY, Cormac (1933–)
American novelist
Child of God (1973) F
Suttree (1979) F
Blood Meridian, or the Evening Redness in the West (1985) F
All the Pretty Horses (1992) F
The Crossing (1994) F
The Stonemason (1994) F
Cities of the Plain (1998) F

McCARTHY, Justin (1830–1912)
Irish politician, historian, and novelist
A Fair Saxon (1873) F

Linley Rochford (1874) F
Dear Lady Disdain (1875) F
Miss Misanthrope (1878) F
A History of Our Own Times [vols. i, ii; vol. iii, 1880) (1879) NF
The Epoch of Reform 1830–50 (1882) NF
The Right Honourable (1886) F
The Ladies' Gallery (1888) F
Modern England (1899) NF
Reminiscences (1899) NF

McCARTHY, Mary [Therese] (1912–1989)
American novelist, short-story writer, and critic
The Company She Keeps (1942) F
The Oasis (1949) F
Cast a Cold Eye (1950) F SS
The Groves of Academe (1952) F
A Charmed Life (1955) F
Venice Observed (1956) NF
Memories of a Catholic Girlhood (1957) NF
The Stones of Florence (1959) NF
On the Contrary (1961) NF
The Group (1963) F
Vietnam (1967) NF
The Writing on the Wall (1970) NF
Birds of America (1971) F
Medina (1972) NF
The Mask of State (1974) NF
Cannibals and Missionaries (1979) F
Ideas and the Novel (1980) NF
How I Grew (1987) NF

McCOURT, Frank (1930–)
Irish writer
Angela's Ashes (1996) NF
'Tis (1999) NF

McCULLERS, Carson [Smith] (1917–1967)
American novelist
The Heart is a Lonely Hunter (1940) F
Reflections in a Golden Eye (1941) F
The Member of the Wedding (1946) F
The Ballad of the Sad Café (1951) F SS
The Square Root of Wonderful (1958) F
Clock Without Hands (1961) F

'MACDIARMID, Hugh' [Christopher Murray Grieve] (1892–1978)
Scottish poet
Annals of the Five Senses (1923) V
Sangscaw (1925) V
A Drunk Man Looks at the Thistle (1926) V
Penny Wheep (1926) V
To Circumjack Cencrastus; or, The Curly Snake (1930) V
First Hymn to Lenin and Other Poems (1931) V
At the Sign of the Thistle (1934) NF
Stony Limits, and Other Poems (1934) V
Second Hymn to Lenin, and Other Poems (1935) V
Lucky Poet (1943) NF
Poems of the East-West Synthesis (1946) V
In Memoriam James Joyce (1955) V
The Battle Continues (1957) V
The Kind of Poetry I Want (1961) V
Bracken Hills in Autumn (1962) V
The Company I've Kept (1966) NF
A Lap of Honour (1967) V
The Uncanny Scot (1968) NF
A Clyack-Sheaf (1969) V

MacDONAGH, Donagh (1912–1968)
Irish poet and dramatist
Happy as Larry (1946) V D

MacDONALD, George (1824–1905)
Scottish poet and novelist
Within and Without (1855) V
Phantastes (1858) F
David Elginbrod (1863) F
Adela Cathcart (1864) F
The Portent (1864) F
Alec Forbes of Howglen (1865) F
Annals of a Quiet Neighbourhood (1867) F
Dealings with the Faeries (1867) F
The Disciple, and Other Poems (1867) V
Guild Court (1868) F
Robert Falconer (1868) F
The Seaboard Parish (1868) F
At the Back of the North Wind (1870) F
Ranald Bannerman's Boyhood (1871) F CH
The Princess and the Goblin (1872) F CH
The Vicar's Daughter (1872) F
Wilfred Cumbermede (1872) F
Gutta-Percha Willie, the Working Genius (1873) F CH
Malcolm (1875) F
St George and St Michael (1876) F
Thomas Wingfold, Curate (1876) F
The Marquis of Lossie (1877) F
Paul Faber, Surgeon (1879) F
Sir Gibbie (1879) F
Mary Marston (1881) F
Castle Warlock (1882) F CH
The Gifts of the Child Christ, and Other Tales (1882) F SS
Weighed and Wanting (1882) F
Donal Grant (1883) F
The Princess and Curdie (1883) F CH
What's Mine's Mine (1886) F
The Light Princess, and Other Fairy Stories (1890) F SS
The Flight of the Shadow (1891) F
There and Back (1891) F
Heather and Snow (1893) F
Lilith (1895) F

MacDONALD, John D[ann] (1916–1986)
American crime writer
The Brass Cupcake (1950) F
Cape Fear (1953) F
The Deep Blue Goodbye [first Travis McGee novel] (1964) F
Condominium (1977) F

'MacDONALD, Ross' [Kenneth Millar] (1915–1983)
American crime writer
The Moving Target [first Lew Archer novel] (1949) F
The Drowning Pool (1950) F
The Zebra-Striped Hearse (1962) F
The Goodbye Look (1969) F
Lords and Masters (1936) F
Autobiography of a Cad (1938) F
The Spanish Pistol, and Other Stories (1939) F SS

MacDONELL, A[rchibald] G[ordon] (1895–1941)
British novelist
England, Their England (1933) F
The Shakespeare Murders [as 'Neil Gordon'] (1933) F

McEWAN, Ian [Russell] (1948–)
British novelist and dramatist
First Love, Last Rites (1975) F SS
The Cement Garden (1978) F
In Between the Sheets (1978) F SS
The Comfort of Strangers (1981) F
The Child in Time (1987) F
The Innocent; or, The Special Relationship (1990) F
Black Dogs (1992) F
The Daydreamer (1994) F
Enduring Love (1997) F
Amsterdam (1998) F

McFALL, Frances Elizabeth *see* SARAH GRAND

McGAHERN, John (1934–)
Irish novelist and short-story writer
The Barracks (1963) F
The Dark (1965) F
Nightlines (1970) F SS
The Pornographer (1979) F
High Ground (1985) F SS
Amongst Women (1990) F

McGONAGALL, William (1830–1902)
Scottish versifier
Poetic Gems (1890)

McGOUGH, Roger (1937–)
British poet and dramatist
Frinck; A Day in the Life Of; and Summer with Monica (1967) F V
Watchwords (1969) V
Holiday on Death Row (1979) V
Waving at Trains (1982) V
Defying Gravity (1992) V

McGRATH, John [Peter] (1935–)
British dramatist
Events While Guarding the Bofors Gun (1966) D

McGUCKIAN, Medbh (1950–)
Irish poet
The Flower Master (1982) V
Venus and the Rain (1984) V
On Ballycastle Beach (1988) V
Marconi's Cottage (1991) V
Captain Lavender (1994) V

MACHEN, Arthur [Arthur Llewellyn Jones] (1863–1947)
British novelist and short-story writer
The Anatomy of Tobacco; or, Smoking Methodised (1884) NF
The Chronicle of Clemendy; or, The History of the IX Joyous Journeys (1888) F SS
The Great God Pan, and The Inmost Light (1894) F
The Three Impostors; or, The Transmutations (1895) F SS
The House of Souls (1906) F
The Hill of Dreams (1907) F
The Angels of Mons, The Bowmen, and Other Legends of the War (1915) F
The Great Return (1915) F
The Terror (1917) F
Far Off Things (1922) NF
Things Near and Far (1923) NF
The Shining Pyramid (1924) F SS
The Green Round (1933) F
The Children of the Pool, and Other Stories (1936) F SS
The Cosy Room, and Other Stories (1936) F SS

MACHIAVELLI, Niccolò (1469–1527)
Italian statesman and political philosopher
The Art of War [*Dell'Arte della guerra*] (1521) NF
The Prince [*Il principe*; first Eng. trn, 1560] (1532) NF

McILVANNEY, William [Angus] (1936–)
Scottish novelist
Docherty (1975) F
The Big Man (1985) F
Walking Wounded (1989) F SS

McINERNEY, Jay (1955–)
American novelist
Bright Lights, Big City (1983) F
Ransom (1985) F
Story of My Life (1988) F
Brightness Falls (1992) F

MacINNES, Colin (1914–1976)
British novelist and journalist
To the Victors the Spoils (1950) F
City of Spades (1957) F
Absolute Beginners (1959) F
Mr Love and Justice (1960) F

MACKENZIE, [Sir Edward Montague] Compton (1883–1972)
British novelist
The Passionate Elopement (1911) F
Carnival (1912) F
Sinister Street [vol. i] (1913) F
Sinister Street [vol. ii] (1914) F
Guy and Pauline (1915) F
The Early Life and Adventures of Sylvia Scarlett (1918) F
Sylvia and Michael (1919) F
Poor Relations (1920) F

The Vanity Girl (1920) F
Rich Relatives (1921) F
The Altar Steps (1922) F
The Parson's Progress (1923) F
The Seven Ages of Woman (1923) F
The Old Men of the Sea (1924) F
Coral (1925) F
Rogues and Vagabonds (1927) F
Vestal Fire (1927) F
Extraordinary Women (1928) F
Gallipoli Memories (1929) NF
First Athenian Memories (1931) NF
Our Street (1931) F
Greek Memories (1932) NF
Literature in My Time (1933) NF
Reaped and Bound (1933) NF
Water on the Brain (1933) F
The East Wind of Love (1937) F
The South Wind of Love (1937) F
West to North (1940) F
The West Wind of Love (1940) F
The Red Tapeworm (1941) F
Wind of Freedom (1943) NF
The North Wind of Love: Book One (1944) F
The North Wind of Love: Book Two (1945) F
Whisky Galore (1947) F
All Over the Place (1948) NF
Hunting the Fairies (1949) F
The Rival Monster (1952) F
Thin Ice (1956) F
Mezzotint (1961) F
The Stolen Soprano (1965) F
Paper Lives (1966) F

MacKENZIE, Henry (1745–1831)
Scottish novelist and essayist
The Man of Feeling (1771) F
The Man of the World (1773) F
The Prince of Tunis (1773) D
Julia de Roubigné (1777) F

McKERROW, R[onald] B[runlees] (1872–1940)
British bibliographer, textual scholar, and editor
An Introduction to Bibliography for Literary Students (1927) NF

MACKINTOSH, Elizabeth *see* JOSEPHINE TEY

MACKLIN, Charles (1699?–1797)
British actor and dramatist
Love à la Mode (1759) D
The Man of the World (1781) D

MACLAREN-ROSS, J[ulian] (1912–1964)
British novelist and short-story writer
The Stuff to Give the Troops (1944) F SS
Better Than a Kick in the Pants (1945) F SS
Of Love and Hunger (1947) F
Memoirs of the Forties (1965) NF

MacLAVERTY, Bernard (1942–)
Northern Irish novelist and short-story writer
Secrets, and Other Stories (1977) F SS
Lamb (1980) F
A Time to Dance, and Other Stories (1982) F SS
Cal (1983) F
The Great Profundo, and Other Stories (1987) F SS
Walking the Dog (1994) F SS
Grace Notes (1997) F

McLAVERTY, Michael (1904–1992)
Irish novelist and short-story writer
Call My Brother Back (1939) F
Lost Fields (1941) F
The White Mare (1943) F SS
The Game Cock, and Other Stories (1947) F SS
The Road to the Shore (1976) F SS

MACLEAN, Alistair [Stuart] (1923–1987)
British thriller writer
The Guns of Navarone (1957) F
Ice Station Zebra (1963) F
Where Eagles Dare (1967) F

MacLEAN, Sorley [Somhairle MacGill-Eain] 1911–)
Gaelic poet
Spring Tide and Neap Tide [Reothairt is Contraigh] [Gaelic and English] (1977) V

MacLEISH, Archibald (1892–1982)
American poet, critic, and dramatist
Towers of Ivory (1917) V
The Happy Marriage (1924) V
The Pot of Earth (1925) V
Nobodaddy (1926) V D
Streets in the Moon (1926) V
The Hamlet of A. MacLeish (1928) V
New Found Land (1930) V
Conquistador (1932) V
Frescoes for Mr Rockefeller's City (1933) V
Panic (1935) V D
Public Speech (1936) V
The Fall of the City (1937) V
Air Raid (1938) V
America Was Promises (1939) V
The Irresponsibles (1940) NF
The American Cause (1941) NF
A Time to Speak (1941) NF
Colloquy for the States (1943) V
A Time to Act (1943) NF
The American Story (1944) NF
Actfive (1948) V
Poetry and Opinion (1950) NF
This Music Crept by Me Upon the Waters (1953) V D
Songs for Eve (1954) V
J.B. (1958) V
Poetry and Experience (1960) NF
Herakles (1967) V
A Continuing Journey (1968) NF
The Great American Fourth of July Parade (1975) V
Riders on the Earth (1978) NF

MacLENNAN, [John] Hugh (1907–1990)
Canadian novelist and essayist
Barometer Rising (1941) F
Two Solitudes (1945) F

The Precipice (1948) F
Cross Country (1949) NF
Thirty and Three (1954) NF
The Watch That Ends the Night (1959) F
Scotchman's Return, and Other Essays (1960) NF
Return of the Sphinx (1967) F
Voices in Time (1980) F

MACLEOD, Fiona *see* WILLIAM SHARP

McLUHAN, [Herbert] Marshall (1911–1980)
Canadian critic
The Mechanical Bride (1951) NF
The Gutenberg Galaxy (1962) NF
Understanding Media (1964) NF
The Medium is the Message (1967) NF
Verbi-voco-Visual Explorations (1967) NF
Peace and War in the Global Village (1968) NF
Counterblast (1969) NF
Culture is Our Business (1970) NF
The City as Classroom (1977) NF

McMURTY, Larry [Jeff] (1936–)
American novelist
Horseman, Pass By (1961) F
Leaving Cheyenne (1963) F
The Last Picture Show (1966) F
Terms of Endearment (1975) F
Somebody's Darling (1978) F
Cadillac Jack (1982) F
The Desert Rose (1983) F
Lonesome Dove (1985) F
Anything for Billy (1988) F
Buffalo Girls (1990) F
The Evening Star (1992) F
Streets of Laredo (1993) F

MacNEICE, [Frederick] Louis (1907–1963)
Anglo-Irish poet and dramatist
Blind Fireworks (1929) V
The Agamemnon of Aechylus (1936) V
The Earth Compels (1938) V
I Crossed the Minch (1938) V P
Modern Poetry (1938) NF
Autumn Journal (1939) V
The Last Ditch (1940) V
Plant and Phantom (1941) V
Christopher Columbus (1944) D
Springboard (1944) V
The Dark Tower, and Other Radio Scripts (1947) D
Holes in the Sky (1948) V
Goethe's Faust: Parts 1 and 2 [abridged version] (1951) V
Ten Burnt Offerings (1952) V
Autumn Sequel (1954) V
Visitations (1957) V
Eighty-Five Poems (1959) V
Solstices (1961) V
The Burning Perch (1963) V
The Strings Are False (1965) NF
Persons From Porlock, and Other Plays for Radio (1969) D

McNEILE, Herman Cyril *see* 'SAPPER'

MACPHERSON, James (1736–1796)
Scottish poet and translator
The Highlander (1758) V
Fragments of Ancient Poetry (1760) V
Fingal (1762) V
Temora (1763) V
The Works of Ossian (1765) V

MACPHERSON, Jay (1931–)
British-born Canadian poet
Nineteen Poems (1952) V
O Earth Return (1954) V
The Boatman [enlarged 1968] (1957) V
Welcoming Disaster (1974) V

McTAGGART, John [McTaggart Ellis] (1866–1925)
Scottish philosopher
Studies in Hegelian Cosmology (1901) NF
Some Dogmas of Religion (1906) NF
A Commentary on Hegel's Logic (1910) NF
The Nature of Existence (1921) NF

McWILLIAM, Candia (1955–)
Scottish novelist, short-story writer, and poet
A Case of Knives (1988) F
A Little Stranger (1989) F
Debatable Land (1994) F
Change of Use (1997) F SS
Wait Till I Tell You (1997) F SS

MADGE, Charles [Henry] (1912–1996)
South African born poet and sociologist
Mass-Observation (1937) NF
The Disappearing Castle (1937) V
The Father Found (1941) V
Of Love, Time, and Places (1994) V

MAETERLINCK, [Count] Maurice (1862–1949)
Belgian dramatist
The Princess Maleine (1889) D
Pelleas and Melisande (1892) D
The Blue Bird (1908) D

MAHON, Derek (1941–)
Northern Irish poet and dramatist
Night-Crossing (1968) V
Beyond Howth Head (1970) V
The Man Who Built His City in Snow (1975) V
Light Music (1977) V
Courtyards in Delft (1981) V
A Kensington Notebook (1984) V
Antarctica (1985) V
The Yaddo Letter (1994) V

MAHY, Margaret (1936–)
New Zealand children's writer
The Haunting (1982) F CH
The Changeover (1984) F CH
Aliens in the Family (1986) F CH
The Tricksters (1986) F CH
Memory (1987) F CH

MAILER, Norman (1923–)
American novelist and journalist
The Naked and the Dead (1948) F
Barbary Shore (1951) F
The Deer Park (1955) F
The White Negro (1957) F
Advertisements for Myself (1959) F NF
Death for the Ladies, and Other Disasters (1962) V
An American Dream (1965) F
Cannibals and Christians (1966) NF
Why Are We in Vietnam? (1967) F
The Armies of the Night (1968) NF
Miami and the Siege of Chicago (1968) NF
Of a Fire on the Moon (1970) NF
The Prisoner of Sex (1971) NF
Marilyn (1973) NF
The Fight (1975) NF
The Executioner's Song (1979) F
Of Women and Their Elegance (1980) NF
Ancient Evenings (1983) F
Tough Guys Don't Dance (1984) F
Harlot's Ghost (1991) F
Oswald's Tale (1995) F
The Gospel According to the Son (1997) F
The Time of Our Time (1998) F

MAITLAND, F[rederic] W[illiam] (1850–1906)
British historian and jurist
The History of English Law Before the Time of Edward I (1895) NF
Roman Canon Law in the Church of England (1898) NF

MAITLAND, Sara (1950–)
British novelist and short-story writer
Daughter of Jerusalem (1978) F
Telling Tales (1983) F SS
Virgin Territory (1984) F SS
Three Times Table (1990) F
Home Truths (1993) F
Women Fly When Men Aren't Watching (1993) F SS

MALAMUD, Bernard (1914–1986)
American novelist
The Natural (1952) F
The Assistant (1957) F
The Magic Barrel (1958) F SS
A New Life (1961) F
Idiots First (1963) F SS
The Fixer (1967) F
Pictures of Fidelman (1969) F
The Tenants (1971) F
Rembrandt's Hat (1973) F SS
Dubin's Lives (1979) F
God's Grace (1982) F

'MALET, Lucas' [Mary St Leger Harrison], ***née*** **Kingsley** (1852–1931)
British novelist
Mrs Lorimer (1883) F
Colonel Enderby's Wife (1885) F
The Wages of Sin (1891) F
The Carissima (1896) F
The Gateless Barrier (1900) F
The History of Sir Richard Calmady (1901) F

MALLARMÉ, Stéphane (1842–1898)
French Symbolist poet
'L'Apres-midi d'un faune' ['The Afternoon of a Faun'] (1876) V
Les Dieux antiques ['The Ancient Gods'] (1880) V
Vers et prose (1893) V
Poésies (1899) V

MALLET, David [originally **Malloch]** (1705?–1765)
Scottish poet and dramatist
The Excursion (1728) V
Eurydice (1731) D
Of Verbal Criticism (1733) V
Mustapha (1739) D
Amyntor and Theodora; or, The Hermit (1747) V
Alfred (1751) D
Britannia (1755) D
Elvira (1763) D

MALLOCK, W[illiam] H[urrell] (1849–1923)
British novelist and writer on philosophy and politics
The New Republic (1877) F
The New Paul and Virginia; or, Positivism on an Island (1878) F
A Romance of the Nineteenth Century (1881) F
Atheism and the Value of Life (1884) NF
The Old Order Changes (1886) F
A Human Document (1892) F
Labour and the Popular Welfare (1893) NF
The Heart of Life (1895) F
Studies of Contemporary Superstition (1895) NF
The Individualist (1899) F
The Veil of the Temple (1904) F

MALONE, Edmond (1741–1812)
British critic and editor of Shakespeare
A Supplement to the Edition of Shakespeare Published by Johnson and Steevens (1780) EDN
Cursory Observations on the Poems Attributed to Thomas Rowley (1782) NF
The Plays and Poems of William Shakespeare (1790) EDN
An Inquiry into the Authenticity of Certain Miscellaneous Papers [on the Ireland forgeries] (1796) NF

MALOUF, David (1934–)
Australian novelist and poet
Bicycle, and Other Poems [US: *The Year of the Foxes*] (1970) V
Neighbours in a Thicket (1974) V
Johnno (1975) F
An Imaginary Life (1978) F
First Things Last (1980) V
Wild Lemons (1980) V
Harland's Half-Acre (1984) F
Antipodes (1985) F
The Great World (1990) F
Remembering Babylon (1993) F
Dream Stuff (2000) F

MALRAUX, André (1901–1976)
French novelist and critic
The Conquerors [*Les Conquérants*] (1928) F
Man's Fate [*Le Condition humaine*] (1933) F
Man's Hope [*L'Espoir*] (1937) F
Attenburg (1947) F
The Psychology of Art [*La Psychologie de l'art*] (1947) NF
The Voices of Silence [*Les Voix du silence*] (1951) NF

MALTHUS, T[homas] R[obert] (1766–1834)
British economist
An Essay on the Principle of Population (1798) NF
Observations on the Effect of the Corn Laws (1814) NF
An Inquiry into the Nature and Progress of Rent (1815) NF
Principles of Political Economy Considered (1820) NF
The Measure of Value Stated and Illustrated (1823) NF
Definitions in Political Economy (1827) NF

MAMET, David [Alan] (1947–)
American dramatist, critic, and novelist
Duck Variations (1974) D
Sexual Perversity in Chicago (1974) D
American Buffalo (1975) D
Reunion (1976) D
Dark Pony (1977) D
A Life in the Theater (1977) D
The Woods (1977) D
Shoeshine (1979) D
Edmond (1982) D
Glengarry Glen Ross (1984) D
Writing in Restaurants (1986) NF
Speed-the-Plow (1988) D
Some Freaks (1989) NF
Oleander (1992) D
The Cabin (1993) NF
The Village (1994) F
Wilson: A Consideration of the Sources (2000) F

MANDEVILLE, Bernard (1670?–1733)
Dutch-born satirist
Some Fables After Monsieur de la Fontaine (1703) V
Typhon; or, The Wars Between the Gods and Giants (1704) V
The Grumbling Hive; or, Knaves Turn'd Honest (1705) V
The Virgin Unmask'd (1709) V
The Fable of the Bees; or, Private Vices, Publick Benefits (1714) NF

MANLEY, Mary Delariviere (1663–1724)
English dramatist and author
Letters Written by Mrs Manley (1696) NF
The Lost Lover; or, The Jealous Husband (1696) D
The Royal Mischief (1696) D
The Secret History of Queen Zarah and the Zarazians (1705) F
Almyna; or, The Arabian Vow (1706) D
The Lady's Paquet of Letters (1707) F
Secret Memoirs and Manners of Several Persons of Quality (1709) F
Memoirs of Europe Towards the Close of the Eighth Century (1710) F
Court Intrigues (1711) F
The Adventures of Rivella (1714) F
Lucius, the First Christian King of Britain (1717) D
The Power of Love (1720) F

MANN, Thomas (1875–1955)
German novelist
Buddenbrooks (1901) F
Tonio Kröger (1903) F
Tristan (1903) F
Death in Venice [*Der Tod in Venedig*] (1912) F
Das Wunderkind (1914) F
Reflections of a Non-Political Man [*Betrachtungen eines Unpolitischen*] (1918) NF
The Magic Mountain [*Der Zauberberg*] (1924) F
Mario and the Magician [*Mario und der Zauberer*] (1930) F
Joseph and his Brothers [*Joseph und seine Brüder*; tetralogy] (1933–42) F
Lotte in Weimar (1939) F
Doctor Faustus [*Doktor Faustus*] (1947) F
The Holy Sinner [*Der Erwählte*] (1951) F
The Black Swan [*Die Betrogene*] (1953) F
Confessions of Felix Krull, Confidence Man [*Bekenntnisse des Hochstaplers Felix Krull*] (1954) F

MANNING, Henry Edward (1808–1892)
British cardinal
The Unity of the Church (1842) NF
The Grounds of Faith (1852) NF
The Temporal Mission of the Holy Ghost (1865) NF
National Education (1872) NF
The Vatican Decrees (1875) NF
The Eternal Priesthood (1883) NF

MANNING, Olivia [Mary] (1908–1980)
British novelist
The Wind Changes (1937) F
Growing Up (1948) F SS
Artist Among the Missing (1949) F
School for Love (1951) F
A Different Face (1953) F
The Doves of Venus (1955) F
My Husband Cartwright (1956) F SS
The Great Fortune (1960) F
The Spoilt City (1962) F
Friends and Heroes (1965) F
A Romantic Hero, and Other Stories (1967) F SS
The Play Room [US: *The Camperlea Girls*] (1969) F
The Rain Forest (1974) F
The Danger Tree (1977) F
The Battle Lost and Won (1978) F
The Sum of Things (1980) F

'MANSFIELD, Katherine' [Kathleen Mansfield Beauchamp] (1888–1923)
New Zealand short-story writer
In a German Pension (1911) F SS
Prelude (1918) F
Bliss,and Other Stories (1920) F SS
The Garden-Party, and Other Stories (1922) F SS

The Dove's Nest (1923) F SS
Something Childish, and Other Stories (1924) F SS
Journal (1927) NF SS
Novels and Novelists (1930) NF SS

MANTEL, Hilary [Mary] (1952–)
British novelist
Every Day is Mother's Day (1985) F
Vacant Posession (1986) F
Eight Months on Ghazzah Street (1988) F
Fludd (1989) F
A Place of Greater Safety (1992) F
A Change of Climate (1994) F
An Experiment in Love (1995) F
The Giant, O'Brien (1998) F

MANZONI, Allessandro (1785–1873)
Italian novelist and poet
The Fifth of May (1821) F
The Betrothed (1827) F

MARCUS, Frank (1928–)
British dramatist and critic
The Killing of Sister George (1965) D

MARK, Jan[et] [Marjorie] (1943–)
British children's writer
Thunder and Lightnings (1976) F CH
The Ennead (1978) F CH
Divide and Rule (1979) F CH
Nothing to Be Afraid Of (1980) F SS CH
Aquarius (1982) F CH
Handles (1983) F CH

MARKHAM, E[dward] A[rchibald] (1939–)
Caribbean British poet and short-story writer
Crossfire (1972) V
Human Rites (1984) V
Living in Disguise (1986) V
Something Unusual (1986) F SS
Towards the End of the Century (1989) V
Letter From Ulster and the Hugo Poems (1993) V

MARKHAM, Gervase or Jervis (1568?–1637)
English miscellaneous author
A Discource of Horsmanshippe (1593) NF
Sir Richard Grinvile, Knight (1595) D
The Poem of Poems; or, Sions Muse (1596) V
The Teares of the Beloved; or, The Lamentation of Saint John (1600) V
Marie Magdalens Lamentations for the Losse of Her Master Jesus (1601) V
Cavelarice; or, The English Horseman (1607) NF
The English Arcadia [pt. i; pt. ii 1613] (1607) F
Rodomonths Infernall; or, The Divell Conquered (1607) V
The Dumbe Knight (1608) D
The Famous Whore, or Noble Curtizan (1609) V
Markhams Maister-peece; or, What Doth a Horse-man Lacke (1610) NF
The English Husbandman (1613) NF
Cheape and Good Husbandry (1614) NF
The True Tragedy of Herod and Antipater (1622) D
The Souldiers Accidence; or, An Introduction into Military Discipline (1625) NF
Markhams Faithful Farrier (1629) NF

MARLOWE, Christopher (1564–1593)
English poet and dramatist
Tamburlane the Great (1590) D
The Massacre at Paris: with the Death of the Duke of Guise (1594) D
The Tragedie of Dido Queene of Carthage (1594) D
The Troublesome Raigne and Lamentable Death of Edward the Second (1594) D
Hero and Leander (1598) V
All Ovids Elegies (1599) V
Lucans First Booke Translated (1600) V
The Tragicall History of Dr Faustus (1604) D
The Famous Tragedy of the Rich Jew of Malta (1633) D

MARMION, Shackerley (1603–1639)
English dramatist and poet
Hollands Leaguer (1632) D
A Fine Companion (1633) D
The Legend of Cupid and Psyche; or, Cupid and his Mistris (1637) V
The Antiquary (1641) D

'MARPRELATE, Martin'
Collaborative pseudonym
The Epistle (1588) NF
The Epitome (1588) NF
Hay Any Worke for Cooper (1589) NF
Martin Junior (1589) NF
Martin Senior (1589) NF
The Minerալls (1589) NF
The Protestatyon of Martin Marprelat (1589) NF

MARQUAND, John P[hillips] (1893–1960)
American popular novelist
The Late George Apley (1937) F
Wickford Point (1939) F
Point of No Return (1949) F

MARRYAT, [Captain] Frederick (1792–1848)
British novelist and children's writer
The Naval Officer; or, Scenes and Adventures in the Life of Frank Mildmay (1829) F
The King's Own (1830) F
Newton Forster; or, The Merchant Service (1832) F
Peter Simple (1833) F
Jacob Faithful (1834) F
The Pacha of Many Tales (1835) F SS
Japhet in Search of a Father (1836) F
Mr Midshipman Easy (1836) F
The Pirate and the Three Cutters (1836) F
Snarleyvow; or, The Dog Fiend (1837) F
A Diary in America, with Remarks on its Institutions (1839) NF
The Phantom Ship (1839) F
Olla Podrida (1840) MISC
Poor Jack (1840) F
Joseph Rushbrook; or, The Poacher (1841) F
Masterman Ready; or, The Wreck of the Pacific (1841–2) F CH

Percival Keene (1842) F
Narrative of the Travels and Adventures of Monsieur Violet (1843) F
The Settlers in Canada (1844) F CH
The Mission; or, Scenes in Africa (1845) F CH
The Privateer's-Man (1846) F
The Children of the New Forest (1847) F CH
The Little Savage (1848–9) F
Valerie (1849) F

MARSH, [Dame] Ngaio (1899–1982)
New Zealand writer of detective fiction
A Man Lay Dead (1934) F
Enter a Murderer (1935) F
Vintage Murder (1937) F
Artists in Crime (1938) F
Overture to Death (1939) F
Death at the Bar (1940) F
Surfeit of Lampreys [US: *Death of a Peer*] (1941) F
Died in the Wool (1945) F
Final Curtain (1947) F
Swing, Brother, Swing [US: *A Wreath for Rivera*] (1949) F
Opening Night [US: *Night at the Vulcan*] (1951) F
Off With His Head (1957) F
Singing in the Shrouds (1958) F
Clutch of Constables (1968) F
Grave Mistake (1978) F
Light Thickens (1982) F

MARS-JONES, Adam (1954–)
British novelist and short-story writer
Lantern Lecture [US: *Fabrications*] (1981) F SS
Monopolies of Loss (1992) F SS
The Waters of Thirst (1993) F

MARSTON, John (1576–1634)
English dramatist and poet
The Metamorphosis of Pigmalions Image (1598) V
The Scourge of Villanie [as 'William Kinsayder'] (1598) V
Jacke Drums Entertainment; or, The Comedie of Pasquill and Katherine (1601) D
Antonio and Mellida: The First Part (1602) D
Antonio's Revenge: The Second Part (1602) D
The Malcontent (1604) D
The Dutch Courtezan (1605) D
Parasitaster; or, The Fawne (1606) D
The Wonder of Women; or, The Tragedie of Sophonisba (1606) D
What You Will (1607) D
Histrio-Mastix; or, The Player Whipt (1610) D

MARSTON, Philip Bourke (1850–1887)
British poet
Song-Tide, and Other Poems (1871) V
All in All (1875) V
Wind-Voices (1883) V

MARTIN, Violet Florence *see* 'SOMERVILLE AND ROSS'

MARTIN DU GARD, Roger (1881–1958)
French novelist and dramatist
Becoming [*Devenir*] (1909) F
Jean Barois (1913) F
The Thibault [*Les Thibault*; 8-novel series] (1922–40) F

MARTINEAU, Harriet (1802–1876)
British novelist, economist, and woman of letters
Five Years of Youth; or, Sense and Sentiment (1831) F
Illustrations of Political Economy (1832) NF
Society in America (1837) NF
Deerbrook (1839) F
The Hour and the Man (1841) F
The Playfellow (1841) F SS
Life in the Sick-Room; or, Essays by an Invalid (1844) NF
Dawn Island (1845) F
Letters on Mesmerism (1845) NF
The Billow and the Rock (1846) F
Eastern Life, Past and Present (1848) NF
Household Education (1849) NF
Letters from Ireland (1853) NF
The Positive Philosophy of August Comte (1853) NF
Complete Guide to the Lakes (1854) NF
England and Her Soldiers (1859) NF
Biographical Sketches (1869) NF
Autobiography (1877) NF

MARVELL, Andrew (1621–1678)
English poet
The First Anniversary of the Government Under the Lord Protector (1655) V
The Character of Holland (1665) V
The Rehearsal Transpros'd [pt. i; pt. ii, 1673] (1672) NF
Miscellaneous Poems (1681) V

MASEFIELD, John [Edward] (1878–1967)
British poet, novelist, and children's writer
Salt-Water Ballads (1902) V
Ballads (1903) V
A Mainsail Haul (1905) F SS
A Tarpaulin Muster (1907) F SS
Captain Margaret (1908) F
Multitude and Solitude (1909) F
The Tragedy of Nan, and Other Plays (1909) D
Ballads and Poems (1910) V
Martin Hyde, the Duke's Messenger (1910) F CH
The Everlasting Mercy (1911) V
Jim Davis; or, The Captive of Smugglers (1911) F CH
Dauber (1913) V
Philip the King, and Other Poems (1914) V
Good Friday (1916) V D
Lollingdon Downs, and Other Poems (1917) V
Enslaved, and Other Poems (1920) V
King Cole, and Other Poems (1923) V
A King's Daughter (1923) V
The Taking of Helen (1923) F SS
Tristan and Isolt (1923) V D
Sard Harker (1924) F
The Trial of Jesus (1925) V D

Odtaa (1926) F
The Midnight Folk (1927) F CH
The Coming of Christ (1928) V D
Midsummer Night, and Other Tales in Verse (1928) V
The Hawbucks (1929) F
Minnie Maylow's Story, and Other Tales and Scenes (1931) V
A Tale of Troy (1932) V
The Bird of Dawning; or, The Fortune of the Sea (1933) F
End and Beginning (1933) D
The Taking of the Gry (1934) F
The Box of Delights; or, When the Wolves Were Running (1935) F CH
A Letter From Pontus, and Other Verse (1936) V
Dead Ned (1938) F
Gautama the Enlightened, and Other Verse (1941) V
Wonderings (1943) V
Reynard the Fox (1946) V
On the Hill (1949) V
So Long to Learn (1952) NF
Bluebells, and Other Verse (1961) V
Old Raiger, and Other Verse (1964) V
Grace Before Ploughing (1966) NF

MASON, A[lfred] E[dward] W[oodley] (1865–1948)
British novelist and short-story writer
A Romance of Wastdale (1895) F
The Courtship of Morrice Buckler (1896) F
Lawrence Clavering (1897) F
The Philanderers (1897) F
Miranda of the Balcony (1899) F
The Watchers (1899) F
Clementina (1901) F
Ensign Knightley, and Other Stories (1901) F SS
The Four Feathers (1902) F
The Broken Road (1907) F
At the Villa Rose (1910) F
The Four Corners of the World (1917) F SS
The Summons (1920) F
The Winding Stair (1923) F
The House of the Arrow (1924) F
No Other Tiger (1927) F
The Prisoner in the Opal (1928) F
The Three Gentlemen (1932) F
Dilemmas (1934) F SS
Fire Over England (1936) F
Konigsmark (1938) F
Musk and Amber (1942) F
The House in Lordship Lane (1946) F

MASON, Richard (1919–1997)
British novelist
The World of Suzie Wong (1957) F

MASON, William (1724–1797)
British poet, dramatist, and musician
Musaeus (1747) V
Isis (1749) V
Elfrida (1752) V
Caractacus (1759) V
Elegies (1763) V
The English Garden [bk i; bk ii, 1776] (1772) V
The Dean and the 'Squire' (1782) V
King Stephen's Watch (1782) V

MASSIE, Allan [Johnstone] (1938–)
Scottish novelist, biographer, and critic
Change and Decay in All Around I See (1978) F
The Last Peacock (1980) F
The Death of Men (1981) F
One Night in Winter (1984) F
Augustus (1986) F
A Question of Loyalties (1989) F
The Hanging Tree (1990) F
Tiberius (1990) F
The Sins of the Father (1991) F
Caesar (1993) F
These Enchanted Woods (1993) F
The Ragged Lion (1994) F
King David (1995) F
Antony (1997) F
Shadows of Empire (1997) F

MASSINGER, Philip (1583–1640)
English dramatist
The Virgin Martir (1622) D
The Duke of Millaine (1623) D
The Bond-Man (1624) D
The Roman Actor (1629) D
The Picture (1630) D
The Renegado (1630) D
The Emperour of the East (1632) D
The Fatal Dowry (1632) D
The Maid of Honour (1632) D
A New Way to Pay Old Debts (1633) D
The Great Duke of Florence (1636) D
The Unnaturall Combat (1639) D
The City-Madam (1658) D

MASSON, David (1822–1907)
Scottish literary scholar and biographer and founder of *Macmillan's Magazine*
Essays Biographical and Critical, Chiefly on English Poets (1856) NF
British Novelists and Their Styles (1859) NF
The Life of John Milton (1859) NF
Wordsworth, Shelley, Keats, and Other Essays (1874) NF
De Quincey (1881) NF
Memories of London in the 'Forties (1908) NF

MASTERS, Brian (1939–)
British biographer and author
Now Barabbas Was a Rotter (1978) NF
Killing for Company (1985) NF
The Passion of John Aspinall (1988) NF
The Shrine of Jeffrey Dahmer (1993) NF
The Evil That Men Do (1996) NF

MASTERS, Edgar Lee (1868–1950)
American poet and novelist
A Book of Verses (1898) V
Maximilian (1902) V

Spoon River Anthology (1915) V
Songs and Satires (1916) V
Toward the Gulf (1918) V
Starved Rock (1919) V
Domesday Book (1920) V
Children of the Market Place (1922) F
Skeeters Kirby (1923) F
Mirage (1924) F
The New Spoon River (1924) V
Jack Kelso (1928) V
The Fate of the Jury (1929) V
Lichee Nuts (1930) V
Godbey (1931) V
Invisible Landscapes (1935) V
The New World (1937) V
The Tide of Time (1937) F
Illinois Poems (1941) V

MASTERS, John (1914–1973)
British novelist and author
Nightrunners of Bengal (1951) F
The Deceivers (1952) F
Bhowani Junction (1954) F

MATHER, Cotton (1663–1728)
American Puritan minister
Memorable Providences, Relating to Witchcrafts and Possessions (1689) NF
The Wonders of the Invisible World (1693) NF
Political Fables (1697) F
Magnalia Christi Americana (1702) NF
The Christian Philosopher (1721) NF

MATHER, Increase (1639–1723)
American Puritan minister
The Day of Trouble is Near (1674) NF
A Brief History of the War with the Indians (1676) NF
Remarkable Providences (1684) NF
Cases of Conscience Concerning Evil Spirits (1693) NF

MATHER, Richard (1596–1669)
Puritan minister and father of Increase Mather
Church-Government and Church-Covenant Discussed (1643) NF
A Platform of Church-Discipline (1649) NF

MATHERS, Peter (1931–)
British-born Australian novelist and dramatist
Trap (1966) F
The Wort Papers (1972) F
A Change for the Better (1984) F SS

MATURIN, C[harles] R[obert] (1782–1824)
Irish novelist and dramatist
Fatal Revenge; or, The Family of Montorio (1807) F
The Wild Irish Boy (1808) F
The Milesian Chief (1812) F
Bertram; or, The Castle of St Aldobrand (1816) D
Manuel (1817) D
Women; or, Pour et contre (1818) F
Fredolfo (1819) D
Melmoth the Wanderer (1820) F
The Albigenses (1824) F

'MAUGHAM, Robin' [Robert Cecil Romer Maugham] (1916–1981)
British novelist, dramatist, and author
The Servant (1948) F

MAUGHAM, [William] Somerset (1874–1965)
British novelist, short-story writer, and dramatist
Liza of Lambeth (1897) F
The Making of a Saint (1898) F
Orientations (1899) F SS
The Hero (1901) F
Mrs Craddock (1902) F
A Man of Honour (1903) D
The Merry-Go-Round (1904) F
The Bishop's Apron (1906) F
The Explorer (1908) D
The Magician (1908) F
Jack Straw (1911) D
Lady Frederick (1911) D
Of Human Bondage (1915) F
The Moon and Sixpence (1919) F
The Circle (1921) D
The Trembling of a Leaf (1921) F SS
On a Chinese Screen (1922) NF
Loaves and Fishes (1924) D
The Painted Veil (1925) F
The Casuarina Tree (1926) F SS
Ashenden; or, The British Agent (1928) F SS
The Breadwinner (1930) D
Cakes and Ale; or, The Skeleton in the Cupboard (1930) F
The Gentleman in the Parlour (1930) NF
Six Stories Written in the First Person Singular (1931) F SS
The Narrow Corner (1932) F
Ah King (1933) F SS
Don Fernando; or, Variations on Some Spanish Themes (1935) NF
The Mixture As Before (1940) F SS
Up at the Villa (1941) F
The Razor's Edge (1944) F
Creatures of Circumstance (1947) F SS
Catalina (1948) F
A Writer's Notebook (1949) NF
The Vagrant Mood (1952) NF
Points of View (1958) NF

MAUPASSANT, Guy de (1850–1893)
French novelist and short-story writer
Boule-de-Suif ['Ball of Tallow'] (1880) F
The House of Madame Tellier [*La Maison Tellier*] (1881) F SS
Mademoiselle Fifi (1882) F SS
A Woman's Life [*Une Vie*] (1883) F
Bel-Ami (1885) F
Yvette (1885) F
Monsieur Parent (1886) F SS
Le Horla (1887) F
Pierre et Jean (1888) F

MAUPIN, Armistead (1944–)
American novelist
Tales of the City (1978) F
The Night Listener (2000) F

MAURIAC, François (1885–1970)
French novelist
L'Enfant chargéde chaines (1913) F
Le Baiser au lépreux (1922) F
Thérèse Desqueyroux (1927) F
La Fin de la nuit (1935) F
Les Anges noirs (1936) F
Le Sagouin (1950) F

MAURICE, [John] F[rederick] D[enison] (1805–1872)
British theologian and author
Eustace Conway; or, The Brother and Sister (1834) F
The Kingdom of Christ (1838) NF
Moral and Metaphysical Philosophy (1845) NF
Theological Essays (1853) NF
The Doctrine of Sacrifice (1854) NF
The Claims of the Bible and Science (1863) NF
The Conscience (1868) NF
Social Morality (1869) NF

MAVOR, Osborne Henry *see* JAMES BRIDIE

MAXWELL, Gavin (1914–1969)
British traveller, conservationist, and natural history writer
Harpoon at a Venture (1952) NF
A Reed Shaken by the Wind (1956) NF
Ring of Bright Water (1960) NF
The Rocks Remain (1963) NF
Raven Seek Thy Brother (1968) NF

MAY, Thomas (1595–1650)
English poet, dramatist, translator, and historian
The Heire (1622) D
Lucan's Pharsalia; or, The Civill Warres of Rome [bks i-iii] (1626) V
Lucan's Pharsalia; or, The Civill Warres of Rome [bks i-x] (1627) V
Virgil's Georgicks (1628) V
Selected Epigrams of Martial (1629) V
The Mirrour of Mindes [trn of Barclay's *Icon Animarum* 1614] (1631) NF
The Tragedy of Antigone, the Theban Princesse (1631) D
The Reigne of King Henry the Second (1633) V
The Victorious Reigne of King Edward the Third (1635) V
The Tragedie of Cleopatra Queen of Aegypt (1639) D
The Tragedie of Julia Agrippina, Empresse of Rome (1639) D
History of the Parliament of England (1647) NF
The Old Couple (1658) D

MAY, Sir Thomas Erskine, 1st Baron Farnborough (1815–1886)
British jurist and historian
A Treatise on the Law Privileges, Proceedings and Usage of Parliament (1844) NF

MAYHEW, Henry (1812–1887)
British journalist, novelist, and philanthropist
1851; or, The Adventures of Mr and Mrs Sandboys (1851) F
London Labour and the London Poor (1851) NF

MAYNE, William [Cyril] (1928–)
British children's writer
Follow the Footprints (1953) F CH
The World Upside Down (1954) F CH
A Swarm in May (1955) F CH
Chorister's Cake (1956) F CH
The Member for the Marsh (1956) F CH
The Blue Boat (1957) F CH
A Grass Rope (1957) F CH
The Rolling Season (1958) F CH
Underground Alley (1958) F CH
The Thumbstick (1959) F CH
On the Stepping Stones (1963) F CH
A Parcel of Trees (1963) F CH
A Day Without Wind (1964) F CH
Sand (1964) F CH
No More School (1965) F CH
Pig in the Middle (1965) F CH
Earthfasts (1966) F CH
The Battlefield (1967) F CH
Over the Hills and Far Away (1968) F CH
A Game of Dark (1971) F CH
A Year and a Day (1976) F CH
It (1977) F CH
All the King's Men (1982) F SS CH

MAYOR, F[lora] M[acdonald] (1872–1932)
British novelist and short-story writer
The Third Miss Symons (1913) F
The Rector's Daughter (1924) F

MEADE, Mrs L.T. [Elizabeth Thomasina Meade, later Toulmin Smith] (1854–1915)
British popular novelist and short story writer
Great St Benedict's (1876) F
Stories From the Diary of a Doctor [1st ser.] (1894) F SS
A Princess of the Gutter (1895) F
The Cleverest Woman in England (1898) F
The Brotherhood of the Seven Kings (1899) F
The Sorceress of the Strand (1903) F
A Maid of Mystery (1904) F

MELMOTH, Courtney *see* SAMUEL JACKSON PRATT

MELVILLE, Herman (1819–1891)
American novelist, short-story writer, and poet
Typee (1846) F
Omoo (1847) F
Mardi (1849) F
Redburn (1849) F
White-Jacket (1850) F
Moby-Dick (1851) F
Pierre (1852) F
Israel Potter (1855) F
The Piazza Tales (1856) F SS
The Confidence Man (1857) F

Battle-Pieces and Aspects of the War (1866) V
Clarel (1876) V
John Marr and Other Sailors (1888) V
Timoleon (1891) V

MENCKEN, H[enry] L[ouis] (1880–1956)
American essayist, editor, and critic
Ventures into Verse (1903) V
The American Language (1919) NF
Prejudices [6 series] (1919–27) NF
Notes on Democracy (1926) NF

MERCER, Cecil William *see* DORNFORD YATES

MERCER, David (1928–1980)
British dramatist
A Suitable Case for Treatment (1962) D
After Haggerty (1970) D

MEREDITH, George (1828–1909)
British novelist and poet
Poems (1851) V
The Shaving of Shagpat (1856) F
Farina (1857) F
The Ordeal of Richard Feverel (1859) F
Evan Harrington; or, He Would Be a Gentleman (1860) F
Modern Love and Poems of the English Roadside (1862) V
Emilia in England (1864) F
Rhoda Fleming (1865) F
Vittoria (1867) F
The Adventures of Harry Richmond (1871) F
Beauchamp's Career (1876) F
The Egoist (1879) F
The Tragic Comedians (1880) F
Poems and Lyrics of the Joy of Earth (1883) V
Diana of the Crossways (1885) F
Sandra Belloni (1886) F
Ballads and Poems of Tragic Life (1887) V
A Reading of Earth (1888) V
One of Our Conquerors (1891) F
Modern Love: A Reprint (1892) V
Lord Ormont and His Aminta (1894) F
The Amazing Marriage (1895) F
The Tale of Chloe, and Other Stories (1895) F SS
An Essay on Comedy and the Uses of the Comic Spirit (1897) NF
A Reading of Life, with Other Poems (1901) V

MEREDITH, Owen *see* EDWARD ROBERT BULWER LYTTON

MERES, Francis (1565–1647)
English clergyman and author
Gods Arithmeticke (1597) NF
Palladis Tamia: Wits Treasury (1598) V

MÉRIMÉE, Prosper (1803–1870)
French novelist and short-story writer
Mateo Falcone (1833) F
The Venus of Ille [*La Vénus d'Ille*] (1837) F
Colomba (1841) F
The Abbé Aubain [*L'Abbé Aubain*] (1846) F
Carmen (1847) F
Arsène Guillot (1852) F
La Chambre bleue ['The Blue Room'] (1866) F
Lokis (1870) F

MERRILL, James [Ingram] (1926–)
American poet and dramatist
The Country of a Thousand Years of Peace (1959) V
The Bait (1960) D
Water Street (1962) V
Nights and Days (1966) V
The Fire Screen (1969) V
Braving the Elements (1972) V
The Yellow Pages (1974) V
Divine Comedies (1976) V
Mirabell (1978) V
Scripts for the Pageant (1980) V
Late Settings (1985) V
The Inner Room (1988) V

'MERRIMAN, Henry Seton' [Hugh Stowell Scott] (1862–1903)
British novelist
The Phantom Future (1888) F
From One Generation to Another (1892) F
The Slave of the Lamp (1892) F
With Edged Tools (1894) F
The Grey Lady (1895) F
Flotsam (1896) F
The Sowers (1896) F
In Kedar's Tents (1897) F
Roden's Corner (1898) F
The Isle of Unrest (1900) F
The Velvet Glove (1901) F
Barlasch of the Guard (1903) F
The Last Hope (1904) F
Tomaso's Fortune, and Other Stories (1904) F SS

METALIOUS, Grace (1924–1964)
American novelist
Peyton Place (1956) F

MEW, Charlotte [Mary] (1869–1928)
British poet and short-story writer
The Farmer's Bride (1916) V
The Rambling Sailor (1929) V

MEYNELL, Alice [Christiana Gertrude], *née* Thompson (1847–1922)
British poet and essayist
Preludes (1875) V
The Rhythm of Life (1893) NF
The Colour of Life, and Other Essays (1896) NF
Other Poems (1896) V
The Spirit of Place, and Other Essays (1899) NF
Ceres' Runaway, and Other Essays (1909) NF
Poems on the War (1916) V
A Father of Women, and Other Poems (1917) V
Second Person Singular, and Other Essays (1921) NF

MICHENER, James A[lbert] (1907–)
American novelist
Tales of the South Pacific (1947) F SS
The Fires of Spring (1949) F
Return to Paradise (1951) F NF
The Bridges at Toko-ri (1953) F

Sayonara (1954) F
Hawaii (1959) F
Caravans (1963) F
The Source (1965) F
The Drifters (1971) F
Centennial (1974) F
Chesapeake (1978) F
The Covenant (1980) F
Space (1982) F
Poland (1983) F
Texas (1985) F
Legacy (1987) F
Alaska (1988) F
Caribbean (1989) F
Recessional (1994) F

MIDDLETON, [John] Christopher (1926–)
British poet, translator, and editor
Torse 3 (1962) V
Our Flowers and Nice Bones (1969) V
The Lonely Suppers of W.V. Balloon (1975) V
Carminalenia (1980) V
Wooden Dogs (1982) V
Serpentine (1984) V
The Balcony Tree (1993) V
Ballad of the Putrefaction (1994) V

MIDDLETON, Richard (1882–1911)
British poet and short-story writer
The Ghost Ship, and Other Stories (1912) F SS

MIDDLETON, Stanley (1919–)
British novelist
A Short Answer (1958) F
Harris's Requiem (1960) F
A Man Made of Smoke (1973) F
Holiday (1974) F
The Daysman (1984) F
Necessary Ends (1999) F

MIDDLETON, Thomas (1580–1627)
English dramatist and poet
The Mayor of Quinborough (1596?) D
The Wisdome of Solomon Paraphrased (1597) V
Blurt Master-Constable; or, The Spaniards Night-Walke (1602) D
The Ant, and the Nightingale; or, Father Hubburds Tales (1604) F SS
The Black Booke (1604) F
Michaelmas Terme (1607) D
The Phoenix (1607) D
The Puritaine; or, The Widdow of Watling-streete (1607) D
The Famelie of Love (1608) D
A Mad World, My Masters (1608) D
A Tricke to Catch the Old-One (1608) D
Your Five Gallants (1608) D
The Roaring Girle; or, Moll Cut-Purse (1611) D
A Faire Quarrell (1617) D
The Inner-Temple Masque: or Masque of Heroes (1619) D
The Triumphs of Love and Antiquity (1619) D
The World Tost at Tennis (1620) D
The Sunne in Aries (1621) D
A Game at Chess (1625) D
A Chast Mayd in Cheape-side (1630) D
The Widdow (1652) D
The Changeling (1653) D
The Spanish Gipsie (1653) D
No Wit, Help Like a Woman's (1657) D
Women, Beware Women [in *Two New Playes*] (1657)

MILES, Josephine (1911–1985)
American poet and critic
Lines at Intersection (1939) V
Local Measures (1946) V
Prefabrications (1955) V
Kinds of Affection (1967) V
Fields of Learning (1968) V
To All Appearances (1974) V
Coming to Terms (1979) V

MILL, James (1773–1836)
British Utilitarian philosopher and historian
Commerce Defended (1807) NF
The History of British India (1817) NF
Elements of Political Economy (1821) NF

MILL, J[ohn] S[tuart] (1806–1873)
British philosopher and economist
A System of Logic, Ratiocinative and Inductive (1843) NF
Essays on Some Unsettled Questions of Political Economy (1844) NF
Principles of Political Economy (1848) NF
Dissertations and Discussions (1859) NF
On Liberty (1859) NF
Thoughts on Parliamentary Reform (1859) NF
Considerations on Representative Government (1861) NF
Utilitarianism (1863) NF
Auguste Comte and Positivism (1865) NF
An Examination of Hamilton's Philosophy (1865) NF
England and Ireland (1868) NF
The Subjection of Women (1869) NF
Chapters and Speeches on the Irish Land Question (1870) NF
Autobiography (1873) NF

MILLAR, Kenneth *see* ROSS MACDONALD

MILLER, Arthur (1915–)
American dramatist
The Man Who Had All the Luck (1944) D
Focus (1945) F
All My Sons (1947) D
Death of a Salesman (1949) D
The Crucible (1953) D
A View From the Bridge (1955) D
The Misfits (1961) F
After the Fall (1964) D
Incident at Vichy (1965) D
I Don't Need You Anymore (1967) F SS
The Price (1968) D
Theater Essays (1978) NF
The American Clock (1980) D
Playing for Time (1981) D

Timebends (1987) NF
Broken Glass (1994) D

MILLER, Henry [Valentine] (1891–1980)
American novelist, critic, autobiographer, and dramatist
Tropic of Cancer (1934) F
Aller Retour New York (1935) F
Black Spring (1936) F
The Cosmological Eye (1939) F NF
Tropic of Capricorn (1939) F
The Colossus of Maroussi (1941) NF
The Wisdom of the Heart (1941) F NF
The Air-Conditioned Nightmare (1945) NF
Remember to Remember (1947) NF
The Smile at the Foot of the Ladder (1948) F
Sexus (1949) NF
The Books in My Life (1952) NF
Plexus (1953) NF
Nights of Love and Laughter (1955) F SS
The Time of the Assassins (1956) NF
Big Sur and the Oranges of Hieronymus Bosch (1957) NF
Nexus (1960) NF
Stand Still Like a Hummingbird (1962) NF
Just Wild About Harry (1963) D

MILLER, Walter M[ichael] Jr (1922–)
American science fiction writer
A Canticle for Liebowitz (1960) F

MILMAN, Henry Hart (1791–1868)
British historian and poet
Fazio (1815) D
Samor: Lord of the Bright City (1818) V
The Fall of Jerusalem (1820) V
Belshazzar (1822) V
The Martyr of Antioch (1822) V
Anne Boleyn (1826) V D
The History of the Jews (1829) NF
The History of Christianity to the Abolition of Paganism (1840) NF
History of Latin Christianity (1854–5) NF

MILNE, A[lan] A[lexander] (1882–1956)
British novelist, dramatist, essayist, poet, and children's writer
Lovers in London (1905) F
The Day's Play (1910) MISC
Once a Week (1914) F
Once on a Time (1917) F CH
Not That It Matters (1919) NF
The Sunny Side (1921) MISC
The Red House Mystery (1922) F
When We Were Very Young (1924) V CH
Winnie-the-Pooh (1926) F CH
Now We Are Six (1927) V CH
The House at Pooh Corner (1928) F CH
Toad of Toad Hall (1929) D CH
When I Was Very Young (1930) NF
Two People (1931) F
Behind the Lines (1940) V
A Table Near the Band, and Other Stories (1950) F SS

MILNES, Richard Monckton, 1st Baron Houghton (1809–1885)
British poet and biographer of Keats
Memorials of a Tour in Some Parts of Greece (1834) V
Poems of Many Years (1840) V
Poetry for the People, and Other Poems (1840) V
Memorials of Many Scenes (1844) V
Palm Leaves (1844) V
The Life, Letters and Literary Remains of John Keats (1848) NF

MILTON, John (1608–1674)
English poet and author
Comus [*A Maske Presented at Ludlow Castle, 1634*] (1637) D
'Lycidas' [in Cambridge memorial volume to Edward King] (1638)
Animadversions Upon the Remonstrants Defence, Against Smectymnuus (1641) NF
Of Prelatical Episcopacy (1641) NF
Of Reformation Touching Church-Discipline in England (1641) NF
The Reason of Church-government Urg'd Against Prelaty (1642) NF
The Doctrine and Discipline of Divorce (1643) NF
Areopagitica (1644) NF
Colasterion (1645) NF
Poems of Mr John Milton, Both English and Latin (1645) V
Tetrachordon (1645) NF
Eikonoklastes (1649) NF
The Tenure of Kings and Magistrates (1649) NF
The Readie & Easie Way to Establish a Free Commonwealth (1660) NF
Paradise Lost [bks i-x] (1667) V
The History of Britain (1670) NF
Paradise Regain'd. To which is added Samson Agonistes (1671) V
Paradise Lost [bks i–xii] (1674) V
A Brief History of Moscovia (1682) NF

MISTRY, Rohinton (1952–)
Indian novelist and short-story writer
Tales From a Firozsha Bag (1987) F SS
Such a Long Journey (1991) F
A Fine Balance (1996) F

MITCHEL, John (1815–1875)
Irish patriotic writer
Jail Journal (1854) NF

MITCHELL, Adrian (1932–)
British poet, dramatist, children's writer, and novelist
Peace is Milk (1966) V
Out Loud (1968) V
The Apeman Cometh (1975) V
For Beauty Douglas (1982) V

MITCHELL, [Charles] Julian (1935–)
British novelist and dramatist
Imaginary Toys (1961) F
The White Father (1964) F
The Undiscovered Country (1968) F
Another Country (1981) D

MITCHELL, Gladys [Maude Winifred] (1901–1983)
British detective novelist
Speedy Death [first Mrs Bradley novel] (1929) F
The Saltmarsh Murders (1932) F
Laurels Are Poison (1942) F
The Rising of the Moon (1945) F
Tom Brown's Body (1949) F
Watson's Choice (1955) F
Spotted Hemlock (1958) F

MITCHELL, Margaret (1900–1949)
American novelist
Gone With the Wind (1936) F
Lost Laysen (1996) F

MITCHELL, W[illiam] O[rmond] (1914–)
Canadian novelist and dramatist
Who Has Seen the Wind (1947) F
The Kite (1962) F
The Vanishing Point (1973) F
How I Spent My Holidays (1981) F

MITCHISON, Naomi [Mary Margaret], *née* Haldane (1897–1999)
British novelist, short-story writer, children's author, and biographer
The Conquered (1923) F
When the Bough Breaks, and Other Stories (1924) F SS
Cloud Cuckoo Land (1925) F CH
Black Sparta (1928) F SS
The Corn King and the Spring Queen (1931) F CH
The Blood of the Martyrs (1939) F CH
Memoirs of a Spacewoman (1962) F

MITFORD, Jessica [Lucy] (1917–1996)
British memoirist, journalist, and social critic
Hons and Rebels [US: *Daughters and Rebels*] (1960) NF

MITFORD, Mary Russell (1787–1855)
British novelist, poet, and dramatist
Christina, the Maid of the South Seas (1811) V
Blanche of Castile (1812) V
Watlington Hill (1812) V
Narrative Poems on the Female Character (1813) V
Julian (1823) D
Our Village [5 vols; 1824, 1826, 1828, 1830, 1832] (1824–32) F
Foscari (1826) D
Dramatic Scenes, Sonnets, and Other Poems (1827) V
Rienzi (1828) D
Mary, Queen of Scots (1831) V
Charles the First (1834) D
Belford Regis; or, Sketches of a Country Town (1835) F
Country Stories (1837) F SS
Recollections of a Literary Life (1852) NF
Atherton, and Other Tales (1854) F SS

MITFORD, Nancy [Freeman] (1904–1973)
British novelist and biographer
Highland Fling (1931) F
Wigs on the Green (1935) F
The Pursuit of Love (1945) F
Love in a Cold Climate (1949) F
Madame de Pompadour (1954) NF
Noblesse Oblige (1956) NF
Voltaire in Love (1957) NF
Don't Tell Alfred (1960) F
The Sun King (1966) NF

MITTELHOLZER, Edgar (1909–1965)
Guyanese-born British novelist
Corentyne Thunder (1941) F
Shadows Move Among Them (1951) F
The Children of Kaywana (1952) F
The Harrowing of Hubertus [repub. as *Hubertus*, 1955, and *Kaywana Stock*, 1968] (1954) F
Kaywana Blood [repub. as *The Old Blood*, 1958] (1958) F

MO, Timothy (1950–)
Anglo-Chinese novelist
The Monkey King (1978) F
Sour Sweet (1982) F
An Insular Possession (1986) F
The Redundancy of Courage (1991) F
Brownout on Breadfruit Boulevard (1995) F

MOGGACH, Deborah (1948–)
British novelist, short-story writer, and screenwriter
Hot Water Man (1982) F
Porky (1983) F
To Have and to Hold (1986) F
Driving in the Dark (1988) F
Changing Babies (1995) F
Tulip Fever (1999) F

MOLESWORTH, Mary Louisa, *née* Stewart (1839–1921)
British novelist, short-story writer, and children's author
Lover and Husband (1869) F
Not Without Thorns [as 'Ennis Graham'] (1873) F
Cicely [as 'Ennis Graham'] (1874) F
'Carrots' [as 'Ennis Graham'] (1876) F
The Cuckoo Clock [as 'Ennis Graham'] (1877) F
Hathercourt Rectory (1878) F
The Tapestry Room (1879) F CH
A Christmas Child (1880) F CH
Miss Bouverie (1880) F
Christmas-Tree Land (1884) F CH
'Us' (1885) F CH
Four Ghost Stories (1888) F SS
The Third Miss St Quentin (1889) F
The Children of the Castle (1890) F CH
The Green Casket, and Other Stories (1890) F CH
An Enchanted Garden (1892) F CH
Studies and Stories (1893) F SS
The Carved Lions (1895) F
Uncanny Tales (1896) F SS
The Laurel Walk (1898) F
The House That Grew (1900) F CH
The Blue Baby, and Other Stories (1901) F CH
Fairies Afield (1911) F CH

MOLIÈRE [Jean-Baptiste Poquelin] (1622–1673)
French comic dramatist
The School for Wives [*L'École des femmes*] (1662) D

Don Juan (1665) D
The Doctor In Spite of Himself [*Le Médecin malgré lui*] (1666) D
The Misanthrope [*Le Misanthrope*] (1666) D
The Imposter [*L'Imposteur*; 1st version, 1664, as *Le Tartuffe*] (1667) D
Amphitryon (1668) D
George Dandin (1668) D
The Miser [*L'Avare*] (1668) D
Monsieur de Pourceaugnac (1669) D
The Would-Be Gentleman [*Le Bourgeois gentilhomme*] (1670) D
The Learned Ladies [*Les Femmes savantes*] (1672) D
The Imaginary Invalid [*Le Malade imaginaire*] (1673) D

MONRO, Harold [Edward] (1879–1932)
British poet and publisher
Before Dawn (1911) V
Children of Love (1914) V
Strange Meetings (1917) V
The Earth For Sale (1928) V

MONSARRAT, Nicholas [John Turney] (1910–1979)
British novelist
This is the Schoolroom (1939) F
The Cruel Sea (1951) F
The Ship That Died of Shame, and Other Stories (1959) F SS

MONTAGU, Lady Mary Wortley, *née* Pierrepont (1689–1762)
English traveller and author
Court Poems (1716) V
Verses Address'd to the Imitator of Horace (1733) V
The Dean's Provocation for Writing the Lady's Dressing-Room (1734) V
Six Town Eclogues (1747) V
Letters (1763) NF

MONTAGUE, C[harles] E[dward] (1867–1928)
Anglo-Irish novelist, essayist, and journalist
A Hind Let Loose (1910) F
Dramatic Values (1911) NF
The Morning's War (1913) F
Disenchantment (1922) NF
Fiery Particles (1923) F SS
Rough Justice (1926) F
Action, and Other Stories (1928) F SS

MONTAIGNE, Michel [Eyquem] de (1533–1592)
French essayist
Essays [bks i-ii; enlarg. 1588] (1580) NF

MONTGOMERY, L[ucy] M[aud] (1874–1942)
Canadian novelist and children's writer
Anne of Green Gables (1908) F CH
Anne of Avonlea (1909) F CH
The Story Girl (1911) F SS CH
Anne of the Island (1915) F CH
The Watchman, and Other Poems (1916) V
Anne's House of Dreams (1917) F CH
Rainbow Valley (1919) F CH
Rilla of Ingleside (1921) F CH
Emily of New Moon (1923) F CH
Emily Climbs (1925) F CH
The Blue Castle (1926) F
Emily's Quest (1927) F CH
A Tangled Web (1931) F
Pat of Silver Bush (1933) F CH
Mistress Pat (1935) F CH
Anne of Windy Poplars (1936) F CH
Jane of Lantern Hill (1937) F CH
Anne of Ingleside (1939) F CH

MONTGOMERY, Robert Bruce *see* EDMUND CRISPIN

MOODIE, Susanna, *née* Strickland (1803–1885)
British-born Canadian poet, novelist and essayist
Enthusiasm, and Other Poems (1831) V
Roughing It in the Bush; or, Life in Canada (1852) NF
Geoffrey Monckton; or, The Faithless Guardian (1853) F
Mark Hurdlestone; or, the Gold Worshipper (1853) F
Flora Lyndsay; or, Passages in an Eventful Life (1854) F

MOORCOCK, Michael (1939–)
British 'New Wave' science fiction writer and novelist
Stormbringer (1965) F
Behold the Man (1969) F
The Final Programme [first of the 'Cornelius Chronicle'] (1969) F
The Eternal Champion (1970) F
A Cure for Cancer (1971) F
An Alien Heart [first of *The Dancers at the End of Time* trilogy] (1972) F
The English Assassin (1972) F
The Hollow Lands (1974) F
The End of All Songs (1976) F
The Condition of Muzak (1977) F
Gloriana; or, The Unfulfill'd Queen (1978) F
Byzantium Endures [first of the 'Pyat' series] (1981) F
The Brothel in Rosenstrasse (1982) F
The Laughter of Carthage (1984) F
Mother London (1988) F
Jerusalem Commands (1992) F
Blood (1995) F
King of the City (2000) F

MOORE, Brian (1921–)
Irish novelist and dramatist
Judith Hearne [US: *The Lonely Passion of Judith Hearne*] (1955) F
The Feast of Lupercal (1958) F
The Luck of Ginger Coffey (1960) F
An Answer From Limbo (1963) F
The Emperor of Ice-Cream (1965) F
I Am Mary Dunne (1968) F
Fergus (1970) F
Catholics (1972) F
The Great Victorian Collection (1975) F
The Doctor's Wife (1976) F
The Mangan Inheritance (1979) F
Cold Heaven (1983) F

Black Robe (1985) F
The Colour of Blood (1987) F
Lies of Silence (1990) F
No Other Life (1993) F
The Magician's Wife (1997) F

MOORE, Edward (1712–1757)
British poet and dramatist
Fables for the Female Sex (1744) V
The Foundling (1748) D
The Trial of Selim the Persian (1748) V
The Gamester (1753) D
Poems, Fables, and Plays (1756) V

MOORE, Francis *see* 'Old Moore'

MOORE, George [Augustus] (1852–1933)
Anglo-Irish novelist, poet, and dramatist
Flowers of Passion (1878) V
Pagan Poems (1881) V
A Modern Lover (1883) F
A Mummer's Wife (1885) F
A Drama in Muslin (1886) F
A Mere Accident (1887) F
Parnell and His Island (1887) NF
Confessions of a Young Man (1888) NF
Spring Days (1888) F
Mike Fletcher (1889) F
Impressions and Opinions (1891) NF
The Strike at Arlingford (1893) D
Esther Waters (1894) F
Celibates (1895) F
Evelyn Innes (1898) F
The Bending of the Bough (1900) D
Sister Teresa (1901) F
The Untilled Field (1903) F SS
The Lake (1905) F
Memoirs of My Dead Life (1906) NF
Reminiscences of the Impressionist Painters (1906) NF
The Apostle (1911) D
Ave [first of the *Hail and Farewell* trilogy] (1911) NF
Salve (1912) NF
Elizabeth Cooper (1913) D
Vale (1914) NF
The Brook Kerith (1916) F
Lewis Seymour and Some Women (1917) F
Avowals (1921) NF
Conversations in Ebury Street (1924) NF
Héloise and Abelard (1925) F
Celibate Lives (1927) F
A Story-Teller's Holiday (1928) F
Aphrodite in Aulis (1930) F

MOORE, G[eorge] E[dward] (1873–1958)
British philosopher
Principia Ethica (1903) NF
Ethics (1912) NF
Philosophical Studies (1922) NF
Some Main Problems of Philosophy (1953) NF
Philosophical Papers (1959) NF

MOORE, John (1729–1802)
British physician, novelist, and traveller
A View of Society and Manners in France, Switzerland, and Germany (1779) NF
A View of Society and Manners in Italy (1781) NF
Zeluco (1789) F
A Journal During a Residence in France (1792) NF
A View of the Causes and Progress of the French Revolution (1795) NF
Edward (1796) F
Mordaunt (1800) F

MOORE, Marianne [Craig] (1887–1972)
American poet
Observations (1924) V
The Pangolin, and Other Verse (1936) V
What Are Years (1941) V
Nevertheless (1944) V
Predilections (1955) NF
Like a Bulwark (1956) V
O To Be a Dragon (1959) V
Tell Me, Tell Me (1966) V NF

MOORE, Nicholas (1918–1986)
British poet
The Glass Tower (1944) V
Recollections of the Gala (1950) V

MOORE, Thomas (1779–1852)
British poet
Odes of Anacreon (1800) V
Corruption, and Intolerance (1801) V
The Poetical Works of the Late Thomas Little, Esq. (1801) V
Epistles, Odes and Other Poems (1806) V
A Selection of Irish Melodies [pts. i, ii] (1808) V
The Sceptic (1809) V
MP; or, The Blue-Stocking (1811) D
Intercepted Letters; or, The Two Penny Post Bag [as 'Thomas Brown the Younger'] (1813) V
Sacred Songs [No. i] (1816) V
Lalla Rookh (1817) V
The Fudge Family in Paris [as 'Thomas Brown the Younger'] (1818) V
Irish Melodies (1821) V
Fables for the Holy Alliance [as 'Thomas Brown the Younger'] (1823) V
The Loves of the Angels (1823) V
Memoirs of Captain Rock, the Celebrated Irish Chieftain (1824) NF
Sacred Songs [No. ii] (1824) V
Memoirs of Richard Brinsley Sheridan (1825) NF
The Epicurean (1827) F
Letters and Journals of Lord Byron (1830) NF
Travels of an Irish Gentleman in Search of a Religion (1833) NF
The Fudges in England (1835) V
Alciphron (1839) V

MOORE, T[homas] Sturge (1870–1944)
British poet and illustrator
The Vinedresser, and Other Poems (1899) V
The Centaur's Booty (1903) V

The Gazelles, and Other Poems (1904) V
Pan's Prophecy (1904) V
The Sea is Kind (1914) V
Armour for Aphrodite (1929) NF
The Unknown Known, and a Dozen Odd Poems (1939) V

MORAVIA, Alberto (1907–1990)
Italian novelist
The Indifferent Ones [*Gli indifferenti*] (1929) F
Agostino (1944) F
The Woman of Rome [*La romana*] (1947) F
Conjugal Love [*L'amore coniugale*] (1949) F
Roman Tales [*Raconti romani*] (1954) F SS
Two Women [*La ciociara*] (1957) F
The Lie [*L'attenzione*] (1965) F
Time of Desecration [*La vita interiore*] (1978) F
The Voyeur [*L'uomo che guarda*] (1985) F

MORE, Hannah (1745–1833)
British poet and author
A Search After Happiness (1766) V D
The Inflexible Captive (1774) V
Sir Eldred of the Bower, and The Bleeding Rock (1776) V
Essays on Various Subjects (1777) NF
Percy (1778) D
The Fatal Falsehood (1779) D
Sacred Dramas (1782) V
Florio; and The Bas Bleu (1786) V
Slavery (1788) V
Village Politics (1793) NF
Coelebs in Search of a Wife (1808) F
Practical Piety (1811) NF
Christian Morals (1813) NF
Moral Sketches of Prevailing Opinions and Manners (1819) NF
Bible Rhymes (1821) V

MORE, Henry (1614–1687)
English philosopher and poet
Psychodia Platonica; or, A Platonicall Song of the Soul (1642) V
Democritus Platonissans (1646) NF
Philosophicall Poems (1647) V
An Antidote Against Atheisme (1653) NF
Conjectura Cabbalistica (1653) NF
Enthusiasmus Triumphatus (1656) NF
The Immortality of the Soul (1659) NF
An Explanation of the Grand Mystery of Godliness (1660) NF
A Modest Enquiry into the Mystery of Iniquity (1664) NF
Divine Dialogues (1668) NF
A Plain and Continued Exposition of the Prophecies of Daniel (1681) NF
Tetractys Anti-Astrologica (1681) NF
Paralipomena Prophetica (1685) NF

MORE, Sir Thomas (1478–1535)
Lord Chancellor and humanist
Utopia [Latin] (1516) NF
A Dialogue Concernynge Heresyes & Matters of Religion (1529) NF
The Supplycacyon of Soulys (1529?) NF
The Confutacyon of Tyndales Answere (1532) NF
The Apologye of Syr Thomas More Knyght (1533) NF
The Debellacyon of Salem and Bizance (1533) NF
The Second Parte of the Confutacyon of Tyndales Answere (1533) NF
Lady Fortune (1540?) V
Utopia [English] (1551) NF
A Dialoge of Comfort Against Tribulacion (1553) NF

MORGAN, Charles [Langbridge] (1894–1958)
British novelist and dramatist
The Gunroom (1919) F
Portrait in a Mirror (1929) F
The Fountain (1932) F
Sparkenbroke (1936) F
The Flashing Stream (1938) D
The Voyage (1940) F
Reflections in a Mirror [1st ser.; 2nd ser., 1946] (1944) NF
The Judge's Story (1947) F
A Breeze of Morning (1951) F
Challenge to Venus (1957) F

MORGAN, Edwin [George] (1920–)
Scottish poet, critic, and translator
The Vision of Cathkin Braes (1952) V
Sealwear (1966) V
The Second Life (1968) V
Glasgow Sonnets (1972) V
From Glasgow to Saturn (1973) V
Sonnets From Scotland (1984) V
From the Video Box (1986) V
Themes on a Variation (1988) V
Hold Hands Among the Atoms (1991) V

MORGAN, Kenneth O[wen] (1934–)
British historian
Keir Hardie (1967) NF
Consensus and Disunity (1979) NF
Rebirth of a Nation: Wales, 1880–1980 (1981) NF
Labour in Power, 1945–1951 (1984) NF
Labour People (1987) NF
The People's Peace (1990) NF

MORGAN, Lady Sydney, *née* Owenson (1783?–1859)
Irish novelist and poet
St Clair; or, The Heiress of Desmond (1803) F
The Novice of St Dominick (1806) F
The Wild Irish Girl (1806) F
The Lay of an Irish Harp; or, Metrical Fragments (1807) V
The Missionary (1811) F
O'Donnel (1814) F
Florence Macarthy (1818) F
The O'Briens and the O'Flahertys (1827) F
The Princess; or, The Beguine (1835) F

MORIER, David [Richard] (1784–1877)
British traveller and novelist
Photo the Suliote (1857) F

MORIER, James [Justinian] (1780–1849)
British diplomat, traveller, and novelist
A Journey Through Persia, Armenia and Asia Minor (1812) NF
A Second Journey Through Persia, Armenia and Asia Minor (1818) NF
The Adventures of Hajji Baba, of Ispahan (1824) F
The Adventures of Hajji Baba, of Ispahan, in England (1828) F
Zohrab the Hostage (1832) F
Ayesha, the Maid of Kars (1834) F
Abel Allnutt (1837) F
The Mirza (1841) F
Misselmah (1847) F
Martin Toutrond; or, The Frenchman in London (1849) F

MORLEY, Henry (1822–1894)
British scholar, editor, and novelist
Palissy the Potter (1852) NF
Fables and Fairy Tales (1860) F CH
Oberon's Horn (1861) F CH
A First Sketch of English Literature (1873) NF

MORLEY, John, 1st Viscount Morley of Blackburn (1838–1923)
British statesman, critic, and biographer
Critical Miscellanies [1st ser.] (1871) NF
Voltaire (1872) NF
Rousseau (1873) NF
The Struggle for National Education (1873) NF
Edmund Burke (1879) NF
The Life of Richard Cobden (1881) NF
Studies in Literature (1890) NF
Oliver Cromwell (1900) NF
The Life of William Ewart Gladstone (1903) NF
Literary Essays (1906) NF
Recollections (1917) NF

MORRIS, Jan [formerly **James Morris**] (1926–)
British travel writer
Coast to Coast (1956) NF
Coronation Everest (1958) NF
Venice (1960) NF
The Presence of Spain (1964) NF
Pax Britannica (1968) NF
Heaven's Command (1973) NF
Conundrum (1974) NF
Farewell the Trumpets (1978) NF
The Matter of Wales (1984) NF
Hong Kong (1988) NF

MORRIS, William (1834–1896)
British poet, artist, and craftsman
The Defence of Guenevere, and Other Poems (1858) V
The Life and Death of Jason (1867) V
The Earthly Paradise [pts. i & ii] (1868) V
Grettis Saga: The Story of Grettir the Strong [with E. Magnússon] (1869) V
The Earthly Paradise [pt. iii] (1870) V
The Earthly Paradise [pt. iv] (1870) V
Volsung Saga: The Story of the Volsungs and Niblungs [with E. Magnússon] (1870) V
Three Northern Love Stories, and Other Tales [with E. Magnússon] (1875) F SS
The Story of Sigurd the Volsung, and the Fall of the Niblungs (1877) V
The Decorative Arts (1878) NF
Hopes and Fears for Art (1882) NF
A Summary of the Principles of Socialism (1884) NF
Chants for Socialists (1885) V
The Manifesto of the Socialist League (1885) NF
Useful Work Versus Useless Toil (1886) NF
The Aims of Art (1887) NF
The Odyssey of Homer (1887) V
The Tables Turned; or, Nupkins Awakened (1887) D
A Dream of John Ball; and A King's Lesson (1888) F
Signs of Change (1888) NF
A Tale of the House of the Wolfings and All the Kindreds of the Mark (1889) F V
Monopoly; or, How Labour is Robbed (1890) NF
The Roots of the Mountains (1890) F
News from Nowhere; or, An Epoch of Rest (1891) F
Poems By the Way (1891) V
The Story of the Glittering Plain (1891) F
Gothic Architecture (1893) NF
Socialism (1893) NF
The Wood Beyond the World (1894) F
The Tale of Beowulf (1895) V
The Well at the World's End (1896) F
Art and the Beauty of Earth (1898) NF

MORRISON, Arthur (1863–1945)
British novelist and short-story writer
Martin Hewitt, Investigator (1894) F SS
Tales of Mean Streets (1894) F SS
Chronicles of Martin Hewitt (1895) F SS
Adventures of Martin Hewitt (1896) F SS
A Child of the Jago (1896) F
The Dorrington Deed-Box (1897) F
To London Town (1899) F
Cunning Murrell (1900) F
The Hole in the Wall (1902) F
The Red Triangle (1903) F SS
The Green Eye of Goona (1904) F SS
Green Ginger (1909) F SS

MORRISON, [Philip] Blake (1950–)
British poet and critic
Dark Glasses (1984) V
The Ballad of the Yorkshire Ripper (1987) V

MORRISON, Toni [Chloe Anthony] (1931–)
African-American novelist
The Bluest Eye (1970) F
Sula (1973) F
Song of Solomon (1977) F
Tar Baby (1981) F
Beloved (1987) F
Jazz (1992) F
Playing in the Dark (1992) NF
Paradise (1998) NF

MORTIMER, John [Clifford] (1923–)
British novelist, short-story writer, and dramatist
A Voyage Round My Father (1963) D

Rumpole of the Bailey (1978) F SS
Clinging to the Wreckage (1982) NF
Paradise Postponed (1985) F
Summer's Lease (1988) F
Titmuss Regained (1990) F
Dunster (1992) F
The Sound of Trumpets (1998) F

MORTIMER, Penelope [Ruth], *née* Fletcher (1918–1999)
British novelist, biographer, and film critic
A Villa in Summer (1954) F
The Bright Prison (1956) F
Daddy's Gone-a-Hunting [US: *Cave of Ice*] (1958) F
Saturday Lunch With the Brownings (1960) F SS
The Pumpkin Eater (1962) F
The Home (1971) F
Long Distance (1974) F
The Handyman (1983) F

MORTON, J[ohn] [Cameron Andrieu] B[ingham] [Michael] (1893–1979)
British humorist and biographer
The Barber of Putney (1919) F
A Diet of Thistles [as 'Beachcomber'] (1938) F
The Tibetan Venus [as 'Beachcomber'] (1951) F

MORTON, Nathaniel (1612–1685)
American colonial historian
New England's Memorial (1669) NF

MORTON, Thomas (1764?–1838)
British dramatist, father of J.M. Morton
Speed the Plough [introduced the character of 'Mrs Grundy'] (1798) D

MOSLEY, Nicholas, 3rd Baron Ravensdale (1923–)
British novelist and biographer
Spaces of the Dark (1951) F
The Rainbearers (1955) F
Meeting Place (1962) F
Accident (1965) F
Impossible Object (1969) F
Catastrophe Practice (1979) F
Imago Bird (1980) F
Serpent (1981) F
Judith (1986) F
Hopeful Monsters (1990) F
Children of Darkness and Light (1996) F

MOSLEY, Walter (1952–)
African-American novelist
Devil in a Blue Dress (1990) F
A Red Death (1991) F
White Butterfly (1992) F
Black Betty (1994) F
A Little Yellow Dog (1996) F
Always Outnumbered, Always Outgunned (1997) F

MOTION, Andrew [Peter] (1952–)
British Poet Laureate, biographer, critic, and novelist
The Pleasure Steamers (1978) V
Independence (1981) V
Secret Narratives (1983) V
Dangerous Play (1984) V
Natural Causes (1987) V
Love in a Life (1991) V
Philip Larkin (1993) NF
The Price of Everything (1994) V
Keats (1997) NF
Salt Water (1997) V

MOTTRAM, R[alph] H[ale] (1883–1971)
British novelist and author
The Spanish Farm (1924) F
Sixty-Four, Ninety-Four! (1925) F
The Crime at the Vanderlynden's (1926) F

MOWAT, Farley [McGill] (1921–)
Canadian author and children's writer
People of the Deer (1952) NF
The Desperate People (1959) NF
The Grey Seas Under (1959) NF
Ordeal by Ice (1960) NF
Never Cry Wolf (1963) NF
Lost in the Barrens (1965) NF CH
The Polar Passion (1967) NF
Siber: My Discovery of Siberia (1970) NF
Tundra (1973) NF
The Black Joke (1974) NF CH
Curse of the Viking's Grave (1974) NF CH

MUIR, Edwin (1887–1959)
Scottish poet, critic, translator, and novelist
We Moderns [as 'Edward Moore'] (1918) NF
First Poems (1925) V
Chorus of the Newly Dead (1926) V
Transition (1926) NF
The Marionette (1927) F
The Structure of the Novel (1928) NF
The Three Brothers (1931) F
Poor Tom (1932) F
Variations on a Time Theme (1934) V
Scottish Journey (1935) NF
Journeys and Places (1937) V
The Story and the Fable (1940) NF
The Narrow Place (1943) V
The Voyage, and Other Poems (1946) V
Essays on Literature and Society (1949) NF
The Labyrinth (1949) V
One Foot in Eden (1956) V
The Estate of Poetry (1962) NF

MULCASTER, Richard (1530?–1611)
English schoolmaster and author
Positions (1581) NF
The First Part of the Elementarie (1582) NF

MULDOON, Paul (1951–)
Northern Irish poet
Knowing My Place (1971) V
New Weather (1973) V
Mules (1977) V
Why Brownlee Left (1980) V
Out of Siberia (1982) V
Quoof (1983) V
Meeting the British (1987) V
Madoc (1990) V

The Annals of Chile (1994) V
The Prince of Quotidian (1994) V
Hay (1998) V

MULHOLLAND, Rosa [Lady Gilbert] (1841–1921)
Irish novelist, short-story writer, and poet
Dunmara (1864) F
Hester's History (1869) F
Eldergowan; or, Twelve Months of My Life, and Other Tales (1874) F SS
Marcella Grace (1886) F SS
A Fair Emigrant (1889) F
The Haunted Organist of Hurly Burly, and Other Stories (1891) F SS

MUNDAY, Anthony (1560–1633)
English poet, dramatist, and translator
The Mirrour of Mutabilitie (1579) V
The Paine of Pleasure (1580) V
Zelauto: The Fountaine of Fame (1580) P
The English Romayne Lyfe (1582) NF
Fedele and Fortunio [from Luigi Pasquaglio] (1585) D
A Banquet of Daintie Conceits (1588) V
Palladine of England [from French] (1588) F
Palmerin D'Oliva [pt. i; pt. ii 1597] (1588) F
The Historie of Palmendos [from Francisco de Moraes] (1589) F
Amadis of Gaule [pt. i; from a French trn of Spanish original] (1590) F
Archaioplutos; or, The Riches of Elder Ages [from French] (1592) NF
Palmerin of England [pt. i; pt. ii, 1596; pt. iii, 1602] (1596) F
Sir John Old-castle (1600) D
The Death of Robert, Earle of Huntington. Otherwise Called Robin Hood (1601) D
The True Knowledge of a Mans Owne Selfe [from Philippe de Mornay] (1602) NF

MUNRO, Alice, *née* Laidlaw (1931–)
Canadian short-story writer
Dance of the Happy Shades (1968) F SS
Lives of Girls and Women (1971) F
Something I've Been Meaning to Tell You (1974) F SS
Who Do You Think You Are? [US/UK: *The Beggar Maid*] (1978) F SS
The Moons of Jupiter (1982) F SS
The Progress of Love (1986) F SS
Friend of My Youth (1990) F SS
Open Secrets (1994) F SS
Love of a Good Woman (1998) F SS
The Beggar Maid: Stories of Flo and Rose (1999) F

MUNRO, Hector Hugh *see* 'SAKI'

MURDOCH, [Dame] Iris [Jean] (1919–1999)
British novelist and philosopher
Under the Net (1954) F
The Flight From the Enchanter (1956) F
The Sandcastle (1956) F
The Bell (1958) F
A Severed Head (1961) F
An Unofficial Rose (1962) F
The Unicorn (1963) F
The Italian Girl (1964) F
The Red and the Green (1965) F
The Time of the Angels (1966) F
The Nice and the Good (1968) F
Bruno's Dream (1969) F
The Sovereignty of Good (1970) NF
An Accidental Man (1971) F
The Black Prince (1973) F
The Sacred and Profane Love Machine (1974) F
A World Child (1975) F
Henry and Cato (1976) F
The Fire and the Sun (1977) NF
The Sea, the Sea (1978) F
Nuns and Soldiers (1980) F
The Philosopher's Pupil (1983) F
The Good Apprentice (1985) F
The Book and the Brotherhood (1987) F
The Message to the Planet (1989) F
Something Special (1990) V SS
Metaphysics as a Guide to Morals (1992) NF
The Green Knight (1993) F
Jackson's Dilemma (1996) F

MURPHY, Arthur (1727–1805)
Irish barrister, actor, and dramatist
The Upholsterer; or, What News? (1758) D

MURPHY, Dervla [Dervilla Maria] (1931–)
Irish travel writer
Full Tilt: Ireland to India by Bicycle (1965) NF
Tibetan Foothold (1966) NF
Where the Indus is Young (1977) NF
Wheels Within Wheels (1979) NF
Eight Feet in the Andes (1983) NF
Muddling Through in Madagascar (1985) NF
Cameroon with Egbert (1989) NF
One Foot in Laos (1999) NF

MURPHY, Richard (1927–)
Irish poet
Sailing to an Island (1955) V
The Woman of the House (1959) V
The Battle of Aughrim and the God Who Eats Corn (1968) V
High Island (1974) V
The Price of Stone (1985) V
The Mirror Wall (1989) V

MURPHY, Tom [Thomas] (1935–)
Irish dramatist
The Morning After Optimism (1971) D
The Sanctuary Lamp (1975) D
The Gigli Concert (1983) D
Bailegangáire (1985) D
A Whistle in the Dark, and Other Plays (1989) D
Too Late For Logic (1990) D

MURRAY, David Christie (1847–1907)
British journalist and novelist
Joseph's Coat (1881) F
Coals of Fire, and Other Stories (1882) F SS
Val Strange (1882) F
By the Gate of the Sea (1883) F
Rainbow Gold (1885) F

Aunt Rachel (1886) F
A Novelist's Note Book (1887) NF
The Weaker Vessel (1888) F
John Vale's Guardian (1890) F
The Making of a Novelist (1894) NF
A Rising Star (1894) F
My Contemporaries in Fiction (1897) NF
The Brangwyn Mystery (1906) F

MURRAY, Les[lie] [Allan] (1938–)
Australian poet
The Ilex Tree (1965) V
The Weatherboard Cathedral (1969) V
Poems Against Economics (1972) V
Lunch & Counterlunch (1974) V
The Vernacular Republic (1976) V
Ethnic Radio (1977) V
The Peasant Mandarin (1978) NF
The Boys Who Stole the Funeral (1980) V
The People's Otherworld (1983) V
Persistence in Folly (1984) NF
The Daylight Moon (1987) V
Blocks and Tackles (1990) NF
Dog Fox Field (1990) V
The Paperbark Tree (1992) NF
Translations From the Natural World (1992) V
Conscious and Verbal (2000) V

MURRAY, T[homas] C[ornelius] (1873–1959)
Irish dramatist
Birthright (1910) D
Autumn Fire (1924) D

MURRY, John Middleton (1889–1957)
British critic, editor, novelist, and poet
Still Life (1916) F
Aspects of Literature (1920) NF
The Evolution of an Intellectual (1920) NF
Countries of the Mind (1922) NF
The Problem of Style (1922) NF
The Things We Are (1922) F
To the Unknown God (1924) NF
The Voyage (1924) F
Keats and Shakespeare (1925) NF
The Life of Jesus (1926) NF
Things to Come (1928) NF
Son of Woman (1931) NF
The Necessity of Communism (1932) NF
Between Two Worlds (1935) NF
Marxism (1935) NF
The Necessity of Pacifism (1937) NF
The Pledge of Peace (1938) NF
The Free Society (1948) NF
Katherine Mansfield, and Other Literary Portraits (1949) NF
Unprofessional Essays (1956) NF
Love, Freedom and Society (1957) NF

MYERS, L[eopold] H[amilton] (1881–1944)
British novelist and poet
Arvat (1908) V
The Near and the Far (1929) F
Prince Jali (1931) F
The Root and the Flower (1935) F
The Pool of Vishnu (1940) F
From One Generation to Another (1892) F
The Slave of the Lamp (1892) F
With Edged Tools (1894) F
The Grey Lady (1895) F
Flotsam (1896) F
The Sowers (1896) F
In Kedar's Tents (1897) F
Roden's Corner (1898) F
The Isle of Unrest (1900) F
The Velvet Glove (1901) F
Barlasch of the Guard (1903) F
The Last Hope (1904) F
Tomaso's Fortune, and Other Stories (1904) F SS

N

NABOKOV, Vladimir (1899–1977)
Russian-born American novelist
Camera Obscura [US: *Laughter in the Dark*] (1936) F
The Real Life of Sebastian Knight (1941) F
Bend Sinister (1947) F
Conclusive Evidence [rev. 1966 as *Speak, Memory*] (1951) NF
Pnin (1957) F
Lolita (1958) F
Invitation to a Beheading (1959) F
Pale Fire (1962) F
The Gift (1963) F
The Defense (1964) F
The Eye (1965) F
Despair (1966) F
The Waltz Invention (1966) D
King, Queen, Knave (1968) F
Ada or Ardor (1969) F
Mary (1970) F
Glory (1971) F
Poems and Problems (1971) V
Transparent Things (1972) F
Strong Opinions (1973) NF
Look at the Harlequins! (1974) F

NAIPAUL, Shiva[dhar Srinivasa] (1945–1985)
Trinidadian novelist and travel writer
Fireflies (1970) F
The Chip-Chip Gatherers (1973) F
North of South [US: *Journey to Nowhere*] (1978) NF
A Hot Country [US: *Death in a Hot Country*] (1983) F

NAIPAUL, V[idiadhar] S[urajprasad] (1932–)
Trinidadian-born British novelist and travel writer
The Mystic Masseur (1957) F
The Suffrage of Elvira (1958) F
Miguel Street (1959) F
A House For Mr Biswas (1961) F
The Middle Passage (1962) NF
An Area of Darkness (1964) NF
The Mimic Men (1967) NF
In a Free State (1971) F
Guerillas (1975) F
India (1977) NF
A Bend in the River (1979) F

The Enigma of Arrival (1987) F
A Way in the World (1994) F
Beyond Belief (1998) NF

NAMIER, Sir Lewis [Bernstein] (1888–1960)
British historian
The Structure of Politics at the Accession of George III (1929) NF
England in the Age of the American Revolution (1930) NF
Conflicts (1942) NF
Europe in Decay (1950) NF
In the Nazi Era (1952) NF

NAPIER, Sir William [Francis Patrick] (1785–1860)
British historian
History of the War in the Peninsula (1828) NF
English Battles and Sieges in the Peninsula (1852) NF

NARAYAN, R[asipuram] K[rishnaswami] (1907–)
Indian novelist
Swami and Friends (1935) F
The Bachelor of Arts (1937) F
The Dark Room (1938) F
The English Teacher [US: *Grateful to Life and Death*] (1945) F
An Astrologer's Day, and Other Stories (1947) F SS
Mr Sampath [US: *The Printer of Malgudi*] (1949) F
The Financial Expert (1952) F
Lawley Road (1956) F SS
The Guide (1958) F
The Man-Eater of Malgudi (1961) F
The Vendor of Sweets (1967) F
A Horse and Two Goats (1970) F SS
My Days (1974) NF
The Painter of Signs (1977) F
Malgudi Days (1982) F SS
A Tiger for Malgudi (1983) F
The World of Nagaraj (1990) F

NASH, Ogden (1902–1971)
American poet
Cricket of Cavador (1925) V
Free Wheeling (1931) V
Happy Days (1933) V
The Primrose Path (1935) V
The Bad Parents' Garden of Verse (1936) V
I'm a Stranger Here Myself (1938) V
The Face is Familiar (1940) V
Many Long Years Ago (1945) V
Versus (1949) V
Family Reunion (1950) V
Parents Keep Out (1951) V
The Private Dining Room (1953) V
You Can't Get There From Here (1957) V
Everyone But Thee and Me (1962) V

NASHE, Thomas (1567–1601)
English satirist, dramatist, and pamphleteer
The Anatomie of Absurditie (1589) NF
Pierce Penilesse his Supplication to the Divell (1592) NF
Strange Newes, of the Intercepting Certaine Letters (1592) NF
Christs Teares Over Jerusalem (1593) NF
The Terrors of the Night; or, A Discourse of Apparitions (1594) NF
The Unfortunate Traveller; or, The Life of Jacke Wilton (1594) F
Have With You to Saffron-walden (1596) NF
Nashes Lenten Stuffe (1599) NF
Summers Last Will and Testament (1600) D

NATHAN, Robert (1894–1985)
American novelist and screenwriter
Portrait of Jennie (1940) F

NAUGHTON, Bill (1910–1992)
British dramatist, novelist, and short-story writer
Spring and Port Wine (1964) D
Alfie [from play of the same name, perf. 1963] (1966) F

NAYLOR, Gloria (1952–)
African-American novelist
The Women of Brewster Place (1982) F

NEAL, John (1793–1876)
American novelist
Keep Cool (1817) F
A Family History (1822) F
Errata; or, The Works of Will. Adams (1823) F
Randolph (1823) F
Seventy-Six (1823) F
Brother Jonathan (1825) F
Rachel Dyer (1828) F
Authorship (1830) F
The Down-Easters (1833) F
True Womanhood (1859) F

NEALE, J[ohn] M[ason] (1818–1866)
British hymn-writer and novelist
A Few Words to Churchwardens on Churches and Church Ornaments (1841) NF
Herbert Tresham (1842) F
Agnes de Tracy (1843) F
Ayton Priory; or, The Restored Monastery (1843) F
A Few Words to the Parish Clerks and Sextons of Country Parishes (1843) NF
Hymns for the Sick (1843) NF
Shepperton Manor (1845) F
Stories of the Crusades (1846) F
The Unseen World (1847) NF
Duchenier; or, The Revolt of La Vendée (1848) F
Deeds of Faith (1850) NF
Victories of the Saints (1850) F
The Egyptian Wanderers (1854) F
Theodora Phranza; or, The Fall of Constantinople (1857) F
Seatonian Poems (1864) V
Sequences, Hymns, and Other Ecclesiastical Verses (1866) V

NEMEROV, Howard (1920–)
American poet, novelist, short-story writer, and critic
The Image and the Law (1947) V
The Melodramatists (1949) F
Guide to the Ruins (1950) V

Federigo; or, The Power of Love (1954) F
The Salt Garden (1955) V
The Homecoming Game (1957) F
Mirrors and Windows (1958) V
A Commodity of Dreams (1959) F SS
Poetry and Fiction (1963) NF
The Next Room of the Dream (1964) V
Journal of the Fictive Life (1966) NF
The Blue Swallows (1967) V
Gnomes & Occasions (1973) V
The Western Approaches (1976) V
Figures of Thought (1978) NF
Inside the Onion (1984) V
The Oak and the Acorn (1987) NF
War Stories (1987) V

NERUDA, Pablo (1904–1973)
Chilean poet
Twenty Love Poems and a Song of Despair [*Veinte poemas de amor y una canción desesperada*] (1924) V
'*Residence on Earth*' [*Residencia en la Tierra*] (1933–47) V
The Heights of Macchu Picchu [*Alturas de Macchu Picchu*] (1945) V
Canto General (1950) V
Elementary Odes [*Odas elementales*] (1954) V

'NERVAL, Gérard de' [Gérard Labrunie] (1808–1855)
French poet
Faust, et le Second Faust [from Goethe] (1840) D
Le Marquis de Fayolle (1849) F
Contes et facéties ['Stories and Jests'] (1853) F SS
Sylvie (1853) F
Daughters of Fire [*Les Filles du feu*] (1854) F SS
Aurélia (1855) NF
La Bohème galante ['Gallant Bohemian Life'] (1855) NF V

NESBIT, E[dith], later **Bland,** then **Tucker** (1858–1924)
British novelist, children's author, and poet
Lays and Legends [1st ser.] (1886) V
The Lily and the Cross (1887) V
Leaves of Life (1888) V
Sweet Lavender (1892) V
Grim Tales (1893) F SS
Something Wrong (1893) F SS
A Pomander of Verse (1895) V
The Secret of Kyriels (1898) F
Songs of Love and Empire (1898) V
The Story of the Treasure Seekers (1899) F CH
The Book of Dragons (1900) F CH
Nine Unlikely Tales for Children (1901) F CH
The Would-Begoods (1901) F CH
Five Children—and It (1902) F CH
The Red House (1902) F
The Literary Sense (1903) F SS
The New Treasure Seekers (1904) F CH
The Phoenix and the Carpet (1904) F CH
Oswald Bastable—and Others (1905) F CH
The Rainbow and the Rose (1905) V
The Incomplete Amorist (1906) F
Man and Maid (1906) F
The Railway Children (1906) F CH
The Story of the Amulet (1906) F CH
The Enchanted Castle (1907) F CH
Ballads and Lyrics of Socialism (1908) V
The House of Arden (1908) F CH
Daphne in Fitzroy Street (1909) F
Harding's Luck (1909) F
The Magic City (1910) F CH
Ballads and Verses of the Spiritual Life (1911) V
The Wonderful Garden; or, The Three C's (1911) F CH
The Magic World (1912) F SS
Many Voices (1922) V
Five of Us—and Madeline (1925) F CH
The Complete History of the Bastable Family (1928) F CH

NEWBOLT, Sir Henry [John] (1862–1938)
British poet and novelist
Taken From the Enemy (1892) F
Mordred (1895) V
Admirals All, and Other Verses (1897) V
The Island Race (1898) V
The Sailing of the Long Ships, and Other Poems (1902) V
Songs of the Sea (1904) V
Songs of Memory and Hope (1909) V
The Twymans (1911) F
Poems: New and Old (1912) V
A New Study of English Poetry (1917) NF
St George's Day, and Other Poems (1918) V

NEWBY, [George] Eric (1919–)
British travel writer
A Short Walk in the Hindu Kush (1958) NF

NEWBY, P[ercy] H[oward] (1918–1997)
British novelist
A Journey to the Interior (1945) F
Agents and Witnesses (1947) F
Mariner Dances (1948) F
The Snow Pasture (1949) F
A Season in England (1951) F
The Picnic at Sakkara (1955) F
Revolution and Roses (1957) F
Ten Miles From Anywhere, and Other Stories (1958) F SS
A Guest and His Going (1959) F
The Retreat (1959) F
The Barbary Light (1962) F
One of the Founders (1965) F
Something to Answer For (1968) F
A Lot to Ask (1973) F
Leaning in the Wind (1986) F
Coming in With the Tide (1991) F
Something About Women (1995) F

NEWMAN, Andrea (1938–)
British novelist
A Share of the World (1964) F

A Bouquet of Barbed Wire (1969) F
An Evil Streak (1977) F
Triangles (1990) F

NEWMAN, John Henry (1801–1890)
British cardinal, poet, and theological writer
The Arians of the Fourth Century (1833) NF
Lyra Apostolica [inc. poems by R.H. Froude and John Keble] (1834) V
Lectures on the Prophetical Office of the Church (1837) NF
Lectures on Justification (1838) NF
An Essay on the Development of Christian Doctrine (1845) NF
Loss and Gain (1848) F
Callista (1856) F
Lectures and Essays on University Subjects (1859) NF
Apologia Pro Vita Sua (1864) V
The Dream of Gerontius (1866) V
Two Essays on Scripture Miracles and on Ecclesiastical (1870) NF
Essays Critical and Historical (1872) NF
Historical Essays (1872) NF
The Idea of a University (1873) NF
Tracts Theological and Ecclesiastical (1874) NF
The Via Media of the Anglican Church (1877) NF
Mr Kingsley and Dr Newman (1864) NF

NEWTON, John (1725–1807)
British Evangelical divine, poet, and hymn-writer
Cardiphonia; or, The Utterance of the Heart (1781) NF
Apologia (1784) NF
Messiah (1786) NF
Thoughts Upon the African Slave Trade (1788) NF
Letters to a Wife (1793) NF

NEWTON, Sir Isaac (1642–1727)
English mathematician and scientist
Philosophiae Naturalis Principia Mathematica [in Latin] (1687) NF
Opticks (1704) NF
Arithmetica Universalis (1707) NF

NICHOLS, Peter [Richard] (1927–)
British dramatist
A Day in the Death of Joe Egg (1967) D
The National Health; or, Nurse Norton's Affair (1969) D
Privates on Parade (1977) D
Born in the Gardens (1979) D
Feeling You're Behind (1984) NF

NICHOLS, Robert [Malise Bowyer] (1893–1944)
British poet, dramatist, and novelist
Invocation (1915) V
Ardours and Endurances (1917) V
Aurelia (1920) V
Fisbo; or, The Looking Glass Loaned (1934) V
A Spanish Triptych (1936) V

NICHOLSON, Norman [Cornthwaite] (1914–1987)
British poet and novelist
Man and Literature (1943) NF
The Fire of the Lord (1944) F
Five Rivers (1944) V
The Old Man of the Mountains (1945) D
The Green Shore (1947) F
Rock Face (1948) V
The Pot Geranium (1954) V
A Local Habitation (1972) V
Cloud on Black Combe (1975) V
The Shadow on Black Combe (1978) V
Sea to the West (1981) V

NICOLSON, Nigel (1917–)
British biographer and editor
Portrait of a Marriage (1973) NF

NICOLSON, Sir Harold [George] (1886–1968)
British diplomatist and author
Sweet Waters (1921) F
The Development of English Biography (1927) NF
Some People (1927) NF
Public Faces (1932) F
Diplomacy (1939) NF
Friday Mornings 1941–4 (1944) NF
Good Behaviour (1955) NF
Diaries and Letters 1930–62 (1966) NF

NIETZSCHE, Friedrich Wilhelm (1844–1900)
German philosopher and poet
The Birth of Tragedy [*Die Geburt der Tragödie*] (1872) NF
Thoughts Out of Season [*Unzeitgemässe Betrachtungen*] (1873–6) NF
The Joyful Wisdom [*Die Fröhliche Wissenschaft*] (1882) NF
Thus Spake Zarathustra [*Also sprach Zarathustra*] (1883–92) NF
Beyond Good and Evil [*Jenseits von Gut und Böse*] (1886) NF
On the Genealogy of Morals [*Zur Genealogie der Moral*] (1887) NF
Ecce Homo (1908) NF

'NIMROD' *see* CHARLES JAMES APPERLEY

NIN, Anaïs (1903–1977)
French-born American, novelist, diarist, and critic
House of Incest (1936) F
Winter of Artifice (1939) F
Under a Glass Bell (1944) F SS
This Hunger (1945) F SS
Ladders to Fire (1946) F SS
Realism and Reality (1946) NF
On Writing (1947) NF
The Four-Chambered Heart (1950) F
A Spy in the House of Love (1954) F
Cities of the Interior (1959) F
Collages (1964) F
Journals (1966–83) NF
The Novel of the Future (1968) NF
A Woman Speaks (1975) NF
In Favour of the Sensitive Man (1976) NF
Delta of Venus (1977) F

NISBET, Hume (1849–1921?)
Australian novelist
Ashes (1890) F
'Bail Up!' (1890) F
A Bush Girl's Romance (1894) F
The Haunted Station, and Other Stories (1894) F SS
Paths of the Dead (1899) F
The Empire Makers (1900) F HF
A Colonial King (1905) F

NIVEN, Larry [Lawrence van Cott Niven] (1938–)
American science fiction writer
World of Ptavvs (1966) F
Neutron Star (1968) F
The Shape of Space (1969) F
Ringworld (1970) F
Protector (1973) F
The Mote in God's Eye (1974) F
Oath of Fealty (1981) F
N-Space (1990) F SS
Playgrounds of the Mind (1992) F SS

NOBBS, David (1935–)
British novelist and TV dramatist
A Piece of the Sky is Missing (1965) F
The Death of Reginald Perrin (1975) F
The Return of Reginald Perrin (1977) F
The Better World of Reginald Perrin (1978) F
Second From Last in the Sack Race (1983) F
A Bit of a Do (1986) F
Pratt of the Argus (1988) F

NOLAN, Christopher (1965–)
Irish writer
Under the Eye of the Clock (1987) NF

NOONAN, Robert P. *see* ROBERT TRESSELL

NORRIS, [Benjamin] Frank[lin] (1870–1902)
American novelist
Moran of the Lady Letty (1898) F
Blix (1899) F
McTeague (1899) F
A Man's Woman (1900) F
The Octopus (1901) F
A Deal in Wheat (1903) F SS
The Pit (1903) F
The Responsibilities of the Novelist (1903) NF
The Joyous Miracle (1906) F
The Third Circle (1909) F SS
Vandover and the Brute (1914) F

NORTH, Christopher *see* JOHN WILSON

NORTH, Sir Thomas (1535–1601?)
English translator
The Diall of Princes [from Antonio de Guevara] (1557) NF
The Morall Philosophie of Doni [from Antonio Francesco Doni] (1570) NF
The Lives of the Noble Grecians and Romanes [from a French trn of Plutarch] (1579) NF

NORTON [the Hon.] Caroline Elizabeth Sarah, *née* Sheridan, later **Lady Stirling-Maxwell** (1808–1877)
British poet, novelist, and polemicist
The Sorrows of Rosalie (1829) V
The Coquette, and Other Tales and Sketches (1830) F SS
The Undying One, and Other Poems (1830) V
The Wife and Woman's Reward (1835) F
A Voice From the Factories (1836) V
The Child of the Islands (1845) V
Stuart of Danleath (1851) F
The Lady of La Garaye (1862) V
Lost and Saved (1863) F
Old Sir Douglas (1868) F

NORTON, Mary (1903–1992)
British children's writer
The Magic Bedknob (1943) F CH
Bonfires and Broomsticks (1947) F CH
The Borrowers (1952) F CH
The Borrowers Afield (1955) F CH
The Borrowers Afloat (1959) F CH
The Borrowers Aloft (1961) F CH
The Borrowers Avenged (1982) F CH

NORTON, Thomas (1532–1584)
English statesman, poet, and dramatist
The Institution of the Christian Religion [from Calvin] (1561) NF
Gorboduc (1565) D

NORWAY, Nevil Shute *see* NEVIL SHUTE

NOYES, Alfred (1880–1958)
British poet, novelist, and critic
The Loom of Years (1902) V
The Flower of Old Japan (1903) V
Drake [vol. i; vol. ii, 1908] (1906) V
Forty Singing Seamen, and Other Poems (1907) V
The Enchanted Island, and Other Poems (1909) V
Tales of the Mermaid Tavern (1913) V
A Salute From the Fleet, and Other Poems (1915) V
Open Boats (1917) V
The Elfin Artist, and Other Poems (1920) V
The Watchers of the Sky (1922) V
Some Aspects of Modern Poetry (1924) NF
Songs of Shadow-of-a-Leaf, and Other Poems (1924) V
The Book of the Earth (1925) V
The Last Voyage (1930) V
The Torch-Bearers (1937) V
The Last Man (1940) F
Two Worlds For Memory (1953) NF
The Devil Takes a Holiday (1955) F
A Letter to Lucian, and Other Poems (1956) V

NYE, Robert [Thomas] (1939–)
British novelist, poet, editor, and children's writer
Doubtfire (1968) F
Darker Ends (1969) V
Divisions on a Ground (1976) V
Falstaff (1976) F
Merlin (1978) F

Faust (1980) F
The Facts of Life, and Other Fictions (1983) F SS
The Memoirs of Lord Byron (1989) F
The Life and Death of My Lord Gilles de Rais (1990) F
Mrs Shakespeare (1993) F
The Late Mr Shakespeare (1998) F

O

OATES, Joyce Carol (1938–)
American novelist, poet, short-story writer, and critic
By the North Gate (1963) F SS
With Shuddering Fall (1964) F
Upon the Sweeping Flood (1966) F SS
A Garden of Earthly Delights (1967) F
Expensive People (1968) F
Women in Love (1968) V
them (1969) F
The Wheel of Love (1970) F SS
The Edge of Impossibility (1971) NF
Wonderland (1971) F
Marriages and Infidelities (1972) F SS
Angel Fire (1973) V
Do With Me What You Will (1973) F
Dreaming America (1973) V
The Hostile Sun (1973) NF
The Goddess and Other Women (1974) F SS
The Hungry Ghosts (1974) F SS
New Heaven, New Earth (1974) NF
Where Are You Going, Where Have You Been? (1974) F SS
The Assassins (1975) F
The Poisoned Kiss (1975) F SS
The Seduction (1975) F SS
The Childwold (1976) F
Crossing the Border (1976) F SS
Night-Side (1977) F SS
The Triumph of the Spider Monkey (1978) F
Women Whose Lives Are Food, Men Whose Lives Are Money (1978) V
Bellefleur (1980) F
Contraries (1981) NF
A Bloodsmoor Romance (1982) F
Last Days (1984) F
Solstice (1985) F
Marya, a Life (1986) F
On Boxing (1987) NF
Raven's Wing (1987) F
You Must Remember This (1987) F
American Appetites (1989) F
Because It Is Bitter, and Because It Is My Heart (1990) F
I Lock the Door Upon Myself (1990) F
Black Water (1992) F
Foxfire (1993) F
Haunted (1994) F SS
What I Lived For (1994) F
Broke Heart Blues (1999) F
Blonde: A Novel (2000) F

O'BRIAN, Patrick [originally Richard Patrick Russ] (1914–2000)
British historical novelist and biographer
The Golden Ocean (1956) F
Master and Commander [first of the Aubrey-Maturin series] (1970) F
Post Captain (1972) F
HMS Surprise (1973) F
Desolation Island (1978) F
The Mauritius Command (1978) F
The Fortune of War (1979) F
The Surgeon's Mate (1980) F
The Ionian Mission (1981) F
Treason's Harbour (1982) F
The Far Side of the World (1984) F
The Reverse of the Medal (1986) F
The Letter of Marque (1988) F
The Thirteen Gun Salute (1989) F
The Letter of Marque (1990) F
The Nutmeg of Consolation (1991) F
Clarissa Oakes (1992) F
The Wine-Dark Sea (1993) F
The Commodore (1994) F
The Yellow Admiral (1997) F
The Hundred Days (1998) F
Blue at the Mizzen (1999) F

O'BRIEN, Connor Cruise (1917–)
Irish critic and political commentator
States of Ireland (1972) NF
The Siege (1986) NF
The Great Melody (1993) NF

'O'BRIEN, Flann' [Brian O'Nolan] (1911–1966)
Irish novelist and humorist
At Swim-Two-Birds (1939) F
The Hard Life (1961) F
The Dalkey Archive (1964) F
The Third Policeman (1967) F

O'BRIEN, [Josephine] Edna (1932–)
Irish novelist and short-story writer
The Country Girls (1960) F
The Lonely Girl (1962) F
Girls in Their Married Bliss (1964) F
August is a Wicked Month (1965) F
Casualties of Peace (1966) F
The Love Object (1968) F SS
A Pagan Place (1970) F
Night (1972) F
A Scandalous Woman (1974) F SS
Johnnie, I Hardly Knew You [US: *I Hardly Knew You*] (1977) F
Mrs Reinhardt, and Other Stories (1978) F SS
Returning (1982) F SS
The High Road (1988) F
Lantern Slides (1990) F SS
Time and Tide (1992) F
The House of Splendid Isolation (1994) F
Wild Decembers (1999) F

O'BRIEN, Kate (1897–1974)
Irish novelist and dramatist
Distinguished Villa (1926) D
Without My Cloak (1931) F
The Ante-Room (1934) F
Mary Lavelle (1936) F
Farewell Spain (1937) NF
The Land of Spices (1941) F
That Lady [US: *For One Sweet Grape*] (1946) F

O'BRIEN, Sean (1952–)
British poet and critic
The Indoor Park (1983) V
The Frighteners (1987) V
HMS Glasshouse (1991) V
Ghost Train (1995) V
The Deregulated Muse (1998) NF

O'BRIEN, [William] Tim[othy] (1946–)
American novelist and journalist
If I Die in a Combat Zone, Box Me Up and Ship Me Home (1973) NF
Going After Cacciato (1978) F

O'CASEY, Sean [John Casey] (1880–1964)
Irish dramatist
Juno and the Paycock [with *The Shadow of a Gunman*, 1923] (1924) D
The Plough and the Stars (1926) D
The Silver Tassie (1928) D
Windfalls (1934) F V D
Within the Gates (1934) D
The Flying Wasp (1937) NF
I Knock at the Door (1939) NF
Purple Dust (1940) D
The Star Turns Red (1940) D
Pictures in the Hallway (1942) NF
Red Roses for Me (1942) D
Drums Under the Window (1945) NF
Cock-a-Doodle Dandy (1949) D
Inishfallen, Fare Thee Well (1949) NF
Rose and Crown (1952) NF
The Bishop's Bonfire (1955) D
The Green Crow (1957) NF
The Drums of Father Ned (1958) D
Under a Coloured Cap (1963) NF

'O'CONNOR, Frank' [Michael Francis O'Donovan] (1903–1966)
Irish short-story writer, critic, and novelist
Guests of the Nation (1931) F SS
The Saint and Mary Kate (1932) F
Bones of Contention, and Other Stories (1936) F SS
Dutch Interior (1940) F
Crab Apple Jelly (1944) F SS
The Common Chord (1947) F SS
Traveller's Samples (1951) F SS
The Mirror in the Roadway (1956) NF
Domestic Relations (1957) F SS
The Lonely Voice (1963) NF
The Backward Look (1967) NF

O'CONNOR, [Mary] Flannery (1925–1964)
American short-story writer and novelist
Wise Blood (1952) F
A Good Man is Hard to Find [UK: *The Artificial Nigger*] (1955) F SS
The Violent Bear It Away (1960) F
Everything That Rises Must Converge (1965) F SS

ODELL, Eric *see* BARRY PAIN

ODETS, Clifford (1906–1963)
American dramatist
Awake and Sing! (1935) D
Paradise Lost (1935) D
Till the Day I Die (1935) D
Waiting for Lefty (1935) D
Golden Boy (1937) D
Rocket to the Moon (1938) D
Night Music (1940) D
Clash by Night (1941) D
The Big Knife (1948) D
The Country Girl (1950) D
The Flowering Peach (1954) D

O'FAOLAIN, Julia (1932–)
Irish novelist and short-story writer
We Might See Sights! and Other Stories (1968) F SS
Godded and Codded (1970) F
Man in the Cellar, and Other Stories (1974) F SS
Women in the Wall (1975) F
Melancholy Baby, and Other Stories (1978) F SS
No Country For Young Men (1980) F
The Obedient Wife (1982) F SS
The Judas Cloth (1992) F

O'FAOLÁIN, Seán [John Francis Whelan] (1900–1991)
Irish short-story writer and novelist
Midsummer Night Madness, and Other Stories (1932) F SS
A Nest of Simple Folk (1933) F
Bird Alone (1936) F
A Purse of Coppers (1937) F SS
Come Back to Erin (1940) F
Teresa, and Other Stories (1947) F SS
The Short Story (1948) NF
The Heat of the Sun (1966) F SS
The Talking Trees, and Other Stories (1971) F SS
Foreign Affairs, and Other Stories (1976) F SS

O'FLAHERTY, Liam (1897–1984)
Irish novelist and short-story writer
Thy Neighbour's Wife (1923) F
The Black Soul (1924) F
Spring Sowing (1924) F SS
The Informer (1925) F
Mr Gilhooley (1926) F
The Assassin (1928) F
Red Barbara, and Other Stories (1928) F SS
The Mountain Tavern, and Other Stories (1929) F SS
The Return of the Brute (1929) F
The Puritan (1931) F
Skerrett (1932) F

The Wild Swan, and Other Stories (1932) F SS
The Martyr (1933) F
Shame the Devil (1934) NF
Famine (1937) F
Two Lovely Beasts, and Other Stories (1948) F SS
Insurrection (1950) F
The Pedlar's Revenge, and Other Stories (1976) F SS

O'GRADY, Standish [James] (1846–1928)
Irish journalist and novelist
Red Hugh's Captivity [rev. 1897 as *The Flight of the Eagle*] (1889) F
Finn and His Companions (1892) F
The Bog of Stars, and Other Stories and Sketches of Elizabethan Ireland (1893) F SS
The Coming of Cuchulain (1894) F
Lost on Du Corrig; or, 'Twixt Earth and Ocean (1894) F
The Chain of Gold; or, In Crannied Rocks (1895) F CH
Ulrick the Ready; or, The Chieftain's Last Rally (1896) F
The Flight of the Eagle (1897) F
The Queen of the World; or, Under the Tyranny (1900) F

O'HANLON, Redmond [Douglas] (1947–)
British travel writer
Into the Heart of Borneo (1984) NF

O'HARA, Frank (1926–1966)
American poet and dramatist
A City Winter, and Other Poems (1952) V
Meditations in an Emergency (1957) V
Second Avenue (1960) V
Lunch Poems (1964) V
Art Chronicles (1975) NF

O'HARA, John [Henry] (1905–1970)
American novelist and short-story writer
Appointment in Samarra (1934) F
Butterfield 8 (1935) F
The Doctor's Son (1935) F SS
Hope of Heaven (1938) F
Files on Parade (1939) F SS
Pal Joey [later dramatized as a musical comedy] (1940) F
Pipe Night (1945) F SS
Hellbox (1947) F SS
A Rage to Live (1949) F
The Farmers Hotel (1951) F
Ten North Frederick (1955) F
A Family Party (1956) F
From the Terrace (1958) F
Ourselves to Know (1960) F
Sermons and Soda Water (1960) F SS
The Big Laugh (1962) F
The Cape Cod Lighter (1962) F SS
Elizabeth Appleton (1963) F
The Hat on the Bed (1963) F SS
The Horse Knows the Way (1964) F SS
The Lockwood Concern (1965) F
The Instrument (1967) F
Lovey Childs (1970) F
The Ewings (1972) F

O'HARA, Mary [Mary O'Hara Alsop] (1885–1980)
American children's writer
My Friend Flicka (1941) F CH

O'KEEFFE, John (1747–1833)
Irish poet, actor, and dramatist
Tony Lumpkin in Town (1778) D
Peeping Tom of Coventry (1784) D
Patrick in Prussia; or, Love in a Camp (1786) D

OKRI, Ben[jamin] (1959–)
Nigerian novelist, poet, and short-story writer
Incidents at the Shrine (1986) F SS
The Famished Road (1991) F
An African Elegy (1992) V
Songs of Enchantment (1993) F
Astonishing the Gods (1995) F
Dangerous Love (1996) F
Infinite Riches (1998) F

'OLD MOORE' [Francis Moore] (1657–1714)
English astrologer and physician
Vox Stellarum: An Almanac for 1701 [The first *Old Moore's Almanac*] (1700) NF

OLDHAM, John (1653–1683)
English poet and translator
Upon the Marriage of the Prince of Orange with the Lady Mary (1677) V
Garnets Ghost (1679) V
Satyrs Upon the Jesuits (1681) V

OLDMIXON, John (1673–1742)
English historian, pamphleteer, poet, and critic
Amintas (1698) D
Reflections on the Stage and Mr Collier's Defence of the Short View (1699) NF
The Grove; or, Love's Paradise (1700) D
Amores Britannici (1703) V
The Governour of Cyprus (1703) D
The Secret History of Europe [pts. i, ii; pt. iii, 1713; pt. iv, 1715] (1712) NF
Memoirs of Ireland from the Restoration, to the Present Times (1716) NF
The Critical History of England, Ecclesiastical and Civil (1724) NF
Clarendon and Whitlock Compar'd (1727) NF
An Essay on Criticism (1728) NF
The History of England [vol. i] (1729) NF
The History of England [vol. ii] (1735) NF
The History of England [vol. iii] (1739) NF
Memoirs of the Press (1742) NF

OLIPHANT, Laurence (1829–1888)
British novelist
A Journey to Khatmandu with the Camp of Jung Bahadoor (1852) NF
Piccadilly (1870) F
Altiora Peto (1883) F
Massollam: A Problem of the Period (1886) F
Fashionable Philosophy (1887) F SS

OLIPHANT, Margaret Oliphant, *née* Wilson (1828–1897)
British novelist and short-story writer
Passages in the Life of Mrs Margaret Maitland, of Sunnyside (1849) F
Merkland (1850) F
Caleb Field (1851) F
John Drayton (1851) F
Katie Stewart (1852) F
The Melvilles (1852) F
Memoirs and Resolutions of Adam Graeme of Mossgray (1852) F
Alieford (1853) F
Harry Muir (1853) F
Magdalen Hepburn (1854) F
The Quiet Heart (1854) F
Lilliesleaf (1855) F
Christian Melville (1856) F
Zaidee (1856) F
The Athelings; or, The Three Gifts (1857) F
The Days of My Life (1857) F
Orphans (1858) F
Lucy Crofton (1859) F
The House on the Moor (1861) F
The Last of the Mortimers (1862) F
The Rector and The Doctor's Family (1862) F
Salem Chapel (1863) F
The Perpetual Curate (1864) F
Agnes (1865) F
A Son of the Soil (1865) F
Madonna Mary (1866) F
Miss Marjoribanks (1866) F
Brownlows (1868) F
The Minister's Wife (1869) F
The Three Brothers (1870) F
A Rose in June (1874) F
The Story of Valentine and His Brother (1875) F
Whiteladies (1875) F
The Curate in Charge (1876) F
An Odd Couple (1876) F
Phoebe Junior (1876) F
Carità (1877) F
Young Musgrave (1877) F
A Beleagured City (1879) F
Within the Precincts (1879) F
He That Will Not When He May (1880) F
Harry Joscelyn (1881) F
In Trust (1881) F
A Little Pilgrim in the Unseen (1882) F SS
The Lady's Walk (1883) F
Madam (1884) F
The Wizard's Son (1884) F
The Land of Darkness (1888) F SS
Kirsteen (1890) F
Sons and Daughters (1890) F
The Marriage of Elinor (1891) F
The Railway Man and His Children (1891) F
Diana Trelawny (1892) F
A House in Bloomsbury (1894) F
Old Mr Tredgold (1895) F
The Ways of Life (1897) F SS
A Widow's Tale, and Other Stories (1898) F
Autobiography and Letters (1899) NF

OLSEN, Tillie (1913–)
American short-story writer and novelist
Tell Me a Riddle (1962) F SS
Yonnondio (1974) F
Silences (1978) NF

OLSON, Charles (1910–1970)
American poet
Call Me Ishmael (1947) NF
In Cold Hell, in Thicket (1953) V
The Maximus Poems 1–10 [11–23, 1956; combined, 1960] (1953) V
The Distances (1960) V
Maximus IV, V, VI (1968) V
The Maximus Poem (1975) V

ONDAATJE, Michael (1943–)
Sri-Lankan born Canadian novelist and poet
The Dainty Monsters (1967) V
The Man With Seven Toes (1969) V
The Collected Works of Billy the Kid (1970) V
Coming Through Slaughter (1979) F
There's a Trick With a Knife I'm Learning to Do (1979) V
In the Skin of a Lion (1987) F
The English Patient (1991) F
Anil's Ghost (1999) F

O'NEILL, Eugene [Gladstone] (1888–1953)
American dramatist
Bound East for Cardiff (1916) D
The Moon of the Caribbees (1918) D
Beyond the Horizon (1920) D
Chris Christopherson [rewritten 1921 as *Anna Christie*] (1920) D
Diff'rent (1920) D
The Emperor Jones (1920) D
Gold (1921) D
The Straw (1921) D
The First Man (1922) D
The Hairy Ape (1922) D
All God's Chillun Got Wings (1924) D
Desire Under the Elms (1924) D
The Fountain (1925) D
The Great God Brown (1926) D
Lazarus Laughed (1927) D
Marco Millions (1928) D
Strange Interlude (1928) D
Dynamo (1929) D
Mourning Becomes Electra (1931) D
Ah! Wilderness (1932) D
Days Without End (1934) D
The Iceman Cometh (1946) D
A Moon for the Misbegotten (1947, written 1943) D
Long Day's Journey into Night (1956, written 1940–1) D

ONIONS, C[harles] T[albut] (1873–1965)
British lexicographer
A Shakespeare Glossary (1911) NF

ONIONS, [George] Oliver (1873–1961)
British novelist and short-story writer
Widdershins (1911) F SS
Ghosts in Daylight (1924) F SS
The Painted Face (1929) F SS
The Story of Ragged Robyn (1945) F
Poor Man's Tapestry (1946) F HF
Arras of Youth (1949) F HF
A Penny for the Harp (1952) F HF

OPIE, Amelia, *née* Alderson (1769–1853)
British novelist and poet
Dangers of Coquetry (1790) F
The Father and Daughter (1801) F V
Adeline Mowbray; or, The Mother and Daughter (1805) F
Simple Tales (1806) F
The Warrior's Return, and Other Poems (1808) V
Temper; or, Domestic Scenes (1812) F
Tales of Real Life (1813) F
Valentine's Eve (1816) F
New Tales (1818) F
Tales of the Heart (1820) F SS
Madeline (1822) F
The Negro Boy's Tale: A Poem (1824) V
Illustrations of Lying, In All its Branches (1825) NF
Tales of the Pemberton Family (1825) F CH
The Black Man's Lament; or, How to Make Sugar (1826) V
Detraction Displayed (1828) NF
Lays for the Dead (1834) V

OPIE, Peter [Mason] (1918–1982) and **Iona [Margaret Balfour]** (1923–)
British folklorists
The Oxford Dictionary of Nursery Rhymes (1951) NF

OPPENHEIM, E[dward] Phillips (1866–1946)
British novelist and short-story writer
The Mysterious Mr Sabin (1898) F
The Man and His Kingdom (1899) F
A Millionaire of Yesterday (1900) F
The World's Great Snare (1900) F
The Survivor (1901) F
A Prince of Sinners (1903) F
A Maker of History (1905) F
The Secret (1907) F
The Double Four (1911) F
Mr Grex of Monte Carlo (1915) F
The Kingdom of the Blind (1917) F
The Great Impersonation (1920) F
The Mystery Road (1924) F
The Treasure House of Martin Hews (1929) F
The Ostrakoff Jewels (1932) F
Envoy Extraordinary (1937) F

ORAGE, A[lfred] R[ichard] (1873–1934)
British social critic and editor
Friedrich Nietzsche (1906) NF
Consciousness (1907) NF
An Alphabet of Economics (1917) NF
Readers and Writers 1917–21 (1922) NF

ORCZY, [Emma Magdalena Rosalia Maria Josefa Barbara] Baroness, later **Mrs Montagu Barstow** (1865–1947)
Hungarian-born British novelist and short-story writer
The Emperor's Candlesticks (1899) F
By the Gods Beloved (1905) F
The Scarlet Pimpernel (1905) F
A Son of the People (1906) F
Beau Brocade (1907) F
The Tangled Skein (1907) F
The Elusive Pimpernel (1908) F
The Nest of the Sparrowhawk (1909) F
The Old Man in the Corner (1909) F SS
Lady Molly of Scotland Yard (1910) F SS
The League of the Scarlet Pimpernel (1919) F
The Triumph of the Scarlet Pimpernel (1922) F
Sir Percy Hits Back (1927) F
The Way of the Scarlet Pimpernel (1933) F
Mam'zelle Guillotine (1940) F

'ORINDA' *see* KATHERINE PHILIPS

ORTON, Joe [John Kingsley] (1933–1967)
British dramatist and novelist
Entertaining Mr Sloane (1964) D
Crimes of Passion (1967) D
Loot (1967) D
What the Butler Saw (1969) D
Funeral Games [with *The Good and Faithful Servants*] (1970) D
Head to Toe (1971) F
Between Us Girls (1998) F
The Boy Hairdresser and Lord Cucumber (1999) F

'ORWELL, George' [Eric Arthur Blair] (1903–1950)
British novelist and social critic
Down and Out in Paris and London (1933) NF
Burmese Days (1934) F
A Clergyman's Daughter (1935) F
Keep the Aspidistra Flying (1936) F
The Road to Wigan Pier (1937) NF
Homage to Catalonia (1938) NF
Coming Up For Air (1939) F
Inside the Whale, and Other Essays (1940) F
The Lion and the Unicorn (1941) NF
Animal Farm (1945) F
Critical Essays (1946) NF
Nineteen Eighty-Four (1949) F
Shooting an Elephant, and Other Essays (1950) NF
Luther (1961) D
Plays For England [*The Blood of the Bambergs*; *Under Plain Cover*] (1963) D
Inadmissible Evidence (1964) D
A Patriot For Me (1965) D
Time Present; [with *Hotel in Amsterdam*] (1968) D
West of Suez (1971) D
A Sense of Detachment (1973) D
Watch It Come Down (1975) D
A Better Class of Person (1981) F
Almost a Gentleman (1991) F
Déja Vu (1991) D

OSBORNE, John [James] (1929–1994)
British dramatist
Look Back in Anger (1956) D
The Entertainer (1957) D

O'SHAUGHNESSY, Arthur [William Edgar] (1844–1881)
British poet
An Epic of Women, and Other Poems (1870) V
Lays of France (1872) V
Music and Moonlight (1874) V

OSTROVSKY, Alexander Nikolaevich (1823–1886)
Russian dramatist
The Poor Bride (1853) D
The Storm (1860) D
Snow Maiden (1873) D

OTWAY, Thomas (1652–1685)
English dramatist and poet
Alcibiades (1675) D
Don Carlos, Prince of Spain (1676) D
Titus and Berenice (1676?) D
Friendship in Fashion (1678) D
The History and Fall of Caius Marius (1679) D
The Orphan; or, The Unhappy Marriage (1680) D
The Poet's Complaint of his Muse; or, A Satyr Against Libells (1680) V
The Souldiers Fortune (1680) D
Venice Preserv'd; or, A Plot Discover'd (1682) D
The Atheist; or, The Second Part of the Souldiers Fortune (1683) D
Windsor Castle, in a Monument to Our Late Sovereign Charles II (1685) V

'OUIDA' [Marie Louise de la Ramée, originally **Louise Ramé]** (1839–1908)
British novelist and short-story writer
Held in Bondage (1863) F
Stratmore (1865) F
Chandos (1866) F
Cecil Castlemaine's Gage, and Other Novelettes (1867) F SS
Idalia; or, The Unfortunate Mistress (1867) F
Under Two Flags (1867) F
Puck (1869) F
Tricotrin (1869) F
Folle Farine (1871) F
A Dog of Flanders, and Other Stories (1872) F SS
Pascarel (1873) F
Two Little Wooden Shoes (1874) F
Signa (1875) F
In a Winter City (1876) F
Ariadne (1877) F
Friendship (1878) F
Moths (1880) F
Pipistrello, and Other Stories (1880) F SS
A Village Commune (1881) F
In Maremma (1882) F
Wanda (1883) F
Princess Napraxine (1884) F
Othmar (1885) F
Don Gesualdo (1886) F
A House Party (1887) F
Guilderoy (1889) F
Ruffino (1890) F
Santa Barbara (1891) F SS
The Tower of Taddeo (1892) F
Two Offenders, and Other Tales (1894) F SS
Le Selve, and Other Tales (1896) F SS
The Massarenes (1897) F
La Strega, and Other Stories (1899) F SS
The Waters of Edera (1900) F
Street Dust, and Other Stories (1901) F SS

OWEN, Robert (1771–1858)
British social reformer
A New View of Society (1813) NF
Observations on the Effect of the Manufacturing System (1815) NF
Manifesto (1840) NF
Letters on Education (1849) NF
The Future of the Human Race (1853) NF

OWEN, Wilfred [Edward Salter] (1893–1918)
British poet
Poems (1920) V
Collected Poems (1963) V

OWENSON, Sydney *see* LADY SYDNEY MORGAN

OZ, Amos (1939–)
Israeli novelist, short-story writer, and essayist
Where the Jackals Howl, and Other Stories (1965) F SS
Elsewhere, Perhaps (1966) F
My Michael (1968) F
Touch the Water, Touch the Wind (1973) F
The Hill of Evil Counsel (1976) F
Black Box (1987) F
The Third State (1991) F

OZICK, Cynthia (1928–)
American novelist and critic
Trust (1966) F
The Pagan Rabbi, and Other Stories (1971) F SS
Bloodshed (1976) F
Levitation (1982) F
Art and Ardor (1983) NF
The Cannibal Galaxy (1983) F
Metaphor and Memory (1987) NF
Metaphor and Myth (1989) NF
The Shawl (1989) F

P

PAGE, Thomas Nelson (1853–1922)
American novelist and short-story writer
In Ole Virginia (1887) F SS
Elsket, and Other Stories (1891) F SS
On Newfound River (1891) F
The Old South (1892) NF
The Burial of the Guns (1894) F SS
The Old Gentleman of the Black Stock (1897) F
Red Rock (1898) F
Gordon Keith (1903) F
Bred in the Bone (1904) F SS
John Marvel, Assistant (1909) F

PAGET, Violet *see* VERNON LEE

'PAIN, Barry' [Eric Odell] (1864–1928)
British journalist, humorist, novelist, and short-story writer
In a Canadian Canoe (1891) F SS
Stories and Interludes (1892) F
Playthings and Parodies (1893) NF
Eliza (1900) F
Nothing Serious (1901) F
Stories in the Dark (1901) F SS
Eliza's Husband (1903) F
Wilhemina in London (1906) F
Eliza Getting On (1911) F
Here and Hereafter (1911) F SS
Stories in Grey (1911) F SS
Exit Eliza (1912) F
Eliza's Son (1913) F
Mrs Murphy (1913) F
Edwards (1915) F
The Confessions of Alphonse (1917) F
Marge Askinfort (1920) F
If Summer Don't (1922) F

PAINE, Thomas (1737–1809)
British political writer
Common Sense (1776) NF
'The Crises' (1776) NF
Rights of Man [pt. i; pt. ii, 1792] (1791) NF
The Age of Reason [pt. i; pt. ii, 1795] (1794) NF
Dissertation on the First-Principles of Government (1795) NF

PAINTER, William (1540?–1594)
English translator
The Palace of Pleasure [vol. i] (1566) F
The Second Tome of the Palace of Pleasure (1567) F

PALEY, Grace [Goodside] (1922–)
American short-story writer and poet
The Little Disturbances of Man (1959) F SS
Later the Same Day (1985) F SS

PALEY, William (1743–1805)
British theological and philosophical writer
The Principles of Moral and Political Philosophy (1785) NF
Horae Paulinae; or, The Truth of the Scripture History of St Paul Evinced (1790) NF
A View of the Evidences of Christianity (1794) NF
Natural Theology; or, Evidences of the Existence and Attributes of the Deity (1802) NF

PALGRAVE, Francis Turner (1824–1897)
British poet, novelist, and anthologist
Preciosa (1852) F
Idyls and Songs (1854) V
The Passionate Pilgrim; or, Eros and Anteros (1858) V
The Golden Treasury of Songs and Lyrics (1861) ANTH
Essays on Art (1866) NF
Hymns (1867) V
Lyrical Poems (1871) V
The Children's Treasury of English Song (1875) ANTH
The Visions of England (1881) V
The Treasury of Sacred Song (1889) ANTH
Amenophis, and Other Poems (1892) V

PALLISER, Charles (1947–)
American-born British author
The Quincunx (1989) F

PALTOCK, Robert (1697–1767)
British novelist
The Life and Adventures of Peter Wilkins, a Cornish Man (1751) F

PARDOE, Julia (1806–1862)
British novelist and miscellaneous author
Confessions of a Pretty Woman (1846) F

PARETSKY, Sara (1947–)
American crime novelist
Indemnity Only [first V.I. Warshawski novel] (1982) F
Deadlock (1984) F
Killing Orders (1985) F
Bitter Medicine (1987) F
Blood Shot (1988) F
Burn Marks (1990) F
Guardian Angel (1991) F
Tunnel Vision (1994) F
Hard Time (1999) F

PARGETER, Edith Mary *see* ELLIS PETERS

PARK, Mungo (1771–1806)
British explorer and author
Travels in the Interior of Africa (1799) NF

PARKER, Dorothy [Rothschild] (1893–1967)
American poet, short-story writer, and critic
Enough Rope (1926) V
Sunset Gun (1928) V
Laments for the Living (1930) F SS
Death and Taxes (1931) V
After Such Pleasures (1933) F SS

PARKER, Eric [Frederick Moore Searle] (1870–1955)
British journalist and author
The Sinner and the Problem (1901) F
The Promise of Arden (1912) F
Eton in the 'Eighties (1914) NF

PARKER, Robert B[rown] (1932–)
American crime writer
God Save the Child (1974) F
The Godwulf Manuscript (1974) F
Mortal Stakes (1975) F
Promised Land (1976) F
The Judas Goat (1978) F
Looking for Rachel Wallace (1980) F
Valediction (1984) F
A Catskill Eagle (1985) F
Perchance to Dream [sequel to Raymond Chandler's *The Big Sleep*] (1991) F

PARKINSON, John (1567–1650)
English apothecary and herbalist
Paradisi in sole Paradisus terrestris; or, A Garden of Flowers (1629) NF
Theatrum Botanicum: The Theater of Plants (1640) NF

PARKS, Tim[othy Harold] (1954–)
British novelist and translator
Tongues of Flame (1985) F
Loving Roger (1986) F
Family Planning (1989) F
Cara Massimina [as 'John MacDowell'; US: *Juggling the Stars*] (1990) F
Goodness (1991) F
Mimi's Ghost (1995) F
Destiny (1999) F

PARNELL, Thomas (1679–1718)
Anglo-Irish poet
An Essay on the Different Stiles of Poetry (1713) V
Homer's Battle of the Frogs and Mice (1717) V
Poems on Several Occasions (1722) V

PARSONS, Eliza, *née* Phelp (1748–1811)
British novelist
The History of Miss Meredith (1790) F
The Errors of Education (1791) F
The Castle of Wolfenbach (1793) F
Ellen and Julia (1793) F
Woman as She Should Be; or, Memoirs of Mrs Menville (1793) F
Lucy (1794) F
The Voluntary Exile (1795) F
The Mysterious Warning (1796) F
Women as They Are (1796) F
The Girl of the Mountains (1797) F
An Old Friend with a New Face (1797) F
The Valley of St Gothard (1799) F

PARTRIDGE, Eric [Honeywood] (1894–1979)
British lexicographer, etymologist, and historian of slang
A Dictionary of Slang and Unconventional English (1937) NF

PASTERNAK, Boris [Leonidovich] (1890–1960)
Russian novelist and poet
Dr Zhivago (1957) F

PATCHEN, Kenneth (1911–1971)
American poet and novelist
Before the Brave (1936) V
First Will and Testament (1939) V
The Teeth of the Lion (1942) V
Cloth of the Tempest (1943) V
An Astonished Eye Looks Out of the Air (1945) V
Memoirs of Shy Pornographer (1945) F
Sleepers Awake (1946) V
See You in the Morning (1948) F
Red Wine & Yellow Hair (1949) V
Hurrah for Anything (1957) V
Because It Is (1960) V

PATER, Walter [Horatio] (1839–1894)
British scholar and critic
Studies in the History of the Renaissance (1873) NF
Marius the Epicurean (1885) F
Imaginary Portraits (1887) P
Appreciations (1889) NF
Plato and Platonism (1893) NF
Greek Studies (1895) NF
Miscellaneous Studies (1895) NF

PATERSON, A[ndrew] B[arton] 'Banjo' (1864–1941)
Australian poet, journalist, and novelist
The Man From Snowy River, and Other Verses (1895) V
Rio Grande's Last Race, and Other Verse (1902) V
Old Bush Songs (1905) V
An Outback Marriage (1906) F
Saltbush Bill J.P., and Other Verses (1917) V
Three Elephant Power, and Other Stories (1917) F SS
The Shearer's Colt (1936) F

PATMORE, Coventry [Kersey Dighton] (1823–1896)
British poet
Tamerton Church-Tower and Other Poems (1853) V
The Angel in the House: The Betrothal (1854) V
The Espousals [*The Angel in the House* ii] (1856) V
Faithful For Ever [*The Angel in the House* iii] (1860) V
The Victories of Love [*The Angel in the House* iv] (1862) V
The Unknown Eros, and Other Odes (1877) V
The Rod, the Root, and the Flower (1895) V

PATON, Alan [Stewart] (1903–1988)
South African novelist and short-story writer
Cry, the Beloved Country (1948) F
Too Late the Phalarope (1953) F
Debbie Go Home (1961) F SS
Apartheid and the Archbishop: The Life and Times of Geoffrey Clayton (1973) NF
Ah, But Your Land is Beautiful (1981) F
Shakespeare's Bawdy (1947) NF
Origins (1958) NF
A Dictionary of Catch Phrases (1977) NF

PATTEN, Brian (1946–)
British poet, dramatist, and children's writer
Little Johnny's Confession (1967) V
Notes to the Hurrying Man (1969) V
The Homecoming (1970) V
And Sometimes It Happens (1972) V
The Unreliable Nightingale (1973) V
Vanishing Trick (1976) V
Grave Gossip (1979) V
Love Poems (1981) V
Gargling with Jelly (1985) F CH
Storm Damage (1988) V
Grinning Jack (1990) V
Thawing Frozen Frogs (1990) F CH
The Magic Bicycle (1993) V

PATTERSON, Harry *see* JACK HIGGINS

PATTISON, Mark (1813–1884)
British scholar and biographer
Milton (1879) NF
Memoirs (1885) NF
Essays (1889) NF

PAULIN, Tom [Thomas Neilson] (1949–)
Northern Irish poet, critic, and dramatist
A State of Justice (1977) V
Personal Column (1978) V
The Strange Museum (1980) V
The Book of Juniper (1981) V
Liberty Tree (1983) V
Ireland and the English Crisis (1984) NF
Fivemiletown (1987) V
Minotaur (1992) NF
Walking a Line (1994) V

PAYN, James (1830–1898)
British journalist and novelist
Lost Sir Massingberd (1864) F
Married Beneath Him (1865) F
Lights and Shadows of London Life (1867) F
Bentinck's Tutor, One of the Family (1868) F
Blondel Parva (1868) F
Not Wooed, But Won (1871) F
Walter's Word (1875) F
Fallen Fortunes (1876) F
What He Cost Her (1877) F
By Proxy (1878) F
Less Black Than We're Painted (1878) F
The Canon's Ward (1884) F
Some Literary Recollections (1884) NF
The Luck of the Darrells (1885) F
The Talk of the Town (1885) F
The Heir of the Ages (1886) F
The Burnt Million (1890) F
A Stumble on the Threshold (1892) F
The Disappearance of George Driffell (1896) F

PEACHAM, Henry, the Elder (fl.1577)
English author
The Garden of Eloquence (1577) NF

PEACHAM, Henry, the Younger (1578?–1642?)
English essayist
The Art of Drawing with the Pen, and Limming in Water Colours (1606) NF
The More the Merrier (1608) V
Minerva Britanna; or, A Garden of Heroical Devises (1612) V
Prince Henrie Revived; or, A Poeme (1615) V
Thalias Banquet (1620) V
The Compleat Gentleman (1622) NF
The Truth of Our Times (1638) NF
The Art of Living in London (1642) NF

PEACOCK, Thomas Love (1785–1866)
British novelist, poet, and critic
Palmyra and Other Poems (1806) V
The Genius of the Thames (1810) V
The Philosophy of Melancholy (1812) V
Sir Hornbrook; or, Childe Launcelot's Expedition (1814) V
Sir Proteus [as 'P.M. O'Donovan'] (1814) V
Headlong Hall (1816) F
Melincourt (1817) F
Nightmare Abbey (1818) F
Rhododaphne; or, The Thessalian Spell (1818) V
Maid Marian (1822) F
The Misfortunes of Elphin (1829) F
Crotchet Castle (1831) F
Gryll Grange (1861) MISC

PEAKE, Mervyn [Laurence] (1911–1968)
British fantasy writer, children's author, poet, and illustrator
Rhymes Without Reason (1944) V
Titus Groan (1946) F
The Glassblowers (1950) V
Gormenghast (1950) F
Mr Pye (1953) F
Titus Alone (1959) F
The Rhyme of the Flying Bomb (1962) V

PEARCE, Philippa (1920–)
British children's writer
Minnow on the Say (1955) F CH
Tom's Midnight Garden (1958) F CH
A Dog So Small (1962) F CH
The Shadow-Cage, and Other Tales of the Supernatural (1977) F SS CH
The Battle of Bubble and Squeak (1978) F CH
The Way to Sattin Shore (1983) F CH
The Tooth Ball (1987) F CH
The Rope (2000) F CH

PEARS, Iain (1955–)
British novelist
An Instance of the Fingerpost (1997) F

PEARSON, John (1613–1686)
English theologian and Bishop of Chester
Exposition of the Apostles Creed (1659) NF

PEDERSEN, Knut *see* KNUT HAMSUN

PEELE, George (1556–1596)
English dramatist
The Araygnment of Paris (1584) D
The Famous Chronicle of King Edward the First (1593) D
The Battell of Alcazar (1594) D
The Old Wives Tale (1595) D
The Love of King David and Fair Bethsabe (1599) D

PEMBERTON, [Sir] Max (1863–1950)
British journalist, novelist, and short-story writer
The Iron Pirate (1893) F
The Sea Wolves (1894) F
The Impregnable City (1895) F
The Little Huguenot (1895) F
A Gentleman's Gentleman (1896) F
A Puritan's Wife (1896) F
Kronstadt (1898) F
The Phantom Army (1898) F

The Garden of Swords (1899) F
The House Under the Sea (1902) F
The Show Girl (1909) F
Captain Black (1911) F
War and the Woman (1912) F
The Great White Army (1915) F
Her Wedding Night, and Other Stories (1918) F SS

PENN, William (1644–1718)
English Quaker and founder of Pennsylvania
The Sandy Foundations Shaken (1668) NF
Truth Exalted (1668) NF
Innocency with her Open Face (1669) NF
No Cross, No Crown (1669) NF
The Great Case of Liberty of Conscience Once More Debated (1670) NF
A Serious Apology for the Principles and Practices of the People Called Quakers (1671) NF
The Spirit of Truth Vindicated (1672) NF
The Christian-Quaker and His Divine Testimony Vindicated (1674) NF
A Brief Account of the Province of Pennsylvania (1681) NF
Some Fruits of Solitude (1693) NF
Primitive Christianity Revived (1696) NF
Fruits of a Father's Love (1726) NF

PENNANT, Thomas (1726–1798)
British naturalist and traveller
A Tour in Scotland (1771) NF
Literary Life of the Late Thomas Pennant (1793) NF

PERCY, Thomas (1729–1811)
British antiquary and poet
Hau Kiou Choaan; or, The Pleasing History (1761) F
Five Pieces of Runic Poetry from the Icelandic Language (1763) V
Reliques of Ancient English Poetry (1765) V
Northern Antiquities (1770) MISC
The Hermit of Warkworth, a Northumbrian Ballad (1771) V
An Essay on the Origin of the English Stage (1793) NF

PERCY, Walker (1916–1990)
American novelist
The Moviegoer (1961) F
The Last Gentleman (1966) F
Love in the Ruins (1971) F
The Message in the Bottle (1975) NF
Lancelot (1977) F
The Second Coming (1980) F
Lost in the Cosmos (1983) NF
The Thanatos Syndrome (1987) F

PERELMAN, S[idney] J[oseph] (1904–1979)
American humorist
Dawn Ginsbergh's Revenge (1929) MISC
Parlor, Bedlam, and Bath (1930) MISC
Strictly From Huner (1937) MISC
Look Who's Talking (1940) MISC
The Dream Department (1943) MISC
One Touch of Venus (1943) D
Keep It Crisp (1946) MISC
Westward Ha! (1948) MISC
Listen to the Mocking Bird (1949) MISC
The Ill-Tempered Clavichord (1953) MISC
The Road to Milltown; or, Under the Spreading Atrophy (1957) MISC
The Rising Gorge (1961) MISC
Chicken Inspector No. 23 (1966) MISC
Baby, It's Cold Inside (1970) MISC
Vinegar Puss (1975) MISC

PERKINS, William (1558–1602)
English Puritan theologian
The Foundation of Christian Religion (1590) NF
A Golden Chaine; or, The Description of Theologie (1591) NF
An Exposition of the Lords Prayer (1592) NF
A Salve for a Sicke Man; or, The Right Manner of Dying Well (1595) NF
A Declaration of the True Manner of Knowing Christ Crucified (1596) NF
The Cases of Conscience [pt. i] (1604) NF
The Whole Treatise of the Cases of Conscience (1606) NF
A Discourse of the Damned Art of Witchcraft (1608) NF

PERRAULT, Charles (1628–1703)
French poet and critic
Tales of Mother Goose ['*Contes de ma mère l'Oye*'] (1697) F CH

'PETERS, Ellis' [Edith Mary Pargeter] (1913–)
British crime writer and historical novelist
Hortensius, Friend of Nero (1936) F CF
The Heaven Tree (1960) F
The Green Branch (1962) F
The Scarlet Seed (1963) F
A Morbid Taste for Bones [first of the Cadfael series] (1977) F
One Corpse Too Many (1979) F
Monk's-Hood (1980) F
The Leper of Saint Giles (1981) F
Saint Peter's Fair (1981) F
The Virgin in the Ice (1982) F
The Sanctuary Sparrow (1983) F
Dead Man's Ransom (1984) F
The Devil's Novice (1984) F
The Pilgrim of Hate (1984) F
The Raven in the Foregate (1986) F
The Hermit of Eyton Forest (1987) F
The Heretic's Apprentice (1989) F
The Potter's Field (1989) F
The Holy Thief (1992) F
Brother Cadfael's Penance (1994) F

PETRY, Ann [Lane] (1908–)
African-American novelist, short-story writer, journalist, and children's writer
The Street (1946) F
The Country Place (1947) F
In Darkness and Confusion (1947) F
Miss Muriel, and Other Stories (1971) F SS

PETTIE, George (1548–1589)
English poet
A Petite Pallace of Pettie his Pleasure (1576) F

PEYTON, K.M. [Kathleen Wendy], *née* Herald (1929–)
British children's writer
Sabre, the Horse From the Sea (1948) F CH
Flambards (1967) F CH
Pennington's Seventeenth Summer (1970) F CH
A Pattern of Roses (1973) F CH

PHILALETHES, Eugenius *see* THOMAS VAUGHAN

PHILIPS, Ambrose (1674–1749)
English poet and dramatist
Persian Tales [from the French] (1709) V
Pastoral Tales (1710) V
The Distrest Mother [tr. from Racine] (1712) D
The Briton (1722) D
Humfrey, Duke of Gloucester (1723) D
Pastorals, Epistles, Odes and Other Original Poems (1748) V

PHILIPS, John (1676–1709)
English poet
The Sylvan Dream; or, The Mourning Muse (1701) V
Blenheim (1705) V
The Splendid Shilling (1705) V
Cerealia [also attrib. to Elijah Fenton] (1706) V
Cyder (1708) V

PHILIPS, Katherine ['Orinda'] (1632–1664)
English poet and dramatist
Pompey [tr. from Corneille] (1663) D
Poems by . . . the Matchless Orinda (1667) V

PHILLIPS, Caryl (1958–)
West Indian-born British dramatist and novelist
Strange Fruit (1980) D
Where There is Darkness (1982) D
The Shelter (1983) D
The Final Passage (1985) F
Cambridge (1991) F
Crossing the River (1993) F

PHILLIPS, John (1631–1706)
English poet and satirist
A Satyr Against Hypocrites (1655) V
Montelion, 1660; or, The Propheticall Almanack (1660) V
Typhon; or, The Gyants War with the Gods (1665) V
Maronides; or, Virgil Travestie [paraphrase of Virgil's *Aeneid*; tr. from Scarron] (1672) V
Jockey's Downfall (1679) V
Advice to a Painter (1688) V
A Reflection on Our Modern Poetry (1695) NF

PHILLIPS, Stephen (1864–1915)
British poet and verse-dramatist
Eremus (1894) V
Christ in Hades (1896) V
Paolo and Francesca (1898) D
Herod (1901) D
Ulysses (1902) V
Nero (1906) D
The New Inferno (1911) V
Armageddon (1915) D
Panama (1915) V
Harold (1927) D

PHILLPOTTS, Eden (1862–1960)
British novelist, playwright, and poet
The End of a Life (1891) F
Folly and Fresh Airs (1892) F
A Tiger's Cub (1892) F
Some Every-day Folks (1894) F
A Deal With the Devil (1895) F
Down Dartmoor Way (1895) F
My Laughing Philosopher (1896) F
Lying Prophets (1897) F
Children of the Mist (1898) F
The Human Boy (1899) F CH
Sons of the Morning (1900) F
The Good Red Earth (1901) F
The River (1902) F
The Golden Fetich (1903) F
The American Prisoner (1904) F
The Farm of the Dagger (1904) F
The Secret Woman (1905) F
Wild Fruit (1905) V
The Human Boy Again (1908) F CH
The Mother (1908) F
The Thief of Virtue (1910) F
The Iscariot (1912) V
Widecombe Fair (1913) F
The Human Boy and the War (1916) F CH
The Grey Room (1921) F
A Voice From the Dark (1925) F
The Jury (1927) F
A Deed Without a Name (1941) F
The Fall of the House of Heron (1948) F

PINCHERLE, Alberto *see* ALBERTO MORAVIA

PINERO, [Sir] Arthur Wing (1855–1934)
British actor and dramatist
The Magistrate (1885) D
The Schoolmistress (1886) D
Dandy Dick (1887) D
Sweet Lavender (1888) D
The Profligate (1889) D
The Cabinet Minister (1890) D
The Times (1891) D
The Second Mrs Tanqueray (1893) D
The Notorious Mrs Ebbsmith (1895) D
The Princess and the Butterfly; or, The Fantastics (1897) D
Trelawny of the 'Wells' (1898) D
The Gay Lord Quex (1899) D
Iris (1901) D
The Thunderbolt (1908) D
Mid-Channel (1909) D

PINTER, Harold (1930–)
British dramatist and poet
The Birthday Party, and Other Plays [*Birthday Party* perf. 1958] (1960) D

The Caretaker (1960) D
A Slight Ache, and Other Plays (1961) D
The Homecoming (1965) D
Tea Party, and Other Plays (1967) D
Landscape, and Silence (1969) D
Five Screenplays [*The Caretaker, The Servant, The Pumpkin Eater, Accident, The Quiller Memorandum*] (1971) D
Old Times (1971) D
No Man's Land (1975) D
Betrayal (1978) D
The Hothouse (1980) D
A Kind of Alaska (1982) D
Other Places (1982) D
One For the Road (1985) D
Mountain Language (1988) D
The Heat of the Day (1989) D
Party Time (1991) D
Moonlight (1993) D
Various Voices (1998) V NF

PIOZZI, Hester Lynch [Mrs Thrale] (1741–1821)
British author and memorialist of Samuel Johnson
Anecdotes of the Late Samuel Johnson (1786) NF
Letters To and From the Late Samuel Johnson (1788) NF

PIRANDELLO, Luigi (1867–1936)
Italian dramatist and short-story writer
The Late Mattia Pascal [*Il Fu Mattia Pascal*] (1904) F SS
Shoot [*Si Gira*] (1916) F SS
Six Characters in Search of an Author [*Sei personaggi in cerca d'autore*] (1921) D
Henry IV [*Enrico IV*] (1922) D
As You Desire Me [*Come Tu Mi Vuoi*] (1931) D

PIRSIG, Robert [Maynard] (1928–)
American novelist
Zen and the Art of Motorcycle Maintenance (1974) F
Lila: An Enquiry into Morals (1991) F

PITT-KETHLEY, Fiona (1954–)
British poet and novelist
London (1984) V
Rome (1985) V
Sky Ray Lolly (1986) V
Private Parts (1987) V
The Perfect Man (1989) V
Dogs (1993) V

PITTER, Ruth (1897–1992)
British poet
First Poems (1920) V
A Mad Lady's Garland (1934) V
A Trophy of Arms (1936) V
The Spirit Watches (1939) V
The Rude Potato (1941) V
The Bridge (1945) V
The Ermine (1953) V
Still By Choice (1966) V
End of Drought (1975) V
A Heaven to Find (1987) V

PIX, Mary (1666–1709)
English dramatist
Ibrahim, the Thirteenth Emperour of the Turks (1696) D
The Inhumane Cardinal; or, Innocence Betray'd (1696) F
Queen Catharine; or, The Ruines of Love (1698) D
The False Friend; or, The Fate of Disobedience (1699) D
The Double Distress (1701) D
Violenta; or, The Rewards of Virtue [from Boccaccio] (1704) V
The Conquest of Spain (1705) D
The Adventures in Madrid (1706) D

'PLAIDY, Jean' [Eleanor Alice Hibbert, *née* Burford, 'Victoria Holt', 'Philippa Carr'] (1906–1993)
British historical and romantic novelist
Together They Ride (1945) F
Madame Serpent (1951) F
The Spanish Bridegroom (1954) F
Passage to Pontefract (1981) F
The Sun in Splendour (1982) F
Myself My Enemy (1983) F
Queen of the Realm (1984) F
Victoria Victorious (1985) F
The Lady in the Tower (1986) F
The Courts of Love (1987) F
In the Shadow of the Crown (1988) F
The Reluctant Queen (1990) F

PLATER, Alan [Frederick] (1935–)
British dramatist, scriptwriter, and novelist
Close the Coalhouse Door (1969) D
The Beiderbecke Affair (1985) F

PLATH, Sylvia (1932–1963)
American poet and novelist
The Colossus, and Other Poems (1960) V
The Bell Jar [as 'Victoria Lucas'] (1963) F
Ariel (1965) F
Crossing the Water (1971) V
Winter Trees (1971) V
Letters Home (1975) NF
Johnny Panic and the Bible of Dreams, and Other Prose Writings (1977) P
The Journals of Sylvia Plath (1982) NF

PLOMER, William [Charles Franklyn] (1903–1973)
South African-born novelist, short-story writer, and poet
Turbott Wolfe (1926) F
I Speak of Africa (1927) F SS
The Family Tree (1929) V
Paper Houses (1929) F SS
Sado (1931) F
The Case is Altered (1932) F
The Fivefold Screen (1932) V
The Child of Queen Victoria, and Other Stories (1933) F SS
The Invaders (1934) F
Visiting the Caves (1936) V

Double Lives (1943) NF
The Dorking Thigh, and Other Satires (1945) V
Four Countries (1949) F SS
Museum Pieces (1952) F
Taste and Remember (1966) V
The Planes of Bedford Square (1971) V
Celebrations (1972) V

PLUMPTRE, James (1771–1832)
British dramatist, critic, and traveller
The Coventry Act (1793) D

POE, Edgar Allan (1809–1849)
American short-story writer and poet
Tamerlane, and Other Poems (1827) V
Al Aaraff (1829) V
Poems by Edgar A. Poe (1831) V
Narrative of Arthur Gordon Pym, of Nantucket (1838) F
Tales of the Grotesque and Arabesque (1840) F SS
The Raven, and Other Poems (1845) V
Tales (1845) F SS
Eureka: A Prose Poem (1848) V

POHL, Frederik (1919–)
American science fiction writer
Danger Moon [as 'James MacCreigh'] (1953) F SS
The Space Merchants (1953) F
Gladiator-at-Law (1955) F
Alternating Currents (1956) F SS
Tomorrow Times Seven (1959) F SS
Wolfbane (1959) F
The Man Who Ate the World (1960) F SS
Turn Left at Thursday (1961) F SS
The Reefs of Space (1964) F
Starchild (1965) F
The Age of the Pussyfoot (1969) F
Rogue Star (1969) F
Beyond the Blue Event Horizon (1980) F
The Coming of the Quantum Cats (1986) F
Chernobyl (1987) F
The Day the Martians Came (1988) F
Outnumbering the Dead (1991) F

POLIAKOFF, Stephen (1952–)
British dramatist
Hitting Town; and City Sugar (1976) D
Strawberry Fields (1977) D
Shout Across the River (1978) D
American Days (1979) D
The Summer Party (1979) D
Favourite Nights (1981) D
Breaking the Silence (1985) D
Coming in to Land (1987) D
Playing with Trains (1989) D
Siena Red (1992) D

POLLARD, A[lbert] F[rederick] (1869–1948)
British historian
Factors in Modern History (1907) NF
The History of England (1912) NF
The Commonwealth at War (1917) NF
The Evolution of Parliament (1920) NF
Wolsey (1929) NF

POLLARD, A[lfred] W[illiam] (1859–1944)
British bibliographer and literary scholar
Shakespeare Folios and Quartos (1909) NF
Shakespeare's Fight With the Pirates (1917) NF
A Short-Title Catalogue of Books [with G.R. Redgrave] *1475–1640* (1926) NF

POLLOCK, Sharon (1936–)
Canadian dramatist
A Compulsory Option (1972) D
Walsh (1974) D
Out Goes You (1975) D
The Komagata Man Incident (1978) D
Blood Relations (1980) D
Generations (1980) D
One Tiger to a Hill (1980) D

POMFRET, John (1667–1702)
English poet
The Sceptical Muse; or, A Paradox on Human Understanding (1699) V
The Choice (1700) V
Reason (1700) V

POPE, Alexander (1688–1744)
English poet and translator
An Essay on Criticism (1711) V
Miscellaneous Poems and Translations [inc. 2-canto version of 'The Rape of the Lock'] (1712) V
Ode for Musick (1713) V
Windsor-Forest (1713) V
The Rape of the Lock (1714) V
The Iliad of Homer [vol. i: bks i-iv] (1715) V
The Temple of Fame (1715) V
The Iliad of Homer [vol. ii: bks v-viii] (1716) V
The Iliad of Homer [vol. iii: bks ix-xii] (1717) V
The Iliad of Homer [vol. iv: bks xiii-xvi] (1718) V
The Iliad of Homer [vol. v: bks xvii-xxi] (1720) V
The Iliad of Homer [vol. vi: bks xxii-xxiv] (1720) V
The Odyssey of Homer [vols. i, ii, iii: bks i-xiv] (1725) V
The Works of Shakespear (1725) EDN
The Odyssey of Homer [vols. iv, v: bks xv-xxiv] (1726) V
The Dunciad (1728) V
The Dunciad, Variorum (1729) V
An Epistle to the Right Honourable Richard Earl of Burlington (1731) V
An Epistle to the Right Honourable Richard Lord Visct. Cobham ['Of the Knowledge and Characters of Men'] (1733) V
The First Satire of the Second Book of Horace (1733, 1734) V
The Impertinent; or, A Visit to the Court (1733) V
Of the Use of Riches (1733) V
An Essay on Man [4 epistles pub. separately; pub. together 1734] (1733–4) V
An Epistle to Dr Arbuthnot (1734) V
Sober Advice From Horace (1734) V
Of the Characters of Women (1735) V
The First Epistle of the Second Book of Horace, Imitated (1737) V
Horace His Ode to Venus (1737) V

Letters of Mr Alexander Pope, and Several of his Friends (1737) NF
The Second Epistle of the Second Book of Horace, Imitated (1737) V
The First Epistle of the First Book of Horace Imitated (1738) V
The Sixth Epistle of the First Book of Horace Imitated (1738) V
The Universal Prayer (1738) V

POPE, Dudley [Bernard Egerton] (1925–)
British naval historian and novelist
Ramage (1965) F

POPE-HENNESSY, [Richard] James [Arthur] (1916–1974)
British biographer and travel writer
London Fabric (1939) NF
Monckton Milnes: The Years of Promise (1949) NF
Monckton Milnes: The Flight of Youth (1951) NF
The Baths of Absalom (1954) NF
Verandah (1964) NF
Sins of the Fathers (1967) NF
Half-Crown Colony (1969) NF

POPPER, Sir Karl [Raimund] (1902–1994)
Austrian-born philosopher of science
The Open Society and its Enemies (1945) NF
The Poverty of Historicism (1957) NF
The Logic of Scientific Discovery (1959) NF
Objective Knowledge (1972) NF
A World of Propensities (1990) NF

POQUELIN, Jean-Baptiste *see* MOLIÈRE

PORTER, Anna Maria (1780–1832)
British novelist and poet
Artless Tales (1793) F SS
Walsh Colville; or, A Young Man's First Entrance into Life (1797) F
Octavia (1798) F
The Lake of Killarney (1804) F
The Hungarian Brothers (1807) F
Don Sebastian; or, The House of Braganza (1809) F
Ballad Romances, and Other Poems (1811) V
The Recluse of Norway (1814) F
The Knight of St John (1817) F
The Feast of St Magdalen (1818) F
The Village of Mariendorpt (1821) F
Roche-Blanche; or, The Hunters of the Pyrenees (1822) F
Honor O'Hara (1826) F
Tales Round a Winter Hearth (1826) F SS
Coming Out; and The Field of the Forty Footsteps (1828) F
The Barony (1830) F
The Tuileries (1831) F

PORTER, Hal (1911–1984)
Australian short-story writer, novelist, dramatist, and autobiographer
The Hexagon (1956) V
A Handful of Pennies (1958) F
The Tilted Cross (1961) F
A Bachelor's Children (1962) F SS
The Watcher on the Cast-Iron Balcony (1963) NF
The Cats of Venice (1965) F SS
The Paper Chase (1966) NF
Elijah's Ravens (1968) V
Mr Butterfry and Other Tales of New Japan (1970) F SS
The Right Thing (1971) F
Fredo Fuss Love Life (1974) F SS
In an Australian Country Graveyard (1974) V
The Extra (1975) NF
The Clairvoyant Goat (1981) F SS

PORTER, Jane (1776–1850)
British novelist
Thaddeus of Warsaw (1803) F
The Scottish Chiefs (1810) F
The Pastor's Fire-Side (1817) F
Duke Christian of Luneburg; or, Tradition From the Harz (1824) F

PORTER, Katherine Anne (1890–1980)
American short-story writer and novelist
Flowering Judas, and Other Stories (1930) F SS
Hacienda (1934) F
Pale Horse, Pale Rider (1939) F SS
The Leaning Tower (1944) F SS
The Old Order: Stories of the South (1944) F SS
The Days Before (1952) NF
Ship of Fools (1962) F
The Never-Ending Wrong (1977) NF

PORTER, Peter [Neville Frederick] (1929–)
Australian-born poet
Once Bitten, Twice Bitten (1961) V
Poems Ancient & Modern (1964) V
Words Without Music (1968) V
A Porter Folio (1969) V
The Last of England (1970) V
Preaching to the Converted (1972) V
Living in a Calm Country (1975) V
The Cost of Seriousness (1978) V
English Subtitles (1981) V
Fast Forward (1984) V
The Automatic Oracle (1987) V
Possible Worlds (1989) V
The Chair of Babel (1992) V
Millenial Fables (1994) V

PORTER, William Sydney *see* O. HENRY

POTTER, Dennis [Christopher George] (1935–1994)
British dramatist
The Nigel Barton Plays (1968) D
Son of Man (1970) D
Brimstone and Treacle (1978) D
Pennies From Heaven (1981) F
Waiting for the Boat [Inc. *Joe's Ark*, *Blue Remembered Hills*, and *Cream in My Coffee*] (1984) D
The Singing Detective (1986) D
Blackeyes (1987) F
Lipstick on Your Collar (1993) D

POTTER, [Helen] Beatrix (1866–1943)
British children's author and illustrator
The Tale of Peter Rabbit (1902) F CH
The Tailor of Gloucester (1903) F CH
The Tale of Squirrel Nutkin (1903) F CH
The Tale of Benjamin Bunny (1904) F CH
The Tale of Mrs Tiggy-Winkle (1905) F CH
The Tale of Mr Jeremy Fisher (1906) F CH
The Tale of Tom Kitten (1907) F CH
The Tale of Jemima Puddle-Duck (1908) F CH
The Tale of Pigling Bland (1913) F CH
The Tale of Little Pig Robinson (1930) F CH

POTTER, Stephen [Meredith] (1900–1969)
British humorist, radio producer, and critic
The Muse in Chains (1937) NF
The Theory and Practice of Gamesmanship (1947) NF
Some Notes on Lifemanship (1950) NF
One-Upmanship (1952) NF
Supermanship; or, How to Continue to Stay on Top Without Actually Falling Apart (1958) NF
Steps into Immaturity (1959) NF

POUND, Ezra [Weston Loomis] (1885–1972)
American poet
A Lume Spento (1908) V
Exultations (1909) V
Personae (1909) V
Provença (1910) V
The Spirit of Romance (1910) NF
Canzoni (1911) V
Ripostes (1912) V
The Sonnets and Ballate of Guido Cavalcanti (1912) V
Cathay [trn from the Chinese] (1915) V
Lustra (1916) V
Pavannes and Divisions (1918) NF
Qui Pauper Amavi (1919) V
Hugh Selwyn Mauberley (1920) V
Instigations (1920) NF
Umbra (1920) V
Indiscretions (1923) NF
ABC of Economics (1933) NF
ABC of Reading (1934) NF
Polite Essays (1937) NF
Pavannes and Divagations (1958) NF
Cantos [final collected edn] (1970) V

POWELL, Anthony [Dymoke] (1905–2000)
British novelist, critic, and autobiographer
Afternoon Men (1931) F
Venusberg (1932) F
From a View to a Death (1933) F
Agents and Patients (1936) F
What's Become of Waring? (1939) F
A Question of Upbringing [first of the *Dance to the Music of Time* series] (1951) F
A Buyer's Market [vol. 2 of *Dance to the Music of Time*] (1952) F
The Acceptance World [vol. 3 of *Dance to the Music of Time*] (1955) F
At Lady Molly's [vol. 4 of *Dance to the Music of Time*] (1957) F
Casanova's Chinese Restaurant [vol. 5 of *Dance to the Music of Time*] (1960) F
The Kindly Ones [vol. 6 of *Dance to the Music of Time*] (1962) F
The Valley of Bones [vol. 7 of *Dance to the Music of Time*] (1964) F
The Soldier's Art [vol. 8 of *Dance to the Music of Time*] (1966) F
The Military Philosophers [vol. 9 of *Dance to the Music of Time*] (1968) F
Books Do Furnish a Room [vol. 10 of *Dance to the Music of Time*] (1971) F
Temporary Kings [vol. 11 of *Dance to the Music of Time*] (1973) F
Hearing Secret Harmonies [vol. 12 of *Dance to the Music of Time*] (1975) F
Infants of the Spring (1976) NF
Messengers of Day (1978) NF
Faces In My Time (1980) NF
The Strangers All Are Gone (1982) NF
O, How the Wheel Becomes It! (1983) F
The Fisher King (1986) F
Miscellaneous Verdicts [Writings on writers 1946–1989] (1990) NF
Journals, 1982–1986 (1995) NF

POWYS, John Cooper (1872–1963)
British novelist, poet, and essayist
Odes, and Other Poems (1896) V
Wood and Stone (1915) F
Ducdame (1925) F
Wolf Solent (1929) F
The Meaning of Culture (1930) NF
In Defence of Sensuality (1930) NF
A Glastonbury Romance (1932) F
A Philosophy of Solitude (1933) NF
Autobiography (1934) NF
Weymouth Sands [UK: 1935, as *Jobber Skald*] (1934) F
Maiden Castle (1936) F
Morwyn; or, The Vengeance of God (1937) F
Owen Glendower (1940) F
Mortal Strife (1942) NF
Porius (1951) F
The Inmates (1952) F
Atlantis (1954) F
The Brazen Head (1956) F
All or Nothing (1960) F

POWYS, Llewelyn (1884–1939)
British essayist and novelist
Skin for Skin (1925) NF
The Cradle of God (1929) NF
Apples Be Ripe (1930) F
Impassioned Clay (1931) NF
A Pagan's Pilgrimage (1931) NF
Dorset Essays (1935) NF
Love and Death (1939) F

POWYS, T[heodore] F[rancis] (1875–1953)
British essayist and novelist
Black Bryony (1923) F

The Left Leg (1923) F SS
Mr Tasker's Gods (1925) F
Innocent Birds (1926) F
The House with the Echo (1928) F SS
Mr Weston's Good Wine (1928) F
Kindness in a Corner (1930) F
The White Paternoster, and Other Stories (1930) F SS
Unclay (1931) F
Captain Patch (1935) F SS
Bottle's Path, and Other Stories (1946) F SS
God's Eyes a-Twinkle (1947) F SS
Rosie Plum, and Other Stories (1966) F SS
The Strong Wooer (1970) F
Father Adam (1990) F

PRAED, Rosa Caroline, *née* Murray-Prior [Mrs Campbell Praed] (1851–1935)
Australian-born novelist
Policy and Passion (1881) F
Nadine (1882) F
Zéro (1884) F
Affinities (1885) F
The Other Mrs Jacobs (1903) F

PRATCHETT, Terry (1948–)
British fantasy novelist
The Colour of Magic [first of the Discworld series] (1983) F
The Light Fantastic (1986) F
Mort (1987) F
Sourcery (1988) F
Eric (1989) F
Guards! Guards! (1989) F
Pyramids (1989) F
Moving Pictures (1990) F
Reaper Man (1991) F
Small Gods (1992) F
Men at Arms (1993) F
Soul Music (1995) F
Feet of Clay (1996) F
Carpe Jugulum (1998) F
The Last Continent (1998) F
The Fifth Elephant (1999) F
The Truth (2000) F

PRATT, E[dwin] J[ohn] (1882–1964)
Canadian poet
Newfoundland Verse (1923) V
The Witches' Brew (1925) V
The Iron Door (1927) V
Verses of the Sea (1930) V
Titanic (1935) V
The Fable of the Goats (1937) V
Brébuf and his Brethren (1940) V
Still Life (1943) V
Towards the Last Spike (1952) V

PRATT, Samuel Jackson ['Courtney Melmoth'] (1749–1814)
British poet, novelist, and dramatist
Liberal Opinions Upon Animals, Man, and Providence [as 'Courtney Melmoth'] (1775) F
Observations on the Night Thoughts of Dr Young [as 'Courtney Melmoth'] (1776) NF
The Pupil of Pleasure; or, The New System Illustrated [as 'Courtney Melmoth'] (1776) F
Charles and Charlotte (1777) D
Travels for the Heart [as 'Courtney Melmoth'] (1777) F
Shenstone-Green; or, The New Paradise Lost [as 'Courtney Melmoth'] (1779) F
The Tutor of Truth (1779) F
Emma Corbett; or, The Miseries of Civil War (1780) F
The Fair Circassian (1781) D
Sympathy; or, A Sketch of the Social Passion (1781) V
Family Secrets, Literary and Domestic (1797) F

PRESTON, Thomas (1537–1598)
English dramatist
Cambises King of Percia (1570) D

PRÉVOST, Antoine-François [Abbé Prévost] (1697–1763)
French novelist
Manon Lescaut (1731) F

PRICE, Richard (1723–1791)
Welsh writer on ethics, politics, and economics
A Review of the Principal Questions and Difficulties in Morals (1758) NF
Observations on the Nature of Civil Liberty (1776) NF
An Essay on the Population of England (1780) NF

PRIESTLEY, J[ohn] B[oynton] (1894–1984)
British novelist, dramatist, critic, and essayist
Brief Diversions (1922) MISC
Figures in Modern Literature (1924) NF
Adam in Moonshine (1927) F
Benighted (1927) F
The English Novel (1927) NF
Apes and Angels (1928) NF
The Good Companions (1929) F
Angel Pavement (1930) F
Dangerous Corner (1932) D
Far Away (1932) F
Laburnum Grove (1933) D
Wonder Hero (1933) F
English Journey (1934) NF
I Have Been Here Before (1937) D
Midnight on the Desert (1937) NF
Time and the Conways (1937) D
The Doomsday Men (1938) F
When We Are Married (1938) D
Let the People Sing (1939) F
Rain Upon Godshill (1939) NF
Daylight on Saturday (1943) F
Three Men in New Suits (1945) F
Bright Day (1946) F
An Inspector Calls (1946) D
The Arts Under Socialism (1947) NF
Festival at Farbridge (1951) F
The Other Place, and Other Stories of the Same Sort (1953) F SS
The Magicians (1954) F
Literature and Western Man (1960) NF
Saturn Over the Water (1961) F
Margin Released (1962) NF

The Shapes of Sleep (1962) F
Lost Empires (1965) F
The Moments, and Other Pieces (1966) NF

PRIESTLEY, Joseph (1733–1804)
British theologian and scientist
The Rudiments of English Grammar (1761) NF
A Course of Lectures on the Theory of Language, and Universal Grammar (1762) NF
An Essay on a Course of Liberal Education (1765) NF
The History and Present State of Electricity (1767) NF
An Essay on the First Principles of Government (1768) NF
The History and Present State of Discoveries Relating to Vision, Light, and Colours (1772) NF
Experiments and Observations on Different Kinds of Air (1774–86) NF
Hartley's Theory of the Human Mind (1775) NF
Disquisitions Relating to Matter and Spirit (1777) NF
The Doctrine of Philosophical Necessity Illustrated (1777) NF
An History of the Corruptions of Christianity (1782) NF

PRINCE, F[rank] T[empleton] (1912–)
South African-born British poet and scholar
Soldiers Bathing, and Other Poems (1945) V
The Doors of Stone (1963) V
Drypoints of the Hasidim (1975) V
Afterword on Rupert Brooke (1976) V
Later On (1983) V
Walks in Rome (1987) V

PRINGLE, Thomas (1789–1834)
Scottish poet and anti-slavery campaigner
Ephemerides (1828) V

PRIOR, Matthew (1664–1721)
English poet and diplomat
The Hind and the Panther Transvers'd (1687) V
Poems on Several Occasions (1709) V
The Dove (1717) V
The Conversation (1720) V
Down-Hall (1723) V

PRITCHETT, [Sir] V[ictor] S[awdon] (1900–1997)
British short-story writer, novelist, critic, and essayist
Marching Spain (1928) NF
Clare Drummer (1929) F
The Spanish Virgin, and Other Stories (1930) F SS
Shirley Sanz (1932) F
Nothing Like Leather (1935) F
Dead Man Leading (1937) F
You Make Your Own Life (1938) F SS
In My Good Books (1942) NF
It May Never Happen, and Other Stories (1945) F SS
The Living Novel (1946) NF
Mr Beluncle (1951) F
Books in General (1953) NF
The Spanish Temper (1954) NF
When My Girl Comes Home (1961) F SS
The Key to My Heart (1963) F SS
The Working Novelist (1965) NF
A Cab at the Door (1968) NF
Blind Love, and Other Stories (1969) F SS
Midnight Oil (1971) NF
The Camberwell Beauty, and Other Stories (1974) F SS
The Myth Makers (1979) NF
On the Edge of the Cliff (1979) F SS
The Tale Bearers (1980) NF
Man of Letters (1986) NF
A Careless Widow, and Other Stories (1989) F SS

PROCTER, Adelaide Anne (1825–1864)
British poet and campaigner for women's rights
Legends and Lyrics [1st ser.; 2nd ser., 1861] (1858) V
The Victoria Regia (1861) ANTH
A Chaplet of Verses (1862) V

PROCTER, Bryan Waller *see* BARRY CORNWALL

PROULX, E[dna] Annie (1935–)
American novelist and short-story writer
Heart Songs, and Other Stories (1988) F SS
Postcards (1992) F
The Shipping News (1993) F
Accordion Crimes (1996) F

PROUST, Marcel (1871–1922)
French novelist
Swann's Way [*Du côté de chez Swann*; *A la recherche du temps perdu* i] (1913) F
Within a Budding Grove [*A l'ombre des jeunes filles en fleurs*; *A la recherche du temps perdu* ii] (1919) F
The Guermantes' Way [*Le Côté de Guermantes*; *A la recherche du temps perdu* iii] (1920–1) F
The Cities of the Plain [*Sodome et Gomorrhe*; *A la recherche du temps perdu* iv] (1921–2) F
The Captive [*La Prisonnière*; *A la recherche du temps perdu* v] (1923) F
The Sweet Cheat Gone [*Albertine disparue*; *A la recherche du temps perdu* vi] (1925) F
Time Regained [*Le Temps retrouvé*; *A la recherche du temps perdu* vii] (1927) F
Jean Santeuil (1952) F

PRYNNE, J[eremy] H[alvard] (1936–)
British poet and academic
Kitchen Poems (1968) V
The White Stones (1969) V
High Pink on Chrome (1975) V
The Oval Window (1983) V
Word Order (1989) V
Triodes (2000) V

PRYNNE, William (1600–1669)
English Puritan pamphleteer
Histrio-mastix (1633) NF
The Opening of the Great Seale of England (1643) NF
The Popish Royall Favourite (1643) NF
The Soveraigne Power of Parliaments and Kingdomes (1643) NF
A Breviate of the Life of William Laud (1644) NF
The Levellers Levelled to the Very Ground (1647) NF
Open the Sky (1934) V

PUDNEY, John [Sleigh] (1909–1977)
British poet, novelist and children's writer
Dispersal Point, and Other Air Poems (1942) V

Beyond This Disregard (1943) V
Almanack of Hope (1944) V
Low Life (1947) V
The Net (1952) F
The Trampoline (1959) V
Thin Air (1961) F

PUGH, Edwin [William] (1874–1930)
British novelist
A Street in Suburbia (1895) F
A Man of Straw (1897) F
King of Circumstance (1898) F
The Enchantress (1908) F

PUGIN, A[ugustus] W[elby] N[orthmore] (1812–1852)
British architect and ecclesiologist
Gothic Furniture in the Style of the 15th Century (1835) NF
The True Principles of Pointed or Christian Architecture (1841) NF
An Apology for the Revival of Christian Architecture in England (1843) NF

PURCHAS, Samuel (1577–1626)
English traveller and author
Purchas His Pilgrimage (1613) NF
Purchas His Pilgrim (1619) NF
Hakluytus Posthumus; or, Purchas His Pilgrimes (1625) NF

PURDY, Al[fred] [Wellington] (1918–)
Canadian poet and novelist
The Enchanted Echo (1944) V
Emu, Remember (1955) V
Pressed on Sand (1955) V
The Crafte So Longe to Lerne (1959) V
Poems for all the Annettes (1962) V
Cariboo Horses (1965) V
North of Summer (1967) V
Wild Grape Wine (1968) V
In Search of Owen Roblin (1974) V
Being Alive (1978) V
The Stone Bird (1981) V

PURDY, James (1923–)
American novelist and short-story writer
Don't Call Me By My Right Name, and Other Stories (1956) F SS
Color of Darkness (1957) F SS
Malcolm (1959) F
The Nephew (1960) F
Cabot Wright Begins (1964) F
Eustace Chisholm and the Works (1967) F
Jeremy's Version (1970) F
I Am Elijah Thrush (1972) F
The House of the Solitary Maggot (1974) F
Narrow Rooms (1978) F
Sleep Tight (1979) F SS
Mourners Below (1981) F
On Glory's Course (1984) F
The Candles of Your Eyes (1985) F SS
In the Hollow of His Hand (1986) F
Garments the Living Wear (1989) F
Out with the Stars (1993) F

PUSEY, E[dward] B[ouverie] (1800–1882)
British theologian and tractarian
The Doctrine of the Real Presence (1855) NF
The Minor Prophets (1860) NF
Daniel the Prophet (1864) NF
An Eirenicon [pt. i; pt. ii, 1869; pt. iii, 1870] (1865) NF
What is of Faith as to Everlasting Punishment? (1880) NF

PUSHKIN, Alexander [Sergeevich] (1799–1837)
Russian poet, dramatist, and short-story writer
Ruslan and Ludmilla (1820) V
The Prisoner of the Caucasus (1820–1) V
The Fountain of Bakhchisarai (1822) V
Eugene Onegin (1823–31) V
The Gypsies (1824) V
Boris Godunov (1825) D
Count Nulin (1825) V
Poltava (1829) V
The Little House in Kolomna (1830) V
The Tales of Belkin (1830) F SS
The Bronze Horseman (1833) V
The Queen of Spades (1834) F
The Captain's Daughter (1836) F

PUTTENHAM, George (1530?–1590)
English critic
The Arte of English Poesie (1589) NF

PUZO, Mario (1920–)
American novelist
The Dark Arena (1955) F
The Fortunate Pilgrim (1965) F
The Godfather (1969) F
Fools Die (1978) F
The Sicilian (1984) F
The Fourth K. (1991) F
Omertà (2000) F

PYE, Henry James (1745–1813)
British poet, Poet Laureate, and dramatist
Beauty (1766) V
The Triumph of Fashion (1771) V
Farringdon Hill (1774) V
Amusement (1790) V
The Siege of Meaux (1794) D
Naucratia; or, Naval Dominion (1798) V
The Aristocrat (1799) F
Adelaide (1800) D
Alfred (1801) V

PYLE, Howard (1853–1911)
American children's writer and illustrator
The Merry Adventures of Robin Hood of Great Renown in Nottinghamshire (1883) F CH
Men of Iron (1892) F CH

PYM, Barbara [Mary Crampton] (1913–1980)
British novelist
Some Tame Gazelle (1950) F
Excellent Women (1952) F
Jane and Prudence (1953) F

Less Than Angels (1955) F
A Glass of Blessings (1959) F
Quartet in Autumn (1977) F
The Sweet Dove Died (1978) F
A Few Green Leaves (1980) F
An Unsuitable Attachment (1982) F
An Academic Question (1986) F

PYNCHON, Thomas (1937–)
American novelist
V. (1963) F
The Crying of Lot 49 (1966) F
Gravity's Rainbow (1973) F
Vineland (1990) F
Mason & Dixon (1997) F

Q

QUARLES, Francis (1592–1644)
English poet
A Feast for Wormes (1620) V
Hadassa; or, The History of Queene Ester (1621) V
Job Militant (1624) V
Sions Elegies, Wept by Jeremie the Prophet (1624) V
Sions Sonets (1625) V
Argalus and Parthenia (1629) V
Divine Poems (1630) V
The Historie of Samson (1631) V
Divine Fancies (1632) V
Emblemes (1635) V
Hieroglyphikes of the Life of Man (1638) V
Enchyridion (1640) V

'QUEEN, Ellery' [Frederic Dannay (1905–1982) and **Manfred B. Lee** (1905–1971)**]**
American crime writers
The Roman Hat Mystery (1929) F
The French Powder Mystery (1930) F
The Dutch Shoe Mystery (1931) F
The Greek Coffin Mystery (1932) F
The Chinese Orange Mystery (1934) F
The Spanish Cape Mystery (1935) F
The Four of Hearts (1938) F
And On the Eighth Day (1964) F
A Fine and Private Place (1971) F

QUENEAU, Raymond (1903–1976)
French novelist and poet
The Bark Tree [Le Chiendent] (1933) F
Pierrot [Pierrot Mon Ami] (1942) F
Exercises in Style [Exercices de style] (1947) MISC
Saint Glinglin (1948) F
Zazie [Zazie dans le Métro] (1959) F
One Hundred Million Million Poems [Cent mille milliards de poèmes] (1961) V

QUENNELL, Peter [Courtney] (1905–1993)
British biographer, critic, essayist, and novelist
Byron: The Years of Fame (1935) NF
Byron in Italy (1941) NF
Four Portraits (1945) NF
The Singular Preference (1952) NF
Casanova in London, and Other Essays (1971) NF
The Marble Foot (1976) NF

QUILLER-COUCH, Sir Arthur [Thomas] ['Q'] (1863–1944)
British novelist, short-story writer, and literary scholar
Dead Man's Rock (1887) F
The Astonishing History of Troy Town (1888) F
The Splendid Spur (1889) F
The Blue Pavilions (1891) F
Noughts and Crosses (1891) F SS
I Saw Three Ships, and Other Winter's Tales (1892) F SS
The Delectable Duchy (1893) F SS
Green Bays (1893) V
Wandering Heath (1895) F SS
Adventures in Criticism (1896) NF
Ia (1896) F
Poems and Ballads (1896) V
The Ship of Stars (1899) F
Old Fires and Profitable Ghosts (1900) F SS
The Oxford Book of English Verse 1250–1900 (1900) ANTH
The Laird's Luck, and Other Fireside Tales (1901) F SS
The White Wolf, and Other Fireside Tales (1902) F SS
The Adventures of Harry Revel (1903) F
Hetty Wesley (1903) F
Two Sides of the Face (1903) F SS
Fort Amity (1904) F
Shakespeare's Christmas, and Other Stories (1905) F SS
Shining Ferry (1905) F
From a Cornish Window (1906) F
The Mayor of Troy (1906) F
Sir John Constantine (1906) F
Major Vigoureux (1907) F
Merry-Garden, and Other Stories (1907) F SS
Poison Island (1907) F
True Tilda (1909) F
Corporal Sam, and Other Stories (1910) F SS
Lady Good-for-Nothing (1910) F SS
The Oxford Book of Ballads (1910) ANTH
The Oxford Book of Victorian Verse (1912) ANTH
News From the Duchy (1913) F
On the Art of Writing (1916) NF
Mortallone and Aunt Trinidad (1917) F SS
On the Art of Reading (1920) NF
The Oxford Book of English Prose (1925) ANTH
Memories and Opinions (1944) NF

QUOIREZ, Françoise *see* FRANÇOISE SAGAN

R

RABAN, Jonathan (1942–)
British travel writer, critic, and novelist
The Technique of Modern Fiction (1968) NF
The Society of the Poem (1971) NF
Soft City (1973) NF

Arabia Through the Looking-Glass (1979) NF
Old Glory: An American Voyage (1981) NF
Foreign Land (1985) F
Coasting (1986) NF
For Love and Money (1987) NF
Hunting Mister Heartbreak (1990) NF
Passage to Juneau (1999) NF

RABELAIS, François (1494?–1553?)
French physician, humanist, and satirist
Pantagruel [as 'Alcofribas Nasier'] (1532/3) F
Gargantua [as 'Alcofribas Nasier'] (1534) F
Tiers Livre ['Third Book'] (1546) F
Quart Livre ['Fourth Book'] (1548–52) F
Cinquième Livre ['Fifth Book'] (1562–4) F

RACINE, Jean (1639–1699)
French dramatist and poet
La Thébaïde; ou Les Frères ennemis ['The Thebaid; or, The Enemy Brothers'] (1664) D
Alexander the Great [*Alexandre le grand*] (1665) D
Andromache [*Andromaque*] (1667) D
The Litigants [*Les Plaideurs*] (1668) D
Britannicus (1669) D
Bérénice (1670) D
Bajazet (1672) D
Mithridates [*Mithridate*] (1673) D
Iphigénie (1675) D
Phaedrus and Hippolytus [*Phèdre et Hippolyte*] (1677) D

RADCLIFFE, Ann, *née* Ward (1764–1823)
British novelist and poet
The Castles of Athlin and Dunbayne (1789) F
A Sicilian Romance (1790) F
The Romance of the Forest (1791) F
The Mysteries of Udolpho (1794) F
A Journey Made in the Summer of 1794 (1795) NF
The Italian; or, The Confessional of the Black Penitents (1797) F
Gaston de Blondeville; or, The Court of Henry III (1826) F V

RAINE, Craig [Anthony] (1944–)
British poet and editor
The Onion, Memory (1978) V
A Martian Sends a Postcard Home (1979) V
Rich (1984) V
Haydn and the Valve Trumpet (1990) NF
History: The Home Movie (1994) V
Clay: Whereabouts Unknown (1996) V
A la recherche du temps perdu (2000) V

RAINE, Kathleen [Jessie] (1908–)
British poet and critic
Stone and Flower (1943) V
Living in Time (1946) V
The Pythoness, and Other Poems (1949) V
The Year One (1952) V
The Hollow Hill, and Other Poems 1960–4 (1965) V
Defending Ancient Springs (1967) NF
Six Dreams, and Other Poems (1968) V
On a Deserted Shore (1973) V
The Oval Portrait, and Other Poems (1977) V
The Oracle in the Heart, and Other Poems 1975–1978 (1980) V
To the Sun (1988) V
Living With Mystery (1992) V

RALEGH [or **RALEIGH] Sir Walter** (1554–1618)
English statesman, soldier, historian, and poet
A Report of the Truth of the Fight About the Iles of the Açores (1591) NF
The Discoverie of the Large, Rich, and Bewtiful Empyre of Guiana (1596) NF
The History of the World (1614) NF
The Prerogative of Parlaments in England (1628) NF
Sir Walter Raleighs Instructions to his Sonne and to Posterity (1632) NF
The Prince; or, Maxims of State (1642) NF
To day a Man, To morrow None (1644) NF
Judicious and Select Essayes and Observations (1650) NF
Sir Walter Raleigh's Sceptick, or Speculations (1651) NF

RALEIGH, Sir Walter [Alexander] (1861–1922)
British literary scholar
The English Novel (1891) NF
Robert Louis Stevenson (1895) NF
Style (1897) NF
Milton (1900) NF
Wordsworth (1903) NF
Shakespeare (1907) NF
Six Essays on Johnson (1910) NF

RAMÉE, Marie Louise de la *see* 'OUIDA'

RAMSAY, Allan (1686–1758)
Scottish poet
Christ's Kirk on the Green [canto i supposedly by James I] (1718) V
Content (1719) V
A Poem on the South Sea (1720) V
Poems (1720) V
Fables and Tales (1722) V
The Fair Assembly (1723) V
The Tea-Table Miscellany [vol. i; vol. ii, 1726; vol. iii, 1727; vol. iv, 1737] (1723) V
Health (1724) V
The Gentle Shepherd (1725) V

RAND, Ayn (1905–1982)
Russian-born American novelist and critic
The Night of January 16th (1935) D
We, the Living (1936) F
Anthem (1938) F
The Fountainhead (1943) F
Atlas Shrugged (1957) F
For the New Intellectual (1961) NF
The Romantic Manifesto (1969) NF

RANDOLPH, Thomas (1605–1635)
English poet and dramatist
Aristippus; or, The Joviall Philosopher (1630) V
The Jealous Lovers (1632) D
Poems, with the Muses Looking-Glasse: and Amyntas (1638) V

RANKIN, Ian (1960–)
Scottish crime writer
The Flood (1986) F
Knots and Crosses (1987) F
Hide and Seek (1991) F
A Good Hanging, and Other Stories (1992) F SS
Strip Jack (1992) F
Tooth and Nail [originally titled *Wolfman*] (1992) F
The Black Book (1993) F
Mortal Causes (1994) F
Let It Bleed (1996) F
Black and Blue (1997) F
Death is Not the End (1998) F
The Hanging Garden (1998) F
Dead Souls (1999) F
Rebus: The Early Years [compilation] (1999) F
Set in Darkness (2000) F

RANSOM, John Crowe (1888–1974)
American poet and critic
Poems About God (1919) V
Chills and Fever (1924) V
Two Gentlemen in Bonds (1927) V
God Without Thunder (1930) NF
The World's Body (1938) NF
Beating the Bushes (1972) NF

RANSOME, Arthur [Michell] (1884–1967)
British author, journalist, children's writer, and illustrator
Bohemia in London (1907) NF
The Hoofmarks of the Faun (1911) F SS
Old Peter's Russian Tales (1916) F CH
Six Weeks in Russia in 1919 (1919) NF
'Racundra's' First Cruise (1923) NF
Swallows and Amazons (1930) F CH
Swallowdale (1931) F CH
Pigeon Post (1936) F CH
We Didn't Mean to Go to Sea (1937) F CH
The Big Six (1940) F CH

RAO, Raja (1909–)
Indian novelist
Kanthapura (1938) F
The Cow of the Barricade, and Other Stories (1947) F SS
The Serpent and the Rope (1960) F
The Cat and Shakespeare (1965) F
Comrade Kirillov (1976) F
The Policeman and the Rose (1978) F SS
On the Ganga Ghat (1989) F SS

RAPHAEL, Frederic [Michael] (1931–)
American-born novelist, dramatist, and critic
Obbligato (1956) F
The Limits of Love (1960) F
A Wild Surmise (1961) F
The Trouble With England (1962) F
Lindmann (1963) F
Orchestra and Beginners (1967) F
Like Men Betrayed (1970) F
Who Were You With Last Night? (1971) F
Richard's Things (1973) F
California Time (1975) F
The Glittering Prizes (1976) F
Oxbridge Blues, and Other Stories (1980) F SS
Oxbridge Blues, and Other Plays for Television (1984) D
Think of England (1986) F SS
After the War (1988) F
A Double Life (1993) F
The Latin Lover, and Other Stories (1994) F SS
Old Scores (1995) F
All His Sons (1999) F SS

RASPE, Rudolph Erich (1737–1794)
German novelist
The Adventures of Baron Münchausen (1785) F SS

RATTIGAN, [Sir] Terence [Mervyn] (1911–1977)
British dramatist
French Without Tears (1936) D
After the Dance (1939) D
Flare Path (1942) D
While the Sun Shines (1943) D
Love in Idleness (1944) D
The Winslow Boy (1946) D
The Browning Version (1948) D
Harlequinade (1948) D
Adventure Story (1949) D
Who is Sylvia? (1950) D
The Deep Blue Sea (1952) D
The Sleeping Prince (1953) D
Separate Tables [*Table by the Window*; *Table Number Seven*] (1954) D
Variations on a Theme (1958) D
Ross (1960) D
Cause Célèbre (1975) D

RATUSHINSKAYA, Irina (1954–)
Russian poet
I'm Not Afraid (1986) V
Grey is the Colour of Hope (1989) NF
In the Beginning (1991) NF
Dance With a Shadow (1992) V

RAVEN, Simon [Arthur Noel] (1927–)
British novelist and dramatist
The Feathers of Death (1959) F
Doctors Wear Scarlet (1960) F
Close of Play (1962) F
Boys Will be Boys, and Other Essays (1963) NF
The Rich Pay Late [first of the *Alms for Oblivion* series] (1964) F
Friends in Low Places (1965) F
The Sabre Squadron (1966) F
Fielding Gray (1967) F
The Judas Boy (1968) F
Places Where They Sing (1970) F
Sound the Retreat (1971) F
Come Like Shadows (1972) F
Bring Forth the Body (1974) F
The Survivors (1976) F
Morning Star [first of *The First-Born of Egypt* series] (1984) F
The Face of the Waters (1985) F

Before the Cock Crow (1986) F
New Seed for Old (1988) F
Blood of My Bone (1989) F
In the Image of God (1990) F
The Troubadour (1992) F

RAVENSCROFT, Edward (1644–1704)
English dramatist
The Citizen Turn'd Gentleman (1672) D
The Careless Lovers (1673) D
The Wrangling Lovers; or, The Invisible Mistress (1676) D
The Italian Husband (1677) D
King Edgar and Alfreda (1677) D
Scaramouch, a Philosopher, Harlequin, a School-boy, Bravo, Merchant and Magician (1677) D
Titus Andronicus; or, The Rape of Lavinia [altered from Shakespeare] (1677) D
The London Cuckolds (1681) D
The Anatomist; or, The Sham Doctor (1696) D

RAVERAT, Gwen[dolen] [Mary] (1885–1957)
British autobiographer
Period Piece: A Cambridge Childhood (1952) NF

RAWLINGS, Marjorie [Kinnan] (1896–1953)
American novelist
South Moon Under (1933) F
Golden Apples (1935) F
The Yearling (1938) F
Whippoorwill (1940) F SS
Cross Creek (1942) F

RAYMOND, Ernest (1888–1974)
British novelist
Tell England (1922) F

REACH, Angus Bethune (1821–1856)
British journalist and novelist
Clement Lorimer; or, The Book with the Iron Clasps (1849) F

READ, Sir Herbert [Edward] (1893–1968)
British poet and critic
Songs of Chaos (1915) V
Eclogues (1919) V
In Retreat (1925) NF
Reason and Romanticism (1926) NF
English Prose Style (1928) NF
The Sense of Glory (1929) NF
The Meaning of Art (1931) NF
Form in Modern Poetry (1932) NF
Art Now (1933) NF
Art and Industry (1934) NF
The Green Child (1935) F
In Defence of Shelley, and Other Essays (1936) NF
Art and Society (1937) NF
Poetry and Anarchism (1938) NF
Annals of Innocence and Experience (1940) NF
A World Within a War (1944) V
The Philosophy of Modern Art (1952) NF
The True Voice of Feeling (1953) NF
Anarchy and Order (1954) NF
Moon's Farm, and Poems Mostly Elegaic (1955) V
The Tenth Muse (1957) NF
The Form of Things Unknown (1960) NF
To Hell with Culture, and Other Essays on Art and Society (1963) NF
Poetry and Experience (1967) NF
The Cult of Sincerity (1968) NF

'READ, Miss' [Dora Jessie Saint] (1913–)
British novelist
Village School (1955) F
Thrush Green (1959) F
The Fairacre Festival (1969) F
The Christmas Mouse (1973) F
No Holly for Miss Quin (1976) F

READ, Piers Paul (1941–)
British novelist
A Game in Heaven with Tussy Marx (1966) F
Monk Dawson (1969) F
The Professor's Daughter (1971) F
The Upstart (1973) F
A Married Man (1979) F
The Villa Golitsyn (1981) F
A Season in the West (1988) F
On the Third Day (1990) F

READE, Charles (1814–1884)
British novelist and dramatist
Christie Johnstone (1853) F
Peg Woffington (1853) F
The King's Rival (1854) D
Masks and Faces; or, Before and Behind the Curtain (1854) D
Two Loves and a Life (1854) D
'It Is Never Too Late To Mend' (1856) F
Poverty and Pride (1856) D
The Course of True Love Never Did Run Smooth (1857) F SS
White Lies (1857) F
'Love Me Little, Love Me Long' (1859) F
The Cloister and the Hearth (1861) F
Hard Cash [US: *Very Hard Cash*] (1863) F
Griffith Gaunt; or, Jealousy (1866) F
Put Yourself in His Place (1870) F
A Terrible Temptation (1871) F
A Simpleton (1873) F
A Woman-Hater (1877) F
Singleheart and Double Face (1882) F
Good Stories of Man and Other Animals [US: *Good Stories*] (1884) F SS
The Jilt, and Other Stories (1884) F SS
A Perilous Secret (1884) F

READE, William Winwood (1838–75)
British poet, novelist, and controversialist
Charlotte and Myra (1859) F
Liberty Hall, Oxon. (1860) F
The Martyrdom of Man (1872) V
The Outcast (1875) F

READING, Peter (1946–)
British poet
For the Municipality's Elderly (1974) V
Nothing For Anyone (1977) V
Tom O' Bedlam's Beauties (1981) V
Ukelele Music (1985) V
Stet (1986) V
Final Demands (1988) V
Perduta Gente (1989) V
Evagatory (1992) V
Ob (1999) V
Apopthegmatic (1999) V
Marfan (2000) V

REDGROVE, Peter [William] (1932–)
British poet, novelist, dramatist, and critic
The Collector, and Other Poems (1959) V
At the White Monument, and Other Poems (1963) V
The Force, and Other Poems (1966) V
The Mother, the Daughter and the Sighing Bridge (1970) V
Dr Faust's Sea-Spiral Spirit, and Other Poems (1972) V
In the Country of the Skin (1973) F
From Every New Chink of the Ark, and Other New Poems (1977) V
The Weddings at Nether Powers, and Other New Poems (1979) V
The Beekeepers (1980) F
The Apple Broadcast, and Other New Poems (1981) V
A Man Named East, and Other New Poems (1985) V
In the Hall of the Saurians (1987) V
Dressed as For a Tarot Pack (1990) V
Under the Reservoir (1992) V
My Father's Trapdoor (1994) V
The Lessons of the War (1970) V

REED, Henry (1914–1986)
British poet, dramatist, and critic
A Map of Verona [inc. 'Naming of Parts'] (1946) V
The Novel Since 1939 (1946) NF
Hilda Tablet, and Other Plays (1971) D
The Streets of Pompeii, and Other Plays (1971) D

REED, Jeremy (1954–)
British poet, novelist, and translator
Bleecker Street (1980) V
No Refuge Here (1981) V
A Man Afraid (1982) V
By the Fisheries (1984) V
The Lipstick Boys (1984) F
Nero (1985) V
Engaging Form (1988) V
Nineties (1990) V
Isidore (1991) F
Black Sugar (1992) V
When the Whip Comes Down (1992) F
Turkish Delight (1993) V
Diamond Nebula (1994) F
Kicks (1994) V

REED, Talbot Baines (1852–1893)
British boy's writer
The Adventures of a Three-Guinea Watch (1880) F CH
The Fifth Form at St Dominic's (1882) F CH
My Friend Smith (1882) F CH
The Willougby Captains (1887) F CH
Roger Ingleton Minor (1891) F CH
The Master of the Shell (1894) F CH

REEVE, Clara (1729–1807)
British novelist
The Champion of Virtue (1777) F
The Old English Baron [2nd edn of *The Champion of Virtue*] (1778) F
The Two Mentors (1783) F
The Progress of Romance (1785) NF
The Exiles; or, Memoirs of the Count de Cronstadt (1788) F
The School for Widows (1791) F
Memoirs of Sir Roger de Clarendon (1793) F
Destination; or, Memoirs of a Private Family (1799) F

REEVES, James [John Morris] (1909–1978)
British poet, critic, and children's writer
The Natural Need (1935) V
The Imprisoned Sea (1949) V
The Wandering Moon (1950) V CH
The Blackbird in the Lilac (1952) V CH
The Password, and Other Poems (1952) V
Pigeons and Princesses (1956) F CH
The Talking Skull (1958) V
Sailor Rumbelow and Britannia (1962) F CH
The Questioning Tiger (1964) V
Subsong (1969) V

REID, Christopher [John] (1949–)
British poet
Arcadia (1979) V
Pea Soup (1982) V
Katerina Brac (1985) V
In the Echoey Tunnel (1991) V
Universe (1994) V

REID, Forrest (1875–1947)
Ulster novelist
The Kingdom of Twilight (1904) F
The Garden God (1905) F
The Bracknels [rev. 1947 as *Denis Bracknel*] (1911) F
Following Darkness [rev. 1937 as *Peter Waring*] (1912) F
The Gentle Lover (1913) F
At the Door of the Gate (1915) F
Pirates of the Spring (1919) F
Apostate (1926) NF
Demophon (1927) F
Uncle Stephen (1931) F
The Retreat; or, The Machinations of Henry (1936) F
Private Road (1940) NF
Young Tom; or, Very Mixed Company (1944) F

REID, Thomas (1710–1796)
Scottish philosopher
An Inquiry into the Human Mind (1764) NF
Essays on the Intellectual Powers of Man (1785) NF
Essays on the Active Powers of Man (1788) NF

REID, [Captain] [Thomas] Mayne (1818–1883)
British boys' writer
The Rifle Rangers; or Adventures of an Officer in Southern Mexico (1850) F
The Scalp Hunters; or, Romantic Adventures in Northern Mexico (1851) F
The Boy Hunters; or, Adventures in Search of a White Buffalo (1852) F CH
The Desert Home; or, The Adventures of a Lost Family in the Wilderness [subtitled 'The English Family Robinson'] (1852) F
The Forest Exiles; or, The Perils of a Peruvian Family Amid the Wilds of the Amazon (1855) F
The Hunters' Feast; or, Conversations Around the Camp-Fire (1855) F
The White Huntress (1861) F
The Maroon (1862) F
Lost Lenore; or, The Adventures of a Rolling Stone (1864) F
The Headless Horseman (1866) F CH
The Giraffe Hunters (1867) F
The Child Wife (1868) F
The Castaways (1870) F CH
The Death Shot (1873) F
Gwen Wynn (1877) F

REID, V[ictor] S[tafford] (1913–1987)
Jamaican novelist
New Day (1949) F
The Leopard (1958) F

'REMARQUE, Erich Maria' [Erich Paul Remark] (1898–1970)
German novelist
All Quiet on the Western Front [*Im Westen nichts Neues*] (1929) F
The Road Back [*Der Weg zurück*] (1931) F
Flotsam (1941) F
Arch of Triumph [*Arc de Triomphe*] (1946) F
The Black Obelisk [*Der schwartz Obelisk*] (1956) F
The Night in Lisbon [*Die Nacht von Lisbon*] (1962) F

'RENAULT, Mary' [Eileen Mary Challans] (1905–1983)
British novelist
Purposes of Love (1939) F
The Charioteer (1953) F
The Last of the Wine (1956) F
The King Must Die (1958) F
The Bull From the Sea (1962) F
The Mask of Apollo (1966) F
Fire From Heaven [first of the *Alexander Trilogy*] (1969) F
The Persian Boy (1972) F
Funeral Games (1981) F

RENDELL, Ruth [Barbara], *née* Grasemann ['Barbara Vine'] (1930–)
British writer of detective fiction and psychological thrillers
From Doon With Death [first Inspector Wexford novel] (1964) F
To Fear a Painted Devil (1965) F
Wolf to the Slaughter (1967) F
The Best Man to Die (1969) F
A Guilty Thing Surprised (1970) F
No More Dying, Then (1971) F
A Judgement in Stone (1977) F
The Lake of Darkness (1980) F
Master of the Moor (1982) F
The Speaker of Mandarin (1983) F
An Unkindness of Ravens (1985) F
A Dark Adapted Eye [as 'Barbara Vine'] (1986) F
A Fatal Inversion [as 'Barbara Vine'] (1987) F
Gallowglass [as 'Barbara Vine'] (1990) F
Kissing the Gunner's Daughter (1992) F
The Crocodile Bird (1993) F
Simisola (1994) F
The Brimstone Wedding [as 'Barbara Vine'] (1996) F
The Keys to the Street (1996) F
Road Rage (1997) F
The Chimney-Sweeper's Boy [as 'Barbara Vine'] (1998) F
A Sight for Sore Eyes (1998) F
Harm Done (1999) F
The Grasshopper [as 'Barbara Vine'] (2000) F

REXROTH, Kenneth (1905–1982)
American poet and non-fiction writer
In What Hour (1940) V
The Phoenix and the Tortoise (1944) V
The Signature of All Things (1949) V
Beyond the Mountains (1951) V
In Defence of the Earth (1956) V
Bird in the Bush (1959) NF
Assays (1961) NF
Natural Numbers (1963) V
The Alternative Society (1971) NF
With Eye and Ear (1971) NF
The Elastic Retort (1974) NF

REYNOLDS, J[ohn] H[amilton] (1796–1852)
British poet
The Eden of the Imagination (1814) V
Safie (1814) V
The Naiad: A Tale, with Other Poems (1816) V
Benjamin the Waggoner (1819) V
Peter Bell (1819) V
The Garden of Florence, and Other Poems (1821) V
The Press; or, Literary Chit-Chat (1822) V

REYNOLDS, Sir Joshua (1723–1792)
British painter and author
A Discourse, Delivered at the Opening of the Royal Academy [the first of Reynolds' *Discourses*; the fifteenth and last pub. 1791; collected 1820] (1769) NF

'RHYS, Jean' [Ella Gwendolyn Rees Williams] (1890–1979)
British novelist
The Left Bank, and Other Stories (1927) F SS
Postures [US: *Quartet*] (1928) F
After Leaving Mr Mackenzie (1931) F
Voyage in the Dark (1934) F
Good Morning, Midnight (1939) F
Wide Sargasso Sea (1966) F
Tigers Are Better Looking (1968) F SS
Sleep it Off, Lady (1976) F SS
Smile Please (1979) NF

RICARDO, David (1772–1823)
British political economist
Proposals for an Economical and Secure Currency (1816) NF
On the Principles of Political Economy and Taxation (1817) NF

RICE, Anne, *née* O'Brien (1941–)
American novelist
Interview with the Vampire [first of the Vampire Chronicles] (1976) F
The Claiming of Sleeping Beauty [as 'A.N. Roquelaure'] (1983) F
Beauty's Punishment [as 'A.N. Roquelaure'] (1984) F
Beauty's Release [as 'A.N. Roquelaure'] (1985) F
The Vampire Lestat (1985) F
The Queen of the Damned (1988) F
The Mummy; or, Ramses the Damned (1989) F
The Witching Hour (1990) F
Taltos (1994) F
The Servant of the Bones (1996) F
Vittorio (1999) F

RICE, Elmer [Elmer Leopold Reizenstein] (1892–1967)
American playwright and novelist
On Trial (1914) D
Morningside Plays (1917) D
Wake Up, Jonathan (1921) D
The Adding Machine (1923) D
Close Harmony (1929) D
See Naples and Die (1929) D
Street Scene (1929) D
A Voyage to Purilia (1930) F
We, the People (1933) D
Between Two Worlds (1934) D
Judgment Day (1934) D
Imperial City (1937) F
American Landscape (1938) D
Two on an Island (1940) D
Flight to the West (1941) D
A New Life (1943) D
The Show Must Go On (1949) F
The Living Theatre (1959) NF
Minority Report (1963) NF

RICH, Adrienne [Cecile] (1929–)
American poet
A Change of World (1951) V
The Diamond Cutters (1955) V
Snapshots of a Daughter-in-Law (1963) V
Necessities of Life (1966) V
Leaflets (1969) V
The Will to Change (1971) V
Diving into the Wreck (1973) V
Of Woman Born (1976) NF
The Dream of a Common Language (1978) V
A Wild Patience Has Taken Me This Far (1981) V
The Fact of a Doorframe (1984) V
Your Native Land, Your Life (1986) V
Blood, Bread, and Poetry (1987) NF
Time's Power (1989) V

RICH, Barnabe (1542–1617)
English romance writer, pamphleteer, and soldier
A Dialogue, Betwene Mercury and an English Souldier (1574) F
Allarme to England (1578) NF
Riche his Farewell to Militarie Profession (1581) F
The Straunge and Wonderfull Adventures of Don Simonides, [vol. i; vol. ii 1584] (1581) F
A Path-way to Military Practise (1587) NF
The Adventures of Brusanus, Prince of Hungaria (1592) F
A New Description of Ireland (1610) NF
The Excellency of Good Women (1613) NF

'RICHARDS, Frank' [Charles Harold St John Hamilton] (1876–1961)
British writer of school stories and creator of Billy Bunter
Billy Bunter of Greyfriars School [the first Billy Bunter book] (1947) F

RICHARDS, I[vor] A[rmstrong] (1893–1979)
British critic and poet
The Meaning of Meaning (1923) NF
Principles of Literary Criticism (1924) NF
Science and Poetry (1926) NF
Practical Criticism (1929) NF
Mencius on the Mind (1932) NF
Coleridge on Imagination (1934) NF
Speculative Instruments (1955) NF
Goodbye Earth, and Other Poems (1958) V
The Screens, and Other Poems (1960) V
Internal Colloquies (1972) V

RICHARDSON, Dorothy M[iller] (1873–1957)
British novelist
Pointed Roofs (1915) F
Backwater (1916) F
Honeycomb (1917) F
Interim (1919) F
The Tunnel (1919) F
Deadlock (1921) F
Revolving Lights (1923) F
The Trap (1925) F
Oberland (1927) F
Dawn's Left Hand (1931) F

Clear Horizon (1935) F
Pilgrimage (1938) F

'RICHARDSON, Henry Handel' [Ethel Florence Lindesay Robertson, *née* Richardson] (1870–1946)
Australian novelist
Maurice Guest (1908) F
The Getting of Wisdom (1910) F
Australia Felix [first of *The Fortunes of Richard Mahony* trilogy] (1917) F
The Way Home (1925) F
Ultima Thule (1929) F
Two Studies (1931) F SS
The End of a Childhood (1934) F SS
The Adventures of Cuffy Mahoney (1979) F SS

RICHARDSON, Samuel (1689–1761)
English novelist
Letters Written to and for Particular Friends [known as *The Familiar Letter*] (1741) NF
Pamela; or, Virtue Rewarded [vols. i, ii] (1741) F
Pamela; or, Virtue Rewarded [vols. iii, iv] (1742) F
Clarissa; or, The History of a Young Lady [vols. i, ii] (1748) F
The History of Sir Charles Grandison (1754) F

RICHLER, Mordecai (1931–)
Canadian novelist and non-fiction writer
The Acrobats (1954) F
Son of a Smaller Hero (1955) F
A Choice of Enemies (1957) F
The Apprenticeship of Duddy Kravitz (1959) F
The Incomparable Atuk [US: *Stick Your Neck Out*] (1963) F
Cocksure (1968) F
Hunting Tigers Under Glass (1968) NF
St Urbain's Horseman (1971) F
Shovelling Trouble (1972) NF
Notes on an Endangered Species (1974) NF
Joshua Then and Now (1980) F
Home Sweet Home (1984) NF
Solomon Gursky Was Here (1989) F
This Year in Jerusalem (1994) NF
Barney's Version (1997) F

RICHTER, Conrad [Michael] (1890–1968)
American novelist
The Sea of Grass (1937) F
The Trees (1940) F
Tacey Cromwell (1942) F
The Free Man (1943) F
The Fields (1946) F
Always Young and Fair (1947) F
The Town (1950) F
Light in the Forest (1953) F
The Lady (1957) F
The Waters of Kronos (1960) F
A Simple Honorable Man (1962) F
The Grandfathers (1964) F
The Rawhide Knot (1978) F SS
Writing to Survive (1988) NF

RICKS, Christopher (1933–)
British literary critic and editor
Milton's Grand Style (1963) NF
Keats and Embarrassment (1974) NF

RICKWORD, [John] Edgell (1898–1982)
British poet, critic, and editor
Behind the Eyes (1921) V
Rimbaud (1924) NF
Invocations to Angels (1928) V

RIDDELL, Charlotte Elizabeth Lawson, *née* Cowan [Mrs J.H. Riddell] (1832–1906)
British novelist and short-story writer
The Moors and the Fens (1858) F
Too Much Alone [as 'F.G. Trafford'] (1860) F
City and Suburb [as 'F.G. Trafford'] (1861) F
George Geith of Fen Court [as 'F.G. Trafford'] (1864) F
Maxwell Drewitt [as 'F.G. Trafford'] (1865) F
The Race for Wealth (1866) F
Austin Friars (1870) F
A Life's Assize (1871) F
The Earl's Promise (1873) F
Home, Sweet Home (1873) F
Frank Sinclair's Wife, and Other Stories (1874) F SS
Mortomley's Estate (1874) F
Above Suspicion (1876) F
Her Mother's Darling (1877) F
Fairy Water (1878) F
The Mystery in Palace Gardens (1880) F
Alaric Spenceley; or, A High Ideal (1881) F
The Senior Partner (1881) F
Daisies and Buttercups (1882) F
The Prince of Wales's Garden Party, and Other Stories (1882) F SS
A Struggle for Fame (1883) F
Berna Boyle (1884) F
Susan Drummond (1884) F
Weird Stories (1884) F SS
Mitre Court (1885) F
Miss Gascoigne (1887) F
Idle Tales (1888) F SS
The Nun's Curse (1888) F
Princess Sunshine, and Other Stories (1889) F SS
The Head of the Firm (1892) F
A Silent Tragedy (1893) F
Did He Deserve It? (1897) F
A Rich Man's Daughter (1897) F
Handsome Phil, and Other Stories (1899) F SS
Poor Fellow! (1902) F

RIDGE, William Pett (1860–1930)
British novelist
Eighteen of Them (1894) F SS
A Clever Wife (1895) F
The Second Opportunity of Mr Staplehurst (1896) F
Secretary to Bayne, M.P. (1897) F
Mord Em'ly (1898) F
A Son of the State (1899) F
A Breaker of Laws (1900) F
Erb (1903) F

Mrs Galer's Business (1905) F
Sixty-nine Birnam Road (1908) F
Nine to Six-Thirty (1910) F

RIDING, Laura (1901–1991)
American-born poet, novelist, and critic
The Close Chaplet (1926) V
A Survey of Modernist Poetry (1927) NF
Contemporaries and Snobs (1928) NF
Love as Love, Death as Death (1928) V
Poet: A Lying Word (1933) V
Progress of Stories (1935) F SS
A Trojan Ending (1937) F
Lives of Wives (1939) F

RIDLER, Anne [Barbara], *née* Bradby (1912–)
British poet, dramatist, and anthologist
The Nine Bright Shiners (1943) V
Henry Bly, and Other Plays (1950) D
The Golden Bird, and Other Poems (1951) V
The Trial of Thomas Cranmer (1956) D
A Matter of Life and Death (1959) V
Some Time After, and Other Poems (1972) V
Italian Prospect (1976) V

RIDLEY, James (1736–1765)
British fiction writer
The History of James Lovegrove, Esquire (1761) F
The Tales of the Genii (1764) F

RIMBAUD, [Jean-Nicholas-] Arthur (1854–1891)
French poet
The Drunken Boat [*Le Bateau ivre*] (1871) V
A Season in Hell [*Une saison en enfer*] (1873) V
Les Illuminations [prose and verse poems] (1886) V

RITCHIE, Lady Anne Isabella, *née* Thackeray (1837–1919)
British novelist, biographer, and essayist
The Story of Elizabeth (1863) F
The Village on the Cliff (1867) F
Old Kensington (1873) F
Bluebeard's Keys, and Other Stories (1874) F SS
Miss Angel (1875) F
Mrs Dymond (1885) F
Records of Tennyson, Ruskin, Robert and Elizabeth Browning (1892) NF
Alfred, Lord Tennyson and His Friends (1893) NF
Chapters From Some Memoirs (1894) NF

RIVERA, José Eustacio (1889–1928)
Colombian novelist
The Vortext [*La Vorágine*] (1924) F

ROBBE-GRILLET, Alain (1922–)
French novelist and critic
The Erasers [*Les Gommes*] (1953) F
In the Labyrinth [*Dans le labyrinthe*] (1959) F
Last Year at Marienbad [*L'Année dernière à Marienbad*; film scenario] (1961)
Towards a New Novel [*Pour un nouveau roman*] (1963) NF

ROBBINS, Harold (1912–)
American popular novelist
Never Love a Stranger (1948) F
The Dream Merchants (1949) F
A Stone for Danny Fisher (1952) F
The Carpetbaggers (1961) F
The Betsy (1971) F
The Pirate (1974) F

ROBBINS, Tom [Thomas Eugene] (1936–)
American novelist
Another Roadside Attraction (1971) F
Even Cowgirls Get the Blues (1976) F
Still Life with Woodpecker (1980) F
Jitterbug Perfume (1984) F
Skinny Legs and All (1990) F
Half Asleep in Frog Pajamas (1994) F

ROBERTS, Sir Charles G[eorge] D[ouglas] (1860–1943)
Canadian poet, novelist, and short-story writer
Orion, and Other Poems (1880) V
In Divers Tones (1886) V
Songs of the Common Day (1893) V
Earth's Enigmas (1896) F SS
The Forge in the Forest (1896) F
New York Nocturnes, and Other Poems (1898) V
A Sister to Evangeline (1898) F
By the Marshes of Minas (1900) F SS
The Heart of the Ancient Wood (1900) F
Barbara Ladd (1902) F
The Kindred of the Wild (1902) F SS
The Book of the Rose (1903) V
The Prisoner of Mademoiselle (1904) F
The Watchers of the Trails (1904) F SS
Red Fox (1905) F SS
The Heart That Knows (1906) F
The Haunters of the Silences (1907) F SS
In the Deep of the Snow (1907) F
The House in the Water (1908) F SS
The Backwoods-men (1909) F
Kings in Exile (1910) F SS
More Kindred of the Wild (1911) F SS
Neighbours Unknown (1911) F SS
Babes of the Wild (1912) F SS
The Feet of the Furtive (1912) F SS
Hoof and Claw (1914) F SS
The Secret Trails (1914) F SS
The Ledge on Bald Face (1918) F SS
Wisdom of the Wilderness (1922) F SS
They Who Walk in the Wild (1924) F SS
The Vagrant of Time (1927) V
Eyes of the Wilderness (1933) F
The Iceberg, and Other Poems (1934) V
Canada Speaks of Britain, and Other Poems of the War (1941) V

ROBERTS, Michael [William Edward] (1902–1948)
British poet, critic, and editor
These Our Matins (1930) V
Critique of Poetry (1934) NF
The Faber Book of Modern Verse (1936) NF

The Modern Mind (1937) NF
Orion Marches (1939) V
The Recovery of the West (1941) NF

ROBERTS, Michèle [Brigitte] (1949-)
British novelist and poet
A Piece of the Night (1978) F
The Visitation (1983) F
The Wild Girl (1984) F
The Book of Mrs Noah (1987) F
In the Red Kitchen (1990) F
Psyche and the Hurricane (1991) F
Daughters of the House (1992) F
During Mother's Absence (1993) F
Flesh and Blood (1994) F
Impossible Saints (1997) F
The Looking Glass (2000) F

ROBERTSON, Ethel Florence Lindesay *see* HENRY HANDEL RICHARDSON

ROBERTSON, T[homas] W[illiam] (1829-1871)
British dramatist
Society (1865) D
Ours (1866) D
Caste (1867) D

ROBERTSON, William (1721-1793)
Scottish historian
The History of Scotland During the Reigns of Mary and James VI (1759) NF
The History of the Reign of the Emperor Charles V (1769) NF
The History of America (1777) NF

ROBINSON, Edwin Arlington (1869-1935)
American poet
The Torrent, and the Night Before (1896) V
The Children of the Night (1897) V
Captain Craig (1902) V
The Town Down the River (1910) V
Van Zorn (1914) D
The Man Against the Sky (1916) V
Merlin (1917) V
Lancelot (1920) V
The Three Taverns (1920) V
Avon's Harvest (1921) V
Roman Bartholow (1923) V
The Man Who Died Twice (1924) V
Tristram (1927) V
Cavender's House (1929) V
The Glory of the Nightingales (1930) V
Matthias at the Door (1931) V
Nicodemus (1932) V
Talifer (1933) V
Amaranth (1934) V
King Jasper (1935) V

ROBINSON, Emma (1814-1890)
British novelist
Whitefriars; or, The Days of Charles the Second (1844) F
Whitehall; or, The Days of Charles the First (1845) F
Caesar Borgia (1846) F
The Maid of Orleans (1849) F
Owen Tudor (1849) F
The Gold Worshippers; or, The Days We Live In (1851) F
The City Banker; or, Love or Money (1856) F
Mauleverer's Divorce (1858) F

ROBINSON, [Esmé Stuart] Lennox (1886-1958)
Irish dramatist and theatre manager
The Cross-Roads (1909) D
Two Plays [Harvest; The Clancy Name] (1911) D
The Whiteheaded Boy (1920) D
Crabbed Youth and Age (1924) D
The Big House (1928) D
The Far-Off Hills (1931) D
Is Life Worth Living? (1933) D

ROBINSON, Henry Crabb (1775-1867)
British lawyer, journalist, and diarist
The Diary, Reminiscences, and Correspondence of Henry Crabb Robinson (1869) NF

ROBINSON, Mary [Mrs Thomas], *née* Darby ['Perdita'] (1758-1800)
British actress, novelist, and poet
Captivity: A Poem; and Celadon and Lydia: A Tale (1777) V
Vancenza; or, The Dangers of Credulity (1792) F
The Widow (1794) F
Angelina (1796) F
Hubert de Sevrac (1796) F
Sappho and Phaon (1796) V
Walsingham; or, The Pupil of Nature (1797) F
The False Friend (1799) F
A Letter to the Women of England on the Injustice of Mental Subordination [as 'Anne Frances Randall'] (1799) NF
The Natural Daughter (1799) F
Lyrical Tales (1800) V

ROCHESTER, 2nd Earl of *see* JOHN WILMOT

RODENBACH, Georges (1855-1898)
Belgian poet and novelist
Bruges-la-morte (1892) F

RODGERS, W[illiam] R[obert] (1909-1969)
Northern Irish poet, critic, and novelist
Awake! and Other Poems (1941) V
Europa and the Bull, and Other Poems (1952) V
Irish Literary Portraits (1972) NF

ROETHKE, Theodore [Huebner] (1908-1963)
American poet
Open House (1941) V
The Lost Son (1948) V
Praise to the End! (1951) V
The Waking (1953) V
Words for the Wind (1958) V
I Am! Says the Lamb (1961) V
The Far Field (1964) V

ROGERS, Jane (1952–)
British novelist
Separate Tracks (1983) F
Her Living Image (1984) F
The Ice is Singing (1987) F
Mr Wroe's Virgins (1991) F
Promised Lands (1995) F

ROGERS, Samuel (1763–1855)
British poet
An Ode to Superstition, with Some Other Poems (1786) V
The Pleasures of Memory (1792) V
An Epistle to a Friend, with Other Poems (1798) V
The Voyage of Columbus (1810) V
Poems (1812) V
Human Life (1819) V
Italy: A Poem. Part the First (1822) V
Italy: A Poem. Part the Second (1828) V
Recollections of the Table-Talk of Samuel Rogers, with a Memoir (1856) V

ROGERS, Will[iam] [Penn Adair] (1879–1935)
American actor and humorist
The Cowboy Philosopher on Prohibition (1919) NF
The Illiterate Digest (1924) NF

'ROHMER, Sax' [Arthur Henry Sarsfield Ward] (1883–1959)
British popular thriller writer
The Mystery of Dr Fu-Manchu [US: *The Insidious Dr Fu-Manchu*] (1913) F
The Devil Doctor [US: *The Return of Dr Fu-Manchu*] (1916) F
Brood of the Witch-Queen (1918) F

ROLFE, Frederick William [Serafino Austin Lewis Mary, 'Baron Corvo'] (1860–1913)
British novelist and author
Stories Toto Told Me (1898) F SS
Chronicles of the House of Borgia (1901) NF
In His Own Image (1901) F SS
Hadrian the Seventh (1904) F
Don Tarquinio (1905) F
The Desire and Pursuit of the Whole (1934) F
Hubert's Arthur (1935) F

ROMER, Stephen (1957–)
British poet
Idols (1986) V
Plato's Ladder (1992) V

RONSARD, Pierre de (1524–1585)
French poet
Odes (1550) V
Amours ['Love Poems'] (1552) V
Bocage ['Grove'] (1554) V
Hymnes (1555) V
Amours [conclusion] (1556) V
La Franciade ['The Hymn of France'; unfinished] (1572) V

ROSCOE, William [Stanley] (1753–1831)
British historian and poet
Mount Pleasant (1777) V
The Wrongs of Africa (1787) V
The Butterfly's Ball and the Grasshopper's Feast (1807) V CH

ROSENBERG, Isaac (1890–1918)
British poet and painter
Night and Day (1912) V
Youth (1915) V
Moses (1916) D V
Collected Works (1937) MISC

ROSENTHAL, Jack [Morris] (1931–)
British dramatist and television writer
The Evacuees (1975) D
Barmitzvah Boy (1976) D
Spend, Spend, Spend (1977) D
London's Burning (1986) D

ROSS, Alan [John] (1922–)
British poet and editor
Summer Thunder (1941) V
The Derelict Day (1947) V
Time Was Away (1948) NF
The Forties (1950) NF
The Bandit on the Billiard Table (1954) NF
Something of the Sea (1954) V
To Whom It May Concern (1958) V
African Negatives (1962) V
North From Sicily (1965) V
Tropical Ice (1972) V
The Taj Express (1973) V
Open Sea (1975) V
After Pusan (1995) V

ROSS, [James] Sinclair (1908–)
Canadian novelist and short-story writer
As For Me and My House (1941) F
The Well (1958) F
The Lamp at Noon, and Other Stories (1968) F SS
Whir of Gold (1970) F
Sawbones Memorial (1974) F
The Race, and Other Stories (1982) F SS

ROSSETTI, Christina [Georgina] (1830–1894)
British poet
Verses by Christina G. Rossetti (1847) V
Goblin Market, and Other Poems (1862) V
The Prince's Progress, and Other Poems (1866) V
Commonplace, and Other Short Stories (1870) F SS
Sing-Song (1872) V
Called to be Saints (1881) NF V
A Pageant, and Other Poems (1881) V
Time Flies (1885) NF V
Poems (1890) V
The Face of the Deep (1892) NF V
New Poems, Hitherto Unpublished and Uncollected (1896) V

ROSSETTI, Dante Gabriel (1828–1882)
British poet and artist
The Early Italian Poets (1861) V
Poems (1870) V
Ballads and Sonnets (1881) V

ROSSETTI, W[illiam] M[ichael] (1829–1910)
British critic and biographer
Swinburne's Poems and Ballads (1866) NF
Lives of Famous Poets (1878) NF
Memoir of Percy Bysshe Shelley (1886) NF
Dante Gabriel Rossetti as Designer and Writer (1889) NF

ROSTAND, Edmond (1868–1918)
French poet and dramatist
Les Musardises ['Dawdlings'] (1890) V
Cyrano de Bergerac (1897) D
L'Aiglon (1900) D
Chantecler (1910) D

ROSTEN, Leo (1908–)
American novelist, anthologist, and social scientist
*The Education of H*y*m*a*n K*a*p*l*a*n* [as 'Leonard Q. Ross'] (1937) F
*The Return of H*y*m*a*n K*a*p*l*a*n* [as 'Leonard Q. Ross'] (1959) F
Captain Newman, M.D. (1961) F
The Joys of Yiddish (1968) NF
*O K*a*p*l*a*n! My K*a*p*l*a*n!* [as 'Leonard Q. Ross'] (1976) F

ROTH, Henry (1906–1995)
American novelist
Call It Sleep (1934) F

ROTH, Philip (1933–)
American novelist
Goodbye, Columbus, and Five Short Stories (1959) F SS
Letting Go (1962) F
When She Was Good (1967) F
Portnoy's Complaint (1969) F
Our Gang (Starring Tricky and His Friends) (1971) F
The Breast (1972) F
The Great American Novel (1973) F
My Life as a Man (1974) F
The Professor of Desire (1977) F
The Ghost Writer (1979) F
Zuckerman Unbound (1981) F
The Anatomy Lesson (1984) F
Zuckerman Bound (1985) F
The Counterlife (1987) F
Deception (1990) F
Operation Shylock: A Confession (1993) F

ROUSSEAU, Jean-Jacques (1712–1778)
French novelist and social philosopher
A Discourse on the Arts and Sciences [*Discours sur les sciences et les arts*] (1750) NF
Discourse on Inequality [*Discours sur l'origine de l'inégalité*] (1755) NF
A Letter to M. Alembert [*Lettre à d'Almebert sur les spectacles*] (1758) NF
Julie; or, The New Eloise [*Julie; ou la Nouvelle Héloïse*] (1761) F
Émile (1762) F
The Social Contract [*Du contrat social*] (1762) NF
The Confessions [*Les Confessions*] (1781–8) NF
The Reveries of a Solitary Walker [*Les Rêveries du promeneur solitaire*] (1782) NF

ROWE, Nicholas (1674–1718)
English Poet Laureate and dramatist
The Ambitious Step-Mother (1700) D
Tamerlane (1701) D
The Fair Penitent (1703) D
Ulysses (1705) D
The Royal Convert (1707) D
The Works of Mr William Shakespear, Revis'd and Corrected (1709) MISC
The Tragedy of Jane Shore (1714) D
The Tragedy of the Lady Jane Grey (1715) D

ROWLANDS, Samuel (1570?–1630?)
English poet and satirist
The Betraying of Christ (1598) V
The Letting of Humors Blood in the Head-vaine (1600) V
Tis Merrie When Gossips Meete (1602) V
Diogines Lanthorne (1607) V
Humors Looking Glasse (1608) V
Good Newes and Bad Newes (1622) V

ROWLEY, Samuel (d. 1624)
English dramatist
When You See Me, You Know Me; or, The Famous Chronicle Historie of King Henry the Eight (1605) D
The Noble Souldier; or, A Contract Broken, Justly Reveng'd (1634) D

ROWLEY, William (1585?–1626)
English dramatist
A Search for Money (1609) D
A New Wonder; a Woman Never Vext (1632) D
All's Lost by Lust (1633) D
A Match at Mid-night (1633) D
A Shoo-Maker a Gentleman (1637) D
The Witch of Edmonton (1658) D

ROWLING, J[oanne] K. (1965–)
British children's author
Harry Potter and the Philosopher's Stone (1997) F CH
Harry Potter and the Chamber of Secrets (1998) F CH
Harry Potter and the Prisoner of Azkaban (1999) F CH
Harry Potter and the Goblet of Fire (2000) F CH

ROWSE, A[lfred] L[eslie] (1903–1997)
British historian and autobiographer
A Cornish Childhood (1942) NF
The English Spirit (1944) NF
The Use of History (1946) NF
The English Past (1951) NF
An Elizabethan Garland (1953) NF
William Shakespeare (1963) NF
Shakespeare's Sonnets (1964) EDN
Shakespeare the Man (1973) NF
Simon Forman (1974) NF

ROWSON, Susanna, *née* Haswell (1762–1824)
British-born American novelist, dramatist, and actress
Victoria (1786) F

The Inquisitor; or, Invisible Rambler (1788) F
Charlotte [later retitled *Charlotte Temple*] (1791) F
Mentoria; or, The Young Lady's Friend (1791) F
The Fille de Chambre [reprtd 1814 as *Rebecca; or, The Fille de Chambre*] (1792) F
Reuben and Rachel; or, Tales of Old Times (1799) F

RUBENS, Bernice [Ruth] (1923–)
British novelist
Madame Sousatzka (1962) F
The Elected Member [US: *The Chosen People*] (1969) F
Sunday Best (1971) F
I Sent a Letter to My Love (1975) F
The Ponsonby Post (1977) F
A Five Year Sentence [US: *Favours*] (1978) F
Spring Sonata (1979) F
Birds of Passage (1981) F
The Brothers (1983) F
Mr Wakefield's Crusade (1985) F
Our Father (1987) F
Kingdom Come (1990) F
A Solitary Grief (1991) F
Mother Russia (1992) F
Autobiopsy (1993) F
Yesterday in the Back Lane (1995) F
The Waiting Game (1997) F
I, Dreyfus (1999) F

RUCK, Berta [Amy Roberta] (1878–1978)
British romantic novelist
His Official Fiancée (1914) F
The Courtship of Rosamond Fayre (1915) F
Arabella the Awful (1918) F
The Girl Who Proposed! (1918) F

RUDKIN, [James] David (1936–)
British dramatist
Afore Night Come (1960) D
Ashes (1974) D
The Sons of Light (1976) D

RULE, Jane (1931–)
Canadian novelist and short-story writer
Desert of the Heart (1964) F
This Is Not For You (1970) F
Against the Season (1971) F
Lesbian Images (1975) NF
Themes for Diverse Instruments (1975) F SS
The Young in One Another's Arms (1977) F
Contract with the World (1980) F
Outlander (1981) F SS
Inland Passages (1985) F SS
Memory Board (1987) F

RUMENS, Carol[-Ann] (1944–)
British poet, novelist, and editor
A Strange Girl in Bright Colours (1973) V
A Necklace of Mirrors (1978) V
Unplayed Music (1981) V
Star Whisper (1983) V
Direct Dialling (1985) V
Plato Park (1987) F
The Greening of Snow Beach (1988) V
From Berlin to Heaven (1990) V

RUNCIMAN, Sir [James Cochran] Steven[son] (1903–)
British historian
The Emperor Romanus Lecapenus (1929) NF
The First Bulgarian Empire (1930) NF
Byzantine Civilisation (1933) NF
A History of the Crusades (1951–4) NF
The Eastern Schism (1955) NF
The Sicilian Vespers (1958) NF
The Fall of Constantinople (1965) NF
The Last Byzantine Renaissance (1970) NF
A Traveller's Alphabet (1991) NF

RUNYON, Damon [Alfred] (1884–1946)
American short-story writer
Guys and Dolls (1931) F SS
Take It Easy (1938) F SS
My Wife Ethel (1940) F SS
Runyon à la Carte (1944) F SS
In Our Town (1946) F SS
Short Takes (1946) F SS

RUSHDIE, [Ahmed] Salman (1947–)
British novelist
Grimus (1975) F
Midnight's Children (1981) F
Shame (1983) F
The Satanic Verses (1988) F
Haroun and the Sea of Stories (1990) F CH
Imaginary Homelands (1991) NF
East, West (1994) F SS
The Moor's Last Sigh (1995) F
The Ground Beneath Her Feet (1999) F

RUSKIN, John (1819–1900)
British art critic, artist, and social reformer
Modern Painters: [vol. i] (1843) NF
Modern Painters: [vol. ii] (1846) NF
The Seven Lamps of Architecture (1849) NF
The King of the Golden River; or, The Black Brothers (1851) F CH
Pre-Raphaelitism (1851) NF
The Stones of Venice: [vol. i] (1851) NF
The Stones of Venice: [vols. ii, iii] (1853) NF
Lectures on Architecture and Painting (1854) NF
Modern Painters: Volume III (1856) NF
Modern Painters: Volume IV (1856) NF
The Elements of Drawing (1857) NF
The Political Economy of Art (1857) NF
The Two Paths (1859) NF
Modern Painters: Volume V (1860) NF
'Unto This Last' (1862) NF
Sesame and Lilies (1865) NF
The Crown of Wild Olive (1866) NF
The Ethics of the Dust (1866) NF
Time and Tide, by Weare and Tyne (1867) NF
The Queen of the Air (1869) NF
Fors Clavigera (1871) NF
Aratra Pentelici (1872) NF
Munera Pulveris (1872) NF
Mornings in Florence (1875) NF
The Art of England (1884) NF

The Pleasures of England (1884) NF
On the Old Road (1885) NF
Dilecta (1886) NF
Praeterita [vol. i] (1886) NF
Praeterita [vol. ii] (1887) NF
Praeterita [vol. iii] (1888) NF

RUSS, Joanna (1937–)
American science-fiction writer
Picnic on Paradise (1968) F
The Female Man (1975) F
Alyx (1976) F
We Who Are about To . . . (1977) F
The Two of Them (1978) F
The Zanzibar Cat (1983) F SS
The Hidden Side of the Moon (1987) F SS

RUSS, Richard Patrick *see* PATRICK O'BRIAN

RUSSELL, Bertrand [Arthur William], 3rd Earl Russell (1872–1970)
British philosopher
The Principles of Mathematics (1903) NF
Philosophical Essays (1910) NF
Principia Mathematica (1910) NF
Principles of Social Reconstruction (1916) NF
Mysticism and Logic, and Other Essays (1918) NF
Roads to Freedom (1918) NF
Introduction to Mathematical Philosophy (1919) NF
The Practice and Theory of Bolshevism (1920) NF
The Analysis of Mind (1921) NF
The Problem of China (1922) NF
The ABC of Atoms (1923) NF
The Prospects of Industrial Civilization (1923) NF
Icarus; or, The Future of Science (1924) NF
The ABC of Relativity (1925) NF
What I Believe (1925) NF
The Analysis of Matter (1927) NF
Sceptical Essays (1928) NF
Marriage and Morals (1929) NF
The Scientific Outlook (1931) NF
Education and the Social Order (1932) NF
In Praise of Idleness, and Other Essays (1935) NF
Religion and Science (1935) NF
Power (1938) NF
An Inquiry into Meaning and Truth (1940) NF
A History of Western Philosophy (1945) NF
Human Knowledge (1948) NF
Unpopular Essays (1950) NF
Satan in the Suburbs, and Other Stories (1953) F SS
Nightmares of Eminent Persons, and Other Stories (1954) F SS
Portraits from Memory, and Other Essays (1956) NF
Common Sense and Nuclear Warfare (1959) NF
Autobiography (1967) NF

RUSSELL, George William ['Æ'] (1867–1935)
Irish poet, essayist, dramatist, and painter
Homeward (1894) V
The Earth Breath, and Other Poems (1897) V
Deirdre (1903) D
The Nuts of Knowledge (1903) V
The Divine Vision, and Other Poems (1904) V
The Mask of Apollo, and Other Stories (1905) F SS
By Still Waters (1906) NF
Some Irish Essays (1906) NF
Co-operation and Nationality (1912) NF
Gods of War, with Other Poems (1915) V
Imaginations and Reveries, 1915 (1915) V
Salutation (1917) V
The Candle of Vision (1918) NF
The Inner and the Outer Ireland (1921) NF
Ireland, Past and Future (1922) NF
Vale, and Other Poems (1931) V
The Avatars (1933) F
The House of the Tirans, and Other Poems (1934) V

RUSSELL, W[illiam] Clark (1844–1911)
British nautical novelist, short-story writer, and biographer
As Innocent as a Baby (1874) F
John Holdsworth, Chief Mate (1875) F
The Wreck of the 'Grosvenor' (1877) F
My Watch Below; or, Yarns Spun When Off Duty (1882) F SS
Round the Galley Fire (1883) F SS
The Frozen Pirate (1887) F
The Golden Hope (1887) F
The Death Ship (1888) F
An Ocean Tragedy (1890) F
Marooned (1891) F
The Emigrant Ship (1893) F
List, Ye Landsmen! (1893) F
The Convict Ship (1895) F
The Phantom Death, and Other Stories (1895) F SS
The Honour of the Flag, and Other Stories (1896) F SS
An Atlantic Tragedy, and Other Stories (1905) F SS

RUSSELL, Willy [William Martin] (1947–)
British dramatist
John Paul George Ringo . . . and Bert (1974) D
Breezeblock Park (1975) D
Stags and Hens (1978) D
Educating Rita (1980) D
Blood Brothers (1986) D
Shirley Valentine (1986) D
The Wrong Boy (2000) F

'RUTHERFORD, Mark' [William Hale White] (1831–1913)
British novelist
The Autobiography of Mark Rutherford, Dissenting Minister (1881) F
Mark Rutherford's Deliverance (1885) F
The Revolution in Tanner's Lane (1887) F
Miriam's Schooling, and Other Papers (1890) F SS
Catharine Furze (1893) F
Clara Hopgood (1896) F
Pages from a Journal, with Other Papers (1900) NF
More Pages from a Journal (1910) NF
Last Pages from a Journal (1915) NF

RYMER, James Malcolm *see* MALCOLM J. ERRYM

RYMER, Thomas (1641–1713)
English poet, critic, archaeologist, and historiographer
The Tragedies of the Last Age Consider'd (1677) NF
Edgar; or, The English Monarch (1678) D
A Short View of Tragedy (1693) NF

S

SABATINI, Rafael (1875–1950)
Anglo-Italian historical novelist
The Tavern Knight (1904) F
Bardelys the Magnificent (1906) F
St Martin's Summer (1909) F
The Sea-Hawk (1915) F
The Historical Nights' Entertainment (1918) F SS
Scaramouche (1921) F
Captain Blood, His Odyssey (1922) F
The Carolinian (1925) F
The Hounds of God (1928) F
The Black Swan (1932) F
King in Prussia (1944) F

SACKLER, Howard (1929–1982)
American dramatist, director, and actor
The Great White Hope (1968) D

SACKVILLE-WEST, Vita [Victoria Mary] (1892–1962)
British poet and novelist
Poems of East and West (1917) V
Orchard and Vineyard (1921) V
The Heir (1922) F SS
The Land (1926) V
The Edwardians (1930) F
All Passion Spent (1931) F
The Garden (1946) V
No Signposts in the Sea (1961) F

SADE, Donatien Alphonse François, Marquis de (1740–1814)
French libertine and author
The Hundred and Twenty Days of Sodom [*Les 120 Journées de Sodome*] (1784) F
Justine; or, The Misfortunes of Virtue [*Justine; ou, les Malheurs de la vertu*] (1791) F
Juliette (1798) F

SADLEIR [orig. **SADLER**], **Michael** (1888–1957)
British bibliographer and novelist
Excursions in Victorian Bibliography (1922) NF
Fanny by Gaslight (1940) F
Nineteenth-Century Fiction (1951) NF

'SAGAN, Françoise' [Françoise Quoirez] (1935–)
French novelist
Bonjour Tristesse (1954) F
A Certain Smile [*Un Certain Sourie*] (1956) F
Those Without Shadows [*Dans un mois, dans un an*] (1957) F
Aimez-vous Brahms . . . (1959) F
Château en Suède ['Castle in Sweden'] (1960) D
La Chamade (1966) F
L'Echarde ['The Splinter'] (1966) F
The Unmade Bed [*Le Lit défait*] (1977) F
The Painted Lady [*La Femme Fardée*] (1981) F
The Still Storm [*Un orage immobile*] (1983) F

SAID, Edward (1935–)
Palestinian critic
Beginnings (1975) NF
Orientalism (1978) NF
The Question of Palestine (1979) NF
Culture and Imperialism (1993) NF
The Politics of Dispossession (1994) NF
Representations of the Intellectual [Reith lectures 1993] (1994) NF

SAINT, Dora Jessie *see* 'Miss Read'

ST AUBIN DE TERÁN, Lisa (1953–)
British novelist
The Keepers of the House (1982) F
The Slow Train to Milan (1983) F
The Tiger (1984) F
The Bay of Silence (1986) F
Black Idol (1987) F
The Marble Mountain, and Other Stories (1988) F SS
Joanna (1990) F
Nocturne (1992) F

SAINT-EXUPÉRY, Antoine de (1900–1944)
French novelist
Courrier-Sud ['Southbound Mail'] (1928) F
Night Flight [*Vol de nuit*] (1931) F
Wind, Sand and Stars [*Terre des Hommes*] (1939) F
Flight to Arras [*Pilote de guerre*] (1942) F
The Little Prince [*Le Petit Prince*] (1943) F CH

SAINT-JOHN, Henry, 1st Viscount Bolingbroke (1678–1751)
English statesman and author
A Dissertation upon Parties (1735) NF
Remarks on the History of England (1743) NF
Letters on the Spirit of Patriotism (1749) NF
Letters on the Study and Use of History (1752) NF
Philosophical Works (1754) NF

'SAINT-JOHN PERSE' [Marie René Auguste Alexis Saint-Léger Léger] (1887–1975)
French poet and diplomat
Éloges ['Eulogies'] (1911) V
Amitiés du prince ['The Prince's Friendships'] (1924) V
Anabasis [*Anabase*] (1924) V
Exil ['Exile'] (1942) V
Pluies ['Rain'] (1944) V
Seamarks [*Amers*] (1957) V
Chroniques (1960) V

SAINTE-BEUVE, Charles-Augustin (1804–1869)
French poet, novelist, and critic
Vie, poésies, et pensées de Joseph Delorme ['Life and Poems of Joseph Delorme'] (1829) V
Les Consolations (1830) V
Volupté ['Voluptuousness'] (1834) F

Critiques et portraits littéraires ['Literary Portraits and Critical Essays'] (1836–46) NF
Pensées d'août ['Thoughts of August'] (1837) V
Port-Royal (1840–59) NF
Portraits de femmes ['Portraits of Women'] (1844) NF
Portraits contemporains ['Contemporary Portraits'] (1846) NF
Causeries du lundi ['Monday Chats'] (1851–2) NF
Chateaubriand et son groupe littéraire sous l'Empire ['Chateaubriand and his Literary Set'] (1861) NF

SAINTSBURY, George [Edward Bateman] (1845–1933)
British literary scholar and critic
A Short History of French Literature (1882) NF
A History of Elizabethan Literature, 1560–1665 (1887) NF
Miscellaneous Essays (1892) NF
A History of Nineteenth-Century Literature, 1780–1895 (1896) NF
A Short History of English Literature (1898) NF
Matthew Arnold (1899) NF
The History of Criticism and Literary Taste in Europe (1900) NF
A History of English Prosody (1906) NF
A History of English Prose Rhythm (1912) NF
The Peace of the Augustans (1916) NF
A History of the French Novel (1917) NF

'SAKI' [Hector Hugh Munro] (1870–1916)
British novelist and short-story writer
The Westminster Alice (1902) NF
Reginald (1904) F SS
Reginald in Russia, and Other Sketches (1910) F SS
The Chronicles of Clovis (1912) F SS
The Unbearable Bassington (1912) F
Beasts and Super-Beasts (1914) F SS
When William Came (1914) F
The Toys of Peace, and Other Papers (1919) F SS

SALA, George Augustus (1828–1895)
British journalist, caricaturist, and novelist
A Journey Due North (1858) NF
Gaslight and Daylight (1859) F
Twice Round the Clock (1859) F
The Baddington Peerage (1860) F
Lady Chesterfield's Letters to Her Daughter (1860) NF
Looking at Life; or, Thoughts and Things (1860) F
Make Your Game; or, The Adventures of the Stout Gentleman, the Slim Gentleman, and the Man with the Iron Chest (1860) F
The Seven Sons of Mammon (1862) F
The Ship Chandler, and Other Tales (1862) F SS
Breakfast in Bed; or, Philosophy Between the Sheets (1863) NF
The Perfidy of Captain Slyboots, and Other Tales (1863) F SS
The Strange Adventures of Captain Dangerous (1863) F
The Life and Adventures of George Augustus Sala (1895) NF

SALINGER, J[erome] D[avid] (1919–)
American novelist and short-story writer
The Catcher in the Rye (1951) F
Nine Stories (1953) F SS
Franny and Zooey (1961) F
Raise High the Roof-Beam, Carpenters; and Seymour: An Introduction (1963) F SS

'SALTEN, Felix' [Siegmund Salzmann] (1869–1947)
Hungarian-born Austrian novelist and essayist
Bambi (1923) F
Bambi's Children [*Bambis Kinder*] (1940) F

SALZMANN, Siegmund *see* FELIX SALTEN

'SAND, George' [Amandine Aurore Lucie Dupin, Baronne Dudevant] (1804–1876)
French novelist and dramatist
Indiana (1832) F
Valentine (1832) F
Lélia (1833) F
Jacques (1834) F
Mauprat (1837) F
Spiridion (1838–9) F
Cosima (1840) D
Consuelo (1842) F
The Countess of Rudolstadt [*La Comtesse de Rudolstadt*] (1843) F
Jeanne (1843) F
The Miller of Angibault [*Le Meunier d'Angibault*] (1845) F
The Haunted Marsh [*La Mare au diable*] (1846) F
Francis the Waif [*François le Champi*] (1848) F
Little Fadette [*La Petite Fadette*] (1848) F
The Gallant Lords of Bois-Doré [*Les Beaux Messieurs de Bois-Doré*] (1858) F
The Marquis of Villemer [*Le Marquis de Villemer*] (1860–1) F
Mademoiselle La Quintinie (1863) F

SANDBURG, Carl [August] (1878–1967)
American poet, biographer, journalist, and children's writer
Reckless Ecstasy (1904) V
Chicago Poems (1916) V
Cornhuskers (1918) V
The Chicago Race Riots (1919) NF
Smoke and Steel (1920) V
Rootabaga Stories (1922) F CH
Slabs of the Sunburnt West (1922) V
Rootabaga Pigeons (1923) F CH
Abraham Lincoln: The Prairie Years (1926) NF
The American Songbag (1927) ANTH
Good Morning, America (1928) V
Potato Face (1930) F CH
The People, Yes (1936) V
Abraham Lincoln: The War Years (1939) NF
Storm Over the Land (1942) NF
Remembrance Rock (1948) F
Always the Young Strangers (1953) NF

Harvest Poems (1960) V
Wind Song (1960) V
Honey and Salt (1963) V

SANDYS, George (1578–1644)
English traveller, poet, and translator
A Relation of a Journey Begun 1610 (1615) NF
The First Five Books of Ovid's Metamorphosis (1621) V
Ovid's Metamorphosis (1626) V
A Paraphrase Upon the Psalmes of David (1636) V
A Paraphrase Upon the Divine Poems (1637) V
Christs Passion [tr. from Hugo Grotius] (1640) D

SANSOM, William [Norman Trevor Sansom] (1912–1976)
British short-story writer and novelist
Fireman Flower, and Other Stories (1944) F SS
Three (1946) F SS
Something Terrible, Something Lovely (1948) F SS
The Body (1949) F
The Passionate North (1950) F SS
The Face of Innocence (1951) F
A Touch of the Sun (1952) F
Pleasures Strange and Simple (1953) NF
A Bed of Roses (1954) F
Lord Love Us (1954) F SS
A Contest of Ladies (1956) F
The Loving Eye (1956) F
Among the Dahlias, and Other Stories (1957) F SS
The Cautious Heart (1958) F
The Last Hours of Sandra Lee (1961) F
The Ulcerated Milkman (1966) F SS
The Vertical Ladder, and Other Stories (1969) F SS
The Marmalade Bird (1973) F SS
A Young Wife's Tale (1974) F

SANTAYANA, George (1863–1952)
Spanish-born American philosopher and man of letters
The Sense of Beauty (1896) NF
Lucifer: A Theological Tragedy (1899) D V
Interpretations of Poetry and Religion (1900) NF
A Hermit of Carmel (1901) V
The Life of Reason (1905–6) NF
Three Philosophical Poets (1910) NF
Winds of Doctrine (1913) NF
Egotism in German Philosophy (1916) NF
Philosophical Opinion in America (1918) NF
Character and Opinion in the United States (1920) NF
Soliloquies in England (1922) NF
Scepticism and Animal Faith (1923) NF
Dialogues in Limbo (1925) NF
Platonism and the Spiritual Life (1927) NF
The Realm of Essence [first of *The Realms of Being* series] (1927) NF
The Realm of Matter (1930) NF
The Genteel Tradition at Bay (1931) NF
Some Turns of Thought in Modern Philosophy (1933) NF
The Last Puritan (1935) F
Obiter Scripta (1936) NF
The Realm of Truth (1937) NF
The Realm of Spirit (1940) NF
The Backgrounds of My Life (1944) NF
The Middle Span (1945) NF
The Idea of Christ in the Gospels (1946) NF
My Host the World (1953) NF

'SAPPER' [Herman Cyril McNeile] (1888–1937)
British popular thriller writer
Men, Women, and Guns (1916) F SS
Bull-Dog Drummond (1920) F
The Black Gang (1922) F
The Dinner Club (1923) F SS
The Third Round [US: *Bull-Dog Drummond's Third Round*] (1924) F SS
The Female of the Species [US: *Bulldog Drummond Meets . . .*] (1928) F
The Return of Bull-Dog Drummond [US: *Bulldog Drummond Returns*] (1932) F
Ronald Standish (1933) F
Bull-Dog Drummond at Bay (1935) F

SARDOU, Victorien (1831–1908)
French dramatist
The Meadows of Saint-Gervais [*Les Prés Saint-Gervais*] (1860) D
Monsieur Garat (1860) D
Les Pattes du monde ['The World's Legs'] (1860) D
Our Friends [*Nos Intimes*] (1861) D
Odette (1882) D
Fédora (1883) D
Tosca [*La Tosca*] (1887) D

SARGESON, Frank (1903–1982)
New Zealand short-story writer and novelist
Conversations With My Uncle (1936) F SS
A Man and His Wife (1940) F SS
That Summer, and Other Stories (1946) F SS
I Saw in My Dream (1949) F
Memoirs of a Peon (1965) F
Joy of the Worm (1969) F
Once is Enough (1973) NF
More Than Enough (1975) NF
Never Enough! (1977) NF

SAROYAN, William (1908–1981)
American dramatist, novelist, and short-story writer
The Daring Young Man on the Flying Trapeze (1934) F SS
Inhale and Exhale (1936) F SS
Three Times Three (1936) F SS
Little Children (1937) F SS
Love, Here is My Hat (1938) F SS
A Native American (1938) F SS
The Trouble with Tigers (1938) F SS
My Heart's in the Highland (1939) D
Peace, It's Wonderful (1939) F SS
The Time of Your Life (1939) D
My Name is Aram (1940) F SS
The Beautiful People (1941) D
Fables (1941) F SS
Love's Old Sweet Song (1941) D
Razzle-Dazzle (1942) D

The Human Comedy (1943) F
Dear Baby (1944) F SS
Get Away Old Man (1944) D
The Adventures of Wesley Jackson (1946) F
Jim Dandy, Fat Man in a Famine (1947) D
Don't Go Away Mad (1949) D
Rock Wagram (1951) F
The Bicycle Rider in Beverley Hills (1952) NF
Mama, I Love You (1956) F
The Whole Voyald (1956) F SS
Papa, You're Crazy (1957) F
The Cave Dwellers (1958) D
Here Comes, There Goes, You Know Who (1962) NF
Boys and Girls Together (1963) F
Not Dying (1963) NF
One Day in the Afternoon of the World (1964) F
Short Drive, Sweet Chariot (1966) NF
I Used To Believe I Had Forever, Now I'm Not So Sure (1967) [short stories, short plays, essays, and poems]
Days of Life and Death and Escape to the Moon (1970) NF
Places Where I've Done Time (1972) NF
Sons Come and Go, Mothers Hang In Forever (1976) NF
Chance Meetings (1978) NF
Obituaries (1979) NF

SARTRE, Jean-Paul (1905–1980)
French philosopher, novelist, critic, and dramatist
Nausea [*La Nausée*] (1938) F
The Wall, and Other Stories [*Le Mur*] (1939) F SS
Being and Nothingness [*L'Être et le néant*] (1943) NF
The Flies [*Les Mouches*] (1943) D
In Camera [*Huis clos*] (1944) D
The Age of Reason [*L'Âge de raison*] (1945) F
The Reprieve [*Le Sursis*] (1945) F
Existentialism and Humanism [*L'Existentialisme est un humanisme*] (1946) NF
Baudelaire (1947) NF
Les Jeux son faits [screenplay] (1947) D
Dirty Hands [also tran as *Crime passionel*] [*Les Mains Sales*] (1948) D
Iron in the Soul [*La Mort dans l'âme*] (1949) F
Loser Wins [*Les Séquestres d'Altona*] (1959) D
The Words [*Les Mots*] (1966) NF

SASSOON, Siegfried [Loraine] (1886–1967)
British poet, novelist, and autobiographer
The Old Huntsman, and Other Poems (1917) V
Counter-Attack, and Other Poems (1918) V
Picture Show (1919) V
The War Poems of Siegfried Sassoon (1919) V
Satirical Poems (1926) V
The Heart's Journey (1928) V
Memoirs of a Fox-Hunting Man (1928) F
Memoirs of an Infantry-Officer (1930) F
The Road to Ruin (1933) V
Vigils (1935) V
Sherston's Progress (1936) F
The Complete Memoirs of George Sherston (1937) F
The Old Century and Seven More Years (1938) NF
The Weald of Youth (1942) NF
Siegfried's Journey 1916–20 (1945) NF
Sequences (1956) V

SAVAGE, Marmion W. (1803–1872)
British journalist and novelist
The Falcon Family; or, Young Ireland (1845) F
The Bachelor of the Albany (1847) F
The Woman of Business; or, The Lady and the Lawyer (1870) F

SAVAGE, Richard (1697?–1743)
English poet, dramatist, and satirist
The Convocation; or, A Battle of Pamphlets (1717) V
Love in a Veil (1718) D
The Tragedy of Sir Thomas Overbury (1723) D
The Authors of the Town (1725) V
The Bastard (1728) MISC
The Wanderer (1729) V
The Progress of a Divine (1735) V

SAVILE, Sir George, Marquis of Halifax (1633–1695)
English politician and author
Observations Upon a Late Libel (1681) NF
A Letter to a Dissenter (1687) NF
The Anatomy of an Equivalent (1688) NF
The Lady's New-Years Gift; or, Advice to a Daughter (1688) NF
A Rough Draft of a New Model at Sea (1694) NF

SAYERS, Dorothy L[eigh] (1893–1957)
British writer of detective fiction, anthologist, and translator
Whose Body? (1923) F
Clouds of Witness (1926) F
Unnatural Death [US: *The Dawson Pedigree*] (1927) F
Great Short Stories of Detection, Mystery and Horror [1st ser.] (1928) ANTH
Lord Peter Views the Body (1928) F SS
The Unpleasantness at the Bellona Club (1928) F
The Documents in the Case (1930) F
Strong Poison (1930) F
The Five Red Herrings [US: *Suspicious Characters*] (1931) F
Great Short Stories of Detection, Mystery and Horror [2nd ser.] (1931) ANTH
Have His Carcase (1932) F
Hangman's Holiday (1933) F SS
Murder Must Advertise (1933) F
The Nine Tailors (1934) F
Gaudy Night (1935) F
Busman's Honeymoon (1937) F
In the Teeth of the Evidence, and Other Stories (1939) F SS
The Man Born To Be King (1943) D
The Divine Comedy [from Dante] (1949–62) V

SCANNELL, Vernon (1922–)
British poet, novelist, and critic
Graves and Resurrections (1948) V
The Face of the Enemy (1961) F
A Sense of Danger (1962) V
Walking Wounded (1965) V
The Winter Man (1973) V

Not Without Glory: Poets of the Second World War (1976) NF
Ring of Truth (1983) F
Argument of Kings (1987) F
Funeral Games, and Other Poems (1987) V
Soldiering On (1989) V

SCHAMA, Simon [Michael] (1945–)
British historian
Patriots and Liberators (1977) NF
The Two Rothschilds and the Land of Israel (1979) NF
The Embarrassment of Riches (1987) NF
Citizens (1989) NF
Rembrandt's Eyes (1999) NF
A History of Britain (2000) NF

SCHLESINGER, Arthur [Meier] Jr (1917–)
American historian
The Age of Jackson (1945) NF
The Crisis of the Old Order (1957) NF
The Coming of the New Deal (1959) NF
The Politics of Upheaval (1960) NF
A Thousand Days (1965) NF
The Bitter Heritage (1967) NF

SCHREINER, Olive [Emilie Albertina], later Cronwright (1855–1920)
South African novelist and author
The Story of an African Farm [as 'Ralph Iron'] (1883) F
Dreams (1891) NF
Dream Life and Real Life [as 'Ralph Iron'] (1893) F SS
Trooper Peter Halket of Mashonaland (1897) F
Woman and Labour (1911) NF

SCHWARTZ, Delmore (1913–1966)
American poet, critic, and short-story writer
In Dreams Begin Responsibilities (1938) V
Shenandoah (1941) V D
Genesis (1943) F V
The World is a Wedding (1948) F SS
Vaudeville for a Princess (1950) V
Summer Knowledge (1959) V
Successful Love (1961) F SS

SCOT [or **SCOTT**], **Reginald** (1538?–1599)
English writer on witchcraft
The Discoverie of Witchcraft (1584) NF

SCOTT, Hugh Stowell *see* HENRY SETON MERRIMAN

SCOTT, Paul [Mark] (1920–1978)
British novelist and dramatist
Johnnie Sahib (1952) F
The Alien Sky [US: *Six Days in Marapore*] (1953) F
A Male Child (1956) F
The Mark of the Warrior (1958) F
The Chinese Love Pavilion [US: *The Love Pavilion*] (1960) F
The Birds of Paradise (1962) F
The Bender (1963) F
The Corrida at San Feliu (1964) F
The Jewel in the Crown (1966) F
The Day of the Scorpion (1968) F
The Towers of Silence (1971) F
A Division of the Spoils (1975) F
Staying On (1977) F

SCOTT, Robert Falcon (1868–1912)
British explorer
The Voyage of the 'Discovery' (1905) NF

SCOTT, Sir Walter (1771–1832)
Scottish poet and novelist
The Chase, and William and Helen (1796) V
Goetz of Berlichingen, with The Iron Hand: A Tragedy [trn from Goethe] (1799) V
The Eve of Saint John (1800) V
Minstrelsy of the Scottish Border (1802) V
Sir Tristrem [by Thomas of Ercildoune] (1804) V
The Lay of the Last Minstrel (1805) V
Ballads and Lyrical Pieces (1806) V
Marmion (1808) V
English Minstrelsy (1810) V
The Lady of the Lake (1810) V
The Vision of Don Roderick (1811) V
The Bridal of Triermain; or, The Vale of St John (1813) V
Rokeby (1813) V
Waverley; or, 'tis Sixty Years Since (1814) F
The Field of Waterloo (1815) V
Guy Mannering; or, The Astrologer (1815) F
The Lord of the Isles (1815) V
The Antiquary (1816) F
Tales of My Landlord [1st ser.] (1816) F
Harold the Dauntless (1817) V
Rob Roy (1818) F
Tales of My Landlord [2nd ser.; contains 'The Heart of Midlothian'] (1818) F
Tales of My Landlord [3rd ser.; contains 'The Bride of Lammermoor'] (1819) F
The Abbot (1820) F
Ivanhoe (1820) F
The Monastery (1820) F
Kenilworth (1821) F
The Fortunes of Nigel (1822) F
Peveril of the Peak (1822) F
The Pirate (1822) F
Quentin Durward (1823) F
Redgauntlet (1824) F
St Ronan's Well (1824) F
Tales of the Crusaders [inc. 'The Betrothed' and 'The Talisman'] (1825) F
Woodstock; or, The Cavalier (1826) F
Chronicles of the Canongate [1st ser.] (1827) F
The Life of Napoleon Buonaparte (1827) NF
Chronicles of the Canongate [2nd ser.; inc. 'The Fair Maid of Perth'] (1828) F
Tales of a Grandfather [1st ser.] (1828) NF
Anne of Geierstein; or, The Maiden of the Mist (1829) F
Tales of a Grandfather [2nd ser.] (1829) NF
Letters on Demonology and Witchcraft (1830) NF
Tales of a Grandfather [3rd ser.] (1830) NF
Tales of a Grandfather [4th ser.] (1831) NF

Tales of My Landlord: Fourth and Last Series (1832) F

SCOVELL, E[dith] J[oy] (1907–)
British poet
Shadows of Chrysanthemums, and Other Poems (1944) V
Midsummer Meadows, and Other Poems (1946) V
The River Steamer, and Other Poems (1956) V
The Space Between (1982) V
Listening to Collared Doves (1986) V

SCUPHAM, [John] Peter (1933–)
British poet
The Snowing Globe (1972) V
Prehistories (1975) V
The Hinterland (1977) V
Summer Palaces (1980) V
Winter Quarters (1983) V
Under the Barrage (1985) V
Out Late (1986) V
The Air Show (1988) V
Watching the Perseids (1990) V
The Ark (1994) V

SEARLE, Ronald (1920–)
British artist and author
Hurrah for St Trinian's (1948) F CH

SEDGWICK, Catherine Maria (1789–1867)
American novelist
A New-England Tale (1822) F
Hope Leslie; or, Early Times in the Massachusetts (1827) F
Clarence; or, A Tale of Our Own Times (1830) F
The Linwoods; or, 'Sixty Years Since' in America (1835) F
Married or Single? (1857) F

SEDLEY, Sir Charles (1639–1701)
English poet and dramatist
Pompey the Great (1664) D
The Mulberry-Garden (1668) D
Antony and Cleopatra (1677) D
Bellamira; or, The Mistress (1687) D

SEELEY, Sir John Robert (1834–1895)
British historian and essayist
Ecce Homo (1866) NF
The Expansion of England (1883) NF

SEGAL, Erich (1937–)
American novelist
Love Story (1970) F

SELBY, Hubert Jr (1928–)
American novelist and short-story writer
Last Exit to Brooklyn (1964) F
The Room (1971) F
The Demon (1976) F
Requiem for a Dream (1978) F
Song of the Silent Snow (1986) F SS

SELDEN, John (1584–1634)
English jurist and antiquary
The Duello or Single Combat (1610) NF
Titles of Honor (1614) NF
The Historie of Tithes (1618) NF
The Priviledges of the Baronage of England (1642) NF
Theanthropos; or, God Made Man (1661) NF
Englands Epinomis (1683) NF
Table-Talk (1689) NF

SELF, Will[iam] (1961–)
British novelist
The Quantity Theory of Insanity (1991) F
Cock & Bull (1992) F
My Idea of Fun (1993) F
Grey Area, and Other Stories (1994) F SS
Great Apes (1997) F
Tough, Tough Toys for Tough, Tough Boys (1998) F SS
How the Dead Live (2000) F

SELINCOURT, Ernest de (1870–1943)
British literary scholar, critic, and biographer
Dorothy Wordsworth (1933) NF
Oxford Lectures on Poetry (1934) NF

SELVON, Samuel [Selvon] (1923–1994)
Trinidadian novelist, short-story writer, poet, and dramatist
A Brighter Sun (1952) F
An Island is a World (1955) F
The Lonely Londoners (1956) F
Moses Ascending (1975) F
Moses Migrating (1983) F

SENDAK, Maurice [Bernard] (1928–)
American children's writer and illustrator
Kenny's Window (1956) F CH
The Sign on Rosie's Door (1960) F CH
Where the Wild Things Are (1963) F CH
In the Night Kitchen (1970) F CH

SENIOR, Nassau [William] (1790–1864)
British economist and essayist
An Outline of the Science of Political Economy (1836) NF
A Journal Kept in Turkey and Greece in 1857 and 1858 (1859) NF
Suggestions on Popular Education (1861) NF
Biographical Sketches (1863) NF
Essays on Fiction (1864) NF

SERVICE, Robert W[illiam] (1876–1958)
Canadian poet and novelist
Songs of a Sourdough (1907) V
The Spell of the Yukon (1907) V
Ballads of a Cheechako (1909) V
The Trail of Ninety-Eight (1910) F
Rhymes of a Rolling Stone (1912) V
The Pretender (1914) F
Rhymes of a Red Cross Man (1916) V
Ballads of a Bohemian (1921) V
The Poisoned Paradise (1922) F
The Roughneck (1923) F
The Master of the Microbe (1926) F
The House of Fear (1927) F
Twenty Bath-Tub Ballads (1939) V
Bar-Room Ballads (1940) V

Songs of a Sun-Lover (1949) V
Rhymes of a Roughneck (1950) V
Lyrics of a Lowbrow (1951) V
Rhymes of a Rebel (1952) V
Songs for My Supper (1953) V
Carols of an Old Codger (1954) V
Rhymes for My Rags (1956) V

SETH, Vikram (1952–)
Indian novelist, poet, and travel writer
From Heaven Lake (1983) NF
The Humble Administrator's Garden (1985) V
The Golden Gate (1986) V
All You Who Sleep Tonight (1990) V
A Suitable Boy (1993) F
An Equal Music (1999) F

SETON, Ernest Thompson (1860–1946)
Canadian naturalist
Wild Animals I Have Known (1898) F SS
Lobo, Rag, and Vixen (1899) F SS
The Biography of a Grizzly (1900) F
Lives of the Hunted (1901) F SS
Monarch, the Big Bear of Tallac (1904) F
Animal Heroes (1905) F SS
Legend of the White Reindeer (1915) F
The Slum Cat (1915) F
Woodland Tales (1921) F SS
Chink, and Other Stories (1927) F SS
Foam, the Razor-Back (1927) F
Johnny Bear, and Other Stories (1927) F SS
Krag, the Kootenay Ram, and Other Stories (1929) F SS
Cute Coyote, and Other Stories (1930) F SS

SETTLE, Elkanah (1648–1724)
English dramatist and poet
Mare Clausum; or, A Ransack for the Dutch (1666) V
Cambyses King of Persia (1667) D
The Empress of Morocco (1673) D
The Conquest of China, by the Tartars (1675) D
Love and Revenge (1675) D
Ibrahim the Illustrious Bassa (1676) D
Pastor Fido; or, The Faithful Shepherd (1676) D
Fatal Love; or, The Forc'd Inconstancy (1680) D
The Female Prelate (1680) D
Absalom Senior; or, Achitophel Transpros'd (1682) V
The Heir of Morocco, with the Death of Gayland (1682) D
Distress'd Innocence; or, The Princess of Persia (1690) D
The Fairy Queen (1692) D
The Notorious Impostor (1692) F
The Ambitious Slave; or, A Generous Revenge (1694) D
Philaster; or, Love Lies A-Bleeding (1695) D
The World in the Moon (1697) D
The Virgin Prophetesse; or, The Fate of Troy (1701) D
The City-Ramble; or, A Play-house Wedding (1711) D

'SEUSS, Dr' [Theodor Giesel] (1904–1991)
American children's writer and illustrator
The Cat in the Hat (1957) F CH
How the Grinch Stole Christmas (1957) F CH
Green Eggs and Ham (1960) F CH

SEWARD, Anna (1747–1809)
British poet and author
Elegy on Captain Cook (1780) V
Monody on Major André (1781) MISC
Louisa (1784) V
Llangollen Vale, with Other Poems (1796) V
Original Sonnets on Various Subjects (1799) V

SEWELL, Anna (1820–1878)
British children's novelist
Black Beauty (1877) F CH

SEXTON, Anne (1928–1974)
American poet
To Bedlam and Part of the Way Back (1961) V
All My Pretty Ones (1962) V
Live or Die (1966) V

SHADWELL, Thomas (1642?–1692)
English dramatist and Poet Laureate
The Sullen Lovers; or, The Impertinents (1668) D
The Royal Shepherdess (1669) D
The Humorists (1670) D
Epsom-Wells (1672) D
The Miser (1672) D
The Tempest; or, The Enchanted Island (1674) D
The Libertine (1675) D
Psyche (1675) D
The Virtuoso (1676) D
The History of Timon of Athens, the Man-hater (1678) D
A True Widow (1678) D
The Woman-Captain (1679) D
The Lancashire-Witches, and Tegue o Divelly the Irish Priest (1681) D
The Medal of John Bayes (1682) V
The Tenth Satyr of Juvenal (1687) V
The Squire of Alsatia (1688) D
The Amorous Bigotte; with the Second Part of Tegue o Divelly (1689) D
Bury-Fair (1689) D
The Scowrers (1690) D
The Volunteers; or, The Stock-Jobbers (1692) D

SHAFFER, Anthony (1926–)
British dramatist
Sleuth (1970) D

SHAFFER, Peter [Levin] (1926–)
British dramatist
Five Finger Exercise (1958) D
The Royal Hunt of the Sun (1964) D
White Liars, and Black Comedy (1968) D
The Battle of Shrivings (1970) D
Equus (1973) D
Amadeus (1979) D
Lettice and Lovage (1987) D
The Gift of the Gorgon (1993) D

SHAKESPEARE, William (1564–1616)
English dramatist and poet
Richard the Third (1592/3) D
Venus and Adonis (1593) V
Henry VI, Part 2 (1594) D

Lucrece (1594) V
Titus Andronicus (1594) D
Henry VI, Part 3 (1595) D
Richard the Second (1597) D
Romeo and Juliet (1597) D
Henry IV, Part 1 (1598) D
Love's Labour's Lost (1598) D
The Passionate Pilgrime (1599) V
Henry IV, Part 2 (1600) D
Henry the Fifth (1600) D
The Merchant of Venice (1600) D
A Midsummer Night's Dream (1600) D
Much Ado About Nothing (1600) D
The Merry Wives of Windsor (1602) D
Hamlet (1603) D
Othello, the Moor of Venice (1604) D
King Lear (1608) D
Pericles, Prince of Tyre (1609) D
Sonnets (1609) V
Troilus and Cressida (1609) D
Comedies, Histories, & Tragedies [the First Folio] (1623) D:
The Two Gentlemen of Verona (written *c.* 1592) D
The Taming of the Shrew (written *c.* 1592) D
Henry VI Part I (written *c.* 1592) D
Richard III (written *c.* 1592/3) D
The Comedy of Errors (written *c.* 1594) D
King John (written *c.* 1596) D
Julius Caesar (written *c.* 1599) D
As You Like It (written *c.* 1600) D
Twelfth Night (written 1601) D
Measure for Measure (written 1604) D
Othello (written 1602/4) D
All's Well that Ends Well (written 1604/5) D
Timon of Athens (written 1607) D
King Lear (written 1604/5) D
Macbeth (written 1606) D
Antony and Cleopatra (written 1606/7) D
Coriolanus (written 1608) D
Cymbeline (written *c.* 1609/10) D
The Winter's Tale (written 1610/11) D
The Tempest (written 1611) D
The Two Noble Kinsmen (1634) D

SHAPIRO, Karl [Jay] (1913–)
American poet and critic
Person, Place and Thing (1942) V
V-Letter (1944) V
Trial of a Poet (1947) V
Beyond Criticism (1953) NF
Poems of a Jew (1958) V
The Bourgeois Poet [prose poems] (1964) V
To Abolish Children (1968) NF
White-Haired Lover (1968) V
Edsel (1971) F
The Poetry Wreck (1975) NF
Adult Bookstore (1976) V
Love and War, Art and God (1984) V
The Younger Son: Poet (1988) NF
Reports of My Death (1990) NF
The Old Horsefly (1992) V

SHARP, William ['Fiona Macleod'] (1855–1905)
Scottish poet and novelist
The Human Inheritance, The New Hope, Motherhood (1882) V
Children of To-morrow (1889) F
Pharais [as 'Fiona Macleod'] (1894) F
The Mountain Lovers [as 'Fiona Macleod'] (1895) F
Green Fire [as 'Fiona Macleod'] (1896) F
The Sin Eater, and Other Tales [as 'Fiona Macleod'] (1896) F SS
The Dominion of Dreams [as 'Fiona Macleod'] (1899) F
Silence Farm (1899) F

SHARPE, Tom [Thomas Ridley Sharpe] (1928–)
British comic novelist
Riotous Assembly (1971) F
Indecent Exposure (1973) F
Porterhouse Blue (1974) F
Blott on the Landscape (1975) F
Wilt (1976) F
The Wilt Alternative (1979) F
Ancestral Vices (1980) F
Wilt on High (1984) F

SHAW, George Bernard (1856–1950)
Irish dramatist, novelist, and social critic
Cashel Byron's Profession (1886) F
An Unsocial Socialist (1887) F
The Quintessence of Ibsenism (1891) NF
Widowers' Houses (1892) D
Mrs Warren's Profession (1898) D
The Perfect Wagnerite (1898) NF
Plays Pleasant and Unpleasant (1898) D
Fabianism and the Empire (1900) NF
Love Among the Artists (1900) F
Three Plays for Puritans [*The Devil's Disciple*, *Caesar and Cleopatra*, *Captain Brassbound's Conversion*] (1901) D
Man and Superman (1903) D
The Common Sense of Municipal Trading (1904) NF
The Irrational Knot (1905) F
John Bull's Other Island, and Major Barbara (1907) D
The Sanity of Art (1908) NF
Press Cuttings (1909) D
The Doctor's Dilemma, Getting Married, and The Shewing-Up of Blanco Posnet (1911) D
Common Sense About the War (1914) NF
Misalliance, The Dark Lady of the Sonnets, and Fanny's First Play (1914) D
Androcles and the Lion, Overruled, Pygmalion (1916) D
How to Settle the Irish Question (1917) NF
Heartbreak House, Great Catherine, and Playlets of the War (1919) D
Peace Conference Hints (1919) NF
Back to Methuselah (1920) D
Saint Joan (1923) D
Table-Talk of G.B.S. (1925) NF

Translations and Tomfooleries (1926) NF
Do We Agree? (1928) NF
The Intelligent Woman's Guide to Socialism and Capitalism (1928) NF
The Apple Cart (1929) D
Immaturity (1930) F
Ellen Terry and Bernard Shaw (1931) NF
The Adventures of the Black Girl in Her Search for God (1932) F
Too True To Be Good; Village Wooing; and On the Rocks (1932) D
Prefaces (1934) NF
Short Stories, Scraps and Shavings (1934) MISC
The Simpleton, The Six, and The Millionairess (1936) D
London Music in 1888–89 (1937) NF
Geneva (1938) D
In Good King Charles's Golden Days (1939) D
Pygmalion [screen version] (1941) D
Everybody's Political What's What (1944) NF
Major Barbara [screen version] (1946) D
Buoyant Billions (1948) D
Sixteen Self Sketches (1949) NF
Buoyant Billions, Farfetched Fables, and Shakes Versus Shav (1951) D
Bernard Shaw and Mrs Patrick Campbell [correspondence] (1952) NF
My Dear Dorothea (1956) NF
An Unfinished Novel (1958) F

SHAW, Irwin (1913–1984)
American novelist, dramatist, and short-story writer
Bury the Dead (1936) D
Siege (1937) D
The Gentle People: A Brooklyn Fable (1939) D
Sailor Off the Bremen (1939) F SS
Retreat to Pleasure (1940) D
Welcome to the City (1941) F SS
The Assassin (1944) D
Sons and Soldiers (1944) D
Act of Faith (1946) F SS
The Young Lions (1948) F
Mixed Faith (1950) F SS
The Troubled Air (1951) F
Lucy Crown (1956) F
Tip on a Dead Jockey (1957) F SS
Two Weeks in Another Town (1960) F
Children From their Games (1963) D
In the Company of Dolphins (1964) NF
Love on a Dark Street (1965) F SS
Voices of a Summer Day (1965) F
Rich Man, Poor Man (1970) F
Evening in Byzantium (1973) F
God Was Here But He Left Early (1973) F SS
Nightwork (1975) F
Beggarman Thief (1977) F
Paris! Paris! (1977) NF
Five Decades (1978) F SS
The Top of the Hill (1979) F
Bread Upon the Waters (1981) F
Acceptable Losses (1982) F

SHEFFIELD, John, Earl of Mulgrave, Marquis of Normanby, Duke of Buckingham (1648–1721)
English politician and poet
An Essay upon Poetry (1682) V
The Temple of Death (1695) V
The Character of Charles II, King of England (1696) V

SHEIL, Richard Lalor (1791–1851)
Irish politician and dramatist
Adelaide; or, The Emigrants (1814) D
The Apostate (1817) D
Bellamira; or, The Fall of Tunis (1818) D
Evadne; or, The Statue (1819) D
Damon and Pythias (1821) D

SHELDON, Sidney (1917–)
American popular novelist
The Naked Face (1970) F
The Other Side of Midnight (1974) F
A Stranger in the Mirror (1976) F
Bloodline (1977) F
The Master of the Game (1982) F
If Tomorrow Comes (1985) F
The Sands of Time (1988) F

SHELLEY, Mary [Wollstonecraft], *née* Godwin (1797–1851)
British novelist
History of a Six Weeks' Tour Through a Part of France, Switzerland, Germany, and Holland (1817) NF
Frankenstein; or, The Modern Prometheus (1818) F
Valperga; or, The Life and Adventures of Castruccio, Prince of Lucca (1823) F
The Last Man (1826) F
The Fortunes of Perkin Warbeck (1830) F
Lodore (1835) F
Falkner (1837) F
Rambles in Germany and Italy, in 1840, 1842, and 1843 (1844) NF

SHELLEY, P[ercy] B[ysshe] (1792–1822)
British poet
Original Poetry by Victor and Cazire [by Shelley and his sister Elizabeth] (1810) V
Posthumous Fragments of Margaret Nicholson (1810) V
Zastrozzi (1810) F
The Necessity of Atheism (1811) NF
St Irvyne; or, The Rosicrucian (1811) F
An Address to the Irish People (1812) NF
Queen Mab (1813) V
A Vindication of Natural Diet (1813) NF
A Refutation of Deism: in a Dialogue (1814) NF
Alastor; or, The Spirit of Solitude, and Other Poems (1816) V
A Proposal for Putting Reform to the Vote Throughout the Kingdom [by 'The Hermit of Marlow'] (1817) NF
Laon and Cythna; or, The Revolution of the Golden City [reissued 1818 as *The Revolt of Islam*] (1818) V
The Cenci (1819) V D
Rosalind and Helen: A Modern Eclogue, with Other Poems (1819) V

Oedipus Tyrannus; or, Swellfoot the Tyrant (1820) V D
Prometheus Unbound: A Lyrical Drama, with Other Poems (1820) V D
Adonais (1821) V
Epipsychidion (1821) V
Hellas (1822) V
Posthumous Poems [inc. 'Julian and Maddalo', 'The Witch of Atlas', and 'Mont Blanc'] (1824) V
The Masque of Anarchy (1832) V
Essays, Letters from Abroad, Translations and Fragments (1840) MISC

SHENSTONE, William (1714–1763)
British poet and landscape gardener
Poems Upon Various Occasions [inc. early version of 'The School-Mistress'] (1737) V
The Judgment of Hercules (1741) V
The School-Mistress (1742) V

SHERIDAN, Frances, *née* Chamberlaine (1724–1766)
Irish novelist and dramatist
Memoirs of Miss Sidney Bidulph (1761) F
The Discovery (1763) D
The History of Nourjahad (1767) F
Eugenia and Adelaide (1791) F

SHERIDAN, Richard Brinsley (1753–1816)
Irish dramatist
The Rivals (1775) D
The School for Scandal (1777) D
A Trip to Scarborough [altered from Vanbrugh's *The Relapse*] (1777) D
The Critic; or, A Tragedy Rehearsed (1779) D
Pizarro [from Kotzebue] (1799) D

SHERLOCK, Thomas (1678–1761)
English prelate and author
The Tryal of the Witnesses of the Resurrection of Jesus (1729) NF

SHERLOCK, William (1641?–1707)
English prelate and religious controversialist
A Preservative Against Popery. First Part (1688) NF
A Practical Discourse Concerning Death (1689) NF
A Vindication of the Doctrine of the Holy and Ever Blessed Trinity (1690) NF
The Case of the Allegiance Due to Sovereign Powers (1691) NF

SHERRIFF, R[obert] C[edric] (1896–1975)
British dramatist and novelist
Journey's End (1928) D
Greengates (1936) F
The Hopkins Manuscript (1939) F
Another Year (1948) F
The White Carnation (1953) D

SHERWOOD, Mary Martha (1775–1851)
British writer for children
The History of the Fairchild Family (1818) F CH
Idiot's Delight (1936) D
Tovarich (1936) D
Abe Lincoln in Illinois (1938) D
There Shall Be No Night (1940) D
Roosevelt and Hopkins (1948) NF

SHERWOOD, Robert E[mmet] (1896–1955)
American dramatist
The Love Nest (1927) D
The Road to Rome (1927) D
This is New York (1930) D
Waterloo Bridge (1930) D
Reunion in Vienna (1931) D
The Virtuous Knight (1931) F
The Petrified Forest (1935) D

SHIEL, M[atthew] P[hipps] (1865–1947)
West Indian-born fantasy and detective novelist
Prince Zaleski (1895) F SS
The Rajah's Saphire (1896) F
The Yellow Danger (1898) F
The Lord of the Sea (1901) F
The Purple Cloud (1901) F
The Lost Viol (1905) F

SHIELDS, Carol, *née* Warner (1935–)
American-Canadian author
Small Ceremonies (1976) F
The Box Garden (1977) F
Happenstance: The Husband's Story (1980) F
Various Miracles (1985) F SS
Swann: A Mystery (1987) F
The Orange Fish (1989) F SS
The Republic of Love (1992) F
The Stone Diaries (1993) F
A Fairly Conventional Woman (1982) F
Happenstance: The Wife's Story (1982) F
Larry's Party (1997) F
Dressing Up for the Carnival (2000) F

SHIRLEY, James (1596–1666)
English poet and dramatist
The Wedding (1629) D
The Gratefull Servant (1630) D
The Schoole of Complement (1631) D
Changes; or, Love in a Maze (1632) D
The Bird in a Cage (1633) D
A Contention for Honour and Riches (1633) D
The Triumph of Peace (1633) D
The Wittie Faire One (1633) D
The Traytor (1635) D
The Dukes Mistris (1636) D
The Example (1637) D
The Gamester (1637) D
Hide Parke (1637) D
The Lady of Pleasure (1637) D
The Young Admirall (1637) D
The Royall Master (1638) D
The Maides Revenge (1639) D
The Arcadia (1640) D
The Constant Maid (1640) D
The Coronation (1640) D
The Humorous Courtier (1640) D
Loves Crueltie (1640) D
The Opportunitie (1640) D
Cupid and Death (1653) D

The Gentleman of Venice (1655) D
The Politician (1655) D

SHOLOKHOV, Mikhail [Alexandrovich] (1905–1984)
Russian novelist
And Quiet Flows the Don (1928–40) F

SHORTHOUSE, J[oseph] H[enry] (1834–1903)
British novelist
John Inglesant (1881) F
The Little Schoolmaster Mark (1883) F
Sir Percival (1886) F
The Countess Eve (1888) F
A Teacher of the Violin, and Other Tales (1888) F SS
Blance, Lady Falaise (1891) F

SHOWALTER, Elaine (1941–)
American cultural and feminist critic
A Literature of Their Own [rev. 1982] (1977) NF
Alternative Alcott (1985) NF
The Female Malady (1987) NF
Sexual Anarchy (1990) NF
Sister's Choice (1991) NF

'SHUTE, Nevil' [Nevil Shute Norway] (1899–1960)
British novelist
Marazan (1926) F
So Disdained [US: *Mysterious Aviator*] (1928) F
Pied Piper (1941) F
No Highway (1948) F
A Town Like Alice [US: *The Legacy*] (1950) F
On the Beach (1957) F

SIDGWICK, Henry (1838–1900)
British philosopher
The Ethics of Conformity and Subscription (1870) NF
The Methods of Ethics (1874) NF
The Principles of Political Economy (1883) NF
The Scope and Method of Economic Science (1885) NF
Outline of the History of Ethics (1886) NF
The Elements of Politics (1891) NF

SIDNEY, Sir Philip (1554–1586)
English poet, romance writer, and soldier
The Countesse of Pembrokes Arcadia [bks i-iii] (1590) F
Astrophel and Stella (1591) V
The Countesse of Pembrokes Arcadia [bks i-v] (1593) F
The Defence of Poesie (1595) NF
The Countesse of Pembrokes Arcadia [3rd edn with additional poems] (1598) F

SIENKIEWICZ, Henryk (1846–1916)
Polish novelist
In Vain (1872) F
With Fire and Sword (1884) F
The Deluge (1886) F
Quo Vadis? (1896) F

SIGERSON, Dora, later **Shorter** (1866–1918)
British poet and short-story writer
The Fairy Changeling (1897) V
Ballads and Poems (1898) V
The Father Confessor (1900) F SS
The Woman Who Went to Hell (1902) V
The Country House Party (1905) V
Madge Linsey (1913) V
Love of Ireland (1916) V
The Sad Years (1918) V
Sixteen Dead Men, and Other Ballads of Easter Week (1919) V

SILKIN, Jon (1930–1997)
British poet and editor
The Peaceable Kingdom (1954) V
The Re-Ordering of the Stones (1961) V
Nature With Man (1965) V
Poetry of the Committed Individual (1973) ANTH
The Principle of Water (1974) V
The Little Time-Keeper (1976) V
The Psalms With Their Spoils (1980) V
The Ship's Pasture (1986) V
The Lens-Breakers (1992) V

SILLITOE, Alan (1928–)
British novelist, poet, and dramatist
Saturday Night and Sunday Morning (1958) F
The Loneliness of the Long-Distance Runner (1959) F SS
The General (1960) F
Key to the Door (1961) F
The Ragman's Daughter (1963) F SS
The Death of William Posters (1965) F
A Tree on Fire (1967) F
A Start in Life (1970) F
Raw Material (1972) F
Flame of Life (1974) F
The Widower's Son (1976) F
Her Victory (1982) F
Life Goes On (1985) F
The Far Side of the Street (1988) F SS
The Open Door (1989) F SS
Last Loves (1990) F
Snow Stop (1993) F
Alligator Playground (1997) F SS
The Broken Chariot (1998) F
The German Numbers Woman (1999) F

SILVERBERG, Robert (1935–)
American novelist and short-story writer
Revolt on Alpha C (1955) F
The 13th Immortal (1957) F
Thorns (1967) F
Hawksbill Station (1968) F
The Masks of Time (1968) F
Nightwings (1969) F
Downward to the Earth (1970) F
Tower of Glass (1970) F
The Book of Skulls (1971) F
Moonferns and Starsongs (1971) F SS
Son of Man (1971) F
A Time of Changes (1971) F
The World Inside (1971) F
Dying Inside (1972) F
Capricorn Games (1976) F SS

The Conglomeroid Cocktail Party (1984) F SS
Tom O'Bedlam (1985) F
Hot Sky at Midnight (1994) F

SIMAK, Clifford D[onald] (1904–1988)
American science fiction writer and journalist
City (1952) F
Way Station (1963) F
All Flesh is Grass (1965) F
A Choice of Gods (1972) F
The Fellowship of the Talisman (1978) F
Where the Evil Dwells (1982) F

SIMENON, Georges [Joseph Christian] (1903–1989)
Belgian novelist
The Death of Monsieur Gallet [*M. Gallet décède*; first Maigret story] (1931) F

SIMMS, William Gilmore (1806–1870)
American novelist, short-story writer, and poet
Atlantis: A Story of the Sea (1832) V
Martin Faber (1833) F
Guy Rivers (1834) F
The Partisan (1835) F
The Yemassee (1835) F
Mellichampe (1836) F
Pelayo (1838) F
Richard Hurdis (1838) F
The Damsel of Darien (1839) F
Border Beagles (1840) F
The Kinsmen [rev. as *The Scout*, 1854] (1841) F
Beauchampe (1842) F
Count Julian (1845) F
Helen Halsey; or, the Swamp State of Conelachita (1845) F
Katharine Walton (1851) F
The Sword and the Distaff [rev. as *Woodcraft*, 1854] (1853) F
Vasconselos (1853) F
The Forayers (1855) F
Charlemont (1856) F
Eutaw (1856) F
The Cassique of Kiawah (1859) F

SIMON, Claudee [Eugène Henri] (1913–)
French novelist
The Wind [*Le Vent*] (1957) F
The Flanders Road [*La Route des Flandres*] (1960) F

SIMON, [Marvin] Neil (1927–)
American dramatist
Come Blow Your Horn (1961) D
Little Me (1962) D
Barefoot in the Park (1963) D
The Odd Couple (1965) D
The Star-Spangled Girl (1966) D
Sweet Charity (1966) D
Plaza Suite (1968) D
Promises, Promises (1968) D
Last of the Red-Hot Lovers (1969) D
The Gingerbread Lady (1970) D
The Prisoner of Second Avenue (1972) D
The Sunshine Boys (1972) D
California Suite (1976) D
They're Playing Our Song (1979) D
Brighton Beach Memoirs (1983) D
Biloxi Blues (1984) D
Broadway Bound (1986) D

SIMPSON, Louis [Aston Marantz] (1923–)
American poet, dramatist, novelist, and critic
The Arrivistes (1949) V
Good News of Death (1955) V
A Dream of Governors (1959) V
Riverside Drive (1962) F
At the End of the Open Road (1963) V
Adventures of the Letter I (1971) V
North of Jamaica (1972) NF
Searching for the Ox (1976) V
Caviare at the Funeral (1980) V
A Company of Poets (1981) NF
People Live Here (1983) V
The Best Hour of the Night (1984) V
The Character of the Poet (1986) NF

SIMPSON, N[orman] F[rederick] (1919–)
British dramatist
A Resounding Tinkle (1957) D
One-Way Pendulum (1959) D
The Cresta Run (1965) D

SIMS, George R[obert] (1847–1922)
British journalist, poet, and short story writer
The Dagonet Ballads (1879) V
Ballads of Babylon (1880) V
Zeph, and Other Stories (1880) F SS
The Theatre of Life (1881) F SS
How the Poor Live (1883) NF
Stories in Black and White (1885) F SS
The Land of Gold, and Other Poems (1888) V
Tales of Today (1889) F SS
Dramas of Life (1890) F
The Ten Commandments (1896) F
Dorcas Dene, Detective (1897) F SS
A Blind Marriage, and Other Stories (1901) F SS
London by Night (1906) NF
The Mysteries of Modern London (1906) F SS
Anna of the Underworld (1916) F

SINCLAIR, Andrew [Annandale] (1935–)
British novelist, biographer, and cultural historian
The Breaking of Bumbo (1959) F
Gog (1967) F
Magog (1972) F
King Ludd (1988) F

SINCLAIR, May [Mary Amelia St Clair] (1863–1946)
British novelist, short-story writer, and poet
Essays in Verse (1891) V
Audrey Craven (1897) F
Mr and Mrs Nevill Tyson (1898) F
Two Sides of a Question (1901) F
The Divine Fire (1904) F
The Helpmate (1907) F
Kitty Tailleur (1908) F

Feminism (1912) NF
The Judgement of Eve, and Other Stories (1914) F SS
The Three Sisters (1914) F
A Defence of Idealism (1917) NF
The Tree of Heaven (1917) F
Mary Olivier (1919) F
Ann Severn and the Fieldings (1922) F
Life and Death of Harriet Frean (1922) F
Uncanny Stories (1923) F SS
The History of Anthony Waring (1927) F
The Intercessor, and Other Stories (1931) F SS

SINCLAIR, Upton [Beall] (1878–1968)
American novelist and non-fiction writer
Springtime and Harvest [retitled *King Midas*, 1901] (1901) F
The Journal of Arthur Stirling (1903) F
Prince Hagen (1903) F
Manassas (1904) F
The Jungle (1906) F
The Metropolis (1908) F
King Coal (1917) F
The Profits of Religion (1918) NF
The Brass Check (1919) NF
Jimmie Higgins (1919) F
They Call Me Carpenter (1922) F
The Goose-Step (1923) NF
Mammonmart (1925) NF
Money Writes! (1927) NF
Oil! (1927) F
Boston (1928) F
Mountain City (1930) F
The Wet Parade (1931) F
American Outpost (1932) NF
The Flivver King (1937) F
World's End (1940) F
Between Two Worlds (1941) F
Dragon's Teeth (1942) F
Wide is the Gate (1943) F
Presidential Agent (1944) F
Dragon Harvest (1945) F
A World to Win (1946) F
Presidential Mission (1947) F
One Clear Call (1948) F
O Shepherd, Speak! (1949) F
The Return of Lanny Budd (1953) F
It Happened to Didymus (1958) F
My Lifetime in Letters (1960) NF

SINGER, Isaac Bashevis (1904–1991)
Polish-born American Yiddish novelist
The Family Moskat (1950) F
Satan in Goray (1955) F
Gimpel the Fool (1957) F SS
The Magician of Lublin (1960) F
The Spinoza of Market Street (1961) F SS
The Slave (1962) F
Short Friday (1964) F SS
In My Father's Court (1966) NF
Zlateh the Goat (1966) F SS
The Manor (1967) F
The Séance (1968) F SS
When Shlemiel Went to Warsaw (1968) F CH
The Estate (1969) F
Enemies (1970) F
A Friend of Kafka (1970) F SS
A Crown of Feathers (1973) F SS
Passions (1978) F SS
Shosha (1978) F
Lost in America (1981) NF
The Penitent (1983) F
Love and Exile (1984) NF
Scum (1991) F
The Certificate (1992) F
Meshugah (1994) F

SISSON, C[harles] H[ubert] (1914–)
British poet, critic, novelist, and translator
An Asiatic Romance (1953) F
The London Zoo (1961) V
Christopher Homm (1965) F
Numbers (1965) V
The Disincarnation (1967) V
Roman Poems (1968) V
English Poetry 1900–1950 (1971) NF
In the Trojan Ditch (1974) V
The Corridor (1975) V
Anchises (1976) V
The Avoidance of Literature (1978) NF
The Divine Comedy [from Dante] (1980) V
Exactions (1980) V
Anglican Essays (1983) NF
The Aeneid [from Virgil] (1986) V
God Bless Karl Marx (1987) V
Antidotes (1991) V
Pattern (1993) V
What and Who (1994) V

SITWELL, [Dame] Edith [Louisa] (1887–1964)
British poet and author
The Mother, and Other Poems (1915) V
Twentieth-Century Harlequinade, and Other Poems (1916) V
Clowns' Houses (1918) V
The Wooden Pegasus (1920) V
Façade (1922) V
Bucolic Comedies (1923) V
Poetry and Criticism (1925) NF
Gold Coast Customs (1929) V
Aspects of Modern Poetry (1934) NF
Victoria of England (1936) NF
Street Songs (1942) V
A Poet's Notebook (1943) NF
Green Song, and Other Poems (1944) V
The Song of the Cold (1945) V
The Shadow of Cain (1947) V
The Canticle of the Rose (1949) V
Poor Men's Music (1950) V
Gardeners and Astronomers (1953) V

SITWELL, Sir [Francis] Osbert [Sacheverell] (1892–1969)
British poet, novelist, and autobiographer
Argonaut and Juggernaut (1919) V

The Winstonburg Line (1919) V
Out of the Flame (1923) V
Triple Fugue (1924) F SS
Before the Bombardment (1926) F
England Reclaimed (1927) V
The Man Who Lost Himself (1929) F
Left Hand, Right Hand! (1944) NF
The Scarlet Tree (1946) NF
Great Morning (1947) NF
Laughter in the Next Room (1948) NF
Noble Essences; or, Courteous Revelations (1950) NF
Wrack at Tidesend (1952) V
On the Continent (1958) V
Tales My Father Taught Me (1962) NF

SITWELL, Sir Sacheverell (1897–1988)
British poet and art historian
The People's Palace (1918) V
The Hundred and One Harlequins (1922) V
The Thirteenth Caesar, and Other Poems (1924) V
The Cyder Feast, and Other Poems (1927) V
Far From My Home (1931) F SS
Canons of Giant Art (1933) V
Conversation Pieces (1936) NF
Dance of the Quick and the Dead (1936) NF
British Architects and Craftsmen (1945) NF
Journey to the Ends of Time (1959) NF

SKEAT, W[alter] W[illiam] (1835–1912)
British philologist
The Vision of William Concerning Piers Plowman (1867) EDN
The Holy Gospels in Anglo-Saxon, Northumbrian and Old Mercian Versions (1871) EDN
An Etymological Dictionary of the English Language (1879) NF
Aelfric's Lives of the Saints (1881) NF

SKELTON, John (1460?–1529)
English priest, royal tutor, poet, and dramatist
The Bowge of Courte (1499?) V
A Ballade of the Scottysshe Kynge (1513) V
The Tunnying of Eleynour Rummyng (1521?) V
The Garland of Laurel (1523) V
Diverse Ballads (1528?) V
A Replication (1528)V
Collyn Clout (1531?) V
Magnyfycence (1533?) D
Phyllyp Sparowe (1545?) V
Why Come Ye Nat to Courte (1545?) V

SLAUGHTER, Carolyn (1946–)
British novelist
The Story of the Weasel (1976) F
Columba (1977) F
Magdalene (1978) F
Dreams of the Kalahari (1981) F
The Banquet (1983) F
A Perfect Woman (1984) F
The Widow (1989) F

SLAUGHTER, Frank G[ill] (1908–)
American crime and thriller writer
Spencer Brade, MD (1942) F
Air Surgeon (1943) F
Battle Surgeon (1944) F
In a Dark Garden (1946) F
The Stubborn Heart (1950) F
The Healer (1955) F
Sword and Scalpel (1957) F
Epidemic (1961) F
Plague Ship (1977) F
Gospel Fever (1980) F
Transplant (1986) F

SMART, Christopher (1722–1771)
British poet
Poems on Several Occasions (1752) V
The Hilliad (1753) V
Hymn to the Supreme Being (1756) V
A Song to David (1763) V
Hannah (1764) D
Hymns and Spiritual Songs (1765) V
The Psalms of David (1765) V
The Works of Horace Translated into Verse (1767) V
The Parables of Our Lord and Saviour Jesus Christ (1768) V CH
Hymns, for the Amusement of Children (1772) V

SMART, Elizabeth (1913–1986)
Canadian novelist and poet
By Grand Central Station I Sat Down and Wept (1945) F
A Bonus (1977) V
The Assumption of the Rodues and Rascals (1978) F
Eleven Poems (1982) V
In the Mean Time (1984) V

SMART, [Henry] Hawley (1833–1893)
British novelist
The Great Tontine (1881) F

SMEDLEY, Francis [Frank] Edward (1818–1864)
British novelist
Frank Fairlegh; or, Scenes From the Life of a Private Pupil (1850) F
Lewis Arundel; or, The Railroad of Life (1852) F
Harry Coverdale's Courtship (1855) F

SMILES, Samuel (1812–1904)
British biographer and advocate of self-help
The Life of George Stephenson, Railway Engineer (1857) NF
Self-Help (1859) NF
Industrial Biography (1863) NF
Lives of Boulton and Watt (1865) NF
Lives of the Engineers (1867) NF
Character (1871) NF
Duty (1880) NF
Life and Labour: or, Characteristics of Men of Industry, Culture, and Genius (1887) NF
The Autobiography of Samuel Smiles (1905) NF

SMILEY, Jane (1949–)
American novelist
Barn Blind (1980) F

At Paradise Gate (1981) F SS
The Age of Grief (1987) F SS
The Greenlanders (1988) F SS
A Thousand Acres (1992) F SS
Moo (1995) F

SMITH, Adam (1723–1790)
British political economist
The Theory of Moral Sentiments (1759) NF
An Inquiry into the Nature and Causes of the Wealth of Nations (1776) NF
Essays on Philosophical Subjects (1795) NF

SMITH, Alexander (1830–1867)
Scottish poet and essayist
A Life Drama (1853) V
City Poems (1857) V
Dreamthorp (1863) NF

SMITH, Charlotte, *née* Turner (1749–1806)
British poet and novelist
Elegaic Sonnets, and Other Essays (1784) V
Manon Lescaut; or, The Fatal Attachment [from A.F. Prévost] (1785) F
The Romance of Real Life (1787) F
Emmeline; or, The Orphan of the Castle (1788) F
Ethelinde; or, The Recluse of the Lake (1789) F
Celestina (1791) F
Desmond (1792) F
The Emigrants (1793) V
The Old Manor House (1793) F
The Banished Man (1794) F
The Wanderings of Warwick (1794) F
Montalbert (1795) F
Marchmont (1796) F
Elegaic Sonnets, and Other Poems [vol. ii] (1797) V
The Young Philosopher (1798) F
The Letters of a Solitary Wanderer [vols. i-iii; vols. iv, v, 1802] (1799) F SS
Beachy Head, with Other Poems (1807) V

SMITH, Dodie [Dorothy Gladys Smith] (1896–1990)
British dramatist and novelist
Autumn Crocus [as 'C.L. Anthony'] (1931) D
Service [as 'C.L. Anthony'] (1932) D
Touch Wood [as 'C.L. Anthony'] (1934) D
Call It a Day (1935) D
Bonnet Over the Windmill (1937) D
Dear Octopus (1938) D
I Capture the Castle (1949) F
Letter from Paris (1952) D
One Hundred and One Dalmatians (1956) F CH
The New Moon with the Old (1963) F
The Town in Bloom (1965) F
A Tale of Two Families (1970) F
The Girl From the Candle-Lit Bath (1978) F

SMITH, E[dward] E[lmer] 'Doc' Smith (1890–1965)
American science fiction writer
The Skylark of Space [in *Amazing magazine*; book form 1946] (1928) F
Triplanetary (1948) F
First Lensman (1950) F
Galactic Patrol (1950) F
Gray Lensman (1951) F
Second Stage Lensman (1953) F
Children of the Lens (1954) F
The Vortex Blaster (1960) F

SMITH, Ernest Bramah *see* ERNEST BRAMAH

SMITH, Frederick R. *see* JOHN ACKWORTH

SMITH, Horatio [always known as **Horace**] (1779–1849)
British poet, novelist, and journalist
The Runaway (1800) F
Trevanion; or, Matrimonial Ventures (1801) F
Horatio; or, Memoirs of the Davenport Family (1807) F
Rejected Addresses; or, The New Theatrum Poetarum (1812) V
Horace in London (1813) V
Brambletye House; or, Cavaliers and Roundheads (1826) F
Reuben Apsley (1827) F
Zillah (1828) F
The Moneyed Man (1841) F
Love and Mesmerism (1845) F

SMITH, Iain Crichton [Iain Mac a'Ghobhainn] (1928–)
Scottish poet, dramatist, and novelist
The Long River (1955) V
Deer on the High Hills (1960) V
The Law and the Grace (1965) V
Consider the Lilies [US: *The Alien Light*] (1968) F
From Bourgeois Land (1969) V
My Last Duchess (1971) F
Love Poems and Elegies (1972) V
Goodbye Mr Dixon (1974) F
Notebooks of Robinson Crusoe, and Other Poems (1975) V
An End to Autumn (1978) F
Murdo, and Other Stories (1981) F SS
Exiles (1984) V
The Tenement (1985) F
A Life (1986) V
Towards the Human (1986) NF
The Village, and Other Poems (1989) V
Listening to the Voice (1993) F SS
Ends and Beginnings (1994) V

SMITH, Ken[neth John] (1938–)
British poet
The Pity (1967) V
The Poet Reclining (1982) V
Terra (1986) V
Wormwood (1987) V
The Heart, the Border (1990) V
Tender to the Queen of Spades (1993) V

SMITH, [Lloyd] Logan Pearsall (1865–1946)
American-born essayist
The Youth of Parnassus, and Other Stories (1895) F SS
Trivia (1918) NF

More Trivia (1922) NF
Words and Idioms (1925) NF
The Prospects of Literature (1927) NF
Afterthoughts (1931) NF
Unforgotten Years (1938) NF
Milton and his Modern Critics (1940) NF

SMITH, Martin Cruz (1942–)
American thriller writer
Nightwing (1978) F
Gorky Park (1981) F
Havanna Bay (1999) F

SMITH, Stevie [Florence Margaret Smith] (1902–1971)
British poet and novelist
Novel on Yellow Paper (1936) F
A Good Time Was Had by All (1937) V
Tender Only to One (1938) V
Over the Frontier (1939) F
Mother, What is Man? (1942) V
The Holiday (1949) F
Harold's Leap (1950) V
Not Waving But Drowning (1957) V
The Frog Prince, and Other Poems (1966) V
Scorpion, and Other Poems (1972) V

SMITH, Sydney (1771–1845)
British clergyman and author
Elementary Sketches of Moral Philosophy (1804) NF
The Letters of Peter Plymley on the Subject of the Catholics (1807–8) NF
Three Letters on the Ecclesiastical Commission (1837–9) NF

SMITH, Sydney Goodsir (1915–1975)
New Zealand-born Scottish poet
Skail Wind (1941) V
The Deevil's Waltz (1946) V
Carotid Cornucopius (1947) F
Under the Eildon Tree (1948) V
So Late into the Night (1952) V
Cokkils (1953) V
Figs and Thistles (1959) V
The Wallace (1960) D
Girl with a Violin (1968) V

SMITH, Wilbur [Addison] (1933–)
South African popular novelist
When the Lion Feeds (1964) F
Shout at the Devil (1966) F
The Dark of the Sun (1968) F
Gold Mine (1970) F
The Diamond Hunters (1971) F
The Sunbird (1972) F
The Eye of the Tiger (1975) F
Cry Wolf (1976) F
A Sparrow Falls (1977) F
A Falcon Flies (1980) F
Men of Men (1981) F
The Leopard Hunts in Darkness (1984) F
Elephant Song (1991) F

SMITH, William Robertson (1846–1894)
Scottish theologian and orientalist
The Old Testament in the Jewish Church (1881) NF

SMITH, Zadie (1975–)
British novelist
White Teeth (2000) F

SMOLLETT, Tobias [George] (1721–1771)
British novelist, poet, and dramatist
Advice (1746) V
Reproof (1747) V
The Adventures of Roderick Random (1748) F
The Adventures of Gil Blas of Santillane (1749) F
The Regicide; or, James the First of Scotland (1749) D
The Adventures of Peregrine Pickle (1751) F
The Adventures of Ferdinand Count Fathom (1753) F
The History and Adventures of the Renowned Don Quixote [from Cervantes] (1755) F
The Reprisal; or, The Tars of Old England (1757) D
The Life and Adventures of Sir Launcelot Greaves (1762) F
Travels Through France and Italy (1766) NF
The History and Adventures of an Atom (1769) F
The Expedition of Humphrey Clinker (1771) F

SNODGRASS, W[illiam] D[e Witt] (1926–)
American poet
Heart's Needle (1959) V
After Experience (1968) V
In Radical Pursuit (1975) NF
The Fuhrer Bunker (1977) V

SNOW, C[harles] P[ercy] Baron Snow of Leicester (1905–1980)
British novelist and non-fiction writer
Death Under Sail (1932) F
New Lives For Old (1933) F
The Search (1934) F
Strangers and Brothers (1940) F
The Light and the Dark (1947) F
Time of Hope (1949) F
The Masters (1951) F
The New Men (1954) F
Homecomings (1956) F
The Conscience of the Rich (1958) F
The Two Cultures and the Scientific Revolution (1959) NF
The Affair (1960) F
Science and Government (1961) NF
Corridors of Power (1964) F
The Two Cultures; and A Second Look (1964) NF
Variety of Men (1967) NF
The Sleep of Reason (1968) F
Last Things (1970) F
The Malcontents (1972) F
In Their Wisdom (1974) F
A Coat of Varnish (1978) F

SNYDER, Gary [Sherman] (1930–)
American poet
Riprap (1959) V
Myths and Texts (1960) V

Six Sections from Mountains and Rivers Without End (1965) V
The Back Country (1968) V
Earth House Hold (1969) NF
Regarding Wave (1970) V
Turtle Island (1974) V
Left Out in the Rain (1986) V

SOLZHENITSYN, Alexander [Isayevich] (1918–)
Russian novelist and author
One Day in the Life of Ivan Denisovich (1962) F
The Cancer Ward (1968) F
The First Circle (1968) F
August, 1914 (1971) F
The Gulag Archipelago (1973–6) NF
The Oak and the Calf (1975) NF
Rebuilding Russia (1990) NF

SOMERVILLE, Edith Anna Oenone *see* 'SOMERVILLE AND ROSS'

'SOMERVILLE and **ROSS' [Edith Anna Oenone Somerville** (1858–1949) and **Violet Florence Martin]** (1862–1915)
Irish novelists
An Irish Cousin (1889) F
Naboth's Vineyard (1891) F
The Real Charlotte (1894) F
The Silver Fox (1897) F
Some Experiences of an Irish R.M. (1899) F SS
All on the Irish Shore (1903) F SS
Further Experiences of an Irish R.M. (1908) F SS
Dan Russel the Fox (1911) F
In Mr Knox's Country (1915) F
Mount Music (1919) F
An Enthusiast (1921) F
The Big House of Inver (1925) F

SONTAG, Susan (1933–)
American critic, novelist, and short-story writer
The Benefactor (1963) F
Against Interpretation (1966) NF
Death Kit (1967) F
Trip to Hanoi (1968) NF
Styles of Radical Will (1969) NF
On Photography (1977) NF
I, etcetera (1978) F SS
Illness as Metaphor (1978) NF
Under the Sign of Saturn (1980) NF
AIDS and its Metaphors (1988) NF
The Volcano Lover (1992) F
Alice in Bed (1993) D
In America (2000) F

SOPHOCLES (*c.* 496–*c.* 406 BC)
Greek tragic dramatist
Ajax D
Antigone (441 BC) D
Oedipus the King [*Oedipus Tyrannus*] D
The Women of Trachis [*Trachiniae*] D
Electra D
Philoctetes (409 BC) D
Oedipus at Colonus [*Oedipus Coloneus*; probably written 406–5] (401 BC) D

SORLEY, C[harles] H[amilton] (1895–1915)
Scottish poet
Marlborough, and Other Poems (1916) V

SOTHEBY, William (1757–1833)
British poet and translator
Oberon [from Wieland] (1798) V
The Battle of the Nile (1799) V
Georgics [from Virgil] (1800) V
Julian and Agnes; or, The Monks of the Great St Bernard (1800) D
The Siege of Cuzco (1800) V
A Poetical Epistle to Sir George Beaumont (1801) V
Oberon; or, Huon de Bourdeaux; and Orestes: A Tragedy (1802) D
Saul (1807) V
Constance of Castille (1810) V
Farewell to Italy, and Occasional Poems (1818) V
Iliad [from Homer] (1831) V

SOUTAR, William (1898–1943)
Scottish poet
Conflict (1931) V
Seeds in the Wind (1933) V CH
The Solitary Way (1934) V
A Handful of Earth (1936) V
But the Earth Abideth (1943) V
The Expectant Silence (1944) V

SOUTHERN, R[ichard] W[illiam] (1912–)
British medieval historian
The Making of the Middle Ages (1953) NF
Candy (1958) F

SOUTHERN, Terry (1924–)
American novelist
Flash and Filigree (1958) F
The Magic Christian (1960) F
Lollipop (1962) F
Red-Dirt Marijuana (1967) F SS
Blue Movie (1970) F

SOUTHERNE, Thomas (1659–1746)
English dramatist
The Loyal Brother; or, The Persian Prince (1682) D
The Disappointment; or, The Mother in Fashion (1684) D
Sir Anthony Love; or, The Rambling Lady (1690) D
The Wives Excuse; or, Cuckolds Make Themselves (1691) D
The Maids Last Prayer; or Any, Rather Than Fail (1693) D
The Fatal Marriage; or, The Innocent Adultery (1694) D
Oroonoko (1695) D
The Fate of Capua (1700) D
The Spartan Dame (1719) D
Money the Mistress (1726) D

SOUTHEY, Robert (1774–1843)
British poet, biographer, translator, and historian
Poems [with Robert Lovell] (1795) V
Joan of Arc (1796) V
Poems (1796) V

Letters Written During a Short Residence in Spain and Portugal . . . (1797) NF
Poems . . . The Second Volume (1799) V
Thalaba the Destroyer (1801) V
Amadis of Gaul [from Vasco Lobeira] (1803) F
Madoc (1805) V
Metrical Tales, and Other Poems (1805) V
Letters from England (1807) NF
Palmerin of England [from Francisco de Moraes] (1807) F
Chronicles of the Cid, from the Spanish (1808) NF
The Geographical, Natural, and Civil History Of Chili [from the Italian of J. Ignatius Molina] (1809) NF
The Curse of Kehama (1810) V
History of Brazil . . . Part the First (1810) NF
The Life of Nelson (1813) NF
Roderick, the Last of the Gauls (1814) V
The Lay of the Laureate: Carmen Nuptiale (1816) V
The Poet's Pilgrimage to Waterloo (1816) V
History of Brazil . . . Part the Second (1817) NF
Wat Tyler (1817) V
History of Brazil . . . Part the Third (1819) NF
The Life of Wesley, and the Rise and Progress of Methodism (1820) NF
A Vision of Judgement (1821) V
History of the Peninsular War [vol. i] (1823) NF
The Book of the Church (1824) NF
A Tale of Paraguay (1825) V
Vindiciae Ecclesiae Anglicanae (1826) NF
History of the Peninsular War [vol. ii] (1827) NF
Sir Thomas More; or, Colloquies on the Progress and Prospects of Society (1829) NF
Select Works of the British Poets (1831) ANTH
Essays, Moral and Political (1832) NF
History of the Peninsular War [vol. iii] (1832) NF
Lives of the British Admirals [vols. i, ii] (1833) NF
The Doctor [vols. i, ii] (1834) NF
Lives of the British Admirals [vol. iii] (1834) NF
The Doctor [vol. iii] (1835) NF
The Doctor [vol. iv] (1837) NF
Lives of the British Admirals [vol. iv] (1837) NF
The Doctor [vol. v] (1838) NF
The Doctor [vols. vi, vii] (1847) NF
Common-place Book [*1st and 2nd ser.*] (1849) MISC
Common-place Book [*3rd and 4th ser.*] (1849) MISC

SOUTHWELL, Robert (1561?–1595)
English Jesuit and poet
An Epistle of Comfort (1587) NF
Marie Magdalens Funeral Teares (1591) NF
Moeniae (1595) V
Saint Peters Complaint, with Other Poemes (1595) NF
The Triumphs Over Death; or, A Consolatorie Epistle (1595) NF

SOYINKA, Wole [Akinwande Oluwole Soyinka] (1934–)
Nigerian novelist, dramatist, and poet
The Inventor (1957) D
The Swamp Dwellers (1958) D
The Trials of Brother Jero (1961) D
The Lion and the Jewel (1963) D
Kongi's Harvest (1964) D
The Road (1965) D
Idanre, and Other Poems (1967) V
Poems From Prison (1969) V
The Interpreters (1970) F
Madmen and Specialists (1970) D
A Shuttle in the Crypt (1972) V
The Man Died: Prison Notes (1973) NF
Season of Anomy (1973) F
Jero's Metamorphosis (1974) D
Death and the King's Horseman (1975) D
Myth, Literature and the African World (1976) NF
Ogun Abibiman (1976) V
A Play of Giants (1984) D
Requiem for a Futurologist (1985) D
Art, Dialogue and Outrage (1988) NF
Mandela's Earth (1989) V
The Beatification of Area Boy (1995) D

SPARK, Muriel [Sarah], *née* Camberg (1918–)
British novelist, short-story writer, poet, and dramatist
The Comforters (1957) F
The Go-Away Bird, and Other Stories (1958) F SS
Robinson (1958) F
Memento Mori (1959) F
The Bachelors (1960) F
The Ballad of Peckham Rye (1960) F
The Prime of Miss Jean Brodie (1961) F
The Girls of Slender Means (1963) F
The Mandelbaum Gate (1965) F
The Public Image (1968) F
The Driver's Seat (1970) F
Not to Disturb (1971) F
The Hothouse by the River (1972) F
The Abbess of Crewe (1974) F
The Takeover (1976) F
Territorial Rights (1979) F
Loitering With Intent (1981) F
Bang-Bang You're Dead, and Other Stories (1982) F SS
Going Up to Sotheby's, and Other Poems (1982) V
The Only Problem (1984) F
A Far Cry From Kensington (1988) F
Symposium (1990) F
Curriculum Vitae (1992) NF
Aiding and Abetting (2000) F

SPEED, John (1552?–1629)
English antiquary and cartographer
The Genealogies Recorded in the Sacred Scriptures (1611) NF
The History of Great Britaine (1611) NF
The Theatre of the Empire of Great Britaine (1611) NF

SPEKE, John Hanning (1827–1864)
British explorer
Journal of the Discovery of the Source of the Nile (1863) NF

SPENCER, [Charles] Bernard (1909–1963)
British poet
Aegean Islands, and Other Poems (1946) V
With Luck Lasting (1963) V

SPENCER, Elizabeth (1921–)
American novelist and short-story writer
Fire in the Morning (1948) F
This Crooked Way (1952) F
The Voice at the Back Door (1956) F
The Light in the Piazza (1960) F
Knights and Dragons (1965) F
Ship Island (1968) F SS
The Snare (1972) F
Marilee (1981) F SS
The Salt Line (1984) F
Jack of Diamonds (1988) F SS

SPENCER, Herbert (1820–1903)
British philosopher
Social Statics; or, The Conditions Essential to Human Happiness Specified (1851) NF
A New Theory of Population (1852) NF
Principles of Psychology (1855) NF
Essays Scientific, Political, and Speculative [1st ser.; 2nd ser., 1863] (1858) NF
A System of Synthetic Philosophy (1860) NF
The Study of Sociology (1873) NF
Principles of Sociology [vol. i; vol. ii, 1882; vol. iii, 1896] (1876) NF
The Man Versus the State (1884) NF
Principles of Ethics [vol. i; vol. ii, 1893] (1892) NF
The Inadequacy of Natural Selection (1893) NF

SPENDER, Sir Stephen [Harold] (1909–1995)
British poet, dramatist, and translator
Twenty Poems (1930) V
Poems (1933) V
Vienna (1934) V
The Destructive Element (1935) NF
The Burning Cactus (1936) F SS
Forward From Liberalism (1937) NF
Trial of a Judge (1938) D
The Still Centre (1939) V
The Backward Son (1940) F
Life and the Poet (1942) NF
Ruins and Visions (1942) V
Citizens in War—and After (1945) NF
European Witness (1946) NF
Poems of Dedication (1946) V
Returning to Vienna (1947) V
The Edge of Being (1949) V
World Within World (1951) NF
The Creative Element (1953) NF
The Making of a Poem (1955) NF
The Struggle of the Modern (1963) NF
The Generous Days (1971) V
Love-Hate Relations (1974) NF
The Thirties and After (1978) NF
Dolphins (1994) V

SPENSER, Edmund (1552–1599)
English poet
The Shepheardes Calender (1579) V
The Faerie Queene [bks i-iii] (1590) V
Complaints (1591) V
Daphnaida (1591) V
Amoretti and Epithalamion (1595) V
Colin Clouts Come Home Againe (1595) V
Fowre Hymnes (1596) V
Prothalamion; or, A Spousall Verse (1596) V
The Second Part of the Faerie Queene [bks iv-vi, with revised bks i-iii] (1596) V

SPILLANE, Mickey [Frank Morrison Spillane] (1918–)
American crime writer
I, the Jury [first Mike Hammer story] (1947) F
Vengeance is Mine! (1950) F
The Big Kill (1951) F
The Girl Hunters (1952) F
Kiss Me, Deadly (1952) F
Day of the Guns (1964) F
Bloody Sunrise (1965) F
The Body Lovers (1967) F
The Delta Factor (1967) F
The Last Cop Out (1973) F

SPINRAD, Norman (1940–)
American science fiction writer
Bug Jack Barron (1969) F
The Iron Dream (1972) F

SPRING, Christopher St John *see* CHRISTOPHER CAUDWELL

SPRING, [Robert] Howard (1889–1965)
British novelist and dramatist
Shabby Tiger (1934) F
O Absalom! [US: *My Son, My Son!*] (1938) F
Heaven Lies About Us (1939) NF
Fame is the Spur (1940) F
In the Meantime (1942) NF
Hard Facts (1944) F
And Another Thing . . . (1946) NF
There is No Armour (1948) F
The Houses in Between (1951) F
I Met a Lady (1961) F
Winds of the Day (1964) F

SPURGEON, Charles [Haddon] (1834–1892)
British preacher and theologian
John Ploughman's Talks (1869) NF
John Ploughman's Pictures (1880) NF

SPYRI, Johanna (1827–1901)
Swiss novelist
Heidi (1881) F

SQUIRE, [Sir] J[ohn] C[ollings] (1884–1958)
British poet, humourist, and editor
Imaginary Speeches and Other Parodies in Prose and Verse (1912) MISC
The Three Hills, and Other Poems (1913) V
The Lily of Malud, and Other Poems (1917) V
American Poems, and Others (1923) V
The Grub Street Nights Entertainment (1924) F SS
A Face in the Candlelight, and Other Poems (1932) V

STABLEFORD, Brian M[ichael] (1948–)
British science fiction writer and critic
Cradle of the Sun (1969) F
Man in a Cage (1975) F

The Realms of Tartarus (1977) F
The Walking Shadow (1979) F
Scientific Romance in Britain (1985) NF
The Empire of Fear (1988) F
The Werewolves of London (1990) F
The Angel of Pain (1991) F
The Carnival of Destruction (1994) F

STACPOOLE, Henry de Vere (1863–1951)
Irish novelist and poet
The Intended (1894) F
Pierrot! (1896) F
Death, the Knight and the Lady (1897) F
The Bourgeois (1901) F
The Crimson Azaleas (1907) F
The Blue Lagoon (1908) F
The Pools of Silence (1909) F
Poems and Ballads (1910) V
The North Sea, and Other Poems (1915) V
The Starlit Garden (1917) F
The Man Who Lost Himself (1918) F

STAËL, Madame de [Anne Louise Germaine Necker, Baronne de Staël-Holstein] (1766–1817)
French author
Réflexions sur la paix intérieure ['Reflections on Civil Peace'] (1795) NF
The Influence of Literature Upon Society [*De la littérature considérée dans ses rapports avec les institutions sociales*] (1800) NF
Delphine (1802) F
Memoirs of the Private Life of My Father [*Du caracttère de M. Necker et sa vie privée*] (1804) NF
Corinne (1807) F
Germany [*De l'Allemagne*] (1810) NF
Considerations on the Principal Events of the French Revolution [*Considérations sur les principaux événements de la Révolution française*] (1818) NF
Ten Years' Exile [*Dix Années d'exil*] (1821) NF

STAFFORD, Jean (1915–1979)
American novelist and short-story writer
Boston Adventure (1944) F
Mountain Lion (1947) F
The Catherine Wheel (1952) F
Children Are Bored on Sunday (1954) F SS
A Winter's Tale (1954) F
Bad Characters (1964) F SS
A Mother in History (1966) NF

STALLWORTHY, Jon [Howie] (1935–)
British poet, critic, and editor
The Astronomy of Love (1961) V
Out of Bounds (1963) V
Root and Branch (1969) V
Hand in Hand (1974) V
Wilfred Owen (1974) NF
A Familiar Tree (1978) V
The Anzac Sonata (1986) V
The Guest From the Future (1989) V
Louis MacNeice (1995) NF
Rounding the Horn (1998) V
Singing School (1999) V

STANHOPE, Philip Dormer, 4th Earl of Chesterfield (1694–1773)
English statesman and letter writer
Letters Written to his Son (1774) NF
Lord Chesterfield's Maxims; or, A New Plan of Education (1774) NF
Characters of Eminent Personages of His Own Time (1777) NF

STANLEY, Arthur Penrhyn (1815–1881)
British churchman, historian, and biographer
Life of Dr Arnold (1844) NF
Lectures on the History of the Jewish Church (1863) NF
Essays, Chiefly on Questions of Church and State (1870) NF
Christian Institutions (1881) NF

STANLEY, Henry Morton (1841–1904)
British explorer, administrator, author, and journalist
How I Found Livingstone (1872) NF
Through the Dark Continent; or, The Sources of the Nile (1878) NF
In Darkest Africa (1890) NF

STANLEY, Thomas, the Elder (1625–1678)
English classical scholar and poet
Aurora, & The Prince (1647) F V
Poems and Translations (1647) V
Europa. Cupid Crucified. Venus Vigils (1649) V
The History of Philosophy (1655) NF

STAPLEDON, W[illiam] Olaf (1886–1950)
British science fiction writer
Last and First Men (1930) F
Last Men in London (1931) F
Odd John (1935) F
Star Maker (1937) F
Sirius (1944) F
Man Divided (1950) F

STARK, [Dame] Freya [Madeline] (1893–1993)
British travel writer
The Valleys of the Assassins, and Other Persian Travels (1934) NF
The Southern Gates of Arabia (1936) NF
Baghdad Sketches (1937) NF
Letters From Syria (1942) NF
Perseus in the Wind (1948) NF
Traveller's Prelude (1950) NF
Beyond Euphrates (1951) NF
The Coast of Incense (1953) NF
Ionia (1954) NF
The Lycian Shore (1956) NF
Dust in the Lion's Paw (1961) NF

STEAD, C[hristian] K[arlson] (1932–)
New Zealand critic, poet, novelist, and short-story writer
The New Poetic (1964) NF
Smith's Dream (1971) F
Crossing the Bar (1972) V
Queseda (1978) V

Walking Westwards (1978) V
Five for the Symbol (1981) F SS
In the Glass Case (1981) NF
Geographies (1982) V
All Visitors Ashore (1984) F
Pound, Yeats, Eliot, and the Modern Movement (1985) NF
The Death of the Body (1986) F
Between (1988) V
Sister Hollywood (1989) F
Voices (1990) V
End of the World at the End of the Century (1992) F

STEAD, Christina [Ellen] (1902–1983)
Australian-born novelist and short-story writer
The Salzburg Tales (1934) F SS
Seven Poor Men of Sydney (1934) F
The Beauties and the Furies (1936) F
House of All Nations (1938) F
The Man Who Loved Children (1940) F
For Love Alone (1944) F
Letty Fox: her Luck (1946) F
A Little Tea, a Little Chat (1948) F
The People with the Dogs (1952) F
Cotter's England [US: *Dark Places of the Heart*] (1966) F
The Puzzleheaded Girl (1967) F SS
The Little Hotel (1973) F
Miss Herbert (1976) F
Ocean of Story (1985) F SS
I'm Dying Laughing (1986) F

STEEL, Danielle (1947–)
American popular novelist
Going Home (1973) F
The Promise (1977) F
Now and Forever (1978) F
Season of Passion (1979) F
A Perfect Stranger (1982) F
Daddy (1989) F
Mirror Image (1998) F
Irresistible Forces (1999) F
The Wedding (2000) F

STEEL, Flora Annie, *née* Webster (1847–1929)
British novelist and short story writer
Wide Awake Stories (1884) F SS
Miss Stuart's Legacy (1893) F
The Flower of Forgiveness (1894) F SS
The Potter's Thumb (1894) F
Red Rowans (1895) F
On the Face of the Waters (1896) F HF
In the Permanent Way, and Other Stories (1897) F SS
The Hosts of the Lord (1900) F
In the Guardianship of God (1903) F
Marmaduke (1917) F

STEELE, Sir Richard (1672–1729)
English essayist, dramatist, and poet
The Christian Hero (1701) NF
The Funeral; or, Grief a-la-mode (1701) D
The Lying Lover; or, The Ladies Friendship (1703) D
The Tender Husband; or, The Accomplish'd Fools (1705) D
The Tatler (1709–10) PER
The Spectator (1711–12) PER
The Crisis; or, A Discourse Representing the Just Causes of the Late Happy Revolution (1714) NF
The Public Spirit of the Tories (1714) NF
The Crisis of Property (1720) NF
A Nation a Family (1720) NF
The Conscious Lovers (1722) D

STEEVENS, George (1736–1800)
British Shakespeare scholar
Twenty of the Plays of Shakespeare Publish'd from the Originals (1766) EDN
The Plays of William Shakespeare (1773) EDN

STEGNER, Wallace [Earle] (1909–1993)
American novelist, historian, and biographer
Remembering Laughter (1937) F
On a Darkling Plain (1940) F
The Big Rock Candy Mountain (1943) F
Second Growth (1947) F
The Preacher and the Slave (1950) F
Beyond the Hundredth Meridian [biog. of John Wesley Powell] (1954) NF
A Shooting Star (1961) F
Wolf Willow (1962) NF
The Gathering of Zion (1964) NF
All the Little Live Things (1967) F
Angle of Repose (1971) F
The Spectator Bird (1976) F
Recapitulation (1979) F
Crossing to Safety (1987) F

STEIN, Gertrude (1874–1946)
American novelist, poet, dramatist, and critic
Three Lives: The Story of the Good Anna, Melanctha, and the Gentle Lena (1909) F
Tender Buttons (1914) V
Geography and Plays (1922) NF
The Making of Americans (1925) F
Composition as Explanation (1926) NF
Lucy Church Amiably (1930) F
A Long Gay Book (1932) F
The Autobiography of Alice B. Toklas (1933) NF
Four Saints in Three Acts (1934) OP
Lectures in America (1935) NF
Narration (1935) NF
The Geographical History of America (1936) NF
Everybody's Autobiography (1937) NF
Picasso (1938) NF
Paris France (1940) NF
Ida (1941) F
Wars I Have Seen (1945) NF
Brewsie and Willie (1946) F
Yes Is For a Very Young Man (1946) D

STEINBECK, John [Ernst] (1902–1968)
American novelist
Cup of Gold (1929) F
The Pastures of Heaven (1932) F SS
To a God Unknown (1933) F

Tortilla Flat (1935) F
In Dubious Battle (1936) F
Of Mice and Men [dramatized 1938] (1937) F
The Red Pony (1937) F SS
The Long Valley (1938) F SS
The Grapes of Wrath (1939) F
The Sea of Cortez (1941) NF
Bombs Away (1942) NF
The Moon is Down [dramatized 1942] (1942) F
Cannery Row (1945) F
The Wayward Bus (1947) F
The Pearl (1948) F
A Russian Journal (1948) NF
Burning Bright (1950) F
East of Eden (1952) F
Sweet Thursday (1954) F
The Short Reign of Pippin IV (1957) F
Once There Was a War (1958) NF
The Winter of Our Discontent (1961) F
Travels with Charley in Search of America (1962) NF

STEINEM, Gloria (1934–)
American feminist critic
Marilyn (1986) NF
Revolution From Within (1992) NF

STEINER, [Francis] George (1929–)
Austrian-born literary and cultural critic
Tolstoy or Dostoevsky (1959) NF
Language and Silence (1967) NF
In Bluebeard's Castle (1971) NF
After Babel (1975) NF
The Portage to San Cristobal of A.H. (1981) F
Real Presences (1989) NF

'STENDHAL' [Henri Marie Beyle] (1783–1842)
French novelist and critic
Rome, Naples et Florence en 1817 (1817) NF
On Love [*De l'amour*] (1822) NF
Armance (1827) F
Scarlet and Black [*Le Rouge et le Noir*] (1830) F
L'Abbesse de Castro ['The Abbess of Castro'] (1839) F
The Charterhouse of Parma [*La Chartreuse de Parme*] (1839) F

STEPHEN, Sir James (1789–1859)
British statesman, historian, and biographer
Essays in Ecclesiastical Biography (1849) NF
Lectures on the History of France (1851) NF

STEPHEN, Sir Leslie (1832–1904)
British biographer, editor, and man of letters
Peaks, Passes, and Glaciers (1862) NF
The Playground of Europe (1871) NF
Essays on Freethinking and Plainspeaking (1873) NF
Hours in a Library [1st ser.; 2nd ser., 1876; 3rd ser., 1879] (1874) NF
History of English Thought in the Eighteenth Century (1876) NF
Samuel Johnson (1878) NF
Alexander Pope (1880) NF
The Science of Ethics (1882) NF
Swift (1882) NF
An Agnostic's Apology, and Other Essays (1893) NF
Social Rights and Duties (1896) NF
The English Utilitarians (1900) NF
George Eliot (1902) NF
Robert Louis Stevenson (1902) NF
English Literature and Society in the Eighteenth Century (1904) NF
Hobbes (1904) NF

STEPHENS, James (1882–1950)
Irish poet, novelist, and short-story writer
Insurrections (1909) V
The Charwoman's Daughter (1912) F
The Crock of Gold (1912) F
The Hill of Vision (1912) V
Here Are Ladies (1913) F SS
The Demi-Gods (1914) F
The Adventures of Seumas Beg; The Rocky Road to Dublin (1915) V
Songs From the Clay (1915) V
The Insurrection in Dublin (1916) NF
Reincarnations (1918) V
Irish Fairy Tales (1920) F SS
Deirdre (1923) F
Etched in Moonlight (1928) F SS
Strict Joy (1931) V
Kings and the Moon (1938) V

STERN, G[ladys] B[ronwyn] (1890–1973)
British novelist
Tents of Israel [US: *The Matriarch*] (1924) F
A Deputy Was King (1926) F
Petruchia [US: *Modesta*] (1929) F
Shining and Free (1935) F
The Young Matriarch (1942) F

STERNE, Laurence (1713–1768)
British novelist and author
The Life and Opinions of Tristram Shandy, Gentleman [vols. i, ii] (1760) F
The Sermons of Mr Yorick [vols. i, ii] (1760) NF
The Life and Opinions of Tristram Shandy, Gentleman [vols. iii, iv] (1761) F
The Life and Opinions of Tristram Shandy, Gentleman [vols. v, vi] (1762) F
The Life and Opinions of Tristram Shandy, Gentleman [vols. vii, viii] (1765) F
The Sermons of Mr Yorick [vols. iii, iv] (1766) NF
The Life and Opinions of Tristram Shandy, Gentleman [vol. ix] (1767) F
A Sentimental Journey Through France and Italy (1768) P
Sermons by the Late Rev. Mr Sterne [*Sermons of Mr Yorick*, vols. v, vi, vii] (1769) NF
Letters from Yorick to Eliza (1773) NF

STEVENS, Wallace (1879–1955)
American poet
Harmonium [enlarged edn, 1931] (1923) V

Ideas of Order (1935) V
Owl's Clover (1936) V
The Man With the Blue Guitar (1937) V
Notes Toward a Supreme Fiction (1942) V
Parts of a World (1942) V
Transport to Summer (1947) V
The Auroras of Autumn (1950) V
The Necessary Angel (1951) NF
Opus Posthumous (1957) MISC

STEVENSON, Anne [Katherine] (1933–)
British poet
Living in America (1965) V
Reversals (1969) V
Correspondences (1974) V
Travelling Behind Glass (1974) V
Enough of Green (1977) V
Minute by Glass Minute (1982) V
The Fiction-Makers (1985) V
Bitter Fame [biography of Sylvia Plath] (1989) NF
The Other House (1990) V
Four and a Half Dancing Men (1992) V

STEVENSON, Robert Louis (1850–1894)
Scottish poet, novelist, and essayist
Edinburgh: Picturesque Notes (1878) NF
An Inland Voyage (1878) NF
Travels with a Donkey in the Cévennes (1879) NF
Virginibus Puerisque, and Other Papers (1881) NF
Familiar Studies of Men and Books (1882) NF
New Arabian Nights (1882) F SS
The Silverado Squatters (1883) F
Treasure Island (1883) F CH
A Child's Garden of Verses (1885) V CH
More New Arabian Nights: The Dynamiter (1885) F SS
Prince Otto (1885) F
Kidnapped (1886) F CH
Strange Case of Dr Jekyll and Mr Hyde (1886) F
Memories and Portraits (1887) NF
The Merry Men, and Other Tales and Fables (1887) F SS
Underwoods (1887) V
The Black Arrow (1888) F CH
The Master of Ballantrae (1889) F CH
The Wrong Box (1889) F
Ballads (1890) V
Across the Plains, with Other Memories and Essays (1892) NF
A Footnote to History (1892) NF
The Wrecker (1892) F
Catriona (1893) F
Island Nights' Entertainments (1893) F SS
The Ebb-Tide (1894) F
Vailima Letters (1895) NF
Songs of Travel, and Other Verses (1896) V
Weir of Hermiston [unfinished] (1896) F
St Ives [unfinished; completed by Sir A. Quiller-Couch] (1898) F

STEWART, Dugald (1753–1828)
Scottish philosopher
Elements of the Philosophy of the Human Mind [vol. i; vol. ii, 1827; vol. iii, 1847] (1792) NF
Outlines of Moral Philosophy (1793) NF
Philosophical Essays (1810) NF
The Philosophy of the Active and Moral Powers (1828) NF

STEWART, J[ohn] I[nnes] M[ackintosh] ['Michael Innes'] (1906–1994)
British academic, critic, and novelist
Death at the President's Lodging [as 'Michael Innes'. US: *Seven Suspects*] (1936) F
Hamlet, Revenge! [as 'Michael Innes'] (1937) F
Lament for a Maker [as 'Michael Innes'] (1938) F
Stop Press [as 'Michael Innes'. US: *The Spider Strikes*] (1939) F
Appleby on Ararat [as 'Michael Innes'] (1941) F
The Daffodil Affair [as 'Michael Innes'] (1942) F
Appleby's End [as 'Michael Innes'] (1945) F
A Private View [as 'Michael Innes'. US: *One-Man Show*] (1952) F
Appleby Talking [as 'Michael Innes'] (1954) F SS
Mark Lambert's Supper (1954) F
Appleby Plays Chicken [as 'Michael Innes'. US: *Death on a Quiet Day*] (1956) F
Appleby Talks Again [as 'Michael Innes'] (1956) F SS
A Use of Riches (1957) F
The Man Who Wrote Detective Stories, and Other Stories (1959) F SS
Eight Modern Writers (1963) NF
An Acre of Grass (1965) F
Appleby at Allington [as 'Michael Innes'] (1968) F
Cucumber Sandwiches, and Other Stories (1969) F SS
The Gaudy (1974) F
Young Patullo (1975) F
A Memorial Service (1976) F
The Madonna of the Astrolabe (1977) F
Full Term (1978) F

STOKER, Bram [Abraham] (1847–1912)
Anglo-Irish theatre manager, novelist, and short-story writer
Under the Sunset (1881) F SS
The Snake's Pass (1890) F
The Shoulder of Shasta (1895) F
Dracula (1897) F
The Mystery of the Sea (1902) F
The Jewel of the Seven Stars (1903) F
The Man (1905) F
Personal Reminiscences of Henry Irving (1906) NF
Lady Athlyne (1908) F
The Lady of the Shroud (1909) F
The Lair of the White Worm (1911) F
Dracula's Guest, and Other Weird Stories (1914) F SS

STOKES, Adrian [Durham] (1902–1972)
British art critic, painter, and poet
The Quattro Cento (1932) NF
Stones of Rimini (1934) NF

Colour and Form (1937) NF
Three Essays on the Painting of Our Time (1961) NF

STONE, Irving [orig. **Irving Tennenbaum]** (1903–1989)
American novelist
Lust for Life (1934) F
Sailor on Horseback (1938) F
Love is Eternal (1954) F
The Agony and the Ecstasy (1961) F

STONE, Louis (1871–1935)
British-born Australian novelist and dramatist
Jonah (1911) F
Betty Wayside (1915) F
The Lap of the Gods (1923) D
The Watch That Wouldn't Go (1926) D

STOPPARD, Tom [born **Tomas Straussler]** (1937–)
Czechoslovakian-born British dramatist
Lord Malquist and Mr Moon (1966) F
Rosencrantz and Guildenstern Are Dead (1966) D
Enter a Free Man (1968) D
The Real Inspector Hound (1968) D
Albert's Bridge; and If You're Glad I'll Be Frank (1969) D
After Magritte (1970) D
Jumpers (1972) D
Artist Descending a Staircase; and Where Are They Now? (1973) D
Travesties (1974) D
Dirty Linen (1976) D
New-Found-Land (1976) D
Every Good Boy Deserves Favour (1977) D
Professional Foul [tv] (1977) D
Night and Day (1978) D
Dogg's Hamlet; Cahoot's Macbeth (1979) D
On the Razzle (1981) D
The Dog It Was That Died (1982) D
The Real Thing (1982) D
Rough Crossing (1984) D
Hapgood (1988) D
Plays for Radio 1964–1983 (1990) D
Arcadia (1993) D
Indian Ink (1994) D
The Invention of Love (1997) D

STOREY, David [Malcolm] (1933–)
British novelist, dramatist, and poet
This Sporting Life (1960) F
Flight into Camden (1961) F
Radcliffe (1963) F
The Restoration of Arnold Middleton (1966) D
The Contractor (1969) D
In Celebration (1969) D
The Changing Room (1971) D
Pasmore (1972) F
Cromwell (1973) D
A Temporary Life (1973) F
Saville (1976) F
Mother's Day (1977) D
Early Days (1980) D
A Prodigal Child (1982) F
Present Times (1984) F
Storey's Lives (1992) V
A Serious Man (1998) F

STOUT, Rex [Todhunter] (1886–1975)
American crime writer
Fer-de-Lance [first 'Nero Wolfe' novel] (1934) F
The Red Box (1937) F
Some Buried Caesar [alternative US title: *The Red Bull*] (1938) F
Too Many Cooks (1938) F
The Silent Speaker (1946) F
And Be a Villain [UK: *More Deaths Than One*] (1948) F
The Second Confession (1949) F
Gambit (1962) F
Death of a Doxy (1966) F
A Family Affair (1975) F

STOW, John (1525–1605)
English chronicler and antiquary
A Summarie of Englyshe Chronicles (1565) NF
The Chronicles of England, from Brute Unto this Present Yeare 1580 (1580) NF
The Annales of England Until 1592 (1592) NF
A Survay of London (1598) NF

STOW, Randolph (1935–)
Australian novelist, poet, and children's writer
A Haunted Land (1956) F
Act One (1957) V
The Bystander (1957) F
To the Islands (1958) F
Outrider (1962) V
The Merry-Go-Round by the Sea (1965) F
Midnite (1967) F CH
Visitants (1979) F
The Girl Green as Elderflower (1980) F
The Suburbs of Hell (1984) F

STOWE, Harriet [Elizabeth] Beecher (1811–1896)
American novelist
Uncle Tom's Cabin; or, Life Among the Lowly (1852) F
A Key to Uncle Tom's Cabin (1853) NF
Sunny Memories of Foreign Lands (1854) NF
Dred: A Tale of the Great Dismal Swamp (1856) F
The Minister's Wooing (1859) F
Agnes of Sorrento (1862) F
The Pearl of Orr's Island (1862) F
Oldtown Folks (1869) F
Lady Byron Vindicated (1870) NF
My Wife and I (1871) F
Pink and White Tyranny (1871) F
Sam Lawson's Oldtown Fireside Stories (1872) F SS
Palmetto-Leaves (1873) NF
We and Our Neighbors (1875) F
Poganuc People (1878) F

STRACHEY, [Giles] Lytton (1880–1932)
British critic and biographer
Landmarks in French Literature (1912) NF
Eminent Victorians (1918) NF
Queen Victoria (1921) NF
Books and Characters, French and English (1922) NF

Elizabeth and Essex (1928) NF
Portraits in Miniature, and Other Essays (1931) NF
Characters and Commentaries (1933) NF

STRAUB, Peter (1943–)
American novelist
If You Could See Me Now (1977) F
Ghost Story (1979) F
Shadow Land (1980) F
Floating Dragon (1983) F
The Talisman (1984) F
Koko (1988) F
Mystery (1989) F
The Throat (1993) F

STREATFEILD, Noel (1895–1986)
British children's writer
Ballet Shoes (1936) F CH
Tennis Shoes (1937) F CH
The Circus is Coming (1938) F CH
The Children of Primrose Lane (1941) F CH
Curtain Up (1944) F CH
Party Frock (1945) F CH
The Painted Garden (1949) F CH
White Boots (1951) F CH
The Bell Family (1954) F CH
New Town (1960) F CH
Gemma (1968) F CH
Ballet Shoes for Anna (1972) F CH

STRIBLING, T[heodore] S[igismund] (1881–1965)
American novelist
The Forge (1931) F
The Store (1932) F
Unfinished Cathedral (1934) F

STRICKLAND, Agnes (1796–1874)
British poet and biographer
The Seven Ages of Woman, and Other Poems (1827) V
Tales and Stories from History (1836) V

STRINDBERG, [Johan] August (1849–1912)
Swedish dramatist and novelist
The Red Room (1879) F
Master Olof (1881) D
Getting Married [2 vols.] (1884–5) F SS
The Son of a Servant (1886) NF
The Father (1887) D
The People of Hemsö (1887) F
Miss Julie (1888) D
Creditors (1889) D
Inferno (1898) NF
To Damascus (1898–1901) D
Erik XIV (1899) D
Gustav Vasa (1899) D
The Dance of Death (1901) D
A Dream Play (1902) D
The Ghost Sonata (1907) D

STRODE, William (1602–1645)
English poet and dramatist
The Floating Island (1655) D

STRONG, L[eonard] A[lfred] G[eorge] (1896–1958)
Anglo-Irish novelist, poet, and biographer
Dublin Days (1921) V
The Lowery Road (1923) V
Dewer Rides (1929) F
Sea Wall (1933) F
Travellers (1945) F SS
Deliverance (1955) F

STRYPE, John (1643–1737)
English ecclesiastical historian
Memorials of Thomas Cranmer (1694) NF
Annals of the Reformation and Establishment of Religion (1709) NF
The Life and Acts of Matthew Parker (1711) NF
The Life and Acts of John Whitgift (1718) NF
Ecclesiastical Memorials (1721) NF

STUART, [Henry] Francis [Montgomery] (1902–)
Irish novelist and poet
Women and God (1931) F
The Coloured Dome (1932) F
Pigeon Irish (1932) F
The Angel of Pity (1935) F
The White Hare (1936) F
The Pillar of Cloud (1948) F
Redemption (1949) F
The Flowering Cross (1950) F
Black List, Section H (1971) F
A Hole in the Head (1977) F
A Compendium of Lovers (1990) F

STUBBS (or **STUBBES), Philip** (fl. 1581–1593)
English Puritan pamphleteer
The Anatomie of Abuses (1583) NF
A Christal Glass for Christian Women (1591) NF

STUBBS, William (1825–1901)
British historian and bishop
Registrum Sacrum Anglicanum (1858) NF
Select Charters and Other Illustrations of English Constitutional History (1866) NF
The Constitutional History of England [vol. i; vol. ii, 1875; vol. iii, 1878] (1873) NF
Seventeen Lectures on the Study of Mediaeval and Modern History (1886) NF

STUKELEY, William (1687–1765)
English antiquary
Itinerarium Curiosum (1724) NF
Palaeographia Sacra; or, Discourses on Monuments of Antiquity (1736) NF
Stonehenge (1740) NF
Abury: A Temple of the British Druids (1743) NF

STURGEON, Theodore [Hamilton] (1918–1985)
American science fiction and fantasy writer
Without Sorcery (1948) F SS
The Dreaming Jewels (1950) F
E Pluribus Unicorn (1953) F
More Than Human (1953) F
A Touch of Strange (1958) F
Venus Plus X (1960) F

STURGIS, H[oward] O[vering] (1855–1920)
British-born American novelist
Tim (1891) F CH
Belchamber (1904) F

STYRON, William [Clark] (1925–)
American novelist
Lie Down in Darkness (1951) F
The Long March (1953) F
Set This House on Fire (1960) F
The Confessions of Nat Turner (1967) F
In the Clap Shack (1972) F
Sophie's Choice (1979) F
This Quiet Dust (1982) NF
Darkness Visible: A Memoir of Madness (1990) NF
A Tidewater Morning (1993) F SS

SUCKLING, Sir John (1609–1642)
English poet and dramatist
Aglaura (1638) D
Fragmenta Aurea [letters, poems, and plays] (1646) MISC

SUE, [Marie Joseph] Eugène (1804–1857)
French novelist
Les Mystères de Paris ['The Mysteries of Paris'] (1843) F
Le Juif errant ['The Wandering Jew'] (1845) F
Les Mystères du peuple ['Mysteries of the People'] (1849) F
Les Sept péchés capitaux ['The Seven Deadly Sins'] (1849) F

SURTEES, R[obert] S[mith] (1805–1864)
British sporting novelist
Jorrocks' Jaunts and Jollities (1838) F
Handley Cross; or, The Spa Hunt (1843) F
Hillingdon Hall; or, The Cockney Squire (1845) F
Hawbuck Grange; or, The Sporting Adventures of Thomas Scott, Esq. (1847) F
Mr Sponge's Sporting Tour (1853) F
'Ask Mamma'; or, The Richest Commoner in England (1858) F
Plain or Ringlets? (1860) F
Mr Facey Romford's Hounds (1865) F

SUSANN, Jacqueline (1921–1974)
American popular novelist
Valley of the Dolls (1966) F

SUTCLIFF, Rosemary (1920–)
British children's writer
The Chronicles of Robin Hood (1950) F CH
The Queen Elizabeth Story (1950) F CH
The Armourer's House (1951) F CH
Brother Dusty-Feet (1952) F CH
Simon (1953) F CH
The Eagle of the Ninth (1954) F CH
Outcast (1955) F CH
The Shield King (1956) F CH
The Silver Branch (1957) F CH
Warrior Scarlet (1958) F CH
The Lantern Bearers (1959) F CH
Knight's Fee (1960) F CH
Dawn Wind (1961) F CH
The Mark of the Horse Lord (1965) F CH
Blood Feud (1977) F CH
Sun Horse, Moon Horse (1977) F CH
The Light Beyond the Forest (1979) F CH
Frontier Wolf (1980) F CH
The Sword and the Circle (1981) F CH
Blue Remembered Hills (1983) NF

SUTHERLAND, Robert Garioch *see* ROBERT GARIOCH

SWEET, Henry (1845–1912)
British phonetician and comparative philologist
An Anglo-Saxon Reader in Prose and Verse (1876) NF
A Handbook of Phonetics (1877) NF
An Anglo-Saxon Primer (1882) NF
First Middle English Primer (1884) NF
Second Middle English Primer (1886) NF
A Second Anglo-Saxon Reader, Archaic and Dialectal (1887) NF

SWIFT, Graham [Colin] (1949–)
British novelist
The Sweet-Shop Owner (1980) F
Shuttlecock (1981) F
Learning to Swim (1982) F SS
Waterland (1983) F
Out of This World (1988) F
Ever After (1992) F
Last Orders (1996) F

SWIFT, Jonathan (1667–1745)
Irish satirist and poet
The Contests and Dissensions Between the Nobles and the Commons in Athens and Rome (1701) NF
A Tale of a Tub [with 'The Battle of the Books'] (1704) NF
Predictions for the Year 1708 (1708) NF
Baucis and Philemon (1709) V
A Famous Prediction of Merlin, the British Wizard (1709) V
A Project for the Advancement of Religion, and the Reformation of Manners (1709) NF
A Meditation Upon a Broom-Stick (1710) P
Miscellanies in Prose and Verse (1711) MISC
The Conduct of the Allies in Beginning and Carrying on the Present War (1712) P
A Proposal for Correcting, Improving and Ascertaining the English Tongue (1712) P
The First Ode of the Second Book of Horace Paraphras'd (1714) V
The Publick Spirit of the Whigs (1714) NF
A Proposal for the Universal Use of Irish Manifacture (1720) P
The Bubble (1721) V
A Letter to the Shop-Keepers, Tradesmen, Farmers and Common-People of Ireland [by 'M.B. Drapier'] (1724) NF
A Letter to the Whole People of Ireland [by 'M.B. Drapier'] (1724) NF
Fraud Detected; or, The Hibernian Patriot (1725) NF
Cadenus and Vanessa (1726) V

Travels into Several Remote Nations of the World, by Lemuel Gulliver [4 pts.] (1726) F
A Modest Proposal for Preventing the Children of Poor People from being a Burthen to their Parents (1729) NF
The Lady's Dressing-Room (1732) V
The Life and Genuine Character of Doctor Swift, Written by Himself (1733) V
On Poetry (1733) V
A Beautiful Young Nymph Going to Bed, Written for the Honour of the Fair Sex (1734) V
Miscellanies in Prose and Verse: Volume the Fifth (1735) MISC
A Complete Collection of Genteel and Ingenious Conversation (1738) NF
Verses on the Death of Dr Swift, Written by Himself (1739) V

SWINBURNE, Algernon Charles (1837–1909)
British poet and critic
The Queen-Mother; Rosamond (1860) D
Atalanta in Calydon (1865) V
Chastelard (1865) V
Notes on Poems and Reviews (1866) NF
Poems and Ballads [1st ser.] (1866) V
A Song of Italy (1867) V
Siena (1868) V
William Blake (1868) NF
Christabel and the Lyrical and Imaginative Poems of S.T. Coleridge (1869) NF
Ode on the Proclamation of the French Republic (1870) V
Songs Before Sunrise (1871) V
Under the Microscope (1872) NF
Bothwell (1874) V D
Essays and Studies (1875) NF
George Chapman (1875) NF
Songs of Two Nations (1875) V
Erechtheus (1876) V D
Note of an English Republican on the Muscovite Crusade (1876) NF
A Note on Charlotte Brontë (1877) NF
Poems and Ballads: Second Series (1878) V
The Heptalogia; or, The Seven Against Sense (1880) V
Songs of the Springtides (1880) V
Studies in Song (1880) V
A Study of Shakespeare (1880) NF
Mary Stuart (1881) V D
Tristram of Lyonesse, and Other Poems (1882) V
A Century of Roundels (1883) V
A Midsummer Holiday, and Other Poems (1884) V
Marino Faliero (1885) V D
A Study of Victor Hugo (1886) NF
Locrine (1887) V D
Poems and Ballads: Third Series (1889) V
A Study of Ben Jonson (1889) NF
The Sisters (1892) V D
Astrophel, and Other Poems (1894) V
Studies in Prose and Poetry (1894) NF
The Tale of Balen (1896) V
A Channel Passage (1899) V
Rosamund, Queen of the Lombards (1899) V D
A Channel Passage, and Other Poems (1904) V
Love's Cross-Currents (1905) F
The Age of Shakespeare (1908) NF
The Duke of Gandia (1908) V D

SWINNERTON, Frank [Arthur] (1884–1982)
British novelist and critic
The Merry Heart (1909) F
The Young Idea (1910) F
The Casement (1911) F
The Happy Family (1912) F
On the Staircase (1914) F
The Chaste Wife (1916) F
Nocturne (1917) F
Shops and Houses (1918) F
September (1919) F
Young Felix (1923) F
The Georgian Literary Scene (1934) NF
Harvest Comedy (1937) F
Death of a Highbrow (1961) F
Figures in the Foreground (1963) NF

SYLVESTER, Joshua (1563–1618)
English poet and translator
Bartas His Devine Weekes & Workes Translated [from Guillaume de Salustre du Bartas] (1605) V
The Parliament of Vertues Royal [from Jean Bertaut et al.] (1614) V
Tobacco Battered; & the Pipes Shattered (1617) V

SYMONDS, John Addington (1840–1893)
British poet, critic, and translator
An Introduction to the Study of Dante (1872) NF
The Renaissance in Italy (1875) NF
Many Moods (1878) V
Shelley (1878) NF
Sketches and Studies in Italy (1879) NF
New and Old (1880) V
Sir Philip Sidney (1886) NF
The Life of Benvenuto Cellini (1888) NF
Essays Speculative and Suggestive (1890) NF
In the Key of Blue, and Other Prose Essays (1893) NF
Walt Whitman (1893) NF

SYMONS, A[lphonse] J[ames] A[lbert] (1900–1941)
British biographer
The Quest for Corvo (1934) NF

SYMONS, Arthur [William] (1865–1945)
British poet and critic
Days and Nights (1889) V
Silhouettes (1892) V
London Nights (1895) V
Amoris Victima (1897) V
Studies in Two Literatures (1897) NF
Aubrey Beardsley (1898) NF
Images of Good and Evil (1899) V
The Symbolist Movement in Literature (1899) NF
Cities (1903) NF
Spiritual Adventures (1905) NF
The Fool of the World, and Other Poems (1906) V
William Blake (1907) NF

The Romantic Movement in English Poetry (1909) NF
Dante Gabriel Rossetti (1910) NF
Tragedies [contains 'The Death of Aggrippa', 'Cleopatra in Judaea', 'The Harvesters'] (1916) D
Charles Baudelaire (1920) NF
Studies in the Elizabethan Drama (1920) NF
The Café Royal, and Other Essays (1923) NF
From Catullus, Chiefly Concerning Lesbia (1924) V
From Toulouse-Lautrec to Rodin, with Some Personal Impressions (1929) NF
A Study of Oscar Wilde (1930) NF
Jezebel Mort, and Other Poems (1931) V
A Study of Walter Pater (1932) NF

SYMONS, Julian [Gustave] (1912–1995)
British crime novelist, poet, and critic
Confusions About X (1939) V
The Second Man (1943) V
The Immaterial Murder Case (1945) F
A Man Called Jones (1947) F
The Progress of a Crime (1960) F
The Thirties (1960) NF
The End of Solomon Grundy (1964) F
Francis Quarles Investigates (1965) F SS
Critical Occasions (1966) NF
Bloody Murder: From the Detective Story to the Crime Novel [3rd edn, 1992] (1972) NF
The Object of an Affair, and Other Poems (1974) V
The Blackheath Poisonings (1978) F

SYNGE, [Edmund] J[ohn] M[illington] (1871–1909)
Irish dramatist and poet
The Shadow of the Glen (1903) D
Riders to the Sea (1904) D
The Aran Islands (1907) NF
The Playboy of the Western World (1907) D
Deirdre of the Sorrows [unfinished] (1909) D
Poems and Translations (1909) V
The Tinker's Wedding (1909) D
In Wicklow, West Kerry, and Connemara (1911) NF
The Well of the Saints (1905) D

T

TAGORE, Rabindranath (1861–1941)
Bengali poet, novelist, short-story writer, critic, and dramatist
A Poet's Tale (1878) V
Binodini (1902) F
Gora (1910) F
Gitanjali (1912) V
Chitra (1913) D
The Crescent Moon (1913) V
The Gardner (1913) V
The King of the Dark Chamber (1914) D
Hungry Stones (1916) F SS
Lover's Gift, and Crossing (1918) V
The Home and the World (1919) F
Broken Ties (1925) F SS

TALBOT, Catherine (1721–1770)
English essayist and letter writer
Reflections on the Seven Days of the Week (1770) NF
Essays on Various Subjects (1772) NF

TALFOURD, Thomas Noon (1795–1854)
British judge, dramatist, and critic
Ion (1835) D
The Athenian Captive (1838) D
Vacation Rambles and Thoughts (1845) NF
The Castilian (1853) D

TAN, Amy (1952–)
American novelist
The Joy Luck Club (1989) F
The Kitchen-God's Wife (1991) F
The Moon Lady (1992) F
The Chinese Siamese Cat (1994) F
The Year of No Flood (1995) F
The Hundred Secret Senses (1995) F

TANNAHILL, Robert (1774–1810)
Scottish poet
The Soldier's Return (1807) V

TARKINGTON, [Newton] Booth (1869–1946)
American novelist, dramatist, and children's writer
The Gentleman From Indiana (1899) F
Monsieur Beaucaire (1900) F
The Conquest of Canaan (1905) F
Guest of Quesnay (1908) F
Penrod (1914) F
The Turmoil (1915) F
Penrod and Sam (1916) F
Seventeen (1916) F
The Magnificent Ambersons (1918) F
Alice Adams (1921) F
The Midlander (1923) F
The Plutocrat (1927) F
The World Does Move (1928) NF
Penrod Jashber (1929) F
Rumbin Galleries (1937) F
The Heritage of Hatcher Ide (1941) F
Kate Fennigate (1943) F
The Image of Josephine (1945) F

TASSO, Torquato (1544–1595)
Italian poet
Rinaldo (1562) V
Aminta (1573) D
Gerusalemme Liberata [Eng. trn as *Godfrey of Bulloigne; or, The Recoverie of Jerusalem*, 1600] (1580) V
King Torrismond [*Il Re Torrismondo*] (1586) D

TATE, [John Orley] Allen (1899–1979)
American poet and critic
The Golden Mean, and Other Poems (1923) V
Mr Pope, and Other Poems (1928) V
The Mediterranean, and Other Poems (1936) V
The Fathers [rev. 1977] (1938) F
Essays of Four Decades (1969) NF
The Swimmers, and Other Poems (1971) V
Memoirs and Opinions (1975) NF

TATE, Nahum (1652–1715)
English dramatist and Poet Laureate
Brutus of Alba; or, The Enchanted Lovers (1678) D
The Loyal General (1679) D
The History of King Lear (1681) D
The History of King Richard the Second (1681) D
The Ingratitude of a Common-wealth; or, The Fall of Caius Martius Coriolanus (1681) D
A Duke and No Duke (1684) D
The Island-Princess (1687) D
A New Version of the Psalms of David (1696) V
Panacea (1700) V
The Kentish Worthies (1701) V
Injur'd Love; or, The Cruel Husband (1707) D
The Triumph of Union (1707) V

TAWNEY, R[ichard] H[enry] (1880–1962)
British historian
The Agrarian Problem in the Sixteenth Century (1912) NF
Poverty as an Industrial Problem (1913) NF
The Acquisitive Society (1920) NF
Religion and the Rise of Capitalism (1926) NF
Equality (1931) NF

TAYLOR, A[lan] J[ohn] P[ercivale] (1906–1990)
British historian
The Habsburg Monarchy 1815–1918 (1941) NF
From Napoleon to Stalin (1950) NF
Rumours of War (1952) NF
The Struggle for Mastery in Europe (1954) NF
Englishmen and Others (1956) NF
The Trouble Makers (1957) NF
The Origins of the Second World War (1961) NF
Politics in Wartime, and Other Essays (1964) NF
English History 1914–45 (1965) NF
A Personal History (1983) NF

TAYLOR, [James] Bayard (1825–1878)
American travel-writer, novelist, and poet
Ximena (1844) V
Views A-foot (1846) NF
Rhymes of Travel, Ballads and Poems (1849) V
A Journey to Central Africa (1854) NF
The Lands of the Saracen (1855) NF
Poems of the Orient (1855) V
A Visit to India, China, and Japan in the Year 1853 (1855) NF
Northern Travel (1858) NF
Travels in Greece and Russia (1859) NF
At Home and Abroad (1860) NF
Hannah Thurston (1863) F
John Godfrey's Fortunes (1864) F
Joseph and His Friend (1870) F
Lars: A Pastoral of Norway (1873) V
The Echo Club, and Other Literary Diversions (1876) V

TAYLOR, Elizabeth (1912–1975)
British novelist and short-story writer
At Mrs Lippincote's (1945) F
A Game of Hide and Seek (1951) F
Hester Lilly, and Other Stories (1954) F SS
Angel (1957) F
The Blush, and Other Stories (1958) F SS
In a Summer Season (1961) F
The Soul of Kindness (1964) F
A Dedicated Man, and Other Stories (1965) F SS
The Wedding Group (1968) F
Mrs Palfrey at the Claremont (1971) F
The Devastating Boys, and Other Stories (1972) F SS
Blaming (1976) F

TAYLOR, Sir Henry (1800–1886)
British poet and dramatist
Philip van Artevelde (1834) V D
Edwin the Fair (1842) V D
The Eve of the Conquest, and Other Poems (1847) V
A Sicilian Summer; St Clement's Eve; and Minor Poems (1875) V

TAYLOR, Jane (1783–1824)
British poet
Essays in Rhyme, on Morals and Manners (1816) V

TAYLOR, Jeremy (1613–1667)
Bishop of Down and Connor and devotional writer
A Sermon Preached Upon the Anniversary of the Gunpowder-treason (1638) NF
Of the Sacred Order and Offices of Episcopacy (1642) NF
A Discourse Concerning Prayer (1646) NF
The Great Exemplar of Sanctity and Holy Life (1649) NF
The Rule and Exercises of Holy Living (1650) NF
The Rule and Exercises of Holy Dying (1651) NF
Twenty-Eight Sermons Preached at Golden-Grove (1651) NF
The Golden Grove; or, A Manuall of Daily Prayers and Letanies (1655) NF
Deus Justificatus (1656) NF
Ductor Dubitantium; or, The Rule of Conscience in all her General Measures (1660) NF
The Worthy Communicant (1660) NF
The Righteousness Evangelicall Describ'd (1663) NF
A Choice Manual, Containing What is To Be Believed (1664) NF
A Dissuasive from Popery to the People of Ireland [pt. i; pt. ii, 1667] (1664) NF
Antiquitates Christianae (1675) NF

TAYLOR, John [the 'Water Poet'] (1580–1653)
English poet
The Sculler, Rowing from Tiber to Thames (1612) V
The Pennyles Pilgrimage (1618) V
The Praise, Antiquity, and Commodity, of Beggery, Beggers, and Begging (1621) V
Superbiae Flagellum; or, The Whip of Pride (1621) V
A Memorial of all the English Monarchs (1622) V
Divers Crabtree Lectures (1639) V
A Juniper Lecture (1639) V

TAYLOR, [Captain] Philip Meadows (1808–1876)
British Indian Army officer and novelist
The Confessions of a Thug (1839) F
Tippoo Sultaun (1840) F

Tara (1863) F
Ralph Darnell (1865) F
Seeta (1872) F
A Noble Queen (1878) F

TAYLOR, Thomas ['The Platonist'] (1758–1835)
British philosophical author and translator
Concerning the Beautiful [from Plotinus] (1787) NF
A Vindication of the Rights of Brutes (1792) NF
The Works of Plato (1804) NF

TAYLOR, Tom (1817–1880)
British dramatist
The Fool's Revenge (1850) D
Still Waters Run Deep (1855) D
Our American Cousin (1858) D
The Overland Route (1860) D
Joan of Arc (1871) D
The Theatre in England (1871) NF
Leicester Square (1874) D

TEMPLE, Sir William (1628–1699)
English statesman and author
Upon the Death of Mrs Catherine Philips (1664) V
An Essay upon the Advancement of Trade in Ireland (1673) NF
Observations upon the United Provinces of the Netherlands (1673) NF
Miscellanea: The First Part (1680) NF
Miscellanea: The Second Part (1690) NF
Memoirs of What Past in Christendom, From 1672 to 1679 (1692) NF
An Introduction to the History of England (1695) NF
Letters to the Earl of Arlington and Sir John Trevor (1699) NF
Letters Written by Sir W. Temple and Other Ministers of State [ed. Jonathan Swift] (1700) NF
Miscellanea: The Third Part [ed. Jonathan Swift] (1701) NF
Memoirs: From 1679 to the Author's Retirement from Publick Business (1709) NF

TEMPLE, William (1881–1944)
British churchman and Archbishop of Canterbury
The Faith and Modern Thought (1910) NF
Church and Nation (1915) NF
Mens Creatrix (1917) NF
Christus Veritas (1924) NF
Personal Religion and the Life of Fellowship (1926) NF
Christian Faith and Life (1931) NF
Nature, Man and God (1934) NF
Christianity and Social Order (1942) NF
The Church Looks Forward (1944) NF

TENNANT, Emma [Christina] (1937–)
British novelist and journalist
The Time of the Crack (1973) F
The Last of the Country House Murders (1974) F
Hotel de Dream (1976) F
The Bad Sister (1978) F
Wild Nights (1979) F
Alice Fell (1980) F
Queen of Stones (1982) F
Woman Beware Woman (1983) F
The Adventures of Robina, By Herself (1986) F
The House of Hospitalities (1987) F
A Wedding of Cousins (1988) F
Two Women of London: The Strange Case of Mrs Jekyll and Mrs Hyde (1989) F
Sisters and Strangers (1990) F
Faustine (1991) F
Pemberley [sequel to Jane Austen's *Pride and Prejudice*] (1993) F
Tess (1993) F
An Unequal Marriage [continuation of Jane Austen's *Pride and Prejudice*] (1994) F

TENNANT, William (1784–1848)
Scottish poet and scholar
The Thane of Fife (1822) V
Cardinal Beaton (1823) D
John Balliol (1825) D

TENNYSON, Alfred, 1st Baron Tennyson (1809–1892)
British poet and Poet Laureate
Timbuctoo (1829) V
Poems, Chiefly Lyrical [inc. 'Mariana', 'The Kraken'] (1830) V
Poems [inc. 'The Lady of Shalott', 'Mariana in the South', 'Oenone'] (1833) V
The Princess (1847) V
In Memoriam (1850) V
Ode on the Death of the Duke of Wellington (1852) V
Maud, and Other Poems [inc. 'The Charge of the Light Brigade'] (1855) V
Idylls of the King (1859) V
The Sailor Boy (1861) V
Enoch Arden (1864) V
Gareth and Lynette (1872) V
Queen Mary (1875) D
Harold (1877) D
The Lover's Tale (1879) V
Ballads, and Other Poems (1880) V
Early Spring (1883) V
Becket (1884) D
Tiresias, and Other Poems (1885) V
Locksley Hall Sixty Years After (1886) V
Demeter, and Other Poems (1889) V
The Death of Oenone, Akbar's Dream, and Other Poems (1892) V
The Foresters (1892) D

TERESA OF AVILA, St [Teresa Sánchez de Cepeda y Ahumada] (1515–1582)
Spanish Carmelite mystic
The Interior Castle [*El castillo interior*; also known as *Las moradas*] (1577) NF

TERKEL, Studs [Louis] (1912–)
American broadcaster and social historian
Giants of Jazz (1957) NF
Amazing Grace (1959) D
Division Street: America (1966) NF
Hard Times (1970) NF
Working (1974) NF

Talking to Myself (1977) NF
American Dreams: Lost and Found (1980) NF
The Good War (1984) NF

'TEY, Josephine' [Elizabeth Mackintosh] (1897–1952)
Scottish writer of detective fiction
The Man in the Queue [as 'Gordon Daviot'. US: *Killer in the Crowd*] (1929) F
A Shilling for Candles (1936) F CF
Miss Pym Disposes (1946) F CF
The Franchise Affair (1948) F CF
To Love and Be Wise (1950) F CF
The Daughter of Time (1952) F CF
The Singing Sands (1952) F CF

THACKERAY, Anne Isabella *see* LADY ANNE RITCHIE

THACKERAY, William Makepeace ['M[ichael] A[ngelo] Titmarsh'] (1811–1863)
British novelist and essayist
The Yellowplush Correspondence (1838) F
The Paris Sketch Book [as 'M.A. Titmarsh'] (1840) NF
Comic Tales and Sketches [as 'M.A. Titmarsh'] (1841) F SS
The Second Funeral of Napoleon [as 'M.A. Titmarsh'] (1841) MISC
The Irish Sketch-Book [as 'M.A. Titmarsh'] (1843) NF
Notes of a Journey from Cornhill to Grand Cairo [as 'M.A. Titmarsh'] (1846) NF
Mrs Perkins's Ball [as 'M.A. Titmarsh'] (1847) F
The Book of Snobs (1848) NF
The Great Hoggarty Diamond (1848) F
Our Street [as 'M.A. Titmarsh'] (1848) F
Vanity Fair (1848) F
Doctor Birch and His Young Friends [as 'M.A. Titmarsh'] (1849) F
The History of Pendennis (1850) F
The Kickleburys on the Rhine [as 'M.A. Titmarsh'] (1850) F
Rebecca and Rowena [as 'M.A. Titmarsh'] (1850) F
The History of Henry Esmond, Esq. (1852) F
The English Humourists of the Eighteenth Century (1853) NF
The Newcomes [ed. 'Arthur Pendennis'] (1854) F
The Rose and the Ring; or, The History of Prince Giglio and Prince Bulbo [as 'M.A. Titmarsh'] (1855) F
The Memoirs of Barry Lyndon, Esq., of the Kingdom of Ireland [US: *The Luck of Barry Lyndon*, 1853] (1856) F
The Virginians (1858) F
Lovel the Widower (1860) F
The Four Georges (1861) NF
The Adventures of Philip on His Way Through the World (1862) F
Roundabout Papers (1863) NF
Denis Duval [unfinished] (1867) F

THEOBALD, Lewis (1688–1744)
British poet, translator, dramatist, and editor of Shakespeare
The Persian Princess; or, The Royal Villain (1708) D
The Life and Character of Marcus Portius Cato (1713) NF
The Mausoleum (1714) V
The Perfidious Brother (1716) D
Decius and Paulina (1718) D
Orestes (1718) D
Pan and Syrinx (1718) D
The Tragedy of King Richard the Second (1719) D
Shakespeare Restored (1726) NF
Double Falsehood; or, The Distrest Lovers (1727) D
The Rape of Proserpine (1727) D
Perseus and Andromeda (1730) D
The Fatal Secret (1733) D
The Works of Shakespeare (1733) EDN

THEROUX, Paul [Edward] (1941–)
American-born novelist and travel writer
The Great Railway Bazaar (1975) NF
The Family Arsenal (1976) F
Picture Palace (1978) F
The Old Patagonian Express (1979) NF
World's End, and Other Stories (1980) F SS
The Mosquito Coast (1981) F
The Kingdom by the Sea (1983) NF
Doctor Slaughter (1984) F
Sailing Through China (1984) NF
Sunrise with Seamonsters (1985) NF
O-Zone (1986) F
Riding the Iron Rooster (1988) NF
My Secret History (1989) F
Chicago Loop (1990) F
The Happy Isles of Oceania (1992) NF
Millroy the Magician (1993) F

THESIGER, Wilfred [Patrick] (1910–)
British travel writer
Arabian Sands (1959) NF
The Marsh Arabs (1964) NF

THIBAULT, Jacques-Anatole-François *see* ANATOLE FRANCE

THIRKELL, Angela [Margaret] (1890–1961)
British novelist
Ankle Deep (1933) F
Wild Strawberries (1934) F
Pomfret Towers (1938) F
The Brandons (1939) F
Cheerfulness Breaks In (1940) F
Peace Breaks Out (1946) F
Private Enterprise (1947) F
Love Among the Ruins (1948) F
Coronation Summer (1953) F

THIRLWALL, Connop (1797–1875)
British historian and bishop
Critical Essay on the Gospel of St Luke (1825) NF
Letter on the Admission of Dissenters to Academical Degrees (1834) NF
A History of Greece (1835) NF

THOMAS, Augustus (1857–1934)
American dramatist
Alabama (1891) D
In Mizzoura (1893) D

The Capitol (1895) D
Arizona (1899) D
The Witching Hour (1907) D
The Harvest Moon (1909) D
As a Man Thinks (1911) D
The Copperhead (1918) D

THOMAS, Bertram [Sidney] (1892–1950)
Arabist and travel writer
Arabia Felix [foreword by T.E. Lawrence] (1932) NF

THOMAS, Craig (1942–)
British thriller writer
Firefox (1977) F

THOMAS, D[onald] M[ichael] (1935–)
British novelist, poet, and translator
The Honeymoon Voyage (1978) V
The Flute-Player (1979) F
Dreaming in Bronze (1981) V
The White Hotel (1981) F
Ararat (1983) F
Swallow (1984) F
Sphinx (1986) F
Summit (1987) F
Lying Together (1990) F
Flying in to Love (1992) F

THOMAS, Dylan [Marlais] (1914–1953)
Welsh poet
Eighteen Poems (1934) V
Twenty-five Poems (1936) V
The Map of Love (1939) V NF
Portrait of the Artist as a Young Dog (1940) F SS
New Poems (1943) V
Deaths and Entrances (1946) V
In Country Sleep (1952) V
Quite Early One Morning (1954) MISC
Under Milk Wood (1954) D
Adventures in the Skin Trade (1955) F SS

THOMAS, Leslie [John] (1931–)
Anglo-Welsh novelist
The Virgin Soldiers (1966) F
Arthur McCann and All His Women (1970) F
Onward Virgin Soldiers (1971) F
Tropic of Ruislip (1974) F
Stand Up Virgin Soldiers (1975) F
Dangerous Davies (1976) F

THOMAS, [Philip] Edward (1878–1917)
British poet, critic, and topographical writer
The Woodland Life (1897) NF
Horae Solitariae (1902) NF
Rose Acre Papers (1904) F
Beautiful Wales (1905) NF
The Heart of England (1906) NF
Richard Jefferies (1909) NF
The South Country (1909) NF
Rest and Unrest (1910) F
Light and Twilight (1911) NF
The Tenth Muse (1911) NF
George Borrow (1912) NF
The Happy-Go-Lucky Morgans (1913) F
The Icknield Way (1913) NF
Walter Pater (1913) NF
In Pursuit of Spring (1914) NF
Four-and-Twenty Blackbirds (1915) F
A Literary Pilgrim in England (1917) NF
Last Poems (1918) V

THOMAS, R[onald] S[tuart] (1913–2000)
Welsh poet
The Stones of the Fields (1946) V
An Acre of Land (1952) V
The Minister (1953) V
Song at the Year's Turning (1955) V
Poetry for Supper (1958) V
Tares (1961) V
The Bread of Truth (1963) V
Pietà (1966) V
Not That He Brought Flowers (1968) V
Laboratories of the Spirit (1975) V
Frequencies (1978) V
Between Here and Now (1981) V
Experimenting With an Amen (1986) V
Counterpoint (1990) V
Mass for Hard Times (1992) V

THOMAS, Sir Keith [Vivian] (1933–)
British historian
Religion and the Decline of Magic (1971) NF
Man and the Natural World (1983) NF

THOMPSON, Edward [John] (1886–1946)
British poet, translator, and historian
John in Prison (1912) V
Mesopotamian Verses (1919) V

THOMPSON, E[dward] P[almer] (1924–1993)
British historian
The Making of the English Working Class (1963) NF

THOMPSON, Flora [Jane], *née* Timms (1877–1947)
British rural writer
Bog-Myrtle and Peat (1921) V
Lark Rise (1939) F
Over to Candleford (1941) F
Candleford Green (1943) F
Lark Rise to Candleford [the complete trilogy] (1945) F

THOMPSON, Francis (1859–1907)
British poet
Poems (1893) V
Sister Songs (1895) V
New Poems (1897) V
Health and Holiness (1905) NF
Shelley (1909) NF

THOMPSON, Hunter S[tockton] (1939–)
American journalist and novelist
Hell's Angels: A Strange and Terrible Saga (1966) NF
Fear and Loathing in Las Vegas (1971) F
Fear and Loathing on the Campaign Trail '72 (1973) F
The Curse of Lono (1977) NF

The Great Shark Hunt (1979) NF
Better Than Sex: Confessions of a Political Junkie (1994) NF

THOMPSON, Jim (1906–1977)
American crime writer
Nothing More Than Murder (1949) F
The Killer Inside Me (1952) F
Savage Night (1953) F
A Hell of a Woman (1954) F
The Nothing Man (1954) F
After Dark, My Sweet (1955) F
The Getaway (1959) F
The Grifters (1963) F
Pop. 1280 (1964) F

THOMSON, James (1700–1748)
Scottish poet and dramatist
Winter (1726) V
Summer (1727) V
Spring (1728) V
Britannia (1729) V
The Tragedy of Sophonisba (1729) D
The Seasons (1730) V
Antient and Modern Italy Compared [*Liberty* pt. i] (1735) V
Greece [*Liberty* pt. ii] (1735) V
Rome [*Liberty* pt. iii] (1735) V
Britain [*Liberty* pt. iv] (1736) V
The Prospect [*Liberty* pt. v] (1736) V
Agamemnon (1738) D
Liberty (1738) V
Edward and Eleonora (1739) D
Tancred and Sigismunda (1745) D
The Castle of Indolence (1748) V

THOMSON, James (1834–1882)
British poet
The City of Dreadful Night, and Other Poems (1880) V
Vane's Story, Weddah and Om-el-Bonain, and Other Poems (1881) V
Alfred (1740) D

THOREAU, Henry David (1817–1862)
American author
A Week on the Concord and Merrimack Rivers (1849) NF
Walden; or, A Life in the Woods (1854) NF
Excursions (1863) NF
The Maine Woods (1864) NF
Cape Cod (1865) NF
A Yankee in Canada (1866) NF
Early Spring in Massachusetts (1881) NF
Summer (1884) NF
Winter (1888) NF

THRALE, [Mrs] Hester Lynch *see* HESTER LYNCH PIOZZI

THUBRON, Colin [Gerald Dryden] (1939–)
British novelist and travel writer
Mirror to Damascus (1967) NF
The Hills of Adonis (1968) NF
Jerusalem (1969) NF
The God in the Mountain (1977) F
Emperor (1978) F
Among the Russians (1983) NF
A Cruel Madness (1984) F
Behind the Wall (1987) NF
Turning Back the Sun (1991) F
The Lost Heart of Asia (1994) NF
In Siberia (1999) NF

THURBER, James [Grover] (1894–1961)
American humorist and cartoonist
Is Sex Necessary? (1929) F NF
The Owl in the Attic, and Other Perplexities (1931) F NF
The Seal in the Bedroom, and Other Predicaments (1932) F NF
My Life and Hard Times (1933) NF
The Middle-Aged Man on the Flying Trapeze (1935) F NF
Let Your Mind Alone! (1937) NF
The Last Flower (1939) F
Fables For Our Time, and Famous Poems Illustrated (1940) F
My World—and Welcome To It [inc. 'The Secret Life of Walter Mitty'] (1942) F NF
Many Moons (1943) F CH
The Great Quillow (1944) F CH
The Thurber Carnival (1945) F NF
The White Deer (1945) F CH
The Beast in Me and Other Animals (1948) F NF
The Thirteen Clocks (1950) F CH
Thurber Country (1953) F NF
Further Fables for Our Time (1956) F NF
Alarms and Diversions (1957) F NF
The Wonderful O (1957) F CH
Credos and Curios (1961) F NF
Lanterns & Lances (1961) NF

THWAITE, Ann (1932–)
British biographer, children's author, and editor
The House in Turner Square (1960) F CH
Toby Stays with Jane (1962) F CH
Waiting for the Party [biography of Frances Hodgson Burnett] (1974) NF
Edmund Gosse: A Literary Landscape (1984) NF
A.A. Milne: His Life (1990) NF

THWAITE, Anthony [Simon] (1930–)
British poet, critic, and editor
Home Truths (1957) V
The Owl in the Tree (1963) V
The Stones of Emptiness (1967) V
Points (1972) V
Jack (1973) V
Poetry Today 1960–1973 (1973) NF
New Confessions (1974) V
A Portion for Foxes (1977) V
Twentieth-Century English Poetry (1978) NF
Victorian Voices (1980) V
Telling Tales (1983) V
Letter from Tokyo (1987) V
The Dust of the World (1994) V

TICKELL, Thomas (1686–1740)
English poet
Oxford (1707) V
Kensington Garden (1722) V
To Sir Godfrey Kneller, at his Country Seat (1722) V

TILLICH, Paul [Johannes Oskar] (1886–1965)
German-born American theologian
The Religious Situation (1932) NF
The Interpretation of History (1936) NF
The Protestant Era (1948) NF
Systematic Theology (1951–63) NF
The Courage to Believe (1952) NF
Love, Power, and Justice (1954) NF
Biblical Religion and the Search for Ultimate Reality (1955) NF
Dynamics of Faith (1956) NF
Theology of Culture (1959) NF
The Eternal Now (1963) NF

TILLYARD, E[ustace] M[andeville] W[etenhall] (1889–1962)
British literary scholar and critic
Milton (1930) NF
Poetry Direct and Oblique (1934) NF
Shakespeare's Last Plays (1938) NF
The Personal Heresy (1939) NF
The Elizabethan World-Picture (1943) NF
Shakespeare's History Plays (1944) NF
The English Epic and its Background (1954) NF
The Muse Unchained (1958) NF

TILSEY, Frank (1904–1957)
British novelist
The Plebian's Progress (1933) F

TINDAL, Matthew (1657–1733)
English deist and religious writer
An Essay Concerning the Laws of Nations and the Rights of Sovereigns (1693) NF
The Liberty of the Press (1698) NF
The Rights of the Christian Church Asserted (1706) NF
A Defence of the Rights of the Christian Church (1707) NF
The Defection Considered (1717) NF
A Defence of Our Present Happy Establishment (1722) NF
Christianity as Old as the Creation (1730) NF

TOCQUEVILLE, Alexis, Comte de (1805–1859)
French politician and writer
De la démocracie en Amérique (1835) NF

TODD, Ruthven (1914–1978)
British novelist, poet, critic, and children's writer
Over the Mountain (1939) F
The Lost Traveller (1943) F
Space Cat (1952) F CH

TÓIBÍN, Colm (1955–)
Irish journalist and novelist
The South (1990) F
The Heather Blazing (1993) F
The Blackwater Lightship (1999) F

TOLKEIN, J[ohn] R[onald] R[euel] (1892–1973)
British philologist and fantasy author
Beowulf: The Monsters and the Critics (1936) NF
The Hobbit; or, There and Back Again (1937) F CH
Farmer Giles of Ham (1949) F CH
The Fellowship of the Ring [*The Lord of the Rings* pt. i] (1954) F
The Two Towers [*The Lord of the Rings* pt. ii] (1954) F
The Return of the King [*The Lord of the Rings* pt. iii] (1955) F
The Adventures of Tom Bombadil, and Other Verses from the Red Book (1962) V CH
Tree and Leaf (1964) NF F
The Lord of the Rings [all 3 pts.] (1966) F
The Road Goes Ever On (1967) V
The Silmarrillion (1977) F
Unfinished Tales of Numenor and Middle Earth (1980) F
The Book of Lost Tales Part 1 (1983) F
The Book of Lost Tales Part 2 (1984) F
The Book of Lost Tales Part 3 (1985) F

TOLSTOY, Count Leo [Nikolayevich] (1828–1910)
Russian novelist
Childhood (1852) F
Boyhood (1854) F
Sebastopol (1855–6) F
Youth (1856) F
War and Peace (1863–9) F
Anna Karenina (1874–6) F
A Confession (1884) F
My Religion (1885) NF
The Death of Ivan Ilyitch (1886) F
The Kreutzer Sonata (1889) F
The Kingdom of God is Within You (1893–4) NF
Master and Man (1894) NF
What is Art? (1898) NF
Resurrection (1899) NF

TOMALIN, Claire (1933–)
British biographer
The Life and Death of Mary Wollstonecraft (1974) NF
The Invisible Woman [biography of Nelly Ternan] (1990) NF
Mrs Jordan's Profession (1994) NF

TOMLINSON, [Alfred] Charles (1927–)
British poet, translator, editor, and graphic artist
The Necklace (1955) V
Solo for a Glass Harmonica (1957) V
A Peopled Landscape (1963) V
American Scenes, and Other Poems (1966) V
To Be Engraved on the Skull of a Cormorant (1968) V
The Way of a World (1969) V
Written on Water (1972) V
The Shaft (1978) V
Notes From New York, and Other Poems (1984) V
The Return (1987) V
Annunciations (1989) V

The Door in the Wall (1992) V
Jubilation (1995) V
The Vineyard Above the Sea (2000) V

TOMLINSON, H[enry] M[ajor] (1873–1958)
British travel writer and novelist
The Sea and the Jungle (1912) NF
London River (1921) NF
Gallion's Reach (1927) F NF
All Our Yesterdays (1930) F
The Trumpet Shall Sound (1957) F

TOOKE, John Horne (1736–1812)
British radical politician and author
Epea Pteroenta; or, The Diversions of Purley (1786) NF
Proceedings on Trial of Tooke for High Treason (1795) NF

TOOLE, John Kennedy (1937–1969)
American novelist
A Confederacy of Dunces (1980) F

TOOMER, Jean [Nathan Eugene] (1894–1967)
African-American writer
Cain (1923) F V

TOPLADY, Augustus Montague (1740–1778)
British divine and poet
Poems on Sacred Subjects (1759) V
A Letter to the Rev. Mr Wesley (1770) NF
Psalms and Hymns for Public and Private Worship (1776) V

TOURGÉE, Albion W[inegar] (1838–1905)
American novelist
'Toinette [repub. 1881 as *A Royal Gentleman*] (1874) F
Figs and Thistles (1879) F
A Fool's Errand (1879) F
Bricks Without Straw (1880) F
John Eax and Mamelon (1882) F
Hot Plowshares (1883) F
Pactolus Prime (1890) F

TOURNEUR, Cyril (1575–1626)
English dramatist and poet
The Transformed Metamorphosis (1600) V
The Revenger's Tragedy (1607) D
The Atheist's Tragedie; or, The Honest Man's Revenge (1611) D

TOURTEL, Mary (1874–1948)
British children's writer and illustrator
The Adventures of Rupert the Little Bear (1921) F CH

TOWNSEND, Sue (1946–)
British novelist and dramatist
The Secret Diary of Adrian Mole Aged 13¾ (1982) F
The Growing Pains of Adrian Mole (1984) F
The Queen and I (1992) F
Ghost Children (1997) F
Adrian Mole: The Cappuccino Years (1999) F

TOWNSHEND, Aurelian (1583?–1651?)
English poet and dramatist
Albions Triumph (1631) D
Tempe Restored (1632) D

TOYNBEE, Arnold [Joseph] (1889–1975)
British historian
Nationality and the War (1915) NF
A Study of History (1934) NF
Civilization on Trial (1948) NF
The World and the West (1953) NF
An Historian's Approach to Religion (1956) NF
Hellenism (1959) NF
Between Oxus and Jumna (1961) NF
Change and Habit (1966) NF

TOYNBEE, [Theodore] Philip (1916–1981)
British novelist, poet, critic, and diarist
Tea With Mrs Goodman [US: *Prothalamium*] (1947) F
The Garden to the Sea (1953) F
Pantaloon; or, The Valediction (1961) V
Two Brothers (1964) V
A Learned City (1966) V
Views From a Lake (1968) V

TRAHERNE, Thomas (1637–1674)
English poet and author
Roman Forgeries; or, A True Account of False Records (1673) NF
Christian Ethicks; or, Divine Morality Opening the Way to Blessedness (1675) NF V
A Serious and Patheticall Contemplation of the Mercies of God (1699) NF
Hexameron; or, Meditations on the Six Days of Creation (1717) NF V
Poetical Works [ed. Bertam Dobell] (1903) V
Centuries of Meditations [ed. Bertam Dobell] (1908) MISC
Traherne's Poems of Felicity [ed. Idris Bell] (1910) V

TRANTER, Nigel [Godwin] (1909–2000)
Scottish historical novelist
The Master of Gray (1961) F
The Courtesan (1963) F
Past Master (1965) F
The Steps to the Empty Throne (1969) F
The Path of the Hero King (1970) F
The Price of the King's Peace (1971) F

TRAPIDO, Barbara (1941–)
South African-born British novelist
Brother of the More Famous Jack (1982) F
Noah's Ark (1984) F
Temples of Delight (1990) F
Juggling (1994) F
The Travelling Hornplayer (1998) F

'TRAVEN, B.' [Albert Otto Fiege] (1890–1969)
Pseudonymous Polish-German novelist and short-story writer
The Treasure of the Sierra Madre (1934) F

TRAVERS, Ben[jamin] (1886–1980)
British dramatist and novelist
A Cuckoo in the Nest [adapted for the stage 1925] (1922) F
Rookery Nook [adapted for the stage 1926] (1923) F

TRAVERS, P[amela] L[yndon] (1906–)
Australian-born children's writer
Mary Poppins (1934) F CH

TREASE, Geoffrey (1909–1998)
British children's writer, novelist, and historian
Bows Against the Barons (1934) F CH
Aunt Augusta's Elephany (1969) F CH
The Popinjay Mystery (1973) F CH

TREECE, Henry (1911–1966)
British poet, novelist, children's author, and editor
The New Apocalypse (1939) ANTH
The White Horseman (1941) ANTH
The Black Seasons (1945) V
The Crown and the Sickle (1945) ANTH
How I See Apocalypse (1946) NF
The Haunted Garden (1947) V
The Dark Island (1952) F
The Exiles (1952) V
The Rebels (1953) F
Legions of the Eagle (1954) F CH
Viking's Dawn (1955) F CH
The Golden Strangers (1956) F
Red Queen, White Queen (1958) F
The Green Man (1966) F

TRELAWNY, E[dward] J[ohn] (1792–1881)
British adventurer and biographer
Adventures of a Younger Son (1831) NF
Recollections of the Last Days of Shelley and Byron (1858) NF

TREMAIN, Rose (1943–)
British novelist, short-story writer, and dramatist
Sadler's Birthday (1976) F
Letter to Sister Benedicta (1978) F
The Cupboard (1981) F
The Colonel's Daughter, and Other Stories (1984) F SS
The Swimming-Pool Season (1985) F
The Garden of the Villa Mollini, and Other Stories (1987) F SS
Restoration (1989) F
Sacred Country (1992) F
Evangelista's Fan, and Other Stories (1994) F SS
Music and Silence (1999) F SS

TRENCH, Richard Chenevix (1807–1886)
British philologist, theologian, and poet
The Story of Justin Martyr, and Other Poems (1835) V

'TRESSELL, Robert' [Robert P. Noonan] (1870–1911)
Irish novelist
The Ragged Trousered Philanthropist [abridged; full version, 1955] (1914) F

'TREVANIAN' [Rodney Whitaker] (1925–)
American spy novelist
The Eiger Sanction (1972) F
The Loo Sanction (1973) F

TREVELYAN, G[eorge] M[acaulay] (1876–1962)
British historian
England Under the Stuarts (1904) NF
Garibaldi's Defence of the Roman Republic 1848–9 (1907) NF
Garibaldi and the Thousand (1909) NF
Garibaldi and the Making of Italy (1911) NF
History of England [rev. 1937] (1926) NF
English Social History (1942) NF

TREVELYAN, Sir George Otto, OM, 2nd Baronet (1838–1928)
British statesman and historian
Cawnpore (1865) NF
The Life and Letters of Lord Macaulay (1876) NF
The American Revolution (1899) NF

TREVOR, Elleston *see* ADAM HALL

'TREVOR, William' [William Trevor Cox] (1928–)
Irish novelist, short-story writer, and dramatist
A Standard of Behaviour (1958) F
The Old Boys (1964) F
The Boarding House (1965) F
The Love Department (1966) F
The Day We Got Drunk on Cake (1967) F
Mrs Eckdorf in O'Neill's Hotel (1969) F
Miss Gomez and the Brethren (1971) F
The Ballroom of Romance (1972) F
Elizabeth Alone (1973) F
Angels at the Ritz, and Other Stories (1975) F SS
The Children of Dynmouth (1976) F
Lovers of Their Time, and Other Stories (1978) F SS
Other People's Worlds (1980) F
Beyond the Pale (1981) F SS
Fools of Fortune (1983) F
The News From Ireland, and Other Stories (1986) F SS
The Silence in the Garden (1988) F
Family Sins, and Other Stories (1990) F SS
Two Lives (1991) F
Felicia's Journey (1994) F
Death in Summer (1998) F
The Hill Bachelors (2000) F

TREVOR-ROPER, Hugh [Redwald], Baron Dacre (1914–)
British historian
Archbishop Laud (1940) NF
The Last Days of Hitler (1947) NF
Historical Essays (1957) NF
The Rise of Christian Europe (1965) NF
Religion, the Reformation and Social Change, and Other Essays (1967) NF
The Philby Affair (1968) NF
A Hidden Life (1976) NF
Princes and Artists (1976) NF

TRILLING, Lionel (1905–1975)
American literary critic
Matthew Arnold (1939) NF
E.M. Forster (1943) NF
The Middle of the Journey (1947) F
The Liberal Imagination (1950) NF
The Opposing Self (1955) NF
Freud and the Crisis of Our Culture (1956) NF
A Gathering of Fugitives (1956) NF

Beyond Culture (1965) NF
Sincerity and Authenticity (1972) NF
Mind in the Modern World (1973) NF

TROLLOPE, Anthony (1815–1882)
British novelist and short-story writer
The Macdermots of Ballycloran (1847) F
The Kelleys and the O'Kellys; or, Landlords and Tenants (1848) F
La Vendée (1850) F
The Warden (1855) F
Barchester Towers (1857) F
Doctor Thorne (1858) F
The Three Clerks (1858) F
The Bertrams (1859) F
Castle Richmond (1860) F
Framley Parsonage (1861) F
Tales of All Countries [1st ser.] (1861) F SS
North America (1862) NF
Orley Farm (1862) F
The Struggles of Brown, Jones, and Robinson (1862) F
Rachel Ray (1863) F
Tales of All Countries [2nd ser.] (1863) F SS
The Small House at Allington (1864) F
Can You Forgive Her? (1864–5) F
Hunting Sketches (1865) NF
Miss Mackenzie (1865) F
The Belton Estate (1866) F
Clergymen of the Church of England (1866) NF
Travelling Sketches (1866) NF
The Claverings (1867) F
The Last Chronicle of Barset (1867) F
Lotta Schmidt, and Other Stories (1867) F SS
Nina Balatka (1867) F
Linda Tressel (1868) F
He Knew He Was Right (1869) F
Phineas Finn; the Irish Member (1869) F
The Vicar of Bullhampton (1870) F
Ralph the Heir (1871) F
Sir Harry Hotspur of Humblethwaite (1871) F
The Golden Lion of Granpere (1872) F
Australia and New Zealand (1873) NF
The Eustace Diamonds (1873) F
Harry Heathcote of Gangoil (1874) F
Lady Anna (1874) F
Phineas Redux (1874) F
The Way We Live Now (1875) F
The Prime Minister (1876) F
The American Senator (1877) F
How the'Mastiffs' Went to Iceland (1878) NF
Is He Popenjoy? (1878) F
South Africa (1878) NF
Cousin Henry (1879) F
An Eye for an Eye (1879) F
John Caldigate (1879) F
Thackeray (1879) NF
The Duke's Children (1880) F
Ayala's Angel (1881) F
Dr Wortle's School (1881) F
The Fixed Period (1882) F
Kept in the Dark (1882) F
Marion Fay (1882) F
Palmerston (1882) NF
Why Frau Frohmann Raised Her Prices, and Other Stories (1882) F SS
An Autobiography (1883) NF
The Landleaguers (1883) F
Mr Scarborough's Family (1883) F
An Old Man's Love (1884) F

TROLLOPE, Frances, *née* Milton (1780–1863)
British novelist and travel writer
Domestic Manners of the Americans (1832) NF
The Refugee in America (1832) F
The Abbess (1833) F
The Mother's Manual; or, Illustrations of Matrimonial Economy (1833) V
Belgium and Western Germany in 1833 (1834) NF
Tremordyn Cliff (1835) F
The Life and Adventures of Jonathan Jefferson Whitlaw (1836) F
Paris and the Parisians in 1835 (1836) NF
The Vicar of Wrexhill (1837) F
A Romance of Vienna (1838) F
The Widow Barnaby (1839) F
The Life and Adventures of Michael Armstrong, the Factory Boy (1840) F
The Widow Married (1840) F
Charles Chesterfield; or, The Adventures of a Youth of Genius (1841) F
The Barnabys in America; or, Adventures of the Widow Wedded (1843) F
Hargrave; or, The Adventures of a Man of Fashion (1843) F
The Laurringtons; or, Superior People (1844) F
The Robertses on their Travels (1846) F
Father Eustace (1847) F
Petticoat Government (1850) F
The Life and Adventures of a Clever Woman (1854) F
Fashionable Life; or, Paris and London (1856) F

TROLLOPE, Joanna (1943–)
British novelist
Parson Harding's Daughter [US: *Mistaken Virtues*] (1979) F
Leaves From the Valley (1980) F
The City of Gems (1981) F
The Steps of the Sun (1983) F
The Choir (1988) F
A Village Affair (1989) F
The Best of Friends (1995) F
Next of Kin (1996) F
Other People's Children (1998) F
Marrying the Mistress (2000) F

TROLLOPE, T[homas] Adolphus (1810–1892)
British novelist and journalist
Filippo Strozzi (1860) F
Giulio Malatesta (1863) F
Beppo the Conscript (1864) F SS
Leonora Casaloni (1868) F
Durnton Abbey (1871) F

Diamond Cut Diamond (1875) F SS
A Family Party in the Piazza of St Peter, and Other Stories (1877) F SS
What I Remember (1887) NF

TUCHMAN, Barbara (1912–1989)
American historian
The Zimmerman Telegram (1958) NF
The Guns of August (1962) NF
The Proud Tower (1965) NF

TUCKER, Abraham (1705–1774)
British amateur philosopher
The Light of Nature Pursued [by 'Edward Search'] (1768–77) NF

TUPPER, Martin Farquhar (1810–1889)
British versifier and dramatist
Proverbial Philosophy (1838) V
The Crock of Gold (1844) F

TURGENEV, Ivan [Sergeevich] (1818–1883)
Russian novelist
Parasha (1843) V
Russian Life in the Interior (1852) NF
Rudin (1856) F
A Nest of Gentlefolk (1859) F
On the Eve (1860) F
Fathers and Sons (1862) F
Smoke (1867) F
A Lear of the Steppes (1870) F SS
Virgin Soil (1877) F

TUROW, Scott (1949–)
American novelist
Presumed Innocent (1987) F
The Burden of Proof (1990) F
Pleading Guilty (1993) F
Personal Injuries (1999) F

TUSSER, Thomas (1524?–1580)
English agricultural author and poet
A Hundreth Good Pointes of Husbandrie (1557) V
Five Hundreth Points of Good Husbandry (1573) V

'TWAIN, Mark' [Samuel Langhorne Clemens] (1835–1910)
American novelist, short-story writer, and essayist
The Celebrated Jumping Frog of Calaveras County, and Other Sketches (1867) F
The Innocents Abroad; or, The New Pilgrim's Progress (1869) NF
Roughing It (1872) NF
The Gilded Age (1873) F
The Adventures of Tom Sawyer (1876) F
A Tramp Abroad (1880) NF
The Prince and the Pauper (1882) F CH
Life on the Mississippi (1883) NF
Adventures of Huckleberry Finn (1884) F
A Connecticut Yankee in King Arthur's Court (1889) F
The American Claimant (1892) F
Tom Sawyer Abroad (1894) F
The Tragedy of Pudd'nhead Wilson (1894) F
Personal Recollections of Joan of Arc [supposedly trn by 'Jean François Alden'] (1896) F
Tom Sawyer, Detective (1896) F
Following the Equator (1897) NF
The Man That Corrupted Hadleyburg (1900) F
Christian Science (1907) NF
Is Shakespeare Dead? (1909) NF

TYLER, Anne (1941–)
American novelist
If Morning Ever Comes (1965) F
The Tin Can Tree (1966) F
A Slipping Down Life (1970) F
The Clock Winder (1973) F
Celestial Navigation (1975) F
Searching for Caleb (1976) F
Earthly Possessions (1977) F
Morgan's Passing (1980) F
Dinner at the Homesick Restaurant (1982) F
The Accidental Tourist (1985) F
Breathing Lessons (1988) F
Saint Maybe (1992) F
Ladder of Years (1995) F
A Patchwork Planet (1998) F

TYLER, Royall (1757–1826)
American dramatist and novelist
The Contrast (1787) D
The Algerine Captive (1797) F
Yankey in London (1809) F

TYNAN, Katharine, *née* Hinkson (1861–1931)
Irish poet and novelist
Louise de la Vallière, and Other Poems (1885) V
Shamrocks (1887) V
Ballads and Lyrics (1891) V
Cuckoo Songs (1894) V
An Isle in the Water (1895) F
The Way of a Maid (1895) F
Led By a Dream, and Other Stories (1899) F SS
That Sweet Enemy (1901) F
The Handsome Quaker, and Other Stories (1902) F SS
The French Wife (1904) F
Innocencies (1905) V
The Adventures of Alicia (1906) F
The Yellow Domino, and Other Stories (1906) F SS
Irish Poems (1913) V
The Holy War (1916) V

TYNAN, Kenneth [Peacock] (1927–1980)
British drama critic and theatre producer
Curtains (1961) NF
A View of the English Stage 1944–63 (1975) NF

TYNDALE, William (1494?–1536)
English humanist, translator of the Bible, and Protestant martyr
The New Testament [first complete edn] (1526) NF
The Obedience of a Christen Man (1528) NF
The Pentateuch (1530) NF
The Practyse of Prelates (1530) NF
An Answere unto Sir Thomas Mores Dialogue (1531) NF

TYRWHITT, Thomas (1730–1786)
English classical commentator and literary scholar
Observations and Conjectures Upon Some Passages of Shakespeare (1766) NF

The Canterbury Tales of Chaucer (1775) EDN
A Vindication of the Appendix to the Poems, called Rowley's (1782) NF

U

UDALL, Nicholas (1505?–1556)
English dramatist and scholar
Floures for Latine Spekynge [from Terence] (1533) NF
Apopthegmes [from Erasmus] (1542) NF
The Sacrament of the Lord's Supper [from Peter Martyr] (1550) NF
Ralph Roister Doister (1566?) D

UNDERHILL, Evelyn [afterwards **Mrs Stuart Moore]** (1875–1941)
British writer on mysticism and spirituality
Mysticism (1911) NF
The Mystic Way (1913) NF
The Essentials of Mysticism, and Other Essays (1920) NF
The Life of the Spirit and the Life of To-day (1922) NF
The Mystics of the Church (1925) NF
Man and the Supernatural (1927) NF
The Fruits of the Spirit (1942) NF

UNSWORTH, Barry [Forster] (1930–)
British novelist
The Greeks Have a Word For It (1967) F
The Hide (1970) F
The Big Day (1976) F
Pascali's Island [US: *Idol Hunter*] (1980) F
Stone Virgin (1985) F
Sugar and Rum (1988) F
Sacred Hunger (1992) F
Morality Play (1995) F
Losing Nelson (1999) F

UPDIKE, John [Hoyer] (1932–)
American novelist, short-story writer, and poet
The Carpenter Hen, and Other Tame Creatures (1958) V
The Poorhouse Fair (1959) F
The Same Door (1959) F SS
Rabbit, Run (1960) F
Pigeon Feathers (1962) F SS
The Centaur (1963) F
Telephone Poles (1963) V
Of the Farm (1965) F
The Music School (1966) F SS
Couples (1968) F
Midpoint (1969) V
Bech: A Book (1970) F
Rabbit Redux (1971) F
Museums and Women (1972) F SS
A Month of Sundays (1975) F
Picking Up Pieces (1975) NF
Marry Me (1976) F
Tossing and Turning (1977) V
The Coup (1979) F
Problems (1979) F SS
Too Far To Go (1979) F SS
Rabbit is Rich (1981) F
Bech is Back (1982) F
Hugging the Shore (1983) NF
The Witches of Eastwick (1984) F
Facing Nature (1985) V
Roger's Version (1986) F
Trust Me (1987) F SS
Just Looking (1989) NF
Self-Consciousness (1989) NF
Rabbit at Rest (1990) F
Odd Jobs (1991) NF
Memoirs of the Ford Administration (1992) F
The After Life, and Other Stories (1994) F SS
Brazil (1994) F
In the Beauty of the Lilies (1996) F

UPWARD, Allen (1863–1926)
British novelist
The Prince of Balkistan (1895) F
The Secrets of the Courts of Europe (1897) F SS

UPWARD, Edward [Falaise] (1903–)
British novelist and short-story writer
Journey to the Border (1938) F
In the Thirties (1962) F
The Railway Accident, and Other Stories (1969) F SS
The Rotten Elements (1969) F
No Home But the Struggle (1977) F SS
The Spiral Ascent (1977) F
The Night Walk, and Other Stories (1987) F SS
The Mortmere Stories (1994) F SS
An Unmentionable Man (1994) F SS

URIS, Leon [Marcus] (1924–)
American novelist
Battle Cry (1953) F
The Angry Hills (1955) F
Exodus (1957) F
Armageddon (1964) F
Topaz (1967) F
The Haj (1984) F

URQUHART, Fred[erick Burrows] (1912–1995)
Scottish short-story writer and novelist
I Fell For a Sailor (1940) F SS
The Ploughing Match (1968) F SS
Proud Lady in a Cage (1980) F SS
Full Score (1989) F SS

URQUHART, Sir Thomas (1611–1660)
Scottish author and translator
Epigrams: Divine and Moral (1641) V
Trissotetras; or, A Most Exquisite Table for Resolving Triangles (1645) V
The Discoverie of a Most Exquisite Jewel (1652) V
Pantochronochanon; or, A Peculiar Promptuary of Time (1652) NF
The First/Second Book of Mr Francis Rabelais [3rd bk, 1693] (1653) V

USSHER, James (1581–1656)
Irish ecclesiastic and scholar
The Original of Bishops and Metropolitans (1641) NF
A Body of Divinitie; or, The Summe and Substance of Christian Religion (1645) NF
The Annals of the World (1658) NF

'UTTLEY, Allison' [Alice Jane Uttley] (1884–1976)
British children's writer
The Squirrel, the Hare, and the Little Grey Rabbit [first of the 'Little Grey Rabbit' books] (1929) F CH
A Traveller in Time (1939) F CH
Sam Pig (1940) F CH

V

'VALENTINE, Douglas' [George Valentine Williams] (1883–1946)
British thriller writer
The Man With the Club Foot (1918) F

VALÉRY, Paul-Ambroise (1871–1945)
French poet, critic, and essayist
An Evening with Monsieur Teste [*La Soirée avec Monsieur Teste*] (1896) F
The Young Fate [*La Jeune Parque*] (1917) V
Charms [*Charmes*] (1922) V
Dance and the Soul [*L'Âme et la danse*] (1924) V
Eupalinos (1924) V

VANBRUGH, Sir John (1664–1726)
English dramatist and architect
The Relapse; or, Virtue in Danger (1696) D
Aesop (1696–7) D
The Provok'd Wife (1697) D
The Country House (1698) D
A Short Vindication of 'The Relapse' and 'The Provok'd Wife' (1698) NF
The Pilgrim (1700) D
The False Friend (1702) D
The Confederacy (1705) D
The Mistake (1705) D

VANCE, Jack [John Holbrook] (1916–)
American science fiction and fantasy writer
The Dying Earth (1950) F
Big Planet (1957) F
The Dragon Masters (1963) F
Lyonesse (1983) F

VAN DER POST, Sir Laurens [Jan] (1906–1996)
South African novelist and author
In a Province (1934) F
Venture to the Interior (1952) NF
The Face Beside the Fire (1953) F
The Dark Eye in Africa (1955) NF
Flamingo Feather (1955) F
The Lost World of the Kalahari (1958) NF
The Heart of the Hunter (1961) NF
The Seed and the Sower (1963) F
Journey into Russia (1964) NF
The Hunter and the Whale (1967) F
A Portrait of all the Russias (1967) NF
A Portrait of Japan (1968) NF
The Night of the New Moon (1970) NF
Jung and the Story of Our Time (1975) NF
A Mantis Carol (1975) F
Yet Being Someone Other (1982) NF
A Walk With a White Bushman (1986) NF
The Voice of the Thunder (1993) NF

'VAN DINE, S.S.' [Willard Huntington Wright] (1888–1939)
American detective novelist and art critic
The Benson Murder Case [first Philo Vance novel] (1926) F
The Canary Murder Case (1927) F
The Greene Murder Case (1928) F
The Bishop Murder Case (1929) F
The Scarab Murder Case (1930) F

VANSITTART, Peter (1920–)
British novelist
I Am the World (1942) F
The Friends of God [US: *The Siege*] (1963) F
Lancelot (1978) F
The Death of Robin Hood (1981) F
Three Six Seven (1983) F
Parsifal (1988) F
The Wall (1990) F
A Choice of Murder (1992) F

VAN VOGHT, A[lfred] E[lton] (1912–)
Canadian-born science fiction writer
Slan [rev. 1951] (1948) F
The Weapon Shops of Ishar (1951) F
The Weapon Makers (1956) F

VARGAS LLOSA, Mario (1936–)
Peruvian novelist
The Time of the Hero [*La ciudad y los perros*] (1962) F
The Green House [*La casa verde*] (1965) F
Conversation in the Cathedral [*Conversación en la catedral*] (1969) F
Captain Pantoja and the Special Service [*Pantaléon y las visitadoras*] (1973) F
Aunt Julia and the Scriptwriter [*La tia Julia y el escribidor*] (1977) F
The War of the End of the World [*La guerra del fin del mundo*] (1981) F
The Real Life of Alejandro Mayta [*La Historia de Alejandro Mayta*] (1984) F

VAUGHAN, Henry ['Silurist'] (1622–1695)
Welsh poet
Poems, with the Tenth Satyre of Juvenal Englished (1646) V
Silex Scintillans; or, Sacred Poems and Private Ejaculations (1650) V
Olor Iscanus (1651) V NF
The Mount of Olives; or, Solitary Devotions (1652) NF
Flores Solitudinis (1654) NF
Hermetical Physick [from Heinrich Nolle] (1655) NF
Silex Scintillans [2nd edn] (1655) V

The Chymists Key [from Heinrich Nolle] (1657) NF
Thalia Rediviva (1678) V

VAUGHAN, Thomas ['Eugenius Philalethes'] (1622–1666)
Welsh alchemist and poet, twin brother of Henry Vaughan
Anthroposophia Theomagica [as 'Eugenius Philalethes'] (1650) V
Magia Adamica; or, The Antiquitie of Magic [as 'Eugenius Philalethes'] (1650) NF
Lumen de Lumine; or, A New Magicall Light Discovered [as 'Eugenius Philalethes'] (1651) NF
Aula Lucis; or, The House of Light (1652) NF
Euphrates; or, The Waters of the East [as 'Eugenius Philalethes'] (1655) NF

VEGA, Lope de [Lope Félix de Vega Carpio] (1562–1635)
Spanish dramatist and poet
Arcadia (1598) F
La Dragontea (1598) V
Angelica [written 1588] (1602) V
Rhymes [*Rimas*] (1604) V
The Gardener's Dog [*El perro del hortelano*] (1613–15) D
Fuenteovejuna (1619) D
La Dorotea (1632) V
The Knight of Olmedo [*El caballero de Olmedo*; written 1620–5] (1641) D

VERLAINE, Paul (1844–1896)
French poet
Poèmes saturniens ['Saturnine Poems'] (1866) V
Gallant Parties [*Fêtes galantes*] (1869) V
La bonne chanson ['The Pretty Song'] (1870) V
Romances Without Words [*Romances sans paroles*] (1874) V
Sagesse ['Wisdom'] (1881) V
Les Poètes maudits ['Accursed Poets'] (1884) V
Parallèlement ['In Parallel'] (1889) V
Élégies ['Elegies'] (1893) V

VERNE, Jules (1828–1905)
French fantasy novelist
Five Weeks in a Balloon [*Cinq Semaines en ballon*] (1863) F
A Journey to the Centre of the Earth [*Voyage au centre de la terre*] (1864) F
From the Earth to the Moon [*De la Terre à la Lune*] (1865) F
Twenty Thousand Leagues Under the Sea [*Vingt mille lieues sous les mers*] (1869) F
Around the World in Eighty Days [*Le Tour du monde en quatre-vingts jours*] (1873) F

VIAUD, Julien *see* PIERRE LOTI

VIDAL, Gore (1925–)
American novelist, essayist, and dramatist
Williwaw (1946) F
In a Yellow Wood (1947) F
The City and the Pillar (1948) F
The Season of Comfort (1949) F
Dark Green, Bright Red (1950) F
A Search for the King (1950) F
The Judgment of Paris [rev. 1965] (1952) F
Messiah [rev. 1965] (1954) F
A Thirsty Evil (1956) F SS
Julian (1964) F
Washington, DC (1967) F
Myra Breckinridge (1968) F
Two Sisters (1970) F
Burr (1973) F
Myron (1975) F
1876 (1976) F
Matters of Fact and of Fiction (1977) NF
Kalki (1978) F
Creation (1981) F
Pink Triangle and Yellow Star, and Other Essays (1982) NF
The Second American Revolution (1982) NF
Duluth (1983) F
Lincoln (1984) F
Armageddon, and Other Essays (1987) NF
Empire (1987) F
At Home (1988) NF
Hollywood (1990) F
Golgotha (1992) F
Screening History (1992) NF
Palimpsest: A Memoir (1995) NF

VILLON, François (*c.* 1431–post 1463)
French poet
Petit Testament [also known as the *Lais*] (1456) V
Grand Testament [written 1461–2] (1489) V

VINE, Barbara *see* RUTH RENDELL

VIRGIL [Publius Vergilius Maro] (70–19 BC)
Roman poet
Eclogues (37 BC) V
Aeneid [incomplete at Virgil's death] (19 BC) V
Georgics (29 BC) V

'VOLTAIRE' [François-Marie Arouet] (1694–1778)
French philosopher and novelist
La Ligue, ou Henri le Grand (1723) V
Letters Concerning the English Nation [*Lettres écrites de Londres sur les Anglais*] (1734) NF
The Elements of Newton's Philosophy [*Eléments de la philosophie de Newton*] (1738) NF
Mahomet (1741) D
Mérope (1743) D
Zadig (1747) F
The Age of Louis XIV [*Siècle de Louis Quatorze*] (1751) NF
The General History and State of Europe [*Les Moeurs et l'esprit des nations*] (1756) NF
Candide (1759) F
The Philosophical Dictionary for the Pocket [*Dictionnaire philosophique portatif*] (1764) NF

VON ARNIM, 'Elizabeth' [Mary Annette Gräfin, *née* Beauchamp, later **Countess Russell]** (1866–1941)
New Zealand-born novelist

Elizabeth and Her German Garden (1898) F
The Solitary Summer (1899) F
The Benefactress (1901) F
The Adventures of Elizabeth in Rügen (1904) F
Fräulein Schmidt and Mr Anstruther (1907) F
The Caravaners (1909) F
The Pastor's Wife (1914) F

VONNEGUT, Kurt Jr (1922–)
American novelist, short-story writer, and dramatist
Player Piano (1952) F
The Sirens of Titan (1959) F
Canary in a Cat House (1961) F SS
Mother Night (1961) F
Cat's Cradle (1963) F
God Bless You, Mr Rosewater (1965) F
Welcome to the Monkey House (1968) F NF
Slaughterhouse-Five; or, The Children's Crusade (1969) F
Happy Birthday, Wanda Jane (1970) D
Breakfast of Champions; or, Goodbye Blue Monday! (1973) F
Wampeters, Foma, and Granfalloons (1974) NF
Slapstick; or, Lonesome No More! (1976) F
Jailbird (1979) F
Palm Sunday (1981) NF
Deadeye Dick (1982) F
Galapagos (1985) F
Bluebeard (1987) F
Hocus Pocus (1990) F
Timequake (1994) F

VOYNICH, Ethel Lilian, *née* Boole (1864–1947?)
Irish novelist
The Gadfly (1897) F
An Interrupted Friendship (1910) F
Put Off Thy Shoes (1945) F

W

WADDELL, Helen [Jane] (1889–1965)
British scholar, translator, and author
The Wandering Scholars [rev. 1932, 1934] (1927) NF
Mediaeval Latin Lyrics (1929) ANTH
Peter Abelard (1933) F
The Desert Fathers [from Latin] (1936) NF

WADE, Thomas (1805–1875)
British poet and dramatist
Tasso and the Sisters (1825) V
Woman's Love; or, The Triumph of Patience (1829) D
The Jew of Arragon; or, The Hebrew Queen (1830) D
Prothanasia, and Other Poems (1839) V

WAIN, John [Barrington] (1925–1994)
British poet, novelist, short-story writer, and critic
Mixed Feelings (1951) V
Hurry On Down [US: *Born in Captivity*] (1953) F
Living in the Present (1955) F
The Contenders (1958) F
A Travelling Woman (1959) F
Nuncle, and Other Stories (1960) F SS
Weep Before God (1961) V
Strike the Father Dead (1962) F
Wildtrack (1965) V
Death of the Hind Legs, and Other Stories (1966) F SS
The Smaller Sky (1967) F
A Winter in the Hills (1970) F
The Lifeguard, and Other Stories (1971) F SS
Samuel Johnson (1974) NF
Professing Poetry (1977) NF
King Caliban, and Other Stories (1978) F SS
Young Shoulders (1982) F
Open Country (1987) V
Where the Rivers Meet (1988) F
Comedies (1990) F
Hungry Generations (1994) F

WAINWRIGHT, Jeffrey (1944–)
British poet
The Important Man (1970) V
Heart's Desire (1978) V
The Red-Headed Pupil, and Other Poems (1994) V

WAKE, William (1657–1737)
English prelate and Archbishop of Canterbury
The Principles of the Christian Religion Explained (1699) NF
The State of the Church and Clergy of England (1703) NF

WAKEFIELD, Tom (1935–)
British novelist and short-story writer
Trixie Trash, Star Ascending (1977) F
Isobel Quirk in Orbit (1978) F
The Love Siege (1979) F
Mates (1983) F
Drifters (1984) F SS
Lot's Wife (1989) F
War Paint (1993) F

WALCOTT, Derek [Alton] (1930–)
Caribbean poet and dramatist
Henri Christophe (1950) D
In a Green Night (1962) V
The Castaway (1965) V
The Dream on Monkey Mountain, and Other Plays (1970) D
The Star-Apple Kingdom (1979) V
The Fortunate Traveller (1981) V
The Arkansas Testament (1987) V
Omeros (1990) V
What the Twilight Says (1999) NF

WALEY, Arthur [David] (1889–1966)
British poet and translator
A Hundred and Seventy Chinese Poems (1918) V
Japanese Poetry: the 'Uta' (1919) V
More Translations From the Chinese (1919) V
The Temple and Other Poems (1923) V
The Analects of Confucius (1938) NF
Monkey [from Wu Ch'eng-en] (1942) P
The Opium War Through Chinese Eyes (1958) NF

WALFORD, L[ucy] B[erthia], *née* Colquhoun (1845–1915)
British novelist, short-story writer, biographer, and journalist
Mr Smith (1874) F
Her Great Idea, and Other Stories (1888) F SS
The Mischief of Monica (1891) F
The Matchmaker (1894) F
A Fair Rebel, and Other Stories (1906) F SS
Memories of Victorian London (1912) NF

WALKER, Alice [Malsenior] (1944–)
African-American novelist, short-story writer, and poet
Once (1968) V
The Third Life of Grange Copeland (1970) F
In Love and Trouble (1973) F SS
Revolutionary Petunias, and Other Poems (1973) V
Meridian (1976) F
Good Night, Willie Lee, I'll See You in the Morning (1979) V
You Can't Keep a Good Woman Down (1981) F SS
The Color Purple (1982) F
In Search of Our Mothers' Gardens (1983) NF
Horses Make a Landscape Look More Beautiful (1984) V
Living by the Word (1988) NF
The Temple of My Familiar (1989) F
Her Blue Body Everything We Know (1991) V
Possessing the Secret of Joy (1992) F
By the Light of My Father's Smile (1999) F

WALKER, Patricius *see* WILLIAM ALLINGHAM

WALLACE, Alfred Russel, OM (1823–1913)
British naturalist
Travels on the Amazon and the Rio Negro (1853) NF
Contributions to the Theory of Natural Selection (1870) NF
The Geographical Distribution of Animals (1876) NF
Darwinism (1889) NF
Studies, Scientific and Social (1900) NF
Man's Place in the Universe (1903) NF
My Life (1905) NF

WALLACE, Lew[is] (1827–1905)
American novelist
The Fair God (1873) F
Ben-Hur (1880) F
The Boyhood of Christ (1888) F
The Prince of India (1893) F
The Wooing of Malkatoon (1898) V

WALLACE, [Richard Horatio] Edgar (1875–1932)
British journalist, thriller and short-story writer
The Four Just Men (1905) F
'Smithy' (1905) F
The Duke in the Suburbs (1909) F
Sanders of the River (1911) F SS
The River of Stars (1913) F
The Man Who Bought London (1915) F
The Adventures of Heine (1919) F SS
Room 13 (1924) F
The Mind of Mr J.G. Reeder [US: *The Murder Book of Mr J.G. Reeder*] (1925) F
The Guv'nor, and Other Stories (1932) F SS

WALLACE-CRABBE, Chris[topher] [Keith] (1934–)
Australian poet and critic
The Music of Division (1959) V
In Light and Darkness (1964) V
The Rebel General (1967) V
Melbourne or the Bush (1973) NF
Act in the Noon (1974) V
The Foundations of Joy (1976) V
Toil and Spin (1979) NF
Splinters (1981) F
The Amorous Cannibal (1985) V
Falling into Language (1990) NF
For Crying Out Loud (1990) V
Rungs of Time (1993) V

WALLANT, Edward [Lewis] (1926–1962)
American novelist
The Human Season (1960) F
The Pawnbroker (1961) F
The Tenants of Moonbloom (1963) F
The Children at the Gate (1964) F

WALLER, Edmund (1606–1687)
English poet
Poems (1645) V
A Panegyrick to my Lord Protector (1655) V
Upon the Late Storme and Death of His Highness (1658) V
A Poem on St James's Park (1661) V
Instructions to a Painter (1666) V
Divine Poems (1685) V
The Maid's Tragedy Altered (1690) V
The Second Part of Mr Waller's Poems (1690) V

WALMSLEY, Leo [Lionel] (1892–1966)
British novelist and dramatist
Three Fevers (1932) F
Phantom Lobster (1933) F
Foreigners (1935) F
Sally Lunn (1937) F
Love in the Sun (1939) F
The Happy Ending (1957) F
The Sound of the Sea (1959) F
Paradise Creek (1963) F
Angler's Moon (1965) F

WALPOLE, Horace, 4th Earl of Orford (1717–1797)
English author and letter writer
The Lessons for the Day (1742) NF
The Beauties (1746) V
A Catalogue of the Royal and Noble Authors of England (1758) NF
Fugitive Pieces in Verse and Prose (1758) MISC
Anecdotes of Painting in England (1762–3) NF
The Castle of Otranto (1765) F
Historic Doubts on the Life and Reign of King Richard III (1768) NF
The Mysterious Mother (1768) D

A Description of the Villa of Horace Walpole at Strawberry-Hill (1774) NF
Memoirs of the Last Ten Years of the Reign of George II (1822) NF
Journal of the Reign of King George the Third (1859) NF

WALPOLE, [Sir] Hugh Seymour (1884–1941)
New Zealand-born novelist and short-story writer
The Wooden Horse (1909) F
Maradick at Forty (1910) F
Mr Perrin and Mr Traill (1911) F
The Prelude to Adventure (1912) F
Fortitude (1913) F
The Golden Scarecrow (1915) F SS
The Dark Forest (1916) F
The Green Mirror (1918) F
Jeremy (1919) F
The Secret City (1919) F
The Captives (1920) F
The Thirteen Travellers (1921) F SS
The Cathedral (1922) F
Jeremy and Hamlet (1923) F
The Old Ladies (1924) F
Portrait of a Man with Red Hair (1925) F
Harmer John (1926) F
Jeremy at Crale (1927) F
Wintersmoon (1928) F
Rogue Herries (1930) F
Above the Dark Circus (1931) F
Judith Paris (1931) F
The Fortress (1932) F
All Souls' Night (1933) F SS
Vanessa (1933) F
The Inquisitor (1935) F
John Cornelius (1937) F
Head in Green Bronze, and Other Stories (1938) F SS
The Bright Pavilions (1940) F
Roman Fountain (1940) NF
The Killer and the Slain (1942) F
Mr Huffam, and Other Stories (1948) F SS

WALSH, William (1663–1708)
English poet and critic
A Dialogue Concerning Women (1691) NF
Letters and Poems, Amorous and Gallant (1692) V
Squire Trelooby [from Molière] (1704) D

WALSH, Jill [Gillian] Paton (1937–)
British children's writer and novelist
Hengest's Tale (1966) F CH
The Dolphin Crossing (1967) F CH
Fireweed (1969) F CH
Wordhoard (1969) F CH
Farewell Great King (1972) F
Goldengrove (1972) F CH
The Emperor's Winding-Sheet (1974) F
Unleaving (1976) F CH
Crossing to Salamis (1977) F CH
A Chance Child (1978) F CH
Babylon (1982) F CH
Knowledge of Angels (1994) F

WALTON, Izaak (1593–1683)
English angler and biographer
'The Life of Sir Henry Wotton' [in *Reliquiae Wottonianae*] (1651) NF
The Compleat Angler; or, The Contemplative Man's Recreation (1653) NF
The Life of John Donne (1658) NF
The Life of Mr Richard Hooker (1665) NF
The Life of Mr George Herbert (1670) NF
The Life of Dr Sanderson (1678) NF

WAMBAUGH, Joseph (1937–)
American crime writer
The Onion Field (1973) F
The Choirboys (1975) F

WANLEY, Nathaniel (1634–1680)
English compiler and poet
The Wonders of the Little World; or, A General History of Man (1678) NF

'WARD, Artemus' [Charles Farrar Browne] (1834–1867)
American humorist
Artemus Ward, His Book (1862) NF

WARD, Arthur Henry Sarsfield *see* SAX ROHMER

WARD, Edward (1667–1731)
English versifier and humorist
The London Spy (1698–1700) NF
A Trip to New-England (1699) NF V
A Step to the Bath (1700) NF V
Hudibras Redivivius; or, A Burlesque Poem on the Times (1705) V
The Tipling Philosophers (1710) V
The Delights of the Bottle; or, The Compleat Vintner (1720) V

WARD, Mrs T. Humphrey [Mary Augusta Ward, *née* Arnold] (1851–1920)
British novelist
Miss Bretherton (1884) F
Robert Elsmere (1888) F
The History of David Grieve (1892) F
Marcella (1894) F
The Story of Bessie Costrell (1895) F
Sir George Tressady (1896) F
Helbeck of Bannisdale (1898) F
Eleanor (1900) F
Lady Rose's Daughter (1903) F
The Marriage of William Ashe (1905) F
Fenwick's Career (1906) F
Diana Mallory (1908) F
Daphne; or, Marriage à la Mode [US: *Marriage a la Mode*] (1909) F
Canadian Born [US: *Lady Merton, Colonist*] (1910) F
The Case of Richard Meynell (1911) F
The Coryston Family (1913) F
The Mating of Lydia (1913) F
Delia Blanchflower (1915) F
England's Effort (1916) NF
A Great Success (1916) F
Lady Connie (1916) F

Towards the Goal (1917) NF
A Writer's Recollections (1918) NF
Fields of Victory (1919) NF

WARD, Nathaniel (1578–1652)
American Puritan author
The Simple Cobler of Aggawam [by 'Theodore de la Guard'] (1647) NF

WARD, Robert Plumer (1765–1846)
British novelist
Tremaine; or, The Man of Refinement (1825) F
De Vere; or, The Man of Independence (1827) F
De Clifford; or, The Constant Man (1841) F

WARD-THOMAS, Evelyn *see* EVELYN ANTHONY

WARNER, Charles Dudley (1829–1900)
American novelist and essayist
My Summer in a Garden (1870) NF
Saunterings (1872) NF
Backlog Studies (1873) NF
The Gilded Age (1873) F
Baddeck (1874) NF
My Winter on the Nile (1876) NF
Being a Boy (1878) NF
On Horseback (1888) NF
A Little Journey in the World (1889) F
As We Were Saying (1891) NF
Our Italy (1891) NF
The Golden House (1894) F
That Fortune (1899) F

WARNER, Marina [Sarah] (1946–)
British novelist, critic, and cultural historian
Alone of All Her Sex (1976) NF
In a Dark Wood (1977) F
Joan of Arc (1981) NF
The Skating Party (1982) F
Monuments and Maidens (1985) NF
The Lost Father (1988) F
Indigo (1992) F
L'Atalante (1993) F
Mermaids in the Basement (1993) F SS
From the Beast to the Blonde (1994) NF
Modern Myths (1994) NF
No Go the Bogeyman (1998) F

WARNER, Rex [Ernest] (1905–1986)
British poet, novelist, and translator
The Wild Goose Chase (1937) F
The Professor (1938) F
The Aerodrome (1941) F
Why Was I Killed? (1943) F
Poems and Contradictions (1945) V
Men of Stones (1949) F
Escapade (1953) F
The Young Caesar (1958) F
Imperial Caesar (1960) F
Pericles the Athenian (1963) F
The Converts (1967) F

WARNER, Sylvia Townsend (1893–1978)
British novelist, poet, and short-story writer
The Espalier (1925) V
Lolly Willowes; or, The Loving Huntsman (1926) F
Mr Fortune's Maggot (1927) F
Time Importuned (1928) V
The True Heart (1929) F
A Moral Ending, and Other Stories (1931) F SS
The Salutation (1932) F SS
More Joy in Heaven, and Other Stories (1935) F SS
Summer Will Show (1936) F
After the Death of Don Juan (1938) F
A Garland of Straw, and Other Stories (1943) F SS
The Museum of Cheats, and Other Stories (1947) F SS
The Corner That Held Them (1948) F
The Flint Anchor (1954) F
Winter in the Air, and Other Stories (1955) F SS
A Spirit Rises (1962) F SS
A Stranger With a Bag, and Other Stories [US: *Swans on an Autumn River*] (1966) F SS
The Innocent and the Guilty (1971) F SS
Kingdoms of Elfin (1977) F SS
One Thing Leading to Another, and Other Stories (1984) F SS

WARNER, William (1558?–1609)
English poet
Pan his Syrinx, or Pipe (1584) F
Albions England; or, Historicall Map of the Same Island (1586) V
Menaecmi (1595) D
A Continuance of Albions England (1606) D

WARREN, Mercy Otis (1728–1814)
American dramatist
The Adulateur (1773) D
The Group (1775) D
History of the Rise, Progress, and Termination of the American Revolution (1805) NF

WARREN, Robert Penn (1905–1989)
American novelist, poet, and critic
John Brown, the Making of a Martyr (1929) NF
Thirty-Six Poems (1935) V
Understanding Poetry (1938) NF
Night Rider (1939) F
Eleven Poems on the Same Theme (1942) V
At Heaven's Gate (1943) F
All the King's Men (1946) F
The Circus in the Attic (1947) F SS
World Enough and Time (1950) F
Brother to Dragons [rev. 1979] (1953) V
Band of Angels (1955) F
Segregation: The Inner Conflict in the South (1956) NF
Promises (1957) V
The Cave (1959) F
You, Emperors, and Others (1960) V
The Legacy of the Civil War (1961) NF
Wilderness (1961) F
Flood (1964) F
Who Speaks for the Negro? (1965) NF

Incarnations (1968) V
Audubon: A Vision (1969) V
Homage to Theodore Dreiser (1971) NF
Meet Me in the Green Glen (1971) F
Democracy and Poetry (1975) NF
Or-Else Poem (1975) V
A Place To Come To (1977) F
Now and Then (1978) V
Being Here (1980) V
Rumor Verified (1981) V
Chief Joseph of the Nez Percé (1983) V

WARREN, Samuel (1807–1877)
British novelist
Ten Thousand a Year (1841) F

WARTON, Joseph (1722–1800)
British poet and critic
The Enthusiast; or, The Lover of Nature (1744) V
Odes on Various Subjects (1746) V
Ranleagh House (1747) NF
An Ode to Evening (1749) V
An Essay on the Writings and Genius of Pope [vol. i] (1756) NF
An Essay on the Writings and Genius of Pope [vol. ii] (1782) NF

WARTON, Thomas, the Elder (1688?–1745)
English poet
Poems on Several Occasions (1748) V

WARRTON, Thomas, the Younger (1728–1790)
British poet and literary scholar
The Pleasures of Melancholy (1747) V
The Triumphs of Isis (1749) V
Newmarket (1751) V
The Union; or, Select Scots and English Poems (1753) V
Observations on the Faerie Queene of Spenser (1754) NF
The History of English Poetry (1774–81) NF
Poems (1777) V
An Enquiry into the Authenticity of the Poems Attributed to Thomas Rowley (1782) NF
Essays on Gothic Architecture (1800) NF

WASHINGTON, Booker T[aliaferro] (1856–1915)
African-American leader and author
The Future of the American Negro (1899) NF
Up From Slavery (1901) NF

WATERHOUSE, Keith [Spencer] (1929–)
British novelist, dramatist, and journalist
There is a Happy Land (1957) F
Billy Liar (1959) F
The Bucket Shop (1968) F
Billy Liar on the Moon (1975) F
Office Life (1978) F
Maggie Muggins; or, Spring in Earl's Court (1981) F
Our Song (1988) F
Jeffrey Bernard is Unwell (1989) D
Bimbo (1990) F
Sharon and Tracey and the Rest (1992) NF
Unsweet Charity (1992) F
City Lights (1994) NF

WATKINS, Vernon [Phillips] (1906–1967)
Welsh poet
The Ballad of Mari Lwyd, and Other Poems (1941) V
The Lamp and the Veil (1945) V
The Lady With the Unicorn (1948) V
The Death Bell (1954) V
Cypress and Acacia (1959) V
Affinities (1962) V
Fidelities (1968) V
Uncollected Poems (1969) V
The Influences (1976) D

WATSON, Sheila (1909–)
Canadian novelist
The Double Hook (1959) F
Four Stories (1979) F SS
Wordsworth's Grave, and Other Poems (1890) V
Lachrymae Musarum (1892) V
Odes, and Other Poems (1894) V
The Father of the Forest, and Other Poems (1895) V
The Purple East (1896) V
The Hope of the World, and Other Poems (1898) V
For England (1904) V
Sable and Purple, with Other Poems (1910) V
The Muse in Exile (1913) V
The Man Who Saw, and Other Poems Arising Out of the War (1917) V
Retrogression, and Other Poems (1917) V
The Superhuman Antagonists, and Other Poems (1919) V
Poems Brief and New (1925) V

WATSON, Thomas (1557?–1592)
English poet and translator
The Hekatompathia; or, Passionate Centurie of Love (1582) V
The Lamentations of Amyntas for the Death of Phillis [trn from Watson's Latin by Abraham Fraunce] (1587) V

WATSON, Sir William (1858–1935)
British poet
The Prince's Quest, and Other Poems (1880) V

WATTS, Isaac (1674–1748)
English poet, hymn-writer, and theological writer
Horae Lyricae (1706) V
Hymns and Spiritual Songs (1707) V
Divine Songs Attempted in Easy Language for the Use of Children (1715) V
A Guide to Prayer (1715) NF
The Psalms of David (1719) V
Death and Heaven; or, The Last Enemy Conquer'd, and Separate Spirits Made Perfect (1722) NF
Catechisms; or, Instructions in the Principles of the Christian Religion (1730) NF
Philosophical Essays on Various Subjects (1733) NF
The World To Come; or, Discourses on the Joys and Sorrows of Departed Souls (1739) NF

WATTS-DUNTON, [Walter] Theodore (1832–1914)
British critic, poet, and novelist
The Coming of Love, and Other Poems (1898) V
Aylwin (1899) F
Vesprie Towers (1916) F

WAUGH, Alec [Alexander Raban] (1898–1981)
British novelist and poet
The Loom of Youth (1917) F
Resentment (1918) V
The Prisoners of Mainz (1919) F
Pleasure (1921) F SS
The Lonely Unicorn (1922) F
Myself When Young (1923) NF
Card Castle (1924) F
Kept (1925) F
Love in These Days (1926) F
On Doing What One Likes (1926) NF
The Last Chukka (1928) F SS
Three Score and Ten (1929) F
'Sir', She Said [rev. 1977 as *Love in Conflict*] (1930) F
Leap Before You Look (1932) F
Playing With Fire (1933) F
Wheels Within Wheels (1933) F
The Balliols (1934) F
Eight Short Stories (1937) F SS
No Truce with Time (1941) F
His Second War (1944) F
Unclouded Summer (1948) F
Island in the Sun (1955) F
Fuel for the Flame (1960) F
The Early Years of Alec Waugh (1962) NF
My Brother Evelyn, and Other Profiles (1967) NF
A Spy in the Family (1970) F
A Fatal Gift (1973) F
Married to a Spy (1976) F

WAUGH, Auberon [Alexander] (1939–2001)
British journalist, critic, and novelist
The Foxglove Saga (1960) F
Consider the Lilies (1968) F

WAUGH, Evelyn [Arthur St John] (1903–1966)
British novelist, essayist, and biographer
Decline and Fall (1928) F
Vile Bodies (1930) F
Remote People (1931) NF
Black Mischief (1932) F
A Handful of Dust (1934) F
Mr Loveday's Little Outing, and Other Sad Stories (1936) F SS
Waugh in Abyssinia (1936) NF
Scoop (1938) F
Robbery Under Law [US: *Mexico: An Object Lesson*] (1939) NF
Put Out More Flags (1942) F
Work Suspended (1942) F
Brideshead Revisited (1945) F
The Loved One (1948) F
Helena (1950) F
The Holy Places (1952) NF
Men at Arms (1952) F
Love Among the Ruins (1953) F
Officers and Gentlemen (1955) F
The Ordeal of Gilbert Pinfold (1957) F
The Life of Ronald Knox (1959) NF
A Tourist in Africa (1960) NF
Unconditional Surrender (1961) F
Basil Seal Rides Again; or, The Rake's Regress (1963) F
A Little Learning (1964) NF
Sword of Honour [cont. *Men at Arms*, *Officers and Gentlemen*, and *Unconditional Surrender*] (1965) F

WEBB, Beatrice [Martha], *née* Potter (1858–1943)
British political reformer
My Apprenticeship (1926) NF
Our Partnership (1948) NF

WEBB, Mary [Gladys], *née* Meredith (1881–1927)
British novelist
The Golden Arrow (1916) F
Gone to Earth (1917) F
Seven for a Secret (1922) F
Precious Bane (1924) F
Armour Wherein He Trusted (1929) F

WEBB, Phyllis (1921–)
Canadian poet
Even Your Right Eye (1956) V
The Sea is Also a Garden (1962) V
Naked Poems (1965) V
Wilson's Bowl (1980) V
Sunday Water (1982) V
The Vision Tree (1982) V

WEBB, Sidney [James], 1st Baron Passfield (1859–1947)
British writer on sociology and political reform
Socialism in England (1890) NF
London Education (1904) NF

WEBB, Sidney [James], 1st Baron Passfield (1859–1947), and **Beatrice [Martha], *née* Potter** (1858–1943)
British writers on sociology and political reform
The History of Trade Unionism (1894) NF
Industrial Democracy (1897) NF
Problems of Modern Industry (1898) NF
English Local Government (1906–29) NF
The State and the Doctor (1910) NF
A Constitution for the Socialist Commonwealth of Great Britain (1920) NF
The Decay of Capitalist Civilisation (1923) NF
Soviet Communism (1935) NF

WEBBE, William (fl.1568–1591)
English critic and translator
A Discourse of English Poetrie (1586) NF

WEBSTER, John (1580?–1635?)
English dramatist
The White Divel; or, The Tragedy of Paulo Giordano Ursini (1612) D
The Devils Law-Case (1623) D
The Tragedy of the Dutchesse of Malfy (1623) D

Appius and Virginia (1654) D
A Cure for a Cuckold (1661) D

WEDDE, Ian (1946–)
New Zealand poet, novelist, and critic
Homage to Matisse (1971) V
Made Over (1974) V
Earthly: Sonnets for Carlos (1975) V
Pathway to the Sea (1975) V
Dick Seddon's Great Dive (1976) F
Castaly (1980) V
Survival Arts (1981) F
Georgicon (1984) V
Tales of Gotham City (1984) V
Symmes Hole (1986) F
Driving into the Storm (1987) V
Tendering (1989) V
The Drummer (1993) V

WEDGWOOD, [Dame] C[icely] V[eronica] (1910–)
British historian
The King's Peace 1637–41 (1955) NF
The King's War 1641–7 (1958) NF

WEEVER, John (1576–1632)
English poet and antiquary
Epigrammes in the Oldest Cut, and Newest Fashion (1599) V
Faunus and Melliflora; or, The Original of Our English Satyres (1600) V
An Agnus Dei (1601) V
The Mirror of Martyrs; or, The Life and Death of Sir John Old-castle (1601) V

WEINSTEIN, Nathan Wallenstein *see* NATHANAEL WEST

WELCH, [Maurice] Denton (1915–1948)
British novelist and short-story writer
Maiden Voyage (1943) NF
In Youth is Pleasure (1944) F
Brave and Cruel, and Other Stories (1948) F SS
A Last Sheaf (1951) F SS
Fragments of a Life Story (1987) F SS

WELDON, Fay [Franklin], *née* Birkinshaw (1931–)
British novelist, playwright, and screenwriter
The Fat Woman's Joke (1967) F
Down Among the Women (1971) F
Female Friends (1975) F
Remember Me (1976) F
Little Sisters (1978) F
Praxis (1978) F
Puffball (1980) F
Watching Me, Watching You (1981) F SS
The Life and Loves of a She-Devil (1983) F
Polaris, and Other Stories (1985) F SS
Heart of the Country (1987) F
Leader of the Band (1988) F
The Cloning of Joanna May (1989) F
Darcy's Utopia (1990) F
Moon Over Minneapolis (1991) F
Growing Rich (1992) F
Affliction (1994) F
Splitting (1995) F
Big Women (1998) F
Goddess in Eden (2000) NF
Rhode Island Blues (2000) F

WELLESLEY, Mary *see* MARY WESLEY

WELLS, H[erbert] G[eorge] (1866–1946)
British novelist, short-story writer and social critic
The Stolen Bacillus, and Other Incidents (1895) F SS
The Time Machine (1895) F
The Wonderful Visit (1895) F
The Island of Dr Moreau (1896) F
The Wheels of Chance (1896) F
The Invisible Man (1897) F
The Plattner Story, and Others (1897) F SS
Certain Personal Matters (1898) NF
The War of the Worlds (1898) F
When the Sleeper Wakes (1899) F
Love and Mr Lewisham (1900) F
Tales of Space and Time (1900) F SS
The First Men in the Moon (1901) F
The Sea Lady (1902) F
Mankind in the Making (1903) NF
Twelve Stories and a Dream (1903) F SS
The Food of the Gods, and How It Came to Earth (1904) F
Kipps (1905) F
A Modern Utopia (1905) F
The Future in America (1906) NF
In the Days of the Comet (1906) F
First and Last Things (1908) NF
New Worlds for Old (1908) NF
The War in the Air (1908) F
Ann Veronica (1909) F
Tono-Bungay (1909) F
The History of Mr Polly (1910) F
The New Machiavelli (1910) F
The Country of the Blind, and Other Stories (1911) F SS
The Great State (1912) NF
Marriage (1912) F
The Passionate Friends (1913) F
The War That Will End War (1914) NF
The Wife of Sir Isaac Harman (1914) F
The World Set Free (1914) F
Bealby (1915) F
Mr Britling Sees It Through (1916) F
What is Coming? (1916) NF
God the Invisible King (1917) NF
The Soul of a Bishop (1917) F
Joan and Peter (1918) F
The Undying Fire (1919) F
The Outline of History (1920) NF
The Salvaging of Civilization (1921) NF
The Secret Places of the Heart (1922) F
A Short History of the World (1922) NF
Men Like Gods (1923) F
The Dream (1924) F
Christina Alberta's Father (1925) F

The World of William Clissold (1926) F
Meanwhile (1927) F
Mr Blettsworthy on Rampole Island (1928) F
The Open Conspiracy (1928) NF
The Science of Life (1929) NF
The Autocracy of Mr Parham (1930) F
The Shape of Things to Come (1933) F
Experiment in Autobiography (1934) NF
The New America (1935) NF
The Anatomy of Frustration (1936) NF
The Croquet Player (1936) F
Brynhild (1937) F
The Camford Visitation (1937) F
Star Begotten (1937) F
Apropos of Dolores (1938) F
The Brothers (1938) F
The Holy Terror (1939) F
All Aboard for Ararat (1940) F
Babes in the Darkling Wood (1940) F
Guide to the New World (1941) NF
'42 to '44 (1944) NF
The Happy Turning (1945) NF
Mind at the End of its Tether (1945) NF

WELSH, Irvine (1957–)
British novelist
Trainspotting (1993) F
The Acid House (1994) F SS
Ecstasy (1996) F SS
Filth (1998) F

WELTY, Eudora (1909–)
American short-story writer and novelist
A Curtain of Green, and Other Stories (1941) F SS
The Robber Bridegroom (1942) F
The Wide Net (1943) F SS
Delta Wedding (1946) F
The Golden Apples (1949) F SS
The Ponder Heart (1954) F
The Bride of the Innisfallen (1955) F SS
The Shoe Bird (1964) F CH
Losing Battles (1970) F
The Optimist's Daughter (1972) F
The Eye of the Story (1978) NF
Moon Lake (1980) F SS

WENDT, Albert (1939–)
Western Samoan novelist, short-story writer, critic, and poet
Sons for the Return Home (1973) F
Pouliuli (1977) F
Leaves of the Banyan Tree (1979) F

WERTENBAKER, Timberlake (1951–)
Anglo-American dramatist
New Anatomies (1981) D
The Grace of Mary Traverse (1985) D
Our Country's Good [from Thomas Kenneally's *The Playmaker*] (1988) D
The Love of the Nightingale (1989) D
Three Birds Alighting on a Field (1991) D
After Darwin (1998) D

WESCOTT, Glenway (1901–1987)
American novelist and poet
The Bitterns (1920) V
The Apple of the Eye (1924) F
Natives of Rock (1925) V
The Grandmothers [UK: *A Family Portrait*] (1927) F
Good-Bye, Wisconsin (1928) F SS
The Pilgrim Hawk (1940) F
Images of the Truth (1962) NF
The Best of All Possible Worlds (1975) NF

WESKER, Arnold (1932–)
British dramatist and short-story writer
Chicken Soup with Barley (1958) D
Roots (1959) D
I'm Talking About Jerusalem (1960) D
Chips With Everything (1962) D
The Four Seasons (1965) D
Their Very Own and Golden City (1965) D
The Friends (1970) D
Six Sundays in January (1971) F SS
The Old Ones (1972) D
Caritas (1981) D
The King's Daughters (1998) F SS

WESLEY, Charles (1707–1788)
British Methodist and hymn-writer
Hymns and Sacred Poems (1749) V
Journal (1849) NF

WESLEY, John (1703–1791)
British clergyman, diarist, and founder of Methodism
A Collection of Psalms and Hymns (1737) V
Journal (1739–91) NF
The Character of a Methodist (1742) NF
The Principles of a Methodist (1742) NF
The Principles of a Methodist Farther Explain'd (1746) NF
A Plain Account of the People Called Methodists (1749) NF
Serious Thoughts upon the Perseverance of Saints (1751) NF
An Address to the Clergy (1756) NF
The Doctrine of Original Sin (1757) NF
A Survey of the Wisdom of God in the Creation (1763) NF
A Plain Account of Christian Perfection (1766) NF
Thoughts upon Slavery (1774) NF
A Calm Address to Our American Colonies (1775) NF
Reflections on the Rise and Progress of the American Rebellion (1780) NF

'WESLEY, Mary' [Mary Wellesley] (1912–)
British novelist
The Sixth Seal (1969) F
Jumping the Queue (1983) F
The Camomile Lawn (1984) F
Harnessing Peacocks (1985) F
The Vacillations of Poppy Carew (1986) F
Not That Sort of Girl (1987) F
Second Fiddle (1988) F
A Sensible Life (1990) F

A Dubious Legacy (1992) F
An Imaginative Experience (1994) F

WEST, Morris [Langlo] (1916–)
Australian novelist
Gallows on the Sand (1955) F
Children of the Sun (1957) F
The Second Victory (1958) F
The Devil's Advocate (1959) F
The Shoes of the Fisherman (1963) F
The Ambassador (1965) F
The Tower of Babel (1968) F
The Salamander (1973) F
The Clowns of God (1981) F
The World is Made of Glass (1983) F
Lazarus (1990) F
The Lovers (1993) F

'WEST, Nathanael' [Nathan Wallenstein Weinstein] (1903–1940)
American novelist
The Dream Life of Balso Snell (1931) F
Miss Lonelyhearts (1933) F
A Cool Million (1934) F
The Day of the Locust (1939) F

'WEST, [Dame] Rebecca' [Cicily Isabel Andrews, *née* Fairfield] (1892–1983)
British novelist and political essayist
The Return of the Soldier (1918) F
The Judge (1922) F
The Strange Necessity (1928) NF
Harriet Hume (1929) F
St Augustine (1933) NF
The Thinking Reed (1936) F
Black Lamb and Grey Falcon (1941) NF
The Meaning of Treason [rev. 1964 as *The New Meaning of Treason*] (1947) NF
A Train of Powder (1955) NF
The Fountain Overflows (1956) F
The Birds Fall Down (1966) F
Sunflower (1986) F
This Real Night (1987) F
The Only Poet, and Other Stories (1992) F SS

WESTALL, Robert (1929–1993)
British children's writer
The Machine-Gunners (1975) F CH
The Wind Eye (1976) F CH
The Watch House (1977) F CH
The Devil in the Road (1979) F CH
Fathom Five (1979) F CH
The Scarecrows (1981) F CH
Futuretrack 5 (1983) F CH
The Kingdom by the Sea (1992) F CH

WEYMAN, Stanley [John] (1855–1928)
British novelist
The House of the Wolf (1890) F
A Gentleman of France (1893) F HF
The Man in Black (1894) F
My Lady Rotha (1894) F
Under the Red Robe (1894) F
From the Memoirs of a Minister of France (1895) F
The Red Cockade (1895) F
The Castle Inn (1898) F
Shrewsbury (1898) F
Count Hannibal (1901) F
In King's Byways (1902) F SS
The Long Night (1903) F
The Abbess of Vlaye (1904) F
Starvecrow Farm (1905) F
The Great House (1919) F
Ovington's Bank (1922) F

WHARTON, Edith [Newbold] (1862–1937)
American novelist and short-story writer
The Greater Inclination (1899) F SS
The Touchstone [UK: *A Gift From the Grave*] (1900) F
Crucial Instances (1901) F SS
The Valley of Decision (1902) F
Sanctuary (1903) F
The Descent of Man (1904) F SS
The House of Mirth (1905) F
Italian Backgrounds (1905) NF
The Fruit of the Tree (1907) F
Madame de Treymes (1907) F
The Hermit and the Wild Woman (1908) F SS
A Motor-Flight Through France (1908) NF
Artemis to Acteon (1909) V
Tales of Men and Ghosts (1910) F SS
Ethan Frome (1911) F
The Reef (1912) F
The Custom of the Country (1913) F SS
Fighting France, From Dunkerque to Belfort (1915) NF
Xingu, and Other Stories (1916) F SS
Summer (1917) F
The Marne (1918) F
The Age of Innocence (1920) F
In Morocco (1920) NF
The Glimpses of the Moon (1922) F
A Son at the Front (1923) F
Old New York (1924) F SS
The Mother's Recompense (1925) F
The Writing of Fiction (1925) NF
Here and Beyond (1926) F SS
Twilight Sleep (1927) F
The Children (1928) F
Hudson River Bracketed (1929) F
Certain People (1930) F SS
The Gods Arrive (1932) F
Human Nature (1933) F SS
A Backward Glance (1934) NF
The World Over (1936) F SS
Ghosts (1937) F SS
The Buccaneers [unfinished] (1938) F

WHEATLEY, Dennis [Yates] (1897–1977)
British popular novelist
The Forbidden Territory (1933) F
Such Power is Dangerous (1933) F
The Devil Rides Out (1935) F
Murder Off Miami (1936) F
They Found Atlantis (1936) F
The Man Who Missed the War (1945) F

The Haunting of Toby Jugg (1948) F
To the Devil—A Daughter (1953) F
The Ka of Gifford Hillary (1956) F
The Irish Witch (1973) F

WHELAN, John Francis *see* SEÁN O'FAOLÁIN

WHETSTONE, George (c. 1551–1587)
English poet and author
The Rocke of Regard (1576) V
Promos and Cassandra (1578) D
A Heptamaron of Civill Discourses [2nd edn, 1593, as *Aurelia*] (1582) F
A Mirour for Magestrates of Cyties (1584) NF
The Honorable Reputation of a Souldier (1585) NF
The English Myrror (1586) NF
Sir Philip Sidney, his Honorable Life, his Valiant Death, and his True Vertues (1587) V

WHEWELL, William (1794–1866)
British philosopher and scientist
The History of the Inductive Sciences (1837) NF
The Philosophy of the Inductive Sciences (1840) NF
Lectures on the History of Moral Philosophy in England (1852) NF
On the Plurality of Worlds (1853) NF

WHITAKER, Rodney *see* 'TREVANIAN'

'WHITE, Antonia' [Eirene Botting] (1899–1980)
British novelist and translator
Frost in May (1933) F
The Lost Traveller (1950) F
The Sugar House (1952) F
Beyond the Glass (1954) F

WHITE, Edmund (1940–)
American novelist
Forgetting Elena (1973) F
Nocturnes for the King of Naples (1978) F
States of Desire (1980) NF
A Boy's Own Story (1982) F
Caracole (1985) F
The Darker Proof [inc. stories by Adam Mars-Jones] (1987) F SS
The Beautiful Room is Empty (1988) F
The Married Man (2000) F

WHITE, E[lwyn] B[rooks] (1899–1985)
American journalist, essayist, and children's writer
The Lady is Cold (1929) V
Alice Through the Cellophane (1933) NF
Every Day is Saturday (1934) NF
The Fox of Peapack (1938) V
One Man's Meat (1942) NF
Stuart Little (1945) F CH
The Wild Flag (1946) NF
Charlotte's Web (1952) F CH
The Second Tree from the Corner (1954) NF V
The Points of My Compass (1962) NF

WHITE, Gilbert (1720–1793)
British naturalist
The Natural History and Antiquities of Selborne (1789) NF
A Naturalist's Calendar (1795) NF

WHITE, Joseph Blanco [formerly **José Maria Blanco]** (1775–1841)
Spanish poet and theological author
Second Travels of an Irish Gentleman in Search of a Religion (1833)NF
Observations on Heresy and Orthodoxy (1835) NF
The Life of Joseph Blanco White, Written by Himself (1845) NF

WHITE, Kenneth (1936–)
Scottish poet, critic, and travel writer
Wild Coal (1963) V
The Cold Wind of Dawn (1966) V
The Most Difficult Area (1968) V
A Walk Along the Shore (1977) V
Travels in the Drifting Dawn (1989) NF
The Blue Road (1990) NF
Pilgrim of the Void (1990) NF

WHITE, Patrick [Victor Martindale] (1912–1990)
Australian novelist, short-story writer, and dramatist
The Ploughman (1935) V
The Happy Valley (1939) F
The Living and the Dead (1941) F
The Aunt's Story (1948) F
The Tree of Man (1955) F
Voss (1957) F
Riders in the Chariot (1961) F
The Burnt Ones (1964) F SS
The Solid Mandala (1966) F
The Vivisector (1970) F
The Eye of the Storm (1973) F
The Cockatoos (1974) F SS
A Fringe of Leaves (1976) F
Big Toys (1977) D
The Twyborn Affair (1979) F
Memoirs of Many in One (1986) F
Three Uneasy Pieces (1987) NF

WHITE, T[erence] H[anbury] (1906–1964)
British novelist and poet
Loved Helen, and Other Poems (1929) V
Dead Mr Nixon (1931) F
Darkness at Pemberley (1932) F
Gone to Ground (1935) F
England Have My Bones (1936) NF
The Sword in the Stone (1938) F
The Witch in the Wood (1939) F
The Ill-Made Knight (1941) F
Mistress Masham's Repose (1946) F
The Age of Scandal (1950) NF
The Goshawk (1951) NF
The Once and Future King [complete] (1958) F
The Godstone and the Blackymor (1959) NF

WHITE, William Hale *see* MARK RUTHERFORD

WHITEHEAD, A[lfred] N[orth] (1861–1947)
British mathematician and philosopher
An Enquiry Concerning the Principles of Natural Knowledge (1919) NF
The Concept of Nature (1920) NF
The Principle of Relativity (1922) NF

Science and the Modern World (1925) NF
Process and Reality (1929) NF

WHITEHEAD, Charles (1804–1862)
British poet and novelist
The Solitary (1831) V
The Autobiography of Jack Ketch (1834) F
Richard Savage (1842) F
The Earl of Essex (1843) F
Smiles and Tears (1847) F SS

WHITEHEAD, William (1715–1785)
English dramatist and Poet Laureate
An Essay on Ridicule (1743) V
The Roman Father (1750) D
Crëusa, Queen of Athens (1754) D
A Charge to the Poets (1762) V
The School for Lovers (1762) D
Variety (1776) V

WHITEING, Richard (1840–1928)
British engraver, journalist, and novelist
The Island; or, An Adventure of a Person of Quality (1888) F
No.5 John Street (1899) F

WHITING, John [Robert] (1917–1963)
British dramatist
A Penny for a Song (1951) D
Marching Song (1954) D
The Gates of Summer (1956) D
The Devils (1961) D
Saint's Day (1963) D
John Whiting on Theatre (1966) NF

WHITMAN, Walt[er] (1819–1892)
American poet
Franklin Evans; or, The Inebriate (1842) F
Leaves of Grass [first edn] (1855) V
Drum-Taps (1865) V
Sequel to Drum-Taps (1865–6) V
Democratic Vistas (1871) NF
Passage to India (1871) V
Memoranda During the War (1875) NF
Two Rivulets [inc. *Democratic Vistas*, 1871] (1876) NF V
November Boughs (1888) V
Good-Bye, My Fancy (1891) NF/V

WHITTIER, John Greenleaf (1807–1892)
American poet
Legends of New-England in Prose and Verse (1831) F V
Mogg Megone (1836) V
Poems Written During the Progress of the Abolition Questions (1838) V
Lays of My Home, and Other Poems (1843) V
Voices of Freedom (1846) V
Leaves from Margaret Smith's Journal (1849) F
Old Portraits and Modern Sketches (1850) NF
Songs of Labor (1850) V
The Chapel of the Hermits (1853) V
Literary Recreations and Miscellanies (1854) NF
The Panorama, and Other Poems (1856) V
Home Ballads, Poems and Lyrics (1860) V
In War Time, and Other Poems (1864) V
Snow-Bound (1866) V
The Tent of the Beach (1867) V
Among the Hills (1869) V
Miriam, and Other Poems (1871) V
Hazel-Blossoms (1875) V
The Vision of Echard (1878) V
St Gregory's Guest (1886) V
At Sundown (1890) V

WHYTE-MELVILLE, G[eorge] J[ohn] (1821–1878)
British novelist
Digby Grand (1853) F
Tilbury Nogo; or, Passages in the Life of an Unsuccessful Man (1854) F
Kate Coventry (1856) F
The Interpreter (1858) F
Holmby House (1860) F
Market Harborough; or, How Mr Sawyer Went to the Shires (1861) F
The Gladiators (1863) F
Cerise (1866) F
The True Cross (1873) V
Uncle John (1874) F
Katerfelto (1875) F
Sister Louise; or, The Story of a Woman's Repentance (1876) F

WIGGIN, Kate Douglas, *née* Smith (1856–1923)
American children's writer
Rebecca of Sunnybrook Farm (1903) F CH
Mother Carey's Chickens (1911) F CH

WILBUR, Richard [Purdy] (1921–)
American poet
The Beautiful Changes (1947) V
Ceremony (1950) V
A Bestiary (1955) V
Things of This World (1956) V
Advice to a Prophet (1961) V
Walking to Sleep (1969) V
The Mind-Reader (1976) V
Responses (1976) NF
Andromache [from Racine] (1982) D

WILDE, Lady Jane Francisca, *née* Elgee (1826–1896)
Irish poet and author
Ancient Legends, Mystic Charms and Superstitions of Ireland (1887) NF
Ancient Cures, Charms and Usages of Ireland (1890) NF
Notes on Men, Women and Books (1891) NF

WILDE, Oscar [Fingal O'Flahertie Wills] (1854–1900)
Irish poet, dramatist, short-story writer, and novelist
Ravenna (1878) V
Vera; or, The Nihilists (1880) D
Poems (1881) V
The Happy Prince, and Other Tales (1888) F SS
A House of Pomegranates (1891) F SS

Intentions (1891) NF
Lord Arthur Savile's Crime, and Other Stories (1891) F SS
The Picture of Dorian Gray (1891) F
Lady Windermere's Fan (1892) D
A Woman of No Importance (1893) D
Salomé (1894) D
The Sphinx (1894) V
An Ideal Husband (1895) D
The Importance of Being Earnest (1895) D
The Soul of Man (1895) NF
The Ballad of Reading Gaol [by 'C.3.3'] (1898) V
De Profundis (1905) NF

WILDER, Laura Ingalls (1867–1957)
American children's writer
Little House in the Big Woods (1932) F CH
Little House on the Prairie (1935) F CH

WILDER, Thornton [Niven] (1897–1975)
American dramatist and novelist
The Cabala (1926) F
The Bridge of San Luis Rey (1927) F
The Angel That Troubled the Waters (1928) D
The Woman of Andros (1930) F
The Long Christmas Dinner (1931) D
Heaven's My Destination (1935) F
The Merchant of Yonkers [rev. 1954 as *The Matchmaker* and adapted 1963 as *Hello, Dolly!*] (1938) D
Our Town (1938) D
The Skin of Our Teeth (1942) D
The Ides of March (1948) F
Plays for Bleecker Street (1962) D
The Eighth Day (1967) F
Theophilus North (1973) F

WILDING, Michael (1942–)
British-born Australian short-story writer, novelist, and critic
Aspects of the Dying Process (1972) F SS
Living Together (1974) F
The Short Story Embassy (1975) F
The West Midland Underground (1975) F SS
The Phallic Forest (1978) F SS
Pacific Highway (1982) F
Reading the Signs (1984) F
The Man of Slow Feeding (1985) F SS
The Paraguayan Experiment (1985) F
Under Saturn (1988) F SS
Great Climate (1990) F SS
Book of the Reading (1994) F SS
This is For You (1994) F SS

WILKINSON, Iris Guiver *see* ROBIN HYDE

WILLEY, Basil (1897–1978)
British literary critic and scholar
The Seventeenth-Century Background (1934) NF
The Eighteenth-Century Background (1940) NF
The English Moralists (1964) NF

WILLIAMS, Charles [Walter Stansby] (1886–1945)
British novelist, poet, and dramatist
The Silver Stair (1912) V
Poems of Conformity (1917) V
Heroes and Kings (1930) V
War in Heaven (1930) F
Many Dimensions (1931) F
The Place of the Lion (1931) F
The Greater Trumps (1932) F
Shadows of Ecstasy (1933) F
Descent into Hell (1937) F
Taliessen Through Logres (1938) V
The Descent of the Dove (1939) NF
Witchcraft (1941) NF
The Region of the Summer Stars (1944) V
All Hallows' Eve (1945) F
Seed of Adam, and Other Plays (1948) D

WILLIAMS, Ella Gwendolyn Rees *see* JEAN RHYS

WILLIAMS, George Valentine *see* DOUGLAS VALENTINE

WILLIAMS, Heathcote (1941–)
British poet, dramatist, and novelist
The Speakers (1964) F
AC/DC (1970) D
Falling for a Dolphin (1988) V
Whale Nation (1988) V
Sacred Elephant (1989) V
Autogeddon (1991) V

WILLIAMS, Helen Maria (1762–1827)
British political writer, poet, and novelist
Edwin and Eltruda (1782) V
Peru (1784) V
Julia (1790) F V
Letters Written in France, in the Summer of 1790 (1790) NF
Paul and Virginia [from Bernadin de St Pierre] (1796) F
A Tour in Switzerland (1798) NF
Perourou, the Bellows-Mender (1799) F
Sketches of the State of Manners and Opinions in the French Republic (1801) NF
Letters on Events in France since the Restoration (1819) NF

WILLIAMS, Hugo [Mordaunt] (1942–)
British poet
Symptoms of Loss (1965) V
Sugar Daddy (1970) V
Some Sweet Day (1975) V
Writing Home (1985) V
Self-Portrait With a Slide (1990) V

WILLIAMS, Isaac (1802–1865)
British poet
The Cathedral; or, The Catholic and Apostolic Church in England (1838) V
The Christian Scholar (1849) V
The Seven Days; or, The Old and New Creation (1850) V
The Christian Seasons (1854) V

WILLIAMS, John [Alfred] (1925–)
African-American novelist
The Angry Ones (1960) F
Night Song (1961) F
Sissie (1963) F
This is My Country Too (1965) NF
The Man Who Cried I Am (1967) F
Sons of Darkness, Sons of Light (1969) F
Captain Blackman (1972) F
Mothersill and the Foxes (1975) F
The Junior Bachelor Society (1976) F
The Berhama Account (1985) F
Jacob's Ladder (1987) F

WILLIAMS, Nigel (1948–)
British novelist and dramatist
My Life Closed Twice (1977) F
Jack Be Nimble (1980) F
Star Turn (1985) F
Witchcraft (1987) F
The Wimbledon Poisoner (1990) F
They Came From SW19 (1992) F
Scenes From a Poisoner's Life (1994) F SS
Fortysomething (1999) F

WILLIAMS, Raymond [Henry] (1921–1988)
British critic and novelist
Culture and Society 1780–1950 (1958) NF
Border Country (1960) F
Second Generation (1964) F
The Country and the City (1973) NF

WILLIAMS, 'Tennessee' [Thomas Lanier] (1911–1983)
American dramatist and novelist
American Blues (1939) D
Battle of Angels (1940) D
The Glass Menagerie (1944) D
A Streetcar Named Desire (1947) D
You Touched Me! (1947) D
One Arm (1948) F SS
Summer and Smoke [rev. as *The Eccentricities of a Nightingale*, 1964] (1948) D
The Roman Spring of Mrs Stone (1950) F
The Rose Tattoo (1950) D
I Rise in Flame, Cried the Phoenix (1951) D
Camino Real (1953) D
Hard Candy (1954) F SS
Cat on a Hot Tin Roof (1955) D
Baby Doll [film script] (1956) D
In the Winter of Cities (1956) V
Garden District [*Suddenly Last Summer*, and *Something Unspoken*] (1958) D
Sweet Bird of Youth (1959) D
Triple Play (1959) D
Period of Adjustment (1960) D
The Night of the Iguana (1962) D
Slapstick Tragedy [*The Mutilated*, and *The Gnaidige Fräulein*] (1965) D
The Knightly Quest (1966) F
Kingdom of Earth (1968) D
In the Bar of a Tokyo Hotel (1969) D
The Two-Character Play [rev. as *Outcry*, 1973] (1969) D
Small Craft Warning (1972) D
Eight Mortal Ladies Possessed (1974) F SS
Moise and the World of Reason (1975) F
Androgyne, Mon Amour (1977) V

WILLIAMS, William Carlos (1883–1963)
American poet, critic, novelist, and short-story writer
The Tempers (1913) V
Al Que Quiere! (1917) V
Kora in Hell [prose poems] (1920) V
Sour Grapes (1921) V
Spring and All (1922) V
The Great American Novel (1923) NF
In the American Grain (1925) NF
A Voyage to Pagany (1928) F
The Knife of the Times (1932) F SS
An Early Martyr (1935) V
Adam & Eve & the City (1936) V
White Mule (1937) F
Life Along the Passaic River (1938) F SS
In the Money (1940) F
The Broken Span (1941) V
The Wedge (1944) V
Paterson (1946–58) V
Make Light of It (1950) F SS
The Build-Up (1952) F
The Desert Music (1954) V
Journey to Love (1955) V
The Farmers' Daughters (1961) F SS
Many Loves (1961) D
Pictures from Brueghel (1963) V

WILLIAMSON, David [Keith] (1942–)
Australian dramatist
The Coming of Stork (1970) D
Don's Party (1971) D
The Removalists (1971) D
The Department (1975) D
A Handful of Friends (1976) D
The Club (1978) D
Travelling North (1980) D
Sons of Cain (1985) D
Emerald City (1987) D
Top Silk (1989) D
Siren (1991) D
Money & Friends (1992) D
Brilliant Lies (1993) D
Sanctuary (1994) D

WILLIAMSON, Henry (1895–1977)
British novelist and author
The Beautiful Years (1921) F
Dandelion Days (1922) F
The Peregrine's Saga, and Other Stories of the Country Green (1923) F SS
The Dream of Fair Women (1924) F
Tarka the Otter (1927) F
The Pathway (1928) F
The Linhay on the Downs (1929) NF

The Village Book (1930) NF
The Labouring Life (1932) NF
The Star-Born (1933) F
Salar the Salmon (1935) F
The Dark Lantern (1951) F
Tales of Moorland and Estuary (1953) F SS
The Gale of the World (1969) F

WILLS, William Gorman (1828–1891)
Irish artist, dramatist, and novelist
Notice to Quit (1861) F
The Wife's Evidence (1864) F
David Chantrey (1865) F
Charles the First (1872) D

WILMOT, John, 2nd Earl of Rochester (1647–1680)
English poet
A Satyr Against Mankind (1675?) V
A Letter From Artemiza in the Town to Chloë in the Country (1679) V
Upon Nothing (1679) V
A Very Heroical Epistle From My Lord All-Pride to Dol-Common (1679) V
Poems on Several Occasions (1680) V
Valentinian (1685) D
Poems, &c. on Several Occasions (1691) V

WILSON, A[ndrew] N[orman] (1950–)
British novelist and biographer
The Sweets of Pimlico (1977) F
Unguarded Hours (1978) F
Kindly Light (1979) F
The Healing Art (1980) F
The Laird of Abbotsford (1980) NF
Wise Virgin (1982) F
The Life of John Milton (1983) NF
Scandal (1983) F
Gentlemen in England (1985) F
How Can We Know? (1985) NF
Love Unknown (1986) F
Stray (1987) F CH
Incline Our Hearts (1988) F
Penfriends From Porlock (1988) NF
Against Religion (1990) NF
A Bottle in the Smoke (1990) F
C.S. Lewis (1990) NF
Daughters of Albion (1991) F
Jesus (1992) NF
The Vicar of Sorrows (1993) F
Hearing Voices (1995) F
Watch in the Night (1996) F
Dream Children (1998) F
God's Funeral (1999) NF

WILSON, [Sir] Angus [Frank Johnstone] (1913–1991)
British novelist, short-story writer, and critic
The Wrong Set, and Other Stories (1949) F SS
Such Darling Dodos, and Other Stories (1950) F SS
Hemlock and After (1952) F
Anglo-Saxon Attitudes (1956) F
A Bit Off the Map, and Other Stories (1957) F SS
The Middle Age of Mrs Eliot (1958) F
The Old Men at the Zoo (1961) F
The Wild Garden; or, Speaking of Writing (1963) NF
Late Call (1964) F
No Laughing Matter (1967) F
As If By Magic (1973) F
Setting the World on Fire (1980) F
Diversity and Depth in Fiction (1983) NF
Reflections in A Writer's Eye (1986) NF

WILSON, Colin (1931–)
British critic and novelist
The Outsider (1956) NF

WILSON, Edmund (1895–1972)
American critic, novelist, poet, and dramatist
The Undertaker's Garland (1922) V
Discordant Encounters (1926) D
I Thought of Daisy (1929) F
Poets, Farewell! (1929) V NF
Axel's Castle (1931) NF
The American Jitters: A Year of the Slump (1932) NF
Travels in Two Democracies (1936) NF
This Room and This Gin and These Sandwiches (1937) D
The Triple Thinkers (1938) NF
To the Finland Station (1940) NF
The Boys in the Back Room (1941) NF
The Wound and the Bow (1941) NF
Note-Books of Night (1942) V NF
Memoirs of Hecate County (1946) F SS
Europe Without Baedeker (1947) NF
Classics and Commercials (1950) NF
The Little Blue Light (1950) D
The Shores of Light (1952) NF
A Piece of My Mind (1956) NF
Red, Black, Blond, and Olive (1956) NF
The American Earthquake (1958) NF
Apologies to the Iroquois (1960) NF
Patriotic Gore (1962) NF
The Cold War and the Income Tax (1963) NF
The Bit Between My Teeth (1965) NF
O Canada (1965) NF
A Prelude (1967) NF
The Duke of Palermo (1969) D
Upstate (1971) NF
A Window on Russia (1972) NF
The Devils and Canon Barham (1973) NF
The Twenties (1975) NF
The Sixties: The Last Journal (1993) NF

WILSON, John (1627?–1696)
English dramatist and recorder of Londonderry
Andronicus Commenius (1664) D
The Cheats (1664) D
The Projectors (1665) D
Belphegor; or, The Marriage of the Devil (1691) D

WILSON, John ['Christopher North'] (1785–1854)
British poet, novelist, journalist, and essayist
The Isle of Palms, and Other Poems (1812) V
The City of the Plague, and Other Poems (1816) V
Lights and Shadows of Scottish Life (1822) F

The Trials of Margaret Lyndsay (1823) F
The Foresters (1825) F
The Recreations of Christopher North (1842) NF
Essays, Critical and Imaginative (1866) NF

WILSON, John Anthony Burgess *see* ANTHONY BURGESS

WILSON, John Dover (1881–1969)
British Shakespeare scholar and editor
The Essential Shakespeare (1932) NF
What Happens in Hamlet (1935) NF
The Fortunes of Falstaff (1943) NF

WILSON, Margaret (1882–1973)
American novelist, poet, and short-story writer
The Able McLaughlins (1923) F

WILSON, Robert (fl.1572–1600)
English dramatist
The Three Ladies of London (1584) D
The Three Lordes and Ladies of London (1590) D
The Coblers Prophesie (1594) D
The Pedlers Prophecie (1595) D

WILSON, Thomas (1525?–1581)
English diplomat and scholar
The Rule of Reason (1551) NF

WINKWORTH, Catherine (1827–1878)
British poet and translator
Lyra Germanica: [1st ser.] (1855) V
Lyra Germanica: [2nd ser.] (1858) V

WINSOR, Kathleen (1919–)
American popular novelist
Forever Amber (1944) F

WINTERS, [Arthur] Yvor (1900–1968)
American poet and critic
The Immobile Wind (1921) V
The Magpie's Shadow (1922) V
The Bare Hills (1927) V
The Proof (1930) V
The Journey (1931) V
Before Disaster (1934) V
Primitivism and Decadence (1937) NF
Maule's Curse (1938) NF
The Anatomy of Nonsense (1943) NF
The Giant Weapon (1943) V
The Function of Criticism (1957) NF
Forms of Discovery (1967) NF

WINTERSON, Jeanette (1959–)
British novelist
Boating for Beginners (1985) F
Oranges Are Not the Only Fruit (1985) F
The Passion (1987) F
Sexing the Cherry (1989) F
Written on the Body (1992) F
Art and Lies (1994) F
The World and Other Places (1998) F
The PowerBook (2000) F

WINTHROP, Theodore (1826–1861)
American novelist and travel-writer
Cecil Dreeme (1861) F
Edwin Brothertoft (1862) F
John Brent (1862) F
The Canoe and the Saddle (1863) NF

WISEMAN, Nicholas Patrick Stephen (1802–1865)
British cardinal and Archbishop of Westminster
High Church Claims; or, A Series of Papers on the Oxford Controversy (1841) NF
The Social and Intellectual State of England (1850) NF
Three Lectures on the Catholic Hierarchy (1850) NF
Fabiola; or, The Church of the Catacombs (1855) F
The Witch of Rosenburg (1866) D

WISTER, Owen (1860–1938)
American novelist and short-story writer
Red Man and White (1896) F SS
Lin McLean (1898) F SS
The Jimmyjohn Boss (1900) F SS
Lady Baltimore (1906) F

WITHER, George (1588–1667)
English poet and pamphleteer
Abuses Stript, and Whipt; or, Satirical Essayes (1613) V
Fidelia (1615) V
The Shepherds Hunting (1615) V
The Hymnes and Songs of the Church [music by Orlando Gibbons] (1623) V
The Schollers Purgatory (1624) NF
Britain's Remembrancer (1628) V
A Collection of Emblemes, Ancient and Moderne (1635) V
Haleluiah; or, Britains Second Remembrancer (1641) V
Campo-Musae (1643) V
The Dark Lantern (1653) V
The Protector (1655) V
Speculum Speculatiuum; or, A Considering-Glass (1660) V
The Prisoners Plea (1661) V
Tuba-Pacifica (1664) V
Sigh for the Pitchers (1666) V
Divine Poems on the Ten Commandments (1688) V

WITTGENSTEIN, Ludwig [Joseph Johann] (1889–1951)
Austrian-born British philosopher
Tractatus Logico-Philosophicus (1921) NF
Philosophical Investigations (1953) NF

WODEHOUSE, [Sir] P[elham] G[renville] (1881–1975)
British novelist and dramatist
Love Among the Chickens (1906) F
Mike (1909) F
A Gentleman of Leisure (1910) F
Psmith in the City (1910) F
Picadilly Jim (1918) F

A Damsel in Distress (1919) F
My Man Jeeves (1919) F SS
The Indiscretions of Archie (1921) F SS
The Clicking of Cuthbert (1922) F SS
The Adventures of Sally (1923) F
The Inimitable Jeeves (1923) F SS
Ukridge (1924) F SS
Carry On, Jeeves! (1925) F SS
Meet Mr Mulliner (1927) F SS
Money For Nothing (1928) F
Mr Mulliner Speaking (1929) F SS
Summer Lightning [US: *Fish Preferred*] (1929) F
Very Good, Jeeves (1930) F SS
Heavy Weather (1933) F
Mulliner Nights (1933) F SS
Right Ho, Jeeves (1934) F
Thank You, Jeeves (1934) F
Blandings Castle and Elsewhere (1935) F SS
The Luck of the Bodkins (1935) F
Laughing Gas (1936) F
Lord Emsworth and Others [US: *The Crime Wave at Blandings*] (1937) F SS
Summer Moonshine (1937) F
The Code of the Woosters (1938) F
Uncle Fred in the Springtime (1939) F
Uncle Dynamite (1948) F
The Old Reliable (1951) F
Pigs Have Wings (1952) F
Ring for Jeeves [US: *The Return of Jeeves*] (1953) F
Jeeves and the Feudal Spirit [US: *Bertie Wooster Sees It Through*] (1954) F
Jeeves in the Offing (1960) F
Stiff Upper Lip, Jeeves (1963) F
Frozen Assets (1964) F
Galahad at Blandings [US: *The Brinkmanship of Galahad Threepwood*] (1965) F
A Pelican at Blandings (1969) F
Much Obliged, Jeeves [US: *Jeeves and the Ties That Bind*] (1971) F
Sunset at Blandings [unfinished] (1977) F

WOLFE, Thomas [Clayton] (1900–1938)
American novelist and dramatist
Welcome to Our City (1923) D
Look Homeward, Angel (1929) F
From Death to Morning (1935) F SS
Of Time and the River (1935) F
The Story of a Novel (1936) F
The Web and the Rock (1939) F
You Can't Go Home Again (1940) F
The Hills Beyond [unfinished] (1941) F

WOLFE, Tom [Thomas] [Kennerly] (1930–)
American novelist and journalist
The Kandy-Kolored Tangerine Flake Streamline Baby (1966) NF
The Electric Kool-Aid Acid Test (1968) NF
The Pump House Gang (1968) NF
Radical Chic and Mau-Mauing the Flak Catchers (1970) NF
The New Journalism (1973) NF
The Painted Word (1975) NF
Mauve Gloves and Madmen (1976) NF SS
The Right Stuff (1979) NF
From Bauhaus to Our House (1981) NF
The Bonfire of the Vanities (1987) F
A Man in Full (1998) F

WOLFF, Tobias (1945–)
American short-story writer
In the Garden of the North American Martyrs [UK: *Hunters in the Snow*] (1981) F SS
The Barracks Thief (1984) F
Back in the World (1985) F SS
In Pharaoh's Army: Memories of the Lost War (1994) NF

WOLLSTONECRAFT, Mary, later Godwin (1759–1797)
British novelist and essayist
Thoughts on the Education of Daughters (1787) NF
Mary (1788) F
Of the Importance of Religious Opinions [from J. Necker] (1788) NF
Original Stories, from Real Life (1788) F SS
Elements of Morality for the Use of Children [from C.G. Salzmann] (1790) NF
A Vindication of the Rights of Men (1790) NF
A Vindication of the Rights of Women (1792) NF
An Historical and Moral View of the French Revolution (1794) NF
Letters Written During a Short Residence in Sweden, Norway and Denmark (1796) NF
The Wrongs of Woman [unfinished] (1798) F

WOOD, Anthony à (1632–1695)
English antiquary
Historia et Antiquitates Universitatis Oxoniensis [English trn 1786–96] (1674) NF
Athenae Oxonienses [vol. ii, 1692] (1691) NF

WOOD, Mrs Henry [Ellen Wood], *née* Price (1814–1887)
British novelist and short-story writer
Danesbury House (1860) F
East Lynne (1861) F
The Channings (1862) F
Mrs Halliburton's Troubles (1862) F
The Shadow of Ashlydyat (1863) F
Lord Oakburn's Daughters (1864) F
Lady Adelaide's Oath (1867) F
A Life's Secret (1867) F
Orville College (1867) F
Anne Hereford (1868) F
The Red Court Farm (1868) F
Roland Yorke (1869) F
George Canterbury's Will (1870) F
Dene Hollow (1871) F
Johnny Ludlow [1st ser.] (1874) F
Told in the Twilight (1875) F SS
Adam Grainger (1876) F
Pomeroy Abbey (1878) F
Court Netherleigh (1881) F
Lady Grace, and Other Stories (1887) F SS
The Story of Charles Strange (1888) F
The House of Halliwell (1890) F

The Unholy Wish, and Other Stories (1890) F SS
Ashley, and Other Stories (1897) F SS

WOODHAM-SMITH, Cecil [Blanche] (1896–1977)
British historian and biographer
Florence Nightingale (1950) NF
The Reason Why (1953) NF
The Great Hunger (1962) NF

WOOLF, [Adeline] Virginia, *née* Stephen (1882–1941)
British novelist and essayist
The Voyage Out (1915) F
The Mark on the Wall (1919) F
Night and Day (1919) F
Jacob's Room (1922) F
The Common Reader [1st ser.] (1925) NF
Mrs Dalloway (1925) F
To the Lighthouse (1927) F
Orlando (1928) F
A Room of One's Own (1929) NF
The Waves (1931) F
The Common Reader [2nd ser.] (1932) NF
Flush (1933) NF
The Years (1937) F
Three Guineas (1938) NF
Roger Fry (1940) NF
Between the Acts (1941) F
The Death of the Moth, and Other Essays (1942) NF
A Haunted House, and Other Short Stories (1943) F SS
The Moment, and Other Essays (1947) NF
The Captain's Death Bed, and Other Essays (1950) NF
A Writer's Diary (1953) NF
Granite and Rainbow (1958) NF
Contemporary Writers (1965) NF

WOOLF, Leonard [Sidney] (1880–1969)
British author and publisher
The Village in the Jungle (1913) F
The Wise Virgins (1914) F
Economic Imperialism (1920) NF
Socialism and Co-operation (1921) NF
Imperialism and Civilization (1928) NF
After the Deluge (1931) NF
Quack, Quack! (1935) NF
Barbarians at the Gate (1939) NF
Principia Politica (1953) NF
Sowing (1960) NF
Growing (1961) NF
Beginning Again (1964) NF
Downhill all the Way (1967) NF
The Journey Not the Arrival Matters (1969) NF

WOOLLEY, Sir [Charles] Leonard (1880–1960)
British archaeologist and author
Ur of the Chaldees (1929) NF
Digging Up the Past (1930) NF

WOOLRICH, Cornell ['George Hopley', 'William Irish'] (1903–1968)
American crime and mystery writer
The Bride Wore Black [also pub. as *Beware the Lady*] (1940) F
Phantom Lady [as 'William Irish'] (1942) F
The Night Has a Thousand Eyes [as 'George Hopley'] (1945) F
Rendezvous in Black (1948) F

WOOLSEY, Sarah Chauncy *see* SUSAN COOLIDGE

WORDSWORTH, William (1770–1850)
British poet and Poet Laureate
Descriptive Sketches (1793) V
An Evening Walk (1793) V
Lyrical Ballads, with a Few Other Poems (1798) V
Lyrical Ballads, with Other Poems [inc. poems by Coleridge and new preface] (1800) V
Lyrical Ballads, with Pastoral and Other Poems [with expanded preface] (1802) V
Lyrical Ballads, with Pastoral and Other Poems [last edn to include Coleridge's poems] (1805) V
Poems, in Two Volumes (1807) V
Concerning the Relations of Great Britain, Spain, and Portugal [on the Convention of Cintra] (1809) NF
The Excursion (1814) V
The White Doe of Rylstone; or, The Fate of the Nortons (1815) V
Peter Bell (1819) V
The Waggoner (1819) V
The River Duddon (1820) V
A Description of the Scenery of the Lakes in the North of England (1822) NF
Ecclesiastical Sonnets (1822) V
Memorials of a Tour on the Continent, 1820 (1822) NF
A Guide Through the District of the Lakes in the North of England . . . (1835) NF
Yarrow Revisited, and Other Poems (1835) V
The Prelude; or, Growth of a Poet's Mind (1850) V
The Recluse (1888) V

WOTTON, Sir Henry (1568–1639)
English diplomat and poet
The Elements of Architecture (1624) NF
Reliquiae Wottonianae; or, A Collection of Lives, Letters, Poems (1651) MISC

WOTTON, William (1666–1727)
English scholar
Reflections Upon Ancient and Modern Learning (1694) NF
The History of Rome (1701) NF
A Discourse Concerning the Confusion of Languages at Babel (1730) NF

WOUK, Herman (1915–)
American novelist
Aurora Dawn (1947) F
The City Boy (1948) F
The Traitor (1949) D
The Caine Mutiny (1951) F
Marjorie Morningstar (1955) F
Nature's Way (1957) D
This is My God (1959) NF
Youngblood Hawke (1962) F

Don't Stop the Carnival (1965) F
The Winds of War (1971) F
War and Remembrance (1978) F
Inside, Outside (1985) F
The Hope (1993) F
The Glory (1994) F

WREN, P[ercival] C[hristopher] (1885–1941)
British popular novelist
Beau Geste (1924) F
Beau Sabreur (1926) F
Beau Ideal (1928) F

WRIGHT, David [John Murray] (1920–1994)
South African-born British poet, editor, and translator
Moral Stories (1954) V
Monologue of a Deaf Man (1958) V
Adam at Evening (1965) V
To the Gods the Shades (1976) V
Metrical Observations (1980) V

WRIGHT, Richard (1908–1960)
African-American novelist and social critic
Uncle Tom's Children (1938) F SS
Native Son (1940) F
Black Boy (1945) NF
The Outsider (1953) F
Black Power (1954) NF
Pagan Spain (1957) NF
The Long Dream (1958) F
Eight Men (1961) F SS
Lawd Today (1963) F
American Hunger (1977) NF

WRIGHT, Thomas (1810–1877)
British antiquary
Biographia Britannica Literaria [vol. i] (1842) NF
Narratives of Sorcery and Magic (1851) NF
The Celt, the Roman, and the Saxon (1852) NF
Dictionary of Obsolete and Provincial English (1857) NF
Womankind in Western Europe (1869) NF

WYATT, Sir Thomas (1503?–1542)
English poet
The Quyete of Mynde [from Plutarch] (1528) NF
Certayne Psalmes Chosen Out of the Psalter of David (1549) V

WYCHERLEY, William (1641–1716)
English dramatist and poet
Love in a Wood; or, St James's Park (1671) D
The Gentleman Dancing-Master (1672) D
The Country-Wife (1675) D
The Plain-Dealer (1676) D

WYCLIFFE or **WICLIF, John** (d. 1384)
English religious reformer
Wycklyffes Wicket (1546) NF

'WYNDHAM, John' [John Wyndham Parkes Lucas Beynon Harris] (1903–1969)
British novelist and short-story writer
The Day of the Triffids (1951) F SF
The Kraken Wakes (1953) F SF
Jizzle (1954) F SS
The Chrysalids (1955) F SF
The Midwich Cuckoos [filmed as *Village of the Damned*, 1960] (1957) F SF
The Seeds of Time (1959) F SS
Trouble With Lichen (1960) F
Consider Her Ways (1961) F SS
Chocky (1968) F

WYSS, Johann [David] (1743–1818)
Swiss novelist
The Swiss Family Robinson [Der schweizerische Robinson; completed by Johan Rudolf Wyss] (1812–13) F

Y

'YATES, Dornford' [Cecil William Mercer] (1885–1960)
British popular novelist
The Brother of Daphne (1914) F SS
The Courts of Idleness (1920) F SS
Berry and Co. (1921) F SS
Jonah and Co. (1922) F SS
The Stolen March (1926) F
Blind Corner (1927) F
Perishable Goods (1928) F
Maiden Stakes (1929) F SS
And Berry Came Too (1936) F SS
The House That Berry Built (1945) F

YATES, Edmund [Hodgson] (1831–1894)
British journalist, novelist, and short-story writer
My Haunts and their Frequenters (1854) NF
After Office Hours (1861) F SS
Broken to Harness (1865) F
The Business of Pleasure (1865) NF
Running the Gauntlet (1865) F
Kissing the Rod (1866) F
Land at Last (1866) F
Black Sheep! (1867) F
The Rock Ahead (1868) F
A Righted Wrong (1870) F
Dr Wainwright's Patient (1871) F
Nobody's Fortune (1872) F
A Silent Witness (1875) F

YATES, [Dame] Frances [Amelia] (1899–1981)
British cultural historian
Giordano Bruno and the Hermetic Tradition (1964) NF
The Rosicrucian Enlightenment (1972) NF
The Occult Philosophy in the Elizabethan Age (1979) NF

YEATS, W[illiam] B[utler] (1865–1939)
Irish poet and dramatist
Mosada (1886) V
The Wanderings of Oisin, and Other Poems (1889) V
John Sherman and Dhoya [as 'Ganconagh'] (1891) F

The Countess Cathleen, and Various Legends and Lyrics (1892) V
The Celtic Twilight (1893) NF
The Land of Heart's Desire (1894) V D
Poems (1895) V
The Secret Rose (1897) F
The Wind Among the Reeds (1899) V
The Shadowy Waters (1900) V
Cathleen ni Hoolihan (1902) D
Ideas of Good and Evil (1903) NF
In the Seven Woods (1903) V
Where There is Nothing [*Plays for an Irish Theatre* vol. i] (1903) D
The Hour-Glass, Cathleen ni Houlihan, The Pot of Broth [*Plays for an Irish Theatre* vol. ii] (1904) D
The King's Threshold, and On Baile's Strand [*Plays for an Irish Theatre* vol. iii] (1904) D
Stories of Red Hanrahan (1904) F
The Tables of the Law, and The Adoration of the Magi (1904) F
Poems, 1899–1905 (1906) V
The Poetical Works of William B. Yeats [vol. i: *Lyrical Poems*] (1906) V
Deirdre [*Plays for an Irish Theatre* vol. iv] (1907) D
Discoveries (1907) NF
The Poetical Works of William B. Yeats [vol. ii: *Dramatical Poems*] (1907) V
The Unicorn From the Stars, and Other Plays (1908) NF
Poems: Second Series (1909) V
The Green Helmet, and Other Poems (1910) V
J.M. Synge and the Ireland of His Time (1911) NF
Easter, 1916 (1916) V
Responsibilities, and Other Poems (1916) V
The Wild Swans at Coole, Other Verses and a Play in Verse (1917) V
Nine Poems (1918) V
Per Amica Silentia Lunae (1918) V
Two Plays for Dancers ['The Dreaming of the Bones', and 'The Only Jealousy of Emer'] (1919) V
The Wild Swans at Coole (1919) V
Michael Robartes and the Dancer (1920) NF
Four Plays for Dancers [adds 'At the Hawk's Well' and 'Calvary' to *Two Plays for Dancers*] (1921) V
Later Poems (1922) V
The Player Queen (1922) V D
The Trembling of the Veil (1922) NF
The Cat and the Moon, and Certain Poems (1924) NF
A Vision [rev. 1937] (1925) NF
October Blast [inc. 'Sailing to Byzantium'] (1927) V
Stories of Red Hanrahan and the Secret Rose (1927) F SS
The Tower (1928) V
Words for Music Perhaps, and Other Poems (1932) V
The Winding Stair, and Other Poems (1933) V
The King of the Great Clock Tower (1934) V
Wheels and Butterflies (1934) V
The Words Upon the Window Pane (1934) D
Dramatis Personae (1935) NF
The Herne's Egg (1938) D
New Poems (1938) V
Last Poems and Two Plays (1939) V D

YERBY, Frank [Garvin] (1916–1991)
African-American novelist
The Foxes of Harrow (1946) F
A Woman Called Fancy (1951) F
The Garfield Honor (1961) F
An Odor of Sanctity (1965) F
Goat Song (1967) F
Judas, My Brother (1968) F
A Darkness at Ingraham's Crest (1979) F
Western (1982) F
Devilseed (1984) F
McKenzie's Hundred (1985) F

YEVTUSHENKO, Yevgeny [Aleksandrovich] (1933–)
Russian poet, dramatist, and novelist
Zima Junction (1956) V
Babi Yar (1962) V
Wild Berries (1982) F

YEZIERSKA, Anzia (*c.* 1885–1970)
Polish-born Jewish-American novelist
Hungry Hearts (1920) F
Bread Givers (1925) F

YIN, Leslie Charles Bowyer *see* LESLIE CHARTERIS

YONGE, Charlotte M[ary] (1823–1901)
British novelist and children's author
Abbeychurch; or, Self-control and Self-conceit (1844) F
The Heir of Redclyffe (1853) F
Heartsease; or, The Brother's Wife (1854) F
The Little Duke; or, Richard the Fearless (1854) F
The Lances of Lynwood (1855) F
The Railroad Children (1855) F CH
The Daisy Chain; or, Aspirations (1856) F
Dynevor Terrace; or, The Clue of Life (1857) F
Hopes and Fears; or, Scenes from the Life of a Spinster (1860) F
Countess Kate (1862) F CH
Sea Spleenwort, and Other Stories (1862) F SS
The Trial (1864) F
The Clever Woman of the Family (1865) F
The Dove in the Eagle's Nest (1866) F CH
The Chaplet of Pearls; or, The White and Black Ribaumont (1868) F
The Pillars of the House; or, Under Wode, Under Rode (1873) F
Stray Pearls (1883) F
Beechcroft at Rockstone (1888) F
The Long Vacation (1895) F
Modern Broods; or, Developments Unlooked For (1900) F

YORKE, Henry Vincent *see* HENRY GREEN

YOUNG, Andrew] [John] (1885–1971)
Scottish poet
Songs of Night (1910) V
Boaz and Ruth (1920) V

Winter Harvest (1933) V
Nicodemus (1937) V D
Speak to the Earth (1939) V
The Green Man (1947) V
Out of the World and Back (1958) V
The Poet and the Landscape (1962) NF

YOUNG, Arthur (1741–1820)
British agriculturalist and author
The Theatre of the Present War in North America (1758) NF
Reflections on the Present State of Affairs at Home and Abroad (1759) NF
The Adventures of Emmera; or, The Fair American (1767) F
A Farmer's Letters to the People of England (1767) NF
A Six Weeks' Tour Through the Southern Counties of England and Wales (1768) NF
A Course of Experimental Agriculture (1770) NF
The Farmer's Tour Through the East of England (1770) NF
A Six Months' Tour Through the North of England (1770) NF
A Tour in Ireland (1780) NF
Travels During the Years 1787, 1788, and 1790 (1792) NF

YOUNG, Edward (1683–1765)
British poet
An Epistle to the Right Honourable the Lord Lansdowne (1713) V
A Poem on the Last Day (1713) V
The Force of Religion; or, Vanquish'd Love (1714) V
Busiris, King of Egypt (1719) D
The Revenge (1721) D
The Universal Passion (1725) V
Ocean (1728) V
A Vindication of Providence; or, A True Estimate of Human Life (1728) NF
Two Epistles to Mr Pope (1730) V
The Complaint; or, Night-Thoughts on Life, Death and Immortality [collected edn, 1750] (1742–6) V
The Brothers (1753) D
The Centaur Not Fabulous (1755) NF
Conjectures on Original Composition (1759) NF
Resignation (1762) V

YOUNG, E[mily] H[ilda] (1880–1949)
British novelist
The Bridge Dividing [repub. 1927 as *The Misses Mallett*] (1922) F
William (1925) F
Miss Mole (1930) F
Jenny Wren (1932) F
The Curate's Life (1934) F
Chatterton Square (1948) F

YOUNG, Francis Brett (1884–1954)
British novelist
Deep Sea (1914) F
The Iron Age (1916) F
The Crescent Moon (1918) F
The Young Physician (1919) F
The Black Diamond (1921) F
The Red Knight (1921) F
Portrait of Clare [US: *Love is Enough*] (1927) F
My Brother Jonathan (1928) F
Dr Bradley Remembers Mr and Mrs Pennington (1931) F
The Cage Bird, and Other Stories (1933) F SS
White Ladies (1935) F
Dr Bradley Remembers (1938) F
The City of Gold (1939) F
Cotswold Honey, and Other Stories (1940) F SS
The Island (1944) V

YOUNG, Gavin (1928–)
British travel writer
Return to the Marshes (1977) NF
Iraq: Land of Two Rivers (1980) NF
Slow Boats to China (1981) NF
Slow Boats Home (1985) NF

YOUNG, G[eorge] M[alcolm] (1882–1959)
British historian
Early Victorian England (1934) NF
Victorian England (1936) NF

Z

ZANGWILL, Israel (1864–1926)
British novelist, short-story writer, and dramatist
The Big Bow Mystery (1892) F
Children of the Ghetto (1892) F
Ghetto Tragedies (1893) F
'Merely Mary Ann' (1893) F
The King of Schnorrers (1894) F
The Master (1895) F
Dreamers of the Ghetto (1898) NF
'They That Walk in Darkness' (1899) F
The Mantle of Elijah (1900) F
The Grey Wig (1903) F SS
Ghetto Comedies (1907) F
Four for Tomorrow (1967) F SS
Lord of Light (1967) F

ZELAZNY, Roger [Joseph] (1937–)
American science fiction writer
This Immortal (1966) F
The Dream Master (1966) F

ZEPHANIAH, Benjamin (1958–)
British poet and dramatist
Pen Rhythm (1980) V
The Dread Affair (1985) V
A Rasta Time in Palestine (1987) V
Hurricane Dub (1988) D
Job Rocking (1989) D
City Psalms (1992) V

ZIEGLER, Philip [Sandeman] (1929–)
British historian and biographer
The Black Death (1968) NF
William IV (1971) NF
Melbourne (1976) NF

Diana Cooper (1981) NF
Mountbatten (1985) NF
The Sixth Great Power (1988) NF
King Edward VIII (1990) NF
London at War, 1939–1945 (1995) NF

ZOLA, Émile (1840–1902)
French novelist
Stories for Ninon [*Contes à Ninon*] (1864) F SS
My Hatreds [*Mes Haines*] (1866) NF
Madeleine Férat (1868) F
Thérèse Raquin (1868) F
The Fortune of the Rougons [*La Fortune des Rougon*; first of the 20-vol. *Les Rougon-Macquart* cycle] (1871) F
The Rush for the Spoils [*La Curée*] (1872) F
Le Ventre de Paris (1873) F
The Conquest of Plassans [*La Conquête de Plassans*] (1874) F
Abbé Mouret's Transgression [*La Faute de l'abbé Mouret*] (1875) F
His Excellency Eugène Rougon [*Son Excellence Eugène Rougon*] (1876) F
L'Assommoir (1877) F
The Experimental Novel [*Le Roman expérimental*] (1880) NF
Nana (1880) F
Piping Hot! [*Pot-Bouille*] (1882) F
The Ladies' Paradise [*Au bonheur des dames*] (1883) F
How Jolly Life Is! [*La Joie de vivre*] (1884) F
Germinal (1885) F
The Masterpiece [*L'Oeuvre*] (1886) F
The Soil [*La Terre*] (1887) F
The Dream [*Le Rêve*] (1888) F
The Human Beast [*La Bête humaine*] (1890) F
Money [*L'Argent*] (1891) F
The Downfall [*La Débâcle*] (1892) F
Doctor Pascal [*Le Docteur Pascal*; final vol. in *Les Rougon-Macquart* cycle] (1893) F
Lourdes (1894) F
Rome (1896) F
J'accuse [on the Dreyfus affair] (1898) NF
Paris (1898) F
Fruitfulness [*Fécondité*] (1899) F
Work [*Travail*] (1901) F
Truth [*Vérité*] (1903) F

Title Index

A

A.A. Milne (1990) **Ann Thwaite** (1932)
A for Andromeda (1962) **Sir Fred Hoyle** (1915)
'A' is for Alibi (1982) **Sue Grafton** (1940)
A Lume Spento (1908) **Ezra Pound** (1885)
A Propos of Lady Chatterley's Lover (1930) **D.H. Lawrence** (1885)
Aaron the Jew (1894) **B.L. Farjeon** (1838)
Aaron's Rod (1922) **D.H. Lawrence** (1885)
Abba Abba (1977) **'Anthony Burgess' [John Anthony Burgess Wilson]** (1917)
Abbé Aubain, The [*L'Abbé Aubain*] (1846) **Prosper Mérimée** (1803)
Abbé Mouret's Transgression [*La Faute de l'abbé Mouret*] (1875) **Émile Zola** (1840)
Abbess of Crewe, The (1974) **Muriel Spark** (1918)
Abbess of Vlaye, The (1904) **Stanley J. Weyman** (1855)
Abbess, The (1799) **William-Henry Ireland** (1777)
Abbess, The (1833) **Frances Trollope** (1780)
Abbesse de Castro, L' ['The Abbess of Castro'] (1839) **'Stendhal' [Henri Marie Beyle]** (1783)
Abbey of Innismoyle, The (1828) **Selina Bunbury** (1802)
Abbeychurch (1844) **Charlotte M. Yonge** (1823)
Abbot, The (1820) **Sir Walter Scott** (1771)
Abbots Verney (1906) **Rose Macaulay** (1881)
ABC Murders, The (1936) **Agatha Christie** (1890)
ABC of Atoms, The (1923) **Bertrand Russell** (1872)
ABC of Economics (1933) **Ezra Pound** (1885)
ABC of Plain Words (1951) **Sir Ernest Gowers** (1880)
ABC of Reading (1934) **Ezra Pound** (1885)
ABC of Relativity, The (1925) **Bertrand Russell** (1872)
Abdelazar (1676) **Aphra Behn** (1640?)
Abduction, The (1971) **Maxine Kumin** (1925)
Abductors, The (1970) **Stuart Cloete** (1897)
Abe Lincoln in Illinois (1938) **Robert E. Sherwood** (1896)
Abel Allnutt (1837) **James Morier** (1780)
Abel Redevivus (1651) **Thomas Fuller** (1608) and others
Abhorrence (1990) **Ed Dorn** (1929)
Abigail's Party (1979) **Mike Leigh** (1943)
Abinger Harvest (1936) **E.M. Forster** (1879)
Able McLaughlins, The (1923) **Margaret Wilson** (1882)
Abortion, The (1971) **Richard Brautigan** (1935)
About a Boy (1998) **Nick Hornby** (1957)
About Looking (1980) **John Berger** (1926)
About Paris (1895) **Richard Harding Davis** (1864)
About the House (1966) **W.H. Auden** (1907)
About the Theatre (1886) **William Archer** (1856)
About Time (1970) **P.J. Kavanagh** (1931)
Above Suspicion (1876) **Mrs J.H. Riddell** (1832)
Above the Dark Circus (1931) **Sir Hugh Walpole** (1884)
Abra (1978) **Joan Barfoot** (1946)
Abraham Lincoln (1918) **John Drinkwater** (1882)
Abraham Lincoln: The Prairie Years (1926) **Carl Sandburg** (1878)
Abraham Lincoln: The War Years (1939) **Carl Sandburg** (1878)
Abridgement of the Histories of Trogus Pompeius, The (1564) **Arthur Golding** (1536) (tr.)
Absalom, Absalom! (1936) **William Faulkner** (1897)
Absalom and Achitophel [pt. i] (1681) **John Dryden** (1631)
Absalom Senior (1682) **Elkanah Settle** (1648)
Absence of War (1993) **David Hare** (1947)
Absentee, The (1812) **Maria Edgeworth** (1767)
Absolute and Abitofhell (1915) **Ronald Knox** (1888)
Absolute Beginners (1959) **Colin MacInnes** (1914)
Absolute Truths (1994) **Susan Howatch** (1940)
Absolute Unlawfulness of the Stage-Entertainment, The (1726) **William Law** (1686)
Absolute Zero (1978) **Helen Cresswell** (1934)
Abury (1743) **William Stukeley** (1687)
Abuses Stript, and Whipt (1613) **George Wither** (1588)
AC/DC (1970) **Heathcote Williams** (1941)
Academic Graffiti (1971) **W.H. Auden** (1907)
Academic Question, An (1986) **Barbara Pym** (1913–80)
Academic Year (1955) **D.J. Enright** (1920)
Acceptable Losses (1982) **Irwin Shaw** (1913)
Acceptance World, The (1955) **Anthony Powell** (1905)
Accident (1965) **Nicholas Mosley** (1923)
Accidental Death of an Anarchist (1970) **Dario Fo** (1926)
Accidental Man, An (1971) **Iris Murdoch** (1919)
Accidental Tourist, The (1985) **Anne Tyler** (1941)
Accidental Woman, The (1987) **Jonathan Coe** (1961)
Accomplish'd Rake, The (1727) **Mary Davys** (1674)
Accordian Crimes (1996) **E. Annie Proulx** (1935)
According to Jennings (1954) **Anthony Buckeridge** (1912)
According to Mark (1984) **Penelope Lively** (1933)
According to Queenie (2000) **Beryl Bainbridge** (1934)
Accosting Profiles (1989) **Walter Allen** (1911)
Account of Corsica, An (1768) **James Boswell** (1740)
Account of the Life of Mr Richard Savage, An (1744) **Samuel Johnson** (1709)
Account Rendered (1911) **E.F. Benson** (1867)
Achilles (1700) **Abel Boyer** (1667)
Achilles (1733) **John Gay** (1685)
Achilles in Scyros (1890) **Robert Bridges** (1844)
Achilles' Shield (1598) **George Chapman** (1559?)
Acid House, The (1994) **Irvine Welsh** (1957)
Acis and Galatea [music by Handel] (1732) **John Gay** (1685)
Acolyte, The (1972) **Thea Astley** (1925)
Acquisitive Society, The (1920) **R.H. Tawney** (1880)
Acre of Grass, An (1965) **J.I.M. Stewart** (1906)

Acre of Land, An (1952) **R.S. Thomas** (1913)
Acrobats, The (1954) **Mordecai Richler** (1931)
Across Patagonia (1880) **Lady Florence Dixie** (1857)
Across the Black Waters (1940) **Mulk Raj Anand** (1905)
Across the City (1980) **Wendy Cope** (1945)
Across the Common (1964) **Elizabeth Berridge** (1921)
Across the Plains (1892) **Robert Louis Stevenson** (1850)
Across the River and Into the Trees (1950) **Ernest Hemingway** (1898)
Across the Sea Wall [rev. 1982] (1965) **C. J. Koch** (1932)
Across the Stream (1919) **E.F. Benson** (1867)
Act in a Backwater, An (1903) **E.F. Benson** (1867)
Act in the Noon (1974) **Chris Wallace-Crabbe** (1934)
Act of Darkness (1982) **Francis King** (1923)
Act of Faith (1946) **Irwin Shaw** (1913)
Act of Grace [as 'William Coyle'] (1988) **Thomas Keneally** (1935)
Act of Terror, An (1991) **André Brink** (1935)
Act of Will (1986) **Barbara Taylor Bradford** (1933)
Act One (1957) **Randolph Stow** (1935)
Actes and Monuments [known as *The Book of Martyrs*] (1563) **John Foxe** (1517)
Actfive (1948) **Archibald MacLeish** (1892)
Action (1928) **C.E. Montague** (1867)
Action, The (1978) **Francis King** (1923)
Actions and Reactions (1909) **Rudyard Kipling** (1865)
Active Service (1899) **Stephen Crane** (1871)
Acts of English Votaries, The (1546) **John Bale** (1495)
Ada or Ardor (1969) **Vladimir Nabokov** (1899)
Ada Reis (1823) **Lady Caroline Lamb** (1785)
Ada the Betrayed [sometimes attrib. to T.P. Prest] (1842) **'Malcolm J. Errym' [James Malcolm Rymer]** (1804)
Adages [Adagia] (1500) **Erasmus** (c.1467)
Adalgisa (1944) **Carlo Emilio Gadda** (1893)
Adam and Eve and Pinch Me (1921) **A.E. Coppard** (1878)
Adam at Evening (1965) **David Wright** (1920)
Adam Bede (1859) **'George Eliot' [Mary Ann Evans]** (1819)
Adam Cast Forth (1908) **Charles Doughty** (1843)
Adam & Eve & the City (1936) **William Carlos Williams** (1883)
Adam Grainger (1876) **Mrs Henry Wood** (1814)
Adam in Moonshine (1927) **J.B. Priestley** (1894)
Adam's Breed (1926) **Radclyffe Hall** (1880)
Adamastor Poems (1930) **Roy Campbell** (1901)
Adaptable Man, The (1965) **Janet Frame** (1924)
Addictions (1962) **D.J. Enright** (1920)
Adding Machine, The (1986) **William S. Burroughs** (1914)
Adding Machine, The (1923) **Elmer Rice** (1892)
Address to the Clergy, An (1756) **John Wesley** (1703)
Address to the Irish People, An (1812) **P.B. Shelley** (1792)
Address to the Negroes of the State of New York, An (1787) **Jupiter Hammon** (1720)
Addresses and Lectures (1849) **Ralph Waldo Emerson** (1803)
Adela Cathcart (1864) **George MacDonald** (1824)
Adelaide (1800) **Henry James Pye** (1745)
Adelaide; or, The Emigrants (1814) **Richard Lalor Sheil** (1791)
Adele (1858) **Julia Kavanagh** (1824)
Adelgitha (1806) **M.G. Lewis** (1775)
Adeline Mowbray (1805) **Amelia Opie** (1769)
Adelmorn the Outlaw (1801) **M.G. Lewis** (1775)
Admirable Crichton, The (1914) **[Sir] J.M. Barrie** (1860)
Admirable Tinker, The (1904) **Edgar Jepson** (1863)
Admiral Guinea (1884) **W.E. Henley** (1849) [with R.L. Stevenson]
Admirals All (1897) **Sir Henry Newbolt** (1862)
Admissions and Asides About Life and Literature (1905) **A. St John Adcock** (1864)
Admonition, The (1571) **George Buchanan** (1506)
Adolphe (1816) **Benjamin Constant** (1767)
Adonais (1821) **P.B. Shelley** (1792)
Adonis and the Alphabet (1956) **Aldous Huxley** (1894)
Adrastus [etc] (1823) **R.C. Dallas** (1754)
Adrian Mole: The Cappuccino Years (1999) **Sue Townsend** (1946)
Adrian Rome (1899) **Ernest Dowson** (1867) [and Arthur Moore]
Adulateur, The (1773) **Mercy Otis Warren** (1728)
Adult Bookstore (1976) **Karl Shapiro** (1913)
Adult Life of Toulouse Lautrec, The (1978) **Kathy Acker** (1948)
Advancement and Reformation of Modern Poetry, The (1701) **John Dennis** (1657)
Advancement of Learning, An (1971) **Reginald Hill** (1936)
Advancement of Learning, Divine and Human, The (1605) **Sir Francis Bacon** (1561)
Adventure Story (1949) **Terence Rattigan** (1911)
Adventures in Criticism (1896) **Sir A.T. Quiller-Couch** (1863)
Adventures in Madrid, The (1706) **Mary Pix** (1666)
Adventures in the Skin Trade (1955) **Dylan Thomas** (1914–53)
Adventures of a Beauty, The (1852) **Catherine Crowe** (1790)
Adventures of a Supercargo, The (1906) **Louis Becke** (1855)
Adventures of a Three-Guinea Watch, The (1880) **Talbot Baines Reed** (1852)
Adventures of a Young Man (1939) **John Dos Passos** (1896)
Adventures of a Younger Son, The (1831) **E.J. Trelawny** (1792)
Adventures of Alicia, The (1906) **Katharine Tynan** (1861)
Adventures of an Aide-de-Camp (1848) **James Grant** (1822)

Adventures of Anthony Varnish, The (1786) **Charles Johnstone** (1719)
Adventures of Augie March, The (1947) **Saul Bellow** (1915)
Adventures of Barney Mahoney, The (1832) **T. Crofton Croker** (1798)
Adventures of Baron de Faeneste, The [Adventures du baron de Faeneste] (1617) **Théodore-Agrippa D'Aubigné** (1552)
Adventures of Baron Münchausen, The (1785) **Rudolph Erich Raspe** (1737)
Adventures of Brusanus, Prince of Hungaria, The (1592) **Barnabe Rich** (1542)
Adventures of Captain Bonneville, The (1837) **Washington Irving** (1783)
Adventures of Captain Kettle, The (1898) **C.J. Cutcliffe Hyne** (1865)
Adventures of Christian Rosy Cross, The (1986) **David Foster** (1944)
Adventures of Covent-Garden, The (1699) **George Farquhar** (1678)
Adventures of Cuffy Mahoney, The (1979) **'Henry Handel Richardson' [Ethel Florence Robertson]** (1870–1946)
Adventures of David Simple, The (1744) **Sarah Fielding** (1710)
Adventures of David Simple: Volume the Last, The (1753) **Sarah Fielding** (1710)
Adventures of Elizabeth in Rügen, The (1904) **'Elizabeth' [Mary Annette Gräfin] von Arnim** (1866)
Adventures of Emmera, The (1767) **Arthur Young** (1741)
Adventures of Eovaai, The (1736) **Eliza Haywood** (*c.* 1693)
Adventures of Ferdinand Count Fathom, The (1753) **Tobias George Smollett** (1721)
Adventures of Gerard (1903) **A. Conan Doyle** (1859)
Adventures of Gil Blas of Santillane, The (1749) **Tobias George Smollett** (1721) (tr.)
Adventures of Hajii Baba, in England, The (1828) **James Morier** (1780–1844)
Adventures of Hajii Baba, The (1824) **James Morier** (1780)
Adventures of Harry Revel, The (1903) **Sir A.T. Quiller-Couch** (1863)
Adventures of Harry Richmond, The (1871) **George Meredith** (1828)
Adventures of Heine, The (1919) **Edgar Wallace** (1875)
Adventures of Huckleberry Finn (1884) **'Mark Twain' [Samuel Langhorne Clemens]** (1835)
Adventures of Hugh Trevor, The [vols. i–iii] (1794) **Thomas Holcroft** (1745)
Adventures of Hugh Trevor, The [vols. iv–vi] (1797) **Thomas Holcroft** (1745)
Adventures of Martin Hewitt (1896) **Arthur Morrison** (1863)
Adventures of Mr Verdant Green, The (1853) **'Cuthbert Bede B.A.' [Edward Bradley]** (1827)
Adventures of Peregrine Pickle, The (1751) **Tobias George Smollett** (1721)
Adventures of Philip, The (1862) **W.M. Thackeray** (1811)
Adventures of Rivella, The (1714) **Mary Delariviere Manley** (1663)
Adventures of Robin Day, The (1839) **Robert Bird** (1806)
Adventures of Robina, The (1986) **Emma Tennant** (1937)
Adventures of Roderick Random, The (1748) **Tobias George Smollett** (1721)
Adventures of Romney Pringle, The (1902) **R. Austin Freeman** (1862)
Adventures of Rupert the Little Bear, The (1921) **Mary Tourtel** (1874)
Adventures of Sally, The (1923) **P.G. Wodehouse** (1881)
Adventures of Seumas Beg, The (1915) **James Stephens** (1882)
Adventures of Sherlaw Kombs, The [as 'Luke Sharp'] (1892) **Robert Barr** (1850)
Adventures of Sherlock Holmes, The (1892) **A. Conan Doyle** (1859)
Adventures of Speedfall, The (1985) **John Fuller** (1937)
Adventures of Susan Hopley (1841) **Catherine Crowe** (1790)
Adventures of Telemachus, The [Les Aventures de Télémaque] (1699) **François Fénelon** (1651)
Adventures of the Black Girl in Her Search for God, The (1932) **Bernard Shaw** (1856)
Adventures of the Comte de la Muette (1898) **Bernard Capes** (1850?)
Adventures of the Letter I (1971) **Louis Simpson** (1923)
Adventures of Tom Bombadil, The (1962) **J.R.R. Tolkein** (1892)
Adventures of Tom Sawyer, The (1876) **'Mark Twain' [Samuel Langhorne Clemens]** (1835)
Adventures of Wesley Jackson, The (1946) **William Saroyan** (1908)
Advertisement to the Jury-Men of England, An (1653) **Sir Robert Filmer** (1588?)
Advertisements for Myself (1959) **Norman Mailer** (1923)
Advice (1746) **Tobias George Smollett** (1721)
Advice to a Lady (1733) **George Lyttelton, 1st Baron Lyttelton** (1709)
Advice to a Painter (1688) **John Phillips** (1631)
Advice to a Prophet (1961) **Richard Wilbur** (1921)
Advice to the Poets (1706) **Sir Richard Blackmore** (1654)
Advice to the Poets (1731) **Aaron Hill** (1685)
Adzuma (1893) **Sir Edwin Arnold** (1832)
Aegean Islands (1946) **Bernard Spencer** (1909)
Aelfric's Lives of the Saints (1881) **W.W. Skeat** (1835) (ed.)
Aeneid [incomplete at Virgil's death] (19 BC) **Virgil** (70–19 BC)
Aeneid, The [from Virgil] (1986) **C.H. Sisson** (1914) (tr.)

Aeneid Books VII to IX (1924) **Ronald Knox** (1888) (ed. and tr.)
Aeneid of Virgil, The (1952) **C. Day Lewis** (1904) (tr.)
Aerius Redivivus (1670) **Peter Heylyn** (1600–62)
Aerodrome, The (1941) **Rex Warner** (1905)
Aeschylus: The Oresteia (1999) **Ted Hughes** (1930–98) (tr.)
Aesop (1696–7) **Sir John Vanbrugh** (1664)
Affair of Dishonour, An (1910) **William De Morgan** (1839)
Affair, The (1960) **C.P. Snow** (1905)
Affaire Lerouge, L' (1866) **Émile Gaboriau** (1832)
Affairs of the Heart (1900) **Violet Hunt** (1866)
Affinities (1885) **Mrs Campbell Praed** (1851)
Affinities (1962) **Vernon Watkins** (1906)
Affirmations (1898) **Havelock Ellis** (1859)
Affliction (1989) **Russell Banks** (1940)
Affliction (1994) **Fay Weldon** (1931)
Affluent Society, The (1955) **J.K. Galbraith** (1908)
Afloat and Ashore (1844) **James Fenimore Cooper** (1789)
Afoot in England (1909) **W.H. Hudson** (1841)
Afore Night Come (1960) **David Rudkin** (1936)
African Elegy, An (1992) **Ben Okri** (1959)
African Millionaire, An (1897) **Grant Allen** (1848)
African Negatives (1962) **Alan Ross** (1922)
African Queen, The (1935) **C.S. Forester** (1899)
African Stories (1964) **Doris Lessing** (1919)
African Witch, The (1936) **Joyce Cary** (1888)
After (1973) **Robert W. Anderson** (1917)
After 1903—What? (1938) **Robert Benchley** (1889)
After Babel (1975) **George Steiner** (1929)
After Bakhtin (1990) **David Lodge** (1935)
After Dark (1856) **Wilkie Collins** (1824)
After Dark, My Sweet (1955) **Jim Thompson** (1906)
After Darwin (1998) **Timberlake Wertenbaker** (1951)
After Every Green Thing (1949) **Dannie Abse** (1923)
After Experience (1968) **W.D. Snodgrass** (1926)
After Haggerty (1970) **David Mercer** (1928)
After Henry (1992) **Joan Didion** (1934)
After Julius (1965) **Elizabeth Jane Howard** (1923)
After Leaving Mr Mackenzie (1931) **'Jean Rhys' [Ella Gwendolyn Rees Williams]** (1890)
After Life, The (1994) **John Updike** (1932)
After London (1885) **Richard Jefferies** (1848)
After Magritte (1970) **Tom Stoppard** (1937)
After Many a Summer [US: *After Many a Summer Dies the Swan*] (1939) **Aldous Huxley** (1894)
After October (1936) **Rodney Ackland** (1908)
After Office Hours (1861) **Edmund Yates** (1831)
After Paradise (1887) **Edward Robert Bulwer Lytton** (1831)
After Puritanism 1850–1900 (1929) **'Hugh Kingsmill' [Hugh Kingsmill Lunn]** (1889)
After Pusan (1995) **Alan Ross** (1922)
After Sixty Years (1931) **Shan F. Bullock** (1865)
After Strange Gods (1934) **T.S. Eliot** (1888)
After Such Pleasures (1933) **Dorothy Parker** (1893)
After the Bombing (1949) **Edmund Blunden** (1896)
After the Cries of the Birds (1967) **Lawrence Ferlinghetti** (1920)
After the Dance (1939) **Terence Rattigan** (1911)
After the Death of Don Juan (1938) **Sylvia Townsend Warner** (1893)
After the Deluge (1931) **Leonard Woolf** (1880)
After the Fall (1964) **Arthur Miller** (1915)
After the First Death (1979) **Robert Cormier** (1925)
After the War (1988) **Frederic Raphael** (1931)
Aftermath (1896) **James Lane Allen** (1849)
Afternoon Men (1931) **Anthony Powell** (1905)
Afternoon of a Good Woman (1976) **Nina Bawden** (1925)
Afternoon of an Author (1958) **F. Scott Fitzgerald** (1896–1940)
Afterthoughts (1931) **Logan Pearsall Smith** (1865)
Afterword on Rupert Brooke (1976) **F.T. Prince** (1912)
Against Interpretation (1966) **Susan Sontag** (1933)
Against Nature [*Arebours*] (1884) **J.K. Huysmans** (1848)
Against Religion (1990) **A.N. Wilson** (1950)
Against the Season (1971) **Jane Rule** (1931)
Agamemnon (1738) **James Thomson** (1700)
Agamemnon; Choephptpe; Eumenidies [*Oresteia* trilogy] (458 BC) **Aeschylus** (525 BC)
Agamemnon of Aechylus, The (1936) **Louis MacNeice** (1907) (tr.)
Agate's Folly (1925) **James Evershed Agate** (1877)
Agatha (1973) **Isabel Colegate** (1931)
Agatha (1869) **'George Eliot' [Mary Ann Evans]** (1819)
Agatha's Husband (1853) **Dinah Maria Craik** (1826)
Age, An (1967) **Brian Aldiss** (1925)
Age of Anxiety, The (1948) **W.H. Auden** (1907)
Age of Bronze, The (1823) **George Gordon, Lord Byron** (1788)
Age of Capital, The (1975) **Eric Hobsbawm** (1917)
Age of Consent (1938) **Norman Lindsay** (1879)
Age of Empire, The (1987) **Eric Hobsbawm** (1917)
Age of Grief, The (1987) **Jane Smiley** (1949)
Age of Innocence, The (1920) **Edith Wharton** (1862)
Age of Iron (1990) **J.M. Coetzee** (1940)
Age of Jackson, The (1945) **Arthur Schlesinger** (1917)
Age of Longing, The (1951) **Arthur Koestler** (1905)
Age of Louis XIV, The [*Siècle de Louis Quatorze*] (1751) **'Voltaire' [François-Marie Arouet]** (1694)
Age of Reason, The [pt. i; pt. ii, 1795] (1794) **Thomas Paine** (1737)
Age of Reason, The [*L'Âge de raison*] (1945) **Jean-Paul Sartre** (1905)
Age of Revolution: Europe, The (1962) **Eric Hobsbawm** (1917)
Age of Scandal, The (1950) **T.H. White** (1906)
Age of Shakespeare, The (1908) **A.C. Swinburne** (1837)
Age of the Dragon, The (1951) **John Lehmann** (1907)
Age of the Pussyfoot, The (1969) **Frederik Pohl** (1919)
Age, The (1858) **Philip James Bailey** (1816)
Agents and Patients (1936) **Anthony Powell** (1905)

Agents and Witnesses (1947) **P.H. Newby** (1918)
Agincourt (1844) **G.P.R. James** (1799)
Agis (1758) **John Home** (1722)
Aglaura (1638) **Sir John Suckling** (1609)
Agnes (1865) **Margaret Oliphant** (1828)
Agnes de Tracy (1843) **John Mason Neale** (1818)
Agnes Grey (1847) **Anne Brontë** (1820)
Agnes Grey [Brontë]: see *Wuthering Heights*
Agnes of Sorrento (1862) **Harriet Beecher Stowe** (1811)
Agnes Sorel (1853) **G.P.R. James** (1799)
Agnes Waring (1856) **Mrs A.H. Alexander** (1825)
Agnostic's Apology, An (1893) **Sir Leslie Stephen** (1832)
Agnus Dei, An (1601) **John Weever** (1576)
Agony and the Ecstasy, The (1961) **Irving Stone** (1903)
Agostino (1944) **'Alberto Moravia' [Alberto Pincherle]** (1907)
Agrarian Problem in the Sixteenth Century, The (1912) **R.H. Tawney** (1880)
Agreeable Caledonian, The [pt. i] (1728) **Eliza Haywood** (*c.* 1693)
Ah, But Your Land is Beautiful (1981) **Alan Paton** (1903)
Ah King (1933) **Somerset Maugham** (1874)
Ah Sin (1877) **Bret Harte** (1836)
Ah! Wilderness (1932) **Eugene O'Neill** (1888)
Aiding and Abeting (2000) **Muriel Spark** (1918)
AIDS and its Metaphors (1988) **Susan Sontag** (1933)
Aids to Reflection (1825) **S.T. Coleridge** (1772)
Aiglon, L' (1900) **Edmond Rostand** (1868)
Aimez-vous Brahms . . . (1959) **'Françoise Sagan' [Françoise Quoirez]** (1935)
Aims of Art, The (1887) **William Morris** (1834)
Air and Angels (1991) **Susan Hill** (1942)
Air and Chill Earth (1971) **Molly Holden** (1927)
Air de l'eau, L' (1934) **André Breton** (1896)
Air Raid (1938) **Archibald MacLeish** (1892)
Air Show, The (1988) **Peter Scupham** (1933)
Air Surgeon (1943) **Frank G. Slaughter** (1908)
Air-Conditioned Nightmare, The (1945) **Henry Miller** (1891)
Airport (1968) **Arthur Hailey** (1920)
Airs and Tributes (1989) **Dennis Brutus** (1924)
Airs of Earth, The (1963) **Brian Aldiss** (1925)
Airways, Inc. (1928) **John Dos Passos** (1896)
Aissa Saved (1932) **Joyce Cary** (1888)
Ajax **Sophocles** (*c.* 496 BC)
Akenfield (1969) **Ronald Blythe** (1922)
Al Aaraff (1829) **Edgar Allan Poe** (1809)
A la recherche du temps perdu (2000) **Craig Raine** (1944)
Al Que Quiere! (1917) **William Carlos Williams** (1883)
Alabama (1891) **Augustus Thomas** (1857)
Alabaster Box, The (1923) **James Lane Allen** (1849)
Alabaster Box, The (1900) **Sir Walter Besant** (1836)
Aladdin's Lamp [*La Lampe d'Aladin*] (1909) **Jean Cocteau** (1889)
Alamein to Zem Zem (1946) **Keith Douglas** (1920–44)
Alan (1924) **E.F. Benson** (1867)
Alanna Autumnal (1933) **George Barker** (1913)
Alaric at Rome (1840) **Matthew Arnold** (1822)
Alaric Spenceley (1881) **Mrs J.H. Riddell** (1832)
Alarms and Discursions (1910) **G.K. Chesterton** (1874)
Alarms and Diversions (1957) **James Thurber** (1894)
Alarum Against Usurers, An (1584) **Thomas Lodge** (1558)
Alarums and Excursions (1922) **James Evershed Agate** (1877)
Alas! (1890) **Rhoda Broughton** (1840)
Alaska (1988) **James A. Michener** (1907)
Alastor (1816) **P.B. Shelley** (1792)
Albatross Muff, The (1977) **Barbara Hanrahan** (1939)
Albatross, The (1971) **Susan Hill** (1942)
Albert Angelo (1964) **B.S. Johnson** (1933)
Albert Lunel (1844) **Henry, Lord Brougham** (1778)
Albert's Bridge; and If You're Glad I'll Be Frank (1969) **Tom Stoppard** (1937)
Albertus (1832) **Théophile Gautier** (1811)
Albigenses, The (1824) **C.R. Maturin** (1782)
Albina, Countess Raimond (1779) **Hannah Cowley** (1743)
Albion and Albanius (1685) **John Dryden** (1631)
Albions England (1586) **William Warner** (1558?)
Albions Triumph (1631) **Aurelian Townshend** (1583?)
Albovine, The Tragedy of (1629) **Sir William Davenant** (1606)
Album Verses (1830) **Charles Lamb** (1775)
Alcestis [from Euripides] (1999) **Ted Hughes** (1930–98) (tr.)
Alchemist, The (1610) **Ben Jonson** (1572)
Alchemy (1920) **Robert Hillyer** (1895)
Alchemy of Thought, The (1910) **L.P. Jacks** (1860)
Alchymist's Journal, The (1991) **Evan S. Connell, Jr** (1924)
Alcibiades (1675) **Thomas Otway** (1652)
Alciphron (1732) **George Berkeley** (1685)
Alciphron (1839) **Thomas Moore** (1779)
Alcools (1913) **'Guillaume Apollinaire' [Wilhelm de Kostrowitsky]** (1880)
Alcuin (1798) **Charles Brockden Brown** (1771)
Alderman Ralph [as 'Adam Hornbrook'] (1853) **Thomas Cooper** (1805)
Aldous Huxley (1973) **Sybille Bedford** (1911)
Alec Forbes of Howglen (1865) **George MacDonald** (1824)
Aleck Maury, Sportsman (1934) **Caroline Gordon** (1895)
Aleph, The [*El Aleph*] (1949) **Jorge Luis Borges** (1899)
Alexander, Campaspe, and Diogenes (1584) **John Lyly** (1554)
Alexander Pope (1880) **Sir Leslie Stephen** (1832)
Alexander the Great [*Alexandre le grand*] (1665) **Jean Racine** (1639)
Alexander's Bridge (1912) **Willa Cather** (1873)
Alexander's Feast (1697) **John Dryden** (1631)

Alexandrian Quartet, The [*Justine, Balthazar, Mountolive, Clea*] (1962) **Lawrence Durrell** (1912)
Alfie [from play of the same name, perf. 1963] (1966) **Bill Naughton** (1910)
Alfonso, King of Castile (1801) **M.G. Lewis** (1775)
Alfred (1723) **Sir Richard Blackmore** (1654)
Alfred (1740) **James Thomson** (1700) [with David Mallet]
Alfred (1751) **David Mallet** (1705?)
Alfred (1778) **John Home** (1722)
Alfred (1801) **Henry James Pye** (1745)
Alfred, Lord Tennyson and His Friends (1893) **Lady Anne Ritchie** (1837)
Algeria (1985) **Kathy Acker** (1948)
Algerine Captive, The (1797) **Royall Tyler** (1757)
Alhambra, The (1832) **Washington Irving** (1783)
Alias Grace (1996) **Margaret Atwood** (1939)
Alias Madame Doubtfire (1987) **Anne Fine** (1947)
Alice (1838) **Edward Bulwer-Lytton** (1803)
Alice Adams (1921) **Booth Tarkington** (1869)
Alice and the Lost Novel (1929) **Sherwood Anderson** (1876)
Alice and Thomas and Jane (1930) **Enid Bagnold** (1889)
Alice Fell (1980) **Emma Tennant** (1937)
Alice in Bed (1993) **Susan Sontag** (1933)
Alice in Wormland (1987) **Dorothy Hewett** (1923)
Alice Learmont (1852) **Dinah Maria Craik** (1826)
Alice Lorraine (1875) **R.D. Blackmore** (1825)
Alice Stanley (1868) **Anna Maria [Mrs S.C.] Hall** (1800)
Alice Through the Cellophane (1933) **E.B. White** (1899)
Alice's Adventures in Wonderland (1865) **'Lewis Carroll' [Charles Lutwidge Dodgson]** (1832)
Alice's Adventures Under Ground (1994) **Christopher Hampton** (1946)
Alice-For-Short (1907) **William Frend De Morgan** (1839)
Alieford (1853) **Margaret Oliphant** (1828)
Alien Heart, An [first of *The Dancers at the End of Time* trilogy] (1972) **Michael Moorcock** (1939)
Alien Sky, The [US: *Six Days in Marapore*] (1953) **Paul Scott** (1920)
Aliens in the Family (1986) **Margaret Mahy** (1936)
All Aboard for Ararat (1940) **H.G. Wells** (1866)
All About H. Hatterr (1948) **G.V. Desani** (1909)
All Along the River (1893) **M.E. Braddon** (1835)
All But a Rib (1973) **Alex Comfort** (1920)
All Creatures Great and Small (1972) **James Herriot** (1916)
All Flesh is Grass (1965) **Clifford D. Simak** (1904)
All Fools (1605) **George Chapman** (1559?)
All for Love (1677) **John Dryden** (1631)
All for the Better (1720) **Charles Gildon** (1665)
All God's Children Need Traveling Shoes (1986) **Maya Angelou** (1928)
All God's Chillun Got Wings (1924) **Eugene O'Neill** (1888)
All Good Men; and, Absolute Beginners (1977) **Trevor Griffiths** (1935)
All Hallows' Eve (1945) **Charles Williams** (1886)
All He Fears (1993) **Howard Barker** (1946)
All His Sons (1999) **Frederic Raphael** (1931)
All I Survey (1933) **G.K. Chesterton** (1874)
All in a Garden Fair (1883) **Sir Walter Besant** (1836)
All in a Lifetime [US title: *Threescore and Ten*] (1959) **Walter Allen** (1911)
All in All (1875) **Philip Bourke Marston** (1850)
All in the Dark (1866) **J.S. le Fanu** (1814)
All is Grist (1931) **G.K. Chesterton** (1874)
All Men Are Brothers (1933) **Pearl S. Buck** (1892)
All Men Are Enemies (1933) **Richard Aldington** (1892)
All Men Are Ghosts (1913) **L.P. Jacks** (1860)
All Men Are Mortal [*Tous les hommes sont mortels*] (1946) **Simone de Beauvoir** (1908)
All My Little Ones (1978) **Gavin Ewart** (1916)
All My Men (1977) **Bernard Ashley** (1935)
All My Pretty Ones (1962) **Anne Sexton** (1928)
All My Sons (1947) **Arthur Miller** (1915)
All Night Long (1942) **Erskine Caldwell** (1903)
All on the Irish Shore (1903) **'Somerville and Ross' [Edith Somerville** (1858) and **Violet Martin]** (1862)
All or Nothing (1960) **John Cooper Powys** (1872)
All Our Yesterdays (1930) **H.M. Tomlinson** (1873)
All Over (1971) **Edward Albee** (1928)
All Over the Place (1948) **Compton Mackenzie** (1883)
All Ovids Elegies (1599) **Christopher Marlowe** (1564–93) (tr.) [with Sir John Davies]
All Passion Spent (1931) **Vita Sackville-West** (1892)
All Points North (1998) **Simon Armitage** (1963)
All Quiet on the Western Front [*Im Westen nichts Neues*] (1929) **'Erich Maria Remarque' [Erich Paul Remark]** (1898)
All Religions Are One [1788?] **William Blake** (1757)
All Roads Lead to Calvary (1919) **Jerome K. Jerome** (1859)
All Said and Done [*Tout compte fait*] (1972) **Simone de Beauvoir** (1908)
All Shot Up (1960) **Chester Himes** (1909)
All Sorts and Conditions of Men (1882) **Sir Walter Besant** (1836)
All Souls' Night (1933) **Sir Hugh Walpole** (1884)
All Strange Away [limited edn 1976] (1979) **Samuel Beckett** (1906)
All Summer Long (1953) **Robert W. Anderson** (1917)
All That Fall (1957) **Samuel Beckett** (1906)
All That Glitters (1981) **Michael Anthony** (1932)
All That Remains (1992) **Patricia Cornwell** (1956)
All That Swagger (1936) **Miles Franklin** (1879)
All the Conspirators (1928) **Christopher Isherwood** (1904)
All the Days of My Life (1984) **Hilary Bailey** (1936)
All the King's Men (1982) **William Mayne** (1928)
All the King's Men (1946) **Robert Penn Warren** (1905)
All the Little Live Things (1967) **Wallace Stegner** (1909)
All the Pretty Horses (1992) **Cormac McCarthy** (1933)

All the Sad Young Men (1926) **F. Scott Fitzgerald** (1896)
All Things Bright and Beautiful (1974) **James Herriot** (1916)
All Things Considered (1908) **G.K. Chesterton** (1874)
All Things Nice (1969) **Rachel Billington** (1942)
All Things Wise and Wonderful (1977) **James Herriot** (1916)
All Visitors Ashore (1984) **C.K. Stead** (1932)
All Watched Over by Machines of Loving Grace (1967) **Richard Brautigan** (1935)
All What Jazz (1970) **Philip Larkin** (1922)
All You Need (1989) **Elaine Feinstein** (1930)
All You Who Sleep Tonight (1990) **Vikram Seth** (1952)
All You've Ever Wanted (1953) **Joan Aiken** (1924)
All's Lost by Lust (1633) **William Rowley** (1585?-1626)
Allan and the Ice-Gods (1927) **Sir H. Rider Haggard** (1856–1925)
Allan Quatermain (1887) **Sir H. Rider Haggard** (1856)
Allan's Wife (1889) **Sir H. Rider Haggard** (1856)
Allarme to England (1578) **Barnabe Rich** (1542)
Allegory of Love, The (1936) **C.S. Lewis** (1898)
Allegro Postillions (1983) **Jonathan Keates** (1946)
Allen Verbatim (1974) **Allen Ginsberg** (1926)
Aller Retour New York (1935) **Henry Miller** (1891)
Allerton and Dreux (1851) **Jean Ingelow** (1820)
Alley Sheridan (1858) **William Carleton** (1794)
Alleys of Eden, The (1981) **Robert Olen Butler** (1945)
Alligator Playground (1997) **Alan Sillitoe** (1928)
Alluring Problem, The (1986) **D.J. Enright** (1920)
Almanack of Hope (1944) **John Pudney** (1909)
Almayer's Folly (1895) **Joseph Conrad** (1857)
Almeyda (1796) **Sophia Lee** (1750)
Almost a Gentleman (1991) **John Osborne** (1929)
Almyna (1706) **Mary Delariviere Manley** (1663)
Alnilam (1987) **James Dickey** (1923)
Alnwick Castle (1827) **Fitz-Greene Halleck** (1790)
Alone (1980) **Beverley Farmer** (1941)
Alone of All Her Sex (1976) **Marina Warner** (1946)
Along the Road (1913) **A.C. Benson** (1862)
Along the Road (1925) **Aldous Huxley** (1894)
Along the Trail (1898) **Richard Hovey** (1864)
Alonzo (1773) **John Home** (1722)
Alpha List, The (1979) **Ted Allbeury** (1917)
Alphabet of Economics, An (1917) **A.R. Orage** (1873)
Alphabet Soup (1972) **Gavin Ewart** (1916)
Alphabetical Africa (1974) **Walter Abish** (1931)
Alphabetical Order (1975) **Michael Frayn** (1933)
Alphbeings and Other Seasyours (1976) **Earle Birney** (1904)
Altar Fire, The (1907) **A.C. Benson** (1862)
Altar Steps, The (1922) **Compton Mackenzie** (1883)
Alteration, The (1976) **Kingsley Amis** (1922)
Altered States (1996) **Anita Brookner** (1928)
Alternating Currents (1956) **Frederik Pohl** (1919)
Alternative Alcott (1985) **Elaine Showalter** (1941)
Alternative Society, The (1971) **Kenneth Rexroth** (1905)
Altiora Peto (1883) **Laurence Oliphant** (1829)
Alton Locke (1850) **Charles Kingsley** (1819)
Always Coming Home (1986) **Ursula K. Le Guin** (1929)
Always Outnumbered, Always Outgunned (1997) **Walter Mosley** (1952)
Always the Young Strangers (1953) **Carl Sandburg** (1878)
Always Young and Fair (1947) **Conrad Richter** (1890)
Alwyn (1780) **Thomas Holcroft** (1745)
Alyx (1976) **Joanna Russ** (1937)
Alzira (1736) **Aaron Hill** (1685)
Amadeus (1979) **Peter Shaffer** (1926)
Amadis of Gaul [from Vasco Lobeira] (1803) **Robert Southey** (1774) (tr.)
Amadis of Gaule [pt. i; from a French trn of Spanish original] (1590) **Anthony Munday** (1560) (tr.)
Amalgamemnon (1984) **Christine Brooke-Rose** (1926)
Amaranth (1934) **Edwin Arlington Robinson** (1869)
Amaryllis at the Fair (1887) **Richard Jefferies** (1848)
Amateur Cracksman, The (1899) **E.W. Hornung** (1866)
Amateur Gentleman, The (1913) **Jeffery Farnol** (1878)
Amateur Poacher, The (1879) **Richard Jefferies** (1848)
Amateurs (1976) **Donald Barthelme** (1931)
Amazing Grace (1959) **Studs Terkel** (1912)
Amazing Marriage, The (1895) **George Meredith** (1828)
Ambarvalia (1849) **A.H. Clough** (1819)
Ambassador, The (1965) **Morris West** (1916)
Ambassador's Wife, The (1842) **Mrs C.F. Gore** (1799)
Ambassadors, The (1903) **Henry James** (1843)
Ambition (1929) **W.H. Davies** (1871)
Ambitious Slave, The (1694) **Elkanah Settle** (1648)
Ambitious Statesman, The (1679) **John Crowne** (d. 1703)
Ambitious Step-Mother, The (1700) **Nicholas Rowe** (1674)
Amboyna (1673) **John Dryden** (1631)
Amédée (1954) **Eugène Ionesco** (1909)
Amelia (1732) **Henry Carey** (1687?)
Amelia (1751) **Henry Fielding** (1707)
Amen Corner, The (1955) **James Baldwin** (1924)
Amendments of Mr Collier's False and Imperfect Citations (1698) **William Congreve** (1670)
Amends for Ladies (1618) **Nathan Field** (1587)
Amenities of Literature (1841) **Isaac D'Israeli** (1766)
Amenophis (1892) **Francis Turner Palgrave** (1824)
America (1793) **William Blake** (1757)
America [*Amerika*] (1927) **Franz Kafka** (1883–1924)
America and Cosmic Man (1948) **Wyndham Lewis** (1882)
America Hispaña (1931) **Waldo Frank** (1889)
America is Worth Saving (1941) **Theodore Dreiser** (1871)
America Was Promises (1939) **Archibald MacLeish** (1892)
American Appetites (1989) **Joyce Carol Oates** (1938)
American Blues (1939) **'Tennessee' [Thomas Lanier] Williams** (1911)
American Buffalo (1975) **David Mamet** (1947)

American Capitalism (1952) **J.K. Galbraith** (1908)
American Cause, The (1941) **Archibald MacLeish** (1892)
American Citizen (1944) **Kay Boyle** (1903)
American Claimant, The (1892) **'Mark Twain' [Samuel Langhorne Clemens]** (1835)
American Clock, The (1980) **Arthur Miller** (1915)
American Commonwealth, The (1888) **James Bryce** (1838)
American Conflict, The (1864–6) **Horace Greeley** (1811)
American Dad (1981) **Tama Janowitz** (1957)
American Days (1979) **Stephen Poliakoff** (1952)
American Dream, An (1965) **Norman Mailer** (1923)
American Dream Girl, An (1950) **James T. Farrell** (1904)
American Dream, The (1960) **Edward Albee** (1928)
American Dreams: Lost and Found (1980) **Studs Terkel** (1912)
American Earth (1931) **Erskine Caldwell** (1903)
American Earthquake, The (1958) **Edmund Wilson** (1895)
American Ghosts and Old World Wonders (1993) **Angela Carter** (1940–92)
American Gothic (1974) **Robert Bloch** (1917)
American Hunger (1977) **Richard Wright** (1908–60)
American Jitters, The (1932) **Edmund Wilson** (1895)
American Journey (1972) **Robert Gittings** (1911)
American Landscape (1938) **Elmer Rice** (1892)
American Language, The (1919) **H.L. Mencken** (1880)
American Notes (1842) **Charles Dickens** (1812)
American Outpost (1932) **Upton Sinclair** (1878)
American Poems (1923) **J.C. Squire** (1884)
American Prisoner, The (1904) **Eden Phillpotts** (1862)
American Psycho (1991) **Bret Easton Ellis** (1964)
American Revolution, The (1899) **Sir George Otto Trevelyan** (1838)
American Scene, The (1907) **Henry James** (1843)
American Scenes (1966) **Charles Tomlinson** (1927)
American Scholar, The (1837) **Ralph Waldo Emerson** (1803)
American Senator, The (1877) **Anthony Trollope** (1815)
American Shore, The (1978) **Samuel R. Delany** (1942)
American Songbag, The (1927) **Carl Sandburg** (1878) (ed.)
American Story, The (1944) **Archibald MacLeish** (1892)
American Tabloid (1995) **James Ellroy** (1948)
American, The (1946) **Howard Fast** (1914)
American, The (1877) **Henry James** (1843)
American Tragedy, An (1925) **Theodore Dreiser** (1871)
American Village, The (1772) **Philip Freneau** (1752)
American Visitor, An (1933) **Joyce Cary** (1888)
American Wives, and Others (1904) **Jerome.K. Jerome** (1859)
Americana (1971) **Don Delillo** (1936)
Amethyst (1891) **C[hristabel] R[ose] Coleridge** (1843)
Aminta (1573) **Torquato Tasso** (1544)
Amintas (1698) **John Oldmixon** (1673)
Amitiés du prince ['The Prince's Friendships'] (1924) **'Saint-John Perse' [Alexis Saint-Léger Léger]** (1887)
Among My Books [1st ser.; 2nd ser., 1876] (1870) **James Russell Lowell** (1819)
Among People (1915) **Maxim Gorky** (1868)
Among the Dahlias (1957) **William Sansom** (1912)
Among the Hills (1869) **John Greenleaf Whittier** (1807)
Among the Lost People (1934) **Conrad Potter Aiken** (1889)
Among the Russians (1983) **Colin Thubron** (1939)
Amongst Thistles and Thorns (1965) **Austin Clarke** (1932)
Amongst Women (1990) **John McGahern** (1934)
Amores (1916) **D.H. Lawrence** (1885)
Amores Britannici (1703) **John Oldmixon** (1673)
Amoretti and Epithalamion (1595) **Edmund Spenser** (1552?)
Amoris Victima (1897) **Arthur Symons** (1865)
Amorous Bigotte; with the Second Part of Tegue o Divelly, The (1689) **Thomas Shadwell** (1642?)
Amorous Cannibal, The (1985) **Chris Wallace-Crabbe** (1934)
Amorous Prince, The (1671) **Aphra Behn** (1640?)
Amour, la poésie, L' (1929) **'Paul Éluard' [Eugène Grindel]** (1895)
Amours ['Love Poems'] (1552) **Pierre de Ronsard** (1524)
Amours [conclusion] (1556) **Pierre de Ronsard** (1524)
Amours de Voyage (1858) **A.H. Clough** (1819)
Amours of Alcippus and Leucippe, The (1704) **Mary Davys** (1674)
Amours of Philander and Sylvia, The [*Love-letters Between a Nobleman and his Sister* pt. iii] (1687) **Aphra Behn** (1640?)
Amphitryon (1668) **'Molière' [Jean-Baptiste Poquelin]** (1622)
Amphitryon 38 (1929) **Jean Giraudoux** (1882)
Amphityron (1690) **John Dryden** (1631)
Ample Proposition, The (1966) **John Lehmann** (1907)
Amsterdam (1998) **Ian McEwan** (1948)
Amurath to Amurath (1911) **Gertrude Bell** (1868)
Amusement (1790) **Henry James Pye** (1745)
Amy's View (1997) **David Hare** (1947)
Amymone (1848) **E. Lynn Linton** (1822)
Amyntas [from Tasso] (1820) **Leigh Hunt** (1784) (tr.)
Amyntor and Theodora (1747) **David Mallet** (1705?)
Anabasis [*Anabase*] (1924) **'Saint-John Perse' [Alexis Saint-Léger Léger]** (1887)
Analects of Confucius, The (1938) **Arthur Waley** (1889) (tr.)
Analogy of Religion, The (1736) **Joseph Butler** (1692)
Analysis of Matter, The (1927) **Bertrand Russell** (1872)
Analysis of Mind, The (1921) **Bertrand Russell** (1872)
Analysis of the Influence of Natural Religion on the Temporal Happiness of Mankind [as 'Philip Beauchamp'] (1822) **George Grote** (1794)

Analysis of the Laws of England, An (1756) **Sir William Blackstone** (1723)
Anarchy and Order (1954) **Sir Herbert Read** (1893)
Anarchy of a Limited or Mixed Monarchy, The (1648) **Sir Robert Filmer** (1588?)
Anarchy of the Ranters and Other Libertines, The (1676) **Robert Barclay** (1648)
Anathemata, The (1952) **David Jones** (1895)
Anathomie of Sinne, The (1603) **Joseph Hall** (1574) [attrib.]
Anatomie of Absurditie, The (1589) **Thomas Nashe** (1567)
Anatomie of Abuses, The (1583) **Philip Stubbs** (fl. 1581)
Anatomist, The (1931) **'James Bridie' [Osborne Henry Mavor]** (1888)
Anatomist, The (1696) **Edward Ravenscroft** (1644)
Anatomy Lesson, The (1957) **Evan S. Connell, Jr** (1924)
Anatomy Lesson, The (1984) **Philip Roth** (1933)
Anatomy of an Equivalent, The (1688) **Sir George Savile, Marquis of Halifax** (1633)
Anatomy of Criticism (1957) **Northrop Frye** (1912)
Anatomy of Divorce, The (1988) **George MacBeth** (1932)
Anatomy of Frustration, The (1936) **H.G. Wells** (1866)
Anatomy of Melancholy, The (1621) **Robert Burton** (1577)
Anatomy of Nonsense, The (1943) **Yvor Winters** (1900)
Anatomy of Play, The (1651) **Sir John Denham** (1615)
Anatomy of Power, The (1983) **J.K. Galbraith** (1908)
Anatomy of the World, An (1611) **John Donne** (1572)
Anatomy of Tobacco, The (1884) **Arthur Machen** (1863)
Ancestral Footstep, The (1883) **Nathaniel Hawthorne** (1804–64)
Ancestral Vices (1980) **Tom Sharpe** (1928)
Anchises (1976) **C.H. Sisson** (1914)
Ancient Allan, The (1920) **Sir H. Rider Haggard** (1856)
Ancient Cures, Charms and Usages of Ireland (1890) **Jane Francisca, Lady Wilde** (1826)
Ancient Evenings (1983) **Norman Mailer** (1923)
Ancient Law, The (1908) **Ellen Glasgow** (1874)
Ancient Legends, Mystic Charms and Superstitions of Ireland (1887) **Jane Francisca, Lady Wilde** (1826)
Ancient Lights and Certain New Reflections (1911) **Ford Madox Ford** (1873)
Ancient Roman Empire and the British Empire in India, The (1914) **James Bryce** (1838)
Ancient Scottish Poems (1770) **Sir David Dalrymple, Lord Hailes** (1726) (ed.)
Ancient Sorceries (1927) **Algernon Blackwood** (1869)
Ancient Wisdom, The (1897) **Annie Besant** (1847)
& (1925) **E.E. cummings** (1894)
And Another Thing . . . (1946) **Howard Spring** (1889)
And Be a Villain [UK: *More Deaths Than One*] (1948) **Rex Stout** (1886)
And Berry Came Too (1936) **'Dornford Yates' [Cecil William Mercer]** (1885)
And Even Now (1920) **Max Beerbohm** (1872)
And in the Human Heart (1940) **Conrad Potter Aiken** (1889)
And Never Said a Word [*Und sagte kein einziges Wort*] (1953) **Heinrich Böll** (1917)
And Now Good-bye (1931) **James Hilton** (1900)
And On the Eighth Day (1964) **'Ellery Queen' [Frederic Dannay** (1905) and **Manfred B. Lee**] (1905)
And Quiet Flows the Don (1928–40) **Mikhail Sholokhov** (1905)
And Shall Trelawney Die? (1897) **Joseph Hocking** (1860)
And Sometimes It Happens (1972) **Brian Patten** (1946)
And Still I Rise (1978) **Maya Angelou** (1928)
And What if the Pretender Should Come? (1713) **Daniel Defoe** (1660)
Anderby Wold (1923) **Winifred Holtby** (1898)
André Cornélis (1887) **Paul Bourget** (1852)
Andrea of Hungary, and Giovanna of Naples (1839) **Walter Savage Landor** (1775)
Androcles and the Lion, Overruled, Pygmalion (1916) **Bernard Shaw** (1856)
Androgyne, Mon Amour (1977) **'Tennessee' [Thomas Lanier] Williams** (1911)
Andromache (*c.* 426) **Euripides** (480 BC)
Andromache [Andromaque] (1667) **Jean Racine** (1639)
Andromache [from Racine] (1982) **Richard Wilbur** (1921) (tr.)
Andromeda (1858) **Charles Kingsley** (1819)
Andromeda Strain, The (1969) **Michael Crichton** (1942)
Andromède (1650) **Pierre Corneille** (1606)
Andronicus (1646) **Thomas Fuller** (1608)
Andronicus Commenius (1664) **John Wilson** (1627?)
Anecdotes of Destiny (1958) **'Isak Dinesen' [Karen Blixen]** (1885)
Anecdotes of Painting in England (1762–3) **Horace Walpole** (1717) (ed.)
Anecdotes of the Delborough Family (1792) **Susannah Gunning** (1740)
Anecdotes of the Late Samuel Johnson (1786) **Hester Lynch Piozzi** (1741)
Anecdotes of the Turf, the Chase, the Ring and the Stage (1827) **Pierce Egan [the elder]** (1772)
Ange Pitou (1853) **Alexandre Dumas ['père']** (1802)
Angel (1957) **Elizabeth Taylor** (1912)
Angel and the Author, The (1908) **Jerome. K. Jerome** (1859)
Angel at My Table, An (1984) **Janet Frame** (1924)
Angel at the Gate, The (1982) **Wilson Harris** (1921)
Angel Fire (1973) **Joyce Carol Oates** (1938)
Angel in the House, The: The Betrothal (1854) **Coventry Patmore** (1823)
Angel of Pain, The (1906) **E.F. Benson** (1867)

Angel of Pain, The (1991) **Brian M. Stableford** (1948)
Angel of Pity, The (1935) **Francis Stuart** (1902)
Angel of the World, The (1820) **George Croly** (1780)
Angel Pavement (1930) **J.B. Priestley** (1894)
Angel That Troubled the Waters, The (1928) **Thornton Wilder** (1897)
Angel World, The (1850) **Philip James Bailey** (1816)
Angela's Ashes (1996) **Frank McCourt** (1930)
Angelica [written 1588] (1602) **Lope de Vega** (1562)
Angelica's Grotto (1999) **Russell Hoban** (1925)
Angelina (1796) **Mary Robinson** (1758)
Angelo (1835) **Victor Hugo** (1802)
Angelo (1856) **Geraldine Jewsbury** (1812)
Angels and Circles (1974) **Geoffrey Grigson** (1905)
Angels and Insects (1992) **A.S. Byatt** (1936)
Angels and Ministers (1921) **Laurence Housman** (1865)
Angels at the Ritz (1975) **'William Trevor' [William Trevor Cox]** (1928)
Angels Falling (1969) **Janice Elliott** (1931)
Angels of Mons, The [etc] (1915) **Arthur Machen** (1863)
Angels' Revolt, The [*La Révolte des anges*] (1914) **'Anatole France' [Jacques-Anatole-François Thibault]** (1844)
Angels' Wings (1898) **Edward Carpenter** (1844)
Anges noirs, Les (1936) **François Mauriac** (1885)
Angle of Repose (1971) **Wallace Stegner** (1909)
Angler, The (1804) **William-Henry Ireland** (1777)
Angler's Moon (1965) **Leo Walmsley** (1892)
Anglican Essays (1983) **C.H. Sisson** (1914)
Anglo-Irish of the Nineteenth Century, The (1828) **John Banim** (1798)
Anglo-Saxon Attitudes (1956) **Angus Wilson** (1913)
Anglo-Saxon Primer, An (1882) **Henry Sweet** (1845)
Anglo-Saxon Reader in Prose and Verse, An (1876) **Henry Sweet** (1845)
Angry Hills, The (1955) **Leon Uris** (1924)
Angry Mountain, The (1950) **'Hammond Innes' [Ralph Hammond-Innes]** (1913)
Angry Ones, The (1960) **John Williams** (1925)
Angry Summer, The (1943) **Idris Davies** (1905)
Anil's Ghost (1999) **Michael Ondaatje** (1943)
Animadversions Upon the Remonstrants Defence (1641) **John Milton** (1608)
Animal Farm (1945) **George Orwell** (1903)
Animal Heroes (1905) **Ernest Thompson Seton** (1860)
Animals in That Country, The (1968) **Margaret Atwood** (1939)
Animula (1929) **T.S. Eliot** (1888)
Ankle Deep (1933) **Angela Thirkell** (1890)
Ankor Wat (1968) **Allen Ginsberg** (1926)
Ann at Highwood Hall (1964) **Robert Graves** (1895)
Ann Lee's (1926) **Elizabeth Bowen** (1899)
Ann Severn and the Fieldings (1922) **May Sinclair** (1863)
Ann Veronica (1909) **H.G. Wells** (1866)
Ann Vickers (1933) **Sinclair Lewis** (1885)
Anna Apparent (1972) **Nina Bawden** (1925)
Anna Karenina (1874–6) **Leo Tolstoy** (1828)
Anna Karenina, and Other Essays (1967) **F.R. Leavis** (1895)
Anna Livia Plurabelle (1928) **James Joyce** (1882)
Anna of the Five Towns (1902) **Arnold Bennett** (1867)
Anna of the Underworld (1916) **George R. Sims** (1847)
Anna Papers, The (1989) **Ellen Gilchrist** (1935)
Anna St Ives (1792) **Thomas Holcroft** (1745)
Annales of England Untill 1592, The (1592) **John Stow** (1525)
Annals of a Quiet Neighbourhood (1867) **George MacDonald** (1824)
Annals of an Eventful Life (1870) **Sir George Webbe Dasent** (1817)
Annals of Chile, The (1994) **Paul Muldoon** (1951)
Annals of Innocence and Experience (1940) **Sir Herbert Read** (1893)
Annals of Scotland [vol. i; vol. ii, 1779] (1776) **Sir David Dalrymple, Lord Hailes** (1726)
Annals of the Five Senses (1923) **'Hugh MacDiarmid' [Christopher Murray Grieve]** (1892)
Annals of the Parish (1821) **John Galt** (1779)
Annals of the Reformation and Establishment of Religion (1709) **John Strype** (1643)
Annals of the World, The (1658) **James Ussher** (1581)
Annan Water (1883) **Robert Williams Buchanan** (1841)
Anne Boleyn (1826) **Henry Hart Milman** (1791)
Anne Hereford (1868) **Mrs Henry Wood** (1814)
Anne Mauleverer (1899) **'Iota' [Kathleen Mannington Caffyn]** (1855?)
Anne of Avonlea (1909) **L.M. Montgomery** (1874)
Anne of Geierstein (1829) **Sir Walter Scott** (1771)
Anne of Green Gables (1908) **L.M. Montgomery** (1874)
Anne of Ingleside (1939) **L.M. Montgomery** (1874)
Anne of the Island (1915) **L.M. Montgomery** (1874)
Anne of the Thousand Days (1948) **Maxwell Anderson** (1888)
Anne of Windy Poplars (1936) **L.M. Montgomery** (1874)
Anne's House of Dreams (1917) **L.M. Montgomery** (1874)
Année terrible, L' ['The Terrible Year'] (1872) **Victor Hugo** (1802–85)
Annette (1973) **Erskine Caldwell** (1903)
Annette and Bennett (1922) **Gilbert Cannan** (1884)
Annie Kilburn (1889) **William Dean Howells** (1837)
Annie Magdalene (1985) **Barbara Hanrahan** (1939)
Anniversary and Vigil (1971) **Ian Hamilton** (1938)
Anno Domini MCMXXI (1921) **'Anna Akhmatova' [Anna Andreevna Gorenko]** (1889)
Anno Domino (1983) **George Barker** (1913)
Anno Forty-Two (1987) **Tony Harrison** (1937)
Annual Miscellany for the Year 1694 [fourth part of Miscellany Poems] (1694) **John Dryden** (1631) and others
Annunciation, The (1983) **Ellen Gilchrist** (1935)
Annunciations (1989) **Charles Tomlinson** (1927)
Annus Mirabilis (1667) **John Dryden** (1631)
Anonymity (1925) **E.M. Forster** (1879)

Another Country (1962) **James Baldwin** (1924)
Another Country (1981) **Julian Mitchell** (1935)
Another Family Christmas (1998) **Clare Boylan** (1948)
Another Full Moon (1976) **Ruth Fainlight** (1931)
Another Future of Poetry (1926) **Robert Graves** (1895)
Another Part of the Forest (1946) **Lillian Hellman** (1907)
Another Part of the Wood (1969) **Beryl Bainbridge** (1934)
Another Roadside Attraction (1971) **Tom Robbins** (1936)
Another September (1958) **Thomas Kinsella** (1928)
Another Time (1940) **W.H. Auden** (1907)
Another Time, Another Place (1983) **Jessie Kesson** (1916)
Another World (1998) **Pat Barker** (1943)
Another Year (1948) **R.C. Sherriff** (1896)
Anowa (1970) **Ama Ata Aidoo** (1942)
Answer From Limbo, An (1963) **Brian Moore** (1921)
Answer to the Arguments of the Jews, An (1661) **George Fox** (1624)
Answere unto Sir Thomas Mores Dialogue, An (1531) **William Tyndale** (1494?)
Answered Prayers (1986) **Truman Capote** (1924–1984)
Answering Glory, The (1932) **R.C. Hutchinson** (1907)
Ant and the Nightingale, The (1604) **Thomas Middleton** (1580)
Ant Colony, The (1991) **Francis King** (1923)
Antarctica (1985) **Derek Mahon** (1941)
Ante-Room, The (1934) **Kate O'Brien** (1897)
Anteros (1873) **G.A. Lawrence** (1827)
Anthem (1938) **Ayn Rand** (1905)
Anthills of the Savannah (1987) **Chinua Achebe** (1930)
Anthony Adverse (1933) **Hervey Allen** (1889)
Anthony John (1923) **Jerome. K. Jerome** (1859)
Anthony Trollope (1992) **Victoria Glendinning** (1937)
Anthroposophia Theomagica [as 'Eugenius Philalethes'] (1650) **Thomas Vaughan** (1622)
Anti-Death League, The (1966) **Kingsley Amis** (1922)
Anti-Thelyphthora (1781) **William Cowper** (1731)
Antic Hay (1923) **Aldous Huxley** (1894)
Antidote Against Atheisme, An (1653) **Henry More** (1614)
Antidotes (1991) **C.H. Sisson** (1914)
Antient and Modern Italy Compared [*Liberty* pt. i] (1735) **James Thomson** (1700)
Antigone (441 BC) **Sophocles** (*c*. 496 BC)
Antigone (1944) **Jean Anouilh** (1910)
Antiphon, The (1958) **Djuna Barnes** (1892)
Antipodes (1985) **David Malouf** (1934)
Antipodes, The (1640) **Richard Brome** (1590?)
Antiquary, The (1641) **Shackerley Marmion** (1603–1639)
Antiquary, The (1816) **Sir Walter Scott** (1771)
Antiquitates Christianae (1675) **Jeremy Taylor** (1613–1667)
Antiquities of Berkshire, The (1719) **Elias Ashmole** (1617–1692)
Antiquities of England and Wales, The (1773–6) **Francis Grose** (1731)
Antiquities of Scotland, The [inc. Burns's 'Tam O'Shanter'] (1789–91) **Francis Grose** (1731?)
Antiquities of the Anglo-Saxon Church, The (1806) **John Lingard** (1771)
Antiquities of Warwickshire, The (1656) **Sir William Dugdale** (1605)
Antonina (1850) **Wilkie Collins** (1824)
Antonio (1800) **William Godwin** (1756)
Antonio and Mellida: The First Part (1602) **John Marston** (1576)
Antonio's Revenge: The Second Part (1602) **John Marston** (1576)
Antony (1831) **Alexandre Dumas ['père']** (1802)
Antony (1997) **Allan Massie** (1938)
Antony and Cleopatra (1677) **Sir Charles Sedley** (1639)
Antony and Octavius (1856) **Walter Savage Landor** (1775)
Anvil, The (1916) **Laurence Binyon** (1869)
Anxiety of Influence, The (1973) **Harold Bloom** (1930)
Any Excuse for a Party (1991) **A.L. Barker** (1918)
Any Friend of Nicholas Nickleby's is a Friend of Mine (1968) **Ray Bradbury** (1920)
Any Old Iron (1989) **'Anthony Burgess' [John Anthony Burgess Wilson]** (1917)
Any Woman's Blues (1994) **Erica Jong** (1942)
Anyhow Stories (1882) **Lucy [Mrs W.K.] Clifford** (1853)
Anything for Billy (1988) **Larry McMurty** (1936)
Anzac Sonata, The (1986) **Jon Stallworthy** (1935)
Apartheid and the Archbishop (1973) **Alan Paton** (1903)
Ape and Essence (1949) **Aldous Huxley** (1894)
Apeman Cometh, The (1975) **Adrian Mitchell** (1932)
Apes and Angels (1928) **J.B. Priestley** (1894)
Apes of God, The (1930) **Wyndham Lewis** (1882)
Aphorisms Political (1659) **James Harrington** (1611)
Aphrodite (1998) **Isabel Allende** (1942)
Aphrodite in Aulis (1930) **George Moore** (1852)
Apollo Café (1990) **Stephen Gray** (1941)
Apologia (1784) **John Newton** (1725)
Apologia Pro Vita Sua (1864) **J.H. Newman** (1801)
Apologie for the Royal Party, An (1659) **John Evelyn** (1620)
Apologies to the Iroquois (1960) **Edmund Wilson** (1895)
Apology for a Hero (1950) **A.L. Barker** (1918)
Apology for Actors, An (1612) **Thomas Heywood** (1574?)
Apology for the Life of Mr Colley Cibber, An (1740) **Colley Cibber** (1671)
Apology for the Life of Mrs Shamela Andrews, An (1741) **Henry Fielding** (1707)
Apology for the Revival of Christian Architecture in England, An (1843) **A.W.N. Pugin** (1812)
Apology for the True Christian Divinity, An (1678) **Robert Barclay** (1648)
Apology for the True Christian Divinity Vindicated (1679) **Robert Barclay** (1648)

Apology, The (1761) **Charles Churchill** (1731)
Apologye of Syr Thomas More, The (1533) **Sir Thomas More** (1478)
Apophthegmatic (1999) **Peter Reading** (1946)
Apophthegms (1625) **Sir Francis Bacon** (1561)
Apopthegmes [from Erasmus] (1542) **Nicholas Udall** (1505?) (tr.)
Apostate (1926) **Forrest Reid** (1875)
Apostate, The (1817) **Richard Lalor Sheil** (1791)
Apostle, The (1911) **George Moore** (1852)
Apostolic Age, The (1892) **Joseph Barber Lightfoot** (1828)
Apostolic Fathers, The [pt. i, 1885] (1869) **Joseph Barber Lightfoot** (1828)
Apparition (1971) **A. Alvarez** (1929) (ed.)
Appassionata (1996) **Jilly Cooper** (1937)
Appeal from the New to the Old Whigs, An (1791) **Edmund Burke** (1729)
Appeal of Injured Innocence, The (1659) **Thomas Fuller** (1608)
Appearance and Reality (1893) **F.H. Bradley** (1846)
Appearance is Against Them (1785) **Elizabeth Inchbald** (1753)
Appel au soldat, L' (1900) **Maurice Barrès** (1862)
Appius and Virginia (1709) **John Dennis** (1657)
Appius and Virginia (1654) **John Webster** (1580?-1635?)
Apple Broadcast, The (1981) **Peter Redgrove** (1932)
Apple Cart, The (1929) **Bernard Shaw** (1856)
Apple Fall, The (1983) **Helen Dunmore** (1952)
Apple of the Eye, The (1924) **Glenway Wescott** (1901)
Apple, The (1961) **Jack Gelber** (1932)
Apple Tree, The [US: *Kiss Me Again, Stranger*] (1952) **Daphne du Maurier** (1907)
Appleby at Allington [as 'Michael Innes'] (1968) **J.I.M. Stewart** (1906)
Appleby on Ararat [as 'Michael Innes'] (1941) **J.I.M. Stewart** (1906)
Appleby Plays Chicken [as 'Michael Innes'. US: Death on a Quiet Day] (1956) **J.I.M. Stewart** (1906)
Appleby Talking [as 'Michael Innes'] (1954) **J.I.M. Stewart** (1906)
Appleby Talks Again [as 'Michael Innes'] (1956) **J.I.M. Stewart** (1906)
Appleby's End [as 'Michael Innes'] (1945) **J.I.M. Stewart** (1906)
Apples Be Ripe (1930) **Llewelyn Powys** (1884)
Appointment in Samarra (1934) **John O'Hara** (1905)
Appointment with Death (1938) **Agatha Christie** (1890)
Appreciations (1889) **Walter Pater** (1839)
Apprenticeship of Duddy Kravitz, The (1959) **Mordecai Richler** (1931)
Approach to 'Hamlet', An (1960) **L.C. Knights** (1906)
Approach to Murano (1992) **Jack Clemo** (1916)
'Apres-midi d'un faune, L'' ['The Afternoon of a Faun'] (1876) **Stéphane Mallarmé** (1842)
April Galleons (1987) **John Ashbery** (1927)
April Hopes (1888) **William Dean Howells** (1837)
April Morning (1961) **Howard Fast** (1914)
April Twilights (1903) **Willa Cather** (1873)
Apropos of Dolores (1938) **H.G. Wells** (1866)
Aquarium (1923) **Sir Harold Acton** (1904)
Aquarius (1982) **Jan Mark** (1943)
Arabella Stuart (1844) **G.P.R. James** (1799)
Arabella the Awful (1918) **Berta Ruck** (1878)
Arabesques (1835) **Nikolai Vasilevich Gogol** (1809)
Arabia, Egypt, India (1879) **Lady Isabel Burton** (1831)
Arabia Felix [foreword by T.E. Lawrence] (1932) **Bertram Thomas** (1892)
Arabia Infelix (1929) **Aldous Huxley** (1894)
Arabia Through the Looking-Glass (1979) **Jonathan Raban** (1942)
Arabian Nights' Entertainments, The (1885) **Sir Richard Burton** (1821) (tr.)
Arabian Nights Murder, The (1936) **John Dickson Carr** (1906)
Arabian Sands (1959) **Wilfred Thesiger** (1910)
Aran Islands, The (1907) **J.M. Synge** (1871)
Ararat (1983) **D.M. Thomas** (1935)
Aratra Pentelici (1872) **John Ruskin** (1819)
Arawata Bill (1953) **Denis Glover** (1912)
Araygnment of Paris, The (1584) **George Peele** (1556)
Arbasto (1584) **Robert Greene** (1558)
Arbiter, The (1901) **Mrs Hugh Bell** (1851)
Arbor of Amitie, The (1568) **Thomas Howell** (fl. 1568)
Arbour of Amorous Devises, The (1597) **Nicholas Breton** (1545?)
Arcadia (1598) **Lope de Vega** (1562)
Arcadia, The (1640) **James Shirley** (1596)
Arcadia (1979) **Christopher Reid** (1949)
Arcadia (1992) **Jim Crace** (1946)
Arcadia (1993) **Tom Stoppard** (1937)
Arcadia, One Mile (1998) **Dannie Abse** (1923)
Arcadian Adventures with the Idle Rich (1914) **Stephen Leacock** (1869)
Arcadian Rhetorike, The (1588) **Abraham Fraunce** (?1558–1592/3)
Arcady and Other Places (1966) **Vincent Buckley** (1925)
Arch of Triumph [*Arc de Triomphe*] (1946) **'Erich Maria Remarque' [Erich Paul Remark]** (1898)
Archaic Figure (1987) **Amy Clampitt** (1920)
Archaioplutos [from French] (1592) **Anthony Munday** (1560) (tr.)
Archarnians, The (425 BC) **Aristophanes** (*c.* 445–386 BC)
Archbishop Laud (1940) **Hugh Trevor-Roper** (1914)
Archetypal Patterns in Poetry (1934) **Maud Bodkin** (1875)
Archibald Malmaison (1884) **Julian Hawthorne** (1846)
Archimedes and the Seagle (1984) **David Ireland** (1927)
Arctic Summer (1980) **E.M. Forster** (1879–1970)
Ardath (1889) **Marie Corelli** (1855)
Ardèle (1948) **Jean Anouilh** (1910)
Ardours and Endurances (1917) **Robert Nichols** (1893)
Are You Listening, Rabbi Löw (1987) **J.P. Donleavy** (1926)

Are You There, God? It's Me, Margaret (1970) **Judy Blume** (1938)
Area of Darkness, An (1964) **V.S. Naipaul** (1932)
Aren't We All? (1923) **'Frederick Lonsdale' [Lionel Frederick Leonard]** (1881)
Areopagitica (1644) **John Milton** (1608)
Arethusa, The (1837) **Captain Chamier** (1796)
Arfive (1971) **A.B. Guthrie** (1901)
Argalus and Parthenia (1629) **Francis Quarles** (1592)
Argenis [Latin; tr. into English 1625] (1621) **John Barclay** (1582)
Argonaut and Juggernaut (1919) **Sir Osbert Sitwell** (1892)
Argument of Kings (1987) **Vernon Scannell** (1922)
Ariadne (1877) **'Ouida'** (1839–1908)
Ariadne auf Naxos ['Ariadne on Naxos'; music by Richard Strauss] (1912) **Hugo von Hofmannsthal** (1874)
Arians of the Fourth Century, The (1833) **J.H. Newman** (1801)
Arias From a Love Opera (1969) **Robert Conquest** (1917)
Ariel (1965) **Sylvia Plath** (1932–63)
Arilla Sun Down (1976) **Virginia Hamilton** (1936)
Aristippus (1630) **Thomas Randolph** (1605)
Aristocracy (1892) **Bronson Howard** (1842)
Aristocrat, The (1799) **Henry James Pye** (1745)
Aristotle (1864) **G.H. Lewes** (1817)
Arithmetica Universalis (1707) **Isaac Newton** (1642)
Arizona (1899) **Augustus Thomas** (1857)
The Arizona Game (1996) **Georgina Hammick** (1939)
Ark, The (1994) **Peter Scupham** (1933)
Arkansas Testament, The (1987) **Derek Walcott** (1930)
Armadale (1866) **Wilkie Collins** (1824)
Armadillo (1998) **William Boyd** (1952)
Armageddon (1915) **Stephen Phillips** (1864)
Armageddon (1964) **Leon Uris** (1924)
Armageddon (1987) **Gore Vidal** (1925)
Armance (1827) **'Stendhal' [Henri Marie Beyle]** (1783)
Armenia (1854) **Robert Curzon** (1810)
Armies of the Night, The (1968) **Norman Mailer** (1923)
Arminell (1890) **S. Baring-Gould** (1834)
Armorel of Lyonesse (1890) **Sir Walter Besant** (1836)
Armour for Aphrodite (1929) **T. Sturge Moore** (1870)
Armour Wherein He Trusted (1929) **Mary Webb** (1881)
Armourer's House, The (1951) **Rosemary Sutcliff** (1920)
Arms and the Women (2000) **Reginald Hill** (1936)
Armstrong's Last Goodnight (1964) **John Arden** (1930)
Army Doctor's Romance, An (1894) **Grant Allen** (1848)
Around Cinemas (1946) **James Evershed Agate** (1877)
Around the Mountain (1967) **Hugh Hood** (1928)
Around the World in Eighty Days [*Le Tour du monde en quatre-vingts jours*] (1873) **Jules Verne** (1828)
Arragh na-Pogue (1864) **Dion Boucicault** (1820?)
Arraignment of Popery, The (1667) **George Fox** (1624)
Arras of Youth (1949) **Oliver Onions** (1873)
Arrest, The [*L'Arrestation*] (1974) **Jean Anouilh** (1910)
Arrival and Departure (1943) **Arthur Koestler** (1905)
Arrivants, The [cont. *Rites of Passage, Masks, Islands*] (1973) **Edward Brathwaite** (1930)
Arrivistes, The (1949) **Louis Simpson** (1923)
Arrogant History of White Ben, The (1939) **'Clemence Dane' [Winifred Ashton]** (1888)
Arrow in the Blue (1952) **Arthur Koestler** (1905)
Arrow of God (1964) **Chinua Achebe** (1930)
Arrow of Gold, The (1919) **Joseph Conrad** (1857)
Arrowsmith (1925) **Sinclair Lewis** (1885)
Ars Poetica [*The Art of Poetry*] (8 BC?) **Horace** (*Quintus Horatius Flaccus*, 65–8 BC)
Arsène Guillot (1852) **Prosper Mérimée** (1803)
Art (1914) **Clive Bell** (1881)
Art and Ardor (1983) **Cynthia Ozick** (1928)
Art and Industry (1934) **Sir Herbert Read** (1893)
Art and Lies (1994) **Jeanette Winterson** (1959)
Art and Society (1937) **Sir Herbert Read** (1893)
Art and the Beauty of Earth (1898) **William Morris** (1834)
Art Chronicles (1975) **Frank O'Hara** (1926)
Art, Dialogue and Outrage (1988) **Wole Soyinka** (1934)
Art Maguire (1845) **William Carleton** (1794)
Art Now (1933) **Sir Herbert Read** (1893)
Art of Being Ruled, The (1926) **Wyndham Lewis** (1882)
Art of Creation, The (1904) **Edward Carpenter** (1844)
Art of Drawing with the Pen, The (1606) **Henry Peacham the younger** (1578?)
Art of England, The (1884) **John Ruskin** (1819)
Art of Fiction, The (1884) **Sir Walter Besant** (1836)
Art of Hunger, The (1991) **Paul Auster** (1947)
Art of Living in London, The (1642) **Henry Peacham the younger** (1578?)
Art of Living, The (1981) **John Gardner** (1933)
Art of Living, The (1959) **F.L. Lucas** (1894)
Art of Love, The (1975) **Kenneth Koch** (1925)
Art of Preserving Health, The (1744) **John Armstrong** (1709)
Art of Seeing, The (1943) **Aldous Huxley** (1894)
Art of War, The [*Dell'Arte della guerra*] (1521) **Niccolò Machiavelli** (1469)
Art romantique, L' ['Romantic Art'] (1869) **Charles Baudelaire** (1821–67)
Artamonov Business, The (1925) **Maxim Gorky** (1868)
Arte of Divine Meditation, The (1606) **Joseph Hall** (1574)
Arte of English Poesie, The (1589) **George Puttenham** (1530?)
Arte of Love, The [from Ovid] (1625) **Thomas Heywood** (1574?) (tr.)
Arte of Navigation, The (1561) **Richard Eden** (1521?) (tr.)
Artemis to Acteon (1909) **Edith Wharton** (1862)

Artemus Ward, His Book (1862) **'Artemus Ward' [Charles Farrar Browne]** (1834)
Arthur (1923) **Laurence Binyon** (1869)
Arthur Fitz-Albini (1798) **Sir Samuel Egerton Brydges** (1762)
Arthur McCann and All His Women (1970) **Leslie Thomas** (1931)
Arthur Mervyn (1799) **Charles Brockden Brown** (1771)
Arthur O'Leary (1844) **Charles Lever** (1806)
Arthur Rex (1978) **Thomas Berger** (1924)
Arthurian Torso (1948) **C.S. Lewis** (1898) [with Charles Williams]
Articulate Energy (1955) **Donald Davie** (1922)
Artificial Princess, The (1934) **Ronald Firbank** (1886–1926)
Artificios (1944) **Jorge Luis Borges** (1899)
Artillery Garden, The (1616) **Thomas Dekker** (1572?)
Artist Among the Missing (1949) **Olivia Manning** (1908)
Artist Descending a Staircase; and Where Are They Now? (1973) **Tom Stoppard** (1937)
Artist of the Floating World, An (1986) **Kazuo Ishiguro** (1954)
Artist's Proof, An (1864) **Alfred Austin** (1835)
Artists in Crime (1938) **Ngaio Marsh** (1899)
Artists in Uniform (1934) **Max Eastman** (1883)
Artless Tales (1793) **Anna Maria Porter** (1780)
Arts Under Socialism, The (1947) **J.B. Priestley** (1894)
Arundel (1789) **Richard Cumberland** (1732)
Arvat (1908) **L.H. Myers** (1881)
As a Man Thinks (1911) **Augustus Thomas** (1857)
As Ever (1977) **Allen Ginsberg** (1926)
As For Me and My House (1941) **Sinclair Ross** (1908)
As For the Woman [as 'Francis Iles'] (1939) **Anthony Berkeley Cox** (1893)
As From the Thirties (1983) **Roy Fuller** (1912)
As I Lay Dying (1930) **William Faulkner** (1897)
As I Walked Down New Grub Street (1981) **Walter Allen** (1911)
As I Walked Out One Midsummer Morning (1969) **Laurie Lee** (1914)
As I Was Going Down Sackville Street (1937) **Oliver St Gogarty** (1878)
As I Was Saying (1936) **G.K. Chesterton** (1874)
As If By Magic (1973) **Angus Wilson** (1913)
As Innocent as a Baby (1874) **W. Clark Russell** (1844)
As It Was (1979) **Bruce Beaver** (1928)
As It Was (1990) **Sybille Bedford** (1911)
As It Was Written [as 'Sydney Luska'] (1885) **Henry Harland** (1861)
As Time Goes By (1988) **Hilary Bailey** (1936)
As We Are (1932) **E.F. Benson** (1867)
As We Are and As We May Be (1903) **Sir Walter Besant** (1836)
As We Know (1979) **John Ashbery** (1927)
As We Were (1930) **E.F. Benson** (1867)
As We Were Saying (1891) **Charles Dudley Warner** (1829)
As You Desire Me [*Come Tu Mi Vuoi*] (1931) **Luigi Pirandello** (1867)
Ascent of F.6, The (1936) **W.H. Auden** (1907) [with Christopher Isherwood]
Ascent of Man, The (1889) **Mathilde Blind** (1841)
Ascent to Omai (1970) **Wilson Harris** (1921)
Ash on a Young Man's Sleeve (1954) **Dannie Abse** (1923)
Ash-Wednesday (1930) **T.S. Eliot** (1888)
Ashenden (1928) **Somerset Maugham** (1874)
Ashes (1890) **Hume Nisbet** (1849)
Ashes (1974) **David Rudkin** (1936)
Ashley (1897) **Mrs Henry Wood** (1814–87)
Ashtaroth (1867) **Adam Lindsay Gordon** (1833)
Asiatic Romance, An (1953) **C.H. Sisson** (1914)
'Ask Mamma' (1858) **R.S. Surtees** (1805)
Ask Me Tomorrow (1940) **James Gould Cozzens** (1903)
Ask Me Tomorrow (1962) **Stan Barstow** (1928)
Ask the Bloody Horse (1986) **Dannie Abse** (1923)
Ask Your Mama (1961) **Langston Hughes** (1902)
Asmodeus at Large (1833) **Edward Bulwer-Lytton** (1803)
Asolando (1890) **Robert Browning** (1812–89)
Aspects of Literature (1920) **John Middleton Murry** (1889)
Aspects of Love (1955) **David Garnett** (1892)
Aspects of Modern Poetry (1934) **Edith Sitwell** (1887)
Aspects of the Dying Process (1972) **Michael Wilding** (1942)
Aspects of the Novel (1927) **E.M. Forster** (1879)
Aspects of the Theory of Syntax (1965) **Noam Chomsky** (1928)
Aspen Court (1855) **Charles William Shirley Brooks** (1816)
Aspern Papers, The (1888) **Henry James** (1843)
Asphalt Jungle, The (1949) **W.R. Burnett** (1899)
Asphodel (1881) **M.E. Braddon** (1835)
Aspidistra in Babylon, An (1960) **H.E. Bates** (1905)
Assassin, The (1928) **Liam O'Flaherty** (1897)
Assassin, The (1944) **Irwin Shaw** (1913)
Assassin (1970) **'Evelyn Anthony' [Evelyn Ward-Thomas]** (1928)
Assassins, The (1975) **Joyce Carol Oates** (1938)
Assays (1961) **Kenneth Rexroth** (1905)
Assembly of the Gods, The [written post 1422] (1498) **John Lydgate** (1370?-1449)
Assignation, The (1672) **John Dryden** (1631)
Assistant, The (1957) **Bernard Malamud** (1914)
Assommoir, L' (1877) **Émile Zola** (1840)
Assorted Articles (1930) **D.H. Lawrence** (1885)
Assumption of the Rodues and Rascals, The (1978) **Elizabeth Smart** (1913)
Astercote (1970) **Penelope Lively** (1933)
Astonished Eye Looks Out of the Air, An (1945) **Kenneth Patchen** (1911)
Astonishing History of Troy Town, The (1888) **Sir A.T. Quiller-Couch** (1863)
Astonishing the Gods (1995) **Ben Okri** (1959)
Astoria (1836) **Washington Irving** (1783) [with Pierre Irving]
Astraea Redux (1660) **John Dryden** (1631)
Astrologer's Day, An (1947) **R.K. Narayan** (1907)

Astronomy of Love, The (1961) **Jon Stallworthy** (1935)
Astrophel (1894) **A.C. Swinburne** (1837)
Astrophel and Stella (1591) **Sir Philip Sidney** (1554)
At a Winter's Fire (1899) **Bernard Capes** (1850?)
At Bertram's Hotel (1965) **Agatha Christie** (1890)
At Dead Low Water (1949) **Allen Curnow** (1911)
At Fault (1890) **Kate Chopin** (1851)
At Freddie's (1982) **Penelope Fitzgerald** (1916)
At Half-past Eight (1923) **James Evershed Agate** (1877)
At Heaven's Gate (1943) **Robert Penn Warren** (1905)
At Home (1988) **Gore Vidal** (1925)
At Home and Abroad (1860) **Bayard Taylor** (1825)
At Lady Molly's (1957) **Anthony Powell** (1905)
At Large (1908) **A.C. Benson** (1862)
At Market Value (1894) **Grant Allen** (1848)
At Midnight (1897) **Ada Cambridge** (1844)
At Mrs Lippincote's (1945) **Elizabeth Taylor** (1912)
At My Heart's Core (1950) **Robertson Davies** (1913)
At Paradise Gate (1981) **Jane Smiley** (1949)
At Prior Park (1912) **Austin Dobson** (1840)
At Sundown (1890) **John Greenleaf Whittier** (1807)
At Swim-Two-Birds (1939) **'Flann O'Brien' [Brian O'Nolan]** (1911)
At the Back of the North Wind (1870) **George MacDonald** (1824)
At the Bar (1866) **Charles Allston Collins** (1828)
At the Crossroads (1965) **Evan S. Connell, Jr** (1924)
At the Door of the Gate (1915) **Forrest Reid** (1875)
At the Edge (1972) **Elaine Feinstein** (1930)
At the End of the Open Road (1963) **Louis Simpson** (1923)
At the Gate of the Convent (1885) **Alfred Austin** (1835)
At the Jerusalem (1967) **Paul Bailey** (1937)
At the Mountain of Madness (1964) **H.P. Lovecraft** (1890–1937)
At the Sign of the Lyre (1885) **Austin Dobson** (1840)
At the Sign of the Thistle (1934) **'Hugh MacDiarmid' [Christopher Murray Grieve]** (1892)
At the Time of Peony Blossoming (1983) **Robert Bly** (1926)
At the Villa Rose (1910) **A.E.W. Mason** (1865)
At the White Monument (1963) **Peter Redgrove** (1932)
At the Works (1907) **Lady Florence [Mrs Hugh] Bell** (1851)
Atala (1801) **François-René, vicomte de Chateaubriand** (1768)
Atalanta in Calydon (1865) **A.C. Swinburne** (1837)
Atalante, L' (1993) **Marina Warner** (1946)
Atheism and the Value of Life (1884) **W.H. Mallock** (1849)
Atheist, The (1683) **Thomas Otway** (1652)
Atheist's Tragedie, The (1611) **Cyril Tourneur** (1575?)
Athelings, The (1857) **Margaret Oliphant** (1828)
Athelwold (1731) **Aaron Hill** (1685)
Athena (1995) **John Banville** (1945)
Athenae Oxonienses [vol. ii, 1692] (1691) **Anthony à Wood** (1632)
Athenaid, The (1787) **Richard Glover** (1712–85)
Athenian Captive, The (1838) **Thomas Noon Talfourd** (1795)
Atherton (1854) **Mary Russell Mitford** (1787)
Atlantic Avenue (1956) **Albert Halper** (1904)
Atlantic Crossing (1974) **David Helwig** (1938)
Atlantic Fury (1962) **'Hammond Innes' [Ralph Hammond-Innes]** (1913)
Atlantic Tragedy, An (1905) **W. Clark Russell** (1844)
Atlantis (1954) **John Cooper Powys** (1872)
Atlantis: A Story of the Sea (1832) **William Gilmore Simms** (1806)
Atlas Shrugged (1957) **Ayn Rand** (1905)
Atonement of Leam Dundas, The (1876) **E. Lynn Linton** (1822)
Atrocity Exhibition, The (1970) **J.G. Ballard** (1930)
Atta Troll [*Atta Troll: Ein Somernachtstraum*] (1847) **Heinrich Heine** (1797)
Attaché; or, Sam Slick in England, The [1st ser.; 2nd ser., 1844] (1843) **T. C. Haliburton** (1796)
Attack Alarm (1941) **'Hammond Innes' [Ralph Hammond-Innes]** (1913)
Attempt to Shew the Folly and Danger of Methodism, An (1809) **Leigh Hunt** (1784)
Attenburg (1947) **André Malraux** (1901)
Attila (1907) **Laurence Binyon** (1869)
Attila (1837) **G.P.R. James** (1799)
Au service de l'Allemagne (1905) **Maurice Barrès** (1862)
Aubrey (1804) **R.C. Dallas** (1754)
Aubrey Beardsley (1898) **Arthur Symons** (1865)
Aucassin and Nicolete (1887) **Andrew Lang** (1844) (tr.)
Auction Sale, The (1949) **C.H.B. Kitchin** (1895)
Audience (1991) **Michael Frayn** (1933)
Audit of War, The (1986) **Correlli Barnett** (1927)
Audrey Craven (1897) **May Sinclair** (1863)
Audubon: A Vision (1969) **Robert Penn Warren** (1905)
August, 1914 (1971) **Alexander Solzhenitsyn** (1918)
August is a Wicked Month (1965) **Edna O'Brien** (1932)
Auguste Comte and Positivism (1865) **J.S. Mill** (1806)
Augustus (1986) **Allan Massie** (1938)
Augustus John: The Years of Experience (1975) **Michael Holroyd** (1935)
Augustus John: The Years of Innocence (1974) **Michael Holroyd** (1935)
Aula Lucis (1652) **Thomas Vaughan** (1622)
Auld Licht Idylls (1888) **[Sir] J.M. Barrie** (1860)
Auld Reekie (1773) **Robert Fergusson** (1750)
Aunt Augusta's Elephany (1969) **Geoffrey Trease** (1909)
Aunt Judy's Letters (1862) **Margaret [Mrs Alfred] Gatty** (1809)
Aunt Judy's Tales (1859) **Margaret [Mrs Alfred] Gatty** (1809)

Aunt Julia and the Scriptwriter [*La tia Julia y el escribidor*] (1977) **Mario Vargas Llosa** (1936)
Aunt Rachel (1886) **David Christie Murray** (1847)
Aunt Sally's Life (1865) **Margaret [Mrs Alfred] Gatty** (1809)
Aunt's Story, The (1948) **Patrick White** (1912)
Aura (1962) **Carlos Fuentes** (1928)
Aurélia (1855) **'Gérard de Nerval' [Gérard Labrunie]** (1808)
Aurelia (1920) **Robert Nichols** (1893)
Aurélien (1944) **Louis Aragon** (1897)
Aureng-Zebe (1675) **John Dryden** (1631)
Auriol (1850) **W.H. Ainsworth** (1805)
Aurora (1604) **Sir William Alexander** (1567?)
Aurora Dawn (1947) **Herman Wouk** (1915)
Aurora Floyd (1863) **M.E. Braddon** (1835)
Aurora Leigh (1857) **E.B. Browning** (1806)
Aurora, & The Prince [from Juan Pérez de Montalbán] (1647) **Thomas Stanley the elder** (1625) (tr.)
Auroras of Autumn, The (1950) **Wallace Stevens** (1879)
Austin Elliot (1863) **Henry Kingsley** (1830)
Austin Friars (1870) **Mrs J.H. Riddell** (1832)
Australia and New Zealand (1873) **Anthony Trollope** (1815)
Australia Felix [first of *The Fortunes of Richard Mahony* trilogy] (1917) **'Henry Handel Richardson' [Ethel Florence Robertson]** (1870)
Australians, The (1920) **Arthur Henry Adams** (1872)
Australians, The (1966) **George Johnston** (1912)
Authentic Account of the Shakespear Manuscripts, An (1796) **William-Henry Ireland** (1777)
Author of Beltraffio, The (1885) **Henry James** (1843)
Author, The (1763) **Charles Churchill** (1731)
Author, The (1757) **Samuel Foote** (1720)
Author's Craft, The (1914) **Arnold Bennett** (1867)
Author's Farce, The (1730) **Henry Fielding** (1707)
Authoress of the Odyssey, The (1897) **Samuel Butler** (1835)
Authors Dead and Living (1926) **F.L. Lucas** (1894)
Authors of the Town, The (1725) **Richard Savage** (1697?)
Authorship (1830) **John Neal** (1793)
Auto da Fé [*Die Blendung*] (1935) **Elias Canetti** (1905)
Autobiographic Memoirs (1911) **Frederic Harrison** (1831)
Autobiographic Sketches [i] (1853) **Thomas De Quincey** (1785)
Autobiographic Sketches [ii] (1854) **Thomas De Quincey** (1785)
Autobiography (1902) **Sir Walter Besant** (1836)
Autobiography (1834) **Sir Samuel Egerton Brydges** (1762)
Autobiography (1827) **William Gifford** (1756–1826)
Autobiography (1833) **John Galt** (1779)
Autobiography (1850) **Leigh Hunt** (1784)
Autobiography (1873) **J.S. Mill** (1806–73)
Autobiography (1877) **Harriet Martineau** (1802–76)
Autobiography (1934) **John Cooper Powys** (1872)
Autobiography (1936) **G.K. Chesterton** (1874)
Autobiography (1967) **Bertrand Russell** (1872)
Autobiography (1971) **Adrian Henri** (1932)
Autobiography, An (1883) **Anthony Trollope** (1815–82)
Autobiography, An (1893) **Annie Besant** (1847)
Autobiography and Letters (1899) **Margaret Oliphant** (1828)
Autobiography of a Cad (1938) **A.G. Macdonell** (1895)
Autobiography of a Gordon, The (1968) **Rodney Hall** (1935)
Autobiography of a Saint (1958) **Ronald Knox** (1888) (tr.)
Autobiography of a Super-Tramp, The (1908) **W.H. Davies** (1871)
Autobiography of Alice B. Toklas, The (1933) **Gertrude Stein** (1874)
Autobiography of an Ex-Colored Man, The (1912) **James Weldon Johnson** (1871)
Autobiography of Christopher Kirkland, The (1885) **E. Lynn Linton** (1822)
Autobiography of Douglas, The (1929) **Lord Alfred Douglas** (1870)
Autobiography of Jack Ketch, The (1834) **Charles Whitehead** (1804)
Autobiography of Mark Rutherford, The (1881) **'Mark Rutherford' [William Hale White]** (1831)
Autobiography of Miss Jane Pitman, The (1971) **Ernest J. Gaines** (1933)
Autobiography of Samuel Smiles, The (1909) **Samuel Smiles** (1812)
Autobiopsy (1993) **Bernice Rubens** (1923)
Autocracy of Mr Parham, The (1930) **H.G. Wells** (1866)
Autocrat of the Breakfast Table, The (1858) **Oliver Wendell Holmes** (1809)
Autogeddon (1991) **Heathcote Williams** (1941)
Automatic Oracle, The (1987) **Peter Porter** (1929)
Autumn Crocus [as 'C.L. Anthony'] (1931) **Dodie Smith** (1896)
Autumn Fire (1924) **T.C. Murray** (1873)
Autumn Garden, The (1908) **Sir Edmund Gosse** (1849)
Autumn Garden, The (1951) **Lillian Hellman** (1907)
Autumn Journal (1939) **Louis MacNeice** (1907)
Autumn of the Patriarch, The [*El otoño del patriarca*] (1975) **Gabriel García Márquez** (1928)
Autumn Sequel (1954) **Louis MacNeice** (1907)
Autumn Testament (1972) **James K. Baxter** (1926)
Autumn to Autumn and Selected Poems (1978) **A. Alvarez** (1929)
Available for Dreams (1989) **Roy Fuller** (1912)
Avalanche (1943) **Kay Boyle** (1903)
Avatars, The (1933) **George William Russell ['AE']** (1867)
Ave [first of the '*Hail and Farewell*' trilogy] (1911) **George Moore** (1852)
Aventures de Télémaque, Les (1922) **Louis Aragon** (1897)

Avenue of Stone, An (1947) **Pamela Hansford Johnson** (1912)
Avillion (1853) **Dinah Maria Craik** (1826)
Avocado Baby (1982) **Joihn Burningham** (1926)
Avoidance of Literature, The (1978) **C.H. Sisson** (1914)
Avon's Harvest (1921) **Edwin Arlington Robinson** (1869)
Avowals (1921) **George Moore** (1852)
Avril (1904) **Hilaire Belloc** (1870)
Awake! (1941) **W.R. Rodgers** (1909)
Awake and Rehearse (1929) **Louis Bromfield** (1896)
Awake and Sing! (1935) **Clifford Odets** (1906)
Awakening (1920) **John Galsworthy** (1867)
Awakening of Balthazar, The (1935) **F.L. Lucas** (1894)
Awakening of George Darroch, The (1985) **Robin Jenkins** (1912)
Awakening, The (1899) **Kate Chopin** (1851)
Awfully Big Adventure, An (1989) **Beryl Bainbridge** (1934)
Awkward Age, The (1899) **Henry James** (1843)
Awkward Squads, The (1893) **Shan F. Bullock** (1865)
Axel's Castle (1931) **Edmund Wilson** (1895)
Ayala's Angel (1881) **Anthony Trollope** (1815)
Ayesha (1905) **Sir H. Rider Haggard** (1856)
Ayesha, the Maid of Kars (1834) **James Morier** (1780)
Aylwin (1899) **Theodore Watts-Dunton** (1832)
Ayrshire Legatees, The (1821) **John Galt** (1779)
Ayton Priory (1843) **John Mason Neale** (1818)
Azemia (1797) **William Beckford** (1760)
Azeth the Egyptian (1847) **E. Lynn Linton** (1822)
Aziyadé (1879) **'Pierre Loti' [Julien Viaud]** (1850)

B

'B' is for Burglar (1985) **Sue Grafton** (1940)
Baal (1922) **Bertolt Brecht** (1898)
'Bab' Ballads, The (1869) **W.S. Gilbert** (1836)
Babbitt (1922) **Sinclair Lewis** (1885)
Babbling April (1925) **Graham Greene** (1904)
Babe, B.A., The (1897) **E.F. Benson** (1867)
Babe in Bohemia, A (1889) **'Frank Danby' [Julia Frankau]** (1864)
Babel to Byzantium (1968) **James Dickey** (1923)
Babel Tower (1996) **A.S. Byatt** (1936)
Babel 17 (1966) **Samuel R. Delany** (1942)
Babes in the Bush (1900) **'Rolf Boldrewood' [Thomas Alexander Browne]** (1826)
Babes in the Darkling Wood (1940) **H.G. Wells** (1866)
Babes of the Wild (1912) **Sir Charles G.D. Roberts** (1860)
Babi Yar (1962) **Yevgeny Yevtushenko** (1933)
Baboo Jabberjee, BA (1897) **'F. Anstey' [Thomas Anstey Guthrie]** (1856)
Baby Doll [film script] (1956) **'Tennessee' [Thomas Lanier] Williams** (1911)
Baby in the Icebox, The (1981) **James M. Cain** (1892–1977)
Baby, It's Cold Inside (1970) **S.J. Perelman** (1904)
Baby Love (1973) **David Edgar** (1948)
Babylon (1982) **Jill Paton Walsh** (1937)
Babylon South (1989) **Jon Cleary** (1917)
Babyons, The (1928) **'Clemence Dane' [Winifred Ashton]** (1888)
Bacchus in Tuscany [from the Italian] (1825) **Leigh Hunt** (1784) (tr.)
Bachelor of Arts, The (1937) **R.K. Narayan** (1907)
Bachelor of the Albany, The (1847) **Marmion W. Savage** (1803)
Bachelor's Children, A (1962) **Hal Porter** (1911)
Bachelor's Wife, The (1824) **John Galt** (1779)
Bachelors, The (1960) **Muriel Spark** (1918)
Back (1946) **'Henry Green' [Henry Vicent Yorke]** (1905)
Back at the Spike (1994) **David Constantine** (1944)
Back Country, The (1968) **Gary Snyder** (1930)
Back in the World (1985) **Tobias Wolff** (1945)
Back of Sunset (1959) **Jon Cleary** (1917)
Back to Bool Bool [as 'Brent of Bin Bin'] (1931) **Miles Franklin** (1879)
Back to Methuselah (1920) **Bernard Shaw** (1856)
Background for Venus (1934) **James Laver** (1899)
Backgrounds of My Life, The (1944) **George Santayana** (1863)
Backlog Studies (1873) **Charles Dudley Warner** (1829)
Backward Glance, A (1934) **Edith Wharton** (1862)
Backward Look, The (1967) **'Frank O'Connor' [Michael Francis O'Donovan']** (1903)
Backward Shadow, The (1970) **Lynne Reid Banks** (1929)
Backward Son, The (1940) **Sir Stephen Spender** (1909)
Backwater (1916) **Dorothy M. Richardson** (1873)
Backwoods-men, The (1909) **Sir Charles G.D. Roberts** (1860)
Bad Behaviour (1988) **Mary Gaitskill** (1954)
Bad Box, The (1987) **Alison Fell** (1944)
Bad Characters (1964) **Jean Stafford** (1915)
Bad Child's Book of Beasts, The (1896) **Hilaire Belloc** (1870)
Bad Girls (1984) **Mary Flanagan** (1943)
Bad Luck (1877) **Albany de Fonblanque** (1793–1872)
Bad Man, A (1967) **Stanley Elkin** (1930)
Bad Manners (1938) **James Evershed Agate** (1877)
Bad Parents' Garden of Verse, The (1936) **Ogden Nash** (1902)
Bad Place, The (1990) **Dean Koontz** (1945)
Bad Seed, The (1955) **Maxwell Anderson** (1888)
Bad Sister, The (1978) **Emma Tennant** (1937)
Baddeck (1874) **Charles Dudley Warner** (1829)
Baddington Peerage, The (1860) **George Augustus Sala** (1828)
Badlands (1986) **Elaine Feinstein** (1930)
Bag of Farthings, A (1893) **C[hristabel] R[ose] Coleridge** (1843)
Baghdad Sketches (1937) **Freya Stark** (1893)
Bagpipe Muzak (1991) **Liz Lochhead** (1947)
Bagthorpes Abroad (1984) **Helen Cresswell** (1934)
Bagthorpes Haunted (1985) **Helen Cresswell** (1934)

Bagthorpes Unlimited (1978) **Helen Cresswell** (1934)
Bagthorpes v. the World (1979) **Helen Cresswell** (1934)
Bahama Crisis (1980) **Desmond Bagley** (1923)
Baikie Charivari, The (1952) **'James Bridie' [Osborne Henry Mavor]** (1888)
'Bail Up!' (1890) **Hume Nisbet** (1849)
Bailegangáire (1985) **Tom Murphy** (1935)
Baiser au lépreux, Le (1922) **François Mauriac** (1885)
Bait, The (1960) **James Merrill** (1926)
Bajazet (1672) **Jean Racine** (1639)
Balcony Tree, The (1993) **Christopher Middleton** (1926)
Bald Soprano, The (1950) **Eugène Ionesco** (1909)
Balder (1853) **Sydney Dobell** (1824)
Baldwin (1820) **R.H. Barham** (1788)
Balisand (1924) **Joseph Hergesheimer** (1880)
Ball and the Cross, The (1910) **G.K. Chesterton** (1874)
Ballad and the Source, The (1944) **Rosamond Lehmann** (1903)
Ballad Book, The (1864) **William Allingham** (1824) (ed.)
Ballad of Beau Brocade, The (1892) **Austin Dobson** (1840)
Ballad of Bill Spinks' Bedstead, The (1981) **Pam Ayres** (1947)
Ballad of Mari Lwyd, The (1941) **Vernon Watkins** (1906)
Ballad of Peckham Rye, The (1960) **Muriel Spark** (1918)
Ballad of Reading Gaol, The [by 'C.3.3'] (1898) **Oscar Wilde** (1854)
Ballad of St Barbara, The (1922) **G.K. Chesterton** (1874)
Ballad of the Putrefaction (1994) **Christopher Middleton** (1926)
Ballad of the Sad Café, The (1951) **Carson McCullers** (1917)
Ballad of the White Horse, The (1911) **G.K. Chesterton** (1874)
Ballad of the Yorkshire Ripper, The (1987) **Blake Morrison** (1950)
Ballad of William Sycamore, The (1923) **Stephen Vincent Benét** (1889)
Ballad Romances (1846) **R.H. Horne** (1803)
Ballad Romances (1811) **Anna Maria Porter** (1780)
Ballade of the Scottysshe Kynge, A (1513) **John Skelton** (1460?)
Ballads [prints designed and engraved by William Blake] (1805) **William Hayley** (1745)
Ballads (1855) **W.H. Ainsworth** (1805)
Ballads (1890) **Robert Louis Stevenson** (1850)
Ballads (1903) **John Masefield** (1878)
Ballads and Lyrical Pieces (1806) **Sir Walter Scott** (1771)
Ballads and Lyrics (1891) **Katharine Tynan** (1861)
Ballads and Lyrics of Old France (1872) **Andrew Lang** (1844)
Ballads and Lyrics of Socialism (1908) **E[dith] Nesbit** (1858)
Ballads and Other Poems (1841) **Henry Wadsworth Longfellow** (1807)
Ballads and Other Poems (1847) **Mary Howitt** (1799)
Ballads, and Other Poems (1880) **Alfred, Lord Tennyson** (1809)
Ballads and Poems (1898) **Dora Sigerson** (1866)
Ballads and Poems (1910) **John Masefield** (1878)
Ballads and Poems of Tragic Life (1887) **George Meredith** (1828)
Ballads and Songs (1894) **John Davidson** (1857)
Ballads and Sonnets (1881) **Dante Gabriel Rossetti** (1828–1882)
Ballads and Verses of the Spiritual Life (1911) **E[dith] Nesbit** (1858)
Ballads for Sale (1927) **Amy Lowell** (1874)
Ballads from Manuscripts (1868) **F.J. Furnivall** (1825) (ed.)
Ballads of a Bohemian (1921) **Robert W. Service** (1876)
Ballads of a Cheechako (1909) **Robert W. Service** (1876)
Ballads of Babylon (1880) **George R. Sims** (1847)
Ballads of Life, Love and Humour (1882) **Robert Williams Buchanan** (1841)
Ballads of Lost Haven (1895) **William Bliss Carman** (1861)
Ballads of Lost Haven (1895) **William Bliss Carman** (1861)
Ballads of Scotland, The (1858) **W.E. Aytoun** (1813)
Ballerina (1958) **Vicki Baum** (1888)
Ballet Shoes (1936) **Noel Streatfeild** (1895)
Ballet Shoes for Anna (1972) **Noel Streatfeild** (1895)
Balliols, The (1934) **Alec Waugh** (1898)
Ballroom of Romance, The (1972) **'William Trevor' [William Trevor Cox]** (1928)
Balme of Gilead, The (1646) **Joseph Hall** (1574)
Balthasar (1889) **'Anatole France' [Jacques-Anatole-François Thibault]** (1844)
Balthazar (1958) **Lawrence Durrell** (1912)
Bambi (1923) **'Felix Salten' [Siegmund Salzmann]** (1869)
Bambi's Children [*Bambis Kinder*] (1940) **'Felix Salten' [Siegmund Salzmann]** (1869)
Band of Angels (1955) **Robert Penn Warren** (1905)
Band Rotunda, The (1967) **James K. Baxter** (1926)
Bandit on the Billiard Table, The (1954) **Alan Ross** (1922)
Bandits (1987) **Elmore Leonard** (1925)
Banditti, The (1686) **Thomas D'Urfey** (1653)
Bang-Bang You're Dead (1982) **Muriel Spark** (1918)
Banished Man, The (1794) **Charlotte Smith** (1749)
Bank Holiday (1967) **Michael Horovitz** (1935)
Banker's Wife, The (1843) **Mrs C.F. Gore** (1799)
Bankrupt, The (1773) **Samuel Foote** (1720)
Banks of Wye, The (1811) **Robert Bloomfield** (1766)
Banquet of Daintie Conceits, A (1588) **Anthony Munday** (1560)
Banquet of Sapience, The (1539) **Sir Thomas Elyot** (1490?)
Banquet, The (1983) **Carolyn Slaughter** (1946)
Baptist Lake (1894) **John Davidson** (1857)

Bar Sinister, The (1864) **Charles Allston Collins** (1828)
Bar Sinister, The (1903) **Richard Harding Davis** (1864)
Bar-Room Ballads (1940) **Robert W. Service** (1876)
Barabbas (1893) **Marie Corelli** (1855)
Barbara Ladd (1902) **Sir Charles G.D. Roberts** (1860)
Barbara, Lady's Maid and Peeress (1897) **Mrs A.H. Alexander** (1825)
Barbara Rebell (1905) **Mrs Belloc Lowndes** (1868)
Barbara's History (1864) **Amelia B. Edwards** (1831)
Barbarians (1979) **Douglas Dunn** (1942)
Barbarians at the Gate (1939) **Leonard Woolf** (1880)
Barbarism and Sexual Freedom (1948) **Alex Comfort** (1920)
Barbary Light, The (1962) **P.H. Newby** (1918)
Barbary Shore (1951) **Norman Mailer** (1923)
Barber of Putney, The (1919) **J.B. Morton** ('Beachcomber', 1893)
Barber of Seville, The [*Le Barbier de Séville*] (1775) **Pierre Augustin Caron de Beaumarchais** (1732)
Barber's Trade Union, The (1944) **Mulk Raj Anand** (1905)
Barcellona (1710) **George Farquhar** (1678–1707)
Barchester Pilgrimage (1935) **Ronald Knox** (1888)
Barchester Towers (1857) **Anthony Trollope** (1815)
Barclay Family Theatre, The (1981) **Jack Hodgins** (1938)
Bardelys the Magnificent (1906) **Rafael Sabatini** (1875)
Bare Hills, The (1927) **Yvor Winters** (1900)
Barefoot in Athens (1951) **Maxwell Anderson** (1888)
Barefoot in the Head (1969) **Brian Aldiss** (1925)
Barefoot in the Park (1963) **Neil Simon** (1927)
Barford Abbey (1768) **Susannah Gunning** (1740)
Barham Downs (1784) **Robert Bage** (1728)
Bark Tree, The [*Le Chiendent*] (1933) **Raymond Queneau** (1903)
Barlasch of the Guard (1903) **'Henry Seton Merriman' [Hugh Stowell Scott]** (1862)
Barmitzvah Boy (1976) **Jack Rosenthal** (1931)
Barn Blind (1980) **Jane Smiley** (1949)
Barnaby Rudge (1841) **Charles Dickens** (1812)
Barnabys in America, The (1843) **Frances Trollope** (1780)
Barney's Version (1997) **Mordechai Richler** (1931)
Barometer Rising (1941) **Hugh MacLennan** (1907)
Baron in the Trees, The [*Il Barone rampante*] (1957) **Italo Calvino** (1923)
Baron Rudolph (1881) **Bronson Howard** (1842)
Baron's Little Daughter, The (1848) **Mrs C.F. Alexander** (1818)
Baronage of England, The (1675) **Sir William Dugdale** (1605)
Barony, The (1830) **Anna Maria Porter** (1780)
Barrack-Room Ballads (1892) **Rudyard Kipling** (1865)
Barracks, The (1963) **John McGahern** (1934)
Barracks Thief, The (1984) **Tobias Wolff** (1945)
Barren Fig-Tree, The (1673) **John Bunyan** (1628)
Barren Ground (1925) **Ellen Glasgow** (1874)
Barren Honour (1862) **G.A. Lawrence** (1827)
Barrington (1863) **Charles Lever** (1806)
Barrons Wars, The (1603) **Michael Drayton** (1563)
Barrys, The (1899) **Shan F. Bullock** (1865)
Bartas His Devine Weekes & Workes [from Guillaume de Salustre du Bartas] (1605) **Joshua Sylvester** (1563) (tr.)
Bartholomew Fayre [with *The Divell is an Asse* and *The Staple of Newes*; first pub. in Jonson's *Works* 1616] (1614) **Ben Jonson** (1572)
Basement Room, The (1935) **Graham Greene** (1904)
Basil (1852) **Wilkie Collins** (1824)
Basil Netherby (1926) **A.C. Benson** (1862–1925)
Basil Seal Rides Again (1963) **Evelyn Waugh** (1903)
Basil Street Blues: A Family Story (1999) **Michael Holroyd** (1935)
Basilikon Doron (1599) **James I** (1566)
Basset-Table, The (1705) **Susanna Centlivre** (1669?)
Bassett (1934) **Stella Gibbons** (1902)
Bastard of Mauleon, The [*Le Bâtard de Mauléon*] (1846) **Alexandre Dumas ['père']** (1802)
Bastard, The (1728) **Richard Savage** (1697?)
Bath Comedy, The (1900) **Egerton Smith Castle** (1858–) and **Agnes Castle** (*c.* 1860)
Bath-Intrigues (1725) **Eliza Haywood** (*c.* 1693)
Baths of Absalom, The (1954) **James Pope-Hennessy** (1916)
Batrachomyomachia [from Homer] (1624) **George Chapman** (1559?) (tr.)
Battaile of Agincourt, The (1627) **Michael Drayton** (1563)
Battell of Alcazar, The (1594) **George Peele** (1556)
Battery and the Boiler, The (1883) **R.M. Ballantyne** (1825)
Battle (1915) **Wilfrid Gibson** (1878)
Battle Continues, The (1957) **'Hugh MacDiarmid' [Christopher Murray Grieve]** (1892)
Battle Cry (1953) **Leon Uris** (1924)
Battle Day, The (1855) **Ernest Charles Jones** (1819)
Battle for Christabel, The (1991) **Margaret Forster** (1938)
'Battle Hymn of the Republic, The' [in the *Atlantic Monthly*] (1862) **Julia Ward Howe** (1819)
Battle Lost and Won, The (1978) **Olivia Manning** (1908)
Battle of Angels (1940) **'Tennessee' [Thomas Lanier] Williams** (1911)
Battle of Aughrim and the God Who Eats Corn, The (1968) **Richard Murphy** (1927)
Battle of Bubble and Squeak, The (1978) **Philippa Pearce** (1920)
Battle of Bunkers-Hill, The (1776) **Hugh Henry Brackenridge** (1748)
Battle of Dorking, The (1871) **General Sir George Tomkyns Chesney** (1830)
Battle of Largs, The (1804) **John Galt** (1779)
Battle of Life, The (1846) **Charles Dickens** (1812)
Battle of Marathon, The (1820) **E.B. Browning** (1806)
Battle of Pollocks Crossing, The (1985) **J.L. Carr** (1912)

Battle of Ramillia, The (1706) **John Dennis** (1657)
Battle of Shrivings, The (1970) **Peter Shaffer** (1926)
Battle of the Nile, The (1799) **William Sotheby** (1757)
Battle of the Villa Fiorita, The (1963) **Rumer Godden** (1907)
Battle Surgeon (1944) **Frank G. Slaughter** (1908)
Battle-Ground, The (1902) **Ellen Glasgow** (1874)
Battle-Pieces and Aspects of the War (1866) **Herman Melville** (1819)
Battlefield, The (1967) **William Mayne** (1928)
Baucis and Philemon (1709) **Jonathan Swift** (1667)
Baudelaire (1947) **Jean-Paul Sartre** (1905)
Baumgartner's Bombay (1988) **Anita Desai** (1937)
Baviad, The (1791) **William Gifford** (1756)
Bay (1919) **D.H. Lawrence** (1885)
Bay of Contented Men, The (1989) **Robert Drewe** (1943)
Bay of Noon, The (1970) **Shirley Hazzard** (1931)
Bay of Silence, The (1986) **Lisa St Aubin de Terán** (1953)
Bayard from Bengal, A (1902) **'F. Anstey' [Thomas Anstey Guthrie]** (1856)
Bayou Folk (1894) **Kate Chopin** (1851)
Be Angry at the Sun (1941) **Robinson Jeffers** (1887)
Be Cool (1999) **Elmore Leonard** (1925)
Beachcombers, The (1972) **Helen Cresswell** (1934)
Beachmasters (1985) **Thea Astley** (1925)
Beachy Head (1807) **Charlotte Smith** (1749–1806)
Bealby (1915) **H.G. Wells** (1866)
Beany-Eye (1935) **David Garnett** (1892)
Bear (1976) **Marian Engel** (1933–1985)
Bear Called Paddington, A (1958) **Michael Bond** (1926)
Beard's Roman Women (1976) **'Anthony Burgess' [John Anthony Burgess Wilson]** (1917)
Bearing Breast, The (1976) **Patric Dickinson** (1914)
Beast in Me and Other Animals, The (1948) **James Thurber** (1894)
Beast Must Die, The (1938) **'Nicholas Blake' [C. Day Lewis]** (1904)
Beastly Beatitudes of Balthasar B, The (1969) **J.P. Donleavy** (1926)
Beasts and Super-Beasts (1914) **'Saki' [Hector Hugh Munro]** (1870)
Beatification of Area Boy, The (1995) **Wole Soyinka** (1934)
Beating the Bushes (1972) **John Crowe Ransom** (1888)
Beatrice (1890) **Sir H. Rider Haggard** (1856)
Beatrice Tyldesley (1878) **W.H. Ainsworth** (1805)
Beau Austin (1884) **W.E. Henley** (1849) [with R.L. Stevenson]
Beau Brocade (1907) **Baroness Orczy** (1865)
Beau Geste (1924) **P.C. Wren** (1885)
Beau Ideal (1928) **P.C. Wren** (1885)
Beau Nash (1879) **W.H. Ainsworth** (1805)
Beau Nash (1834) **Douglas Jerrold** (1803)
Beau Sabreur (1926) **P.C. Wren** (1885)
Beauchamp's Career (1876) **George Meredith** (1828)
Beauchampe (1842) **William Gilmore Simms** (1806)
Beaufort Sisters, The (1979) **Jon Cleary** (1917)
Beauties, The (1746) **Horace Walpole** (1717)
Beautiful and the Damned, The (1922) **F. Scott Fitzgerald** (1896)
Beauties and the Furies, The (1936) **Christina Stead** (1902)
Beautiful Changes, The (1947) **Richard Wilbur** (1921)
Beautiful End (1918) **Constance Holme** (1881)
Beautiful Losers (1966) **Leonard Cohen** (1934)
Beautiful People, The (1941) **William Saroyan** (1908)
Beautiful Rebel, A (1909) **Wilfred Campbell** (1858)
Beautiful Room is Empty, The (1988) **Edmund White** (1940)
Beautiful Visit, The (1950) **Elizabeth Jane Howard** (1923)
Beautiful Wales (1905) **Edward Thomas** (1878)
Beautiful Years, The (1921) **Henry Williamson** (1895)
Beautiful Young Nymph Going to Bed, A (1734) **Jonathan Swift** (1667)
Beauty (1766) **Henry James Pye** (1745)
Beauty and the Beast (1943) **John Heath-Stubbs** (1918)
Beauty and the Beast [*La Belle et la Bête*; film] (1945) **Jean Cocteau** (1889)
Beauty of the Dead, The (1940) **H.E. Bates** (1905)
Beauty's Punishment [as 'A.N. Roquelaure'] (1984) **Anne Rice** (1941)
Beauty's Release [as 'A.N. Roquelaure'] (1985) **Anne Rice** (1941)
Beaux' Stratagem, The (1707) **George Farquhar** (1678)
Because I Was Flesh (1964) **Edward Dahlberg** (1900)
Because It Is (1960) **Kenneth Patchen** (1911)
Because It Is Bitter, and Because It Is My Heart (1990) **Joyce Carol Oates** (1938)
Because of the Cats (1963) **Nicholas Freeling** (1927)
Because the Night (1985) **James Ellroy** (1948)
Bech: A Book (1970) **John Updike** (1932)
Bech is Back (1982) **John Updike** (1932)
Becker Wives, The (1946) **Mary Lavin** (1912)
Becket (1959) **Jean Anouilh** (1910)
Becket (1884) **Alfred, Lord Tennyson** (1809)
Beckoning Hand, The (1887) **Grant Allen** (1848)
Beckoning Lady, The [US: *The Estate of the Beckoning Lady*] (1955) **Margery Allingham** (1904)
Beckside Lights (1897) **'John Ackworth' [Frederick R. Smith]** (1845)
Becoming [*Devenir*] (1909) **Roger Martin du Gard** (1881)
Bed of Roses, A (1954) **William Sansom** (1912)
Bed, The (1981) **John Ash** (1948)
Bedrock (1990) **Lisa Alther** (1944)
Beds in the East (1959) **'Anthony Burgess' [John Anthony Burgess Wilson]** (1917)
Bee, The (1759) **Oliver Goldsmith** (1728)
Beechcroft at Rockstone (1888) **Charlotte M. Yonge** (1823)
Beechen Vigil (1925) **C. Day Lewis** (1904)
Beekeepers, The (1980) **Peter Redgrove** (1932)
Beet Queen, The (1986) **Louise Erdrich** (1954)

Before Adam (1906) **'Jack London' [John Griffith Chaney]** (1876)
Before Dawn (1911) **Harold Monro** (1879)
Before Disaster (1934) **Yvor Winters** (1900)
Before She Met Me (1982) **Julian Barnes** (1946)
Before the Bombardment (1926) **Sir Osbert Sitwell** (1892)
Before the Brave (1936) **Kenneth Patchen** (1911)
Before the Cock Crow (1986) **Simon Raven** (1927)
Before the Curfew (1888) **Oliver Wendell Holmes** (1809)
Before the Fact [as 'Francis Iles'] (1932) **Anthony Berkeley Cox** (1893)
Before the Gringo Came (1894) **Gertrude Atherton** (1857)
Before the Party (1949) **Rodney Ackland** (1908)
Beggar Maid, The (1999) **Alice Munro** (1931)
Beggar My Neighbour (1964) **Dan Jacobson** (1929)
Beggar's Opera, The (1728) **John Gay** (1685)
Beggarman Thief (1977) **Irwin Shaw** (1913)
Beggars (1909) **W.H. Davies** (1871)
Beggars Bush, The (1661) **Francis Beaumont** (1585?-1616) [with John Fletcher]
Beginner, A (1894) **Rhoda Broughton** (1840)
Beginners, The (1966) **Dan Jacobson** (1929)
Beginning, A (1955) **Walter de la Mare** (1873)
Beginning Again (1964) **Leonard Woolf** (1880)
Beginning and the End, The (1963) **Robinson Jeffers** (1887–62)
Beginning of Spring, The (1988) **Penelope Fitzgerald** (1916–2000)
Beginning of Wisdom, The (1921) **Stephen Vincent Benét** (1889)
Beginnings (1975) **Edward Said** (1935)
Behemoth (1679) **Thomas Hobbes** (1588)
Behind the Arras (1895) **William Bliss Carman** (1861)
Behind the Eyes (1921) **Edgell Rickword** (1898)
Behind the Lines (1940) **A.A. Milne** (1882)
Behind the Wall (1987) **Colin Thubron** (1939)
Behold, Here's Poison! (1936) **Georgette Heyer** (1902)
Behold the Man (1969) **Michael Moorcock** (1939)
Behold, This Dreamer! (1939) **Walter de la Mare** (1873) (ed.)
Beiderbecke Affair, The (1985) **Alan Plater** (1935)
Being a Boy (1878) **Charles Dudley Warner** (1829)
Being Alive (1978) **Al Purdy** (1918)
Being and Nothingness [*L'être et le néant*] (1943) **Jean-Paul Sartre** (1905)
Being Dead (1999) **Jim Crace** (1946)
Being Here (1980) **Robert Penn Warren** (1905)
Being Invisible (1987) **Thomas Berger** (1924)
Bel-Ami (1885) **Guy de Maupassant** (1850)
Belchamber (1904) **H.O. Sturgis** (1855)
Beleagured City, A (1879) **Margaret Oliphant** (1828)
Belford Regis (1835) **Mary Russell Mitford** (1787)
Belfry of Bruges, The (1845) **Henry Wadsworth Longfellow** (1807)
Belgium and Western Germany in 1833 (1834) **Frances Trollope** (1780)
Belinda (1801) **Maria Edgeworth** (1767)
Belinda (1883) **Rhoda Broughton** (1840)
Belinda (1928) **Hilaire Belloc** (1870)
Bell Call (1965) **Sylvia Ashton-Warner** (1908)
Bell Family, The (1954) **Noel Streatfeild** (1895)
Bell for Adano, A (1944) **John Hersey** (1914)
Bell Harry (1963) **Christopher Hassall** (1912)
Bell, The (1958) **Iris Murdoch** (1919)
Bell Jar, The [as 'Victoria Lucas'] (1963) **Sylvia Plath** (1932)
Bell of St Paul's, The (1889) **Sir Walter Besant** (1836)
Bella (1976) **Jilly Cooper** (1937)
Bella (1926) **Jean Giraudoux** (1882)
Bella Donna (1909) **Robert Hichens** (1864)
Bellamira (1687) **Sir Charles Sedley** (1639)
Bellamira (1818) **Richard Lalor Sheil** (1791)
Bellarmine Jug, The (1984) **Nicholas Hasluck** (1942)
Bellarosa Connection, The (1989) **Saul Bellow** (1915)
Belle Assemblé, La [from Madeleine, Mme de Gomez] (1724) **Eliza Haywood** (*c.* 1693) (tr.)
Belle Jenny, La ['Beautiful Jenny'] (1865) **Théophile Gautier** (1811)
Belle of a Season, The (1840) **Marguerite, Countess of Blessington** (1789)
Belle's Stratagem, The (1780) **Hannah Cowley** (1743)
Bellefleur (1980) **Joyce Carol Oates** (1938)
Belles Images, Les (1966) **Simone de Beauvoir** (1908)
Bells and Grass (1941) **Walter de la Mare** (1873)
Bells and Pomegranates i: Pippa Passes (1841) **Robert Browning** (1812)
Bells and Pomegranates ii: King Victor and King Charles (1842) **Robert Browning** (1812)
Bells and Pomegranates iii: Dramatic Lyrics (1842) **Robert Browning** (1812)
Bells and Pomegranates iv: The Return of the Druses (1843) **Robert Browning** (1812)
Bells and Pomegranates v: A Blot on the 'Scutcheon (1843) **Robert Browning** (1812)
Bells and Pomegranates vi: Colombe's Birthday (1844) **Robert Browning** (1812)
Bells and Pomegranates vii: Dramatic Romances and Lyrics (1845) **Robert Browning** (1812)
Bells and Pomegranates viii and Last: Luria; and A Soul's Tragedy (1846) **Robert Browning** (1812)
Bells, The (1855) **Thomas Bailey Aldrich** (1836)
Belman of London, The (1608) **Thomas Dekker** (1572?)
Beloved (1987) **Toni Morrison** (1931)
Beloved Stranger (1999) **Clare Boylan** (1948)
Below Loughrigg (1979) **Fleur Adcock** (1934)
Belphegor (1691) **John Wilson** (1627?)
Belshazzar (1822) **Henry Hart Milman** (1791)
Belshazzar's Feast [*La cena del rey Baltasar*] (1632) **Pedro Calderón de la Barca** (1600)
Beltane the Smith (1915) **Jeffery Farnol** (1878)
Belton Estate, The (1866) **Anthony Trollope** (1815)
Ben Brace (1836) **Captain Chamier** (1796–1820)
Ben Burton (1871) **W.H.G. Kingston** (1814)
Ben, in the World (2000) **Doris Lessing** (1919)
Ben-Hur (1880) **Lew Wallace** (1827)
Benchley Beside Himself (1943) **Robert Benchley** (1889)
Bend in the River, A (1979) **V.S. Naipaul** (1932)

Bend Sinister (1947) **Vladimir Nabokov** (1899)
Bender, The (1963) **Paul Scott** (1920)
Bending of the Bough, The (1900) **George Moore** (1852)
Bendish (1913) **Maurice Hewlett** (1861)
Beneath the Visiting Moon (1923) **Mary** (1865) and Jane (1866) Findlater
Benefactor, The (1905) **Ford Madox Ford** (1873)
Benefactor, The (1963) **Susan Sontag** (1933)
Benefactors (1984) **Michael Frayn** (1933)
Benefactress, The (1901) **'Elizabeth' [Mary Annette Gräfin] von Arnim** (1866)
Benefits Forgot (1892) **Wolcott Balestier** (1861)
Benighted (1927) **J.B. Priestley** (1894)
Benita (1906) **Sir H. Rider Haggard** (1856)
Benjamin the Waggoner (1819) **J.H. Reynolds** (1796)
Benson Murder Case, The [first 'Philo Vance' novel] (1926) **'S.S. van Dine' [Willard Huntington Wright]** (1888)
Bentinck's Tutor (1868) **James Payn** (1830)
Beowulf (1921) **R.W. Chambers** (1874)
Beowulf (tr.) (1999) **Seamus Heaney** (1939)
Beowulf: The Monsters and the Critics (1936) **J.R.R. Tolkein** (1892)
Beppo (1818) **George Gordon, Lord Byron** (1788)
Beppo the Conscript (1864) **T. Adolphus Trollope** (1810)
Bérénice (1670) **Jean Racine** (1639)
Berhama Account, The (1985) **John Williams** (1925)
Beric the Briton (1893) **G.A. Henty** (1832)
Berlin Bertie (1992) **Howard Brenton** (1942)
Berlin Game (1983) **Len Deighton** (1929)
Berlin Stories, The (1946) **Christopher Isherwood** (1904)
Berna Boyle (1884) **Mrs J.H. Riddell** (1832)
Bernard Clare (1946) **James T. Farrell** (1904)
Bernard Shaw (1907) **Holbrook Jackson** (1874)
Bernard Shaw and Mrs Patrick Campbell [correspondence] (1952) **Bernard Shaw** (1856–1950)
Bernicia (1895) **Amelia Barr** (1831)
Berry and Co. (1921) **'Dornford Yates' [Cecil William Mercer]** (1885)
Berryman's Sonnets (1967) **John Berryman** (1914)
Bertha, and Other Plays (1966) **Kenneth Koch** (1925)
Bertha and the Racing Pigeon (1979) **Pam Ayres** (1947)
Bertram (1816) **Sir Samuel Egerton Brydges** (1762)
Bertram (1816) **C.R. Maturin** (1782)
Bertram Cope's Year (1919) **Henry Blake Fuller** (1857)
Bertrams, The (1859) **Anthony Trollope** (1815)
Beryl of the Biplane (1917) **William le Queux** (1864)
Beside Myself (1990) **Russell Haley** (1934)
Beside Still Waters (1907) **A.C. Benson** (1862)
Beside the Fire (1890) **Douglas Hyde** (1860)
Beside the Ocean of Time (1994) **George Mackay Brown** (1921)
Best Hour of the Night, The (1984) **Louis Simpson** (1923)
Best Man to Die, The (1969) **Ruth Rendell** (1930)
Best Name of Silence, The (1972) **David Helwig** (1938)
Best Name on Earth, The (1657) **Thomas Fuller** (1608)
Best of All Possible Worlds, The (1975) **Glenway Wescott** (1901)
Best of Friends, The (1995) **Joanna Trollope** (1943)
Best Times, The (1966) **John Dos Passos** (1896)
Bestiaire, Le ['The Bestiary'] (1911) **'Guillaume Apollinaire' [Wilhelm de Kostrowitsky]** (1880)
Bestiary, A (1955) **Richard Wilbur** (1921)
Bethel Merriday (1940) **Sinclair Lewis** (1885)
Betrayal (1978) **Harold Pinter** (1930)
Betrayal, The (1966) **L.P. Hartley** (1895)
Betraying of Christ, The (1598) **Samuel Rowlands** (1570?)
Betrothed, The (1827) **Alessandro Manzoni** (1785)
Betsy, The (1971) **Harold Robbins** (1912)
Better Class of Person, A (1981) **John Osborne** (1929)
Better Dead (1887) **[Sir] J.M. Barrie** (1860)
Better Sort, The (1903) **Henry James** (1843)
Better Than a Kick in the Pants (1945) **J. Maclaren-Ross** (1912)
Better Than Sex (1994) **Hunter S. Thompson** (1939)
Better World of Reginald Perrin, The (1978) **David Nobbs** (1935)
Betty Wayside (1915) **Louis Stone** (1871)
Between (1988) **C.K. Stead** (1932)
Between Here and Now (1981) **R.S. Thomas** (1913)
Between Mars and Venus (1962) **Robert Conquest** (1917)
Between Oxus and Jumna (1961) **Arnold Toynbee** (1889)
Between Tears and Laughter (1973) **Mulk Raj Anand** (1905)
Between the Acts (1941) **Virginia Woolf** (1882)
Between the Woods and the Water (1985) **Patrick Leigh Fermor** (1915)
Between Two Loves (1886) **Amelia Barr** (1831)
Between Two Stools (1912) **Rhoda Broughton** (1840)
Between Two Tides (1952) **R. D. FitzGerald** (1902)
Between Two Worlds (1935) **John Middleton Murry** (1889)
Between Two Worlds (1934) **Elmer Rice** (1892)
Between Two Worlds (1941) **Upton Sinclair** (1878)
Between Us Girls (1998) **Joe Orton** (1933–67)
Beulah Land (1949) **H.L. Davis** (1896)
Bevis (1882) **Richard Jefferies** (1848)
Beware, Soul-Brother (1971) **Chinua Achebe** (1930)
Bewick Bestiary, A (1971) **James Kirkup** (1923)
Bewitched Crossroad, A (19984) **Bessie Head** (1937)
Beyond a Boundary (1963) **C.L.R. James** (1901)
Beyond All This Fiddle (1968) **A. Alvarez** (1929)
Beyond Atonement (1896) **A. St John Adcock** (1864)
Beyond Belief (1998) **V.S. Naipaul** (1932)
Beyond Criticism (1953) **Karl Shapiro** (1913)
Beyond Culture (1965) **Lionel Trilling** (1905)
Beyond Desire (1932) **Sherwood Anderson** (1876)
Beyond Euphrates (1951) **Freya Stark** (1893)
Beyond Good and Evil [*Jenseits von Gut und Böse*] (1886) **Friedrich Wilhelm Nietzsche** (1844)
Beyond Howth Head (1970) **Derek Mahon** (1941)

Beyond Personality (1944) **C.S. Lewis** (1898)
Beyond Power (1985) **Marilyn French** (1929)
Beyond the Blue Event Horizon (1980) **Frederik Pohl** (1919)
Beyond the Dreams of Avarice (1895) **Sir Walter Besant** (1836)
Beyond the Fringe (1962) **Alan Bennett** (1934) **et al.** [with Peter Cook, Dudley Moore, and Jonathan Miller]
Beyond the Glass (1954) **'Antonia White' [Eirene Botting]** (1899)
Beyond the Hills of Dream (1899) **Wilfred Campbell** (1858)
Beyond the Horizon (1920) **Eugene O'Neill** (1888)
Beyond the Hundredth Meridian [biog. of John Wesley Powell] (1954) **Wallace Stegner** (1909)
Beyond the Mountains (1951) **Kenneth Rexroth** (1905)
Beyond the Pale (1981) **'William Trevor' [William Trevor Cox]** (1928)
Beyond the Palisade (1944) **James K. Baxter** (1926)
Beyond the Rocks (1906) **Elinor Glyn** (1864)
Beyond the Wall of Sleep (1943) **H.P. Lovecraft** (1890)
Beyond These Voices (1910) **M.E. Braddon** (1835)
Beyond This Disregard (1943) **John Pudney** (1909)
Beyond This Place (1953) **A.J. Cronin** (1896)
BFG, The (1982) **Roald Dahl** (1916)
Bhowani Junction (1954) **John Masters** (1914)
Bianca Capello (1843) **Edward Bulwer-Lytton** (1803)
Biathanatos (1644) **John Donne** (1572–1631)
Bib Ballads (1915) **Ring Lardner** (1885)
Bible in Spain, The (1843) **George Borrow** (1803)
Bible Rhymes (1821) **Hannah More** (1745)
Bible Tragedies (1881) **R.H. Horne** (1803)
Biblical Religion and the Search for Ultimate Reality (1955) **Paul Tillich** (1886)
Bibliographical Decameron, The (1817) **Thomas Frognall Dibdin** (1776)
Bibliographical Tour in France and Germany, A (1821) **Thomas Frognall Dibdin** (1776)
Bibliographical Tour in the Northern Counties of England and Scotland, A (1838) **Thomas Frognall Dibdin** (1776–1847)
Bibliography of the English Printed Drama to the Restoration, A (1939) **W.W. Greg** (1875)
Bibliomania, The (1809) **Thomas Frognall Dibdin** (1776)
Bibliophobia (1832) **Thomas Frognall Dibdin** (1776–1847)
Bicentential Man, The (1976) **Isaac Asimov** (1920)
Biches, Les [music by Darius Milhaud and Francis Poulenc] (1924) **Jean Cocteau** (1889)
Bicycle, and Other Poems [US: *The Year of the Foxes*] (1970) **David Malouf** (1934)
Bicycle Rider in Beverley Hills, The (1952) **William Saroyan** (1908)
Bid for Fortune, A (1895) **Guy Boothby** (1867)
Bid Me to Live (1960) **Hilda Doolittle** (1886)
Bien Venu (1606) **John Davies of Hereford** (1565)
Big as Life (1966) **E.L. Doctorow** (1931)
Big Bow Mystery, The (1892) **Israel Zangwill** (1864)
Big Chapel, The (1971) **Thomas Kilroy** (1934)
Big Day, The (1976) **Barry Unsworth** (1930)
Big Heart, The (1945) **Mulk Raj Anand** (1905)
Big House of Inver, The (1925) **'Somerville and Ross' [Edith Somerville** (1858) and **Violet Martin]** (1862)
Big House, The (1958) **Brendan Behan** (1923)
Big House, The (1928) **Lennox Robinson** (1886)
Big Kill, The (1951) **Mickey Spillane** (1918)
Big Knife, The (1948) **Clifford Odets** (1906)
Big Laugh, The (1962) **John O'Hara** (1905)
Big Man, The (1985) **William McIlvanney** (1936)
Big Money, The (1936) **John Dos Passos** (1896)
Big Music, The (1971) **'Robert Garioch' [Robert Garioch Sutherland]** (1909)
Big Nowhere, The (1988) **James Ellroy** (1948)
Big Otter, The (1887) **R.M. Ballantyne** (1825)
Big Planet (1957) **Jack Vance** (1916)
Big Rock Candy Mountain, The (1943) **Wallace Stegner** (1909)
Big Sea, The (1940) **Langston Hughes** (1902)
Big Season, The (1962) **Maurice Gee** (1931)
Big Six, The (1940) **Arthur Ransome** (1884)
Big Sky, The (1947) **A.B. Guthrie** (1901)
Big Sleep, The (1939) **Raymond Chandler** (1888)
Big Sur (1962) **Jack Kerouac** (1922)
Big Sur and the Oranges of Hieronymus Bosch (1957) **Henry Miller** (1891)
Big Town, The (1921) **Ring Lardner** (1885)
Big Toys (1977) **Patrick White** (1912)
Big Women (1998) **Fay Weldon** (1931)
Big Woods (1955) **William Faulkner** (1897)
Bigger Light, The (1975) **Austin Clarke** (1932)
Biggles Flies Again (1934) **W.E. Johns** (1893)
Biggles Flies East (1935) **W.E. Johns** (1893)
Biggles Flies North (1939) **W.E. Johns** (1893)
Biggles Flies South (1938) **W.E. Johns** (1893)
Biggles Flies West (1937) **W.E. Johns** (1893)
Biggles in Africa (1936) **W.E. Johns** (1893)
Biggles in Borneo (1943) **W.E. Johns** (1893)
Biggles in the Baltic (1940) **W.E. Johns** (1893)
Biggles in the Jungle (1942) **W.E. Johns** (1893)
Biggles in the Orient (1945) **W.E. Johns** (1893)
Biggles of the Camel Squadron (1934) **W.E. Johns** (1893)
Biggles—Secret Agent (1940) **W.E. Johns** (1893)
Biggles Sees It Through (1941) **W.E. Johns** (1893)
Biggles Sees Too Much (1970) **W.E. Johns** (1893)
Biglow Papers, The [1st ser.; 2nd ser., 1867] (1848) **James Russell Lowell** (1819)
Bill Bailey (1986) **Catherine Cookson** (1906)
Bill Bailey's Daughter (1988) **Catherine Cookson** (1906)
Bill Bailey's Lot (1987) **Catherine Cookson** (1906)
Bill Bergsen, Master Detective (1946) **Astrid Lindgren** (1907)
Bill of Billabong (1931) **Mary Grant Bruce** (1878)
Bill of Divorcement, A (1921) **'Clemence Dane' [Winifred Ashton]** (1888)

Billabong Adventures (1927) **Mary Grant Bruce** (1878)
Billabong's Daughter (1924) **Mary Grant Bruce** (1878)
Billiards at Half-Past Nine [*Und sagte kein einziges Wort*] (1959) **Heinrich Böll** (1917)
Billicks (1909) **Arthur St John Adcock** (1864)
Billion Dollar Brain, The (1966) **Len Deighton** (1929)
Billion Year Spree (1973) **Brian Aldiss** (1925)
Billow and the Rock, The (1846) **Harriet Martineau** (1802)
Billy Bathgate (1989) **E.L. Doctorow** (1931)
Billy Budd [music by Benjamin Britten] (1951) **E.M. Forster** (1879)
Billy Bunter of Greyfriars School [the first 'Billy Bunter' book] (1947) **'Frank Richards' [Charles Harold St John Hamilton]** (1876)
Billy Liar (1959) **Keith Waterhouse** (1929)
Billy Liar on the Moon (1975) **Keith Waterhouse** (1929)
Billy Phelan's Greatest Game (1978) **William Joseph Kennedy** (1928)
Biloxi Blues (1984) **Neil Simon** (1927)
Bimbo (1990) **Keith Waterhouse** (1929)
Bingo (1973) **Edward Bond** (1934)
Bingo (1988) **Rita Mae Brown** (1944)
Bingo Palace, The (1994) **Louise Erdrich** (1954)
Binodini (1902) **Rabindranath Tagore** (1861)
Biographer's Moustache, The (1995) **Kingsley Amis** (1922)
Biographer's Tale, The (2000) **A.S. Byatt** (1936)
Biographia Britannica Literaria [vol. i] (1842) **Thomas Wright** (1810)
Biographia Literaria (1817) **S.T. Coleridge** (1772)
Biographical Dictionary of the Celebrated Women of Every Age and Country, A (1804) **Mary Matilda Betham** (1776)
Biographical Sketches (1863) **Nassau Senior** (1790–1864)
Biographical Sketches (1869) **Harriet Martineau** (1802)
Biographical Studies (1881) **Walter Bagehot** (1826–77)
Biography for Beginners (1905) **E.C. Bentley** (1875)
Biography of a Grizzly, The (1900) **Ernest Thompson Seton** (1860)
Birchwood (1973) **John Banville** (1945)
Bird Alone (1936) **'Seán O'Faoláin' [John Francis Whelan]** (1900)
Bird in a Cage, The (1633) **James Shirley** (1596)
Bird in Hand (1927) **John Drinkwater** (1882)
Bird in the Bush (1959) **Kenneth Rexroth** (1905)
Bird in the House, A (1970) **Margaret Laurence** (1926)
Bird in the Tree, The (1940) **Elizabeth Goudge** (1900)
Bird of Dawning, The (1933) **John Masefield** (1878)
Bird of Night, The (1972) **Susan Hill** (1942)
Bird of Paradise (1914) **Ada Leverson** (1862)
Bird of Paradise, The (1914) **W.H. Davies** (1871)
Bird's Nest, The (1954) **Shirley Jackson** (1919)
Birds and Flowers and Other Country Things (1838) **Mary Howitt** (1799)
Birds, Beasts and Flowers (1923) **D.H. Lawrence** (1885)
Birds Fall Down, The (1966) **'Rebecca West' [Cicily Isabel Andrews]** (1892)
Birds in a Village (1893) **W.H. Hudson** (1841)
Birds in London (1898) **W.H. Hudson** (1841)
Birds of America (1971) **Mary McCarthy** (1912)
Birds of Aristophanes, The (1824) **Henry Cary** (1772) (tr.)
Birds of Paradise, The (1962) **Paul Scott** (1920)
Birds of Passage (1895) **Mathilde Blind** (1841)
Birds of Passage (1981) **Bernice Rubens** (1923)
Birds of Prey (1867) **M.E. Braddon** (1835)
Birds of the Air, The (1980) **'Alice Thomas Ellis' [Anna Margaret Haycraft]** (1932)
Birds on the Trees, The (1970) **Nina Bawden** (1925)
Birds Reconvened (1980) **John Heath-Stubbs** (1918)
Birds, The (414BC) **Aristophanes** (*c.* 445 BC)
Birdsong (1994) **Sebastian Faulks** (1953)
Birmingham River (1994) **Roy Fisher** (1930)
Birth (1918) **Zona Gale** (1874)
Birth of a Hero (1951) **Herbert Gold** (1924)
Birth of a World (1951) **Waldo Frank** (1889)
Birth of the Muse, The (1698) **William Congreve** (1670)
Birth of Tragedy, The [*Die Geburt der Tragödie*] (1872) **Friedrich Wilhelm Nietzsche** (1844)
Birthday (1934) **Rodney Ackland** (1908)
Birthday Book for Children, The [verses by Mrs Sales Barker] (1880) **Kate Greenaway** (1846)
Birthday Boys, The (1991) **Beryl Bainbridge** (1934)
Birthday Letters (1998) **Ted Hughes** (1930)
Birthday Party, The [perf. 1958] (1960) **Harold Pinter** (1930)
Birthright (1910) **T.C. Murray** (1873)
Birthright, The (1844) **Mrs C.F. Gore** (1799)
Births, Deaths and Marriages (1839) **Theodore Hook** (1788)
Biscuits and Grog (1848) **James Hannay** (1827)
Bishop Burnet's History of His Own Time [vol. i; vol. ii, 1734] (1724) **Gilbert Burnet** (1643–1715)
Bishop Murder Case, The (1929) **'S.S. van Dine' [Willard Huntington Wright]** (1888)
Bishop of Bangor's Late Sermon Answer'd, The (1717) **William Law** (1686)
Bishop of Hell, The (1949) **'Marjorie Bowen' [Gabrielle Margaret Vere Campbell]** (1886)
Bishop Percy's Folio Manuscript (1867) **F.J. Furnivall** (1825) [with J.W. Hales]
Bishop's Apron, The (1906) **Somerset Maugham** (1874)
Bishop's Bonfire, The (1955) **Sean O'Casey** (1880)
Bishop's Crime, The (1940) **H.C. Bailey** (1878)
Bishop's Dilemma, The (1898) **Ella D'Arcy** (1851)
Bishop's Secret, The (1900) **Fergus Hume** (1859)
Bit Between My Teeth, The (1965) **Edmund Wilson** (1895)
Bit o' Writin', The (1838) **John Banim** (1798)

Bit of a Do, A (1986) **David Nobbs** (1935)
Bit of Singing and Dancing, A (1973) **Susan Hill** (1942)
Bit Off the Map, A (1957) **Angus Wilson** (1913)
Bitch, The (1979) **Jackie Collins** (1939)
Bitter Fame [biography of Sylvia Plath] (1989) **Anne Stevenson** (1933)
Bitter Heritage, The (1967) **Arthur Schlesinger** (1917)
Bitter Lemons (1957) **Lawrence Durrell** (1912)
Bitter Medicine (1987) **Sara Paretsky** (1947)
Bitter Sweet (1929) **Noel Coward** (1899)
Bitterns, The (1920) **Glenway Wescott** (1901)
Black Album, The (1995) **Hanif Kureishi** (1954)
Black and Blue (1997) **Ian Rankin** (1960)
Black and Blues (1976) **Edward Brathwaite** (1930)
Black and White Keys (1982) **Hugh Hood** (1928)
Black Arrow, The (1888) **Robert Louis Stevenson** (1850)
Black Baby (1988) **Clare Boylan** (1948)
Black Bagatelles (1978) **Rodney Hall** (1935)
Black Bartlemy's Treasure (1920) **Jeffery Farnol** (1878)
Black Beauty (1877) **Anna Sewell** (1820)
Black Beetles in Amber (1892) **Ambrose Bierce** (1842)
Black Bethlehem (1947) **Lettice Cooper** (1897)
Black Betty (1994) **Walter Mosley** (1952)
Black Book, The (1938) **Lawrence Durrell** (1912)
Black Book, The (1993) **Ian Rankin** (1960)
Black Booke, The (1604) **Thomas Middleton** (1580)
Black Box (1987) **Amos Oz** (1939)
Black Boxer, The (1932) **H.E. Bates** (1905)
Black Boy (1945) **Richard Wright** (1908)
Black Bryony (1923) **T.F. Powys** (1875)
Black Country, The (1946) **Walter Allen** (1911)
Black Dahlia, The (1987) **James Ellroy** (1948)
Black Daisies for the Bride (1993) **Tony Harrison** (1937)
Black Death, The (1968) **Philip Ziegler** (1929)
Black Diamond, The (1921) **Francis Brett Young** (1884)
Black Dog, The (1923) **A.E. Coppard** (1878)
Black Dogs (1992) **Ian McEwan** (1948)
Black Douglas, The (1899) **S.R. Crockett** (1860)
Black Faces, White Faces (1975) **Jane Gardam** (1928)
Black Gang, The (1922) **'Sapper' [Herman Cyril McNeile]** (1888)
Black Heart and White Heart (1900) **Sir H. Rider Haggard** (1856)
Black Hearts in Battersea (1964) **Joan Aiken** (1924)
Black Idol (1987) **Lisa St Aubin de Terán** (1953)
Black Ivory (1873) **R.M. Ballantyne** (1825)
Black Jack (1968) **Leon Garfield** (1921)
Black Joke, The (1974) **Farley Mowat** (1921)
Black Knight, The (1926) **Ethel M. Dell** (1881)
Black Lamb and Grey Falcon (1941) **'Rebecca West' [Cicily Isabel Andrews]** (1892)
Black List, Section H (1971) **Francis Stuart** (1902)
Black Magic (1909) **'Marjorie Bowen' [Gabrielle Margaret Vere Campbell]** (1886)
Black Magic (1969) **LeRoi Jones** (1934)
Black Man's Lament, The (1826) **Amelia Opie** (1769)
Black Marsden (1972) **Wilson Harris** (1921)
Black Mask, The (1901) **E.W. Hornung** (1866)
Black Minute, The (1929) **Pamela Frankau** (1908)
Black Mischief (1932) **Evelyn Waugh** (1903)
Black Monk, The [sometimes attrib. to T.P. Prest] (1844) **'Malcolm J. Errym' [James Malcolm Rymer]** (1804)
Black Moth, The (1921) **Georgette Heyer** (1902)
Black Narcissus (1939) **Rumer Godden** (1907)
Black Notice (1999) **Patricia Cornwell** (1956)
Black Obelisk, The [*Der schwartz Obelisk*] (1956) **'Erich Maria Remarque' [Erich Paul Remark]** (1898)
Black Oxen (1923) **Gertrude Atherton** (1857)
Black Poodle, The (1884) **'F. Anstey' [Thomas Anstey Guthrie]** (1856)
Black Power (1954) **Richard Wright** (1908)
Black Prince, The (1903) **Maurice Baring** (1874)
Black Prince, The (1955) **Shirley Ann Grau** (1929)
Black Prince, The (1973) **Iris Murdoch** (1919)
Black Prophet, The (1847) **William Carleton** (1794)
Black Reconstruction (1935) **W.E.B. Du Bois** (*c.* 1868)
Black Riders, The (1895) **Stephen Crane** (1871)
Black Robe, The (1881) **Wilkie Collins** (1824)
Black Robe (1985) **Brian Moore** (1921)
Black Rock, The (1928) **John Gould Fletcher** (1886)
Black Seasons, The (1945) **Henry Treece** (1911)
Black Sheep! (1867) **Edmund Yates** (1831)
Black Soul, The (1924) **Liam O'Flaherty** (1897)
Black Sparta (1928) **Naomi Mitchison** (1897)
Black Spring (1936) **Henry Miller** (1891)
Black Sugar (1992) **Jeremy Reed** (1954)
Black Sunday (1975) **Thomas Harris** (1940)
Black Swan, The (1932) **Rafael Sabatini** (1875)
Black Swan, The [*Die Betrogene*] (1953) **Thomas Mann** (1875)
Black Tower, The (1975) **P.D. James** (1920)
Black Tulip, The [*La Tulipe noire*] (1850) **Alexandre Dumas ['père']** (1802)
Black Velvet Gown, The (1984) **Catherine Cookson** (1906)
Black Venus [US: *Saints and Strangers*] (1985) **Angela Carter** (1940)
Black Water (1992) **Joyce Carol Oates** (1938)
Black-Eyed Susan (1829) **Douglas Jerrold** (1803)
Blackbird in the Lilac, The (1952) **James Reeves** (1909)
Blackboard Jungle, The [as Evan Hunter] (1954) **'Ed McBain' [Evan Hunter]** (1926)
Blacke Bookes Messenger, The (1592) **Robert Greene** (1558)
Blackeyes (1987) **Dennis Potter** (1935)
Blackground (1989) **Joan Aiken** (1924)
Blackheath Poisonings, The (1978) **Julian Symons** (1912)
Blackmailer, The (1958) **Isabel Colegate** (1931)
Blacks, The [*Les Nègres*] (1958) **Jean Genet** (1910)
Blackthorn Winter, and Other Stories (1936) **J.D. Beresford** (1873)
Blackwater Lightship, The (1999) **Colm Tóibín** (1955)
Blade Runner: A Movie (1979) **William S. Burroughs** (1914)

Blade-o'Grass (1871) **B.L. Farjeon** (1838)
Bladys of the Stewponey (1897) **S. Baring-Gould** (1834)
Blake (1995) **Peter Ackroyd** (1949)
Blame the Dead (1973) **Gavin Lyall** (1932)
Blaming (1976) **Elizabeth Taylor** (1912)
Blance, Lady Falaise (1891) **J.H. Shorthouse** (1834)
Blanche (1967) **Louis Aragon** (1897)
Blanche of Brandywine (1846) **George Lippard** (1822)
Blanche of Castile (1812) **Mary Russell Mitford** (1787)
Blandings Castle and Elsewhere (1935) **P.G. Wodehouse** (1881)
Blank Verse (1798) **Charles Lamb** (1775–1834) [with Charles Lloyd]
Blanket of the Dark, The (1931) **John Buchan** (1875)
Blasting and Bombarding (1937) **Wyndham Lewis** (1882)
Bleak House (1853) **Charles Dickens** (1812)
Bleak Spring (1993) **Jon Cleary** (1917)
Bleecker Street (1980) **Jeremy Reed** (1954)
Bleeding Heart, The (1980) **Marilyn French** (1929)
Blenheim (1728) **George Lyttelton, 1st Baron Lyttelton** (1709)
Blenheim (1705) **John Philips** (1676)
Blessed Above Women (1936) **Pamela Hansford Johnson** (1912)
Blessed are the Rich (1924) **James Evershed Agate** (1877)
Blessing Way, The (1970) **Tony Hillerman** (1925)
Blind Assassin, The (2000) **Margaret Atwood** (1939)
Blind Beggar of Alexandria, The (1598) **George Chapman** (1559?)
Blind Corner (1927) **'Dornford Yates' [Cecil William Mercer]** (1885)
Blind Fireworks (1929) **Louis MacNeice** (1907)
Blind Lion, The (1974) **Paula Gunn Allen** (1939)
Blind Love (1890) **Wilkie Collins** (1824–89)
Blind Love (1969) **V.S. Pritchett** (1900)
Blind Man's Ditch (1939) **Walter Allen** (1911)
Blind Marriage, A (1901) **George R. Sims** (1847)
Blind-Beggar of Bednal-Green, The (1659) **John Day** (*c.* 1574–1640) and Henry Chettle (1560?–1607)
Blindman's World, The (1898) **Edward Bellamy** (1850)
Blindness (1926) **'Henry Green' [Henry Vicent Yorke]** (1905)
Bliss (1981) **Peter Carey** (1943)
Bliss (1920) **'Katherine Mansfield' [Kathleen Mansfield Beauchamp]** (1888)
Blithe Spirit (1941) **Noel Coward** (1899)
Blithedale Romance, The (1852) **Nathaniel Hawthorne** (1804)
Blix (1899) **Frank Norris** (1870)
Blizzard, The (1834) **Sergei Timofeyevich Aksakov** (1791)
Blocks and Tackles (1990) **Les Murray** (1938)
Blonde: A Novel (2000) **Joyce Carol Oates** (1938)
Blondel (1927) **'Hugh Kingsmill' [Hugh Kingsmill Lunn]** (1889)
Blondel Parva (1868) **James Payn** (1830)
Blood (1995) **Michael Moorcock** (1939)
Blood and Guts in High School (1984) **Kathy Acker** (1948)
Blood and Ice (1982) **Liz Lochhead** (1947)
Blood, Bread, and Poetry (1987) **Adrienne Rich** (1929)
Blood Brothers (1986) **Willy Russell** (1947)
Blood Feud (1977) **Rosemary Sutcliff** (1920)
Blood for a Stranger (1942) **Randall Jarrell** (1914)
Blood Knot, The (1960) **Athol Fugard** (1932)
Blood Meridian (1985) **Cormac McCarthy** (1933)
Blood of My Bone (1989) **Simon Raven** (1927)
Blood of Others, The [*Le Sang des autres*] (1945) **Simone de Beauvoir** (1908)
Blood of the Lamb, The (1962) **Peter De Vries** (1910)
Blood of the Martyrs, The (1939) **Naomi Mitchison** (1897)
Blood on the Moon (1984) **James Ellroy** (1948)
Blood Poetry (1985) **Howard Brenton** (1942)
Blood Rain (1999) **Michael Dibdin** (1947)
Blood Red, Sister Rose (1974) **Thomas Keneally** (1935)
Blood Relations (1980) **Sharon Pollock** (1936)
Blood Royal (1893) **Grant Allen** (1848)
Blood Shot (1988) **Sara Paretsky** (1947)
Blood Vote, The (1985) **Jack Lindsay** (1900)
Blood Wedding [*Bodas de sangre*] (1933) **Federico García Lorca** (1898)
Bloodfather (1987) **David Ireland** (1927)
Bloodline (1977) **Sidney Sheldon** (1917)
Bloodshed (1976) **Cynthia Ozick** (1928)
Bloodsmoor Romance, A (1982) **Joyce Carol Oates** (1938)
Bloodstock (1954) **Margaret Irwin** (1889)
Bloody Brother, The (1639) **John Fletcher** (1579–1625)
Bloody Chamber, The (1979) **Angela Carter** (1940)
Bloody Chasm, The (1881) **John W. de Forest** (1826)
Bloody Murder [3rd edn, 1992] (1972) **Julian Symons** (1912)
Bloody Sunrise (1965) **Mickey Spillane** (1918)
Bloom of Candles, The (1947) **Laurie Lee** (1914)
Bloomsbury: A House of Lions (1979) **Leon Edel** (1907)
Blossoming World, The (1971) **H.E. Bates** (1905)
Blott on the Landscape (1975) **Tom Sharpe** (1928)
Blow Your House Down (1984) **Pat Barker** (1943)
Blown to Bits (1889) **R.M. Ballantyne** (1825)
Blubber (1974) **Judy Blume** (1938)
Blue (1988) **Adam Lively** (1961)
Blue Afternoon, The (1993) **William Boyd** (1952)
Blue at the Mizzen (1999) **Patrick O'Brian** (1914)
Blue Baby, The (1901) **Mary Louisa Molesworth** (1839)
Blue Bamboo (1994) **James Kirkup** (1923)
Blue Bird, The (1908) **Maurice Maeterlinck** (1862)
Blue Boat, The (1957) **William Mayne** (1928)
Blue Castle, The (1926) **L.M. Montgomery** (1874)
Blue Fairy Book, The (1889) **Andrew Lang** (1844) (ed.)
Blue Flower, The (1995) **Penelope Fitzgerald** (1916)
Blue Guitar, The (1980) **Nicholas Hasluck** (1942)

Blue Lagoon, The (1908) **Henry de Vere Stacpoole** (1863)
Blue Lights (1888) **R.M. Ballantyne** (1825)
Blue Movie (1970) **Terry Southern** (1924)
Blue Pavilions, The (1891) **Sir A.T. Quiller-Couch** (1863)
Blue Remembered Hills (1983) **Rosemary Sutcliff** (1920)
Blue Road, The (1990) **Kenneth White** (1936)
Blue Swallows, The (1967) **Howard Nemerov** (1920)
Blue Voyage (1927) **Conrad Potter Aiken** (1889)
Blue Woman, The (1994) **Mary Flanagan** (1943)
Blue-Fly in His Head, The (1962) **John Heath-Stubbs** (1918)
Bluebeard (1987) **Kurt Vonnegut** (1922)
Bluebeard's Castle (1972) **Roy Fisher** (1930)
Bluebeard's Egg (1983) **Margaret Atwood** (1939)
Bluebeard's Keys (1874) **Lady Anne Ritchie** (1837)
Bluebells (1961) **John Masefield** (1878)
Blues for Mister Charley (1964) **James Baldwin** (1924)
Blues People (1963) **LeRoi Jones** (1934)
Blues, The (1823) **George Gordon, Lord Byron** (1788)
Bluest Eye, The (1970) **Toni Morrison** (1931)
Bluette (1990) **Ronald Frame** (1953)
Blunderer, The (1954) **Patricia Highsmith** (1921)
Blunt Instrument, A (1938) **Georgette Heyer** (1902)
Blurt Master-Constable (1602) **Thomas Middleton** (1580)
Blush, The (1958) **Elizabeth Taylor** (1912)
Boadicea (1753) **Richard Glover** (1712)
Boadicea (1927) **Laurence Binyon** (1869)
Boarding House Blues (1961) **James T. Farrell** (1904)
Boarding House, The (1965) **'William Trevor' [William Trevor Cox]** (1928)
Boat Load of Home Folk, A (1968) **Thea Astley** (1925)
Boat, The (1949) **L.P. Hartley** (1895)
Boating for Beginners (1985) **Jeanette Winterson** (1959)
Boatman, The (1864) **Edward Bulwer-Lytton** (1803)
Boatman, The [enlarged 1968] (1957) **Jay Macpherson** (1931)
Boats of the 'Glen Carrig', The (1907) **William Hope Hodgson** (1877)
Boaz and Ruth (1920) **Andrew Young** (1885)
Bobbin Up (1959) **Dorothy Hewett** (1923)
Bocage ['Grove'] (1554) **Pierre de Ronsard** (1524)
Bodies of Work: Essays (1997) **Kathy Acker** (1948)
Bodily Harm (1981) **Margaret Atwood** (1939)
Bodily Harm (1992) **Rachel Billington** (1942)
Body, The (1949) **William Sansom** (1912)
Body Farm, The (1994) **Patricia Cornwell** (1956)
Body in the Library, The (1942) **Agatha Christie** (1890)
Body in the Silo, The (1933) **Ronald Knox** (1888)
Body Lovers, The (1967) **Mickey Spillane** (1918)
Body of Divinitie, A (1645) **James Ussher** (1581)
Body of Evidence (1991) **Patricia Cornwell** (1956)
Body of Water, A (1990) **Beverley Farmer** (1941)
Body Servant, The (1971) **James Kirkup** (1923)
Bodysurfers, The (1983) **Robert Drewe** (1943)
Boesman and Lena (1969) **Athol Fugard** (1932)
Bog of Stars, The (1893) **Standish O'Grady** (1846)
Bog-Land Studies (1892) **Jane Barlow** (1857)
Bog-Myrtle and Peat (1895) **S.R. Crockett** (1860–1914)
Bog-Myrtle and Peat (1921) **Flora Thompson** (1877)
Bogle Corbet (1831) **John Galt** (1779–1779)
Bohème galante, La ['Gallant Bohemian Life'] (1855) **'Gérard de Nerval' [Gérard Labrunie]** (1808)
Bohemia in London (1907) **Arthur Ransome** (1884)
Bold Stroke for a Husband, A (1783) **Hannah Cowley** (1743)
Bold Stroke for a Wife, A (1718) **Susanna Centlivre** (1669?)
Bomb, The (1908) **'Frank' Harris** (1856)
Bombed Happiness, The (1942) **J.F. Hendry** (1912)
Bomber Gipsy, The (1918) **A.P. Herbert** (1890)
Bombs Away (1942) **John Steinbeck** (1902)
Bon Ton (1775) **David Garrick** (1717)
Bon Voyage (1967) **Noel Coward** (1899)
Bonaventure (1888) **George Washington Cable** (1844)
Bond Slaves (1893) **Isabella [Mrs G. Linnaeus] Banks** (1821)
Bond-Man, The (1624) **Philip Massinger** (1583)
Bondman, The (1890) **Hall Caine** (1853)
Bone People, The (1984) **Keri Hulme** (1947)
Bones of Contention (1936) **'Frank O'Connor' [Michael Francis O'Donovan']** (1903)
Bonfire, A (1981) **Pamela Hansford Johnson** (1912)
Bonfire of the Vanities, The (1987) **Tom Wolfe** (1930)
Bonfires and Broomsticks (1947) **Mary Norton** (1903)
Bongleweed, The (1973) **Helen Cresswell** (1934)
Bonjour Tristesse (1954) **'Françoise Sagan' [Françoise Quoirez]** (1935)
bonne chanson, La ['The Pretty Song'] (1870) **Paul Verlaine** (1844)
Bonnet Over the Windmill (1937) **Dodie Smith** (1896)
Bons-Bons and Roses for Dolly (1972) **Dorothy Hewett** (1923)
Bonus, A (1977) **Elizabeth Smart** (1913)
Book, A (1923) **Djuna Barnes** (1892)
Book About Billie, A (1972) **David Helwig** (1938)
Book About Myself, A (1922) **Theodore Dreiser** (1871)
Book and the Brotherhood, The (1987) **Iris Murdoch** (1919)
Book Class, The (1984) **Louis Auchinloss** (1917)
Book for Boys and Girls, A (1686) **John Bunyan** (1628)
Book of Ahania, The (1795) **William Blake** (1757)
Book of Ballads, A (1931) **A.P. Herbert** (1890)
Book of Ballads, The (1845) **'Bon Gaultier' [W.E. Aytoun]** (1813)
Book of Caricatures, A (1907) **Max Beerbohm** (1872)
Book of Common Prayer, A (1977) **Joan Didion** (1934)
Book of Daniel, The (1971) **E.L. Doctorow** (1931)
Book of Dragons, The (1900) **E[dith] Nesbit** (1858)
Book of Dreams and Ghosts, The (1897) **Andrew Lang** (1844)

Book of Evidence, The (1989) **John Banville** (1945)
Book of Fallacies (1824) **Jeremy Bentham** (1748)
Book of Ghosts, A (1904) **S. Baring-Gould** (1834)
Book of Guys, The (1993) **Garrison Keillor** (1942)
Book of Household Management, The (1861) **Isabella Beeton** (1836)
Book of Jamaica, The (1980) **Russell Banks** (1940)
Book of Juniper, The (1981) **Tom Paulin** (1949)
Book of Life, The (1960) **C.H.B. Kitchin** (1895)
Book of Los, The (1795) **William Blake** (1757)
Book of Lost Tales Part 1, The (1983) **J.R.R. Tolkein** (1892–1973)
Book of Lost Tales Part 2, The (1984) **J.R.R. Tolkein** (1892–1973)
Book of Lost Tales Part 3, The (1985) **J.R.R. Tolkein** (1892–1973)
Book of Martyrs, The [**Foxe**]: see *Actes and Monuments*
Book of Matches (1993) **Simon Armitage** (1963)
Book of Mediterranean Food, A (1950) **Elizabeth David** (1913)
Book of Miracles, A (1939) **Ben Hecht** (1894)
Book of Mrs Noah, The (1987) **Michèle Roberts** (1949)
Book of Nonsense, A (1846) **Edward Lear** (1812)
Book of Nonsense and More Nonsense, A (1862) **Edward Lear** (1812)
Book of Poems [*Libro de poemas*] (1921) **Federico García Lorca** (1898)
The Book of Prefaces (2000) **Alasdair Grey** (1934)
Book of Repulsive Women, The (1948) **Djuna Barnes** (1892)
The Book of Ruth (1998) **Jane Hamilton**
Book of Sand, The [*El libro de arena*] (1975) **Jorge Luis Borges** (1899)
Book of Skulls, The (1971) **Robert Silverberg** (1935)
Book of Snobs, The (1848) **W.M. Thackeray** (1811)
Book of Songs [*Das Buch der Lieder*] (1827) **Heinrich Heine** (1797)
Book of Sun-Dials, The (1872) **Margaret [Mrs Alfred] Gatty** (1809)
Book of the Church, The (1824) **Robert Southey** (1774)
Book of the Earth, The (1925) **Alfred Noyes** (1880)
Book of the Hours, A (1979) **David Helwig** (1938)
Book of the Reading (1994) **Michael Wilding** (1942)
Book of the Rhymers' Club, The (1892) **Lionel Johnson** (1867)
Book of the Rose, The (1903) **Sir Charles G.D. Roberts** (1860)
Book of the Seasons, The (1831) **Mary Howitt** (1799) [with William Howitt]
Book of the Sword (1884) **Sir Richard Burton** (1821)
Book of Thel, The (1789) **William Blake** (1757)
Book of Verses, A (1888) **W.E. Henley** (1849)
Book of Verses, A (1898) **Edgar Lee Masters** (1868)
Book of Were Wolves, The (1890) **S. Baring-Gould** (1834)
Book of Wonder, The (1912) **Lord Dunsany** (1878)
Books and Bookmen (1886) **Andrew Lang** (1844)
Books and Characters (1922) **Lytton Strachey** (1880)
Books Do Furnish a Room (1971) **Anthony Powell** (1905)
Books in General (1953) **V.S. Pritchett** (1900)
Books in My Life, The (1952) **Henry Miller** (1891)
Books of Bale (1988) **John Arden** (1930)
Books of Blood [vols. i–iii] (1984, 1985) **Clive Barker** (1952)
Bookshop, The (1978) **Penelope Fitzgerald** (1916)
Border and Bastille (1863) **G.A. Lawrence** (1827)
Border Beagles (1840) **William Gilmore Simms** (1806)
Border Country (1960) **Raymond Williams** (1921)
Border Crossing (2000) **Pat Barker** (1943)
Border, The (1984) **Elaine Feinstein** (1930)
Borderlands (1914) **Wilfrid Gibson** (1878)
Borgia (1929) **Zona Gale** (1874)
Boris Godunov (1825) **Alexander Pushkin** (1799)
Borka (1963) **Joihn Burningham** (1926)
Born in Exile (1892) **George Gissing** (1857)
Born in the Gardens (1979) **Peter Nichols** (1927)
Born of Man (1989) **Stephen Gray** (1941)
Borough, The (1810) **George Crabbe** (1754)
Borrowers Afield, The (1955) **Mary Norton** (1903)
Borrowers Afloat, The (1959) **Mary Norton** (1903)
Borrowers Aloft, The (1961) **Mary Norton** (1903)
Borrowers Avenged, The (1982) **Mary Norton** (1903)
Borrowers, The (1952) **Mary Norton** (1903)
Borstal Boy (1958) **Brendan Behan** (1923)
Boscobel (1872) **W.H. Ainsworth** (1805)
Bosom Friends (1910) **Angela Brazil** (1869)
Boss Cupid (2000) **Thom Gunn** (1929)
Boss of Taroomba, The (1894) **E.W. Hornung** (1866)
Bostock and Harris (1979) **Leon Garfield** (1921)
Boston (1928) **Upton Sinclair** (1878)
Boston Adventure (1944) **Jean Stafford** (1915)
Bostonians, The (1886) **Henry James** (1843)
Boswell (1964) **Stanley Elkin** (1930)
Botanic Garden, The (1790) **Erasmus Darwin** (1731)
Both Your Houses (1933) **Maxwell Anderson** (1888)
Bothie of Toper-na-Fuosich, The (1848) **A.H. Clough** (1819)
Bothwell (1856) **W.E. Aytoun** (1813)
Bothwell (1851) **James Grant** (1822)
Bothwell (1874) **A.C. Swinburne** (1837)
Bottle Factory Outing, The (1974) **Beryl Bainbridge** (1934)
Bottle in the Smoke, A (1990) **A.N. Wilson** (1950)
Bottle's Path (1946) **T.F. Powys** (1875)
Bottom Dogs (1929) **Edward Dahlberg** (1900)
Boule-de-Suif ['Ball of Tallow'] (1880) **Guy de Maupassant** (1850)
Bound East for Cardiff (1916) **Eugene O'Neill** (1888)
Bounty Hunters, The (1953) **Elmore Leonard** (1925)
Bouquet of Barbed Wire, A (1969) **Andrea Newman** (1938)
Bourbons of Naples 1734–1825, The (1956) **Sir Harold Acton** (1904)
Bourbons of Naples 1825–61, The (1961) **Sir Harold Acton** (1904)
Bourgeois, The (1901) **Henry de Vere Stacpoole** (1863)
Bourgeois Poet, The [prose poems] (1964) **Karl Shapiro** (1913)

Bourne Identity, The (1980) **Robert Ludlum** (1927)
Bourne Supremacy, The (1986) **Robert Ludlum** (1927)
Bourne Ultimatum, The (1990) **Robert Ludlum** (1927)
Bouvard et Pécuchet [unfinished] (1881) **Gustave Flaubert** (1821–80)
Bow of Orange Ribbon, The (1886) **Amelia Barr** (1831)
Bowge of Courte, The (1499?) **John Skelton** (1460?)
Bows Against the Barons (1934) **Geoffrey Trease** (1909)
Box (1968) **Edward Albee** (1928)
Box (1990) **Adrian Henri** (1932)
Box and Cox (1847) **J.M. Morton** (1811)
Box Garden, The (1977) **Carol Shields** (1935)
Box of Delights, The (1935) **John Masefield** (1878)
Boxiana (1818) **Pierce Egan [the elder]** (1772)
Boy (1900) **Marie Corelli** (1855)
Boy (1931) **James Hanley** (1901)
Boy and the Monkey, The (1969) **Leon Garfield** (1921)
Boy Hairdresser and Lord Cucumber, The (1999) **Joe Orton** (1933–67) [with Kenneth Halliwell]
Boyhood: Scenes from Provincial Life (1997) **J.M. Coetzee** (1940)
Boy Hunters, The (1852) **Mayne Reid** (1818)
Boy Life on the Prairie (1899) **Hamlin Garland** (1860)
Boy With a Cart, The—Cuthman, Saint of Sussex (1937) **Christopher Fry [Christopher Fry Harris]** (1907)
Boy's Own Story, A (1982) **Edmund White** (1940)
Boy's Will, A (1913) **Robert Frost** (1874)
Boyfriends and Girlfriends (1994) **Douglas Dunn** (1942)
Boyhood (1854) **Leo Tolstoy** (1828)
Boyhood of Christ, The (1888) **Lew Wallace** (1827)
Boyne Water, The (1826) **John Banim** (1798)
Boys and Girls Come Out to Play (1949) **Nigel Dennis** (1912)
Boys and Girls Together (1963) **William Saroyan** (1908)
Boys From Brazil, The (1976) **Ira Levin** (1929)
Boys from the Black Stuff, The (1985) **Alan Bleasdale** (1946)
Boys in the Back Room, The (1941) **Edmund Wilson** (1895)
Boys in the Island, The [rev. 1974] (1958) **C.J. Koch** (1932)
Boys Who Stole the Funeral, The (1980) **Les Murray** (1938)
Boys Will be Boys (1963) **Simon Raven** (1927)
Bracebridge Hall [by 'Geoffrey Crayon'] (1822) **Washington Irving** (1783)
Bracken Hills in Autumn (1962) **'Hugh MacDiarmid' [Christopher Murray Grieve]** (1892)
Bracknels, The [rev. 1947 as Denis Bracknel] (1911) **Forrest Reid** (1875)
Brakespeare (1868) **G.A. Lawrence** (1827)
Brambletye House (1826) **Horace Smith** (1779)
Bramleighs of Bishop's Folly, The (1868) **Charles Lever** (1806)
Branch of Dodona, The (1970) **David Campbell** (1915)
Branches of Adam (1926) **John Gould Fletcher** (1886)
Branching Stairs, The (1984) **John Ash** (1948)
Brand (1865) **Henrik Ibsen** (1828)
Brand New Life, A (1972) **James T. Farrell** (1904)
Branded (1888) **Mrs Caroline Bray** (1814)
Brandons, The (1939) **Angela Thirkell** (1890)
Brangane: A Memoir (1926) **Martin Boyd** (1893)
Brangwyn Mystery, The (1906) **David Christie Murray** (1847)
Brass Bottle, The (1900) **'F. Anstey' [Thomas Anstey Guthrie]** (1856)
Brass Butterfly, The (1958) **William Golding** (1911)
Brass Check, The (1919) **Upton Sinclair** (1878)
Brass Cupcake, The (1950) **John D. MacDonald** (1916)
Brassneck (1973) **Howard Brenton** (1942) [with David Hare]
Brava, La (1983) **Elmore Leonard** (1925)
Brave and Cruel (1948) **Denton Welch** (1915)
Brave Lady, A (1870) **Dinah Maria Craik** (1826)
Brave New World (1932) **Aldous Huxley** (1894)
Brave New World Revisited (1958) **Aldous Huxley** (1894)
Bravery of Earth, A (1930) **Richard Eberhart** (1904)
Braving the Elements (1972) **James Merrill** (1926)
Bravo, The (1831) **James Fenimore Cooper** (1789)
Bravo of Venice, The (1805) **M.G. Lewis** (1775)
Brazen Age, The (1613) **Thomas Heywood** (1574?)
Brazen Head, The (1956) **John Cooper Powys** (1872)
Brazen Lyre, The (1911) **E.V. Knox** (1881)
Brazen Tower, The (1974) **Ralph Gustafson** (1909)
Brazil (1994) **John Updike** (1932)
Brazil on the Move (1963) **John Dos Passos** (1896)
Brazilian Adventure (1933) **Peter Fleming** (1907)
Brazzaville Beach (1990) **William Boyd** (1952)
Bread Givers (1925) **Anzia Yezierska** (*c.* 1885)
Bread of Truth, The (1963) **R.S. Thomas** (1913)
Bread Rather Than Blossoms (1956) **D.J. Enright** (1920)
Bread Upon the Waters (1852) **Dinah Maria Craik** (1826)
Bread Upon the Waters (1981) **Irwin Shaw** (1913)
Bread-Winners, The (1884) **John Hay** (1838)
Breadwinner, The (1930) **Somerset Maugham** (1874)
Breaker of Laws, A (1900) **W. Pett Ridge** (1860)
Breakers and Granite (1921) **John Gould Fletcher** (1886)
Breakfast at Tiffany's (1958) **Truman Capote** (1924)
Breakfast in Bed (1863) **George Augustus Sala** (1828)
Breakfast of Champions (1973) **Kurt Vonnegut** (1922)
Breaking a Butterfly (1869) **G.A. Lawrence** (1827)
Breaking Ground (1984) **Alison Brackenbury** (1953)
Breaking of Bumbo, The (1959) **Andrew Sinclair** (1935)
Breaking Point, The (1907) **Edward Garnett** (1868)
Breaking Point, The [inc.'The Birds'] (1959) **Daphne du Maurier** (1907)

Breaking the Silence (1985) **Stephen Poliakoff** (1952)
Breast, The (1972) **Philip Roth** (1933)
Breath of Air, A (1950) **Rumer Godden** (1907)
Breath of French Air, A (1959) **H.E. Bates** (1905)
Breathing Lessons (1988) **Anne Tyler** (1941)
Brébuf and his Brethren (1940) **E.J. Pratt** (1882)
Bred in the Bone (1904) **Thomas Nelson Page** (1853)
Breeze of Morning, A (1951) **Charles Morgan** (1894)
Breezeblock Park (1975) **Willy Russell** (1947)
Bresant (1873) **Julian Hawthorne** (1846)
Brethren, The (1904) **Sir H. Rider Haggard** (1856)
Brethren, The (2000) **John Grisham** (1955)
Breviate of the Life of Margaret [Baxter], A (1681) **Richard Baxter** (1615)
Breviate of the Life of William Laud, A (1644) **William Prynne** (1600)
Brewsie and Willie (1946) **Gertrude Stein** (1874)
Brian Boroihme (1812) **James Sheridan Knowles** (1784)
Briary-Bush, The (1921) **Floyd Dell** (1887)
Brickfield, The (1964) **L.P. Hartley** (1895)
Bricks Without Straw (1880) **Albion W. Tourgée** (1838)
Bridal of Triermain, The (1813) **Sir Walter Scott** (1771)
Bridal Pond (1930) **Zona Gale** (1874)
Bride, The (1828) **Joanna Baillie** (1762)
Bride Comes to Evensford, The (1949) **H.E. Bates** (1905)
Bride for the Unicorn, A (1933) **Denis Johnston** (1901)
Bride from the Bush, A (1890) **E.W. Hornung** (1866)
Bride from the Sea, A (1904) **Guy Boothby** (1867)
Bride of Abydos, The (1813) **George Gordon, Lord Byron** (1788)
Bride of the Innisfallen, The (1955) **Eudora Welty** (1909)
Bride of the Mistletoe, The (1909) **James Lane Allen** (1849)
Bride of Zante, The (1861) **Mrs C.F. Gore** (1799)
Bride Price, The (1976) **Buchi Emecheta** (1944)
Bride Wore Black, The [also pub. as *Beware the Lady*] (1940) **Cornell Woolrich** (1903)
Bride's Tragedy, The (1822) **Thomas Lovell Beddoes** (1803)
Bridegroom Cometh, The (1939) **Waldo Frank** (1889)
Brides of Reason (1955) **Donald Davie** (1922)
Brideshead Revisited (1945) **Evelyn Waugh** (1903)
Bridge, The (1986) **Iain Banks** (1954)
Bridge, The (1930) **Hart Crane** (1899)
Bridge, The (1945) **Ruth Pitter** (1897)
Bridge, The (1957) **Pamela Frankau** (1908)
Bridge Dividing, The [repub. 1927 as *The Misses Mallett*] (1922) **E.H. Young** (1880)
Bridge of Fire, The (1907) **James Elroy Flecker** (1884)
Bridge of Lost Desire, The (1987) **Samuel R. Delany** (1942)
Bridge of San Luis Rey, The (1927) **Thornton Wilder** (1897)
Bridge Over the River Kwai, The [*Le Pont sur la Rivière Kwai*] (1952) **Pierre Boulle** (1912)
Bridgehead (1957) **Waldo Frank** (1889)
Bridges at Toko-ri, The (1953) **James A. Michener** (1907)
Bridget (1877) **Matilda Betham-Edwards** (1836)
Bridle the Wind (1983) **Joan Aiken** (1924)
Brief Account of the Province of Pennsylvania, A (1681) **William Penn** (1644)
Brief Candles (1930) **Aldous Huxley** (1894)
Brief Diversions (1922) **J.B. Priestley** (1894)
Brief History of Moscovia, A (1682) **John Milton** (1608–74)
Brief History of the War with the Indians, A (1676) **Increase Mather** (1639)
Brief Lives (1990) **Anita Brookner** (1928)
Brief Lives [**Aubrey**]: see *Lives of Eminent Men*
Brief Reflections Relative to the Emigrant French Clergy (1793) **Frances Burney** (1752)
Briefe and True Report of the New Found Land of Virginia, A (1588) **Thomas Harriot** (1560)
Briefe of the Art of Rhetorique, A [from Aristotle] (1637) **Thomas Hobbes** (1588) (tr.)
Briefing For a Descent into Hell (1971) **Doris Lessing** (1919)
Briefings (1971) **A.R. Ammons** (1926)
Brigadier and the Golf Widow, The (1964) **John Cheever** (1912)
Briggflatts (1966) **Basil Bunting** (1900)
Bright Day (1946) **J.B. Priestley** (1894)
Bright Lights, Big City (1983) **Jay McInerney** (1955)
Bright November (1947) **Kingsley Amis** (1922)
Bright Pavilions, The (1940) **Sir Hugh Walpole** (1884)
Bright Prison, The (1956) **Penelope Mortimer** (1918)
Brighter Sun, A (1952) **Samuel Selvon** (1923)
Brightfount Diaries, The (1955) **Brian Aldiss** (1925)
Brightness Falls (1992) **Jay McInerney** (1955)
Brightness to Cast Shadows, A (1980) **David Constantine** (1944)
Brighton Beach Memoirs (1983) **Neil Simon** (1927)
Brighton Rock (1938) **Graham Greene** (1904)
Brilliant Lies (1993) **David Williamson** (1942)
Brimstone and Treacle (1978) **Dennis Potter** (1935)
Brimstone Wedding, The [as 'Barbara Vine'] (1996) **Ruth Rendell** (1930)
Bring Back the Bells (1943) **A.P. Herbert** (1890)
Bring! Bring! (1925) **Conrad Potter Aiken** (1889)
Bring Forth the Body (1974) **Simon Raven** (1927)
Bring Larks and Heroes (1967) **Thomas Keneally** (1935)
Bring the Monkey (1933) **Miles Franklin** (1879)
Briseis (1896) **William Black** (1841)
Britain [*Liberty* pt. iv] (1736) **James Thomson** (1700)
Britain and Her Army (1970) **Correlli Barnett** (1927)
Britain's Ida (1628) **Phineas Fletcher** (1582)
Britain's Remembrancer (1628) **George Wither** (1588)
Britannia [tr. Philemon Holland; first pub. in Latin 1586] (1610) **William Camden** (1551)
Britannia (1729) **James Thomson** (1700)
Britannia (1755) **David Mallet** (1705?)
Britannia and Batavia (1740) **George Lillo** (1693)
Britannia Rediviva (1688) **John Dryden** (1631)

Britannia Triumphans (1638) **Sir William Davenant** (1606) [and Inigo Jones]
Britannia Victrix (1919) **Robert Bridges** (1844)
Britannia's Pastorals (1613) **William Browne of Tavistock** (1590?)
Britannia's Pastorals: The Second Book (1616) **William Browne of Tavistock** (1590?)
Britannicus (1669) **Jean Racine** (1639)
British Architects and Craftsmen (1945) **Sir Sacheverell Sitwell** (1897)
British Barbarians, The (1895) **Grant Allen** (1848)
British Bibliographer, The (1810) **Sir Samuel Egerton Brydges** (1762)
British Campaign in France and Flanders, The [vol. i] (1916, 1917, 1918, 1919, 1920) **A. Conan Doyle** (1859)
British Constitution, The (1844) **Henry, Lord Brougham** (1778)
British Drama, The (1945) **'James Bridie' [Osborne Henry Mavor]** (1888)
British Museum is Falling Down, The (1965) **David Lodge** (1935)
British Novelists and Their Styles (1859) **David Masson** (1822)
British Novelists, The (1810) **Anna Laetitia Barbauld** (1743) (ed.)
British Philippic, A (1738) **Mark Akenside** (1721)
British Prison Ship, The (1781) **Philip Freneau** (1752)
British Recluse, The (1722) **Eliza Haywood** (*c.*1693)
British Theatre, The (1808) **Elizabeth Inchbald** (1753) (ed.)
British Way in Warfare, The (1932) **Sir Basil Liddell Hart** (1895)
Briton, The (1722) **Ambrose Philips** (1674)
Broad Highway, The (1910) **Jeffery Farnol** (1878)
Broad-Stone of Honour, The (1822) **Kenelm Henry Digby** (1796?)
Broadcast Minds (1932) **Ronald Knox** (1888)
Broadcast Talks (1942) **C.S. Lewis** (1898)
Broadway Bound (1986) **Neil Simon** (1927)
Brodgar Poems (1992) **George Mackay Brown** (1921)
Broke Heart Blues (1999) **Joyce Carol Oates** (1938)
Broken Bridge, The (1994) **Lynne Reid Banks** (1929)
Broken Chariot, The (1998) **Alan Sillitoe** (1928)
Broken Dishes (1929) **Martin Flavin** (1883)
Broken Glass (1994) **Arthur Miller** (1915)
Broken Halo, The (1913) **Florence Barclay** (1862)
Broken Heart, The (1633) **John Ford** (1586)
Broken Journey, A (1932) **Morley Callaghan** (1903)
Broken Music (1914) **Phyllis Bottome** (1884)
Broken Necks (1924) **Ben Hecht** (1894)
Broken Places, The (1963) **George MacBeth** (1932)
Broken Record (1934) **Roy Campbell** (1901)
Broken Road, The (1907) **A.E.W. Mason** (1865)
Broken Span, The (1941) **William Carlos Williams** (1883)
Broken Ties (1925) **Rabindranath Tagore** (1861)
Broken to Harness (1865) **Edmund Yates** (1831)
Broker of Bogotá, The (1834) **Robert Bird** (1806)
Bronwen, the Traw, and the Shape-Shifter (1986) **James Dickey** (1923)
Bronze Horseman, The (1833) **Alexander Pushkin** (1799)
Brood of the Witch-Queen (1918) **'Sax Rohmer' [Arthur Henry Sarsfield Ward]** (1883)
Brook Kerith, The (1916) **George Moore** (1852)
Broom Squire, The (1896) **S. Baring-Gould** (1834)
Broome Stages (1931) **'Clemence Dane' [Winifred Ashton]** (1888)
Broomsticks (1925) **Walter de la Mare** (1873)
Brothel in Rosenstrasse, The (1982) **Michael Moorcock** (1939)
Brother and Sister [as Marian Lewes] (1869) **'George Eliot' [Mary Ann Evans]** (1819)
Brother Cadfael's Penance (1994) **'Ellis Peters' [Edith Mary Pargeter]** (1913)
Brother Dusty-Feet (1952) **Rosemary Sutcliff** (1920)
Brother Gabriel (1878) **Matilda Betham-Edwards** (1836)
'Brother Jacob' (1864) **George Eliot** (1819)
Brother Jonathan (1825) **John Neal** (1793)
Brother of Daphne, The (1914) **'Dornford Yates' [Cecil William Mercer]** (1885)
Brother of the More Famous Jack (1982) **Barbara Trapido** (1941)
Brother to Dragons [rev. 1979] (1953) **Robert Penn Warren** (1905)
Brother's Tale, A (1980) **Stan Barstow** (1928)
Brotherhood of Man (1949) **Richard Eberhart** (1904)
Brotherhood of the Seven Kings, The (1899) **Mrs L.T. Meade** (1854) [with 'Robert Eustace' (Robert Eustace Barton)]
Brothers and Sisters (1929) **I. Compton-Burnett** (1884)
Brothers and Sisters [from Frederika Bremer] (1848) **Mary Howitt** (1799) (tr.)
Brothers, The (1753) **[Edward Young]** (1683)
Brothers, The (1769) **Richard Cumberland** (1732)
Brothers, The (1938) **H.G. Wells** (1866)
Brothers, The (1983) **Bernice Rubens** (1923)
Brothers Karamazov, The (1880) **Fyodor Mikhailovich Dostoevsky** (1821)
Brown Fairy Book, The (1904) **Andrew Lang** (1844) (ed.)
Brown on Resolution [US: *Single-Handed*] (1929) **C.S. Forester** (1899)
Brown, V.C. (1899) **Mrs A.H. Alexander** (1825)
Brownie of Bodsbeck, The (1818) **James Hogg** (1770)
Brownies, The (1870) **Mrs J.H. Ewing** (1841)
Browning Version, The (1948) **Terence Rattigan** (1911)
Brownlows (1868) **Margaret Oliphant** (1828)
Brownout on Breadfruit Boulevard (1995) **Timothy Mo** (1950)
Brownsmith's Boy (1886) **George Manville Fenn** (1831)
Brownstone Eclogues (1942) **Conrad Potter Aiken** (1889)
Bruce, The (1571) **John Barbour** (*c.* 1320)
Bruges-la-Morte (1892) **Georges Rodenbach** (1855)
Bruno's Dream (1969) **Iris Murdoch** (1919)
Brutus of Alba (1678) **Nahum Tate** (1652)

Brutus's Orchard (1957) **Roy Fuller** (1912)
Brynhild (1937) **H.G. Wells** (1866)
Bubble, The (1721) **Jonathan Swift** (1667)
Bubble, The (1984) **Mulk Raj Anand** (1905)
Buccaneer, The (1832) **Anna Maria [Mrs S.C.] Hall** (1800)
Buccaneer, The (1925) **Maxwell Anderson** (1888) [with Laurence Stallings]
Buccaneers, The [unfinished] (1938) **Edith Wharton** (1862)
Buckdancer's Choice (1965) **James Dickey** (1923)
Bucket Shop, The (1968) **Keith Waterhouse** (1929)
Bucolic Comedies (1923) **Edith Sitwell** (1887)
Buddenbrooks (1901) **Thomas Mann** (1875)
Buddha of Suburbia, The (1990) **Hanif Kureishi** (1954)
Budget of the Bubble Family, The (1840) **Edward Bulwer-Lytton** (1803)
Buff (1965) **Roy Fuller** (1912)
Buffalo Girls (1990) **Larry McMurty** (1936)
Buffalo Hunters, The (1891) **R.M. Ballantyne** (1825)
Bug Jack Barron (1969) **Norman Spinrad** (1940)
Build-Up, The (1952) **William Carlos Williams** (1883)
Builders, The (1919) **Ellen Glasgow** (1874)
Building of Jalna, The (1944) **Mazo de la Roche** (1879)
Building Speculation [*La speculazione edilizia*] (1957) **Italo Calvino** (1923)
Bull From the Sea, The (1962) **'Mary Renault' [Eileen Mary Challans]** (1905)
Bull-Dog Drummond (1920) **'Sapper' [Herman Cyril McNeile]** (1888)
Bull-Dog Drummond at Bay (1935) **'Sapper' [Herman Cyril McNeile]** (1888)
Bullet Park (1969) **John Cheever** (1912)
Buln-Buln and the Brolga, The (1944) **Joseph Furphy** (1843–1912)
Bulwark, The (1946) **Theodore Dreiser** (1871)
Bumblebee Flies Anyway, The (1985) **Robert Cormier** (1925)
Bunch of Keys, A (1883) **Charles Hale Hoyt** (1860)
Bundle, The (1978) **Edward Bond** (1934)
Bunyip Land (1884) **George Manville Fenn** (1831)
Buoyant Billions (1948) **Bernard Shaw** (1856)
Buoyant Billions, Farfetched Fables, and Shakes Versus Shav (1951) **Bernard Shaw** (1856–1950)
Burden of Proof, The (1990) **Scott Turow** (1949)
Burger's Daughter (1979) **Nadine Gordimer** (1923)
Burglar Bill (1977) **Alan Ahlberg** (1938)
Burglar of the Zodiac, The (1918) **William Rose Benét** (1886)
Burial of the Guns, The (1894) **Thomas Nelson Page** (1853)
Buried Alive (1908) **Arnold Bennett** (1867)
Buried Day, The (1960) **C. Day Lewis** (1904)
Buried For Pleasure (1948) **'Edmund Crispin'** (1921)
Buried Land, A (1963) **Madison Jones** (1925)
Burlesque upon Burlesque (1675) **Charles Cotton** (1630)
Burmese Days (1934) **'George Orwell'** (1903)
Burn [adaptation of *Image in the Clay* 1964] (1974) **David Ireland** (1927)
Bùrn is Aran [in Gaelic] (1960) **Iain Crichton Smith [Iain Mac a'Ghobhainn]** (1928)
Burn Marks (1990) **Sara Paretsky** (1947)
Burn, The (1991) **James Kelman** (1946)
Burning Book, The (1983) **Maggie Gee** (1948)
Burning Boy, The (1990) **Maurice Gee** (1931)
Burning Boys, The (1989) **John Fuller** (1937)
Burning Bright (1950) **John Steinbeck** (1902)
Burning Bush, The (1967) **Richard Church** (1893)
Burning Cactus, The (1936) **Sir Stephen Spender** (1909)
Burning Chrome (1986) **William Gibson** (1948)
Burning Cone, The (1970) **George MacBeth** (1932)
Burning Daylight (1910) **'Jack London' [John Griffith Chaney]** (1876)
Burning in Water, Drowning in Flame (1974) **Charles Bukowski** (1920)
Burning Mountain, The (1946) **John Gould Fletcher** (1886)
Burning Mystery of Anna in 1951, The (1979) **Kenneth Koch** (1925)
Burning of the Leaves, The (1944) **Laurence Binyon** (1869–1943)
Burning Oracle, The (1939) **G. Wilson Knight** (1897)
Burning Perch, The (1963) **Louis MacNeice** (1907)
Burning Spear, The (1919) **John Galsworthy** (1867)
Burning Wheel, The (1916) **Aldous Huxley** (1894)
Burning Your Boats (1995) **Angela Carter** (1940–92)
Burns (1854) **Thomas Carlyle** (1795)
Burnt House, The (1989) **Adam Lively** (1961)
Burnt Million, The (1890) **James Payn** (1830)
Burnt Norton (1941) **T.S. Eliot** (1888)
Burnt Ones, The (1964) **Patrick White** (1912)
Burnt Pages, The (1991) **John Ash** (1948)
Burnt-Out Case, A (1961) **Graham Greene** (1904)
Burr (1973) **Gore Vidal** (1925)
Burr Oaks (1947) **Richard Eberhart** (1904)
Bury My Heart at W.H. Smith's (1990) **Brian Aldiss** (1925)
Bury the Dead (1936) **Irwin Shaw** (1913)
Bury-Fair (1689) **Thomas Shadwell** (1642?)
Bus Stop (1955) **William Inge** (1913)
Busconductor Hines, The (1984) **James Kelman** (1946)
Bush Ballads and Galloping Rhymes (1870) **Adam Lindsay Gordon** (1833)
Bush Garden, The (1971) **Northrop Frye** (1912)
Bush Girl's Romance, A (1894) **Hume Nisbet** (1849)
Bush Studies (1902) **Barbara Baynton** (1857)
Bushrangers, The (1853) **Charles Harpur** (1813)
Busie Body, The (1709) **Susanna Centlivre** (1669?)
Business of Pleasure, The (1865) **Edmund Yates** (1831)
Business, The (1999) **Iain Banks** (1954)
Busiris (1719) **Edward Young** (1683)
Busman's Honeymoon (1937) **Dorothy L. Sayers** (1893)
Bussy D'Ambois (1607) **George Chapman** (1559?)
But Gentlemen Marry Brunettes (1928) **Anita Loos** (1893)

But It Still Goes On (1930) **Robert Graves** (1895)
But the Earth Abideth (1943) **William Soutar** (1898)
But Who Wakes the Burglar? (1940) **Peter de Vries** (1910)
Butcher's Broom (1934) **Neil M. Gunn** (1891)
Butcher's Dozen (1972) **Thomas Kinsella** (1928)
Butler's Ghost (1682) **Thomas d'Urfey** (1653)
Butley (1971) **Simon Gray** (1936)
Butterfield 8 (1935) **John O'Hara** (1905)
Butterflies (1973) **Ian Hamilton Finlay** (1925)
Butterfly, The (1947) **James M. Cain** (1892)
Butterfly Plague, The (1969) **Timothy Findley** (1930)
Butterfly's Ball and the Grasshopper's Feast, The (1807) **William Roscoe** (1753)
Buyer's Market, A (1952) **Anthony Powell** (1905)
Buying a Heart (1977) **George MacBeth** (1932)
Buzz Buzz (1981) **John Heath Stubbs** (1918)
By Avon River (1949) **Hilda Doolittle** (1886)
By Beach and Bog-Land (1905) **Jane Barlow** (1857)
By Celia's Arbour (1878) **Sir Walter Besant** (1836) [with James Rice]
By Grand Central Station I Sat Down and Wept (1945) **Elizabeth Smart** (1913)
By Love Possessed (1957) **James Gould Cozzens** (1903)
By Pike and Dyke (1890) **G.A. Henty** (1832)
By Proxy (1878) **James Payn** (1830)
By Reef and Palm (1894) **Louis Becke** (1855)
By Request [US: *Peggy by Request*] (1927) **Ethel M. Dell** (1881)
By Right of Conquest (1891) **G.A. Henty** (1832)
By Still Waters (1906) **George William Russell ['AE']** (1867)
By the Fisheries (1984) **Jeremy Reed** (1954)
By the Gate of the Sea (1883) **David Christie Murray** (1847)
By the Gods Beloved (1905) **Baroness Orczy** (1865)
By the Ionian Sea (1901) **George Gissing** (1857)
By the Light of My Father's Smile (1999) **Alice Walker** (1944)
By the Marshes of Minas (1900) **Sir Charles G.D. Roberts** (1860)
By the North Gate (1963) **Joyce Carol Oates** (1938)
By the Pricking of My Thumbs (1968) **Agatha Christie** (1890)
By the Sound (1991) **Ed Dorn** (1929)
By Thrasna River (1895) **Shan F. Bullock** (1865)
Bye-Bye Blackbird (1971) **Anita Desai** (1937)
Bylow Hill (1902) **George Washington Cable** (1844)
Byron in Italy (1941) **Peter Quennell** (1905)
Byron: The Years of Fame (1935) **Peter Quennell** (1905)
Bystander, The (1957) **Randolph Stow** (1935)
Byzantine Achievement, The (1929) **Robert Byron** (1905)
Byzantine Civilisation (1933) **Sir Steven Runciman** (1903
Byzantium Endures [first of the 'Pyat' series] (1981) **Michael Moorcock** (1939)

C

'C' is for Corpse (1986) **Sue Grafton** (1940)
'C' (1924) **Maurice Baring** (1874)
Cab at the Door, A (1968) **V.S. Pritchett** (1900)
Cabal (1988) **Clive Barker** (1952)
Cabala, The (1926) **Thornton Wilder** (1897)
Cabbages and Kings (1904) **'O. Henry' [William Sydney Porter]** (1862)
Cabbagetown [complete text pub. 1968] (1950) **Hugh Garner** (1913)
Cabin Fever (1990) **Elizabeth Jolley** (1923)
Cabin, The (1993) **David Mamet** (1947)
Cabinet Minister, The (1839) **Mrs C.F. Gore** (1799)
Cabinet Minister, The (1890) **Arthur Wing Pinero** (1855)
Cabinet Secret, A (1901) **Guy Boothby** (1867)
Cabot Wright Begins (1964) **James Purdy** (1923)
Cactus on Carmel (1967) **Jack Clemo** (1916)
Cadences (1915) **F.S. Flint** (1885)
Cadenus and Vanessa (1726) **Jonathan Swift** (1667)
Cadillac Jack (1982) **Larry McMurty** (1936)
Caesar (1993) **Allan Massie** (1938)
Caesar and Pompey (1631) **George Chapman** (1559?)
Caesar Borgia (1679) **Nathaniel Lee** (1649?)
Caesar Borgia (1846) **Emma Robinson** (1814)
Caesar in Aegypt (1725) **Colley Cibber** (1671)
Caesar's Camp (1755) **Stephen Duck** (1705)
Café Royal, The (1923) **Arthur Symons** (1865)
Cage Bird, The (1933) **Francis Brett Young** (1884)
Cage Without Grievance (1942) **W.S. Graham** (1918)
Cages (1966) **Ruth Fainlight** (1931)
Cahiers d'André Walter, Les (1891) **André Gide** (1869)
Cain (1923) **Jean Toomer** (1894)
Caine Mutiny, The (1951) **Herman Wouk** (1915)
Caius Gracchus (1815) **James Sheridan Knowles** (1784)
Cakes and Ale (1842) **Douglas Jerrold** (1803)
Cakes and Ale (1930) **Somerset Maugham** (1874)
Cal (1983) **Bernard MacLaverty** (1942)
Calamiterror (1937) **George Barker** (1913)
Calamities of Authors (1812) **Isaac D'Israeli** (1766)
Calavar (1834) **Robert Bird** (1806)
Caleb Field (1851) **Margaret Oliphant** (1828)
Caleb Williams [**Godwin**]: see *Things as They Are*
Caledonia (1706) **Daniel Defoe** (1660)
Calendar of Love, A (1967) **George Mackay Brown** (1921)
Caliban in Grub Street (1930) **Ronald Knox** (1888)
Calico Shoes (1934) **James T. Farrell** (1904)
California Suite (1976) **Neil Simon** (1927)
California Time (1975) **Frederic Raphael** (1931)
Californians, The [rev. 1935] (1898) **Gertrude Atherton** (1857)
Californians (1916) **Robinson Jeffers** (1887)
Caligula (1698) **John Crowne** (d. 1703)
Caligula (1938) **Albert Camus** (1913)
Calisto (1675) **John Crowne** (d. 1703)
Call, A (1910) **Ford Madox Ford** (1873)

Call for the Dead (1961) **'John le Carré' [David John Moore Cornwell]** (1931)
Call If You Need Me (2000) **Raymond Carver** (1939–1988)
Call It a Day (1935) **Dodie Smith** (1896)
Call It Sleep (1934) **Henry Roth** (1906)
Call Me Ishmael (1947) **Charles Olson** (1910)
Call Mr Fortune (1920) **H.C. Bailey** (1878)
Call My Brother Back (1939) **Michael McLaverty** (1904)
Call of the Blood, The (1906) **Robert Hichens** (1864)
Call of the South, The (1909) **Louis Becke** (1855)
Call of the Toad, The [*Die Unkenrufe*] (1992) **Günter Grass** (1927)
Call of the Valley (1968) **Gillian Avery** (1926)
Call of the Wild, The (1903) **'Jack London' [John Griffith Chaney]** (1876)
Call-Girls, The (1972) **Arthur Koestler** (1905)
Called to be Saints (1881) **Christina Rossetti** (1830)
Calligrammes (1918) **'Guillaume Apollinaire' [Wilhelm de Kostrowitsky]** (1880)
Callista (1856) **J.H. Newman** (1801)
Calm Address to Our American Colonies, A (1775) **John Wesley** (1703)
Caltrop's Desire (1980) **Stephen Gray** (1941)
Calvary (1792) **Richard Cumberland** (1732)
Camberwell Beauty, The (1974) **V.S. Pritchett** (1900)
Camberwell Miracle, The (1933) **J.D. Beresford** (1873)
Cambises King of Percia (1570) **Thomas Preston** (1537)
Cambridge (1991) **Caryl Phillips** (1958)
Cambridge Bibliography of English Literature, The (1940) **F.W. Bateson** (1901) (ed.)
Cambyses King of Persia (1667) **Elkanah Settle** (1648)
Camels Are Coming, The (1932) **W.E. Johns** (1893)
Cameos (1896) **Marie Corelli** (1855)
Camera Always Lies, The (1967) **Hugh Hood** (1928)
Camera Obscura [US: *Laughter in the Dark*] (1936) **Vladimir Nabokov** (1899)
Cameron Hill (1957) **Martin Flavin** (1883)
Cameronians, The (1881) **James Grant** (1822)
Cameroon with Egbert (1989) **Dervla Murphy** (1931)
Camford Visitation, The (1937) **H.G. Wells** (1866)
Camilla (1796) **Frances Burney** (1752)
Camino Real (1953) **'Tennessee' [Thomas Lanier] Williams** (1911)
Camomile Lawn, The (1984) **'Mary Wesley' [Mary Wellesley]** (1912)
Camp Concentration (1968) **Thomas M. Disch** (1940)
Campaign, The (1705) **Joseph Addison** (1672)
Campaigners, The (1698) **Thomas D'Urfey** (1653)
Campbell's Kingdom (1952) **'Hammond Innes' [Ralph Hammond-Innes]** (1913)
Campo-Musae (1643) **George Wither** (1588)
Can All This Grandeur Perish? (1937) **James T. Farrell** (1904)
Can Grande's Castle (1918) **Amy Lowell** (1874)
Can Such Things Be? (1893) **Ambrose Bierce** (1842)
Can Wrong Be Right? (1862) **Anna Maria [Mrs S.C.] Hall** (1800)
Can You Forgive Her? (1864–1865) **Anthony Trollope** (1815)
Can You See Me Yet? (1976) **Timothy Findley** (1930)
Can't Pay? Won't Pay! (1970) **Dario Fo** (1926)
Canaan (1996) **Geoffrey Hill** (1932)
Canada Speaks of Britain (1941) **Sir Charles G.D. Roberts** (1860)
Canadian Born (1903) **Pauline Johnson** (1862)
Canadian Born [US: *Lady Merton, Colonist*] (1910) **Mrs T. Humphry Ward** (1851)
Canaries Sometimes Sing (1929) **'Frederick Lonsdale' [Lionel Frederick Leonard]** (1881)
Canary in a Cat House (1961) **Kurt Vonnegut** (1922)
Canary Murder Case, The (1927) **'S.S. van Dine' [Willard Huntington Wright]** (1888)
Cancer Ward, The (1968) **Alexander Solzhenitsyn** (1918)
Candidate for Truth, A (1912) **J.D. Beresford** (1873)
Candidate, The (1764) **Charles Churchill** (1731)
Candidate, The (1780) **George Crabbe** (1754)
Candide (1759) **'Voltaire' [François-Marie Arouet]** (1694)
Candle for St Jude, A (1948) **Rumer Godden** (1907)
Candle in the Cabin, The (1926) **Vachel Lindsay** (1879)
Candle in the Wind (1941) **Maxwell Anderson** (1888)
Candle of Vision, The (1918) **George William Russell ['AE']** (1867)
Candleford Green (1943) **Flora Thompson** (1877)
Candles of Your Eyes, The (1985) **James Purdy** (1923)
Candy (1958) **Terry Southern** (1924)
Cannery Row (1945) **John Steinbeck** (1902)
Cannibal Galaxy, The (1983) **Cynthia Ozick** (1928)
Cannibal in Manahattan, A (1987) **Tama Janowitz** (1957)
Cannibals and Christians (1966) **Norman Mailer** (1923)
Cannibals and Missionaries (1979) **Mary McCarthy** (1912)
Cannon Between My Knees, A (1981) **Paula Gunn Allen** (1939)
Canoe and the Saddle, The (1863) **Theodore Winthrop** (1826)
Canolles (1877) **John Cooke** (1830)
Canon (1717) **Charles Gildon** (1665)
Canon's Ward, The (1884) **James Payn** (1830)
Canons of Giant Art (1933) **Sir Sacheverell Sitwell** (1897)
Canopy of Time, The (1959) **Brian Aldiss** (1925)
Canterbury Tales for the Year 1797 (1797) **Harriet Lee** (1756)
Canterbury Tales of Chaucer, The (1775) **Thomas Tyrwhitt** (1730) (ed.)
Canterbury Tales, The [pub. by Caxton] (1477) **Geoffrey Chaucer** (1340?-1400)
Canterbury Tales, The [pub. by Pynson] (1526) **Geoffrey Chaucer** (1340?-1400)
Canticle for Liebowitz, A (1960) **Walter M. Miller Jr** (1922)

Canticle of the Rose, The (1949) **Edith Sitwell** (1887)
Canticles on the Skin (1970) **Robert Adamson** (1943)
Cantique à Elsa ['Song to Elsa'] (1942) **Louis Aragon** (1897)
Canto General (1950) **Pablo Neruda** (1904)
Cantos [final collected edn] (1970) **Ezra Pound** (1885)
Canzoni (1911) **Ezra Pound** (1885)
Cape Cod (1865) **Henry David Thoreau** (1817–62)
Cape Cod Lighter, The (1962) **John O'Hara** (1905)
Cape Drives (1974) **Christopher Hope** (1944)
Cape Fear (1953) **John D. MacDonald** (1916)
Capel Sion (1916) **Caradoc Evans** (1878)
Capitaine Fracasse, Le (1863) **Théophile Gautier** (1811)
Capital Letters (1983) **Gavin Ewart** (1916)
Capitale de la douleur (1926) **'Paul Éluard' [Eugène Grindel]** (1895)
Capitalism and Freedom (1962) **Milton Friedman** (1912)
Capitol, The (1895) **Augustus Thomas** (1857)
Caprice (1917) **Ronald Firbank** (1886)
Caprices et Zig-zags ['Whims and Zig-Zags'] (1845) **Théophile Gautier** (1811)
Capricorn Games (1976) **Robert Silverberg** (1935)
Capricornia (1938) **Xavier Herbert** (1901)
Capsina, The (1899) **E.F. Benson** (1867)
Capt'n Davy's Honeymoon [etc] (1893) **Hall Caine** (1853)
Captain and the Enemy, The (1988) **Graham Greene** (1904)
Captain and the Kings, The (1972) **Jennifer Johnston** (1930)
Captain Black (1911) **Max Pemberton** (1863)
Captain Blackman (1972) **John Williams** (1925)
Captain Blood, His Odyssey (1922) **Rafael Sabatini** (1875)
Captain Cobler (1850) **Thomas Cooper** (1805)
Captain Corelli's Mandolin (1994) **Louis de Bernières** (1954)
Captain Craig (1902) **Edwin Arlington Robinson** (1869)
Captain From Connecticut, The (1941) **C.S. Forester** (1899)
Captain Hornblower, R.N. (1965) **C.S. Forester** (1899)
Captain Jim (1919) **Mary Grant Bruce** (1878)
Captain Lavender (1994) **Medbh McGuckian** (1950)
Captain Macklin (1902) **Richard Harding Davis** (1864)
Captain Margaret (1908) **John Masefield** (1878)
Captain Neal MacDougal and the Naked Goddess (1982) **Milton Acorn** (1923)
Captain Newman, M.D. (1961) **Leo Rosten** (1908)
Captain of the Gray-Horse Troop, The (1902) **Hamlin Garland** (1860)
Captain of the Polestar, The (1890) **A. Conan Doyle** (1859)
Captain of the Vulture, The (1863) **M.E. Braddon** (1835)
Captain Pantoja and the Special Service [*Pantaleón y las visitadoras*] (1973) **Mario Vargas Llosa** (1936)
Captain Patch (1935) **T.F. Powys** (1875)
Captain Singleton [**Defoe**]: see *The Life, Adventures and Pyracies of the Famous Captain Singleton*
Captain Sword and Captain Pen (1835) **Leigh Hunt** (1784)
Captain's Daughter, The (1836) **Alexander Pushkin** (1799)
Captain's Death Bed, The (1950) **Virginia Woolf** (1882–1941)
Captain's Room, The (1883) **Sir Walter Besant** (1836)
Captains All (1905) **W.W. Jacobs** (1863)
'Captains Courageous' (1897) **Rudyard Kipling** (1865)
Captive of Fez, The (1830) **Thomas Aird** (1802)
Captive Shrew, The (1932) **Julian Huxley** (1887)
Captive, The [*La Prisonnière*; *A la recherche du temps perdu* v] (1923) **Marcel Proust** (1871–1922)
Captives, The (1724) **John Gay** (1685)
Captives, The (1920) **Sir Hugh Walpole** (1884)
Captivity Captive (1988) **Rodney Hall** (1935)
Captivity [with *Celadon* and *Lydia*] (1777) **Mary Robinson** (1758)
Cara Massimina [as 'John MacDowell'; US: *Juggling the Stars*] (1990) **Tim Parks** (1954)
Caracole (1985) **Edmund White** (1940)
Caractacus (1759) **William Mason** (1724)
Caravaners, The (1909) **'Elizabeth' [Mary Annette Gräfin] von Arnim** (1866)
Caravans (1963) **James A. Michener** (1907)
Card Castle (1924) **Alec Waugh** (1898)
Card, The (1911) **Arnold Bennett** (1867)
Cardboard Crown, The (1952) **Martin Boyd** (1893)
Cardinal Beaton (1823) **William Tennant** (1784)
Cardinal of the Kremlin, The (1988) **Tom Clancy** (1947)
Cardinal Pole (1863) **W.H. Ainsworth** (1805)
Cardinal's Snuff-Box, The (1900) **Henry Harland** (1861)
Cardiphonia; or, The Utterance of the Heart (1781) **John Newton** (1725)
Cards of Identity (1955) **Nigel Dennis** (1912)
Care of Time, The (1981) **Eric Ambler** (1909)
Career of Katherine Bush, The (1917) **Elinor Glyn** (1864)
Careful and Strict Enquiry into the Modern Prevailing Notions of Freedom and Will, A (1754) **Jonathan Edwards** (1703)
Careless Husband, The (1704) **Colley Cibber** (1671)
Careless Lovers, The (1673) **Edward Ravenscroft** (1644)
Careless Shepherdess, The (1656) **Thomas Goffe** (1591–1629)
Careless Widow, and Other Stories, A (1989) **V.S. Pritchett** (1900)
Caretaker, The (1960) **Harold Pinter** (1930)
Caribbean (1989) **James A. Michener** (1907)
Caribbean Mystery, A (1964) **Agatha Christie** (1890)
Cariboo Horses (1965) **Al Purdy** (1918)
Caricatures of Twenty-Five Gentlemen (1896) **Max Beerbohm** (1872)

Carissima, The (1896) **'Lucas Malet' [Mary St Leger Harrison]** (1852)
Carità (1877) **Margaret Oliphant** (1828)
Caritas (1981) **Arnold Wesker** (1932)
Carlyle (1887) **Richard Garnett** (1835)
Carmelite, The (1784) **Richard Cumberland** (1732)
Carmen (1847) **Prosper Mérimée** (1803)
Carmen (1914) **Aleksandr Blok** (1880)
Carmen Deo Nostro (1652) **Richard Crashaw** (1612/13–1649)
Carmen Elegiacum (1876) **Robert Bridges** (1844)
Carminalenia (1980) **Christopher Middleton** (1926)
Carnacki the Ghost-Finder (1913) **William Hope Hodgson** (1877)
Carnal Myth, The (1968) **Edward Dahlberg** (1900)
Carnival (1912) **Compton Mackenzie** (1883)
Carnival (1985) **Wilson Harris** (1921)
Carnival of Destruction, The (1994) **Brian M. Stableford** (1948)
Carnival of Florence, The (1915) **'Marjorie Bowen' [Gabrielle Margaret Vere Campbell]** (1886)
Caroline of Lichtfield [from the French] (1786) **Thomas Holcroft** (1745) (tr.)
Carolinian, The (1925) **Rafael Sabatini** (1875)
Carols of an Old Codger (1954) **Robert W. Service** (1876)
Carotid Cornucopius (1947) **Sydney Goodsir Smith** (1915)
Carpathians, The (1988) **Janet Frame** (1924)
Carpe Jugulum (1998) **Terry Pratchett** (1948)
Carpenter Hen, The (1958) **John Updike** (1932)
Carpenter's Gothic (1985) **William Gaddis** (1922)
Carpetbaggers, The (1961) **Harold Robbins** (1912)
Carr of Carrlyon (1862) **Charles Hamilton Aïdé** (1826)
Carrie (1973) **Stephen King** (1947)
Carrie's War (1973) **Nina Bawden** (1925)
'Carrots' [as 'Ennis Graham'] (1876) **Mary Louisa Molesworth** (1839)
Carry On, Jeeves! (1925) **P.G. Wodehouse** (1881)
Cartload of Clay, A (1971) **George Johnston** (1912)
Carved Lions, The (1895) **Mary Louisa Molesworth** (1839)
Casa Guidi Windows (1851) **E.B. Browning** (1806)
Casanova in London (1971) **Peter Quennell** (1905)
Casanova's Chinese Restaurant (1960) **Anthony Powell** (1905)
Case Examined, A (1965) **A.L. Barker** (1918)
Case is Altered, The (1598?) **Ben Jonson** (1572)
Case is Altered, The (1932) **William Plomer** (1903)
Case of Conscience, A (1958) **James Blish** (1921)
Case of Conscience Resolved, A (1683) **John Bunyan** (1628)
Case of Knives, A (1988) **Candia McWilliam** (1955)
Case of Mr Lucraft, The (1876) **Sir Walter Besant** (1836) [with James Rice]
Case of Reason, The (1731) **William Law** (1686)
Case of Rebellious Susan, The (1894) **Henry Arthur Jones** (1851)
Case of Richard Meynell, The (1911) **Mrs T. Humphry Ward** (1851)
Case of Samples, A (1956) **Kingsley Amis** (1922)
Case of the Allegiance Due to Sovereign Powers, The (1691) **William Sherlock** (1641?)
Case of the Black-Eyed Blonde, The (1944) **Erle Stanley Gardner** (1889)
Case of the Careless Cupid, The (1968) **Erle Stanley Gardner** (1889)
Case of the Constant Suicides, The (1941) **John Dickson Carr** (1906)
Case of the Curious Bride, The (1934) **Erle Stanley Gardner** (1889)
Case of the Gilded Fly, The [US: *Obsequies at Oxford*] (1944) **'Edmund Crispin' [Robert Bruce Montgomery]** (1921)
Case of the Grinning Gorilla, The (1952) **Erle Stanley Gardner** (1889)
Case of the Haunted Husband, The (1941) **Erle Stanley Gardner** (1889)
Case of the Lonely Heiress, The (1948) **Erle Stanley Gardner** (1889)
Case of the Postponed Murder, The [last 'Perry Mason' novel] (1977) **Erle Stanley Gardner** (1889)
Case of the Shoplifter's Shoe, The (1938) **Erle Stanley Gardner** (1889)
Case of the Sulky Girl, The (1933) **Erle Stanley Gardner** (1889)
Case of the Velvet Claws, The [first 'Perry Mason' novel] (1933) **Erle Stanley Gardner** (1889)
Case-Book of Sherlock Holmes, The (1927) **A. Conan Doyle** (1859)
Casement, The (1911) **Frank Swinnerton** (1884)
Cases of Conscience, The [pt. i] (1604) **William Perkins** (1558–1602)
Cases of Conscience Concerning Evil Spirits (1693) **Increase Mather** (1639)
Cashel Byron's Profession (1886) **Bernard Shaw** (1856)
Casimir Maremma (1870) **Sir Arthur Helps** (1813)
Casino (1978) **John Ash** (1948)
Casino Royale (1953) **Ian Fleming** (1908)
Cask, The (1920) **Freeman Wills Crofts** (1879)
Cass Timberlane (1945) **Sinclair Lewis** (1885)
Cassique of Kiawah, The (1859) **William Gilmore Simms** (1806)
Cast a Cold Eye (1950) **Mary McCarthy** (1912)
Cast the First Stone (1952) **Chester Himes** (1909)
Cast Up by the Sea (1868) **Sir Samuel White Baker** (1821)
Castaly (1980) **Ian Wedde** (1946)
Castara (1634) **William Habington** (1605)
Castaway (1934) **James Gould Cozzens** (1903)
Castaway, The (1965) **Derek Walcott** (1930)
Castaways, The (1870) **Mayne Reid** (1818)
Caste (1867) **T.W. Robertson** (1829)
Castilian Days (1871) **John Hay** (1838)
Castilian, The (1853) **Thomas Noon Talfourd** (1795)
Casting Off (1995) **Elizabeth Jane Howard** (1923)
Castle Corner (1938) **Joyce Cary** (1888)

Castle Gay (1930) **John Buchan** (1875)
Castle Inn, The (1898) **Stanley J. Weyman** (1855)
Castle of Ehrenstein The (1847) **G.P.R. James** (1799)
Castle of Health, The (1537) **Sir Thomas Elyot** (1490?)
Castle of Indolence, The (1748) **James Thomson** (1700)
Castle of Labour, The (1505) **Alexander Barclay** (1475?) (tr.)
Castle of Otranto, The (1765) **Horace Walpole** (1717)
Castle of Udine, The [*Il castello di Udine*] (1934) **Carlo Emilio Gadda** (1893)
Castle of Wolfenbach, The (1793) **Eliza Parsons** (1748)
Castle Rackrent (1800) **Maria Edgeworth** (1767)
Castle Richmond (1860) **Anthony Trollope** (1815)
Castle Spectre, The (1797) **M.G. Lewis** (1775)
Castle, The [*Das Schloss*] (1926) **Franz Kafka** (1883–1924)
Castle to Castle [*D'un château l'autre*] **'Céline Louis-Ferdinand' [L.F. Destouches]** (1894)
Castle Warlock (1882) **George MacDonald** (1824)
Castleford Case, The (1862) **Frances Browne** (1816)
Castles (1926) **Sir Charles Oman** (1860)
Castles in Spain (1912) **Ruby M. Ayres** (1883)
Castles of Athlin and Dunbayne, The (1789) **Ann Radcliffe** (1764)
Casual Acquaintance, A (1976) **Stan Barstow** (1928)
Casual Commentary, A (1925) **Rose Macaulay** (1881)
Casualties of Peace (1966) **Edna O'Brien** (1932)
Casuarina Tree, The (1926) **Somerset Maugham** (1874)
Cat, The [*La Chatte*] (1933) **Colette** (1873)
Cat and Mouse [*Katz und Maus*] (1961) **Günter Grass** (1927)
Cat and Shakespeare, The (1965) **Raja Rao** (1908)
Cat and the Moon, The (1924) **W.B. Yeats** (1865)
Cat in the Hat, The (1957) **'Dr Seuss' [Theodor Giesel]** (1904)
Cat Jumps, The (1934) **Elizabeth Bowen** (1899)
Cat of Bubastis, The (1888) **G.A. Henty** (1832)
Cat on a Hot Tin Roof (1955) **'Tennessee' [Thomas Lanier] Williams** (1911)
Cat's Cradle (1925) **Maurice Baring** (1874)
Cat's Cradle (1963) **Kurt Vonnegut** (1922)
Cat's Eye (1988) **Margaret Atwood** (1939)
Cat's Pyjamas, The [and *Witch's Milk*] (1968) **Peter de Vries** (1910)
Cat's Tail, The (1831) **Caroline Bowles** (1786)
Cat-in-the-Manger (1923) **Phyllis Bentley** (1894)
Catalina (1948) **Somerset Maugham** (1874)
Catalogue of the Peers of the Kingdome of England, A (1661) **Elias Ashmole** (1617)
Catalogue of the Royal and Noble Authors of England, A (1758) **Horace Walpole** (1717)
Catastrophe Practice (1979) **Nicholas Mosley** (1923)
Catch-22 (1961) **Joseph Heller** (1923)
Catcher in the Rye, The (1951) **J.D. Salinger** (1919)
Catching It (1983) **Lauris Edmond** (1924)
Catechism and Confession of Faith, A (1673) **Robert Barclay** (1648)
Catechisms (1730) **Isaac Watts** (1674)
Catharine Furze (1893) **'Mark Rutherford' [William Hale White]** (1831)
Cathay [trns from the Chinese] (1915) **Ezra Pound** (1885) (tr.)
Cathedral, The (1838) **Isaac Williams** (1802)
Cathedral, The (1869) **James Russell Lowell** (1819)
Cathedral, The (1922) **Sir Hugh Walpole** (1884)
Cathedral (1984) **Raymond Carver** (1939)
Catherine and Petruchio [from Shakespeare's *The Taming of the Shrew*] (1756) **David Garrick** (1717)
Catherine Carmier (1964) **Ernest J. Gaines** (1933)
Catherine Carter (1952) **Pamela Hansford Johnson** (1912)
Catherine Foster (1929) **H.E. Bates** (1905)
Catherine Herself (1920) **James Hilton** (1900)
Catherine Wheel, The (1952) **Jean Stafford** (1915)
Catherine Wheel, The (1960) **Elizabeth Harrower** (1928)
Cathleen ni Hoolihan (1902) **W.B. Yeats** (1865)
Catholic Church and Conversion, The (1926) **G.K. Chesterton** (1874)
Catholick Theologie (1675) **Richard Baxter** (1615)
Catholics (1972) **Brian Moore** (1921)
Catiline his Conspiracy (1611) **Ben Jonson** (1572)
Cato (1713) **Joseph Addison** (1672)
Catriona (1893) **Robert Louis Stevenson** (1850)
Cats of the Temple, The (1986) **Brad Leithauser** (1953)
Cats of Venice, The (1965) **Hal Porter** (1911)
Catskill Eagle, A (1985) **Robert B. Parker** (1932)
Cattle Brands (1906) **Andy Adams** (1859)
Caucasian Chalk Circle, The [*Der kaukasische Kreidekreis*] (1948) **Bertolt Brecht** (1898)
Caught (1943) **'Henry Green' [Henry Vicent Yorke]** (1905)
Cause and Cure of a Wounded Conscience, The (1647) **Thomas Fuller** (1608)
Cause Célèbre (1975) **Terence Rattigan** (1911)
Cause for Alarm (1938) **Eric Ambler** (1909)
Cause of Death (1996) **Patricia Cornwell** (1956)
Causeries du lundi ['Monday Chats'] (1851–2) **Charles-Augustin Sainte-Beuve** (1804)
Cautionary Tales for Children (1907) **Hilaire Belloc** (1870)
Cautious Amorist, The (1932) **Norman Lindsay** (1879)
Cautious Heart, The (1958) **William Sansom** (1912)
Cavalcade (1931) **Noel Coward** (1899)
Cavalier, The (1901) **George Washington Cable** (1844)
Cavalleria Rusticana and Other Stories [from Giovanni Verga] (1928) **D.H. Lawrence** (1885) (tr.)
Cavanagh, Forest Ranger (1910) **Hamlin Garland** (1860)
Cave Birds (1978) **Ted Hughes** (1930)
Cave Dwellers, The (1958) **William Saroyan** (1908)
Cave, The (1959) **Robert Penn Warren** (1905)
Cave with Echoes (1962) **Janice Elliott** (1931)
Cavelarice (1607) **Gervaise Markham** (1568?)

Cavender's House (1929) **Edwin Arlington Robinson** (1869)
Caves of Steel, The (1954) **Isaac Asimov** (1920)
Caviare at the Funeral (1980) **Louis Simpson** (1923)
Cawdor (1928) **Robinson Jeffers** (1887)
Cawnpore (1865) **Sir George Otto Trevelyan** (1838)
Caxtoniana (1863) **Edward Bulwer-Lytton** (1803)
Caxtons, The (1849) **Edward Bulwer-Lytton** (1803)
Cecil (1841) **Mrs C.F. Gore** (1799)
Cecil a Peer (1841) **Mrs C.F. Gore** (1799)
Cecil Castlemaine's Gage (1867) **'Ouida'** (1839–1908)
Cecil Dreeme (1861) **Theodore Winthrop** (1826)
Cécile (1951) **Benjamin Constant** (1767–1830)
Cecilia (1782) **Frances Burney** (1752)
Cecilia de Noel (1891) **'Lanoe Falconer' [Mary Elizabeth Hawker]** (1848)
Cefal (1947) **Lawrence Durrell** (1912)
Celebrants, The (1973) **Elaine Feinstein** (1930)
Celebrated Jumping Frog of Calaveras County, The (1867) **'Mark Twain' [Samuel Langhorne Clemens]** (1835)
Celebrations (1972) **William Plomer** (1903)
Celebrity at Home, The (1904) **Violet Hunt** (1866)
Celebrity, The (1898) **Winston Churchill** (1871)
Celebrity's Daughter, The (1913) **Violet Hunt** (1866)
Celestial Navigation (1975) **Anne Tyler** (1941)
Celestial Omnibus, The (1911) **E.M. Forster** (1879)
Celestina (1791) **Charlotte Smith** (1749)
Celibate Lives (1927) **George Moore** (1852)
Celibates (1895) **George Moore** (1852)
Cell Mates (1995) **Simon Gray** (1936)
Celt, the Roman, and the Saxon, The (1852) **Thomas Wright** (1810)
Celt's Paradise, The (1821) **John Banim** (1798)
Celtic Psaltery, A (1917) **A.P. Graves** (1846) (tr.)
Celtic Twilight, The (1893) **W.B. Yeats** (1865)
Cement Garden, The (1978) **Ian McEwan** (1948)
Cenci, The (1819) **P.B. Shelley** (1792)
Censura Literaria (1805) **Sir Samuel Egerton Brydges** (1762)
Centaur, The (1911) **Algernon Blackwood** (1869)
Centaur, The (1963) **John Updike** (1932)
Centaur Not Fabulous, The (1755) **Edward Young** (1683)
Centaur's Booty, The (1903) **T. Sturge Moore** (1870)
Centenary at Jalna (1958) **Mazo de la Roche** (1879)
Centennial (1974) **James A. Michener** (1907)
Central Italian Painters, The (1897) **Bernard Berenson** (1865)
Central Mischief (1992) **Elizabeth Jolley** (1923)
Central Questions of Philosophy, The (1973) **A.J. Ayer** (1910)
Centuries of Meditations [ed. Bertam Dobell] (1908) **Thomas Traherne** (1637–74)
Century of Roundels, A (1883) **A.C. Swinburne** (1837)
Century Shakespeare, The (1908) **F.J. Furnivall** (1825) (ed.)
Century's Daughter, The (1986) **Pat Barker** (1943)
Cerealia [also attrib. to Elijah Fenton] (1706) **John Philips** (1676)
Ceremony (1950) **Richard Wilbur** (1921)
Ceres' Runaway (1909) **Alice Meynell** (1847)
Cerise (1866) **G.J. Whyte-Melville** (1821)
Cerise Swimsuit, The (1992) **Adrian Henri** (1932)
Certain Hour, The (1916) **James Branch Cabell** (1879)
Certain Justice, A (1997) **P.D. James** (1920)
Certain Miscellany Tracts (1683) **Sir Thomas Browne** (1605–82)
Certain People (1930) **Edith Wharton** (1862)
Certain Personal Matters (1898) **H.G. Wells** (1866)
Certain Smile, A [Un Certain Sourie] (1956) **'Françoise Sagan' [Françoise Quoirez]** (1935)
Certaine Learned and Elegant Workes (1633) **Fulke Greville, Lord Brooke** (1554–1628)
Certaine Small Poems (1605) **Samuel Daniel** (1562)
Certaine Small Workes (1607) **Samuel Daniel** (1562)
Certaine Tragicall Discourses (1567) **Sir Geoffrey Fenton** (1539?) (tr.)
Certayne Psalmes Chosen Out of the Psalter of David (1549) **Sir Thomas Wyatt** (1503?) (tr.)
Certificate, The (1992) **Isaac Bashevis Singer** (1904–91)
César Birotteau (1837) **Honoré de Balzac** (1799)
Cetawayo and His White Neighbours (1882) **Sir H. Rider Haggard** (1856)
Cézanne (1927) **Roger Fry** (1866)
Chain Bearers, The (1845) **James Fenimore Cooper** (1789)
Chain of Days (1985) **James Berry** (1924)
Chain of Gold, The (1895) **Standish O'Grady** (1846)
Chain of Voices, A (1982) **André Brink** (1935)
Chains (1927) **Theodore Dreiser** (1871)
Chair Molle ['Weak Flesh'] (1885) **Paul Adam** (1862)
Chair of Babel, The (1992) **Peter Porter** (1929)
Chairs, The (1952) **Eugène Ionesco** (1909)
Chalk Face (1924) **Waldo Frank** (1889)
Chalk Garden, The (1956) **Enid Bagnold** (1889)
Challenge for Beautie, A (1636) **Thomas Heywood** (1574?)
Challenge to Clarissa (1931) **'E.M. Delafield' [E.E.M. de la Pasture]** (1890)
Challenge to Venus (1957) **Charles Morgan** (1894)
Challoners, The (1904) **E.F. Benson** (1867)
Chamade, La (1966) **'Françoise Sagan' [Françoise Quoirez]** (1935)
Chamber Music (1907) **James Joyce** (1882)
Chamber, The (1994) **John Grisham** (1955)
Chambers of Imagery [1st ser.] (1907) **Gordon Bottomley** (1874)
Chambre bleue, La ['The Blue Room'] (1866) **Prosper Mérimée** (1803)
Champion From Far Away, The (1931) **Ben Hecht** (1894)
Champion of Virtue, The (1777) **Clara Reeve** (1729)
Champion, The (1739) **Henry Fielding** (1707)
Chance (1913) **Joseph Conrad** (1857)
Chance Acquaintance, A (1873) **William Dean Howells** (1837)
Chance Child, A (1978) **Jill Paton Walsh** (1937)
Chance Meetings (1978) **William Saroyan** (1908)

Chance of a Lifetime, The (1907) **Nat Gould** (1857)
Chancer, A (1985) **James Kelman** (1946)
Chandos (1866) **'Ouida'** (1839)
Change and Decay in All Around I See (1978) **Allan Massie** (1938)
Change and Habit (1966) **Arnold Toynbee** (1889)
Change for the Better, A (1969) **Susan Hill** (1942)
Change for the Better, A (1984) **Peter Mathers** (1931)
Change Here for Babylon (1955) **Nina Bawden** (1925)
Change in the Cabinet, A (1909) **Hilaire Belloc** (1870)
Change of Air, A (1893) **'Anthony Hope' [Sir Anthony Hope Hawkins]** (1863)
Change of Climate, A (1994) **Hilary Mantel** (1952)
Change of Hearts, A (1973) **Kenneth Koch** (1925)
Change of Skin, A [Cambio de piel] (1967) **Carlos Fuentes** (1928)
Change of Use (1997) **Candia McWilliam** (1955)
Change of World, A (1951) **Adrienne Rich** (1929)
Change, The (1991) **Germaine Greer** (1939)
Change the World (1937) **'Michael Gold' [Irwin Granich]** (1893)
Change Upon Change [US: *A Reed Shaken with the Wind*] (1868) **Emily Faithfull** (1836)
Changed Man, A (1913) **Thomas Hardy** (1840)
The Changeling (1653) **Thomas Middleton** (1580)
Changeling, The (1898) **Sir Walter Besant** (1836)
Changeling, The (1958) **Robin Jenkins** (1912)
Changeover, The (1984) **Margaret Mahy** (1936)
Changes (1991) **Ama Ata Aidoo** (1942)
Changes (1632) **James Shirley** (1596)
Changing Babies (1995) **Deborah Moggach** (1948)
Changing Places (1975) **David Lodge** (1935)
Changing Room, The (1971) **David Storey** (1933)
Changing the Past (1990) **Thomas Berger** (1924)
Channel Passage, A (1899) **A.C. Swinburne** (1837)
Channel Passage, A (1904) **A.C. Swinburne** (1837)
Channings, The (1862) **Mrs Henry Wood** (1814)
Chant of Jimmie Blacksmith, The (1972) **Thomas Keneally** (1935)
Chantecler (1910) **Edmond Rostand** (1868)
Chantic Bird, The (1968) **David Ireland** (1927)
Chants for Socialists (1885) **William Morris** (1834)
Chants Secrets ['Secret Songs'] (1947) **Jean Genet** (1910)
Chaos and Order in Industry (1920) **G.D.H. Cole** (1889)
Chapel of the Hermits, The (1853) **John Greenleaf Whittier** (1807)
Chapel Perilous, The (1971) **Dorothy Hewett** (1923)
Chaplain of the Fleet, The (1881) **Sir Walter Besant** (1836) [with James Rice]
Chaplet of Pearls, The (1868) **Charlotte M. Yonge** (1823)
Chaplet of Verses, A (1862) **Adelaide Procter** (1825)
Chapter House: Dune (1985) **Frank Herbert** (1920)
Chapters and Speeches on the Irish Land Question (1870) **J.S. Mill** (1806)
Chapters From Some Memoirs (1894) **Lady Anne Ritchie** (1837)
Chapters of an Autobiography (1930) **A.J. Balfour** (1848–1930)
Character (1871) **Samuel Smiles** (1814)
Character and Comedy (1907) **E.V. Lucas** (1868)
Character and Opinion in the United States (1920) **George Santayana** (1863)
Character of a London Diurnall, The (1644) **John Cleveland** (1613)
Character of a Methodist, The (1742) **John Wesley** (1703)
Character of Charles II, The (1696) **John Sheffield, duke of Buckingham** (1648)
Character of England, A (1659) **John Evelyn** (1620)
Character of Holland, The (1665) **Andrew Marvell** (1621)
Character of the Poet, The (1986) **Louis Simpson** (1923)
Characteristics (1823) **William Hazlitt** (1778)
Characteristics (1877) **Thomas Carlyle** (1795)
Characteristics of French Art (1932) **Roger Fry** (1866)
Characteristics of Women, Moral, Poetical and Historical (1832) **Anna Jameson** (1794)
Characters and Commentaries (1933) **Lytton Strachey** (1880–1932)
Characters of Eminent Personages of His Own Time (1777) **Philip Dormer Stanhope, Earl of Chesterfield** (1694–1773)
Characters of Shakespear's Plays (1817) **William Hazlitt** (1778)
Characters of Vertues and Vices (1608) **Joseph Hall** (1574)
Charge to the Poets, A (1762) **William Whitehead** (1715)
Charioteer, The (1953) **'Mary Renault' [Eileen Mary Challans]** (1905)
Charitesse (1911) **Elizabeth Daryush** (1887)
Charity (1912) **R.B. Cunninghame Graham** (1852)
Charity and its Fruits (1738) **Jonathan Edwards** (1703)
Charlemont (1856) **William Gilmore Simms** (1806)
Charles and Charlotte (1777) **Samuel Jackson Pratt** (1749)
Charles Baudelaire (1920) **Arthur Symons** (1865)
Charles Chesterfield (1841) **Frances Trollope** (1780)
Charles Demailly (1868) **Edmond de Goncourt** (1822–1896) and **Jules de Goncourt** (1830)
Charles Dickens (1898) **George Gissing** (1857)
Charles Dickens (1906) **G.K. Chesterton** (1874)
Charles O'Malley (1841) **Charles Lever** (1806)
Charles the First (1834) **Mary Russell Mitford** (1787)
Charles the First (1872) **William Gorman Wills** (1828)
Charley is My Darling (1940) **Joyce Cary** (1888)
Charlie and the Chocolate Factory (1964) **Roald Dahl** (1916)
Charlie to the Rescue (1890) **R.M. Ballantyne** (1825)
Charlotte [later retitled *Charlotte Temple*] (1791) **Susanna Rowson** (1762)
Charlotte and Myra (1859) **William Winwood Reade** (1838)
Charlotte Gray (1998) **Sebastian Faulks** (1953)
Charlotte's Inheritance (1868) **M.E. Braddon** (1835)
Charlotte's Row (1931) **H.E. Bates** (1905)

Charlotte's Web (1952) **E.B. White** (1899)
Charm Against the Toothache, A (1954) **John Heath-Stubbs** (1918)
Charmed Life (1977) **Diana Wynne Jones** (1934)
Charmed Life, A (1955) **Mary McCarthy** (1912)
Charmed Lives (1988) **Bruce Beaver** (1928)
Charmers, The (1965) **Stella Gibbons** (1902)
Charms [*Charmes*] (1922) **Paul-Ambroise Valéry** (1871)
Charnel Rose, The [etc] (1918) **Conrad Potter Aiken** (1889)
Chart for Rough Water (1940) **Waldo Frank** (1889)
Charterhouse of Parma, The [*La Chartreuse de Parme*] (1839) **'Stendhal' [Henri Marie Beyle]** (1783)
Chartism (1839) **Thomas Carlyle** (1795)
Charwoman's Daughter, The (1912) **James Stephens** (1882)
Chase, The (1796) **Sir Walter Scott** (1771) (tr.)
Chast Mayd in Cheape-side, A (1630) **Thomas Middleton** (1580–1627)
Chaste Wife, The (1916) **Frank Swinnerton** (1884)
Chastelard (1865) **A. C. Swinburne** (1837)
Château d'Harmenthal, The [*Le Château d'Harmenthal*] (1843) **Alexandre Dumas ['père']** (1802)
Château en Suède [*Castle in Sweden*] (1960) **'Françoise Sagan' [Françoise Quoirez]** (1935)
Chateaubriand et son groupe littéraire ['Chateaubriand and his Literary Set'] (1861) **Charles-Augustin Sainte-Beuve** (1804)
Chatelaine of La Trinité, The (1892) **Henry Blake Fuller** (1857)
Châtiments, Les ['The Punishments'] (1853) **Victor Hugo** (1802)
Chatterton (1987) **Peter Ackroyd** (1949)
Chatterton Square (1948) **E.H. Young** (1880)
Chaucer (1932) **G.K. Chesterton** (1874)
Chaunt of the Cholera, The (1831) **John Banim** (1798) [with Michael Banim]
Cheap Jack Zita (1893) **S. Baring-Gould** (1834)
Cheape and Good Husbandry (1614) **Gervaise Markham** (1568?)
Cheats, The (1664) **John Wilson** (1627?)
Checkmate (1871) **J.S. le Fanu** (1814)
Checkmate (1975) **Dorothy Dunnett** (1923)
Cheek (1970) **Howard Barker** (1946)
Cheerfulness Breaks In (1940) **Angela Thirkell** (1890)
Chelkash (1895) **Maxim Gorky** (1868)
Chelsea Girl, A (1988) **Barbara Hanrahan** (1939)
Chelsea Householder, A (1882) **Hon. Emily Lawless** (1845)
Chéri (1920) **Colette** (1873)
Chérie (1885) **Edmond de Goncourt** (1822)
Chernobyl (1987) **Frederik Pohl** (1919)
Cherry Orchard, The (1904) **Anton Chekhov** (1860)
Cherry Ripe (1935) **A.E. Coppard** (1878)
Cherwell Water-Lily, The (1840) **Frederick William Faber** (1814)
Chesapeake (1978) **James A. Michener** (1907)
Chetwynd Calverley (1876) **W.H. Ainsworth** (1805)
Chevalier des touches, Le (1864) **J.-A. Barbey-d'Aurevilly** (1808)
Chevalier of Pensieri-Vani, The [as 'Stanton Page'] (1890) **Henry Blake Fuller** (1857)
Cheveley (1839) **Edward Bulwer-Lytton** (1803)
Chicago Loop (1990) **Paul Theroux** (1941)
Chicago Poems (1916) **Carl Sandburg** (1878)
Chicago Race Riots, The (1919) **Carl Sandburg** (1878)
Chicken Inspector No. 23 (1966) **S.J. Perelman** (1904)
Chicken Soup with Barley (1958) **Arnold Wesker** (1932)
Chief Joseph of the Nez Percé (1983) **Robert Penn Warren** (1905)
Chief of Staff [as 'William Coyle'] (1991) **Thomas Keneally** (1935)
Chief Promises of God unto Man, The (1577) **John Bale** (1495–1563)
Chikkin Hazard (1881) **Sir F.C. Burnand** (1836)
Child Buyer, The (1960) **John Hersey** (1914)
Child From the Sea, The (1970) **Elizabeth Goudge** (1900)
Child in Time, The (1987) **Ian McEwan** (1948)
Child Lovers (1916) **W.H. Davies** (1871)
Child of God (1973) **Cormac McCarthy** (1933)
Child of Pleasure, The [*Il piacere*] (1890) **Gabriele D'Annunzio** (1863)
Child of Queen Victoria, The (1933) **William Plomer** (1903)
Child of Storm (1913) **Sir H. Rider Haggard** (1856)
Child of the Age, A (1894) **Francis Adams** (1862)
Child of the Century, A (1954) **Ben Hecht** (1894)
Child of the Dawn, The (1912) **A.C. Benson** (1862)
Child of the Islands, The (1845) **Caroline Norton** (1808)
Child of the Jago, A (1896) **Arthur Morrison** (1863)
Child Possessed, A (1964) **R.C. Hutchinson** (1907)
Child Wife, The (1868) **Mayne Reid** (1818)
Child's Day, A (1912) **Walter de la Mare** (1873)
Child's Garden of Verses, A (1885) **Robert Louis Stevenson** (1850)
Child's History of England, A (1853) **Charles Dickens** (1812)
Childe Harold's Pilgrimage [i–ii] (1812) **George Gordon, Lord Byron** (1788)
Childe Harold's Pilgrimage [i–iv] (1819) **George Gordon, Lord Byron** (1788)
Childe Harold's Pilgrimage [iii] (1816) **George Gordon, Lord Byron** (1788)
Childe Harold's Pilgrimage [iv] (1818) **George Gordon, Lord Byron** (1788)
Childermass, The (1928) **Wyndham Lewis** (1882)
Childhood (1852) **Leo Tolstoy** (1828)
Childhood (1913) **Maxim Gorky** (1868)
Childhood is Not Forever (1969) **James T. Farrell** (1904)
Childhood Years of Bagrova-grandchild (1858) **Sergei Timofeyevich Aksakov** (1791)
Childhood's End (1953) **Arthur C. Clarke** (1917)
Childlike Life of the Black Tarantula, The (1975) **Kathy Acker** (1948)
Children, The (1928) **Edith Wharton** (1862)

Children, The (1937) **Howard Fast** (1914)
Children and Others (1964) **James Gould Cozzens** (1903)
Children Are Bored on Sunday (1954) **Jean Stafford** (1915)
Children at the Gate, The (1964) **Edward Wallant** (1926–62)
Children From their Games (1963) **Irwin Shaw** (1913)
Children of Albion (1969) **Michael Horovitz** (1935) (ed.)
Children of Darkness and Light (1996) **Nicholas Mosley** (1923)
Children of Dune (1976) **Frank Herbert** (1920)
Children of Dynmouth, The (1976) **'William Trevor' [William Trevor Cox]** (1928)
Children of Gibeon (1886) **Sir Walter Besant** (1836)
Children of Green Knowe, The (1954) **Lucy Boston** (1892)
Children of Kaywana, The (1952) **Edgar Mittelholzer** (1909)
Children of Love (1914) **Harold Monro** (1879)
Children of Primrose Lane, The (1941) **Noel Streatfeild** (1895)
Children of the Castle, The (1890) **Mary Louisa Molesworth** (1839)
Children of the Ghetto (1892) **Israel Zangwill** (1864)
Children of the King, The (1893) **F. Marion Crawford** (1854)
Children of the Lens (1954) **E.E.'Doc' Smith** (1890)
Children of the Market Place (1922) **Edgar Lee Masters** (1868)
Children of the Mist (1898) **Eden Phillpotts** (1862)
Children of the Moon (1923) **Martin Flavin** (1883)
Children of the New Forest, The (1847) **Frederick Marryat** (1792)
Children of the Night, The (1897) **Edwin Arlington Robinson** (1869)
Children of the Pool, The (1936) **Arthur Machen** (1863)
Children of the Rose (1975) **Elaine Feinstein** (1930)
Children of the Sun (1957) **Morris West** (1916)
Children of To-morrow (1889) **William Sharp** (1855)
Children's Bach, The (1986) **Helen Garner** (1942)
Children's Hour, The (1934) **Lillian Hellman** (1907)
Children's Treasury of English Song, The (1875) **Francis Turner Palgrave** (1824) (ed.)
Childwold, The (1976) **Joyce Carol Oates** (1938)
Chills and Fever (1924) **John Crowe Ransom** (1888)
Chiltern Hundreds, The (1947) **William Douglas Home** (1912)
Chimera (1972) **John Barth** (1930)
Chimes, The (1844) **Charles Dickens** (1812)
Chimney-Sweeper's Boy, The [as 'Barbara Vine'] (1998) **Ruth Rendell** (1930)
Chimneys of Green Knowe, The (1958) **Lucy Boston** (1892)
China Poems (1970) **Dennis Brutus** (1924)
Chinese Love Pavilion, The [US: *The Love Pavilion*] (1960) **Paul Scott** (1920)
Chinese Nightingale, The (1917) **Vachel Lindsay** (1879)
Chinese Orange Mystery, The (1934) **'Ellery Queen' [Frederic Dannay** (1905) and **Manfred B. Lee** (1905)**]**
Chinese Siamese Cat, The (1994) **Amy Tan** (1952)
Chink (1927) **Ernest Thompson Seton** (1860)
Chip-Chip Gatherers, The (1973) **Shiva Naipaul** (1945)
Chips With Everything (1962) **Arnold Wesker** (1932)
Chita (1889) **Lafcadio Hearn** (1850)
Chitra (1913) **Rabindranath Tagore** (1861)
Chitty-Chitty-Bang-Bang: The Magical Car (1964) **Ian Fleming** (1908)
Chivalry (1909) **James Branch Cabell** (1879)
Chivalry of the Sea, The (1916) **Robert Bridges** (1844)
Chocky (1968) **'John Wyndham' [John Wyndham Harris]** (1903)
Chocolate War, The (1974) **Robert Cormier** (1925)
Choice , The (1700) **John Pomfret** (1667)
Choice Collection of New Songs and Ballads, A (1699) **Thomas d'Urfey** (1653)
Choice Manual, A (1664) **Jeremy Taylor** (1613)
Choice New Songs (1684) **Thomas d'Urfey** (1653)
Choice of Books, The (1886) **Frederic Harrison** (1831)
Choice of Enemies, A (1957) **Mordecai Richler** (1931)
Choice of Enemies, A (1973) **Ted Allbeury** (1917)
Choice of Enemies, A (1984) **George V. Higgins** (1939)
Choice of Gods, A (1972) **Clifford D. Simak** (1904)
Choice of Murder, A (1992) **Peter Vansittart** (1920)
Choice of Straws (1965) **E.R. Braithwaite** (1912)
Choice or Chance (1934) **Edmund Blunden** (1896)
Choir Invisible, The (1897) **James Lane Allen** (1849)
Choir, The (1988) **Joanna Trollope** (1943)
Choirboys, The (1975) **Joseph Wambaugh** (1937)
Choleric Man, The (1774) **Richard Cumberland** (1732)
Choric Plays and a Comedy (1939) **Gordon Bottomley** (1874)
Chorister's Cake (1956) **William Mayne** (1928)
Chorle and the Birde, The [written *c.* 1400] (1477?) **John Lydgate** (1370?-1449)
Chorus of Disapproval, A (1984) **Alan Ayckbourn** (1939)
Chorus of the Newly Dead (1926) **Edwin Muir** (1887)
Chorus Poetarum (1694) **[Charles Gildon]** (1665) (ed.)
Chosen Country (1951) **John Dos Passos** (1896)
Chouans, The [*Les Chouans*] (1829) **Honoré de Balzac** (1799)
Chrestomathia (1816) **Jeremy Bentham** (1748)
Chris Christopherson [rewritten 1921 as *Anna Christie*] (1920) **Eugene O'Neill** (1888)
Chris of All-Sorts (1903) **S. Baring-Gould** (1834)
Christ in Hades (1896) **Stephen Phillips** (1864)
Christ's Company (1861) **Richard Watson Dixon** (1833)
Christ's Kirk on the Green [canto i supposedly by James I] (1718) **Allan Ramsay** (1686)
Christabel and the Poems of S.T. Coleridge (1869) **A.C. Swinburne** (1837)

Christabel; Kubla Khan: A Vision; The Pains of Sleep (1816) **S.T. Coleridge** (1772)
Christal Glass for Christian Women, A (1591) **Philip Stubbs** (fl.1581)
Christian, The (1897) **Hall Caine** (1853)
Christian Astrology (1647) **William Lilly** (1602)
Christian Behaviour (1663) **John Bunyan** (1628)
Christian Behaviour (1943) **C.S. Lewis** (1898)
Christian Captives, The (1890) **Robert Bridges** (1844)
Christian Ethicks (1675) **Thomas Traherne** (1637–1674)
Christian Ethics and Modern Problems (1930) **W.R. Inge** (1860)
Christian Faith and Life (1931) **William Temple** (1881)
Christian Hero, The (1701) **Sir Richard Steele** (1672)
Christian Hero, The (1735) **George Lillo** (1863)
Christian Institutions (1881) **Arthur Penrhyn Stanley** (1815)
Christian Melville (1856) **Margaret Oliphant** (1828)
Christian Moderation (1640) **Joseph Hall** (1574)
Christian Morals (1716) **Sir Thomas Browne** (1605–82)
Christian Morals (1813) **Hannah More** (1745)
Christian Mysticism (1899) **W.R. Inge** (1860)
Christian Philosopher, The (1721) **Cotton Mather** (1663)
Christian Reflections (1967) **C.S. Lewis** (1898–1963)
Christian Scholar, The (1849) **Isaac Williams** (1802)
Christian Science (1907) **'Mark Twain' [Samuel Langhorne Clemens]** (1835)
Christian Seasons, The (1854) **Isaac Williams** (1802)
Christian Year, The (1827) **John Keble** (1792)
Christian's Mistake (1865) **Dinah Maria Craik** (1826)
Christian-Quaker and His Divine Testimony Vindicated, The (1674) **William Penn** (1644)
Christianism (1832) **Leigh Hunt** (1784)
Christianity and Social Order (1942) **William Temple** (1881)
Christianity as Old as the Creation (1730) **Matthew Tindal** (1657)
Christie in Love, and Other Plays (1969) **Howard Brenton** (1942)
Christie Johnstone (1853) **Charles Reade** (1814)
Christie Malry's Own Double Entry (1973) **B.S. Johnson** (1933)
Christina Alberta's Father (1925) **H.G. Wells** (1866)
Christina, the Maid of the South Seas (1811) **Mary Russell Mitford** (1787)
Christine (1983) **Stephen King** (1947)
Christmas at Cold Comfort Farm (1940) **Stella Gibbons** (1902)
Christmas Carol in Prose, A (1843) **Charles Dickens** (1812)
Christmas Child, A (1880) **Mary Louisa Molesworth** (1839)
Christmas Formula (1932) **Stella Benson** (1892)
Christmas Garland, A (1912) **Max Beerbohm** (1872)
Christmas Hirelings, The (1894) **M.E. Braddon** (1835)
Christmas, his Masque (1616) **Ben Jonson** (1572)
Christmas Memory, A (1966) **Truman Capote** (1924)
Christmas Mouse, The (1973) **'Miss Read' [Dora Jessie Saint]** (1913)
Christmas Poems (1984) **George Mackay Brown** (1921)
Christmas Poems (1931) **John Drinkwater** (1882)
Christmas Roses (1988) **Alison Brackenbury** (1953)
Christmas-Eve and Easter-Day (1850) **Robert Browning** (1812)
Christmas-Tree Land (1884) **Mary Louisa Molesworth** (1839)
Christopher and His Kind 1929–39 (1977) **Christopher Isherwood** (1904)
Christopher Columbus (1944) **Louis MacNeice** (1907)
Christopher Homm (1965) **C.H. Sisson** (1914)
Christowell (1882) **R.D. Blackmore** (1825)
Christs Passion [tr. from Hugo Grotius] (1640) **George Sandys** (1578) (tr.)
Christs Teares Over Jerusalem (1593) **Thomas Nashe** (1567)
Christs Victorie, and Triumph (1610) **Giles Fletcher, the younger** (1549)
Christus (1872) **Henry Wadsworth Longfellow** (1807)
Christus Veritas (1924) **William Temple** (1881)
Chronicle Historie of Perkin Warbeck, The (1634) **John Ford** (1586)
Chronicle of Clemendy, The (1888) **Arthur Machen** (1863)
Chronicle of the Conquest of Granada, A (1829) **Washington Irving** (1783)
Chronicles and Characters (1868) **Edward Robert Bulwer Lytton** (1831)
Chronicles of a Death Foretold [Crónica de una muerte anunciada] (1981) **Gabriel García Márquez** (1928)
Chronicles of Clovernook, The (1846) **Douglas Jerrold** (1803)
Chronicles of Clovis, The (1912) **'Saki' [Hector Hugh Munro]** (1870)
Chronicles of Count Antonio, The (1895) **'Anthony Hope' [Sir Anthony Hope Hawkins]** (1863)
Chronicles of England, Scotlande, and Irelande (1577) **Raphael Holinshed** (d. 1580?)
Chronicles of England, The (1580) **John Stow** (1525)
Chronicles of Golden Friars (1871) **J.S. Le Fanu** (1814)
Chronicles of Martin Hewitt (1895) **Arthur Morrison** (1863)
Chronicles of Robin Hood, The (1950) **Rosemary Sutcliff** (1920)
Chronicles of the Canongate [1st ser.] (1827) **Sir Walter Scott** (1771)
Chronicles of the Canongate [2nd ser.; inc. 'The Fair Maid of Perth'] (1828) **Sir Walter Scott** (1771)
Chronicles of the Cid (1808) **Robert Southey** (1774) (tr.)
Chronicles of the House of Borgia (1901) **Frederick William Rolfe** (1860)
Chroniques (1960) **'Saint-John Perse' [Alexis Saint-Léger Léger]** (1887)
Chrysal (1760) **Charles Johnstone** (1719?)

Chrysalids, The (1955) **'John Wyndham' [John Wyndham Harris]** (1903)

Chuckles on a Cairn (1949) **'Robert Garioch' [Robert Garioch Sutherland]** (1909)

Chums [retitled *Hearts of Oak*, 1880] (1879) **James A. Herne** (1839)

Church, The [*L'Église*] (1933) **'Louis-Ferdinand Céline' [L.F. Destouches]** (1894)

Church and Nation (1915) **William Temple** (1881)

Church in Bondage, The (1914) **Ronald Knox** (1888)

Church Looks Forward, The (1944) **William Temple** (1881)

Church Poems (1981) **Sir John Betjeman** (1906)

Church-Government and Church-Covenant Discussed (1643) **Richard Mather** (1596)

Church-History of Britain, The (1655) **Thomas Fuller** (1608)

Churchyard's Round (1566) **Thomas Churchyard** (1520?)

Churchyardes Farewell (1566) **Thomas Churchyard** (1520?)

Churchyards Good Will (1604) **Thomas Churchyard** (1520?)

Chymists Key, The [from Heinrich Nolle] (1657) **Henry Vaughan** (1622) (tr.)

Cicadas, The (1931) **Aldous Huxley** (1894)

Cicely [as 'Ennis Graham'] (1874) **Mary Louisa Molesworth** (1839)

Ciceronis Amor: Tullies Love (1589) **Robert Greene** (1558)

Cid, Le (1637) **Pierre Corneille** (1606)

Cider House Rules, The (1985) **John Irving** (1942)

Cider With Rosie [US: *The Edge of Day*] (1959) **Laurie Lee** (1914)

Cigarette-Maker's Romance, A (1890) **F. Marion Crawford** (1854)

Cimarron (1930) **Edna Ferber** (1885)

Cinder Path, The (1978) **Catherine Cookson** (1906)

Cinna (1640) **Pierre Corneille** (1606)

Cinna's Conspiracy (1713) **Colley Cibber** (1671)

Cinquième Livre ['Fifth Book'] (1562–1564) **François Rabelais** (1494?-1553?)

Cipango's Hinder Door (1966) **Edward Dahlberg** (1900)

Circe (1867) **M.E. Braddon** (1835)

Circle, The (1970) **Elaine Feinstein** (1930)

Circle, The (1921) **Somerset Maugham** (1874)

Circle Game, The (1966) **Margaret Atwood** (1939)

Circle of Friends (1990) **Maeve Binchy** (1940)

Circles of Deceit (1987) **Nina Bawden** (1925)

Circuit Rider, The (1874) **Edward Eggleston** (1837)

Circus in the Attic, The (1947) **Robert Penn Warren** (1905)

Circus is Coming, The (1938) **Noel Streatfeild** (1895)

Citadel, The (1937) **A.J. Cronin** (1896)

Cities (1903) **Arthur Symons** (1865)

Cities in Flight (1970) **James Blish** (1921)

Cities of the Interior (1959) **Anaïs Nin** (1903)

Cities of the Plain (1998) **Cormac McCarthy** (1933)

Cities of the Plain, The [*Sodome et Gomorrhe; A la recherche du temps perdu* iv] (1921–2) **Marcel Proust** (1871)

Cities of the Red Night (1981) **William S. Burroughs** (1914)

Cities, Plains and People (1946) **Lawrence Durrell** (1912)

Citizen of the World, The (1760) **Oliver Goldsmith** (1728)

Citizen Tom Paine (1943) **Howard Fast** (1914)

Citizen Turn'd Gentleman, The (1672) **Edward Ravenscroft** (1644)

Citizens (1989) **Simon Schama** (1945)

Citizens in War—and After (1945) **Sir Stephen Spender** (1909)

City, The (1904–8) **Aleksandr Blok** (1880)

City (1952) **Clifford D. Simak** (1904)

City (1961) **Roy Fisher** (1930)

City and Suburb [as 'F.G. Trafford'] (1861) **Mrs J.H. Riddell** (1832)

City and the Pillar, The (1948) **Gore Vidal** (1925)

City and the Stars, The (1956) **Arthur C. Clarke** (1917)

City as Classroom, The (1977) **Marshall McLuhan** (1911)

City Banker, The (1856) **Emma Robinson** (1814)

City Block (1922) **Waldo Frank** (1889)

City Boy, The (1948) **Herman Wouk** (1915)

City Hedges (1977) **Adrian Henri** (1932)

City Life (1970) **Donald Barthelme** (1931)

City Lights (1994) **Keith Waterhouse** (1929)

City Music (1990) **Elaine Feinstein** (1930)

City of Bells, A (1936) **Elizabeth Goudge** (1900)

City of Dreadful Night, The (1880) **James Thomson** (1834)

City of Dreams, The (1888) **Robert Williams Buchanan** (1841)

City of Fading Light (1985) **Jon Cleary** (1917)

City of Gems, The (1981) **Joanna Trollope** (1943)

City of Glass (1985) **Paul Auster** (1947)

City of God, The [*De Civitate Dei*] (413–26) **St Augustine of Hippo** (354)

City of Gold, The (1939) **Francis Brett Young** (1884)

City of Pleasure, The (1907) **Arnold Bennett** (1867)

City of Refuge, The (1896) **Sir Walter Besant** (1836)

City of Spades (1957) **Colin MacInnes** (1914)

City of the Mind (1991) **Penelope Lively** (1933)

City of the Plague, The (1816) **John Wilson** (1785)

City of the Soul, The (1899) **Lord Alfred Douglas** (1870)

City of Women (1981) **David Ireland** (1927)

City on a Hill, A (1975) **George V. Higgins** (1939)

City Poems (1857) **Alexander Smith** (1830)

City Politiques (1683) **John Crowne** (d. 1703)

City Primeval (1980) **Elmore Leonard** (1925)

City Psalms (1992) **Benjamin Zephaniah** (1958)

City Winter, and Other Poems, A (1952) **Frank O'Hara** (1926)

City Without Walls (1969) **W.H. Auden** (1907)

City-Heiress, The (1682) **Aphra Behn** (1640?)

City-Madam, The (1658) **Philip Massinger** (1583–1640)
City-Ramble, The (1711) **Elkanah Settle** (1648)
Civic Sermons to the People (1792) **Anna Laetitia Barbauld** (1743)
Civile Wares Betweene the House of Lancaster and Yorke Corrected and Continued, The (1609) **Samuel Daniel** (1562)
Civilisation (1969) **Kenneth Clark** (1903)
Civilization (1928) **Clive Bell** (1881)
Civilization: Its Cause and Cure, and Other Essays (1889) **Edward Carpenter** (1844)
Civilization on Trial (1948) **Arnold Toynbee** (1889)
Claiming of Sleeping Beauty, The [as 'A.N. Roquelaure'] (1983) **Anne Rice** (1941)
Claims of the Bible and Science, The (1863) **F.D. Maurice** (1805)
Clair de terre (1923) **André Breton** (1896)
Claire Clairmont and the Shelleys (1992) **Robert Gittings** (1911) [with Jo Manton]
Clairvoyant Goat, The (1981) **Hal Porter** (1911)
Clan of the Cave Bear, The (1980) **Jean M. Auel** (1936)
Clandara (1963) **'Evelyn Anthony' [Evelyn Ward-Thomas]** (1928)
Clandestine Marriage, The (1766) **George Colman, the Elder** (1732) [with David Garrick]
Clara Hopgood (1896) **'Mark Rutherford' [William Hale White]** (1831)
Clara Howard (1801) **Charles Brockden Brown** (1771)
Clara Lennox (1797) **Harriet Lee** (1756)
Clara Vaughan (1864) **R.D. Blackmore** (1825)
Clare Drummer (1929) **V.S. Pritchett** (1900)
Clarel (1876) **Herman Melville** (1819)
Claremont (1715) **Sir Samuel Garth** (1661)
Clarence (1830) **Catharine Maria Sedgwick** (1789)
Clarendon and Whitlock Compar'd (1727) **John Oldmixon** (1673)
Clarice (1905) **William Gillette** (1855)
Clarissa [vols. i, ii] (1748) **Samuel Richardson** (1689)
Clarissa Oakes (1992) **Patrick O'Brian** (1914)
Clark's Field (1914) **Robert Herrick** (1868)
Clarkton (1947) **Howard Fast** (1914)
Clash by Night (1941) **Clifford Odets** (1906)
Classic Records Reviewed or Deciphered (1859) **Thomas de Quincey** (1785)
Classical Dictionary of the Vulgar Tongue, A (1785) **Francis Grose** (1731)
Classical Education, A (1985) **Richard Cobb** (1917)
Classical Landscape with Figures (1947) **Osbert Lancaster** (1908)
Classics and Commercials (1950) **Edmund Wilson** (1895)
Claudelle Inglish (1958) **Erskine Caldwell** (1903)
Claudine and Annie [*Claudine s'en va*] (1903) **Colette** (1873)
Claudine at School [*Claudine à l'école*] (1900) **Colette** (1873)
Claudine in Paris [*Claudine à Paris*] (1901) **Colette** (1873)
Claudine Married [*Claudine en ménage*] (1902) **Colette** (1873)
Claudius the God and his Wife Messalina (1934) **Robert Graves** (1895)
Claverings, The (1867) **Anthony Trollope** (1815)
Clavigo (1774) **Johann Wolfgang von Goethe** (1749)
Clay Verge, The (1951) **Jack Clemo** (1916)
Clay: Whereabouts Unknown (1996) **Craig Raine** (1944)
Clayhanger (1910) **Arnold Bennett** (1867)
Clayhanger Family, The (1925) **Arnold Bennett** (1867)
Clé des champs, La (1953) **André Breton** (1896)
Clea (1960) **Lawrence Durrell** (1912)
Clean Dark, The (1989) **Robert Adamson** (1943)
Clean Straw for Nothing (1969) **George Johnston** (1912)
Clear and Present Danger (1989) **Tom Clancy** (1947)
Clear Horizon (1935) **Dorothy M. Richardson** (1873)
Clear Light of Day (1980) **Anita Desai** (1937)
Cleaver Gardens, The (1986) **George MacBeth** (1932)
Cleft Stick, The (1937) **Walter Greenwood** (1903)
Cleg Kelly (1896) **S.R. Crockett** (1860–1914)
Clemenceau Affair, The [*L'Affaire Clemenceau*] (1864) **Alexandre Dumas ['fils']** (1824)
Clement Lorimer (1849) **Angus Bethune Reach** (1821)
Clementina (1771) **Hugh Kelly** (1739)
Clementina (1901) **A.E.W. Mason** (1865)
Cleomelia (1727) **Eliza Haywood** (c.1693)
Cleomenes (1692) **John Dryden** (1631)
Cleon (1855) **Robert Browning** (1812)
Cleopatra (1889) **Sir H. Rider Haggard** (1856)
Cleopatra's Sister (1993) **Penelope Lively** (1933)
Clergyman's Daughter, A (1935) **'George Orwell'** (1903)
Clergymen of the Church of England (1866) **Anthony Trollope** (1815)
Clerihews Complete (1951) **E.C. Bentley** (1875)
Clever Wife, A (1895) **W. Pett Ridge** (1860)
Clever Woman of the Family, The (1865) **Charlotte M. Yonge** (1823)
Cleverest Woman in England, The (1898) **Mrs L.T. Meade** (1854)
Clevinger's Trial (1974) **Joseph Heller** (1923)
Clicking of Cuthbert, The (1922) **P.G. Wodehouse** (1881)
Client, The (1993) **John Grisham** (1955)
Cliff-Dwellers, The (1893) **Henry Blake Fuller** (1857)
Cliffs of Fall (1945) **Dan Davin** (1913)
Cliffs of Fall (1963) **Shirley Hazzard** (1931)
Climate of Courage, The [also titled *Naked in the Night*] (1954) **Jon Cleary** (1917)
Climates (1983) **Ruth Fainlight** (1931)
Climber, The (1908) **E.F. Benson** (1867)
Clinging to the Wreckage (1982) **John Mortimer** (1923)
Clitandre (1632?) **Pierre Corneille** (1606)
Clock Winder, The (1973) **Anne Tyler** (1941)

Clock Without Hands (1961) **Carson McCullers** (1917)
Clockmaker, The [1st ser.; 2nd ser., 1838; 3rd ser., 1840] (1836) **T. C. Haliburton** (1796)
Clocks, The (1963) **Agatha Christie** (1890)
Clockwork Orange, A (1962) **'Anthony Burgess' [John Anthony Burgess Wilson]** (1917)
Clockwork Testament, The (1974) **'Anthony Burgess' [John Anthony Burgess Wilson]** (1917)
Clogshop Chronicles (1896) **'John Ackworth' [Frederick R. Smith]** (1845–1919?)
Cloister and the Hearth, The (1861) **Charles Reade** (1814)
Cloning of Joanna May, The (1989) **Fay Weldon** (1931)
Clorinda Walks in Heaven (1922) **A.E. Coppard** (1878)
Close Chaplet, The (1926) **Laura Riding** (1901)
Close Harmony (1929) **Elmer Rice** (1892) [with Dorothy Parker]
Close of Play (1962) **Simon Raven** (1927)
Close of Play (1979) **Simon Gray** (1936)
Close Quarters (1987) **William Golding** (1911)
Close Ring, A (1907) **Matilda Betham-Edwards** (1836)
Close the Coalhouse Door (1969) **Alan Plater** (1935)
Close to the Sun Again (1977) **Morley Callaghan** (1903)
Closed Eye, A (1991) **Anita Brookner** (1928)
Closer to the Sun (1960) **George Johnston** (1912)
Closing the Ring (1984) **Maxine Kumin** (1925)
Closing Time (1994) **Joseph Heller** (1923)
Cloth of Gold (1874) **Thomas Bailey Aldrich** (1836)
Cloth of the Tempest (1943) **Kenneth Patchen** (1911)
Clothes in the Wardrobe, The (1987) **'Alice Thomas Ellis' [Anna Margaret Haycraft]** (1932)
Cloud and Silver (1916) **E.V. Lucas** (1868)
Cloud Cuckoo Land (1925) **Naomi Mitchison** (1897)
Cloud Nine (1979) **Caryl Churchill** (1938)
Cloud on Black Combe (1975) **Norman Nicholson** (1914)
CloudCuckooLand (1997) **Simon Armitage** (1963)
Cloudesley (1830) **William Godwin** (1756)
Cloudless May (1943) **Storm Jameson** (1897)
Clouds (1976) **Michael Frayn** (1933)
Clouds of Witness (1926) **Dorothy L. Sayers** (1893)
Clouds, The (423BC) **Aristophanes** (*c.* 445 BC)
Cloven Foot, The (1879) **M.E. Braddon** (1835)
Cloven Viscount, The [*Il visconte dimezzato*] (1952) **Italo Calvino** (1923)
Clover (1888) **'Susan Coolidge' [Sarah Chauncy Woolsey]** (1845)
Clowns' Houses (1918) **Edith Sitwell** (1887)
Clowns of God, The (1981) **Morris West** (1916)
Club of Queer Trades, The (1905) **G.K. Chesterton** (1874)
Club, The (1978) **David Williamson** (1942)
Clubbable Woman, A [first 'Dalziel and Pascoe' novel] (1970) **Reginald Hill** (1936)
Clues From a Detective's Camera (1893) **'Headon Hill' [Francis Edward Grainger]** (1857)
Clutch of Constables (1968) **Ngaio Marsh** (1899)
Clyack Sheaf, A (1969) **'Hugh MacDiarmid' [Christopher Murray Grieve]** (1892)
Clytemnestra [etc] [as 'Owen Meredith'] (1855) **Edward Robert Bulwer Lytton** (1831)
Co-operation and Nationality (1912) **George William Russell ['AE']** (1867)
Coals of Fire (1882) **David Christie Murray** (1847)
Coast of Incense, The (1953) **Freya Stark** (1893)
Coast of Trees, A (1981) **A.R. Ammons** (1926)
Coast to Coast (1956) **Jan Morris** (1926)
Coasting (1986) **Jonathan Raban** (1942)
Coat of Varnish, A (1978) **C.P. Snow** (1905)
Coat Without Seam, The (1929) **Maurice Baring** (1874)
Coblers Prophesie, The (1594) **Robert Wilson** (fl.1572)
Cobwebs From an Empty Skull (1874) **Ambrose Bierce** (1842)
Cocaine Nights (1996) **J.G. Ballard** (1930)
Cock and Anchor, The (1845) **J.S. le Fanu** (1814)
Cock & Bull (1992) **Will Self** (1961)
Cock Lane and Common-Sense (1894) **Andrew Lang** (1844)
Cock Pit (1928) **James Gould Cozzens** (1903)
Cock-a-Doodle Dandy (1949) **Sean O'Casey** (1880)
Cockatoos [as 'Brent of Bin Bin'] (1974) **Miles Franklin** (1879–1954)
Cockatoos, The (1974) **Patrick White** (1912)
Cocksure (1968) **Mordecai Richler** (1931)
Cocktail Party, The (1949) **T.S. Eliot** (1888)
Code of the Woosters, The (1938) **P.G. Wodehouse** (1881)
Codrus and Mynalcas (1521?) **Alexander Barclay** (1475?)
Coelebs in Search of a Wife (1808) **Hannah More** (1745)
Coelum Brittanicum (1634) **Thomas Carew** (1595)
Cogan's Trade (1974) **George V. Higgins** (1939)
Cogs Tyrannic (1991) **John Arden** (1930)
Cokkils (1953) **Sydney Goodsir Smith** (1915)
Colasterion (1645) **John Milton** (1608)
Cold Comfort Farm (1932) **Stella Gibbons** (1902)
Cold Coming, A (1991) **Tony Harrison** (1937)
Cold Hand in Mine (1975) **Robert Aickman** (1914)
Cold Heaven (1983) **Brian Moore** (1921)
Cold Spring, A (1955) **Elizabeth Bishop** (1911)
Cold War and the Income Tax, The (1963) **Edmund Wilson** (1895)
Cold Wind of Dawn, The (1966) **Kenneth White** (1936)
Coleridge on Imagination (1934) **I.A. Richards** (1893)
Colette Baudoche (1909) **Maurice Barrès** (1862)
Colin (1923) **E.F. Benson** (1867)
Colin Clouts Come Home Againe (1595) **Edmund Spenser** (1552?)
Colin II (1925) **E.F. Benson** (1867)
Collages (1964) **Anaïs Nin** (1903)
Collapse of British Power, The (1972) **Correlli Barnett** (1927)
Collected Ewart 1933–1980, The (1980) **Gavin Ewart** (1916)
Collected Poems (1914) **Ford Madox Ford** (1873)

Collected Poems [1st ser.] (1916) **W.H. Davies** (1871)
Collected Poems [2nd ser.] (1923) **W.H. Davies** (1871)
Collected Poems (1928) **W.H. Davies** (1871)
Collected Poems (1930) **Robert Frost** (1874)
Collected Poems (1933) **Hart Crane** (1899–1932)
Collected Poems (1951) **Keith Douglas** (1920–44)
Collected Poems (1960) **Lawrence Durrell** (1912)
Collected Poems (1976) **Elizabeth Daryush** (1887)
Collected Poems (1990) **Donald Davie** (1922)
Collected Poems (1990) **Padraic Fallon** (1906–74)
Collected Poems (1963) **Wilfred Owen** (1893–1918)
Collected Poems 1909–1935 (1936) **T.S. Eliot** (1888)
Collected Poems 1909–1962 (1963) **T.S. Eliot** (1888)
Collected Poems 1929–33 (1935) **C. Day Lewis** (1904)
Collected Poems 1929–36 (1949) **C. Day Lewis** (1904)
Collected Poems 1936–1961 (1962) **Roy Fuller** (1912)
Collected Poems 1942–1977 (1979) **W.S. Graham** (1918)
Collected Poems: 1948–1998 (1998) **D.J. Enright** (1920)
Collected Poems 1980–1991 (1991) **Gavin Ewart** (1916)
Collected Poems of C. Day Lewis (1954) **C. Day Lewis** (1904)
Collected Poems (1911) **Sir Edmund Gosse** (1849)
Collected Poems of Rupert Brooke (1918) **Rupert Brooke** (1887–1915)
Collected Prose (1920) **James Elroy Flecker** (1884–1915)
Collected Pruse [sic] (1967) **Patrick Kavanagh** (1904)
Collected Stories for Children (1947) **Walter de la Mare** (1873)
Collected Works (1937) **Isaac Rosenberg** (1890–1918)
Collected Works of Billy the Kid, The (1970) **Michael Ondaatje** (1943)
Collection of Curious Discourses, A (1720) **Thomas Hearne** (1678)
Collection of Emblemes, A (1635) **George Wither** (1588)
Collection of Psalms and Hymns, A (1737) **John Wesley** (1703)
Collection of Several Tracts and Discourses, A (1685) **Gilbert Burnet** (1643)
Collector, The (1963) **John Fowles** (1926)
Collector, The (1959) **Peter Redgrove** (1932)
Colleen Bawn, The (1860) **Dion Boucicault** (1820?)
College Window, The (1904) **George Ade** (1866)
Collegians, The (1829) **Gerald Griffin** (1803)
Collin's Walk Through London and Westminster (1690) **Thomas D'Urfey** (1653)
Colline inspirée, La (1913) **Maurice Barrès** (1862)
Colloquia (1518) **Erasmus** (c.1467)
Colloquy for the States (1943) **Archibald MacLeish** (1892)
Collyn Clout (1531?) **John Skelton** (1460?-1529)
Colmain (1963) **Simon Gray** (1936)
Colomba (1841) **Prosper Mérimée** (1803)
Colombe (1951) **Jean Anouilh** (1910)
Colonel Chabert [*Le Colonel Chabert*] (1832) **Honoré de Balzac** (1799)
Colonel Enderby's Wife (1885) **'Lucas Malet' [Mary St Leger Harrison]** (1852)
Colonel Jack [**Defoe**]: see *The History and Remarkable Life of Colonel Jacque*
Colonel Julian (1951) **H.E. Bates** (1905)
Colonel Quaritch, V.C. (1888) **Sir H. Rider Haggard** (1856)
Colonel Starbottle's Client (1892) **Bret Harte** (1836)
Colonel Stow (1908) **H.C. Bailey** (1878)
Colonel Sun (1968) **Kingsley Amis** (1922)
Colonel's Daughter, The (1931) **Richard Aldington** (1892)
Colonel's Daughter, The (1984) **Rose Tremain** (1943)
Colonel's Dream, The (1905) **Charles W. Chesnutt** (1858)
Colonial Innocency (1982) **Austin Clarke** (1932)
Colonial King, A (1905) **Hume Nisbet** (1849)
Colonial Reformer, A (1890) **'Rolf Boldrewood' [Thomas Alexander Browne]** (1826)
Color and Democracy (1945) **W.E.B. du Bois** (c.1868)
Color of a Great City, The (1923) **Theodore Dreiser** (1871)
Color of Darkness (1957) **James Purdy** (1923)
Color Purple, The (1982) **Alice Walker** (1944)
Colossus of Maroussi, The (1941) **Henry Miller** (1891)
Colossus, The (1960) **Sylvia Plath** (1932)
Colour and Form (1937) **Adrian Stokes** (1902)
Colour Blind (1953) **Catherine Cookson** (1906)
Colour of Blood, The (1987) **Brian Moore** (1921)
Colour of Life, The (1896) **Alice Meynell** (1847)
Colour of Magic, The [first of the *Discworld* series] (1983) **Terry Pratchett** (1948)
Coloured Dome, The (1932) **Francis Stuart** (1902)
Coloured Lands, The (1938) **G.K. Chesterton** (1874–1936)
Colours of War, The (1977) **Matt Cohen** (1942)
Columba (1977) **Carolyn Slaughter** (1946)
Columbus (1857) **John Brougham** (1810)
Columbus and the Fat Lady (1972) **Matt Cohen** (1942)
Columella (1779) **Richard Graves** (1715)
Colville of the Guards (1885) **James Grant** (1822)
Combat of the Thirty, The (1859) **W.H. Ainsworth** (1805)
Come and Go (1965) **Samuel Beckett** (1906)
Come Back, Dr Caligari (1964) **Donald Barthelme** (1931)
Come Back Little Sheba (1950) **William Inge** (1913)
Come Back to Erin (1940) **'Seán O'Faoláin' [John Francis Whelan]** (1900)
Come Blow Your Horn (1961) **Neil Simon** (1927)
Come Hither (1923) **Walter de la Mare** (1873) (ed.)
Come Like Shadows (1972) **Simon Raven** (1927)
Come to Think of It (1930) **G.K. Chesterton** (1874)
Come & Welcome to Jesus Christ (1678) **John Bunyan** (1628)
Come Wind, Come Weather (1940) **Daphne du Maurier** (1907)
Comedians (1975) **Trevor Griffiths** (1935)
Comedians, The (1966) **Graham Greene** (1904)
Comédie de la mort, La ['The Comedy of Death'] (1838) **Théophile Gautier** (1811)

Comedies (1990) **John Wain** (1925)
Comedies and Tragedies [inc. *The Parson's Wedding*] (1664) **Thomas Killigrew** (1612)
Comedies & Errors (1898) **Henry Harland** (1861)
Comedies, Histories, & Tragedies [the *First Folio*] (1623) **William Shakespeare** (1564–1616)
Comedies of Courtship (1896) **'Anthony Hope' [Sir Anthony Hope Hawkins]** (1863)
Comedy in Spasms, A (1895) **'Iota' [Kathleen Mannington Caffyn]** (1855?)
Comedy of Masks, A (1893) **Ernest Dowson** (1867) [with Arthur Moore]
Cometh Up as a Flower (1867) **Rhoda Broughton** (1840)
Comfort Me with Apples (1956) **Peter de Vries** (1910)
Comfort of Strangers, The (1981) **Ian McEwan** (1948)
Comforte of Lovers, The (1515) **Stephen Hawes** (d. 1523?)
Comforters, The (1957) **Muriel Spark** (1918)
Comic Blackstone, A (1846) **Gilbert Abbott a Beckett** (1811)
Comic Dramas (1817) **Maria Edgeworth** (1767)
Comic History of England, A (1847) **Gilbert Abbott a Beckett** (1811)
Comic History of Rome, A (1852) **Gilbert Abbott a Beckett** (1811)
Comic Tales and Sketches [as 'M.A. Titmarsh'] (1841) **W.M. Thackeray** (1811)
Comical History of Don Quixote: Part 1, The (1694) **Thomas d'Urfey** (1653)
Comical History of Don Quixote: Part the Second, The (1694) **Thomas d'Urfey** (1653)
Comical History of Don Quixote: The Third Part, The (1696) **Thomas d'Urfey** (1653)
Comical Revenge, The (1664) **Sir George Etherege** (1635)
Comicall Historie of Alphonsus, King of Aragon, The (1599) **Robert Greene** (1558–92)
Coming Forth by Day of Osiris Jones, The (1931) **Conrad Potter Aiken** (1889)
Coming From Behind (1983) **Howard Jacobson** (1942)
Coming in to Land (1987) **Stephen Poliakoff** (1952)
Coming in With the Tide (1991) **P.H. Newby** (1918)
Coming of Christ, The (1928) **John Masefield** (1878)
Coming of Cuchulain, The (1894) **Standish O'Grady** (1846)
Coming of Love, The (1898) **Theodore Watts-Dunton** (1832)
Coming of Stork, The (1970) **David Williamson** (1942)
Coming of the Fairies, The (1922) **A. Conan Doyle** (1859)
Coming of the Kings, The (1970) **Ted Hughes** (1930)
Coming of the New Deal, The (1959) **Arthur Schlesinger** (1917)
Coming of the Quantum Cats, The (1986) **Frederik Pohl** (1919)
Coming Out; and The Field of the Forty Footsteps (1828) **Anna Maria** (1780) **Porter** [with **Jane Porter**]
Coming Out Fighting (1969) **Philip Hobsbaum** (1932)
Coming Race, The (1871) **Edward Bulwer-Lytton** (1803)
Coming Through Slaughter (1979) **Michael Ondaatje** (1943)
Coming to Terms (1979) **Josephine Miles** (1911)
Coming Up For Air (1939) **George Orwell** (1903)
Commandmant, The (1975) **Jessica Anderson** (1925)
Commentaries on the Laws of England (1765) **Sir William Blackstone** (1723)
Commentary, A (1908) **John Galsworthy** (1867)
Commentary on Hegel's Logic, A (1910) **John McTaggart** (1866)
Commentary on St Paul's Epistle to the Colossians (1875) **Joseph Barber Lightfoot** (1828)
Commentary on St Paul's Epistle to the Philippians (1868) **Joseph Barber Lightfoot** (1828)
Commerce Defended (1807) **James Mill** (1773)
Commitments, The (1987) **Roddy Doyle** (1958)
Commodity of Dreams, A (1959) **Howard Nemerov** (1920)
Commodore, The [US: *Commodore Hornblower*] (1945) **C.S. Forester** (1899)
Commodore, The (1994) **Patrick O'Brian** (1914)
Common Asphodel, The (1949) **Robert Graves** (1895)
Common Chord, The (1914) **Phyllis Bottome** (1884)
Common Chord, The (1947) **'Frank O'Connor' [Michael Francis O'Donovan']** (1903)
Common Grace, A (1960) **Norman MacCaig** (1910)
Common Lot, The (1904) **Robert Herrick** (1868)
Common People, The (1938) **G.D.H. Cole** (1889) and R.W. Postgage (1896)
Common Pursuit, The (1952) **F.R. Leavis** (1895)
Common Pursuit, The (1984) **Simon Gray** (1936)
Common Reader, The [1st ser.] (1925) **Virginia Woolf** (1882)
Common Reader, The [2nd ser.] (1932) **Virginia Woolf** (1882)
Common Rights of Subjects Defended, The (1719) **Benjamin Hoadly** (1676)
Common Sense (1776) **Thomas Paine** (1737)
Common Sense About the War (1914) **Bernard Shaw** (1856)
Common Sense and Nuclear Warfare (1959) **Bertrand Russell** (1872)
Common Sense of Municipal Trading, The (1904) **Bernard Shaw** (1856)
Common Touch, The (1926) **James Evershed Agate** (1877)
Common-place Book: First Series (1849) **Robert Southey** (1774–1843)
Common-place Book: Fourth Series (1850) **Robert Southey** (1774–1843)
Common-place Book: Second Series (1849) **Robert Southey** (1774–1843)
Common-place Book: Third Series (1850) **Robert Southey** (1774–1843)
Common-Sense Ethics (1921) **C.E.M. Joad** (1891)
Common-wealth of Oceana, The (1656) **James Harrington** (1611)

Common-wealth of Women, A (1685) **Thomas d'Urfey** (1653)
Commonplace (1870) **Christina Rossetti** (1830)
Commonwealth at War, The (1917) **A.F. Pollard** (1869)
Communicating Doors (1995) **Alan Ayckbourn** (1939)
Communication Cord, The (1982) **Brian Friel** (1929)
Communion of Labour, The (1856) **Anna Jameson** (1794)
Communism (1927) **Harold Laski** (1893)
Companion to Mr Wells's Outline of History, A (1926) **Hilaire Belloc** (1870)
Companions of Pickle, The (1898) **Andrew Lang** (1844)
Companions of the Day and Night (1975) **Wilson Harris** (1921)
Company I've Kept, The (1966) **'Hugh MacDiarmid' [Christopher Murray Grieve]** (1892)
Company of Poets, A (1981) **Louis Simpson** (1923)
Company Parade (1934) **Storm Jameson** (1897)
Company She Keeps, The (1942) **Mary McCarthy** (1912)
Comparison Between the Two Stages, A (1702) **Charles Gildon** (1665)?
Compass Error, A (1968) **Sybille Bedford** (1911)
Compass Rose, The (1982) **Ursula K. le Guin** (1929)
Compendium of Lovers, A (1990) **Francis Stuart** (1902)
Complaint of the Black Knight, The (1508) **John Lydgate** (1370?-1449)
Complaint; or, Night-Thoughts: Night the First, The [collected edition, 1750] (1742–6) **Edward Young** (1683)
Complaints (1591) **Edmund Spenser** (1552?)
Complaints of the Poor People of England, The (1793) **George Dyer** (1755)
Complaisant Lover, The (1959) **Graham Greene** (1904)
Compleat Angler, The (1653) **Izaak Walton** (1593)
Compleat Gamester, The (1674) **Charles Cotton** (1630)
Compleat Gard'ner, The (1693) **John Evelyn** (1620) (tr.)
Compleat Gentleman, The (1622) **Henry Peacham the Elder** (1578?)
Compleat Key to the Dispensary, A (1714) **Sir Samuel Garth** (1661)
Complete Art of Poetry, The (1718) **Charles Gildon** (1665)
Complete Collection of Genteel and Ingenious Conversation, A (1738) **Jonathan Swift** (1667)
Complete Concordance to Shakespeare, The (1845) **Mary Cowden Clarke** (1809)
Complete Concordance to the Holy Scriptures, A (1738) **Alexander Cruden** (1701)
Complete Guide to the Lakes (1854) **Harriet Martineau** (1802)
Complete History of the Bastable Family, The (1928) **E[dith] Nesbit** (1858)
Complete History of the English Stage, A (1797–1800) **Charles Dibdin** (1745)
Complete Memoirs of George Sherston, The (1937) **Siegfried Sassoon** (1886)
Complete Poems (1969) **Walter de la Mare** (1873–56)
Complete Sherlock Holmes Long Stories (1929) **A. Conan Doyle** (1859)
Complete Sherlock Holmes Short Stories (1928) **A. Conan Doyle** (1859)
Composed on the Tongue (1980) **Allen Ginsberg** (1926)
Composition as Explanation (1926) **Gertrude Stein** (1874)
Compulsory Option, A (1972) **Sharon Pollock** (1936)
Comrade Kirillov (1976) **Raja Rao** (1908)
Comte's Philosophy of the Sciences (1853) **G.H. Lewes** (1817)
Comus (1637) **John Milton** (1608)
Conan the Barbarian (1954) **Robert E. Howard** (1906)
Conceived in Liberty (1939) **Howard Fast** (1914)
Concept of Nature, The (1920) **A.N. Whitehead** (1861)
Concept of the Person, The (1963) **A.J. Ayer** (1910)
Concepts and Categories (1978) **Sir Isaiah Berlin** (1909)
Concerning a Vow (1914) **Rhoda Broughton** (1840)
Concerning Children (1900) **Charlotte Perkins Gilman** (1860)
Concerning Isabel Carnaby (1898) **Ellen Thorneycroft Fowler** (1860)
Concerning Revelation, Prophecy, Measures and Rule (1676) **George Fox** (1624)
Concerning the Beautiful [from Plotinus] (1787) **Thomas Taylor** (1758) (tr.)
Concerning the Eccentricities of Cardinal Pirelli (1926) **Ronald Firbank** (1886)
Concerning the Living God of Truth (1680) **George Fox** (1624)
Concerning the Relations of Great Britain, Spain, and Portugal [on the Convention of Cintra] (1809) **William Wordsworth** (1770)
Concerning Virgins (1990) **Clare Boylan** (1948)
Concert Pitch (1913) **'Frank Danby' [Julia Frankau]** (1864)
Conciones ad Populum (1795) **S.T. Coleridge** (1772)
Concise Oxford Dictionary of Current English, The (1911) **H.W. Fowler** (1858) and **F.G. Fowler** (1870)
Concluding (1948) **'Henry Green' [Henry Vicent Yorke]** (1905)
Conclusive Evidence [rev. 1966 as *Speak, Memory*] (1951) **Vladimir Nabokov** (1899)
Concrete Island (1974) **J.G. Ballard** (1930)
Concubine, The (1966) **Elechi Amadi** (1934)
Condeferate General from Big Sur, A (1964) **Richard Brautigan** (1935)
Condemned Playground, The (1945) **Cyril Connolly** (1903)
Condensed Novels (1867) **Bret Harte** (1836)
Condition of Muzak, The (1977) **Michael Moorcock** (1939)
Condition of the Working Class in England, The [*Die Lage der arbeitenden Klassen in England*] (1845) **Friedrich Engels** (1820)
Conditions (1969) **G.S. Fraser** (1915)

Conditions of Peace (1942) **E.H. Carr** (1892)
Condominium (1977) **John D. MacDonald** (1916)
Condor and the Cows, The (1948) **Christopher Isherwood** (1904)
Condor Passes, The (1971) **Shirley Ann Grau** (1929)
Conduct of Life, The (1860) **Ralph Waldo Emerson** (1803)
Conduct of Major Maxim, The (1983) **Gavin Lyall** (1932)
Conduct of the Allies, The (1712) **Jonathan Swift** (1667)
Cone-Gatherers, The (1955) **Robin Jenkins** (1912)
Coney Island of the Mind, A (1958) **Lawrence Ferlinghetti** (1920)
Confederacy of Dunces, A (1980) **John Kennedy Toole** (1937–69)
Confederacy, The (1705) **Sir John Vanbrugh** (1664)
Confederates (1979) **Thomas Keneally** (1935)
Conference at Cold Comfort Farm (1949) **Stella Gibbons** (1902)
Confession Amantis (1390) **John Gower** (c.1330)
Conference, The (1763) **Charles Churchill** (1731)
Confessio Juvenis (1925) **Richard Hughes** (1900)
Confession, A (1884) **Leo Tolstoy** (1828)
Confession de Sancy (1660) **Théodore-Agrippa D'Aubigné** (1552–1630)
Confession of a Lover (1976) **Mulk Raj Anand** (1905)
Confession of a Rebel (1949) **Jack Clemo** (1916)
Confession of Faith, The (1641) **Sir Francis Bacon** (1561–1626)
Confession of John Whitlock, The (1891) **E.W. Howe** (1853)
Confession of My Faith, A (1672) **John Bunyan** (1628)
Confession of Stephen Whapshare, The (1898) **E[mma] F[rances] Brooke** (1859?)
Confessions (c. 400) **St Augustine of Hippo** (354)
Confessions, The [*Les Confessions*] (1781–8) **Jean-Jacques Rousseau** (1712–78)
Confessions and Histories (1964) **Edward Lucie-Smith** (1933)
Confessions of a Pretty Woman (1846) **Julia Pardoe** (1806)
Confessions of a Thug, The (1839) **Captain Meadows Taylor** (1808)
Confessions of a Young Man (1888) **George Moore** (1852)
Confessions of Alphonse, The (1917) **'Barry Pain' [Eric Odell]** (1864)
Confessions of an Elderly Gentleman, The (1836) **Marguerite, Countess of Blessington** (1789)
Confessions of an Elderly Lady, The (1838) **Marguerite, Countess of Blessington** (1789)
Confessions of an English Opium Eater (1856) **Thomas De Quincey** (1785)
Confessions of an Irish Rebel (1965) **Brendan Behan** (1923–64)
Confessions of Con. Cregan (1849) **Charles Lever** (1806)
Confessions of Felix Krull, Confidence Man [*Bekenntnisse des Hochstaplers Felix Krull*] (1954) **Thomas Mann** (1875)
Confessions of Harry Lorrequer, The (1839) **Charles Lever** (1806)
Confessions of Joseph Baisz, The (1977) **Dan Jacobson** (1929)
Confessions of Nat Turner, The (1967) **William Styron** (1925)
Confessions of the Nun of St Omer, The (1805) **Charlotte Dacre** (1782?)
Confessions (1805) **William-Henry Ireland** (1777)
Confidence (1880) **Henry James** (1843)
Confidence Man, The (1857) **Herman Melville** (1819)
Confidence Man, The (1978) **Leon Garfield** (1921)
Confidences (1859) **Charles Hamilton Aïdé** (1826)
Confidential Agent, The (1939) **Graham Greene** (1904)
Confidential Chats With Boys (1982) **Alan Hollinghurst** (1954)
Confidential Clerk, The (1954) **T.S. Eliot** (1888)
Conflict (1931) **William Soutar** (1898)
Conflict, The (1903) **M.E. Braddon** (1835)
Conflicts (1942) **Sir Lewis Namier** (1888)
Conflicts of Spring (1981) **Ralph Gustafson** (1909)
Confusion (1924) **James Gould Cozzens** (1903)
Confusion (1993) **Elizabeth Jane Howard** (1923)
Confusions About X (1939) **Julian Symons** (1912)
Confutacyon of Tyndales Answere, The (1532) **Sir Thomas More** (1478)
Confutation of Atheism, A [*pt. i*] (1692) **Richard Bentley** (1662)
Confutation of Atheism, A [*pt. ii*] (1692) **Richard Bentley** (1662)
Conglomeroid Cocktail Party, The (1984) **Robert Silverberg** (1935)
Congo (1980) **Michael Crichton** (1942)
Congo, The (1914) **Vachel Lindsay** (1879)
Coningsby (1844) **Benjamin Disraeli** (1804)
Conjectura Cabbalistica (1653) **Henry More** (1614)
Conjectures on Original Composition (1759) **Edward Young** (1683)
Conjugal Love [*L'amore coniugale*] (1949) **'Alberto Moravia' [Alberto Pincherle]** (1907)
Conjure Wife (1953) **Fritz Leiber** (1910)
Conjure Woman, The (1899) **Charles W. Chesnutt** (1858)
Connecticut Yankee in King Arthur's Court, A (1889) **'Mark Twain' [Samuel Langhorne Clemens]** (1835)
Connection, The (1959) **Jack Gelber** (1932)
Connections (2000) **Hilary Bailey** (1936)
Connoisseur, The (1974) **Evan S. Connell, Jr** (1924)
Connoisseur, The (1926) **Walter de la Mare** (1873)
Conquered, The (1923) **Naomi Mitchison** (1897)
Conqueror, The (1902) **Gertrude Atherton** (1857)
Conquerors, The [*Les Conquérants*] (1928) **André Malraux** (1901)
Conquest of Canaan, The (1785) **Timothy Dwight** (1752)
Conquest of Canaan, The (1905) **Booth Tarkington** (1869)
Conquest of China, The (1675) **Elkanah Settle** (1648)
Conquest of Granada by the Spaniards, The (1670) **John Dryden** (1631)

Conquest of Plassans, The [*La Conquête de Plassans*] (1874) **Émile Zola** (1840)
Conquest of Spain, The (1705) **Mary Pix** (1666)
Conquistador (1932) **Archibald MacLeish** (1892)
Conquistadors, The (1969) **'Hammond Innes' [Ralph Hammond-Innes]** (1913)
Conquistadors (1973) **Meridel Le Sueur** (1900)
Conscience, The (1868) **F.D. Maurice** (1805)
Conscience of the Rich, The (1958) **C.P. Snow** (1905)
Conscious and Verbal, (2000) **Les Murray** (1938)
Conscious Lovers, The (1722) **Sir Richard Steele** (1672)
Consciousness (1907) **A.R. Orage** (1873)
Consecration of Hetty Fleet, The (1898) **Arthur St John Adcock** (1864)
Consensus and Disunity (1979) **Kenneth O. Morgan** (1934)
Consenting Adults (1980) **Peter de Vries** (1910)
Consequently I Rejoice (1977) **Elizabeth Jennings** (1926)
Conservationist, The (1974) **Nadine Gordimer** (1923)
Consider Her Ways (1947) **Frederick Grove** (1879)
Consider Her Ways (1961) **'John Wyndham' [John Wyndham Harris]** (1903)
Consider Phlebas (1987) **Iain M. Banks** (1954)
Consider the Lilies [US: *The Alien Light*] (1968) **Iain Crichton Smith [Iain Mac a'Ghobhainn]** (1928)
Consider the Lilies (1968) **Auberon Waugh** (1939)
Considerations on Representative Government (1861) **J.S. Mill** (1806)
Considerations on the Principal Events of the French revolution [*Considérations sur les principaux événements de la Révolution française*] (1818) **Madame de Staël** (1766–1817)
Consolation of Philosophy, The [from Boethius] (1478?) **Geoffrey Chaucer** (1340?-1400) (tr.)
Consolations, Les (1830) **Charles-Augustin Sainte-Beuve** (1804)
Consolidated Comedies (1981) **Roy Fisher** (1930)
Constable de Bourbon, The (1866) **W.H. Ainsworth** (1805)
Constable of France, The (1866) **James Grant** (1822)
Constable of St Nicholas, The (1894) **Edwin Lester Arnold** (1857)
Constable of the Tower, The (1861) **W.H. Ainsworth** (1805)
Constance (1982) **Lawrence Durrell** (1912)
Constance Herbert (1855) **Geraldine Jewsbury** (1812)
Constance of Castille (1810) **William Sotheby** (1757)
Constance Sherwood (1865) **Lady Georgiana Fullerton** (1812)
Constancia (1989) **Carlos Fuentes** (1928)
Constant Couple, The (1699) **George Farquhar** (1678)
Constant Maid, The (1640) **James Shirley** (1596)
Constant Nymph, The (1924) **Margaret Kennedy** (1896)
Constantine the Great (1683) **Nathaniel Lee** (1649?)
Constitution for the Socialist Commonwealth of Great Britain, A (1920) **Sidney Webb** (1859) and **Beatrice Webb** (1858)
Constitutional History of England , The [vol. i; vol. ii, 1875; vol. iii, 1878] (1873) **William Stubbs** (1825)
Constitutional History of England, The (1827) **Henry Hallam** (1777)
Consuelo (1842) **'George Sand' [Auore Dupin]** (1804)
Contarini Fleming (1832) **Benjamin Disraeli** (1804)
Contemplations, Les ['Contemplations'] (1856) **Victor Hugo** (1802)
Contemplations, Moral and Divine (1678) **Sir Matthew Hale** (1609–76)
Contemplations Upon the Principall Passages of the Holy Storie (1612) **Joseph Hall** (1574)
Contemporaries and Snobs (1928) **Laura Riding** (1901)
Contemporary Portraits (1975) **Murray Bail** (1941)
Contemporary Writers (1965) **Virginia Woolf** (1882–1941)
Contenders, The (1958) **John Wain** (1925)
Content (1719) **Allan Ramsay** (1686)
Contention for Honour and Riches, A (1633) **James Shirley** (1596)
Contes et Facéties ['Stories and Jests'] (1853) **'Gérard de Nerval' [Gérard Labrunie]** (1808)
Contest of Ladies, A (1956) **William Sansom** (1912)
Contests and Dissensions Between the Nobles and the Commons in Athens and Rome, The (1701) **Jonathan Swift** (1667)
Continent (1986) **Jim Crace** (1946)
Continental Drift (1985) **Russell Banks** (1940)
Continual Dew (1937) **Sir John Betjeman** (1906)
Continuance of Albions England, A (1606) **William Warner** (1558?)
Continuation of Early Lessons (1814) **Maria Edgeworth** (1767)
Continuing Journey, A (1968) **Archibald MacLeish** (1892)
Continuous (1981) **Tony Harrison** (1937)
Continuum (1988) **Allen Curnow** (1911)
Contract with the World (1980) **Jane Rule** (1931)
Contractor, The (1969) **David Storey** (1933)
Contraries (1981) **Joyce Carol Oates** (1938)
Contrary View, The (1974) **Geoffrey Grigson** (1905)
Contrast, The (1787) **Royall Tyler** (1757)
Contrast, The (1923) **Hilaire Belloc** (1870)
Contrast, The (1913) **Elinor Glyn** (1864)
Contributions to the Theory of Natural Selection (1870) **Alfred Russel Wallace** (1823)
Contrivances, The (1715) **Henry Carey** (1687?)
Conundrum (1974) **Jan Morris** (1926)
Convention and Revolt in Poetry (1919) **John Livingston Lowes** (1867)
Conventional Weapons (1961) **Jocelyn Brooke** (1908)
Conventionalists, The (1908) **R.H. Benson** (1871)
Convercyon of Swerers, The (1509) **Stephen Hawes** (d. 1523?)
Conversation (1940) **Conrad Potter Aiken** (1889)

Conversation in the Cathedral [*Conversación en la catedral*] (1969) **Mario Vargas Llosa** (1936)
Conversation Pieces (1936) **Sir Sacheverell Sitwell** (1897)
Conversation, The (1720) **Matthew Prior** (1664)
Conversation with a Cat and Others, A (1931) **Hilaire Belloc** (1870)
Conversation with an Angel, A (1928) **Hilaire Belloc** (1870)
Conversations in Bloomsbury (1981) **Mulk Raj Anand** (1905)
Conversations in Ebury Street (1924) **George Moore** (1852)
Conversations of James Northcote (1830) **William Hazlitt** (1778)
Conversations of Lord Byron with the Countess of Blessington (1834) **Marguerite, Countess of Blessington** (1789)
Conversations With My Uncle (1936) **Frank Sargeson** (1903)
Conversion of Winckelmann, The (1897) **Alfred Austin** (1835)
Converts, The (1967) **Rex Warner** (1905)
Convict Ship, The (1895) **W. Clark Russell** (1844)
Convict's Appeal, The (1818) **Bernard Barton** (1784)
Convivio [unfinished] (1304–1308) **Dante Alighieri** (1265)
Convocation, The (1717) **Richard Savage** (1697?)
Cool Million, A (1934) **'Nathanael West' [Nathan Wallenstein Weinstein]** (1903)
Cool Thoughts on the Present Situation of Our Public Affairs (1764) **Benjamin Franklin** (1706)
Coolie Odyssey (1988) **David Dabydeen** (1956)
Coolie, The (1936) **Mulk Raj Anand** (1905)
Coombe Abbey (1844) **Selina Bunbury** (1802)
Coopers Hill [unauthorized] (1642) **Sir John Denham** (1615)
Coopers Hill [first authorized edn] (1655) **Sir John Denham** (1615)
Copenhagen (1998) **Michael Frayn** (1933)
Cop Hater (1956) **'Ed McBain' [Evan Hunter]** (1926)
Cophetua (1911) **John Drinkwater** (1882)
Copper Beach, The (1990) **Maeve Binchy** (1940)
Copperhead, The (1893) **Harold Frederic** (1856)
Copperhead, The (1918) **Augustus Thomas** (1857)
Cops and Robbers (1978) **Alan Ahlberg** (1938)
Coquette in Crape, A (1907) **'Frank Danby' [Julia Frankau]** (1864)
Coquette, The (1830) **Caroline Norton** (1808)
Coral (1925) **Compton Mackenzie** (1883)
Coral Island, The (1858) **R.M. Ballantyne** (1825)
Corayda (1860) **Ernest Charles Jones** (1819)
Corde au cou, La (1873) **Émile Gaboriau** (1832)
Cords of Vanity, The (1909) **James Branch Cabell** (1879)
Corduroy (1930) **Adrian Bell** (1901)
Corentyne Thunder (1941) **Edgar Mittelholzer** (1909)
Corinne (1807) **Madame de Staël** (1766–1817)
Cork Street, Next to the Hatter's (1965) **Pamela Hansford Johnson** (1912)
Corker's Freedom (1964) **John Berger** (1926)
Corleone (1897) **F. Marion Crawford** (1854)
Cormorant Crag (1895) **George Manville Fenn** (1831)
Corn in Egypt (1941) **Warwick Deeping** (1877)
Corn King and the Spring Queen, The (1931) **Naomi Mitchison** (1897)
Corn Law Rhymes: The Ranter (1830) **Ebenezer Elliott** (1781)
Cornelia [from Robert Garnier] (1594) **Thomas Kyd** (1558) (tr.)
Corner That Held Them, The (1948) **Sylvia Townsend Warner** (1893)
Corners in Glass (1977) **Ralph Gustafson** (1909)
Cornhuskers (1918) **Carl Sandburg** (1878)
Cornish Ballads (1869) **R.S. Hawker** (1803)
Cornish Childhood, A (1942) **A.L. Rowse** (1903)
Cornish Dancer, The (1982) **Geoffrey Grigson** (1905)
Coromandel Sea Change (1991) **Rumer Godden** (1907)
Coronation Everest (1958) **Jan Morris** (1926)
Coronation Summer (1953) **Angela Thirkell** (1890)
Coronation, The (1640) **James Shirley** (1596)
Corporal Cat (1941) **Martin Flavin** (1883)
Corporal Sam (1910) **Sir A.T. Quiller Couch** (1863)
Correct Compassion, A (1952) **James Kirkup** (1923)
Correspondence and Table-Talk (1876) **Benjamin Robert Haydon** (1786–1846)
Correspondences (1974) **Anne Stevenson** (1933)
Corrida at San Feliu, The (1964) **Paul Scott** (1920)
Corridor, The (1975) **C.H. Sisson** (1914)
Corridors of Power (1964) **C.P. Snow** (1905)
Corruption (1984) **Penelope Lively** (1933)
Corruption, and Intolerance (1801) **Thomas Moore** (1779)
Corsair, The (1814) **George Gordon, Lord Byron** (1788)
Corsican Brothers, The (1852) **Dion Boucicault** (1820?)
Corsons Inlet (1965) **A.R. Ammons** (1926)
Coryats Crambe (1611) **Thomas Coryate** (1577?)
Coryats Crudities (1611) **Thomas Coryate** (1577?)
Coryston Family, The (1913) **Mrs T. Humphry Ward** (1851)
Cosima (1840) **'George Sand' [Auore Dupin]** (1804)
Cosmo Cosmolino (1992) **Helen Garner** (1942)
Cosmo de'Medici (1837) **R.H. Horne** (1803)
Cosmographie (1652) **Peter Heylyn** (1600)
Cosmological Eye, The (1939) **Henry Miller** (1891)
Cosmopolis (1893) **Paul Bourget** (1852)
Cost of Caergwyn, The (1864) **Mary Howitt** (1799)
Cost of Seriousness, The (1978) **Peter Porter** (1929)
Cost of Wings, The [as 'Richard Dehan'] (1914) **Clo Graves** (1863)
Costumes by Eros (1928) **Conrad Potter Aiken** (1889)
Cosy Room, The (1936) **Arthur Machen** (1863)
Cotswold Honey (1940) **Francis Brett Young** (1884)
Cottagers of Glenburnie, The (1808) **Elizabeth Hamilton** (1758)

Cotter's England [US: *Dark Places of the Heart*] (1966) **Christina Stead** (1902)
Couching at the Door (1942) **D.K. Broster** (1878)
Count Belisarius (1938) **Robert Graves** (1895)
Count Bruga (1926) **Ben Hecht** (1894)
Count Fathom [**Smollett**]: see *The Adventures of Ferdinand Count Fathom*
Count Hannibal (1901) **Stanley J. Weyman** (1855)
Count Julian (1812) **Walter Savage Landor** (1775)
Count Julian (1845) **William Gilmore Simms** (1806)
Count Nulin (1825) **Alexander Pushkin** (1799)
Count of Monte Cristo, The [*Le Comte de Monte-Cristo*] (1844) **Alexandre Dumas ['père']** (1802)
Count Your Enemies and Economise Your Expenditure (1862) **Walter Bagehot** (1826)
Count Zero (1986) **William Gibson** (1948)
Countenance of Truth (1990) **Shirley Hazzard** (1931)
Counter-Attack (1918) **Siegfried Sassoon** (1886)
Counter-blaste to Tobacco, A (1604) **[King James I]** (1566)
Counterblast (1969) **Marshall McLuhan** (1911)
Counterfeiters, The [*Les Faux-Monnayeurs*] (1926) **André Gide** (1869)
Counterlife, The (1987) **Philip Roth** (1933)
Counterparts (1954) **Roy Fuller** (1912)
Counterpoint (1990) **R.S. Thomas** (1913)
Countess Cathleen, and Various Legends and Lyrics, The (1892) **W.B. Yeats** (1865)
Countess Eve, The (1888) **J.H. Shorthouse** (1834)
Countess Glika (1919) **Warwick Deeping** (1877)
Countess Kate (1862) **Charlotte M. Yonge** (1823)
Countess of Lowndes Square, The (1920) **E.F. Benson** (1867)
Countess of Rudolstadt, The [*La Comtesse de Rudolstadt*] (1843) **'George Sand' [Auore Dupin]** (1804)
Countess Tekla, The (1899) **Robert Barr** (1850)
Countesse of Pembrokes Arcadia, The [bks i-iii] (1590, 1593, 1598) **Sir Philip Sidney** (1554)
Countesse of Pembrokes Emanuel, The (1591) **Abraham Fraunce** (fl.1582–1633)
Countesse of Pembrokes Ivychurch, The (1591) **Abraham Fraunce** (fl.1582–1633)
Counting Small Boned Bodies (1979) **Robert Bly** (1926)
Counting the Ways (1976) **Edward Albee** (1928)
Countries of the Mind (1922) **John Middleton Murry** (1889)
Country and the City, The (1973) **Raymond Williams** (1921)
Country Comets (1928) **C. Day Lewis** (1904)
Country Doctor, A (1884) **Sarah Orne Jewett** (1849)
Country Dressmaker, The (1907) **George Fitzmaurice** (1878)
Country Girl, The [from Wycherley] (1766) **David Garrick** (1717)
Country Girl, The (1950) **Clifford Odets** (1906)
Country Girls, The (1960) **Edna O'Brien** (1932)
Country House, The (1907) **John Galsworthy** (1867)
Country House, The (1698) **Sir John Vanbrugh** (1664)
Country House Party, The (1905) **Dora Sigerson** (1866)
Country Life (1978) **Peter Ackroyd** (1949)
Country of a Thousand Years of Peace, The (1959) **James Merrill** (1926)
Country of Marriage, The (1962) **Jon Cleary** (1917)
Country of the Blind, The (1911) **H.G. Wells** (1866)
Country of the Pointed Firs, The (1896) **Sarah Orne Jewett** (1849)
Country Over, The (1975) **Molly Holden** (1927)
Country Place, The (1947) **Ann Petry** (1908)
Country Quarters (1850) **Marguerite, Countess of Blessington** (1789)
Country Sentiment (1920) **Robert Graves** (1895)
Country Stories (1837) **Mary Russell Mitford** (1787)
Country Town Savings (1911) **E.W. Howe** (1853)
Country Without Music, The (1990) **Nicholas Hasluck** (1942)
Country-Wife, The (1675) **William Wycherley** (1641)
Coup, The (1979) **John Updike** (1932)
Couples (1968) **John Updike** (1932)
Courage to Believe, The (1952) **Paul Tillich** (1886)
Couragious Turke, The (1632) **Thomas Goffe** (1591–1629)
Courrier-Sud ['Southbound Mail'] (1928) **Antoine de Saint-Exupéry** (1900)
Cours de philosophie positive (1830–42) **Auguste Comte** (1798)
Course of Experimental Agriculture, A [*Containing an exvarious soils . . .*] (1770) **Arthur Young** (1741)
Course of Lectures on the Theory of Language (1762) **Joseph Priestley** (1733)
Course of True Love Never Did Run Smooth, The (1857) **Charles Reade** (1814)
Court Intrigues (1711) **Mary Delariviere Manley** (1663)
Court Netherleigh (1881) **Mrs Henry Wood** (1814)
Court of Death, The (1695) **John Dennis** (1657)
Court Poems (1716) **Lady Mary Wortley Montagu** (1689)
Court Royal (1886) **S. Baring-Gould** (1834)
Courtenay of Walreddon (1844) **Anna Eliza Bray** (1790)
Courtesan, The (1963) **Nigel Tranter** (1909)
Courtesy Dame, The (1900) **Robert Murray Gilchrist** (1868)
Courtier, The [*Il libro del cortegiano*] (1528) **Baldassare Castiglione** (1478)
Courting of Susie Brown, The (1952) **Erskine Caldwell** (1903)
Courts of Idleness, The (1920) **'Dornford Yates' [Cecil William Mercer]** (1885)
Courts of Love, The (1987) **'Jean Plaidy' [Eleanor Hibbert]** (1906)
Courts of the Morning, The (1929) **John Buchan** (1875)
Courtship of Miles Standish, The (1858) **Henry Wadsworth Longfellow** (1807)
Courtship of Morrice Buckler, The (1896) **A.E.W. Mason** (1865)

Courtship of Rosamond Fayre, The (1915) **Berta Ruck** (1878)

Courtyards in Delft (1981) **Derek Mahon** (1941)

Cousin Bette [*La Cousine Bette*] (1846) **Honoré de Balzac** (1799)

Cousin from Fiji, The (1945) **Norman Lindsay** (1879)

Cousin Henry (1879) **Anthony Trollope** (1815)

Cousin Honoré (1940) **Storm Jameson** (1897)

Cousin Phillis (1865) **Elizabeth Gaskell** (1810–1865)

Cousin Pons [*Le Cousin Pons*] (1846) **Honoré de Balzac** (1799)

Couteau entre les Dents, Le ['Knife Between the Teeth'] (1921) **Henri Barbusse** (1873)

Covenant, The (1980) **James A. Michener** (1907)

Covenant, The (1984) **Dick Davis** (1945)

Covent-Garden Tragedy, The (1732) **Henry Fielding** (1707)

Coventry Act, The (1793) **James Plumptre** (1771)

Cover Her Face (1962) **P.D. James** (1920)

Cow of the Barricade, The (1947) **Raja Rao** (1909)

Coward, The (1912) **R.H. Benson** (1871)

Cowboy Philosopher on Prohibition, The (1919) **Will Rogers** (1879)

Coxswain's Bride, The (1891) **R.M. Ballantyne** (1825)

Coyote's Daylight Trip (1978) **Paula Gunn Allen** (1939)

Crab Apple Jelly (1944) **'Frank O'Connor' [Michael Francis O'Donovan]** (1903)

Crabbed Youth and Age (1924) **Lennox Robinson** (1886)

Crack-Up, The (1945) **F. Scott Fitzgerald** (1896–1940)

Cradle of God, The (1929) **Llewelyn Powys** (1884)

Cradle of the Sun (1969) **Brian M. Stableford** (1948)

Cradock Nowell (1866) **R.D. Blackmore** (1825)

Craft of Fiction, The (1921) **Percy Lubbock** (1879)

Crafte So Longe to Lerne, The (1959) **Al Purdy** (1918)

Craig's Wife (1925) **George Kelly** (1887)

Crane Bag, The (1969) **Robert Graves** (1895)

Cranford (1853) **Elizabeth Gaskell** (1810)

Cranmer (1839) **Thomas Frognall Dibdin** (1776)

Crash! (1973) **J.G. Ballard** (1930)

Crater, The (1848) **James Fenimore Cooper** (1789)

Crater, The (1992) **Pam Ayres** (1947)

Craven House (1926) **Patrick Hamilton** (1904)

Crayon Miscellany, The (1835) **Washington Irving** (1783)

Crazy Hunter, The (1940) **Kay Boyle** (1903)

Crazy in Berlin (1958) **Thomas Berger** (1924)

Crazy Kill, The (1959) **Chester Himes** (1909)

Cream of the Jest, The (1917) **James Branch Cabell** (1879)

Creation (1712) **Sir Richard Blackmore** (1654)

Creation (1981) **Gore Vidal** (1925)

Creation, The (1720) **Aaron Hill** (1685)

Creative Effort (1920) **Norman Lindsay** (1879)

Creative Element, The (1953) **Sir Stephen Spender** (1909)

Creative Evolution [*L'Évolution créatice*] (1907) **Henri Bergson** (1859)

Creative Experiment, The (1949) **Maurice Bowra** (1898)

Creatures of Circumstance (1947) **Somerset Maugham** (1874)

Creditors (1889) **August Strindberg** (1849)

Credo (1996) **Melvyn Bragg** (1939)

Credos and Curios (1961) **James Thurber** (1894–1961)

Creed of a Layman, The (1907) **Frederic Harrison** (1831)

Creel of Irish Stories, A (1897) **Jane Barlow** (1857)

Crescendo (1958) **Phyllis Bentley** (1894)

Crescent Moon, The (1913) **Rabindranath Tagore** (1861)

Crescent Moon, The (1918) **Francis Brett Young** (1884)

Crest on the Silver, The (1950) **Geoffrey Grigson** (1905)

Cresta Run, The (1965) **N.F. Simpson** (1919)

Cretan Lover, The (1980) **'Jack Higgins' [Harry Patterson]** (1929)

Crëusa, Queen of Athens (1754) **William Whitehead** (1715)

Crève-Coeur, Le ['Heartbreak'] (1941) **Louis Aragon** (1897)

Crew of the Water Wagtail, The (1889) **R.M. Ballantyne** (1825)

Crewe Train (1926) **Rose Macaulay** (1881)

Crichton (1837) **W.H. Ainsworth** (1805)

Cricket in the Road (1973) **Michael Anthony** (1932)

Cricket of Cavador (1925) **Ogden Nash** (1902)

Cricket on the Hearth, The (1845) **Charles Dickens** (1812)

Criers and Kibitzers, Kibitzers and Criers (1966) **Stanley Elkin** (1930)

Crilley (1945) **James Hanley** (1901)

Crime and Punishment (1866) **Fyodor Mikhailovich Dostoevsky** (1821)

Crime at Black Dudley, The [the first 'Albert Campion' mystery] (1929) **Margery Allingham** (1904)

Crime at the Vanderlynden's, The (1926) **R.H. Mottram** (1883)

Crime d'Orcival, Le (1867) **Émile Gaboriau** (1832)

Crime of Sylvester Bonnard, The [*Le Crime de Sylvestre Bonnard*] (1881) **'Anatole France' [Jacques-Anatole-François Thibault]** (1844)

Crime of the Congo, The (1909) **A. Conan Doyle** (1859)

Crime Wave (1999) **James Ellroy** (1948)

Crimes in Hot Countries (1985) **Howard Barker** (1946)

Crimes of England, The (1915) **G.K. Chesterton** (1874)

Crimes of Passion (1967) **Joe Orton** (1933)

Crimes of the Heart (1978) **Beth Henley** (1952)

Criminal Code, The (1929) **Martin Flavin** (1883)

Crimson Azaleas, The (1907) **Henry de Vere Stacpoole** (1863)

Crimson Witch, The (1971) **Dean Koontz** (1945)

Cripps the Carrier (1876) **R.D. Blackmore** (1825)

'Crises, The' (1776) **Thomas Paine** (1737)

Crisis (1939) **Christopher Hassall** (1912)
Crisis of Our Civilization, The (1937) **Hilaire Belloc** (1870)
Crisis of Property, The (1720) **Sir Richard Steele** (1672)
Crisis of the Old Order, The (1957) **Arthur Schlesinger** (1917)
Crisis, The (1714) **Sir Richard Steele** (1672)
Critic, The (1779) **Richard Brinsley Sheridan** (1753)
Critical Account of the Philosophy of Kant, A (1877) **Edward Caird** (1835)
Critical and Historical Essays (1843) **T.B. Macaulay** (1800)
Critical and Miscellaneous Essays (1839) **Thomas Carlyle** (1795)
Critical Attitude, The (1911) **Ford Madox Ford** (1873)
Critical Dissertation on the Poems of Ossian, A (1763) **Hugh Blair** (1718)
Critical Essay on the Gospel of St Luke (1825) **Connop Thirlwall** (1797)
Critical Essays (1946) **George Orwell** (1903)
Critical Essays on the Performers of the London Theatres (1807) **Leigh Hunt** (1784)
Critical Fable, A (1922) **Amy Lowell** (1874)
Critical History of England, The (1724) **John Oldmixon** (1673)
Critical History of English Literature, A (1960) **David Daiches** (1912)
Critical Miscellanies [1st ser.] (1871) **John Morley, 1st Viscount Moreley of Blackburn** (1838)
Critical Observations on the Sixth Book of the Aeneid (1770) **Edward Gibbon** (1737)
Critical Occasions (1966) **Julian Symons** (1912)
Critical Philosophy of Immanuel Kant, The (1889) **Edward Caird** (1835)
Critical Review, The (1759) **Oliver Goldsmith** (1728)
Critical Suggestions on Style and Rhetoric (1859) **Thomas de Quincey** (1785)
Criticism (1932) **Desmond MacCarthy** (1877)
Criticism and Fiction (1891) **William Dean Howells** (1837)
Criticisms on Contemporary Thought and Thinkers (1894) **R.H. Hutton** (1826)
Critique of Logical Positivism, A (1950) **C.E.M. Joad** (1891)
Critique of Poetry (1934) **Michael Roberts** (1902)
Critiques et portraits littéraires ['Literary Portraits and Critical Essays'] (1836–46) **Charles-Augustin Sainte-Beuve** (1804)
Crock of Gold, The (1844) **Martin Tupper** (1810)
Crock of Gold, The ([1899]) **S. Baring-Gould** (1834)
Crock of Gold, The (1912) **James Stephens** (1882)
Crocodile Bird, The (1993) **Ruth Rendell** (1930)
Cromartie v the God Shiva (1997) **Rumer Godden** (1907)
Crome Yellow (1921) **Aldous Huxley** (1894)
Cromwell (1827) **Victor Hugo** (1802)
Cromwell (1843) **Matthew Arnold** (1822)
Cromwell (1913) **John Drinkwater** (1882)
Cromwell (1973) **David Storey** (1933)
Crooked Coronet, The (1937) **'Michael Arlen' [Dikran Kouyoumdjian]** (1895)
Crooked Furrow, The (1937) **Jeffery Farnol** (1878)
Crooked Stick, The (1895) **'Rolf Boldrewood' [Thomas Alexander Browne]** (1826)
Croppy, The (1828) **Michael Banim** (1796)
Croquet Player, The (1936) **H.G. Wells** (1866)
Cross Channel (1996) **Julian Barnes** (1946)
Cross Country (1949) **Hugh MacLennan** (1907)
Cross Creek (1942) **Marjorie Rawlings** (1896)
Cross Currents in English Literature of the XVIIth century (1929) **H.J.C. Grierson** (1866)
Cross Purpose [*La Malentendu*] (1945) **Albert Camus** (1913)
Cross the Border (1977) **Robert Adamson** (1943)
Cross-Roads, The (1909) **Lennox Robinson** (1886)
Crossfire (1972) **E.A. Markham** (1939)
Crossing, The (1971) **Howard Fast** (1914)
Crossing, The (1994) **Cormac McCarthy** (1933)
Crossing the Bar (1972) **C.K. Stead** (1932)
Crossing the Border (1976) **Joyce Carol Oates** (1938)
Crossing the Gap (1987) **C.J. Koch** (1932)
Crossing the River (1993) **Caryl Phillips** (1958)
Crossing the Water (1971) **Sylvia Plath** (1932–63)
Crossing to Safety (1987) **Wallace Stegner** (1909)
Crossing to Salamis (1977) **Jill Paton Walsh** (1937)
Crossriggs (1908) **Mary** (1865) and **Jane** (1866) **Findlater**
Crotchet Castle (1831) **Thomas Love Peacock** (1785)
Crotty Shinkwin (1932) **A.E. Coppard** (1878)
Crow (1970) **Ted Hughes** (1930)
Crow Road, The (1992) **Iain Banks** (1954)
Crowded Street, The (1924) **Winifred Holtby** (1898)
Crowds and Power [*Masse und Macht*] (1960) **Elias Canetti** (1905)
Crown and Sickle (1944) **J.F. Hendry** (1912) [with Henry Treece]
Crown and the Sickle, The (1945) **Henry Treece** (1911) (ed.) [with J.F. Hendry]
Crown Jewel (1952) **Ralph de Bossière** (1907)
Crown of Columbus, The (1991) **Louise Erdrich** (1954) [with Michael Dorris]
Crown of Feathers, A (1973) **Isaac Bashevis Singer** (1904)
Crown of Life, The (1899) **George Gissing** (1857)
Crown of Life, The (1947) **G. Wilson Knight** (1897)
Crown of Wild Myrtle, A (1962) **H.E. Bates** (1905)
Crown of Wild Olive, The (1866) **John Ruskin** (1819)
Crucial Instances (1901) **Edith Wharton** (1862)
Crucible, The (1953) **Arthur Miller** (1915)
Crucifix in a Deathhand (1965) **Charles Bukowski** (1920)
Crucifixion, The [*La Crucifixion*] (1946) **Jean Cocteau** (1889)
Crucifying of the World, by the Cross of Christ, The (1658) **Richard Baxter** (1615)
Cruel and Unusual (1993) **Patricia Cornwell** (1956)
Cruel Gift, The (1716) **Susanna Centlivre** (1669?)
Cruel Madness, A (1984) **Colin Thubron** (1939)
Cruel Sea, The (1951) **Nicholas Monsarrat** (1910)

Cruel Solstice, The (1943) **Sidney Keyes** (1922–43)
Cruelest Month, The (1963) **Ernest Buckler** (1908)
Cruell Brother, The (1630) **Sir William Davenant** (1606)
Cruelty of the Spaniards in Peru, The (1658) **Sir William Davenant** (1606)
Cruise of the Breadwinner, The (1946) **H.E. Bates** (1905)
Cruise of the Condor, The (1933) **W.E. Johns** (1893)
Cruise of the Frolic, The (1860) **W.H.G. Kingston** (1814)
Cruise of the 'Nona', The (1925) **Hilaire Belloc** (1870)
Crumbling Idols (1894) **Hamlin Garland** (1860)
Crump Folk Going Home (1913) **Constance Holme** (1881)
Crumpled Leaf, The (1911) **Mrs A.H. Alexander** (1825)
Crusades, The (1816) **John Galt** (1779)
Crusoe's Daughter (1985) **Jane Gardam** (1928)
Cry, The (1754) **Sarah Fielding** (1710) [with Jane Collier]
Cry in the Jungle Bar, A (1979) **Robert Drewe** (1943)
Cry of Absence, A (1971) **Madison Jones** (1925)
Cry of Children, A (1952) **John Horne Burns** (1916)
Cry, the Beloved Country (1948) **Alan Paton** (1903)
Cry Wolf (1976) **Wilbur Smith** (1933)
Crying Embers, The (1971) **Martin Booth** (1944)
Crying Game, The (1968) **John Braine** (1922)
Crying of Lot 49, The (1966) **Thomas Pynchon** (1937)
Crystal Age, A (1887) **W.H. Hudson** (1841)
Crystal and Fox (1968) **Brian Friel** (1929)
Crystal Rooms (1992) **Melvyn Bragg** (1939)
Crystal World, The (1937) **Richard Aldington** (1892)
Crystal World, The (1966) **J.G. Ballard** (1930)
C.S. Lewis (1990) **A.N. Wilson** (1950)
Cub at Newmarket, The (1762) **James Boswell** (1740)
Cuba in War Time (1897) **Richard Harding Davis** (1864)
Cuba Libre (1961) **LeRoi Jones** (1934)
Cuba Libre (1998) **Elmore Leonard** (1925)
Cuba: Prophetic Island (1961) **Waldo Frank** (1889)
Cuban and the Porto Rican Campaigns, The (1898) **Richard Harding Davis** (1864)
Cuban Passage (1982) **Norman Lewis** (1918)
Cuban Thing, The (1969) **Jack Gelber** (1932)
Cuckoo Clock, The [as 'Ennis Graham'] (1877) **Mary Louisa Molesworth** (1839)
Cuckoo in the Nest, A [adapted for the stage 1925] (1922) **Ben Travers** (1886)
Cuckoo Songs (1894) **Katharine Tynan** (1861)
Cuckoo Tree, The (1971) **Joan Aiken** (1924)
Cucumber Sandwiches, and Other Stories (1969) **J.I.M. Stewart** (1906)
Cujo (1981) **Stephen King** (1947)
Cult of Sincerity, The (1968) **Sir Herbert Read** (1893)
Culture and Anarchy (1869) **Matthew Arnold** (1822)
Culture and Imperialism (1993) **Edward Said** (1935)
Culture and Society 1780–1950 (1958) **Raymond Williams** (1921)
Culture and the Coming Peril (1927) **G.K. Chesterton** (1874)
Culture is Our Business (1970) **Marshall McLuhan** (1911)
Culture of Contentment, The (1992) **J.K. Galbraith** (1908)
Cunning Man, The (1995) **Robertson Davies** (1913)
Cunning Murrell (1900) **Arthur Morrison** (1863)
Cup of Gold (1929) **John Steinbeck** (1902)
Cup of Tea for Mr Thorgill, A (1957) **Storm Jameson** (1897)
Cupboard, The (1981) **Rose Tremain** (1943)
Cupid and Commonsense (1909) **Arnold Bennett** (1867)
Cupid and Death (1653) **James Shirley** (1596)
Cupid's Revenge (1615) **Francis Beaumont** (1585?) [with John Fletcher]
Curate in Bohemia, A (1913) **Norman Lindsay** (1879)
Curate in Charge, The (1876) **Margaret Oliphant** (1828)
Curate's Life, The (1934) **E.H. Young** (1880)
Curb of Honour, The (1893) **Matilda Betham-Edwards** (1836)
Cure for a Cuckold, A (1661) **John Webster** (1580?-1635?) [with William Rowley]
Cure for Cancer, A (1971) **Michael Moorcock** (1939)
Curé of Tours, The [*Le Curé de Tours*] (1832) **Honoré de Balzac** (1799)
Cured Arno, The (1995) **Jack Clemo** (1916)
Curiosities of Literature [1st ser., vol. i] (1791, 1793) **Isaac D'Israeli** (1766)
Curiosities of Literature [1st ser., vol. iii] (1817) **Isaac D'Israeli** (1766)
Curious Myths of the Middle Ages (1866) **S. Baring-Gould** (1834)
Currents of Space, The (1952) **Isaac Asimov** (1920)
Curriculum Vitae (1992) **Muriel Spark** (1918)
Curse of Kehama, The (1810) **Robert Southey** (1774)
Curse of Lono, The (1977) **Hunter S. Thompson** (1939)
Curse of Minerva, The (1812) **George Gordon, Lord Byron** (1788)
Curse of the Viking's Grave (1974) **Farley Mowat** (1921)
Cursory Observations on the Poems Attributed to Thomas Rowley (1782) **Edmond Malone** (1741)
Curtain of Green, A (1941) **Eudora Welty** (1909)
Curtain Up (1944) **Noel Streatfeild** (1895)
Curtains (1961) **Kenneth Tynan** (1927)
Curtmantle (1961) **Christopher Fry [Christopher Fry Harris]** (1907)
Curve and the Tusk, The (1953) **Stuart Cloete** (1897)
Custom and Myth (1884) **Andrew Lang** (1844)
Custom House, The (1961) **Francis King** (1923)
Custom of the Country, The (1913) **Edith Wharton** (1862)
Cut and Come Again (1935) **H.E. Bates** (1905)
Cut Pages, The (1971) **Roy Fisher** (1930)
Cut-Rate Kingdom, The (1980) **Thomas Keneally** (1935)
Cute Coyote, and Other Stories (1930) **Ernest Thompson Seton** (1860)

Cuts (1987) **Malcolm Bradbury** (1932)
Cutter of Coleman-Street (1663) **Abraham Cowley** (1618)
Cutting Edge, The (1978) **Penelope Gilliatt** (1932)
Cutting Green Hay (1983) **Vincent Buckley** (1925)
Cyder (1708) **John Philips** (1676)
Cyder Feast, The (1927) **Sir Sacheverell Sitwell** (1897)
Cymbeline [from Shakespeare] (1762) **David Garrick** (1717)
Cymon (1767) **David Garrick** (1717)
Cynthia (1947) **Laurence Housman** (1865)
Cynthia's Revel's [**Jonson**]: see *The Fountaine of Self-love*
Cypress and Acacia (1959) **Vernon Watkins** (1906)
Cyprian Woman, The (1955) **George Johnston** (1912)
Cyprianus Anglicanus (1668) **Peter Heylyn** (1600–1662)
Cyrano de Bergerac (1897) **Edmond Rostand** (1868)
Cyril Thornton (1827) **Thomas Hamilton** (1789)
Cytherea (1922) **Joseph Hergesheimer** (1880)
Dun château l'autre [*D'un château l'autre*] (1957) **'Louis-Ferdinand Céline' [L.F. Destouches]** (1894)
The Cognizance of Sorrow [*Cognizione del dolore*] (1963) **Carlo Emilio Gadda** (1893)

D

'D' is for Deadbeat (1987) **Sue Grafton** (1940)
Da (1973) **'Hugh Leonard' [Johns Keyes Byrne]** (1926)
Daddy (1989) **Danielle Steel** (1947)
Daddy Darwin's Dovecote (1884) **Mrs J.H. Ewing** (1841)
Daddy We Hardly Knew You (1989) **Germaine Greer** (1939)
Daddy's Gone A-Hunting (1921) **Zoë Akins** (1886)
Daddy's Gone-a-Hunting [US: *Cave of Ice*] (1958) **Penelope Mortimer** (1918)
Daedalus (1924) **J.B.S. Haldane** (1892)
Daemonologie (1597) **King James I** (1566)
Daffodil Affair, The [as 'Michael Innes'] (1942) **J.I.M. Stewart** (1906)
Daffodil Sky, The (1955) **H.E. Bates** (1905)
Daggers and Javelins (1984) **LeRoi Jones** (1934)
Dagon, and Other Macabre Tales (1965) **H.P. Lovecraft** (1890–1937)
Dagonet Ballads, The (1879) **George R. Sims** (1847)
Dain Curse, The (1929) **Dashiell Hammett** (1894)
Dainty Monsters, The (1967) **Michael Ondaatje** (1943)
Daisies and Buttercups (1882) **Mrs J.H. Riddell** (1832)
Daisies in the Grass (1865) **Isabella [Mrs G. Linnaeus] Banks** (1821)
Daisy Burns (1853) **Julia Kavanagh** (1824)
Daisy Chain, The (1856) **Charlotte M. Yonge** (1823)
Daisy Mayme (1926) **George Kelly** (1887)
Daisy Miller (1878) **Henry James** (1843)
Daisy's Aunt (1910) **E.F. Benson** (1867)
Dalkey Archive, The (1964) **Flann O'Brien** (1911)
Dalva (1989) **Jim Harrison** (1937)
Dame of Sark, The (1974) **William Douglas Home** (1912)
Dame's Delight (1964) **Margaret Forster** (1938)
Damnation Game, The (1985) **Clive Barker** (1952)
Damnation of Theron Ware, The (1896) **Harold Frederic** (1856)
Damoiselles à la Mode, The (1667) **Richard Flecknoe** (*c.* 1620)
Damon and Delia (1784) **William Godwin** (1756)
Damon and Pithias (1571) **Richard Edwards** (1523?–66)
Damon and Pythias (1821) **John Banim** (1798)
Damon and Pythias (1821) **Richard Lalor Sheil** (1791)
Damsel and the Sage, The (1903) **Elinor Glyn** (1864)
Damsel in Distress, A (1919) **P.G. Wodehouse** (1881)
Damsel of Darien, The (1839) **William Gilmore Simms** (1806)
Dan Leno and the Limehouse Golem (1994) **Peter Ackroyd** (1949)
Dan Russel the Fox (1911) **'Somerville and Ross' [Edith Somerville** (1858) and **Violet Martin]** (1862)
Dan the Dollar (1907) **Shan F. Bullock** (1865)
Dance and the Soul [*L'Âme et la danse*] (1924) **Paul-Ambroise Valéry** (1871)
Dance Hall of the Dead (1973) **Tony Hillerman** (1925)
Dance in the Sun, A (1956) **Dan Jacobson** (1929)
Dance of Death, The (1901) **August Strindberg** (1849)
Dance of Life, The (1923) **Havelock Ellis** (1859)
Dance of the Dwarfs (1968) **Geoffrey Household** (1900)
Dance of the Happy Shades (1968) **Alice Munro** (1931)
Dance of the Quick and the Dead (1936) **Sir Sacheverell Sitwell** (1897)
Dance With a Shadow (1992) **Irina Ratushinskaya** (1954)
Dance With No Music (1930) **Rodney Ackland** (1908)
Dancer in Red, The (1906) **Fergus Hume** (1859)
Dancers in Mourning [US: *Who Killed Chloe?*] (1937) **Margery Allingham** (1904)
Dancers Inherit the Party, The (1960) **Ian Hamilton Finlay** (1925)
Dancing at Lughnasa (1990) **Brian Friel** (1929)
Dancing Dodo, The (1978) **John Gardner** (1926)
Dancing Floor, The (1926) **John Buchan** (1875)
Dancing Girls (1977) **Margaret Atwood** (1939)
Dancing in the Dark (1982) **Joan Barfoot** (1946)
Dandelion Clocks (1887) **Mrs J.H. Ewing** (1841)
Dandelion Days (1922) **Henry Williamson** (1895)
Dandelion Wine (1957) **Ray Bradbury** (1920)
Dandy Dick (1887) **Arthur Wing Pinero** (1855)
Danesbury House (1860) **Mrs Henry Wood** (1814)
Danger! (1918) **A. Conan Doyle** (1859)
Danger Moon [as 'James MacCreigh'] (1953) **Frederik Pohl** (1919)
Danger of Being a Gentleman, The (1939) **Harold Laski** (1893)

Danger Tree, The (1977) **Olivia Manning** (1908)
Dangerous Ages (1921) **Rose Macaulay** (1881)
Dangerous Corner (1932) **J.B. Priestley** (1894)
Dangerous Davies (1976) **Leslie Thomas** (1931)
Dangerous Love (1996) **Ben Okri** (1959)
Dangerous Pilgrimages (1994) **Malcolm Bradbury** (1932)
Dangerous Play (1984) **Andrew Motion** (1952)
Dangerous Woman, A (1957) **James T. Farrell** (1904)
Dangerous Years, The (1956) **Richard Church** (1893)
Dangers of Coquetry (1790) **Amelia Opie** (1769)
Dangers of Obedience, The (1930) **Harold Laski** (1893)
Dangling in the Tournefortia (1981) **Charles Bukowski** (1920)
Dangling Man (1944) **Saul Bellow** (1915)
Daniel Deronda (1876) **'George Eliot' [Mary Ann Evans]** (1819)
Daniel Jazz, The (1920) **Vachel Lindsay** (1879)
Daniel Martin (1977) **John Fowles** (1926)
Daniel the Prophet (1864) **E.B. Pusey** (1800)
Danse Macabre (1981) **Stephen King** (1947)
Dante (1929) **T.S. Eliot** (1888)
Dante (1961) **LeRoi Jones** (1934)
Dante Gabriel Rossetti (1910) **Arthur Symons** (1865)
Dante Gabriel Rossetti as Designer and Writer (1889) **W.M. Rossetti** (1829)
Dante's Drum-Kit (1993) **Douglas Dunn** (1942)
Danton (1899) **Hilaire Belloc** (1870)
Danvers Jewels, The (1887) **Mary Cholmondeley** (1859)
Daphnaida (1591) **Edmund Spenser** (1552?)
Daphne [US: *Marriage à la Mode*] (1909) **Mrs T. Humphry Ward** (1851)
Daphne Adeane (1926) **Maurice Baring** (1874)
Daphne du Maurier (1993) **Margaret Forster** (1938)
Daphne in Fitzroy Street (1909) **E[dith] Nesbit** (1858)
Daphne Laureola (1949) **'James Bridie' [Osborne Henry Mavor]** (1888)
Darcy's Utopia (1990) **Fay Weldon** (1931)
Dariel (1897) **R.D. Blackmore** (1825)
Daring Young Man on the Flying Trapeze, The (1934) **William Saroyan** (1908)
Darius, King of Persia (1688) **John Crowne** (d. 1703)
Dark Adapted Eye, A [as 'Barbara Vine'] (1986) **Ruth Rendell** (1930)
Dark Ann (1927) **'Marjorie Bowen' [Gabrielle Margaret Vere Campbell]** (1886)
Dark Arena, The (1955) **Mario Puzo** (1920)
Dark As the Grave Wherein My Friend is Laid (1968) **Malcolm Lowry** (1909–57)
Dark at the Top of the Stairs, The (1957) **William Inge** (1913)
Dark Avenues (1946) **Ivan Bunin** (1870)
Dark Carnival (1947) **Ray Bradbury** (1920)
Dark Entries (1964) **Robert Aickman** (1914)
Dark Eye in Africa, The (1955) **Sir Laurens van der Post** (1906)
Dark Flower, The (1913) **John Galsworthy** (1867)
Dark Forest, The (1916) **Sir Hugh Walpole** (1884)
Dark Frontier, The (1936) **Eric Ambler** (1909)
Dark Glasses (1976) **Hugh Hood** (1928)
Dark Glasses (1984) **Blake Morrison** (1950)
Dark Glasses, The (1954) **Francis King** (1923)
Dark Green, Bright Red (1950) **Gore Vidal** (1925)
Dark Half, The (1989) **Stephen King** (1947)
Dark Horse, The (1899) **Nat Gould** (1857)
Dark House, The (1941) **Warwick Deeping** (1877)
Dark is Light Enough, The (1954) **Christopher Fry [Christopher Fry Harris]** (1907)
Dark Island, The (1952) **Henry Treece** (1911)
Dark Lady, The (1977) **Louis Auchinloss** (1917)
Dark Lantern, The (1653) **George Wither** (1588)
Dark Lantern, The (1951) **Henry Williamson** (1895)
Dark Laughter (1925) **Sherwood Anderson** (1876)
Dark Light Years, The (1964) **Brian Aldiss** (1925)
Dark Lord of Savaika, The (1980) **Alistair Campbell** (1925)
Dark Mile, The (1929) **D.K. Broster** (1878)
Dark Mother, The (1920) **Waldo Frank** (1889)
Dark Night's Work, A (1863) **Elizabeth Gaskell** (1810)
Dark o' the Moon, The (1902) **S.R. Crockett** (1860)
Dark of Summer, The (1956) **Eric Linklater** (1899)
Dark of the Sun, The (1968) **Wilbur Smith** (1933)
Dark Pony (1977) **David Mamet** (1947)
Dark Princess, The (1928) **W.E.B. Du Bois** (*c.* 1868)
Dark River, The (1941) **Rodney Ackland** (1908)
Dark Room, The (1938) **R.K. Narayan** (1907)
Dark Shore, The (1965) **Susan Howatch** (1940)
Dark Summer (1992) **Jon Cleary** (1917)
Dark, The (1980) **James Herbert** (1943)
Dark, The (1965) **John McGahern** (1934)
Dark Tide, The (1923) **Vera Brittain** (1893)
Dark Tower, The (1947) **Louis MacNeice** (1907)
Darker Ends (1969) **Robert Nye** (1939)
Darker Proof, The [inc. stories by Adam Mars-Jones] (1987) **Edmund White** (1940)
Darkling Plain, The (1950) **John Heath-Stubbs** (1918)
Darkness and Dawn (1891) **Frederic W. Farrar** (1831)
Darkness and Day (1951) **I. Compton-Burnett** (1884)
Darkness at Ingraham's Crest, A (1979) **Frank Yerby** (1916)
Darkness at Noon (1940) **Arthur Koestler** (1905)
Darkness at Pemberley (1932) **T.H. White** (1906)
Darkness Comes (1984) **Dean Koontz** (1945)
Darkness Falls From the Air (1942) **Nigel Balchin** (1908)
Darkness Outside, The (1959) **George Johnston** (1912)
Darkness Visible (1979) **William Golding** (1911)
Darkness Visible (1990) **William Styron** (1925)
Darkwater (1920) **W.E.B. Du Bois** (*c.* 1868)
Darling Buds of May, The (1958) **H.E. Bates** (1905)
Darnley (1830) **G.P.R. James** (1799)
Dartmoor (1821) **Felicia Dorothea Hemans** (1793)
Dartmoor Idylls (1896) **S. Baring-Gould** (1834)
Darwinism (1889) **Alfred Russel Wallace** (1823)
Darwinism in Morals and Other Essays (1872) **Frances Power Cobbe** (1822)

Dash for Karthoum, The (1892) **G.A. Henty** (1832)
Date with Darkness (1947) **Donald Hamilton** (1916)
Dauber (1913) **John Masefield** (1878)
Daughter Buffalo (1972) **Janet Frame** (1924)
Daughter of Fife, A (1886) **Amelia Barr** (1831)
Daughter of Fortune (1999) **Isabel Allende** (1942)
Daughter of Heth, A (1871) **William Black** (1841)
Daughter of Jerusalem (1978) **Sara Maitland** (1950)
Daughter of Jorio, The [*La figlia di Jorio*] (1904) **Gabriele D'Annunzio** (1863)
Daughter of the Middle Border, A (1921) **Hamlin Garland** (1860)
Daughter of the Snows, A (1902) **'Jack London' [John Griffith Chaney]** (1876)
Daughter of Time, The (1952) **'Josephine Tey' [Elizabeth Mackintosh]** (1897)
Daughters and Sons (1937) **I. Compton-Burnett** (1884)
Daughters of Albion (1991) **A.N. Wilson** (1950)
Daughters of Earth (1972) **D.J. Enright** (1920)
Daughters of England, The (1842) **Sarah [Mrs William] Ellis** (1812)
Daughters of Fire [*Les Filles du feu*] (1854) **'Gérard de Nerval' [Gérard Labrunie]** (1808)
Daughters of the House (1992) **Michèle Roberts** (1949)
Daughters Who Have Not Revolted, The (1894) **C[hristabel] R[ose] Coleridge** (1843)
Davenport Dunn (1859) **Charles Lever** (1806)
David (1942) **Earle Birney** (1904)
David Blaize (1916) **E.F. Benson** (1867)
David Blaize and the Blue Door (1918) **E.F. Benson** (1867)
David Chantrey (1865) **William Gorman Wills** (1828)
David Elginbrod (1863) **George MacDonald** (1824)
David Hume (1878) **T.H. Huxley** (1825)
David of King's (1924) **E.F. Benson** (1867)
Davideis (1712) **Thomas Ellwood** (1639)
Davids Hainous Sinne (1631) **Thomas Fuller** (1608)
Davids Teares (1622) **Sir John Hayward** (1564?)
Davies (1985) **David Constantine** (1944)
Dawn (1931) **Theodore Dreiser** (1871)
Dawn (1884) **Sir H. Rider Haggard** (1856)
Dawn Ginsbergh's Revenge (1929) **S.J. Perelman** (1904)
Dawn in Russia (1932) **Waldo Frank** (1889)
Dawn Island (1845) **Harriet Martineau** (1802)
Dawn O'Hara, the Girl Who Laughed (1911) **Edna Ferber** (1885)
Dawn of Britain, The (1906) **Charles Doughty** (1843)
Dawn of Liberation, The (1945) **Sir Winston Churchill** (1874)
Dawn of Reckoning, The (1925) **James Hilton** (1900)
Dawn of the Gods, The (1968) **Jacquetta Hawkes** (1910)
Dawn Wind (1961) **Rosemary Sutcliff** (1920)
Dawn's Left Hand (1931) **Dorothy M. Richardson** (1873)
Day, A (1761) **John Armstrong** (1709)
Day After Judgment, The (1970) **James Blish** (1921)
Day and Night Songs (1854) **William Allingham** (1824)
Day and Night Stories (1917) **Algernon Blackwood** (1869)
Day Before Tomorrow, The (1971) **David Helwig** (1938)
Day by Day (1977) **Robert Lowell** (1917)
Day Gone By, The (1990) **Richard Adams** (1920)
Day in Autumn, A (1820) **Bernard Barton** (1784)
Day in Summer, A (1963) **J.L. Carr** (1912)
Day in the Dark, A (1965) **Elizabeth Bowen** (1899)
Day in the Death of Joe Egg, A (1967) **Peter Nichols** (1927)
Day of Atonement (1991) **A. Alvarez** (1929)
Day of Creation, The (1987) **J.G. Ballard** (1930)
Day of Deliverance (1944) **William Rose Benét** (1886)
Day of Reckoning (2000) **'Jack Higgins' [Harry Patterson]** (1929)
Day of the Dog, The (1962) **Michael Frayn** (1933)
Day of the Guns (1964) **Mickey Spillane** (1918)
Day of the Jackal, The (1971) **Frederick Forsyth** (1938)
Day of the Locust, The (1939) **'Nathanael West' [Nathan Wallenstein Weinstein]** (1903)
Day of the Scorpion, The (1968) **Paul Scott** (1920)
Day of the Triffids, The (1951) **'John Wyndham' [John Wyndham Harris]** (1903)
Day of Trouble is Near, The (1674) **Increase Mather** (1639)
Day the Martians Came, The (1988) **Frederik Pohl** (1919)
Day We Got Drunk on Cake, The (1967) **'William Trevor' [William Trevor Cox]** (1928)
Day Will Come, The (1889) **M.E. Braddon** (1835)
Day Without Wind, A (1964) **William Mayne** (1928)
Day's End (1928) **H.E. Bates** (1905)
Day's Play, The (1910) **A.A. Milne** (1882)
Day's Ride, A (1864) **Charles Lever** (1806)
Day's Work, The (1898) **Rudyard Kipling** (1865)
Daydreamer, The (1994) **Ian McEwan** (1948)
Daylight Moon, The (1987) **Les Murray** (1938)
Daylight on Saturday (1943) **J.B. Priestley** (1894)
Days (1974) **Eva Figes** (1932)
Days and Nights (1975) **Edward Brathwaite** (1930)
Days and Nights (1889) **Arthur Symons** (1865)
Days Before, The (1952) **Katherine Anne Porter** (1890)
Days Between, The (1965) **Robert W. Anderson** (1917)
Days Departed (1828) **William Lisle Bowles** (1762)
Days of Bruce, The (1852) **Grace Aguilar** (1816–47)
Days of Life and Death and Escape to the Moon (1970) **William Saroyan** (1908)
Days of My Life, The (1857) **Margaret Oliphant** (1828)
Days Run Away Like Wild Horses Over the Hills, The (1969) **Charles Bukowski** (1920)
Days to Come (1936) **Lillian Hellman** (1907)
Days Without End (1934) **Eugene O'Neill** (1888)

Daysman, The (1984) **Stanley Middleton** (1919)
Dazzled (1990) **Judith Krantz** (1928)
De Arte Graphica [from C.A. de Fresnoy] (1695) **John Dryden** (1631) (tr.)
De Brassier (1852) **Ernest Charles Jones** (1819)
De Clifford (1841) **Robert Plumer Ward** (1765)
De Corpore Politico (1650) **Thomas Hobbes** (1588)
De Foix (1826) **Anna Eliza Bray** (1790)
De l'Orme (1830) **G.P.R. James** (1799)
De la démocracie en Amérique (1835) **Alexis de Tocqueville** (1805)
De Magntete [in Latin] (1600) **William Gilbert** (1544)
De Monarchia (1309–12) **Dante Alighieri** (1265)
De Montfort (1807) **Joanna Baillie** (1762)
De Profundis (1905) **Oscar Wilde** (1854)
De Quincey (1881) **David Masson** (1822)
De Senectute (1923) **Frederic Harrison** (1831)
De Trinitate (400–16) **St Augustine of Hippo** (354)
De Vere (1827) **Robert Plumer Ward** (1765)
Deacon Brodie (1888) **W.E. Henley** (1849) [with R.L. Stevenson]
Dead and Alive (1946) **'Hammond Innes' [Ralph Hammond-Innes]** (1913)
Dead Babies (1975) **Martin Amis** (1949)
Dead Cert (1962) **Dick Francis** (1920)
Dead City, The [*La Città morta*] (1898) **Gabriele D'Annunzio** (1863)
Dead Father, The (1975) **Donald Barthelme** (1931)
Dead Fingers Talk (1963) **William S. Burroughs** (1914)
Dead Head (1987) **Howard Brenton** (1942)
Dead Lecturer, The (1964) **LeRoi Jones** (1934)
Dead Letters (1910) **Maurice Baring** (1874)
Dead Letters (1997) **Francis King** (1923)
Dead Love Has Chains (1907) **M.E. Braddon** (1835)
Dead Man in Deptford, A (1993) **'Anthony Burgess' [John Anthony Burgess Wilson]** (1917)
Dead Man Leading (1937) **V.S. Pritchett** (1900)
Dead Man Over All [US: *The Square Peg*] (1950) **Walter Allen** (1911)
Dead Man's Ransom (1984) **'Ellis Peters' [Edith Mary Pargeter]** (1913)
Dead Man's Rock (1887) **Sir A.T. Quiller-Couch** (1863)
Dead Men Tell No Tales (1899) **E.W. Hornung** (1866)
Dead Men's Shoes (1876) **M.E. Braddon** (1835)
Dead Mr Nixon (1931) **T.H. White** (1906)
Dead Ned (1938) **John Masefield** (1878)
Dead of Jericho, The (1981) **Colin Dexter** (1930)
Dead on Time (1988) **H.R.F. Keating** (1926)
Dead Sea Fruit (1868) **M.E. Braddon** (1835)
Dead Sea Poems, The (1955) **Simon Armitage** (1963)
Dead Seagull, The (1950) **George Barker** (1913)
Dead Secret, A (1957) **Rodney Ackland** (1908)
Dead Secret, The (1857) **Wilkie Collins** (1824)
Dead Soldiers (1981) **James Fenton** (1949)
Dead Souls (1842) **Nikolai Vasilevich Gogol** (1809)
Dead Souls (1999) **Ian Rankin** (1960)
Dead Yesterdays (1916) **Mary Agnes Hamilton** (1884)
Dead Zone, The (1979) **Stephen King** (1947)
Deadeye Dick (1982) **Kurt Vonnegut** (1922)
Deadheads (1984) **Reginald Hill** (1936)
Deadlock (1921) **Dorothy M. Richardson** (1873)
Deadlock (1984) **Sara Paretsky** (1947)
Deal in Wheat, A (1903) **Frank Norris** (1870)
Deal With the Devil, A (1895) **Eden Phillpotts** (1862)
Dealings with the Faeries (1867) **George MacDonald** (1824)
Dean and the 'Squire', The (1782) **William Mason** (1724)
Dean of St Patrick's, The (1903) **Mrs Hugh Bell** (1851)
Dean's Daughter, The (1853) **Mrs C.F. Gore** (1799)
Dean's December, The (1982) **Saul Bellow** (1915)
Dean's Provocation for Writing the Lady's Dressing-Room, The (1734) **Lady Mary Wortley Montagu** (1689)
Dear Antoine [*Cher Antoine*] (1969) **Jean Anouilh** (1910)
Dear Baby (1944) **William Saroyan** (1908)
Dear Deceit, The (1960) **Christine Brooke-Rose** (1926)
Dear Faustina (1897) **Rhoda Broughton** (1840)
Dear Judas (1929) **Robinson Jeffers** (1887)
Dear Lady Disdain (1875) **Justin McCarthy** (1830)
Dear Lovely Death (1931) **Langston Hughes** (1902)
Dear Octopus (1938) **Dodie Smith** (1896)
Dear Shrink (1982) **Helen Cresswell** (1934)
Dearest Idol [as 'Walter Beckett'] (1929) **Martin Boyd** (1893)
Death and Birth of David Markand, The (1934) **Waldo Frank** (1889)
Death and Heaven (1722) **Isaac Watts** (1674)
Death and Taxes (1931) **Dorothy Parker** (1893)
Death and the King's Horseman (1975) **Wole Soyinka** (1934)
Death and the Lover [*Narziss und Goldmund*] (1930) **Hermann Hesse** (1877)
Death at the Bar (1940) **Ngaio Marsh** (1899)
Death at the President's Lodging [as 'Michael Innes'. US: *Seven Suspects*] (1936) **'Michael Innes' [J.I.M. Stewart]** (1906)
Death Bell, The (1954) **Vernon Watkins** (1906)
Death Comes for the Archbishop (1927) **Willa Cather** (1873)
Death for the Ladies (1962) **Norman Mailer** (1923)
Death in Don Mills (1975) **Hugh Garner** (1913)
Death in Paris (1978) **Richard Cobb** (1917)
Death in Summer (1998) **'William Trevor' [William Trevor Cox]** (1928)
Death in the Afternoon (1932) **Ernest Hemingway** (1898)
Death in the Family, A (1957) **James Agee** (1909)
Death in the Stocks [US: *Merely Murder*] (1935) **Georgette Heyer** (1902)
Death in the Woods (1933) **Sherwood Anderson** (1876)
Death in Venice [*Der Tod in Venedig*] (1912) **Thomas Mann** (1875)
Death is a Lonely Business (1985) **Ray Bradbury** (1920)
Death is Not the End (1998) **Ian Rankin** (1960)
Death Kit (1967) **Susan Sontag** (1933)
Death of a Citizen (1960) **Donald Hamilton** (1916)

Death of a Doxy (1966) **Rex Stout** (1886)
Death of a Ghost (1934) **Margery Allingham** (1904)
Death of a Hero (1929) **Richard Aldington** (1892)
Death of a Hero (1963) **Mulk Raj Anand** (1905)
Death of a Highbrow (1961) **Frank Swinnerton** (1884)
Death of a Huntsman (1957) **H.E. Bates** (1905)
Death of a Lady's Man (1978) **Leonard Cohen** (1934)
Death of a Man (1936) **Kay Boyle** (1903)
Death of a Naturalist (1966) **Seamus Heaney** (1939)
Death of a Salesman (1949) **Arthur Miller** (1915)
Death of Adam, The (1903) **Laurence Binyon** (1869)
Death of an Aryan [US: *The African Poison Murders*] (1939) **Elspeth Huxley** (1907)
Death of an Expert Witness (1977) **P.D. James** (1920)
Death of Artemio Cruz, The (1962) **Carlos Fuentes** (1928)
Death of Bessie Smith, The (1959) **Edward Albee** (1928)
Death of Captain Nemo, The (1949) **Robert Hillyer** (1895)
Death of Che Guevara, The (1983) **Jay Cantor** (1948)
Death of General Montgomery, The (1777) **Hugh Henry Brackenridge** (1748)
Death of Ivan Ilyitch, The (1886) **Leo Tolstoy** (1828)
Death of Leander, The (1906) **John Drinkwater** (1882)
Death of Marlowe, The (1837) **R.H. Horne** (1803)
Death of Men, The (1981) **Allan Massie** (1938)
Death of Monsieur Gallet, The [*M. Gallet décède;* first 'Maigret' story] (1931) **George Simenon** (1903)
Death of My Aunt (1929) **C.H.B. Kitchin** (1895)
Death of Nora Ryan, The (1978) **James T. Farrell** (1904)
Death of Oenone, The (1892) **Alfred, Lord Tennyson** (1809–92)
Death of Pompey, The [*La Mort de Pompée*] (1643) **Pierre Corneille** (1606)
Death of Reginald Perrin, The (1975) **David Nobbs** (1935)
Death of Robert, Earle of Huntington, The (1601) **Anthony Munday** (1560) [with Henry Chettle]
Death of Robin Hood, The (1981) **Peter Vansittart** (1920)
Death of the Body, The (1986) **C.K. Stead** (1932)
Death of the Heart, The (1938) **Elizabeth Bowen** (1899)
Death of the Hind Legs (1966) **John Wain** (1925)
Death of the Moth, The (1942) **Virginia Woolf** (1882–1941)
Death of Titian, The [*Der Tod des Tizian*] (1892) **Hugo von Hofmannsthal** (1874)
Death of Wallenstein, The (1800) **S.T. Coleridge** (1772) (tr.)
Death of William Posters, The (1965) **Alan Sillitoe** (1928)
Death on the Instalment Plan [*Mort à crédit*] (1936) **'Louis-Ferdinand Céline' [L.F. Destouches]** (1894)
Death on the Nile (1937) **Agatha Christie** (1890)
Death on the Way [US: *Double Death*] (1932) **Freeman Wills Crofts** (1879)
Death Ship, The (1888) **W. Clark Russell** (1844)
Death Shot, The (1873) **Mayne Reid** (1818)
Death, the Knight and the Lady (1897) **Henry de Vere Stacpoole** (1863)
Death Under Sail (1932) **C.P. Snow** (1905)
Death's Directives (1978) **Bruce Beaver** (1928)
Death's Jest-Book (1850) **Thomas Lovell Beddoes** (1803–49)
Deaths and Entrances (1946) **Dylan Thomas** (1914)
Deaths and Pretty Cousins (1975) **David Campbell** (1915)
Deaths Duell (1632) **John Donne** (1572–1631)
Debatable Land (1994) **Candia McWilliam** (1955)
Debbie Go Home (1961) **Alan Paton** (1903)
Debellacyon of Salem and Bizance, The (1533) **Sir Thomas More** (1478)
Debenham's Vow (1870) **Amelia B. Edwards** (1831)
Debits and Credits (1926) **Rudyard Kipling** (1865)
Deborah (1913) **Lascelles Abercrombie** (1881)
Débutante, The (1846) **Mrs C.F. Gore** (1799)
Decadence (1908) **A.J. Balfour** (1848)
Decadence (1981) **Steven Berkoff** (1937)
Decades of the New Worlde, The (1555) **Richard Eden** (1521?) (tr.)
Decameron, The (1349–1351) **Giovanni Boccaccio** (1313)
Decameron Physiologicum (1678) **Thomas Hobbes** (1588)
Decay and Renewal (1976) **Jack Lindsay** (1900)
Decay of Capitalist Civilisation, The (1923) **Sidney Webb** (1859) and **Beatrice Webb** (1858)
Decaying Magician, The [*L'Enchanteur pourrissant*] (1909) **'Guillaume Apollinaire' [Wilhelm de Kostrowitsky]** (1880)
Deceits of Time (1988) **Isabel Colegate** (1931)
Deceivers, The (1952) **John Masters** (1914)
December Tales (1823) **W.H. Ainsworth** (1805)
Deception (1990) **Philip Roth** (1933)
Deceptive Grin of the Gravel Porters, The (1968) **Gavin Ewart** (1916)
Decisive Wars of History, The (1929) **Sir Basil Liddell Hart** (1895)
Decius and Paulina (1718) **Lewis Theobald** (1688)
Declaration Against all Popery, A (1655) **George Fox** (1624)
Declaration of the True Manner of Knowing Christ Crucified, A (1596) **William Perkins** (1558)
Déclassé (1919) **Zoë Akins** (1886)
Decline and Fall (1928) **Evelyn Waugh** (1903)
Decline and Fall of the Romantic Ideal, The (1936) **F.L. Lucas** (1894)
Decorations in Verse and Prose (1899) **Ernest Dowson** (1867)
Decorative Arts, The (1878) **William Morris** (1834)
Dedicated Man, A (1965) **Elizabeth Taylor** (1912)
Deed Without a Name, A (1941) **Eden Phillpotts** (1862)
Deeds of Faith (1850) **John Mason Neale** (1818)
Deemster, The (1887) **Hall Caine** (1853)

Deenie (1973) **Judy Blume** (1938)
Deep, The (1976) **Peter Benchley** (1940)
Deep Blue Goodbye, The [first Travis McGee novel] (1964) **John D. MacDonald** (1916)
Deep Blue Sea, The (1952) **Terence Rattigan** (1911)
Deep Down (1867) **R.M. Ballantyne** (1825)
Deep Range, The (1957) **Arthur C. Clarke** (1917)
Deep Sea (1914) **Francis Brett Young** (1884)
Deep Water (1957) **Patricia Highsmith** (1921)
Deephaven (1877) **Sarah Orne Jewett** (1849)
Deer on the High Hills (1960) **Iain Crichton Smith [Iain Mac a'Ghobhainn]** (1928)
Deer Park, The (1955) **Norman Mailer** (1923)
Deerbrook (1839) **Harriet Martineau** (1802)
Deerslayer, The (1841) **James Fenimore Cooper** (1789)
Deevil's Waltz, The (1946) **Sydney Goodsir Smith** (1915)
Defeat of an Ideal (1973) **Shirley Hazzard** (1931)
Defeat of Youth, The (1918) **Aldous Huxley** (1894)
Defection Considered, The (1717) **Matthew Tindal** (1657)
Defence of Britain, The (1939) **Sir Basil Liddell Hart** (1895)
Defence of Good Women, The (1540) **Sir Thomas Elyot** (1490?)
Defence of Guenevere, The (1858) **William Morris** (1834)
Defence of Idealism, A (1917) **May Sinclair** (1863)
Defence of Our Present Happy Establishment, A (1722) **Matthew Tindal** (1657)
Defence of Philosophic Doubt, A (1879) **A.J. Balfour** (1848)
Defence of Poesie, The (1595) **Sir Philip Sidney** (1554)
Defence of Sir Fopling Flutter, A (1722) **John Dennis** (1657)
Defence of Tarascon, The [*La Défense de Tarascon*] (1886) **Alphonse Daudet** (1840)
Defence of the Doctrine of Justification, by Faith, A (1672) **John Bunyan** (1628)
Defence of the French Language [*La Deffence et illustration de la langue françoyse*] (1549) **Joachim du Bellay** (1522)
Defence of the Rights of the Christian Church, A (1707) **Matthew Tindal** (1657)
Defence of the Short View of the Profaneness and Immorality of the English Stage, A (1699) **Jeremy Collier** (1650)
Defence of Usury (1787) **Jeremy Bentham** (1748)
Defendant, The (1901) **G.K. Chesterton** (1874)
Defender of the Faith (1911) **'Marjorie Bowen' [Gabrielle Margaret Vere Campbell]** (1886)
Defending Ancient Springs (1967) **Kathleen Raine** (1908)
Defense, The (1964) **Vladimir Nabokov** (1899)
Definitions in Political Economy (1827) **T.R. Malthus** (1766)
Deformed Transformed, The (1824) **George Gordon, Lord Byron** (1788)
Defying Gravity (1992) **Roger McGough** (1937)
Degrees [*Degrés*] (1960) **Michel Butor** (1926)
Deirdre (1903) **George William Russell ['AE']** (1867)
Deirdre [*Plays for an Irish Theatre* vol. iv] (1907) **W.B. Yeats** (1865)
Deirdre (1923) **James Stephens** (1882)
Deirdre of the Sorrows [unfinished] (1909) **J.M. Synge** (1871–1909)
Deist's Manual, The (1705) **Charles Gildon** (1665)
Déja Vu (1991) **John Osborne** (1929)
Dekker his Dreame (1620) **Thomas Dekker** (1572?)
Delectable Duchy, The (1893) **Sir A.T. Quiller-Couch** (1863)
Delia (1592) **Samuel Daniel** (1562)
Delia and Rosamond Augmented (1594) **Samuel Daniel** (1562)
Delia Blanchflower (1915) **Mrs T. Humphry Ward** (1851)
Delicate Balance, A (1966) **Edward Albee** (1928)
Delicate Diet, for Daintiemouthde Droonkardes, A (1576) **George Gascoigne** (1542?)
Delicate Episode, A (1988) **Paul Bowles** (1910)
Delight (1926) **Mazo de la Roche** (1879)
Delights of the Bottle, The (1720) **Edward Ward** (1667)
Deliverance, The (1904) **Ellen Glasgow** (1874)
Deliverance (1955) **L.A.G. Strong** (1896)
Deliverance (1970) **James Dickey** (1923)
Delmour (1823) **Edward Bulwer-Lytton** (1803)
Deloraine (1833) **William Godwin** (1756)
Delphine (1802) **Madame de Staël** (1766)
Delta Factor, The (1967) **Mickey Spillane** (1918)
Delta of Venus (1977) **Anaïs Nin** (1903–77)
Delta Wedding (1946) **Eudora Welty** (1909)
Deluge, The (1886) **Henryk Sienkiewicz** (1846)
Delusions, etc. (1972) **John Berryman** (1914–72)
Delves (1796) **Susannah Gunning** (1740)
Demagogue, The (1764) **William Falconer** (1732)
Demeter (1905) **Robert Bridges** (1844)
Demeter, and Other Poems (1889) **Alfred, Lord Tennyson** (1809)
Demi-Gods, The (1914) **James Stephens** (1882)
Demi-monde, Le (1855) **Alexandre Dumas ['fils']** (1824)
Demian (1919) **Hermann Hesse** (1877)
Democracy (1880) **Henry Adams** (1838)
Democracy (1984) **Joan Didion** (1934)
Democracy and Leadership (1924) **Irving Babbit** (1865)
Democracy and Poetry (1975) **Robert Penn Warren** (1905)
Democratic Vistas (1871) **Walt Whitman** (1819)
Democritus Platonissans (1646) **Henry More** (1614)
Demon Lover, The [US: *Ivy Gripped the Steps*] (1945) **Elizabeth Bowen** (1899)
Demon of Progress in the Arts, The (1954) **Wyndham Lewis** (1882)
Demon, The (1976) **Hubert Selby Jr** (1928)
Demoniac, The (1890) **Sir Walter Besant** (1836)
Demophon (1927) **Forrest Reid** (1875)
Demos (1886) **George Gissing** (1857)
Dene Hollow (1871) **Mrs Henry Wood** (1814)

Denis Duval [unfinished] (1867) **W.M. Thackeray** (1811–63)
Denis O'Shaughnessy Going to Maynooth (1845) **William Carleton** (1794)
Denise (1885) **Alexandre Dumas ['fils']** (1824)
Denounced, The (1830) **John Banim** (1798)
Denzil Quarrier (1892) **George Gissing** (1857)
Deontology; or, Science of Morality (1834) **Jeremy Bentham** (1748–1832)
Department, The (1975) **David Williamson** (1942)
Department of Queer Complaints, The [as 'Carter Dickson'] (1940) **John Dickson Carr** (1906)
Departmental Ditties (1886) **Rudyard Kipling** (1865)
Deputy Was King, A (1926) **G.B. Stern** (1890)
Déracinés, Les (1897) **Maurice Barrès** (1862)
Deregulated Muse, The (1998) **Sean O'Brien** (1952)
Derek (1982) **Edward Bond** (1934)
Derelict Day, The (1947) **Alan Ross** (1922)
Derelict, The (1901) **C.J. Cutcliffe Hyne** (1865)
Derval Hampton (1881) **James Grant** (1822)
Descant for Gossips, A (1960) **Thea Astley** (1925)
Descendant, The (1897) **Ellen Glasgow** (1874)
Descent into Hell (1937) **Charles Williams** (1886)
Descent into the Cave, The (1957) **James Kirkup** (1923)
Descent of Liberty, The (1815) **Leigh Hunt** (1784)
Descent of Man, The (1871) **Charles Darwin** (1809)
Descent of Man, The (1904) **Edith Wharton** (1862)
Descent of the Dove, The (1939) **Charles Williams** (1886)
Descent to the Dead (1931) **Robinson Jeffers** (1887)
Description of the Scenery of the Lakes, A (1822) **William Wordsworth** (1770)
Description of the Villa of Horace Walpole at Strawberry-Hill, A (1774) **Horace Walpole** (1717)
Descriptive Sketches (1793) **William Wordsworth** (1770)
Desert and the Sown [US: *Syria: The Desert and the Sown*] (1907) **Gertrude Bell** (1868)
Desert Fathers, The [from Latin] (1936) **Helen Waddell** (1889) (tr.)
Desert Generals, The (1960) **Correlli Barnett** (1927)
Desert Home, The [subtitled 'The English Family Robinson'] (1852) **Mayne Reid** (1818)
Desert Music, The (1954) **William Carlos Williams** (1883)
Desert of the Heart (1964) **Jane Rule** (1931)
Desert Rose, The (1983) **Larry McMurty** (1936)
Deserted Village, The (1770) **Oliver Goldsmith** (1728)
Deserter, The (1773) **Charles Dibdin** (1745)
Design for Living (1933) **Noel Coward** (1899)
Designated Heir, The (1974) **Maxine Kumin** (1925)
Designs by Mr R. Bentley, for Six Poems by Mr T. Gray [inc. 'Ode on the Death of a Favourite Cat', 'Ode on a Distant Prospect of Eton College'] (1753) **Thomas Gray** (1716)
Desire and Pursuit of the Whole, The (1934) **Frederick William Rolfe** (1860–1913)
Desire Under the Elms (1924) **Eugene O'Neill** (1888)
Desmond (1792) **Charlotte Smith** (1749)
Desolation Angels (1965) **Jack Kerouac** (1922)
Desolation Island (1978) **Patrick O'Brian** (1914)
Desolation of America, The (1777) **Thomas Day** (1748)
Desolation of Eyam, The (1827) **Mary Howitt** (1799) [with William Howitt]
Despair (1966) **Vladimir Nabokov** (1899)
Desperadoes, The (1961) **Stan Barstow** (1928)
Desperate People, The (1959) **Farley Mowat** (1921)
Desperate Remedies (1871) **Thomas Hardy** (1840)
Despotism (1811) **Isaac D'Israeli** (1766)
Dessous d'une vie, Les (1926) **'Paul Éluard' [Eugène Grindel]** (1895)
Destination (1799) **Clara Reeve** (1729)
Destination Biafra (1982) **Buchi Emecheta** (1944)
Destinies of Darcy Dancer, Gentleman, The (1977) **J.P. Donleavy** (1926)
Destiny (1831) **Susan Edmonstone Ferrier** (1782)
Destiny (1976) **David Edgar** (1948)
Destiny (1999) **Tim Parks** (1954)
Destiny of Nathalie 'X', The (1995) **William Boyd** (1952)
Destroy, She Said [*Détruitre, dit-elle*; text and film] (1969) **'Marguerite Duras' [Marguerite Donnadieu]** (1914)
Destruction of Jerusalem, The (1677) **John Crowne** (d. 1703)
Destruction of Troy, The [from Virgil] (1656) **Sir John Denham** (1615) (tr.)
Destructive Element, The (1935) **Sir Stephen Spender** (1909)
Detached Retina, The (1994) **Brian Aldiss** (1925)
Detection of the Doings of Mary Queen of Scots, A (1571) **George Buchanan** (1506)
Detection Unlimited (1953) **Georgette Heyer** (1902)
Deterrent or Defence (1960) **Sir Basil Liddell Hart** (1895) (ed.)
Detraction Displayed (1828) **Amelia Opie** (1769)
Deuce is in Him, The (1763) **George Colman, the Elder** (1732)
Deus Justificatus (1656) **Jeremy Taylor** (1613)
Devastating Boys, The (1972) **Elizabeth Taylor** (1912)
Development of English Biography, The (1927) **Sir Harold Nicolson** (1886)
Devereux (1829) **Edward Bulwer-Lytton** (1803)
Devices and Desires (1989) **P.D. James** (1920)
Devil and Daniel Webster, The [libretto] (1939) **Stephen Vincent Benét** (1889)
Devil and Mr Mulcahy, The (1967) **James K. Baxter** (1926)
Devil and the Deep Sea, The (1910) **Rhoda Broughton** (1840)
Devil by the Sea (1957) **Nina Bawden** (1925)
Devil Came From Dublin, The (1951) **Paul Vincent Carroll** (1900)
Devil Doctor, The [US: *The Return of Dr Fu-Manchu*] (1916) **'Sax Rohmer' [Arthur Henry Sarsfield Ward]** (1883)
Devil Finds Work, The (1976) **James Baldwin** (1924)
Devil in a Blue Dress (1990) **Walter Mosley** (1952)
Devil in the Road, The (1979) **Robert Westall** (1929)

Devil, Maggot and Son (1956) **Christopher Logue** (1926)
Devil of a State (1961) **'Anthony Burgess' [John Anthony Burgess Wilson]** (1917)
Devil Rides Out, The (1935) **Dennis Wheatley** (1897)
Devil Takes a Holiday, The (1955) **Alfred Noyes** (1880)
Devil Upon Two Sticks in England, The (1790) **William Combe** (1742)
Devil upon Two Sticks, The (1768) **Samuel Foote** (1720–77)
Devil We Know, The (1939) **Pamela Frankau** (1908)
Devil's Advocate, The (1959) **Morris West** (1916)
Devil's Charter, The (1607) **Barnabe Barnes** (1571)
Devil's Children, The (1970) **Peter Dickinson** (1927)
Devil's Cub (1934) **Georgette Heyer** (1902)
Devil's Dictionary, The [first pub. 1906 as *The Cynic's Word Book*] (1911) **Ambrose Bierce** (1842)
Devil's Die, The (1888) **Grant Allen** (1848)
Devil's Elixir, The [*Die Elixiere des Teufels*] (1815–1816) **E.T.A. Hoffmann** (1776)
Devil's Mode, The (1989) **'Anthony Burgess' [John Anthony Burgess Wilson]** (1917)
Devil's Novice, The (1984) **'Ellis Peters' [Edith Mary Pargeter]** (1913)
Devil's Rock (1974) **David Campbell** (1915)
Devil's Stocking, The (1983) **Nelson Algren** (1909–1981)
Devil's Walk, The (1830) **S.T. Coleridge** (1772) [with Robert Southey]
Devil-in-the-Fog (1966) **Leon Garfield** (1921)
Devils, The (1872) **Fyodor Mikhailovich Dostoevsky** (1821)
Devils, The (1961) **John Whiting** (1917)
Devils and Canon Barham, The (1973) **Edmund Wilson** (1895–1972)
Devils Law-Case, The (1623) **John Webster** (1580?)
Devils of Loudon, The (1952) **Aldous Huxley** (1894)
Devilseed (1984) **Frank Yerby** (1916)
Devious Ways (1910) **Gilbert Cannan** (1884)
Devlin the Barber (1888) **B.L. Farjeon** (1838)
Devon Boys, The (1886) **George Manville Fenn** (1831)
Devoted Ladies [as 'M.J. Farrell'] (1934) **Molly Keane** (1905)
Devotee, A (1897) **Mary Cholmondeley** (1859)
Devotional Verses (1826) **Bernard Barton** (1784)
Devotions Upon Emergent Occasions (1624) **John Donne** (1572)
Devout Soul, The (1644) **Joseph Hall** (1574)
Dewer Rides (1929) **L.A.G. Strong** (1896)
Dewy Morn, The (1884) **Richard Jefferies** (1848)
Dhalgren (1975) **Samuel R. Delany** (1942)
Dharma Bums, The (1958) **Jack Kerouac** (1922)
D.H. Lawrence, Novelist (1955) **F.R. Leavis** (1895)
Diable boiteux, Le ['The Devil with a Limp'] (1707) **Alain-René Lesage** (1668)
Diaboliad, The (1777) **William Combe** (1742)
Diaboliques, Les (1874) **J.A. Barbey-d'Aurevilly** (1808)
Diall of Princes, The [from Antonio de Guevara] (1557) **Sir Thomas North** (1535) (tr.)
Dialogue, Betwene Mercury and an English Souldier, A (1574) **Barnabe Rich** (1542)
Dialogue Concerning Women, A (1691) **William Walsh** (1663)
Dialogue Concernynge Heresyes & Matters of Religion, A (1529) **Sir Thomas More** (1478)
Dialoge of Comfort Against Tribulacion, A (1553) **Sir Thomas More** (1478–1535)
Dialogues in Limbo (1925) **George Santayana** (1863)
Dialogues of the Dead (1699) **William King** (1663)
Dialogues of the Dead (1760) **George Lyttelton, 1st Baron Lyttelton** (1709)
Dialstone Lane (1904) **W.W. Jacobs** (1863)
Diamond Cut Diamond (1875) **T. Adolphus Trollope** (1810)
Diamond Cut Paste (1909) **Egerton** (1858) and **Agnes Castle** (*c.* 1860)
Diamond Cutters, The (1955) **Adrienne Rich** (1929)
Diamond Dust (1865) **Eliza Cook** (1818)
Diamond Dust (2000) **Anita Desai** (1937)
Diamond Hunters, The (1971) **Wilbur Smith** (1933)
Diamond Nebula (1994) **Jeremy Reed** (1954)
Diamonds Are Forever (1956) **Ian Fleming** (1908)
Diana Cooper (1981) **Philip Ziegler** (1929)
Diana Mallory (1908) **Mrs T. Humphry Ward** (1851)
Diana of Dobson's (1908) **Cicely Mary Hamilton** (1872)
Diana of the Crossways (1885) **George Meredith** (1828)
Diana Tempest (1893) **Mary Cholmondeley** (1859)
Diana Trelawny (1892) **Margaret Oliphant** (1828)
Diaries and Letters (1966) **Sir Harold Nicolson** (1886)
Diarium, The (1656) **Richard Flecknoe** (*c.* 1620)
Diary Illustrative of the Times of George the Fourth (1838) **Lady Charlotte Bury** (1775)
Diary in America, A (1839) **Frederick Marryat** (1792)
Diary of a Drug Fiend, The (1932) **'Aleister' [Edward Alexander] Crowley** (1875)
Diary of a Good Neighbour, The [as 'Jane Somers'] (1983) **Doris Lessing** (1919)
Diary of a Nobody, The (1892) **George** (1847) and **Weedon** (1854) **Grossmith**
Diary of a Pilgrimage (1891) **Jerome. K. Jerome** (1859)
Diary of a Provincial Lady (1930) **'E.M. Delafield' [E.E.M. de la Pasture]** (1890)
Diary of a Rapist, The (1966) **Evan S. Connell, Jr** (1924)
Diary of a Yuppie (1986) **Louis Auchinloss** (1917)
Diary of Samuel Marchbanks, The (1947) **Robertson Davies** (1913)
Diary, Reminiscences, and Correspondence (1869) **Henry Crabb Robinson** (1775–1867)
Diary Without Dates, A (1918) **Enid Bagnold** (1889)
Dichtung und Wahreit [*Poetry and Truth*; autobiography] (1811–33) **Johann Wolfgang von Goethe** (1749)
Dick Deterred (1974) **David Edgar** (1948)
Dick Gibson Show, The (1971) **Stanley Elkin** (1930)

Dick o' the Fens (1887) **George Manville Fenn** (1831)
Dick Seddon's Great Dive (1976) **Ian Wedde** (1946)
Dickens (1990) **Peter Ackroyd** (1949)
Dickens the Novelist (1970) **F.R. Leavis** (1895) [with Q.D. Leavis]
Dictator Resigns, The (1936) **C.E.M. Joad** (1891)
Dictator, The (1904) **Richard Harding Davis** (1864)
Dictator's Daughter, The (1902) **Edgar Jepson** (1863)
Dictionary of Archaic and Provincial Words, A (1846) **J.O. Halliwell-Phillipps** (1820)
Dictionary of Catch Phrases, A (1977) **Eric Partridge** (1894)
Dictionary of Every-Day Cookery, A (1865) **Isabella Beeton** (1836)
Dictionary of Modern English Usage, A (1926) **H.W. Fowler** (1858) [planned with F.G. Fowler]
Dictionary of Music and Musicians, A (1879) **Sir George Grove** (1820) (ed.)
Dictionary of Obsolete and Provincial English (1857) **Thomas Wright** (1810)
Dictionary of Old English Plays, A (1860) **J.O. Halliwell-Phillipps** (1820)
Dictionary of Phrase and Fable, A (1870) **E. Cobham Brewer** (1810)
Dictionary of Slang and Unconventional English, A (1937) **Eric Partridge** (1894)
Dictionary of Syr Thomas Eliot, The (1538) **Sir Thomas Elyot** (1490?)
Dictionary of the Bible, A (1898) **James Hastings** (1862) (ed.)
Dictionary of the English Language, A (1755) **Samuel Johnson** (1709)
Did He Deserve It? (1897) **Mrs J.H. Riddell** (1832)
Did She? (1934) **Elinor Glyn** (1864)
Diderot at the Hermitage (2000) **Malcolm Bradbury** (1932)
Died in the Wool (1945) **Ngaio Marsh** (1899)
Died on a Rainy Sunday (1972) **Joan Aiken** (1924)
Diet of Thistles, A [as 'Beachcomber'] (1938) **J.B. Morton** (1893)
Dieux antiques, Les ['The Ancient Gods'] (1880) **Stéphane Mallarmé** (1842)
Differences in Judgment About Water-Baptism, No Bar to Communion (1673) **John Bunyan** (1628)
Different Drummer, A (1986) **Jack Clemo** (1916)
Different Face, A (1953) **Olivia Manning** (1908)
Different Kind of Christmas, A (1988) **Alex Haley** (1921)
Different Kinds of Love (1987) **Leland Bardwell** (1928)
Difficult Man, The [*Der Schwierige*] (1921) **Hugo von Hofmannsthal** (1874)
Difficult Young Man, A (1955) **Martin Boyd** (1893)
Difficulties With Girls (1988) **Kingsley Amis** (1922)
Diff'rent (1920) **Eugene O'Neill** (1888)
Dig Up My Heart (1983) **Milton Acorn** (1923)
Digby Grand (1853) **G.J. Whyte-Melville** (1821)
Digger's Game, The (1973) **George V. Higgins** (1939)
Digging Up the Past (1930) **Sir Leonard Woolley** (1880)
Dilecta (1886) **John Ruskin** (1819)
Dilemma, The (1876) **General Sir George Tomkyns Chesney** (1830)
Dilemma of a Ghost, The (1964) **Ama Ata Aidoo** (1942)
Dilemmas (1895) **Ernest Dowson** (1867)
Dilemmas (1934) **A.E.W. Mason** (1865)
Dimboola (1969) **Jack Hibberd** (1940)
Dimetos (1976) **Athol Fugard** (1932)
Dinarbas (1790) **Ellis Cornelia Knight** (1758)
Ding Dong Bell (1924) **Walter de la Mare** (1873)
Dinner at Antoine's (1948) **Frances Parkinson Keyes** (1885)
Dinner at the Homesick Restaurant (1982) **Anne Tyler** (1941)
Dinner Club, The (1923) **'Sapper' [Herman Cyril McNeile]** (1888)
Dinner of Herbs, A (1985) **Catherine Cookson** (1906)
Diogines Lanthorne (1607) **Samuel Rowlands** (1570?)
Diplomacy (1939) **Sir Harold Nicolson** (1886)
Direct Dialling (1985) **Carol Rumens** (1944)
Dirk Gently's Holistic Detective Agency (1987) **Douglas Adams** (1952)
Dirty Hands [also translated as *Crime Passionel*] [*Les Mains Sales*] (1948) **Jean-Paul Sartre**
Dirty Linen (1976) **Tom Stoppard** (1937)
Dirty Story (1967) **Eric Ambler** (1909)
Dirty Tricks (1991) **Michael Dibdin** (1947)
Disaffection, A (1989) **James Kelman** (1946)
Disappearance (1993) **David Dabydeen** (1956)
Disappearance of George Driffell, The (1896) **James Payn** (1830)
Disappearing Castle, The (1937) **Charles Madge** (1912)
Disappointment, The (1684) **Thomas Southerne** (1659)
Disaster Area, The (1967) **J.G. Ballard** (1930)
Discarded Image, The (1964) **C.S. Lewis** (1898–1963)
Disciple, Le (1889) **Paul Bourget** (1852)
Disciple, The (1867) **George MacDonald** (1824)
Discipline (1814) **Mary Brunton** (1778)
Discipline (1868) **Charles Kingsley** (1819)
Disclosure (1994) **Michael Crichton** (1942)
Discordant Encounters (1926) **Edmund Wilson** (1895)
Discords (1894) **'George Egerton' [Mary Chavelita Dunne]** (1859)
Discource of Horsmanshippe, A (1593) **Gervaise Markham** (1568?)
Discourse Concerning Prayer, A (1646) **Jeremy Taylor** (1613)
Discourse Concerning the Confusion of Languages at Babel, A (1730) **William Wotton** (1666–1727)
Discourse Concerning the True Notion of the Lords Supper, A (1642) **Ralph Cudworth** (1617)
Discourse Concerning the Vegetation of Plants, A (1661) **Sir Kenelm Digby** (1603)

Discourse, Delivered at the Opening of the Royal Academy, A [the first of Reynolds' *Discourses*; the fifteenth and last pub. 1791; collected 1820] (1769) **Sir Joshua Reynolds** (1723)
Discourse of a Discoverie for a New Passage to Cataia, A (1576) **Sir Humphrey Gilbert** (1539?)
Discourse of English Poetrie, A (1586) **William Webbe** (fl.1568–91)
Discourse of Free-thinking, A (1713) **Anthony Collins** (1676)
Discourse of Rebellion, A (1570) **Thomas Churchyard** (1520?)
Discourse of the Civile Warres in Fraunce, A (1570) **Sir Geoffrey Fenton** (1539?) (tr.)
Discourse of the Damned Art of Witchcraft, A (1608) **William Perkins** (1558–1602)
Discourse of the Grounds and Reasons of the Christian Religion, A (1724) **Anthony Collins** (1676)
Discourse of the Pastoral Care, A (1692) **Gilbert Burnet** (1643)
Discourse on Antient and Modern Learning, A (1734) **Joseph Addison** (1672–1719)
Discourse on Inequality [*Discours sur l'origine de l'inégalité*] (1755) **Jean Jacques Rousseau** (1712)
Discourse on the Arts and Sciences, A [*Discours sur les sciences et les arts*] (1750) **Jean-Jacques Rousseau** (1712)
Discourse on the Memory of Sir Robert Fletcher, A (1665) **Gilbert Burnet** (1643)
Discourse on the Plurality of Worlds [*Entretiens sur la pluralité des mondes*] (1686) **Bernard le Bovier Fontenelle** (1657)
Discourse on the Study of Law, A (1758) **Sir William Blackstone** (1723)
Discourse Upon the Pharisee and the Publicane, A (1685) **John Bunyan** (1628)
Discourses in America (1885) **Matthew Arnold** (1822)
Discoverie of a Most Exquisite Jewel, The (1652) **Sir Thomas Urquhart** (1611) (tr.)
Discoverie of the Large, Rich, and Bewtiful Empyre of Guiana, The (1596) **Sir Walter Ralegh** (1554)
Discoverie of the True Causes Why Ireland was Never Entirely Subdued, A (1612) **Sir John Davies** (1569)
Discoverie of Witchcraft, The (1584) **Reginald Scot** (1538?)
Discoveries (1907) **W.B. Yeats** (1865)
Discovery (1932) **John Drinkwater** (1882)
Discovery, The (1763) **Frances Sheridan** (1724)
Disenchantment (1922) **C.E. Montague** (1867)
Disentanglers, The (1902) **Andrew Lang** (1844)
Disgrace (1999) **J.M. Coetzee** (1940)
Disincarnation, The (1967) **C.H. Sisson** (1914)
Disinherited, The (1933) **Jack Conroy** (1899)
Disinherited, The (1974) **Matt Cohen** (1942)
Disobedience (2000) **Jane Hamilton**
Disorderly Knights, The (1966) **Dorothy Dunnett** (1923)
Disowned, The (1828) **Edward Bulwer-Lytton** (1803)
Disowned, The (1852) **Edward Bulwer-Lytton** (1803)
Dispensary, The (1699) **Sir Samuel Garth** (1661)
Dispersal Point (1942) **John Pudney** (1909)
Dispossessed, The (1948) **John Berryman** (1914)
Dispossessed, The (1975) **Ursula K. le Guin** (1929)
Disquiet and Peace (1956) **'William Cooper' [Harry Summerfield Hoff]** (1910)
Disquisitions Relating to Matter and Spirit (1777) **Joseph Priestley** (1733)
Dissuasive from Popery, A [pt. i; pt. ii, 1667] (1664) **Jeremy Taylor** (1613)
Dissenters Answer to the High-Church Challenge, The (1704) **Daniel Defoe** (1660)
Dissertation on Liberty and Necessity, A (1725) **Benjamin Franklin** (1706)
Dissertation on the First-Principles of Government (1795) **Thomas Paine** (1737)
Dissertation upon Parties, A (1735) **Henry Saint-John, Viscount Bolingbroke** (1678)
Dissertation upon the Epistles of Phalaris; with an Answer to Boyle, A (1697) **Richard Bentley** (1662)
Dissertations and Discussions (1859) **J.S. Mill** (1806)
Dissertations Moral and Critical (1783) **James Beattie** (1735)
Distances, The (1960) **Charles Olson** (1910)
Distant Likeness, A (1973) **Paul Bailey** (1937)
Distant Relations (1980) **Carlos Fuentes** (1928)
Distant Stars (1981) **Samuel R. Delany** (1942)
Distant Trumpet, A (1960) **Paul Horgan** (1903)
Distinguished Marks of a Work of the Spirit of God, The (1741) **Jonathan Edwards** (1703)
Distinguished Villa (1926) **Kate O'Brien** (1897)
Distress'd Innocence (1690) **Elkanah Settle** (1648)
Distress'd Wife, The (1743) **John Gay** (1685–1732)
Distrest Mother, The [tr. from Racine] (1712) **Ambrose Philips** (1674)
Disturbing Element (1963) **Xavier Herbert** (1901)
Divers Crabtree Lectures (1639) **John Taylor** (1580)
Divers Voyages Touching the Discoverie of America (1582) **Richard Hakluyt** (1552?)
Diverse Ballads (1528?) **John Skelton** (1460?)
Diversifications (1975) **A.R. Ammons** (1926)
Diversions of Purley (1987) **Peter Ackroyd** (1949)
Diversity and Depth in Fiction (1983) **Angus Wilson** (1913)
Diversity of Creatures, A (1917) **Rudyard Kipling** (1865)
Diverting History of John Gilpin, The (1782) **William Cowper** (1731)
Divide and Rule (1979) **Jan Mark** (1943)
Divided Self, The (1960) **R.D. Laing** (1927)
Divided Ways, The (1946) **John Heath-Stubbs** (1918)
Dividing Stream, The (1951) **Francis King** (1923)
Divina Commedia (1307–21?) **Dante Alighieri** (1265)
Divine and Supernatural Light (1734) **Jonathan Edwards** (1703)
Divine Century of Spiritual Sonnets, A (1595) **Barnabe Barnes** (1571)
Divine Comedies (1976) **James Merrill** (1926)

Divine Comedy, The [from Dante] (1949–1962) **Dorothy L. Sayers** (1893) (tr.)
Divine Comedy, The [from Dante] (1980) **C.H. Sisson** (1914) (tr.)
Divine Dialogues (1668) **Henry More** (1614)
Divine Fancies (1632) **Francis Quarles** (1592)
Divine Fire, The (1904) **May Sinclair** (1863)
Divine Invasion, The (1981) **Philip K. Dick** (1928)
Divine Life, The (1664) **Richard Baxter** (1615)
Divine Poem of Musaeus, The (1616) **George Chapman** (1559?) (tr.)
Divine Poems (1630) **Francis Quarles** (1592)
Divine Poems (1685) **Edmund Waller** (1606)
Divine Poems of John Donne, The (1972) **Helen Gardner** (1908) (ed.)
Divine Poems on the Ten Commandments (1688) **George Wither** (1588–1667)
Divine Songs for the Use of Children (1715) **Isaac Watts** (1674)
Divine Vision, The (1904) **George William Russell ['AE']** (1867)
Diviner, The (1983) **Brian Friel** (1929)
Diviners, The (1974) **Margaret Laurence** (1926)
Diving for Pearls (1989) **Howard Brenton** (1942)
Diving into the Wreck (1973) **Adrienne Rich** (1929)
Division of the Spoils, A (1975) **Paul Scott** (1920)
Division Street: America (1966) **Studs Terkel** (1912)
Divisions on a Ground (1976) **Robert Nye** (1939)
Divorce, Un (1904) **Paul Bourget** (1852)
Djinn in the Nightingale's Eye, The (1994) **A.S. Byatt** (1936)
Do Androids Dream of Electric Sheep? (1969) **Philip K. Dick** (1928)
Do Me a Favour (1963) **Susan Hill** (1942)
Do These Bones Live? (1941) **Edward Dahlberg** (1900)
Do We Agree? (1928) **Bernard Shaw** (1856)
Do With Me What You Will (1973) **Joyce Carol Oates** (1938)
Docherty (1975) **William McIlvanney** (1936)
Doctor , The [vols. i–vii] (1834–1847) **Robert Southey** (1774)
Doctor Birch and His Young Friends [as 'M.A. Titmarsh'] (1849) **W.M. Thackeray** (1811)
Doctor Copernicus (1976) **John Banville** (1945)
Doctor Cupid (1886) **Rhoda Broughton** (1840)
Doctor Dido (1938) **F.L. Lucas** (1894)
Doctor Faustus [*Doktor Faustus*] (1947) **Thomas Mann** (1875)
Doctor Frigo (1974) **Eric Ambler** (1909)
Doctor In Spite of Himself, The [*Le Médecin malgré lui*] (1666) **'Molière' [Jean-Baptiste Poquelin]** (1622)
Doctor is Sick, The (1960) **'Anthony Burgess' [John Anthony Burgess Wilson]** (1917)
Doctor Jacob (1864) **Matilda Betham-Edwards** (1836)
Doctor Mirabilis (1964) **James Blish** (1921)
Doctor Nikola (1896) **Guy Boothby** (1867)
Doctor Nikola's Experiment (1899) **Guy Boothby** (1867)
Doctor Pascal [*Le Docteur Pascal*; final vol. in *Les Rougon-Macquart* cycle] (1893) **Émile Zola** (1840)
Doctor Sax (1959) **Jack Kerouac** (1922)
Doctor Slaughter (1984) **Paul Theroux** (1941)
Doctor Therne (1898) **Sir H. Rider Haggard** (1856)
Doctor Thorne (1858) **Anthony Trollope** (1815)
Doctor Zhivago [screenplay] (1966) **Robert Bolt** (1924)
Doctor's Christmas Eve, The (1910) **James Lane Allen** (1849)
Doctor's Dilemma [etc], *The* (1911) **Bernard Shaw** (1856)
Doctor's Son, The (1935) **John O'Hara** (1905)
Doctor's Wife, The (1864) **M.E. Braddon** (1835)
Doctor's Wife, The (1976) **Brian Moore** (1921)
Doctors Wear Scarlet (1960) **Simon Raven** (1927)
Doctrinall of Princis, The (1534) **Sir Thomas Elyot** (1490?) (tr.)
Doctrine and Discipline of Divorce , The (1643) **John Milton** (1608)
Doctrine of Knowledge [*Wissenschaftslehre*] (1794) **Johann Gottlieb Fichte** (1762)
Doctrine of Original Sin, The (1757) **John Wesley** (1703)
Doctrine of Philosophical Necessity Illustrated, The (1777) **Joseph Priestley** (1733)
Doctrine of Sacrifice, The (1854) **F.D. Maurice** (1805)
Doctrine of the Law and Grace Unfolded, The (1659) **John Bunyan** (1628)
Doctrine of the Real Presence, The (1855) **E.B. Pusey** (1800)
Documents in the Case, The (1930) **Dorothy L. Sayers** (1893) [with Robert Eustace]
Documents Relating to the Sentimental Agents in the Volyen Empire (1983) **Doris Lessing** (1919)
Dodd Family Abroad, The (1854) **Charles Lever** (1806)
Dodgem (1981) **Bernard Ashley** (1935)
Dodo (1893) **E.F. Benson** (1867)
Dodo the Second (1914) **E.F. Benson** (1867)
Dodo Wonders (1921) **E.F. Benson** (1867)
Dodsworth (1929) **Sinclair Lewis** (1885)
Does She Like Word-Games? (1988) **Wendy Cope** (1945)
Dog Beneath the Skin, The (1935) **W.H. Auden** (1907) [with Christopher Isherwood]
Dog Crusoe, The (1861) **R.M. Ballantyne** (1825)
Dog Fox Field (1990) **Les Murray** (1938)
Dog It Was That Died, The (1982) **Tom Stoppard** (1937)
Dog of Flanders, A (1872) **'Ouida' [Marie Louise de la Ramée]** (1839)
Dog Rock (1985) **David Foster** (1944)
Dog So Small, A (1962) **Philippa Pearce** (1920)
Dog Years [*Hundejahre*] (1963) **Günter Grass** (1927)
Dogg's Hamlet; Cahoot's Macbeth (1979) **Tom Stoppard** (1937)
Dogs (1993) **Fiona Pitt-Kethley** (1954)
Dogs Bark, The (1973) **Truman Capote** (1924)
Dogs of War, The (1974) **Frederick Forsyth** (1938)
Dogsbody (1975) **Diana Wynne Jones** (1934)

Doings and Dealings (1913) **Jane Barlow** (1857)
Doings of Raffles Haw, The (1892) **A. Conan Doyle** (1859)
Doktor Faust in Rose Street (1973) **'Robert Garioch' [Robert Garioch Sutherland]** (1909)
Doll's House, A (1879) **Henrik Ibsen** (1828)
Dollars and Deficit (1968) **Milton Friedman** (1912)
Dolliver Romance, The (1876) **Nathaniel Hawthorne** (1804–64)
Dollmaker, The (1954) **Harriette Arnow** (1908)
Dolly and the Cookie Bird [US: *Murder in the Round*] (1970) **Dorothy Dunnett** (1923)
Dolly and the Doctor Bird [US: *Match for a Murderer*] (1971) **Dorothy Dunnett** (1923)
Dolly and the Singing Bird [US: *The Photogenic Soprano*] (1968) **Dorothy Dunnett** (1923)
Dolly and the Starry Bird [US: *Murder in Focus*] (1973) **Dorothy Dunnett** (1923)
Dolly Dialogues, The (1894) **'Anthony Hope' [Sir Anthony Hope Hawkins]** (1863)
Dolores (1911) **I. Compton-Burnett** (1884)
Dolphin Crossing, The (1967) **Jill Paton Walsh** (1937)
Dolphins (1973) **Robert Lowell** (1917)
Dolphins (1994) **Sir Stephen Spender** (1909)
Domain (1984) **James Herbert** (1943)
Dombey and Son (1848) **Charles Dickens** (1812)
Dome of Many-Coloured Glass, A (1912) **Amy Lowell** (1874)
Domesday Book (1920) **Edgar Lee Masters** (1868)
Domestic Affections, The (1812) **Felicia Dorothea Hemans** (1793)
Domestic Animal, A (1970) **Francis King** (1923)
Domestic Manner and Private Life of Sir Walter Scott, The (1834) **James Hogg** (1770)
Domestic Manners of the Americans (1832) **Frances Trollope** (1780)
Domestic Relations (1957) **'Frank O'Connor' [Michael Francis O'Donovan']** (1903)
Dominion of Dreams, The [as 'Fiona Macleod'] (1899) **William Sharp** (1855)
Domitia (1898) **S. Baring-Gould** (1834)
Don Carlos, Prince of Spain (1676) **Thomas Otway** (1652)
Don Fernando (1935) **Somerset Maugham** (1874)
Don Gesualdo (1886) **'Ouida' [Marie Louise de la Ramée]** (1839)
Don John (1881) **Jean Ingelow** (1820)
Don Juan (1665) **'Molière' [Jean-Baptiste Poquelin]** (1622)
Don Juan (1813) **E.T.A. Hoffmann** (1776)
Don Juan [cantos i-ii] (1819, 1821, 1823, 1824) **George Gordon, Lord Byron** (1788)
Don Orsino (1893) **F. Marion Crawford** (1854)
Don Quixote [*El ingenioso hidalgo Don Quixote de la Mancha*, pt. i] (1605) **Miguel de Cervantes Saavedra** (1547)
Don Quixote [pt. ii] (1615) **Miguel de Cervantes Saavedra** (1547)
Don Quixote (1986) **Kathy Acker** (1948)
Don Quixote in England (1734) **Henry Fielding** (1707)
Don Sebastian (1809) **Anna Maria Porter** (1780)
Don Sebastian, King of Portugal (1690) **John Dryden** (1631)
Don Tarquinio (1905) **Frederick William Rolfe** (1860)
Don's Party (1971) **David Williamson** (1942)
Don't (1998) **Jenny Diski** (1947)
Don't Call Me By My Right Name (1956) **James Purdy** (1923)
Don't Stop the Carnival (1965) **Herman Wouk** (1915)
Don't Tell Alfred (1960) **Nancy Mitford** (1904)
Don't Tell the Grown-Ups (1990) **Alison Lurie** (1926)
Donal Grant (1883) **George MacDonald** (1824)
Donald Ross of Heimra (1891) **William Black** (1841)
Donkeys' Years (1976) **Michael Frayn** (1933)
Don't Go Away Mad (1949) **William Saroyan** (1908)
Doomed Oasis, The (1960) **'Hammond Innes' [Ralph Hammond-Innes]** (1913)
Doomsday (1614) **Sir William Alexander** (1567?)
Doomsday Book, A (1965) **George MacBeth** (1932)
Doomsday Men, The (1938) **J.B. Priestley** (1894)
Door in the Wall, The (1992) **Charles Tomlinson** (1927)
Door into the Dark (1969) **Seamus Heaney** (1939)
Doors of Perception, The (1954) **Aldous Huxley** (1894)
Doors of Stone, The (1963) **F.T. Prince** (1912)
Dop Doctor, The [as 'Richard Dehan'] (1896) **Clo Graves** (1863)
Dora (1868) **Julia Kavanagh** (1824)
Dorando (1767) **James Boswell** (1740)
Dorcas Dene, Detective (1897) **George R. Sims** (1847)
Dorinda and Her Daughter (1910) **'Iota' [Kathleen Mannington Caffyn]** (1855?)
Dorking Thigh, The (1945) **William Plomer** (1903)
Dorotea, La (1632) **Lope de Vega** (1562)
Dorothy and the Wizard of Oz (1908) **L. Frank Baum** (1856)
Dorothy Forster (1884) **Sir Walter Besant** (1836)
Dorothy South (1902) **George Cary Eggleston** (1839)
Dorothy Wordsworth (1933) **Ernest de Selincourt** (1870)
Dorrington Deed-Box, The (1897) **Arthur Morrison** (1863)
Dorset Essays (1935) **Llewelyn Powys** (1884)
Dossier 113, Le (1867) **Émile Gaboriau** (1832)
Dostoevsky (1931) **E.H. Carr** (1892)
Dot and Tot of Merryland (1901) **L. Frank Baum** (1856)
Doting (1952) **'Henry Green' [Henry Vicent Yorke]** (1905)
Double Agent, The (1935) **R.P. Blackmur** (1904)
Double Axe, The (1948) **Robinson Jeffers** (1887)
Double Cross (1986) **Thomas Kilroy** (1934)
Double Cross Purposes (1937) **Ronald Knox** (1888)
Double Distress, The (1701) **Mary Pix** (1666)
Double Dream of Spring, The (1970) **John Ashbery** (1927)
Double Event, The (1891) **Nat Gould** (1857)
Double Falsehood (1727) **Lewis Theobald** (1688)
Double Four, The (1911) **E. Phillips Oppenheim** (1866)

Double Gallant, The (1707) **Colley Cibber** (1671)
Double Honeymoon (1976) **Evan S. Connell, Jr** (1924)
Double Hook, The (1959) **Sheila Watson** (1909)
Double Indemnity (1936) **James M. Cain** (1892)
Double Life, A (1993) **Frederic Raphael** (1931)
Double Lives (1943) **William Plomer** (1903)
Double PP, The (1606) **Thomas Dekker** (1572?)
Double Prophecy, The (1862) **William Carleton** (1794)
Double Star (1956) **Robert A. Heinlein** (1907)
Double Thread, A (1899) **Ellen Thorneycroft Fowler** (1860)
Double Tongue, The (1995) **William Golding** (1911–93)
Double Yoke (1982) **Buchi Emecheta** (1944)
Double-Dealer, The (1693) **William Congreve** (1670)
Doubleman, The (1985) **C. J. Koch** (1932)
Doubling the Point (1992) **J.M. Coetzee** (1940)
Doubtfire (1968) **Robert Nye** (1939)
Douglas (1757) **John Home** (1722)
Douleur, La (1945) **'Marguerite Duras' [Marguerite Donnadieu]** (1914)
Dove (1982) **Barbara Hanrahan** (1939)
Dove in the Eagle's Nest, The (1866) **Charlotte M. Yonge** (1823)
Dove, The (1717) **Matthew Prior** (1664)
Dove's Nest, The (1923) **'Katherine Mansfield' [Kathleen Mansfield Beauchamp]** (1888)
Doves of Venus, The (1955) **Olivia Manning** (1908)
Dowager, The (1840) **Mrs C.F. Gore** (1799)
Down all the Days (1970) **Christy Brown** (1932)
Down Among the Women (1971) **Fay Weldon** (1931)
Down and Out in Paris and London (1933) **'George Orwell' [Eric Arthur Blair]** (1903)
Down Dartmoor Way (1895) **Eden Phillpotts** (1862)
Down in the City (1957) **Elizabeth Harrower** (1928)
Down the Long Table (1955) **Earle Birney** (1904)
Down There on a Visit (1962) **Christopher Isherwood** (1904)
Down Where the Moon is Small (1966) **'Richard Llewellyn' [Richard Llewellyn Lloyd]** (1907)
Down-Adown-Derry (1922) **Walter de la Mare** (1873)
Down-Easters, The (1833) **John Neal** (1793)
Down-Hall (1723) **Matthew Prior** (1664)
Downfall, The [*La Débâcle*] (1892) **Émile Zola** (1840)
Downhill all the Way (1967) **Leonard Woolf** (1880)
Downstream (1962) **Thomas Kinsella** (1928)
Downward to the Earth (1970) **Robert Silverberg** (1935)
Doxie Dent (1899) **'John Ackworth' [Frederick R. Smith]** (1845)
Dr Bradley Remembers (1938) **Francis Brett Young** (1884)
Dr Bradley Remembers Mr and Mrs Pennington (1931) **Francis Brett Young** (1884)
Dr Breen's Practice (1881) **William Dean Howells** (1837)
Dr Brodie's Report [*El informe de Brodie*]] (1971) **Jorge Luis Borges** (1899)
Dr Claudius (1883) **F. Marion Crawford** (1854)
Dr Criminale (1992) **Malcolm Bradbury** (1932)
Dr Dolittle's Zoo (1925) **Hugh Lofting** (1886)
Dr Dolittle's Circus (1924) **Hugh Lofting** (1886)
Dr Dolittle's Post Office (1923) **Hugh Lofting** (1886)
Dr Dolittle's Return (1933) **Hugh Lofting** (1886)
Dr Faust's Sea-Spiral Spirit (1972) **Peter Redgrove** (1932)
Dr Fischer of Geneva (1980) **Graham Greene** (1904)
Dr Grimshawe's Secret (1883) **Nathaniel Hawthorne** (1804–64)
Dr Gruber's Daughter (1986) **Janice Elliott** (1931)
Dr Heidenhoff's Process (1880) **Edward Bellamy** (1850)
Dr Martino (1934) **William Faulkner** (1897)
Dr No (1958) **Ian Fleming** (1908)
Dr Palliser's Patient (1889) **Grant Allen** (1848)
Dr Phillips (1887) **'Frank Danby' [Julia Frankau]** (1864)
Dr Sevier (1885) **George Washington Cable** (1844)
Dr Thorndyke's Case-Book [US: *The Blue Scarab*] (1923) **R. Austin Freeman** (1862)
Dr Wainwright's Patient (1871) **Edmund Yates** (1831)
Dr Wortle's School (1881) **Anthony Trollope** (1815)
Dr Zhivago (1957) **Boris Pasternak** (1890)
Dracula (1897) **Bram Stoker** (1847)
Dracula Unbound (1991) **Brian Aldiss** (1925)
Dracula's Guest (1914) **Bram Stoker** (1847)
Dragon and the Raven, The (1886) **G.A. Henty** (1832)
Dragon Apparent, A (1951) **Norman Lewis** (1918)
Dragon, Dragon (1975) **John Gardner** (1933)
Dragon Harvest (1945) **Upton Sinclair** (1878)
Dragon in the Sea, The (1956) **Frank Herbert** (1920)
Dragon Laughed, A (1930) **Eric Linklater** (1899)
Dragon Masters, The (1963) **Jack Vance** (1916)
Dragon of Wantley, The (1737) **Henry Carey** (1687?)
Dragon Rampant (1939) **'Robin Hyde' [Iris Guiver Wilkinson]** (1906)
Dragon Seed (1941) **Pearl S. Buck** (1892)
Dragon's Teeth (1891) **Clo Graves** (1863)
Dragon's Teeth (1942) **Upton Sinclair** (1878)
Dragons at the Party (1987) **Jon Cleary** (1917)
Dragontea, La (1598) **Lope de Vega** (1562)
Drake [vol. i; vol. ii, 1908] (1906) **Alfred Noyes** (1880)
Drama (1940) **Desmond MacCarthy** (1877)
Drama and Society in the Age of Jonson (1937) **L.C. Knights** (1906)
Drama and the Weather (1958) **Paul Green** (1894)
Drama in Muslin, A (1886) **George Moore** (1852)
Dramas in Miniature (1891) **Mathilde Blind** (1841)
Dramas Must Explain Themselves (1975) **Ursula K. le Guin** (1929)
Dramas of Life (1890) **George R. Sims** (1847)
Dramatic Historiographer, The (1735) **Eliza Haywood** (*c.* 1693)
Dramatic Idyls [1st ser.] (1879) **Robert Browning** (1812)
Dramatic Idyls [2nd ser.] (1880) **Robert Browning** (1812)
Dramatic Scenes, and Other Poems (1819) **'Barry Cornwall' [Bryan Waller Procter]** (1787)

Dramatic Scenes (1827) **Mary Russell Mitford** (1787)
Dramatic Values (1911) **C.E. Montague** (1867)
Dramatis Personae (1864) **Robert Browning** (1812)
Dramatis Personae (1935) **W.B. Yeats** (1865)
Drayneflete Revealed (1949) **Osbert Lancaster** (1908)
Dread Affair, The (1985) **Benjamin Zephaniah** (1958)
Dread Beat and Blood (1975) **Linton Kwesi Johnson** (1952)
Dread Voyage, The (1898) **Wilfred Campbell** (1858)
Dream, The (1924) **H.G. Wells** (1866)
Dream, The [*Le Rêve*] (1888) **Émile Zola** (1840)
Dream Children (1998) **A.N. Wilson** (1950)
Dream Days (1898) **Kenneth Grahame** (1859)
Dream Department, The (1943) **S.J. Perelman** (1904)
Dream House, The (1976) **Kevin Crossley-Holland** (1941)
Dream in Hawaii, A (1978) **Bhabani Bhattacharya** (1906)
Dream Keeper, The (1932) **Langston Hughes** (1902)
Dream Life and Real Life [as 'Ralph Iron'] (1893) **Olive Schreiner** (1855)
Dream Life of Balso Snell, The (1931) **'Nathanael West' [Nathan Wallenstein Weinstein]** (1903)
Dream Master, The (1966) **Roger Zelazny** (1937)
Dream Merchants, The (1949) **Harold Robbins** (1912)
Dream of a Common Language, The (1978) **Adrienne Rich** (1929)
Dream of Eugene Aram, The (1831) **Thomas Hood** (1799)
Dream of Fair Women, The (1924) **Henry Williamson** (1895)
Dream of Gerontius, The (1866) **J.H. Newman** (1801)
Dream of Governors, A (1959) **Louis Simpson** (1923)
Dream of John Ball [and *A King's Lesson*], *A* (1888) **William Morris** (1834)
Dream of Spring, A (1980) **Elizabeth Jennings** (1926)
Dream on Monkey Mountain, The (1970) **Derek Walcott** (1930)
Dream People (1987) **Barbara Hanrahan** (1939)
Dream Play, A (1902) **August Strindberg** (1849)
Dream Songs, The (1969) **John Berryman** (1914)
Dream Stuff (2000) **David Malouf** (1934)
Dream The (1927) **Richard Church** (1893)
Dream-Charlotte, The (1896) **Matilda Betham-Edwards** (1836)
Dreamer and the Worker, The (1851) **R.H. Horne** (1803)
Dreamer's Tales, A (1910) **Lord Dunsany** (1878)
Dreamers of Dreams (1948) **Holbrook Jackson** (1874)
Dreamers of the Ghetto (1898) **Israel Zangwill** (1864)
Dreaming (1988) **Herbert Gold** (1924)
Dreaming America (1973) **Joyce Carol Oates** (1938)
Dreaming Frankenstein and Collected Poems (1984) **Liz Lochhead** (1947)
Dreaming in Bronze (1981) **D.M. Thomas** (1935)
Dreaming Jewels, The (1950) **Theodore Sturgeon** (1918)
Dreaming of Babylon (1977) **Richard Brautigan** (1935)
Dreamland (1977) **George V. Higgins** (1939)
Dreams (1891) **Olive Schreiner** (1855)
Dreams of a Summer Night (1966) **George Barker** (1913)
Dreams of Power (1981) **Alison Brackenbury** (1953)
Dreams of the Kalahari (1981) **Carolyn Slaughter** (1946)
Dreams, Waking Thoughts and Incidents (1783) **William Beckford** (1760)
Dreams, Yellow Lions (1975) **Alistair Campbell** (1925)
Dreamthorp (1863) **Alexander Smith** (1830)
Dreamtigers [*El Hacedor*] (1960) **Jorge Luis Borges** (1899)
Dred (1856) **Harriet Beecher Stowe** (1811)
Dreiser Looks at Russia (1928) **Theodore Dreiser** (1871)
Dressed as For a Tarot Pack (1990) **Peter Redgrove** (1932)
Dressed to Kill (1994) **Douglas Dunn** (1942)
Dressing of Diamond (1974) **Nicholas Freeling** (1927)
Dressing Up for the Carnival (2000) **Carol Shields** (1935)
Dressing Up (1979) **Peter Ackroyd** (1949)
Dressmaker, The (1973) **Beryl Bainbridge** (1934)
Drift (1861) **Mrs C.L. Balfour** (1808)
Drift (1930) **James Hanley** (1901)
Drifters, The (1971) **James A. Michener** (1907)
Drifters (1984) **Tom Wakefield** (1935)
Driver's Seat, The (1970) **Muriel Spark** (1918)
Driving in the Dark (1988) **Deborah Moggach** (1948)
Driving into the Storm (1987) **Ian Wedde** (1946)
Driving West (1975) **Patricia Beer** (1924)
Droome of Doomes Day, The (1576) **George Gascoigne** (1542?)
Drought, The (1965) **J.G. Ballard** (1930)
Drowned Sailor, The (1947) **James Kirkup** (1923)
Drowned World, The (1963) **J.G. Ballard** (1930)
Drowning Pool, The (1950) **'Ross MacDonald' [Kenneth Millar]** (1915)
Drowning with Others (1962) **James Dickey** (1923)
Drum-Taps (1865) **Walt Whitman** (1819)
Drummer Boy, The (1969) **Leon Garfield** (1921)
Drummer, The (1716) **Joseph Addison** (1672)
Drummer, The (1993) **Ian Wedde** (1946)
Drums in the Night [*Trommeln in der Nacht*] (1922) **Bertolt Brecht** (1898)
Drums of Father Ned, The (1958) **Sean O'Casey** (1880)
Drums Under the Window (1945) **Sean O'Casey** (1880)
Drunk Man Looks at the Thistle, A (1926) **'Hugh MacDiarmid' [Christopher Murray Grieve]** (1892)
Drunk with Love (1986) **Ellen Gilchrist** (1935)
Drunken Boat, The [*Le Bateau ivre*] (1871) **Arthur Rimbaud** (1854)

Dry Salvages, The (1941) **T.S. Eliot** (1888)
Dry Sticks, Fagoted (1858) **Walter Savage Landor** (1775)
Dry White Season, A (1979) **André Brink** (1935)
Dryaides (1712) **William Diaper** (1685)
Drypoints of the Hasidim (1975) **F.T. Prince** (1912)
Dual Cactus, The (1957) **Michael Hamburger** (1924)
Dubin's Lives (1979) **Bernard Malamud** (1914)
Dubious Legacy, A (1992) **'Mary Wesley' [Mary Wellesley]** (1912)
Dublin Days (1921) **L.A.G. Strong** (1896)
Dubliners (1914) **James Joyce** (1882)
Ducdame (1925) **John Cooper Powys** (1872)
Duchenier (1848) **John Mason Neale** (1818)
Duchess de la Valliere, The (1836) **Edward Bulwer-Lytton** (1803)
Duchess Laura (1929) **Mrs Belloc Lowndes** (1868)
Duchess of Malfi, The [**Webster**]: see *The Tragedy of the Dutchesse of Malfy*
Duchess of Powysland, The (1892) **Grant Allen** (1848)
Duchess of Rosemary Lane, The (1876) **B.L. Farjeon** (1838)
Duck Variations (1974) **David Mamet** (1947)
Ductor Dubitantium (1660) **Jeremy Taylor** (1613)
Duel of Angels [from Giraudoux, *Pour Lucrece*] (1958) **Christopher Fry [Christopher Fry Harris]** (1907)
Duel of Angels [tr. 1958 by Christopher Fry as *Duel of Angels*] (1953) **Jean Giraudoux** (1882–1944)
Duel Site (1970) **Walter Abish** (1931)
Duell of the Staggs, The (1668) **Sir Robert Howard** (1626)
Duellist, The (1764) **Charles Churchill** (1731)
Duello, The (1610) **John Selden** (1584)
Duet for Three (1985) **Joan Barfoot** (1946)
Duet With an Occasional Chorus, A (1899) **A. Conan Doyle** (1859)
Duffy [as 'Dan Kavanagh'] (1980) **Julian Barnes** (1946)
Duke, The (1931) **Philip Guedalla** (1889)
Duke and No Duke, A (1684) **Nahum Tate** (1652)
Duke Christian of Luneburg (1824) **Jane Porter** (1776)
Duke in the Suburbs, The (1909) **Edgar Wallace** (1875)
Duke of Gandia, The (1908) **A.C. Swinburne** (1837)
Duke of Guise, The (1682) **John Dryden** (1631) [with Nathaniel Lee]
Duke of Millaine, The (1623) **Philip Massinger** (1583)
Duke of Palermo, The (1969) **Edmund Wilson** (1895)
Duke, the Lost Engine (1970) **Revd W.V. Awdry** (1911)
Duke's Children, The (1880) **Anthony Trollope** (1815)
Dukes Mistris, The (1636) **James Shirley** (1596)
Dulcie Everton (1896) **E. Lynn Linton** (1822)
Duluth (1983) **Gore Vidal** (1925)
Dumaresq's Daughter (1891) **Grant Allen** (1848)
Dumbe Knight, The (1608) **Gervaise Markham** (1568?) [with Lewis Machin]
Dumbfounding, The (1966) **Margaret Avison** (1918)
Dunciad, The (1728) **Alexander Pope** (1688)
Dunciad, Variorum, The (1729) **Alexander Pope** (1688)
Dune (1965) **Frank Herbert** (1920)
Dune Messiah (1969) **Frank Herbert** (1920)
Dunky Fitlow (1933) **A.E. Coppard** (1878)
Dunmara (1864) **Rosa Mulholland** (1841)
Dunne Family, The (1976) **James T. Farrell** (1904)
Dunster (1992) **John Mortimer** (1923)
Dunwich Horror and Others, The (1963) **H.P. Lovecraft** (1890–1937)
Duo (1934) **Colette** (1873)
Duplicate Death (1951) **Georgette Heyer** (1902)
Duplications, The (1977) **Kenneth Koch** (1925)
Duplicity (1781) **Thomas Holcroft** (1745)
During Her Majesty's Pleasure (1908) **M.E. Braddon** (1835)
During Mother's Absence (1993) **Michèle Roberts** (1949)
Durnton Abbey (1871) **T. Adolphus Trollope** (1810)
Dusk of Dawn (1940) **W.E.B. du Bois** (*c.* 1868)
Dusklands (1974) **J.M. Coetzee** (1940)
Dust in the Lion's Paw (1961) **Freya Stark** (1893)
Dust of the World, The (1994) **Anthony Thwaite** (1930)
Dust on the Paw (1961) **Robin Jenkins** (1912)
Dust or Polish? (1950) **Norman Lindsay** (1879)
Dust Which Is God, The (1941) **William Rose Benét** (1886)
Dusty Answer (1927) **Rosamond Lehmann** (1903)
Dusty Diamonds Cut and Polished (1884) **R.M. Ballantyne** (1825)
Dutch Courtezan, The (1605) **John Marston** (1576)
Dutch Interior (1940) **'Frank O'Connor' [Michael Francis O'Donovan]** (1903)
Dutch Lover, The (1673) **Aphra Behn** (1640?)
Dutch Shoe Mystery, The (1931) **'Ellery Queen' [Frederic Dannay]** (1905) and **Manfred B. Lee** (1905)
Dutchman (1964) **LeRoi Jones** (1934)
Duties of Women, The (1881) **Frances Power Cobbe** (1822)
Dutiful Daughter, A (1971) **Thomas Keneally** (1935)
Duty (1880) **Samuel Smiles** (1812)
Duty and Inclination (1838) **Letitia Elizabeth Landon** (1802)
Dwale Bluth, The [etc] (1876) **Oliver Madox Brown** (1855–74)
Dwarf Kingdom, A (1996) **Nicholas Freeling** (1927)
Dwarf's Chamber, The (1896) **Fergus Hume** (1859)
Dwarves of Death, The (1990) **Jonathan Coe** (1961)
Dweller on the Threshold, The (1911) **Robert Hichens** (1864)
Dyer's Hand, The (1963) **W.H. Auden** (1907)
Dyet of Poland, The (1705) **Daniel Defoe** (1660)
Dying Earth, The (1950) **Jack Vance** (1916)
Dying Gaul, The (1978) **David Jones** (1895)
Dying, in Other Words (1981) **Maggie Gee** (1948)
Dying Inside (1972) **Robert Silverberg** (1935)

Dying Negro, The (1773) **Thomas Day** (1748)
Dying of the Light, The (1993) **Michael Dibdin** (1947)
Dynamics of Faith (1956) **Paul Tillich** (1886)
Dynamo (1929) **Eugene O'Neill** (1888)
Dynasts, The [pt. i] (1904, 1906, 1908) **Thomas Hardy** (1840)
Dynevor Terrace (1857) **Charlotte M. Yonge** (1823)

E

'E' is for Evidence (1988) **Sue Grafton** (1940)
Each Peach Pear Plum (1978) **Alan Ahlberg** (1938)
Eagle and the Chicken, and Other Stories, The (1986) **Ama Ata Aidoo** (1942)
Eagle Cliff, The (1889) **R.M. Ballantyne** (1825)
Eagle Has Landed, The (1975) **'Jack Higgins' [Harry Patterson]** (1929)
Eagle Has Two Heads, The [*L'Aigle a deux têtes*] (1946) **Jean Cocteau** (1889)
Eagle of the Ninth, The (1954) **Rosemary Sutcliff** (1920)
Eagle's Shadow, The (1904) **James Branch Cabell** (1879)
Earl of Essex, The (1761) **Henry Brooke** (1703)
Earl of Essex, The (1843) **Charles Whitehead** (1804)
Earl's Promise, The (1873) **Mrs J.H. Riddell** (1832)
Earlham (1922) **Percy Lubbock** (1879)
Early Autumn (1926) **Louis Bromfield** (1896)
Early Days (1980) **David Storey** (1933)
Early H.G. Wells, The (1961) **Bernard Bergonzi** (1929)
Early History of Jacob Stahl, The (1911) **J.D. Beresford** (1873)
Early in the Morning (1986) **Charles Causley** (1917)
Early Italian Poets, The (1861) **Dante Gabriel Rossetti** (1828) (tr.)
Early Kings of Norway, The (1875) **Thomas Carlyle** (1795)
Early Lessons (1801) **Maria Edgeworth** (1767)
Early Life and Adventures of Sylvia Scarlett, The (1918) **Compton Mackenzie** (1883)
Early Life of Stephen Hind, The (1966) **Storm Jameson** (1897)
Early Martyr, An (1935) **William Carlos Williams** (1883)
Early Spring (1883) **Alfred, Lord Tennyson** (1809)
Early Spring in Massachusetts (1881) **Henry David Thoreau** (1817–62)
Early Victorian England (1934) **G.M. Young** (1882) (ed.)
Early Worm, The (1927) **Robert Benchley** (1889)
Early Years of Alec Waugh, The (1962) **Alec Waugh** (1898)
Earnest Invitation, An (1673) **Joseph Glanvill** (1636)
Earth Breath, The (1897) **George William Russell ['AE']** (1867)
Earth Compels, The (1938) **Louis MacNeice** (1907)
Earth For Sale, The (1928) **Harold Monro** (1879)
Earth House Hold (1969) **Gary Snyder** (1930)
Earth of Cualann (1917) **Joseph Campbell** (1879)
Earth Out of Earth (1939) **Daniel Corkery** (1878)
Earth to Earth [as 'Richard Dehan'] (1916) **Clo Graves** (1863)
Earth Triumphant (1914) **Conrad Potter Aiken** (1889)
Earth's Enigmas (1896) **Sir Charles G.D. Roberts** (1860)
Earthfasts (1966) **William Mayne** (1928)
Earthlight (1955) **Arthur C. Clarke** (1917)
Earthly Paradise, The [pt. iii] (1870) **William Morris** (1834)
Earthly Paradise, The [pts. i & ii] (1868) **William Morris** (1834)
Earthly Possessions (1977) **Anne Tyler** (1941)
Earthly Powers (1980) **'Anthony Burgess' [John Anthony Burgess Wilson]** (1917)
Earthly: Sonnets for Carlos (1975) **Ian Wedde** (1946)
Earthman, Come Home (1955) **James Blish** (1921)
Earthquake, The (1820) **John Galt** (1779)
Earthworks (1964) **Tony Harrison** (1937)
Earthworks (1965) **Brian Aldiss** (1925)
East (1975) **Steve[n] Berkoff** (1937)
East Coker (1940) **T.S. Eliot** (1888)
East End Idylls (1897) **A. St John Adcock** (1864)
East Indian, The (1799) **M.G. Lewis** (1775)
East into Upper East (1998) **Ruth Prawer Jhabvala** (1927)
East Lynne (1861) **Mrs Henry Wood** (1814)
East of Eden (1952) **John Steinbeck** (1902)
East, West (1994) **Salman Rushdie** (1947)
East Wind (1926) **Amy Lowell** (1874)
East Wind of Love, The (1937) **Compton Mackenzie** (1883)
East Wind, West Wind (1930) **Pearl S. Buck** (1892)
Easter, 1916 (1916) **W.B. Yeats** (1865)
Eastern Life, Past and Present (1848) **Harriet Martineau** (1802)
Eastern Schism, The (1955) **Sir Steven Runciman** (1903
Eastward Hoe (1605) **George Chapman** (1559?), **Ben Jonson** (1573?), and **John Marston** (1575?)
Eaten Heart, The (1933) **Richard Aldington** (1892)
Eating People is Wrong (1959) **Malcolm Bradbury** (1932)
Ebb-Tide, The (1894) **Robert Louis Stevenson** (1850) [with Lloyd Osbourne]
Eben Erskine (1833) **John Galt** (1779)
Ebony Tower, The [novellas] (1974) **John Fowles** (1926)
Ecce Homo (1866) **Sir John Seeley** (1834)
Ecce Homo (1908) **Friedrich Wilhelm Nietzsche** (1844)
Ecclesia (1840) **R.S. Hawker** (1803)
Ecclesia Restaurata (1661) **Peter Heylyn** (1600)
Ecclesia Vindicata (1657) **Peter Heylyn** (1600)
Ecclesiastical History of Great Britain, An [vol. i; vol. ii, 1714] (1708) **Jeremy Collier** (1650)
Ecclesiastical Memorials (1721) **John Strype** (1643)
Ecclesiastical Sketches (1822) **William Wordsworth** (1770)
Echarde, L' ['The Splinter'] (1966) **'Françoise Sagan' [Françoise Quoirez]** (1935)

Echo, The (1844) **Charles Fenno Hoffman** (1806)
Echo Club, The (1876) **Bayard Taylor** (1825)
Echo Gate, The (1979) **Michael Longley** (1939)
Echo's Bones and Other Precipitates (1935) **Samuel Beckett** (1906)
Echoing Green, The (1983) **Peter Levi** (1931)
Echoing Grove, The (1953) **Rosamond Lehmann** (1903)
Eclipse (2000) **John Banville** (1945)
Eclipse Fever (1993) **Walter Abish** (1931)
Eclogues (37 BC) **Virgil** (70 BC)
Eclogues (1530?) **Alexander Barclay** (1475?–1529)
Eclogues (1919) **Sir Herbert Read** (1893)
Eclogues of Virgil, The (1963) **C. Day Lewis** (1904) (tr.)
École des femmes, L' (1929) **André Gide** (1869)
Economic Consequences of Mr Churchill, The (1925) **J.M. Keynes** (1883)
Economic Consequences of the Peace, The (1919) **J.M. Keynes** (1883)
Economic Imperialism (1920) **Leonard Woolf** (1880)
Economic Studies (1880) **Walter Bagehot** (1826–77)
Economics and the Public Purpose (1973) **J.K. Galbraith** (1908)
Economy of Love, The (1736) **John Armstrong** (1709)
Ecstasy (1996) **Irvine Walsh** (1957)
Ecstasy Collection (1918) **'Anna Akhmatova' [Anna Andreevna Gorenko]** (1889)
Ecstasy of Dr Miriam Garner, The (1976) **Elaine Feinstein** (1930)
Eden (1891) **Robert Bridges** (1844)
Eden of the Imagination, The (1814) **J.H. Reynolds** (1796)
Edgar (1678) **Thomas Rymer** (1641)
Edgar Huntly (1799) **Charles Brockden Brown** (1771)
Edge of Being, The (1949) **Sir Stephen Spender** (1909)
Edge of Impossibility, The (1971) **Joyce Carol Oates** (1938)
Edge of the Alphabet, The (1962) **Janet Frame** (1924)
Edge of the Sea, The (1955) **Rachel Carson** (1907)
Edge-Hill (1767) **Richard Jago** (1715)
Edgewater People (1918) **Mary Wilkins Freeman** (1852)
Edible Woman, The (1969) **Margaret Atwood** (1939)
Edinburgh: Picturesque Notes (1878) **Robert Louis Stevenson** (1850)
Editorial Problem in Shakespeare, The (1942) **W.W. Greg** (1875)
Edmond (1982) **David Mamet** (1947)
Edmund Burke (1879) **John Morley** (1838)
Edmund Gosse (1984) **Ann Thwaite** (1932)
Edna, His Wife (1935) **Margaret Ayer Barnes** (1886)
Edom of Gordon (1755) **Sir David Dalrymple, Lord Hailes** (1726) (ed.)
Edsel (1971) **Karl Shapiro** (1913)
Educacion or Bringinge up of Children, The [from Plutarch] (1530) **Sir Thomas Elyot** (1490?) (tr.)
Educating Rita (1980) **Willy Russell** (1947)
Education and the Social Order (1932) **Bertrand Russell** (1872)
*Education of H*y*m*a*n K*a*p*l*n, The* [as 'Leonard Q. Ross'] (1937) **Leo Rosten** (1908)
Education of Henry Adams, The (1907) **Henry Adams** (1838)
Education of the Whole Man, The (1931) **L.P. Jacks** (1860)
Education of Uncle Paul, The (1909) **Algernon Blackwood** (1869)
Education of Young Gentlewomen, The [*Traité de l'education des filles*] (1678) **François Fénelon** (1651)
Edward (1796) **John Moore** (1729)
Edward and Eleonora (1739) **James Thomson** (1700)
Edward Barry, South Sea Pearler (1900) **Louis Becke** (1855)
Edward Fitzgerald (1905) **A.C. Benson** (1862)
Edward Marsh (1959) **Christopher Hassall** (1912)
Edward, the Blue Engine (1954) **Revd W. V. Awdry** (1911)
Edward Thomas in Heaven (1974) **P.J. Kavanagh** (1931)
Edwardians, The (1930) **Vita Sackville-West** (1892)
Edwards (1915) **'Barry Pain' [Eric Odell]** (1864)
Edwin and Eltruda (1782) **Helen Maria Williams** (1762)
Edwin Brothertoft (1862) **Theodore Winthrop** (1826)
Edwin the Fair (1842) **Sir Henry Taylor** (1800)
Effi Briest (1895) **Theodor Fontane** (1819)
Effie Hetherington (1896) **Robert Williams Buchanan** (1841)
Eglogs, Epytaphes, and Sonettes (1563) **Barnaby Googe** (1540)
Egmont (1788) **Johann Wolfgang von Goethe** (1749)
Ego (1935) **James Evershed Agate** (1877)
Egoist, The (1879) **George Meredith** (1828)
Egotism in German Philosophy (1916) **George Santayana** (1863)
Egyptian Journal, An (1985) **William Golding** (1911)
Egyptian Wanderers, The (1854) **John Mason Neale** (1818)
Eh Joe, and Other Writings (1967) **Samuel Beckett** (1906)
Eiffel Tower Wedding Party, The [*Les Mariés de la Tour Eiffel*] (1921) **Jean Cocteau** (1889)
Eiger Sanction, The (1972) **'Trevanian' [Rodney Whitaker]** (1925)
Eight Books of the Peloponnesian War [from Thucidides] (1629) **Thomas Hobbes** (1588) (tr.)
Eight Cousins (1875) **Louisa M. Alcott** (1832)
Eight Days of Luke (1975) **Diana Wynne Jones** (1934)
Eight Feet in the Andes (1983) **Dervla Murphy** (1931)
Eight Men (1961) **Richard Wright** (1908–60)
Eight Modern Writers (1963) **J.I.M. Stewart** (1906)
Eight Months on Ghazzah Street (1988) **Hilary Mantel** (1952)
Eight Mortal Ladies Possessed (1974) **'Tennessee' [Thomas Lanier] Williams** (1911)
Eight Short Stories (1937) **Alec Waugh** (1898)

Eight Victorian Poets [enlarg. as *Ten Victorian Poets* 1940] (1930) **F.L. Lucas** (1894)
Eight Years' Wanderings in Ceylon (1855) **Sir Samuel White Baker** (1821)
Eighteen Fifty One (1851) **Henry Mayhew** (1812) [with John Binny]
Eighteen Hundred and Eleven (1812) **Anna Laetitia Barbauld** (1743)
Eighteen Nineties, The (1913) **Holbrook Jackson** (1874)
Eighteen of Them (1894) **W. Pett Ridge** (1860)
Eighteen Poems (1934) **Dylan Thomas** (1914)
Eighteen Poems From 1966 (1967) **Ruth Fainlight** (1931)
Eighteen Seventy-Six (1976) **Gore Vidal** (1925)
Eighteenth-Century Studies (1912) **Austin Dobson** (1840)
Eighteenth Century Vignettes [1st ser.] (1892, 1894, 1896) **Austin Dobson** (1840)
Eighteenth-Century Background, The (1940) **Basil Willey** (1897)
Eighth Day, The (1967) **Thornton Wilder** (1897)
Eighty Sermons (1640) **John Donne** (1572–1631)
Eighty-Five Poems (1959) **Louis MacNeice** (1907)
Eikonoklastes (1649) **John Milton** (1608)
Eimi (1933) **E.E. Cummings** (1894)
Einstein Intersection, The (1967) **Samuel R. Delany** (1942)
Einstein's Monsters (1987) **Martin Amis** (1949)
Eirenicon, An [pt. i; pt. ii, 1869; pt. iii, 1870] (1865) **E.B. Pusey** (1800)
Elastic Retort, The (1974) **Kenneth Rexroth** (1905)
Elbow Room (1939) **Oliver St Gogarty** (1878)
Elder Brother, The (1637) **John Fletcher** (1579–1625)
Elder Conklin (1894) **'Frank' Harris** (1856)
Elder Statesman, The (1959) **T.S. Eliot** (1888)
Eldergowan (1874) **Rosa Mulholland** (1841)
Elders and Betters (1944) **I. Compton-Burnett** (1884)
Eleanor (1900) **Mrs T. Humphry Ward** (1851)
Eleanor's Victory (1863) **M.E. Braddon** (1835)
Eleanore, and Other Poems (1856) **Charles Hamilton AÏdé** (1826)
Elected Member, The [US: *The Chosen People*] (1969) **Bernice Rubens** (1923)
Elective Affinities [*Die Wahlverwandtschaften*] (1809) **Johann Wolfgang von Goethe** (1749)
Electra **Sophocles** (*c.* 496 BC)
Electra (*c.* 413) **Euripides** (480 BC)
Electra [*Elektra*] (1903) **Hugo von Hofmannsthal** (1874)
Électre (1937) **Jean Giraudoux** (1882)
Electric Kool-Aid Acid Test, The (1968) **Tom Wolfe** (1930)
Electricity (1995) **Victoria Glendinning** (1937)
Elegaic Sonnets [vol. ii] (1797) **Charlotte Smith** (1749)
Elegaic Sonnets, and Other Essays (1784) **Charlotte Smith** (1749)
Elegies (1763) **William Mason** (1724)
Elegies (1985) **Douglas Dunn** (1942)
Élégies ['Elegies'] (1893) **Paul Verlaine** (1844)
Elegy, An (1937) **Edmund Blunden** (1896)
Elegy for John Donne (1967) **Joseph Brodsky** (1940)
Elegy on Captain Cook (1780) **Anna Seward** (1747)
Elegy on Spain (1939) **George Barker** (1913)
Elegy on the Death of Prince Henry, An (1612) **Sir William Alexander** (1567?)
Elegy Upon King Charles the I, An (1648) **Henry King** (1592)
Elegy Wrote in a Country Church Yard, An (1751) **Thomas Gray** (1716)
Element of Doubt (1992) **A.L. Barker** (1918)
Elementals (1998) **A.S. Byatt** (1936)
Elementary Odes [*Odas elementales*] (1954) **Pablo Neruda** (1904)
Elementary Sketches of Moral Philosophy (1804) **Sydney Smith** (1771)
Elements of Architecture, The (1624) **Sir Henry Wotton** (1568)
Elements of Criticism (1762) **Henry Home, Lord Kames** (1696)
Elements of Drawing , The (1857) **John Ruskin** (1819)
Elements of Law [**Hobbes**]: see *De Corpore Politico*
Elements of Moral Science (1790) **James Beattie** (1735)
Elements of Morality for the Use of Children [from C.G. Salzmann] (1790) **Mary Wollstonecraft** (1759) (tr.)
Elements of Newton's Philosophy, The [*Eléments de la philosophie de Newton*] (1738) **'Voltaire' [François-Marie Arouet]** (1694)
Elements of Political Economy (1821) **James Mill** (1773)
Elements of Politics, The (1891) **Henry Sidgwick** (1838)
Elements of the Common Laws of England, The (1630) **Sir Francis Bacon** (1561–1626)
Elements of the Philosophy of the Human Mind [vol. i; vol. ii, 1827; vol. iii, 1847] (1792) **Dugald Stewart** (1753)
Eleonora (1692) **John Dryden** (1631)
Elephant Song (1991) **Wilbur Smith** (1933)
Elephant War, The (1960) **Gillian Avery** (1926)
Elephants Can Remember (1972) **Agatha Christie** (1890)
Eleven Essays in the European Novel (1964) **R.P. Blackmur** (1904)
Eleven Poems (1965) **Seamus Heaney** (1939)
Eleven Poems (1982) **Elizabeth Smart** (1913)
Eleven Poems on the Same Theme (1942) **Robert Penn Warren** (1905)
Elfin Artist, The (1920) **Alfred Noyes** (1880)
Elfrid (1710) **Aaron Hill** (1685)
Elfrida (1752) **William Mason** (1724)
Elia: Essays [1st ser.] (1823) **Charles Lamb** (1775)
Elia: Essays [2nd ser.; unauthorized] (1828) **Charles Lamb** (1775)
Elidor (1965) **Alan Garner** (1934)
Elijah's Ravens (1968) **Hal Porter** (1911)
Eliot (1885) **William Ellery Channing** (1780)
Elisa [*La File Élisa*] (1878) **Edmond de Goncourt** (1822)
Eliza (1705) **Sir Richard Blackmore** (1654)

Eliza (1900) **'Barry Pain' [Eric Odell]** (1864)
Eliza Getting On (1911) **'Barry Pain' [Eric Odell]** (1864)
Eliza's Husband (1903) **'Barry Pain' [Eric Odell]** (1864)
Eliza's Son (1913) **'Barry Pain' [Eric Odell]** (1864)
Elizabeth (1960) **'Evelyn Anthony' [Evelyn Ward-Thomas]** (1928)
Elizabeth Alone (1973) **'William Trevor' [William Trevor Cox]** (1928)
Elizabeth and Essex (1928) **Lytton Strachey** (1880)
Elizabeth and her German Garden (1898) **'Elizabeth' [Mary Annette Gräfin] von Arnim** (1866)
Elizabeth Appleton (1963) **John O'Hara** (1905)
Elizabeth Cooper (1913) **George Moore** (1852)
Elizabeth the Queen (1930) **Maxwell Anderson** (1888)
Elizabeth Visits America (1909) **Elinor Glyn** (1864)
Elizabeth's Pretenders (1895) **Charles Hamilton AÏdé** (1826)
Elizabethan Garland, An (1953) **A.L. Rowse** (1903)
Elizabethan Stage, The (1923) **Sir E.K. Chambers** (1866)
Elizabethan World-Picture, The (1943) **E.M.W. Tillyard** (1889)
Ellen and Julia (1793) **Eliza Parsons** (1748)
Ellen and the Queen (1972) **Gillian Avery** (1926)
Ellen Fitzarthur (1820) **Caroline Bowles** (1786)
Ellen Gray (1823) **William Lisle Bowles** (1762)
Ellen Middleton (1844) **Lady Georgiana Fullerton** (1812)
Ellen Rogers (1941) **James T. Farrell** (1904)
Ellen Terry and Bernard Shaw (1931) **Bernard Shaw** (1856)
Ellen's Birthday (1971) **Gillian Avery** (1926)
Elmer Gantry (1927) **Sinclair Lewis** (1885)
Elmerick (1740) **George Lillo** (1693–1739)
Éloges ['Eulogies'] (1911) **'Saint-John Perse' [Alexis Saint-Léger Léger]** (1887)
Eloquence of the British Senate, The (1807) **William Hazlitt** (1778)
Elsa (1959) **Louis Aragon** (1897)
Elsewhere, Perhaps (1966) **Amos Oz** (1939)
Elsie and the Child (1924) **Arnold Bennett** (1867)
Elsie Venner (1861) **Oliver Wendell Holmes** (1809)
Elsket, and Other Stories (1891) **Thomas Nelson Page** (1853)
Elusive Pimpernel, The (1908) **Baroness Orczy** (1865)
Elvira (1763) **David Mallet** (1705?)
E.M. Forster (1943) **Lionel Trilling** (1905)
Emancipated, The (1890) **George Gissing** (1857)
Émaux et camées ['Enamels and Cameos'] (1852) **Théophile Gautier** (1811)
Embarrassment of Riches, The (1987) **Simon Schama** (1945)
Embarrassments (1896) **Henry James** (1843)
Embezzler, The (1966) **Louis Auchinloss** (1917)
Emblemes (1635) **Francis Quarles** (1592)
Emblems of Love (1912) **Lascelles Abercrombie** (1881)
Emerald City (1987) **David Williamson** (1942)
Emergence of Jewish Statehood, The (1978) **Martin Gilbert** (1936)
Emigrant Ship, The (1893) **W. Clark Russell** (1844)
Emigrants of Ahadarra, The (1848) **William Carleton** (1794)
Emigrants, The (1793) **Gilbert Imlay** (1754)
Emigrants, The (1954) **George Lamming** (1927)
Emigrants, The (1793) **Charlotte Smith** (1749)
Emigré, L' ['The Emigrant'] (1907) **Paul Bourget** (1852)
Emil and the Detectives [*Emil und die Detektive*] (1928) **Erich Kästner** (1899)
Émile (1762) **Jean-Jacques Rousseau** (1712)
Emilia in England (1864) **George Meredith** (1828)
Emily (1975) **Jilly Cooper** (1937)
Emily Climbs (1925) **L.M. Montgomery** (1874)
Emily of New Moon (1923) **L.M. Montgomery** (1874)
Emily's Quest (1927) **L.M. Montgomery** (1874)
Eminent Victorians (1918) **Lytton Strachey** (1880)
Emma (1815) **Jane Austen** (1775)
Emma Corbett (1780) **Samuel Jackson Pratt** (1749)
Emmanuel Burden (1904) **Hilaire Belloc** (1870)
Emmeline (1819) **Mary Brunton** (1778–1818)
Emmeline (1788) **Charlotte Smith** (1749)
Emotions and the Will, The (1859) **Alexander Bain** (1818)
Empathy Experiment, The (1977) **David Foster** (1944)
Empedocles on Etna (1852) **Matthew Arnold** (1822)
Emperor (1978) **Colin Thubron** (1939)
Emperor Jones, The (1920) **Eugene O'Neill** (1888)
Emperor of Ice-Cream, The (1965) **Brian Moore** (1921)
Emperor of the Moon, The (1687) **Aphra Behn** (1640?)
Emperor Romanus Lecapenus, The (1929) **Sir Steven Runciman** (1903
Emperor's Candlesticks, The (1899) **Baroness Orczy** (1865)
Emperor's Snuffbox, The (1942) **John Dickson Carr** (1906)
Emperor's Winding-Sheet, The (1974) **Jill Paton Walsh** (1937)
Emperour of the East, The (1632) **Philip Massinger** (1583)
Empire (1987) **Gore Vidal** (1925)
Empire in the East, An (1993) **Norman Lewis** (1918)
Empire Makers, The (1900) **Hume Nisbet** (1849)
Empire of Fear, The (1988) **Brian M. Stableford** (1948)
Empire of the Senseless (1988) **Kathy Acker** (1948)
Empire of the Sun (1984) **J.G. Ballard** (1930)
Empire of the World (1910) **C.J. Cutcliffe Hyne** (1865)
Empress of Morocco, The (1673) **Elkanah Settle** (1648)
Empty House, The (1906) **Algernon Blackwood** (1869)
Empty Mirror (1960) **Allen Ginsberg** (1926)
Emu, Remember (1955) **Al Purdy** (1918)
En 18.. (1851) **Edmond** (1822) and **Jules** (1830) **de Goncourt**
En ménage (1881) **J.K. Huysmans** (1848)
En rade (1887) **J.K. Huysmans** (1848)

Encaenia (1623) **John Donne** (1572)
Enchafed Flood, The (1951) **W.H. Auden** (1907)
Enchanted, The (1947) **Martin Flavin** (1883)
Enchanted Castle, The (1907) **E[dith] Nesbit** (1858)
Enchanted Doll, The (1849) **Mark Lemon** (1809)
Enchanted Echo, The (1944) **Al Purdy** (1918)
Enchanted Garden, An (1892) **Mary Louisa Molesworth** (1839)
Enchanted Island, The (1909) **Alfred Noyes** (1880)
Enchanted Woods, The (1905) **'Vernon Lee' [Violet Paget]** (1856)
Enchantment, An (1991) **P.J. Kavanagh** (1931)
Enchantress, The (1908) **Edwin Pugh** (1874)
Enchiridion Militis Christiani (1503) **Erasmus** (*c.* 1467)
Enchyridion (1640) **Francis Quarles** (1592)
Enclosure, The (1961) **Susan Hill** (1942)
Encounters (1923) **Elizabeth Bowen** (1899)
Encouragement to Colonies, An (1624) **Sir William Alexander** (1567?)
Encyclopedia [Encyclopédie, ou Dictionnaire Raisonné des Sciences, des Arts et des Métiers] (1751) **Denis Diderot** (1713) (ed.)
End and a Beginning, An (1958) **James Hanley** (1901)
End and Beginning (1933) **John Masefield** (1878)
End of a Childhood, The (1934) **'Henry Handel Richardson' [Ethel Florence Robertson]** (1870)
End of a Life, The (1891) **Eden Phillpotts** (1862)
End of All Songs, The (1976) **Michael Moorcock** (1939)
End of an Age, The (1948) **W.R. Inge** (1860)
End of Desire, The (1931) **Robert Herrick** (1868)
End of Drought (1975) **Ruth Pitter** (1897)
End of Elfintown, The (1894) **Jane Barlow** (1857)
End of Eternity, The (1955) **Isaac Asimov** (1920)
End of Her Honeymoon, The (1914) **Mrs Belloc Lowndes** (1868)
End of It, The (1958) **A. Alvarez** (1929)
End of Solomon Grundy, The (1964) **Julian Symons** (1912)
End of the Affair, The (1951) **Graham Greene** (1904)
End of the Beginning, The (1943) **Sir Winston Churchill** (1874)
End of the Chapter (1935) **John Galsworthy** (1867)
End of the House of Alard, The (1923) **Sheila Kaye-Smith** (1887)
End of the Road, The (1958) **John Barth** (1930)
End of the World at the End of the Century (1992) **C.K. Stead** (1932)
End of the World News, The (1982) **'Anthony Burgess' [John Anthony Burgess Wilson]** (1917)
End of the World, The (1872) **Edward Eggleston** (1837)
End of the World, The (1973) **Mavis Gallant** (1922)
End to Autumn, An (1978) **Iain Crichton Smith [Iain Mac a'Ghobhainn]** (1928)
End to Torment [biography of Ezra Pound] (1958) **Hilda Doolittle** (1886)
End Zone (1972) **Don deLillo** (1936)
Enderby Outside (1968) **'Anthony Burgess' [John Anthony Burgess Wilson]** (1917)
Enderby's Dark Lady (1984) **'Anthony Burgess' [John Anthony Burgess Wilson]** (1917)
Endgame [pub. in French 1957] (1958) **Samuel Beckett** (1906)
Endimion and Phoebe (1595) **Michael Drayton** (1563)
Endimion, the Man in the Moone (1591) **John Lyly** (1554)
Ending Up (1974) **Kingsley Amis** (1922)
Endless Life (1981) **Lawrence Ferlinghetti** (1920)
Ends and Beginnings (1994) **Iain Crichton Smith [Iain Mac a'Ghobhainn]** (1928)
Enduring Love (1997) **Ian McEwan** (1948)
Enduring Spirit (1998) **Isabel Allende** (1942)
Endymion (1880) **Benjamin Disraeli** (1804)
Endymion (1818) **John Keats** (1795)
Enemies (1970) **Isaac Bashevis Singer** (1904)
Enemies of Promise (1938) **Cyril Connolly** (1903)
Enemies of the System (1978) **Brian Aldiss** (1925)
Enemy, The (1978) **Desmond Bagley** (1923)
Enemy at Green Knowe, An (1964) **Lucy Boston** (1892)
Enemy in the Blanket, The (1958) **'Anthony Burgess' [John Anthony Burgess Wilson]** (1917)
Enemy of the People, An (1882) **Henrik Ibsen** (1828)
Enemy of the Stars (1932) **Wyndham Lewis** (1882)
Enemy's Country, The (1991) **Geoffrey Hill** (1932)
Energy of Slaves, The (1972) **Leonard Cohen** (1934)
Enfant chargéde chaines, L' (1913) **François Mauriac** (1885)
Enfant d'Austerlitz, L' ['The Child of Austerlitz'] (1902) **Paul Adam** (1862)
Enfants Terribles, Les (1929) **Jean Cocteau** (1889)
Engage the Enemy More Closely (1991) **Correlli Barnett** (1927)
Engaging Form (1988) **Jeremy Reed** (1954)
England (1926) **W.R. Inge** (1860)
England and Her Soldiers (1859) **Harriet Martineau** (1802)
England and Ireland (1868) **J.S. Mill** (1806)
England, and Other Poems (1909) **Laurence Binyon** (1869)
England and Spain (1808) **Felicia Dorothea Hemans** (1793)
England and the English (1833) **Edward Bulwer-Lytton** (1803)
England and the Italian Question (1859) **Matthew Arnold** (1822)
England, England (1998) **Julian Barnes** (1946)
England Have My Bones (1936) **T.H. White** (1906)
England in the Age of the American Revolution (1930) **Sir Lewis Namier** (1888)
England in Time of War (1856) **Sydney Dobell** (1824)
England Made Me (1935) **Graham Greene** (1904)
England, My England (1922) [UK: *1924*] **D.H. Lawrence** (1885)
England Reclaimed (1927) **Sir Osbert Sitwell** (1892)
England, Their England (1933) **A.G. Macdonell** (1895)

England Under the Stuarts (1904) **G.M. Trevelyan** (1876)
England Under the Tudors (1955) **G.R. Elton** (1921)
England's Effort (1916) **Mrs T. Humphry Ward** (1851)
England's Ideal (1887) **Edward Carpenter** (1844)
England's Mourning Garment (1603) **Henry Chettle** (1560?)
England's Peril (1899) **William le Queux** (1864)
Englands Elizabeth (1631) **Thomas Heywood** (1574?)
Englands Epinomis (1683) **John Selden** (1584–1634)
Englands Heroicall Epistles (1597) **Michael Drayton** (1563)
English Agent, The (1969) **F.L. Lucas** (1894)
English Arcadia, The [pt. i; pt. ii 1613] (1607) **Gervaise Markham** (1568?)
English Assassin, The (1972) **Michael Moorcock** (1939)
English Bards, and Scotch Reviewers (1809) **[George Gordon, Lord Byron]** (1788)
English Battles and Sieges in the Peninsula (1852) **Sir William Napier** (1785)
English Bread and Yeast Cooking (1977) **Elizabeth David** (1913)
English Constitution, The (1867) **Walter Bagehot** (1826)
English Costume of the Eighteenth Century (1931) **James Laver** (1899)
English Dramatists of Today (1882) **William Archer** (1856)
English Epic and its Background, The (1954) **E.M.W. Tillyard** (1889)
English Excursions (1960) **Geoffrey Grigson** (1905)
English Frier, The (1690) **John Crowne** (d. 1703)
English Garden, The [bk i; bk ii 1776] (1772) **William Mason** (1724)
English Girl, An (1907) **Ford Madox Ford** (1873)
English History 1914–1945 (1965) **A.J.P. Taylor** (1906)
English Hours (1905) **Henry James** (1843)
English Humourists of the Eighteenth Century, The (1853) **W.M. Thackeray** (1811)
English Husbandman, The (1613) **Gervaise Markham** (1568?)
English in Ireland in the Eighteenth Century, The (1872) **J.A. Froude** (1818)
English in the West Indies, The (1888) **J.A. Froude** (1818) (ed.)
English Journey (1934) **J.B. Priestley** (1894)
English Literature and Society in the Eighteenth Century (1904) **Sir Leslie Stephen** (1832)
English Literature in Our Time and the University (1969) **F.R. Leavis** (1895)
English Literature in the Sixteenth Century (1954) **C.S. Lewis** (1898)
English Local Government (1906–29) **Sidney Webb** (1859) and **Beatrice Webb** (1858)
English Lover, The [*L'Amante anglaise*] (1967) **'Marguerite Duras' [Marguerite Donnadieu]** (1914)
English Madam, An (1982) **Paul Bailey** (1937)
English Merchant, The (1767) **George Colman, the Elder** (1732)
English Minstrelsy (1810) **Sir Walter Scott** (1771) (ed.)
English Misrule and Irish Deeds (1848) **Aubrey Thomas de Vere** (1814)
English Moralists, The (1964) **Basil Willey** (1897)
English Music (1992) **Peter Ackroyd** (1949)
English Myrror, The (1586) **George Whetstone** (*c.* 1551)
English Novel, The (1891) **Sir Walter Raleigh** (1861)
English Novel, The (1927) **J.B. Priestley** (1894)
English Novel, The (1954) **Walter Allen** (1911)
English Past, The (1951) **A.L. Rowse** (1903)
English Patient, The (1991) **Michael Ondaatje** (1943)
English Physitian Enlarged, The (1653) **Nicholas Culpeper** (1616)
English Poems (1892) **Richard le Gallienne** (1866)
English Poems (1926) **Edmund Blunden** (1896)
English Poetry (1950) **F.W. Bateson** (1901)
English Poetry 1900–1950 (1971) **C.H. Sisson** (1914)
English Prose Style (1928) **Sir Herbert Read** (1893)
English Rogue, The (1665) **Richard Head** (1637?)
English Romayne Lyfe, The (1582) **Anthony Munday** (1560)
English Social History (1942) **G.M. Trevelyan** (1876)
English Songs (1832) **'Barry Cornwall' [Bryan Waller Procter]** (1787)
English Spirit, The (1944) **A.L. Rowse** (1903)
English Squire, An (1881) **C[hristabel] R[ose] Coleridge** (1843)
English Subtitles (1981) **Peter Porter** (1929)
English Teacher, The [US: *Grateful to Life and Death*] (1945) **R.K. Narayan** (1907)
English Traits (1856) **Ralph Waldo Emerson** (1803)
English Traveller, The (1633) **Thomas Heywood** (1574?)
English Utilitarians, The (1900) **Sir Leslie Stephen** (1832)
English Women of Letters (1863) **Julia Kavanagh** (1824)
Englishman Abroad, An (1982) **Alan Bennett** (1934)
Englishman in Paris, The (1753) **Samuel Foote** (1720)
Englishman Returned from Paris, The (1756) **Samuel Foote** (1720)
Englishmans Docter, The [from Joannes de Mediolano] (1607) **Sir John Harington** (1560) (tr.)
Englishmen and Others (1956) **A.J.P. Taylor** (1906)
Englishwoman's Cooking-Book, The (1862) **Isabella Beeton** (1836)
Englishwoman's Family Library, The (1843) **Sarah [Mrs William] Ellis** (1812)
Englishwoman's Love Letters, An (1900) **Laurence Housman** (1865)
Engrafted Rose, The (1899) **E[mma] F[rances] Brooke** (1859?)
Enigma of Arrival, The (1987) **V.S. Naipaul** (1932)
Enigmaticall Characters (1658) **Richard Flecknoe** (*c.* 1620)
Enjoy (1980) **Alan Bennett** (1934)
Enjoyment of Laughter (1936) **Max Eastman** (1883)

Enjoyment of Poetry (1913) **Max Eastman** (1883)
Ennead, The (1978) **Jan Mark** (1943)
Enoch Arden (1864) **Alfred, Lord Tennyson** (1809)
Enormous Room, The (1922) **E.E. Cummings** (1894)
Enough of Green (1977) **Anne Stevenson** (1933)
Enough Rope (1926) **Dorothy Parker** (1893)
Enquirer, The (1797) **William Godwin** (1756)
Enquiry (1969) **Dick Francis** (1920)
Enquiry Concerning the Principles of Morals, An (1751) **David Hume** (1711)
Enquiry Concerning the Principles of Natural Knowledge, An (1919) **A.N. Whitehead** (1861)
Enquiry Concerning the Principles of Political Justice, An (1793) **William Godwin** (1756)
Enquiry into the Authenticity of the Poems Attributed to Thomas Rowley, An (1782) **Thomas Warton, the Younger** (1728)
Enquiry into the Causes of the Late Increase of Robbers, An (1751) **Henry Fielding** (1707)
Enquiry into the Occasional Conformity of Dissenters, An (1698) **Daniel Defoe** (1660)
Enquiry into the Present State of Polite Learning in Europe, An (1759) **Oliver Goldsmith** (1728)
Ensign Knightley (1901) **A.E.W. Mason** (1865)
Enslaved (1920) **John Masefield** (1878)
Ensorcelée, L' (1854) **J.A. Barbey-D'Aurevilly** (1808)
Entail, The (1823) **John Galt** (1779)
Entangled (1885) **E[mma] F[rances] Brooke** (1859?)
Enter a Free Man (1968) **Tom Stoppard** (1937)
Enter a Murderer (1935) **Ngaio Marsh** (1899)
Enter the Saint (1930) **'Leslie Charteris' [Leslie Charles Yin]** (1907)
Entertainer, The (1957) **John Osborne** (1929)
Entertaining Mr Sloane (1964) **Joe Orton** (1933)
Entertaining Strangers (1986) **David Edgar** (1948)
Enthusiasm (1751) **John Byrom** (1692)
Enthusiasm (1950) **Ronald Knox** (1888)
Enthusiasm (1831) **Susanna Moodie** (1803)
Enthusiasms of Robertson Davies, The (1979) **Robertson Davies** (1913)
Enthusiasmus Triumphatus (1656) **Henry More** (1614)
Enthusiast, An (1921) **'Somerville and Ross' [Edith Somerville]** (1858) and **Violet Martin** (1862)
Enthusiast, The (1744) **Joseph Warton** (1722)
Envious Casca (1941) **Georgette Heyer** (1902)
Environment (1922) **Phyllis Bentley** (1894)
Envoy Extraordinary (1937) **E. Phillips Oppenheim** (1866)
Envoy From Mirror City, The (1985) **Janet Frame** (1924)
Eothen (1844) **A.W. Kinglake** (1809)
Épaves, Les (1866) **Charles Baudelaire** (1821)
Epea Pteroenta; or, The Diversions of Purley (1786) **John Horne Tooke** (1736)
Ephemera Critica (1901) **John Churton Collins** (1848)
Ephemerides (1828) **Thomas Pringle** (1789)
Ephemerides of Phialo, The (1579) **Stephen Gosson** (1554)
Epic, The (1914) **Lascelles Abercrombie** (1881)
Epic and Romance (1897) **W.P. Ker** (1855)
Epic of Arkansas, The (1936) **John Gould Fletcher** (1886)
Epic of Women, An (1870) **Arthur O'Shaughnessy** (1844)
Epicoene (1609/10) **Ben Jonson** (1572)
Epicurean, The (1827) **Thomas Moore** (1779)
Epidemic (1961) **Frank G. Slaughter** (1908)
Epigrammes (1599) **John Weever** (1576)
Epigrams (1669) **Richard Flecknoe** (*c.* 1620)
Epigrams (1641) **Sir Thomas Urquhart** (1611)
Epigrams Both Pleasant and Serious (1615) **Sir John Harington** (1560–1612)
Epipsychidion (1821) **P.B. Shelley** (1792)
Episcopacie by Divine Right Asserted (1640) **Joseph Hall** (1574)
Episode in Palmetto (1950) **Erskine Caldwell** (1903)
Epistle from a Nobleman to a Doctor of Divinity, An (1733) **John Hervey, 2nd Baron Hervey** (1696)
Epistle of Comfort, An (1587) **Robert Southwell SJ** (1561?)
Epistle, The [Oct. 1588] (1588) **'Martin Marprelate'**
Epistle to a Friend, An (1798) **Samuel Rogers** (1763)
Epistle to Admirall Keppel (1779) **William Hayley** (1745)
Epistle to a Godson (1972) **W.H. Auden** (1907)
Epistle to Curio, An (1744) **Mark Akenside** (1721)
Epistle to Dr Arbuthnot, An (1734) **Alexander Pope** (1688)
Epistle to Mr Pope, An (1730) **George Lyttelton, 1st Baron Lyttelton** (1709)
Epistle to Peter Pindar (1800) **William Gifford** (1756)
Epistle to the Right Honourable Richard Earl of Burlington, An (1731) **Alexander Pope** (1688)
Epistle to the Right Honourable Richard Lord Visct. Cobham, An ['Of the Knowledge and Characters of Men'] (1733) **Alexander Pope** (1688)
Epistle to the Right Honourable the Lord Lansdowne, An (1713) **Edward Young** (1683)
Epistle to William Hogarth, An (1763) **Charles Churchill** (1731)
Epistles [bk i] (20 BC) **Horace (Quintus Horatius Flaccus**, 65–8 BC)
Epistles [bk ii] (14 BC?) **Horace (Quintus Horatius Flaccus**, 65–8 BC)
Epistles, Odes and Other Poems (1806) **Thomas Moore** (1779)
Epistles on Women (1810) **Lucy Aikin** (1781)
Epistles the First Volume [vol. ii, 1608] (1608) **Joseph Hall** (1574)
Epistles to Several Persons (1973) **John Fuller** (1937)
Epitaph for a Spy (1938) **Eric Ambler** (1909)
Epitaph of Sir Phillip Sidney, The (1586) **Thomas Churchyard** (1520?)
Epitaphs and Occasions (1940) **Roy Fuller** (1912)
Epithalamium in Time of War (1941) **Ralph Gustafson** (1909)
Epitome, The [Nov. 1588] (1588) **'Martin Marprelate'**
E. Pluribus Unicorn (1953) **Theodore Sturgeon** (1918)
Epoch of Reform 1830–1850, The (1882) **Justin McCarthy** (1830)

Epodes (30 BC) **Horace** (Quintus Horatius Flaccus, 65–8 BC)
Epping Hunt, The (1829) **Thomas Hood** (1799)
Epsom Downs (1977) **Howard Brenton** (1942)
Epsom-Wells (1672) **Thomas Shadwell** (1642?)
Epullia (1855) **R.D. Blackmore** (1825)
Equal Distance (1985) **Brad Leithauser** (1953)
Equal Skies, The (1980) **Norman MacCaig** (1910)
Equality (1931) **R.H. Tawney** (1880)
Equinox (1966) **Eva Figes** (1932)
Equal Music, An (1999) **Vikram Seth** (1952)
Equus (1973) **Peter Shaffer** (1926)
Erasers, The [*Les Gommes*] (1953) **Alain Robbe-Grillet** (1922)
Erb (1903) **W. Pett Ridge** (1860)
Erechtheus (1876) **A. C. Swinburne** (1837)
Erema (1877) **R.D. Blackmore** (1825)
Eremus (1894) **Stephen Phillips** (1864)
Erewhon (1872) **Samuel Butler** (1835)
Erewhon Revisited (1901) **Samuel Butler** (1835)
Eric (1989) **Terry Pratchett** (1948)
Eric (1858) **Frederic W. Farrar** (1831)
Eric Brighteyes (1891) **Sir H. Rider Haggard** (1856)
Erik Dorn (1921) **Ben Hecht** (1894)
Erik XIV (1899) **August Strindberg** (1849)
Erin (1822) **Thomas Haynes Bayly** (1797)
Erling the Bold (1869) **R.M. Ballantyne** (1825)
Ermine, The [*L'Hermine*] (1932) **Jean Anouilh** (1910)
Ermine, The [*Poems*] (1953) **Ruth Pitter** (1897)
Erminia (1661) **Richard Flecknoe** (*c.* 1620)
Ernest Maltravers (1837) **Edward Bulwer-Lytton** (1803)
Eros and Psyche (1885) **Robert Bridges** (1844)
Eros in Dogma (1944) **George Barker** (1913)
Errata (1823) **John Neal** (1793)
Errata of Ovid, The (1983) **Ian Hamilton Finlay** (1925)
Error of Judgement, An (1962) **Pamela Hansford Johnson** (1912)
Errors of Ecstasie, The (1822) **George Darley** (1795)
Errors of Education, The (1791) **Eliza Parsons** (1748)
Errors of Innocence, The (1786) **Harriet Lee** (1756)
Escapade (1953) **Rex Warner** (1905)
Escape (1926) **John Galsworthy** (1867)
Escape on Venus (1946) **Edgar Rice Burroughs** (1875)
Escape to Reality (1977) **David Foster** (1944)
Esclaves de Paris, Les (1869) **Émile Gaboriau** (1832)
Esmerelda (1881) **William Gillette** (1855)
Esmond in India (1958) **Ruth Prawer Jhabvala** (1927)
Esoteric Christianity (1901) **Annie Besant** (1847)
Espalièr, The (1925) **Sylvia Townsend Warner** (1893)
Espousals, The [*The Angel in the House* ii] (1856) **Coventry Patmore** (1823)
Esprit de corps (1957) **Lawrence Durrell** (1912)
Esprit nouveau et les poètes, L' ['The New Spirit and the Poets'] (1946) **'Guillaume Apollinaire' [Wilhelm de Kostrowitsky]** (1880–1918)
Essais (1883) **Paul Bourget** (1852)
Essay Concerning Humane Understanding, An (1690) **John Locke** (1632)
Essay Concerning Preaching, An (1678) **Joseph Glanvill** (1636)
Essay Concerning the Laws of Nations and the Rights of Sovereigns, An (1693) **Matthew Tindal** (1657)
Essay on a Course of Liberal Education , An (1765) **Joseph Priestley** (1733)
Essay on Acting, An (1744) **David Garrick** (1717) attrib.
Essay on Comedy, An (1897) **George Meredith** (1828)
Essay on Criticism, An (1728) **John Oldmixon** (1673)
Essay on Criticism, An (1711) **Alexander Pope** (1688)
Essay on Epic Poetry, An (1782) **William Hayley** (1745)
Essay on History, An (1780) **William Hayley** (1745)
Essay on Man, An [4 epistles pub. separately; pub. together 1734] (1733–4) **Alexander Pope** (1688)
Essay on Metaphysics, An (1940) **R.G. Collingwood** (1889)
Essay on Mind, An (1826) **E.B. Browning** (1806)
Essay on Philosophical Method, An (1933) **R.G. Collingwood** (1889)
Essay on Revolutions [*Essai sur les révolutions anciennes et modernes*] (1797) **François-René, vicomte de Chateaubriand** (1768)
Essay on Ridicule, An (1743) **William Whitehead** (1715)
Essay on Sculpture, An (1800) **William Hayley** (1745)
Essay on Sepulchres (1809) **William Godwin** (1756)
Essay on the Development of Christian Doctrine, An (1845) **J.H. Newman** (1801)
Essay on the Different Stiles of Poetry, An (1713) **Thomas Parnell** (1679)
Essay on the First Book of De Rerum Natura, An (1656) **John Evelyn** (1620)
Essay on the First Principles of Government, An (1768) **Joseph Priestley** (1733)
Essay on the History and Reality of Apparitions, An (1727) **Daniel Defoe** (1660)
Essay on the History of Civil Society, An (1767) **Adam Ferguson** (1723)
Essay on the History of Parties, and Persecution in Britain, An (1711) **Daniel Defoe** (1660)
Essay on the Manners and Genius of the Literary Character, An (1795) **Isaac D'Israeli** (1766)
Essay on the Memory of the Late Queen, An (1695) **Gilbert Burnet** (1643)
Essay on the Nature and Immutability of Truth, An (1770) **James Beattie** (1735)
Essay on the Nature of Contemporary England, A (1937) **Hilaire Belloc** (1870)
Essay on the Opera's After the Italian Manner, An (1706) **John Dennis** (1657)
Essay on the Origin of the English Stage, An (1793) **Thomas Percy** (1729)
Essay on the Population of England, An (1780) **Richard Price** (1723)
Essay on the Principle of Population, An (1798) **T.R. Malthus** (1766)

Essay on the Principles of Human Action, An (1805) **William Hazlitt** (1778)
Essay on the Regulation of the Press, An (1704) **Daniel Defoe** (1660)?
Essay on the Slavery and Commerce of the Human Species, An (1786) **Thomas Clarkson** (1760)
Essay on the South-Sea Trade, An (1711) **Daniel Defoe** (1660)
Essay on the Writings and Genius of Pope, An [vol. i] (1756, 1782) **Joseph Warton** (1722)
Essay on Translated Verse, An (1684) **Wentworth Dillon, 4th earl of Roscommon** (1633)
Essay Towards a New Theory of Vision, An (1709) **George Berkeley** (1685)
Essay Towards a Theory of Art, An (1922) **Lascelles Abercrombie** (1881)
Essay Towards Preventing the Ruin of Great Britain, An (1721) **George Berkeley** (1685)
Essay Upon Literature; An (1726) **Daniel Defoe** (1660)
Essay upon Poetry, An (1682) **John Sheffield, duke of Buckingham** (1648)
Essay Upon Projects, An (1697) **Daniel Defoe** (1660)
Essay Upon Publick Spirit, An (1711) **John Dennis** (1657)
Essay upon the Advancement of Trade in Ireland, An (1673) **Sir William Temple** (1628)
Essay upon the Genius and Writings of Shakespear, An (1712) **John Dennis** (1657)
Essay Upon Two of Virgil's Eclogues, An (1658) **James Harrington** (1611) (tr.)
Essayes in Divinity (1651) **John Donne** (1572–1631)
Essayes of a Prentise, The (1584) **King James I** (1566)
Essayes or Morall Politicke and Militaire Discourses, The [Montaigne] (1603) **John Florio** (1553)
Essays [bks i-ii; enlarg. 1588] (1580) **Michel de Montaigne** (1533)
Essays (1597) **Sir Francis Bacon** (1561)
Essays (1612) **Sir Francis Bacon** (1561)
Essays (1765) **Oliver Goldsmith** (1728)
Essays (1841) **Ralph Waldo Emerson** (1803)
Essays (1889) **Mark Pattison** (1813–84)
Essays Ancient and Modern (1936) **T.S. Eliot** (1888)
Essays and Historiettes (1903) **Sir Walter Besant** (1836)
Essays and Interviews (1984) **Joan Didion** (1934)
Essays and Studies (1895) **John Churton Collins** (1848)
Essays and Studies (1875) **A.C. Swinburne** (1837)
Essays and Treatises on Several Subjects (1753–1756) **David Hume** (1711)
Essays Biographical and Critical (1856) **David Masson** (1822)
Essays, Chiefly on Questions of Church and State (1870) **Arthur Penrhyn Stanley** (1815)
Essays Critical and Historical (1872) **J.H. Newman** (1801)
Essays, Critical and Imaginative (1866) **John Wilson** (1785–1854)
Essays in Biography (1933) **J.M. Keynes** (1883)
Essays in Common Sense Philosophy (1919) **C.E.M. Joad** (1891)
Essays in Critical Dissent (1972) **F.W. Bateson** (1901)
Essays in Criticism [1st ser.] (1865) **Matthew Arnold** (1822)
Essays in Criticism [2nd ser.] (1888) **Matthew Arnold** (1822)
Essays in Criticism: Third Series (1910) **Matthew Arnold** (1822–88)
Essays in Ecclesiastical Biography (1849) **Sir James Stephen** (1789)
Essays in London and Elsewhere (1893) **Henry James** (1843)
Essays in Persuasion (1931) **J.M. Keynes** (1883)
Essays in Positive Economics (1953) **Milton Friedman** (1912)
Essays in Rhyme (1816) **Jane Taylor** (1783)
Essays in Verse (1891) **May Sinclair** (1863)
Essays in Wartime (1916) **Havelock Ellis** (1859)
Essays, Letters from Abroad, Translations and Fragments (1840) **P.B. Shelley** (1792–1822)
Essays Moral and Political [vol. i] (1741) **David Hume** (1711)
Essays, Moral and Political (1832) **Robert Southey** (1774)
Essays of a Biologist (1923) **Julian Huxley** (1887)
Essays of a Catholic Layman in England (1931) **Hilaire Belloc** (1870)
Essays of a Humanist (1964) **Julian Huxley** (1887)
Essays of an Ex-librarian (1901) **Richard Garnett** (1835)
Essays of Four Decades (1969) **Allen Tate** (1899)
Essays on Art (1866) **Francis Turner Palgrave** (1824)
Essays on Fiction (1864) **Nassau Senior** (1790)
Essays on Freethinking and Plainspeaking (1873) **Sir Leslie Stephen** (1832)
Essays on Gothic Architecture (1800) **Thomas Warton, the Younger** (1728–90) et al.
Essays on Life, Art and Science (1904) **Samuel Butler** (1835–1902)
Essays on Literature and Philosophy (1892) **Edward Caird** (1835)
Essays on Literature and Society (1949) **Edwin Muir** (1887)
Essays on Philosophical Subjects (1795) **Adam Smith** (1723–90)
Essays on Professional Education (1809) **Richard Lovell Edgeworth** (1744) [with Maria Edgeworth]
Essays on Several Important Subjects (1676) **Joseph Glanvill** (1636)
Essays on Some Unsettled Questions of Political Economy (1844) **J.S. Mill** (1806)
Essays on the Active Powers of Man (1788) **Thomas Reid** (1710)
Essays on the Intellectual Powers of Man (1785) **Thomas Reid** (1710)
Essays on the Nature and Principles of Taste (1790) **Archibald Alison** (1757)
Essays on the Principles of Human Action (1836) **William Hazlitt** (1778–1830)

Essays on the Principles of Morality and Natural Religion (1751) **Henry Home, Lord Kames** (1696)
Essays on Truth and Reality (1914) **F.H. Bradley** (1846)
Essays on Various Subjects (1772) **Catherine Talbot** (1721–70)
Essays on Various Subjects (1777) **Hannah More** (1745)
Essays or Counsels, Civll and Moral, The (1625) **Sir Francis Bacon** (1561)
Essays Sceptical and Anti-sceptical (1858) **Thomas de Quincey** (1785)
Essays Scientific, Political, and Speculative [1st ser.; 2nd ser., 1863] (1858) **Herbert Spencer** (1820)
Essays Speculative and Political (1920) **A.J. Balfour** (1848)
Essays Speculative and Suggestive (1890) **John Addington Symonds** (1840)
Essays Theological and Literary (1871) **R.H. Hutton** (1826)
Essays Upon Several Subjects Concerning British Antiquities (1747) **Henry Home, Lord Kames** (1696)
Essence of Christianity, The [as Marian Evans] (1854) **'George Eliot' [Mary Ann Evans]** (1819) (tr.)
Essence of Christianity, The [*Das Wesen des Christentums*] (1841) **Ludwig Feuerbach** (1804)
Essential Shakespeare, The (1932) **John Dover Wilson** (1881)
Essentials of Mysticism, The (1920) **Evelyn Underhill** (1875)
Essentials of Spiritual Unity, The (1918) **Ronald Knox** (1888)
Essex Poems (1969) **Donald Davie** (1922)
Estate, The (1969) **Isaac Bashevis Singer** (1904)
Estate of Poetry, The (1962) **Edwin Muir** (1887)
Esther (1884) **Henry Adams** (1838)
Esther (1887) **Rosa Nouchette Carey** (1840)
Esther, Love Lyrics, and Natalia's Resurrection (1892) **Wilfrid Scawen Blunt** (1840)
Esther Waters (1894) **George Moore** (1852)
Estimates of Some Englishmen and Scotchmen (1858) **Walter Bagehot** (1826)
Esto Perpetua (1906) **Hilaire Belloc** (1870)
Estrangement (1986) **Elechi Amadi** (1934)
Estuary, The (1971) **Patricia Beer** (1924)
Et Cetera (1930) **Augustine Birrell** (1850)
Etape, L' ['The Halting-Place'] (1902) **Paul Bourget** (1852)
Etched in Moonlight (1928) **James Stephens** (1882)
Eternal Champion, The (1970) **Michael Moorcock** (1939)
Eternal City, The (1901) **Hall Caine** (1853)
Eternal Moment, The (1928) **E.M. Forster** (1879)
Eternal Now, The (1963) **Paul Tillich** (1886)
Eternal Priesthood, The (1883) **Henry Edward Manning** (1808)
Eternity to Season (1954) **Wilson Harris** (1921)
Ethan Frome (1911) **Edith Wharton** (1862)
Ethel Churchill [as 'L.E.L.'] (1837) **Letitia Elizabeth Landon** (1802)
Ethelinda (1789) **Charlotte Smith** (1749)
Ethelstan (1841) **George Darley** (1795)
Ethical Studies (1876) **F.H. Bradley** (1846)
Ethics (1912) **G.E. Moore** (1873)
Ethics of Conformity and Subscription, The (1870) **Henry Sidgwick** (1838)
Ethics of the Dust, The (1866) **John Ruskin** (1819)
Ethnic Radio (1977) **Les Murray** (1938)
Eton and King's (1926) **M.R. James** (1862)
Eton in the 'Eighties (1914) **Eric Parker** (1870)
Etruscan Places (1932) **D.H. Lawrence** (1885–1930)
Etymological Dictionary of the English Language, An (1879) **W.W. Skeat** (1835)
Eudemian Ethics **Aristotle** (384 BC)
Eugene Aram (1832) **Edward Bulwer-Lytton** (1803)
Eugene Onegin (1823–1831) **Alexander Pushkin** (1799)
Eugenia and Adelaide (1791) **Frances Sheridan** (1724–66)
Eugenics, and Other Evils (1922) **G.K. Chesterton** (1874)
Eugénie (1767) **Pierre Augustin Caron de Beaumarchais** (1732)
Eugénie Grandet (1833) **Honoré de Balzac** (1799)
Eugenius (1785) **Richard Graves** (1715)
Eupalinos (1924) **Paul-Ambroise Valéry** (1871)
Euphemia (1790) **Charlotte Lennox** (1720)
Euphorion (1884) **'Vernon Lee' [Violet Paget]** (1856)
Euphranor (1851) **Edward FitzGerald** (1809)
Euphrates [as 'Eugenius Philalethes'] (1655) **Thomas Vaughan** (1622)
Euphrosyne [vol. i] (1776) **Richard Graves** (1715)
Euphues (1578) **John Lyly** (1554)
Euphues and his England (1580) **John Lyly** (1554)
Euphues his Censure to Philautus (1587) **Robert Greene** (1558)
Euphues Shadow, the Battaile of the Sences (1592) **Thomas Lodge** (1558)
Eureka: A Prose Poem (1848) **Edgar Allan Poe** (1809)
Europa and the Bull (1952) **W.R. Rodgers** (1909)
Europa [etc] (1649) **Thomas Stanley the elder** (1625)
Europa's Lover (1982) **Douglas Dunn** (1942)
Europe (1794) **William Blake** (1757)
Europe (1809) **Reginald Heber** (1783)
Europe and the Faith (1920) **Hilaire Belloc** (1870)
Europe in Decay (1950) **Sir Lewis Namier** (1888)
Europe in the Looking-Glass (1926) **Robert Byron** (1905)
Europe Without Baedeker (1947) **Edmund Wilson** (1895)
European Powers, The (1965) **Martin Gilbert** (1936)
European Witness (1946) **Sir Stephen Spender** (1909)
Europeans, The (1878) **Henry James** (1843)
Eurydice (1731) **David Mallet** (1705?)
Eustace and Hilda (1947) **L.P. Hartley** (1895)
Eustace Chisholm and the Works (1967) **James Purdy** (1923)

Eustace Conway; or, The Brother and Sister (1834) **F.D. Maurice** (1805)
Eustace Conyers (1855) **James Hannay** (1827)
Eustace Diamonds, The (1873) **Anthony Trollope** (1815)
Eutaw (1856) **William Gilmore Simms** (1806)
Eva [etc] (1842) **Edward Bulwer-Lytton** (1803)
Eva Luna (1987) **Isabel Allende** (1942)
Eva St Clair (1843) **G.P.R. James** (1799)
Eva Trout (1968) **Elizabeth Bowen** (1899)
Evacuees, The (1975) **Jack Rosenthal** (1931)
Evadne (1819) **Richard Lalor Sheil** (1791)
Evagatory (1992) **Peter Reading** (1946)
Evan Harrington (1860) **George Meredith** (1828)
Evangeline (1847) **Henry Wadsworth Longfellow** (1807)
Evangelist, The [*L'Évangéliste*] (1883) **Alphonse Daudet** (1840)
Evangelista's Fan (1994) **Rose Tremain** (1943)
Evans Country, The (1962) **Kingsley Amis** (1922)
Eve (1888) **S. Baring-Gould** (1834)
Eve (1867) **Pierce Egan, the Younger** (1814)
Eve of Saint John, The (1800) **Sir Walter Scott** (1771)
Eve of St Mark, The (1942) **Maxwell Anderson** (1888)
Eve of St Venus, The (1964) **'Anthony Burgess' [John Anthony Burgess Wilson]** (1917)
Eve of the Conquest, The (1847) **Sir Henry Taylor** (1800)
Eve's Ransom (1895) **George Gissing** (1857)
Evelina (1778) **Frances Burney** (1752)
Evelyn (1849) **Selina Bunbury** (1802)
Evelyn Byrd (1904) **George Cary Eggleston** (1839)
Evelyn Innes (1898) **George Moore** (1852)
Even Cowgirls Get the Blues (1976) **Tom Robbins** (1936)
Even Your Right Eye (1956) **Phylllis Webb** (1921)
Evening (1912) **'Anna Akhmatova' [Anna Andreevna Gorenko]** (1889)
Evening (1821) **T.B. Macaulay** (1800)
Evening in Byzantium (1973) **Irwin Shaw** (1913)
Evening News, The (1990) **Arthur Hailey** (1920)
Evening of Adam, The (1994) **'Alice Thomas Ellis' [Anna Margaret Haycraft]** (1932)
Evening of the Holiday, The (1966) **Shirley Hazzard** (1931)
Evening Star, The (1992) **Larry McMurty** (1936)
Evening Thought, An (1760) **Jupiter Hammon** (1720)
Evening under the Lamplight (1959) **David Campbell** (1915)
Evening Walk, An (1793) **William Wordsworth** (1770)
Evening with Monsieur Teste, An [*La Soirée avec Monsieur Teste*] (1896) **Paul-Ambroise Valéry** (1871)
Evening's Love, An (1668) **John Dryden** (1631)
Evenings at Home (1792) **Anna Laetitia Barbauld** (1743)
Evenings on a Farm Near Dikanka (1831–2) **Nikolai Vasilevich Gogol** (1809)
Events and Wisdoms (1964) **Donald Davie** (1922)
Events While Guarding the Bofors Gun (1966) **John McGrath** (1935)
Ever After (1992) **Graham Swift** (1949)
Ever-Interesting Topic, The (1953) **'William Cooper' [Harry Summerfield Hoff]** (1910)
Everlasting Man, The (1925) **G.K. Chesterton** (1874)
Everlasting Mercy, The (1911) **John Masefield** (1878)
Every Day is Mother's Day (1985) **Hilary Mantel** (1952)
Every Day is Saturday (1934) **E.B. White** (1899)
Every Good Boy Deserves Favour (1977) **Tom Stoppard** (1937)
Every Living Thing (1992) **James Herriot** (1916)
Every Man for Himself (1996) **Beryl Bainbridge** (1934)
Every Man in His Humor (1598) **Ben Jonson** (1572)
Every Man in His Humour (1752) **David Garrick** (1717)
Every Man in his Own Way (1741) **Stephen Duck** (1705)
Every Man Out of his Humor (1599) **Ben Jonson** (1572)
Every One Has His Fault (1793) **Elizabeth Inchbald** (1753)
Everybody's Autobiography (1937) **Gertrude Stein** (1874)
Everybody's Political What's What (1944) **Bernard Shaw** (1856)
Everyman [*Jedermann*] (1912) **Hugo von Hofmannsthal** (1874)
Everyone But Thee and Me (1962) **Ogden Nash** (1902)
Everything That Rises Must Converge (1965) **Flannery O'Connor** (1925)
Everything to Live For (1968) **Paul Horgan** (1903)
Everything You Need (1999) **A.L. Kennedy** (1965)
Evesong (1975) **Maureen Duffy** (1933)
Evidence as to Man's Place in Nature (1863) **T.H. Huxley** (1825)
Evidence for the Resurrection of Jesus Christ, The (1865) **Samuel Butler** (1835)
Evidence of Love (1974) **Shirley Ann Grau** (1929)
Evidence of Love (1960) **Dan Jacobson** (1929)
Evidences of the Christian Religion (1786) **James Beattie** (1735)
Evil Eye, The (1860) **William Carleton** (1794)
Evil Genius, The (1886) **Wilkie Collins** (1824)
Evil May-Day (1882) **William Allingham** (1824)
Evil Streak, An (1977) **Andrea Newman** (1938)
Evil That Men Do, The (1996) **Brian Masters** (1939)
Evil Under the Sun (1941) **Agatha Christie** (1890)
Evil Was Abroad (1938) **John Lehmann** (1907)
Evolution (1942) **Julian Huxley** (1887)
Evolution and Ethics (1893) **T.H. Huxley** (1825)
Evolution in Action (1953) **Julian Huxley** (1887)
Evolution of an Intellectual, The (1920) **John Middleton Murry** (1889)
Evolution of Modesty, The (1899) **Havelock Ellis** (1859)
Evolution of Parliament, The (1920) **A.F. Pollard** (1869)
Evolution of Religion, The (1893) **Edward Caird** (1835)
Evolution of Theology in the Greek Philosophers, The (1904) **Edward Caird** (1835)

Evolution, Old and New (1879) **Samuel Butler** (1835)
Ewart Quarto, The (1984) **Gavin Ewart** (1916)
Ewings, The (1972) **John O'Hara** (1905)
Ex Voto (1888) **Samuel Butler** (1835)
Exact Catalogue of all the Comedies That Were Ever Printed or Published, An (1680) **Gerard Langbaine the younger** (1656)
Exact Name, The (1965) **Nissim Ezekiel** (1924)
Exactions (1980) **C.H. Sisson** (1914)
Examen Miscellaneum (1702) **Charles Gildon** (1665) (ed.)
Examen Poeticum: Being the Third Part of Miscellany Poems (1693) **John Dryden** (1631) and others
Examination and Death of the Martyr Sir John Oldcastle, The (1544) **John Bale** (1495)
Examination of Hamilton's Philosophy, An (1865) **J.S. Mill** (1806)
Examination of Mr Pope's Essay on Man [from J.P. Crousaz] (1739) **Elizabeth Carter** (1717) (tr.)
Example of Virtue, The (1504?) **Stephen Hawes** (d. 1523?)
Example, The (1637) **James Shirley** (1596)
Excellency of Good Women, The (1613) **Barnabe Rich** (1542)
Excellent Women (1952) **Barbara Pym** (1913)
Except the Lord (1953) **Joyce Cary** (1888)
Excursion, The (1728) **David Mallet** (1705?)
Excursion, The (1777) **Frances Brooke** (1724)
Excursion, The (1814) **William Wordsworth** (1770)
Excursions (1863) **Henry David Thoreau** (1817–62)
Excursions in Victorian Bibliography (1922) **Michael Sadleir** (1888)
Execration Against Vulcan (1640) **Ben Jonson** (1572–1637)
Execution of Sir Charles Baldwin, The (1772) **Thomas Chatterton** (1752–70)
Executioner Waits, The (1934) **Josephine Herbst** (1897)
Executioner's Song, The (1979) **Norman Mailer** (1923)
Exemplarie Novells (1640) **James Mabbe** (1572) (tr.)
Exemplary Novels [*Novelas ejemplares*] (1613) **Miguel de Cervantes Saavedra** (1547)
Exemplary Theatre, The (1922) **Harley Granville-Barker** (1877)
Exercises in Style [*Exercices de style*] (1947) **Raymond Queneau** (1903)
Exhumations (1966) **Christopher Isherwood** (1904)
Exil ['Exile'] (1942) **'Saint-John Perse' [Alexis Saint-Léger Léger]** (1887)
Exile (1923) **Richard Aldington** (1892)
Exile, An (1967) **Madison Jones** (1925)
Exile and the Kingdom [*L'Exil et le royaume*] (1958) **Albert Camus** (1913)
Exiled (1929) **John Galsworthy** (1867)
Exiles, The (1894) **Richard Harding Davis** (1864)
Exiles (1918) **James Joyce** (1882)
Exiles, The (1952) **Henry Treece** (1911)
Exiles (1984) **Iain Crichton Smith [Iain Mac a'Ghobhainn]** (1928)
Exiles and Emigrés (1970) **Terry Eagleton** (1943)
Exiles, The (1788) **Clara Reeve** (1729)
Existentialism and Humanism [*L'Existentialisme est un humanisme*] (1946) **Jean-Paul Sartre** (1905)
Exit Eliza (1912) **'Barry Pain' [Eric Odell]** (1864)
Exocet (1983) **'Jack Higgins' [Harry Patterson]** (1929)
Exodus (1957) **Leon Uris** (1924)
Exorcist, The (1971) **William Peter Blatty** (1928)
Expansion of England, The (1883) **Sir John Seeley** (1834)
Expectant Silence, The (1944) **William Soutar** (1898–1943)
Expedition of Humphrey Clinker, The (1771) **Tobias George Smollett** (1721)
Expense of Greatness, The (1940) **R.P. Blackmur** (1904)
Expensive People (1968) **Joyce Carol Oates** (1938)
Expensive Place to Die, An (1967) **Len Deighton** (1929)
Experience [memoirs] (2000) **Martin Amis** (1949)
Experiment in Autobiography (1934) **H.G. Wells** (1866)
Experiment in Criticism, An (1961) **C.S. Lewis** (1898)
Experiment in Love, An (1995) **Hilary Mantel** (1952)
Experiment with Time, An (1927) **J.W. Dunne** (1875)
Experimental Novel, The [*Le Roman expérimental*] (1880) **Émile Zola** (1840)
Experimenting With an Amen (1986) **R.S. Thomas** (1913)
Experiments and Observations on Different Kinds of Air (1774–1786) **Joseph Priestley** (1733)
Experiments and Observations on Electricity (1751–1754) **Benjamin Franklin** (1706)
Explanation of the Grand Mystery of Godliness, An (1660) **Henry More** (1614)
Explanations (1845) **Robert Chambers** (1802)
Expletives Deleted (1992) **Angela Carter** (1940)
Exploded View, An (1973) **Michael Longley** (1939)
Exploding English (1990) **Bernard Bergonzi** (1929)
Exploits of Brigadier Gerard, The (1896) **A. Conan Doyle** (1859)
Explorations (1946) **L.C. Knights** (1906)
Explorer, The (1908) **Somerset Maugham** (1874)
Explorers of the Dawn (1922) **Mazo de la Roche** (1879)
Exposition, The (1851) **Charles William Shirley Brooks** (1816)
Exposition of the Apostles Creed (1659) **John Pearson** (1613)
Exposition of the Lords Prayer, An (1592) **William Perkins** (1558)
Exposition of the New Testament, An (1790) **William Gilpin** (1724)
Exposition on the Church-Catechism, An (1685) **Thomas Ken** (1637)
Expression of the Emotions in Man and Animals, The (1872) **Charles Darwin** (1809)
Expressions of Sea Level (1964) **A.R. Ammons** (1926)

Extending the Territory (1985) **Elizabeth Jennings** (1926)
Exterminator! (1973) **William S. Burroughs** (1914)
Extra, The (1975) **Hal Porter** (1911)
Extraordinary Confessions of Diana Please, The (1904) **Bernard Capes** (1850?)
Extraordinary Women (1928) **Compton Mackenzie** (1883)
Exultations (1909) **Ezra Pound** (1885)
Eye for an Eye, An (1879) **Anthony Trollope** (1815)
Eye in the Door, The (1993) **Pat Barker** (1943)
Eye of Istar, The (1897) **William le Queux** (1864)
Eye of Osiris, The [US: *The Vanishing Man*] (1911) **R. Austin Freeman** (1862)
Eye of the Hurricane, The (1964) **Fleur Adcock** (1934)
Eye of the Needle [US: *Storm Island*] (1978) **Ken Follett** (1949)
Eye of the Scarecrow, The (1965) **Wilson Harris** (1921)
Eye of the Storm, The (1973) **Patrick White** (1912)
Eye of the Story, The (1978) **Eudora Welty** (1909)
Eye of the Tiger, The (1975) **Wilbur Smith** (1933)
Eye, The (1965) **Vladimir Nabokov** (1899)
Eye-Beaters, The (1970) **James Dickey** (1923)
Eyebright (1879) **'Susan Coolidge' [Sarah Chauncy Woolsey]** (1845)
Eyeless in Gaza (1936) **Aldous Huxley** (1894)
Eyes of Max Carrados, The (1923) **Ernest Bramah** (1868)
Eyes of the Wilderness (1933) **Sir Charles G.D. Roberts** (1860)
Eyewitness (1967) **Rodney Hall** (1935)
Ezra Pound and His World (1980) **Peter Ackroyd** (1949)

F

'F' is for Fugitive (1989) **Sue Grafton** (1940)
Faber Book of Modern Verse, The (1936) **Michael Roberts** (1902) (ed.)
Faber Book of Twentieth-Century Verse, The (1953) **John Heath-Stubbs** (1918) (ed.) [with David Wright]
Fabianism and the Empire (1900) **Bernard Shaw** (1856)
Fabiola (1855) **Nicholas Patrick S. Wiseman** (1802)
Fable, A (1954) **William Faulkner** (1897)
Fable for Critics, A (1848) **James Russell Lowell** (1819)
Fable of the Bees, The (1714) **Bernard Mandeville** (1670)
Fable of the Goats, The (1937) **E.J. Pratt** (1882)
Fabled Shore (1949) **Rose Macaulay** (1881)
Fables [*Fables choisies, mises en vers*; vol. ii, 1679–94] (1668) **Jean de La Fontaine** (1621)
Fables (1727) **John Gay** (1685)
Fables (1941) **William Saroyan** (1908)
Fables Ancient and Modern (1700) **John Dryden** (1631)
Fables Ancient and Modern (1805) **William Godwin** (1756)
Fables and Dialogues of the Dead [*Dialogues des Morts anciens et modernes*] (1713) **François Fénelon** (1651)
Fables and Fairy Tales (1860) **Henry Morley** (1822)
Fables and Tales (1722) **Allan Ramsay** (1686)
Fables For Our Time, and Famous Poems Illustrated (1940) **James Thurber** (1894)
Fables for the Female Sex (1744) **Edward Moore** (1712)
Fables for the Holy Alliance [as 'Thomas Brown the Younger'] (1823) **Thomas Moore** (1779)
Fables in Slang (1899) **George Ade** (1866)
Fables in Song (1874) **Edward Robert Bulwer Lytton** (1831)
Fables: Volume the Second (1738) **John Gay** (1685)
Fabulists, The (1915) **Bernard Capes** (1850?)
Fabulous Mrs V, The (1964) **H.E. Bates** (1905)
Façade (1922) **Edith Sitwell** (1887)
Face and the Mask, The (1894) **Robert Barr** (1850)
Face Beside the Fire, The (1953) **Sir Laurens van der Post** (1906)
Face in the Candlelight, A (1932) **J.C. Squire** (1884)
Face is Familiar, The (1940) **Ogden Nash** (1902)
Face of England, The (1932) **Edmund Blunden** (1896)
Face of Innocence, The (1951) **William Sansom** (1912)
Face of the Deep, The (1892) **Christina Rossetti** (1830)
Face of the Enemy, The (1961) **Vernon Scannell** (1922)
Face of the Night, The (1904) **Ford Madox Ford** (1873)
Face of the Waters, The (1985) **Simon Raven** (1927)
Face of Time, The (1953) **James T. Farrell** (1904)
Face of War, The (1959) **Martha Gellhorn** (1908)
Face to Face (1949) **Nadine Gordimer** (1923)
Faceache (1971) **Howard Barker** (1946)
Faces In My Time (1980) **Anthony Powell** (1905)
Faces in the Water (1962) **Janet Frame** (1924)
Facing Death (1883) **G.A. Henty** (1832)
Facing Nature (1985) **John Updike** (1932)
Fact and Faith (1934) **J.B.S. Haldane** (1892)
Fact of a Doorframe, The (1984) **Adrienne Rich** (1929)
Factors in Modern History (1907) **A.F. Pollard** (1869)
Factotum (1975) **Charles Bukowski** (1920)
Facts of Life, The (1983) **Robert Nye** (1939)
Faerie Queene, The [bks i-iii] (1590) **Edmund Spenser** (1552?)
Fahrenheit 451 (1953) **Ray Bradbury** (1920)
Faina (1906–1908) **Aleksandr Blok** (1880)
Fair Assembly, The (1723) **Allan Ramsay** (1686)
Fair Barbarian, A (1881) **Frances Hodgson Burnett** (1849)
Fair Captive, The (1721) **Eliza Haywood** (*c.* 1693)
Fair Circassian, The (1781) **Samuel Jackson Pratt** (1749)

Fair Country Maid, A (1883) **E[mma] F[rances] Brooke** (1859?)
Fair Device, A (1886) **Wolcott Balestier** (1861)
Fair Emigrant, A (1889) **Rosa Mulholland** (1841)
Fair Exchange (1998) **Lynne Reid Banks** (1929)
Fair God, The (1873) **Lew Wallace** (1827)
Fair Haven, The (1873) **Samuel Butler** (1835)
Fair Hebrew, The (1729) **Eliza Haywood** (*c.* 1693)
Fair Jilt, The (1688) **Aphra Behn** (1640?)
'Fair Maid of Perth, The' [**Scott**]: see *Chronicles of the Chanongate [2nd ser.]*
Fair Maid of the West, The [2 pts, 1631] (1631) **Thomas Heywood** (1574?)
Fair Margaret (1907) **Sir H. Rider Haggard** (1856)
Fair Penitent, The (1703) **Nicholas Rowe** (1674)
Fair Rebel, A (1906) **L[ucy] B[erthia] Walford** (1845)
Fair Rosamond (1844) **Pierce Egan, the Younger** (1814)
Fair Saxon, A (1873) **Justin McCarthy** (1830)
Fair Slaughter (1977) **Howard Barker** (1946)
Fair Stood the Wind for France (1944) **H.E. Bates** (1905)
Fair Syrian, The (1787) **Robert Bage** (1728)
Fairacre Festival, The (1969) **'Miss Read' [Dora Jessie Saint]** (1913)
Faire Quarrell, A (1617) **Thomas Middleton** (1580) [with William Rowley]
Fairfax (1868) **John Cooke** (1830)
Fairground Music (1961) **John Fuller** (1937)
Fairies, The [from Shakespeare's *A Midsummer Night's Dream*] (1755) **David Garrick** (1717)
Fairies, The (1883) **William Allingham** (1824)
Fairies Afield (1911) **Mary Louisa Molesworth** (1839)
Fairies and Fusiliers (1917) **Robert Graves** (1895)
Fairly Conventional Woman, A (1982) **Carol Shields** (1935)
Fairly Good Time, A (1970) **Mavis Gallant** (1922)
Fairy Book, The (1863) **Dinah Maria Craik** (1826)
Fairy Changeling, The (1897) **Dora Sigerson** (1866)
Fairy Godmothers, The (1851) **Margaret [Mrs Alfred] Gatty** (1809)
Fairy Legends and Traditions of the South of Ireland [vol. i; inc. 4 stories by William Maginn] (1826, 1828) **T. Crofton Croker** (1798)
Fairy Queen, The (1692) **Elkanah Settle** (1648)
Fairy Tale of New York, A (1973) **J.P. Donleavy** (1926)
Fairy Water (1878) **Mrs J.H. Riddell** (1832)
Faith (1994) **Len Deighton** (1929)
Faith (1909) **R.B. Cunninghame Graham** (1852)
Faith and Modern Thought, The (1910) **William Temple** (1881)
Faith Doctor, The (1891) **Edward Eggleston** (1837)
Faith Fox (1996) **Jane Gardam** (1928)
Faith Healer (1979) **Brian Friel** (1929)
Faith, Reason and Civilization (1944) **Harold Laski** (1893)
Faithful For Ever [The Angel in the House iii] (1860) **Coventry Patmore** (1823)
Faithful Narrative of the Surprising Work of God, A (1737) **Jonathan Edwards** (1703)
Faithful Stranger (1938) **Sheila Kaye-Smith** (1887)
Faithfull Shepheardesse, The (1610) **John Fletcher** (1579)
Faithless Lollybird, The (1977) **Joan Aiken** (1924)
Falcon Family, The (1845) **Marmion W. Savage** (1803)
Falcon Flies, A (1980) **Wilbur Smith** (1933)
Falconer (1977) **John Cheever** (1912)
Falconer of God, The (1914) **William Rose Benét** (1886)
Falkland (1827) **Edward Bulwer-Lytton** (1803)
Falkner (1837) **Mary Shelley** (1797)
Falkner Lyle (1866) **Mark Lemon** (1809)
Fall, The (1940) **'Hugh Kingsmill' [Hugh Kingsmill Lunn]** (1889)
Fall, The [La Chute] (1956) **Albert Camus** (1913)
Fall by Fury (1978) **Earle Birney** (1904)
Fall In, Ghosts (1932) **Edmund Blunden** (1896)
Fall of America, The (1973) **Allen Ginsberg** (1926)
Fall of an Eagle, The (1964) **Jon Cleary** (1917)
Fall of Constantinople, The (1965) **Sir Steven Runciman** (1903
Fall of Jerusalem, The (1820) **Henry Hart Milman** (1791)
Fall of Kelvin Walker, The (1985) **Alasdair Gray** (1934)
Fall of Nineveh, The (1828) **Edwin Atherstone** (1788)
Fall of Princes, The [tr. *c.* 1431–8 from Boccaccio] (1494) **John Lydgate** (1370?–49) (tr.)
Fall of Robespierre, The (1794) **S.T. Coleridge** (1772) [with Robert Southey]
Fall of Somerset, The (1877) **W.H. Ainsworth** (1805)
Fall of the City, The (1937) **Archibald MacLeish** (1892)
Fall of the House of Heron, The (1948) **Eden Phillpotts** (1862)
Fall of the Monarchy of Charles I, The (1882) **S. R. Gardiner** (1829)
Fallen Angels (1925) **Noel Coward** (1899)
Fallen Fortunes (1876) **James Payn** (1830)
Fallen Idol, A (1886) **'F. Anstey' [Thomas Anstey Guthrie]** (1856)
Fallen Leaves, The (1879) **Wilkie Collins** (1824)
Falling (1999) **Elizabeth Jane Howard** (1923)
Falling for a Dolphin (1988) **Heathcote Williams** (1941)
Falling into Language (1990) **Chris Wallace-Crabbe** (1934)
Falling Star (1934) **Vicki Baum** (1888)
Falling Towards England (1985) **Clive James** (1939)
Fallow Land, The (1932) **H.E. Bates** (1905)
False Alarm, The (1770) **Samuel Johnson** (1709)
False Count, The (1681) **Aphra Behn** (1640?)
False Delicacy (1768) **Hugh Kelly** (1739)
False Friend, The (1699) **Mary Pix** (1666)
False Friend, The (1702) **Sir John Vanbrugh** (1664)
False Friend, The (1799) **Mary Robinson** (1758)
False Heir, The (1843) **G.P.R. James** (1799)
Falstaff (1976) **Robert Nye** (1939)

Fame and Fiction (1901) **Arnold Bennett** (1867)
Fame is the Spur (1940) **Howard Spring** (1889)
Famelie of Love, The (1608) **Thomas Middleton** (1580)
Fames Memoriall (1606) **John Ford** (1586)
Familiar Faces, The (1962) **David Garnett** (1892)
Familiar Letters (1747) **Sarah Fielding** (1710)
Familiar Passions (1979) **Nina Bawden** (1925)
Familiar Spirits (1994) **Elizabeth Jennings** (1926)
Familiar Studies of Men and Books (1882) **Robert Louis Stevenson** (1850)
Familiar Tree, A (1978) **Jon Stallworthy** (1935)
Family (1981) **Herbert Gold** (1924)
Family (1989) **Susan Hill** (1942)
Family Affair, A (1975) **Rex Stout** (1886)
Family and a Fortune, A (1939) **I. Compton-Burnett** (1884)
Family and Friends (1985) **Anita Brookner** (1928)
Family Arsenal, The (1976) **Paul Theroux** (1941)
Family Chronicle, A (1846–1856) **Sergei Timofeyevich Aksakov** (1791)
Family Feud, The [as 'Adam Hornbrook'] (1855) **Thomas Cooper** (1805)
Family From One End Street, The (1937) **Eve Garnett** (1900)
Family History, A (1822) **John Neal** (1793)
Family Instructor, The (1715) **Daniel Defoe** (1660)
Family Legend, The (1810) **Joanna Baillie** (1762)
Family Life (1974) **Russell Banks** (1940)
Family Likeness, A (1985) **Mary Lavin** (1912)
Family Madness, A (1985) **Thomas Keneally** (1935)
Family Matters (1980) **Elizabeth Berridge** (1921)
Family Money (1991) **Nina Bawden** (1925)
Family Moskat, The (1950) **Isaac Bashevis Singer** (1904)
Family News (1990) **Joan Barfoot** (1946)
Family Party, A (1956) **John O'Hara** (1905)
Family Party in the Piazza of St Peter, A (1877) **T. Adolphus Trollope** (1810)
Family Picture, The (1783) **Thomas Holcroft** (1745)
Family Pictures (1764) **Susannah Gunning** (1740)
Family Planning (1989) **Tim Parks** (1954)
Family Reunion (1950) **Ogden Nash** (1902)
Family Reunion, The (1939) **T.S. Eliot** (1888)
Family Romance, A (1993) **Anita Brookner** (1928)
Family Secrets (1797) **Samuel Jackson Pratt** (1749)
Family Sins (1990) **'William Trevor' [William Trevor Cox]** (1928)
Family Tree, The (1929) **William Plomer** (1903)
Famine (1937) **Liam O'Flaherty** (1897)
Famished Road, The (1991) **Ben Okri** (1959)
Famous Chronicle of King Edward the First, The (1593) **George Peele** (1556)
Famous History of Sir Thomas Wyat, The (1607) **Thomas Dekker** (1572?) [with John Webster]
Famous Last Words (1981) **Timothy Findley** (1930)
Famous Prediction of Merlin, A (1709) **Jonathan Swift** (1667)
Famous Tragedy of the Queen of Cornwall at Tintagel in Lyonesse, The (1923) **Thomas Hardy** (1840)
Famous Tragedy of the Rich Jew of Malta, The (1633) **Christopher Marlowe** (1564–93)
Famous Whore, The (1609) **Gervaise Markham** (1568?)
Fan, The (1714) **John Gay** (1685)
Fan [as 'Henry Harford'] (1892) **W.H. Hudson** (1841)
Fanchette (1883) **John Cooke** (1830)
Fanciad, The (1743) **Aaron Hill** (1685)
Fancies and Goodnights (1951) **John Collier** (1901)
Fancies, Chast and Noble, The (1638) **John Ford** (1586)
Fancies Versus Fads (1923) **G.K. Chesterton** (1874)
Fancy, The (1943) **Monica Dickens** (1915)
Fancy's Following (1896) **M.E. Coleridge** (1861)
Fancy's Guerdon (1897) **M.E. Coleridge** (1861)
Fanfarlo, La (1847) **Charles Baudelaire** (1821)
Fanfrolico and After (1962) **Jack Lindsay** (1900)
Fanny (1819) **Fitz-Greene Halleck** (1790)
Fanny (1980) **Erica Jong** (1942)
Fanny by Gaslight (1940) **Michael Sadleir** (1888)
Fanny Hill [**Cleland**]: see *Memoirs of a Woman of Pleasure*
Fanny McBride (1959) **Catherine Cookson** (1906)
Fanshawe (1828) **Nathaniel Hawthorne** (1804)
Fanshen (1975) **David Hare** (1947)
Fantasia of the Unconscious (1923) **D.H. Lawrence** (1885)
Fantasies [Fantasiestücke] (1814–15) **E.T.A. Hoffmann** (1776)
Fantasies (1898) **'George Egerton' [Mary Chavelita Dunne]** (1859)
Fantastic Mr Fox (1970) **Roald Dahl** (1916)
Fantasy and Fugue (1954) **Roy Fuller** (1912)
Fantazius Mallare (1922) **Ben Hecht** (1894)
Fantomina (1725) **Eliza Haywood** (*c.* 1693)
Far Away (1932) **J.B. Priestley** (1894)
Far Away and Long Ago (1889) **Frances [Fanny] Kemble** (1809)
Far Away and Long Ago (1918) **W.H. Hudson** (1841)
Far Cry (1943) **Norman MacCaig** (1910)
Far Cry From Kensington, A (1988) **Muriel Spark** (1918)
Far Face of the Moon, The (1965) **George Johnston** (1912)
Far Field, The (1964) **Theodore Roethke** (1908–63)
Far From Cibola (1938) **Paul Horgan** (1903)
Far From My Home (1931) **Sir Sacheverell Sitwell** (1897)
Far From the Madding Crowd (1874) **Thomas Hardy** (1840)
Far Journey of Oudin, The (1961) **Wilson Harris** (1921)
Far Off Things (1922) **Arthur Machen** (1863)
Far Pavilions, The (1978) **M.M. Kaye** (1908)
Far Road, The (1962) **George Johnston** (1912)
Far Side of the Street, The (1988) **Alan Sillitoe** (1928)
Far Side of the World, The (1984) **Patrick O'Brian** (1914)
Far-Off Hills, The (1931) **Lennox Robinson** (1886)
Faraway Drums, The (1981) **Jon Cleary** (1917)
Fardorougha the Miser (1839) **William Carleton** (1794)

Farewell, The (1764) **Charles Churchill** (1731)
Farewell, Aggie Weston (1951) **Charles Causley** (1917)
Farewell Great King (1972) **Jill Paton Walsh** (1937)
Farewell, My Lovely (1940) **Raymond Chandler** (1888)
'Farewell, Nikola' (1901) **Guy Boothby** (1867)
Farewell Party, The (1976) **Milan Kundera** (1929)
Farewell Spain (1937) **Kate O'Brien** (1897)
Farewell the Trumpets (1978) **Jan Morris** (1926)
Farewell to Arms, A (1929) **Ernest Hemingway** (1898)
Farewell to Italy, (1818) **William Sotheby** (1757)
Farewell to Poesy (1910) **W.H. Davies** (1871)
Farina [A lege] (1857) **George Meredith** (1828)
Farm of the Dagger, The (1904) **Eden Phillpotts** (1862)
Farm, The (1933) **Louis Bromfield** (1896)
Farmer (1976) **Jim Harrison** (1937)
Farmer Giles of Ham (1949) **J.R.R. Tolkein** (1892)
Farmer's Boy, The (1800) **Robert Bloomfield** (1766)
Farmer's Bride, The (1916) **Charlotte Mew** (1869)
Farmer's Daughter, The (1795) **Christopher Anstey** (1724)
Farmer's Letters to the People of England, A (1767) **Arthur Young** (1741)
Farmer's Tour Through the East of England, The (1770) **Arthur Young** (1741)
Farmer's Year, A (1899) **Sir H. Rider Haggard** (1856)
Farmers' Daughters, The (1961) **William Carlos Williams** (1883)
Farmers Hotel, The (1951) **John O'Hara** (1905)
Faro's Daughter (1941) **Georgette Heyer** (1902)
Farringdon Hill (1774) **Henry James Pye** (1745)
Farringdons, The (1900) **Ellen Thorneycroft Fowler** (1860)
Farther Adventures of Robinson Crusoe, The (1719) **Daniel Defoe** (1660)
Farther Off From Heaven (1947) **William Inge** (1913)
Farther Vindication of the Short View of the Profaneness and Immorality of the English Stage, A (1708) **Jeremy Collier** (1650)
Farthest Shore, The (1972) **Ursula K. Le Guin** (1929)
Fashion in Shrouds, The (1938) **Margery Allingham** (1904)
Fashionable Involvements (1800) **Susannah Gunning** (1740)
Fashionable Life; or, Paris and London (1856) **Frances Trollope** (1780)
Fashionable Lover, The (1772) **Richard Cumberland** (1732)
Fashionable Philosophy (1887) **Laurence Oliphant** (1829)
Fast Forward (1984) **Peter Porter** (1929)
Fasting, Feasting (1999) **Anita Desai** (1937)
Fat Man in History, The (1974) **Peter Carey** (1943)
Fat Woman's Joke, The (1967) **Fay Weldon** (1931)
Fatal Curiosity (1736) **George Lillo** (1693)
Fatal Discovery, The (1769) **John Home** (1722)
Fatal Dowry, The (1632) **Philip Massinger** (1583) [with Nathan Field]
Fatal Falsehood, The (1779) **Hannah More** (1745)
Fatal Gift, A (1973) **Alec Waugh** (1898)
Fatal Inversion, A [as 'Barbara Vine'] (1987) **Ruth Rendell** (1930)
Fatal Landscape, The (1941) **G.S. Fraser** (1915)
Fatal Love (1680) **Elkanah Settle** (1648)
Fatal Marriage, The (1694) **Thomas Southerne** (1659)
Fatal Revenge (1807) **C.R. Maturin** (1782)
Fatal Secret, The (1733) **Lewis Theobald** (1688)
Fatal Secret, The (1724) **Eliza Haywood** (*c.* 1693)
Fatal Three, The (1888) **M.E. Braddon** (1835)
Fatal Vision, The (1716) **Aaron Hill** (1685)
Fatality in Fleet Street [as Christopher St John Sprigg] (1933) **'Christopher Caudwell' [Christopher St John Sprigg]** (1907)
Fate Cries Out (1935) **'Clemence Dane' [Winifred Ashton]** (1888)
Fate of Adelaide, The [as 'L.E.L.'] (1821) **Letitia Elizabeth Landon** (1802)
Fate of Capua, The (1700) **Thomas Southerne** (1659)
Fate of Sparta, The (1788) **Hannah Cowley** (1743)
Fate of the Jury, The (1929) **Edgar Lee Masters** (1868)
Fated to be Free (1875) **Jean Ingelow** (1820)
Father, The (1887) **August Strindberg** (1849)
Father Adam (1990) **T.F. Powys** (1875–1953)
Father and Daughter, The (1801) **Amelia Opie** (1769)
Father and His Fate, A (1957) **I. Compton-Burnett** (1884)
Father and Son (1940) **James T. Farrell** (1904)
Father and Son (1907) **Sir Edmund Gosse** (1849)
Father Anthony (1898) **Robert Williams Buchanan** (1841)
Father Butler; [and] *The Lough Dearg Pilgrim* (1829) **William Carleton** (1794)
Father Christmas (1973) **Raymond Briggs** (1934)
Father Christmas Goes on Holiday (1975) **Raymond Briggs** (1934)
Father Confessor, The (1900) **Dora Sigerson** (1866)
Father Connell (1842) **Michael Banim** (1796)
Father Eustace (1847) **Frances Trollope** (1780)
Father Found, The (1941) **Charles Madge** (1912)
Father of the Family, The [*Le Père de famille*] (1758) **Denis Diderot** (1713)
Father of the Forest, The (1895) **Sir William Watson** (1858)
Father of Women, A (1917) **Alice Meynell** (1847)
Father Payne (1915) **A.C. Benson** (1862)
Father Stafford (1891) **'Anthony Hope' [Sir Anthony Hope Hawkins]** (1863)
Father's Comedy, The (1961) **Roy Fuller** (1912)
Father's Curse, The (1848) **Anna Eliza Bray** (1790)
Fathers (1967) **Herbert Gold** (1924)
Fathers and Sons (1862) **Ivan Turgenev** (1818)
Fathers, The [rev. 1977] (1938) **Allen Tate** (1899)
Fathom Five (1979) **Robert Westall** (1929)
Faulkener (1807) **William Godwin** (1756)
Faulkner at Nagano (1956) **William Faulkner** (1897)
Faulkner at West Point (1964) **William Faulkner** (1897–1962)

Faulkner in the University (1959) **William Faulkner** (1897)
Fault of Angels, The (1933) **Paul Horgan** (1903)
Fauns and Ladies (1923) **Jack Lindsay** (1900)
Faunus and Melliflora (1600) **John Weever** (1576)
Faust [pt i; pt ii pub. 1832] (1808) **Johann Wolfgang von Goethe** (1749)
Faust (1980) **Robert Nye** (1939)
Faust Book, A (1979) **D.J. Enright** (1920)
Faust [from Goethe] (1840) **'Gérard de Nerval' [Gérard Labrunie]** (1808) (tr.)
Faustine (1991) **Emma Tennant** (1937)
Favourite Game, The (1963) **Leonard Cohen** (1934)
Favourite Nights (1981) **Stephen Poliakoff** (1952)
Favourite of the Gods, A (1963) **Sybille Bedford** (1911)
Fawn of Spring-Vale, The (1841) **William Carleton** (1794)
Fayre Mayde of the Exchange, The (1607) **Thomas Heywood** (1574?)
Fazio (1815) **Henry Hart Milman** (1791)
Fear and Loathing in Las Vegas (1971) **Hunter S. Thompson** (1939)
Fear and Loathing on the Campaign Trail (1973) **Hunter S. Thompson** (1939)
Fear of Fifty (1994) **Erica Jong** (1942)
Fear of Flying (1974) **Erica Jong** (1942)
Fear, The (1965) **Thomas Keneally** (1935)
Feare of Losing the Old Light (1646) **Thomas Fuller** (1608)
Fearful Joy, A (1949) **Joyce Cary** (1888)
Fearful Pleasures (1946) **A.E. Coppard** (1878)
Fearful Responsibility, A (1881) **William Dean Howells** (1837)
Fearful Symmetry (1947) **Northrop Frye** (1912)
Fears in Solitude [Inc. 'France, an Ode', and 'Frost at Midnight'] (1798) **S.T. Coleridge** (1772)
Feast for Wormes, A (1620) **Francis Quarles** (1592)
Feast of Bacchus, The (1889) **Robert Bridges** (1844)
Feast of Belshazzar, The (1852) **Sir Edwin Arnold** (1832)
Feast of Euridice, The (1980) **Elaine Feinstein** (1930)
Feast of July, The (1954) **H.E. Bates** (1905)
Feast of Lupercal, The (1958) **Brian Moore** (1921)
Feast of St Magdalen, The (1818) **Anna Maria Porter** (1780)
Feast of the Poets, The (1814) **Leigh Hunt** (1784)
Feathers in the Fire (1971) **Catherine Cookson** (1906)
Feathers of Death, The (1959) **Simon Raven** (1927)
Fedele and Fortunio [from Luigi Pasquaglio] (1585) **Anthony Munday** (1560) (tr.)
Federigo (1954) **Howard Nemerov** (1920)
Fédora (1883) **Victorien Sardou** (1831)
Feeling You're Behind (1984) **Peter Nichols** (1927)
Feet of Clay (1996) **Terry Pratchett** (1948)
Feet of the Furtive, The (1912) **Sir Charles G.D. Roberts** (1860)
Feign'd Curtizans, The (1679) **Aphra Behn** (1640?)
Felicia's Journey (1994) **'William Trevor' [William Trevor Cox]** (1928)
Felicity of Queen Elizabeth, The (1651) **Sir Francis Bacon** (1561–1626)
Felix Holt (1866) **'George Eliot' [Mary Ann Evans]** (1819)
Fellowship of the Ring, The [The Lord of the Rings pt. i] (1954) **J.R.R. Tolkein** (1892)
Fellowship of the Talisman, The (1978) **Clifford D. Simak** (1904)
Female Advocate, The (1686) **Sarah Egerton** (1670)
Female Eunuch, The (1970) **Germaine Greer** (1939)
Female Friends (1975) **Fay Weldon** (1931)
Female Malady, The (1987) **Elaine Showalter** (1941)
Female Man, The (1975) **Joanna Russ** (1937)
Female of the Species, The [US: *Bulldog Drummond Meets . . .*] (1928) **'Sapper' [Herman Cyril McNeile]** (1888)
Female Prelate, The (1680) **Elkanah Settle** (1648)
Female Quixote, The (1752) **Charlotte Lennox** (1720)
Female Speaker, The (1811) **Anna Laetitia Barbauld** (1743) (ed.)
Femina Real (1971) **A.L. Barker** (1918)
Feminism (1912) **May Sinclair** (1863)
Femme de Claude, La (18[illegible]) **Alexandre Dumas ['fils']** (1824)
Femmes damnées (1978) **Philip Larkin** (1922)
Fen (1983) **Caryl Churchill** (1938)
Fenny (1953) **Lettice Cooper** (1897)
Fenton's Quest (1871) **M.E. Braddon** (1835)
Fenwick's Career (1906) **Mrs T. Humphry Ward** (1851)
Fer-de-Lance [first 'Nero Wolfe' novel] (1934) **Rex Stout** (1886)
Fergus (1970) **Brian Moore** (1921)
Fergus Lamont (1979) **Robin Jenkins** (1912)
Ferishtah's Fancies (1884) **Robert Browning** (1812)
Fermata, The (1994) **Nicholson Baker** (1957)
Fervour of Buenos Aires [*Fervor de Buenos Aires*] (1923) **Jorge Luis Borges** (1899)
Festival at Farbridge (1951) **J.B. Priestley** (1894)
Festival Nights (1984) **Gavin Ewart** (1916)
Festus (1839) **Philip James Bailey** (1816)
Fetish (1951) **Wilson Harris** (1921)
Feu de joie ['Bonfire'] (1921) **Louis Aragon** (1897)
Feud, The (1864) **Adam Lindsay Gordon** (1833)
Feud, The (1983) **Thomas Berger** (1924)
Feuilles d'automne, Les ['Autumn Leaves'] (1831) **Victor Hugo** (1802)
Fever Pitch (1992) **Nick Hornby**
Few Fair Days, A (1971) **Jane Gardam** (1928)
Few Flowers for Shiner, A (1950) **'Richard Llewellyn' [Richard Llewellyn Lloyd]** (1907)
Few Green Leaves, A (1980) **Barbara Pym** (1913–80)
Few Late Chrysanthemums, A (1954) **Sir John Betjeman** (1906)
Few Sighs from Hell, A (1658) **John Bunyan** (1628)
Few Words to Churchwardens, A (1841) **J[ohn] M[ason] Neale** (1818)
Few Words to the Parish Clerks and Sextons, A (1843) **John Mason Neale** (1818)

Fiction and the Figures of Life (1970) **William H. Gass** (1924)
Fiction As She Is Wrote (1923) **E.V. Knox** (1881)
Fiction-Makers, The (1985) **Anne Stevenson** (1933)
Fictions [Ficciónes] (1945) **Jorge Luis Borges** (1899)
Fictive Certainties (1985) **Robert Duncan** (1919)
Fiddle City (1981) **Julian Barnes** (1946)
Fiddler's House, The (1907) **Padraic Colum** (1881)
Fidelia (1615) **George Wither** (1588)
Fidelities (1968) **Vernon Watkins** (1906–67)
Field and Hedgerow (1889) **Richard Jefferies** (1848–87)
Field God, The (1927) **Paul Green** (1894)
Field of 13 (1998) **Dick Francis** (1920)
Field of Mustard, The (1926) **A.E. Coppard** (1878)
Field of Vision, A (1988) **Charles Causley** (1917)
Field of Waterloo, The (1815) **Sir Walter Scott** (1771)
Field Work (1979) **Seamus Heaney** (1939)
Fielding Gray (1967) **Simon Raven** (1927)
Fields, The (1946) **Conrad Richter** (1890)
Fields of Grace (1972) **Richard Eberhart** (1904)
Fields of Learning (1968) **Josephine Miles** (1911)
Fields of Victory (1919) **Mrs T. Humphry Ward** (1851)
Fields of Vision (1988) **D.J. Enright** (1920)
Fields of Wonder (1947) **Langston Hughes** (1902)
Fiend's Delight, The (1873) **Ambrose Bierce** (1842)
Fiery Dawn, The (1901) **M.E. Coleridge** (1861)
Fiery Particles (1923) **C.E. Montague** (1867)
Fiesta, The (1978) **Geoffrey Grigson** (1905)
Fifine at the Fair (1872) **Robert Browning** (1812)
Fifteen Decisive Battles of the World (1851) **Sir Edward Creasy** (1812)
Fifteen Poems From Centre City (1990) **Thomas Kinsella** (1928)
Fifteen Sermons Preached at the Rolls Chapel (1726) **Joseph Butler** (1692)
Fifteen Streets, The (1952) **Catherine Cookson** (1906)
Fifteen to Infinity (1983) **Ruth Fainlight** (1931)
Fifth Business (1970) **Robertson Davies** (1913)
Fifth Child, The (1988) **Doris Lessing** (1919)
Fifth Column and the Firsty Forty-Nine Stories, The (1938) **Ernest Hemingway** (1898)
Fifth Elephant, The (1999) **Terry Pratchett** (1948)
Fifth Form at St Dominic's, The (1882) **Talbot Baines Reed** (1852)
Fifth of May, The (1821) **Alessandro Manzoni** (1785)
Fifth Queen and How She Came to Court, The (1906) **Ford Madox Ford** (1873)
Fifth Queen Crowned, The (1908) **Ford Madox Ford** (1873)
Fifty Caricatures (1913) **Max Beerbohm** (1872)
Fifty Modern Poems (1865) **William Allingham** (1824)
Fifty Poems (1940) **E.E. Cummings** (1894)
Fifty Poems (1990) **Ian Hamilton** (1938)
Fifty Sermons (1649) **John Donne** (1572–1631)
Fifty-Five, and Other Stories (1936) **Pamela Frankau** (1908)
Fifty-One Tales (1915) **Lord Dunsany** (1878)
Fig for Momus, A (1595) **Thomas Lodge** (1558)
Figaro at Hastings, St Leonards (1877) **'Cuthbert Bede' [Edward Bradley]** (1827)
Fight, The (1975) **Norman Mailer** (1923)
Fight With Fortune, A (1876) **Mortimer Collins** (1827)
Fighting France, From Dunkerque to Belfort (1915) **Edith Wharton** (1862)
Fighting Terms (1954) **Thom Gunn** (1929)
Fighting the Flames (1867) **R.M. Ballantyne** (1825)
Figs and Thistles (1879) **Albion W. Tourgée** (1838)
Figs and Thistles (1959) **Sydney Goodsir Smith** (1915)
Figure of 8 (1969) **Charles Causley** (1917)
Figures in a Landscape (1967) **David Helwig** (1938)
Figures in a Landscape (1940) **Paul Horgan** (1903)
Figures in Modern Literature (1924) **J.B. Priestley** (1894)
Figures in the Foreground (1963) **Frank Swinnerton** (1884)
Figures of Earth (1921) **James Branch Cabell** (1879)
Figures of Thought (1978) **Howard Nemerov** (1920)
Files on Parade (1939) **John O'Hara** (1905)
Filibusters in Barbary (1932) **Wyndham Lewis** (1882)
Filippo Strozzi (1860) **T. Adolphus Trollope** (1810)
Fille de chambre, The [reprtd 1814 as *Rebecca*; or, *The Fille de Chambre*] (1792) **Susanna Rowson** (1762)
Fils naturel, Le (1858) **Alexandre Dumas ['fils']** (1824)
Filth (1998) **Irvine Welsh** (1957)
Filthy Lucre (1986) **Beryl Bainbridge** (1934)
Fin de la nuit, La (1935) **François Mauriac** (1885)
Final Curtain (1947) **Ngaio Marsh** (1899)
Final Demands (1988) **Peter Reading** (1946)
Final Diagnosis, The (1959) **Arthur Hailey** (1920)
Final Edition (1940) **E.F. Benson** (1867)
Final Passage, The (1985) **Caryl Phillips** (1958)
Final Programme, The [first of the 'Cornelius Chronicle'] (1969) **Michael Moorcock** (1939)
Financial Expert, The (1952) **R.K. Narayan** (1907)
Finch's Fortune (1931) **Mazo de la Roche** (1879)
Finding the Sun (1982) **Edward Albee** (1928)
Fine and Private Place, A (1975) **Morley Callaghan** (1903)
Fine and Private Place, A (1971) **'Ellery Queen' [Frederic Dannay** (1905) and **Manfred B. Lee]** (1905)
Fine Balance, A (1996) **Rohinton Mistry** (1952)
Fine Clothes to the Jew (1927) **Langston Hughes** (1902)
Fine Companion, A (1633) **Shackerley Marmion** (1603)
Finer Grain, The (1910) **Henry James** (1843)
Fingal (1762) **James Macpherson** (1736)
Finish to the Adventures of Tom, Jerry and Logic (1828) **Pierce Egan [the elder]** (1772)
Finished (1917) **Sir H. Rider Haggard** (1856)
Finishing Touch, The (1963) **Brigid Brophy** (1929)
Finn and His Companions (1892) **Standish O'Grady** (1846)

Finnegans Wake (1939) **James Joyce** (1882)
Fire and Hemlock (1985) **Diana Wynne Jones** (1934)
Fire and the Sun, The (1977) **Iris Murdoch** (1919)
Fire and the Wood, The (1940) **R.C. Hutchinson** (1907)
Fire Down Below (1989) **William Golding** (1911)
Fire From Heaven [first of the *Alexander* Trilogy] (1969) **'Mary Renault' [Eileen Mary Challans]** (1905)
Fire in Heaven (1956) **Dannie Abse** (1923)
Fire in the Morning (1948) **Elizabeth Spencer** (1921)
Fire Next Time, The (1963) **James Baldwin** (1924)
Fire of Driftwood, A (1932) **D.K. Broster** (1878)
Fire of the Lord, The (1944) **Norman Nicholson** (1914)
Fire on Stone (1974) **Ralph Gustafson** (1909)
Fire on the Mountain (1977) **Anita Desai** (1937)
Fire Over England (1936) **A.E.W. Mason** (1865)
Fire Screen, The (1969) **James Merrill** (1926)
Fire Ships, The (1861) **W.H.G. Kingston** (1814)
Fire-Dwellers, The (1969) **Margaret Laurence** (1926)
Fire-Gap, The (1985) **Tony Harrison** (1937)
Fire-Seekers, The (1911) **'Iota' [Kathleen Mannington Caffyn]** (1855?)
Firebug (1961) **Robert Bloch** (1917)
Fireflies (1970) **Shiva Naipaul** (1945)
Firefly Summer (1987) **Maeve Binchy** (1940)
Firefox (1977) **Craig Thomas** (1942)
Fireman Flower (1944) **William Sansom** (1912)
Fires (1912) **Wilfrid Gibson** (1878)
Fires (1984) **Raymond Carver** (1939)
Fires of Spring, The (1949) **James A. Michener** (1907)
Fireside and Sunshine (1906) **E.V. Lucas** (1868)
Fireside Travels (1864) **James Russell Lowell** (1819)
Firestarter (1980) **Stephen King** (1947)
Firewalkers, The [as 'Frank Cauldwell'] (1956) **[Francis King]** (1923)
Fireweed (1969) **Jill Paton Walsh** (1937)
Fireworks (1974) **Angela Carter** (1940)
Firm of Girdlestone, The (1890) **A. Conan Doyle** (1859)
Firm, The (1991) **John Grisham** (1955)
Firmilian (1854) **'T. Percy Jones' [W.E. Aytoun]** (1813)
First Among Equals (1984) **Jeffrey Archer** (1940)
First and Last (1911) **Hilaire Belloc** (1870)
First and Last (1934) **Ring Lardner** (1885)
First and Last Loves (1952) **Sir John Betjeman** (1906)
First and Last Things (1908) **H.G. Wells** (1866)
First [and Second] Anniversarie (1612) **John Donne** (1572)
First Anniversary of the Government, The (1655) **Andrew Marvell** (1621)
First Athenian Memories (1931) **Compton Mackenzie** (1883)
First Blast of the Trumpet Against the Monstruous Regiment of Women, The (1558) **John Knox** (1505)
First Blues (1975) **Allen Ginsberg** (1926)
First Book of Airs, The (1613) **Thomas Campion** (1567)
First Book of Odes (1966) **Basil Bunting** (1900)
First Book of Poetry, The (1810) **Charles Lamb** (1775) [with Mary Lamb]
First Book of Urizen, The (1794) **William Blake** (1757)
First Booke of Songes or Ayres of Fowre Partes, The (1597) **John Dowland** (1563)
First Bulgarian Empire, The (1930) **Sir Steven Runciman** (1903
First Circle, The (1968) **Alexander Solzhenitsyn** (1918)
First Eagle (1999) **Tony Hillerman** (1925)
First Epistle of the First Book of Horace Imitated, The (1738) **Alexander Pope** (1688)
First Epistle of the Second Book of Horace, The (1737) **Alexander Pope** (1688)
First Five Books of Ovid's Metamorphosis, The (1621) **George Sandys** (1578) (tr.)
First Fleet Family, A (1896) **Louis Becke** (1855)
First Flight (1925) **Maxwell Anderson** (1888) [with Laurence Stallings]
First Fowre Bookes of the Civile Warres, The (1595) **Samuel Daniel** (1562)
First Gentleman of America (1942) **James Branch Cabell** (1879)
First Great Civilizations, The (1973) **Jacquetta Hawkes** (1910)
First Hundred Thousand, The (1915) **'Ian Hay' [John Hay Beith]** (1876)
First Hymn to Lenin (1931) **'Hugh MacDiarmid' [Christopher Murray Grieve]** (1892)
First Lensman (1950) **E.E.'Doc' Smith** (1890)
First Light (1989) **Peter Ackroyd** (1949)
First Love (1795) **Richard Cumberland** (1732)
First Love [pub. in French 1970] (1973) **Samuel Beckett** (1906)
First Love and Last Love (1868) **James Grant** (1822)
First Love and Other Sorrows (1958) **Harold Brodkey** (1930)
First Love, Last Rites (1975) **Ian McEwan** (1948)
First Lover, The (1933) **Kay Boyle** (1903)
First Man, The (1922) **Eugene O'Neill** (1888)
First Men in the Moon, The (1901) **H.G. Wells** (1866)
First Middle English Primer (1884) **Henry Sweet** (1845)
First Mrs Fraser, The (1929) **St John Ervine** (1883)
First Ode of the Second Book of Horace Paraphras'd, The (1714) **Jonathan Swift** (1667)
First Part of the Elementarie, The (1582) **Richard Mulcaster** (1530?)
First Part of the Historie of England, The (1612) **Samuel Daniel** (1562)
First Part of the Life and Raigne of King Henrie the IIII, The (1599) **Sir John Hayward** (1564?)
First Poems (1920) **Ruth Pitter** (1897)
First Poems (1925) **Edwin Muir** (1887)
First Russia, Then Tibet (1933) **Robert Byron** (1905)
First Satire of the Second Book of Horace, Imitated, The (1734) **Alexander Pope** (1688)
First Satire of the Second Book of Horace, The (1733) **Alexander Pope** (1688)
First Sermon Preached to King Charles, The (1625) **John Donne** (1572)

First Sketch of English Literature, A (1873) **Henry Morley** (1822)
First Term at Malory Towers (1946) **Enid Blyton** (1897)
First Testament (1955) **Christopher Logue** (1926)
First Things Last (1980) **David Malouf** (1934)
First Violin, The (1877) **Jessie Fothergill** (1851)
First Will and Testament (1939) **Kenneth Patchen** (1911)
First World War, The (1993) **Martin Gilbert** (1936)
First/Second Book of of Mr Francis Rabelais, The [3rd book, 1693] (1653) **Sir Thomas Urquhart** (1611) (tr.)
Firstborn, The (1946) **Christopher Fry [Christopher Fry Harris]** (1907)
Fisbo (1934) **Robert Nichols** (1893)
Fisher King, The (1986) **Anthony Powell** (1905)
Fishermen with Ploughs (1971) **George Mackay Brown** (1921)
Fishmonger's Fiddle (1925) **A.E. Coppard** (1878)
Fitz of Fitz-Ford (1830) **Anna Eliza Bray** (1790)
Five Acre Virgin (1976) **Elizabeth Jolley** (1923)
Five Books of Youth, The (1920) **Robert Hillyer** (1895)
Five Children—and It (1902) **E[dith] Nesbit** (1858)
Five Decades (1978) **Irwin Shaw** (1913)
Five Finger Exercise (1958) **Peter Shaffer** (1926)
Five for the Symbol (1981) **C.K. Stead** (1932)
Five Hundreth Points of Good Husbandry (1573) **Thomas Tusser** (1524?)
Five Jars, The (1922) **M.R. James** (1862)
Five Little Pigs [US: *Murder in Retrospect*] (1942) **Agatha Christie** (1890)
Five Minutes in heaven (1995) **Lisa Alther** (1944)
Five Nations, The (1903) **Rudyard Kipling** (1865)
Five of Us—and Madeline (1925) **E[dith] Nesbit** (1858)
Five on Treasure Island (1942) **Enid Blyton** (1897)
Five Pieces of Runic Poetry (1763) **Thomas Percy** (1729) (tr.)
Five Plays (1914) **George Fitzmaurice** (1878)
Five Red Herrings, The [US: *Suspicious Characters*] (1931) **Dorothy L. Sayers** (1893)
Five Rivers (1944) **Norman Nicholson** (1914)
Five Screenplays [*The Caretaker, The Servant, The Pumpkin Eater, Accident, The Quiller Memorandum*] (1971) **Harold Pinter** (1930)
Five Sermons Upon Speciall Occasions (1626) **John Donne** (1572)
Five Tales (1918) **John Galsworthy** (1867)
Five Weeks in a Balloon [*Cinq Semaines en ballon*] (1863) **Jules Verne** (1828)
Five Year Sentence, A [US: *Favours*] (1978) **Bernice Rubens** (1923)
Five Years of It (1858) **Alfred Austin** (1835)
Five Years of Youth (1831) **Harriet Martineau** (1802)
Five Years' Tryst, A (1902) **Sir Walter Besant** (1836)
Fivefold Screen, The (1932) **William Plomer** (1903)
Fivemiletown (1987) **Tom Paulin** (1949)
Fixed Period, The (1882) **Anthony Trollope** (1815)
Fixer, The (1967) **Bernard Malamud** (1914)
Flagons and Apples (1912) **Robinson Jeffers** (1887)
Flambards (1967) **K.M. Peyton** (1929)
Flame and Shadow (1976) **David Campbell** (1915)
Flame of Life (1974) **Alan Sillitoe** (1928)
Flame of Life, The [*Il fuoco*] (1900) **Gabriele D'Annunzio** (1863)
Flame Trees of Thika, The (1959) **Elspeth Huxley** (1907)
Flames (1897) **Robert Hichens** (1864)
Flaming Terrapin, The (1924) **Roy Campbell** (1901)
Flamingo Feather (1955) **Sir Laurens van der Post** (1906)
Flanders Road, The [*La Route des Flandres*] (1960) **Claude Simon** (1913)
Flappers and Philosophers (1920) **F. Scott Fitzgerald** (1896)
Flare Path (1942) **Terence Rattigan** (1911)
Flash and Filigree (1958) **Terry Southern** (1924)
Flash for Freedom (1971) **George MacDonald Fraser** (1925)
Flashing Stream, The (1938) **Charles Morgan** (1894)
Flashman (1969) **George MacDonald Fraser** (1925)
Flashman and the Mountain of Light (1990) **George MacDonald Fraser** (1925)
Flashman and the Tiger (1999) **George MacDonald Fraser** (1925)
Flashman at the Charge (1973) **George MacDonald Fraser** (1925)
Flat Iron for a Farthing, A (1872) **Mrs J.H. Ewing** (1841)
Flaubert's Parrot (1984) **Julian Barnes** (1946)
Flawless Jade (1989) **Barbara Hanrahan** (1939)
Flea of Sodom (1950) **Edward Dahlberg** (1900)
Fleece, The (1757) **John Dyer** (1699)
Fleeing Atalanta, The (1975) **David Foster** (1944)
Fleet Street (1909) **John Davidson** (1857)
Fleet Street Eclogues [1st ser.] (1893) **John Davidson** (1857)
Fleet Street Eclogues [2nd ser.] (1896) **John Davidson** (1857)
Fleeting, The (1933) **Walter de la Mare** (1873)
Fleetwood (1805) **William Godwin** (1756)
Flesh (1962) **Brigid Brophy** (1929)
Flesh and Blood (1994) **Michèle Roberts** (1949)
Flesheaters, The (1972) **David Ireland** (1927)
Fleshly School of Poetry, The (1872) **Robert Williams Buchanan** (1841)
Fleshweathercock (1973) **Carol Ann Duffy** (1955)
Les Fleurs du mal (1857) **Charles Baudelaire** (1821)
Flies in Amber (1905) **'George Egerton' [Mary Chavelita Dunne]** (1859)
Flies, The [*Les Mouches*] (1943) **Jean-Paul Sartre** (1905)
Flight From the Enchanter, The (1956) **Iris Murdoch** (1919)
Flight into Camden (1961) **David Storey** (1933)
Flight into Darkness (1944) **Ralph Gustafson** (1909)
Flight of Chariots, A (1963) **Jon Cleary** (1917)
Flight of the Eagle, The (1897) **Standish O'Grady** (1846)
Flight of the Falcon, The (1965) **Daphne du Maurier** (1907)

Flight of the Heron, The (1925) **D.K. Broster** (1878)
Flight of the Shadow, The (1891) **George MacDonald** (1824)
Flight to Arras [*Pilote de guerre*] (1942) **Antoine de Saint-Exupéry** (1900)
Flight to Lucifer, The (1979) **Harold Bloom** (1930)
Flight to the West (1941) **Elmer Rice** (1892)
Flim-flams! (1805) **Isaac Disraeli** (1766)
Flint Anchor, The (1954) **Sylvia Townsend Warner** (1893)
Flint and Feather (1912) **Pauline Johnson** (1862)
Flirtation (1827) **Lady Charlotte Bury** (1775)
Flitch of Bacon, The (1854) **W.H. Ainsworth** (1805)
Flivver King, The (1937) **Upton Sinclair** (1878)
Floating Dragon (1983) **Peter Straub** (1943)
Floating Island, The (1673) **Richard Head** (1637?)
Floating Island, The (1655) **William Strode** (1602–45)
Floating Light of the Goodwin Sands, The (1870) **R.M. Ballantyne** (1825)
Floating Opera, The (1956) **John Barth** (1930)
Flodden Field (1903) **Alfred Austin** (1835)
Flood (1964) **Robert Penn Warren** (1905)
Flood, The (1986) **Ian Rankin** (1960)
Flood of Life, The (1917) **Richard Church** (1893)
Flood of Thessaly, The (1823) **'Barry Cornwall' [Bryan Waller Procter]** (1787)
Flora Lyndsay (1854) **Susanna Moodie** (1803)
Florence Macarthy (1818) **Lady Sydney Morgan** (1783?)
Florence Manvers (1865) **Selina Bunbury** (1802)
Florence Nightingale (1950) **Cecil Woodham-Smith** (1896)
Florentine Dagger, The (1923) **Ben Hecht** (1894)
Florentine Painters, The (1896) **Bernard Berenson** (1865)
Flores Solitudinis (1654) **Henry Vaughan** (1622)
Florida Poems (1989) **Richard Eberhart** (1904)
Florio; and The Bas Bleu (1786) **Hannah More** (1745)
Florio His Firste Fruites (1578) **John Florio** (1553)
Florios Second Frutes (1591) **John Florio** (1553)
Florizel and Perdita [from Shakespeare's *A Winter's Tale*] (1758) **David Garrick** (1717)
Flotsam (1896) **'Henry Seton Merriman' [Hugh Stowell Scott]** (1862)
Flotsam (1941) **'Erich Maria Remarque' [Erich Paul Remark]** (1898)
Flounder, The [Der Butt] (1977) **Günter Grass** (1927)
Floures for Latine Spekynge [from Terence] (1533) **Nicholas Udall** (1505?) (tr.)
Flow Chart (1991) **John Ashbery** (1927)
Flow My Tears, the Policeman Said (1974) **Philip K. Dick** (1928)
Flower and Thorn (1877) **Thomas Bailey Aldrich** (1836)
Flower and Weed (1882) **M.E. Braddon** (1835)
Flower and Weed, and Other Tales (1883) **M.E. Braddon** (1835)
Flower Babies (1993) **Anne Fine** (1947)
Flower Master, The (1982) **Medbh McGuckian** (1950)
Flower of Forgiveness, The (1894) **Flora Annie Steel** (1847)
Flower of Old Japan, The (1903) **Alfred Noyes** (1880)
Flower Pieces (1888) **William Allingham** (1824)
Flower Pieces (1938) **Padraic Colum** (1881)
Flowering Cherry (1957) **Robert Bolt** (1924)
Flowering Cross, The (1950) **Francis Stuart** (1902)
Flowering Judas (1930) **Katherine Anne Porter** (1890)
Flowering of the Rod (1946) **Hilda Doolittle** (1886)
Flowering Peach, The (1954) **Clifford Odets** (1906)
Flowering Reeds (1933) **Roy Campbell** (1901)
Flowering Rifle (1939) **Roy Campbell** (1901)
Flowering Wilderness (1932) **John Galsworthy** (1867)
Flowers for Hitler (1964) **Leonard Cohen** (1934)
Flowers for Mrs Harris (1958) **Paul Gallico** (1897)
Flowers for the Judge [US: *Legacy in Blood*] (1936) **Margery Allingham** (1904)
Flowers in the Attic (1979) **Virginia Andrews** (1933)
Flowers of Darkness (1981) **Matt Cohen** (1942)
Flowers of Passion (1878) **George Moore** (1852)
Flowers of the Forest, The (1955) **David Garnett** (1892)
Flowres of Sion (1623) **William Drummond of Hawthornden** (1585)
Fludd (1989) **Hilary Mantel** (1952)
Fluke (1977) **James Herbert** (1943)
Flush (1933) **Virginia Woolf** (1882)
Flute and Violin (1891) **James Lane Allen** (1849)
Flute-Player, The (1979) **D.M. Thomas** (1935)
Fly and the Bed Bug, The (1984) **Leland Bardwell** (1928)
Fly in the Ointment, The (1989) **'Alice Thomas Ellis' [Anna Margaret Haycraft]** (1932)
Fly Leaves (1872) **C.S. Calverley** (1831)
Fly on the Wall (1971) **Tony Hillerman** (1925)
Flyaway (1979) **Desmond Bagley** (1923)
Flying Finish (1966) **Dick Francis** (1920)
Flying Goat, The (1939) **H.E. Bates** (1905)
Flying Hero Class (1991) **Thomas Keneally** (1935)
Flying in a Red Kite (1962) **Hugh Hood** (1928)
Flying in to Love (1992) **D.M. Thomas** (1935)
Flying Inn, The (1914) **G.K. Chesterton** (1874)
Flying to Nowhere (1983) **John Fuller** (1937)
Flying Visit, The (1940) **Peter Fleming** (1907)
Flying Wasp, The (1937) **Sean O'Casey** (1880)
Flyting of Dunbar and Kennedy, The (1508) **William Dunbar** (1460?)
Foam, the Razor-Back (1927) **Ernest Thompson Seton** (1860)
Focus (1945) **Arthur Miller** (1915)
Foe (1986) **J.M. Coetzee** (1940)
Foes in Law (1900) **Rhoda Broughton** (1840)
Fog, The (1975) **James Herbert** (1943)
Folding Star, The (1994) **Alan Hollinghurst** (1954)
Foliage (1818) **Leigh Hunt** (1784)
Folks That Live on the Hill, The (1990) **Kingsley Amis** (1922)
Folle Farine (1871) **'Ouida' [Marie Louise de la Ramée]** (1839)
Follow the Footprints (1953) **William Mayne** (1928)

Following Darkness [rev. 1937 as Peter Waring] (1912) **Forrest Reid** (1875)
Following of the Star, The (1911) **Florence Barclay** (1862)
Following the Equator (1897) **'Mark Twain' [Samuel Langhorne Clemens]** (1835)
Folly and Fresh Airs (1892) **Eden Phillpotts** (1862)
Folly Calling (1932) **E.V. Knox** (1881)
Folly of Atheism, The (1692) **Richard Bentley** (1662)
Folly of Eustace, The (1896) **Robert Hichens** (1864)
Foma Gordeyev (1899) **Maxim Gorky** (1868)
Fond Adventures (1905) **Maurice Hewlett** (1861)
Fond Husband, A (1677) **Thomas D'Urfey** (1653)
Food of the Gods, The (1904) **H.G. Wells** (1866)
Fool Errant, The (1905) **Maurice Hewlett** (1861)
Fool i' the Forest, A (1925) **Richard Aldington** (1892)
Fool in Her Folly, A (1920) **Rhoda Broughton** (1840)
Fool of Nature, A (1896) **Julian Hawthorne** (1846)
Fool of Quality, The (1765) **Henry Brooke** (1703)
Fool of the Family, The (1930) **Margaret Kennedy** (1896)
Fool of the World, The (1906) **Arthur Symons** (1865)
Fool Turn'd Critick, The (1676) **Thomas D'Urfey** (1653)
Fool upon Fool (1600) **Robert Armin** (1565?)
Fool's Alphabet, A (1992) **Sebastian Faulks** (1953)
Fool's Errand, A (1879) **Albion W. Tourgée** (1838)
Fool's Preferment, A (1688) **Thomas D'Urfey** (1653)
Fool's Revenge, The (1850) **Tom Taylor** (1817)
Fool's Sanctuary (1987) **Jennifer Johnston** (1930)
Fools Die (1978) **Mario Puzo** (1920)
Fools of Fortune (1983) **'William Trevor' [William Trevor Cox]** (1928)
Foolscap Rose, The (1934) **Joseph Hergesheimer** (1880)
Foot of Clive, The (1962) **John Berger** (1926)
Footnote to History, A (1892) **Robert Louis Stevenson** (1850)
Footsteps at the Lock, The (1928) **Ronald Knox** (1888)
For Beauty Douglas (1982) **Adrian Mitchell** (1932)
For Continuity (1933) **F.R. Leavis** (1895)
For Crying Out Loud (1990) **Chris Wallace-Crabbe** (1934)
For England (1904) **Sir William Watson** (1858)
For England's Sake (1900) **W.E. Henley** (1849)
For Faith and Freedom (1889) **Sir Walter Besant** (1836)
For Lancelot Andrewes (1928) **T.S. Eliot** (1888)
For Lilias (1885) **Rosa Nouchette Carey** (1840)
For Lizzie and Harriet (1973) **Robert Lowell** (1917)
For Love (1918) **Ruby M. Ayres** (1883)
For Love Alone (1944) **Christina Stead** (1902)
For Love and Money (1987) **Jonathan Raban** (1942)
For Love of Imabelle [reissued as A Rage in Harlem (1965)] (1957) **Chester Himes** (1909)
For Mamie's Sake (1886) **Grant Allen** (1848)
For Maurice (1927) **'Vernon Lee' [Violet Paget]** (1856)
For One and the World (1889) **Matilda Betham-Edwards** (1836)
For the Islands I Sing (1997) **George Mackay Brown** (1921–96)
For the Municipality's Elderly (1974) **Peter Reading** (1946)
For the New Intellectual (1961) **Ayn Rand** (1905)
For the Rest of Our Lives (1947) **Dan Davin** (1913)
For the Time Being (1945) **W.H. Auden** (1907)
For the Unfallen (1959) **Geoffrey Hill** (1932)
For the Union Dead (1964) **Robert Lowell** (1917)
For To End Yet Again (1976) **Samuel Beckett** (1906)
For Want of a Nail (1965) **Melvyn Bragg** (1939)
For Whom the Bell Tolls (1940) **Ernest Hemingway** (1898)
For Your Eyes Only (1960) **Ian Fleming** (1908)
Forayers, The (1855) **William Gilmore Simms** (1806)
Forbidden Territory, The (1933) **Dennis Wheatley** (1897)
Forbidden to Marry (1883) **Isabella [Mrs G. Linnaeus] Banks** (1821)
Forc'd Marriage, The (1670) **Aphra Behn** (1640?)
Force, La ['The Power'] (1899) **Paul Adam** (1862)
Force du mal, La ['The Force of Evil'] (1896) **Paul Adam** (1862)
Force of Circumstance [*La Force des choses*] (1963) **Simone de Beauvoir** (1908)
Force of Friendship, The (1710) **Charles Johnson** (1679)
Force of Religion, The (1714) **Edward Young** (1683)
Force, The (1966) **Peter Redgrove** (1932)
The Ford (1917) **Mary Austin** (1868)
Forecast, a Fable, A (1958) **Ruth Fainlight** (1931)
Foregone Conclusion, A (1875) **William Dean Howells** (1837)
Foreign Affairs (1984) **Alison Lurie** (1926)
Foreign Affairs (1976) **'Seán O'Faoláin' [John Francis Whelan]** (1900)
Foreign Land (1985) **Jonathan Raban** (1942)
Foreigners (1935) **Leo Walmsley** (1892)
Forest Exiles, The (1855) **Mayne Reid** (1818)
Forest Lovers, The (1898) **Maurice Hewlett** (1861)
Forest Minstrel, The (1823) **Mary Howitt** (1799) [with William Howitt]
Forest of the Night (1960) **Madison Jones** (1925)
Forest of the South, The (1945) **Caroline Gordon** (1895)
Forest Sanctuary, The (1825) **Felicia Dorothea Hemans** (1793)
Foresters, The (1796) **Elizabeth Gunning** (1769)
Foresters, The (1825) **John Wilson** (1785)
Foresters, The (1892) **Alfred, Lord Tennyson** (1809)
Forests of the Night (1963) **Jon Cleary** (1917)
Forever (1975) **Judy Blume** (1938)
Forever Amber (1944) **Kathleen Winsor** (1919)
Forever Panting (1975) **Peter De Vries** (1910)
Forever Young (1941) **Zoë Akins** (1886)
Forge, The (1924) **Radclyffe Hall** (1880)
Forge, The (1931) **T.S. Stribling** (1881)
Forge in the Forest, The (1896) **Sir Charles G.D. Roberts** (1860)
Forgetting Elena (1973) **Edmund White** (1940)

Forgive Me, Sire (1950) **Norman Cameron** (1905)
Forgotten Life (1988) **Brian Aldiss** (1925)
Forgotten Life (1998) **Brian Aldiss** (1925)
Form in Modern Poetry (1932) **Sir Herbert Read** (1893)
Form of Things Unknown, The (1960) **Sir Herbert Read** (1893)
Forms of Discovery (1967) **Yvor Winters** (1900)
Forms of Fiction, The (1961) **John Gardner** (1933)
Fors Clavigera (1871) **John Ruskin** (1819)
Forsyte Saga, The (1922) **John Galsworthy** (1867)
Fort Amity (1904) **Sir A.T. Quiller-Couch** (1863)
Fortescue (1847) **James Sheridan Knowles** (1784)
Forth Feasting (1617) **William Drummond of Hawthornden** (1585)
Forties, The (1950) **Alan Ross** (1922)
Fortitude (1913) **Sir Hugh Walpole** (1884)
Fortress, The (1932) **Sir Hugh Walpole** (1884)
Fortunate Foundlings, The (1744) **Eliza Haywood** (*c.* 1693)
Fortunate Isles and their Union, The (1625) **Ben Jonson** (1572)
Fortunate Mistress, The [i.e. *Roxana*] (1724) **Daniel Defoe** (1660)
Fortunate Pilgrim, The (1965) **Mario Puzo** (1920)
Fortunate Traveller, The (1981) **Derek Walcott** (1930)
Fortunatus the Pessimist (1892) **Alfred Austin** (1835)
Fortune (1986) **Robert Drewe** (1943)
Fortune at Stake, A (1913) **Nat Gould** (1857)
Fortune by Land and Sea (1655) **Thomas Heywood** (1574?-1641) [with William Rowley]
Fortune, My Foe (1949) **Robertson Davies** (1913)
Fortune of the Rougons, The [*La Fortune des Rougon*; first of the 20-vol. *Les Rougon-Macquart cycle*] (1871) **Émile Zola** (1840)
Fortune of War, The (1979) **Patrick O'Brian** (1914)
Fortunes and Misfortunes of the Famous Moll Flanders, The (1722) **Daniel Defoe** (1660)
Fortunes of Colonel Torlogh O'Brien, The (1847) **J.S. le Fanu** (1814)
Fortunes of Falstaff, The (1943) **John Dover Wilson** (1881)
Fortunes of Glencore, The (1857) **Charles Lever** (1806)
Fortunes of Nigel, The (1822) **Sir Walter Scott** (1771)
Fortunes of Perkin Warbeck, The (1830) **Mary Shelley** (1797)
Fortunes of Philippa, The (1906) **Angela Brazil** (1869)
Forty Beads on a Hangman's Rope (1963) **Rodney Hall** (1935)
Forty Modern Fables (1901) **George Ade** (1866)
Forty Singing Seamen (1907) **Alfred Noyes** (1880)
Forty Stories (1987) **Donald Barthelme** (1931)
Forty Years On (1968) **Alan Bennett** (1934)
Forty-Five Guardsman, The [*Les Quarante-cinq*] (1848) **Alexandre Dumas ['père']** (1802)
Forty-One Poems (1925) **E.E. Cummings** (1894)
Forty-Second Parallel, The (1930) **John Dos Passos** (1896)
Forty-two to Forty-four (1944) **H.G. Wells** (1866)
Fortysomething (1999) **Nigel Williams** (1948)
Forward From Liberalism (1937) **Sir Stephen Spender** (1909)
Foscari (1826) **Mary Russell Mitford** (1787)
Fossil Snake, The (1975) **Lucy Boston** (1892)
Foucault's Pendulum (1988) **Umberto Eco** (1932)
Found in the Street (1986) **Patricia Highsmith** (1921)
Foundation (1951) **Isaac Asimov** (1920)
Foundation and Earth (1986) **Isaac Asimov** (1920)
Foundation and Empire (1952) **Isaac Asimov** (1920)
Foundation of Christian Religion, The (1590) **William Perkins** (1558)
Foundation's Edge (1982) **Isaac Asimov** (1920)
Foundations of a Creed, The (1873) **G.H. Lewes** (1817)
Foundations of Belief, The (1895) **A.J. Balfour** (1848)
Foundations of Empirical Knowledge, The (1940) **A.J. Ayer** (1910)
Foundations of Joy, The (1976) **Chris Wallace-Crabbe** (1934)
Foundling, The (1748) **Edward Moore** (1712)
Foundry, The (1934) **Albert Halper** (1904)
Fountain, The (1925) **Eugene O'Neill** (1888)
Fountain, The (1932) **Charles Morgan** (1894)
Fountain of Bakhchisarai, The (1822) **Alexander Pushkin** (1799)
Fountain Overflows, The (1956) **'Rebecca West' [Cicily Isabel Andrews]** (1892)
Fountain Sealed, A (1897) **Sir Walter Besant** (1836)
Fountaine of Selfe-love, The (1600) **Ben Jonson** (1572)
Fountainhead, The (1943) **Ayn Rand** (1905)
Fountains in the Sand (1912) **Norman Douglas** (1868)
Fountains of Paradise, The (1979) **Arthur C. Clarke** (1917)
Four and a Half Dancing Men (1992) **Anne Stevenson** (1933)
Four Banks of the River of Space, The (1990) **Wilson Harris** (1921)
Four Beauties, The (1968) **H.E. Bates** (1905)
Four Corners of the World, The (1917) **A.E.W. Mason** (1865)
Four Countries (1949) **William Plomer** (1903)
Four Discourses (1694) **Gilbert Burnet** (1643)
Four Dissertations (1757) **David Hume** (1711)
Four Faultless Felons (1930) **G.K. Chesterton** (1874)
Four Feathers, The (1902) **A.E.W. Mason** (1865)
Four for Tomorrow (1967) **Roger Zelazny** (1937)
Four Forsyte Stories (1929) **John Galsworthy** (1867)
Four Generations (1934) **Naomi Jacob** (1884)
Four Georges, The (1861) **W.M. Thackeray** (1811)
Four Ghost Stories (1888) **Mary Louisa Molesworth** (1839)
Four Just Men, The (1905) **Edgar Wallace** (1875)
Four Loves, The (1960) **C.S. Lewis** (1898)
Four Million, The (1906) **'O. Henry' [William Sydney Porter]** (1862)
Four New Plays [*The Surprisal, The Committee, The Indian Queen, The Vestal Virgin*] (1665) **Sir Robert Howard** (1626)
Four Novellas (1977) **Samuel Beckett** (1906)

Four of Hearts, The (1938) **'Ellery Queen' [Frederic Dannay** (1905) and **Manfred B. Lee]** (1905)
Four Past Midnight (1990) **Stephen King** (1947)
Four Plays (1913) **Gilbert Cannan** (1884)
Four Plays for Dancers [adds 'At the Hawk's Well' and 'Calvary' to *Two Plays for Dancers*] (1921) **W.B. Yeats** (1865)
Four Poems in Measure (1973) **John Heath-Stubbs** (1918)
Four Portraits (1945) **Peter Quennell** (1905)
Four Quartets (1944) **T.S. Eliot** (1888)
Four Red Nightcaps (1890) **C.J. Cutcliffe Hyne** (1865)
Four Saints in Three Acts (1934) **Gertrude Stein** (1874)
Four Seasons, The (1965) **Arnold Wesker** (1932)
Four Short Plays (1922) **Lascelles Abercrombie** (1881)
Four Stories (1979) **Sheila Watson** (1919)
Four-and-Twenty Blackbirds (1915) **Edward Thomas** (1878)
Four-Chambered Heart, The (1950) **Anaïs Nin** (1903)
Four-Dimensional Nightmare, The (1963) **J.G. Ballard** (1930)
Four-Fifty From Paddington (1957) **Agatha Christie** (1890)
Four-Gated City, The (1969) **Doris Lessing** (1919)
Foure Birds of Noahs Arke (1609) **Thomas Dekker** (1572?)
Foure Bookes of Husbandry [from Conrad Heresbach] (1577) **Barnaby Googe** (1540) (tr.)
Foure PP, The (1544?) **John Heywood** (1497?)
Foure Prentises of London, The (1615) **Thomas Heywood** (1574?)
Foure Sermons Upon Speciall Occasions (1625) **John Donne** (1572)
Fourteen Sisters of Emilio Monez O'Brien, The (1993) **Oscar Hijuelos** (1951)
Fourteen Sonnets (1789) **William Lisle Bowles** (1762)
Fourteenth Chronicle, The (1973) **John Dos Passos** (1896–1970)
Fourth Generation, The (1900) **Sir Walter Besant** (1836)
Fourth Horseman of Miami Beach, The (1966) **Albert Halper** (1904)
Fourth K., The (1991) **Mario Puzo** (1920)
Fourth Protocol, The (1984) **Frederick Forsyth** (1938)
Fowler, The (1899) **Beatrice Harraden** (1864)
Fowre Hymnes (1596) **Edmund Spenser** (1552?)
Fox in the Attic, The (1961) **Richard Hughes** (1900)
Fox of Peapack, The (1938) **E.B. White** (1899)
Foxes of Harrow, The (1946) **Frank Yerby** (1916)
Foxfire (1993) **Joyce Carol Oates** (1938)
Foxglove Manor (1884) **Robert Williams Buchanan** (1841)
Foxglove Saga, The (1960) **Auberon Waugh** (1939)
Foxybaby (1985) **Elizabeth Jolley** (1923)
Fra Rupert (1840) **Walter Savage Landor** (1775)
Fractured Circles (1979) **James Berry** (1924)
Fragment (1969) **John Ashbery** (1927)
Fragment on Government, A (1776) **Jeremy Bentham** (1748)
Fragmenta Aurea [letters, poems, and plays] (1646) **Sir John Suckling** (1609–42)
Fragments of a Life Story (1987) **Denton Welch** (1915–48)
Fragments of Ancient Poetry (1760) **James Macpherson** (1736)
Framley Parsonage (1861) **Anthony Trollope** (1815)
Francesca Carrara [as 'L.E.L.'] (1834) **Letitia Elizabeth Landon** (1802)
Francesca da Rimini (1901) **Gabriele D'Annunzio** (1863)
Franchise Affair, The (1948) **'Josephine Tey' [Elizabeth Mackintosh]** (1897)
Franchiser, The (1976) **Stanley Elkin** (1930)
Franciade, La ['The Hymn of France'; unfinished] (1572) **Pierre de Ronsard** (1524)
Francis Quarles Investigates (1965) **Julian Symons** (1912)
Francis the First (1832) **Frances [Fanny] Kemble** (1809)
Francis the Waif [*François le Champi*] (1848) **'George Sand' [Auore Dupin]** (1804)
Frangipani Gardens, The (1980) **Barbara Hanrahan** (1939)
Frank (1822) **Maria Edgeworth** (1767)
Frank Fairlegh (1850) **Frank Smedley** (1818)
Frank Hilton (1855) **James Grant** (1822)
Frank Sinclair's Wife (1874) **Mrs J.H. Riddell** (1832)
Frankenstein (1818) **Mary Shelley** (1797)
Frankenstein Unbound (1974) **Brian Aldiss** (1925)
Franklin Evans (1842) **Walt Whitman** (1819)
Franny and Zooey (1961) **J.D. Salinger** (1919)
Fraternity (1909) **John Galsworthy** (1867)
Frau Jenny Treibel (1892) **Theodor Fontane** (1819)
Frau ohne Schatten, Die ['The Woman Without a Shadow'; music by Richard Strauss] (1919) **Hugo von Hofmannsthal** (1874)
Fraud (1992) **Anita Brookner** (1928)
Fraud Detected; or, The Hibernian Patriot (1725) **Jonathan Swift** (1667)
Fräulein Schmidt and Mr Anstruther (1907) **'Elizabeth' [Mary Annette Gräfin] von Arnim** (1866)
Freaks of Mayfair, The (1916) **E.F. Benson** (1867)
Freaky Deaky (1988) **Elmore Leonard** (1925)
Freddy's Book (1980) **John Gardner** (1933)
Frederick, Duke of Brunswick-Lunenburgh (1729) **Eliza Haywood** (*c.* 1693)
Fredo Fuss Love Life (1974) **Hal Porter** (1911)
Fredolfo (1819) **C.R. Maturin** (1782)
Free (1918) **Theodore Dreiser** (1871)
Free and Clear (1983) **Robert W. Anderson** (1917)
Free Fall (1959) **William Golding** (1911)
Free Fishers, The (1934) **John Buchan** (1875)
Free Joe (1887) **Joel Chandler Harris** (1848)
Free Man, The (1943) **Conrad Richter** (1890)
Free Press, The (1918) **Hilaire Belloc** (1870)
Free Society, The (1948) **John Middleton Murry** (1889)

Free Thoughts on Faith (1746) **Aaron Hill** (1685)
Free Thoughts on Public Affairs (1806) **William Hazlitt** (1778)
Free Thoughts on Reviving the Dissenting Interest (1730) **Philip Doddridge** (1702)
Free Wheeling (1931) **Ogden Nash** (1902)
Freedom of the City, The (1973) **Brian Friel** (1929)
Freedom of the Poet, The (1976) **John Berryman** (1914–72)
Freedom Road (1944) **Howard Fast** (1914)
Freedom Trap, The (1971) **Desmond Bagley** (1923)
Freelands, The (1915) **John Galsworthy** (1867)
Freeman, The (1902) **Ellen Glasgow** (1874)
French Eton, A (1864) **Matthew Arnold** (1822)
French Gardiner, The (1658) **John Evelyn** (1620) (tr.)
French Girls Are Vicious (1956) **James T. Farrell** (1904)
French Lieutenant's Woman, The (1969) **John Fowles** (1926)
French Nan (1905) **Egerton** (1858) and **Agnes** (*c.* 1860) **Castle**
French Poets and Novelists (1878) **Henry James** (1843)
French Powder Mystery, The (1930) **'Ellery Queen' [Frederic Dannay** (1905) and **Manfred B. Lee]** (1905)
French Revolution, The (1911) **Hilaire Belloc** (1870)
French Revolution, The (1791) **William Blake** (1757)
French Revolution, The (1837) **Thomas Carlyle** (1795)
French Studies and Reviews (1926) **Richard Aldington** (1892)
French Wife, The (1904) **Katharine Tynan** (1861)
French Without Tears (1936) **Terence Rattigan** (1911)
French Women of Letters (1862) **Julia Kavanagh** (1824)
Frenchman Must Die, A (1946) **Kay Boyle** (1903)
Frenchman's Creek (1941) **Daphne du Maurier** (1907)
Frenzied Fiction (1918) **Stephen Leacock** (1869)
Frequencies (1978) **R.S. Thomas** (1913)
Frequent Hearses [US: *Double Death*] (1950) **'Edmund Crispin'** (1921)
Frescoes for Mr Rockefeller's City (1933) **Archibald MacLeish** (1892)
Freud and the Crisis of Our Culture (1956) **Lionel Trilling** (1905)
Friar Jerome's Beautiful Book (1881) **Thomas Bailey Aldrich** (1836)
Friday (1982) **Robert A. Heinlein** (1907)
Friday Book, The (1984) **John Barth** (1930)
Friday Mornings 1941–4 (1944) **Sir Harold Nicolson** (1886)
Friedrich Nietzsche (1906) **A.R. Orage** (1873)
Friend From England, A (1987) **Anita Brookner** (1928)
Friend of Heraclitus (1993) **Patricia Beer** (1924)
Friend of Kafka, A (1970) **Isaac Bashevis Singer** (1904)
Friend of My Youth (1990) **Alice Munro** (1931)
Friend, The (1809) **S.T. Coleridge** (1772)
Friendly Tree, The (1936) **C. Day Lewis** (1904)
Friends (1916) **Wilfrid Gibson** (1878)
Friends, The (1970) **Arnold Wesker** (1932)
Friends and Heroes (1965) **Olivia Manning** (1908)
Friends and Relations (1931) **Elizabeth Bowen** (1899)
Friends in Low Places (1965) **Simon Raven** (1927)
Friends of Eddie Coyle, The (1972) **George V. Higgins** (1939)
Friends of God, The [US: *The Siege*] (1963) **Peter Vansittart** (1920)
Friends Over the Water (1879) **Matilda Betham-Edwards** (1836)
Friendship (1878) **'Ouida' [Marie Louise de la Ramée]** (1839)
Friendship and Love (1745) **Mark Akenside** (1721)
Friendship in Fashion (1678) **Thomas Otway** (1652)
Friendship's Garland (1871) **Matthew Arnold** (1822)
Frigate Bird, The (1989) **Alistair Campbell** (1925)
Frighteners, The (1987) **Sean O'Brien** (1952)
Frinck; Summer with Monica (1967) **Roger McGough** (1937)
Fringe of Leaves, A (1976) **Patrick White** (1912)
Fringilla (1895) **R.D. Blackmore** (1825)
Frobishers, The (1901) **S. Baring-Gould** (1834)
Frog Prince, The (1966) **Stevie Smith** (1902)
Frogs, The (405BC) **Aristophanes** (*c.* 445 BC)
Frolic of His Own, A (1994) **William Gaddis** (1922)
From a College Window (1906) **A.C. Benson** (1862)
From a Cornish Window (1906) **Sir A.T. Quiller-Couch** (1863)
From a View to a Death (1933) **Anthony Powell** (1905)
From Adam's Peak to Elephanta (1892) **Edward Carpenter** (1844)
From an Unknown Isle (1924) **John Drinkwater** (1882)
From Authority to Freedom (1920) **L.P. Jacks** (1860)
From Bauhaus to Our House (1981) **Tom Wolfe** (1930)
From Bed to Worse (1934) **Robert Benchley** (1889)
From Berlin to Heaven (1990) **Carol Rumens** (1944)
From Billabong to London (1915) **Mary Grant Bruce** (1878)
From Bourgeois Land (1969) **Iain Crichton Smith [Iain Mac a'Ghobhainn]** (1928)
From Catullus, Chiefly Concerning Lesbia (1924) **Arthur Symons** (1865)
From Centre City (1994) **Thomas Kinsella** (1928)
From Death to Morning (1935) **Thomas Wolfe** (1900)
From Doon With Death [first 'Inspector Wexford' novel] (1964) **Ruth Rendell** (1930)
From Door to Door (1900) **Bernard Capes** (1850?)
From Every New Chink of the Ark (1977) **Peter Redgrove** (1932)
From Feathers to Iron (1931) **C. Day Lewis** (1904)
From Flushing to Calvary (1932) **Edward Dahlberg** (1900)
From Glasgow to Saturn (1973) **Edwin Morgan** (1920)
From Gloucester Out (1964) **Ed Dorn** (1929)

From Heaven Lake (1983) **Vikram Seth** (1952)
From Here to Eternity (1951) **James Jones** (1921)
From Inland (1907) **Ford Madox Ford** (1873)
From Jordan's Delight (1937) **R.P. Blackmur** (1904)
From Moor Isles (1888) **Jessie Fothergill** (1851)
From My Window [*De ma fenêtre*] (1942) **Colette** (1873)
From Napoleon to Stalin (1980) **E.H. Carr** (1892)
From Napoleon to Stalin (1950) **A.J.P. Taylor** (1906)
From One Generation to Another (1892) **'Henry Seton Merriman' [Hugh Stowell Scott]** (1862)
From Ponkapog to Pesth (1883) **Thomas Bailey Aldrich** (1836)
From Potter's Field (1995) **Patricia Cornwell** (1956)
From Russia With Love (1957) **Ian Fleming** (1908)
From Sea to Sea (1899) **Rudyard Kipling** (1865)
From Six Books (1940) **'Anna Akhmatova' [Anna Andreevna Gorenko]** (1889)
From the Beast to the Blonde (1994) **Marina Warner** (1946)
From the Diary of a Snail (1972) **Günter Grass** (1927)
From the Earth to the Moon [*De la Terre à la Lune*] (1865) **Jules Verne** (1828)
From the Fifteenth District (1979) **Mavis Gallant** (1922)
From the Four Winds [by 'John Sinjohn'] (1897) **John Galsworthy** (1867)
From the Hidden Way (1916) **James Branch Cabell** (1879)
From the Joke Shop (1975) **Roy Fuller** (1912)
From the Land of the Shamrock (1901) **Jane Barlow** (1857)
From the Loveless Matel (1980) **Adrian Henri** (1932)
From the Memoirs of a Minister of France (1895) **Stanley J. Weyman** (1855)
From the School of Eloquence (1978) **Tony Harrison** (1937)
From the Terrace (1958) **John O'Hara** (1905)
From the Video Box (1986) **Edwin Morgan** (1920)
From Toulouse-Lautrec to Rodin (1929) **Arthur Symons** (1865)
From Whose Bourne (1893) **Robert Barr** (1850)
Fromont Junior and Risler Senior [*Fromont jeune et Risler aîné*] (1874) **Alphonse Daudet** (1840)
Front Page, The (1928) **Ben Hecht** (1894)
Frontier Wolf (1980) **Rosemary Sutcliff** (1920)
Frost in May (1933) **'Antonia White' [Eirene Botting]** (1899)
Frozen Assets (1964) **P.G. Wodehouse** (1881)
Frozen Deep, The (1874) **Wilkie Collins** (1824)
Frozen Earth, The (1935) **Winifred Holtby** (1898)
Frozen Pirate, The (1887) **W. Clark Russell** (1844)
Fruit Man, the Meat Man, and the Manager, The (1971) **Hugh Hood** (1928)
Fruit of the Tree, The (1907) **Edith Wharton** (1862)
Fruitful Sayings of David, The (1508) **John Fisher** (1459?)
Fruitfulness [Fécondité] (1899) **Émile Zola** (1840)
Fruits of a Father's Love (1726) **William Penn** (1644–1718)
Fruits of the Earth (1933) **Frederick Grove** (1879)
Fruits of the Spirit, The (1942) **Evelyn Underhill** (1875)
Fudge Family in Paris, The [as 'Thomas Brown the Younger'] (1818) **Thomas Moore** (1779)
Fudges in England, The (1835) **Thomas Moore** (1779)
Fuel for the Flame (1960) **Alec Waugh** (1898)
Fuenteovejuna (1619) **Lope de Vega** (1562)
Fugitive Pieces (1806) **George Gordon, Lord Byron** (1788)
Fugitive Pieces (1810) **James Sheridan Knowles** (1784)
Fugitive Pieces in Verse and Prose (1758) **Horace Walpole** (1717)
Fugitive, The (1705) **Mary Davys** (1674)
Fugitive, The (1913) **John Galsworthy** (1867)
Fugitives, The (1887) **R.M. Ballantyne** (1825)
Fugue in Time, A (1945) **Rumer Godden** (1907)
Fuhrer Bunker, The (1977) **W.D. Snodgrass** (1926)
Full and True Account of the Wonderful Mission of Earl Lavender, A (1895) **John Davidson** (1857)
Full Score (1989) **Fred Urquhart** (1912)
Full Swing (1914) **'Frank Danby' [Julia Frankau]** (1864)
Full Term (1978) **J.I.M. Stewart** (1906)
Full Tilt: Ireland to India by Bicycle (1965) **Dervla Murphy** (1931)
Full Vindication of the Dutchess Dowager of Marlborough, A (1742) **Henry Fielding** (1707)
Fumifugium (1661) **John Evelyn** (1620)
Function of Criticism, The (1957) **Yvor Winters** (1900)
Fundamental Disch (1980) **Thomas M. Disch** (1940)
Funeral Games [with *The Good and Faithful Servants*] (1970) **Joe Orton** (1933)
Funeral Games (1981) **'Mary Renault' [Eileen Mary Challans]** (1905)
Funeral Games (1987) **Vernon Scannell** (1922)
Funeral in Berlin (1964) **Len Deighton** (1929)
Funeral Rites [Pompes funèbres] (1947) **Jean Genet** (1910)
Funeral, The (1701) **Sir Richard Steele** (1672)
Funerall Poeme uppon . . . the Late Earle of Devonshyre, A (1606) **Samuel Daniel** (1562)
Fungus the Bogeyman (1975) **Raymond Briggs** (1934)
Funland (1973) **Dannie Abse** (1923)
Funny Thing Happened on the Way to the Forum, A (1961) **Larry Gelbart** (1923) [with Burt Shevelove]
Furious Seasons (1977) **Raymond Carver** (1939)
Furmetary, The (1699) **William King** (1663)
Further Adventures of Captain Kettle, The (1899) **C.J. Cutcliffe Hyne** (1865)
Further Adventures of Mr Verdant Green, The (1853) **'Cuthbert Bede B.A.' [Edward Bradley]** (1827)
Further Adventures of the Family From One End Street (1956) **Eve Garnett** (1900)
Further Experiences of an Irish R.M. (1908) **'Somerville and Ross' [Edith Somerville** (1858) and **Violet Martin]** (1862)
Further Explorations (1965) **L.C. Knights** (1906)
Further Fables for Our Time (1956) **James Thurber** (1894)

Further Foolishness (1916) **Stephen Leacock** (1869)
Further Range, A (1936) **Robert Frost** (1874)
Further Records (1890) **Frances [Fanny] Kemble** (1809)
Further Studies in a Dying Culture (1949) **'Christopher Caudwell'** (1907)
Furys, The (1935) **James Hanley** (1901)
Futility (1922) **William Gerhardie** (1895)
Future in America, The (1906) **H.G. Wells** (1866)
Future Indefinite (1954) **Noel Coward** (1899)
Future of English Poetry, The (1913) **Sir Edmund Gosse** (1849)
Future of Islam, The (1882) **Wilfrid Scawen Blunt** (1840)
Future of the American Negro, The (1899) **Booker T. Washington** (1856)
Future of the Human Race, The (1853) **Robert Owen** (1771)
Futuretrack 5 (1983) **Robert Westall** (1929)

G

G (1972) **John Berger** (1926)
'G' is for Gumshoe (1990) **Sue Grafton** (1940)
Gaberlunzie's Wallet, The (1843) **James Ballantine** (1808)
Gabriel Conroy (1876) **Bret Harte** (1836)
Gabriel Denver (1873) **Oliver Madox Brown** (1855)
Gabriel Tolliver (1902) **Joel Chandler Harris** (1848)
Gabriel's Lament (1986) **Paul Bailey** (1937)
Gadfly, The (1897) **Ethel Voynich** (1864)
Gaily, Gaily (1963) **Ben Hecht** (1894)
Galactic Patrol (1950) **E.E.'Doc' Smith** (1890)
Galahad at Blandings [US: *The Brinkmanship of Galahad Threepwood*] (1965) **P.G. Wodehouse** (1881)
Galahad Jones (1910) **Arthur Henry Adams** (1872)
Galapagos (1985) **Kurt Vonnegut** (1922)
Galatea (1953) **James M. Cain** (1892)
Galatea, La (1585) **Miguel de Cervantes Saavedra** (1547)
Gale of the World, The (1969) **Henry Williamson** (1895)
Galilee (1998) **Clive Barker** (1952)
Galilee Hitch-Hiker, The (1958) **Richard Brautigan** (1935)
Gallant Lords of Bois-Doré, The [*Les Beaux Messieurs de Bois-Doré*] (1858) **'George Sand' [Auore Dupin]** (1804)
Gallant Parties [*Fêtes galantes*] (1869) **Paul Verlaine** (1844)
Gallantry (1907) **James Branch Cabell** (1879)
Gallathea (1592) **John Lyly** (1554)
Gallegher (1891) **Richard Harding Davis** (1864)
Gallery, A (1924) **Philip Guedalla** (1889)
Gallery, The (1947) **John Horne Burns** (1916)
Gallery of Literary Portraits [2nd ser., 1850; 3rd ser., 1854] (1845) **George Gilfillan** (1813)
Gallery of Women, A (1929) **Theodore Dreiser** (1871)
Gallic Wars [Caesar] (1565) **Arthur Golding** (1536) (tr.)
Gallion's Reach (1927) **H.M. Tomlinson** (1873)
Gallipoli Memories (1929) **Compton Mackenzie** (1883)
Gallowglass [as 'Barbara Vine'] (1990) **Ruth Rendell** (1930)
Gallows on the Sand (1955) **Morris West** (1916)
Gambit (1962) **Rex Stout** (1886)
Gambling Man, The (1975) **Catherine Cookson** (1906)
Game, The (1905) **'Jack London' [John Griffith Chaney]** (1876)
Game, The (1967) **A.S. Byatt** (1936)
Game and the Candle, The (1899) **Rhoda Broughton** (1840)
Game at Cha, A (1625) **Thomas Middleton** (1580)
Game Cock, The (1947) **Michael McLaverty** (1904)
Game in Heaven with Tussy Marx, A (1966) **Piers Paul Read** (1941)
Game of Dark, A (1971) **William Mayne** (1928)
Game of Hide and Seek, A (1951) **Elizabeth Taylor** (1912)
Game of Kings (1962) **Dorothy Dunnett** (1923)
Game of Love and Death, The (1990) **John Heath-Stubbs** (1918)
Game of Touch, A (1970) **Hugh Hood** (1928)
Gamekeeper at Home, The (1878) **Richard Jefferies** (1848)
Gamekeeper, The (1975) **Barry Hines** (1939)
Games at Twilight (1978) **Anita Desai** (1937)
Games Were Coming, The (1963) **Michael Anthony** (1932)
Gamester, The (1705) **Susanna Centlivre** (1669?)
Gamester, The (1753) **Edward Moore** (1712)
Gamester, The (1637) **James Shirley** (1596)
Gap in the Curtain, The (1932) **John Buchan** (1875)
Garbage (1993) **A.R. Ammons** (1926)
Garbage Man, The (1925) **John Dos Passos** (1896)
Garden, The (1946) **Vita Sackville-West** (1892)
Garden District [*Suddenly Last Summer*, and *Something Unspoken*] (1958) **'Tennessee' [Thomas Lanier] Williams** (1911)
Garden God, The (1905) **Forrest Reid** (1875)
Garden of Adonis, The (1937) **Caroline Gordon** (1895)
Garden of Allah, The (1904) **Robert Hichens** (1864)
Garden of Bees, The (1905) **Joseph Campbell** (1879)
Garden of Earthly Delights, A (1967) **Joyce Carol Oates** (1938)
Garden of Eloquence, The (1577) **Henry Peacham the elder** (fl.1577)
Garden of Florence, The (1821) **J.H. Reynolds** (1796)
Garden of Swords, The (1899) **Max Pemberton** (1863)
Garden of the Villa Mollini, The (1987) **Rose Tremain** (1943)
Garden Revisited, A (1931) **John Lehmann** (1907)
Garden That I Love, The (1894) **Alfred Austin** (1835)
Garden to the Sea, The (1953) **Philip Toynbee** (1916)
Garden-Party, The (1922) **'Katherine Mansfield' [Kathleen Mansfield Beauchamp]** (1888)
Gardener's Dog, The [*El perro del hortelano*] (1613–15) **Lope de Vega** (1562)

Gardeners and Astronomers (1953) **Edith Sitwell** (1887)
Gardens of this World (1929) **Henry Blake Fuller** (1857–1929)
Gardner, The (1913) **Rabindranath Tagore** (1861)
Gareth and Lynette (1872) **Alfred, Lord Tennyson** (1809)
Garfield Honor, The (1961) **Frank Yerby** (1916)
Garfield's Apprentices [series of 12 short novels] (1976–8) **Leon Garfield** (1921)
Gargantua [as 'Alcofribas Nasier'] (1534) **François Rabelais** (1494?)
Gargling with Jelly (1985) **Brian Patten** (1946)
Gargoyles (1922) **Ben Hecht** (1894)
Garibaldi (1861) **M.E. Braddon** (1835)
Garibaldi and the Making of Italy (1911) **G.M. Trevelyan** (1876)
Garibaldi and the Thousand (1909) **G.M. Trevelyan** (1876)
Garibaldi's Defence of the Roman Republic (1907) **G.M. Trevelyan** (1876)
Garland of Good Will, The (1628) **Thomas Deloney** (1543?-1600)
Garland of Laurel, The (1523) **John Skelton** (1460?)
Garland of Straw, A (1943) **Sylvia Townsend Warner** (1893)
Garments the Living Wear (1989) **James Purdy** (1923)
Garnets Ghost (1679) **John Oldham** (1653)
Garrick Year, The (1964) **Margaret Drabble** (1939)
Garry Owen; and Poor Bob (1832) **Maria Edgeworth** (1767)
Garstons (1930) **H.C. Bailey** (1878)
Garth (1877) **Julian Hawthorne** (1846)
Gas-House McGinty (1933) **James T. Farrell** (1904)
Gascoyne, the Sandal-Wood Trader (1864) **R.M. Ballantyne** (1825)
Gaslight and Daylight (1859) **George Augustus Sala** (1828)
Gaston de Blondeville (1826) **Ann Radcliffe** (1764–1823)
Gate of Angels, The (1990) **Penelope Fitzgerald** (1916)
Gate of Death, The (1909) **A.C. Benson** (1862)
Gate of Smaragdus, The (1904) **Gordon Bottomley** (1874)
Gate, The (1962) **C. Day Lewis** (1904)
Gateless Barrier, The (1900) **'Lucas Malet' [Mary St Leger Harrison]** (1852)
Gates, The (1973) **Jennifer Johnston** (1930)
Gates of Ivory, The (1991) **Margaret Drabble** (1939)
Gates of Summer, The (1956) **John Whiting** (1917)
Gates of the Compass, The (1930) **Robert Hillyer** (1895)
Gates of Wrath, The (1903) **Arnold Bennett** (1867)
Gates of Wrath, The (1973) **Allen Ginsberg** (1926)
Gather Together in My Name (1974) **Maya Angelou** (1928)
Gathering Clouds (1895) **Frederic W. Farrar** (1831)
Gathering of Brother Hilarius, The (1901) **'Michael Fairless' [Margaret Fairless Barber]** (1869)
Gathering of Fugitives, A (1956) **Lionel Trilling** (1905)
Gathering of Old Men, A (1983) **Ernest J. Gaines** (1933)
Gathering of Zion, The (1964) **Wallace Stegner** (1909)
Gathering Storm, The (1940) **Sir William Empson** (1906)
Gaudete (1977) **Ted Hughes** (1930)
Gaudy, The (1974) **J.I.M. Stewart** (1906)
Gaudy Night (1935) **Dorothy L. Sayers** (1893)
Gautama the Enlightened (1941) **John Masefield** (1878)
Gaverocks, The (1887) **S. Baring-Gould** (1834)
Gay Lord Quex, The (1899) **Arthur Wing Pinero** (1855)
Gay Science, The (1866) **E.S. Dallas** (1828)
Gaze of the Gorgon, The (1992) **Tony Harrison** (1937)
Gazelles, The (1904) **T. Sturge Moore** (1870)
Gebir (1798) **Walter Savage Landor** (1775)
Gedichte ['Poems'] (1821) **Heinrich Heine** (1797)
Gemini (2000) **Dorothy Dunnett** (1923)
Geetanjali (1912) **Rabindranath Tagore** (1861)
Gemel in London (1928) **James Evershed Agate** (1877)
Gemma (1968) **Noel Streatfeild** (1895)
Genealogies Recorded in the Sacred Scriptures, The (1611) **John Speed** (1552?)
General, The (1936) **C.S. Forester** (1899)
General, The (1960) **Alan Sillitoe** (1928)
General Description of Nova Scotia, A (1823) **T. C. Haliburton** (1796)
General Gage's Confession (1775) **Philip Freneau** (1752)
General Gage's Soliloquy (1775) **Philip Freneau** (1752)
General History and State of Europe, The [Les Moeurs et l'esprit des nations] (1756) **'Voltaire' [François-Marie Arouet]** (1694)
General History of Trade, A (1713) **Daniel Defoe** (1660)
General Theory of Employment, Interest and Money, The (1936) **J.M. Keynes** (1883)
General William Booth Enters into Heaven (1913) **Vachel Lindsay** (1879)
Generall Historie of the Turkes, The (1603) **Richard Knolles** (1550?)
Generally Speaking (1928) **G.K. Chesterton** (1874)
Generation Without Farewell (1959) **Kay Boyle** (1903)
Generations (1980) **Sharon Pollock** (1936)
Generous Days, The (1971) **Sir Stephen Spender** (1909)
Genesis (1943) **Delmore Schwartz** (1913)
Geneva (1938) **Bernard Shaw** (1856)
Génie du lieu, Le ['The Spirit of Place'] (1958–88) **Michel Butor** (1926)
Génie du Rhin, Le (1921) **Maurice Barrès** (1862)
'Genius', The (1915) **Theodore Dreiser** (1871)
Genius and the Goddess, The (1955) **Aldous Huxley** (1894)
Genius Loci (1899) **'Vernon Lee' [Violet Paget]** (1856)

Genius of Christianity, The [*Le Génie du christianisme*] (1802) **François-René, vicomte de Chateaubriand** (1768)
Genius of the Thames, The (1810) **Thomas Love Peacock** (1785)
Genocides, The (1965) **Thomas M. Disch** (1940)
Genteel Tradition at Bay, The (1931) **George Santayana** (1863)
Gentian Hill (1949) **Elizabeth Goudge** (1900)
Gentle Craft, The (1597) **Thomas Deloney** (1543?)
Gentle Grafter, The (1908) **'O. Henry' [William Sydney Porter]** (1862)
Gentle Island, The (1971) **Brian Friel** (1929)
Gentle Jack (1963) **Robert Bolt** (1924)
Gentle Libertine, The [*L'Ingénue libertine*] (1909) **Colette** (1873)
Gentle Lover, The (1913) **Forrest Reid** (1875)
Gentle People, The (1939) **Irwin Shaw** (1913)
Gentle Shepherd, The (1725) **Allan Ramsay** (1686)
Gentleman Adventurer, The (1914) **H.C. Bailey** (1878)
Gentleman and Ladies (1968) **Susan Hill** (1942)
Gentleman Dancing-Master, The (1672) **William Wycherley** (1641)
Gentleman From Indiana, The (1899) **Booth Tarkington** (1869)
Gentleman from San Francisco, The (1914) **Ivan Bunin** (1870)
Gentleman, I Address You Privately (1933) **Kay Boyle** (1903)
Gentleman in the Parlour, The (1930) **Somerset Maugham** (1874)
Gentleman of France, A (1893) **Stanley J. Weyman** (1855)
Gentleman of Leisure, A (1910) **P.G. Wodehouse** (1881)
Gentleman of the Old School, The (1839) **G.P.R. James** (1799)
Gentleman of Venice, The (1655) **James Shirley** (1596)
Gentleman Usher, The (1606) **George Chapman** (1559?)
Gentleman's Gentleman, A (1896) **Max Pemberton** (1863)
Gentlemen at Gyang Gyang [as 'Brent of Bin Bin'] (1956) **Miles Franklin** (1879–1954)
Gentlemen in England (1985) **A.N. Wilson** (1950)
Gentlemen Prefer Blondes (1925) **Anita Loos** (1893)
Geoffrey Monckton (1853) **Susanna Moodie** (1803)
Geographical Distribution of Animals, The (1876) **Alfred Russel Wallace** (1823)
Geographical History of America, The (1936) **Gertrude Stein** (1874)
Geographical, Natural, and Civil History Of Chili, The [from the Italian of J. Ignatius Molina] (1809) **Robert Southey** (1774) (tr.)
Geographies (1982) **C.K. Stead** (1932)
Geography (1965) **Ed Dorn** (1929)
Geography and Plays (1922) **Gertrude Stein** (1874)
Geography III (1976) **Elizabeth Bishop** (1911)
Geological Observations on South America (1846) **Charles Darwin** (1809)
Geological Observations on Volcanic Islands (1844) **Charles Darwin** (1809)
George Bernard Shaw: The Last Laugh (1992) **Michael Holroyd** (1935)
George Bernard Shaw: The Lure of Fantasy (1991) **Michael Holroyd** (1935)
George Bernard Shaw: The Pursuit of Power (1989) **Michael Holroyd** (1935)
George Bernard Shaw: The Search for Love (1988) **Michael Holroyd** (1935)
George Borrow (1912) **Edward Thomas** (1878)
George Canterbury's Will (1870) **Mrs Henry Wood** (1814)
George Chapman (1875) **A. C. Swinburne** (1837)
George Dandin (1668) **'Molière' [Jean-Baptiste Poquelin]** (1622)
George Eliot (1902) **Sir Leslie Stephen** (1832)
George Geith of Fen Court [as 'F.G. Trafford'] (1864) **Mrs J.H. Riddell** (1832)
George Lovell (1846) **James Sheridan Knowles** (1784)
George Mills (1982) **Stanley Elkin** (1930)
George St George Julian (1841) **Henry Cockton** (1807)
George Stephenson (1857) **Samuel Smiles** (1812)
George the Fourth (1822) **Charlotte Dacre** (1782?)
George's Marvellous Medicine (1981) **Roald Dahl** (1916)
George's Mother (1896) **Stephen Crane** (1871)
George's Wife, The (1993) **Elizabeth Jolley** (1923)
Georgiad, The (1931) **Roy Campbell** (1901)
Georgian Literary Scene, The (1934) **Frank Swinnerton** (1884)
Georgicon (1984) **Ian Wedde** (1946)
Georgics (29 BC) **Virgil** (70 BC)
Georgics [from Virgil] (1800) **William Sotheby** (1757) (tr.)
Georgics of Hesiod, The (1618) **George Chapman** (1559?) (tr.)
Georgics of Virgil, The (1940) **C. Day Lewis** (1904) (tr.)
Georgy Girl (1965) **Margaret Forster** (1938)
Gerald's Party (1986) **Robert Coover** (1932)
Gerard (1891) **M.E. Braddon** (1835)
German Numbers Woman, The (1999) **Alan Sillitoe** (1928)
German Peril, The (1915) **Frederic Harrison** (1831)
German Requiem, A (1981) **James Fenton** (1949)
German Romance (1827) **Thomas Carlyle** (1795)
German War, The (1911) **A. Conan Doyle** (1859)
Germany [De l'Allemagne] (1810) **Madame de Staël** (1766)
Germany: A Winter's Tale [*Deutschland: Ein Wintermärchen*] (1844) **Heinrich Heine** (1797)
Germinal (1885) **Émile Zola** (1840)
Germinie Lacerteux (1864) **Edmond** (1822) and Jules (1830) de Goncourt
Gertrud (1910) **Hermann Hesse** (1877)
Gertrude of Wyoming (1809) **Thomas Campbell** (1777)
Gerusalemme Liberata [Eng trn as *Godfrey of Bulloigne*; or, *The Recoverie of Jerusalem*, 1600] (1580) **Torquato Tasso** (1544)

Gestern ['Yesterday'] (1891) **Hugo von Hofmannsthal** (1874)
Get Away Old Man (1944) **William Saroyan** (1908)
Get Shorty (1990) **Elmore Leonard** (1925)
Getaway, The (1959) **Jim Thompson** (1906)
Getting into Death (1973) **Thomas M. Disch** (1940)
Getting It Right (1982) **Elizabeth Jane Howard** (1923)
Getting Licked (1999) **Howard Jacobson** (1942)
Getting Married [2 vols] (1884–5) **August Strindberg** (1849)
Getting of Wisdom, The (1910) **'Henry Handel Richardson' [Ethel Florence Robertson]** (1870)
Getting On (1971) **Alan Bennett** (1934)
Getting Up and Going Home (1978) **Robert W. Anderson** (1917)
Ghastly Good Taste (1933) **Sir John Betjeman** (1906)
Ghetto Comedies (1907) **Israel Zangwill** (1864)
Ghetto Tragedies (1893) **Israel Zangwill** (1864)
Ghost Camp, The (1902) **'Rolf Boldrewood' [Thomas Alexander Browne]** (1826)
Ghost Children (1997) **Sue Townsend** (1946)
Ghost Downstairs, The (1972) **Leon Garfield** (1921)
Ghost in the Machine, The (1967) **Arthur Koestler** (1905)
Ghost Kings, The (1908) **Sir H. Rider Haggard** (1856)
Ghost of Monsieur Scarron, The (1956) **Janet Lewis** (1899)
Ghost of Napoleon, The (1933) **Sir Basil Liddell Hart** (1895)
Ghost of Thomas Kempe, The (1973) **Penelope Lively** (1933)
Ghost Orchid (1995) **Michael Longley** (1939)
Ghost Pirates, The (1909) **William Hope Hodgson** (1877)
Ghost Road, The (1995) **Pat Barker** (1943)
Ghost Ship, The (1912) **Richard Middleton** (1882–1911)
Ghost Sonata, The (1907) **August Strindberg** (1849)
Ghost Stories and Tales of Mystery (1851) **J.S. Le Fanu** (1814)
Ghost Stories of an Antiquary (1904) **M.R. James** (1862)
Ghost Story (1979) **Peter Straub** (1943)
Ghost , The [bks i-ii; bk iii, 1762; bk iv, 1763] (1762) **Charles Churchill** (1731)
Ghost, The (1907) **Arnold Bennett** (1867)
Ghost Train (1995) **Sean O'Brien** (1952)
Ghost Writer, The (1979) **Philip Roth** (1933)
Ghost-Bereft (1901) **Jane Barlow** (1857)
Ghost-Hunter and His Family, The (1833) **Michael Banim** (1796)
Ghosts (1881) **Henrik Ibsen** (1828)
Ghosts (1937) **Edith Wharton** (1862)
Ghosts (1986) **Paul Auster** (1947)
Ghosts (1988) **Eva Figes** (1932)
Ghosts (1993) **John Banville** (1945)
Ghosts and Family Legends (1859) **Catherine Crowe** (1790)
Ghosts in Daylight (1924) **Oliver Onions** (1873)
Ghosts of Sleath, The (1994) **James Herbert** (1943)
Giant (1952) **Edna Ferber** (1885)
Giant, O'Brien, The (1998) **Hilary Mantel** (1952)
Giant of the North, The (1882) **R.M. Ballantyne** (1825)
Giant Weapon, The (1943) **Yvor Winters** (1900)
Giant's Robe, The (1884) **'F. Anstey' [Thomas Anstey Guthrie]** (1856)
Giants of Jazz (1957) **Studs Terkel** (1912)
Giaour, The (1813) **George Gordon, Lord Byron** (1788)
Gibraltar (1705) **John Dennis** (1657)
Gideon (1749) **Aaron Hill** (1685)
Gideon Planish (1943) **Sinclair Lewis** (1885)
Gift of Black Folk, The (1924) **W.E.B. du Bois** (*c.* 1868)
Gift of Stones, The (1988) **Jim Crace** (1946)
Gift of the Gorgon, The (1993) **Peter Shaffer** (1926)
Gift, The (1963) **Vladimir Nabokov** (1899)
Gifts of the Child Christ, The (1882) **George MacDonald** (1824)
Gigi (1944) **Colette** (1873)
Gigli Concert, The (1983) **Tom Murphy** (1935)
Gil Blas (1715–35) **Alain-René Lesage** (1668)
Gilbert Gurney (1836) **Theodore Hook** (1788)
Gildas Salvianus (1656) **Richard Baxter** (1615)
Gilded Age, The (1873) **'Mark Twain' [Samuel Langhorne Clemens]** (1835) [with **C.D. Warner**]
Gilded Age, The (1873) **Charles Dudley Warner** (1829) [with Mark Twain]
Gilead Balm, Knight Errant (1911) **Bernard Capes** (1850?)
Giles Corey, Yeoman (1893) **Mary Wilkins Freeman** (1852)
Giles Goat-Boy (1966) **John Barth** (1930)
Gilly of Christ, The (1907) **Joseph Campbell** (1879)
Gimpel the Fool (1957) **Isaac Bashevis Singer** (1904)
Ginger Man, The (1955) **J.P. Donleavy** (1926)
Ginger, You're Barmy (1962) **David Lodge** (1935)
Gingerbread Lady, The (1970) **Neil Simon** (1927)
Gioconda [La Gioconda] (1899) **Gabriele D'Annunzio** (1863)
Gioconda Smile, The (1948) **Aldous Huxley** (1894)
Giordano Bruno and the Hermetic Tradition (1964) **Frances Yates** (1899)
Giovanni's Room (1956) **James Baldwin** (1924)
Gipsy, The (1835) **G.P.R. James** (1799)
Gipsy Countess, The (1799) **Elizabeth Gunning** (1769)
Giraffe Hunters, The (1867) **Mayne Reid** (1818)
Girdle of Venus (1939) **Pamela Hansford Johnson** (1912)
Girl, The (1939) **Meridel Le Sueur** (1900)
Girl, 20 (1971) **Kingsley Amis** (1922)
Girl at the Lion d'Or, The (1989) **Sebastian Faulks** (1953)
Girl From the Candle-Lit Bath, The (1978) **Dodie Smith** (1896)
Girl Green as Elderflower, The (1980) **Randolph Stow** (1935)
Girl Hunters, The (1952) **Mickey Spillane** (1918)
Girl in the Head, A (1967) **J.G. Farrell** (1935)

Girl in a Swing, The (1980) **Richard Adams** (1920)
Girl in Winter, A (1947) **Philip Larkin** (1922)
Girl of the Mountains, The (1797) **Eliza Parsons** (1748)
Girl of the Period [and other essays], The (1883) **E. Lynn Linton** (1822)
Girl of the Period, The (1868) **E. Lynn Linton** (1822)
Girl of the Sea of Cortez, The (1982) **Peter Benchley** (1940)
Girl on a Bicycle (1977) **Leland Bardwell** (1928)
Girl Who Proposed!, The (1918) **Berta Ruck** (1878)
Girl with a Monkey (1958) **Thea Astley** (1925)
Girl with a Violin (1968) **Sydney Goodsir Smith** (1915)
Girlhood of Shakespeare's Heroines, The (1850) **Mary Cowden Clarke** (1809)
Girls and Yanga Marshall, The (1987) **James Berry** (1924)
Girls at War (1972) **Chinua Achebe** (1930)
Girls in Their Married Bliss (1964) **Edna O'Brien** (1932)
Girls of Slender Means, The (1963) **Muriel Spark** (1918)
Girls on the Run (2000) **John Ashbery** (1927)
Girondin, The (1911) **Hilaire Belloc** (1870)
Gisippus (1842) **Gerald Griffin** (1803–40)
Giulio Malatesta (1863) **T. Adolphus Trollope** (1810)
Give Us This Day (1989) **Stan Barstow** (1928)
Give Your Heart to the Hawks (1933) **Robinson Jeffers** (1887)
Giving Birth to One's Own Mother (1991) **Jay Cantor** (1948)
Glad Day, A (1938) **Kay Boyle** (1903)
Glad Eye, The (1978) **Stan Barstow** (1928)
Gladiator, The (1831) **Robert Bird** (1806)
Gladiator-at-Law (1955) **Frederik Pohl** (1919) [with C.M. Kornbluth]
Gladiators, The (1863) **G.J. Whyte-Melville** (1821)
Glamorous Nights [music by Ivor Novello] (1935) **Christopher Hassall** (1912)
Glamorous Powers (1988) **Susan Howatch** (1940)
Glances at Europe (1851) **Horace Greeley** (1811)
Glasgow Beasts an' a Burd (1961) **Ian Hamilton Finlay** (1925)
Glasgow Sonnets (1972) **Edwin Morgan** (1920)
Glass Alembic, The [US: *The Crystal Garden*] (1973) **Elaine Feinstein** (1930)
Glass Canoe, The (1976) **David Ireland** (1927)
Glass Key, The (1931) **Dashiell Hammett** (1894)
Glass Knight, The (1976) **David Helwig** (1938)
Glass Lake, The (1994) **Maeve Binchy** (1940)
Glass Menagerie, The (1944) **'Tennessee' [Thomas Lanier] Williams** (1911)
Glass Mender, The (1910) **Maurice Baring** (1874)
Glass of Blessings, a (1959) **Barbara Pym** (1913)
Glass Slipper, The (1944) **Eleanor Farjeon** (1881)
Glass Tower, The (1944) **Nicholas Moore** (1918)
Glass-Blowers, The (1963) **Daphne du Maurier** (1907)
Glassblowers, The (1950) **Mervyn Peake** (1911)
Glasse of Governement, The (1575) **George Gascoigne** (1542?)
Glassy Sea, The (1978) **Marian Engel** (1933)
Glastonbury Romance, A (1932) **John Cooper Powys** (1872)
Glaucus (1855) **Charles Kingsley** (1819)
Gleam in the North, The (1927) **D.K. Broster** (1878)
Glenarvon (1816) **Lady Caroline Lamb** (1785)
Glenaveril; or, The Metamorphoses (1885) **Edward Robert Bulwer Lytton** (1831)
Glenfell (1820) **John Galt** (1779)
Glengarry's Glen Ross (1984) **David Mamet** (1947)
Glide Time (1976) **Roger Hall** (1939)
Glimpse, The (1909) **Arnold Bennett** (1867)
Glimpses of the Moon, The (1922) **Edith Wharton** (1862)
Glitter of Mica (1963) **Jessie Kesson** (1916)
Glittering Images (1987) **Susan Howatch** (1940)
Glittering Prizes, The (1976) **Frederic Raphael** (1931)
Glitz (1985) **Elmore Leonard** (1925)
Gloria Mundi (1898) **Harold Frederic** (1856)
Gloriana (1890) **Lady Florence Dixie** (1857)
Gloriana (1676) **Nathaniel Lee** (1649?)
Gloriana (1978) **Michael Moorcock** (1939)
Glorious Fortune, A (1883) **Sir Walter Besant** (1836)
Glory (1877) **Isabella [Mrs G. Linnaeus] Banks** (1821)
Glory (1971) **Vladimir Nabokov** (1899)
Glory, The (1994) **Herman Wouk** (1915)
Glory of Hera, The (1972) **Caroline Gordon** (1895)
Glory of the Humming-Bird, The (1975) **Peter De Vries** (1910)
Glory of the Nightingales, The (1930) **Edwin Arlington Robinson** (1869)
Glory That Was Grub Street, The (1928) **A. St John Adcock** (1864)
Gnomes & Occasions (1973) **Howard Nemerov** (1920)
Go Down, Moses (1942) **William Faulkner** (1897)
Go Saddle the Sea (1977) **Joan Aiken** (1924)
Go Tell It on the Mountain (1953) **James Baldwin** (1924)
Go to the Widow-Maker (1967) **James Jones** (1921)
Go-Away Bird, The (1958) **Muriel Spark** (1918)
Go-Between, The (1953) **L.P. Hartley** (1895)
Goat Song (1967) **Frank Yerby** (1916)
Goblin Market (1862) **Christina Rossetti** (1830)
Goblins and Pagodas (1916) **John Gould Fletcher** (1886)
Gobseck (1830) **Honoré de Balzac** (1799)
God and His Gifts, A (1963) **I. Compton-Burnett** (1884)
God and Mammon (1907) **John Davidson** (1857)
God and Mr Wells (1917) **William Archer** (1856) (ed.)
God and the Astronomers (1933) **W.R. Inge** (1860)
God and the Atom (1945) **Ronald Knox** (1888)
God and the Bible (1875) **Matthew Arnold** (1822)
God and the King (1911) **'Marjorie Bowen' [Gabrielle Margaret Vere Campbell]** (1886)
God and the Man (1881) **Robert Williams Buchanan** (1841)

God Beneath the Sea, The (1970) **Leon Garfield** (1921) [with Edward Blishen]
God Bless Karl Marx (1987) **C.H. Sisson** (1914)
God Bless You, Mr Rosewater (1965) **Kurt Vonnegut** (1922)
God Glorified in the Work of Redemption (1731) **Jonathan Edwards** (1703)
God in the Car, The (1894) **'Anthony Hope' [Sir Anthony Hope Hawkins]** (1863)
God in the Mountain, The (1977) **Colin Thubron** (1939)
God Knows (1984) **Joseph Heller** (1923)
God Likes Them Plain (1935) **Eric Linklater** (1899)
God of Clay, The (1908) **H.C. Bailey** (1878)
God on the Rocks (1978) **Jane Gardam** (1928)
God Save the Child (1974) **Robert B. Parker** (1932)
God Seeker, The (1949) **Sinclair Lewis** (1885)
God the Invisible King (1917) **H.G. Wells** (1866)
God the Known and God the Unknown (1909) **Samuel Butler** (1835–1902)
God Was Here But He Left Early (1973) **Irwin Shaw** (1913)
God Without Thunder (1930) **John Crowe Ransom** (1888)
God's Eyes a-Twinkle (1947) **T.F. Powys** (1875)
God's Funeral (1999) **A.N. Wilson** (1950)
God's Good Man (1904) **Marie Corelli** (1855)
God's Grace (1982) **Bernard Malamud** (1914)
God's Little Acre (1933) **Erskine Caldwell** (1903)
God's Outcast (1898) **Silas K. Hocking** (1850)
God's Promises (1547) **John Bale** (1495)
God's Providence House (1865) **Isabella [Mrs G. Linnaeus] Banks** (1821)
God-Emperor of Dune (1980) **Frank Herbert** (1920)
Godbey (1931) **Edgar Lee Masters** (1868)
Godded and Codded (1970) **Julia O'Faolain** (1932)
Goddess and Other Women, The (1974) **Joyce Carol Oates** (1938)
Goddess Named Gold, A (1960) **Bhabani Bhattacharya** (1906)
Godfather, The (1969) **Mario Puzo** (1920)
Godfrey of Bulloigne [from Tasso's *Gerusalemme Liberata*, 1580–1] (1600) **Edward Fairfax** (*c.* 1580) (tr.)
Godfrida (1898) **John Davidson** (1857)
Godless in Eden (2000) **Fay Weldon** (1931)
Godlie Treatise Declaryng the Benefites of Prayer, A (1560) **John Fisher** (1459?-1535)
Godolphin (1833) **Edward Bulwer-Lytton** (1803)
Gods and Their Makers (1897) **Laurence Housman** (1865)
Gods Are Thirsty, The [*Les Dieux ont soif*] (1912) **'Anatole France' [Jacques-Anatole-François Thibault]** (1844)
Gods Arithmeticke (1597) **Francis Meres** (1565)
Gods Arrive, The (1932) **Edith Wharton** (1862)
Gods of Modern Grub Street (1923) **A. St John Adcock** (1864)
Gods of the Lightning (1928) **Maxwell Anderson** (1888) [with Harold Hickerson]
Gods of War (1915) **George William Russell ['AE']** (1867)
Gods Themselves, The (1972) **Isaac Asimov** (1920)
Godstone and the Blackymor, The (1959) **T.H. White** (1906)
Godwulf Manuscript, The (1974) **Robert B. Parker** (1932)
Goethe (1877) **Thomas Carlyle** (1795)
Goethe's Faust: Parts 1 and 2 [abridged version] (1951) **Louis MacNeice** (1907) (tr.)
Goetz of Berlichingen [tr. from Goethe] (1799) **Sir Walter Scott** (1771) (tr.)
Gog (1967) **Andrew Sinclair** (1935)
Goggle Eyes (1982) **Anne Fine** (1947)
Going Abroad (1934) **Rose Macaulay** (1881)
Going After Cacciato (1978) **Tim O'Brien** (1946)
Going Home (1973) **Danielle Steel** (1947)
Going into a Dark House (1994) **Jane Gardam** (1928)
Going to Meet the Man (1965) **James Baldwin** (1924)
Going to the Dogs [as 'Dan Kavanagh'] (1987) **Julian Barnes** (1946)
Going to the Territory (1986) **Ralph Ellison** (1914)
Going Up to Sotheby's (1982) **Muriel Spark** (1918)
Gold (1921) **Eugene O'Neill** (1888)
Gold and Iron (1918) **Joseph Hergesheimer** (1880)
Gold Coast (1980) **Elmore Leonard** (1925)
Gold Coast Customs (1929) **Edith Sitwell** (1887)
Gold in the Sea, The (1966) **Brian Friel** (1929)
Gold Mine (1970) **Wilbur Smith** (1933)
Gold Worshippers, The (1851) **Emma Robinson** (1814)
Gold-Digger, The (1872) **Lady Georgiana Fullerton** (1812)
Golden Age Restor'd, The (1616) **Ben Jonson** (1572)
Golden Age, The (1794) **Erasmus Darwin** (1731)
Golden Age, The (1871) **Alfred Austin** (1835)
Golden Age, The (1895) **Kenneth Grahame** (1859)
Golden Age, The (1611) **Thomas Heywood** (1574?)
Golden Aphroditis, The (1577) **John Grange** (*c.* 1577)
Golden Apples (1935) **Marjorie Rawlings** (1896)
Golden Apples, The (1949) **Eudora Welty** (1909)
Golden Apples of the Sun, The (1953) **Ray Bradbury** (1920)
Golden Arrow, The (1916) **Mary Webb** (1881)
Golden Ass, The [**Apuleius**]: see *Metamorphoses*
Golden Bird, The (1951) **Anne Ridler** (1912)
Golden Book of St John Chrysostom, The (1659) **John Evelyn** (1620) (tr.)
Golden Bough, The (1890) **Sir J.G. Frazer** (1854)
Golden Bowl, The (1904) **Henry James** (1843)
Golden Boy (1937) **Clifford Odets** (1906)
Golden Builders (1976) **Vincent Buckley** (1925)
Golden Butterfly, The (1876) **Sir Walter Besant** (1836) [with James Rice]
Golden Calf, The (1883) **M.E. Braddon** (1835)
Golden Calves, The (1987) **Louis Auchinloss** (1917)
Golden Chaine, A (1591) **William Perkins** (1558)
Golden Chains, The (1968) **George Barker** (1913)
Golden Chalice, The (1935) **Ralph Gustafson** (1909)
Golden Child, The (1977) **Penelope Fitzgerald** (1916)

Golden Cuckoo, The (1939) **Denis Johnston** (1901)
Golden Dream, The (1861) **R.M. Ballantyne** (1825)
Golden Earth (1952) **Norman Lewis** (1918)
Golden Echo, The (1953) **David Garnett** (1892)
Golden Epistles (1575) **Sir Geoffrey Fenton** (1539?) (tr.)
Golden Fetich, The (1903) **Eden Phillpotts** (1862)
Golden Fetters (1868) **Mark Lemon** (1809)
Golden Fleece, The [US: *Hercules, My Shipmate*] (1944) **Robert Graves** (1895)
Golden Gate, The (1986) **Vikram Seth** (1952)
Golden Grove, The (1655) **Jeremy Taylor** (1613)
Golden Hope, The (1887) **W. Clark Russell** (1844)
Golden House, The (1894) **Charles Dudley Warner** (1829)
Golden Journey to Samarkand, The (1913) **James Elroy Flecker** (1884)
Golden Keel, The (1963) **Desmond Bagley** (1923)
Golden Legend, The (1851) **Henry Wadsworth Longfellow** (1807)
Golden Lion of Granpere, The (1872) **Anthony Trollope** (1815)
Golden Magnet, The (1884) **George Manville Fenn** (1831)
Golden Mean, The (1923) **Allen Tate** (1899) [with Ridley Wills]
Golden Notebook, The (1962) **Doris Lessing** (1919)
Golden Ocean, The (1956) **Patrick O'Brian** (1914)
Golden Poems [*Poèmes dorés*] (1873) **'Anatole France' [Jacques-Anatole-François Thibault]** (1844)
Golden Pot, The [*Der goldene Topf*] (1814) **E.T.A. Hoffmann** (1776)
Golden Remaines (1659) **John Hales** (1584–1656)
Golden Room, The (1928) **Wilfrid Gibson** (1878)
Golden Sabre, The (1981) **Jon Cleary** (1917)
Golden Scarecrow, The (1915) **Sir Hugh Walpole** (1884)
Golden Shadow, The (1973) **Leon Garfield** (1921)
Golden Sovereign, The (1957) **Richard Church** (1893)
Golden Spy, The (1709) **Charles Gildon** (1665)
Golden Strangers, The (1956) **Henry Treece** (1911)
Golden Targe, The (1508) **William Dunbar** (1460?)
Golden Treasury, The (1861) **Francis Turner Palgrave** (1824) (ed.)
Golden Violet, The [as 'L.E.L.'] (1827) **Letitia Elizabeth Landon** (1802)
Golden Watch, The (1953) **Albert Halper** (1904)
Golden Whales of California, The (1920) **Vachel Lindsay** (1879)
Goldengrove (1972) **Jill Paton Walsh** (1937)
Goldfinger (1959) **Ian Fleming** (1908)
Goldsmith's Wife, The (1875) **W.H. Ainsworth** (1805)
Goldsworthy Lowes Dickinson (1934) **E.M. Forster** (1879)
Golgotha [US: *The Last Trump*] (1980) **John Gardner** (1926)
Golgotha (1992) **Gore Vidal** (1925)
Gombo Zhêbes (1885) **Lafcadio Hearn** (1850)
Gondibert (1651) **Sir William Davenant** (1606)
Gondoliers, The [music by Sir Arthur Sullivan] (1889) **W.S. Gilbert** (1836)
Gone to Earth (1917) **Mary Webb** (1881)
Gone to Ground (1935) **T.H. White** (1906)
Gone With the Wind (1936) **Margaret Mitchell** (1900)
Gone Wrong (1881) **Sir F.C. Burnand** (1836)
Good Apprentice, The (1985) **Iris Murdoch** (1919)
Good as Gold (1979) **Joseph Heller** (1923)
Good Behaviour (1955) **Sir Harold Nicolson** (1886)
Good Behaviour (1981) **Molly Keane** (1905)
Good Bones (1994) **Margaret Atwood** (1939)
Good Companions, The (1929) **J.B. Priestley** (1894)
Good Day to Die, A (1973) **Jim Harrison** (1937)
Good Earth, The (1931) **Pearl S. Buck** (1892)
Good European, The (1947) **R.P. Blackmur** (1904)
Good Fight, The (1973) **Thomas Kinsella** (1928)
Good Friday (1916) **John Masefield** (1878)
Good Girl is Hard to Find, A (1958) **LeRoi Jones** (1934)
Good Hanging, A (1992) **Ian Rankin** (1960)
Good Luck, Miss Wyckoff (1970) **William Inge** (1913)
Good Man in Africa, A (1981) **William Boyd** (1952)
Good Man is Hard to Find, A [UK: *The Artificial Nigger*] (1955) **Flannery O'Connor** (1925)
Good Morning, America (1928) **Carl Sandburg** (1878)
Good Morning, Midnight (1939) **'Jean Rhys' [Ella Gwendolyn Rees Williams]** (1890)
Good Natur'd Man, The (1768) **Oliver Goldsmith** (1728)
Good Newes and Bad Newes (1622) **Samuel Rowlands** (1570?)
Good News for the Vilest of Men (1688) **John Bunyan** (1628)
Good News of Death (1955) **Louis Simpson** (1923)
Good News of God, The (1859) **Charles Kingsley** (1819)
Good Night, Mr Moon (1992) **Barbara Hanrahan** (1939–91)
Good Night, Willie Lee, I'll See You in the Morning (1979) **Alice Walker** (1944)
Good Old Times, The (1873) **W.H. Ainsworth** (1805)
Good Red Earth, The (1901) **Eden Phillpotts** (1862)
Good Scent From a Strange Mountain, A (1992) **Robert Olen Butler** (1945)
Good Shepherd, The (1955) **C.S. Forester** (1899)
Good Soldier, The (1915) **Ford Madox Ford** (1873)
Good St Louis and His Times, The (1870) **Anna Eliza Bray** (1790)
Good Stories of Man and Other Animals [US: *Good Stories*] (1884) **Charles Reade** (1814)
Good Terrorist, The (1985) **Doris Lessing** (1919)
Good Thoughts in Bad Times (1645) **Thomas Fuller** (1608)
Good Thoughts in Worse Times (1647) **Thomas Fuller** (1608)
Good Tidings (1804) **Robert Bloomfield** (1766)
Good Time Was Had by All, A (1937) **Stevie Smith** (1902)
Good War, The (1984) **Studs Terkel** (1912)
Good Wife from a Bad, A (1602) **Thomas Heywood** (1574?)
Good Wives (1869) **Louisa M. Alcott** (1832)

Good Woman, A (1927) **Louis Bromfield** (1896)
Good Woman of Setzuan, The [*Der Gute Mensch von Sezuan*] (1938–41) **Bertolt Brecht** (1898)
Good-Bye Mr Chips (1934) **James Hilton** (1900)
Good-Bye, My Fancy (1891) **Walt Whitman** (1819)
Good-bye, Sweetheart (1872) **Rhoda Broughton** (1840)
Good-Bye, Wisconsin (1928) **Glenway Wescott** (1901)
Goodbye, Columbus (1959) **Philip Roth** (1933)
Goodbye Earth, and Other Poems (1958) **I.A. Richards** (1893)
Goodbye Hamilton (1984) **Catherine Cookson** (1906)
Goodbye Look, The (1969) **'Ross MacDonald' [Kenneth Millar]** (1915)
Goodbye Mr Dixon (1974) **Iain Crichton Smith [Iain Mac a'Ghobhainn]** (1928)
Goodbye to All That (1929) **Robert Graves** (1895)
Goodbye to Berlin (1939) **Christopher Isherwood** (1904)
Goodness (1991) **Tim Parks** (1954)
Goose Cathedral, The (1950) **Jocelyn Brooke** (1908)
Goose on Your Grave, A (1987) **Joan Aiken** (1924)
Goose-Step, The (1923) **Upton Sinclair** (1878)
Gooseboy, The (1987) **A.L. Barker** (1918)
Gor Saga (1981) **Maureen Duffy** (1933)
Gora (1910) **Rabindranath Tagore** (1861)
Gorboduc (1565) **Thomas Norton** (1532) [with Thomas Sackville]
Gordian Knot, The (1859) **Charles William Shirley Brooks** (1816)
Gordon Keith (1903) **Thomas Nelson Page** (1853)
Gordon, the Big Engine (1953) **Revd W.V. Awdry** (1911)
Gorilla Hunters, The (1861) **R.M. Ballantyne** (1825)
Gorky Park (1981) **Martin Cruz Smith** (1942)
Gormenghast (1950) **Mervyn Peake** (1911)
Gorse Blooms Pale, The (1947) **Dan Davin** (1913)
Gorse Fires (1991) **Michael Longley** (1939)
Goshawk, The (1951) **T.H. White** (1906)
Goslings (1913) **J.D. Beresford** (1873)
Gospel According to the Son, The (1997) **Norman Mailer** (1923)
Gospel Fever (1980) **Frank G. Slaughter** (1908)
Gospel of Atheism, The (1877) **Annie Besant** (1847)
Gospel of Freedom, The (1898) **Robert Herrick** (1868)
Gospel of the Pentateuch, The (1863) **Charles Kingsley** (1819)
Gospels of Anarchy (1908) **'Vernon Lee' [Violet Paget]** (1856)
Gossip From the Forest (1975) **Thomas Keneally** (1935)
Gossip in a Library (1891) **Sir Edmund Gosse** (1849)
Gotham [bk i; bks ii-iii, 1764] (1764) **Charles Churchill** (1731)
Gothic Architecture (1893) **William Morris** (1834)
Gothic Furniture in the Style of the 15th Century (1835) **A.W.N. Pugin** (1812)
Gothic Revival, The (1928) **Kenneth Clark** (1903)
Götz of Berlichingen with the Iron Hand [*Götz von Berlichingen mit der eisernen Hand*] (1773) **Johann Wolfgang von Goethe** (1749)
Governaunce of Kynges, The [tr. *c.* 1370 from Aristotle; also known as *Secrets of the Old Philisoffres*] (1511) **John Lydgate** (1370?-1449)
Governess, The (1839) **Marguerite, Countess of Blessington** (1789)
Governess, The (1749) **Sarah Fielding** (1710)
Government of the Tongue, The (1988) **Seamus Heaney** (1939)
Governor, The (1531) **Sir Thomas Elyot** (1490?)
Governor of England, The (1913) **'Marjorie Bowen' [Gabrielle Margaret Vere Campbell]** (1886)
Governour of Cyprus, The (1703) **John Oldmixon** (1673)
Grace (1988) **Maggie Gee** (1948)
Grace Abounding to the Chief of Sinners (1666) **John Bunyan** (1628)
Grace Before Ploughing (1966) **John Masefield** (1878)
Grace Notes (1997) **Bernard MacLaverty** (1942)
Grace of Mary Traverse, The (1985) **Timberlake Wertenbaker**
Gradations of Grandeur (1982) **Ralph Gustafson** (1909)
Graham Hamilton (1822) **Lady Caroline Lamb** (1785)
Grammar of Politics, A (1925) **Harold Laski** (1893)
Grammar of the English Tongue, A (1699) **Charles Gildon** (1665) [with John Brightland]
Grand Babylon Hotel, The (1902) **Arnold Bennett** (1867)
Grand Design, The (1949) **John Dos Passos** (1896)
Grand Escort, The [*Le Grand Écart*] (1923) **Jean Cocteau** (1889)
Grand Hotel (1930) **Vicki Baum** (1888)
Grand Man, A (1954) **Catherine Cookson** (1906)
Grand Meaulnes, Le (1913) **'Alain-Fournier' [Henri-Alban Fournier]** (1886)
Grand Testament [written 1461–2] (1489) **François Villon** (*c.* 1431)
Grandfather's Chair (1841) **Nathaniel Hawthorne** (1804)
Grandfathers, The (1964) **Conrad Richter** (1890)
Grandison Mather (1889) **Henry Harland** (1861)
Grandissimes, The (1880) **George Washington Cable** (1844)
Grandmothers of the Light (1991) **Paula Gunn Allen** (1939)
Grandmothers, The [UK: *A Family Portrait*] (1927) **Glenway Wescott** (1901)
Grandpa (1984) **Joihn Burningham** (1926)
Grange Garden, The (1876) **Henry Kingsley** (1830)
Grania (1892) **Emily Lawless** (1845)
Granite (1926) **'Clemence Dane' [Winifred Ashton]** (1888)
Granite and Rainbow (1958) **Virginia Woolf** (1882–1941)
Granny's Wonderful Chair (1857) **Frances Browne** (1816)
Grantley Manor (1847) **Lady Georgiana Fullerton** (1812)
Grapes of Wrath, The (1939) **John Steinbeck** (1902)
Grasp Your Nettle (1865) **E. Lynn Linton** (1822)

Grass Harp, The (1951) **Truman Capote** (1924)
Grass is Singing, The (1950) **Doris Lessing** (1919)
Grass of Parnassus (1888) **Andrew Lang** (1844)
Grass Rope, A (1957) **William Mayne** (1928)
Grasshopper, The [as 'Barbara Vine'] (2000) **Ruth Rendell** (1930)
Grasshoppers Come, The (1931) **David Garnett** (1892)
Gratefull Servant, The (1630) **James Shirley** (1596)
Grave, The (1743) **Robert Blair** (1699)
Grave Gossip (1979) **Brian Patten** (1946)
Grave Mistake (1978) **Ngaio Marsh** (1899)
Grave of the Last Saxon, The (1822) **William Lisle Bowles** (1762)
Grave of Truth, The (1979) **'Evelyn Anthony' [Evelyn Ward-Thomas]** (1928)
Gravel Ponds, The (1960) **Peter Levi** (1931)
Graves and Resurrections (1948) **Vernon Scannell** (1922)
Graveyard for Lunatics, A (1990) **Ray Bradbury** (1920)
Gravity's Rainbow (1973) **Thomas Pynchon** (1937)
Gray (1882) **Sir Edmund Gosse** (1849)
Gray Lensman (1951) **E.E. 'Doc' Smith** (1890)
Graysons, The (1888) **Edward Eggleston** (1837)
Great Adventure, The (1913) **Arnold Bennett** (1867)
Great American Fourth of July Parade, The (1975) **Archibald MacLeish** (1892)
Great American Jackpot, The (1969) **Herbert Gold** (1924)
Great American Novel, The (1973) **Philip Roth** (1933)
Great American Novel, The (1923) **William Carlos Williams** (1883)
Great and Secret Show, The (1989) **Clive Barker** (1952)
Great Apes (1997) **Will Self** (1961)
Great Boer War, The (1900) **A. Conan Doyle** (1859)
Great Case of Liberty of Conscience, The (1670) **William Penn** (1644)
Great Christian Doctrine of Original Sin Defended, The (1758) **Jonathan Edwards** (1703)
Great Circle (1933) **Conrad Potter Aiken** (1889)
Great Climate (1990) **Michael Wilding** (1942)
Great Code, The (1982) **Northrop Frye** (1912)
Great Companions (1959) **Max Eastman** (1883)
Great Contemporaries (1937) **Sir Winston Churchill** (1874)
Great Crash, The (1961) **J.K. Galbraith** (1908)
Great Days (1979) **Donald Barthelme** (1931)
Great Days (1914) **'Frank' Harris** (1856)
Great Days, The (1958) **John dos Passos** (1896)
Great Duke of Florence, The (1636) **Philip Massinger** (1583)
Great Exemplar of Sanctity and Holy Life, The (1649) **Jeremy Taylor** (1613)
Great Exhibition, The (1972) **David Hare** (1947)
Great Expectations (1982) **Kathy Acker** (1948)
Great Expectations (1861) **Charles Dickens** (1812)
Great Favourite, The (1668) **Sir Robert Howard** (1626)
Great Fight, The (1908) **William Henry Drummond** (1854–1907)
Great Fire of London, The (1982) **Peter Ackroyd** (1949)
Great Fortune, The (1960) **Olivia Manning** (1908)
Great Game, The (1939) **H.C. Bailey** (1878)
Great Gatsby, The (1925) **F. Scott Fitzgerald** (1896)
Great God Brown, The (1926) **Eugene O'Neill** (1888)
Great God Pan [and *The Inmost Light*], The (1894) **Arthur Machen** (1863)
Great Hoggarty Diamond, The (1848) **W.M. Thackeray** (1811)
Great House, The (1919) **Stanley J. Weyman** (1855)
Great Hunger, The (1942) **Patrick Kavanagh** (1904)
Great Hunger, The (1962) **Cecil Woodham-Smith** (1896)
Great Impersonation, The (1920) **E. Phillips Oppenheim** (1866)
Great Jones Street (1973) **Don Delillo** (1936)
Great Magoo, The (1933) **Ben Hecht** (1894) [with Gene Fowler]
Great Man, A (1904) **Arnold Bennett** (1867)
Great Melody, The (1993) **Connor Cruise O'Brien** (1917)
Great Miss Driver, The (1908) **'Anthony Hope' [Sir Anthony Hope Hawkins]** (1863)
Great Morning (1947) **Sir Osbert Sitwell** (1892)
Great Mysterie of Godliness, The (1652) **Joseph Hall** (1574)
Great Mystery of the Great Whore Unfolded, The (1659) **George Fox** (1624)
Great Occasion, The (1962) **Isabel Colegate** (1931)
Great Ponds, The (1969) **Elechi Amadi** (1934)
Great Porter Square (1885) **B.L. Farjeon** (1838)
Great Praises (1957) **Richard Eberhart** (1904)
Great Profundo, The (1983) **Bernard MacLaverty** (1942)
Great Quillow, The (1944) **James Thurber** (1894–1961)
Great Railway Bazaar, The (1975) **Paul Theroux** (1941)
Great Return, The (1915) **Arthur Machen** (1863)
Great Shadow, The (1892) **A. Conan Doyle** (1859)
Great Shark Hunt, The (1979) **Hunter S. Thompson** (1939)
Great Short Stories of Detection, Mystery and Horror [1st ser.] (1928) **Dorothy L. Sayers** (1893) (ed.)
Great Short Stories of Detection, Mystery and Horror [2nd ser.] (1931) **Dorothy L. Sayers** (1893) (ed.)
Great Skene Mystery, The (1907) **Bernard Capes** (1850?)
Great St Benedict's (1876) **Mrs L.T. Meade** (1854)
Great State, The (1912) **H.G. Wells** (1866)
Great Success, A (1916) **Mrs T. Humphry Ward** (1851)
Great Terror, The (1968) **Robert Conquest** (1917)
Great Theatre of the World, The [*El gran teatro del mundo*] (1645–1650) **Pedro Calderón de la Barca** (1600)
Great Tontine, The (1881) **Hawley Smart** (1833)
Great Tradition, The (1948) **F.R. Leavis** (1895)
Great Victorian Collection, The (1975) **Brian Moore** (1921)

Great War in England in 1897, The (1894) **William le Queux** (1864)
Great War, The (1979) **Correlli Barnett** (1927)
Great White Army, The (1915) **Max Pemberton** (1863)
Great White Hope, The (1968) **Howard Sackler** (1929)
Great White Wall, The (1916) **William Rose Benét** (1886)
Great World and Timothy Colt, The (1956) **Louis Auchinloss** (1917)
Great World, The (1990) **David Malouf** (1934)
Greater Apollo, The (1927) **R.D. FitzGerald** (1902)
Greater Britain (1868) **Sir Charles Wentworth Dilke** (1843)
Greater Inclination, The (1899) **Edith Wharton** (1862)
Greater Trumps, The (1932) **Charles Williams** (1886)
Greater Wave, The (1967) **Mary Lavin** (1912)
Greatest Gresham, The (1962) **Gillian Avery** (1926)
Greatest People in the World, The (1942) **H.E. Bates** (1905)
Grecian History, The (1774) **Oliver Goldsmith** (1728–74)
Greece [*Liberty* pt. ii] (1735) **James Thomson** (1700)
Greek Christian Poets and the English Poets, The (1862) **E.B. Browning** (1806–61)
Greek Coffin Mystery, The (1932) **'Ellery Queen' [Frederic Dannay** (1905) and **Manfred B. Lee]** (1905)
Greek Memories (1932) **Compton Mackenzie** (1883)
Greek Myths, The (1955) **Robert Graves** (1895)
Greek Studies (1895) **Walter Pater** (1839–94)
Greek View of Life, The (1896) **Goldsworthy Lowes Dickinson** (1862)
Greek Wedding (1970) **Jane Aiken Hodge** (1917)
Greeks Had a Word For It, The (1929) **Zoë Akins** (1886)
Greeks Have a Word For It, The (1967) **Barry Unsworth** (1930)
Green Apple Harvest (1920) **Sheila Kaye-Smith** (1887)
Green Arras (1895) **Laurence Housman** (1865)
Green Bay Tree, The (1924) **Louis Bromfield** (1896)
Green Bays (1893) **Sir A.T. Quiller-Couch** (1863)
Green Bough, A (1933) **William Faulkner** (1897)
Green Branch, The (1962) **'Ellis Peters' [Edith Mary Pargeter]** (1913)
Green Carnation, The (1894) **Robert Hichens** (1864)
Green Casket, The (1890) **Mary Louisa Molesworth** (1839)
Green Centuries (1941) **Caroline Gordon** (1895)
Green Child, The (1935) **Sir Herbert Read** (1893)
Green Crow, The (1957) **Sean O'Casey** (1880)
Green Curtain, The (1911) **M.E. Braddon** (1835)
Green Days by the River (1967) **Michael Anthony** (1932)
Green Dolphin Country (1944) **Elizabeth Goudge** (1900)
Green Eggs and Ham (1960) **'Dr Seuss'** (1904)
Green Eye of Goona, The (1904) **Arthur Morrison** (1863)
Green Fairy Book, The (1892) **Andrew Lang** (1844) (ed.)
Green Fire [as 'Fiona Macleod'] (1896) **William Sharp** (1855)
Green Flag, The (1900) **A. Conan Doyle** (1859)
Green Fool, The (1938) **Patrick Kavanagh** (1904)
Green Gene, The (1973) **Peter Dickinson** (1927)
Green Ginger (1909) **Arthur Morrison** (1863)
Green Goddess, The (1921) **William Archer** (1856)
Green Graves of Balgowrie, The (1896) **Jane Findlater** (1866)
Green, Green My Valley Now (1975) **'Richard Llewellyn' [Richard Llewellyn Lloyd]** (1907)
Green Hat, The (1924) **'Michael Arlen' [Dikran Kouyoumdjian]** (1895)
Green Helmet, The (1957) **Jon Cleary** (1917)
Green Helmet, The (1910) **W.B. Yeats** (1865)
Green Hills of Africa (1935) **Ernest Hemingway** (1898)
Green Hills of Earth, The (1951) **Robert A. Heinlein** (1907)
Green House, The [*La casa verde*] (1965) **Mario Vargas Llosa** (1936)
Green Knight, The (1993) **Iris Murdoch** (1919)
Green Man, The (1947) **Andrew Young** (1885)
Green Man, The (1952) **Storm Jameson** (1897)
Green Man, The (1966) **Henry Treece** (1911)
Green Man, The (1969) **Kingsley Amis** (1922)
Green Mansions (1904) **W.H. Hudson** (1841)
Green Mirror, The (1918) **Sir Hugh Walpole** (1884)
Green Overcoat, The (1912) **Hilaire Belloc** (1870)
Green Parrot, The (1908) **Bernard Capes** (1850?)
Green Pastures and Piccadilly (1877) **William Black** (1841)
Green Round, The (1933) **Arthur Machen** (1863)
Green Shadow, White Whale (1992) **Ray Bradbury** (1920)
Green Shore, The (1947) **Norman Nicholson** (1914)
Green Song (1944) **Edith Sitwell** (1887)
Green Water, Green Sky (1959) **Mavis Gallant** (1922)
Greene Ferne Farm (1880) **Richard Jefferies** (1848)
Greene Murder Case, The (1928) **'S.S. van Dine' [Willard Huntington Wright]** (1888)
Greenes Farewell to Folly (1591) **Robert Greene** (1558)
Greenes Groats-worth of Witte (1592) **Robert Greene** (1558–92)
Greenes Mourning Garment (1590) **Robert Greene** (1558)
Greenes Never Too Late (1590) **Robert Greene** (1558)
Greenes Orpharion (1599) **Robert Greene** (1558–1592)
Greenfield Hill (1794) **Timothy Dwight** (1752)
Greengage Summer, The (1958) **Rumer Godden** (1907)
Greengates (1936) **R.C. Sherriff** (1896)
Greenheart (1990) **Alan Jenkins** (1955)
Greenhouse (1979) **Dorothy Hewett** (1923)
Greening of Snow Beach, The (1988) **Carol Rumens** (1944)
Greenlanders, The (1988) **Jane Smiley** (1949)

Greenmantle (1916) **John Buchan** (1875)
Greenstone (1966) **Sylvia Ashton-Warner** (1908)
Greenvoe (1972) **George Mackay Brown** (1921)
Greenwood Hat, The (1937) **[Sir] J.M. Barrie** (1860)
Gregory VII (1840) **R.H. Horne** (1803)
Greifenstein (1889) **F. Marion Crawford** (1854)
Grendel (1971) **John Gardner** (1933)
Gretta (1955) **Erskine Caldwell** (1903)
Grettir the Outlaw (1890) **S. Baring-Gould** (1834)
Grettis Saga: The Story of Grettir the Strong [with E. Magnússon] (1869) **William Morris** (1834) (tr.)
Greville (1841) **Mrs C.F. Gore** (1799)
Grey Among the Green, The (1988) **John Fuller** (1937)
Grey Area (1994) **Will Self** (1961)
Grey Fairy Book, The (1900) **Andrew Lang** (1844) (ed.)
Grey is the Colour of Hope (1989) **Irina Ratushinskaya** (1954)
Grey Lady, The (1895) **'Henry Seton Merriman' [Hugh Stowell Scott]** (1862)
Grey Man, The (1896) **S.R. Crockett** (1860)
Grey Room, The (1921) **Eden Phillpotts** (1862)
Grey Roses (1895) **Henry Harland** (1861)
Grey Seas Under, The (1959) **Farley Mowat** (1921)
Grey Weather (1899) **John Buchan** (1875)
Grey Wig, The (1903) **Israel Zangwill** (1864)
Grey Woman, The (1865) **Elizabeth Gaskell** (1810)
Greybeards at Play (1900) **G.K. Chesterton** (1874)
Greyhound for Breakfast (1987) **James Kelman** (1946)
Greyslaer (1840) **Charles Fenno Hoffman** (1806)
Grief Observed, A [as 'N.W. Clerk'] (1961) **C.S. Lewis** (1898)
Grif (1870) **B.L. Farjeon** (1838)
Griffith Gaunt (1866) **Charles Reade** (1814)
Grifters, The (1963) **Jim Thompson** (1906)
Grim Smile of the Five Towns, The (1907) **Arnold Bennett** (1867)
Grim Tales (1893) **E[dith] Nesbit** (1858)
Grimm Sisters, The (1981) **Liz Lochhead** (1947)
Grimm's Fairy Tales [*Kinder- und Hausmärchen*; first pub. in English as *German Popular Stories*] (1812–1814) **Jacob Ludwig Carl** (1785) and **Wilhelm Carl Grimm** (1786)
Grimus (1975) **Salman Rushdie** (1947)
Grinning Jack (1990) **Brian Patten** (1946)
Griselda (1856) **Sir Edwin Arnold** (1832)
Griselda (1893) **Wilfrid Scawen Blunt** (1840)
Grisly Wife, The (1993) **Rodney Hall** (1935)
Grotto, The (1733) **Matthew Green** (1696)
Ground Beneath Her Feet, The (1999) **Salman Rushdie** (1947)
Ground We Stand On, The (1941) **John Dos Passos** (1896)
Ground Work II (1987) **Robert Duncan** (1919)
Grounds and Reasons of Christian Regeneration, The (1739) **William Law** (1686)
Grounds of Criticism in Poetry, The (1704) **John Dennis** (1657)
Grounds of Faith, The (1852) **Henry Edward Manning** (1808)
Group of Noble Dames, A (1891) **Thomas Hardy** (1840)
Group Portrait with Lady [*Gruppenbild mit Dame*] (1971) **Heinrich Böll** (1917)
Group, The (1775) **Mercy Otis Warren** (1728)
Group, The (1963) **Mary McCarthy** (1912)
Grove, The (1700) **John Oldmixon** (1673)
Groves of Academe, The (1952) **Mary McCarthy** (1912)
Growing (1961) **Leonard Woolf** (1880)
Growing Pains [US: *Myself When Young*] (1977) **Daphne du Maurier** (1907)
Growing Pains of Adrian Mole, The (1984) **Sue Townsend** (1946)
Growing Points (1975) **Elizabeth Jennings** (1926)
Growing Rich (1992) **Fay Weldon** (1931)
Growing Up (1948) **Olivia Manning** (1908)
Growing Up Stupid Under the Union (1980) **Austin Clarke** (1932)
Grown Ups, The (1989) **Victoria Glendinning** (1937)
Growth of a Man (1938) **Mazo de la Roche** (1879)
Growth of Love, The (1876) **Robert Bridges** (1844)
Growth of the English Constitution, The (1872) **E.A. Freeman** (1823)
Growth of the Soil (1917) **Knut Hamsun** (1859)
Gruach (1921) **Gordon Bottomley** (1874)
Grub Street Nights Entertainment, The (1924) **J.C. Squire** (1884)
Grumbling Hive, The (1705) **Bernard Mandeville** (1670)
Gryll Grange (1861) **Thomas Love Peacock** (1785–1866)
Guard of Honor (1948) **James Gould Cozzens** (1903)
Guardian, The (1650) **Abraham Cowley** (1618)
Guardian, The (1759) **David Garrick** (1717)
Guardian Angel (1991) **Sara Paretsky** (1947)
Guardian Angel, The (1867) **Oliver Wendell Holmes** (1809)
Guards Came Through, The (1919) **A. Conan Doyle** (1859)
Guards! Guards! (1989) **Terry Pratchett** (1948) [with Gray Jolliffe]
Guavas the Tinner (1897) **S. Baring-Gould** (1834)
Guerillas (1975) **V.S. Naipaul** (1932)
Guermantes' Way, The [*Le Côté de Guermantes*; *A la recherche du temps perdu iii*] (1920–1) **Marcel Proust** (1871)
Guerre de Troie n'aura pas lieu, La [tr. 1955 by Christopher Fry as *Tiger at the Gate*] (1935) **Jean Giraudoux** (1882)
Guest and His Going, A (1959) **P.H. Newby** (1918)
Guest From the Future, The (1989) **Jon Stallworthy** (1935)
Guest of Honour, A (1970) **Nadine Gordimer** (1923)
Guest of Quesnay (1908) **Booth Tarkington** (1869)
Guests of the Nation (1931) **'Frank O'Connor' [Michael Francis O'Donovan']** (1903)
Guests of War (1956) **Robin Jenkins** (1912)
Guide for the Bedevilled, A (1944) **Ben Hecht** (1894)
Guide, The (1958) **R.K. Narayan** (1907)
Guide Through the District of the Lakes, A (1835) **William Wordsworth** (1770)

Guide to Modern Thought (1933) **C.E.M. Joad** (1891)
Guide to Modern Wickedness (1939) **C.E.M. Joad** (1891)
Guide to Prayer, a (1715) **Isaac Watts** (1674)
Guide to the New World (1941) **H.G. Wells** (1866)
Guide to the Ruins (1950) **Howard Nemerov** (1920)
Guiding Thread, The (1916) **Beatrice Harraden** (1864)
Guignol's Band I (1944) **'Louis-Ferdinand Céline' [L.F. Destouches]** (1894)
Guignol's Band II (1964) **'Louis-Ferdinand Céline' [L.F. Destouches]** (1894–1961)
Guild Court (1868) **George MacDonald** (1824)
Guilderoy (1889) **'Ouida' [Marie Louise de la Ramée]** (1839)
Guillotine Party (1935) **James T. Farrell** (1904)
Guilty Mother, The [L'Autre Tartufe; ou, la Mère coupable] (1792) **Pierre Augustin Caron de Beaumarchais** (1732)
Guilty Pleasures (1974) **Donald Barthelme** (1931)
Guilty River, The (1886) **Wilkie Collins** (1824)
Guilty Thing Surprised, A (1970) **Ruth Rendell** (1930)
Gulag Archipelago, The (1973–6) **Alexander Solzhenitsyn** (1918)
Gulf Between Us, The (1992) **Trevor Griffiths** (1935)
Gulf Coast Stories (1956) **Erskine Caldwell** (1903)
Gullible's Travels (1917) **Ring Lardner** (1885)
Gulliver's Travels [**Swift**]: see *Travels into Several Remote Nations of the World*
Guls Horne-book, The (1609) **Thomas Dekker** (1572?)
Gun, The (1933) **C.S. Forester** (1899)
Gun for Sale, A (1936) **Graham Greene** (1904)
Gunroom, The (1919) **Charles Morgan** (1894)
Guns of August, The (1962) **Barbara Tuchman** (1912)
Guns of Navarone, The (1957) **Alistair Maclean** (1923)
Gunslinger (1968–72) **Ed Dorn** (1929)
Gunslinger, The (1982) **Stephen King** (1947)
Gurney Married (1838) **Theodore Hook** (1788)
Gustav Vasa (1899) **August Strindberg** (1849)
Gutenberg Galaxy, The (1962) **Marshall McLuhan** (1911)
Gutta-Percha Willie (1873) **George MacDonald** (1824)
Guv'nor, The (1932) **Edgar Wallace** (1875)
Guy and Pauline (1915) **Compton Mackenzie** (1883)
Guy Deverell (1865) **J.S. le Fanu** (1814)
Guy Fawkes (1841) **W.H. Ainsworth** (1805)
Guy Livingstone (1857) **G.A. Lawrence** (1827)
Guy Mannering (1815) **Sir Walter Scott** (1771)
Guy Mervyn (1891) **Florence Barclay** (1862)
Guy Rivers (1834) **William Gilmore Simms** (1806)
Guys and Dolls (1931) **Damon Runyon** (1884)
Guzman (1693) **Roger Boyle, earl of Orrery** (1621–1679)
Gwalia Deserta (1938) **Idris Davies** (1905)
Gwen Wynn (1877) **Mayne Reid** (1818)
Gwendolen (1989) **Buchi Emecheta** (1944)
Gwydonius (1584) **Robert Greene** (1558)
Gyfford of Weare (1928) **Jeffery Farnol** (1878)
Gynaikeion (1624) **Thomas Heywood** (1574?)
Gypsies Metamorphos'd, The (1621) **Ben Jonson** (1572)
Gypsies, The (1824) **Alexander Pushkin** (1799)
Gypsy Ballads [Romancero gitano] (1928) **Federico García Lorca** (1898)
Gypsy, Gypsy (1940) **Rumer Godden** (1907)

H

Ha! Ha! Among the Trumpets (1945) **Alun Lewis** (1915–44)
Habeas Corpus (1973) **Alan Bennett** (1934)
Habit of Empire, The (1941) **Paul Horgan** (1903)
Habitant, The (1897) **William Henry Drummond** (1854)
Habitations of the World (1985) **William H. Gass** (1924)
Habsburg Monarchy 1815–1918, The (1941) **A.J.P. Taylor** (1906)
Hacedor, El [**Borges**]: see *Dreamtiger*
Hacienda (1934) **Katherine Anne Porter** (1890)
Hackenfeller's Ape (1953) **Brigid Brophy** (1929)
Hadassa (1621) **Francis Quarles** (1592)
Hadrian the Seventh (1904) **Frederick William Rolfe** (1860)
Hag's Nook (1933) **John Dickson Carr** (1906)
Hagar of the Pawn-Shop (1898) **Fergus Hume** (1859)
Hagarene (1874) **G.A. Lawrence** (1827)
Hairy Ape, The (1922) **Eugene O'Neill** (1888)
Haj, The (1984) **Leon Uris** (1924)
Hakluytus Posthumus (1625) **Samuel Purchas** (1577)
Halcyone (1912) **Elinor Glyn** (1864)
Haleluiah (1641) **George Wither** (1588)
Half a Hero (1893) **'Anthony Hope' [Sir Anthony Hope Hawkins]** (1863)
Half a Million of Money (1866) **Amelia B. Edwards** (1831)
Half a Minute's Silence (1925) **Maurice Baring** (1874)
Half Asleep in Frog Pajamas (1994) **Tom Robbins** (1936)
'Half Moon', The (1909) **Ford Madox Ford** (1873)
Half-Crown Colony (1969) **James Pope Hennessy** (1916)
Half-Hearted, The (1900) **John Buchan** (1875)
Half-Sisters, The (1848) **Geraldine Jewsbury** (1812)
Halfway (1961) **Maxine Kumin** (1925)
Halfway House (1932) **Edmund Blunden** (1896)
Halfway House (1908) **Maurice Hewlett** (1861)
Halfway to Anywhere (1947) **Norman Lindsay** (1879)
Hall of Hellingsley, The (1821) **Sir Samuel Egerton Brydges** (1762)
Halloween Tree, The (1968) **Ray Bradbury** (1920)
Halt in the Garden, The (1925) **Robert Hillyer** (1895)
Ham on Rye (1982) **Charles Bukowski** (1920)
Hamilton Stark (1978) **Russell Banks** (1940)
Hamiltons, The (1834) **Mrs C.F. Gore** (1799)
Hamlet (1603) **William Shakespeare** (1564)
Hamlet, The (1940) **William Faulkner** (1897)
Hamlet Had an Uncle (1940) **James Branch Cabell** (1879)

Hamlet of A. MacLeish, The (1928) **Archibald MacLeish** (1892)
Hamlet, Revenge! [as 'Michael Innes'] (1937) **J.I.M. Stewart** (1906)
Hammer and Rapier (1871) **John Cooke** (1830)
Hampdenshire Wonder, The [US: *The Wonder*] (1911) **J.D. Beresford** (1873)
Hampshire Days (1903) **W.H. Hudson** (1841)
Han of Iceland [*Han d'Islande*] (1823) **Victor Hugo** (1802)
Hanbury Mills (1872) **C[hristabel] R[ose] Coleridge** (1843)
Hand in Hand (1974) **Jon Stallworthy** (1935)
Hand of Ethelberta, The (1876) **Thomas Hardy** (1840)
Hand of Mary Constable, The (1964) **Paul Gallico** (1897)
Hand That Cradles the Rock, The (1971) **Rita Mae Brown** (1944)
Hand That Feeds You, The (1982) **Nicholas Hasluck** (1942)
Hand-Book for Travellers in Spain, A (1845) **Richard Ford** (1796)
Hand-Made Fables (1920) **George Ade** (1866)
Hand-Reared Boy, The (1970) **Brian Aldiss** (1925)
Handbook of Phonetics, A (1877) **Henry Sweet** (1845)
Handel: The Man and his Music (1985) **Jonathan Keates** (1946)
Handful of Dust, A (1934) **Evelyn Waugh** (1903)
Handful of Earth, A (1936) **William Soutar** (1898)
Handful of Friends, A (1976) **David Williamson** (1942)
Handful of Pennies, A (1958) **Hal Porter** (1911)
Handles (1983) **Jan Mark** (1943)
Handley Cross (1843) **R.S. Surtees** (1805)
Handmaid's Tale, The (1985) **Margaret Atwood** (1939)
Hands to Dance (1951) **Charles Causley** (1917)
Hands Up! (1964) **Ed Dorn** (1929)
Handsome Heart, The (1943) **Peter de Vries** (1910)
Handsome Humes, The (1893) **William Black** (1841)
Handsome Phil (1899) **Mrs J.H. Riddell** (1832)
Handsome Quaker, The (1902) **Katharine Tynan** (1861)
Handy Andy (1842) **Samuel Lover** (1797)
Handyman, The (1983) **Penelope Mortimer** (1918)
Hang of the Gaol, The (1978) **Howard Barker** (1946)
Hanging and Marriage (1722) **Henry Carey** (1687?)
Hanging Garden, The (1998) **Ian Rankin** (1960)
Hanging On (1974) **Dean Koontz** (1945)
Hanging Tree, The (1990) **Allan Massie** (1938)
Hangman's Holiday (1933) **Dorothy L. Sayers** (1893)
Hangover Square (1941) **Patrick Hamilton** (1904)
Hangsaman (1951) **Shirley Jackson** (1919)
Hannah (1872) **Dinah Maria Craik** (1826)
Hannah (1764) **Christopher Smart** (1722)
Hannah Hewit (1792) **Charles Dibdin** (1745)
Hannah Massey (1964) **Catherine Cookson** (1906)
Hannah Thurston (1863) **Bayard Taylor** (1825)
Hannibal (1999) **Thomas Harris** (1940)
Hapgood (1988) **Tom Stoppard** (1937)
Happenstance: The Husband's Story (1980) **Carol Shields** (1935)
Happenstance: The Wife's Story (1982) **Carol Shields** (1935)
Happier Life, The (1972) **Douglas Dunn** (1942)
Happily Ever After (1991) **Jenny Diski** (1947)
Happiness of the Present Establishment, The (1708) **Benjamin Hoadly** (1676)
Happy as Larry (1946) **Donagh MacDonagh** (1912)
Happy Birthday, Wanda Jane (1970) **Kurt Vonnegut** (1922)
Happy Days (1961) **Samuel Beckett** (1906)
Happy Days (1933) **Ogden Nash** (1902)
Happy Ending, The (1957) **Leo Walmsley** (1892)
Happy Episode, The (1927) **Robert Hillyer** (1895)
Happy Family, The (1912) **Frank Swinnerton** (1884)
Happy Foreigner, The (1920) **Enid Bagnold** (1889)
Happy Harvest, The (1939) **Jeffery Farnol** (1878)
Happy Hypocrite, The (1897) **Max Beerbohm** (1872)
Happy Isles of Oceania, The (1992) **Paul Theroux** (1941)
Happy Man, A (1972) **P.J. Kavanagh** (1931)
Happy Marriage, The (1924) **Archibald MacLeish** (1892)
Happy Prince, The (1888) **Oscar Wilde** (1854)
Happy Return, The [US: *Beat to Quarters*. The first 'Hornblower' novel.] (1937) **C.S. Forester** (1899)
Happy Thoughts (1866) **Sir F.C. Burnand** (1836)
Happy to Be Here (1981) **Garrison Keillor** (1942)
Happy Turning, The (1945) **H.G. Wells** (1866)
Happy Valley, The (1939) **Patrick White** (1912)
Happy-Go-Lucky Morgans, The (1913) **Edward Thomas** (1878)
Happy-Thought Hall (1872) **Sir F.C. Burnand** (1836)
Hard Blue Sky, The (1958) **Shirley Ann Grau** (1929)
Hard Candy (1954) **'Tennessee' [Thomas Lanier] Williams** (1911)
Hard Cash [US: *Very Hard Cash*] (1863) **Charles Reade** (1814)
Hard Facts (1944) **Howard Spring** (1889)
Hard Feelings (1976) **Francis King** (1923)
Hard Life, The (1961) **'Flann O'Brien'** (1911)
Hard Time (1999) **Sara Paretsky** (1947)
Hard Times (1970) **Studs Terkel** (1912)
Hard Times (1854) **Charles Dickens** (1812)
Hard Woman, A (1895) **Violet Hunt** (1866)
Hard Words (1981) **Ursula K. le Guin** (1929)
Harding's Luck (1909) **E[dith] Nesbit** (1858)
Hargrave (1843) **Frances Trollope** (1780)
Harland's Half-Acre (1984) **David Malouf** (1934)
Harlequin (2000) **Bernard Cornwell** (1944)
Harlequinade (1948) **Terence Rattigan** (1911)
Harlot's Ghost (1991) **Norman Mailer** (1923)
Harm (1994) **Alan Jenkins** (1955)
Harm Done (1999) **Ruth Rendell** (1930)
Harmer John (1926) **Sir Hugh Walpole** (1884)
Harmonie of the Church, The (1591) **Michael Drayton** (1563)
Harmonium [enlarged edn, 1931] (1923) **Wallace Stevens** (1879)

Harnessing Peacocks (1985) **'Mary Wesley' [Mary Wellesley]** (1912)
Harold (1848) **Edward Bulwer-Lytton** (1803)
Harold (1927) **Stephen Phillips** (1864–1915)
Harold (1877) **Alfred, Lord Tennyson** (1809)
Harold the Dauntless (1817) **Sir Walter Scott** (1771)
Harold's Leap (1950) **Stevie Smith** (1902)
Haroun and the Sea of Stories (1990) **Salman Rushdie** (1947)
Harp of a Thousand Strings (1947) **H.L. Davis** (1896)
Harp of Aeolus, The (1947) **Geoffrey Grigson** (1905)
Harp of Fishbones, A (1972) **Joan Aiken** (1924)
Harpoon at a Venture (1952) **Gavin Maxwell** (1914)
Harriet (1977) **Jilly Cooper** (1937)
Harriet Hume (1929) **'Rebecca West' [Cicily Isabel Andrews]** (1892)
Harriet Said . . . (1972) **Beryl Bainbridge** (1934)
Harrington; and Ormond (1817) **Maria Edgeworth** (1767)
Harris's Requiem (1960) **Stanley Middleton** (1919)
Harrowing of Hubertus, The [repub. as *Hubertus*, 1955, and *Kaywana Stock*, 1968] (1954) **Edgar Mittelholzer** (1909)
Harry and Lucy Concluded (1825) **Maria Edgeworth** (1767)
Harry Coverdale's Courtship (1855) **Frank Smedley** (1818)
Harry Heathcote of Gangoil (1874) **Anthony Trollope** (1815)
Harry Joscelyn (1881) **Margaret Oliphant** (1828)
Harry Muir (1853) **Margaret Oliphant** (1828)
Harry Ogilvie (1856) **James Grant** (1822)
Harry Potter and the Chamber of Secrets (1998) **J.K. Rowling** (1965)
Harry Pottter and the Goblet of Fire (2000) **J.K. Rowling** (1965)
Harry Potter and the Philosopher's Stone (1997) **J.K. Rowling** (1965)
Harry Potter and the Prisoner of Azkaban (1999) **J.K. Rowling** (1965)
Hartland Forest (1871) **Anna Eliza Bray** (1790)
Hartley's Theory of the Human Mind (1775) **Joseph Priestley** (1733)
Harvest Comedy (1937) **Frank Swinnerton** (1884)
Harvest Moon, The (1909) **Augustus Thomas** (1857)
Harvest of Sorrow, The (1986) **Robert Conquest** (1917)
Harvest Poems (1960) **Carl Sandburg** (1878)
Harvey (1944) **Mary Chase** (1907)
Hassan (1922) **James Elroy Flecker** (1884–1915)
Haste to the Wedding (1962) **Alex Comfort** (1920)
Hat on the Bed, The (1963) **John O'Hara** (1905)
Hat on the Letter O, The (1978) **Nicholas Hasluck** (1942)
Hate Begins at Home (1967) **Joan Aiken** (1924)
Hated Nightfall; [and] *Wounds to the Face* (1994) **Howard Barker** (1946)
Hathercourt Rectory (1878) **Mary Louisa Molesworth** (1839)
Hatter's Castle (1931) **A.J. Cronin** (1896)
Hau Kiou Choaan (1761) **Thomas Percy** (1729)
Haunch of Venison, The (1776) **Oliver Goldsmith** (1728–74)
Haunt, The (1999) **A.L. Barker** (1918)
Haunted (1988) **James Herbert** (1943)
Haunted (1994) **Joyce Carol Oates** (1938)
Haunted and the Haunters, The (1857) **Edward Bulwer-Lytton** (1803)
Haunted Garden, The (1947) **Henry Treece** (1911)
Haunted Hotel, The [with 'My Lady's Money'] (1878) **Wilkie Collins** (1824)
Haunted House, A (1943) **Virginia Woolf** (1882–1941)
Haunted House, The (1927) **Hilaire Belloc** (1870)
Haunted Land, A (1956) **Randolph Stow** (1935)
Haunted Lives (1868) **J.S. le Fanu** (1814)
Haunted Man and the Ghost's Bargain, The (1848) **Charles Dickens** (1812)
Haunted Marsh, The [*La Mare au diable*] (1846) **'George Sand' [Auore Dupin]** (1804)
Haunted Organist of Hurly Burly, The (1891) **Rosa Mulholland** (1841)
Haunted Station, The (1894) **Hume Nisbet** (1849)
Haunters of the Silences, The (1907) **Sir Charles G.D. Roberts** (1860)
Haunting, The (1982) **Margaret Mahy** (1936)
Haunting of Hill House, The (1959) **Shirley Jackson** (1919)
Haunting of Lamb House, The (1991) **Joan Aiken** (1924)
Haunting of Toby Jugg, The (1948) **Dennis Wheatley** (1897)
Hauntings (1890) **'Vernon Lee' [Violet Paget]** (1856)
Haunts of Ancient Peace (1902) **Alfred Austin** (1835)
Havanna Bay (1999) **Martin Cruz Smith** (1942)
Have His Carcase (1932) **Dorothy L. Sayers** (1893)
Have the Men Had Enough? (1989) **Margaret Forster** (1938)
Have With You to Saffron-walden (1596) **Thomas Nashe** (1567)
Having a Ball (1981) **Alan Bleasdale** (1946)
Haw Lantern, The (1987) **Seamus Heaney** (1939)
Hawaii (1959) **James A. Michener** (1907)
Hawbuck Grange (1847) **R.S. Surtees** (1805)
Hawbucks, The (1929) **John Masefield** (1878)
Hawk in the Rain, The (1957) **Ted Hughes** (1930)
Hawkfall (1974) **George Mackay Brown** (1921)
Hawkins Monster, The (1974) **Richard Brautigan** (1935)
Hawks of Hawk-Hollow, The (1835) **Robert Bird** (1806)
Hawksbill Station (1968) **Robert Silverberg** (1935)
Hawksmoor (1985) **Peter Ackroyd** (1949)
'Haworth's' (1879) **Frances Hodgson Burnett** (1849)
Hawthorn and Lavender (1899) **W.E. Henley** (1849)
Hawthorn Tree, The (1943) **Paul Green** (1894)
Hay (1998) **Paul Muldoon** (1951)
Hay Any Worke for Cooper (1589) **Martin Marprelate**
Hay Fever (1925) **Noel Coward** (1899)

Haydn and the Valve Trumpet (1990) **Craig Raine** (1944)
Hazard (1930) **Wilfrid Gibson** (1878)
Hazard of New Fortunes, A (1890) **William Dean Howells** (1837)
Hazel-Blossoms (1875) **John Greenleaf Whittier** (1807)
Hazelwood Hall (1823) **Robert Bloomfield** (1766)
He Knew He Was Right (1869) **Anthony Trollope** (1815)
He Should Have Died Hereafter [US: *Untimely Death*] (1958) **'Cyril Hare' [A.A.G. Clark]** (1900)
He That Will Not When He May (1880) **Margaret Oliphant** (1828)
He Who Rides the Tiger (1954) **Bhabani Bhattacharya** (1906)
He/She (1980) **Herbert Gold** (1924)
Head in Green Bronze (1938) **Sir Hugh Walpole** (1884)
Head of the Family, The (1852) **Dinah Maria Craik** (1826)
Head of the Firm, The (1892) **Mrs J.H. Riddell** (1832)
Head to Toe (1971) **Joe Orton** (1933)
Headless Angel (1940) **Vicki Baum** (1888)
Headless Horseman, The (1866) **Mayne Reid** (1818)
Headlong (1999) **Michael Frayn** (1933)
Headlong Hall (1816) **Thomas Love Peacock** (1785)
Headquarter Recruit, The [as 'Richard Dehan'] (1913) **Clo Graves** (1863)
Headsman, The (1833) **James Fenimore Cooper** (1789)
Healer, The (1911) **Robert Herrick** (1868)
Healer, The (1955) **Frank G. Slaughter** (1908)
Healey (1875) **Jessie Fothergill** (1851)
Healing Art, The (1980) **A.N. Wilson** (1950)
Health (1724) **Allan Ramsay** (1686)
Health and Holiness (1905) **Francis Thompson** (1859)
Hear Us, O Lord, From Heaven Thy Dwelling Place (1961) **Malcolm Lowry** (1909)
Hearing Secret Harmonies (1975) **Anthony Powell** (1905)
Hearing Voices (1995) **A.N. Wilson** (1950)
Heart and Science (1883) **Wilkie Collins** (1824)
Heart for the Gods of Mexico, A (1939) **Conrad Potter Aiken** (1889)
Heart is a Lonely Hunter, The (1940) **Carson McCullers** (1917)
Heart of a Child, The (1908) **'Frank Danby' [Julia Frankau]** (1864)
Heart of a Stranger (1976) **Margaret Laurence** (1926)
Heart of a Woman, The (1981) **Maya Angelou** (1928)
'Heart of Darkness, The' (1902) **Joseph Conrad** (1857)
Heart of England, The (1906) **Edward Thomas** (1878)
Heart of Life, The (1895) **W.H. Mallock** (1849)
Heart of London, The (1961) **Monica Dickens** (1915)
'Heart of Midlothian, The' [**Scott**]: see *Tales of My Landlord [2nd ser.]*
Heart of Penelope, The (1904) **Mrs Belloc Lowndes** (1868)
Heart of Princess Osra, The (1896) **'Anthony Hope' [Sir Anthony Hope Hawkins]** (1863)
Heart of the Ancient Wood, The (1900) **Sir Charles G.D. Roberts** (1860)
Heart of the Country, The (1906) **Ford Madox Ford** (1873)
Heart of the Country (1987) **Fay Weldon** (1931)
Heart of the Family, The (1953) **Elizabeth Goudge** (1900)
Heart of the Hunter, The (1961) **Sir Laurens van der Post** (1906)
Heart of the Matter, The (1948) **Graham Greene** (1904)
Heart of the West (1907) **'O. Henry' [William Sydney Porter]** (1862)
Heart of the World (1896) **Sir H. Rider Haggard** (1856)
Heart Songs (1988) **E. Annie Proulx** (1935)
Heart That Knows, The (1906) **Sir Charles G.D. Roberts** (1860)
Heart, the Border, The (1990) **Ken Smith** (1938)
Heart's Desire (1978) **Jeffrey Wainwright** (1944)
Heart's Highway, The (1900) **Mary Wilkins Freeman** (1852)
Heart's Journey, The (1928) **Siegfried Sassoon** (1886)
Heart's Needle (1959) **W.D. Snodgrass** (1926)
Heartbreak House, Great Catherine, and Playlets of the War (1919) **Bernard Shaw** (1856)
Heartland (1964) **Wilson Harris** (1921)
Heartlanders (1989) **David Edgar** (1948)
Hearts in Atlantis (1999) **Stephen King** (1947)
Hearts of Alsace (1916) **Matilda Betham-Edwards** (1836)
Heartsease (1969) **Peter Dickinson** (1927)
Heartsease (1854) **Charlotte M. Yonge** (1823)
Heat and Dust (1975) **Ruth Prawer Jhabvala** (1927)
Heat of the Day, The (1949) **Elizabeth Bowen** (1899)
Heat of the Day, The (1989) **Harold Pinter** (1930)
Heat of the Sun, The (1966) **'Seán O'Faoláin' [John Francis Whelan]** (1900)
Heat Wave (1996) **Penelope Lively** (1933)
Heathcliff and the Great Hunger (1995) **Terry Eagleton** (1943)
Heather and Snow (1893) **George MacDonald** (1824)
Heather Blazing, The (1993) **Colm Tóibín** (1955)
Heaven and Hell (1956) **Aldous Huxley** (1894)
Heaven, in a Way (1970) **Rodney Hall** (1935)
Heaven Lies About Us (1939) **Howard Spring** (1889)
Heaven on Earth (1975) **Janice Elliott** (1931)
Heaven to Find, A (1987) **Ruth Pitter** (1897)
Heaven Tree, The (1960) **'Ellis Peters' [Edith Mary Pargeter]** (1913)
Heaven Upon Earth (1606) **Joseph Hall** (1574)
Heaven's Command (1973) **Jan Morris** (1926)
Heaven's My Destination (1935) **Thornton Wilder** (1897)
Heavenly City, Earthly City (1947) **Robert Duncan** (1919)
Heavenly Twins, The (1893) **'Sarah Grand' [Frances Elizabeth McFall]** (1854)
Heavy Feather, A (1978) **A.L. Barker** (1918)

Heavy Water (1998) **Martin Amis** (1949)
Heavy Weather (1933) **P.G. Wodehouse** (1881)
Hebrew Melodies (1815) **George Gordon, Lord Byron** (1788)
Hedda Gabler (1890) **Henrik Ibsen** (1828)
Hedgehog, The (1936) **Hilda Doolittle** (1886)
Hedylus (1928) **Hilda Doolittle** (1886)
Heel of Achilles, The (1921) **'E.M. Delafield' [E.E.M. de la Pasture]** (1890)
Heemskerck Shoals (1949) **R. D. FitzGerald** (1902)
Hegel (1883) **Edward Caird** (1835)
Heidenmauer, The (1832) **James Fenimore Cooper** (1789)
Heidi (1881) **Johanna Spyri** (1827)
Heights of Macchu Picchu, The [Alturas de Macchu Picchu] (1945) **Pablo Neruda** (1904)
Heir at Law, The (1797) **George Colman the Younger** (1762)
Heir of Gaymount, The (1870) **John Cooke** (1830)
Heir of Linne, The (1888) **Robert Williams Buchanan** (1841)
Heir of Morocco, The (1682) **Elkanah Settle** (1648)
Heir of Redclyffe, The (1853) **Charlotte M. Yonge** (1823)
Heir of the Ages, The (1886) **James Payn** (1830)
Heir, The (1922) **Vita Sackville-West** (1892)
Heir Without a Heritage (1887) **E[mma] F[rances] Brooke** (1859?)
Heire, The (1622) **Thomas May** (1595)
Heiress of Red Dog, An (1878) **Bret Harte** (1836)
Heiress, The (1786) **John Burgoyne** (1722)
Hekatompathia, The (1582) **Thomas Watson** (1557?)
Helbeck of Bannisdale (1898) **Mrs T. Humphry Ward** (1851)
Held by the Enemy (1886) **William Gillette** (1855)
Held Fast for England (1892) **G.A. Henty** (1832)
Held in Bondage (1863) **'Ouida' [Marie Louise de la Ramée]** (1839)
Helen (1834) **Maria Edgeworth** (1767)
Helen (c. 412 BC) **Euripides** (480 BC)
Helen Adair (1903) **Louis Becke** (1855)
Helen Halsey (1845) **William Gilmore Simms** (1806)
Helen in Egypt (1961) **Hilda Doolittle** (1886–1961)
Helen in Egypt, and Other Plays (1958) **John Heath-Stubbs** (1918)
Helen of Troy (1882) **Andrew Lang** (1844)
Helen With the High Hand (1910) **Arnold Bennett** (1867)
Helena (1950) **Evelyn Waugh** (1903)
Helga's Web (1970) **Jon Cleary** (1917)
Heliodora (1924) **Hilda Doolittle** (1886)
Hell of a Woman, A (1954) **Jim Thompson** (1906)
Hell! Said the Duchess (1934) **'Michael Arlen' [Dikran Kouyoumdjian]** (1895)
Hell's Angels (1966) **Hunter S. Thompson** (1939)
Hellas (1822) **P.B. Shelley** (1792)
Hellbound Heart, The (1988) **Clive Barker** (1952)
Hellbox (1947) **John O'Hara** (1905)
Hellenics , The (1847) **Walter Savage Landor** (1775)
Hellenism (1959) **Arnold Toynbee** (1889)
Helliconia Spring (1982) **Brian Aldiss** (1925)
Helliconia Summer (1983) **Brian Aldiss** (1925)
Helliconia Winter (1985) **Brian Aldiss** (1925)
Hello America (1981) **J.G. Ballard** (1930)
Hello and Goodbye (1965) **Athol Fugard** (1932)
Hello, I'm Erica Long (1984) **Kathy Acker** (1948)
Hello La Jolla (1978) **Ed Dorn** (1929)
Hellow Towns! (1929) **Sherwood Anderson** (1876)
Helmets (1964) **James Dickey** (1923)
Héloise and Abelard (1925) **George Moore** (1852)
Helpmate, The (1907) **May Sinclair** (1863)
Hemlock and After (1952) **Angus Wilson** (1913)
Hence (1989) **Brad Leithauser** (1953)
Henderson the Rain King (1959) **Saul Bellow** (1915)
Hengest's Tale (1966) **Jill Paton Walsh** (1937)
Henri Christophe (1950) **Derek Walcott** (1930)
Henrietta (1758) **Charlotte Lennox** (1720)
Henrietta Temple (1836) **Benjamin Disraeli** (1804)
Henrietta, The (1887) **Bronson Howard** (1842)
Henry (1795) **Richard Cumberland** (1732)
Henry Bly, and Other Plays (1950) **Anne Ridler** (1912)
Henry Brocken (1904) **Walter de la Mare** (1873)
Henry de Pomeroy (1842) **Anna Eliza Bray** (1790)
Henry Dunbar (1864) **M.E. Braddon** (1835)
Henry and Cato (1976) **Iris Murdoch** (1919)
Henry III [Henri III et sa cour] (1829) **Alexandre Dumas ['père']** (1802)
Henry Irving (1883) **William Archer** (1856)
Henry IV [Enrico IV] (1922) **Luigi Pirandello** (1867)
Henry IV, Part 1 (1598) **William Shakespeare** (1564)
Henry IV, Part 2 (1600) **William Shakespeare** (1564)
Henry James (1953–72) **Leon Edel** (1907)
Henry James (1914) **Ford Madox Ford** (1873)
Henry Masterton (1832) **G.P.R. James** (1799)
Henry Smeaton (1851) **G.P.R. James** (1799)
Henry St John, Gentleman (1859) **John Cooke** (1830)
Henry the Fifth (1600) **William Shakespeare** (1564)
Henry, the Green Engine (1951) **Revd W.V. Awdry** (1911)
Henry VI, Part 2 (1594) **William Shakespeare** (1564)
Henry VI, Part 3 (1595) **William Shakespeare** (1564)
Henry's Fate (1977) **John Berryman** (1914–72)
Heptalogia, The (1880) **A.C. Swinburne** (1837)
Heptamaron of Civill Discourses, A [2nd edn, 1593, as Aurelia] (1582) **George Whetstone** (c. 1551)
Her (1974) **A. Alvarez** (1929) (ed.)
Her (1960) **Lawrence Ferlinghetti** (1920)
Her Benny (1879) **Silas K. Hocking** (1850)
Her Blue Body Everything We Know (1991) **Alice Walker** (1944)
Her Convict (1907) **M.E. Braddon** (1835)
Her Dearest Foe (1876) **Mrs A.H. Alexander** (1825)
Her Great Idea (1888) **L[ucy] B[erthia] Walford** (1845)
Her Ladyship's Conscience (1913) **Ellen Thorneycroft Fowler** (1860)
Her Living Image (1984) **Jane Rogers** (1952)
Her Majesty the Queen (1873) **John Cooke** (1830)

Her Mother's Darling (1877) **Mrs J.H. Riddell** (1832)
Her Mother's Daughter (1987) **Marilyn French** (1929)
Her Story (1987) **Dan Jacobson** (1929)
Her Victory (1982) **Alan Sillitoe** (1928)
Her Wedding Night (1918) **Max Pemberton** (1863)
Héraclius (1646) **Pierre Corneille** (1606)
Herakles (1967) **Archibald MacLeish** (1892)
Herb Basket, An (1950) **Richard Eberhart** (1904)
Herb of Grace (1901) **Rosa Nouchette Carey** (1840)
Herb of Grace, The (1948) **Elizabeth Goudge** (1900)
Herball or Generall Historie of Plantes (1597) **John Gerard** (1545)
Herbert Tresham (1842) **John Mason Neale** (1818)
Hercules Furens [from Seneca] (1561) **Jasper Heywood** (1535) (tr.)
Here (1993) **Michael Frayn** (1933)
Here and Beyond (1926) **Edith Wharton** (1862)
Here and Hereafter (1911) **'Barry Pain' [Eric Odell]** (1864)
Here Are Ladies (1913) **James Stephens** (1882)
Here Be Dragons (1956) **Stella Gibbons** (1902)
Here Comes a Candle (1967) **Jane Aiken Hodge** (1917)
Here Comes Everybody (1965) **'Anthony Burgess' [John Anthony Burgess Wilson]** (1917)
Here Comes, There Goes, You Know Who (1962) **William Saroyan** (1908)
Here Comes Thursday (1966) **Michael Bond** (1926)
Here Was a Man (1936) **Norah Lofts** (1904)
Here We Go Round the Round House (1976) **Charles Causley** (1917)
Heredity and Politics (1938) **J.B.S. Haldane** (1892)
Heretic's Apprentice, The (1989) **'Ellis Peters' [Edith Mary Pargeter]** (1913)
Heretics (1905) **G.K. Chesterton** (1874)
Heretics of Dune (1982) **Frank Herbert** (1920)
Hereward the Wake (1866) **Charles Kingsley** (1819)
Heritage and its History, A (1959) **I. Compton-Burnett** (1884)
Heritage of Hatcher Ide, The (1941) **Booth Tarkington** (1869)
Heritage of Symbolism, The (1943) **Maurice Bowra** (1898)
Herland (1915) **Charlotte Perkins Gilman** (1860)
Hermann und Dorothea (1797) **Johann Wolfgang von Goethe** (1749)
Hermes Flew to Olympus (1968) **Christopher Logue** (1926)
Hermetic Definition (1972) **Hilda Doolittle** (1886–1961)
Hermetical Physick [from Heinrich Nolle] (1655) **Henry Vaughan** (1622) (tr.)
Hermione (1981) **Hilda Doolittle** (1886–1961)
Hermit, The (1770) **Susannah Gunning** (1740)
Hermit and the Wild Woman, The (1908) **Edith Wharton** (1862)
Hermit of Carmel, A (1901) **George Santayana** (1863)
Hermit of Eyton Forest, The (1987) **'Ellis Peters' [Edith Mary Pargeter]** (1913)
Hermit of Warkworth, The (1771) **Thomas Percy** (1729)
Hermit's Tale, A (1787) **Sophia Lee** (1750)
Hermsprong (1796) **Robert Bage** (1728)
Hernani (1830) **Victor Hugo** (1802)
Herne's Egg, The (1938) **W.B. Yeats** (1865)
Hero, The (1901) **Somerset Maugham** (1874)
Hero and Leander (1598) **Christopher Marlowe** (1564–93)
Hero and Leander, and Bacchus and Ariadne (1819) **Leigh Hunt** (1784)
Hero of Our Time, A (1840) **Mikhail Lermontov** (1814)
Hero Rises Up, The (1968) **John Arden** (1930) [with Margaretta D'Arcy]
Herod (1901) **Stephen Phillips** (1864)
Herod the Great (1694) **Roger Boyle, Earl of Orrery** (1621)
Heroes and Kings (1930) **Charles Williams** (1886)
Heroes and Villains (1969) **Angela Carter** (1940)
Heroes of Asgard, The (1857) **Annie Keary** (1825) [with Eliza Keary]
Heroes of Smokeover (1926) **L.P. Jacks** (1860)
Heroes, The (1856) **Charles Kingsley** (1819)
Heroes' Twilight (1965) **Bernard Bergonzi** (1929)
Heroic Idyls (1863) **Walter Savage Landor** (1775)
Heroick Portraits (1660) **Richard Flecknoe** (*c.* 1620)
Herr Paulus (1888) **Sir Walter Besant** (1836)
Herself Surprised (1941) **Joyce Cary** (1888)
Herzog (1964) **Saul Bellow** (1915)
Hesiod's Works and Days (1913) **Samuel Butler** (1835–1902) (tr.)
Hesperides (1648) **Robert Herrick** (1591)
Hessian, The (1972) **Howard Fast** (1914)
Hester Lilly (1954) **Elizabeth Taylor** (1912)
Hester's History (1869) **Rosa Mulholland** (1841)
Hetty (1871) **Henry Kingsley** (1830)
Hetty Wesley (1903) **Sir A.T. Quiller-Couch** (1863)
Heu-Heu (1924) **Sir H. Rider Haggard** (1856)
Hexagon, The (1956) **Hal Porter** (1911)
Hexameron; or, Meditations on the Six Days of Creation (1717) **Thomas Traherne** (1637–74)
Hey Rub-a-Dub-Dub (1920) **Theodore Dreiser** (1871)
Hiawatha (1855) **Henry Wadsworth Longfellow** (1807)
Hickory, Dickory, Dock [US: *Hickory, Dickory, Death*] (1955) **Agatha Christie** (1890)
Hidden Ireland, The (1925) **Daniel Corkery** (1878)
Hidden Laughter (1990) **Simon Gray** (1936)
Hidden Life, A (1976) **Hugh Trevor-Roper** (1914)
Hidden Lives (1995) **Margaret Forster** (1938)
Hidden Side of the Moon, The (1987) **Joanna Russ** (1937)
Hidden Sin, The (1866) **Frances Browne** (1816)
Hide and Seek (1854) **Wilkie Collins** (1824)
Hide and Seek (1991) **Ian Rankin** (1960)
Hide Parke (1637) **James Shirley** (1596)
Hide, The (1970) **Barry Unsworth** (1930)
Hideaway (1992) **Dean Koontz** (1945)
Hierarchie of the Blessed Angells, The (1635) **Thomas Heywood** (1574?)

Hieroglyphikes of the Life of Man (1638) **Francis Quarles** (1592)
High and Low (1966) **Sir John Betjeman** (1906)
High Church Claims (1841) **Nicholas Patrick S. Wiseman** (1802)
High Commissioner, The (1966) **Jon Cleary** (1917)
High Country Weather (1984) **Lauris Edmond** (1924)
High Fidelity (1995) **Nick Hornby** (1957)
High Flyer, The (1999) **Susan Howatch** (1940)
High Ground (1985) **John McGahern** (1934)
High Hearts (1986) **Rita Mae Brown** (1944)
High Island (1974) **Richard Murphy** (1927)
High Life Below Stairs (1759) **David Garrick** (1717)
High Notes From When I Was Rolling in Moss (1966) **Michael Horovitz** (1935)
High Pavement Blues (1983) **Bernard Ashley** (1935)
High Pink on Chrome (1975) **J.H. Prynne** (1936)
High Place, The (1923) **James Branch Cabell** (1879)
High Rise (1975) **J.G. Ballard** (1930)
High Road, The (1988) **Edna O'Brien** (1932)
High Road to China (1977) **Jon Cleary** (1917)
High Sierra (1940) **W.R. Burnett** (1899)
High Spirits (1982) **Robertson Davies** (1913)
High Stakes (1975) **Dick Francis** (1920)
High Tide in the Garden (1971) **Fleur Adcock** (1934)
High Tor (1937) **Maxwell Anderson** (1888)
High Wind in Jamaica, A [US: *The Innocent Voyage*] (1929) **Richard Hughes** (1900)
High Window, The (1942) **Raymond Chandler** (1888)
High Windows (1974) **Philip Larkin** (1922)
Highgate Road (1977) **A.R. Ammons** (1926)
Highland Call, The (1941) **Paul Green** (1894)
Highland Cousins (1894) **William Black** (1841)
Highland Fling (1931) **Nancy Mitford** (1904)
Highland River (1937) **Neil M. Gunn** (1891)
Highlander, The (1758) **James Macpherson** (1736)
Highwayman, The (1915) **H.C. Bailey** (1878)
Hilary St Ives (1870) **W.H. Ainsworth** (1805)
Hilda Lessways (1911) **Arnold Bennett** (1867)
Hilda Strafford; and The Remittance Man (1897) **Beatrice Harraden** (1864)
Hilda Tablet (1971) **Henry Reed** (1914)
Hilda Wade, Hospital Nurse (1900) **Grant Allen** (1848–99)
The Hill Bachelors (2000) **William Trevor** (1928)
Hill of Devi, The (1953) **E.M. Forster** (1879)
Hill of Dreams, The (1907) **Arthur Machen** (1863)
Hill of Evil Counsel, The (1976) **Amos Oz** (1939)
Hill of Trouble, The (1903) **A.C. Benson** (1862)
Hill of Vision, The (1912) **James Stephens** (1882)
Hill Station, The (1981) **J.G. Farrell** (1935–79)
Hilliad, The (1753) **Christopher Smart** (1722)
Hillingdon Hall (1845) **R.S. Surtees** (1805)
Hills and the Sea (1906) **Hilaire Belloc** (1870)
Hills Beyond, The [unfinished] (1941) **Thomas Wolfe** (1900–38)
Hills Give Promise, The (1923) **Robert Hillyer** (1895)
Hills of Adonis, The (1968) **Colin Thubron** (1939)
Hillyars and the Burtons, The (1865) **Henry Kingsley** (1830)
Hilt to Hilt (1869) **John Cooke** (1830)
him (1927) **E.E. Cummings** (1894)
Him With His Foot in His Mouth (1984) **Saul Bellow** (1915)
Hind and the Panther, The (1687) **John Dryden** (1631)
Hind and the Panther Transvers'd , The (1687) **Matthew Prior** (1664) [with Charles Montagu]
Hind Let Loose, A (1910) **C.E. Montague** (1867)
Hindle Wakes (1912) **Stanley Houghton** (1881)
Hindoo Holiday (1932) **J.R. Ackerley** (1896)
Hint to Husbands, A (1806) **Richard Cumberland** (1732)
Hinterland, The (1977) **Peter Scupham** (1933)
Hints From Horace (1831) **George Gordon, Lord Byron** (1788–1824)
Hippolytus Temporizes (1927) **Hilda Doolittle** (1886)
Hips and Haws (1922) **A.E. Coppard** (1878)
Hired Man, The (1969) **Melvyn Bragg** (1939)
Hireling, The (1957) **L.P. Hartley** (1895)
Hiroshima (1946) **John Hersey** (1914)
Hiroshima mon amour [screenplay] (1959) **'Marguerite Duras' [Marguerite Donnadieu]** (1914)
His Darling Sin (1899) **M.E. Braddon** (1835)
His Excellency Eugène Rougon [*Son Excellence Eugène Rougon*] (1876) **Émile Zola** (1840)
His Fatal Beauty (1917) **E.V. Lucas** (1868)
His Fellow Men (1952) **Lord Dunsany** (1878)
His Hour (1910) **Elinor Glyn** (1864)
His Human Majesty (1949) **Kay Boyle** (1903)
His Last Bow (1917) **A. Conan Doyle** (1859)
His Last Sebastian (1922) **James Laver** (1899)
His Majesties Poeticall Exercises at Vacant Houres (1591) **King James I** (1566)
His Majesty (1928) **Harley Granville-Barker** (1877)
His Monkey Wife (1930) **John Collier** (1901)
His Native Wife (1896) **Louis Becke** (1855)
His Natural Life (1875) **Marcus Clarke** (1846)
His Official Fiancée (1914) **Berta Ruck** (1878)
His Religion and Hers (1923) **Charlotte Perkins Gilman** (1860)
His Second War (1944) **Alec Waugh** (1898)
His Toy, His Dream, His Rest (1968) **John Berryman** (1914)
His Worship the Mayor (1934) **Walter Greenwood** (1903)
Histoire comique des états et empires de la lune (1656) **Cyrano de Bergerac** (1619–55)
Histoire comique des états et empires du soleil (1661) **Cyrano de Bergerac** (1619–55)
Histoire du romantisme ['History of Romanticism'] (1874) **Théophile Gautier** (1811–72)
Historia animalium **Aristotle** (384 BC)
Historia et Antiquitates Universitatis Oxoniensis [Eng trn. 1786–96] (1674) **Anthony à Wood** (1632)
Historian's Approach to Religion, An (1956) **Arnold Toynbee** (1889)
Historic Doubts on the Life and Reign of King Richard III (1768) **Horace Walpole** (1717)
Historical and Biographical Essays (1858) **John Forster** (1812)

Historical and Moral View of the French Revolution, An (1794) **Mary Wollstonecraft** (1759)
Historical and Statistical Account of Nova Scotia, A (1829) **T.C. Haliburton** (1796)
Historical Essays [1st ser.] (1871) **E.A. Freeman** (1823)
Historical Essays (1872) **J.H. Newman** (1801)
Historical Essays (1957) **Hugh Trevor-Roper** (1914)
Historical Essays and Studies (1907) **Lord Acton** (1834–1902)
Historical Essays: Fourth Series (1892) **E.A. Freeman** (1823)
Historical Essays: Second Series (1873) **E.A. Freeman** (1823)
Historical Essays: Third Series (1879) **E.A. Freeman** (1823)
Historical Geography of Europe, The (1881) **E.A. Freeman** (1823)
Historical Inevitability (1954) **Sir Isaiah Berlin** (1909)
Historical Narration Concerning Heresie, An (1680) **Thomas Hobbes** (1588–1679)
Historical Nights' Entertainment, The (1918) **Rafael Sabatini** (1875)
Historical Odes (1864) **Richard Watson Dixon** (1833)
Historical Register for the Year 1736, The (1737) **Henry Fielding** (1707)
Historical Review of the Constitution and Government of Pennsylvania, An (1759) **Benjamin Franklin** (1706)
Historical Sketches of Statesmen [1st and 2nd ser.] (1839) **Henry, Lord Brougham** (1778)
Historical Sketches of Statesmen [3rd ser.] (1842) **Henry, Lord Brougham** (1778)
Historie of Edward the Fourth, The (1640) **William Habington** (1605)
Historie of Guicciardin, The (1579) **Sir Geoffrey Fenton** (1539?) (tr.)
Historie of Palmendos, The [from Francisco de Moraes] (1589) **Anthony Munday** (1560) (tr.)
Historie of Samson, The (1631) **Francis Quarles** (1592)
Historie of the Holy Warre, The (1639) **Thomas Fuller** (1608)
Histories of Lady Frances S— and Lady Caroline S—, The (1763) **Susannah Gunning** (1740)
History (1973) **Robert Lowell** (1917)
History and Adventures of an Atom, The (1769) **Tobias George Smollett** (1721)
History and Adventures of the Renowned Don Quixote, The [from Cervantes] (1755) **Tobias George Smollett** (1721) (tr.)
History and Conquests of the Saracens, The (1856) **E.A. Freeman** (1823)
History and Fall of Caius Marius, The (1679) **Thomas Otway** (1652)
History and Present State of Discoveries Relating to Vision, Light, and Colours, The (1772) **Joseph Priestley** (1733)
History and Present State of Electricity, The (1767) **Joseph Priestley** (1733)
History and Remarkable Life of Colonel Jacque, The [*Colonel Jack*] (1723) **Daniel Defoe** (1660)
History Maker, A (1994) **Alasdair Gray** (1934)
History Man, The (1975) **Malcolm Bradbury** (1932)
History of a Flirt, The (1840) **Lady Charlotte Bury** (1775)
History of a Six Weeks' Tour (1817) **Mary Shelley** (1797) [with P.B. Shelley]
History of America, The (1777) **William Robertson** (1721)
History of an Adopted Child, The (1852) **Geraldine Jewsbury** (1812)
History of Anthony Waring, The (1927) **May Sinclair** (1863)
History of Architecture, A (1849) **E.A. Freeman** (1823)
History of Arsaces, The (1774) **Charles Johnstone** (1719?)
History of Brazil . . . Part the First (1810) **Robert Southey** (1774)
History of Brazil . . . Part the Second (1817) **Robert Southey** (1774)
History of Brazil . . . Part the Third (1819) **Robert Southey** (1774)
History of Britain, The (1670) **John Milton** (1608)
History of Britain, A (2000) **Simon Schama** (1945)
History of British India, The (1817) **James Mill** (1773)
History of Charles the Eighth of France, The (1672) **John Crowne** (d. 1703)
History of Christianity to the Abolition of Paganism, The (1840) **Henry Hart Milman** (1791)
History of Civilization in England (1857–61) **Henry Thomas Buckle** (1821)
History of Criticism and Literary Taste in Europe , The (1900) **George Saintsbury** (1845)
History of David Grieve, The (1892) **Mrs T. Humphry Ward** (1851)
History of Eighteenth-Century Literature, A (1889) **Sir Edmund Gosse** (1849)
History of Elizabethan Literature, A (1887) **George Saintsbury** (1845)
History of Emily Montague, The (1769) **Frances Brooke** (1724)
History of England, The [vol. i] (1729, 1735, 1739) **John Oldmixon** (1673)
History of England (1764) **Oliver Goldsmith** (1728)
History of England,, The (1771) **Oliver Goldsmith** (1728)
History of England [rev. 1937] (1926) **G.M. Trevelyan** (1876)
History of England 1603–16 (1863) **S.R. Gardiner** (1829)
History of England 1603–42 (1883) **S.R. Gardiner** (1829)
History of England 1624–8 (1875) **S.R. Gardiner** (1829)
History of England, from Julius Caesar to VII, The (1762) **David Hume** (1711)
History of England from the Accession of James II, The [vols. i, ii] (1849) **T.B. Macaulay** (1800)

History of England from the Accession of James II , The [vols. iii, iv] (1855) **T.B. Macaulay** (1800)
History of England from the Fall of Wolsey to the Death of Elizabeth (1856) **J.A. Froude** (1818)
History of England, The (1912) **A.F. Pollard** (1869)
History of England to the Accession of Henry VIII, The (1819) **John Lingard** (1771)
History of England, Under the House of Tudor, The (1759) **David Hume** (1711)
History of English Law Before the Time of Edward I, The (1895) **F.W. Maitland** (1850) [with Frederick Pollock]
History of English Poetry, The (1774–81) **Thomas Warton, the Younger** (1728)
History of English Prose Rhythm, A (1912) **George Saintsbury** (1845)
History of English Prosody, A (1906) **George Saintsbury** (1845)
History of English Thought in the Eighteenth Century (1876) **Sir Leslie Stephen** (1832)
History of Europe During the French Revolution (1832–42) **Sir Archibald Alison** (1792)
History of Federal Government (1863) **E.A. Freeman** (1823)
History of France [*Histoire de France*] (1831) **François-René, vicomte de Chateaubriand** (1768)
History of Frederick II of Prussia [vols. i-iv] (1858) **Thomas Carlyle** (1795)
History of Frederick II of Prussia [vols. v-vi] (1865) **Thomas Carlyle** (1795)
History of Freedom, The (1907) **Lord Acton** (1834–1902)
History of Great Britain, The [vol. i] (1754) **David Hume** (1711)
History of Great Britain, The [vol. ii] (1757) **David Hume** (1711)
History of Great Britaine, The (1611) **John Speed** (1552?)
History of Greece, A (1835) **Connop Thirlwall** (1797)
History of Greece, A (1845) **George Grote** (1794)
History of Henry Esmond, The (1852) **W.M. Thackeray** (1811)
History of Him (1980) **Geoffrey Grigson** (1905)
History of Imbanking and Drayning of Divers Fenns and Marshes, The (1662) **Sir William Dugdale** (1605)
History of Italian Literature (1897) **Richard Garnett** (1835)
History of James Lovegrove, The (1761) **James Ridley** (1736)
History of Jenny and Jemmy Jessamy, The (1753) **Eliza Haywood** (*c.* 1693)
'History of John Bull, The' [5 separate pamphlets] (1712) **John Arbuthnot** (1667)
History of John Juniper, The (1781) **[Charles Johnstone** (1719?)**]**
History of Johnny Quae Genus, The (1822) **William Combe** (1742)
History of King Lear, The (1681) **Nahum Tate** (1652)
History of King Richard the Second, The (1681) **Nahum Tate** (1652)
History of Lady Julia Mandeville, The (1763) **Frances Brooke** (1724)
History of Latin Christianity (1854–5) **Henry Hart Milman** (1791)
History of Life and Death, The (1638) **Sir Francis Bacon** (1561–1626)
History of Miss Betty Thoughtless, The (1751) **Eliza Haywood** (*c.* 1693)
History of Miss Meredith, The (1790) **Eliza Parsons** (1748)
History of Mr Polly, The (1910) **H.G. Wells** (1866)
History of Napoleon, The (1841) **R.H. Horne** (1803)
History of New York, A [by 'Diedrich Knickerbocker'] (1809) **Washington Irving** (1783)
History of Nineteenth-Century Literature, A (1896) **George Saintsbury** (1845)
History of Nourjahad, The (1767) **Frances Sheridan** (1724–66)
History of Old Robin Gray, The (1783) **Lady Anne Barnard** (1750)
History of Ophelia, The (1760) **Sarah Fielding** (1710)
History of Oracles, The [*Histoire des oracles*] (1687) **Bernard le Bovier Fontenelle** (1657)
History of Our Own Times, A [vols. i, ii; vol. iii, 1880)] (1879) **Justin McCarthy** (1830)
History of Pendennis, The (1850) **W.M. Thackeray** (1811)
History of Philosophy, The (1655) **Thomas Stanley the Elder** (1625)
History of Pompey the Little, The (1751) **Francis Coventry** (1725)
History of Rome, The (1701) **William Wotton** (1666)
History of Rome (1838–43) **Thomas Arnold** (1795)
History of Sandford and Merton, The (1783) **Thomas Day** (1748)
History of Scotland, The (1655) **William Drummond of Hawthornden** (1585–1649)
History of Scotland, The (1759) **William Robertson** (1721)
History of Sir Charles Grandison, The (1754) **Samuel Richardson** (1689)
History of Sir Richard Calmady, The (1901) **'Lucas Malet' [Mary St Leger Harrison]** (1852)
History of Socialist Thought, A (1953) **G.D.H. Cole** (1889)
History of Soviet Russia, A (1950–78) **E.H. Carr** (1892)
History of Sr Francis Drake, The (1659) **Sir William Davenant** (1606)
History of St Giles and St James, The (1851) **Douglas Jerrold** (1803)
History of St Paul's Cathedral, The (1658) **Sir William Dugdale** (1605)
History of the Abolition of the African Slave-Trade , The (1808) **Thomas Clarkson** (1760)
History of the Adventures of Joseph Andrews, The (1742) **Henry Fielding** (1707)
History of the American Revolution (1805) **Mercy Otis Warren** (1728)
History of the Art of War, A (1898) **Sir Charles Oman** (1860)

History of the Commonwealth of England (1824) **William Godwin** (1756)
History of the Corruptions of Christianity, An (1782) **Joseph Priestley** (1733)
History of the Countess of Dellwyn, The (1759) **Sarah Fielding** (1710)
History of the Crusades, A (1951–4) **Sir Steven Runciman** (1903
History of the Decline and Fall of the Roman Empire [vol. i] (1776) **Edward Gibbon** (1737)
History of the Decline and Fall of the Roman Empire [vols. ii, iii] (1781) **Edward Gibbon** (1737)
History of the Decline and Fall of the Roman Empire [vols. iv, v, vi] (1788) **Edward Gibbon** (1737)
History of the Earth and Animated Nature, An (1774) **Oliver Goldsmith** (1728–74)
History of the English-Speaking Peoples, A (1956) **Sir Winston Churchill** (1874)
History of the Fairchild Family, The (1818) **Mary Martha Sherwood** (1775)
History of the French Novel , A (1917) **George Saintsbury** (1845)
History of the Inductive Sciences, The (1837) **William Whewell** (1794)
History of the Jews, The (1812) **Hannah Adams** (1755)
History of the Jews, The (1829) **Henry Hart Milman** (1791)
History of the Life and Voyages of Christopher Columbus (1828) **Washington Irving** (1783)
History of the Life of Thomas Ellwood, The (1714) **Thomas Ellwood** (1639–1713)
History of the Lives and Deaths of the Most Eminent Martyrs, An (1764) **Oliver Goldsmith** (1728)
History of the Marquis of Lussa and Isabella, The (1764) **Charlotte Lennox** (1720)
History of the Norman Conquest of England, The (1867) **E.A. Freeman** (1823)
History of the Nun, The (1689) **Aphra Behn** (1640?-1689)
History of the Parliament of England (1647) **Thomas May** (1595)
History of the Peninsular War [vol. i] (1823) **Robert Southey** (1774)
History of the Peninsular War [vol. ii] (1827) **Robert Southey** (1774)
History of the Peninsular War [vol. iii] (1832) **Robert Southey** (1774)
History of the Peninsular War, A (1902) **Sir Charles Oman** (1860)
History of the Progress and Termination of the Roman Republic, The (1783) **Adam Ferguson** (1723)
History of the Reformation of Religion Within the Realm of Scotland, The (1587) **John Knox** (1505–72)
History of the Reformation of the Church of England, The [vol. i; vol. ii, 1681; vol. iii, 1715] (1679) **Gilbert Burnet** (1643)
History of the Reign of King Henry the Seventh, The (1622) **Sir Francis Bacon** (1561)
History of the Reign of Queen Anne, The (1703) **Abel Boyer** (1667)
History of the Reign of the Emperor Charles V, The (1769) **William Robertson** (1721)
History of the Sabbath, The (1636) **Peter Heylyn** (1600)
History of the Second World War (1970) **Sir Basil Liddell Hart** (1895)
History of the Thirteen [Histoire des Treize] (1883–1885) **Honoré de Balzac** (1799)
History of the Troubles and Tryal of William Laud, The (1695) **William Laud** (1573–1645)
History of the Two Maids of More-clack, The (1609) **Robert Armin** (1565?)
History of the Union of Great Britain, The (1709) **Daniel Defoe** (1660)
History of the United States (1889–91) **Henry Adams** (1838)
History of the Unreformed Parliament, The (1860) **Walter Bagehot** (1826)
History of the Voice (1984) **Edward Brathwaite** (1930)
History of the War in the Peninsula (1828) **Sir William Napier** (1785)
History of the World in 10 ½ Chapters, A (1989) **Julian Barnes** (1946)
History of the World, The (1614) **Sir Walter Ralegh** (1554)
History of the Worthies of England, The (1662) **Thomas Fuller** (1608)
History of Timon of Athens, The (1678) **Thomas Shadwell** (1642?)
History of Tithes, The (1618) **John Selden** (1584)
History of Tom Jones, The (1749) **Henry Fielding** (1707)
History of Trade Unionism, The (1894) **Sidney Webb** (1859) and Beatrice Webb (1858)
History of Twelve Caesars, The [from Suetonius] (1606) **Philemon Holland** (1552) (tr.)
History of Western Philosophy, A (1945) **Bertrand Russell** (1872)
History: The Home Movie (1994) **Craig Raine** (1944)
Histrio-Mastix (1610) **John Marston** (1576)?
Histrio-mastix (1633) **William Prynne** (1600)
Hitch-Hiker's Guide to the Galaxy, The (1979) **Douglas Adams** (1952)
Hitler: A Study in Tyranny (1952) **Alan Bullock** (1914)
Hitler and Stalin (1991) **Alan Bullock** (1914)
Hitler Cult, The (1939) **Wyndham Lewis** (1882)
Hitler Dances (1972) **Howard Brenton** (1942)
Hitting the Wall [two novellas] (1989) **David Foster** (1944)
Hitting Town; and City Sugar (1976) **Stephen Poliakoff** (1952)
HMS Glasshouse (1991) **Sean O'Brien** (1952)
HMS Pinafore [music by Sir Arthur Sullivan] (1878) **W.S. Gilbert** (1836)
HMS Surprise (1973) **Patrick O'Brian** (1914)
Hobbes (1904) **Sir Leslie Stephen** (1832)
Hobbit, The (1937) **J.R.R. Tolkein** (1892)
Hobson's Choice (1915) **Harold Brighouse** (1882)

Hocus Pocus (1990) **Kurt Vonnegut** (1922)
Hodge and His Masters (1880) **Richard Jefferies** (1848)
Hogarth's Blacks (1985) **David Dabydeen** (1956)
Hohenzollerns in America, The (1919) **Stephen Leacock** (1869)
Holcroft Covenant, The (1977) **Robert Ludlum** (1927)
Hold Hands Among the Atoms (1991) **Edwin Morgan** (1920)
Hold the Dream (1985) **Barbara Taylor Bradford** (1933)
Holden's Performance (1987) **Murray Bail** (1941)
Hölderlin's Madness (1938) **David Gascoyne** (1916)
Hole in the Head, A (1977) **Francis Stuart** (1902)
Hole in the Wall, The (1902) **Arthur Morrison** (1863)
Holes in the Sky (1948) **Louis MacNeice** (1907)
Holiday (1923) **Waldo Frank** (1889)
Holiday, The (1949) **Stevie Smith** (1902)
Holiday (1974) **Stanley Middleton** (1919)
Holiday at Dew Drop Inn (1962) **Eve Garnett** (1900)
Holiday on Death Row (1979) **Roger McGough** (1937)
Holiday Snaps (1985) **Adrian Henri** (1932)
Hollands Leaguer (1632) **Shackerley Marmion** (1603)
Hollow Hill, The (1965) **Kathleen Raine** (1908)
Hollow Land, The (1981) **Jane Gardam** (1928)
Hollow Lands, The (1974) **Michael Moorcock** (1939)
Hollow Sea (1938) **James Hanley** (1901)
Hollywood (1990) **Gore Vidal** (1925)
Hollywood Wives (1983) **Jackie Collins** (1939)
Holmby House (1860) **G.J. Whyte-Melville** (1821)
Holocaust, The (1986) **Martin Gilbert** (1936)
Holy Bible, The [abridgement and rearrangement] (1936) **Ronald Knox** (1888) (ed.)
Holy Bible, The [tr. from the Latin Vulgate] (1955) **Ronald Knox** (1888) (tr.)
Holy City, The (1665) **John Bunyan** (1628)
Holy Commonwealth, A (1659) **Richard Baxter** (1615)
Holy Deadlock (1934) **A.P. Herbert** (1890)
Holy Face (1929) **Aldous Huxley** (1894)
Holy Flower, The (1915) **Sir H. Rider Haggard** (1856)
Holy Gospels in Anglo-Saxon, Northumbrian and Old Mercian Versions, The (1871) **W.W. Skeat** (1835) (ed.)
Holy Graal, The (1907) **Richard Hovey** (1864)
Holy Observations (1607) **Joseph Hall** (1574)
Holy Orders (1908) **Marie Corelli** (1855)
Holy Pictures (1983) **Clare Boylan** (1948)
Holy Places, The (1952) **Evelyn Waugh** (1903)
Holy Raptures (1652) **Joseph Hall** (1574)
Holy Roman Empire, The (1864) **James Bryce** (1838)
Holy Roode, The (1609) **John Davies of Hereford** (1565)
Holy Rose, The (1890) **Sir Walter Besant** (1836)
Holy Sinner, The [*Der Erwählte*] (1951) **Thomas Mann** (1875)
Holy State, The (1642) **Thomas Fuller** (1608)
Holy Terror, The (1939) **H.G. Wells** (1866)
Holy Thief, The (1992) **'Ellis Peters' [Edith Mary Pargeter]** (1913)
Holy War, The (1916) **Katharine Tynan** (1861)
Holy War, The (1682) **John Bunyan** (1628)
Homage to Catalonia (1938) **George Orwell** (1903)
Homage to Clio (1960) **W.H. Auden** (1907)
Homage to John Dryden (1924) **T.S. Eliot** (1888)
Homage to Matisse (1971) **Ian Wedde** (1946)
Homage to Mistress Bradstreet (1956) **John Berryman** (1914)
Homage to QWERTYUIOP (1985) **'Anthony Burgess' [John Anthony Burgess Wilson]** (1917)
Homage to Theodore Dreiser (1971) **Robert Penn Warren** (1905)
Hombre (1961) **Elmore Leonard** (1925)
Home (1966) **LeRoi Jones** (1934)
Home and Dry (1984) **Roy Fuller** (1912)
Home, The (1904) **Charlotte Perkins Gilman** (1860)
Home, The (1971) **Penelope Mortimer** (1918)
Home and the World, The (1919) **Rabindranath Tagore** (1861)
Home as Found (1838) **James Fenimore Cooper** (1789)
Home Ballads, Poems and Lyrics (1860) **John Greenleaf Whittier** (1807)
Home Before Night (1979) **'Hugh Leonard' [Johns Keyes Byrne]** (1926)
Home From the Hill (1958) **William Humphrey** (1924)
Home Influence (1847) **Grace Aguilar** (1816)
Home (1836) **Sarah [Mrs William] Ellis** (1812)
Home, The [from Frederika Bremer] (1843) **Mary Howitt** (1799) (tr.)
Home Rule (1992) **Clare Boylan** (1948)
Home Scenes and Heart Studies (1853) **Grace Aguilar** (1816–47)
Home Sweet Home (1984) **Mordecai Richler** (1931)
Home, Sweet Home (1873) **Mrs J.H. Riddell** (1832)
Home Time (1985) **Beverley Farmer** (1941)
Home to My Valley (1969) **Paul Green** (1894)
Home Town (1940) **Sherwood Anderson** (1876)
Home Town Elegy (1944) **G.S. Fraser** (1915)
Home Truths (1957) **Anthony Thwaite** (1930)
Home Truths (1981) **Mavis Gallant** (1922)
Home Truths (1993) **Sara Maitland** (1950)
Homecoming Game, The (1957) **Howard Nemerov** (1920)
Homecoming, The (1965) **Harold Pinter** (1930)
Homecoming, The (1970) **Brian Patten** (1946)
Homecomings (1956) **C.P. Snow** (1905)
Homely Lilla (1923) **Robert Herrick** (1868)
Homer and His Age (1906) **Andrew Lang** (1844)
Homer and the Epic (1893) **Andrew Lang** (1844)
Homer Prince of Poets (1609) **George Chapman** (1559?) (tr.)
Homer's Battle of the Frogs and Mice (1717) **Thomas Parnell** (1679)
Homer's Daughter (1955) **Robert Graves** (1895)
Homeric Hymns, The (1899) **Andrew Lang** (1844) (tr.)
Homers Odyssey (1614) **George Chapman** (1559?) (tr.)
Homes, Sweet Homes (1939) **Osbert Lancaster** (1908)

Homesickness (1980) **Murray Bail** (1941)
Homeward (1894) **George William Russell ['AE']** (1867)
Homeward Bound (1838) **James Fenimore Cooper** (1789)
Homilies and Recreations (1926) **John Buchan** (1875)
Homme libre, Un (1889) **Maurice Barrès** (1862)
Hommes de lettres, Les ['The Men of Letters'] (1860) **Edmond de Goncourt** (1822) and **Jules** (1830) **de Goncourt**
Homogenic Love and its Place in a Free Society (1894) **Edward Carpenter** (1844)
Hondo (1953) **Louis L'Amour** (1908)
Honest John Vane (1875) **John W. de Forest** (1826)
Honest Whore, The (1604) **Thomas Dekker** (1572?) [with Thomas Middleton]
Honest Yorkshireman, The (1735) **Henry Carey** (1687?)
Honey and Salt (1963) **Carl Sandburg** (1878)
Honey for the Bears (1963) **'Anthony Burgess' [John Anthony Burgess Wilson]** (1917)
Honey in the Horn (1935) **H.L. Davis** (1896)
Honeycomb (1917) **Dorothy M. Richardson** (1873)
Honeymoon Festival, The (1970) **Marian Engel** (1933)
Honeymoon Voyage, The (1978) **D.M. Thomas** (1935)
Hong Kong (1988) **Jan Morris** (1926)
Hong Kong House, A (1962) **Edmund Blunden** (1896)
Honor O'Hara (1826) **Anna Maria Porter** (1780)
Honorable Historie of Frier Bacon, and Frier Bongay, The (1594) **Robert Greene** (1558–92)
Honorable Man (1985) **Louis Auchinloss** (1917)
Honorable Reputation of a Souldier, The (1585) **George Whetstone** (*c.* 1551)
Honorary Consul, The (1973) **Graham Greene** (1904)
Honorary White (1975) **E.R. Braithwaite** (1912)
Honour Among Thieves (1993) **Jeffrey Archer** (1940)
Honour and Other People's Children [two novellas] (1980) **Helen Garner** (1942)
Honour of the Flag, The (1896) **W. Clark Russell** (1844)
Honourable Intentions (1999) **Gavin Lyall** (1932)
Honourable Mr Tawnish, The (1913) **Jeffery Farnol** (1878)
Honourable Schoolboy, The (1977) **'John le Carré' [David John Moore Cornwell]** (1931)
Hons and Rebels [US: *Daughters and Rebels*] (1960) **Jessica Mitford** (1917)
Hoof and Claw (1914) **Sir Charles G.D. Roberts** (1860)
Hoofmarks of the Faun, The (1911) **Arthur Ransome** (1884)
Hoosier Holiday, A (1916) **Theodore Dreiser** (1871)
Hoosier Schoolboy, The (1883) **Edward Eggleston** (1837)
Hoosier Schoolmaster, The (1871) **Edward Eggleston** (1837)
Hopalong Cassidy and the Riders of High Rock [as 'Tex Burns'] (1951) **Louis L'Amour** (1908)
Hope (1796) **William Lisle Bowles** (1762)
Hope (1910) **R.B. Cunninghame Graham** (1852)
Hope (1995) **Len Deighton** (1929)
Hope, The (1993) **Herman Wouk** (1915)
Hope Against Hope (1931) **Stella Benson** (1892)
Hope for Poetry, A (1934) **C. Day Lewis** (1904)
Hope Leslie (1827) **Catharine Maria Sedgwick** (1789)
Hope of Heaven (1938) **John O'Hara** (1905)
Hope of the World, The (1898) **Sir William Watson** (1858)
Hopeful Monsters (1990) **Nicholas Mosley** (1923)
Hopes and Fears (1860) **Charlotte M. Yonge** (1823)
Hopes and Fears for Art (1882) **William Morris** (1834)
Hopes and Impediments (1988) **Chinua Achebe** (1930)
Hopkins Manuscript, The (1939) **R.C. Sherriff** (1896)
Horace (1640) **Pierre Corneille** (1606)
Horace His Ode to Venus (1737) **Alexander Pope** (1688)
Horace in London (1813) **Horace Smith** (1779) [with James Smith]
Horace's Art of Poetry (1680) **Wentworth Dillon, 4th Earl of Roscommon** (1633) (tr.)
Horae Lyricae (1706) **Isaac Watts** (1674)
Horae Paulinae (1790) **William Paley** (1743)
Horae Solitariae (1902) **Edward Thomas** (1878)
Horae Vacivae (1646) **John Hall, of Durham** (1627)
Horatio (1807) **Horace Smith** (1779)
Horla, Le (1887) **Guy de Maupassant** (1850)
Hornblower and the Atropos (1953) **C.S. Forester** (1899)
Hornblower in the West Indies [US: *Admiral Hornblower in the West Indies*] (1958) **C.S. Forester** (1899)
Hornby Mills (1872) **Henry Kingsley** (1830)
Hornet's Nest (1997) **Patricia Cornwell** (1956)
Horse and His Boy, The (1954) **C.S. Lewis** (1898)
Horse and Two Goats, A (1970) **R.K. Narayan** (1907)
Horse Knows the Way, The (1964) **John O'Hara** (1905)
Horse the Ghoos & the Sheep, The [written post 1436] (1477?) **John Lydgate** (1370?-1449)
Horse Under Water (1963) **Len Deighton** (1929)
Horse's Mouth, The (1944) **Joyce Cary** (1888)
Horse-Shoe Robinson (1835) **John Pendleton Kennedy** (1795)
Horseman, Pass By (1961) **Larry McMurty** (1936)
Horses and Men (1923) **Sherwood Anderson** (1876)
Horses Make a Landscape Look More Beautiful (1984) **Alice Walker** (1944)
Hortensius, Friend of Nero (1936) **'Ellis Peters' [Edith Mary Pargeter]** (1913)
Hortus Vitae (1904) **'Vernon Lee' [Violet Paget]** (1856)
Hospital Sketches (1863) **Louisa M. Alcott** (1832)
Hostage, The (1958) **Brendan Behan** (1923)
Hostages to Fortune (1984) **William Humphrey** (1924)
Hostile Sun, The (1973) **Joyce Carol Oates** (1938)
Hosts of the Lord, The (1900) **Flora Annie Steel** (1847)

Hot Country, A [US: *Death in a Hot Country*] (1983) **Shiva Naipaul** (1945)
Hot Earth, Cold Earth (1995) **James Berry** (1924)
Hot Fudge (1990) **Caryl Churchill** (1938)
Hot Gates, The (1965) **William Golding** (1911)
Hot Irons (1995) **Howard Brenton** (1942)
Hot Money (1987) **Dick Francis** (1920)
Hot Plowshares (1883) **Albion W. Tourgée** (1838)
Hot Sky at Midnight (1994) **Robert Silverberg** (1935)
Hot Spring, The (1965) **Bruce Beaver** (1928)
Hot Swamp, The (1892) **R.M. Ballantyne** (1825)
Hot Water Man (1982) **Deborah Moggach** (1948)
Hotel, The (1927) **Elizabeth Bowen** (1899)
Hotel (1965) **Arthur Hailey** (1920)
Hotel d'Angleterre, The (1891) **'Lanoe Falconer' [Mary Elizabeth Hawker]** (1848)
Hotel de Dream (1976) **Emma Tennant** (1937)
Hotel du Lac (1984) **Anita Brookner** (1928)
Hotel Lautréamont (1993) **John Ashbery** (1927)
Hotel New Hampshire, The (1981) **John Irving** (1942)
Hothouse, The (1980) **Harold Pinter** (1930)
Hothouse by the River, The (1972) **Muriel Spark** (1918)
Hotspur (1986) **Fleur Adcock** (1934)
Hottentot Venus (1979) **Stephen Gray** (1941)
Hound of Death, The (1933) **Agatha Christie** (1890)
Hound of the Baskervilles, The (1902) **A. Conan Doyle** (1859)
Hounds of Banba, The (1920) **Daniel Corkery** (1878)
Hounds of God, The (1928) **Rafael Sabatini** (1875)
Hour and the Man, The (1841) **Harriet Martineau** (1802)
Hour of Magic, The (1922) **W.H. Davies** (1871)
Hour-Glass, The; Cathleen ni Houlihan, The Pot of Broth [*Plays for an Irish Theatre* vol. ii] (1904) **W.B. Yeats** (1865)
Hours in a Library [1st ser.; 2nd ser., 1876; 3rd ser., 1879] (1874) **Sir Leslie Stephen** (1832)
Hours of Idleness (1807) **George Gordon, Lord Byron** (1788)
Hours of Solitude (1805) **Charlotte Dacre** (1782?)
House and its Head, A (1935) **I. Compton-Burnett** (1884)
House at Old Vine, The (1961) **Norah Lofts** (1904)
House at Pooh Corner, The (1928) **A.A. Milne** (1882)
House at Sunset, The (1963) **Norah Lofts** (1904)
House Behind the Cedars, The (1900) **Charles W. Chesnutt** (1858)
House, Bridge, Fountain, Gate (1975) **Maxine Kumin** (1925)
House by the Churchyard, The (1863) **J.S. le Fanu** (1814)
House Divided, A (1935) **Pearl S. Buck** (1892)
House For Mr Biswas, A (1961) **V.S. Naipaul** (1932)
House in Bloomsbury, A (1894) **Margaret Oliphant** (1828)
House in Demetrius Road, The (1914) **J.D. Beresford** (1873)
House in Lordship Lane, The (1946) **A.E.W. Mason** (1865)
House in Marylebone, The (1917) **Lucy [Mrs W.K.] Clifford** (1853)
House in Order, A (1966) **Nigel Dennis** (1912)
House in Paris, The (1935) **Elizabeth Bowen** (1899)
House in the Uplands (1946) **Erskine Caldwell** (1903)
House in the Water, The (1908) **Sir Charles G.D. Roberts** (1860)
House in Turner Square, The (1960) **Ann Thwaite** (1932)
House Mother Normal (1971) **B.S. Johnson** (1933)
House of All Nations (1938) **Christina Stead** (1902)
House of Arden, The (1908) **E[dith] Nesbit** (1858)
House of Bernada Alba, The [*La casa de Bernada Alba*] (1935) **Federico García Lorca** (1898)
House of Children, A (1941) **Joyce Cary** (1888)
House of Cobwebs, The (1906) **George Gissing** (1857–1903)
House of Connelly, The (1931) **Paul Green** (1894)
House of Dies Drear, The (1968) **Virginia Hamilton** (1936)
House of Doctor Dee, The (1993) **Peter Ackroyd** (1949)
House of Dust, The (1920) **Conrad Potter Aiken** (1889)
House of Fame, The (1483) **Geoffrey Chaucer** (1340?-1400)
House of Fear, The (1927) **Robert W. Service** (1876)
House of Five Talents, The (1960) **Louis Auchinloss** (1917)
House of Gair, The (1953) **Eric Linklater** (1899)
House of Halliwell, The (1890) **Mrs Henry Wood** (1814–87)
House of Hospitalities, The (1987) **Emma Tennant** (1937)
House of Incest (1936) **Anaïs Nin** (1903)
House of Madame Tellier, The [*La Maison Tellier*] (1881) **Guy de Maupassant** (1850)
House of Many Voices, The (1911) **Bernard Capes** (1850?)
House of Menerdue, The (1925) **A.C. Benson** (1862)
House of Mirth, The (1905) **Edith Wharton** (1862)
House of Pomegranates, A (1891) **Oscar Wilde** (1854)
House of Quiet, The (1904) **A.C. Benson** (1862)
House of Sleep, The (1997) **Jonathan Coe** (1961)
House of Souls, The (1906) **Arthur Machen** (1863)
House of Spies, The (1913) **Warwick Deeping** (1877)
House of Splendid Isolation, The (1994) **Edna O'Brien** (1932)
House of the Arrow, The (1924) **A.E.W. Mason** (1865)
House of the Four Winds, The (1935) **John Buchan** (1875)
House of the Seven Gables, The (1851) **Nathaniel Hawthorne** (1804)
House of the Solitary Maggot, The (1974) **James Purdy** (1923)
House of the Spirits, The (1982) **Isabel Allende** (1942)
House of the Tirans, The (1934) **George William Russell ['AE']** (1867)
House of the Wolf, The (1890) **Stanley J. Weyman** (1855)
House of White Shadows, The (1884) **B.L. Farjeon** (1838)

House of Women, A (1936) **H.E. Bates** (1905)
House of Women, The (1927) **Louis Bromfield** (1896)
House on Cherry Street, The (1909) **Amelia Barr** (1831)
House on Coliseum Street, The (1961) **Shirley Ann Grau** (1929)
House on the Borderland, The (1908) **William Hope Hodgson** (1877)
House on the Moor, The (1861) **Margaret Oliphant** (1828)
House on the Strand, The (1969) **Daphne du Maurier** (1907)
House Party, A (1887) **'Ouida' [Marie Louise de la Ramée]** (1839)
House That Berry Built, The (1945) **'Dornford Yates' [Cecil William Mercer]** (1885)
House That Grew, The (1900) **Mary Louisa Molesworth** (1839)
House Under the Sea, The (1902) **Max Pemberton** (1863)
House with Four Rooms, A (1989) **Rumer Godden** (1907)
House with the Apricot, The (1933) **H.E. Bates** (1905)
House with the Echo, The (1928) **T.F. Powys** (1875)
House with the Green Shutters, The [as 'George Douglas'] (1901) **George Douglas Brown** (1869)
Houseboat Days (1977) **John Ashbery** (1927)
Houseboat on the Styx, A (1896) **John Kendrick Bangs** (1862)
Housebreaker of Shady Hill, The (1958) **John Cheever** (1912)
Houseguest, The (1988) **Thomas Berger** (1924)
Household Education (1849) **Harriet Martineau** (1802)
Household Fairy, The (1870) **Edward Bulwer-Lytton** (1803)
Household Ghosts (1961) **James Kennaway** (1928)
Household Verses (1845) **Bernard Barton** (1784)
Householder, The (1960) **Ruth Prawer Jhabvala** (1927)
Housepy (1978) **Maureen Duffy** (1933)
Houses by the Sea (1952) **'Robin Hyde' [Iris Guiver Wilkinson]** (1906–39)
Houses in Between, The (1951) **Howard Spring** (1889)
How Can We Know? (1985) **A.N. Wilson** (1950)
How Far Can You Go? [US: *Souls and Bodies*] (1980) **David Lodge** (1935)
How German Is It? (1980) **Walter Abish** (1931)
How Green Was My Valley (1939) **'Richard Llewellyn' [Richard Llewellyn Lloyd]** (1907)
How I Became a Holy Mother (1976) **Ruth Prawer Jhabvala** (1927)
How I Found Livingstone (1872) **Sir Henry Morton Stanley** (1841)
How I Grew (1987) **Mary McCarthy** (1912)
How I See Apocalypse (1946) **Henry Treece** (1911)
How I Spent My Holidays (1981) **W.O. Mitchell** (1914)
How It Is (1964) **Samuel Beckett** (1906)
How Jolly Life Is! [*La Joie de vivre*] (1884) **Émile Zola** (1840)
How Late it Was, How Late (1994) **James Kelman** (1946)
How Many Children Had Lady Macbeth? (1933) **L.C. Knights** (1906)
How Many Miles to Babylon? (1967) **Paula Fox** (1923)
How Many Miles to Babylon? (1974) **Jennifer Johnston** (1930)
How Sleep the Brave (1943) **H.E. Bates** (1905)
How the Dead Live (2000) **Will Self** (1961)
How the Grinch Stole Christmas (1957) **'Dr Seuss'** (1904)
How the 'Mastiffs' Went to Iceland (1878) **Anthony Trollope** (1815)
How the Other Half Loves (1969) **Alan Ayckbourn** (1939)
How the Poor Live (1883) **George R. Sims** (1847)
How to Do Things with Words (1962) **J.L. Austin** (1911–60)
How to Live on 24 Hours a Day (1908) **Arnold Bennett** (1867)
How to Read a Novel (1957) **Caroline Gordon** (1895)
How To Save Your Own Life (1977) **Erica Jong** (1942)
How to Settle the Irish Question (1917) **Bernard Shaw** (1856)
How to Travel with a Salmon (1994) **Umberto Eco** (1932)
How to Write Short Stories (1924) **Ring Lardner** (1885)
Howards End (1910) **E.M. Forster** (1879)
Howl (1956) **Allen Ginsberg** (1926)
Howrah Bridge (1961) **James K. Baxter** (1926)
Hubert de Sevrac (1796) **Mary Robinson** (1758)
Hubert's Arthur (1935) **Frederick William Rolfe** (1860–1913)
Hudibras Redivivius (1705) **Edward Ward** (1667)
Hudibras: The First Part (1663) **Samuel Butler** (1612)
Hudibras: The Second Part (1664) **Samuel Butler** (1612)
Hudibras: The Third and Last Part (1678) **Samuel Butler** (1612)
Hudson River Bracketed (1929) **Edith Wharton** (1862)
Hudson's Bay (1848) **R.M. Ballantyne** (1825)
Hugging the Shore (1983) **John Updike** (1932)
Hugh (1915) **A.C. Benson** (1862)
Hugh Selwyn Mauberley (1920) **Ezra Pound** (1885)
Hugo (1906) **Arnold Bennett** (1867)
Huguenot, The (1839) **G.P.R. James** (1799)
Human Beast, The [*La Bête humaine*] (1890) **Émile Zola** (1840)
Human Boy Again, The (1908) **Eden Phillpotts** (1862)
Human Boy and the War, The (1916) **Eden Phillpotts** (1862)
Human Boy, The (1899) **Eden Phillpotts** (1862)
Human Chord, The (1910) **Algernon Blackwood** (1869)
Human Comedy, The (1943) **William Saroyan** (1908)
Human Document, A (1892) **W.H. Mallock** (1849)
Human Drift, The (1917) **'Jack London' [John Griffith Chaney]** (1876)
Human Element, The (1969) **Stan Barstow** (1928)
Human Face Divine, The (1860) **Margaret [Mrs Alfred] Gatty** (1809)
Human Factor, The (1978) **Graham Greene** (1904)

Human Inheritance, The (1882) **William Sharp** (1855)
Human Interest, The (1899) **Violet Hunt** (1866)
Human Knowledge (1948) **Bertrand Russell** (1872)
Human Life (1819) **Samuel Rogers** (1763)
Human Machine, The (1908) **Arnold Bennett** (1867)
Human Nature (1933) **Edith Wharton** (1862)
Human Odds and Ends (1898) **George Gissing** (1857)
Human Rites (1984) **E.A. Markham** (1939)
Human Season, The (1960) **Edward Wallant** (1926)
Human Shows, Far Phantasies (1925) **Thomas Hardy** (1840)
Human Toll (1902) **Barbara Baynton** (1857)
Human Tragedy, The (1876) **Alfred Austin** (1835)
Human Voices (1980) **Penelope Fitzgerald** (1916)
Humane Nature (1650) **Thomas Hobbes** (1588)
Humble Administrator's Garden, The (1985) **Vikram Seth** (1952)
Humble Attempt to Promote Visible Union of God's People, An (1747) **Jonathan Edwards** (1703)
Humble Enterprise, A (1896) **Ada Cambridge** (1844)
Humble Inquiry into the Rules of the Word of God, An (1749) **Jonathan Edwards** (1703)
Humble Remonstrance to the High Court of Parliament, An (1641) **Joseph Hall** (1574)
Humble Romance, A (1887) **Mary Wilkins Freeman** (1852)
Humboldt's Gift (1975) **Saul Bellow** (1915)
Humdrum (1928) **Sir Harold Acton** (1904)
Humfrey, Duke of Gloucester (1723) **Ambrose Philips** (1674)
Humorists, The (1670) **Thomas Shadwell** (1642?)
Humorous Courtier, The (1640) **James Shirley** (1596)
Humorous Day's Mirth, A (1599) **George Chapman** (1559?)
Humors Looking Glasse (1608) **Samuel Rowlands** (1570?)
Humour of Homer, The (1913) **Samuel Butler** (1835–1902)
Humour Out of Breath (1608) **John Day** (*c.* 1574)
Humours Heav'n on Earth (1609) **John Davies of Hereford** (1565)
Humours of the Court, The (1893) **Robert Bridges** (1844)
Humphrey Clinker [**Smollett**]: see *The Expedition of Humphrey Clinker*
Humpty Dumpty (1924) **Ben Hecht** (1894)
Hunchback, The (1832) **James Sheridan Knowles** (1784)
Hunchback of Notre-Dame, The [*Notre Dame de Paris*] (1831) **Victor Hugo** (1802)
Hundred and Fifty-Eight Pound Marriage, The (1974) **John Irving** (1942)
Hundred and One Harlequins, The (1922) **Sir Sacheverell Sitwell** (1897)
Hundred and Seventy Chinese Poems, A (1918) **Arthur Waley** (1889) (tr.)
Hundred and Ten Considerations of Valdesso, The (1638) **Nicholas Ferrar** (1592–1637) (tr.)
Hundred and Twenty Days of Sodom, The [*Les 120 Journées de Sodome*] (1784) **Marquis de Sade** (1740)
Hundred Days, The (1998) **Patrick O'Brian** (1914)
Hundred Secret Senses, The (1995) **Amy Tan** (1952)
Hundreds of Fireflies (1982) **Brad Leithauser** (1953)
Hundredth Chance, The (1917) **Ethel M. Dell** (1881)
Hundreth Good Pointes of Husbandrie, A (1557) **Thomas Tusser** (1524?)
Hundreth Sundrie Flowres, A (1573) **George Gascoigne** (1542?)
Hungarian Brothers, The (1807) **Anna Maria Porter** (1780)
Hunger (1890) **'Knut Hamsun' [Knut Pedersen]** (1859)
Hunger and Thirst (1964) **Eugène Ionesco** (1909)
Hungerfield (1945) **Robinson Jeffers** (1887)
Hungry Generations (1994) **John Wain** (1925)
Hungry Ghosts, The (1974) **Joyce Carol Oates** (1938)
Hungry Hearts (1920) **Anzia Yezierska** (*c.* 1885)
Hungry Hill (1943) **Daphne du Maurier** (1907)
Hungry Stones (1916) **Rabindranath Tagore** (1861)
Hunt (1978) **A. Alvarez** (1929)
Hunt for Red October, The (1984) **Tom Clancy** (1947)
Hunted and Harried (1892) **R.M. Ballantyne** (1825)
Hunter and the Whale, The (1967) **Sir Laurens van der Post** (1906)
Hunter's Horn, The (1949) **Harriette Arnow** (1908)
Hunters' Feast, The (1855) **Mayne Reid** (1818)
Hunting Mister heartbreak (1990) **Jonathan Raban** (1942)
Hunting of Badlewe, The (1814) **James Hogg** (1770)
Hunting of the Snark, The (1876) **'Lewis Carroll' [Charles Lutwidge Dodgson]** (1832)
Hunting Reminiscences (1842) **Charles James Apperley** (1779)
Hunting Sketches (1865) **Anthony Trollope** (1815)
Hunting Stuart [written 1955] (1972) **Robertson Davies** (1913)
Hunting the Fairies (1949) **Compton Mackenzie** (1883)
Hunting the Wild Pineapple (1979) **Thea Astley** (1925)
Hunting Tigers Under Glass (1968) **Mordecai Richler** (1931)
Huntingtower (1922) **John Buchan** (1875)
Hurrah for Anything (1957) **Kenneth Patchen** (1911)
Hurrah for St Trinian's (1948) **Ronald Searle** (1920)
Hurricane (1919) **Richard Church** (1893)
Hurricane Dub (1988) **Benjamin Zephaniah** (1958)
Hurrish (1886) **Emily Lawless** (1845)
Hurry On Down [US: *Born in Captivity*] (1953) **John Wain** (1925)
Hurt (1970) **Elizabeth Jennings** (1926)
Husbands, The (1994) **Christopher Logue** (1926)
Hwomely Rhymes (1859) **William Barnes** (1801)
Hydriotaphia: Urn-Burial (1658) **Sir Thomas Browne** (1605)
Hygiasticon (1634) **George Herbert** (1593–1633) (tr.)
Hymen (1921) **Hilda Doolittle** (1886)
Hymenai (1606) **Ben Jonson** (1572)
Hymens Triumph (1615) **Samuel Daniel** (1562)
Hymn to the Pillory, A (1703) **Daniel Defoe** (1660)

Hymn to the Rising Sun (1936) **Paul Green** (1894)
Hymn to the Supreme Being (1756) **Christopher Smart** (1722)
Hymn to Victory, A (1704) **Daniel Defoe** (1660)
Hymnes (1555) **Pierre de Ronsard** (1524)
Hymnes and Songs of the Church, The [music by Orlando Gibbons] (1623) **George Wither** (1588) (ed.)
Hymns (1848) **Frederick William Faber** (1814)
Hymns (1867) **Francis Turner Palgrave** (1824)
Hymns (1827) **Reginald Heber** (1783–1826)
Hymns and Fire-side Verses (1839) **Mary Howitt** (1799)
Hymns and Sacred Poems (1749) **Charles Wesley** (1707)
Hymns and Spiritual Songs (1765) **Christopher Smart** (1722)
Hymns and Spiritual Songs (1707) **Isaac Watts** (1674)
Hymns Descriptive and Devotional for the Use of School (1858) **Mrs C.F. Alexander** (1818)
Hymns for Childhood (1834) **Felicia Dorothea Hemans** (1793)
Hymns for Little Children (1848) **Mrs C.F. Alexander** (1818)
Hymns, for the Amusement of Children (1772) **Christopher Smart** (1722)
Hymns for the Sick (1843) **John Mason Neale** (1818)
Hymns in Darkness (1976) **Nissim Ezekiel** (1924)
Hymns in Prose for Children (1781) **Anna Laetitia Barbauld** (1743)
Hymns of Astraea (1599) **Sir John Davies** (1569)
Hypatia (1853) **Charles Kingsley** (1819)
Hyperborea (1928) **Norman Lindsay** (1879)
Hyperion (1797–9) **Friedrich HÖlderlin** (1770)
Hyperion (1839) **Henry Wadsworth Longfellow** (1807)
Hystorye, Sege and Dystruccyon of Troye, The [paraphrased from Guido delle Colonne] (1513) **John Lydgate** (1370?-1449) (tr.)

I

I Am Elijah Thrush (1972) **James Purdy** (1923)
I Am Mary Dunne (1968) **Brian Moore** (1921)
I Am My Brother (1960) **John Lehmann** (1907)
I Am! Says the Lamb (1961) **Theodore Roethke** (1908)
I Am the Cheese (1977) **Robert Cormier** (1925)
I Am the World (1942) **Peter Vansittart** (1920)
I Can't Stay Long (1975) **Laurie Lee** (1914)
I Cannot Get You Close Enough [novellas] (1990) **Ellen Gilchrist** (1935–)
I Capture the Castle (1949) **Dodie Smith** (1896)
I, Claudius (1934) **Robert Graves** (1895)
I Crossed the Minch (1938) **Louis MacNeice** (1907)
I Don't Need You Anymore (1967) **Arthur Miller** (1915)
I, Dreyfus (1999) **Bernice Rubens** (1923)
I, etcetera (1978) **Susan Sontag** (1933)
I Fell For a Sailor (1940) **Fred Urquhart** (1912)
I Have Been Here Before (1937) **J.B. Priestley** (1894)
I Hear America Swinging (1976) **Peter de Vries** (1910)
I Knock at the Door (1939) **Sean O'Casey** (1880)
I Know Why the Caged Bird Sings (1970) **Maya Angelou** (1928)
I Like It Here (1958) **Kingsley Amis** (1922)
I Lock the Door Upon Myself (1990) **Joyce Carol Oates** (1938)
I Met a Gypsy (1935) **Norah Lofts** (1904)
I Met a Lady (1961) **Howard Spring** (1889)
I Never Sang for My Father (1968) **Robert W. Anderson** (1917)
I Pose (1915) **Stella Benson** (1892)
I Rise in Flame, Cried the Phoenix (1951) **'Tennessee' [Thomas Lanier] Williams** (1911)
I, Robot (1950) **Isaac Asimov** (1920)
I Saw in My Dream (1949) **Frank Sargeson** (1903)
I Saw Three Ships (1892) **Sir A.T. Quiller-Couch** (1863)
'I Say No' (1884) **Wilkie Collins** (1824)
I Sent a Letter to My Love (1975) **Bernice Rubens** (1923)
I Shall Not Be Moved (1990) **Maya Angelou** (1928)
I Shout Love, and On Shaving off His Beard (1971) **Milton Acorn** (1923)
I Sing the Body Electric (1969) **Ray Bradbury** (1920)
I Sing the Body Electric (1993) **Adam Lively** (1961)
I Speak of Africa (1927) **William Plomer** (1903)
I, the Jury [first 'Mike Hammer' story] (1947) **Mickey Spillane** (1918)
I, the King (1966) **Frances Parkinson Keyes** (1885)
I Thought of Daisy (1929) **Edmund Wilson** (1895–1972)
I Used To Believe I Had Forever, Now I'm Not So Sure (1967) **William Saroyan** (1908)
I Want It Now (1968) **Kingsley Amis** (1922)
I Want To Go To Moscow (1973) **Maureen Duffy** (1933)
I Will Maintain (1910) **'Marjorie Bowen' [Gabrielle Margaret Vere Campbell]** (1886)
I Wonder as I Wander (1956) **Langston Hughes** (1902)
I'll Take Manhattan (1986) **Judith Krantz**
I'm a Stranger Here Myself (1938) **Ogden Nash** (1902)
I'm Dying Laughing (1986) **Christina Stead** (1902)
I'm Not Afraid (1986) **Irina Ratushinskaya** (1954)
I'm Talking About Jerusalem (1960) **Arnold Wesker** (1932)
I'm the King of the Castle (1970) **Susan Hill** (1942)
I've Tasted My Blood (1969) **Milton Acorn** (1923)
Ia (1896) **Sir A.T. Quiller-Couch** (1863)
Ian of the Orcades (1906) **Wilfred Campbell** (1858)
Ibant Obscuri (1916) **Robert Bridges** (1844)
Ibrahim (1696) **Mary Pix** (1666)
Ibrahim the Illustrious Bassa (1676) **Elkanah Settle** (1648)
Icarus (1924) **Bertrand Russell** (1872)
Icarus Agenda, The (1988) **Robert Ludlum** (1927)
Ice Age, The (1977) **Margaret Drabble** (1939)
Ice and Fire (1986) **Andrea Dworkin** (1946)
Ice Cod Bell and Stone (1962) **Earle Birney** (1904)
Ice Cream (1989) **Caryl Churchill** (1938)
Ice Cream (2000) **Helen Dunmore** (1952)

Ice House, The (1983) **Nina Bawden** (1925)
Iceman Cometh, The (1946) **Eugene O'Neill** (1888)
Ice is Singing, The (1987) **Jane Rogers** (1952)
Ice Station Zebra (1963) **Alistair Maclean** (1923)
Ice-Cream Headache, The (1968) **James Jones** (1921)
Ice-Cream War, An (1982) **William Boyd** (1952)
Iceberg, The (1934) **Sir Charles G.D. Roberts** (1860)
Iceland Fisherman, An [*Pêcheur d'Islande*] (1886) **'Pierre Loti' [Julien Viaud]** (1850)
Ichabod! (1848) **Bernard Barton** (1784)
Iciest Sin, The (1990) **H.R.F. Keating** (1926)
Icknield Way, The (1913) **Edward Thomas** (1878)
Icon Animorum [Latin; tr. into English 1631 as *The Mirror of Minds*] (1614) **John Barclay** (1582–1621)
Ida (1941) **Gertrude Stein** (1874)
Idalia (1723) **Eliza Haywood** (*c.* 1693)
Idalia (1867) **'Ouida' [Marie Louise de la Raminée]** (1839)
Idanre (1967) **Wole Soyinka** (1934)
Idea (1593) **Michael Drayton** (1563)
Idea of a Christian Society, The (1939) **T.S. Eliot** (1888)
Idea of a University, The (1873) **J.H. Newman** (1801)
Idea of Christ in the Gospels, The (1946) **George Santayana** (1863)
Idea of Great Poetry, The (1925) **Lascelles Abercrombie** (1881)
Idea of History, The (1946) **R.G. Collingwood** (1889–1943)
Idea of the Perfection of Painting, An (1668) **John Evelyn** (1620) (tr.)
Ideal Husband, An (1895) **Oscar Wilde** (1854)
Ideala (1888) **'Sarah Grand' [Frances Elizabeth McFall]** (1854)
Ideas About India (1885) **Wilfrid Scawen Blunt** (1840)
Ideas and Places (1953) **Cyril Connolly** (1903)
Ideas and the Novel (1980) **Mary McCarthy** (1912)
Ideas Mirrour (1594) **Michael Drayton** (1563)
Ideas of Good and Evil (1903) **W.B. Yeats** (1865)
Ideas of Order (1935) **Wallace Stevens** (1879)
Idées de Madame Aubray, Les (1867) **Alexandre Dumas ['fils']** (1824)
Identity of Yeats, The (1951) **Richard Ellmann** (1918)
Ideology: An Introduction (1991) **Terry Eagleton** (1943)
Ideology of the Aesthetic, The (1990) **Terry Eagleton** (1943)
Ides of March, The (1948) **Thornton Wilder** (1897)
Idiot, The (1895) **John Kendrick Bangs** (1862)
Idiot, The (1868) **Fyodor Mikhailovich Dostoevsky** (1821)
Idiot's Delight (1936) **Robert E. Sherwood** (1896)
Idiots First (1963) **Bernard Malamud** (1914)
Idle Days in Patagonia (1893) **W.H. Hudson** (1841)
Idle Ideas in 1905 (1905) **Jerome K. Jerome** (1859)
Idle Tales (1888) **Mrs J.H. Riddell** (1832)
Idle Thoughts of an Idle Fellow, The (1886) **Jerome K. Jerome** (1859)
Idler in France, The (1841) **Marguerite, Countess of Blessington** (1789)
Idler in Italy, The (1839) **Marguerite, Countess of Blessington** (1789)
Idol of the Clownes, The (1654) **John Cleveland** (1613)
Idols, The (1928) **Laurence Binyon** (1869)
Idols (1986) **Stephen Romer** (1957)
Idyll in the Desert (1931) **William Faulkner** (1897)
Idylls of the King (1859) **Alfred, Lord Tennyson** (1809)
Idyls and Legends of Inverburn (1865) **Robert Williams Buchanan** (1841)
Idyls and Songs (1854) **Francis Turner Palgrave** (1824)
If (1921) **Lord Dunsany** (1878)
If Beale Street Could Talk (1974) **James Baldwin** (1924)
If He Hollers Let Him Go (1945) **Chester Himes** (1909)
If I Die in a Combat Zone, Box Me Up and Ship Me Home (1973) **Tim O'Brien** (1946)
If I Were a Dictator (1934) **Julian Huxley** (1887)
If It Be Not Good, the Divel Is In It (1612) **Thomas Dekker** (1572?)
If Morning Ever Comes (1965) **Anne Tyler** (1941)
If Not Now, When? [*Se non ora, quando?*] (1982) **Primo Levi** (1919)
If Summer Don't (1922) **'Barry Pain' [Eric Odell]** (1864)
If the Old Could [as 'Jane Somers'] (1984) **Doris Lessing** (1919)
If There Be Thorns (1981) **Virginia Andrews** (1933)
If This Is a Man [*Se questo è un uomo*] (1947) **Primo Levi** (1919)
If Tomorrow Comes (1985) **Sidney Sheldon** (1917)
If You Could See Me Now (1977) **Peter Straub** (1943)
If You Know Not Me, You Know No Bodie (1605) **Thomas Heywood** (1574?)
If You Know Not Me, You Know No Bodie [pt. ii] (1606) **Thomas Heywood** (1574?)
Ignatius his Conclave (1611) **[John Donne]** (1572)
Ikons, The (1966) **Lawrence Durrell** (1912)
Ile of Guls, The (1606) **John Day** (*c.* 1574)
Ilex Tree, The (1965) **Les Murray** (1938) [with Geoffrey Lehmann]
Iliad, The **Homer** (8th century BC)
Iliad [from Homer] (1831) **William Sotheby** (1757) (tr.)
Iliad and the Odyssey, The (1791) **William Cowper** (1731) (tr.)
Iliad of Homer, The (1898) **Samuel Butler** (1835) (tr.)
Iliad of Homer, The (1611) **George Chapman** (1559?) (tr.)
Iliad of Homer, The [vol. i: bks i-iv] (1715–1720) **Alexander Pope** (1688) (tr.)
Iliads and Odyssey of Homer, The (1673) **Thomas Hobbes** (1588) (tr.)
Ill-Governed Coast, An (1976) **Roy Fuller** (1912)
Ill-Made Knight, The (1941) **T.H. White** (1906)
Ill-Tempered Clavichord, The (1953) **S.J. Perelman** (1904)
Illinois Poems (1941) **Edgar Lee Masters** (1868)
Illiterate Digest, The (1924) **Will Rogers** (1879)
Illness as Metaphor (1978) **Susan Sontag** (1933)

Illuminations, Les [prose and verse poems] (1886) **Arthur Rimbaud** (1854)
Illusion and Reality (1937) **'Christopher Caudwell'** (1907)
Illustrated Excursions in Italy (1846) **Edward Lear** (1812)
Illustrated Man, The (1951) **Ray Bradbury** (1920)
Illustrations of Lying (1825) **Amelia Opie** (1769)
Illustrations of Political Economy (1832) **Harriet Martineau** (1802)
Illywhacker (1985) **Peter Carey** (1943)
Image and the Law, The (1947) **Howard Nemerov** (1920)
Image in the Clay (1964) **David Ireland** (1927)
Image in the Sand, The (1905) **E.F. Benson** (1867)
Image of a Society (1956) **Roy Fuller** (1912)
Image of Governance, The (1541) **Sir Thomas Elyot** (1490?)
Image of Josephine, The (1945) **Booth Tarkington** (1869)
Images 1910–15 (1915) **Richard Aldington** (1892)
Images of Desire (1919) **Richard Aldington** (1892)
Images of Good and Evil (1899) **Arthur Symons** (1865)
Images of the Truth (1962) **Glenway Wescott** (1901)
Images of War (1919) **Richard Aldington** (1892)
Imaginary Conversations of Greeks and Romans (1853) **Walter Savage Landor** (1775)
Imaginary Conversation of King Carlo-Alberto and the Duchess Belgioioso (1848) **Walter Savage Landor** (1775)
Imaginary Conversations [vols. i, ii] (1824, 1828, 1829) **Walter Savage Landor** (1775)
Imaginary Friends (1967) **Alison Lurie** (1926)
Imaginary Homelands (1991) **Salman Rushdie** (1947)
Imaginary Invalid, The [*Le Malade imaginaire*] (1673) **'Molière' [Jean-Baptiste Poquelin]** (1622)
Imaginary Life, An (1978) **David Malouf** (1934)
Imaginary Love Affair, An (1974) **Gavin Ewart** (1916)
Imaginary Portraits (1887) **Walter Pater** (1839)
Imaginary Speeches and Other Parodies in Prose and Verse (1912) **J.C. Squire** (1884)
Imaginary Toys (1961) **Julian Mitchell** (1935)
Imagination and Fancy (1844) **Leigh Hunt** (1784)
Imaginations and Reveries, 1915 (1915) **George William Russell ['AE']** (1867)
Imaginative Experience, An (1994) **'Mary Wesley' [Mary Wellesley]** (1912)
Imaginative Man, An (1895) **Robert Hichens** (1864)
Imagine Dead Imagine (1965) **Samuel Beckett** (1906)
Imagined Life, An (1992) **Richard Hoggart** (1918)
Imago Bird (1980) **Nicholas Mosley** (1923)
Imajica (1991) **Clive Barker** (1952)
Imitation (1961) **Robert Lowell** (1917)
Imitation of the Seventeenth Epistle of the First Book of Horace (1714) **William Diaper** (1685)
Immaculate Mistake, An (1990) **Paul Bailey** (1937)
Immaterial Murder Case, The (1945) **Julian Symons** (1912)
Immaturity (1930) **Bernard Shaw** (1856)
Immobile Wind, The (1921) **Yvor Winters** (1900)
Immolation of Aleph, The (1985) **John Heath-Stubbs** (1918)
Immoralist, The [L'Immoraliste] (1902) **André Gide** (1869)
Immortality at Any Price (1991) **'William Cooper' [Harry Summerfield Hoff]** (1910)
Immortality of the Soul, The (1659) **Henry More** (1614)
Imogen (1784) **William Godwin** (1756)
Imogen (1978) **Jilly Cooper** (1937)
Impartial Critic, The (1693) **John Dennis** (1657)
Impassioned Clay (1931) **Llewelyn Powys** (1884)
Imperative Duty, An (1893) **William Dean Howells** (1837)
Imperial Caesar (1960) **Rex Warner** (1905)
Imperial City (1937) **Elmer Rice** (1892)
Imperial Earth (1975) **Arthur C. Clarke** (1917)
Imperial Highness (1953) **'Evelyn Anthony' [Evelyn Ward-Thomas]** (1928)
Imperial Palace (1930) **Arnold Bennett** (1867)
Imperial Theme, The (1931) **G. Wilson Knight** (1897)
Imperial Tragedy, The (1669) **Sir William Killigrew** (1606)
Imperial Women (1956) **Pearl S. Buck** (1892)
Imperialism and Civilization (1928) **Leonard Woolf** (1880)
Impersonators, The (1980) **Jessica Anderson** (1925)
Impertinent, The (1733) **Alexander Pope** (1688)
Impertubable Duchess, The (1923) **J.D. Beresford** (1873)
Implements in Their Places (1977) **W.S. Graham** (1918)
Importance of Being Earnest, The (1895) **Oscar Wilde** (1854)
Important Man, Thr (1970) **Jeffrey Wainwright** (1944)
Imported Bridegroom, The (1898) **Abraham Cahan** (1860)
Impossible Marriage, An (1954) **Pamela Hansford Johnson** (1912)
Impossible Object (1969) **Nicholas Mosley** (1923)
Impossible Saints (1997) **Michèle Roberts** (1949)
Imposter, The [*L'Imposteur*; 1st version, 1664, as *Le Tartuffe*] (1667) **'Molière' [Jean-Baptiste Poquelin]** (1622)
Imposters (1986) **George V. Higgins** (1939)
Impregnable City, The (1895) **Max Pemberton** (1863)
Impressions and Experiences (1896) **William Dean Howells** (1837)
Impressions and Opinions (1891) **George Moore** (1852)
Impressions of South Africa (1897) **James Bryce** (1838)
Impresssions of Theophrastus Such (1879) **'George Eliot' [Mary Ann Evans]** (1819)
Imprisoned Sea, The (1949) **James Reeves** (1909)
Impromptu in Moribundia (1939) **Patrick Hamilton** (1904)
Improper People (1930) **Rodney Ackland** (1908)
Improvasitore, The [Eng. trn, 1845] (1835) **Hans Christian Andersen** (1805)

Improvisatore, The (1821) **Thomas Lovell Beddoes** (1803)
Improvisatrice, The [as 'L.E.L.'] (1824) **Letitia Elizabeth Landon** (1802)
Impudent Ones, The [*Les Impudents*] (1942) **'Marguerite Duras' [Marguerite Donnadieu]** (1914)
In a Canadian Canoe (1891) **'Barry Pain' [Eric Odell]** (1864)
In a Dark Garden (1946) **Frank G. Slaughter** (1908)
In a Dark Wood (1977) **Marina Warner** (1946)
In a Free State (1971) **V.S. Naipaul** (1932)
In a German Pension (1911) **'Katherine Mansfield' [Kathleen Mansfield Beauchamp]** (1888)
In a Glass Darkly (1872) **J.S. Le Fanu** (1814)
In a Green Eye (1966) **Elaine Feinstein** (1930)
In a Green Night (1962) **Derek Walcott** (1930)
In a Music-Hall (1891) **John Davidson** (1857)
In a Province (1934) **Sir Laurens van der Post** (1906)
In a Silver Sea (1886) **B.L. Farjeon** (1838)
In a Steamer Chair [as 'Luke Sharp'] (1892) **Robert Barr** (1850)
In a Summer Season (1961) **Elizabeth Taylor** (1912)
In a Time of Violence (1994) **Eavan Boland** (1944)
In a Winter City (1876) **'Ouida' [Marie Louise de la Ramée]** (1839)
In a Yellow Wood (1947) **Gore Vidal** (1925)
In Abraham's Bosom [first version pub. 1924] (1927) **Paul Green** (1894)
In All Countries (1934) **John Dos Passos** (1896)
In All Shades (1886) **Grant Allen** (1848)
In America (2000) **Susan Sontag** (1933)
In an Australian Country Graveyard (1974) **Hal Porter** (1911)
In Bad Company (1901) **'Rolf Boldrewood' [Thomas Alexander Browne]** (1826)
In Between the Sheets (1978) **Ian McEwan** (1948)
In Black and White (1888) **Rudyard Kipling** (1865)
In Bluebeard's Castle (1971) **George Steiner** (1929)
In Brief Authority (1915) **'F. Anstey' [Thomas Anstey Guthrie]** (1856)
In Camera [*Huis clos*] (1944) **Jean-Paul Sartre** (1905)
In Celebration (1969) **David Storey** (1933)
In Chancery (1920) **John Galsworthy** (1867)
In Cold Blood (1966) **Truman Capote** (1924)
In Cold Hell, in Thicket (1953) **Charles Olson** (1910)
In Country Sleep (1952) **Dylan Thomas** (1914)
In Custody (1984) **Anita Desai** (1937)
In Darkest Africa (1890) **Sir Henry Morton Stanley** (1841)
In Darkest England, and the Way Out (1890) **William Booth** (1829)
In Darkness and Confusion (1947) **Ann Petry** (1908)
In Deacon's Orders (1895) **Sir Walter Besant** (1836)
In Deep Country (1987) **Maxine Kumin** (1925)
In Defence of Sensuality (1930) **John Cooper Powys** (1872)
In Defence of Shelley (1936) **Sir Herbert Read** (1893)
In Defence of the Earth (1956) **Kenneth Rexroth** (1905)
In Dewisland (1904) **S. Baring-Gould** (1834)
In Divers Tones (1886) **Sir Charles G.D. Roberts** (1860)
In Dreams Begin Responsibilities (1938) **Delmore Schwartz** (1913)
In Dubious Battle (1936) **John Steinbeck** (1902)
In Evil Hour [*La mala hora*] (1966) **Gabriel García Márquez** (1928)
In Exitu Israel (1870) **S. Baring-Gould** (1834)
In Far Lochaber (1888) **William Black** (1841)
In Favour of the Sensitive Man (1976) **Anaïs Nin** (1903)
In Fires of No Return (1958) **James K. Baxter** (1926)
In Flashlight (1965) **Michael Hamburger** (1924)
In Good King Charles's Golden Days (1939) **Bernard Shaw** (1856)
In Greek Waters (1893) **G.A. Henty** (1832)
In Haste and at Leisure (1895) **E. Lynn Linton** (1822)
In Hazard (1938) **Richard Hughes** (1900)
In Her Day (1976) **Rita Mae Brown** (1944)
In Her Own Image (1980) **Eavan Boland** (1944)
In High Places (1898) **M.E. Braddon** (1835)
In High Places (1962) **Arthur Hailey** (1920)
In His Own Image (1901) **Frederick William Rolfe** (1860)
In Honour Bound (1961) **Nina Bawden** (1925)
In Kedar's Tents (1897) **'Henry Seton Merriman' [Hugh Stowell Scott]** (1862)
In King's Byways (1902) **Stanley J. Weyman** (1855)
In Light and Darkness (1964) **Chris Wallace-Crabbe** (1934)
In Love and Trouble (1973) **Alice Walker** (1944)
In Luck at Last (1884) **Sir Walter Besant** (1836)
In Maremma (1882) **'Ouida' [Marie Louise de la Ramée]** (1839)
In Memoriam (1850) **Alfred, Lord Tennyson** (1809)
In Memoriam James Joyce (1955) **'Hugh MacDiarmid' [Christopher Murray Grieve]** (1892)
In Memoriam to Identity (1990) **Kathy Acker** (1948)
In Mio's Country (1917) **Jane Barlow** (1857)
In Mizzoura (1893) **Augustus Thomas** (1857)
In Morocco (1920) **Edith Wharton** (1862)
In Mr Knox's Country (1915) **'Somerville and Ross' [Edith Somerville** (1858) and **Violet Martin** (1862)**]**
In My End is My Beginning (1931) **Maurice Baring** (1874)
In My Father's Court (1966) **Isaac Bashevis Singer** (1904)
In My Father's Den (1972) **Maurice Gee** (1931)
In My Father's House (1978) **Ernest J. Gaines** (1933)
In My Good Books (1942) **V.S. Pritchett** (1900)
In Ole Virginia (1887) **Thomas Nelson Page** (1853)
In Our Terribleness (1971) **LeRoi Jones** (1934)
In Our Time (1925) **Ernest Hemingway** (1898)
In Our Town (1946) **Damon Runyon** (1884)
In Parenthesis (1937) **David Jones** (1895)
In Patagonia (1977) **Bruce Chatwin** (1940)
In Pharaoh's Army (1994) **Tobias Wolff** (1945)
In Praise of Idleness (1935) **Bertrand Russell** (1872)
In Pursuit of Spring (1914) **Edward Thomas** (1878)

In Radical Pursuit (1975) **W.D. Snodgrass** (1926)
In Retreat (1966) **Philip Hobsbaum** (1932)
In Retreat (1925) **Sir Herbert Read** (1893)
In Russet and Silver (1894) **Sir Edmund Gosse** (1849)
In Search of a Character (1961) **Graham Greene** (1904)
In Search of J.D. Salinger (1988) **Ian Hamilton** (1938)
In Search of Love and Beauty (1983) **Ruth Prawer Jhabvala** (1927)
In Search of Myself (1946) **Frederick Grove** (1879)
In Search of Our Mothers' Gardens (1983) **Alice Walker** (1944)
In Search of Owen Roblin (1974) **Al Purdy** (1918)
In Siberia (1999) **Colin Thubron** (1939)
In Silk Attire (1869) **William Black** (1841)
In Spite of the Czar (1905) **Guy Boothby** (1867)
In the Absence of Mrs Petersen (1966) **Nigel Balchin** (1908)
In the American Grain (1925) **William Carlos Williams** (1883)
In the American Jungle (1937) **Waldo Frank** (1889)
In the Bar of a Tokyo Hotel (1969) **'Tennessee' [Thomas Lanier] Williams** (1911)
In the Beauty of the Lilies (1996) **John Updike** (1932)
In the Beginning (1991) **Irina Ratushinskaya** (1954)
In the Cage (1898) **Henry James** (1843)
In the Castle of My Skin (1953) **George Lamming** (1927)
In the Clap Shack (1972) **William Styron** (1925)
In the Clearing (1962) **Robert Frost** (1874)
In the Company of Dolphins (1964) **Irwin Shaw** (1913)
In The Country of Last Things (1987) **Paul Auster** (1947)
In the Country of the Skin (1973) **Peter Redgrove** (1932)
In the Cruel Arcade (1994) **Alan Brownjohn** (1931)
In the Days of My Youth (1873) **Amelia B. Edwards** (1831)
In the Days of the Comet (1906) **H.G. Wells** (1866)
In the Deep of the Snow (1907) **Sir Charles G.D. Roberts** (1860)
In the Distance (1975) **Dick Davis** (1945)
In the Ditch (1972) **Buchi Emecheta** (1944)
In the Echoey Tunnel (1991) **Christopher Reid** (1949)
In the Frame (1976) **Dick Francis** (1920)
In the Future Perfect (1977) **Walter Abish** (1931)
In the Garden of the North American Martyrs [UK: *Hunters in the Snow*] (1981) **Tobias Wolff** (1945)
In the Glass Case (1981) **C.K. Stead** (1932)
In the Green Tree (1948) **Alun Lewis** (1915–44)
In the Guardianship of God (1903) **Flora Annie Steel** (1847)
In the Hall of the Saurians (1987) **Peter Redgrove** (1932)
In the Harbor (1882) **Henry Wadsworth Longfellow** (1807)
In the Heart of the Country (1942) **H.E. Bates** (1905)
In the Heart of the Country (1977) **J.M. Coetzee** (1940)
In the Heart of the Heart of the Country (1968) **William H. Gass** (1924)
In the Heat of the Night (1965) **John Ball** (1911)
In the High Valley (1890) **'Susan Coolidge' [Sarah Chauncy Woolsey]** (1845)
In the Hollow of His Hand (1986) **James Purdy** (1923)
In the Hot-House (1988) **Alan Jenkins** (1955)
In the Image of God (1898) **A. St John Adcock** (1864)
In the Image of God (1990) **Simon Raven** (1927)
In the Key of Blue (1893) **John Addington Symonds** (1840)
In the Labyrinth [*Dans le labyrinthe*] (1959) **Alain Robbe-Grillet** (1922)
In the Land of Dreamy Dreams (1981) **Ellen Gilchrist** (1935)
In the Mean Time (1984) **Elizabeth Smart** (1913)
In the Meantime (1942) **Howard Spring** (1889)
In the Meantime (1997) **Elizabeth Jennings** (1926)
In the Middle Air (1975) **Lauris Edmond** (1924)
In the Midst of Alarms (1894) **Robert Barr** (1850)
In the Money (1940) **William Carlos Williams** (1883)
In the Name of the Bodleian (1905) **Augustine Birrell** (1850)
In the Nazi Era (1952) **Sir Lewis Namier** (1888)
In the Net of the Stars (1909) **F.S. Flint** (1885)
In the Night Kitchen (1970) **Maurice Sendak** (1928)
In the Permanent Way (1897) **Flora Annie Steel** (1847)
In the Purely Pagan Sense (1976) **John Lehmann** (1907)
In the Red Kitchen (1990) **Michèle Roberts** (1949)
In the Roar of the Sea (1892) **S. Baring-Gould** (1834)
In the Seven Woods (1903) **W.B. Yeats** (1865)
In the Shadow of the Crown (1988) **'Jean Plaidy' [Eleanor Hibbert]** (1906)
In the Skin of a Lion (1987) **Michael Ondaatje** (1943)
In the Springtime of the Year (1974) **Susan Hill** (1942)
In the Stopping Train (1980) **Donald Davie** (1922)
In the Teeth of the Evidence (1939) **Dorothy L. Sayers** (1893)
In the Thirties (1962) **Edward Upward** (1903)
In the Track of the Troops (1876) **R.M. Ballantyne** (1825)
In the Trojan Ditch (1974) **C.H. Sisson** (1914)
In the Valley (1890) **Harold Frederic** (1856)
In the Valley (1928) **Paul Green** (1894)
In the Wake of War (1900) **A. St John Adcock** (1864)
In the Winter of Cities (1956) **'Tennessee' [Thomas Lanier] Williams** (1911)
In the Wrong Paradise (1886) **Andrew Lang** (1844)
In the Year of the Jubilee (1894) **George Gissing** (1857)
In Their Wisdom (1974) **C.P. Snow** (1905)
In This House of Brede (1969) **Rumer Godden** (1907)
In This Our Life (1941) **Ellen Glasgow** (1874)
In Time of Mistrust (1939) **Robert Hillyer** (1895)
In Transit (1969) **Brigid Brophy** (1929)
In Trust (1881) **Margaret Oliphant** (1828)
In Two Years' Time (1879) **Ada Cambridge** (1844)
In Vain (1872) **Henryk Sienkiewicz** (1846)
In Varying Moods (1894) **Beatrice Harraden** (1864)
In Vein of Iron (1935) **Ellen Glasgow** (1874)
In Veronica's Garden (1895) **Alfred Austin** (1835)

In Virginia (1913) **Ellen Glasgow** (1874)
In War Time (1864) **John Greenleaf Whittier** (1807)
In Watermelon Sugar (1968) **Richard Brautigan** (1935)
In What Hour (1940) **Kenneth Rexroth** (1905)
In Wicklow, West Kerry, and Connemara (1911) **J.M. Synge** (1871–1909)
In Youth is Pleasure (1944) **Denton Welch** (1915)
Inadequacy of Natural Selection, The (1893) **Herbert Spencer** (1820)
Inadmissible Evidence (1964) **John Osborne** (1929)
Inalienable Heritage, The (1914) **Emily Lawless** (1845–1913)
Incarnations (1968) **Robert Penn Warren** (1905)
Incense to Idols (1960) **Sylvia Ashton-Warner** (1908)
Incident at Vichy (1965) **Arthur Miller** (1915)
Incident Book, The (1986) **Fleur Adcock** (1934)
Incidental Bishop, The (1898) **Grant Allen** (1848)
Incidents at the Shrine (1986) **Ben Okri** (1959)
Incidents in the Rue Laugier (1995) **Anita Brookner** (1928)
Inclinations (1916) **Ronald Firbank** (1886)
Incline Our Hearts (1988) **A.N. Wilson** (1950)
Incognita (1692) **William Congreve** (1670)
Incomparable Atuk, The [US: *Stick Your Neck Out*] (1963) **Mordecai Richler** (1931)
Incomparable Bellairs, The (1904) **Egerton Smith Castle**(1858) and **Agnes Castle neé Sweetman** (*c.* 1860)
Incompleat Etonian, An (1909) **'Frank Danby' [Julia Frankau]** (1864)
Incomplete Amorist, The (1906) **E[dith] Nesbit** (1858)
Inconstant, The (1702) **George Farquhar** (1678)
Incorrigible Music, An (1979) **Allen Curnow** (1911)
Incredible Adventures (1914) **Algernon Blackwood** (1869)
Incredulity of Father Brown, The (1926) **G.K. Chesterton** (1874)
Incurable, The (1971) **Nell Dunn** (1936)
Indecent Exposure (1973) **Tom Sharpe** (1928)
Indemnity Only [first 'V.I. Warshawski' novel] (1982) **Sara Paretsky** (1947)
Independence (1764) **Charles Churchill** (1731)
Independence (1981) **Andrew Motion** (1952)
Independent Member (1950) **A.P. Herbert** (1890)
India (1977) **V.S. Naipaul** (1932)
India Song [text and film] (1973) **'Marguerite Duras' [Marguerite Donnadieu]** (1914)
India Speaks (1943) **Mulk Raj Anand** (1905)
Indian Ass, An (1925) **Sir Harold Acton** (1904)
Indian Boyhood, An (1902) **Charles Eastman** (1858)
Indian Emperour, The (1665) **John Dryden** (1631)
Indian in the Cupboard, The (1980) **Lynne Reid Banks** (1929)
Indian Ink (1994) **Tom Stoppard** (1937)
Indian Journals (1970) **Allen Ginsberg** (1926)
Indian Summer (1886) **William Dean Howells** (1837)
Indiana (1832) **'George Sand' [Auore Dupin]** (1804)
Indifferent Children, The (1947) **Louis Auchinloss** (1917)
Indigo (1992) **Marina Warner** (1946)
Indirect Method (1980) **Francis King** (1923)
Indiscreet Toys, The [*Les Bijoux indiscrets*] (1748) **Denis Diderot** (1713)
Indiscretion of the Duchess, The (1894) **'Anthony Hope' [Sir Anthony Hope Hawkins]** (1863)
Indiscretions (1923) **Ezra Pound** (1885)
Indiscretions of Archie, The (1921) **P.G. Wodehouse** (1881)
Individualist, The (1899) **W.H. Mallock** (1849)
Indoor Park, The (1983) **Sean O'Brien** (1952)
Industry of Souls, The (1998) **Martin Booth** (1944)
Industrial Biography (1863) **Samuel Smiles** (1812)
Industrial Democracy (1897) **Sidney Webb** (1859) and Beatrice Webb (1858)
Inebriety (1775) **George Crabbe** (1754)
Inequality of Man, The (1932) **J.B.S. Haldane** (1892)
Infants of the Spring (1976) **Anthony Powell** (1905)
Infernal Desire Machines of Doctor Hoffman, The [US: *The War of Dreams*] (1972) **Angela Carter** (1940)
Infernal Machine, The [*La Machine infernale*] (1934) **Jean Cocteau** (1889)
Infernal World of Branwell Bronte, The (1960) **Daphne du Maurier** (1907)
Inferno (1898) **August Strindberg** (1849)
Inferno of Dante, The (1805) **Henry Cary** (1772) (tr.)
Infidel, The (1900) **Mary Elizabeth Braddon** (1835)
Infidel, The (1835) **Robert Bird** (1806)
Infinite Plan, The (1993) **Isabel Allende** (1942)
Infinite Rehearsal, The (1987) **Wilson Harris** (1921)
Infinite Riches (1998) **Ben Okri** (1959)
Infinity of Mirrors, An (1964) **Richard Condon** (1915)
Inflexible Captive, The (1774) **Hannah More** (1745)
Influence of Literature Upon Society, The [*De la littérature considérée dans ses rapports avec les institutions sociales*] (1800) **Madame de Staël** (1766)
Influence of Natural Religion upon the Temporal Happiness of Mankind, The (1822) **Jeremy Bentham** (1748)
Influences, The (1976) **Vernon Watkins** (1906–67)
Information, The (1995) **Martin Amis** (1949)
Informer, The (1925) **Liam O'Flaherty** (1897)
Informers, The (1994) **Bret Easton Ellis** (1964)
Ingestion of Ice-Cream (1969) **Geoffrey Grigson** (1905)
Inglan is a Bitch (1980) **Linton Kwesi Johnson** (1952)
Ingoldsby Legends, The [1st ser.] (1840) **R.H. Barham** (1788)
Ingoldsby Legends, The [2nd ser.] (1842, 1847) **R.H. Barham** (1788)
Ingratitude of a Common-wealth, The (1681) **Nahum Tate** (1652)
Inhale and Exhale (1936) **William Saroyan** (1908)
Inheritance, The (1824) **Susan Edmonstone Ferrier** (1782)

Inheritance (1931) **John Drinkwater** (1882)
Inheritance (1932) **Phyllis Bentley** (1894)
Inheritor, The (1930) **E.F. Benson** (1867)
Inheritors, The (1901) **Joseph Conrad** (1857) [with F.M. Hueffer]
Inheritors, The (1957) **Richard Church** (1893)
Inheritors, The (1955) **William Golding** (1911)
Inhumane Cardinal, The (1696) **Mary Pix** (1666)
Inimitable Jeeves, The (1923) **P.G. Wodehouse** (1881)
Inisfail (1863) **Aubrey Thomas de Vere** (1814)
Inishfallen, Fare Thee Well (1949) **Sean O'Casey** (1880)
Injur'd Love (1707) **Nahum Tate** (1652)
Injured Princess, The (1682) **Thomas d'Urfey** (1653)
Injury Time (1977) **Beryl Bainbridge** (1934)
Injustice Collectors, The (1950) **Louis Auchinloss** (1917)
Ink Truck, The (1969) **William Joseph Kennedy** (1928)
Inland Passages (1985) **Jane Rule** (1931)
Inland Voyage, An (1878) **Robert Louis Stevenson** (1850)
Inmates, The (1952) **John Cooper Powys** (1872)
Inn at the Edge of the World, The (1990) **'Alice Thomas Ellis' [Anna Margaret Haycraft]** (1932)
Inn of Tranquillity, The (1912) **John Galsworthy** (1867)
Inner and the Outer Ireland, The (1921) **George William Russell ['AE']** (1867)
Inner Harbour, The (1979) **Fleur Adcock** (1934)
Inner Life of Syria, Palestine, and the Holy Land, The (1875) **Lady Isabel Burton** (1831)
Inner Room, The (1988) **James Merrill** (1926)
Inner-Temple Masque, The (1619) **Thomas Middleton** (1580)
Innocence (1986) **Penelope Fitzgerald** (1916)
Innocence is Drowned (1938) **Walter Allen** (1911)
Innocence of Father Brown, The (1911) **G.K. Chesterton** (1874)
Innocencies (1905) **Katharine Tynan** (1861)
Innocency with her Open Face (1669) **William Penn** (1644)
Innocent (1914) **Marie Corelli** (1855)
Innocent, The (1957) **Madison Jones** (1925)
Innocent and the Guilty, The (1971) **Sylvia Townsend Warner** (1893)
Innocent Anthropologist, The (1983) **Nigel Barley** (1947)
Innocent Birds (1926) **T.F. Powys** (1875)
Innocent Blood (1980) **P.D. James** (1920)
Innocent, The (1990) **Ian McEwan** (1948)
Innocents, The (1917) **Sinclair Lewis** (1885)
Innocents (1947) **A.L. Barker** (1918)
Innocents Abroad, The (1869) **'Mark Twain' [Samuel Langhorne Clemens]** (1835)
Inquiry into Meaning and Truth, An (1940) **Bertrand Russell** (1872)
Inquiry into the Authenticity of Certain Miscellaneous Papers, An [on the Ireland forgeries] (1796) **Edmond Malone** (1741)
Inquiry into the Colonial Policy of the European Powers, An (1803) **Henry, Lord Brougham** (1778)
Inquiry into the Human Mind, An (1764) **Thomas Reid** (1710)
Inquiry into the Nature and Causes of the Wealth of Nations, An (1776) **Adam Smith** (1723)
Inquiry into the Nature and Progress of Rent, An (1815) **T.R. Malthus** (1766)
Inquisitor, The (1935) **Sir Hugh Walpole** (1884)
Inquisitor, The (1788) **Susanna Rowson** (1762)
Inside Benchley (1942) **Robert Benchley** (1889)
Inside Mr Enderby (1963) **'Anthony Burgess' [John Anthony Burgess Wilson]** (1917)
Inside, Outside (1985) **Herman Wouk** (1915)
Inside the Easter Egg (1975) **Marian Engel** (1933)
Inside the Onion (1984) **Howard Nemerov** (1920)
Inside the Whale (1940) **George Orwell** (1903)
Inspector Calls, An (1946) **J.B. Priestley** (1894)
Inspector French's Greatest Case (1925) **Freeman Wills Crofts** (1879)
Inspector Ghote Draws a Line (1979) **H.R.F. Keating** (1926)
Inspector Ghote's Good Crusade (1966) **H.R.F. Keating** (1926)
Instance of the Fingerpost, An (1997) **Iain Pears** (1955)
Instant Chronicles (1985) **D.J. Enright** (1920)
The Instant Gardener (2000) **John Le Carré** (1931)
Instant in the Wind, An (1976) **André Brink** (1935)
Instigations (1920) **Ezra Pound** (1885)
Institute, The (1976) **James M. Cain** (1892)
Institutes of Moral Philosophy (1769) **Adam Ferguson** (1723)
Institution and Life of Cyrus, The [Xenophon: *Cyropaedia*]] (1632) **Philemon Holland** (1552) (tr.)
Institution, Laws and Ceremonies of the Order of the Garter, The (1672) **Elias Ashmole** (1617)
Institution of the Christian Religion, The [from Calvin] (1561) **Thomas Norton** (1532) (tr.)
Institutiones Piae (1630) **Lancelot Andrewes** (1555)
Instruction for the Ignorant (1675) **John Bunyan** (1628)
Instructions to a Painter (1666) **Edmund Waller** (1606)
Instrument, The (1967) **John O'Hara** (1905)
Insular Possession, An (1986) **Timothy Mo** (1950)
Insulted and the Injured, The (1861) **Fyodor Mikhailovich Dostoevsky** (1821)
Insurance Man, The (1986) **Alan Bennett** (1934)
Insurrection (1950) **Liam O'Flaherty** (1897)
Insurrection in Dublin, The (1916) **James Stephens** (1882)
Insurrections (1909) **James Stephens** (1882)
Intellectual Origins of the English Revolution, The (1965) **Christopher Hill** (1912)
Intellectual Things (1930) **Stanley J. Kunitz** (1905)
Intelligent Woman's Guide to Socialism and Capitalism, The (1928) **Bernard Shaw** (1856)
Intended, The (1894) **Henry de Vere Stacpoole** (1863)

Intended, The (1990) **David Dabydeen** (1956)
Intensity (1995) **Dean Koontz** (1945)
Intensive Care (1970) **Janet Frame** (1924)
Intentions (1891) **Oscar Wilde** (1854)
Inter Arma (1916) **Sir Edmund Gosse** (1849)
Intercepted Letters [as 'Thomas Brown the Younger'] (1813) **Thomas Moore** (1779)
Intercessor, The (1931) **May Sinclair** (1863)
Intercom Conspiracy, The (1970) **Eric Ambler** (1909)
Intercourse (1987) **Andrea Dworkin** (1946)
Interest of Great Britain Considered with Regard to Her Colonies, The (1760) **Benjamin Franklin** (1706)
Interfaces (1980) **Ursula K. le Guin** (1929)
Interim (1919) **Dorothy M. Richardson** (1873)
Interior Castle, The [*El castillo interior*; also known as *Las moradas*] (1577) **St Teresa of Ávila** (1515)
Interludes (1872) **Alfred Austin** (1835)
Interludes and Poems (1908) **Lascelles Abercrombie** (1881)
Interlunar (1984) **Margaret Atwood** (1939)
Intermediate Sex, The (1908) **Edward Carpenter** (1844)
Intermezzo (1933) **Jean Giraudoux** (1882)
Internal Colloquies (1972) **I.A. Richards** (1893)
International Episode, An (1879) **Henry James** (1843)
Interplay (1908) **Beatrice Harraden** (1864)
Interpretation of History, The (1936) **Paul Tillich** (1886)
Interpretations of Poetry and Religion (1900) **George Santayana** (1863)
Interpreter, The (1858) **G.J. Whyte-Melville** (1821)
Interpreters, The (1970) **Wole Soyinka** (1934)
Interrupted Friendship, An (1910) **Ethel Voynich** (1864)
Interview with the Vampire [first of the *Vampire* Chronicles] (1976) **Anne Rice** (1941)
Intimacy (1998) **Hanif Kureishi** (1954)
Into Battle (1941) **Sir Winston Churchill** (1874)
Into the Heart of Borneo (1984) **Redmond O'Hanlon** (1947)
Into the Lap of Atlas (1979) **Richard Hughes** (1900–76)
Into the Stone, and Other Poems (1960) **James Dickey** (1923)
Into Your Tent I'll Creep (1971) **Peter De Vries** (1910)
Intrigues at Versailles, The (1697) **Thomas d'Urfey** (1653)
Intriguing Chambermaid, The (1734) **Henry Fielding** (1707)
Introduced to Society (1884) **Charles Hamilton Aïdé** (1826)
Introduction to Bibliography for Literary Students, An (1927) **R.B. McKerrow** (1872)
Introduction to Mathematical Philosophy (1919) **Bertrand Russell** (1872)
Introduction to Metaphysics, An [by Henri Bergson] (1913) **T.E. Hulme** (1883) (tr.)
Introduction to Modern Philosophy (1924) **C.E.M. Joad** (1891)
Introduction to Rare and Valuable Editions of the Greek and Roman Classics (1802) **Thomas Frognall Dibdin** (1776)
Introduction to the Art of Thinking (1761) **Henry Home, Lord Kames** (1696)
Introduction to the History of England, An (1695) **Sir William Temple** (1628)
Introduction to the Literature of Europe (1837) **Henry Hallam** (1777)
Introduction to the Principles of Morals and Legislation, An (1789) **Jeremy Bentham** (1748)
Introduction to the Study of Dante, An (1872) **John Addington Symonds** (1840)
Introduction to the Study of English History (1881) **S.R. Gardiner** (1829)
Intruder in the Dust (1948) **William Faulkner** (1897)
Intruders, The (1976) **Hugh Garner** (1913)
Intrusions (1980) **Robert Aickman** (1914)
Intrusions of Peggy, The (1902) **'Anthony Hope' [Sir Anthony Hope Hawkins]** (1863)
Invader of His Country, The (1720) **John Dennis** (1657)
Invaders, The (1948) **Waldo Frank** (1889)
Invasion, The (1832) **Gerald Griffin** (1803)
Invasion, The (1932) **Janet Lewis** (1899)
Invaders, The (1934) **William Plomer** (1903)
Invasion 1940 (1957) **Peter Fleming** (1907)
Invasion of 1910, The (1906) **William le Queux** (1864)
Invasion of the Crimea, The [vols. i, ii] (1863, 1887) **A.W. Kinglake** (1809)
The Invention of Solitude (1982) **Paul Auster** (1947)
Invention of the World, The (1977) **Jack Hodgins** (1938)
Inventions of the March Hare (1998) **T.S. Eliot** (1888–1965)
Inventor, The (1957) **Wole Soyinka** (1934)
Invisible Cities [*Le città invisibili*] (1972) **Italo Calvino** (1923)
Invisible Event, The (1915) **J.D. Beresford** (1873)
Invisible Landscapes (1935) **Edgar Lee Masters** (1868)
Invisible Man, The (1952) **Ralph Ellison** (1914)
Invisible Man, The (1897) **H.G. Wells** (1866)
Invisible Swords (1971) **James T. Farrell** (1904)
Invisible Woman, The [biography of Nelly Ternan] (1990) **Claire Tomalin** (1933)
Invisible World, The (1659) **Joseph Hall** (1574–1656)
Invisible Worm, The (1991) **Jennifer Johnston** (1930)
Invisible Writing, The (1954) **Arthur Koestler** (1905)
Invitation to a Beheading (1959) **Vladimir Nabokov** (1899)
Invitation to the Waltz (1932) **Rosamond Lehmann** (1903)
Invocation (1915) **Robert Nichols** (1893)
Invocation to Music (1895) **Robert Bridges** (1844)
Invocations to Angels (1928) **Edgell Rickword** (1898)
Inward Companion (1950) **Walter de la Mare** (1873)
Inward Eye, The (1946) **Norman MacCaig** (1910)
Iola Lerot; or, Shadows Uplifted (1892) **Frances E. Harper** (1825)

Iolanthe [music by Sir Arthur Sullivan] (1885) **W.S. Gilbert** (1836)
Iolaus (1902) **Edward Carpenter** (1844) (ed.)
Ion (1835) **Thomas Noon Talfourd** (1795)
Ion of Euripides, The (1937) **Hilda Doolittle** (1886) (tr.)
Ione (1883) **E. Lynn Linton** (1822)
Ionia (1954) **Freya Stark** (1893)
Ionian Mission, The (1981) **Patrick O'Brian** (1914)
Ionica (1858) **William [Johnson] Cory** (1823)
Ionica II (1877) **William [Johnson] Cory** (1823)
Ipané, The (1899) **R.B. Cunninghame Graham** (1852)
Ipcress File, The (1962) **Len Deighton** (1929)
Iphigenia (1700) **John Dennis** (1657)
Iphigenia in Delphi (1890) **Richard Garnett** (1835)
Iphigenia in Tauris [*Iphigenie auf Tauris*] (1787) **Johann Wolfgang von Goethe** (1749)
Iphigénie (1675) **Jean Racine** (1639)
Ira and Isabella (1807) **William Hill Brown** (1765)
Iranian Nights (1989) **Howard Brenton** (1942) and Tariq Ali (1943)
Iraq: Land of Two Rivers (1980) **Gavin Young** (1928)
Ireland (1897) **Lionel Johnson** (1867)
Ireland and the English Crisis (1984) **Tom Paulin** (1949)
Ireland, Past and Future (1922) **George William Russell ['AE']** (1867)
Irene (1749) **Samuel Johnson** (1709)
Irene the Missionary (1879) **John W. De Forest** (1826)
Iris (1901) **Arthur Wing Pinero** (1855)
Iris in Her Garden (1992) **Barbara Hanrahan** (1939–1991)
Irish Artifice (1728) **Eliza Haywood** (*c.* 1693)
Irish Cousin, An (1889) **'Somerville and Ross' [Edith Somerville** (1858) and **Violet Martin** (1862)**]**
Irish Elegies (1961) **Padraic Colum** (1881)
Irish Essays (1882) **Matthew Arnold** (1822)
Irish Fairy Tales (1920) **James Stephens** (1882)
Irish Folk-History Plays (1912) **Lady Gregory** (1852)
Irish Idylls (1892) **Jane Barlow** (1857)
Irish Land Question, The (1881) **Henry George** (1839)
Irish Literary and Musical Studies (1913) **A.P. Graves** (1846)
Irish Literary Portraits (1972) **W.R. Rodgers** (1909)
Irish Melodies (1821) **Thomas Moore** (1779)
Irish Neighbours (1907) **Jane Barlow** (1857)
Irish Pastorals (1901) **Shan F. Bullock** (1865)
Irish Poems (1913) **Katharine Tynan** (1861)
Irish Sketch-Book, The [as 'M.A. Titmarsh'] (1843) **W.M. Thackeray** (1811)
Irish Ways (1909) **Jane Barlow** (1857)
Irish Widow, The (1772) **David Garrick** (1717)
Irish Witch, The (1973) **Dennis Wheatley** (1897)
Iron Age, The [2 pts., 1632] (1632) **Thomas Heywood** (1574?)
Iron Age, The (1916) **Francis Brett Young** (1884)
Iron and Smoke (1928) **Sheila Kaye-Smith** (1887)
Iron Chest, The (1796) **George Colman the Younger** (1762)
Iron Cousin, The (1854) **Mary Cowden Clarke** (1809)
Iron Door, The (1927) **E.J. Pratt** (1882)
Iron Dream, The (1972) **Norman Spinrad** (1940)
Iron Gate, The (1880) **Oliver Wendell Holmes** (1809)
Iron Heel, The (1908) **'Jack London' [John Griffith Chaney]** (1876)
Iron Horse (1973) **Allen Ginsberg** (1926)
Iron Horse, The (1871) **R.M. Ballantyne** (1825)
Iron in the Soul [*La Mort dans l'âme*] (1949) **Jean-Paul Sartre** (1905)
Iron John (1990) **Robert Bly** (1926)
Iron Laurel, The (1942) **Sidney Keyes** (1922)
Iron Man, The (1968) **Ted Hughes** (1930)
Iron Pirate, The (1893) **Max Pemberton** (1863)
Iron Wolf, The (1980) **Richard Adams** (1920)
Ironweed (1983) **William Joseph Kennedy** (1928)
Irradiations (1915) **John Gould Fletcher** (1886)
Irrational Knot, The (1905) **Bernard Shaw** (1856)
Irréparable, L' (1884) **Paul Bourget** (1852)
Irresistible Forces (1999) **Danielle Steel** (1947)
Irresponsibles, The (1940) **Archibald MacLeish** (1892)
is five (1926) **E.E. Cummings** (1894)
Is He Popenjoy? (1878) **Anthony Trollope** (1815)
Is Life Worth Living? (1933) **Lennox Robinson** (1886)
Is Sex Necessary? (1929) **James Thurber** (1894) [with E.B. White]
Is Shakespeare Dead? (1909) **'Mark Twain' [Samuel Langhorne Clemens]** (1835)
Isabel Clarendon (1886) **George Gissing** (1857)
Isabelle de Bavière (1836) **Alexandre Dumas ['père']** (1802)
Iscariot, The (1912) **Eden Phillpotts** (1862)
Ishmael (1884) **M.E. Braddon** (1835)
Ishmael Pengelly (1893) **Joseph Hocking** (1860)
Isidro (1905) **Mary Austin** (1868)
Isidore (1991) **Jeremy Reed** (1954)
Isis (1749) **William Mason** (1724)
Island, The (1944) **Francis Brett Young** (1884)
Island (1962) **Aldous Huxley** (1894)
Island, The (1979) **Peter Benchley** (1940)
Island and Time (1941) **Allen Curnow** (1911)
Island in the Atlantic (1946) **Waldo Frank** (1889)
Island in the Sun (1955) **Alec Waugh** (1898)
Island is a World, An (1955) **Samuel Selvon** (1923)
Island Magic (1934) **Elizabeth Goudge** (1900)
Island Means Minago, The (1975) **Milton Acorn** (1923)
Island Nights' Entertainments (1893) **Robert Louis Stevenson** (1850)
Island of Dr Moreau, The (1896) **H.G. Wells** (1866)
Island of Sheep, The (1936) **John Buchan** (1875)
Island of the Day Before, The (1994) **Umberto Eco** (1932)
Island of the Mighty, The (1972) **John Arden** (1930) [with Margaretta D'Arcy]
Island of the Women, The (1998) **George Mackay Brown** (1921–96)
Island Pharisees, The (1904) **John Galsworthy** (1867)
Island Queen, The (1885) **R.M. Ballantyne** (1825)

Island Race, The (1898) **Sir Henry Newbolt** (1862)
Island, The (1823) **George Gordon, Lord Byron** (1788)
Island, The (1888) **Richard Whiteing** (1840)
Island-Princess, The (1687) **Nahum Tate** (1652)
Islands (1969) **Edward Brathwaite** (1930)
Islands (1978) **Liz Lochhead** (1947)
Islands in the Stream (1970) **Ernest Hemingway** (1898–1961)
Isle in the Water, An (1895) **Katharine Tynan** (1861)
Isle of Palms, The (1812) **John Wilson** (1785)
Isle of Penguins, the [*L'île des pingouins*] (1908) **'Anatole France' [Jacques-Anatole-François Thibault]** (1844)
Isle of Unrest, The (1900) **'Henry Seton Merriman' [Hugh Stowell Scott]** (1862)
Isles of Scilly, The (1946) **Geoffrey Grigson** (1905)
Isles of Sunset, The (1904) **A.C. Benson** (1862)
Ismael (1820) **Edward Bulwer-Lytton** (1803)
Ismailia (1874) **Sir Samuel White Baker** (1821)
Isobel Quirk in Orbit (1978) **Tom Wakefield** (1935)
Isola (1902) **Lady Florence Dixie** (1857)
Israel in Egypt (1861) **Edwin Atherstone** (1788)
Israel Potter (1855) **Herman Melville** (1819)
It (1977) **William Mayne** (1928)
It (1986) **Stephen King** (1947)
It All Adds Up (1994) **Saul Bellow** (1915)
It, and Other Stories (1927) **Elinor Glyn** (1864)
It Can Never Happen Again (1909) **William De Morgan** (1839)
It Can't Happen Here (1935) **Sinclair Lewis** (1885)
It Catches My Heart in Its Hands (1963) **Charles Bukowski** (1920)
It Happened to Didymus (1958) **Upton Sinclair** (1878)
It Is Always Summer (1982) **David Helwig** (1938)
'It Is Never Too Late To Mend' (1856) **Charles Reade** (1814)
It Isn't This Time of Year at All! (1954) **Oliver St Gogarty** (1878)
It May Never Happen (1945) **V.S. Pritchett** (1900)
It Should Happen to a Vet (1972) **James Herriot** (1916)
It Takes All Kinds (1939) **Louis Bromfield** (1896)
It's a Battlefield (1934) **Graham Greene** (1904)
It's About Time (1974) **Stephen Gray** (1941)
It's Never Over (1930) **Morley Callaghan** (1903)
It's Not the End of the World (1972) **Judy Blume** (1938)
It's Raining in Mango (1988) **Thea Astley** (1925)
Italian Backgrounds (1905) **Edith Wharton** (1862)
Italian Food (1954) **Elizabeth David** (1913)
Italian Girl, The (1964) **Iris Murdoch** (1919)
Italian Hours (1909) **Henry James** (1843)
Italian Husband, The (1677) **Edward Ravenscroft** (1644)
Italian Journeys (1991) **Jonathan Keates** (1946)
Italian Letters (1784) **William Godwin** (1756)
Italian Painters of the Renaissance, The [prev. 4 titles collected] (1930) **Bernard Berenson** (1865)
Italian Prospect (1976) **Anne Ridler** (1912)
Italian Spring, The (1964) **Gillian Avery** (1926)
Italian Taylor, and his Boy, The (1609) **Robert Armin** (1565?)
Italian, The (1797) **Ann Radcliffe** (1764)
Italian Verses, The (1909) **Aleksandr Blok** (1880)
Italian Visit, An (1953) **C. Day Lewis** (1904)
Italics , The (1848) **Walter Savage Landor** (1775)
Italy (1834) **William Beckford** (1760)
Italy: Part the First (1822) **Samuel Rogers** (1763)
Italy: Part the Second (1828) **Samuel Rogers** (1763)
Item From the Late News, An (1982) **Thea Astley** (1925)
Itinerarium Curiosum (1724) **William Stukeley** (1687)
Itinerary of John Leland the Antiquary, The (1710) **Thomas Hearne** (1678) (ed.)
Ivan Greet's Masterpiece (1893) **Grant Allen** (1848)
Ivanhoe (1820) **Sir Walter Scott** (1771)
Ivanov (1887) **Anton Chekhov** (1860)
Ivory Child, The (1916) **Sir H. Rider Haggard** (1856)
Ivory Gate, The (1892) **Sir Walter Besant** (1836)
Ivory Gate, The (1869) **Mortimer Collins** (1827)
Ivory Tower, The (1917) **Henry James** (1843–1916)
Ivy and Stevie (1971) **Kay Dick** (1915)
Ixion's Wheel (1969) **Ralph Gustafson** (1909)
The Indifferent Ones [*Gli indifferenti*] (1929) **'Alberto Moravia' [Alberto Pincherle]** (1907)

J

'J' is for Judgment (1993) **Sue Grafton** (1940)
Jabez Easterbrook (1890) **Joseph Hocking** (1860)
Jacaranda Tree, The (1949) **H.E. Bates** (1905)
J'accuse [on the Dreyfus affair] (1898) **Émile Zola** (1840–1902)
J'accuse (1982) **Graham Greene** (1904)
Jack (1973) **Anthony Thwaite** (1930)
Jack Adams, the Mutineer (1838) **Captain Chamier** (1796)
Jack and Jill (1880) **Louisa M. Alcott** (1832)
Jack Ashore (1840) **Edward Howard** (1793?)
Jack Be Nimble (1980) **Nigel Williams** (1948)
Jack Brag (1837) **Theodore Hook** (1788)
Jack Hinton, the Guardsman (1845) **Charles Lever** (1806)
Jack Holborn (1964) **Leon Garfield** (1921)
Jack Juggler and the Emperor's Whore (1996) **John Arden** (1930)
Jack Kelso (1928) **Edgar Lee Masters** (1868)
Jack Maggs (1997) **Peter Carey** (1943)
Jack o'Lanthorn (1889) **C[hristabel] R[ose] Coleridge** (1843)
Jack of Diamonds (1988) **Elizabeth Spencer** (1921)
Jack of Eagles (1952) **James Blish** (1921)
Jack Sheppard (1839) **W.H. Ainsworth** (1805)
Jack Straw (1911) **Somerset Maugham** (1874)
Jack Straw's Castle (1976) **Thom Gunn** (1929)
Jack Tier (1848) **James Fenimore Cooper** (1789)
Jackanapes (1883) **Mrs J.H. Ewing** (1841)
Jackdaw Cake (1985) **Norman Lewis** (1918)

Jacke Drums Entertainment (1601) **John Marston** (1576)
Jackets (1989) **Edward Bond** (1934)
Jacklight (1984) **Louise Erdrich** (1954)
Jacko (1993) **Thomas Keneally** (1935)
Jackpine Sonnets (1977) **Milton Acorn** (1923)
Jackpot (1940) **Erskine Caldwell** (1903)
Jackson's Dilemma (1996) **Iris Murdoch** (1919)
Jacob Faithful (1834) **Frederick Marryat** (1792)
Jacob Street Mystery, The [the last 'Dr Thorndyke' novel] (1942) **R. Austin Freeman** (1862)
Jacob's Ladder (1987) **John Williams** (1925)
Jacob's Room (1922) **Virginia Woolf** (1882)
Jacobean Poets, The (1894) **Sir Edmund Gosse** (1849)
Jacquerie, The (1841) **G.P.R. James** (1799)
Jacques (1834) **'George Sand' [Auore Dupin]** (1804)
Jacquetta (1890) **S. Baring-Gould** (1834)
Jade Eye, The (1903) **Fergus Hume** (1859)
Jail Diary of Albee Sachs, The (1978) **David Edgar** (1948)
Jail Journal (1854) **John Mitchel** (1815)
Jailbird (1979) **Kurt Vonnegut** (1922)
Jake's Thing (1978) **Kingsley Amis** (1922)
Jalna (1927) **Mazo de la Roche** (1879)
Jamaica Inn (1936) **Daphne du Maurier** (1907)
James and the Giant Peach (1961) **Roald Dahl** (1916)
James Bond Dossier, The (1965) **Kingsley Amis** (1922)
James Joyce (1959) **Richard Ellmann** (1918)
James Joyce: The Last Journey (1947) **Leon Edel** (1907)
James Merle (1864) **William Black** (1841)
James the Fatalist [*Jacques le fataliste*] (1796) **Denis Diderot** (1713–84)
James, the Red Engine (1948) **Revd W. V. Awdry** (1911)
James the Second (1848) **W.H. Ainsworth** (1805)
James Wallace (1788) **Robert Bage** (1728)
James Without Thomas (1959) **Gillian Avery** (1926)
Jan of the Windwill (1876) **Mrs J.H. Ewing** (1841)
Jan Vedder's Wife (1885) **Amelia Barr** (1831)
Jane (1897) **Marie Corelli** (1855)
Jane and Prudence (1953) **Barbara Pym** (1913)
Jane Annie (1893) **Florence Barclay** (1862)
Jane Clegg (1914) **St John Ervine** (1883)
Jane Eyre (1847) **Charlotte Bronte** (1816)
Jane Field (1893) **Mary Wilkins Freeman** (1852)
Jane of Lantern Hill (1937) **L.M. Montgomery** (1874)
Jane Oglander (1911) **Mrs Belloc Lowndes** (1868)
Jane Seton (1853) **James Grant** (1822)
Jane Talbot (1801) **Charles Brockden Brown** (1771)
Jane Treachel (1899) **Charles Hamilton Aïdé** (1826)
Jane's Career (1914) **H.G. De Lisser** (1878)
Janet March (1923) **Floyd Dell** (1887)
Janey (1985) **Bernard Ashley** (1935)
January Divan, The (1980) **John Fuller** (1937)
Janus (1935) **George Barker** (1913)
Japanese Garland (1928) **Edmund Blunden** (1896)
Japanese Poetry: the 'Uta' (1919) **Arthur Waley** (1889) (tr.)
Japanese Umbrella, The (1964) **Francis King** (1923)
Japhet in Search of a Father (1836) **Frederick Marryat** (1792)
Jar of Honey from Mount Hybla, A (1848) **Leigh Hunt** (1784)
Jardin de Bérénice, Le (1891) **Maurice Barrès** (1862)
Jardín de senderos que se bifurcan, El (1941) **Jorge Luis Borges** (1899)
Jardin sur l'Oronte, Un (1922) **Maurice Barrès** (1862)
Jarwin and Cuffy (1878) **R.M. Ballantyne** (1825)
Jasbo Brown (1931) **DuBose Heyward** (1885)
Jason and Medeia (1973) **John Gardner** (1933)
Jason Edwards (1892) **Hamlin Garland** (1860)
Java Head (1919) **Joseph Hergesheimer** (1880)
Jawbreakers (1963) **Milton Acorn** (1923)
Jaws (1974) **Peter Benchley** (1940)
Jay of Italy, A (1905) **Bernard Capes** (1850?)
Jazz (1992) **Toni Morrison** (1931)
Jazz and Jasper (1928) **William Gerhardie** (1895)
JB (1958) **Archibald MacLeish** (1892)
Jealous God, The (1964) **John Braine** (1922)
Jealous Lovers, The (1632) **Thomas Randolph** (1605)
Jealous Wife, The (1761) **George Colman, the Elder** (1732)
Jean Barois (1913) **Roger Martin du Gard** (1881)
Jean Huguenot (1923) **Stephen Vincent Benét** (1889)
Jean Santeuil (1952) **Marcel Proust** (1871–1922)
Jeanne (1843) **'George Sand' [Auore Dupin]** (1804)
Jeeves and the Feudal Spirit [US: *Bertie Wooster Sees It Through*] (1954) **P.G. Wodehouse** (1881)
Jeeves in the Offing (1960) **P.G. Wodehouse** (1881)
Jeff Briggs's Love Story (1880) **Bret Harte** (1836)
Jeffrey Bernard is Unwell (1989) **Keith Waterhouse** (1929)
Jennie (1950) **Paul Gallico** (1897)
Jennie Baxter, Journalist (1899) **Robert Barr** (1850)
Jennie Gerhardt (1911) **Theodore Dreiser** (1871)
Jennifer (1979) **David Helwig** (1938)
Jennings and Darbishire (1952) **Anthony Buckeridge** (1912)
Jennings' Diary (1953) **Anthony Buckeridge** (1912)
Jennings Follows a Clue (1951) **Anthony Buckeridge** (1912)
Jennings Goes to School (1950) **Anthony Buckeridge** (1912)
Jennings' Little Hut (1951) **Anthony Buckeridge** (1912)
Jenny by Nature (1961) **Erskine Caldwell** (1903)
Jenny Wren (1932) **E.H. Young** (1880)
Jeremy (1919) **Sir Hugh Walpole** (1884)
Jeremy and Hamlet (1923) **Sir Hugh Walpole** (1884)
Jeremy at Crale (1927) **Sir Hugh Walpole** (1884)
Jeremy Taylor (1903) **Sir Edmund Gosse** (1849)
Jeremy's Version (1970) **James Purdy** (1923)
Jero's Metamorphosis (1974) **Wole Soyinka** (1934)
Jerome, a Poor Man (1897) **Mary Wilkins Freeman** (1852)
Jerry of the Islands (1917) **'Jack London' [John Griffith Chaney]** (1876)
Jersey Lily, A (1880) **'Susan Coolidge' [Sarah Chauncy Woolsey]** (1845)

Jerusalem (dated 1804) **William Blake** (1757)
Jerusalem (1969) **Colin Thubron** (1939)
Jerusalem Commands (1992) **Michael Moorcock** (1939)
Jerusalem Sonnets (1970) **James K. Baxter** (1926)
Jerusalem the Golden (1967) **Margaret Drabble** (1939)
Jess (1887) **Sir H. Rider Haggard** (1856)
Jest of God, A [UK: *Now I Lay Me Down*] (1966) **Margaret Laurence** (1926)
Jesting Pilate (1926) **Aldous Huxley** (1894)
Jests to Make You Merie (1607) **Thomas Dekker** (1572?) [with George Wilkins]
Jesus (1992) **A.N. Wilson** (1950)
Jeux son faits, Les [screenplay] (1947) **Jean-Paul Sartre** (1905)
Jew in Love, A (1930) **Ben Hecht** (1894)
Jew in Our Day, The (1944) **Waldo Frank** (1889)
Jew of Arragon, The (1830) **Thomas Wade** (1805)
Jew, The (1794) **Richard Cumberland** (1732)
Jewel in the Crown, The (1966) **Paul Scott** (1920)
Jewel of the Seven Stars, The (1903) **Bram Stoker** (1847)
Jewel-Hinged Jaw, The (1977) **Samuel R. Delany** (1942)
Jewish Faith, The (1846) **Grace Aguilar** (1816)
Jews, The (1922) **Hilaire Belloc** (1870)
Jews, The (1939) **Wyndham Lewis** (1882)
Jews Without Money (1930) **'Michael Gold' [Irwin Granich]** (1893)
Jezebel Mort (1931) **Arthur Symons** (1865)
Jezebel's Daughter (1880) **Wilkie Collins** (1824)
Jig for the Gypsy, A (1954) **Robertson Davies** (1913)
Jig of Forslin, The (1916) **Conrad Potter Aiken** (1889)
Jigsaw (1989) **Sybille Bedford** (1911)
Jill (1946) **Philip Larkin** (1922)
Jilt, The (1884) **Charles Reade** (1814)
Jim and the Beanstalk (1970) **Raymond Briggs** (1934)
Jim and Wally (1916) **Mary Grant Bruce** (1878)
Jim Dandy, Fat Man in a Famine (1947) **William Saroyan** (1908)
Jim Davis (1911) **John Masefield** (1878)
Jimbo (1909) **Algernon Blackwood** (1869)
Jimmie Higgins (1919) **Upton Sinclair** (1878)
Jimmyjohn Boss, The (1900) **Owen Wister** (1860)
Jitterbug Perfume (1984) **Tom Robbins** (1936)
Jizzle (1954) **'John Wyndham' [John Wyndham Harris]** (1903)
J.M. Synge and the Ireland of His Time (1911) **W.B. Yeats** (1865)
Jo's Boys (1886) **Louisa M. Alcott** (1832)
Joan (1876) **Rhoda Broughton** (1840)
Joan and Peter (1918) **H.G. Wells** (1866)
Joan Brotherhood (1900) **Bernard Capes** (1850?)
Joan Haste (1895) **Sir H. Rider Haggard** (1856)
Joan of Arc (1796) **Robert Southey** (1774)
Joan of Arc (1871) **Tom Taylor** (1817)
Joan of Arc (1981) **Marina Warner** (1946)
Joan of Lorraine (1947) **Maxwell Anderson** (1888)
Joan of the Sword Hand (1900) **S.R. Crockett** (1860)
Joanna (1990) **Lisa St Aubin de Terán** (1953)
Joanna Godden (1921) **Sheila Kaye-Smith** (1887)
Joanna Godden Married (1926) **Sheila Kaye-Smith** (1887)
Joanne (1975) **Marian Engel** (1933)
Job Militant (1624) **Francis Quarles** (1592)
Job Rocking (1989) **Benjamin Zephaniah** (1958)
Job, The (1917) **Sinclair Lewis** (1885)
Joby (1964) **Stan Barstow** (1928)
Jocelyn [by 'John Sinjohn'] (1898) **John Galsworthy** (1867)
Jockey's Downfall (1679) **John Phillips** (1631)
Jocoseria (1883) **Robert Browning** (1812)
Johan Johan (1533) **John Heywood** (1497?)
Johanna at Daybreak (1969) **R.C. Hutchinson** (1907)
John Andross (1874) **Rebecca Harding Davis** (1831)
John Balliol (1825) **William Tennant** (1784)
John Barleycorn (1913) **'Jack London' [John Griffith Chaney]** (1876)
John Brent (1862) **Theodore Winthrop** (1826)
John Brown (1909) **W.E.B. Du Bois** (*c.* 1868)
John Brown and the Heroes of Harper's Ferry (1886) **William Ellery Channing** (1780)
John Brown, the Making of a Martyr (1929) **Robert Penn Warren** (1905)
John Brown's Body (1969) **A.L. Barker** (1918)
John Brown's Body (1928) **Stephen Vincent Benét** (1889)
John Bull (1803) **George Colman the Younger** (1762)
John Bull's Other Island, and Major Barbara (1907) **Bernard Shaw** (1856)
John Burnet of Barns (1898) **John Buchan** (1875)
John Caldigate (1879) **Anthony Trollope** (1815)
John Cornelius (1937) **Sir Hugh Walpole** (1884)
John de Lancaster (1809) **Richard Cumberland** (1732)
John Diamond (1980) **Leon Garfield** (1921)
John Deth (1930) **Conrad Potter Aiken** (1889)
John Drayton (1851) **Margaret Oliphant** (1828)
John Eax and Mamelon (1882) **Albion W. Tourgée** (1838)
John Ferguson (1915) **St John Ervine** (1883)
John Gabriel Borkman (1896) **Henrik Ibsen** (1828)
John Godfrey's Fortunes (1864) **Bayard Taylor** (1825)
John Greswold (1864) **Caroline Clive** (1801)
John Halifax, Gentleman (1856) **Dinah Maria Craik** (1826)
John Herring (1883) **S. Baring-Gould** (1834)
John Holdsworth (1875) **W. Clark Russell** (1844)
John in Prison (1912) **Edward Thompson** (1886)
John Ingerfield (1894) **Jerome K. Jerome** (1859)
John Inglesant (1881) **J.H. Shorthouse** (1834)
John Jerome: His Thoughts and Ways (1886) **Jean Ingelow** (1820)
John Keats (1895) **Robert Bridges** (1844)
John Keats (1917) **Sir Sidney Colvin** (1845)
John Keats (1968) **Robert Gittings** (1911)
John Kemp's Wager (1925) **Robert Graves** (1895)

John Knox (1949) **'James Bridie' [Osborne Henry Mavor]** (1888)
John Law (1864) **W.H. Ainsworth** (1805)
John Macnab (1925) **John Buchan** (1875)
John March, Southerner (1894) **George Washington Cable** (1844)
John Marchmont's Legacy (1863) **M.E. Braddon** (1835)
John Marr and Other Sailors (1888) **Herman Melville** (1819)
John Marvel, Assistant (1909) **Thomas Nelson Page** (1853)
John o' the Green (1935) **Jeffery Farnol** (1878)
John of Jingalo (1912) **Laurence Housman** (1865)
John Paul George Ringo . . . and Bert (1974) **Willy Russell** (1947)
John Ploughman's Talks (1869) **Charles Spurgeon** (1834)
John Ploughman's Pictures (1880) **Charles Spurgeon** (1834)
John Ruskin (1902) **Frederic Harrison** (1831)
John Sherman and Dhoya [as 'Ganconagh'] (1891) **W.B. Yeats** (1865)
John Silence (1908) **Algernon Blackwood** (1869)
John the Baptist's Preaching (1547) **John Bale** (1495)
John Thorndyke's Cases [US: *Dr Thorndyke's Cases*] (1909) **R. Austin Freeman** (1862)
John Vale's Guardian (1890) **David Christie Murray** (1847)
John Webb's End (1891) **Francis Adams** (1862)
John Webster and the Elizabethan Drama (1916) **Rupert Brooke** (1887–1915)
John Whiting on Theatre (1966) **John Whiting** (1917–1963)
John Woodvil (1802) **Charles Lamb** (1775)
Johnnie Courteau (1901) **William Henry Drummond** (1854)
Johnnie, I Hardly Knew You [US: *I Hardly Knew You*] (1977) **Edna O'Brien** (1932)
Johnnie Sahib (1952) **Paul Scott** (1920)
Johnno (1975) **David Malouf** (1934)
Johnny Alleluia (1961) **Charles Causley** (1917)
Johnny Appleseed (1928) **Vachel Lindsay** (1879)
Johnny Bear (1927) **Ernest Thompson Seton** (1860)
Johnny Crackle Sings (1971) **Matt Cohen** (1942)
Johnny Gibb of Gushetneuk (1871) **William Alexander** (1826)
Johnny Johnson (1937) **Paul Green** (1894) [with Kurt Weill]
Johnny Ludlow [1st ser.] (1874) **Mrs Henry Wood** (1814)
Johnny Panic and the Bible of Dreams, and Other Prose Writings (1977) **Sylvia Plath** (1932–63)
Joining Charles (1929) **Elizabeth Bowen** (1899)
Joke, The (1967) **Milan Kundera** (1929)
Jolly Postman, The (1986) **Alan Ahlberg** (1938)
Jonah (1911) **Louis Stone** (1871)
Jonah, The (1981) **James Herbert** (1943)
Jonah and Co. (1922) **'Dornford Yates' [Cecil William Mercer]** (1885)
Jonah's Gourd Vine (1934) **Zora Neale Hurston** (1903)
Jonathan Swift (1998) **Victoria Glendinning** (1937)
Jorkens Borrows Another Whiskey (1954) **Lord Dunsany** (1878)
Jorkens Remembers Africa (1934) **Lord Dunsany** (1878)
Jorrocks' Jaunts and Jollities (1838) **R.S. Surtees** (1805)
Joseph and his Brothers [*Joseph und seine Brüder*; tetralogy] (1933–42) **Thomas Mann** (1875)
Joseph and His Friend (1870) **Bayard Taylor** (1825)
Joseph Balsamo (1846–8) **Alexandre Dumas ['père']** (1802)
Joseph in Jeopardy (1912) **'Frank Danby' [Julia Frankau]** (1864)
Joseph Rushbrook (1841) **Frederick Marryat** (1792)
Joseph Vance (1906) **William De Morgan** (1839)
Joseph's Coat (1881) **David Christie Murray** (1847)
Joseph's Party-coloured Coat (1640) **Thomas Fuller** (1608)
Joshua Haggard's Daughter (1876) **M.E. Braddon** (1835)
Joshua Marvel (1871) **B.L. Farjeon** (1838)
Joshua Then and Now (1980) **Mordecai Richler** (1931)
Journal, A (1694) **George Fox** (1624–91)
Journal (1739–91) **John Wesley** (1703)
Journal (1835) **Frances [Fanny] Kemble** (1809)
Journal (1849) **Charles Wesley** (1707–88)
Journal (1927) **'Katherine Mansfield' [Kathleen Mansfield Beauchamp]** (1888)
Journal, 1929 (1930) **Arnold Bennett** (1867)
Journal 1936–1937 (1980) **David Gascoyne** (1916)
Journal During a Residence in France, A (1792) **John Moore** (1729)
Journal Kept in Turkey and Greece, A (1859) **Nassau Senior** (1790)
Journal of a Disappointed Man, The (1919) **'W.N.P. Barbellion' [Bruce Frederick Cumming]** (1889)
Journal of a Landscape Painter in Corsica (1870) **Edward Lear** (1812)
Journal of a Residence at the Cape of Good Hope (1840) **Lady Anne Barnard** (1750–1825)
Journal of a Tour Through the Netherlands to Paris (1822) **Marguerite, Countess of Blessington** (1789)
Journal of a Tour to the Hebrides with Samuel Johnson, The (1785) **James Boswell** (1740)
Journal of a Voyage to Lisbon, The (1755) **Henry Fielding** (1707–54)
Journal of Arthur Stirling, The (1903) **Upton Sinclair** (1878)
Journal of Researches into Geology and Natural History (1839) **Charles Darwin** (1809)
Journal of the Discovery of the Source of the Nile (1863) **John Hanning Speke** (1827)
Journal of the Fictive Life (1966) **Howard Nemerov** (1920)
Journal of the Heart (1830) **Lady Charlotte Bury** (1775)

Journal of the Plague Year, A (1722) **Daniel Defoe** (1660)
Journal of the Reign of King George the Third (1859) **Horace Walpole** (1717–97)
Journal Under the Terror 1938 (1938) **F.L. Lucas** (1894)
Journalism for Women (1898) **Arnold Bennett** (1867)
Journals (1966–83) **Anaïs Nin** (1903)
Journals (1977) **Allen Ginsberg** (1926)
Journals, 1982–1986 (1995) **Anthony Powell** (1905)
Journals (1982) **Sylvia Plath** (1932–63)
Journals of a Landscape Painter in Albania, Illyria (1851) **Edward Lear** (1812)
Journals of a Landscape Painter in S. Calabria (1852) **Edward Lear** (1812)
Journals of Susanna Moodie, The (1970) **Margaret Atwood** (1939)
Journey, The (1931) **Yvor Winters** (1900)
Journey Among the Dead (1981) **Eugène Ionesco** (1909)
Journey Due North, A (1858) **George Augustus Sala** (1828)
Journey From the North (1969) **Storm Jameson** (1897)
Journey in the Dark (1943) **Martin Flavin** (1883)
Journey into Fear (1940) **Eric Ambler** (1909)
Journey into Russia (1964) **Sir Laurens van der Post** (1906)
Journey Made in the Summer of 1794, A (1795) **Ann Radcliffe** (1764)
Journey Not the Arrival Matters, The (1969) **Leonard Woolf** (1880)
Journey of the Magi (1927) **T.S. Eliot** (1888)
Journey, The (1986) **Eavan Boland** (1944)
Journey Through Economic Time, A (1994) **J.K. Galbraith** (1908)
Journey Through Persia, Armenia and Asia Minor , A (1812) **James Morier** (1780)
Journey Through the War Mind (1940) **C.E.M. Joad** (1891)
Journey Through Tomorrow (1947) **George Johnston** (1912)
Journey to a War (1939) **Christopher Isherwood** (1904) [with W.H. Auden]
Journey to Central Africa, A (1854) **Bayard Taylor** (1825)
Journey to Ithaca (1995) **Anita Desai** (1937)
Journey to Jerusalem (1940) **Maxwell Anderson** (1888)
Journey to Khatmandu, A (1852) **Laurence Oliphant** (1829)
Journey to Love (1955) **William Carlos Williams** (1883)
Journey to the Border (1938) **Edward Upward** (1903)
Journey to the Centre of the Earth, A [*Voyage au centre de la terre*] (1864) **Jules Verne** (1828)
Journey to the End of Night [*Voyage au bout de la nuit*] (1932) **'Louis-Ferdinand Céline' [L.F. Destouches]** (1894)
Journey to the Ends of Time (1959) **Sir Sacheverell Sitwell** (1897)
Journey to the Interior, A (1945) **P.H. Newby** (1918)
Journey to the Western Islands of Scotland, A (1775) **Samuel Johnson** (1709)
Journey Without Maps (1936) **Graham Greene** (1904)
Journey's End (1928) **R.C. Sherriff** (1896) [novelized, with V. Bartlett, 1930]
Journeyman (1935) **Erskine Caldwell** (1903)
Journeys (1982) **Dorothy Hewett** (1923)
Journeys and Places (1937) **Edwin Muir** (1887)
Journeys Between Wars (1938) **John Dos Passos** (1896)
Journeys of Celia Fiennes, The [definitive edition, ed. Christopher Morris] (1947) **Celia Fiennes** (1662–1741)
Jovial Crew, A (1652) **Richard Brome** (1590?)
Joy in Tribulation (1632) **Phineas Fletcher** (1582)
Joy Luck Club, The (1989) **Amy Tan** (1952)
Joy of Sex, The (1972) **Alex Comfort** (1920)
Joy of the Worm (1969) **Frank Sargeson** (1903)
Joy-Ride and After, The (1963) **A.L. Barker** (1918)
Joyful Wisdom, The [*Die Fröliche Wissenschaft*] (1882) **Friedrich Wilhelm Nietzsche** (1844)
Joyous Gard (1913) **A.C. Benson** (1862)
Joyous Miracle, The (1906) **Frank Norris** (1870)
Joys of Motherhood, The (1979) **Buchi Emecheta** (1944)
Joys of Yiddish, The (1968) **Leo Rosten** (1908)
Joysprick (1973) **'Anthony Burgess' [John Anthony Burgess Wilson]** (1917)
JR (1976) **William Gaddis** (1922)
Juan in America (1931) **Eric Linklater** (1899)
Juan in China (1937) **Eric Linklater** (1899)
Jubilation (1995) **Charles Tomlinson** (1927)
Jud Süss (1925) **Lion Feuchtwanger** (1884)
Judah (1890) **Henry Arthur Jones** (1851)
Judas Boy, The (1968) **Simon Raven** (1927)
Judas Cloth, The (1992) **Julia O'Faolain** (1932)
Judas Country (1975) **Gavin Lyall** (1932)
Judas de Jésus, Le ['Jesus' Judas'] (1927) **Henri Barbusse** (1873)
Judas Factor, The (1984) **Ted Allbeury** (1917)
Judas Goat, The (1978) **Robert B. Parker** (1932)
Judas Iscariot (1848) **R.H. Horne** (1803)
Judas Kiss, The (1998) **David Hare** (1947)
Judas, My Brother (1968) **Frank Yerby** (1916)
Judas Tree, The (1961) **A.J. Cronin** (1896)
Judas Window, The [as 'Carter Dickson'; US: *The Crossbow Murder*] (1938) **John Dickson Carr** (1906)
Jude the Obscure (1896) **Thomas Hardy** (1840)
Judge, The (1922) **'Rebecca West' [Cicily Isabel Andrews]** (1892)
Judge's Story, The (1947) **Charles Morgan** (1894)
Judgement Books, The (1895) **E.F. Benson** (1867)
Judgement Day (1980) **Penelope Lively** (1933)
Judgement in Stone, A (1977) **Ruth Rendell** (1930)
Judgement of Dr Johnson, The (1927) **G.K. Chesterton** (1874)
Judgement of Eve, The (1914) **May Sinclair** (1863)
Judgement on Deltchev (1951) **Eric Ambler** (1909)
Judgment Day (1934) **Elmer Rice** (1892)

Judgment of Deke Hunter, The (1976) **George V. Higgins** (1939)
Judgment of Hercules, The (1741) **William Shenstone** (1714)
Judgment of Paris, The (1765) **James Beattie** (1735)
Judgment of Paris, The [rev. 1965] (1952) **Gore Vidal** (1925)
Judicious and Select Essayes (1650) **Sir Walter Ralegh** (1554–1618)
Judith (1574) **Guillaume de Salluste Du Bartas** (1544)
Judith (1931) **Jean Giraudoux** (1882)
Judith (1974) **James T. Farrell** (1904)
Judith (1986) **Nicholas Mosley** (1923)
Judith and Holofernes (1896) **Thomas Bailey Aldrich** (1836)
Judith Hearne [US: *The Lonely Passion of Judith Hearne*] (1955) **Brian Moore** (1921)
Judith Paris (1931) **Sir Hugh Walpole** (1884)
Judith Shakespeare (1884) **William Black** (1841)
Juggernaut (1891) **George Cary Eggleston** (1839)
Juggernaut (1911) **E.F. Benson** (1867)
Juggling (1994) **Barbara Trapido** (1941)
Jugurthine War (1520) **Alexander Barclay** (1475?) (tr.)
Juif errant, Le ['The Wandering Jew'] (1845) **Eugène Sue** (1804)
Julia (1790) **Helen Maria Williams** (1762)
Julia de Roubigné (1777) **Henry Mackenzie** (1745)
Julia France and Her Times (1912) **Gertrude Atherton** (1857)
Julian (1823) **Mary Russell Mitford** (1787)
Julian (1964) **Gore Vidal** (1925)
Julian and Agnes (1800) **William Sotheby** (1757)
Julian Home (1859) **Frederic W. Farrar** (1831)
Juliana (1671) **John Crowne** (d. 1703)
Julie de Carneilhan (1941) **Colette** (1873)
Julie; or, The New Eloise [*Julie; ou la Nouvelle Héloïse*] (1761) **Jean-Jacques Rousseau** (1712)
Juliet Grenville (1774) **Henry Brooke** (1703)
Juliette (1798) **Marquis de Sade** (1740)
July's People (1981) **Nadine Gordimer** (1923)
Jumbo Afloat (1966) **Helen Cresswell** (1934)
Jumbo and the Big Dig (1968) **Helen Cresswell** (1934)
Jumbo Back to Nature (1965) **Helen Cresswell** (1934)
Jumbo Spencer (1963) **Helen Cresswell** (1934)
Jumpers (1972) **Tom Stoppard** (1937)
Jumping Joan (1954) **C.H.B. Kitchin** (1895)
Jumping the Queue (1983) **'Mary Wesley' [Mary Wellesley]** (1912)
June 30th, June 30th (1978) **Richard Brautigan** (1935)
Jung and the Story of Our Time (1975) **Sir Laurens van der Post** (1906)
Jungle, The (1906) **Upton Sinclair** (1878)
Jungle Book, The (1894) **Rudyard Kipling** (1865)
Junior Bachelor Society, The (1976) **John Williams** (1925)
Juniper Lecture, A (1639) **John Taylor** (1580)
Junius: Stat Nominis Umbra (1772) **'Junius' [probably Sir Philip Francis]** (1740)
Junkie (1953) **William S. Burroughs** (1914)
Juno and the Paycock [with *The Shadow of a Gunman*, 1923] (1924) **Sean O'Casey** (1880)
Jurassic Park (1990) **Michael Crichton** (1942)
Jure Divino (1706) **Daniel Defoe** (1660)
Jurgen (1919) **James Branch Cabell** (1879)
Jury, The (1927) **Eden Phillpotts** (1862)
Just Above My Head (1979) **James Baldwin** (1924)
Just and the Unjust, The (1942) **James Gould Cozzens** (1903)
Just as I Am (1880) **M.E. Braddon** (1835)
Just Give Me a Cool Drink of Water 'fore I Die (1971) **Maya Angelou** (1928)
Just Italian, The (1630) **Sir William Davenant** (1606)
Just Let Me Go [repub. 1990 as *You, the Jury*] (1950) **Jon Cleary** (1917)
Just Like a Lady (1960) **Nina Bawden** (1925)
Just Like the Resurrection (1967) **Patricia Beer** (1924)
Just Looking (1989) **John Updike** (1932)
Just Man's Funeral, The (1649) **Thomas Fuller** (1608)
Just Out of College (1905) **George Ade** (1866)
Just Relations (1982) **Rodney Hall** (1935)
Just So Stories (1902) **Rudyard Kipling** (1865)
Just to Get Married (1911) **Cicely Mary Hamilton** (1872)
Just Wild About Harry (1963) **Henry Miller** (1891)
Just—William (1922) **'Richmal Crompton' [Richmal Crompton Lamburn]** (1890)
Just You Wait and See (1986) **Stan Barstow** (1928)
Justice (1910) **John Galsworthy** (1867)
Justice and Liberty (1908) **Goldsworthy Lowes Dickinson** (1862)
Justin Bayard [also titled *Dust in the Sun*] (1955) **Jon Cleary** (1917)
Justine (1957) **Lawrence Durrell** (1912)
Justine [*Justine; ou, les Malheurs de la vertu*] (1791) **Marquis de Sade** (1740)
Justine's Lovers (1878) **John W. de Forest** (1826)
Juvenilia (1633) **John Donne** (1572–1631)

K

'K' is for Killer (1994) **Sue Grafton** (1940)
Ka of Gifford Hillary, The (1956) **Dennis Wheatley** (1897)
Kai Lung Beneath the Mulberry Tree (1940) **Ernest Bramah** (1868)
Kail Lung Unrolls His Mat (1928) **Ernest Bramah** (1868)
Kalki (1978) **Gore Vidal** (1925)
Kandy-Kolored Tangerine Flake Streamline Baby, The (1966) **Tom Wolfe** (1930)
Kane and Abel (1979) **Jeffrey Archer** (1940)
Kangaroo (1923) **D.H. Lawrence** (1885)
Kanthapura (1938) **Raja Rao** (1908)
Kapiti (1972) **Alistair Campbell** (1925)
Karl Marx (1934) **E.H. Carr** (1892)
Karl Marx (1939) **Sir Isaiah Berlin** (1909)
Karl of Erbach (1903) **H.C. Bailey** (1878)

Kate and Emma (1964) **Monica Dickens** (1915)
Kate Beaumont (1872) **John W. de Forest** (1826)
Kate Coventry (1856) **G.J. Whyte-Melville** (1821)
Kate Fennigate (1943) **Booth Tarkington** (1869)
Kate Hannigan (1950) **Catherine Cookson** (1906)
Kate Vernon (1854) **Mrs A.H. Alexander** (1825)
Katerfelto (1875) **G.J. Whyte-Melville** (1821)
Katerina Brac (1985) **Christopher Reid** (1949)
Katharine Frensham (1903) **Beatrice Harraden** (1864)
Katharine Regina (1887) **Sir Walter Besant** (1836)
Katharine Walton (1851) **William Gilmore Simms** (1806)
Katherine Mansfield, and Other Literary Portraits (1949) **John Middleton Murry** (1889)
Kathy Goes to Haiti (1978) **Kathy Acker** (1948)
Katie Mulholland (1967) **Catherine Cookson** (1906)
Katie Stewart (1852) **Margaret Oliphant** (1828)
Kavanagh (1849) **Henry Wadsworth Longfellow** (1807)
Kaywana Blood [repub. as *The Old Blood*, 1958] (1958) **Edgar Mittelholzer** (1909)
Keats [*English Men of Letters* series] (1887) **Sidney Colvin** (1845)
Keats (1997) **Andrew Motion** (1952)
Keats and Embarrassment (1974) **Christopher Ricks** (1933)
Keats and Shakespeare (1925) **John Middleton Murry** (1889)
Keep Cool (1817) **John Neal** (1793)
Keep It Crisp (1946) **S.J. Perelman** (1904)
Keep the Aspidistra Flying (1936) **George Orwell** (1903)
Keeper of the Door, The (1915) **Ethel M. Dell** (1881)
Keepers of the Flame (1992) **Ian Hamilton** (1938)
Keepers of the House, The (1964) **Shirley Ann Grau** (1929)
Keepers of the House, The (1982) **Lisa St Aubin de Terán** (1953)
Keepers of the House, The (1987) **George Mackay Brown** (1921)
Keepers of the People, The (1898) **Edgar Jepson** (1863)
Keeping Henry (1988) **Nina Bawden** (1925)
Kehinde (1994) **Buchi Emecheta** (1944)
Keir Hardie (1967) **Kenneth O. Morgan** (1934)
Kelleys and the O'Kellys, The (1848) **Anthony Trollope** (1815)
Kemps Nine Daies Wonder (1600) **William Kemp** (fl.1600)
Kenelm Chillingly (1873) **Edward Bulwer-Lytton** (1803)
Kenilworth (1821) **Sir Walter Scott** (1771)
Kennedy for the Defense (1980) **George V. Higgins** (1939)
Kenny's Window (1956) **Maurice Sendak** (1928)
Kensington Garden (1722) **Thomas Tickell** (1686)
Kensington Mass, The (1975) **David Jones** (1895)
Kensington Notebook, A (1984) **Derek Mahon** (1941)
Kentish Worthies, The (1701) **Nahum Tate** (1652)
Kentucky Cardinal, A (1894) **James Lane Allen** (1849)
Kentucky Warbler, The (1918) **James Lane Allen** (1849)
Kepler (1981) **John Banville** (1945)
Kept (1925) **Alec Waugh** (1898)
Kept in the Dark (1882) **Anthony Trollope** (1815)
Kéramos (1878) **Henry Wadsworth Longfellow** (1807)
Kerrigan's Quality (1894) **Jane Barlow** (1857)
Kestrel for a Knave, A [repub. 1974 as *Kes*; film 1974] (1968) **Barry Hines** (1939)
Kewpie Doll (1984) **Barbara Hanrahan** (1939)
Key Largo (1939) **Maxwell Anderson** (1888)
Key to My Heart, The (1963) **V.S. Pritchett** (1900)
Key to Rebecca, The (1980) **Ken Follett** (1949)
Key to the Door (1961) **Alan Sillitoe** (1928)
Key to Uncle Tom's Cabin, A (1853) **Harriet Beecher Stowe** (1811)
Keynotes (1893) **'George Egerton' [Mary Chavelita Dunne]** (1859)
Keys of the Kingdom, The (1942) **A.J. Cronin** (1896)
Keys to the Street, The (1996) **Ruth Rendell** (1930)
Keziah (1967) **Sue Grafton** (1940)
Kickleburys on the Rhine, The [as 'M.A. Titmarsh'] (1850) **W.M. Thackeray** (1811)
Kicks (1994) **Jeremy Reed** (1954)
Kid (1992) **Simon Armitage** (1963)
Kid, The (1947) **Conrad Potter Aiken** (1889)
Kidnapped (1886) **Robert Louis Stevenson** (1850)
Kidnapper, The (1954) **Robert Bloch** (1917)
Killer, The (1958) **Eugène Ionesco** (1909)
Killer and the Slain, The (1942) **Sir Hugh Walpole** (1884)
Killer Inside Me, The (1952) **Jim Thompson** (1906)
Killer Mine (1947) **'Hammond Innes' [Ralph Hammond-Innes]** (1913)
Killing Bottle, The (1932) **L.P. Hartley** (1895)
Killing for Company (1985) **Brian Masters** (1939)
Killing of Sister George, The (1965) **Frank Marcus** (1928)
Killing Orders (1985) **Sara Paretsky** (1947)
Killing Time (1967) **Thomas Berger** (1924)
Killing Time (1999) **Simon Armitage** (1963)
The Killjoy (1986) **Anne Fine** (1947)
Killshot (1989) **Elmore Leonard** (1925)
Kilmeny (1870) **William Black** (1841)
Kim (1901) **Rudyard Kipling** (1865)
Kind Harts Dreame (1593) **Henry Chettle** (1560?)
Kind Keeper, The (1678) **John Dryden** (1631)
Kind of Alaska, A (1982) **Harold Pinter** (1930)
Kind of Anger, A (1964) **Eric Ambler** (1909)
Kind of Homecoming, A (1962) **E.R. Braithwaite** (1912)
Kind of Loving, A (1960) **Stan Barstow** (1928)
Kind of Poetry I Want, The (1961) **'Hugh MacDiarmid' [Christopher Murray Grieve]** (1892)
Kind of Wild Justice, A (1978) **Bernard Ashley** (1935)
Kindly Light (1979) **A.N. Wilson** (1950)
Kindly Ones, The (1962) **Anthony Powell** (1905)
Kindness Cup, A (1974) **Thea Astley** (1925)
Kindness in a Corner (1930) **T.F. Powys** (1875)

Kindness of Women, The (1991) **J.G. Ballard** (1930)
Kindred of the Wild, The (1902) **Sir Charles G.D. Roberts** (1860)
Kinds of Affection (1967) **Josephine Miles** (1911)
Kinflicks (1976) **Lisa Alther** (1944)
Kinfolk (1949) **Pearl S. Buck** (1892)
King (1999) **John Berger** (1926)
King Alfred (1937) **Ralph Gustafson** (1909)
King and Joker (1976) **Peter Dickinson** (1927)
King and No King, A (1619) **Francis Beaumont** (1585?–1616) [with John Fletcher]
King Arthur (1697) **Sir Richard Blackmore** (1654)
King Arthur (1849) **Edward Bulwer-Lytton** (1803)
King Arthur (1886) **Dinah Maria Craik** (1826)
King Arthur (1691) **John Dryden** (1631)
King Caliban (1978) **John Wain** (1925)
King Coal (1917) **Upton Sinclair** (1878)
King Coffin (1935) **Conrad Potter Aiken** (1889)
King Cole (1923) **John Masefield** (1878)
King David (1923) **Stephen Vincent Benét** (1889)
King David (1995) **Allan Massie** (1938)
King Dobbs (1849) **James Hannay** (1827)
King Edgar and Alfreda (1677) **Edward Ravenscroft** (1644)
King Edward the Fourth (1599) **Thomas Heywood** (1574?)
King Edward VII: A Biography [vol. i only] (1925) **Sir Sidney Lee** (1859)
King Edward VIII (1990) **Philip Ziegler** (1929)
King in Prussia (1944) **Rafael Sabatini** (1875)
King Jasper (1935) **Edwin Arlington Robinson** (1869)
King Jesus (1946) **Robert Graves** (1895)
King Lear (1608) **William Shakespeare** (1564)
King Liveth, The (1943) **Jeffery Farnol** (1878)
King Log (1968) **Geoffrey Hill** (1932)
King Ludd (1988) **Andrew Sinclair** (1935)
King Must Die, The (1958) **'Mary Renault' [Eileen Mary Challans]** (1905)
King of a Rainy Country, The (1956) **Brigid Brophy** (1929)
King of Alsander, The (1914) **James Elroy Flecker** (1884)
King of Britain's Daughter, The (1993) **Gillian Clarke** (1937)
King of Circumstance (1898) **Edwin Pugh** (1874)
King of Elfland's Daughter, The (1924) **Lord Dunsany** (1878)
King of Folly Island, The (1888) **Sarah Orne Jewett** (1849)
King of Ireland's Son, The (1916) **Padraic Colum** (1881)
King of Nowhere, The (1938) **'James Bridie' [Osborne Henry Mavor]** (1888)
King of Schnorrers, The (1894) **Israel Zangwill** (1864)
King of the City (2000) **Michael Moorcock** (1939)
King of the Dark Chamber, The (1914) **Rabindranath Tagore** (1861)
King of the Golden River, The (1851) **John Ruskin** (1819)
King of the Great Clock Tower, The (1934) **W.B. Yeats** (1865)
King of the Rainy Country, The (1966) **Nicholas Freeling** (1927)
King of the Two Lands (1966) **Jacquetta Hawkes** (1910)
King Poppy (1892) **Edward Robert Bulwer Lytton** (1831–91)
King, Queen, Knave (1968) **Vladimir Nabokov** (1899)
King Rat (1962) **James Clavell** (1924)
King Solomon's Mines (1885) **Sir H. Rider Haggard** (1856)
King Stephen's Watch (1782) **William Mason** (1724)
King, The (1990) **Donald Barthelme** (1931–89)
King Torrismond [Il Re Torrismondo] (1586) **Torquato Tasso** (1544)
King Was in his Counting House, The (1938) **James Branch Cabell** (1879)
King With Two Faces, The (1897) **M.E. Coleridge** (1861)
King's Achievement, The (1905) **R.H. Benson** (1871)
King's Daughter, A (1923) **John Masefield** (1878)
King's Daughters, The (1998) **Arnold Wesker** (1932)
King's English, The (1906) **H.W. Fowler** (1858) and **F.G. Fowler** (1870)
King's Evil, The (1981) **David Helwig** (1938)
King's General, The (1946) **Daphne du Maurier** (1907)
King's Indian, The (1974) **John Gardner** (1933)
King's Jackal, The (1898) **Richard Harding Davis** (1864)
King's Own, The (1830) **Frederick Marryat** (1792)
King's Peace, The (1955) **C.V. Wedgwood** (1910)
King's Rival, The (1854) **Charles Reade** (1814) [with Tom Taylor]
King's Threshold, The; On Baile's Strand [Plays for an Irish Theatre vol. iii] (1904) **W.B. Yeats** (1865)
King's War, The (1958) **C.V. Wedgwood** (1910)
Kingdom, A (1978) **James Hanley** (1901)
Kingdom by the Sea, The (1983) **Paul Theroux** (1941)
Kingdom by the Sea, The (1992) **Robert Westall** (1929)
Kingdom Come (1980) **Melvyn Bragg** (1939)
Kingdom Come (1990) **Bernice Rubens** (1923)
Kingdom of Christ, The (1838) **F.D. Maurice** (1805)
Kingdom of Earth (1968) **'Tennessee' [Thomas Lanier] Williams** (1911)
Kingdom of Evil, The (1924) **Ben Hecht** (1894)
Kingdom of God is Within You, The (1893–4) **Leo Tolstoy** (1828)
Kingdom of the Blind, The (1917) **E. Phillips Oppenheim** (1866)
Kingdom of the Wicked, The (1985) **'Anthony Burgess' [John Anthony Burgess Wilson]** (1917)
Kingdom of Twilight, The (1904) **Forrest Reid** (1875)
Kingdoms for Horses (1936) **James Evershed Agate** (1877)
Kingdoms of Elfin (1977) **Sylvia Townsend Warner** (1893)

Kingfisher, The (1977) **William Douglas Home** (1912)
Kingfisher, The (1983) **Amy Clampitt** (1920)
Kings (1990) **Christopher Logue** (1926)
Kings and the Moon (1938) **James Stephens** (1882)
Kings in Exile (1910) **Sir Charles G.D. Roberts** (1860)
Kings of Infinite Space (1967) **Nigel Balchin** (1908)
Kings Prophecie, The (1603) **Joseph Hall** (1574)
Kingsblood Royal (1947) **Sinclair Lewis** (1885)
Kinsmen, The [rev. as The Scout, 1854] (1841) **William Gilmore Simms** (1806)
Kipps (1905) **H.G. Wells** (1866)
Kirsteen (1890) **Margaret Oliphant** (1828)
Kiss Before Dying, A (1953) **Ira Levin** (1929)
Kiss Kiss (1960) **Roald Dahl** (1916)
Kiss Me, Deadly (1952) **Mickey Spillane** (1918)
Kisses for Mayakovsky (1984) **Alison Fell** (1944)
Kisses of the Enemy (1987) **Rodney Hall** (1935)
Kissing the Gunner's Daughter (1992) **Ruth Rendell** (1930)
Kissing the Rod (1866) **Edmund Yates** (1831)
Kit and Kitty (1889) **R.D. Blackmore** (1825)
Kit Bam's Adventures (1849) **Mary Cowden Clarke** (1809)
Kit Brandon (1936) **Sherwood Anderson** (1876)
Kit Kennedy (1899) **S.R. Crockett** (1860)
Kit-Cats, The (1708) **Sir Richard Blackmore** (1654)
Kitchen Fugue (1945) **Sheila Kaye-Smith** (1887)
Kitchen Poems (1968) **J.H. Prynne** (1936)
Kitchen-God's Wife, The (1991) **Amy Tan** (1952)
Kite, The (1962) **W.O. Mitchell** (1914)
Kith and Kin (1881) **Jessie Fothergill** (1851)
Kitty (1869) **Matilda Betham-Edwards** (1836)
Kitty Alone (1894) **S. Baring-Gould** (1834)
Kitty and Virgil (1998) **Paul Bailey** (1937)
Kitty Costello (1904) **Mrs A.H. Alexander** (1825)
Kitty Tailleur (1908) **May Sinclair** (1863)
Klosterheim (1832) **Thomas de Quincey** (1785)
Knack, The (1961) **Anne Jellicoe** (1927)
Knave of Diamonds, The (1913) **Ethel M. Dell** (1881)
Kneel to the Rising Sun (1935) **Erskine Caldwell** (1903)
Knickerbocker Holiday [music by Kurt Weill] (1938) **Maxwell Anderson** (1888)
Knife of the Times, The (1932) **William Carlos Williams** (1883)
Knight of Gwynne, The (1847) **Charles Lever** (1806)
Knight of Olmedo, The [*El caballero de Olmedo*; written 1620–5] (1641) **Lope de Vega** (1562–1635)
Knight of Spain, A (1913) **'Marjorie Bowen' [Gabrielle Margaret Vere Campbell]** (1886)
Knight of St John, The (1817) **Anna Maria Porter** (1780)
Knight of the Burning Pestle, The (1613) **Francis Beaumont** (1585?) [with John Fletcher]
Knight of the Nets, A (1896) **Amelia Barr** (1831)
Knight on Wheels, A (1914) **'Ian Hay' [John Hay Beith]** (1876)
Knight's Fee (1960) **Rosemary Sutcliff** (1920)
Knight's Gambit (1949) **William Faulkner** (1897)
Knightly Quest, The (1966) **'Tennessee' [Thomas Lanier] Williams** (1911)
Knights and Dragons (1965) **Elizabeth Spencer** (1921)
Knights Conjuring, A (1607) **Thomas Dekker** (1572?)
Knights, The (424BC) **Aristophanes** (*c.* 445BC)
Knights, The (1808) **R.C. Dallas** (1754)
Knot, The (1990) **Ruth Fainlight** (1931)
Knot, The (1996) **Eva Figes** (1932)
Knots (1970) **R.D. Laing** (1927)
Knots and Crosses (1987) **Ian Rankin** (1960)
Knowing My Place (1971) **Paul Muldoon** (1951)
Knowledge of Angels (1994) **Jill Paton Walsh** (1937)
Knuckle (1974) **David Hare** (1947)
Knulp (1915) **Hermann Hesse** (1877)
Ko (1959) **Kenneth Koch** (1925)
Koko (1988) **Peter Straub** (1943)
Komagata Man Incident, The (1978) **Sharon Pollock** (1936)
Konek Landing (1969) **Eva Figes** (1932)
Kongi's Harvest (1964) **Wole Soyinka** (1934)
Konigsmark (1938) **A.E.W. Mason** (1865)
Konovalov (1903) **Maxim Gorky** (1868)
Kora in Hell [prose poems] (1920) **William Carlos Williams** (1883)
Korsoniloff (1969) **Matt Cohen** (1942)
Krag, the Kootenay Ram (1929) **Ernest Thompson Seton** (1860)
Kraken Wakes, The (1953) **'John Wyndham' [John Wyndham Harris]** (1903)
Krapp's Last Tape; Embers (1959) **Samuel Beckett** (1906)
Krazy Kat (1987) **Jay Cantor** (1948)
Kreutzer Sonata, The (1889) **Leo Tolstoy** (1828)
Krindlesdyke (1922) **Wilfrid Gibson** (1878)
Kronstadt (1898) **Max Pemberton** (1863)
Kruger's Alp (1984) **Christopher Hope** (1944)
Kumquat for John Keats, A (1981) **Tony Harrison** (1937)

L

'L' is for Lawless (1996) **Sue Grafton** (1940)
Là-bas (1891) **J.K. Huysmans** (1848)
Labor and Genius (1768) **Richard Jago** (1715)
Laboratories of the Spirit (1975) **R.S. Thomas** (1913)
Laboryouse Journey and Serche of Johan Leylande, The (1549) **John Leland** (1506?)
Labour and the Popular Welfare (1893) **W.H. Mallock** (1849)
Labour in Power, 1945–1951 (1984) **Kenneth O. Morgan** (1934)
Labour Leader, The (1920) **Daniel Corkery** (1878)
Labour People (1987) **Kenneth O. Morgan** (1934)
Labouring Life, The (1932) **Henry Williamson** (1895)
Labouring Men (1964) **Eric Hobsbaum** (1917)
Labours of Idleness, The [as 'Guy Penseval'] (1826) **George Darley** (1795)
Laburnum Grove (1933) **J.B. Priestley** (1894)
Laburnum Tree, The (1935) **James Laver** (1899)

Labyrinth, The (1949) **Edwin Muir** (1887)
Lachrymae Musarum (1892) **Sir William Watson** (1858)
LAConfidential (1990) **James Ellroy** (1948)
Lacquer Lady, The (1929) **F. Tennyson Jesse** (1888)
Ladder of Years (1995) **Anne Tyler** (1941)
Ladders to Fire (1946) **Anaïs Nin** (1903)
Ladies and Gentlemen (1932) **Hilaire Belloc** (1870)
Ladies and Gentlemen (1939) **Ben Hecht** (1894) [with Charles MacArthur]
Ladies' Gallery, The (1888) **Justin McCarthy** (1830) [with Mrs Campbell Praed]
Ladies' Paradise, The [*Au bonheur des dames*] (1883) **Émile Zola** (1840)
Ladies Triall, The (1639) **John Ford** (1586)
Ladies Whose Bright Eyes (1911) **Ford Madox Ford** (1873)
Lads' Love (1897) **S.R. Crockett** (1860)
Lady, The (1957) **Conrad Richter** (1890)
Lady Adelaide's Oath (1867) **Mrs Henry Wood** (1814)
Lady Anna (1874) **Anthony Trollope** (1815)
Lady Anne Granard (1847) **Letitia Elizabeth Landon** (1802–38)
Lady Athlyne (1908) **Bram Stoker** (1847)
Lady Audley's Secret (1862) **M.E. Braddon** (1835)
Lady Baltimore (1906) **Owen Wister** (1860)
Lady Betty (1870) **C[hristabel] R[ose] Coleridge** (1843)
Lady Byron Vindicated (1870) **Harriet Beecher Stowe** (1811)
Lady Chatterley's Lover [1st edn] [privately prtd Florence] (1928) **D.H. Lawrence** (1885)
Lady Chatterley's Lover [1st expurgated English edn] (1932) **D.H. Lawrence** (1885–1930)
Lady Chatterley's Lover [1st English unexpurgated edn] (1960) **D.H. Lawrence** (1885–1930)
Lady Chesterfield's Letters to Her Daughter (1860) **George Augustus Sala** (1828)
Lady Connie (1916) **Mrs T. Humphry Ward** (1851)
Lady Fortune (1540?) **Sir Thomas More** (1478)
Lady Frederick (1911) **Somerset Maugham** (1874)
Lady from Dubuque, The (1979) **Edward Albee** (1928)
Lady from Nowhere, The (1900) **Fergus Hume** (1859)
Lady From the Sea, The (1888) **Henrik Ibsen** (1828)
Lady Good-for Nothing (1910) **Sir A.T. Quiller-Couch** (1863)
Lady Grace (1887) **Mrs Henry Wood** (1814)
Lady in the Car, The (1908) **William le Queux** (1864)
Lady in the Lake, The (1943) **Raymond Chandler** (1888)
Lady in the Tower, The (1986) **'Jean Plaidy' [Eleanor Hibbert]** (1906)
Lady in the Van, The (1990) **Alan Bennett** (1934)
Lady into Fox (1922) **David Garnett** (1892)
Lady is Cold, The (1929) **E.B. White** (1899)
Lady Jim of Curzon Street (1905) **Fergus Hume** (1859)
Lady Lisle, The (1861) **M.E. Braddon** (1835)
Lady Molly of Scotland Yard (1910) **Baroness Orczy** (1865)
Lady Noggs Intervenes (1908) **Edgar Jepson** (1863)
Lady Noggs, Peeress, The (1906) **Edgar Jepson** (1863)
Lady of Blossholme, The (1909) **Sir H. Rider Haggard** (1856)
Lady of Fashion, The (1856) **Lady Charlotte Bury** (1775)
Lady of La Garaye, The (1862) **Caroline Norton** (1808)
Lady of Lynn, The (1901) **Sir Walter Besant** (1836)
Lady of Lyons, The (1839) **Edward Bulwer-Lytton** (1803)
Lady of Pleasure, The (1637) **James Shirley** (1596)
Lady of Quality (1972) **Georgette Heyer** (1902)
Lady of Situations, The (1990) **Louis Auchinloss** (1917)
Lady of the Aroostock, The (1879) **William Dean Howells** (1837)
Lady of the Barge, The [contains 'The Monkey's Paw'] (1902) **W.W. Jacobs** (1863)
Lady of the Island, The (1909) **Guy Boothby** (1867)
Lady of the Lake, The (1810) **Sir Walter Scott** (1771)
Lady of the Shroud, The (1909) **Bram Stoker** (1847)
Lady on the Drawing-room Floor, The (1906) **M.E. Coleridge** (1861)
Lady Oracle (1976) **Margaret Atwood** (1939)
Lady Paramount, The (1902) **Henry Harland** (1861)
Lady Rose's Daughter (1903) **Mrs T. Humphry Ward** (1851)
Lady Silverdale's Sweetheart (1876) **William Black** (1841)
Lady Susan [in J.E. Austen-Leigh's *Memoir*; written 1793–4] (1871) **Jane Austen** (1775–1817)
Lady Susan and Life (1923) **Storm Jameson** (1897)
Lady Windermere's Fan (1892) **Oscar Wilde** (1854)
Lady with the Camelias, The [*La Dame aux camélias*] (1848) **Alexandre Dumas ['fils']** (1824)
Lady With the Unicorn, The (1948) **Vernon Watkins** (1906)
Lady's Dressing-Room, The (1732) **Jonathan Swift** (1667)
Lady's Maid (1990) **Margaret Forster** (1938)
Lady's Mile, The (1866) **M.E. Braddon** (1835)
Lady's New-Years Gift, The (1688) **Sir George Savile, Marquis of Halifax** (1633)
Lady's Not for Burning, The (1948) **Christopher Fry [Christopher Fry Harris]** (1907)
Lady's Paquet of Letters, The (1707) **Mary Delariviere Manley** (1663)
Lady's Walk, The (1883) **Margaret Oliphant** (1828)
Lady-Bird (1852) **Lady Georgiana Fullerton** (1812)
Ladybird, The [etc] (1923) **D.H. Lawrence** (1885)
Lagoon, The (1951) **Janet Frame** (1924)
Lair (1979) **James Herbert** (1943)
Lair of the White Worm, The (1911) **Bram Stoker** (1847)
Laird of Abbotsford, The (1980) **A.N. Wilson** (1950)
Laird's Luck, The (1901) **Sir A.T. Quiller-Couch** (1863)
Lajwanti (1966) **Mulk Raj Anand** (1905)
Lake, The (1905) **George Moore** (1852)
Lake Effect Country (1983) **A.R. Ammons** (1926)
Lake Lyrics, and Other Poems (1889) **Wilfred Campbell** (1858)

Lake of Darkness, The (1980) **Ruth Rendell** (1930)
Lake of Geneva, The (1832) **Sir Samuel Egerton Brydges** (1762)
Lake of Killarney, The (1804) **Anna Maria Porter** (1780)
Lake Wobegon Days (1985) **Garrison Keillor** (1942)
Lalla Rookh (1817) **Thomas Moore** (1779)
Lamb (1980) **Bernard MacLaverty** (1942)
Lame Englishman, The (1910) **Warwick Deeping** (1877)
Lame Lover, The (1770) **Samuel Foote** (1720)
Lament and Triumph (1940) **George Barker** (1913)
Lament for a Maker [as'Michael Innes'] (1938) **J.I.M. Stewart** (1906)
Lament for the Death of a Bullfighter [*Llanto por la muerte de Ignacio Sánchez Mejías*] (1934) **Federico García Lorca** (1898)
Lament of Tasso, The (1817) **George Gordon, Lord Byron** (1788)
Lament on the Death of a Master of Arts (1939) **Mulk Raj Anand** (1905)
Lamentations of Amyntas for the Death of Phillis, The [trn. from Watson's Latin by Abraham Fraunce] (1587) **Thomas Watson** (1557?)
Laments for the Living (1930) **Dorothy Parker** (1893)
Lamia, Isabella, The Eve of St Agnes (1820) **John Keats** (1795)
Lamia's Winter-Quarters (1898) **Alfred Austin** (1835)
Lamp and the Veil, The (1945) **Vernon Watkins** (1906)
Lamp at Noon, The (1968) **Sinclair Ross** (1908)
Lamp for Nightfall, A (1952) **Erskine Caldwell** (1903)
Lamp in the Desert, The (1919) **Ethel M. Dell** (1881)
Lanark (1981) **Alasdair Gray** (1934)
Lancashire Witches, The (1849) **W.H. Ainsworth** (1805)
Lancashire-Witches, The (1681) **Thomas Shadwell** (1642?)
Lancelot (1920) **Edwin Arlington Robinson** (1869)
Lancelot (1977) **Walker Percy** (1916)
Lancelot (1978) **Peter Vansittart** (1920)
Lances of Lynwood, The (1855) **Charlotte M. Yonge** (1823)
Land, The (1905) **Padraic Colum** (1881)
Land, The (1926) **Vita Sackville-West** (1892)
Land, A [plates by Henry Moore] (1951) **Jacquetta Hawkes** (1910)
Land at Last (1866) **Edmund Yates** (1831)
Land of Darkness, The (1888) **Margaret Oliphant** (1828)
Land of Gold, The (1888) **George R. Sims** (1847)
Land of Green Ginger, The (1927) **Winifred Holtby** (1898)
Land of Heart's Desire, The (1894) **W.B. Yeats** (1865)
Land of Little Rain, The (1903) **Mary Austin** (1868)
Land of Mist, The (1926) **A. Conan Doyle** (1859)
Land of Nod (1976) **Paul Green** (1894)
Land of Plenty, The (1934) **Robert Cantwell** (1908)
Land of Spices, The (1941) **Kate O'Brien** (1897)
Land of Unlikeness (1944) **Robert Lowell** (1917)
Land That Time Forgot, The (1924) **Edgar Rice Burroughs** (1875)
Landing on the Sun, A (1991) **Michael Frayn** (1933)
Landleaguers, The (1883) **Anthony Trollope** (1815–1882)
Landlocked (1965) **Doris Lessing** (1919)
Landlord at Lion's Head, The (1897) **William Dean Howells** (1837)
Landmark, The (1925) **James Lane Allen** (1849)
Landmarks (1914) **E.V. Lucas** (1868)
Landmarks in French Literature (1912) **Lytton Strachey** (1880)
Landor (1881) **Sidney Colvin** (1845)
Lands of the Saracen, The (1855) **Bayard Taylor** (1825)
Landscape, and Silence (1969) **Harold Pinter** (1930)
Landscape into Art (1949) **Kenneth Clark** (1903)
Landscape West of Eden (1934) **Conrad Potter Aiken** (1889)
Landscape Without Rain (1980) **Ralph Gustafson** (1909)
Landslide (1967) **Desmond Bagley** (1923)
Language and Silence (1967) **George Steiner** (1929)
Language as Gesture (1951) **R.P. Blackmur** (1904)
Language of Clothes, The (1981) **Alison Lurie** (1926)
Language of Fiction, The (1966) **David Lodge** (1935)
Language of the Night, The (1978) **Ursula K. Le Guin** (1929)
Language, Truth and Logic (1936) **A.J. Ayer** (1910)
Languages of Love, The (1957) **Christine Brooke-Rose** (1926)
Lantana Lane (1959) **Eleanor Dark** (1901)
Lantern Bearers, The (1959) **Rosemary Sutcliff** (1920)
Lantern Lecture [US: *Fabrications*] (1981) **Adam Mars-Jones** (1954)
Lantern Slides (1990) **Edna O'Brien** (1932)
Lantern-Bearers, The (1999) **Ronald Frame** (1953)
Lanterns & Lances (1961) **James Thurber** (1894)
Lanthorne and Candle-light (1608) **Thomas Dekker** (1572?)
Laodicean, A (1881) **Thomas Hardy** (1840)
Laon and Cythna [reissued 1818 as *The Revolt of Islam*] (1818) **P.B. Shelley** (1792)
Lap of Honour, A (1967) **'Hugh MacDiarmid' [Christopher Murray Grieve]** (1892)
Lap of the Gods, The (1923) **Louis Stone** (1871)
Lara (1814) **George Gordon, Lord Byron** (1788)
Larger Than Life (1963) **Xavier Herbert** (1901)
Lark Rise (1939) **Flora Thompson** (1877)
Lark Rise to Candleford [the complete trilogy] (1945) **Flora Thompson** (1877)
Lark, The [*L'Alouette*] (1953) **Jean Anouilh** (1910)
Lark, The [from Anouilh, *L'alouette*] (1955) **Christopher Fry [Christopher Fry Harris]** (1907) (tr.)
Larme du diable, Une ['A Tear From the Devil'] (1839) **Théophile Gautier** (1811)
Larry's Party (1977) **Carol Shields** (1935)
Lars: A Pastoral of Norway (1873) **Bayard Taylor** (1825)
Lars Porsena (1927) **Robert Graves** (1895)

Lasselia (1723) **Eliza Haywood** (*c.* 1693)
Last Adam, The [UK: *A Cure of Flesh*] (1933) **James Gould Cozzens** (1903)
Last Analysis, The (1965) **Saul Bellow** (1915)
Last and First Men (1930) **W. Olaf Stapledon** (1886)
Last and the First, The (1971) **I. Compton-Burnett** (1892–1969)
Last Ballad, The (1899) **John Davidson** (1857)
Last Battle, The (1956) **C.S. Lewis** (1898)
Last Boer War, The (1899) **Sir H. Rider Haggard** (1856)
Last Bouquet, The (1932) **'Marjorie Bowen' [Gabrielle Margaret Vere Campbell]** (1886)
Last Bus to Woodstock (1975) **Colin Dexter** (1930)
Last Byzantine Renaissance, The (1970) **Sir Steven Runciman** (1903
Last Chance, The (1905) **'Rolf Boldrewood' [Thomas Alexander Browne]** (1826)
Last Chronicle of Barset, The (1867) **Anthony Trollope** (1815)
Last Chukka, The (1928) **Alec Waugh** (1898)
Last Continent, The (1998) **Terry Pratchett** (1948)
Last Cop Out, The (1973) **Mickey Spillane** (1918)
Last Cycle, The (1946) **Stephen Vincent Benét** (1889)
Last Days (1984) **Joyce Carol Oates** (1938)
Last Days of Herculaneum, The (1821) **Edwin Atherstone** (1788)
Last Days of Hitler, The (1947) **Hugh Trevor-Roper** (1914)
Last Days of Pompeii, The (1834) **Edward Bulwer-Lytton** (1803)
Last Ditch, The (1940) **Louis MacNeice** (1907)
Last Essays of Elia, The (1833) **Charles Lamb** (1775)
Last Essays on Church and Religion (1877) **Matthew Arnold** (1822)
Last Exit to Brooklyn (1964) **Hubert Selby Jr** (1928)
Last Flower, The (1939) **James Thurber** (1894)
Last Frontier, The (1941) **Howard Fast** (1914)
Last Fruit Off an Old Tree, The (1853) **Walter Savage Landor** (1775)
Last Galley, The (1911) **A. Conan Doyle** (1859)
Last Generation, The (1908) **James Elroy Flecker** (1884)
Last Gentleman, The (1966) **Walker Percy** (1916)
Last Hope, The (1904) **'Henry Seton Merriman' [Hugh Stowell Scott]** (1862)
Last Hours of Sandra Lee, The (1961) **William Sansom** (1912)
Last House Party, The (1982) **Peter Dickinson** (1927)
Last Inspection, The (1942) **Alun Lewis** (1915)
Last Lectures (1939) **Roger Fry** (1866–1934)
Last Legend of Smokeover, The (1939) **L.P. Jacks** (1860)
Last Letters (1904) **Aubrey Beardsley** (1872–98)
Last Letters of Jacopo Ortis [*Ultime lettere di Jacopo Ortis*] (1802) **Ugo Foscolo** (1778)
Last Loves (1990) **Alan Sillitoe** (1928)
Last Man, The (1826) **Mary Shelley** (1797)
Last Man, The (1940) **Alfred Noyes** (1880)
Last Man's Head, The (1970) **Jessica Anderson** (1925)
Last Medici, The (1932) **Sir Harold Acton** (1904)
Last Men in London (1931) **Olaf Stapledon** (1886)
Last Night of the Earth Poems, The (1992) **Charles Bukowski** (1920)
Last of Chéri, The [*La Fin de Chéri*] (1926) **Colette** (1873)
Last of England, The (1970) **Peter Porter** (1929)
Last of the Abencérages, The [*Les Aventures du dernier des Abencérages*] (1826) **François-René, vicomte de Chateaubriand** (1768–1848)
Last of the Barons, The (1843) **Edward Bulwer-Lytton** (1803)
Last of the Country House Murders, The (1974) **Emma Tennant** (1937)
Last of the Crazy People, The (1967) **Timothy Findley** (1930)
Last of the Lairds, The (1826) **John Galt** (1779)
Last of the Mohicans, The (1826) **James Fenimore Cooper** (1789)
Last of the Mortimers, The (1862) **Margaret Oliphant** (1828)
Last of the Red-Hot Lovers (1969) **Neil Simon** (1927)
Last of the Wine, The (1956) **'Mary Renault' [Eileen Mary Challans]** (1905)
Last Orders (1996) **Graham Swift** (1949)
Last Pages from a Journal (1915) **'Mark Rutherford' [William Hale White]** (1831–1913)
Last Peacock, The (1980) **Allan Massie** (1938)
Last Picture Show, The (1966) **Larry McMurty** (1936)
Last Poems (1862) **E.B. Browning** (1806–61)
Last Poems (1905) **Richard Watson Dixon** (1833–1900)
Last Poems (1918) **Edward Thomas** (1878–1917)
Last Poems (1922) **A.E. Housman** (1859)
Last Poems (1933) **D.H. Lawrence** (1885–1930)
Last Poems (1993) **Roy Fuller** (1912–91)
Last Poems and Two Plays (1939) **W.B. Yeats** (1865)
Last Post (1928) **Ford Madox Ford** (1873)
Last Puritan, The (1935) **George Santayana** (1863)
Last Refuge, The (1900) **Henry Blake Fuller** (1857)
The Last Resort (1998) **Alison Lurie** (1926)
Last Resorts (1984) **Clare Boylan** (1948)
Last Seen Wearing (1976) **Colin Dexter** (1930)
Last September, The (1929) **Elizabeth Bowen** (1899)
Last Sheaf, A (1951) **Denton Welch** (1915–48)
Last Songs from Vagabondia (1895) **William Bliss Carman** (1861) [with Richard Hovey]
Last Studies (1897) **Hubert Crackanthorpe** (1870–96)
Last Supper, The (1988) **Howard Barker** (1946)
Last Tales (1957) **'Isak Dinesen' [Karen Blixen]** (1885)
Last Temptation of Christ, The (1955) **Nikos Kazantzakis** (1883)
Last Testament of Oscar Wilde, The (1983) **Peter Ackroyd** (1949)
Last Things (1970) **C.P. Snow** (1905)
Last Tycoon, The (1941) **F. Scott Fitzgerald** (1896–1940)
Last Voyage of Somebody the Sailor, The (1991) **John Barth** (1930)

Last Voyage, The (1930) **Alfred Noyes** (1880)
Last Word, The (1990) **Graham Greene** (1904)
Last Words of Dutch Schultz, The (1975) **William S. Burroughs** (1914)
Last Year at Marienbad [*L'Année dernière à Marienbad*; film scenario] (1961) **Alain Robbe-Grillet** (1922)
Late and Soon (1943) **'E.M. Delafield' [E.E.M. de la Pasture]** (1890)
Late Bourgeois World, The (1966) **Nadine Gordimer** (1923)
Late Call (1964) **Angus Wilson** (1913)
Late George Apley, The (1937) **John P. Marquand** (1893)
Late Harvest (1946) **Norman Douglas** (1868)
Late in the Afternoon (1971) **Lettice Cooper** (1897)
Late Lyrics and Earlier (1922) **Thomas Hardy** (1840)
Late Mattia Pascal, The [*Il Fu Mattia Pascal*] (1904) **Luigi Pirandello** (1867)
Late Mr Shakespeare, The (1998) **Robert Nye** (1939)
Late Night Bulletin (1969) **Dorothy Hewett** (1923)
Late Pickings (1987) **Gavin Ewart** (1916)
Late Settings (1985) **James Merrill** (1926)
Late-Winter Child (1979) **Vincent Buckley** (1925)
Latecomers (1988) **Anita Brookner** (1928)
Later Hogarth (1945) **Michael Hamburger** (1924)
Later On (1983) **F.T. Prince** (1912)
Later Poems (1922) **W.B. Yeats** (1865)
Later Poems 1925–35 (1941) **T.S. Eliot** (1888)
Later the Same Day (1985) **Grace Paley** (1922)
Latest Literary Essays and Addresses (1891) **James Russell Lowell** (1819)
Latin and Italian Poems of Milton (1808) **William Cowper** (1731–1800)
Latin Lover, The (1994) **Frederic Raphael** (1931)
Latin-Quarter Romance, A [as 'Sydney Luska'] (1889) **Henry Harland** (1861)
Latter-Day Pamphlets (1850) **Thomas Carlyle** (1795)
Latter-Day Psalms (1982) **Nissim Ezekiel** (1924)
Lauds and Plaints (1974) **Bruce Beaver** (1928)
Laugh and Lie Down (1931) **Robert Cantwell** (1908)
Laughable Lyrics (1877) **Edward Lear** (1812)
Laughing Gas (1936) **P.G. Wodehouse** (1881)
Laughing Hyena, The (1953) **D.J. Enright** (1920)
Laughter in the Next Room (1948) **Sir Osbert Sitwell** (1892)
Laughter of Carthage, The (1984) **Michael Moorcock** (1939)
Laura Richmond (1901) **Jean Ingelow** (1820)
Laureate of Peace (1954) **G. Wilson Knight** (1897)
Laurel Walk, The (1898) **Mary Louisa Molesworth** (1839)
Laurels Are Poison (1942) **Gladys Mitchell** (1901)
Laurence Bloomfield in Ireland (1864) **William Allingham** (1824)
Laurentia (1861) **Lady Georgiana Fullerton** (1812)
Laurringtons, The (1844) **Frances Trollope** (1780)
Laurus Nobilis (1909) **'Vernon Lee' [Violet Paget]** (1856)
Lavengro (1851) **George Borrow** (1803)
Lavinia (1902) **Rhoda Broughton** (1840)
Law and the Grace, The (1965) **Iain Crichton Smith [Iain Mac a'Ghobhainn]** (1928)
Law and the Lady, The (1875) **Wilkie Collins** (1824)
Law at Heart's Desire, The (1982) **Robert Adamson** (1943)
Law for the Lion, A (1953) **Louis Auchinloss** (1917)
Law of Karma, The (1968) **Rodney Hall** (1935)
Law-Trickes (1608) **John Day** (*c.* 1574)
Lawd Today (1963) **Richard Wright** (1908–60)
Lawiers Logike, The (1588) **Abraham Fraunce** (fl.1582–1633)
Lawless Road, The (1939) **Graham Greene** (1904)
Lawley Road (1956) **R.K. Narayan** (1907)
Lawrence and the Arabs (1927) **Robert Graves** (1895)
Lawrence Clavering (1897) **A.E.W. Mason** (1865)
Lawrence of Arabia (1955) **Richard Aldington** (1892)
Lawrie Todd (1830) **John Galt** (1779)
Lawton Girl, The (1890) **Harold Frederic** (1856)
Laxdale Hall (1951) **Eric Linklater** (1899)
Lay Anthony, The (1914) **Joseph Hergesheimer** (1880)
Lay of an Irish Harp, The (1807) **Lady Sydney Morgan** (1783?)
Lay of Marie, The (1816) **Mary Matilda Betham** (1776)
Lay of the Last Minstrel, The (1805) **Sir Walter Scott** (1771)
Lay of the Laureate, The [*Carmen Nuptiale*] (1816) **Robert Southey** (1774)
Lay Thoughts of a Dean (1926) **W.R. Inge** (1860)
Lays and Legends [1st ser.] (1886) **E[dith] Nesbit** (1858)
Lays for the Dead (1834) **Amelia Opie** (1769)
Lays of a Wild Harp (1835) **Eliza Cook** (1818)
Lays of Ancient Rome (1842) **T.B. Macaulay** (1800)
Lays of France (1872) **Arthur O'Shaughnessy** (1844)
Lays of Many Lands (1825) **Felicia Dorothea Hemans** (1793)
Lays of My Home (1843) **John Greenleaf Whittier** (1807)
Lays of the Scottish Cavaliers (1849) **W.E. Aytoun** (1813)
Lays of the Western Gael (1864) **Sir Samuel Ferguson** (1810) (ed.)
Layton Court Mystery, The (1925) **Anthony Berkeley Cox** (1893)
Lazarus (1990) **Morris West** (1916)
Lazarus Laughed (1927) **Eugene O'Neill** (1888)
Le Forester (1802) **Sir Samuel Egerton Brydges** (1762)
Leader of the Band (1988) **Fay Weldon** (1931)
Leaders in Literature (1858) **Thomas de Quincey** (1785)
Leaf Storm [*La hojarasca*] (1955) **Gabriel García Márquez** (1928)
Leaflets (1969) **Adrienne Rich** (1929)
League of Frightened Philistines, The (1945) **James T. Farrell** (1904)

League of the Scarlet Pimpernel, The (1919) **Baroness Orczy** (1865)
Leaguer of Lathom, The (1876) **W.H. Ainsworth** (1805)
Lean Tales (1985) **Alasdair Gray** (1934) [with James Kelman and Agnes Owen]
Leaning in the Wind (1986) **P.H. Newby** (1918)
Leaning Tower, The (1944) **Katherine Anne Porter** (1890)
Leap Before You Look (1932) **Alec Waugh** (1898)
Lear of the Steppes, A (1870) **Ivan Turgenev** (1818)
Learned City, A (1966) **Philip Toynbee** (1916)
Learned Discourse of Justification, A (1612) **Richard Hooker** (1554–1600)
Learned Ladies, The [Les Femmes savantes] (1672) **'Molière' [Jean-Baptiste Poquelin]** (1622)
Learned Sermon of the Nature of Pride, A (1612) **Richard Hooker** (1554–1600)
Learning to Swim (1982) **Graham Swift** (1949)
Leather Stocking and Silk (1854) **John Cooke** (1830)
Leatherwood God, The (1916) **William Dean Howells** (1837)
Leaven of Malice (1954) **Robertson Davies** (1913)
Leaves and Fruit (1927) **Sir Edmund Gosse** (1849)
Leaves from Margaret Smith's Journal (1849) **John Greenleaf Whittier** (1807)
Leaves From the Valley (1980) **Joanna Trollope** (1943)
Leaves of Grass [first edition] (1855) **Walt Whitman** (1819)
Leaves of Life (1888) **E[dith] Nesbit** (1858)
Leaves of the Banyan Tree (1979) **Albert Wendt** (1939)
Leaves of the Tree, The (1911) **A.C. Benson** (1862)
Leaves Without a Tree (1953) **G.S. Fraser** (1915)
Leaving Cheyenne (1963) **Larry McMurty** (1936)
Leaving Home (1987) **Garrison Keillor** (1942)
Lecture on the Study of History, A (1895) **Lord Acton** (1834)
Lectures and Essays on University Subjects (1859) **J.H. Newman** (1801)
Lectures Chiefly on the Dramatic Literature of the Age of Elizabeth (1820) **William Hazlitt** (1778)
Lectures in America (1935) **Gertrude Stein** (1874)
Lectures on Architecture and Painting (1854) **John Ruskin** (1819)
Lectures on Justification (1838) **J.H. Newman** (1801)
Lectures on Political Science (1919) **Annie Besant** (1847)
Lectures on Psychical Research (1962) **C.D. Broad** (1887)
Lectures on Rhetoric and Belles Lettres (1783) **Hugh Blair** (1718)
Lectures on the Catechism of the Church of England (1779) **William Gilpin** (1724)
Lectures on the English Comic Writers (1819) **William Hazlitt** (1778)
Lectures on the English Poets (1818) **William Hazlitt** (1778)
Lectures on the French Revolution (1910) **Lord Acton** (1834–1902)
Lectures on the History of France (1851) **Sir James Stephen** (1789)
Lectures on the History of Moral Philosophy in England (1852) **William Whewell** (1794)
Lectures on the History of the Jewish Church (1863) **Arthur Penrhyn Stanley** (1815)
Lectures on the Prophetical Office of the Church (1837) **J.H. Newman** (1801)
Led By a Dream (1899) **Katharine Tynan** (1861)
Leda (1920) **Aldous Huxley** (1894)
Ledge on Bald Face, The (1918) **Sir Charles G.D. Roberts** (1860)
Left Bank, The (1927) **'Jean Rhys' [Ella Gwendolyn Rees Williams]** (1890)
Left Hand, Right Hand! (1944) **Sir Osbert Sitwell** (1892)
Left Leg, The (1923) **T.F. Powys** (1875)
Left Out in the Rain (1986) **Gary Snyder** (1930)
Left Wings Over Europe (1936) **Wyndham Lewis** (1882)
Left-Handed Liberty (1965) **John Arden** (1930)
Legacy, The (1956) **Sybille Bedford** (1911)
Legacy, The (1972) **A. Alvarez** (1929)
Legacy (1987) **James A. Michener** (1907)
Legacy for Young Ladies, A (1826) **Anna Laetitia Barbauld** (1743–1825)
Legacy of Cain, The (1888) **Wilkie Collins** (1824)
Legacy of the Civil War, The (1961) **Robert Penn Warren** (1905)
Legend (1919) **'Clemence Dane' [Winifred Ashton]** (1888)
Legend of Cupid and Psyche, The (1637) **Shackerley Marmion** (1603)
Legend of Florence, A (1840) **Leigh Hunt** (1784)
Legend of Great Cromwel, The (1607) **Michael Drayton** (1563)
Legend of Jubal, The (1874) **'George Eliot' [Mary Ann Evans]** (1819)
Legend of the Golden Prayers, The (1859) **Mrs C.F. Alexander** (1818)
Legend of the White Reindeer (1915) **Ernest Thompson Seton** (1860)
Légende des siècles, La ['Legend of the Centuries'] (1859) **Victor Hugo** (1802)
Legends (1921) **Amy Lowell** (1874)
Legends and Lyrics [1st ser.; 2nd ser., 1861] (1858) **Adelaide Procter** (1825)
Legends of New-England in Prose and Verse (1831) **John Greenleaf Whittier** (1807)
Legends of Smokeover (1922) **L.P. Jacks** (1860)
Legends of the Fall (1978) **Jim Harrison** (1937)
Legends of the Madonna (1852) **Anna Jameson** (1794)
Legends of the Monastic Orders (1850) **Anna Jameson** (1794)
Legends of the Saints (1848) **Anna Jameson** (1794)
Legends of Vancouver (1911) **Pauline Johnson** (1862)
Legions of the Eagle (1954) **Henry Treece** (1911)
Legs (1975) **William Joseph Kennedy** (1928)
Leicester (1885) **Francis Adams** (1862)
Leicester Square (1874) **Tom Taylor** (1817)
Leighton Court (1866) **Henry Kingsley** (1830)

Leila (1910) **Antonio Fogazzaro** (1842)
Leila (1983) **J.P. Donleavy** (1926)
Leila; [and] *Calderon the Courtier* (1838) **Edward Bulwer-Lytton** (1803)
Lélia (1833) **'George Sand' [Auore Dupin]** (1804)
Lemon Farm, The (1935) **Martin Boyd** (1893)
Lenient God, The (1937) **Naomi Jacob** (1884)
Lens-Breakers, The (1992) **Jon Silkin** (1930)
Léocadia (1940) **Jean Anouilh** (1910)
Leoline and Sydanis (1642) **Sir Francis Kynaston** (1587)
Leonardo's Last Supper [with *Noonday Demons*] (1970) **Peter Barnes** (1931)
Leonidas (1737) **Richard Glover** (1712)
Leonora (1806) **Maria Edgeworth** (1767)
Leonora (1903) **Arnold Bennett** (1867)
Leonora Casaloni (1868) **T. Adolphus Trollope** (1810)
Leonora d'Orco (1857) **G.P.R. James** (1799)
Leopard Hunts in Darkness, The (1984) **Wilbur Smith** (1933)
Leopard, The [*Il Gattopardo*] (1958) **Giuseppi Lampedusa** (1896–1957)
Leopard, The (1958) **V.S. Reid** (1913)
Leper of Saint Giles, The (1981) **'Ellis Peters' [Edith Mary Pargeter]** (1913)
Lepidus the Centurion (1901) **Edwin Lester Arnold** (1857)
Lesbian Images (1975) **Jane Rule** (1931)
Less Black Than We're Painted (1878) **James Payn** (1830)
Less Deceived, The (1955) **Philip Larkin** (1922)
Less Than Angels (1955) **Barbara Pym** (1913)
Less Than One (1986) **Joseph Brodsky** (1940)
Less Than the Dust (1912) **Mary Agnes Hamilton** (1884)
Less Than Zero (1985) **Bret Easton Ellis** (1964)
Lessness [pub. in French 1969] (1971) **Samuel Beckett** (1906)
Lesson, The (1951) **Eugène Ionesco** (1909)
Lesson Before Dying, A (1993) **Ernest J. Gaines** (1933)
Lesson from Aloes, A (1979) **Athol Fugard** (1932)
Lesson of the Master, The (1892) **Henry James** (1843)
Lessons for Children of Two to Three Years Old (1778) **Anna Laetitia Barbauld** (1743)
Lessons for the Day, The (1742) **Horace Walpole** (1717)
Lessons of the War, The (1970) **Henry Reed** (1914)
Lesters, The (1893) **General Sir George Tomkyns Chesney** (1830)
Leszko the Bastard (1877) **Alfred Austin** (1835)
Let Dons Delight (1939) **Ronald Knox** (1888)
Let It Bleed (1996) **Ian Rankin** (1960)
Let It Come Down (1952) **Paul Bowles** (1910)
Let Me Count the Ways (1965) **Peter de Vries** (1910)
Let Sleeping Vets Lie (1973) **James Herriot** (1916)
Let the People Sing (1939) **J.B. Priestley** (1894)
Let the Roof Fall In (1910) **'Frank Danby' [Julia Frankau]** (1864)
Let Us Compare Mythologies (1956) **Leonard Cohen** (1934)
Let Us Now Praise Famous Men [photographs by Walker Evans] (1941) **James Agee** (1909)
Let Your Mind Alone! (1937) **James Thurber** (1894)
Letter About Liberty and Necessity, A (1676) **Thomas Hobbes** (1588)
Letter Concerning Toleration, A (1689) **John Locke** (1632)
Letter from a Far Country (1982) **Gillian Clarke** (1937)
Letter from Artemiza, A (1679) **John Wilmot, earl of Rochester** (1647)
Letter from Li Po, A (1955) **Conrad Potter Aiken** (1889)
Letter from Paris (1952) **Dodie Smith** (1896)
Letter from Pontus, A (1936) **John Masefield** (1878)
Letter from Tokyo (1987) **Anthony Thwaite** (1930)
Letter from Ulster and the Hugo Poems (1993) **E.A. Markham** (1939)
Letter of Marque, The (1988) **Patrick O'Brian** (1914)
Letter of Marque, The (1990) **Patrick O'Brian** (1914)
Letter on the Admission of Dissenters to Academical Degrees (1834) **Connop Thirlwall** (1797)
Letter to a Dissenter, A (1687) **Sir George Savile, Marquis of Halifax** (1633)
Letter to John Farr and John Harris on the Affairs of America (1777) **Edmund Burke** (1729)
Letter to Lucian, A (1956) **Alfred Noyes** (1880)
Letter to M. Alembert, A [*Lettre à d'Almebert sur les spectacles*] (1758) **Jean-Jacques Rousseau** (1712)
Letter to Mr Addison, A (1714) **Laurence Eusden** (1688)
Letter to Sir Samuel Romilly (1818) **Henry, Lord Brougham** (1778)
Letter to Sister Benedicta (1978) **Rose Tremain** (1943)
Letter to the Rev. Mr Wesley, A (1770) **Augustus Montague Toplady** (1740)
Letter to the Shop-Keepers, Tradesmen, Farmers and Common-People of Ireland, A [by 'M.B. Drapier'] (1724) **Jonathan Swift** (1667)
Letter to the Whole People of Ireland, A [by 'M.B. Drapier'] (1724) **Jonathan Swift** (1667)
Letter to the Women of England, A [as 'Anne Frances Randall'] (1799) **Mary Robinson** (1758)
Letter-Writers, The (1731) **Henry Fielding** (1707)
Letterbag of the Great Western, The (1840) **T.C. Haliburton** (1796)
Letters (1979) **John Barth** (1930)
Letters (1763) **Lady Mary Wortley Montagu** (1689–1762)
Letters and Journals of Lord Byron (1830) **Thomas Moore** (1779) (ed.)
Letters and Poems (1692) **William Walsh** (1663)
Letters and Remains (1865) **A.H. Clough** (1819–61)
Letters and Social Aims (1876) **Ralph Waldo Emerson** (1803)
Letters Concerning the English Nation [*Lettres écrites de Londres sur les Anglais*] (1734) **'Voltaire' [François-Marie Arouet]** (1694)
Letters for Literary Ladies (1795) **Maria Edgeworth** (1767)

Letters from a Persian in England to his Friend at Isphahan (1735) **George Lyttelton, 1st Baron Lyttelton** (1709)
Letters from America (1916) **Rupert Brooke** (1887–1915)
Letters from England (1807) **Robert Southey** (1774)
Letters from Hamnavoe (1975) **George Mackay Brown** (1921)
Letters from Iceland (1937) **W.H. Auden** (1907) [with Louis MacNeice]
Letters from Ireland (1853) **Harriet Martineau** (1802)
Letters from Juliet, Lady Catesby (1760) **Frances Brooke** (1724)
Letters from London (1995) **Julian Barnes** (1946)
Letters from My Mill [Lettres de mon moulin] (1869) **Alphonse Daudet** (1840)
Letters from Syria (1942) **Freya Stark** (1893)
Letters from the Levant (1813) **John Galt** (1779)
Letters from the South (1837) **Thomas Campbell** (1777)
Letters from Yorick to Eliza (1773) **Laurence Sterne** (1713–68)
Letters Home (1975) **Sylvia Plath** (1932–63)
Letters of a Conservative, The (1836) **Walter Savage Landor** (1775)
Letters of a Solitary Wanderer, The [vols. i–iii; vols. iv, v, 1802] (1799) **Charlotte Smith** (1749)
Letters of Advice to a Young American (1818) **William Godwin** (1756)
'Letters of Jonathan Oldstyle, Gent., The' [pub. in the *Morning Chronicle*] (1803) **Washington Irving** (1783)
Letters of Mr Alexander Pope, and Several of his Friends (1737) **Alexander Pope** (1688)
Letters of Peter Plymley, The (1807–8) **Sydney Smith** (1771)
Letters of Queen Victoria, The (1907) **A.C. Benson** (1862)
Letters of Travel (1920) **Rudyard Kipling** (1865)
Letters of Verax to the Editors of the Morning Chronicle (1815) **William Godwin** (1756)
Letters on Demonology and Witchcraft (1830) **Sir Walter Scott** (1771)
Letters on Education (1849) **Robert Owen** (1771)
Letters on Events in France since the Restoration (1819) **Helen Maria Williams** (1762)
Letters on Literature (1899) **Andrew Lang** (1844)
Letters on Mesmerism (1845) **Harriet Martineau** (1802)
Letters on the Character and Poetical Genius of Lord Byron (1824) **Sir Samuel Egerton Brydges** (1762)
Letters on the Elementary Principles of Education (1801) **Elizabeth Hamilton** (1758)
Letters on the Improvement of the Mind (1773) **Hester Chapone** (1727)
Letters on the Spirit of Patriotism (1749) **Henry Saint-John, Viscount Bolingbroke** (1678)
Letters on the Study and Use of History (1752) **Henry Saint-John, Viscount Bolingbroke** (1678–1751)
Letters on Various Interesting and Important Subjects (1799) **Philip Freneau** (1752)
Letters to a Wife (1793) **John Newton** (1725)
Letters to a Young Man Whose Education Has Been Neglected (1860) **Thomas De Quincey** (1785–1859)
Letters to and from the Late Samuel Johnson (1788) **Hester Lynch Piozzi** (1741)
Letters to Dead Authors (1886) **Andrew Lang** (1844)
Letters to Live Poets (1969) **Bruce Beaver** (1928)
Letters to Malcolm (1964) **C.S. Lewis** (1898–1963)
Letters to Martha (1968) **Dennis Brutus** (1924)
Letters to Severall Persons of Honour (1651) **John Donne** (1572–1631)
Letters to the Daughter of a Nobleman (1806) **Elizabeth Hamilton** (1758)
Letters to the Earl of Arlington and Sir John Trevor (1699) **Sir William Temple** (1628)
Letters Written by Mrs Manley (1696) **Mary Delariviere Manley** (1663)
Letters Written by Sir W. Temple and Other Ministers of State [ed. Jonathan Swift] (1700) **Sir William Temple** (1628–99)
Letters Written During a Short Residence in Spain and Portugal . . . (1797) **Robert Southey** (1774)
Letters Written During a Short Residence in Sweden, Norway and Denmark (1796) **Mary Wollstonecraft** (1759)
Letters Written in France, in the Summer of 1790 (1790) **Helen Maria Williams** (1762)
Letters Written to and for Particular Friends [known as *The Familiar Letters*] (1741) **Samuel Richardson** (1689)
Letters Written to his Son (1774) **Philip Dormer Stanhope, Earl of Chesterfield** (1694–1773)
Lettice and Lovage (1987) **Peter Shaffer** (1926)
Letting Go (1962) **Philip Roth** (1933)
Letting in the Rumour (1989) **Gillian Clarke** (1937)
Letting of Humors Blood in the Head-vaine, The (1600) **Samuel Rowlands** (1570?)
Letty Fox: her Luck (1946) **Christina Stead** (1902)
Leurs figures (1902) **Maurice Barrès** (1862)
Levanter, The (1972) **Eric Ambler** (1909)
Levellers Levelled to the Very Ground, The (1647) **William Prynne** (1600)
Leviathan (1992) **Paul Auster** (1947)
Leviathan (1651) **Thomas Hobbes** (1588)
Levine (1956) **James Hanley** (1901)
Levitation (1982) **Cynthia Ozick** (1928)
Levkas Man (1971) **'Hammond Innes' [Ralph Hammond-Innes]** (1913)
Lewis Arundel (1852) **Frank Smedley** (1818)
Lewis Percy (1989) **Anita Brookner** (1928)
Lewis Seymour and Some Women (1917) **George Moore** (1852)
Leyton Hall (1867) **Mark Lemon** (1809)
Liar, The [Le Menteur] (1643) **Pierre Corneille** (1606)
Liars, The (1897) **Henry Arthur Jones** (1851)

Libbie Marsh's Three Eras (1850) **Elizabeth Gaskell** (1810)
Liber Amoris (1823) **William Hazlitt** (1778)
Liberal Imagination, The (1950) **Lionel Trilling** (1905)
Liberal Opinions Upon Animals, Man, and Providence [as 'Courtney Melmoth'] (1775) **Samuel Jackson Pratt** (1749)
Liberality (1788) **Christopher Anstey** (1724)
Libertas Triumphans (1708) **Charles Gildon** (1665)
Libertine, The (1675) **Thomas Shadwell** (1642?)
Libertine, The (1807) **Charlotte Dacre** (1782?)
Liberty (1738) **James Thomson** (1700)
Liberty Asserted (1704) **John Dennis** (1657)
Liberty Hall, Oxon. (1860) **William Winwood Reade** (1838)
Liberty of the Press, The (1698) **Matthew Tindal** (1657)
Liberty To-day (1934) **C.E.M. Joad** (1891)
Liberty Tree (1841) **Nathaniel Hawthorne** (1804)
Liberty Tree (1983) **Tom Paulin** (1949)
Libra (1988) **Don DeLillo** (1936)
Library Companion, The (1824) **Thomas Frognall Dibdin** (1776)
Library, The (1781) **George Crabbe** (1754)
Licensed Renewed (1981) **John Gardner** (1926)
Lichee Nuts (1930) **Edgar Lee Masters** (1868)
Licia (1593) **Giles Fletcher the Elder** (1549?)
Licking Hitler (1978) **David Hare** (1947)
Lie Down in Darkness (1951) **William Styron** (1925)
Lie, The [*L'attenzione*] (1965) **'Alberto Moravia' [Alberto Pincherle]** (1907)
Lies and Secrets (1979) **John Fuller** (1937)
Lies of Silence (1990) **Brian Moore** (1921)
Lieut. Gulliver Jones, His Vacation (1905) **Edwin Lester Arnold** (1857)
Life, A (1979) **'Hugh Leonard' [Johns Keyes Byrne]** (1926)
Life, A (1986) **Iain Crichton Smith [Iain Mac a'Ghobhainn]** (1928)
Life, Adventures and Pyracies of the Famous Captain Singleton, The (1720) **Daniel Defoe** (1660)
Life Along the Passaic River (1938) **William Carlos Williams** (1883)
Life and Acts of John Whitgift, The (1718) **John Strype** (1643)
Life and Acts of Matthew Parker, The (1711) **John Strype** (1643)
Life and Adventures of a Clever Woman, The (1854) **Frances Trollope** (1780)
Life and Adventures of George Augustus Sala, The (1895) **George Augustus Sala** (1828)
Life and Adventures of John Marston Hall, The (1834) **G.P.R. James** (1799)
Life and Adventures of Jonathan Jefferson Whitlaw, The (1836) **Frances Trollope** (1780)
Life and Adventures of Martin Chuzzlewit, The (1844) **'Boz' [Charles Dickens]** (1812)
Life and Adventures of Michael Armstrong, The (1840) **Frances Trollope** (1780)
Life and Adventures of Miss Robinson Crusoe, The (1846) **Douglas Jerrold** (1803)
Life and Adventures of Nicholas Nickleby, The (1839) **'Boz' [Charles Dickens]** (1812)
Life and Adventures of Oliver Goldsmith (1848) **John Forster** (1812)
Life and Adventures of Peter Wilkins, The (1751) **Robert Paltock** (1697)
Life and Adventures of Sir Launcelot Greaves, The (1762) **Tobias George Smollett** (1721)
Life and Adventures of the Lady Lucy, The (1726) **Penelope Aubin** (*c.* 1685)
Life and Adventures of Valentine Vox, The (1840) **Henry Cockton** (1807)
Life and Adventures of Young Count Albertus, The (1728) **Penelope Aubin** (*c.* 1685)
Life and Amorous Adventures of Lucinda, The (1722) **Penelope Aubin** (*c.* 1685)
Life and Character of Marcus Portius Cato, The (1713) **Lewis Theobald** (1688) (tr.)
Life and Death in the Charity Ward (1973) **Charles Bukowski** (1920)
Life and Death of Harriet Frean (1922) **May Sinclair** (1863)
Life and Death of Jason, The (1867) **William Morris** (1834)
Life and Death of Mary Wollstonecraft, The (1974) **Claire Tomalin** (1933)
Life and Death of Mother Shipton, The (1677) **Richard Head** (1637?)
Life and Death of Mr Badman, The (1680) **John Bunyan** (1628)
Life and Death of My Lord Gilles de Rais, The (1990) **Robert Nye** (1939)
Life and Death of Queen Elizabeth, The (1639) **Thomas Heywood** (1574?)
Life and Death of Richard Yea-and-Nay, The (1900) **Maurice Hewlett** (1861)
Life and Death of Sir Matthew Hale, The (1682) **Gilbert Burnet** (1643)
Life and Death of William Long Beard, The (1593) **Thomas Lodge** (1558)
Life and Gabriella (1916) **Ellen Glasgow** (1874)
Life and Genuine Character of Doctor Swift, The (1733) **Jonathan Swift** (1667)
Life and Habit (1878) **Samuel Butler** (1835)
Life and Labour: or, Characteristics of Men of Industry, Culture, and Genius (1887) **Samuel Smiles** (1812)
Life and Letters of J.G. Lockhart, The (1897) **Andrew Lang** (1844)
Life and Letters of Lord Macaulay, The (1876) **Sir George Otto Trevelyan** (1838)
Life and Loves of a She-Devil, The (1983) **Fay Weldon** (1931)
Life and Mary Ann (1962) **Catherine Cookson** (1906)
Life and Opinions of Tristram Shandy, The (9 vols., 1759–67) [note that vol. i was pub. in Dec 1759 but dated 1760] (1760, 1762, 1765, 1777) **Laurence Sterne** (1713)
Life and Phantasy (1889) **William Allingham** (1824)
Life and Posthumous Writings of Cowper, The (1803) **William Hayley** (1745)

Life, and Raigne of King Edward the Sixt, The (1630) **Sir John Hayward** (1564?)

Life and Strange Surprizing Adventures of Mr Daniel DeFoe, The (1719) **Charles Gildon** (1665)

Life and Strange Surprizing Adventures of Robinson Crusoe, The (1719) **Daniel Defoe** (1660)

Life and the Poet (1942) **Sir Stephen Spender** (1909)

Life and Times of Frederick Douglass (1881) **Frederick Douglass** (1817)

Life and Times of Lord Brougham, The (1871) **Henry, Lord Brougham** (1778–1868)

Life and Times of Michael K, The (1983) **J.M. Coetzee** (1940)

Life and Works of Goethe, The (1855) **G.H. Lewes** (1817)

Life at the Top (1962) **John Braine** (1922)

Life Before Death (1979) **P.J. Kavanagh** (1931)

Life Before Man (1979) **Margaret Atwood** (1939)

Life Drama, A (1853) **Alexander Smith** (1830)

Life Everlasting, The (1911) **Marie Corelli** (1855)

Life for a Life, A (1859) **Dinah Maria Craik** (1826)

Life Full of Holes, A (1964) **Paul Bowles** (1910)

Life Goes On (1985) **Alan Sillitoe** (1928)

Life in London (1821) **Pierce Egan [the elder]** (1772)

Life in the Red Brigade (1873) **R.M. Ballantyne** (1825)

Life in the Sick-Room (1844) **Harriet Martineau** (1802)

Life in the Theater, A (1977) **David Mamet** (1947)

Life in the West (1998) **Brian Aldiss** (1925)

Life Interest, A (1888) **Mrs A.H. Alexander** (1825)

Life is a Dream [La vida es sueño] (1635) **Pedro Calderón de la Barca** (1600)

Life is Elsewhere (1973) **Milan Kundera** (1929)

Life, Letters and Literary Remains of John Keats, The (1848) **Richard Monckton Milnes** (1809)

Life of a Lover, The (1804) **Sophia Lee** (1750)

Life of a Sailor, The (1832) **Captain Chamier** (1796)

Life of a Sportsman, The (1842) **Charles James Apperley** (1779)

Life of a Useless Man, The (1917) **Maxim Gorky** (1868)

Life of Arsenev, The (1927–9) **Ivan Bunin** (1870)

Life of Benvenuto Cellini, The (1888) **John Addington Symonds** (1840) (tr.)

Life of Blake (1863) **Alexander Gilchrist** (1828–61)

Life of Captain Sir Richard F. Burton, The (1893) **Isabel, Lady Burton** (1831)

Life of Charles Dickens, The (1872) **John Forster** (1812)

Life of Charlotta du Pont, The (1723) **Penelope Aubin** (*c.* 1685)

Life of Charlotte Brontë, The (1887) **Augustine Birrell** (1850)

Life of Charlotte Brontë, The (1857) **Elizabeth Gaskell** (1810)

Life of Christ, The (1874) **Frederic W. Farrar** (1831)

Life of David Hume, The (1777) **David Hume** (1711–76)

Life of Dr Arnold (1844) **Arthur Penrhyn Stanley** (1815)

Life of Dr Sanderson, The (1678) **Izaak Walton** (1593)

Life of Edward Lord Herbert of Cherbury, Written by Himself (1764) **Edward Herbert, Lord Herbert of Cherbury** (1583–1648)

Life of Edward White Benson (1899) **A.C. Benson** (1862)

Life of Faith, The (1660) **Richard Baxter** (1615)

Life of Frances Power Cobbe (1894) **Frances Power Cobbe** (1822)

Life of Friedrich Schiller, The (1825) **Thomas Carlyle** (1795)

Life of Galileo, The [Leben des Galilei] (1937–9) **Bertolt Brecht** (1898)

Life of Geoffrey Chaucer (1803) **William Godwin** (1756)

The Life of George Stephenson, Railway engineer (1857) **Samuel Smiles** (1812)

Life of Harriot Stuart, The (1750) **Charlotte Lennox** (1720)

Life of Haydon, The (1853) **Benjamin Robert Haydon** (1786–1846)

Life of Henry St John (1770) **Oliver Goldsmith** (1728)

Life of Jesus, The (1846) **'George Eliot' [Mary Ann Evans]** (1819) (tr.)

Life of Jesus, The (1926) **John Middleton Murry** (1889)

Life of John Buncle, Esq., The (1756) **Thomas Amory** (1691?)

Life of John Donne, The (1658) **Izaak Walton** (1593)

Life of John Milton, The (1859) **David Masson** (1822)

Life of John Milton, The (1983) **A.N. Wilson** (1950)

Life of John Stirling, The (1851) **Thomas Carlyle** (1795)

Life of Joseph Blanco White, The (1845) **Joseph Blanco White** (1775–1841)

Life of Klim Samgin, The (1925–36) **Maxim Gorky** (1868)

Life of Lord Byron, The (1830) **John Galt** (1779)

Life of Madam de Beaumont, The (1721) **Penelope Aubin** (*c.* 1685)

Life of Merlin, The (1641) **Thomas Heywood** (1574?)

Life of Milton (1796) **William Hayley** (1745)

Life of Mr George Herbert, The (1670) **Izaak Walton** (1593)

Life of Mr Jonathan Wild the Great, The (1759) **Henry Fielding** (1707)

Life of Mr Richard Hooker, The (1665) **Izaak Walton** (1593)

Life of Mr Thomas Betterton, The (1710) **Charles Gildon** (1665)

Life of Mrs Siddons (1834) **Thomas Campbell** (1777)

Life of Nancy, The (1895) **Sarah Orne Jewett** (1849)

Life of Napoleon Buonaparte, The (1827) **Sir Walter Scott** (1771) (ed.)

Life of Napoleon Buonaparte , The [vols. i, ii] (1828) **William Hazlitt** (1778)

Life of Napoleon Buonaparte, The [vols. iii, iv] (1830) **William Hazlitt** (1778)

Life of Nelson, The (1813) **Robert Southey** (1774)

Life of Percy Bysshe Shelley, The (1886) **Edward Dowden** (1843)

Life of Philip Henry Gosse, The (1890) **Sir Edmund Gosse** (1849)

Life of Reason, The (1905–6) **George Santayana** (1863)
Life of Richard Cobden, The (1881) **John Morley, 1st Viscount Morley of Blackburn** (1838)
Life of Richard Nash, The (1762) **Oliver Goldsmith** (1728)
Life of Ronald Knox, The (1959) **Evelyn Waugh** (1903)
Life of Samuel Johnson, The (1791) **James Boswell** (1740)
'Life of Sir Henry Wotton, The' [in *Reliquiae Wottonianae*] (1651) **Izaak Walton** (1593)
Life of Sir Philip Sidney, The (1652) **Fulke Greville, Lord Brooke** (1554–1628)
Life of the Fields, The (1884) **Richard Jefferies** (1848)
Life of the Land, The (1983) **Patricia Beer** (1924)
Life of the Spirit and the Life of To-day, The (1922) **Evelyn Underhill** (1875)
Life of Thomas More, The (1998) **Peter Ackroyd** (1949)
Life of Thomas Parnell, The (1770) **Oliver Goldsmith** (1728)
Life of Washington (1855–9) **Washington Irving** (1783)
Life of Wesley, The (1820) **Robert Southey** (1774)
Life of William Ewart Gladstone, The (1903) **John Morley, 1st Viscount Morley of Blackburn** (1838)
Life of William Shakespeare, A (1898) **Sir Sidney Lee** (1859)
Life of William Shakespeare, The (1848) **J.O. Halliwell-Phillipps** (1820)
Life on the Mississippi (1883) **'Mark Twain' [Samuel Langhorne Clemens]** (1835)
Life Quest (1935) **Richard Aldington** (1892)
Life Rarely Tells (1958) **Jack Lindsay** (1900)
Life Romantic, The (1901) **Richard le Gallienne** (1866)
Life Sentence (1935) **Mary Agnes Hamilton** (1884)
Life Stories (1981) **A.L. Barker** (1918)
Life Story (1948) **Phyllis Bentley** (1894)
Life Studies (1959) **Robert Lowell** (1917)
Life the Accuser (1896) **E[mma] F[rances] Brooke** (1859?)
Life, the Universe and Everything (1982) **Douglas Adams** (1952)
Life to Come, The (1972) **E.M. Forster** (1879–1970)
Life's Assize, A (1871) **Mrs J.H. Riddell** (1832)
Life's Handicap (1891) **Rudyard Kipling** (1865)
Life's Little Ironies (1894) **Thomas Hardy** (1840)
Life's Morning, A (1888) **George Gissing** (1857)
Life's Progress Through the Passions (1748) **Eliza Haywood** (*c.* 1693)
Life's Secret, A (1867) **Mrs Henry Wood** (1814)
Lifeboat, The (1864) **R.M. Ballantyne** (1825)
Lifeguard, The (1971) **John Wain** (1925)
Lifelines (1974) **Lawrence Durrell** (1912)
'Lifted Veil, The' (1859) **George Eliot** (1819)
Light (1981) **Eva Figes** (1932)
Light a Penny Candle (1982) **Maeve Binchy** (1940)
Light and Darkness (1850) **Catherine Crowe** (1790)
Light and the Dark, The (1947) **C.P. Snow** (1905)
Light and Twilight (1911) **Edward Thomas** (1878)
Light Around the Body, The (1967) **Robert Bly** (1926)
Light Beyond the Forest, The (1979) **Rosemary Sutcliff** (1920)
Light Can Be Both Wave and Particle (1989) **Ellen Gilchrist** (1935)
Light Fantastic, The (1986) **Terry Pratchett** (1948)
Light for Them That Sit in Darkness (1675) **John Bunyan** (1628)
Light Freights (1901) **W.W. Jacobs** (1863)
Light in August (1932) **William Faulkner** (1897)
Light in the Forest (1953) **Conrad Richter** (1890)
Light in the Piazza, The (1960) **Elizabeth Spencer** (1921)
Light Music (1977) **Derek Mahon** (1941)
Light of Asia, The (1879) **Sir Edwin Arnold** (1832)
Light of Day, The [US: *Topkapi*] (1962) **Eric Ambler** (1909)
Light of Nature Pursued, The [by 'Edward Search'] (1768–77) **Abraham Tucker** (1705)
Light of the World, The (1891) **Sir Edwin Arnold** (1832)
Light on a Dark Horse (1951) **Roy Campbell** (1901)
Light Princess, The (1890) **George MacDonald** (1824)
Light Shining in Buckinghamshire (1976) **Caryl Churchill** (1938)
Light That Failed, The (1891) **Rudyard Kipling** (1865)
Light the Lights (1945) **A.P. Herbert** (1890)
Light Thickens (1982) **Ngaio Marsh** (1899)
Light Years (1985) **Maggie Gee** (1948)
Light Years, The (1990) **Elizabeth Jane Howard** (1923)
Lightbody on Liberty (1936) **Nigel Balchin** (1908)
Lighted Room, The (1925) **Lettice Cooper** (1897)
Lighthouse, The (1865) **R.M. Ballantyne** (1825)
Lightning (1988) **Dean Koontz** (1945)
Lightning Tree, The (1980) **Joan Aiken** (1924)
Lights and Shadows of London Life (1867) **James Payn** (1830)
Lights and Shadows of Scottish Life (1822) **John Wilson** (1785)
Ligue, La (1723) **'Voltaire' [François-Marie Arouet]** (1694)
Like a Bulwark (1956) **Marianne Moore** (1887)
Like and Unlike (1887) **M.E. Braddon** (1835)
Like It Or Not (1992) **Gavin Ewart** (1916)
Like Men Betrayed (1970) **Frederic Raphael** (1931)
Like Mother (1988) **Jenny Diski** (1947)
Likely Lad, A (1971) **Gillian Avery** (1926)
Likely Story, A (1911) **William De Morgan** (1839)
Lila: An Enquiry into Morals (1991) **Robert Pirsig** (1928)
Lilac and Flag (1990) **John Berger** (1926)
Lilac Fairy Book, The (1910) **Andrew Lang** (1844) (ed.)
Lilac Sunbonnet, The (1894) **S.R. Crockett** (1860)
Lilacs Out of the Dead Land (1971) **Rachel Billington** (1942)
Lilian (1922) **Arnold Bennett** (1867)
Lilias Lee (1871) **James Ballantine** (1808)
Lilith (1895) **George MacDonald** (1824)
Lilla (1916) **Mrs Belloc Lowndes** (1868)

Lilliesleaf (1855) **Margaret Oliphant** (1828)
Lilliput (1757) **David Garrick** (1717)
Lily and the Cross, The (1887) **E[dith] Nesbit** (1858)
Lily of Malud, The (1917) **J.C. Squire** (1884)
Limbo (1920) **Aldous Huxley** (1894)
Limbo (1897) **'Vernon Lee' [Violet Paget]** (1856)
Limbo Dancer in Dark Glasses (1983) **John Agard** (1949)
Limestone Tree, The (1931) **Joseph Hergesheimer** (1880)
Limit, The (1911) **Ada Leverson** (1862)
Limitations (1896) **E.F. Benson** (1867)
Limits and Renewals (1932) **Rudyard Kipling** (1865)
Limits of Love, The (1960) **Frederic Raphael** (1931)
Lin McLean (1898) **Owen Wister** (1860)
Lincoln (1984) **Gore Vidal** (1925)
Linda Condon (1919) **Joseph Hergesheimer** (1880)
Linda Tressel (1868) **Anthony Trollope** (1815)
Linda's Lie (1982) **Bernard Ashley** (1935)
Lindmann (1963) **Frederic Raphael** (1931)
Line of Life, A (1620) **John Ford** (1586)
Line of Fire (1955) **Donald Hamilton** (1916)
Line of Love, The (1905) **James Branch Cabell** (1879)
Lines at Intersection (1939) **Josephine Miles** (1911)
Linhay on the Downs, The (1929) **Henry Williamson** (1895)
Linley Rochford (1874) **Justin McCarthy** (1830)
Linnet (1898) **Grant Allen** (1848)
Linny Lockwood (1854) **Catherine Crowe** (1790)
Linwoods, The (1835) **Catharine Maria Sedgwick** (1789)
Lion and the Fox, The (1927) **Wyndham Lewis** (1882)
Lion and the Honeycomb, The (1955) **R.P. Blackmur** (1904)
Lion and the Jewel, The (1963) **Wole Soyinka** (1934)
Lion and the Unicorn, The (1899) **Richard Harding Davis** (1864)
Lion and the Unicorn, The (1941) **George Orwell** (1903)
Lion in Love, The (1960) **Shelagh Delaney** (1939)
Lion of Boaz-Jachin and Jachin-Boaz, The (1973) **Russell Hoban** (1925)
Lion, the Witch, and the Wardrobe, The (1950) **C.S. Lewis** (1898)
Lion's Share, The (1916) **Arnold Bennett** (1867)
Lionel Lincoln (1825) **James Fenimore Cooper** (1789)
Lions and Shadows (1938) **Christopher Isherwood** (1904)
Lions' Mouths, The (1967) **Alan Brownjohn** (1931)
Lipstick Boys, The (1984) **Jeremy Reed** (1954)
Lipstick on Your Collar (1993) **Dennis Potter** (1935)
Liquidator, The (1964) **John Gardner** (1926)
Lisa & Co (1981) **Jilly Cooper** (1937)
List, Ye Landsmen! (1893) **W. Clark Russell** (1844)
Listen to the Mocking Bird (1949) **S.J. Perelman** (1904)
Listener, The (1907) **Algernon Blackwood** (1869)
Listener's Lure (1906) **E.V. Lucas** (1868)
Listeners, The (1912) **Walter de la Mare** (1873)
Listening (1976) **Edward Albee** (1928)
Listening to Collared Doves (1986) **E.J. Scovell** (1907)
Listening to the Voice (1993) **Iain Crichton Smith [Iain Mac a'Ghobhainn]** (1928)
Literary Essays (1906) **John Morley, 1st Viscount Morley of Blackburn** (1838)
Literary History of Ireland, A (1899) **Douglas Hyde** (1860)
Literary Lapses (1910) **Stephen Leacock** (1869)
Literary Life of the Late Thomas Pennant (1793) **Thomas Pennant** (1726)
Literary Life, The [*La Vie littéraire*] (1888–92) **'Anatole France' [Jacques-Anatole-François Thibault]** (1844)
Literary Mind, The (1931) **Max Eastman** (1883)
Literary Pilgrim in England, A (1917) **Edward Thomas** (1878)
Literary Pocket-Book (1818) **Leigh Hunt** (1784)
Literary Recreations and Miscellanies (1854) **John Greenleaf Whittier** (1807)
Literary Sense, The (1903) **E[dith] Nesbit** (1858)
Literary Studies (1879) **Walter Bagehot** (1826–1877)
Literary Taste (1909) **Arnold Bennett** (1867)
Literary Theory (1983) **Terry Eagleton** (1943)
Literature and Dogma (1873) **Matthew Arnold** (1822)
Literature and Life (1902) **William Dean Howells** (1837)
Literature and Morality (1947) **James T. Farrell** (1904)
Literature and Psychology (1951) **F.L. Lucas** (1894)
Literature and the American College (1908) **Irving Babbit** (1865)
Literature and Western Man (1960) **J.B. Priestley** (1894)
Literature in My Time (1933) **Compton Mackenzie** (1883)
Literature of Their Own, A [rev. 1982] (1977) **Elaine Showalter** (1941)
Litigants, The [*Les Plaideurs*] (1668) **Jean Racine** (1639)
Little Anna Mark (1900) **S.R. Crockett** (1860)
Little Big Man (1964) **Thomas Berger** (1924)
Little Black Bobtail [**Bannerman**]: see *The Story of Little Black Bobtail*
Little Black Mingo [**Bannerman**]: see *The Story of Little Black Mingo*
Little Black Princess, The (1905) **Jeannie Gunn** (1870)
Little Black Quasha [**Bannerman**]: see *The Story of Little Black Quasha*
Little Black Quibba [**Bannerman**]: see *The Story of Little Black Quibba*
Little Black Sambo [**Bannerman**]: see *The Story of Little Black Sambo*
Little Blue Light, The (1950) **Edmund Wilson** (1895)
Little Book of Profitable Tales, A (1889) **Eugene Field** (1850)
Little Book of Western Verse, A (1889) **Eugene Field** (1850)
Little Bookworm, The (1955) **Eleanor Farjeon** (1881)
Little Brother (1912) **Gilbert Cannan** (1884)
Little Bush Maid, A (1910) **Mary Grant Bruce** (1878)
Little Caesar (1929) **W.R. Burnett** (1899)
Little Children (1937) **William Saroyan** (1908)

Little Company, The (1945) **Eleanor Dark** (1901)
Little Degchie-Head (1903) **Helen Bannerman** (1863)
Little Dinners with the Sphinx (1909) **Richard le Gallienne** (1866)
Little Disturbances of Man, The (1959) **Grace Paley** (1922)
Little Dorrit (1857) **Charles Dickens** (1812)
Little Drummer Girl, The (1983) **'John le Carré'** [David John Moore Cornwell] (1931)
Little Duke, The (1854) **Charlotte M. Yonge** (1823)
Little Essays of Love and Virtue (1922) **Havelock Ellis** (1859)
Little Eyolf (1894) **Henrik Ibsen** (1828)
Little Fadette [*La Petite Fadette*] (1848) **'George Sand' [Auore Dupin]** (1804)
Little Foxes, The (1939) **Lillian Hellman** (1907)
Little Friend, Little Friend (1945) **Randall Jarrell** (1914)
Little Gidding (1942) **T.S. Eliot** (1888)
Little Girls, The (1964) **Elizabeth Bowen** (1899)
Little Horses of Tarquinia, The [*Les Petits Chevaux de Tarquinia*] (1953) **'Marguerite Duras' [Marguerite Donnadieu]** (1914)
Little Hotel, The (1973) **Christina Stead** (1902)
Little House in Kolomna, The (1830) **Alexander Pushkin** (1799)
Little House in the Big Woods (1932) **Laura Ingalls Wilder** (1867)
Little House on the Prairie (1935) **Laura Ingalls Wilder** (1867)
Little Huguenot, The (1895) **Max Pemberton** (1863)
Little Johnny's Confession (1967) **Brian Patten** (1946)
Little Journey in the World, A (1889) **Charles Dudley Warner** (1829)
Little Learning, A (1964) **Evelyn Waugh** (1903)
Little Loot, A (1920) **E.V. Knox** (1881)
Little Lord Fauntleroy (1886) **Frances Hodgson Burnett** (1849)
Little Man, The (1915) **John Galsworthy** (1867)
Little Me (1962) **Neil Simon** (1927)
Little Men (1871) **Louisa M. Alcott** (1832)
Little Mexican (1924) **Aldous Huxley** (1894)
Little Minister, The (1891) **[Sir] J.M. Barrie** (1860)
Little Mr Bouncer and His Friend, Verdant Green (1873) **'Cuthbert Bede' [Edward Bradley]** (1827)
Little Noddy Goes to Toyland (1949) **Enid Blyton** (1897)
Little Norsk, A (1892) **Hamlin Garland** (1860)
Little Novels (1887) **Wilkie Collins** (1824)
Little Novels of Italy (1899) **Maurice Hewlett** (1861)
Little of What You Fancy, A (1970) **H.E. Bates** (1905)
Little People (1942) **Albert Halper** (1904)
Little Pilgrim in the Unseen, A (1882) **Margaret Oliphant** (1828)
Little Plays for Children (1827) **Maria Edgeworth** (1767)
Little Plays of Mahatma Gandhi (1990) **Mulk Raj Anand** (1905)
Little Plays of St Francis [2nd ser., 1931] (1922) **Laurence Housman** (1865)
Little Prince, The [*Le Petit Prince*] (1943) **Antoine de Saint-Exupéry** (1900)
Little Princess, A (1905) **Frances Hodgson Burnett** (1849)
Little Regiment, The [UK: *Pictures of War*] (1896) **Stephen Crane** (1871)
Little Savage, The (1848–9) **Frederick Marryat** (1792)
Little Schoolmaster Mark, The (1883) **J.H. Shorthouse** (1834)
Little Sister, The (1949) **Raymond Chandler** (1888)
Little Sisters (1978) **Fay Weldon** (1931)
Little Stone, A (1950) **Paul Bowles** (1910)
Little Stranger, A (1989) **Candia McWilliam** (1955)
Little Tea. a Little Chat, A (1948) **Christina Stead** (1902)
Little Time-Keeper, The (1976) **Jon Silkin** (1930)
Little White Bird, The (1902) **[Sir] J.M. Barrie** (1860)
Little Wilson and Big God (1987) **'Anthony Burgess' [John Anthony Burgess Wilson]** (1917)
Little Women (1868) **Louisa M. Alcott** (1832)
Little World, A (1877) **George Manville Fenn** (1831)
Little World of the Past, The [*Piccolo mondo antico*] (1895) **Antonio Fogazzaro** (1842)
Little World, The (1925) **Stella Benson** (1892)
Little Yellow Dog, A (1996) **Walter Mosley** (1952)
Live and Let Die (1954) **Ian Fleming** (1908)
Live or Die (1966) **Anne Sexton** (1928)
Livelihood (1917) **Wilfrid Gibson** (1878)
Lives and Characters of the English Dramatick Poets, The (1699) **Charles Gildon** (1665)
Lives of Animals, The (1999) **J.M. Coetzee** (1940)
Lives of Boulton and Watt (1865) **Samuel Smiles** (1812)
Lives of Eminent Men ['Brief Lives'] (1813) **John Aubrey** (1626–97)
Lives of Famous Poets (1878) **W.M. Rossetti** (1829)
Lives of Girls and Women (1971) **Alice Munro** (1931)
Lives of the British Admirals [vol. i] (1833–1837) **Robert Southey** (1774)
Lives of the Engineers (1867) **Samuel Smiles** (1812)
Lives of the English Poets [**Johnson**]: see *Prefaces, Biographical and Critical*
Lives of the Hunted (1901) **Ernest Thompson Seton** (1860)
Lives of the Most Eminent British Painters, Sculptors and Architects (1829) **Allan Cunningham** (1784)
Lives of the Necromancers (1834) **William Godwin** (1756)
Lives of the Noble Grecians and Romanes, The [from a French trn of Plutarch] (1579) **Sir Thomas North** (1535) (tr.)
Lives of the Poet (1984) **E.L. Doctorow** (1931)
Lives of the Three Normans, Kings of England (1613) **Sir John Hayward** (1564?)
Lives of Wives (1939) **Laura Riding** (1901)
Livia (1978) **Lawrence Durrell** (1912)
Living (1929) **'Henry Green' [Henry Vicent Yorke]** (1905)
Living Alone (1919) **Stella Benson** (1892)
Living and the Dead, The (1941) **Patrick White** (1912)

Living by the Word (1988) **Alice Walker** (1944)
Living End, The (1979) **Stanley Elkin** (1930)
Living in a Calm Country (1975) **Peter Porter** (1929)
Living in America (1965) **Anne Stevenson** (1933)
Living in Disguise (1986) **E.A. Markham** (1939)
Living in the Maniototo (1979) **Janet Frame** (1924)
Living in the Present (1955) **John Wain** (1925)
Living in Time (1946) **Kathleen Raine** (1908)
Living Novel, The (1946) **V.S. Pritchett** (1900)
Living of Charlotte Perkins Gilman, The (1935) **Charlotte Perkins Gilman** (1860)
Living Quarters (1977) **Brian Friel** (1929)
Living Room, The (1953) **Graham Greene** (1904)
Living Space (1940) **Walter Allen** (1911)
Living Theatre, The (1959) **Elmer Rice** (1892)
Living Together (1974) **Michael Wilding** (1942)
Living With Mystery (1992) **Kathleen Raine** (1908)
Liza of Lambeth (1897) **Somerset Maugham** (1874)
Lizzie Dripping (1973) **Helen Cresswell** (1934)
Lizzie Dripping Again (1974) **Helen Cresswell** (1934)
Lizzie Dripping and the Little Angel (1974) **Helen Cresswell** (1934)
Lizzie Dripping by the Sea (1974) **Helen Cresswell** (1934)
Lizzie Leigh (1854) **Elizabeth Gaskell** (1810)
Lizzie Lorton of Greyrigg (1866) **E. Lynn Linton** (1822)
Llangollen Vale (1796) **Anna Seward** (1747)
Lloyd George Knew My Father (1972) **William Douglas Home** (1912)
Loading Mercury with a Pitchfork (1976) **Richard Brautigan** (1935)
Loaves and Fishes (1906) **Bernard Capes** (1850?)
Loaves and Fishes (1924) **Somerset Maugham** (1874)
Loaves and Fishes (1959) **George Mackay Brown** (1921)
Lob Lie-by-the-Fire (1874) **Mrs J.H. Ewing** (1841)
Lobo, Rag, and Vixen (1899) **Ernest Thompson Seton** (1860)
Local Anaesthetic [*Örtlich betäubt*] (1969) **Günter Grass** (1927)
Local Color (1950) **Truman Capote** (1924)
Local Colour (1975) **Stephen Gray** (1941)
Local Habitation, A (1972) **Norman Nicholson** (1914)
Local Habitation, A (1988) **Richard Hoggart** (1918)
Local Measures (1946) **Josephine Miles** (1911)
Lochinvar (1897) **S.R. Crockett** (1860)
Locked Room, The (1986) **Paul Auster** (1947)
Locksley Hall Sixty Years After (1886) **Alfred, Lord Tennyson** (1809)
Lockwood Concern, The (1965) **John O'Hara** (1905)
Locrine (1887) **A.C. Swinburne** (1837)
Locustae (The Locusts) [Latin and English] (1627) **Phineas Fletcher** (1582)
Lodger, The (1913) **Mrs Belloc Lowndes** (1868)
Lodore (1835) **Mary Shelley** (1797)
Log of a Cowboy, The (1903) **Andy Adams** (1859)
Logic of Scientific Discovery, The (1959) **Sir Karl Popper** (1902)
Logoi Threskia (1670) **Joseph Glanvill** (1636)
Logue's ABC (1966) **Christopher Logue** (1926)
Loiners, The (1970) **Tony Harrison** (1937)
Lois the Witch (1861) **Elizabeth Gaskell** (1810)
Loiterer's Harvest (1913) **E.V. Lucas** (1868)
Loitering With Intent (1981) **Muriel Spark** (1918)
Lokis (1870) **Prosper Mérimée** (1803)
Lolita (1958) **Vladimir Nabokov** (1899)
Lollingdon Downs (1917) **John Masefield** (1878)
Lollipop (1962) **Terry Southern** (1924)
Lolly Madonna War, The (1969) **Sue Grafton** (1940)
Lolly Willowes; or, The Loving Huntsman (1926) **Sylvia Townsend Warner** (1893)
Lombard Street (1873) **Walter Bagehot** (1826)
London (1739) **Richard Glover** (1712)
London (1738) **Samuel Johnson** (1709)
London (1984) **Fiona Pitt-Kethley** (1954)
London Assurance (1841) **Dion Boucicault** (1820?)
London at War (1995) **Philip Ziegler** (1929)
London by Night (1906) **George R. Sims** (1847)
London Cuckolds, The (1681) **Edward Ravenscroft** (1644)
London Education (1904) **Sidney Webb** (1859)
London Fabric (1939) **James Pope-Hennessy** (1916)
London Fields (1989) **Martin Amis** (1949)
London in the Nineteenth Century (1909) **Sir Walter Besant** (1836)
London Labour and the London Poor (1851) **Henry Mayhew** (1812)
London Lavender (1912) **E.V. Lucas** (1868)
London Lickpenny (1973) **Peter Ackroyd** (1949)
London Life, A (1889) **Henry James** (1843)
London Life (1924) **Arnold Bennett** (1867)
London Match (1985) **Len Deighton** (1929)
London Merchant, The (1731) **George Lillo** (1693)
London Music in 1888–89 (1937) **Bernard Shaw** (1856)
London Nights (1895) **Arthur Symons** (1865)
London Observed (1990) **Doris Lessing** (1919)
London Plane-Tree, A (1889) **Amy Levy** (1861)
London Poems (1866) **Robert Williams Buchanan** (1841)
London Pride (1941) **Phyllis Bottome** (1884)
London Pride (1896) **M.E. Braddon** (1835)
London Revisited (1916) **E.V. Lucas** (1868)
London River (1921) **H.M. Tomlinson** (1873)
London Spy, The (1698–1700) **Edward Ward** (1667)
London to Ladysmith via Pretoria (1900) **Sir Winston Churchill** (1874)
London Venture, The (1920) **'Michael Arlen' [Dikran Kouyoumdjian]** (1895)
London Volunteers (1893) **W.E. Henley** (1849)
London Zoo, The (1961) **C.H. Sisson** (1914)
London's Burning (1986) **Jack Rosenthal** (1931)
London's Heart (1873) **B.L. Farjeon** (1838)
Londoners, The (1898) **Robert Hichens** (1864)
Londoners (1964) **Gavin Ewart** (1916)
Londoners (1983) **Maureen Duffy** (1933)
Loneliest Mountain, The (1939) **W.H. Davies** (1871)
Loneliness (1915) **R.H. Benson** (1871)
Loneliness of the Long-Distance Runner, The (1959) **Alan Sillitoe** (1928)

Lonely, The (1947) **Paul Gallico** (1897)
Lonely Crusade (1947) **Chester Himes** (1909)
Lonely Dancer, The (1914) **Richard loe Gallienne** (1866)
Lonely for the Future (1966) **James T. Farrell** (1904)
Lonely Girl, The (1962) **Edna O'Brien** (1932)
Lonely House, The (1920) **Mrs Belloc Lowndes** (1868)
Lonely Island, The (1880) **R.M. Ballantyne** (1825)
Lonely Lady of Dulwich, The (1934) **Maurice Baring** (1874)
Lonely Londoners, The (1956) **Samuel Selvon** (1923)
Lonely Plough, The (1914) **Constance Holme** (1881)
Lonely Queen, The (1911) **H.C. Bailey** (1878)
Lonely Suppers of W.V. Balloon, The (1975) **Christopher Middleton** (1926)
Lonely Unicorn, The (1922) **Alec Waugh** (1898)
Lonely Voice, The (1963) **'Frank O'Connor' [Michael Francis O'Donovan']** (1903)
Lonesome Dove (1985) **Larry McMurty** (1936)
Lonesome Road (1926) **Paul Green** (1894)
Lonesome Traveler (1960) **Jack Kerouac** (1922–69)
Lonesome-Like (1911) **Harold Brighouse** (1882)
Long Ago, The (1944) **Mary Lavin** (1912)
Long Approach, The (1985) **Maxine Kumin** (1925)
Long Christmas Dinner, The (1931) **Thornton Wilder** (1897)
Long Dark Tea-Time of the Soul, The (1988) **Douglas Adams** (1952)
Long Day's Journey into Night (1956) **Eugene O'Neill** (1888)
Long Desire, A (1979) **Evan S. Connell, Jr** (1924)
Long Distance (1974) **Penelope Mortimer** (1918)
Long Divorce, The [US: *A Noose for Her*] (1951) **Edmund Crispin** (1921)
Long Dream, The (1958) **Richard Wright** (1908)
Long Gay Book, A (1932) **Gertrude Stein** (1874)
Long Goodbye, The (1953) **Raymond Chandler** (1888)
Long Lankin (1970) **John Banville** (1945)
Long March, The (1953) **William Styron** (1925)
Long March, The [*La Longue Marche*] (1957) **Simone de Beauvoir** (1908)
Long Night, The (1903) **Stanley J. Weyman** (1855)
Long Prospect, The (1958) **Elizabeth Harrower** (1928)
Long Pursuit, The (1967) **Jon Cleary** (1917)
Long Reach, The (1984) **Richard Eberhart** (1904)
Long Retrospect, A (1936) **'F. Anstey' [Thomas Anstey Guthrie]** (1856)
Long River, The (1955) **Iain Crichton Smith [Iain Mac a'Ghobhainn]** (1928)
Long Shadow, The (1949) **Jon Cleary** (1917)
Long Shadows, The (1997) **Alan Brownjohn** (1931)
Long Silence, A (1971) **Nicholas Freeling** (1927)
Long Traverse, The (1941) **John Buchan** (1875–1940)
Long Vacation, The (1895) **Charlotte M. Yonge** (1823)
Long Valley, The (1938) **John Steinbeck** (1902)
Long View, The (1956) **Elizabeth Jane Howard** (1923)
Long Weekend with Marcel Proust, A (1986) **Ronald Frame** (1953)
Longest Journey, The (1907) **E.M. Forster** (1879)
Longhand (1989) **Murray Bail** (1941)
Longshot (1990) **Dick Francis** (1920)
Loo Sanction, The (1973) **'Trevanian' [Rodney Whitaker]** (1925)
Look at All Those Roses (1941) **Elizabeth Bowen** (1899)
Look at Me (1983) **Anita Brookner** (1928)
Look at the Harlequins! (1974) **Vladimir Nabokov** (1899)
Look Back in Anger (1956) **John Osborne** (1929)
Look Before You Leap (1865) **Mrs A.H. Alexander** (1825)
Look Homeward, Angel (1929) **Thomas Wolfe** (1900)
Look Look (1990) **Michael Frayn** (1933)
Look Round Literature, A (1887) **Robert Williams Buchanan** (1841)
Look Round the Estate, A (1967) **Kingsley Amis** (1922)
Look, Stranger! (1936) **W.H. Auden** (1907)
Look to the Lady [US: *The Gyrth Chalice Mystery*] (1931) **Margery Allingham** (1904)
Look Twice (1991) **John Fuller** (1937)
Look! We Have Come Through (1917) **D.H. Lawrence** (1885)
Look Who's Talking (1940) **S.J. Perelman** (1904)
Looking at Life (1860) **George Augustus Sala** (1828)
Looking Back (1933) **Norman Douglas** (1868)
Looking Back (1997) **Fleur Adcock** (1934)
Looking Backward (1888) **Edward Bellamy** (1850)
Looking for Luck (1993) **Maxine Kumin** (1925)
Looking for Rachel Wallace (1980) **Robert B. Parker** (1932)
Looking For the Possible Dance (1993) **A.L. Kennedy** (1965)
Looking Glass, The (2000) **Michèle Roberts** (1949)
Looking on Darkness (1974) **André Brink** (1935)
Looking-Glass War, The (1965) **'John le Carré' [David John Moore Cornwell]** (1931)
Looks and Smiles (1981) **Barry Hines** (1939)
Loom of Years, The (1902) **Alfred Noyes** (1880)
Loom of Youth, The (1917) **Alec Waugh** (1898)
Loon Lake (1980) **E.L. Doctorow** (1931)
Loop in Lone Kauri Road, The (1986) **Allen Curnow** (1911)
Loose Hints Upon Education (1781) **Henry Home, Lord Kames** (1696)
Loot (1967) **Joe Orton** (1933)
Loot of Cities, The (1905) **Arnold Bennett** (1867)
Loquitur (1965) **Basil Bunting** (1900)
Lord and Mary Ann, The (1956) **Catherine Cookson** (1906)
Lord Arthur Savile's Crime (1891) **Oscar Wilde** (1854)
Lord Brackenbury (1880) **Amelia B. Edwards** (1831)
Lord Byron and Some of His Contemporaries (1828) **Leigh Hunt** (1784)
Lord Byron: Christian Virtues (1952) **G. Wilson Knight** (1897)
Lord Chesterfield's Maxims (1774) **Philip Dormer Stanhope, Earl of Chesterfield** (1694–1773)
Lord Emsworth and Others [US: *The Crime Wave at Blandings*] (1937) **P.G. Wodehouse** (1881)

Lord Fitzhenry (1794) **Elizabeth Gunning** (1769)
Lord God Made Them All, The (1981) **James Herriot** (1916)
Lord, I Was Afraid (1947) **Nigel Balchin** (1908)
Lord Jim (1900) **Joseph Conrad** (1857)
Lord Kilgobbin (1872) **Charles Lever** (1806)
Lord Love Us (1954) **William Sansom** (1912)
Lord M. (1954) **Lord David Cecil** (1902)
Lord Malquist and Mr Moon (1966) **Tom Stoppard** (1937)
Lord Mayor of London, The (1862) **W.H. Ainsworth** (1805)
Lord Oakburn's Daughters (1864) **Mrs Henry Wood** (1814)
Lord of Light (1967) **Roger Zelazny** (1937)
Lord of the Flies (1954) **William Golding** (1911)
Lord of the Forest and His Vassals, The (1848) **Mrs C.F. Alexander** (1818)
Lord of the Harvest, The (1899) **Matilda Betham-Edwards** (1836)
Lord of the Isles, The (1815) **Sir Walter Scott** (1771)
Lord of the Manor, The (1780) **John Burgoyne** (1722)
Lord of the Rings, The [all 3 pts] (1966) **J.R.R. Tolkein** (1892)
Lord of the Sea, The (1901) **M.P. Shiel** (1865)
Lord Ormont and His Aminta (1894) **George Meredith** (1828)
Lord Peter Views the Body (1928) **Dorothy L. Sayers** (1893)
Lord Raingo (1926) **Arnold Bennett** (1867)
Lord Vyet (1895) **A.C. Benson** (1862)
Lord Weary's Castle (1946) **Robert Lowell** (1917)
Lord's Will, The (1925) **Paul Green** (1894)
Lords and Masters (1936) **A.G. Macdonell** (1895)
Lords of Limit, The (1984) **Geoffrey Hill** (1932)
Lorimer (1814) **Lucy Aikin** (1781)
Lorna Doone (1869) **R.D. Blackmore** (1825)
Loser Takes All (1955) **Graham Greene** (1904)
Loser Wins [Les Séquestres d'Altona] (1959) **Jean-Paul Sartre** (1905)
Losing Battles (1970) **Eudora Welty** (1909)
Losing Nelson (1999) **Barry Unsworth** (1930)
Losing Touch (1990) **Tony Harrison** (1937)
Loss and Gain (1848) **J.H. Newman** (1801)
Loss of Roses, A (1959) **William Inge** (1913)
Loss of the Magyar (1959) **Patricia Beer** (1924)
Losses (1948) **Randall Jarrell** (1914)
Lost and Saved (1863) **Caroline Norton** (1808)
Lost Boy, The (1987) **Paula Fox** (1923)
Lost Child, The (1934) **Mulk Raj Anand** (1905)
Lost Childhood, The (1951) **Graham Greene** (1904)
Lost Children (1994) **Maggie Gee** (1948)
Lost Continent, The (1900) **C.J. Cutcliffe Hyne** (1865)
Lost Diaries (1913) **Maurice Baring** (1874)
Lost Eden, A (1904) **M.E. Braddon** (1835)
Lost Empires (1965) **J.B. Priestley** (1894)
Lost Endeavour, A (1895) **Guy Boothby** (1867)
Lost Face (1910) **'Jack London' [John Griffith Chaney]** (1876)
Lost Father, The (1988) **Marina Warner** (1946)
Lost Fields (1941) **Michael McLaverty** (1904)
Lost for Love (1874) **M.E. Braddon** (1835)
Lost Galleon, The (1867) **Bret Harte** (1836)
Lost Girl, The (1920) **D.H. Lawrence** (1885)
Lost Heart of Asia, The (1994) **Colin Thubron** (1939)
Lost Honour of Katherina Blum, The [Die verlorene Ehre der Katherina Blum] (1974) **Heinrich Böll** (1917)
Lost Horizon (1933) **James Hilton** (1900)
Lost Illusions [Illusions perdues] (1837[-43]) **Honoré de Balzac** (1799)
Lost in America (1981) **Isaac Bashevis Singer** (1904)
Lost in the Barrens (1965) **Farley Mowat** (1921)
Lost in the Cosmos (1983) **Walker Percy** (1916)
Lost in the Funhouse (1968) **John Barth** (1930)
Lost in the Stars (1948) **Maxwell Anderson** (1888)
Lost Lady, A (1923) **Willa Cather** (1873)
Lost Lady of Old Years, A (1899) **John Buchan** (1875)
Lost Laysen (1996) **Margaret Mitchell** (1900)
Lost Lenore (1864) **Mayne Reid** (1818)
Lost Lover, The (1696) **Mary Delariviere Manley** (1663)
Lost Name, A (1868) **J.S. le Fanu** (1814)
Lost on Du Corrig (1894) **Standish O'Grady** (1846)
Lost Ones, The [pub. in French 1971] (1972) **Samuel Beckett** (1906)
Lost Possessions (1985) **Keri Hulme** (1947)
Lost Princess of Oz, The (1917) **L. Frank Baum** (1856)
Lost Railway, The (1980) **Gillian Avery** (1926)
Lost Season, A (1944) **Roy Fuller** (1912)
Lost Sir Massingberd (1864) **James Payn** (1830)
Lost Son, The (1948) **Theodore Roethke** (1908)
Lost Stradivarius, The (1895) **J. Meade Falkner** (1858)
Lost Tales of Miletus, The (1866) **Edward Bulwer-Lytton** (1803)
Lost Traveller, The (1943) **Ruthven Todd** (1914)
Lost Traveller, The (1950) **'Antonia White' [Eirene Botting]** (1899)
Lost Upon the Roundabouts (1964) **A.L. Barker** (1918)
Lost Valley, The (1910) **Algernon Blackwood** (1869)
Lost Victory, The (1995) **Correlli Barnett** (1927)
Lost Village, The (1992) **George Mackay Brown** (1921)
Lost Viol, The (1905) **M.P. Shiel** (1865)
Lost World of the Kalahari, The (1958) **Sir Laurens van der Post** (1906)
Lost World, The (1995) **Michael Crichton** (1942)
Lost World, The (1912) **A. Conan Doyle** (1859)
Lost World, The (1965) **Randall Jarrell** (1914)
Lot to Ask, A (1973) **P.H. Newby** (1918)
Lot's Wife (1989) **Tom Wakefield** (1935)
Lothair (1870) **Benjamin Disraeli** (1804)
Lotta Schmidt (1867) **Anthony Trollope** (1815)
Lotte in Weimar (1939) **Thomas Mann** (1875)
Lottery, The (1732) **Henry Fielding** (1707)
Lottery, The (1949) **Shirley Jackson** (1919)
Lottery of Life, The (1842) **Marguerite, Countess of Blessington** (1789)
Lotus and the Robot, The (1960) **Arthur Koestler** (1905)
Loud Boy's Life, The (1980) **Howard Barker** (1946)

Loughsiders, The (1924) **Shan F. Bullock** (1865)
Louis MacNeice (1995) **Jon Stallworthy** (1935)
Louisa (1784) **Anna Seward** (1747)
Louise de la Vallière (1885) **Katharine Tynan** (1861)
Louisiana (1880) **Frances Hodgson Burnett** (1849)
Lourdes (1894) **Émile Zola** (1840)
Love (1823) **Ebenezer Elliott** (1781)
Love (1971) **Angela Carter** (1940)
Love [L'Amour] (1971) **'Marguerite Duras' [Marguerite Donnadieu]** (1914)
Love à la Mode (1759) **Charles Macklin** (1699?)
Love Adept, The (1969) **L.P. Hartley** (1895)
Love, Again (1996) **Doris Lessing** (1919)
Love Among the Artists (1900) **Bernard Shaw** (1856)
Love Among the Chickens (1906) **P.G. Wodehouse** (1881)
Love Among the Lions (1898) **'F. Anstey' [Thomas Anstey Guthrie]** (1856)
Love Among the Ruins (1904) **Warwick Deeping** (1877)
Love Among the Ruins (1948) **Angela Thirkell** (1890)
Love Among the Ruins (1953) **Evelyn Waugh** (1903)
Love and a Bottle (1698) **George Farquhar** (1678)
Love and Business (1701) **George Farquhar** (1678)
Love and Death (1939) **Llewelyn Powys** (1884)
Love and Exile (1984) **Isaac Bashevis Singer** (1904)
Love and Fame (1970) **John Berryman** (1914)
Love and Friendship (1962) **Alison Lurie** (1926)
Love and Glory (1983) **Melvyn Bragg** (1939)
Love and Hatred (1917) **Mrs Belloc Lowndes** (1868)
Love and Honour (1649) **Sir William Davenant** (1606)
Love and Liberty (1709) **Charles Johnson** (1679)
Love and Like (1960) **Herbert Gold** (1924)
Love and Mary Ann (1961) **Catherine Cookson** (1906)
Love and Mesmerism (1845) **Horace Smith** (1779)
Love and Mirage (1885) **Matilda Betham-Edwards** (1836)
Love and Money (1957) **Phyllis Bentley** (1894)
Love and Money (1954) **Erskine Caldwell** (1903)
Love and Mr Lewisham (1900) **H.G. Wells** (1866)
Love and Revenge (1675) **Elkanah Settle** (1648)
Love and Revolution (1965) **Max Eastman** (1883)
Love—and the Philosopher (1923) **Marie Corelli** (1855)
Love and War, Art and God (1984) **Karl Shapiro** (1913)
Love as Love, Death as Death (1928) **Laura Riding** (1901)
Love at a Venture (1706) **Susanna Centlivre** (1669?)
Love at First Sight (1797) **Susannah Gunning** (1740)
Love at Second Sight (1916) **Ada Leverson** (1862)
Love Child (1971) **Maureen Duffy** (1933)
Love Conquers All (1922) **Robert Benchley** (1889)
Love Department, The (1966) **'William Trevor' [William Trevor Cox]** (1928)
Love, Etc (2000) **Julian Barnes** (1946)
Love Eternal (1918) **Sir H. Rider Haggard** (1856)
Love For an Hour is Love Forever (1892) **Amelia Barr** (1831)
Love for Love (1695) **William Congreve** (1670)
Love for Lydia (1952) **H.E. Bates** (1905)
Love For Money (1691) **Thomas D'Urfey** (1653)
Love, Freedom and Society (1957) **John Middleton Murry** (1889)
Love Gods (1925) **Martin Boyd** (1893)
Love Has No Resurrection (1939) **'E.M. Delafield' [E.E.M. de la Pasture]** (1890)
Love, Here is My Hat (1938) **William Saroyan** (1908)
Love in a Cold Climate (1949) **Nancy Mitford** (1904)
Love in a Forest (1723) **Charles Johnson** (1679)
Love in a Life (1991) **Andrew Motion** (1952)
Love in a Riddle (1729) **Colley Cibber** (1671)
Love in a Veil (1718) **Richard Savage** (1697?)
Love in a Village (1762) **Isaac Bickerstaffe** (1733)
Love in a Wood (1671) **William Wycherley** (1641)
Love in Amsterdam [US: *Murder in Amsterdam*] (1962) **Nicholas Freeling** (1927)
Love in Excess (1719) **Eliza Haywood** (*c.* 1693)
Love in Idleness (1944) **Terence Rattigan** (1911)
Love in London (1906) **Arthur St John Adcock** (1864)
Love in Several Masques (1728) **Henry Fielding** (1707)
Love in the Days of Rage (1988) **Lawrence Ferlinghetti** (1920)
Love in the Ruins (1971) **Walker Percy** (1916)
Love in the Sun (1939) **Leo Walmsley** (1892)
Love in the Time of Cholera [El amor en los tiempos de coléra] (1988) **Gabriel García Márquez** (1928)
Love in These Days (1926) **Alec Waugh** (1898)
Love in Winter (1935) **Storm Jameson** (1897)
Love is a Dog From Hell (1977) **Charles Bukowski** (1920)
Love is Eternal (1954) **Irving Stone** (1903)
Love Lies Bleeding (1948) **Edmund Crispin** (1921)
Love Lyrics and Songs of Proteus, The (1892) **Wilfrid Scawen Blunt** (1840)
Love Makes a Man (1700) **Colley Cibber** (1671)
Love Match, The (1922) **Arnold Bennett** (1867)
'Love Me Little, Love Me Long' (1859) **Charles Reade** (1814)
Love Medicine (1984) **Louise Erdrich** (1954)
Love Nest, The (1926) **Ring Lardner** (1885)
Love Nest, The (1927) **Robert E. Sherwood** (1896)
Love Object, The (1968) **Edna O'Brien** (1932)
Love of a Good Man, The (1978) **Howard Barker** (1946)
Love of a Good Woman (1998) **Alice Munro** (1931)
Love of Fat Men (1997) **Helen Dunmore** (1952)
Love of Gain, The (1799) **M.G. Lewis** (1775)
Love of Ireland (1916) **Dora Sigerson** (1866)
Love of King David and Fair Bethsabe, The (1599) **George Peele** (1556)
Love of Life (1907) **'Jack London' [John Griffith Chaney]** (1876)
Love of Long Ago, The (1920) **Marie Corelli** (1855)
Love of Order, The (1773) **Richard Graves** (1715)
Love of Others, The (1962) **James Kirkup** (1923)
Love of Robert Dennison, The (1921) **Ruby M. Ayres** (1883)

Love of the Nightingale, The (1989) **Timberlake Wertenbaker**
Love on a Dark Street (1965) **Irwin Shaw** (1913)
Love on the Coast (1973) **'William Cooper' [Harry Summerfield Hoff]** (1910)
Love on the Dole (1933) **Walter Greenwood** (1903)
Love on the Supertax (1944) **Marghanita Laski** (1915)
Love or Marriage (1868) **William Black** (1841)
Love or Nothing (1974) **Douglas Dunn** (1942)
Love Poems (1981) **Brian Patten** (1946)
Love Poems and Elegies (1972) **Iain Crichton Smith [Iain Mac a'Ghobhainn]** (1928)
Love Poems and Others (1913) **D.H. Lawrence** (1885)
Love Poems, Hate Poems (1982) **Stephen Gray** (1941)
Love, Power, and Justice (1954) **Paul Tillich** (1886)
Love Restored (1612) **Ben Jonson** (1572)
Love Siege, The (1979) **Tom Wakefield** (1935)
Love Songs of a Connacht, The (1893) **Douglas Hyde** (1860)
Love Sonnets of Proteus, The (1880) **Wilfrid Scawen Blunt** (1840)
Love Story (1970) **Erich Segal** (1937)
Love Triumphant (1694) **John Dryden** (1631)
Love Unknown (1986) **A.N. Wilson** (1950)
Love's Calendar (1847) **Charles Fenno Hoffman** (1806)
Love's Coming-of-Age (1896) **Edward Carpenter** (1844) (ed.)
Love's Contrivance (1703) **Susanna Centlivre** (1669?)
Love's Cross-Currents (1905) **A.C. Swinburne** (1837)
Love's Dominion (1654) **Richard Flecknoe** (*c.* 1620)
Love's Kingdom (1664) **Richard Flecknoe** (*c.* 1620)
Loves Labors Lost [first play to be published under Shakespeare's name] (1598) **William Shakespeare** (1564)
Love's Last Shift (1696) **Colley Cibber** (1671)
Love's Lovely Counterfeit (1942) **James M. Cain** (1892)
Love's Old Sweet Song (1941) **William Saroyan** (1908)
Love's Provocations (1855) **Edward Bradley** (1827)
Love's Shadow (1908) **Ada Leverson** (1862)
Love's Victim (1701) **Charles Gildon** (1665)
Love's Victory (1658) **William Chamberlayne** (1619)
Love-Chase, The (1837) **James Sheridan Knowles** (1784)
Love-Hate Relations (1974) **Sir Stephen Spender** (1909)
Love-Letters Between a Noble-man and His Sister [pt. i] (1684–1685) **Aphra Behn** (1640?)
Love-Letters of a Worldly Woman (1891) **Lucy [Mrs W.K.] Clifford** (1853)
Loved and Envied, The (1951) **Enid Bagnold** (1889)
Loved and the Lost, The (1951) **Morley Callaghan** (1903)
Loved at Last (1864) **Mark Lemon** (1809)
Loved Helen, and Other Poems (1929) **T.H. White** (1906)
Loved One, The (1948) **Evelyn Waugh** (1903)
Lovel the Widower (1860) **W.M. Thackeray** (1811)
Lovelines for a Goat-Born Lady (1990) **John Agard** (1949)
Lovels of Arden, The (1871) **M.E. Braddon** (1835)
Lovely Lady, The (1932) **D.H. Lawrence** (1885–1930)
Lovely Ship, The (1927) **Storm Jameson** (1897)
Lover, The [*L'Amant*] (1984) **'Marguerite Duras' [Marguerite Donnadieu]** (1914)
Lover and Husband (1869) **Mary Louisa Molesworth** (1839)
Lover's Gift, and Crossing (1918) **Rabindranath Tagore** (1861)
Lover's Revolt, A (1898) **John W. De Forest** (1826)
Lover's Tale, The (1879) **Alfred, Lord Tennyson** (1809)
Lovers, The [*Les Amoureuses*] (1858) **Alphonse Daudet** (1840)
Lovers (1967) **Brian Friel** (1929)
Lovers, The (1993) **Morris West** (1916)
Lovers and Cohorts (1986) **Herbert Gold** (1924)
Lovers in London (1905) **A.A. Milne** (1882)
Lovers Melancholy, The (1629) **John Ford** (1586)
Lovers of Their Time (1978) **'William Trevor' [William Trevor Cox]** (1928)
Lovers' Vows (1798) **Elizabeth Inchbald** (1753)
Loves Crueltie (1640) **James Shirley** (1596)
Loves Maistresse (1636) **Thomas Heywood** (1574?)
Loves Metamorphosis (1601) **John Lyly** (1554)
Loves of Cass McGuire, The (1966) **Brian Friel** (1929)
Loves of Miss Anne, The (1904) **S.R. Crockett** (1860)
Loves of the Angels, The (1823) **Thomas Moore** (1779)
Loves of the Plants, The (1789) **Erasmus Darwin** (1731)
Loves of the Poets (1829) **Anna Jameson** (1794)
Loves Riddle (1638) **Abraham Cowley** (1618)
Loves Sacrifice (1633) **John Ford** (1586)
Lovey Childs (1970) **John O'Hara** (1905)
Loving (1945) **'Henry Green' [Henry Vicent Yorke]** (1905)
Loving and Giving (1988) **Molly Keane** (1905)
Loving Brecht (1992) **Elaine Feinstein** (1930)
Loving Eye, The (1956) **William Sansom** (1912)
Loving Roger (1986) **Tim Parks** (1954)
Loving Spirit, The (1931) **Daphne du Maurier** (1907)
Low Life (1947) **John Pudney** (1909)
Low Tide on Grand Pré (1895) **[William] Bliss Carman** (1861)
Low-Flying Aircraft (1976) **J.G. Ballard** (1930)
Lower Depths, The (1902) **Maxim Gorky** (1868)
Lowery Road, The (1923) **L.A.G. Strong** (1896)
Lowest Trees Have Tops, The (1969) **Martha Gellhorn** (1908)
Lowland Venus, The (1938) **Stella Gibbons** (1902)
Loyal Brother, The (1682) **Thomas Southerne** (1659)
Loyal General, The (1679) **Nahum Tate** (1652)
Loyalties (1919) **John Drinkwater** (1882)
Loyalties (1922) **John Galsworthy** (1867)
LSD (1844) **Samuel Lover** (1797)
L-Shaped Room, The (1960) **Lynne Reid Banks** (1929)

Lucan's Pharsalia [bks i-iii] (1626–1627) **Thomas May** (1595) (tr.)
Lucans First Booke Translated (1600) **Christopher Marlowe** (1564–93) (tr.)
Lucia in London (1927) **E.F. Benson** (1867)
Lucia's Progress (1935) **E.F. Benson** (1867)
Luciano's Luck (1981) **'Jack Higgins' [Harry Patterson]** (1929)
Lucifer: A Theological Tragedy (1899) **George Santayana** (1863)
Lucifer with a Book (1949) **John Horne Burns** (1916)
Lucile [as 'Owen Meredith'] (1860) **Edward Robert Bulwer Lytton** (1831)
Lucinda (1920) **'Anthony Hope' [Sir Anthony Hope Hawkins]** (1863)
Lucinda Brayford (1946) **Martin Boyd** (1893)
Lucius (1717) **Mary Delariviere Manley** (1663)
Lucius Davoren (1873) **M.E. Braddon** (1835)
Lucius Junius Brutus (1680) **Nathaniel Lee** (1649?)
Luck and Pluck (1867) **Horatio Alger** (1832)
Luck of Ginger Coffey, The (1960) **Brian Moore** (1921)
Luck of Private Foster, The (1900) **A. St John Adcock** (1864)
Luck of the Bodkins, The (1935) **P.G. Wodehouse** (1881)
Luck of the Darrells, The (1885) **James Payn** (1830)
Luck of the Roaring Camp, The (1870) **Bret Harte** (1836)
Luck of the Vails, The (1901) **E.F. Benson** (1867)
Lucky Chance, The (1686) **Aphra Behn** (1640?)
Lucky Jim (1953) **Kingsley Amis** (1922)
Lucky Penny, The (1858) **Anna Maria [Mrs S.C.] Hall** (1800)
Lucky Poet (1943) **'Hugh MacDiarmid' [Christopher Murray Grieve]** (1892)
Lucrece [running title: *The Rape of Lucrece*] (1594) **William Shakespeare** (1564)
Lucretia (1846) **Edward Bulwer-Lytton** (1803)
Lucretia Borgia [*Lucrèce Borgia*] (1833) **Victor Hugo** (1802)
Lucubrations (1786) **Richard Graves** (1715)
Lucy (1794) **Eliza Parsons** (1748)
Lucy Church Amiably (1930) **Gertrude Stein** (1874)
Lucy Crofton (1859) **Margaret Oliphant** (1828)
Lucy Crown (1956) **Irwin Shaw** (1913)
Lucy Gayheart (1935) **Willa Cather** (1873)
Lucy in Her Pink Jacket (1954) **A.E. Coppard** (1878)
Lucy's Letters and Loving (1982) **James Berry** (1924)
Ludmilla (1955) **Paul Gallico** (1897)
Luigo (1990) **Penelope Gilliatt** (1932)
Lumen de Lumine [as 'Eugenius Philalethes'] (1651) **Thomas Vaughan** (1622)
Luna de enfrente (1925) **Jorge Luis Borges** (1899)
Lunar Attractions (1979) **Clark Blaise** (1940)
Lunar Caustic (1968) **Malcolm Lowry** (1909–57)
Lunatic Villas [UK: *The Year of the Child*] (1981) **Marian Engel** (1933)
Lunch & Counterlunch (1974) **Les Murray** (1938)
Lunch Poems (1964) **Frank O'Hara** (1926)
Lung, The (1965) **J.G. Farrell** (1935)
Lupercal (1960) **Ted Hughes** (1930)
Lusiad, The (1655) **Sir Richard Fanshawe** (1608) (tr.)
Lusiads, The [*Os Luciadas*] (1572) **Luis de Camoëns** (1524)
Lust for Life (1934) **Irving Stone** (1903)
Lustra (1916) **Ezra Pound** (1885)
Lusts (1983) **Clark Blaise** (1940)
Luther (1961) **John Osborne** (1929)
Luttrell of Arran (1865) **Charles Lever** (1806)
Lux Orientalis (1662) **Joseph Glanvill** (1636)
Lyar, The (1762) **Samuel Foote** (1720)
Lycian Shore, The (1956) **Freya Stark** (1893)
'Lycidas' (1638) **John Milton** (1608)
Lyf of Our Lady, The (1484) **John Lydgate** (1370?-1449)
Lying Days, The (1953) **Nadine Gordimer** (1923)
Lying Lover, The (1703) **Sir Richard Steele** (1672)
Lying Prophets (1897) **Eden Phillpotts** (1862)
Lying Together (1990) **D.M. Thomas** (1935)
Lying Valet, The (1741) **David Garrick** (1717)
Lyonesse (1983) **Jack Vance** (1916)
Lyra Apostolica [inc. poems by R.H. Froude and John Keble] (1834) **J.H. Newman** (1801) et al.
Lyra Germanica [1st series] (1855) **Catherine Winkworth** (1827)
Lyra Germanica: Second Series (1858) **Catherine Winkworth** (1827)
Lyra Innocentium (1846) **John Keble** (1792)
Lyre and Lancet (1895) **'F. Anstey' [Thomas Anstey Guthrie]** (1856)
Lyre of Orpheus, The (1988) **Robertson Davies** (1913)
Lyric Plays (1932) **Gordon Bottomley** (1874)
Lyric Poems (1894) **Laurence Binyon** (1869)
Lyrical Ballads, with a Few Other Poems (1798) **William Wordsworth** (1770) [with S.T. Coleridge]
Lyrical Ballads, with Other Poems [inc. poems by Coleridge and new preface] (1800) **William Wordsworth** (1770)
Lyrical Ballads, with Pastoral and Other Poems [with expanded preface] (1802) **William Wordsworth** (1770)
Lyrical Ballads, with Pastoral and Other Poems [last edn to include Coleridge's poems] (1805) **William Wordsworth** (1770)
Lyrical Poems (1871) **Francis Turner Palgrave** (1824)
Lyrical Tales (1800) **Mrs Mary Robinson** (1758)
Lyrics (1895) **A.C. Benson** (1862)
Lyrics (1935) **Lord Alfred Douglas** (1870)
Lyrics and Unfinished Poems (1940) **Lascelles Abercrombie** (1881–1938)
Lyrics for the Dog Hour (1968) **Maureen Duffy** (1933)
Lyrics of a Lowbrow (1951) **Robert W. Service** (1876)
Lyrics Unromantic (1942) **Ralph Gustafson** (1909)
Lyrisches Intermezzo ['Lyrical Intermezzo'] (1823) **Heinrich Heine** (1797)
Lysbeth (1901) **Sir H. Rider Haggard** (1856)
Lysistrata (411 BC) **Aristophanes** (*c.* 445 BC)
Lytton Strachey: The New Biography (1994) **Michael Holroyd** (1935)

Lytton Strachey: The Unknown Years (1967) **Michael Holroyd** (1935)
Lytton Strachey: The Years of Achievement (1968) **Michael Holroyd** (1935)

M

'M' is for Malice (1996) **Sue Grafton** (1940)
Mac Flecknoe (1682) **John Dryden** (1631)
Macaire (1885) **W.E. Henley** (1849) [with R.L. Stevenson]
Macbeth [from Shakespeare] (1674) **Sir William Davenant** (1606–68)
Macbett (1972) **Eugène Ionesco** (1909)
Macdermots of Ballycloran, The (1847) **Anthony Trollope** (1815)
MacGuffin, The (1991) **Stanley Elkin** (1930)
Machine-Gunners, The (1975) **Robert Westall** (1929)
Machineries of Joy, The (1964) **Ray Bradbury** (1920)
Mackerel Plaza, The (1958) **Peter De Vries** (1910)
Macleod of Dare (1878) **William Black** (1841)
Mad Barbara (1908) **Warwick Deeping** (1877)
Mad Cyclist, The (1970) **Leland Bardwell** (1928)
Mad Forest (1990) **Caryl Churchill** (1938)
Mad Lady's Garland, A (1934) **Ruth Pitter** (1897)
Mad Puppetstown [as 'M.J. Farrell'] (1931) **Molly Keane** (1905)
Mad Shepherds and Other Human Studies (1909) **L.P. Jacks** (1860)
Mad Sir Uchtred of the Hills (1894) **S.R. Crockett** (1860)
Mad Willoughbys, The (1875) **E. Lynn Linton** (1822)
Mad Woman's Underclothes, The (1986) **Germaine Greer** (1939)
Mad World, My Masters, A (1608) **Thomas Middleton** (1580)
Madagascar (1638) **Sir William Davenant** (1606)
Madam (1884) **Margaret Oliphant** (1828)
Madam Crowl's Ghost [ed. M.R. James] (1923) **J.S. le Fanu** (1814–73)
Madam Life's Lovers (1929) **Norman Lindsay** (1879)
Madame Bovary (1857) **Gustave Flaubert** (1821)
Madame Butterfly (1900) **David Belasco** (1853) [with John L. Long]
Madame Chrysanthème (1887) **'Pierre Loti' [Julien Viaud]** (1850)
Madame de Pompadour (1954) **Nancy Mitford** (1904)
Madame de Treymes (1907) **Edith Wharton** (1862)
Madame Delphine (1881) **George Washington Cable** (1844)
Madame Fears the Dark (1935) **Margaret Irwin** (1889)
Madame Fickle (1676) **Thomas D'Urfey** (1653)
Madame Gervaisais (1869) **Edmond** (1822) and Jules (1830) de Goncourt
Madame Serpent (1951) **'Jean Plaidy' [Eleanor Hibbert]** (1906)
Madame Sousatzka (1962) **Bernice Rubens** (1923)
Madcap Violet (1876) **William Black** (1841)
Madder (1987) **David Constantine** (1944)
Madder Music (1977) **Peter de Vries** (1910)
Made or Marred (1881) **Jessie Fothergill** (1851)
Made Over (1974) **Ian Wedde** (1946)
Madeleine (1848) **Julia Kavanagh** (1824)
Madeleine Férat (1868) **Émile Zola** (1840)
Madeline (1938) **Ludwig Bemelmans** (1898)
Madeline (1822) **Amelia Opie** (1769)
Mademoiselle de Maupin (1835) **Théophile Gautier** (1811)
Mademoiselle Fifi (1882) **Guy de Maupassant** (1850)
Mademoiselle Ixe (1891) **'Lanoe Falconer' [Mary Elizabeth Hawker]** (1848)
Mademoiselle la Quintinie (1863) **'George Sand' [Auore Dupin]** (1804)
Mademoiselle Mathilde (1868) **Henry Kingsley** (1830)
Mademoiselle Miss (1893) **Henry Harland** (1861)
Madge Linsey (1913) **Dora Sigerson** (1866)
Madman and the Pirate, The (1883) **R.M. Ballantyne** (1825)
Madmen and Specialists (1970) **Wole Soyinka** (1934)
Madness of David Baring, The (1900) **Joseph Hocking** (1860)
Madness of George III, The (1992) **Alan Bennett** (1934)
Madoc (1805) **Robert Southey** (1774)
Madoc (1990) **Paul Muldoon** (1951)
Madoc of the Moor (1816) **James Hogg** (1770)
Madonna (1991) **Thomas Kinsella** (1928)
Madonna Mary (1866) **Margaret Oliphant** (1828)
Madonna of the Astrolabe, The (1977) **J.I.M. Stewart** (1906)
Madonna of the Future, The (1879) **Henry James** (1843)
Madras House, The (1910) **Harley Granville-Barker** (1877)
Madwoman of Chaillot, The [*La Folle de Chaillot*] (1945) **Jean Giraudoux** (1882–1944)
Maelcho (1894) **Emily Lawless** (1845)
Maeviad, The (1795) **William Gifford** (1756)
Magdalen Hepburn (1854) **Margaret Oliphant** (1828)
Magdalene (1978) **Carolyn Slaughter** (1946)
Maggie: A Girl of the Streets (1893) **Stephen Crane** (1871)
Maggie Cassidy (1959) **Jack Kerouac** (1922)
Maggie Muggins (1981) **Keith Waterhouse** (1929)
Maggie Rowan (1954) **Catherine Cookson** (1906)
Maggot, A (1985) **John Fowles** (1926)
Magia Adamica [as 'Eugenius Philalethes'] (1650) **Thomas Vaughan** (1622)
Magic and Religion (1901) **Andrew Lang** (1844)
Magic Apple Tree, The (1971) **Elaine Feinstein** (1930)
Magic Apple Tree, The (1983) **Susan Hill** (1942)
Magic Barrel, The (1958) **Bernard Malamud** (1914)
Magic Bedknob, The (1943) **Mary Norton** (1903)
Magic Bicycle, The (1993) **Brian Patten** (1946)
Magic Christian, The (1960) **Terry Southern** (1924)
Magic City, The (1910) **E[dith] Nesbit** (1858)
Magic Cottage, The (1986) **James Herbert** (1943)
Magic Faraway Tree, The (1943) **Enid Blyton** (1897)
Magic Glasses, The (1913) **George Fitzmaurice** (1878)

Magic Ink The (1892) **William Black** (1841)
Magic Lantern, The (1822) **Marguerite, Countess of Blessington** (1789)
Magic Mountain, The [Der Zauberberg] (1924) **Thomas Mann** (1875)
Magic Pudding, The (1918) **Norman Lindsay** (1879)
Magic Toyshop, The (1967) **Angela Carter** (1940)
Magic Will, The (1971) **Herbert Gold** (1924)
Magic World, The (1912) **E[dith] Nesbit** (1858)
Magic Wreath, The (1835) **Grace Aguilar** (1816)
Magician, The (1908) **Somerset Maugham** (1874)
Magician of Lublin, The (1960) **Isaac Bashevis Singer** (1904)
Magician's Nephew, The (1955) **C.S. Lewis** (1898)
Magician's Wife, The (1997) **Brian Moore** (1921)
Magicians, The (1954) **J.B. Priestley** (1894)
Magicians of Caprona, The (1980) **Diana Wynne Jones** (1934)
Magister Ludi [Der Glasperlenspiel] (1943) **Hermann Hesse** (1877)
Magistrate, The (1885) **Arthur Wing Pinero** (1855)
Magnalia Christi Americana (1702) **Cotton Mather** (1663)
Magnetic Mountain, The (1933) **C. Day Lewis** (1904)
Magnificent Ambersons, The (1918) **Booth Tarkington** (1869)
Magnus (1973) **George Mackay Brown** (1921)
Magnus Merriman (1934) **Eric Linklater** (1899)
Magnyfycence (1533?) **John Skelton** (1460?-1529)
Magog (1972) **Andrew Sinclair** (1935)
Magpie's Shadow, The (1922) **Yvor Winters** (1900)
Magus, The (1965) **John Fowles** (1926)
Mahatma and the Hare, The (1911) **Sir H. Rider Haggard** (1856)
Mahomet (1741) **'Voltaire' [François-Marie Arouet]** (1694)
Maia (1984) **Richard Adams** (1920)
Maid in Waiting (1931) **John Galsworthy** (1867)
Maid Marian (1822) **Thomas Love Peacock** (1785)
Maid of Aragon, The (1780) **Hannah Cowley** (1743)
Maid of Buttermere, The (1987) **Melvyn Bragg** (1939)
Maid of Elvar, The (1833) **Allan Cunningham** (1784)
Maid of Honour, The (1632) **Philip Massinger** (1583)
Maid of Killeena, The (1874) **William Black** (1841)
Maid of Maiden Lane, The (1900) **Amelia Barr** (1831)
Maid of Mystery, A (1904) **Mrs L.T. Meade** (1854)
Maid of Orleans, The (1849) **Emma Robinson** (1814)
Maid of Sker, The (1872) **R.D. Blackmore** (1825)
Maid of the Mill, The (1765) **Isaac Bickerstaffe** (1733)
Maid of the Oaks, The (1774) **John Burgoyne** (1722)
Maid of Warsaw, The (1854) **Ernest Charles Jones** (1819)
Maid's Tragedy Altered, The (1690) **Edmund Waller** (1606–87)
Maid's Tragedy, The (1619) **Francis Beaumont** (1585?-1616) [with John Fletcher]
Maiden Castle (1936) **John Cooper Powys** (1872)
Maiden Stakes (1929) **'Dornford Yates' [Cecil William Mercer]** (1885)
Maiden Voyage (1943) **Denton Welch** (1915)
Maiden's Progress, The (1894) **Violet Hunt** (1866)
Maidens of the Rocks, The [Le Vergini delle rocce] (1896) **Gabriele D'Annunzio** (1863)
Maides Revenge, The (1639) **James Shirley** (1596)
Maids, The [Les Bonnes] (1946) **Jean Genet** (1910)
Maids in a Market Garden (1894) **Clo Graves** (1863)
Maids Last Prayer, The (1693) **Thomas Southerne** (1659)
Mail From Anywhere, The (1990) **Brad Leithauser** (1953)
Main Street (1920) **Sinclair Lewis** (1885)
Main-Travelled Roads (1891) **Hamlin Garland** (1860)
Maine Poems (1988) **Richard Eberhart** (1904)
Maine Woods, The (1864) **Henry David Thoreau** (1817–62)
Mainly On the Air (1946) **Max Beerbohm** (1872)
Mainsail Haul, A (1905) **John Masefield** (1878)
Maiwa's Revenge (1888) **Sir H. Rider Haggard** (1856)
Majolo, The (1815) **John Galt** (1779)
Major Barbara [screen version] (1946) **Bernard Shaw** (1856)
Major Lawrence, F.L.S. (1887) **Emily Lawless** (1845)
Major Vigoureux (1907) **Sir A.T. Quiller-Couch** (1863)
Majorca Observed (1965) **Robert Graves** (1895)
Makar Chudra (1892) **Maxim Gorky** (1868)
Make and Break (1980) **Michael Frayn** (1933)
Make Light of It (1950) **William Carlos Williams** (1883)
Make Your Game (1860) **George Augustus Sala** (1828)
Maker of History, A (1905) **E. Phillips Oppenheim** (1866)
Maker of Nations, A (1900) **Guy Boothby** (1867)
Making Cocoa for Kingsley Amis (1986) **Wendy Cope** (1945)
Making History (1988) **Brian Friel** (1929)
Making of a Novelist, The (1894) **David Christie Murray** (1847)
Making of a Poem, The (1955) **Sir Stephen Spender** (1909)
Making of a Saint, The (1898) **Somerset Maugham** (1874)
Making of a Statesman, The (1902) **Joel Chandler Harris** (1848)
Making of Americans, The (1925) **Gertrude Stein** (1874)
Making of England, The (1881) **J[ohn] R[ichard] Green** (1837)
Making of English, The (1904) **Henry Bradley** (1845)
Making of Religion, The (1898) **Andrew Lang** (1844)
Making of the English Working Class, The (1963) **E.P. Thompson** (1924)
Making of the Middle Ages, The (1953) **R.W. Southern** (1912)
Making of the Representative for Planet 8, The (1982) **Doris Lessing** (1919)
Malacia Tapestry, The (1976) **Brian Aldiss** (1925)
Malcolm (1875) **George MacDonald** (1824)

Malcolm (1959) **James Purdy** (1923)
Malcolm Mooney's Land (1970) **W.S. Graham** (1918)
Malcontent, The (1604) **John Marston** (1576)
Malcontent, The (1684) **Thomas D'Urfey** (1653)
Malcontents, The (1972) **C.P. Snow** (1905)
Male Child, A (1956) **Paul Scott** (1920)
Male Cross-Dresser Support Group, The (1992) **Tama Janowitz** (1957)
Male Impersonator, The (1929) **E.F. Benson** (1867)
Malefactors, The (1956) **Caroline Gordon** (1895)
Malgudi Days (1982) **R.K. Narayan** (1907)
Malice Aforethought [as 'Francis Iles'] (1931) **Anthony Berkeley Cox** (1893)
Malice of Men, The (1938) **Warwick Deeping** (1877)
Mallen Girl, The (1973) **Catherine Cookson** (1906)
Mallen Litter, The (1974) **Catherine Cookson** (1906)
Mallen Streak, The (1973) **Catherine Cookson** (1906)
Malone Dies [pub. in French 1951] (1956) **Samuel Beckett** (1906)
Maltese Falcon, The (1930) **Dashiell Hammett** (1894)
Malvina of Brittany (1916) **Jerome K. Jerome** (1859)
Mam'zelle Guillotine (1940) **Baroness Orczy** (1865)
Mama, I Love You (1956) **William Saroyan** (1908)
Mamba's Daughters (1929) **DuBose Heyward** (1885) [dramatized, with Dorothy Heyward, 1939]
Mambo Kings Play Songs of Love, The (1989) **Oscar Hijuelos** (1951)
Mamelles de Tirésias, Les ['The Breasts of Tiresias'] (1918) **'Guillaume Apollinaire' [Wilhelm de Kostrowitsky]** (1880)
Mamillia (1583) **Robert Greene** (1558)
Mamista (1991) **Len Deighton** (1929)
Mamma (1908) **Rhoda Broughton** (1840)
Mammon (1855) **Mrs C.F. Gore** (1799)
Mammon and the Black Goddess (1965) **Robert Graves** (1895)
Mammon & Co (1899) **E.F. Benson** (1867)
Mammonmart (1925) **Upton Sinclair** (1878)
Mammoth Hunters, The (1985) **Jean M. Auel** (1936)
Man, The (1905) **Bram Stoker** (1847)
Man Afraid, A (1982) **Jeremy Reed** (1954)
Man Against the Sky, The (1916) **Edwin Arlington Robinson** (1869)
Man and His Kingdom, The (1899) **E. Phillips Oppenheim** (1866)
Man and His Wife, A (1940) **Frank Sargeson** (1903)
Man and Literature (1943) **Norman Nicholson** (1914)
Man and Maid (1906) **E[dith] Nesbit** (1858)
Man and Maid—Renaissance (1922) **Elinor Glyn** (1864)
Man and Superman (1903) **Bernard Shaw** (1856)
Man and the Natural World (1983) **Sir Keith Thomas** (1933)
Man and the Supernatural (1927) **Evelyn Underhill** (1875)
Man and Wife (1870) **Wilkie Collins** (1824)
Man and Wife (1769) **George Colman, the Elder** (1732)
Man and Woman (1890) **Havelock Ellis** (1859)
Man as He Is (1792) **Robert Bage** (1728)
Man Born To Be King, The (1943) **Dorothy L. Sayers** (1893)
Man Called Jones, A (1947) **Julian Symons** (1912)
Man Could Stand Up, A (1926) **Ford Madox Ford** (1873)
Man Died, The (1973) **Wole Soyinka** (1934)
Man Divided (1950) **Olaf Stapledon** (1886)
Man Does, Woman Is (1964) **Robert Graves** (1895)
Man for All Seasons, A (1960) **Robert Bolt** (1924)
Man From Blankley's, The (1893) **'F. Anstey' [Thomas Anstey Guthrie]** (1856)
Man from Downing Street, The (1904) **William le Queux** (1864)
Man From Elsewhere, A (1963) **J.G. Farrell** (1935)
Man From Mukinupin, The (1979) **Dorothy Hewett** (1923)
Man From Snowy River, The (1895) **A.B. 'Banjo' Paterson** (1864)
Man From the North, A (1898) **Arnold Bennett** (1867)
Man in a Cage (1975) **Brian M. Stableford** (1948)
Man in Black, The (1894) **Stanley J. Weyman** (1855)
Man in the Black Coat Turns, The (1981) **Robert Bly** (1926)
Man in the Cellar (1974) **Julia O'Faolain** (1932)
Man in the High Castle, The (1962) **Philip K. Dick** (1928)
Man in the Honeysuckle, The (1979) **David Campbell** (1915)
Man in the Queue, The [as 'Gordon Daviot'. US: *Killer in the Crowd*] (1929) **'Josephine Tey' [Elizabeth Mackintosh]** (1897)
Man in the Zoo, A (1924) **David Garnett** (1892)
Man is Man [Mann ist Mann] (1927) **Bertolt Brecht** (1898)
Man Lay Dead, A (1934) **Ngaio Marsh** (1899)
Man Lying on a Wall (1976) **Michael Longley** (1939)
Man Made of Money, A (1849) **Douglas Jerrold** (1803)
Man Made of Smoke, A (1973) **Stanley Middleton** (1919)
Man Made World (1911) **Charlotte Perkins Gilman** (1860)
Man Named East, A (1985) **Peter Redgrove** (1932)
Man of Business, The (1774) **George Colman, the Elder** (1732)
Man of Devon, A [by 'John Sinjohn'] (1901) **John Galsworthy** (1867)
Man of Feeling, The (1771) **Henry Mackenzie** (1745)
Man of Fortune, The (1842) **Mrs C.F. Gore** (1799)
Man of his Time, A (1966) **Phyllis Bentley** (1894)
Man of Honour, A (1873) **George Cary Eggleston** (1839)
Man of Honour, A (1903) **Somerset Maugham** (1874)
Man of Letters (1986) **V.S. Pritchett** (1900)
Man of Mark, A (1890) **'Anthony Hope' [Sir Anthony Hope Hawkins]** (1863)

Man of Mode, The (1676) **Sir George Etherege** (1635)
Man of Power, A (1960) **Isabel Colegate** (1931)
Man of Property, The (1906) **John Galsworthy** (1867)
Man of Slow Feeding, The (1985) **Michael Wilding** (1942)
Man of Sorrow, The [as 'Alfred Allendale'] (1808) **Theodore Hook** (1788)
Man of Straw, A (1897) **Edwin Pugh** (1874)
Man of the Moment (1988) **Alan Ayckbourn** (1939)
Man of the People, A (1966) **Chinua Achebe** (1930)
Man of the World, The (1773) **Henry Mackenzie** (1745)
Man of the World, The (1781) **Charles Macklin** (1699?)
Man on Earth (1954) **Jacquetta Hawkes** (1910)
Man on the Rock, The (1957) **Francis King** (1923)
Man on the White Horse, The (1934) **Warwick Deeping** (1877)
Man Over Forty, A (1963) **Eric Linklater** (1899)
Man Possessed (1927) **William Rose Benét** (1886)
Man Shakespeare and His Tragic Life Story, The (1909) **'Frank' Harris** (1856)
Man That Corrupted Hadleyburg, The (1900) **'Mark Twain' [Samuel Langhorne Clemens]** (1835)
Man to Pan (1982) **John Agard** (1949)
Man Versus the State, The (1884) **Herbert Spencer** (1820)
Man Who Ate the World, The (1960) **Frederik Pohl** (1919)
Man Who Bought London, The (1915) **Edgar Wallace** (1875)
Man Who Built His City in Snow, The (1975) **Derek Mahon** (1941)
Man Who Cried I Am, The (1967) **John Williams** (1925)
Man Who Cried, The (1979) **Catherine Cookson** (1906)
Man Who Died, The (1931) **D.H. Lawrence** (1885)
Man Who Died Twice, The (1924) **Edwin Arlington Robinson** (1869)
Man Who Had All the Luck, The (1944) **Arthur Miller** (1915)
Man Who Had No Idea, The (1982) **Thomas M. Disch** (1940)
Man Who Had Three Arms, The (1982) **Edward Albee** (1928)
Man Who Knew Coolidge, The (1928) **Sinclair Lewis** (1885)
Man Who Knew Too Much, The (1922) **G.K. Chesterton** (1874)
Man Who Lost Himself, The (1929) **Sir Osbert Sitwell** (1892)
Man Who Lost Himself, The (1918) **Henry de Vere Stacpoole** (1863)
Man Who Loved Children, The (1940) **Christina Stead** (1902)
Man Who Missed the War, The (1945) **Dennis Wheatley** (1897)
Man Who Saw, The (1917) **Sir William Watson** (1858)
Man Who Sold the Moon, The (1950) **Robert A. Heinlein** (1907)
Man Who Was Not With It, The (1956) **Herbert Gold** (1924)
Man Who Was Thursday, The (1908) **G.K. Chesterton** (1874)
Man Who Wasn't There, The (1989) **Pat Barker** (1943)
Man Who Went Back, The (1940) **Warwick Deeping** (1877)
Man Who Wins, The (1897) **Robert Herrick** (1868)
Man Who Wrote Detective Stories, The (1959) **J.I.M. Stewart** (1906)
Man With a Past, A (1911) **Arthur. St John Adcock** (1864)
Man With Night Sweats, The (1992) **Thom Gunn** (1929)
Man With Seven Toes, The (1969) **Michael Ondaatje** (1943)
Man With the Blue Guitar, The (1937) **Wallace Stevens** (1879)
Man With the Club Foot, The (1918) **'Douglas Valentine' [George Valentine Williams]** (1883)
Man With the Golden Arm, The (1949) **Nelson Algren** (1909)
Man With the Golden Gun, The (1965) **Ian Fleming** (1908)
Man with the President's Mind, The (1977) **Ted Allbeury** (1917)
Man Within, The (1929) **Graham Greene** (1904)
Man's Estate [also titled *The Ninth Marquess*] (1972) **Jon Cleary** (1917)
Man's Fate [*Le Condition humaine*] (1933) **André Malraux** (1901)
Man's Hope [*L'Espoir*] (1937) **André Malraux** (1901)
Man's Life, A (1929) **Arthur Henry Adams** (1872)
Man's Life is This Meat (1936) **David Gascoyne** (1916)
Man's Man, A (1909) **'Ian Hay' [John Hay Beith]** (1876)
Man's Place in the Universe (1903) **Alfred Russel Wallace** (1823)
Man's the Master, The (1669) **Sir William Davenant** (1606–68)
Man's Unconquerable Mind (1939) **R.W. Chambers** (1874)
Man's Woman, A (1900) **Frank Norris** (1870)
Man-Eater of Malgudi, The (1961) **R.K. Narayan** (1907)
Man-Eaters of Kumaon, The (1946) **Jim Corbett** (1875)
Manalive (1912) **G.K. Chesterton** (1874)
Manassas (1904) **Upton Sinclair** (1878)
Manchester Man, The (1876) **Isabella [Mrs G. Linnaeus] Banks** (1821)
Manchurian Candidate, The (1959) **Richard Condon** (1915)
Mandarins, The [Les Mandarins] (1954) **Simone de Beauvoir** (1908)
Mandela's Earth (1989) **Wole Soyinka** (1934)
Mandelbaum Gate, The (1965) **Muriel Spark** (1918)
Mandeville (1817) **William Godwin** (1756)
Mandoa! Mandoa! (1933) **Winifred Holtby** (1898)

Manette Salomon (1867) **Edmond** (1822) and **Jules** (1830) **de Goncourt**
Manfred (1817) **George Gordon, Lord Byron** (1788)
Mangan Inheritance, The (1979) **Brian Moore** (1921)
Mangle House, The (1902) **'John Ackworth' [Frederick R. Smith]** (1845)
Manhattan Transfer (1925) **John Dos Passos** (1896)
Mani (1958) **Patrick Leigh Fermor** (1915)
Manifesto (1840) **Robert Owen** (1771)
Manifesto of the Socialist League, The (1885) **William Morris** (1834)
Manila Envelope (1989) **James Fenton** (1949)
Mankind in the Making (1903) **H.G. Wells** (1866)
Manliness of Christ, The (1879) **Thomas Hughes** (1822)
Manoeuvring Mother, The (1842) **Lady Charlotte Bury** (1775)
Manon Lescaut (1731) **Antoine-François Prévost** (1697)
Manon Lescaut [from A.F. Prévost] (1785) **Charlotte Smith** (1749) (tr.)
Manor, The (1967) **Isaac Bashevis Singer** (1904)
Manor of Northstead, The (1954) **William Douglas Home** (1912)
Mansart Builds a School (1959) **W.E.B. Du Bois** (*c.* 1868)
Manservant and Maidservant (1947) **I. Compton-Burnett** (1884)
Mansfield Park (1814) **Jane Austen** (1775)
Mansfield Revisited (1984) **Joan Aiken** (1924)
Mansion, The (1960) **William Faulkner** (1897)
Manticore , The (1972) **Robertson Davies** (1913)
Mantis Carol, A (1975) **Sir Laurens van der Post** (1906)
Mantissa (1982) **John Fowles** (1926)
Mantle of Elijah, The (1900) **Israel Zangwill** (1864)
Manual of Prayers, A (1674) **Thomas Ken** (1637)
Manuel (1817) **C.R. Maturin** (1782)
Manxman, The (1894) **Hall Caine** (1853)
Many Cargoes (1896) **W.W. Jacobs** (1863)
Many Colored Coat, The (1960) **Morley Callaghan** (1903)
Many Dimensions (1931) **Charles Williams** (1886)
Many Inventions (1893) **Rudyard Kipling** (1865)
Many Long Years Ago (1945) **Ogden Nash** (1902)
Many Loves (1961) **William Carlos Williams** (1883)
Many Marriages (1923) **Sherwood Anderson** (1876)
Many Moods (1878) **John Addington Symonds** (1840)
Many Moons (1943) **James Thurber** (1894–1961)
Many Voices (1922) **E[dith] Nesbit** (1858)
Mao II (1991) **Don DeLillo** (1936)
Map of Clay, The (1961) **Jack Clemo** (1916)
Map of Love, The (1939) **Dylan Thomas** (1914)
Map of the World, A (1982) **David Hare** (1947)
A Map of the World (1994) **Jane Hamilton**
Map of Verona, A [inc. 'Naming of Parts'] (1946) **Henry Reed** (1914)
Mapmakers (1983) **André Brink** (1935)
Mapp and Lucia (1931) **E.F. Benson** (1867)
Mappa Mundi (1984) **David Constantine** (1944)
Mara and Dann (1999) **Doris Lessing** (1919)
Maracot Deep, The (1929) **A. Conan Doyle** (1859)
Maradick at Forty (1910) **Sir Hugh Walpole** (1884)
Marazan (1926) **'Nevil Shute' [Nevil Shute Norway]** (1899)
Marble Faun, The (1860) **Nathaniel Hawthorne** (1804)
Marble Faun, The (1924) **William Faulkner** (1897)
Marble Foot, The (1976) **Peter Quennell** (1905)
Marble Mountain, The (1988) **Lisa St Aubin de Terán** (1953)
Marbles (1989) **Joseph Brodsky** (1940)
Marcella (1894) **Mrs T. Humphry Ward** (1851)
Marcella Grace (1886) **Rosa Mulholland** (1841)
March Hares (1896) **Harold Frederic** (1856)
Marching Men (1917) **Sherwood Anderson** (1876)
Marching Soldier (1945) **Joyce Cary** (1888)
Marching Song (1954) **John Whiting** (1917)
Marching Spain (1928) **V.S. Pritchett** (1900)
Marchmont (1796) **Charlotte Smith** (1749)
Marcian Colonna (1820) **'Barry Cornwall' [Bryan Waller Procter]** (1787)
Marco Millions (1928) **Eugene O'Neill** (1888)
Marconi's Cottage (1991) **Medbh McGuckian** (1950)
Marcus Flaminius (1792) **Ellis Cornelia Knight** (1758)
Mardi (1849) **Herman Melville** (1819)
Mare Clausum (1666) **Elkanah Settle** (1648)
Marfan (2000) **Peter Reading** (1946)
Margaret de Navarre [*La Reine Margot*] (1845) **Alexandre Dumas ['père']** (1802)
Margaret Denzil's History (1864) **Frederick Greenwood** (1830)
Margaret Fleming (1890) **James A. Herne** (1839)
Margaret Howth (1862) **Rebecca Harding Davis** (1831)
Margaret Ogilvy (1896) **[Sir] J.M. Barrie** (1860)
Margarite of America, A (1596) **Thomas Lodge** (1558)
Marge Askinfort (1920) **'Barry Pain' [Eric Odell]** (1864)
Margery of Quether (1891) **S. Baring-Gould** (1834)
Margin Released (1962) **J.B. Priestley** (1894)
Marian (1788) **Frances Brooke** (1724)
Marian (1840) **Anna Maria [Mrs S.C.] Hall** (1800)
Marian Withers (1851) **Geraldine Jewsbury** (1812)
Marie (1912) **Sir H. Rider Haggard** (1856)
Marie Magdalens Funeral Teares (1591) **Robert Southwell SJ** (1561?)
Marie Magdalens Lamentations (1601) **Gervaise Markham** (1568?)
Marie Tudor (1834) **Victor Hugo** (1802)
Marigold Garden (1885) **Kate Greenaway** (1846)
Marilee (1981) **Elizabeth Spencer** (1921)
Marilyn (1973) **Norman Mailer** (1923)
Marilyn (1986) **Gloria Steinem** (1934)
Marimarusa (1978) **J.F. Hendry** (1912)
Marina (1738) **George Lillo** (1693)
Marina (1930) **T.S. Eliot** (1888)
Mariner Dances (1948) **P.H. Newby** (1918)

Marino Faliero (1885) **A.C. Swinburne** (1837)
Marino Faliero (1821) **George Gordon, Lord Byron** (1788)
Mario and the Magician [*Mario und der Zauberer*] (1930) **Thomas Mann** (1875)
Marion Delorme (1831) **Victor Hugo** (1802)
Marion Fay (1882) **Anthony Trollope** (1815)
Marionette, The (1927) **Edwin Muir** (1887)
Marital Rites (1981) **Margaret Forster** (1938)
Marius the Epicurean (1885) **Walter Pater** (1839)
Marjorie Daw and Other People (1873) **Thomas Bailey Aldrich** (1836)
Marjorie Morningstar (1955) **Herman Wouk** (1915)
Mark Hurdlestone (1853) **Susanna Moodie** (1803)
Mark Lambert's Supper (1954) **J.I.M. Stewart** (1906)
Mark of Cain, The (1886) **Andrew Lang** (1844)
Mark of the Horse Lord, The (1965) **Rosemary Sutcliff** (1920)
Mark of the Warrior, The (1958) **Paul Scott** (1920)
Mark on the Wall, The (1919) **Virginia Woolf** (1882)
Mark Rutherford's Deliverance (1885) **'Mark Rutherford' [William Hale White]** (1831)
Marked Man, A (1890) **Ada Cambridge** (1844)
Market Harborough (1861) **G.J. Whyte-Melville** (1821)
Market Place, The (1899) **Harold Frederic** (1856)
Markhams Faithful Farrier (1629) **Gervaise Markham** (1568?)
Markhams Maister-peece (1610) **Gervaise Markham** (1568?)
Marking Time (1991) **Elizabeth Jane Howard** (1923)
Marlborough (1933) **Sir Winston Churchill** (1874)
Marlborough (1916) **C.H. Sorley** (1895–1915)
Marmaduke (1917) **Flora Annie Steel** (1847)
Marmaduke Herbert (1847) **Marguerite, Countess of Blessington** (1789)
Marmalade Bird, The (1973) **William Sansom** (1912)
Marmion (1808) **Sir Walter Scott** (1771)
Marne, The (1918) **Edith Wharton** (1862)
Marnie (1961) **Winston Graham** (1910)
Maronides [paraphrase of Virgil's *Aeneid*; tr. from Scarron] (1672) **John Phillips** (1631)
Maroon, The (1862) **Mayne Reid** (1818)
Marooned (1891) **W. Clark Russell** (1844)
Marquis de Fayolle, Le (1849) **'Gérard de Nerval' [Gérard Labrunie]** (1808)
Marquis of Lossie, The (1877) **George MacDonald** (1824)
Marquis of Villemer, The [*Le Marquis de Villemer*] (1860–1) **'George Sand' [Auore Dupin]** (1804)
Marriage (1818) **Susan Edmonstone Ferrier** (1782)
Marriage (1912) **H.G. Wells** (1866)
Marriage and Mary Ann (1964) **Catherine Cookson** (1906)
Marriage and Morals (1929) **Bertrand Russell** (1872)
Marriage as a Trade (1909) **Cicely Mary Hamilton** (1872)
Marriage by Capture, A (1896) **Robert Williams Buchanan** (1841)
Marriage in a Free Society (1894) **Edward Carpenter** (1844) (ed.)
Marriage of a Rebel, The (1980) **Jack Clemo** (1916)
Marriage of Elinor, The (1891) **Margaret Oliphant** (1828)
Marriage of Figaro, The [*Le Mariage de Figaro*] (1784) **Pierre Augustin Caron de Beaumarchais** (1732)
Marriage of Harlequin, The (1927) **Pamela Frankau** (1908)
Marriage of Heaven and Hell, The [1793?] **William Blake** (1757)
Marriage of William Ashe, The (1905) **Mrs T. Humphry Ward** (1851)
Marriage-a-la-Mode (1672) **John Dryden** (1631)
Marriage-Hater Match'd, The (1692) **Thomas D'Urfey** (1653)
Marriages and Infidelities (1972) **Joyce Carol Oates** (1938)
Marriages Between Zones Three, Four and Five, The (1980) **Doris Lessing** (1919)
Married Beau, The (1694) **John Crowne** (d. 1703)
Married Beneath Him (1865) **James Payn** (1830)
Married Man, A (1979) **Piers Paul Read** (1941)
Married Man, The (2000) **Edmund White** (1940)
Married or Single? (1857) **Catharine Maria Sedgwick** (1789)
Married to a Spy (1976) **Alec Waugh** (1898)
Marrow of Tradition, The (1901) **Charles W. Chesnutt** (1858)
Marry Me (1976) **John Updike** (1932)
Marrying of Ann Leete, The (1902) **Harley Granville-Barker** (1877)
Marrying the Mistress (2000) **Joanna Trollope** (1943)
Marsden Case, The (1923) **Ford Madox Ford** (1873)
Marsena, and Other Stories (1894) **Harold Frederic** (1856)
Marsh Arabs, The (1964) **Wilfred Thesiger** (1910)
Marsh Island, A (1885) **Sarah Orne Jewett** (1849)
Marston (1846) **George Croly** (1780)
Marstons, The (1868) **Charles Hamilton Aïdé** (1826)
Martha Quest (1952) **Doris Lessing** (1919)
Martha Rose, Teacher (1906) **Matilda Betham-Edwards** (1836)
Martian Chronicles, The [UK: *The Silver Locusts*] (1950) **Ray Bradbury** (1920)
Martian Sends a Postcard Home, A (1979) **Craig Raine** (1944)
Martian, The (1897) **George du Maurier** (1834–96)
Martian Time-Slip (1964) **Philip K. Dick** (1928)
Martin Chuzzlewit [**Dickens**]: see *The Life and Adventures of Martin Chuzzlewit*
Martin Eden (1909) **'Jack London' [John Griffith Chaney]** (1876)
Martin Faber (1833) **William Gilmore Simms** (1806)
Martin Hewitt, Investigator (1894) **Arthur Morrison** (1863)
Martin Hyde (1910) **John Masefield** (1878)
Martin Junior [22 July 1589] (1589) **Martin Marprelate**

Martin Make-Believe (1930) **Gilbert Frankau** (1884)
Martin Pippin in the Apple Orchard (1921) **Eleanor Farjeon** (1881)
Martin Rattler (1858) **R.M. Ballantyne** (1825)
Martin Senior [29 July 1589] (1589) **'Martin Marprelate'**
Martin Toutrond (1849) **James Morier** (1780)
Martyr of Alabama, The (1894) **Frances E. Harper** (1825)
Martyr of Antioch, The (1822) **Henry Hart Milman** (1791)
Martyr, The (1826) **Joanna Baillie** (1762)
Martyr, The (1933) **Liam O'Flaherty** (1897)
Martyr to Mammon, A (1886) **Mrs Louisa Baldwin** (1845)
Martyrdom of Madeline, The (1882) **Robert Williams Buchanan** (1841)
Martyrdom of Man, The (1872) **William Winwood Reade** (1838)
Martyrdom of St Sebastian, The [*Le Martyre de Saint Sébastien; music by Debussy*] (1911) **Gabriele D'Annunzio** (1863)
Martyrdom of Theodora, The (1687) **[Roger Boyle, Earl of Orrery]** (1621)
Martyrs, The [*Les Martyrs ou le Triomphe de la religion chrétienne*] (1809) **François-René, vicomte de Chateaubriand** (1768)
Maru (1971) **Bessie Head** (1937)
Marvellous Land of Oz, The (1904) **L. Frank Baum** (1856)
Marx, Lenin, and the Science of Revolution (1926) **Max Eastman** (1883)
Marxism (1935) **John Middleton Murry** (1889)
Marxism: Is it Science? (1940) **Max Eastman** (1883)
Marxist Philosophy and the Sciences, The (1938) **J.B.S. Haldane** (1892)
Mary (1788) **Mary Wollstonecraft** (1759)
Mary (1916) **M.E. Braddon** (1835–1915)
Mary (1970) **Vladimir Nabokov** (1899)
Mary Anerley (1880) **R.D. Blackmore** (1825)
Mary Ann and Bill (1967) **Catherine Cookson** (1906)
Mary Ann's Angels (1965) **Catherine Cookson** (1906)
Mary Anne (1954) **Daphne du Maurier** (1907)
Mary Barnes (1978) **David Edgar** (1948)
Mary Barton (1848) **Elizabeth Gaskell** (1810)
Mary de Clifford (1792) **Sir Samuel Egerton Brydges** (1762)
Mary Deare, The (1956) **'Hammond Innes' [Ralph Hammond-Innes]** (1913)
'Mary Had a Little Lamb' [**Hale**]: see *Poems For Our Children*
Mary Lavelle (1936) **Kate O'Brien** (1897)
Mary Marston (1881) **George MacDonald** (1824)
Mary O'Grady (1950) **Mary Lavin** (1912)
Mary of Burgundy (1833) **G.P.R. James** (1799)
Mary of Scotland (1933) **Maxwell Anderson** (1888)
Mary Olivier (1919) **May Sinclair** (1863)
Mary Pechell (1912) **Mrs Belloc Lowndes** (1868)
Mary Poppins (1934) **P.L. Travers** (1906)
Mary Queen of Scots (1969) **Lady Antonia Fraser** (1932)
Mary, Queen of Scots (1831) **Mary Russell Mitford** (1787)
Mary Queen of Scots Got Her Head Chopped Off (1987) **Liz Lochhead** (1947)
Mary Stuart (1921) **John Drinkwater** (1882)
Mary Stuart (1881) **A.C. Swinburne** (1837)
Mary Wakefield (1949) **Mazo de la Roche** (1879)
Marya, a Life (1986) **Joyce Carol Oates** (1938)
Mask of Apollo, The (1966) **'Mary Renault' [Eileen Mary Challans]** (1905)
Mask of Apollo, The (1905) **George William Russell ['AE']** (1867)
Mask of Dimitrios, The [US: *A Coffin for Dimitrios*] (1939) **Eric Ambler** (1909)
Mask of State, The (1974) **Mary McCarthy** (1912)
Mask of the Andes [also titled *The Liberators*] (1971) **Jon Cleary** (1917)
Mask, The (1905) **William Le Queux** (1864)
Mask, The (1981) **Dean Koontz** (1945)
Masked Days, The [*Los dias enmascarados*] (1954) **Carlos Fuentes** (1928)
Masks (1968) **Edward Brathwaite** (1930)
Masks and Faces (1854) **Charles Reade** (1814) [with Tom Taylor]
Masks of Time (1925) **Edmund Blunden** (1896)
Masks of Time, The (1968) **Robert Silverberg** (1935)
Masks or Faces? (1888) **William Archer** (1856)
Mason & Dixon (1997) **Thomas Pynchon** (1937)
Masque of Anarchy, The (1832) **P.B. Shelley** (1792–1822)
Masque of Dead Florentines, A (1895) **Maurice Hewlett** (1861)
Masque of Edinburgh, The (1954) **'Robert Garioch' [Robert Garioch Sutherland]** (1909)
Masque of Kings, The (1936) **Maxwell Anderson** (1888)
Masque of Mercy, A (1947) **Robert Frost** (1874)
Masque of Pandora, The (1875) **Henry Wadsworth Longfellow** (1807)
Masque of Reason, A (1945) **Robert Frost** (1874)
Masquerade, The (1728) **Henry Fielding** (1707)
Masquerade (1842) **Mikhail Lermontov** (1814)
Masqueraders, The (1724) **Eliza Haywood** (*c.* 1693)
Mass for Hard Times (1992) **R.S. Thomas** (1913)
Mass-Observation (1937) **Charles Madge** (1912) [with Tom Harrisson]
Massacre of Paris, The (1689) **Nathaniel Lee** (1649?)
Massacre at Paris, The (1594) **Christopher Marlowe** (1564)
Massarenes, The (1897) **'Ouida' [Marie Louise de la Ramée]** (1839)
Massollam (1886) **Laurence Oliphant** (1829)
Mast of Hankies, A (1975) **Ian Hamilton Finlay** (1925)
Master, The (1895) **Israel Zangwill** (1864)
Master and Commander [first of the 'Aubrey-Maturin' series] (1970) **Patrick O'Brian** (1914)
Master and Man (1894) **Leo Tolstoy** (1828)
Master Builder, The (1892) **Henrik Ibsen** (1828)

Master Craftsman, The (1896) **Sir Walter Besant** (1836)
Master Georgie (1998) **Beryl Bainbridge** (1934)
Master Harold and the Boys (1982) **Athol Fugard** (1932)
Master Hope, The (1904) **Phyllis Bottome** (1884)
Master Humphrey's Clock [vol. i] (1840) **Charles Dickens** (1812)
Master of Ballantrae, The (1889) **Robert Louis Stevenson** (1850)
Master of Craft, A (1900) **W.W. Jacobs** (1863)
Master of Gray, The (1903) **H.C. Bailey** (1878)
Master of Gray, The (1961) **Nigel Tranter** (1909)
Master of Jalna, The (1933) **Mazo de la Roche** (1879)
Master of Man, The (1921) **Hall Caine** (1853)
Master of St Petersburg, The (1994) **J.M. Coetzee** (1940)
Master of the Ceremonies, The (1886) **[George Manville Fenn]** (1831)
Master of the Game, The (1982) **Sidney Sheldon** (1917)
Master of the Inn, The (1908) **Robert Herrick** (1868)
Master of the Microbe, The (1926) **Robert W. Service** (1876)
Master of the Mill, The (1944) **Frederick Grove** (1879)
Master of the Mine, The (1885) **Robert Williams Buchanan** (1841)
Master of the Moor (1982) **Ruth Rendell** (1930)
Master of the Shell, The (1894) **Talbot Baines Reed** (1852)
Master of Warlock, The (1903) **George Cary Eggleston** (1839)
Master Olof (1881) **August Strindberg** (1849)
Master Poisoner, The (1918) **Ben Hecht** (1894) [with Maxwell Bodenheim]
Master-Christian, The (1900) **Marie Corelli** (1855)
Masterman Ready; or, The Wreck of the Pacific (1841–2) **Frederick Marryat** (1792)
Masterpiece, The [*L'Oeuvre*] (1886) **Émile Zola** (1840)
Masters in Israel (1961) **Vincent Buckley** (1925)
Masters of Modern French Criticism (1912) **Irving Babbit** (1865)
Masters, The (1951) **C.P. Snow** (1905)
Masterson (1926) **Gilbert Frankau** (1884)
Matador of the Five Towns, The (1912) **Arnold Bennett** (1867)
Match at Mid-night, A (1633) **William Rowley** (1585?-1626)
Match Mee in London (1631) **Thomas Dekker** (1572?)
Matchmaker, The (1894) **L[ucy] B[erthia] Walford** (1845)
Matelot (1893) **'Pierre Loti' [Julien Viaud]** (1850)
Mateo Falcone (1833) **Prosper Mérimée** (1803)
Materfamilias (1898) **Ada Cambridge** (1844)
Mates (1983) **Tom Wakefield** (1935)
Mates of Mars (1991) **David Foster** (1944)
Matilda (1594) **Michael Drayton** (1563)
Matilda (1988) **Roald Dahl** (1916)
Mating of Lydia, The (1913) **Mrs T. Humphry Ward** (1851)
Matisse Stories, The (1993) **A.S. Byatt** (1936)
Matter and Memory [*Matière et mémoire*] (1896) **Henri Bergson** (1859)
Matter and Motion Cannot Think (1692) **Richard Bentley** (1662)
Matter of Life and Death, A (1959) **Anne Ridler** (1912)
Matter of Money, A (1916) **Cicely Mary Hamilton** (1872)
Matter of Wales, The (1984) **Jan Morris** (1926)
Matters of Fact and of Fiction (1977) **Gore Vidal** (1925)
Matthew Arnold (1899) **George Saintsbury** (1845)
Matthew Arnold (1928) **'Hugh Kingsmill' [Hugh Kingsmill Lunn]** (1889)
Matthew Arnold (1939) **Lionel Trilling** (1905)
Matthias at the Door (1931) **Edwin Arlington Robinson** (1869)
Mattins and Muttons (1866) **'Cuthbert Bede' [Edward Bradley]** (1827)
Maud, and Other Poems [inc.'The Charge of the Light Brigade'] (1855) **Alfred, Lord Tennyson** (1809)
Maule's Curse (1938) **Yvor Winters** (1900)
Maulever Hall (1964) **Jane Aiken Hodge** (1917)
Mauleverer's Divorce (1858) **Emma Robinson** (1814)
Mauprat (1837) **'George Sand' [Auore Dupin]** (1804)
Maureen's Fairing (1895) **Jane Barlow** (1857)
Maurice (1971) **E.M. Forster** (1879–1970)
Maurice Dering (1864) **G.A. Lawrence** (1827)
Maurice Guest (1908) **'Henry Handel Richardson' [Ethel Florence Robertson]** (1870)
Maurice Tiernay (1861) **Charles Lever** (1806)
Mauritius Command, The (1978) **Patrick O'Brian** (1914)
Mausoleum (1613) **William Drummond of Hawthornden** (1585) and others
Mausoleum, The (1714) **Lewis Theobald** (1688)
Mauve Gloves and Madmen (1976) **Tom Wolfe** (1930)
Mavis Belfrage (1996) **Alasdair Gray** (1934)
Max Carrados (1914) **Ernest Bramah** (1868)
Maximilian (1902) **Edgar Lee Masters** (1868)
Maxims of the Saints Explained, The [*Explication des maximes des saints sur la vie intérieure*] (1697) **François Fénelon** (1651)
Maximum Bob (1991) **Elmore Leonard** (1925)
Maximus IV, V, VI (1968) **Charles Olson** (1910)
Maximus Poem, The (1975) **Charles Olson** (1910)
Maximus Poems 1–10, The [11–23, 1956; combined, 1960] (1953) **Charles Olson** (1910)
Maxwell (1830) **Theodore Hook** (1788)
Maxwell Drewitt [as 'F.G. Trafford'] (1865) **Mrs J.H. Riddell** (1832)
May Carols (1857) **Aubrey Thomas de Vere** (1814)
May Day (1611) **George Chapman** (1559?)
May Day with the Muses (1822) **Robert Bloomfield** (1766)
May Fair (1925) **'Michael Arlen' [Dikran Kouyoumdjian]** (1895)
May We Borrow Your Husband? (1967) **Graham Greene** (1904)
May Week Was in June (1990) **Clive James** (1939)
May-Day, and Other Pieces (1867) **Ralph Waldo Emerson** (1803)

Maydays (1983) **David Edgar** (1948)

Mayden-head Well Lost, A (1634) **Thomas Heywood** (1574?)

Mayor of Casterbridge, The (1886) **Thomas Hardy** (1840)

Mayor of Quinborough, The (1596?) **Thomas Middleton** (1580–1627)

Mayor of Troy, The (1906) **Sir A.T. Quiller-Couch** (1863)

Mayor of Windgap, The (1835) **Michael Banim** (1796)

Mayor of Zalamea, The [*El Alcalde de Zalamea*] (c. 1643) **Pedro Calderón de la Barca** (1600)

Mazeppa (1819) **George Gordon, Lord Byron** (1788)

M.C. Higgins the Great (1974) **Virginia Hamilton** (1936)

McKenzie's Hundred (1985) **Frank Yerby** (1916)

McTeague (1899) **Frank Norris** (1870)

Mea Culpa (1891) **Henry Harland** (1861)

Meadows of Saint-Gervais, The [*Les Prés Saint-Gervais*] (1860) **Victorien Sardou** (1831)

Mean Time (1993) **Carol Ann Duffy** (1955)

Meaning of Art, The (1931) **Sir Herbert Read** (1893)

Meaning of Culture, The (1929) **John Cowper Powys** (1872)

Meaning of Dreams, The (1924) **Robert Graves** (1895)

Meaning of History, The (1894) **Frederic Harrison** (1831)

Meaning of Meaning, The (1923) **I.A. Richards** (1893) [with C.K. Ogden]

Meaning of Treason, The [rev. 1964 as *The New Meaning of Treason*] (1947) **'Rebecca West' [Cicily Isabel Andrews]** (1892)

Meaning of Truth, The (1909) **William James** (1842)

Means of Escape, The (2000) **Penelope Fitzgerald** (1916)

Meanwhile (1927) **H.G. Wells** (1866)

Measure for Measure [from Shakespeare] (1699) **Charles Gildon** (1665)

Measure of Value Stated and Illustrated, The (1823) **T.R. Malthus** (1766)

Mechanical Body, The (1991) **John Fuller** (1937)

Mechanical Bride, The (1951) **Marshall McLuhan** (1911)

Medal of John Bayes, The (1682) **Thomas Shadwell** (1642?)

Medall, The (1682) **John Dryden** (1631)

Medea (431 BC) **Euripides** (480 BC)

Medea (1761) **Richard Glover** (1712)

Medea [*Médée*] (1946) **Jean Anouilh** (1910)

Médée (1634/5) **Pierre Corneille** (1606)

Mediaeval Latin Lyrics (1929) **Helen Waddell** (1889) (tr.)

Mediaeval Stage, The (1903) **Sir E.K. Chambers** (1866)

Medieval Scenes (1950) **Robert Duncan** (1919)

Medina (1972) **Mary McCarthy** (1912)

Meditation for Melancholy, A [UK: *The Day it Rained Forever*] (1959) **Ray Bradbury** (1920)

Meditation Upon a Broom-Stick, A (1710) **Jonathan Swift** (1667)

Meditations Among the Tombs (1746) **James Hervey** (1714)

Meditations and Contemplations (1748) **James Hervey** (1714)

Meditations and Vowes (1605) **Joseph Hall** (1574)

Meditations in an Emergency (1957) **Frank O'Hara** (1926)

Mediterranean, The (1936) **Allen Tate** (1899)

Medium is the Message, The (1967) **Marshall McLuhan** (1911)

Medusa (1988) **'Hammond Innes' [Ralph Hammond-Innes]** (1913)

Meet Me in the Green Glen (1971) **Robert Penn Warren** (1905)

Meet Mr Mulliner (1927) **P.G. Wodehouse** (1881)

Meet My Maker the Mad Molecule (1964) **J.P. Donleavy** (1926)

Meet the Tiger [first of the many 'Simon Templar'/ 'Saint' novels] (1928) **'Leslie Charteris' [Leslie Charles Yin]** (1907)

Meeting at Telgte, The [*Das Treffen in Telgte*] (1979) **Günter Grass** (1927)

Meeting by the River, A (1967) **Christopher Isherwood** (1904)

Meeting Evil (1992) **Thomas Berger** (1924)

Meeting of Gallants at an Ordinarie, The (1604) **Thomas Dekker** (1572?)

Meeting Place (1962) **Nicholas Mosley** (1923)

Meeting Place, The (1929) **J.D. Beresford** (1873)

Meeting Point, The (1967) **Austin Clarke** (1932)

Meeting the British (1987) **Paul Muldoon** (1951)

Meeting the Comet (1988) **Fleur Adcock** (1934)

Mefisto (1986) **John Banville** (1945)

Meg (1981) **Maurice Gee** (1931)

Mehalah (1880) **S. Baring-Gould** (1834)

Mein Kampf (1925) **Adolf Hitler** (1889)

Melaia (1840) **Eliza Cook** (1818)

Melancholy Baby (1978) **Julia O'Faolain** (1932)

Melbourne (1976) **Philip Ziegler** (1929)

Melbourne or the Bush (1973) **Chris Wallace-Crabbe** (1934)

Melbournians, The (1892) **Francis Adams** (1862)

Melchior's Dream (1862) **Mrs J.H. Ewing** (1841)

Melincourt (1817) **Thomas Love Peacock** (1785)

Mélite (1629?) **Pierre Corneille** (1606)

Mellichampe (1836) **William Gilmore Simms** (1806)

Melmoth the Wanderer (1820) **C.R. Maturin** (1782)

Melodramatists, The (1949) **Howard Nemerov** (1920)

Melon (1987) **Simon Gray** (1936)

Melvilles, The (1852) **Margaret Oliphant** (1828)

Member for the Marsh, The (1956) **William Mayne** (1928)

Member of the Third House, A (1892) **Hamlin Garland** (1860)

Member of the Wedding, The (1946) **Carson McCullers** (1917)

Member, The (1832) **John Galt** (1779)

Memento Mori (1959) **Muriel Spark** (1918)

Memo for Spring (1972) **Liz Lochhead** (1947)

Memoir of Percy Bysshe Shelley (1886) **W.M. Rossetti** (1829)
Mémoires d'un fou (1838) **Gustave Flaubert** (1821)
Memoirs (1717) **Elias Ashmole** (1617–92)
Memoirs (1823) **William Hayley** (1745–1820)
Memoirs (1885) **Mark Pattison** (1813–84)
Memoirs (1965) **Sir Basil Liddell Hart** (1895)
Memoirs (1990) **Kingsley Amis** (1922)
Memoirs and Opinions (1975) **Allen Tate** (1899)
Memoirs and Resolutions of Adam Graeme of Mossgray (1852) **Margaret Oliphant** (1828)
Memoirs: Containing the Lives of Several Ladies of Great Britain (1755) **Thomas Amory** (1691?)
Memoirs: From 1679 (1709) **Sir William Temple** (1628–99)
Memoirs of a Cavalier (1720) **Daniel Defoe** (1660)?
Memoirs of a Certain Island Adjacent to the Kingdom of Utopia (1725) **Eliza Haywood** (*c.* 1693)
Memoirs of a Coxcomb (1751) **John Cleland** (1709)
Memoirs of a Dutiful Daughter [*Mémoires d'une jeune fille rangée*] (1958) **Simone de Beauvoir** (1908)
Memoirs of a femme de chambre, The (1846) **Marguerite, Countess of Blessington** (1789)
Memoirs of a Fox-Hunting Man (1928) **Siegfried Sassoon** (1886)
Memoirs of a London Doll [as 'Mrs Fairstar'] (1846) **R.H. Horne** (1803)
Memoirs of a Magdalen (1767) **Hugh Kelly** (1739)
Memoirs of a Midget (1921) **Walter de la Mare** (1873)
Memoirs of a Muscovite (1844) **Edward Bulwer-Lytton** (1803)
Memoirs of a New Man (1966) **'William Cooper' [Harry Summerfield Hoff]** (1910)
Memoirs of a Peon (1965) **Frank Sargeson** (1903)
Memoirs of a Polyglot (1931) **William Gerhardie** (1895)
Memoirs of a Protestant, The [tr. from Jean Marteilhe] (1758) **Oliver Goldsmith** (1728) (tr.)
Memoirs of a Spacewoman (1962) **Naomi Mitchison** (1897)
Memoirs of a Survivor, The (1974) **Doris Lessing** (1919)
Memoirs of a Woman of Pleasure [vol. i; vol. ii, 1749] (1748) **John Cleland** (1709)
Memoirs of an Aesthete (1948) **Sir Harold Acton** (1904)
Memoirs of an Infantry-Officer (1930) **Siegfried Sassoon** (1886)
Memoirs of Bryan Perdue (1805) **Thomas Holcroft** (1745)
Memoirs of Captain Rock (1824) **Thomas Moore** (1779)
Memoirs of Dr Burney (1832) **Frances Burney** (1752)
Memoirs of Europe Towards the Close of the Eighth Century (1710) **Mary Delariviere Manley** (1663)
Memoirs of Hecate County (1946) **Edmund Wilson** (1895–1972)
Memoirs of Ireland (1716) **John Oldmixon** (1673)
Memoirs of John Evelyn [first edn of Evelyn's diary, ed. W. Bray] (1818) **John Evelyn** (1620–1706)
Memoirs of Lord Byron, The (1989) **Robert Nye** (1939)
Memoirs of Many in One (1986) **Patrick White** (1912)
Memoirs of Marau Taaroa, Last Queen of Tahiti (1893) **Henry Adams** (1838)
Memoirs of Martinus Scriblerus, The (1741) **John Arbuthnot** (1667–1735)
Memoirs of Mary (1793) **Susannah Gunning** (1740)
Memoirs of Miss Sidney Bidulph (1761) **Frances Sheridan** (1724)
Memoirs of Modern Philosophers (1800) **Elizabeth Hamilton** (1758)
Memoirs of My Dead Life (1906) **George Moore** (1852)
Memoirs of Richard Brinsley Sheridan (1825) **Thomas Moore** (1779)
Memoirs of Richard Lovell Edgeworth (1820) **Maria Edgeworth** (1767)
Memoirs of Sherlock Holmes, The (1893) **A. Conan Doyle** (1859)
Memoirs of Shy Pornographer (1945) **Kenneth Patchen** (1911)
Memoirs of Sir Roger de Clarendon (1793) **Clara Reeve** (1729)
Memoirs of the Celebrated Female Sovereigns (1831) **Anna Jameson** (1794)
Memoirs of the Court of King Charles the First (1833) **Lucy Aikin** (1781)
Memoirs of the Court of King James the First (1822) **Lucy Aikin** (1781)
Memoirs of the Court of Queen Elizabeth (1818) **Lucy Aikin** (1781)
Memoirs of the Ford Administration (1992) **John Updike** (1932)
Memoirs of the Forties (1965) **J. Maclaren-Ross** (1912–64)
Memoirs of the Last Ten Years of the Reign of George II (1822) **Horace Walpole** (1717–97)
Memoirs of the Late Thomas Holcroft (1816) **Thomas Holcroft** (1745–1809)
Memoirs of the Life of Mrs Elizabeth Carter (1807) **Elizabeth Carter** (1717–1806)
Memoirs of the Life of the Count de Grammont (1714) **Anthony Hamilton** (1646?)
Memoirs of the Life of William Collins (1848) **Wilkie Collins** (1824)
Memoirs of the Life of William Wycherley (1718) **Charles Gildon** (1665) (ed.)
Memoirs of the Press (1742) **John Oldmixon** (1673)
Memoirs of the Private Life of My Father [*Du caractère de M. Necker et sa vie privée*] (1804) **Madame de Staël** (1766)
Memoirs of the Reign of George the Second (1848) **John Hervey, 2nd Baron Hervey** (1696–1743)
Memoirs of What Past in Christendom, From 1672 to 1679 (1692) **Sir William Temple** (1628)
Memorable Providences (1689) **Cotton Mather** (1663)
Memoranda During the War (1875) **Walt Whitman** (1819)
Memorial of all the English Monarchs, A (1622) **John Taylor** (1580)
Memorial Service, A (1976) **J.I.M. Stewart** (1906)

Memorial, The (1932) **Christopher Isherwood** (1904)
Memorials of a Tour in Some Parts of Greece (1834) **Richard Monckton Milnes** (1809)
Memorials of a Tour on the Continent, 1820 (1822) **William Wordsworth** (1770)
Memorials of Jane Welsh Carlyle (1883) **J.A. Froude** (1818) (ed.)
Memorials of Many Scenes (1844) **Richard Monckton Milnes** (1809)
Memorials of the Quick and the Dead (1979) **Maureen Duffy** (1933)
Memorials of Thomas Cranmer (1694) **John Strype** (1643)
Memories (1953) **Desmond MacCarthy** (1877–1952)
Memories [vol. i; vol ii, 1973] (1970) **Julian Huxley** (1887)
Memories and Adventures (1924) **A. Conan Doyle** (1859)
Memories and Friends (1924) **A.C. Benson** (1862)
Memories and Notes of Persons and Places (1921) **Sir Sidney Colvin** (1845)
Memories and Opinions (1944) **Sir A.T. Quiller-Couch** (1863–1944)
Memories and Portraits (1887) **Robert Louis Stevenson** (1850)
Memories From Beyond the Grave [*Mémoires d'outre-tombe*] (1849–50) **François-René, vicomte de Chateaubriand** (1768–1848)
Memories of a Catholic Girlhood (1957) **Mary McCarthy** (1912)
Memories of London in the 'Forties (1908) **David Masson** (1822–907)
Memories of the Future (1923) **Ronald Knox** (1888)
Memories of Victorian London (1912) **L[ucy] B[erthia] Walford** (1845)
Memory (1938) **Walter de la Mare** (1873)
Memory (1987) **Margaret Mahy** (1936)
Memory Board (1987) **Jane Rule** (1931)
Memory Box, The (1999) **Margaret Forster** (1938)
Memory of War and Children in Exile (1983) **James Fenton** (1949)
Memory-Hold-the-Door (1940) **John Buchan** (1875)
Men and Brethren (1936) **James Gould Cozzens** (1903)
Men and Their Boring Arguments (1988) **Wendy Cope** (1945)
Men and Wives (1931) **I. Compton-Burnett** (1884)
Men and Women (1855) **Robert Browning** (1812)
Men and Women (1844) **Catherine Crowe** (1790)
Men at Arms (1993) **Terry Pratchett** (1948)
Men at Arms (1952) **Evelyn Waugh** (1903)
Men Dislike Women (1931) **'Michael Arlen' [Dikran Kouyoumdjian]** (1895)
Men Like Gods (1923) **H.G. Wells** (1866)
Men of Capital (1846) **Mrs C.F. Gore** (1799)
Men of Character (1838) **Douglas Jerrold** (1803)
Men of Deep Waters (1914) **William Hope Hodgson** (1877)
Men of Iron (1892) **Howard Pyle** (1853)
Men of Men (1981) **Wilbur Smith** (1933)
Men of Ness, The (1932) **Eric Linklater** (1899)
Men of Stones (1949) **Rex Warner** (1905)
Men of the Moss-Hags, The (1895) **S.R. Crockett** (1860)
Men of the Mountain, The (1909) **S.R. Crockett** (1860)
Men Who Made the Nation (1957) **John Dos Passos** (1896)
Men Without Art (1934) **Wyndham Lewis** (1882)
Men Without Women (1927) **Ernest Hemingway** (1898)
Men, Women, and Books (1847) **Leigh Hunt** (1784)
Men, Women, and Ghosts (1916) **Amy Lowell** (1874)
Men, Women, and Guns (1916) **'Sapper' [Herman Cyril McNeile]** (1888)
Menaecmi (1595) **William Warner** (1558?)
Menagerie, The (1958) **Catherine Cookson** (1906)
Menaphon (1589) **Robert Greene** (1558)
Mencius on the Mind (1932) **I.A. Richards** (1893)
Mendel (1916) **Gilbert Cannan** (1884)
Menhardoc (1884) **George Manville Fenn** (1831)
Mens Creatrix (1917) **William Temple** (1881)
Mental and Moral Science (1868) **Alexander Bain** (1818)
Mentoria (1791) **Susanna Rowson** (1762)
Mer de glace (1991) **Alison Fell** (1944)
Mercedes, and Later Lyrics (1884) **Thomas Bailey Aldrich** (1836)
Mercenary Lover, The (1726) **Eliza Haywood** (*c.* 1693)
Merchant of Venice, The (1600) **William Shakespeare** (1564)
Merchant of Yonkers, The [rev. 1954 as *The Matchmaker* and adapted 1963 as *Hello, Dolly!*] (1938) **Thornton Wilder** (1897)
Merchants from Cathay (1913) **William Rose Benét** (1886)
Mercian Hymns (1971) **Geoffrey Hill** (1932)
Mercier and Camier [pub. in French 1970] (1974) **Samuel Beckett** (1906)
Mercurie Vindicated (1616) **Ben Jonson** (1572)
Mercy (1990) **Andrea Dworkin** (1946)
Mere Accident, A (1887) **George Moore** (1852)
Mere Chance, A (1882) **Ada Cambridge** (1844)
Mere Christianity (1952) **C.S. Lewis** (1898)
Meredith (1843) **Marguerite, Countess of Blessington** (1789)
'Merely Mary Ann' (1893) **Israel Zangwill** (1864)
Meridian (1976) **Alice Walker** (1944)
Merkland (1850) **Margaret Oliphant** (1828)
Merle's Crusade (1889) **Rosa Nouchette Carey** (1840)
Merlin (1917) **Edwin Arlington Robinson** (1869)
Merlin (1978) **Robert Nye** (1939)
Merlinus Anglicus Junior (1644) **William Lilly** (1602)
Mermaids in the Basement (1993) **Marina Warner** (1946)
Mermoirs of Barry Lyndon, The [US: *The Luck of Barry Lyndon*, 1853] (1856) **W.M. Thackeray** (1811)
Merope (1858) **Matthew Arnold** (1822)
Mérope (1743) **'Voltaire' [François-Marie Arouet]** (1694)

Meropé (1749) **Aaron Hill** (1685)
Merry Adventures of Robin Hood , The (1883) **Howard Pyle** (1853)
Merry England (1874) **W.H. Ainsworth** (1805)
Merry Heart, The (1909) **Frank Swinnerton** (1884)
Merry Men, The (1887) **Robert Louis Stevenson** (1850)
Merry Month of May, The (1971) **James Jones** (1921)
Merry Wives of Windsor, The (1602) **William Shakespeare** (1564)
Merry-Garden (1907) **Sir A.T. Quiller-Couch** (1863)
Merry-Go-Round, The (1904) **Somerset Maugham** (1874)
Merry-Go-Round by the Sea, The (1965) **Randolph Stow** (1935)
Mervyn Clitheroe (1858) **W.H. Ainsworth** (1805)
Meshugah (1994) **Isaac Bashevis Singer** (1904–91)
Mesmerists, The (1900) **B.L. Farjeon** (1838)
Mesopotamian Verses (1919) **Edward Thompson** (1886)
Message in the Bottle, The (1975) **Walker Percy** (1916)
Message to the Planet, The (1989) **Iris Murdoch** (1919)
Messengers of Day (1978) **Anthony Powell** (1905)
Messiah (1786) **John Newton** (1725)
Messiah [rev. 1965] (1954) **Gore Vidal** (1925)
Metamora (1847) **John Brougham** (1810)
Metamorphoses [Eng trn as *The Golden Ass*, 1566] **Apuleius** (fl.*c.* AD 155)
Metamorphosis [from Ovid; bks i-iv] (1565) **Arthur Golding** (1536) (tr.)
Metamorphosis [from Ovid; bks 1-xv] (1567) **Arthur Golding** (1536) (tr.)
'Metamorphosis, The' ['Die Verwandlung'] (1915) **Franz Kafka** (1883)
Metamorphosis of Pigmalions Image, The (1598) **John Marston** (1576)
Metaphor and Memory (1987) **Cynthia Ozick** (1928)
Metaphor and Myth (1989) **Cynthia Ozick** (1928)
Metaphysical Lyrics and Poems of the Seventeenth Century (1921) **H.J.C. Grierson** (1866) (ed.)
Metaphysics **Aristotle** (384 BC)
Metaphysics and Common Sense (1969) **A.J. Ayer** (1910)
Metaphysics as a Guide to Morals (1992) **Iris Murdoch** (1919)
Methods of Ethics, The (1874) **Henry Sidgwick** (1838)
Methods of Historical Study, The (1886) **E.A. Freeman** (1823)
Methuselah's Children (1958) **Robert A. Heinlein** (1907)
Metrical Effusions (1812) **Bernard Barton** (1784)
Metrical Legends of Exalted Characters (1821) **Joanna Baillie** (1762)
Metrical Observations (1980) **David Wright** (1920)
Metrical Tales (1860) **Samuel Lover** (1797)
Metrical Tales (1805) **Robert Southey** (1774)
Metroland (1980) **Julian Barnes** (1946)
Metropolis, The (1908) **Upton Sinclair** (1878)
Mettle of the Pasture, The (1903) **James Lane Allen** (1849)
Mexico Bay (1982) **Paul Horgan** (1903)
Mexico City Blues (1959) **Jack Kerouac** (1922–69)
Mexico Set (1984) **Len Deighton** (1929)
Mezzanine, The (1989) **Nicholson Baker** (1957)
Mezzotint (1961) **Compton Mackenzie** (1883)
MF (1971) **'Anthony Burgess' [John Anthony Burgess Wilson]** (1917)
Mi Amigo (1959) **W.R. Burnett** (1899)
Miami (1987) **Joan Didion** (1934)
Miami and the Siege of Chicago (1968) **Norman Mailer** (1923)
Mianserin Sonnets (1984) **Roy Fuller** (1912)
Micah Clarke (1889) **A. Conan Doyle** (1859)
Michael Robartes and the Dancer (1920) **W.B. Yeats** (1865)
Michael Scarlett (1925) **James Gould Cozzens** (1903)
Michaelmas Terme (1607) **Thomas Middleton** (1580)
Mickelsson's Ghosts (1982) **John Gardner** (1933)
Micro-cosmographie (1628) **John Earle** (1601?)
Microcosmos (1603) **John Davies of Hereford** (1565)
Microcosmus (1621) **Peter Heylyn** (1600)
Mid-American Chants (1918) **Sherwood Anderson** (1876)
Mid-Channel (1909) **Arthur Wing Pinero** (1855)
Mid-night and Daily Thoughts (1694) **Sir William Killigrew** (1606)
Mid-night Thoughts (1681) **Sir William Killigrew** (1606)
Midas (1592) **John Lyly** (1554)
Midcentury (1961) **John Dos Passos** (1896)
Middle Age of Mrs Eliot, The (1958) **Angus Wilson** (1913)
Middle East 1940–2 (1944) **Philip Guedalla** (1889)
Middle Ground, The (1980) **Margaret Drabble** (1939)
Middle of a War, The (1942) **Roy Fuller** (1912)
Middle of the Journey, The (1947) **Lionel Trilling** (1905)
Middle Passage, The (1962) **V.S. Naipaul** (1932)
Middle Span, The (1945) **George Santayana** (1863)
Middle Years, The (1917) **Henry James** (1843–1916)
Middle-Aged Man on the Flying Trapeze, The (1935) **James Thurber** (1894)
Middle-Aged Spread (1977) **Roger Hall** (1939)
Middlemarch (1871) **'George Eliot' [Mary Ann Evans]** (1819)
Middlemen, The (1961) **Christine Brooke-Rose** (1926)
Middy and Ensign (1883) **George Manville Fenn** (1831)
Middy and the Moors, The (1888) **R.M. Ballantyne** (1825)
Midlander, The (1923) **Booth Tarkington** (1869)
Midnight (1989) **Dean Koontz** (1945)
Midnight All Day (1999) **Hanif Kureishi** (1954)
Midnight Bell, The (1929) **Patrick Hamilton** (1904)
Midnight Folk, The (1927) **John Masefield** (1878)
Midnight is a Place (1974) **Joan Aiken** (1924)
Midnight Oil (1971) **V.S. Pritchett** (1900)
Midnight on the Desert (1937) **J.B. Priestley** (1894)

Midnight Plus One (1965) **Gavin Lyall** (1932)
Midnight's Children (1981) **Salman Rushdie** (1947)
Midnights Trance, A (1619) **William Drummond of Hawthornden** (1585)
Midnite (1967) **Randolph Stow** (1935)
Midpoint (1969) **John Updike** (1932)
Midsummer Night's Dream, A (1600) **William Shakespeare** (1564)
Midsummer Day's Dream, A (1824) **Edwin Atherstone** (1788)
Midsummer Holiday, A (1884) **A.C. Swinburne** (1837)
Midsummer Meadows (1946) **E.J. Scovell** (1907)
Midsummer Morning Jog Log (1986) **Michael Horovitz** (1935) (ed.)
Midsummer Night (1928) **John Masefield** (1878)
Midsummer Night Madness (1932) **'Seán O'Faoláin' [John Francis Whelan]** (1900)
Midwich Cuckoos, The [filmed as Village of the Damned, 1960] (1957) **'John Wyndham' [John Wyndham Harris]** (1903)
Midwinter (1923) **John Buchan** (1875)
Mighty and Their Fall, The (1961) **I. Compton-Burnett** (1884)
Mighty Atom, The (1896) **Marie Corelli** (1855)
Mighty Waltzer, The (1999) **Howard Jacobson** (1942)
Mignon (1962) **James M. Cain** (1892)
Miguel Street (1959) **V.S. Naipaul** (1932)
Mikado, The [music by Sir Arthur Sullivan] (1885) **W.S. Gilbert** (1836)
Mike (1909) **P.G. Wodehouse** (1881)
Mike (1916) **E.F. Benson** (1867)
Mike Fletcher (1889) **George Moore** (1852)
Mildred Pierce (1941) **James M. Cain** (1892)
Miles Wallingford (1844) **James Fenimore Cooper** (1789)
Milesian Chief, The (1812) **C.R. Maturin** (1782)
Milestones ([1912]) **Arnold Bennett** (1867)
Military Orchid, The (1948) **Jocelyn Brooke** (1908)
Military Philosophers, The (1968) **Anthony Powell** (1905)
Milk (1983) **Beverley Farmer** (1941)
Milk and Honey (1984) **Elizabeth Jolley** (1923)
Mill on the Floss, The (1860) **'George Eliot' [Mary Ann Evans]** (1819)
Millennial Fables (1994) **Peter Porter** (1929)
Miller of Angibault, The [*Le Meunier d'Angibault*] (1845) **'George Sand' [Auore Dupin]** (1804)
Miller of Deanhaugh, The (1844) **James Ballantine** (1808)
Miller of Old Church, The (1911) **Ellen Glasgow** (1874)
Millionaire of Yesterday, A (1900) **E. Phillips Oppenheim** (1866)
Millroy the Magician (1993) **Paul Theroux** (1941)
Mills of the Kavanaughs, The (1951) **Robert Lowell** (1917)
Millstone, The (1965) **Margaret Drabble** (1939)
Milly Darrell (1873) **M.E. Braddon** (1835)
Milton (dated 1804) **William Blake** (1757)
Milton (1879) **Mark Pattison** (1813)
Milton (1900) **Sir Walter Raleigh** (1861)
Milton (1930) **E.M.W. Tillyard** (1889)
Milton (1935) **Hilaire Belloc** (1870)
Milton and his Modern Critics (1940) **Logan Pearsall Smith** (1865)
Milton in America (1996) **Peter Ackroyd** (1949)
Milton's God (1961) **Sir William Empson** (1906)
Milton's Grand Style (1963) **Christopher Ricks** (1933)
Milton's Prosody (1893) **Robert Bridges** (1844)
Mimesis (1953) **Erich Auerbach** (1892)
Mimi's Ghost (1995) **Tim Parks** (1954)
Mimic Men, The (1967) **V.S. Naipaul** (1932)
Mind and Body (1873) **Alexander Bain** (1818)
Mind and its Place in Nature, The (1925) **C.D. Broad** (1887)
Mind and its Workings, The (1927) **C.E.M. Joad** (1891)
Mind at the End of its Tether (1945) **H.G. Wells** (1866)
Mind Breaths (1977) **Allen Ginsberg** (1926)
Mind Has Mountains, The (1966) **Elizabeth Jennings** (1926)
Mind in the Modern World (1973) **Lionel Trilling** (1905)
Mind of Man, The (1940) **John Gawsworth** (1912)
Mind of Mr J.G. Reeder, The [US. *The Murder Book of Mr J.G. Reeder*] (1925) **Edgar Wallace** (1875)
Mind to Murder, A (1963) **P.D. James** (1920)
Mind's Eye, The (1934) **Edmund Blunden** (1896)
Mind-Reader, The (1976) **Richard Wilbur** (1921)
Minds Meet (1975) **Walter Abish** (1931)
Mine Boy (1946) **Peter Abrahams** (1919)
Mine Eyes Dazzle (1950) **Alistair Campbell** (1925)
Mine of Serpents, A (1949) **Jocelyn Brooke** (1908)
Mine Own Executioner (1945) **Nigel Balchin** (1908)
Miner's Right, The (1890) **'Rolf Boldrewood' [Thomas Alexander Browne]** (1826)
Mineralls, The (1589) **Martin Marprelate**
Minerva Britanna (1612) **Henry Peacham the younger** (1578?)
Mingo and Other Sketches (1884) **Joel Chandler Harris** (1848)
Minister, The (1797) **M.G. Lewis** (1775)
Minister, The (1953) **R.S. Thomas** (1913)
Minister's Charge, The (1887) **William Dean Howells** (1837)
Minister's Wife, The (1869) **Margaret Oliphant** (1828)
Minister's Wooing, The (1859) **Harriet Beecher Stowe** (1811)
Ministry of Fear, The (1943) **Graham Greene** (1904)
Minna's Holiday (1876) **Matilda Betham-Edwards** (1836)
Minne (1904) **Colette** (1873)
Minnie Maylow's Story (1931) **John Masefield** (1878)
Minnow on the Say (1955) **Philippa Pearce** (1920)
Minor, The (1760) **Samuel Foote** (1720)
Minor Poet, A (1884) **Amy Levy** (1861)
Minor Prophets, The (1860) **E.B. Pusey** (1800)
Minority Report (1963) **Elmer Rice** (1892)
Minotaur (1992) **Tom Paulin** (1949)

Minstrel, The [bk i] (1771,1774) **James Beattie** (1735)
Minstrelsy of the Scottish Border (1802) **Sir Walter Scott** (1771) (ed.)
Minty Alley (1936) **C.L.R. James** (1901)
Minute by Glass Minute (1982) **Anne Stevenson** (1933)
Mirabell (1978) **James Merrill** (1926)
Miracle of Mullion Hill, The (1956) **David Campbell** (1915)
Miracle of the Rose [Miracle de la rose] (1946) **Jean Genet** (1910)
Miracles (1947) **C.S. Lewis** (1898)
Miracles by Arrangement [US: *Mr Gresham and Olympus*] (1932) **Norman Lindsay** (1879)
Mirage (1924) **Edgar Lee Masters** (1868)
Miranda (1913) **M.E. Braddon** (1835)
Miranda of the Balcony (1899) **A.E.W. Mason** (1865)
Mirandola (1821) **'Barry Cornwall' [Bryan Waller Procter]** (1787)
Mirgorod (1835) **Nikolai Vasilevich Gogol** (1809)
Miriam, and Other Poems (1871) **John Greenleaf Whittier** (1807)
Miriam Rozella (1898) **B.L. Farjeon** (1838)
Miriam Sedley (1851) **Edward Bulwer-Lytton** (1803)
Miriam's Schooling (1890) **'Mark Rutherford' [William Hale White]** (1831)
Mirour for Magestrates of Cyties, A (1584) **George Whetstone** (*c.* 1551)
Mirror Crack'd From Side to Side, The [US: *The Mirror Crack'd*] (1962) **Agatha Christie** (1890)
Mirror Image (1998) **Danielle Steel** (1947)
Mirror in the Roadway, The (1956) **'Frank O'Connor' [Michael Francis O'Donovan]** (1903)
Mirror of Good Manners, The (1523) **Alexander Barclay** (1475?) (tr.)
Mirror of Martyrs, The (1601) **John Weever** (1576)
Mirror of the Months, The (1925) **Sheila Kaye-Smith** (1887)
Mirror of the Sea, The (1906) **Joseph Conrad** (1857)
Mirror to Damascus (1967) **Colin Thubron** (1939)
Mirror Wall, The (1989) **Richard Murphy** (1927)
Mirrors and Windows (1958) **Howard Nemerov** (1920)
Mirrour of Mindes, The [trn of Barclay's *Icon Animarum* 1614] (1631) **Thomas May** (1595) (tr.)
Mirrour of Mutabilitie, The (1579) **Anthony Munday** (1560)
Mirum in Modum (1602) **John Davies of Hereford** (1565)
Mirza, The (1841) **James Morier** (1780)
Misalliance, A (1986) **Anita Brookner** (1928)
Misalliance, The Dark Lady of the Sonnets, and Fanny's First Play (1914) **Bernard Shaw** (1856)
Misanthrope, The [*Le Misanthrope*] (1666) **'Molière' [Jean-Baptiste Poquelin]** (1622)
Miscellanea: The First Part (1680) **Sir William Temple** (1628)
Miscellanea: The Second Part (1690) **Sir William Temple** (1628)
Miscellanea: The Third Part [ed. Jonathan Swift] (1701) **Sir William Temple** (1628–99)
Miscellaneous Essays (1892) **George Saintsbury** (1845)
Miscellaneous Observations on the Tragedy of Macbeth (1745) **Samuel Johnson** (1709)
Miscellaneous Poems (1681) **Andrew Marvell** (1621–78)
Miscellaneous Poems and Translations [inc. 2-canto version of 'The Rape of the Lock'] (1712) **Alexander Pope** (1688) and others
Miscellaneous Studies (1895) **Walter Pater** (1839–94)
Miscellaneous Verdicts [Writings on writers 1946–1989] (1990) **Anthony Powell** (1905)
Miscellaneous Works (1796) **Edward Gibbon** (1737–94)
Miscellaneous Writings (1797) **R.C. Dallas** (1754)
Miscellania (1653) **Richard Flecknoe** (*c.* 1620)
Miscellanies (1696) **John Aubrey** (1626)
Miscellanies (1743) **Henry Fielding** (1707)
Miscellanies (1859) **Charles Kingsley** (1819)
Miscellanies [i] (1854) **Thomas De Quincey** (1785)
Miscellanies in Prose and Verse (1775) **Hester Chapone** (1727)
Miscellanies in Prose and Verse [Supplement pub. 1784] (1778) **Thomas Chatterton** (1752–70)
Miscellanies in Prose and Verse (1711) **Jonathan Swift** (1667) and others
Miscellanies in Prose and Verse: Volume the Fifth (1735) **Jonathan Swift** (1667) and others
Miscellanies (1796) **Isaac D'Israeli** (1766)
Miscellany of Men, A (1912) **G.K. Chesterton** (1874)
Miscellany of Sense and Nonsense, A (1923) **Jerome K. Jerome** (1859)
Miscellany Poems (1684) **John Dryden** (1631) and others
Miscellany Poems on Several Occasions (1713) **Anne Finch, Countess of Winchilsea** (1661)
Miscellany Poems upon Several Occasions (1692) **Charles Gildon** (1665) (ed.)
Mischief of Monica, The (1891) **L[ucy] B[erthia] Walford** (1845)
Miser, The [*L'Avare*] (1668) **'Molière' [Jean-Baptiste Poquelin]** (1622)
Miser, The (1672) **Thomas Shadwell** (1642?)
Miser, The (1733) **Henry Fielding** (1707)
Miser's Daughter, The (1842) **W.H. Ainsworth** (1805)
Misérables, Les (1862) **Victor Hugo** (1802)
Misery (1987) **Stephen King** (1947)
Misfits, The (1961) **Arthur Miller** (1915)
Misfortunes of Elphin, The (1829) **Thomas Love Peacock** (1785)
Misleading Cases in the Common Law (1929) **A.P. Herbert** (1890)
Miss Angel (1875) **Lady Anne Ritchie** (1837)
Miss Armstrong's and Other Circumstances (1896) **John Davidson** (1857)
Miss Bouverie (1880) **Mary Louisa Molesworth** (1839)

Miss Bretherton (1884) **Mrs T. Humphry Ward** (1851)
Miss Brown (1884) **'Vernon Lee' [Violet Paget]** (1856)
Miss Carew (1865) **Amelia B. Edwards** (1831)
Miss Cayley's Adventures (1899) **Grant Allen** (1848)
Miss Cheyne of Essilmont (1883) **James Grant** (1822)
Miss Civilization (1906) **Richard Harding Davis** (1864)
Miss Fallowfield's Fortune (1908) **Ellen Thorneycroft Fowler** (1860)
Miss Gascoigne (1887) **Mrs J.H. Riddell** (1832)
Miss Gomez and the Brethren (1971) **'William Trevor' [William Trevor Cox]** (1928)
Miss Herbert (1976) **Christina Stead** (1902)
Miss in Her Teens (1747) **David Garrick** (1717)
Miss Julie (1888) **August Strindberg** (1849)
Miss Lonelyhearts (1933) **'Nathanael West' [Nathan Wallenstein Weinstein]** (1903)
Miss Ludington's Sister (1884) **Edward Bellamy** (1850)
Miss Lulu Bett (1920) **Zona Gale** (1874)
Miss Mackenzie (1865) **Anthony Trollope** (1815)
Miss Mapp (1922) **E.F. Benson** (1867)
Miss Marjoribanks (1866) **Margaret Oliphant** (1828)
Miss Meredith (1889) **Amy Levy** (1861)
Miss Misanthrope (1878) **Justin McCarthy** (1830)
Miss Mole (1930) **E.H. Young** (1880)
Miss Muriel (1971) **Ann Petry** (1908)
Miss or Mrs? (1873) **Wilkie Collins** (1824)
Miss Owen is at Home (1969) **Margaret Forster** (1938)
Miss Peabody's Inheritance (1983) **Elizabeth Jolley** (1923)
Miss Pym Disposes (1946) **'Josephine Tey' [Elizabeth Mackintosh]** (1897)
Miss Quillet (1902) **S. Baring-Gould** (1834)
Miss Ravenel's Conversion from Secession to Loyalty (1867) **John W. de Forest** (1826)
Miss Stuart's Legacy (1893) **Flora Annie Steel** (1847)
Miss Tod and the Prophets (1898) **Mrs Hugh Bell** (1851)
Miss Tommy (1884) **Dinah Maria Craik** (1826)
Miss Zilphia Gant (1932) **William Faulkner** (1897)
Misselmah (1847) **James Morier** (1780)
Missing the Midnight (1997) **Jane Gardam** (1928)
Mission, The (1845) **Frederick Marryat** (1792)
Missionaries, The (1988) **Norman Lewis** (1918)
Missionary, The (1811) **Lady Sydney Morgan** (1783?)
Missionary, The (1813) **William Lisle Bowles** (1762)
Missionary Travels and Researches in South Africa (1857) **David Livingstone** (1813)
Mist in the Mirror, The (1992) **Susan Hill** (1942)
Mistake, The (1705) **Sir John Vanbrugh** (1664)
Mister Johnson (1939) **Joyce Cary** (1888)
Mister White Eyes (1984) **Herbert Gold** (1924)
Mistral's Daughter (1982) **Judith Krantz**
Mistress and Maid (1863) **Dinah Maria Craik** (1826)
Mistress Masham's Repose (1946) **T.H. White** (1906)
Mistress of Royalty, The (1814) **Pierce Egan [the elder]** (1772)
Mistress of Shenstone, The (1910) **Florence Barclay** (1862)
Mistress Pat (1935) **L.M. Montgomery** (1874)
Mistresse, The (1647) **Abraham Cowley** (1618)
Mithraic Emblems (1936) **Roy Campbell** (1901)
Mithridates [Mithridate] (1673) **Jean Racine** (1639)
Mithridates King of Pontus (1678) **Nathaniel Lee** (1649?)
Mitre Court (1885) **Mrs J.H. Riddell** (1832)
Mixed Essays (1879) **Matthew Arnold** (1822)
Mixed Faith (1950) **Irwin Shaw** (1913)
Mixed Feelings (1951) **John Wain** (1925)
Mixed Marriage (1911) **St John Ervine** (1883)
Mixt Contemplations in Better Times (1660) **Thomas Fuller** (1608)
Mixture As Before, The (1940) **Somerset Maugham** (1874)
Mixture of Frailties, A (1958) **Robertson Davies** (1913)
Mob, The (1914) **John Galsworthy** (1867)
Mobile (1963) **Michel Butor** (1926)
Moby-Dick (1851) **Herman Melville** (1819)
Moccasin Maker, The (1913) **Pauline Johnson** (1862)
Mock Beggar Hall (1924) **Robert Graves** (1895)
Mock Doctor, The (1732) **Henry Fielding** (1707)
Mock-Mourners, The (1702) **Daniel Defoe** (1660)
Moderato cantabile (1958) **'Marguerite Duras' [Marguerite Donnadieu]** (1914)
Modern American Novel, The (1983) **Malcolm Bradbury** (1932)
Modern Arabian Nights, The (1877) **Gilbert Abbott a Beckett** (1811)
Modern Broods (1900) **Charlotte M. Yonge** (1823)
Modern Buccaneer, A (1894) **'Rolf Boldrewood' [Thomas Alexander Browne]** (1826)
Modern Chivalry (1792–1815) **Hugh Henry Brackenridge** (1748)
Modern Chivalry (1843) **W.H. Ainsworth** (1805)
Modern Comedy, A (1929) **John Galsworthy** (1867)
Modern Cookery (1845) **Eliza Acton** (1799)
Modern Criticism and Theory (1988) **David Lodge** (1935) (ed.)
Modern Democrats (1921) **James Bryce** (1838)
Modern England (1899) **Justin McCarthy** (1830)
Modern Greece (1817) **Felicia Dorothea Hemans** (1793)
Modern Griselda, The (1805) **Maria Edgeworth** (1767)
Modern Husband, The (1732) **Henry Fielding** (1707)
Modern Instance, A (1882) **William Dean Howells** (1837)
Modern Instances (1898) **Ella D'Arcy** (1851)
Modern Love: A Reprint (1892) **George Meredith** (1828)
Modern Love and Poems of the English Roadside (1862) **George Meredith** (1828)
Modern Lover, A (1883) **George Moore** (1852)
Modern Mephistopheles, A (1877) **Louisa M. Alcott** (1832)

Modern Mind, The (1937) **Michael Roberts** (1902)
Modern Mythology (1897) **Andrew Lang** (1844)
Modern Myths (1994) **Marina Warner** (1946)
Modern Novel Writing (1796) **William Beckford** (1760)
Modern Painters [vol. i] (1843) **John Ruskin** (1819)
Modern Painters (1846) **John Ruskin** (1819)
Modern Painters (1856) **John Ruskin** (1819)
Modern Painters (1856) **John Ruskin** (1819)
Modern Painters (1860) **John Ruskin** (1819)
Modern Poetry (1938) **Louis MacNeice** (1907)
Modern Poetry and the Tradition (1939) **Cleanth Brooks** (1906)
Modern Rack, The (1889) **Frances Power Cobbe** (1822)
Modern Society (1885) **Edward Carpenter** (1844) (ed.)
Modern Symposium, A (1905) **Goldsworthy Lowes Dickinson** (1862)
Modern Tragedy, A (1934) **Phyllis Bentley** (1894)
Modern Traveller, The (1898) **Hilaire Belloc** (1870)
Modern Utopia, A (1905) **H.G. Wells** (1866)
Modern Way, The (1906) **Lucy [Mrs W.K.] Clifford** (1853)
Modern World, The (1988) **Malcolm Bradbury** (1932)
Modern Writer and His World, The (1953) **G.S. Fraser** (1915)
Modernism in Literature (1938) **W.R. Inge** (1860)
Modest Enquiry into the Mystery of Iniquity, A (1664) **Henry More** (1614)
Modest Proposal, A (1729) **Jonathan Swift** (1667)
Moeniae (1595) **Robert Southwell SJ** (1561?)
Mogg Megone (1836) **John Greenleaf Whittier** (1807)
Mogreb-el-Acksa (1898) **R.B. Cunninghame Graham** (1852)
Mogul Tale, A (1784) **Elizabeth Inchbald** (1753)
Mohawks (1886) **M.E. Braddon** (1835)
Mohicans of Paris, The [*Les Mohicans de Paris*] (1854–7) **Alexandre Dumas ['père']** (1802)
Mohocks, The (1712) **John Gay** (1685)
Mohun (1869) **John Cooke** (1830)
Moise and the World of Reason (1975) **'Tennessee' [Thomas Lanier] Williams** (1911)
Moll Flanders [**Defoe**]: see *The Fortunes and Misfortunes of the Famous Moll Flanders*
Molloy [pub. in French 1951] (1955) **Samuel Beckett** (1906)
Molly Sweeney (1994) **Brian Friel** (1929)
Moly (1971) **Thom Gunn** (1929)
Moment After, The (1890) **Robert Williams Buchanan** (1841)
Moment in Time, A (1964) **H.E. Bates** (1905)
Moment of Cubism, The (1969) **John Berger** (1926)
Moment of Eclipse, The (1971) **Brian Aldiss** (1925)
Moment of Time, A (1926) **Richard Hughes** (1900)
Moment of Truth, The (1949) **Storm Jameson** (1897)
Moment of War, A (1991) **Laurie Lee** (1914)
Moment, The (1947) **Virginia Woolf** (1882–1941)
Moments of Grace (1979) **Elizabeth Jennings** (1926)
Moments of Vision (1917) **Thomas Hardy** (1840)
Moments, The (1966) **J.B. Priestley** (1894)
Mona Lisa Overdrive (1988) **William Gibson** (1948)
Monarch of Mincing Lane, The (1871) **William Black** (1841)
Monarch, the Big Bear of Tallac (1904) **Ernest Thompson Seton** (1860)
Monarchick Tragedies, The (1604) **Sir William Alexander** (1567?)
Monas Hieroglyphica (1564) **Dr John Dee** (1527)
Monastery, The (1820) **Sir Walter Scott** (1771)
Monckton Milnes: The Flight of Youth (1951) **James Pope-Hennessy** (1916)
Monckton Milnes: The Years of Promise (1949) **James Pope-Hennessy** (1916)
Monday Night (1938) **Kay Boyle** (1903)
Monday Stories [*Contes du lundi*] (1873) **Alphonse Daudet** (1840)
Money (1840) **Edward Bulwer-Lytton** (1803)
Money [L'Argent] (1891) **Émile Zola** (1840)
Money (1984) **Martin Amis** (1949)
Money for Love (1929) **Josephine Herbst** (1897)
Money For Nothing (1928) **P.G. Wodehouse** (1881)
Money & Friends (1992) **David Williamson** (1942)
Money Market, The (1898) **E.F. Benson** (1867)
Money Moon, The (1911) **Jeffery Farnol** (1878)
Money the Mistress (1726) **Thomas Southerne** (1659)
Money Writes! (1927) **Upton Sinclair** (1878)
Moneychangers, The (1975) **Arthur Hailey** (1920)
Money-Spider, The (1911) **William le Queux** (1864)
Moneyed Man, The (1841) **Horace Smith** (1779)
Monk and the Hangman's Daughter, The (1892) **Ambrose Bierce** (1842)
Monk Dawson (1969) **Piers Paul Read** (1941)
Monk, The (1796) **M.G. Lewis** (1775)
Monk's-Hood (1980) **'Ellis Peters' [Edith Mary Pargeter]** (1913)
Monkey [from Wu Ch'eng-en] (1942) **Arthur Waley** (1889) (tr.)
Monkey Grip (1977) **Helen Garner** (1942)
Monkey King, The (1978) **Timothy Mo** (1950)
Monkey's Uncle (1994) **Jenny Diski** (1947)
Monks of Monk Hall, The (1844) **George Lippard** (1822)
Monks of Thelema, The (1878) **Sir Walter Besant** (1836) [with James Rice]
Monochromes (1895) **Ella D'Arcy** (1851)
Monodromos [reissued as *One-Way Street*, 1975] (1973) **Marian Engel** (1933)
Monody on Major André (1781) **Anna Seward** (1747)
Monologue of a Deaf Man (1958) **David Wright** (1920)
Monophylo (1572) **Sir Geoffrey Fenton** (1539?) (tr.)
Monopolies of Loss (1992) **Adam Mars-Jones** (1954)
Monopolist, The (1795) **Christopher Anstey** (1724)
Monopoly (1890) **William Morris** (1834)
Monsieur (1974) **Lawrence Durrell** (1912)
Monsieur Alphonse (1873) **Alexandre Dumas ['fils']** (1824)
Monsieur Beaucaire (1900) **Booth Tarkington** (1869)

Monsieur Bergeret in Paris [*Monsieur Bergeret à Paris*] (1901) **'Anatole France' [Jacques-Anatole-François Thibault]** (1844)
Monsieur D'Olive (1606) **George Chapman** (1559?)
Monsieur de Pourceaugnac (1669) **'Molière' [Jean-Baptiste Poquelin]** (1622)
Monsieur Garat (1860) **Victorien Sardou** (1831)
Monsieur Judas (1891) **Fergus Hume** (1859)
Monsieur Lecoq (1869) **Émile Gaboriau** (1832)
Monsieur Parent (1886) **Guy de Maupassant** (1850)
Monsieur Pichelmère (1905) **S. Baring-Gould** (1834)
Monsieur Quixote (1982) **Graham Greene** (1904)
Monsieur Thomas (1639) **John Fletcher** (1579–1625)
Monster, The (1899) **Stephen Crane** (1871)
Monstre Gai; Malign Fiesta (1955) **Wyndham Lewis** (1882)
Mont-Saint-Michel and Chartres (1904) **Henry Adams** (1838)
Montage of a Dream Deferred (1951) **Langston Hughes** (1902)
Montaigne's Tower (1984) **Geoffrey Grigson** (1905)
Montalbert (1795) **Charlotte Smith** (1749)
Montelion, 1660 (1660) **John Phillips** (1631)
Montes the Matador (1900) **'Frank' Harris** (1856)
Montezuma's Daughter (1893) **Sir H. Rider Haggard** (1856)
Montforts, The [as 'Martin Mills'] (1928) **Martin Boyd** (1893)
Month in the Country, A (1980) **J.L. Carr** (1912)
Month of Sundays, A (1975) **John Updike** (1932)
Months, The (1821) **Leigh Hunt** (1784)
Montrose (1928) **John Buchan** (1875)
Monument, The (1702) **John Dennis** (1657)
Monuments and Maidens (1985) **Marina Warner** (1946)
Moo (1995) **Jane Smiley** (1949)
Moods (1865) **Louisa M. Alcott** (1832)
Moods, Cadenced and Declaimed (1926) **Theodore Dreiser** (1871)
Moon (1985) **James Herbert** (1943)
Moon and Sixpence, The (1919) **Somerset Maugham** (1874)
Moon at Perigee [UK: *Monsoon*] (1948) **George Johnston** (1912)
Moon Endureth, The (1912) **John Buchan** (1875)
Moon for the Misbegotten, A (1947) **Eugene O'Neill** (1888)
Moon in the Yellow River, The (1931) **Denis Johnston** (1901)
Moon is a Harsh Mistress, The (1967) **Robert A. Heinlein** (1907)
Moon is Down, The [dramatized 1942] (1942) **John Steinbeck** (1902)
Moon is Feminine, The (1938) **'Clemence Dane' [Winifred Ashton]** (1888)
Moon Lady, The (1992) **Amy Tan** (1952)
Moon Lake (1980) **Eudora Welty** (1909)
Moon of Gomrath, The (1963) **Alan Garner** (1934)
Moon of Israel (1918) **Sir H. Rider Haggard** (1856)
Moon of the Caribbees, The (1918) **Eugene O'Neill** (1888)
Moon on a Fencepost, The (1988) **Robert Bly** (1926)
Moon Over Minneapolis (1991) **Fay Weldon** (1931)
Moon Palace (1989) **Paul Auster** (1947)
Moon Tiger (1987) **Penelope Lively** (1933)
Moon's Farm (1955) **Sir Herbert Read** (1893)
Moon's Ottery (1978) **Patricia Beer** (1924)
Moon-Calf (1920) **Floyd Dell** (1887)
Moondial (1987) **Helen Cresswell** (1934)
Moonferns and Starsongs (1971) **Robert Silverberg** (1935)
Moonfleet (1898) **J. Meade Falkner** (1858)
Moonlight (1993) **Harold Pinter** (1930)
Moonlight Acre (1938) **R.D. FitzGerald** (1902)
Moonlight, The (1946) **Joyce Cary** (1888)
Moonlite (1981) **David Foster** (1944)
Moonraker (1955) **Ian Fleming** (1908)
Moons of Grandeur (1920) **William Rose Benét** (1886)
Moons of Jupiter, The (1982) **Alice Munro** (1931)
Moonstone, The (1868) **Wilkie Collins** (1824)
Moor's Last Sigh, The (1995) **Salman Rushdie** (1947)
Moorland Cottage, The (1850) **Elizabeth Gaskell** (1810)
Moorland Idylls (1896) **Grant Allen** (1848)
Moors and the Fens, The (1858) **Mrs J.H. Riddell** (1832)
Moortown (1979) **Ted Hughes** (1930)
Mopsa the Fairy (1869) **Jean Ingelow** (1820)
Moral Alphabet, The (1899) **Hilaire Belloc** (1870)
Moral and Metaphysical Philosophy (1845) **F.D. Maurice** (1805)
Moral Ending, and Other Stories, A (1931) **Sylvia Townsend Warner** (1893)
Moral Law Expounded, The (1642) **Lancelot Andrewes** (1555)
Moral Sketches of Prevailing Opinions and Manners (1819) **Hannah More** (1745)
Moral Songs (1849) **Mrs C.F. Alexander** (1818)
Moral Stories (1954) **David Wright** (1920)
Moral Tales for Young People (1801) **Maria Edgeworth** (1767)
Morality of Stage-Plays, The (1757) **Adam Ferguson** (1723)
Morality Play (1995) **Barry Unsworth** (1930)
Morall Faibillis of Esope, The (1570) **Robert Henryson** (*c.* 1430–*c.* 1505) (tr.)
Morall Philosophie of Doni, The [from Antonio Francesco Doni] (1570) **Sir Thomas North** (1535) (tr.)
Moran of the Lady Letty (1898) **Frank Norris** (1870)
Morando the Tritameron of Love (1584) **Robert Greene** (1558)
Morbid Taste for Bones, A [first of the 'Cadfael' series] (1977) **'Ellis Peters' [Edith Mary Pargeter]** (1913)
Mord Em'ly (1898) **W. Pett Ridge** (1860)
Mordaunt (1800) **John Moore** (1729)
Mordred (1895) **Sir Henry Newbolt** (1862)
More (1899) **Max Beerbohm** (1872)
More 'Bab' Ballads (1873) **W.S. Gilbert** (1836)
More Beasts—For Worse Children (1897) **Hilaire Belloc** (1870)

More Die of Heartbreak (1987) **Saul Bellow** (1915)
More Essays of Love and Virtue (1931) **Havelock Ellis** (1859)
More Ghost Stories of an Antiquary (1911) **M.R. James** (1862)
More Joy in Heaven (1937) **Morley Callaghan** (1903)
More Joy in Heaven (1935) **Sylvia Townsend Warner** (1893)
More Joy of Sex (1973) **Alex Comfort** (1920)
More Kindred of the Wild (1911) **Sir Charles G.D. Roberts** (1860)
More Little Ones (1982) **Gavin Ewart** (1916)
More Memoirs of an Aesthete (1970) **Sir Harold Acton** (1904)
More New Arabian Nights (1885) **Robert Louis Stevenson** (1850) [with Fanny Van der Grift Stevenson]
More Nonsense, Pictures, Rhymes Botany (1872) **Edward Lear** (1812)
More Obiter Dicta (1924) **Augustine Birrell** (1850)
More Pages from a Journal (1910) **'Mark Rutherford' [William Hale White]** (1831)
More Peers (1911) **Hilaire Belloc** (1870)
More Poems (1936) **A.E. Housman** (1859–1936)
More Poems (1961) **Robert Graves** (1895)
More Poems for People (1972) **Milton Acorn** (1923)
More Pricks Than Kicks (1934) **Samuel Beckett** (1906)
More Short-Ways with the Dissenters (1704) **Daniel Defoe** (1660)
More Songs from Vagabondia (1895) **William Bliss Carman** (1861) [with Richard Hovey]
More Spook Stories (1934) **E.F. Benson** (1867)
More Tales of the Unexpected (1980) **Roald Dahl** (1916)
More Than Enough (1975) **Frank Sargeson** (1903)
More Than Human (1953) **Theodore Sturgeon** (1918)
More Than Time (1970) **Patric Dickinson** (1914)
More the Merrier, The (1608) **Henry Peacham the younger** (1578?)
More Translations From the Chinese (1919) **Arthur Waley** (1889) (tr.)
More Trivia (1922) **Logan Pearsall Smith** (1865)
More Ways Than One (1783) **Hannah Cowley** (1743)
More William (1922) **'Richmal Crompton' [Richmal Crompton Lamburn]** (1890)
More Women Than Men (1933) **I. Compton-Burnett** (1884)
Moreau's Other Island (1980) **Brian Aldiss** (1925)
Morgan's Daughter (1953) **H.G. de Lisser** (1878)
Morgan's Passing (1980) **Anne Tyler** (1941)
Morgante Maggiore (1823) **George Gordon, Lord Byron** (1788) (tr.)
Morlands, The (1805) **R.C. Dallas** (1754)
Morlas, The (1853) **Caroline Clive** (1801)
Morning After Optimism, The (1971) **Tom Murphy** (1935)
Morning at Jalna (1960) **Mazo de la Roche** (1879)
Morning Face (1968) **Mulk Raj Anand** (1905)
Morning, Noon and Night (1968) **James Gould Cozzens** (1903)
Morning Song of Lord Zero, The (1963) **Conrad Potter Aiken** (1889)
Morning Star (1910) **Sir H. Rider Haggard** (1856)
Morning Star [first of *The First-Born of Egypt* series] (1984) **Simon Raven** (1927)
Morning Tide (1930) **Neil M. Gunn** (1891)
Morning Watch, The (1951) **James Agee** (1909)
Morning Yet on Creation Day (1975) **Chinua Achebe** (1930)
Morning's War, The (1913) **C.E. Montague** (1867)
Mornings in Florence (1875) **John Ruskin** (1819)
Mornings in Mexico (1927) **D.H. Lawrence** (1885)
Morningside Plays (1917) **Elmer Rice** (1892)
Moronic Inferno, The (1986) **Martin Amis** (1949)
Mors et Vita (1923) **Shan F. Bullock** (1865)
Mort (1987) **Terry Pratchett** (1948)
Mort d'Agrippine, La (1653) **Cyrano de Bergerac** (1619)
Mortal Antipathy, A (1885) **Oliver Wendell Holmes** (1809)
Mortal Causes (1994) **Ian Rankin** (1960)
Mortal Coils (1922) **Aldous Huxley** (1894)
Mortal Matters (1983) **Penelope Gilliatt** (1932)
Mortal Stakes (1975) **Robert B. Parker** (1932)
Mortal Storm, The (1937) **Phyllis Bottome** (1884)
Mortal Strife (1942) **John Cooper Powys** (1872)
Mortallone and Aunt Trinidad (1917) **Sir A.T. Quiller-Couch** (1863)
Morte Arthur, Le (1864) **F.J. Furnivall** (1825) (ed.)
Mortimeriados (1596) **Michael Drayton** (1563)
Mortmere Stories, The (1994) **Edward Upward** (1903) [with Christopher Isherwood]
Mortomley's Estate (1874) **Mrs J.H. Riddell** (1832)
Morwyn (1937) **John Cooper Powys** (1872)
Mosada (1886) **W.B. Yeats** (1865)
Mosby's Memoirs (1968) **Saul Bellow** (1915)
Moscow Gold (1990) **Howard Brenton** (1942) and Tariq Ali (1943)
Moscow, Moscow (1990) **Christopher Hope** (1944)
Moscow Quadrille (1976) **Ted Allbeury** (1917)
Moses (1875) **Edward Carpenter** (1844)
Moses (1916) **Isaac Rosenberg** (1890)
Moses Ascending (1975) **Samuel Selvon** (1923)
Moses Migrating (1983) **Samuel Selvon** (1923)
Moses, Prince of Egypt (1958) **Howard Fast** (1914)
Mosquito Coast, The (1981) **Paul Theroux** (1941)
Mosquitoes (1927) **William Faulkner** (1897)
Moss Troopers, The (1912) **S.R. Crockett** (1860)
Mosses From an Old Manse (1846) **Nathaniel Hawthorne** (1804)
Most Beautiful World, The (1981) **Rodney Hall** (1935)
Most Dangerous Game, The (1963) **Gavin Lyall** (1932)
Most Difficult Area, The (1968) **Kenneth White** (1936)
Most Joyfull Songe, A (1586) **Thomas Deloney** (1543?)
Most Likely to Succeed (1954) **John Dos Passos** (1896)
Mote in God's Eye, The (1974) **Larry Niven** (1938) [with Jerry Pournelle]
Moth and Rust (1902) **Mary Cholmondeley** (1859)
Moth, The (1948) **James M. Cain** (1892)

Moth, The (1986) **Catherine Cookson** (1906)
Mother, The (1934) **Pearl S. Buck** (1892)
Mother (1925) **E.F. Benson** (1867)
Mother, The (1907) **Maxim Gorky** (1868)
Mother, The (1908) **Eden Phillpotts** (1862)
Mother and Son (1955) **I. Compton-Burnett** (1884)
Mother Bombie (1594) **John Lyly** (1554)
Mother Can You Hear Me? (1979) **Margaret Forster** (1938)
Mother Carey's Chickens (1911) **Kate Douglas Wiggin** (1856)
Mother Courage [*Mutter Courage*] (1941) **Bertolt Brecht** (1898)
Mother Goose (1881) **Kate Greenaway** (1846)
Mother Goose in Prose (1897) **L. Frank Baum** (1856)
Mother in History, A (1966) **Jean Stafford** (1915)
Mother London (1988) **Michael Moorcock** (1939)
Mother Night (1961) **Kurt Vonnegut** (1922)
Mother of the Muses, The (1989) **Tony Harrison** (1937)
Mother of Three, A (1909) **Clo Graves** (1863)
Mother Poem (1977) **Edward Brathwaite** (1930)
Mother Russia (1992) **Bernice Rubens** (1923)
Mother, The (1915) **Edith Sitwell** (1887)
Mother, the Daughter and the Sighing Bridge, The (1970) **Peter Redgrove** (1932)
Mother, What is Man? (1942) **Stevie Smith** (1902)
Mother's Blessing, The (1602) **Nicholas Breton** (1545?)
Mother's Book of Poetry, The (1872) **Margaret [Mrs Alfred] Gatty** (1809) (ed.)
Mother's Boys (1994) **Margaret Forster** (1938)
Mother's Day (1977) **David Storey** (1933)
Mother's Girl (1988) **Elaine Feinstein** (1930)
Mother's Manual, The (1833) **Frances Trollope** (1780)
Mother's Marvel (1949) **Caradoc Evans** (1878)
Mother's Recompense, A (1851) **Grace Aguilar** (1816–47)
Mother's Recompense, The (1925) **Edith Wharton** (1862)
Mothers and Children (1918) **'Frank Danby' [Julia Frankau]** (1864)
Mothers and Daughters (1831) **Mrs C.F. Gore** (1799)
Mothersill and the Foxes (1975) **John Williams** (1925)
Moths (1880) **'Ouida' [Marie Louise de la Ramée]** (1839)
Motley, A (1910) **John Galsworthy** (1867)
Motley (1918) **Walter de la Mare** (1873)
Motor-Flight Through France, A (1908) **Edith Wharton** (1862)
Mound Builders, The (1974) **Meridel Le Sueur** (1900)
Mount Henneth (1781) **Robert Bage** (1728)
Mount Music (1919) **'Somerville and Ross' [Edith Somerville** (1858) and **Violet Martin]** (1862)
Mount of Olives, The (1652) **Henry Vaughan** (1622)
Mount Pleasant (1777) **William Roscoe** (1753)
Mount Royal (1882) **M.E. Braddon** (1835)
Mount Zion (1931) **Sir John Betjeman** (1906)
Mountain and the Valley, The (1952) **Ernest Buckler** (1908)
Mountain Bard, The (1807) **James Hogg** (1770)
Mountain Beast, The (1930) **Stella Gibbons** (1902)
Mountain Blood (1915) **Joseph Hergesheimer** (1880)
Mountain City (1930) **Upton Sinclair** (1878)
Mountain in the Sea, The (1975) **John Fuller** (1937)
Mountain Interval (1916) **Robert Frost** (1874)
Mountain Language (1988) **Harold Pinter** (1930)
Mountain Lion (1947) **Jean Stafford** (1915)
Mountain Lovers, The [as 'Fiona Macleod'] (1895) **William Sharp** (1855)
Mountain Path, The (1936) **Harriette Arnow** (1908)
Mountain Tavern, The (1929) **Liam O'Flaherty** (1897)
Mountainy Singer, The (1909) **Joseph Campbell** (1879)
Mountbatten (1985) **Philip Ziegler** (1929)
Mountolive (1958) **Lawrence Durrell** (1912)
Mourners Below (1981) **James Purdy** (1923)
Mourning Becomes Electra (1931) **Eugene O'Neill** (1888)
Mourning Bride, The (1697) **William Congreve** (1670)
Mourning Muse of Alexas, The (1695) **William Congreve** (1670)
Mourning Remembrance, A (1509) **John Fisher** (1459?)
Mouse and his Child, The (1967) **Russell Hoban** (1925)
Mousetrap, The (1956) **Agatha Christie** (1890)
Mouth of Hell, The [*Le Trou de l'enfer*] (1850–1) **Alexandre Dumas ['père']** (1802)
Mouthful of Air, A (1992) **'Anthony Burgess' [John Anthony Burgess Wilson]** (1917)
Mouvement perpétuel, Le ['Perpetual Motion'] (1926) **Louis Aragon** (1897)
Moveable Feast, A (1964) **Ernest Hemingway** (1898–1961)
Moviegoer, The (1961) **Walker Percy** (1916)
Moving Pictures (1990) **Terry Pratchett** (1948)
Moving Target, A (1982) **William Golding** (1911)
Moving Target, The [first 'Lew Archer' novel] (1949) **'Ross MacDonald' [Kenneth Millar]** (1915)
Moving the Mountain (1911) **Charlotte Perkins Gilman** (1860)
Moving Toyshop, The (1946) **Edmund Crispin** (1921)
Moyses in a Map of his Miracles (1604) **Michael Drayton** (1563)
Mozart and the Wolf Gang (1991) **'Anthony Burgess' [John Anthony Burgess Wilson]** (1917)
MP; or, The Blue-Stocking (1811) **Thomas Moore** (1779)
Mr and Mrs Faulconbridge (1864) **Charles Hamilton Aïdé** (1826)
Mr Apollo (1908) **Ford Madox Ford** (1873)
Mr Balcony (1927) **C.H.B. Kitchin** (1895)
Mr Barrett's Secret (1993) **Kingsley Amis** (1922)
Mr Belloc Still Objects to Mr Wells's Outline of History (1926) **Hilaire Belloc** (1870)
Mr Beluncle (1951) **V.S. Pritchett** (1900)
Mr Biff the Boxer (1980) **Alan Ahlberg** (1938)

Mr Blettsworthy on Rampole Island (1928) **H.G. Wells** (1866)
Mr Bone's Retreat (1971) **Margaret Forster** (1938)
Mr Bridge (1969) **Evan S. Connell, Jr** (1924)
Mr Britling Sees It Through (1916) **H.G. Wells** (1866)
Mr Clutterbuck's Election (1908) **Hilaire Belloc** (1870)
Mr Corbett's Ghost (1968) **Leon Garfield** (1921)
Mr Facey Romford's Hounds (1865) **R.S. Surtees** (1805)
Mr Fleight (1913) **Ford Madox Ford** (1873)
Mr Fortune Objects (1935) **H.C. Bailey** (1878)
Mr Fortune's Maggot (1927) **Sylvia Townsend Warner** (1893)
Mr Fortune's Practice (1923) **H.C. Bailey** (1878)
Mr Gilhooley (1926) **Liam O'Flaherty** (1897)
Mr Grex of Monte Carlo (1915) **E. Phillips Oppenheim** (1866)
Mr Gumpy's Motor Car (1973) **Joihn Burningham** (1926)
Mr Gumpy's Outing (1970) **Joihn Burningham** (1926)
Mr H. (1813) **Charles Lamb** (1784)
Mr Huffam (1948) **Sir Hugh Walpole** (1884)
Mr Ingleside (1910) **E.V. Lucas** (1868)
Mr Isaacs (1882) **F. Marion Crawford** (1854)
Mr Ives' Christmas (1995) **Oscar Hijuelos** (1951)
Mr Justice Raffles (1909) **E.W. Hornung** (1866)
Mr Kingsley and Dr Newman (1864) **John Henry Newman** (1801)
Mr Littlejohn (1940) **Martin Flavin** (1883)
Mr Love and Justice (1960) **Colin MacInnes** (1914)
Mr Loveday's Little Outing (1936) **Evelyn Waugh** (1903)
Mr Meeson's Will (1888) **Sir H. Rider Haggard** (1856)
Mr Midshipman Easy (1836) **Frederick Marryat** (1792)
Mr Mulliner Speaking (1929) **P.G. Wodehouse** (1881)
Mr Murder (1993) **Dean Koontz** (1945)
Mr Norris Changes Trains [US: *The Last of Mr Norris*] (1935) **Christopher Isherwood** (1904)
Mr Perrin and Mr Traill (1911) **Sir Hugh Walpole** (1884)
Mr Petre (1925) **Hilaire Belloc** (1870)
Mr Pisistratus Brown, M.P., in the Highlands (1871) **William Black** (1841)
Mr Pope (1928) **Allen Tate** (1899)
Mr Prohack (1922) **Arnold Bennett** (1867)
Mr Punch's Pocket Ibsen (1893) **'F. Anstey' [Thomas Anstey Guthrie]** (1856)
Mr Pye (1953) **Mervyn Peake** (1911)
Mr Rabbit at Home (1895) **Joel Chandler Harris** (1848)
Mr Sammler's Planet (1964) **Saul Bellow** (1915)
Mr Sampath [US: *The Printer of Malgudi*] (1949) **R.K. Narayan** (1907)
Mr Scarborough's Family (1883) **Anthony Trollope** (1815–82)
Mr Scobie's Riddle (1983) **Elizabeth Jolley** (1923)
Mr Smith (1874) **L[ucy] B[erthia] Walford** (1845)
Mr Sponge's Sporting Tour (1853) **R.S. Surtees** (1805)
Mr Standfast (1918) **John Buchan** (1875)
Mr Tasker's Gods (1925) **T.F. Powys** (1875)
Mr Teddy (1917) **E.F. Benson** (1867)
Mr Tennyson and Mr Browning (1863) **Edward Dowden** (1843)
Mr Verdant Green, Married and Done For (1857) **'Cuthbert Bede B.A.' [Edward Bradley]** (1827)
Mr Vertigo (1994) **Paul Auster** (1947)
Mr Wakefield's Crusade (1985) **Bernice Rubens** (1923)
Mr Weston's Good Wine (1928) **T.F. Powys** (1875)
Mr William Shakespeare His Comedies, Histories and Tragedies (1767) **Edward Capell** (1713) (ed.)
Mr Wilson's War (1963) **John Dos Passos** (1896)
Mr Wray's Cash Box (1852) **Wilkie Collins** (1824)
Mr Wroe's Virgins (1991) **Jane Rogers** (1952)
Mr Wrong (1975) **Elizabeth Jane Howard** (1923)
Mrs Ames (1912) **E.F. Benson** (1867)
Mrs and Mrs Nevill Tyson (1898) **May Sinclair** (1863)
Mrs Armytage (1836) **Mrs C.F. Gore** (1799)
Mrs Bligh (1892) **Rhoda Broughton** (1840)
Mrs Bridge (1959) **Evan S. Connell, Jr**(1924)
Mrs Carteret Receives (1971) **L.P. Hartley** (1895)
Mrs Caudle's Curtain Lectures (1846) **Douglas Jerrold** (1803)
Mrs Cradock (1902) **Somerset Maugham** (1874)
Mrs Curgenven of Curgenven (1893) **S. Baring-Gould** (1834)
Mrs Dalloway (1925) **Virginia Woolf** (1882)
Mrs Dane's Defence (1900) **Henry Arthur Jones** (1851)
Mrs De Winter [sequel to Daphne du Maurier's Rebecca (1938)] (1993) **Susan Hill** (1942)
Mrs Duke's Million (1977) **Wyndham Lewis** (1882–1957)
Mrs Dymond (1885) **Lady Anne Ritchie** (1837)
Mrs Eckdorf in O'Neill's Hotel (1969) **'William Trevor' [William Trevor Cox]** (1928)
Mrs Fisher (1928) **Robert Graves** (1895)
Mrs Gailey (1951) **Sheila Kaye-Smith** (1887)
Mrs Galer's Business (1905) **W. Pett Ridge** (1860)
Mrs Gerald's Niece (1869) **Lady Georgiana Fullerton** (1812)
Mrs Halliburton's Troubles (1862) **Mrs Henry Wood** (1814)
Mrs Harter (1924) **'E.M. Delafield' [E.E.M. de la Pasture]** (1890)
Mrs Jordan's Profession (1994) **Claire Tomalin** (1933)
Mrs Keith's Crime (1885) **Lucy [Mrs W.K.] Clifford** (1853)
Mrs Leicester's School (1808) **Charles Lamb** (1775) [with Mary Lamb]
Mrs Lorimer (1883) **'Lucas Malet' [Mary St Leger Harrison]** (1852)
Mrs Markham's New History of England (1926) **Hilaire Belloc** (1870)
Mrs Martin's Company (1895) **Jane Barlow** (1857)
Mrs Martin's Man (1914) **St John Ervine** (1883)
Mrs Murphy (1913) **'Barry Pain' [Eric Odell]** (1864)
Mrs Oliver Cromwell (1940) **Margaret Irwin** (1889)

Mrs Overtheway's Remembrances (1869) **Mrs J.H. Ewing** (1841)
Mrs Palfrey at the Claremont (1971) **Elizabeth Taylor** (1912)
Mrs Parkinson (1943) **Louis Bromfield** (1896)
Mrs Peixada [as 'Sydney Luska'] (1886) **Henry Harland** (1861)
Mrs Perkins's Ball [as 'M.A. Titmarsh'] (1847) **W.M. Thackeray** (1811)
Mrs Reinhardt (1978) **Edna O'Brien** (1932)
Mrs Shakespeare (1993) **Robert Nye** (1939)
Mrs Skagg's Husbands (1873) **Bret Harte** (1836)
Mrs Wallop (1970) **Peter de Vries** (1910)
Mrs Warren's Profession (1898) **Bernard Shaw** (1856)
Mrs Winthrop (1882) **Bronson Howard** (1842)
Much Ado About Nothing (1600) **William Shakespeare** (1564)
Much Obliged, Jeeves [US: *Jeeves and the Ties That Bind*] (1971) **P.G. Wodehouse** (1881)
Muddling Through in Madagascar (1985) **Dervla Murphy** (1931)
Mudfog Papers, The (1880) **Charles Dickens** (1812–70)
Mulatto (1936) **Langston Hughes** (1902)
Mulberry-Garden, The (1668) **Sir Charles Sedley** (1639)
Mules (1977) **Paul Muldoon** (1951)
Mulliner Nights (1933) **P.G. Wodehouse** (1881)
Multitude and Solitude (1909) **John Masefield** (1878)
Mum and Mr Armitage (1985) **Beryl Bainbridge** (1934)
Mummer's Wife, A (1885) **George Moore** (1852)
Mummy, The (1989) **Anne Rice** (1941)
Munera Pulveris (1872) **John Ruskin** (1819)
Munster Twilight, A (1916) **Daniel Corkery** (1878)
Murder at the Vicarage, The (1930) **Agatha Christie** (1890)
Murder Has Your Number (1978) **Hugh Garner** (1913)
Murder in Mesopotamia (1936) **Agatha Christie** (1890)
Murder in the Cathedral (1935) **T.S. Eliot** (1888)
Murder is Announced, A (1950) **Agatha Christie** (1890)
Murder Must Advertise (1933) **Dorothy L. Sayers** (1893)
Murder Must Appetize (1975) **H.R.F. Keating** (1926)
Murder of Delicia, The (1896) **Marie Corelli** (1855)
Murder of Quality, A (1962) **'John le Carré' [David John Moore Cornwell]** (1931)
Murder of Roger Ackroyd, The (1926) **Agatha Christie** (1890)
Murder of the Maharajah, The (1980) **H.R.F. Keating** (1926)
Murder Off Miami (1936) **Dennis Wheatley** (1897)
Murder on Safari (1938) **Elspeth Huxley** (1907)
Murder on the Links (1923) **Agatha Christie** (1890)
Murder on the Orient Express [US: *Murder on the Calais Coach*] (1934) **Agatha Christie** (1890)
Murder Song (1990) **Jon Cleary** (1917)
Murder Twice Told (1950) **Donald Hamilton** (1916)
Murdo, and Other Stories (1981) **Iain Crichton Smith [Iain Mac a'Ghobhainn]** (1928)
Murmuring Judges (1991) **David Hare** (1947)
Murphy (1938) **Samuel Beckett** (1906)
Murther and Walking Spirits (1991) **Robertson Davies** (1913)
Murtzoufle (1826) **Thomas Aird** (1802)
Musaeus (1747) **William Mason** (1724)
Musardises, Les ['Dawdlings'] (1890) **Edmond Rostand** (1868)
Muse in Chains, The (1937) **Stephen Potter** (1900)
Muse in Exile, The (1913) **Sir William Watson** (1858)
Muse Unchained, The (1958) **E.M.W. Tillyard** (1889)
Muses are Heard, The (1956) **Truman Capote** (1924)
Muses Elizium, The (1630) **Michael Drayton** (1563)
Muses Sacrifice, The (1612) **John Davies of Hereford** (1565)
Muses-Teares, The (1613) **John Davies of Hereford** (1565)
Museum of Cheats, The (1947) **Sylvia Townsend Warner** (1893)
Museum Pieces (1952) **William Plomer** (1903)
Museums and Women (1972) **John Updike** (1932)
Music and Moonlight (1874) **Arthur O'Shaughnessy** (1844)
Music and Silence (1999) **Rose Tremain** (1943)
Music at Night (1931) **Aldous Huxley** (1894)
Music for Chameleons (1980) **Truman Capote** (1924)
Music for Mohini (1952) **Bhabani Bhattacharya** (1906)
Music From Behind the Moon, The (1926) **James Branch Cabell** (1879)
The Music of Chance (1990) **Paul Auster** (1947)
Music of Division, The (1959) **Chris Wallace-Crabbe** (1934)
Music School, The (1966) **John Updike** (1932)
Music-Master, The (1855) **William Allingham** (1824)
Musk and Amber (1942) **A.E.W. Mason** (1865)
Mustapha (1739) **David Mallet** (1705?)
Mustard Ball, The (1858) **John Brougham** (1810)
Mustard Seed, The (1953) **Vicki Baum** (1888)
Mutable Many, The (1897) **Robert Barr** (1850)
Mutineer, The (1898) **Louis Becke** (1855)
Mutius Scaevola (1801) **William-Henry Ireland** (1777)
Mutual Flame, The (1955) **G. Wilson Knight** (1897)
My Antonia (1918) **Willa Cather** (1873)
My Apprenticeship (1926) **Beatrice Webb** (1858)
My Aunt's Rhinoceros (1956) **Peter Fleming** (1907)
My Beautiful Launderette (1986) **Hanif Kureishi** (1954)
My Bondage and My Freedom (1855) **Frederick Douglass** (1817)
My Brilliant Career (1901) **Miles Franklin** (1879)
My Brother Evelyn (1967) **Alec Waugh** (1898)
My Brother Jack (1964) **George Johnston** (1912)
My Brother Jonathan (1928) **Francis Brett Young** (1884)
My Brother Yves [*Mon frère Yves*] (1883) **'Pierre Loti' [Julien Viaud]** (1850)

My Career Goes Bung (1946) **Miles Franklin** (1879)
My Children! My Africa! (1989) **Athol Fugard** (1932)
My City (1929) **Theodore Dreiser** (1871)
My Confessional (1934) **Havelock Ellis** (1859)
My Contemporaries in Fiction (1897) **David Christie Murray** (1847)
My Cousin Rachel (1951) **Daphne du Maurier** (1907)
My Dark Places (1996) **James Ellroy** (1948)
My Days (1974) **R.K. Narayan** (1907)
My Days and Dreams (1916) **Edward Carpenter** (1844) (ed.)
My Days of Anger (1943) **James T. Farrell** (1904)
My Dear Dorothea (1956) **Bernard Shaw** (1856–1950)
My Discovery of England (1922) **Stephen Leacock** (1869)
My Dog Tulip (1956) **J.R. Ackerley** (1896–1967)
My Early Life (1930) **Sir Winston Churchill** (1874)
My Family and Other Animals (1956) **Gerald Durrell** (1925)
My Father and Myself (1968) **J.R. Ackerley** (1896–1967)
My Father's Moon (1989) **Elizabeth Jolley** (1923)
My Father's Trapdoor (1994) **Peter Redgrove** (1932)
My Fellow Devils (1951) **L.P. Hartley** (1895)
My Friend Flicka (1941) **'Mary O'Hara' [Mary O'Hara Alsop]** (1885)
My Friend Prospero (1904) **Henry Harland** (1861)
My Friend, Remember (1914) **Arthur Henry Adams** (1872)
My Friend Smith (1882) **Talbot Baines Reed** (1852)
My Friend's Book [*Le Livre de mon ami*] (1885) **'Anatole France' [Jacques-Anatole-François Thibault]** (1844)
My Glorious Brothers (1948) **Howard Fast** (1914)
My Guardian (1878) **Ada Cambridge** (1844)
My Hatreds [*Mes Haines*] (1866) **Émile Zola** (1840–1902)
My Haunts and their Frequenters (1854) **Edmund Yates** (1831)
My Head! My Head! (1925) **Robert Graves** (1895)
My Heart for Hostage (1942) **Robert Hillyer** (1895)
My Heart is Broken [UK: *An Unmarried Man's Summer*] (1964) **Mavis Gallant** (1922)
My Heart's in the Highland (1939) **William Saroyan** (1908)
My Heart's Right There (1914) **Florence Barclay** (1862)
My Host the World (1953) **George Santayana** (1863–1952)
My Husband Cartwright (1956) **Olivia Manning** (1908)
My Idea of Fun (1993) **Will Self** (1961)
My Lady Caprice [US: *The Chronicles of the Imp*] (1907) **Jeffery Farnol** (1878)
My Lady Nicotine (1890) **[Sir] J.M. Barrie** (1860)
My Lady of Orange (1901) **H.C. Bailey** (1878)
My Lady Pokahontas (1885) **John Cooke** (1830)
My Lady Rotha (1894) **Stanley J. Weyman** (1855)
My Lady's Sonnets (1887) **Richard Le Gallienne** (1866)
My Last Duchess (1971) **Iain Crichton Smith [Iain Mac a'Ghobhainn]** (1928)
My Last Two Thousand Years (1972) **Herbert Gold** (1924)
My Laughing Philosopher (1896) **Eden Phillpotts** (1862)
My Left Foot (1954) **Christy Brown** (1932)
My Life (1905) **Alfred Russel Wallace** (1823)
My Life [*Ma Vie (Le Cahier rouge)*] (1907) **Benjamin Constant** (1767–1830)
My Life (1939) **Havelock Ellis** (1859)
My Life and Hard Times (1933) **James Thurber** (1894)
My Life and Loves (1922) **'Frank' Harris** (1856)
My Life and Times (1926) **Jerome K. Jerome** (1859)
My Life as a Man (1974) **Philip Roth** (1933)
My Life Closed Twice (1977) **Nigel Williams** (1948)
My Lifetime in Letters (1960) **Upton Sinclair** (1878)
My Literary Life (1899) **E. Lynn Linton** (1822–98)
My Little Girl (1873) **Sir Walter Besant** (1836) [with James Rice]
My Lord Duke (1897) **E.W. Hornung** (1866)
My Lord of Wrybourne (1948) **Jeffery Farnol** (1878)
'My Love!' (1881) **E. Lynn Linton** (1822)
My Man Jeeves (1919) **P.G. Wodehouse** (1881)
My Many-Coated Man (1955) **Laurie Lee** (1914)
My Michael (1968) **Amos Oz** (1939)
My Mortal Enemy (1926) **Willa Cather** (1873)
My Name is Aram (1940) **William Saroyan** (1908)
My Neighbours (1920) **Caradoc Evans** (1878)
My Next Bride (1934) **Kay Boyle** (1903)
'My Novel' (1853) **Edward Bulwer-Lytton** (1803)
My Own Fairy Book (1895) **Andrew Lang** (1844)
My Own Master (1961) **Adrian Bell** (1901)
My People (1915) **Caradoc Evans** (1878)
My Religion (1885) **Leo Tolstoy** (1828)
My Run Home (1897) **'Rolf Boldrewood' [Thomas Alexander Browne]** (1826)
My Sad Captains (1961) **Thom Gunn** (1929)
My Secret History (1989) **Paul Theroux** (1941)
My Silver Shoes (1966) **Nell Dunn** (1936)
My Son is a Splendid Driver (1971) **William Inge** (1913)
My Strange Search for Mensonge (1987) **Malcolm Bradbury** (1932)
My Study Windows (1871) **James Russell Lowell** (1819)
My Summer in a Garden (1870) **Charles Dudley Warner** (1829)
My Ten Years in a Quandary (1936) **Robert Benchley** (1889)
My Turn to Make the Tea (1951) **Monica Dickens** (1915)
My Uncle Florimond [as 'Sydney Luska'] (1888) **Henry Harland** (1861)
My Uncle Oswald (1979) **Roald Dahl** (1916)
My Uncle Silas (1939) **H.E. Bates** (1905)
My Universities (1923) **Maxim Gorky** (1868)
My Watch Below (1882) **W. Clark Russell** (1844)
My Wife and I (1871) **Harriet Beecher Stowe** (1811)
My Wife Ethel (1940) **Damon Runyon** (1884)

My Wife's the Least of It (1938) **William Gerhardie** (1895)
My World—and Welcome To It [inc.'The Secret Life of Walter Mitty'] (1942) **James Thurber** (1894)
My Year in a Log Cabin (1893) **William Dean Howells** (1837)
Myddleton Pomfret (1868) **W.H. Ainsworth** (1805)
Myra Breckenridge (1968) **Gore Vidal** (1925)
Myron (1975) **Gore Vidal** (1925)
Myrrour for Man, A (1552) **Thomas Churchyard** (1520?)
Myrrour of Modestie, The (1584) **Robert Greene** (1558)
Myself (1967) **Sylvia Ashton-Warner** (1908)
Myself My Enemy (1983) **'Jean Plaidy' [Eleanor Hibbert]** (1906)
Myself When Young (1923) **Alec Waugh** (1898)
Mystère de la chambre jaune, Le ['The Mystery of the Yellow Room'] (1907) **Gaston Leroux** (1868)
Mystère des foules, Le ['The Mystery of the Masses'] (1895) **Paul Adam** (1862)
Mystères de Paris, Les ['The Mysteries of Paris'] (1843) **Eugène Sue** (1804)
Mystères du peuple, Les ['Mysteries of the People'] (1849) **Eugène Sue** (1804)
Mysteries (1892) **'Knut Hamsun' [Knut Pedersen]** (1859)
Mysteries and Adventures (1889) **A. Conan Doyle** (1859)
Mysteries of Modern London, The (1906) **George R. Sims** (1847)
Mysteries of Udolpho, The (1794) **Ann Radcliffe** (1764)
Mysterious Affair at Styles, The (1920) **Agatha Christie** (1890)
Mysterious Mother, The (1768) **Horace Walpole** (1717)
Mysterious Mr Bull, The (1938) **Wyndham Lewis** (1882)
Mysterious Mr Miller, The (1906) **William le Queux** (1864)
Mysterious Mr Sabin, The (1898) **E. Phillips Oppenheim** (1866)
Mysterious Warning, The (1796) **Eliza Parsons** (1748)
Mystery (1989) **Peter Straub** (1943)
Mystery in Palace Gardens, The (1880) **Mrs J.H. Riddell** (1832)
Mystery of a Hansom Cab, The (1886) **Fergus Hume** (1859)
Mystery of a Motor Cab, The (1908) **Fergus Hume** (1859)
Mystery of Cloomber, The (1888) **A. Conan Doyle** (1859)
Mystery of Dr Fu-Manchu, The [US: *The Insidious Dr Fu-Manchu*] (1913) **'Sax Rohmer' [Arthur Henry Sarsfield Ward]** (1883)
Mystery of Edwin Drood, The [unfinished] (1870) **Charles Dickens** (1812–70)
Mystery of Iniquity Unvailed, The (1672) **Gilbert Burnet** (1643)
Mystery of Landy Court, The (1894) **Fergus Hume** (1859)
Mystery of M. Felix, The (1890) **B.L. Farjeon** (1838)
Mystery of Mary Stuart, The (1901) **Andrew Lang** (1844)
Mystery of Metropolisville, The (1873) **Edward Eggleston** (1837)
Mystery of the Blue Train, The (1928) **Agatha Christie** (1890)
Mystery of the Charity of Charles Péguy, The (1983) **Geoffrey Hill** (1932)
Mystery of the Clasped Hands, The (1901) **Guy Boothby** (1867)
Mystery of the Sea, The (1902) **Bram Stoker** (1847)
Mystery Road, The (1924) **E. Phillips Oppenheim** (1866)
Mystic Masseur, The (1957) **V.S. Naipaul** (1932)
Mystic, The (1855) **Philip James Bailey** (1816)
Mystic Way, The (1913) **Evelyn Underhill** (1875)
Mystical Paths (1992) **Susan Howatch** (1940)
Mysticism (1911) **Evelyn Underhill** (1875)
Mysticism and Logic (1918) **Bertrand Russell** (1872)
Mysticism in Religion (1947) **W.R. Inge** (1860)
Mystics of the Church, The (1925) **Evelyn Underhill** (1875)
Myth, Literature and the African World (1976) **Wole Soyinka** (1934)
Myth Makers, The (1979) **V.S. Pritchett** (1900)
Myth of Modernism and Twentieth-Century Literature, The (1986) **Bernard Bergonzi** (1929)
Myth of Sisyphus, The [*Le Mythe de Sisyphe*] (1942) **Albert Camus** (1913)
Myth, Ritual and Religion (1887) **Andrew Lang** (1844)
Myths and Texts (1960) **Gary Snyder** (1930)
Myths of the Near Future (1982) **J.G. Ballard** (1930)

N

'N' is for Noose (1998) **Sue Grafton** (1940)
Nabob, The [*Le Nabab*] (1877) **Alphonse Daudet** (1840)
Naboth's Vineyard (1891) **'Somerville and Ross' [Edith Somerville** (1858) and **Violet Martin** (1862)**]**
Naboth's Vineyard in Pawn (1913) **Ronald Knox** (1888)
Nada the Lily (1892) **Sir H. Rider Haggard** (1856)
Nadine (1882) **Mrs Campbell Praed** (1851)
Nadja (1928) **André Breton** (1896)
Naggletons, The (1875) **Charles William Shirley Brooks** (1816)
Naiad, The (1816) **J.H. Reynolds** (1796)
Nail in the Head, A (1983) **Clare Boylan** (1948)
Naked and the Dead, The (1948) **Norman Mailer** (1923)
Naked Face, The (1970) **Sidney Sheldon** (1917)
Naked Lunch (1959) **William S. Burroughs** (1914)
Naked Poems (1965) **Phylllis Webb** (1921)
Naked Sun, The (1957) **Isaac Asimov** (1920)
Name and Nature of Poetry, The (1933) **A.E. Housman** (1859–1936)
Name of Action, The (1930) **Graham Greene** (1904)

Name of the Rose, The [*Il nome della rosa*] (1980) **Umberto Eco** (1932)
Names, The (1982) **Don Delillo** (1936)
Nana (1880) **Émile Zola** (1840)
Nancy (1873) **Rhoda Broughton** (1840)
Nancy (1739) **Henry Carey** (1687?)
Napoleon (1822) **Bernard Barton** (1784)
Napoleon of Notting Hill , The (1904) **G.K. Chesterton** (1874)
Napoleon Symphony (1974) **'Anthony Burgess' [John Anthony Burgess Wilson]** (1917)
Narcissus (1873) **Edward Carpenter** (1844)
Narration (1935) **Gertrude Stein** (1874)
Narrative Hymns for Village Schools (1853) **Mrs C.F. Alexander** (1818)
Narrative of a Journey Through India (1828) **Reginald Heber** (1783–1826)
Narrative of Arthur Gordon Pym (1838) **Edgar Allan Poe** (1809)
Narrative of the Life of Frederick Douglass [rev. 1892] (1845) **Frederick Douglass** (1817)
Narrative of the Travels and Adventures of Monsieur Violet (1843) **Frederick Marryat** (1792)
Narrative Poems (1803) **Isaac D'Israeli** (1766)
Narrative Poems on the Female Character (1813) **Mary Russell Mitford** (1787)
Narratives of Sorcery and Magic (1851) **Thomas Wright** (1810)
Narrow Corner, The (1932) **Somerset Maugham** (1874)
Narrow Place, The (1943) **Edwin Muir** (1887)
Narrow Road to the Deep North (1968) **Edward Bond** (1934)
Narrow Rooms (1978) **James Purdy** (1923)
Nashes Lenten Stuffe (1599) **Thomas Nashe** (1567)
Nat the Naturalist (1883) **George Manville Fenn** (1831)
Nathalie (1850) **Julia Kavanagh** (1824)
Nathalie Granger [text and film] (1972) **'Marguerite Duras' [Marguerite Donnadieu]** (1914)
Nation a Family, A (1720) **Sir Richard Steele** (1672)
National Advocate, The (1795) **William Hayley** (1745)
National and Social Problems (1908) **Frederic Harrison** (1831)
National Apostasy (1833) **John Keble** (1792)
National Education (1872) **Henry Edward Manning** (1808)
National Health, The (1969) **Peter Nichols** (1927)
National Lyrics and Songs for Music (1834) **Felicia Dorothea Hemans** (1793)
National Provincial (1938) **Lettice Cooper** (1897)
National Tales (1827) **Thomas Hood** (1799)
National Theatre, The (1975) **David Edgar** (1948)
'National Velvet' (1935) **Enid Bagnold** (1889)
Nationality and the War (1915) **Arnold Toynbee** (1889)
Nationalization of Health, The (1892) **Havelock Ellis** (1859)
Native American, A (1938) **William Saroyan** (1908)
Native Argosy, A (1929) **Morley Callaghan** (1903)
Native Land (1907–16) **Aleksandr Blok** (1880)
Native of Winby, A (1893) **Sarah Orne Jewett** (1849)
Native Son (1940) **Richard Wright** (1908)
Natives of Milton (1902) **Robert Murray Gilchrist** (1868)
Natives of My Person (1972) **George Lamming** (1927)
Natives of Rock (1925) **Glenway Wescott** (1901)
Natural Affection (1963) **William Inge** (1913)
Natural and Experimental History of Winds, The (1653) **Sir Francis Bacon** (1561–1626)
Natural Causes (1987) **Andrew Motion** (1952)
Natural Curiosity, A (1989) **Margaret Drabble** (1939)
Natural Daughter, The [*Die natürliche Tochter*] (1803) **Johann Wolfgang von Goethe** (1749)
Natural Daughter, The (1799) **Mary Robinson** (1758)
Natural History and Antiquities of Selborne, The (1789) **Gilbert White** (1720)
Natural History of Intellect (1893) **Ralph Waldo Emerson** (1803–82)
Natural History [from Pliny] (1601) **Philemon Holland** (1552) (tr.)
Natural Need, The (1935) **James Reeves** (1909)
Natural Numbers (1963) **Kenneth Rexroth** (1905)
Natural Son, The [*Le Fils naturel*] (1757) **Denis Diderot** (1713)
Natural Son, The (1784) **Richard Cumberland** (1732)
Natural, The (1952) **Bernard Malamud** (1914)
Natural Theology (1728) **Sir Richard Blackmore** (1654)
Natural Theology (1802) **William Paley** (1743)
Naturalism in English Poetry (1920) **Stopford Brooke** (1832)
Naturalist in La Plata, The (1892) **W.H. Hudson** (1841)
Naturalist on the Amazon, The (1863) **Henry Walter Bates** (1825)
Naturalist's Calendar, A (1795) **Gilbert White** (1720–93)
Nature (1836) **Ralph Waldo Emerson** (1803)
Nature and Art (1796) **Mrs [Elizabeth] Inchbald** (1753)
Nature, and Danger, of Infidel Philosophy, The (1798) **Timothy Dwight** (1752)
Nature and Human Nature (1855) **T.C. Haliburton** (1796)
Nature in Downland (1900) **W.H. Hudson** (1841)
Nature in English Literature (1929) **Edmund Blunden** (1896)
Nature, Man and God (1934) **William Temple** (1881)
Nature of a Crime, The (1924) **Joseph Conrad** (1857) [with F.M. Hueffer]
Nature of Biography, The (1978) **Robert Gittings** (1911)
Nature of Existence, The (1921) **John McTaggart** (1866)
Nature of Man, The (1711) **Sir Richard Blackmore** (1654)
Nature of Mass Poverty, The (1979) **J.K. Galbraith** (1908)

Nature of Passion, The (1956) **Ruth Prawer Jhabvala** (1927)
Nature of the Kingdom or Church of Christ, The (1717) **Benjamin Hoadly** (1676)
Nature Poems and Others (1908) **W.H. Davies** (1871)
Nature With Man (1965) **Jon Silkin** (1930)
Nature's Music (1808) **Robert Bloomfield** (1766)
Nature's Way (1957) **Herman Wouk** (1915)
Naucratia (1798) **Henry James Pye** (1745)
Nausea [La Nausée] (1938) **Jean-Paul Sartre** (1905)
Naval Officer, The (1829) **Frederick Marryat** (1792)
Near and Far (1929) **Edmund Blunden** (1896)
Near and the Far, The (1929) **L.H. Myers** (1881)
Near Home (1858) **William Ellery Channing** (1780)
Near the Ocean (1967) **Robert Lowell** (1917)
Nearer the Grass Roots (1929) **Sherwood Anderson** (1876)
Nebo the Nailer (1902) **S. Baring-Gould** (1834)
Nebuly Coat, The (1903) **J. Meade Falkner** (1858)
Necessary Angel, The (1951) **Wallace Stevens** (1879)
Necessary Ends (1999) **Stanley Middleton** (1919)
Necessary Rites (1990) **Janice Elliott** (1931)
Necessities of Life (1966) **Adrienne Rich** (1929)
Necessity of Atheism, The (1811) **P.B. Shelley** (1792)
Necessity of Communism, The (1932) **John Middleton Murry** (1889)
Necessity of Pacifism, The (1937) **John Middleton Murry** (1889)
Necessity of Poetry, The (1918) **Robert Bridges** (1844)
Necessity of the Absolute Power of Kings, The (1648) **Sir Robert Filmer** (1588?)
Necklace of Mirrors, A (1978) **Carol Rumens** (1944)
Necklace, The (1955) **Charles Tomlinson** (1927)
Necromancers, The (1909) **R.H. Benson** (1871)
Ned Kelly and the City of the Bees (1978) **Thomas Keneally** (1935)
Ned Myers (1843) **James Fenimore Cooper** (1789)
Needful Things (1991) **Stephen King** (1947)
Needle, The (1975) **Francis King** (1923)
Needle's Eye, The (1972) **Margaret Drabble** (1939)
Negro, The (1915) **W.E.B. du Bois** (*c.* 1868)
Negro Boy's Tale, The (1824) **Amelia Opie** (1769)
Negro Mother, The (1931) **Langston Hughes** (1902)
Neighbors (1980) **Thomas Berger** (1924)
Neighbours, The [from Frederika Bremer] (1842) **Mary Howitt** (1799) (tr.)
Neighbours in a Thicket (1974) **David Malouf** (1934)
Neighbours Unknown (1911) **Sir Charles G.D. Roberts** (1860)
Nellie's Memories (1868) **Rosa Nouchette Carey** (1840)
Nelly Nowlan (1865) **Anna Maria [Mrs S.C.] Hall** (1800)
Nelly's Version (1977) **Eva Figes** (1932)
Nemesis (1989) **Isaac Asimov** (1920)
Nemesis of Faith, The [as 'Zeta'] (1849) **J.A. Froude** (1818)
Neon Wilderness, The (1947) **Nelson Algren** (1909)
Nephew, The (1960) **James Purdy** (1923)
Nereides (1712) **William Diaper** (1685)
Nero (1906) **Stephen Phillips** (1864)
Nero (1985) **Jeremy Reed** (1954)
Nero, Emperour of Rome (1674) **Nathaniel Lee** (1649?)
Nero: Part 1 (1885) **Robert Bridges** (1844)
Nero: Part 2 (1894) **Robert Bridges** (1844)
Nerve, The (1971) **Melvyn Bragg** (1939)
Nest of Gentlefolk, A (1859) **Ivan Turgenev** (1818)
Nest of Ninnies, A (1608) **Robert Armin** (1565?)
Nest of Ninnies, A (1969) **John Ashbery** (1927) [with James Schuyler]
Nest of Simple Folk, A (1933) **'Seán O'Faoláin' [John Francis Whelan]** (1900)
Nest of the Sparrowhawk, The (1909) **Baroness Orczy** (1865)
Nest of Tigers, A (1968) **John Lehmann** (1907)
Net, The (1952) **John Pudney** (1909)
Nether World, The (1889) **George Gissing** (1857)
Nettles (1930) **D.H. Lawrence** (1885)
Neuromancer (1984) **William Gibson** (1948)
Neutron Star (1968) **Larry Niven** (1938)
Never Come Morning (1942) **Nelson Algren** (1909)
Never Cry Wolf (1963) **Farley Mowat** (1921)
Never Enough! (1977) **Frank Sargeson** (1903)
Never Love a Stranger (1948) **Harold Robbins** (1912)
Never-Ending Wrong, The (1977) **Katherine Anne Porter** (1890)
Nevermore (1892) **'Rolf Boldrewood' [Thomas Alexander Browne]** (1826)
Nevertheless (1944) **Marianne Moore** (1887)
New Abelard, The (1884) **Robert Williams Buchanan** (1841)
New America, The (1935) **H.G. Wells** (1866)
New Anatomies (1981) **Timberlake Wertenbaker** (1951)
New and Collected Poems 1934–1984 (1985) **Roy Fuller** (1912)
New and Old (1880) **John Addington Symonds** (1840)
New Apocalypse, The (1939) **J.F. Hendry** (1912) (ed.) [with Henry Treece]
New Apocalypse, The (1939) **Henry Treece** (1911) (ed.) [with J.F. Hendry]
New Arabian Nights (1882) **Robert Louis Stevenson** (1850)
New Athens, A (1977) **Hugh Hood** (1928)
New Atlantis, The (1627) **Sir Francis Bacon** (1561–1626)
New Atlantis, The [Bacon]: see Sylva Sylvarum
New Ballads (1897) **John Davidson** (1857)
New Bath Guide, The (1766) **Christopher Anstey** (1724)
New Bats in Old Belfries (1945) **Sir John Betjeman** (1906)
New Bearings in English Poetry (1932) **F.R. Leavis** (1895)
New Canterbury Tales, The (1901) **Maurice Hewlett** (1861)
New Cautionary Tales (1930) **Hilaire Belloc** (1870)
New Chum, The (1909) **Arthur Henry Adams** (1872)
New Collected Rhymes (1905) **Andrew Lang** (1844)

New Collection of Songs and Poems, A (1683) **Thomas D'Urfey** (1653)
New Comedies [*The Bogie Men; The Full Moon; Coats; Damer's Gold; McDonough's Wife*] (1913) **Lady Gregory** (1852)
New Confessions (1974) **Anthony Thwaite** (1930)
New Confessions, The (1987) **William Boyd** (1952)
New Cronycles of Englande and of Fraunce, The (1516) **Robert Fabyan** (d. 1513)
New Day (1949) **V.S. Reid** (1913)
New Description of Ireland, A (1610) **Barnabe Rich** (1542)
New Dialogues of the Dead [*Nouveaux dialogue des morts*] (1683) **Bernard le Bovier Fontenelle** (1657)
New Dominion, A (1972) **Ruth Prawer Jhabvala** (1927)
New Echoes (1864) **Eliza Cook** (1818)
New England Nun, A (1891) **Mary Wilkins Freeman** (1852)
New England's Memorial (1669) **Nathaniel Morton** (1612)
New Found Land (1930) **Archibald MacLeish** (1892)
New Grub Street (1891) **George Gissing** (1857)
New Hampshire (1923) **Robert Frost** (1874)
New Heaven, New Earth (1974) **Joyce Carol Oates** (1938)
New History of Sandford and Merton, The (1872) **Sir F.C. Burnand** (1836)
New House, The (1936) **Lettice Cooper** (1897)
New Immortality, The (1938) **J.W. Dunne** (1875)
New Industrial State, The (1967) **J.K. Galbraith** (1908)
New Inferno, The (1911) **Stephen Phillips** (1864)
New Inne, The (1629) **Ben Jonson** (1572)
New Journalism, The (1973) **Tom Wolfe** (1930)
New Laokoon, The (1910) **Irving Babbit** (1865)
New Letter of Notable Contents, A (1593) **Gabriel Harvey** (1550)
New Life, A (1943) **Elmer Rice** (1892)
New Life, A (1961) **Bernard Malamud** (1914)
New Lives For Old (1933) **C.P. Snow** (1905)
New Machiavelli, The (1910) **H.G. Wells** (1866)
New Magdalen, The (1873) **Wilkie Collins** (1824)
New Maps of Hell (1961) **Kingsley Amis** (1922)
New Men, The (1954) **C.P. Snow** (1905)
New Metamorphosis, The [trn of *The Golden Ass* by Apuleius] (1708) **Charles Gildon** (1665) (tr.)
New Miscellany of Original Poems, A (1701) **Charles Gildon** (1665) (ed.)
New Mistress, The (1883) **George Manville Fenn** (1831)
New Moon with the Old, The (1963) **Dodie Smith** (1896)
New Numbers (1970) **Christopher Logue** (1926)
New Orleans Sketches (1958) **William Faulkner** (1897)
New Oxford Book of English Verse, The (1972) **Helen Gardner** (1908) (ed.)
New Oxford Book of Light Verse, The (1978) **Kingsley Amis** (1922) (ed.)
New Paths in Genetics (1941) **J.B.S. Haldane** (1892)
New Paul and Virginia, The (1878) **W.H. Mallock** (1849)
New Pilgrimage, A (1889) **Wilfrid Scawen Blunt** (1840)
New Poems (1690) **Thomas D'Urfey** (1653)
New Poems [Neue Gedichte] (1844) **Heinrich Heine** (1797)
New Poems (1867) **Matthew Arnold** (1822)
New Poems (1879) **Sir Edmund Gosse** (1849)
New Poems (1897) **Francis Thompson** (1859)
New Poems (1910) **Richard le Gallienne** (1866)
New Poems (1913) **Robert Browning** (1812–89)
New Poems (1918) **D.H. Lawrence** (1885)
New Poems (1938) **W.B. Yeats** (1865)
New Poems (1943) **Dylan Thomas** (1914)
New Poems (1962) **Robert Graves** (1895)
New Poems (1968) **Roy Fuller** (1912)
New Poems, Hitherto Unpublished and Uncollected (1896) **Christina Rossetti** (1830–1894)
New Poetic, The (1964) **C.K. Stead** (1932)
New Poetry, The (1962) **A. Alvarez** (1929) (ed.)
New Prince Fortunatus, The (1890) **William Black** (1841)
New Rehearsal, A (1714) **Charles Gildon** (1665)
New Republic, The (1877) **W.H. Mallock** (1849)
New Revelation, The (1918) **A. Conan Doyle** (1859)
New Rome, The (1899) **Robert Williams Buchanan** (1841)
New Seed for Old (1988) **Simon Raven** (1927)
New Sentimental Journey, A (1859) **Charles Allston Collins** (1828)
New Sketch Book, The [as 'Geoffrey Crayon jun.'] (1829) **George Darley** (1795)
New Society, The (1951) **E.H. Carr** (1892)
New Song, A (1938) **Langston Hughes** (1902)
New Spirit of the Age, A (1844) **R.H. Horne** (1803) [with E.B. Browning]
New Spirit, The (1890) **Havelock Ellis** (1859)
New Spoon River, The (1924) **Edgar Lee Masters** (1868)
New Studies in Literature (1895) **Edward Dowden** (1843)
New Study of English Poetry, A (1917) **Sir Henry Newbolt** (1862)
New Tales (1818) **Amelia Opie** (1769)
New Territory (1967) **Eavan Boland** (1944)
New Testament, The [first complete edn] (1526) **William Tyndale** (1494?) (tr.)
New Testament of Our Lord and Saviour Jesus Christ, The (1945) **Ronald Knox** (1888) (tr.)
New Theory of Population, A (1852) **Herbert Spencer** (1820)
New Timon, The (1846) **Edward Bulwer-Lytton** (1803)
New Town (1960) **Noel Streatfeild** (1895)
New Treasure Seekers, The (1904) **E[dith] Nesbit** (1858)
New Verse (1939) **Geoffrey Grigson** (1905) (ed.)
New Verse Written in 1921 (1925) **Robert Bridges** (1844)

New Version of the Psalms, A (1696) **Nahum Tate** (1652) [with Nicholas Brady]
New View of Society, A (1813) **Robert Owen** (1771)
New Voyage Round the World, A (1697) **William Dampier** (1652)
New Voyage Round the World, A (1724) **Daniel Defoe** (1660)
New Way to Pay Old Debts, A (1633) **Philip Massinger** (1583)
New Weather (1973) **Paul Muldoon** (1951)
New Wonder, A (1632) **William Rowley** (1585?-1626)
New World, The (1918) **Laurence Binyon** (1869)
New World, The (1937) **Edgar Lee Masters** (1868)
New Worlds for Old (1908) **H.G. Wells** (1866)
New Year Letter [US: *The Double Man*] (1941) **W.H. Auden** (1907)
New Year's Eve, 1929 (1967) **James T. Farrell** (1904)
New Year's Eve, A (1828) **Bernard Barton** (1784)
New York: Its Upper Ten and Lower Million (1853) **George Lippard** (1822)
New York Nocturnes (1898) **Sir Charles G.D. Roberts** (1860)
New-England Tale, A (1822) **Catharine Maria Sedgwick** (1789)
New-Found-Land (1976) **Tom Stoppard** (1937)
Newcomes, The [ed. 'Arthur Pendennis'] (1854) **W.M. Thackeray** (1811)
Newes from Graves-end (1604) **Thomas Dekker** (1572?)
Newes from Hell (1606) **Thomas Dekker** (1572?)
Newes from the New World Discover'd in the Moone (1621) **Ben Jonson** (1572)
Newfoundland Verse (1923) **E.J. Pratt** (1882)
Newly Fallen, The (1961) **Ed Dorn** (1929)
Newmarket (1751) **Thomas Warton, the Younger** (1728)
News From Ireland, The (1986) **'William Trevor' [William Trevor Cox]** (1928)
News from Nowhere (1891) **William Morris** (1834)
News From Tartary (1936) **Peter Fleming** (1907)
News From the Duchy (1913) **Sir A.T. Quiller-Couch** (1863)
News From the Mountain (1932) **Richard Church** (1893)
News of the World (1950) **George Barker** (1913)
News-Paper, The (1785) **George Crabbe** (1754)
Newspaper of Claremont Street, The (1981) **Elizabeth Jolley** (1923)
Newton Forster (1832) **Frederick Marryat** (1792)
Newton Letter, The (1982) **John Banville** (1945)
Next Generation, The (1932) **J.D. Beresford** (1873)
Next of Kin (1991) **Stan Barstow** (1928)
Next of Kin (1996) **Joanna Trollope** (1943)
Next of Kin Wanted (1887) **Matilda Betham-Edwards** (1836)
Next Room of the Dream, The (1964) **Howard Nemerov** (1920)
Next to Nature, Art (1982) **Penelope Lively** (1933)
Next to Nothing (1981) **Paul Bowles** (1910)
Next-to-Last Things (1985) **Stanley J. Kunitz** (1905)
Nexus (1960) **Henry Miller** (1891)
Niccolò Rising (1986) **Dorothy Dunnett** (1923)
Nice and the Good, The (1968) **Iris Murdoch** (1919)
Nice Place to Visit, A (1970) **Hugh Garner** (1913)
Nice Work (1988) **David Lodge** (1935)
Nicest Girl in the School, The (1909) **Angela Brazil** (1869)
Nicholas and Mary (1899) **Robert Murray Gilchrist** (1868)
Nicholas Nickleby (1980) **David Edgar** (1948)
Nick of the Woods (1837) **Robert Bird** (1806)
Nickel Mountain (1973) **John Gardner** (1933)
Nicodemus (1932) **Edwin Arlington Robinson** (1869)
Nicodemus (1937) **Andrew Young** (1885)
Nicomachean Ethics **Aristotle** (384)
Nicomède (1651) **Pierre Corneille** (1606)
Nigel Barton Plays, The (1968) **Dennis Potter** (1935)
Nigger of the 'Narcissus', The (1898) **Joseph Conrad** (1857)
Night (1761) **Charles Churchill** (1731)
Night (1818) **Ebenezer Elliott** (1781)
Night (1972) **Edna O'Brien** (1932)
Night Among the Horses, A (1929) **Djuna Barnes** (1892)
Night and Day (1912) **Isaac Rosenberg** (1890)
Night and Day (1919) **Virginia Woolf** (1882)
Night and Day (1978) **Tom Stoppard** (1937)
Night and Morning (1841) **Edward Bulwer-Lytton** (1803)
Night and Silence! Who is Here? (1963) **Pamela Hansford Johnson** (1912)
Night Chills (1977) **Dean Koontz** (1945)
Night Fears (1924) **L.P. Hartley** (1895)
Night Feed (1982) **Eavan Boland** (1944)
Night Flight [Vol de nuit] (1931) **Antoine de Saint-Exupéry** (1900)
Night Flights (1978) **Matt Cohen** (1942)
Night Geometry and the Garscadden Trains (1990) **A.L. Kennedy** (1965)
Night Has a Thousand Eyes, The [as 'George Hopley'] (1945) **Cornell Woolrich** (1903)
Night Hurling (1983) **James Dickey** (1923)
Night in Acadie, A (1897) **Kate Chopin** (1851)
Night in Bombay (1940) **Louis Bromfield** (1896)
Night in Lisbon, The [*Die Nacht von Lisbon*] (1962) **'Erich Maria Remarque' [Erich Paul Remark]** (1898)
Night in the Gazebo, A (1980) **Alan Brownjohn** (1931)
Night in Tunisia (1976) **Neil Jordan** (1950)
Night Land, The (1912) **William Hope Hodgson** (1877)
Night Listener, The (2000) **Armistead Maupin** (1944)
Night Music (1940) **Clifford Odets** (1906)
Night of January 16th, The (1935) **Ayn Rand** (1905)
Night of Stones, The (1968) **George MacBeth** (1932)
Night of the Fox (1986) **'Jack Higgins' [Harry Patterson]** (1929)
Night of the Iguana, The (1962) **'Tennessee' [Thomas Lanier] Williams** (1911)

Night of the New Moon, The (1970) **Sir Laurens van der Post** (1906)
Night of the Party (1938) **Martin Boyd** (1893)
Night of the Ripper (1984) **Robert Bloch** (1917)
Night of Their Own, A (1965) **Peter Abrahams** (1919)
Night Over Taos (1932) **Maxwell Anderson** (1888)
Night Rider (1939) **Robert Penn Warren** (1905)
Night Shift (1976) **Stephen King** (1947)
Night Song (1961) **John Williams** (1925)
Night Thoughts (1956) **David Gascoyne** (1916)
Night Train (1997) **Martin Amis** (1949)
Night Violet, The (1906) **Aleksandr Blok** (1880)
Night Walk, The (1987) **Edward Upward** (1903)
Night Walker (1954) **Donald Hamilton** (1916)
Night Watches (1914) **W.W. Jacobs** (1863)
Night-Comers, The [US: *State of Siege*] (1956) **Eric Ambler** (1909)
Night-Crossing (1968) **Derek Mahon** (1941)
Night-Pieces [*Nachtstücke*] (1817) **E.T.A. Hoffmann** (1776)
Night-Side (1977) **Joyce Carol Oates** (1938)
Night-Side of Nature, The (1848) **Catherine Crowe** (1790)
Night-Thoughts [**Young**]: see *The Complaint*
Night-Walker, The (1640) **John Fletcher** (1579–1625)
Night-Watchmen, The (1969) **Helen Cresswell** (1934)
Nightbirds in Nantucket (1966) **Joan Aiken** (1924)
Nightfishing, The (1955) **W.S. Graham** (1918)
Nightingale Valley [as 'Giraldus'] (1860) **William Allingham** (1824) (ed.)
Nightlines (1970) **John McGahern** (1934)
Nightmare Abbey (1818) **Thomas Love Peacock** (1785)
Nightmare at Noon (1940) **Stephen Vincent Benét** (1889)
Nightmare Factory, The (1970) **Maxine Kumin** (1925)
Nightmares of Eminent Persons (1954) **Bertrand Russell** (1872)
Nightrunners of Bengal (1951) **John Masters** (1914)
Nights and Days (1966) **James Merrill** (1926)
Nights at the Circus (1984) **Angela Carter** (1940)
Nights of Love and Laughter (1955) **Henry Miller** (1891)
Nights with Uncle Remus (1883) **Joel Chandler Harris** (1848)
Nightspawn (1971) **John Banville** (1945)
Nightwalker (1967) **Thomas Kinsella** (1928)
Nightwing (1978) **Martin Cruz Smith** (1942)
Nightwings (1969) **Robert Silverberg** (1935)
Nightwood (1936) **Djuna Barnes** (1892)
Nightwork (1975) **Irwin Shaw** (1913)
Nile Tributaries of Abbyssinia, The (1867) **Sir Samuel White Baker** (1821)
Nimrod's Hunting Tours (1835) **Charles James Apperley** (1779)
Nimrod's Northern Tour (1838) **Charles James Apperley** (1779)
Nina Balatka (1867) **Anthony Trollope** (1815)
Nine African Stories (1968) **Doris Lessing** (1919)
Nine Bright Shiners, The (1943) **Anne Ridler** (1912)
Nine Poems (1918) **W.B. Yeats** (1865)
Nine Poems by 'V' (1840) **Caroline Clive** (1801)
Nine Stories (1953) **J.D. Salinger** (1919)
Nine Tailors, The (1934) **Dorothy L. Sayers** (1893)
Nine to Six-Thirty (1910) **W. Pett Ridge** (1860)
Nine Unlikely Tales for Children (1901) **E[dith] Nesbit** (1858)
Nineteen Eighty-Five (1978) **'Anthony Burgess' [John Anthony Burgess Wilson]** (1917)
Nineteen Eighty-Four (1949) **'George Orwell'** (1903)
Nineteen Impressions (1918) **J.D. Beresford** (1873)
Nineteen Nineteen (1932) **John Dos Passos** (1896)
Nineteen Poems (1952) **Jay Macpherson** (1931)
Nineteen Stories (1947) **Graham Greene** (1904)
Nineteen-Fourteen and Other Poems (1915) **Rupert Brooke** (1887–1915)
Nineteenth Century, The (1900) **Havelock Ellis** (1859)
Nineteenth Eighty-Two, Janine (1984) **Alasdair Gray** (1934)
Nineteenth-Century Fiction (1951) **Michael Sadleir** (1888)
Nineties (1990) **Jeremy Reed** (1954)
Ninety-Five Poems (1958) **E.E. Cummings** (1894)
Ninety-Nine Novels (1984) **'Anthony Burgess' [John Anthony Burgess Wilson]** (1917)
Ninety-Nine: The New Meaning (1990) **Walter Abish** (1931)
Ninety-Three [*Quatre-vingt-treize*] (1873) **Victor Hugo** (1802)
Ninth Directive, The (1966) **'Adam Hall' [Elleston Trevor]** (1920)
Nip in the Air, A (1974) **Sir John Betjeman** (1906)
Nixey's Harlequin (1931) **A.E. Coppard** (1878)
No Barrier (1953) **Eleanor Dark** (1901)
No, But I Saw the Movie (1952) **Peter De Vries** (1910)
No Clouds of Glory [reissued as *Sara Bastard's Notebook*, 1974] (1968) **Marian Engel** (1933)
No Continuing City (1969) **Michael Longley** (1939)
No Country For Young Men (1980) **Julia O'Faolain** (1932)
No Cross, No Crown (1669) **William Penn** (1644)
No Directions (1943) **James Hanley** (1901)
No End of Blame (1981) **Howard Barker** (1946)
No Enemy But Time (1987) **'Evelyn Anthony' [Evelyn Ward-Thomas]** (1928)
No Fool Like an Old Fool (1976) **Gavin Ewart** (1916)
'No Friend Like a Sister' (1906) **Rosa Nouchette Carey** (1840)
No Go the Bogeyman (1998) **Marina Warner** (1946)
No Heroics, Please (1991) **Raymond Carver** (1939)
No Highway (1948) **'Nevil Shute' [Nevil Shute Norway]** (1899)
No Holly for Miss Quin (1976) **'Miss Read' [Dora Jessie Saint]** (1913)
No Home But the Struggle (1977) **Edward Upward** (1903)
No Laughing Matter (1967) **Angus Wilson** (1913)
No Longer at Ease (1960) **Chinua Achebe** (1930)
No Man's Land (1975) **Harold Pinter** (1930)
No Man's Meat (1931) **Morley Callaghan** (1903)
No More Dying, Then (1971) **Ruth Rendell** (1930)
No More Hiroshimas (1982) **James Kirkup** (1923)

No More Meadows (1953) **Monica Dickens** (1915)
No More Mister Nice Guy (1998) **Howard Jacobson** (1942)
No More Parades (1925) **Ford Madox Ford** (1873)
No More School (1965) **William Mayne** (1928)
No Mother to Guide Her (1961) **Anita Loos** (1893)
No Name (1862) **Wilkie Collins** (1824)
No Name in the Street (1972) **James Baldwin** (1924)
No, Not Bloomsbury (1987) **Malcolm Bradbury** (1932)
No One Writes to the Colonel [*El coronel no tiene quien le escriba*] (1961) **Gabriel García Márquez** (1928)
No Other Life (1993) **Brian Moore** (1921)
No Other Tiger (1927) **A.E.W. Mason** (1865)
No Other Way (1902) **Sir Walter Besant** (1836)
No Quarter Given (1935) **Paul Horgan** (1903)
No Refuge Here (1981) **Jeremy Reed** (1954)
No Resting Place (1989) **William Humphrey** (1924)
No Saddles for Kangaroos (1964) **Ralph de Bossière** (1907)
No Signposts in the Sea (1961) **Vita Sackville-West** (1892)
No Star is Lost (1938) **James T. Farrell** (1904)
No Sweetness Here (1970) **Ama Ata Aidoo** (1942)
No Thanks (1935) **E.E. Cummings** (1894)
No Time (1990) **Margaret Avison** (1918)
No Truce with Time (1941) **Alec Waugh** (1898)
No Wind of Blame (1939) **Georgette Heyer** (1902)
No Wit, Help Like a Woman's (1657) **Thomas Middleton** (1580–1627)
No's Knife (1967) **Samuel Beckett** (1906)
No-Good Friday (1958) **Athol Fugard** (1932)
Noah and the Waters (1936) **C. Day Lewis** (1904)
Noah's Ark (1984) **Barbara Trapido** (1941)
Noble Arte of Venerie or Hunting, The [from J. de Fouilloux; formerly attrib. to George Turbeville] (1575) **George Gascoigne** (1542?) (tr.)
Noble Essences; or, Courteous Revelations (1950) **Sir Osbert Sitwell** (1892)
Noble House (1981) **James Clavell** (1924)
Noble in Reason (1955) **Phyllis Bentley** (1894)
Noble Life, A (1866) **Dinah Maria Craik** (1826)
Noble Queen, A (1878) **Captain Meadows Taylor** (1808–76)
Noble Slaves, The (1722) **Penelope Aubin** (*c.* 1685)
Noble Souldier, The (1634) **Samuel Rowley** (d. 1634)
Noblesse Oblige (1944) **James Evershed Agate** (1877)
Noblesse Oblige (1956) **Nancy Mitford** (1904) [with A.S.C. Ross et al.]
Nobodaddy (1926) **Archibald MacLeish** (1892)
Nobody Knows My Name (1961) **James Baldwin** (1924)
Nobody Lives Forever (1943) **W.R. Burnett** (1899)
Nobody's Business (1972) **Penelope Gilliatt** (1932)
Nobody's Fortune (1872) **Edmund Yates** (1831)
Nocturne (1917) **Frank Swinnerton** (1884)
Nocturne (1992) **Lisa St Aubin de Terán** (1953)
Nocturne of Remembered Spring (1917) **Conrad Potter Aiken** (1889)
Nocturnes for the King of Naples (1978) **Edmund White** (1940)
Noémi (1895) **S. Baring-Gould** (1834)
Noise From the Zoo, The (1991) **Janice Elliott** (1931)
Noise of History, The (1934) **John Lehmann** (1907)
Noises Off (1982) **Michael Frayn** (1933)
Non-Combatants and Others (1916) **Rose Macaulay** (1881)
Non-Existent Knight, The [*Il cavaliere inesistente*] (1959) **Italo Calvino** (1923)
Non-Juror, The (1717) **Colley Cibber** (1671)
Non-Stop (1958) **Brian Aldiss** (1925)
Non-Stop Connolly Show, The (1977) **John Arden** (1930) [with Margaretta D'Arcy]
None But the Lonely Heart (1943) **'Richard Llewellyn' [Richard Llewellyn Lloyd]** (1907)
None Genuine Without this Signature (1980) **Hugh Hood** (1928)
None Other Gods (1910) **R.H. Benson** (1871)
None Shall Look Back (1937) **Caroline Gordon** (1895)
None Turn Back (1936) **Storm Jameson** (1897)
Nones (1952) **W.H. Auden** (1907)
Nongogo (1959) **Athol Fugard** (1932)
Nonsense Novels (1911) **Stephen Leacock** (1869)
Nonsense Songs, Stories, Botany and Alphabets (1871) **Edward Lear** (1812)
Nor the Years Condemn (1938) **'Robin Hyde' [Iris Guiver Wilkinson]** (1906)
Norman Conquests, The [*Table Manners*; *Living Together*; *Round and Round the Garden*] (1973) **Alan Ayckbourn** (1939)
Norman Sinclair (1861) **W.E. Aytoun** (1813)
Norsemen in the West, The (1872) **R.M. Ballantyne** (1825)
North [Nord] (1960) **'Louis-Ferdinand Céline' [L.F. Destouches]** (1894)
North (1975) **Seamus Heaney** (1939)
North America (1862) **Anthony Trollope** (1815)
North American Education, A (1973) **Clark Blaise** (1940)
North and South (1855) **Elizabeth Gaskell** (1810)
North and South (1946) **Elizabeth Bishop** (1911)
North Atlantic Turbine, The (1967) **Ed Dorn** (1929)
North Coast, and Other Poems (1868) **Robert Williams Buchanan** (1841)
North From Sicily (1965) **Alan Ross** (1922)
North Italian Painters, The (1907) **Bernard Berenson** (1865)
North of Boston (1914) **Robert Frost** (1874)
North of Jamaica (1972) **Louis Simpson** (1923)
North of South [US: *Journey to Nowhere*] (1978) **Shiva Naipaul** (1945)
North of Summer (1967) **Al Purdy** (1918)
North of Thursday (1960) **Jon Cleary** (1917)
North Sea, The (1915) **Henry de Vere Stacpoole** (1863)
North Ship, The (1945) **Philip Larkin** (1922)
North South West [three novellas] (1973) **David Foster** (1944)
North Star (1974) **'Hammond Innes' [Ralph Hammond-Innes]** (1913)

North Star, The (1941) **Laurence Binyon** (1869)
North Star Country (1945) **Meridel le Sueur** (1900)
North Wind of Love, The: Book One (1944) **Compton Mackenzie** (1883)
North Wind of Love, The: Book Two (1945) **Compton Mackenzie** (1883)
North-ward Hoe (1607) **Thomas Dekker** (1572?) [with John Webster]
Northanger Abbey; and Persuasion (1818) **Jane Austen** (1775–1817)
Northern Antiquities (1770) **Thomas Percy** (1729) (ed.)
Northern Heiress, The (1716) **Mary Davys** (1674)
Northern Lasse, The (1632) **Richard Brome** (1590?)
Northern Light, The (1958) **A.J. Cronin** (1896)
Northern Roses (1868) **Sarah [Mrs William] Ellis** (1812)
Northern Travel (1858) **Bayard Taylor** (1825)
Northfield Poems (1965) **A.R. Ammons** (1926)
Northlight (1988) **Douglas Dunn** (1942)
Northwood (1827) **Sarah Hale** (1788)
Nosce Teipsum [also 1602, 1619] (1599) **Sir John Davies** (1569)
Nostromo (1904) **Joseph Conrad** (1857)
Not a Penny More, Not a Penny Less (1976) **Jeffrey Archer** (1940)
Not After Midnight [US: *Don't Look Now*] (1971) **Daphne du Maurier** (1907)
Not Dying (1963) **William Saroyan** (1908)
Not Fade Away (1994) **Adrian Henri** (1932)
Not Honour More (1955) **Joyce Cary** (1888)
Not in Narrow Seas (1939) **Allen Curnow** (1911)
Not Like Other Girls (1884) **Rosa Nouchette Carey** (1840)
Not Not While the Giro (1983) **James Kelman** (1946)
Not on the Screen (1930) **Henry Blake Fuller** (1857–1929)
Not That He Brought Flowers (1968) **R.S. Thomas** (1913)
Not That It Matters (1919) **A.A. Milne** (1882)
Not That Sort of Girl (1987) **'Mary Wesley' [Mary Wellesley]** (1912)
Not to Disturb (1971) **Muriel Spark** (1918)
Not Under Forty (1936) **Willa Cather** (1873)
Not Waving But Drowning (1957) **Stevie Smith** (1902)
Not Wisely But Too Well (1867) **Rhoda Broughton** (1840)
Not Without Glory (1976) **Vernon Scannell** (1922)
Not Without Laughter (1930) **Langston Hughes** (1902)
Not Without Thorns [as 'Ennis Graham'] (1873) **Mary Louisa Molesworth** (1839)
Not Wooed, But Won (1871) **James Payn** (1830)
Notable Discovery of Coosenage, A [running-title: *The Art of Cony-catching*] (1591) **Robert Greene** (1558)
Note in Music, A (1930) **Rosamond Lehmann** (1903)
Note of an English Republican on the Muscovite Crusade (1876) **A.C. Swinburne** (1837)
Note on Charlotte Bronte, A (1877) **A.C. Swinburne** (1837)
Note-Books of Night (1942) **Edmund Wilson** (1895–1972)
Notebooks 1967–68 (1969) **Robert Lowell** (1917)
Notebooks of Robinson Crusoe (1975) **Iain Crichton Smith [Iain Mac a'Ghobhainn]** (1928)
Notes and Various Readings to Shakespeare (1779) **Edward Capell** (1713)
Notes for a New Culture (1976) **Peter Ackroyd** (1949)
Notes from a Bottle Found on the Beach at Carmel (1963) **Evan S. Connell, Jr** (1924)
Notes from New York, and Other Poems (1984) **Charles Tomlinson** (1927)
Notes from the House of the Dead (1860–1) **Fyodor Mikhailovich Dostoevsky** (1821)
Notes from the Land of the Dead (1972) **Thomas Kinsella** (1928)
Notes from Underground (1864) **Fyodor Mikhailovich Dostoevsky** (1821)
Notes of a Camp-Follower on the Western Front (1919) **E.W. Hornung** (1866)
Notes of a Dirty Old Man (1973) **Charles Bukowski** (1920)
Notes of a Journey from Cornhill to Grand Cairo [as 'M.A. Titmarsh'] (1846) **W.M. Thackeray** (1811)
Notes of a Journey Through France and Italy (1826) **William Hazlitt** (1778)
Notes of a Native Son (1955) **James Baldwin** (1924)
Notes of a Son and Brother (1914) **Henry James** (1843)
Notes of a War Correspondent (1910) **Richard Harding Davis** (1864)
Notes on an Endangered Species (1974) **Mordecai Richler** (1931)
Notes on Democracy (1926) **H.L. Mencken** (1880)
Notes on Life and Letters (1921) **Joseph Conrad** (1857)
Notes on Men, Women and Books (1891) **Lady Jane Francisca Wilde** (1826)
Notes on Novelists (1914) **Henry James** (1843)
Notes on Poems and Reviews (1866) **A.C. Swinburne** (1837)
Notes to the Hurrying Man (1969) **Brian Patten** (1946)
Notes Toward a Supreme Fiction (1942) **Wallace Stevens** (1879)
Notes Towards the Definition of Culture (1948) **T.S. Eliot** (1888)
Notes Upon Some of Shakespeare's Plays (1882) **Frances [Fanny] Kemble** (1809)
Nothing (1950) **'Henry Green' [Henry Vicent Yorke]** (1905)
Nothing Dies (1940) **J.W. Dunne** (1875)
Nothing Ever Breaks Except the Heart (1966) **Kay Boyle** (1903)
Nothing For Anyone (1977) **Peter Reading** (1946)
Nothing is Sacred (1928) **Josephine Herbst** (1897)
Nothing Like Leather (1935) **V.S. Pritchett** (1900)
Nothing Like the Sun (1964) **'Anthony Burgess' [John Anthony Burgess Wilson]** (1917)
Nothing Man, The (1954) **Jim Thompson** (1906)
Nothing Missing But the Samovar (1978) **Penelope Lively** (1933)

Nothing More Than Murder (1949) **Jim Thompson** (1906)
Nothing Natural (1986) **Jenny Diski** (1947)
Nothing New (1857) **Dinah Maria Craik** (1826)
Nothing of the Sort (1971) **Lucy Boston** (1892)
Nothing Sacred (1982) **Angela Carter** (1940)
Nothing Serious (1901) **'Barry Pain' [Eric Odell]** (1864)
Nothing to Be Afraid Of (1980) **Jan Mark** (1943)
Nothing to Pay (1930) **Caradoc Evans** (1878)
Notice to Quit (1861) **William Gorman Wills** (1828)
Notorious Impostor, The (1692) **Elkanah Settle** (1648)
Notorious Mrs Ebbsmith, The (1895) **Arthur Wing Pinero** (1855)
Notwithstanding (1913) **Mary Cholmondeley** (1859)
Noughts and Crosses (1891) **Sir A.T. Quiller-Couch** (1863)
Nouveaux essais de psychologie contemporaine ['New Essays on Contemporary Psychology'] (1886) **Paul Bourget** (1852)
Nova (1968) **Samuel R. Delany** (1942)
Nova Express (1964) **William S. Burroughs** (1914)
Novel in Contemporary Life, The (1938) **Storm Jameson** (1897)
Novel Notes (1893) **Jerome K. Jerome** (1859)
Novel Now, The (1967) **'Anthony Burgess' [John Anthony Burgess Wilson]** (1917)
Novel of the Future, The (1968) **Anaïs Nin** (1903)
Novel on Yellow Paper (1936) **Stevie Smith** (1902)
Novel Since 1939, The (1946) **Henry Reed** (1914)
Novel Today, The (1955) **Walter Allen** (1911)
Novel Today, The (1963) **'Anthony Burgess' [John Anthony Burgess Wilson]** (1917)
Novelette, with Other Stories (1951) **A.L. Barker** (1918)
Novelist at the Crossroads, The (1971) **David Lodge** (1935)
Novelist's Note Book, A (1887) **David Christie Murray** (1847)
Novelist's Responsibility, The (1967) **L.P. Hartley** (1895)
Novels and Novelists (1930) **'Katherine Mansfield' [Kathleen Mansfield Beauchamp]** (1888)
November [*Novembre*] (1842) **Gustave Flaubert** (1821)
November Boughs (1888) **Walt Whitman** (1819)
November Walk Near False Creek Mouth (1964) **Earle Birney** (1904)
Novice of St Dominick, The (1806) **Lady Sydney Morgan** (1783?)
Novissima Verba (1920) **Frederic Harrison** (1831)
Novum Organum (1620) **Sir Francis Bacon** (1561)
Now and Forever (1978) **Danielle Steel** (1947)
Now and Then (1978) **Robert Penn Warren** (1905)
Now and Then, Amen (1988) **Jon Cleary** (1917)
'Now Barabbas . . . ' (1947) **William Douglas Home** (1912)
Now Barabbas Was a Rotter (1978) **Brian Masters** (1939)
Now in Wintry Delights (1903) **Robert Bridges** (1844)
Now is Time (1945) **Earle Birney** (1904)
Now or Never (1662) **Richard Baxter** (1615)
Now or Never (1859) **Matilda Betham-Edwards** (1836)
Now Sheba Sings the Song (1987) **Maya Angelou** (1928)
Now Sleeps the Crimson Petal (1961) **H.E. Bates** (1905)
Now That April's Here (1936) **Morley Callaghan** (1903)
Now That You're Back (1994) **A.L. Kennedy** (1965)
Now Wait for Last Year (1966) **Philip K. Dick** (1928)
Now We Are Six (1927) **A.A. Milne** (1882)
Now You Know (1992) **Michael Frayn** (1933)
Nowhere (1985) **Thomas Berger** (1924)
Nowhere City, The (1965) **Alison Lurie** (1926)
N-Space (1990) **Larry Niven** (1938)
Nude, The (1956) **Kenneth Clark** (1903)
Numa Roumestan (1881) **Alphonse Daudet** (1840)
Number Five John Street (1899) **Richard Whiteing** (1840)
Number of the Beast, The (1980) **Robert A. Heinlein** (1907)
Number One (1943) **John Dos Passos** (1896)
Number Seventeen (1875) **Henry Kingsley** (1830)
Numbers (1965) **C.H. Sisson** (1914)
Numismata (1697) **John Evelyn** (1620)
Nun, The [*La Religieuse*] (1796) **Denis Diderot** (1713–84)
Nun's Curse, The (1888) **Mrs J.H. Riddell** (1832)
Nuncle (1960) **John Wain** (1925)
Nunquam (1970) **Lawrence Durrell** (1912)
Nuns and Soldiers (1980) **Iris Murdoch** (1919)
Nuns in Jeopardy (1940) **Martin Boyd** (1893)
Nursery Rhymes of England, The (1842) **J.O. Halliwell-Phillipps** (1820) (ed.)
Nursery Rhymes of London Town (1916) **Eleanor Farjeon** (1881)
Nurture (1989) **Maxine Kumin** (1925)
Nutmeg of Consolation, The (1991) **Patrick O'Brian** (1914)
Nuts in May (1976) **Mike Leigh** (1943)
Nuts of Knowledge, The (1903) **George William Russell ['AE']** (1867)
Nymph Errant (1932) **James Laver** (1899)

O

O Absalom! [US: *My Son, My Son!*] (1938) **Howard Spring** (1889)
O Canada (1965) **Edmund Wilson** (1895)
O Earth Return (1954) **Jay Macpherson** (1931)
O, Evening Star (1936) **Zoë Akins** (1886)
O, How the Wheel Becomes It! (1983) **Anthony Powell** (1905)
'O' is for Outlaw (1999) **Sue Grafton** (1940)
O Jones, O Jones (1970) **Dannie Abse** (1923)
*O K*a*p*l*a*n! My K*a*p*l*a*n!* [as 'Leonard Q. Ross'] (1976) **Leo Rosten** (1908)
O Lovely England (1953) **Walter de la Mare** (1873)
O Pioneers! (1913) **Willa Cather** (1873)
O Shepherd, Speak! (1949) **Upton Sinclair** (1878)
O To Be a Dragon (1959) **Marianne Moore** (1887)

O'Briens and the O'Flahertys, The (1827) **Lady Sydney Morgan** (1783?)
O'Donnel (1814) **Lady Sydney Morgan** (1783?)
O'Donoghue, The (1845) **Charles Lever** (1806)
O'Neill (1827) **Edward Bulwer-Lytton** (1803)
O-Zone (1986) **Paul Theroux** (1941)
Oak and the Acorn, The (1987) **Howard Nemerov** (1920)
Oak and the Calf, The (1975) **Alexander Solzhenitsyn** (1918)
Oak Openings, The (1848) **James Fenimore Cooper** (1789)
Oakfield [as 'Punjabee'] (1853) **William Delafield Arnold** (1828)
Oasis, The (1949) **Mary McCarthy** (1912)
Oath of Fealty (1981) **Larry Niven** (1938) [with Jerry Pournelle]
OB (1999) **Peter Reading** (1946)
Obbligato (1956) **Frederic Raphael** (1931)
Obedience of a Christen Man, The (1528) **William Tyndale** (1494?)
Obedient Wife, The (1982) **Julia O'Faolain** (1932)
Oberland (1927) **Dorothy M. Richardson** (1873)
Oberon [from Wieland] (1798) **William Sotheby** (1757) (tr.)
Oberon; and Orestes (1802) **William Sotheby** (1757)
Oberon's Horn (1861) **Henry Morley** (1822)
Obiter Dicta [1st ser.] (1884) **Augustine Birrell** (1850)
Obiter Dicta [2nd ser.] (1887) **Augustine Birrell** (1850)
Obiter Scripta (1918) **Frederic Harrison** (1831)
Obiter Scripta (1936) **George Santayana** (1863–1952)
Obituaries (1979) **William Saroyan** (1908)
Object of an Affair, The (1974) **Julian Symons** (1912)
Objective Knowledge (1972) **Sir Karl Popper** (1902)
Oblomov (1859) **Ivan Aleksandrovich Goncharov** (1812)
Obscure Destinies (1932) **Willa Cather** (1873)
Observation Car, The (1990) **Alan Brownjohn** (1931)
Observations (1924) **Marianne Moore** (1887)
Observations (1925) **Max Beerbohm** (1872)
Observations and Conjectures Upon Some Passages of Shakespeare (1766) **Thomas Tyrwhitt** (1730)
Observations Concerning the Originall of Government (1652) **Sir Robert Filmer** (1588?)
Observations in the Art of English Poesy (1602) **Thomas Campion** (1567)
Observations of Henry, The (1901) **Jerome K. Jerome** (1859)
Observations on a Late State of the Nation (1769) **Edmund Burke** (1729)
Observations on Heresy and Orthodoxy (1835) **Joseph Blanco White** (1775)
Observations on Man, his Frame, his Duty, and his Expectations (1749) **David Hartley** (1705)
Observations on the Effect of the Corn Laws (1814) **T.R. Malthus** (1766)
Observations on the Effect of the Manufacturing System (1815) **Robert Owen** (1771)
Observations on the Faerie Queene of Spenser (1754) **Thomas Warton, the Younger** (1728)
Observations on the Nature of Civil Liberty (1776) **Richard Price** (1723)
Observations on the Night Thoughts of Dr Young [as 'Courtney Melmoth'] (1776) **Samuel Jackson Pratt** (1749)
Observations on the River Wye, and Several Parts of South Wales (1782) **William Gilpin** (1724)
Observations on the Writings of the Craftsman (1730) **John Hervey, 2nd Baron Hervey** (1696)
Observations, Relative Chiefly to Picturesque Beauty . . . Particularly the Mountains, and Lakes of Cumberland, and Westmoreland (1786) **William Gilpin** (1724)
Observations, Relative Chiefly to Picturesque Beauty . . . Particularly the High-lands of Scotland (1789) **William Gilpin** (1724)
Observations Upon a Late Libel (1681) **Sir George Savile, Marquis of Halifax** (1633)
Observations Upon Aristotles Politiques (1652) **Sir Robert Filmer** (1588?)
Observations upon Historie (1641) **William Habington** (1605)
Observations upon Religio Medici (1643) **Sir Kenelm Digby** (1603)
Observations upon the United Provinces of the Netherlands (1673) **Sir William Temple** (1628)
Obstacle Race, The (1979) **Germaine Greer** (1939)
Occam's Razor (1993) **Maureen Duffy** (1933)
Occasion for Loving (1963) **Nadine Gordimer** (1923)
Occasional Verses (1665) **Edward Herbert, Lord Herbert of Cherbury** (1583)
Occasionall Meditations (1630) **Joseph Hall** (1574)
Occasions and Protests (1964) **John Dos Passos** (1896)
Occasions of Poetry, The (1982) **Thom Gunn** (1929)
Occult Philosophy in the Elizabethan Age, The (1979) **Frances Yates** (1899)
Occupations; The Big House (1970) **Trevor Griffiths** (1935)
Occupying Power, The (1973) **'Evelyn Anthony' [Evelyn Ward-Thomas]** (1928)
Ocean (1728) **Edward Young** (1683)
Ocean of Story (1985) **Christina Stead** (1902–83)
Ocean, The (1941) **James Hanley** (1901)
Ocean Tragedy, An (1890) **W. Clark Russell** (1844)
Oceana; or, England and Her Colonies (1886) **J.A. Froude** (1818) (ed.)
Octavia (1798) **Anna Maria Porter** (1780)
Octavia (1977) **Jilly Cooper** (1937)
October (1920) **Robert Bridges** (1844)
October Blast [inc. 'Sailing to Byzantium'] (1927) **W.B. Yeats** (1865)
October Country (1955) **Ray Bradbury** (1920)
October Light (1976) **John Gardner** (1933)
Octopus, The (1901) **Frank Norris** (1870)
Octopus Frontier, The (1960) **Richard Brautigan** (1935)
Odd Couple, An (1876) **Margaret Oliphant** (1828)
Odd Couple, The (1965) **Neil Simon** (1927)

Odd Flamingo, The (1954) **Nina Bawden** (1925)
Odd Girl Out (1972) **Elizabeth Jane Howard** (1923)
Odd Jobs (1991) **John Updike** (1932)
Odd John (1935) **Olaf Stapledon** (1886)
Odd Man Out, The (1912) **Harold Brighouse** (1882)
Odd Women, The (1893) **George Gissing** (1857)
Ode for Musick (1713) **Alexander Pope** (1688)
Ode for the Bicentenary Commemoration of Henry Purcell (1896) **Robert Bridges** (1844)
Ode on a Distant Prospect of Eton College (1747) **Thomas Gray** (1716)
Ode on Solitude (1755) **James Grainger** (1721)
Ode on the Death of Mr Henry Purcell (1696) **John Dryden** (1631)
Ode on the Death of the Duke of Wellington (1852) **Alfred, Lord Tennyson** (1809)
Ode on the Departing Year (1796) **S.T. Coleridge** (1772)
Ode on the Proclamation of the French Republic (1870) **A.C. Swinburne** (1837)
Ode to Evening, An (1749) **Joseph Warton** (1722)
Ode to General Kosciusko (1797) **Henry Cary** (1772)
Ode to Napoleon Buonaparte (1814) **George Gordon, Lord Byron** (1788)
Ode to Superstition, An (1786) **Samuel Rogers** (1763)
Ode to the Country Gentlemen of England (1758) **Mark Akenside** (1721)
Ode to the Dodo (1981) **Christopher Logue** (1926)
Ode to the Duke of Wellington (1819) **R.C. Dallas** (1754)
Ode to the Earl of Huntingdon (1748) **Mark Akenside** (1721)
Ode to the Late Thomas Edwards, An (1766) **Mark Akenside** (1721)
Odes (23 BC) **Horace** [Quintus Horatius Flaccus] (65–8 BC)
Odes [bk iv] (14 BC?) **Horace [Quintus Horatius Flaccus]** (65–8 BC)
Odes (1894) **Sir William Watson** (1858)
Odes (1550) **Pierre de Ronsard** (1524)
Odes (1757) **Thomas Gray** (1716)
Odes (1822) **Victor Hugo** (1802)
Odes (1896) **John Cooper Powys** (1872)
Odes and Days (1975) **Bruce Beaver** (1928)
Odes et Ballades (1826) **Victor Hugo** (1802)
Odes of Anacreon (1800) **Thomas Moore** (1779) (tr.)
Odes of Horace, The (1894) **W.E. Gladstone** (1809) (tr.)
Odes on Several Subjects (1745) **Mark Akenside** (1721)
Odes on Various Subjects (1746) **Joseph Warton** (1722)
Odessa File, The (1972) **Frederick Forsyth** (1938)
Odette (1882) **Victorien Sardou** (1831)
Odette d'Antrevernes; and A Study in Temperament (1905) **Ronald Firbank** (1886)
Odo, Count of Lingen (1824) **Sir Samuel Egerton Brydges** (1762)
Odor of Sanctity, An (1965) **Frank Yerby** (1916)
Odtaa (1926) **John Masefield** (1878)
Odyssey, The **Homer** (8th century BC)
Odyssey of Homer, The (1887) **William Morris** (1834) (tr.)
Odyssey of Homer, The [vols. i, ii, iii: bks i-xiv] (1725, 1726) **Alexander Pope** (1688) (tr.)
Odyssey of Homer, The (1879) **Andrew Lang** (1844) (tr.) [with S.H. Butcher]
Odyssey, The (1900) **Samuel Butler** (1835) (tr.)
Oedipus [Oedipe] (1659) **Pierre Corneille** (1606)
Oedipus (1678) **John Dryden** (1631) [with Nathaniel Lee]
Oedipe (1930) **André Gide** (1869)
Oedipus and the Sphinx [*Oedipus und die Sphinx*] (1906) **Hugo von Hofmannsthal** (1874)
Oedipus at Colonus [*Oedipus Coloneus*; probably written 406/5] (401 BC) **Sophocles** (*c.* 496–*c.* 406 BC)
Oedipus the King [*Oedipus Tyrannus*] **Sophocles** (*c.* 496 BC)
Oedipus Tyrannus (1820) **P.B. Shelley** (1792)
Of a Fire on the Moon (1970) **Norman Mailer** (1923)
Of All Things (1921) **Robert Benchley** (1889)
Of Demons and Darkness (1965) **John Collier** (1901)
Of Dramatick Poesie (1668) **John Dryden** (1631)
Of Human Bondage (1915) **Somerset Maugham** (1874)
Of Justification by Faith and Works (1760) **William Law** (1686)
Of Libertie and Necessitie (1654) **Thomas Hobbes** (1588)
Of Liberty and Servitude (1649) **John Evelyn** (1620) (tr.)
Of Love and Dust (1967) **Ernest J. Gaines** (1933)
Of Love and Hunger (1947) **J. Maclaren-Ross** (1912)
Of Love and Other Demons (1995) **Gabriel García Márquez** (1928)
Of Love and Shadows (1984) **Isabel Allende** (1942)
Of Love, Time, and Places (1994) **Charles Madge** (1912)
Of Mice and Men [dramatized 1938] (1937) **John Steinbeck** (1902)
Of Mortal Love (1936) **William Gerhardie** (1895)
Of Places and Poetry (1976) **R.D. FitzGerald** (1902)
Of Population (1820) **William Godwin** (1756)
Of Prelatical Episcopacy (1641) **John Milton** (1608)
Of Reformation Touching Church-Discipline (1641) **John Milton** (1608)
Of Resolutions and Decisions of Divers Practicall Cases (1649) **Joseph Hall** (1574)
Of Sepulchres [*Dei Sepolcri*] (1807) **Ugo Foscolo** (1778)
Of the Characters of Women (1735) **Alexander Pope** (1688)
Of the Evidences of Christianity (1743) **Philip Doddridge** (1702)
Of the Farm (1965) **John Updike** (1932)
Of the Importance of Religious Opinions [from J. Necker] (1788) **Mary Wollstonecraft** (1759) (tr.)
Of the Lawes of Ecclesiasticall Politie [fifth book pub. 1597] (1593) **Richard Hooker** (1554)
Of the Reasonableness of the Christian Religion (1650) **Henry Hammond** (1605)

Of the Russe Common Wealth (1591) **Giles Fletcher the Elder** (1549?)
Of the Sacred Order and Offices of Episcopacy (1642) **Jeremy Taylor** (1613)
Of the Use of Riches (1733) **Alexander Pope** (1688)
Of Time and Stars (1972) **Arthur C. Clarke** (1917)
Of Time and the River (1935) **Thomas Wolfe** (1900)
Of Verbal Criticism (1733) **David Mallet** (1705?)
Of Woman Born (1976) **Adrienne Rich** (1929)
Of Women and Their Elegance (1980) **Norman Mailer** (1923)
Off the Skelligs (1872) **Jean Ingelow** (1820)
Off With His Head (1957) **Ngaio Marsh** (1899)
Offering of Swans, An (1923) **Oliver St Gogarty** (1878)
Office Life (1978) **Keith Waterhouse** (1929)
Officers and Gentlemen (1955) **Evelyn Waugh** (1903)
Official Aptitude Maximised—Expense Minimised (1831) **Jeremy Bentham** (1748)
Offshore (1979) **Penelope Fitzgerald** (1916)
Ogilvies, The (1849) **Dinah Maria Craik** (1826)
Ogun Abibiman (1976) **Wole Soyinka** (1934)
Oh Pray My Wings Are Gonna Fit Me Well (1975) **Maya Angelou** (1928)
Oh! To Be in England (1963) **H.E. Bates** (1905)
Oh What a Paradise It Seems (1982) **John Cheever** (1912)
Oi for England (1982) **Trevor Griffiths** (1935)
Oil! (1927) **Upton Sinclair** (1878)
Old Adam, The (1965) **D.J. Enright** (1920)
Old Bachelor, The (1693) **William Congreve** (1670)
Old Blastus of Bandicoot (1931) **Miles Franklin** (1879)
Old Boys, The (1964) **'William Trevor' [William Trevor Cox]** (1928)
Old Bush Songs (1905) **A.B. 'Banjo' Paterson** (1864)
Old Calabria (1915) **Norman Douglas** (1868)
Old Century and Seven More Years, The (1938) **Siegfried Sassoon** (1886)
Old Commodore, The (1837) **Edward Howard** (1793?)
Old Country, The (1977) **Alan Bennett** (1934)
Old Couple, The (1658) **Thomas May** (1595–1650)
Old Court (1867) **W.H. Ainsworth** (1805)
Old Court Suburb, The (1855) **Leigh Hunt** (1784)
Old Creole Days (1879) **George Washington Cable** (1844)
Old Curiosity Shop, The (1841) **Charles Dickens** (1812)
Old Debauchess, The (1732) **Henry Fielding** (1707)
Old Devils, The (1986) **Kingsley Amis** (1922)
Old Dovecote, The (1928) **David Garnett** (1892)
Old Drama and the New, The (1923) **William Archer** (1856)
Old English Baron, The [2nd edn of *The Champion of Virtue*] (1778) **Clara Reeve** (1729)
Old Fashioned Fairy Tales (1882) **Mrs J.H. Ewing** (1841)
Old Fires and Profitable Ghosts (1900) **Sir A.T. Quiller-Couch** (1863)
Old Flea-Pit, The (1987) **Alan Brownjohn** (1931)
Old Fortunatus (1600) **Thomas Dekker** (1572?)
Old Friend with a New Face, An (1797) **Eliza Parsons** (1748)
Old Friends (1890) **Andrew Lang** (1844)
Old Friends (1956) **Clive Bell** (1881)
Old Gentleman of the Black Stock, The (1897) **Thomas Nelson Page** (1853)
Old Glory, The (1965) **Robert Lowell** (1917)
Old Glory: An American Voyage (1981) **Jonathan Raban** (1942)
Old Goriot [*Le Père Goriot*] (1835) **Honoré de Balzac** (1799)
Old Gray Homestead, The (1919) **Frances Parkinson Keyes** (1885)
Old Gringo, The (1985) **Carlos Fuentes** (1928)
Old Guard, The (1843) **Dion Boucicault** (1820?)
Old Heads and Young Hearts (1849) **Dion Boucicault** (1820?)
Old Horsefly, The (1992) **Karl Shapiro** (1913)
Old Huntsman, The (1917) **Siegfried Sassoon** (1886)
Old Indian Days (1907) **Charles Eastman** (1858)
Old Jest, The (1979) **Jennifer Johnston** (1930)
Old Judge, The (1849) **T.C. Haliburton** (1796)
Old Kensington (1873) **Lady Anne Ritchie** (1837)
Old Kensington Palace (1910) **Austin Dobson** (1840)
Old Ladies, The (1924) **Sir Hugh Walpole** (1884)
Old Lamps for New (1911) **E.V. Lucas** (1868)
Old Lights for New Chancels (1940) **Sir John Betjeman** (1906)
Old Love Letters (1878) **Bronson Howard** (1842)
Old Maid, The (1935) **Zoë Akins** (1886)
Old Man and the Sea, The (1952) **Ernest Hemingway** (1898)
Old Man in the Corner, The (1909) **Baroness Orczy** (1865)
Old Man of the Mountains, The (1945) **Norman Nicholson** (1914)
Old Man Rubbing His Eyes (1975) **Robert Bly** (1926)
Old Man Taught Wisdom, An (1735) **Henry Fielding** (1707)
Old Man's Folly, An (1926) **Floyd Dell** (1887)
Old Man's Love, An (1884) **Anthony Trollope** (1815–82)
Old Manor House, The (1793) **Charlotte Smith** (1749)
Old Men and Comets (1993) **D.J. Enright** (1920)
Old Men at the Zoo, The (1961) **Angus Wilson** (1913)
Old Men of the Sea, The (1924) **Compton Mackenzie** (1883)
Old Mole (1914) **Gilbert Cannan** (1884)
Old Moore's Almanac: see *Vox Stellerum*
Old Mr Tredgold (1895) **Margaret Oliphant** (1828)
Old Negatives (1989) **Alasdair Gray** (1934)
Old New York (1924) **Edith Wharton** (1862)
Old Ones, The (1972) **Arnold Wesker** (1932)
Old Order Changes, The (1886) **W.H. Mallock** (1849)
Old Order, The (1944) **Katherine Anne Porter** (1890)
Old Patagonian Express, The (1979) **Paul Theroux** (1941)
Old Peter's Russian Tales (1916) **Arthur Ransome** (1884)
Old Portraits and Modern Sketches (1850) **John Greenleaf Whittier** (1807)

Old Possum's Book of Practical Cats (1939) **T.S. Eliot** (1888)
Old Pybus (1928) **Warwick Deeping** (1877)
Old Raiger (1964) **John Masefield** (1878)
Old Red (1963) **Caroline Gordon** (1895)
Old Reliable, The (1951) **P.G. Wodehouse** (1881)
Old Road From Spain, The (1916) **Constance Holme** (1881)
Old Road, The (1904) **Hilaire Belloc** (1870)
Old Saint Paul's (1841) **W.H. Ainsworth** (1805)
Old Scores (1995) **Frederic Raphael** (1931)
Old Ships, The (1915) **James Elroy Flecker** (1884)
Old Sir Douglas (1868) **Caroline Norton** (1808)
Old Soldiers (1980) **Paul Bailey** (1937)
Old South, The (1892) **Thomas Nelson Page** (1853)
Old Stories (1992) **Thom Gunn** (1929)
Old Testament, The [tr. from the Latin Vulgate] (1949) **Ronald Knox** (1888) (tr.)
Old Testament in the Jewish Church, The (1881) **William Robertson Smith** (1846)
Old Times (1971) **Harold Pinter** (1930)
Old Town by the Sea, An (1893) **Thomas Bailey Aldrich** (1836)
Old Wine and New (1932) **Warwick Deeping** (1877)
Old Wives Tale, The (1595) **George Peele** (1556)
Old Wives Tale, The (1908) **Arnold Bennett** (1867)
Old Woman and the Cow, The [repub. as *Gauri*, 1960] (1960) **Mulk Raj Anand** (1905)
Old-Fashioned Girl, An (1870) **Louisa M. Alcott** (1832)
Olde Religion, The (1628) **Joseph Hall** (1574)
Older Hardy, The (1979) **Robert Gittings** (1911)
Oldest Confession, The (1958) **Richard Condon** (1915)
Oldtown Folks (1869) **Harriet Beecher Stowe** (1811)
Oleander (1992) **David Mamet** (1947)
Oleander, Jacaranda (1994) **Penelope Lively** (1933)
Olive (1850) **Dinah Maria Craik** (1826)
Olive, L' (1549–50) **Joachim du Bellay** (1522)
Olive of Minerva, The (1976) **Edward Dahlberg** (1900)
Olive Tree, The (1936) **Aldous Huxley** (1894)
Oliver Cromwell (1900) **John Morley 1st Viscount Morley of Blackburn** (1838)
Oliver Cromwell (1921) **John Drinkwater** (1882)
Oliver Cromwell (1927) **Hilaire Belloc** (1870)
Oliver Cromwell (1934) **John Buchan** (1875)
Oliver Cromwell's Letters and Speeches (1845) **Thomas Carlyle** (1795) (ed.)
Oliver Goldsmith (1840) **Washington Irving** (1783)
Oliver, the Western Engine (1969) **Revd W.V. Awdry** (1911)
Oliver Twist (1838) **'Boz' [Charles Dickens]** (1812)
Oliver's Daughter (1930) **Richard Church** (1893)
Olla Podrida (1840) **Frederick Marryat** (1792)
Olney Hymns (1779) **William Cowper** (1731) [with John Newton]
Olor Iscanus (1651) **Henry Vaughan** (1622)
Ombilic des limbes, L' ['The Umbilicus of Limbo'] (1925) **Antonin Artaud** (1896)
Ombú, El (1902) **W.H. Hudson** (1841)
Omelette and a Glass of Wine, An (1984) **Elizabeth David** (1913)
Omen, The (1825) **John Galt** (1779)
Omensetter's Luck (1966) **William H. Gass** (1924)
Omeros (1990) **Derek Walcott** (1930)
Omertà (2000) **Mario Puzo** (1920)
Ommateum with Doxology (1955) **A.R. Ammons** (1926)
Omniana (1809) **S.T. Coleridge** (1772) [with Robert Southey]
Omoo (1847) **Herman Melville** (1819)
On a Chinese Screen (1922) **Somerset Maugham** (1874)
On a Darkling Plain (1940) **Wallace Stegner** (1909)
On a Deserted Shore (1973) **Kathleen Raine** (1908)
On Actors and the Art of Acting (1875) **G.H. Lewes** (1817)
On Anything (1910) **Hilaire Belloc** (1870)
On Approval (1926) **'Frederick Lonsdale' [Lionel Frederick Leonard]** (1881)
On Ballycastle Beach (1988) **Medbh McGuckian** (1950)
On Being Blue (1976) **William H. Gass** (1924)
On Being Creative (1932) **Irving Babbit** (1865)
On Boxing (1987) **Joyce Carol Oates** (1938)
On Democracy (1884) **James Russell Lowell** (1819)
On Doing What One Likes (1926) **Alec Waugh** (1898)
On Dramatic Method (1931) **Harley Granville-Barker** (1877)
On Eucharistic Adoration (1857) **John Keble** (1792)
On Everything (1909) **Hilaire Belloc** (1870)
On Forsyte Change (1930) **John Galsworthy** (1867)
On Glory's Course (1984) **James Purdy** (1923)
On Her Majesty's Secret Service (1963) **Ian Fleming** (1908)
On Heroes, Hero-Worship, and the Heroic in History (1841) **Thomas Carlyle** (1795)
On Horseback (1888) **Charles Dudley Warner** (1829)
On Liberty (1859) **J.S. Mill** (1806)
On Living in a Revolution (1944) **Julian Huxley** (1887)
On Love [De l'amour] (1822) **'Stendhal' [Henri Marie Beyle]** (1783)
On Moral Fiction (1978) **John Gardner** (1933)
On Mr Abraham Cowley His Death (1667) **Sir John Denham** (1615)
On Newfound River (1891) **Thomas Nelson Page** (1853)
On Nothing and Kindred Subjects (1908) **Hilaire Belloc** (1870)
On Photography (1977) **Susan Sontag** (1933)
On Poetry (1733) **Jonathan Swift** (1667)
On Races, Species and their Origin (1860) **T.H. Huxley** (1825)
On Seeming to Presume (1948) **Lawrence Durrell** (1912)
On Something (1910) **Hilaire Belloc** (1870)
On Ten Plays of Shakespeare (1905) **Stopford Brooke** (1832)
On the Art of Reading (1920) **Sir A.T. Quiller-Couch** (1863)

On the Art of Writing (1916) **Sir A.T. Quiller-Couch** (1863)
On the Beach (1957) **'Nevil Shute' [Nevil Shute Norway]** (1899)
On the Black Hill (1982) **Bruce Chatwin** (1940)
On the Constitution of the Church and State (1830) **S.T. Coleridge** (1772)
On the Continent (1958) **Sir Osbert Sitwell** (1892)
On the Contrary (1993) **André Brink** (1935)
On the Contrary (1961) **Mary McCarthy** (1912)
On the Death of Mrs Behn (1689) **Nathaniel Lee** (1649?)
On the Deity of Jesus of Nazareth (1873) **Annie Besant** (1847)
On the Edge (1930) **Walter de la Mare** (1873)
On the Edge (1986) **Kenneth Koch** (1925)
On the Edge of the Cliff (1979) **V.S. Pritchett** (1900)
On the Educational Value of the Natural History Sciences (1854) **T.H. Huxley** (1825)
On the Eve (1860) **Ivan Turgenev** (1818)
On the Evening Road (1994) **Dannie Abse** (1923)
On the Face of the Waters (1896) **Flora Annie Steel** (1847)
On the Frontier (1938) **W.H. Auden** (1907) [with Christopher Isherwood]
On the Ganga Ghat (1989) **Raja Rao** (1908)
On the Genealogy of Morals [Zur Genealogie der Moral] (1887) **Friedrich Wilhelm Nietzsche** (1844)
On the Heavens **Aristotle** (384)
On the Hill (1949) **John Masefield** (1878)
On the Irrawaddy (1897) **G.A. Henty** (1832)
On the Makaloa Mat (1919) **'Jack London' [John Griffith Chaney]** (1876–1916)
On the Margin (1923) **Aldous Huxley** (1894)
On the Nature and Existence of God (1875) **Annie Besant** (1847)
On the Old Road (1885) **John Ruskin** (1819)
On the Origin of Fables [De l'origine des fables] (1724) **Bernard le Bovier Fontenelle** (1657)
On the Place of Chesterton in English Letters (1940) **Hilaire Belloc** (1870)
On the Plurality of Worlds (1853) **William Whewell** (1794)
On the Principles of Political Economy and Taxation (1817) **David Ricardo** (1772)
On the Pulse of the Morning (1993) **Maya Angelou** (1928)
On the Razzle (1981) **Tom Stoppard** (1937)
On the Road (1957) **Jack Kerouac** (1922)
On the Shore (1934) **Albert Halper** (1904)
On the Soul **Aristotle** (384)
On the Staircase (1914) **Frank Swinnerton** (1884)
On the Stairs (1918) **Henry Blake Fuller** (1857)
On the Stepping Stones (1963) **William Mayne** (1928)
On the Study of Celtic Literature (1867) **Matthew Arnold** (1822)
On the Third Day (1990) **Piers Paul Read** (1941)
On the Way to the Depot (1967) **P.J. Kavanagh** (1931)
On the Yankee Station (1981) **William Boyd** (1952)
On Translating Homer (1861) **Matthew Arnold** (1822)
On Translating Homer: Last Words (1862) **Matthew Arnold** (1822)
On Trial (1914) **Elmer Rice** (1892)
On Tyranny (1789) **Vittorio Alfieri** (1759)
On Wings of Song (1979) **Thomas M. Disch** (1940)
On Writing (1947) **Anaïs Nin** (1903)
Once (1968) **Alice Walker** (1944)
Once a Week (1914) **A.A. Milne** (1882)
Once and Future King, The [complete] (1958) **T.H. White** (1906)
Once Bitten, Twice Bitten (1961) **Peter Porter** (1929)
Once in Europa (1987) **John Berger** (1926)
Once is Enough (1973) **Frank Sargeson** (1903)
Once on a Time (1917) **A.A. Milne** (1882)
Once There Was a War (1958) **John Steinbeck** (1902)
Ondine (1939) **Jean Giraudoux** (1882)
One and Last Love, The (1981) **John Braine** (1922)
One and One (1959) **P.J. Kavanagh** (1931)
One and Only, The (1994) **Francis King** (1923)
One Arm (1948) **'Tennessee' [Thomas Lanier] Williams** (1911)
One by One (1965) **Penelope Gilliatt** (1932)
One Christmas (1983) **Truman Capote** (1924)
One Clear Call (1948) **Upton Sinclair** (1878)
One Corpse Too Many (1979) **'Ellis Peters' [Edith Mary Pargeter]** (1913)
One Day in the Afternoon of the World (1964) **William Saroyan** (1908)
One Day in the Life of Ivan Denisovich (1962) **Alexander Solzhenitsyn** (1918)
One Day, When I Was Lost (1973) **James Baldwin** (1924)
One Fat Englishman (1963) **Kingsley Amis** (1922)
One Flew Over the Cuckoo's Nest (1962) **Ken Kesey** (1935)
One Foot in Eden (1956) **Edwin Muir** (1887)
One Foot in Laos (1999) **Dervla Murphy** (1931)
One For the Road (1985) **Harold Pinter** (1930)
One Hundred and One Dalmatians (1956) **Dodie Smith** (1896)
One Hundred and Twenty Million (1929) **'Michael Gold' [Irwin Granich]** (1893)
One Hundred Million Million Poems [Cent mille milliards de poèmes] (1961) **Raymond Queneau** (1903)
One Hundred Years of Solitude [Cien años de soledad] (1967) **Gabriel García Márquez** (1928)
One I Knew the Best of All, The (1893) **Frances Hodgson Burnett** (1849)
One in a Thousand (1835) **G.P.R. James** (1799)
One Life, One Love (1890) **M.E. Braddon** (1835)
One Man in His Time (1922) **Ellen Glasgow** (1874)
One Man's Initiation: 1917 (1920) **John Dos Passos** (1896)
One Man's Meat (1942) **E.B. White** (1899)
One Night in Winter (1984) **Allan Massie** (1938)
One of Our Conquerors (1891) **George Meredith** (1828)
One of Our Girls (1885) **Bronson Howard** (1842)
One of Ours (1922) **Willa Cather** (1873)
One of the Family (1993) **Monica Dickens** (1915)

One of the Founders (1965) **P.H. Newby** (1918)
One of Them (1861) **Charles Lever** (1806)
One Pair of Feet (1942) **Monica Dickens** (1915)
One Pair of Hands (1939) **Monica Dickens** (1915)
One Thing Leading to Another (1984) **Sylvia Townsend Warner** (1893–1978)
One Thing More (1986) **Christopher Fry [Christopher Fry Harris]** (1907)
One Thing Needful (1886) **M.E. Braddon** (1835)
One Tiger to a Hill (1980) **Sharon Pollock** (1936)
One Too Many, The (1894) **E. Lynn Linton** (1822)
One Touch of Venus (1943) **S.J. Perelman** (1904) [with Ogden Nash]
One True Santa, The (1985) **Alan Ahlberg** (1938)
One Twentieth (1936) **E.E. Cummings** (1894)
One, Two, Buckle My Shoe [US: The Patriotic Murders] (1940) **Agatha Christie** (1890)
One Who Forgot, The (1919) **Ruby M. Ayres** (1883)
One Woman's Life (1913) **Robert Herrick** (1868)
One Year (1976) **Adrian Henri** (1932)
One's Company (1934) **Peter Fleming** (1907)
One-Upmanship (1952) **Stephen Potter** (1900)
One Way Pendulum (1959) **N.F. Simpson** (1919)
One-Way Ticket (1949) **Langston Hughes** (1902)
Onion Eaters, The (1971) **J.P. Donleavy** (1926)
Onion Field, The (1973) **Joseph Wambaugh** (1937)
Onion, Memory, The (1978) **Craig Raine** (1944)
Onlookers (1983) **Gillian Avery** (1926)
Only a Clod (1865) **M.E. Braddon** (1835)
Only an Inch From Glory (1943) **Albert Halper** (1904)
Only By Mistake (1986) **P.J. Kavanagh** (1931)
Only Child, The (1957) **James Kirkup** (1923)
Only Child, The (1978) **Nell Dunn** (1936)
Only Children (1979) **Alison Lurie** (1926)
The Only Daughter [UK title: *The Impersonators*] (1980) **Jessica Anderson** (1925)
Only Poet, and Other Stories, The (1992) **'Rebecca West' [Cicily Isabel Andrews]** (1892)
Only Problem, The (1984) **Muriel Spark** (1918)
Only the Governess (1888) **Rosa Nouchette Carey** (1840)
Only When I Larf (1968) **Len Deighton** (1929)
Onward to Victory (1944) **Sir Winston Churchill** (1874)
Onward Virgin Soldiers (1971) **Leslie Thomas** (1931)
Open Air, The (1885) **Richard Jefferies** (1848)
Open at Random (1967) **Bruce Beaver** (1928)
Open Boat, The (1898) **Stephen Crane** (1871)
Open Boats (1917) **Alfred Noyes** (1880)
Open Confession (1925) **Marie Corelli** (1855)
Open Conspiracy, The (1928) **H.G. Wells** (1866)
Open Country (1909) **Maurice Hewlett** (1861)
Open Country (1987) **John Wain** (1925)
Open Door, The (1989) **Alan Sillitoe** (1928)
Open Eye, Open Heart (1973) **Lawrence Ferlinghetti** (1920)
Open House (1941) **Theodore Roethke** (1908)
Open Night, The (1952) **John Lehmann** (1907)
Open Road, The (1899) **E.V. Lucas** (1868)
Open Sea (1975) **Alan Ross** (1922)
Open Secrets (1994) **Alice Munro** (1931)
Open Society and its Enemies, The (1945) **Sir Karl Popper** (1902)
Open the Sky (1934) **John Pudney** (1909)
Open Verdict, An (1878) **M.E. Braddon** (1835)
Open-Eyed Conspiracy, An (1897) **William Dean Howells** (1837)
Opened Ground (1998) **Seamus Heaney** (1939)
Opening Day (1933) **David Gascoyne** (1916)
Opening Night [US: *Night at the Vulcan*] (1951) **Ngaio Marsh** (1899)
Opening of the Field, The (1960) **Robert Duncan** (1919)
Opening of the Great Seale of England, The (1643) **William Prynne** (1600)
Opera of Operas, The [*Tom Thumb the Great*] (1733) **Eliza Haywood** (*c.* 1693) [with William Hatchett]
Opera, The (1832) **Mrs C.F. Gore** (1799)
Operation Shylock (1993) **Philip Roth** (1933)
Opinions of Jerome Coignard, The [*Les Opinions de Jérôme Coignard*] (1893) **'Anatole France' [Jacques-Anatole-François Thibault]** (1844)
Opinions of the Tomcat Murr [*Lebensansichten des Katers Murr*] (1821–2) **E.T.A. Hoffmann** (1776)
Opium War Through Chinese Eyes, The (1958) **Arthur Waley** (1889)
Opportunitie, The (1640) **James Shirley** (1596)
Opposing Self, The (1955) **Lionel Trilling** (1905)
Opticks (1704) **Sir Isaac Newton** (1642)
Optimist, The (1959) **Herbert Gold** (1924)
Optimist's Daughter, The (1972) **Eudora Welty** (1909)
Options (1909) **'O. Henry' [William Sydney Porter]** (1862)
Opus Posthumous (1957) **Wallace Stevens** (1879–1955)
Or-Else Poem (1975) **Robert Penn Warren** (1905)
Oracle in the Heart, The (1980) **Kathleen Raine** (1908)
Oralloossa, Son of the Incas (1832) **Robert Bird** (1806)
Orange Fairy Book, The (1906) **Andrew Lang** (1844) (ed.)
Orange Fish, The (1989) **Carol Shields** (1935)
Orange Girl, The (1899) **Sir Walter Besant** (1836)
Oranges Are Not the Only Fruit (1985) **Jeanette Winterson** (1959)
Orators, The (1762) **Samuel Foote** (1720)
Orators, The (1932) **W.H. Auden** (1907)
Orchard and Vineyard (1921) **Vita Sackville-West** (1892)
Orchard Pavilion, The (1914) **A.C. Benson** (1862)
Orchestra (1596) **Sir John Davies** (1569)
Orchestra and Beginners (1967) **Frederic Raphael** (1931)
Orchestral Mountain, The (1943) **J.F. Hendry** (1912)
Ordeal by Ice (1960) **Farley Mowat** (1921)
Ordeal of Gilbert Pinfold, The (1957) **Evelyn Waugh** (1903)
Ordeal of Mansart, The (1957) **W.E.B. du Bois** (*c.* 1868)
Ordeal of Richard Feverel, The (1859) **George Meredith** (1828)
Order and Progress (1875) **Frederic Harrison** (1831)

Ordinary Jack (1977) **Helen Cresswell** (1934)
Ordinary Lunacy, An (1963) **Jessica Anderson** (1925)
Ordinary Story, An (1847) **Ivan Aleksandrovich Goncharov** (1812)
Ordways, The (1965) **William Humphrey** (1924)
Orestes (408 BC) **Euripides** (480 BC)
Orestes (1718) **Lewis Theobald** (1688)
Organon [6 treatises] **Aristotle** (384 BC)
Orient Express (1927) **John Dos Passos** (1896)
Oriental Assembly (1939) **T.E. Lawrence** (1888–1935)
Orientalism (1978) **Edward Said** (1935)
Orientations (1899) **Somerset Maugham** (1874)
Origin of Species by Natural Selection, The Oh (1859) **Charles Darwin** (1809)
Origin of the Brunists, The (1965) **Robert Coover** (1932)
Origin of the Knights of the Bath, The (1725) **Laurence Eusden** (1688)
Original Bliss (1997) **A.L. Kennedy** (1965)
Original of Bishops and Metropolitans, The (1641) **James Ussher** (1581)
Original Poems and Translations (1760) **James Beattie** (1735)
Original Poetry by Victor and Cazire [by Shelley and his sister Elizabeth] (1810) **P.B. Shelley** (1792)
Original Sin (1994) **P.D. James** (1920)
Original Sins (1981) **Lisa Alther** (1944)
Original Sonnets on Various Subjects (1799) **Anna Seward** (1747)
Original Stories, from Real Life (1788) **Mary Wollstonecraft** (1759)
Origins (1958) **Eric Partridge** (1894)
Origins of Cathleen (1971) **R.C. Hutchinson** (1907)
Origins of Religion, The (1908) **Andrew Lang** (1844)
Origins of the Second World War, The (1961) **A.J.P. Taylor** (1906)
Orion (1843) **R.H. Horne** (1803)
Orion (1880) **Sir Charles G.D. Roberts** (1860)
Orion Marches (1939) **Michael Roberts** (1902)
Orlandino (1848) **Maria Edgeworth** (1767)
Orlando (1928) **Virginia Woolf** (1882)
Orlando at the Brazen Threshold (1971) **Isabel Colegate** (1931)
Orlando Furioso (1516–32) **Ludovico Ariosto** (1474)
Orlando Furioso [from *Ariosto*] (1591) **Sir John Harington** (1560) (tr.)
Orlando King (1968) **Isabel Colegate** (1931)
Orlando Poems, The (1971) **George MacBeth** (1932)
Orley Farm (1862) **Anthony Trollope** (1815)
Ormond (1799) **Charles Brockden Brown** (1771)
Ornifle (1955) **Jean Anouilh** (1910)
Oroonoko (1695) **Thomas Southerne** (1659)
Oroonoko (1688) **Aphra Behn** (1640?)
Orphan, The (1680) **Thomas Otway** (1652)
Orphans (1858) **Margaret Oliphant** (1828)
Orphans of Snowden, The (1797) **Elizabeth Gunning** (1769)
Orphans of the Sky (1963) **Robert A. Heinlein** (1907)
Orpheus [*Orphée*] (1927) **Jean Cocteau** (1889)
Orpheus and Eurydice (1508?) **Robert Henryson** (*c.* 1430–*c.* 1505)
Orpheus in Mayfair (1909) **Maurice Baring** (1874)
Orra (1822) **William Barnes** (1801)
Orrie's Story (1990) **Thomas Berger** (1924)
Orsinian Tales (1976) **Ursula K. le Guin** (1929)
Orthodoxy (1909) **G.K. Chesterton** (1874)
Orthuriel (1840) **Thomas Aird** (1802)
Orval; or, The Fool of Time (1869) **Edward Robert Bulwer Lytton** (1831)
Orville College (1867) **Mrs Henry Wood** (1814)
Osbornes, The (1910) **E.F. Benson** (1867)
Oscar and Lucinda (1988) **Peter Carey** (1943)
Oscar Wilde (1918) **'Frank' Harris** (1856)
Oscar Wilde (1988) **Richard Ellmann** (1918)
Oscar Wilde and Myself (1914) **Lord Alfred Douglas** (1870)
Osterman Weekend, The (1973) **Robert Ludlum** (1927)
Ostrakoff Jewels, The (1932) **E. Phillips Oppenheim** (1866)
Oswald Bastable—and Others (1905) **E[dith] Nesbit** (1858)
Oswald's Tale (1995) **Norman Mailer** (1923)
Othello; the Moor of Venice (1604) **William Shakespeare** (1564–1616)
Other Exiles (1975) **Edward Brathwaite** (1930)
Other Eyes Than Ours (1926) **Ronald Knox** (1888)
Other House, The (1896) **Henry James** (1843)
Other House, The (1990) **Anne Stevenson** (1933)
Other Main-Travelled Roads (1910) **Hamlin Garland** (1860)
Other Mrs Jacobs, The (1903) **Mrs Campbell Praed** (1851)
Other Paris, The (1956) **Mavis Gallant** (1922)
Other People (1981) **Martin Amis** (1949)
Other People's Children (1998) **Joanna Trollope** (1943)
Other People's Lives (1897) **Rosa Nouchette Carey** (1840)
Other People's Worlds (1980) **'William Trevor' [William Trevor Cox]** (1928)
Other Place, The (1953) **J.B. Priestley** (1894)
Other Places (1982) **Harold Pinter** (1930)
Other Poems (1896) **Alice Meynell** (1847)
Other Side of Midnight, The (1974) **Sidney Sheldon** (1917)
Other Side of Silence, The (1981) **Ted Allbeury** (1917)
Other Side of the Fire, The (1983) **'Alice Thomas Ellis' [Anna Margaret Haycraft]** (1932)
Other Side of the Hill, The (1948) **Sir Basil Liddell Hart** (1895)
Other Voices, Other Rooms (1948) **Truman Capote** (1924)
Other Women (1985) **Lisa Alther** (1944)
Others to Adorn (1938) **Oliver St Gogarty** (1878)
Otherwise Engaged (1975) **Simon Gray** (1936)
Otherworld (1920) **F.S. Flint** (1885)
Othmar (1885) **'Ouida' [Marie Louise de la Ramée]** (1839)
Othon (1664) **Pierre Corneille** (1606)
Othon the Archer [*Othon l'archer*] (1840) **Alexandre Dumas ['père']** (1802)

Ottilie (1883) **'Vernon Lee' [Violet Paget]** (1856)
Our Admirable Betty (1918) **Jeffery Farnol** (1878)
Our Adversary (1909) **M.E. Braddon** (1835)
Our America (1919) **Waldo Frank** (1889)
Our American Adventure (1923) **A. Conan Doyle** (1859)
Our American Cousin (1858) **Tom Taylor** (1817)
Our Blood (1976) **Andrea Dworkin** (1946)
Our Country's Good [from Thomas Kenneally's *The Playmaker*] (1988) **Timberlake Wertenbaker**
Our Daily Bread (1928) **Frederick Grove** (1879)
Our English Cousins (1894) **Richard Harding Davis** (1864)
Our Family Affairs (1920) **E.F. Benson** (1867)
Our Father (1987) **Bernice Rubens** (1923)
Our Father (1994) **Marilyn French** (1929)
Our Flowers and Nice Bones (1969) **Christopher Middleton** (1926)
Our Friend Jennings (1955) **Anthony Buckeridge** (1912)
Our Friend the Charlatan (1901) **George Gissing** (1857)
Our Friends [*Nos Intimes*] (1861) **Victorien Sardou** (1831)
Our Friends in the North (1982) **Peter Flannery** (1951)
Our Game (1995) **'John le Carré' [David John Moore Cornwell]** (1931)
Our Gang (1971) **Philip Roth** (1933)
Our Ground Time Here Will Be Brief (1982) **Maxine Kumin** (1925)
Our House in the Last World (1983) **Oscar Hijuelos** (1951)
Our Irish Theatre (1913) **Lady Gregory** (1852)
Our Italy (1891) **Charles Dudley Warner** (1829)
Our Lady of Darkness (1899) **Bernard Capes** (1850?)
Our Lady of Darkness (1977) **Fritz Leiber** (1910)
Our Lady of the Flowers [*Notre-Dame-des-fleurs*] (1944) **Jean Genet** (1910)
Our Living John (1979) **Patric Dickinson** (1914)
Our Man in Havana (1958) **Graham Greene** (1904)
Our Mr Wrenn (1914) **Sinclair Lewis** (1885)
Our Mutual Friend (1865) **Charles Dickens** (1812)
Our New Rector (1861) **'Cuthbert Bede' [Edward Bradley]** (1827)
Our Old Home (1863) **Nathaniel Hawthorne** (1804)
Our Own People (1977) **David Edgar** (1948)
Our Own Story (1856) **Selina Bunbury** (1802)
Our Partnership (1948) **Beatrice Webb** (1858–1943)
Our Second American Adventure (1924) **A. Conan Doyle** (1859)
Our Sister Killjoy (1977) **Ama Ata Aidoo** (1942)
Our Song (1988) **Keith Waterhouse** (1929)
Our Street [as 'M.A. Titmarsh'] (1848) **W.M. Thackeray** (1811)
Our Street (1931) **Compton Mackenzie** (1883)
Our Sunshine (1991) **Robert Drewe** (1943)
Our Time is Gone (1940) **James Hanley** (1901)
Our Town (1938) **Thornton Wilder** (1897)
Our Uncle the Traveller's Stories (1859) **Frances Browne** (1816)
Our Village [5 vols: 1824, 1826, 1828, 1830, 1832] (1824–32) **Mary Russell Mitford** (1787)
Our Warrior Women (1916) **Beatrice Harraden** (1864)
Our Western Furniture (1968) **James Fenton** (1949)
Ours (1866) **T.W. Robertson** (1829)
Ourselves (1870) **E. Lynn Linton** (1822)
Ourselves to Know (1960) **John O'Hara** (1905)
Out (1964) **Christine Brooke-Rose** (1926)
Out After Dark (1989) **'Hugh Leonard' [Johns Keyes Byrne]** (1926)
Out Goes You (1975) **Sharon Pollock** (1936)
Out Late (1986) **Peter Scupham** (1933)
Out Loud (1968) **Adrian Mitchell** (1932)
Out of Africa (1937) **'Isak Dinesen' [Karen Blixen]** (1885)
Out of Bounds (1963) **Jon Stallworthy** (1935)
Out of Danger (1993) **James Fenton** (1949)
Out of Ireland (1987) **Thomas Kinsella** (1928)
Out of Siberia (1982) **Paul Muldoon** (1951)
Out of the Flame (1923) **Sir Osbert Sitwell** (1892)
Out of the Shelter (1970) **David Lodge** (1935)
Out of the Silent Planet (1938) **C.S. Lewis** (1898)
Out of the World and Back (1958) **Andrew Young** (1885)
Out of the Wreck I Rise (1912) **Beatrice Harraden** (1864)
Out of This World (1988) **Graham Swift** (1949)
Out on the Pampas (1870) **G.A. Henty** (1832)
Out with the Stars (1993) **James Purdy** (1923)
Outback Marriage, An (1906) **A.B. 'Banjo' Paterson** (1864)
Outbreak of Love (1957) **Martin Boyd** (1893)
Outbreak of the War of 1914–18, The (1919) **Sir Charles Oman** (1860)
Outcast, The (1875) **William Winwood Reade** (1838)
Outcast (1955) **Rosemary Sutcliff** (1920)
Outcast of the Islands, An (1896) **Joseph Conrad** (1857)
Outcry, The (1911) **Henry James** (1843)
Outlander (1981) **Jane Rule** (1931)
Outlanders, The (1970) **Helen Cresswell** (1934)
Outlandish Knight, The (1999) **Richard Adams** (1920)
Outlandish Proverbs (1640) **George Herbert** (1593)
Outlaw, The (1835) **Anna Maria [Mrs S.C.] Hall** (1800)
Outlaws (1987) **George V. Higgins** (1939)
Outlet, The (1905) **Andy Adams** (1859)
Outline of English History (1881) **S. R. Gardiner** (1829)
Outline of History, The (1920) **H.G. Wells** (1866)
Outline of Sanity, The (1926) **G.K. Chesterton** (1874)
Outline of the History of Ethics (1886) **Henry Sidgwick** (1838)
Outline of the Science of Political Economy, An (1836) **Nassau Senior** (1790)
Outlines of Astronomy (1841) **Sir John Herschel** (1792)
Outlines of Moral Philosophy (1793) **Dugald Stewart** (1753)
Outnumbering the Dead (1991) **Frederik Pohl** (1919)

Outre-Mer (1833–4) **Henry Wadsworth Longfellow** (1807)
Outrider (1962) **Randolph Stow** (1935)
Outside History (1990) **Eavan Boland** (1944)
Outside the Canon (1986) **Roy Fuller** (1912)
Outsider, The (1953) **Richard Wright** (1908)
Outsider, The (1956) **Colin Wilson** (1931)
Outsider and Others, The (1939) **H.P. Lovecraft** (1890–1937)
Outspoken Essays [1st ser.] (1919) **W.R. Inge** (1860)
Outspoken Essays [2nd ser.] (1922) **W.R. Inge** (1860)
Outward Bound; or, A Merchant's Adventures (1838) **Edward Howard** (1793?)
Oval Portrait, The (1977) **Kathleen Raine** (1908)
Oval Window, The (1983) **J.H. Prynne** (1936)
Over Bemerton's (1908) **E.V. Lucas** (1868)
Over Praries Trails (1922) **Frederick Grove** (1879)
Over the Border (1903) **Robert Barr** (1850)
Over the Brazier (1916) **Robert Graves** (1895)
Over the Bridge (1955) **Richard Church** (1893)
Over the Frontier (1939) **Stevie Smith** (1902)
Over the Hills and Far Away (1968) **William Mayne** (1928)
Over the Mountain (1939) **Ruthven Todd** (1914)
Over the River (1933) **John Galsworthy** (1867)
Over the Teacups (1891) **Oliver Wendell Holmes** (1809)
Over There (1915) **Arnold Bennett** (1867)
Over to Candleford (1941) **Flora Thompson** (1877)
Over to You (1946) **Roald Dahl** (1916)
Overland (1871) **John W. De Forest** (1826)
Overland Route, The (1860) **Tom Taylor** (1817)
Overload (1979) **Arthur Hailey** (1920)
Overnight to Many Distant Cities (1984) **Donald Barthelme** (1931)
Overture to Death (1939) **Ngaio Marsh** (1899)
Overtures to Death (1938) **C. Day Lewis** (1904)
Ovid's Banquet of Sense (1595) **George Chapman** (1559?)
Ovid's Epistles (1680) **John Dryden** (1631) and others (tr.)
Ovid's Metamorphosis (1626) **George Sandys** (1578) (tr.)
Ovingdean Grange (1860) **W.H. Ainsworth** (1805)
Ovington's Bank (1922) **Stanley J. Weyman** (1855)
Owen Glendower (1940) **John Cooper Powys** (1872)
Owen Tudor (1849) **Emma Robinson** (1814)
Owl in the Attic, The (1931) **James Thurber** (1894)
Owl in the Tree, The (1963) **Anthony Thwaite** (1930)
Owl Service, The (1967) **Alan Garner** (1934)
Owl's Clover (1936) **Wallace Stevens** (1879)
Owle, The (1604) **Michael Drayton** (1563)
Owls and Artificers (1971) **Roy Fuller** (1912)
Owls Do Cry (1957) **Janet Frame** (1924)
Ownerless Earth (1973) **Michael Hamburger** (1924)
Owners (1972) **Caryl Churchill** (1938)
Ox Bells and Fireflies (1968) **Ernest Buckler** (1908)
Oxbridge Blues, and Other Plays for Television (1984) **Frederic Raphael** (1931)
Oxbridge Blues, and Other Stories (1980) **Frederic Raphael** (1931)
Oxford (1707) **Thomas Tickell** (1686)
Oxford Addresses on Poetry (1962) **Robert Graves** (1895)
Oxford Book of Ballads, The (1910) **Sir A.T. Quiller-Couch** (1863) (ed.)
Oxford Book of English Prose, The (1925) **Sir A.T. Quiller-Couch** (1863) (ed.)
Oxford Book of English Verse, The (1900) **Sir A.T. Quiller-Couch** (1863) (ed.)
Oxford Book of Greek Verse in Translation, The (1938) **Maurice Bowra** (1898) (ed.)
Oxford Book of Seventeenth-Century Verse, The (1934) **H.J.C. Grierson** (1866) (ed.) [with Geoffrey Bullough]
Oxford Book of Twentieth-Century Verse, The (1973) **Philip Larkin** (1922) (ed.)
Oxford Book of Victorian Verse, The (1912) **Sir A.T. Quiller-Couch** (1863) (ed.)
Oxford Companion to English Literature, The (1985) **Margaret Drabble** (1939) (ed.)
Oxford Companion to Twentieth-Century Poetry in English, The (1994) **Ian Hamilton** (1938) (ed.)
Oxford Dictionary of Nursery Rhymes, The (1951) **Peter** (1918) and **Iona** (1923) **Opie**
Oxford Lectures on Poetry (1909) **A.C. Bradley** (1851)
Oxford Lectures on Poetry (1934) **Ernest de Selincourt** (1870)
Oxford University Chest, An (1938) **Sir John Betjeman** (1906)
Ozma of Oz (1907) **L. Frank Baum** (1856)

P

Pabo the Priest (1899) **S. Baring-Gould** (1834)
Pacchiarotta and How He Worked in Distemper (1876) **Robert Browning** (1812)
Pacha of Many Tales, The (1835) **Frederick Marryat** (1792)
Pacific Highway (1982) **Michael Wilding** (1942)
Pacificator, The (1700) **Daniel Defoe** (1660)
Pack My Bag (1940) **'Henry Green' [Henry Vincent Yorke]** (1905)
Pack of Cards (1986) **Penelope Lively** (1933)
Packet, The (1794) **Elizabeth Gunning** (1769)
Pactolus Prime (1890) **Albion W. Tourgée** (1838)
Paddy Clarke Ha Ha Ha (1993) **Roddy Doyle** (1958)
Padlock, The (1768) **Isaac Bickerstaffe** (1733)
Paean Triumphall, A (1604) **Michael Drayton** (1563)
Pagan Papers (1893) **Kenneth Grahame** (1859)
Pagan Place, A (1970) **Edna O'Brien** (1932)
Pagan Poems (1881) **George Moore** (1852)
Pagan Rabbi, The (1971) **Cynthia Ozick** (1928)
Pagan Spain (1957) **Richard Wright** (1908)
Pagan's Pilgrimage, A (1931) **Llewelyn Powys** (1884)
Pageant, A (1881) **Christina Rossetti** (1830)
Pages from a Journal (1900) **'Mark Rutherford' [William Hale White]** (1831)
Pages From an Old Volume of Life (1883) **Oliver Wendell Holmes** (1809)
Paid Servant (1962) **E.R. Braithwaite** (1912)

Paine of Pleasure, The (1580) **Anthony Munday** (1560)
Painted Bird, The (1965) **Jerzy Kosinski** (1933)
Painted Devil, A (1975) **Rachel Billington** (1942)
Painted Face, The (1929) **Oliver Onions** (1873)
Painted Garden, The (1949) **Noel Streatfeild** (1895)
Painted Lady, The [*La Femme Fardée*] (1981) **'Françoise Sagan' [Françoise Quoirez]** (1935)
Painted Princess, The (1936) **Martin Boyd** (1893)
Painted Veil, The (1925) **Somerset Maugham** (1874)
Painted Word, The (1975) **Tom Wolfe** (1930)
Painter of Our Time, A (1958) **John Berger** (1926)
Painter of Signs, The (1977) **R.K. Narayan** (1907)
Painting Room, The (1988) **Kevin Crossley-Holland** (1941)
Pair of Blue Eyes, A (1873) **Thomas Hardy** (1840)
Pal Joey [later dramatized as a musical comedy] (1940) **John O'Hara** (1905)
Palace and Mosque at Ukhaidir, The (1914) **Gertrude Bell** (1868)
Palace of Minos at Knossos, The (1922–35) **Sir Arthur Evans** (1851)
Palace of Pleasure, The [vol. i] (1566) **William Painter** (1540?)
Palace of the Peacock (1960) **Wilson Harris** (1921)
Palace Without Chairs (1978) **Brigid Brophy** (1929)
Palaeographia Sacra (1736) **William Stukeley** (1687)
Pale Blue Crochet Coathanger Cover, The (1988) **David Foster** (1944)
Pale Fire (1962) **Vladimir Nabokov** (1899)
Pale Horse, Pale Rider (1939) **Katherine Anne Porter** (1890)
Pale View of Hills, A (1982) **Kazuo Ishiguro** (1954)
Paleface (1929) **Wyndham Lewis** (1882)
Paleface and Redskin (1898) **'F. Anstey' [Thomas Anstey Guthrie]** (1856)
Palestine Plays (1942) **Laurence Housman** (1865)
Palfrey, The (1842) **Leigh Hunt** (1784)
Palice of Honour, The (1535) **Gavin Douglas** (1474?-1522)
Palicio (1890) **Robert Bridges** (1844)
Palimpsest: A Memoir (1995) **Gore Vidal** (1925)
Palinode (1977) **Michael Hamburger** (1924)
Palissy the Potter (1852) **Henry Morley** (1822)
Palladine of England [from French] (1588) **Anthony Munday** (1560) (tr.)
Palladis Tamia (1598) **Francis Meres** (1565)
Palm Leaves (1844) **Richard Monckton Milnes** (1809)
Palm Sunday (1981) **Kurt Vonnegut** (1922)
Palmerin D'Oliva [pt. i; pt. ii, 1597] (1588) **Anthony Munday** (1560) (tr.)
Palmerin of England [pt. i; pt. ii, 1596; pt iii, 1602] (1596) **Anthony Munday** (1560) (tr.)
Palmerin of England [from Francisco de Moraes] (1807) **Robert Southey** (1774) (tr.)
Palmerston (1882) **Anthony Trollope** (1815)
Palmetto-Leaves (1873) **Harriet Beecher Stowe** (1811)
Palmyra (1806) **Thomas Love Peacock** (1785)
Palomar (1983) **Italo Calvino** (1923)
Palomino (1980) **Elizabeth Jolley** (1923)
Palomino Blonde [US: *Omega Minus*] (1975) **Ted Allbeury** (1917)
Pamela [vols. i, ii] (1741, 1742) **Samuel Richardson** (1689)
Pampinea (1861) **Thomas Bailey Aldrich** (1836)
Pan (1894) **Knut Hamsun** (1859)
Pan and Syrinx (1718) **Lewis Theobald** (1688)
Pan his Syrinx, or Pipe (1584) **William Warner** (1558?)
Pan in the Parlour (1933) **Norman Lindsay** (1879)
Pan's Garden (1912) **Algernon Blackwood** (1869)
Pan's Prophecy (1904) **T. Sturge Moore** (1870)
Panacea (1700) **Nahum Tate** (1652)
Panama (1915) **Stephen Phillips** (1864)
Pandora (1662) **Sir William Killigrew** (1606)
Pandosto (1588) **Robert Greene** (1558)
Panegyric to Charles the Second, A (1661) **John Evelyn** (1620)
Panegyrick to my Lord Protector, A (1655) **Edmund Waller** (1606)
Panegyrick to the King's Most Excellent Majesty, A (1660) **Charles Cotton** (1630)
Panegyrike , A [inc. 'A Defence of Rhyme'] (1603) **Samuel Daniel** (1563)
Panel, The (1912) **Ford Madox Ford** (1873)
Pangolin, The (1936) **Marianne Moore** (1887)
Pangs of Love, The (1983) **Jane Gardam** (1928)
Panic (1935) **Archibald MacLeish** (1892)
Panopticon (1791) **Jeremy Bentham** (1748)
Panorama, and Other Poems, The (1856) **John Greenleaf Whittier** (1807)
Pansies (1929) **D.H. Lawrence** (1885)
Pantagruel [as 'Alcofribas Nasier'] (1532/3) **François Rabelais** (1494?)
Pantaloon (1961) **Philip Toynbee** (1916)
Pantheon, The (1747) **Sir William Blackstone** (1723)
Pantochronochanon (1652) **Sir Thomas Urquhart** (1611)
Paolo and Francesca (1898) **Stephen Phillips** (1864)
Papa La Fleur (1933) **Zona Gale** (1874)
Papa, You're Crazy (1957) **William Saroyan** (1908)
Pape, Le ['The Pope'] (1878) **Victor Hugo** (1802–85)
Paper Chase, The (1966) **Hal Porter** (1911)
Paper Houses (1929) **William Plomer** (1903)
Paper Lives (1966) **Compton Mackenzie** (1883)
Paper Men, The (1984) **William Golding** (1911)
Paper Roses (1916) **Ruby M. Ayres** (1883)
Paper Windows (1968) **James Kirkup** (1923)
Paperbark Tree, The (1992) **Les Murray** (1938)
Papers Upon Codification and Public Instruction (1817) **Jeremy Bentham** (1748)
Parables from Nature (1861) **Margaret [Mrs Alfred] Gatty** (1809)
Parables from Nature, Third and Fourth Series (1865) **Margaret [Mrs Alfred] Gatty** (1809)
Parables of Our Lord and Saviour Jesus Christ, The (1768) **Christopher Smart** (1722)
Paracelsus (1835) **Robert Browning** (1812)
Parachutes and Kisses (1984) **Erica Jong** (1942)

Parade [ballet] (1917) **Jean Cocteau** (1889)
Paradine Case, The (1933) **Robert Hichens** (1864)
Paradise (1986) **Donald Barthelme** (1931)
Paradise (1998) **Toni Morrison** (1931)
Paradise Creek (1963) **Leo Walmsley** (1892)
Paradise Illustrated (1978) **D.J. Enright** (1920)
Paradise Lost [bks i-x] (1667) **John Milton** (1608)
Paradise Lost [bks i-xii] (1674) **John Milton** (1608)
Paradise Lost (1935) **Clifford Odets** (1906)
Paradise News (1991) **David Lodge** (1935)
Paradise Place (1949) **Warwick Deeping** (1877)
Paradise Postponed (1985) **John Mortimer** (1923)
Paradise Regain'd [with *Samson Agonistes*] (1671) **John Milton** (1608)
Paradisi in sole Paradisus terrestris (1629) **John Parkinson** (1567)
Paradox Players, The (1967) **Maureen Duffy** (1933)
Paradoxes (1650) **John Hall, of Durham** (1627)
Paradoxes [etc] (1652) **John Donne** (1572–1631)
Paradoxes of Mr Pond, The (1937) **G.K. Chesterton** (1874–1936)
Paradyse of Daynty Devises, The (1576) **Richard Edwards** (1523?-66) and others
Paraenesis to the Prince, A (1604) **Sir William Alexander** (1567?)
Paraguayan Experiment, The (1985) **Michael Wilding** (1942)
Parallèlement ['In Parallel'] (1889) **Paul Verlaine** (1844)
Paraphrase, and Annotations Upon all the Books of the New Testament, A (1653) **Henry Hammond** (1605)
Paraphrase on the First Twenty Psalms (1627) **George Buchanan** (1506–82)
Paraphrase Upon the Divine Poems, A (1637) **George Sandys** (1578) (tr.)
Paraphrase Upon the Psalmes of David, A (1636) **George Sandys** (1578) (tr.)
Parasha (1843) **Ivan Turgenev** (1818)
Parasitaster (1606) **John Marston** (1576)
Parasite, The (1894) **A. Conan Doyle** (1859)
Parasites of Heaven (1966) **Leonard Cohen** (1934)
Parcel of Trees, A (1963) **William Mayne** (1928)
Pardoner and the Friar, The (1533) **John Heywood** (1497?)
Parent's Assistant, The (1796) **Maria Edgeworth** (1767)
Parents and Children (1941) **I. Compton-Burnett** (1884)
Parents Keep Out (1951) **Ogden Nash** (1902)
Pariah, The (1889) **'F. Anstey' [Thomas Anstey Guthrie]** (1856)
Paris (1900) **Hilaire Belloc** (1870)
Paris (1898) **Émile Zola** (1840)
Paris and the Parisians in 1835 (1836) **Frances Trollope** (1780)
Paris France (1940) **Gertrude Stein** (1874)
Paris Journal (1978) **David Gascoyne** (1916)
Paris! Paris! (1977) **Irwin Shaw** (1913)
Paris Sketch Book, The [as 'M.A. Titmarsh'] (1840) **W.M. Thackeray** (1811)
Paris Visit, A (1985) **Robert Duncan** (1919)
Parisians, The (1873) **Edward Bulwer-Lytton** (1803)
Parisina [music by Mascagni] (1913) **Gabriele D'Annunzio** (1863)
Park, The (1968) **Margaret Forster** (1938)
Parker Pyne Investigates [US: *Mr Parker Pyne, Detective*] (1934) **Agatha Christie** (1890)
Parliament of Bees, The (1641) **John Day** (*c.* 1574)
Parliament of Birds, A (1975) **John Heath-Stubbs** (1918)
Parliament of Fowls, The (1477?) **Geoffrey Chaucer** (1340?-1400)
Parliament of Vertues Royal, The [from Jean Bertaut et al.] (1614) **Joshua Sylvester** (1563) (tr.)
Parliamentary Government in England (1938) **Harold Laski** (1893)
Parliamentary Letters (1818) **Thomas Haynes Bayly** (1797)
Parliamentary Reform (1859) **Walter Bagehot** (1826)
Parlor, Bedlam, and Bath (1930) **S.J. Perelman** (1904)
Parnell and His Island (1887) **George Moore** (1852)
Parnell and the Englishwoman (1990) **'Hugh Leonard' [Johns Keyes Byrne]** (1926)
'Parodies Regained' (1921) **E.V. Knox** (1881)
Parra Sashta (1845) **William Carleton** (1794)
Parsifal (1988) **Peter Vansittart** (1920)
Parsifal Mosaic, The (1982) **Robert Ludlum** (1927)
Parson Harding's Daughter [US: *Mistaken Virtues*] (1979) **Joanna Trollope** (1943)
Parson Kelly (1900) **Andrew Lang** (1844) [with A.E.W. Mason]
Parson's Daughter, The, (1987) **Catherine Cookson** (1906)
Parson's Progress, The (1923) **Compton Mackenzie** (1883)
Part of Speech, A (1980) **Joseph Brodsky** (1940)
Parthenissa (1651) **Roger Boyle, earl of Orrery** (1621)
Parthenophil and Parthenophe (1593) **Barnabe Barnes** (1571)
Partial Portraits (1888) **Henry James** (1843)
Parting of the Ways, The (1888) **Matilda Betham-Edwards** (1836)
Partisan, The (1835) **William Gilmore Simms** (1806)
Partner, The (1997) **John Grisham** (1955)
Partridge in a Pear Tree, A (1988) **John Heath-Stubbs** (1918)
Parts of a World (1942) **Wallace Stevens** (1879)
Party Frock (1945) **Noel Streatfeild** (1895)
Party Going (1939) **'Henry Green' [Henry Vincent Yorke]** (1905)
Party, The (1973) **Trevor Griffiths** (1935)
Party Time (1991) **Harold Pinter** (1930)
Pasmore (1972) **David Storey** (1933)
Pas perdus, Les (1924) **André Breton** (1896)
Pascali's Island [US: *Idol Hunter*] (1980) **Barry Unsworth** (1930)
Pascarel (1873) **'Ouida' [Marie Louise de la Ramée]** (1839)

Pasquil the Playne (1532) **Sir Thomas Elyot** (1490?)
Pasquil's Mad-cap (1600) **Nicholas Breton** (1545?)
Pasquil's Mistress (1600) **Nicholas Breton** (1545?)
Pasquin (1736) **Henry Fielding** (1707)
Passage de Milan (1954) **Michel Butor** (1926)
Passage of Arms (1959) **Eric Ambler** (1909)
Passage Perilous, A (1903) **Rosa Nouchette Carey** (1840)
Passage to India (1871) **Walt Whitman** (1819)
Passage to India, A (1924) **E.M. Forster** (1879)
Passage to Juneau (1999) **Jonathan Raban** (1942)
Passage to Pontefract (1981) **'Jean Plaidy' [Eleanor Hibbert]** (1906)
Passages in the History of a Shilling (1862) **Mrs C.L. Balfour** (1808)
Passages in the Life of a Lady (1887) **Charles Hamilton Aïdé** (1826)
Passages in the Life of Mrs Margaret Maitland (1849) **Margaret Oliphant** (1828)
Passages of Joy, The (1982) **Thom Gunn** (1929)
Passenger (1979) **Thomas Keneally** (1935)
Passing of a Hero, The (1953) **Jocelyn Brooke** (1908)
Passing of the Third Floor Back, The (1907) **Jerome K. Jerome** (1859)
Passing On (1989) **Penelope Lively** (1933)
Passing Through Gehenna (1978) **Madison Jones** (1925)
Passing Time [L'emploi du temps] (1956) **Michel Butor** (1926)
Passion, The (1987) **Jeanette Winterson** (1959)
Passion Flowers (1854) **Julia Ward Howe** (1819)
Passion in Rome, A (1961) **Morley Callaghan** (1903)
Passion of John Aspinall, The (1988) **Brian Masters** (1939)
Passion of New Eve, The (1977) **Angela Carter** (1940)
Passionate Elopement, The (1911) **Compton Mackenzie** (1883)
Passionate Friends, The (1913) **H.G. Wells** (1866)
Passionate North, The (1950) **William Sansom** (1912)
Passionate Pilgrim, A (1875) **Henry James** (1843)
Passionate Pilgrim, The (1858) **'Henry J. Thurstan' [Francis Turner Palgrave]** (1824)
Passionate Pilgrime, The (1599) **William Shakespeare** (1564)
Passionate Shepherd, The (1604) **Nicholas Breton** (1545?)
Passions, The (1811) **Charlotte Dacre** (1782?)
Passions (1978) **Isaac Bashevis Singer** (1904)
Passions of the Mind (1991) **A.S. Byatt** (1936)
Passions of the Spirit, The (1599) **Nicholas Breton** (1545?)
Passions of Uxport, The (1968) **Maxine Kumin** (1925)
Passive Obedience (1712) **George Berkeley** (1685)
Passport to Hell (1936) **'Robin Hyde' [Iris Guiver Wilkinson]** (1906)
Passport to the War (1940) **Stanley J. Kunitz** (1905)
Password, The (1952) **James Reeves** (1909)
Past All Dishonor (1946) **James M. Cain** (1892)
Past and Present (1843) **Thomas Carlyle** (1795)
Past Master (1965) **Nigel Tranter** (1909)
Past, The (1980) **Neil Jordan** (1950)
Paston Carew (1886) **E. Lynn Linton** (1822)
Pastor fido, Il ['Fido the Shepherd'] (1589) **Giovanni Battista Guarini** (1538)
Pastor Fido (1676) **Elkanah Settle** (1648)
Pastor Fido, Il [expanded 1648] (1647) **Sir Richard Fanshawe** (1608) (tr.)
Pastor's Fire-Side, The (1817) **Jane Porter** (1776)
Pastor's Wife, The (1914) **'Elizabeth' [Mary Annette Gräfin] von Arnim** (1866)
Pastoral Tales (1710) **Ambrose Philips** (1674)
Pastorals (1916) **Edmund Blunden** (1896)
Pastorals, Epistles, Odes (1748) **Ambrose Philips** (1674)
Pastors and Masters (1925) **I. Compton-Burnett** (1884)
Pastures of Heaven, The (1932) **John Steinbeck** (1902)
Pastyme of Pleasure, The (1509) **Stephen Hawes** (d. 1523?)
Pat and the Spider (1904) **Helen Bannerman** (1863)
Pat Hoby Stories, The (1962) **F. Scott Fitzgerald** (1896–1940)
Pat of Silver Bush (1933) **L.M. Montgomery** (1874)
Patchwork (1981) **Michael Longley** (1939)
Patchwork Planet, A (1998) **Anne Tyler** (1941)
Paterson (1946–58) **William Carlos Williams** (1883)
Path and Goal (1900) **Ada Cambridge** (1844)
Path by the Window, The (1952) **Adrian Bell** (1901)
Path of Roses, The (1859) **Frederick Greenwood** (1830)
Path of the Hero King, The (1970) **Nigel Tranter** (1909)
Path of the Just, The (1857) **S. Baring-Gould** (1834)
Path of the King, The (1921) **John Buchan** (1875)
Path to the Nest of Spiders, The [Il sentiero dei nidi di ragno] (1947) **Italo Calvino** (1923)
Path of Thunder (1948) **Peter Abrahams** (1919)
Path to Rome, The (1902) **Hilaire Belloc** (1870)
Path-way to Military Practise, A (1587) **Barnabe Rich** (1542)
Pathfinder, The (1840) **James Fenimore Cooper** (1789)
Paths of the Dead (1899) **Hume Nisbet** (1849)
Pathway, The (1928) **Henry Williamson** (1895)
Pathway to the Sea (1975) **Ian Wedde** (1946)
Patience [music by Sir Arthur Sullivan] (1881) **W.S. Gilbert** (1836)
Patient Grissill (1603) **Henry Chettle** (1560?) [with Thomas Dekker and William Haughton]
Patient, The (1992) **George MacBeth** (1932)
Patriarcha (1680) **Sir Robert Filmer** (1588?-1653)
Patriarchal Attitudes (1970) **Eva Figes** (1932)
Patricia Kemball (1875) **E. Lynn Linton** (1822)
Patrician, The (1911) **John Galsworthy** (1867)
Patrick in Prussia (1786) **John O'Keefe** (1747)
Patrick Pearse Motel, The (1971) **'Hugh Leonard' [Johns Keyes Byrne]** (1926)
Patriot For Me, A (1965) **John Osborne** (1929)
Patriot Game, The (1982) **George V. Higgins** (1939)
Patriot Games (1987) **Tom Clancy** (1947)
Patriot, The (1774) **Samuel Johnson** (1709)

Patriot, The (1960) **Evan S. Connell, Jr** (1924)
Patriot, The [from Nathaniel Lee's *Lucius Junius Brutus* (1681)] (1703) **Charles Gildon** (1665)
Patriotic Gore (1962) **Edmund Wilson** (1895)
Patriots and Liberators (1977) **Simon Schama** (1945)
Patron, The (1764) **Samuel Foote** (1720)
Patronage (1814) **Maria Edgeworth** (1767)
Pattern, The (1979) **Vincent Buckley** (1925)
Pattern (1993) **C.H. Sisson** (1914)
Pattern of a Day (1940) **Robert Hillyer** (1895)
Pattern of Catechistical Doctrine, A (1630) **Lancelot Andrewes** (1555)
Pattern of Roses, A (1973) **K.M. Peyton** (1929)
Pattes du monde, Les ['The World's Legs'] (1860) **Victorien Sardou** (1831)
Paul (1906) **E.F. Benson** (1867)
Paul and Virginia [from Bernadin de St Pierre] (1796) **Helen Maria Williams** (1762) (tr.)
Paul Bradley (1876) **Mrs Caroline Bray** (1814)
Paul Claudel: Five Great Odes (1967) **Edward Lucie-Smith** (1933) (tr.)
Paul Clifford (1830) **Edward Bulwer-Lytton** (1803)
Paul Faber, Surgeon (1879) **George MacDonald** (1824)
Paul Ferroll (1855) **Caroline Clive** (1801)
Paul Gosslett's Confessions (1868) **Charles Lever** (1806)
Paul Jones (1826) **Allan Cunningham** (1784)
Paul Jones, the Pirate (1842) **Pierce Egan, the Younger** (1814)
Paul Kelver (1902) **Jerome K. Jerome** (1859)
Paul Patoff (1887) **F. Marion Crawford** (1854)
Paul the Minstrel (1911) **A.C. Benson** (1862)
Paula (1995) **Isabel Allende** (1942)
Pauline (1833) **Robert Browning** (1812)
Pausanias the Spartan (1876) **Edward Bulwer-Lytton** (1803–73)
Pavannes and Divagations (1958) **Ezra Pound** (1885)
Pavannes and Divisions (1918) **Ezra Pound** (1885)
Pawn in Frankincense (1969) **Dorothy Dunnett** (1923)
Pawnbroker, The (1961) **Edward Wallant** (1926)
Pawns [The Storm, The God of Quiet, A Night of the Trojan War] (1917) **John Drinkwater** (1882)
Pax Britannica (1968) **Jan Morris** (1926)
Paying Guest, The (1895) **George Gissing** (1857)
Paying Guests (1929) **E.F. Benson** (1867)
Paysan de Paris, Le ['The Peasant of Paris'] (1926) **Louis Aragon** (1897)
Pea Soup (1982) **Christopher Reid** (1949)
Peace (421BC) **Aristophanes** (*c.* 445 BC)
Peace (1905) **A.C. Benson** (1862)
Peace and War (1854) **William Allingham** (1824)
Peace and War in the Global Village (1968) **Marshall McLuhan** (1911)
Peace Breaks Out (1946) **Angela Thirkell** (1890)
Peace Conference Hints (1919) **Bernard Shaw** (1856)
'Peace in Our Time' (1947) **Noel Coward** (1899)
Peace is Milk (1966) **Adrian Mitchell** (1932)
Peace, It's Wonderful (1939) **William Saroyan** (1908)
Peace Ode Written on the Conclusion of the Three Years' War (1903) **Robert Bridges** (1844)
Peace of the Augustans, The (1916) **George Saintsbury** (1845)
Peace-Maker, The (1645) **Joseph Hall** (1574)
Peaceable Kingdom, The (1954) **Jon Silkin** (1930)
Peach Groves, The (1979) **Barbara Hanrahan** (1939)
Peach Stone, The (1967) **Paul Horgan** (1903)
Peacock House, The (1963) **Gillian Avery** (1926)
Peacock Pie (1913) **Walter de la Mare** (1873)
Peacock Spring, The (1975) **Rumer Godden** (1907)
Peakland Faggot, A (1897) **Robert Murray Gilchrist** (1868)
Peaks, Passes, and Glaciers (1862) **Sir Leslie Stephen** (1832)
Pear Tree, The (1977) **Lauris Edmond** (1924)
Pearl, The (1948) **John Steinbeck** (1902)
Pearl of Orr's Island, The (1862) **Harriet Beecher Stowe** (1811)
Pearl-Maiden (1903) **Sir H. Rider Haggard** (1856)
Pearla (1883) **Matilda Betham-Edwards** (1836)
Pearls of the Faith (1883) **Sir Edwin Arnold** (1832)
Peasant Mandarin, The (1978) **Les Murray** (1938)
Peau de tigre, La ['The Tiger's Skin'] (1852) **Théophile Gautier** (1811)
Pebble in the Sky (1950) **Isaac Asimov** (1920)
Peccavi (1900) **E.W. Hornung** (1866)
Peckham's Marbles (1986) **Peter de Vries** (1910)
Pédant joué, Le (1653) **Cyrano de Bergerac** (1619)
Pedlar's Revenge, The (1976) **Liam O'Flaherty** (1897)
Pedlers Prophecie, The (1595) **Robert Wilson** (fl.1572–1600)
Peeping Tom (1984) **Howard Jacobson** (1942)
Peeping Tom of Coventry (1784) **John O'Keefe** (1747)
Peer Gynt (1867) **Henrik Ibsen** (1828)
Peer's Daughters, The (1849) **Edward Bulwer-Lytton** (1803)
Peerage and Baronetage (1826) **John Burke** (1787)
Peers and Parvenus (1846) **Mrs C.F. Gore** (1799)
Peg Woffington (1853) **Charles Reade** (1814)
Pegasus (1957) **C. Day Lewis** (1904)
Pegnitz Junction, The (1973) **Mavis Gallant** (1922)
Peintres cubistes, Les ['The Cubist Painters'] (1913) **'Guillaume Apollinaire' [Wilhelm de Kostrowitsky]** (1880)
Pelagea (1926) **A.E. Coppard** (1878)
Pelayo (1838) **William Gilmore Simms** (1806)
Pelham (1828) **Edward Bulwer-Lytton** (1803)
Pelican at Blandings, A (1969) **P.G. Wodehouse** (1881)
Pelican Brief, The (1992) **John Grisham** (1955)
Pelicans, The (1918) **'E.M. Delafield' [E.E.M. de la Pasture]** (1890)
Pelleas and Melisande (1892) **Maurice Maeterlinck** (1862)
Pemberley [sequel to Jane Austen's Pride and Prejudice] (1993) **Emma Tennant** (1937)
Pembroke (1894) **Mary Wilkins Freeman** (1852)
Pen Rhythm (1980) **Benjamin Zephaniah** (1958)
Penance for Jerry Kennedy (1985) **George V. Higgins** (1939)

Penance of John Logan, The (1889) **William Black** (1841)
Pending Heaven (1930) **William Gerhardie** (1895)
Penelope's Hat (1989) **Ronald Frame** (1953)
Penelopes Web (1587) **Robert Greene** (1558)
Penfriends From Porlock (1988) **A.N. Wilson** (1950)
Penhally (1931) **Caroline Gordon** (1895)
Penitent, The (1983) **Isaac Bashevis Singer** (1904)
Penmarric (1971) **Susan Howatch** (1940)
Pennies From Heaven (1981) **Dennis Potter** (1935)
Penniless Till Doomsday (1962) **Rodney Hall** (1935)
Pennington's Seventeenth Summer (1970) **K.M. Peyton** (1929)
Penny Arcade (1983) **Adrian Henri** (1932)
Penny Fiddle, The (1960) **Robert Graves** (1895)
Penny for a Song, A (1951) **John Whiting** (1917)
Penny for the Harp, A (1952) **Oliver Onions** (1873)
Penny Monypenny (1911) **Mary** (1865) and **Jane** (1866) **Findlater**
Penny Wheep (1926) **'Hugh MacDiarmid' [Christopher Murray Grieve]** (1892)
Penny-wise Pound-foolish (1631) **Thomas Dekker** (1572?)
Pennycomequicks, The (1889) **S. Baring-Gould** (1834)
Pennyles Pilgrimage, The (1618) **John Taylor** (1580)
Penrod (1914) **Booth Tarkington** (1869)
Penrod and Sam (1916) **Booth Tarkington** (1869)
Penrod Jashber (1929) **Booth Tarkington** (1869)
Penruddock (1873) **Charles Hamilton Aïdé** (1826)
Pensées d'août ['Thoughts of August'] (1837) **Charles-Augustin Sainte-Beuve** (1804)
Pentameron and Pentalogia, The (1837) **Walter Savage Landor** (1775)
Pentateuch, The (1530) **William Tyndale** (1494?) (tr.)
Pentecost (1995) **David Edgar** (1948)
Pentimento (1973) **Lillian Hellman** (1907)
Penultimate Poems (1989) **Gavin Ewart** (1916)
Peonies and Ponies (1941) **Sir Harold Acton** (1904)
People and Places (1985) **Richard Cobb** (1917)
People Are Curious (1938) **James Hanley** (1901)
People for Lunch (1987) **Georgina Hammick** (1939)
People in Glass Houses (1967) **Shirley Hazzard** (1931)
People Live Here (1983) **Louis Simpson** (1923)
People of Hemsö, The (1887) **August Strindberg** (1849)
People of the Abyss, The (1903) **'Jack London' [John Griffith Chaney]** (1876)
People of the Deer (1952) **Farley Mowat** (1921)
People of the Mist, The (1894) **Sir H. Rider Haggard** (1856)
People with the Dogs, The (1952) **Christina Stead** (1902)
People, Yes, The (1936) **Carl Sandburg** (1878)
People You Know (1903) **George Ade** (1866)
People's Otherworld, The (1983) **Les Murray** (1938)
People's Palace, The (1918) **Sir Sacheverell Sitwell** (1897)
People's Peace, The (1990) **Kenneth O. Morgan** (1934)
Peopled Landscape, A (1963) **Charles Tomlinson** (1927)
Peppered Moth, The (2001) **Margaret Drabble** (1939)
Peppermint Pig, The (1975) **Nina Bawden** (1925)
Per Amica Silentia Lunae (1918) **W.B. Yeats** (1865)
Perception, Physics and Reality (1914) **C.D. Broad** (1887)
Perchance to Dream [sequel to Raymond Chandler's *The Big Sleep*] (1991) **Robert B. Parker** (1932)
Percival (1801) **R.C. Dallas** (1754)
Percival Keene (1842) **Frederick Marryat** (1792)
Percy (1778) **Hannah More** (1745)
Percy, the Small Engine (1956) **Revd W. V. Awdry** (1911)
Perduta Gente (1989) **Peter Reading** (1946)
Peregrine Bunce; or, Settled at Last (1842) **Theodore Hook** (1788–1841)
Peregrine Pickle [**Smollett**]: see *The Adventures of Peregrine Pickle*
Peregrine's Saga, The (1923) **Henry Williamson** (1895)
Perelandra (1943) **C.S. Lewis** (1898)
Perennial (1946) **Oliver St Gogarty** (1878)
Perfect Happiness (1983) **Penelope Lively** (1933)
Perfect Man, The (1989) **Fiona Pitt-Kethley** (1954)
Perfect Murder, The [the first 'Inspector Ghote' novel] (1964) **H.R.F. Keating** (1926)
Perfect Spy, A (1986) **'John le Carré' [David John Moore Cornwell]** (1931)
Perfect Stranger, The (1966) **P.J. Kavanagh** (1931)
Perfect Stranger, A (1982) **Danielle Steel** (1947)
Perfect Wagnerite, The (1898) **Bernard Shaw** (1856)
Perfect Woman, A (1955) **L.P. Hartley** (1895)
Perfect Woman, A (1984) **Carolyn Slaughter** (1946)
Perfection (1836) **Thomas Haynes Bayly** (1797)
Perfervid (1890) **John Davidson** (1857)
Perfidious Brother, The (1716) **Lewis Theobald** (1688)
Perfidy (1961) **Ben Hecht** (1894)
Perfidy of Captain Slyboots, The (1863) **George Augustus Sala** (1828)
Perhaps Women (1931) **Sherwood Anderson** (1876)
Pericles and Aspasia (1836) **Walter Savage Landor** (1775)
Pericles, Prince of Tyre (1609) **William Shakespeare** (1564)
Pericles the Athenian (1963) **Rex Warner** (1905)
Peril (1884) **Jessie Fothergill** (1851)
Perilous Secret, A (1884) **Charles Reade** (1814–84)
Perimedes the Blacke-Smith (1588) **Robert Greene** (1558)
Period of Adjustment (1960) **'Tennessee' [Thomas Lanier] Williams** (1911)
Period Piece (1952) **Gwen Raverat** (1885)
Periodic Table, The [*Il sistemo periodico*] (1984) **Primo Levi** (1919)
Perishable Goods (1928) **'Dornford Yates' [Cecil William Mercer]** (1885)
Perjur'd Husband, The (1700) **Susanna Centlivre** (1669?)
Perlycross (1894) **R.D. Blackmore** (1825)
Permanent Red [US: *Towards Reality*] (1960) **John Berger** (1926)
Permit Me Voyage (1934) **James Agee** (1909)

Perourou, the Bellows-Mender (1799) **Helen Maria Williams** (1762)
Perpetua (1897) **S. Baring-Gould** (1834)
Perpetual Curate, The (1864) **Margaret Oliphant** (1828)
Perplex'd Dutchess, The (1727) **Eliza Haywood** (*c.* 1693)
Perplex'd Lovers, The (1712) **Susanna Centlivre** (1669?)
Perry Mason novels: see under Erle Stanley Gardner
Persephone in Winter (1937) **'Robin Hyde' [Iris Guiver Wilkinson]** (1906)
Perseus and Andromeda (1730) **Lewis Theobald** (1688)
Perseus in the Wind (1948) **Freya Stark** (1893)
Persian Boy, The (1972) **'Mary Renault' [Eileen Mary Challans]** (1905)
Persian Princess, The (1708) **Lewis Theobald** (1688)
Persian Tales [from the French] (1709) **Ambrose Philips** (1674) (tr.)
Persians, The (472 BC) **Aeschylus** (525–456BC)
Persistence in Folly (1984) **Les Murray** (1938)
Person of Quality's Answer to Mr Collier's Letter, The (1704) **[John Dennis]** (1657)
Person, Place and Thing (1942) **Karl Shapiro** (1913)
Personae (1909) **Ezra Pound** (1885)
Personal Column (1978) **Tom Paulin** (1949)
Personal Government of Charles I, The (1877) **S. R. Gardiner** (1829)
Personal Heresy, The (1939) **E.M.W. Tillyard** (1889) [with C.S. Lewis]
Personal History, A (1983) **A.J.P. Taylor]** (1906)
Personal History of David Copperfield, The (1850) **Charles Dickens** (1812)
Personal Injuries (1999) **Scott Turow** (1949)
Personal Narrative of a Pilgrimage to El-Medinah and Meccah (1855) **Sir Richard Burton** (1821)
Personal Recollections of Joan of Arc [supposedly tr. by 'Jean François Alden'] (1896) **'Mark Twain' [Samuel Langhorne Clemens]** (1835)
Personal Religion and the Life of Fellowship (1926) **William Temple** (1881)
Personal Reminiscences in Book-Making (1893) **R.M. Ballantyne** (1825)
Personal Reminiscences of Henry Irving (1906) **Bram Stoker** (1847)
Persons From Porlock (1969) **Louis MacNeice** (1907–63)
Persuasion [**Austen**]: see *Northanger Abbey*
Peru (1784) **Helen Maria Williams** (1762)
Petals on the Wind (1980) **Virginia Andrews** (1933)
Peter (1922) **E.F. Benson** (1867)
Peter Abelard (1933) **Helen Waddell** (1889)
Peter and Wendy (1911) **[Sir] J.M. Barrie** (1860)
Peter Ashley (1932) **DuBose Heyward** (1885)
Peter Bell (1819) **J.H. Reynolds** (1796)
Peter Bell (1819) **William Wordsworth** (1770)
Peter Camenzind (1904) **Hermann Hesse** (1877)
Peter Faultless to His Brother Simon (1820) **Ebenezer Elliott** (1781)
Peter Homunculus (1909) **Gilbert Cannan** (1884)
Peter Ibbetson (1892) **George du Maurier** (1834)
Peter Pan in Kensington Gardens (1906) **[Sir] J.M. Barrie** (1860)
Peter Simple (1833) **Frederick Marryat** (1792)
Peter Smart's Confessions (1977) **Paul Bailey** (1937)
Peter the Whaler (1851) **W.H.G. Kingston** (1814)
Peter's Pence (1974) **Jon Cleary** (1917)
Petit chose, Le (1868) **Alphonse Daudet** (1840)
Petit Testament [also known as the *Lais*] (1456) **François Villon** (*c.* 1431)
Petite Pallace of Pettie his Pleasure, A (1576) **George Pettie** (1548)
Petits poèmes en prose ['Little Poems in Prose'] (1869) **Charles Baudelaire** (1821–67)
Petrarch's Seven Penitential Psalms (1612) **George Chapman** (1559?) (tr.)
Petrified Forest, The (1935) **Robert E. Sherwood** (1896)
Petruchia [US: *Modesta*] (1929) **G.B. Stern** (1890)
Petticoat Government (1850) **Frances Trollope** (1780)
Peveril of the Peak (1822) **Sir Walter Scott** (1771)
Peyton Place (1956) **Grace Metalious** (1924)
Phaedrus and Hippolytus [*Phèdre et Hippolyte*] (1677) **Jean Racine** (1639)
Phaeton (1698) **Charles Gildon** (1665)
Phaeton (1852) **Charles Kingsley** (1819)
Phallic Forest, The (1978) **Michael Wilding** (1942)
Phantasmagoria (1869) **'Lewis Carroll' [Charles Lutwidge Dodgson]** (1832)
Phantasmion (1837) **Sara Coleridge** (1802)
Phantastes (1858) **George MacDonald** (1824)
Phantom Army, The (1898) **Max Pemberton** (1863)
Phantom Death, The (1895) **W. Clark Russell** (1844)
Phantom Fortune (1883) **M.E. Braddon** (1835)
Phantom Future, The (1888) **'Henry Seton Merriman' [Hugh Stowell Scott]** (1862)
Phantom Lady [as 'William Irish'] (1942) **Cornell Woolrich** (1903)
Phantom Lobster (1933) **Leo Walmsley** (1892)
Phantom Lover, A (1886) **'Vernon Lee' [Violet Paget]** (1856)
Phantom of Manhattan, The (1999) **Frederick Forsyth** (1938)
Phantom of the Opera, The [*Le Fantôme de l'Opéra*] (1911) **Gaston Leroux** (1868)
Phantom Regiment, The (1856) **James Grant** (1822)
Phantom 'Rickshaw, The (1888) **Rudyard Kipling** (1865)
Phantom Ship, The (1839) **Frederick Marryat** (1792)
Phantoms (1983) **Dean Koontz** (1945)
Pharais [as 'Fiona Macleod'] (1894) **William Sharp** (1855)
Pharaohs, Fellahs, and Explorers (1891) **Amelia B. Edwards** (1831)
Pharisees and Publicans (1926) **E.F. Benson** (1867)
Pharonnida (1659) **William Chamberlayne** (1619)
Pharos and Pharillon (1923) **E.M. Forster** (1879)
Pharsalia [*Lucan*] (1614) **Sir Arthur Gorges** (1577?) (tr.)
Phèdre [music by Georges Auric] (1950) **Jean Cocteau** (1889)

Phedre (1998) **Ted Hughes** (1930) (tr.)
Phil-o-Rum's Canoe, and Madeleine de Verchères (1898) **William Henry Drummond** (1854)
Philadelphia, Here I Come! (1964) **Brian Friel** (1929)
Philadelphia Negro, The (1899) **W.E.B. du Bois** (*c.* 1868)
Philander (1758) **Charlotte Lennox** (1720)
Philanderers, The (1897) **A.E.W. Mason** (1865)
Philanthropist, The (1970) **Christopher Hampton** (1946)
Philaster (1695) **Elkanah Settle** (1648)
Philby Affair, The (1968) **Hugh Trevor-Roper** (1914)
Philidore and Placentia (1727) **Eliza Haywood** (*c.* 1693)
Philip Augustus (1831) **G.P.R. James** (1799)
Philip Larkin (1975) **Alan Brownjohn** (1931)
Philip Larkin (1993) **Andrew Motion** (1952)
Philip Rollo (1854) **James Grant** (1822)
Philip the King (1914) **John Masefield** (1878)
Philip van Artevelde (1834) **Sir Henry Taylor** (1800)
Philistines (1902) **Maxim Gorky** (1868)
Phillis (1593) **Thomas Lodge** (1558)
Philocothonista (1635) **Thomas Heywood** (1574?)
Philoctetes (409 BC) **Sophocles** (*c.* 496 BC)
Philomela (1592) **Robert Greene** (1558)
Philosopher Jack (1880) **R.M. Ballantyne** (1825)
Philosopher's Pupil, The (1983) **Iris Murdoch** (1919)
Philosophia Pia (1671) **Joseph Glanvill** (1636)
Philosophiae Naturalis Principia Mathematica [in Latin] (1687) **Sir Isaac Newton** (1642)
Philosophical Dictionary for the Pocket, The [*Dictionnaire philosophique portatif*] (1764) **'Voltaire' [François-Marie Arouet]** (1694)
Philosophical Discourse of Earth, A (1676) **John Evelyn** (1620)
Philosophical Enquiry Concerning Human Liberty (1715) **Anthony Collins** (1676)
Philosophical Enquiry into the Sublime and Beautiful, A (1757) **Edmund Burke** (1729)
Philosophical Essays (1810) **Dugald Stewart** (1753)
Philosophical Essays (1910) **Bertrand Russell** (1872)
Philosophical Essays Concerning Human Understanding (1748) **David Hume** (1711)
Philosophical Essays on Various Subjects (1733) **Isaac Watts** (1674)
Philosophical, Historical and Moral Essay on Old Maids, A (1785) **William Hayley** (1745)
Philosophical Investigations (1953) **Ludwig Wittgenstein** (1889–51)
Philosophical Opinion in America (1918) **George Santayana** (1863)
Philosophical Papers (1959) **G.E. Moore** (1873–1958)
Philosophical Rudiments Concerning Government and Society (1651) **Thomas Hobbes** (1588)
Philosophical Studies (1922) **G.E. Moore** (1873)
Philosophical Thoughts [*Pensées philosophiques*] (1746) **Denis Diderot** (1713–84)
Philosophical Works (1754) **Henry Saint-John, Viscount Bolingbroke** (1678–1751)
Philosophicall Poems (1647) **Henry More** (1614)
Philosophie, Commonlie Called, the Morals, The [Plutarch: *Moralia*] (1603) **Philemon Holland** (1552) (tr.)
Philosophy of Common Sense, The (1907) **Frederic Harrison** (1831)
Philosophy of Melancholy, The (1812) **Thomas Love Peacock** (1785)
Philosophy of Modern Art, The (1952) **Sir Herbert Read** (1893)
Philosophy of Plotinus, The (1918) **W.R. Inge** (1860)
Philosophy of Solitude, A (1933) **John Cooper Powys** (1872)
Philosophy of the Active and Moral Powers, The (1828) **Dugald Stewart** (1753)
Philosophy of the Inductive Sciences, The (1840) **William Whewell** (1794)
Phineas Finn (1869) **Anthony Trollope** (1815)
Phineas Redux (1874) **Anthony Trollope** (1815)
Phoebe Junior (1876) **Margaret Oliphant** (1828)
Phoenician Women, The (*c.* 410) **Euripides** (480 BC)
Phoenix, The (1607) **Thomas Middleton** (1580)
Phoenix (1923) **Lascelles Abercrombie** (1881)
Phoenix [posthumous papers] (1936) **D.H. Lawrence** (1885–1930)
Phoenix and the Carpet, The (1904) **E[dith] Nesbit** (1858)
Phoenix and the Tortoise, The (1944) **Kenneth Rexroth** (1905)
Phoenix Too Frequent, A (1946) **Christopher Fry [Christopher Fry Harris]** (1907)
Phoenix Tree, The (1984) **Jon Cleary** (1917)
Photo the Suliote (1857) **David Morier** (1784)
Phylaster (1620) **Francis Beaumont** (1585?-1616) [with John Fletcher]
Phyllyp Sparowe (1545?) **John Skelton** (1460?–1529)
Physician to His Own Honour [*El médico de su honra*] (1635) **Pedro Calderón de la Barca** (1600)
Physics and Politics (1872) **Walter Bagehot** (1826)
Physiology of Taste, The [*Physiologie du goût ou Méditations sur la gastronomie transcendente*] (1825) **Anthelme Brillat-Savarin** (1755)
Phytologia (1800) **Erasmus Darwin** (1731)
Pianoplayers, The (1986) **'Anthony Burgess' [John Anthony Burgess Wilson]** (1917)
Piazza Tales, The (1856) **Herman Melville** (1819)
Pic (1971) **Jack Kerouac** (1922–69)
Picasso (1938) **Gertrude Stein** (1874)
Piccadilly Jim (1918) **P.G. Wodehouse** (1881)
Piccadilly (1870) **Laurence Oliphant** (1829)
Piccadilly Puzzle, The (1889) **Fergus Hume** (1859)
Piccolomini, The (1800) **S.T. Coleridge** (1772) (tr.)
Picking Up Pieces (1975) **John Updike** (1932)
Pickle the Spy (1897) **Andrew Lang** (1844)
Picnic, The (1937) **Martin Boyd** (1893)
Picnic (1953) **William Inge** (1913)
Picnic at Sakkara, The (1955) **P.H. Newby** (1918)
Picnic on Paradise (1968) **Joanna Russ** (1937)
Picture, The (1630) **Philip Massinger** (1583)
Picture, The (1766) **Susannah Gunning** (1740) [with Margaret Minifie]
Picture, The (1803) **William Lisle Bowles** (1762)
Picture and Text (1893) **Henry James** (1843)

Picture of Dorian Gray, The (1891) **Oscar Wilde** (1854)
Picture Palace (1978) **Paul Theroux** (1941)
Picture Show (1919) **Siegfried Sassoon** (1886)
Picture This (1988) **Joseph Heller** (1923)
Picturegoers, The (1960) **David Lodge** (1935)
Pictures from Brueghel (1963) **William Carlos Williams** (1883)
Pictures from Italy (1846) **Charles Dickens** (1812)
Pictures From the Gone World (1955) **Lawrence Ferlinghetti** (1920)
Pictures in the Fire (1958) **John Collier** (1901)
Pictures in the Hallway (1942) **Sean O'Casey** (1880)
Pictures of Fidelman (1969) **Bernard Malamud** (1914)
Pictures of the Floating World (1919) **Amy Lowell** (1874)
Pictures of Travel [*Reisebilder*; vols. i, ii] (1826–7) **Heinrich Heine** (1797)
Pictures of Travel [*Reisebilder*; vols. iii, iv] (1830–1) **Heinrich Heine** (1797)
Picturesque Remarks on Western Parts of England and the Isle of Wight (1798) **William Gilpin** (1724)
Pie-Dish, The (1908) **George Fitzmaurice** (1878)
Piece of My Heart, A (1976) **Richard Ford** (1944)
Piece of My Mind, A (1956) **Edmund Wilson** (1895)
Piece of the Night, A (1978) **Michèle Roberts** (1949)
Piece of the Sky is Missing, A (1965) **David Nobbs** (1935)
Pied Piper (1941) **'Nevil Shute' [Nevil Shute Norway]** (1899)
Pied Piper of Lovers (1935) **Lawrence Durrell** (1912)
Piemakers, The (1967) **Helen Cresswell** (1934)
Pier-Glass, The (1921) **Robert Graves** (1895)
Pierce Penilesse his Supplication to the Divell (1592) **Thomas Nashe** (1567)
Pierces Supererogation (1593) **Gabriel Harvey** (1550)
Pierre (1852) **Herman Melville** (1819)
Pierre et Jean (1888) **Guy de Maupassant** (1850)
Pierre Nozière (1899) **'Anatole France' [Jacques-Anatole-François Thibault]** (1844)
Pierrot [*Pierrot Mon Ami*] (1942) **Raymond Queneau** (1903)
Pierrot! (1896) **Henry de Vere Stacpoole** (1863)
Pierrot of the Minute, The (1897) **Ernest Dowson** (1867)
Piers Plainnes Seaven Yeres Prentiship (1595) **Henry Chettle** (1560?)
Piers Ploughman [**Langland**]: see *The Vision of Pierce Plowman*
Pietà (1966) **R.S. Thomas** (1913)
Pietro Ghisleri (1893) **F. Marion Crawford** (1854)
Pig Earth (1979) **John Berger** (1926)
Pig in the Middle (1965) **William Mayne** (1928)
Pig Island Letters (1966) **James K. Baxter** (1926)
Pigeon Feathers (1962) **John Updike** (1932)
Pigeon Irish (1932) **Francis Stuart** (1902)
Pigeon Post (1936) **Arthur Ransome** (1884)
Pigeons and Princesses (1956) **James Reeves** (1909)
Pigs Have Wings (1952) **P.G. Wodehouse** (1881)
Pigs in Clover (1902) **'Frank Danby' [Julia Frankau]** (1864)
Pike County Ballads (1871) **John Hay** (1838)
Pilgermann (1983) **Russell Hoban** (1925)
Pilgrim, The (1775) **Charles Johnstone** (1719?)
Pilgrim, The (1700) **Sir John Vanbrugh** (1664)
Pilgrim Hawk, The (1940) **Glenway Wescott** (1901)
Pilgrim of Glencoe, The (1842) **Thomas Campbell** (1777)
Pilgrim of Hate, The (1984) **'Ellis Peters' [Edith Mary Pargeter]** (1913)
Pilgrim of the Void (1990) **Kenneth White** (1936)
Pilgrim's Progress From This World, The (1678) **John Bunyan** (1628)
Pilgrim's Progress: The Second Part, The (1684) **John Bunyan** (1628)
Pilgrim's Regress, The (1933) **C.S. Lewis** (1898)
Pilgrimage (1938) **Dorothy M. Richardson** (1873)
Pilgrimage of Festus, The (1923) **Conrad Potter Aiken** (1889)
Pilgrimage to Paradise, The (1592) **Nicholas Breton** (1545?)
Pilgrimes Solace, A (1612) **John Dowland** (1563)
Pilgrims in a Foreign Land (1942) **Caradoc Evans** (1878)
Pilgrims of the Rhine, The (1834) **Edward Bulwer-Lytton** (1803)
Pilgrims of the Sun, The (1815) **James Hogg** (1770)
Pill Versus the Springfield Mine Disaster, The (1968) **Richard Brautigan** (1935)
Pillar of Cloud, The (1948) **Francis Stuart** (1902)
Pillar of State (1972) **Elizabeth Longford** (1906)
Pillar to Post (1938) **Osbert Lancaster** (1908)
Pillars of Gold (1992) **'Alice Thomas Ellis' [Anna Margaret Haycraft]** (1932)
Pillars of the House, The (1873) **Charlotte M. Yonge** (1823)
Pilot, The (1823) **James Fenimore Cooper** (1789)
Pin to See the Peepshow, A (1934) **F. Tennyson Jesse** (1888)
Pin-Money (1831) **Mrs C.F. Gore** (1799)
Pinch of Snuff, A (1978) **Reginald Hill** (1936)
Pincher Martin [US: *The Two Deaths of Christopher Martin*] (1956) **William Golding** (1911)
Pindar in English Verse (1833) **Henry Cary** (1772) (tr.)
Pink and White Tyranny (1871) **Harriet Beecher Stowe** (1811)
Pink Fairy Book, The (1897) **Andrew Lang** (1844) (ed.)
Pink Triangle and Yellow Star (1982) **Gore Vidal** (1925)
Pinocchio (1883) **'Carlo Collodi' [Carlo Lorenzini]** (1826)
Pioneers on Parade (1939) **Miles Franklin** (1879) [with Dymphna Cusak]
Pioneers, The, (1872) **R.M. Ballantyne** (1825)
Pioneers, The (1823) **James Fenimore Cooper** (1789)
'Pip' (1907) **'Ian Hay' [John Hay Beith]** (1876)
Pipe Night (1945) **John O'Hara** (1905)
Pipers and a Dancer (1924) **Stella Benson** (1892)
Piping Hot! [Pot-Bouille] (1882) **Émile Zola** (1840)
Pipistrello (1880) **'Ouida' [Marie Louise de la Ramée]** (1839)
Pippa Passes (1994) **Rumer Godden** (1907)

Pippi Longstocking (1945) **Astrid Lindgren** (1907)
Pique (1850) **Sarah [Mrs William] Ellis** (1812)
Pirate, The (1822) **Sir Walter Scott** (1771)
Pirate, The (1974) **Harold Robbins** (1912)
Pirate and the Three Cutters, The (1836) **Frederick Marryat** (1792)
Pirate City, The (1874) **R.M. Ballantyne** (1825)
Pirates of Penzance, The [music by Sir Arthur Sullivan] (1879) **W.S. Gilbert** (1836)
Pirates of the Spring (1919) **Forrest Reid** (1875)
Pisgah-Sight of Palestine, A (1650) **Thomas Fuller** (1608)
Pistol, The (1959) **James Jones** (1921)
Pit, The (1903) **Frank Norris** (1870)
Pity Is Not Enough (1933) **Josephine Herbst** (1897)
Pity, The (1967) **Ken Smith** (1938)
Pizarro [from Kotzebue] (1799) **Richard Brinsley Sheridan** (1753)
Place Among People, A (1975) **Rodney Hall** (1935)
Place at Whitton, The (1964) **Thomas Keneally** (1935)
Place Called Estherville, A (1949) **Erskine Caldwell** (1903)
Place in England, A (1970) **Melvyn Bragg** (1939)
Place of English Literature in the Modern University, The (1913) **Sir Sidney Lee** (1859)
Place of Greater Safety, A (1992) **Hilary Mantel** (1952)
Place of the Dead Roads, The (1984) **William S. Burroughs** (1914)
Place of the Lion, The (1931) **Charles Williams** (1886)
Place To Come To, A (1977) **Robert Penn Warren** (1905)
Place Where Souls Are Born, The (1992) **Thomas Keneally** (1935)
Place with the Pigs, A (1987) **Athol Fugard** (1932)
Place's Fault, The (1964) **Philip Hobsbaum** (1932)
Places Where I've Done Time (1972) **William Saroyan** (1908)
Places Where They Sing (1970) **Simon Raven** (1927)
Placid Pug, The (1906) **Lord Alfred Douglas** (1870)
Plague Court Murders, The (1934) **John Dickson Carr** (1906)
Plague Dogs, The (1977) **Richard Adams** (1920)
Plague Ship (1977) **Frank G. Slaughter** (1908)
Plague, The [*La Peste*] (1947) **Albert Camus** (1913)
Plagued by the Nightingale (1931) **Kay Boyle** (1903)
Plain Account of Christian Perfection, A (1766) **John Wesley** (1703)
Plain Account of the Nature and End of the Sacrament, A (1735) **Benjamin Hoadly** (1676)
Plain Account of the People Called Methodists, A (1749) **John Wesley** (1703)
Plain and Continued Exposition of the Prophecies of Daniel, A (1681) **Henry More** (1614)
Plain Brown Rapper (1976) **Rita Mae Brown** (1944)
Plain Frances Mowbray (1889) **Emily Lawless** (1845)
Plain Jane (1927) **A.P. Herbert** (1890)
Plain Living (1898) **'Rolf Boldrewood' [Thomas Alexander Browne]** (1826)
Plain or Ringlets? (1860) **R.S. Surtees** (1805)
Plain Pleasures (1966) **Jane Bowles** (1917)
Plain Speaker, The (1825) **William Hazlitt** (1778)
Plain Tales From the Hills (1888) **Rudyard Kipling** (1865)
Plain Truth (1747) **Benjamin Franklin** (1706)
Plain Words (1948) **Sir Ernest Gowers** (1880)
Plain-Dealer, The (1676) **William Wycherley** (1641)
Plains of Cement, The (1934) **Patrick Hamilton** (1904)
Plains of Passage, The (1990) **Jean M. Auel** (1936)
Plan of a Dictionary of the English Language, The (1747) **Samuel Johnson** (1709)
Planes of Bedford Square, The (1971) **William Plomer** (1903)
Planet News (1968) **Allen Ginsberg** (1926)
Planet of Junior Brown, The (1971) **Virginia Hamilton** (1936)
Planet of the Apes [*La Planete des Singes*] (1959) **Pierre Boulle** (1912)
Planetomachia (1585) **Robert Greene** (1558)
Plant and Phantom (1941) **Louis MacNeice** (1907)
Plantain (1921) **'Anna Akhmatova' [Anna Andreevna Gorenko]** (1889)
Planters Manual, The (1675) **Charles Cotton** (1630)
Platform of Church-Discipline, A (1649) **Richard Mather** (1596)
Plato and Platonism (1893) **Walter Pater** (1839)
Plato and the Other Companions of Sokrates (1865) **George Grote** (1794)
Plato Papers, The (1999) **Peter Ackroyd** (1949)
Plato Park (1987) **Carol Rumens** (1944)
Plato's Ladder (1992) **Stephen Romer** (1957)
Platonick Lady, The (1706) **Susanna Centlivre** (1669?)
Platonick Lovers, The (1636) **Sir William Davenant** (1606)
Platonism and the Spiritual Life (1927) **George Santayana** (1863)
Plattner Story, and Others, The (1897) **H.G. Wells** (1866)
Play Actress, The (1894) **S.R. Crockett** (1860)
Play it as it Lays (1970) **Joan Didion** (1934)
Play of Giants, A (1984) **Wole Soyinka** (1934)
Play of Love, A (1534) **John Heywood** (1497?)
Play of the Wether, The (1533) **John Heywood** (1497?)
Play Resumed (1999) **D.J. Enright** (1920)
Play Room, The [US. *The Camperlea Girls*] (1969) **Olivia Manning** (1908)
Play-Making (1912) **William Archer** (1856)
Playback (1958) **Raymond Chandler** (1888)
Playboy of the Western World, The (1907) **J.M. Synge** (1871)
Player King, The (1952) **Christopher Hassall** (1912)
Player of Games, The (1988) **Iain M. Banks** (1954)
Player Piano (1952) **Kurt Vonnegut** (1922)
Player Queen, The (1922) **W.B. Yeats** (1865)
Players (1977) **Don DeLillo** (1936)
Playes Confuted in Five Actions (1582) **Stephen Gosson** (1554)
Playfellow, The (1841) **Harriet Martineau** (1802)

Playground of Europe, The (1871) **Sir Leslie Stephen** (1832)
Playgrounds of the Mind (1992) **Larry Niven** (1938)
Playing a Dazzler (1996) **James Berry** (1924)
Playing for Time (1981) **Arthur Miller** (1915)
Playing in the Dark (1992) **Toni Morrison** (1931)
Playing the Mischief (1875) **John W. De Forest** (1826)
Playing with Fire (1887) **James Grant** (1822)
Playing With Fire (1933) **Alec Waugh** (1898)
Playing with Trains (1989) **Stephen Poliakoff** (1952)
Playland (1992) **Athol Fugard** (1932)
Playmaker, The (1987) **Thomas Keneally** (1935)
Plays (1894) **John Davidson** (1857)
Plays and Poems of William Shakespeare, The (1790) **Edmond Malone** (1741) (ed.)
Plays and Puritans (1873) **Charles Kingsley** (1819)
Plays for Bleecker Street (1962) **Thornton Wilder** (1897)
Plays For England [The Blood of the Bambergs; Under Plain Cover] (1963) **John Osborne** (1929)
Plays for Plain People (1944) **'James Bridie' [Osborne Henry Mavor]** (1888)
Plays for Public Places (1972) **Howard Brenton** (1942)
Plays for Radio 1964–1983 (1990) **Tom Stoppard** (1937)
Plays of Gods and Men (1917) **Lord Dunsany** (1878)
Plays of the Natural and the Supernatural (1916) **Theodore Dreiser** (1871)
Plays of William Shakespeare, The (1765) **Samuel Johnson** (1709) (ed.)
Plays of William Shakespeare, The (1773) **George Steevens** (1736) (ed)
Plays on the Passions [vol. i] (1798, 1802, 1812) **Joanna Baillie** (1762)
Plays: One (1987) **David Edgar** (1948)
Plays Pleasant and Unpleasant (1898) **Bernard Shaw** (1856)
Plays: Two (1989) **David Edgar** (1948)
Plays: Three (1991) **David Edgar** (1948)
Playthings and Parodies (1893) **'Barry Pain' [Eric Odell]** (1864)
Plaza Suite (1968) **Neil Simon** (1927)
Plea for the Constitution, A (1803) **Jeremy Bentham** (1748)
Plea of the Midsummer Fairies, The (1827) **Thomas Hood** (1799)
Pleading Guilty (1993) **Scott Turow** (1949)
Pleasant Historie of Jack of Newberie, The (1597) **Thomas Deloney** (1543?)
Pleasant History of John Winchcomb, The (1619) **Thomas Deloney** (1543?-1600)
Pleasant Valley (1945) **Louis Bromfield** (1896)
Pleasure (1921) **Alec Waugh** (1898)
Pleasure Dome, The (1972) **Graham Greene** (1904)
Pleasure Garden, The (1976) **Leon Garfield** (1921)
Pleasure of Ruins (1953) **Rose Macaulay** (1881)
Pleasure Steamers, The (1978) **Andrew Motion** (1952)
Pleasures of England, The (1884) **John Ruskin** (1819)
Pleasures of Exile, The (1960) **George Lamming** (1927)
Pleasures of Hope, The (1799) **Thomas Campbell** (1777)
Pleasures of Imagination, The (1744) **Mark Akenside** (1721)
Pleasures of Melancholy, The (1747) **Thomas Warton, the Younger** (1728)
Pleasures of Memory, The [A Poem in Two Parts] (1792) **Samuel Rogers** (1763)
Pleasures of Peace, The (1969) **Kenneth Koch** (1925)
Pleasures of the Flesh (1966) **Gavin Ewart** (1916)
Pleasures Strange and Simple (1953) **William Sansom** (1912)
Plebian's Progress, The (1933) **Frank Tilsey** (1904)
Pledge of Peace, The (1938) **John Middleton Murry** (1889)
Plenty (1978) **David Hare** (1947)
Plexippus (1790) **Richard Graves** (1715)
Plexus (1953) **Henry Miller** (1891)
Plot and No Plot, A (1697) **John Dennis** (1657)
Plough and Furrow (1963) **Paul Green** (1894)
Plough and the Stars, The (1926) **Sean O'Casey** (1880)
Ploughing Match, The (1968) **Fred Urquhart** (1912)
Ploughman, The (1935) **Patrick White** (1912)
Ploughman (1936) **Patrick Kavanagh** (1904)
Pluck and Luck (1925) **Robert Benchley** (1889)
Pluies ['Rain'] (1944) **'Saint-John Perse' [Alexis Saint-Léger Léger]** (1887)
Plumb (1978) **Maurice Gee** (1931)
Plumbum (1983) **David Foster** (1944)
Plumed Serpent, The (1926) **D.H. Lawrence** (1885)
Pluralistic Universe, A (1909) **William James** (1842)
Plus Ultra (1668) **Joseph Glanvill** (1636)
Plutocrat, The (1927) **Booth Tarkington** (1869)
Plutonian Ode (1981) **Allen Ginsberg** (1926)
Plutus (382BC) **Aristophanes** (*c.* 445BC)
Pnin (1957) **Vladimir Nabokov** (1899)
Poacher, The (1935) **H.E. Bates** (1905)
Pocket Mirror, The (1967) **Janet Frame** (1924)
Pocketful of Rye, A (1953) **Agatha Christie** (1890)
Pocketful of Rye, A (1969) **A.J. Cronin** (1896)
Poellenberg Inheritance, The (1972) **'Evelyn Anthony' [Evelyn Ward-Thomas]** (1928)
Poem of Poems, The (1596) **Gervaise Markham** (1568?)
Poem on St James's Park, A (1661) **Edmund Waller** (1606)
Poem on the Marriage of the Duke of Newcastle, A (1717) **Laurence Eusden** (1688)
Poem on the South Sea, A (1720) **Allan Ramsay** (1686)
Poem on the the Last Day, A (1713) **Edward Young** (1683)
Poem to the Memory of John Cunningham (1773) **Robert Fergusson** (1750)
Poem Without a Hero (1960) **'Anna Akhmatova' [Anna Andreevna Gorenko]** (1889)
Poemes Lyrick and Pastorall (1606) **Michael Drayton** (1563)
Poèmes saturniens ['Saturnine Poems'] (1866) **Paul Verlaine** (1844)
Poems (1605) **Michael Drayton** (1563)
Poems (1645) **Edmund Waller** (1606)

Poems (1717) **Wentworth Dillon, 4th earl of Roscommon** (1633–85) and others
Poems (1720) **Allan Ramsay** (1686)
Poems (1768) **Thomas Gray** (1716)
Poems (1773) **Robert Fergusson** (1750)
Poems (1777) **Thomas Warton, the Younger** (1728)
Poems (1786) **Philip Freneau** (1752)
Poems (1792) **George Dyer** (1755)
Poems (1795) **Robert Southey** [with Robert Lovell] (1774)
Poems, (1796) **Robert Southey** (1774)
Poems (1812) **Samuel Rogers** (1763)
Poems (1817) **John Keats** (1795)
Poems [inc. 'The Lady of Shalott', 'Mariana in the South', Oenone'] (1833) **Alfred, Lord Tennyson** (1809)
Poems (1843) **William Ellery Channing** (1780)
Poems (1851) **George Meredith** (1828)
Poems (1863) **Jean Ingelow** (1820)
Poems (1870) **Dante Gabriel Rossetti** (1828)
Poems (1876) **Edward Dowden** (1843)
Poems (1881) **Oscar Wilde** (1854)
Poems (1890) **Christina Rossetti** (1830)
Poems (1893) **Francis Thompson** (1859)
Poems (1895) **W.B. Yeats** (1865)
Poems [ed. Robert Bridges] (1918) **Gerard Manley Hopkins** (1844–89)
Poems (1920) **Wilfred Owen** (1893–1918)
Poems (1933) **Sir Stephen Spender** (1909)
Poems (1939) **Roy Fuller** (1912)
Poems (1974) **Padraic Fallon** (1906–74)
Poems, 1899–1905 (1906) **W.B. Yeats** (1865)
Poems 1901 to 1918 (1920) **Walter de la Mare** (1873)
Poems 1909–25 (1925) **T.S. Eliot** (1888)
Poems 1914–26 (1927) **Robert Graves** (1895)
Poems 1919 to 1934 (1935) **Walter de la Mare** (1873)
Poems 1926–1930 (1931) **Robert Graves** (1895)
Poems 1930–32 (1933) **'John Gawsworth' [Terence Ian Fytton Armstrong]** (1912)
Poems 1930–1933 (1933) **Robert Graves** (1895)
Poems 1937–1942 (1943) **David Gascoyne** (1916)
Poems 1938–1945 (1946) **Robert Graves** (1895)
Poems 1949–57 (1957) **Allen Curnow** (1911)
Poems: 1950 (1950) **Basil Bunting** (1900)
Poems 1953 (1953) **Robert Graves** (1895)
Poems 1955–1980 (1980) **Roy Fisher** (1930)
Poems 1960–2000 (2000) **Fleur Adcock**
Poems 1965–1968 (1968) **Robert Graves** (1895)
Poems: A New Edition (1853) **Matthew Arnold** (1822)
Poems About God (1919) **John Crowe Ransom** (1888)
Poems Against Economics (1972) **Les Murray** (1938)
Poems Ancient & Modern (1964) **Peter Porter** (1929)
Poems and Ballads [1st ser.] (1866) **A.C. Swinburne** (1837)
Poems and Ballads (1896) **Sir A.T. Quiller-Couch** (1863)
Poems and Ballads (1910) **Henry de Vere Stacpoole** (1863)
Poems and Ballads of Goethe (1859) **W.E. Aytoun** (1813) (tr.)
Poems and Ballads of Schiller, The (1844) **Edward Bulwer-Lytton** (1803)
Poems and Ballads: Second Series (1878) **A.C. Swinburne** (1837)
Poems and Ballads: Third Series (1889) **A.C. Swinburne** (1837)
Poems and Contradictions (1945) **Rex Warner** (1905)
Poems and Critical Essays (1802) **George Dyer** (1755)
Poems and Lyrics of the Joy of Earth (1883) **George Meredith** (1828)
Poems and Poets (1969) **Geoffrey Grigson** (1905)
Poems and Problems (1971) **Vladimir Nabokov** (1899)
Poems and Satires (1951) **Robert Graves** (1895)
Poems and Songs (1939) **Gavin Ewart** (1916)
Poems and Translations (1647) **Thomas Stanley the Elder** (1625)
Poems and Translations (1668) **Sir John Denham** (1615)
Poems and Translations (1812) **Reginald Heber** (1783)
Poems and Translations (1909) **J.M. Synge** (1871)
Poems and Versions (1983) **Padraic Fallon** (1906–74)
Poems at White-Nights (1899) **Gordon Bottomley** (1874)
Poems Before Congress (1860) **E.B. Browning** (1806)
Poems Brief and New (1925) **Sir William Watson** (1858)
Poems by Currer, Ellis and Acton Bell (1846) **Charlotte** (1816), Emily (1818), and Anne (1820) Brontë
Poems by Edgar A. Poe (1831) **Edgar Allan Poe** (1809)
Poems by Emily Dickinson (1890) **Emily Dickinson** (1830–86)
Poems (1633) **John Donne** (1572–1631)
Poems by Melanter (1853) **R.D. Blackmore** (1825)
Poems by . . . the Matchless Orinda (1667) **Katherine Philips** (1632–64)
Poems By the Way (1891) **William Morris** (1834)
Poems (1614) **William Drummond of Hawthornden** (1585)
Poems, &c. on Several Occasions (1691) **John Wilmot, earl of Rochester** (1647–80)
Poems Chiefly in the Scottish Dialect (1786) **Robert Burns** (1759)
Poems, Chiefly Lyrical [inc. 'Mariana', 'The Kraken'] (1830) **Alfred, Lord Tennyson** (1809)
Poems Descriptive of Rural Life and Scenery (1820) **John Clare** (1793)
Poems, Elegies, Paradoxes, and Sonnets (1657) **Henry King** (1592)
Poems, Fables, and Plays (1756) **Edward Moore** (1712)
Poems for all the Annettes (1962) **Al Purdy** (1918)
Poems for Music (1947) **Robert Hillyer** (1895)
Poems For Our Children [inc. 'Mary Had a Little Lamb'] (1830) **Sarah Hale** (1788)
Poems for Pictures and for Notes of Music (1900) **Ford Madox Ford** (1873)

Poems for Young Ladies (1767) **Oliver Goldsmith** (1728)
Poems From Algiers (1970) **Dennis Brutus** (1924)
Poems From Prison (1969) **Wole Soyinka** (1934)
Poems from the Arabic and Persian (1800) **Walter Savage Landor** (1775) (tr.)
Poems, Golders Green (1962) **Dannie Abse** (1923)
Poems in Burlesque (1692) **John Dennis** (1657)
Poems in the Porch (1954) **Sir John Betjeman** (1906)
Poems, in Two Volumes (1807) **William Wordsworth** (1770)
Poems in Wartime (1940) **C. Day Lewis** (1904)
Poems: New and Old (1912) **Sir Henry Newbolt** (1862)
Poems of a Jew (1958) **Karl Shapiro** (1913)
Poems of Arthur Conan Doyle, The (1922) **A. Conan Doyle** (1859)
Poems of Conformity (1917) **Charles Williams** (1886)
Poems of Dedication (1946) **Sir Stephen Spender** (1909)
Poems of East and West (1917) **Vita Sackville-West** (1892)
Poems of Five Decades (1954) **Max Eastman** (1883)
Poems of Impudence (1926) **E.V. Knox** (1881)
Poems of John Donne, The (1912) **H.J.C. Grierson** (1866) (ed.)
Poems of Love and Death (1980) **George MacBeth** (1932)
Poems of Love and Earth (1912) **John Drinkwater** (1882)
Poems of Many Years (1840) **Richard Monckton Milnes** (1809)
Poems of Many Years (1957) **Edmund Blunden** (1896)
Poems of Men and Hours (1911) **John Drinkwater** (1882)
Poems of Mr John Milton, Both English and Latin (1645) **John Milton** (1608)
Poems of Places and People (1971) **George Barker** (1913)
Poems of Rural Life in Common English (1868) **William Barnes** (1801)
Poems of Rural Life in the Dorset Dialect (1844) **William Barnes** (1801)
Poems of the East-West Synthesis (1946) **'Hugh MacDiarmid' [Christopher Murray Grieve]** (1892)
Poems of the Orient (1855) **Bayard Taylor** (1825)
Poems of the Past and Present (1910) **Radclyffe Hall** (1880)
Poems of the Past and the Present (1901) **Thomas Hardy** (1840)
Poems of Thirty Years (1925) **Gordon Bottomley** (1874)
Poems of Two Years (1935) **Christopher Hassall** (1912)
Poems on Miscellaneous Subjects (1854) **Frances E. Harper** (1825)
Poems on Sacred Subjects (1759) **Augustus Montague Toplady** (1740)
Poems on Several Occasions (1680) **John Wilmot, earl of Rochester** (1647)
Poems on Several Occasions (1703) **Sarah Egerton** (1670)
Poems on Several Occasions (1709) **Matthew Prior** (1664)
Poems on Several Occasions (1720) **John Gay** (1685)
Poems on Several Occasions (1722) **Thomas Parnell** (1679)
Poems on Several Occasions (1724) **Eliza Haywood** (*c.* 1693)
Poems on Several Occasions (1736) **Stephen Duck** (1705)
Poems on Several Occasions (1748) **Thomas Warton, the Elder** (1688?)
Poems on Several Occasions (1752) **Christopher Smart** (1722)
Poems on Several Occasions (1889) **Austin Dobson** (1840)
Poems on Several Subjects (1730) **Stephen Duck** (1705)
Poems on Slavery (1842) **Henry Wadsworth Longfellow** (1807)
Poems on the War (1916) **Alice Meynell** (1847)
Poems on Various Subjects (1779) **Robert Fergusson** (1750–1774)
Poems on Various Subjects (1796) **S.T. Coleridge** (1772)
Poems Original and Translated (1808) **George Gordon, Lord Byron** (1788)
Poems, Partly of Rural Life (1846) **William Barnes** (1801)
Poems, Scots and English (1917) **John Buchan** (1875)
Poems: Second Edition [ed. Charles Williams] (1930) **Gerard Manley Hopkins** (1844–89)
Poems: Second Series (1855) **Matthew Arnold** (1822)
Poems: Second Series (1891) **Emily Dickinson** (1830–86)
Poems: Second Series (1848) **James Russell Lowell** (1819)
Poems: Second Series (1909) **W.B. Yeats** (1865)
Poems, Supposed to Have Been Written by Thomas Rowley (1777) **Thomas Chatterton** (1752–70)
Poems . . . The Second Volume (1799) **Robert Southey** (1774)
Poems: Third Series (1885) **Jean Ingelow** (1820)
Poems: Third Series (1896) **Emily Dickinson** (1830–86)
Poems to Poets (1976) **Richard Eberhart** (1904)
Poems Upon Various Occasions [inc. early version of 'The School-Mistress'] (1737) **William Shenstone** (1714)
Poems, with the Muses Looking-Glasse: and Amyntas (1638) **Thomas Randolph** (1605–35)
Poems, with the Tenth Satyre of Juvenal (1646) **Henry Vaughan** (1622)
Poems Written Between the Years 1768 and 1794 (1795) **Philip Freneau** (1752)
Poems Written During the Progress of the Abolition Questions (1838) **John Greenleaf Whittier** (1807)
Poésies (1899) **Stéphane Mallarmé** (1842–1898)

Poet: A Lying Word (1933) **Laura Riding** (1901)
Poet and Dancer (1993) **Ruth Prawer Jhabvala** (1927)
Poet and Peer (1880) **Charles Hamilton Aïdé** (1826)
Poet and the Landscape, The (1962) **Andrew Young** (1885)
Poet and the Lunatics, The (1929) **G.K. Chesterton** (1874)
Poet at the Breakfast-Table, The (1872) **Oliver Wendell Holmes** (1809)
Poet in the Family, A (1974) **Dannie Abse** (1923)
Poet Reclining, The (1982) **Ken Smith** (1938)
Poet Turns on Himself, The (1982) **James Dickey** (1923)
Poet's Alphabet, A (1925) **W.H. Davies** (1871)
Poet's Calendar, A (1927) **W.H. Davies** (1871)
Poet's Child, The (1903) **E[mma] F[rances] Brooke** (1859?)
Poet's Complaint of his Muse, The (1680) **Thomas Otway** (1652)
Poet's Fate, The (1797) **George Dyer** (1755)
Poet's Notebook, A (1943) **Edith Sitwell** (1887)
Poet's Pilgrimage, A (1918) **W.H. Davies** (1871)
Poet's Pilgrimage to Waterloo, The (1816) **Robert Southey** (1774)
Poet's Tale, A (1878) **Rabindranath Tagore** (1861)
Poetaster (1601) **Ben Jonson** (1572)
Poètes maudits, Les ['Accursed Poets'] (1884) **Paul Verlaine** (1844)
Poetic Craft and Principle (1967) **Robert Graves** (1895)
Poetic Gems (1890) **William McGonagall** (1830)
Poetic Image, The (1947) **C. Day Lewis** (1904)
Poetic Unreason, and Other Studies (1925) **Robert Graves** (1895)
Poetic Vigils (1824) **Bernard Barton** (1784)
Poetical Blossomes (1633) **Abraham Cowley** (1618)
Poetical Epistle to an Eminent Painter, A (1778) **William Hayley** (1745)
Poetical Epistle to Sir George Beaumont, A (1801) **William Sotheby** (1757)
Poetical Pieces (1820) **William Barnes** (1801)
Poetical Sketches (1783) **William Blake** (1757)
Poetical Tales by Sir Gregory Gander (1778) **George Ellis** (1753)
Poetical Works [ed. Bertam Dobell] (1903) **Thomas Traherne** (1637–74)
Poetical Works [vol. i: *Lyrical Poems*] (1906) **W.B. Yeats** (1865)
Poetical Works [vol. ii: *Dramatical Poems*] (1907) **W.B. Yeats** (1865)
Poetical Works of the Late Thomas Little (1801) **Thomas Moore** (1779)
Poeticall Essayes (1599) **Samuel Daniel** (1562)
Poetics (1852) **E.S. Dallas** (1828)
Poetry and Anarchism (1938) **Sir Herbert Read** (1893)
Poetry and Criticism (1925) **Edith Sitwell** (1887)
Poetry and Experience (1960) **Archibald MacLeish** (1892)
Poetry and Experience (1967) **Sir Herbert Read** (1893)
Poetry and Fiction (1963) **Howard Nemerov** (1920)
Poetry and Ireland (1908) **Lionel Johnson** (1867–1902) [with W.B. Yeats]
Poetry and Opinion (1950) **Archibald MacLeish** (1892)
Poetry and the Age (1953) **Randall Jarrell** (1914)
Poetry by the Author of Gebir (1802) **Walter Savage Landor** (1775)
Poetry Chronicle, A (1973) **Ian Hamilton** (1938)
Poetry Direct and Oblique (1934) **E.M.W. Tillyard** (1889)
Poetry for Children (1809) **Charles Lamb** (1775) [with Mary Lamb]
Poetry for Supper (1958) **R.S. Thomas** (1913)
Poetry for the People (1840) **Richard Monckton Milnes** (1809)
Poetry: Its Music and Meaning (1932) **Lascelles Abercrombie** (1881)
Poetry of the Committed Individual (1973) **Jon Silkin** (1930) (ed.)
Poetry of the Period, The (1870) **Alfred Austin** (1835)
Poetry of the Present (1949) **Geoffrey Grigson** (1905)
Poetry Today (1973) **Anthony Thwaite** (1930)
Poetry Wreck, The (1975) **Karl Shapiro** (1913)
Poets and Dreamers (1903) **Lady Gregory** (1852)
Poets' Corner, The (1904) **Max Beerbohm** (1872)
Poets, Farewell! (1929) **Edmund Wilson** (1895–1972)
Poganuc People (1878) **Harriet Beecher Stowe** (1811)
Point Counter Point (1928) **Aldous Huxley** (1894)
Point du jour (1934) **André Breton** (1896)
Point of No Return (1949) **John P. Marquand** (1893)
Pointed Roofs (1915) **Dorothy M. Richardson** (1873)
Points (1972) **Anthony Thwaite** (1930)
Points for a Compass Rose (1973) **Evan S. Connell, Jr** (1924)
Points of My Compass, The (1962) **E.B. White** (1899)
Points of View (1958) **Somerset Maugham** (1874)
Poirot Investigates (1924) **Agatha Christie** (1890)
Poison Belt, The (1913) **A. Conan Doyle** (1859)
Poison Island (1907) **Sir A.T. Quiller-Couch** (1863)
Poison Oracle, The (1974) **Peter Dickinson** (1927)
Poisoned Chocolates Case, The [as 'Anthony Berkeley'] (1929) **Anthony Berkeley Cox** (1893)
Poisoned Kiss, The (1975) **Joyce Carol Oates** (1938)
Poisoned Paradise, The (1922) **Robert W. Service** (1876)
Poland (1831) **Thomas Campbell** (1777)
Poland (1983) **James A. Michener** (1907)
Poland, Homer, and Other Poems (1832) **W.E. Aytoun** (1813)
Polar Passion, The (1967) **Farley Mowat** (1921)
Polaris (1985) **Fay Weldon** (1931)
Policeman and the Rose, The (1978) **Raja Rao** (1909)
Policy and Passion (1881) **Mrs Campbell Praed** (1851)
Policy and Police (1972) **G.R. Elton** (1921)

Polish Spy, The [Les Blancs et les Bleus] (1868) **Alexandre Dumas ['père']** (1802)
Polite Essays (1937) **Ezra Pound** (1885)
Polite Farces for the Drawing-Room (1899) **Arnold Bennett** (1867)
Political Contest, The [pt. i] (1769) **'Junius'** [probably **Sir Philip Francis]** (1740)
Political Discourses (1660) **James Harrington** (1611)
Political Discourses (1752) **David Hume** (1711)
Political Economy of Art, The (1857) **John Ruskin** (1819)
Political Essays (1819) **William Hazlitt** (1778)
Political Essays (1888) **James Russell Lowell** (1819)
Political Fable, A (1980) **Robert Coover** (1932)
Political Fables (1697) **Cotton Mather** (1663)
Political History of the Devil, The (1726) **Daniel Defoe** (1660)
Politician, The (1655) **James Shirley** (1596)
Politics **Aristotle** (384BC)
Politics and Literature (1929) **G.D.H. Cole** (1889)
Politics in Wartime (1964) **A.J.P. Taylor** (1906)
Politics of Dispossession, The (1994) **Edward Said** (1935)
Politics of Experience, The (1967) **R.D. Laing** (1927)
Politics of Upheaval, The (1960) **Arthur Schlesinger** (1917)
Polly (1729) **John Gay** (1685)
Polly Honeycombe (1760) **George Colman, the Elder** (1732)
Polly Oliver (1935) **A.E. Coppard** (1878)
Polly Put the Kettle On (1975) **Hilary Bailey** (1936)
Polo (1991) **Jilly Cooper** (1937)
Polonaise (1987) **Jane Aiken Hodge** (1917)
Poltava (1829) **Alexander Pushkin** (1799)
Poly-Olbion [pt. i] (1612) **Michael Drayton** (1563)
Polyeucte (1641?) **Pierre Corneille** (1606)
Polyglots, The (1925) **William Gerhardie** (1895)
Pomander of Verse, A (1895) **E[dith] Nesbit** (1858)
Pomeroy Abbey (1878) **Mrs Henry Wood** (1814)
Pomes Penyeach (1927) **James Joyce** (1882)
Pomfret Towers (1938) **Angela Thirkell** (1890)
Pomp and Circumstance (1960) **Noel Coward** (1899)
Pompeii (1819) **T.B. Macaulay** (1800)
Pompey [tr. from Corneille] (1663) **Katherine Philips** (1632) (tr.)
Pompey the Great [from the French] (1664) **Sir Charles Sedley** (1639) and others (tr.)
Ponder Heart, The (1954) **Eudora Welty** (1909)
Pongo and the Bull (1910) **Hilaire Belloc** (1870)
Ponkapog Papers (1903) **Thomas Bailey Aldrich** (1836)
Ponsonby Post, The (1977) **Bernice Rubens** (1923)
Pool of Vishnu, The (1940) **L.H. Myers** (1881)
Pools of Silence, The (1909) **Henry de Vere Stacpoole** (1863)
Poor Bitos [*Pauvre Bitos*] (1956) **Jean Anouilh** (1910)
Poor Bride, The (1853) **Alexander Nikolaevich Ostrovsky** (1823)
Poor Caroline (1931) **Winifred Holtby** (1898)
Poor Clare (1968) **L.P. Hartley** (1895)
Poor Cow (1967) **Nell Dunn** (1936)
Poor Fellow (1902) **Mrs J.H. Riddell** (1832)
Poor Fellow My Country (1975) **Xavier Herbert** (1901)
Poor Incumbent, The (1858) **Margaret [Mrs Alfred] Gatty** (1809)
Poor Jack (1840) **Frederick Marryat** (1792)
Poor Man, The (1922) **Stella Benson** (1892)
Poor Man's Plea, The (1698) **Daniel Defoe** (1660)
Poor Man's Tapestry (1946) **Oliver Onions** (1873)
Poor Max (1898) **'Iota' [Kathleen Mannington Caffyn]** (1855?)
Poor Men's Music (1950) **Edith Sitwell** (1887)
Poor Miss Finch (1872) **Wilkie Collins** (1824)
Poor Relations (1920) **Compton Mackenzie** (1883)
Poor Richard's Almanack (1733–58) **Benjamin Franklin** (1706)
Poor Things (1992) **Alasdair Gray** (1934)
Poor Tom (1932) **Edwin Muir** (1887)
Poor Vulcan (1778) **Charles Dibdin** (1745)
Poor White (1920) **Sherwood Anderson** (1876)
Poorhouse Fair, The (1959) **John Updike** (1932)
Pop. 1280 (1964) **Jim Thompson** (1906)
Pope Jacynth (1904) **'Vernon Lee' [Violet Paget]** (1856)
Pope's Wedding, The (1962) **Edward Bond** (1934)
Popinjay Mystery, The (1973) **Geoffrey Trease** (1909)
Popish Kingdome, The [from Thomas Kirchmeyer] (1570) **Barnaby Googe** (1540) (tr.)
Popish Royall Favourite, The (1643) **William Prynne** (1600)
Popular Tales (1804) **Maria Edgeworth** (1767)
Popular Tales from the Norse (1859) **Sir George Webbe Dasent** (1817) (tr.)
Porch, The (1937) **Richard Church** (1893)
Porcupine, The (1992) **Julian Barnes** (1946)
Porgy (1925) **DuBose Heyward** (1885) [dramatized, with Dorothy Heyward, 1927; opera by George Gershwin, as *Porgy and Bess*, 1935]
Porius (1951) **John Cooper Powys** (1872)
Porky (1983) **Deborah Moggach** (1948)
Pornographer, The (1979) **John McGahern** (1934)
Pornography and Obscenity (1929) **D.H. Lawrence** (1885)
Pornography: Men Possessing Women (1981) **Andrea Dworkin** (1946)
Porphyrion (1898) **Laurence Binyon** (1869)
Port of Saints (1973) **William S. Burroughs** (1914)
Port Tarascon (1890) **Alphonse Daudet** (1840)
Port-Royal (1840–59) **Charles-Augustin Sainte-Beuve** (1804)
Portage to San Cristobal of A.H., The (1981) **George Steiner** (1929)
Portage, Wisconsin (1928) **Zona Gale** (1874)
Portent, The (1864) **George MacDonald** (1824)
Porter Folio, A (1969) **Peter Porter** (1929)
Porterhouse Blue (1974) **Tom Sharpe** (1928)
Portion for Foxes, A (1977) **Anthony Thwaite** (1930)
Portion of Labor, The (1901) **Mary Wilkins Freeman** (1852)
Portnoy's Complaint (1969) **Philip Roth** (1933)
Portrait, The (1910) **Ford Madox Ford** (1873)

Portrait of an Eye: Three Novels (1992) **Kathy Acker** (1948)
Portrait in a Mirror (1929) **Charles Morgan** (1894)
Portrait in Brownstone (1962) **Louis Auchinloss** (1917)
Portrait of a Genius, But . . . (1950) **Richard Aldington** (1892)
Portrait of a Lady, The (1881) **Henry James** (1843)
Portrait of a Man with Red Hair (1925) **Sir Hugh Walpole** (1884)
Portrait of a Marriage (1973) **Nigel Nicolson** (1917)
Portrait of all the Russias, A (1967) **Sir Laurens van der Post** (1906)
Portrait of Clare [US: *Love is Enough*] (1927) **Francis Brett Young** (1884)
Portrait of Edith Wharton (1947) **Percy Lubbock** (1879)
Portrait of Japan, A (1968) **Sir Laurens van der Post** (1906)
Portrait of Jennie (1940) **Robert Nathan** (1894)
Portrait of the Artist as a Young Dog (1940) **Dylan Thomas** (1914)
Portrait of the Artist as a Young Man (1916) **James Joyce** (1882)
Portrait of the Artist as an Old Man (2000) **Joseph Heller** (1923)
Portraits (1931) **Desmond MacCarthy** (1877)
Portraits and Sketches (1912) **Sir Edmund Gosse** (1849)
Portraits contemporains ['Contemporary Portraits'] (1846) **Charles-Augustin Sainte-Beuve** (1804)
Portraits de femmes ['Portraits of Women'] (1844) **Charles-Augustin Sainte-Beuve** (1804)
Portraits et souvenirs littéraires ['Literary Portraits and Recollections'] (1875) **Théophile Gautier** (1811)
Portraits from Memory (1956) **Bertrand Russell** (1872)
Portraits in Miniature (1931) **Lytton Strachey** (1880)
Portraits in Oil and Vinegar (1925) **James Laver** (1899)
Portraits of Places (1883) **Henry James** (1843)
Portraiture of Quakerism, A (1806) **Thomas Clarkson** (1760)
Poseidon Adventure, The (1969) **Paul Gallico** (1897)
Posies of George Gascoigne, The (1575) **George Gascoigne** (1542?)
Positions (1581) **Richard Mulcaster** (1530?)
Positive Evolution of Religion, The (1913) **Frederic Harrison** (1831)
Positive Philosophy of August Comte, The (1853) **Harriet Martineau** (1802) (tr. and ed.)
Possessing the Secret of Joy (1992) **Alice Walker** (1944)
Possession (1923) **Mazo de la Roche** (1879)
Possession (1925) **Louis Bromfield** (1896)
Possession (1990) **A.S. Byatt** (1936)
Possibilities (1973) **Malcolm Bradbury** (1932)
Possibilities, The (1987) **Howard Barker** (1946)
Possible Worlds (1927) **J.B.S. Haldane** (1892)
Possible Worlds (1989) **Peter Porter** (1929)
Post Captain (1972) **Patrick O'Brian** (1914)
Post Haste (1880) **R.M. Ballantyne** (1825)
Post Liminium (1911) **Lionel Johnson** (1867–1902)
Post Office (1971) **Charles Bukowski** (1920)
Postcards (1992) **E. Annie Proulx** (1935)
Postcards from Surfers (1985) **Helen Garner** (1942)
Posthumous Fragments of Margaret Nicholson (1810) **P.B. Shelley** (1792) [with Thomas Jefferson Hogg]
Posthumous Papers of the Pickwick Club, The (1837) **'Boz' [Charles Dickens]** (1812)
Posthumous Poems [inc. 'Julian and Maddalo'. 'The Witch of Atlas', and 'Mont Blanc'] (1824) **P.B. Shelley** (1792–1822)
Postman Always Rings Twice, The (1934) **James M. Cain** (1892)
Postmortem (1990) **Patricia Cornwell** (1956)
Postscripts (1923) **O. Henry' [William Sydney Porter** (1862–1910)]
Postures [US: *Quartet*] (1928) **'Jean Rhys' [Ella Gwendolyn Rees Williams]** (1890)
Pot Boils, The (1919) **Storm Jameson** (1897)
Pot Geranium, The (1954) **Norman Nicholson** (1914)
Pot of Basil, The (1913) **Bernard Capes** (1850?)
Pot of Earth, The (1925) **Archibald MacLeish** (1892)
Potato Face (1930) **Carl Sandburg** (1878)
Potiphar's Wife (1892) **Sir Edwin Arnold** (1832)
Potter's Field, The (1989) **'Ellis Peters' [Edith Mary Pargeter]** (1913)
Potter's Thumb, The (1894) **Flora Annie Steel** (1847)
Potterism (1920) **Rose Macaulay** (1881)
Potting Shed, The (1958) **Graham Greene** (1904)
Pouliuli (1977) **Albert Wendt** (1939)
Pound, Yeats, Eliot, and the Modern Movement (1985) **C.K. Stead** (1932)
Poverty and Pride (1856) **Charles Reade** (1814)
Poverty as an Industrial Problem (1913) **R.H. Tawney** (1880)
Poverty Castle (1991) **Robin Jenkins** (1912)
Poverty of Historicism, The (1957) **Sir Karl Popper** (1902)
Power (1963) **Howard Fast** (1914)
Power (1938) **Bertrand Russell** (1872)
Power and the Glory, The (1940) **Graham Greene** (1904)
Power of Darkness, The (1958) **Mulk Raj Anand** (1905)
Power of Love, The (1720) **Mary Delariviere Manley** (1663)
Power of Sympathy, The (1789) **William Hill Brown** (1765)
Power of the Dog, The (1984) **Howard Barker** (1946)
Power Politics (1971) **Margaret Atwood** (1939)
Power-House, The (1916) **John Buchan** (1875)
Powers of Darkness (1966) **Robert Aickman** (1914)
Practical Criticism (1929) **I.A. Richards** (1893)
Practical Discourse Concerning Death, A (1689) **William Sherlock** (1641?)
Practical Education (1798) **Richard Lovell Edgeworth** (1744) [with Maria Edgeworth]
Practical Observations Upon the Education of the People (1825) **Henry, Lord Brougham** (1778)
Practical Philosophy (1842) **Henry, Lord Brougham** (1778)

Practical Piety (1811) **Hannah More** (1745)
Practical Treatise upon Christian Perfection, A (1726) **William Law** (1686)
Practicall Catechisme, A (1644) **Henry Hammond** (1605)
Practice and Theory of Bolshevism, The (1920) **Bertrand Russell** (1872)
Practice of the Criminal Law in Scotland (1833) **Sir Archibald Alison** (1792)
Practyse of Prelates, The (1530) **William Tyndale** (1494?)
Praeterita [vol. i] (1886, 1887, 1888) **John Ruskin** (1819)
Pragmatism (1907) **William James** (1842)
Prairie, The (1827) **James Fenimore Cooper** (1789)
Prairie Chief, The (1886) **R.M. Ballantyne** (1825)
Prairie Folk (1893) **Hamlin Garland** (1860)
Praise, Antiquity, and Commodity, of Beggery, Beggers, and Begging, The (1621) **John Taylor** (1580)
Praise of Folly, The [*Encomium Moriae*] (1511) **Erasmus** (*c.* 1467)
Praise of Life, The (1896) **Laurence Binyon** (1869)
Praise to the End! (1951) **Theodore Roethke** (1908)
Prater Violet (1945) **Christopher Isherwood** (1904)
Pratt of the Argus (1988) **David Nobbs** (1935)
Pravda (1985) **Howard Brenton** (1942) [with David Hare]
Praxis (1978) **Fay Weldon** (1931)
Prayer for Owen Meaney, A (1989) **John Irving** (1942)
Pre-Raphaelite Brotherhood, The (1907) **Ford Madox Ford** (1873)
Pre-Raphaelitism (1851) **John Ruskin** (1819)
Preacher and the Slave, The (1950) **Wallace Stegner** (1909)
Preaching to the Converted (1972) **Peter Porter** (1929)
Precaution (1820) **James Fenimore Cooper** (1789)
Precepts and Practice (1840) **Theodore Hook** (1788)
Preces Privatae [**Andrewes**]: see *The Private Devotions*
Preciosa (1852) **Francis Turner Palgrave** (1824)
Precious Bane (1924) **Mary Webb** (1881)
Precipice, The (1948) **Hugh MacLennan** (1907)
Predictions for the Year 1708 (1708) **Jonathan Swift** (1667)
Predilections (1955) **Marianne Moore** (1887)
Prefabrications (1955) **Josephine Miles** (1911)
Preface to a Life (1926) **Zona Gale** (1874)
Preface to a Twenty Volume Suicide Note (1961) **LeRoi Jones** (1934)
Preface to Paradise Lost, A (1942) **C.S. Lewis** (1898)
Preface to the Past (1936) **James Branch Cabell** (1879)
Prefaces (1934) **Bernard Shaw** (1856)
Prefaces, Biographical and Critical, to the Works of the English Poets ['*Lives of the Poets*'] (1779) **Samuel Johnson** (1709)
Prefaces to Shakespeare (1927) **Harley Granville-Barker** (1877)
Prefaces to the Players' Shakespeare (1923) **Harley Granville-Barker** (1877)
Preferment (1840) **Mrs C.F. Gore** (1799)
Prehistories (1975) **Peter Scupham** (1933)
Prejudices [6 series] (1919–27) **H.L. Mencken** (1880)
Prelude (1918) **'Katherine Mansfield' [Kathleen Mansfield Beauchamp]** (1888)
Prelude, A (1967) **Edmund Wilson** (1895)
Prelude, The (1850) **William Wordsworth** (1770)
Prelude to Adventure, The (1912) **Sir Hugh Walpole** (1884)
Prelude to Christopher (1934) **Eleanor Dark** (1901)
Prelude to Waking [as 'Brent of Bin Bin'] (1950) **Miles Franklin** (1879)
Preludes (1875) **Alice Meynell** (1847)
Preludes for Memnon (1931) **Conrad Potter Aiken** (1889)
Preoccupations (1980) **Seamus Heaney** (1939)
Prerogative of Parlaments, The (1628) **Sir Walter Ralegh** (1554–1618)
Prerogative of Popular Government , The (1658) **James Harrington** (1611)
Presence (1987) **P.J. Kavanagh** (1931)
Presence of Spain, The (1964) **Jan Morris** (1926)
Present and the Future, The (1880) **Frederic Harrison** (1831)
Present and the Past, The (1953) **I. Compton-Burnett** (1884)
Present Indicative (1937) **Noel Coward** (1899)
Present Laughter (1942) **Noel Coward** (1899)
Present State of the British Empire , The (1768) **Oliver Goldsmith** (1728)
Present State of Wit, The (1711) **John Gay** (1685)
Present Times (1984) **David Storey** (1933)
Presenting Moonshine (1941) **John Collier** (1901)
Preservation and Restoration of Ancient Monuments, The (1852) **E.A. Freeman** (1823)
Preservative Against Popery, A (1688) **William Sherlock** (1641?)
Preservative Agaynste Deth, A (1545) **Sir Thomas Elyot** (1490?)
Presidential Agent (1944) **Upton Sinclair** (1878)
Presidential Mission (1947) **Upton Sinclair** (1878)
Press Cuttings (1909) **Bernard Shaw** (1856)
Press, The (1822) **J.H. Reynolds** (1796)
Pressed on Sand (1955) **Al Purdy** (1918)
Prester John (1910) **John Buchan** (1875)
Preston Fight (1875) **W.H. Ainsworth** (1805)
Presumed Innocent (1987) **Scott Turow** (1949)
Pretender, The (1914) **Robert W. Service** (1876)
Pretenders, The [*I Suppositi*] (1509) **Ludovico Ariosto** (1474)
Pretending Not to Sleep (1964) **Ian Hamilton** (1938)
Pretty Creatures (1927) **William Gerhardie** (1895)
Pretty Lady, The (1918) **Arnold Bennett** (1867)
Pretty Polly Barlow (1964) **Noel Coward** (1899)
Pretty Tales for Tired People (1965) **Martha Gellhorn** (1908)
Previous Convictions (1963) **Cyril Connolly** (1903)
Prey of the Dragon, The (1912) **Ethel M. Dell** (1881)
Priapus and the Pool (1922) **Conrad Potter Aiken** (1889)
Price, The (1968) **Arthur Miller** (1915)
Price of Diamonds, The (1957) **Dan Jacobson** (1929)

Price of Everything, The (1994) **Andrew Motion** (1952)
Price of Love, The (1914) **Arnold Bennett** (1867)
Price of Stone, The (1985) **Richard Murphy** (1927)
Price of the King's Peace, The (1971) **Nigel Tranter** (1909)
Price of the Ticket, The (1986) **James Baldwin** (1924)
Prick of Noon, The (1985) **Peter De Vries** (1910)
Prick Up Your Ears (1987) **Alan Bennett** (1934)
Pricksongs and Descants (1969) **Robert Coover** (1932)
Pride and Prejudice (1813) **Jane Austen** (1775)
Pride of Eve, The (1914) **Warwick Deeping** (1877)
Pride's Harvest (1991) **Jon Cleary** (1917)
Priest to the Temple, A [first pub. in *Remains*, 1652] (1671) **George Herbert** (1593–1633)
Prima Donna, The (1908) **F. Marion Crawford** (1854)
Prime Minister, The (1876) **Anthony Trollope** (1815)
Prime Minister, The (1845) **W.H.G. Kingston** (1814)
Prime Minister, The (1918) **Hall Caine** (1853)
Prime Minister, The (1977) **Austin Clarke** (1932)
Prime of Miss Jean Brodie, The (1961) **Muriel Spark** (1918)
Primer of English Literature (1876) **Stopford Brooke** (1832)
Primitive, The (1955) **Chester Himes** (1909)
Primitive Christianity Revived (1696) **William Penn** (1644)
Primitive Rebels (1959) **Eric Hobsbaum** (1917)
Primitive Tradition Recognized in Holy Scriptire (1836) **John Keble** (1792)
Primitivism and Decadence (1937) **Yvor Winters** (1900)
Primrose Path, The (1935) **Ogden Nash** (1902)
Prince, The [*El principe*; first Eng. trn, 1560] (1532) **Niccolo Machiavelli** (1469)
Prince, The (1642) **Sir Walter Ralegh** (1554–1618)
Prince and Heretic (1914) **'Marjorie Bowen' [Gabrielle Margaret Vere Campbell]** (1886)
Prince and the Pauper, The (1882) **'Mark Twain' [Samuel Langhorne Clemens]** (1835)
Prince Arthur (1695) **Sir Richard Blackmore** (1654)
Prince Caspian (1951) **C.S. Lewis** (1898)
Prince Charles and the Spanish Marriage 1617–23 (1869) **S. R. Gardiner** (1829)
Prince Charming: A Memoir (1999) **Christopher Logue** (1926)
Prince Dorus (1811) **Charles Lamb** (1775)
Prince Hagen (1903) **Upton Sinclair** (1878)
Prince Henrie Revived (1615) **Henry Peacham the younger** (1578?)
Prince Jali (1931) **L.H. Myers** (1881)
Prince Lucifer (1887) **Alfred Austin** (1835)
Prince of Abissinia, The [*Rasselas*] (1759) **Samuel Johnson** (1709)
Prince of Balkistan, The (1895) **Allen Upward** (1863)
Prince of India, The (1893) **Lew Wallace** (1827)
Prince of Quotidian, The (1994) **Paul Muldoon** (1951)
Prince of Sinners, A (1903) **E. Phillips Oppenheim** (1866)
Prince of the Captivity, A (1933) **John Buchan** (1875)
Prince of Tunis, The (1773) **Henry Mackenzie** (1745)
Prince of Wales v The Examiner, The (1812) **Leigh Hunt** (1784)
Prince of Wales's Garden Party, The (1882) **Mrs J.H. Riddell** (1832)
Prince Otto (1885) **Robert Louis Stevenson** (1850)
Prince Prigio (1889) **Andrew Lang** (1844)
Prince Ricardo of Pantouflia (1893) **Andrew Lang** (1844)
Prince Zaleski (1895) **M.P. Shiel** (1865)
Prince's Progress, The (1866) **Christina Rossetti** (1830)
Prince's Quest, The (1880) **Sir William Watson** (1858)
Prince's Tale, The (1998) **E.M. Forster** (1879–1970)
Prince-Duke and His Page, The (1841) **Edward Bulwer-Lytton** (1803)
Princes and Artists (1976) **Hugh Trevor-Roper** (1914)
Princess, The (1835) **Lady Sydney Morgan** (1783?)
Princess, The (1847) **Alfred, Lord Tennyson** (1809)
Princess and Curdie, The (1883) **George MacDonald** (1824)
Princess and the Butterfly, The (1897) **Arthur Wing Pinero** (1855)
Princess and the Goblin, The (1872) **George MacDonald** (1824)
Princess Casamassima, The (1886) **Henry James** (1843)
Princess Daisy (1980) **Judith Krantz**
Princess Ida [music by Sir Arthur Sullivan] (1884) **W.S. Gilbert** (1836)
Princess Maleine, The (1889) **Maurice Maeterlinck** (1862)
Princess Napraxine (1884) **'Ouida' [Marie Louise de la Ramée]** (1839)
Princess Nobody, The (1884) **Andrew Lang** (1844)
Princess of Cleve, The (1680/81) **Nathaniel Lee** (1649?)
Princess of Cleves, The [*La Princesse de Cleves*] (1678) **Marie-Madeleine La Fayette** (1634)
Princess of Mars, A (1917) **Edgar Rice Burroughs** (1875)
Princess of Montpensier, The [*La Princesse de Montpensier*] (1662) **Marie-Madeleine la Fayette** (1634)
Princess of the Gutter, A (1895) **Mrs L.T. Meade** (1854)
Princess of Thule, A (1874) **William Black** (1841)
Princess Sophia, The (1900) **E.F. Benson** (1867)
Princess Sunshine (1889) **Mrs J.H. Riddell** (1832)
Princess Zoubaroff, The (1920) **Ronald Firbank** (1886)
Principall Navigations, Voiages and Discoveries of the English Nation, The (1589) **Richard Hakluyt** (1552?)
Principia Ethica (1903) **G.E. Moore** (1873)
Principia Mathematica (1910) **Bertrand Russell** (1872) [with A.N. Whitehead]
Principia Politica (1953) **Leonard Woolf** (1880)
Principle of Relativity, The (1922) **A.N. Whitehead** (1861)

Principle of Water, The (1974) **Jon Silkin** (1930)
Principles of a Methodist Farther Explain'd, The (1746) **John Wesley** (1703)
Principles of a Methodist, The (1742) **John Wesley** (1703)
Principles of Art, The (1938) **R.G. Collingwood** (1889)
Principles of Church Reform (1833) **Thomas Arnold** (1795)
Principles of Church Restoration (1846) **E.A. Freeman** (1823)
Principles of English Prosody (1923) **Lascelles Abercrombie** (1881)
Principles of Ethics [vol. i; vol. ii, 1893] (1892) **Herbert Spencer** (1820)
Principles of Literary Criticism (1924) **I.A. Richards** (1893)
Principles of Logic, The (1883) **F.H. Bradley** (1846)
Principles of Mathematics, The (1903) **Bertrand Russell** (1872)
Principles of Moral and Political Philosophy, The (1785) **William Paley** (1743)
Principles of Moral and Political Science (1792) **Adam Ferguson** (1723)
Principles of Political Economy (1848) **J.S. Mill** (1806)
Principles of Political Economy Considered (1820) **T.R. Malthus** (1766)
Principles of Political Economy, The (1883) **Henry Sidgwick** (1838)
Principles of Psychology (1855) **Herbert Spencer** (1820)
Principles of Psychology, The (1890) **William James** (1842)
Principles of Shakespearian Production (1936) **G. Wilson Knight** (1897)
Principles of Social Reconstruction (1916) **Bertrand Russell** (1872)
Principles of Sociology [vol. i; vol. ii, 1882; vol. iii, 1896] (1876) **Herbert Spencer** (1820)
Principles of the Christian Religion Explained, The (1699) **William Wake** (1657)
Principles of the Christian Religion, The (1743) **Philip Doddridge** (1702)
Principles of the Criminal Law of Scotland (1832) **Sir Archibald Alison** (1792)
Prison of Ice (1976) **Dean Koontz** (1945)
Prisoner in the Opal, The (1928) **A.E.W. Mason** (1865)
Prisoner of Chillon, The (1816) **George Gordon, Lord Byron** (1788)
Prisoner of Grace (1952) **Joyce Cary** (1888)
Prisoner of Mademoiselle, The (1904) **Sir Charles G.D. Roberts** (1860)
Prisoner of Second Avenue, The (1972) **Neil Simon** (1927)
Prisoner of Sex, The (1971) **Norman Mailer** (1923)
Prisoner of the Caucasus, The (1820–1) **Alexander Pushkin** (1799)
Prisoner of Zenda, The (1894) **'Anthony Hope' [Sir Anthony Hope Hawkins]** (1863)
Prisoners, Fast Bound in Misery and Iron (1906) **Mary Cholmondeley** (1859)
Prisoners of Mainz, The (1919) **Alec Waugh** (1898)
Prisoners of September, The (1975) **Leon Garfield** (1921)
Prisoners of War, The (1925) **J.R. Ackerley** (1896)
Prisoners Plea, The (1661) **George Wither** (1588)
Prisoners, The (1641) **Thomas Killigrew** (1612)
Private Angelo (1946) **Eric Linklater** (1899)
Private Country, A (1943) **Lawrence Durrell** (1912)
Private Devotions, The [*Preces Privatae*] (1647) **Lancelot Andrewes** (1555)
Private Dining Room, The (1953) **Ogden Nash** (1902)
Private Enterprise (1947) **Angela Thirkell** (1890)
Private Function, A (1985) **Alan Bennett** (1934)
Private Ground (1981) **Peter Levi** (1931)
Private Life, The (1893) **Henry James** (1843)
Private Life (1972) **Janice Elliott** (1931)
Private Life of an Indian Prince (1953) **Mulk Raj Anand** (1905)
Private Lives (1930) **Noel Coward** (1899)
Private Memoirs and Confessions of a Justified Sinner, The (1824) **James Hogg** (1770)
Private Papers (1986) **Margaret Forster** (1938)
Private Papers of Henry Ryecroft, The (1903) **George Gissing** (1857)
Private Parts (1987) **Fiona Pitt-Kethley** (1954)
Private Road (1940) **Forrest Reid** (1875)
Private Secretary, The (1881) **General Sir George Tomkyns Chesney** (1830)
Private Secretary, The (1881) **William Gillette** (1855)
Private View, A [as 'Michael Innes'. US: *One-Man Show*] (1952) **J.I.M. Stewart** (1906)
Private View (1953) **Walter de la Mare** (1873)
Private View, A (1994) **Anita Brookner** (1928)
Private Worlds (1934) **Phyllis Bottome** (1884)
Privateer's-Man, The (1846) **Frederick Marryat** (1792)
Privates on Parade (1977) **Peter Nichols** (1927)
Priviledges of the Baronage of England, The (1642) **John Selden** (1584–1634)
Privilege, The (1965) **Maxine Kumin** (1925)
Privy Seal (1907) **Ford Madox Ford** (1873)
Prizzi's Family (1986) **Richard Condon** (1915)
Prizzi's Honor (1982) **Richard Condon** (1915)
Probation (1879) **Jessie Fothergill** (1851)
Problem of China, The (1922) **Bertrand Russell** (1872)
Problem of Knowledge, The (1956) **A.J. Ayer** (1910)
Problem of Pain, The (1940) **C.S. Lewis** (1898)
Problem of Style, The (1922) **John Middleton Murry** (1889)
Problems (1979) **John Updike** (1932)
Problems of Greater Britain (1890) **Sir Charles Wentworth Dilke** (1843)
Problems of Life and Mind (1873) **G.H. Lewes** (1817)
Problems of Modern Industry (1898) **Sidney Webb** (1859) and **Beatrice Webb** (1858)
Problems of Race Degeneration, The (1911) **Havelock Ellis** (1859)
Procedures for Underground (1970) **Margaret Atwood** (1939)
Proceed, Sergeant Lamb (1941) **Robert Graves** (1895)

Proceedings on Trial of Tooke for High Treason (1795) **John Horne Tooke** (1736)

Process and Reality (1929) **A.N. Whitehead** (1861)

Prodigal Child, A (1982) **David Storey** (1933)

Prodigal Parents, The (1938) **Sinclair Lewis** (1885)

Prodigal Son, The (1904) **Hall Caine** (1853)

Prodigal Son, The (1957) **James Kirkup** (1923)

Product (1977) **R.D. FitzGerald** (1902)

Professing Poetry (1977) **John Wain** (1925)

Professional Foul [tv] (1977) **Tom Stoppard** (1937)

Professional Life of Mr Dibdin, The (1803) **Charles Dibdin** (1745)

Professor, The (1900) **A.C. Benson** (1862)

Professor, The (1857) **Charlotte Bronte** (1816)

Professor, The (1938) **Rex Warner** (1905)

Professor at the Breakfast-Table, The (1860) **Oliver Wendell Holmes** (1809)

Professor of Desire, The (1977) **Philip Roth** (1933)

Professor's Daughter, The (1971) **Piers Paul Read** (1941)

Professor's House, The (1925) **Willa Cather** (1873)

Profits of Religion, The (1918) **Upton Sinclair** (1878)

Profligate, The (1889) **Arthur Wing Pinero** (1855)

Progress (1905) **R.B. Cunninghame Graham** (1852)

Progress and Poverty (1879) **Henry George** (1839)

Progress and Prejudice (1854) **Mrs C.F. Gore** (1799)

Progress of a Biographer, The (1949) **'Hugh Kingsmill' [Hugh Kingsmill Lunn]** (1889)

Progress of a Crime, The (1960) **Julian Symons** (1912)

Progress of a Divine, The (1735) **Richard Savage** (1697?)

Progress of Gallantry, The (1774) **Richard Graves** (1715)

Progress of Honesty, The (1681) **Thomas D'Urfey** (1653)

Progress of Julius, The (1933) **Daphne du Maurier** (1907)

Progress of Love, The (1732) **George Lyttelton, 1st Baron Lyttelton** (1709)

Progress of Love, The (1986) **Alice Munro** (1931)

Progress of Romance, The (1785) **Clara Reeve** (1729)

Progress of Stories (1935) **Laura Riding** (1901)

Project for the Advancement of Religion, and the Reformation of Manners, A (1709) **Jonathan Swift** (1667)

Projectors, The (1665) **John Wilson** (1627?)

Prolegomena to Ethics (1883) **Thomas Hill Green** (1836–82)

Prolegomena to the Study of Greek Religion (1903) **Jane Harrison** (1850) et al.

Prolusions (1760) **Edward Capell** (1713)

Promenades (1980) **Richard Cobb** (1917)

Prometheus Bound **Aeschylus** (525–456 BC)

Prometheus Bound (1833) **E.B. Browning** (1806)

Prometheus the Fire-Bringer (1864) **R.H. Horne** (1803)

Prometheus the Firegiver (1883) **Robert Bridges** (1844)

Prometheus Unbound (1820) **P.B. Shelley** (1792)

Promise, The (1977) **Danielle Steel** (1947)

Promise of Air, The (1918) **Algernon Blackwood** (1869)

Promise of Arden, The (1912) **Eric Parker** (1870)

Promised Land (1976) **Robert B. Parker** (1932)

Promised Lands (1995) **Jane Rogers** (1952)

Promises (1957) **Robert Penn Warren** (1905)

Promises, Promises (1968) **Neil Simon** (1927)

Promos and Cassandra (1578) **George Whetstone** (*c.* 1551)

Proof, The (1930) **Yvor Winters** (1900)

Proper Marriage, A (1954) **Doris Lessing** (1919)

Proper Studies (1927) **Aldous Huxley** (1894)

Prophecy of Famine, The (1763) **Charles Churchill** (1731)

Prophecy of St Oran, The (1881) **Mathilde Blind** (1841)

Prophet, The (1923) **Kahlil Gibran** (1883)

Proposal for Correcting, Improving and Ascertaining the English Tongue, A (1712) **Jonathan Swift** (1667)

Proposal for Promoting Useful Knowledge, A (1743) **Benjamin Franklin** (1706)

Proposal for Putting Reform to the Vote Throughout the Kingdom, A [by 'The Hermit of Marlow'] (1817) **P.B. Shelley** (1792)

Proposal for the Universal Use of Irish Manufacture, A (1720) **Jonathan Swift** (1667)

Proposals for an Economical and Secure Currency (1816) **David Ricardo** (1772)

Proposals Relating to the Education of Youth in Pensilvania (1749) **Benjamin Franklin** (1706)

Proprietors, The (1996) **Jeffrey Archer** (1940)

Prose Idylls (1873) **Charles Kingsley** (1819)

Prose Papers (1917) **John Drinkwater** (1882)

Prospect Before Us, The (1950) **John Dos Passos** (1896)

Prospect Before Us, The (1954) **Herbert Gold** (1924)

Prospect, The [*Liberty* pt. v] (1736) **James Thomson** (1700)

Prospects of a Golden Age (1959) **John Dos Passos** (1896)

Prospects of Industrial Civilization, The (1923) **Bertrand Russell** (1872)

Prospects of Literature, The (1927) **Logan Pearsall Smith** (1865)

Prospectus and Specimen of an Intended National Work (1817) **John Hookham Frere** (1769)

Prospero's Cell (1945) **Lawrence Durrell** (1912)

Protector (1973) **Larry Niven** (1938)

Protector, The (1655) **George Wither** (1588)

Protestant, The (1828) **Anna Eliza Bray** (1790)

Protestant Era, The (1948) **Paul Tillich** (1886)

Protestatyon of Martin Marprelat, The [Sept. 1589] (1589) **Martin Marprelate**

Proteus and Amadeus (1878) **Wilfrid Scawen Blunt** (1840)

Prothalamion (1596) **Edmund Spenser** (1552?)

Prothanasia (1839) **Thomas Wade** (1805)

Proud Flesh (1973) **William Humphrey** (1924)

Proud Lady in a Cage (1980) **Fred Urquhart** (1912)

Proud Tower, The (1965) **Barbara Tuchman** (1912)

Proust (1928) **Clive Bell** (1881)

Proust (1931) **Samuel Beckett** (1906)
Provença (1910) **Ezra Pound** (1885)
Proverbial Philosophy (1838) **Martin Tupper** (1810)
Proverbs [written *c.* 1431–8] (1510?) **John Lydgate** (1370?-1449)
Proverbs in Porcelain (1877) **Austin Dobson** (1840)
Providence (1982) **Anita Brookner** (1928)
Provincial Lady Goes Further, The (1932) **'E.M. Delafield' [E.E.M. de la Pasture]** (1890)
Provincial Lady in America, The (1934) **'E.M. Delafield' [E.E.M. de la Pasture]** (1890)
Provincial Lady in War-Time, The (1940) **'E.M. Delafield' [E.E.M. de la Pasture]** (1890)
Provinciales (1909) **Jean Giraudoux** (1882)
Provok'd Husband, The (1728) **Colley Cibber** (1671)
Provok'd Wife, The (1697) **Sir John Vanbrugh** (1664)
Provost, The (1822) **John Galt** (1779)
Prowlers (1987) **Maurice Gee** (1931)
Prudence (1978) **Jilly Cooper** (1937)
Prudence Palfry (1874) **Thomas Bailey Aldrich** (1836)
Prufrock and Other Observations (1917) **T.S. Eliot** (1888)
Prussian Officer, The (1914) **D.H. Lawrence** (1885)
Psalms and Hymns for Public and Private Worship (1776) **Augustus Montague Toplady** (1740)
Psalms of David, The (1719) **Isaac Watts** (1674) (tr.)
Psalms of David, The (1765) **Christopher Smart** (1722) (tr.)
Psalms, Songs, and Sonnets (1611) **William Byrd** (1543)
Psalms, Sonnets, & Songs of Sadness and Piety (1588) **William Byrd** (1543)
Psalms With Their Spoils, The (1980) **Jon Silkin** (1930)
Psalter or Psalms of David , The (1839) **John Keble** (1792)
Pseudo-Martyr (1610) **John Donne** (1572)
Pseudodoxia Epidemica (1646) **Sir Thomas Browne** (1605)
Psmith in the City (1910) **P.G. Wodehouse** (1881)
Psyche (1648) **Joseph Beaumont** (1616)
Psyche (1675) **Thomas Shadwell** (1642?)
Psyche (1952) **H.G. de Lisser** (1878)
Psyche and the Hurricane (1991) **Michèle Roberts** (1949)
Psyche Apocalypté (1876) **R.H. Horne** (1803)
Psycho (1959) **Robert Bloch** (1917)
Psycho II (1982) **Robert Bloch** (1917)
Psychoanalysis and the Unconscious (1923) **D.H. Lawrence** (1885)
Psychodia Platonica (1642) **Henry More** (1614)
Psychology of Art, The [*La Psychologie de l'art*] (1947) **André Malraux** (1901)
Psychology of Sex (1933) **Havelock Ellis** (1859)
Public Burning, The (1977) **Robert Coover** (1932)
Public Faces (1932) **Sir Harold Nicolson** (1886)
Public Image, The (1968) **Muriel Spark** (1918)
Public Speech (1936) **Archibald MacLeish** (1892)
Public Spirit of the Tories, The (1714) **Sir Richard Steele** (1672)
Publick Spirit of the Whigs, The (1714) **Jonathan Swift** (1667)
Puck (1869) **'Ouida' [Marie Louise de la Ramée]** (1839)
Puck of Pook's Hill (1906) **Rudyard Kipling** (1865)
Puella (1982) **James Dickey** (1923)
Puffball (1980) **Fay Weldon** (1931)
Pulse of Danger, The (1966) **Jon Cleary** (1917)
Pump House Gang, The (1968) **Tom Wolfe** (1930)
Pumpkin Eater, The (1962) **Penelope Mortimer** (1918)
Punch: The Immortal Liar (1921) **Conrad Potter Aiken** (1889)
Punch's Complete Letter-Writer (1845) **Douglas Jerrold** (1803)
Punch's Letters to His Son (1843) **Douglas Jerrold** (1803)
Pupil of Pleasure, The [as 'Courtney Melmoth'] (1776) **Samuel Jackson Pratt** (1749)
Puppet Show, The (1906) **Aleksandr Blok** (1880)
Puppet Show of Memory, The (1922) **Maurice Baring** (1874)
Puppets at Large (1897) **'F. Anstey' [Thomas Anstey Guthrie]** (1856)
Purcell (1995) **Jonathan Keates** (1946)
Purcell Papers, The (1880) **J.S. le Fanu** (1814–73)
Purchas His Pilgrim (1619) **Samuel Purchas** (1577)
Purchas His Pilgrimage (1613) **Samuel Purchas** (1577)
Pure as the Lily (1972) **Catherine Cookson** (1906)
Pure Land, The (1974) **David Foster** (1944)
Purgatory of Suicides, The (1845) **Thomas Cooper** (1805)
Puritaine, The (1607) **Thomas Middleton** (1580)?
Puritan, The (1931) **Liam O'Flaherty** (1897)
Puritan's Wife, A (1896) **Max Pemberton** (1863)
Puritanism and Revolution (1958) **Christopher Hill** (1912)
Purity of Diction in English Verse (1952) **Donald Davie** (1922)
Purple Cloud, The (1901) **M.P. Shiel** (1865)
Purple Dust (1940) **Sean O'Casey** (1880)
Purple East, The (1896) **Sir William Watson** (1858)
Purple Island, The (1633) **Phineas Fletcher** (1582)
Purple Land that England Lost, The (1885) **W.H. Hudson** (1841)
Purple Plain, The (1947) **H.E. Bates** (1905)
Purposes of Love (1939) **'Mary Renault' [Eileen Mary Challans]** (1905)
Purse of Coppers, A (1937) **'Seán O'Faoláin' [John Francis Whelan]** (1900)
Pursuit of Love, The (1945) **Nancy Mitford** (1904)
Pursuit of the Prodigal (1959) **Louis Auchinloss** (1917)
Pushcart at the Kerb, A (1922) **John Dos Passos** (1896)
Pussy, King of the Pirates (1996) **Kathy Acker** (1948)
Put Off Thy Shoes (1945) **Ethel Voynich** (1864)
Put Out More Flags (1942) **Evelyn Waugh** (1903)
Put Yourself in His Place (1870) **Charles Reade** (1814)
Putting the Boot In (1985) **Julian Barnes** (1946)

Puzzle of Dickens's Last Plot, The (1905) **Andrew Lang** (1844)
Puzzleheaded Girl, The (1967) **Christina Stead** (1902)
Pygmalion [screen version] (1941) **Bernard Shaw** (1856)
Pylon (1935) **William Faulkner** (1897)
Pyramid, The (1967) **William Golding** (1911)
Pyramids (1989) **Terry Pratchett** (1948)
Pyrates, The (1983) **George MacDonald Fraser** (1925)
Pyrenees, The (1909) **Hilaire Belloc** (1870)
Pythoness, The (1949) **Kathleen Raine** (1908)

Q

Quack, Quack! (1935) **Leonard Woolf** (1880)
Quadrille (1952) **Noel Coward** (1899)
Quaker, The (1777) **[Charles Dibdin]** (1745)
Quakerism Confirmed (1676) **Robert Barclay** (1648)
Quality of Mercy, The (1892) **William Dean Howells** (1837)
Quality Street (1913) **[Sir] J.M. Barrie** (1860)
Quantity Theory of Insanity, The (1991) **Will Self** (1961)
Quarantine (1997) **Jim Crace** (1946)
Quarantine (1978) **Nicholas Hasluck** (1942)
Quare Fellow, The (1954) **Brendan Behan** (1923)
Quarrels of Authors (1814) **Isaac D'Israeli** (1766)
Quarry, The (1964) **Richard Eberhart** (1904)
Quart Livre ['Fourth Book'] (1548–52) **François Rabelais** (1494?)
Quartermaine's Terms (1981) **Simon Gray** (1936)
Quartet in Autumn (1977) **Barbara Pym** (1913)
Quatre Vents de l'esprit, Les ['The Four Winds of the Spirit'] (1881) **Victor Hugo** (1802–85)
Quattro Cento, The (1932) **Adrian Stokes** (1902)
Queen, The (1653) **John Ford** (1586–1640?)
Queen and I, The (1992) **Sue Townsend** (1946)
Queen Anelida and False Arcite (1477?) **Geoffrey Chaucer** (1340?-1400)
Queen Catharine (1698) **Mary Pix** (1666)
Queen Elizabeth Story, The (1950) **Rosemary Sutcliff** (1920)
Queen Hynde (1825) **James Hogg** (1770)
Queen Lucia (1920) **E.F. Benson** (1867)
Queen Mab (1813) **P.B. Shelley** (1792)
Queen Mary (1875) **Alfred, Lord Tennyson** (1809)
Queen of a Distant Country, The (1972) **John Braine** (1922)
Queen of Cornwall, The [**Hardy**]: see *The Famous Tragedy of the Queen of Cornwall*
Queen of Hearts, The (1859) **Wilkie Collins** (1824)
Queen of Love, The (1894) **S. Baring-Gould** (1834)
Queen of Seven Swords, The (1927) **G.K. Chesterton** (1874)
Queen of Sheba, The (1877) **Thomas Bailey Aldrich** (1836)
Queen of Spades, The (1851) **Dion Boucicault** (1820?)
Queen of Spades, The (1834) **Alexander Pushkin** (1799)
Queen of Stones (1982) **Emma Tennant** (1937)
Queen of the Air, The (1869) **John Ruskin** (1819)
Queen of the Damned, The (1988) **Anne Rice** (1941)
Queen of the Dawn (1925) **Sir H. Rider Haggard** (1856)
Queen of the Realm (1984) **'Jean Plaidy' [Eleanor Hibbert]** (1906)
Queen of the Tambourine, The (1991) **Jane Gardam** (1928)
Queen of the World, The (1900) **'Luke Netterville' [Standish O'Grady]** (1846)
Queen Sheba's Ring (1910) **Sir H. Rider Haggard** (1856)
Queen Victoria (1902) **Sir Sidney Lee** (1859)
Queen Victoria (1921) **Lytton Strachey** (1880)
Queen Who Flew, The (1894) **Ford Madox Ford** (1873)
Queenes Visiting of the Campe at Tilsburie, The (1588) **Thomas Deloney** (1543?)
Queen's Ball, The (1847) **Caroline Clive** (1801)
Queen's Necklace, The [*Le Collier de la reine*] (1849) **Alexandre Dumas ['père']** (1802)
Queen's Quair, The (1904) **Maurice Hewlett** (1861)
Queen's Tragedy, The (1906) **R.H. Benson** (1871)
Queen's Wake, The (1813) **James Hogg** (1770)
Queen-Mother, The [with *Rosamond*] (1860) **A.C. Swinburne** (1837)
Queene of Arragon, The (1640) **William Habington** (1605)
Queenes Arcadia, The (1606) **[Samuel Daniel]** (1562)
Queenes Exchange, The (1657) **Richard Brome** (1590?-1652?)
Queens' Play (1964) **Dorothy Dunnett** (1923)
Queer (1985) **William S. Burroughs** (1914)
Quentin Durward (1823) **Sir Walter Scott** (1771)
Querelle de Brest (1947) **Jean Genet** (1910)
Querer por sola querer (1654) **Sir Richard Fanshawe** (1608) (tr.)
Querist, The (1735) **George Berkeley** (1685)
Queseda (1978) **C.K. Stead** (1932)
Quest for Corvo, The (1934) **A.J.A. Symons** (1900)
Quest of the Golden Girl, The (1896) **Richard Le Gallienne** (1866)
Quest of the Sangraal, The (1863) **R.S. Hawker** (1803)
Quest of Youth, The (1927) **Jeffery Farnol** (1878)
Question of Integrity, A (1994) **Susan Howatch** (1940)
Question of Loyalties, A (1989) **Allan Massie** (1938)
Question of Palestine, The (1979) **Edward Said** (1935)
Question of Power, A (1974) **Bessie Head** (1937)
Question of Proof, A (1935) **'Nicholas Blake' [C. Day Lewis]** (1904)
Question of Upbringing, A [first of the *Dance to the Music of Time* series] (1951) **Anthony Powell** (1905)
Questioning Tiger, The (1964) **James Reeves** (1909)
Questionings on Criticism and Beauty (1909) **A.J. Balfour** (1848)
Questions About the Nature and Perpetuity of the Seventh-Day-Sabbath (1685) **John Bunyan** (1628)
Questions Concerning Liberty, Necessity and Chance, The (1656) **Thomas Hobbes** (1588)
Questions of Travel (1965) **Elizabeth Bishop** (1911)
Qui Pauper Amavi (1919) **Ezra Pound** (1885)

Quiet American, The (1955) **Graham Greene** (1904)
Quiet as a Nun (1977) **Lady Antonia Fraser** (1932)
Quiet Heart, The (1854) **Margaret Oliphant** (1828)
Quiet Life, A (1976) **Beryl Bainbridge** (1934)
Quiller Memorandum, The [US: *The Quiller Memorandum*] (1965) **'Adam Hall' [Elleston Trevor]** (1920)
Quincunx, The (1989) **Charles Palliser** (1947)
Quintessence of Ibsenism, The (1891) **Bernard Shaw** (1856)
Quinx (1985) **Lawrence Durrell** (1912)
Quips upon Questions (1600) **Robert Armin** (1565?)
Quisanté (1900) **'Anthony Hope' [Sir Anthony Hope Hawkins]** (1863)
Quite Early One Morning (1954) **Dylan Thomas** (1914–53)
Quo Vadis? (1617) **Joseph Hall** (1574)
Quo Vadis? (1896) **Henryk Sienkiewicz** (1846)
Quoof (1983) **Paul Muldoon** (1951)
Quorum (1950) **Phyllis Bentley** (1894)
Quotations from Chairman Mao Tse-Tung (1968) **Edward Albee** (1928)
Quyete of Mynde, The [from Plutarch] (1528) **Sir Thomas Wyatt** (1503?) (tr.)

R

Rabbi of Lud (1987) **Stanley Elkin** (1930)
Rabbit at Rest (1990) **John Updike** (1932)
Rabbit is Rich (1981) **John Updike** (1932)
Rabbit Redux (1971) **John Updike** (1932)
Rabbit, Run (1960) **John Updike** (1932)
Race for Wealth, The (1866) **Mrs J.H. Riddell** (1832)
Race of Castlebar, The (1913) **Shan F. Bullock** (1865)
Race, The (1982) **Sinclair Ross** (1908)
Rachel (1926) **Beatrice Harraden** (1864)
Rachel Dene (1894) **Robert Williams Buchanan** (1841)
Rachel Dyer (1828) **John Neal** (1793)
Rachel Gray (1856) **Julia Kavanagh** (1824)
Rachel Papers, The (1973) **Martin Amis** (1949)
Rachel Ray (1863) **Anthony Trollope** (1815)
Racing Demon (1991) **David Hare** (1947)
Racketty Packetty House (1907) **Frances Hodgson Burnett** (1849)
'Racundra's' First Cruise (1923) **Arthur Ransome** (1884)
Radcliffe (1963) **David Storey** (1933)
Radiant Way, The (1987) **Margaret Drabble** (1939)
Radical Chic and Mau-Mauing the Flak Catchers (1970) **Tom Wolfe** (1930)
Radio Romance (1991) **Garrison Keillor** (1942)
Raffles (1901) **E.W. Hornung** (1866)
Rag and Bone Shop (1971) **Earle Birney** (1904)
Rage to Live, A (1949) **John O'Hara** (1905)
Ragged Dick (1867) **Horatio Alger** (1832)
Ragged Lady (1899) **William Dean Howells** (1837)
Ragged Lion, The (1994) **Allan Massie** (1938)
Ragged Trousered Philanthropist, The [abridged; full version, 1955] (1914) **'Robert Tressell' [Robert P. Noonan]** (1870–1911)
Raging Calm, A (1968) **Stan Barstow** (1928)
Raging Turke, The (1631) **Thomas Goffe** (1591–1629)
Ragman's Daughter, The (1963) **Alan Sillitoe** (1928)
Rags of Time, The (1994) **Peter Levi** (1931)
Ragtime (1975) **E.L. Doctorow** (1931)
Rahab (1922) **Waldo Frank** (1889)
Raiders' Dawn (1942) **Alun Lewis** (1915)
Raiders, The (1894) **S.R. Crockett** (1860)
Railings, The (1961) **Alan Brownjohn** (1931)
Railroad Children, The (1855) **Charlotte M. Yonge** (1823)
Railway Accident, The (1969) **Edward Upward** (1903)
Railway Children, The (1906) **E[dith] Nesbit** (1858)
Railway Man and His Children, The (1891) **Margaret Oliphant** (1828)
Rain Forest, The (1974) **Olivia Manning** (1908)
Rain Upon Godshill (1939) **J.B. Priestley** (1894)
Rain-Charm for the Duchy (1992) **Ted Hughes** (1930)
Rainbearers, The (1955) **Nicholas Mosley** (1923)
Rainbirds, The (1968) **Janet Frame** (1924)
Rainbow Gold (1885) **David Christie Murray** (1847)
Rainbow and the Rose, The (1905) **E[dith] Nesbit** (1858)
Rainbow, The (1915) **D.H. Lawrence** (1885)
Rainbow Valley (1919) **L.M. Montgomery** (1874)
Rainbow's End (1975) **James M. Cain** (1892)
Rainforest (1987) **Jenny Diski** (1947)
Rainmaker, The (1995) **John Grisham** (1955)
Rains Came, The (1937) **Louis Bromfield** (1896)
Raise High the Roof-Beam, Carpenters (1963) **J.D. Salinger** (1919)
Raise Race Rays Raze (1971) **LeRoi Jones** (1934)
Raise the Titanic (1976) **Clive Cussler** (1931)
Raisin in the Sun, A (1959) **Lorraine Hansberry** (1930)
Rajah's Saphire, The (1896) **M.P. Shiel** (1865)
Rake's Progress, The (1912) **'Marjorie Bowen' [Gabrielle Margaret Vere Campbell]** (1886)
Ralph Darnell (1865) **Captain Meadows Taylor** (1808)
Ralph Roister Doister (1566?) **Nicholas Udall** (1505?)
Ralph the Bailiff (1862) **M.E. Braddon** (1835)
Ralph the Heir (1871) **Anthony Trollope** (1815)
Ralph Wilton's Weird (1875) **Mrs A.H. Alexander** (1825)
Ralstons, The (1895) **F. Marion Crawford** (1854)
Ramage (1965) **Dudley Pope** (1925)
Rambles Beyond Railways (1851) **Wilkie Collins** (1824)
Rambles by Patricius Walker (1873) **William Allingham** (1824)
Rambles in Germany and Italy (1844) **Mary Shelley** (1797)
Rambles on the Devonshire Coast (1853) **Philip Henry Gosse** (1810)
Rambling Sailor, The (1929) **Charlotte Mew** (1869–1928)
Rameau's Nephew [*Le Neveu de Rameau*] (1804) **Denis Diderot** (1713)

Ramona (1884) **Helen Hunt Jackson** (1830)
Ramuntcho (1897) **'Pierre Loti' [Julien Viaud]** (1850)
Ranald Bannerman's Boyhood (1871) **George MacDonald** (1824)
Ranch on the Beaver, The (1927) **Andy Adams** (1859)
Randolph (1823) **John Neal** (1793)
Random Harvest (1941) **James Hilton** (1900)
Ranleagh House (1747) **Joseph Warton** (1722)
Ransom (1973) **Jon Cleary** (1917)
Ransom (1985) **Jay McInerney** (1955)
Ranson's Folly (1902) **Richard Harding Davis** (1864)
Ranthorpe (1847) **G.H. Lewes** (1817)
Raoul, Gentleman of Fortune (1907) **H.C. Bailey** (1878)
Rape of Clarissa, The (1982) **Terry Eagleton** (1943)
Rape of Lucrece, The (1608) **Thomas Heywood** (1574?)
Rape of Proserpine, The (1727) **Lewis Theobald** (1688)
Rape of Shavi, The (1983) **Buchi Emecheta** (1944)
Rape of Tamar, The (1970) **Dan Jacobson** (1929)
Rape of the Lock, The (1714) **Alexander Pope** (1688)
Rape upon Rape (1730) **Henry Fielding** (1707)
Rapunzel in Suburbia (1975) **Dorothy Hewett** (1923)
Rarahu (1880) **'Pierre Loti' [Julien Viaud]** (1850)
Rasselas **[Johnson]**: see *The Prince of Abyssinia*
Rasta Time in Palestine, A (1987) **Benjamin Zephaniah** (1958)
Rat on Fire, The (1981) **George V. Higgins** (1939)
Rat Race (1970) **Dick Francis** (1920)
Rates of Exchange (1983) **Malcolm Bradbury** (1932)
Rational Primer, A (1799) **Richard Lovell Edgeworth** (1744) [with Maria Edgeworth]
Rationale of Evidence, The (1827) **Jeremy Bentham** (1748
Ratking (1988) **Michael Dibdin** (1947)
Ratner's Star (1976) **Don DeLillo** (1936)
Rats, The (1974) **James Herbert** (1943)
Rats, The [Die Ratten] (1987) **Günter Grass** (1927)
Rattle-Bag, The (1982) **Seamus Heaney** (1939) (ed.) [with Ted Hughes]
Rattlin the Reefer (1836) **Edward Howard** (1793?)
Ravelstein (2000) **Saul Bellow** (1915)
Raven in the Foregate, The (1986) **'Ellis Peters' [Edith Mary Pargeter]** (1913)
Raven Seek Thy Brother (1968) **Gavin Maxwell** (1914)
Raven, The (1845) **Edgar Allan Poe** (1809)
Raven's Brood (1934) **E.F. Benson** (1867)
Raven's Wing (1987) **Joyce Carol Oates** (1938)
Ravenna (1878) **Oscar Wilde** (1854)
Ravenshoe (1862) **Henry Kingsley** (1830)
Ravevens Almanacke, The (1609) **Thomas Dekker** (1572?)
Ravine, The (1869) **Ivan Aleksandrovich Goncharov** (1812)
Ravissement de Lol V. Stein, Le (1964) **'Marguerite Duras' [Marguerite Donnadieu]** (1914)
Raw Edges [inc. the ghost story 'Thurnley Abbey'] (1908) **Perceval Landon** (1869)
Raw Garden, The (1988) **Helen Dunmore** (1952)
Raw Material (1972) **Alan Sillitoe** (1928)
Rawhide Knot, The (1978) **Conrad Richter** (1890)
Rayons et les ombres, Les ['Sunlight and Shadows'] (1840) **Victor Hugo** (1802)
Razor's Edge, The (1944) **Somerset Maugham** (1874)
Razzle-Dazzle (1942) **William Saroyan** (1908)
Re: Colonised Planet 5, Shikasta (1979) **Doris Lessing** (1919)
Re-Discovery of America, The (1928) **Waldo Frank** (1889)
Re-Ordering of the Stones, The (1961) **Jon Silkin** (1930)
Reaching Tin River (1990) **Thea Astley** (1925)
Reactions to the French Revolution (1972) **Richard Cobb** (1917)
Reader, I Married Him (1974) **Patricia Beer** (1924)
Readers and Writers 1917–21 (1922) **A.R. Orage** (1873)
Readie & Easie Way to Establish a Free Commonwealth, The (1660) **John Milton** (1608)
Reading a Novel (1949) **Walter Allen** (1911)
Reading of Earth, A (1888) **George Meredith** (1828)
Reading of Life, A (1901) **George Meredith** (1828)
Reading the Signs (1984) **Michael Wilding** (1942)
Reading the Spirit (1937) **Richard Eberhart** (1904)
Reading the Thirties (1978) **Bernard Bergonzi** (1929)
Reading, Writing and Remembering (1932) **E.V. Lucas** (1868)
Readings for Railways (1849) **Leigh Hunt** (1784)
Readings on Poetry (1810) **Richard Lovell Edgeworth** (1744) [with Maria Edgeworth]
Ready-Money Mortiboy (1872) **Sir Walter Besant** (1836) [with James Rice]
Real Adventures of Robinson Crusoe, The (1892) **Sir F.C. Burnand** (1836)
Real Charlotte, The (1894) **'Somerville and Ross' [Edith Somerville** (1858) and **Violet Martin** (1862)**]**
Real David Copperfield, The (1933) **Robert Graves** (1895)
Real Dreams (1984) **Trevor Griffiths** (1935)
Real Illusions (1985) **Russell Haley** (1934)
Real Inspector Hound, The (1968) **Tom Stoppard** (1937)
Real Life of Alejandro Mayta, The [*La Historia de Alejandro Mayta*] (1984) **Mario Vargas Llosa** (1936)
Real Life of Sebastian Knight, The (1941) **Vladimir Nabokov** (1899)
Real People (1969) **Alison Lurie** (1926)
Real Presences (1989) **George Steiner** (1929)
Real Thing, The (1982) **Tom Stoppard** (1937)
Real Thing, The (1893) **Henry James** (1843)
Real War 1914–18, The (1930) **Sir Basil Liddell Hart** (1895)
Real World, The (1901) **Robert Herrick** (1868)
Realism and Reality (1946) **Anaïs Nin** (1903)
Realities (1851) **[E. Lynn Linton]** (1822)
Reality Sandwiches (1963) **Allen Ginsberg** (1926)
Realm of Essence, The [first of *The Realms of Being* series] (1927) **George Santayana** (1863)

Realm of Matter, The (1930) **George Santayana** (1863)
Realm of Spirit, The (1940) **George Santayana** (1863)
Realm of Truth, The (1937) **George Santayana** (1863)
Realmah (1868) **Sir Arthur Helps** (1813)
Realms of Gold, The (1975) **Margaret Drabble** (1939)
Realms of Tartarus, The (1977) **Brian M. Stableford** (1948)
Reaped and Bound (1933) **Compton Mackenzie** (1883)
Reaper Man (1991) **Terry Pratchett** (1948)
Reaping, A (1909) **E.F. Benson** (1867)
Rear Column, The (1978) **Simon Gray** (1936)
Reason (1700) **John Pomfret** (1667)
Reason and Romanticism (1926) **Sir Herbert Read** (1893)
Reason of Church-government Urg'd Against Prelaty, The (1642) **John Milton** (1608)
Reason Why, The (1953) **Cecil Woodham-Smith** (1896)
Reasonableness of Christianity, The (1695) **John Locke** (1632)
Reasonableness of Conformity to the Church of England, The (1703) **Benjamin Hoadly** (1676)
Rebecca (1938) **Daphne du Maurier** (1907)
Rebecca and Rowena [as 'M.A. Titmarsh'] (1850) **W.M. Thackeray** (1811)
Rebecca Notebook, The (1981) **Daphne du Maurier** (1907)
Rebecca of Sunnybrook Farm (1903) **Kate Douglas Wiggin** (1856)
Rebecca West (1987) **Victoria Glendinning** (1937)
Rebel, The [*L'Homme révolté*] (1951) **Albert Camus** (1913)
Rebel Angels, The (1981) **Robertson Davies** (1913)
Rebel General, The (1967) **Chris Wallace-Crabbe** (1934)
Rebel of the Family, The (1880) **E. Lynn Linton** (1822)
Rebel Queen, The (1893) **Sir Walter Besant** (1836)
Rebellion of Young David, The (1975) **Ernest Buckler** (1908)
Rebels, The (1953) **Henry Treece** (1911)
Rebirth of a Nation (1981) **Kenneth O. Morgan** (1934)
Rebuilding Russia (1990) **Alexander Solzhenitsyn** (1918)
Rebus: The Early Years [compilation] (1999) **Ian Rankin** (1960)
Recapitulation (1979) **Wallace Stegner** (1909)
Recess, The [vol. i; vols. ii and iii, 1785] (1783) **Sophia Lee** (1750)
Recessional (1994) **James A. Michener** (1907)
Reckless Ecstasy (1904) **Carl Sandburg** (1878)
Reckoning, The (1999) **Ted Allbeury** (1917)
Recluse, The (1888) **William Wordsworth** (1770–1850)
Recluse of Norway, The (1814) **Anna Maria Porter** (1780)
Recognitions, The (1955) **William Gaddis** (1922)
Recollections (1917) **John Morley** (1838)
Recollections of a Busy Life (1868) **Horace Greeley** (1811)
Recollections of a Literary Life (1852) **Mary Russell Mitford** (1787)
Recollections of an Excursion to the Monasteries of Alcobaça and Batalha (1835) **William Beckford** (1760)
Recollections of Geoffrey Hamlyn, The (1859) **Henry Kingsley** (1830)
Recollections of the Gala (1950) **Nicholas Moore** (1918)
Recollections of the Last Days of Shelley and Byron (1858) **E.J. Trelawny** (1792)
Recollections of the Life of Lord Byron (1814) **R.C. Dallas** (1754)
Recollections of the Table-Talk of Samuel Rogers (1856) **Samuel Rogers** (1763–1855)
Record of a Girlhood (1878) **Frances [Fanny] Kemble** (1809)
Records of Israel (1844) **Grace Aguilar** (1816)
Records of Later Life (1882) **Frances [Fanny] Kemble** (1809)
Records of Tennyson, Ruskin, Robert and Elizabeth Browning (1892) **Lady Anne Ritchie** (1837)
Records of Woman (1828) **Felicia Dorothea Hemans** (1793)
Recoveries (1964) **Elizabeth Jennings** (1926)
Recovering a Body (1994) **Helen Dunmore** (1952)
Recovery (1973) **John Berryman** (1914–72)
Recovery of Belief, The (1952) **C.E.M. Joad** (1891)
Recovery of the West, The (1941) **Michael Roberts** (1902)
Recreations of Christopher North, The (1842) **John Wilson** (1785)
Recreations with the Muses (1637) **Sir William Alexander** (1567?)
Recruiting Officer, The (1706) **George Farquhar** (1678)
Rector and the Doctor's Family, The (1862) **Margaret Oliphant** (1828)
Rector of Justin, The (1964) **Louis Auchinloss** (1917)
Rector's Daughter, The (1924) **F.M. Mayor** (1872)
Red and the Green, The (1965) **Iris Murdoch** (1919)
Red and White Heather (1894) **Robert Williams Buchanan** (1841)
Red as a Rose is She (1870) **Rhoda Broughton** (1840)
Red Axe, The (1898) **S.R. Crockett** (1860)
Red Badge of Courage, The (1895) **Stephen Crane** (1871)
Red Barbara (1928) **Liam O'Flaherty** (1897)
Red Bird (1979) **Christopher Logue** (1926)
Red, Black, Blond, and Olive (1956) **Edmund Wilson** (1895)
Red Box, The (1937) **Rex Stout** (1886)
Red Bull [**Stout**]: see *Some Buried Caesar*
Red Cap Adventures (1908) **S.R. Crockett** (1860)
Red Cap Tales (1904) **S.R. Crockett** (1860)
Red Cockade, The (1895) **Stanley J. Weyman** (1855)
Red Cotton Night-Cap Country; or, Turf and Towers (1873) **Robert Browning** (1812)
Red Court Farm, The (1868) **Mrs Henry Wood** (1814)

Red Cross Barge, The (1916) **Mrs Belloc Lowndes** (1868)
Red Death, A (1991) **Walter Mosley** (1952)
Red Deer (1884) **Richard Jefferies** (1848)
Red Dragon (1981) **Thomas Harris** (1940)
Red Eric, The (1861) **R.M. Ballantyne** (1825)
Red Eve (1911) **Sir H. Rider Haggard** (1856)
Red Fairy Book, The (1890) **Andrew Lang** (1844) (ed.)
Red Fox (1905) **Sir Charles G.D. Roberts** (1860)
Red Hall (1852) **William Carleton** (1794)
Red Harvest (1929) **Dashiell Hammett** (1894)
Red House Mystery, The (1922) **A.A. Milne** (1882)
Red House, The (1902) **E[dith] Nesbit** (1858)
Red Hugh's Captivity [rev. 1897 as *The Flight of the Eagle*] (1889) **Standish O'Grady** (1846)
Red Hunters and Animal People (1904) **Charles Eastman** (1858)
Red Knight, The (1921) **Francis Brett Young** (1884)
Red Leaf, The (1957) **Christopher Hassall** (1912)
Red Leaguers, The (1904) **Shan F. Bullock** (1865)
Red Lily, The [Le Lys rouge] (1894) **'Anatole France' [Jacques-Anatole-François Thibault]** (1844)
Red Limbo Lingo, The (1971) **Lawrence Durrell** (1912)
Red Man and White (1896) **Owen Wister** (1860)
Red Man's Revenge, The (1880) **R.M. Ballantyne** (1825)
Red Pony, The (1937) **John Steinbeck** (1902)
Red Pottage (1899) **Mary Cholmondeley** (1859)
Red Priest, The (1956) **Wyndham Lewis** (1882)
Red Queen, White Queen (1958) **Henry Treece** (1911)
Red Rock (1898) **Thomas Nelson Page** (1853)
Red Room, The (1879) **August Strindberg** (1849)
Red Rooney (1886) **R.M. Ballantyne** (1825)
Red Roses for Me (1942) **Sean O'Casey** (1880)
Red Rover, The (1827) **James Fenimore Cooper** (1789)
Red Rowans (1895) **Flora Annie Steel** (1847)
Red Shift (1973) **Alan Garner** (1934)
Red Snow and Other Parables from Nature (1862) **Margaret [Mrs Alfred] Gatty** (1809)
Red Spider (1887) **S. Baring-Gould** (1834)
Red Storm Rising (1986) **Tom Clancy** (1947)
Red Tapeworm, The (1941) **Compton Mackenzie** (1883)
Red Thumb Mark, The (1907) **R. Austin Freeman** (1862)
Red Triangle, The (1903) **Arthur Morrison** (1863)
Red Wine & Yellow Hair (1949) **Kenneth Patchen** (1911)
Red-Dirt Marijuana (1967) **Terry Southern** (1924)
Red-Headed Pupil, The (1994) **Jeffrey Wainwright** (1944)
Redback (1986) **Howard Jacobson** (1942)
Redburn (1849) **Herman Melville** (1819)
Redemption (1722) **Sir Richard Blackmore** (1654)
Redemption (1772) **Henry Brooke** (1703)
Redemption (1949) **Francis Stuart** (1902)
Redgauntlet (1824) **Sir Walter Scott** (1771)
Redheap [US: *Every Mother's Son*] (1930) **Norman Lindsay** (1879)
Redimiculum Matellarum (1930) **Basil Bunting** (1900)
Redmond Count O'Hanlon, the Irish Rapparee (1862) **William Carleton** (1794)
Redress of Poetry, The (1990) **Seamus Heaney** (1939)
Redskin and Cowboy (1892) **G.A. Henty** (1832)
Redskins, The (1846) **James Fenimore Cooper** (1789)
Redundancy of Courage, The (1991) **Timothy Mo** (1950)
Reed Anthony, Cowman (1907) **Andy Adams** (1859)
Reed Music (1998) **Peter Levi** (1931)
Reed Shaken by the Wind, A (1956) **Gavin Maxwell** (1914)
Reeds Shaken with the Wind (1843) **R.S. Hawker** (1803)
Reef, The (1912) **Edith Wharton** (1862)
Reefs of Space, The (1964) **Frederik Pohl** (1919)
Reflection on Our Modern Poetry, A (1695) **John Phillips** (1631)
Reflections 1923–1988 (1990) **Graham Greene** (1904)
Reflections at Fifty (1954) **James T. Farrell** (1904)
Reflections Critical and Satyrical (1711) **John Dennis** (1657)
Reflections in a Golden Eye (1941) **Carson McCullers** (1917)
Reflections in a Mirror [1st ser.; 2nd ser., 1846] (1944) **Charles Morgan** (1894)
Reflections in A Writer's Eye (1986) **Angus Wilson** (1913)
Reflections of a Non-Political Man [*Betrachtungen eines Unpolitischen*] (1918) **Thomas Mann** (1875)
Reflections of Ambrosine, The (1902) **Elinor Glyn** (1864)
Reflections on a Marine Venus (1953) **Lawrence Durrell** (1912)
Reflections on a Ravaged Century (1999) **Robert Conquest** (1917)
Reflections on British Painting (1934) **Roger Fry** (1866)
Reflections on the Constitution (1951) **Harold Laski** (1893)
Reflections on the Failure of Socialism (1955) **Max Eastman** (1883)
Reflections on the Golden Bed (1947) **Mulk Raj Anand** (1905)
Reflections on the Present State of Affairs at Home and Abroad (1759) **Arthur Young** (1741)
Reflections on the Psalms (1958) **C.S. Lewis** (1898)
Reflections on the Revolution in France (1790) **Edmund Burke** (1729)
Reflections on the Revolution of Our Time (1943) **Harold Laski** (1893)
Reflections on the Rise and Progress of the American Rebellion (1780) **John Wesley** (1703)
Reflections on the Seven Days of the Week (1770) **Catherine Talbot** (1721–70)
Reflections on the Stage and Mr Collier's Defence of the Short View (1699) **John Oldmixon** (1673)
Reflections Upon Ancient and Modern Learning (1694) **William Wotton** (1666)

Reflections upon the Present State of England (1782) **Thomas Day** (1748)
Réflexions sur la paix intérieure ['Reflections on Civil Peace'] (1795) **Madame de Staël** (1766)
Reform and Reformation (1977) **G.R. Elton** (1921)
Reform'd Coquet, The (1724) **Mary Davys** (1674)
Reformation of Manners (1702) **Daniel Defoe** (1660)
Refugee in America, The (1832) **Frances Trollope** (1780)
Refugees, The (1893) **A. Conan Doyle** (1859)
Refusal, The (1721) **Colley Cibber** (1671)
Refusal to Conform (1963) **James Kirkup** (1923)
Refutation of Deism, A (1814) **P.B. Shelley** (1792)
Regarding Wave (1970) **Gary Snyder** (1930)
Regency Buck (1935) **Georgette Heyer** (1902)
Regeneration (1991) **Pat Barker** (1943)
Regent, The (1913) **Arnold Bennett** (1867)
Regent's Daughter, The [*La Fille du régent*] (1847) **Alexandre Dumas ['père']** (1802)
Reggae or Not! (1981) **LeRoi Jones** (1934)
Regicide, The (1749) **Tobias George Smollett** (1721)
Regiment of Women (1917) **'Clemence Dane' [Winifred Ashton]** (1888)
Regiment of Women (1973) **Thomas Berger** (1924)
Reginald (1904) **'Saki' [Hector Hugh Munro]** (1870)
Reginald Hetherege (1874) **Henry Kingsley** (1830)
Reginald in Russia (1910) **'Saki' [Hector Hugh Munro]** (1870)
Region of the Summer Stars, The (1944) **Charles Williams** (1886)
Region's Violence, The (1976) **Ruth Fainlight** (1931)
Registrum Sacrum Anglicanum (1858) **William Stubbs** (1825)
Regulus (1694) **John Crowne** (d. 1703)
Rehabilitations (1939) **C.S. Lewis** (1898)
Rehearsal (1976) **Jack Gelber** (1932)
Rehearsal at Goatham, The (1754) **John Gay** (1685–1732)
Rehearsal, The [*La Répétition*] (1950) **Jean Anouilh** (1910)
Rehearsal Transpros'd , The [pt. i] (1672) **Andrew Marvell** (1621)
Rehearsal Transpros'd, The [pt. ii] (1673) **Andrew Marvell** (1621)
Reign of Law, The (1900) **James Lane Allen** (1849)
Reign of Sparrows, The (1980) **Roy Fuller** (1912)
Reign of William Rufus and the Accession of Henry the First, The (1882) **E.A. Freeman** (1823)
Reigne of King Henry the Second, The (1633) **Thomas May** (1595)
Reincarnation (1892) **Annie Besant** (1847)
Reincarnations (1918) **James Stephens** (1882)
Reinhart in Love (1962) **Thomas Berger** (1924)
Reinhart's Women (1981) **Thomas Berger** (1924)
Reivers, The (1962) **William Faulkner** (1897)
Rejected Addresses (1812) **Horace Smith** (1779) [with James Smith]
Relapse, The (1696) **Sir John Vanbrugh** (1664)
Relation of a Journey, A (1615) **George Sandys** (1578)
Relation of My Imprisonment, The (1983) **Russell Banks** (1940)
Relation of Ten Years Travells, A (1656) **Richard Flecknoe** (*c.* 1620)
Relation of the Conference Betweene William Lawd . . . and Mr Fisher, A (1639) **William Laud** (1573)
Relative Successes (1984) **A.L. Barker** (1918)
Relative Value of Studies and Accomplishments in the Education of Women, The (1862) **R.H. Hutton** (1826)
Relative Values (1951) **Noel Coward** (1899)
Relatively Speaking (1965) **Alan Ayckbourn** (1939)
Relentless City, The (1903) **E.F. Benson** (1867)
Relic, The (1957) **Robert Hillyer** (1895)
Relics of Shelley (1862) **Richard Garnett** (1835) (ed.)
Religio Laici (1682) **John Dryden** (1631)
Religio Medici (1643) **Sir Thomas Browne** (1605)
Religion and Philosophy (1916) **R.G. Collingwood** (1889)
Religion and Science (1935) **Bertrand Russell** (1872)
Religion and the Decline of Magic (1971) **Sir Keith Thomas** (1933)
Religion and the Rise of Capitalism (1926) **R.H. Tawney** (1880)
Religion of a Literary Man, The (1893) **Richard le Gallienne** (1866)
Religion of Humanity, The (1888) **A.J. Balfour** (1848)
Religion of Protestants a Safe Way to Salvation, The (1637) **William Chillingworth** (1602)
Religion, Philosophy and Psychical Research (1953) **C.D. Broad** (1887)
Religion, the Reformation and Social Change (1967) **Hugh Trevor-Roper** (1914)
Religion Without Revelation (1927) **Julian Huxley** (1887)
Religious Courtship (1722) **Daniel Defoe** (1660)
Religious Situation, The (1932) **Paul Tillich** (1886)
Religious Songs of a Connacht, The (1906) **Douglas Hyde** (1860)
Religious Tendencies of the Age, The (1860) **W.E.H. Lecky** (1838)
Reliquary, The (1836) **Bernard Barton** (1784) [with Lucy Barton]
Reliques of Ancient English Poetry (1765) **Thomas Percy** (1729) (ed.)
Reliques of Irish Poetry (1789) **Charlotte Brooke** (1740?)
Reliquiae Baxterianae (1696) **Richard Baxter** (1615–91)
Reliquiae Bodleianae (1703) **Thomas Hearne** (1678) (ed.)
Reliquiae Wottonianae (1651) **Sir Henry Wotton** (1568–1639)
Reluctant Neighbours (1972) **E.R. Braithwaite** (1912)
Reluctant Peer, The (1964) **William Douglas Home** (1912)
Reluctant Queen, The (1990) **'Jean Plaidy' [Eleanor Hibbert]** (1906)
Remains (1670) **Fulke Greville, Lord Brooke** (1554–1628)
Remains (1652) **George Herbert** (1593–1633)

Remains [pt. i] (1838) **R.H. Froude** (1803–36)
Remains [pt. ii] (1838) **R.H. Froude** (1803–36)
Remains in Verse and Prose (1834) **A.H. Hallam** (1811–33)
Remains of Elmet (1979) **Ted Hughes** (1930)
Remains of the Day, The (1989) **Kazuo Ishiguro** (1954)
Remake (1996) **Christine Brooke-Rose** (1926)
Remaking of Modern Armies, The (1927) **Sir Basil Liddell Hart** (1895)
Remarkable History of Sir Thomas Upmore, The (1884) **R.D. Blackmore** (1825)
Remarkable Providences (1684) **Increase Mather** (1639)
Remarks on 'Clarissa' (1749) **Sarah Fielding** (1710)
Remarks on Forest Scenery (1791) **William Gilpin** (1724)
Remarks on Mr Pope's Rape of the Lock (1728) **John Dennis** (1657)
Remarks on Several Parts of Italy (1705) **Joseph Addison** (1672)
Remarks on the History of England (1743) **Henry Saint-John, Viscount Bolingbroke** (1678)
Remarks on the History of Scotland (1773) **Sir David Dalrymple, Lord Hailes** (1726)
Remarks upon a Late Discourse of Free-thinking (1713) **Richard Bentley** (1662)
Remarks upon Cato (1713) **John Dennis** (1657)
Remarks upon Mr Pope's Translation of Homer (1717) **John Dennis** (1657)
Rembrandt's Eyes (1999) **Simon Schama** (1945)
Rembrandt's Hat (1973) **Bernard Malamud** (1914)
Remedie Against Sorrow and Feare, A (1612) **Richard Hooker** (1554–1600)
Remedy of Discontentment, The (1645) **Joseph Hall** (1574)
Remember Jack Hoxie (1969) **Jon Cleary** (1917)
Remember Me (1976) **Fay Weldon** (1931)
Remember the Alamo (1888) **Amelia Barr** (1831)
Remember to Remember (1947) **Henry Miller** (1891)
Remembering Babylon (1993) **David Malouf** (1934)
Remembering Laughter (1937) **Wallace Stegner** (1909)
Remembrance Day (1993) **Brian Aldiss** (1925)
Remembrance of Crimes Past (1990) **Dannie Abse** (1923)
Remembrance Rock (1948) **Carl Sandburg** (1878)
Reminiscences (1881) **Thomas Carlyle** (1795–1881)
Reminiscences (1899) **Justin McCarthy** (1830)
Reminiscences of a Literary Life (1836) **Thomas Frognall Dibdin** (1776)
Reminiscences of the Impressionist Painters (1906) **George Moore** (1852)
Remnants (1918) **Desmond MacCarthy** (1877)
Remorse (1813) **S.T. Coleridge** (1772)
Remorseful Day, The [last 'Inspector Morse' novel] (1999) **Colin Dexter** (1930)
Remote People (1931) **Evelyn Waugh** (1903)
Removalists, The (1971) **David Williamson** (1942)
Renaissance Fancies and Studies (1895) **'Vernon Lee' [Violet Paget]** (1856)
Renaissance in Italy, The (1875) **John Addington Symonds** (1840)
Rendezvous in Black (1948) **Cornell Woolrich** (1903)
Rendezvous, The (1980) **Daphne du Maurier** (1907)
Rendezvous with Rama (1973) **Arthur C. Clarke** (1917)
René (1802) **François-René, vicomte de Chateaubriand** (1768–1848)
Renée Mauperin (1864) **Edmond** (1822) and **Jules** (1830) **de Goncourt**
Renegado, The (1630) **Philip Massinger** (1583)
Renny's Daughter (1951) **Mazo de la Roche** (1879)
Rent Day, The (1832) **Douglas Jerrold** (1803)
Repealers, The (1833) **Marguerite, Countess of Blessington** (1789)
Replication, A [Honorificatissimo, amplisimo . . . A replycacion agaynst certayne yong scolers] (1528) **John Skelton** (1460?)
Reply to the Essay on Population, A (1807) **William Hazlitt** (1778)
Report of the Truth of the Fight About the Iles of the Açores, A (1591) **Sir Walter Ralegh** (1554)
Report on Probability A (1968) **Brian Aldiss** (1925)
Reports of My Death (1990) **Karl Shapiro** (1913)
Representations of the Intellectual [Reith lectures 1993] (1994) **Edward Said** (1935)
Representative Men (1850) **Ralph Waldo Emerson** (1803)
Reprieve, The [*Le Sursis*] (1945) **Jean-Paul Sartre** (1905)
Reprisal, The (1757) **Tobias George Smollett** (1721)
Reproof (1747) **Tobias George Smollett** (1721)
Republic of Love, The (1992) **Carol Shields** (1935)
Reputations (1928) **Sir Basil Liddell Hart** (1895)
Requiem (1964) **'Anna Akhmatova' [Anna Andreevna Gorenko]** (1889)
Requiem for a Dream (1978) **Hubert Selby Jr** (1928)
Requiem for a Futurologist (1985) **Wole Soyinka** (1934)
Requiem for a Nun (1951) **William Faulkner** (1897)
Required Writing (1983) **Philip Larkin** (1922)
Res Judicatae (1892) **Augustine Birrell** (1850)
Rescue, The (1920) **Joseph Conrad** (1857)
Resentment (1918) **Alec Waugh** (1898)
Reservoir Ravine (1979) **Hugh Hood** (1928)
Reservoir, The (1966) **Janet Frame** (1924)
'Residence on Earth' [*Residencia en la Tierra*] (1933–47) **Pablo Neruda** (1904)
Resident Alien (1986) **Clark Blaise** (1940)
Resignation (1762) **Edward Young** (1683)
Resistible Rise of Arturo Uri, The [*Der aufhaltsame Aufstieg des Arturo Uri*] (1941) **Bertolt Brecht** (1898)
Resolves (1623) **Owen Felltham** (1602?)
Resounding Tinkle, A (1957) **N.F. Simpson** (1919)
Responses (1976) **Richard Wilbur** (1921)
Responsibilities (1914) **W.B. Yeats** (1865)
Responsibilities, and Other Poems (1916) **W.B. Yeats** (1865)
Responsibilities of the Novelist, The (1903) **Frank Norris** (1870–1902)

Responsibility (1919) **James Evershed Agate** (1877)
Responsibility and Culture (1925) **L.P. Jacks** (1860)
Rest and Unrest (1910) **Edward Thomas** (1878)
Rest Harrow (1910) **Maurice Hewlett** (1861)
Restaurant at the End of the Universe, The (1980) **Douglas Adams** (1952)
Restitution (1998) **Maureen Duffy** (1933)
Restless Heart, The [*La Sauvage*] (1938) **Jean Anouilh** (1910)
Restless Human Hearts (1875) **Richard Jefferies** (1848)
Restoration (1989) **Rose Tremain** (1943)
Restoration of Arnold Middleton, The (1966) **David Storey** (1933)
Restoration of the Works of Art to Italy, The (1816) **Felicia Dorothea Hemans** (1793)
Resurrection (1934) **William Gerhardie** (1895)
Resurrection (1899) **Leo Tolstoy** (1828)
Resurrection of Joseph Bourne, The (1980) **Jack Hodgins** (1938)
Resurrection of the Dead, and Eternall Judgement, The (1665) **John Bunyan** (1628)
Resurrection, The (1966) **John Gardner** (1933)
Retaliation (1774) **Oliver Goldsmith** (1728–74)
Retour d l'URSS ['Return to the USSR'] (1937) **André Gide** (1869)
Retour d'Alsace, août 1914 ['Return from Alsace in August 1914'] (1916) **Jean Giraudoux** (1882–1944)
Retour du Tchad ['Return to Chad'] (1928) **André Gide** (1869)
Retreat (1928) **Edmund Blunden** (1896)
Retreat, The (1959) **P.H. Newby** (1918)
Retreat, The (1936) **Forrest Reid** (1875)
Retreat From Love [*La Retraite sentimentale*] (1907) **Colette** (1873)
Retreat to Pleasure (1940) **Irwin Shaw** (1913)
Retrieval System, The (1978) **Maxine Kumin** (1925)
Retrogression (1917) **Sir William Watson** (1858)
Retrospection (1811) **Richard Cumberland** (1732)
Retrospective Reviews (1896) **Richard le Gallienne** (1866)
Return, The (1910) **Walter de la Mare** (1873)
Return, The (1987) **Charles Tomlinson** (1927)
Return of Bull-Dog Drummond, The [US: *Bulldog Drummond Returns*] (1932) **'Sapper' [Herman Cyril McNeile]** (1888)
Return of Don Quixote, The (1927) **G.K. Chesterton** (1874)
*Return of H*y*m*a*n K*a*p*l*a*n, The* [as 'Leonard Q. Ross'] (1959) **Leo Rosten** (1908)
Return of Lanny Budd, The (1953) **Upton Sinclair** (1878)
Return of Reginald Perrin, The (1977) **David Nobbs** (1935)
Return of Sherlock Holmes, The (1905) **A. Conan Doyle** (1859)
Return of Tarzan, The (1915) **Edgar Rice Burroughs** (1875)
Return of the Brute, The (1929) **Liam O'Flaherty** (1897)
Return of the King, The [*The Lord of the Rings* pt. iii] (1955) **J.R.R. Tolkein** (1892)
Return of the Native, The (1878) **Thomas Hardy** (1840)
Return of the O'Mahony, The (1892) **Harold Frederic** (1856)
Return of the Petticoat, The (1909) **Warwick Deeping** (1877)
Return of the Soldier, The (1918) **'Rebecca West' [Cicily Isabel Andrews]** (1892)
Return of the Sphinx (1967) **Hugh MacLennan** (1907)
Return of the Sphinx (1980) **Hugh MacLennan** (1907)
Return of Ulysses, The (1890) **Robert Bridges** (1844)
Return to Coolami (1936) **Eleanor Dark** (1901)
Return to Essentials (1991) **G.R. Elton** (1921)
Return to Jalna (1946) **Mazo de la Roche** (1879)
Return to Paradise (1951) **James A. Michener** (1907)
Return to the Marshes (1977) **Gavin Young** (1928)
Returning (1982) **Edna O'Brien** (1932)
Returning to Vienna (1947) **Sir Stephen Spender** (1909)
Reuben and Rachel (1799) **Mrs [Susanna] Rowson** (1762)
Reuben Apsley (1827) **Horace Smith** (1779)
Reuben, Reuben (1964) **Peter de Vries** (1910)
Reuben Sachs (1888) **Amy Levy** (1861)
Reuben's Luck (1896) **R.M. Ballantyne** (1825–94)
Reunion (1976) **David Mamet** (1947)
Reunion in Vienna (1931) **Robert E. Sherwood** (1896)
Rev Annabel Lee, The (1898) **Robert Williams Buchanan** (1841)
Revaluation (1936) **F.R. Leavis** (1895)
Revaluation of Obscenity, The (1931) **Havelock Ellis** (1859)
Revelations of the Dead-Alive (1824) **John Banim** (1798)
Revelations of the Secret Service (1911) **William le Queux** (1864)
Revenge, The (1795) **Thomas Chatterton** (1752–70)
Revenge, The (1721) **Edward Young** (1683)
Revenge (1919) **H.G. de Lisser** (1878)
Revenge for Love, The (1937) **Wyndham Lewis** (1882)
Revenge of Bussy D'Ambois, The (1613) **George Chapman** (1559?)
Revenge of the Lawn (1971) **Richard Brautigan** (1935)
Revenger's Comedies, The (1989) **Alan Ayckbourn** (1939)
Revenger's Tragedy, The (1607) **Cyril Tourneur** (1575?) [or Thomas Middleton]
Reverberator, The (1888) **Henry James** (1843)
Reverend Griffith Davenport, The (1899) **James A. Herne** (1839)
Reverie, The (1762) **Charles Johnstone** (1719?)
Reveries of a Solitary Walker, The [*Les Rêveries du promeneur solitaire*] (1782) **Jean-Jacques Rousseau** (1712–78)
Reversals (1969) **Anne Stevenson** (1933)
Reverse of the Medal, The (1986) **Patrick O'Brian** (1914)

Review of the Principal Questions and Difficulties in Morals, A (1758) **Richard Price** (1723)
Revision of the Treaty, A (1922) **J.M. Keynes** (1883)
Revizor (1836) **Nikolai Vasilevich Gogol** (1809)
Revolt in 2100 (1953) **Robert A. Heinlein** (1907)
Revolt in the Desert (1927) **T.E. Lawrence** (1888–1935)
Revolt of Hindoostan, The (1857) **Ernest Charles Jones** (1819)
Revolt of Man, The (1882) **Sir Walter Besant** (1836)
Revolt of the Workhouse, The (1834) **Gilbert Abbott a Beckett** (1811)
Revolt on Alpha C (1955) **Robert Silverberg** (1935)
Revolting Garden, The [as 'Rose Blight'] (1979) **Germaine Greer** (1939)
Revolution and Roses (1957) **P.H. Newby** (1918)
Revolution From Within (1992) **Gloria Steinem** (1934)
Revolution in Tanner's Lane, The (1887) **'Mark Rutherford' [William Hale White]** (1831)
Revolution in Warfare, The (1946) **Sir Basil Liddell Hart** (1895)
Revolution in Writing (1935) **C. Day Lewis** (1904)
Revolutionary Petunias (1973) **Alice Walker** (1944)
Revolver à cheveux blancs, Le (1932) **André Breton** (1896)
Revolving Lights (1923) **Dorothy M. Richardson** (1873)
Reward of the Faithfull, The (1623) **Giles Fletcher the Younger** (1588?)
Rewards and Fairies (1910) **Rudyard Kipling** (1865)
Rex (1925) **E.F. Benson** (1867)
Reynard the Fox [*Reineke Fuchs*] (1794) **Johann Wolfgang von Goethe** (1749)
Reynard the Fox (1946) **John Masefield** (1878)
Rezánov (1906) **Gertrude Atherton** (1857)
Rhetoric **Aristotle** (384)
Rhetoric of the Unreal, A (1981) **Christine Brooke-Rose** (1926)
Rhinoceros (1960) **Eugène Ionesco** (1909)
Rhoda Fleming (1865) **George Meredith** (1828)
Rhode Island Blues (2000) **Fay Weldon** (1931)
Rhododaphne (1818) **Thomas Love Peacock** (1785)
Rhyme of the Flying Bomb, The (1962) **Mervyn Peake** (1911)
Rhymes [*Rimas*] (1604) **Lope de Vega** (1562)
Rhymes à la Mode (1885) **Andrew Lang** (1844)
Rhymes for My Rags (1956) **Robert W. Service** (1876)
Rhymes for Young Folk (1887) **William Allingham** (1824)
Rhymes of a Rebel (1952) **Robert W. Service** (1876)
Rhymes of a Red Cross Man (1916) **Robert W. Service** (1876)
Rhymes of a Rolling Stone (1912) **Robert W. Service** (1876)
Rhymes of a Roughneck (1950) **Robert W. Service** (1876)
Rhymes of Travel, Ballads and Poems (1849) **Bayard Taylor** (1825)
Rhymes Without Reason (1944) **Mervyn Peake** (1911)
Rhyming Chronicle, A (1850) **Jean Ingelow** (1820)
Rhythm of Life, The (1893) **Alice Meynell** (1847)
Riceyman Steps (1923) **Arnold Bennett** (1867)
Rich (1984) **Craig Raine** (1944)
Rich Man, Poor Man (1970) **Irwin Shaw** (1913)
Rich Man's Daughter, A (1897) **Mrs J.H. Riddell** (1832)
Rich Pay Late, The [first of the *Alms for Oblivion* series] (1964) **Simon Raven** (1927)
Rich Relatives (1921) **Compton Mackenzie** (1883)
Richard Barton (1873) **Mrs Caroline Bray** (1814)
Richard Cable the Lightshipman (1888) **[S. Baring-Gould]** (1834)
Richard Chatterton, VC (1915) **Ruby M. Ayres** (1883)
Richard Coeur de Lion (1786) **John Burgoyne** (1722)
Richard Dare (1894) **Mrs Louisa Baldwin** (1845)
Richard Darlington (1831) **Alexandre Dumas ['père']** (1802)
Richard Hurdis (1838) **William Gilmore Simms** (1806)
Richard Jefferies (1909) **Edward Thomas** (1878)
Richard Savage (1842) **Charles Whitehead** (1804)
Richard Savage (1891) **[Sir] J.M. Barrie** (1860)
Richard the Second (1597) **William Shakespeare** (1564)
Richard the Third (1592/3) **William Shakespeare** (1564)
Richard's Things (1973) **Frederic Raphael** (1931)
Riche his Farewell to Militarie Profession (1581) **Barnabe Rich** (1542)
Richelieu (1839) **Edward Bulwer-Lytton** (1803)
Richelieu (1829) **G.P.R. James** (1799)
Richer Dust, A (1931) **Storm Jameson** (1897)
Richmond Heiress, The (1693) **Thomas D'Urfey** (1653)
Riddle of the Sands, The (1903) **Erskine Childers** (1870)
Riddle of the Third Mile, The (1983) **Colin Dexter** (1930)
Riddle, The (1923) **Walter de la Mare** (1873)
Riddley Walker (1980) **Russell Hoban** (1925)
Riders (1985) **Jilly Cooper** (1937)
Riders in the Chariot (1961) **Patrick White** (1912)
Riders of the Purple Sage (1912) **Zane Grey** (1872)
Riders on the Earth (1978) **Archibald MacLeish** (1892)
Riders to the Sea (1904) **J.M. Synge** (1871)
Riding Lights (1955) **Norman MacCaig** (1910)
Riding the Iron Rooster (1988) **Paul Theroux** (1941)
Riding the Rap (1995) **Elmore Leonard** (1925)
Rienzi (1828) **Mary Russell Mitford** (1787)
Rienzi (1835) **Edward Bulwer-Lytton** (1803)
Rifle and Hound in Ceylon, The (1854) **Sir Samuel White Baker** (1821)
Rifle Rangers, The (1850) **Mayne Reid** (1818)
Rift in Time, A (1982) **Patric Dickinson** (1914)
Rigby's Romance (1946) **Joseph Furphy** (1843–1912)
Right at Last (1860) **Elizabeth Gaskell** (1810)
Right Ho, Jeeves (1934) **P.G. Wodehouse** (1881)
Right Honourable, The (1886) **Justin McCarthy** (1830) [with Mrs Campbell Praed]
Right or Wrong (1859) **Geraldine Jewsbury** (1812)

'Right Stuff, The' (1908) **'Ian Hay' [John Hay Beith]** (1876)
Right Stuff, The (1979) **Tom Wolfe** (1930)
Right Thing, The (1971) **Hal Porter** (1911)
Right to an Answer, The (1960) **'Anthony Burgess' [John Anthony Burgess Wilson]** (1917)
Right True End, The (1976) **Stan Barstow** (1928)
Righted Wrong, A (1870) **Edmund Yates** (1831)
Righteousness Evangelicall Describ'd, The (1663) **Jeremy Taylor** (1613)
Rightful Heir, The (1868) **Edward Bulwer-Lytton** (1803)
Rights of Man [pt. i; pt. ii, 1792] (1791) **Thomas Paine** (1737)
Rights of the Christian Church Asserted, The (1706) **Matthew Tindal** (1657)
Rigodon (1969) **'Louis-Ferdinand Céline' [L.F. Destouches]** (1894–1961)
Rilla of Ingleside (1921) **L.M. Montgomery** (1874)
Rimbaud (1924) **Edgell Rickword** (1898)
'Rime of the Ancient Mariner, The' [in Wordsworth and Coleridge, *Lyrical Ballads*](1798)
Rinaldo (1562) **Torquato Tasso** (1544)
Rinaldo and Armida (1699) **John Dennis** (1657)
Ring and the Book, The [vols. i, ii] (1868) **Robert Browning** (1812)
Ring and the Book, The [vols. iii, iv] (1869) **Robert Browning** (1812)
Ring for Jeeves [US: *The Return of Jeeves*] (1953) **P.G. Wodehouse** (1881)
Ring o' Rushes (1897) **Shan F. Bullock** (1865)
Ring of Amasis, The [as 'Owen Meredith'] (1863) **Edward Robert Bulwer Lytton** (1831)
Ring of Bright Water (1960) **Gavin Maxwell** (1914)
Ring of Truth (1983) **Vernon Scannell** (1922)
Ring Round the Moon [*L'invitation au château*] (1947) **Jean Anouilh** (1910)
Ring Round the Moon [from Anouilh, *L'invitation au château*] (1950) **Christopher Fry [Christopher Fry Harris]** (1907) (tr.)
Ringan Gilhaize (1823) **John Galt** (1779)
Ringed Castle, The (1972) **Dorothy Dunnett** (1923)
Rings on a Tree (1968) **Norman MacCaig** (1910)
Ringworld (1970) **Larry Niven** (1938)
Rio Grande's Last Race (1902) **A.B. 'Banjo' Paterson** (1864)
Riotous Assembly (1971) **Tom Sharpe** (1928)
Rip Tide (1932) **William Rose Benét** (1886)
Ripeness is All (1935) **Eric Linklater** (1899)
Ripley Under Water (1991) **Patricia Highsmith** (1921)
Ripley Underground (1971) **Patricia Highsmith** (1921)
Ripley's Game (1974) **Patricia Highsmith** (1921)
Ripostes (1912) **Ezra Pound** (1885)
Ripple From the Storm, A (1958) **Doris Lessing** (1919)
Riprap (1959) **Gary Snyder** (1930)
R is for Rocket, S is for Space (1962) **Ray Bradbury** (1920)
Rise and Progress of Religion in the Soul, The (1745) **Philip Doddridge** (1702)
Rise and Progress of the English Constitution, The (1853) **Sir Edward Creasy** (1812)
Rise of Christian Europe, The (1965) **Hugh Trevor-Roper** (1914)
Rise of David Livinsky, The (1917) **Abraham Cahan** (1860)
Rise of Henry Morcar, The (1946) **Phyllis Bentley** (1894)
Rise of Silas Lapham, The (1885) **William Dean Howells** (1837)
Rising (1976) **R.C. Hutchinson** (1907–75)
Rising Gorge, The (1961) **S.J. Perelman** (1904)
Rising of the Moon, The (1945) **Gladys Mitchell** (1901)
Rising Star, A (1894) **David Christie Murray** (1847)
Rising Tide, The [as 'M.J. Farrell'] (1937) **Molly Keane** (1905)
Rita (1856) **Charles Hamilton Aïdé** (1826)
Rite of Passage, The (1965) **Ed Dorn** (1929)
Rites of Passage (1967) **Edward Brathwaite** (1930)
Rites of Passage (1980) **William Golding** (1911)
Ritter Gluck (1809) **E.T.A. Hoffmann** (1776)
Rival Ladies, The (1664) **John Dryden** (1631)
Rival Monster, The (1952) **Compton Mackenzie** (1883)
Rival Queens, The (1677) **Nathaniel Lee** (1649?)
Rivals, The (1668) **Sir William Davenant** (1606)
Rivals, The (1775) **Richard Brinsley Sheridan** (1753)
Rivals (1988) **Jilly Cooper** (1937)
River, The (1902) **Eden Phillpotts** (1862)
River, The (1946) **Rumer Godden** (1907)
River (1983) **Ted Hughes** (1930)
River at Green Knowe, The (1959) **Lucy Boston** (1892)
River Duddon, The (1820) **William Wordsworth** (1770)
River of Stars, The (1913) **Edgar Wallace** (1875)
River Steamer, The (1956) **E.J. Scovell** (1907)
Riverhead (1932) **Robert Hillyer** (1895)
Rivers Among Rocks (1960) **Ralph Gustafson** (1909)
Rivers and Mountains (1966) **John Ashbery** (1927)
Rivers of Ice (1875) **R.M. Ballantyne** (1825)
Riverside Drive (1962) **Louis Simpson** (1923)
Riverside Villas Murder, The (1973) **Kingsley Amis** (1922)
Rivet in Grandfather's Neck, The (1915) **James Branch Cabell** (1879)
Road, The (1961) **Mulk Raj Anand** (1905)
Road, The (1965) **Wole Soyinka** (1934)
Road Back, The [*Der Weg zurück*] (1931) **'Erich Maria Remarque' [Erich Paul Remark]** (1898)
Road Between, The (1949) **James T. Farrell** (1904)
Road From the Monument, The (1962) **Storm Jameson** (1897)
Road Goes Ever On, The (1967) **J.R.R. Tolkein** (1892)
Road Rage (1997) **Ruth Rendell** (1930)
Road Through the Wall, The (1948) **Shirley Jackson** (1919)
Road to Lichfield, The (1977) **Penelope Lively** (1933)
Road to Mecca, The (1984) **Athol Fugard** (1932)
Road to Milltown, The (1957) **S.J. Perelman** (1904)
Road to Oxiana, The (1937) **Robert Byron** (1905)

Road to Rome, The (1927) **Robert E. Sherwood** (1896)

Road to Ruin, The (1792) **Thomas Holcroft** (1745)

Road to Ruin, The (1933) **Siegfried Sassoon** (1886)

Road to the Shore, The (1976) **Michael McLaverty** (1904)

Road to Wigan Pier, The (1937) **George Orwell** (1903)

Road to Xanadu, The (1927) **John Livingston Lowes** (1867)

Roadmender, The (1902) **Margaret Fairless Barber** (1869)

Roads From Home (1949) **Dan Davin** (1913)

Roads of Destiny (1909) **'O. Henry' [William Sydney Porter]** (1862)

Roads to Freedom (1918) **Bertrand Russell** (1872)

Roads to Glory (1930) **Richard Aldington** (1892)

Roaring Girle, The (1611) **Thomas Middleton** (1580) [with Thomas Dekker]

Roaring Queen, The (1973) **Wyndham Lewis** (1882–1957)

Roaring Tower (1937) **Stella Gibbons** (1902)

Roaring Twenties, The (1960) **Jack Lindsay** (1900)

Rob of the Bowl (1838) **John Pendleton Kennedy** (1795)

Rob Roy (1818) **Sir Walter Scott** (1771)

Robber, The (1838) **G.P.R. James** (1799)

Robber Bride, The (1994) **Margaret Atwood** (1939)

Robber Bridegroom, The (1942) **Eudora Welty** (1909)

Robbery Under Arms (1888) **'Rolf Boldrewood' [Thomas Alexander Browne]** (1826)

Robbery Under Law [US: *Mexico: An Object Lesson*] (1939) **Evelyn Waugh** (1903)

Robert (1930) **André Gide** (1869)

Robert Ainsleigh (1872) **M.E. Braddon** (1835)

Robert Browning (1904) **Edward Dowden** (1843)

Robert Crews (1994) **Thomas Berger** (1924)

Robert E. Lee (1923) **John Drinkwater** (1882)

Robert Elsmere (1888) **Mrs T. Humphry Ward** (1851)

Robert Falconer (1868) **George MacDonald** (1824)

Robert Louis Stevenson (1895) **Richard le Gallienne** (1866)

Robert Louis Stevenson (1895) **Sir Walter Raleigh** (1861)

Robert Louis Stevenson (1902) **Sir Leslie Stephen** (1832)

Robert Lowell (1981) **Ian Hamilton** (1938)

Robert of Gloucester's Chronicle (1724) **Thomas Hearne** (1678) (ed.)

Robert Peckham (1930) **Maurice Baring** (1874)

Robert Second Duke of Normandy (1591) **Thomas Lodge** (1558)

Robert Thorne (1907) **Shan F. Bullock** (1865)

Robert's Wife (1938) **St John Ervine** (1883)

Robertses on their Travels, The (1846) **Frances Trollope** (1780)

Robes rouges ['Red Dresses'] (1891) **Paul Adam** (1862)

Robespierre (1901) **Hilaire Belloc** (1870)

Robinson (1958) **Muriel Spark** (1918)

Robinson Crusoe [**Defoe**]: see *The Life and Strange Surprizing Adventures of Robinson Crusoe*

Roche-Blanche (1822) **Anna Maria Porter** (1780)

Rock, The (1934) **T.S. Eliot** (1888)

Rock Ahead, The (1868) **Edmund Yates** (1831)

Rock Face (1948) **Norman Nicholson** (1914)

Rock Pool, The (1936) **Cyril Connolly** (1903)

Rock Springs (1987) **Richard Ford** (1944)

Rock Wagram (1951) **William Saroyan** (1908)

Rocke of Regard, The (1576) **George Whetstone** (*c.* 1551)

Rocket to the Moon (1938) **Clifford Odets** (1906)

Rocks Remain, The (1963) **Gavin Maxwell** (1914)

Rocky Mountain Poems (1960) **Ralph Gustafson** (1909)

Rococo; Vote by Ballot; Farewell to the Theatre (1917) **Harley Granville-Barker** (1877)

Rod for Run-awayes, A (1625) **Thomas Dekker** (1572?)

Rod, the Root, and the Flower, The (1895) **Coventry Patmore** (1823)

Roden's Corner (1898) **'Henry Seton Merriman' [Hugh Stowell Scott]** (1862)

Roderick (1814) **Robert Southey** (1774)

Roderick Hudson (1876) **Henry James** (1843)

Roderick Random [**Smollett**]: see *The Adventures of Roderick Random*

Rodney Stone (1896) **A. Conan Doyle** (1859)

Rodomonths Infernall (1607) **Gervaise Markham** (1568?)

Rody the Rover (1845) **William Carleton** (1794)

Roger Fry (1940) **Virginia Woolf** (1882)

Roger Ingleton Minor (1891) **Talbot Baines Reed** (1852)

Roger's Version (1986) **John Updike** (1932)

Rogue Elephant (1946) **Walter Allen** (1911)

Rogue Herries (1930) **Sir Hugh Walpole** (1884)

Rogue Justice (1982) **Geoffrey Household** (1900)

Rogue Male (1939) **Geoffrey Household** (1900)

Rogue, The [from Matheo Alemán] (1622) **James Mabbe** (1572) (tr.)

Rogue Star (1969) **Frederik Pohl** (1919)

Rogue's Life, A (1879) **Wilkie Collins** (1824)

Rogue's March, The (1896) **E.W. Hornung** (1866)

Rogue's Memoirs, A (1912) **Augustine Birrell** (1850)

Rogues and Vagabonds (1927) **Compton Mackenzie** (1883)

Roi s'amuse, Le [basis of Verdi's *Rigoletto*] (1832) **Victor Hugo** (1802)

Rokeby (1813) **Sir Walter Scott** (1771)

Roland Cashel (1850) **Charles Lever** (1806)

Roland Yorke (1869) **Mrs Henry Wood** (1814)

Roll of Honour (1961) **Eric Linklater** (1899)

Roll, Sweet Chariot (1934) **Paul Green** (1894)

Roll-Call, The (1918) **Arnold Bennett** (1867)

Rolla (1799) **M.G. Lewis** (1775)

Rolling Season, The (1958) **William Mayne** (1928)

Rolling Stones (1913) **O. Henry' [William Sydney Porter]** (1862–1910)

Romaine Persuasion, The (1981) **Bernard Bergonzi** (1929)

Roman, The [as 'Sydney Yendys'] (1850) **Sydney Dobell** (1824)
Roman Actor, The (1629) **Philip Massinger** (1583)
Roman and English Comedy Consider'd and Compar'd, The (1747) **Samuel Foote** (1720)
Roman Balcony (1932) **David Gascoyne** (1916)
Roman Bartholow (1923) **Edwin Arlington Robinson** (1869)
Roman Brides Revenge, The (1697) **[Charles Gildon]** (1665)
Roman Canon Law in the Church of England (1898) **F.W. Maitland** (1850)
Roman Elegies [Römische Elegien; in Schiller's *Die Horen*] (1795) **Johann Wolfgang von Goethe** (1749)
Roman Father, The (1750) **William Whitehead** (1715)
Roman Forgeries (1673) **Thomas Traherne** (1637)
Roman Fountain (1940) **Sir Hugh Walpole** (1884)
Roman Hat Mystery, The (1929) **'Ellery Queen' [Frederic Dannay]** (1905) and **[Manfred B. Lee]** (1905)
Roman Historie, The [from *Ammianus Marcellinus*] (1609) **Philemon Holland** (1552) (tr.)
Roman History, The (1769) **Oliver Goldsmith** (1728)
Roman Pictures (1923) **Percy Lubbock** (1879)
Roman Poems (1968) **C.H. Sisson** (1914)
Roman Road, The (1932) **Robert Gittings** (1911)
Roman Singer, A (1884) **F. Marion Crawford** (1854)
Roman Spring of Mrs Stone, The (1950) **'Tennessee' [Thomas Lanier] Williams** (1911)
Roman Tales [*Raconti romani*] (1954) **'Alberto Moravia' [Alberto Pincherle]** (1907)
Romance (1903) **Joseph Conrad** (1857) [with F.M. Hueffer]
Romance and Reality (1911) **Holbrook Jackson** (1874)
Romance and Reality [as 'L.E.L.'] (1831) **Letitia Elizabeth Landon** (1802)
Romance Island (1906) **Zona Gale** (1874)
Romance of a Plain Man, The (1909) **Ellen Glasgow** (1874)
Romance of a Shop, The (1888) **Amy Levy** (1861)
Romance of a Spahi, The [*Le Roman d'un Spahi*] (1881) **'Pierre Loti' [Julien Viaud]** (1850)
Romance of Canvas Town, A (1898) **'Rolf Boldrewood' [Thomas Alexander Browne]** (1826)
Romance of Dijon, A (1894) **Matilda Betham-Edwards** (1836)
Romance of His Life, The (1921) **Mary Cholmondeley** (1859)
Romance of Isabel, Lady Burton, The (1897) **Isabel, Lady Burton** (1831–96)
Romance of Natural History, The (1860) **Philip Henry Gosse** (1810)
Romance of Real Life, The (1787) **Charlotte Smith** (1749)
Romance of the Forest, The (1791) **Ann Radcliffe** (1764)
Romance of the Nineteenth Century, A (1881) **W.H. Mallock** (1849)
Romance of the Scarlet Leaf, The (1865) **Charles Hamilton Aïdé** (1826)
Romance of Two Worlds, A (1886) **Marie Corelli** (1855)
Romance of Vienna, A (1838) **Frances Trollope** (1780)
Romance of War, The (1846) **James Grant** (1822)
Romance of Wastdale, A (1895) **A.E.W. Mason** (1865)
Romancero [*Romanzero*] (1851) **Heinrich Heine** (1797)
Romances of Real Life (1829) **Mrs C.F. Gore** (1799)
Romances Without Words [*Romances sans paroles*] (1874) **Paul Verlaine** (1844)
Romane Historie , The [from Livy] (1600) **Philemon Holland** (1552) (tr.)
Romano Lavo-Lil (1874) **George Borrow** (1803)
Romans in Britain, The (1980) **Howard Brenton** (1942)
Romantic Adventure (1936) **Elinor Glyn** (1864)
Romantic Ballads (1826) **George Borrow** (1803) (tr.)
Romantic Comedians, The (1926) **Ellen Glasgow** (1874)
Romantic Egoists, The (1954) **Louis Auchinloss** (1917)
Romantic Hero, A (1967) **Olivia Manning** (1908)
Romantic Image, The (1957) **Frank Kermode** (1919)
Romantic Imagination, The (1949) **Maurice Bowra** (1898)
Romantic Lady, The (1921) **'Michael Arlen' [Dikran Kouyoumdjian]** (1895)
Romantic Manifesto, The (1969) **Ayn Rand** (1905)
Romantic Movement in English Poetry, The (1909) **Arthur Symons** (1865)
Romantic Nineties, The (1926) **Richard le Gallienne** (1866)
Romantic School, The [*Die romantische Schule*] (1836) **Heinrich Heine** (1797)
Romantic Tales (1808) **M.G. Lewis** (1775)
Romanticism (1926) **Lascelles Abercrombie** (1881)
Romany Rye, The (1857) **George Borrow** (1803)
Rome [*Liberty* pt. iii] (1735) **James Thomson** (1700)
Rome (1896) **Émile Zola** (1840)
Rome (1985) **Fiona Pitt-Kethley** (1954)
Rome (1992) **Howard Barker** (1946)
Rome, Naples et Florence en 1817 (1817) **'Stendhal' [Henri Marie Beyle]** (1783)
Romeo and Juliet (1750) **David Garrick** (1717)
Romeo and Juliet (1597) **William Shakespeare** (1564)
Roméo et Jeannette (1946) **Jean Anouilh** (1910)
Rommel Drives on Deep into Egypt (1970) **Richard Brautigan** (1935)
Rommel Papers, The (1953) **Sir Basil Liddell Hart** (1895) (ed.)
Romola (1863) **'George Eliot' [Mary Ann Evans]** (1819)
Romulus and Remus (1970) **Rodney Hall** (1935)
Ronald Standish (1933) **'Sapper' [Herman Cyril McNeile]** (1888)

Rookery Nook [adpated for the stage 1926] (1923) **Ben Travers** (1886)
Rookwood (1834) **W.H. Ainsworth** (1805)
Room, The (1965) **C. Day Lewis** (1904)
Room, The (1971) **Hubert Selby Jr** (1928)
Room 13 (1924) **Edgar Wallace** (1875)
Room at the Top (1957) **John Braine** (1922)
Room For a Single Lady (1997) **Clare Boylan** (1948)
Room in the Tower, The (1912) **E.F. Benson** (1867)
Room of One's Own, A (1929) **Virginia Woolf** (1882)
Room Temperature (1990) **Nicholson Baker** (1957)
Room With a View, A (1908) **E.M. Forster** (1879)
Rooms and Houses (1968) **Norman Lindsay** (1879)
Rooney (1957) **Catherine Cookson** (1906)
Roosevelt and Hopkins (1948) **Robert E. Sherwood** (1896)
Root and Branch (1969) **Jon Stallworthy** (1935)
Root and the Flower, The (1935) **L.H. Myers** (1881)
Rootabaga Pigeons (1923) **Carl Sandburg** (1878)
Rootabaga Stories (1922) **Carl Sandburg** (1878)
Roots (1977) **Alex Haley** (1921)
Roots (1959) **Arnold Wesker** (1932)
Roots and Branches (1964) **Robert Duncan** (1919)
Roots in the Air (1991) **Michael Hamburger** (1924)
Roots of Coincidence, The (1972) **Arthur Koestler** (1905)
Roots of the Mountains, The (1890) **William Morris** (1834)
Rope, The (2000) **Philippa Pearce** (1920)
Rope of Gold (1939) **Josephine Herbst** (1897)
Roper's Row (1929) **Warwick Deeping** (1877)
Rory O'More (1837) **Samuel Lover** (1797)
Rosa Amorosa (1901) **'George Egerton' [Mary Chavelita Dunne]** (1859)
Rosa Mundi (1921) **Ethel M. Dell** (1881)
Rosalba's Journal (1915) **Austin Dobson** (1840)
Rosalind and Helen (1819) **P.B. Shelley** (1792)
Rosalynde: Euphues Golden Legacie (1590) **Thomas Lodge** (1558)
Rosamund (1707) **Joseph Addison** (1672)
Rosamond (1821) **Maria Edgeworth** (1767)
Rosamund, Queen of the Lombards (1899) **A.C. Swinburne** (1837)
Rosary, The (1909) **Florence Barclay** (1862)
Rosary, The (1914) **'Anna Akhmatova' [Anna Andreevna Gorenko]** (1889)
Rosary, The (1845) **Frederick William Faber** (1814)
Rosciad, The (1761) **Charles Churchill** (1731)
Rose Acre Papers (1904) **Edward Thomas** (1878)
Rose and Crown (1952) **Sean O'Casey** (1880)
Rose and the Key, The (1871) **J.S. le Fanu** (1814)
Rose and the Ring, The [as 'M.A. Titmarsh'] (1855) **W.M. Thackeray** (1811)
Rose, Blanche, and Violet (1848) **G.H. Lewes** (1817)
Rose for Winter, A (1955) **Laurie Lee** (1914)
Rose in Bloom (1876) **Louisa M. Alcott** (1832)
Rose in June, A (1874) **Margaret Oliphant** (1828)
Rose Leblanc (1862) **Lady Georgiana Fullerton** (1812)
Rose of Dutcher's Coolly (1895) **Hamlin Garland** (1860)
Rose of Life, The (1905) **M.E. Braddon** (1835)
Rose publique, La (1934) **'Paul Éluard' [Eugène Grindel]** (1895)
Rose Reason (1990) **Mary Flanagan** (1943)
Rose Tattoo, The (1950) **'Tennessee' [Thomas Lanier] Williams** (1911)
Rose Under Glass (1961) **Elizabeth Berridge** (1921)
Rosemary's Baby (1967) **Ira Levin** (1929)
Rosencrantz and Guildenstern Are Dead (1966) **Tom Stoppard** (1937)
Rosenkavalier, The ['The Knight of the Rose'; music by Richard Strauss] (1911) **Hugo von Hofmannsthal** (1874)
Roseteague (1874) **Anna Eliza Bray** (1790)
Rosicrucian Enlightenment, The (1972) **Frances Yates** (1899)
Rosie Plum (1966) **T.F. Powys** (1875–1953)
Rosina (1783) **Frances Brooke** (1724)
Rosinante to the Road Again (1922) **John Dos Passos** (1896)
Rosmersholm (1886) **Henrik Ibsen** (1828)
Ross (1960) **Terence Rattigan** (1911)
Ross Poldark (1945) **Winston Graham** (1910)
Rossetti (1904) **A.C. Benson** (1862)
Rossetti (1902) **Ford Madox Ford** (1873)
Rossetti and his Circle (1922) **Max Beerbohm** (1872)
Rosshalde (1914) **Hermann Hesse** (1877)
Rothelan (1824) **John Galt** (1779)
Rotten Elements, The (1969) **Edward Upward** (1903)
Rotting Hill (1951) **Wyndham Lewis** (1882)
Rough Crossing (1984) **Tom Stoppard** (1937)
Rough Draft of a New Model at Sea, A (1694) **Sir George Savile, Marquis of Halifax** (1633)
Rough Justice (1898) **M.E. Braddon** (1835)
Rough Justice (1926) **C.E. Montague** (1867)
Rough Shoot, A (1951) **Geoffrey Household** (1900)
Roughing It (1872) **'Mark Twain' [Samuel Langhorne Clemens]** (1835)
Roughing It in the Bush (1852) **Susanna Moodie** (1803)
Roughneck, The (1923) **Robert W. Service** (1876)
Roumeli (1966) **Patrick Leigh Fermor** (1915)
Round of Applause, A (1962) **Norman MacCaig** (1910)
Round Table, The [inc. 12 essays by Leigh Hunt] (1817) **William Hazlitt** (1778)
Round the Corner (1913) **Gilbert Cannan** (1884)
Round the Fire Stories (1908) **A. Conan Doyle** (1859)
Round the Galley Fire (1883) **W. Clark Russell** (1844)
Round the Red Lamp (1894) **A. Conan Doyle** (1859)
Round the Sofa (1859) **Elizabeth Gaskell** (1810)
Round Tower, The (1968) **Catherine Cookson** (1906)
Round Up (1929) **Ring Lardner** (1885)
Round-Heads, The (1681) **Aphra Behn** (1640?)
Roundabout Papers (1863) **W.M. Thackeray** (1811)
Rounding the Horn (1998) **Jon Stallworthy** (1935)
Rousseau (1873) **John Morley** (1838)
Rousseau and Romanticism (1919) **Irving Babbit** (1865)
Rover, The (1677) **Aphra Behn** (1640?)
Rover, The (1923) **Joseph Conrad** (1857)

Rover I Would Be, A (1928) **E.V. Lucas** (1868)
Rover of the Andes, The (1885) **R.M. Ballantyne** (1825)
Row at the Lyceum, A (1851) **John Brougham** (1810)
Roxana [**Defoe**]: see *The Fortunate Mistress*
Royal Convert, The (1707) **Nicholas Rowe** (1674)
Royal Dictionary, The (1699) **Abel Boyer** (1667)
Royal Flush (1932) **Margaret Irwin** (1889)
Royal George (1901) **S. Baring-Gould** (1834)
Royal Hunt of the Sun, The (1964) **Peter Shaffer** (1926)
Royal Jubilee, The (1822) **James Hogg** (1770)
Royal Mischief, The (1696) **Mary Delariviere Manley** (1663)
Royal Shepherdess, The (1669) **Thomas Shadwell** (1642?)
Royalist, The (1682) **Thomas D'Urfey** (1653)
Royall King, and the Loyall Subject, The (1637) **Thomas Heywood** (1574?)
Royall Master, The (1638) **James Shirley** (1596)
Rubáiyát of Omar Khayyám, The (1859) **Edward FitzGerald** (1809) (tr.)
Rubicon, The (1894) **E.F. Benson** (1867)
Rubyfruit Jungle, The (1973) **Rita Mae Brown** (1944)
Ruddigore [music by Sir Arthur Sullivan] (1887) **W.S. Gilbert** (1836)
Rude Assignment (1950) **Wyndham Lewis** (1882)
Rude Awakening, A (1978) **Brian Aldiss** (1925)
Rude Potato, The (1941) **Ruth Pitter** (1897)
Rudiments of English Grammar, The (1761) **Joseph Priestley** (1733)
Rudiments of Grammar for the English-Saxon Tongue, The (1715) **Elizabeth Elstob** (1683)
Rudin (1856) **Ivan Turgenev** (1818)
Rue (1899) **Laurence Housman** (1865)
Rue With a Difference (1900) **Rosa Nouchette Carey** (1840)
Ruffino (1890) **'Ouida' [Marie Louise de la Ramée]** (1839)
Ruin the Sacred Truths (1989) **Harold Bloom** (1930)
Ruins (1987) **Brian Aldiss** (1925)
Ruins and Visions (1942) **Sir Stephen Spender** (1909)
Ruins of Rome, The (1740) **John Dyer** (1699)
Rule a Wife and Have a Wife (1640) **John Fletcher** (1579–1625)
Rule and Exercises of Holy Living, The (1650) **Jeremy Taylor** (1613)
Rule and Exercises of Holy Dying, The (1651) **Jeremy Taylor** (1613)
Rule Britannia (1972) **Daphne du Maurier** (1907)
Rule of Reason, The (1551) **Thomas Wilson** (1525?)
Rule of the Bone (1995) **Russell Banks** (1940)
Rulers of the Mediterranean, The (1894) **Richard Harding Davis** (1864)
Rules of Attraction (1987) **Bret Easton Ellis** (1964)
Ruling Class, The (1969) **Peter Barnes** (1931)
Ruling Passion (1973) **Reginald Hill** (1936)
Rum and Coca Cola (1956) **Ralph de Bossière** (1907)
Rumbin Galleries (1937) **Booth Tarkington** (1869)
Ruminator, The (1813) **Sir Samuel Egerton Brydges** (1762)
Rumor Verified (1981) **Robert Penn Warren** (1905)
Rumour at Nightfall (1931) **Graham Greene** (1904)
Rumour, The (1971) **Robert Adamson** (1943)
Rumoured City, A (1982) **Douglas Dunn** (1942) (ed.)
Rumours of Rain (1978) **André Brink** (1935)
Rumours of War (1952) **A.J.P. Taylor** (1906)
Rumpole of the Bailey (1978) **John Mortimer** (1923)
Run, River (1964) **Joan Didion** (1934)
Run Silent, Run Deep (1955) **Edward Beach** (1918)
Run to Earth (1868) **M.E. Braddon** (1835)
Runagates Club, The (1928) **John Buchan** (1875)
Runaway, The (1776) **Hannah Cowley** (1743)
Runaway, The (1800) **Horace Smith** (1779)
Runaway (1925) **Floyd Dell** (1887)
Runaway Jury, The (1996) **John Grisham** (1955)
Runaway Soul, The (1991) **Harold Brodkey** (1930)
Runes and Rhymes and Tunes and Chimes (1969) **George Barker** (1913)
Rungs of Time (1993) **Chris Wallace-Crabbe** (1934)
Running Blind (1970) **Desmond Bagley** (1923)
Running Dog (1978) **Don Delillo** (1936)
Running Scared (1986) **Bernard Ashley** (1935)
Running the Gauntlet (1865) **Edmund Yates** (1831)
Running Wild (1988) **J.G. Ballard** (1930)
Runyon à la Carte (1944) **Damon Runyon** (1884)
Rupert Brooke (1964) **Christopher Hassall** (1912–63)
Rupert Godwin (1867) **M.E. Braddon** (1835)
Rupert of Hentzau (1898) **'Anthony Hope' [Sir Anthony Hope Hawkins]** (1863)
Rural Muse, The (1835) **John Clare** (1793)
Rural Rides in the Counties of Surrey, Kent, Sussex . . . (1830) **William Cobbett** (1763)
Rural Sports (1713) **John Gay** (1685)
Rural Tales, Ballads and Songs (1802) **Robert Bloomfield** (1766)
Rush for the Spoils, The [*La Curée*] (1872) **Émile Zola** (1840)
Rush on the Ultimate, A (1961) **H.R.F. Keating** (1926)
Rushing to Paradise (1994) **J.G. Ballard** (1930)
Rushlight, The (1906) **Joseph Campbell** (1879)
Ruskin (1911) **A.C. Benson** (1862)
Ruslan and Ludmilla (1820) **Alexander Pushkin** (1799)
Russia House, The (1989) **'John le Carré' [David John Moore Cornwell]** (1931)
Russian Girl, The (1992) **Kingsley Amis** (1922)
Russian Hide-and-Seek (1980) **Kingsley Amis** (1922)
Russian Interpreter, The (1966) **Michael Frayn** (1933)
Russian Journal, A (1948) **John Steinbeck** (1902)
Russian Life in the Interior (1852) **Ivan Turgenev** (1818)
Russian Thinkers (1978) **Sir Isaiah Berlin** (1909)
Ruth (1853) **Elizabeth Gaskell** (1810)
Ruy Blas (1838) **Victor Hugo** (1802)
Ryder (1928) **Djuna Barnes** (1892)

S

Sabbatical (1982) **John Barth** (1930)

Sabine Zembra (1887) **William Black** (1841)

Sable and Purple (1910) **Sir William Watson** (1858)

Sabre Squadron, The (1966) **Simon Raven** (1927)

Sabre, the Horse From the Sea (1948) **K.M. Peyton** (1929)

Sack (1916) **Harold Brighouse** (1882)

Sacrament (1996) **Clive Barker** (1952)

Sacrament of the Lord's Supper, The [from Peter Martyr] (1550) **Nicholas Udall** (1505?) (tr.)

Sacred and Profane Love (1908) **Alfred Austin** (1835)

Sacred and Profane Love (1905) **Arnold Bennett** (1867)

Sacred and Profane Love Machine, The (1974) **Iris Murdoch** (1919)

Sacred Clowns (1993) **Tony Hillerman** (1925)

Sacred Country (1992) **Rose Tremain** (1943)

Sacred Dramas (1782) **Hannah More** (1745)

Sacred Elephant (1989) **Heathcote Williams** (1941)

Sacred Fount, The (1901) **Henry James** (1843)

Sacred Hunger (1992) **Barry Unsworth** (1930)

Sacred Songs [No. i] (1816) **Thomas Moore** (1779)

Sacred Songs [No. ii] (1824) **Thomas Moore** (1779)

Sacred Wood, The (1920) **T.S. Eliot** (1888)

Sacrificial Egg, The (1962) **Chinua Achebe** (1930)

Sad Dust Glories (1975) **Allen Ginsberg** (1926)

Sad Grave of an Imperial Mongoose (1973) **Geoffrey Grigson** (1905)

Sad Heart at the Supermarket, A (1962) **Randall Jarrell** (1914)

Sad Ires (1975) **D.J. Enright** (1920)

Sad Years, The (1918) **Dora Sigerson** (1866)

Saddest Summer of Samuel S., The (1966) **J.P. Donleavy** (1926)

Sadeian Woman, The (1979) **Angela Carter** (1940)

Sadler's Birthday (1976) **Rose Tremain** (1943)

Sadness (1972) **Donald Barthelme** (1931)

Sadness of Witches, The (1987) **Janice Elliott** (1931)

Sado (1931) **William Plomer** (1903)

Saducismus Triumphatus (1681) **Joseph Glanvill** (1636–1680)

Safe House, The (1975) **Jon Cleary** (1917)

Safe Sex (1987) **Harvey Fierstein** (1954)

Safety Match, A (1911) **'Ian Hay' [John Hay Beith]** (1876)

Safie (1814) **J.H. Reynolds** (1796)

Sag Harbor (1899) **James A. Herne** (1839)

Sagas of Vaster Britain (1914) **Wilfred Campbell** (1858)

Sagesse ['Wisdom'] (1881) **Paul Verlaine** (1844)

Sagouin, Le (1950) **François Mauriac** (1885)

Saigon Rose (1976) **David Edgar** (1948)

Sailing of the Long Ships, The (1902) **Sir Henry Newbolt** (1862)

Sailing Race, The (1952) **Patric Dickinson** (1914)

Sailing Ships, The (1918) **Enid Bagnold** (1889)

Sailing Through China (1984) **Paul Theroux** (1941)

Sailing to an Island (1955) **Richard Murphy** (1927)

Sailing to Byzantium (1969) **Osbert Lancaster** (1908)

Sailor Boy, The (1861) **Alfred, Lord Tennyson** (1809)

Sailor from Gibraltar, The [*Le Marin de Gibraltar*] (1952) **'Marguerite Duras' [Marguerite Donnadieu]** (1914)

Sailor Off the Bremen (1939) **Irwin Shaw** (1913)

Sailor on Horseback (1938) **Irving Stone** (1903)

Sailor Rumbelow and Britannia (1962) **James Reeves** (1909)

Sailor's Bride, A (1899) **Guy Boothby** (1867)

Sailor's Daughter, The (1804) **Richard Cumberland** (1732)

Sailor's Return, The (1925) **David Garnett** (1892)

Sailor's Song (1943) **James Hanley** (1901)

Sailors' Home, A [as 'Richard Dehan'] (1919) **Clo Graves** (1863)

Sailors' Knots (1909) **W.W. Jacobs** (1863)

Saint, The [Il santo] (1905) **Antonio Fogazzaro** (1842)

Saint and Mary Kate, The (1932) **'Frank O'Connor' [Michael Francis O'Donovan']** (1903)

Saint Augustine (1933) **'Rebecca West' [Cicily Isabel Andrews]** (1892)

Saint Augustine's Pigeon (1980) **Evan S. Connell, Jr** (1924)

Saint Clair (1803) **Lady Sydney Morgan** (1783?)

Saint George (1515) **Alexander Barclay** (1475?) (tr.)

Saint George and Saint Michael (1876) **George MacDonald** (1824)

Saint George's Day (1918) **Sir Henry Newbolt** (1862)

Saint Glinglin (1948) **Raymond Queneau** (1903)

Saint Gregory's Guest (1886) **John Greenleaf Whittier** (1807)

Saint Irvyne (1811) **P.B. Shelley** (1792)

Saint Ives [unfinished; completed by Sir A. Quiller-Couch] (1898) **Robert Louis Stevenson** (1850–94)

Saint James's (1844) **W.H. Ainsworth** (1805)

Saint Joan (1923) **Bernard Shaw** (1856)

Saint John in Patmos (1835) **William Lisle Bowles** (1762)

Saint John of the Stockyards [*Die heilige Johanna der Schlachthöfe*] (1929–30) **Bertolt Brecht** (1898)

Saint Katherine's by the Tower (1891) **Sir Walter Besant** (1836)

Saint Kilda's Parliament (1981) **Douglas Dunn** (1942)

Saint Leon (1799) **William Godwin** (1756)

Saint Martin's Summer (1909) **Rafael Sabatini** (1875)

Saint Mawr, Together with The Princess (1925) **D.H. Lawrence** (1885)

Saint Maybe (1992) **Anne Tyler** (1941)

Saint Michael's Mount (1798) **William Lisle Bowles** (1762)

'Saint' novels: see **Leslie Charteris**

Saint or Satyr? [US: *Such Men Are Dangerous*] (1933) **Elinor Glyn** (1864)

Saint Patrick's Eve (1845) **Charles Lever** (1806)

Saint Paul and Protestantism (1870) **Matthew Arnold** (1822)
Saint Peter's Fair (1981) **'Ellis Peters' [Edith Mary Pargeter]** (1913)
Saint Peters Complaint, with Other Poemes (1595) **Robert Southwell SJ** (1561?)
Saint Ronan's Well (1824) **Sir Walter Scott** (1771)
Saint Thomas Aquinas (1933) **G.K. Chesterton** (1874)
Saint Urbain's Horseman (1971) **Mordecai Richler** (1931)
Saint Winifred's (1862) **Frederic W. Farrar** (1831)
Saint's Day (1963) **John Whiting** (1917)
Saint's Tragedy, The (1848) **Charles Kingsley** (1819)
Saints and Sinners (1884) **Henry Arthur Jones** (1851)
Saints' Everlasting Rest, The (1650) **Richard Baxter** (1615)
Salamacis and Hermaphroditus (1602) **Francis Beaumont** (1585?) (tr.)
Salámán and Absál (1856) **Edward FitzGerald** (1809) (tr.)
Salamander, The (1973) **Morris West** (1916)
Salar the Salmon (1935) **Henry Williamson** (1895)
Salathiel (1828) **George Croly** (1780)
Sale of St Thomas, The (1930) **Lascelles Abercrombie** (1881)
Salem Chapel (1863) **Margaret Oliphant** (1828)
Salem's Lot (1975) **Stephen King** (1947)
Saliva Tree, The (1966) **Brian Aldiss** (1925)
Sally Bowles (1937) **Christopher Isherwood** (1904)
Sally Cavanagh (1869) **Charles J. Kickham** (1828)
Sally in our Alley (1830) **Douglas Jerrold** (1803)
Sally Lunn (1937) **Leo Walmsley** (1892)
Salmacida Spolia (1639) **Sir William Davenant** (1606)
Salmagundi (1807–8) **Washington Irving** (1783)
Salomé (1894) **Oscar Wilde** (1854)
Salomon's Divine Arts (1609) **Joseph Hall** (1574)
Salt (1963) **Herbert Gold** (1924)
Salt Garden, The (1955) **Howard Nemerov** (1920)
Salt Line, The (1984) **Elizabeth Spencer** (1921)
Salt Water (1857) **W.H.G. Kingston** (1814)
Salt Water (1997) **Andrew Motion** (1952)
Salt-Water Ballads (1902) **John Masefield** (1878)
Saltbush Bill J.P. (1917) **A.B. 'Banjo' Paterson** (1864)
Salted Almonds (1906) **'F. Anstey' [Thomas Anstey Guthrie]** (1856)
Salthaven (1908) **W.W. Jacobs** (1863)
Saltmarsh Murders, The (1932) **Gladys Mitchell** (1901)
Salutation (1917) **George William Russell ['AE']** (1867)
Salutation, The (1932) **Sylvia Townsend Warner** (1893)
Salute From the Fleet, A (1915) **Alfred Noyes** (1880)
Salute to Spring, and Other Stories (1940) **Meridel le Sueur** (1900)
Salutes and Censures (1984) **Dennis Brutus** (1924)
Salvaging of Civilization, The (1921) **H.G. Wells** (1866)
Salvation of Pisco Gabar, The (1938) **Geoffrey Household** (1900)
Salvation on a String (1946) **Paul Green** (1894)
Salvator (1845) **John Abraham Heraud** (1799)
Salve (1912) **George Moore** (1852)
Salve for a Sicke Man, A (1595) **William Perkins** (1558)
Salvos (1924) **Waldo Frank** (1889)
Salzburg Tales, The (1934) **Christina Stead** (1902)
Salzburger grosse Welttheater, Das ['The Salzburg Great Theatre of the World'] (1922) **Hugo von Hofmannsthal** (1874)
Sam Lawson's Oldtown Fireside Stories (1872) **Harriet Beecher Stowe** (1811)
Sam Pig (1940) **'Alison Uttley' [Alice Jane Uttley]** (1884)
Sam Slick's Wise Saws and Modern Instances (1853) **T.C. Haliburton** (1796)
Same Door, The (1959) **John Updike** (1932)
Samor (1818) **Henry Hart Milman** (1791)
Samuel Johnson (1853) **Thomas Carlyle** (1795)
Samuel Johnson [first of the *English Men of Letters* series] (1878) **Sir Leslie Stephen** (1832)
Samuel Johnson (1933) **'Hugh Kingsmill' [Hugh Kingsmill Lunn]** (1889)
Samuel Johnson (1974) **John Wain** (1925)
Samuel Marchbanks' Almanac (1967) **Robertson Davies** (1913)
Samuel Palmer (1947) **Geoffrey Grigson** (1905)
Sancta Sophia (1657) **'Augustine' [David] Baker** (1575–1641)
Sanctions (1924) **Ronald Knox** (1888)
Sanctuarie of a Troubled Soule, The [pt. i] (1601) **Sir John Hayward** (1564?)
Sanctuary (1903) **Edith Wharton** (1862)
Sanctuary (1931) **William Faulkner** (1897)
Sanctuary (1994) **David Williamson** (1942)
Sanctuary Lamp, The (1975) **Tom Murphy** (1935)
Sanctuary of Spirits (1963) **Alistair Campbell** (1925)
Sanctuary Sparrow, The (1983) **'Ellis Peters' [Edith Mary Pargeter]** (1913)
Sand (1964) **William Mayne** (1928)
Sand Castles (1989) **Nicholas Freeling** (1927)
Sandbox, The (1960) **Edward Albee** (1928)
Sandcastle, The (1956) **Iris Murdoch** (1919)
Sanders of the River (1911) **Edgar Wallace** (1875)
Sandgrains on a Tray (1969) **Alan Brownjohn** (1931)
Sandmouth People (1987) **Ronald Frame** (1953)
Sandra Belloni (1886) **George Meredith** (1828)
Sands of Time, The (1988) **Sidney Sheldon** (1917)
Sandy Foundations Shaken, The (1668) **William Penn** (1644)
Sangscaw (1925) **'Hugh MacDiarmid' [Christopher Murray Grieve]** (1892)
Sanity of Art, The (1908) **Bernard Shaw** (1856)
Sans Merci (1866) **G.A. Lawrence** (1827)
Sant' Ilario (1889) **F. Marion Crawford** (1854)
Santa Barbara (1891) **'Ouida' [Marie Louise de la Ramée]** (1839)
Santa Lucia (1908) **Mary Austin** (1868)
Sapho and Phao (1584) **John Lyly** (1554)
Sapphira and the Slave Girl (1940) **Willa Cather** (1873)

Sapphire Cross, The (1871) **George Manville Fenn** (1831)
Sappho (1884) **Alphonse Daudet** (1840)
Sappho and Phaon (1796) **Mary Robinson** (1758)
Sappho of Green Springs, A (1891) **Bret Harte** (1836)
Sara Crewe (1888) **Frances Hodgson Burnett** (1849)
Saracinesca (1887) **F. Marion Crawford** (1854)
Sarah de Berenger (1879) **Jean Ingelow** (1820)
Saratoga (1870) **Bronson Howard** (1842)
Saratoga Trunk (1941) **Edna Ferber** (1885)
Sard Harker (1924) **John Masefield** (1878)
Sardanapalus [etc.] (1821) **George Gordon, Lord Byron** (1788)
Sarrasine (1830) **Honoré de Balzac** (1799)
Sartor Resartus [privately printed 1834] (1838) **Thomas Carlyle** (1795)
Sartoris (1929) **William Faulkner** (1897)
Satan Absolved (1899) **Wilfrid Scawen Blunt** (1840)
Satan in Goray (1955) **Isaac Bashevis Singer** (1904)
Satan in the Suburbs (1953) **Bertrand Russell** (1872)
Satan, the Waster (1920) **'Vernon Lee' [Violet Paget]** (1856)
Satan's Sergeants (1941) **Josephine Herbst** (1897)
Satanic Verses, The (1988) **Salman Rushdie** (1947)
Satanstoe (1845) **James Fenimore Cooper** (1789)
Satires and Epigrams (1968) **John Heath-Stubbs** (1918)
Satires [bk i] (35 BC) **Horace [Quintus Horatius Flaccus]** 65–8 BC
Satires [bk ii] (30 BC) **Horace [Quintus Horatius Flaccus]** 65–8 BC
Satires of Circumstance (1914) **Thomas Hardy** (1840)
Satires of Decimus Junius Juvenalis, The (1693) **John Dryden** (1631) and others (tr.)
Satires of Juvenal, The (1802) **William Gifford** (1756) (tr.)
Satires of Persius , The (1821) **William Gifford** (1756) (tr.)
Satirical Poems (1926) **Siegfried Sassoon** (1886)
Satiro-Mastix (1602) **Thomas Dekker** (1572?)
Saturday Life, A (1925) **Radclyffe Hall** (1880)
Saturday Lunch With the Brownings (1960) **Penelope Mortimer** (1918)
Saturday Night and Sunday Morning (1958) **Alan Sillitoe** (1928)
Saturday's Children (1927) **Maxwell Anderson** (1888)
Saturdee (1933) **Norman Lindsay** (1879)
Saturn Over the Water (1961) **J.B. Priestley** (1894)
Satyr Against Hypocrites, A (1655) **John Phillips** (1631)
Satyr Against Mankind, A (1675?) **John Wilmot, earl of Rochester** (1647)
Satyr Against Wit, A (1700) **Sir Richard Blackmore** (1654)
Satyrs Upon the Jesuits (1681) **John Oldham** (1653)
Sauce for the Goose (1981) **Peter De Vries** (1910)
Saucer of Larks, The (1962) **Brian Friel** (1929)
Saul (1782) **Vittorio Alfieri** (1759)
Saul (1807) **William Sotheby** (1757)
Saül (1896) **André Gide** (1869)
Sauna Bath Mysteries, The (1978) **Russell Haley** (1934)
Saunter Through the West End, A (1861) **Leigh Hunt** (1784–1859)
Saunterings (1872) **Charles Dudley Warner** (1829)
Sauve qui peut (1966) **Lawrence Durrell** (1912)
Savage Amusement (1978) **Peter Flannery** (1951)
Savage Crows, The (1976) **Robert Drewe** (1943)
Savage God, The (1971) **A. Alvarez** (1929)
Savage Night (1953) **Jim Thompson** (1906)
Savages (1973) **Christopher Hampton** (1946)
Savannah Purchase (1971) **Jane Aiken Hodge** (1917)
Saville (1976) **David Storey** (1933)
Savonarola (1881) **Alfred Austin** (1835)
Savrola (1900) **Sir Winston Churchill** (1874)
Sawbones Memorial (1974) **Sinclair Ross** (1908)
Sayings and Doings [1st ser.] (1824) **Theodore Hook** (1788)
Sayonara (1954) **James A. Michener** (1907)
Scala Coeli (1611) **Lancelot Andrewes** (1555)
Scale of Things, The (1955) **Patric Dickinson** (1914)
Scallywag, The (1893) **Grant Allen** (1848)
Scalp Hunters, The (1851) **Mayne Reid** (1818)
Scandal (1983) **A.N. Wilson** (1950)
Scandal of Father Brown, The (1935) **G.K. Chesterton** (1874)
Scandal of Spring (1934) **Martin Boyd** (1893)
Scandalous Risks (1990) **Susan Howatch** (1940)
Scandalous Woman, A (1974) **Edna O'Brien** (1932)
Scanner Darkly, A (1977) **Philip K. Dick** (1928)
Scapegoat, The (1891) **Hall Caine** (1853)
Scapegoat, The (1948) **Jocelyn Brooke** (1908)
Scapegoat, The (1957) **Daphne du Maurier** (1907)
Scapegoat (2000) **Andrea Dworkin** (1946)
Scarab Murder Case, The (1930) **'S.S. Van Dine' [Willard Huntington Wright]** (1888)
Scaramouch [etc.] (1677) **Edward Ravenscroft** (1644)
Scaramouche (1921) **Rafael Sabatini** (1875)
Scarecrow of Oz, The (1915) **L. Frank Baum** (1856)
Scarecrows, The (1981) **Robert Westall** (1929)
Scarf, The (1947) **Robert Bloch** (1917)
Scarlatti Inheritance, The (1971) **Robert Ludlum** (1927)
Scarlet and Black [Le Rouge et le Noir] (1830) **'Stendhal' [Henri Marie Beyle]** (1783)
Scarlet and Hyssop (1902) **E.F. Benson** (1867)
Scarlet Boy, The (1961) **Arthur Calder-Marshall** (1908)
Scarlet Car, The (1897) **Richard Harding Davis** (1864)
Scarlet Feather (2000) **Maeve Binchy** (1940)
Scarlet Letter, The (1850) **Nathaniel Hawthorne** (1804)
Scarlet Pimpernel, The (1905) **Baroness Orczy** (1865)
Scarlet Seed, The (1963) **'Ellis Peters' [Edith Mary Pargeter]** (1913)
Scarlet Shawl, The (1874) **Richard Jefferies** (1848)
Scarlet Tree, The (1946) **Sir Osbert Sitwell** (1892)

Scarperer, The (1966) **Brendan Behan** (1923)
Scarronides (1664) **Charles Cotton** (1630)
Scenes and Hymns of Life (1834) **Felicia Dorothea Hemans** (1793)
Scenes and Plays (1929) **Gordon Bottomley** (1874)
Scenes From a Poisoner's Life (1994) **Nigel Williams** (1948)
Scenes From an Execution (1984) **Howard Barker** (1946)
Scenes From Death and Life (2000) **'William Cooper' [Harry Summerfield Hoff]** (1910)
Scenes From Later Life (1983) **'William Cooper' [Harry Summerfield Hoff]** (1910)
Scenes From Married Life (1961) **'William Cooper' [Harry Summerfield Hoff]** (1910)
Scenes From Metropolitan Life (1982) **'William Cooper' [Harry Summerfield Hoff]** (1910)
Scenes From Provincial Life (1950) **'William Cooper' [Harry Summerfield Hoff]** (1910)
Scenes From Sesshu (1978) **James Kirkup** (1923)
Scenes From the Alphabet (1978) **Roy Fisher** (1930)
Scenes of Clerical Life (1858) **'George Eliot' [Mary Ann Evans]** (1819)
Scenic Route, The (1974) **Fleur Adcock** (1934)
Scent of Eucalyptus, The (1973) **Barbara Hanrahan** (1939)
Scented Gardens for the Blind (1963) **Janet Frame** (1924)
Sceptic, The (1809) **Thomas Moore** (1779)
Sceptic, The (1820) **Felicia Dorothea Hemans** (1793)
Sceptical Essays (1928) **Bertrand Russell** (1872)
Sceptical Muse, The (1699) **John Pomfret** (1667)
Scepticism and Animal Faith (1923) **George Santayana** (1863)
Scepticisms (1919) **Conrad Potter Aiken** (1889)
Schindler's Ark (1982) **Thomas Keneally** (1935)
Schirmer Inheritance, The (1953) **Eric Ambler** (1909)
Schisme and Schismaticks (1642) **John Hales** (1584)
Scholar Gypsies (1896) **John Buchan** (1875)
Scholar's Daughter, The (1906) **Beatrice Harraden** (1864)
Schollers Purgatory, The (1624) **George Wither** (1588)
School at the Chalet, The (1925) **Elinor M. Brent-Dyer** (1894)
School for Greybeards, A (1786) **Hannah Cowley** (1743)
School for Husbands, The (1852) **Edward Bulwer-Lytton** (1803)
School for Love (1951) **Olivia Manning** (1908)
School for Lovers, The (1762) **William Whitehead** (1715)
School for Scandal, The (1777) **Richard Brinsley Sheridan** (1753)
School for Widows, The (1791) **Clara Reeve** (1729)
School for Wives, The [*L'École des femmes*] (1662) **'Molière' [Jean-Baptiste Poquelin]** (1622)
School for Wives, The (1773) **Hugh Kelly** (1739)
School of Donne, The (1962) **A. Alvarez** (1929)
School of Night, The (1936) **Muriel Bradbrook** (1909)
School on the Loch, The (1946) **Angela Brazil** (1869)
School-Mistress, The (1742) **William Shenstone** (1714)
Schoole of Abuse, The (1579) **Stephen Gosson** (1554)
Schoole of Complement, The (1631) **James Shirley** (1596)
Schoolmaster, The (1570) **Roger Ascham** (1515)
Schoolmistress, The (1886) **Arthur Wing Pinero** (1855)
Schools and Universities on the Continent (1868) **Matthew Arnold** (1822)
Schultz (1979) **J.P. Donleavy** (1926)
Science and Culture (1881) **T.H. Huxley** (1825)
Science and Government (1961) **C.P. Snow** (1905)
Science and Poetry (1926) **I.A. Richards** (1893)
Science and the Modern World (1925) **A.N. Whitehead** (1861)
Science of Ethics, The (1882) **Sir Leslie Stephen** (1832)
Science of Life, The (1929) **H.G. Wells** (1866)
Science of Political Economy (1897) **Henry George** (1839)
Scientific Outlook, The (1931) **Bertrand Russell** (1872)
Scientific Romance in Britain (1985) **Brian M. Stableford** (1948)
Scientific Thought (1923) **C.D. Broad** (1887)
Scillaes Metamorphosis (1589) **Thomas Lodge** (1558)
Scoop (1938) **Evelyn Waugh** (1903)
Scope and Method of Economic Science, The (1885) **Henry Sidgwick** (1838)
Score! (1999) **Jilly Cooper** (1937)
Scornful Lady, The (1616) **Francis Beaumont** (1585?) [with John Fletcher]
Scorpion, and Other Poems (1972) **Stevie Smith** (1902)
Scorpion God, The (1971) **William Golding** (1911)
Scotch Nationality (1824) **Ebenezer Elliott** (1781)
Scotchman's Return, and Other Essays (1960) **Hugh MacLennan** (1907)
Scotland's Lament (1895) **[Sir] J.M. Barrie** (1860)
Scottboro Limited (1932) **Langston Hughes** (1902)
Scottish Bestiary, The (1986) **George Mackay Brown** (1921)
Scottish Cavalier, The (1850) **James Grant** (1822)
Scottish Chiefs, The (1810) **Jane Porter** (1776)
Scottish Journey (1935) **Edwin Muir** (1887)
Scottish Pastorals, Poems, Songs (1801) **James Hogg** (1770)
Scottish Stories (1914) **R.B. Cunninghame Graham** (1852)
Scottish Village, The (1786) **Hannah Cowley** (1743)
Scoundrel Time (1976) **Lillian Hellman** (1907)
Scourge for Rebels, A (1584) **Thomas Churchyard** (1520?)
Scourge of Folly, The (1611) **John Davies of Hereford** (1565)
Scourge of Villanie, The [as 'William Kinsayder'] (1598) **John Marston** (1576)
Scouring of the White Horse, The (1859) **Thomas Hughes** (1822)
Scowrers, The (1690) **Thomas Shadwell** (1642?)

Screening History (1992) **Gore Vidal** (1925)
Screens, The [*Les Paravents*] (1961) **Jean Genet** (1910)
Screens, The (1960) **I.A. Richards** (1893)
Screwtape Letters, The (1942) **C.S. Lewis** (1898)
Screwtape Proposes a Toast, and Other Pieces (1965) **C.S. Lewis** (1898–1963)
Scribbleomania (1815) **William-Henry Ireland** (1777)
Scribblings of an Idle Mind, The (1966) **Norman Lindsay** (1879)
Scripts for the Pageant (1980) **James Merrill** (1926)
'Scrub' (1860) **Mrs C. L. Balfour** (1808)
Scruffy (1962) **Paul Gallico** (1897)
Scruples (1968) **Judith Krantz**
Scrutiny: A Retrospect (1963) **F.R. Leavis** (1895)
Sculler, The (1612) **John Taylor** (1580)
Scully (1975) **Alan Bleasdale** (1946)
Sculptura (1662) **John Evelyn** (1620)
Scum (1991) **Isaac Bashevis Singer** (1904)
Scum of the Earth (1941) **Arthur Koestler** (1905)
Scylla or Charybdis? (1895) **Rhoda Broughton** (1840)
Sea, The (1973) **Edward Bond** (1934)
Sea and the Jungle, The (1912) **H.M. Tomlinson** (1873)
Sea Around Us, The (1951) **Rachel Carson** (1907)
Sea Change, The (1959) **Elizabeth Jane Howard** (1923)
Sea Egg, The (1967) **Lucy Boston** (1892)
Sea Garden (1916) **Hilda Doolittle** (1886)
Sea Green (1974) **Barbara Hanrahan** (1939)
Seagull, The (1895) **Anton Chekhov** (1860)
Sea is Also a Garden, The (1962) **Phylllis Webb** (1921)
Sea is Kind, The (1914) **T. Sturge Moore** (1870)
Sea King's Daughter, The (1991) **George Mackay Brown** (1921)
Sea Lady, The (1902) **H.G. Wells** (1866)
Sea Lions, The (1848) **James Fenimore Cooper** (1789)
Sea of Cortez, The (1941) **John Steinbeck** (1902) [with Edward F. Ricketts]
Sea of Grass, The (1937) **Conrad Richter** (1890)
Sea Spleenwort (1862) **Charlotte M. Yonge** (1823)
Sea Spray and Smoke Drift (1867) **Adam Lindsay Gordon** (1833)
Sea, the Sea, The (1978) **Iris Murdoch** (1919)
Sea to the West (1981) **Norman Nicholson** (1914)
Sea Urchins (1898) **W.W. Jacobs** (1863)
Sea Wall (1933) **L.A.G. Strong** (1896)
Sea Wall, The [*Un barrage contre le Pacifique*] (1950) **'Marguerite Duras' [Marguerite Donnadieu]** (1914)
Sea Whispers (1926) **W.W. Jacobs** (1863)
Sea Wolves, The (1894) **Max Pemberton** (1863)
Sea-Bed, The (1958) **Ian Hamilton Finlay** (1925)
Sea-Captain, The (1839) **Edward Bulwer-Lytton** (1803)
Sea-Grape Tree, A (1970) **Rosamond Lehmann** (1903)
Sea-Hawk, The (1915) **Rafael Sabatini** (1875)
Sea-Kings in England, The (1830) **Edwin Atherstone** (1788)
Sea-Weeds (1846) **Bernard Barton** (1784)
Sea-Wolf, The (1904) **'Jack London' [John Griffith Chaney]** (1876)
Seaboard Parish, The (1868) **George MacDonald** (1824)
Seacliff (1859) **John W. De Forest** (1826)
Seagull on the Step (1955) **Kay Boyle** (1903)
Seal in the Bedroom, The (1932) **James Thurber** (1894)
Seal Woman, The (1992) **Beverley Farmer** (1941)
Sealskin Cloak, The (1896) **'Rolf Boldrewood' [Thomas Alexander Browne]** (1826)
Sealskin Trousers (1947) **Eric Linklater** (1899)
Sealwear (1966) **Edwin Morgan** (1920)
Seaman's Friend, The [UK: *The Seaman's Manual*] (1841) **Richard Henry Dana Jr** (1815)
Seamarks [*Amers*] (1957) **'Saint-John Perse' [Alexis Saint-Léger Léger]** (1887)
Seamy Side, The (1880) **Sir Walter Besant** (1836) [with James Rice]
Séance, The (1968) **Isaac Bashevis Singer** (1904)
Search, The (1934) **C.P. Snow** (1905)
Search After Happiness, A (1766) **Hannah More** (1745)
Search After Prosperine, The (1843) **Aubrey Thomas de Vere** (1814)
Search for America, A (1927) **Frederick Grove** (1879)
Search for Good Sense, The (1958) **F.L. Lucas** (1894)
Search for Money, A (1609) **William Rowley** (1585?)
Search for the King, A (1950) **Gore Vidal** (1925)
Searches and Seizures (1973) **Stanley Elkin** (1930)
Searching for Caleb (1976) **Anne Tyler** (1941)
Searching for Survivors (1975) **Russell Banks** (1940)
Searching for the Ox (1976) **Louis Simpson** (1923)
Searching Wind, The (1944) **Lillian Hellman** (1907)
Seascape (1975) **Edward Albee** (1928)
Seaside and the Fireside, The (1849) **Henry Wadsworth Longfellow** (1807)
Season in England, A (1951) **P.H. Newby** (1918)
Season in Hell, A [*Une saison en enfer*] (1873) **Arthur Rimbaud** (1854)
Season in Hell, A (1989) **'Jack Higgins' [Harry Patterson]** (1929)
Season in Purgatory (1976) **Thomas Keneally** (1935)
Season in Sinji, A (1967) **J.L. Carr** (1912)
Season in the West, A (1988) **Piers Paul Read** (1941)
Season of Adventure (1960) **George Lamming** (1927)
Season of Anomy (1973) **Wole Soyinka** (1934)
Season of Comfort, The (1949) **Gore Vidal** (1925)
Season of Doubt (1968) **Jon Cleary** (1917)
Season of Passion (1979) **Danielle Steel** (1947)
Season of the Strangler (1982) **Madison Jones** (1925)
Season of Violence (1992) **Stephen Gray** (1941)
Season Ticket (1948) **D.J. Enright** (1920)
Season with Eros, A (1971) **Stan Barstow** (1928)
Seasonable Defence of Preaching, A (1678) **Joseph Glanvill** (1636)
Seasonably Alarming and Humiliating Truths (1774) **John Byrom** (1692–1763)

Seasons, The (1730) **James Thomson** (1700)
Seatonian Poems (1864) **John Mason Neale** (1818)
Seawall and Shoreline (1964) **Bruce Beaver** (1928)
Sebastian (1983) **Lawrence Durrell** (1912)
Sebastopol (1855–6) **Leo Tolstoy** (1828)
Second Advice to the Painter, The (1667) **Sir John Denham** (1615)
Second American Revolution, The (1982) **Gore Vidal** (1925)
Second Anglo-Saxon Reader, A (1887) **Henry Sweet** (1845)
Second Avenue (1960) **Frank O'Hara** (1926)
Second Booke of Songs or Ayres, The (1600) **John Dowland** (1563)
Second Bridegroom, The (1991) **Rodney Hall** (1935)
Second Coming, The (1980) **Walker Percy** (1916)
Second Confession, The (1949) **Rex Stout** (1886)
Second Defence of the Short View of the Profaneness and Immorality of the English Stage, A (1700) **Jeremy Collier** (1650)
Second Empire, The (1922) **Philip Guedalla** (1889)
Second Epistle of the Second Book of Horace, The (1737) **Alexander Pope** (1688)
Second Fiddle (1988) **'Mary Wesley' [Mary Wellesley]** (1912)
Second Foundation (1953) **Isaac Asimov** (1920)
Second From Last in the Sack Race (1983) **David Nobbs** (1935)
Second Funeral of Napoleon , The [as 'M.A. Titmarsh'] (1841) **W.M. Thackeray** (1811)
Second Generation (1964) **Raymond Williams** (1921)
Second Growth (1947) **Wallace Stegner** (1909)
Second Hymn to Lenin (1935) **'Hugh MacDiarmid' [Christopher Murray Grieve]** (1892)
Second Identity, A (1969) **Richard Cobb** (1917)
Second Journey Through Persia, Armenia and Asia Minor, A (1818) **James Morier** (1780)
Second Jungle Book, The (1895) **Rudyard Kipling** (1865)
Second Letter Concerning Toleration, A (1690) **John Locke** (1632)
Second Life, The (1968) **Edwin Morgan** (1920)
Second Man, The (1943) **Julian Symons** (1912)
Second Middle English Primer (1886) **Henry Sweet** (1845)
Second Mrs Tanqueray, The (1893) **Arthur Wing Pinero** (1855)
Second Opportunity of Mr Staplehurst, The (1896) **W. Pett Ridge** (1860)
Second Part of Absalom and Achitophel, The [mostly by **Nahum Tate** (1652)] (1682) **John Dryden** (1631)
Second Part of Conny-Catching, The (1591) **Robert Greene** (1558)
Second Part of Mr Waller's Poems, The (1690) **Edmund Waller** (1606)
Second Part of the Faerie Queene, The [bks iv–vi, with revised bks i-iii] (1596) **Edmund Spenser** (1552?)
Second Part of the Honest Whore, The (1630) **Thomas Dekker** (1572?)
Second Part of the Rover, The (1681) **Aphra Behn** (1640?)
Second Part of the Spirit of Love, The (1754) **William Law** (1686)
Second Part, or a Continuance of Poly-Olbion, The (1622) **Michael Drayton** (1563)
Second Parte of the Confutacyon of Tyndales Answere, The (1533) **Sir Thomas More** (1478)
Second Person Singular (1921) **Alice Meynell** (1847)
Second Poems (1945) **W.S. Graham** (1918)
Second Series of Curiosities of Literature, A (1823) **Isaac D'Israeli** (1766)
Second Sex, The [*Le Deuxième Sexe*] (1949) **Simone de Beauvoir** (1908)
Second Shot, The [as 'Anthony Berkeley'] (1930) **Anthony Berkeley Cox** (1893)
Second Stage Lensman (1953) **E.E.'Doc' Smith** (1890)
Second Thoughts (1880) **Rhoda Broughton** (1840)
Second Thoughts of an Idle Fellow, The (1898) **Jerome K. Jerome** (1859)
Second Tome of the Palace of Pleasure, The (1567) **William Painter** (1540?)
Second Tour of Doctor Syntax, The (1820) **William Combe** (1742)
Second Travels of an Irish Gentleman in Search of a Religion (1833) **Joseph Blanco White** (1775)
Second Tree from the Corner, The (1954) **E.B. White** (1899)
Second Victory, The (1958) **Morris West** (1916)
Second World, The (1942) **R.P. Blackmur** (1904)
Second World War, The (1948) **Sir Winston Churchill** (1874)
Second Year of the War, The (1916) **Hilaire Belloc** (1870)
Second Youth of Theodora Desanges, The (1900) **E. Lynn Linton** (1822–98)
Second-Class Citizen (1974) **Buchi Emecheta** (1944)
Secondary Worlds (1969) **W.H. Auden** (1907)
Secret, The (1907) **E. Phillips Oppenheim** (1866)
Secret, The (1920) **Laurence Binyon** (1869)
Secret Agent, The (1907) **Joseph Conrad** (1857)
Secret Battle, The (1919) **A.P. Herbert** (1890)
Secret City, The (1919) **Sir Hugh Walpole** (1884)
Secret Destinations (1984) **Charles Causley** (1917)
Secret Diary of Adrian Mole Aged 13 ¾, The (1982) **Sue Townsend** (1946)
Secret Families, The (1989) **John Gardner** (1926)
Secret Garden, The (1911) **Frances Hodgson Burnett** (1849)
Secret Generations, The (1985) **John Gardner** (1926)
Secret History of Arlus and Odolphus, The (1714) **[Colley Cibber]** (1671)
Secret History of Europe, The [pts. i, ii; pt. iii, 1713; pt. iv, 1715] (1712) **John Oldmixon** (1673)
Secret History of Queen Zarah and the Zarazians, The (1705) **Mary Delariviere Manley** (1663)
Secret History of the Present Intrigues of the Court of Caramania, The (1727) **Eliza Haywood** (*c.* 1693)
Secret Houses, The (1988) **John Gardner** (1926)
Secret Inheritance, A (1887) **B.L. Farjeon** (1838)
Secret Journey, The (1936) **James Hanley** (1901)

Secret Ladder, The (1963) **Wilson Harris** (1921)
Secret Life, The (1923) **Harley Granville-Barker** (1877)
Secret Lives (1932) **E.F. Benson** (1867)
Secret Meaning of Things, The (1969) **Lawrence Ferlinghetti** (1920)
Secret Memoirs and Manners of Several Persons of Quality, (1709) **Mary Delariviere Manley** (1663)
Secret Narratives (1983) **Andrew Motion** (1952)
Secret of Annexe 3, The (1986) **Colin Dexter** (1930)
Secret of Father Brown, The (1927) **G.K. Chesterton** (1874)
Secret of Kyriels, The (1898) **E[dith] Nesbit** (1858)
Secret of Narcisse, The (1892) **Sir Edmund Gosse** (1849)
Secret Pilgrim, The (1991) **'John le Carré' [David John Moore Cornwell]** (1931)
Secret Places (1981) **Janice Elliott** (1931)
Secret Places of the Heart, The (1922) **H.G. Wells** (1866)
Secret Power, The (1921) **Marie Corelli** (1855)
Secret Rapture, The (1990) **David Hare** (1947)
Secret River, The (1909) **Rose Macaulay** (1881)
Secret Rose, The (1897) **W.B. Yeats** (1865)
Secret Servant, The (1980) **Gavin Lyall** (1932)
Secret Service (1895) **William Gillette** (1855)
Secret Seven, The (1949) **Enid Blyton** (1897)
Secret Trails, The (1914) **Sir Charles G.D. Roberts** (1860)
Secret Vengeance for Secret Insult [A secreto agravio secreta venganza] (1636) **Pedro Calderón de la Barca** (1600)
Secret Villages (1985) **Douglas Dunn** (1942)
Secret Way, The (1921) **Zona Gale** (1874)
Secret Woman, The (1905) **Eden Phillpotts** (1862)
Secret World of Polly Flint, The (1982) **Helen Cresswell** (1934)
Secret-Love (1667) **John Dryden** (1631)
Secretary Bird, The (1968) **William Douglas Home** (1912)
Secretary, The (1843) **James Sheridan Knowles** (1784)
Secretary to Bayne, M.P. (1897) **W. Pett Ridge** (1860)
Secrets (1977) **Bernard MacLaverty** (1942)
Secrets of Monte Carlo (1899) **William le Queux** (1864)
Secrets of the Courts of Europe, The (1897) **Allen Upward** (1863)
Secrets of the Foreign Office (1903) **William Le Queux** (1864)
Seduction (1787) **Thomas Holcroft** (1745)
Seduction, The (1975) **Joyce Carol Oates** (1938)
Seduction of Mrs Pendlebury, The (1974) **Margaret Forster** (1938)
See Naples and Die (1929) **Elmer Rice** (1892)
See You in the Morning (1948) **Kenneth Patchen** (1911)
Seed and the Sower, The (1963) **Sir Laurens van der Post** (1906)
Seed of Adam (1948) **Charles Williams** (1886–1945)
Seedling Stars, The (1957) **James Blish** (1921)
Seeds in the Wind (1933) **William Soutar** (1898)
Seeds of Chaos (1944) **Vera Brittain** (1893)
Seeds of Enchantment, The (1921) **Gilbert Frankau** (1884)
Seeds of Time (1921) **John Drinkwater** (1882)
Seeds of Time, The (1959) **'John Wyndham' [John Wyndham Harris]** (1903)
Seeing it Through (1915) **A. St John Adcock** (1864)
Seeing the World (1980) **Dick Davis** (1945)
Seer, The [pt. i; pt. ii, 1841] (1840) **Leigh Hunt** (1784)
Seeress of Prevorst, The [from J.A.C. Kerner] (1845) **Catherine Crowe** (1790) (tr.)
Seeta (1872) **Captain Meadows Taylor** (1808)
Segregation (1956) **Robert Penn Warren** (1905)
Seize the Day (1956) **Saul Bellow** (1915)
Sejanus his Fall (1603) **Ben Jonson** (1572)
Select British Poets (1824) **William Hazlitt** (1778)
Select Charters and Other Illustrations of English Constitutional History (1866) **William Stubbs** (1825)
Select Thoughts (1648) **Joseph Hall** (1574)
Select Works of the British Poets (1831) **Robert Southey** (1774) (ed.)
Selected Epigrams of Martial (1629) **Thomas May** (1595) (tr.)
Selected Essays 1917–1932 (1932) **T.S. Eliot** (1888)
Selected Parts of Horace (1652) **Sir Richard Fanshawe** (1608) (tr.)
Selected Poems (1938) **John Gould Fletcher** (1886)
Selection of Irish Melodies, A [pts. i, ii] (1808) **Thomas Moore** (1779)
Self and its Sheaths, The (1895) **Annie Besant** (1847)
Self and Others, The (1961) **R.D. Laing** (1927)
Self's the Man (1901) **John Davidson** (1857)
Self-Condemned (1954) **Wyndham Lewis** (1882)
Self-Consciousness (1989) **John Updike** (1932)
Self-Control (1811) **Mary Brunton** (1778)
Self-Government in Industry (1917) **G.D.H. Cole** (1889)
Self-Help (1859) **Samuel Smiles** (1812)
Self-Indulgence (1812) **Lady Charlotte Bury** (1775)
Self-interviews (1970) **James Dickey** (1923)
Self-Portrait in a Convex Mirror (1975) **John Ashbery** (1927)
Self-Portrait With a Slide (1990) **Hugo Williams** (1942)
Selling Manhattan (1987) **Carol Ann Duffy** (1955)
Le Selve, and other Tales (1896) **Ouida** (1839)
Semi-Attached Couple, The (1860) **Emily Eden** (1797)
Semi-Detached House, The (1859) **Emily Eden** (1797)
Send No More Roses [US: *The Siege of Villa Lipp*] (1977) **Eric Ambler** (1909)
Seneca and Elizabethan Tragedy (1922) **F.L. Lucas** (1894)
Senior Partner, The (1881) **Mrs J.H. Riddell** (1832)
Señor Vivo and the Coco Lord (1991) **Louis de Bernières** (1954)
Sense and Sensibilia (1962) **J.L. Austin** (1911–60)
Sense and Sensibility (1811) **Jane Austen** (1775)
Sense of Beauty, The (1896) **George Santayana** (1863)
Sense of Danger, A (1962) **Vernon Scannell** (1922)

Sense of Detachment, A (1973) **John Osborne** (1929)
Sense of Glory, The (1929) **Sir Herbert Read** (1893)
Sense of Movement, The (1957) **Thom Gunn** (1929)
Sense of Reality, A (1963) **Graham Greene** (1904)
Sense of the Past, The (1917) **Henry James** (1843–1916)
Sense of the World, A (1958) **Elizabeth Jennings** (1926)
Senses and the Intellect, The (1855) **Alexander Bain** (1818)
Sensible Life, A (1990) **'Mary Wesley' [Mary Wellesley]** (1912)
Sensualists, The (1959) **Ben Hecht** (1894)
Sentimental Education [*L'Éducation sentimentale*] (1869) **Gustave Flaubert** (1821)
Sentimental Journey, A (1768) **Laurence Sterne** (1713)
Sentimental Journey, The (1934) **'Hugh Kingsmill' [Hugh Kingsmill Lunn,]** (1889)
Sentimental Studies (1895) **Hubert Crackanthorpe** (1870)
Sentimental Tommy (1896) **[Sir] J.M. Barrie** (1860)
Sentimentalists, The (1906) **R.H. Benson** (1871)
Separate Development, A (1981) **Christopher Hope** (1944)
Separate Tables [*Table by the Window*; *Table Number Seven*] (1954) **Terence Rattigan** (1911)
Separate Tracks (1983) **Jane Rogers** (1952)
Sept Péchés capitaux, Les ['The Seven Deadly Sins'] (1849) **Eugène Sue** (1804)
September (1919) **Frank Swinnerton** (1884)
September 1989 (1989) **Edward Bond** (1934)
Septimus Felton (1872) **Nathaniel Hawthorne** (1804–64)
Sequel to Drum-Taps (1865–6) **Walt Whitman** (1819)
Sequences (1956) **Siegfried Sassoon** (1886)
Sequences (1979) **Ralph Gustafson** (1909)
Sequences, Hymns, and Other Ecclestiastical Verses (1866) **John Mason Neale** (1818)
Seraph on the Suwanee (1948) **Zora Neale Hurston** (1903)
Seraphim, The (1838) **E.B. Browning** (1806)
Serapion Brothers, The [*Die Serapionsbrüder*] (1819–21) **E.T.A. Hoffmann** (1776)
Serena Blandish (1924) **Enid Bagnold** (1889)
Serenade (1937) **James M. Cain** (1892)
Serenissima (1987) **Erica Jong** (1942)
Serenity House (1992) **Christopher Hope** (1944)
Sergeant Lamb of the Ninth [US: *Serjeant Lamb's America*] (1940) **Robert Graves** (1895)
Serial Universe, The (1934) **J.W. Dunne** (1875)
Serious and Patheticall Contemplation of the Mercies of God, A (1699) **Thomas Traherne** (1637–74)
Serious Apology for the Principles and Practices of the Quakers, A (1671) **William Penn** (1644) [with George Whitehead]
Serious Call to a Devout and Holy Life, A (1728) **William Law** (1686)
Serious Concerns (1992) **Wendy Cope** (1945)
A Serious Man (1998) **David Storey** (1933)
Serious Money (1987) **Caryl Churchill** (1938)
Serious Reflections of Robinson Crusoe (1720) **Daniel Defoe** (1660)
Serious Thoughts upon the Perseverance of Saints (1751) **John Wesley** (1703)
Serjeant Musgrave's Dance (1959) **John Arden** (1930)
Sermon of Christ Crucified, A (1570) **John Foxe** (1517)
Sermon of John the Bysshop of Rochester , The (1521) **John Fisher** (1459?)
Sermon of Reformation, A (1643) **Thomas Fuller** (1608)
Sermon Preached Upon the Anniversary of the Gunpowder-treason, A (1638) **Jeremy Taylor** (1613)
Sermon upon Popery, A (1715) **Richard Bentley** (1662)
Sermons, Academical and Occasional (1847) **John Keble** (1792)
Sermons and Soda Water (1960) **John O'Hara** (1905)
Sermons by the Late Rev. Mr Sterne [*Sermons of Mr Yorick*, vols. v, vi, vii] (1769) **Laurence Sterne** (1713–68)
Sermons for the Times (1855) **Charles Kingsley** (1819)
Sermons, Occasional and Parochial (1868) **John Keble** (1792–1866)
Sermons of Mr Yorick, The [vols. i, ii] (1760) **Laurence Sterne** (1713)
Sermons of Mr Yorick , The [vols. iii, iv] (1766) **Laurence Sterne** (1713)
Sermons on National Subjects [1st ser.] (1852) **Charles Kingsley** (1819)
Sermons on National Subjects: Second Series (1854) **Charles Kingsley** (1819)
Sermons on the Religious Education of Children (1732) **Philip Doddridge** (1702)
Serpent (1981) **Nicholas Mosley** (1923)
Serpent and the Rope, The (1960) **Raja Rao** (1908)
Serpentine (1984) **Christopher Middleton** (1926)
Servant, The (1948) **'Robin Maugham' [Robert Cecil Romer Maugham]** (1916)
Servant of the Bones, The (1996) **Anne Rice** (1941)
Service [as 'C.L. Anthony'] (1932) **Dodie Smith** (1896)
Service of all the Dead (1979) **Colin Dexter** (1930)
Service of Clouds, The (1998) **Susan Hill** (1942)
Servile State, The (1912) **Hilaire Belloc** (1870)
Sesame and Lilies (1865) **John Ruskin** (1819)
Set in Darkness (2000) **Ian Rankin** (1960)
Set of Six, A (1908) **Joseph Conrad** (1857)
Set This House on Fire (1960) **William Styron** (1925)
Seth's Brother's Wife (1887) **Harold Frederic** (1856)
Setting Free the Bears (1969) **John Irving** (1942)
Setting the World on Fire (1980) **Angus Wilson** (1913)
Settlement, The (1986) **Russell Haley** (1934)
Settler and the Savage, The (1876) **R.M. Ballantyne** (1825)
Settlers in Canada, The (1844) **Frederick Marryat** (1792)
Settlers of the Marsh (1925) **Frederick Grove** (1879)
Seven Against Thebes (467 BC) **Aeschylus** (525–456 BC)

Seven Ages of Woman, The (1923) **Compton Mackenzie** (1883)
Seven Ages of Woman, The (1827) **Agnes Strickland** (1796)
Seven Ages, The (1986) **Eva Figes** (1932)
Seven Books of the Iliad of Homer (1598) **George Chapman** (1559?) (tr.)
Seven Days in New Crete (1949) **Robert Graves** (1895)
Seven Days of Jericho, The (1944) **Patric Dickinson** (1914)
Seven Days, The (1850) **Isaac Williams** (1802)
Seven Deadly Sinnes of London, The (1606) **Thomas Dekker** (1572?)
Seven Dials Mystery, The (1929) **Agatha Christie** (1890)
Seven Emus (1959) **Xavier Herbert** (1901)
Seven for a Secret (1922) **Mary Webb** (1881)
Seven Gothic Tales (1934) **'Isak Dinesen' [Karen Blixen]** (1885)
Seven Journeys, The (1944) **W.S. Graham** (1918)
Seven Lamps of Architecture, The (1849) **John Ruskin** (1819)
Seven Lears (1990) **Howard Barker** (1946)
Seven Men (1919) **Max Beerbohm** (1872)
Seven Pillars of Wisdom (1926) **T.E. Lawrence** (1888)
Seven Plays (1923) **Gilbert Cannan** (1884)
Seven Poor Men of Sydney (1934) **Christina Stead** (1902)
Seven Seas, The (1896) **Rudyard Kipling** (1865)
Seven Sermons (1651) **William Laud** (1573–1645)
Seven Short Plays (1909) **Lady Gregory** (1852)
Seven Sleepers of Ephesus, The (1893) **M.E. Coleridge** (1861)
Seven Sons of Mammon, The (1862) **George Augustus Sala** (1828)
Seven Stories (1873) **Lady Georgiana Fullerton** (1812)
Seven Streams, The (1905) **Warwick Deeping** (1877)
Seven Summers (1951) **Mulk Raj Anand** (1905)
Seven Tales and Alexander (1929) **H.E. Bates** (1905)
Seven Temptations, The (1834) **Mary Howitt** (1799)
Seven Types of Ambiguity (1930) **Sir William Empson** (1906)
Seven Years (1860) **Julia Kavanagh** (1824)
Seven-League Crutches, The (1951) **Randall Jarrell** (1914)
Seventeen (1916) **Booth Tarkington** (1869)
Seventeen Lectures on the Study of Mediaeval and Modern History (1886) **William Stubbs** (1825)
Seventeen Poems for 6d. (1940) **'Robert Garioch' [Robert Garioch Sutherland** (1909)**]** [with Sorley Maclean]
Seventeenth-Century Background, The (1934) **Basil Willey** (1897)
Seventeenth-Century Studies (1883) **Sir Edmund Gosse** (1849)
Seventh and Last Canto of the Third Book of Gondibert, The (1685) **Sir William Davenant** (1606–68)
Seventh Hill, The (1928) **Robert Hillyer** (1895)
Seventy-Seven Dream Songs (1964) **John Berryman** (1914)
Seventy-Six (1823) **John Neal** (1793)
Seventy-Three Poems (1963) **E.E. Cummings** (1894–62)
Several Perceptions (1968) **Angela Carter** (1940)
Several Tracts (1677) **John Hales** (1584–1656)
Severed Head, A (1961) **Iris Murdoch** (1919)
Severn and Somme (1917) **Ivor Gurney** (1890)
Sex and Education (1874) **Julia Ward Howe** (1819)
Sex and Subterfuge (1982) **Eva Figes** (1932)
Sexing the Cherry (1989) **Jeanette Winterson** (1959)
Sexual Anarchy (1990) **Elaine Showalter** (1941)
Sexual Behaviour in Society [rev. 1963 as *Sex in Society*] (1950) **Alex Comfort** (1920)
Sexual Inversion (1897) **Havelock Ellis** (1859)
Sexual Perversity in Chicago (1974) **David Mamet** (1947)
Sexus (1949) **Henry Miller** (1891)
Shabby Tiger (1934) **Howard Spring** (1889)
Shades of Eton (1929) **Percy Lubbock** (1879)
Shadow and Act (1964) **Ralph Ellison** (1914)
Shadow and Bone (1989) **Peter Levi** (1931)
Shadow and Substance (1937) **Paul Vincent Carroll** (1900)
Shadow Box, The (1975) **Michael Cristofer** (1945)
Shadow Country (1982) **Paula Gunn Allen** (1939)
Shadow Dance [US: *Honeybuzzard*] (1966) **Angela Carter** (1940)
Shadow From Ladakh (1967) **Bhabani Bhattacharya** (1906)
Shadow Guests, The (1980) **Joan Aiken** (1924)
Shadow Land (1980) **Peter Straub** (1943)
Shadow of a Crime, The (1885) **Hall Caine** (1853)
Shadow of a Gunman, The [**O'Casey**]: see *Juno and the Paycock*
Shadow of a Sun (1964) **A.S. Byatt** (1936)
Shadow of Ashlydyat, The (1863) **Mrs Henry Wood** (1814)
Shadow of Cain, The (1947) **Edith Sitwell** (1887)
Shadow of Hiroshima, The (1995) **Tony Harrison** (1937)
Shadow of Night, The (1594) **George Chapman** (1559?)
Shadow of Shadows (1982) **Ted Allbeury** (1917)
Shadow of the Glen, The (1903) **J.M. Synge** (1871)
Shadow of the Moon (1957) **M.M. Kaye** (1908)
Shadow of the Rope, The (1902) **E.W. Hornung** (1866)
Shadow of the Sword, The (1876) **Robert Williams Buchanan** (1841)
Shadow on Black Combe, The (1978) **Norman Nicholson** (1914)
Shadow on Summer. A (1974) **Christy Brown** (1932)
Shadow on the Blind, The (1895) **Mrs Louisa Baldwin** (1845)
Shadow on the Dial, The (1909) **Ambrose Bierce** (1842)
Shadow Over Innsmouth, The (1936) **H.P. Lovecraft** (1890)
Shadow, The (1929) **Jeffery Farnol** (1878)
Shadow Train (1981) **John Ashbery** (1927)
Shadow-Cage, The (1977) **Philippa Pearce** (1920)
Shadow-Line, The (1917) **Joseph Conrad** (1857)

Shadowed Bed, The (1986) **Jack Clemo** (1916)
Shadows Move Among Them (1951) **Edgar Mittelholzer** (1909)
Shadows of Chrysanthemums (1944) **E.J. Scovell** (1907)
Shadows of Ecstasy (1933) **Charles Williams** (1886)
Shadows of Empire (1997) **Allan Massie** (1938)
Shadows of the Clouds [as 'Zeta'] (1847) **J.A. Froude** (1818)
Shadows on Our Skin (1977) **Jennifer Johnston** (1930)
Shadows on the Grass (1960) **'Isak Dinesen' [Karen Blixen]** (1885)
Shadows on the Rock (1931) **Willa Cather** (1873)
Shadowy Third, The (1923) **Ellen Glasgow** (1874)
Shadowy Waters, The (1900) **W.B. Yeats** (1865)
Shaft, The (1978) **Charles Tomlinson** (1927)
Shagganappi, The (1913) **Pauline Johnson** (1862)
Shaken in the Wind (1948) **Pamela Frankau** (1908)
Shaker, Why Don't You Sing? (1983) **Maya Angelou** (1928)
Shakespeare (1875) **Edward Dowden** (1843)
Shakespeare (1907) **Sir Walter Raleigh** (1861)
Shakespeare (1970) **'Anthony Burgess' [John Anthony Burgess Wilson]** (1917)
Shakespeare and the Goddess of Complete Being (1992) **Ted Hughes** (1930)
Shakespeare and the Modern Stage (1906) **Sir Sidney Lee** (1859)
Shakespeare, Bacon and the Great Unknown (1912) **Andrew Lang** (1844)
Shakespeare First Folio, The (1955) **W.W. Greg** (1875)
Shakespeare Folios and Quartos (1909) **A.W. Pollard** (1859)
Shakespeare Glossary, A (1911) **C.T. Onions** (1873)
Shakespeare in Harlem (1941) **Langston Hughes** (1902)
Shakespeare Key, The (1879) **Mary Cowden Clarke** (1809) [with Charles Cowden Clarke]
Shakespeare Murders, The [as 'Neil Gordon'] (1933) **A.G. Macdonell** (1895)
Shakespeare Primer, A (1877) **Edward Dowden** (1843)
Shakespeare Restored (1726) **Lewis Theobald** (1688)
Shakespeare the Man (1973) **A.L. Rowse** (1903) (ed.)
Shakespeare's Bawdy (1947) **Eric Partridge** (1894)
Shakespeare's Christmas (1905) **Sir A.T. Quiller-Couch** (1863)
Shakespeare's Fight With the Pirates (1917) **A.W. Pollard** (1859)
Shakespeare's History Plays (1944) **E.M.W. Tillyard** (1889)
Shakespeare's Last Plays (1938) **E.M.W. Tillyard** (1889)
Shakespeare's Sonnets (1964) **A.L. Rowse** (1903) (ed.)
Shakespeare's Sonnets Reconsidered (1899) **Samuel Butler** (1835)
Shakespearean Tragedy (1904) **A.C. Bradley** (1851)
Shakesperiana (1841) **J.O. Halliwell-Phillipps** (1820)
Shall India Live or Die? (1925) **Annie Besant** (1847)
Shall Not Be Moved (1990) **Maya Angelou** (1928)
Shall We Tell the President? (1976) **Jeffrey Archer** (1940)
Shame (1983) **Salman Rushdie** (1947)
Shame the Devil (1934) **Liam O'Flaherty** (1897)
Shamrocks (1887) **Katharine Tynan** (1861)
Shandon Bells (1883) **William Black** (1841)
Shane (1951) **A.B. Guthrie** (1901)
Shannon's Way (1948) **A.J. Cronin** (1896)
Shape of Space, The (1969) **Larry Niven** (1938)
Shape of the Table, The (1990) **David Edgar** (1948)
Shape of Things to Come, The (1933) **H.G. Wells** (1866)
Shapes of Clay (1903) **Ambrose Bierce** (1842)
Shapes of Sleep, The (1962) **J.B. Priestley** (1894)
Shaping Spirit, The (1958) **A. Alvarez** (1929)
Shardik (1974) **Richard Adams** (1920)
Shards of Memory (1995) **Ruth Prawer Jhabvala** (1927)
Share of the World, A (1964) **Andrea Newman** (1938)
Sharon and Tracey and the Rest (1992) **Keith Waterhouse** (1929)
Sharpe's Eagle (1981) **Bernard Cornwell**
Sharpe's Trafalgar (2000) **Bernard Cornwell**
Shaving of Shagpat, The (1856) **George Meredith** (1828)
Shawl, The (1989) **Cynthia Ozick** (1928)
She (1887) **Sir H. Rider Haggard** (1856)
She and Allan (1921) **Sir H. Rider Haggard** (1856)
She and I (1930) **Pamela Frankau** (1908)
She Came to Stay [*L'Invitée*] (1943) **Simone de Beauvoir** (1908)
She Made of It (1974) **Alan Brownjohn** (1931)
She Stoops to Conquer (1773) **Oliver Goldsmith** (1728)
She Wou'd and She Wou'd Not (1702) **Colley Cibber** (1671)
She Wou'd If She Cou'd (1668) **Sir George Etherege** (1635)
Sheaf of Verses, A (1908) **Radclyffe Hall** (1880)
Shearer's Colt, The (1936) **A.B. 'Banjo' Paterson** (1864)
Sheepfold Hill (1958) **Conrad Potter Aiken** (1889)
Shelley (1878) **John Addington Symonds** (1840)
Shelley (1909) **Francis Thompson** (1859–1907)
Shelley (1946) **Edmund Blunden** (1896)
Shelley: The Pursuit (1974) **Richard Holmes** (1945)
Shelley's Myth-Making (1959) **Harold Bloom** (1930)
Shells by a Stream (1944) **Edmund Blunden** (1896)
Shelter, The (1983) **Caryl Phillips** (1958)
Sheltered Life, The (1932) **Ellen Glasgow** (1874)
Sheltering Sky, The (1949) **Paul Bowles** (1910)
Shenandoah (1888) **Bronson Howard** (1842)
Shenandoah (1941) **Delmore Schwartz** (1913)
Shenstone-Green [as 'Courtney Melmoth'] (1779) **Samuel Jackson Pratt** (1749)
Shepheardes Calender, The (1579) **Edmund Spenser** (1552?)
Shepherd, The (1922) **Edmund Blunden** (1896)
Shepherd's Artifice, The (1765) **Charles Dibdin** (1745)
Shepherd's Calendar, The (1827) **John Clare** (1793)

Shepherd's Calendar, The (1829) **James Hogg** (1770)
Shepherd's Life, A (1910) **W.H. Hudson** (1841)
Shepherd's Pipe, The (1614) **William Browne of Tavistock** (1590?)
Shepherd's Week, The (1714) **John Gay** (1685)
Shepherds Hunting, The (1615) **George Wither** (1588)
Shepherds in Sackcloth (1930) **Sheila Kaye-Smith** (1887)
Sheppard Lee (1836) **Robert Bird** (1806)
Shepperton Manor (1845) **John Mason Neale** (1818)
Sherlock Holmes [adaptation of Conan Doyle stories] (1899) **William Gillette** (1855)
Sherston's Progress (1936) **Siegfried Sassoon** (1886)
Shield King, The (1956) **Rosemary Sutcliff** (1920)
Shifting of the Fire, The (1892) **Ford Madox Ford** (1873)
Shifting Winds (1866) **R.M. Ballantyne** (1825)
Shifts of Being (1968) **Richard Eberhart** (1904)
Shilling for Candles, A (1936) **'Josephine Tey' [Elizabeth Mackintosh]** (1897)
Shining and Free (1935) **G.B. Stern** (1890)
Shining Ferry (1905) **Sir A.T. Quiller-Couch** (1863)
Shining Pyramid, The (1924) **Arthur Machen** (1863)
Shining Scabbard (1936) **R.C. Hutchinson** (1907)
Shining, The (1976) **Stephen King** (1947)
Ship, The (1943) **C.S. Forester** (1899)
Ship, The (1918) **Oliver St Gogarty** (1878)
Ship Chandler, The (1862) **George Augustus Sala** (1828)
Ship Island (1968) **Elizabeth Spencer** (1921)
Ship of Fools (1962) **Katherine Anne Porter** (1890)
Ship of Fools, The (1509) **Alexander Barclay** (1475?) (tr.)
Ship of Safeguard, The (1569) **Barnaby Googe** (1540)
Ship of Shadows (1979) **Fritz Leiber** (1910)
Ship of Stars, The (1899) **Sir A.T. Quiller-Couch** (1863)
Ship on the Coin, The (1972) **Rodney Hall** (1935)
Ship That Died of Shame, The (1959) **Nicholas Monsarrat** (1910)
Ship's Company (1911) **W.W. Jacobs** (1863)
Ship's Orchestra, The (1966) **Roy Fisher** (1930)
Ship's Pasture, The (1986) **Jon Silkin** (1930)
Shipping News, The (1993) **E. Annie Proulx** (1935)
Ships That Pass in the Night (1893) **Beatrice Harraden** (1864)
Shipwreck, The (1762) **William Falconer** (1732)
Shires, The (1974) **Donald Davie** (1922)
Shirley (1849) **Charlotte Bronte** (1816)
Shirley Sanz (1932) **V.S. Pritchett** (1900)
Shirley Valentine (1986) **Willy Russell** (1947)
Shocks (1935) **Algernon Blackwood** (1869)
Shoe Bird, The (1964) **Eudora Welty** (1909)
Shoemakers Holiday, The (1600) **Thomas Dekker** (1572?)
Shoes of the Fisherman, The (1963) **Morris West** (1916)
Shoeshine (1979) **David Mamet** (1947)
Shogun (1975) **James Clavell** (1924)
Shoo-Maker a Gentleman, A (1637) **William Rowley** (1585?-1626)
Shoot [Si Gira] (1916) **Luigi Pirandello** (1867)
Shoot Me With Flowers (1973) **John Agard** (1949)
Shooting an Elephant (1950) **George Orwell** (1903)
Shooting Niagara: and After? (1867) **Thomas Carlyle** (1795)
Shooting Party, The (1981) **Isabel Colegate** (1931)
Shooting Star (1958) **Robert Bloch** (1917)
Shooting Star, A (1961) **Wallace Stegner** (1909)
Shooting Stars (1992) **James Kirkup** (1923)
Shops and Houses (1918) **Frank Swinnerton** (1884)
Shore Acres (1892) **James A. Herne** (1839)
Shores of Light, The (1952) **Edmund Wilson** (1895)
Short and Sweet (1999) **Simon Armitage** (1963)
Short Answer, A (1958) **Stanley Middleton** (1919)
Short Answer to . . . Smectymnuus, A (1641) **Joseph Hall** (1574)
Short Cruises (1907) **W.W. Jacobs** (1863)
Short Drive, Sweet Chariot (1966) **William Saroyan** (1908)
Short Friday (1964) **Isaac Bashevis Singer** (1904)
Short Story of a Prince, The (1998) **Jane Hamilton**
Short History of English Literature, A (1898) **George Saintsbury** (1845)
Short History of French Literature, A (1882) **George Saintsbury** (1845)
Short History of the British Working Class Movement, A (1925) **G.D.H. Cole** (1889)
Short History of the English People, A (1874) **J[ohn] R[ichard] Green** (1837)
Short History of the World, A (1922) **H.G. Wells** (1866)
Short Poems (1967) **John Berryman** (1914)
Short Reign of Pippin IV, The (1957) **John Steinbeck** (1902)
Short Stories, Scraps and Shavings (1934) **Bernard Shaw** (1856)
Short Story Embassy, The (1975) **Michael Wilding** (1942)
Short Story, The (1948) **'Seán O'Faoláin' [John Francis Whelan]** (1900)
Short Story in English, The (1981) **Walter Allen** (1911)
Short Survey of Surrealism, A (1935) **David Gascoyne** (1916)
Short Takes (1946) **Damon Runyon** (1884)
Short Talks with the Dead and Others (1926) **Hilaire Belloc** (1870)
Short View of the Immorality, and Profaneness of the English Stage, A (1698) **Jeremy Collier** (1650)
Short View of the Late Troubles in England, A (1681) **Sir William Dugdale** (1605)
Short View of Tragedy, A (1693) **Thomas Rymer** (1641)
Short Vindication of 'The Relapse' and 'The Provok'd Wife', A (1698) **Sir John Vanbrugh** (1664)
Short Walk in the Hindu Kush, A (1958) **Eric Newby** (1919)
Short-Title Catalogue of Books 1475–1640, A (1926) **A.W. Pollard** (1859) [with G.R. Redgrave]
Shortest Way to Peace and Union, The (1703) **Daniel Defoe** (1660)
Shortest Way with the Dissenters, The (1702) **Daniel Defoe** (1660)
Shorts (1989) **David Edgar** (1948)

Shosha (1978) **Isaac Bashevis Singer** (1904)
Shot in the Dark, A (1958) **David Garnett** (1892)
Shoulder of Shasta, The (1895) **Bram Stoker** (1847)
Shoulder to Shoulder (1891) **'Lanoe Falconer' [Mary Elizabeth Hawker]** (1848)
Shout, The (1929) **Robert Graves** (1895)
Shout Across the River (1978) **Stephen Poliakoff** (1952)
Shout at the Devil (1966) **Wilbur Smith** (1933)
Shovelling Trouble (1972) **Mordecai Richler** (1931)
Show Girl, The (1909) **Max Pemberton** (1863)
Show Must Go On, The (1949) **Elmer Rice** (1892)
Showboat (1926) **Edna Ferber** (1885)
Showing the Flag (1989) **Jane Gardam** (1928)
Shrapnel (1973) **George MacBeth** (1932)
Shrewsbury (1898) **Stanley J. Weyman** (1855)
Shrimp and the Anenome, The (1944) **L.P. Hartley** (1895)
Shrine, The (1977) **Mary Lavin** (1912)
Shrine of Jeffrey Dahmer, The (1993) **Brian Masters** (1939)
Shropshire Lad, A (1896) **A.E. Housman** (1859)
Shroud for a Nightingale (1971) **P.D. James** (1920)
Shuttle in the Crypt, A (1972) **Wole Soyinka** (1934)
Shuttlecock (1981) **Graham Swift** (1949)
Siamese Twins, The (1831) **Edward Bulwer-Lytton** (1803)
Siber: My Discovery of Siberia (1970) **Farley Mowat** (1921)
Sibyl Falcon (1895) **Edgar Jepson** (1863)
Sicelides a Piscatory (1631) **Phineas Fletcher** (1582)
Sicilian, The (1984) **Mario Puzo** (1920)
Sicilian Romance, A (1790) **Ann Radcliffe** (1764)
Sicilian Specialist, The (1974) **Norman Lewis** (1918)
Sicilian Story, A (1820) **'Barry Cornwall' [Bryan Waller Procter]** (1787)
Sicilian Summer; St Clement's Eve (1875) **Sir Henry Taylor** (1800)
Sicilian Vespers, The (1958) **Sir Steven Runciman** (1903
Sick Heart River (1941) **John Buchan** (1875–1940)
Siddhartha (1922) **Hermann Hesse** (1877)
Side Street (1961) **James T. Farrell** (1904)
Sidmouth Letters, The (1975) **Jane Gardam** (1928)
Sido (1929) **Colette** (1873)
Siege (1937) **Irwin Shaw** (1913)
Siege of Acre, The (1801) **Hannah Cowley** (1743)
Siege of Aquileia, The (1760) **John Home** (1722)
Siege of Corinth, The (1816) **George Gordon, Lord Byron** (1788)
Siege of Cuzco, The (1800) **William Sotheby** (1757)
Siege of Krishnapur, The (1973) **J.G. Farrell** (1935)
Siege of Meaux, The (1794) **Henry James Pye** (1745)
Siege of Memphis, The (1676) **Thomas D'Urfey** (1653)
Siege of Pleasure, The (1932) **Patrick Hamilton** (1904)
Siege of Rhodes, The (1656) **Sir William Davenant** (1606)
Siege of Sinope, The (1781) **Frances Brooke** (1724)
Siege of Valencia, The (1823) **Felicia Dorothea Hemans** (1793)
Siege, The (1986) **Connor Cruise O'Brien** (1917)
Siegfried (1928) **Jean Giraudoux** (1882)
Siegfried's Journey 1916–20 (1945) **Siegfried Sassoon** (1886)
Siena (1868) **A.C. Swinburne** (1837)
Siena Red (1992) **Stephen Poliakoff** (1952)
Sift in an Hourglass (1966) **Ralph Gustafson** (1909)
Sigh for the Pitchers (1666) **George Wither** (1588)
Sight for Sore Eyes, A (1998) **Ruth Rendell** (1930)
Sign in Sidney Brustein's Window, The (1964) **Lorraine Hansberry** (1930)
Sign of Four, The (1890) **A. Conan Doyle** (1859)
Sign of the Gunman, The (1969) **David Helwig** (1938)
Sign on Rosie's Door, The (1960) **Maurice Sendak** (1928)
Signa (1875) **'Ouida' [Marie Louise de la Ramée]** (1839)
Signal to Engage, The (1946) **Alex Comfort** (1920)
Signals of Distress (1994) **Jim Crace** (1946)
Signature of All Things, The (1949) **Kenneth Rexroth** (1905)
Signposters, The (1968) **Helen Cresswell** (1934)
Signs of Change (1888) **William Morris** (1834)
Silas Marner (1861) **'George Eliot' [Mary Ann Evans]** (1819)
Silcote of Silcotes (1867) **Henry Kingsley** (1830)
Silence Among the Weapons (1982) **John Arden** (1930)
Silence Farm (1899) **William Sharp** (1855)
Silence in the Garden, The (1988) **'William Trevor' [William Trevor Cox]** (1928)
Silence in the Snowy Fields (1962) **Robert Bly** (1926)
Silence of History, The (1963) **James T. Farrell** (1904)
Silence of the Lambs, The (1988) **Thomas Harris** (1940)
Silence of the Sea, The (1940) **Hilaire Belloc** (1870)
Silence on the Shore, The (1962) **Hugh Garner** (1913)
Silence Opens, A (1994) **Amy Clampitt** (1920)
Silences (1978) **Tillie Olsen** (1913)
Silent House in Pimlico, The (1899) **Fergus Hume** (1859)
Silent Isle, The (1910) **A.C. Benson** (1862)
Silent Night, Lonely Night (1959) **Robert W. Anderson** (1917)
Silent Speaker, The (1946) **Rex Stout** (1886)
Silent Spring (1963) **Rachel Carson** (1907)
Silent Tragedy, A (1893) **Mrs J.H. Riddell** (1832)
Silent Witness, A (1875) **Edmund Yates** (1831)
Silent World of Nicholas Quinn, The (1977) **Colin Dexter** (1930)
Silex Scintillans (1650) **Henry Vaughan** (1622)
Silex Scintillans [2nd edn] (1655) **Henry Vaughan** (1622)
Silhouettes (1892) **Arthur Symons** (1865)
Silhouettes of American Life (1892) **Rebecca Harding Davis** (1831)
Silk Stocking Murders, The [as 'Anthony Berkeley'] (1928) **Anthony Berkeley Cox** (1893)
Silk-Hat Soldier, The (1915) **Richard le Gallienne** (1866)
Silmarrillion, The (1977) **J.R.R. Tolkein** (1892–1973)

Silver Acre, The (1862) **William Carleton** (1794)
Silver Age, The (1613) **Thomas Heywood** (1574?)
Silver Branch, The (1957) **Rosemary Sutcliff** (1920)
Silver Chair, The (1953) **C.S. Lewis** (1898)
Silver Circus (1928) **A.E. Coppard** (1878)
Silver Cord, The (1861) **Charles William Shirley Brooks** (1816)
Silver Darlings, The (1941) **Neil M. Gunn** (1891)
Silver Domino, The (1892) **Marie Corelli** (1855)
Silver Flame, The (1928) **James Hilton** (1900)
Silver Fox, The (1897) **'Somerville and Ross' [Edith Somerville** (1858) and **Violet Martin** (1862)**]**
Silver King, The (1882) **Henry Arthur Jones** (1851) [with Henry Herman]
Silver Lake (1867) **R.M. Ballantyne** (1825)
Silver Ley (1931) **Adrian Bell** (1901)
Silver Sand (1914) **S.R. Crockett** (1860)
Silver Service (1985) **Liz Lochhead** (1947)
Silver Skull, The (1901) **S.R. Crockett** (1860)
Silver Spoon, The (1926) **John Galsworthy** (1867)
Silver Stair, The (1912) **Charles Williams** (1886)
Silver Stallion, The (1926) **James Branch Cabell** (1879)
Silver Tassie, The (1928) **Sean O'Casey** (1880)
Silverado Squatters, The (1883) **Robert Louis Stevenson** (1850)
Silverland (1873) **G.A. Lawrence** (1827)
Silverpoints (1893) **John Gray** (1866)
Silvia (1870) **Julia Kavanagh** (1824)
Silvia (1730) **George Lillo** (1693)
Simisola (1994) **Ruth Rendell** (1930)
Simon (1953) **Rosemary Sutcliff** (1920)
Simon Dale (1898) **'Anthony Hope' [Sir Anthony Hope Hawkins]** (1863)
Simon Forman (1974) **A.L. Rowse** (1903) (ed.)
Simon le pathétique (1918) **Jean Giraudoux** (1882)
Simonidia (1806) **Walter Savage Landor** (1775)
Simple Cobler of Aggawam, The [by'Theodore de la Guard'] (1647) **Nathaniel Ward** (1578)
Simple Honorable Man, A (1962) **Conrad Richter** (1890)
Simple Lust, A (1973) **Dennis Brutus** (1924)
Simple Speaks his Mind (1950) **Langston Hughes** (1902)
Simple Stakes a Claim (1957) **Langston Hughes** (1902)
Simple Story, A (1791) **Mrs [Elizabeth] Inchbald** (1753)
Simple Takes a Wife (1953) **Langston Hughes** (1902)
Simple Tales (1806) **Amelia Opie** (1769)
Simple's Uncle Sam (1965) **Langston Hughes** (1902)
Simpleton, A (1873) **Charles Reade** (1814)
Simpleton, The [with *The Six*, and *The Millionairess*] (1936) **Bernard Shaw** (1856)
Sin Eater, The (1977) **'Alice Thomas Ellis' [Anna Margaret Haycraft]** (1932)
Sin Eater, The [as 'Fiona Macleod'] (1896) **William Sharp** (1855)
Sin Sniper, The (1970) **Hugh Garner** (1913)
Sinai Sort, The (1957) **Norman MacCaig** (1910)
Since Cézanne (1922) **Clive Bell** (1881)
Since Then (1957) **Denis Glover** (1912)
Sincerity (1912) **Warwick Deeping** (1877)
Sincerity and Authenticity (1972) **Lionel Trilling** (1905)
Sinews of War, The (1906) **Arnold Bennett** (1867)
Sing Me Who You Are (1967) **Elizabeth Berridge** (1921)
Sing-Song (1872) **Christina Rossetti** (1830)
Singapore Grip, The (1978) **J.G. Farrell** (1935)
Singer (1989) **Peter Flannery** (1951)
Singin' and Swingin' and Gettin' Merry Like Christmas (1976) **Maya Angelou** (1928)
Singing Bone, The [US: *The Adventures of Dr Thorndyke*] (1912) **R. Austin Freeman** (1862)
Singing Detective, The (1986) **Dennis Potter** (1935)
Singing in the Shrouds (1958) **Ngaio Marsh** (1899)
Singing Sands, The (1952) **'Josephine Tey' [Elizabeth Mackintosh]** (1897)
Singing School (1999) **Jon Stallworthy** (1935)
Single Eye, The (1964) **Maureen Duffy** (1933)
Single Hound, The (1914) **Emily Dickinson** (1830–86)
Single Man, A (1964) **Christopher Isherwood** (1904)
Single Pilgrim, A (1953) **Norman Lewis** (1918)
Single & Single (1999) **'John le Carré' [David John Moore Cornwell]** (1931)
Single Spies (1988) **Alan Bennett** (1934)
Singleheart and Double Face (1882) **Charles Reade** (1814)
Singleton Fontenoy, RN (1850) **James Hannay** (1827)
Sings Harry (1951) **Denis Glover** (1912)
Singular Man, A (1963) **J.P. Donleavy** (1926)
Singular Preference, The (1952) **Peter Quennell** (1905)
Sinister Street [vol. i] (1913) **Compton Mackenzie** (1883)
Sinister Street [vol. ii] (1914) **Compton Mackenzie** (1883)
Sink the Belgrano! (1986) **Steven Berkoff** (1937)
Sinner and the Problem, The (1901) **Eric Parker** (1870)
Sinners in the Hands of an Angry God (1741) **Jonathan Edwards** (1703)
Sins of the Father, The (1991) **Allan Massie** (1938)
Sins of the Fathers (1967) **James Pope Hennessy** (1916)
Sins of the Government, Sins of the Nation (1793) **Anna Laetitia Barbauld** (1743)
Sions Elegies (1624) **Francis Quarles** (1592)
Sions Sonets (1625) **Francis Quarles** (1592)
Sir Andrew Wylie (1822) **John Galt** (1779)
Sir Anthony Love (1690) **Thomas Southerne** (1659)
Sir Barnaby Whigg (1681) **Thomas D'Urfey** (1653)
Sir Bertram (1773) **Anna Laetitia Barbauld** (1743)
Sir Brooke Fossbrooke (1866) **Charles Lever** (1806)
Sir Charles Danvers (1889) **Mary Cholmondeley** (1859)
Sir Courtly Nice (1685) **John Crowne** (d. 1703)
Sir Eldred of the Bower, and The Bleeding Rock (1776) **Hannah More** (1745)
Sir Francis Darrell (1820) **R.C. Dallas** (1754)

Sir George Tressady (1896) **Mrs T. Humphry Ward** (1851)
Sir George's Objection (1910) **Lucy [Mrs W.K.] Clifford** (1853)
Sir Gibbie (1879) **George MacDonald** (1824)
Sir Giles Goosecap, Knight (1606) **George Chapman** (1559?)
Sir Guy D'Esterre (1858) **Selina Bunbury** (1802)
Sir Harry Hotspur of Humblethwaite (1871) **Anthony Trollope** (1815)
Sir Harry Wildair (1701) **George Farquhar** (1678)
Sir Hornbrook (1814) **Thomas Love Peacock** (1785)
Sir Isaac Newton's Philosophy Explained for the Use of Ladies [from F. Algarotti] (1739) **Elizabeth Carter** (1717) (tr.)
Sir Jasper's Tenant (1865) **M.E. Braddon** (1835)
Sir John Chiverton (1826) **W.H. Ainsworth** (1805)
Sir John Constantine (1906) **Sir A.T. Quiller-Couch** (1863)
Sir John Magill's Last Journey (1930) **Freeman Wills Crofts** (1879)
Sir John Oldcastle (1600) **Anthony Munday** (1560) and others
Sir Lancelot (1844) **Frederick William Faber** (1814)
Sir Launcelot Greaves [**Smollett**]: see *The Life and Adventures of Sir Launcelot Greaves*
Sir Marmaduke Maxwell (1822) **Allan Cunningham** (1784)
Sir Martin Mar-all (1667) **John Dryden** (1631)
Sir Michael Scott (1828) **Allan Cunningham** (1784)
Sir Nigel (1906) **A. Conan Doyle** (1859)
Sir Patient Fancy (1678) **Aphra Behn** (1640?)
Sir Percival (1886) **J.H. Shorthouse** (1834)
Sir Percy Hits Back (1927) **Baroness Orczy** (1865)
Sir Philip Sidney (1886) **John Addington Symonds** (1840)
Sir Philip Sidney (1587) **George Whetstone** (*c.* 1551)
Sir Proteus [as 'P.M. O'Donovan'] (1814) **Thomas Love Peacock** (1785)
Sir Quixote of the Moors (1895) **John Buchan** (1875)
Sir Ralph Esher (1832) **[Leigh Hunt]** (1784)
Sir Richard Grinvile, Knight (1595) **Gervaise Markham** (1568?)
'Sir', She Said [rev. 1977 as *Love in Conflict*] (1930) **Alec Waugh** (1898)
Sir Theodore's Guest (1902) **Grant Allen** (1848–99)
Sir Thomas Browne (1905) **Sir Edmund Gosse** (1849)
Sir Thomas More (1829) **Robert Southey** (1774)
Sir Tristrem [by Thomas of Ercildoune] (1804) **Sir Walter Scott** (1771) (ed.)
Sir Walter Raleigh's Sceptick (1651) **Sir Walter Ralegh** (1554–1618)
Sir Walter Raleigh's Instructions to his Sonne (1632) **Sir Walter Ralegh** (1554–1618)
Sir Walter Scott (1932) **John Buchan** (1875)
Sir William D'Avenant's Voyage to the Other World (1668) **Richard Flecknoe** (*c.* 1620)
Sir Winston Churchill (1966–88) **Martin Gilbert** (1936)
Siren (1991) **David Williamson** (1942)
Siren Land (1911) **Norman Douglas** (1868)
Sirens, Knuckles, Boots (1963) **Dennis Brutus** (1924)
Sirens of Titan, The (1959) **Kurt Vonnegut** (1922)
Sirian Experiments, The (1981) **Doris Lessing** (1919)
Siris (1744) **George Berkeley** (1685)
Sirius (1944) **Olaf Stapledon** (1886)
Sirius (1901) **Ellen Thorneycroft Fowler** (1860)
Sissie (1963) **John Williams** (1925)
Sister, The (1769) **Charlotte Lennox** (1720)
Sister Carrie (1900) **Theodore Dreiser** (1871)
Sister Hollywood (1989) **C.K. Stead** (1932)
Sister Jane: Her Friends and Acquaintances (1896) **Joel Chandler Harris** (1848)
Sister Louise (1876) **G.J. Whyte-Melville** (1821)
Sister Philomène [*Soeur Philomène*] (1861) **Edmond** (1822) and **Jules** (1830) **de Goncourt**
Sister Songs (1895) **Francis Thompson** (1859)
Sister Teresa (1901) **George Moore** (1852)
Sister to Evangeline, A (1898) **Sir Charles G.D. Roberts** (1860)
Sister's Choice (1991) **Elaine Showalter** (1941)
Sisterly Feelings, [and] *Taking Steps* (1979) **Alan Ayckbourn** (1939)
Sisters, The (1892) **A.C. Swinburne** (1837)
Sisters and Strangers (1990) **Emma Tennant** (1937)
Sisters of Charity (1855) **Anna Jameson** (1794)
Sisters, The [etc] (1861) **Aubrey Thomas de Vere** (1814)
Sisters' Tragedy, The (1924) **Richard Hughes** (1900)
Sisters-in-Law, The (1921) **Gertrude Atherton** (1857)
Six Characters in Search of an Author [*Sei personaggi in cerca d'autore*] (1921) **Luigi Pirandello** (1867)
Six Common Things (1893) **E.F. Benson** (1867)
Six Days (1924) **Elinor Glyn** (1864)
Six Dramas of Calderón (1853) **Edward FitzGerald** (1809) (tr.)
Six Dreams (1968) **Kathleen Raine** (1908)
Six Easy Ways of Dodging Debt Collectors (1936) **Denis Glover** (1912)
Six Essays on Johnson (1910) **Sir Walter Raleigh** (1861)
Six Life Studies of Famous Women (1880) **Matilda Betham-Edwards** (1836)
Six Months' Tour Through the North of England, A (1770) **Arthur Young** (1741)
Six of One (1978) **Rita Mae Brown** (1944)
Six Poems on Bruges (1919) **Laurence Binyon** (1869)
Six Political Discourses (1778) **Hugh Henry Brackenridge** (1748)
Six Sections from Mountains and Rivers Without End (1965) **Gary Snyder** (1930)
Six Sermons (1634) **John Donne** (1572–1631)
Six Stories Written in the First Person Singular (1931) **Somerset Maugham** (1874)
Six Sundays in January (1971) **Arnold Wesker** (1932)
Six to One (1878) **Edward Bellamy** (1850)
Six to Sixteen (1875) **Mrs J.H. Ewing** (1841)
Six Town Eclogues (1747) **Lady Mary Wortley Montagu** (1689)
Six Weeks in Russia in 1919 (1919) **Arthur Ransome** (1884)

Six Weeks' Tour Through the Southern Counties of England and Wales, A (1768) **Arthur Young** (1741)
Sixes and Sevens (1911) **O. Henry' [William Sydney Porter]** (1862–1910)
Sixteen Dead Men (1919) **Dora Sigerson** (1866)
Sixteen Self Sketches (1949) **Bernard Shaw** (1856)
Sixteen Sermons (1754) **Benjamin Hoadly** (1676)
Sixth Beatitude, The (1936) **Radclyffe Hall** (1880)
Sixth Epistle of the First Book of Horace Imitated, The (1738) **Alexander Pope** (1688)
Sixth Great Power, The (1988) **Philip Ziegler** (1929)
Sixth Heaven, The (1946) **L.P. Hartley** (1895)
Sixth Seal, The (1969) **'Mary Wesley' [Mary Wellesley]** (1912)
Sixties, The (1993) **Edmund Wilson** (1895–1972)
Sixty Poems (1953) **Nissim Ezekiel** (1924)
Sixty Stories (1981) **Donald Barthelme** (1931)
Sixty-Four, Ninety-Four! (1925) **R.H. Mottram** (1883)
Sixty-nine Birnam Road (1908) **W. Pett Ridge** (1860)
Size of Thoughts, The (1996) **Nicholson Baker** (1957)
Sizwe Banzi is Dead (1972) **Athol Fugard** (1932)
Skail Wind (1941) **Sydney Goodsir Smith** (1915)
Skating Party, The (1982) **Marina Warner** (1946)
Skeeters Kirby (1923) **Edgar Lee Masters** (1868)
Skeleton Crew (1985) **Stephen King** (1947)
Skeleton in the Cupboard, The (1988) **'Alice Thomas Ellis' [Anna Margaret Haycraft]** (1932)
Skeleton Key, The (1919) **Bernard Capes** (1850?-1918)
Skeleton-in-Waiting (1989) **Peter Dickinson** (1927)
Skerrett (1932) **Liam O'Flaherty** (1897)
Sketch Book, The [by 'Geoffrey Crayon'] (1819–20) **Washington Irving** (1783)
Sketches and Studies in Italy (1879) **John Addington Symonds** (1840)
Sketches by 'Boz' [1st ser.] (1836) **Charles Dickens** (1812)
Sketches by 'Boz' [2nd ser.] (1837) **'Boz' [Charles Dickens]** (1812)
Sketches, Critical and Biographic (1857) **Thomas de Quincey** (1785)
Sketches in Lavender, Blue and Green (1897) **Jerome K. Jerome** (1859)
Sketches in London (1838) **James Grant** (1822)
Sketches of American Characters (1829) **Sarah Hale** (1788)
Sketches of English Character (1846) **Mrs C.F. Gore** (1799)
Sketches of Irish Character (1829) **Anna Maria [Mrs S.C.] Hall** (1800)
Sketches of Natural History (1834) **Mary Howitt** (1799)
Sketches of the History of Man (1774) **Henry Home, Lord Kames** (1696)
Sketches of the State of Manners and Opinions in the French Republic (1801) **Helen Maria Williams** (1762)
Skialetheia (1598) **Everard Guilpin** (fl.1598)
Skin Deep [US: *The Glass-Sided Ant's Nest*] (1968) **Peter Dickinson** (1927)
Skin for Skin (1925) **Llewelyn Powys** (1884)
Skin Game, The (1920) **John Galsworthy** (1867)
Skin of Our Teeth, The (1942) **Thornton Wilder** (1897)
Skinny Island (1987) **Louis Auchinloss** (1917)
Skinny Legs and All (1990) **Tom Robbins** (1936)
Skins and Bones (1988) **Paula Gunn Allen** (1939)
Skinwalkers (1986) **Tony Hillerman** (1925)
Skipper's Wooing, The (1897) **W.W. Jacobs** (1863)
Skriker, The (1994) **Caryl Churchill** (1938)
Skull Beneath the Skin, The (1982) **P.D. James** (1920)
Skull in Salop, A (1967) **Geoffrey Grigson** (1905)
Sky Ray Lolly (1986) **Fiona Pitt-Kethley** (1954)
Skylark of Space, The [in *Amazing* magazine; book form 1946] (1928) **E.E.'Doc' Smith** (1890)
Skylight (1995) **David Hare** (1947)
Skylight One (1949) **Conrad Potter Aiken** (1889)
Skyscrapers in the Mist (1946) **George Johnston** (1912)
Slabs of the Sunburnt West (1922) **Carl Sandburg** (1878)
Slade (1943) **Warwick Deeping** (1877)
Slag (1970) **David Hare** (1947)
Slan [rev. 1951] (1948) **A.E. van Voght** (1912)
Slapstick (1976) **Kurt Vonnegut** (1922)
Slapstick Tragedy [*The Mutilated*, and *The Gnaidige Fraulein*] (1965) **'Tennessee' [Thomas Lanier] Williams** (1911)
Slaughterhouse Five; or, *The Children's crusade* (1969) **Kurt Vonnegut** (1922)
Slave, The (1899) **Robert Hichens** (1864)
Slave, The (1962) **Isaac Bashevis Singer** (1904)
Slave, The (1978) **Elechi Amadi** (1934)
Slave Dancer, The (1973) **Paula Fox** (1923)
Slave Girl, The (1977) **Buchi Emecheta** (1944)
Slave King, The [*Bug-Jargal*] (1824) **Victor Hugo** (1802)
Slave of the Lamp, The (1892) **'Henry Seton Merriman' [Hugh Stowell Scott]** (1862)
Slave Ship (1967) **LeRoi Jones** (1934)
Slave Song (1984) **David Dabydeen** (1956)
Slavery (1788) **Hannah More** (1745)
Slaves of New York (1986) **Tama Janowitz** (1957)
Slaves of the Lamp (1965) **Pamela Frankau** (1908)
Sleep (1972) **Jack Gelber** (1932)
Sleep in Peace (1938) **Phyllis Bentley** (1894)
Sleep it Off, Lady (1976) **'Jean Rhys' [Ella Gwendolyn Rees Williams]** (1890)
Sleep of Prisoners, A (1951) **Christopher Fry [Christopher Fry Harris]** (1907)
Sleep of Reason, The (1968) **C.P. Snow** (1905)
Sleep Tight (1979) **James Purdy** (1923)
Sleepers Awake (1946) **Kenneth Patchen** (1911)
Sleeping Beauty (1900) **Richard le Gallienne** (1866)
Sleeping Clergyman, A (1933) **'James Bridie' [Osborne Henry Mavor]** (1888)
Sleeping Fires (1895) **George Gissing** (1857)
Sleeping Lord, The (1974) **David Jones** (1895)
Sleeping Murder (1976) **Agatha Christie** (1890)

Sleeping Prince, The (1953) **Terence Rattigan** (1911)
Sleepless Moon, The (1956) **H.E. Bates** (1905)
Sleepwalkers, The (1959) **Arthur Koestler** (1905)
Sleuth (1970) **Anthony Shaffer** (1926)
Slight Ache, A (1961) **Harold Pinter** (1930)
Slinky Jane (1959) **Catherine Cookson** (1906)
Slip-Shod Sybils (1995) **Germaine Greer** (1939)
Slipping Down Life, A (1970) **Anne Tyler** (1941)
Slouching Towards Bethlehem (1968) **Joan Didion** (1934)
Slouching Towards Kalamazoo (1983) **Peter de Vries** (1910)
Slow Boats Home (1985) **Gavin Young** (1928)
Slow Boats to China (1981) **Gavin Young** (1928)
Slow Dawning (1932) **Eleanor Dark** (1901)
Slow Natives, The (1965) **Thea Astley** (1925)
Slow Night, and Other Poems, The (1949) **Christopher Hassall** (1912)
Slow Train to Milan, The (1983) **Lisa St Aubin de Terán** (1953)
Slum Cat, The (1915) **Ernest Thompson Seton** (1860)
Small Back Room, The (1943) **Nigel Balchin** (1908)
Small Boy and Others, A (1913) **Henry James** (1843)
Small Ceremonies (1976) **Carol Shields** (1935)
Small Craft Warning (1972) **'Tennessee' [Thomas Lanier] Williams** (1911)
Small Desperation, A (1968) **Dannie Abse** (1923)
Small Family Business, A (1987) **Alan Ayckbourn** (1939)
Small g (1995) **Patricia Highsmith** (1921)
Small Gods (1992) **Terry Pratchett** (1948)
Small Handful of Fragrant Flowers, A (1575) **Nicholas Breton** (1545?)
Small House at Allington, The (1864) **Anthony Trollope** (1815)
Small Miracle, The (1952) **Paul Gallico** (1897)
Small Pinch of Weather, A (1969) **Joan Aiken** (1924)
Small Room with Large Windows, A (1962) **Allen Curnow** (1911)
Small Town in Germany, A (1968) **'John le Carré' [David John Moore Cornwell]** (1931)
Small War Made to Order, A (1966) **Norman Lewis** (1918)
Small World (1984) **David Lodge** (1935)
Smaller Sky, The (1967) **John Wain** (1925)
Smile, The (1991) **Ray Bradbury** (1920)
Smile at the Foot of the Ladder, The (1948) **Henry Miller** (1891)
Smile Please (1979) **'Jean Rhys' [Ella Gwendolyn Rees Williams]** (1890)
Smile Please (2000) **Jonathan Keates** (1946)
Smiles and Tears (1847) **Charles Whitehead** (1804)
Smiley's People (1980) **'John le Carré' [David John Moore Cornwell]** (1931)
Smire (1937) **James Branch Cabell** (1879)
Smirt (1934) **James Branch Cabell** (1879)
Smith (1935) **James Branch Cabell** (1879)
Smith (1967) **Leon Garfield** (1921)
Smith and the Pharaohs (1920) **Sir H. Rider Haggard** (1856)
Smith's Dream (1971) **C.K. Stead** (1932)
'Smithy' (1905) **Edgar Wallace** (1875)
Smoke (1867) **Ivan Turgenev** (1818)
Smoke (1982) **Djuna Barnes** (1892)
Smoke and Steel (1920) **Carl Sandburg** (1878)
Smoke Bellew (1912) **'Jack London' [John Griffith Chaney]** (1876)
Smoking Mountain, The (1951) **Kay Boyle** (1903)
Smuggler, The (1831) **John Banim** (1798)
Smuggler, The (1845) **G.P.R. James** (1799)
Snail, The (1991) **Adam Lively** (1961)
Snake's Pass, The (1890) **Bram Stoker** (1847)
Snapper, The (1990) **Roddy Doyle** (1958)
Snapshots of a Daughter-in-Law (1963) **Adrienne Rich** (1929)
Snare of the Fowler, The (1892) **Mrs A.H. Alexander** (1825)
Snare, The (1972) **Elizabeth Spencer** (1921)
Snarleyvow (1837) **Frederick Marryat** (1792)
Sneaky People (1975) **Thomas Berger** (1924)
Snooty Baronet (1932) **Wyndham Lewis** (1882)
Snow Ball, The (1964) **Brigid Brophy** (1929)
Snow Goose, The (1941) **Paul Gallico** (1897)
Snow Light, Water Light (1983) **Frances Horovitz** (1938)
Snow Maiden (1873) **Alexander Nikolaevich Ostrovsky** (1823)
Snow Mask, The (1907) **Aleksandr Blok** (1880)
Snow Pasture, The (1949) **P.H. Newby** (1918)
Snow Poems, The (1977) **A.R. Ammons** (1926)
Snow Stop (1993) **Alan Sillitoe** (1928)
Snow Tiger, The (1975) **Desmond Bagley** (1923)
Snow White (1967) **Donald Barthelme** (1931)
Snow-Bound (1866) **John Greenleaf Whittier** (1807)
Snow-Image, The (1851) **Nathaniel Hawthorne** (1804)
Snowball (1974) **Ted Allbeury** (1917)
Snowcroft Critics, The (1898) **'John Ackworth' [Frederick R. Smith]** (1845)
Snowflakes and Sunbeams (1856) **R.M. Ballantyne** (1825)
Snowflakes and Sunbeams (1888) **Wilfred Campbell** (1858)
Snowing Globe, The (1972) **Peter Scupham** (1933)
Snowman, The (1979) **Raymond Briggs** (1934)
So Big (1924) **Edna Ferber** (1885)
So Brief the Spring (1952) **Walter Greenwood** (1903)
So Disdained [US: *Mysterious Aviator*] (1928) **'Nevil Shute' [Nevil Shute Norway]** (1899)
So Forth (1995) **Joseph Brodsky** (1940)
So Hurt and Humiliated (1959) **Francis King** (1923)
So I Am Glad (1995) **A.L. Kennedy** (1965)
So Late into the Night (1952) **Sydney Goodsir Smith** (1915)
So Long, and Thanks for all the Fish (1984) **Douglas Adams** (1952)
So Long to Learn (1952) **John Masefield** (1878)
So Many Hungers (1947) **Bhabani Bhattacharya** (1906)

So the Wind Won't Blow It All Away (1992) **Richard Brautigan** (1935)
Soames and the Flag (1930) **John Galsworthy** (1867)
Soapbox Omnibus, A (1973) **Rodney Hall** (1935)
Sober Advice From Horace (1734) **Alexander Pope** (1688)
Sociable Plover, A (1957) **Eric Linklater** (1899)
Social and Intellectual State of England, The (1850) **Nicholas Patrick S. Wiseman** (1802)
Social Context of Modern English Literature, The (1971) **Malcolm Bradbury** (1932)
Social Contract, The [*Du contrat social*] (1762) **Jean-Jacques Rousseau** (1712)
Social Diseases and Worse Remedies (1891) **T.H. Huxley** (1825)
Social History of England, A (1983) **Asa Briggs** (1921)
Social Hymns (1840) **Robert Owen** (1771)
Social Morality (1869) **F.D. Maurice** (1805)
Social Philosophy and Religion of Comte, The (1885) **Edward Caird** (1835)
Social Problems (1884) **Henry George** (1839)
Social Rights and Duties (1896) **Sir Leslie Stephen** (1832)
Social Statics (1851) **Herbert Spencer** (1820)
Social Theory (1920) **G.D.H. Cole** (1889)
Socialism (1893) **William Morris** (1834)
Socialism and Co-operation (1921) **Leonard Woolf** (1880)
Socialism in England (1890) **Sidney Webb** (1859)
Society (1865) **T.W. Robertson** (1829)
Society and Solitude (1870) **Ralph Waldo Emerson** (1803)
Society in America (1837) **Harriet Martineau** (1802)
Society of the Poem, The (1971) **Jonathan Raban** (1942)
Sodom et Gomorrhe (1943) **Jean Giraudoux** (1882)
Soeurs Vatard, Les ['The Vatard Sisters'] (1879) **J.K. Huysmans** (1848)
Soft Answers (1932) **Richard Aldington** (1892)
Soft City (1973) **Jonathan Raban** (1942)
Soft Machine, The (1961) **William S. Burroughs** (1914)
Soft Side, The (1900) **Henry James** (1843)
Softcops (1984) **Caryl Churchill** (1938)
Soil, The [*La Terre*] (1887) **Émile Zola** (1840)
Soldier Erect, A (1971) **Brian Aldiss** (1925)
Soldier, The (1944) **Conrad Potter Aiken** (1889)
Soldier, The (1810) **Ebenezer Elliott** (1781)
Soldier's Art, The (1966) **Anthony Powell** (1905)
Soldier's Return, The (1807) **Robert Tannahill** (1774)
Soldier's Return, The (1999) **Melvyn Bragg** (1939)
Soldiering On (1989) **Vernon Scannell** (1922)
Soldiers Bathing (1945) **F.T. Prince** (1912)
Soldiers' Pay (1926) **William Faulkner** (1897)
Soldiers Three (1888) **Rudyard Kipling** (1865)
Soldiers' Women (1961) **Xavier Herbert** (1901)
Sole Survivor (1983) **Maurice Gee** (1931)
Solid Mandala, The (1966) **Patrick White** (1912)
Soliloquies in England (1922) **George Santayana** (1863)
Soliloquies in Song (1882) **Alfred Austin** (1835)
Solitaire/Double Solitaire (1971) **Robert W. Anderson** (1917)
Solitary, The (1831) **Charles Whitehead** (1804)
Solitary Child, The (1956) **Nina Bawden** (1925)
Solitary Grief, A (1991) **Bernice Rubens** (1923)
Solitary Hours (1826) **Caroline Bowles** (1786)
Solitary Summer, The (1899) **'Elizabeth' [Mary Annette Gräfin] von Arnim** (1866)
Solitary Way, The (1934) **William Soutar** (1898)
Solo (1980) **'Jack Higgins' [Harry Patterson]** (1929)
Solo for a Glass Harmonica (1957) **Charles Tomlinson** (1927)
Solomon Gursky Was Here (1989) **Mordecai Richler** (1931)
Solomon's Seal (1980) **'Hammond Innes' [Ralph Hammond-Innes]** (1913)
Solomon's Temple Spiritualized (1688) **John Bunyan** (1628)
Solstice (1985) **Joyce Carol Oates** (1938)
Solstice, and Other Poems (1935) **Robinson Jeffers** (1887)
Solstices (1961) **Louis MacNeice** (1907)
Sombrero Fallout (1976) **Richard Brautigan** (1935)
Some Account of My Cousin Nicholas [by 'Thomas Ingoldsby'] (1841) **R.H. Barham** (1788)
Some Adventures of Captain Simon Suggs (1846) **J.J. Hooper** (1815)
Some Angry Angel (1960) **Richard Condon** (1915)
Some Aspects of Modern Poetry (1924) **Alfred Noyes** (1880)
Some Buried Caesar [alternative US title: *The Red Bull*] (1938) **Rex Stout** (1886)
Some Came Running (1957) **James Jones** (1921)
Some Do Not (1924) **Ford Madox Ford** (1873)
Some Dogmas of Religion (1906) **John McTaggart** (1866)
Some Eighteenth-Century Byways (1908) **John Buchan** (1875)
Some Every-day Folks (1894) **Eden Phillpotts** (1862)
Some Everyday Folk and Dawn (1909) **Miles Franklin** (1879)
Some Experiences of an Irish R.M. (1899) **'Somerville and Ross' [Edith Somerville** (1858) and **Violet Martin** (1862)**]**
Some Fables After Monsieur de la Fontaine (1703) **Bernard Mandeville** (1670)
Some Freaks (1989) **David Mamet** (1947)
Some Fruits of Solitude (1693) **William Penn** (1644)
Some Gorgeous Accident (1967) **James Kennaway** (1928)
Some Gospel-Truths Opened (1656) **John Bunyan** (1628)
Some Irish Essays (1906) **George William Russell ['AE']** (1867)
Some Literary Recollections (1884) **James Payn** (1830)
Some Main Problems of Philosophy (1953) **G.E. Moore** (1873)
Some Men Are Brothers (1960) **D.J. Enright** (1920)
Some More of Me Poetry (1976) **Pam Ayres** (1947)

Some Notes on Lifemanship (1950) **Stephen Potter** (1900)
Some of Me Poetry (1976) **Pam Ayres** (1947)
Some Passages of the Life and Death of the Right Honourable John Earl of Rochester (1680) **Gilbert Burnet** (1643)
Some People (1927) **Sir Harold Nicolson** (1886)
Some People, Places and Things That Will Not Appear in My Next Novel (1961) **John Cheever** (1912)
Some Poems (1940) **W.H. Auden** (1907)
Some Principles of the Elect People of God (1661) **George Fox** (1624)
Some Shakespearean Themes (1959) **L.C. Knights** (1906)
Some Sweet Day (1975) **Hugo Williams** (1942)
Some Tame Gazelle (1950) **Barbara Pym** (1913)
Some Thoughts Concerning Education (1693) **John Locke** (1632)
Some Thoughts Concerning the Present Revival of Religion in New England (1742) **Jonathan Edwards** (1703)
Some Time After (1972) **Anne Ridler** (1912)
Some Trees (1956) **John Ashbery** (1927)
Some Turns of Thought in Modern Philosophy (1933) **George Santayana** (1863)
Some Unease and Angels (1977) **Elaine Feinstein** (1930)
Some Versions of Pastoral (1935) **Sir William Empson** (1906)
Somebody in Boots (1935) **Nelson Algren** (1909)
Somebody's Darling (1978) **Larry McMurty** (1936)
Somehow Good (1908) **William de Morgan** (1839)
Someone Like You (1953) **Roald Dahl** (1916)
Someone Talking to Sometime (1985) **Ama Ata Aidoo** (1942)
Something About Eve (1927) **James Branch Cabell** (1879)
Something About Women (1995) **P.H. Newby** (1918)
Something Childish (1924) **'Katherine Mansfield' [Kathleen Mansfield Beauchamp]** (1888)
Something Happened (1974) **Joseph Heller** (1923)
Something I've Been Meaning to Tell You (1974) **Alice Munro** (1931)
Something in Common (1963) **Langston Hughes** (1902)
Something in Disguise (1969) **Elizabeth Jane Howard** (1923)
Something Leather (1990) **Alasdair Gray** (1934)
Something of the Sea (1954) **Alan Ross** (1922)
Something Short and Sweet (1937) **H.E. Bates** (1905)
Something Special (1990) **Iris Murdoch** (1919)
Something Terrible, Something Lovely (1948) **William Sansom** (1912)
Something to Answer For (1968) **P.H. Newby** (1918)
Something to Remember Me By (1993) **Saul Bellow** (1915)
Something Unusual (1986) **E.A. Markham** (1939)
Something Wicked This Way Comes (1962) **Ray Bradbury** (1920)
Something Wrong (1893) **E[dith] Nesbit** (1858)
Sometime (1933) **Robert Herrick** (1868)
Sometime Never (1948) **Roald Dahl** (1916)
Sometimes a Great Notion (1964) **Ken Kesey** (1935)
Sometimes Island (1968) **Erskine Caldwell** (1903)
Somewhere East of Life (1995) **Brian Aldiss** (1925)
Somewhere is Such a Kingdom (1975) **Geoffrey Hill** (1932)
Somewhere the Tempest Fell (1947) **Josephine Herbst** (1897)
Son at the Front, A (1923) **Edith Wharton** (1862)
Son of a Servant, The (1886) **August Strindberg** (1849)
Son of a Smaller Hero (1955) **Mordecai Richler** (1931)
Son of Hagar, A (1887) **Hall Caine** (1853)
Son of Man (1970) **Dennis Potter** (1935)
Son of Man (1971) **Robert Silverberg** (1935)
Son of Perdition, The (1929) **James Gould Cozzens** (1903)
Son of Royal Langbrith, The (1904) **William Dean Howells** (1837)
Son of Tarzan, The (1917) **Edgar Rice Burroughs** (1875)
Son of the Circus, A (1994) **John Irving** (1942)
Son of the Middle Border, A (1917) **Hamlin Garland** (1860)
Son of the Morning Star (1984) **Evan S. Connell, Jr** (1924)
Son of the People, A (1906) **Baroness Orczy** (1865)
Son of the Soil, A (1865) **Margaret Oliphant** (1828)
Son of the State, A (1899) **W. Pett Ridge** (1860)
Son of the Wolf, The (1900) **'Jack London' [John Griffith Chaney]** (1876)
Son of Woman (1931) **John Middleton Murry** (1889)
Song and Dance, A (1968) **P.J. Kavanagh** (1931)
Song and Idea (1942) **Richard Eberhart** (1904)
Song at the Year's Turning (1955) **R.S. Thomas** (1913)
Song For a Birth or a Death (1961) **Elizabeth Jennings** (1926)
Song for My Time (1977) **Meridel le Sueur** (1900)
Song for Simeon, A (1928) **T.S. Eliot** (1888)
Song for St Cecilia's Day, A (1687) **John Dryden** (1631)
Song of Darkness and Light, A (1898) **Robert Bridges** (1844)
Song of Good Life, A (1975) **Alan Brownjohn** (1931)
Song of Italy, A (1867) **A.C. Swinburne** (1837)
Song of Lazarus, The (1945) **Alex Comfort** (1920)
Song of Life, The (1920) **W.H. Davies** (1871)
Song of Los, The (1795) **William Blake** (1757)
Song of Sixpence, A (1964) **A.J. Cronin** (1896)
Song of Solomon (1977) **Toni Morrison** (1931)
Song of Solomon in the Dorset Dialect, The (1859) **William Barnes** (1801)
Song of Speed, A (1903) **W.E. Henley** (1849)
Song of Stone, A (1997) **Iain Banks** (1954)
Song of the Battle of the Nile (1799) **William Lisle Bowles** (1762)
Song of the City (1945) **Peter Abrahams** (1919)
Song of the Cold, The (1945) **Edith Sitwell** (1887)
Song of the Lark, The (1915) **Willa Cather** (1873)
Song of the Plow, The (1916) **Maurice Hewlett** (1861)

'*Song of the Shirt, The*' [pub. in *Punch*] (1843) **Thomas Hood** (1799)
Song of the Silent Snow (19986) **Hubert Selby Jr** (1928)
Song of the Sword, The (1892) **W.E. Henley** (1849)
Song of the Wren, The (1972) **H.E. Bates** (1905)
Song to David, A (1763) **Christopher Smart** (1722)
Song-Tide, and Other Poems (1871) **Philip Bourke Marston** (1850)
Songlines, The (1987) **Bruce Chatwin** (1940)
Songs (1959) **Christopher Logue** (1926)
Songs and Satires (1916) **Edgar Lee Masters** (1868)
Songs and Sonnets (1893) **Mathilde Blind** (1841)
Songs Before Sunrise (1871) **A.C. Swinburne** (1837)
Songs, Chiefly in the Rural Language of Scotland (1813) **Allan Cunningham** (1784)
Songs for Eve (1954) **Archibald MacLeish** (1892)
Songs for My Supper (1953) **Robert W. Service** (1876)
Songs From Books (1912) **Rudyard Kipling** (1865)
Songs From London (1910) **Ford Madox Ford** (1873)
Songs From the Clay (1915) **James Stephens** (1882)
Songs from Vagabondia (1894) **William Bliss Carman** (1861) [with Richard Hovey]
Songs in Many Keys (1826) **Oliver Wendell Holmes** (1809)
Songs of a Savoyard (1890) **W.S. Gilbert** (1836)
Songs of a Sourdough (1907) **Robert W. Service** (1876)
Songs of a Sun-Lover (1949) **Robert W. Service** (1876)
Songs of Action (1898) **A. Conan Doyle** (1859)
Songs of Chaos (1915) **Sir Herbert Read** (1893)
Songs of Childhood (1902) **Walter de la Mare** (1873)
Songs of Enchantment (1993) **Ben Okri** (1959)
Songs of England (1898) **Alfred Austin** (1835)
Songs of Erin (1892) **A.P. Graves** (1846)
Songs of Innocence (1789) **William Blake** (1757)
Songs of Innocence and of Experience (1794) **William Blake** (1757)
Songs of Joy (1911) **W.H. Davies** (1871)
Songs of Labor (1850) **John Greenleaf Whittier** (1807)
Songs of Love and Empire (1898) **E[dith] Nesbit** (1858)
Songs of Many Seasons (1875) **Oliver Wendell Holmes** (1809)
Songs of Memory and Hope (1909) **Sir Henry Newbolt** (1862)
Songs of Night (1910) **Andrew Young** (1885)
Songs of Old Ireland (1882) **A.P. Graves** (1846)
Songs of Scotland, Ancient and Modern, The (1825) **Allan Cunningham** (1784)
Songs of Shadow-of-a-Leaf (1924) **Alfred Noyes** (1880)
Songs of Sundry Natures (1589) **William Byrd** (1543)
Songs of the Affections (1830) **Felicia Dorothea Hemans** (1793)
Songs of the Army of Night (1888) **Francis Adams** (1862)
Songs of the Common Day (1893) **Sir Charles G.D. Roberts** (1860)
Songs of the Gael (1925) **A.P. Graves** (1846) (tr.)
Songs of the Psyche (1985) **Thomas Kinsella** (1928)
Songs of the Sea (1904) **Sir Henry Newbolt** (1862)
Songs of the Springtides (1880) **A.C. Swinburne** (1837)
Songs of the War (1900) **Arthur St John Adcock** (1864)
Songs of Three Counties (1913) **Radclyffe Hall** (1880)
Songs of Travel (1896) **Robert Louis Stevenson** (1850–94)
Songs of Twilight [*Les Chants du crépuscle*] (1835) **Victor Hugo** (1802)
Songs of Two Nations (1875) **A.C. Swinburne** (1837)
Songs to a Handsome Woman (1973) **Rita Mae Brown** (1944)
Songs Without Music (1882) **Charles Hamilton Aïdé** (1826)
Sonnets (1909) **Lord Alfred Douglas** (1870)
Sonnets (1609) **William Shakespeare** (1564)
Sonnets and Ballate of Guido Cavalcanti, The (1912) **Ezra Pound** (1885) (tr.)
Sonnets and Odes (1788) **Henry Cary** (1772)
Sonnets and Other Lyrics (1917) **Robert Hillyer** (1895)
Sonnets and Other Poems (1785) **Sir Samuel Egerton Brydges** (1762)
Sonnets and Songs by Proteus (1875) **Wilfrid Scawen Blunt** (1840)
Sonnets from Antan (1929) **James Branch Cabell** (1879)
Sonnets From Scotland (1984) **Edwin Morgan** (1920)
Sons (1932) **Pearl S. Buck** (1892)
Sons and Daughters (1890) **Margaret Oliphant** (1828)
Sons and Lovers (1913) **D.H. Lawrence** (1885)
Sons and Soldiers (1944) **Irwin Shaw** (1913)
Sons Come and Go, Mothers Hang In Forever (1976) **William Saroyan** (1908)
Sons for the Return Home (1973) **Albert Wendt** (1939)
Sons of Cain (1985) **David Williamson** (1942)
Sons of Darkness, Sons of Light (1969) **John Williams** (1925)
Sons of Fire (1895) **M.E. Braddon** (1835)
Sons of Light, The (1976) **David Rudkin** (1936)
Sons of the Father (1940) **Albert Halper** (1904)
Sons of the Morning (1900) **Eden Phillpotts** (1862)
Sons of the Soil [*Les Paysans*] (1844) **Honoré de Balzac** (1799)
Sooner or Later (1868) **Charles William Shirley Brooks** (1816)
Sophia (1762) **Charlotte Lennox** (1720)
Sophie's Choice (1979) **William Styron** (1925)
Sophonisba (1675) **Nathaniel Lee** (1649?)
Sophonisbe (1663) **Pierre Corneille** (1606)
Sophy of Kravonia (1906) **'Anthony Hope' [Sir Anthony Hope Hawkins]** (1863)
Sophy, The (1642) **Sir John Denham** (1615)
Soprano (1905) **F. Marion Crawford** (1854)
Sorceress of the Strand, The (1903) **Mrs L.T. Meade** (1854)
Sordello (1840) **Robert Browning** (1812)
Sore-Footed Man, The (1967) **James K. Baxter** (1926)
Sorrell and Son (1925) **Warwick Deeping** (1877)
Sorrow in Sunlight [US: *Prancing Nigger*] (1925) **Ronald Firbank** (1886)

Sorrows of Gentility, The (1856) **Geraldine Jewsbury** (1812)
Sorrows of Priapus, The (1957) **Edward Dahlberg** (1900)
Sorrows of Rosalie, The (1829) **Caroline Norton** (1808)
Sorrows of Satan, The (1895) **Marie Corel** (1855)
Sorrows of Switzerland, The (1801) **William Lisle Bowles** (1762)
Sorrows of Young Werther, The [*Die Leiden des jungen Werther*] (1774) **Johann Wolfgang von Goethe** (1749)
Sort of Clowning, A (1990) **Richard Hoggart** (1918)
Sort of Life, A (1971) **Graham Greene** (1904)
Sort of Traitors, A (1949) **Nigel Balchin** (1908)
Sorties (1971) **James Dickey** (1923)
SOS. . . . 'Ludlow' (1940) **Christopher Hassall** (1912)
Sot-Weed Factor, The (1960) **John Barth** (1930)
Soul For Sale, A (1947) **Patrick Kavanagh** (1904)
Soul Music (1995) **Terry Pratchett** (1948)
Soul of a Bishop, The (1917) **H.G. Wells** (1866)
Soul of Kindness, The (1964) **Elizabeth Taylor** (1912)
Soul of Lilith, The (1892) **Marie Corelli** (1855)
Soul of London, The (1905) **Ford Madox Ford** (1873)
Soul of Man, The (1895) **Oscar Wilde** (1854)
Soul of Melicent, The [revised 1920 as *Domnei*] (1913) **James Branch Cabell** (1879)
Soul of the Indian, The (1911) **Charles Eastman** (1858)
Soul Traps (1985) **Alistair Campbell** (1925)
Soul's Immortal Crown, The (1605) **Nicholas Breton** (1545?)
Souldiers Accidence, The (1625) **Gervaise Markham** (1568?)
Souldiers Fortune, The (1680) **Thomas Otway** (1652)
Souls of Black Folk, The (1903) **W.E.B. du Bois** (*c.* 1868)
Sound and the Fury, The (1929) **William Faulkner** (1897)
Sound Like Laughter, A (1983) **David Helwig** (1938)
Sound of Coaches, The (1974) **Leon Garfield** (1921)
Sound of Lightning, A (1976) **Jon Cleary** (1917)
Sound of the Sea, The (1959) **Leo Walmsley** (1892)
Sound of Trumpets, The (1998) **John Mortimer** (1923)
Sound the Retreat (1971) **Simon Raven** (1927)
Soundings (1997) **Anita Brookner** (1928)
Soundings From the Atlantic (1864) **Oliver Wendell Holmes** (1809)
Sour Grapes (1921) **William Carlos Williams** (1883)
Sour Sweet (1982) **Timothy Mo** (1950)
Source of Embarrassment, A (1974) **A.L. Barker** (1918)
Source, The (1965) **James A. Michener** (1907)
Sourcery (1988) **Terry Pratchett** (1948)
Sous l'oeil des barbares (1888) **Maurice Barrès** (1862)
South, The (1990) **Colm Tóibín** (1955)
South Africa (1878) **Anthony Trollope** (1815)
South America (1912) **James Bryce** (1838)
South American Journey (1943) **Waldo Frank** (1889)
South Country, The (1909) **Edward Thomas** (1878)
South Moon Under (1933) **Marjorie Rawlings** (1896)
South of No North (1973) **Charles Bukowski** (1920)
South Riding (1936) **Winifred Holtby** (1898–1935)
South Sea Bubble (1956) **Noel Coward** (1899)
South Sea Bubble, The (1871) **W.H. Ainsworth** (1805)
South Sea Tales (1911) **'Jack London' [John Griffith Chaney]** (1876)
South Star (1941) **John Gould Fletcher** (1886)
South Wind (1917) **Norman Douglas** (1868)
South Wind of Love, The (1937) **Compton Mackenzie** (1883)
South-most Twelve (1962) **R.D. FitzGerald** (1902)
Southern Cross (1999) **Patricia Cornwell** (1956)
Southern Discomfort (1982) **Rita Mae Brown** (1944)
Southern Gates of Arabia, The (1936) **Freya Stark** (1893)
Southey (1879) **Edward Dowden** (1843)
Southways (1938) **Erskine Caldwell** (1903)
Souvenirs (1980) **Roy Fuller** (1912)
Soveraigne Power of Parliaments and Kingdomes, The (1643) **William Prynne** (1600)
Sovereigns Prerogative, The (1657) **Thomas Fuller** (1608)
Sovereignty of Good, The (1970) **Iris Murdoch** (1919)
Soviet Communism (1935) **Sidney Webb** (1859) and Beatrice Webb (1858)
Soviet Genetics and World Science (1949) **Julian Huxley** (1887)
Soviet Impact on the Western World, The (1946) **E.H. Carr** (1892)
Soviet Poems (1978) **Ralph Gustafson** (1909)
Sowers, The (1896) **'Henry Seton Merriman' [Hugh Stowell Scott]** (1862)
Sowing (1960) **Leonard Woolf** (1880)
Sowing the Wind (1867) **E. Lynn Linton** (1822)
Space (1982) **James A. Michener** (1907)
Space Between Literature and Politics, The (1981) **Jay Cantor** (1948)
Space Between, The (1982) **E.J. Scovell** (1907)
Space Cat (1952) **Ruthven Todd** (1914)
Space Merchants, The (1953) **Frederik Pohl** (1919) [with C.M. Kornbluth]
Space, Time, and Nathaniel (1957) **Brian Aldiss** (1925)
Spaces of the Dark (1951) **Nicholas Mosley** (1923)
Spaewife, The (1823) **John Galt** (1779)
Spanish Balcony (1973) **Patricia Beer** (1924)
Spanish Bawd, The [from Fernando de Rojas] (1631) **James Mabbe** (1572) (tr.)
Spanish Bayonet (1926) **Stephen Vincent Benét** (1889)
Spanish Bridegroom, The (1954) **'Jean Plaidy' [Eleanor Hibbert]** (1906)
Spanish Cape Mystery, The (1935) **'Ellery Queen' [Frederic Dannay** (1905) and **Manfred B. Lee** (1905)**]**
Spanish Character, The (1932) **Irving Babbit** (1865–1933)
Spanish Descent, The (1702) **Daniel Defoe** (1660)
Spanish Farm, The (1924) **R.H. Mottram** (1883)
Spanish Fryar, The (1680) **John Dryden** (1631)
Spanish Gardener, The (1950) **A.J. Cronin** (1896)

Spanish Gipsie, The (1653) **Thomas Middleton** (1580–1627) [with William Rowley]
Spanish Gypsy, The (1868) **'George Eliot' [Mary Ann Evans]** (1819)
Spanish Jade, The (1908) **Maurice Hewlett** (1861)
Spanish Masquerado, The (1589) **Robert Greene** (1558)
Spanish Match, The (1865) **W.H. Ainsworth** (1805)
Spanish Pistol, The (1939) **A.G. Macdonell** (1895)
Spanish Student, The (1843) **Henry Wadsworth Longfellow** (1807)
Spanish Temper, The (1954) **V.S. Pritchett** (1900)
Spanish Tragedie, The (1592) **Thomas Kyd** (1558)
Spanish Triptych, A (1936) **Robert Nichols** (1893)
Spanish Virgin, The (1930) **V.S. Pritchett** (1900)
Spanking the Maid (1982) **Robert Coover** (1932)
Spanner and Pen (1991) **Roy Fuller** (1912)
Sparagus Garden, The (1640) **Richard Brome** (1590?)
Sparkenbroke (1936) **Charles Morgan** (1894)
Sparrow Falls, A (1977) **Wilbur Smith** (1933)
Spartacus (1952) **Howard Fast** (1914)
Spartan Dame, The (1719) **Thomas Southerne** (1659)
Speak to the Earth (1939) **Andrew Young** (1885)
Speak With the Sun (1949) **David Campbell** (1915)
Speaker of Mandarin, The (1983) **Ruth Rendell** (1930)
Speakers, The (1964) **Heathcote Williams** (1941)
Speaking with the Angel (2000) **Nick Hornby** (1957)
Spear, The (1978) **James Herbert** (1943)
Spearfield's Daughter (1982) **Jon Cleary** (1917)
Special Providence (1930) **Mary Agnes Hamilton** (1884)
Specimen Case, The (1924) **Ernest Bramah** (1868)
Specimens of Early English Metrical Romances (1805) **George Ellis** (1753) (ed.)
Specimens of English Dramatic Poets (1808) **Charles Lamb** (1775) (ed.)
Specimens of the Early English Poets (1790) **George Ellis** (1753) (ed.)
Spectator Bird, The (1976) **Wallace Stegner** (1909)
Spectator, The (1711–12) **Sir Richard Steele** (1672) [with Joseph Addison]
Spectre is Haunting Texas, A (1969) **Fritz Leiber** (1910)
Speculation (1780) **Christopher Anstey** (1724)
Speculations (1924) **T.E. Hulme** (1883)
Speculations, Literary and Philosophic (1859) **Thomas de Quincey** (1785)
Speculative Dialogues (1913) **Lascelles Abercrombie** (1881)
Speculative Instruments (1955) **I.A. Richards** (1893)
Speculum Mentis (1924) **R.G. Collingwood** (1889)
Speculum Speculatiuum (1660) **George Wither** (1588)
Speech on American Taxation (1775) **Edmund Burke** (1729)
Speech on Moving his Resolutions for Conciliation with the Colonies (1775) **Edmund Burke** (1729)
Speeches Corrected by Himself (1854) **T.B. Macaulay** (1800)
Speeches to the German Nation [*Reden an die deutsche Nation*] (1814) **Johann Gottlieb Fichte** (1762)
Speed the Plough [introduced the character of 'Mrs Grundy'] (1798) **Thomas Morton** (1764?)
Speed-the-Plow (1988) **David Mamet** (1947)
Speedy Death [first 'Mrs Bradley' novel] (1929) **Gladys Mitchell** (1901)
Spell, The (1998) **Alan Hollinghurst** (1954)
Spell of the Yukon, The (1907) **Robert W. Service** (1876)
Spell of Winter, A (1995) **Helen Dunmore** (1952)
Spencer Brade, MD (1942) **Frank G. Slaughter** (1908)
Spend, Spend, Spend (1977) **Jack Rosenthal** (1931)
Spendthrift, The (1857) **W.H. Ainsworth** (1805)
Sphere (1987) **Michael Crichton** (1942)
Sphere of Glass, The (1944) **John Lehmann** (1907)
Sphere: The Form of a Motion (1974) **A.R. Ammons** (1926)
Sphinx, The (1894) **Oscar Wilde** (1854)
Sphinx (1986) **D.M. Thomas** (1935)
Sphinx of Eaglehawk, The (1895) **'Rolf Boldrewood' [Thomas Alexander Browne]** (1826)
Sphinx's Lawyer, The (1906) **'Frank Danby' [Julia Frankau]** (1864)
Spice Box of Earth, The (1961) **Leonard Cohen** (1934)
Spider and the Flie, The (1556) **John Heywood** (1497?)
Spider's House, The (1955) **Paul Bowles** (1910)
Spiderweb (1998) **Penelope Lively** (1933)
Spies of the Kaiser (1909) **William le Queux** (1864)
Spies on the Wight, The (1899) **'Headon Hill' [Francis Edward Grainger]** (1857)
Spikenard (1898) **Laurence Housman** (1865)
Spinning-Wheel Stories (1884) **Louisa M. Alcott** (1832)
Spinoza of Market Street, The (1961) **Isaac Bashevis Singer** (1904)
Spinster (1958) **Sylvia Ashton-Warner** (1908)
Spiral Ascent, The (1977) **Edward Upward** (1903)
Spire, The (1964) **William Golding** (1911)
Spiridion (1838–9) **'George Sand' [Auore Dupin]** (1804)
Spirit and the Flesh, The (1936) **Pearl S. Buck** (1892)
Spirit in Prison, A (1908) **Robert Hichens** (1864)
Spirit Level, The (1996) **Seamus Heaney** (1939)
Spirit of Discovery, The (1804) **William Lisle Bowles** (1762)
Spirit of Love, The (1752) **William Law** (1686)
Spirit of Peers and People, The (1834) **R.H. Horne** (1803)
Spirit of Place, The (1899) **Alice Meynell** (1847)
Spirit of Prayer, The [pt. i; pt. ii 1750] (1749) **William Law** (1686)
Spirit of Romance, The (1910) **Ezra Pound** (1885)
Spirit of Rome, The (1906) **'Vernon Lee' [Violet Paget]** (1856)
Spirit of the Age, The (1825) **William Hazlitt** (1778)
Spirit of Truth Vindicated, The (1672) **William Penn** (1644)
Spirit Reach (1972) **LeRoi Jones** (1934)
Spirit Rises, A (1962) **Sylvia Townsend Warner** (1893)
Spirit Watches, The (1939) **Ruth Pitter** (1897)
Spiritual Adventures (1905) **Arthur Symons** (1865)

Spiritual Aeneid, A (1918) **Ronald Knox** (1888)
Spiritual Quixote, The (1773) **Richard Graves** (1715)
Spiritualism, and the Age We Live In (1859) **Catherine Crowe** (1790)
Spirituall Consolation, A (1578) **[John Fisher[** (1459?-1535)
Spit Delaney's Island (1976) **Jack Hodgins** (1938)
Spitfire, The (1840) **Captain Chamier** (1796)
Spleen, The (1737) **Matthew Green** (1696)
Splendid Fairing, The (1919) **Constance Holme** (1881)
Splendid Idle Forties, The (1902) **Gertrude Atherton** (1857)
Splendid Lives (1977) **Penelope Gilliatt** (1932)
Splendid Shilling, The (1705) **John Philips** (1676)
Splendid Sin, A (1896) **Grant Allen** (1848)
Splendid Spur, The (1889) **Sir A.T. Quiller-Couch** (1863)
Splendid Village, The [etc] (1833) **Ebenezer Elliott** (1781)
Splinters (1981) **Chris Wallace-Crabbe** (1934)
Split Images (1982) **Elmore Leonard** (1925)
Splitting (1995) **Fay Weldon** (1931)
Spoil of Office, A (1892) **Hamlin Garland** (1860)
Spoilers, The (1969) **Desmond Bagley** (1923)
Spoils, The (1965) **Basil Bunting** (1900)
Spoils of Poynton, The (1897) **Henry James** (1843)
Spoilt (1992) **Georgina Hammick** (1939)
Spoilt City, The (1962) **Olivia Manning** (1908)
Spook House (1987) **Harvey Fierstein** (1954)
Spook Stories (1928) **E.F. Benson** (1867)
Spoon River Anthology (1915) **Edgar Lee Masters** (1868)
Sport of My Mad Mother, The (1956) **Anne Jellicoe** (1927)
Sport of Nature, A (1987) **Nadine Gordimer** (1923)
Sport Royal (1893) **'Anthony Hope' [Sir Anthony Hope Hawkins]** (1863)
Sporting Life, The (1960) **David Storey** (1933)
Sportswriter, The (1986) **Richard Ford** (1944)
Spotted Hemlock (1958) **Gladys Mitchell** (1901)
Spoyle of Antwerpe, The (1576?) **George Gascoigne** (1542?)
Spring (1728) **James Thomson** (1700)
Spring and All (1922) **William Carlos Williams** (1883)
Spring and Port Wine (1964) **Bill Naughton** (1910)
Spring Days (1888) **George Moore** (1852)
Spring of the Ram, The (1987) **Dorothy Dunnett** (1923)
Spring Sonata (1979) **Bernice Rubens** (1923)
Spring Song (1960) **Joyce Cary** (1888)
Spring Sowing (1924) **Liam O'Flaherty** (1897)
Spring Tide and Neap Tide Reothairt is Contraigh [Gaelic and English] (1977) **Sorley MacLean [Somhairle MacGill-Eain]** (1911)
Springboard (1944) **Louis MacNeice** (1907)
Springhaven (1887) **R.D. Blackmore** (1825)
Springtime (1907) **H.C. Bailey** (1878)
Springtime and Harvest [retitled *King Midas*, 1901] (1901) **Upton Sinclair** (1878)
Spy, The (1821) **James Fenimore Cooper** (1789)
Spy Hook (1988) **Len Deighton** (1929)
Spy in the Family, A (1970) **Alec Waugh** (1898)
Spy in the House of Love, A (1954) **Anaïs Nin** (1903)
Spy Line (1989) **Len Deighton** (1929)
Spy Sinker (1990) **Len Deighton** (1929)
Spy Who Came in From the Cold, The (1963) **'John le Carré' [David John Moore Cornwell]** (1931)
Spy Who Loved Me, The (1962) **Ian Fleming** (1908)
Spy's Wife, The (1980) **Reginald Hill** (1936)
Squanders of Castle Squander, The (1852) **William Carleton** (1794)
Square in the Eye (1966) **Jack Gelber** (1932)
Square Peg, The ([UK: *Dead Man Over All* (1950) **Walter Ernest Allen** (1911)
Square Root of Wonderful, The (1958) **Carson McCullers** (1917)
Squatter's Dream, The (1890) **'Rolf Boldrewood' [Thomas Alexander Browne]** (1826)
Squeeze Play (1982) **Paul Auster** (1947)
Squire of Alsatia, The (1688) **Thomas Shadwell** (1642?)
Squire Oldsapp (1678) **Thomas D'Urfey** (1653)
Squire Silchester's Whim (1873) **Mortimer Collins** (1827)
Squire, The (1938) **Enid Bagnold** (1889)
Squire Trelooby [from Molière]] (1704) **William Walsh** (1663) [with Sir John Vanbrugh and William Congreve]
Squireen, The (1903) **Shan F. Bullock** (1865)
Squirrel, the Hare, and the Little Grey Rabbit, The [first of the 'Little Grey Rabbit' books] (1929) **'Alison Uttley' [Alice Jane Uttley]** (1884)
SS Perdition (1931) **James Gould Cozzens** (1903)
SS-GB (1978) **Len Deighton** (1929)
Stabbed in the Dark (1885) **E. Lynn Linton** (1822)
Stage Defended, The (1726) **John Dennis** (1657)
Stage for Poetry, A (1948) **Gordon Bottomley** (1874)
Stage-Coach, The (1704) **George Farquhar** (1678)
Stage-Land (1889) **Jerome.K. Jerome** (1859)
Stags and Hens (1978) **Willy Russell** (1947)
Stalin's Russia (1940) **Max Eastman** (1883)
Stalky & Co. (1899) **Rudyard Kipling** (1865)
Stamboul Train (1932) **Graham Greene** (1904)
Stand Fast, Craig Royston (1891) **William Black** (1841)
Stand Still Like a Hummingbird (1962) **Henry Miller** (1891)
Stand, The (1978) **Stephen King** (1947)
Stand Up Virgin Soldiers (1975) **Leslie Thomas** (1931)
Standard Bearer, The (1898) **S.R. Crockett** (1860)
Standard of Behaviour, A (1958) **'William Trevor' [William Trevor Cox]** (1928)
Standing Female Nude (1985) **Carol Ann Duffy** (1955)
Standing Room Only (1936) **Walter Greenwood** (1903)
Stanley and the Women (1984) **Kingsley Amis** (1922)
Stanley Brereton (1881) **W.H. Ainsworth** (1805)
Stanley Buxton (1832) **John Galt** (1779)

Stans Puer ad Mensam (1476?) **John Lydgate** (1370?-1449)
Star Begotten (1937) **H.G. Wells** (1866)
Star Called Henry, A (1999) **Roddy Doyle** (1958)
Star Maker (1937) **Olaf Stapledon** (1886)
Star of the Coast, The (1844) **Selina Bunbury** (1802)
Star Spangled Virgin (1939) **DuBose Heyward** (1885)
Star Stalker, The (1968) **Robert Bloch** (1917)
Star Turn (1985) **Nigel Williams** (1948)
Star Turns Red, The (1940) **Sean O'Casey** (1880)
Star Wagon, The (1937) **Maxwell Anderson** (1888)
Star Whisper (1983) **Carol Rumens** (1944)
Star-Apple Kingdom, The (1979) **Derek Walcott** (1930)
Star-Born, The (1933) **Henry Williamson** (1895)
Star-Chamber, The (1854) **W.H. Ainsworth** (1805)
'Star-Spangled Banner, The' [pub. in the *Baltimore Patriot*] (1814) **Francis Scott Key** (1779)
Star-Spangled Girl, The (1966) **Neil Simon** (1927)
Starboard Wine (1984) **Samuel R. Delany** (1942)
Starbrace (1909) **Sheila Kaye-Smith** (1887)
Starchild (1965) **Frederik Pohl** (1919)
Starchild (1981) **Paula Gunn Allen** (1939)
Staring at the Sun (1986) **Julian Barnes** (1946)
Stark Munro Letters, The (1895) **A. Conan Doyle** (1859)
Starlight (1967) **Stella Gibbons** (1902)
Starlit Dome, The (1941) **G. Wilson Knight** (1897)
Starlit Eye, The (1952) **Thomas Kinsella** (1928)
Starlit Garden, The (1917) **Henry de Vere Stacpoole** (1863)
Starry Messenger, The (1645) **William Lilly** (1602)
Stars and Bars (1984) **William Boyd** (1952)
Stars in My Pocket Like Grains of Sand (1984) **Samuel R. Delany** (1942)
Stars Look Down, The (1935) **A.J. Cronin** (1896)
Starship Troopers (1959) **Robert A. Heinlein** (1907)
Start in Life, A (1981) **Anita Brookner** (1928)
Start in Life, A (1970) **Alan Sillitoe** (1928)
Starters (1980) **Jack Gelber** (1932)
Starting from Central Station (1973) **David Campbell** (1915)
Starting from San Francisco (1961) **Lawrence Ferlinghetti** (1920)
Starting Point (1937) **C. Day Lewis** (1904)
Starvecrow Farm (1905) **Stanley J. Weyman** (1855)
Starved Rock (1919) **Edgar Lee Masters** (1868)
State and the Doctor, The (1910) **Sidney Webb** (1859) and **Beatrice Webb** (1858)
State in its Relations with the Church, The (1838) **W.E. Gladstone** (1809)
State of Change, A (1967) **Penelope Gilliatt** (1932)
State of France, The (1652) **John Evelyn** (1620)
State of Innocence, and the Fall of Man, The (1677) **John Dryden** (1631)
State of Justice, A (1977) **Tom Paulin** (1949)
State of Peace, A (1971) **Janice Elliott** (1931)
State of Revolution (1977) **Robert Bolt** (1924)
State of Siege, A (1966) **Janet Frame** (1924)
State of the Church and Clergy of England, The (1703) **William Wake** (1657)
State of the Nation (1944) **John Dos Passos** (1896)
Statements After an Arrest Under the Immorality Act (1972) **Athol Fugard** (1932)
States of Desire (1980) **Edmund White** (1940)
States of Emergency (1988) **André Brink** (1935)
States of Ireland (1972) **Connor Cruise O'Brien** (1917)
Statesman's Manual, The (1816) **S.T. Coleridge** (1772)
Station Island (1984) **Seamus Heaney** (1939)
Station, The (1928) **Robert Byron** (1905)
Statue and the Bust, The (1855) **Robert Browning** (1812)
Statue, The (1908) **Arnold Bennett** (1867)
Statues in a Garden (1964) **Isabel Colegate** (1931)
Stay With me Till Morning (1970) **John Braine** (1922)
Staying On (1977) **Paul Scott** (1920)
Steam-Boat, The (1822) **John Galt** (1779)
Steaming (1981) **Nell Dunn** (1936)
Steel Hawk (1968) **Bhabani Bhattacharya** (1906)
Steele Glas, The (1576) **George Gascoigne** (1542?)
Steeple Bush (1947) **Robert Frost** (1874)
Stella Frefelius (1904) **Sir H. Rider Haggard** (1856)
Stendhal (1994) **Jonathan Keates** (1946)
Step to the Bath, A (1700) **Edward Ward** (1667)
Stepford Wives, The (1972) **Ira Levin** (1929)
Stephen D. [adapted from James Joyce] (1962) **'Hugh Leonard' [Johns Keyes Byrne]** (1926)
Stephen Hero (1944) **James Joyce** (1882–1941)
Stepmother, The (1955) **R.C. Hutchinson** (1907)
Steppenwolf [*Die Steppenwolf*] (1927) **Hermann Hesse** (1877)
Stepping Heavenward (1931) **Richard Aldington** (1892)
Stepping Westward (1965) **Malcolm Bradbury** (1932)
Steps into Immaturity (1959) **Stephen Potter** (1900)
Steps of the Sun, The (1983) **Joanna Trollope** (1943)
Steps to the Empty Throne, The (1969) **Nigel Tranter** (1909)
Steps to the Temple (1646) **Richard Crashaw** (1612/13)
Steps to the Temple (1979) **James Kirkup** (1923)
Stet (1986) **Peter Reading** (1946)
Stick (1983) **Elmore Leonard** (1925)
Stickit Minister and Some Common Men, The (1893) **S.R. Crockett** (1860)
Stickit Minister's Wooing, The (1900) **S.R. Crockett** (1860)
Stiff Upper Lip (1958) **Lawrence Durrell** (1912)
Stiff Upper Lip, Jeeves (1963) **P.G. Wodehouse** (1881)
Still By Choice (1966) **Ruth Pitter** (1897)
Still Centre, The (1939) **Sir Stephen Spender** (1909)
Still Dead (1934) **Ronald Knox** (1888)
Still Life (1916) **John Middleton Murry** (1889)
Still Life (1943) **E.J. Pratt** (1882)
Still Life (1983) **Richard Cobb** (1917)
Still Life (1985) **A.S. Byatt** (1936)
Still Life with Woodpecker (1980) **Tom Robbins** (1936)
Still She Wished For Company (1924) **Margaret Irwin** (1889)

Still Storm, The [*Un orage immobile*] (1983) **'Françoise Sagan' [Françoise Quoirez]** (1935)
Still Waters Run Deep (1855) **Tom Taylor** (1817)
Still William (1925) **'Richmal Crompton' [Richmal Crompton Lamburn]** (1890)
Stillwater Tragedy, The (1880) **Thomas Bailey Aldrich** (1836)
Stingaree (1905) **E.W. Hornung** (1866)
Stitch in Time, A (1976) **Penelope Lively** (1933)
Stokeshill Place (1837) **Mrs C.F. Gore** (1799)
Stolen Bacillus, and Other Incidents, The (1895) **H.G. Wells** (1866)
Stolen Child, The (1833) **John Galt** (1779)
Stolen Heiress, The (1702) **Susanna Centlivre** (1669?)
Stolen March, The (1926) **'Dornford Yates' [Cecil William Mercer]** (1885)
Stolen Soprano, The (1965) **Compton Mackenzie** (1883)
Stone and Flower (1943) **Kathleen Raine** (1908)
Stone Angel, The (1964) **Margaret Laurence** (1926)
Stone Bird, The (1981) **Al Purdy** (1918)
Stone Book, The (1976) **Alan Garner** (1934)
Stone Diaries, The (1993) **Carol Shields** (1935)
Stone for Danny Fisher, A (1952) **Harold Robbins** (1912)
Stone Virgin (1985) **Barry Unsworth** (1930)
Stonefolds, The (1907) **Wilfrid Gibson** (1878)
Stonehenge (1740) **William Stukeley** (1687)
Stonemason, The (1994) **Cormac McCarthy** (1933)
Stones of Emptiness, The (1967) **Anthony Thwaite** (1930)
Stones of Florence, The (1959) **Mary McCarthy** (1912)
Stones of Green Knowe, The (1976) **Lucy Boston** (1892)
Stones of Rimini (1934) **Adrian Stokes** (1902)
Stones of the Fields, The (1946) **R.S. Thomas** (1913)
Stones of Venice, The (1851) **John Ruskin** (1819)
Stones of Venice, The [vol. ii] (1853) **John Ruskin** (1819)
Stones of Venice, The [vol. iii] (1853) **John Ruskin** (1819)
Stony Limits (1934) **'Hugh MacDiarmid' [Christopher Murray Grieve]** (1892)
Stooping Lady, The (1907) **Maurice Hewlett** (1861)
Stop Press [as 'Michael Innes'. US: *The Spider Strikes*] (1939) **J.I.M. Stewart** (1906)
Store, The (1932) **T.S. Stribling** (1881)
Storey's Lives (1992) **David Storey** (1933)
Stories and Interludes (1892) **'Barry Pain' [Eric Odell]** (1864)
Stories for Ninon [*Contes à Ninon*] (1864) **Émile Zola** (1840)
Stories From the Diary of a Doctor [1st ser.]] (1894) **Mrs L.T. Meade** (1854) [with 'Clifford Halifax, M.D.' (Edgar Beaumont)]
Stories from the Italian Poets (1846) **Leigh Hunt** (1784)
Stories From the Warm Zone (1987) **Jessica Anderson** (1925)
Stories in an Almost Classical Mode (1988) **Harold Brodkey** (1930)
Stories in Black and White (1885) **George R. Sims** (1847)
Stories in Grey (1911) **'Barry Pain' [Eric Odell]** (1864)
Stories in the Dark (1901) **'Barry Pain' [Eric Odell]** (1864)
Stories in Verse (1855) **Leigh Hunt** (1784)
Stories, Moral and Comical (1707?) **Thomas D'Urfey** (1653)
Stories of John Cheever, The (1978) **John Cheever** (1912)
Stories of Misbegotten Love (1985) **Herbert Gold** (1924)
Stories of Red Hanrahan (1904) **W.B. Yeats** (1865)
Stories of Red Hanrahan and the Secret Rose (1927) **W.B. Yeats** (1865)
Stories of the Crusades (1846) **John Mason Neale** (1818)
Stories of the Irish Peasantry (1850) **Anna Maria [Mrs S.C.] Hall** (1800)
Stories of the Study (1833) **John Galt** (1779)
Stories Revived (1885) **Henry James** (1843)
Stories to be Told to a Child (1865) **Jean Ingelow** (1820)
Stories Toto Told Me (1898) **Frederick William Rolfe** (1860)
Storm, The (1860) **Alexander Nikolaevich Ostrovsky** (1823)
Storm and Treasure (1910) **H.C. Bailey** (1878)
Storm Below (1949) **Hugh Garner** (1913)
Storm Damage (1988) **Brian Patten** (1946)
Storm in a Teacup (1936) **'James Bridie' [Osborne Henry Mavor]** (1888)
Storm of Fortune (1971) **Austin Clarke** (1932)
Storm of Time (1948) **Eleanor Dark** (1901)
Storm Operation (1944) **Maxwell Anderson** (1888)
Storm Over the Land (1942) **Carl Sandburg** (1878)
Storm Passage (1922) **James Hilton** (1900)
Stormbringer (1965) **Michael Moorcock** (1939)
Stormy Hills, The (1929) **Daniel Corkery** (1878)
Stormy Life, A (1867) **Lady Georgiana Fullerton** (1812)
Story and the Fable, The (1940) **Edwin Muir** (1887)
Story Girl, The (1911) **L.M. Montgomery** (1874)
Story of a Bad Boy, The (1870) **Thomas Bailey Aldrich** (1836)
Story of a Country Town, The (1883) **E.W. Howe** (1853)
Story of a Feather, The (1844) **Douglas Jerrold** (1803)
Story of a Marriage, The (1889) **Mrs Louisa Baldwin** (1845)
Story of a Non-Marrying Man, The [US: *The Temptation of Jack Orkney*] (1972) **Doris Lessing** (1919)
Story of a Novel, The (1936) **Thomas Wolfe** (1900)
Story of a Short Life, The (1885) **Mrs J.H. Ewing** (1841)
Story of Al Raoui, The (1799) **William Beckford** (1760)
Story of an African Farm, The [as 'Ralph Iron'] (1883) **Olive Schreiner** (1855)
Story of Art, The (1950) **E.H. Gombrich** (1909)
Story of Babar, The (1931) **Jean de Brunhoff** (1899)
Story of Barbara, The (1880) **M.E. Braddon** (1835)
Story of Bessie Costrell, The (1895) **Mrs T. Humphry Ward** (1851)

Story of Burnt Njal, The (1861) **Sir George Webbe Dasent** (1817) (tr.)
Story of Charles Strange, The (1888) **Mrs Henry Wood** (1814)
Story of Doom, A (1867) **Jean Ingelow** (1820)
Story of Dr Dolittle, The (1920) **Hugh Lofting** (1886)
Story of Early Gaelic Literature, The (1895) **Douglas Hyde** (1860)
Story of Elizabeth, The (1863) **Lady Anne Ritchie** (1837)
Story of Fifine, The (1914) **Bernard Capes** (1850?-1918)
Story of Gisli the Outlaw, The (1866) **Sir George Webbe Dasent** (1817) (tr.)
Story of Hauksgarth Farm, The (1909) **E[mma] F[rances] Brooke** (1859?)
Story of Justin Martyr, The (1835) **Richard Chenevix Trench** (1807)
Story of Lilly Dawson, The (1847) **Catherine Crowe** (1790)
Story of Little Black Bobtail, The (1909) **Helen Bannerman** (1863)
Story of Little Black Quasha, The (1908) **Helen Bannerman** (1863)
Story of Little Black Quibba, The (1902) **Helen Bannerman** (1863)
Story of Little Black Sambo, The (1899) **Helen Bannerman** (1863)
Story of Marie Powell, Wife to Mr Milton, The [US: *Wife to Mr Milton*] (1943) **Robert Graves** (1895)
Story of My Heart, The (1883) **Richard Jefferies** (1848)
Story of My Life (1988) **Jay McInerney** (1955)
Story of Ragged Robyn, The (1945) **Oliver Onions** (1873)
Story of Rimini, The (1816) **Leigh Hunt** (1784)
Story of Rosina, The (1895) **Austin Dobson** (1840)
Story of Sigurd the Volsung, and the Fall of the Niblungs, The (1877) **William Morris** (1834)
Story of the Amulet, The (1906) **E[dith] Nesbit** (1858)
Story of the Gadsbys, The (1888) **Rudyard Kipling** (1865)
Story of the Glittering Plain, The (1891) **William Morris** (1834)
Story of the Malakand Field Force, The (1898) **Sir Winston Churchill** (1874)
Story of the Siren, The (1920) **E.M. Forster** (1879)
Story of the Treasure Seekers, The (1899) **E[dith] Nesbit** (1858)
Story of the Weasel, The (1976) **Carolyn Slaughter** (1946)
Story of Ulla, The (1895) **Edwin Lester Arnold** (1857)
Story of Ursula, The (1895) **Mrs Hugh Bell** (1851)
Story of Valentine and His Brother, The (1875) **Margaret Oliphant** (1828)
Story of Venus and Tannhäuser, The (1907) **Aubrey Beardsley** (1872–98)
Story to Tell, A (1942) **Peter Fleming** (1907)
Story-Teller's Holiday, A (1928) **George Moore** (1852)
Storye of Thebes, The [adapted *c.* 1421–2 from a French source] (1497?) **John Lydgate** (1370?–1449)
Strafford (1837) **Robert Browning** (1812)
Straight Hearts's Delight (1980) **Allen Ginsberg** (1926)
Strains (1975) **Dennis Brutus** (1924)
Strait Gate, The (1676) **John Bunyan** (1628)
Strait is the Gate [*La Porte étroite*] (1909) **André Gide** (1869)
Strands (1992) **Keri Hulme** (1947)
Strange Adventures of a House-Boat (1888) **William Black** (1841)
Strange Adventures of a Phaeton, The (1872) **William Black** (1841)
Strange Adventures of Captain Dangerous, The (1863) **George Augustus Sala** (1828)
Strange Adventures of Israel Pendry, The (1899) **Silas K. Hocking** (1850)
Strange Adventures of the Count de Vinevil and his Family, The (1721) **Penelope Aubin** (*c.* 1685)
Strange Affair of Adelaide Harris, The (1971) **Leon Garfield** (1921)
Strange Case of Dr Jekyll and Mr Hyde (1886) **Robert Louis Stevenson** (1850)
Strange Children, The (1951) **Caroline Gordon** (1895)
Strange Ends and Discoveries (1948) **Laurence Housman** (1865)
Strange Fruit (1928) **Phyllis Bottome** (1884)
Strange Fruit (1980) **Caryl Phillips** (1958)
Strange Fugitive (1928) **Morley Callaghan** (1903)
Strange Girl in Bright Colours, A (1973) **Carol Rumens** (1944)
Strange Histories (1602) **Thomas Deloney** (1543?–1600)
Strange Horse-race, A (1613) **Thomas Dekker** (1572?)
Strange Interlude (1928) **Eugene O'Neill** (1888)
Strange Land, The (1954) **'Hammond Innes' [Ralph Hammond-Innes]** (1913)
Strange Meeting (1971) **Susan Hill** (1942)
Strange Meetings (1917) **Harold Monro** (1879)
Strange Museum, The (1980) **Tom Paulin** (1949)
Strange Necessity, The (1928) **'Rebecca West' [Cicily Isabel Andrews]** (1892)
Strange Newes, of the Intercepting Certaine Letters (1592) **Thomas Nashe** (1567)
Strange Orchestra (1932) **Rodney Ackland** (1908)
Strange Pilgrims [*Doce cuentos peregrinos*] (1992) **Gabriel García Márquez** (1928)
Strange Stories (1884) **Grant Allen** (1848)
Strange Story, A (1862) **Edward Bulwer-Lytton** (1803)
Strange Tales of a Nihilist (1892) **William le Queux** (1864)
Strange World, A (1875) **M.E. Braddon** (1835)
Stranger at Green Knowe, A (1961) **Lucy Boston** (1892)
Stranger in the Mirror, A (1976) **Sidney Sheldon** (1917)
Stranger, The [*L'Étranger*] (1942) **Albert Camus** (1913)

Stranger With a Bag, A [US: *Swans on an Autumn River*] (1966) **Sylvia Townsend Warner** (1893)
Strangers (1986) **Dean Koontz** (1945)
Strangers All Are Gone, The (1982) **Anthony Powell** (1905)
Strangers and Brothers (1940) **C.P. Snow** (1905)
Strangers and Pilgrims (1873) **M.E. Braddon** (1835)
Strangers at Lisconnel (1895) **Jane Barlow** (1857)
Strangers' Gallery, The (1987) **Jonathan Keates** (1946)
Strangers in a Strange Land (1961) **Robert A. Heinlein** (1907)
Strangers on a Train (1950) **Patricia Highsmith** (1921)
Stranleigh's Millions (1909) **Robert Barr** (1850)
Strathcairn (1864) **Charles Allston Collins** (1828)
Strathern (1845) **Marguerite, Countess of Blessington** (1789)
Stratmore (1865) **'Ouida' [Marie Louise de la Ramée]** (1839)
Straunge and Wonderfull Adventures of Don Simonides, The [vol. ii, 1584] (1581) **Barnabe Rich** (1542)
Straw Peter [*Struwwelpeter*] (1847) **Heinrich Hoffmann** (1809)
Straw, The (1921) **Eugene O'Neill** (1888)
Strawberry Fields (1977) **Stephen Poliakoff** (1952)
Straws and Prayer-Books (1924) **James Branch Cabell** (1879)
Stray (1987) **A.N. Wilson** (1950)
Stray Pearls (1883) **Charlotte M. Yonge** (1823)
Strayed Reveller, The (1849) **Matthew Arnold** (1822)
Streamers Waving (1925) **C.H.B. Kitchin** (1895)
Street Dust (1901) **'Ouida' [Marie Louise de la Ramée]** (1839)
Street in Suburbia, A (1895) **Edwin Pugh** (1874)
Street Lawyer, The (1998) **John Grisham** (1955)
Street Scene (1929) **Elmer Rice** (1892)
Street Songs (1942) **Edith Sitwell** (1887)
Street, The (1946) **Ann Petry** (1908)
Streetcar Named Desire, A (1947) **'Tennessee' [Thomas Lanier] Williams** (1911)
Streets in the Moon (1926) **Archibald MacLeish** (1892)
Streets of Conflict (1976) **Michael Anthony** (1932)
Streets of Laredo (1993) **Larry McMurty** (1936)
Streets of Night (1923) **John Dos Passos** (1896)
Streets of Pompeii, The (1971) **Henry Reed** (1914)
Streets of Summer, The (1969) **David Helwig** (1938)
Strega, La (1899) **'Ouida' [Marie Louise de la Ramée]** (1839)
Strength of Fields, The (1970) **James Dickey** (1923)
Stretch of the Imagination, A (1972) **Jack Hibberd** (1940)
Stretton (1869) **Henry Kingsley** (1830)
Stricken Deer, The (1929) **Lord David Cecil** (1902)
Strict Joy (1931) **James Stephens** (1882)
Strictly Business (1910) **'O. Henry' [William Sydney Porter]** (1862)
Strictly From Huner (1937) **S.J. Perelman** (1904)
Strife (1909) **John Galsworthy** (1867)
Strike at Arlingford, The (1893) **George Moore** (1852)
Strike the Father Dead (1962) **John Wain** (1925)
Striker Portfolio, The (1969) **'Adam Hall' [Elleston Trevor]** (1920)
String of Pearls, The (1832) **G.P.R. James** (1799)
Strings Are False, The [An unfinished autobiography] (1965) **Louis MacNeice** (1907–63)
Strip Jack (1992) **Ian Rankin** (1960)
Stripwell, [and] *Claw* [pub. 1977] (1975) **Howard Barker** (1946)
Strode Venturer, The (1965) **'Hammond Innes' [Ralph Hammond-Innes]** (1913)
Strong Dose of Myself, A (1983) **Dannie Abse** (1923)
Strong Hearts (1899) **George Washington Cable** (1844)
Strong Medicine (1984) **Arthur Hailey** (1920)
Strong Opinions (1973) **Vladimir Nabokov** (1899)
Strong Poison (1930) **Dorothy L. Sayers** (1893)
Strong Wooer, The (1970) **T.F. Powys** (1875–1953)
Structure and Distribution of Coral Reefs, The (1842) **Charles Darwin** (1809)
Structure of Complex Words, The (1951) **Sir William Empson** (1906)
Structure of Politics at the Accession of George III, The (1929) **Sir Lewis Namier** (1888)
Structure of the Novel, The (1928) **Edwin Muir** (1887)
Struggle for Fame, A (1883) **Mrs J.H. Riddell** (1832)
Struggle for Mastery in Europe, The (1954) **A.J.P. Taylor** (1906)
Struggle for National Education, The (1873) **John Morley** (1838)
Struggle of the Modern, The (1963) **Sir Stephen Spender** (1909)
Struggles of Brown, Jones, and Robinson, The (1862) **Anthony Trollope** (1815)
Stuart Little (1945) **E.B. White** (1899)
Stuart of Danleath (1851) **Caroline Norton** (1808)
Stubborn Heart, The (1950) **Frank G. Slaughter** (1908)
Stubborn Hope (1978) **Dennis Brutus** (1924)
Stucco House, The (1917) **Gilbert Cannan** (1884)
Student of Padua, The (1836) **Ernest Charles Jones** (1819)
Studies and Stories (1893) **Mary Louisa Molesworth** (1839)
Studies for Stories (1864) **Jean Ingelow** (1820)
Studies in a Dying Culture (1938) **Christopher Caudwell** (1907)
Studies in Classic American Literature (1924) **D.H. Lawrence** (1885)
Studies in Contemporary Biography (1903) **James Bryce** (1838)
Studies in Early French Poetry (1868) **Sir Walter Besant** (1836)
Studies in Early Victorian Literature (1895) **Frederic Harrison** (1831)
Studies in Hegelian Cosmology (1901) **John McTaggart** (1866)
Studies in History and Jurisprudence (1901) **James Bryce** (1838)
Studies in Literature (1890) **John Morley** (1838)

Studies in Literature 1789–1877 (1878) **Edward Dowden** (1843)
Studies in Love and Terror (1913) **Mrs Belloc Lowndes** (1868)
Studies in Poetry (1907) **Stopford Brooke** (1832)
Studies in Poetry and Criticism (1905) **John Churton Collins** (1848)
Studies in Prose and Poetry (1894) **A.C. Swinburne** (1837)
Studies in Secret Records, Personal and Historic (1858) **Thomas de Quincey** (1785)
Studies in Shakespeare (1904) **John Churton Collins** (1848)
Studies in Song (1880) **A.C. Swinburne** (1837)
Studies in the Elizabethan Drama (1920) **Arthur Symons** (1865)
Studies in the History of the Renaissance (1873) **Walter Pater** (1839)
Studies in the Literature of Northern Europe (1879) **Sir Edmund Gosse** (1849)
Studies in the Psychology of Sex (1905) **Havelock Ellis** (1859)
Studies in Two Literatures (1897) **Arthur Symons** (1865)
Studies in Wives (1909) **Mrs Belloc Lowndes** (1868)
Studies of Contemporary Superstition (1895) **W.H. Mallock** (1849)
Studies of the Eighteenth Century in Italy (1880) **'Vernon Lee' [Violet Paget]** (1856)
Studies on Homer and the Homeric Age (1858) **W.E. Gladstone** (1809)
Studies on Thackeray (1869) **James Hannay** (1827)
Studies, Scientific and Social (1900) **Alfred Russel Wallace** (1823)
Study in Scarlet, A (1888) **A. Conan Doyle** (1859)
Study of Ben Jonson, A (1889) **A.C. Swinburne** (1837)
Study of English Literature, The (1891) **John Churton Collins** (1848)
Study of History, A (1934) **Arnold Toynbee** (1889)
Study of Oscar Wilde, A (1930) **Arthur Symons** (1865)
Study of Shakespeare, A (1880) **A.C. Swinburne** (1837)
Study of Sociology, The (1873) **Herbert Spencer** (1820)
Study of Victor Hugo, A (1886) **A.C. Swinburne** (1837)
Study of Walter Pater, A (1932) **Arthur Symons** (1865)
Stuff and Nonsense (1927) **Walter de la Mare** (1873)
Stuff of Dreams, The [*Matière de rêves*] (1975–85) **Michel Butor** (1926)
Stuff of Sleep and Dreams, The (1982) **Leon Edel** (1907)
Stuff to Give the Troops, The (1944) **J. Maclaren-Ross** (1912)
Stumble on the Threshold, A (1892) **James Payn** (1830)
Stung to the Quick (1867) **Isabella [Mrs G. Linnaeus] Banks** (1821)
Style (1897) **Sir Walter Raleigh** (1861)
Styles of Radical Will (1969) **Susan Sontag** (1933)
Styrian Lake, The (1842) **Frederick William Faber** (1814)
Sub Rosa (1968) **Robert Aickman** (1914)
Subjection of Women, The (1869) **J.S. Mill** (1806)
Submerged Village, The (1951) **James Kirkup** (1923)
Submission to Divine Providence in the Death of Children (1737) **Philip Doddridge** (1702)
Subsequent to Summer (1985) **Roy Fuller** (1912)
Subsong (1969) **James Reeves** (1909)
Subterraneans, The (1958) **Jack Kerouac** (1922)
Suburban, The (1912) **H.C. Bailey** (1878)
Suburbs of Hell, The (1984) **Randolph Stow** (1935)
Success (1902) **R.B. Cunninghame Graham** (1852)
Success (1978) **Martin Amis** (1949)
Success Stories (1986) **Russell Banks** (1940)
Successful Love (1961) **Delmore Schwartz** (1913)
Successful Pyrate, The (1712) **Charles Johnson** (1679)
Such a Good Man (1877) **Sir Walter Besant** (1836) [with James Rice]
Such a Long Journey (1991) **Rohinton Mistry** (1952)
Such Counsels You Gave to Me, and Other Poems (1937) **Robinson Jeffers** (1887)
Such Darling Dodos (1950) **Angus Wilson** (1913)
Such is Life (1903) **Joseph Furphy** (1843)
Such is My Beloved (1934) **Morley Callaghan** (1903)
Such Pleasure (1949) **Martin Boyd** (1893)
Such Power is Dangerous (1933) **Dennis Wheatley** (1897)
Such Things Are (1787) **Elizabeth Inchbald** (1753)
Sudden Death (1983) **Rita Mae Brown** (1944)
Sudden View, The [reissued as *A Visit to Don Otavio*, 1960] (1953) **Sybille Bedford** (1911)
Suffolk Courtship, A (1900) **Matilda Betham-Edwards** (1836)
Suffrage of Elvira, The (1958) **V.S. Naipaul** (1932)
Sugar (1987) **A.S. Byatt** (1936)
Sugar and Rum (1988) **Barry Unsworth** (1930)
Sugar Cane (1993) **Paul Bailey** (1937)
Sugar Daddy (1970) **Hugo Williams** (1942)
Sugar for the Horse (1957) **H.E. Bates** (1905)
Sugar House, The (1952) **'Antonia White' [Eirene Botting]** (1899)
Sugar Mother, The (1988) **Elizabeth Jolley** (1923)
Sugar-Cane, The (1764) **James Grainger** (1721)
Suggestions on Popular Education (1861) **Nassau Senior** (1790)
Suicide Hill (1986) **James Ellroy** (1948)
Suitable Boy, A (1993) **Vikram Seth** (1952)
Suitable Case for Treatment, A (1962) **David Mercer** (1928)
Sukhodol (1911) **Ivan Bunin** (1870)
Sula (1973) **Toni Morrison** (1931)
Sullen Lovers, The (1668) **Thomas Shadwell** (1642?)
Sultan of Sulu, The (1902) **George Ade** (1866)
Sultaness, The (1717) **Charles Johnson** (1679)
Sum of All Fears, The (1991) **Tom Clancy** (1947)
Sum of Things, The (1980) **Olivia Manning** (1908)
Sumerian Vistas (1987) **A.R. Ammons** (1926)
Summa Contra Gentiles **St Thomas Aquinas** (*c.* 1225)
Summa Theologica [written 1265-after 1271] **St Thomas Aquinas** (*c.* 1225)

Summa Totalis (1607) **John Davies of Hereford** (1565)
Summarie of Devotions, A (1667) **William Laud** (1573–1645)
Summarie of Englyshe Chronicles, A (1565) **John Stow** (1525)
Summary History of New England, A (1799) **Hannah Adams** (1755)
Summary of the Principles of Socialism, A (1884) **William Morris** (1834) [with H.M. Hydnman]
Summer (1727) **James Thomson** (1700)
Summer (1884) **Henry David Thoreau** (1817–62)
Summer (1888) **Henry David Thoreau** (1817–62)
Summer (1917) **Edith Wharton** (1862)
Summer (1974) **'Hugh Leonard' [Johns Keyes Byrne]** (1926)
Summer After the Funeral, The (1973) **Jane Gardam** (1928)
Summer and Smoke [rev. as *The Eccentricities of a Nightingale*, 1964] (1948) **'Tennessee' [Thomas Lanier] Williams** (1911)
Summer Before the Dark, The (1973) **Doris Lessing** (1919)
Summer Bird-Cage, A (1963) **Margaret Drabble** (1939)
Summer House, The (1954) **Jane Bowles** (1917)
Summer in Arcady (1896) **James Lane Allen** (1849)
Summer Islands (1931) **Norman Douglas** (1868)
Summer Knowledge (1959) **Delmore Schwartz** (1913)
Summer Lightning [US: *Fish Preferred*] (1929) **P.G. Wodehouse** (1881)
Summer Moonshine (1937) **P.G. Wodehouse** (1881)
Summer Near the Arctic Circle (1988) **Lauris Edmond** (1924)
Summer Never Ends (1941) **Waldo Frank** (1889)
Summer of the Royal Visit, The (1991) **Isabel Colegate** (1931)
Summer of the Seventeenth Doll (1955) **Ray Lawler** (1921)
Summer Palaces (1980) **Peter Scupham** (1933)
Summer Party, The (1979) **Stephen Poliakoff** (1952)
Summer Thunder (1941) **Alan Ross** (1922)
Summer to Decide, A (1948) **Pamela Hansford Johnson** (1912)
Summer Will Show (1936) **Sylvia Townsend Warner** (1893)
Summer's Fancy, A (1930) **Edmund Blunden** (1896)
Summer's Lease (1988) **John Mortimer** (1923)
Summers Last Will and Testament (1600) **Thomas Nashe** (1567)
Summit (1987) **D.M. Thomas** (1935)
Summoned by Bells (1960) **Sir John Betjeman** (1906)
Summons, The (1920) **A.E.W. Mason** (1865)
Sun Across the Sky (1937) **Eleanor Dark** (1901)
Sun Also Rises, The (1926) **Ernest Hemingway** (1898)
Sun Circle (1933) **Neil M. Gunn** (1891)
Sun Horse, Moon Horse (1977) **Rosemary Sutcliff** (1920)
Sun in Splendour, The (1982) **'Jean Plaidy' [Eleanor Hibbert]** (1906)
Sun King, The (1966) **Nancy Mitford** (1904)
Sun My Monument, The (1944) **Laurie Lee** (1914)
Sun on the Wall, The [three novellas] (1994) **Ronald Frame** (1953)
Sun Poem (1982) **Edward Brathwaite** (1930)
Sun's Net, The (1976) **George Mackay Brown** (1921)
Sun's-Darling, The (1656) **John Ford** (1586–1640?) [with Thomas Dekker]
Sunbird, The (1972) **Wilbur Smith** (1933)
Sunblue (1978) **Margaret Avison** (1918)
Sunday (1962) **Kay Dick** (1915)
Sunday Best (1971) **Bernice Rubens** (1923)
Sunday Water (1982) **Phylllis Webb** (1921)
Sundial, The (1958) **Shirley Jackson** (1919)
Sundial, The (1978) **Gillian Clarke** (1937)
Sundog (1985) **Jim Harrison** (1937)
Sundowners, The (1952) **Jon Cleary** (1917)
Sunflower (1986) **'Rebecca West' [Cicily Isabel Andrews]** (1892)
Sunken Garden, The (1917) **Walter de la Mare** (1873)
Sunlight Dialogues, The (1972) **John Gardner** (1933)
Sunne in Aries, The (1621) **Thomas Middleton** (1580)
Sunny Memories of Foreign Lands (1854) **Harriet Beecher Stowe** (1811)
Sunny Side, The (1921) **A.A. Milne** (1882)
Sunrise (1880) **William Black** (1841)
Sunrise in Suburbia (1968) **John Ashbery** (1927)
Sunrise with Sea Monster (1995) **Neil Jordan** (1950)
Sunrise with Seamonsters (1985) **Paul Theroux** (1941)
Sunset at Blandings [unfinished] (1977) **P.G. Wodehouse** (1881–1975)
Sunset Gun (1928) **Dorothy Parker** (1893)
Sunshine Boys, The (1972) **Neil Simon** (1927)
Sunshine Sketches of a Little Town (1912) **Stephen Leacock** (1869)
Superbiae Flagellum (1621) **John Taylor** (1580)
Super-Cannes (2000) **J.G. Ballard** (1930)
Superfluous Woman, A (1894) **E[mma] F[rances] Brooke** (1859?)
Superfudge (1980) **Judy Blume** (1938)
Superhuman Antagonists, The (1919) **Sir William Watson** (1858)
Supermanship; or, How to Continue to Stay on Top Without Actually Falling Apart (1958) **Stephen Potter** (1900)
Supers and Supermen (1920) **Philip Guedalla** (1889)
Superstition of Divorce, The (1920) **G.K. Chesterton** (1874)
Superstitions of the Sceptic, The (1925) **G.K. Chesterton** (1874)
Supplement to the Edition of Shakespeare Published by Johnson and Steevens, A (1780) **Edmond Malone** (1741)
Suppliants, The (463 BC) **Aeschylus** (525–456 BC)
Supplicacyon for the Beggers, A (1529) **Simon Fish** (d. 1531)
Supplicants, The (*c.* 422) **Euripides** (480 BC)
Supplycacyon of Soulys, The (1529?) **Sir Thomas More** (1478)
Sure Hand of God, The (1947) **Erskine Caldwell** (1903)

Surfacing (1972) **Margaret Atwood** (1939)
Surfeit of Lampreys [US: *Death of a Peer*] (1941) **Ngaio Marsh** (1899)
Surgeon's Mate, The (1980) **Patrick O'Brian** (1914)
Surprised by Joy (1955) **C.S. Lewis** (1898)
Surprises of Love, The (1764) **John Cleland** (1709)
Surréalisme et la peinture, Le (1928) **André Breton** (1896)
Surroundings (1966) **Norman MacCaig** (1910)
Surry of Eagle's Nest (1866) **John Cooke** (1830)
Survay of London, A (1598) **John Stow** (1525)
Survey of English Literature 1780–1830, A (1912) **Oliver Elton** (1861)
Survey of English Literature 1830–80, A (1920) **Oliver Elton** (1861)
Survey of Experimental Philosophy, A (1776) **Oliver Goldsmith** (1728–74)
Survey of Modernist Poetry, A (1927) **Robert Graves** (1895)
Survey of Modernist Poetry, A (1927) **Laura Riding** (1901) [with Robert Graves]
Survey of the Wisdom of God in the Creation, A (1763) **John Wesley** (1703)
Survival (1972) **Margaret Atwood** (1939)
Survival Arts (1981) **Ian Wedde** (1946)
Survival of the Fittest, The (1968) **Pamela Hansford Johnson** (1912)
Survivals and New Arrivals (1929) **Hilaire Belloc** (1870)
Survivor, The (1901) **E. Phillips Oppenheim** (1866)
Survivor, The (1969) **Thomas Keneally** (1935)
Survivor, The (1976) **James Herbert** (1943)
Survivors, The (1963) **Patricia Beer** (1924)
Survivors, The (1976) **Simon Raven** (1927)
Survivors, The (1982) **Elaine Feinstein** (1930)
Survivor's Leave (1953) **Charles Causley** (1917)
Survivors of the Crossing (1964) **Austin Clarke** (1932)
Susan Drummond (1884) **Mrs J.H. Riddell** (1832)
Susan Proudleigh (1915) **H.G. de Lisser** (1878)
Susannah and the Elders (1940) **'James Bridie' [Osborne Henry Mavor]** (1888)
Suspect in Poetry, The (1964) **James Dickey** (1923)
Suspense (1925) **Joseph Conrad** (1857–1924)
Suspicious Husband, The (1747) **Benjamin Hoadly 'the younger** (1706)
Sussex Gorse (1916) **Sheila Kaye-Smith** (1887)
Susurrium Cum Deo (1651) **Joseph Hall** (1574)
Sut Lovingwood (1867) **George Washington Harris** (1814)
Suttree (1979) **Cormac McCarthy** (1933)
Swallow (1899) **Sir H. Rider Haggard** (1856)
Swallow (1984) **D.M. Thomas** (1935)
Swallow Barn [as 'Mark Littleton'] (1832) **John Pendleton Kennedy** (1795)
Swallowdale (1931) **Arthur Ransome** (1884)
Swallows and Amazons (1930) **Arthur Ransome** (1884)
Swami and Friends (1935) **R.K. Narayan** (1907)
Swamp Dwellers, The (1958) **Wole Soyinka** (1934)
Swamp Riddles (1974) **Robert Adamson** (1943)
Swan Song (1928) **John Galsworthy** (1867)
Swann: A Mystery (1987) **Carol Shields** (1935)
Swann's Way [*Du côté de chez Swann; A la recherche du temps perdu i*] (1913) **Marcel Proust** (1871)
Swarm in May, A (1955) **William Mayne** (1928)
Swarming of the Bees, The (1950) **John Heath-Stubbs** (1918)
Sweeney Agonistes (1932) **T.S. Eliot** (1888)
Sweeney Astray (1984) **Seamus Heaney** (1939)
Sweeney's Flight (1992) **Seamus Heaney** (1939)
Sweet and Twenty (1875) **Mortimer Collins** (1827)
Sweet Anne Page (1868) **Mortimer Collins** (1827)
Sweet Bird of Youth (1959) **'Tennessee' [Thomas Lanier] Williams** (1911)
Sweet Charity (1966) **Neil Simon** (1927)
Sweet Cheat Gone, The [*Albertine disparue; A la recherche du temps perdu vi*] (1925) **Marcel Proust** (1871–1922)
Sweet Dove Died, The (1978) **Barbara Pym** (1913)
Sweet Dreams (1974) **Michael Frayn** (1933)
Sweet Hereafter, The (1991) **Russell Banks** (1940)
Sweet Lavender (1888) **Arthur Wing Pinero** (1855)
Sweet Lavender (1892) **E[dith] Nesbit** (1858)
Sweet Nelly, My Heart's Delight (1879) **Sir Walter Besant** (1836) [with James Rice]
Sweet Second Summer of Kitty Malone, The (1979) **Matt Cohen** (1942)
Sweet Thursday (1954) **John Steinbeck** (1902)
Sweet Waters (1921) **Sir Harold Nicolson** (1886)
Sweet William (1936) **'Richmal Crompton' [Richmal Crompton Lamburn]** (1890)
Sweet William (1975) **Beryl Bainbridge** (1934)
Sweet-Shop Owner, The (1980) **Graham Swift** (1949)
Sweets of Pimlico, The (1977) **A.N. Wilson** (1950)
Swift (1882) **Sir Leslie Stephen** (1832)
Swiftie the Magician (1974) **Herbert Gold** (1924)
Swimmers, The (1971) **Allen Tate** (1899)
Swimming-Pool Library, The (1988) **Alan Hollinghurst** (1954)
Swimming-Pool Season, The (1985) **Rose Tremain** (1943)
Swinburne's Poems and Ballads (1866) **W.M. Rossetti** (1829)
Swindler, The (1914) **Ethel M. Dell** (1881)
Swing, Brother, Swing [US: *A Wreath for Rivera*] (1949) **Ngaio Marsh** (1899)
Swing in the Garden, The (1975) **Hugh Hood** (1928)
Swiss Family Robinson, The [*Der schweizerische Robinson*; completed by Johan Rudolf Wyss] (1812–13) **Johann Wyss** (1743)
Swiss Summer, The (1951) **Stella Gibbons** (1902)
Switch, The (1978) **Elmore Leonard** (1925)
Switch Bitch (1974) **Roald Dahl** (1916)
Switchback, The (1930) **'James Bridie' [Osborne Henry Mavor]** (1888)
Sword and Gown (1859) **G.A. Lawrence** (1827)
Sword and Scalpel (1957) **Frank G. Slaughter** (1908)
Sword and the Circle, The (1981) **Rosemary Sutcliff** (1920)

Sword and the Distaff, The [rev. as Woodcraft, 1854] (1853) **William Gilmore Simms** (1806)
Sword and the Sickle, The (1942) **Mulk Raj Anand** (1905)
Sword Blades and Poppy Seed (1914) **Amy Lowell** (1874)
Sword Decides, The (1908) **'Marjorie Bowen' [Gabrielle Margaret Vere Campbell]** (1886)
Sword in the Stone, The (1938) **T.H. White** (1906)
Sword of Honour [cont. *Men at Arms*, *Officers and Gentlemen*, and *Unconditional Surrender*] (1965) **Evelyn Waugh** (1903)
Sword of Welleran, The (1908) **Lord Dunsany** (1878)
Sword of Youth, The (1915) **James Lane Allen** (1849)
Swordbearers, The (1963) **Correlli Barnett** (1927)
Swords and Ploughshares (1915) **John Drinkwater** (1882)
Swords and Roses (1929) **Joseph Hergesheimer** (1880)
Sybil (1952) **Louis Auchinloss** (1917)
Sybil (1845) **Benjamin Disraeli** (1804)
Sybil's Second Love (1867) **Julia Kavanagh** (1824)
Sybilline Leaves (1817) **S.T. Coleridge** (1772)
Sybils and Others (1980) **Ruth Fainlight** (1931)
Sycamore Tree, The (1958) **Christine Brooke-Rose** (1926)
Sydney-Side Saxon, A (1891) **'Rolf Boldrewood' [Thomas Alexander Browne]** (1826)
Sylva (1664) **John Evelyn** (1620)
Sylva Sylvarum [inc. *The New Atlantis*; pub. sep. 1627] (1626) **Sir Francis Bacon** (1561–1626)
Sylvae (1685) [**John Dryden** and others] (1631)
Sylvan Dream, The (1701) **John Philips** (1676)
Sylvester Sound (1844) **Henry Cockton** (1807)
Sylvia and Michael (1919) **Compton Mackenzie** (1883)
Sylvia's Lovers (1863) **Elizabeth Gaskell** (1810)
Sylvie (1853) **'Gérard de Nerval' [Gérard Labrunie]** (1808)
Sylvie and Bruno (1889) **'Lewis Carroll' [Charles Lutwidge Dodgson]** (1832)
Sylvie and Bruno Concluded (1893) **'Lewis Carroll' [Charles Lutwidge Dodgson]** (1832)
Symbolist Movement in Literature, The (1899) **Arthur Symons** (1865)
Symmes Hole (1986) **Ian Wedde** (1946)
Sympathy (1781) **Samuel Jackson Pratt** (1749)
Symphonies (1897) **'George Egerton' [Mary Chavelita Dunne]** (1859)
Symposium (1990) **Muriel Spark** (1918)
Symptoms of Loss (1965) **Hugo Williams** (1942)
Synagogue, The (1640) **Christopher Harvey** (1597)
Syntactic Structures (1957) **Noam Chomsky** (1928)
System of Dante's Hell, The (1965) **LeRoi Jones** (1934)
System of Logic, A (1843) **J.S. Mill** (1806)
System of Magick, A (1726) **Daniel Defoe** (1660)
System of Synthetic Philosophy, A (1860) **Herbert Spencer** (1820)
Systematic Theology (1951–63) **Paul Tillich** (1886)
The Story of Little Black Mingo (1901) **Helen Bannerman** (1863)

T

Table Near the Band, A (1950) **A.A. Milne** (1882)
Table Talk (1835) **S.T. Coleridge** (1772–1834)
Table Talk (1851) **Leigh Hunt** (1784)
Table Talk of Samuel Marchbanks, The (1949) **Robertson Davies** (1913)
Table-Talk [vol. i] (1821) **William Hazlitt** (1778)
Table-Talk [vol. ii] (1822) **William Hazlitt** (1778)
Table-Talk (1689) **John Selden** (1584–1634)
Table-Talk of G.B.S. (1925) **Bernard Shaw** (1856)
Tables of the Law, and The Adoration of the Magi, The (1904) **W.B. Yeats** (1865)
Tables Turned, The (1887) **William Morris** (1834)
Tacey Cromwell (1942) **Conrad Richter** (1890)
Tai Pan (1966) **James Clavell** (1924)
Tailor of Gloucester, The (1903) **Beatrix Potter** (1866)
Taj Express, The (1973) **Alan Ross** (1922)
Take a Girl Like You (1960) **Kingsley Amis** (1922)
Take Courage [US: *The Power and the Glory*] (1940) **Phyllis Bentley** (1894)
Take It Easy (1938) **Damon Runyon** (1884)
Taken at the Flood (1874) **M.E. Braddon** (1835)
Taken at the Flood [US: *There is a Tide*] (1948) **Agatha Christie** (1890)
Taken From the Enemy (1892) **Sir Henry Newbolt** (1862)
Takeover, The (1976) **Muriel Spark** (1918)
Taking Chances [as 'M.J. Farrell'] (1929) **Molly Keane** (1905)
Taking of Helen, The (1923) **John Masefield** (1878)
Taking of the Gry, The (1934) **John Masefield** (1878)
Taking Shelter (1989) **Jessica Anderson** (1925)
Taking the Devil's Advice (1990) **Anne Fine** (1947)
Talba, The (1830) **Anna Eliza Bray** (1790)
Talbot Harland (1870) **W.H. Ainsworth** (1805)
Talbot Road (1981) **Thom Gunn** (1929)
Talbot's Box (1977) **Thomas Kilroy** (1934)
Tale Bearers, The (1980) **V.S. Pritchett** (1900)
Tale of a Tub, A [with 'The Battle of the Books'] (1704) **Jonathan Swift** (1667)
Tale of Balen, The (1896) **A.C. Swinburne** (1837)
Tale of Benjamin Bunny, The (1904) **Beatrix Potter** (1866)
Tale of Beowulf, The (1895) **William Morris** (1834) (tr.) [with A.J. Wyatt]
Tale of Chloe, The (1895) **George Meredith** (1828)
Tale of Jemima Puddle-Duck, The (1908) **Beatrix Potter** (1866)
Tale of Little Pig Robinson, The (1930) **Beatrix Potter** (1866)
Tale of Mr Jeremy Fisher, The (1906) **Beatrix Potter** (1866)
Tale of Mrs Tiggy-Winkle, The (1905) **Beatrix Potter** (1866)
Tale of Mystery, A (1802) **Thomas Holcroft** (1745)
Tale of Paraguay, A (1825) **Robert Southey** (1774)
Tale of Peter Rabbit, The (1902) **Beatrix Potter** (1866)
Tale of Pigling Bland, The (1913) **Beatrix Potter** (1866)
Tale of Rosamund Gray and Old Blind Margaret, A (1798) **Charles Lamb** (1775)

Tale of Squirrel Nutkin, The (1903) **Beatrix Potter** (1866)
Tale of the House of the Wolfings, A (1889) **William Morris** (1834)
Tale of Tom Kitten, The (1907) **Beatrix Potter** (1866)
Tale of Troy, A (1932) **John Masefield** (1878)
Tale of Two Cities, A (1859) **Charles Dickens** (1812)
Tale of Two Families, A (1970) **Dodie Smith** (1896)
Talent for Loving, A (1961) **Richard Condon** (1915)
Talented Mr Ripley, The (1955) **Patricia Highsmith** (1921)
Tales (1812) **George Crabbe** (1754)
Tales (1845) **Edgar Allan Poe** (1809)
Tales and Historic Scenes (1819) **Felicia Dorothea Hemans** (1793)
Tales and Miscellaneous Pieces (1825) **Maria Edgeworth** (1767)
Tales and Stories from History (1836) **Agnes Strickland** (1796)
Tales Before Midnight (1939) **Stephen Vincent Benét** (1889)
Tales, by the O'Hara Family [1st ser.] (1825) **John Banim** (1798) [with Michael Banim]
Tales by the O'Hara Family [2nd ser.] (1826) **John Banim** (1798) [with Michael Banim]
Tales for Christmas Eve (1873) **Rhoda Broughton** (1840)
Tales From a Firozsha Bag (1987) **Rohinton Mistry** (1952)
Tales From Bective Bridge (1942) **Mary Lavin** (1912)
Tales From Hollywood (1983) **Christopher Hampton** (1946)
Tales from Ovid (1997) **Ted Hughes** (1930)
Tales from Shakespear [14 pieces by Mary Lamb (1764)] (1807) **Charles Lamb [1775]**
Tales from the Telling House (1896) **R.D. Blackmore** (1825)
Tales in Prose (1836) **Mary Howitt** (1799)
Tales My Father Taught Me (1962) **Sir Osbert Sitwell** (1892)
Tales of a Fourth Grade Nothing (1972) **Judy Blume** (1938)
Tales of a Grandfather 1st ser. (1831) **Sir Walter Scott** (1771)
Tales of a Traveller (1824) **Washington Irving** (1783)
Tales of a Wayside Inn [1st ser.; 2nd ser., 1873; 3rd ser., 1874] (1863) **Henry Wadsworth Longfellow** (1807)
Tales of Adventure and Medical Life (1922) **A. Conan Doyle** (1859)
Tales of All Countries [1st ser.] (1861) **Anthony Trollope** (1815)
Tales of All Countries [2nd ser.] (1863) **Anthony Trollope** (1815)
Tales of Belkin, The (1830) **Alexander Pushkin** (1799)
Tales of Chicago Streets (1924) **Ben Hecht** (1894)
Tales of College Life (1856) **'Cuthbert Bede B.A.' [Edward Bradley]** (1827)
Tales of Fashionable Life [vols. i-iii] (1809) **Maria Edgeworth** (1767)
Tales of Fashionable Life [vols. iv, v, vi] (1812) **Maria Edgeworth** (1767)
Tales of Gotham City (1984) **Ian Wedde** (1946)
Tales of Hearsay (1925) **Joseph Conrad** (1857–1924)
Tales of Ireland (1834) **William Carleton** (1794)
Tales of Long Ago (1922) **A. Conan Doyle** (1859)
Tales of Love and Death (1977) **Robert Aickman** (1914)
Tales of Mean Streets (1894) **Arthur Morrison** (1863)
Tales of Men and Ghosts (1910) **Edith Wharton** (1862)
Tales of Moorland and Estuary (1953) **Henry Williamson** (1895)
Tales of Mother Goose ['Contes de ma mère l'Oye'] (1697) **Charles Perrault** (1628)
Tales of My Country (1833) **Selina Bunbury** (1802)
Tales of My Landlord [1st ser.] (1816) **Sir Walter Scott** (1771)
Tales of My Landlord [2nd ser.; contains 'The Heart of Midlothian'] (1818) **Sir Walter Scott** (1771)
Tales of My Landlord [3rd ser.; contains 'The Bride of Lammermoor'] (1819) **Sir Walter Scott** (1771)
Tales of My Neighbourhood (1835) **Gerald Griffin** (1803)
Tales of Olga da Polga, The (1971) **Michael Bond** (1926)
Tales of Pirates and Blue Water (1922) **A. Conan Doyle** (1859)
Tales of Real Life (1813) **Amelia Opie** (1769)
Tales of Soldiers and Civilians [UK: *In the Midst of Life*] (1891) **Ambrose Bierce** (1842)
Tales of Space and Time (1900) **H.G. Wells** (1866)
Tales of Ten Worlds (1962) **Arthur C. Clarke** (1917)
Tales of Terror (1799) **M.G. Lewis** (1775)
Tales of Terror and Mystery (1922) **A. Conan Doyle** (1859)
Tales of the Argonauts (1875) **Bret Harte** (1836)
Tales of the Castle (1785) **Thomas Holcroft** (1745)
Tales of the City (1978) **Armistead Maupin** (1944)
Tales of the Crusaders [inc. 'The Betrothed' and 'The Talisman'] (1825) **Sir Walter Scott** (1771)
Tales of the Early World (1988) **Ted Hughes** (1930)
Tales of the Factories (1833) **Caroline Bowles** (1786)
Tales of the Five Towns (1905) **Arnold Bennett** (1867)
Tales of the Genii, The (1764) **James Ridley** (1736)
Tales of the Grotesque and Arabesque (1840) **Edgar Allan Poe** (1809)
Tales of the Hall (1819) **George Crabbe** (1754)
Tales of the Heart (1820) **Amelia Opie** (1769)
Tales of the Home Folks in Peace and War (1898) **Joel Chandler Harris** (1848)
Tales of the Jazz Age (1922) **F. Scott Fitzgerald** (1896)
Tales of the Mermaid Tavern (1913) **Alfred Noyes** (1880)
Tales of the Pemberton Family (1825) **Amelia Opie** (1769)
Tales of the Ring and Camp (1922) **A. Conan Doyle** (1859)

Tales of the South Pacific (1947) **James A. Michener** (1907)
Tales of the Trains [as 'Tilbury Tramp'] (1845) **Charles Lever** (1806)
Tales of the Uneasy (1911) **Violet Hunt** (1866)
Tales of the Unexpected (1979) **Roald Dahl** (1916)
Tales of the Wars of Montrose (1835) **James Hogg** (1770)
Tales of Three Cities (1884) **Henry James** (1843)
Tales of Three Hemispheres (1920) **Lord Dunsany** (1878)
Tales of Today (1889) **George R. Sims** (1847)
Tales of Toytown (1928) **S.G. Hulme Beaman** (1886)
Tales of Twilight and the Unseen (1922) **A. Conan Doyle** (1859)
Tales of Two People (1907) **'Anthony Hope' [Sir Anthony Hope Hawkins]** (1863)
Tales of Unrest (1898) **Joseph Conrad** (1857)
Tales of War (1918) **Lord Dunsany** (1878)
Tales of Women's Trials (1835) **Anna Maria [Mrs S.C.] Hall** (1800)
Tales of Wonder (1916) **Lord Dunsany** (1878)
Tales of Wonder (1801) **M.G. Lewis** (1775)
Tales Round a Winter Hearth (1826) **Anna Maria Porter** (1780) [with Jane Porter]
Tales Told for Children (1835) **Hans Christian Andersen** (1805)
Taliessen Through Logres (1938) **Charles Williams** (1886)
Talifer (1933) **Edwin Arlington Robinson** (1869)
Talis Qualis (1842) **Gerald Griffin** (1803–40)
Talisman, The (1835) **George Borrow** (1803) (tr.)
Talisman, The (1984) **Peter Straub** (1943) [with Stephen King]
Talk of the Town, The (1885) **James Payn** (1830)
Talking God (1989) **Tony Hillerman** (1925)
Talking Heads 2 (1998) **Alan Bennett** (1934)
Talking Heads (1998) **Alan Bennett** (1934)
Talking Horse, The (1892) **'F. Anstey' [Thomas Anstey Guthrie]** (1856)
Talking It Over (1991) **Julian Barnes** (1946)
Talking Skull, The (1958) **James Reeves** (1909)
Talking to Myself (1977) **Studs Terkel** (1912)
Talking Trees, The (1971) **'Seán O'Faoláin' [John Francis Whelan]** (1900)
Taltos (1994) **Anne Rice** (1941)
'Tam O'Shanter' [**Burns**]: see *The Antiquities of Scotland* [**Grose**]
Tamar (1924) **Robinson Jeffers** (1887)
Tamarind Seed, The (1971) **'Evelyn Anthony' [Evelyn Ward-Thomas]** (1928)
Tamarisk Town (1919) **Sheila Kaye-Smith** (1887)
Tambourines to Glory (1958) **Langston Hughes** (1902)
Tamburlane the Great (1590) **Christopher Marlowe** (1564)
Tamerlane (1701) **Nicholas Rowe** (1674)
Tamerlane (1827) **Edgar Allan Poe** (1809)
Tamerton Church-Tower (1853) **Coventry Patmore** (1823)
Tampico (1926) **Joseph Hergesheimer** (1880)
Tancred (1847) **Benjamin Disraeli** (1804)
Tancred and Sigismunda (1745) **James Thomson** (1700)
Tangled Skein, The (1907) **Baroness Orczy** (1865)
Tangled Web, A (1931) **L.M. Montgomery** (1874)
Tanglewood Tales (1853) **Nathaniel Hawthorne** (1804)
Tapes for the Turn of the Year (1965) **A.R. Ammons** (1926)
Tapestry Room, The (1879) **Mary Louisa Molesworth** (1839)
Taps at Reveille (1935) **F. Scott Fitzgerald** (1896)
Tapster's Tapestry (1938) **A.E. Coppard** (1878)
Taquisara (1896) **F. Marion Crawford** (1854)
Tar: A Midwest Childhood [fictionalized autobiography] (1926) **Sherwood Anderson** (1876)
Tar Baby (1981) **Toni Morrison** (1931)
Tar-Baby and Other Rhymes, The (1904) **Joel Chandler Harris** (1848)
Tara (1863) **Captain Meadows Taylor** (1808)
Tara Road (1998) **Maeve Binchy** (1940)
Tarantella (1885) **Mathilde Blind** (1841)
Tares (1961) **R.S. Thomas** (1913)
Targum (1835) **George Borrow** (1803) (tr.)
Tarka the Otter (1927) **Henry Williamson** (1895)
Tarpaulin Muster, A (1907) **John Masefield** (1878)
Tarr (1918) **Wyndham Lewis** (1882)
Tarry Flynn (1948) **Patrick Kavanagh** (1904)
Tartarin in the Alps [*Tartarin sur les Alpes*] (1885) **Alphonse Daudet** (1840)
Tartarin of Tarascon [*Tartarin de Tarascon*] (1872) **Alphonse Daudet** (1840)
Tartuffe, Le [**Molière**]: see *The Imposter*
Tarzan, Lord of the Jungle (1928) **Edgar Rice Burroughs** (1875)
Tarzan of the Apes (1914) **Edgar Rice Burroughs** (1875)
Task of Social Hygiene, The (1912) **Havelock Ellis** (1859)
Task, The (1785) **William Cowper** (1731)
Tassle-Gentle (1934) **Pamela Frankau** (1908)
Tasso and the Sisters (1825) **Thomas Wade** (1805)
Taste (1753) **John Armstrong** (1709)
Taste (1752) **Samuel Foote** (1720)
Taste and Remember (1966) **William Plomer** (1903)
Taste for Death, A (1986) **P.D. James** (1920)
Taste of Honey, A (1958) **Shelagh Delaney** (1939)
Tatler, The (1709–10) **Sir Richard Steele** (1672) [with Joseph Addison]
Tatooed Woman, The (1985) **Marian Engel** (1933)
Tatter of Scarlet, A (1913) **S.R. Crockett** (1860)
Tatterdemalion (1920) **John Galsworthy** (1867)
Tattered Tom (1871) **Horatio Alger** (1832)
Tatty Hollow Story, The (1975) **Dorothy Hewett** (1923)
Tavare (1787) **Pierre Augustin Caron de Beaumarchais** (1732)
Tavern Knight, The (1904) **Rafael Sabatini** (1875)
Tax Inspector, The (1991) **Peter Carey** (1943)
Taylors, The (1767) **Samuel Foote** (1720)
Te Kaihu: The Windeater (1986) **Keri Hulme** (1947)

'TE Lawrence', in Arabia and After (1934) **Sir Basil Liddell Hart** (1895)
Tea and Sympathy (1953) **Robert W. Anderson** (1917)
Tea Party (1967) **Harold Pinter** (1930)
Tea With Mrs Goodman [US: *Prothalamium*] (1947) **Philip Toynbee** (1916)
Tea-Table Miscellany, The [vol. i; vol. ii, 1726; vol. iii, 1727; vol. iv, 1737] (1723) **Allan Ramsay** (1686)
Tea-Table Talk (1903) **Jerome K. Jerome** (1859)
Tea-Time of Love, The (1969) **Martin Boyd** (1893)
Teacher (1963) **Sylvia Ashton-Warner** (1908)
Teacher of the Violin, A (1888) **J.H. Shorthouse** (1834)
Teares of the Beloved, The (1600) **Gervaise Markham** (1568?)
Teares on the Death of Meliades (1613) **William Drummond of Hawthornden** (1585)
Tears of the Muses, The (1737) **Aaron Hill** (1685)
Technique of Modern Fiction, The (1968) **Jonathan Raban** (1942)
Tedious and Brief (1944) **'James Bridie' [Osborne Henry Mavor]** (1888)
Teendreams (1979) **David Edgar** (1948) [with Susan Todd]
Teeth 'n' Smiles (1975) **David Hare** (1947)
Teeth of the Lion, The (1942) **Kenneth Patchen** (1911)
Tehanua (1990) **Ursula K. le Guin** (1929)
Telephone Poles (1963) **John Updike** (1932)
Tell England (1922) **Ernest Raymond** (1888)
Tell Me a Riddle (1962) **Tillie Olsen** (1913)
Tell Me How Long the Train's Been Gone (1968) **James Baldwin** (1924)
Tell Me, Tell Me (1966) **Marianne Moore** (1887)
Telling Liddy (1998) **Anne Fine** (1947)
Telling Tales (1983) **Sara Maitland** (1950)
Telling Tales (1983) **Anthony Thwaite** (1930)
Temora (1763) **James Macpherson** (1736)
Tempe Restored (1632) **Aurelian Townshend** (1583?)
Temper (1812) **Amelia Opie** (1769)
Tempers, The (1913) **William Carlos Williams** (1883)
Tempest, The [from Shakespeare] (1667) **John Dryden** (1631) [with Sir William Davenant]
Tempest, The [from Shakespeare] (1756) **David Garrick** (1717)
Tempest, The (1674) **Thomas Shadwell** (1642?)
Tempest Tost (1951) **Robertson Davies** (1913)
Temple, The (1633) **George Herbert** (1593–1633)
Temple, The (1923) **Arthur Waley** (1889)
Temple Beau, The (1730) **Henry Fielding** (1707)
Temple of Death, The [from the French of P. Habert] (1695) **John Sheffield, duke of Buckingham** (1648) (tr.)
Temple of Fame, The (1715) **Alexander Pope** (1688)
Temple of Glas, The [written c. 1403] (1477?) **John Lydgate** (1370?-1449)
Temple of Love, The (1635) **Sir William Davenant** (1606) [and Inigo Jones]
Temple of My Familiar, The (1989) **Alice Walker** (1944)
Temple of Nature, The (1803) **Erasmus Darwin** (1731)
Temples of Delight (1990) **Barbara Trapido** (1941)
Temporal Mission of the Holy Ghost, The (1865) **Henry Edward Manning** (1808)
'Temporal Power' (1902) **Marie Corelli** (1855)
Temporary Kings (1973) **Anthony Powell** (1905)
Temporary Life, A (1973) **David Storey** (1933)
Temptation (1849) **John Brougham** (1810)
Temptation and Atonement (1847) **Mrs C.F. Gore** (1799)
Temptation of Our Lord, The (1547) **John Bale** (1495)
Temptation of Saint Anthony, The [*La Tentation de saint Antoine*] (1874) **Gustave Flaubert** (1821)
Temptations of Oedipus, The (1970) **James K. Baxter** (1926)
Ten Burnt Offerings (1952) **Louis MacNeice** (1907)
Ten Commandments, The (1896) **George R. Sims** (1847)
Ten Creeks Run [as 'Brent of Bin Bin'] (1930) **Miles Franklin** (1879)
Ten Letters From a Young Lady of Quality [from Edmé Bursault] (1720) **Eliza Haywood** (*c.* 1693) (tr.)
Ten Little Niggers [US: *And Then There Was None*] (1939) **Agatha Christie** (1890)
Ten Miles From Anywhere (1958) **P.H. Newby** (1918)
Ten More Plays of Shakespeare (1913) **Stopford Brooke** (1832)
Ten North Frederick (1955) **John O'Hara** (1905)
Ten Poems (1932) **Lawrence Durrell** (1912)
Ten Tales Tall and True (1993) **Alasdair Gray** (1934)
Ten Thousand a Year (1841) **Samuel Warren** (1807)
Ten Years' Exile [*Dix Années d'exil*] (1821) **Madame de Staël** (1766–1817)
Ten Years' Tenant, The (1881) **Sir Walter Besant** (1836) [with James Rice]
Tenancy, The (1993) **Eva Figes** (1932)
Tenant of Wildfell Hall, The (1848) **Anne Brontë** (1820)
Tenants, The (1971) **Bernard Malamud** (1914)
Tenants of Malory, The (1867) **J.S. le Fanu** (1814)
Tenants of Moonbloom, The (1963) **Edward Wallant** (1926–62)
Tenants of the House (1957) **Dannie Abse** (1923)
Tendencies in Modern American Poetry (1917) **Amy Lowell** (1874)
Tender Buttons (1914) **Gertrude Stein** (1874)
Tender Husband, The (1705) **Sir Richard Steele** (1672)
Tender is the Night (1934) **F. Scott Fitzgerald** (1896)
Tender Only to One (1938) **Stevie Smith** (1902)
Tender to the Queen of Spades (1993) **Ken Smith** (1938)
Tendering (1989) **Ian Wedde** (1946)
Tenebrae (1978) **Geoffrey Hill** (1932)
Tenement, The (1985) **Iain Crichton Smith [Iain Mac a'Ghobhainn]** (1928)
Tennis Court Oath, The (1962) **John Ashbery** (1927)
Tennis Shoes (1937) **Noel Streatfeild** (1895)

Tennyson, Ruskin, Mill and Other Literary Estimates (1899) **Frederic Harrison** (1831)
Tent of the Beach, The (1867) **John Greenleaf Whittier** (1807)
Tenterhooks (1912) **Ada Leverson** (1862)
Tenth Man, The (1985) **Graham Greene** (1904)
Tenth Millennium: The Beginning Place (1979) **Ursula K. le Guin** (1929)
Tenth Muse, The (1895) **Sir Edwin Arnold** (1832)
Tenth Muse, The (1911) **Edward Thomas** (1878)
Tenth Muse, The [*Essa*] (1957) **Sir Herbert Read** (1893)
Tenth Muse Lately Sprung Up in America, The (1650) **Anne Bradstreet**
Tenth Satyr of Juvenal, The (1687) **Thomas Shadwell** (1642?) (tr.)
Tents of Israel [US: *The Matriarch*] (1924) **G.B. Stern** (1890)
Tents of Shem, The (1889) **Grant Allen** (1848)
Tents of Wickedness, The (1959) **Peter de Vries** (1910)
Tenure of Kings and Magistrates, The (1649) **John Milton** (1608)
Teraminta (1732) **Henry Carey** (1687?)
Teresa (1947) **'Seán O'Faoláin' [John Francis Whelan]** (1900)
Teresa of Watling Street (1904) **Arnold Bennett** (1867)
Terminal Beach, The (1964) **J.G. Ballard** (1930)
Terminal Man, The (1972) **Michael Crichton** (1942)
Terminal Moraine (1972) **James Fenton** (1949)
Terminations (1895) **Henry James** (1843)
Terms of Endearment (1975) **Larry McMurty** (1936)
Terra (1986) **Ken Smith** (1938)
Terra nostra (1975) **Carlos Fuentes** (1928)
Terrible Freedom, A (1966) **Eric Linklater** (1899)
Terrible Shears, The (1973) **D.J. Enright** (1920)
Terrible Temptation, A (1871) **Charles Reade** (1814)
Terrible Tomboy, A (1904) **Angela Brazil** (1869)
Terrible World, The (1907–16) **Aleksandr Blok** (1880)
Territorial Rights (1979) **Muriel Spark** (1918)
Terror, The (1917) **Arthur Machen** (1863)
Terror (1962) **Robert Bloch** (1917)
Terrors of the Night, The (1594) **Thomas Nashe** (1567)
Terry on the Fence (1975) **Bernard Ashley** (1935)
Terry Street (1969) **Douglas Dunn** (1942)
Tess (1993) **Emma Tennant** (1937)
Tess of the d'Urbervilles (1891) **Thomas Hardy** (1840)
Testament (1938) **R.C. Hutchinson** (1907)
Testament of a Man Forbid, The (1901) **John Davidson** (1857)
Testament of a Prime Minister, The (1904) **John Davidson** (1857)
Testament of a Vivisector, The (1901) **John Davidson** (1857)
Testament of an Empire-Builder, The (1902) **John Davidson** (1857)
Testament of Beauty, The (1929) **Robert Bridges** (1844)
Testament of Cresseid, The (1593) **Robert Henryson** (*c.* 1430–*c.* 1505)
Testament of Experience (1957) **Vera Brittain** (1893)
Testament of Friendship (1940) **Vera Brittain** (1893)
Testament of John Davidson, The (1908) **John Davidson** (1857)
Testament of John Lydgate, The (1515?) **John Lydgate** (1370?–1449)
Testament of Youth (1933) **Vera Brittain** (1893)
Testing-Tree, The (1971) **Stanley J. Kunitz** (1905)
Testostero (1987) **David Foster** (1944)
Tethys Festival (1610) **Samuel Daniel** (1562)
Tetrachordon (1645) **John Milton** (1608)
Tetractys Anti-Astrologica (1681) **Henry More** (1614)
Texas (1985) **James A. Michener** (1907)
Texas Nightingale, The [rev. 1923 as *Greatness*] (1922) **Zoë Akins** (1886)
Textermination (1991) **Christine Brooke-Rose** (1926)
Thackeray (1879) **Anthony Trollope** (1815)
Thaddeus of Warsaw (1803) **Jane Porter** (1776)
Thaïs (1890) **'Anatole France' [Jacques-Anatole-François Thibault]** (1844)
Thalaba the Destroyer (1801) **Robert Southey** (1774)
Thalia Rediviva (1678) **Henry Vaughan** (1622)
Thalias Banquet (1620) **Henry Peacham the younger** (1578?)
Thanatos Syndrome, The (1987) **Walker Percy** (1916)
Thane of Fife, The (1822) **William Tennant** (1784)
Thank You (1962) **Kenneth Koch** (1925)
Thank You, Jeeves (1934) **P.G. Wodehouse** (1881)
Thanks to Jennings (1957) **Anthony Buckeridge** (1912)
Thanksgiving Visitor, The (1969) **Truman Capote** (1924)
That Bad Woman (1995) **Clare Boylan** (1948)
That Darcy, That Dancer, That Gentleman (1990) **J.P. Donleavy** (1926)
That Dreadful Mess on the Via Merulana [*Quer pasticciaccio brutto de via Merulana*] (1957) **Carlo Emilio Gadda** (1893)
That Fortune (1899) **Charles Dudley Warner** (1829)
That Good Between Us (1977) **Howard Barker** (1946)
That Hideous Strength (1945) **C.S. Lewis** (1898)
That Lady [US: *For One Sweet Grape*] (1946) **Kate O'Brien** (1897)
That Lass o' Lowries (1877) **Frances Hodgson Burnett** (1849)
That Summer (1946) **Frank Sargeson** (1903)
That Sweet Enemy (1901) **Katharine Tynan** (1861)
That Uncertain Feeling (1955) **Kingsley Amis** (1922)
That Ye Inherit (1968) **W.S. Graham** (1918)
That Yew Tree's Shade [US: *Death Walks the Woods*] (1954) **'Cyril Hare' [A.A.G. Clark]** (1900)
That You Fog: Last Poems (1974) **W.H. Auden** (1907)
That's How It Was (1962) **Maureen Duffy** (1933)
Thatcher's Children (1993) **Trevor Griffiths** (1935)
Thawing Frozen Frogs (1990) **Brian Patten** (1946)
Thealma and Clearchus (1683) **John Chalkhill** (*c.* 1594)

Theanthropos (1661) **John Selden** (1584–1634)
Theater Essays (1978) **Arthur Miller** (1915)
Theatre (1954) **Desmond MacCarthy** (1877–1952)
Theatre and its Double, The [*Le Théâtre et son double*] (1938) **Antonin Artaud** (1896)
Theatre I-XIX (1976) **Robert Adamson** (1943)
Theatre in England, The (1871) **Tom Taylor** (1817)
Theatre of Life, The (1881) **George R. Sims** (1847)
Theatre of the Empire of Great Britaine, The (1611) **John Speed** (1552?)
Theatre of the Present War in North America, The (1758) **Arthur Young** (1741)
Theatrical Illusion, The [*L'Illusion Comique*] (1636) **Pierre Corneille** (1606)
Theatrical 'World', The (1895) **William Archer** (1856) (ed.)
Theatrocrat, The (1905) **John Davidson** (1857)
Theatrum Botanicum: The Theater of Plants (1640) **John Parkinson** (1567)
Theatrum Chemicum Britannicum [in Latin] (1652) **Elias Ashmole** (1617)
Thébaïde, La ['The Thebaid; or, 'The Enemy Brothers'] (1664) **Jean Racine** (1639)
Theft, The (1988) **Saul Bellow** (1915)
Their Eyes Were Watching God (1934) **Zora Neale Hurston** (1903)
Their Heads Are Green and Their Hands Are Blue (1963) **Paul Bowles** (1910)
Their Silver Wedding Journey (1899) **William Dean Howells** (1837)
Their Very Own and Golden City (1965) **Arnold Wesker** (1932)
Their Wedding Journey (1872) **William Dean Howells** (1837)
Theism and Humanism (1915) **A.J. Balfour** (1848)
Theism and Thought (1915) **A.J. Balfour** (1848)
Thelma (1887) **Marie Corelli** (1855)
them (1969) **Joyce Carol Oates** (1938)
Theme is Freedom, The (1956) **John Dos Passos** (1896)
Themes and Variations (1950) **Aldous Huxley** (1894)
Themes for Diverse Instruments (1975) **Jane Rule** (1931)
Themes on a Variation (1988) **Edwin Morgan** (1920)
Themis (1912) **Jane Harrison** (1850) et al.
Then Again (1990) **Jenny Diski** (1947)
Then Again, Maybe I Won't (1971) **Judy Blume** (1938)
Then it All Came Down (1976) **Truman Capote** (1924)
Theo and Matilda (1990) **Rachel Billington** (1942)
Theocritus Translated into English Verse (1869) **C.S. Calverley** (1831)
Theodora Phranza (1857) **John Mason Neale** (1818)
Théodore (1645) **Pierre Corneille** (1606)
Theodosius (1680) **Nathaniel Lee** (1649?)
Theodric (1824) **Thomas Campbell** (1777)
Theological Essays (1853) **F.D. Maurice** (1805)
Theological Position, A (1972) **Robert Coover** (1932)
Theology of Culture (1959) **Paul Tillich** (1886)
Theophilia (1652) **Edward Benlowes** (1602)
Theophilus North (1973) **Thornton Wilder** (1897)
Theory and Practice of Gamesmanship, The (1947) **Stephen Potter** (1900)
Theory of Moral Sentiments, The (1759) **Adam Smith** (1723)
Theory of Poetry, The (1924) **Lascelles Abercrombie** (1881)
Theosophy and the New Psychology (1904) **Annie Besant** (1847)
Power Book, The (2000) **Jeanette Winterson** (1959)
Therapy (1995) **David Lodge** (1935)
There and Back (1891) **George MacDonald** (1824)
There is a Happy Land (1957) **Keith Waterhouse** (1929)
There is a Serpent in Eden (1979) **Robert Bloch** (1917)
There is No Armour (1948) **Howard Spring** (1889)
There is No Natural Religion (1788?) **William Blake** (1757)
There Shall Be No Night (1940) **Robert E. Sherwood** (1896)
There Was a Young Man From Cardiff (1991) **Dannie Abse** (1923)
There We Have Been (1989) **Leland Bardwell** (1928)
There Will Be a Short Interval (1972) **Storm Jameson** (1897)
There's a Trick With a Knife I'm Learning to Do (1979) **Michael Ondaatje** (1943)
Therefore Be Bold (1960) **Herbert Gold** (1924)
Thérèse Desqueyroux (1927) **François Mauriac** (1885)
Thérèse Raquin (1868) **Émile Zola** (1840)
Theron and Aspasio (1755) **James Hervey** (1714)
These 13 (1931) **William Faulkner** (1897)
These Charming People (1923) **'Michael Arlen' [Dikran Kouyoumdjian]** (1895)
These Enchanted Woods (1993) **Allan Massie** (1938)
These Golden Days (1985) **John Braine** (1922)
These Horned Islands (1962) **James Kirkup** (1923)
These Liberties (1923) **E.V. Knox** (1881)
These Our Matins (1930) **Michael Roberts** (1902)
These Thousand Hills (1956) **A.B. Guthrie** (1901)
These Twain (1916) **Arnold Bennett** (1867)
Thésée (1946) **André Gide** (1869)
Thesmophoriazusae (411 BC) **Aristophanes** (*c.* 445)
They (1977) **Kay Dick** (1915)
They and I (1909) **Jerome.K. Jerome** (1859)
They Call Me Carpenter (1922) **Upton Sinclair** (1878)
They Came From SW19 (1992) **Nigel Williams** (1948)
They Do it With Mirrors [US: *Murder With Mirrors*] (1952) **Agatha Christie** (1890)
They Found Atlantis (1936) **Dennis Wheatley** (1897)
They Found Him Dead (1937) **Georgette Heyer** (1902)
They Shall Inherit the Earth (1935) **Morley Callaghan** (1903)
They Sleep Without Dreaming (1985) **Penelope Gilliatt** (1932)
They Stooped to Folly (1929) **Ellen Glasgow** (1874)
'They That Walk in Darkness' (1899) **Israel Zangwill** (1864)
They Went (1920) **Norman Douglas** (1868)

They Went to Portugal (1946) **Rose Macaulay** (1881)
They Were Defeated (1932) **Rose Macaulay** (1881)
They Whisper (1994) **Robert Olen Butler** (1945)
They Who Walk in the Wild (1924) **Sir Charles G.D. Roberts** (1860)
They're Playing Our Song (1979) **Neil Simon** (1927)
Thibault, The [*Les Thibault*; 8-novel series] (1922–40) **Roger Martin du Gard** (1881)
Thicket of Spring, The (1972) **Paul Bowles** (1910)
Thief in the Night, A (1905) **E.W. Hornung** (1866)
Thief of Always, The (1992) **Clive Barker** (1952)
Thief of Virtue, The (1910) **Eden Phillpotts** (1862)
Thief's Journal [*Le Journal du voleur*] (1949) **Jean Genet** (1910)
Thieves' Carnival, The [*Le Bal des Voleurs*] (1938) **Jean Anouilh** (1910)
Thieves in the Night (1946) **Arthur Koestler** (1905)
Thin Air (1961) **John Pudney** (1909)
Thin Ghost, A (1919) **M.R. James** (1862)
Things We Do For Love (1998) **Alan Ayckbourn** (1939)
Thin Ice (1956) **Compton Mackenzie** (1883)
Thin Man, The (1932) **Dashiell Hammett** (1894)
Thin Mountain Air, The (1977) **Paul Horgan** (1903)
Thin Red Line, The (1962) **James Jones** (1921)
Thing About Joe Sullivan, The (1978) **Roy Fisher** (1930)
Things as They Are (1794) **William Godwin** (1756)
Things As They Are (1965) **Paul Horgan** (1903)
Things Fall Apart (1958) **Chinua Achebe** (1930)
Things Near and Far (1923) **Arthur Machen** (1863)
Things New and Old (1923) **Max Beerbohm** (1872)
Things of This World (1956) **Richard Wilbur** (1921)
Things That Are Caesar's, The (1932) **Paul Vincent Carroll** (1900)
Things That Have Interested Me [1st ser.] (1921) **Arnold Bennett** (1867)
Things to Come (1928) **John Middleton Murry** (1889)
Things We Are, The (1922) **John Middleton Murry** (1889)
Things Which Belong, The (1925) **Constance Holme** (1881)
Think of England (1986) **Frederic Raphael** (1931)
Thinking Reed, The (1936) **'Rebecca West' [Cicily Isabel Andrews]** (1892)
Third, The (1958) **Nissim Ezekiel** (1924)
Third and Fourth Book of Airs, The (1617) **Thomas Campion** (1567)
Third and Last Booke of Songs or Aires, The (1603) **John Dowland** (1563)
Third and Last Part of Conny-Catching, The (1592) **Robert Greene** (1558)
Third Circle, The (1909) **Frank Norris** (1870)
Third Class at Miss Kaye's, The (1908) **Angela Brazil** (1869)
Third Eye, The (1940) **Elinor Glyn** (1864)
Third Generation (1954) **Chester Himes** (1909)
Third Hour, The (1937) **Geoffrey Household** (1900)
Third Letter for Toleration, A (1692) **John Locke** (1632)
Third Life of Grange Copeland, The (1970) **Alice Walker** (1944)
Third Man, The [and *The Fallen Idol*] (1950) **Graham Greene** (1904)
Third Mind, The (1978) **William S. Burroughs** (1914)
Third Miss St Quentin, The (1889) **Mary Louisa Molesworth** (1839)
Third Miss Symons, The (1913) **F.M. Mayor** (1872)
Third Part of the Countesse of Pembrokes Ivychurch (1592) **Abraham Fraunce** (fl.1582–1633)
Third Policeman, The (1967) **Flann O'Brien** (1911–66)
Third Round, The [US: *Bull-Dog Drummond's Third Round*] (1924) **'Sapper' [Herman Cyril McNeile]** (1888)
Third State, The (1991) **Amos Oz** (1939)
Third Tour of Doctor Syntax, The (1821) **William Combe** (1742)
Third Violet, The (1897) **Stephen Crane** (1871)
Third World Poems (1983) **Edward Brathwaite** (1930)
Thirsty Evil, A (1956) **Gore Vidal** (1925)
Thirteen Clocks, The (1950) **James Thurber** (1894–1961)
Thirteen Gun Salute, The (1989) **Patrick O'Brian** (1914)
Thirteen O'Clock (1937) **Stephen Vincent Benét** (1889)
Thirteen Problems, The [US: *The Tuesday Club Murders*] (1932) **Agatha Christie** (1890)
Thirteen Stories (1900) **R.B. Cunninghame Graham** (1852)
Thirteen Travellers, The (1921) **Sir Hugh Walpole** (1884)
Thirteenth Caesar, The (1924) **Sir Sacheverell Sitwell** (1897)
Thirteenth Immortal, The (1957) **Robert Silverberg** (1935)
Thirties and After, The (1978) **Sir Stephen Spender** (1909)
Thirties, The (1960) **Julian Symons** (1912)
Thirty and Three (1954) **Hugh MacLennan** (1907)
Thirty Preliminary Poems (1933) **George Barker** (1913)
Thirty Years' War, The (1874) **S.R. Gardiner** (1829)
Thirty-Nine Steps, The (1915) **John Buchan** (1875)
Thirty-One Sonnets (1967) **Richard Eberhart** (1904)
Thirty-Six Poems (1910) **James Elroy Flecker** (1884)
Thirty-Six Poems (1935) **Robert Penn Warren** (1905)
This and That and the Other (1912) **Hilaire Belloc** (1870)
This Bed Thy Centre (1935) **Pamela Hansford Johnson** (1912)
This Body is Made of Camphor and Gopherwood (1977) **Robert Bly** (1926)
This Body the Earth (1935) **Paul Green** (1894)
This Chaos (1930) **Sir Harold Acton** (1904)
This Cold Universe (1964) **Patric Dickinson** (1914)
This Crooked Way (1952) **Elizabeth Spencer** (1921)
This Expanding War (1942) **Sir Basil Liddell Hart** (1895)

This Happy Breed (1942) **Noel Coward** (1899)
This Hunger (1945) **Anaïs Nin** (1903)
This Immortal (1966) **Roger Zelazny** (1937)
This is For You (1994) **Michael Wilding** (1942)
This is My Country Too (1965) **John Williams** (1925)
This is My God (1959) **Herman Wouk** (1915)
This is New York (1930) **Robert E. Sherwood** (1896)
This Is Not For You (1970) **Jane Rule** (1931)
This is the Schoolroom (1939) **Nicholas Monsarrat** (1910)
This Island Now (1967) **Peter Abrahams** (1919)
This Man and This Woman (1951) **James T. Farrell** (1904)
This Man's Wife (1887) **George Manville Fenn** (1831)
This Mortal Coil (1888) **Grant Allen** (1848)
This Music Crept by Me Upon the Waters (1953) **Archibald MacLeish** (1892)
This Night's Orbit (1953) **R.D. FitzGerald** (1902)
This Old Man Comes Rolling Home (1966) **Dorothy Hewett** (1923)
This Our World (1893) **Charlotte Perkins Gilman** (1860)
This Porcelain God (1939) **Naomi Jacob** (1884)
This Proud Heart (1938) **Pearl S. Buck** (1892)
This Quiet Dust (1982) **William Styron** (1925)
This Real Night (1987) **'Rebecca West' [Cicily Isabel Andrews]** (1892)
This Room and This Gin and These Sandwiches (1937) **Edmund Wilson** (1895)
This Side Jordan (1960) **Margaret Laurence** (1926)
This Side of Paradise (1920) **F. Scott Fitzgerald** (1896)
This Son of Vulcan (1876) **Sir Walter Besant** (1836) [with James Rice]
This Sweet Sickness (1960) **Patricia Highsmith** (1921)
This Tree Will Be Here for a Thousand Years (1979) **Robert Bly** (1926)
This Very Earth (1948) **Erskine Caldwell** (1903)
This Was the Old Chief's Country (1951) **Doris Lessing** (1919)
This Way to Heaven (1934) **Caradoc Evans** (1878)
This Year in Jerusalem (1994) **Mordecai Richler** (1931)
Thomas a Becket (1840) **George Darley** (1795)
Thomas Andrews, Shipbuilder (1912) **Shan F. Bullock** (1865)
Thomas Carlyle (1882) **J.A. Froude** (1818)
Thomas Carlyle: A History of his Life in London (1884) **J.A. Froude** (1818) (ed.)
Thomas Hardy (1912) **Lascelles Abercrombie** (1881)
Thomas Muskerry (1910) **Padraic Colum** (1881)
Thomas of Reading (1612) **Thomas Deloney** (1543?–1600)
Thomas the Imposter [*Thomas l'Imposteur*] (1923) **Jean Cocteau** (1889)
Thomas, the Tank Engine (1946) **Revd W.V. Awdry** (1911)
Thomas Wingfold, Curate (1876) **George MacDonald** (1824)
Thorley Weir (1913) **E.F. Benson** (1867)
Thorns (1967) **Robert Silverberg** (1935)
Those Barren Leaves (1925) **Aldous Huxley** (1894)
Those Days (1940) **E.C. Bentley** (1875)
Those United States (1912) **Arnold Bennett** (1867)
Those Who Perish (1934) **Edward Dahlberg** (1900)
Those Without Shadows [*Dans un mois, dans un an*] (1957) **'Françoise Sagan' [Françoise Quoirez]** (1935)
Thou Art the Man (1894) **M.E. Braddon** (1835)
Thou Shell of Death [US: *Shell of Death*] (1936) **'Nicholas Blake' [C. Day Lewis]** (1904)
Thought Power (1911) **Annie Besant** (1847)
Thought, Words and Creativity (1976) **F.R. Leavis** (1895)
Thoughts (1845) **Charles Harpur** (1813)
Thoughts and Adventures (1932) **Sir Winston Churchill** (1874)
Thoughts Occasioned by Dr Parr's Spital Sermon (1801) **William Godwin** (1756)
Thoughts of a Late-Night Knitter (1978) **Pam Ayres** (1947)
Thoughts on Man, his Nature, Productions and Discoveries (1831) **William Godwin** (1756)
Thoughts on Negro Slavery (1826) **Henry, Lord Brougham** (1778)
Thoughts on Parliamentary Reform (1859) **J.S. Mill** (1806)
Thoughts on the Cause of the Present Discontents (1770) **Edmund Burke** (1729)
Thoughts on the Education of Daughters (1787) **Mary Wollstonecraft** (1759)
Thoughts on the Interpretation of Nature [*Pensées sur l'interprétation de la nature*] (1753) **Denis Diderot** (1713)
Thoughts Out of Season [*Unzeitgemässe Betrachtungen*] (1873–6) **Friedrich Wilhelm Nietzsche** (1844)
Thoughts upon Slavery (1774) **John Wesley** (1703)
Thoughts Upon the African Slave Trade (1788) **John Newton** (1725)
Thoughts Upon the Aristocracy of England (1835) **'Isaac Tomkins, Gent.' [Henry, Lord Brougham]** (1778)
Thousand Acres, A (1992) **Jane Smiley** (1949)
Thousand and One Afternoons in Chicago, A (1922) **Ben Hecht** (1894)
Thousand and One Afternoons in New York, A (1941) **Ben Hecht** (1894)
Thousand and One Churches, The (1909) **Gertrude Bell** (1868) [with W.M. Ramsay]
Thousand Days, A (1965) **Arthur Schlesinger** (1917)
Thousand Miles Up the Nile, A (1877) **Amelia B. Edwards** (1831)
Thrasymachus (1925) **C.E.M. Joad** (1891)
Thread of Gold, The (1905) **A.C. Benson** (1862)
Three (1946) **William Sansom** (1912)
Three Admirals, The (1877) **W.H.G. Kingston** (1814)

Three Birds Alighting on a Field (1991) **Timberlake Wertenbaker**
Three Black Pennys, The (1917) **Joseph Hergesheimer** (1880)
Three Books of Duties [Cicero]] (1556) **Nicholas Grimald** (1519?) (tr.)
Three Brothers, The (1931) **Edwin Muir** (1887)
Three Brothers, The (1870) **Margaret Oliphant** (1828)
Three Cheers for the Paraclete (1968) **Thomas Keneally** (1935)
Three Clerks, The (1858) **Anthony Trollope** (1815)
Three Continents (1987) **Ruth Prawer Jhabvala** (1927)
Three Days (1919) **Rose Macaulay** (1881)
Three Dialogues Between Hylas and Philonous (1713) **George Berkeley** (1685)
Three Elephant Power (1917) **A.B. 'Banjo' Paterson** (1864)
Three Essays, Moral and Political (1748) **David Hume** (1711)
Three Essays on Picturesque Beauty (1792) **William Gilpin** (1724)
Three Essays on the Painting of Our Time (1961) **Adrian Stokes** (1902)
Three Feathers (1875) **William Black** (1841)
Three Fevers (1932) **Leo Walmsley** (1892)
Three General Epistles (1664) **George Fox** (1624)
Three Gentlemen, The (1932) **A.E.W. Mason** (1865)
Three Gringos in Venezuela and Central America (1896) **Richard Harding Davis** (1864)
Three Guineas (1938) **Virginia Woolf** (1882)
Three Hills, The (1913) **J.C. Squire** (1884)
Three Homes, The [as 'F.T.L. Hope'] (1873) **Frederic W. Farrar** (1831)
Three Hostages, The (1924) **John Buchan** (1875)
Three Hours After Marriage (1717) **John Gay** (1685) [with Alexander Pope and John Arbuthnot]
Three Hundred and Thirty-Four (1972) **Thomas M. Disch** (1940)
Three Impostors, The (1895) **Arthur Machen** (1863)
Three Ladies of London, The (1584) **Robert Wilson** (fl.1572–1600)
Three Last Plays [*Sancho's Master*; *Dave*; *The Would-Be Gentleman* (from Molière)] (1928) **Lady Gregory** (1852)
Three Laws, The (1548) **John Bale** (1495)
Three Lectures on the Catholic Hierarchy (1850) **Nicholas Patrick S. Wiseman** (1802)
Three Letters, and Certaine Sonnets (1592) **Gabriel Harvey** (1550)
Three Letters on the Ecclesiastical Commission (1837–9) **Sydney Smith** (1771)
Three Lieutenants, The (1874) **W.H.G. Kingston** (1814)
Three Lives (1957) **Lettice Cooper** (1897)
Three Lives (1993) **Louis Auchinloss** (1917)
Three Lives (1909) **Gertrude Stein** (1874)
Three Lordes and Ladies of London, The (1590) **Robert Wilson** (fl.1572–1600)
Three Memorials on French Affairs (1797) **Edmund Burke** (1729)
Three Men in a Boat (1889) **Jerome.K. Jerome** (1859)
Three Men in New Suits (1945) **J.B. Priestley** (1894)
Three Men on the Bummel (1900) **Jerome K. Jerome** (1859)
Three Midshipmen, The (1873) **W.H.G. Kingston** (1814)
Three Miss Kings, The (1891) **Ada Cambridge** (1844)
Three Mulla-Mulgars, The (1910) **Walter de la Mare** (1873)
Three Musketeers, The [Les Trois Mousquetaires] (1844) **Alexandre Dumas ['père']** (1802)
Three Northern Love Stories [with E. Magnússon] (1875) **William Morris** (1834) (tr.)
Three Papers Against Dr Wallis (1671) **Thomas Hobbes** (1588)
Three Perils of Man, The (1822) **James Hogg** (1770)
Three Perils of Woman, The (1823) **James Hogg** (1770)
Three Philosophical Poets (1910) **George Santayana** (1863)
Three Playes [*Selindra*, *Pandora*, and *Ormasdes*] (1665) **Sir William Killigrew** (1606)
Three Plays for Puritans [*The Devil's Disciple*, *Caesar and Cleopatra*, *Captain Brassbound's Conversion*] (1901) **Bernard Shaw** (1856)
Three Poems (1722) **Laurence Eusden** (1688)
Three Poems Upon the Death of . . . Oliver Lord Protector of England (1659) **John Dryden** (1631) [with Edmund Waller and Thomas Sprat]
Three Pretty Men (1916) **Gilbert Cannan** (1884)
Three Proper and Wittie, Familiar Letters (1580) **Gabriel Harvey** (1550)
Three Questor Plays (1967) **Dannie Abse** (1923)
Three Railway Engines, The (1945) **Revd W. V. Awdry** (1911)
Three Rooms (1924) **Warwick Deeping** (1877)
Three Score and Ten (1929) **Alec Waugh** (1898)
Three Sermons Upon Speciall Occasions (1623) **John Donne** (1572)
Three Sisters (1901) **Anton Chekhov** (1860)
Three Sisters, The (1914) **May Sinclair** (1863)
Three Six Seven (1983) **Peter Vansittart** (1920)
Three Soldiers (1921) **John Dos Passos** (1896)
Three Stories and Ten Poems (1923) **Ernest Hemingway** (1898)
Three Tales [*Trois contes*] (1877) **Gustave Flaubert** (1821)
Three Tall Women (1992) **Edward Albee** (1928)
Three Taps, The (1927) **Ronald Knox** (1888)
Three Taverns, The (1920) **Edwin Arlington Robinson** (1869)
Three Times Dead (1854) **M.E. Braddon** (1835)
Three Times Table (1990) **Sara Maitland** (1950)
Three Times Three (1936) **William Saroyan** (1908)
Three Uneasy Pieces (1987) **Patrick White** (1912)
Three Voices of Poetry, The (1953) **T.S. Eliot** (1888)
Three Weeks (1907) **Elinor Glyn** (1864)
Three Wonder Plays [*The Dragon*; *Aristotle's Bellows*; *The Jester*] (1922) **Lady Gregory** (1852)

Threepenny Opera, The [*Die Dreigroschenoper*] (1928) **Bertolt Brecht** (1898)
Threescore and ten [UK: *All in a lifetime*] (1959) **Walter Ernest Allen** (1911)
Threnodia Augustalis (1685) **John Dryden** (1631)
Threnodia Augustalis (1772) **Oliver Goldsmith** (1728)
Threshold of Quiet, The (1917) **Daniel Corkery** (1878)
Throat, The (1993) **Peter Straub** (1943)
Through Dooms of Love (1965) **Maxine Kumin** (1925)
Through Fire to Fortune (1900) **Mrs A.H. Alexander** (1825)
Through Flood and Flame (1868) **[S. Baring-Gould]** (1834)
Through One Administration (1883) **Frances Hodgson Burnett** (1849)
Through the Dark Continent (1878) **Sir Henry Morton Stanley** (1841)
Through the Eye of a Needle (1907) **William Dean Howells** (1837)
Through the Fields of Clover (1961) **Peter de Vries** (1910)
Through the Fog of War (1938) **Sir Basil Liddell Hart** (1895)
Through the Garden Gate (1986) **Susan Hill** (1942)
Through the Kitchen Window (1984) **Susan Hill** (1942)
Through the Long Night (1888) **E. Lynn Linton** (1822)
Through the Looking-Glass, and What Alice Found There (1872) **'Lewis Carroll' [Charles Lutwidge Dodgson]** (1832)
Through the Magic Door (1907) **A. Conan Doyle** (1859)
Through the Wilderness (1977) **Dan Jacobson** (1929)
Thrown to the Woolfs (1978) **John Lehmann** (1907)
Thrown Voices (1986) **Carol Ann Duffy** (1955)
Thru (1975) **Christine Brooke-Rose** (1926)
Thrush Green (1959) **'Miss Read' [Dora Jessie Saint]** (1913)
Thumbstick, The (1959) **William Mayne** (1928)
Thunder and Lightnings (1976) **Jan Mark** (1943)
Thunderball (1961) **Ian Fleming** (1908)
Thunderbolt, The (1908) **Arthur Wing Pinero** (1855)
Thurber Carnival, The (1945) **James Thurber** (1894)
Thurber Country (1953) **James Thurber** (1894)
Thursday Friend, The (1999) **Catherine Cookson** (1906)
Thursday's Children (1984) **Rumer Godden** (1907)
Thurso's Landing (1932) **Robinson Jeffers** (1887)
Thus Spake Zarathustra [*Also Sprach Zarathustra*] (1883–92) **Friedrich Wilhelm Nietzsche** (1844)
Thus to Revisit (1947) **James Evershed Agate** (1877)
Thy Neighbour's Wife (1923) **Liam O'Flaherty** (1897)
Thy Rod and Staff (1912) **A.C. Benson** (1862)
Thyestes [from Seneca] (1560) **Jasper Heywood** (1535) (tr.)
Thyestes (1681) **John Crowne** (d. 1703)
Thyrza (1887) **George Gissing** (1857)
Tiberius (1990) **Allan Massie** (1938)
Tibetan Foothold (1966) **Dervla Murphy** (1931)
Tibetan Venus, The [as 'Beachcomber'] (1951) **J.B. Morton** (1893)
Tick-Tock (1996) **Dean Koontz** (1945)
Ticket That Exploded, The (1962) **William S. Burroughs** (1914)
Ticky (1943) **Stella Gibbons** (1902)
Ticonderoga (1854) **G.P.R. James** (1799)
Tiddledywink Tales (1891) **John Kendrick Bangs** (1862)
Tide of Life, The (1976) **Catherine Cookson** (1906)
Tide of Time, The (1937) **Edgar Lee Masters** (1868)
Tides (1917) **John Drinkwater** (1882)
Tidewater Morning, A (1993) **William Styron** (1925)
Tidewater Tales, The (1987) **John Barth** (1930)
Tiers Livre ['Third Book'] (1546) **François Rabelais** (1494?)
Tiger and the Horse, The (1960) **Robert Bolt** (1924)
Tiger at the Gates [from Giraudoux, *La guerre de Troie n'aura pas lieu*] (1955) **Christopher Fry [Christopher Fry Harris]** (1907)
Tiger for Malgudi, A (1983) **R.K. Narayan** (1907)
Tiger in the Smoke, The (1952) **Margery Allingham** (1904)
Tiger Joy (1925) **Stephen Vincent Benét** (1889)
Tiger, The (1984) **Lisa St Aubin de Terán** (1953)
Tiger's Cub, A (1892) **Eden Phillpotts** (1862)
Tigers (1967) **Fleur Adcock** (1934)
Tigers Are Better Looking (1968) **'Jean Rhys' [Ella Gwendolyn Rees Williams]** (1890)
Tightrope Men, The (1973) **Desmond Bagley** (1923)
Tilbury Nogo (1854) **G.J. Whyte-Melville** (1821)
Till the Day I Die (1935) **Clifford Odets** (1906)
Till We Have Faces (1956) **C.S. Lewis** (1898)
Tilly Trotter (1980) **Catherine Cookson** (1906)
Tilly Trotter Wed (1981) **Catherine Cookson** (1906)
Tilly Trotter Widowed (1982) **Catherine Cookson** (1906)
Tilted Cross, The (1961) **Hal Porter** (1911)
Tim (1891) **H.O. Sturgis** (1855)
Timbuctoo (1829) **Alfred, Lord Tennyson** (1809)
Timbuktu (2000) **Paul Auster** (1947)
Time After Time (1983) **Molly Keane** (1905)
Time and a Place, A (1968) **William Humphrey** (1924)
Time and Eternity (1919) **Gilbert Cannan** (1884)
Time and Free Will [*Essai sur les données immédiates de la conscience*] (1889) **Henri Bergson** (1859)
Time and the Conways (1937) **J.B. Priestley** (1894)
Time and the Gods (1906) **Lord Dunsany** (1878)
Time and Tide (1992) **Edna O'Brien** (1932)
Time and Tide, by Weare and Tyne (1867) **John Ruskin** (1819)
Time and Time Again (1971) **Alan Ayckbourn** (1939)
Time and Time Again (1953) **James Hilton** (1900)
Time and Western Man (1927) **Wyndham Lewis** (1882)
Time Enough for Love (1973) **Robert A. Heinlein** (1907)
Time Flies (1885) **Christina Rossetti** (1830)
Time for a Tiger (1956) **'Anthony Burgess' [John Anthony Burgess Wilson]** (1917)
Time for Judas, A (1983) **Morley Callaghan** (1903)

Time Importuned (1928) **Sylvia Townsend Warner** (1893)
Time in a Red Coast (1984) **George Mackay Brown** (1921)
Time in the Rock (1936) **Conrad Potter Aiken** (1889)
Time Machine, The (1895) **H.G. Wells** (1866)
Time Must Have a Stop (1944) **Aldous Huxley** (1894)
Time of Changes, A (1971) **Robert Silverberg** (1935)
Time of Desecration [*La vita interiore*] (1978) **'Alberto Moravia' [Alberto Pincherle]** (1907)
Time of Gifts, A (1977) **Patrick Leigh Fermor** (1915)
Time of Hope (1949) **C.P. Snow** (1905)
Time of My Life (1992) **Alan Ayckbourn** (1939)
Time of Our Darkness (1988) **Stephen Gray** (1941)
Time of Our Time, The (1998) **Norman Mailer** (1923)
Time of the Angels, The (1966) **Iris Murdoch** (1919)
Time of the Assassins, The (1956) **Henry Miller** (1891)
Time of the Crack, The (1973) **Emma Tennant** (1937)
Time of the Hero, The [*La ciudad y los perros*] (1962) **Mario Vargas Llosa** (1936)
Time of Your Life, The (1939) **William Saroyan** (1908)
Time Present; [with *Hotel in Amsterdam*] (1968) **John Osborne** (1929)
Time Regained [*Le Temps retrouvé; A la recherche du temps perdu* vii] (1927) **Marcel Proust** (1871–1922)
Time to Act, A (1943) **Archibald MacLeish** (1892)
Time to Change, A (1951) **Nissim Ezekiel** (1924)
Time to Dance, A (1990) **Melvyn Bragg** (1939)
Time to Dance, A (1935) **C. Day Lewis** (1904)
Time to Dance, A (1982) **Bernard MacLaverty** (1942)
Time to Dance, No Time to Weep, A (1987) **Rumer Godden** (1907)
Time to Keep, A (1969) **George Mackay Brown** (1921)
Time to Kill, A (1989) **John Grisham** (1955)
Time to Speak, A (1941) **Archibald MacLeish** (1892)
Time Was Away (1948) **Alan Ross** (1922)
Time Works Wonders (1845) **Douglas Jerrold** (1803)
Time Zones (1991) **Fleur Adcock** (1934)
Time's Arrow (1991) **Martin Amis** (1949)
Time's Laughingstocks (1909) **Thomas Hardy** (1840)
Time's Power (1989) **Adrienne Rich** (1929)
Timebends (1987) **Arthur Miller** (1915)
Timeless Land, The (1941) **Eleanor Dark** (1901)
Timeline (1999) **Michael Crichton** (1942)
Timequake (1994) **Kurt Vonnegut** (1922)
Times and Seasons (1992) **Elizabeth Jennings** (1926)
Times, The (1764) **Charles Churchill** (1731)
Times, The (1891) **Arthur Wing Pinero** (1855)
Timoleon (1891) **Herman Melville** (1819)
Timour the Tartar! (1850) **Charles William Shirley Brooks** (1816)
Tin Can Tree, The (1966) **Anne Tyler** (1941)
Tin Drum, The [*Die Blechtrommel*] (1959) **Günter Grass** (1927)
Tin Men, The (1965) **Michael Frayn** (1933)
Tin Pot Foreign General and the Old Iron Woman, The (1984) **Raymond Briggs** (1934)
Tings and Times (1991) **Linton Kwesi Johnson** (1952)
Tinker, Tailor, Soldier, Spy (1974) **'John le Carré' [David John Moore Cornwell]** (1931)
Tinker's Wedding, The (1909) **J.M. Synge** (1871)
Tinted Venus, The (1885) **'F. Anstey' [Thomas Anstey Guthrie]** (1856)
Tiny Alice (1964) **Edward Albee** (1928)
Tiny Luttrell (1893) **E.W. Hornung** (1866)
Tiny Tears (1973) **Roy Fuller** (1912)
Tip on a Dead Jockey (1957) **Irwin Shaw** (1913)
Tipling Philosophers, The (1710) **Edward Ward** (1667)
Tippoo Sultaun (1840) **Captain Meadows Taylor** (1808)
Tiresias (1885) **Alfred, Lord Tennyson** (1809)
Tirra Lirra by the River (1978) **Jessica Anderson** (1925)
'Tis (1999) **Frank McCourt** (1999)
Tis Merrie When Gossips Meete (1602) **Samuel Rowlands** (1570?)
'Tis Pity She's a Whore (1633) **John Ford** (1586)
Tit for Tat (1972) **Sir Harold Acton** (1904)
Titanic (1935) **E.J. Pratt** (1882)
Tithe-Proctor, The (1849) **William Carleton** (1794)
Title, The (1918) **Arnold Bennett** (1867)
Titles of Honor (1614) **John Selden** (1584)
Titmuss Regained (1990) **John Mortimer** (1923)
Titus Alone (1959) **Mervyn Peake** (1911)
Titus and Berenice (1676?) **Thomas Otway** (1652)
Titus Andronicus [altered from Shakespeare] (1677) **Edward Ravenscroft** (1644)
Titus Andronicus (1594) **William Shakespeare** (1564)
Titus Groan (1946) **Mervyn Peake** (1911)
To a God Unknown (1933) **John Steinbeck** (1902)
To Abolish Children (1968) **Karl Shapiro** (1913)
To All Appearances (1974) **Josephine Miles** (1911)
To Be a Pilgrim (1942) **Joyce Cary** (1888)
To Be Engraved on the Skull of a Cormorant (1968) **Charles Tomlinson** (1927)
To Be the Best (1988) **Barbara Taylor Bradford** (1933)
To Bedlam and Part of the Way Back (1961) **Anne Sexton** (1928)
To Call Her Mine (1889) **Sir Walter Besant** (1836)
To Circumjack Cencrastus (1930) **'Hugh MacDiarmid' [Christopher Murray Grieve]** (1892)
To Criticize the Critic (1965) **T.S. Eliot** (1888)
To Cuba and Back (1859) **Richard Henry Dana Jr** (1815)
To Cut a Long Story Short (2000) **Jeffrey Archer** (1940)
To Damascus (1898–1901) **August Strindberg** (1849)
To day a Man, To morrow None (1644) **Sir Walter Ralegh** (1554–1618)
To Fear a Painted Devil (1965) **Ruth Rendell** (1930)
To Go Hidden (1984) **Patric Dickinson** (1914)
To Have and Have Not (1937) **Ernest Hemingway** (1898)

To Have and to Hold (1986) **Deborah Moggach** (1948)
To Hell with Culture (1963) **Sir Herbert Read** (1893)
To Jerusalem and Back (1976) **Saul Bellow** (1915)
To Kill a Mockingbird (1960) **Harper Lee** (1926)
To Leeward (1884) **F. Marion Crawford** (1854)
To Let (1921) **John Galsworthy** (1867)
To London Town (1899) **Arthur Morrison** (1863)
To Love and Be Wise (1950) **'Josephine Tey' [Elizabeth Mackintosh]** (1897)
To Make a Prairie (1979) **Maxine Kumin** (1925)
To Make Me Grieve (1968) **Molly Holden** (1927)
To Meet the Sun (1929) **R.D. FitzGerald** (1902)
To Present the Pretence (1977) **John Arden** (1930)
To Quito and Back (1937) **Ben Hecht** (1894)
To Return to All That (1930) **A.P. Graves** (1846) (tr.)
To Scorch or Freeze (1989) **Donald Davie** (1922)
To See the Matter Clearly (1968) **Ruth Fainlight** (1931)
To Sir Godfrey Kneller (1722) **Thomas Tickell** (1686)
To Sir, With Love (1959) **E.R. Braithwaite** (1912)
To Step Aside (1939) **Noel Coward** (1899)
To Tame a Sister (1961) **Gillian Avery** (1926)
To the Bitter End (1872) **M.E. Braddon** (1835)
To the Devil—A Daughter (1953) **Dennis Wheatley** (1897)
To the Finland Station (1940) **Edmund Wilson** (1895)
To the Gods the Shades (1976) **David Wright** (1920)
To the Hilt (1996) **Dick Francis** (1920)
To the Island (1982) **Janet Frame** (1924)
To the Islands (1958) **Randolph Stow** (1935)
To the Lighthouse (1927) **Virginia Woolf** (1882)
To the Majestie of King James (1603) **Michael Drayton** (1563)
To the North (1932) **Elizabeth Bowen** (1899)
To the Sun (1988) **Kathleen Raine** (1908)
To the Unknown God (1924) **John Middleton Murry** (1889)
To the Victors the Spoils (1950) **Colin MacInnes** (1914)
To the Wedding (1995) **John Berger** (1926)
To the White Sea (1993) **James Dickey** (1923)
To Urania (1988) **Joseph Brodsky** (1940)
To Whom It May Concern (1944) **James T. Farrell** (1904)
To Whom It May Concern (1958) **Alan Ross** (1922)
To Whom She Will (1955) **Ruth Prawer Jhabvala** (1927)
To You, Mr Chips (1938) **James Hilton** (1900)
Toad of Toad Hall (1929) **A.A. Milne** (1882)
Toast to the Lord, A (1972) **Robin Jenkins** (1912)
Tobacco Battered (1617) **Joshua Sylvester** (1563)
Tobacco Road (1932) **Erskine Caldwell** (1903)
Tobit Transplanted [US: *The Far-Away Bride*] (1931) **Stella Benson** (1892)
Toby Stays with Jane (1962) **Ann Thwaite** (1932)
Toby, the Tram Engine (1952) **Revd W.V. Awdry** (1911)
Together (1908) **Robert Herrick** (1868)
Together They Ride (1945) **'Jean Plaidy' [Eleanor Hibbert]** (1906)
Toil and Spin (1979) **Chris Wallace-Crabbe** (1934)
Toilers of Babylon (1888) **B.L. Farjeon** (1838)
Toilers of the Sea [*Les Travailleurs de la mer*] (1866) **Victor Hugo** (1802)
'Toinette [repub. 1881 as *A Royal Gentleman*] (1874) **Albion W. Tourgée** (1838)
Tokyo-Montana Express, The (1980) **Richard Brautigan** (1935)
Told After Supper (1891) **Jerome.K. Jerome** (1859)
Told Again (1927) **Walter de la Mare** (1873)
Told in the Twilight (1875) **Mrs Henry Wood** (1814)
Toll for the Brave (1971) **'Jack Higgins' [Harry Patterson]** (1929)
Tolstoy or Dostoevsky (1959) **George Steiner** (1929)
Tom [satirical ballet] (1935) **E.E. cummings** (1894)
Tom Bowling (1841) **Captain Chamier** (1796)
Tom Brown at Oxford (1861) **Thomas Hughes** (1822)
Tom Brown's Body (1949) **Gladys Mitchell** (1901)
Tom Brown's Schooldays (1857) **Thomas Hughes** (1822)
Tom Burke of 'Ours' (1844) **Charles Lever** (1806)
Tom O' Bedlam's Beauties (1981) **Peter Reading** (1946)
Tom O'Bedlam (1985) **Robert Silverberg** (1935)
Tom Sawyer Abroad (1894) **'Mark Twain' [Samuel Langhorne Clemens]** (1835)
Tom Sawyer, Detective (1896) **'Mark Twain' [Samuel Langhorne Clemens]** (1835)
Tom Thumb (1730) **Henry Fielding** (1707)
Tom's Midnight Garden (1958) **Philippa Pearce** (1920)
Tomaso's Fortune, and Other Stories (1904) **'Henry Seton Merriman' [Hugh Stowell Scott]** (1862)
Tombs of Atuan, The (1971) **Ursula K. le Guin** (1929)
Tommy and Co. (1904) **Jerome K. Jerome** (1859)
Tommy and Grizel (1900) **[Sir] J.M. Barrie** (1860)
Tommy Gallagher's Crusade (1939) **James T. Farrell** (1904)
Tommyknockers, The (1988) **Stephen King** (1947)
Tomorrow Times Seven (1959) **Frederik Pohl** (1919)
Tomorrow's Another Day (1945) **W.R. Burnett** (1899)
Tomorrow-Tamer, The (1963) **Margaret Laurence** (1926)
Tongues of Conscience (1900) **Robert Hichens** (1864)
Tongues of Flame (1985) **Tim Parks** (1954)
Tonight at Noon (1968) **Adrian Henri** (1932)
Tonio Kröger (1903) **Thomas Mann** (1875)
Tono-Bungay (1909) **H.G. Wells** (1866)
Tonto Woman, The (1999) **Elmore Leonard** (1925)
Tony Butler (1865) **Charles Lever** (1806)
Tony Lumpkin in Town (1778) **John O'Keefe** (1747)
Tonypandy (1945) **Idris Davies** (1905)
Too Dear For My Possessing (1940) **Pamela Hansford Johnson** (1912)
Too Far To Go (1979) **John Updike** (1932)
Too Late For Logic (1990) **Tom Murphy** (1935)
Too Late the Phalarope (1953) **Alan Paton** (1903)
Too Many Cooks (1938) **Rex Stout** (1886)
Too Many Ghosts (1961) **Paul Gallico** (1897)

Too Much Alone [as 'F.G. Trafford'] (1860) **Mrs J.H. Riddell** (1832)
Too Much Johnson (1894) **William Gillette** (1855)
Too Strange Not To Be True (1864) **Lady Georgiana Fullerton** (1812)
Too True To Be Good; Village Wooing,;and On the Rocks (1932) **Bernard Shaw** (1856)
Tooth and Nail [originally titled *Wolfman*] (1992) **Ian Rankin** (1960)
Tooth Ball, The (1987) **Philippa Pearce** (1920)
Top Down Bottom Up (1990) **Roy Fisher** (1930)
Top Girls (1982) **Caryl Churchill** (1938)
Top of the Hill, The (1979) **Irwin Shaw** (1913)
Top Silk (1989) **David Williamson** (1942)
Topaz (1967) **Leon Uris** (1924)
Topographical Miscellanies (1792) **Sir Samuel Egerton Brydges** (1762)
Torch Song Trilogy (1981) **Harvey Fierstein** (1954)
Torch-Bearers, The (1922) **George Kelly** (1887)
Torch-Bearers, The (1937) **Alfred Noyes** (1880)
Torquato Tasso (1790) **Johann Wolfgang von Goethe** (1749)
Torquemada (1882) **Victor Hugo** (1802–85)
Torrent, The (1896) **Edwin Arlington Robinson** (1869)
Torrents of Spring, The (1926) **Ernest Hemingway** (1898)
Torse 3 (1962) **Christopher Middleton** (1926)
Tortilla Flat (1935) **John Steinbeck** (1902)
Tortoise by Candlelight (1963) **Nina Bawden** (1925)
Tortoises (1921) **D.H. Lawrence** (1885)
Tory Heaven (1948) **Marghanita Laski** (1915)
Tory Lover, The (1901) **Sarah Orne Jewett** (1849)
Tosca [La Tosca] (1887) **Victorien Sardou** (1831)
Tossing and Turning (1977) **John Updike** (1932)
Total Eclipse (1968) **Christopher Hampton** (1946)
Touch (1967) **Thom Gunn** (1929)
Touch (1987) **Elmore Leonard** (1925)
Touch of Danger, A (1973) **James Jones** (1921)
Touch of Love, A (1989) **Jonathan Coe** (1961)
Touch of Strange, A (1958) **Theodore Sturgeon** (1918)
Touch of the Sun, A (1952) **William Sansom** (1912)
Touch the Devil (1982) **'Jack Higgins' [Harry Patterson]** (1929)
Touch the Water, Touch the Wind (1973) **Amos Oz** (1939)
Touch Wood [as 'C.L. Anthony'] (1934) **Dodie Smith** (1896)
Toucher, The (1993) **Dorothy Hewett** (1923)
Touchstone, The [UK: *A Gift From the Grave*] (1900) **Edith Wharton** (1862)
Tough Guys Don't Dance (1984) **Norman Mailer** (1923)
Tough, Tough Toys for Tough, Tough Boys (1998) **Will Self** (1961)
Tour in Ireland, A (1780) **Arthur Young** (1741)
Tour in Scotland, A (1771) **Thomas Pennant** (1726)
Tour in Switzerland, A (1798) **Helen Maria Williams** (1762)
Tour in Tartan-Land, A (1863) **'Cuthbert Bede' [Edward Bradley]** (1827)
Tour of Dr Syntax in Search of the Picturesque, The (1812) **William Combe** (1742)
Tour of Duty (1946) **John Dos Passos** (1896)
Tour of Europe and Asia, A (1820) **John Galt** (1779)
Tour Thro' the Whole Island of Great Britain, A (1725) **Daniel Defoe** (1660)
Tourist in Africa, A (1960) **Evelyn Waugh** (1903)
Tourmalin's Time Cheques (1891) **'F. Anstey' [Thomas Anstey Guthrie]** (1856)
Tovarich (1936) **Robert E. Sherwood** (1896)
Toward the Gulf (1918) **Edgar Lee Masters** (1868)
Towards a New Novel [*Pour un nouveau roman*] (1963) **Alain Robbe-Grillet** (1922)
Towards Asmara (1988) **Thomas Keneally** (1935)
Towards Democracy [pt. i] (1883) **Edward Carpenter** (1844)
Towards Silence (1968) **Edward Lucie-Smith** (1933)
Towards the End of the Century (1989) **E.A. Markham** (1939)
Towards the End of the Morning (1967) **Michael Frayn** (1933)
Towards the Goal (1917) **Mrs T. Humphry Ward** (1851)
Towards the Human (1986) **Iain Crichton Smith [Iain Mac a'Ghobhainn]** (1928)
Towards the Last Spike (1952) **E.J. Pratt** (1882)
Tower, The [*Der Turm*] (1925) **Hugo von Hofmannsthal** (1874)
Tower, The (1928) **W.B. Yeats** (1865)
Tower Hill (1871) **W.H. Ainsworth** (1805)
Tower of Babel, The (1874) **Alfred Austin** (1835)
Tower of Babel, The (1968) **Morris West** (1916)
Tower of Glass (1970) **Robert Silverberg** (1935)
Tower of London, The (1840) **W.H. Ainsworth** (1805)
Tower of Taddeo, The (1892) **'Ouida' [Marie Louise de la Ramée]** (1839)
Tower of the Dream, The (1865) **Charles Harpur** (1813)
Tower of the Mirrors, The (1914) **'Vernon Lee' [Violet Paget]** (1856)
Towers in the Mist (1938) **Elizabeth Goudge** (1900)
Towers of Ivory (1917) **Archibald MacLeish** (1892)
Towers of Silence, The (1971) **Paul Scott** (1920)
Towers of Trebizond, The (1956) **Rose Macaulay** (1881)
Town, The (1848) **Leigh Hunt** (1784)
Town, The (1950) **Conrad Richter** (1890)
Town, The (1957) **William Faulkner** (1897)
Town and the City, The (1950) **Jack Kerouac** (1922)
Town Before You, The (1794) **Hannah Cowley** (1743)
Town Down the River, The (1910) **Edwin Arlington Robinson** (1869)
Town House, The (1959) **Norah Lofts** (1904)
Town in Bloom, The (1965) **Dodie Smith** (1896)
Town Like Alice, A [US: *The Legacy*] (1950) **'Nevil Shute' [Nevil Shute Norway]** (1899)
Town of the Cascades, The (1864) **Michael Banim** (1796)
Town Traveller, The (1898) **George Gissing** (1857)
Town-Fop, The (1676) **Aphra Behn** (1640?)
Township Plays (1993) **Athol Fugard** (1932)

Toxophilus (1545) **Roger Ascham** (1515)
Toynbee Convector, The (1988) **Ray Bradbury** (1920)
Toys in the Attic (1960) **Lillian Hellman** (1907)
Toys of Peace, The (1919) **'Saki' [Hector Hugh Munro]** (1870–1916)
Tracks (1988) **Louise Erdrich** (1954)
Tract on Monetary Reform, A (1923) **J.M. Keynes** (1883)
Tractatus Logico-Philosophicus (1921) **Ludwig Wittgenstein** (1889)
Tractor and the Corn Goddess, The (1947) **Mulk Raj Anand** (1905)
Tracts Theological and Ecclesiastical (1874) **J.H. Newman** (1801)
Tradition and Dream (1964) **Walter Allen** (1911)
Tradition and Experiment in English Poetry (1979) **Philip Hobsbaum** (1932)
Traditional Tales of the English and Scottish Peasantry (1822) **Allan Cunningham** (1784)
Traffics and Discoveries (1904) **Rudyard Kipling** (1865)
Tragedie of Abrahams Sacrifice, A [from Theodore Beza] (1577) **Arthur Golding** (1536) (tr.)
Tragedie of Cleopatra Queen of Aegypt, The (1639) **Thomas May** (1595)
Tragedie of Darius, The (1603) **Sir William Alexander** (1567?)
Tragedie of Dido Queene of Carthage, The (1594) **Christopher Marlowe** (1564–93)
Tragedie of Julia Agrippina, The (1639) **Thomas May** (1595)
Tragedies [contains 'The Death of Aggrippa', 'Cleopatra in Judaea', 'The Harvesters'] (1916) **Arthur Symons** (1865)
Tragedies of the Last Age Consider'd, The (1677) **Thomas Rymer** (1641)
Tragedy at Law (1942) **'Cyril Hare' [A.A.G. Clark]** (1900)
Tragedy of Antigone, The [Written by T.M.] (1631) **Thomas May** (1595)
Tragedy of Chrononhotonthologos, The (1734) **Henry Carey** (1687?)
Tragedy of Count Alarcos, The (1839) **Benjamin Disraeli** (1804)
Tragedy of Featherstone, The (1887) **B.L. Farjeon** (1838)
Tragedy of Hoffman, The (1631) **Henry Chettle** (1560?-1607)
Tragedy of Jane Shore, The [Written in imitation of Shakespeare's style] (1714) **Nicholas Rowe** (1674)
Tragedy of King Richard the Second, The (1719) **Lewis Theobald** (1688)
Tragedy of King Saul, The (1703) **Roger Boyle, earl of Orrery** (1621–79)
Tragedy of Mariam, The (1613) **Elizabeth Cary, Viscountess Falkland** (1585?)
Tragedy of Medea, The (1730) **Charles Johnson** (1679)
Tragedy of Mustapha, The (1609) **Fulke Greville, Lord Brooke** (1554)
Tragedy of Nan, The (1909) **John Masefield** (1878)
Tragedy of Orestes, The (1633) **Thomas Goffe** (1591–1629)
Tragedy of Pudd'nhead Wilson, The (1894) **'Mark Twain' [Samuel Langhorne Clemens]** (1835)
Tragedy of Sir Thomas Overbury, The (1723) **Richard Savage** (1697?)
Tragedy of Sophonisba, The (1729) **James Thomson** (1700)
Tragedy of the Dutchesse of Malfy, The (1623) **John Webster** (1580?)
Tragedy of the Korosko, The (1898) **A. Conan Doyle** (1859)
Tragedy of the Lady Jane Grey, The (1715) **Nicholas Rowe** (1674)
Tragedy of Thierry King of France, The (1621) **John Fletcher** (1579)
Tragedy of Zara, The (1736) **Aaron Hill** (1685)
Tragic America (1931) **Theodore Dreiser** (1871)
Tragic Comedians, The (1880) **George Meredith** (1828)
Tragic Ground (1944) **Erskine Caldwell** (1903)
Tragic Muse, The (1890) **Henry James** (1843)
Tragicall History of Dr Faustus, The (1604) **Christopher Marlowe** (1564)
Tragicall Legend of Robert Duke of Normandy, The (1596) **Michael Drayton** (1563)
Tragiques, Les (1616) **Théodore-Agrippa D'Aubigné** (1552)
Traherne's Poems of Felicity [ed. Idris Bell] (1910) **Thomas Traherne** (1637–74)
Trail of Ninety-Eight, The (1910) **Robert W. Service** (1876)
Trail of the Dinosaur, The (1955) **Arthur Koestler** (1905)
Trail of the Hawk, The (1915) **Sinclair Lewis** (1885)
Train of Powder, A (1955) **'Rebecca West' [Cicily Isabel Andrews]** (1892)
Trainspotting (1994) **Irvine Welsh** (1957)
Traité du style ['Treatise on Style'] (1928) **Louis Aragon** (1897)
Traitor, The (1949) **Herman Wouk** (1915)
Traitor in London, A (1900) **Fergus Hume** (1859)
Traitor's Purse (1941) **Margery Allingham** (1904)
Traits and Stories of the Irish Peasantry [1st ser.] (1830) **William Carleton** (1794)
Traits and Stories of the Irish Peasantry [2nd ser.] (1833) **William Carleton** (1794)
Traits and Trials of Early Life [as 'L.E.L.'] (1836) **Letitia Elizabeth Landon** (1802)
Tramp Abroad, A (1880) **'Mark Twain' [Samuel Langhorne Clemens]** (1835)
Tramping Methodist, The (1908) **Sheila Kaye-Smith** (1887)
Trampoline, The (1959) **John Pudney** (1909)
Tranquil Life, The [*La Vie Tranquille*] (1944) **'Marguerite Duras' [Marguerite Donnadieu]** (1914)
Trans-Caucasia and Ararat (1877) **James Bryce** (1838)
Transactioneer, The (1700) **William King** (1663)
Transatlantic Sketches (1875) **Henry James** (1843)

Transcripts and Studies (1888) **Edward Dowden** (1843)
Transformation Scene (1971) **Alan Brownjohn** (1931)
Transformations (1926) **Roger Fry** (1866)
Transformed Metamorphosis, The (1600) **Cyril Tourneur** (1575?)
Transit of Venus, The (1980) **Shirley Hazzard** (1931)
Transition (1895) **E[mma] F[rances] Brooke** (1859?)
Transition (1926) **Edwin Muir** (1887)
Transition (1934) **Lawrence Durrell** (1912)
Transitional Poem (1929) **C. Day Lewis** (1904)
Translation of the Letters of a Hindoo Rajah (1796) **Elizabeth Hamilton** (1758)
Translations (1980) **Brian Friel** (1929)
Translations and Tomfooleries (1926) **Bernard Shaw** (1856)
Translations from Camoens and Other Poets (1818) **Felicia Dorothea Hemans** (1793)
Translations From the Natural World (1992) **Les Murray** (1938)
Translations into English and Latin (1866) **C.S. Calverley** (1831)
Transparent Things (1972) **Vladimir Nabokov** (1899)
Transplant (1986) **Frank G. Slaughter** (1908)
Transport to Summer (1947) **Wallace Stevens** (1879)
Transposition and Other Addresses (1949) **C.S. Lewis** (1898)
Trap, The (1925) **Dorothy M. Richardson** (1873)
Trap, The (1955) **Dan Jacobson** (1929)
Trap (1966) **Peter Mathers** (1931)
Travail of Gold (1933) **E.F. Benson** (1867)
Travailes of the Three English Brothers, The (1607) **John Day** (*c.* 1574) [with William Rowley and George Wilkins]
Traveler at Forty, A (1913) **Theodore Dreiser** (1871)
Traveler From Altruria, A (1894) **William Dean Howells** (1837)
Traveller, The [US: *The Burning-Glass*] (1946) **Walter de la Mare** (1873)
Traveller (1988) **Richard Adams** (1920)
Traveller Has Regrets, The (1948) **G.S. Fraser** (1915)
Traveller in Time, A (1939) **'Alison Uttley' [Alice Jane Uttley]** (1884)
Traveller, The (1765) **Oliver Goldsmith** (1728)
Traveller Without Luggage [*Le Voyageur sans bagage*] (1937) **Jean Anouilh** (1910)
Traveller's Alphabet, A (1991) **Sir Steven Runciman** (1903
Traveller's Luck (1930) **E.V. Lucas** (1868)
Traveller's Prelude (1950) **Freya Stark** (1893)
Traveller's Samples (1951) **'Frank O'Connor' [Michael Francis O'Donovan]** (1903)
Traveller's Tree, The (1950) **Patrick Leigh Fermor** (1915)
Travellers (1945) **L.A.G. Strong** (1896)
Travellers Alone (1954) **Alan Brownjohn** (1931)
Travelling Behind Glass (1974) **Anne Stevenson** (1933)
Travelling Companions, The (1892) **'F. Anstey' [Thomas Anstey Guthrie]** (1856)
Travelling Entertainer, The (1979) **Elizabeth Jolley** (1923)
Travelling Grave, The (1948) **L.P. Hartley** (1895)
Travelling Hornplayer, The (1998) **Barbara Trapido** (1941)
Travelling North (1980) **David Williamson** (1942)
Travelling People (1963) **B.S. Johnson** (1933)
Travelling Sketches (1866) **Anthony Trollope** (1815)
Travelling Woman, A (1959) **John Wain** (1925)
Travels During the Years 1787, 1788, and 1790 (1792) **Arthur Young** (1741)
Travels for the Heart [as 'Courtney Melmoth'] (1777) **Samuel Jackson Pratt** (1749)
Travels in Arabia Deserta (1888) **Charles Doughty** (1843)
Travels in Greece and Russia (1859) **Bayard Taylor** (1825)
Travels in Greece, Palestine, Egypt and Barbary [*Itinéraire de Paris à Jerusalem*] (1811) **François-René, vicomte de Chateaubriand** (1768)
Travels in New England and New York (1821–2) **Timothy Dwight** (1752–1817)
Travels in San Francisco (1990) **Herbert Gold** (1924)
Travels in the Drifting Dawn (1989) **Kenneth White** (1936)
Travels in the Interior of Africa (1799) **Mungo Park** (1771)
Travels in the Track of the Ten Thousand Greeks (1844) **William Francis Ainsworth** (1807)
Travels in Two Democracies (1936) **Edmund Wilson** (1895)
Travels in West Africa (1897) **Mary Kingsley** (1862)
Travels into Several Remote Nations of the World, by Lemuel Gulliver [4 pts.] (1726) **Jonathan Swift** (1667)
Travels of an Irish Gentleman in Search of a Religion (1833) **Thomas Moore** (1779)
Travels of Maudie Tipstaff, The (1967) **Margaret Forster** (1938)
Travels of Persiles and Sigismunda, The [*Los trabajos de Persiles y Sigismunda*] (1617) **Miguel de Cervantes Saavedra** (1547–1616)
Travels of Ulysses, The (1673) **Thomas Hobbes** (1588) (tr.)
Travels on the Amazon and the Rio Negro (1853) **Alfred Russel Wallace** (1823)
Travels Through France and Italy (1766) **Tobias George Smollett** (1721)
Travels to Discover the Source of the Nile (1790) **James Bruce** (1730)
Travels with a Donkey in the Cévennes (1879) **Robert Louis Stevenson** (1850)
Travels with Charley in Search of America (1962) **John Steinbeck** (1902)
Travels With My Aunt (1969) **Graham Greene** (1904)
Travels with Myself and Another (1979) **Martha Gellhorn** (1908)
Travesties (1974) **Tom Stoppard** (1937)
Trawl (1966) **B.S. Johnson** (1933)

Traytor, The (1635) **James Shirley** (1596)
Tread the Green Grass (1929) **Paul Green** (1894)
Treason's Harbour (1982) **Patrick O'Brian** (1914)
Treasure House of Martin Hews, The (1929) **E. Phillips Oppenheim** (1866)
Treasure Island (1883) **Robert Louis Stevenson** (1850)
Treasure of Heaven, The (1906) **Marie Corelli** (1855)
Treasure of the Sierra Madre, The (1934) **B. Traven**
Treasurer's Report, The (1930) **Robert Benchley** (1889)
Treasures of Time (1979) **Penelope Lively** (1933)
Treasury of Sacred Song, The (1889) **Francis Turner Palgrave** (1824) (ed.)
Treat 'Em Rough (1918) **Ring Lardner** (1885)
Treatise Concerning Eternal and Immutable Morality, A (1731) **Ralph Cudworth** (1617–88)
Treatise Concerning Religious Affections (1746) **Jonathan Edwards** (1703)
Treatise Concerning the Principles of Human Knowledge, A (1710) **George Berkeley** (1685)
Treatise of Human Nature, A (1739) **David Hume** (1711)
Treatise of the Plague, A [from F. Valleriole] (1603) **Thomas Lodge** (1558) (tr.)
Treatise on Money, A (1930) **J.M. Keynes** (1883)
Treatise on the Fear of God, A (1679) **John Bunyan** (1628)
Treatise on the Law Privileges, Proceedings and Usage of Parliament (1844) **Sir Thomas Erksine May** (1815)
Treats (1976) **Christopher Hampton** (1946)
Treatyse of the New India, A (1553) **Richard Eden** (1521?) (tr.)
Tree and Leaf (1964) **J.R.R. Tolkein** (1892)
Tree Clock, The (1990) **Seamus Heaney** (1939)
Tree of Heaven, The (1917) **May Sinclair** (1863)
Tree of Idleness, The (1955) **Lawrence Durrell** (1912)
Tree of Knowledge, The (1990) **Eva Figes** (1932)
Tree of Man, The (1955) **Patrick White** (1912)
Tree of Night (1949) **Truman Capote** (1924)
Tree of Strings (1977) **Norman MacCaig** (1910)
Tree of the Sun, The (1978) **Wilson Harris** (1921)
Tree on Fire, A (1967) **Alan Sillitoe** (1928)
Tree That Walked, The (1967) **John Fuller** (1937)
Trees, The (1940) **Conrad Richter** (1890)
Trefoil, The (1923) **A.C. Benson** (1862)
Trelawny of the 'Wells' (1898) **Arthur Wing Pinero** (1855)
Trelawny of Trelawne (1837) **Anna Eliza Bray** (1790)
Tremaine (1825) **Robert Plumer Ward** (1765)
Trembling of a Leaf, The (1921) **Somerset Maugham** (1874)
Trembling of the Veil, The (1922) **W.B. Yeats** (1865)
Tremendous Trifles (1909) **G.K. Chesterton** (1874)
Tremendous World in Her Head, A (1989) **Dorothy Hewett** (1923)
Tremor of Intent (1966) **'Anthony Burgess' [John Anthony Burgess Wilson]** (1917)
Tremordyn Cliff (1835) **Frances Trollope** (1780)
Trent Intervenes (1913) **E.C. Bentley** (1875)
Trent's Last Case [US: *The Woman in Black*] (1913) **E.C. Bentley** (1875)
Trespasser, The (1912) **D.H. Lawrence** (1885)
Trespasses (1970) **Paul Bailey** (1937)
Trespassers at Charlecote (1958) **Gillian Avery** (1926)
Trespassing (1991) **George MacBeth** (1932)
Trevanion (1801) **Horace Smith** (1779)
Trewnesse of the Christian Religion, The [from Philippe de Mornay; trn begun by Sir Philip Sydney] (1587) **Arthur Golding** (1536) (tr.)
Trial, The (1864) **Charlotte M. Yonge** (1823)
Trial, The [*Der Prozess*] (1925) **Franz Kafka** (1883–1924)
Trial by Jury [music by Sir Arthur Sullivan] (1875) **W.S. Gilbert** (1836)
Trial of a City (1952) **Earle Birney** (1904)
Trial of a Judge (1938) **Sir Stephen Spender** (1909)
Trial of a Poet (1947) **Karl Shapiro** (1913)
Trial of Jesus, The (1925) **John Masefield** (1878)
Trial of Selim the Persian, The (1748) **Edward Moore** (1712)
Trial of Sören Qvist, The (1947) **Janet Lewis** (1899)
Trial of Thomas Cranmer, The (1956) **Anne Ridler** (1912)
Trials of a Translator, The (1949) **Ronald Knox** (1888)
Trials of Brother Jero, The (1961) **Wole Soyinka** (1934)
Trials of Margaret Lyndsay, The (1823) **John Wilson** (1785)
Trials of the Heart (1839) **Anna Eliza Bray** (1790)
Triangles (1990) **Andrea Newman** (1938)
Tribal Justice (1974) **Clark Blaise** (1940)
Tribune's Visitation, The (1969) **David Jones** (1895)
Tribute to Angels (1945) **Hilda Doolittle** (1886)
Tribute to Freud (1956) **Hilda Doolittle** (1886)
Trick for Trick (1678) **Thomas D'Urfey** (1653)
Trick of It, The (1989) **Michael Frayn** (1933)
Trick of the Light, A (1984) **Sebastian Faulks** (1953)
Tricke to Catch the Old-One, A (1608) **Thomas Middleton** (1580)
Tricksters, The (1986) **Margaret Mahy** (1936)
Tricotrin (1869) **'Ouida' [Marie Louise de la Ramée]** (1839)
Trilby (1894) **George du Maurier** (1834)
Trimblerigg (1924) **Laurence Housman** (1865)
Trimmed Lamp, The (1907) **'O. Henry' [William Sydney Porter]** (1862)
Trio (1993) **Jane Gardam** (1928)
Triodes (2000) **J.H. Prynne** (1936)
Triolets (1893) **Maurice Baring** (1874)
Trip to Calais, A (1778) **Samuel Foote** (1720–77)
Trip to Chinatown, a (1891) **Charles Hale Hoyt** (1860)
Trip to Hanoi (1968) **Susan Sontag** (1933)
Trip to New-England, A (1699) **Edward Ward** (1667)
Trip to Scarborough, A [altered from Vanbrugh's *The Relapse*] (1777) **Richard Brinsley Sheridan** (1753)
Triplanetary (1948) **E.E.'Doc' Smith** (1890)
Triple Fugue (1924) **Sir Osbert Sitwell** (1892)

Triple Play (1959) **'Tennessee' [Thomas Lanier] Williams** (1911)
Triple Thinkers, The (1938) **Edmund Wilson** (1895)
Trissotetras (1645) **Sir Thomas Urquhart** (1611) (tr.)
Tristan (1903) **Thomas Mann** (1875)
Tristan and Isolt (1923) **John Masefield** (1878)
Tristessa (1960) **Jack Kerouac** (1922)
Tristram (1927) **Edwin Arlington Robinson** (1869)
Tristram of Blent (1901) **'Anthony Hope' [Sir Anthony Hope Hawkins]** (1863)
Tristram of Lyonesse (1882) **A.C. Swinburne** (1837)
Triumph of Death, The [*Trionfo della morte*] (1894) **Gabriele D'Annunzio** (1863)
Triumph of Fashion, The (1771) **Henry James Pye** (1745)
Triumph of Infidelity, The (1788) **Timothy Dwight** (1752)
Triumph of Music, The (1804) **William Hayley** (1745)
Triumph of Peace, The (1633) **James Shirley** (1596)
Triumph of the Egg, The (1921) **Sherwood Anderson** (1876)
Triumph of the Muse, The (1958) **John Heath-Stubbs** (1918)
Triumph of the Scarlet Pimpernel, The (1922) **Baroness Orczy** (1865)
Triumph of the Spider Monkey, The (1978) **Joyce Carol Oates** (1938)
Triumph of Time, The (1958) **James Blish** (1921)
Triumph of Time, The (1932) **Storm Jameson** (1897)
Triumph of Union, The (1707) **Nahum Tate** (1652)
Triumphal March (1931) **T.S. Eliot** (1888)
Triumphant Squalitone (1917) **H.G. De Lisser** (1878)
Triumphs of Eugene Valmont, The (1906) **Robert Barr** (1850)
Triumphs of Isis, The (1749) **Thomas Warton, the Younger** (1728)
Triumphs of Love and Antiquity, The (1619) **Thomas Middleton** (1580)
Triumphs of Temper, The (1781) **William Hayley** (1745)
Triumphs of the Prince d'Amour, The (1636) **Sir William Davenant** (1606)
Triumphs Over Death, The (1595) **Robert Southwell SJ** (1561?)
Trivia (1918) **Logan Pearsall Smith** (1865)
Trivial Poems, and Triolets (1771) **Patrick Cary** (1624)
Trixie Trash, Star Ascending (1977) **Tom Wakefield** (1935)
Troas [from Seneca] (1559) **Jasper Heywood** (1535) (tr.)
Troia Britanica (1609) **Thomas Heywood** (1574?)
Troia-Nova Triumphans, London Triumphing (1612) **Thomas Dekker** (1572?)
Troilus and Cressida (1679) **John Dryden** (1631)
Troilus and Cressida (1609) **William Shakespeare** (1564)
Troilus and Criseyde (1483?) **Geoffrey Chaucer** (1340?-1400)
Trojan Brothers, The (1944) **Pamela Hansford Johnson** (1912)
Trojan Ending, A (1937) **Laura Riding** (1901)
Trojan Women, The (415 BC) **Euripides** (480 BC)
Troll Garden, The (1905) **Willa Cather** (1873)
Trooper Peter Halket of Mashonaland (1897) **Olive Schreiner** (1855)
Trophy of Arms, A (1936) **Ruth Pitter** (1897)
Tropic of Cancer (1934) **Henry Miller** (1891)
Tropic of Capricorn (1939) **Henry Miller** (1891)
Tropic of Ruislip (1974) **Leslie Thomas** (1931)
Tropical Childhood, A (1961) **Edward Lucie-Smith** (1933)
Tropical Ice (1972) **Alan Ross** (1922)
Tropical Winter (1933) **Joseph Hergesheimer** (1880)
Troubadour, The (1992) **Simon Raven** (1927)
Troubador, The [etc] [as 'L.E.L.'] (1825) **Letitia Elizabeth Landon** (1802)
Trouble I've Seen, The (1936) **Martha Gellhorn** (1908)
Trouble in July (1940) **Erskine Caldwell** (1903)
Trouble Makers, The (1957) **A.J.P. Taylor** (1906)
Trouble with Donovan Croft, The (1974) **Bernard Ashley** (1935)
Trouble With England, The (1962) **Frederic Raphael** (1931)
Trouble With Lichen (1960) **'John Wyndham' [John Wyndham Harris]** (1903)
Trouble with Tigers, The (1938) **William Saroyan** (1908)
Troubled Air, The (1951) **Irwin Shaw** (1913)
Troubles (1970) **J.G. Farrell** (1935)
Troublesome Offspring of Cardinal Guzman, The (1992) **Louis de Bernières** (1954)
Troublesome Raigne and Lamentable Death of Edward the Second, The (1594) **Christopher Marlowe** (1564)
Trout Fishing in America (1967) **Richard Brautigan** (1935)
Troy Chimneys (1952) **Margaret Kennedy** (1896)
Truant State (1987) **Nicholas Hasluck** (1942)
True Character of Mr Pope, A (1716) **John Dennis** (1657)
True Confession of George Barker, The (1950) **George Barker** (1913)
True Confessions and New Clichés (1985) **Liz Lochhead** (1947)
True Cross, The (1873) **G.J. Whyte-Melville** (1821)
True Declaration of the Troublesome Voyadge of J. Haukins, A (1569) **Sir John Hawkins** (1532)
True Heart, The (1929) **Sylvia Townsend Warner** (1893)
True History of Joshua Davidson, The (1872) **E. Lynn Linton** (1822)
True Intellectual System of the Universe, The (1678) **Ralph Cudworth** (1617)
True Knowledge of a Mans Owne Selfe, The [from Philippe de Mornay] (1602) **Anthony Munday** (1560) (tr.)
True Lawe of Free Monarchies, The (1598) **King James I** (1566)
True Love (1982) **Herbert Gold** (1924)
True Means of Establishing Public Happiness, The (1795) **Timothy Dwight** (1752)
True Patriot, The (1745) **Henry Fielding** (1707)

True Principles of Pointed or Christian Architecture, The (1841) **A.W.N. Pugin** (1812)
True Reformer, A (1874) **General Sir George Tomkyns Chesney** (1830)
True Relation of the Apparition of one Mrs Veal, A (1706) **Daniel Defoe** (1660)?
True Stories (1981) **Margaret Atwood** (1939)
True Tilda (1909) **Sir A.T. Quiller-Couch** (1863)
True to the Old Flag (1885) **G.A. Henty** (1832)
True Tragedy of Herod and Antipater, The (1622) **Gervaise Markham** (1568?) [with William Sampson]
True Traveller, The (1912) **W.H. Davies** (1871)
True Voice of Feeling, The (1953) **Sir Herbert Read** (1893)
True Widow, A (1678) **Thomas Shadwell** (1642?)
True Womanhood (1859) **John Neal** (1793)
True-Born Englishman, The (1701) **Daniel Defoe** (1660)
Trumpet in the Dust, The (1921) **Constance Holme** (1881)
Trumpet Shall Sound, The (1957) **H.M. Tomlinson** (1873)
Trumpet-Major, The (1880) **Thomas Hardy** (1840)
Trust (1966) **Cynthia Ozick** (1928)
Trust (1987) **Mary Flanagan** (1943)
Trust (1989) **George V. Higgins** (1939)
Trust Me (1987) **John Updike** (1932)
Truth, The (2000) **Terry Pratchett** (1948)
Truth [*Vérité*] (1903) **Émile Zola** (1840–1902)
Truth About Lorrin Jones, The (1988) **Alison Lurie** (1926)
Truth and Excellence of the Christian Religion Exhibited, The (1804) **Hannah Adams** (1755)
Truth and Falsehood (1734) **Stephen Duck** (1705)
Truth Exalted (1668) **William Penn** (1644)
Truth is More Sacred (1961) **Edward Dahlberg** (1900)
Truth is Not Sober (1934) **Winifred Holtby** (1898)
Truth Maintained (1643) **Thomas Fuller** (1608)
Truth of Our Times, The (1638) **Henry Peacham the younger** (1578?)
Truth of Poetry, The (1969) **Michael Hamburger** (1924)
Truth Triumphant Through the Spiritual Warfare (1692) **Robert Barclay** (1648–90)
Tryal of the Witnesses of the Resurrection of Jesus, The (1729) **Thomas Sherlock** (1678)
Trying to Save Peggy Sneed (1993) **John Irving** (1942)
TS Eliot (1984) **Peter Ackroyd** (1949)
TS Eliot (1972) **Bernard Bergonzi** (1929)
Tsing-Boum (1969) **Nicholas Freeling** (1927)
Tsotsi (1980) **Athol Fugard** (1932)
Tua Mariit Wemen and the Wedo, The (1507?) **William Dunbar** (1460?)
Tuba-Pacifica (1664) **George Wither** (1588)
Tudor Revolution in Government, The (1953) **G.R. Elton** (1921)
Tuileries, The (1831) **Anna Maria Porter** (1780)
Tulip Fever (1999) **Deborah Moggach** (1948)
Tulips and Chimneys (1923) **E.E. cummings** (1894)
Tulku (1979) **Peter Dickinson** (1927)
Tumatumari (1968) **Wilson Harris** (1921)
Tumbling in the Hay (1939) **Oliver St Gogarty** (1878)
Tunc (1968) **Lawrence Durrell** (1912)
Tundra (1973) **Farley Mowat** (1921)
Tunes of Glory (1956) **James Kennaway** (1928)
Tunnel of Love (1954) **Peter de Vries** (1910)
Tunnel, The (1919) **Dorothy M. Richardson** (1873)
Tunnel Vision (1994) **Sara Paretsky** (1947)
Tunnying of Eleynour Rummyng, The (1521?) **John Skelton** (1460?)
Turandot (1953) **John Ashbery** (1927)
Turbott Wolfe (1926) **William Plomer** (1903)
Turkish Delight (1993) **Jeremy Reed** (1954)
Turmoil, The (1915) **Booth Tarkington** (1869)
Turn Back the Leaves (1930) **'E.M. Delafield' [E.E.M. de la Pasture]** (1890)
Turn Left at Thursday (1961) **Frederik Pohl** (1919)
'*Turn of the Screw , The*' [**Hardy**]: see *The Two Magics*
Turn of the Year, The (1923) **Frederick Grove** (1879)
Turner (1994) **David Dabydeen** (1956)
Turning Back the Sun (1991) **Colin Thubron** (1939)
Turning the Prism (1985) **Roy Fisher** (1930)
Turning Wheels (1937) **Stuart Cloete** (1897)
Turns and Movies (1916) **Conrad Potter Aiken** (1889)
Turtle Diary (1975) **Russell Hoban** (1925)
Turtle Island (1974) **Gary Snyder** (1930)
Turvey (1949) **Earle Birney** (1904)
Tussock Land (1904) **Arthur Henry Adams** (1872)
Tutor of Truth, The (1779) **Samuel Jackson Pratt** (1749)
'Twas in Trafalgar Bay (1879) **Sir Walter Besant** (1836) [with James Rice]
Twelfth Hour, The (1907) **Ada Leverson** (1862)
Twelve Idylls (1928) **Lascelles Abercrombie** (1881)
Twelve Men (1919) **Theodore Dreiser** (1871)
Twelve Red Herrings (1994) **Jeffrey Archer** (1940)
Twelve Stories and a Dream (1903) **H.G. Wells** (1866)
Twelve Tales (1899) **Grant Allen** (1848)
Twelve Types (1902) **G.K. Chesterton** (1874)
Twenties, The (1975) **Edmund Wilson** (1895–1972)
Twentieth Century (1932) **Ben Hecht** (1894)
Twentieth-Century English Poetry (1978) **Anthony Thwaite** (1930)
Twentieth-Century Harlequinade (1916) **Edith Sitwell** (1887) [with Osbert Sitwell]
Twentieth-Century Literary Criticism (1972) **David Lodge** (1935) (ed.)
Twentieth-Century Psalter (1943) **Richard Church** (1893)
Twenty (1918) **Stella Benson** (1892)
Twenty Bath-Tub Ballads (1939) **Robert W. Service** (1876)
Twenty Love Poems and a Song of Despair [*Veinte poemas de amor y una canción desesperada*] (1924) **Pablo Neruda** (1904)
Twenty of the Plays of Shakespeare (1766) **George Steevens** (1736) (ed.)
Twenty Poems (1930) **Stephen Spender** (1909)
Twenty Sermons (1755) **Benjamin Hoadly** (1676)

Twenty Thousand Leagues Under the Sea (1928) **Robert Benchley** (1889)
Twenty Thousand Leagues Under the Sea [*Vingt mille lieues sous les mers*] (1869) **Jules Verne** (1828)
Twenty Years After [*Vingt ans après*] (1845) **Alexandre Dumas ['père']** (1802)
Twenty Years' Crisis, The (1939) **E.H. Carr** (1892)
Twenty-Eight Sermons Preached at Golden-Grove (1651) **Jeremy Taylor** (1613)
Twenty-five Poems (1936) **Dylan Thomas** (1914)
Twenty-Five Village Sermons (1849) **Charles Kingsley** (1819)
Twenty-Seven Tales and Fables, French and English (1729) **François Fénelon** (1651–1715)
Twenty-Seventh Kingdom, The (1982) **'Alice Thomas Ellis' [Anna Margaret Haycraft]** (1932)
Twenty-Six Men and a Girl (1899) **Maxim Gorky** (1868)
Twenty-Six Sermons (1660) **John Donne** (1572–1631)
Twenty-two Ballades in Blue China (1880) **Andrew Lang** (1844)
Twice Bought (1885) **R.M. Ballantyne** (1825)
Twice Round the Clock (1859) **George Augustus Sala** (1828)
Twice Twenty-Two (1966) **Ray Bradbury** (1920)
Twice-Told Tales [enlarged 1842] (1837) **Nathaniel Hawthorne** (1804)
Twilight (1916) **'Frank Danby' [Julia Frankau]** (1864)
Twilight Eyes (1987) **Dean Koontz** (1945)
Twilight in Italy (1916) **D.H. Lawrence** (1885)
Twilight of the Gods, The (1888) **Richard Garnett** (1835)
Twilight Sleep (1927) **Edith Wharton** (1862)
Twin-Rivals, The (1702) **George Farquhar** (1678)
Twinkle, Twinkle Little Spy [US: *Catch a Falling Spy*] (1976) **Len Deighton** (1929)
Twinkling of an Eye, The (1998) **Brian Aldiss** (1925)
Twins at St Clares (1941) **Enid Blyton** (1897)
Twins of Skirlaugh Hall, The (1903) **E[mma] F[rances] Brooke** (1859?)
'Twixt Cup and Lip (1896) **E. Lynn Linton** (1822)
'Twixt Earth and Stars (1906) **Radclyffe Hall** (1880)
'Twixt Land and Sea (1912) **Joseph Conrad** (1857)
Two Bites at a Cherry (1894) **Thomas Bailey Aldrich** (1836)
Two Black Sheep (1933) **Warwick Deeping** (1877)
Two Blind Countries, The (1914) **Rose Macaulay** (1881)
Two Books of Airs (1613) **Thomas Campion** (1567)
Two Brothers (1964) **Philip Toynbee** (1916)
Two by Two (1958) **Martha Gellhorn** (1908)
Two Cheers for Democracy (1951) **E.M. Forster** (1879)
Two Concepts of Liberty (1959) **Sir Isaiah Berlin** (1909)
Two Cultures and the Scientific Revolution, The (1959) **C.P. Snow** (1905)
Two Cultures, The; and *A Second Look* (1964) **C.P. Snow** (1905)
Two Days in Aragon [as 'M.J. Farrell'] (1941) **Molly Keane** (1905)
Two Destinies, The (1876) **Wilkie Collins** (1824)
Two Epistles to Mr Pope (1730) **Edward Young** (1683)
Two Essays on Scripture Miracles and on Ecclesiastical (1870) **J.H. Newman** (1801)
Two for the River (1961) **L.P. Hartley** (1895)
Two Friends, The [*Les Deux Amis*] (1770) **Pierre Augustin Caron de Beaumarchais** (1732)
Two Friends, The (1835) **Marguerite, Countess of Blessington** (1789)
Two Frontiers, The (1930) **John Gould Fletcher** (1886)
Two Generations (1939) **Frederick Grove** (1879)
Two Gentlemen in Bonds (1927) **John Crowe Ransom** (1888)
Two Girls, Fat and Thin (1991) **Mary Gaitskill** (1954)
Two Hundred Epigrammes (1555) **John Heywood** (1497?)
Two in a Train (1935) **Warwick Deeping** (1877)
Two is Lonely (1974) **Lynne Reid Banks** (1929)
Two Leaves and a Bud (1937) **Mulk Raj Anand** (1905)
*Two Letters from Junius to the D*** of G******* (1769) **'Junius' [probably Sir Philip Francis]** (1740)
Two Letters on the Conduct of Our Domestic Parties (1797) **Edmund Burke** (1729)
Two Letters the Proposals for Peace with the Regicide Directory of France (1796) **Edmund Burke** (1729)
Two Letters to Gentlemen in the City of Bristol (1778) **Edmund Burke** (1729)
Two Little Pilgrims' Progress (1895) **Frances Hodgson Burnett** (1849)
Two Little Wooden Shoes (1874) **'Ouida' [Marie Louise de la Ramée]** (1839)
Two Lives (1991) **'William Trevor' [William Trevor Cox]** (1928)
Two Lovely Beasts (1948) **Liam O'Flaherty** (1897)
Two Loves and a Life (1854) **Charles Reade** (1814) [with Tom Taylor]
Two Magics, The [inc.'*The Turn of the Screw*'] (1898) **Henry James** (1843)
Two Marriages (1867) **Dinah Maria Craik** (1826)
Two Men of Sandy Bar (1876) **Bret Harte** (1836)
Two Mentors, The (1783) **Clara Reeve** (1729)
Two Most Worthy and Notable Histories, The [from Sallust] (1608) **Thomas Heywood** (1574?) (tr.)
Two Noble Kinsmen, The (1634) **William Shakespeare** (1564–1616) [with John Fletcher]
Two of a Kind (1933) **Arthur Calder-Marshall** (1908)
Two of Them, The (1978) **Joanna Russ** (1937)
Two of Us, The (1984) **John Braine** (1922)
Two of Us, The (1970) **Michael Frayn** (1933)
Two Offenders (1894) **'Ouida' [Marie Louise de la Ramée]** (1839)
Two on a Tower (1882) **Thomas Hardy** (1840)
Two on an Island (1940) **Elmer Rice** (1892)
Two or Three Graces (1926) **Aldous Huxley** (1894)
Two Paths, The (1859) **John Ruskin** (1819)
Two People (1931) **A.A. Milne** (1882)
Two Plays [*Harvest; The Clancy Name*] (1911) **Lennox Robinson** (1886)
Two Plays and a Preface [*Cards of Identity*, and *The Making of Moo*] (1958) **Nigel Dennis** (1912)

Two Plays for Dancers ['The Dreaming of the Bones', and 'The Only Jealousy of Emer'] (1919) **W.B. Yeats** (1865)
Two Plunges for a Pearl (1872) **Mortimer Collins** (1827)
Two Quiet Lives (1948) **Lord David Cecil** (1902)
Two Rivulets [inc. *Democratic Vistas*, 1871] (1876) **Walt Whitman** (1819)
Two Rothschilds and the Land of Israel, The (1979) **Simon Schama** (1945)
Two Serious Ladies (1943) **Jane Bowles** (1917)
Two Sides of a Question (1901) **May Sinclair** (1863)
Two Sides of the Face (1903) **Sir A.T. Quiller-Couch** (1863)
Two Sisters (1970) **Gore Vidal** (1925)
Two Sisters, The (1926) **H.E. Bates** (1905)
Two Solitudes (1945) **Hugh MacLennan** (1907)
Two Studies (1931) **'Henry Handel Richardson' [Ethel Florence Robertson]** (1870)
Two Supercargoes, The (1877) **W.H.G. Kingston** (1814)
Two Surplices, The (1865) **Ada Cambridge** (1844)
Two Symphonies [*La Symphonie pastorale*] (1919) **André Gide** (1869)
Two Thousand and One: A Space Odyssey (1968) **Arthur C. Clarke** (1917)
Two Towers, The [*The Lord of the Rings* pt. ii] (1954) **J.R.R. Tolkein** (1892)
Two Treatises of Government (1690) **John Locke** (1632)
Two Valleys (1933) **Howard Fast** (1914)
Two Weeks in Another Town (1960) **Irwin Shaw** (1913)
Two Wind Poems (1980) **Ruth Fainlight** (1931)
Two Women [*La ciociara*] (1957) **'Alberto Moravia' [Alberto Pincherle]** (1907)
Two Women of London (1989) **Emma Tennant** (1937)
Two Women or One (1890) **Henry Harland** (1861)
Two Worlds and Their Ways (1949) **I. Compton-Burnett** (1884)
Two Worlds For Memory (1953) **Alfred Noyes** (1880)
Two Years Ago (1857) **Charles Kingsley** (1819)
Two Years Before the Mast (1840) **Richard Henry Dana Jr** (1815)
Two-Character Play, The [rev. as *Outcry*, 1973] (1969) **'Tennessee' [Thomas Lanier] Williams** (1911)
Two-Headed Poems (1978) **Margaret Atwood** (1939)
Twyborn Affair, The (1979) **Patrick White** (1912)
Twymans, The (1911) **Sir Henry Newbolt** (1862)
Tylney Hall (1834) **Thomas Hood** (1799)
Type-Writer Girl, The (1897) **Grant Allen** (1848) [as 'Olive Pratt Rayner']
Typee (1846) **Herman Melville** (1819)
Typhon (1704) **Bernard Mandeville** (1670)
Typhon (1665) **John Phillips** (1631)
Typhoon, and Other Stories (1903) **Joseph Conrad** (1857)
Tyrannick Love (1669) **John Dryden** (1631)
Tyrannus Nix (1969) **Lawrence Ferlinghetti** (1920)

U

U and I (1991) **Nicholson Baker** (1957)
Ugly Anna (1944) **A.E. Coppard** (1878)
Ugly Duchess, The [*Die hässliche Herzogin*] (1923) **Lion Feuchtwanger** (1884)
Ukelele Music (1985) **Peter Reading** (1946)
Ukridge (1924) **P.G. Wodehouse** (1881)
Ulcerated Milkman, The (1966) **William Sansom** (1912)
Ulrick the Ready (1896) **Standish O'Grady** (1846)
Ulterior Motives (1966) **David Garnett** (1892)
Ultima Thule (1880) **Henry Wadsworth Longfellow** (1807)
Ultima Thule (1929) **'Henry Handel Richardson' [Ethel Florence Robertson]** (1870)
Ultimate Good Luck, The (1981) **Richard Ford** (1944)
Ultimate Prizes (1989) **Susan Howatch** (1940)
Ultra-Crepidarius (1823) **Leigh Hunt** (1784)
Ultramarine (1933) **Malcolm Lowry** (1909)
Ulysses (1705) **Nicholas Rowe** (1674)
Ulysses (1902) **Stephen Phillips** (1864)
Ulysses [prtd in France] (1922) **James Joyce** (1882)
Ulysses [*definitive text*] (1986) **James Joyce** (1882)
Umbra (1920) **Ezra Pound** (1885)
Unbearable Bassington, The (1912) **'Saki' [Hector Hugh Munro]** (1870)
Unbearable Lightness of Being, The (1984) **Milan Kundera** (1929)
Unbidden Guest, The (1894) **E.W. Hornung** (1866)
Uncanny Scot, The (1968) **'Hugh MacDiarmid' [Christopher Murray Grieve]** (1892)
Uncanny Stories (1923) **May Sinclair** (1863)
Uncanny Tales (1896) **Mary Louisa Molesworth** (1839)
Uncanny Tales (1911) **F. Marion Crawford** (1854)
Unclassed, The (1884) **George Gissing** (1857)
Unclay (1931) **T.F. Powys** (1875)
Uncle Bernac (1897) **A. Conan Doyle** (1859)
Uncle Dynamite (1948) **P.G. Wodehouse** (1881)
Uncle Fred in the Springtime (1939) **P.G. Wodehouse** (1881)
Uncle Horace (1837) **Anna Maria [Mrs S.C.] Hall** (1800)
Uncle Jack (1885) **Sir Walter Besant** (1836)
Uncle John (1874) **G.J. Whyte-Melville** (1821)
Uncle Remus and Br'er Rabbit (1906) **Joel Chandler Harris** (1848)
Uncle Remus and his Friends (1892) **Joel Chandler Harris** (1848)
Uncle Remus: His Songs and Sayings (1881) **Joel Chandler Harris** (1848)
Uncle Silas (1864) **J.S. le Fanu** (1814)
Uncle Stephen (1931) **Forrest Reid** (1875)
Uncle Tom's Cabin (1852) **Harriet Beecher Stowe** (1811)
Uncle Tom's Children (1938) **Richard Wright** (1908)
Uncle Vanya (1900) **Anton Chekhov** (1860)
Unclouded Summer (1948) **Alec Waugh** (1898)

Uncollected Poems (1969) **Vernon Watkins** (1906–67)
Uncommercial Traveller, The (1861) **Charles Dickens** (1812)
Uncommon Danger [US: *Background to Danger*] (1937) **Eric Ambler** (1909)
Unconditional Surrender (1961) **Evelyn Waugh** (1903)
Unconscious Memory (1880) **Samuel Butler** (1835)
Unconsoled, The (1995) **Kazuo Ishiguro** (1954)
Under a Coloured Cap (1963) **Sean O'Casey** (1880)
Under a Glass Bell (1944) **Anaïs Nin** (1903)
Under Briggflats (1989) **Donald Davie** (1922)
Under Brinkie's Brae (1979) **George Mackay Brown** (1921)
Under Compulsion (1968) **Thomas M. Disch** (1940)
Under Drake's Flag (1883) **G.A. Henty** (1832)
Under Fire [Le Feu] (1916) **Henri Barbusse** (1873)
Under Love's Rule (1897) **M.E. Braddon** (1835)
Under Milk Wood (1954) **Dylan Thomas** (1914–53)
Under My Skin (1994) **Doris Lessing** (1919)
Under Saturn (1988) **Michael Wilding** (1942)
Under Sealed Orders (1895) **Grant Allen** (1848)
Under the Barrage (1985) **Peter Scupham** (1933)
Under the Bridge (1961) **Bruce Beaver** (1928)
Under the Cliff (1943) **Geoffrey Grigson** (1905)
Under the Deodars (1888) **Rudyard Kipling** (1865)
Under the Eildon Tree (1948) **Sydney Goodsir Smith** (1915)
Under the Eye of the Clock (1987) **Christopher Nolan** (1965)
Under the Greenwood Tree (1872) **Thomas Hardy** (1840)
Under the Hill (1904) **Aubrey Beardsley** (1872–98)
Under the Lilacs (1878) **Louisa M. Alcott** (1832)
Under the Microscope (1872) **A.C. Swinburne** (1837)
Under the Net (1954) **Iris Murdoch** (1919)
Under the North Star (1981) **Ted Hughes** (1930)
Under the Red Flag (1883) **M.E. Braddon** (1835)
Under the Red Flag (1886) **M.E. Braddon** (1835)
Under the Red Robe (1894) **Stanley J. Weyman** (1855)
Under the Reservoir (1992) **Peter Redgrove** (1932)
Under the Rose (1894) **'F. Anstey' [Thomas Anstey Guthrie]** (1856)
Under the Sangre de Cristo (1985) **Paul Horgan** (1903)
Under the Sea Wind (1941) **Rachel Carson** (1907)
Under the Sign of Saturn (1980) **Susan Sontag** (1933)
Under the Skin (1964) **Nina Bawden** (1925)
Under the Skylights (1901) **Henry Blake Fuller** (1857)
Under the Sunset (1881) **Bram Stoker** (1847)
Under the Volcano (1947) **Malcolm Lowry** (1909)
Under the Waves (1876) **R.M. Ballantyne** (1825)
Under the Wheel [*Unterm Rad*] (1906) **Hermann Hesse** (1877)
Under the Window (1879) **Kate Greenaway** (1846)
Under Two Flags (1867) **'Ouida' [Marie Louise de la Ramée]** (1839)
Under Western Eyes (1911) **Joseph Conrad** (1857)
Under Which Lord? (1879) **E. Lynn Linton** (1822)
Under World (1988) **Reginald Hill** (1936)
Undercliff (1953) **Richard Eberhart** (1904)
Underground Alley (1958) **William Mayne** (1928)
Underneath the Water (1968) **Charles Causley** (1917)
Understanding Media (1964) **Marshall McLuhan** (1911)
Understanding Poetry (1938) **Robert Penn Warren** (1905)
Undertaker's Garland, The (1922) **Edmund Wilson** (1895) [with John Peale Bishop]
Undertones (1863) **Robert Williams Buchanan** (1841)
Undertones of War (1928) **Edmund Blunden** (1896)
Underwood and After (1991) **Ronald Frame** (1953)
Underwoods (1887) **Robert Louis Stevenson** (1850)
Underworld (1997) **Don Delillo** (1936)
Undine (1816) **E.T.A. Hoffmann** (1776)
Undiscovered Country, The (1880) **William Dean Howells** (1837)
Undiscovered Country, The (1968) **Julian Mitchell** (1935)
Undream'd of Shores (1924) **'Frank' Harris** (1856)
Undue Influence (1999) **Anita Brookner** (1928)
Undying Fire, The (1919) **H.G. Wells** (1866)
Undying One, The (1830) **Caroline Norton** (1808)
Unearthing Suite (1983) **Margaret Atwood** (1939)
Unequal Marriage, An [continuation of Jane Austen's *Pride and Prejudice*] (1994) **Emma Tennant** (1937)
Unexpected Years, The (1937) **Laurence Housman** (1865)
Unfair Arguments with Existence (1962) **Lawrence Ferlinghetti** (1920)
Unfinished Cathedral (1934) **T.S. Stribling** (1881)
Unfinished Man, The (1960) **Nissim Ezekiel** (1924)
Unfinished Martyrdom, and Other Stories, An (1894) **A. St John Adcock** (1864)
Unfinished Novel, An (1958) **Bernard Shaw** (1856–1950)
Unfinished Tales of Numenor and Middle Earth (1980) **J.R.R. Tolkein** (1892–1973)
Unfinished Woman, An (1969) **Lillian Hellman** (1907)
Unforgotten Prisoner, The (1933) **R.C. Hutchinson** (1907)
Unforgotten Years (1938) **Logan Pearsall Smith** (1865)
Unfortunate Lovers, The (1643) **Sir William Davenant** (1606)
Unfortunate Man, The (1835) **Captain Chamier** (1796)
Unfortunate Traveller, The (1594) **Thomas Nashe** (1567)
Unfortunates, The (1969) **B.S. Johnson** (1933)
Ungava (1858) **R.M. Ballantyne** (1825)
Unguarded Hours (1978) **A.N. Wilson** (1950)
Unholy Trinity (1986) **Robert Bloch** (1917)
Unholy Wish, The (1890) **Mrs Henry Wood** (1814–87)
Unicorn, The (1963) **Iris Murdoch** (1919)

Unicorn From the Stars, The (1908) **W.B. Yeats** (1865) [with Lady Gregory]
Union of Christ and the Church, The (1642) **Ralph Cudworth** (1617)
Union Square (1933) **Albert Halper** (1904)
Union, The (1753) **Thomas Warton, the Younger** (1728) (ed.)
Union Street (1957) **Charles Causley** (1917)
Union Street (1982) **Pat Barker** (1943)
Uniqueness of Man, The (1941) **Julian Huxley** (1887)
Unity of the Church, The (1842) **Henry Edward Manning** (1808)
Universal Baseball Association, Inc., The (1968) **Robert Coover** (1932)
Universal Beauty (1735) **Henry Brooke** (1703)
Universal English Short-hand, The (1767) **John Byrom** (1692–1763)
Universal Etymological Dictionary, An (1721) **Nathan Bailey** (d. *c.* 1742)
Universal Gallant, The (1735) **Henry Fielding** (1707)
Universal History [Histoire Universelle] (1616–20) **Théodore-Agrippa D'Aubigné** (1552)
Universal History of Infamy, A [Historia universal de la infamia] (1935) **Jorge Luis Borges** (1899)
Universal Hymn (1867) **Philip James Bailey** (1816)
Universal Passion, The (1725) **Edward Young** (1683)
Universal Prayer, The (1738) **Alexander Pope** (1688)
Universe (1994) **Christopher Reid** (1949)
Unkind Word, The (1870) **Dinah Maria Craik** (1826)
Unkindness of Ravens, An (1985) **Ruth Rendell** (1930)
Unkist, Unkind! (1897) **Violet Hunt** (1866)
Unknown Eros, The (1877) **Coventry Patmore** (1823)
Unknown Industrial Prisoner, The (1971) **David Ireland** (1927)
Unknown Known, The (1939) **T. Sturge Moore** (1870)
Unknown Man No. 89 (1977) **Elmore Leonard** (1925)
Unlawful Assembly (1968) **D.J. Enright** (1920)
Unleaving (1976) **Jill Paton Walsh** (1937)
Unlikely Stories, Mostly (1983) **Alasdair Gray** (1934)
Unlimited Dream Company, The (1979) **J.G. Ballard** (1930)
Unlit Lamp, The (1924) **Radclyffe Hall** (1880)
Unlucky for Pringle (1973) **Wyndham Lewis** (1882–1957)
Unmade Bed, The [Le Lit défait] (1977) **'Françoise Sagan' [Françoise Quoirez]** (1935)
Unmarried Father, An (1927) **Floyd Dell** (1887)
Unmentionable Man, An (1994) **Edward Upward** (1903)
Unnatural Causes (1967) **P.D. James** (1920)
Unnatural Death [US: *The Dawson Pedigree*] (1927) **Dorothy L. Sayers** (1893)
Unnatural Exposure (1997) **Patricia Cornwell** (1956)
Unnaturall Combat, The (1639) **Philip Massinger** (1583)
Unofficial Rose, An (1962) **Iris Murdoch** (1919)
Unpath'd Waters (1913) **'Frank' Harris** (1856)
Unplayed Music (1981) **Carol Rumens** (1944)
Unpleasantness at the Bellona Club, The (1928) **Dorothy L. Sayers** (1893)
Unpopular Essays (1950) **Bertrand Russell** (1872)
Unprofessional Essays (1956) **John Middleton Murry** (1889)
Unpublished Poems (1936) **Emily Dickinson** (1830–86)
Unquiet Grave, The (1944) **Cyril Connolly** (1903)
Unrelenting Struggle, The (1942) **Sir Winston Churchill** (1874)
Unreliable Memoirs (1980) **Clive James** (1939)
Unreliable Nightingale, The (1973) **Brian Patten** (1946)
Unseen World, The (1847) **John Mason Neale** (1818)
Unsocial Socialist, An (1887) **Bernard Shaw** (1856)
Unspeakable Practices, Unnatural Acts (1968) **Donald Barthelme** (1931)
Unspeakable Skipton, The (1959) **Pamela Hansford Johnson** (1912)
Unsuitable Attachment, An (1982) **Barbara Pym** (1913–80)
Unsuitable Job For a Woman, An (1972) **P.D. James** (1920)
Unsweet Charity (1992) **Keith Waterhouse** (1929)
Untilled Field, The (1903) **George Moore** (1852)
'Unto This Last' (1862) **John Ruskin** (1819)
Untouchable (1935) **Mulk Raj Anand** (1905)
Untouchable, The (1997) **John Banville** (1945)
Untrodden Peaks and Unfrequented Valleys (1873) **Amelia B. Edwards** (1831)
Unusual Behaviour (1986) **Lettice Cooper** (1897)
Unusual Life of Tristan Smith, The (1994) **Peter Carey** (1943)
Unvanquished, The (1938) **William Faulkner** (1897)
Unvanquished, The (1942) **Howard Fast** (1914)
Unwelcome Man, The (1917) **Waldo Frank** (1889)
Unwelcome Words (1989) **Paul Bowles** (1910)
Up Above the World (1966) **Paul Bowles** (1910)
Up at the Villa (1941) **Somerset Maugham** (1874)
Up Country (1972) **Maxine Kumin** (1925)
Up From Slavery (1901) **Booker T. Washington** (1856)
Up, Into the Singing Mountain (1963) **'Richard Llewellyn' [Richard Llewellyn Lloyd]** (1907)
Up the Chimney Down (1984) **Joan Aiken** (1924)
Up the Country (1866) **Emily Eden** (1797)
Up the Country [as 'Brent of Bin Bin'] (1928) **Miles Franklin** (1879)
Up the Junction (1963) **Nell Dunn** (1936)
Upas Tree, The (1912) **Florence Barclay** (1862)
Upholsterer, The (1758) **Arthur Murphy** (1727)
Uplands (1970) **A.R. Ammons** (1926)
Upon Nothing (1679) **John Wilmot, earl of Rochester** (1647)
Upon Several Occasions (1953) **Elizabeth Berridge** (1921)
Upon the Death of Mrs Catherine Philips (1664) **Sir William Temple** (1628)
Upon the Late Storme and Death of His Highness (1658) **Edmund Waller** (1606)
Upon the Marriage of the Prince of Orange (1677) **John Oldham** (1653)

Upon the Sweeping Flood (1966) **Joyce Carol Oates** (1938)
Upstart, The (1973) **Piers Paul Read** (1941)
Upstart, The (1996) **Catherine Cookson** (1906)
Upstate (1971) **Edmund Wilson** (1895)
Upton Letters, The (1905) **A.C. Benson** (1862)
Ur of the Chaldees (1929) **Sir Leonard Woolley** (1880)
Urbanal (1975) **Christopher Logue** (1926)
Urgent Copy (1968) **'Anthony Burgess' [John Anthony Burgess Wilson]** (1917)
Urith (1891) **S. Baring-Gould** (1834)
Urn Burial [**Browne**]: see *Hydriotaphia*
Ursule Mirouët (1841) **Honoré de Balzac** (1799)
'Us' (1885) **Mary Louisa Molesworth** (1839)
Use of History, The (1946) **A.L. Rowse** (1903)
Use of Poetry and the Use of Criticism, The (1933) **T.S. Eliot** (1888)
Use of Riches, A (1957) **J.I.M. Stewart** (1906)
Useful Work Versus Useless Toil (1886) **William Morris** (1834)
Usefulness of the Stage, The (1698) **John Dennis** (1657)
Uses of Diversity, The (1920) **G.K. Chesterton** (1874)
Uses of Literacy, The (1957) **Richard Hoggart** (1918)
Ushant (1952) **Conrad Potter Aiken** (1889)
Uther & Igraine (1903) **Warwick Deeping** (1877)
Utilitarianism (1863) **J.S. Mill** (1806)
Utopia [Latin] (1516) **Sir Thomas More** (1478)
Utopia [English] (1551) **Sir Thomas More** (1478–1535)
Uttermost Farthing, The (1908) **Mrs Belloc Lowndes** (1868)
Utz (1988) **Bruce Chatwin** (1940)
Uxmal; Macée de Léodepart (1877) **John Abraham Heraud** (1799)

V

V (1985) **Tony Harrison** (1937)
V. (1963) **Thomas Pynchon** (1937)
Vacant Posession (1986) **Hilary Mantel** (1952)
Vacant Possession, A (1978) **James Fenton** (1949)
Vacation Rambles and Thoughts (1845) **Thomas Noon Talfourd** (1795)
Vacillations of Poppy Carew, The (1986) **'Mary Wesley' [Mary Wellesley]** (1912)
Vagabond, The [*La Vagabonde*] (1910) **Colette** (1873)
Vagaries Malicieux (1975) **Djuna Barnes** (1892)
Vagrant, and Other Poems, A (1950) **David Gascoyne** (1916)
Vagrant Mood, The (1952) **Somerset Maugham** (1874)
Vagrant of Time, The (1927) **Sir Charles G.D. Roberts** (1860)
Vailima Letters (1895) **Robert Louis Stevenson** (1850–94)
Vainglory (1915) **Ronald Firbank** (1886)
Val Strange (1882) **David Christie Murray** (1847)
Valdez is Coming (1969) **Elmore Leonard** (1925)
Vale (1914) **George Moore** (1852)
Vale (1931) **George William Russell ['AE']** (1867)
Vale of Cedars, The (1850) **Grace Aguilar** (1816–47)
Vale of Laughter, The (1967) **Peter de Vries** (1910)
Valediction (1984) **Robert B. Parker** (1932)
Valentine (1832) **'George Sand' [Auore Dupin-rsqb;** (1804)
Valentine M'Clutchy, the Irish Agent (1845) **William Carleton** (1794)
Valentine's Eve (1816) **Amelia Opie** (1769)
Valentinian (1685) **John Wilmot, earl of Rochester** (1647–80)
Valerie (1849) **Frederick Marryat** (1792–1848)
Valis (1981) **Philip K. Dick** (1928)
Valley Forge (1934) **Maxwell Anderson** (1888)
Valley of Bones, The (1964) **Anthony Powell** (1905)
Valley of Decision, The (1902) **Edith Wharton** (1862)
Valley of Fear, The (1915) **A. Conan Doyle** (1859)
Valley of Horses, The (1982) **Jean M. Auel** (1936)
Valley of St Gothard, The (1799) **Eliza Parsons** (1748)
Valley of the Dolls (1966) **Jacqueline Susann** (1921)
Valley of the Moon, The (1913) **'Jack London' [John Griffith Chaney]** (1876)
Valley of the Rea, The (1851) **Caroline Clive** (1801)
Valleys of the Assassins, The (1934) **Freya Stark** (1893)
Valmouth (1919) **Ronald Firbank** (1886)
Valperga (1823) **Mary Shelley** (1797)
Vamp Till Ready (1982) **Roy Fuller** (1912)
Vampire Lestat, The (1985) **Anne Rice** (1941)
Van Bibber and Others (1892) **Richard Harding Davis** (1864)
Van, The (1991) **Roddy Doyle** (1958)
Van Zorn (1914) **Edwin Arlington Robinson** (1869)
Vancenza (1792) **Mary Robinson** (1758)
Vandover and the Brute (1914) **Frank Norris** (1870–1902)
Vane's Story (1881) **James Thomson** (1834)
Vanessa (1933) **Sir Hugh Walpole** (1884)
Vanished World, The (1969) **H.E. Bates** (1905)
Vanishing Point, The (1973) **W.O. Mitchell** (1914)
Vanishing Points (1992) **Thea Astley** (1925)
Vanishing Roads (1915) **Richard le Gallienne** (1866)
Vanishing Trick (1976) **Brian Patten** (1946)
Vanitas (1892) **'Vernon Lee' [Violet Paget]** (1856)
Vanity Fair (1848) **W.M. Thackeray** (1811)
Vanity Girl, The (1920) **Compton Mackenzie** (1883)
Vanity of Dogmatizing, The (1661) **Joseph Glanvill** (1636)
Vanity of Duluoz (1968) **Jack Kerouac** (1922)
Vanity of Human Wishes, The (1749) **Samuel Johnson** (1709)
Variable Winds at Jalna (1954) **Mazo de la Roche** (1879)
Variation of Animals and Plants Under Domestication, The (1868) **Charles Darwin** (1809)
Variations on a Theme (1958) **Terence Rattigan** (1911)
Variations on a Time Theme (1934) **Edwin Muir** (1887)
Varieties of Religious Experience, The (1902) **William James** (1842)

Variety (1776) **William Whitehead** (1715)
Variety of Men (1967) **C.P. Snow** (1905)
Various Miracles (1985) **Carol Shields** (1935)
Various Voices (1998) **Harold Pinter** (1930)
Varney the Vampire; or, The Feast of Blood [sometimes attrib. to T.P. Prest] (1847) **'Malcolm J. Errym' [James Malcolm Rymer]** (1804)
Varying Shore, The (1921) **Zoë Akins** (1886)
Vasconselos (1853) **William Gilmore Simms** (1806)
Vases communicants, Les (1932) **André Breton** (1896)
Vathek [first pub. in French] (1786) **William Beckford** (1760)
Vatican Decrees, The (1875) **Henry Edward Manning** (1808)
Vatican Swindle, The [*Les Caves du Vatican*] (1914) **André Gide** (1869)
Vaudeville for a Princess (1950) **Delmore Schwartz** (1913)
Vaurien (1797) **Isaac D'Israeli** (1766)
Vega (1973) **Lawrence Durrell** (1912)
Vegetable, The (1923) **F. Scott Fitzgerald** (1896)
Veil of the Temple, The (1904) **W.H. Mallock** (1849)
Veil, The (1921) **Walter de la Mare** (1873)
Veiled Man, The (1899) **William le Queux** (1864)
Velvet Glove, The (1901) **'Henry Seton Merriman' [Hugh Stowell Scott]** (1862)
Vendée, La (1850) **Anthony Trollope** (1815)
Vendetta! (1886) **Marie Corelli** (1855)
Vendor of Sweets, The (1967) **R.K. Narayan** (1907)
Venetia (1837) **Benjamin Disraeli** (1804)
Venetia (1958) **Georgette Heyer** (1902)
Venetian Bracelet, The [as 'L.E.L.'] (1828) **Letitia Elizabeth Landon** (1802)
Venetian Life (1866) **William Dean Howells** (1837)
Venetian Painters, The (1894) **Bernard Berenson** (1865)
Venetians, The (1892) **M.E. Braddon** (1835)
Vengeance is Mine! (1950) **Mickey Spillane** (1918)
Venice (1994) **Jonathan Keates** (1946)
Venice (1960) **Jan Morris** (1926)
Venice Observed (1956) **Mary McCarthy** (1912)
Venice Preserv'd (1682) **Thomas Otway** (1652)
Ventre de Paris, Le (1873) **Émile Zola** (1840)
Venture to the Interior (1952) **Sir Laurens van der Post** (1906)
Ventures into Verse (1903) **H.L. Mencken** (1880)
Venus and Adonis (1593) **William Shakespeare** (1564)
Venus and the Rain (1984) **Medbh McGuckian** (1950)
Venus Hunters, The (1980) **J.G. Ballard** (1930)
Venus in Sparta (1958) **Louis Auchinloss** (1917)
Venus Observed (1950) **Christopher Fry [Christopher Fry Harris]** (1907)
Venus of Ille, The [*La Vénus d'Ille*] (1837) **Prosper Mérimée** (1803)
Venus Plus X (1960) **Theodore Sturgeon** (1918)
Venus Touch, The (1971) **Maureen Duffy** (1933)
Venus With Pistol (1969) **Gavin Lyall** (1932)
Venusberg (1932) **Anthony Powell** (1905)
Vera (1880) **Oscar Wilde** (1854)
Vera the Medium (1908) **Richard Harding Davis** (1864)
Verandah (1964) **James Pope Hennessy** (1916)
Veranilda [incomplete] (1904) **George Gissing** (1857–1903)
Verbena Camellia Stephanotis (1892) **Sir Walter Besant** (1836)
Verbi-voco-Visual Explorations (1967) **Marshall McLuhan** (1911)
Verbivore (1990) **Christine Brooke-Rose** (1926)
Vermilion Box, The (1916) **E.V. Lucas** (1868) [with C.L. Graves]
Vernacular Republic, The (1976) **Les Murray** (1938)
Vers et prose (1893) **Stéphane Mallarmé** (1842–1898)
Verses (1896) **Ernest Dowson** (1867)
Verses (1916) **Elizabeth Daryush** (1887)
Verses Address'd to the Imitator of Horace (1733) **Lady Mary Wortley Montagu** (1689)
Verses and Translations (1862) **C.S. Calverley** (1831)
Verses by Christina G. Rossetti (1847) **Christina Rossetti** (1830)
Verses for Children (1888) **Mrs J.H. Ewing** (1841)
Verses from Glenarvon (1819) **Lady Caroline Lamb** (1785)
Verses of the Sea (1930) **E.J. Pratt** (1882)
Verses on the Death of Dr Swift, Written by Himself (1739) **Jonathan Swift** (1667)
Verses on the Death of Percy Bysshe Shelley (1822) **Bernard Barton** (1784)
Verses: Sixth Book (1938) **Elizabeth Daryush** (1887)
Version of the Psalms (1714) **Sir John Denham** (1615–69)
Versus (1949) **Ogden Nash** (1902)
Vertical Ladder, The (1969) **William Sansom** (1912)
Very Good, Jeeves (1930) **P.G. Wodehouse** (1881)
Very Heaven (1937) **Richard Aldington** (1892)
Very Heroical Epistle From My Lord All-Pride to Dol-Common, A (1679) **John Wilmot, earl of Rochester** (1647)
Very Hungry Caterpillar, The (1969) **Eric Carle** (1929)
Very Model of a Man, The (1992) **Howard Jacobson** (1942)
Very Private Life, A (1968) **Michael Frayn** (1933)
Very Private War, A (1980) **Jon Cleary** (1917)
Very Successful! (1856) **Edward Bulwer-Lytton** (1803)
Vespers of Palermo, The (1823) **Felicia Dorothea Hemans** (1793)
Vesprie Towers (1916) **Theodore Watts-Dunton** (1832–1914)
Vestal Fire (1927) **Compton Mackenzie** (1883)
Vestiges of the Natural History of Creation (1844) **Robert Chambers** (1802)
Vets in Harness (1976) **James Herriot** (1916)
Vets Might Fly (1976) **James Herriot** (1916)
Via Media of the Anglican Church, The (1877) **J.H. Newman** (1801)
Viaducs de la Seine-et-Oise, Les (1960) **'Marguerite Duras' [Marguerite Donnadieu]** (1914)
Viaduct Murder, The (1925) **Ronald Knox** (1888)

Vialls of the Wrath of God, The (1654) **George Fox** (1624)
Vicar of Bullhampton, The (1870) **Anthony Trollope** (1815)
Vicar of Morwenstow, The (1876) **S. Baring-Gould** (1834)
Vicar of Sorrows, The (1993) **A.N. Wilson** (1950)
Vicar of Wakefield, The (1766) **Oliver Goldsmith** (1728)
Vicar of Wrexhill, The (1837) **Frances Trollope** (1780)
Vicar's Daughter, The (1872) **George MacDonald** (1824)
Vice filial, Le ['Filial Vice'] (1891) **Paul Adam** (1862)
Vice Versa (1882) **'F. Anstey' [Thomas Anstey Guthrie]** (1856)
Vice-Consul, The [*Le Vice-Consul*] (1966) **'Marguerite Duras' [Marguerite Donnadieu]** (1914)
Viceroy of Ouidah, The (1980) **Bruce Chatwin** (1940)
Vicissitudes of Evangeline, The (1905) **Elinor Glyn** (1864)
Vicomte de Bragelonne, The [*The Vicomte de Bragelonne*] (1848–50) **Alexandre Dumas ['père']** (1802)
Victim, The (1714) **Charles Johnson** (1679)
Victim, The (1944) **Saul Bellow** (1915)
Victim of the Aurora, A (1977) **Thomas Keneally** (1935)
Victim, The (1860) **Mrs C.L. Balfour** (1808)
Victims of Duty (1953) **Eugène Ionesco** (1909)
Victims of Society, The (1837) **Marguerite, Countess of Blessington** (1789)
Victoria (1786) **Susanna Rowson** (1762)
Victoria (1898) **Knut Hamsun** (1859)
Victoria (1960) **'Evelyn Anthony' [Evelyn Ward-Thomas]** (1928)
Victoria of England (1936) **Edith Sitwell** (1887)
Victoria R.I. (1964) **Elizabeth Longford** (1906)
Victoria Regia, The (1861) **Adelaide Procter** (1825) (ed.)
Victoria Regina (1937) **Laurence Housman** (1865)
Victoria Victorious (1985) **'Jean Plaidy' [Eleanor Hibbert]** (1906)
Victorian Age in Literature, The (1913) **G.K. Chesterton** (1874)
Victorian Chaise-Longue, The (1953) **Marghanita Laski** (1915)
Victorian Cities (1963) **Asa Briggs** (1921)
Victorian England (1936) **G.M. Young** (1882)
Victorian People (1954) **Asa Briggs** (1921)
Victorian Son, A (1971) **Stuart Cloete** (1897)
Victorian Things (1988) **Asa Briggs** (1921)
Victorian Voices (1980) **Anthony Thwaite** (1930)
Victories (1990) **George V. Higgins** (1939)
Victories of Love, The [*The Angel in the House* iv] (1862) **Coventry Patmore** (1823)
Victories of the Saints (1850) **John Mason Neale** (1818)
Victorious Reigne of King Edward the Third, The (1635) **Thomas May** (1595)
Victors, The (1902) **Robert Barr** (1850)
Victory (1946) **Sir Winston Churchill** (1874)
Victory (1915) **Joseph Conrad** (1857)
Victory Over Japan (1984) **Ellen Gilchrist** (1935)
Videna (1853) **John Abraham Heraud** (1799)
Vie immédiate, La (1932) **'Paul Éluard' [Eugène Grindel]** (1895)
Vie inquiète, La ['The Anxious Life'] (1875) **Paul Bourget** (1852)
Vie, poésies, et pensées de Joseph Delorme ['Life and Poems of Joseph Delorme'] (1829) **Charles-Augustin Sainte-Beuve** (1804)
Vienna (1934) **Sir Stephen Spender** (1909)
Vietnam (1967) **Mary McCarthy** (1912)
View From a Blind I, The (1962) **George Barker** (1913)
View From Coyoba, The (1985) **Peter Abrahams** (1919)
View From the Bridge, A (1955) **Arthur Miller** (1915)
View of Society and Manners in France, Switzerland, and Germany, A (1779) **John Moore** (1729)
View of Society and Manners in Italy, A (1781) **John Moore** (1729)
View of the Causes and Progress of the French Revolution, A (1795) **John Moore** (1729)
View of the English Stage 1944–63, A (1975) **Kenneth Tynan** (1927)
View of the English Stage, A (1818) **William Hazlitt** (1778)
View of the Evidences of Christianity, A (1794) **William Paley** (1743)
View of the State of Europe During the Middle Ages (1818) **Henry Hallam** (1777)
Views A-foot (1846) **Bayard Taylor** (1825)
Views and Reviews (1890) **W.E. Henley** (1849)
Views and Reviews (1902) **W.E. Henley** (1849)
Views and Reviews (1908) **Henry James** (1843)
Views From a Lake (1968) **Philip Toynbee** (1916)
Vigil of Faith, The (1842) **Charles Fenno Hoffman** (1806)
Vigils (1935) **Siegfried Sassoon** (1886)
Vignettes (1896) **Hubert Crackanthorpe** (1870–96)
Vignettes in Rhyme (1873) **Austin Dobson** (1840)
Vignettes: In Verse (1818) **Mary Matilda Betham** (1776)
Viking's Dawn (1955) **Henry Treece** (1911)
Vikings of the Baltic, The (1875) **Sir George Webbe Dasent** (1817)
Vile Bodies (1930) **Evelyn Waugh** (1903)
Villa Golitsyn, The (1981) **Piers Paul Read** (1941)
Villa in Summer, A (1954) **Penelope Mortimer** (1918)
Villa Rubein [by 'John Sinjohn'] (1900) **John Galsworthy** (1867)
Village Affair, A (1989) **Joanna Trollope** (1943)
Village Book, The (1930) **Henry Williamson** (1895)
Village by the Sea, The (1982) **Anita Desai** (1937)
Village Commune, A (1881) **'Ouida' [Marie Louise de la Ramée]** (1839)
Village Dialogues (1810) **Rowland Hill** (1744)

Village in the Jungle, The (1913) **Leonard Woolf** (1880)
Village Minstrel, The (1821) **John Clare** (1793)
Village of Mariendorpt, The (1821) **Anna Maria Porter** (1780)
Village on the Cliff, The (1867) **Lady Anne Ritchie** (1837)
Village Patriarch, The (1829) **Ebenezer Elliott** (1781)
Village Politics (1793) **Hannah More** (1745)
Village School (1955) **'Miss Read' [Dora Jessie Saint]** (1913)
Village, The (1939) **Mulk Raj Anand** (1905)
Village, The (1910) **Ivan Bunin** (1870)
Village, The (1783) **George Crabbe** (1754)
Village, The (1994) **David Mamet** (1947)
Village, The (1989) **Iain Crichton Smith [Iain Mac a'Ghobhainn]** (1928)
Village Virtues (1796) **M.G. Lewis** (1775)
Villette (1853) **Charlotte Brontë** (1816)
Vindication of Natural Diet, A (1813) **P.B. Shelley** (1792)
Vindication of Natural Society, A (1756) **Edmund Burke** (1729)
Vindication of Providence, A (1728) **Edward Young** (1683)
Vindication of Some Passages in the History of the Decline and Fall of the Roman Empire, A (1779) **Edward Gibbon** (1737)
Vindication of the Appendix to the Poems, called Rowley's, A (1782) **Thomas Tyrwhitt** (1730)
Vindication of the Book Called Some Gospel-Truths Opened, A (1657) **John Bunyan** (1628)
Vindication of the Doctrine of the Holy and Ever Blessed Trinity, A (1690) **William Sherlock** (1641?)
Vindication of the Gospel Doctrine of Justifying Faith, A (1746) **Jonathan Edwards** (1703)
Vindication of the Rights of Brutes, A (1792) **Thomas Taylor** (1758)
Vindication of the Rights of Men, A (1790) **Mary Wollstonecraft** (1759)
Vindication of the Rights of Women, A (1792) **Mary Wollstonecraft** (1759)
Vindiciae Ecclesiae Anglicanae (1826) **Robert Southey** (1774)
Vinedresser, The (1899) **T. Sturge Moore** (1870)
Vinegar Puss (1975) **S.J. Perelman** (1904)
Vinegar Tom (1976) **Caryl Churchill** (1938)
Vineland (1990) **Thomas Pynchon** (1937)
Vineyard Above the Sea, The (2000) **Charles Tomlinson** (1927)
Vinland (1992) **George Mackay Brown** (1921)
Vintage Murder (1937) **Ngaio Marsh** (1899)
Vintage, The (1898) **E.F. Benson** (1867)
Violent Bear It Away, The (1960) **Flannery O'Connor** (1925)
Violenta [from Boccaccio] (1704) **Mary Pix** (1666) (tr.)
Violet Fairy Book, The (1901) **Andrew Lang** (1844) (ed.)
Violins of Saint-Jacques, The (1953) **Patrick Leigh Fermor** (1915)
Viper of Milan, The (1906) **'Marjorie Bowen' [Gabrielle Margaret Vere Campbell]** (1886)
Virgidemiarum, Sixe Bookes (1597) **Joseph Hall** (1574)
Virgil's Aeneis: The Third, Fourth, Fifth and Sixth Books (1659) **James Harrington** (1611) (tr.)
Virgil's Georgicks (1628) **Thomas May** (1595) (tr.)
Virgin and the Gypsy, The (1930) **D.H. Lawrence** (1885)
Virgin in the Garden, The (1978) **A.S. Byatt** (1936)
Virgin in the Ice, The (1982) **'Ellis Peters' [Edith Mary Pargeter]** (1913)
Virgin Martir, The (1622) **Philip Massinger** (1583) [with John Dekker]
Virgin of the Sun, The (1922) **Sir H. Rider Haggard** (1856)
Virgin Prophetesse. The (1701) **Elkanah Settle** (1648)
Virgin Soil (1877) **Ivan Turgenev** (1818)
Virgin Soldiers, The (1966) **Leslie Thomas** (1931)
Virgin Spain (1926) **Waldo Frank** (1889)
Virgin Territory (1984) **Sara Maitland** (1950)
Virgin Unmask'd, The (1709) **Bernard Mandeville** (1670)
Virginia Comedians, The (1854) **John Cooke** (1830)
Virginians, The (1858) **W.M. Thackeray** (1811)
Virginibus Puerisque (1881) **Robert Louis Stevenson** (1850)
Virginius (1820) **James Sheridan Knowles** (1784)
Virginius and Virginia (1792) **Susannah Gunning** (1740)
Virtual Light (1993) **William Gibson** (1948)
Virtue of the Mass, The (1500?) **John Lydgate** (1370?-1449)
Virtuoso, The (1676) **Thomas Shadwell** (1642?)
Virtuous Knight, The (1931) **Robert E. Sherwood** (1896)
Virtuous Wife, The (1679) **Thomas d'Urfey** (1653)
Visible and Invisible (1923) **E.F. Benson** (1867)
Visible People (1977) **Stephen Gray** (1941)
Vision, The (1706) **Daniel Defoe** (1660)
Vision, The (1737) **Stephen Duck** (1705)
Vision, A [rev. 1937] (1925) **W.B. Yeats** (1865)
Vision and Design (1920) **Roger Fry** (1866)
Vision and Rhetoric (1959) **G.S. Fraser** (1915)
Vision of Battlements, A (1965) **'Anthony Burgess' [John Anthony Burgess Wilson]** (1917)
Vision of Beasts and Gods, A (1954) **George Barker** (1913)
Vision of Cathkin Braes, The (1952) **Edwin Morgan** (1920)
Vision of Delight, The (1617) **Ben Jonson** (1572)
Vision of Don Roderick, The (1811) **Sir Walter Scott** (1771)
Vision of Echard, The (1878) **John Greenleaf Whittier** (1807)
Vision of Judgement, A (1821) **Robert Southey** (1774)
Vision of Judgment, The (1822) **George Gordon, Lord Byron** (1788)
Vision of Pierce Plowman, The [*Piers Plowman*; first printing of the the B-text] (1550) **William Langland** (*c.* 1330)

Vision of Sir Launfal, The (1848) **James Russell Lowell** (1819)
Vision of the Great Rememberer, The (1974) **Allen Ginsberg** (1926)
Vision of William Concerning Piers Plowman, The (1867) **W.W. Skeat** (1835) (ed.)
Vision; or, Hell, Purgatory and Paradise of Dante, The (1814) **Henry Cary** (1772) (tr.)
Vision Tree, The (1982) **Phyllis Webb** (1921)
Visionary Company, The (1962) **Harold Bloom** (1930)
Visions and Beliefs in the West of Ireland (1920) **Lady Gregory** (1852) [with two essays and notes by W.B. Yeats]
Visions of England, The (1881) **Francis Turner Palgrave** (1824)
Visions of Gerard (1963) **Jack Kerouac** (1922)
Visions of the Daughters of Albion (1793) **William Blake** (1757)
Visit, The (1970) **Ian Hamilton** (1938)
Visit to India, China, and Japan, A (1855) **Bayard Taylor** (1825)
Visitants (1979) **Randolph Stow** (1935)
Visitation, The (1983) **Michèle Roberts** (1949)
Visitations (1957) **Louis MacNeice** (1907)
Visiting Cards (1990) **Francis King** (1923)
Visiting Mrs Nabokov (1993) **Martin Amis** (1949)
Visiting the Caves (1936) **William Plomer** (1903)
Visitors (1997) **Anita Brookner** (1928)
Visits and Sketches at Home and Abroad (1834) **Anna Jameson** (1794)
Visits of Elizabeth, The (1900) **Elinor Glyn** (1864)
Visits to Monasteries in the Levant (1849) **Robert Curzon** (1810)
Vita (1983) **Victoria Glendinning** (1937)
Vita Nuova (1290–4) **Dante Alighieri** (1265)
Vital Lies (1912) **'Vernon Lee' [Violet Paget]** (1856)
Vital Message, The (1919) **A. Conan Doyle** (1859)
Vittoria (1867) **George Meredith** (1828)
Vittorio (1999) **Anne Rice** (1941)
ViVa (1931) **E.E. Cummings** (1894)
Vivat! Vivat Regina! (1970) **Robert Bolt** (1924)
Vivero Letter, The (1968) **Desmond Bagley** (1923)
Vivia Perpetua (1841) **Sarah Fuller Adams** (1805)
Vivian Grey [vols. i, ii] (1826) **Benjamin Disraeli** (1804)
Vivian Grey [vols. iii, iv, v] (1827) **Benjamin Disraeli** (1804)
Vivian Romance, The (1870) **Mortimer Collins** (1827)
Vivid Air, The (1980) **Ralph Gustafson** (1909)
Vivisector, The (1970) **Patrick White** (1912)
Vixen (1879) **M.E. Braddon** (1835)
V-Letter (1944) **Karl Shapiro** (1913)
Voces Populi [1st ser.] (1890) **'F. Anstey' [Thomas Anstey Guthrie]** (1856)
Voice at the Back Door, The (1956) **Elizabeth Spencer** (1921)
Voice From the Attic, A (1960) **Robertson Davies** (1913)
Voice From the Dark, A (1925) **Eden Phillpotts** (1862)
Voice From the Factories, A (1836) **Caroline Norton** (1808)
Voice of the City, The (1908) **'O. Henry' [William Sydney Porter]** (1862)
Voice of the Heart (1983) **Barbara Taylor Bradford** (1933)
Voice of the People, The (1900) **Ellen Glasgow** (1874)
Voice of the Thunder, The (1993) **Sir Laurens van der Post** (1906)
Voice-Over (1988) **Norman MacCaig** (1910)
Voices (1990) **C.K. Stead** (1932)
Voices in an Empty Room (1984) **Francis King** (1923)
Voices in the City (1965) **Anita Desai** (1937)
Voices in ???? (1980) **Hugh MacLennard** (1907)
Voices of a Summer Day (1965) **Irwin Shaw** (1913)
Voices of Freedom (1846) **John Greenleaf Whittier** (1807)
Voices of Silence, The [*Les Voix du silence*] (1951) **André Malraux** (1901)
Voices of the Living and the Dead (1974) **Linton Kwesi Johnson** (1952)
Voices of the Night (1839) **Henry Wadsworth Longfellow** (1807)
Voices of the Old Sea (1984) **Norman Lewis** (1918)
Voix intérieures, Les ['Inner Voices'] (1837) **Victor Hugo** (1802)
Volcano Lover, The (1992) **Susan Sontag** (1933)
Volcanoes Above Us, The (1957) **Norman Lewis** (1918)
Volpone (1606) **Ben Jonson** (1572)
Volsung Saga: The Story of the Volsungs and Niblungs [with E. Magnússon] (1870) **William Morris** (1834) (tr.)
Voltaire (1872) **John Morley** (1838)
Voltaire in Love (1957) **Nancy Mitford** (1904)
Volumes in Folio (1889) **Richard le Gallienne** (1866)
Voluntary Exile, The (1795) **Eliza Parsons** (1748)
Volunteers (1975) **Brian Friel** (1929)
Volunteers, The (1692) **Thomas Shadwell** (1642?-92)
Volupté ['Voluptuousness'] (1834) **Charles-Augustin Sainte-Beuve** (1804)
Vortex, The (1924) **Noel Coward** (1899)
Vortex (1977) **Jon Cleary** (1917)
Vortex Blaster, The (1960) **E.E.'Doc' Smith** (1890)
Vortext, The [*La Vorágine*] (1924) **José Eustacio Rivera** (1889)
Vortigern [supposedly written by Shakespeare] (1799) **William-Henry Ireland** (1777)
Voss (1957) **Patrick White** (1912)
Votive Tablets (1931) **Edmund Blunden** (1896)
Vow of the Peacock, and Other Poems, The [as 'L.E.L.'] (1835) **Letitia Elizabeth Landon** (1802)
Vox (1992) **Nicholson Baker** (1957)
Vox Stellarum (1700) **'Old Moore' [Francis Moore]** (1657)
Voyage, The (1924) **John Middleton Murry** (1889)
Voyage, The (1940) **Charles Morgan** (1894)
Voyage au Congo (1927) **André Gide** (1869)
Voyage Home, The (1930) **Storm Jameson** (1897)
Voyage Home, The (1964) **Richard Church** (1893)

Voyage in the Dark (1934) **'Jean Rhys' [Ella Gwendolyn Rees Williams]** (1890)
Voyage of Captain Popanilla, The (1828) **Benjamin Disraeli** (1804)
Voyage of Columbus, The (1810) **Samuel Rogers** (1763)
Voyage of Discovery, A (1892) **Charles Hamilton Aïdé** (1826)
Voyage of Ithobal, The (1901) **Sir Edwin Arnold** (1832)
Voyage of Magellan, The (1948) **Laurie Lee** (1914)
Voyage of the Dawn Treader, The (1952) **C.S. Lewis** (1898)
Voyage of the 'Discovery', The (1905) **Robert Falcon Scott** (1868)
Voyage Out, The (1915) **Virginia Woolf** (1882)
Voyage Round My Father, A (1963) **John Mortimer** (1923)
Voyage, The (1946) **Edwin Muir** (1887)
Voyage to Arcturus, A (1920) **David Lindsay** (1876)
Voyage to New Holland, A (1703) **William Dampier** (1652)
Voyage to Pagany, A (1928) **William Carlos Williams** (1883)
Voyage to Purilia, A (1930) **Elmer Rice** (1892)
Voyages (1983) **George Mackay Brown** (1921)
Voyages and Descriptions (1699) **William Dampier** (1652)
Voyages and Travels in the Years 1809, 1810 and 1811 (1812) **John Galt** (1779)
Voyages of Dr Dolittle, The (1922) **Hugh Lofting** (1886)
Voyageur, The (1905) **William Henry Drummond** (1854)
Voyeur, The [L'uomo che guarda] (1985) **'Alberto Moravia' [Alberto Pincherle]** (1907)
Voysey Inheritance, The (1905) **Harley Granville-Barker** (1877)
Vulgar Streak, The (1941) **Wyndham Lewis** (1882)

W

Wages of Sin, The (1891) **'Lucas Malet' [Mary St Leger Harrison]** (1852)
Waggoner, The (1920) **Edmund Blunden** (1896)
Waggoner, The (1819) **William Wordsworth** (1770)
Waif of the River (1952) **Jeffery Farnol** (1878)
Waif's Progress, A (1905) **Rhoda Broughton** (1840)
Waifs and Strays (1917) **O. Henry' [William Sydney Porter]** (1862–1910)
Wait for the End (1863) **Mark Lemon** (1809)
Wait Till I Tell You (1997) **Candia McWilliam** (1955)
Waiting for Cordelia (1977) **Herbert Gold** (1924)
Waiting for Godot [pub. in French 1952] (1955) **Samuel Beckett** (1906)
Waiting for Lefty (1935) **Clifford Odets** (1906)
Waiting for the Barbarians (1980) **J.M. Coetzee** (1940)
Waiting for the Boat [Inc. *Joe's Ark, Blue Remembered Hills*, and *Cream in My Coffee*] (1984) **Dennis Potter** (1935)
Waiting for the Party [biography of Frances Hodgson Burnett] (1974) **Ann Thwaite** (1932)
Waiting for the Verdict (1868) **Rebecca Harding Davis** (1831)
Waiting Game, The (1997) **Bernice Rubens** (1923)
Waiting in the Wings (1960) **Noel Coward** (1899)
Waiting Room, The (1967) **Wilson Harris** (1921)
Wake Up, Jonathan (1921) **Elmer Rice** (1892) [with Hatcher Hughes]
Wakefield's Course (1941) **Mazo de la Roche** (1879)
Waking, The (1953) **Theodore Roethke** (1908)
Walden (1854) **Henry David Thoreau** (1817)
Waldenses, The (1842) **Aubrey Thomas de Vere** (1814)
Waldo Trench and Others (1908) **Henry Blake Fuller** (1857)
Walk Along the Shore, A (1977) **Kenneth White** (1936)
Walk on the Wild Side, A (1956) **Nelson Algren** (1909)
Walk With a White Bushman, A (1986) **Sir Laurens van der Post** (1906)
Walker London (1907) **[Sir] J.M. Barrie** (1860)
Walking (1984) **Edward Albee** (1928)
Walking a Line (1994) **Tom Paulin** (1949)
Walking in the Shade (1997) **Doris Lessing** (1919
Walking Naked (1981) **Nina Bawden** (1925)
Walking on Glass (1985) **Iain Banks** (1954)
Walking Possession (1994) **Ian Hamilton** (1938)
Walking Shadow, The (1979) **Brian M. Stableford** (1948)
Walking to Sleep (1969) **Richard Wilbur** (1921)
Walking Westwards (1978) **C.K. Stead** (1932)
Walking With My Mistress in Deauville (1992) **Ronald Frame** (1953)
Walking Wounded (1965) **Vernon Scannell** (1922)
Walking Wounded (1989) **William McIlvanney** (1936)
Walks in London (1878) **Augustus Hare** (1834)
Walks in Rome (1871) **Augustus Hare** (1834)
Walks in Rome (1987) **F.T. Prince** (1912)
Wall, The (1950) **John Hersey** (1914)
Wall, The [Le Mur] (1939) **Jean-Paul Sartre** (1905)
Wall, The (1990) **Peter Vansittart** (1920)
Wall of the Plague, The (1984) **André Brink** (1935)
Wallace, The (1960) **Sydney Goodsir Smith** (1915)
Wallace's Invocation to Bruce (1819) **Felicia Dorothea Hemans** (1793)
Wallet of Kai Lung, The (1900) **Ernest Bramah** (1868)
Walls Do Not Fall, The (1944) **Hilda Doolittle** (1886)
Walrus Hunters, The (1893) **R.M. Ballantyne** (1825)
Walsh (1974) **Sharon Pollock** (1936)
Walsh Colville (1797) **Anna Maria Porter** (1780)
Walsingham (1797) **Mary Robinson** (1758)
Walt Whitman (1893) **John Addington Symonds** (1840)
Walter Pater (1906) **A.C. Benson** (1862)
Walter Pater (1913) **Edward Thomas** (1878)
Walter Savage Landor (1869) **John Forster** (1812)
Walter's Word (1875) **James Payn** (1830)

Waltz (1813) **George Gordon, Lord Byron** (1788)
Waltz Invention, The (1966) **Vladimir Nabokov** (1899)
Waltz of the Toreadors [*La Valse des toréadors*] (1952) **Jean Anouilh** (1910)
Wampeters, Foma, and Granfalloons (1974) **Kurt Vonnegut** (1922)
Wand and Quadrant (1953) **Christopher Logue** (1926)
Wanda (1883) **'Ouida' [Marie Louise de la Ramée-rsqb;** (1839)
Wanderer in Florence, A (1912) **E.V. Lucas** (1868)
Wanderer in Holland, A (1905) **E.V. Lucas** (1868)
Wanderer in London, A (1906) **E.V. Lucas** (1868)
Wanderer in Paris, A (1909) **E.V. Lucas** (1868)
Wanderer in Venice, A (1914) **E.V. Lucas** (1868)
Wanderer, The (1729) **Richard Savage** (1697?)
Wanderer, The [as 'Owen Meredith'] (1857) **Edward Robert Bulwer Lytton** (1831)
Wanderer, The (1871) **William Ellery Channing** (1780)
Wanderer, The (1964) **Fritz Leiber** (1910)
Wanderer, The (1814) **Frances Burney** (1752)
Wanderer's Necklace, The (1914) **Sir H. Rider Haggard** (1856)
Wandering Heath (1895) **Sir A.T. Quiller-Couch** (1863)
Wandering Jew, The (1820) **John Galt** (1779)
Wandering Moon, The (1950) **James Reeves** (1909)
Wandering Scholars, The [rev. 1932, 1934] (1927) **Helen Waddell** (1889)
Wanderings in Spain [*Voyage en Espagne*] (1845) **Théophile Gautier** (1811)
Wanderings in Spain (1873) **Augustus Hare** (1834)
Wanderings of a Spiritualist, The (1921) **A. Conan Doyle** (1859)
Wanderings of Oisin, The (1889) **W.B. Yeats** (1865)
Wanderings of Warwick, The (1794) **Charlotte Smith** (1749)
Wanting Seed, The (1962) **'Anthony Burgess' [John Anthony Burgess Wilson]** (1917)
Wapshot Chronicle, The (1957) **John Cheever** (1912)
Wapshot Scandal, The (1964) **John Cheever** (1912)
War All the Time (1985) **Charles Bukowski** (1920)
War and Peace (1863–9) **Leo Tolstoy** (1828)
War and Remembrance (1978) **Herman Wouk** (1915)
War and the Woman (1912) **Max Pemberton** (1863)
War Between the Tates, The (1974) **Alison Lurie** (1926)
War Crimes (1979) **Peter Carey** (1943)
War Fever (1990) **J.G. Ballard** (1930)
War Horse, The (1975) **Eavan Boland** (1944)
War in Heaven (1930) **Charles Williams** (1886)
War in South Africa, The (1902) **A. Conan Doyle** (1859)
War in the Air, The (1908) **H.G. Wells** (1866)
War is Kind (1899) **Stephen Crane** (1871)
War Music (1977) **Christopher Logue** (1926)
War of 1870, The (1871) **Lord Acton** (1834)
War of Don Emmanuel's Nether Parts, The (1990) **Louis de Bernières** (1954)
War of the Classes (1905) **'Jack London' [John Griffith Chaney]** (1876)
War of the End of the World, The [*La guerra del fin del mundo*] (1981) **Mario Vargas Llosa** (1936)
War of the Wenuses, The (1898) **E.V. Lucas** (1868) [with C.L. Graves]
War of the Worlds, The (1898) **H.G. Wells** (1866)
War Paint (1993) **Tom Wakefield** (1935)
War Plays, The (1985) **Edward Bond** (1934)
War Poems (1919) **Siegfried Sassoon** (1886)
War Stories (1987) **Howard Nemerov** (1920)
War That Will End War, The (1914) **H.G. Wells** (1866)
War's Embers (1919) **Ivor Gurney** (1890)
Ward of Chancery, A (1894) **Mrs A.H. Alexander** (1825)
Warden, The (1855) **Anthony Trollope** (1815)
Warden's Niece, The (1957) **Gillian Avery** (1926)
Wards of the State (1992) **Robert Adamson** (1943)
Warleigh (1834) **Anna Eliza Bray** (1790)
Warlock (1981) **Jim Harrison** (1937)
Warning Bell, The (1984) **Lynne Reid Banks** (1929)
Warning to the Curious, A (1925) **M.R. James** (1862)
Warrior Scarlet (1958) **Rosemary Sutcliff** (1920)
Warrior's Career (1972) **Alan Brownjohn** (1931)
Warrior's Return, The (1808) **Amelia Opie** (1769)
Wars I Have Seen (1945) **Gertrude Stein** (1874)
Wars, The (1977) **Timothy Findley** (1930)
Warsaw Document, The (1970) **'Adam Hall' [Elleston Trevor]** (1920)
Wartime and Aftermath (1993) **Bernard Bergonzi** (1929)
Washington, DC (1967) **Gore Vidal** (1925)
Washington Square (1881) **Henry James** (1843)
Wasp Factory, The (1984) **Iain Banks** (1954)
Wasps, The (422 BC) **Aristophanes** (*c.* 445 BC)
Waste (1907) **Harley Granville-Barker** (1877)
Waste (1924) **Robert Herrick** (1868)
Waste Land, The (1923) **T.S. Eliot** (1888)
Waste Land and Other Poems, The (1940) **T.S. Eliot** (1888)
Wat Tyler (1817) **Robert Southey** (1774)
Wat Tyler (1841) **Pierce Egan the Younger** (1814)
Watch and Ward (1878) **Henry James** (1843)
Watch House, The (1977) **Robert Westall** (1929)
Watch in the Night (1996) **A.N. Wilson** (1950)
Watch It Come Down (1975) **John Osborne** (1929)
Watch on the Rhine (1941) **Lillian Hellman** (1907)
Watch That Ends the Night, The (1959) **Hugh MacLennan** (1907)
Watch That Wouldn't Go, The (1926) **Louis Stone** (1871)
Watch Tower, The (1966) **Elizabeth Harrower** (1928)
Watcher, The (1894) **J.S. le Fanu** (1814–73)
Watcher by the Threshold, The (1902) **John Buchan** (1875)
Watcher in the Shadows (1960) **Geoffrey Household** (1900)
Watcher on the Cast-Iron Balcony, The (1963) **Hal Porter** (1911)
Watchers, The (1899) **A.E.W. Mason** (1865)

Watchers (1987) **Dean Koontz** (1945)
Watchers of the Sky, The (1922) **Alfred Noyes** (1880)
Watchers of the Trails, The (1904) **Sir Charles G.D. Roberts** (1860)
Watchers on the Shore, The (1966) **Stan Barstow** (1928)
Watchfires (1982) **Louis Auchinloss** (1917)
Watching For Dolphins (1983) **David Constantine** (1944)
Watching Me, Watching You (1981) **Fay Weldon** (1931)
Watching Mrs Gordon (1985) **Ronald Frame** (1953)
Watching the Perseids (1990) **Peter Scupham** (1933)
Watchman, The (1796) **S.T. Coleridge** (1772)
Watchman, The (1916) **L.M. Montgomery** (1874)
Watchman's Flute, The (1978) **John Heath-Stubbs** (1918)
Watchwords (1969) **Roger McGough** (1937)
Water Gipsies, The (1930) **A.P. Herbert** (1890)
Water of Life, The (1867) **Charles Kingsley** (1819)
Water on the Brain (1933) **Compton Mackenzie** (1883)
Water Over Stone (1980) **Frances Horovitz** (1938)
Water Pourer, The (1972) **Robert Coover** (1932)
Water, Rock and Sand (1962) **Peter Levi** (1931)
Water Street (1962) **James Merrill** (1926)
Water Under the Earth (1972) **Robert Bly** (1926)
Water Witch, The (1830) **James Fenimore Cooper** (1789)
Water-Babies, The (1863) **Charles Kingsley** (1819)
Water-Method Man, The (1972) **John Irving** (1942)
Watercress Girl, The (1959) **H.E. Bates** (1905)
Waterfall, The (1969) **Margaret Drabble** (1939)
Waterland (1983) **Graham Swift** (1949)
Waterloo Bridge (1930) **Robert E. Sherwood** (1896)
Waterman, The (1774) **Charles Dibdin** (1745)
Watermarks (1992) **Joseph Brodsky** (1940)
Waters of Babylon, The (1957) **John Arden** (1930)
Waters of Edera, The (1900) **'Ouida' [Marie Louise de la Ramée]** (1839)
Waters of Kronos, The (1960) **Conrad Richter** (1890)
Waters of Thirst, The (1993) **Adam Mars-Jones** (1954)
Watership Down (1972) **Richard Adams** (1920)
Waterslain (1986) **Kevin Crossley-Holland** (1941)
Watersprings (1913) **A.C. Benson** (1862)
Waterway (1938) **Eleanor Dark** (1901)
Watlington Hill (1812) **Mary Russell Mitford** (1787)
Watson's Apology (1984) **Beryl Bainbridge** (1934)
Watson's Choice (1955) **Gladys Mitchell** (1901)
Watsons, The [in J.E. Austen-Leigh's *Memoir*; written *c.* 1804] (1871) **Jane Austen** (1775–1817)
Watt (1953) **Samuel Beckett** (1906)
Waugh in Abyssinia (1936) **Evelyn Waugh** (1903)
Wave, A (1984) **John Ashbery** (1927)
Waverley (1814) **Sir Walter Scott** (1771)
Waves, The (1931) **Virginia Woolf** (1882)
Waving at Trains (1982) **Roger McGough** (1937)
Way Home, The (1925) **'Henry Handel Richardson' [Ethel Florence Robertson]** (1870)
Way in the World, A (1994) **V.S. Naipaul** (1932)
Way of a Maid, The (1895) **Katharine Tynan** (1861)
Way of a World, The (1969) **Charles Tomlinson** (1927)
Way of All Flesh, The (1903) **Samuel Butler** (1835–1902)
Way of an Eagle, The (1911) **Ethel M. Dell** (1881)
Way of Ecben, The (1929) **James Branch Cabell** (1879)
Way of Happiness, The (1670) **Joseph Glanvill** (1636)
Way of Looking, A (1955) **Elizabeth Jennings** (1926)
Way of Marriage, The (1896) **Violet Hunt** (1866)
Way of the Cat, The (1992) **D.J. Enright** (1920)
Way of the Scarlet Pimpernel, The (1933) **Baroness Orczy** (1865)
Way of the Spirit, The (1906) **Sir H. Rider Haggard** (1856)
Way of the World, The (1700) **William Congreve** (1670)
Way Out in the Centre (1981) **Dannie Abse** (1923)
Way Some People Live, The (1943) **John Cheever** (1912)
Way Station (1963) **Clifford D. Simak** (1904)
Way Things Are, The (1927) **'E.M. Delafield' [E.E.M. de la Pasture]** (1890)
Way to Blessedness, The (1632) **Phineas Fletcher** (1582)
Way to Bliss, The (1658) **Elias Ashmole** (1617)
Way to Divine Knowledge, The (1752) **William Law** (1686)
Way to Sattin Shore, The (1983) **Philippa Pearce** (1920)
Way Upstream (1982) **Alan Ayckbourn** (1939)
Way We Live Now, The (1875) **Anthony Trollope** (1815)
Way West, The (1949) **A.B. Guthrie** (1901)
Way You Tell Them, The (1990) **Alan Brownjohn** (1931)
Waynflete (1893) **C[hristabel] R[ose] Coleridge** (1843)
Ways and Means (1788) **George Colman the Younger** (1762)
Ways of Escape (1980) **Graham Greene** (1904)
Ways of Life, The (1897) **Margaret Oliphant** (1828)
Ways of Seeing (1972) **John Berger** (1926)
Ways of the Hour, The (1850) **James Fenimore Cooper** (1789)
Ways of White Folk, The (1934) **Langston Hughes** (1902)
Wayside Courtships (1897) **Hamlin Garland** (1860)
Wayward Bus, The (1947) **John Steinbeck** (1902)
Wayzgoose, The (1928) **Roy Campbell** (1901)
We and Our Neighbors (1875) **Harriet Beecher Stowe** (1811)
We Are For the Dark (1951) **Elizabeth Jane Howard** (1923) [with Robert Aickman]
We Are Still Married (1989) **Garrison Keillor** (1942)
We Are the Living (1933) **Erskine Caldwell** (1903)
We Bombed in New Haven (1968) **Joseph Heller** (1923)
'We Can't Afford It!' (1835) **'Isaac Tomkins, Gent.' [Henry, Lord Brougham]** (1778)

We Didn't Mean to Go to Sea (1937) **Arthur Ransome** (1884)
We Dream of Honour (1988) **John Berryman** (1914–72)
We Europeans (1935) **Julian Huxley** (1887)
We Have Always Lived in the Castle (1962) **Shirley Jackson** (1919)
We Have Come to a Country (1935) **Lettice Cooper** (1897)
We Might See Sights! (1968) **Julia O'Faolain** (1932)
We Moderns [as 'Edward Moore'] (1918) **Edwin Muir** (1887)
We of the Never-Never (1908) **Jeannie Gunn** (1870)
We, the Living (1936) **Ayn Rand** (1905)
We, the People (1933) **Elmer Rice** (1892)
We Think the World of You (1960) **J.R. Ackerley** (1896)
We Who Are about To . . . (1977) **Joanna Russ** (1937)
Weaker Vessel, The (1913) **E.F. Benson** (1867)
Weaker Vessel, The (1888) **David Christie Murray** (1847)
Weald of Youth, The (1942) **Siegfried Sassoon** (1886)
Weapon Makers, The (1956) **A.E. van Voght** (1912)
Weapon Shops of Ishar, The (1951) **A.E. van Voght** (1912)
Weapons of Happiness (1976) **Howard Brenton** (1942)
Weary Blues, The (1926) **Langston Hughes** (1902)
Weather and Season (1963) **Michael Hamburger** (1924)
Weather in Africa, The (1980) **Martha Gellhorn** (1908)
Weather in the Streets, The (1936) **Rosamond Lehmann** (1903)
Weather Shelter, The (1969) **Erskine Caldwell** (1903)
Weatherboard Cathedral, The (1969) **Les Murray** (1938)
Weathermonger, The (1968) **Peter Dickinson** (1927)
Weavers and Weft (1877) **M.E. Braddon** (1835)
Weaveworld (1987) **Clive Barker** (1952)
Web and the Rock, The (1939) **Thomas Wolfe** (1900–38)
Web of Life, The (1900) **Robert Herrick** (1868)
Wedding, The (1629) **James Shirley** (1596)
Wedding, The (2000) **Danielle Steel** (1947)
Wedding Day (1930) **Kay Boyle** (1903)
Wedding Group, The (1968) **Elizabeth Taylor** (1912)
Wedding of Cousins, A (1988) **Emma Tennant** (1937)
Wedding Party, The (1965) **H.E. Bates** (1905)
Wedding-Day, The (1743) **Henry Fielding** (1707)
Weddings at Nether Powers, The (1979) **Peter Redgrove** (1932)
Wedge, The (1944) **William Carlos Williams** (1883)
Wee Wifie (1869) **Rosa Nouchette Carey** (1840)
Wee Willie Winkie (1888) **Rudyard Kipling** (1865)
Weeds of Witchery (1837) **Thomas Haynes Bayly** (1797)
Week on the Concord and Merrimack Rivers, A (1849) **Henry David Thoreau** (1817)
Week, The [*La Semaine*] (1578) **Guillaume de Salluste Du Bartas** (1544)
Weekend with Claude, A (1967) **Beryl Bainbridge** (1934)
Weep Before God (1961) **John Wain** (1925)
Weighed and Wanting (1882) **George MacDonald** (1824)
Weir of Hermiston [unfinished] (1896) **Robert Louis Stevenson** (1850–94)
Weird Stories (1884) **Mrs J.H. Riddell** (1832)
Weirdstone of Brisingamen, The (1960) **Alan Garner** (1934)
Welch Harper, The (1796) **James Sheridan Knowles** (1784)
Welchman's Hose (1925) **Robert Graves** (1895)
Welcome to Hard Times [UK: *Bad Man From Bodie*] (1960) **E.L. Doctorow** (1931)
Welcome to Our City (1923) **Thomas Wolfe** (1900)
Welcome to the City (1941) **Irwin Shaw** (1913)
Welcome to the Monkey House (1968) **Kurt Vonnegut** (1922)
Welcoming Disaster (1974) **Jay Macpherson** (1931)
Well, The (1958) **Sinclair Ross** (1908)
Well, The (1986) **Elizabeth Jolley** (1923)
Well and the Shallows, The (1935) **G.K. Chesterton** (1874)
Well at the World's End, The (1896) **William Morris** (1834)
Well Dressed Explorer, The (1962) **Thea Astley** (1925)
Well of Loneliness, The (1928) **Radclyffe Hall** (1880)
Well of the Saints, The (1905) **J.M. Synge** (1871)
Well-Beloved, The (1897) **Thomas Hardy** (1840)
Well-Meaning Woman, A (1896) **Clo Graves** (1863)
Well-Tempered Critic, The (1963) **Northrop Frye** (1912)
Well-Tempered Critic, The (1981) **Robertson Davies** (1913)
Well-Wishers, The (1974) **Edward Lucie-Smith** (1933)
Well-Wrought Urn, The (1947) **Cleanth Brooks** (1906)
Wellfields, The (1880) **Jessie Fothergill** (1851)
Wellfleet Whale, The (1983) **Stanley J. Kunitz** (1905)
Wellington Letter (1980) **Lauris Edmond** (1924)
Wellington's Army (1912) **Sir Charles Oman** (1860)
Wells Brothers (1911) **Andy Adams** (1859)
Welsh Childhood, A (1990) **'Alice Thomas Ellis' [Anna Margaret Haycraft]** (1932)
Welsh Melodies (1822) **Felicia Dorothea Hemans** (1793)
Wench is Dead, The (1989) **Colin Dexter** (1930)
Wept of Wish-ton-Wish, The (1829) **James Fenimore Cooper** (1789)
Werewolf Trace, The (1977) **John Gardner** (1926)
Werewolves of London, The (1990) **Brian M. Stableford** (1948)
Werner (1823) **George Gordon, Lord Byron** (1788)
Wessex Poems (1898) **Thomas Hardy** (1840)
Wessex Tales (1888) **Thomas Hardy** (1840)

West From a Car Window, The (1892) **Richard Harding Davis** (1864)
West Indian, The (1771) **Richard Cumberland** (1732)
West Midland Underground, The (1975) **Michael Wilding** (1942)
West of Suez (1971) **John Osborne** (1929)
West to North (1940) **Compton Mackenzie** (1883)
West Wind of Love, The (1940) **Compton Mackenzie** (1883)
West-östliche Divan, Der ['East-West Divan'] (1819) **Johann Wolfgang von Goethe** (1749)
West-Running Brook (1928) **Robert Frost** (1874)
West-ward Hoe (1607) **Thomas Dekker** (1572?) [with John Webster]
Western (1982) **Frank Yerby** (1916)
Western Approaches, The (1976) **Howard Nemerov** (1920)
Western Canon, The (1994) **Harold Bloom** (1930)
Western Lands, The (1987) **William S. Burroughs** (1914)
Western Star (1943) **Stephen Vincent Benét** (1889)
Western Wonder, The [reissued 1675 as *O Brazile*] (1674) **Richard Head** (1637?)
Westminster Alice, The (1902) **'Saki' [Hector Hugh Munro]** (1870)
Westminster Sermons (1874) **Charles Kingsley** (1819)
Westward (1990) **Amy Clampitt** (1920)
Westward Ha! (1948) **S.J. Perelman** (1904)
Westward Ho! (1855) **Charles Kingsley** (1819)
Westwood [US: *The Gentle Powers*] (1946) **Stella Gibbons** (1902)
Wet Parade, The (1931) **Upton Sinclair** (1878)
Wetherel Affair, The (1873) **John W de Forest** (1826)
Weymouth Sands [UK: 1935, as *Jobber Skald*] (1934) **John Cooper Powys** (1872)
Whale Nation (1988) **Heathcote Williams** (1941)
What a Carve Up! (1994) **Jonathan Coe** (1961)
What About the People (1961) **Dorothy Hewett** (1923) [with Merv Lilley]
What Am I Doing Here? (1989) **Bruce Chatwin** (1940–89)
What and Who (1994) **C.H. Sisson** (1914)
What Are Years (1941) **Marianne Moore** (1887)
What Became of Jane Austen? (1970) **Kingsley Amis** (1922)
What D'Ye Call It, The (1715) **John Gay** (1685)
What Dare I Think? (1931) **Julian Huxley** (1887)
What Happens in Hamlet (1935) **John Dover Wilson** (1881)
What He Cost Her (1877) **James Payn** (1830)
What I Believe (1939) **E.M. Forster** (1879)
What I Believe (1925) **Bertrand Russell** (1872)
What I Lived For (1994) **Joyce Carol Oates** (1938)
What I Remember (1887) **T. Adolphus Trollope** (1810)
What I Saw in America (1922) **G.K. Chesterton** (1874)
What Is a Novel? (1969) **Malcolm Bradbury** (1932)
What is Art? (1898) **Leo Tolstoy** (1828)
What is Coming? (1916) **H.G. Wells** (1866)
What is History? (1961) **E.H. Carr** (1892)
What is of Faith as to Everlasting Punishment? (1880) **E.B. Pusey** (1800)
What Katy Did (1872) **'Susan Coolidge' [Sarah Chauncy Woolsey]** (1845)
What Katy Did at School (1873) **'Susan Coolidge' [Sarah Chauncy Woolsey]** (1845)
What Katy Did Next (1886) **'Susan Coolidge' [Sarah Chauncy Woolsey]** (1845)
What Maisie Knew (1897) **Henry James** (1843)
What Marx Really Meant (1934) **G.D.H. Cole** (1889)
What of It? (1925) **Ring Lardner** (1885)
What Price Glory? (1924) **Maxwell Anderson** (1888) [with Laurence Stallings]
What the Butler Saw (1969) **Joe Orton** (1933)
What the Light Was Like (1985) **Amy Clampitt** (1920)
What the Public Wants (1909) **Arnold Bennett** (1867)
What the Twilight Says (1999) **Derek Walcott** (1930)
'What, Then, Does Dr Newman Mean?' (1864) **Charles Kingsley** (1819)
What Time Collects (1964) **James T. Farrell** (1904)
What We Talk About When We Talk About Love (1981) **Raymond Carver** (1939)
What Will He Do With It? (1859) **Edward Bulwer-Lytton** (1803)
What You Will (1607) **John Marston** (1576)
What's Become of Waring? (1939) **Anthony Powell** (1905)
What's Bred in the Bone (1891) **Grant Allen** (1848)
What's Bred in the Bone (1985) **Robertson Davies** (1913)
What's It Like Out? (1968) **Penelope Gilliatt** (1932)
What's Mine's Mine (1886) **George MacDonald** (1824)
What's O'Clock? (1925) **Amy Lowell** (1874–1925)
What's Wrong With the World (1910) **G.K. Chesterton** (1874)
Whatever Happened to Gloomy Guts of the Chicago Bears? (1987) **Robert Coover** (1932)
Wheel of Fire, The (1930) **G. Wilson Knight** (1897)
Wheel of Fortune, The (1795) **Richard Cumberland** (1732)
Wheel of God, The (1898) **'George Egerton' [Mary Chavelita Dunne]** (1859)
Wheel of Life, The (1906) **Ellen Glasgow** (1874)
Wheel of Love, The (1970) **Joyce Carol Oates** (1938)
Wheels (1971) **Arthur Hailey** (1920)
Wheels and Butterflies (1934) **W.B. Yeats** (1865)
Wheels of Chance, The (1896) **H.G. Wells** (1866)
Wheels Within Wheels (1933) **Alec Waugh** (1898)
Wheels Within Wheels (1979) **Dervla Murphy** (1931)
When a Man's Single (1888) **'Gavin Ogilvy' [J.M. Barrie]** (1860)
When Blackbirds Sing (1962) **Martin Boyd** (1893)
When Did You Last See My Mother? (1966) **Christopher Hampton** (1946)
When Elephants Last in the Doorway Bloomed (1973) **Ray Bradbury** (1920)

When Ghost Meets Ghost (1914) **William De Morgan** (1839)
When He Was Free and Young and He Used to Wear Silks (1971) **Austin Clarke** (1932)
When I Was Very Young (1930) **A.A. Milne** (1882)
When My Girl Comes Home (1961) **V.S. Pritchett** (1900)
When Rain Clouds Gather (1968) **Bessie Head** (1937)
When She Was Good (1967) **Philip Roth** (1933)
When Shlemiel Went to Warsaw (1968) **Isaac Bashevis Singer** (1904)
When the Bough Breaks (1924) **Naomi Mitchison** (1897)
When the Green Woods Laugh (1960) **H.E. Bates** (1905)
When the Lion Feeds (1964) **Wilbur Smith** (1933)
When the Sleeper Wakes (1899) **H.G. Wells** (1866)
When the Whip Comes Down (1992) **Jeremy Reed** (1954)
When the Wind Blows (1982) **Raymond Briggs** (1934)
When the Wind Blows [US: *The Wind Blows Death*] (1949) **'Cyril Hare' [A.A.G. Clark]** (1900)
When the World Shook (1919) **Sir H. Rider Haggard** (1856)
When Time Was Born (1967) **James T. Farrell** (1904)
When We Are Married (1938) **J.B. Priestley** (1894)
When We Dead Awaken (1899) **Henrik Ibsen** (1828)
When We Were Orphans (2000) **Kazuo Ishiguro** (1954)
When We Were Very Young (1924) **A.A. Milne** (1882)
When William Came (1914) **'Saki' [Hector Hugh Munro]** (1870)
When You See Me, You Know Me (1605) **Samuel Rowley** (d. 1624)
When You Think of Me (1959) **Erskine Caldwell** (1903)
Where Angels Fear to Tread (1905) **E.M. Forster** (1879)
Where Are the Snows? (1991) **Maggie Gee** (1948)
Where Are You Going, Where Have You Been? (1974) **Joyce Carol Oates** (1938)
Where Eagles Dare (1967) **Alistair Maclean** (1923)
Where I Come From (1979) **Robert Adamson** (1943)
Where I'm Calling From (1988) **Raymond Carver** (1939)
Where No Fear Was (1914) **A.C. Benson** (1862)
Where Robot Men and Robot Women Run Round in Robot Towns (1977) **Ray Bradbury** (1920)
Where Shall We Go This Summer? (1975) **Anita Desai** (1937)
Where the Air is Clear (1958) **Carlos Fuentes** (1928)
Where the Apple Ripens (1985) **Jessie Kesson** (1916)
Where the Evil Dwells (1982) **Clifford D. Simak** (1904)
Where the Indus is Young (1977) **Dervla Murphy** (1931)
Where the Jackals Howl (1965) **Amos Oz** (1939)
Where the Queens All Strayed (1978) **Barbara Hanrahan** (1939)
Where the Rivers Meet (1988) **John Wain** (1925)
Where the Wild Things Are (1963) **Maurice Sendak** (1928)
Where the Wind Blows (1966) **Helen Cresswell** (1934)
Where There is Darkness (1982) **Caryl Phillips** (1958)
Where There is Nothing [*Plays for an Irish Theatre* vol. i] (1903) **W.B. Yeats** (1865)
Where Town and Country Meet (1891) **Mrs Louisa Baldwin** (1845)
Where You Belong (2000) **Barbara Taylor Bradford** (1933)
Where Your Treasure Is (1918) **Beatrice Harraden** (1864)
Where's Daddy? (1966) **William Inge** (1913)
Which is the Man? (1782) **Hannah Cowley** (1743)
While the Sun Shines (1943) **Terence Rattigan** (1911)
Whilomville Stories (1900) **Stephen Crane** (1871)
Whims and Oddities in Prose and Verse [1st ser.] (1826) **Thomas Hood** (1799)
Whims and Oddities in Prose and Verse [2nd ser.] (1827) **Thomas Hood** (1799)
Whimsicalities (1844) **Thomas Hood** (1799)
Whip Hand (1979) **Dick Francis** (1920)
Whipper of the Satyre his Pennance, The (1601) **Everard Guilpin** (fl. 1598)
Whipperginny (1923) **Robert Graves** (1895)
Whippoorwill (1940) **Marjorie Rawlings** (1896)
Whir of Gold (1970) **Sinclair Ross** (1908)
Whirligigs (1910) **'O. Henry' [William Sydney Porter]** (1862)
Whirlpool, The (1897) **George Gissing** (1857)
Whisky Galore (1947) **Compton Mackenzie** (1883)
Whispering Gallery, The (1955) **John Lehmann** (1907)
Whispering Mountain, The (1968) **Joan Aiken** (1924)
Whispering Roots, The (1970) **C. Day Lewis** (1904)
Whispers (1980) **Dean Koontz** (1945)
Whistle (1978) **James Jones** (1921)
Whistle in the Dark, A (1989) **Tom Murphy** (1935)
White Album, The (1979) **Joan Didion** (1934)
White Bird Passes, The (1958) **Jessie Kesson** (1916)
White Boots (1951) **Noel Streatfeild** (1895)
White Boy Running (1988) **Christopher Hope** (1944)
White Boy, The (1845) **Anna Maria [Mrs S.C.] Hall** (1800)
White Buildings (1926) **Hart Crane** (1899)
White Butterfly (1992) **Walter Mosley** (1952)
White Carnation, The (1953) **R.C. Sherriff** (1896)
White Chameleon (1991) **Christopher Hampton** (1946)
White Coat, Purple Coat (1989) **Dannie Abse** (1923)
White Company, The (1891) **A. Conan Doyle** (1859)
White Crow, The (1968) **Storm Jameson** (1897)
White Deer, The (1945) **James Thurber** (1894–1961)
White Desert (1923) **Maxwell Anderson** (1888)
White Divel, The (1612) **John Webster** (1580?)
White Doe of Rylstone, The (1815) **William Wordsworth** (1770)
White Dresses (1923) **Paul Green** (1894)
White Fang (1906) **'Jack London' [John Griffith Chaney]** (1876)

White Father, The (1964) **Julian Mitchell** (1935)

White Figure, White Ground (1964) **Hugh Hood** (1928)

White Flock, The (1917) **'Anna Akhmatova' [Anna Andreevna Gorenko]** (1889)

White Gate, The (1913) **Warwick Deeping** (1877)

White Goddess, The (1948) **Robert Graves** (1895)

White Hare, The (1936) **Francis Stuart** (1902)

White Heather (1885) **William Black** (1841)

White Heron, A (1886) **Sarah Orne Jewett** (1849)

White Hoods, The (1828) **Anna Eliza Bray** (1790)

White Horseman, The (1941) **J.F. Hendry** (1912) (ed.) [with Henry Treece]

White Horseman, The (1941) **Henry Treece** (1911) (ed.) [with J.F. Hendry]

White Horses of Vienna, The (1936) **Kay Boyle** (1903)

White Hotel, The (1981) **D.M. Thomas** (1935)

White House by the Sea, The (1857) **Matilda Betham-Edwards** (1836)

White House, The (1906) **M.E. Braddon** (1835)

White Huntress, The (1861) **Mayne Reid** (1818)

White Jazz (1993) **James Ellroy** (1948)

White Ladies (1935) **Francis Brett Young** (1884)

White Lantern, The (1980) **Evan S. Connell, Jr** (1924)

White Liars, and Black Comedy (1968) **Peter Shaffer** (1926)

White Lies (1857) **Charles Reade** (1814)

White Mare, The (1943) **Michael McLaverty** (1904)

White Mice, The (1909) **Richard Harding Davis** (1864)

White Monkey, The (1924) **John Galsworthy** (1867)

White Mule (1937) **William Carlos Williams** (1883)

White Negro, The (1957) **Norman Mailer** (1923)

White Noise (1985) **Don Delillo** (1936)

White Paternoster, The (1930) **T.F. Powys** (1875)

White Peacock, The (1911) **D.H. Lawrence** (1885)

White Plumes of Navarre, The (1906) **S.R. Crockett** (1860)

White Prophet, The (1909) **Hall Caine** (1853)

White Robe, The (1928) **James Branch Cabell** (1879)

White Rose of Withered Leaf (1908) **Violet Hunt** (1866)

White Shroud (1986) **Allen Ginsberg** (1926)

White Sister, The (1909) **F. Marion Crawford** (1854)

White South, The (1949) **'Hammond Innes' [Ralph Hammond-Innes]** (1913)

White Stones, The (1969) **J.H. Prynne** (1936)

White Teeth (2000) **Zadie Smith** (1975)

White Threshold, The (1949) **W.S. Graham** (1918)

White Virgin, The (1894) **George Manville Fenn** (1831)

White Wampum, The (1895) **Pauline Johnson** (1862)

White Wife, The (1865) **'Cuthbert Bede' [Edward Bradley]** (1827)

White Wings (1880) **William Black** (1841)

White Witch of Rosehall, The (1929) **H.G. de Lisser** (1878)

White with Wire Wheels (1967) **Jack Hibberd** (1940)

White Wolf, The (1902) **Sir A.T. Quiller-Couch** (1863)

White Writing (1988) **J.M. Coetzee** (1940)

White-Haired Lover (1968) **Karl Shapiro** (1913)

White-Jacket (1850) **Herman Melville** (1819)

White-Maa's Saga (1929) **Eric Linklater** (1899)

Whitefriars (1844) **Emma Robinson** (1814)

Whitehall (1845) **Emma Robinson** (1814)

Whiteheaded Boy, The (1920) **Lennox Robinson** (1886)

Whiteladies (1875) **Margaret Oliphant** (1828)

Whiteoak Brothers (1953) **Mazo de la Roche** (1879)

Whiteoak Harvest (1936) **Mazo de la Roche** (1879)

Whiteoak Heritage (1940) **Mazo de la Roche** (1879)

Whiteoaks of Jalna (1929) **Mazo de la Roche** (1879)

Whitewater (1970) **Paul Horgan** (1903)

Whitsun Weddings, The (1964) **Philip Larkin** (1922)

Who Are the Friends of Order? (1852) **Charles Kingsley** (1819)

Who Are We Now? (1976) **Lawrence Ferlinghetti** (1920)

Who Calls the Tune (1953) **Nina Bawden** (1925)

Who Do You Think You Are? (1976) **Malcolm Bradbury** (1932)

Who Do You Think You Are? [US/UK: *The Beggar Maid*] (1978) **Alice Munro** (1931)

Who Has Seen the Wind (1947) **W.O. Mitchell** (1914)

Who is Sylvia? (1950) **Terence Rattigan** (1911)

Who is Teddy Villanova? (1977) **Thomas Berger** (1924)

Who Is the Heir? (1865) **Mortimer Collins** (1827)

Who Speaks for the Negro? (1965) **Robert Penn Warren** (1905)

Who Were You With Last Night? (1971) **Frederic Raphael** (1931)

Who's Afraid of Virginia Woolf? (1962) **Edward Albee** (1928)

Who's the Dupe? (1779) **Hannah Cowley** (1743)

Whole Armour, The (1962) **Wilson Harris** (1921)

Whole of the Story, The (1935) **Phyllis Bentley** (1894)

Whole Treatise of the Cases of Conscience, The (1606) **William Perkins** (1558–1602)

Whole Voyald, The (1956) **William Saroyan** (1908)

Whole Workes . . . in Poetrie, The (1623) **Samuel Daniel** (1562–1619)

Whole Works of Homer, The (1616) **George Chapman** (1559?) (tr.)

Whom God Hath Joined (1906) **Arnold Bennett** (1867)

Whore of Babylon, The (1607) **Thomas Dekker** (1572?)

Whoroscopey (1930) **Samuel Beckett** (1906)

Whose Body? (1923) **Dorothy L. Sayers** (1893)

Why Are We in Vietnam? (1967) **Norman Mailer** (1923)

Why Brownlee Left (1980) **Paul Muldoon** (1951)

Why Can't We Live Together Like Civilized Human Beings? (1982) **Maxine Kumin** (1925)

Why Come Ye Nat to Courte (1545?) **John Skelton** (1460?-1529)

Why Didn't They Ask Evans? [US: *The Boomerang Club*] (1934) **Agatha Christie** (1890)

Why Frau Frohmann Raised Her Prices (1882) **Anthony Trollope** (1815)

Why Paul Ferroll Killed His Wife (1860) **Caroline Clive** (1801)
Why Was I Killed? (1943) **Rex Warner** (1905)
Wickford Point (1939) **John P. Marquand** (1893)
Widdershins (1911) **Oliver Onions** (1873)
Widdow, The (1652) **Thomas Middleton** (1580–1627)
Widdow Ranter, The (1689) **Aphra Behn** (1640?-89)
Widdow'sTears, The (1612) **George Chapman** (1559?)
Wide Awake Stories (1884) **Flora Annie Steel** (1847)
Wide Fields (1928) **Paul Green** (1894)
Wide Field (1995) **Günter Grass** (1927)
Wide is the Gate (1943) **Upton Sinclair** (1878)
Wide Net, The (1943) **Eudora Welty** (1909)
Wide Sargasso Sea (1966) **'Jean Rhys' [Ella Gwendolyn Rees Williams]** (1890)
Widecombe Fair (1913) **Eden Phillpotts** (1862)
Widow, The (1794) **Mary Robinson** (1758)
Widow, The (1979) **Nicholas Freeling** (1927)
Widow, The (1989) **Carolyn Slaughter** (1946)
Widow Barnaby, The (1839) **Frances Trollope** (1780)
Widow for One Year, A (1998) **John Irving** (1942)
Widow Married, The (1840) **Frances Trollope** (1780)
Widow's Tale, The (1822) **Caroline Bowles** (1786)
Widow's Tale, A (1827) **Bernard Barton** (1784)
Widow's Tale, A (1898) **Margaret Oliphant** (1828)
Widow's Tears, The (1612) **George Chapman** (1559)
Widower's Son, The (1976) **Alan Sillitoe** (1928)
Widowers' Houses (1892) **Bernard Shaw** (1856)
Widsith (1912) **R.W. Chambers** (1874)
Wieland (1798) **Charles Brockden Brown** (1771)
Wife, The (1833) **James Sheridan Knowles** (1784)
Wife and Woman's Reward, The (1835) **Caroline Norton** (1808)
Wife of Altamont, The (1910) **Violet Hunt** (1866)
Wife of Bath, The (1713) **John Gay** (1685)
Wife of His Youth, The (1899) **Charles W. Chesnutt** (1858)
Wife of Martin Guerre, The (1941) **Janet Lewis** (1899)
Wife of Sir Isaac Harman, The (1914) **H.G. Wells** (1866)
Wife to be Lett, A (1723) **Eliza Haywood** (c.1693)
Wife's Evidence, The (1864) **William Gorman Wills** (1828)
Wigs on the Green (1935) **Nancy Mitford** (1904)
Wigwam Evenings (1909) **Charles Eastman** (1858)
Wild Angels (1974) **Ursula K. le Guin** (1929)
Wild Animals I Have Known (1898) **Ernest Thompson Seton** (1860)
Wild Apples (1928) **Oliver St Gogarty** (1878)
Wild Ass's Skin, The [*La Peau de chagrin*] (1832) **Honoré de Balzac** (1799)
Wild Berries (1982) **Yevgeny Yevtushenko** (1933)
Wild Body; A Soldier of Humour (1927) **Wyndham Lewis** (1882)
Wild Boys, The (1971) **William S. Burroughs** (1914)
Wild Card (1990) **Dorothy Hewett** (1923)
Wild Coal (1963) **Kenneth White** (1936)
Wild Conquest (1951) **Peter Abrahams** (1919)
Wild Decembers (1932) **'Clemence Dane' [Winifred Ashton]** (1888)
Wild Decembers (1999) **Edna O'Brien** (1932)
Wild Duck, The (1884) **Henrik Ibsen** (1828)
Wild Earth (1907) **Padraic Colum** (1881)
Wild Eelin (1898) **William Black** (1841)
Wild Flag, The (1946) **E.B. White** (1899)
Wild Flowers (1806) **Robert Bloomfield** (1766)
Wild Fruit (1905) **Eden Phillpotts** (1862)
Wild Gallant, The (1663) **John Dryden** (1631)
Wild Garden, The (1963) **Angus Wilson** (1913)
Wild Girl, The (1984) **Michèle Roberts** (1949)
Wild Goose Chase, The (1937) **Rex Warner** (1905)
Wild Grape Wine (1968) **Al Purdy** (1918)
Wild Honey (1964) **Alistair Campbell** (1925)
Wild Irish Boy, The (1808) **C.R. Maturin** (1782)
Wild Irish Girl, The (1806) **Lady Sydney Morgan** (1783?)
Wild is the River (1941) **Louis Bromfield** (1896)
Wild Knight, The (1900) **G.K. Chesterton** (1874)
Wild Lemons (1980) **David Malouf** (1934)
Wild Life (1990) **Richard Ford** (1944)
Wild Life in a Southern County (1879) **[Richard Jefferies]** (1848)
Wild Man of the West, The (1863) **R.M. Ballantyne** (1825)
Wild Nights (1979) **Emma Tennant** (1937)
Wild Old Man on the Road, A (1988) **Morley Callaghan** (1903)
Wild Palms, The (1939) **William Faulkner** (1897)
Wild Patience Has Taken Me This Far, A (1981) **Adrienne Rich** (1929)
Wild Pitch (1973) **A.B. Guthrie** (1901)
Wild Proxy, A (1893) **Lucy [Mrs W.K.] Clifford** (1853)
Wild Strawberries (1934) **Angela Thirkell** (1890)
Wild Surmise, A (1961) **Frederic Raphael** (1931)
Wild Swan, The (1932) **Liam O'Flaherty** (1897)
Wild Swans at Coole, The (1919) **W.B. Yeats** (1865)
Wild Swans at Coole, The (1917) **W.B. Yeats** (1865)
Wild Tulip, The (1932) **F.L. Lucas** (1894)
Wild Wales (1862) **George Borrow** (1803)
Wild-Goose Chase, The (1652) **Francis Beaumont** (1585?-1616) [with John Fletcher]
Wilderness (1961) **Robert Penn Warren** (1905)
Wildest Dreams (1991) **Alan Ayckbourn** (1939)
Wilding Graft (1948) **Jack Clemo** (1916)
Wildtrack (1965) **John Wain** (1925)
Wilfred Cumbermede (1872) **George MacDonald** (1824)
Wilfred Owen (1974) **Jon Stallworthy** (1935)
Wilfulness of Woman, The (1844) **Lady Charlotte Bury** (1775)
Wilhelm Meister's Apprenticeship [*Wilhelm Meisters Lehrjahre*] (1795) **Johann Wolfgang von Goethe** (1749)
Wilhelm Meister's Apprenticeship [from Goethe] (1824) **Thomas Carlyle** (1795) (tr.)
Wilhelm Meister's Travels [*Wilhelm Meisters Wanderjahre*] (1821) **Johann Wolfgang von Goethe** (1749)
Wilhemina in London (1906) **'Barry Pain' [Eric Odell]** (1864)
Wilkins' Tooth (1973) **Diana Wynne Jones** (1934)

Will and a Way, A (1881) **Lady Georgiana Fullerton** (1812)
Will and the Way, The (1973) **L.P. Hartley** (1895–1972)
Will to Change, The (1971) **Adrienne Rich** (1929)
Will to Love, A (1919) **'Hugh Kingsmill' [Hugh Kingsmill Lunn]** (1889)
Will Warburton (1905) **George Gissing** (1857–1903)
Will You Be Quiet, Please? (1976) **Raymond Carver** (1939)
Willard and his Bowling Trophies (1975) **Richard Brautigan** (1935)
William (1925) **E.H. Young** (1880)
William (1929) **'Richmal Crompton' [Richmal Crompton Lamburn]** (1890)
William Again (1923) **'Richmal Crompton' [Richmal Crompton Lamburn]** (1890)
William, an Englishman (1919) **Cicely Mary Hamilton** (1872)
William and A.R.P. (1939) **'Richmal Crompton' [Richmal Crompton Lamburn]** (1890)
William and the Evacuees (1940) **'Richmal Crompton' [Richmal Crompton Lamburn]** (1890)
William and the Pop Singers (1965) **'Richmal Crompton' [Richmal Crompton Lamburn]** (1890)
William and the Tramp (1952) **'Richmal Crompton' [Richmal Crompton Lamburn]** (1890)
William and the Witch (1964) **'Richmal Crompton' [Richmal Crompton Lamburn]** (1890)
William Blake (1868) **A.C. Swinburne** (1837)
William Blake (1907) **Arthur Symons** (1865)
William Does His Bit (1941) **'Richmal Crompton' [Richmal Crompton Lamburn]** (1890)
William in Trouble (1927) **'Richmal Crompton' [Richmal Crompton Lamburn]** (1890)
William IV (1971) **Philip Ziegler** (1929)
William Makepeace Thackeray (1978) **Margaret Forster** (1938)
William Shakespeare (1963) **A.L. Rowse** (1903)
William Shakespeare: A Study of Facts and Problems (1930) **Sir E.K. Chambers** (1866)
William Shakespeare, Pedagogue and Poacher (1905) **Richard Garnett** (1835)
William Tell (1825) **James Sheridan Knowles** (1784)
William the Conqueror (1926) **'Richmal Crompton' [Richmal Crompton Lamburn]** (1890)
William the Detective (1935) **'Richmal Crompton' [Richmal Crompton Lamburn]** (1890)
William the Dictator (1938) **'Richmal Crompton' [Richmal Crompton Lamburn]** (1890)
William the Fourth (1924) **'Richmal Crompton' [Richmal Crompton Lamburn]** (1890)
William the Gangster (1934) **'Richmal Crompton' [Richmal Crompton Lamburn]** (1890)
William the Good (1928) **'Richmal Crompton' [Richmal Crompton Lamburn]** (1890)
William the Lawless (1970) **'Richmal Crompton' [Richmal Crompton Lamburn]** (1890)
William the Outlaw (1927) **'Richmal Crompton' [Richmal Crompton Lamburn]** (1890)
William the Pirate (1932) **'Richmal Crompton' [Richmal Crompton Lamburn]** (1890)
William the Rebel (1933) **'Richmal Crompton' [Richmal Crompton Lamburn]** (1890)
William the Superman (1968) **'Richmal Crompton' [Richmal Crompton Lamburn]** (1890)
William Wetmore Story and His Friends (1903) **Henry James** (1843)
Willie Masters' Lonesome Wife (1970) **William H. Gass** (1924)
Willing to Die (1873) **J.S. le Fanu** (1814)
Williwaw (1946) **Gore Vidal** (1925)
Willougby Captains, The (1887) **Talbot Baines Reed** (1852)
Willow Cabin, The (1949) **Pamela Frankau** (1908)
Willowbrake (1898) **Robert Murray Gilchrist** (1868)
Willows Forge (1914) **Sheila Kaye-Smith** (1887)
Willy Reilly and his Dear Coleen Brawn (1855) **William Carleton** (1794)
Wilson: A Consideration of the Sources (2000) **David Mamet** (1947)
Wilson's Bowl (1980) **Phyllis Webb** (1931)
Wilt (1976) **Tom Sharpe** (1928)
Wilt Alternative, The (1979) **Tom Sharpe** (1928)
Wilt on High (1984) **Tom Sharpe** (1928)
Wimbledon Poisoner, The (1990) **Nigel Williams** (1948)
Wind, The [Le Vent] (1957) **Claude Simon** (1913)
Wind Among the Reeds, The (1899) **W.B. Yeats** (1865)
Wind and the Whirlwind, The (1883) **Wilfrid Scawen Blunt** (1840)
Wind Blows Over, The (1936) **Walter de la Mare** (1873)
Wind Changes, The (1937) **Olivia Manning** (1908)
Wind Eye, The (1976) **Robert Westall** (1929)
Wind in the Rose-Bush, The (1903) **Mary Wilkins Freeman** (1852)
Wind in the Willows, The (1908) **Kenneth Grahame** (1859)
Wind of Freedom (1943) **Compton Mackenzie** (1883)
Wind, Sand and Stars [Terre des Hommes] (1939) **Antoine de Saint-Exupéry** (1900)
Wind Song (1960) **Carl Sandburg** (1878)
Wind's Twelve Quarters, The (1975) **Ursula K. le Guin** (1929)
Wind-Voices (1883) **Philip Bourke Marston** (1850)
Windfall (1982) **Desmond Bagley** (1923)
Windfalls (1934) **Sean O'Casey** (1880)
Winding Stair, The (1923) **A.E.W. Mason** (1865)
Winding Stair, The (1933) **W.B. Yeats** (1865)
Windmill Country (1968) **Dorothy Hewett** (1923)
Window in Thrums, A (1889) **[Sir] J.M. Barrie** (1860)
Window on Russia, A (1972) **Edmund Wilson** (1895)
Windows (1922) **John Galsworthy** (1867)
Winds of Doctrine (1913) **George Santayana** (1863)
Winds of the Day (1964) **Howard Spring** (1889)
Winds of War, The (1971) **Herman Wouk** (1915)

Windsor Castle (1843) **W.H. Ainsworth** (1805)
Windsor Castle (1685) **Thomas Otway** (1652)
Windsor-Forest (1713) **Alexander Pope** (1688)
Windy McPherson's Son (1916) **Sherwood Anderson** (1876)
Wine (1708) **John Gay** (1685)
Wine-Dark Sea, The (1993) **Patrick O'Brian** (1914)
Winefred (1900) **S. Baring-Gould** (1834)
Winesburg, Ohio (1919) **Sherwood Anderson** (1876)
Winged Chariot (1951) **Walter de la Mare** (1873)
Wingless Victory, The (1936) **Maxwell Anderson** (1888)
Wings of the Dove, The (1902) **Henry James** (1843)
Winner Take Nothing (1933) **Ernest Hemingway** (1898)
Winnie-the-Pooh (1926) **A.A. Milne** (1882)
Winnowing-Fan, The (1914) **Laurence Binyon** (1869)
Winslow Boy, The (1946) **Terence Rattigan** (1911)
Winsome Winnie (1920) **Stephen Leacock** (1869)
Winston Affair, The (1959) **Howard Fast** (1914)
Winstonburg Line, The (1919) **Sir Osbert Sitwell** (1892)
Winter (1726) **James Thomson** (1700)
Winter (1888) **Henry David Thoreau** (1817)
Winter Evening Tales (1820) **James Hogg** (1770)
Winter Garden (1980) **Beryl Bainbridge** (1934)
Winter Harvest (1933) **Andrew Young** (1885)
Winter Hostages (1980) **Patric Dickinson** (1914)
Winter House, The (1935) **Norman Cameron** (1905)
Winter in Russia, A [Voyage en Russie] (1866) **Théophile Gautier** (1811)
Winter in the Air (1955) **Sylvia Townsend Warner** (1893)
Winter in the Hills, A (1970) **John Wain** (1925)
Winter in the West, A (1835) **Charles Fenno Hoffman** (1806)
Winter Journey (1967) **Eva Figes** (1932)
Winter Journey (1984) **Ronald Frame** (1953)
Winter Journey (1995) **Isabel Colegate** (1931)
Winter Man, The (1973) **Vernon Scannell** (1922)
Winter Moon (1993) **Dean Koontz** (1945)
Winter Movement (1930) **Julian Bell** (1908)
Winter Notes on Summer Impressions (1863) **Fyodor Mikhailovich Dostoevsky** (1821)
Winter of Artifice (1939) **Anaïs Nin** (1903)
Winter of Our Discontent, The (1961) **John Steinbeck** (1902)
Winter of the Birds, The (1975) **Helen Cresswell** (1934)
Winter on the Nile, My (1876) **Charles Dudley Warner** (1829)
Winter Pollen (1994) **Ted Hughes** (1930)
Winter Quarters (1983) **Peter Scupham** (1933)
Winter Song (1950) **James Hanley** (1901)
Winter Studies and Summer Rambles in Canada (1838) **Anna Jameson** (1794)
Winter Sun (1960) **Margaret Avison** (1918)
Winter Talent, A (1957) **Donald Davie** (1922)
Winter Trees (1971) **Sylvia Plath** (1932–63)
Winter Words (1928) **Thomas Hardy** (1840–1928)
Winter's Tale, A (1954) **Jean Stafford** (1915)
Winter's Tales (1942) **'Isak Dinesen' [Karen Blixen]** (1885)
Winterfold (1976) **George Mackay Brown** (1921)
Wintering Out (1972) **Seamus Heaney** (1939)
Wintering Tree, A (1973) **Patric Dickinson** (1914)
Winterset (1935) **Maxwell Anderson** (1888)
Wintersmoon (1928) **Sir Hugh Walpole** (1884)
Wisdom of Father Brown, The (1914) **G.K. Chesterton** (1874)
Wisdom of the Ancients, The (1619) **Sir Francis Bacon** (1561)
Wisdom of the Heart, The (1941) **Henry Miller** (1891)
Wisdom of the Simple, The (1937) **Constance Holme** (1881)
Wisdom of the Wilderness (1922) **Sir Charles G.D. Roberts** (1860)
Wisdom's Daughter (1923) **Sir H. Rider Haggard** (1856)
Wisdom's Gate (1938) **Margaret Ayer Barnes** (1886)
Wisdome of Solomon Paraphrased, The (1597) **Thomas Middleton** (1580)
Wise Blood (1952) **Flannery O'Connor** (1925)
Wise Child (1967) **Simon Gray** (1936)
Wise Children (1991) **Angela Carter** (1940)
Wise Men of the East, The [from the *German of Kotzebue*] (1799) **Elizabeth Inchbald** (1753)
Wise Saws and Modern Instances (1845) **Thomas Cooper** (1805)
Wise Virgin (1982) **A.N. Wilson** (1950)
Wise Virgins, The (1914) **Leonard Woolf** (1880)
Wise Women of Inverness, The (1885) **William Black** (1841)
Wise-Woman of Hogsdon, The (1638) **Thomas Heywood** (1574?)
Wit and Humour (1846) **Leigh Hunt** (1784)
Wit Without Money (1639) **Francis Beaumont** (1585?-1616) [with John Fletcher]
Wit's Private Wealth (1607) **Nicholas Breton** (1545?)
Witch in the Wood, The (1939) **T.H. White** (1906)
Witch of Edmonton, The (1658) **William Rowley** (1585?-1626) [with Thomas Dekker and John Ford]
Witch of Exmoor, The (1996) **Margaret Drabble** (1939)
Witch of Prague, The (1891) **F. Marion Crawford** (1854)
Witch of Rosenburg, The (1866) **Nicholas Patrick S. Wiseman** (1802)
Witch Stories (1861) **E. Lynn Linton** (1822)
Witch Wood (1927) **John Buchan** (1875)
Witch's Head, The (1885) **Sir H. Rider Haggard** (1856)
Witchcraft (1941) **Charles Williams** (1886)
Witchcraft (1987) **Nigel Williams** (1948)
Witchcraft of Salem Village, The (1956) **Shirley Jackson** (1919)
Witches (1981) **Erica Jong** (1942)
Witches, The (1983) **Roald Dahl** (1916)
Witches' Brew, The (1925) **E.J. Pratt** (1882)
Witches of Eastwick, The (1984) **John Updike** (1932)
Witching Hill (1913) **E.W. Hornung** (1866)

Witching Hour, The (1907) **Augustus Thomas** (1857)
Witching Hour, The (1990) **Anne Rice** (1941)
With a Bare Bodkin (1946) **'Cyril Hare' [A.A.G. Clark]** (1900)
With a Silken Thread (1880) **E. Lynn Linton** (1822)
With Both Armies in South Africa (1900) **Richard Harding Davis** (1864)
With Buller to Natal (1900) **G.A. Henty** (1832)
With Clive in India (1884) **G.A. Henty** (1832)
With Edged Tools (1894) **'Henry Seton Merriman' [Hugh Stowell Scott]** (1862)
With Essex in Ireland (1890) **Emily Lawless** (1845)
With Eye and Ear (1971) **Kenneth Rexroth** (1905)
With Fire and Sword (1884) **Henryk Sienkiewicz** (1846)
With Harp and Crown (1875) **Sir Walter Besant** (1836) [with James Rice]
With Her in Ourland (1916) **Charlotte Perkins Gilman** (1860)
With Kitchener in the Sudan (1903) **G.A. Henty** (1832)
With Luck Lasting (1963) **Bernard Spencer** (1909)
With Roberts to Pretoria (1901) **G.A. Henty** (1832)
With Sa'di in the Garden (1888) **Sir Edwin Arnold** (1832) (tr.)
With Shuddering Fall (1964) **Joyce Carol Oates** (1938)
With the Allies (1914) **Richard Harding Davis** (1864)
With the French in France and Salonika (1916) **Richard Harding Davis** (1864)
With the Procession (1895) **Henry Blake Fuller** (1857)
With the Wild Geese (1902) **Emily Lawless** (1845)
With Trumpet and Drum (1892) **Eugene Field** (1850)
With Wolfe in Canada (1887) **G.A. Henty** (1832)
Within a Budding Grove [A l'ombre des jeunes filles en fleurs; A la recherche du temps perdu ii] (1919) **Marcel Proust** (1871)
Within and Without (1855) **George MacDonald** (1824)
Within the Gates (1934) **Sean O'Casey** (1880)
Within the Labyrinth (1950) **Norman Lewis** (1918)
Within the Precincts (1879) **Margaret Oliphant** (1828)
Within the Rim (1919) **Henry James** (1843–1916)
Within the Tides (1915) **Joseph Conrad** (1857)
Within This Present (1933) **Margaret Ayer Barnes** (1886)
Without a Stitch in Time (1972) **Peter de Vries** (1910)
Without My Cloak (1931) **Kate O'Brien** (1897)
Without Sorcery (1948) **Theodore Sturgeon** (1918)
Witness Tree, A (1942) **Robert Frost** (1874)
Wits Bedlam (1617) **John Davies of Hereford** (1565)
Wittes Pilgrimage (1605) **John Davies of Hereford** (1565)
Wittie Faire One, The (1633) **James Shirley** (1596)
Witts, The (1636) **Sir William Davenant** (1606)
Wives and Daughters (1866) **Elizabeth Gaskell** (1810–65)
Wives as They Were and Maids as They Are (1797) **Elizabeth Inchbald** (1753)
Wives Excuse, The (1691) **Thomas Southerne** (1659)
Wizard of Earthsea, A (1968) **Ursula K. le Guin** (1929)
Wizard's Son, The (1884) **Margaret Oliphant** (1828)
Wolf (1971) **Jim Harrison** (1937)
Wolf Solent (1929) **John Cooper Powys** (1872)
Wolf to the Slaughter (1967) **Ruth Rendell** (1930)
Wolf Willow (1962) **Wallace Stegner** (1909)
Wolfbane (1959) **Frederik Pohl** (1919) [with C.M. Kornbluth]
Wolfenburg (1892) **William Black** (1841)
Wolfert's Roost (1855) **Washington Irving** (1783)
Wolfwatching (1989) **Ted Hughes** (1930)
Wolsey (1929) **A.F. Pollard** (1869)
Wolverhampton Wanderer, The (1971) **Michael Horovitz** (1935)
Wolves of Willoughby Chase, The (1962) **Joan Aiken** (1924)
Woman, The (1978) **Edward Bond** (1934)
Woman, and Her Place in a Free Society (1894) **Edward Carpenter** (1844) (ed.)
Woman and Labour (1911) **Olive Schreiner** (1855)
Woman and the Man (1893) **Robert Williams Buchanan** (1841)
Woman as She Should Be (1793) **Eliza Parsons** (1748)
Woman at the Door, The (1937) **Warwick Deeping** (1877)
Woman at the Washington Zoo, The (1960) **Randall Jarrell** (1914)
Woman Beware Woman (1983) **Emma Tennant** (1937)
Woman Called Fancy, A (1951) **Frank Yerby** (1916)
Woman Clothed with the Sun, The (1937) **F.L. Lucas** (1894)
Woman Destroyed, The [La Femme rompue] (1968) **Simone de Beauvoir** (1908)
Woman Hater, The (1920) **Ruby M. Ayres** (1883)
Woman Hater, The (1607) **Francis Beaumont** (1585?) [with John Fletcher]
Woman Hating (1974) **Andrea Dworkin** (1946)
Woman in a Lampshade (1983) **Elizabeth Jolley** (1923)
Woman in Black, The (1983) **Susan Hill** (1942)
Woman in Mind (1985) **Alan Ayckbourn** (1939)
Woman in the Moone, The (1597) **John Lyly** (1554)
Woman in the Sky, A (1973) **James Hanley** (1901)
Woman in White, The (1860) **Wilkie Collins** (1824)
Woman is a Weather-cocke, A (1612) **Nathan Field** (1587)
Woman Kilde with Kindnesse, A (1607) **Thomas Heywood** (1574?)
Woman Lit by Fireflies, The (1991) **Jim Harrison** (1937)
Woman of Andros, The (1930) **Thornton Wilder** (1897)
Woman of Business, The (1870) **Marmion W. Savage** (1803)
Woman of Genius, A (1912) **Mary Austin** (1868)
Woman of Judah, A (1988) **Ronald Frame** (1953)

Woman of Knockaloe, The (1923) **Hall Caine** (1853)
Woman of My Age, A (1967) **Nina Bawden** (1925)
Woman of No Importance, A (1893) **Oscar Wilde** (1854)
Woman of Rome, The [*La romana*] (1947) **'Alberto Moravia' [Alberto Pincherle]** (1907)
Woman of Singular Occupation, A (1988) **Penelope Gilliatt** (1932)
Woman of Substance, A (1980) **Barbara Taylor Bradford** (1933)
Woman of the Future, A (1979) **David Ireland** (1927)
Woman of the Horizon, The (1917) **Gilbert Frankau** (1884)
Woman of the House, The (1959) **Richard Murphy** (1927)
Woman of the Inner Sea (1992) **Thomas Keneally** (1935)
Woman of the World, The (1838) **Mrs C.F. Gore** (1799)
Woman Speaks, A (1975) **Anaïs Nin** (1903)
Woman Who Did, The (1895) **Grant Allen** (1848)
Woman Who Had Imagination, The (1934) **H.E. Bates** (1905)
Woman Who Owned the Shadows, The (1983) **Paula Gunn Allen** (1939)
Woman Who Rode Away, The (1928) **D.H. Lawrence** (1885)
Woman Who Stole Everything, The (1927) **Arnold Bennett** (1867)
Woman Who Talked to Herself, The (1989) **A.L. Barker** (1918)
Woman Who Walked into Doors, The (1996) **Roddy Doyle** (1958)
Woman Who Was God, The (1988) **Francis King** (1923)
Woman Who Went to Hell, The (1902) **Dora Sigerson** (1866)
Woman with the Velvet Necklace, The [*La Femme au collier de velours*] (1851) **Alexandre Dumas ['père']** (1802)
Woman's Age, A (1979) **Rachel Billington** (1942)
Woman's Friendship (1850) **Grace Aguilar** (1816–47)
Woman's Kingdom, The (1869) **Dinah Maria Craik** (1826)
Woman's Life, A [*Une Vie*] (1883) **Guy de Maupassant** (1850)
Woman's Love (1829) **Thomas Wade** (1805)
Woman's Reason, A (1883) **William Dean Howells** (1837)
Woman's Story, A (1857) **Anna Maria [Mrs S.C.] Hall** (1800)
Woman's Thoughts About Women, A (1858) **Dinah Maria Craik** (1826)
Woman-Captain, The (1679) **Thomas Shadwell** (1642?)
Woman-Hater, A (1877) **Charles Reade** (1814)
Womankind in Western Europe (1869) **Thomas Wright** (1810)
Womans Wit (1696) **Colley Cibber** (1671)
Women (1978) **Charles Bukowski** (1920)
Women (1818) **C.R. Maturin** (1782)
Women and Angels (1985) **Harold Brodkey** (1930)
Women and Animals (1972) **Philip Hobsbaum** (1932)
Women and Economics (1898) **Charlotte Perkins Gilman** (1860)
Women and Ghosts (1994) **Alison Lurie** (1926)
Women and God (1931) **Francis Stuart** (1902)
Women Are Like That (1929) **'E.M. Delafield' [E.E.M. de la Pasture]** (1890)
Women Are So Serious (1932) **Pamela Frankau** (1908)
Women As They Are (1830) **Mrs C.F. Gore** (1799)
Women as They Are (1796) **Eliza Parsons** (1748)
Women at Point Sur, The (1927) **Robinson Jeffers** (1887)
Women Beware Women (1986) **Howard Barker** (1946)
Women, Beware Women (1657) **Thomas Middleton** (1580)
Women Fly When Men Aren't Watching (1993) **Sara Maitland** (1950)
Women in Love (1921) **D.H. Lawrence** (1885)
Women in Love (1968) **Joyce Carol Oates** (1938)
Women in the Wall (1975) **Julia O'Faolain** (1932)
Women Must Work (1934) **Richard Aldington** (1892)
Women of Brewster Place, The (1982) **Gloria Naylor** (1952)
Women of England,, The (1839) **Sarah [Mrs William] Ellis** (1812)
Women of Israel, The (1845) **Grace Aguilar** (1816)
Women of Trachis, The [*Trachiniae*] **Sophocles** (*c.* 496 BC)
Women on the Porch, The (1944) **Caroline Gordon** (1895)
Women Whose Lives Are Food, Men Whose Lives Are Money (1978) **Joyce Carol Oates** (1938)
Women's Room, The (1977) **Marilyn French** (1929)
Women's Wrongs (1855) **Ernest Charles Jones** (1819)
Wonder Book, A (1852) **Nathaniel Hawthorne** (1804)
Wonder Hero (1933) **J.B. Priestley** (1894)
Wonder of a Kingdome, The (1636) **Thomas Dekker** (1572?–1634)
Wonder of Women, The (1606) **John Marston** (1576)
Wonder!, The (1714) **Susanna Centlivre** (1669?)
Wonder-Worker, The (1973) **Dan Jacobson** (1929)
Wonder-Working Magician, The [*El mágico prodigioso*] (1637) **Pedro Calderón de la Barca** (1600)
Wonder-Working Providence of Sion's Saviour in New-England, The (1654) **Edward Johnson** (1599?)
Wonderful Adventures of Phra the Phonecian, The (1891) **Edwin Lester Arnold** (1857)
Wonderful Combat Between Christ and Satan, The (1592) **Lancelot Andrewes** (1555)
Wonderful Garden, The (1911) **E[dith] Nesbit** (1858)
Wonderful Ice Cream Suit, The (1965) **Ray Bradbury** (1920)
Wonderful O, The (1957) **James Thurber** (1894–1961)
Wonderful Stories for Children [from Hans Christian Andersen] (1846) **Mary Howitt** (1799) (tr.)

Wonderful Visit, The (1895) **H.G. Wells** (1866)
Wonderful Wizard of Oz, The (1900) **L. Frank Baum** (1856)
Wonderful Years, Wonderful Years (1988) **George V. Higgins** (1939)
Wonderfull Yeare, The (1603) **Thomas Dekker** (1572?)
Wonderings (1943) **John Masefield** (1878)
Wonderland (1971) **Joyce Carol Oates** (1938)
Wonders in the Sun (1706) **Thomas d'Urfey** (1653)
Wonders of the Invisible World, The (1693) **Cotton Mather** (1663)
Wonders of the Little World, The (1678) **Nathaniel Wanley** (1634)
Wonders of the Peake, The (1681) **Charles Cotton** (1630)
Wondrous Tale of Alroy, The [with *The Rise of Iskander*] (1833) **Benjamin Disraeli** (1804)
Wood and Stone (1915) **John Cooper Powys** (1872)
Wood Beyond the World, The (1894) **William Morris** (1834)
Wood Leighton (1836) **Mary Howitt** (1799)
Wood Magic (1880) **Richard Jefferies** (1848)
Wooden Dogs (1982) **Christopher Middleton** (1926)
Wooden Horse, The (1909) **Sir Hugh Walpole** (1884)
Wooden Hunters (1975) **Matt Cohen** (1942)
Wooden Pegasus, The (1920) **Edith Sitwell** (1887)
Wooden Shepherdess, The (1973) **Richard Hughes** (1900)
Woodland Life, The (1897) **Edward Thomas** (1878)
Woodland Tales (1921) **Ernest Thompson Seton** (1860)
Woodlanders, The (1887) **Thomas Hardy** (1840)
Woodman, The (1849) **William Ellery Channing** (1780)
Woodman, The (1849) **G.P.R. James** (1799)
Woods in Winter, The (1970) **Stella Gibbons** (1902)
Woods, The (1977) **David Mamet** (1947)
Woodstock (1826) **Sir Walter Scott** (1771)
Woodwo (1967) **Ted Hughes** (1930)
Wooing O't, The (1873) **Mrs A.H. Alexander** (1825)
Wooing of Malkatoon, The (1898) **Lew Wallace** (1827)
Word Order (1989) **J.H. Prynne** (1936)
Word Over All (1943) **C. Day Lewis** (1904)
Word to the Wise, A (1770) **Hugh Kelly** (1739)
Wordhoard (1969) **Jill Paton Walsh** (1937) [with Kevin Crossley-Holland]
Words and Idioms (1925) **Logan Pearsall Smith** (1865)
Words for Music Perhaps (1932) **W.B. Yeats** (1865)
Words for the Wind (1958) **Theodore Roethke** (1908)
Words, The [*Les Mots*] (1966) **Jean-Paul Sartre** (1905)
Words Upon the Window Pane, The (1934) **W.B. Yeats** (1865)
Words with a Black Orpington (1978) **David Campbell** (1915)
Words Without Music (1968) **Peter Porter** (1929)
Wordsworth (1903) **Sir Walter Raleigh** (1861)
Wordsworth (1954) **F.W. Bateson** (1901)
Wordsworth, Shelley, Keats (1874) **David Masson** (1822)
Wordsworth's Grave (1890) **Sir William Watson** (1858)
Work (1873) **Louisa M. Alcott** (1832)
Work [*Travail*] (1901) **Émile Zola** (1840)
Work for the Winter (1936) **Julian Bell** (1908)
Work of Art (1934) **Sinclair Lewis** (1885)
Work Suspended (1942) **Evelyn Waugh** (1903)
Workaday Woman, The (1906) **Violet Hunt** (1866)
Worke for Armourours (1609) **Thomas Dekker** (1572?)
Workers in the Dawn (1880) **George Gissing** (1857)
Workes of Geffrey Chaucer, The [ed. William Thynne] (1532) **Geoffrey Chaucer** (1340?–1400)
Workes of Geffrey Chaucer, The [ed. John Stow] (1561) **Geoffrey Chaucer** (1340?–1400)
Workes of Our Antient and Lerned English Poet, Geffrey Chaucer, The [ed. Thomas Speght] (1598) **Geoffrey Chaucer** (1340?–1400)
Workhouse Donkey, The (1963) **John Arden** (1930)
Working (1974) **Studs Terkel** (1912)
Working Novelist, The (1965) **V.S. Pritchett** (1900)
Working with Structuralism (1981) **David Lodge** (1935)
Works . . . Newly Augmented (1601) **Samuel Daniel** (1562)
Works of Horace Translated into Verse, The (1767) **Christopher Smart** (1722) (tr.)
Works of Mr William Shakespear (1709) **Nicholas Rowe** (1674) (ed.)
Works of Ossian, The (1765) **James Macpherson** (1736)
Works of Plato, The (1804) **Thomas Taylor** (1758) [with Floyer Sydenham]
Works of Richard Savage , The (1775) **Samuel Johnson** (1709) (ed.)
Works of Shakespear, The (1725) **Alexander Pope** (1688) (ed.)
Works of Shakespeare, The (1733) **Lewis Theobald** (1688) (ed.)
Works of Virgil (1697) **John Dryden** (1631) (tr.)
Works of William Shakespeare , The (1904) **F.J. Furnivall** (1825) (ed.)
World According to Garp, The (1978) **John Irving** (1942)
World Alien, A (1980) **J.F. Hendry** (1912)
World and His Wife, The (1858) **Edward Bulwer-Lytton** (1803)
World and Other Places, The (1998) **Jeanette Winterson** (1959)
World and the West, The (1953) **Arnold Toynbee** (1889)
World As It Goes, The (1779) **William Combe** (1742)
World Child, A (1975) **Iris Murdoch** (1919)
World Crisis, The (1923) **Sir Winston Churchill** (1874)
World Decision, The (1916) **Robert Herrick** (1868)
World Does Move, The (1928) **Booth Tarkington** (1869)

World Enough and Time (1950) **Robert Penn Warren** (1905)
World I Never Made, A (1936) **James T. Farrell** (1904)
World I See, The (1960) **Patric Dickinson** (1914)
World in Ripeness, The (1972) **H.E. Bates** (1905)
World in the Evening, The (1954) **Christopher Isherwood** (1904)
World in the Moon, The (1697) **Elkanah Settle** (1648)
World Inside, The (1971) **Robert Silverberg** (1935)
World is a Wedding, The (1948) **Delmore Schwartz** (1913)
World is Full of Married Men, The (1968) **Jackie Collins** (1939)
World is Made of Glass, The (1983) **Morris West** (1916)
World Jones Made, The (1956) **Philip K. Dick** (1928)
World of Apples, The (1973) **John Cheever** (1912)
World of Chance, The (1893) **William Dean Howells** (1837)
World of Difference, A (1955) **Robert Conquest** (1917)
World of Dreams, The (1911) **Havelock Ellis** (1859)
World of Ice, The (1859) **R.M. Ballantyne** (1825)
World of Labour, The (1913) **G.D.H. Cole** (1889)
World of Love, A (1955) **Elizabeth Bowen** (1899)
World of Nagaraj, The (1990) **R.K. Narayan** (1907)
World of Profit, A (1968) **Louis Auchinloss** (1917)
World of Propensities, A (1990) **Sir Karl Popper** (1902)
World of Ptavvs (1966) **Larry Niven** (1938)
World of Strangers, A (1958) **Nadine Gordimer** (1923)
World of Suzie Wong, The (1957) **Richard Mason** (1919)
World of William Clissold, The (1926) **H.G. Wells** (1866)
World of Wonders (1975) **Robertson Davies** (1913)
World Over, The (1936) **Edith Wharton** (1862)
World Set Free, The (1914) **H.G. Wells** (1866)
World So Wide (1951) **Sinclair Lewis** (1885)
World To Come, The (1739) **Isaac Watts** (1674)
World to Win, A (1935) **Jack Conroy** (1899)
World to Win, A (1946) **Upton Sinclair** (1878)
World Tost at Tennis, The (1620) **Thomas Middleton** (1580) [with William Rowley]
World Turned Upside Down, The (1972) **Christopher Hill** (1912)
World Upside Down, The (1954) **William Mayne** (1928)
World We Live In, The (1944) **Louis Bromfield** (1896)
World Well Lost, The (1877) **E. Lynn Linton** (1822)
World Went Very Well Then, The (1887) **Sir Walter Besant** (1836)
World Within a War, A (1944) **Sir Herbert Read** (1893)
World Within World (1951) **Sir Stephen Spender** (1909)
World's Body, The (1938) **John Crowe Ransom** (1888)
World's Desire, The (1890) **Sir H. Rider Haggard** (1856) [with Andrew Lang]
World's End, The (1877) **Richard Jefferies** (1848)
World's End (1940) **Upton Sinclair** (1878)
World's End (1980) **Paul Theroux** (1941)
World's Fair (1985) **E.L. Doctorow** (1931)
World's Flesh, The (1954) **Vincent Buckley** (1925)
World's Great Snare, The (1900) **E. Phillips Oppenheim** (1866)
World's Room, The (1974) **Norman MacCaig** (1910)
World's Wife, The (1999) **Carol Ann Duffy** (1955)
Worlde of Wordes, A (1598) **John Florio** (1553)
Worldly Hopes (1982) **A.R. Ammons** (1926)
'Worlds Not Realized' (1856) **Margaret [Mrs Alfred] Gatty** (1809)
Worlds of Color (1961) **W.E.B. du Bois** (c.1868)
Wormwood (1890) **Marie Corelli** (1855)
Wormwood (1966) **Thomas Kinsella** (1928)
Wormwood (1987) **Ken Smith** (1938)
Worrals of the WAAF (1941) **W.E. Johns** (1893)
Wort Papers, The (1972) **Peter Mathers** (1931)
Worthy Communicant, The (1660) **Jeremy Taylor** (1613)
Worthy Tract of Paulus Jovius, The (1585) **Samuel Daniel** (1562) (tr.)
Would-Be Gentleman, The [Le Bourgeois gentilhomme] (1670) **'Molière' [Jean-Baptiste Poquelin]** (1622)
Would-Begoods, The (1901) **E[dith] Nesbit** (1858)
Wouldn't Take Nothing For My Journey Now (1993) **Maya Angelou** (1928)
Wound and the Bow, The (1941) **Edmund Wilson** (1895)
Wounded Thammuz (1942) **John Heath-Stubbs** (1918)
Wounds in the Rain (1900) **Stephen Crane** (1871)
Wounds of Civill War, The (1594) **Thomas Lodge** (1558)
Wrack at Tidesend (1952) **Sir Osbert Sitwell** (1892)
Wrangling Lovers, The (1676) **Edward Ravenscroft** (1644)
Wreath for the Enemy, A (1954) **Pamela Frankau** (1908)
Wreath for Udomo, A (1956) **Peter Abrahams** (1919)
Wreck of the Archangel, The (1989) **George Mackay Brown** (1921)
Wreck of the 'Grosvenor', The (1877) **W. Clark Russell** (1844)
Wreck of the Northern Belle, The (1857) **Sir Edwin Arnold** (1832)
Wreckage (1893) **Hubert Crackanthorpe** (1870)
Wreckage of Agathon, The (1970) **John Gardner** (1933)
Wrecker, The (1892) **Robert Louis Stevenson** (1850) [with Lloyd Osbourne]
Wrecker, The (1954) **Saul Bellow** (1915)
Wreckers Must Breathe (1940) **'Hammond Innes' [Ralph Hammond-Innes]** (1913)
Write On (1986) **David Lodge** (1935)
Writer and the Absolute, The (1952) **Wyndham Lewis** (1882)
Writer in Disguise, The (1985) **Alan Bennett** (1934)
Writer's Britain, A (1979) **Margaret Drabble** (1939)

Writer's Capital, A (1974) **Louis Auchinloss** (1917)
Writer's Diary, A (1953) **Virginia Woolf** (1882–1941)
Writer's Notebook, A (1949) **Somerset Maugham** (1874)
Writer's Recollections, A (1918) **Mrs T. Humphry Ward** (1851)
Writing Game, The (1990) **David Lodge** (1935)
Writing Home (1985) **Hugo Williams** (1942)
Writing Home (1994) **Alan Bennett** (1934)
Writing in Restaurants (1986) **David Mamet** (1947)
Writing Lives (1984) **Leon Edel** (1907)
Writing of Fiction, The (1925) **Edith Wharton** (1862)
Writing on the Wall, The (1970) **Mary McCarthy** (1912)
Writing to Survive (1988) **Conrad Richter** (1890)
Written on the Body (1992) **Jeanette Winterson** (1959)
Written on Water (1972) **Charles Tomlinson** (1927)
Wrong Box, The (1889) **Robert Louis Stevenson** (1850) [with Lloyd Osbourne]
Wrong boy, The (2000) **Willy Russell** (1947)
Wrong Information is Being Given Out at Princeton (1998) **J.P. Donleavy** (1926)
Wrong Prescription, The (1893) **'Lanoe Falconer' [Mary Elizabeth Hawker]** (1848)
Wrong Set, The (1949) **Angus Wilson** (1913)
Wrongs of Africa, The (1787) **William Roscoe** (1753)
Wrongs of Woman, The [unfinished] (1798) **Mary Wollstonecraft** (1759)
Wunderkind, Das (1914) **Thomas Mann** (1875)
Wuthering Heights; and Agnes Grey [by 'Ellis and Acton Bell'] (1847) **Emily Brontë** (1818) and **Anne Brontë** (1820)
Wyatt's Hurricane (1966) **Desmond Bagley** (1923)
Wychford Poisoning Case, The [as 'Anthony Berkeley'] (1926) **Anthony Berkeley Cox** (1893)
Wycklyffes Wicket (1546) **John Wycliffe** (d. 1384)
Wylder's Hand (1864) **J.S. Le Fanu** (1814)
Wyllard's Weird (1885) **M.E. Braddon** (1835)
Wyndham Towers (1890) **Thomas Bailey Aldrich** (1836)
Wyvern Mystery, The (1869) **J.S. le Fanu** (1814)

X

Χαιρε (1950) **E.E. Cummings** (1894)
Xanadu (1992) **Simon Armitage** (1963)
Xantippe (1881) **Amy Levy** (1861)
Xerxes (1699) **Colley Cibber** (1671)
Ximena (1844) **Bayard Taylor** (1825)
Ximena (1712) **Colley Cibber** (1671)
Xingu (1916) **Edith Wharton** (1862)
Xorandor (1986) **Christine Brooke-Rose** (1926)
X-Self (1987) **Edward Brathwaite** (1930)

Y

Yaddo Letter, The (1994) **Derek Mahon** (1941)
Yage Letters, The [correspondence with William S. Burroughs] (1963) **Allen Ginsberg** (1926)
Yankee in Canada, A (1866) **Henry David Thoreau** (1817–62)
Yankey in London (1809) **Royall Tyler** (1757)
Yard of Sun, A (1970) **Christopher Fry [Christopher Fry Harris]** (1907)
Yarrow Revisited (1835) **William Wordsworth** (1770)
Year and a Day, A (1976) **William Mayne** (1928)
Year Before Last (1932) **Kay Boyle** (1903)
Year From a Reporter's Note-Book, A (1898) **Richard Harding Davis** (1864)
Year in San Fernando, The (1965) **Michael Anthony** (1932)
Year of Living Dangerously, The (1978) **C.J. Koch** (1932)
Year of No Flood, The (1995) **Amy Tan** (1952)
Year of Space, A (1953) **Eric Linklater** (1899)
Year of the Whale, The (1965) **George Mackay Brown** (1921)
Year of Wonders, The (1737) **Stephen Duck** (1705)
Year One, The (1952) **Kathleen Raine** (1908)
Year or So with Edgar, A (1979) **George V. Higgins** (1939)
Year's Life, A (1841) **James Russell Lowell** (1819)
Yearling, The (1938) **Marjorie Rawlings** (1896)
Years as Catches, The (1966) **Robert Duncan** (1919)
Years Between, The (1919) **Rudyard Kipling** (1865)
Years of Grace (1930) **Margaret Ayer Barnes** (1886)
Years of the Sword (1969) **Elizabeth Longford** (1906)
Years, The (1937) **Virginia Woolf** (1882)
Yeast (1851) **Charles Kingsley** (1819)
Yeats: The Man and the Mask [rev. 1979] (1948) **Richard Ellmann** (1918)
Yekl (1896) **Abraham Cahan** (1860)
Yellow Admiral, The (1997) **Patrick O'Brian** (1914)
Yellow Aster, A (1894) **'Iota' [Kathleen Mannington Caffyn]** (1855?)
Yellow Bittern, The (1920) **Daniel Corkery** (1878)
Yellow Danger, The (1898) **M.P. Shiel** (1865)
Yellow Domino, The (1906) **Katharine Tynan** (1861)
Yellow Fairy Book, The (1894) **Andrew Lang** (1844) (ed.)
Yellow Frigate, The (1855) **James Grant** (1822)
Yellow Gentians and Blue (1927) **Zona Gale** (1874)
Yellow God, The (1909) **Sir H. Rider Haggard** (1856)
Yellow Meads of Asphodel, The (1976) **H.E. Bates** (1905–74)
Yellow Pages, The (1974) **James Merrill** (1926)
Yellow Ticket, The (1914) **'Frank' Harris** (1856)
Yellowplush Correspondence, The (1838) **W.M. Thackeray** (1811)
'Yellow Wallpaper, The' (1892) **Charlotte Perkins Gilman** (1860)
Yemassee, The (1835) **William Gilmore Simms** (1806)
Yerma (1934) **Federico García Lorca** (1898)

Yes Is For a Very Young Man (1946) **Gertrude Stein** (1874)
Yesterday Came Suddenly (1993) **Francis King** (1923)
Yesterday in the Back Lane (1995) **Bernice Rubens** (1923)
Yesterday's Spy (1975) **Len Deighton** (1929)
Yet Again (1909) **Max Beerbohm** (1872)
Yet Being Someone Other (1982) **Sir Laurens van der Post** (1906)
Yet Other Waters (1952) **James T. Farrell** (1904)
Yeux d'Elsa, Les ['Elsa's Eyes'] (1942) **Louis Aragon** (1897)
Yogi and the Commissar, The (1945) **Arthur Koestler** (1905)
Yoke of Life, The (1930) **Frederick Grove** (1879)
Yoke of the Thorah, The [as 'Sydney Luska'] (1887) **Henry Harland** (1861)
Yolande (1883) **William Black** (1841)
Yonnondio (1974) **Tillie Olsen** (1913)
You Are Now Entering the Human Heart (1983) **Janet Frame** (1924)
You Can't Come Back (1966) **Bruce Beaver** (1928)
You Can't Do Both (1994) **Kingsley Amis** (1922)
You Can't Get There From Here (1957) **Ogden Nash** (1902)
You Can't Get There From Here (1972) **Hugh Hood** (1928)
You Can't Go Home Again (1940) **Thomas Wolfe** (1900–38)
You Can't Keep a Good Woman Down (1981) **Alice Walker** (1944)
You Can't See Round Corners (1947) **Jon Cleary** (1917)
You, Emperors, and Others (1960) **Robert Penn Warren** (1905)
You Know I Can't Hear You When the Water's Running (1967) **Robert W. Anderson** (1917)
You Know Me, Al (1914) **Ring Lardner** (1885)
You Make Your Own Life (1938) **V.S. Pritchett** (1900)
You Must Remember This (1987) **Joyce Carol Oates** (1938)
You Only Live Twice (1964) **Ian Fleming** (1908)
You Touched Me! (1947) **'Tennessee' [Thomas Lanier] Williams** (1911)
You Who Have Dreams (1925) **Maxwell Anderson** (1888)
You Who Know (1994) **Nicholas Freeling** (1927)
You Will Know When You Get There (1982) **Allen Curnow** (1911)
You've Had Your Time (1990) **'Anthony Burgess' [John Anthony Burgess Wilson]** (1917)
Young Admirall, The (1637) **James Shirley** (1596)
Young Adolf (1978) **Beryl Bainbridge** (1934)
Young Blood (1898) **E.W. Hornung** (1866)
Young Caesar, The (1958) **Rex Warner** (1905)
Young Diana, The (1918) **Marie Corelli** (1855)
Young Duke, The (1831) **Benjamin Disraeli** (1804)
Young Fate, The [*La Jeune Parque*] (1917) **Paul-Ambroise Valéry** (1871)
Young Felix (1923) **Frank Swinnerton** (1884)
Young Franc-Tireurs, The (1872) **G.A. Henty** (1832)
Young Idea, The (1910) **Frank Swinnerton** (1884)
Young in One Another's Arms, The (1977) **Jane Rule** (1931)
Young King, The (1679) **Aphra Behn** (1640?)
Young Lions, The (1948) **Irwin Shaw** (1913)
Young Lives (1899) **Richard le Gallienne** (1866)
Young Lonigan (1932) **James T. Farrell** (1904)
Young Lovell, The (1913) **Ford Madox Ford** (1873)
Young Man (1951) **Kay Dick** (1915)
Young Man's Year, A (1915) **'Anthony Hope' [Sir Anthony Hope Hawkins]** (1863)
Young Manhood of Studs Lonigan, The (1934) **James T. Farrell** (1904)
Young Matriarch, The (1942) **G.B. Stern** (1890)
Young Melbourne, The (1939) **Lord David Cecil** (1902)
Young Musgrave (1877) **Margaret Oliphant** (1828)
Young Patullo (1975) **J.I.M. Stewart** (1906)
Young People (1958) **'William Cooper' [Harry Summerfield Hoff]** (1910)
Young People's Pride (1922) **Stephen Vincent Benét** (1889)
Young Philosopher, The (1798) **Charlotte Smith** (1749)
Young Physician, The (1919) **Francis Brett Young** (1884)
Young Renny (1935) **Mazo de la Roche** (1879)
Young Shoulders (1982) **John Wain** (1925)
Young Thomas Hardy (1975) **Robert Gittings** (1911)
Young Tom (1944) **Forrest Reid** (1875)
Young Trawler, The (1884) **R.M. Ballantyne** (1825)
Young Visiters, The (1919) **Daisy Ashford** (1881)
Young Widow, The (1789) **William Hayley** (1745)
Young Wife's Tale, A (1974) **William Sansom** (1912)
Youngblood Hawke (1962) **Herman Wouk** (1915)
Younger Brother, The (1793) **Charles Dibdin** (1745)
Younger Generation, The (1910) **Stanley Houghton** (1881)
Younger Son, The (1988) **Karl Shapiro** (1913)
Youngest Camel, The (1939) **Kay Boyle** (1903)
Your Fiery Furnace (1932) **Paul Green** (1894)
Your Five Gallants (1608) **Thomas Middleton** (1580)
Your Native Land, Your Life (1986) **Adrienne Rich** (1929)
Youth (1856) **Leo Tolstoy** (1828)
Youth (1902) **Joseph Conrad** (1857)
Youth (1915) **Isaac Rosenberg** (1890)
Youth and the Bright Medusa (1920) **Willa Cather** (1873)
Youth of Parnassus, The (1895) **Logan Pearsall Smith** (1865)
Yussuf the Guide (1886) **George Manville Fenn** (1831)
Yvette (1885) **Guy de Maupassant** (1850)

Z

Zadig (1747) **'Voltaire' [François-Marie Arouet]** (1694)
Zaïde (1670) **Marie-Madeleine La Fayette** (1634)
Zaidee (1856) **Margaret Oliphant** (1828)

Zambra the Detective (1894) **'Headon Hill' [Francis Edward Grainger]** (1857)
Zanoni (1842) **Edward Bulwer-Lytton** (1803)
Zanzibar Cat, The (1983) **Joanna Russ** (1937)
Zastrozzi (1810) **P.B. Shelley** (1792)
Zazie [*Zazie dans le Métro*] (1959) **Raymond Queneau** (1903)
Zebra-Striped Hearse, The (1962) **'Ross MacDonald' [Kenneth Millar]** (1915)
Zeely (1967) **Virginia Hamilton** (1936)
Zelauto (1580) **Anthony Munday** (1560)
Zella Sees Herself (1917) **'E.M. Delafield' [E.E.M. de la Pasture]** (1890)
Zeluco (1789) **John Moore** (1729)
Zen and the Art of Motorcycle Maintenance (1974) **Robert Pirsig** (1928)
Zen Garden (1973) **James Kirkup** (1923)
Zen There Was Murder (1960) **H.R.F. Keating** (1926)
Zeph (1880) **George R. Sims** (1847)
Zeppelin Nights (1916) **Violet Hunt** (1866) [with Ford Madox Ford]
Zéro (1884) **Mrs Campbell Praed** (1851)
Zillah (1828) **Horace Smith** (1779)
Zima Junction (1956) **Yevgeny Yevtushenko** (1933)
Zimmerman Telegram, The (1958) **Barbara Tuchman** (1912)
Zincali, The (1841) **George Borrow** (1803)
Ziska (1897) **Marie Corelli** (1855)
Zlateh the Goat (1966) **Isaac Bashevis Singer** (1904)
Zodiac of Life, The [bks i-iii; from Palingenius] (1560) **Barnaby Googe** (1540) (tr.)
Zodiac of Life, The [bks i-vi] (1561) **Barnaby Googe** (1540) (tr.)
Zodiac of Life, The [bks i-xii] (1565) **Barnaby Googe** (1540) (tr.)
Zodiac, The (1976) **James Dickey** (1923)
Zoe (1845) **Geraldine Jewsbury** (1812)
Zofloya (1806) **Charlotte Dacre** (1782?)
Zohrab the Hostage (1832) **James Morier** (1780)
Zoo Story, The (1958) **Edward Albee** (1928)
Zoology of the Voyage of HMS Beagle, The (1838–43) **Charles Darwin** (1809) (ed.)
Zoom! (1989) **Simon Armitage** (1963)
Zoonomia (1794) **Erasmus Darwin** (1731)
Zorba the Greek (1946) **Nikos Kazantzakis** (1883)
Zoroaster (1885) **F. Marion Crawford** (1854)
Zuckerman Bound (1985) **Philip Roth** (1933)
Zuckerman Unbound (1981) **Philip Roth** (1933)
Zuleika Dobson (1911) **Max Beerbohm** (1872)

Character Index

A

A., Mr and Mrs
W.H. Auden & Christopher Isherwood: *The Ascent of F6*

Aaron the Moor Lover of *Tamora
William Shakespeare: *Titus Andronicus*

Abdiel The loyal seraph
John Milton: *Paradise Lost*

Abelwhite, Godfrey A barrister and hypocritical philanthropist
Wilkie Collins: *The Moonstone*

Abessa Daughter of *Corceca
Edmund Spenser: *The Faerie Queene*

Abhorson An executioner
William Shakespeare: *Measure for Measure*

Abigail A waiting woman
Francis Beaumont & John Fletcher: *The Scornful Lady*

Absolute, Sir Anthony Father of Captain Jack *Absolute
R.B. Sheridan: *The Rivals*

Absolute, Captain Jack Son of Sir Anthony *Absolute who takes the alias Ensign Beverley to court Lydia *Languish
R.B. Sheridan: *The Rivals*

Achilles Leader of the Greeks
William Shakespeare: *Troilus and Cressida*

Achitophel Meant for the Earl of Shaftesbury
John Dryden: *Absalom and Achitophel*

Acrasia Personification of intemperance
Edmund Spenser: *Faerie Queene*

Acres, Bob A country squire
R.B. Sheridan: *The Rivals*

Adah Cain's wife
Lord Byron: *Cain*

Adam A faithful old servant who accompanies *Orlando into exile
William Shakespeare: *As You Like It*

Adams, [Parson] Abraham Companion of Joseph Andrews
Henry Fielding: *The History of the Adventures of Joseph Andrews*

Adramelech A rebel angel
John Milton: *Paradise Lost*

Adriana Wife of *Antipholus of Ephesus
William Shakespeare: *The Comedy of Errors*

Aegeon Syracusan merchant
William Shakespeare: *The Comedy of Errors*

Aeglamour The sad shepherd, who mourns for the supposed loss of his love *Earine
Ben Jonson: *The Sad Shepherd*

Aetion Possibly meant for Shakespeare
Edmund Spenser: *Colin Clouts Come Home Again*

Affery *see* FLINTWICH, JEREMIAH

Agag
John Dryden: *Absalom and Achitophel*

Agape Mother of Priamond, Diamond, and Triamond
Edmund Spenser: *Faerie Queene*

Agdistes The porter of the Bower of Bliss
Edmund Spenser: *Faerie Queene*

Aguecheek, Sir Andrew Companion of Sir Toby *Belch
William Shakespeare: *Twelfth Night*

Ahab, Monomaniacal one-legged master of the Pequod
Herman Melville: *Moby-Dick*

Aimwell An impoverished younger son, friend of *Archer
George Farquhar: *The Beaux' Stratagem*

Ajax Greek leader of Trojan blood
William Shakespeare: *Troilus and Cressida*

Akela Leader of the wolf pack in which the 'man-cub' *Mowgli is brought up
Rudyard Kipling: *The Jungle Book*

Alarbus A son of *Tamora
William Shakespeare: *Titus Andronicus*

Albany, Duke of Husband of *Goneril
William Shakespeare: *King Lear*

Albovine King of the Lombards
Sir William Davenant: *Albovine*

Aldclyffe, Cytherea Daughter of Captain Aldclyffe [formerly Bradleigh]
Thomas Hardy: *Desperate Remedies*

Alden, Roberta A working-class girl seduced by Clyde *Griffiths
Theodore Dreiser: *An American Tragedy*

Alexas Attendant on *Cleopatra
William Shakespeare: *Antony and Cleopatra*

Alftruda
Charles Kingsley: *Hereward the Wake*

Algarsife One of the two sons of King *Cambuscan
Geoffrey Chaucer: 'The Squire's Tale' [*Canterbury Tales*]

Algrind Meant for Edmuind Grindal, Archbishop of Canterbury
Edmund Spenser: *The Shepheardes Calender*

Aliena Name adopted by *Celia
William Shakespeare: *As You Like It*

Allen, Arabella Friend of Isabella *Wardle; sister of Benjamin *Allen
Charles Dickens: *The Posthumous Papers of the Pickwick Club*

Allen, Benjamin Medical student and friend of Bob *Sawyer
Charles Dickens: *The Posthumous Papers of the Pickwick Club*

Alleyn, [Chief Inspector] Roderick A gentleman police detective
Ngaio Marsh: *Enter a Murderer* [and many others]

Allworth, Tom and Lady
Philip Massinger: *A New Way to Pay Old Debts*

Allworthy, Bridget Sister of Squire *Allworthy,

mother of Tom Jones, who marries Captain *Blifil
Henry Fielding: *Tom Jones*

Allworthy, Squire Benevolent widower who takes in Tom Jones (unaware that he is his nephew)
Henry Fielding: *Tom Jones*

Alma Representing the virgin soul
Edmund Spenser: *The Faerie Queene*

Almeria
William Congreve: *The Mourning Bride*

Almeyda
John Dryden: *Don Sebastian*

Alonso King of Naples
William Shakespeare: *The Tempest*

Alrui
Benjamin Disraeli: *Alroy*

Altamont
Nicholas Rowe: *The Fair Penitent*

Altamont, Colonel Jack [alias **Amory,** alias **Armstrong**] Father of Blanch *Amory
W.M. Thackeray: *Pendennis*

Amanda Wife of *Loveless
Sir John Vanbrugh: *The Relapse*

Amaryllis A shepherdess; meant for Alice Spencer, later Countess of Derby
Edmund Spenser: *Colin Clouts Come Home Again*

Ambrose, Father *see* GLENDINNING, EDWARD

Ambrosio A satanic villain
M.G. Lewis: *The Monk*

Amelia *see* BOOTH, AMELIA

Amidas Brother of *Bracidas
Edmund Spenser: *The Faerie Queene*

Amintor Gentleman betrothed to *Aspatia
Francis Beaumont & John Fletcher: *The Maid's Tragedy*

Amlet, Mrs, and Dick
Sir John Vanbrugh: *The Confederacy*

Amoret Twin sister of *Belphoebe
Edmund Spenser: *The Faerie Queene*

Amory, Blanche [Betsy] The haughty daughter of Lady *Clavering's first marriage to Jack *Altamont
W.M. Thackeray: *Pendennis*

Amory, Jack *see* ALTAMONT, COLONEL JACK

Amphialus Son of *Cecropia
Sir Philip Sidney: *Arcadia*

Amundeville, Lord Henry
Lord Byron: *Don Juan*

Amyas A squire 'of low degree'
Edmund Spenser: *The Faerie Queene*

Amyntas Possibly meant for the Earl of Derby
Edmund Spenser: *Colin Clouts Come Home Again*

Ananias A fanatical Anabaptist
Ben Jonson: *The Alchemist*

Andrews, Joseph Stable-boy to Sir Thomas Booby, finally revealed to be the son of Squire Wilson
Henry Fielding: *The History of the Adventures of Joseph Andrews*

Andrews, Pamela Impoverished central character and principal correspondent, obsessively pursued by Mr B.
Samuel Richardson: *Pamela*

Andrugio, Duke of Genoa
John Marston: *Antonio and Mellida*

Angelica Niece of Foresight, in love with Valentine Legend
William Congreve: *Love for Love*

Angelica, Princess Daughter of King Valoroso of Paflagonia
W.M. Thackeray: *The Rose and the Ring*

Angelo A goldsmith
William Shakespeare: *The Comedy of Errors*

Angelo Deputy to *Vincentio who lusts after *Claudio's sister *Isabella
William Shakespeare: *Measure for Measure*

Annabella Sister of Giovanni, with whom she has an incestuous affair
John Ford: *'Tis Pity She's a Whore*

Anne of Green Gables *see* SHIRLEY, ANNE

Ansell, Stewart A philosopher
E.M. Forster: *The Longest Journey*

Antigonus Husband of *Paulina
William Shakespeare: *The Winter's Tale*

Antipholus, of Ephesus and of Syracuse Twin brothers, sons of *Egeon
William Shakespeare: *The Comedy of Errors*

Antonio The 'changeling' who disguises himself as a lunatic to pursue Isabella
Thomas Middleton and William Rowley: *The Changeling*

Antonio The'merchant of Venice' obliged to borrow money from Shylock for his friend *Bassanio
William Shakespeare: *The Merchant of Venice*

Antonio A sea-captain
William Shakespeare: *Twelfth Night*

Antony, Mark Triumvir of Rome
John Dryden: *All for Love*

Antony, Mark Triumvir of Rome
William Shakespeare: *Antony and Cleopatra*

Anville, Miss Name assumed by Evelina
Frances Burney: *Evelina*

Apemantus A 'churlish philosopher'
William Shakespeare: *Timon of Athens*

Apollyon The angel of the bottomless pit (Rev. 9: 11)
John Bunyan: *Pilgrim's Progress*

Arabin, Revd Francis High Church clergyman and fellow of Lazarus College, Oxford; later Dean of Barchester and second husband of Eleanor *Bold
Anthony Trollope: *Barchester Towers; Framley Parsonage; The Last Chronicle of Barset*

Aragorn [known as **Strider**] Chivalrous companion of Frodo *Baggins and heir of Gondor
J.R.R. Tolkein: *The Lord of the Rings*

Aramis One of three valiant members of Louis

XIII's musketeers, together with *Athos and *Porthos; see also *D'Artagnan
Alexander Dumas [père]: *The Three Musketeers*

Arbaces King of Iberia
Francis Beaumont & John Fletcher: *A King and No King*

Archer One of the two central characters, who pretends to be his friend *Aimwell's servant
George Farquhar: *The Beaux' Stratagem*

Archer, Isabel American heiress who marries Gilbert *Osmond
Henry James: *The Portrait of a Lady*

Archer, Newland A young lawyer engaged (later married) to May *Welland but who is really in love with Ellen *Olenska
Edith Wharton: *The Age of Innocence*

Archibald of Hagenbach
Sir Walter Scott: *Anne of Geierstein*

Archimago/Archimage The great enchanter
Edmund Spenser: *The Faerie Queene*

Arcite A young knight, his friend *Palamon's rival for the love of *Emelye
Geoffrey Chaucer: 'The Knight's Tale' [*Canterbury Tales*]

Arethusa Daughter of the King of Calabria
Francis Beaumont & John Fletcher: *Philaster*

Argante Personification of lust
Edmund Spenser: *The Faerie Queene*

Ariel A rebel angel
John Milton: *Paradise Lost*

Ariel Chief of the sylphs
Alexander Pope: *Rape of the Lock*

Ariel An airy spirit
William Shakespeare: *The Tempest*

Arioch A rebel angel
John Milton: *Paradise Lost*

Armado, Don Adriano de A Spanish braggart
William Shakespeare: *Love's Labour's Lost*

Armine, Ferdinand
Benjamin Disraeli: *Henrietta Temple*

Armstrong *see* ALTAMONT

Armstrong, John
John Arden: *Armstrong's Last Goodnight*

Artegall, Sir Champion of Justice. Representing Lord Grey de Wilton
Edmund Spenser: *The Faerie Queene*

Artful Dodger, The *see* DAWKINS, JACK

Arthur, Prince
Edmund Spenser: *The Faerie Queene*

Arveragus Husband of *Dorigen
Geoffrey Chaucer: 'The Franklin's Tale' [*Canterbury Tales*]

Arviragus Younger son of *Cymbeline, stolen by *Belarius; known as Cadwal
William Shakespeare: *Cymbeline*

Arviragus
Edmund Spenser: *The Faerie Queene*

Asaph In Tate's portion, representing Dryden
John Dryden/Nahum Tate: *Absalom and Achitophel*

Ash, Randolph Henry A fictitious Victorian poet
A.S. Byatt: *Possession*

Ashburnham, Edward Embodiment of the perfect English gentleman but with a fatal weakness for women; his wife, Leonora
Ford Madox Ford: *The Good Soldier*

Ashenden Novelist and secret agent
W. Somerset Maugham: *Ashenden*

Ashton, Sir William, Lady, and Lucy
Sir Walter Scott: *The Bride of Lammermoor*

Aslan A noble lion, Lord of Narnia
C.S. Lewis: *The Lion, the Witch, and the Wardrobe* [and others]

Aspatia
Francis Beaumont & John Fletcher: *The Maid's Tragedy*

Astarte The Phoenician goddess of love; meant for Byron's half-sister, Augusta Leigh
Lord Byron: *Manfred*

Asteria, Mr An 'ichthyologist'
Thomas Love Peacock: *Nightmare Abbey*

Athelstane of Coningsburgh
Sir Walter Scott: *Ivanhoe*

Athos One of three valiant members of Louis XIII's musketeers, together with *Porthos and *Aramis; see also *D'Artagnan
Alexander Dumas [père]: *The Three Musketeers*

Atwater, William In love with Susan Nunnery
Anthony Powell: *Afternoon Men*

Aubery, Jean-Benoît A French gentleman turned pirate
Daphne du Maurier: *Frenchman's Creek*

Audrey A goatherd, betrothed to *Touchstone
William Shakespeare: *As You Like It*

Aufidius, Tullus General of the Volscians
William Shakespeare: *Coriolanus*

Aurelia Loved by Launcelot *Greaves
Tobias Smollett: *Sir Launcelot Greaves*

Autolycus A pedlar
William Shakespeare: *The Winter's Tale*

Avenel, Roland [Roland Graeme]
Sir Walter Scott: *The Abbot*

Avery, Shug A nightclub singer
Alice Walker: *The Color Purple*

Aziz, Dr A young Muslim doctor
E.M. Forster: *A Passage to India*

B

B., Mr The profligate pursuer of Pamela *Andrews
Samuel Richardson: *Pamela*

Backbite, Sir Benjamin A scandal-monger
R.B. Sheridan: *The School for Scandal*

Bacon and Bungay Rival publishers
W.M. Thackeray: *Pendennis*

Badger, Richard Bayham Fashionable Chelsea doctor with whom Richard *Castone briefly studies
Charles Dickens: *Bleak House*

Badgery, Herbert A con-man
Peter Carey: *Illywhacker*

Baggins, Bilbo A hobbit, finder of the 'One Ring'
J.R.R. Tolkein: *The Hobbit;* and *The Lord of the Rings*

Baggins, Frodo A hobbit, nephew of Bilbo *Baggins
J.R.R. Tolkein: *The Lord of the Rings*

Bagheera The Black Panther, friend of *Mowgli
Rudyard Kipling: *The Jungle Book*

Bagnet, Matthew, and Mrs ['the Old Girl'] An ex-artillery man and proprietor of a musical instrument shop
Charles Dickens: *Bleak House*

Bagot, William ['Little Billy'] An art student
George du Maurier: *Trilby*

Bagstock, Major Joseph [Joe] Choleric retired military man
Charles Dickens: *Dombey and Son*

Bailly, Harry Host of the Tabard Inn
Geoffrey Chaucer: *The Canterbury Tales*

Baines, Constance Staid daughter of a Bursley draper and sister of Sophia *Baines; marries Samuel *Povey
Arnold Bennett: *The Old Wives' Tale*

Baines, Sophia The more passionate sister of Constance *Baines who elopes with Gerald *Scales, eventually becoming a Parisian lodging-house keeper
Arnold Bennett: *The Old Wives' Tale*

Bajazeth Emperor of the Turks
Christopher Marlowe: *Tamburlane the Great*

Baker, Nicole Girlfriend of Gary *Gilmore
Norman Mailer: *The Executioner's Song*

Balaam, Sir A corrupt courtier; tentatively identified with the grandfather of William Pitt the Elder
Alexander Pope: *Moral Essays [iii]*

Balchristie, Jenny Housekeeper of the Laird of Dumbiedikes
Sir Walter Scott: *The Heart of Midlothian*

Balderstone, Caleb Manservant of the Ravenswood family
Sir Walter Scott: *The Bride of Lammermoor*

Balfour, David, of Shaws Central character and narrator, left in poverty on the death of his father
R.L. Stevenson: *Kidnapped;* and *Catriona*

Balfour of Burley, John Leader of the Cameronian sect
Sir Walter Scott: *Old Mortality*

Balladino, Antonio Foolish writer of city pageants
Ben Jonson: *The Case is Altered*

Balliol, Mrs
Sir Walter Scott: *Chronicles of the Canongate*

Balmawhapple, The Laird of [surnamed **Falconer]**
Sir Walter Scott: *Waverley*

Baloo A bear who teaches the 'man-cub' *Mowgli
Rudyard Kipling: *The Jungle Book*

Balthazar Name assumed by *Portia
William Shakespeare: *The Merchant of Venice*

Balthazar, Prince Son of the Viceroy of Portugal
Thomas Kyd: *The Spanish Tragedy*

Balwhidder, Revd Mr Minister of Dalmailing, Ayrshire
John Galt: *Annals of the Parish*

Banquo Scottish general and companion of Macbeth
William Shakespeare: *Macbeth*

Bantam, Angelo Cyrus Grand Master of Ceremonies at Bath
Charles Dickens: *The Posthumous Papers of the Pickwick Club*

Baptista Minola Rich gentleman of Padua father of *Katherina, the 'shrew'
William Shakespeare: *The Taming of the Shrew*

Barabas A Jewish merchant
Christopher Marlowe: *The Jew of Malta*

Bardell, Mrs Martha Mr *Pickwick's landlady in Goswell Street
Charles Dickens: *The Posthumous Papers of the Pickwick Club*

Bardolph Soldier and companion of *Falstaff
William Shakespeare: *Henry IV 1* and *2; Henry V; The Merry Wives of Windsor*

Barkis A Yarmouth carrier, a man of few words, who eventually marries Clara *Peggotty
Charles Dickens: *David Copperfield*

Barnacles, The Government officials in the Circumlocution Office
Charles Dickens: *Little Dorrit*

Barnadine A condemned prisoner
William Shakespeare: *Measure for Measure*

Barney Associate of Fagin
Charles Dickens: *Oliver Twist*

Barrymore Caretaker at Baskerville Hall
A. Conan Doyle: *The Hound of the Baskervilles*

Bart, Lily The beautiful but vulnerable central character tragically ambitious for wealth and position in New York society
Edith Wharton: *The House of Mirth*

Bartleby A scrivener
Herman Melville: *The Piazza Tales*

Bartlett, Miss Chaperone to Lucy *Honeychurch
E.M. Forster: *A Room with a View*

Barton, Amos Curate of Shepperton
George Eliot: 'The Sad Fortunes of the Rev. Amos Barton' [*Scenes of Clerical Life*]

Barton, Mary Working-class heroine, daughter of an embittered trade unionist
Elizabeth Gaskell: *Mary Barton*

Basilius Ruler of Arcadia, husband of *Gynecia
Sir Philip Sydney: *Arcadia*

Basilius Rival of Camacho
Cervantes: *Don Quixote*

Bassanio Venetian nobleman, friend of *Antonio, and suitor of *Portia
William Shakespeare: *The Merchant of Venice*

Bassianus Brother of *Saturninus
William Shakespeare: *Titus Andronicus*

Bast, Leonard A clerk
E.M. Forster: *Howards End*

Bastables, The Six motherless children—Dora,

Oswald, Dicky, Alice and Noel (twins), and Horace Octavius
E. Nesbit: *The Treasure Seekers* [and others]

Bateman, Patrick A wealthy psychopathic killer
Bret Easton Ellis: *American Psycho*

Bates, Miss A kind-hearted spinster
Jane Austen: *Emma*

Bates, Charley A pickpocket in Fagin's gang
Charles Dickens: *Oliver Twist*

Bath, Colonel
Henry Fielding: *Amelia*

Batsby, Captain A hunting man
Anthony Trollope: *Ayala's Angel*

Battle, Sarah
Charles Lamb: *Essays of Elia*

Baynes, General, Mrs, and Charlotte
W.M. Thackeray: *The Adventures of Philip*

Bazzard, Mr Mr *Grewgious's clerk
Charles Dickens: *Edwin Drood*

Beadle, Harriet [Tattycoram] A foundling
Charles Dickens: *Little Dorrit*

Bean Lean, Donald A Highland marauder
Sir Walter Scott: *Waverley*

Beatrice Niece of *Leonato and lover of *Benedick
William Shakespeare: *Much Ado About Nothing*

Beatrice-Joanna Daughter of the governor of Alicant, forced to marry Alonzo de Piraquo but in love with Alsemero
Thomas Middleton and William Rowley: *The Changeling*

Beaumanoir, Sir Lucas Grand Master of the Knights Templar
Sir Walter Scott: *Ivanhoe*

Beaver, John
Evelyn Waugh: *A Handful of Dust*

Beck, Madame Headmistress of a girls' school
Charlotte Brontë: *Villette*

Bede, Adam A village carpenter, who marries Dinah *Morris
George Eliot: *Adam Bede*

Bede, Seth Brother of Adam *Bede
George Eliot: *Adam Bede*

Bedonebyasyoudid, Mrs Punisher of bad children, sister of Mrs *Doasyouwouldbedoneby
Charles Kingsley: *The Water Babies*

Beebe, Mr A clergyman resident of the Pensione Bertolini in Florence
E.M. Forster: *A Room with a View*

Beeblebrox, Zaphod A two-headed, three-armed humanoid from Betelgeuse
Douglas Adams: *The Hitch-Hiker's Guide to the Galaxy*

Beecham, Phoebe (née Tozer)
Margaret Oliphant: *Salem Chapel; Phoebe Junior*

Beesley Fellow-lodger of Jim *Dixon
Kingsley Amis: *Lucky Jim*

Beetle Part of a schoolboy trio along with *Stalky and *M'Turk
Rudyard Kipling: *Stalky & Co.*

Bel-Imperia Daughter of the Duke of Castile
Thomas Kyd: *The Spanish Tragedy*

Belarius A banished lord, calling himself Morgan
William Shakespeare: *Cymbeline*

Belch, Sir Toby A roistering humorous knight, kinsman to *Olivia
William Shakespeare: *Twelfth Night*

Belford, John Friend and correspondent of Robert *Lovelace
Samuel Richardson: *Clarissa*

Belforest Father of *Castabella
Cyril Tourneur: *The Atheist's Tragedy*

Belinda Main character
Maria Edgeworth: *Belinda*

Belinda
Sir John Vanbrugh: *The Provok'd Wife*

Belinda Main character
Alexander Pope: *The Rape of the Lock*

Bell, Laura
W.M. Thackeray: *Pendennis* [also, as Laura Pendennis, in *The Newcomes* and *The Adventures of Philip*]

Belladonna, Countess of Mistress of Lord *Steyne
W.M. Thackeray: *Vanity Fair*

Bellair
George Etherege: *The Man of Mode*

Bellario A lawyer and cousin of *Portia
William Shakespeare: *The Merchant of Venice*

Bellario Name assumed by *Euphrasia when disguised as a page
Francis Beaumont & John Fletcher: *Philaster*

Bellaston, Lady
Henry Fielding: *Tom Jones*

Bellenden, Lady Margaret, and Edith Royalist owner of Tillietudlem Castle and her daughter
Sir Walter Scott: *Old Mortality*

Bellingham, Henry The wealthy seducer of Ruth *Hilton
Elizabeth Gaskell: *Ruth*

Belmont, Evelina Abandoned daughter, known as Miss Anville, of Sir John *Belmont
Frances Burney: *Evelina*

Belmont, Sir John *Evelina's father
Frances Burney: *Evelina*

Belphoebe The chaste huntress, daughter of the nymph Chrysogone and twin sister of *Amoret; partly symbolic of Elizabeth I
Edmund Spenser: *The Faerie Queene*

Belvidera Main character
Thomas Otway: *Venice Preserv'd*

Bendrix, Maurice A novelist; lover of Sarah *Miles
Graham Greene: *The End of the Affair*

Benedick A sworn bachelor who falls in love with *Beatrice
William Shakespeare: *Much Ado About Nothing*

Benjamin A donkey
George Orwell: *Animal Farm*

Bennet, Mrs
Henry Fielding: *Amelia*

Bennet, Elizabeth Principal female character; marries Fitzwilliam *Darcy
Jane Austen: *Pride and Prejudice*

Bennet, Jane Sister of Elizabeth *Bennet, marries Charles *Bingley
Jane Austen: *Pride and Prejudice*

Bennet, Lydia Sister of Elizabeth *Bennet who elopes with George *Wickham
Jane Austen: *Pride and Prejudice*

Bennet, Mr and Mrs, and their daughters **Jane, Elizabeth, Mary, Kitty, and Lydia** Principal characters
Jane Austen: *Pride and Prejudice*

Benson, Thurston A Dissenting minister who saves Ruth *Hilton from suicide after her seduction by Henry *Bellingham and takes her into his own house
Elizabeth Gaskell: *Ruth*

Benvolio Friend and cousin of *Romeo
William Shakespeare: *Romeo and Juliet*

Benwick, Captain Guest of the *Harvilles at Lyme Regis
Jane Austen: *Persuasion*

Berengaria, Queen Daughter of the King of Navarre and consort of Richard I
Sir Walter Scott: *The Talisman*

Berenger, Eveline Daughter of the Lord of Garde Doloureuse
Sir Walter Scott: *The Betrothed*

Berinthia An unscrupulous young widow who seeks to tempt *Loveless
Sir John Vanbrugh: *The Relapse*

Berinthia
R.B. Sheridan: *A Trip to Scarborough*

Bernstein, Baroness [formerly **Beatrix Esmond**]
W.M. Thackeray: *The Virginians*

Berowne [or Biron] Lord attending the King of France
William Shakespeare: *Love's Labours Lost*

Bertram, Count of Rousillon Reluctant husband of *Helena
William Shakespeare: *All's Well That Ends Well*

Bertram, Augusta Henry *Pulling's aunt
Graham Greene: *Travels with my Aunt*

Bertram, Edmund Clergyman and second son of Sir Thomas *Bertram who marries Fanny *Price
Jane Austen: *Mansfield Park*

Bertram, Harry
Sir Walter Scott: *Guy Mannering*

Bertram, Julia Youngest daughter of Sir Thomas *Bertram who elopes with John *Yates
Jane Austen: *Mansfield Park*

Bertram, Lady Indolent wife of Sir Thomas *Bertram
Jane Austen: *Mansfield Park*

Bertram, Maria Eldest daughter of Sir Thomas *Bertram who marries James *Rushworth
Jane Austen: *Mansfield Park*

Bertram, Sir Thomas Owner of Mansfield Park
Jane Austen: *Mansfield Park*

Bertram, Tom [Thomas] Eldest son of Sir Thomas *Bertram
Jane Austen: *Mansfield Park*

Bessue A cowardly braggart
Francis Beaumont & John Fletcher: *A King and No King*

Beste-Chetwynde, Hon. Mrs Margot An eccentric millionairess to whom Paul *Pennyfeather proposes
Evelyn Waugh: *Decline and Fall*

Betteredge, Gabriel House-steward of Lady Julia *Verinder
Wilkie Collins: *The Moonstone*

Beverley, Cecilia Central character; the inheritor of a large fortune on the condition that her future husband takes her name
Frances Burney: *Cecilia*

Beverley, Ensign *see* ABSOLUTE, CAPTAIN JACK

Beynon, Butcher, and Gossamer Father and daughter
Dylan Thomas: *Under Milk Wood*

Bianca Sister of *Katharina
William Shakespeare: *The Taming of the Shrew*

Biederman, Arnold [formerly **Count of Geierstein**]
Sir Walter Scott: *Anne of Geierstein*

Biffen, Harold A poor but generous scholar
George Gissing: *New Grub Street*

Big Brother Ubiquitous head of the Party
George Orwell: *Nineteen Eighty-Four*

Bigwig
Richard Adams: *Watership Down*

Billickin, Mrs London landlady to whom Mr *Grewgious takes Rosa *Budd to lodge
Charles Dickens: *The Mystery of Edwin Drood*

Bingley, Caroline Sister of Charles *Bingley
Jane Austen: *Pride and Prejudice*

Bingley, Charles Affable owner of Netherfield who marries Jane *Bennet
Jane Austen: *Pride and Prejudice*

Bingley, Louisa Sister of Charles *Bingley who becomes Mrs Hurst
Jane Austen: *Pride and Prejudice*

Binks, Sir Bingo, and Lady
Sir Walter Scott: *St Ronan's Well*

Birdseye, Miss An aged, altruistic worker for lost causes
Henry James: *The Bostonians*

Birkin, Rupert A school inspector; marries Ursula *Brangwen
D.H. Lawrence: *Women in Love*

Biron *see* BEROWNE

Bitzer A sly, ambitious youth, a pupil at *Gradgrind's school
Charles Dickens: *Hard Times*

Blackacre, The Widow
William Wycherley: *The Plain Dealer*

Blackhouse, Tommy
Evelyn Waugh: *Sword of Honour trilogy*

Blackpool, Stephen A solitary Coketown weaver
Charles Dickens: *Hard Times*

Blackstick, Fairy
W.M. Thackeray: *The Rose and the Ring*

Blackwill and Shakebag Murderers of Arden
Anon: *Arden of Feversham*
Blake, Franklin Nephew of Lady Julia *Verinder, in love with her daughter Rachel
Wilkie Collins: *The Moonstone*
Blakeney, Sir Percy An English aristocrat;'The Scarlet Pimpernel'
Baroness Orczy: *The Scarlet Pimpernel* [and others]
Blanche, Anthony An effeminate but clever aesthete
Evelyn Waugh: *Brideshead Revisited*
Blandamour A youthful knight
Edmund Spenser: *The Faerie Queene*
Blatant Beast, The Personification of the calumnious voice of the world
Edmund Spenser: *The Faerie Queene*
Blattergowl, Mr Minister of Trotcosey
Sir Walter Scott: *The Antiquary*
Bledsoe, Dr A self-made black educator
Ralph Ellison: *Invisible Man*
Blifil, Captain John Brother of Dr Blifil, marries Squire *Allworthy's sister Bridget
Henry Fielding: *Tom Jones*
Blifil, Master Nephew of Squire *Allworthy
Henry Fielding: *Tom Jones*
Blimber, Cornelia Daughter of Dr *Blimber who marries her father's assistant, Mr Feeder
Charles Dickens: *Dombey and Son*
Blimber, Dr Proprietor and headmaster of the Brighton school to which Paul *Dombey is sent
Charles Dickens: *Dombey and Son*
Blofeld, Ernst Stavros An arch-villain and founder of SPECTRE
Ian Fleming: *Thunderball*
Bloom, Leopold and Molly Son of a Hungarian Jew and his wife
James Joyce: *Ulysses*
Bloomfield, Mr and Mrs Parents of Tom, Mary Ann, and Fanny–Agnes Grey's first charges as a governess
Anne Brontë: *Agnes Grey*
Blount, Jake An idealist
Carson McCullers: *The Heart is a Lonely Country*
Blouzelinda A shepherdess
John Gay: *The Shepherd's Week*
Bluffe, Captain
William Congreve: *The Old Bachelor*
Blumine The lady with whom Herr Teufelsdröckh falls in love
Thomas Carlyle: *Sartor Resartus*
Bobadill, Captain A boastful, cowardly soldier
Ben Jonson: *Every Man in his Humour*
Boffin, Mr [Nicodemus ('Noddy')], and Mrs [Henrietta] Kind-hearted servant of the dust-contractor *Harmon and his wife
Charles Dickens: *Our Mutual Friend*
Bois-Guilbert, Sir Brian De A belligerent Knight Templar
Sir Walter Scott: *Ivanhoe*
Bold, Eleanor [*née* Harding] Younger daughter of the Revd Septimus *Harding, sister-in-law of Archdeacon *Grantly, wife (later widow) of John *Bold; finally Mrs *Arabin
Anthony Trollope: *The Warden*
Bold, John Well-to-do Barchester surgeon and reformer, in love with Eleanor Harding
Anthony Trollope: *The Warden*
Boldwood, John A gentleman farmer, obsessively in love with Bathsheba *Everdene, who finally kills Francis *Troy
Thomas Hardy: *Far From the Madding Crowd*
Boles, Meg A boarding-house landlady
Harold Pinter: *The Birthday Party*
Bolton, Fanny Daughter of Mrs Bolton of Shepherd's Inn
W.M. Thackeray: *Pendennis*
Bombastus Intended for Paracelsus
Samuel Butler: *Hudribras*
Bon, Charles Natural child of Thomas *Sutpen
William Faulkner: *Absalom, Absalom!*
Boncassen, Ezekiel An American scholar, father of Isabel
Anthony Trollope: *The Duke's Children*
Bond, James Agent '007'; a member of the British Secret Service, licensed to kill
Ian Fleming: *Casino Royale* [and many others]
Bones, Brom A brawling practical joker
Washington Irving: *The Legend of Sleepy Hollow*
Boniface Landlord of an inn (and hence a generic name for innkeepers)
George Farquhar: *The Beaux' Stratagem*
Boniface Abbot of Kennaquhair
Sir Walter Scott: *The Monastery*
Bonteen, Mr Political rival of Phineas *Finn
Anthony Trollope: *Phineas Finn; The Eustace Diamonds; Phineas Redux*
Bonthron, Anthony A villainous cut-throat
Sir Walter Scott: *The Fair Maid of Perth*
Booby, Sir Thomas, and Lady A country squire and his wife
Henry Fielding: *The History of the Adventures of Joseph Andrews*
Boot, William A writer of nature notes mistakenly sent by Lord *Copper to cover the war in Ishmaelia instead of his cousin, the novelist John Boot
Evelyn Waugh: *Scoop*
Booth, Amelia Wife of Captain Billy *Booth
Henry Fielding: *Amelia*
Booth, [Captain] William [Billy], and Amelia Husband and wife
Henry Fielding: *Amelia*
Bordereau, Miss An elderly spinster living in Venice; Miss Tina, her niece
Henry James: *The Aspern Papers*
Bosola, Daniel de A spy for the duchess's brothers
John Webster: *The Duchess of Malfi*
Bothwell, Sergeant A soldier in Claverhouse's force who claims the name of Francis Stewart
Sir Walter Scott: *Old Mortality*
Bottom, Nick A weaver
William Shakespeare: *A Midsummer Night's Dream*

Bounderby, Josiah Coketown banker, mill-owner, and friend of Mr *Gradgrind
Charles Dickens: *Hard Times*

Bountiful, Lady Mother of Squire Sullen
George Farquhar: *The Beaux' Stratagem*

Bowes, Mrs A crippled fiddler
W.M. Thackeray: *Pendennis*

Bowles, Sally A cabaret club singer in Berlin
Christopher Isherwood: 'Sally Bowles' in *Goodbye to Berlin*

Bowling, George An insurance salesman
George Orwell: *Coming Up for Air*

Bowling, Lt Tom Seafaring maternal uncle of Roderick *Random
Tobias Smollett: *The Adventures of Roderick Random*

Bowzybeus A drunken swain
John Gay: *The Shepherd's Week*

Boxer A noble carthorse
George Orwell: *Animal Farm*

Boyet A lord attending on *Ferdinand
William Shakespeare: *Love's Labour's Lost*

Boyle, Juno Long-suffering wife of 'Captain' Jack Boyle
Sean O'Casey: *Juno and the Paycock*

Boythorn, Lawrence Friend of Mr *Jarndyce and neighbour of Sir Leicester *Dedlock; based on the character of Walter Savage Landor
Charles Dickens: *Bleak House*

Bozzle, Samuel Ex-policeman and private detective hired by Louis *Trevelyan; his wife, Maryanne
Anthony Trollope: *He Knew He Was Right*

Brabantio A Venetian senator, father of *Desdemona
William Shakespeare: *Othello*

Brachiano, Duke of [Paulo Giordano Ursini] Obsessed by love for Vittoria *Corombona
John Webster: *The White Devil*

Bracidas Brother of *Amidas
Edmund Spenser: *The Faerie Queene*

Bracknell, Lady Formidable aunt of Algy *Moncrieff and mother of Gwendolen *Fairfax
Oscar Wilde: *The Importance of Being Earnest*

Bracy, Sir Maurice One of Prince John's knights and a suitor of *Rowena
Sir Walter Scott: *Ivanhoe*

Bradamante A maiden warrior, sister of Rinaldo
Ariosto: *Orlando Furioso*

Bradley, Mrs [later Dame] Beatrice Adela Lestrange Consultant Psychiatrist to the Home Office and detective
Gladys Mitchell: *Speedy Death* [and others]

Bradwardine, Baron Cosmos of Comyne, and Rose, his daughter
Sir Walter Scott: *Waverley*

Brady, Cecilia Principal character; the daughter of a film producer
F. Scott Fitzgerald: *The Last Tycoon*

Braggadochio The typical braggart
Edmund Spenser: *The Faerie Queene*

Brainworm A wily, high-spirited servant
Ben Jonson: *Every Man in his Humour*

Braithwaite, Geoffrey A retired doctor, obsessed by Flaubert
Julian Barnes: *Flaubert's Parrot*

Bramble, Matthew, and Tabitha Father and aunt of Humphrey *Clinker
Tobias Smollett: *The Expedition of Humphrey Clinker*

Brandon, Colonel Friend of Sir John *Middleton; marries Marianne *Dashwood
Jane Austen: *Sense and Sensibility*

Brandt, Margaret The daughter of a poor scholar, in love with *Gerard
Charles Reade: *The Cloister and the Hearth*

Branghtons, The Vulgar relatives of Evelina
Frances Burney: *Evelina*

Brangwen, Tom Son of a Nottinghamshire farmer
D.H. Lawrence: *Women in Love*

Brangwen, Ursula and Gudrun Sisters; respectively, a schoolteacher and art student; both seeking new intellectual and emotional horizons
D.H. Lawrence: *Women in Love*

Brangwen, Will Nephew of Tom *Brangwen married to Anna, daughter of Lydia *Lensky, and father of Ursula and Gudrun *Brangwen
D.H. Lawrence: *Women in Love*

Brass
Sir John Vanbrugh: *The Confederacy*

Brass, Sampson, and Sally *Quilp's lawyer, and his sister
Charles Dickens: *The Old Curiosity Shop*

Brattle, Carry A 'fallen woman' who turns to prostitution
Anthony Trollope: *The Vicar of Bullhampton*

Bray, Madeline Daughter of a deceased former sweetheart of Charles *Cheeryble; finally marries Nicholas *Nickleby
Charles Dickens: *Nicholas Nickleby*

Bray, Walter A selfish and tyrannical invalid, bankrupted by Ralph *Nickleby; father of Madeline *Bray
Charles Dickens: *Nicholas Nickleby*

Brazen, Captain
George Farquhar: *The Recruiting Officer*

Breck, Alan Friend of David *Balfour
R.L. Stevenson: *Kidnapped; Catriona*

Breckinridge, Myra Formerly the [male] film critic Myron Breckinridge
Gore Vidal: *Myra Breckinridge*

Breedlove, Pecola
Toni Morrison: *The Bluest Eye*

Bretton, John [Graham; later **Dr]** Godson of Mrs Maria Bretton, a widow
Charlotte Brontë: *Villette*

Bridehead, Sue [Susanna Florence Mary] Cousin and lover of Jude *Fawley; marries Richard *Phillotson
Thomas Hardy: *Jude the Obscure*

Bridgenorth, Major Ralph, and Alice Widowed

former schoolfellow of Sir Geoffrey *Peveril; his daughter, named after his dead wife
Sir Walter Scott: *Peveril of the Peak*

Brierly, Henry [Harry] A speculator
Edith Wharton: *The Gilded Age*

Brigadore Sir *Guyon's horse, stolen by *Braggadochio
Edmund Spenser: *The Faerie Queene*

Briscoe, Lily A painter
Virginia Woolf: *To the Lighthouse*

Brisk A voluble coxcomb
William Congreve: *The Double Dealer*

Brisk, Fastidious A foppish courtier
Ben Jonson: *Every Man Out of His Humour*

Britomart Daughter of King Ryence of Britain and the female Knight of Chastity
Edmund Spenser: *The Faerie Queene*

Brocklehurst, Mr Head of Lowood school
Charlotte Brontë: *Jane Eyre*

Brodie, Miss Jean Idealistic Edinburgh schoolmistress
Muriel Spark: *The Prime of Miss Jean Brodie*

Bromden, Chief An American-Indian, inmate of a mental institution
Ken Kesey: *One Flew Over the Cuckoo's Nest*

Bronowsky, Count Dmitri A Russian emigré, vizier to the Nawab of Mirat
Paul Scott: *The Raj Quartet*

Bronzomarte Launcelot Greaves's horse
Tobias Smollett: *Sir Launcelot Greaves*

Brooke, Celia Sister of Dorothea; marries Sir James Chettam
George Eliot: *Middlemarch*

Brooke, Dorothea Ardent, idealistic sister of Celia; marries (1) the Revd Edward *Casaubon, (2) Will *Ladislaw
George Eliot: *Middlemarch*

Brookenham, Nanda The central character; a young girl emerging from childhood into the brilliant atmosphere of her mother's London salon
Henry James: *The Awkward Age*

Browdie, John Yorkshire corn-factor who befriends Nicholas *Nickleby
Charles Dickens: *Nicholas Nickleby*

Brown Hotel owner and narrator
Graham Greene: *The Comedians*

Brown, Father A Roman Catholic priest-detective
G.K. Chesterton: *The Innocence of Father Brown* [and others]

Brown, Velvet Daughter of a Sussex butcher
Enid Bagnold: *National Velvet*

Brown, Vic [Victor] Narrator
Stan Barstow: *A Kind of Loving*

Brownlow, Mr Benefactor of Oliver *Twist
Charles Dickens: *Oliver Twist*

Brute, Sir John, and Lady
Sir John Vanbrugh: *The Provok'd Wife*

Brutus, Marcus Friend of Caesar, conspirator, and assassin;'the noblest Roman of them all'
William Shakespeare: *Julius Caesar*

Buchanan, Daisy A Southern belle; married to Tom
F. Scott Fitzgerald: *The Great Gatsby*

Bucket, Inspector Police detective hired by *Tulkinghorn
Charles Dickens: *Bleak House*

Buckingham, Duke of Richard III's ally in murdering Lord Hastings
William Shakespeare: *Richard III*

Bud, Rosa Betrothed as a child to Edwin *Drood
Charles Dickens: *The Mystery of Edwin Drood*

Buffone, Carlo A scurrilous jester
Ben Jonson: *Every Man Out of his Humour*

Bufo A patron of the arts 'fed with soft Dedications all day long'
Alexander Pope: *Epistle to Dr Arbuthnot*

Bulbo, Prince
W.M. Thackeray: *The Rose and the Ring*

'Bull-dog' Drummond *see* DRUMMOND, HUGH

Bullivant, Sir Walter Senior Foreign Office official
John Buchan: *The Thirty-Nine Steps*

Bulstrode, Nicholas A banker
George Eliot: *Middlemarch*

Bultitude, Paul A colonial produce merchant; his sons Dick and 'Roly', his daughter, Barbara
F. Anstey: *Vice Versa*

Bumble, Mr A pompous parish beadle
Charles Dickens: *Oliver Twist*

Bumppo, Natty [also known as **'Leatherstocking','Deerslayer', 'Hawkeye', and 'Pathfinder')** Woodsman and adventurer
J. Fenimore Cooper: *The Pioneer* [and others in the 'Leatherstocking' series]

Bunbury An imaginary character invented by Algy *Moncrieff
Oscar Wilde: *The Importance of Being Earnest*

Bunce, Jack [alias **Frederick Altamont]** Ex-actor and pirate
Sir Walter Scott: *The Pirate*

Bundren, Addie Married to Anse; their children Cash, Darl, Vardaman, and only daughter Dewey Dell
William Faulkner: *As I Lay Dying*

Bundren, Jewel Illegitimate son of Addie *Bundren
William Faulkner: *As I Lay Dying*

Bunny *see* MANNERS, BUNNY

Bunsby, Captain John [Jack] Friend of Captain *Cuttle, a sententious sea-dog
Charles Dickens: *Dombey and Son*

Bunter Former sergeant of Lord Peter *Wimsey, now his manservant and assistant in the investigation of crime
Dorothy L. Sayers: *Whose Body?* [and many others]

Bunthorne, Reginald Caricature of an aesthete
Gilbert and Sullivan: *Patience*

Burbon, Sir Representing Henry of Navarre
Edmund Spenser: *The Faerie Queene*

Burgundy, Duke of Suitor of *Cordelia
William Shakespeare: *King Lear*

Burns, Helen Friend of Jane *Eyre's at Lowood school
Charlotte Brontë: *Jane Eyre*

Burr, Aaron A historical character (1756–1836); a hero of the American Revolution
Gore Vidal: *Burr*

Burton, Florence The demure daughter of Mr Burton, junior partner of Beilby & Burton, civil engineers; engaged to Harry *Clavering
Anthony Trollope: *The Claverings*

Busirane The 'vile Enchaunter', symbolizing unlawful love, who is struck down by *Britomart
Edmund Spenser: *The Faerie Queene*

Butler, Rhett Cynical and worldly third husband of Scarlett *O'Hara
Margaret Mitchell: *Gone With the Wind*

Buzfuz, Mr Serjeant Counsel for the plaintiff in *Bardell v. *Pickwick
Charles Dickens: *The Posthumous Papers of the Pickwick Club*

By-Ends, Mr A hypocrite
John Bunyan: *Pilgrim's Progress*

Byron, Harriet 'The most beautiful woman in England', abducted by Sir Hargreve *Pollexfen, but who finally marries Sir Charles Grandison
Samuel Richardson: *Sir Charles Grandison*

C

Cadfael, Brother A Benedictine monk in the abbey of St Peter and St Paul, Shrewsbury
Ellis Peters: *A Morbid Taste for Bones* [and many others]

Cadwal *see* ARVIRAGUS

Caelia Lady of the House of Holiness, mother of Fidelia, Speranza, and Charissa (Faith, Hope, and Charity)
Edmund Spenser: *The Faerie Queene*

Caius, Dr A French physician
William Shakespeare: *The Merry Wives of Windsor*

Calantha The heroine; daughter of the King of Sparta
John Ford: *The Broken Heart*

Calchas Father of *Cressida who betrays Troy to the Greeks
William Shakespeare: *Troilus and Cressida*

Calcott, Jack An Australian former soldier
D.H. Lawrence: *Kangaroo*

Caldwell, George A Pennsylvanian high-school teacher; his son, Peter
John Updike: *The Centaur*

Caliban A deformed, semi-human slave, son of the witch *Sycorax
William Shakespeare: *The Tempest*

Calidore, Sir The Knight of Courtesy
Edmund Spenser: *The Faerie Queene*

Calista The heroine, loved by 'the gay Lothario'
Nicholas Rowe: *The Fair Penitent*

Calpurnia Caesar's wife
William Shakespeare: *Julius Caesar*

Calvo, Baldesarre Adoptive father of Tito *Melema
George Eliot: *Romola*

Camacho A rich farmer
Cervantes: *Don Quixote*

Cambalo One of the two sons of King *Cambuscan
Geoffrey Chaucer: 'The Squire's Tale' [*Canterbury Tales*]

Cambell [Cambello] Brother of *Canacee
Edmund Spenser: *The Faerie Queene*

Cambuscan, King King of Tartary
Geoffrey Chaucer: 'The Squire's Tale' [*Canterbury Tales*]

Camidius Follower of Mark *Antony
William Shakespeare: *Antony and Cleopatra*

Camilla *see* TYROLD, CAMILLA

Camillo Sexually inadequate husband of Vittoria *Corombona
John Webster: *The White Devil*

Camillo A Sicilian lord
William Shakespeare: *The Winter's Tale*

Camiola The heroine
Philip Massinger: *The Maid of Honour*

Campion, Albert An amateur detective
Margery Allingham: *The Crime at Black Dudley* [and many others]

Canacee A soothsayer, sister of *Cambell
Edmund Spenser: *The Faerie Queene*

Canacee Daughter of King *Cambuscan
Geoffrey Chaucer: 'The Squire's Tale' [*Canterbury Tales*]

Candour, Mrs A scandal-monger
R.B. Sheridan: *The School for Scandal*

Canty, Tom The beggar boy who exchanges clothes with his double, Prince Edward
Mark Twain: *The Prince and the Pauper*

Captain Cat A blind retired seaman
Dylan Thomas: *Under Milk Wood*

Capulet Father of *Juliet and rival of *Montague
William Shakespeare: *Romeo and Juliet*

Carabas, Marquis of A powerful but disappointed politician
Benjamin Disraeli: *Vivian Grey*

Carbury, Sir Felix The handsome, scapegrace son of Lady Matilda *Carbury
Anthony Trollope: *The Way We Live Now*

Carbury, Lady Matilda A shallow but well meaning woman with ambitions to be an author; doting mother of Sir Felix *Carbury
Anthony Trollope: *The Way We Live Now*

Carbury, Roger Cousin of Sir Felix *Carbury; a country squire, the model of an old-fashioned conservative gentleman
Anthony Trollope: *The Way We Live Now*

Cardew, Cecily Jack *Worthing's ward, loved by Algy *Moncrieff
Oscar Wilde: *The Importance of Being Earnest*

Carducis The brilliant and moody Byronic hero
Benjamin Disraeli: *Venetia*

Carker, James Manager of Dombey and Son, perpetually smiling but devoured by resentment
Charles Dickens: *Dombey and Son*

Caro, Avice The shared name of three generations of women—grandmother, mother, and daughter—courted by the sculptor Jocelyn *Pierston
Thomas Hardy: *The Well-Beloved*

Caroline Crippled daughter of a Canadian diplomat
Ian McEwan: *The Comfort of Strangers*

Carr, Katy Principal character; the eldest of widowed Dr Carr's six children
Susan Coolidge: *What Katy Did* [and others]

Carraway Nick Narrator; a young Midwesterner who sells bonds in New York, neighbour of Jay *Gatsby
F. Scott Fitzgerald: *The Great Gatsby*

Carson, Henry A mill-owner's son, involved with Mary *Barton, murdered by her father John Barton
Elizabeth Gaskell: *Mary Barton*

Carstone, Richard A ward in Chancery taken into the home of John *Jarndyce
Charles Dickens: *Bleak House*

Carton, Sydney A young barrister with a striking physical likeness to Charles *Darnay
Charles Dickens: *A Tale of Two Cities*

Casaubon, Revd Edward An elderly and pompous pedant; married Dorothea *Brooke
George Eliot: *Middlemarch*

Casby, Christopher The rack-renting landlord of Bleeding Heart Yard, father of Flora *Finching
Charles Dickens: *Little Dorrit*

Casca A conspirator
William Shakespeare: *Julius Caesar*

Caspar, Billy The adolescent owner of a tame kestral
Barry Hines: *A Kestral for a Knave*

Cass, Dunstan The squire's reprobate son who steals Silas *Marner's gold
George Eliot: *Silas Marner*

Cass, Godfrey Elder brother of Dunstan *Cass and the father of *Eppie
George Eliot: *Silas Marner*

Cassio, Michael A Florentine gentleman, deputy to Othello
William Shakespeare: *Othello*

Cassius Friend of *Brutus and leader of the conspiracy against Caesar
William Shakespeare: *Julius Caesar*

Cassy A mulatto woman
Harriet Beecher Stowe: *Uncle Tom's Cabin*

Castabella Daughter of *Belforest; betrothed to *Charlemont
Cyril Tourneur: *The Atheist's Tragedy*

Castle, Maurice A double agent
Graham Greene: *The Human Factor*

Catherick, Anne The 'woman in white'—half-sister to Laura *Fairlie, to whom she bears a striking resemblance; confined in an asylum by Sir Percival *Glyde
Wilkie Collins: *The Woman in White*

Caulfield, Holden A lonely 16-year-old boy plagued by the 'phoniness' of his moral environment
J.D. Salinger: *The Catcher in the Rye*

Caxon, Jacob A hairdresser employed by Jonathan *Oldbuck
Sir Walter Scott: *The Antiquary*

Cecilia *see* Beverley, Cecilia

Cecropia Wicked sister of *Basilius
Sir Philip Sidney: *Arcadia*

Cedric the Saxon [Cedric of Rotherwood] A proud Saxon nobleman, descended from Hereward, and kinsman of *Rowena
Sir Walter Scott: *Ivanhoe*

Celia Daughter of Duke *Frederick; later disguised as *Aliena
William Shakespeare: *As You Like It*

Cereno, Captain Benito A Spanish sea captain
Herman Melville: *The Piazza Tales*

Cesario Name assumed by *Viola
William Shakespeare: *Twelfth Night*

Chadband Verbose and hypocritical Dissenting minister
Charles Dickens: *Bleak House*

Chaffanbrass, Mr A barrister
Anthony Trollope: *The Three Clerks; Orley Farm; Phineas Redux*

Chainmail, Mr Enamoured of the 12th century
T.L. Peacock: *Crotchet Castle*

Challenger, Professor George Edward A choleric scientist and explorer
A. Conan Doyle: *The Lost World* [and others]

Chamberlayne, Edward, and Lavinia A middle-aged barrister and his wife, trapped in a loveless marriage
T.S. Eliot: *The Cocktail Party*

Chan, Charlie A Chinese detective
Earl Derr Biggers: *The House Without a Key* [and others]

Chance, Nora [Leonora] and Dora Identical twin sisters, illegitimate daughters of the Shakespearean actor Sir Melchior *Hazard
Angela Carter: *Wise Children*

Chancellor, Olive Neurotic feminist cousin of Basil *Ransom
Henry James: *The Bostonians*

Chantry-Pigg, Hon. Father Hugh A retired Anglican priest
Rose Macauley: *The Towers of Trebizond*

Charalois Son of the marshal of Burgundy
Philip Massinger: *The Fatal Dowry*

Charlemont Son of *Montferrers
Cyril Tourneur: *The Atheist's Tragedy*

Charlemont Betrothed to *Castabella
Cyril Tourneur: *The Atheist's Tragedy*

Charmian Attendant on *Cleopatra
William Shakespeare: *Antony and Cleopatra*

Charmond, Felice A wealthy widow
Thomas Hardy: *The Woodlanders*

Charteris, Sir Patrick Provost of Perth
Sir Walter Scott: *The Fair Maid of Perth*

Chauvelin A French revolutionary agent—the deadly foe of Sir Percy *Blakeney
Baroness Orczy: *The Scarlet Pimpernel* [and others]

Cheeryble, Charles and Edwin [Ned] Twin brothers and wealthy merchants who befriend Nicholas *Nickleby
Charles Dickens: *Nicholas Nickleby*

Cherrington, Eustace and Hilda Principal characters: brother and elder sister
L.P. Hartley: *The Shrimp and the Anemone; The Sixth Heaven; Eustace and Hilda*

Cherry and Merry *see* PECKSNIFF, CHARITY AND MERCY

Chester, Sir John A polished but ruthlessly selfish MP for a pocket borough; his son, Edward, the opposite in character, who finally marries Emma *Haredale
Charles Dickens: *Barnaby Rudge*

Chick, Louisa, and John Mr *Dombey's sister and her husband
Charles Dickens: *Dombey and Son*

Chickerell, Ethelberta The daughter of a butler
Thomas Hardy: *The Hand of Ethelberta*

Childe, Joanna A trainee elocution teacher at the May of Teck Club
Muriel Spark: *The Girls of Slender Means*

Chillingworth, Roger The name assumed by the stern, unforgiving husband of Hester *Prynne
Nathaniel Hawthorn: *The Scarlet Letter*

Chillip, Dr The kind and mild-mannered doctor who attends David *Copperfield's birth
Charles Dickens: *David Copperfield*

Chingachgook An Indian chief–'the last of the Mohicans'–and companion of Natty *Bumppo
J. Fenimore Cooper: The 'Leatherstocking' series

Chips, Mr [James Chipping] A housemaster at Brookfield School for boys
James Hilton: *Goodbye, Mr Chips*

Chiron A son of *Tamora
William Shakespeare: *Titus Andronicus*

Chivery, Mr, and 'Young John' The Marshalsea turnkey and his son (who fosters a hopeless passion for Little *Dorrit)
Charles Dickens: *Little Dorrit*

Chowder Tabitha *Bramble's dog
Tobias Smollett: *The Expedition of Humphrey Clinker*

Christmas, Joe Half-caste child left by his brutally racist grandfather, Eupheus Hines, on the steps of a white orphange
William Faulkner: *Light in August*

Chrysaor The sword of Justice wielded by Sir *Artegall
Edmund Spenser: *The Faerie Queene*

Chuffey Anthony *Chuzzlewit's devoted clerk
Charles Dickens: *Martin Chuzzlewit*

Churchill, Frank Son of Mr *Weston by a former marriage
Jane Austen: *Emma*

Chuzzlewit, Anthony Younger brother of Old Martin *Chuzzlewit; a grasping man of business
Charles Dickens: *Martin Chuzzlewit*

Chuzzlewit, Jonas The uncouth and villainous son of Anthony *Chuzzlewit
Charles Dickens: *Martin Chuzzlewit*

Chuzzlewit, Martin Grandson of Old Martin *Chuzzlewit; the personable but selfish hero of the story
Charles Dickens: *Martin Chuzzlewit*

Chuzzlewit, Old Martin Wealthy but miserly grandfather of young Martin *Chuzzlewit
Charles Dickens: *Martin Chuzzlewit*

Clare, Ada A ward in Chancery, taken into the home of John *Jarndyce; companion of Esther *Summerson; eventually married to Richard *Carstone
Charles Dickens: *Bleak House*

Clare, Angel Son of a clergyman, married briefly to Tess *Durbeyfield
Thomas Hardy: *Tess of the D'Urbervilles*

Clarendel, Sir Sedley A fop
Frances Burney: *Camilla*

Claret, Captain Master of the warship Neversink
Herman Melville: *White-Jacket*

Clarke, St John A prolific Edwardian novelist
Anthony Powell: *A Dance to the Music of Time*

Clarke, Tom A lawyer, friend of Launcelot *Greaves
Tobias Smollett: *Sir Launcelot Greaves*

Claudio Brother of *Isabella and betrothed husband of Julietta; sentenced to death by *Angelo for unchastity
William Shakespeare: *Measure for Measure*

Claudio Lover of *Hero
William Shakespeare: *Much Ado About Nothing*

Claudius *Hamlet's uncle, married to his brother's widow *Gertrude
William Shakespeare: *Hamlet*

Clavering, Sir Francis Second husband of the mother of Blanche *Amory
W.M. Thackeray: *Pendennis*

Clavering, Harry A gentleman engineer, engaged to Florence *Burton
Anthony Trollope: *The Claverings*

Clavering, Lady A vulgar social climber, mother of Blanche *Amory by her first husband, Col *Altamont
W.M. Thackeray: *Pendennis*

Claypole, Noah Assistant to *Sowerberry
Charles Dickens: *Oliver Twist*

Cleaver, Fanny *see* JENNY WREN

Clennam, Arthur Principal character who eventually marries Little *Dorrit
Charles Dickens: *Little Dorrit*

Clennam, Mrs The harsh, self righteous mother of Arthur *Clennam, confined to a wheelchair
Charles Dickens: *Little Dorrit*

Cleon Governor of Tarsus
William Shakespeare: *Pericles*

Cleopatra Queen of Egypt
John Dryden: *All for Love*

Cleopatra Queen of Egypt
William Shakespeare: *Antony and Cleopatra*

Clerval, Henry Friend of Victor *Frankenstein
Mary Shelley: *Frankenstein*

Cleveland, Captain Clement A buccaneer captain
Sir Walter Scott: *The Pirate*

Clinker, Humphrey Illegitimate son of Matthew *Bramble
Tobias Smollett: *The Expedition of Humphrey Clinker*

Clorin The faithful shepherdess of Thessaly, dedicated to a life of chastity in memory of her dead lover
John Fletcher: *The Faithful Shepherdess*

Clorinda Pagan daughter of the King of Ethiopia, lost as a baby and suckled by a tigress
Tasso: *Gerusalemme Liberata* [*Jerusalem Delivered*]

Cloten Clownish son of the queen by a former husband, rejected by his step-sister *Imogen
William Shakespeare: *Cymbeline*

Clove A fop
Ben Jonson: *Every Man Out of His Humour*

Clumsy, Sir Tunbelly A country squire
Sir John Vanbrugh: *The Relapse*

Cluppins, Mrs Elizabeth [Betsey] Friend of Mrs *Bardell's, on whose behalf she gives evidence in the case of Bardell v. Pickwick
Charles Dickens: *The Posthumous Papers of the Pickwick Club*

'Coavinses' *see* NECKETT

Codlin and Short Travelling Punch and Judy men
Charles Dickens: *The Old Curiosity Shop*

Coldfield, Rosa Sister-in-law to Thomas *Sutpen
William Faulkner: *Absalom, Absalom!*

Coleman A nihilist
Aldous Huxley: *Antic Hay*

Collins, Revd William A foolish and snobbish young clergyman, cousin of Elizabeth *Bennett,
Jane Austen: *Pride and Prejudice*

Compeyson A professional swindler, though outwardly a gentleman, who jilts Miss *Havisham on their wedding morning and who seeks to ensnare *Magwitch
Charles Dickens: *Great Expectations*

Compson, Benjy, Quentin, Jason, and Candace [Caddy] The children of a degenerate, dysfunctional family of formerly genteel Southern patricians
William Faulkner: *The Sound and the Fury*

Comstock, Gordon A lonely bookshop assistant
George Orwell: *Keep the Aspidistra Flying*

Conachar Highland apprentice of Simon *Glover
Sir Walter Scott: *The Fair Maid of Perth*

Conchis, Maurice A recluse
John Fowles: *The Magus*

Coningsby, Harry Central character; brought up by his grandfather, Lord *Monmouth
Benjamin Disraeli: *Coningsby*

Conscience, Mr The Recorder of Mansoul, deposed by Diabolus
John Bunyan: *The Holy War*

Constantine, Lady The central character who secretly marries Swithin *St Cleeve in the mistaken belief that her disagreeable husband is dead
Thomas Hardy: *Two on a Tower*

Copper, Lord A domineering newspaper magnate and proprietor of *The Beast*
Evelyn Waugh: *Scoop*

Copperfield, Clara David *Copperfield's pretty young mother, widowed before David's birth
Charles Dickens: *David Copperfield*

Copperfield, David Narrator and principal character; a novelist
Charles Dickens: *David Copperfield*

Cora and Clarice Identical twin sisters of Lord *Sepulchrave
Mervyn Peake: *Titus Groan; Gormenghast*

Corah Name for Titus Oates
John Dryden: *Absalom and Achitophel*

Corbaccio A deaf old miser
Ben Jonson: *Volpone*

Corbett, Cassandra An Oxford don
A.S. Byatt: *The Game*

Corceca An old blind woman, mother of *Abessa
Edmund Spenser: *Faerie Queene*

Cordelia Youngest daughter of King *Lear, disinherited by her father
William Shakespeare: *King Lear*

Corflambo Symbolic of lust; carries off *Amoret
Edmund Spenser: *The Faerie Queene*

Coridon A shepherd, in love with *Pastorella
Edmund Spenser: *The Faerie Queene*

Corin An old shepherd
William Shakespeare: *As You Like It*

Corinthian Tom A man about town
Pierce Egan the elder: *Life in London*

Coriolanus The principal character; a Roman aristocrat and soldier
William Shakespeare: *Coriolanus*

Corisande, Lady Eventually marries *Lothair
Benjamin Disraeli: *Lothair*

Corkran, Artie *see* STALKY

Cornelia Mother of *Flamineo and Marcello
John Webster: *The White Devil*

Cornelius A physician
William Shakespeare: *Cymbeline*

Corombona, Vittoria A Venetian lady, wife of *Camillo, seduced by *Brachiano
John Webster: *The White Devil*

Corvino One of *Volpone's would-be heirs
Ben Jonson: *Volpone*

Costard A clown
William Shakespeare: *Love's Labour's Lost*

Costigan, Captain, and Emily ['Miss Fotheringhay'] A disreputable rogue and his actress daughter
W.M. Thackeray: *Pendennis*

Coverdale, Miles The narrator; a minor poet
Nathaniel Hawthorne: *The Blithedale Romance*

Crab *Launce's dog
William Shakespeare: *The Two Gentlemen of Verona*

Crabshaw The cowardly squire of Launcelot *Greaves
Tobias Smollett: *Sir Launcelot Greaves*

Craigdallie The Bailie of Perth
Sir Walter Scott: *The Fair Maid of Perth*

Crane, Edwina Elderly British mission school supervisor in Mayapore
Paul Scott: *The Raj Quartet*

Crane, Ichabod The village schoolmaster of Tarrytown
Washington Irving: *The Legend of Sleepy Hollow*

Cratchit, Bob Clerk to Ebenezer *Scrooge
Charles Dickens: *A Christmas Carol*

Cratchit, Tiny Tim Crippled younger son of Bob *Cratchit
Charles Dickens: *A Christmas Carol*

Craven, Colin A bedridden child, kept hidden in Misselthwaite Manor in Yorkshire by his father, whose life is transformed by Mary *Lennox
Frances Hodgson Burnett: *The Secret Garden*

Crawford, Henry and Mary A wealthy young man and his sister, the one selfish and manipulative, the other snobbish and insensitive
Jane Austen: *Mansfield Park*

Crawford, Lord Commander of the Scottish Archers of the Guard
Sir Walter Scott: *Quentin Durward*

Crawley, Revd Josiah Perpetual curate of Hogglestock; later accused of stealing a cheque made out to Mrs *Arabin
Anthony Trollope: *Framley Parsonage; The Last Chronicle of Barset*

Crawley, Pitt Elder son of Sir Pitt *Crawley
W.M. Thackeray: *Vanity Fair*

Crawley, Sir Pitt A coarse country squire
W.M. Thackeray: *Vanity Fair*

Crawley, Rawdon Younger son of Sir Pitt *Crawley; married to Becky *Sharp
W.M. Thackeray: *Vanity Fair*

Creakle, Mr Brutal and ignorant proprietor and headmaster of Salem House, the school to which David *Copperfield is sent by Mr *Murdstone
Charles Dickens: *David Copperfield*

Cressida Daughter of the traitor *Calchas who herself betrays *Troilus for *Diomedes
William Shakespeare: *Troilus and Cressida*

Crewler, Sophy Fourth of the ten daughters of the Revd Horace Crewler; *Traddles's 'dearest girl in the world'
Charles Dickens: *David Copperfield*

Crich, Gerald Son of the local colliery owner, involved in a destructive relationship with Gudrun *Brangwen
D.H. Lawrence: *Women in Love*

Crichton The perfect manservant, cast away with his employers on a desert island
J.M. Barrie: *The Admirable Crichton*

Crimsworth, William The narrator; an orphan who becomes a Brussels schoolteacher
Charlotte Brontë: *The Professor*

Crisparkle, Septimus Minor canon at Cloisterham Cathedral who takes in Neville *Landless as a pupil
Charles Dickens: *The Mystery of Edwin Drood*

Crispinus A false poet (partly a caricature of John Marston)
Ben Jonson: *The Poetaster*

Croaker Guardian of Miss *Richland
Oliver Goldsmith: *The Good-Natur'd Man*

Crocker-Harris, Andrew A disappointed classics teacher at a public school
Terence Rattigan: *The Browning Version*

Croft, Admiral [and Mrs] A former naval man who rents Kellynch Hall from Sir Walter *Elliot
Jane Austen: *Persuasion*

Croft, Francis A mad poet
Susan Hill: *The Bird of Night*

Crosbie, Adolphus Ambitious secretary to the Board of the General Committee Office who becomes engaged to Lady Alexandrina *De Courcy
Anthony Trollope: *The Small House at Allington*

Crouchback, Guy Only surviving son of an old Catholic family who joins the Royal Corps of Halberdiers at the outbreak of World War Two
Evelyn Waugh: *The Sword of Honour trilogy*

Crowe, Captain Uncle of Tom *Clarke
Tobias Smollett: *Sir Launcelot Greaves*

Cruella de Vil The fur-obsessed villainess who steals the Dalmatian puppies belonging to Mr and Mrs Dearly
Dodie Smith: *The One Hundred and One Dalmatians*

Crummles, Ninetta The 'Infant Phenomenon', daughter of Vincent *Crummles
Charles Dickens: *Nicholas Nickleby*

Crummles, Vincent Theatrical manager of the touring company which Nicholas *Nickleby joins at Portsmouth; his daughter Ninetta *Crummles; his sons Charles and Percy
Charles Dickens: *Nicholas Nickleby*

Cruncher, Jerry [Jeremiah] An odd-job man and messenger for Tellson's Bank
Charles Dickens: *A Tale of Two Cities*

Cuff, Sergeant Richard The rose-growing detective sergeant called in to investigate the theft of the Moonstone
Wilkie Collins: *The Moonstone*

Cullen, Sir Patrick A senior Irish doctor
George Bernard Shaw: *The Doctor's Dilemma*

Curdie *see* PETERSON, CURDIE

Curio Attending on *Orsino
William Shakespeare: *Twelfth Night*

Custance, Christian A widow
Nicholas Udall: *Ralph Roister Doister*

Cute, Alderman A self-satisfied City magistrate
Charles Dickens: *The Chimes*

Cuttle, Captain Alfred [Ned] Retired seafaring man with a hook in place of his right hand
Charles Dickens: *Dombey and Son*

Cymbeline King of Britain
William Shakespeare: *Cymbeline*

Cymochles Husband of *Acrasia and brother of *Pyrochles
Edmund Spenser: *The Faerie Queene*

Cynthia Daughter of Sir Paul *Plyant, affianced to Mellefont
William Congreve: *The Double-Dealer*

Cypress, Mr A caricature of Lord Byron
T.L. Peacock: *Nightmare Abbey*

D

Dol Common Consort of *Subtle
Ben Jonson: *The Alchemist*

Dacier, Hon. Percy A rising young politician
George Meredith: *Diana of the Crossways*

Dacres Guardian of *George, Duke of St James; his daughter, May
Benjamin Disraeli: *The Young Duke*

Daggoo A harpooner
Herman Melville: *Moby-Dick*

Dahlia, Aunt [Mrs Tom Travers] Bertie *Wooster's 'good and deserving aunt', proprietor of the magazine *Milady's Boudoir*
P.G. Wodehouse: *Carry on Jeeves* [and others]

Daisy, Solomon Parish-clerk and bell-ringer of Chigwell and one of the habitués of the Maypole Inn
Charles Dickens: *Barnaby Rudge*

Dale, Isabella [Bell] Elder daughter of Mary *Dale, who lives with her mother and sister Lily *Dale in the Small House at Allington
Anthony Trollope: *The Small House at Allington*

Dale, Mary Proud but poor widowed mother of Isabella and Lily *Dale, befriended by her brother-in-law Christopher Dale, the bachelor squire of Allington
Anthony Trollope: *The Small House at Allington*

Dale, Laetitia In love with Sir Willoughby *Patterne, but passed over by him for Constantia *Durham and Clara *Middleton
George Meredith: *The Egoist*

Dale, Lily [Lillian] Younger daughter of the widowed Mary *Dale of Allington; in love with Adolphus *Crosbie who jilts her for Lady Alexandrina *De Courcy
Anthony Trollope: *The Small House at Allington; The Last Chronicle of Barset*

Dalgarno, Lord A dissembling villain
Sir Walter Scott: *The Fortunes of Nigel*

Dalgetty, Dugald A loquacious soldier of fortune
Sir Walter Scott: *The Legend of Montrose*

Dalgliesh, Adam A police detective and poet
P.D. James: *Cover Her Face* [and many others]

Dalloway, Clarissa The fashionable wife of Richard Dalloway, MP
Virginia Woolf: *The Voyage Out; Mrs Dalloway*

D'Ambois, Bussy A man of insolence and fiery courage, raised from poverty and introduced to the court by the brother of Henri III of France: based on the historical figure of Louis de Bussy-d'Ambois
George Chapman: *Bussy D'Ambois; The Revenge of Bussy D'Ambois*

Dametas A herdsman, husband of *Miso
Sir Philip Sydney: *Arcadia*

Damoetas A base herdsman who becomes a royal favourite
Sir Philip Sydney: *Arcadia*

D'Amville The 'atheist', brother of *Montferrers
Cyril Tourneur: *The Atheist's Tragedy*

Dan Sister of *Una
Rudyard Kipling: *Puck of Pook's Hill*

Dandie Dinmont A sturdy hospitable Liddesdale farmer and the owner of a special breed of terriers
Sir Walter Scott: *Guy Mannering*

Dangerfield A cowardly braggart
Sir Charles Sedley: *Bellamira*

Dangerfield, Sebastian Central character
J.P. Donleavy: *The Ginger Man*

Dangle
R.B. Sheridan: *The Critic*

Dannisburgh, Lord Cited by Mr Warwick in the divorce proceedings against his wife, the former Diana *Merion; based on Lord Melbourne
George Meredith: *Diana of the Crossways*

Danvers, Mrs The sinister housekeeper at Manderley
Daphne du Maurier: *Rebecca*

Dapper and Drugger Dupes of *Subtle's; a clerk and a tobaccoman, respectively
Ben Jonson: *The Alchemist*

Darbishire, Charles Edwin Jeremy The less adventurous companion of *Jennings at Linbury Court Preparatory School
Anthony Buckeridge: *Jennings Goes to School* [and many others]

Darcy, Fitzwilliam Friend of Charles *Bingley, marries Elizabeth *Bennet
Jane Austen: *Pride and Prejudice*

Darley, L.G. The narrator
Lawrence Durrell: *The Alexandria Quartet*

Darnay, Charles The assumed English name of Charles D'Aulnais, nephew and heir of the Marquis *St Evremonde; saved from the guillotine by Sydney *Carton
Charles Dickens: *A Tale of Two Cities*

D'Artagnan A poor Gascon gentleman who becomes the companion of the Three Musketeers—*Athos, *Porthos, and *Aramis
Alexander Dumas père: *The Three Musketeers*

Dartle, Rosa Companion and distant relation of the widowed Mrs Steerforth who harbours a frustrated passion for James *Steerforth
Charles Dickens: *David Copperfield*

Dashwood, Elinor The level-headed sister of Marianne *Dashwood; marries Edward *Ferrars
Jane Austen: *Sense and Sensibility*

Dashwood, Fanny [*née* Ferrars] Daughter of Mrs Ferrars and wife of John *Dashwood
Jane Austen: *Sense and Sensibility*

Dashwood, John Stepson of the widowed Mrs Henry Dashwood; half-brother to Elinor and Marianne *Dashwood
Jane Austen: *Sense and Sensibility*

Dashwood, Marianne Emotionally demonstrative sister of Elinor *Dashwood; marries Colonel *Brandon
Jane Austen: *Sense and Sensibility*

Datchery, Dick A mysterious stranger with white hair and black eyebrows
Charles Dickens: *The Mystery of Edwin Drood*

Daubeny, Mr MP for East Barsetshire and Prime Minister
Anthony Trollope: *Phineas Finn; Phineas Redux; The Prime Minister*

Dauphine Eugenie, Sir Nephew of *Morose
Ben Jonson: *Epicene*

Davers, Lady Supercilious sister of Mr *B.
Samuel Richardson: *Pamela*

Davey, Francis Albino vicar of Altarnum
Daphne du Maurier: *Jamaica Inn*

Davies, Mac A tramp
Harold Pinter: *The Caretaker*

Daw, Sir John A cowardly braggart
Ben Jonson: *Epicene*

Dawkins, Jack 'The Artful Dodger', a member of *Fagin's gang
Charles Dickens: *Oliver Twist*

Day, Fancy The pretty but capricious sweetheart of Dick *Dewy
Thomas Hardy: *Under the Greenwood Tree*

Dean, Nelly Housekeeper at Thrushcross Grange
Emily Brontë: *Wuthering Heights*

Dean, Nelly [Ellen] Lifelong retainer of the *Earnshaws
Emily Brontë: *Wuthering Heights*

Deane, Mr and Lucy Uncle and cousin of Maggie *Tulliver
George Eliot: *The Mill on the Floss*

Deans, David ['Douce Davie'] The stern father of Effie *Deans
Sir Walter Scott: *The Heart of Midlothian*

Deans, Effie [Euphemia] Imprisoned in the old Edinburgh Tolbooth on a charge of child-murder
Sir Walter Scott: *The Heart of Midlothian*

Deans, Jeannie Devoted half-sister of Effie *Deans
Sir Walter Scott: *The Heart of Midlothian*

de Bois, Sir Rowland Father of *Oliver, *Orlando, and *Jaques
William Shakespeare: *As You Like It*

de Bourgh, Lady Catharine The arrogant aristocratic aunt of Fitzwilliam *Darcy and patron of the Revd *Collins
Jane Austen: *Pride and Prejudice*

De Courcy, Earl Whig nobleman of West Barsetshire; his wife Countess Rosina; sons George and John; daughters Alexandrina, Amelia, Margaretta, Maria, and Rosina
Anthony Trollope: *The Small House at Allington; Barchester Towers; Doctor Thorne; The Last Chronicle of Barset*

Decretas Follower of Antony
William Shakespeare: *Antony and Cleopatra*

de Croye, Countess Isabelle A Burgundian heiress
Sir Walter Scott: *Quentin Durward*

Dedalus, Stephen Central character
James Joyce: *Portrait of the Artist as a Young Man; Ulysses*

Dedlock, Lady Honoria Wife of Sir Leicester *Dedlock who secretly bears an illegitimate child, Esther *Summerson, to her lover Captain *Hawdon
Charles Dickens: *Bleak House*

Dedlock, Sir Leicester A Lincolnshire baronet, passionately in love with his wife, Lady Honoria *Dedlock
Charles Dickens: *Bleak House*

Deedles A banker, of Deedles Brothers, who commits suicide
Charles Dickens: *The Chimes*

Defarge, Ernest, and Thérèse Keeper of a Parisian wine-shop in the Quartier St Antoine and his formidable wife, both implacable revolutionaries
Charles Dickens: *A Tale of Two Cities*

De Flores A villain employed by *Beatrice-Joanna
Thomas Middleton and William Rowley: *The Changeling*

Delville, Mortimer Son of Cecilia *Beverley's guardian
Frances Burney: *Cecilia*

Demetrius Follower of *Antony
William Shakespeare: *Antony and Cleopatra*

Demetrius A Grecian gentleman, in love with *Hermia
William Shakespeare: *A Midsummer Night's Dream*

Demetrius A son of *Tamora the Goth
William Shakespeare: *Titus Andronicus*

Dempster, Mr, and Janet A hectoring, drunken lawyer and his long-suffering wife
George Eliot: 'Janet's Repentance' [*Scenes From Clerical Life*]

Dennis, Ned The public hangman who takes a grotesque pride in his trade
Charles Dickens: *Barnaby Rudge*

Dennison, Jenny Attendant on Edith *Bellenden
Sir Walter Scott: *Old Mortality*

Dent, Arthur
Douglas Adams: *The Hitch-Hiker's Guide to the Galaxy*

Deputy [aka **Winks]** The urchin employed by

*Durdles and a servant at Cloisterham's Travellers' Two-penny
Charles Dickens: *The Mystery of Edwin Drood*

Deronda, Daniel An idealistic young man, revealed to be the son of a famous Jewish singer, who becomes Gwendolen *Harleth's spiritual adviser
George Eliot: *Daniel Deronda*

Derriman, Festus A boorish yeoman, suitor of Anne *Garland
Thomas Hardy: *The Trumpet Major*

Desdemona Wife of Othello the Moor and daughter of *Brabantio
William Shakespeare: *Othello*

de Vere, Arthur
Sir Walter Scott: *Anne of Geierstein*

de Vionnet, Comtesse In love with Chadwick *Newsome
Henry James: *The Ambassadors*

de Winter, Max The owner of Manderley, husband of the deceased Rebecca
Daphne du Maurier: *Rebecca*

Dewy, Dick Son of the local carrier, in love with Fancy *Day
Thomas Hardy: *Under the Greenwood Tree*

Diana Daughter of Widow *Capilet
William Shakespeare: *All's Well That Ends Well*

Dick, Mr [i.e. **Richard Babley]** Devoted elderly companion of Betsey *Trotwood, saved by her from the lunatic asylum
Charles Dickens: *David Copperfield*

Diddler, Jeremy Chief character—continually borrowing money which he does not repay
James Kenney: *Raising the Wind*

Dimmesdale, Revd Arthur A young minister, lover of Hester *Prynne
Nathaniel Hawthorne: *The Scarlet Letter*

Diomed Attendant on *Cleopatra
William Shakespeare: *Antony and Cleopatra*

Diomedes A Greeek leader, Troilus' rival for *Cressida
William Shakespeare: *Troilus and Cressida*

Dionyza Wife of Cleon, governor of Tarsus, to whom *Pericles entrusts his daughter *Marina
William Shakespeare: *Pericles*

Diver, Dick A handsome doctor
F. Scott Fitzgerald: *Tender is the Night*

Dixon, Jim A university lecturer
Kingsley Amis: *Lucky Jim*

Doasyouwouldbedoneby, Mrs The rewarder of good deeds, sister of Mrs *Bedonebyasyoudid
Charles Kingsley: *The Water Babies*

Dobbin, Colonel William Loyal friend of George *Osborne, secretly in love with Amelia *Sedley
W.M. Thackeray: *Vanity Fair*

Dobson, Zuleika Daughter of the Warden of Judas College, Oxford, who inspires suicide in the undergraduate population during Eights Week
Max Beerbohm: *Zuleika Dobson*

Dods, Meg Landlady of the Cleikum Inn
Sir Walter Scott: *St Ronan's Well*

Dodson and Fogg Firm of unscrupulous solicitors who represent Mrs *Bardell in her breach-of-promise action against Mr *Pickwick
Charles Dickens: *The Posthumous Papers of the Pickwick Club*

Dogberry A constable, a precursor of Mrs *Malaprop in his gift of misapplying words; his colleague, *Verges
William Shakespeare: *Much Ado About Nothing*

Dolabella Follower of *Octavius
William Shakespeare: *Antony and Cleopatra*

Dolabella
John Dryden: *All for Love*

Doll Tearsheet *Falstaff's tavern mistress
William Shakespeare: *Henry IV 2*

Dombey, Florence Elder child of Paul *Dombey, rejected by her father
Charles Dickens: *Dombey and Son*

Dombey, Little Paul Second child and first son of Paul *Dombey
Charles Dickens: *Dombey and Son*

Dombey, Paul Head of the City merchant-house of Dombey and Son
Charles Dickens: *Dombey and Son*

Donn, Arabella A handsome but coarse barmaid who traps Jude *Fawley into marriage by feigning pregnancy
Thomas Hardy: *Jude the Obscure*

Donners, Sir Magnus A wealthy industrialist and patron of the arts
Anthony Powell: *A Dance to the Music of Time*

Donnithorne, Arthur Squire of Donnithrone Chase
George Eliot: *Adam Bede*

Doolittle, Eliza A Cockney flower-seller whom Professor Henry *Higgins attempts to turn into an imitation of a duchess
G.B. Shaw: *Pygmalion*

Doone, Carver The unredeemed villain of the Doone clan of Bagworthy who shoots Lorna *Doone at the altar on her wedding day
R.D. Blackmore: *Lorna Doone*

Doone, Lorna Kidnapped as a child by the Doones of Bagworthy, revealed finally to be a wealthy heiress
R.D. Blackmore: *Lorna Doone*

Dora *see* SPENLOW, DORA

Dorigen
Geoffrey Chaucer: 'The Franklin's Tale' [*Canterbury Tales*]

Dorimont A character based on John Wilmot, Earl of Rochester
Sir George Etherege: *The Man of Mode*

Dormer, Egbert, Lucy, and Ayala Artist and his daughters
Anthony Trollope: *Ayala's Angel*

Dorrit, Amy Third child of William *Dorrit, born in the Marshalsea debtors' prison
Charles Dickens: *Little Dorrit*

Dorrit, William Imprisoned for debt in the

Marshalsea prison; his children Edward ['Tip'], Fanny, and Amy ['Little Dorrit']
Charles Dickens: *Little Dorrit*

Douglas, Ellen Daughter of the outlawed Lord James of Douglas
Sir Walter Scott: *The Lady of the Lake*

Dousterswivel, Herman A charlatan
Sir Walter Scott: *The Antiquary*

Dowell, John and Florence American husband and wife, involved with Edward and Leonora *Ashburnham
Ford Madox Ford: *The Good Soldier*

Doyce, Daniel An engineer and friend of *Meagles
Charles Dickens: *Little Dorrit*

Drawcansir A character parodying Almanzor in Dryden's *The Conquest of Granada*
George Villiers, Duke of Buckingham: *The Rehearsal*

Driffield, Edward A caricature of the 'great writer'—often taken to be based on Thomas Hardy; his young wife and amanuensis, Rosie
W. Somerset Maugham: *Cakes and Ale*

Dromio, of Ephesus and of Syracuse Twin brothers, bondmen of the *Antipholus twins
William Shakespeare: *The Comedy of Errors*

Drood, Edwin Nephew of John *Jasper, betrothed as a child to Rosa *Bud
Charles Dickens: *The Mystery of Edwin Drood*

Droogs, The A murderous amoral gang
Anthony Burgess: *A Clockwork Orange*

Drummle, Bentley Fellow-pupil of *Pip's at Mr Pocket's; a selfish boor who marries *Estella
Charles Dickens: *Great Expectations*

Drummond, Hugh ['Bull-dog'] A xenophobic British ex-army officer who foils the machinations of Carl *Peterson
Sapper: *Bull-Dog Drummond*

Dryasdust, Dr Jonas A fictitious prosy antiquarian to whom Sir Walter Scott addresses the prefaces of some of his novels

DuBois, Blanche A former schoolteacher, raped by Stanley *Kowalski
Tennessee Williams: *A Streetcar Named Desire*

Duessa The daughter of Deceit and Shame—Falsehood in general
Edmund Spenser: *The Faerie Queene*

Duke Senior The banished duke
William Shakespeare: *As You Like It*

Dull, Anthony A constable
William Shakespeare: *Love's Labour's Lost*

Dumaine One of three lords attending the King of Navarra
William Shakespeare: *All's Well That Ends Well*

Dumaine Attending on *Ferdinand
William Shakespeare: *Love's Labour's Lost*

Dumbello, Lady The married name of Griselda, daughter of Archdeacon *Grantly
Anthony Trollope: *The Small House at Allington*, *The Warden*, *Barchester Towers*, and others

Dumbledikes, The Laird of (1) The grasping landlord of the widow Butler and Davie *Deans; (2) his son
Sir Walter Scott: *The Heart of Midlothian*

Duncan King of Scotland, murdered in his sleep by *Macbeth
William Shakespeare: *Macbeth*

Dundreary, Lord An eccentric English aristocrat with prominent side-whiskers
Tom Taylor: *Our American Cousin*

Dupin C. Auguste A brilliant and eccentric detective who solves mysteries by the power of deductive thought
Edgar Allan Poe: 'The Mystery of Marie Roget', 'The Murders in the Rue Morgue', 'The Purloined Letter'

D'Urberville, Alec A young man of means who seduces Tess *Durbeyfield
Thomas Hardy: *Tess of the D'Urbervilles*

Durbeyfield, Tess Daughter of a poor villager of Blackmoor Vale who discovers she is descended from the ancient D'Urberville family
Thomas Hardy: *Tess of the D'Urbervilles*

Durdles A surly drunken stonemason
Charles Dickens: *The Mystery of Edwin Drood*

Durham, Constantia Sir Willoughby *Patterne's second choice of wife who throws him over for Harry Oxford
George Meredith: *The Egoist*

E

Eames, Johnny The energetic, impetuous son of the widowed Mrs *Dale who is constantly rebuffed by her daughter Lily *Dale
Anthony Trollope: *The Small House at Allington*

Earine The shepherdess loved by *Aeglamour
Ben Jonson: *The Sad Shepherd*

Earlforward, Henry A secondhand bookseller; his wife, Violet
Arnold Bennett: *Riceyman Steps*

Earnshaw, Catherine The passionate and wilful sister of Hindley *Earnshaw, married to Edgar *Linton, but tragically entangled by deeper ties to *Heathcliff
Emily Brontë: *Wuthering Heights*

Earnshaw, Hareton Son of Hindley *Earnshaw, adopted by *Heathcliff after the death of his father
Emily Brontë: *Wuthering Heights*

Earnshaw, Hindley, The bitter master of Wuthering Heights and brother of Catherine *Earnshaw
Emily Brontë: *Wuthering Heights*

Earwicker, Humphrey Chimpden A Dublin tavern-keeper
James Joyce: *Finnegans Wake*

Easy, John [Jack] A naval midshipman, known as 'Equality Jack'
Frederick Marryat: *Mr Midshipman Easy*

Echidna Mother of the *Blatant Beast
Edmund Spenser: *The Faerie Queene*

Edgar The honest and legitimate elder son of the Earl of *Gloucester who is banished by his father
William Shakespeare: *King Lear*

Edith of Lorn Affianced to Lord *Ronald
Sir Walter Scott: *The Lord of the Isles*

Edmund The villainous bastard son of the Earl of *Gloucester
William Shakespeare: *King Lear*

Egeon A merchant of Syracuse, father of the *Antipholus twins
William Shakespeare: *The Comedy of Errors*

Eglamour Agent for *Silvia in her escape
William Shakespeare: *The Two Gentlemen of Verona*

Eglantine, Madame The prioress
Geoffrey Chaucer: *The Canterbury Tales*

Egremont, Charles The hero; younger brother of the pitiless landowner Lord Marney
Benjamin Disraeli: *Sybil*

Elbow A constable
William Shakespeare: *Measure for Measure*

Eliasson, Gerard Central character; a skilled but impoverished scribe
Charles Reade: *The Cloister and the Hearth*

Elliot, Anne Second daughter of Sir Walter *Elliot, persuaded by Lady *Russell to break off her engagement to Captain *Wentworth
Jane Austen: *Persuasion*

Elliot, Sir Walter Baronet and widower, of Kellynch Hall
Jane Austen: *Persuasion*

Elliott, Kirstie Housekeeper and relative of Archie *Weir, and sister of Robert, Gilbert, Clement, and Andrew—the 'Black Elliotts' who hunted down their father's murderer
R.L. Stevenson: *Weir of Hermiston*

Elton, Revd Philip The mercenary young vicar whom Emma *Woodhouse hopes to match with Harriet Smith
Jane Austen: *Emma*

Em'ly, Little Niece of Daniel *Peggotty, loved by her cousin Ham, who elopes with David Copperfield's glamorous friend *Steerforth
Charles Dickens: *David Copperfield*

Emelye Loved by *Palamon and *Arcite
Geoffrey Chaucer: 'The Knight's Tale' [*Canterbury Tales*]

Emilia The plain-spoken wife of *Iago
William Shakespeare: *Othello*

Emilia Peregrine's love
Tobias Smollett: *Peregrine Pickle*

Enobarbus, Domitius Close companion and friend of *Antony
William Shakespeare: *Antony and Cleopatra*

Eppie The natural daughter of Godfrey *Cass and Nancy Lammeter, adopted by Silas *Marner
George Eliot: *Silas Marner*

Eros Faithful attendant of *Anthony who kills himself to avoid killing his master
William Shakespeare: *Antony and Cleopatra*

Errol, Cedric The young grandson of an English earl, raised in New York by his American mother, who becomes Lord Fauntleroy
Frances Hodgson Burnett: *Little Lord Fauntleroy*

Escalus An old lord
William Shakespeare: *Measure for Measure*

Estella The beautiful but haughty young girl whom *Pip meets as a boy at Miss *Havisham's and with whom he falls in love
Charles Dickens: *Great Expectations*

Estragon A bowler-hatted tramp, companion of *Vladimir
Samuel Beckett: *Waiting for Godot*

Euarchus The just ruler of Macedon
Sir Philip Sydney: *Arcadia*

Euphrasia Daughter of Dion, a lord
Francis Beaumont & John Fletcher: *Philaster*

Eustace, Father Sub-prior of Kennaquhair
Sir Walter Scott: *The Monastery*

Eustace, Sir Florian Wealthy but ailing dupe who marries Lizzie Greystock, convinced of her purity and innocence
Anthony Trollope: *The Eustace Diamonds*

Eustace, Lady Lizzie [*née* Greystock] The brilliantly dishonest widow of Sir Florian *Eustace who attempts to defraud her late husband's estate
Anthony Trollope: *The Eustace Diamonds*

Eva, Little [Evangeline St Clare] The impossibly angelic child of Augustine St Clare whose life is saved by Uncle *Tom
Harriet Beecher Stowe: *Uncle Tom's Cabin*

Evans, Sir Hugh A Welsh parson
William Shakespeare: *The Merry Wives of Windsor*

Evans, Joey Night-club host and raconteur
John O'Hara: *Pal Joey*

Evelina *see* BELMONT, EVELINA

Everard, Colonel Markham Nephew of the gallant old cavalier Sir Henry Lee who adopts the parliamentary cause for reasons of conscience
Sir Walter Scott: *Woodstock*

Everdene, Bathsheba Young and spirited owner of the farm on which Gabriel *Oak works as a shepherd
Thomas Hardy: *Far From the Madding Crowd*

Ewart, Nanty Captain of the smuggler's brig
Sir Walter Scott: *Redgauntlet*

Eyre, Jane An orphaned governess who comes to work for Mr *Rochester at Thornfield Hall
Charlotte Brontë: *Jane Eyre*

F

Fabian Member of *Olivia's household
William Shakespeare: *Twelfth Night*

Face *Love-Wit's servant; a rogue
Ben Jonson: *The Alchemist*

Fagan, Dr Augustus Snobbish headmaster of Llanabba Castle School
Evelyn Waugh: *Decline and Fall*

Faggus, Tom An Exmoor highwayman
R.D. Blackmore: *Lorna Doone*

Fagin A receiver of stolen goods and organizer of a gang of juvenile pickpockets
Charles Dickens: *Oliver Twist*

Fainall, and Mrs Lover of Mrs *Marwood and pretended friend of *Mirabell
William Congreve: *The Way of the World*

Fair Maid of Perth, The *see* GLOVER

Fairfax, Gwendolen Daughter of Lady *Bracknell and cousin of Algy *Moncrieff, loved by Jack *Worthington ['Ernest']
Oscar Wilde: *The Importance of Being Earnest*

Fairfax, Jane An orphan, the niece of Miss *Bates
Jane Austen: *Emma*

Fairford, Alan Friend of Darsie *Latimer
Sir Walter Scott: *Redgauntlet*

Fairlie, Frederick The valetudinarian master of Limmeridge House and uncle of Laura *Fairlie
Wilkie Collins: *The Woman in White*

Fairlie, Laura Half-sister to her double Anne *Catherick and to Marian *Halcombe, married to Sir Percivcal *Glyde
Wilkie Collins: *The Woman in White*

Fairservice, Andrew A sanctimonious and self-important gardener at Osbaldistone Hall
Sir Walter Scott: *Rob Roy*

Fakredeen A dissembling and brilliant emir
Benjamin Disraeli: *Tancred*

Falkland An idealistic and benevolent country squire who becomes changed by events into the vindictive pursuer of Caleb *Williams
William Godwin: *Caleb Williams*

Fallow, Peter An alcoholic English journalist
Tom Wolfe: *The Bonfire of the Vanities*

Falstaff, Sir John A fat and witty old knight, one-time companion of Prince *Hal
William Shakespeare: *Henry IV 1* and *2; The Merry Wives of Windsor*

Fancyfull, Lady A jealous and affected mischief-maker
Sir John Vanbrugh: *The Provok'd Wife*

Fang, Mr A harsh, bullying magistrate before whom Oliver *Twist is brought on a charge of theft
Charles Dickens: *Oliver Twist*

Fanny A milkmaid, eventually revealed to be well born, who marries Joseph *Andrews
Henry Fielding: *The History of the Adventures of Joseph Andrews*

Fanshawe, Ginevra A wealthy student at Madame Beck's school
Charlotte Brontë: *Villette*

Farange, Beale and Ida An idle, spendthrift, self-absorbed English couple who become divorced when their daughter Maisie is six years old
Henry James: *What Maisie Knew*

Farange, Masie Daughter of Beale and Ida *Farange, forced by her parents' divorce to live with them alternately for six-month periods
Henry James: *What Maisie Knew*

Farfrae, Donald A corn merchant, rival in business and love of Michael *Henchard
Thomas Hardy: *The Mayor of Casterbridge*

Fashion, Sir Novelty [Lord Foppington] The perfect beau
Sir John Vanbrugh: *The Relapse*

Fat Boy, The [Joe] Somnolent page of Mr *Wardle
Charles Dickens: *The Posthumous Papers of the Pickwick Club*

Fawley, Jude A young Wessex villager with intellectual ambitions; cousin of Sue *Bridehead
Thomas Hardy: *Jude the Obscure*

Feathernest, Mr A caricature of Robert Southey
T.L. Peacock: *Melincourt*

Feeble A 'woman's tailor'; one of the recruits brought before *Falstaff
William Shakespeare: *Henry IV 2*

Feenix, Cousin Nephew of Mrs *Skewton: a superannuated man-about-town and clubman
Charles Dickens: *Dombey and Son*

Felix
Coventry Patmore: *The Angel in the House*

Fen, Gervaise An Oxford professor of English Language and Literature turned detective
Edmund Crispin: *The Case of the Gilded Fly* [and others]

Fenton A spendthrift young gentleman in love with Anne *Page
William Shakespeare: *The Merry Wives of Windsor*

Fenwick, Revd Frank The imprudent but well-meaning vicar of Bullhampton
Anthony Trollope: *The Vicar of Bullhampton*

Ferdinand Brother of the duchess
John Webster: *The Duchess of Malfi*

Ferdinand King of Navarre
William Shakespeare: *Love's Labour's Lost*

Ferdinand Son of *Alonso and lover of *Miranda
William Shakespeare: *The Tempest*

Fern, Will A country labourer who comes to London seeking work and falls foul of Alderman *Cute
Charles Dickens: *The Chimes*

Ferrars, Edward Brother of Fanny *Dashwood; marries Elinor Dashwood
Jane Austen: *Sense and Sensibility*

Ferret A misanthropic charlatan
Tobias Smollett: *The Life and Adventures of Sir Launcelot Greaves*

Ferrex and Porrex Sons of Gorboduc and Videna who quarrel over the division of the kingdom, as a result of which Ferrex is killed by Porrex and the latter is murdered by his mother
Thomas Norton and Thomas Sackville: *Gorboduc*

Feste *Olivia's jester, prime mover in the plot to gull *Malvolio
William Shakespeare: *Twelfth Night*

Feverel, Richard Son of Sir Austin Feverel, who

subjects his son to an authoritarian system of home education
George Meredith: *The Ordeal of Richard Feverel*

Feversham, Harry The central character; a soldier accused of cowardice by his fellow officers
A.E.W. Mason: *The Four Feathers*

Fevvers A winged trapeze artist
Angela Carter: *Nights at the Circus*

Fezziwig, Mr, and Mrs A tradesman to whom *Scrooge was apprenticed as a young man, and his wife
Charles Dickens: *A Christmas Carol*

Fidele Name assumed by *Imogen when disguised as a man
William Shakespeare: *Cymbeline*

Fidessa Name assumed by the false *Duessa
Edmund Spenser: *The Faerie Queene*

Fielding, Cyril Hard-bitten former principal of the Government College, friend of *Aziz
E.M. Forster: *A Passage to India*

Fielding, May Former schoolfriend of Bertha *Plummer and sweetheart of Bertha's brother, Edward
Charles Dickens: *The Cricket on the Hearth*

Filario Friend of *Posthumus Leonatus
William Shakespeare: *Cymbeline*

Finch, Atticus A widowed white lawyer, father of Scout and Jem Finch, who defends Tom *Robinson
Harper Lee: *To Kill a Mockingbird*

Finching, Flora Daughter of Christopher *Casby and a former sweetheart of Arthur *Clennam
Charles Dickens: *Little Dorrit*

Finchley, Sondra Daughter of a wealthy industrialist who becomes involved in the murder of Roberta *Alden
Theodore Dreiser: *An American Tragedy*

Fink-Nottle, Gussie [Augustus] Friend of Bertie *Wooster's, infatuated for a time with Madeline Bassett
P.G. Wodehouse: *Right Ho, Jeeves* [and others]

Finlay, Dr A young doctor in the Scottish town of Tannochbrae
A.J. Cronin: *Beyond This Place* [and others]

Finn, Phineas Son of an Irish doctor and a young Liberal politician
Anthony Trollope: *Phineas Finn; Phineas Redux; The Prime Minister; The Duke's Children*

Firmin, Dr George Brand A fashionable doctor; father of Philip
W.M. Thackeray: *The Adventures of Philip*

Fisher, Mary The rich and successful novelist who has an affair with *Ruth's husband
Fay Weldon: *The Life and Loves of a She-Devil*

Fisker, Hamilton K. Dapper American entrepreneur
Anthony Trollope: *The Way We Live Now*

FitzBoodle, George Savage Name and character (a bachelor clubman) assumed by Thackeray
W.M. Thackeray: *The Fitzboodle Papers*

Fitzgerald, Burgo Handsome and impetuous young man who tries to elope with Lady Glencora M'Cluskie [later Lady *Palliser]
Anthony Trollope: *Can You Forgive Her?*

Fitzpiers, Edred A young doctor, lured away from Grace *Melbury by Felice *Charmond
Thomas Hardy: *The Woodlanders*

Fitzpompey, Lord Foolish and vain uncle of *George, Duke of St James
Benjamin Disraeli: *The Young Duke*

Fiver A rabbit with with premonitory powers, brother of *Hazel,
Richard Adams: *Watership Down*

Fizkin, Horatio An unsuccessful candidate in the Eatanswill election
Charles Dickens: *The Posthumous Papers of the Pickwick Club*

Flamineo Machiavellian brother of Vittoria *Corombona
John Webster: *The White Devil*

Flaming Tinman, The A tinker
George Borrow: *Lavengro*

Flanders, Moll An abandoned child, brought up in the house of the compassionate mayor of Colchester, who after many vicissitudes becomes a successful plantation owner in Virginia
Daniel Defoe: *The Fortunes and Misfortunes of the Famous Moll Flanders*

Flashman, Harry A brutal public-school bully (also, as Sir Harry Flashman, the anti-hero of a series of humorous adventures by George Macdonald Fraser)
Thomas Hughes: *Tom Brown's Schooldays*

Flavius A faithful steward
William Shakespeare: *Timon of Athens*

Flay, Mr Loyal servant of Lord Sepulchrave, earl of Gormenghast
Mervyn Peake: *Titus Groan; Gormenghast*

Fleane Son of *Banquo
William Shakespeare: *Macbeth*

Fledgeby, 'Fascination' Proprietor of Pubsey & Co., moneylenders and bill-brokers
Charles Dickens: *Our Mutual Friend*

Fleetwood, Lord
George Meredith: *The Amazing Marriage*

Fleming, Agnes Sister of Rose *Maylie and mistress of Edwin *Leeford who dies in the workhouse after giving birth to his son, Oliver *Twist
Charles Dickens: *Oliver Twist*

Fleming, Henry A young inexperienced soldier facing his first battle
Stephen Crane: *The Red Badge of Courage*

Flintwinch, Jeremiah Servant, clerk, and eventually business-partner of Mrs Clennam; his wife, Affery
Charles Dickens: *Little Dorrit*

Flite, Miss A crazy but kindly old woman who

befriends Esther *Summerson at the Chancery Court
Charles Dickens: *Bleak House*

Flora Sickly, illegitimate daughter of Lord Monmouth
Benjamin Disraeli: *Coningsby*

Flora One of the governess's two young orphaned charges at Bly, sister of *Miles
Henry James: 'The Turn of the Screw'

Florence, Duke of
William Shakespeare: *All's Well That Ends Well*

Florimell The type of chastity and virtue in women
Edmund Spenser: *The Faerie Queene*

Florizel Prince of Bohemia who falls in love with *Perdita
William Shakespeare: *The Winter's Tale*

Flosky, Mr A transcendentalist; a caricature of Coleridge
T.L. Peacock: *Nightmare Abbey*

Fluellen A pedantic but courageous Welsh captain
William Shakespeare: *Henry V*

Flute A bellows-mender who takes the part of Thisbe in the play of 'Pyramus and Thisbe'
William Shakespeare: *A Midsummer Night's Dream*

Flutter, Sir Fopling The 'prince of fops' who gives the drama its name
Sir George Etherege: *The Man of Mode*

Flyte, Sebastian Second son of Lord Marchmain and his wife Lady Teresa: his brother, the Earl of Brideshead; his sisters, Cordelia and Julia; his teddy-bear, Aloysius
Evelyn Waugh: *Brideshead Revisited*

Fogg, Phileas Principal character
Jules Verne: *Around the World in Eighty Days*

Foible Maidservant to Lady *Wishfort
William Congreve: *The Way of the World*

Foker, Harry Heir to a brewing fortune who marries Blanch *Amory
W.M. Thackeray: *Pendennis*

Folliott, Revd Dr An amiable but reactionary clergyman
T.L. Peacock: *Crotchet Castle*

Fondlewife An uxorious old banker
William Congreve: *The Old Bachelor*

Foppington, Lord *see* FASHION, SIR NOVELTY

Ford, Mistress Alice One of the'merry wives', the wife of Master Frank Ford, a prosperous gentleman
William Shakespeare: *The Merry Wives of Windsor*

Foresight A foolish old astrologer
William Congreve: *Love for Love*

Forester, Sylvan An idealistic radical thinker, partly based on P.B. Shelley
T.L. Peacock: *Melincourt*

Fortinbras Militaristic prince of Norway
William Shakespeare: *Hamlet*

Fortnum, Charley British Consul in a small Argentinian posting
Graham Greene: *The Honorary Consul*

Fosco, Count Isidor Ottavio Baldassare A villainous Italian count, in league with Sir Percival *Glyde
Wilkie Collins: *The Woman in White*

Fotheringay, Miss Stage name of Emily *Costigan
W.M. Thackeray: *Pendennis*

Fox, Allie Eccentric and idealistic inventor who removes his family to the Honduran coast
Paul Theroux: *The Mosquito Coast*

Fradubio 'The doubter', the lover of *Fraelissa
Edmund Spenser: *The Faerie Queene*

Fraelissa Transformed into a tree by *Duessa
Edmund Spenser: *The Faerie Queene*

Francesca A nun
William Shakespeare: *Measure for Measure*

Frankenstein, Victor An idealistic Genevan student of natural philosophy who discovers the secret of imparting life to inanimate matter
Mary Shelley: *Frankenstein*

Frederick, Duke The usurper
William Shakespeare: *As You Like It*

Froth A foolish gentleman
William Shakespeare: *Measure for Measure*

Fungoso A foolish law student
Ben Jonson: *Every Man Out of His Humour*

Fuschia Daughter of Lord Sepulchrave and Countess *Gertrude and sister of Titus *Groan
Mervyn Peake: *Titus Groan; Gormenghast; Titus Alone*

G

Galeotti Astrologer of Louis XI
Sir Walter Scott: *Quentin Durward*

Gallus Follower of *Octavius
William Shakespeare: *Antony and Cleopatra*

Galore, Pussy
Ian Fleming: *Goldfinger*

Gama, King Father of Princess *Ida
Lord Tennyson: *The Princess*

Gamp, Mrs Sarah ['Sairey'] Slatternly and drunken old nurse and midwife hired to nurse *Lewsome in his fever
Charles Dickens: *Martin Chuzzlewit*

Gandalf A wizard
J.R.R. Tolkein: *The Hobbit; The Lord of the Rings*

Gantry, Elmer An evangelical preacher and former football player
Sinclair Lewis: *Elmer Gantry*

Ganymede Name adopted by *Rosalind
William Shakespeare: *As You Like It*

Gargery, Joe A village blacksmith, *Pip's sweet-tempered and ever loyal brother-in-law, married to Mrs Joe, a relentless virago
Charles Dickens: *Great Expectations*

Garland, Anne Central character; loved by John and Bob *Loveday
Thomas Hardy: *The Trumpet Major*

Garland, Mr and Mrs A kindly, elderly couple who employ Kit *Nubbles as their groom
Charles Dickens: *The Old Curiosity Shop*

Garter, Polly Romantic and fecund inhabitant of Donkey Street
Dylan Thomas: *Under Milk Wood*

Gashford Lord George Gordon's secretary and evil genius
Charles Dickens: *Barnaby Rudge*

Gatsby, Jay Enigmatic central character whose wealth has been built on bootlegging and other criminal activities
F. Scott Fitzgerald: *The Great Gatsby*

Gautier, Marguerite The central character; a courtesan in love with Armand Duval
Alexandre Dumas [fils]: *La Dame aux Camélias*

Gay, Walter The cheerful, self-reliant nephew of Sol *Gills who works as a clerk at Dombey and Son's and falls in love with Florence *Dombey
Charles Dickens: *Dombey and Son*

General, Mrs Absurdly genteel widow of a commissariat officer engaged by Mr *Dorrit as a chaperone and 'polisher' for Fanny and Amy
Charles Dickens: *Little Dorrit*

George, Duke of St James The 'Young Duke', an orphan placed under the guardianship of *Dacres
Benjamin Disraeli: *The Young Duke*

Gerard *see* ELIASSON, GERARD

Gerard, Brigadier Étienne A dashing soldier in Napoleon's army
A. Conan Doyle: *The Exploits of Brigadier Gerard* [and others]

Gerard, Sybil The beautiful daughter of Walter Gerard loved by Stephen Morley
Benjamin Disraeli: *Sybil*

Gerard, Walter The Chartist father of Sybil *Walter
Benjamin Disraeli: *Sybil*

Gerhardt, Jennie A poor young girl from Columbus, Ohio, who has an affair with Senator Brander and is left with their child Vesta when he dies
Theodore Dreiser: *Jennie Gerhardt*

Gertrude Widow of *Hamlet's father; married to her former brother-in-law *Claudius
William Shakespeare: *Hamlet*

Gertrude, Countess Mother of Titus *Groan, married to Lord *Sepulchrave
Mervyn Peake: *Titus Groan, Gormenghast*

Geryoneo A three-bodied giant (representing the power of Philip II of Spain)
Edmund Spenser: *The Faerie Queene*

Ghote, Inspector Ganesh A timid and indecisive plain-clothes detective in the Bombay CID
H.R.F. Keating: *The Perfect Murder* [and others]

Giacomo Friend of *Filario
William Shakespeare: *Cymbeline*

Gibson, Molly Daughter of Dr *Gibson who finally marries Roger *Hamley
Elizabeth Gaskell: *Wives and Daughters*

Gibson, Mr A widowed doctor in the small country town of Hollingford; father of Molly *Gibson
Elizabeth Gaskell: *Wives and Daughters*

Gibson, Mrs [formerly Kirkpatrick] The widowed governess in the family of Lord Cumnor who becomes the second wife of Mr *Gibson
Elizabeth Gaskell: *Wives and Daughters*

Gills, Solomon [Sol] A dealer in nautical instruments and devoted uncle of Walter *Gay
Charles Dickens: *Dombey and Son*

Gilmore, Gary An actual murderer, executed in 1987
Norman Mailer: *The Executioner's Song*

Glascock, Charles Eldest son of Lord Peterborough, twice rejected by Nora *Rowley, who finally marries Caroline Spalding
Anthony Trollope: *He Knew He Was Right*

Glegg, Mrs The strong-minded sister of Mrs Tulliver
George Eliot: *The Mill on the Floss*

Glendinning, Edward Abbot of Kennaquhair [Father Ambrose]
Sir Walter Scott: *The Abbot*

Gloucester, Earl of Father of *Edgar and the bastard *Edmund whose eyes are put out by the Duke of Cornwall, husband of *Regan
William Shakespeare: *King Lear*

Glover, Simon An honest burgher, father of Catharine, the 'Fair Maid of Perth'
Sir Walter Scott: *The Fair Maid of Perth*

Glowry, Scythrop A gloomy and melancholic young writer, based on P.B. Shelley
T.L. Peacock: *Nightmare Abbey*

Glumdalclitch A farmer's daughter who attends on *Gulliver during his visit to Brobdingnag
Jonathan Swift: *Gulliver's Travels*

Glyde, Sir Percival The villain of the piece who marries Laura *Fairlie for her money
Wilkie Collins: *The Woman in White*

Gobbo, Launcelot Servant to *Shylock
William Shakespeare: *The Merchant of Venice*

Goesler, Marie [Mme Max] The clever, beautiful, and fashionable friend of Lady Glencora *Palliser and the love of both the Duke of Omnium and Phineas *Finn
Anthony Trollope: *Phineas Finn; Phineas Redux; The Prime Minister; The Duke's Children; The Eustace Diamonds*

Golightly, Holly Glamorous former teenage hillbilly and playgirl living in a New York brownstone apartment
Truman Capote: *Breakfast at Tiffany's*

Gollum An underground creature obsessed with the magical ring
J.R.R. Tolkein: *The Hobbit; The Lord of the Rings*

Goneril Eldest daughter of King *Lear
William Shakespeare: *King Lear*

Gonzalo An honest old counsellor loyal to *Prospero
William Shakespeare: *The Tempest*

Gordeloup, Sophie Franco-Polish companion of Lady *Ongar
Anthony Trollope: *The Claverings*

Gostanzo
George Chapman: *All Fools*

Gostrey, Maria Expatriate American, friend of Lambert *Strether
Henry James: *The Ambassadors*

Gotobed, Elias The senator of the title
Anthony Trollope: *The American Senator*

Gould, Charles English owner of the San Tomé silver mine
Joseph Conrad: *Nostromo*

Gowan, Henry A dilettante artist and worthless young snob who marries Pet *Meagles
Charles Dickens: *Little Dorrit*

Gradgrind, Thomas MP for Coketown; a rigid Utilitarian with a passion for facts; his wastrel son, Tom
Charles Dickens: *Hard Times*

Graeme, Magdalen Grandmother of Roland *Avenel
Sir Walter Scott: *The Abbot*

Graeme, Roland *see* AVENEL, ROLAND

Graham, Helen A young widow and painter who takes up residence at Wildfell Hall with her young son Arthur
Anne Brontë: *The Tenant of Wildfell Hall*

Graham, Mary Gentle and beautiful companion to old Martin *Chuzzlewit; in love with young Martin but secretly loved by Tom *Pinch
Charles Dickens: *Martin Chuzzlewit*

Grandcourt, Henleigh The arrogant and cold-hearted husband of Gwendolen *Harleth
George Eliot: *Daniel Deronda*

Grandison, Sir Charles A 'faultily faultless' English gentleman who eventually marries Harriet *Byron
Samuel Richardson: *Sir Charles Grandison*

Granger, Edith The beautiful widow who marries Paul *Dombey
Charles Dickens: *Dombey and Son*

Grantly, Susan Eldest daughter of Septimus Harding, wife of Theophilus *Grantly
Anthony Trollope: *The Warden*

Grantly, Dr Theophilus Archdeacon of Barchester and rector of Plumstead Episcopi
Anthony Trollope: *The Warden*

Gratiano One of *Antonio's friends, who marries *Portia's servant Nerissa
William Shakespeare: *The Merchant of Venice*

Gray, Cordelia A private detective
P.D. James: *An Unsuitable Job for a Woman* [and others]

Gray, Cytherea A lady's maid in love with Edward *Springrove but unaware that he is already engaged
Thomas Hardy: *Desperate Remedies*

Greaves, Sir Launcelot A quixotic and idealistic knight-errant, in love with *Aurelia
Tobias Smollett: *Sir Launcelot Greaves*

Grewgious, Hiram Rosa *Bud's guardian
Charles Dickens: *Edwin Drood*

Grey, Richard A clergyman; Agnes' father
Anne Brontë: *Agnes Grey*

Greystock, Frank Young Conservative MP for Bobsborough
Anthony Trollope: *The Eustace Diamonds*

Gride, Arthur An aged usurer and associate of Ralph *Nickleby's in various shady transactions
Charles Dickens: *Nicholas Nickleby*

Grieux, Chevalier des The principal character, who elopes with Manon *Lescaut
Abbé Prevost: *Manon Lescaut*

Griffiths, Clyde Socially aspiring son of Kansas City street evangelists who murders Roberta *Alden
Theodore Dreiser: *An American Tragedy*

Grimes, Peter A vicious, sadistic fisherman who brings about the death of three workhouse boys
George Crabbe: *The Borough*

Grimes, Thomas A chimney-sweep, Tom's employer
Charles Kingsley: *The Water-Babies*

Grimwig, Mr Friend of Mr *Brownlow
Charles Dickens: *Oliver Twist*

Grip Barnaby *Rudge's pet raven
Charles Dickens: *Barnaby Rudge*

Gripe A rich usurer
Sir John Vanbrugh: *The Confederacy*

Groan, Titus The 77th Earl of Gormenghast
Mervyn Peake: *Titus Groan*

Grueby, John Loyal servant to Lord George Gordon
Charles Dickens: *Barnaby Rudge*

Grumio Faithful servant to *Petruchio
William Shakespeare: *The Taming of the Shrew*

Grundy, Mrs Symbol of a rigid conventional propriety
Thomas Morton: *Speed the Plough*

Guest, Stephen The rich suitor of Lucy *Deane who falls in love with her cousin Maggie *Tulliver
George Eliot: *The Mill on the Floss*

Guiderius Son of *Cymbeline, stolen by *Belarius; known as Polydore
William Shakespeare: *Cymbeline*

Gummidge, Mrs The widow of Daniel *Peggotty's late partner constantly complaining that she is 'a lone lorn creetur'
Charles Dickens: *David Copperfield*

Gunn, Ben The sole inhabitant of Treasure Island, marooned there by his fellow pirates
R.L. Stevenson: *Treasure Island*

Guppy, William Brash and vulgar clerk to Conversation *Kenge who proposes to Esther *Summerson
Charles Dickens: *Bleak House*

Guster, Augusta Servant to Mrs *Snagsby
Charles Dickens: *Bleak House*

Guyon, Sir The Knight of Temperance
Edmund Spenser: *The Faerie Queene*

Gynecia Wife of *Basilius
Sir Philip Sydney: *Arcadia*

H

Hal, Prince Prince of Wales, the future Henry V
William Shakespeare: *Henry IV 1* and *2*

Halcombe, Marian The courageous and resourceful heroine who unmasks the plot by Count *Fosco and Sir Percival *Glyde to obtain Laura *Fairlie's money
Wilkie Collins: *The Woman in White*

Haldin, Victor A former student turned terrorist who, after assassinating a minister of state, seeks help from *Razumov
Joseph Conrad: *Under Western Eyes*

Hale, Margaret Daughter of a Hampshire clergyman whose religious doubts force him to resign his living
Elizabeth Gaskell: *North and South*

Halifax, John A poor honest orphan who rises to gentlemanly status by his own integrity and worth
Dinah Maria Craik: *John Halifax, Gentleman*

Hamel, Isadore Sculptor, married to Lucy *Dormer
Anthony Trollope: *Ayala's Angel*

Hamlet Principal character, disillusioned by his mother's marriage to his uncle *Claudius
William Shakespeare: *Hamlet*

Hamley, Squire Proud and hot-tempered father of Osborne and Roger *Hamley
Elizabeth Gaskell: *Wives and Daughters*

Hamley, Osborne Handsome elder son of Squire *Hamley and brother of Roger who is secretly married to a French nursery-maid
Elizabeth Gaskell: *Wives and Daughters*

Hamley, Roger The younger son of Squire *Hamley who, engaged for a time to Cynthia *Kirkpatrick, finally marries Molly *Gibson
Elizabeth Gaskell: *Wives and Daughters*

Hanaud, Inspector Agent of the French Sûreté
A.E.W. Mason: *At the Villa Rose* [and others]

Hannay, Richard Central character
John Buchan: *The Thirty-Nine Steps* [and others]

Hardcastle, Squire Richard A country squire, father-in-law of Tony *Lumpkin; his wife, Dorothy; his daughter, Kate
Oliver Goldsmith: *She Stoops to Conquer*

Harding, Eleanor *see* BOLD, ELEANOR

Harding, Septimus Warden of Hiram's Hospital, Barchester, and incumbent of Crabtree Parva; father of Susan *Grantly and Eleanor *Bold
Anthony Trollope: *The Warden*

Haredale, Emma Daughter of deceased Reuben Hardedale, eventually married to Edward *Chester
Charles Dickens: *Barnaby Rudge*

Harker, Jonathan A young solicitor sent on business to Count Dracula
Bram Stoker: *Dracula*

Harleth, Gwendolen The high-spirited and self-confident heroine who marries Henleigh *Grandcourt
George Eliot: *Daniel Deronda*

Harley, Adrian Cynical tutor of Richard *Feverel
George Meredith: *The Ordeal of Richard Feverel*

Harlowe, Clarissa The central character, abducted by *Lovelace
Samuel Richardson: *Clarissa*

Harmon, John [alias **John Rokesmith**] Son of Old Harmon, the miserly dust-contractor
Charles Dickens: *Our Mutual Friend*

Harpagon A miser
Molière: *L'Avare*

Harrison, Dr A kindly parson
Henry Fielding: *Amelia*

Harthouse, James [Jem] A bored, unprincipled man about town who comes to Coketown as its prospective parliamentary candidate
Charles Dickens: *Hard Times*

Hartright, Walter A drawing-teacher
Wilkie Collins: *The Woman in White*

Harville, Captain and Mrs Friends of Captain *Wentworth
Jane Austen: *Persuasion*

Hastings, Captain Arthur Ex-army assistant and chronicler of Hercule *Poirot
Agatha Christie: *The Mysterious Affair at Styles* [and many others]

Hastings, George Companion of *Marlow, in love with Constance Neville
Oliver Goldsmith: *She Stoops to Conquer*

Hatchway, Lieutenant Friend of Peregrine Pickle
Tobias Smollett: *The Adventures of Peregrine Pickle*

Hatfield, Mr Rector of Horton
Anne Brontë: *Agnes Grey*

Hatteraick, Dirk A smuggler captain
Sir Walter Scott: *Guy Mannering*

Haut-ton, Sir Oran An orang-utan whom Sylvan *Forester has educated to everything except speech
T.L. Peacock: *Melincourt*

Havisham, Miss An elderly recluse, daughter of a wealthy brewer, jilted on her wedding morning by *Compeyson
Charles Dickens: *Great Expectations*

Hawdon, Captain ['Nemo'] Impoverished former lover of Lady *Dedlock and Esther *Summerson's father
Charles Dickens: *Bleak House*

Hawk, Sir Mulberry A dissolute parasite who sets out to fleece Lord Verisopht
Charles Dickens: *Nicholas Nickleby*

Hawkeye A name used by Natty *Bumppo
J.F. Cooper: *The Last of the Mohicans*

Hawkins, Jim The boy narrator and hero, whose mother keeps the Admiral Benbow inn
R.L. Stevenson: *Treasure Island*

Hawthorn, Jerry
Pierce Egan the elder: *Life in London*

Hayston, Frank The Laird of Bucklaw
Sir Walter Scott: *The Bride of Lammermoor*

Hazard, Sir Melchior A flamboyant Shakespearean actor of the old school
Angela Carter: *Wise Children*

Hazel The rabbit who leads the Sandleford rabbits in search of a new home
Richard Adams: *Watership Down*

Headrigg, Cuddie Ploughman to Lady Margaret *Bellenden
Sir Walter Scott: *Old Mortality*

Headrigg, Mause Zealous covenanting mother of Cuddie, the ploughman
Sir Walter Scott: *Old Mortality*

Headstone, Bradley A schoolmaster who falls obsessively in love with Lizzie *Hexam
Charles Dickens: *Our Mutual Friend*

Heartwell The surly old bachelor
William Congreve: *The Old Bachelor*

Heaslop, Ronnie City Magistrate of Chandrapore, engaged to Adela *Quested
E.M. Forster: *A Passage to India*

Heathcliff A waif of unknown parentage picked up in the streets of Liverpool by Catharine and Hindley *Earnshaw's father, bullied and humiliated as a child by Hindley, destructively obsessed with Catherine
Emily Brontë: *Wuthering Heights*

Heep, Uriah Clerk to Mr *Wickfield who covers his machinations with a veneer of obsequious humility
Charles Dickens: *David Copperfield*

Helen An orphan
William Shakespeare: *All's Well That Ends Well*

Helen Attending on *Imogen
William Shakespeare: *Cymbeline*

Helena The heroine; a physician's daughter in love with *Bertam
William Shakespeare: *All's Well That Ends Well*

Helena An Athenian maid, in love with *Demetrius; the taller of the two heroines
William Shakespeare: *A Midsummer Night's Dream*

Helstone, Caroline The gentle and retiring cousin of Robert Gérard *Moore
Charlotte Brontë: *Shirley*

Henchard, Michael The mayor of Casterbridge; a former hay-trusser who, whilst drunk at a fair, sold his wife and child
Thomas Hardy: *The Mayor of Casterbridge*

Henri, Frances An Anglo-Swiss pupil-teacher and lace mender loved by William *Crimsworth
Charlotte Brontë: *The Professor*

Hermegild
Sir William Davenant: *Albovine*

Hermia Daughter of Egeus, in love with *Lysander; the shorter of the two heroines
William Shakespeare: *A Midsummer Night's Dream*

Hermione Queen of Sicilia, wife of the jealous *Leontes, and mother of *Perdita
William Shakespeare: *The Winter's Tale*

Hero Daughter of *Leonato and cousin of *Beatrice
William Shakespeare: *Much Ado About Nothing*

Herries of Birrenswork Fanatical Jacobite uncle of Darsie *Latimer who kidnaps his nephew to promote his cause
Sir Walter Scott: *Redgauntlet*

Hexam, Jesse [Gaffer] A Thames waterman who robs drowned corpses for a living
Charles Dickens: *Our Mutual Friend*

Hexam, Lizzie Daughter of Gaffer *Hexam who finally marries Eugene *Wrayburn
Charles Dickens: *Our Mutual Friend*

Hiawatha The son of *Mudjekeewis and *Wenonah, reared by his grandmother *Nokomis on the shores of Lake Superior
Henry Wadsworth Longfellow: *The Song of Hiawatha*

Hieronimo Marshal of Spain
Thomas Kyd: *The Spanish Tragedy*

Higden, Betty A fiercely independent old woman who struggles to keep herself out of the workhouse
Charles Dickens: *Our Mutual Friend*

Higgins, Henry A phonetician who attempts to transform the flower-seller Eliza *Doolittle
G.B. Shaw: *Pygmalion*

Hilton, Ruth The central character; a young orphaned dressmaker
Elizabeth Gaskell: *Ruth*

Hines, Eupheus A fanatical racist who murders the father of his daughter's child, Joe *Christmas, because he believes he has Negro blood
William Faulkner: *Light in August*

Holmes, Sherlock A private consulting detective
A. Conan Doyle: *A Study in Scarlet* [and many others]

Holofernes A pedantic schoolmaster
William Shakespeare: *Love's Labour's Lost*

Holt, Father A Jesuit priest and Jacobite spy
W.M. Thackeray: *The History of Henry Esmond*

Honeychurch, Lucy A guest at the Pensione Bertolini
E.M. Forster: *A Room with a View*

Honeythunder, Luke A bullying 'Professor of Philanthropy', guardian of the *Landless twins
Charles Dickens: *The Mystery of Edwin Drood*

Honeywood, Mr A foolishly good-natured young man, in love with Miss *Richland
Oliver Goldsmith: *The Good-Natur'd Man*

Honoria
Coventry Patmore: *The Angel in the House*

Hook, Captain An old Etonian pirate, with a hook instead of a right hand
J.M. Barrie: *Peter Pan*

Horatio University friend of *Hamlet
William Shakespeare: *Hamlet*

Hornblower, Horatio A courageous young naval officer who rises to the rank of admiral during the Napoleonic wars
C.S. Forester: *The Happy Return* [and many others]

Horner A witty libertine who spreads a false report that he is impotent
William Wycherley: *The Country Wife*

Hortensio Friend to *Petruchio and suitor of *Bianca
William Shakespeare: *The Taming of the Shrew*

Howe, Anna Principal correspondent of Clarissa *Harlowe
Samuel Richardson: *Clarissa*

Hoyden, Miss Daughter of Sir Tunbelly *Clumsy
Sir John Vanbrugh: *The Relapse*

Hudibras, Sir A grotesque Presbyterian knight
Samuel Butler: *Hudibras*

Hugh Ostler of the Maypole Inn
Charles Dickens: *Barnaby Rudge*

Humbert, Humbert A Swiss literary historian who, obsessed by Lolita, seduces and marries her mother
Vladimir Nabokov: *Lolita*

Humgudgeon, Corporal Grace-be-here
Sir Walter Scott: *Woodstock*

Huncamunca
Henry Fielding: *Tom Thumb*

Hunter, Mrs, and Mr Leo A lion-hunting hostess and her husband, residents of 'The Den' at Eatanswill
Charles Dickens: *The Posthumous Papers of the Pickwick Club*

I

Iachimo A villainous Roman courtier
William Shakespeare: *Cymbeline*

Iago A dissembling and cynical villain, jealous of Othello
William Shakespeare: *Othello*

Ida, Princess Daughter of King *Gama; a devotee of women's rights who founds a university
Lord Tennyson: *The Princess*

Ilex, Miss An accomplished spinster
T.L. Peacock: *Gryll Grange*

Imlac A much-travelled old philosopher
Samuel Johnson: *The Prince of Abissinia [Rasselas]*

Imogen [more properly **Innogen]** Daughter of *Cymbeline
William Shakespeare: *Cymbeline*

Infant Phenomenon, The *see* CRUMMLES, NINETTA

Innogen *see* IMOGEN

Iras Attendant on *Cleopatra
William Shakespeare: *Antony and Cleopatra*

Irena Personification of Ireland
Edmund Spenser: *The Faerie Queene*

Irene, Princess The king's only daughter, 'with eyes like two bits of night-sky, each with a star dissolved in the blue'
George MacDonald: *The Princess and the Goblin; The Princess and Curdie*

Isabella A novice nun, sister of *Claudio; the object of *Angelo's passion
William Shakespeare: *Measure for Measure*

Isabella Wife of *Hieronimo
Thomas Kyd: *The Spanish Tragedy*

Ishmael The narrator who ships on the whaler Pequod with Captain *Ahab
Herman Melville: *Moby-Dick*

Ivanhoe, Wilfred of Son and heir of *Cedric the Saxon who eventually marries the Lady *Rowena
Sir Walter Scott: *Ivanhoe*

J

Jabberwock A terrifying monster
Lewis Carroll: *Through the Looking-Glass*

Jacynta Daughter of *Juliano
William Rowley: *All's Lost by Lust*

Jaffeir A noble Venetian youth
Thomas Otway: *Venice Preserv'd*

Jaggers, Mr Formidable legal adviser to Miss *Havisham and *Pip's guardian
Charles Dickens: *Great Expectations*

Jakin, Bob A packman, loyal childhood friend of Maggie *Tulliver
George Eliot: *The Mill on the Floss*

James, Colonel
Henry Fielding: *Amelia*

Jane
Coventry Patmore: *The Angel in the House*

Jaquenetta A country wench loved by *Armado
William Shakespeare: *Love's Labour's Lost*

Jaques A discontented lord attending the banished duke
William Shakespeare: *As You Like It*

Jarley, Mrs Proprietress of a travelling waxwork show who employs Nell *Trent and her grandfather
Charles Dickens: *The Old Curiosity Shop*

Jarndyce, John Owner of Bleak House who takes in the young Chancery wards, Richard *Carstone and Ada *Clare
Charles Dickens: *Bleak House*

Jarvie, Bailie Nicol Glaswegian companion of Francis *Osbaldistone
Sir Walter Scott: *Rob Roy*

Jasper, John Uncle of Edwin *Drood and choirmaster of Cloisterham Cathedral
Charles Dickens: *The Mystery of Edwin Drood*

Jeavons, Lady Molly A socialite
Anthony Powell: *A Dance to the Music of Time* series

Jeeves The omniscient and resourceful valet of Bertie *Wooster
P.G. Wodehouse: *The Inimitable Jeeves* [and many others]

Jellyby, Mrs A lady devoted to philanthropic actitivity, especially to the welfare of the natives of Borrioboola-Gha; her daughter Caroline ['Caddy']
Charles Dickens: *Bleak House*

Jenkins, Revd Eli Poet and preacher
Dylan Thomas: *Under Milk Wood*

Jenkins, Nicholas The narrator, successively a publisher, screenwriter, novelist, and biographer
Anthony Powell: *A Dance to the Music of Time* series

Jenkyns, Deborah and Matilda Central characters; the formidable Miss Deborah and her gentle sister Matty, daughters of the former rector; their long-lost brother, Peter
Elizabeth Gaskell: *Cranford*

Jennings, Mrs Widowed friend of the *Dashwood family
Jane Austen: *Sense and Sensibility*

Jennings, John Christopher Timothy
Anthony Buckeridge: *Jennings Goes to School* [and many others]

Jenny Wren [Fanny Cleaver] A young crippled doll-maker
Charles Dickens: *Our Mutual Friend*

Jervis, Mrs Housekeeper and ally of Pamela *Andrews
Samuel Richardson: *Pamela*

Jessel, Miss Former governess at Bly who died in mysterious circumstances connected with the evil valet Peter *Quint
Henry James: 'The Turn of the Screw'

Jessica Daughter of *Shylock
William Shakespeare: *The Merchant of Venice*

Jewkes, Mrs Servant to Mr *B. and an accomplice in his subjugation of Pamela *Andrews
Samuel Richardson: *Pamela*

Jim A runaway slave
Mark Twain: *The Adventures of Huckleberry Finn*

Jimson, Gulley The Bohemian artist-hero
Joyce Carey: *The Horse's Mouth*

Jingle, Alfred A plausible rogue who imposes himself on the Pickwickians
Charles Dickens: *The Posthumous Papers of the Pickwick Club*

Jiniwin, Mrs *Quilp's mother-in-law
Charles Dickens: *The Old Curiosity Shop*

Jo The illiterate, vagrant crossing-sweeper boy who lives in Tom-All-Alone's
Charles Dickens: *Bleak House*

Joad family Expropriated Oklahoma farmers from the Dust Bowl region who set out in search of a better life in California
John Steinbeck: *The Grapes of Wrath*

Jobling, Tony A poor law-writer who lives above *Krook's shop
Charles Dickens: *Bleak House*

Joe *see* FAT BOY, THE

Jollifant, Inigo A former schoolmaster
J.B. Priestley: *The Good Companions*

Jones, Mr The farmer
George Orwell: *Animal Farm*

Jones, Tom The adopted son of Squire *Allworthy, revealed in the end to be Tom's uncle
Henry Fielding: *Tom Jones*

Jones, Wash A poor white squatter on Thomas *Sutpen's estate
William Faulkner: *Absalom, Absalom!*

Jorkins, Mr Junior partner in the firm of Jorkins and *Spenlow
Charles Dickens: *David Copperfield*

Jorrocks, Mr John A sporting Cockney grocer
R.S. Surtees: *Jorrocks's Jaunts and Jollities* [and others]

Julia Faithful lover of *Proteus
William Shakespeare: *The Two Gentlemen of Verona*

Juliano Principal general of *Roderigo
William Rowley: *All's Lost by Lust*

Julie The heroine; loved by *Saint-Preux
J.J. Rousseau: *Julie; or, The New Eloise*

Juliet Betrothed to *Claudio
William Shakespeare: *Measure for Measure*

Juliet Daughter of *Capulet in love with *Romeo, son of her father's rival *Montague
William Shakespeare: *Romeo and Juliet*

Jupe, Cissy [Cecilia] Daughter of Signor Jupe, a performer in *Sleary's circus
Charles Dickens: *Hard Times*

K

Karasmé
Benjamin Disraeli: *Alroy*

Karla A Russian spymaster
John le Carré: *Tinker, Tailor, Soldier, Spy* [and others]

Kastril The rustic lad who comes to London to learn the speech of the roaring boys
Ben Jonson: *The Alchemist*

Katherina Shrewish daughter of *Baptista of Padua
William Shakespeare: *The Taming of the Shrew*

Katherine Daughter of the King of France
William Shakespeare: *Henry V*

Katherine Attending on the Princess of France
William Shakespeare: *Love's Labour's Lost*

Keeldar, Shirley A young heiress of independent spirit
Charlotte Brontë: *Shirley*

Kehaar A black-headed gull
Richard Adams: *Watership Down*

Keith, Willie A spoiled Princeton graduate who joins the minesweeper Caine as a midshipman
Herman Wouk: *The Caine Mutiny*

Kenge, Conversation Partner in the solicitors' firm of Kenge and Carboy
Charles Dickens: *Bleak House*

Kennedy, Lady Laura [*née* Standish] Daughter of the Whig politician the Earl of Brentford and the wife of Robert Kennedy MP, philanthropist and millionaire
Anthony Trollope: *Phineas Finn; Phineas Redux*

Kenneth, Sir The hero; the Knight of the Leopard
Sir Walter Scott: *The Talisman*

Kent, Earl of Banished but loyal follower of King *Lear
William Shakespeare: *King Lear*

Kenwigs, Mr and Mrs An ivory-turner; his wife (Susan) niece of Mr *Lillyvick
Charles Dickens: *Nicholas Nickleby*

Kettledrummle, Revd Gabriel A fanatical Covenanting divine
Sir Walter Scott: *Old Mortality*

Kipps, Arthur An assistant in a draper's shop whose life is transformed by an inheritance
H.G. Wells: *Kipps*

Kipps, Arthur A young lawyer
Susan Hill: *The Woman in Black*

Kirby, Carinthia and Chillon Brother and sister, children of Captain Kirby, the 'Old Buccaneer'
George Meredith: *The Amazing Marriage*

Kirk, Dr Howard Lecturer in sociology at Watermouth University
Malcolm Bradbury: *The History Man*

Kirkpatrick, Cynthia The beautiful but unprincipled daughter of Mrs *Gibson [the former Mrs Kirkpatrick]
Elizabeth Gaskell: *Wives and Daughters*

Kite, Sergeant Resourceful sergeant of Captain *Plume
George Farquhar: *The Recruiting Officer*

Kitely A merchant, irrationally jealous of his young wife
Ben Jonson: *Every Man in His Humour*

Klaius
See STREPHON AND KLAIUS

Klebb, Rosa A Russian colonel in SMERSH and anatagonist of James *Bond
Ian Fleming: *From Russia in Love*

Klugman, Neil A Jewish boy from Newark who has a summer love affair with Brenda Patimkin, the daughter of wealthy parents
Philip Roth: *Goodbye, Columbus*

Knag, Miss Chief assistant to Madame *Mantalini
Charles Dickens: *Nicholas Nickleby*

Knight, Henry Friend and patron of Stephen *Smith
Thomas Hardy: *A Pair of Blue Eyes*

Knight of the Leopard, The *see* KENNETH, SIR

Knightley, George Bachelor owner of Donwell Abbey and Emma *Woodhouse's brother-in-law who eventually proposes to her
Jane Austen: *Emma*

Knockdunder, The Captain of The Duke of Argyl's agent
Sir Walter Scott: *The Heart of Midlothian*

Knowell, Edward Son of a father with an excessive concern for his morals
Ben Jonson: *Every Man in His Humour*

Knox, Flurry A well-to-do rogue from whom Major *Yates rents Shreelane
Somerville and Ross: *Some Experiences of an Irish R.M.*

Kowalski, Stanley Brother-in-law of Blanch *DuBois
Tennessee Williams: *A Streetcar Named Desire*

Krook A rag-and-bone merchant, known as the 'Lord Chancellor', and landlord of Miss *Flite
Charles Dickens: *Bleak House*

Kumar, Hari A middle-class Hindu given an English public school education by his Anglophile father; in love with Daphne *Manners
Paul Scott: *The Raj Quarter*

Kurtz Half-English, half-French agent for an ivory trading company who becomes deified by the local natives and as a result confronts a condition of primitive depravity within himself
Joseph Conrad: 'Heart of Darkness'

L

La Creevy, Miss A painter of miniatures
Charles Dickens: *Nicholas Nickleby*

La Fleur *Yorick's French servant
Lawrence Sterne: *A Sentimental Journey*

La Foote, Sir Amorous A foolish, chattering courtier
Ben Jonson: *Epicene*

Ladislaw, Will[iam] Cousin of Edward *Casaubon who eventually marries his widow, Dorothea *Brooke
George Eliot: *Middlemarch*

Lady Bountiful *see* BOUNTIFUL, LADY

Laertes Brother of *Ophelia
William Shakespeare: *Hamlet*

Lafeu An old lord
William Shakespeare: *All's Well That Ends Well*

Lammle, Alfred An unscrupulous adventurer who marries Sophronia Akershem believing her to be wealthy
Charles Dickens: *Our Mutual Friend*

La Motte, Christabel A fictitious Victorian poet
A.S. Byatt: *Possession*

Landless, Neville, and Helena Orphaned twins, born in Ceylon
Charles Dickens: *The Mystery of Edwin Drood*

Languish, Lydia The romantic heroine, niece of Mrs *Malaprop, loved by Captain *Absolute
R.B. Sheridan: *The Rivals*

Larkin, Pop [Sidney] and Ma A happy-go-lucky rural family living on a ramshackle farm in Kent; their children Mariette, Montgomery, Petunia, Primrose, Victoria, and Zinnia
H.E. Bates: *The Darling Buds of May* [and others]

Latimer, Darsie [Sir Arthur Darsie Redgauntlet] Nephew of *Herries of Birrenswork
Sir Walter Scott: *Redgauntlet*

Launce Clownish servant to *Proteus
William Shakespeare: *The Two Gentlemen of Verona*

Laurence, Friar Counsellor and confessor to the lovers, who performs their marriage
William Shakespeare: *Romeo and Juliet*

Lavatch A clown
William Shakespeare: *All's Well That Ends Well*

Lavinia Daughter of *Titus, who is raped and mutilated
William Shakespeare: *Titus Andronicus*

Lavish, Miss A lady novelist and resident of the Pensione Bertolini in Florence
E.M. Forster: *A Room with a View*

Leamas, Alec A British agent
John le Carré: *The Spy Who Came in from the Cold*

Lear, King King of Britain; his three daughters *Goneril, *Regan, and *Cordelia
William Shakespeare: *King Lear*

Leatherstocking Nickname of Natty *Bumppo
J.F. Cooper: The 'Leatherstocking' series

Lecter, Dr Hannibal A cannibalistic murderer
Thomas Harris: *The Silence of the Lambs; Hannibal*

Leeford, Edwin Deceased father of *Monks and of Oliver *Twist
Charles Dickens: *Oliver Twist*

Legree, Simon A brutal, drunken, degenerate slave-owner who beats Uncle *Tom to death
Harriet Beecher Stowe: *Uncle Tom's Cabin*

Leigh, Sir Amyas
Charles Kingsley: *Westward Ho!*

Leiter, Felix CIA agent
Ian Fleming: *Goldfinger* [and others]

Leithen, Sir Edward Barrister and MP
John Buchan: *Sick Heart River* [and others]

Lennox, Mary A sickly and spoilt orphaned daughter of a British official in India who discovers the secret garden at Misselthwaite Hall
Frances Hodgson Burnett: *The Secret Garden*

Lensky, Lydia Widowed and impoverished Polish aristocrat who marries Tom *Brangwen; her daughter, Anna
D.H. Lawrence: *The Rainbow*

Leonato Governor of Messina, uncle of *Beatrice, and father of *Hero
William Shakespeare: *Much Ado About Nothing*

Leontes King of Sicilia, jealous husband of *Hermione
William Shakespeare: *The Winter's Tale*

Lepidus Triumvir of Rome
William Shakespeare: *Antony and Cleopatra*

Lescaut, Manon An intended nun who elopes with the chevalier des *Grieux
Abbé Prevost: *Manon Lescaut*

Lestrade, Inspector A Scotland Yard detective
A. Conan Doyle: *A Study in Scarlet* [and others]

Levellier, Lord
George Meredith: *The Amazing Marriage*

Levidulcia Second wife of *Belforest
Cyril Tourneur: *The Atheist's Tragedy*

Lewsome A young apothecary, friend of John *Westlock, whose poverty drives him to supply Jonas *Chuzzlewit with drugs
Charles Dickens: *Martin Chuzzlewit*

Light, Christina Leading female character
Henry James: *Roderick Hudson* [also *The Princess Casamassima*]

Lightwood, Mortimer An idle young barrister
Charles Dickens: *Our Mutual Friend*

Lillyvick, Mr Wealthy bachelor uncle of Mrs *Kenwigs
Charles Dickens: *Nicholas Nickleby*

Limberham, Mr An impotent masochist
John Dryden: *The Kind Keeper*

Linkinwater, Tim Loyal chief clerk of the *Cheeryble brothers
Charles Dickens: *Nicholas Nickleby*

Linton, Edgar Gentle husband of Catherine *Earnshaw, the antithesis of *Heathcliff
Emily Brontë: *Wuthering Heights*

Lismahago, Obadiah A disputatious Scotsman
Tobias Smollett: *The Expedition of Humphrey Clinker*

Littimer, Mr *Steerforth's manservant
Charles Dickens: *David Copperfield*

'Little Billee' A student friend of *Trilby O'Ferrall
George du Maurier: *Trilby*

Little Billy *see* Bagot, William

Little Dorrit *see* Dorrit, Amy

Little Eva *see* Eva, Little

Little Nell *see* Trent, Nell

Lochinvar Hero of an interpolated ballad; a dashing lover who carries off the fair Ellen on her wedding day
Sir Walter Scott: *Marmion*

Locke, Alton A tailor
Charles Kingsley: *Alton Locke*

Lockit, Lucy Daughter of the warder of Newgate prison
John Gay: *The Beggar's Opera*

Lockwood The narrator
Emily Brontë: *Wuthering Heights*

Loman, Willy An unsuccessful travelling salesman
Arthur Miller: *Death of a Salesman*

Long John Silver A rascally one-legged buccaneer
R.L. Stevenson: *Treasure Island*

Longueville Attending on *Ferdinand
William Shakespeare: *Love's Labour's Lost*

Lorenzo Lover of *Jessica
William Shakespeare: *The Merchant of Venice*

Lorenzo Son of the Duke of Castile
Thomas Kyd: *The Spanish Tragedy*

Lorry, Jarvis Confidential clerk in Tellson's bank
Charles Dickens: *A Tale of Two Cities*

Lothair Principal character; a wealthy nobleman caught between the claims of Catholicism and Anglicanism
Benjamin Disraeli: *Lothair*

Lothario A heartless libertine [proverbial as 'the Gay Lothario']
Nicholas Rowe: *The Fair Penitent*

Love-Wit
Ben Jonson: *The Alchemist*

Loveday, Bob A sailor, brother of John *Loveday and his rival for the love of Anne *Garland
Thomas Hardy: *The Trumpet Major*

Loveday, John A miller's son, Bob *Loveday's brother: the trumpet-major, in love with Anne *Garland
Thomas Hardy: *The Trumpet Major*

Lovelace, Robert A handsome, dashing rake who abducts Clarissa *Harlowe under the pretence of delivering her from parental tyranny
Samuel Richardson: *Clarissa*

Loveless A reformed libertine
Sir John Vanbrugh: *The Relapse*

Lucas, Charlotte Friend and neighbour of Elizabeth *Bennett who accepts a proposal of marriage from the Revd William *Collins
Jane Austen: *Pride and Prejudice*

Lucas, 'Lucia' [Emmeline, later **Mrs Georgie Pilson]** The pretentious social rival of Miss *Mapp
E.F. Benson: *Mapp and Mucia* [and others]

Lucentio The successful suitor of *Bianca
William Shakespeare: *The Taming of the Shrew*

Lucetta Waiting-woman to *Julia
William Shakespeare: *The Two Gentlemen of Verona*

Lucia *see* LUCAS, 'LUCIA'

Luciana Sister of *Adriana
William Shakespeare: *The Comedy of Errors*

Lucifera Symbol of baseless pride and worldliness
Edmund Spenser: *The Faerie Queene*

Lucio A 'fantastic'
William Shakespeare: *Measure for Measure*

Lucius A son of *Titus
William Shakespeare: *Titus Andronicus*

Lucius, Caius Roman ambassador, later general
William Shakespeare: *Cymbeline*

Lumpkin, Tony Son of Mrs *Hardcastle by a former marriage
Oliver Goldsmith: *She Stoops to Conquer*

Luna, Mrs Widowed sister of Oliver *Chancellor who pursues Basil *Ransom
Henry James: *The Bostonians*

Lussurioso Lecherous son and heir of the duke
Cyril Tourneur: *The Revenger's Tragedy*

Lydgate, Tertius An ambitious and idealistic country doctor
George Eliot: *Middlemarch*

Lyle, Annot
Sir Walter Scott: *The Legend of Montrose*

Lynmere, Indiana Cousin of Camilla *Tyrold
Frances Burney: *Camilla*

Lyon, Esther Supposed daughter of an Independent minister, but in fact the heir to the Transome estate
George Eliot: *Felix Holt, the Radical*

Lysander A young Grecian, in love with *Hermia but who is mistaken by *Puck for *Demetrius
William Shakespeare: *A Midsummer Night's Dream*

M

'M' Head of the British Secret Service to whom James Bond reports
Ian Fleming: *Casino Royale* [and others]

Macbeth A Scottish general who, spurred on by his wife, Lady Macbeth, murders *Duncan, King of Scotland, and assumes the crown
William Shakespeare: *Macbeth*

Macduff Thane of Fife
William Shakespeare: *Hamlet*

Macheath A gallant highwayman
John Gay: *The Beggar's Opera*

MacIntyre, Captain Hector Nephew of Jonathan *Oldbuck
Sir Walter Scott: *The Antiquary*

Mackaye, Saunders and Lillian Father and daughter
Charles Kingsley: *Alton Locke*

Macmorris, Captain An Irish captain
William Shakespeare: *Henry V*

Macro Evil agent of Tiberius
Ben Jonson: *Sejanus*

MacSarcasm, Sir Archy
Charles Macklin: *Love à la Mode*

Macstinger, Mrs Captain *Cuttle's termigant landlady
Charles Dickens: *Dombey and Son*

MacTurk [Turkey] Member of a schoolboy gang together with *Stalky and *Beetle
Rudyard Kipling: *Stalky & Co.*

Maecenas Follower of *Octavius
William Shakespeare: *Antony and Cleopatra*

Magiot, Dr A black doctor
Graham Greene: *The Comedians*

Magnus, Peter Jealous suitor of Miss Witherfield
Charles Dickens: *The Posthumous Papers of the Pickwick Club*

Magwitch, Abel An escaped convict, aided surreptitiously by *Pip, who subsequently becomes the boy's unknown benefactor; eventually revealed to be the father of *Estella
Charles Dickens: *Great Expectations*

Malaprop, Mrs Aunt and guardian of Lydia *Languish, noted for her solecisms
R.B. Sheridan: *The Rivals*

Maldon, Jack Idle and sponging cousin of Annie *Strong
Charles Dickens: *David Copperfield*

Malecasta The lady of Castle Joyeous
Edmund Spenser: *The Faerie Queene*

Malengin Personification of guile
Edmund Spenser: *The Faerie Queene*

Malvolio The morose and joyless steward to *Olivia
William Shakespeare: *Twelfth Night*

Mammon, Sir Epicure A voluptuous gourmandizing knight
Ben Jonson: *The Alchemist*

Mandlebert, Edgar Suitor of Camilla *Tyrold
Frances Burney: *Camilla*

Manette, Dr Alexandre A French physician confined in the Bastille; his devoted daughter, Lucie
Charles Dickens: *A Tale of Two Cities*

Manly An honest but misanthropic sea-captain
William Wycherley: *The Plain Dealer*

Manly Sensible friend of Lord *Townly
Sir John Vanbrugh/Colley Cibber: *The Provok'd Husband*

Manners, Bunny Former public school fag and companion of *Raffles
E.W. Hornung: *The Amateur Cracksman* [and others]

Manners, Daphne Niece of the governor of Mayapore who has a tragic love affair with Hari *Kumar
Paul Scott: *The Raj Quarter*

Mantalini, [formerly **Muntle]** **Alfred, and Madame** A Mayfair dressmaker who lives on his wife
Charles Dickens: *Nicholas Nickleby*

Mapp, Elizabeth [later **Mrs Mapp-Flint]** A leading light in Tilling society until the arrival of Emmeline *Lucas ['Lucia']
E.F. Benson: *Mapp and Mucia* [and others]

Marcelia The heroine; beloved wife of Lodovico Sforza
Philip Massinger: *The Duke of Milan*

March family Mr March, a teacher; his wife Marmee; his daughters Meg, Josephine ['Jo'], Beth, and Amy
Louisa M. Alcott: *Little Women* [and others]

Marchioness, The Servant to Sampson and Sally *Brass, cruelly treated by them
Charles Dickens: *The Old Curiosity Shop*

Marchmain Family name of the *Flytes of Brideshead
Evelyn Waugh: *Brideshead Revisited*

Marcus Andronicus Tribune of the people; brother of *Titus
William Shakespeare: *Titus Andronicus*

Mardian A eunuch, attending on *Cleopatra
William Shakespeare: *Antony and Cleopatra*

Margaret A gentlewoman attendant on *Hero
William Shakespeare: *Much Ado About Nothing*

Maria Attending on the *Princess of France
William Shakespeare: *Love's Labour's Lost*

Maria The ward of Sir Peter *Teazle who is loved by Charles *Surface
R.B. Sheridan: *The School for Scandal*

Maria Waiting-gentlewoman to *Olivia
William Shakespeare: *Twelfth Night*

Mariana A Florentine girl
William Shakespeare: *All's Well That Ends Well*

Mariana Betrothed to *Angelo
William Shakespeare: *Measure for Measure*

Marina Daughter of *Pericles and *Thaisa
William Shakespeare: *Pericles*

Markham, Gilbert The narrator; a young farmer in love with Helen *Graham
Anne Brontë: *The Tenant of Wildfell Hall*

Markleham, Mrs Mother of Annie *Strong
Charles Dickens: *David Copperfield*

Marley, Jacob Deceased partner of Ebenezer *Scrooge who appears to him as a ghost
Charles Dickens: *A Christmas Carol*

Marlow, ['Charlie'] The partly autobiographical narrator of four of Conrad's works
Joseph Conrad: *Youth*; *Heart of Darkness*; *Lord Jim*; *Chance*

Marlow The bashful suitor of Kate *Hardcastle, friend of George *Hastings
Oliver Goldsmith: *She Stoops to Conquer*

Marner, Silas The linen-weaver of Raveloe who adopts *Eppie
George Eliot: *Silas Marner*

Marple, Jane An elderly spinster and amateur detective of genius
Agatha Christie: *Murder at the Vicarage* [and many others]

Marplot A blundering busybody (now proverbial)
Susanna Centlivre: *The Busie Body*

Martext, Sir Oliver A country clergyman
William Shakespeare: *As You Like It*

Martius A son of *Titus
William Shakespeare: *Titus Andronicus*

Marwood, Mrs A vindictive hypocrite, rejected by *Mirabell
William Congreve: *The Way of the World*

Mary Mr *Nupkins's pretty housemaid, who marries Sam *Weller
Charles Dickens: *The Posthumous Papers of the Pickwick Club*

Mary, Queen of Scots *see* Stuart, Mary

Maskwell The'double-dealer'—supposed friend of *Mellefont
William Congreve: *The Double-Dealer*

Mason, Lady Mary Middle-aged widow of Sir Joseph Mason who forges her late husband's will in order that Orley Farm will be left to their son Lucius
Anthony Trollope: *Orley Farm*

Masters, Mary
Anthony Trollope: *The American Senator*

Matthews, Miss A courtesan
Henry Fielding: *Amelia*

Matty, Miss *see* Jenkyns, Deborah and Matilda

Maugrabin, Hayraddin An African Moor
Sir Walter Scott: *Quentin Durward*

Maule, Matthew The character whose curse at the point of execution for witchcraft condemns the house of Pyncheon for its persecution of him
Nathaniel Hawthorne: *The House of the Seven Gables*

Maylie, Rose Sister of Oliver *Twist's mother Agnes *Fleming, adopted by Mrs Maylie as a child
Charles Dickens: *Oliver Twist*

Mayo, Diana The English girl kidnapped by the Sheik
E.M. Hull: *The Sheik*

Meagles, Mr and Mrs A warm-hearted elderly couple; their daughter, Minnie ['Pet']
Charles Dickens: *Little Dorrit*

Melbury, Grace Daughter of a well-to-do timber merchant, betrothed to Giles *Winterbourne
Thomas Hardy: *The Woodlanders*

Melema, Tito A social and political climber, adopted by Baldesarre *Calvo
George Eliot: *Romola*

Melford, Jerry A young squire, nephew of Matthew *Bramble
Tobias Smollett: *The Expedition of Humphrey Clinker*

Mell, Charles Assistant master at Salem House school who is treated wretchedly by *Creakle
Charles Dickens: *David Copperfield*

Mellefont Nephew and heir of Lord Touchwood, engaged to *Cynthia
William Congreve: *The Double-Dealer*

Mellors, Oliver Gamekeeper to Sir Clifford Chatterley who begins an affair with Sir Clifford's wife, Constance
D.H. Lawrence: *Lady Chatterley's Lover*

Melmotte, Augustus An unscrupulous financial speculator; his daughter, Marie
Anthony Trollope: *The Way We Live Now*

Melvil, Count de Benefactor of Ferdinand; his son, Renaldo
Tobias Smollett: *The Adventurers of Ferdinand Count Fathom*

Melville, Julia Friend of Lydia *Languish
R.B. Sheridan: *The Rivals*

Menas Friend of *Pompey
William Shakespeare: *Antony and Cleopatra*

Menecrates Friend of *Pompey
William Shakespeare: *Antony and Cleopatra*

Mercutio Cynical friend of *Romeo, killed in a brawl by *Juliet's cousin *Tybalt
William Shakespeare: *Romeo and Juliet*

Merdle, Mr A crooked financier the failure of whose schemes leads him eventually to commit suicide
Charles Dickens: *Little Dorrit*

Merion, Diana A beautiful and impulsive Irish girl, based on Caroline Norton, married to dull Mr Warwick
George Meredith: *Diana of the Crossways*

Merle, Madame Calculating and cosmopolitan friend of Isabel *Archer and former mistress of Gilbert *Osmond
Henry James: *Portrait of a Lady*

Merrick, Ronald Cold and calculating police superintendent in Mayapore
Paul Scott: *The Raj Quarter*

Merrilies, Meg An old gypsy woman
Sir Walter Scott: *Guy Mannering*

Mertoun, Basil A misanthropical recluse; his son, Mordaunt
Sir Walter Scott: *The Pirate*

Merygreeke, Mathewe
Nicholas Udall: *Ralph Roister Doister*

Metroland, Margot [formerly **Margot Beste-Chetwynde**] A glamorous socialite
Evelyn Waugh: *Decline and Fall* [and others]

Micawber, Wilkins A optimistic and good-natured adventurer who lives from hand to mouth with his ever loyal wife, Emma, and four children—Wilkins, the twins, and the baby
Charles Dickens: *David Copperfield*

Middleton, Clara Sir Willoughby *Patterne's third choice of wife who finally extricates herself from the engagement
George Meredith: *The Egoist*

Miggs Sycophantic maid to Mrs Varden
Charles Dickens: *Barnaby Rudge*

Mignon A fairy-like child rescued by Wilhelm from a troupe of rope-dancers
Goethe: *Wilhelm Meister's Apprenticeship*

Milan, Duke of
William Shakespeare: *The Two Gentlemen of Verona*

Milborough,
Anthony Trollope: *He Knew He Was Right*

Miles An unusually charming young boy who, with his sister *Flora, is believed by the governess to be in communication with the spirits of the evil ex-valet Peter *Quint and her own predecessor Miss *Jessel
Henry James: 'The Turn of the Screw'

Miles, Sarah Wife of a civil servant who embarks on an affair with the novelist Maurice *Bendrix
Graham Greene: *The End of the Affair*

Milestone, Marmaduke A landscape gardener (based on Humphrey Repton)
T.L. Peacock: *Headlong Hall*

Millamant Niece of Lady *Wishfort, finally married to *Millamant
William Congreve: *The Way of the World*

Millbank, Oswald Son of a Lancashire manufacturer whose life is saved at Eton by Harry *Coningsby
Benjamin Disraeli: *Coningsby*

Mills, Julia Friend and confidante of Dora *Spenlow
Charles Dickens: *David Copperfield*

Milvain, Jasper A shallow but facile author who accepts the materialistic conditions of literary success
George Gissing: *New Grub Street*

Minty An unsuccessful journalist
Graham Greene: *England Made Me*

Mirabell In love with *Millamant
William Congreve: *The Way of the World*

Miranda Daughter of *Prospero, loved by *Ferdinand
William Shakespeare: *The Tempest*

Mirobolant A temperamental French chef who falls in love with Blanche *Amory
W.M. Thackeray: *Pendennis*

Miso Wife of *Dametas
Sir Philip Sydney: *Arcadia*

Moncrieff, Algernon [Algy] Man about town and friend of Jack *Worthington ['Ernest']; in love with Jack's ward, Cecily *Cardew
Oscar Wilde: *The Importance of Being Earnest*

Monkbarns, Laird of *see* OLDBUCK, JONATHAN

Monks Alias of Edward Leeford, half-brother of Oliver *Twist
Charles Dickens: *Oliver Twist*

Monmouth, Lord Grandfather of Harry *Coningsby; representative of the old type of oppressive Tory
Benjamin Disraeli: *Coningsby*

Montague Father of *Romeo and deadly rival of *Capulet
William Shakespeare: *Romeo and Juliet*

Montferrers Brother of *D'Amville, father of *Charlemont
Cyril Tourneur: *The Atheist's Tragedy*

Moody, Zenobia *see* ZENOBIA

Moore, Mrs An elderly Englishwoman who comes to India to visit her son Ronny *Heaslop, Adela *Quested's fiancé
E.M. Forster: *A Passage to India*

Moore, Robert Gérard A half-English, half-Belgian mill owner who proposes to Shirley *Keeldar
Charlotte Brontë: *Shirley*

Mopsa Daughter of *Dametas and *Miso
Sir Philip Sydney: *Arcadia*

Morden, Colonel Cousin of Clarissa *Harlowe who finally kills *Lovelace in a duel
Samuel Richardson: *Clarissa*

Morgan Name assumed by *Belarius
William Shakespeare: *Cymbeline*

Morgan Major Pendennis's valet
W.M. Thackeray: *Pendennis*

Moriarty, Professor Deadly criminal enemy of Sherlock *Holmes
A. Conan Doyle: *The Memoirs of Sherlock Holmes* [and others]

Morland, Catherine Central character; the daughter of a well-to-do clergyman
Jane Austen: *Northanger Abbey*

Morley, Stephen Radical and atheist
Benjamin Disraeli: *Sybil*

Morose A crabbed and egotistic old bachelor who hates noise
Ben Jonson: *Epicene*

Morris, Dinah Niece of Mrs *Poyser, marries Adam *Bede
George Eliot: *Adam Bede*

Morton, Henry, of Milnwood The young and courageous hero
Sir Walter Scott: *Old Mortality*

Morton, John English Secretary of Legation in Washington
Anthony Trollope: *The American Senator*

Morton, Reginald
Anthony Trollope: *The American Senator*

Morton, Silas
Sir Walter Scott: *Old Mortality*

Mosby Lover of Mistress Arden
Anon.: *Arden of Feversham*

Mosca *Volpone's parasite and confederate
Ben Jonson: *Volpone*

Moth Page to Don Adriano de *Armado
William Shakespeare: *Love's Labour's Lost*

Moth One of the fairies
William Shakespeare: *A Midsummer Night's Dream*

Mottram, Rex Ex-Canadian army veteran and British MP who marries Lady Julia *Flyte
Evelyn Waugh: *Brideshead Revisited*

Mould, Mr An undertaker
Charles Dickens: *Martin Chuzzlewit*

Mouldy, Ralph One of *Falstaff's recruits
William Shakespeare: *Henry IV 2*

Mountjoy The French herald
William Shakespeare: *Henry V*

Mowcher, Miss A travelling chiropodist and supplier of cosmetics of small stature
Charles Dickens: *David Copperfield*

Mowgli A'man-cub' brought up by wolves
Rudyard Kipling: *The Jungle Book*

Mucklewrath, Habakkuk A fanatical preacher
Sir Walter Scott: *Old Mortality*

Mudjekeewis The immortal father of *Hiawatha whose name means'the West Wind'
Henry Wadsworth Longfellow: *The Song of Hiawatha*

Mulliner Butler to the Hon. Mrs Jamieson
Elizabeth Gaskell: *Cranford*

Mulliner, Mr The inexhaustible raconteur of the Anglers' Rest
P.G. Wodehouse: *Meet Mr Mulliner* [and others]

Mulymamen King of Barbary
William Rowley: *All's Lost by Lust*

Mundungus An ill-tempered author
Laurence Sterne: *A Sentimental Journey*

Munera Daughter of the Saracen Pollente, the personification of ill-gotten wealth
Edmund Spenser: *The Faerie Queene*

Murdstone, Edward, and Jane David *Copperfield's cruel stepfather and his equally unpleasant sister
Charles Dickens: *David Copperfield*

Murray, Rosalie The eldest charge of Agnes Grey; a heartless coquette
Anne Brontë: *Agnes Grey*

Musgrave An army deserter
John Arden: *Sergeant Musgrave's Dance*

Musgrove, Charles Married to Mary, youngest daughter of Sir Walter *Elliott
Jane Austen: *Persuasion*

Musidorus The young duke of Thessalia
Sir Philip Sydney: *Arcadia*

'My Lord' A flamboyant and nameless aristocrat who plots to ensnare Amelia
Henry Fielding: *Amelia*

Mystic, Mr Moley A caricature of Coleridge
T.L. Peacock: *Melincourt*

N

Nana The Darling family's Newfoundland dog
J.M. Barrie: *Peter Pan*

Nancy A prostitute under *Fagin's control who lives with Bill *Sikes
Charles Dickens: *Oliver Twist*

Nandy, John Edward ['Old Nandy'] The father of Mrs *Plornish
Charles Dickens: *Little Dorrit*

Napoleon The chief pig
George Orwell: *Animal Farm*

Narcissa Loved by Roderick
Tobias Smollett: *The Adventures of Roderick Random*

Nathaniel, Sir A curate and friend to *Holofernes
William Shakespeare: *Love's Labour's Lost*

Natty Bumppo *see* BUMPPO, NATTY

Neckett A sherriff's officer employed to follow debtors; referred to as 'Coavinses', from the name of the sponging-house he keeps; his daughter, Charlotte
Charles Dickens: *Bleak House*

Nectabanus A dwarf
Sir Walter Scott: *The Talisman*

Nekayah Sister of Rasselas
Samuel Johnson: *The Prince of Abissinia* [*Rasselas*]

Nemo Name assumed by *Hawdon as an impoverished law writer
Charles Dickens: *Bleak House*

Nemo, Captain Master of the submarine *Nautilus*
Jules Verne: *Twenty Thousand Leagues Under the Sea*

Nerissa *Portia's waiting-woman who marries *Gratiano
William Shakespeare: *The Merchant of Venice*

Neroni, Signora Madeline [*née* Stanhope] Beautiful but crippled and mischief-making younger daughter of Dr Vesey *Stanhope
Anthony Trollope: *Barchester Towers*

Neville, Constance Niece of Dorothy *Hardcastle
Oliver Goldsmith: *She Stoops to Conquer*

Neville, Major [Lovel]
Sir Walter Scott: *The Antiquary*

Newman, Christopher A wealthy American on a visit to Paris
Henry James: *The American*

Newsome, Mrs A wealthy Massachusetts widow; her son Chad, who has spent several years in Europe and has fallen under the spell of the Countess de Vionnet
Henry James: *The Ambassadors*

Nickleby, Nicholas Son of Nicholas Nickleby senior, deceased brother of Ralph *Nickleby; his sister Kate, apprenticed to Mrs *Mantalini
Charles Dickens: *Nicholas Nickleby*

Nickleby, Ralph A moneylender; uncle to Nicholas *Nickleby
Charles Dickens: *Nicholas Nickleby*

Nidderdale, Lord A well-connected Liberal MP and man about town
Anthony Trollope: *The Duke's Children*

Nipper, Susan Florence *Dombey's acerbic maid
Charles Dickens: *Dombey and Son*

Noggs, Newman Ralph *Nickleby's confidential clerk
Charles Dickens: *Nicholas Nickleby*

Nokomis Daughter of the Moon, mother of *Wenonah, and grandmother of *Hiawatha
Henry Wadsworth Longfellow: *The Song of Hiawatha*

Norris, Mrs Spiteful and selfish sister of Lady *Bertram
Jane Austen: *Mansfield Park*

Nubbles, Christopher ['Kit'] A youth employed as an odd-job boy at the Old Curiosity Shop, devoted to Little Nell *Trent
Charles Dickens: *The Old Curiosity Shop*

Nupkins, George Self-important mayor and chief magistrate of Ipswich
Charles Dickens: *The Posthumous Papers of the Pickwick Club*

Nurse Loquacious and humorous attendant of *Juliet who acts as a go-between for the lovers
William Shakespeare: *Romeo and Juliet*

Nym, Corporal A rogue and a thief, obsessed with 'humours'
William Shakespeare: *The Merry Wives of Windsor; Henry V*

O

Oak, Gabriel A shepherd working for Bathsheba *Everdene, whom he loves and finally marries
Thomas Hardy: *Far From the Madding Crowd*

Obadiah Manservant of the Shandy family
Lawrence Sterne: *The Life and Opinions of Tristram Shandy*

Oberon The king of the fairies who quarrels with his wife *Titania
William Shakespeare: *A Midsummer Night's Dream*

O'Brallaghan, Callaghan
Charles Macklin: *Love à la Mode*

Octavia Sister of *Octavius Caesar and wife of *Antony
William Shakespeare: *Antony and Cleopatra*

Octavius Caesar Triumvir of Rome
William Shakespeare: *Antony and Cleopatra*

O'Dowd, Major, and Mrs
W.M. Thackeray: *Vanity Fair*

Og Dryden's name for Shadwell
John Dryden: *Absalom and Achitophel*

O'Hara, Scarlett A beautiful and impetuous Southern belle; married for the third time to Rhett *Butler
Margaret Mitchell: *Gone With the Wind*

'Old Buccaneer, The' Captain Kirby, father of Carinthia and Chillon *Kirby
George Meredith: *The Amazing Marriage*

Oldbuck, Jonathan Laird of Monkbarns; the antiquary
Sir Walter Scott: *The Antiquary*

Olenska, Ellen May *Welland's cousin; the separated wife of a dissolute Polish count who falls in love with May's fiancé Newland *Archer
Edith Wharton: *The Age of Innocence*

Olindo The lover of Sofronia
Tasso: *Gerusalemme Liberata*

Oliver Son of Sir Rowland *de Bois, brother of *Orlando and *Jaques
William Shakespeare: *As You Like It*

Olivia Principal character; a wealthy Illyrian countess
William Shakespeare: *Twelfth Night*

Olivia Faithless lover of *Manly
William Wycherley: *The Plain-Dealer*

Olivia Elder daughter of Dr Primrose, seduced by Squire Thornhill
Oliver Goldsmith: *The Vicar of Wakefield*

Omer, Mr A Yarmouth undertaker
Charles Dickens: *David Copperfield*

Omnium, Duke and Duchess of *see* PALLISER, PLANTAGENET

Ongar, Lady Julia [*née* Brabazon] Widow of the debauched Lord Ongar and an old flame of Harry *Clavering
Anthony Trollope: *The Claverings*

Ophelia Daughter of *Polonius
William Shakespeare: *Hamlet*

Orgilus Betrothed to *Penthea
John Ford: *The Broken Heart*

Orgon A credulous dupe
Molière: *The Imposter* [*Le Tartuffe*]

Orkborne, Dr A grotesque tutor
Frances Burney: *Camilla*

Orlando Son of Sir Rowland *de Bois, brother of *Oliver and *Jaques
William Shakespeare: *As You Like It*

Orlick, Dolge Joe *Gargery's vindictive and resentful journeyman who harbours a deep-seated grudge against *Pip
Charles Dickens: *Great Expectations*

Orsino Duke of Illyria
William Shakespeare: *Twelfth Night*

Orville, Lord The hero, who eventually marries Evelina
Frances Burney: *Evelina*

Osbaldistone, Francis Son of a rich London merchant who refuses to adopt his father's profession and is banished to the house of his uncle, Sir Hildebrand Osbaldistone
Sir Walter Scott: *Rob Roy*

Osborne, Colonel Frederic Bachelor, MP, and friend of Sir Marmaduke *Rowley
Anthony Trollope: *He Knew He Was Right*

Osborne, George Vain and shallow son of a City magnate, killed at Waterloo
W.M. Thackeray: *Vanity Fair*

Osmond, Gilbert A worthless and spiteful dilettante
Henry James: *The Portrait of a Lady*

Osric An affected courtier
William Shakespeare: *Hamlet*

O'Trigger, Lucius A fiery Irishman
R.B. Sheridan: *The Rivals*

Otter, Captain Thomas, and Mistress A henpecked and drunken former sea-captain and his snobbish wife
Ben Jonson: *Epicene*

Outhouse, Revd Oliphant Rector of St Diddulph's-in-the-East, a poor working-class parish
Anthony Trollope: *He Knew He Was Right*

Overdo, Justice Adam The busy seeker-out of 'enormities'
Ben Jonson: *Bartholomew Fair*

Overdone, Mistress A bawd
William Shakespeare: *Measure for Measure*

Overreach, Sir Giles A cruel and rapacious London merchant
Philip Massinger: *A New Way to Pay Old Debts*

P

Page, Anne Daughter of the Pages who rejects her parents' choice of suitors for *Fenton
William Shakespeare: *The Merry Wives of Windsor*

Page, Mistress Meg One of the 'merry wives'; mother of Anne *Page
William Shakespeare: *The Merry Wives of Windsor*

Palamon Friend of *Arcite, the first of the two friends to fall in love with *Emelye
Geoffrey Chaucer: 'The Knight's Tale' [*Canterbury Tales*]

Palliser, Lady Glencora [*née* M'Cluskie] The reigning queen of the Palliser series, an heriess pushed into a marriage of interest to Plantagenet *Palliser, heir of the Duke of Omnium
Anthony Trollope: *Can You Forgive Her?* [and others]

Palliser, Plantangenet Nephew of the old Duke of Omnium, later duke himself and prime minister; married to Lady Glencora *Palliser [*née* M'Cluskie]
Anthony Trollope: *The Small House at Allington; Can You Forgive Her?; Phineas Redux; The Prime Minister; The Duke's Children*

Pamela *see* ANDREWS, PAMELA

Pamela Daughter of *Basilius, sister of *Philoclea, and heir to the dukedom of Arcadia
Sir Philip Sydney: *Arcadia*

Pancks *Casby's agent and rent-collector
Charles Dickens: *Little Dorrit*

Pandarus Immoral uncle of *Cressida and her go-between with *Troilus
William Shakespeare: *Troilus and Cressida*

Pandulph, Cardinal Papal legate
William Shakespeare: *King John*

Panthino Servant to *Antonio
William Shakespeare: *The Two Gentlemen of Verona*

Panurge A voluble and dissolute buffoon
Rabelais: *Pantagruel*

Paradine
Sir William Davenant: *Albovine*

Pardiggle, Mrs Philanthropical friend of Mrs *Jellyby
Charles Dickens: *Bleak House*

Paridell A false and libertine knight
Edmund Spenser: *The Faerie Queene*

Paris, Count A Capulet and suitor of *Juliet
William Shakespeare: *Romeo and Juliet*

Parolles Cowardly follower of *Reynaldo
William Shakespeare: *All's Well That Ends Well*

Pastorella A shepherdess loved by *Coridon and Sir *Calidore
Edmund Spenser: *The Faerie Queene*

Pateroff, Count Édouard Parasitical brother of Sophie *Gordeloup who pursues Lady *Ongar
Anthony Trollope: *The Claverings*

Pathfinder, The Nickname of Natty *Bumppo
J.F. Cooper: The *Leatherstocking* series

Patroclus A Greek commander and close companion ot *Achilles
William Shakespeare: *Troilus and Cressida*

Patterne, Crossjay Poor relation of Sir Willoughby *Patterne, a pupil of Vernon *Whitford
George Meredith: *The Egoist*

Patterne, Sir Willoughby Central character; rich and handsome—the Egoist himself
George Meredith: *The Egoist*

Pattieson, Peter A schoolmaster
Sir Walter Scott: *Tales of My Landlord*

Patullo, Duncan An Oxford academic and playwright
J.I.M. Stewart: *A Staircase in Surrey* series

Paul Emmanuel, M. A waspish but good-hearted professor in the Belgian school where Lucy *Snowe teaches
Charlotte Brontë: *Villette*

Paulina Wife of *Antigonus and loyal defender of *Hermione
William Shakespeare: *The Winter's Tale*

Peachum, Polly Wife of Captain *Macheath
John Gay: *The Beggar's Opera*

Pecksniff, Charity and Mercy [Cherry and Merry] The two daughters of Seth *Pecksniff, the one mean-minded and sour, the other pretty and vain
Charles Dickens: *Martin Chuzzlewit*

Pecksniff, Seth Sleek and unctuous member of the Chuzzlewit family, professedly an architect
Charles Dickens: *Martin Chuzzlewit*

Pecunia A rich heiress
Ben Jonson: *The Staple of News*

Pedro, Don Prince of Aragon who woos *Hero on *Claudio's behalf
William Shakespeare: *Much Ado About Nothing*

Peebles, Peter A crazy litigant
Sir Walter Scott: *Redgauntlet*

Peerybingle, John An honest country carrier, devoted husband of the much younger Mary ['Dot']
Charles Dickens: *The Cricket on the Hearth*

Peggotty, Clara Devoted servant of David *Copperfield's mother who marries *Barkis the carrier
Charles Dickens: *David Copperfield*

Peggotty, Daniel A Yarmouth fisherman, brother of Clara *Peggotty, who lives on a beached boat on the sands with his nephew Ham *Peggotty, Little *Em'ly, and Mrs *Gummidge
Charles Dickens: *David Copperfield*

Peggotty, Ham A boat-builder; the orphaned nephew of Daniel *Peggoty, in love with Little *Em'ly
Charles Dickens: *David Copperfield*

Pegler, Mrs Mother of Josiah *Bounderby
Charles Dickens: *Hard Times*

Pell, Solomon A shady lawyer practising in the Insolvent Court
Charles Dickens: *The Posthumous Papers of the Pickwick Club*

Penfeather, Lady Penelope A leading member of the idle fashionable society of the Scottish spa town of St Ronan's Well
Sir Walter Scott: *St Ronan's Well*

Pennyfeather, Paul The central character, a former student of Scone College, Oxford, who becomes a personal tutor and falls in love with his pupil's mother, Margot *Beste-Chetwynde
Evelyn Waugh: *Decline and Fall*

Penthea A Spartan lady betrothed to *Orgilus but forced by her brother Ithocles to marry the contemptible Bassanes
John Ford: *The Broken Heart*

Perdita Daughter of *Leontes and *Hermione, brought up in Bohemia
William Shakespeare: *The Winter's Tale*

Pericles Prince of Tyre, father of *Marina
William Shakespeare: *Pericles*

Perker, Mr Amiable solicitor of both *Wardle and Mr *Pickwick
Charles Dickens: *The Posthumous Papers of the Pickwick Club*

Perrin, Vincent A faded and disappointed master at Moffatt's boys' school
Hugh Walpole: *Mr Perrin and Mr Traill*

Perrot, Dick Principal character, brought up in an East End slum off Shoreditch High Street
Arthur Morrison: *A Child of the Jago*

Peter, Friar Confidant of *Vincentio
William Shakespeare: *Measure for Measure*

Peterson, Carl An international criminal; the antagonist of Hugh 'Bull-dog' *Drummond
Sapper: *Bull-dog Drummond*

Peterson, Curdie A young miner who rescues Princess *Irene from the goblins
George MacDonald: *The Princess and the Goblin; The Princess and Curdie*

Peto A crony of *Falstaff's
William Shakespeare: *Henry IV* 1 and 2

Petowker, Henrietta Daughter of a theatrical

fireman and a member of Vincent *Crummles's company
Charles Dickens: *Nicholas Nickleby*

Petrie, Miss Wallachia American agitator for women's rights
Anthony Trollope: *He Knew He Was Right*

Petruchio A Veronese gentleman determined to tame *Katherina
William Shakespeare: *The Taming of the Shrew*

Peveril, Sir Geoffrey Derbyshire nobleman and royalist, father of Julian *Peveril
Sir Walter Scott: *Peveril of the Peak*

Peveril, Julian Page to the Countess of Derby; childhood companion to Alice *Bridgenorth
Sir Walter Scott: *Peveril of the Peak*

Pew A blind buccanner
R.L. Stevenson: *Treasure Island*

Phaedria The Lady of the Lake, symbolizing immodest mirth
Edmund Spenser: *The Faerie Queene*

Philharmonus A soothsayer
William Shakespeare: *Cymbeline*

Philisides A melancholy poet
Sir Philip Sydney: *Arcadia*

Phillotson, Richard A schoolmaster who encourages Jude *Fawley to pursue his intellectual ambititions and who eventually marries Sue *Bridehead
Thomas Hardy: *Jude the Obscure*

Philoclea Daughter of *Basilius, sister of *Pamela
Sir Philip Sydney: *Arcadia*

Phoebe A shepherdess who marries *Silvius
William Shakespeare: *As You Like It*

Phunky, Mr A junior barrister in the case of Bardell v. Pickwick
Charles Dickens: *The Posthumous Papers of the Pickwick Club*

Pickwick, Samuel Retired businessman, bachelor, and founder of the Pickwick Club
Charles Dickens: *The Posthumous Papers of the Pickwick Club*

Piero, Duke of Venice
John Marston: *Antonio and Mellida*

Pierston, Jocelyn An idealistic sculptor
Thomas Hardy: *The Well-Beloved*

Pinch, Doctor Schoolmaster and exorcist
William Shakespeare: *The Comedy of Errors*

Pinch, Tom A shy and unworldly former pupil of Seth *Pecksniff's exploited as an unpaid servant
Charles Dickens: *Martin Chuzzlewit*

Pinchwife, Jack A jealous husband
William Wycherley: *The Country Wife*

Pinfold, Gilbert A successful middle-aged novelist
Evelyn Waugh: *The Ordeal of Gilbert Pinfold*

Pip [Philip Pirrip] The hero-narrator; an orphan brought up by his shrewish sister and her large-hearted husband Joe *Gargery
Charles Dickens: *Great Expectations*

Pipchin, Mrs A widowed boarding-house keeper in Brighton
Charles Dickens: *Dombey and San*

Pirrip, Philip *see* Pip

Pisanio Servant of *Posthumus Leonatus
William Shakespeare: *Cymbeline*

Pistol, Ancient or Ensign One of *Falstaff's associates: a braggart with a fine command of bombastic language
William Shakespeare: *Henry IV 2; Henry V*

Plagiary, Sir Fretful A caricature of Richard Cumberland
R.B. Sheridan: *The Critic*

Pliant, Dame A rich widow and sister of *Kastril
Ben Jonson: *The Alchemist*

Plornish, Thomas A good-natured plasterer living in Bleeding-Heart Yard; his wife, Sally
Charles Dickens: *Little Dorrit*

Pluck, Mr Parasitic friend of Sir Mulberry *Hawk and his constant companion Pyke
Charles Dickens: *Nicholas Nickleby*

Plume, Captain Principal character; an officer of limited means, in love with *Sylvia
George Farquhar: *The Recruiting Officer*

Plummer, Bertha Blind daughter of Caleb Plummer the toymaker
Charles Dickens: *The Cricket on the Hearth*

Plyant, Sir Paul Father of *Cynthia; a foolish and uxorious old knight
William Congreve: *The Double-Dealer*

Pocket, Herbert Friend and room-mate of *Pip whose father Matthew is appointed Pip's tutor
Charles Dickens: *Great Expectations*

Pocock, Sarah Sister of Chadwick *Newsome
Henry James: *The Ambassadors*

Podsnap, Mr Pompously self-satisfied and opinionated marine insurance broker
Charles Dickens: *Our Mutual Friend*

Poins A companion of Prince Henry
William Shakespeare: *Henry IV 1* and *2*

Poirot, Hercule A former Belgian police detective with a prominent waxed moustache living in retirement in England
Agatha Christie: *The Mysterious Affair at Styles* [and many others]

Politic Would-be, Sir and Lady A foolish traveller and his loquacious wife
Ben Jonson: *Volpone*

Polixines King of Bohemia
William Shakespeare: *The Winter's Tale*

Pollexfen, Sir Hargreve An unscrupulous libertine who abducts Harriet *Byron
Samuel Richardson: *Sir Charles Grandison*

Pollitt, Big Daddy A rich and ruthless cotton planter; his favourite son Brick, and Brick's wife Maggie
Tennessee Williams: *Cat on a Hot Tin Roof*

Polly, Alfred The central character; a draper
H.G. Wells: *The History of Mr Polly*

Polonius The Lord Chamberlain, father of *Ophelia and *Laertes
William Shakespeare: *Hamlet*

Polydore *see* GUIDERIUS

Pompey Servant to Mistress *Overdone
William Shakespeare: *Measure for Measure*

Pompey, Sextus
William Shakespeare: *Antony and Cleopatra*

Pontifex, Ernest The awkward and unhappy great-grandson of a village carpenter whose childhood is blighted by the oppressive regime instigated by his father, Theobald *Pontifex
Samuel Butler: *The Way of All Flesh*

Pontifex, Theobald An authoritarian and sanctimonious Evangelical clergyman, father of Ernest *Pontifex
Samuel Butler: *The Way of All Flesh*

Poole, Grace Seamstress at Thornfield Hall and Mrs *Rochester's keeper
Charlotte Brontë: *Jane Eyre*

Pooter, Charles The anxiously genteel suburban protagonist
George and Weedon Grossmith: *The Diary of a Nobody*

Poppyseed, Miss Philomela An author of romantic novels (based on Amelia Opie)
T.L. Peacock: *Headlong Hall*

Porthos One of three valiant members of Louis XIII's musketeers, together with *Athos and *Aramis; see also *D'Artagnan
Alexander Dumas père: *The Three Musketeers*

Portia Wife of *Brutus
William Shakespeare: *Julius Caesar*

Portia Venetian heiress in love with *Bassanio
William Shakespeare: *The Merchant of Venice*

Poste, Flora Visiting relative of the *Starkadders at Cold Comfort Farm
Stella Gibbons: *Cold Comfort Farm*

Posthumus Leonatus Husband of *Imogen
William Shakespeare: *Cymbeline*

Pott, Mr Conscientious editor of the Tory Eatanswill Gazette
Charles Dickens: *The Posthumous Papers of the Pickwick Club*

Poundtext, Revd Peter A Presbyterian divine
Sir Walter Scott: *Old Mortality*

Povey, Samuel Estimable but superficially insignificant shop assistant who marries Constance *Baines
Arnold Bennett: *The Old Wives' Tale*

Power, Paula A vacillating young woman
Thomas Hardy: *A Laodicean*

Poyser, Martin A farmer; uncle of Hetty *Sorrel; married to Rachel, aunt of Dinah *Morris
George Eliot: *Adam Bede*

Premium, Mr Name assumed by Sir Oliver *Surface
R.B. Sheridan: *The School for Scandal*

Price, Fanny Impecunious niece of Sir Thomas and Lady *Bertram
Jane Austen: *Mansfield Park*

Prig, Betsey Nurse at St Bartholomew's Hospital and friend of Mrs *Gamp's
Charles Dickens: *Martin Chuzzlewit*

Primrose, Dr The vicar of Wakefield; his wife Deborah; his daughters *Olivia and Sophia; his sons George and Moses, and two younger boys
Oliver Goldsmith: *The Vicar of Wakefield*

Princess of France
William Shakespeare: *Love's Labour's Lost*

Pringle, Guy and Harriet Principal characters
Olivia Manning: *The Balkan Trilogy; The Levant Trilogy*

Pringle, Dr Zachariah A minister
John Galt: *The Ayrshire Legatees*

Prism, Miss Cecily *Cardew's governess
Oscar Wilde: *The Importance of Being Earnest*

Proculeius Follower of *Octavius
William Shakespeare: *Antony and Cleopatra*

Prospero The rightful Duke of Milan with magical powers living in exile on a island with his daughter *Miranda
William Shakespeare: *The Tempest*

Pross, Miss Devoted nurse of Lucie *Manette
Charles Dickens: *A Tale of Two Cities*

Proteus One of the'two gentlemen'; see also *Valentine
William Shakespeare: *The Two Gentlemen of Verona*

Proudfute, Oliver A bonnet-maker
Sir Walter Scott: *The Fair Maid of Perth*

Proudie, Mrs The severe Sabbatarian wife of Bishop *Proudie; their spirited daughter, Olivia
Anthony Trollope: *Barchester Towers; The Last Chronicle of Barset*

Proudie, Thomas Hen-pecked bishop of Barchester
Anthony Trollope: *Barchester Towers; Framlet Parsonage; The Last Chronicle of Barset*

Provis The alias used by *Magwitch when he returns illegally to England
Charles Dickens: *Great Expectations*

Prunesquallor, Dr, and Irma Physician to the Groans, and his vain flat-chested sister
Mervyn Peake: *Titus Groan; Gormenghast*

Prynne, Hester The young wife of Roger *Chillingworth, condemned for adultery
Nathaniel Hawthorne: *The Scarlet Letter*

Pryor, Mrs Governess and companion of Shirley *Keeldar and estranged mother of Caroline *Helstone
Charlotte Brontë: *Shirley*

Publius Son of *Marcus Andronicus
William Shakespeare: *Titus Andronicus*

Puck Mischievous fairy servant of *Oberon
William Shakespeare: *A Midsummer Night's Dream*

Puff, Mr Author of the ludicrous tragedy *The Spanish Armada*
R.B. Sheridan: *The Critic*

Pugh, Mr and Mrs The village schoolmaster and his wife
Dylan Thomas: *Under Milk Wood*

Pullet, Mrs Favourite sister of Mrs *Tulliver
George Eliot: *The Mill on the Floss*

Pulling, Henry A retired bank manager
Graham Greene: *Travels with my Aunt*

Pumblechook, Mr Joe *Gargery's pompous and self-satisfied uncle who is the means of introducing *Pip to Miss *Havisham
Charles Dickens: *Great Expectations*

Puntarvolo A boastful, quixotic knight
Ben Jonson: *Every Man Out of His Humour*

Pyncheon, Hepzibah Descendant of the executed Matthew *Maule
Nathaniel Hawthorne: *The House of the Seven Gables*

Pyrochles Brother of *Cymochles, symbolizing rage
Edmund Spenser: *The Faerie Queene*

Pyrocles A prince
Sir Philip Sydney: *Arcadia*

Q

Quatermain, Allan Big-game hunter and explorer
Sir H. Rider Haggard: *King Solomon's Mines* [and others]

Queeg, Captain Brutal captain of the minesweeper *Caine*
Herman Wouk: *The Caine Mutiny*

Queequeg A Polynesian harpooner
Herman Melville: *Moby-Dick*

Quelch, Mr [Henry Samuel] Form master of the Remove at Greyfriars School
Frank Richards: *Billy Bunter of Greyfriars School* [and many others]

Quested, Adela A young and charmless English girl who accompanies her prospective mother-in-law, Mrs *Moore, to the Caves of Marabar and who accuses Dr *Aziz of sexually assaulting her
E.M. Forster: *A Passage to India*

Quickly, Mistress Hostess of the Boar's Head Tavern in Eastcheap, betrothed to *Falstaff
William Shakespeare: *Henry IV* 1 and 2

Quiggin, J.G. A Marxist critic and reviewer, later publisher
Anthony Powell: *A Dance to the Music of Time*

Quilp, Daniel A diabolically malevolent dwarf
Charles Dickens: *The Old Curiosity Shop*

Quince, Mary Maid to Maud *Ruthyn
J.S. Le Fanu: *Uncle Silas*

Quint, Peter Former valet to the master of Bly who appears, apparently as a ghost, to the new governess
Henry James: 'The Turn of the Screw'

Quintus A son of *Titus
William Shakespeare: *Titus Andronicus*

Quirk, Jason A cunning young lawyer, son of Thady *Quirk
Maria Edgeworth: *Castle Rackrent*

Quirk, Thady Steward to the *Rackrents
Maria Edgeworth: *Castle Rackrent*

Quiverful, Mr Rector of Puddingdale whose large family stretches his modest income to breaking point
Anthony Trollope: *The Last Chronicle of Barset* [and others]

Quixote, Don A poor and aimiable gentleman of La Mancha whose wits have been disordered by his devotion to tales of chivalry
Cervantes: *Don Quixote*

R

Rackrent, Sir Condy The current Rackrent heir, married to Isabella Moneygawl
Maria Edgeworth: *Castle Rackrent*

Raddle, Mrs Mary Anne Sister of Mrs *Cluppins and friend of Mrs *Bardell's who keeps a lodging-house in Lant Street
Charles Dickens: *The Posthumous Papers of the Pickwick Club*

Radigund Queen of the Amazons
Edmund Spenser: *The Faerie Queene*

Raffles, A.J. A gentleman criminal
E.W. Hornung: *The Amateur Cracksman* [and others]

Raffles, John Agent of Mr *Bulstrode's downfall
George Eliot: *Middlemarch*

Ralph One of the leaders of the group of boys stranded on a desert island after a plane crash
William Golding: *Lord of the Flies*

Ralpho Sir *Hudibras's sectarian squire
Samuel Butler: *Hudibras*

Ramorny, Sir John Villainous Master of the Horse who assists the Duke of *Rothsay in his attempt to abduct Catherine *Glover
Sir Walter Scott: *The Fair Maid of Perth*

Ramsay, Mr and Mrs A self-centred, self-pitying philosopher and his maternal and capable wife
Virginia Woolf: *To the Lighthouse*

Random Roderick Central character; surgeon's mate and general rogue; marries Narcissa Topehall
Tobias Smollett: *The Adventures of Roderick Random*

Ranger A rakish man of fashion
William Wycherley: *Love in a Wood*

Ransom, Basil A young Mississippi lawyer
Henry James: *The Bostonians*

Ransom, Michael Forsyth A scholarly man of action and leader of a doomed expedition to climb F6, a mountain in disputed colonial territory
W.H. Auden & Christopher Isherwood: *The Ascent of F6*

Rassendyll, Rudolf An English gentleman who bears an uncanny resemblance to the King of Ruritania and who foils a plot by the King's half brother, Duke Michael, to depose him
Anthony Hope: *The Prisoner of Zenda; Rupert of Hentzau*

Ratcliffe, James A notorious thief who becomes a warder in the Edinburgh Tolbooth
Sir Walter Scott: *The Heart of Midlothian*

Razumov, Kirylo Sidorovitch A Russian philosophy student who betrays Victor *Haldin to the police and thereby becomes their pawn
Joseph Conrad: *Under Western Eyes*

Ready, Masterman A veteran seaman, shipwrecked with the Seagrave family on a desert island in the Pacific
Frederick Marryat: *Masterman Ready*

Reardon, Edwin A gifted but unsuccessful author, driven to an early grave by his poverty; his wife, Amy
George Gissing: *New Grub Street*

Rebecca *see* DE WINTER, MAX

Rebecca The beautiful and courageous daughter of Isaac the Jew of York
Sir Walter Scott: *Ivanhoe*

Redcrosse Knight, The St George, the patron saint of England and champion of Holiness
Edmund Spenser: *The Faerie Queene*

Redlaw, Mr A lecturer in chemistry haunted by a phantom alter ego
Charles Dickens: *The Haunted Man*

Redworth, Thomas The faithful and devoted admirer of Diana *Merion who eventually marries her
George Meredith: *Diana of the Crossways*

Reed, Mrs Cruel aunt of the orphaned Jane *Eyre; her children, Eliza, Georgiana, and John
Charlotte Brontë: *Jane Eyre*

Regan Second daughter of King *Lear, married to Cornwall
William Shakespeare: *King Lear*

Reuter, Zoraide Manipulative headmistress of the Brussels school where William *Crimsworth teaches
Charlotte Brontë: *The Professor*

Reynaldo Steward to the Countess of *Roussillon
William Shakespeare: *All's Well That Ends Well*

Rhodolinda Wife of *Albovine
Sir William Davenant: *Albovine*

Riah A venerable old Jew who works as an agent for *Fledeby
Charles Dickens: *Our Mutual Friend*

Rice, Archie A bitter and cynical music-hall artist
John Osborne: *The Entertainer*

Richardson, Jake A sexually troubled Oxford don
Kingsley Amis: *Jake's Thing*

Richland, Miss The heroine; a lady of fortune
Oliver Goldsmith: *The Good-Natur'd Man*

Ridd, John The narrator; deadly rival of Carver *Doone; in love from childhood with Lorna, whom he finally marries
R.D. Blackmore: *Lorna Doone*

Riderhood, 'Rogue' [Roger] A shady waterside character and former partner of Gaffer *Hexam's
Charles Dickens: *Our Mutual Friend*

Rigaud [aka **Blandois and L'Agnier]** A French criminal who becomes a friend of Henry *Gowan's
Charles Dickens: *Little Dorrit*

Rigby, Right Hon. Nicholas A Tory MP and Lord *Monmouth's political factotum
Benjamin Disraeli: *Coningsby*

Rintherout, Jenny Servant to Jonathan *Oldbuck
Sir Walter Scott: *The Antiquary*

Ripley, Tom A charming but completely amoral psychopath
Patricia Highsmith: *The Talented Mr Ripley* [and others]

Rivers, St John Clergyman cousin of Jane *Eyre; his sisters, Diana and Mary
Charlotte Brontë: *Jane Eyre*

Robarts, Revd Mark Vicar of Famley and eldest son of Dr Robarts of Exeter who succeeds Dr Vesey *Stanhope as prebendary of Barchester; his sister, Lucy; his wife, Fanny [*née* Monsell]
Anthony Trollope: *Framley Parsonage; The Last Chronicle of Barset*

Roberta, Peter, and Phyllis The children of the title whose father has been falsely imprisoned
E. Nesbit: *The Railway Children*

Robertson, George *see* STAUNTON, SIR GEORGE

Robinson, Tom The black man falsely accused of raping a white girl who is defended by Atticus *Finch
Harper Lee: *To Kill a Mockingbird*

Robson, Uncle Brother of Mrs *Bloomfield
Anne Brontë: *Agnes Grey*

Rochester, Edward Fairfax The sardonic and mysterious master of Thornfield Hall who employs Jane *Eyre as a governess for his daughter Adèle
Charlotte Brontë: *Jane Eyre*

Roderigo King of Spain
William Rowley: *All's Lost by Lust*

Roderigo *Iago's gull
William Shakespeare: *Othello*

Rokesmith, John *see* HARMON, JOHN

Romeo Son of *Montague
William Shakespeare: *Romeo and Juliet*

Ronald, Lord The Lord of the Isles, engaged to *Edith of Lorn but for a time in love with Isabella, sister of Robert the Bruce
Sir Walter Scott: *The Lord of the Isles*

Rosalind Daughter of *Duke Senior; later disguised as *Ganymede
William Shakespeare: *As You Like It*

Rosaline Attending on the *Princess of France
William Shakespeare: *Love's Labour's Lost*

Rosaline Niece of *Capulet with whom *Romeo is in love before he sees *Juliet (mentioned but never seen in the play)
William Shakespeare: *Romeo and Juliet*

Rosencrantz and Guildenstern Former schoolfriends of *Hamlet sent by the king to spy on him
William Shakespeare: *Hamlet*

Rosinante Don *Quixote's horse
Cervantes: *Don Quixote*

Rothsay, Duke of Profligate son of Robert III
Sir Walter Scott: *The Fair Maid of Perth*

Rougierre, Maud *Ruthyn's sinister French governess
J.S. Le Fanu: *Uncle Silas*

Rouncewell, Mrs The widowed housekeeper of the Dedlocks at Chesney Wold
Charles Dickens: *Bleak House*

Rousard Husband of *Castabella
Cyril Tourneur: *The Atheist's Tragedy*

Roussillon, Dowager Countess of Mother of *Bertram and guardian of *Helena
William Shakespeare: *All's Well That Ends Well*

Rowena, Lady Kinswoman and ward of *Cedric the Saxon who eventually marries *Ivanhoe
Sir Walter Scott: *Ivanhoe*

Rowley, Sir Marmaduke Colonial governor of the Mandarin Islands
Anthony Trollope: *He Knew He Was Right*

Rowley, Nora Second of Sir Marmaduke *Rowley's eight daughters who leaves the Mandarin Islands to live with her married elder sister Emily *Trevelyan in England
Anthony Trollope: *He Knew He Was Right*

Rudge, Barnaby Feeble-minded son of Reuben Hardedale's steward who becomes the dupe of the Gordon rioters
Charles Dickens: *Barnaby Rudge*

Rufford, Lord
Anthony Trollope: *The American Senator*

Rumpole, Horace An Old Bailey defence barrister and frequenter of Pommeroy's Wine Bar; married to Hilda
John Mortimer: *Rumpole of the Bailey* [and many others]

Rupert of Hentzau Villainous antagonist of Rudolf *Rassendyll
Anthony Hope: *The Prisoner of Zenda; Rupert of Hentzau*

Rushworth, James Wealthy friend of Tom *Bertram who unadvisedly marries Tom's sister Maria
Jane Austen: *Mansfield Park*

Russell, Lady Widowed neighbour of Sir Walter *Elliot and godmother to his daughter Anne
Jane Austen: *Persuasion*

Ruth *see* Hilton, Ruth

Ruth The antithesis of Mary *Fisher who wreaks revenge on Mary for having an affair with her husband
Fay Weldon: *The Life and Loves of a She-Devil*

Ruthyn, Maud Central character and narrator; the daughter of Austin Ruthyn of Knowl
J.S. Le Fanu: *Uncle Silas*

Ruthyn, Silas Aylmer Villainous but plausible uncle and next of kin of Maud *Ruthyn who plots to marry her for her fortune
J.S. Le Fanu: *Uncle Silas*

Ryder, Charles The narrator; a former friend of Sebastian *Flyte's at Oxford whose life becomes enmeshed with Sebastian's aristocratic Roman Catholic family
Evelyn Waugh: *Brideshead Revisited*

S

Saint Aubert, Emily An orphan carried off by her aunt's villainous husband Montoni to a remote castle in the Apennines
Ann Radcliffe: *The Mysteries of Udolpho*

Saint Cleeve, Swithin An astronomer who unknowingly enters into a bigamous marriage to Lady *Constantine
Thomas Hardy: *Two on a Tower*

Saint Evremonde, Marquis de Father of Charles *Darnay; a brutal French aristocrat
Charles Dickens: *A Tale of Two Cities*

Saint-Preux The lover of *Julie
J.J. Rousseau: *Julie; or, The New Eloise*

Salanio and Salarino Friends of *Antonio and *Bassanio
William Shakespeare: *The Merchant of Venice*

Samgrass, Mr A history don at All Soul's, Oxford
Evelyn Waugh: *Brideshead Revisited*

Sancho Panza The shrewed but credulous rustic who serves as squire to Don *Quixote
Cervantes: *Don Quixote*

Sanglier, Sir A wicked knight who cuts off his lady's head and is forced by Sir *Artegall to bear the head before him as a token of his shame
Edmund Spenser: *The Faerie Queene*

Sansfoy, Sansjoy, and Sansloy Three brothers; 'Faithless', 'Joyless', and 'Lawless'
Edmund Spenser: *The Faerie Queene*

Santiago An old Cuban fisherman
Ernest Hemingway: *The Old Man and the Sea*

Sapsea, Thomas A pompous auctioneer who eventually becomes mayor of Cloisterham
Charles Dickens: *The Mystery of Edwin Drood*

Saturninus Eldest son of the late Emperor of Rome (and later emperor himself) and marries *Tamora
William Shakespeare: *Titus Andronicus*

Satyrane, Sir Son of a satyr and the nymph Thyamis
Edmund Spenser: *The Faerie Queene*

Sawyer, Bob Medical student at Guy's Hospital and friend of Benjamin *Allen
Charles Dickens: *The Posthumous Papers of the Pickwick Club*

Scales, Gerald The unprincipled commercial traveller who comes into a fortune and elopes with Sophia *Baines
Arnold Bennett: *The Old Wives' Tale*

Scarlet Pimpernel, The *see* Blakeney, Sir Percy

Scarus Follower of *Antony
William Shakespeare: *Antony and Cleopatra*

Scrooge, Ebenezer Usurer and miser, former partner of Jacob *Marley
Charles Dickens: *A Christmas Carol*

Scrub A man-of-all-work in Lady *Bountiful's household
George Farquhar: *The Beaux' Stratagem*

Scudamour, Sir The lover of *Amoret
Edmund Spenser: *The Faerie Queene*

Scythrop [Glowry] A satirical portrait of P.B. Shelley
T.L. Peacock: *Nightmare Abbey*

Sebastian Brother of Alonso, whom he tries to murder
William Shakespeare: *The Tempest*

Sebastian Twin brother of *Viola
William Shakespeare: *Twelfth Night*

Sedley, Amelia Sheltered child of a rich City merchant, educated with Becky *Sharp at Miss Pinkerton's Academy, and loved by William *Dobbin
W.M. Thackeray: *Vanity Fair*

Selden, Lawrence A bookish New York lawyer
Edith Wharton: *The House of Mirth*

Seleucus Attendant on *Cleopatra
William Shakespeare: *Antony and Cleopatra*

Self, John A film producer who becomes overwhelmed by his urban lifestyle
Martin Amis: *Money*

Sempronius Kinsman of *Marcus Andronicus
William Shakespeare: *Titus Andronicus*

Sepulchrave, Lord Seventy-sixth Earl of Gormenghast and father of Titus *Groan, killed by owls in the Tower of Flints
Mervyn Peake: *Titus Groan*

Seyton, Catherine Attending on Mary Queen of Scots
Sir Walter Scott: *The Abbot*

Shakebag *see* Black Will and Shakebag

Shallow A foolish country justice
William Shakespeare: *Henry IV 2; The Merry Wives of Windsor*

Shandon, Captain A debt-ridden Irish journalist
W.M. Thackeray: *Pendennis*

Shandy, Captain Tobias Tristram's benign and practical Uncle Toby
Lawrence Sterne: *The Life and Opinions of Tristram Shandy*

Sharp, Becky [Rebecca] The resourceful and socially ambitious orphan of an artist and a French opera dancer
W.M. Thackeray: *Vanity Fair*

Shirley *see* Keeldar, Shirley

Shirley, Anne An orphan adopted by Matthew and Marilla Cuthbert
L.M. Montgomery: *Anne of Green Gables* [and others]

Shylock A Jewish merchant who lends *Bassanio 3000 ducats
William Shakespeare: *The Merchant of Venice*

Sidrophel An astrologer
Samuel Butler: *Hudibras*

Sikes, Bill A brutal housebreaker
Charles Dickens: *Oliver Twist*

Silas, Uncle *see* Ruthyn, Silas

Silence A country justice and cousin to *Shallow
William Shakespeare: *Henry IV 2*

Silver, Long John *see* Long John Silver

Silvia Daughter of the Duke of *Milan
William Shakespeare: *The Two Gentlemen of Verona*

Silvius A young shepherd, in love with *Phoebe
William Shakespeare: *As You Like It*

Simcox, Revd Simeon The Red Rector of Rapstone Fanner
John Mortimer: *Paradise Postponed; Titmuss Regained*

Simonides King of Pentapolis, father of *Thaisa
William Shakespeare: *Pericles*

Sisson, Aaron An amateur flautist who leaves his wife and his job to pursue his musical ambitions
D.H. Lawrence: *Aaron's Rod*

Skewton, The Hon. Mrs The vain and heartless mother of Edith *Granger
Charles Dickens: *Dombey and Son*

Skimpole, Harold A dilettante artist and sponger, based on the character of Leigh Hunt
Charles Dickens: *Bleak House*

Slammer, Dr An irascible military surgeon who challenges *Jingle to a duel
Charles Dickens: *The Posthumous Papers of the Pickwick Club*

Slawkenbergius Author of a Latin treatise on noses
Lawrence Sterne: *The Life and Opinions of Tristram Shandy*

Sleary A kind-hearted circus proprietor who gives sanctuary to Tom *Gradgrind
Charles Dickens: *Hard Times*

Slender, Abraham Cousin of *Shallow's and unsuccessful lover of Anne *Page
William Shakespeare: *The Merry Wives of Windsor*

Slipslop, Mrs Waiting-woman and chambermaid to Lady *Booby
Henry Fielding: *The History of the Adventures of Joseph Andrews*

Slop, Dr An incompetent and argumentative physician
Lawrence Sterne: *The Life and Opinions of Tristram Shandy*

Slope, Revd Obadiah The scheming evangelical domestic chaplain to Bishop *Proudie
Anthony Trollope: *Barchester Tower*

Slowboy, Tilly Mrs *Peerybingle's maid-of-all-work
Charles Dickens: *The Cricket on the Hearth*

Slumkey, The Hon. Samuel The Blue candidate in the Eatanswill election
Charles Dickens: *The Posthumous Papers of the Pickwick Club*

Sly, Christopher A drunken tinker for whom the play is performed
William Shakespeare: *The Taming of the Shrew*

Slyme, Chevy Down-at-heel nephew of Old Martin *Chuzzlewit
Charles Dickens: *Martin Chuzzlewit*

Smallweed, Joshua; and Mrs A geriatric money-lender and brother-in-law of *Krook; his senile wife
Charles Dickens: *Bleak House*

Smee The bosun in Captain *Hook's pirate crew
J.M. Barrie: *Peter Pan*

Smelfungus A caricature of Smollett
Lawrence Sterne: *A Sentimental Journey*

Smike Ralph *Nickleby's only child by a secret marriage to the widow of a Leicestershire squire
Charles Dickens: *Nicholas Nickleby*

Smiley, George A British secret agent
John le Carré: *Call for the Dead; Tinker, Tailor, Soldier, Spy* [and others]

Smith, Harriet A pretty and pliant young girl who becomes the object of Emma *Woodhouse's matchmaking schemes
Jane Austen: *Emma*

Smith, Stephen A young architect
Thomas Hardy: *A Pair of Blue Eyes*

Smorltork, Count A foreign guest at Mrs Leo *Hunter's fête champêtre
Charles Dickens: *The Posthumous Papers of the Pickwick Club*

Snagsby A good-natured law stationer; his wife, Sarah
Charles Dickens: *Bleak House*

Snailsfoot, Bryce A pedlar
Thomas Hardy: *The Pirate*

Sneerwell, Lady One of the scandal-mongers
R.B. Sheridan: *The School for Scandal*

Snevellicci, Miss *Crummles's flirtatious leading lady; her father, an alcoholic broken-down actor
Charles Dickens: *Nicholas Nickleby*

Snodgrass, Augustus The aspiring poet of the Pickwick Club
Charles Dickens: *The Posthumous Papers of the Pickwick Club*

Snout, Tom An Athenian tinker cast as Pyramus's father in the play of 'Pyramus and Thisbe'
William Shakespeare: *A Midsummer Night's Dream*

Snowball An idealistic pig
George Orwell: *Animal Farm*

Snowe, Lucy The narrator; a poor, plain girl teaching in a Belgian girls' school
Charlotte Brontë: *Villette*

Snubbin, Mr Serjeant Mr Pickwick's defending counsel in the case of Bardell v. Pickwick
Charles Dickens: *The Posthumous Papers of the Pickwick Club*

Snug A joiner who takes the part of the lion in the play 'Pyramus and Thisbe'
William Shakespeare: *A Midsummer Night's Dream*

Solinus Duke of Ephesus
William Shakespeare: *The Comedy of Errors*

Solmes The wealthy gentleman whom Clarissa *Harlowe's family decide she must marry but whom she detests
Samuel Richardson: *Clarissa*

Sorrel, Hetty Niece of Martin *Poyser
George Eliot: *Adam Bede*

South, Marty A village girl in love with Giles *Winterbourne
Thomas Hardy: *The Woodlanders*

Sowerberry, Mr An undertaker to whom Oliver *Twist is apprenticed after he leaves the workhouse
Charles Dickens: *Oliver Twist*

Spade, Sam A tough but instinctively honourable San Francisco private eye
Dashiell Hammett: *The Maltese Falcon*

Spalding, Caroline [Carry] A young American
Anthony Trollope: *He Knew He Was Right*

Sparkler, Edmund Asinine step-son of Mr *Merdle
Charles Dickens: *Little Dorrit*

Sparsit, Mrs Josiah *Bounderby's housekeeper
Charles Dickens: *Hard Times*

Spearman, Rosann A reformed thief, housemaid to Lady Julia *Verinder
Wilkie Collins: *The Moonstone*

Speed Servant to *Valentine
William Shakespeare: *The Two Gentlemen of Verona*

Spenlow, Dora Only child of Francis Spenlow, senior partner in Spenlow and Jorkins, and 'child-wife' of David *Copperfield
Charles Dickens: *David Copperfield*

Springrove, Edward In love with Cytherea *Gray
Thomas Hardy: *Desperate Remedies*

Spurio The duke's bastard son
Cyril Tourneur: *The Revenger's Tragedy*

Squeers, Wackford The brutal and illiterate one-eyed owner of Dotheboys Hall school
Charles Dickens: *Nicholas Nickleby*

Stagmantle A newspaper magnate
W.H. Auden & Christopher Isherwood: *The Ascent of F6*

Stalky [Artie Corkran] Leader of a schoolboy gang that also include *Beetle and *M'Turk
Rudyard Kipling: *Stalky & Co.*

Stanbury, Jemima, and Hugh Aunt and nephew (a journalist)
Anthony Trollope: *He Knew He Was Right*

Stanhope, Dr Vesey Minister of three Barsetshire parishes (Crabtree Canonicorum, Stogpingum, and Eiderdown) who resides in Italy
Anthony Trollope: *Barchester Towers; The Warden*

Stareleigh, Mr Justice The judge in the case of Bardell v. Pickwick
Charles Dickens: *The Posthumous Papers of the Pickwick Club*

Stark, Willie The self-educated Southern back-country man who becomes governor of his state
Robert Penn Warren: *Allo the King's Men*

Starkadder Name of the gloomily rural family visited by Flora *Poste
Stella Gibbons: *Cold Comfort Farm*

Starling, Clarice An FBI trainee who has to build up a relationship with Hannibal *Lecter in pursuit of the serial killer known as 'Buffalo Bill'
Thomas Harris: *The Silence of the Lambs*

Starveling A tailor, cast for the part of Thisbe's mother in the play of 'Pyramus and Thisbe'
William Shakespeare: *A Midsummer Night's Dream*

Staunton, Sir George [alias **George Robertson**] Lover and subsequently husband of Effie *Deans
Sir Walter Scott: *The Heart of Midlothian*

Steenson, Willie A blind fiddler
Sir Walter Scott: 'Wandering Willie's Tale' [in *Redgauntlet*]

Steerforth, James Protector and patron of David *Copperfield as a boy at Salem House who seduces and elopes with Little *Em'ly
Charles Dickens: *David Copperfield*

Steerpike The evil and unprincipled former cook's boy who plots obsessively and tirelessly to overthrow the Groans of Gormenghast
Mervyn Peake: *Titus Groan; Gormenghast*

Stephano A drunken butler
William Shakespeare: *The Tempest*

Steyne, Lord [George Augustus Gaunt] A dissolute aristocrat
W.M. Thackeray: *Vanity Fair*

Stiggins, Mr A Dissenting preacher at the Emmanuel Chapel, Dorking
Charles Dickens: *The Posthumous Papers of the Pickwick Club*

Strap, Hugh Roderick's old school-fellow and later companion
Tobias Smollett: *The Adventures of Roderick Random*

Strephon and Klaius Shepherds
Sir Philip Sydney: *Arcadia*

Strether, Lambert A magazine editor engaged by Mrs *Newsome to bring her son Chad home from Europe
Henry James: *The Ambassadors*

Strider *see* ARAGORN

Stringham, Charles Schoolfriend of Nicholas *Jenkins who becomes private secretary to Sir Magnus *Donners
Anthony Powell: *A Dance to the Music of Time*

Strong, Dr Elderly headmaster and proprietor of the school at Canterbury to which David *Copperfield is sent by Betsey *Trotwood
Charles Dickens: *David Copperfield*

Strong, Annie Married to the elderly Dr *Strong
Charles Dickens: *David Copperfield*

Stryver, Mr A rising young barrister and *Darnay's defending counsel
Charles Dickens: *A Tale of Two Cities*

Stuart, Mary, Queen of Scots
Sir Walter Scott: *The Abbot*

Stubbs, Jonathan Youngest colonel in the British Army
Anthony Trollope: *Ayala's Angel*

Subtle The false alchemist and astrologer
Ben Jonson: *The Alchemist*

Summerson, Esther Lady *Dedlock's illegitimate daughter, adopted by John *Jarndyce
Charles Dickens: *Bleak House*

Surface, Charles A good-natured, reckless spendthrift
R.B. Sheridan: *The School for Scandal*

Surface, Joseph A sanctimonious hypocrite
R.B. Sheridan: *The School for Scandal*

Surface, Sir Oliver Rich uncle of Joseph and Charles *Surface
R.B. Sheridan: *The School for Scandal*

Surly A choleric gamester
Ben Jonson: *The Alchemist*

Sutpen, Thomas A Mississippi plantation owner
William Faulkner: *Absalom, Absalom!*

Svengali A German-Polish musician who uses his mesmeric powers to train *Trilby O'Ferrall as a singer
George du Maurier: *Trilby*

Swancourt, Elfride The blue-eyed daughter of the vicar of Endlestow
Thomas Hardy: *A Pair of Blue Eyes*

Sweedlepipe, Poll [Paul]; Mrs *Gamp's landlord: a barber and dealer in birds
Charles Dickens: *Martin Chuzzlewit*

Swiveller, Richard [Dick] Convivial but feckless friend of Fred *Trent's
Charles Dickens: *The Old Curiosity Shop*

Sycorax A witch, mother of *Caliban
William Shakespeare: *The Tempest*

Sylvia An heiress
George Farquhar: *The Recruiting Officer*

Symkyn, Symond The miller of Trumpington
Geoffrey Chaucer: 'The Reeve's Tale' [*Canterbury Tales*]

Syntax, Dr An absurd clergyman and schoolmaster who sets out in search of the picturesque; his horse, Grizzle
William Combe: *The Tour of Dr Syntax in Search of the Picturesque* [and others]

T

Tackleton Proprietor of Gruff and Tackleton, toy-makers
Charles Dickens: *The Cricket on the Hearth*

Talent, Keith The central character; a TV-addicted jack-of-all-trades in West London who aspires to become a darts champion
Martin Amis: *London Fields*

Tamburlaine A ruthless and ambitious Scythian shepherd-robber who rises to a position of supreme political and military power
Christopher Marlowe: *Tamburlaine the Great*

Tamora Queen of the Goths; later wife of *Saturninus
William Shakespeare: *Titus Andronicus*

Tanqueray, Paula [*née* Ray] The second wife of

Aubrey Tanqueray who commits suicide because of her sexual past
Sir Arthur Pinero: *The Second Mrs Tanqueray*

Tapley, Mark Servant at the Dragon Inn who becomes the devoted attendant of young Martin *Chuzzlewit during his American tour
Charles Dickens: *Martin Chuzzlewit*

Tappertit, Simon ['Sim'] Gabriel *Varden's apprentice
Charles Dickens: *Barnaby Rudge*

Tarrant, Verena Daughter of a charlatan faith-healer
Henry James: *The Bostonians*

Tartar An ex-naval lieutenant, formerly *Crisparkle's 'fag' at school
Charles Dickens: *The Mystery of Edwin Drood*

Tattle A vain, half-witted beau
William Congreve: *Love for Love*

Tattycoram *see* BEADLE, HARRIET

Tearsheet, Doll *see* DOLL TEARSHEET

Teazle, Sir Peter, and Lady An elderly gentleman (guardian of *Maria) and his young wife
R.B. Sheridan: *The School for Scandal*

Temple, Miss The kindly superintendent at Lowood School who befriends Jane
Charlotte Brontë: *Jane Eyre*

Templer, Peter Schoolfriend of Nicholas *Jenkins
Anthony Powell: *A Dance to the Music of Time*

Teufelsdröckh, Herr Diogenes A fictitious German philosopher from the University of Weissnichtwo
Thomas Carlyle: *Sartor Resartus*

Thaisa Daughter of *Simonides who gives birth to *Pericles' daughter *Marina during a storm at sea and is thought to have died
William Shakespeare: *Pericles*

Theale, Milly A gentle, immensely rich orphan
Henry James: *The Wings of the Dove*

Theodora A passionate Italian patriot
Benjamin Disraeli: *Lothair*

Thersites Achilles' bawdy fool
William Shakespeare: *Troilus and Cressida*

Thidias Follower of *Octavius
William Shakespeare: *Antony and Cleopatra*

Thorne, Mary Illegitimate niece of Dr Thomas *Thorne
Anthony Trollope: *Doctor Thorne*

Thorne, Dr Thomas Greshambury doctor, formerly of Barchester, and second cousin of Squire Thorne of Ullathorne
Anthony Trollope: *Doctor Thorne; The Last Chronicle of Barset*

Thornhill, Squire A scheming and immoral country squire who seduces and abandons Olivia *Primrose
Oliver Goldsmith: *The Vicar of Wakefield*

Thorpe, Isabella, and John Vulgar friend of Catherine *Morland engaged to Catherine's brother, and her foolish brother
Jane Austen: *Northanger Abbey*

Thrasher, Justice
Henry Fielding: *Amelia*

Thurio Rival to *Valentine
William Shakespeare: *Two Gentlemen of Verona*

Thwackum A brutish chaplain and tutor to Tom *Jones
Henry Fielding: *Tom Jones*

Tietjens, Christopher A Tory Yorkshire squire and younger son
F.M. Ford: *Parade's End* Tetralogy

Tigg, Montague A seedy swindler and associate of Chevy *Slyme
Charles Dickens: *Martin Chuzzlewit*

Tilburnia The heroine of Mr Puff's tragedy 'The Spanish Armada' who observes that even an oyster may be crossed in love
R.B. Sheridan: *The Critic*

Tilney, Captain Elder son of General Tilney
Jane Austen: *Northanger Abbey*

Tilney, Eleanor The pleasant sister of General *Tilney
Jane Austen: *Northanger Abbey*

Tilney, General An eccentric military man
Jane Austen: *Northanger Abbey*

Tilney, Henry Younger son of General *Tilney, in love with Catherine *Morland
Jane Austen: *Northanger Abbey*

Timias Prince Arthur's squire
Edmund Spenser: *The Faerie Queene*

Tiny Tim *see* CRATCHIT, TINY TIM

Titania Queen of the fairies and wife of *Oberon
William Shakespeare: *A Midsummer Night's Dream*

Titmuss, The Right Hon. Leslie
John Mortimer: *Paradise Postponed; Titmuss Regained*

Titus Andronicus Roman nobleman and general against the Goths
William Shakespeare: *Titus Andronicus*

Titus Groan *see* GROAN, TITUS

Toby, Uncle *see* SHANDY, CAPTAIN TOBIAS

Todgers, Mrs Proprietess of the Commercial Boarding House where *Pecksniff and his daughters stay in London
Charles Dickens: *Martin Chuzzlewit*

Tolland, Lady Isobel Daughter of Lord Warminster who marries Nicholas *Jenkins
Anthony Powell: *A Dance to the Music of Time*

Tom, Uncle A noble, devoutly Christian black slave in the kindly Shelby family, finally flogged to death on the orders of Simon *Legree
Harriet Beecher Stowe: *Uncle Tom's Cabin*

Toodle, Polly, and Robin Paul *Dombey's wet-nurse and her son ['Rob the Grinder']
Charles Dickens: *Dombey and Son*

Toots, Mr Head Boy at Dr *Blimber's academy
Charles Dickens: *Dombey and Son*

Touchett, Mr and Mrs An American banker and his repellent wife; their invalid son, Ralph
Henry James: *The Portrait of a Lady*

Touchstone Jester to the exiled Duke Frederick; betrothed to *Audrey
William Shakespeare: *As You Like It*

Tow-wouse, Mr, and Mrs An inn-keeper and his wife
Henry Fielding: *The History of the Adventures of Joseph Andrews*

Townly, Lord The 'provok'd husband', driven to desperation by his wife's extravagance
Sir John Vanbrugh/Colley Cibber: *The Provok'd Husband*

Traddles, Tommy One of David *Copperfield's schoolfellows at Salem House
Charles Dickens: *David Copperfield*

Traill, Mr The 'new man' at Moffatt's school for boys
Hugh Walpole: *Mr Perrin and Mr Traill*

Tranio *Lucentio's servant
William Shakespeare: *The Taming of the Shrew*

Transome, Harold One of the central characters who inherits the family estate on the death of his elder brother and stands as a Radical candidate but who is revealed not to have been his father's son
George Eliot: *Felix Holt, the Radical*

Trefoil, Arabella A determined but increasingly shopworn husband-hunter
Anthony Trollope: *The American Senator*

Trelawny, Rose A young actress
Sir Arthur Pinero: *Trelawny of the 'Wells'*

Trenor, Gus A rich and unscrupulous speculator who gains financial power over Lily *Bart
Edith Wharton: *The House of Mirth*

Trent, Nell The child-heroine who seeks to rescue her grandfather from the clutches of *Quilp; her scapegrace elder brother, Fred
Charles Dickens: *The Old Curiosity Shop*

Trent, Philip An artist turned amateur detective
E.C. Bentley: *Trent's Last Case*

Trevelyan, Emily [*née* Rowley] Daughter of Sir Marmaduke *Rowley; married to Louis *Trevelyan
Anthony Trollope: *He Knew He Was Right*

Trevelyan, Louis A wealthy man about town, married to Emily, daughter of Sir Marmaduke *Rowley
Anthony Trollope: *He Knew He Was Right*

Triamond The Knight of Friendship
Edmund Spenser: *The Faerie Queene*

Tribulation A puritan
Ben Jonson: *The Alchemist*

Trilby O'Ferrall An artist's model in Paris who falls under the mesmeric spell of *Svengali
George du Maurier: *Trilby*

Trim, Corporal Devoted servant of Captain *Shandy
Lawrence Sterne: *The Life and Opinions of Tristram Shandy*

Trinculo Companion to *Stephano
William Shakespeare: *The Tempest*

Tringle, Sir Thomas [Tom] A rich financier
Anthony Trollope: *Ayala's Angel*

Troilus A Trojan warrior, son of King Priam, in love with *Cressida
William Shakespeare: *Troilus and Cressida*

Trotter, Job Sly manservant of Alfred *Jingle
Charles Dickens: *The Posthumous Papers of the Pickwick Club*

Trotwood, Betsey Eccentric, strong-minded aunt of David *Copperfield
Charles Dickens: *David Copperfield*

Troy, Sergeant Francis The dashing, morally flawed husband of Bathsheba *Everdene, killed by John *Boldwood
Thomas Hardy: *Far From the Madding Crowd*

Truewit The gallant and chief wit
Ben Jonson: *Epicene*

Trulliber, Parson A sanctimonious and prosperous clergyman
Henry Fielding: *The History of the Adventures of Joseph Andrews*

Trunnion, Commodore Hawser, and Mrs Friends of Peregrine's parents
Tobias Smollett: *The Adventures of Peregrine Pickle*

Tulkinghorn, Mr Lawyer to the *Dedlocks
Charles Dickens: *Bleak House*

Tulliver, Maggie The highly strung and emotional sister of Tom *Tulliver who turns for intellectual and emotional companionship to Philip *Wakem
George Eliot: *The Mill on the Floss*

Tulliver, Mr The honest but obstinate miller of Dorlcote Mill; father of Tom and Maggie; his wife, Bessy
George Eliot: *The Mill on the Floss*

Tulliver, Tom Prosaic and unimaginative brother of Maggie *Tulliver
George Eliot: *The Mill on the Floss*

Tupman, Tracy A stout bachelor member of the Pickwick Club who attempts to woo Rachel *Wardle
Charles Dickens: *The Posthumous Papers of the Pickwick Club*

Turveydrop, Mr An indolent elderly Regency buck; his son Prince, an impecunious dancing-master
Charles Dickens: *Bleak House*

Twentyman, Larry A young farmer
Anthony Trollope: *The American Senator*

Twist, Oliver The illegitimate son of Edwin Leeford and Agnes Fleming, and half-brother of *Monks
Charles Dickens: *Oliver Twist*

Twitcher, Jemmy An associate of *Macheath's who betrays him
John Gay: *The Beggar's Opera*

Tybalt Quarrelsome and cynical nephew of Lady Capulet, killed by *Romeo
William Shakespeare: *Romeo and Juliet*

Tyrold, Camilla Principal character
Frances Burney: *Camilla*
Tyrrel An arrogant and tyrannical country squire, murdered by *Falkland
William Godwin: *Caleb Williams*

U

Ulrica The old sibyl who sets fire to the castle of Torquilstone
Sir Walter Scott: *Ivanhoe*
Ulysses A Greek commander
William Shakespeare: *Troilus and Cressida*
Umbriel A 'dusky melancholy sprite'
Alexander Pope: *The Rape of the Lock*
Una Symbolic of the true religion; separated from the *Redcrosse Knight by the wiles of *Archimago
Edmund Spenser: *The Faerie Queene*
Una Sister of *Dan
Rudyard Kipling: *Puck of Pook's Hill*
Ursini, Paulo Giordano *see* BRACHIANO, DUKE OF
Ursula A pig-woman
Ben Jonson: *Bartholomew Fair*
Ursula *Hero's maidservant
William Shakespeare: *Much Ado About Nothing*

V

Valancourt Lover of Emily St Aubert
Ann Radcliffe: *The Mysteries of Udolpho*
Valdaura Wife of *Paradine
Sir William Davenant: *Albovine*
Valentine Kinsman of *Marcus Andronicus
William Shakespeare: *Titus Andronicus*
Valentine Attending on *Orsino
William Shakespeare: *Twelfth Night*
Valentine One of the 'two gentlemen'; see also *Proteus
William Shakespeare: *The Two Gentlemen of Verona.*
van Helsing, Abraham A Dutch physician and vampire hunter
Bram Stoker: *Dracula*
Vanderbank A young government official, with whom both Nanda *Brockenham and her mother are infatuated
Henry James: *The Awkward Age*
Vane, Harriet A writer of detective stories acquitted of murder through the efforts of Lord Peter *Wimsey, whom she eventually marries
Dorothy L. Sayers: *Strong Poison* [and others]
Varden, Dolly Daughter of Gabriel *Varden and friend of Emma *Haredale
Charles Dickens: *Barnaby Rudge*
Varden, Gabriel, and Martha A worthy locksmith and his wife, a Protestant fanatic and domestic tyrant
Charles Dickens: *Barnaby Rudge*
Varrius Friend of *Pompey
William Shakespeare: *Antony and Cleopatra*
Varrius Friend to *Vincentio
William Shakespeare: *Measure for Measure*
Vautrin A master criminal
Balzac: *Le Père Goriot* [and others]
Veneering, Hamilton A newly wealthy self-made man; his wife, Anastasia
Charles Dickens: *Our Mutual Friend*
Venn, Diggory A reddleman on Egdon Heath
Thomas Hardy: *The Return of the Native*
Ventidius Follower of *Antony
William Shakespeare: *Antony and Cleopatra*
Venus, Mr A taxidermist
Charles Dickens: *Our Mutual Friend*
Verges A constable, along with *Dogbery
William Shakespeare: *Much Ado About Nothing*
Verinder, Lady Julia [*née* Herncastle] Widow of Sir John Verinder
Wilkie Collins: *The Moonstone*
Verinder, Rachel Daughter of Lady Julia *Verinder who marries Franklin *Blake
Wilkie Collins: *The Moonstone*
Verisopht, Lord Frederick A foolish and wealthy young aristocrat, the dupe of Sir Mulberry *Hawk
Charles Dickens: *Nicholas Nickleby*
Verloc, Adolf A half-hearted anarchist who lives by betraying his fellow revolutionaries
Joseph Conrad: *The Secret Agent*
Vernon, Diana High-spirited niece of Sir Hildebrand *Osbaldistone
Sir Walter Scott: *Rob Roy*
Verver, Adam A widowed American in Europe with his daughter Maggie
Henry James: *The Golden Bowl*
Vholes, Mr Richard *Carstone's sinister solicitor
Charles Dickens: *Bleak House*
Vincentio Duke of Vienna
William Shakespeare: *Measure for Measure*
Vincy, Fred and Rosamond Son and daughter of the mayor of Middlemarch
George Eliot: *Middlemarch*
Viola Principal character, sister of *Sebastian
William Shakespeare: *Twelfth Night*
Virgilia Wife of *Coriolanus
William Shakespeare: *Coriolanus*
Vladimir The fellow-tramp of *Estragon—both trapped in an endless waiting for the arrival of the mysterious Godot
Samuel Beckett: *Waiting for Godot*
Volpone Principal character; a rich Venetian (whose name means 'the fox')
Ben Jonson: *Volpone*
Volumnia Mother of *Coriolanus
William Shakespeare: *Coriolanus*
Vye, Eustacia The wild, capricious heroine who in a brief infatuation marries Clym *Yeobright
Thomas Hardy: *The Return of the Native*
Vyse, Cecil A cultured dilettante engaged to Lucy *Honeychurch
E.M. Forster: *A Room with a View*

W

Wackles, Mrs, and the Misses Melissa, Sophy, and Jane Owner of a day-school in Chelsea and her daughters
Charles Dickens: *The Old Curiosity Shop*

Wade, Miss A self-tormented woman, born illegitimate, who maliciously conceals papers relating to Little Dorrit
Charles Dickens: *Little Dorrit*

Wagg, Mr A parasitical journalist and diner-out
W.M. Thackeray: *Vanity Fair; Pendennis*

Waitwell Manservant to *Mirabell
William Congreve: *The Way of the World*

Wardle, Mr Owner of Manor Farm, Dingley Dell, whose hospitality Mr *Pickwick and his friends enjoy; his daughter Rachel
Charles Dickens: *The Posthumous Papers of the Pickwick Club*

Wardour, Isabella Daughter of Sir Arthur Wardour
Sir Walter Scott: *The Antiquary*

Wart, Thomas One of *Falstaff's recruits
William Shakespeare: *Henry IV 2*

Watson, Dr John A retired army medical doctor, the companion of Sherlock *Homes
A. Conan Doyle: *A Study in Scarlet* [and many others]

Welland, May A wealthy but strictly educated New York girl of 'abysmal purity' who marries Newland *Archer
Edith Wharton: *The Age of Innocence*

Wellbred A gallant, brother-in-law of *Kitely
Ben Jonson: *Every Man in His Humour*

Weller, Samuel Devoted manservant of Samuel *Pickwick; his father, Toby—an old stage-coachman
Charles Dickens: *The Posthumous Papers of the Pickwick Club*

Wemmick Clerk to the lawyer *Jaggers who takes *Pip under his wing
Charles Dickens: *Great Expectations*

Wenonah Mother of *Hiawatha
Henry Wadsworth Longfellow: *The Song of Hiawatha*

Wentworth, Captain Frederick Naval officer and brother of Mrs *Croft who eventually marries Anne *Elliot
Jane Austen: *Persuasion*

Western, Sophia The beautiful and sweet-natured daughter of Squire Western loved by Tom *Jones since childhood
Henry Fielding: *Tom Jones*

Westlock, John Pupil of *Pecksniff's and friend of Tom *Pinch
Charles Dickens: *Martin Chuzzlewit*

Weston, Mr A curate, who finally marries Agnes
Anne Brontë: *Agnes Grey*

Weston, Mr [formerly **Captain**] Neighbour of the *Woodhouse family living at Randalls; father of Frank *Churchill
Jane Austen: *Emma*

Whitford, Vernon A poor and earnest young scholar
George Meredith: *The Egoist*

Whorehound, Sir Walter A dissolute knight
Thomas Middleton: *A Chaste Maid in Cheapside*

Wickfield, Mr, and Agnes Betsey *Trotwood's Canterbury solicitor and his devoted daughter who finally marries David *Copperfield
Charles Dickens: *David Copperfield*

Wickham, George Handsome but irresponsible officer who elopes with Lydia *Bennet
Jane Austen: *Pride and Prejudice*

Widmerpool, Kenneth A figure of fun at his school who rises to become a Labour MP and eventually a peer
Anthony Powell: *A Dance to the Music of Time*

Wildeve, Damon A former engineer turned publican married to Thomasin *Yeobright
Thomas Hardy: *The Return of the Native*

Wilfer, Bella Second youngest daughter of Reginald Wilfer, clerk in the firm of Chickley, Veneering, and Stubbles, who goes to live with the *Boffins
Charles Dickens: *Our Mutual Friend*

Willet, John Host of the Maypole Inn; his son Joe, finally the successful wooer of Dolly *Varden
Charles Dickens: *Barnaby Rudge*

William A countryman, in love with *Audrey
William Shakespeare: *As You Like It*

Williams, Caleb Self-educated son of humble parents and secretary to *Falkland
William Godwin: *Caleb Williams*

Willoughby, Sir Clement The persistent lover of Evelina *Belmont
Frances Burney: *Evelina*

Willoughby, John The impecunious and unprincipled young man with whom Marianne *Dashwood unwisely falls in love
Jane Austen: *Sense and Sensibility*

Wilson, Alison Housekeeper of Silas *Morton
Sir Walter Scott: *Old Mortality*

Wimsey, Lord Peter A gentleman-detective, younger brother of the Duke of Denver
Dorothy L. Sayers: *Whose Body?* [and many others]

Winks *see* DEPUTY

Winterbourne, Giles A woodlander who loves Grace *Melbury
Thomas Hardy: *The Woodlanders*

Wishfort, Lady Aunt of *Millamant
William Congreve: *The Way of the World*

Wititterly, Henry and Julia Pretentious residents of fashionable Belgravia who employ Kate *Nickleby
Charles Dickens: *Nicholas Nickleby*

Woodcourt, Allan A young doctor who falls in love with Esther *Summerson
Charles Dickens: *Bleak House*

Woodhouse, Emma The clever but self-satisfied and interfering heroine, finally humbled by marriage to Mr *Knightley
Jane Austen: *Emma*

Woodhouse, Mr A valetudinarain; father of Emma *Woodhouse
Jane Austen: *Emma*

Woodseer, Mr, and Gower Father and son, the latter based on R.L. Stevenson
George Meredith: *The Amazing Marriage*

Wooster, Bertie [Bertram] Amiable but vacuous young man-about-town; the employer of *Jeeves
P.G. Wodehouse: *The Inimitable Jeeves* [and many others]

Wopsle, Mr Parish clerk and friend of the *Gargerys who turns actor
Charles Dickens: *Great Expectations*

Worthing, John [Jack] Known in town as Ernest; adopted son of a wealthy philanthropist, found as a baby in a handbag at Victorian Station; in pursuit of Algy *Moncrieff's cousin Gwendolen *Fairfax
Oscar Wilde: *The Importance of Being Earnest*

Wrayburn, Eugene The indolent and aimless friend of Mortimer *Lightwood's who becomes attracted by Lizzie *Hexam
Charles Dickens: *Our Mutual Friend*

Wren, Jenny *see* JENNY WREN

Y

Yates, Major The resident magistrate
Somerville and Ross: *Some Experiences of an Irish R.M.*

Yates, John Friend of Tom *Bertram who elopes with Tom's sister Julia
Jane Austen: *Mansfield Park*

Yellowhammer A rich goldsmith
Thomas Middleton: *A Chaste Maid in Cheapside*

Yeobright, Clym [Clement] A former diamond merchant who, after returning to his native Egdon Heath, falls in love with and marries Eustacia *Vye
Thomas Hardy: *The Return of the Native*

Yeobright, Thomasin Gentle cousin of Clym *Yeobright who rejects her humble suitor Diggory *Venn for Damon *Wildeve
Thomas Hardy: *The Return of the Native*

Yorick The king's jester whose skull the grave-diggers throw up when digging *Ophelia's grave
William Shakespeare: *Hamlet*

Yorick A parson of Danish descent
Lawrence Sterne: *A Sentimental Journey*

Yossarian, Captain John A US airman stationed on the Mediterranean island of Pianosa during the last months of World War II who, appalled by his experiences, makes desperate attempts to avoid further combat
Joseph Heller: *Catch-22*

Yule, Alfred A learned pedant; his daughter and assistant, Marian, shabbily abandoned by Jasper *Milvain
George Gissing: *New Grub Street*

Z

Zapp, Morris J. An American university lecturer
David Lodge: *Changing Places* [and others]

Zeal-of-the-Land Busy A canting, gluttonous Puritan
Ben Jonson: *Bartholomew Fair*

Zelmane The name assumed by *Pyrocles when disguised as a woman
Sir Philip Sydney: *Arcadia*

Zenobia [Zenobia Moody] An exotic and wealthy resident of Blithedale Farm who becomes infatuated with Miles *Coverdale and who drowns herself after she is rejected
Nathaniel Hawthorne: *The Blithedale Romance*

Zenocrate Daughter of the Soldan of Egypt and wife of *Tamburlaine
Christopher Marlowe: *Tamburlaine the Great*

Zimri Name for the Duke of Buckingham
John Dryden: *Absalom and Achitophel*

Zuleika The heroine
Byron: *The Bride of Abydos*

Zuniga, Hector A narcotics agent with the Drug Enforcement Administration
Thomas Pynchon: *Vineland*